Authors

The Manual of Accounting – UK GAAP 2012 is written by the UK Accounting Consulting Services team of PricewaterhouseCoopers LLP.

Writing team led by
Barry Johnson
Peter Holgate

Authors, contributors and reviewers

Michelle Amjad
Erin Bennett
Dasa Brynjolffssen
Claire Burke
Jo Clarke
Howard Crossland
Luis de Leon Ortiz
Ilaria Evans
Michael Gaull
Imre Guba
Rodney Hamill
Margaret Heneghan
Mike Higgs
Peter Hogarth
Claire Howells
Jayne Kerr
Hannah King
Sabine Koch
Sheetal Kumar
Marian Lovelace
Elizabeth Lynn
Joanna Malvern
Avni Mashru
Helen McCann
Malcolm J Millar
Michelle Millar
Janet Milligan
Armon Nakhai
Peter Piga
Olaf Pusch
Tom Quinn
Iain Selfridge
Alfredo Ramirez
Richard Tattershall
Laura Taylor
Sandra Thompson
Sarah Troughton
Gail Tucker
Simon Whitehead
Ian Wilkinson
Barbara Willis
Michelle Winarto
Katie Woods

Foreword

By Roger Marshall
Chairman
UK Accounting Standards Board

Since 2005, large parts of the world have used IFRS and a number of other major countries are likely to adopt IFRS in the next few years. The credit crunch and associated economic difficulties have, in the last three years, put increased spotlight on accounting standards, especially those dealing with financial instruments. Politicians have interested themselves in accounting like never before. Difficult though these issues have been, they have underlined the immense need for and importance of high quality accounting standards.

Another matter which has been questioned is whether the true and fair view concept continues to apply. The ASB has confirmed that, both under IFRS and under UK GAAP, the true and fair view is central to the preparation of accounts.

IFRS has of course spawned a simplified version – IFRS for SMEs – and the UK ASB has been working hard to develop a new version of UK GAAP based on IFRS for SMEs. This work is in its final stages and is likely to be implemented over the next three or so years. In the meantime, the existing UK GAAP – the SSAPs and FRSs, as well as the accounting provisions of the Companies Act 2006 – continues to be used by hundreds of thousands of UK companies.

The current UK GAAP – the subject of this Manual – is based partly on the application of rules and partly on principles and judgement. Judgement is, of course, most likely to be sound when it is based on experience. In today's rapidly changing environment, I commend this Manual of Accounting and its sister edition Manual of Accounting IFRS for the UK 2012, which gives preparers and practitioners the benefits of the extensive experience and professional judgement of PricewaterhouseCoopers.

October 2011

Foreword

Preface

PricewaterhouseCoopers' Manual of Accounting – UK GAAP 2012 is a practical guide to UK accounting law and practice. It encompasses: the accounting provisions of the Companies Act 2006; the requirements of accounting standards; Urgent Issues Task Force Abstracts; and other Generally Accepted Accounting Principles. The Manual includes practical advice based on our work in PricewaterhouseCoopers LLP's UK Accounting Consulting Services team in advising the firm's clients, partners and staff.

The Manual deals with accounting principles and rules and company reporting. It covers diverse areas of accounting, from disclosure of financial instruments to accounting for deferred taxation. It explains in detail the rules that apply to preparing consolidated financial statements and considers other statements that appear in annual reports, such as cash flow statements. The Manual also considers a number of concessions given to smaller companies and overseas companies. Chapter 6 of the Manual explains how financial instruments are accounted for in the UK and is supplemented by Manual of Accounting – Financial instruments 2012. This explains the international financial reporting standard rules that apply to financial instruments, which are almost identical in certain situations to the rules that apply to companies that use UK GAAP.

This Manual is also accompanied by Manual of Accounting – Narrative reporting, which includes aspects of financial reporting that remain the same for entities reporting under either IFRS or UK GAAP. These areas are often referred to as the 'front half' of financial statements and cover the operating and financial review, directors' report and the remuneration report and corporate governance.

Even in a work of this size it is not possible to cover every aspect of company reporting. For example, the manual does not cover the specific accounting requirements that apply to banking and insurance companies, although much of the advice given in the text will assist them.

Furthermore, as international accounting has become increasingly important, we have also written a sister publication, Manual of Accounting – IFRS for the UK, which follows a similar format to this Manual and explains the rules that apply to UK listed companies and to other UK companies that choose to apply IFRS.

We hope that finance directors, accountants, auditors, analysts and other users of financial statements will find this Manual useful.

Barry Johnson, Peter Holgate
PricewaterhouseCoopers LLP
London
October 2011

Preface

PricewaterhouseCoopers' Manual of Accounting – UK GAAP 2012 is a practical guide to the accounting and reporting requirements of the Companies Act 2006, the requirements of accounting standards, Urgent Issues Task Force Abstracts, and other Generally Accepted Accounting Principles. The Manual includes practical advice based on our work in PricewaterhouseCoopers LLP's UK Accounting Consulting Services team in advising the firm's clients, partners and staff.

The Manual deals with accounting principles and financial reporting. It sets out the areas of accounting, from the issue of financial instruments to accounting for deferred taxation. It explains in detail the rules that apply to preparing consolidated financial statements and considers other statements that appear in annual reports such as cash flow statements. The Manual also considers a number of concessions given to smaller companies and overseas companies. Chapter 6 of the Manual explains how financial instruments are accounted for in the UK and is supplemented by Manual of Accounting – Financial instruments 2012. This explains the international financial reporting standard rules relating to financial instruments, which are almost identical in their application to the rules that apply to companies that use UK GAAP.

This Manual is also supplemented by Manual of Accounting – Narrative reporting, which addresses aspects of financial reporting that contain the rules for narrative reporting under either IFRS or UK GAAP. These areas are often referred to as the 'front half' of financial statements and cover the operating and financial review, directors' report and the remuneration report, and corporate governance.

In a work of this size it is not possible to cover every aspect of company reporting. For example, the Manual does not cover the specific accounting requirements that apply to banking and insurance companies, although much of the advice given in the text will assist them.

Furthermore, as international accounting has become increasingly important, we have also written a sister publication, Manual of Accounting – IFRS for the UK, which follows a similar format to this Manual and explains the rules that apply to UK listed companies and other UK companies that choose to apply IFRS.

We hope that finance directors, accountants, auditors, analysts and other users of financial statements will find this Manual useful.

Barry Johnson, Peter Holgate
PricewaterhouseCoopers LLP
London
October 2011

Contents

Manual of accounting – Financial instruments

This separate book is part of this Manual of Accounting and includes the following chapters:

Abbreviations and terms used

AAPA	Association of Authorised Public Accountants
ABI	Association of British Insurers
AC	Appeal Cases, law reports
Accounts	financial statements
ADR	american depositary receipts
AESOP	all employee share ownership plan
the 1985 Act	the Companies Act 1985 (as amended by the Companies Act 1989)
the 1989 Act	the Companies Act 1989
the 2006 Act	the Companies Act 2006
ACCA	Association of Chartered Certified Accountants
ACT	advance corporation tax
AFS	available-for-sale
AG	Application Guidance
AGM	Annual General Meeting
AIM	Alternative Investment Market
AIMR	Alternative Investment Market Rules
AITC	Association of Investment Trust Companies
All ER	All England Law Reports
AMPS	auction market preferred shares
APB	Auditing Practices Board
APC	Auditing Practices Committee
App	Application note of a Financial Reporting Standard
App	Appendix
ARC	Accounting Regulatory Committee
ARSs	auction rate securities
ASB	Accounting Standards Board
ASC	Accounting Standards Committee
BBA	British Bankers' Association
BC	Basis for Conclusions (to an accounting standard)
BCLC	Butterworths Company Law Cases
BERR	Department for Business, Enterprise and Regulatory Reform (formerly the DTI and now BIS)
BIS	Department for Business, Innovation and Skills (formerly BERR before that DTI)
BNA 1985	Business Names Act 1985
BOT	build-operate-transfer
C	currency unit
CA85	the Companies Act 1985
CA06	the Companies Act 2006
CCA	current cost accounting
CCAB	Consultative Committee of Accountancy Bodies Limited

CC	The Combined Code – Principles of good governance and code of best practice
CC(CP)	Companies Consolidation (Consequential Provisions) Act 1985
CEO	chief executive officer
CESR	Committee of European Securities Regulators
CGAA	Co-ordinating Group on Audit and Accounting Issues
CGU	cash-generating unit
Ch	Chancery Division, law reports
Chp	Chapter
chapter (1)	'PricewaterhouseCoopers' Manual of accounting' – chapter (1)
CIF	cost, insurance, freight
CIMA	Chartered Institute of Management Accountants
CIPFA	Chartered Institute of Public Finance and Accountancy
CISCO	The City Group for Smaller Companies
Cmnd	Command Paper
CBO	collateralised bond obligation
CDO	collateralised debt obligation
CLO	collateralised loan obligation
CMO	collateralised mortgage obligation
CODM	chief operating decision maker
COSO	Committee of Sponsoring Organisations of the Treadway Commission
CPP	current purchasing power
CR	Report of the committee on The Financial Aspects of Corporate Governance (the 'Cadbury Report')
CSR	corporate social responsibility
CTD	cumulative translation difference
CUV	continuing use value
DCF	discounted cash flow
DG XV	Directorate General XV
the 7th Directive	EC 7th Directive on Company Law
DP	discussion paper
DRC	depreciated replacement cost
DTI	Department of Trade and Industry
DTR	Disclosure and Transparency Rules
EASDAQ	European Association of Securities Dealers Automated Quotation
EBIT	earnings before interest and tax
EBITDA	earnings before interest, tax, depreciation and amortisation
EC	European Community
ECU	european currency unit
ED	exposure draft
EEE	electrical and electronic equipment
EFRAG	European Financial Reporting Advisory Group
EGM	extraordinary general meeting
EITF	Emerging Issues Task Force (US)
EPS	earnings per share
ESOP	employee share ownership plan
ESOT	employee share ownership trust

ERP	enterprise resource planning
EU	European Union
EU 2005 Regulation	Regulation (EC) No 1606/2002 on the application of International Accounting Standards
EUV	existing use value
FASB	Financial Accounting Standards Board (US)
FEE	The European Federation of Accountants
FIFO	first-in, first-out
financial statements	Accounts
FLA	Finance and Leasing Association
FM	facilities management
FOB	free on board
FPI	foreign private investors (US-listed)
FRAG	Financial Reporting and Auditing Group of the ICAEW
Framework	Framework for the preparation and presentation of financial statements
FRED	Financial Reporting Exposure Draft
FRA	forward rate agreement
FRC	Financial Reporting Council
FRN	floating rate note
FRRP	Financial Reporting Review Panel
FRS	Financial Reporting Standard
FRSSE	Financial Reporting Standard for Smaller Entities
FSA	Financial Services Authority
FVTPL	at fair value through profit or loss
GAAP	generally accepted accounting principles (and practices)
GAAS	generally accepted auditing standards
GB	Great Britain
GCFR	Going Concern and Financial Reporting — published by the joint working group of the Hundred Group of finance directors, ICAEW and ICAS
GDP	gross domestic product
GRI guidelines	Global Reporting Initiative guidelines
HMSO	Her Majesty's Stationery Office
HP	hire purchase
HMRC	HM Revenue & Customs
IAASB	International Auditing and Assurance Standards Board
IAS	International Accounting Standard (see also IFRS)
IASB	International Accounting Standards Board
IASC	International Accounting Standards Committee
IBF	Irish Bankers' Federation
IBNR	incurred but not reported
ICAEW	Institute of Chartered Accountants in England and Wales
ICAI	Institute of Chartered Accountants in Ireland
ICAS	Institute of Chartered Accountants of Scotland
ICFR	Internal Control and Financial Reporting — published by the joint working group of the Hundred Group of finance directors, ICAEW and ICAS

ICR	Industrial Cases Reports
ICSA	Institute of Chartered Secretaries and Administrators
IFAC	International Federation of Accountants
IFRIC	International Financial Reporting Interpretations Committee
IFRS	International Financial Reporting Standard (see also IAS)
IG	Implementation Guidance (to an accounting standard)
IGU	income-generating unit
IIMR	Institute of Investment Management and Research (see SIP)
IoD	Institute of Directors
IOSCO	International Organisation of Securities Commissions
IPO	initial public offering
IPR&D	in-process research and development
IR	Statement on interim reporting issued by ASB
ISA	International Standard on Auditing
ISA (UK & Ire)	International Standard on Auditing (UK and Ireland)
ISDA	International Swap Dealers Association
ISP	internet service provider
IVSC	International Valuation Standards Committee
JWG	Joint Working Group
LIBID	London inter-bank bid rate
LIBOR	London inter-bank offered rate
LIFFE	the London International Financial Futures and Options Exchange
LIFO	last-in, first-out
LR	UK Listing Authority's Listing Rules
MBO	management buy-out
MD&A	management's discussion and analysis
MR	Master of the Rolls
NASDAQ	National Association of Securities Dealers Automated Quotations
NCI	non-controlling interest
NCU	national currency unit
NIC	national insurance contributions
NPV	net present value
OFR	operating and financial review
OEICs	open-ended investment companies
OIAC	Oil Industry Accounting Committee
OTC	over-the-counter market
PA	preliminary announcement
para(s)	paragraph(s) of Schedules to the Companies Acts, or IFRSs or IASs or FRSs, or SSAPs, or FREDs, or EDs, or DPs, or text
PCAOB	Public Company Accounting Oversight Board (US)
PE	price-earnings
PFI	Private Finance Initiative
PLUSR	Plus Rules for Issuers (for PLUS-quoted entities)
PPE	property, plant and equipment

PPERA	Political Parties, Elections and Referendums Act 2000
PPF	Pension Protection Fund
PRAG	Pensions Research Accountants Group
PS	Practice Statements
QC	Queen's Counsel
QUEST	qualifying employee share ownership trust
R&D	research and development
RDG	regional development grant
Reg	regulation of a statutory instrument (for example, SI 1995/2092 Reg 5 = regulation 5 of The Companies (Summary Financial Statements) Regulations 1995)
RICS	Royal Institution of Chartered Surveyors
ROT	rehabilitate-operate-transfer
RS	Reporting Standard
SAC	the Standards Advisory Council
SAS	Statement of Auditing Standards
SC	Session Cases
Sch	Schedule to the Companies Act 1985 (eg CA85 4A Sch 85 = Schedule 4A, paragraph 85)
SDC	Standards Development Committee
SEC	Securities and Exchange Commission (US)
Sec(s)	Section(s) of the 1985 Act/Sections(s) of the 2006 Act
SEE	social, environmental and ethical
SERPS	State earnings related pension scheme
SFAC	Statement of Financial Accounting Concepts issued in the US
SFAS	Statement of Financial Accounting Standards issued in the US
SI	Statutory Instrument
SIC	Standing Interpretation Committee of the IASC (see IFRIC)
SIP	Society of Investment Professionals (formerly IIMR)
SIPs	share incentive plans
SMEs	small and medium-sized entities
SOI	Statement of Intent
SoP	Statement of principles
SORIE	statement of recognised income and expense
SORP	Statement of Recommended Practice
SPE	special purpose entity
SPV	special purpose vehicle
SSAP	Statement of Standard Accounting Practice
Stock Exchange (or LSE)	the London Stock Exchange
STRGL	statement of total recognised gains and losses
TR	Technical Release of the ICAEW
TUPE	Transfer of Undertakings (Protection of Employment) Regulations
UITF	Urgent Issues Task Force
UK	United Kingdom
US	United States of America

VAT	value added tax
VIE	variable interest entity
WACC	weighted average cost of capital
WEEE	Waste electrical and electronic equipment
WLR	Weekly Law Reports
xBRL	extensible business reporting language

Chapter 1

Introduction

Chapter 1

Introduction

UK GAAP today

1.1 In the listed company arena, and in the press, there is now so much emphasis on international financial reporting standards (IFRS) that it is easy to forget that there is, in the UK, another type of accounting commonly practiced – and that is UK GAAP. UK GAAP is still used by most unlisted companies and groups and by many individual entities – parent entities and UK subsidiaries – in listed groups. Hence, by number at least, the majority of entities in the UK use UK GAAP. This Manual is addressed to their needs.

1.2 UK GAAP has developed over many years and includes both company law and UK accounting standards – SSAPs and FRSs. But the nature of UK GAAP has changed considerably in the past few years. Until about the year 2000, UK GAAP was, albeit internationally influenced to some degree, essentially home-grown. The last conventional UK accounting standard was FRS 19 on deferred tax, which was published in December 2000. But nearly all the standards since then are almost exact copies of IFRSs. Hence the role of the UK Accounting Standards Board has changed fundamentally from one of developing and improving UK GAAP to one of implementing IFRS into UK GAAP.

1.3 The development of IFRS for global application and its partial implementation into the UK are major trends. Three major factors underlie them. First, the case for harmonisation is compelling. Global businesses and international investors need to have accounting information that they can understand when running businesses and making investment decisions. Despite the different histories and cultural backgrounds that have led to the many national GAAPs found today, there is an overwhelming need for accounting principles to be harmonised worldwide.

1.4 Secondly, the International Accounting Standards Board (IASB) has been a major player in the quest for global convergence and harmonisation. But as the last decade has progressed, the IASB has worked more and more with the US standard-setter, the Financial Accounting Standards Board (FASB). The two bodies have an extensive joint work programme to which they are devoting considerable effort. Yet convergence with US GAAP is a complex endeavour, partly because US GAAP is so much more prescriptive than IFRS and partly because the rest of the world – much of which uses IFRS – does not necessarily see the case for increasing US influence.

1.5 Thirdly, the factor that most directly affects accounting in the UK is the June 2002 European Commission Regulation that required all EU listed companies from 2005 to prepare their consolidated financial statements using

IFRS, rather than national GAAP. The preparation of consolidated financial statements of listed companies under IFRS is now well-established.

1.6 Whilst IFRS is compulsory for the consolidated financial statements of listed companies, the regime is permissive for other entities. Some entities adopted IFRS in 2005, but more remained on UK GAAP. Concerns about the effect of IFRS on distributable profits have been the main factor behind this retention of UK GAAP.

1.7 After some years of uncertainty, the future for accounting in the UK for entities other than listed groups now looks clearer. Following the finalisation by the IASB of its 'IFRS for SMEs', the UK ASB published preliminary proposals in 2009 followed by exposure drafts (FREDs 43 and 44) in October 2010. The likely outcome is a three-tier approach. Most medium and large but unlisted entities would adopt a version of IFRS for SMEs that is slightly changed for UK purposes. This would become, in effect, the new UK GAAP for all entities in the middle tier – that is those that are not 'publicly accountable' (they would do full IFRS) and that are not 'small' as defined by the Companies Act (they would continue to use the FRSSE). Under this plan, the existing SSAPs and FRSs would be swept away and replaced by a version of IFRS for SMEs. The timetable for this is not entirely clear, but looks unlikely to be before calendar 2014.

1.8 As the years pass, the case for having a separate set of rules called UK GAAP for UK companies that are outside the listed sector looks less and less tenable. The three-tier approach, based in part on a simplified version of IFRS, on the other hand, has substantial appeal, not only in the UK but in many other countries where full IFRS would introduce too much complexity, too many disclosures and would generally not be fit for purpose.

The approach in this Manual

1.9 Questions about how UK GAAP develops and how and when IFRS for SMEs affects it are important, but are for the future. For the moment, there are many aspects of UK GAAP that demand analysis and interpretation and the remainder of this work seeks to provide helpful guidance in that regard. We discuss the requirements of company law, accounting standards and UITF abstracts. We also give our views on what is good accounting in the many areas in which there are no rules or guidance. As part of that approach, this Manual contains hundreds of examples and extracts from financial statements. This Manual also has a strong company law bias: we are aware from practical experience that many of the questions that arise in practice cannot be answered based solely on accounting principles, but that many of them have to be answered at the interface of accounting and company law. Many of the chapters that follow reflect this. This work is also available in electronic form on pwcinform.com, where it is hypertext linked to the originating source regulations such as the Companies Act and accounting standards.

1.10 Chapter 6 of the Manual explains how financial instruments are accounted for in the UK under what is sometimes called 'old UK GAAP'. This is supplemented by Manual of Accounting – Financial instruments. This explains the international financial reporting standard rules that apply to financial instruments, which are almost identical to the rules that apply to certain companies that use UK GAAP.

1.11 The 'PricewaterhouseCoopers' Manual of Accounting – Narrative Reporting', which supports this Manual, provides UK companies with guidance on the legal and other regulatory requirements that impact elements of reporting that are common to users of both IFRS and UK GAAP, often referred to as the 'front half' of the annual report. The sister edition of this book, 'PricewaterhouseCoopers' Manual of Accounting – IFRS for the UK', sets out detailed guidance on how IFRS affects UK listed groups and other UK entities that opt into IFRS.

Chapter 2

Accounting principles and rules

Chapter 2

Accounting principles and rules

Introduction

2.1 As discussed in chapter 1, the accounting framework in the UK is subject to a greater number of increasingly complicated rules. The sources of accounting principles and rules in the UK range from legislation and accounting standards to customs practised by professionals over many years. In addition, accounting under UK standards is increasingly influenced by practice overseas, for example, in the US and the IASB. International developments in particular are now a crucial source of UK GAAP: the UK ASB has accelerated its agenda of convergence with IFRS and, in 2009, the ASB issued a Consultation Paper proposing to replace existing UK GAAP with the new IFRS for small and medium entities. In October 2010, the UK ASB issued FRED 43 and 44 outlining the future for UK financial reporting. The proposals in FRED 43 and 44 recognise that one size of accounting standard does not fit all entities. It proposes a tier system for financial reporting that requires entities to prepare financial statements in one of three tiers. See further from paragraph 2.63.

2.2 This chapter explores the framework and sources of authority for the generally accepted accounting principles in the UK and how the Companies Act and accounting standards impact on the overriding requirement for financial statements to give a true and fair view.

[The next paragraph is 2.4.]

2.4 The ASB's convergence policy was prompted by the requirement for many companies to adopt IFRS in 2005. The EU approved a Regulation in June 2002 that requires all listed companies in the EU (including banks and insurance companies) to prepare their consolidated financial statements under EU-adopted IFRS ('IFRS') for financial years beginning on or after 1 January 2005. Member States had the option to extend this requirement to unlisted companies and to individual company financial statements. From 2005, any UK company (with the exception of charities) is permitted to prepare its financial statements using IFRS. It is, however, required that a consistent framework should be adopted within UK groups in most circumstances (see further para 2.22.5). Companies that do not choose to use IFRS will continue to prepare their financial statements under UK GAAP.

UK GAAP

The meaning and composition of UK GAAP

2.5 Generally Accepted Accounting Principles in the United Kingdom (UK GAAP) is a much-used, but undefined term. The components of UK GAAP vary according to the type of company or entity in question. However, in general terms, UK GAAP can be described as follows. The components are divided into elements that are mandatory (in law or in practice) and elements that are not mandatory. The core *mandatory* elements are:

- The Companies Act 2006.
- Accounting standards. That is:
  - Statements of Standard Accounting Practice (SSAPs) developed originally by the Accounting Standards Committee (ASC) and adopted in 1990 by the Accounting Standards Board (ASB).
  - Financial Reporting Standards (FRSs) issued by the ASB since 1990.
- Abstracts issued by the ASB's Urgent Issues Task Force (UITF).
- For listed companies, the Listing Rules.

2.6 Other elements of UK GAAP are authoritative to varying degrees but non-mandatory. These include:

- The ASB's Statement of principles for financial reporting. The Statement does not have the status of an accounting standard. Nevertheless, it is authoritative in two senses. First, the main purpose of the Statement of principles is to provide a frame of reference to guide the ASB in its development of standards. Therefore, it should be helpful in guiding companies and auditors as to the meaning and intention of individual accounting standards, if they are not clear. Secondly, the Statement is intended to provide a valuable source of reference in connection with the accounting treatment of transactions for which there is no specific GAAP.
- Other statements issued by the ASB. These include:
  - 'Half-yearly financial reports' — this was published as a non-mandatory document, but compliance with it was encouraged.
  - 'Preliminary announcements' — the ASB's guidance on preliminary announcements has been issued as a non-mandatory statement.
  - 'Operating and financial review' — in January 2006, the ASB published a best practice reporting statement on the operating and financial review (OFR), which builds on the ASB's previous 2003 statement of best practice on the OFR. See further chapter 2 in the Manual of Accounting — IFRS and UK Supplement.

- Statements and recommendations from the professional bodies. Examples are ICAEW Technical Releases (previously called 'FRAGs') such as Tech 02/10, 'Guidance on the determination of realised profits and losses in the context of distributions under the Companies Act 2006', and ICAEW accounting recommendations such as the members' handbook statements on materiality and 'Accounting for goods sold subject to reservation of title'.

- Established practice. Quite literally, practices that are generally accepted, even though not codified in official literature, can be regarded as part of UK GAAP. Much of this practice is set out in the guidance from leading accounting firms, such as in this Manual.

2.7 A key question is whether the output of the Financial Reporting Review Panel (FRRP) constitutes part of UK GAAP. The practical answer to the question is that it does. As discussed from paragraph 2.85, the FRRP does not issue rules, but announces its findings in relation to individual companies. In general, the companies in question have changed their accounting practices or given additional disclosure, following discussion with the Panel. The Panel generally issues formal statements only where it has concluded that companies have deviated from existing requirements of the Act or accounting standards. However, in some cases, the Panel's views have added to, or modified, the previous understanding of UK GAAP. For example, the Review Panel's press release on the financial statements of Trafalgar House led to the UITF issuing an Abstract on accounting for transfers from current assets to fixed assets. Consequently, companies and auditors should pay particular heed to the announcements from the Panel.

2.8 In addition, there are elements of UK GAAP that relate to specific sectors. Examples are the accounting requirements contained in legislation for banks, housing associations, and charities. Some sector-specific guidance is non-mandatory, and much of this appears in the form of Statements of recommended practice (SORPs), which are discussed from paragraph 2.74.

2.9 The Companies Act 2006 does not define the term 'generally accepted accounting principles', but makes reference in section 853(4) (definition of realised profits and realised losses). In addition, the Companies Act 2006 includes a requirement for companies to state whether the financial statements have been prepared in accordance with applicable Accounting standards and to give particulars of any material departures and the reasons for them (see also from para 2.41). [SI 2008/410 1 Sch 45].

[The next paragraph is 2.21.]

The Companies Act 2006

2.21 Although many detailed accounting rules have been added to companies legislation in recent years, its most important accounting requirements are, perhaps unsurprisingly, those that have been there longest (although not in exactly the same words), namely the requirement for companies to prepare financial statements and the true and fair requirement.

The requirement to prepare financial statements

2.22 The directors are required to prepare financial statements for the company for each financial year that are in compliance with section 395 of the Companies Act 2006. These financial statements may be 'Companies Act individual financial statements' or 'IAS individual financial statements'. Companies Act individual financial statements must comprise a balance sheet as at the last day of the financial year and a profit and loss account for the financial year. [CA06 Sec 396]. The balance sheet must give a true and fair view of the company's state of affairs as at the end of the financial year; and the profit and loss account must give a true and fair view of the company's profit or loss for the financial year. In addition, the financial statements must comply with the provision made by the Secretary of State by regulations as to form and content and additional information provided by way of notes to the financial statements. [CA06 Sec 396(3)].

2.22.1 Companies preparing IAS individual financial statements are simply required to prepare financial statements in accordance with international accounting standards (and to state that they have done so in the note to the financial statements). [CA06 Sec 397]. 'International accounting standards' means IFRS as endorsed by the EU. [CA06 Sec 474]. The general rules and formats, accounting principles and disclosure requirements as outlined in Schedule 1 to SI 2008/410 do not apply to IAS individual financial statements. Financial statements prepared under EU-adopted IFRS are dealt with in the Manual of Accounting — IFRS for the UK.

2.22.2 In addition, if, at the end of the financial year, the company is a parent company within the meaning of the Companies Act 2006, the directors must also prepare consolidated financial statements for the group for the year, unless the company is exempt from that requirement. [CA06 Sec 399(2)].

2.22.3 Companies required to prepare consolidated financial statements under the Act that have any security listed on a regulated market within the EU are required to prepare those consolidated financial statements under EU-adopted IFRS (see para 2.4). These financial statements will be 'IFRS consolidated financial statements'. Companies that are not required to prepare consolidated IFRS financial statements may choose to do so. These financial statements will also be prepared in accordance with EU-adopted IFRS. Where the directors of a parent company prepare IFRS consolidated financial statements, they must state in the notes that the financial statements have been prepared in accordance with international accounting standards. [CA06 Sec 406].

2.22.4 Companies that are parent companies and that do not prepare IFRS consolidated financial statements are required to prepare 'Companies Act consolidated financial statements'. Such financial statements must give a true and fair view of the state of affairs at the end of the financial year and of the profit or loss for the financial year of the undertakings included in the consolidation as a whole, so far as concerns the parent company's members and should consist of a consolidated balance sheet dealing with the state of affairs of the parent company and its subsidiaries as at the last date of the financial year and a profit and loss account for the financial year. In addition, the financial statements must comply with the provision made by the Secretary of State by regulations as to form and content and additional information provided by way of notes to the financial statements. [CA06 Sec 404(3)]. The exemptions from the requirement to prepare consolidated financial statements provided in the Act are discussed in chapter 24.

2.22.5 In most cases, companies have a free choice for financial years beginning on or after 1 January 2005 as to whether they prepare their *individual* financial statements under EU-adopted IFRS or under UK GAAP. Similarly, UK companies whose securities are not traded on a regulated market may prepare their *consolidated* financial statements under EU-adopted IFRS or under UK GAAP. However, the government has implemented some restrictions and conditions:

- Once a company has prepared its financial statements under EU-adopted IFRS, it cannot revert to UK GAAP in a later financial year, unless there is a *"relevant change in circumstance"*. A relevant change in circumstance occurs if the company becomes a subsidiary of an undertaking that is not preparing its individual financial statements under EU-adopted IFRS; if the company ceases to be a subsidiary undertaking; or if the company (or its parent) ceases to have its securities admitted to trading on a regulated market in an EEA state. [CA06 Sec 395(3)(4)].

- A parent company may elect to prepare its individual financial statements under UK GAAP even if it elects to use EU-adopted IFRS in its consolidated financial statements.

- Where the parent company prepares group accounts, companies in the same group must adopt the same accounting framework as each other, unless there are *"good reasons"* not do so. That is, the parent must ensure that all UK companies in the group use either EU-adopted IFRS or UK GAAP. There is an exception to this requirement: where a parent adopts EU-adopted IFRS in both its consolidated financial statements and its individual financial statements, it will not be required to ensure that all its subsidiaries use EU-adopted IFRS too. [CA06 Sec 407]. The Department of Business, Innovation and Skills ('BIS') (formerly the DTI and the BERR) has issued guidance notes on these rules, including an explanation of when there might be 'good reasons' (see para 2.22.6 below).

- Building societies are subject to the same requirements as companies in that they have the option of adopting IFRS in their individual and consolidated financial statements.

- Charitable companies may not prepare financial statements under IFRS. IFRS does not specifically address charity sector transactions and the government believes that the direct application of IFRS without modification through a SORP might create 'interpretational issues'. In addition, there are no plans to permit unincorporated charities to use IFRS; adoption of IFRS by charitable corporations would, therefore, lead to inconsistency within the charity sector.

2.22.6 The BIS has issued guidance notes to help companies to apply these rules and these include an explanation of where there might be 'good reasons' for the directors not to prepare all the individual financial statements within a group by using the same accounting framework. The provision is intended to allow a degree of flexibility where there are genuine, including cost/benefit, grounds for not using the same framework. Such reasons would include:

- An IFRS group acquires a subsidiary that does not use IFRS. In the year of acquisition, it might not be practicable for the newly-acquired subsidiary to switch to IFRS straight away.
- A group might include subsidiaries that are themselves publicly traded, in which case market pressures or regulatory requirements to use IFRS might come into play, without necessarily justifying a switch to IFRS by the non-publicly traded subsidiaries.
- Where a subsidiary or a parent is planning to list and so might wish to convert to IFRS in advance, but the rest of the group is not intending to list.
- The group might include small subsidiaries where the cost of switching the accounting framework might outweigh the benefits from doing so.

It is essential that if the parent's directors decide to adopt a different framework for any entities within the group that they are able to justify any inconsistency to shareholders, regulators or other interested parties. [BIS Guidance para 4.16].

2.22.7 The BIS guidance notes do not make any specific mention of tax as a 'good reason' for adopting a different framework for one or more subsidiaries within a group. In commercial terms, tax is a business cost like any other. We have sought advice from legal counsel as to whether tax may be a good reason. The question is one of degree, depends on individual facts and circumstances, and the directors must weigh up various matters in reaching their conclusion.

2.22.7.1 In the case of existing arrangements or structures, where a transition from UK GAAP to EU-adopted IFRS would result in a significant increase or potential volatility in taxable profits, or a significant acceleration of tax cash outflows, or introduce a significant new tax exposure compared with the company continuing to use UK GAAP, the tax consequences may well be a 'good reason' to keep one or more subsidiaries on UK GAAP. For example, a company's revenue recognition might be accelerated under IFRS and thus tax payments might also be accelerated. In this context, 'significant' might be in absolute terms or relative to the size of the company affected. However, a trivial tax effect should not be used as an excuse to keep a company on UK GAAP. Similarly if as a result of a company using EU-adopted IFRS the group could no longer claim the benefits of existing tax planning (or the benefits would be significantly reduced or new tax risks would arise under EU-adopted IFRS such that the planning would not have been entered into with companies using EU-adopted IFRS), the tax effect of using EU-adopted IFRS may be a good reason for one or subsidiaries to remain on UK GAAP. However, as noted above, it is also necessary to weigh up other matters in reaching the conclusion on whether tax may be a good reason, such as comparability with the rest of the group.

2.22.7.2 In contrast, where the accounting frameworks of subsidiaries in a group are currently aligned, the burden of proof to justify departing from this situation is more onerous. The main purpose of having aligned accounting frameworks is to enable shareholders (among other interested parties) to understand the accounts and compare them with the accounts of other companies in the group. In considering whether there are good reasons to adopt different accounting frameworks, the directors must ask how obscure or difficult to understand different accounting frameworks would make the accounts in comparison to the rest of the group. Other factors include how certain it is that any tax planning arrangements put in place will lead to tax benefit, the size of any ensuing tax saving and reputational risk.

2.22.8 Further guidance on which companies are required to use IFRS and which companies may optionally use it is given in chapter 2 of the Manual of Accounting — IFRS for the UK.

The true and fair requirement

2.23 In relation to Companies Act individual accounts, in addition to requiring companies to prepare accounts, the Companies Act 2006 section 396 specifies that the financial statements must:

- *"in the case of the balance sheet, give a true and fair view of the state of affairs of the company as at the end of the financial year; and, in the case of the profit and loss account, give a true and fair view of the profit or loss of the company for the financial year."* [CA06 Sec 396(2)].
- *"...comply with provision made by the Secretary of State by regulations as to the form and content of the balance sheet and profit and loss account and additional information to be provided by way of notes to the accounts."* [CA06 Sec 396(3)].

2.24 In most cases, companies are able to comply with both of these sub-sections at the same time. That is, compliance with the provisions made by the Secretary of State is consistent with the requirement to give a true and fair view.

2.25 However, this will not always be the case. The Act makes clear that the true and fair requirement is overriding, and sets this out in the following way:

- The Companies Act 2006 section 396(4) provides that:

"If compliance with the regulations and any other provision made by or under this Act as to the matters to be included in a company's individual accounts or in notes to those accounts, would not be sufficient to give a true and fair view, the necessary additional information must be given in the accounts or in a note to them."

- The Companies Act 2006 section 396(5) adds that:

"If in special circumstances compliance with any of those provisions is inconsistent with the requirement to give a true and fair view, the directors must depart from that provision to the extent necessary to give a true and fair view."

- The Companies Act 2006 section 396(5) notes that:

"Particulars of any such departure, the reasons for it and its effect must be given in a note to the accounts."

[The next paragraph is 2.27.]

2.27 Section 396(4) of the Companies Act 2006 can be seen as saying merely that compliance with the specific requirements of regulation and other parts of the Act is the minimum requirement. There may be a number of situations in which additional information has to be given, for example, to explain a somewhat unusual transaction. Without that explanation, the financial statements could not be said to give a true and fair view; but with the explanation added they do. Adding the information is the obvious solution and there is no need to consider departing from the specific rules. An example might be that, in order to give a true and fair view, it might be necessary to give information about a transaction with a related party.

2.28 Section 396(5), on the other hand, comes into operation when, owing to 'special circumstances', the accounting treatment otherwise required by the Act does not give a true and fair view, that is, if the treatment otherwise required by the Act (even with the provision of additional information) is inconsistent with a true and fair view.

2.29 Sub-sections 396(4) and 396(5) can, therefore, be seen not so much as sequential provisions, but as alternative provisions to assist in achieving a true and fair view. Each has a role in its own circumstances: sub-section 396(4) of the Companies Act 2006 comes into play where there is *insufficient* information; sub-section 396(5) of the Companies Act 2006 comes into play where there is the *wrong kind* of accounting treatment.

2.30 Although the notion of departing from the otherwise specific rules in order to give a true and fair view is a powerful and important one, that does not mean it is something that should be done frequently or cavalierly. Indeed, it is a treatment to be adopted sparingly. As sub-section 396(5) makes clear, it is only to be used 'in special circumstances'. This means that it is not intended to be used as a route through which all companies can disregard a specific rule of the Act.

2.31 With few exceptions, such as SSAP19 (where companies are required to value investment properties rather than depreciate them, which is what the Act requires), the general understanding is that the override should only be used in the special circumstances of an individual company that has a different situation from most other companies. In practice, this can be extended to a class of companies, for example, in a particular industry, which has considerations that differ from the generality of companies. An example here is that in the past it has been regarded as acceptable for companies in the securities industry to use the override to 'mark to market' their current asset investments and take the resultant gains to the profit and loss account rather than, as the Act required, to the revaluation reserve. The reason it was acceptable for these types of companies is that, because of the nature of their businesses, this treatment gave a true and fair view of their performance, whereas the Act's treatment did not generally do so. However, other types of companies that adopted that practice had to demonstrate that they have special circumstances of their own. (The Act's rules have now been changed to permit fair value accounting for certain financial instruments — see further chapter 6.)

2.32 The majority of departures from the Act's accounting provisions in practice derive from requirements of accounting standards where the applicable accounting standard is inconsistent with the Act — for example, non-amortisation of goodwill with indefinite life (FRS 10).

2.33 Sub-section 396(5) requires certain disclosures to be given when the override is used. These disclosures are detailed in paragraph 2.42.

2.34 As discussed above, Companies Act consolidated financial statements are also required to give a true and fair view. [CA06 Sec 404(2)]. Sub-sections 404(4) and 404(5) contain identical provisions with respect to consolidated financial statements as sub-sections 396(4) and 396(5) respectively. Therefore, the discussion above applies equally to Companies Act consolidated financial statements.

Compliance with accounting standards and UITF abstracts

2.35 FRS 18, 'Accounting policies', recognises that the Act's requirement to give a true and fair view is paramount:

> "*An entity should adopt accounting policies that enable its financial statements to give a true and fair view. Those accounting policies should be consistent with the requirements of accounting standards, Urgent Issues Task Force (UITF) Abstracts and companies legislation.*" [FRS 18 para 14].

2.36 There is a general presumption that compliance with accounting standards is required to meet the true and fair requirement. The legal opinion supporting this presumption is discussed from paragraph 2.78. In addition, paragraph 45 of Schedule 1 to SI 2008/410 requires companies to state in their financial statements whether they have been prepared in accordance with applicable accounting standards and to give the particulars and reasons for any material departures from those standards. Table 2.1 contains an example of a paragraph 45 statement.

Table 2.1 — Eleco plc — Annual report and financial statements — 30 June 2006

1 Accounting policies (extract)

The financial statements have been prepared in accordance with applicable accounting standards in the United Kingdom.

A summary of the more important Group accounting policies, which have been applied consistently, is set out below.

[The next paragraph is 2.38.]

2.38 While compliance with accounting standards and UITF Abstracts is usually required in order for financial statements to give a true and fair view, in exceptional circumstances a departure from an accounting standard or UITF Abstract may be necessary to meet the true and fair requirement. Where compliance with the requirements of an accounting standard or UITF Abstract is inconsistent with the requirement to give a true and fair view, FRS 18 requires a departure to the extent necessary to give a true and fair view. [FRS 18 para 15].

2.39 FRS 18's true and fair override in respect of accounting standards and UITF Abstracts is similar to the Act's true and fair override in respect of the Act's accounting provisions and applies to all types of entities whose financial statements are intended to give a true and fair view. Departures from accounting standards are, however, very rare indeed and should be handled with great care. The ASB's Foreword to Accounting Standards emphasises that compliance with accounting standards will normally be necessary to give a true and fair view because they are formulated with the objective of ensuring that the resulting financial information faithfully represents the underlying commercial activity.

2.40 FRS 18 explicitly provides a sequential approach to the true and fair override. First, entities need to consider what can be achieved by additional disclosure. A departure from an accounting standard is a last resort when a true and fair view cannot be achieved by additional disclosure. [FRS 18 para 16].

True and fair override disclosures

2.41 Where a company departs from any of the Act's accounting provisions in order to give a true and fair view, the Act requires that "*. . .particulars of any such departure, the reasons for it and its effect shall be given in a note to the accounts*". [CA06 Sec 396(5)].

2.42 The true and fair override disclosures required by FRS 18 give a more precise meaning to particulars, reasons and effect and bring together equivalent disclosures in respect of departures from the accounting provisions of the Companies Act or other relevant legislation, accounting standards and UITF Abstracts. The disclosures should include:

- A clear and unambiguous statement that there has been a departure from the requirements of an accounting standard, a UITF Abstract or companies legislation and that the departure is necessary to give a true and fair view.
- A statement of the treatment that would normally be required in the circumstances and a description of the treatment actually adopted.
- A statement as to why the treatment prescribed would not give a true and fair view.
- A description of how the position shown in the financial statements is different as a result of the departure, normally with quantification of the difference (except where quantification is self-evident or cannot reasonably be made, in which latter case the circumstances should be explained).

[FRS 18 para 62]

2.43 The disclosures referred to in the previous paragraph should be given considerable prominence. They should either be included in the note that discloses compliance with applicable accounting standards under paragraph 45 of Schedule 1 to SI 2008/410, or that note should include a cross reference to where such disclosures can be found. [FRS 18 para 64]. As explained earlier, the most common uses of the 'true and fair override' are overrides of company law that are required by accounting standards. In these cases, the applicable accounting standards have of course been complied with.

2.44 It should be noted that the fact that quantification of the effect may be regarded as misleading or meaningless is not, under FRS 18 or the Act, an acceptable reason for omitting it. To give an example of an override that cannot reasonably be quantified, it is not normally possible to quantify the effect of departing from the Companies Act where goodwill on an acquisition is not amortised — by ascribing an indefinite life (as permitted by FRS 10 in special circumstances), there is no benchmark for calculating an amortisation charge required by the Act.

The UK financial reporting structure

2.45 In the UK, the detail of accounting standards remains outside of legislation. However, UK legislation includes certain relevant requirements:

- For all large companies, directors are required to state in the notes to the financial statements whether they are drawn up in accordance with applicable accounting standards and to draw attention to any material departures, explaining the reasons for the departures.

- Certain authorised bodies or the Secretary of State have the statutory power to apply to the courts for an order requiring the revision of financial statements that do not give a true and fair view.

2.46 The task of devising accounting standards is discharged by the Accounting Standards Board (ASB) that issues standards on its own authority. The Financial Reporting Council (FRC) provides guidance to the ASB on priorities for its work programme and on issues of public interest and acts as an instrument for promoting good practice in relation to accounting standards. In securing compliance with accounting standards in support of the 'true and fair' requirement, the Financial Reporting Review Panel [FRRP] exists to examine contentious departures from accounting standards by large companies.

2.47 UK company law includes procedures enabling directors voluntarily to revise financial statements that are discovered to be defective. [CA06 Sec 454]. Further enabling provisions permit the Secretary of State to improve the enforcement of accounting provisions by requiring an explanation from directors of apparent failures to prepare financial statements that comply with the Act. [CA06 Sec 455(1) to (3)]. If a satisfactory explanation is not received, the Secretary of State may apply to the court for a declaration that a company's financial statements do not comply with the Act and to order them to be revised. [CA06 Sec 455(4)]. The Act's provisions relating to the revision of defective financial statements are dealt with in chapter 8 of the Manual of Accounting — Management reports and governance.

The Financial Reporting Council

2.48 The Financial Reporting Council Limited (FRC) was established in 1990 with, at the time, two subsidiaries, the Accounting Standards Board Limited and the Financial Reporting Review Panel Limited. The purpose of these bodies is to provide an institutional framework to underpin financial reporting in the UK. The accountancy profession, the City and the government share in the funding of these bodies.

2.49 The FRC is the single independent accountancy regulator. It comprises a Board and six operating bodies. The organisation of the FRC is represented in the following diagram:

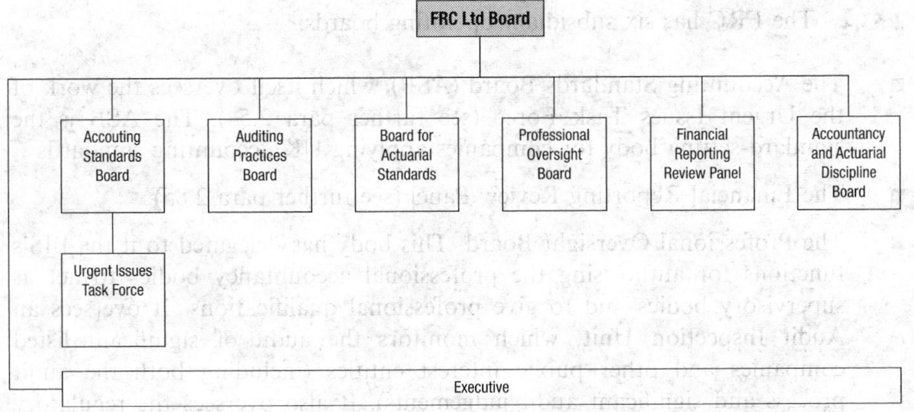

[The next paragraph is 2.53.2].

2.53.2 Since November 2007, the FRC has operated with a single governing body, the Board. The Board has sixteen members, being eight non-executive members, the six chairs of the operating boards, the CEO and the chairman.

2.53.3 The chair and deputy chair of the FRC Board are appointed by the Secretary of State for Business, Innovation and Skills, other directors are appointed by the FRC Board. The Board:

- Determines the FRC's strategy and priorities.
- Sets the FRC's budget, secures the necessary funding and monitors expenditure.
- Oversees the delivery by each operating body of their functions through regular reports from the operating body chairs.
- Oversees the performance of the Executive through regular reports from the CEO.
- Makes appointments to the Board, the operating bodies and senior management.
- Monitors the UK Corporate Governance Code and approves any changes to the Code and related guidance.
- Approves any significant structural changes to the FRC.
- Ensures that the FRC and its operating bodies achieve high levels of accountability and transparency.
- Undertakes an annual assessment of the risks to the FRC's overall success and oversees the necessary risk mitigation plan.
- Undertakes annual evaluation of the FRC's performance and that of its committees against its objectives, including a review of the schedule of matters reserved for the Board.

[FRC web site 2011].

2.53.4 The FRC has six subsidiary operating boards:

- The Accounting Standards Board (ASB), which itself oversees the work of the Urgent Issues Task Force (see further para 2.54). The ASB is the standard-setting body for companies applying UK accounting standards.
- The Financial Reporting Review Panel (see further para 2.85).
- The Professional Oversight Board. This body has delegated to it the BIS's functions for authorising the professional accountancy bodies to act as supervisory bodies and to give professional qualifications. It oversees an Audit Inspection Unit, which monitors the audit of significant listed companies and other public interest entities (including both the audit process and significant audit judgements). It also oversees the regulatory activities of the professional accountancy bodies.
- The Auditing Practices Board (APB). The APB's responsibilities have increased and now encompass setting ethical standards for auditors as well as setting auditing standards.
- The Accountancy and Actuarial Discipline Board (the AADB). This body is responsible for investigating significant public interest disciplinary cases, including sanctioning those found guilty of misconduct.
- The Board for Actuarial Standards (BAS). This body has the objective of promoting competence and transparency of actuarial practice and will do this by establishing and improving actuarial standards and ensuring that they are coherent, consistent and comprehensive.

In addition, the Committee on Corporate Governance, whose members are drawn from the FRC, assists it in its work on corporate governance.

2.53.5 The operating bodies:

- Make regulatory decisions for which they are responsible in a way that has regard to the FRC's regulatory strategy, plan and budget.
- Keep under review any emerging risks or other matters that could affect those aspects of confidence in corporate reporting and governance that fall within their remit.
- Make appointments to working groups and committees, in consultation, where appropriate, with the Chair of the FRC.
- Undertake annual evaluations of their own performance and that of their sub-committees.

[FRC web site 2011].

2.53.6 In applying their regulatory strategy, the FRC aims to:

- Work on the basis that a well-informed market is the best regulator, but in relation to some of its responsibilities, it has been given significant powers and it does not hesitate to use them when appropriate.
- Targeting the use of its powers, taking a proactive, risk-based and proportionate approach.
- Emphasising principles and clarity in its standard-setting and rule-making.
- Being consultative — involving preparers, auditors, users of corporate reports and other regulatory organisations in its decision-making and allowing adequate time for consultation, without compromising its independence or confidentiality.
- Recognising the importance of professional judgement in the way in which standards and rules are applied and enforced.
- Where discharging a judicial or quasi-judicial function, to do so in accordance with the FRC's formal powers and the rules of natural justice.
- Being transparent, accountable and efficient in its work, and ensuring that it receives appropriate publicity.

[FRC web site 2011].

2.53.7 The FRC notes that companies and pension funds, supported by their professional advisors and encouraged by the investor community, have the primary responsibility for achieving high standards of reporting and governance and that an ethical approach to business should make the achievement of these standards more likely. Furthermore, the FRC notes that no system of regulation can ever eliminate the possibility of corporate reporting or governance failures; it believes that it is impossible to achieve zero failure and any attempt to do so would destroy wealth rather than facilitate its creation.

The Accounting Standards Board

2.54 The Accounting Standards Board (ASB) is the authority that has been prescribed by statutory instrument as the standard making body for the purposes of section 464(1) of the Companies Act 2006. The accounting standards (designated FRSs) that it issues, amends and withdraws are 'accounting standards' for the purpose of the Act's accounting requirements. This is in contrast to the accounting standards that were set by the ASB's predecessor, the ASC, that were designated as SSAPs. Previously neither the ASC nor its SSAPs were given statutory recognition. At its inception, the ASB adopted the SSAPs extant at that time so that, until they are withdrawn by the ASB, they now have the same authority and statutory backing as FRSs.

2.55 Unlike the ASC, the ASB is totally independent and needs no outside approval for its actions either from the Council, from government, or from any other source. The ASC had been criticised as being slow in setting standards since agreement for a new standard was required from all its sponsoring bodies. These sponsoring bodies were the six accountancy bodies making up the CCAB. The ASB has a full-time chairman and full-time technical director and is supported by greater staff resources than the ASC. However, the Board has fewer members than the ASC. In addition, other part-time Board members are drawn from industry and commerce, investor institutions and others with an interest in financial reporting as well as the accountancy profession. Membership of the ASB is limited to ten and since a majority of seven is needed for any decision to adopt, revise or withdraw an accounting standard, the standard setting process is designed be more streamlined.

2.56 However, the ASB has stated that it wishes to ensure wide consultation and to be as open as possible in its dealings. As well as issuing exposure drafts of proposed FRSs (FREDs), it publishes discussion papers on topics as they reach an appropriate stage of development and, in exceptional circumstances, it may hold public hearings about a particular problem.

2.57 The ASB has published a 'Statement of aims' which sets out its approach to the task of setting standards and lists the guidelines it will follow in conducting its affairs. The ASB intends to achieve its aims by:

- Developing principles to guide it in establishing standards and providing a framework within which others can exercise judgement in resolving accounting issues.
- Issuing new accounting standards, or amending existing ones, in response to evolving business practices, new economic developments and deficiencies being identified in current practice.
- Addressing urgent issues promptly.

[Statement of aims].

2.58 The ASB works under a conceptual framework of financial reporting principles called the Statement of principles. The content of the Statement of principles is discussed from paragraph 2.191. The effort to create such a framework placed much more emphasis on the underlying concepts. The Statement of principles also supports the ASB's expectation that the spirit and reasoning of accounting standards should be followed, not merely the rules contained within them.

2.59 The ASB has had a strategy of convergence with international developments for some time. Indeed, one of its aims (issued in July 1991) is *"To ensure that through a process of regular communication, accounting standards are produced with due regard to international developments"*. [Statement of aims]. Accounting standards published since 1994 have had an appendix detailing compliance with international accounting standards and many standards published have been broadly in line with international developments. This process has, however, been accelerated and more formally set out in recent years, primarily because of the EU 2005 Regulation (see para 2.4).

2.60 In March 2005, the ASB issued an exposure draft, 'Accounting standard-setting in a changing environment: the role of the Accounting Standards Board'. This confirmed the proposal in the March 2004 discussion paper that the ASB planned to converge UK GAAP to IFRS, over the four years to 2009.

2.61 The convergence of UK GAAP with IFRS is proving controversial, not least because of the IASB's own plans to converge with US GAAP. In May 2006, the ASB began a consultation process to consider the future application of reporting requirements for UK companies. This requested views on the future application of IFRS for UK companies. The ASB considered a number of options, depending on the type of company.

2.62 In October 2006, the ASB posted onto its web site feedback on the tentative proposals. The responses to the press notice broadly support a two-tier approach. Under this approach full IFRS would be applied to UK quoted and other publicly accountable companies and the lower level of small and medium-sized companies would potentially (and ideally) be subject to a suite of standards based on the IASB's SME project. However, the feedback statement made clear that the ASB would not come to a firm view on the convergence of UK standards with IFRS until there was a much clearer understanding on the IASB's proposals on accounting for SMEs.

2.63 In October 2010, the UK ASB issued FRED 43 and 44 outlining the future for UK financial reporting. The proposals in these FREDs recognised that one size of accounting standard does not fit all entities. They propose a tier system for financial reporting that requires entities to prepare financial statements in one of the following three tiers (an entity may voluntarily elect to adopt a higher tier):

Tier	Description	Type of accounting
Tier 1	Listed companies and other publicly accountable entities	Full EU-adopted IFRS
Tier 2	All other entities	The ASB's Financial Reporting Standard for Medium-sized Entities
Tier 3	Small companies (as defined by company law)	The ASB's Financial Reporting Standard for Smaller Entities (FRSSE)

The comment period for this proposal closed on 30 April 2011. The ASB proposes an effective date of accounting periods beginning on or after 1 July 2013, with earlier application permitted

2.63.1 In March 2011 the Accounting Standards Board (ASB) published Financial Reporting Exposure Draft (FRED) 45 setting out proposals for a Financial Reporting Standard for Public Benefit Entities (FRSPBE) to accompany the proposed Financial Reporting Standard for Medium-size Entities (FRSME). The comment period for this proposal closed on 31 July 2011.

2.63.2 In July 2011 following its tentative decision to remove the definition of public accountability, the ASB discussed the need for a revised definition of a qualifying subsidiary, that is those eligible to apply the reduced disclosure framework, as well as any additional disclosures that should be added to the FRSME for those entities that will no longer be forced into Tier 1 (EU IFRS) such as listed entities that are not on a regulated market or entities that hold assets in a fiduciary capacity. The ASB considered how their recent tentative decisions would affect the draft impact assessment set out in FRED 43, noting that its tentative decisions represented a significant change from its proposals in the FRED and that in contrast to its proposals in the FRED the implementation costs should be reduced. The Board considered it should review the project's objectives at a future meeting in view of changes being made to the proposals.

2.63.3 Since July 2011 the ASB have made several tentative decisions that fundamentally change the proposals set out in the FRED documents, namely.

- Application of 'EU IFRS' will not be extended beyond current requirements in law. That is Tier 1 (EU IFRS) will be restricted to groups listed on a regulated exchange.
- The requirement for other publicly accountable entities to use EU IFRS has been removed.
- Guidance for Tier 2, the FRSME, will be expanded to include areas such as segment reporting, EPS and interim reporting; and additional disclosure requirements for financial institutions.
- Principles for amending the IFRS for SME will be changed to permit certain accounting options that exist in current UK GAAP, such as the revaluation of property, plant and equipment; and capitalisation of development costs and/or borrowing costs.
- The effective date will be deferred to periods beginning on or after 1 January 2014.

All subsidiaries will be permitted to take advantage of the reduced disclosure regime. The FREDs had restricted this to qualifying subsidiaries only (entities that are not publicly accountable). Subsidiaries that are financial institutions will not be exempt from IFRS 7, 'Financial instruments: Disclosures'.

2.64 In addition to issuing accounting and reporting standards, the ASB may, from time to time, issue other forms of guidance on best practice. The ASB is attempting to create a virtuous circle where companies are encouraged to provide more informative financial statements. For instance, non-mandatory statements of best practice have been issued on the contents of half-yearly reports and preliminary announcements of full year results.

FRSs and SSAPs

2.65 For entities operating under the Companies Act and standards issued by the ASB (that is, those entities not adopting IFRS), FRSs and SSAPs are applicable to all financial statements of an entity that are intended to give a true and fair view. These accounting standards also apply to consolidated financial statements, including amounts relating to overseas entities that are included in the consolidation.

2.66 However, accounting standards need not be applied to immaterial items. Accounting standards also do not override exemptions from disclosure given by law to certain types of entity. For example, groups that are exempt by virtue of their size from the Companies Act requirements to prepare consolidated financial statements, are not expected to comply with accounting standards dealing with consolidated financial statements.

2.67 In addition, accounting standards themselves may exclude certain entities from their scope. For example, the requirements of SSAP 25, 'Segmental reporting', that are additional to the statutory segmental disclosure requirements and certain disclosure requirements of SSAP 13, 'Accounting for research and development', do not apply to private limited companies unless they exceed the criteria, multiplied in each case by 10, for defining a medium-sized company under section 465 of the Companies Act 2006.

2.68 The application of accounting standards to smaller entities has been a controversial issue for a number of years. Various studies were carried out and recommendations made. In the mid 1990's a new approach emerged, that small companies should comply with a single simplified accounting standard designed specifically for them. The ASB issued the 'Financial reporting standard for smaller entities' (FRSSE) in November 1997 and has revised and updated it periodically (see chapter 32).

2.69 The Foreword to accounting standards states that the prescription of accounting requirements for the public sector in the UK is a matter for government. The government's requirements with regard to public sector bodies that prepare financial statements may or may not refer to accounting standards. Therefore public sector bodies are not specifically required to comply with accounting standards although there is an expectation that they should do so if their financial statements are required to give a true and fair view, unless the government considers it inappropriate.

2.70 The ASB has stated that, in general, when a new accounting standard is issued, it should be applied to all material transactions regardless of the date they were entered into. This would prevent similar transactions being accounted for in different ways in the same financial statements depending on when they occurred. It would also aid comparability between the financial statements of different entities.

2.71 However, the ASB accepts that in a few instances the application of a new accounting standard to past transactions would involve considerable work and may result in information that would be difficult for users to interpret. In these instances, the ASB may exclude transactions that took place before the standard came into force from its scope. FRS 6 and FRS 7, for example, applied in respect of business combinations first accounted for in financial statements relating to accounting periods commencing on or after 23 December 1994. Therefore, the accounting treatment of acquisitions and mergers that were first accounted for before these standards came into effect was not changed.

2.72 The ASB states in the Foreword that until an exposure draft (or discussion paper) is converted into a standard, the requirements of any existing standard that would be affected by the proposals remain in force. FRS 18 reiterates the position that entities should not adopt new proposals if they conflict with existing accounting standards or UITF Abstracts. Exposure drafts are subject to amendment and even more amendment can be expected to proposals contained in discussion papers. Companies wishing to incorporate new proposals into their financial statements may do so as long as the new proposal does not conflict with an existing accounting standard. Alternatively, additional information could be provided in a supplementary form such as in *pro forma* financial statements. [Foreword paras 31, 32; FRS 18 para 47]

2.73 Accounting standards are kept under review and are revised from time to time to reflect changes in the business environment and in accounting thinking. However, it has been the ASB's practice to ensure that standards are given an appropriate period to become established before they are subject to review.

SORPs

2.74 Specific industry groups are recognised by the ASB to develop Statements of Recommended Practice (SORPs) under a code of practice. SORPs give guidance on the application of accounting standards to specialised industries and non-profit-making sectors. Whilst the ASB does not approve or frank SORPs, it monitors their development and, if satisfied, provides a negative assurance statement confirming that the SORP does not appear to contain any fundamental points of principle that are unacceptable in the context of current accounting practice or conflict with existing accounting standards.

2.75 The sectors for which SORPs are presently in issue, or under development, are:

- Authorised funds.
- Banking (see para 2.77.1 below).
- Charities.
- Further and higher education institutions.
- Insurance.

- Investment trusts.
- Local authorities.
- Oil and gas.
- Pension schemes.
- Registered social landlords.
- Unit trusts.
- Leasing.
- Open-ended investment companies (OEICs).
- Limited liability partnerships.

2.76 Although SORPs are themselves non-mandatory, their status in UK GAAP was enhanced by the publication of FRS 18. FRS 18 indicates that if accounting practices set out in a SORP are generally followed in an industry, they will be particularly persuasive in the selection of the most appropriate accounting policies by entities in the industry. FRS 18 also introduced a requirement for entities that fall within the scope of a SORP to provide a compliance statement in their financial statements. Such entities should:

- State the title of the SORP and whether the financial statements have been prepared in accordance with the SORP's provisions currently in effect.
- If the financial statements do not comply with the SORP, give a brief description of the departure, including:
  - the reasons why any treatment that is not in accordance with the SORP is judged more appropriate to the entity's particular circumstances, and
  - details of any disclosures recommended by the SORP that have been omitted and reasons for the omission.

[FRS 18 para 58].

2.77 Other relevant authorities may also encourage compliance with SORPs. For example, the Occupational Pension Schemes (Requirement to obtain Audited Accounts and a Statement from the Auditor) Regulations 1996 require pension schemes to which the regulations apply to state whether the financial statements have been prepared in accordance with the relevant SORP and to disclose any material departures.

2.77.1 In January 2006, the British Bankers' Association (BBA) announced that its four SORPs on financial instruments (covering advances, commitments and contingencies, derivatives and securities) are superseded on adoption of FRS 26, 'Financial instruments: Measurement'. Wording has been added to the four SORPs such that on adopting FRS 26, the non-compliance statement required by FRS 18 (see para 2.76) no longer applies. The BBA's SORP on segmental reporting remains in place for companies reporting under UK GAAP, until UK and international standards converge.

Counsel's opinion on true and fair view and role of accounting standards

2.78 As discussed from paragraph 2.23 above, the Act's overriding requirement is that 'Companies Act' financial statements must give a true and fair view of the entity's state of affairs at the balance sheet date and its profit and loss for the financial period ending on that date. The question then arises as to what is meant by a 'true and fair view'. In particular, there is the question of whether the requirement that all financial statements should give a true and fair view includes compliance with the relevant accounting standards. True and fair is a legal concept that can only be interpreted by the courts.

2.79 In 1993, the ASB obtained an opinion from Mary Arden QC on the relationship between compliance with accounting standards and the requirement that all financial statements should give a true and fair view.

2.80 To obtain a full understanding of Counsel's arguments, the opinion should be read in its entirety. However, the opinion makes the following important points.

- Although the question of whether financial statements satisfy the true and fair requirement is a matter of law, the court cannot interpret the requirement without evidence as to the practices and views of accountants. The more authoritative these practices and views are, the more ready the court will be to follow them.
- Accounting standards initially identify proper accounting practice for the benefit of preparers and auditors of financial statements. However, because financial statements commonly comply with accounting standards, the effect of the standards is to create a common understanding between users and preparers about how particular items are dealt with and to create an expectation that financial statements will comply with applicable accounting standards, unless there is a good reason not to comply.
- The Companies Act gives statutory recognition to the existence of accounting standards. The court infers from company law that statutory policy favours both the issue of accounting standards (by a body prescribed by regulation) and compliance with them. The court also infers from company law that, since there is a requirement to disclose particulars of non-compliance, financial statements that meet the true and fair requirement will generally follow rather than depart from accounting standards. Therefore, the likelihood is increased that the courts will hold that, in general, compliance with applicable accounting standards is necessary to meet the true and fair requirement.
- Company law envisages the possibility of a departure from applicable accounting standards, provided that particulars of the departure and the

reasons for it are disclosed in the financial statements. However, the departure must be appropriate in the particular circumstances of the company. If the court is satisfied that an accounting standard should have been followed to meet the true and fair requirement, then non-compliance, even with the necessary disclosure, will result in a breach of the true and fair requirement.

2.80.1 Since then, the financial reporting environment has changed significantly, with the introduction of IFRS in 2005 and the implementation of the Companies Act 2006 in 2008, as well as changes to UK GAAP. As a result, there have been some questions over the continuing applicability of these earlier opinions. In particular, some users of financial statements have questioned whether the requirement in IFRS to 'present fairly' is the equal of 'showing a true and fair view'. To address these concerns, the FRC sought an opinion from Martin Moore QC on whether the requirements of the Companies Act 2006 or EU legislation (including the application of IFRS to EU listed companies and the subsequent endorsement of international standards and interpretations) require any revisions to the 1993 Arden opinion. Martin Moore QC confirmed that the previous opinion remains valid. In particular, he noted that:

- The requirement in IFRS for financial statements to 'present fairly' is not different from the Companies Act requirement to give a true and fair view: it is a different articulation of the same concept.
- The requirement for financial statements to give a true and fair view (or a fair presentation) is paramount.
- Like UK GAAP, IFRS permits the departure from an accounting standard, if required, in order to preserve the true and fair view, but only under limited circumstances.
- Although compliance with accounting standards (either IFRS or UK GAAP) is highly likely to result in a true and fair view (or fair presentation), their application should not be a mechanical process as this outcome cannot be guaranteed.
- The concept of 'true and fair' (or 'fair presentation') comes into play, for example: in the way a standard is applied, in consideration of whether, in extremely rare circumstances, a standard should be departed from, in choices where two or more relevant but incompatible standards could be applied and in determining the accounting where no relevant standard exists.
- The requirement contained in the EU Transparency Obligations Directive for half-yearly reports to give a true and fair view does not change the analysis of what is a true and fair view.
- The provisions of the Companies Act 2006 have served to underline and reinforce the centrality of the true and fair requirement to the preparation of financial statements.

2.80.2 In his opinion, Martin Moore QC notes that *"Compliance with accounting standards is not an end in itself, but the means to an end"*.

The Urgent Issues Task Force

2.81 Although not envisaged by the revisions to the Act, the ASB also issues UITF Abstracts that set out the consensus reached by its committee, the Urgent Issues Task Force. The main role of the UITF is not to write new accounting standards, but to assist in areas where an accounting standard or Companies Act provision exists, but where unsatisfactory or conflicting interpretations have developed or seem likely to develop. In addition, the ASB may seek the UITF's view on significant accounting developments in areas where there is no extant legal provision or accounting standard.

2.82 The UITF seeks to reach a consensus among its fifteen voting members who are drawn from the accounting profession and the wider business community. Eleven voting members constitute a quorum at meetings and a consensus is achieved if not more than two of the voting members present at a meeting dissent. Although the UITF exposes draft Abstracts, the time for comment is generally much shorter than for accounting standards. Therefore, the UITF should be able to respond more quickly to emerging issues than the ASB. However, since the consultation time is reduced, the ASB ensures that matters on the UITF's agenda and other information about its activities are published.

2.83 The ASB regards UITF Abstracts as generally accepted accounting practice in the areas they address and as part of the body of accounting pronouncements that must be followed in order for financial statements to give a true and fair view. The ASB expects to adopt a UITF consensus, unless it conflicts with law, accounting standards or the ASB's policy or future plans.

2.84 The status of UITF Abstracts is considered in the ASB's legal opinion (see para 2.79). This opinion sets out the process of creating UITF Abstracts and their consideration and publishing by the ASB. It then argues that since the CCAB, the ASB and the profession expect UITF Abstracts to be followed and this expectation has been borne out in practice, there will be a readiness on the part of the court to accept that compliance with UITF Abstracts is also necessary to meet the true and fair requirement.

The Financial Reporting Review Panel

2.85 The Financial Reporting Review Panel (FRRP) sits alongside the ASB. Its role is to examine material departures from the Act's accounting requirements, including the accounting standards. The Companies Act 2006 provides for the Secretary of State to enquire into the accounts of companies (s455) and, where necessary, to apply for a court order requiring their revision (s456). The Secretary of State has the power to authorise others to apply to the Court (s457). The FRRP was given this authority by The Companies (Defective Accounts and Directors' Reports) (Authorised Person) and Supervision of Accounts and

Reports (Prescribed Body) Order (SI 2008 No. 623). Pursuant to its Operating Procedures the Panel handles cases involving public and large private companies [FRRP website 2011]. All other cases fall to the Department of Business, Innovation and Skills (BIS). The following types of company fall within the FRRP's authority:

- Public limited companies, unless they are subsidiaries in small or medium-sized groups.
- Companies within a group headed by a public limited company.
- Any private company that does not qualify as small or medium-sized as defined by section 381 and 465 of the Companies Act 2006.
- Any private company within a group that does not qualify as small or medium-sized.

[FRRP operating procedures para 11].

2.86 The FRRP, in addition to responding to complaints, selects financial statements on the basis of risk. It will select reports, *"by methods which take into account the Panel's assessment of the risk of non-compliance and the consequence of non-compliance"*. [FRRP operating procedures para 3]. The panel focuses its activities on the financial statements in specific industries, following its risk-based assessment and after discussions with the FSA and the panel's Standing Advisory Group. The panel also conducts targeted reviews to check compliance with specific accounting requirements.

2.86.1 The panel is authorised to issue an order regarding compliance with the Act in respect of the directors' report of large and medium-sized companies. The panel is also now empowered to examine all financial information published by listed companies, including interim reports and preliminary announcements. The FRRP will liaise with the FSA in this respect and has signed a memorandum of understanding with the FSA in order to facilitate co-operation and sharing of information.

2.86.2 The Companies Act 2006 allows HM Revenue & Customs (HMRC) to disclose information to the panel that will assist the panel in its investigations. [CA06 Sec 458]. The panel has agreed a memorandum of understanding (MoU) with HMRC. This MoU is more restrictive than the one agreed with the FSA, in line with the provisions of the Act. HMRC may only disclose information to the panel that relates to issues of apparent non-compliance with the Act and accounting standards and it will discuss its concerns with the company concerned and will tell the company that it is contacting the panel. There are no provisions for the panel to disclose any information to HMRC with regard to accounting, tax or any other issues.

2.86.3 Although the FRRP now has an MoU setting out how it will work with the FSA, the FSA itself has traditionally not been involved with enforcement of accounting standards in the UK, since that responsibility has been undertaken by the FRRP. The FSA is part of the Committee of European Securities Regulators (CESR) and since the EU 2005 Regulation applies to listed entities in the EU, CESR has decided to set standards on enforcement of IFRS. CESR issued its first standard on financial information, 'Enforcement of standards on financial information in Europe', in April 2003. The standard sets out 21 high level principles. The main points are that:

- Member States should set up competent independent authorities to take responsibility for enforcement.
- The competent authority should comply with standards on enforcement issued by CESR.
- Enforcers cannot use a purely rotational or reactive approach to selection of information for review: it should at least include a risk-based approach, preferably with sampling or rotation as well.
- Ex-post enforcement is the normal procedure, but this does not preclude pre-clearance. However, *"CESR recognises that it is important that pre-clearance should not result in enforcers becoming standard setters"*.
- Enforcers should be able to take appropriate corrective action, normally by asking for public restatement of errors.
- Co-ordination of decisions taken by the independent authorities will take place.

The principles allow for a body such as the UK FRRP to continue to exist, as the competent independent authority, in the more proactive, risk-based role that it takes. However, the principles apply only to those companies whose securities are admitted (or who are applying for admission) to trading on a regulated market. The FRRP, as the UK's competent independent authority also enforces accounting standards for those entities that are currently within the FRRP's constituency, but are not listed, that is, large private companies.

2.86.4 No outside approval, either from the FRC or from the company's directors, is required for the FRRP's actions. Members of the FRRP are selected by the appointments committee of the FRC, which attempts to ensure that its membership is drawn from the wider business community. Generally, a group of five or more members, drawn from its membership of approximately 20, is assembled to investigate individual cases.

2.87 The FRRP normally attempt to seek a voluntary agreement with the company's directors about any necessary revisions to the financial statements in question. This allows the directors to follow the rules regarding the voluntary revision of defective financial statements rather than those for revision by court order. [CA06 Sec 454]. However, if the FRRP cannot reach an agreement with the company's directors, it has authority from the Secretary of State for Business, Innovation and Skills to use the Act's powers to compel the revision of financial statements if the court finds that they are defective. [CA06 Sec 455]. It also has funds available to it to fund any legal proceedings. To date, all cases examined by the FRRP have been resolved without involving adjudication by the courts.

Companies Act and FRS 18 — accounting principles

Introduction

2.88 Certain basic accounting principles and concepts are contained in FRS 18, 'Accounting policies', and the ASB's 'Statement of principles for financial reporting'.

2.89 Many of the accounting principles and rules that are included in accounting standards overlap with those in Schedule 1 to SI 2008/410.

2.90 Part 2 of Schedule 1 to SI 2008/410 is divided into four sections:

- Accounting principles. This section sets out some basic principles, which have to some extent been refined in FRS 18:
  - Going concern.
  - Consistency.
  - Prudence and realisation.
  - Accruals basis.
  - Separate valuation of assets and liabilities.
- Historical cost accounting rules. This section covers accounting bases, specific accounting rules, depreciation and amounts necessary to write down cost to a lower net realisable value.
- Alternative accounting rules. This section deals with the accounting treatment of items where the accounting rules applied are designed to take account, in some way, of either inflation or other fluctuations in value (such as, the change in a property's value).
- Fair value accounting rules. This section permits companies to use fair value accounting for certain financial instruments (including derivative financial instruments and certain commodity contracts) in both their individual and consolidated financial statements. Companies that do not use fair value accounting are required to disclose the fair value of any derivative financial instruments that they hold. See further chapter 6.

2.91 Schedule 6 to SI 2008/410 deals exclusively with the provisions concerning consolidated financial statements. The Schedule covers, *inter alia*: the elimination of intra-group transactions; acquisition and merger accounting; the treatment of minority interests; interests of subsidiary undertakings excluded from consolidation; and the consolidation of joint ventures and associated companies.

2.92 The first four accounting principles in the Act are not as paramount in FRS 18. FRS 18 replaced these with a framework that requires accounting policies to be selected against the objectives of relevance, reliability, comparability and understandability (these are the core qualities of financial information set out in the Statement of principles). FRS 18 nevertheless regards the going concern and accruals concepts as distinct concepts that play a pervasive role in financial statements. Prudence and consistency, however, are treated as qualities that contribute to the reliability and comparability, respectively, of financial information.

2.93 The Act permits a company's directors to depart from any of the five accounting principles (that is, going concern, consistency, prudence, accruals and separate valuation) where there are special reasons to do so. If they do so, however, the notes to the financial statements must give particulars of the material departure, the directors' reasons for it, and its effect. [SI 2008/410 1 Sch 10(2)]. FRS 18 requires disclosures about the particulars, reasons and effect that are equivalent to the 'true and fair override' disclosures in respect of a departure from the requirements of an accounting standard, UITF Abstract or companies legislation (see para 2.41 above). [FRS 18 para 65].

Going concern

2.94 One of the accounting principles contained in the Act is that *"the company is presumed to be carrying on business as a going concern"*. [SI 2008/410 1 Sch 11]. The presumption can be rebutted if there are special reasons for doing so. The Act does not explain the circumstances that might give rise to special reasons for departing from the going concern principle, but requires the particulars, reasons and effect to be disclosed in the notes.

2.95 FRS 18 is more explicit. An entity should prepare its financial statements on a going concern basis, unless:

- the entity is being liquidated or has ceased trading; or
- the directors either intend to liquidate the entity or to cease trading, or have no realistic alternative but to do so.

[FRS 18 para 21 as amended by FRS 21].

2.96 The going concern concept is reflected in the principles used to determine the amounts recognised in financial statements. Both assets and liabilities are usually recorded on the basis that their carrying amounts will be recovered or discharged in the normal course of business. For example, the carrying values of fixed assets (such as depreciated cost or recoverable amount) reflect costs or values that the business expects to recover from future cash flows relating to their continued use and ultimate disposal. If, however, the business is not a going concern, the fixed assets should be valued at their 'break-up' value.

2.97 The following example illustrates this:

Example – Use of break-up values

A company that manufactures a particular children's toy has the following fixed assets:

	Cost	Depreciation	Net book value	Break-up value
	C'000	C'000	C'000	C'000
Factory buildings	500	25	475	350
Plant and machinery	150	75	75	10
	650	100	550	360

The net book value of the fixed assets is C550,000 whereas their break-up value is C360,000. This difference results from two facts. First, in order to adapt the factory from its present use to a different use, it would need to be altered considerably. Secondly, the plant and machinery would have only a scrap value if the company ceased to manufacture the toy.

So long as the company is a going concern, the financial statements will properly reflect the fixed assets at their net book value of C550,000 (assuming their recoverable amount exceeds this figure). If, however, the company ran into severe financial difficulty (so that it could no longer be regarded as a going concern), the fixed assets would have to be written down to their break-up value of C360,000.

2.98 In the circumstances described in paragraph 2.95, FRS 18 states *"the entity should prepare its financial statements on a basis other than that of a going concern"*. [FRS 18 para 21 as amended by FRS 21]. Any financial statements prepared in such circumstances should reflect the amounts recoverable from a quick sale or scrap, that is the current 'break-up' values of assets. Provisions may be necessary for closure costs and losses to the date of termination, including redundancies and penalties for early termination of contracts. In addition, fixed assets and long-term liabilities would need to be reclassified as current assets and liabilities.

2.99 It should be noted that FRS 18 takes an 'entity' view of the going concern basis. A subsidiary that is no longer a going concern may be part of a group that continues to be a going concern. In such circumstances, whereas the subsidiary's financial statements would be prepared on a 'break-up' basis, the consolidated financial statements would be prepared on a going concern basis.

2.100 For all entities, FRS 18 requires the directors to assess the entity's ability to continue as a going concern at the time the financial statements are prepared. [FRS 18 para 23]. If there are significant doubts about the entity's ability to continue as a going concern, details of the uncertainties should be disclosed (see para 2.102). It should be noted, however, that if the directors believe there are significant doubts about the entity's ability to continue as a going concern, the FRS nevertheless requires the financial statements to be prepared on a going concern basis, unless a cessation is intended, occurring or cannot realistically be avoided.

2.101 Events that occur after the balance sheet date may indicate that the entity is no longer a going concern — for example, a deterioration in performance or a breach of loan covenants. In a situation where the directors might have believed at the year end that a company was a going concern, but their post-year end assessment leads them to decide that there is no realistic alternative but to liquidate the entity or to cease trading, rebuttal of the going concern assumption in any financial statements that are prepared after that assessment (including the financial statements in respect of which the directors are making the assessment) is consistent with FRS 21 (IAS 10), 'Events after the balance sheet date'. FRS 21 brings in almost all the requirements of the international standard IAS 10 to UK GAAP, though it retains the disclosures required by FRS 18, 'Accounting policies', in respect of going concern (see para 2.102). FRS 21 does not state which adjustments need to be made where financial statements are not prepared on a going concern basis; it states that if the going concern basis is not appropriate then this requires a fundamental change in the basis of accounting.

Disclosures

2.102 Clearly, apart from the accounting implications, the directors' assessment of the risks of a business becoming insolvent is relevant information for investors. FRS 18 requires disclosure of:

- Any material uncertainties, of which the directors are aware in making their assessment, related to events or conditions that may cast significant doubt upon the entity's ability to continue as a going concern.
- Where the foreseeable future considered by the directors has been limited to a period of less than one year from the date of approval of the financial statements, that fact.
- Where the financial statements are not prepared on a going concern basis, that fact, and the basis on which they are prepared and the reason why the entity is not regarded as a going concern.

[FRS 18 para 61; FRS 21 para 16].

2.103 More detailed guidance on going concern reporting for listed companies is found in The UK Corporate Governance Code issued in May 2010 and, for auditors, in the auditing standards ISA (UK and Ireland) 570, 'Going concern', and ISA (UK and Ireland) 700, 'The auditor's report on financial statements'. According to ISA (UK and Ireland) 700, where there is a fundamental uncertainty for instance about the validity of the going concern basis, auditors are required to draw attention, by means of an explanatory note, to the note to the financial statements that explains the uncertainty. ISA (UK and Ireland) 570, a more specific auditing standard dealing with going concern, contains a list of factors that may need to be disclosed in relation to such an uncertainty.

2.104 It is generally understood that the going concern concept embodies the assumption that an entity will *"continue in operational existence for the foreseeable future"*. FRS 18 uses these words, but does not define what is meant by the 'foreseeable future'. ISA (UK and Ireland) 570 acknowledges that it would be impossible to specify a minimum length for the future period the directors should consider particularly in assessing going concern. The appropriate period of time that the directors should consider will depend on many factors such as the company's reporting and budgeting systems and the nature of the business and industry in which it operates.

2.105 However, the auditing standard considers that, where the directors have paid particular attention to a period less than one year from the date of approval of the financial statements in assessing going concern, they will need to ask management to extend the period covered by their review to 12 months from the balance sheet date. Disclosure in the financial statements is now an explicit requirement of FRS 18.

2.106 The requirement in the UK Corporate Governance Code for directors to confirm that the going concern basis is appropriate has, in effect, changed it from a presumption to an explicit statement for listed companies. Code provision C.1.3 says that *"The directors should report in annual and half-yearly financial statements that the business is a going concern, with supporting assumptions or qualifications as necessary"*. This requirement is also contained in the Listing Rules. [LR 9.8.6 R(3)]. The guidance that directors should use to interpret this requirement, 'Going Concern and Liquidity Risk: Guidance for Directors of UK Companies 2009' was issued by the FRC in November 2009. It applies to accounting periods ending on or after 31 December 2009; supersedes the guidance issued in 1994 for directors of listed companies; and extends the application of the guidance to all sizes of company for annual and half-yearly financial statements. Principle 3 of the guidance states *"Directors should make balanced, proportionate and clear disclosures about going concern for the financial statements to give a true and fair view. Directors should disclose if the period that they have reviewed is less than twelve months from the date of approval of annual and half-yearly financial statements and explain their justification for limiting their review period."*. The detailed guidance includes examples with respect to going concern disclosures from paragraph 59, in appendix I (small companies) and appendix II (companies other than small companies (including for subsidiary companies of large private or listed groups)). The UK Corporate Governance Code requirements are discussed in detail in chapter 4 of the 'Manual of Accounting – Narrative Reporting'. As far as unlisted companies and other entities are concerned, FRS 18 does not require disclosure of a positive going concern opinion.

2.107 In some situations, the effect on the balance sheet of ceasing to regard the business as a going concern may be negligible. Nevertheless FRS 18 requires the financial statements to disclose that the entity is no longer regarded as a going concern. Unless there is a statement to the contrary, the FRS allows a reader to *presume* that an entity is carrying on business as a going concern. Consequently, where necessary, the company should state that it has prepared its financial statements on a break-up basis, even if the effect of doing so has not been significant.

Accruals

2.108 The accruals basis of accounting is a longstanding fundamental accounting concept and a basic accounting principle in the Act. FRS 18 contains an explicit requirement for all entities whose financial statements are intended to give a true and fair view to adopt the accruals basis. [FRS 18 para 26].

2.109 FRS 18 specifies that the accruals basis should reflect the 'asset and liability' approach advocated in the ASB's Statement of Principles.

2.110 FRS 18's description of the accruals basis excludes any reference to matching revenues and costs, because the ASB believes that is an inappropriate accounting principle: *"The accrual basis of accounting requires the non-cash effects of transactions and other events to be reflected, as far as is possible, in the financial statements for the accounting period in which they occur…"*.

The Statement of principles explains that revenue/expenditure matching should be restricted so that only items that meet the definitions of assets and liabilities, and satisfy their respective recognition criteria, should be recognised in the balance sheet. This in turn affects how revenues and costs are recognised in the profit and loss account. Revenue recognition issues are discussed in detail in chapter 7.

2.111 FRS 18's positioning of the accruals concept means that the former matching aspect of the accruals concept can no longer be used to justify deferring costs that are not assets. Examples of the purging of revenue/expenditure matching appear in accounting pronouncements: UITF Abstract 24 prevents start-up costs from being deferred and matched with future revenues; FRS 12 prevents gains on the expected disposal of assets from being taken into account in measuring a restructuring provision, even if the sale of assets is part of the restructuring.

Prudence and realisation

2.112 The Act requires a company to use a prudent basis in determining the amount of any item that it includes in its financial statements. [SI 2008/410 1 Sch 13]. The Act specifies two particular rules in relation to this. The first is that the profit and loss account may include only those profits that have been realised at the balance sheet date. [SI 2008/410 1 Sch 13(a)]. This principle acts as a constraint on the selection of accounting policies in areas such as revenue recognition. The directors can depart from this principle only if it appears to them that there are special reasons. For this purpose, realised profits are defined as:

> *"Such profits ... of the company as fall to be treated as realised in accordance with principles generally accepted, at the time when the accounts are prepared, with respect to the determination for accounting purposes of realised profits..."* [CA06 Sec 853(4)].

2.113 Realisation is, therefore, an accounting rather than a legal concept. In the present legal and accounting framework, companies (and auditors) need guidance on determining realised profits because:

- Directors need to know what profits recognised in the financial statements are realised so that they can determine the amount of profits available for lawful distribution.
- Companies need to comply with paragraph 10(2) of Schedule 1 to SI 2008/410 if there is a departure from the accounting principle of including in the profit and loss account only those profits that are realised — this requires the effect of the departure to be quantified.
- The law assumes that accountants will be in a position to determine what is meant by realised.

2.114 Before FRS 18, realisation was embedded in the fundamental concept of prudence in FRS 18's predecessor, SSAP 2. Under FRS 18, prudence is no longer a fundamental concept in its own right (see para 2.131), and realisation no longer features as a pre-requisite for the recognition of assets and gains when they are uncertain. Instead, the focus is on whether assets and gains can be evidenced with sufficient reliability. Nevertheless, FRS 18 preserves the status quo by stating (albeit as an explanatory note) the underlying principle of what is 'generally accepted' by the accounting profession to be realised, that is *"when realised in the form either of cash or of other assets the ultimate cash realisation of which can be assessed with reasonable certainty"*. [FRS 18 para 28]. The ICAEW and ICAS have developed detailed guidance (Tech 01/09) on determining realised profits in the context of distributions under the Companies Act 2006. This is *de facto* GAAP on what constitutes a realised profit (see chapter 9). The concepts of 'realised' and 'distributable' profits are considered further in chapters 9 and 23.

2.114.1 Furthermore, where a company uses the fair value accounting rules in Section D of Part 2 of Schedule 1 to SI 2008/410, the Act requires that, despite the rule in paragraph 13(a) of Schedule 1 to SI 2008/410 (whereby only realised profits can be taken to the profit and loss account), changes in the fair value of financial instruments or other assets must be included in the profit and loss account, except in certain specified circumstances (see further chapter 6).

2.115 The second rule that the Companies Act 2006 specifies in connection with the prudence concept relates to liabilities. A company must take account of all liabilities that have arisen in respect of either the financial year in question or a previous financial year. Moreover, they must be included even when they become apparent only in the period between the balance sheet date and the date on which the directors sign the financial statements. [SI 2008/410 1 Sch 13(b)]. However, this requirement deals with liabilities relating to the financial year in question, or a previous financial year and does not extend to anticipating liabilities relating to future years. Accounting standards, in particular FRS 3, FRS 7 and FRS 12, contain more specific rules in this area.

Separate valuation

2.116 When a company is determining the aggregate amount of any item, it must determine separately the amount of each individual asset or liability that makes up that item. [SI 2008/410 1 Sch 15].

2.117 The treatment of investments in subsidiaries is a good example of the separate valuation principle, although the general principle applies equally to other items, such as stocks. In the parent's own financial statements, investments in subsidiaries will normally be accounted for at cost, less write-downs for any permanent diminution in value. Before the implementation of the separate valuation rules, investments (and particularly parents' investments in subsidiaries) were sometimes considered as a whole. If one investment had a market value that was less than book value, and all the other investments had an excess of market value over book value that more than compensated, it was argued that the investments as a whole were not overstated at book value and, therefore, no provision against the one overstated investment was necessary.

2.118 However, under the 2006 Act, investments have to be considered individually. By law, a provision must be made against an investment if there is a permanent diminution in value below cost. This applies irrespective of the value and the quality of the other investments.

2.119 The only statutory exception to the separate valuation rule is that tangible assets and raw materials and consumables may, in certain circumstances, be included in the financial statements at a fixed quantity and value. [SI 2008/410 1 Sch 26].

2.120 Where there is a legal right of set-off, assets and liabilities should, in some circumstances, be netted because they do not constitute separate assets and liabilities. The rules concerning the set off of assets and liabilities have been reinforced by FRS 5. This is considered in detail in chapter 3.

Accounting policies

2.121 FRS 18's stated objectives are to ensure

- Accounting policies are adopted that are judged by the entity to be the most appropriate for giving a true and fair view. This is a black letter requirement.
- Accounting policies are reviewed regularly and changed when a new policy becomes more appropriate.

- Disclosures are given that enable users to understand the accounting policies adopted and how they have been applied.

[FRS 18 para 1].

2.122 FRS 18 defines accounting policies as the principles, bases, conventions, rules and practices for recognising, selecting measurement bases for, and presenting assets, liabilities, gains, losses and changes to shareholders' funds. [FRS 18 para 4]. Accounting policies are distinguished from estimation techniques (see para 2.139). The FRS aims to clarify the distinction between a change of accounting policy (requiring a prior year adjustment) and a change of estimate (requiring the effects to be dealt with wholly in the current year).

2.123 Examples of accounting policies involving different recognition practices are:

- Capitalising or writing-off interest relating to the construction of fixed assets.
- Capitalising or writing-off development expenditure.

2.124 Measurement bases are defined as monetary attributes such as historical cost, net realisable value or current replacement cost, or a combination of such attributes such as the lower of cost and net realisable value, or recoverable amount (the higher of value in use and net realisable value). [FRS 18 para 4]. Examples of accounting policies involving different measurement bases are:

- Measuring fixed assets at depreciated historical cost or at current value.
- Measuring deferred tax liabilities on a discounted or undiscounted basis.
- Measuring the cost of fungible stocks on a weighted average or FIFO basis. (FRS 18 explicitly describes these as different measurement bases and, hence, different accounting policies. For non-fungible stocks, they would be different estimation techniques rather than different accounting policies).

2.125 Examples of different presentation policies are:

- Classifying depreciation charges within cost of sales or administrative expenses.
- Reclassifying fixed assets to be disposed of as current assets or retaining them within fixed assets until disposal.

2.126 The Companies Act 2006 requires disclosure of the accounting policies the company has adopted in determining the amounts to be included in the financial statements. [SI 2008/410 1 Sch 44]. Legal advice obtained by the FRRP confirmed that this requirement is separate from, and in addition to, the requirement in paragraph 45 of Schedule 1 to SI 2008/410 to state in the financial statements whether they have been prepared in accordance with applicable accounting standards and to give the particulars and reasons for any material departures from these standards (see para 2.36). Therefore, in addition to the paragraph 45 requirement, there must be stated in the financial statements both the accounting policies adopted as the result of applying accounting standards and those, not covered by standards, that a company chooses to adopt.

2.127 FRS 18 requires a description of each of the accounting policies that is material in the context of an entity's financial statements and is more explicit in respect of the level of disclosure required where a particular accounting policy is or is not prescribed in an accounting standard. The level of disclosure should be sufficiently informative to enable users to understand the accounting policies adopted. A 'succinct description' of the policy is sufficient where the policy is prescribed by, and fully described in, an accounting standard, a UITF Abstract or companies legislation. A fuller description is required where no policy is prescribed or where alternative policies are allowed, so that users can make proper comparisons of the financial statements of different entities. [FRS 18 paras 55, 56].

Selecting most appropriate accounting policies

2.128 Where an accounting standard allows more than one accounting policy or where a policy is not specified in an accounting standard, an entity should select the policy that is judged to be *"most appropriate to its particular circumstances for the purpose of giving a true and fair view"*. [FRS 18 para 17]. The most appropriate accounting policies should be selected against the objectives of relevance, reliability, comparability and understandability. [FRS 18 para 30]. These are the core qualities of financial information set out in Chapter 3 of the ASB's Statement of principles (see para 2.195). In addition, when selecting from alternative policies, entities should take into account how the cost of providing information compares with the likely benefit of such information to users. [FRS 18 para 31].

2.129 The first objective is relevance. Relevant information helps users make economic decisions and is provided in time to influence those decisions. It has predictive value (that is, it helps users to evaluate future prospects), confirmatory value (that is, it helps users to confirm or correct their previous evaluations and assessments), or both. The priority given to relevance when selecting accounting policies could be construed as steering entities towards policies that use current values. However, the ASB clarified this issue by stating that FRS 18 does not restrict legitimate options to report assets at historical cost, as provided in FRS 15. [FRS 18 App IV para 34].

2.130 The second objective is reliability. Reliable information has the following qualities:

- Faithful representation of what it purports to represent or could reasonably be expected to represent (that is, accounting policies should make the financial statements reflect the substance of transactions or events).
- Freedom from deliberate or systematic bias.

- Freedom from material error.
- Completeness within the bounds of materiality.
- Prudence under conditions of uncertainty.

[FRS 18 para 35].

2.131 FRS 18 reflects the repositioning of the role of prudence in the Statement of principles. Rather than being a fundamental accounting concept in its own right, prudence is now a quality that contributes to the reliability of financial information where risks and uncertainties are involved. Appropriate accounting policies require more confirmatory evidence about the existence of an asset or a gain than of a liability or loss. Similarly, greater reliability of measurement is expected for assets and gains than for liabilities and losses. For liabilities and losses, prudent estimates should be made but deliberate overstatement should be avoided. This philosophy is applied in more detail in FRS 12. Similarly, deliberate understatement of assets and gains should be avoided. [FRS 18 paras 37, 38].

2.132 The third objective is comparability. FRS 18 places considerable weight on comparability in the selection of accounting policies and, in effect, obliges directors to consider whether particular policies are widely accepted in the industry and how the entity's policies compare. If the entity's policies deviate from accepted industry practices, the directors may need to be able to demonstrate why the entity's policies are judged more appropriate to its particular circumstances than the accepted industry practices. The FRS notes that industry practices will be particularly persuasive if they are set out in a SORP that has been generally accepted by an industry or sector (see also para 2.74). [FRS 18 para 40].

2.133 The fourth objective is understandability. Understandability is achieved if information is presented in a way that enables its significance to be perceived by users that have a reasonable knowledge of business and economic activities and accounting and are willing to study the information with reasonable diligence. [FRS 18 para 41].

2.134 The discussion in FRS 18 of how the objectives of relevance, reliability, comparability and understandability interrelate shows that much judgement is involved, for example as regards assessing the entity's particular circumstances. But there is an implied requirement for boards to be able to demonstrate that they have evaluated the appropriateness of alternative policies where more than one policy could give a true and fair view. Different entities will have different views as to where they are positioned with regard to matters such as trading off relevance and reliability, costs and benefits. The discussion of this aspect of the FRS in the development section (paras 28 to 34 of Appendix IV) attempts to allay some commentators' fears about these requirements by indicating that judgements ought to be valid if they are arrived at in good faith, even if it later becomes clear that a different judgement would have been more appropriate.

Disclosing accounting policies

2.134.1 FRS 18 requires disclosure in the notes to the financial statements of *"a description of each of the accounting policies that is material in the context of the entity's financial statements"*. [FRS 18 para 55(a)].

2.134.2 The purpose of this disclosure is to enable users to understand the accounting policies applied in the preparation of financial statements. It is assumed that users have a reasonable knowledge of business and accounting issues. Consequently, where an entity is applying an accounting policy that is prescribed by an accounting standard, the description need not be detailed. However, where a particular accounting treatment is not prescribed by accounting standards, a more detailed description will be needed. [FRS 18 para 56].

2.134.3 Certain accounting standards permit a choice of accounting policies. For example, FRS 15, 'Tangible fixed assets', permits certain finance costs to be either included in the cost of the asset or recognised as an expense immediately. Here, adequate disclosure is required to make it clear which of the two available options has been chosen.

2.134.4 Where accounting policies are not prescribed by accounting standards, or are specific to the reporting entity (for example, a revenue accounting policy) the disclosure of the policy will need to be detailed.

2.134.5 For some accounting policies, extensive disclosure will be required in order to enable users to understand financial statements. For example, it is expected that an entity's revenue recognition accounting policy would address as a minimum, for each principal source of revenue:

- The timing of the recognition of revenue.
- The measurement of revenue.
- The treatment of discounts offered to customers.
- The method of allocation of revenue between different components of the same transaction (where different recognition policies are applied to the components).

Reviewing and changing accounting policies

2.135 Accounting policies should be reviewed regularly to ensure that they remain the most appropriate. [FRS 18 para 45]. It follows from the general requirement to adopt the most appropriate accounting policies that an accounting policy should not be changed unless the new policy is judged to be more appropriate to the entity's particular circumstances than the old policy. The disclosures required when an accounting policy is changed are covered in chapter 8.

2.136 FRS 18 does not, however, encourage frequent changes to accounting policies, because users would find it more difficult to compare the financial statements from one year to another. Therefore, the impact on comparability is a factor that should be taken into account when considering whether or not a policy should be changed. For example, a change to an accounting policy is probably best avoided if it is likely that a further change will be required in the near future. But consistency is not an end in itself. [FRS 18 para 49].

2.137 FRS 18 makes it clear that the 'most appropriate' test does not require new accounting standards to be adopted ahead of their effective dates. However, it is unlikely that a change to (or adoption of) a new policy could be justified if it conflicts with a new FRS that has not yet become mandatory. [FRS 18 para 46].

2.138 Entities cannot adopt new proposals in exposure drafts or discussion papers if they conflict with existing accounting standards or UITF abstracts, because compliance with existing standards is an overriding requirement. But an entity would need to consider adopting a policy proposed in an exposure draft (that does not conflict with any existing standards) if, say, that policy was already widely adopted in the industry.

Consistency — issues for groups

2.138.1 Where both the consolidated financial statements and the individual financial statements of the parent and subsidiaries are being prepared under UK accounting standards, questions may arise as to whether FRS 18 makes it necessary for consistent accounting policies to be adopted in the different sets of financial statements.

2.138.2 For consolidated financial statements, the Companies Act 2006 and FRS 2 require that, other than in exceptional circumstances, uniform group accounting policies should be used. Where any subsidiaries have adopted different accounting policies in their individual financial statements, appropriate consolidation adjustments should be made to achieve uniformity. But the Act (SI 2008/410 6 Sch 3(2)) and FRS 2 paragraph 41 envisage that there may be special reasons for departing from this basic principle and retaining different accounting policies adopted by different entities in the group. In those circumstances, the Act requires that particulars of the departure, the reasons for it and its effect should be disclosed in the notes to the consolidated financial statements. Given the objectives of relevance, reliability, comparability and understandability set out in FRS 18, it is hard to envisage situations where different policies are retained in the consolidated financial statements and could both be considered to be most appropriate, or where the cost of providing information on a consistent basis in the consolidated financial statements would outweigh the benefits to users of consistency. In practice, therefore, it is most unlikely that circumstances will arise that will justify a departure from the principle of adopting uniform accounting policies in consolidated financial statements.

2.138.3 Concerning the individual financial statements of the parent and its subsidiaries, neither the Act nor FRS 2 requires the accounting policies of the parent, the subsidiaries and the group to be the same. Indeed, paragraph 4 of Schedule 6 to SI 2008/410 requires any differences between the accounting policies used in the parent's own financial statements and the group financial statements to be disclosed and the reasons given.

2.138.4 Overseas subsidiaries that do not prepare individual financial statements under UK GAAP are beyond the jurisdiction of FRS 18 and so the issue does not arise, unless there are equivalent local requirements for determining the most appropriate accounting policies. Even then, local GAAP (or IFRS) may permit the use of accounting policies that are not permitted by UK GAAP (or vice versa). For example, in UK GAAP, LIFO stock valuations are considered in SSAP 9 to be likely to be incompatible with the requirement to give a true and fair view. Such valuations are, however, allowed by GAAP in some other countries (for example, the US). So there may be good reasons for subsidiaries in different jurisdictions having different policies.

2.138.5 For each entity that reports individually under UK GAAP, the FRS requires the directors to go through the same accounting policy selection process as for the consolidated financial statements. Each entity should select accounting policies that enable its financial statements to give a true and fair view. If more than one policy can give a true and fair view (for example, where the law or accounting standards allow choices), each entity should select the policies that are judged to be most appropriate to their particular circumstances. In so doing, they should balance the objectives of relevance, reliability, comparability and understandability. They should also balance the cost of providing information with its likely benefit to the financial statement users. Since the factors that the parent entity's directors would take into account in determining the most appropriate accounting policies for the group's consolidated financial statements would generally also apply to the individual entities, in most cases it would be reasonable to expect that the same accounting policies would be selected for the group, the parent and the subsidiaries reporting under UK GAAP.

2.138.6 There may be special reasons, however, for adopting different policies. The particular circumstances of different reporting entities, or the cost-benefit equations between different reporting entities and their users, may differ significantly. As an example, comparability with other GAAPs might score highly in the selection of accounting policies for the consolidated financial statements, but might be less of an issue, however, for the users of the individual entities' financial statements and so other factors, such as the effect of different accounting policies on subsidiaries' distributable profits, may weigh more heavily in the selection of the most appropriate accounting policies for them.

2.138.7 Deciding to adopt consistent or different policies to some extent involves the judgements of different boards of directors. If different policies are adopted, an entity should be able to justify this with sound business or commercial reasons.

2.138.8 The issue of whether companies within a group should have consistent accounting policies when they are all reporting under UK GAAP may be distinguished from a situation (as in the UK) where legislation permits entities to use UK GAAP for the parent and subsidiary individual financial statements, with IFRS being used only for the consolidated financial statements (see para 2.22 onwards). In such situations, the use of UK GAAP for the parent and subsidiaries will clearly mean that the policies will not be consistent in many cases with the IFRS policies used in the consolidated financial statements.

Estimation techniques

2.139 FRS 18 defines estimation techniques as: *"The methods adopted by an entity to arrive at estimated monetary amounts, corresponding to the measurement bases selected, for assets, liabilities, gains, losses and changes to shareholders' funds"*. [FRS 18 para 4].

2.140 Estimation techniques are used as a proxy for making best estimates where the values of items being measured are unknown. They might be used to measure the following items:

- Depreciation of fixed assets (methods such as straight-line or reducing balance).
- Provisions (statistical methods such as 'expected value' used to measure large populations).
- After-tax revenue recognition methods for finance leases (such as actuarial-after-tax and investment period methods).
- Cost of stocks or work-in-progress (measurement methods such as FIFO or weighted average cost for non-fungible stocks). Note that for *non-fungible* stocks the change in measurement method is a change of estimate, but for *fungible* stocks the change in measurement method is a change in accounting policy as noted in example 5 in Appendix I to FRS 18.
- Cost of stocks or work-in-progress (methods of attributing overheads).
- Long-term contracts (methods of estimating turnover and profits attributable to the stage of completion).
- Fair values (market value-based or discounted cash flow methods).
- Asset provisions (methods used to calculate provisions for slow-moving stocks or bad debts).
- Sales returns provisions.
- Impairment of fixed assets and goodwill (methods of grouping assets under income generating units for the purpose of impairment reviews).

2.141 The selection of estimation techniques is given almost the same importance as the selection of accounting policies. The selected estimation techniques should enable the financial statements to give a true and fair view and they should be consistent with the requirements of accounting standards, UITF Abstracts and companies legislation. Where a number of estimation techniques are available, an entity should select those estimation techniques that are judged to be most appropriate to its particular circumstances for the purpose of giving a true and fair view. [FRS 18 paras 50, 51]. Cost-benefit considerations also come into play — techniques can be refined to achieve greater accuracy, but unless there is a material improvement in accuracy, the additional cost may not be justified.

2.142 FRS 18 requires a description of significant estimation techniques. Significance should be assessed by considering if the range of reasonable amounts at which an item could be measured is so large that a different amount from within that range could materially affect the view shown by the financial statements. [FRS 18 para 57]. Entities need to consider whether the range of possible estimates is large and how sensitive the numbers are to different assumptions underlying the techniques. The thrust of the emphasis in paragraph 57 appears to be on disclosure where an estimate is sensitive to the underlying assumptions. It also indicates that the description of any significant estimation technique will include disclosure of underlying assumptions to which the measurement of the relevant item is particularly sensitive. For example, where estimates involve present value measurements, the discount rate is likely to be a key assumption.

2.143 Many accounting standards specifically require such disclosures, for example:

- FRS 15, 'Tangible fixed assets', requires depreciation methods (estimation techniques) and the useful economic lives or depreciation rates (underlying assumptions) to be disclosed.
- FRS 10, 'Goodwill and intangible assets', requires methods (estimation techniques) and periods (underlying assumptions) of amortisation of goodwill and intangible assets to be disclosed.
- FRS 11, 'Impairment of fixed assets and goodwill', requires the discount rate underlying an impairment loss measured by reference to value in use (estimation technique) to be disclosed.
- FRS 17, 'Retirement benefits', requires the main financial assumptions used in the measurement of pension scheme liabilities to be disclosed. On 7 December 2006, the ASB published an amendment to FRS 17, 'Retirement benefits' which requires additional disclosure of the principal actuarial assumptions used as at the balance sheet date.
- FRS 12, 'Provisions, contingent liabilities and contingent assets', requires the major assumptions made concerning future events in the measurement of provisions to be disclosed.

Accounting conventions

2.144 All accounting systems depend on the capital maintenance concept adopted, the basis used to value assets and the unit of measurement used. The different options available for each of these components are considered briefly in this section.

Capital maintenance concepts

2.145 Capital maintenance is linked with the measurement of total accounting profit. Disregarding additions to capital or repayments of capital and distributions, accounting profit is the difference between a company's capital at the start of the period and at the end of the period. A company can only be considered to have made a profit if it has increased its net assets, which are represented by its capital, over and above that necessary to maintain its opening capital. Thus total accounting profit can be measured only once a definition has been established as to what capital is to be maintained.

2.146 There are at least two different concepts of capital maintenance: operating capital maintenance and financial capital maintenance. Operating capital maintenance, although it can be measured in a variety of different ways, generally seeks to ensure that the business' physical operating capacity is preserved. Financial capital maintenance attempts to conserve the value of the funds that shareholders have invested in the business. Financial capital maintained can either be the monetary value of capital attributable to shareholders or a value adjusted by a general purchasing power index to maintain capital as a fund of real purchasing power. Consider the following example.

Example – Different concepts of capital maintenance

A sole trader starts a business buying and selling second-hand cars. In his first year of trading he buys one car for C1,000 and sells it for C2,000. At the time he sells the car, the cost of buying an equivalent car is C1,200 and general inflation between the dates of buying and selling is 10%. Under monetary capital maintenance, maintenance of the general purchasing power of financial capital and operating capital maintenance the trader's profit and loss account would be as follows:

Capital maintenance concepts	Financial capital maintenance		
	Monetary capital	General purchasing power	Operating capital maintenance
	C	C	C
Sales	2,000	2,000	2,000
Cost of sales	(1,000)	(1,000)	(1,200)
Operating profit	1,000	1,000	800
Inflation adjustment to opening capital	–	(100)	–
Total gain	1,000	900	800

Monetary financial capital maintenance, which is the basis most commonly used in accounting, takes no account of the effects of inflation. The profit of C1,000 is the amount in excess of the original capital of the business. In the second column the inflation adjustment shows the effect of the general increase in prices on the opening financial capital of C1,000 and seeks to ensure that profit is only measured after preserving the opening capital in the business in terms of its general purchasing power. The profit of C900 leaves capital of C1,100 in the business to maintain its purchasing power. Operating capital maintenance, on the other hand, is concerned with preserving the productive capacity of the business. In this example, this is the trader's ability to replace the item of stock sold. Under operating capital maintenance, the trader has a profit of C800 and capital in the business of C1,200 which is sufficient to purchase a car to begin the next period's trade.

Valuation bases

2.147 The measurement of profit is also affected by the valuation basis chosen. There are a variety of valuation bases, including historical cost, current cost and market value. Valuation bases are considered further in chapter 16.

Units of measurement

2.148 The unit of measurement chosen affects how profit is determined. Reporting can be in nominal currency or in units of constant purchasing power. Financial statements for two different years may be denominated in nominal currency, but because of inflation, the purchasing power of this nominal currency is not the same. The use of a unit of constant purchasing power eliminates these difficulties in comparability. One method is the unit of *current* purchasing power. All non-monetary assets and liabilities relating to dates prior to the reporting date are restated by reference to movements in a general price index, such as the retail price index, into the value of the currency at the reporting date.

Conventions

2.149 Capital maintenance concepts, asset valuation bases, and the units of measurement used can be combined in different ways to create different accounting conventions. Theoretically the options outlined above would result in many different accounting conventions, but not all the combinations are sensible. The more common conventions are summarised below.

Historical cost convention

2.150 The most common accounting convention is the historical cost convention. This convention values assets at their historical cost, operates financial capital maintenance and uses the nominal currency as its unit of measurement. Although this convention is familiar to all accountants, when prices are rising, historical cost accounting may distort reported profits and balance sheet values. Historical cost accounting, being simple and relatively well understood, is useful for preparing stewardship accounts. It is perhaps less useful for making investment decisions or decisions about amounts to distribute. In the example in paragraph 2.146 above, if the trader had taken the profit of C1,000 for his own use, there would not be sufficient funds in the business for it to continue to trade at the same level.

Modified historical cost convention

2.151 Sometimes the historical cost convention is modified by the revaluation of certain fixed assets. Modified historical cost accounting operates financial capital maintenance and uses the nominal currency as its unit of measurement, but certain fixed assets, usually land and buildings, are included at a valuation above historical cost. This gives some indication of the value to the business of some of the assets employed. The unrealised gains as a result of revaluing assets are generally not recognised in the profit and loss account. This suggests that the gain is an element of the capital of the business that must be retained in order to maintain the business' operating capacity, although no formalised attempt is made to employ operating capital maintenance. In addition, not all companies revalue their assets and, in the past, not all companies that revalued their assets did so on a regular basis. Therefore, comparability between different companies is reduced and, if valuations are allowed to become out of date, their usefulness as an indication of the value of the assets to the business diminishes. The ASB has considered these problems when it developed FRS 15, which is discussed in chapter 16.

Fair value convention

2.151.1 Recent years have seen accounting move towards something that might be termed the 'fair value convention'. Although it has never been explicitly stated in any framework it is clear from recent standards that the basis of accounting is changing. The fair value convention may be said to have the following features: it is balance sheet based, focusing on performance being the result of changes in the carrying values of assets and liabilities rather than a matching between income and expenditure. It focuses on the fair values of assets and liabilities. Fair value is defined in FRS 25 (IAS 32), 'Financial instruments: Disclosure and presentation', as *"the amount for which an asset could be exchanged, or a liability settled, between knowledgeable, willing parties in an arm's length transaction"*. [FRS 25 para 11].

2.151.2 Fair values are 'current' values at any balance sheet date. They are, in essence, based on discounted future cash flows. Proponents of fair values argue that their use gives users of financial statements more useful information, as it is more up to date and reflective of the real value and cost of an entity's assets and liabilities at any point in time. There are difficulties, however, in the practical application of this apparently simple concept, both in terms of its definition and its measurement.

2.151.3 Another feature of the fair value model is that changes in fair value are recorded through the profit and loss account. A full fair value model, in which all assets and liabilities would be fair valued, perhaps including internally generated intangible assets, is some way off. Not least this is because the convention is already at the edge of the sophistication of markets and of most financial statement users and preparers. The convention has, however, come closer to being achieved in the past ten years and the IASB has been a particular advocate. Standards that incorporate the use of fair values include IAS 19 on post-retirement benefits, IAS 39 on financial instruments, IAS 41 on biological assets and IFRS 2, which deals with share-based payment.

2.151.4 In terms of the fair value convention becoming part of UK GAAP, FRS 17 includes the requirement to measure pension plan assets at fair value for defined benefit schemes, IFRS 2 has been introduced as FRS 20 and much of IAS 39 has been introduced as FRS 26 (although it is not compulsory for all companies). To allow this to take place the legal framework of accounting has had to change, with permission to fair value being implemented by the Fair Value Directive (see para 2.20.2).

Current purchasing power

2.152 The current purchasing power (CPP) convention also values assets at their historical cost and operates financial capital maintenance. CPP, however, uses a unit of constant purchasing power rather than the nominal currency for measurement. Therefore, all non-monetary items in the financial statements, including capital, are restated by reference to a general price index. While this maintains capital in terms of what shareholders can do with their funds in the economy as a whole, the general price index used may not move the same way as the input prices specific to the company. Therefore, the resulting asset values may bear no relationship to their current value to the business; moreover, the capital maintained may be either too much or too little to maintain the operating capacity of the business. In the example in paragraph 2.146 above, the increase in the general price index was less than the increase specific to second hand cars. As a result, if the trader had taken all the CPP profit out of the business, he would not have had sufficient capital to replace his stock.

2.153 The principal current example of the use of CPP accounting is in the countries that experience hyper-inflation. UITF Abstract 9, 'Accounting for operations in hyper-inflationary economies', and FRS 24 (IAS 29), 'Financial reporting in hyper-inflationary economies', give guidance in this area (see also chapter 7).

Current cost accounting

2.154 Current cost accounting conventions value assets at their current value to the business. Although this is often combined with operating capital maintenance and measurement in nominal currency it can also be combined with financial capital maintenance and units of constant purchasing power. Since combining current costs with nominal currency usually results in useful information, the additional complexity introduced by using units of constant purchasing power is often not warranted except in trend information. Current cost operating profit shows the current trading margin achieved by the business since it charges the costs incurred at the prices applying when the sales were made. Put another way, it takes inflationary 'holding gains' out of the measurement of income. It gives an indication of the companies' ability to generate profits from its current operations and also maintains its current operating capacity. In the operating capital maintenance example in paragraph 2.146, the operating profit is lower than under financial capital maintenance. This allows sufficient capital to be retained to replace stock and continue trading and may also give a more forward-looking perspective on future profits.

[The next paragraph is 2.191.]

Frameworks for setting accounting standards

The ASB's Statement of principles

2.191 The ASB's Statement of principles for financial reporting is based on the IASB's framework. The statement sets out the ground rules that the ASB will follow when developing new standards. It is also intended to help preparers and auditors resolve issues that are not covered by specific rules.

2.192 The Statement of principles is not an accounting standard and does not override the requirements of any accounting standard or the law. In fact, there are some significant conflicts between the principles as set out in the statement and companies legislation in the UK. The eight chapters in the final Statement, which are discussed in the following paragraphs, are:

- Objective of financial statements.
- The reporting entity.

- Qualitative characteristics of financial information.
- Elements of financial statements.
- Recognition in financial statements.
- Measurement in financial statements.
- Presentation of financial information.
- Accounting for interests in other entities.

Objective

2.193 The ASB identifies present and potential investors as the target (or the proxy for other targets) of financial statements. The ASB has included in the objective the role of financial statements for assessing the stewardship of management as well as their usefulness for making economic decisions. The ASB specifically identifies information on 'financial adaptability' as being useful for economic decisions. Financial adaptability is described as the ability of an enterprise to alter its cash flows so that it can respond to unexpected needs or opportunities.

The reporting entity

2.194 The focus of this chapter is on determining the boundary of the reporting entity, particularly in the case of group accounts. This boundary is determined by the extent of the entity's direct and indirect control.

- Control is stated to have two aspects: the ability to deploy economic resources and the ability to benefit or suffer from their deployment.
- Direct control is said to determine the boundary of single entity accounts, while direct plus indirect control determines the boundary of the group accounts.
- The principles and discussion in this chapter is expanded upon in chapter 8 of the Statement, which deals with interests in other entities.

Qualitative characteristics

2.195 The ASB identifies relevance and reliability as the primary characteristics relating to the content of financial information. Relevance has predictive and confirmatory aspects and requires information to be provided in time to influence decisions. Reliability requires faithful representation (which requires an emphasis on substance), neutrality (that is, freedom from bias), prudence, freedom from material error and completeness.

2.196 Primary characteristics relating to how information is presented in financial statements, which follow from the above two, are comparability (which includes consistency and disclosure of policies and changes in them) and understandability.

2.197 The ASB recognises the need to trade relevance off against reliability, partly by considering timeliness and the most appropriate measurement base. Nevertheless, the importance of relevance seems to imply a move towards current values rather than historical costs.

Materiality

2.198 Materiality sets the threshold for determining whether an item is relevant. The Statement of principles explains materiality as follows: *"An item of information is material to the financial statements if its misstatement or omission might reasonably be expected to influence the economic decisions of users of those financial statements, including their assessments of management's stewardship. Whether information is material will depend on the size and nature of the item in question judged in the particular circumstances of the case"*. [SoP para 3.30 and 3.31].

2.199 An item that is not material is not relevant, it cannot influence the decisions of a user and need not be reported in financial statements. Indeed, if immaterial items are reported in financial statements, they can interfere with decision making because they may obscure the relevant information amid excessive detail. However, determining what is material is a matter of professional judgement and it would be inappropriate to set fixed monetary limits or rules.

2.200 In view of the increasing emphasis on materiality due to the Statement of principles and the public interest in materiality as a result of certain FRRP decisions, the Financial Reporting Committee of the ICAEW issued a statement in June 2008 that replaced the existing guidance on materiality in the ICAEW Members' Handbook. The statement, Tech 03/08, contains guidance to help those preparing financial statements decide what information is material, in the context of the principle that an item is material if it could influence users' economic decisions. This is an update of the previous statement on materiality, Tech 32/96.

2.201 The statement stresses that any guidelines on determining what is material cannot substitute for careful consideration by preparers of how information could influence users' economic decisions such as whether to hold or sell investments or whether to reappoint or replace management. Judgements should be based on the needs of knowledgeable and diligent investors who are reasonable in their use of financial information.

2.202 The statement considers that there are three aspects to consider when deciding whether an item is material and then discusses each aspect in turn. These aspects are:

- Size. While the monetary value of items needs to be taken into account, materiality can never be judged purely on the basis of absolute size, and no specific rule of thumb tests are recommended. In some cases, size may in fact be irrelevant – for example, where the quality of management stewardship or corporate governance is at issue.

- Nature. Consideration needs to be given to the events or transactions giving rise to the item as well as their legality, sensitivity, normality and potential consequences. In addition, the identity of the parties involved in the events or transactions and the accounts captions and disclosure affected may also impact on users' decisions.

- Circumstances. When preparers consider the potential impact of information on users, they should not take a narrow view of the financial statements for a single period. They will often need to modify their views on the materiality of an item in the light of comparative figures, expected future trends, the financial statements of comparable entities and other information relating to the economic and industry background.

2.203 The statement emphasises management's responsibility by encouraging companies to develop internal guidelines on assessing materiality. These would provide relatively objective rebuttable presumptions against which subsequent judgements about particular situations can be gauged. The statement suggests guidelines can be developed by addressing the following questions:

- Who are the relevant users?
- What are their decision-making needs?
- What types of financial information are likely to influence the decisions of the users?
- For a given item, what is the appropriate context for assessing its materiality?
- In what range of values do items become critical in terms of materiality?
- How should particular items in these critical ranges be decided and reported?

2.204 Some practical examples are given of situations where preparers should be particularly sensitive in their judgements because critical thresholds are reached. These are where trends reverse, profits become losses, technical insolvency occurs, compliance with debt covenants is in doubt or where it is known that individuals are deciding whether or not to buy or sell shares.

Elements

2.205 The ASB identifies seven elements: assets; liabilities; ownership interest; gains; losses; contributions from owners; and distributions to owners. All the other definitions depend on those of asset and liability which are:

"Assets are rights or other access to future economic benefits controlled by an entity as a result of past transactions or events."

"Liabilities are obligations of an entity to transfer economic benefits as a result of past transactions or events."

2.206 These definitions are also repeated in FRS 5, which is considered in chapter 3. Ownership interest is the residual net assets.

2.207 The language used by the ASB is somewhat unusual. 'Gains', for this purpose includes revenues and other income, while 'losses' includes expenses write-downs and other losses.

2.208 Leaving aside transfers to and from owners in their capacity as owners (for example, dividends), gains and losses can be defined as increases or decreases in ownership interest.

2.209 The definitions still leave room for interpretation and may in due course lead to changes in specific accounting standards. For example, it is not altogether clear what sort of element is the deferred income which is shown as a credit balance as a result of a government grant.

Recognition

2.210 An element (as defined above) should be recognised when there is sufficient evidence (for example, as a result of a transaction or a contract) that there has been a change in assets or liabilities which can be measured with sufficient reliability. As with the previous chapters of the statement of principles, there are implicit challenges to existing practices. For example, are SSAP 21's operating leases recognisable assets and liabilities? They appear to fit the definitions of the elements and to meet the 'evidence' threshold for recognition. Yet the discussion of unperformed contracts in the Statement indicates that such rights and obligations result in a net position that will not require recognition until an imbalance between these rights and obligations arises. The appropriate treatment of unperformed contracts is the subject of much debate internationally and has yet to be resolved.

2.211 Chapter 5 of the Statement of principles also deals with de-recognition, (which should occur when the asset or liability has been eliminated or when the criteria for recognition is no longer met) and revenue recognition in the case of a transaction involving the provision of services or goods for a net gain, (which requires the occurrence of the critical event in the operating cycle involved). The discussion of revenue recognition is confusing and appears to be an attempt to fit existing long-standing accounting practices, where revenue recognition is linked to the concepts of matching and realisation, into the accounting framework adopted by the Statement, where revenue recognition is linked to the recognition and measurement of assets and liabilities.

Measurement

2.212 Chapter 6 of the Statement of principles describes the pros and cons of historical cost versus current value accounting. The ASB, in the original draft Statement, declared its hand by stating that practice should develop by evolving in the direction of greater use of current values, which it believes are more relevant than historical costs for depicting a company's resources, subject to reliability and cost-benefit considerations. Criticism of this by respondents to the first draft Statement clearly had an impact on the ASB, as their preference for current values is much more veiled in the final Statement. Indeed, according to this Statement, the ASB now apparently supports the mixed measurement system currently used in practice, whilst noting the potential for evolution towards greater use of current values as markets develop and current values become more relevant and reliable.

Presentation

2.213 Chapter 7 of the Statement of principles examines considerations that should guide the presentation of financial statements: communication, structure, aggregation and classification.

2.214 The chapter discusses each of the primary financial statements. For example, in the statement of financial performance (such as the profit and loss account or the statement of recognised gains and losses) components should be classified by reference to a combination of function and the nature of the item, amounts that are affected in different ways by changes in economic conditions or business activity should be distinguished, as should items that are unusual in amount or incidence or that have special characteristics. In the balance sheet, for example, the entity's resource structure and its financial structure should be delineated.

Accounting for interests in other entities

2.215 The last chapter expands the discussion in chapter 2 on the reporting entity to briefly cover consolidated accounts, equity accounting and accounting for investments where there is little or no control. Essentially, this chapter contains an overview of how to apply the principles set out in chapter 2, based upon present accounting practice.

Chapter 3

Reporting the substance of transactions

Reporting the substance of transactions

Scope and basic principles

Scope

3.1 This chapter deals with the requirements of FRS 5, 'Reporting the substance of transactions'. FRS 5 applies to all transactions of a company, subject only to the exclusion of certain specific transactions given in FRS 5 paragraph 12 (see further para 3.2) and transactions to which the recognition and derecognition of financial assets and financial liabilities within the scope of FRS 26 apply (see further para 3.6) FRS 5 also applies to transactions undertaken by other unincorporated entities, such as partnerships, where their financial statements are required to give a true and fair view. However, by 'transaction' the FRS means both single transactions and also arrangements that cover a series of transactions that are designed to have an overall commercial effect. [FRS 5 para 11].

3.2 No exemptions for particular types of undertaking are given in the FRS, although subsequent to its issue both insurance brokers and insurance companies have been exempted from FRS 5's requirements in relation to specific transactions. The FRS does, however, exclude certain specific transactions from its scope, which are:

- Forward contracts.
- Futures contracts.
- Foreign exchange.
- Interest rate swaps.
- Expenditure commitments.
- Orders.
- Contracts for differences.
- Employment contracts.

[FRS 5 para 12].

3.3 All of the transactions listed above are contracts for future performance and have been removed by the ASB from the scope of FRS 5 except in situations where they form part of a transaction (or series of transactions) that falls within the standard's scope. The standard cites as an example an interest rate swap forming part of a securitisation. In this case the swap is an integral component of the overall securitisation transaction which needs to be considered under the standard's rules (see further para 3.156), whereas a swap that is merely part of a company's treasury management does not come within the standard's scope.

3.4 Expenditure commitments and orders fall outside the scope until they are either delivered or paid for, whichever happens first. Contracts for differences, which are contracts where a net amount will be paid or received based on the movement in a price or an index, also fall outside the standard's scope.

3.5 Employment contracts are sometimes termed 'executory contracts' and generally involve agreements where performance by both parties lies in the future. Unless a person's salary is paid in advance, no asset is recognised in the employer's balance sheet in respect of the future benefit of the employee's service. Similarly, no liability is recognised in respect of the future payment that the employer has contracted to make. There is a remote contingent liability in relation to the person's employment, but this will only crystallise into a liability, for example, when the decision is taken to make the person redundant and would only be provided for where necessary in accordance with the requirements of FRS 12, 'Provisions, contingent liabilities and contingent assets'.

3.6 Entities within the scope of FRS 26, 'Financial instruments: Recognition and measurement', should apply the derecognition requirements in FRS 26 to financial assets and liabilities (see further chapter 6) and the derecognition principles of FRS 5 to non-financial assets and liabilities. [FRS 5 para 13B]. Entities that are not within the scope of FRS 26 should continue to apply FRS 5 to the recognition and derecognition of both *financial and non-financial* assets and liabilities.

3.7 The following transactions dealt with in FRS 5 fall within FRS 26's scope:

- Debt factoring.
- Securitisation of assets.
- Loan transfers.
- Sale and repurchase agreements, where the transaction falls within the scope of paragraphs 14 to 42 of FRS 26.

[The next paragraph is 3.42.1]

Interaction with the Act and accounting standards

3.42.1 The Companies Act requirement that a company's and a group's financial statements must give a 'true and fair view' is fundamental. It overrides the detailed rules on the form and content of company, and group, financial statements and the Act's other requirements concerning matters to be included in the financial statements. The Act requires that, if necessary, either additional disclosure should be made or, in special circumstances, the financial statements should depart from the detailed rules

3.42.2 Where the 'true and fair override' is used to depart from the Act's other provisions, the financial statements must disclose, in accordance with sections 396 and 404 of the Companies Act 2006, particulars of the departure, the reasons for it, and its effect. FRS 5, does not require the transaction's legal form to be disclosed in the notes to the financial statements (where that is different from its substance), although there is a general disclosure requirement which requires the financial statements to disclose enough information for users to understand the transaction's commercial effect.

3.43 Where transactions fall within FRS 5's scope and also directly within the scope of other accounting standards or legislation (for example, leasing) the FRS states that the standard or legislation that contains the more specific provisions should be applied. [FRS 5 para 13]. But there is a subtle implication here because the provisions of that more specific standard or legislation have to be applied to the *transaction's substance* and not to its legal form and for that purpose the general provisions of FRS 5 apply. [FRS 5 para 3.].

3.44 There are two areas where these provisions become particularly important. The first is with pension schemes where clearly FRS 17 has specific provisions that deal with how companies should account for pension obligations. Although FRS 17 does not deal specifically with the consolidation of pension schemes into the employing company's financial statements, the ASB contends that such schemes should not be consolidated as quasi-subsidiaries (see further para 3.100). [FRS 5 para 3]. FRS 5 does, however, apply to certain pension scheme transactions, for example, where a scheme enters into a sale and leaseback arrangement for the employing company's properties.

3.45 The second area where there is considerable interaction is leasing. Generally for stand-alone leases the more specific provisions will be contained in SSAP 21. But it is now even clearer that the classification of such leases as either finance or operating should be made according to their substance. This should have been the case under SSAP 21, but in practice there has tended to be undue reliance on arithmetical analysis and insufficient attention to the substance. That is, FRS 5 confirms that it is not acceptable to look only to the 90 per cent test, but that all other aspects of the transaction must also be considered to determine the transaction's substance. The term 'stand-alone' refers to simple leasing arrangements, which are not complicated by options and buy-back clauses. However, for some leases, an example being sale and leaseback arrangements where there is also an option for the lessee to repurchase the asset, FRS 5's provisions are more specific. Generally, more complex leasing arrangements where there are a number of elements will fall within FRS 5's scope. [FRS 5 para 3]. Indeed this was confirmed by an FRRP ruling issued in February 1997 in respect of the accounting treatment of a sale and leaseback transaction undertaken by Associated Nursing Services plc (see further para 3.128.1). Table 3.1 below illustrates a situation where a group has brought leasing transactions back on balance sheet where the group retains the risks and rewards of ownership.

Table 3.1 — Inchcape plc — Annual Report & Accounts — 31 December 1994

accounting policies (extract)

b Basis of Group accounts (extract)

Following the adoption of Financial Reporting Standard 5 (FRS 5) Reporting the Substance of Transactions comparative figures in the balance sheet, cash flow statement and relevant notes to the financial statements have been adjusted but there was no material effect on reported profit.

notes to the accounts (extract)

notes to the accounts (extract)	Freehold and leasehold land and buildings	Plant, machinery and equipment	Total
14 Fixed assets-tangible assets (extract)	**£m**	**£m**	**£m**
Cost or valuation at 1st January 1994	**422.0**	**451.1**	**873.1**
FRS 5 adjustment	–	**40.3**	**40.3**
Cost or valuation at 1st January 1994 — restated	**422.0**	**491.4**	**913.4**
Exchange adjustments	**(2.6)**	**0.8**	**(1.8)**
Assets of subsidiaries acquired	**22.1**	**32.1**	**54.2**
Assets of subsidiaries sold	**(26.8)**	**(43.0)**	**(69.8)**
Additions	**18.1**	**81.0**	**99.1**
Disposals	**(9.1)**	**(72.4)**	**(81.5)**
Transfers (including assets held for resale)	**(10.4)**	**8.8**	**(1.6)**
Cost or valuation at 31st December1994	**413.3**	**498.7**	**912.0**

The book value of plant, machinery and equipment includes £36.5m (1993 — £22.8m) in respect of assets held under finance leases, and £Nil (1993 — £27.2m) of assets relating to contract hire operations. The FRS 5 adjustment relates to motor vehicles leased to customers where the Group retains the risk and rewards of ownership, and includes £34.0m in respect of KCVR UK which was sold in December 1994.

3.46 This means that, for the time being, straightforward operating leases will remain off the lessee's balance sheet. There is, however, a conflict between the partial derecognition rules included in the standard (see further para 3.67) and SSAP 21. For example, if the partial derecognition rules were applied to operating leases, the effect would be that the lessor would derecognise the whole asset, but would recognise new assets representing the entitlement to a stream of receivables and a residual asset. This conflict will remain unless SSAP 21 is revised to fall in line with FRS 5. In the meantime, the provisions of SSAP 21 are generally more specific for a straightforward lease. For an example of how the interaction between FRS 5 and SSAP 21 applies see examples 1 and 2 in paragraph 3.78.

Principles of FRS 5

Objective

3.47 The standard's overriding objective is to ensure that the substance of an entity's transactions is reported in its financial statements. That means that the commercial effect of the undertaking's transactions and any resulting assets, liabilities, gains or losses should be faithfully represented in its financial statements. [FRS 5 para 1].

3.48 The objective is simply stated and the standard's provisions are simple to apply where the transaction is itself simple in nature. However, determining how to account in practice for more complex transactions in accordance with their substance is fraught with difficulties. The nature of the accounting decisions made will inevitably be subjective and the resulting accounting treatment will differ depending upon the perception of the transaction's substance and its effect in practice. The answer to whether an item is on or off balance sheet under the standard will not necessarily be clear even after analysing the transaction in detail following the standard's guidance. The standard places particular emphasis on the transaction's *commercial effect in practice.* It is not adequate to review the transaction from a theoretical standpoint; it is what is likely to happen in practice and what actually happens in practice that is important.

3.49 The commercial effect in practice of a complex transaction might change from year to year as the actual or likely economic outcome becomes clearer. At the outset, the transaction has to be analysed and the likely outcome in practice determined in accordance with the facts and best estimates where future factors of the transaction are uncertain. After the transaction is initially recorded in accordance with its substance, the actual or likely outcome will have to be monitored in future accounting periods to determine whether the transaction's substance changes in practice. Where there is a subsequent change in the transaction's substance, that change will have to be accounted for when it becomes apparent.

3.50 The basic principles concerning reporting the substance of transactions can be summarised under five heads:

- Identifying and recognising assets and liabilities.
- Transactions in previously recognised assets.
- Linked presentation for non-recourse transactions.
- Offset rules.
- Accounting for quasi-subsidiaries.

Each of these is explained in the paragraphs below.

Identifying and recognising assets and liabilities

3.51 FRS 5's identification and recognition principles can be illustrated in a flow diagram (see diagram 1). As can be seen from the diagram, the steps to recognise an asset or liability are relatively straightforward in principle. It is simply a matter of analysing the relevant transactions to ascertain whether they give rise to new assets or liabilities that need to be recognised on the balance sheet or give rise to changes in existing assets and liabilities. Once an asset or liability has been identified and there is sufficient evidence that it exists *and* it can be measured sufficiently reliably, it should be recognised in the financial statements. [FRS 5 para 20]. These steps are considered in more detail below.

Diagram 1 — Recognising the substance of transactions

The numbers in square brackets refer to paragraphs of the standard.

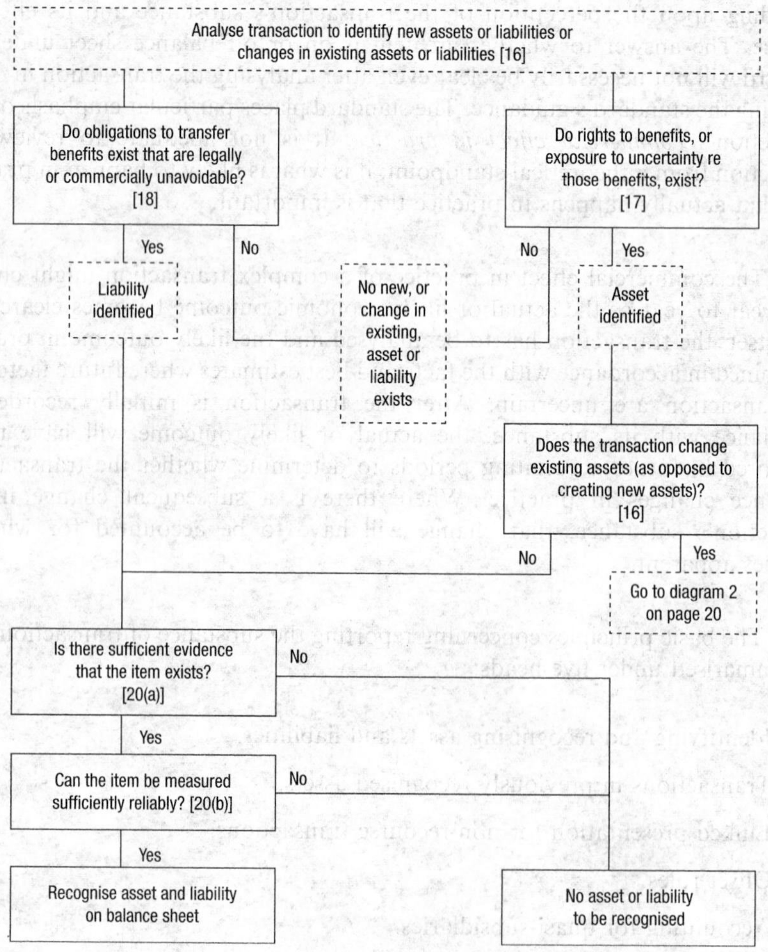

Analysing complex transactions

3.52 The first step in the process outlined above is to analyse the transaction. The most important aspect of analysing complex transactions is to consider carefully the reasons why each of the parties has entered into the transaction. What is the true commercial effect of the transaction? Is the transaction being entered into for tax reasons? Is one of the parties intending to acquire or dispose of an asset or is it intending to raise finance? What is the role of the other party? Once the commercial reason for the arrangement has been ascertained it may become obvious whether one of the parties to the transaction is merely receiving a lender's return. If this is so, then the transaction will almost certainly be a financing arrangement. More complex transactions often include the severance of legal title from the transaction's benefits and risks, some form of linkage with other transactions and put or call options.

Severance of legal title

3.53 Although the legal title to an asset may pass from a company because it enters into a particular transaction, the benefits and obligations associated with the asset often remain with the company. An example of such a transaction is a sale and repurchase of stock, where the seller agrees to repurchase stock at a price based on the original sales price. The title to the stocks passes, but the mark up in the buy-back price in substance represents a finance charge. Therefore, to accord with the standard's principles, such a transaction should remain on the seller's balance sheet with the receipt recorded as a liability. The mark up would be charged to the profit and loss account as a finance cost over the term of the transaction. Similarly, goods sold under reservation of title enable the selling company to have a lien on the goods until the purchaser has paid for them, although the benefits and risks in the goods have been transferred to the purchaser. It is common practice for the purchaser to account for the arrangement's substance and recognise such stocks in its balance sheet, although the supplier retains legal title to the goods. The supplier will treat the transaction as a sale. Conversely, with a finance lease, the lessor retains the legal title, but the transaction's substance is such that the asset and related obligation are recorded in the lessee's books.

Linkage with other transactions

3.54 A transaction is often linked with other transactions so that the commercial effect cannot be understood without considering the transactions as a whole. A simple example would be a transaction where a company sells an asset, but enters into a separate agreement to repurchase the asset at some time in the future. The commitment to repurchase is clearly linked to the sale and, therefore, the commercial outcome of the transaction should be considered as if they were a single transaction. This might, depending on the repurchase conditions, result in the transactions being accounted for as a financing arrangement rather than a sale of the asset with a separate repurchase.

Options and conditions

3.55 Simple options, such as an option to purchase shares, generally represent assets in their own right. A share option of this nature represents the right to purchase the shares at a future date and does not represent the actual shares that will be acquired on exercising the option. But with more complex transactions, options are often used in conjunction with the transaction's other aspects to give one party access to the future benefits associated with an asset, although that party might not have legal ownership of the asset.

3.56 Often options or conditions are included in the terms of a transaction which, by their nature, are almost certain to be fulfilled. In such transactions it is common for the company entering into the agreement to suffer an economic penalty if the option or condition is not fulfilled (or to receive an economic benefit if it is fulfilled). This economic penalty or benefit may be so great that the option or condition will inevitably be taken up by the entity. In determining the outcome of options in practice, greater weight should be given to those aspects and implications that are *more likely to have a commercial effect in practice*. The option's likely outcome has to be considered carefully, for example:

- Where there is no genuine commercial possibility that the option *will* be exercised, it should be ignored.
- Where there is no genuine commercial possibility that the option *will not* be exercised, its future exercise should be assumed.

[FRS 5 para 61].

3.57 In between these two extremes it will be a matter of judgement and the overall transaction's true commercial effect, including the option's likely impact, will have to be considered very carefully. As a consequence, the standard states that where a transaction incorporates one or more options, guarantees or conditional provisions, their commercial effect should be assessed in the context of all aspects and implications of the transaction in practice in order to determine what assets and liabilities exist. [FRS 5 para 19]. This does not mean, however, that the effect of an option should be judged on its probable outcome. In certain situations it might be assessed that the party's obligations and access to benefits are genuinely optional or conditional, in which case the option can be ignored. [FRS 5 para 61]. In other circumstances, the operation of options might indicate that one party has obligations (liabilities) or access to benefits (assets) that require to be recognised in its financial statements. The standard also points out that it should be assumed in the transaction's analysis that each of the parties will act in accordance with its economic interests. [FRS 5 para 62].

3.58 The following examples illustrate the application of these rules:

- Where the cost of exercising an option is expected to be lower than the benefits obtained by its exercise, it will generally be exercised and so in analysing the transaction the option's exercise should be assumed.

- If the cost of exercising an option is expected to be higher than the benefits obtained then generally it can be assumed that it will not be exercised and it can be ignored when analysing the transaction.

- Where the seller of an asset retains a call option over the asset and the buyer retains a put option, then it is almost certain that either the seller will call back the asset or the buyer will put it back to the seller. If for example, the asset is sold for £100,000 and the options are both priced at £110,000, then if the value of the asset decreases to (say) £90,000, the buyer will put it back to the seller at £110,000. Conversely, if the value moves up to £115,000, the seller will call back the asset for £110,000. In this case the asset should remain on the seller's balance sheet as a financing arrangement as the seller continues to bear the risks and rewards of ownership.

- Where the seller of an asset retains a call option over the asset and the buyer does not have an option to put the asset back to the seller the intentions of the seller and the rationale for including the option will have to be considered very carefully. As in the first two examples, the price of the option might indicate whether or not it will be exercised.

Identifying assets and liabilities

3.59 Once the transaction's commercial purpose has been ascertained it is then necessary to determine whether the transaction gives rise to new assets or liabilities or changes the entity's existing assets or liabilities.

Assets

3.60 Assets are defined in the standard as:

> *"Rights or other access to future economic benefits controlled by an entity as a result of past transactions or events."* [FRS 5 para 2].

3.61 Control over the rights to economic benefits means the ability to obtain the future economic benefits relating to an asset and the ability to restrict the access of others to those benefits. [FRS 5 para 3]. Control can be contrasted with management, which is the ability to direct the use of the item that generates the benefits. An example is a unit trust manager, who has day-to-day management of the trust's portfolio of investments, but it is the unit holders who gain the economic benefits from those assets, not the manager.

3.62 There will often be uncertainty regarding the amount of benefit flowing from an asset and this is the risk associated with the benefit. [FRS 5 para 5]. The standard uses the word 'benefit' to encompass also the risks that the benefit will be greater or smaller than expected and to cover the risks associated with the timing of the benefit's receipt. Risk is also defined in terms of the uncertainty of the amount of the benefits, including both the potential for gain and the exposure to loss. [FRS 5 para 5]. However, generally people understand and refer to benefits and risks (or risks and rewards) rather than using the term benefits to cover both.

The party who has access to the benefits of an asset will also generally be subject to the risk that they will turn out to be different from expected. Therefore, evidence of whether an entity is exposed to risks associated with an asset (that is, whether it is exposed to a loss) is evidence that the entity has access to the asset's future economic benefits.

Liabilities

3.63 Liabilities are defined as:

> *"An entity's obligations to transfer economic benefits as a result of past transactions or events."* [FRS 5 para 3].

An entity, therefore, has a liability if it has an obligation which will result in an outflow of funds. Such an obligation will exist if the entity is unable to avoid either legally or commercially an outflow of benefits. [FRS 5 para 18].

3.64 Where an entity's obligation is contingent on the outcome of one or more future events which are uncertain, a liability should not necessarily be recognised. Such an obligation should be accounted for in accordance with FRS 12 and will only give rise to a liability where it is probable that a future event will confirm a loss which can be estimated with reasonable accuracy at the date the financial statements are approved for publication. [FRS 5 para 58]. As a consequence, generally guarantees will not give rise to liabilities that require to be recognised in the financial statements unless a loss is foreseen (but they may prevent derecognition of previously recognised assets — see further para 3.67 onwards). But the commercial effects of guarantees do need to be considered very carefully as part of the overall transaction. Furthermore, some guarantees might operate in a similar way to options. Where this is so, they will need to be considered in the context of the overall transaction (see para 3.55).

Recognition of assets and liabilities

3.65 Once an asset or liability has been identified it should be recognised in the entity's balance sheet if both of the following conditions are satisfied:

- There is sufficient evidence of the item's existence.
- The item can be measured at a monetary amount with sufficient reliability.

3.66 Recognition is defined in the standard as the *"process of incorporating an item into the primary financial statements under the appropriate heading. It involves depiction of the item in words and by a monetary amount and inclusion of that amount in the statement totals"*. [FRS 5 para 6].

Transactions in previously recognised assets

3.67 FRS 5 includes rules concerning when a previously recognised asset can be taken off balance sheet (discontinued recognition, or derecognition). Before a previously recognised asset can be derecognised there must be an effective sale or disposal of the particular asset. That is, *all significant* benefits and risks relating to the asset must be transferred to another party. On the other hand, if after a transaction has been entered into by the company there has been no significant change in the entity's benefits or risks associated with a previously recognised asset, there has been no sale and the relevant asset should remain on the balance sheet.

3.68 In between these two extremes, FRS 5 contains rules to deal with the middle ground. These new rules (called in this chapter 'partial derecognition') deal with situations where:

- Part of an asset has been transferred to another party.
- All of the asset has been transferred, but for only part of its life.
- All of the asset has been transferred for all of its life, but where some significant benefits and risks are retained.

3.69 These rules mean that where there is a significant change in the entity's rights to benefits *and* exposure to risks, but the entity has not got rid of all significant rights and/or significant exposure to risks, then the original asset should be derecognised. But in its place there should be shown a new asset and corresponding liability reflecting the benefits and risks retained by the entity after the transaction. This can be contrasted with the use of the linked presentation (see para 3.83); the linked presentation typically applies in situations where significant benefits and risks are retained which are associated with the performance of the *gross* asset in question (see further para 3.84). The situations that can arise are shown in diagram 2 and are explained in more detail below.

Diagram 2 — Transactions in previously recognised assets

The numbers in square brackets refer to paragraphs of the standard.

Continued recognition of the asset on balance sheet [18]	
Rewards retained	**Risks retained**
All significant	All significant
All significant	Some or none
Some or none	All significant
Ceasing to recognise the asset in its entirety — derecognition [22]	
Rewards retained	**Risks retained**
No significant	No significant
Special cases — partial derecognition [23]	
Rewards retained	**Risks retained**
Some	Some
No significant	Some
Some	No significant

3.70 The term 'significant' is not included in the list of the standard's definitions, but in respect of these rules it should be judged in relation to the benefits and risks that are likely to occur in practice and not in relation to the total possible benefits and risks. [FRS 5 para 25]. This again emphasises the importance of the transaction's commercial effect in practice. The problem in practice will be deciding what benefits and risks are significant and this will be a matter of judgement. The standard illustrates the principle using an example: an entity sells debts of £100 million and bad debts are expected to be £2 million. There is recourse to the seller for the first £5 million of bad debts. In this case, the seller has retained all significant risks of non-payment.

Continued recognition

3.71 As can be seen from diagram 2, an asset should remain on balance sheet where there is no significant change to the entity's rights or benefits relating to the asset. Similarly, unless there is also a significant change in the risks associated with the asset, the entity's asset still has to be retained on balance sheet. [FRS 5 para 21]. Therefore if the entity retains all significant benefits *or* all significant risks (or both) the asset should remain on balance sheet.

3.72 For those entities not applying FRS 26 the standard cites a debt factoring arrangement where the entity selling the debts retains the bad debt risk and slow payment risk as an example of a transaction where the debts clearly cannot be derecognised. In that example, the entity retains the significant risks associated with the transaction and the factor is merely supplying finance and receiving a lender's return, even though the legal title to the debts may have passed. Furthermore, the example illustrates that derecognition is not allowed where the transaction finances the entity's existing assets, even where the finance is non-recourse. With such an arrangement the entity is left with the same benefits and risks relating to the asset that existed before the financing, but in addition the transaction creates an obligation (a liability) to repay the finance, which must be recognised on the balance sheet. The only exception to this rule is where the transaction is a financing arrangement and the conditions for the linked presentation are met (see further para 3.83). [FRS 5 para 67].

Full derecognition

3.73 A previously recognised asset can only be derecognised in its entirety (without being replaced by another asset — see para 3.74) where all significant benefits *and* all significant risks relating to the asset have been transferred. For those entities not applying FRS 26, this situation will arise where an asset is sold for a single non-returnable cash payment where there is no recourse by the buyer to the entity's other assets and no further entitlements to rights on the part of the seller (for example, in a sale of a subsidiary where part of the consideration is deferred). [FRS 5 para 69].

Partial derecognition

3.74 The standard indicates that partial derecognition only applies where there is a significant change in the entity's rights to benefits *and* exposure to risks. It should be borne in mind that the type of situations where partial derecognition applies are few in number; generally previously recognised assets will either have to be retained on the balance sheet or, if they meet the criteria, derecognised in their entirety. Partial derecognition might arise where the transaction takes the form of a transfer of:

- Part of the asset.
- All of the asset for part of its life.
- All of the asset for all its life, but where the entity retains significant benefits or risks.

3.75 The principles can be illustrated as follows:

- Transfer of part of the asset — proportionate share

  For those entities not applying FRS 26, a loan transfer might involve the transfer of a proportionate share of a loan (including rights to interest and principal) such that cash flows and profits and losses are shared by the transferee and transferor in fixed proportions. In this case, the proportionate share transferred should be derecognised.

- Transfer of part of the asset — splitting benefit streams.

  For those entities not applying FRS 26, the interest benefit stream is stripped from a loan being held as an asset such that one party has the benefits and risks associated with the interest stream and the other has the benefits and risks associated with the principal. In this case, the party retaining the investment in the principal should derecognise the original asset and in its place recognise a new asset namely an investment in the non-interest bearing principal. The original carrying amount would have to be allocated to the principal and the interest stream. If the element of cost allocated to the interest stream equals the proceeds, then no profit or loss arises and the remainder is allocated to the principal. However, in principle the principal is recognised at a different amount than its original carrying value. The amount at which the principal is recorded would then earn interest, which would be added to the principal each year and credited to the profit and loss account, until the loan is redeemed at its full amount. For example, if an interest strip is made on a loan, and the amount received is £50,000, the amount of the original carrying value of the principal allocated to the interest may also be £50,000 (and would probably be arrived at by discounting the interest receivable). Therefore, no gain or loss arises on the transaction. The discount of £50,000 would be deducted from the balance of the loan and credited to the profit and loss account over the remaining term of the loan, thereby building up the loan to its redemption amount at the end of its term.

- Transfer of asset for part of its life.

  An entity sells a car, but agrees to repurchase it towards the end of its life at a value that fairly reflects the usage and depreciation over the period to repurchase. The entity now only has an interest in the residual, and also has a liability, which is its obligation to repurchase the item. Any profit or loss on sale will be the difference between the proceeds and the old book value. Whether accounting for a residual asset and liability is actually appropriate depends on the likely commercial outcome. If repurchase is intended or likely, the residual asset and liability should be recognised; and if a loss is likely on repurchase, that would be accounted for at the start by recording a residual liability in excess of a residual asset (that is, by making a provision against the asset to reduce it to its recoverable amount). But if, as for example with some manufacturer's buy-back guarantees, the manufacturer agrees to buy back an asset after say five years, but does so only at a low price such that it is much more likely that the customer will retain the asset or sell it to a third party, it would not be appropriate to record a residual asset or liability. All that is necessary in such situations is for the manufacturer to make provision for any loss that might arise on the (relatively few) units that are expected to be returned.

- Transfer of asset for all of its life where some benefit or risk is retained.

  A subsidiary might be sold with an earn-out (that is, an amount of deferred performance-related consideration), in which case the original asset (the subsidiary) would be derecognised and something else would appear in its place, namely a debtor, being a prudent estimate of the amount of further proceeds under the earn-out, discounted if appropriate.

  Another example is where an asset has been sold subject to a warranty agreement. The party selling the asset has disposed of the benefits and risks associated with the asset and can derecognise it, but has retained a liability which is the obligation under the warranty agreement. Whether this liability will be recognised will depend on the circumstances and where necessary an adequate provision should be made in accordance with the requirements of FRS 12. If a provision is necessary, a corresponding loss is recognised in the profit and loss account.

3.76 Under the partial derecognition rules, where there is a significant change in the entity's rights to benefits and exposure to risks, the original asset should be derecognised in its entirety and a different asset recognised in its place, together with a liability representing any obligations assumed. If there is no new asset, then it is necessary to provide for any liability for loss if an obligation is likely to arise.

3.77 In this type of situation, where an asset has been derecognised in its entirety a profit or loss will arise and this should be recognised on a prudent basis. For example, where the resulting profit or loss is uncertain, the standard requires that full provision should be made for any probable loss and, to the extent that any gain is in doubt, it should be deferred. [FRS 5 para 24].

3.78 The examples that follow illustrate situations where the partial derecognition rules apply and also show how the standard's provisions interact with those of SSAP 21.

Example 1

A vehicle contract hire company buys cars and enters into three-year operating leases with lessees. Economically, what was a single asset (a car) has become two assets: (a) a stream of receivables over three years; and (b) a risk on the residual value at year three. The lessor then sells the stream of rentals to a bank (with the bank taking the bad debt risk); the lessor is left with the residual position.

Following FRS 5's partial derecognition rules, the asset would be split in two (as above), the receivables would be regarded as having been sold and there would remain a different asset, namely a three-year residual, on the balance sheet. This assumes that the lessor would hold the asset at that time or would buy it back at a pre-agreed price. In these circumstances there would be an equivalent liability for the funding of the residual or the repurchase obligation.

Example 2

A slightly different example to that above is where a lessor enters into arrangements with a third party such that the lessor does not buy back the car, but merely guarantees to make good a shortfall if the market value at year three was not as great as the expected amount and, similarly, benefits from any increase in the market value above the guaranteed amount. In this circumstance, the asset would be the extent (if any) to which the market value might exceed the guaranteed amount (this would probably be booked as nil initially on prudence grounds). The obligation would be the provision (if any) that the lessor needs to make in respect of the loss that is likely to occur, which would be recognised and taken to the profit and loss account in accordance with the requirements of FRS 12.

3.79 Thus there seems to be a difference, under the partial de-recognition approach, between cases where the lessor actually holds the asset or will (or may) buy it back (that is, a new asset, the residual, is shown on the balance sheet) and cases where the lessor merely guarantees the residual value (that is, no asset is likely to arise on the balance sheet, but a provision will be required for any expected loss).

3.80 Where there is an overlap with the provisions of FRS 5 and SSAP 21, the standard states that the statement that contains the more specific provisions should be applied. In the examples above, the provisions of FRS 5 are more specific than those of SSAP 21 and hence should be applied in the way indicated.

3.81 In Table 3.2, J Bibby & Sons PLC has brought back on balance sheet following the introduction of FRS 5, repurchase obligations to re-acquire certain equipment at the end of its primary lease period.

Table 3.2 — J. Bibby & Sons PLC — Annual Report and Accounts 24 September 1994

Financial Review (extract)

FRS 5

The implementation of FRS 5 (Reporting the Substance of Transactions), which applies to accounting periods ending after 22nd September 1994, has resulted in bills and leases discounted with recourse and repurchase obligations for equipment sold being included on the balance sheet. All the transactions which gave rise to these items were entered into entirely within the normal course of business and have been included in debtors or stocks on the one hand and creditors on the other hand. The amounts are as follows:

	1994			1993		
	Total	Recourse commitments	Repurchase obligations	Total	Recourse commitments	Repurchase obligations
	£000's	£000's	£000's	£000's	£000's	£000's
Under one year	25,477	21,241	4,236	27,195	25,296	1,899
Over one year	12,593	508	12,085	6,989	1,253	5,736
	38,070	21,749	16,321	34,184	26,549	7,635

The repurchase obligations enable our Capital Equipment and Materials Handling Divisions to re-acquire equipment, which has usually been maintained by themselves, at the end of primary periods thus providing opportunities in the used equipment market.

Insurance

3.82 It is often wrongly thought that insuring against the risks associated with a particular transaction might enable the company concerned to derecognise the related assets on the basis that it has transferred significant risks associated with the asset. This is a misconception because the risks associated with the asset (for example, bad debt risk) remain with the company and the company has a counter claim against its insurer should that risk arise (for example, when a debt is bad). In practice, this counter claim may or may not be met by the insurance company depending on whether the company has complied with its insurance conditions. It is only possible to derecognise an asset if the significant risks and benefits have been sold to another party and the risks and rewards have been transferred to that same party. However, if that other party itself insures against the same risks that the company would have insured against, then it may be possible for the transaction to be derecognised, because the company has successfully transferred its significant risks.

Linked presentation

General rules

3.83 Following representations made to the ASB by the banking industry and others, the ASB developed the 'linked presentation' for certain specialised transactions such as securitisations where non-recourse finance is involved. The only recourse allowed to the provider of the finance in such a transaction is to the specific assets being financed and not to the entity's other assets. The specific assets are, therefore, 'ring-fenced'. There must be *no recourse whatsoever* to other assets of the entity. The linked presentation represents a compromise which allows certain assets and their related finance to be 'linked' on the face of the balance sheet, whereby the finance is deducted from the asset. The presentation is said not to offend the Act's offset rules because, under the standard's principles, the asset that is being recognised on the face of the balance sheet is the net item and not the gross amount. Furthermore, as the amount of finance received is non-refundable, it does not meet the standard's definition of a liability. The gross asset and liability are being disclosed on the face of the balance sheet merely as additional information to enable the user to appreciate the full extent of the transaction.

3.84 An important condition of using this presentation is that the provider of the finance must only be repaid from the benefits generated by the assets or from the realisation of the assets themselves. The entity can retain rights to any surplus benefits that remain after repayment of the finance, but it must not have any right or obligation to keep the assets or to repay the finance from its own resources. Often in such transactions, the entity will be exposed to certain benefits and risks that will have a commercial effect in practice. This might arise, for example, because the future outcome measured in both terms of profits and cash flows will often be dependent on the performance of the gross assets transferred to the other party (for example, in the case of receivables, the performance will be affected by the amount of bad debts and the timing of payment). The ASB contends that it is the retention of these *significant* benefits or risks associated with the gross asset that distinguish this type of non-recourse financing from transactions that can be partially derecognised; where there is a transfer of the whole asset for part of its life or a transfer of part of the asset for all of its life (see para 3.74). This is an important distinction, as without it all transactions eligible for linked presentation might alternatively be partially derecognised. Where significant benefits or risks are retained and the transaction is in the nature of a financing arrangement it is still only eligible for the linked presentation if the strict conditions set out in paragraph 3.89 below can be satisfied.

3.85 The following example illustrates these points for those entities not applying FRS 26.

Example

If a company has debtors of £10m it might factor these and in return receive non-returnable proceeds of £9m. As the debtors are collected it will recover the balance of £1m less the factor's fees, but it is still subject to credit risk (that is, bad debt risk) up to a maximum of £1m on the full amount of the debt of £10m. If the bad debt risk is expected to be £0.5m it is likely to receive only a further £0.5m from the factor. In addition, the factor will charge a financing fee for providing the £9m of funds to the company which varies depending on the speed of collection (late payment risk). Consequently, the company still retains the significant risks associated with the debts (the bad debt risk and the late payment risk), albeit it has transferred the risk of catastrophe (which is negligible) to the factor. The factor's risk of loss would arise only if the bad debts exceeded £1m, which is highly unlikely. Therefore, the company has retained significant risks relating to the whole of the assets and, as a consequence, they cannot be partially derecognised, but (because the £9m is non-returnable and assuming the other criteria are met) the assets are eligible for the linked presentation. The transaction is precluded from being partially derecognised, because the company still bears the risk associated with the *gross* amount of the portfolio of debts and in practice bears the same bad debt risk before and after the transaction (albeit after the sale, it has transferred the risk of catastrophe). If, for example, the company had sold 90% of *each* debt then its risks have changed significantly and its bad debt risk on the portfolio will be very different before and after the sale. In this latter circumstance, the transaction might be eligible for the partial derecognition rules and if so it could be appropriate to derecognise the part of the debt that has been sold (that is, 90% of each debt) and retain on balance sheet the balance (that is, 10% of each debt).

If the transaction complies with the conditions for the linked presentation it would be disclosed on the face of the balance sheet in the following way:

Balance sheet (extract)	£m	£m
Current assets		
Debtors		
Trade debtors		50.0
Trade debtors subject to financing arrangements	9.5	
Less: non-returnable amounts received	9.0	0.5
Total trade debtors		50.5

The trade debtors of £9.5m is made up of the total debtors of £10m less the expected bad debt provision of £0.5m. The required disclosure clearly shows the asset of £0.5m to which the entity is exposed separately from other debtors, there being no other recourse from the providers of the finance to other assets of the entity.

If subsequently, one of the debtors that owes £3m goes into liquidation and the debt is bad, it will be necessary to reduce the gross trade debtors by this amount. However, because part of this debt is covered by non-returnable funds received from the factor it is possible to reduce the liability to the factor by £2m. Of the difference of £1m, £0.5m would be charged to the profit and loss account and the balance of £0.5m used to reduce the provision. In effect, the net presentation is carried through to the profit and loss account, the loss that falls to the company is only £0.5m: of the remainder of the loss, £2m is borne by the factor as a result of the £9m being non-returnable and £0.5m has already been provided for. Therefore, at this stage, the company has provided in full for the risks relating to the debtors of £1m that are not covered by non-recourse finance (that is, £0.5m initial bad debt provision and an additional provision of £0.5m). The linked presentation would then show gross debtors of £7m (£10m less £3m) less a gross liability of the same amount (£9m less £2m) coming to a net balance of nil. Even though the net balance is nil, the linked presentation disclosing the gross figures still has to be shown on the face of the balance sheet.

3.86 The amount of funding received may not always equate exactly to the non-returnable amount as happened in the example above. This is illustrated in the example in paragraph 3.91.

3.87 Another important restriction is that the linked presentation cannot be used where the finance relates to a business unit or to assets that are used in conjunction with other assets of the entity to generate the funds to repay the finance. Therefore, for example, a company cannot use the linked presentation for the debt it might raise to finance the company's operating properties. However, it will be a matter of judgement as to how far this rule should be taken. For example, can a property investment company use the linked presentation for an investment property that it has financed ring-fenced? The answer is probably no, because even if the company is funding the repayment of the finance from the asset's rental income, if it has the right to retain the asset at the end of its life it falls foul of one of the linked presentation conditions mentioned below.

Conditions in detail

3.88 Under the rules in the standard the linked presentation can only be used where a transaction involving a previously recognised asset is in substance a financing, but the company 'ring-fences' the asset such that:

- The finance will be repaid only from proceeds generated by the specific item it finances (or by transfer of the item itself) and there is *no possibility whatsoever* of a claim on the entity being established other than against funds generated by that item (or against the item itself).
- There is *no* provision whereby the entity may either keep the item on repayment of the finance or re-acquire it at any time.

[FRS 5 para 26].

3.89 Following these initial requirements the standard then sets down detailed conditions that must be met before the linked presentation can be used:

- The finance must relate to a specific item (or portfolio of similar items) and, in the case of a loan, must be secured on that item, but not on any other assets of the entity. [FRS 5 para 27(a)].

  The linked presentation cannot be used where the finance relates to two or more assets that are not part of a portfolio or to a portfolio covering assets that would otherwise be shown under different balance sheet captions.

- The provider of the finance must have no recourse whatsoever, either explicit or implicit, to the other assets of the entity for losses and the entity must have no obligation whatsoever to repay the provider of the finance. [FRS 5 para 27(b)].

  This means that there must be no obligation whatsoever (not even a moral one) to fund losses on the assets being financed. For example, a moral obligation on an originator in a mortgage securitisation might arise if the originator were to fund a mortgage interest rate increase which could not be borne by the mortgagors (the borrowers).

- The entity's directors must state explicitly in each set of financial statements where a linked presentation is used that the entity is not obliged to support any losses, nor does it intend to do so (see for example Table 3.3). [FRS 5 para 27(c)].

- The provider of the finance must agree in writing (in the finance documentation or otherwise) that it will seek repayment of the finance, as to both principal and interest, only to the extent that sufficient funds are generated by the specific item it has financed and that it will not seek recourse in any other form, and such agreement is noted in each set of financial statements where a linked presentation is used (see also Table 3.3). [FRS 5 para 27(d)].

- If the funds generated by the item are insufficient to pay off the provider of the finance, this must not constitute an event of default for the entity. [FRS 5 para 27(e)].

  This means, for example, that where an originator in a securitisation transaction has other funds lent to it by the provider of the finance, if there are insufficient funds from the securitisation transaction to repay the finance for that deal, the provider of the finance should not be able to regard that as constituting a default on the other funds lent to the originator and, as a consequence, require their repayment. The provision would also extend to a different lender where there is a cross-default clause linked to all the company's borrowings including the securitisation.

- There must be no provision whatsoever, either in the financing arrangement or otherwise, whereby the entity has a right or an obligation either to keep the item upon repayment of the finance or (where title to the item has been transferred) to re-acquire it at any time. Accordingly:
  - where the item is one (such as a monetary receivable) that directly generates cash, the provider of the finance must be repaid out of the resulting cash receipts (to the extent these are sufficient); or
  - where the item is one (such as a physical asset) that does not directly generate cash, there is a definite point at which either the item must be sold to a third party and the provider of the finance repaid from the proceeds (to the extent these are sufficient) or the item must be transferred to the provider of the finance in full and final settlement.

[FRS 5 para 27(f)].

Even where there is merely an understanding between the parties that the seller will re-acquire the asset at some time in the future, this fact is enough for this condition to be breached. This clearly illustrates that all of the aspects of the transaction need to be considered including the intentions of the parties even where these are not evidenced in writing. Put and call options are commonly used to effect a repurchase and where these exist in a transaction, the linked presentation should not be used.

3.90 It is necessary to analyse a transaction very carefully to establish whether there are any recourse provisions, because recourse can come in different forms, such as:

- Substitution clauses whereby good debts are substituted for non-performing debts (see further para 3.162).

- Guarantees for performance, proceeds or other support.
- Put options to transfer assets back to the originating entity.
- Swap arrangements (see para 3.156).
- Penalty arrangements.

Warranties in relation to the condition of the assets when the arrangement is being entered into (for example, the seller has good title or has delivered the asset or warrants that the assets are in good condition) do not preclude use of the linked presentation, but warranties relating to the future condition or performance (for example, payment or speed of payment) of the assets do preclude use of the linked presentation. [FRS 5 para 83].

Linking part of the finance

3.91 If the conditions hold for only part of the finance, then the linked presentation is still used by those entities not applying FRS 26 for that part of the finance for which all the conditions are met.

Example

A company sells its debtors of £10m to a third party and receives in return an amount of £9m. Of the £9m, £7.5m is non-returnable, but £1.5m of the finance is returnable depending on the performance of the debtors. The bad debts are expected on past experience to be £0.5m. In effect, the company retains the risks associated with the first £2.5m of losses and as £1.5m is potentially returnable it cannot be included in the linked presentation and must be shown as a liability. The transaction would be disclosed in the balance sheet in the following way.

Balance sheet (extract)	£m	£m
Current assets		
Debtors		
Trade debtors		50.0
Trade debtors subject to financing arrangements	9.5	
Less: non-returnable amounts received	7.5	2.0
Total trade debtors		52.0
Creditors		
Financing of trade debtors		1.5

It would be necessary for the notes to the financial statements to explain fully the implications of the transaction and in particular to indicate that certain of the finance related to it is returnable and is included in creditors.

3.92 An example of a company that has non-recourse finance for part of its debts is given in Table 3.3.

Table 3.3 — WPP Group plc — Annual Report and Accounts — 31 December 2000

Consolidated balance sheet (extract)

As at 31 December 2000

	Notes	2000 £m	1999 £m
Current assets			
Stocks and work in progress	16	**241.1**	**113.5**
Debtors	17	**2,181.0**	**1,068.4**
Debtors within working capital facility:	18		
Gross debts		**464.9**	**345.7**
Non-returnable proceeds		**(231.6)**	**(214.1)**
		233.3	**131.6**

Notes to the consolidated balance sheet

Debtors within working capital facility

The following are included in debtors within the Group's working capital facilities:

	2000 £m	1999 £m
Gross debts	**464.9**	**345.7**
Non-returnable proceeds	**(231.6)**	**(214.1)**
	233.3	**131.6**

Within the Group's overall working capital facilities, certain trade debts have been assigned as security against the advance of cash. This security is represented by the assignment of a pool of trade debts, held by one of the Group's subsidiaries, to a trust for the benefit of the providers of this working capital facility. The financing provided against this pool takes into account, inter alia, the risks that may be attached to individual debtors and the expected collection period.

The Group is not obliged (and does not intend) to support any credit-related losses arising from the assigned debts against which cash has been advanced. The providers of the finance have confirmed in writing that, in the event of default in payment by a debtor, they will only seek repayment of cash advanced from the remainder of the pool of debts in which they hold an interest, and that repayment will not be sought from the Group in any other way.

Profit recognition

3.93 Much of FRS 5 is aimed at the balance sheet and how assets and liabilities should be recognised there, but for linked presentations there is also some guidance on when profits and losses should be recognised. At the inception of the transaction a gain will only arise to the extent that the non-returnable proceeds received exceed the asset's previous carrying value. [FRS 5 para 28]. During the transaction's life, a profit or loss will arise to the extent that the income from the asset is different from the amount due to the financier. Finally, if the transaction is such that the asset is eventually sold at the end of the transaction a further profit or loss may arise, but this amount can only be recognised in the period that the onward sale takes place. Furthermore, where for example the asset generates income and there is a cost of finance in a period, it will be the net amount of profit or loss that is generally recognised in the profit and loss account (as these amounts should also be linked in a similar way to the balance sheet items from which they are generated). The gross components should be given in a note to the financial statements, unless in order to give a true and fair view it is necessary to show the gross amounts linked on the face of the profit and loss account. This latter situation might arise where the transaction is of such significance to the company's trading results that the net presentation alone does not give the transaction sufficient prominence.

3.94 What the standard does not discuss is where to show such profits and losses in the profit and loss account. On the inception of the transaction, although it is a financing arrangement, there will be a one off gain or loss that arises in effect on the transfer of benefits and risks to the other party, which is akin to a sale of an asset. For example, if debtors of £10,000 are sold for £9,000, which is non-returnable and further amounts receivable are prudently estimated at nil, a loss of £1,000 should be charged to the profit and loss account and included in the format item 'interest payable and similar charges', because it is in substance a finance charge.

3.95 During the life of a simple financing arrangement, it would seem sensible to show any net losses in an accounting period as part of the company's cost of finance and record it in the profit and loss account as interest payable and similar charges. Where the transaction generates a net profit this is similarly a finance item and should also be included within 'other interest receivable and similar income' in the profit and loss account.

3.96 If on the eventual outcome of the transaction there is a sale of the linked assets then the profit or loss arising on this part of the transaction should be accounted for in accordance with the normal rules for such profits or losses on the sale of fixed or current assets (see further chapter 8).

Offset rules

3.97 The detailed rules in FRS 5 relating to the offset of financial assets and liabilities have been replaced by those in FRS 25, 'Financial instruments: Presentation', which are considered in detail in chapter 6. For non-financial assets and liabilities, no offset it permitted: debit and credit balances may only be aggregated into a single net item where they do not constitute separate assets and liabilities. [FRS 5 para 29].

[The next paragraph is 3.100.]

Accounting for quasi-subsidiaries

3.100 Over time several revisions to the Companies Act have widened the definition of subsidiary, such that it is likely that many entities that were considered to be quasi-subsidiaries in past will today meet the definition of full legal subsidiaries. The Companies Act and FRS 2 definitions of subsidiary are considered in chapter 24.

3.101 However, the ASB has retained the notion of quasi-subsidiaries to close any remaining loopholes. For example, it is not clear under the Act whether trusts come within the definition of subsidiary, although it can be argued that they do. However, it is quite clear that even if they did fall outside the scope of the Act's definition, they are covered by FRS 5's definition of quasi-subsidiary.

3.102 A quasi-subsidiary is defined in FRS 5 as:

> *". . . a company, trust, partnership or other vehicle that, though not fulfilling the definition of a subsidiary, is directly or indirectly controlled by the reporting entity and gives rise to benefits for that entity that are in substance no different from those that would arise were the vehicle a subsidiary ."* [FRS 5 para 7].

3.103 In determining whether a company controls another entity, regard should be had to who in practice directs the entity's financial and operating policies. [FRS 5 para 8]. The rules here are the same as those in FRS 2 where control is defined in terms of the ability of a company to direct, or have the power to direct, the entity's financial and operating policies. The ability to prevent others from enjoying the benefits arising from the vehicle's net assets is also evidence of control. However, a company will not control another entity where there is another party that has the ability to determine all major issues of policy. Consequently, if it is obvious that another party controls the entity, then it cannot be a quasi-subsidiary.

3.104 The quasi-subsidiary definition focuses on the control over the entity where that control is direct or indirect and this definition has not been changed following the amendments to FRS 2 and the Act. Now that the definition in FRS 2 and the Companies Act includes 'power to control', it will be necessary to consider the control relationship carefully, because whether the control is direct or indirect, it might arise because of a power to control. If this is the case the entity will be a full legal subsidiary rather than a quasi-subsidiary. But there might still be situations where the entity fails the revised definition of subsidiary in FRS 2 and the Act. In such a case, the entity may still be a quasi-subsidiary where the benefits the investor receives are no different from those that would arise if the entity were a subsidiary. The benefits that are of concern are those that arise from the vehicle's net assets, as with any normal subsidiary, and similarly any exposure to risks will relate again to the benefits associated with the vehicle's net assets.

3.105 Because of the inclusion of 'power to control' in the revised definitions in FRS 2 and the Companies Act, it might be argued that all entities that were treated as quasi-subsidiaries prior to the change in definition of subsidiary should now be treated as full legal subsidiaries. However, one of the reasons that the provisions in FRS 5 were introduced was to deal with arrangements where the operating and financial provisions were pre-determined (contractually or otherwise). In this type of circumstance, neither party to the contract might seem to have day-to-day control of the vehicle's financial and operating policies, but the contract might specify and determine who gains the benefits and who is exposed to the risks related to the entity. This is typically the case with special purpose vehicles (SPV) used in securitisation schemes. In these situations after the SPV has been established none of the parties to the arrangement can change the operating and financial policies and the arrangement unwinds like clockwork.

3.106 It can be argued in these circumstances that none of the parties to the arrangement control the operating and financial policies on a day to day basis (that is, they cannot be changed). Hence, FRS 5 makes reference to these types of arrangements as 'indirect control', because none of the parties to the arrangement have control or have the power to control the operating and financial policies once the arrangement has been established. Under FRS 5 the party that gains the majority of the benefits from the net assets of the entity should consolidate it as a quasi-subsidiary. If this argument is pursued, if the entity is judged to be a quasi-subsidiary and it complies with the conditions in FRS 5 for linked presentation (see para 3.113), this basis of accounting can still be used. Hence, it will be necessary to look at the detail of an arrangement very carefully to determine where the SPV is subject to control, power to control or indirect control.

Conflict with the law?

3.107 If an entity is a quasi-subsidiary it cannot be a legal subsidiary (and *vice versa*). As the Act only requires subsidiaries to be consolidated the question arises as to whether consolidation of a quasi-subsidiary as required by FRS 5 is a departure from the Act. The ASB contends that consolidation of quasi-subsidiaries represents the provision of additional information in accordance with section 404(4) of the Companies Act 2006, without which the consolidated financial statements would not give a true and fair view. Therefore, accepting ASB's reasoning, consolidation of a quasi-subsidiary is not regarded as a departure from the Act's provisions in order to give a true and fair view (section 404(5) of the Companies Act 2006). As a consequence, consolidation of quasi-subsidiaries does not constitute a true and fair override and, therefore, the resulting disclosures required by the Act and FRS 18 do not have to be made.

Accounting treatment

3.108 Quasi-subsidiaries should be consolidated into the group's financial statements in the same way as for other subsidiaries and the same types of consolidation adjustments should be made (for example, the elimination of intragroup trading and profits). Therefore, the consolidated financial statements should include the quasi-subsidiary's assets, liabilities, profits, losses and cash flows in the same way as if it was a subsidiary. [FRS 5 para 35].

3.109 If a company does not have any legal subsidiaries and, therefore, does not prepare consolidated financial statements, it should provide, along with its individual financial statements, consolidated financial statements including the quasi-subsidiary. Those consolidated financial statements should be presented with equal prominence to the company's individual financial statements. [FRS 5 para 35]

3.110 An intermediate holding company does not have to prepare consolidated financial statements in certain situations where, for example, it is wholly-owned by another company that prepares its financial statements in accordance with the 7th Directive (see chapter 24). It might be inferred from the wording in paragraph 36 of the standard that, because such an intermediate holding company does not need to deal in its individual financial statements with its subsidiaries (other than by giving the normal disclosures concerning such investments) that it would similarly not need to deal with its quasi-subsidiaries in those financial statements. This, however, does not appear to be so, because as explained in the application note on securitisation (Application Note D), such an intermediate holding company will have to determine whether it has assets and liabilities, including those in the quasi-subsidiary, that need to be recognised in its own financial statements. There are three possible ways of dealing with the assets and liabilities of the quasi-subsidiary:

- The individual company need not recognise any of the quasi-subsidiary's assets and liabilities in its financial statements, because they can be regarded as completely derecognised by the company.
- The individual company should adopt the linked presentation in its financial statements, where the conditions for its use are met (see para 3.113).
- The individual company should record its interest in the assets and liabilities of the quasi-subsidiary gross.

3.111 The accounting treatment of a quasi-subsidiary's transactions in the individual company's financial statements, the group's financial statement and in the quasi-subsidiary's financial statements is considered in more detail from paragraph 3.143.

3.112 The rules concerning exclusions of a quasi-subsidiary from consolidation work in the same way as for normal subsidiaries. Quasi-subsidiaries need not be consolidated if they are immaterial or where the quasi-subsidiary is held exclusively with a view to subsequent resale and has not been previously consolidated. Where there are severe long-term restrictions that substantially hinder the exercise of the company's rights over the assets or the management of the other entity, this indicates that the company does not have the requisite control over that other entity for it to be a quasi-subsidiary. The other exceptions from consolidation given in the Companies Act, that is disproportionate expense and undue delay and where there are significant differences between the activities of the quasi-subsidiary and the rest of the group, cannot be used under the standard to justify the non-consolidation of a quasi-subsidiary, just as they cannot be used under FRS 2 (see further chapter 24).

Linked presentation of quasi-subsidiaries

3.113 In certain circumstances, a quasi-subsidiary's assets and liabilities can be consolidated into the group's consolidated financial statements using the linked presentation. The circumstances where the linked presentation can be used are where a company (the originator) puts some of its assets into a vehicle to be financed and where the vehicle is a quasi-subsidiary and effectively 'ring-fences' the transaction. If there is no recourse whatsoever to the group's other assets and the other conditions for linked presentation (set out in para 3.89 above) are met from the group's point of view, the group may account for the quasi-subsidiary in its consolidated financial statements using the linked presentation. The noteholders in the quasi-subsidiary may well have recourse to the quasi-subsidiary's other assets and this will often preclude the use of the linked presentation in its financial statements. However, the important issue from the group's point of view is that, for it to be eligible to use the linked presentation in its consolidated financial statements, there must be no recourse to the group's assets other than those within the securitised vehicle itself.

3.114 This presentation has been designed specifically for securitisation schemes, but may also apply to other schemes. In a securitisation, assets such as mortgages or credit card receivables are in effect sold to a thinly capitalised vehicle. The vehicle raises debt finance to pay for the mortgages or receivables. This debt may come in more than one form. For example, the majority may be raised from third parties on a non-recourse basis (that is, debt is secured solely on the vehicle's assets). In addition, to provide greater security to the third parties and thereby to reduce the cost of that third party debt, the originator may lend to the vehicle, for example investing in a zero coupon bond issued by the vehicle. In this situation the originator's loan will typically be subordinated to the third party debt; thus the originator will bear the first tranche of losses. Moreover, the originator will participate in any residual profits earned by the vehicle. That is, the originator will still have the benefits and risks associated with the vehicle and as a result the vehicle will be a quasi-subsidiary of the originator. Despite its being a quasi-subsidiary, where the conditions for the linked presentation can be met by the group (that is, the quasi-subsidiary is ring-fenced from the group's point of view), it does not have an asset equal to the gross amount of the vehicle's assets, nor does it have a liability for the full amount of the finance. The vehicle is a quasi-subsidiary and, in accordance with FRS 5, additional information concerning the quasi-subsidiary has to be given in the consolidated financial statements in order to give a true and fair view. In this case, the additional information is that required by the linked presentation and not that required by full consolidation.

Subordinated debt and credit enhancement

3.115 The originator may enhance the credit rating of quasi-subsidiaries (and hence the debt that the quasi-subsidiary issues to the public) by using a number of techniques varying from participation via subordinated debt or zero coupon loans to insurance against bad debts. If the originator participates via subordinated debt or a zero coupon loan, such debt will be eliminated in the group's consolidated financial statements. This will have the effect that, where the linked presentation is used, the group will recognise in its consolidated financial statements an amount of securitised assets greater than the amount of linked finance. The resulting asset is in effect financed by the company's subordinated debt or zero coupon loan and is the amount on which the group is at risk. A participation by an originator of this nature does not preclude the use of the linked presentation in the group's consolidated financial statements.

3.116 Another form of credit enhancement that is often used is 'over-collateralisation', which basically means financing a pool of assets by a smaller amount of external debt. For example, the pool of securitised assets might be worth £1 million, but loan notes of only £900,000 are issued to finance the assets. The difference of £100,000 provides a cushion against bad debts and also may cover the costs of the SPV.

Securitising in a legal subsidiary

3.117 If a similar securitisation scheme to that using a SPV is entered into, but using a legal subsidiary instead of a quasi-subsidiary, the same rationale and treatment as described above does *not* necessarily apply. This is because the entity is a legal subsidiary and is required to be consolidated in full by the Act. It will also not generally be possible in a subsidiary to link the finance with the securitised assets in a way that satisfies the standard's conditions, because the providers of the finance will often have recourse to other assets of the subsidiary (see further para 3.143). The only situation where the same result would be achieved is where the subsidiary meets the conditions for linked presentation in its own financial statements. Then on consolidation the linked presentation used by the subsidiary will be retained in the group's financial statements.

Accounting treatment in the parent's financial statements

3.118 Where a company has put some of its assets into a quasi-subsidiary under a securitisation and a linked presentation applies on consolidation, the accounting treatment adopted in that company's individual financial statements will have to be considered carefully. In contrast to a subsidiary where the parent's financial statements merely record the investment in the subsidiary, with a quasi-subsidiary three different presentations might apply (as explained in para 3.110) and it will be necessary to determine which presentation should be adopted. These presentations are considered in more detail in paragraph 3.143 onwards.

Disclosure

3.119 Where one or more quasi-subsidiaries are included in the consolidated financial statements it is necessary to disclose that fact in the financial statements and to give a summary of the financial statements of each quasi-subsidiary in the notes (quasi-subsidiaries of a similar nature may be combined). The summarised financial statements must show separately each main heading in the balance sheet, profit and loss account, statement of total recognised gains and losses and cash flow statement for which there is a material item, together with comparative figures. An example of the type of disclosure required is shown in Table 3.5. This example is unusual in that it consolidates fixed assets and non-recourse finance held in a quasi-subsidiary using the linked presentation, whereas the linked presentation is more generally used for debt factoring arrangements or securitisations (see Table 3.9 and Table 3.10).

Table 3.5 — NFC plc — ANNUAL REPORT & ACCOUNTS — 1 October 1994

Accounting Policies (extract)

a **Accounting Convention (extract)**

Under FRS 5 "Reporting the Substance of Transactions" the accounts of two companies, previously accounted for as associated undertakings, are now consolidated as quasi-subsidiaries using the linked presentation provided for in FRS 5.

Group Balance Sheet (extract)
at 1 October 1994

	Note	**1.10.94**		2.10.93	
				As restated	
		£m	**£m**	£m	£m
Fixed assets					
Tangible assets	*12*		**587.6**		542.0
Tangible assets subject to financing arrangements	*13*	**43.5**		27.6	
Non-recourse debt		**(36.5)**		(26.6)	
			7.0		1.0
Investments	*14*		**28.5**		26.5
			623.1		569.5

Notes to the Accounts (extract)

13 Tangible fixed assets subject to financing arrangements

As noted under accounting policy *a*, under FRS 5 two companies previously accounted for as associated companies become quasi-subsidiaries. They are consolidated using a linked presentation and the comparative figures have been restated accordingly, with no effects on the prior year's profit or shareholders' funds.

The tangible assets subject to financing arrangements are revenue earning vehicles on hire to third parties. The principal quasi-subsidiary is NFC Finance 1991 (S) Limited, the shares in which are owned equally by NFC plc and Ebbgate Investments Limited, a subsidiary of Barclays PLC. The other quasi-subsidiary is NFC Contracts Limited which is a wholly-owned subsidiary of NFC Finance 1991 (S) Limited. The group has entered into interest rate cap agreements on normal commercial terms to limit the interest rate exposure of these companies.

The directors confirm that there is no obligation on any part of the group to support any losses that may be incurred, in respect of the assets being financed, in excess of the net amount shown in the balance sheet and they do not intend to support any such losses in the unlikely event that they were to be incurred. The providers of the finance have agreed in writing that they will seek repayment of principal and interest only to the extent that sufficient funds are generated by the assets being financed and they will not seek recourse in any other form.

The summarised combined accounts of the quasi-subsidiaries are as follows:

Profit and loss account		
	1994	1993
	£m	£m
Turnover	**23.2**	9.8
Operating profit after management charges	**3.8**	1.2
Interest	**(3.8)**	(1.2)
Profit on ordinary activities before taxation	—	—
Taxation	—	—
Profit for the financial year	—	—

There are no recognised gains and losses other than the profit for the financial year.

	1994		1993	
Cash flow statement	**£m**	**£m**	£m	£m
Net cash inflow from operating activities		**16.7**		3.9
Interest paid		**(3.8)**		(1.2)
Net cash inflow before investing and financing		**12.9**		2.7
Investing activities				
Purchases of tangible fixed assets	**(39.5)**		(37.0)	
Disposals of tangible fixed assets	**7.5**		3.5	
Net cash outflow from investing activities	—	**(32.0)**	—	(33.5)
Net cash outflow before financing		**(19.1)**		(30.8)
Financing				
Allotment of shares	**0.5**		—	
New loans	**40.5**		37.0	
Repayment of loans	**(14.5)**		(3.0)	
Net cash inflow from financing		**26.5**		34.0
Increase in cash and cash equivalents		**7.4**		3.2

Balance sheet	**1.10.94**	2.10.93
	£m	£m
Tangible fixed assets	**43.5**	27.6

Cash at bank and in hand		**10.6**	3.2
Debtors:	Amounts due from NFC group companies	**6.8**	3.5
Creditors:	Amounts falling due within one year	**(22.4)**	(12.3)
	Amounts due to NFC group companies	**(6.5)**	(1.0)
	Other amounts falling due after more than one year	**(31.5)**	(21.0)
		0.5	—
Share capital		**0**	—
Reserves		—	—
Shareholders' funds		**0.5**	—

Note: This example pre-dates the changes made to the definition of subsidiary in both the Act and FRS 2, which have effect for accounting periods beginning on 1 January 2005. Hence, it is possible that these entities may no longer be quasi-subsidiaries.

[The next paragraph is 3.119.1]

Trade loans

Obligations in respect of trade loans

3.119.1 Trade loans are common in a number of industries, a typical example being the brewing industry. Trade loans are often given by brewers to their tied houses and in consideration for the loan the tied house will agree to take a certain quantity of beer from the brewer. Such arrangements can be financed in a variety of ways, for example, by advances from the brewer, or from a bank. FRS 5 requires the substance of the arrangement to be accounted for and so, depending on the circumstances of the particular agreement, the obligation in respect of the trade loans may have to be shown on the brewer's balance sheet.

3.119.2 From the 1994 financial statements of Bass PLC, it can be seen that the trade loans and related obligations have been brought on balance sheet following the introduction of FRS 5 (see Table 3.5.1). The liability has been included within the total for 'other borrowings'.

Table 3.5.1 — Bass PLC — Annual Report — 30 September 1994

Accounting Policies (extract)

iii) Investments

Fixed asset investments are stated individually at cost less any provision for permanent diminution in value. Fixed asset investments comprise trade loans and advances, trade investments in the equity of other undertakings, quoted securities and debentures. Trade loans are principally advances made to operators of UK on-licensed outlets by the Brewing division, either directly or through an arrangement with a bank. They are advanced in order to obtain a beer supply agreement and are generally cancellable at three months' notice.

Notes to the Financial Statements

13 Fixed asset investments (extract)

To comply with FRS 5 arrangements entered into by the Group with a number of banks to advance loans to third party outlets are now incorporated within both fixed asset investments and borrowings (see note 20). Trade loans and advances cost at 30 September 1993 has been restated accordingly by £80m.

3.119.3 An example of a company in a different industry recognising obligations in respect of trade loans to third parties, as a result of FRS 5, is Burmah Castrol plc (see Table 3.5.2). Obligations to banks in respect of the provision of financial assistance to customers in the group's fuel and marketing operations have been brought on balance sheet.

Table 3.5.2 — Burmah Castrol plc — Annual Report — 31 December 1994

FINANCIAL REVIEW (extract)

Accounting policies (extract)

The group's lubricants and fuels marketing operations sometimes entail entering into agreements whereby customers receive financial assistance from banks. The group has an obligation to banks in respect of such loans, which are normally serviced and repaid by the withholding of sales rebates. At 31 December 1994, the total amount outstanding under such obligations was £76 million (1993, £60 million). In accordance with FRS5, which came into effect in 1994, these amounts have been incorporated into the group's consolidated balance sheet, both as an asset under trade advances and similar arrangements, and as a liability under obligations to banks in respect of trade advances. The costs and benefits to the group of these arrangements continue to be included in operating profit.

NOTES TO THE ACCOUNTS

2 Changes to corresponding figures (extract)

(b) In compliance with FRS5, certain obligations relating to the provision of financial assistance to third parties have been included in the group's consolidated balance sheet. Corresponding figures for 1993 have been adjusted, increasing fixed asset investments by £60.3 million, creditors falling due within one year by £16.1 million and creditors falling due after one year by £44.2 million. Also, retained on balance sheet are bills discounted with recourse, which at 31 December 1993 amounted to £6.9 million. Current assets and creditors falling due within one year have been adjusted by this amount.

3.119.4 As mentioned above, there are various forms that trade loans can take and some will clearly be on balance sheet and some clearly off balance sheet. However, there are a number of grey areas where the risks and rewards will have to be considered very carefully to determine whether such loans are on or off balance sheet. Consider the following situations using brewers as an example:

Example 1

A bank makes a loan to a brewer and the brewer makes a loan to its tied house at a lower interest rate than that charged by the bank.

In such circumstances, it is clear that both loans should be on the brewer's balance sheet, one as an asset and the other as a liability.

Example 2

A bank makes a loan to the tied house which is guaranteed by the brewer. In consideration for the guarantee, the tied house agrees to take a certain quantity of beer from the brewer on normal commercial terms.

This type of transaction is likely to be off the brewer's balance sheet, because the fact that it has guaranteed the loan would not of itself result in a liability that needs to be recorded on its balance sheet. The guarantee would be disclosed as a contingent liability in accordance with FRS 12.

Example 3

The facts are the same as the example above, but the brewer subsidises part of the interest cost on the loan to the tied house. This is done either by making payments direct to the bank or by making payments to the tied house.

It can be argued that the substance of this arrangement is a subsidised loan made from the brewer to the tied house. Consequently, the brewer's position is no different from the situation where the bank makes a loan to the brewer and the brewer then lends those funds to the tied house at a subsidised rate (example 1). The risks and rewards to the brewer are identical. If the tied house defaults on the loan then the bank has full recourse *via* the guarantee to the brewer. The brewer also bears the interest differential. Alternatively, it can be argued that this transaction is similar to example 2 above and its substance is that of a contingent liability arising from the guarantee and the interest subsidy is a way of giving the tied house a trade discount. These are finely balanced arguments and strictly in accordance with FRS 5 this type of arrangement should probably be accounted for as a financing transaction.

Example 4

The bank makes a loan to the tied house which is guaranteed by the brewer. The brewer does not subsidise the interest payments, but the tied house agrees to take a certain quantity of beer from the brewer and is given a trade discount (which is not normally available).

Again, the substance of such a transaction would have to be considered very carefully. If the substance is similar to that in example 3 above, because there is a strong correlation between the amount of the loan and the amount of business (such that the amount of the trade discount is similar to the amount which would have been paid as interest subsidy), then there seems to be an argument for saying that the substance is a financing and the full amount of the loan should be recorded as a liability on the brewer's balance sheet. If, however, there is little or no correlation between the amount of business and the loan, such that the discount given differs from the amount that would have been paid as interest subsidy, then there is an argument for saying that the substance has changed and the loan should not be recognised on the brewer's balance sheet.

3.119.5 Alternatively, there may be ways whereby the trade loans can be structured so that the risks to the brewer are capped. If, for example, the brewer's portfolio of trade loans was £100 million and the bank advances (say) £80 million of non-recourse finance, the bank would be protected if the bad debts on the portfolio are expected to be only £5 million. The brewer is still exposed to the bad debt risk, but its downside risk is capped at £20 million and the bank is exposed merely to the unlikely risk of catastrophe. In this circumstance, it might be possible to use the linked presentation. The non-recourse finance could then be deducted from the trade loans it finances on the face of the balance sheet; the difference (£20 million in the example) less a provision for bad debts (say £5 million) is the asset included in the balance sheet totals. The presentation would be as follows:

	£m	£m
Trade loans	95	
Less: Non-recourse finance	80	
		15

3.119.6 This presentation could only be justified, however, if the finance is to be repaid from the specific item it finances and there is no possibility whatsoever of a claim on the brewer being established other than against funds generated by the trade loans. Furthermore, the strict linked presentation conditions in paragraph 27 of FRS 5 would also have to be met before this approach could be used.

Application notes

3.120 FRS 5's principles have to be applied to the recognition and presentation in financial statements of all transactions although, as noted earlier, FRS 5 will tend to make a difference only to the accounting for complex transactions, including those where the substance and form differ. This section considers the transactions covered by the application notes in FRS 5. Brief descriptions are given below and in chapter 9, but reference should be made to the application notes themselves for a full appreciation of the analysis. The application notes are included within FRS 5 and cover:

A Consignment stock.

B Sale and repurchase agreements.

C Debt factoring.

D Securitised assets.

E Loan transfers.

F Private finance initiative and similar contracts.

G Revenue recognition (see chapter 9).

3.121 Application notes A to F each includes a table that summarises how the FRS's principles should be applied in the analysis of the transactions. These tables are reproduced below or in chapter 20 for consignment stock in each of the sections that deal with the particular application notes.

Consignment stock

3.122 Arrangements where goods are supplied from a manufacturer to a dealer on a consignment basis are common in certain industries, particularly in the motor vehicle trade. Application Note A to FRS 5 shows how the principles of recognising assets and liabilities should be applied to these arrangements and these matters are fully considered in chapter 20.

Sale and repurchase agreements

3.123 For those entities applying FRS 26 and where the transaction falls within the scope of paragraphs 14 to 42 of FRS 26, FRS 5 Application Note B is not relevant, and the recognition and derecognition principles in FRS 26 should be applied (see further chapter 6). For those entities not within the scope of FRS 26, FRS 5's provisions should be applied to sale and repurchase agreements and the guidance in FRS 5 Application Note B is relevant. Sale and repurchase agreements are arrangements where one party sells assets to another on terms that permit, or commit, it to repurchase those assets at some future date, for example, through the use of put and/or call options. Although in some sale and repurchase agreements, the initial transaction should be accounted for as a sale, equally such agreements have been developed quite widely as methods of raising finance for assets such as properties and development land banks. Sale and repurchase arrangements also cover bed and breakfast deals (see further para 3.243). The seller often remains in control of the use or disposal of the asset, because it may continue to be used in the seller's business during the period of the agreement.

Principal sources of benefits and risks

3.124 The principles involved in analysing these transactions are relatively straightforward. The objective is to determine whether the transaction's commercial effect is that of a sale or that of a secured loan. Under the standard's provisions the main features of such transactions need to be analysed and greater weight given to those aspects that are more likely to have a commercial effect in practice. The application note identifies the main features that need to be considered in this type of transaction as:

- The sale price.
- The nature of the repurchase provision.
- The repurchase price.
- Other relevant provisions (for example, the seller's continued use of the asset).

[FRS 5 App B para B2].

3.125 The principal sources of benefits and risks arising from the main features listed above are considered in detail in the application note and the principles stemming from that discussion are then summarised in a table. The summary table is reproduced below, but with the principal features added as headings; also references are included to the paragraphs of the application note that give the narrative explanation:

Indicates sale of original asset (seller may retain a different asset)	**Indicates no sale of original asset (secured loan)**
Sale price [App B para B].	Sale price does not equal market value at date of sale.
Nature of repurchase provision	
No commitment for seller to repurchase asset, for example: — call option where there is a real possibility the option will fail to be exercised. [App B para B12].	Commitment for seller to repurchase asset, for example: — put and call option with the same exercise price [App B para B12]; — either a put or a call option with no genuine commercial possibility that the option will fail to be exercised [App B para B12]; or — seller requires asset back to use in its business, or asset is in effect the only source of seller's future sales. [App B para B11].
Repurchase price [App B para B13].	
Risk of changes in asset value borne by buyer such that buyer does not receive solely a lender's return, for example: — both sale and repurchase price equal market value at date of sale/ repurchase.	Risk of changes in asset value borne by seller such that buyer receives solely a lender's return, for example: — repurchase price equals sale price plus costs plus interest; — original purchase price adjusted retrospectively to pass variations in the value of the asset to the seller; — seller provides residual value guarantee to buyer or subordinated debt to protect buyer from falls in the value of the asset.
Other relevant provisions	
Nature of the asset is such that it will be used over the life of the agreement, and seller has no rights to determine its use. Seller has no rights to determine asset's development or future sale. [App B Para B15].	Seller retains right to determine asset's use, development or sale, or rights to profits therefrom. [App B paras B15, B17].

3.126 Important points of guidance drawn from the application note are summarised as follows:

- It is necessary to consider all the features of the agreement (particularly the terms of options and any guarantees) that are likely to have a commercial effect in practice, in order to understand them individually and how they interact.
- Determining which party is exposed to, or protected from, a fall in the value of the assets transferred is normally central to the analysis of whether there is really a sale of an asset or whether it is in substance a refinancing.
- A transaction structured so that in practice the purchaser secures just a lender's return on the purchase price without genuine exposure to, or benefit from, changes in value of the underlying assets should be treated as a financing arrangement.

3.127 Following the analysis summarised above, the true commercial effect of a transaction is a sale if the seller genuinely relinquishes control of significant benefits and transfers the exposure to significant risks associated with the asset to the buyer. In a sale, the exposure to changes in the market value of the underlying asset will in practice be passed to the buyer.

3.128 If the repurchase price in an option to repurchase is the market value at the date of exercise, it is probable that the buyer acquires both the opportunity to benefit from any increase in the value of the asset and the risk of loss due to an adverse change in its value. In terms of FRS 5's asset recognition tests, the asset has been transferred to the buyer. If, however, the repurchase price is predetermined so that, however it is formulated, it assures the buyer of a return of the original price together with the cost of holding and financing the asset, the agreement is likely to be in substance a secured borrowing. That is because the principal benefits and risks associated with holding the asset remain with the seller. The buyer (probably a financial institution) is not taking any significantly greater risk than if it made a loan secured on the asset concerned.

3.128.1 An FRRP ruling issued in February 1997 concerned a sale and leaseback undertaken by Associated Nursing Services plc. The complex sale and leaseback arrangement involved a 25-year lease, renewable for a further 25 years, with a call option held by Associated Nursing Services plc. The FRRP's view was that the nature of the transaction was such that not all the significant rights and not all the significant exposure to the risk relating to the asset had been transferred to the purchaser. Therefore, in accordance with FRS 5, an asset should have remained on the balance sheet and the sale proceeds should have been included in borrowings. As outlined above, indicators that a substance of a sale and leaseback is a financing arrangement include an initial sale not at market value and/or an option to repurchase based on a pre-determined price (rather than market price at the date of repurchase).

3.129 The application note recognises that, in more complex situations, it may be determined that a sale and repurchase agreement is not in substance a financing transaction and that the seller only retains access to some of the benefits of the original asset. In this circumstance, the partial derecognition rules in paragraph 23 of the standard might apply (see para 3.74). [FRS 5 App B para B14]. If, for example, the buyer receives more than merely a lender's return, as other benefits and risks associated with the asset have been transferred to the buyer, the seller will not have retained the original asset. In this situation, the original asset should be derecognised and the analysis should determine whether another asset should be recognised in its place. For example, the seller might have an interest in the asset's residual value at the end of its life, in which case this asset and/or liability should be recognised in the seller's balance sheet.

Accounting treatment

3.130 Where the analysis of the particular sale and repurchase transaction shows that it is in substance a secured loan, the original asset should continue to be recognised and the proceeds received from the buyer should be shown as a liability (often under a separate heading), but if the amount were considered material separate disclosure might be appropriate. No profit or loss should be recognised on the transaction's sale as, in substance, no sale has been made. Interest on the liability should be accrued and the finance cost of the liability might, for example, represent the difference between the proceeds received and the repurchase price of the asset. Therefore, the liability would be built up over its life to equal the amount at which the liability will be repaid (which is, in legal form, the repurchase of the asset). The asset's value should be reviewed for diminution in value in the normal way and, if it is a depreciable asset, it should be depreciated. Sale and finance leasebacks would also be accounted for in this manner as explained in paragraphs 153 to 155 of the guidance notes to SSAP 21 (see Tables 3.6 and 3.7).

Table 3.6 — Ladbroke Group PLC — Report and Accounts — 31 December 1994

Financial review (extract)

Financial Reporting Standard 5

Under Financial Reporting Standard 5 (FRS 5), a change is required in the reporting of certain sale and leaseback transactions entered into by the group in prior years. The leases of five hotels and one property, previously accounted for as operating leases, are now included in the accounts with the properties shown as assets and the sale proceeds as borrowings in the balance sheet; rental charges are now shown as interest in the profit and loss account, calculated at the effective rate over the period of the leases. The effect of these presentational changes on the balance sheet is the recognition of £233 million of future lease rental obligations as liabilities at 31st December 1994 and an increase of £172 million in assets, with appropriate changes to the revaluation reserve and retained earnings. In the profit and loss account, operating profits for the year have been increased by £11.8 million (1993: £12.2 million), representing the amount of lease payments, and the interest charge has increased by £23.1 million (1993: £22.9 million). Comparative figures have been restated accordingly and the financial commentary in these financial statements is based upon the restated figures.

Table 3.7 — Arjo Wiggins Appleton p.l.c. — Directors' Report and Financial Statements — 31 December 1994

Notes to the financial statements (extract)

1. Change in presentation of the financial statements

Hitherto, obligations under finance leases have been included in 'Other creditors' in the balance sheet. Following the sale and lease-back arrangement explained in notes 13 and 17, the directors consider that it is more appropriate to treat all finance lease obligations as a form of borrowing and, consequently, these liabilities are now included within 'Short-term borrowings' and 'Medium-term and long-term borrowings', as appropriate, in the balance sheet, with a corresponding change in the presentation of prior year comparative figures. The related security deposit is deducted in arriving at the Group's net debt figure shown in note 26.

13. Security desposit

In December, 1994, the Group entered into a sale and lease-back arrangement in relation to the No. 7 paper machine situated at Locks mill and operated by Appleton Papers. This has been accounted for as a finance lease in accordance with Statement of Standard Accounting Practice (SSAP) 21. The lease has a primary period of 28 years, but can be terminated at any time by the Group. The lease obligation recorded at 31 December, 1994 resulting from this transaction amounted to £65.8 million.

The Group was able to secure lower lease-financing costs by providing a deposit as security for the lease obligations. This deposit, which bears interest at LIBOR minus 3/16% must be maintained at a minimum of 92.5% of the obligations under the lease in order to retain the benefit of the lower finance charges. These obligations have, in addition, been guaranteed by the Company as set out in note 28.

17 Borrowings (extract)

The finance lease obligations include an amount of £65.8 million (1993: nil) in respect of the lease of the No. 7 paper machine situated at Locks mill and operated by Appleton Papers. A deposit of £62.5 million (1993:nil) by a subsidiary and a guarantee by the Company have been provided as security (see notes 13 and 28).

3.131 The notes to the financial statements should include the following information concerning all sale and repurchase transactions:

- The transaction's principal features. [FRS 5 App B para B19].
- The asset's status. [FRS 5 App B para B19].

  For example, this requirement presumably means disclosure that an asset has been legally sold to another party, but has been retained on balance sheet.
- The relationship between the asset and the liability. [FRS 5 App B para B19].

  Again, where an asset has been legally sold, but has been retained on balance sheet because the transaction is considered to be a financing arrangement, the notes should explain how the finance is connected with the asset (for example, whether it is non-recourse).

3.132 In some cases a sale and repurchase transaction might entitle the seller to repurchase certain rights associated with the asset rather than the entire asset. In this type of situation, where the seller has derecognised an asset, but has in its place recognised another asset or liability, because it has retained some benefits or risks, it should deal with the liability, following the provisions of FRS 12. This means, for example, that where there is some remaining obligation it should be determined whether it should be provided for in accordance with FRS 12. In addition, where there are any doubts about the amount of profit or loss that might arise from derecognising the original asset, adequate provision should be made for any expected loss. If there is an entitlement to a residual profit, that should be recognised as an asset, but in practice, it is very likely that it should be recognised at a value of nil on prudence grounds. Also, the notes to the financial statements should give the similar information to that outlined in paragraph 3.130, noting also the terms of any provisions for repurchase or any guarantees. [FRS 5 App B para B21].

Examples of required analysis

3.133 The application note provides examples of arrangements where a property developer finances its land bank by a straightforward sale and repurchase arrangement and by a similar arrangement that makes use of a special purpose vehicle.

3.134 The following example, which is not one included in the application note, illustrates the type of analysis under FRS 5 that needs to be applied.

Example

A scheme was set up two years ago, whereby a newly incorporated company (company A) acquired a number of properties from a property development company and raised £20m of finance to make the purchase. The property company sold sufficient properties (at a discount of 10% to their market value at the time of the sale) to company A to utilise the amount raised from shareholders. The properties were let by company A on assured tenancies. An independent firm of property managers was appointed to be responsible for the day to day letting and management of the properties.

After four years company A will start to sell the properties with a view to selling them all by shortly after the end of the fifth year. company A will then be put into members' voluntary liquidation and the net assets distributed in cash to investors to provide a guaranteed return. Any surpluses over the guaranteed return will also be distributed to investors. If the properties have not been sold by the distribution date at a price sufficient to provide the guaranteed return, company A will put the properties back to the property development company at a price that guarantees the required return to the investors in company A

The principal benefits and risks of the transaction can be analysed as follows from the point of view of the property company:

	Off B/sheet	On B/sheet
Sale price		
Sold to company A at 10% below market price.		✓
Nature of repurchase provision		
The company must re-acquire the properties should their value be below the amount necessary to provide the guaranteed return to the investors.		✓
Repurchase price		
Risk of fall in the asset's value is borne by the seller as it provides a residual value guarantee.		✓
Benefit in increase in asset's value accrues to investors.	✓	
Other relevant provisions		
Properties are not managed and are not occupied by the property development company	✓	

In determining the presentation it is not merely a matter of looking at how many ticks are in the left-hand column and how many are in the right-hand column. It is necessary to consider which of the parties bears the benefits and risks of ownership. In this example, the property development company has retained risks in the form of the residual guarantee. Whether it will be called upon to fulfil its obligation under the guarantee will depend on how the property market performs over the five years and how optimistically the guarantee price is set. Certainly over the past few years it has been difficult to determine how property prices will move and, hence, it cannot be assumed in the present market that such a guarantee will not be called.

It seems relatively clear from the analysis that the transaction's substance is that of a deferred sale (that is, the property should remain on the property development company's balance sheet until there is no further obligation under the guarantee). This is because there has been no significant change in the property development company's exposure to risks because of the existence of the guarantee. Therefore, partial derecognition cannot be justified in this case.

Furthermore, if the properties cost £80m and they were sold to company A at £90m being 10% less than their market value of £100m at the date of sale, then the potential profit on sale to the property company would be £10m. However, this profit cannot be recognised, because in substance no sale has taken place. Therefore, the entries in the property development company's books would be as follows:

	£m	£m
Dr Cash	90	
Cr Liabilities		90
To record the financing of the properties.		

The properties would be retained at their cost of £80m. If the guaranteed repurchase price is £120m, then the difference between the £90m and the £120m would represent a finance cost on the obligation of £90m. Hence this finance cost should be charged as interest to the profit and loss account at a constant rate on the outstanding amount of the obligation (as required by FRS 4 and FRS 26) and credited to increase the obligation to £120m over the term of the scheme. If this line or argument is followed, then, if the guarantee is called, the obligation will be fully provided for and be settled at £120m and the properties retained at a cost of £80m until they are sold. If the guarantee is not called, the sale of the properties is in substance complete and a profit of £40m can be recognised, which is the difference between the outstanding obligation of £120m and the cost of the properties of £80m. This might seem a curious result, because in the latter situation, the finance cost is being charged to the profit and loss account over the five years and a substantial profit on sale is recognised at the end of year five. However, it can be rationalised as follows. The property company did not sell the properties in substance until year five. It received cash in advance at year one. Economically, such an advance payment earns interest, which matches the finance cost on the obligation. Moreover, the value of the properties at year five was clearly at least £120m, so it is right that a profit based on selling at that value should be recognised given that the sale occurred in substance at year five.

3.135 An illustration of the accounting treatment of a BES scheme (similar to the scheme described above) is given in Table 3.8.

Table 3.8 — Persimmon plc — Report & Accounts — 31 December 1997

NOTES TO THE FINANCIAL STATEMENTS

for the year ended 31 December 1997 (extract)

26 Contingent liabilities (extract)

The company has guaranteed the return to investors in the companies formed under the Business Expansion Scheme and has indemnified the company's bankers who have provided guarantees of up to £40,500,000 in support of these obligations.

27 Properties in Business Expansion Scheme (BES) companies

The group sold properties into BES companies set up under BES assured tenancy schemes from 1989 to 1993.

Persimmon plc has guaranteed the return to investors in the companies formed under the BES (see note 26). Because the company has guaranteed that the BES companies will have sufficient cash resources at scheme maturity to pay the guaranteed return to investors, the proceeds received for the properties are treated as loans under BES advances on the balance sheet. The finance cost implicit in the BES arrangements, calculated by reference to the difference between the sales proceeds received and the guaranteed distribution to investors, is being charged in the profit and loss account over the appropriate term. In addition, the net rental income arising in the BES companies is recognised in the profit and loss account in the appropriate period.

Turnover does not include properties sold to BES companies until the schemes mature, the properties being held at cost on the balance sheet as BES assets until the sale is recognised.

At 31 December 1997 only two schemes now remain, all obligations under the previous schemes having been fulfilled. The maturity dates of the two remaining schemes are 5 March 1998 and 24 January 1999. The company acts on behalf of the BES companies in the sale of the properties prior to the scheme maturity date in accordance with the original scheme rules. The company has the right to exercise its option to repurchase any properties that remain unsold at maturity date in fulfilling its obligations under the guarantees.

Debt factoring

3.136 For those entities applying FRS 26, FRS 5 Application Note C is not relevant, and the recognition and derecognition principles in FRS 26 should be applied (see further chapter 6). For those entities not within the scope of FRS 26, FRS 5's provisions should be applied to debt factoring arrangements and the guidance in FRS 5 Application Note C is relevant.

3.136.1 Factoring is a transaction which is capable of different accounting treatments. It involves raising money from the sale of a company's debtor balances before the debt is collected. Debt factoring is considered in Application Note C of FRS 5 and also encompasses invoice discounting. Factoring arrangements come with many different features; at their simplest they might, for example, feature a clean sale of debts at a fixed price without recourse. More complex arrangements might feature a sale of debts on terms where there is both recourse to the seller in respect of non-payment (bad debt or credit risk) and the price received for the debts varies according to the actual period the debts remain unpaid (slow payment risk).

3.136.2 In the former case, the seller has no further interest in the debts so they can be removed from the balance sheet by crediting them with the proceeds from the factor. In the latter case, the seller clearly retains a significant economic interest in the underlying debts and the arrangement should be accounted for as a financing with the debts remaining on balance sheet. In addition, there is now a middle ground where significant, but not all, benefits and risks have been transferred to the factor. In such a transaction, the company might be eligible to use the linked presentation where the conditions in paragraph 27 of FRS 5 are met. Partial derecognition is not an option for such transactions, because they are financing arrangements.

3.136.3 Some of the arguments contained in the application note for and against asset recognition are finely balanced and there are likely to be grey areas in practice. Therefore, individual arrangements will need to be carefully reviewed. The three accounting treatments that might apply are:

- Derecognition — where no significant benefits or risks are retained.
- Linked presentation — where the company retains significant benefits and/or risks associated with the factored debts, but the downside exposure to loss is limited to a fixed amount and the other conditions for use of the linked presentation are met.
- Separate presentation — showing the factored debts and the related finance separately (not linked) on the balance sheet, where the company retains significant benefits and/or risks relating to the assets and the conditions for the linked presentation cannot be met.

3.136.4 The application note lists the main benefits and risks of factoring arrangements as:

- The benefit arising from the future cash flows due to the payment of the debts.
- The risk of slow payment.
- The risk of non payment — credit risk.

[FRS 5 App C para C5].

Main benefits and risks

3.136.5 The main benefits and risks set out above are considered in detail in the application note and the principles stemming from that discussion are then summarised in a table. The summary table is reproduced below, but with the main benefits and risks added as headings; also included are references to the paragraphs of the application note that give the narrative explanation:

Indicates derecognition	Indicates linked presentation	Indicates separate presentation
Cash flow benefit and slow payment risk		
Transfer is for a single, non-returnable fixed sum. [App C para C6].	Some non-returnable proceeds received, but seller has rights to further sums from the factor (or *vice versa*) whose amount depends on whether or when debtors pay. [App C para C15].	Finance cost varies with speed of collection of debts, for example: — by adjustment to consideration for original transfer [App C para C8]; or — subsequent transfers priced to recover costs of earlier transfers. [App C para C8].
Credit risk		
There is no recourse to the seller for losses. [App C para C9].	There is no recourse for losses, or such recourse has a fixed monetary ceiling. [App C para C15].	There is full recourse to the seller for losses. [App C para C9].
Other indicators		
Factor is paid all amounts received from the factored debts (and no more). Seller has no rights to further sums from the factor. [App C para C12].	Factor is paid only out of amounts collected from the factored debts, and seller has no right or obligation to repurchase debts. [App C para C15].	Seller is required to repay amounts received from the factor on or before a set date, regardless of timing or amounts of collections from debtors. [App C para C6].

3.136.6 Debt factoring, as opposed to just invoice discounting, not only involves the discounting of invoices, but often includes the factor administering the sales ledger and collecting the debts on behalf of the company. Generally, for debt factoring the administration arrangements will not affect the analysis of the transaction significantly for accounting purposes provided they are at arm's length. However, with arrangements where the factor is only administering the sales ledger (that is, service-only factoring), the seller will retain access to the benefits and risks associated with the debts and hence they should remain on balance sheet.

3.136.7 In order for factored debts to be derecognised (that is, completely taken off the balance sheet), the seller cannot retain any significant benefits or risks associated with those debts. Derecognition is, therefore, only appropriate where all of the following apply:

- The transaction takes place at an arm's length price for an outright sale.
- The transaction is for a fixed amount of consideration and there is no recourse either implicit or explicit.

Warranties given in respect of the conditions of the debts (for example, to their existence) at the time of transfer are allowed, but warranties concerning the condition of the debts in the future or their future performance (for example, payment or speed of payment) are not allowed.

- The seller will not benefit or suffer if the debts perform better or worse than expected.

[FRS 5 App C para C12].

3.136.8 Derecognition cannot be used where the seller retains significant benefits or risks, but in such a situation it might be possible to use the linked presentation. The linked presentation would normally be appropriate where the downside exposure to risk is limited to a fixed monetary amount and where the conditions for the linked presentation are met. However, the linked presentation should not be used where the factored debts cannot be separately identified.

3.136.9 It is possible in factoring arrangements where the linked presentation is used, for old debts to be replaced by new debts as long as the conditions in FRS 5, paragraph 27(b) (no recourse to other assets) and 27(f) (finance to be repaid out of the cash receipt from debt) are satisfied. The practical problems associated with achieving the linked presentation in this situation are explained in relation to credit card receivable securitisations from paragraph 3.159.

Accounting treatment

Derecognition

3.136.10 If, after analysing the transaction, it is determined that the assets can be derecognised, a loss (and in certain circumstances a profit) will arise which will simply be the difference between the carrying value of the debts and the net proceeds received from the factor. [FRS 5 App C para C18]. This amount will generally represent a finance cost and should be included within interest in the profit and loss account.

Linked presentation

3.136.11 Where the conditions for linked presentation are met, the finance should be deducted from the related debts on the face of the balance sheet, after providing for any bad debts. The interest element of the factor's charge should be accrued as it is incurred. In addition, the notes to the financial statements should include the following information:

- The main terms of the arrangement. [FRS 5 App C para C19].
- The gross amount of the outstanding factored debts at the balance sheet date. [FRS 5 App C para C19].

  Although not stated explicitly in the FRS, the amount to be disclosed is presumably before deducting bad debt provisions as otherwise this additional disclosure would appear unnecessary, because the amount of the debts factored (after deducting bad debt provisions) will be disclosed anyway in the balance sheet linked presentation, although at some point a bad debt must be written off and, therefore, eliminated from both sides.
- The factoring charges recognised in the period, analysed between interest and other charges. [FRS 5 App C para C19].
- A statement by the directors that the company is not obliged and does not intend to support any losses beyond the recourse to the specific debts linked under the scheme. [FRS 5 para 27(c)].
- A note that the factor has agreed in writing that it will seek recourse to both principal and interest only to the extent that sufficient funds are generated by the specific debts it has financed. [FRS 5 para 27(d)].

3.136.12 An example of disclosure of the statements in the last two bullet points above is seen in Table 3.8.1 in relation to hire purchase trade debtors discounted with banks, subject to strictly limited recourse.

Table 3.8.1 — Inchcape plc — Annual Report & Accounts — 31 December 1994

Consolidated balance sheet (extract)

		1994		1993 restated
	£m	**£m**	£m	£m
Current assets:				
Stocks		**1,112.1**		876.8
Debtors		**1,379.1**		1,220.5
Trade debtors subject to limited recourse financing	**34.8**		36.3	
less: non-returnable amounts received	**(24.8)**		(26.1)	
		10.0		10.2
Cash at bank and in hand		**427.3**		354.9
		2,928.5		2,462.4

> **17 Debtors (extract)**
>
> Trade debtors subject to limited recourse financing represent hire purchase debtors discounted with banks in the ordinary course of business, subject to strictly limited recourse so that the majority of cash received by the Group on discounting is not returnable, and which carry interest at variable rates. The returnable element of the proceeds is recorded as bank loans and overdrafts due within one year and after one year as appropriate. The Group will not make good any losses over and above the agreed recourse limit and the relevant banks have confirmed their acceptance of this position in writing.
>
> The Group figures also include the effects of implementing FRS5 in respect of bills of exchange, trade debtors and hire purchase debtors discounted with recourse, at variable rates of interest, to banks and finance houses in the ordinary course of business. These balances have been included within trade debtors due within one year £6.0m (1993 — £32.2m) and net investment in finance leases and hire purchase contracts £0.4m due within one year and £4.0m due after one year respectively (1993 — £0.4m and £3.7m).

Separate presentation

3.136.13 Where the analysis indicates that separate presentation should be used for the transaction, the amount of the debts factored should remain in debtors on the balance sheet (net of any provisions for bad debts). The proceeds received from the factor should be recorded as a liability under the heading of, for example, 'amounts due in respect of factored receivables'. In addition, the interest element of the factor's charges should be accrued and shown as interest in the profit and loss account. Also the notes to the financial statements should show the amount of the factored debts outstanding at the balance sheet date. [FRS 5 App C para C20].

3.136.14 An example of disclosure of trade debtors and hire purchase debtors discounted with recourse is seen in Table 3.8.1 above.

Examples of required analysis

3.136.15 The application note provides two examples of factoring arrangements: one where the factor has recourse and continued recognition is required; and another where the factor has limited recourse and the linked presentation is used.

3.136.16 The following example, which is not one of those included in the application note, also illustrates the FRS 5 principles as they apply to factoring arrangements:

> **Example**
>
> A company has a number of large trade debtors totalling £1m, which are very unlikely to default, but are long-dated. The company decides to sell these debtors to a factoring company. Because the debtors are sound companies, there are unlikely to be any bad debts and the risk of slow payment is minimal. Even so, the seller has given the factor a guarantee up to a total of 10% of the debtors' balance in respect of credit and slow payment risk. In past experience, over the last ten years, the company has never had to provide against any balances with these customers.

Some might try to argue that such a transaction should be accounted for as a sale of assets and recognition of a new asset or liability (partial derecognition). In this case, the recognition would be of an obligation to repay the factor if the debtors go bad (which is extremely unlikely). This argument appears to be supported by paragraph 73 of FRS 5 which illustrates a similar situation; *"…an entity may sell equipment subject to a warranty in respect of the condition of the equipment at the time of sale, or subject to a guarantee of its residual value. This would normally transfer all significant rights to benefits and some significant exposure to risks to the buyer…, but leave the seller with some significant risk in the form of obligations relating to the equipment's future performance or residual value. The seller would therefore cease to recognise the equipment as an asset, but would recognise a liability for its warranty obligation or guarantee (with the liability being accounted for in accordance with the provisions of FRS 12)"*. This paragraph would seem to support the argument that the obligation in the example is so remote that it does not need to be recognised and, as a consequence, the transaction can be treated as an outright sale. However, there is one primary objection to this argument, which is that partial derecognition is not available for financing transactions and this transaction is clearly a financing arrangement. In any case, paragraphs 12 and 13 of Application Note C only allow three possible accounting treatments for debt factoring: full derecognition where the transaction is an outright sale and there is no recourse; linked presentation where there is recourse and the conditions for that presentation are met; and separate presentation. *Partial derecognition is not an option.*

Therefore, using the principles of Application Note C, the benefits and risks of the transaction can be analysed as follows:

	Off B/sheet	**Linked**	**On B/sheet**
Cash flow benefit and slow payment risk The transfer is for a fixed sum, but part may have to be repaid if the guarantee is called.		✓	
Credit risk The factor has recourse via the guarantee to the company for losses, which has a fixed monetary ceiling, but is unlikely to be called.		✓	
Other indicators The factor is only paid out of the amounts collected from the debtors and the seller has no right or obligation to repurchase the debtors.		✓	

The company has retained significant risks associated with the debtors, because it is still liable to fund bad debts up to a limit of 10%. The company might contend, in practice, that its risk of bad debts is nil (because of past experience). This is true, but it still has retained the same significant risk that it had prior to undertaking the transaction, because it is exposed to the risk of bad debts on the gross amount of the debtors it has transferred. It has merely transferred to the factor the risk of catastrophe (the risk of bad debts exceeding the 10% limit). Consequently, the analysis above indicates that the linked presentation is the appropriate accounting treatment for this transaction, but it can only be used where the conditions for its use are met. If those conditions cannot be met, then separate presentation must be used.

The accounting treatment using the linked presentation would be as follows:

Balance sheet (extract)	£'m	£'m
Current assets		
Debtors		
Trade debtors (say)		10.0
Trade debtors subject to financing arrangements	1.0	
Less: non-returnable amounts received	0.9	
		0.1
Total trade debtors		10.1
Creditors		
Financing of trade debtors		0.1
(comprising the amount of finance with recourse)		

Securitised assets

3.137 For those entities applying FRS 26, FRS 5 Application Note D is not relevant, and the recognition and derecognition principles in FRS 26 should be applied (see further chapter 6). For those entities not within the scope of FRS 26, FRS 5's provisions should be applied to the securitisation of assets and the guidance in FRS 5 Application Note D is relevant. Securitisation of assets is a method, first used by originators of mortgage loans, to package assets together to sell as a block or pool to a thinly capitalised vehicle (known as a special purpose vehicle (SPV)). The SPV finances its purchase by issuing loan notes or other marketable debt instruments to outside investors that are secured solely on the assets securitised. Also other pools of debts, such as credit card receivables, hire purchase loans and trade debtors, are securitised in a similar way to mortgages (for example see the example concerning debt factoring in chapter 6).

3.138 The originator of the securitised assets may or may not hold an equity investment in the issuing vehicle. The loan notes issued by the SPV are attractive to investors because, by covering any risks associated with the scheme with some form of credit enhancement, the asset-backed debt provides a very high level of security. The credit enhancement used (covering most risks associated with the assets apart from catastrophe), varies in form from insurance for bad debts to the originator investing in a deep discounted bond or in subordinated debt, whose repayment at the end of the scheme depends on the liquidity of the SPV (see further para 3.115). Many of these schemes hinge on Standard & Poors (a US rating entity) giving the loan notes AAA rating, a higher credit rating than would be available for a debt issued by the originator. Consequently, the note holders' instrument can be given a lower rate of interest because of the debt's high security.

3.139 The SPVs are often companies that are owned by a charitable trust. The charitable purpose of the trust is normally 'obscure', as it is not generally the intention of such schemes that the charitable trust would benefit greatly from the business of its subsidiary. It is merely a convenient way of structuring the scheme. The trust exists to own legally the SPV in order to assist in 'ring-fencing' the transaction.

3.140 The commercial reasons for companies securitising their assets are varied. Securitisation is a means of both tapping alternative markets for funds at very competitive funding rates and permitting the institutions to take on more business by removing their risk exposure for regulatory purposes on substantial tranches of long-term receivables. The sums of money involved in securitisation schemes (particularly mortgage securitisations) are substantial. Consequently, the commercial impact of the accounting treatment is very significant.

3.141 Developing an acceptable accounting treatment was difficult, because the original lender normally retains some economic interest in the gross assets transferred and also in the issuing vehicle. For example, the originator in a mortgage securitisation may continue to administer the mortgages and take the majority of the vehicle's profit, although the vehicle may be structured so that the originator does not control it.

3.142 The ASB developed the linked presentation specifically to apply to securitisation schemes where the originator retains significant benefits and risks associated with the assets securitised, but where the downside exposure to risk is capped. The linked presentation also lends itself to other complex transactions, such as factoring (see chapter 6).

3.143 If consolidation of the SPV as a full legal subsidiary is not appropriate (see para 3.100 onwards) and the SPV has been assessed to be a quasi-subsidiary then the securitisation should be accounted for in accordance with FRS 5. Because securitisations make use of SPVs it is necessary to consider the accounting treatment in three sets of financial statements: the originator's individual financial statements; the SPV's financial statements; and the originator group's consolidated financial statements. The SPV's financial statements are probably the simplest to deal with as separate presentation of the transaction is normally appropriate. This is because the SPV often has access to all of the future benefits and risks related to the securitised assets and the noteholders usually have recourse to all of the vehicle's assets (which would include assets other than the pool of assets being securitised, such as cash balances). In the originator's individual financial statements and its group's financial statements there are three possible accounting treatments:

- Derecognition — where *no* significant benefits *or* risks are retained.
- Linked presentation — where significant benefits and/or risks are retained, but the downside exposure to loss is limited to a fixed amount and the other conditions for use of the linked presentation are met.
- Separate presentation — where significant benefits and/or risks are retained and the conditions for the linked presentation cannot be met.

Originator's financial statements

3.144 The benefits and risks associated with securitisations are considered in detail in the application note and the principles stemming from that discussion are then summarised in a table. The summary table is reproduced below, but split in two. The first section of the table below considers the analysis necessary to determine the accounting treatment in the originator's financial statements and includes references to the paragraphs of the application note that give the narrative explanation:

Indicates derecognition	Indicates linked presentation	Indicates separate presentation
Transaction price is arm's length price for an outright sale. [App D para D8].	Transaction price is not arm's length price for an outright sale.	Transaction price is not arm's length price for an outright sale.
Transfer is for a single, non-returnable fixed sum. [App D para D8].	Some non-returnable proceeds received, but originator has rights to further sums from the issuer, the amount of which depends on the performance of the securitised assets. [App D para D9].	Proceeds received are returnable, or there is a provision whereby the originator may keep the securitised asset on repayment of the loan notes or re-acquire them. [App D para D 14].
There is no recourse to the originator for losses. [App D para D8].	There is either no recourse for losses, or such recourse has a fixed monetary ceiling. [App D para D 10].	There is or may be full recourse to the originator for losses, for example: — originator's directors are unable or unwilling to state that it is not obliged to fund any losses; — noteholders have not agreed in writing that they will seek repayment only from funds generated by the securitised assets. [App D para D 14].

3.145 In order for securitised assets to be derecognised in the originator's individual financial statements, the originator must not retain any significant benefits or risks associated with those assets. Derecognition is, therefore, only appropriate where all of the following apply:

- The transaction takes place at an arm's length price for an outright sale.
- The transaction is for a fixed amount of consideration and there is no recourse (other than to the securitised assets) either implicit or explicit. Warranties given in respect of the asset's condition (for example, to good title or to the completeness/correctness of the documentation relating to the asset) at the time of transfer are allowed, but warranties concerning the condition of the assets in the future, or their future performance (for example, payment or speed of payment), are not allowed.
- The originator will not benefit or suffer if the assets perform better or worse than expected.

[FRS 5 App D para D8].

3.146 Derecognition cannot be used in the originator's financial statements where the originator retains significant benefits or risks, but in such a situation the linked presentation might apply. Again, as with factoring, 'significant' is judged in relation to those benefits and risks that are likely to occur in practice and not in relation to the total possible benefits and risks. It is common in securitisation schemes for the originator to retain some benefits related to the securitised assets, for example, *via* involvement in management of the securitised assets or *via* a residual interest in the SPV. Furthermore, as explained in paragraph 3.115, the linked presentation can still be used where the originator has an interest in the SPV by way of a subordinated loan or a zero coupon loan. The important point is that the linked presentation is only appropriate where the downside exposure to risk is limited to a fixed monetary amount and where the conditions for the linked presentation are met (see para 3.88).

3.147 The linked presentation should not, however, be used where the assets that have been securitised cannot be separately identified. There must generally be no provision for the originator to repurchase the securitised assets. Where there is such a provision, but for only part of the securitised assets, the maximum payment that could result should be excluded from the amount of finance deducted from the securitised assets on the face of the balance sheet and this amount should be shown separately as a liability.

Disclosure requirements

3.148 Where the originator derecognises the securitised assets, they will no longer be recognised in the balance sheet and a profit or loss will arise on their sale, which will equal the difference between their carrying amount and the proceeds of sale. Where separate gross presentation is deemed to be necessary, no profit or loss should be recognised when the securitisation transaction is entered into, unless there is a need to reassess the carrying value of the assets securitised. The notes to the financial statements should disclose the gross amount of the assets securitised at the balance sheet date.

3.149 Where the conditions for the linked presentation are satisfied, the proceeds of the note issue should be deducted from the securitised assets on the face of the balance sheet. In addition, the following disclosures should be given:

- A description of the asset securitised. [FRS 5 App D para D22(a)].
- The amount of any income or expense recognised in the period, analysed as appropriate. [FRS 5 App D para D22(b)].
- The terms of any options for the originator to repurchase assets or to transfer additional assets to the issuer. [FRS 5 App D para D22(c)].

  Where the originator can repurchase the assets, this would invalidate the use of the linked presentation and, therefore, this would seem to make the first disclosure of this requirement redundant, because the linked presentation would be precluded.
- The terms of any interest rate swap or interest rate cap agreements between the issuer and the originator that meet the conditions set out in paragraph 3.157 below. [FRS 5 App D para D22(d)].
- A description of the priority and amount of claims on the proceeds generated by the assets, including any rights of the originator to proceeds from the assets in addition to the non-recourse amounts already received. [FRS 5 App D para D22(e)].
- The ownership of the issuer. [FRS 5 App D para D22(f)].
- A statement by the directors that the company is not obliged and does not intend to support any losses beyond the recourse to the specific assets linked under the scheme. [FRS 5 para 27(c)].
- A note explaining that the noteholders have subscribed to a prospectus or offering circular that clearly stated that the originator will not support any losses of either the issuer or the noteholders. [FRS 5 App D para D10].

3.150 The standard only allows aggregation on the face of the balance sheet and in the notes where a company enters into more than one securitisation which relates to a single type of asset. Where securitisation schemes relate to different types of asset, the balance sheet disclosures and those outlined above should not be aggregated.

Group's financial statements

3.151 The table below is taken from the table given in the application note and considers the analysis necessary to determine the accounting treatment in the group's financial statements and includes references to the paragraphs of the application note that give the narrative explanation:

Indicates derecognition	Indicates linked presentation	Indicates separate presentation
Issuer is owned by an independent third party that made a substantial capital investment, has control of the issuer, and has the benefits and risks of its net assets. [App D para D19].	Issuer is a quasi-subsidiary of the originator, but the conditions for a linked presentation are met from the point of view of the group. [App D para D20].	Issuer is a subsidiary of the originator. [App D para D17].

3.152 Where the special purpose vehicle meets the definition of a subsidiary under the Act and FRS 2, it should be consolidated in the group's financial statements in the normal way (that is, separate presentation, unless the linked presentation is possible in the subsidiary – see para 3.117). Often, SPVs used in securitisation schemes may fall within the definition of a quasi-subsidiary (see from para 3.100). This is likely to be so where the vehicle's financial and operating policies are predetermined as explained in paragraph 3.105.

3.153 Furthermore, it should be presumed that a vehicle, which is not a legal subsidiary, is a quasi-subsidiary where either of the following apply:

- The originator has rights to the benefits generated by the securitised assets that remain after meeting the claims of noteholders and other expenses of the issue.
- The originator has the risks inherent in those benefits. That is, where the benefits are greater or less than expected, the originator gains or suffers.

[FRS 5 App D para D18].

Disclosure requirements

3.154 Where the undertaking is a quasi-subsidiary and the conditions for the linked presentation (see para 3.88) are met at the group level, that presentation should be used in the consolidated financial statements. Where the linked presentation is used in the consolidated financial statements, then the same disclosures as outlined in paragraph 3.149 should be given. Where the conditions are not met at the group level, then the quasi-subsidiary should be accounted for in the same way as a legal subsidiary, that is, by full consolidation (see para 3.108).

3.155 An illustration of a company that has used the linked presentation for a mortgage securitisation scheme is given below in Table 3.9 and an example of a group using the linked presentation for securitising rent receivables is given in Table 3.10.

Table 3.9 — Legal & General Group plc — Annual Reports & Accounts — 31 December 1994

Consolidated Balance Sheet (extract)

on 31 December 1994

	1994	1993	
	£m	£m	Notes
ASSETS			
Investments	29,204	29,110	11a
Mortgage lending and related assets	416	338	11b
other assets	982	951	11c
	30,602	30,400	
Securitised mortgages and related assets	149	228	20
Non-recourse borrowings	(149)	(228)	20

Notes to Financial Statements (extract)

20. SECURITISED MORTGAGES AND RELATED ASSETS

During 1989 and 1991 Legal & General Mortgage Services Limited (LGMSL) sold £298m of mortgages, via Temple Court Originations Limited (TCO) to Temple Court Mortgages (No. 1) Plc and Temple Court Mortgages (No. 2) Plc (TCM 1&2). TCM2 redeemed all of its securities during 1994. These companies issued debt to purchase the mortgages, the written terms of which provide no recourse to LGMSL. Neither LGMSL nor any other member of the Group is obliged, or intends, to support any losses in respect of the sold mortgages. Mortgage payments (interest and principal) in respect of the portfolio are used to pay the capital and interest due on borrowings and other administration expenses. Any residue is payable as deferred consideration to LGMSL. During 1994 this amounted to £3.9m (1993, £5.3m) and is reported within the mortgage lending result under Other Operations. TCO and TCM 1&2 are quasi subsidiaries of the Group and their summarised financial statements at 31 December, which form the basis of the linked presentation in the consolidated balance sheet are:

	Assets	Liabilities	Assets	Liabilities
	1994	1994	1993	1993
	£m	£m	£m	£m
Securitised mortgages	152	—	234	—
Other related assets	7	—	10	—
Non-recourse borrowings	—	(159)	—	(244)
Share capital and reserves	—	0	—	0
Amount reported by quasi subsidiaries	159	(159)	244	(244)
Mortgage backed securities purchased by LGMSL*	(10)	—	16	—
Borrowings for mortgage lending*	—	10	—	16
Amounts shown in linked presentation	149	(149)	228	(228)

The quasi subsidiaries had gross financial income and expenses of approximately £16m (1993, £22.3m). At 31 December 1994 LGMSL held as investments £10m of notes issued by TCM1.

*These investments have been included as mortgage lending and related assets and the related borrowings have been included in borrowings for financing mortgage lending.

Note: This example pre-dates the changes made to the definition of subsidiary in both the Act and FRS 2. Hence, it is possible that these entities may no longer be quasi-subsidiaries.

Table 3.10 — Zeneca Group PLC — Annual Report and Accounts — 31 December 1994

Notes relating to the accounts (extract)

2 BASIS OF PRESENTATION OF FINANCIAL INFORMATION (extract)

In accordance with the provisions of FRS 5 "Reporting the Substance of Transactions", the financial statements include the securitisation of rent receivables from a property which had been effected by Stauffer Chemical Company in 1984, prior to its acquisition by the Group in 1987 (see Note 15). The net effect of these transactions was recorded in the accounts as part of the acquisition accounting in 1987. The adoption of FRS 5 also resulted in recognition of an insurance liability and its related reinsurance recovery, with separate recording in debtors and creditors.

Balance sheets (extract)

			Group			Company	
As at 31 December			*1994*		**1993*	*1994*	*1993*
	Notes		*£m*		*£m*	*£m*	*£m*
Current assets							
Stocks	14		776		776	—	—
Debtors	15		1,396		1,483	1,765	1,483
Securitised rent receivables	15	56		58		—	—
Less: Non-recourse Secured Notes	15	(54)	2	(57)	1	—	—
Short-term investments	16		594		925	—	401
Cash	16		141		124	—	—
			2,909		3,309	1,765	1,884

15 DEBTORS (extract)

Included in debtors are amounts totalling £177m (1993 £145m) in respect of the Group's insurance subsidiaries relating to reinsurance contracts.

Rent receivables in respect of a property were securitised under an arrangement established by Stauffer Chemical Company (SCC) in 1984. The receivables were securitised under a Trust Indenture in connection with the issue of $245m of non-recourse Zero Coupon Secured Notes due 1994-2018 on behalf of SCC. SCC's interest in the receivables and its obligations under the Trust Indenture were vested in Zeneca Holdings Inc. (ZHI) by way of an assignment and assumption agreement. Neither SCC as the issuer of the notes nor ZHI as assignee of SCC's interest is obliged to support any losses of the assets pledged under the trust indenture, nor does either intend to do so. Repayment of the finance is solely secured by rent receivables from the property, payment of which is further secured by an irrecoverable letter of credit drawn on a first class bank. The net present value of these arrangements amounts to a net asset of £6m — this asset was recorded in the accounts as part of the acquisition accounting of Stauffer since 1987. Under FRS 5 this is now reported as an asset of £56m and a liability of £54m, using a linked presentation, with £4m included in cash and short-term investments. The net income recorded in the Group accounts amounted to £1m (1993 £1m). A summary of the financial statements of Stauffer Chemical Company Trust is set out below.

Stauffer Chemical Company Trust	*1994* *£m*	*1993* *£m*
Income and Expenditure account		
Surplus for the financial year	1	1
Trust distributions	(1)	—
Surplus retained for the year	—	1
Balance sheet		
Debtors	56	58
Cash and short-term investments	4	5
Total assets	60	63
Creditors	(54)	(57)
Net assets	6	6
Cash flow		
Increase in cash and cash equivalents	—	—

Note: This example pre-dates the changes made to the definition of subsidiary in both the Act and FRS 2. Hence, it is possible that these entities may no longer be quasi-subsidiaries.

Interest rate swaps

3.156 Often securitisation schemes originated by banks make use of interest rate swaps between the originator and the issuer. The British Bankers Association (BBA) made representations to the ASB to deal specifically with interest rate swaps in the standard, because it was concerned that under the proposals in FRED 4 the linked presentation could not be used for many securitisations undertaken by banks. Swaps have a number of benefits in securitisation schemes as, from the point of view of the issuer, they provide a way in which noteholders can receive an interest stream in a form that accommodates their needs (for example, payment at a rate based on LIBOR, rather than a bank's mortgage rate). In addition, a swap can help the originator to manage its own interest rate position. For example, a bank might have a portfolio of mortgages on which it is receiving a fixed rate. A bank would normally hedge this interest rate exposure. Hence when it sells the mortgages to the securitisation vehicle, without further action the bank's interest rate position becomes unmatched. If the bank arranges a swap with the issuer, such that it receives a fixed rate and pays a rate based on LIBOR, the bank's interest rate position is restored. The issuer will then receive fixed rate interest on the mortgages which it will pay to the bank and receive in return a rate based on LIBOR, which will cover its liability to its noteholders. This type of arrangement provides a cost-effective way of protecting a bank's position. Therefore, in such circumstances, it can be argued that the interest rate swap does not expose the bank to additional risk.

3.157 As a result of its discussions with the BBA and others, the ASB confirmed that the conditions for the linked presentation can be regarded as being met notwithstanding the existence of an interest rate swap, provided all of the following conditions are met:

- The swap is on arm's length market-related terms and the obligations of the issuer under the swap are not subordinated to any of its obligations under the loan notes.

  The words 'arm's length market-related terms' have been used rather than just merely 'arm's length' to allow originator banks to provide the interest rate swap instrument for their own securitisation schemes. If this wording was not included, originator banks would have to look to outside third parties to provide swap instruments.

- The variable interest rates that are swapped are determined by reference to publicly quoted rates that are not under the originator's control.

  Again, this condition has been made to ensure that if an originator bank provides the interest swap it does so at arm's length prices.

- At the time of transfer of the assets to the issuer, the originator had hedged exposures relating to these assets (either individually or as part of a larger portfolio) and entering into the swap effectively restores the hedge position left open by their transfer. Thereafter, where the hedging of the originator's exposure under the swap requires continuing management, any necessary adjustments to the hedging position are made on an ongoing basis.

[FRS 5 App D para D11].

[The next paragraph is 3.159.]

Revolving assets

3.159 There are many examples of credit card securitisations in the US. Because of the fluctuating nature of credit card balances, a special structure is used in the US to effect the securitisation. A trust is set up which acquires the rights to the credit card balances from the originator (usually a bank). The balances are then split in two: the first element is a fixed amount; and the second element is the balance of the credit card receivables, which fluctuates. A SPV issues loan notes to investors and finances the fixed amount of the credit card receivables, the fluctuating balance is financed by the originator as illustrated in the graph below. Some form of credit enhancement will also be used. The originator's staff normally administer the receivables.

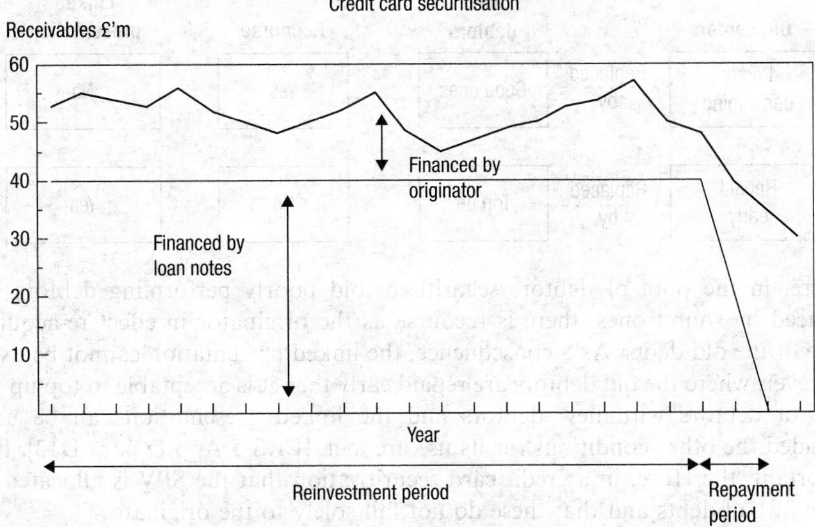

3.160 Generally, in the US, the monies collected, being the repayment of principal and interest, are applied in proportion to the outstanding fixed and fluctuating balances. The proportion of interest collected allocated to the fixed amount is used by the SPV to pay interest on its loan notes. The interest differential between that charged on the receivables and that paid on the loan notes is considerable and the excess is used to finance expenses of the SPV and its bad debts. The amount of principal collected is initially, during the reinvestment period, invested in new receivables such that the balance securitised remains constant. After a set period (typically five years) the amount of principal received stops being used to reinvest in new receivables and is instead used to repay the loan notes during the repayment period.

3.161 In the UK the requirements of FRS 5, have precluded the use of the linked presentation for US-style credit card securitisations, because it has proved difficult for companies to satisfy two of the linked presentation conditions. The two problematical conditions are: condition (b) in paragraph 27, which requires the provider of the finance to have no recourse (implicit or explicit) and the originator no obligation to repay the finance; and condition (f) in paragraph 27, which seeks to ensure that the originator has no obligation or right to re-acquire the securitised assets. These conditions need to be considered carefully.

Reinvestment period

3.162 During the reinvestment period the proceeds from old balances are reinvested in new credit card receivables to maintain the fixed amount finance by the SPV. It is important, during this period, that there is no recourse to the originator (which is the condition in paragraph 27(b) of the standard); this can happen if poorly performing debts are replaced in the SPV by good ones. Consider the following diagram:

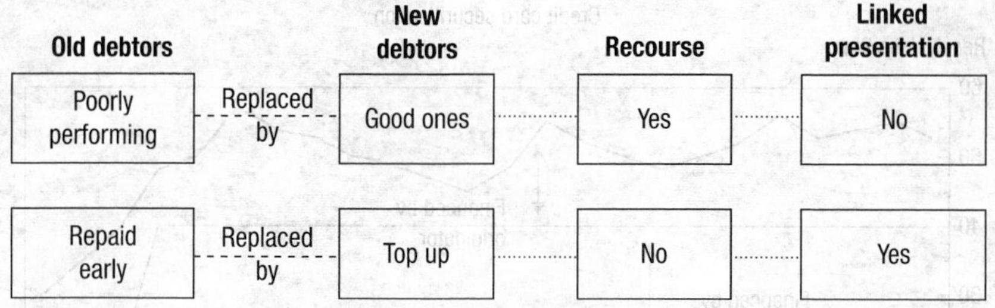

Where, in the pool of debtors securitised, old poorly performing debtors are replaced by sound ones, there is recourse as the originator in effect re-acquires some of the old debts. As a consequence, the linked presentation cannot be used. However, where the old debtors are repaid early then it is acceptable to top up the pool of debtors with new debtors and the linked presentation can be used provided the other conditions for its use are met. [FRS 5 App D para D13]. It is important, therefore, in a credit card securitisation that the SPV is allocated its share of bad debts and that these do not fall solely to the originator.

Repayment period

3.163 As mentioned above, in a credit card securitisation the loan notes are usually repaid from proceeds received during the repayment period. The monies collected during that period arise from balances existing at the beginning of the repayment period and new balances arising subsequently that continue to be financed by the originator. In the US schemes, the proceeds from the repayment of principal relating both to old and to new balances are allocated in proportion to the fixed amount and to the fluctuating balance of the receivables that arises at the beginning of the repayment period. However, in practice, this proportion will change significantly during the repayment period as the old balances financed by the SPV are repaid. For example, if the proportion of fixed to fluctuating debt is 80:20 at the beginning of the repayment period, it can soon become (say) 40:60. If the SPV is still being allocated 80 per cent (and in some US schemes they allocate an arbitrary 99 per cent) of the cash balances received, when it should only be receiving 40 per cent, the effect is that the noteholders are being repaid out of proceeds of the new balances as well as the old ones that existed at the beginning of the repayment period. Therefore, because of this apportionment, the noteholders are being repaid partly out of assets belonging to the originator and only partly out of the assets they were financing at the beginning of the repayment period. As a consequence, the condition in paragraph 27(f) is not met, because the noteholders are not being repaid solely out of the cash receipts generated by the balances that existed at the start of the repayment period.

3.164 In order for conditions (b) and (f) to be satisfied, only the cash collected from the old balances can be used to repay the loan notes during the repayment period. This is necessary to ensure that the issuer is allocated its proper share of losses on those old balances so they do not fall to the originator. [FRS 5 App D para D12]. Therefore, in order for such a scheme to work in the UK it is necessary to analyse the amounts collected during the repayment period on an actual basis such that the SPV only receives its proportion based on the original balances and hence bears its share of losses arising on those balances.

3.165 The type of situation that can arise is illustrated by the following example:

Example

An originator sells the rights to a pool of £600,000 credit card receivables to a SPV, of which £400,000 is funded by noteholders and the balance £200,000 by a loan from the originator. The rights to all new receivables generated during a reinvestment period will be offered for sale to and purchased by the SPV. Increases in the balances of rights to receivables bought by the SPV are to be funded by the originator. The funding by noteholders remains constant. Initially the securitisation covers the rights to a portfolio of 400 debtors and soon after the initial securitisation a number of the card holders have increased their balances as follows:

Pool debtors		On securitisation	Shortly thereafter
		£	£
1		100	450
2		500	500
3		1,200	1,200
4		750	750
5		240	280
6 — 400		597,210	696,820
		600,000	700,000
Funded by:			
Originator		200,000	300,000
Noteholders		400,000	400,000
		600,000	700,000
Originator's interest in debtor 3 (for example)			
On securitisation			
1,200 ×	200,000 / 600,000	400	
Shortly thereafter			
1,200 ×	300,000 / 700,000		514

If the debtor of £1,200 went bad, then the originator would bear £400 of the loss initially, but after the increase in the pool would bear a loss of £514. The example shows that the originator is exposed to a bigger loss on the original asset, which breaches paragraphs 27(f) as it seems that in effect it has re-acquired part of its interest in the debtor of £1,200. This outcome might seem to indicate that it would not be possible under that standard to securitise credit card receivables in this way. However, it can be argued in this case, that this is purely an arithmetic result rather than a matter of principle and in reality the originator's participation will move up and down over the life of the credit card scheme and so fluctuations of this nature can be ignored. This is a pragmatic argument and one that would probably be accepted in practice. What is important is that new credit card balances introduced to the scheme in this period are only used to top up the scheme and not to replace bad debts. Furthermore, in the repayment period, where there is a desire to unwind the scheme and repay the loan notes as fast as possible, it is necessary to ensure that sufficient cash is generated from those balances that existed at the beginning of the repayment period, to make the relevant repayments to the noteholders; or that, if there is not, the relevant part of any loss falls to the noteholders.

Multi-originator programmes

3.166 In certain securitisation schemes, the SPV might serve a number of originators. Such arrangements are often structured so that the originator's benefits and risks are based on the performance of a defined pool of assets (that is, those that it has transferred to the SPV). Where this is so, and the originator is shielded from the benefits and risks on the other assets held by the SPV, the originator should include as an asset in its financial statements the pool of mortgages from which its benefits and risks arise. The related finance can be linked on the face of the balance sheet provided the conditions for that presentation are met, otherwise it should be recorded separately as a liability. [FRS 5 App D para D15].

Example of required analysis

3.167 Application note D unfortunately provides no examples of securitisation transactions to illustrate its provision. The example below illustrates the principles as they apply to a credit card securitisation:

Example

Company A owns credit card receivables that it wishes to securitise. A third party company, company B, acquires the rights from company A to the credit card receivables. Company C is a SPV owned by a charitable trust. The rights sold to company B entitle it to all present and future credit card receivables on those accounts. The legal ownership remains with company A. The transaction is illustrated in the diagram below.

Company A services the accounts and charges company B a fee for doing so and is also entitled to a share of the profits of company B during the first five years of the scheme. The acquisition of the rights to the credit card balances by company B is funded partly by company B issuing loan notes to company C and partly by company B raising money from a third party bank. The total amount funded equals the book value of the debts whose rights are transferred. Company B's loan notes held by company C entitle company C to a share of the cash flows generated by the receivables. Company C's share is a fixed amount which does not fluctuate with the change of the amounts due on the credit card receivables. Company C funds its acquisition of the loan notes in company B by issuing loan notes to third party investors. The amount of the bank's share of the receivables varies and is the difference between company C's share and the total of the receivables.

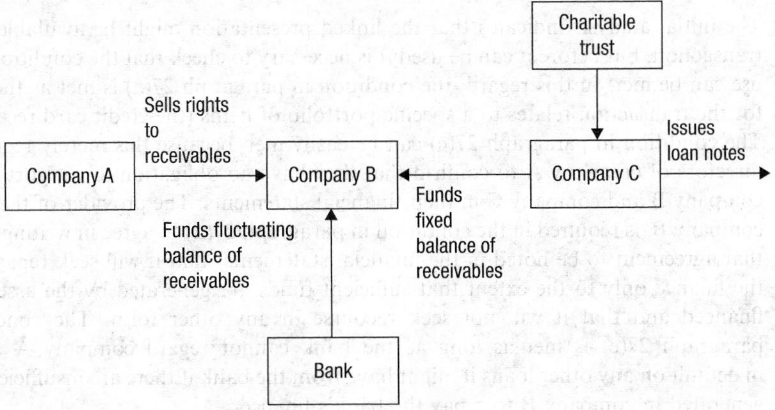

During the scheme's first five years, repayments in respect of principal are reinvested in new credit card receivables. The level of funding provided by company C remains constant, any variations being funded by the bank. After year five the repayment period starts and company C's loan to company B is repaid from its proportionate share of the principal of the receivables collected. The bank's funding will reduce, but at a slower rate than that of company A, so that eventually the bank will fund whatever receivables are left in company B, which will continue to fall.

In analysing the transaction it is necessary to consider how the transaction should be accounted for in company A's financial statements and in company A's group consolidated financial statements. In company A's financial statements, there are three possible treatments: derecognition of the credit card receivables in their entirety; linked presentation where the conditions for its use are satisfied; and full gross presentation on the balance sheet. Using the principles of Application Note D, the benefits and risks of the transaction can be analysed as follows:

	Off B/sheet	**Linked**	**On B/sheet**
Transaction price The transaction price is arm's length, because company B's acquisition of the rights is based on the receivable's book value.	✓		
Amount of non-returnable proceeds Company A receives non-returnable proceeds for the disposal of its rights to the credit card receivables to company B, but retains a right to further sums, which will depend on the performance of the debts.		✓	
Recourse to the originator for losses There is recourse to company A for losses to the extent that there is a variation in the profits of company B that it shares in, however, the recourse is limited to that share.		✓	

The initial analysis indicates that the linked presentation might be available for this transaction, but before it can be used it is necessary to check that the conditions for its use can be met. In this regard, the condition in paragraph 27(a) is met as the finance for the transaction relates to a specific portfolio of items (the credit card receivables). The condition in paragraph 27(c) can be easily met, because this merely requires the directors of company A to confirm that they have no obligation to support losses of company B and company C in their financial statements. The provider of the finance, company B, is required in the condition in paragraph 27(d) to agree in writing (and for that agreement to be noted in the financial statements) that it will seek repayment of the finance only to the extent that sufficient funds are generated by the assets it has financed and that it will not seek recourse in any other form. The condition in paragraph 27(e) is met as long as the bank cannot regard company A as being in default on any other loans it might have from the bank if there are insufficient funds generated in company B to repay the bank's finance.

The problematical conditions with regard to credit card securitisations are those in paragraphs 27(b) and 27(f) as explained in paragraph 3.161. In typical credit card securitisations in the US, there is recourse to the originator, and the originator in effect reacquires a proportion of bad balances, because the allocation of proceeds from the repayment of the principal might include a share of the losses on the balances that are outstanding at the beginning of the repayment period. This is because the originator generally finances the fluctuating balance of the receivables. However, in this example, the bank takes that risk and, as a consequence, there is no recourse to the originator. In conclusion, therefore, it appears that company A can present this securitisation using the linked presentation in its individual financial statements. It would show the finance provided by company B deducted from the credit card receivables on the face of its balance sheet (that is, all of it, not just that from company C's loan notes).

With regard to the presentation in the group's consolidated financial statements, it seems that company B and company C may be quasi-subsidiaries of company A as long as it has been ascertained that company B and company C are not controlled by company A and hence, are not full legal subsidiaries. Then, following the arguments above, the conditions for the linked presentation can also be justified at the group level. In the consolidated financial statements, the same presentation would be given as in company A's individual financial statements, except that the description of the finance would change and the loan from company B would be replaced by a loan from the bank and the loan notes issued to third parties.

Loan transfers

3.168 For those entities applying FRS 26, FRS 5 Application Note E is not relevant, and the recognition and derecognition principles in FRS 26 should be applied (see further chapter 6). For those entities not within the scope of FRS 26, FRS 5's provisions should be applied to loan transfers and the guidance in FRS 5 Application Note E is relevant. Application Note E deals with other types of loan transfers that do not involve the use of SPVs. The principles involved in analysing these transactions closely follow those applicable to securitisation schemes and factoring. The application note refers to three methods under which the benefits and risks associated with loans can be transferred to a third party:

- Novation — where with the consent of the parties a new contract is substituted for an existing one, generally, in this context, having the effect of changing the party who is the lender.

- Assignment — where rights to interest and repayment of principal (but not obligations) are transferred to a third party (assignee—sub-participant). There are two types of assignment. First, a statutory assignment which must relate to the whole loan and comply with certain conditions before it will be a valid statutory assignment. For instance, the assignment must take the form of an out and out transfer which deprives the assignor of all further interest in the loan. In addition, notice in writing must be given to the borrower and guarantors. Secondly, an equitable assignment (which may only relate to part of the loan and does not require all the legal formalities of a statutory assignment). No particular form is required to constitute a valid equitable assignment.

- Sub-participation — where the lender enters into an agreement with a third party (sub-participant) for that party to deposit an amount equal to the whole or part of the loan with the lender on a non-recourse basis. The sub-participant receives an interest in the cash flows arising on the loan, but the loan itself is not transferred. The sub-participant, therefore, assumes a risk exposure to the original borrower, because it only receives its share of the interest and principal if the borrower performs on the loan. The sub-participant is also exposed to the original lender, because the cash flows are often routed through the lender.

3.169 As with securitisation schemes, there are three possible treatments in the lender's financial statements:

- Derecognition — where the loan or part of it is removed from the balance sheet and no liability is shown in respect of the amounts received from the transferee.

- Linked presentation — where the liability in respect of the amounts received from the transferee is deducted from the amount of the loan on the face of the balance sheet.

- Separate presentation — where the loan continues to be shown as an asset and the amount received from the transferee is shown as a liability.

3.170 The benefits to the lender associated with such loan transfers remain the cash flows of interest and principal received from the borrower, although these will eventually be paid to the transferee. The risks associated with such transactions are:

- Credit risk — risk of bad debts.

- Slow payment risk.

- Interest rate risk — risk that the interest rate received from the borrower will not match the rate paid to the transferee.

- Reinvestment/early redemption risk — risk that interest earned on amounts received and reinvested by the lender, before repayment to the transferee, are lower than those payable to the transferee.
- Moral risk — risk that the lender is morally obliged to fund any losses on the loans, because of its association with them.

[FRS 5 App E para E6].

3.171 These main benefits and risks are considered in detail in the application note and the principles stemming from that discussion are then summarised in a table. The summary table is reproduced below; also included are references to the paragraphs of the application note that give the narrative explanation:

Indicates derecognition	Indicates linked presentation	Indicates separate presentation
[App E para E15].	[App E para E17].	[App E para E18].
Transfer is for a single, non-returnable fixed sum.	Some non-returnable proceeds received, but lender has rights to further sums whose amount depends on whether or when the borrowers pay.	The proceeds received are returnable in the event of losses occurring on the loans.
There is no recourse to the lender for losses from any cause.	There is either no recourse for losses, or such recourse has a fixed monetary ceiling.	There is full recourse to the lender for losses.
Transferee is paid all amounts received from the loans (and no more), as and when received. Lender has no rights to further sums from the loans or the transferee.	Transferee is paid only out of amounts received from the loans, and lender has no right or obligation to repurchase them.	Lender is required to repay amounts received from the transferee on or before a set date, regardless of the timing or amount of payments by the borrowers.

3.172 In order for loans to be derecognised in the lender's financial statements, the lender must not retain any significant benefits *or* risks associated with the loan. Derecognition is, therefore, only appropriate where all of the following apply:

- The transaction takes place at an arm's length price for an outright sale.
- The transaction is for a fixed amount of consideration and there is no recourse (other than to the loan itself) either implicit or explicit.

  Warranties given in respect of the loan's condition (for example, that the loan is not in arrears) at the time of transfer are allowed, but warranties concerning the loan's condition in the future or its future performance (for example, the loan will not move into arrears) are not allowed.
- The lender will not benefit or suffer if the loans perform better or worse than expected.

[FRS 5 App E para E15].

3.173 Generally, whether or not the lender continues to administer the loans will be of no consequence unless, for example, its servicing fee is not priced at arm's length. This might indicate that the lender has retained significant benefits and risks.

3.174 Normally, in novation agreements all the significant benefits and risks are transferred and the loan can be derecognised (subject to any side agreements). Also in assignments, all significant benefits and risks might be transferred as long as there are no outstanding obligations (for example, to supply additional funds if the loan is restructured), no side agreements and doubts concerning intervening equitable rights can be satisfied. [FRS 5 App E para E14].

3.175 With sub-participations, derecognition might be appropriate, but only where the lender's obligation to pay amounts to the transferee eliminates its access to benefits from the loans, but extends only to those benefits. There must be no possibility that the lender could be required to pay amounts to the sub-participant, where it has not received equivalent amounts from the borrower. If the lender has an obligation to agree to rescheduling the loan without a similar undertaking by the sub-participant, derecognition is not appropriate. [FRS App E para E14].

3.176 Where derecognition is inappropriate the linked presentation may be used, but only if there is absolutely no doubt that the lender's downside exposure to loss is limited to a fixed monetary amount and the linked presentation conditions can be met. If these conditions are not met then the lender will have to adopt separate presentation.

3.177 In some loan transfers only part of the loan is transferred to the sub-participant. In this circumstance, part of the loan might be able to be derecognised or linked with the related finance, but only where the principles of the standard apply. Such arrangements are considered in detail in paragraphs E19 and E20 of Application Note D.

Disclosure requirements

3.178 Where the conditions for the linked presentation are met and that presentation is given on the face of the balance sheet, the notes to the financial statements should also disclose:

- The arrangement's main terms. [FRS 5 App E para E23].
- The gross amount of the loans transferred and outstanding at the balance sheet date. [FRS 5 App E para E23].

  This information will normally already be given on the face of the balance sheet as part of the linked presentation, unless there are any provisions against the loan to cover irrecoverability.

- Any profit or loss recognised in the period, analysed as appropriate. [FRS 5 App E para E23].

- A statement by the directors that the company is not obliged and does not intend to support any losses beyond the recourse to the specific loans linked under the scheme. [FRS 5 para 27(c)].

- A note that the sub-participant has agreed in writing that it will seek recourse to both principal and interest only to the extent that sufficient funds are generated by the specific loans it has financed. [FRS 5 para 27(d)].

3.178.1 Where the conditions for the linked presentation cannot be met and derecognition is not appropriate, separate presentation should be adopted and the gross loans should be shown on the face of the balance sheet (but not linked). The notes to the financial statements should also disclose the amount of the loans subject to transfer agreements that are outstanding at the balance sheet date. [FRS 5 App E para E24].

Companies Act 2006 — Off balance sheet arrangements

3.178.2 Following the transposition into UK law of the requirements of the EU Corporate Reporting Directive (2006/46/EC), the Companies Act 2006 requires the disclosure of 'off-balance sheet' arrangements for financial years beginning on or after 6 April 2008. These requirements are considered further in chapter 4.

Private Finance Initiative and Public Private Partnership

3.179.1 The Private Finance Initiative (PFI) and Public Private Partnerships (PPP) were developed to allow the public sector to procure the provision of services from the private sector. The objective of PFI and PPP is to give the public sector a value for money service. Therefore, value for money is intended to be the key determinant of whether a project should go ahead, not the accounting treatment. In particular, the public sector has been directed to focus on how the procurement of services can achieve the transfer of risk in a way that optimises value for money, so they should not transfer risks to the operator at the expense of value for money. The accounting issue is determining whether or not the risks and rewards relating to the assets included within the contract are retained by the service provider or have been transferred to the public sector purchaser. The most specific accounting standard that applies to PFI and similar transactions is FRS 5, but SSAP 21 is also relevant.

3.179.2 In 1998, the ASB published a further application note 'F' to FRS 5 entitled 'Private finance initiative and similar contracts'. Whilst the application note was written with PFI contracts in mind, its principles can be applied to PPP and other similar contracts. In addition, the Treasury Taskforce published new guidance in Technical Note No. 1 (Revised): How to Account for PFI Transaction [TT TN 1 (revised)] that provides additional guidance for public sector entities when applying the FRS 5 application note principles.

3.179.3 FRS 5's objective is to ensure that the substance of an entity's transactions is reported in its financial statements. This is done by considering the risks and rewards associated with a transaction to determine whether assets and liabilities arise which need to be reflected in the entity's financial statements. Typically, the public sector is provided with a service for which it pays a unitary amount (that is, the single payment made for both the use of the asset and any facilities management (FM) services). In PFI contracts, the unitary payment covers both the cost of the asset and the cost of the other ancillary services being provided.

3.179.4 As mentioned above, the key question in accounting for PFI is who should include on their balance sheet the assets used to fulfil the contract. In essence, the application note requires that, unless the contract contains a stand-alone lease (in which case SSAP 21 should apply), this question should be answered by looking at the extent to which each party bears variations in profits and losses. The problem is which payments and variations should be taken into account and whether the contract should be separated into different elements or regarded as a whole.

[The next paragraph is 3.179.6.]

3.179.6 It is also important to note that the ASB's application note applies also to contracts that are similar to PFI transactions, such as, capital intensive outsourcing/franchising arrangements.

3.179.7 There are a number of stages that have to be considered in establishing on whose balance sheet the PFI assets will reside and these are considered in the paragraphs that follow.

Contract separability

3.179.8 In many schemes it is possible to see clearly how the unitary payment is made up because, for example, the asset element is indexed by a different factor to the ancillary service element. Where such an analysis can be made, the rules in SSAP 21 are easily applied to the asset element and an evaluation of these payments will often result in the conclusion that the transaction is a full pay-out finance lease, which should be on the public sector's balance sheet.

3.179.9 Where it is possible to see through the unitary payment and identify the element that relates to the property and the element that relates to the provision of the facilities management (FM) service, the property element should be analysed using SSAP 21 principles (as it represents a stand-alone lease) and the service element should be ignored. [FRS 5 App F paras F11, F12]. The discount rate to be applied in the SSAP 21 net present value test should not be the return from the entire PFI contract, but should be estimated by reference to the rate that would be expected on a similar lease. [FRS 5 App F para F16]. The minimum lease payments to be taken into account include the expected PFI payments for the property, less any amounts for which there is a genuine possibility of non-payment. [FRS 5 App F para F17]. (See chapter 19 for further explanation concerning lease evaluation under SSAP 21.) The application note lists three examples of situations where a contract may be separable as explained in the paragraphs that follow.

3.179.10 The standard says the contract will be separable where an element of the payment stream varies according to the availability of the property and another element varies according to the usage or performance of services. [FRS 5 App F para F10(a)]. However, as explained above, the underlying intention in most PFI schemes is that individual elements of the unitary payment should not be related to the delivery of specific inputs and should not contain an element designed to cover the debt service costs of the operator with no variation for performance.

3.179.11 The Treasury guidance categorises the more common payment mechanisms used in PFI transactions into three broad models. Model A is where the unitary payment is based on the number of available places, for example, prisoner places. For a 'place' to be available, not only must there be a physical space available, there must also be associated core services, such as heating and food. There are no separate payment streams for any non-core services, but deductions from the unitary payment will be made for substandard performance of these services. This payment model is regarded as non-separable. [TT TN 1 (revised) para 3.4].

3.179.12 Under model B, which is also considered to be non-separable, the unitary payment is based on the full provision of an overall accommodation requirement, which is divided into different units. Availability is defined in terms of being usable and accessible and, in common with model A, will include some associated core services such as heating. There will be no separate payments for any non-core services but, as with model A, substandard performance leads to payment deductions. [TT TN 1 (revised) para 3.5].

3.179.13 In contrast to models A and B, model C is considered to be separable. Under this model, unitary payment is a combination of an availability payment stream and a separate performance related facilities management payment stream. The availability payment stream relates to areas, divided into units, that are attributed a different deduction percentage for unavailability according to their importance. Availability is defined in terms of being usable accessible and may include some associated core services. The facilities management payment stream is made up of the combination of a performance payment for each required service, with deductions for failure to meet the required performance levels. [TT TN 1 (revised) para 3.6]

3.179.14 Another example of separability is where different parts of the contract run for different periods or can be terminated separately, which might arise where a particular service element can be terminated independently. [FRS 5 App F para F10(b)]. An example is where an accommodation contract running for 25 years includes provision of IT services, but this element of the service may be renegotiated at the end of 10 years and/or may be terminated at any time for persistent poor performance without affecting the continuation of the rest of the contract. [TT TN 1 (revised) para 3.7]. However, changes to the service requirements during the contract term that result in the entire unitary payment being renegotiated would not indicate separability.

3.179.15 A further example of separability is where different parts of the contract can be renegotiated separately. This covers market testing and would apply where a service element is market tested and *some or all* of the cost increases or reductions are passed on to the purchaser in such a way that the part of the unitary payment that relates specifically to that service can be identified. [FRS 5 App F para F10(c)]. This applies regardless of whether the market testing is undertaken by the purchaser or the operator. If the purchaser market tests what it pays for an element of an individual service, with an adjustment made to that payment, then there will be a separately identifiable payment stream for that service and hence the contract will be separable. Another situation is where the operator market tests what it pays to subcontractors for an element of an individual service and passes on some or all of the cost increases or decreases to the purchaser, by means of an adjustment made to the unitary payment rather than a separately identifiable payment stream. In this situation, although the part of the payment by the purchaser for that service element may not be separately identified from the contract itself, the substance is that the purchaser has effectively renegotiated what it is paying for an individual service element and hence the contract is separable. However, the fact that the purchaser or operator, at their own volition, conduct market testing of some aspects of the service and, as a result, the parties voluntarily renegotiate the contract does not, in itself, render the contract separable. [TT TN 1 (revised) paras 3.8 to 3.11].

3.179.16 For other contracts where there are some non-separable service elements, the provisions of FRS 5 and application note F should be applied.

How to apply FRS 5

3.179.17 PFI contracts involve the delivery of outputs to a definable standard for the payment of a unitary amount. Generally, the unitary payment varies depending on a number of measurable deliverables. For example, if the demand for the service (demand risk) is greater or less than predicted or expected, this is likely to impact on the unitary payment. If the service is not being performed to a high enough standard (performance risk) then this will probably also have an impact on the unitary payment. Similarly, if the service is not available (availability risk) this would normally reduce the amount paid by the public sector purchaser. Contracts often have performance and availability criteria that are not related purely to services. Criteria set at such a high level that they never affect the amount paid by the public sector purchaser should not be taken into account in the analysis. If the contract is truly the provision of an integrated service then it is reasonable that it should not be paid for, or there should be a reduction in the payment, if that integrated service is not provided or it is not up to the specified standard. So, under PFI a service provider could provide, for example, heat and light to definable standards or provide serviced office accommodation, with demand, availability and performance criteria set realistically.

3.179.18 From an accounting view point, FRS 5 is concerned with what actually happens in practice. The accounting treatment not only takes into account whether the performance and availability criteria have been set at realistic levels of performance and availability, it also considers whether those targets are measurable and whether this measurement actually takes place in practice. There is growing expertise in this area and very sophisticated measurement techniques are now being applied effectively.

3.179.19 The party that should recognise the asset on its balance sheet is the one that has access to the asset's benefits and exposure to its risks. In this analysis it is necessary to look at the potential variations in property profits (or losses) that each party bears. Any profit variations that relate purely to service should be ignored. For example, penalties arising from the inadequacy in the training of prison security staff or from the standard of food used in catering facilities should not be taken into account even if those penalties affect the whole of the unitary payment. [FRS 5 App F para F20].

3.179.20 After excluding variations related to service, there may still be a significant number of property factors that need to be considered. In this analysis, greater weight should be given to those factors that are more likely to have a commercial effect in practice. [FRS 5 App F para F21]. It is not appropriate to focus on one feature in isolation, rather the combined effect of all relevant factors should be considered for a range of reasonable possible scenarios. [FRS 5 App F para F49]. It is necessary to consider both the probability of any future profit variation arising from a property factor and its likely financial effect. For example, if it is cheaper to correct a problem rather than to incur a much larger penalty, the relevant variation to consider is the rectification cost. [FRS 5 App F para F21].

3.179.21 Furthermore, a financing transaction will be indicated where, in the event that the contract is terminated early, the bank financing will be paid in full by the purchaser under all events of default. [FRS 5 App F para F50].

3.179.22 Hence it is clear from the above that to establish on whose balance sheet the assets associated with the PFI contract should lie, the analysis should focus on the variations in property profits and losses that each of the parties to the contract bear. While the application note gives no guidance on how this should be done in practice, the Treasury guidance does, by providing a methodology for undertaking a quantitative risk analysis. This involves identifying the key commercial risks borne by each party, evaluating the net present value of the potential variations in property profits of each party and then comparing the two. This gives a quantitative indicator of which party has an asset of the property. The guidance contains two simplified examples of how this is done. These examples are set out in paragraph 3.179.56. However, the Treasury guidance warns that care must be taken to ensure that the quantitative risk analysis model is not applied in a mechanistic way. The validity of the results depends on the accuracy, certainty and completeness of the inputs and assumptions made regarding those inputs. Therefore, the results of the quantitative risk analysis must be assessed together with those risks that are not quantifiable, that is, the qualitative indicators and those risks that may not be capable of meaningful quantification, because of the high level of uncertainty surrounding them. [TT TN 1 (revised) paras 4.1 to 4.58].

3.179.23 In general, where the majority (that is, more than 50 per cent) of these risks and rewards remain with the operator, then the assets should remain as fixed assets on the operator's balance sheet. The purchaser would in this case merely record the unitary payment. Where in contrast the majority of the risks and rewards associated with the property lie with the purchaser, the purchaser would record the assets in its balance sheet (based on the fair value of the asset) and an equivalent obligation. The operator in this situation would record a receivable (similar to a finance lease receivable) representing the present value of the property element of the minimum unitary payments it would receive over the term of the contract, which should equate to the market value of the property. Any additional amounts (that is, in addition to the property-related element of the unitary payments) should be treated as revenue by the operator and expenses by the purchaser.

3.179.24 The analysis, therefore, will concentrate on the variation in profits and losses that arise from the property related risks and rewards. These risks and rewards are considered in the paragraphs that follow.

Property factors to be considered

Demand risk

3.179.25 Demand risk is the risk that the demand for the property will be greater or less than predicted or expected. [FRS 5 App F para F24]. Where demand risk is insignificant little weight should be given to it in the analysis. Longer term contracts create greater demand risk, because of the uncertainties concerning demand in the future. Demand risk might be insignificant even, where there is uncertainty over demand for a particular type of property in the long-term, if the purchaser would fill the PFI property in preference to non-PFI properties. [FRS 5 App F para F27].

3.179.26 Demand risk is significant and borne by the *operator*, for example, where the payments between the operator and the purchaser vary proportionately to reflect usage of the property over all reasonably likely levels of demand — the purchaser will not have to pay the operator for the property to the extent it is not used. Another indication would be where the operator gains if future demand is greater than expected. [FRS 5 App F para F28].

3.179.27 It should be relatively obvious who bears the demand risk from the contract terms and how this impacts on the analysis. For example, where the operator bears the demand risk the unitary payment will vary with demand, but the operator's cost base may stay substantially the same or vary in a non-proportionate way, such that operator bears these variations in profits and losses. Where the purchaser bears demand risk, the operator's revenue is protected and the operator can pass on variations in its costs to the purchaser.

3.179.28 Certain types of PFI transaction have significantly less demand risk, for example with a prison contract or a contract for a hospital the variation in demand may not be very great. In these circumstances, the assets associated with such contracts might be judged to be on the public sector's balance sheet, unless there are significant variations in the profits and losses stemming from the property which arise from the other risks associated with the transaction, which are considered below.

Third party revenues

3.179.29 An indication that a property is an asset of the operator is if there are extensive third party revenues, which are necessary for the operator to cover its costs. Significant restrictions on third party usage might on the other hand indicate that the asset is the property of the purchaser. In addition, where there is a guarantee of the operator's property income this indicates that the asset should be on the purchaser's balance sheet. [FRS 5 App F para F32-F34].

3.179.30 Third party revenues that can be taken into the analysis are those that are expected to cover the operator's property costs and flow from features of the property. This might include, for example, income from a car park provided for hospital patients.

Who determines the nature of the property

3.179.31 If the purchaser determines the key features of how the property is to be built and how it will be operated, then this is an indication that it should be on the purchaser's balance sheet as it bears the design risk [FRS 5 App F para 35]. However, the fact that the key features of the property are recorded in the PFI contract, which is agreed by the purchaser, does not necessarily mean that the purchaser has determined those key features. [TT TN 1 (revised) para 4.11].

3.179.32 The purchaser may implicitly determine the key features of the property. For example, a road contract might specify that the road should revert to the purchaser in a predefined state after a short operating period. This might indicate that the operator has no discretion over the standard of road built and how it will be maintained. [FRS 5 App F para F35]

3.179.33 Conversely, where the operator has significant and ongoing discretion over how to fulfil the PFI contract and makes the key decisions on what property is built and how it is operated, bearing the consequent costs and risks, this is an indication that the property is the operator's asset. For example, in a PFI contract to design and build a road and operate it for a long period, the operator may have complete discretion over the balance between the quality of the original road built and the consequent level of maintenance costs. [FRS 5 App para F36].

3.179.34 Although design risk is a key indicator, it is the costs flowing from the design that will impact the analysis. For example, even where the property is designed by the purchaser, if the design is faulty then this will have an impact on running costs. It will then be the party that bears these cost variations which will have an impact on the analysis. If the costs incurred through faulty design can be passed straight onto the purchaser, then the purchaser clearly has this risk. However, if no matter who specifies the design, costs associated with faulty design are borne by the operator, then this indicates that the assets should remain on the operator's balance sheet.

3.179.35 Construction risk refers to who bears the financial implications of cost and time overruns during the construction period and is generally not relevant in the analysis, because such risk has no impact during the property's operational life. But where the purchaser bears construction risk and the property is claimed to be that of the operator it is necessary to consider carefully whether the property is actually the purchaser's asset. [FRS 5 App F para F37].

3.179.36 Where, however, a delay in completing the property means that the unitary payment will not start on the expected date, this variation in the operator's revenue should be taken into account in the analysis.

3.179.37 Also, while construction risk is generally not relevant to the analysis, some risks during construction phase will relate to design risk rather than construction risk. For example the operator may have the freedom to make the design changes during the construction period that, whilst not being necessary to meet the contract requirements, are made in the expectation of reducing expected operating and life cycle costs. Where the financial implications of such changes cannot be quantified, this should be considered as one of the qualitative factors. [TT TN 1 (revised) para 4.40].

Penalties for under-performance or non-availability

3.179.38 Only those penalties for under-performance or non-availability that are significant and have a reasonable possibility of occurring should be taken into the analysis. For example, significant penalties on the operator arising from lane closures for more than a minimal period in a road contract should be taken into account and are an indication that the property is an asset of the operator. [FRS 5 App F para F38, F39].

3.179.39 Clearly, where it is more cost effective for the operator to rectify a problem rather than incur a significant penalty, the cost of the rectification should come into the analysis rather than the penalty. [FRS 5 App F para F21]. This in based on the FRS 5 principle that only those matters that are likely to have an impact in practice should be taken into account.

3.179.40 It is also necessary to distinguish service related penalties, which are irrelevant, from property related penalties, which are relevant. For example, in a PFI contract for a catering service, deductions caused by a leaking kitchen roof are relevant, but deductions due to meals being too small are not. [TT TN 1 (revised) para 4.42].

Changes in relevant costs

3.179.41 Where significant increases in future costs are passed onto the purchaser this is an indication that the asset should be on its balance sheet. For example, this would be the case where the PFI payments vary with specific indices to reflect the operator's increased costs, but this would not be so where the payments vary with a general price index, such as the RPI. [FRS 5 App F paras F40,F41].

3.179.42 It is also necessary to determine which costs should be taken into the analysis. Clearly the costs should be those that relate to the property, but the distinction between the costs associated with the asset and those related to the service might not be obvious. The costs will include capital expenditure to be incurred in replacing the asset over the term of the contract, which would include those costs associated with the buildings, equipment and furniture and fittings. Furthermore, operating costs associated with repairing the fixed assets would also be included. As explained in paragraph 3.179.33 above, the costs associated with rectifying design faults will need to be taken into account, but other costs associated with design might also be relevant. For example, if the design of serviced accommodation specified single-glazed windows, then variations in heating costs and who bears those variations are relevant to the analysis as they stem from a feature of the property.

3.179.43 Other costs that are totally independent of the property, for example, the costs of the raw materials and consumables in a catering facility which is part of a hospital contract, should be excluded from the analysis where they relate purely to services.

Obsolescence and changes in technology

3.179.44 Where the potential for obsolescence or changes in technology are significant who bears the costs and gains any associated benefits will be an indication of who should recognise the asset. [FRS 5 App F para F42]. Although separately identified in the standard, this is just another cost variation that needs to be taken into account in the analysis together with the other cost variations mentioned above.

Contract termination and residual value risk

3.179.45 PFI contracts are generally for the long term, primary terms of 25 to 30 years are typical. Such long periods might indicate that the arrangement is a full payout one for the asset. There is also a problem with what happens to the asset at the end of the term. Often the asset reverts back to the public sector for nil or a nominal sum. Some argue that the residual should not matter over such a long term, because its discounted value will be minimal. However, reversion back to the public sector for a nominal amount could equally be viewed as further evidence that the public sector is buying an asset over the contract term.

3.179.46 Residual value risk is explained in the standard as the risk that the actual residual value of the property at the end of the contract will be different from that expected. The risk is obviously more significant the shorter the contract term. Where residual value risk is significant the purchaser will bear it if it has agreed to purchase the property for a substantially fixed or nominal amount; or if the asset is transferred to a new operator selected by the purchaser for a substantially fixed or nominal amount; or if payments over the contract term are sufficiently large for the operator not to rely on an uncertain residual value. The practical effect of options for the purchaser to acquire the asset or for the operator to 'walk' from the contract need to be considered carefully. [FRS 5 para F44-F48]. Where the purchaser has an option to purchase or walk away and there is no genuine possibility that the purchase option will be exercised, this indicates that the residual value risk is borne by the operator. Alternatively, where there is no genuine possibility that the walk option will be exercised, this indicates that the residual value risk with the purchaser. [TT TN 1 (revised) para 4.52].

3.179.47 However, residual value risk will not have a significant impact on the analysis if, the public sector is to acquire the asset during the term of the contract or at the end of the contract, based on a market value payment for the asset. Alternatively, there could be arrangements whereby the public sector body can re-negotiate an extension of the service term. Sometimes, there are clauses that allow other service providers to re-compete for a subsequent term of the contract. If any transfer of assets to the new service provider is made at market value then the risks associated with assets do not reside with the public sector.

3.179.48 When evaluating residual value risk, a distinction needs to be made between specialised properties, for which there are no practical alternative uses (for example, hospitals and prisons) and alternative use properties, for which there is an alternative use, whether or not such use involves the provision of the same service (for example, office accommodation in areas where there is demand from other users). In the case of specialised properties, in most cases it is unlikely that the operator will accept residual value risk at an acceptable price and, therefore, this risk is usually borne by the purchaser. [TT TN 1 (revised) paras 4.54 to 4.58].

Summary of risks to consider

3.179.49 The principles stemming from the above discussion are summarised in application note F in a table. The summary table is reproduced below; also included are references to the paragraphs of the application note that include the narrative explanation.

Variations in profits/losses for the property, in transactions falling directly within FRS 5 rather than SSAP 21

Three principles govern the assessment of the indications set out below:

- Only variations in property profits/losses are relevant.
- The overall effect of all of the factors taken together must be considered.
- Greater weight should be given to those factors that are more likely to have a commercial effect in practice.

Indications that the property is an asset of the purchaser	Indications that the property is an asset of the operator
Demand risk is significant and borne by the purchaser, for example:	Demand risk is significant and borne by the operator, for example:
■ The payments between the operator and the purchaser will not reflect usage of the property so that the purchaser, will have to pay the operator for the property whether or not it is used. [App F para F28(a)].	■ The payments between the operator and the purchaser will vary proportionately to reflect usage of the property over all reasonably likely levels of demand so that the purchaser will not have to pay the operator for the property to the extent it is not used. [App F para F28(a)].
■ The purchaser gains where future demand is greater than expected. [App F para F28(b)].	■ The operator gains where future demand is greater than expected. [App F para F28(b)].
There is genuine scope for significant third-party use of the property but the purchaser significantly restricts such use. [App F para F33].	The property can be used, and paid for, to a significant extent by third parties and such revenues are necessary for the operator to cover its costs. [App F para F32].
	The purchaser does not guarantee the operator's property income. [App F para F33].
The purchaser determines the key features of the property and how it will be operated. [App F para F35].	The operator has significant ongoing discretion over what property is to be built and how it will be replaced. [App F para F36].
Potential penalties for under-performance or non-availability of the property are either not significant or are unlikely to occur. [App F para F38].	Potential penalties for under-performance or non-availability of the property are significant and have a reasonable possibility of occurring. [App F para F39].
Relevant costs are both significant and highly uncertain and all potential material cost variations will be passed on to the purchaser. [App F para F40].	Relevant costs are both significant and highly uncertain and all potential material cost variations will be borne by the operator. [App F para F41].

Obsolescence or changes in technology are significant and the purchaser will bear the costs and any associated benefits. [App F para F43].	Obsolescence or changes in technology are significant and the operator will bear the costs and any associated benefits. [App F para F43].
Residual value risk is significant (the term of the PFI contract is materially less than the useful economic life of the property) and borne by the purchaser. [App F para F44-48].	Residual value risk is significant (the term of the PFI contract is materially less than the useful economic life of the property) and borne by the operator. [App F para F44-48].
The position of the parties to the transaction is consistent with the property being an asset of the purchaser, for example: ■ The operator's debt funding is such that it implies the contract is in effect a financing arrangement. [App F para F50]. ■ The bank financing would be fully paid out by the purchaser if the contract is terminated under all events of default including operator default. [App F para F50].	The position of the parties to the transaction is consistent with the property being an asset of the operator, for example: ■ The operator's funding includes a significant amount of equity. [App F para F50]. ■ The bank financing would be fully paid out by the purchaser only in the event of purchaser default or limited force majeure circumstances. [App F para F50].

Accounting treatment

Assets recognised by the operator — accounting by the operator

3.179.50 Where the analysis indicates that the asset should be recognised by the operator, then the property will be capitalised as a fixed asset. The normal capitalisation rules of FRS 15 will apply. Depending upon the operator's accounting policy, qualifying interest costs may be capitalised during the asset's construction.

3.179.51 Depreciation will be charged on the asset so that the asset is depreciated to its residual value over its useful economic life which, depending upon the circumstances, may be a different period to the contract term.

3.179.52 It is sometimes argued that the annuity method of depreciation could be used in PFI and PPP type contracts. The annuity method of depreciation involves calculating the annual depreciation charge by taking into account the cost of financing the asset. In the early years of the asset's life the notional capital invested is high, which gives high interest charges. This method provides that such interest and depreciation combined remain approximately the same over the period and hence depreciation in the early years is low.

3.179.53 The annuity method may be appropriate where an entity's rate of consumption of the economic benefits of an asset increases over its life. This may be the case where there is a separable operating lease and the operator is acting as a lessor. However, in general, the annuity method of depreciation should not be used.

Assets recognised by the operator — accounting by the purchaser

3.179.54 Where it is concluded that the purchaser does not have an asset of the property, then the purchaser will simply record the unitary payments as an expense as they are incurred by the purchaser. However, there may be other assets and liabilities for example residuals and contributions that need to be accounted for. These are considered further below in paragraphs 3.179.55.15 and 3.179.55.18.

Assets recognised by the purchaser — accounting by the operator

3.179.55 Where it is concluded that the operator does not have a physical asset of the property, it will, instead have a financial asset. This financial asset is a debt due from the purchaser for the fair value of the property. The asset is recorded at the outset and is reduced in subsequent years as payments are received from the purchaser. In addition, finance income on the financial asset is recognised using a property specific rate. Guidance on determining the property specific rate is given in paragraph F16 to the application note in FRS 5. A rate based upon the return for the entire PFI contract may not be an appropriate rate to use as it will include an allowance for risk on the service element of the contract. Where sufficient information is not available to derive a property specific rate from the PFI contract, the rate can be estimated by reference to the rates that would be expected on a similar lease.

3.179.55.1 Application note F does not provide detailed guidance on how the financial asset should be recognised. Three methods of recognising the asset have been suggested.

- Debit costs directly to the financial asset.

  All costs incurred in constructing assets under the PFI contract are debited directly to a financial asset balance. This is consistent with the idea that the operator is building a property on behalf of the purchaser and will recover the costs it incurs over time. In principle, the operator's asset is an interest yielding financial receivable.

  It may be possible to recognise interest income on the financial asset from day one. However, the operator will have to review the contract to ensure that there is sufficient certainty over recovery of this income. It seems unlikely that the operator should recognise interest income in excess of the interest costs it has incurred in the construction period.

  This approach to recognising the financial asset will in most cases be the most appropriate as it reflects the fact that the operator does not have the benefits and risks associated with the property.

- Initial recognition as work in progress.

  Under this approach all costs incurred are debited directly to work in progress. On completion of the asset the work in progress balance is transferred to financial assets. This could be achieved in one of two ways either:

- A direct balance sheet transfer from work in progress to financial assets.

  Dr Financial assets

  Cr Work in progress

  Or

- A transfer *via* the profit and loss account. That is:

  Dr Profit and loss account (cost of sales)

  Cr Work in progress

  Dr Finance receivable

  Cr Profit and loss account (sales)

  The second method is the correct method as it recognises that the asset has been sold by the operator to a third party in return for a finance receivable.

  In certain limited cases, where it is possible to determine the fair value of the property constructed, it may be possible to recognise a manufacturer's profit on completion of the property. Also, in certain limited situations, it may be possible to recognise turnover, costs and profits during the construction phase using principles similar to those used in long-term contract accounting under SSAP 9. However, whenever it is proposed to recognise a profit, it is necessary to consider the recoverability of the resulting finance receivable and to ensure that any profit recognised does not result in an artificially low return on the service element of the contract.

  Initial recognition of the property as work in progress may be appropriate where the operator has significant property risks during the construction phase of the contract that reduce once construction has been completed.

- Initial recognition as a fixed asset

  Under this approach all costs incurred are debited directly to fixed assets. On completion of the asset, the fixed asset is transferred to financial assets.

  This is not an acceptable way to recognise the financial asset. Fixed assets are defined as assets intended for continuing use within a business. It is difficult to see how an asset whose benefits and risks rest with another party (the purchaser) could be described as being intended for continuing use within the operator's business.

3.179.55.2 Once the financial asset has been recognised, the question arises as to how the balance should be amortised. In a PFI type contract, the operator will receive a single unitary payment. This payment is intended both to reward the operator for the services it provides and to allow it to collect the receivable in respect of the property it has constructed. The unitary payment must, therefore, be split between earning a return on the financial asset, collection of the financial asset and turnover in respect of the service element of the arrangement. This is illustrated below with an example.

Example

Company A is a PFI operator. The asset constructed by company A is being accounted for as a financial asset. In year 5, a unitary payment of £100 is received of which £10 is interest on the financial asset, £60 is collection of the financial asset and £30 is in respect of services provided. The correct way to account for this receipt is as follows:

Dr Cash	100	
Cr Financial asset		60
Cr Interest income		10
Cr Turnover		30

The receipt in respect of the financial asset is a collection of a debtor, so it would not be appropriate to show the £60 flowing through the profit and loss account.

Assets recognised by the purchaser — accounting by the purchaser

3.179.55.3 Where it is concluded that the purchaser has an asset of the property and a liability to pay for it, these should be initially recorded on the purchaser's balance sheet at the fair value of the property. The asset will be depreciated over its useful economic life in accordance with FRS 15. The liability will be reduced as payments for the property are made. In addition, an imputed finance charge on the liability will be recorded in the purchaser's profit and loss account. The charge will be calculated using a property specific rate. The remainder of the PFI payments (that is, the full payments, less the capital repayment and the imputed finance charge) should be recorded as an operating cost in respect of the service element of the arrangement. Again an example will help to illustrate.

Example

Company B is a PFI purchaser. The asset constructed by the operator will be recorded on company B's balance sheet. In year 5, company B makes a unitary payment of £100 of which £10 is interest payable on the outstanding liability, £60 is repayment of that liability and £30 is in respect of services provided by the operator to Company B. In addition, depreciation of £15 is charged on the property. The double entry is as follows:

Dr Interest payable (profit and loss account)	10	
Dr Operating costs	30	
Dr Creditors	60	
Cr Cash		100

To recognise the payment of the unitary charge.

Dr Operating costs	15	
Cr Accumulated depreciation		15

To recognise depreciation on the property.

3.179.55.4 There may be practical problems with this treatment where, for instance, there is a significant variation in the unitary payment due to a service related issue.

Example

Under a small PFI contract, where the purchaser has recognised the asset and the operator has recognised a finance receivable, the normal monthly unitary payment is £1,000, which is, split between a finance cost of £100, a repayment of capital of £700 and the balance attributable to the provision of the integrated service of £200. During, a particular month there is a complete breakdown in the service provision, which has a significant impact on the unitary payment. Instead of £1,000, only £600 is payable for the month. The question then arises as to how to allocate the reduced payment. If £700 is treated as a capital repayment and £100 the finance cost, a credit of £200 would have to be recorded in the purchaser's profit and loss account for the service element. This might be the appropriate treatment over the term of the contract if the credit represents a claw-back of the element of the unitary payment that relates to service. It will, however, in practice be necessary to determine whether or not the reduced payment has an impact on the value of the asset. It might indicate, for example, that there is an impairment and that it is necessary for the purchaser to provide against the asset's carrying value. If the impairment is likely to impact further unitary payments, it might be appropriate to reduce both the asset and the corresponding liability.

3.179.55.5 The point at which the purchaser recognises the asset will usually be when it comes into use, unless the purchaser bears significant construction risk in which case it should recognise the property as it is constructed.

Use of SSAP 9

3.179.55.6 Some operators in PFI type transactions have sought to argue that the principles of SSAP 9 for long-term contract accounting could be applied to the PFI or PPP contract as a whole (rather than just the construction phase as described above in paragraph 3.179.55.1.

3.179.55.7 SSAP 9 defines a long-term contract as *"a contract entered into for the design, manufacture or construction of a single substantial asset or the provision of a service (or of a combination of assets or services which together constitute a single project) where the time taken substantially to complete the contract is such that the contract activity falls into different accounting periods"*. [SSAP 9 para 22].

3.179.55.8 It is difficult to support the use of SSAP 9 when the asset would be on the operator's balance sheet under FRS 5. SSAP 9 is designed to account for assets or services that are sold to another party. If the substance of the transaction is such that the risks and rewards of ownership of the asset are with the operator then the asset has not been sold and should be treated as a fixed asset.

3.179.55.9 It can be argued that there is more scope for applying SSAP 9 when the constructed asset is off the operator's balance sheet as clearly a sale of some description has taken place. However, paragraph F60 of the application note to FRS 5 states that where the operator does not have an asset of the property, the operator should recognise a financial asset, being a debt due from the purchaser for the fair value of the property. This statement appears to preclude the use of SSAP 9 for the contract as a whole.

[The next paragraph is 3.179.55.12.]

Pre-contract costs

3.179.55.12 Entities involved in PFI and PPP type arrangements often incur significant costs in bidding for and securing contracts. UITF Abstract 34 requires that directly attributable pre-contract costs are recognised as an asset only when it is virtually certain that a contract will be obtained and the contract is expected to result in future net cash inflows with a present value not less than all amounts recognised as an asset. All other pre-contract costs should be expensed as incurred. [UITF 34 para 15(a)]. The reinstatement of costs incurred before the virtual certainty condition is met is not permitted by the abstract. [UITF 34 para 15(b)].

3.179.55.13 It should be noted that 'virtual certainty' is a very high test to meet. For the recovery of the pre-contract costs to be virtually certain, it is essential that the entity has been awarded sole preferred bidder status. However, preferred bidder status on its own is not sufficient. The abstract notes that *"virtual certainty is not achieved if the award of the contract is subject to uncertain future events not wholly within the control of the entity or the purchaser (such as the need for regulatory approval or the likelihood of legal challenge)"*. PFI projects can often be subject to some form of legal challenge. However, we believe that the wording in the abstract should be interpreted as meaning a substantive legal challenge, that is, a challenge that could affect either the viability of the contract as a whole or one that could lead to the contract not being finally awarded to the bidder in question.

3.179.55.14 The abstract also requires that the recovery by consortium members of pre-contract costs from a SPV should reflect the same principles as those used by the SPV itself. This is probably best illustrated with an example:

Example

In each of the following scenarios, assume the following:

- Costs incurred before the virtual certainty test is met £60,000
- Costs incurred after the virtual certainty test is met £40,000
- Company A has a 25% stake in the contracting SPV and equity accounts for its investment
- The SPV is entirely debt funded

Scenario 1 – SPV incurs the costs directly

SPV entity financial statements

The SPV will expense the costs incurred before the virtual certainty test has been met (£60,000) and record the remaining £40,000 of costs as an asset.

Company A's financial statements

In its consolidated financial statements, company A will account for its share of the SPV's loss (25% of £60,000 = £15,000) and its share of the SPV's net liabilities (£15,000).

Scenario 2 – Company A incurs the costs and recharges at cost to the SPV once the virtual certainty test has been met

SPV entity financial statements

The costs incurred by the SPV can be viewed in one of two ways:

- It could be argued that, as the SPV is so closely related to company A, it should reflect the accounting that would have been required had the SPV incurred the costs itself. That is, record an asset of £40,000 and an expense of £60,000.
- Alternatively, as far as the SPV is concerned, all the costs have been incurred after the virtual certainty test has been met. Therefore, the SPV will capitalise the full amount as an asset (£100,000).

Whilst both approaches are probably acceptable, the first approach is the preferred method as it simplifies the treatment in the consolidated financial statements (see below).

Company A's entity financial statements

Before recharging the costs to the SPV, company A in its entity financial statements will have:

- expensed £60,000 for costs incurred before the virtual certainty test had been met; and
- recorded an asset of £40,000.

The treatment of the reimbursement from the SPV will depend upon the substance of the payment. If the receipt from the SPV is in any way repayable or gives rise to any continuing obligations in company A, then the full amount of the receipt (£100,000) should be treated as a financing and held as deferred income. £60,000 of this amount would be amortised to the profit and loss account over the contract term and £40,000 would be amortised to match the depreciation of the asset. It should be noted that if company A guarantees the debt of the SPV, then the reimbursement is in substance repayable.

If, however, the receipt is not repayable and does not give rise to any continuing obligations in company A, then company A will credit the amount received from the SPV (£100,000) to recovery of the asset (£40,000) and then to its profit and loss account (£60,000) – offsetting the previously recognised expense.

Company A's consolidated financial statements (assuming the receipt from the SPV has not been treated as deferred income)

The treatment in A's consolidated financial statements will depend upon the treatment that has been adopted in the SPV's entity financial statements.

Where the SPV has expensed pre-virtual certainty costs, company A will simply account for its share of the loss of the SPV (25% of £60,000 = £15,000) and its share of the SPV's net liabilities (£15,000). It should be noted that this approach would also result in the other SPV members recognising as an expense an appropriate share of the pre-virtual certainty costs in their consolidated financial statements.

Where the SPV has recognised the full amount recharged by company A as an asset, paragraph 13 of UITF 34 requires an additional consolidation adjustment to be made.

In accordance with FRS 9, in its consolidated financial statements company A will equity account for its share of the SPV's results (£nil) and its share of the SPV's net assets (£nil — that is 25% of £100,000 asset less cash outflow £100,000). On consolidation, company A will make a consolidation adjustment to ensure that the group's share of the pre-contract costs (that is, 25% of £60,000 = £15,000) is debited to the profit and loss account in accordance with the UITF abstract and credit deferred income. The deferred income being released to the profit and loss account over the term on the contract.

Whichever approach is adopted, the net loss for the group is £15,000, which is the same as in scenario 1 above.

Company A's consolidated financial statements (assuming the receipt from the SPV has been treated as deferred income)

Where the SPV has recognised the full amount recharged by company A as an asset, no consolidation adjustments would be required, because company A's individual financial statements will already show pre-contract costs as an expense, which will flow through to the consolidated financial statements.

Scenario 3 – Company A incurs the costs and recharges £120,000 to the SPV once the virtual certainty test has been met

We believe that any profit recharged by company A is in substance an advance on the profits of contract as a whole and should be deferred and recognised over the contract term in both the entity and the consolidated financial statements of company A.

Contributions — accounting by the operator

3.179.55.15 A public sector organisation may sometimes contribute land and/or other assets to a PFI operator. Where the land is simply leased to the operator and it is required for the operator to carry out his obligations under the contract, then the full value of the land should remain on the balance sheet of the purchaser. However, where the land is transferred to the operator and/or the land is not required under the contract, the accounting is more complex. The effect of these types of contributions is illustrated in the following examples:

Example 1

Terms

A purchaser wishes to make an upfront payment to an operator. This may be done directly or through a third party. The purchaser will often require that the funds injected are used to meet the costs of construction to demonstrate that it is receiving full value from the contribution. In the event of default by the operator, the asset and any amounts remaining from the upfront payment will be returned to the purchaser.

Accounting treatment

Under FRS 5, the accounting treatment would follow the substance of the transaction. It is assumed initially that the new asset being constructed under the PFI contract is on the balance sheet of the operator. Thus the total capital costs of the project would be debited to the fixed asset account in the operator's balance sheet. The accounting standard on government grants (SSAP 4) and paragraph 17 of Schedule 1 to SI 2008/410) requires that a fixed asset should be recorded at its 'purchase price or production cost' — meaning that (apart from depreciation) the cost cannot be reduced by other adjustments such as grants received or other similar contributions. Hence it requires that a grant received should not be netted against the cost of the asset, but should instead be shown separately as a deferred income; this deferred income is then released into income over a period. A contribution in a PFI scheme is treated in the same way.

As a result of the above, the accounting treatment to be followed by the operator is as follows. The total capital costs are recorded as fixed assets and depreciated in the normal way. The contribution is recorded separately as deferred income, which is released into income over a period. Often (for example, with a grant) the deferred income is released into income over the life of the related asset.

Where the physical asset is off the operator's balance sheet and hence the operator instead has a financial receivable, the requirements of the Companies Act as noted above do not apply (as they apply only to fixed assets and to stock). Hence, the operator initially sets up a receivable for the total amount of its investment and any contribution received will be credited to this receivable. Where the amount of the contribution exceeds the financial receivable, the excess should be recognised as a liability in the balance sheet. This liability will be reduced by subsequent investment in the property by the operator. This treatment reflects the substance of the contribution, which is effectively an upfront loan to fund the construction of the property.

Example 2

Terms

A purchaser wishes to contribute land to a PFI project involving say, the construction of a property on a new site (site A). The purchaser agrees that once the building on the new site can be occupied the old site (site B) will be vacated and title will pass to the operator. The operator takes title to site B at the end of the construction phase and sells it at some later date. The calculation of the unitary charge assumes a sale of site B for £5m.

Accounting treatment

The accounting treatment would be similar to that set out in example 1 above in the situation where a cash contribution has been received upfront. The total costs of the new development would be shown gross in the operator's financial statements. When site B is contributed, it will be recorded by debiting land and crediting deferred income with the fair value of the land at the time of its transfer to the operator. As in example 1, the deferred income would be released into income usually over the contract term.

An additional point is that the operator will have to monitor the carrying value of site B for possible impairment, under FRS 11, 'Impairment of fixed assets'. Under FRS 11, any loss on an asset is required to be recorded when the loss is known. Recoveries of value are also recorded. Hence the carrying value of the site may fluctuate until the time its value is established by sale.

Alternatively, where the operator carries a financial asset rather than a physical asset, as with example 1, the value attributed to site B would be taken to reduce the carrying value of the financial receivable, that is, debit land and credit financial receivable.

Contributions — accounting by the purchaser

3.179.55.16 The required accounting by the purchaser for contributions is described in paragraph F54 to application note F of FRS 5. Where the contributions give rise to reduced service payments going forward, the carrying value of the property will be reclassified as a prepayment. The prepayment will be amortised to the profit and loss account over the period of reduced PFI payments.

3.179.55.17 Where no future benefit accrues to the purchaser, the carrying value of the contributed asset will be charged to the profit and loss account when the contribution is made.

Accounting for residuals — asset on the operator's balance sheet

3.179.55.18 In some PFI transactions, all or part of the property will pass to the purchaser at the end of the contract. If the contract requires the transfer to take place at market value at the date of the transfer then no accounting is required until the date of transfer.

3.179.55.19 If the contract specifies the amount at which the transfer is to take place then any difference between the price specified by the contract and the expected fair value of the residual must be accounted for over the life of the contract in the financial statements of both the operator and the purchaser. This is illustrated in the following example:

Example

Contract term	30 years
Expected residual value at year 30	£20m
Contract specified price	£30m

The operator will recognise income over the contract term and build up an asset, that is:

Dr Long-term receivable	10	
Cr P&L	10	

At the end of the contract the operator will have a fixed asset with a carrying value of £20m and a long-term receivable balance of £10m. On sale of the asset to the purchaser, the operator will make the following entries:

Dr Cash	30	
Cr Fixed assets		20
Cr Long-term receivable		10

It might appear that an alternative is to depreciate the fixed asset down to its expected proceeds of 30, as opposed to the open market residual of 20. However, this only works if there will be one asset throughout the whole contract term, for example, a single property. It will not work if there is a series of shorter life assets, as the final asset in the series (but not the others) would be depreciated at a different rate. Therefore, the method set out above is preferred as it spreads the effect over the whole contract term rather than the life of the final asset in the series.

Accounting by the purchaser is as follows:

Over the contract term:		
Dr P&L	10	
Cr Provisions		10
On purchase of the asset:		
Dr Fixed assets	20	
Dr Provisions	10	
Cr Cash		30

This accounting ensures that the correct charge is recognised in the profit and loss account of the purchaser and the correct income is recognised in the accounts of the operator.

3.179.55.20 In cases where the expected residual value is greater than the price specified by the contract the accounting will be reversed. That is the operator will build up a provision whilst the purchaser will build up an asset over the contract term.

Accounting for residuals — asset on the purchaser's balance sheet

3.179.55.21 Where the transfer is to take place at market value, the operator will amortise the finance receivable down to the expected residual value of the asset over the life of the contract. The purchaser will amortise the creditor it recognises in a similar way. The payment made by the purchaser for the residual will, therefore, be used to pay off the outstanding balance on the creditor.

3.179.55.22 Any difference between the residual payment required by the contract and the expected fair value of the residual will be built up in the similar way to that illustrated in paragraph 3.179.55.19 above.

Methods of amortising the financial asset

3.179.55.23 In general, a financial asset will be amortised using principles similar to those used by lessors under SSAP 21. However, in some situations the substance of the contract may require different methods of amortising the financial asset to be considered. For example, it may be clear from the profile of cash receipts that payments for the asset element of the contract are being accelerated or deferred. In which case, it may be necessary to consider increasing or decreasing the amount allocated to repayment of the financial asset in any given year.

[The next paragraph is 3.179.56.]

Example of quantitative analysis

3.179.56 The following examples are reproduced from the Treasury Taskforce Technical Note 1 (revised) Annex A.

Example 1

Stage 1 — Identify the key commercial risks borne by each party

For illustration purposes assume that the key risks in the PFI contract can be allocated as follows:

Risk/Principal factor	Borne by purchaser	Borne by operator
Demand risk	✓	
Third party revenues		✓
Design risk		✓
Penalties for under performance		✓

Penalties for non-availability		✓
Potential changes in relevant costs		✓
Obsolescence		✓
Residual value	✓	

Stage 2 — Evaluate the NPV of the potential variations in property profits/losses for the operator

A range of modelling techniques can be used to perform the risk analysis depending on the size and complexity of the project. These techniques include sensitivity analyses, scenario analyses or a Monte Carlo simulation. For this example a Monte Carlo simulation has been performed which automatically gives greatest weight to those factors which are likely to have the greatest commercial effect in practice. One of the key features which needs to be borne in mind when assigning probability distributions to the different risks/principal factors, is the requirement to identify whether there are any interdependencies between the probability distributions or whether the risks are independent of others.

Risk/principal factor	Min (cost)/ revenue	Most probable (cost)/revenue	Max (cost)/ revenue	Probability Distribution
	NPV	NPV	NPV	
	£m	£m	£m	
Third party revenues	0	20	40	Normal: SD = 10 mean = 20
Design risk	(30)	(25)	(10)	Triangular: most likely = (25), min = (30), max = (10)
Penalties for under-performance	(30)	(10)	0	Triangular most likely = (10), min = (30), max = 0
Penalties for non-availability	(60)	(40)	0	Triangular: most likely = (40), min = (60), max = 0
Relevant costs	(30)	(20)	(10)	Normal: SD = 5, mean = (20)
Obsolescence	(30)	(25)	(20)	Triangular: most likely = (25), min = (30), max = (20)

The Monte Carlo simulation gives the following results, where the lower and upper limits are at the 5%/95% ends of the distribution.

Lower limit	£(123)m
Mean	£(93)m
Upper limit	£(62)m

Stage 3 — Evaluate the NPV of the potential variations in property profits/losses for the purchaser

Risk/principal factor	Min (cost)/ revenue NPV £m	Most probable (cost)/revenue NPV £m	Max (cost)/ revenue NPV £m	Probability Distribution
Demand risk	(20)	(10)	0	Normal: SD = 5, mean = (10)
Residual value	0	10	20	Triangular: most likely = 10, min = 0, max = 20

The Monte Carlo simulation gives the following results:

Lower limit	£(10)m
Mean	£nil
Upper limit	£11m

Stage 4 — Compare the potential variations in property profits/losses for both the operator and the purchaser to determine which party has an asset of the property

The end product of the detailed risk analysis can be summarised as follows:

Operator
- Expected NPV of property profits/losses £(93)m
- 95% lower limit £(123)m
- 95% upper limit £(63)m
- Range (95% confidence interval) £61m

Purchaser
- Expected NPV of property profits/losses £nil
- 95% lower limit £(10)m
- 95% upper limit £11m
- Range (95% confidence interval) £21m

The total potential variation in property profits/losses is therefore £82m, of which the purchaser bears £21m (26%) and the operator £61m (74%). The results of the quantitative risk analysis would therefore indicate that the operator has an asset of the property. However, as noted in paragraphs 3.179.22, the results of the quantitative risk analysis should always be assessed in the context of the qualitative indicators and those risks which may not be capable of meaningful quantification for inclusion in the quantitative risk analysis.

Example 2

Stage 1 – Identify the key commercial risks borne by each party

For illustration purposes assume that the key risks in the PFI contract can be allocated as follows:

Risk/principal factor	Borne by purchaser	Borne by operator
Demand risk	✓	
Third party revenues		✓
Design risk	✓	✓
Penalties for under performance		✓
Penalties for non-availability		✓
Potential changes in relevant costs		✓
Obsolescence	✓	✓
Residual value	✓	

Stage 2 – Evaluate the NPV of the potential variations in property profit/losses for the operator

Risk/principal factor	Min (cost)/ revenue	Most probable (cost)/revenue	Max (cost)/ revenue	Profitability Distribution
	NPV	NPV	NPV	
	£m	£m	£m	
Third party revenues	10	20	30	Normal: SD = 5, mean = 20
Design risk	(15)	(10)	(5)	Triangular: most likely = (10), min = (15), max = (5)
Penalties for under-performance	(30)	(20)	0	Triangular: most likely = (10), min = (30), max = 0
Penalties for non-availability	(30)	(20)	(5)	Triangular: most likely (20), min = (30), max = (5)
Relevant costs	(30)	(20)	(10)	Normal: SD = 5, mean = 20
Obsolescence	0	0	0	

The Monte Carlo simulation gives the following results, where the lower and upper limits are at the 5%/95% ends of the distribution:

Lower limit	£(59)m
Mean	£(42)m
Upper limit	£(24)m

Stage 3 – Evaluate the NPV of the potential variations in property profits/losses for the purchaser

Risk/principal factor	Min (cost)/ revenue	Most probable (cost)/revenue	Max (cost)/ revenue	Profitability Distribution
	NPV	NPV	NPV	
	£m	£m	£m	
Demand risk	(60)	(30)	—	Normal: SD = 15, mean = (30)
Design risk	(15)	(10)	(5)	Triangular: most likely = (10), min = (15), max = (5)
Residual value	0	20	40	Triangular: most likely 20, min = (30), max = 0

The Monte Carlo simulation gives the following results:

Lower limit	£(47)m
Mean	£(20)m
Upper limit	£8m

Stage 4 – Compare the potential variations in property profits/losses for both the operator and the purchaser to determine which party has an asset of the property.

The end product of the detailed risk analysis can be summarised as follows:

Operator – Expected NPV of property profits/losses £(42)m
– 95% lower limit £(59)m
– 95% upper limit £(24)m
– Range (95% confidence interval) £35m

Purchaser – Expected NPV of property profits/losses £(20)m
– 95% lower limit £(47)m
– 95% upper limit £8m
– Range (95% confidence interval) £55m

The total potential variation in property profits/losses is therefore £90m, of which the purchaser bears £55m (61%) and the operator £35 (39%). The results of the quantitative risk analysis would therefore indicate that the purchaser has an asset of the property. Moreover, the results of the quantitative risk analysis should always be assessed in the context of the qualitative indicators and those risks which may not be capable of meaningful quantification for inclusion in the quantitative risk analysis.

[The next paragraph is 3.180.]

Practical issues

3.180 The implications of FRS 5's provisions are very wide; potentially they can have an effect on *any* transaction. A considerable amount of thought and work was undertaken by the ASB and others in developing the guidance concerning six complex transactions included in the application notes, that is: consignment stock; sale and repurchase agreements; debt factoring; securitised assets; loan transfers and transactions arising from PFI. These transactions are considered from paragraph 3.120. As accountants have considered the standard's implications it has become clearer what other transactions are affected by it. A number of these types of transactions are considered in the paragraphs that follow and might cause some surprises; for example, few would have thought that discounted bills of exchange would come back on balance sheet under the standard's requirements. This section also considers the implications of the standard for a number of particular industries.

Partial derecognition

3.181 One aspect of FRS 5's provisions is that, in certain special situations, an asset can be derecognised and in its place another asset recorded. A simple example is where a company sells an asset, but retains an interest in its residual. This might mean that the asset is derecognised and in its place is recognised another asset — its interest in the residual. These rules are explained in more detail in paragraph 3.67 onwards and the example that follows illustrates how the standard's rules might apply in practice:

Example

Company A has a property that cost £75m whose market value is £90m. It is sold at £90m to a joint venture company which is partly financed by company A and partly by company B. Company B, as a consequence, acquires some significant benefits and risks associated with the asset. The idea is that the joint venture will sell the asset in five years and that there is a sharing of risks and rewards. The likely range of outcomes as to the value in year five is (say) £70m to £120m (that is, any reduction in value below £70m is considered remote).

The agreement is that if the value in year five:

- Is above £90m, company A benefits from 60% of the excess and company B from 40%.

- Falls between £80m to £90m, company A and company B share the loss.
- Is worth less than £80m, company B will bear the loss.

Company A's position is that it gains 60% of any excess above £90m and suffers 50% of the loss in the range £80m to £90m. Company B gains 40% of the excess above £90m, bears 50% of the loss in the range £80m to £90m and bears 100% of the loss below £80m (but a value below £70m is considered remote).

In analysing the above transaction it has to be established whether the investee is a quasi-subsidiary of company A, but if company A does not have the requisite control over the investee then it will be a joint venture under FRS 9 (assuming there is shared control). In the transaction some, but not all, significant benefits and risks have been transferred from company A to company B. Therefore, it appears that it is acceptable under FRS 5's rules for company A to derecognise the asset and to recognise another one in its place. However, the question then arises as to what type of asset and liability should be recognised on the balance sheet in its place. If partial derecognition is considered in isolation, then because there is sufficient uncertainty concerning the risks and rewards to company A, it can be argued that the new asset is a contingent one and that it should be prudently measured at nil. Therefore, only when profits arise in the joint venture should they be taken into account by company A. Furthermore, if subsequently the directors of company A believe that the property is worth only (say) £80m, they should make a provision for the 50% of the loss, that is £5m. But the partial derecognition rules cannot be considered in isolation in this circumstance, because the properties are held by a joint venture which should be equity accounted in company A's consolidated financial statements. In that case, company A will recognise, through equity accounting, its share of any subsequent profits or losses of the joint venture. Consequently, where in this type or arrangement the entity holding the assets and related finance is a joint venture of the group, its treatment under equity accounting arrives at the same result as required under the partial derecognition rules.

With regard to the profit to be recognised on the disposal of the properties to the joint venture, if initially the property is worth £90m on transfer, the company would recognise a profit on the disposal which represents the proportion acquired by the other party to the joint venture, that is, 50% of the total profit of £15, but less if it is thought it likely to be worth say £80m.

In conclusion, the result under FRS 5 is that, albeit certain risks and rewards are retained, the asset and liability will be taken off balance sheet, except to the extent that there is a need to make provision for subsequent diminution in value. If, however, it were company A's intention to re-acquire the asset, then the answer would be different and the standard's Application Note B (on sale and repurchase transactions) would apply. Also another factor that might have an impact on the accounting treatment would be if company A continued to occupy the property. In that situation, it would be harder to justify removing the property from the balance sheet.

3.182 It is also important to remember that partial derecognition cannot be used where the transaction is of a financing nature. For example, it cannot be used for securitisation transactions or factoring arrangements (see para 3.137 and 3.136). This is why the tables at the end of Application Notes C and D do not include columns for partial derecognition.

[The next paragraph 3.184.]

Insubstance debt defeasance

3.184 Where a company irrevocably places cash or other essentially risk-free monetary assets in a trust solely for satisfying a debt, is known in the US as 'insubstance defeasance of debt'. The essence of insubstance debt defeasance is that the assets put into trust are ring-fenced such that they can only be used to repay the loan in due course, further recourse to the company is remote. Typically the creditor is not aware of the arrangement.

3.185 Under FRS 5 it is not possible to derecognise such debt, because these arrangements do not meet FRS 25's offset rules as the company cannot insist on net settlement. In addition, it is not possible to use the linked presentation for such arrangements unless the conditions for the linked presentation are met, which is unlikely because, for one reason, the creditor will usually have recourse to the company's other assets.

> **Example**
>
> A company has a fixed interest sterling Eurobond in issue and has invested in fixed interest gilts to match exactly the repayment of interest and principal on the Eurobond. The company wishes to offset these two balances and considers that this should be acceptable because as the asset is a gilt, and a sterling one, there is no settlement risk attached to the transaction. In addition, there is no interest rate risk because both interest rates are fixed and matched.
>
> Although these transactions appear to be perfectly matched, it is not possible to offset the balances under FRS 25 because the company cannot insist on net settlement. In addition, the Eurobond holders on liquidation of the company would have recourse to the company's other assets. Therefore, also the linked presentation is denied in such an arrangement. In fact it is unlikely that it would ever be possible to link a Eurobond with an asset it finances, because it would be difficult to get the Eurobond holders' consent in writing that they would seek repayment of the finance only to the extent that sufficient funds are generated by the specific assets it has financed.

[The next paragraph is 3.219.]

Repurchase agreements — Repos

3.219 Repo agreements are transactions involving the sale of a security with a simultaneous agreement to repurchase the same or a substantially identical security at a specified future date. The main accounting issue, therefore, is whether the repo should be accounted for as a sale or a financing transaction. Whilst a repo transfers legal title to the securities from the seller to the buyer, the accounting treatment depends on whether the risks and rewards of ownership have in substance been transferred.

3.220 Such transactions clearly fall within the scope of FRS 5's Application Note B (see para 3.123). For those entities applying FRS 26 and where the transaction falls within the scope of paragraphs 14 to 42 of FRS 26, FRS 5

Application Note B is not relevant and the recognition and derecognition principles in FRS 26 should be applied (see further chapter 6). For those entities not within the scope of FRS 26, FRS 5's provision should be applied to sales and repurchase agreement and the guidance in FRS 5 Application Note B is relevant. They are also dealt with in the BBA SORP, 'Securities' and the treatment required by the SORP is consistent with the requirements of FRS 5, which in effect has superseded the SORP in this respect. The standard's application note states that in a straightforward situation, the substance of a sale and repurchase agreement will be that of a secured loan. It goes on to say that the seller in such a transaction should account for the arrangement by showing the original asset on its balance sheet together with a liability for the amounts received from the buyer. Some repo transactions are complex and the guidance in the application note is useful in determining whether the instrument's buyer is merely receiving a lender's return. If it is, then, in substance, no sale has been made and the asset and related finance should be retained on the seller's balance sheet.

3.221 Even in repo transactions where different securities are returned to the seller, if they are substantially similar, such that the risks and rewards are unchanged, the substance of the transaction will still be that of a financing. Therefore, generally the securities subject to a repo should be retained on the seller's balance sheet and valued in accordance with the company's normal accounting policy for its legally owned securities (which would normally be market value). The cash advanced by the buyer would be recorded as a liability and termed, for example, 'securities sold under agreements to repurchase'. Where material the liability should be disclosed separately on the face of the balance sheet. The interest expense (in whatever legal form) should then be charged to the profit and loss account over the life of the agreement.

3.222 From the buyer's point of view, in substance it has not bought an asset, therefore, it will not record the security in its balance sheet or recognise any profits or losses arising from changes in its market value. The cash it has advanced to the seller should be shown as an asset and termed, for example, 'securities purchased under agreements to resell'. The interest income (in whatever legal form) should be accrued over the life of the instrument. The notes to the financial statements and accounting policies of both the seller and the buyer would have to explain the treatment they have adopted.

3.223 It is also necessary to consider the accounting treatment of any additional collateral that passes between the seller and the buyer as a result of changes in the market value of the securities underlying the repo. Collateral takes one of two forms: cash or securities. To the extent that cash collateral is used, this should be treated as a separate asset or liability unless the relevant conditions for offset can be met (see para 3.97) in which case it should be offset against the amount of the repo. If additional securities are used, then these should be treated consistently with those of the original repo.

3.224 For some more complex repo arrangements it is possible that the criteria for derecognition could be met, that is where the seller transfers all significant benefits and all significant risks of ownership to the buyer. This might arise, for example, if the agreement incorporates terms whereby the buyer assumes price risk or in the case of repos to maturity where the repo's maturity date coincides with that of the underlying securities. In such circumstances, the transaction should be treated as a sale. However, if material the nature of the repurchase commitment should still be disclosed in the financial statements.

[The next paragraph is 3.228.]

Contract purchase arrangements

3.228 In a typical hire purchase contract, the substance of the transaction is a sale of an asset where the price is paid over a period of time, with interest charged on the outstanding balance. However, the legal form is that of a hire of the asset to the purchaser with the rentals being equivalent to the purchase price plus interest on the outstanding balance. The title to the goods remains with the vendor and the purchaser is given an option to acquire the asset for a nominal amount (normally for £1) at the end of the hire term and it is at this stage that the title to the asset passes. It is clear, however, in a hire purchase agreement that the risks and rewards of ownership rest with the purchaser and the asset is consequently reflected in its financial statements, with its obligation to the vendor shown as a liability.

3.229 In a contract *hire* arrangement, the hirer does not take title to the goods at the end of the contract term, but the goods are returned to the lessor and are either relet by him or more commonly sold to another party. Such arrangements are clearly operating leases under SSAP 21 as the residual risk remains with the lessor. The hired assets will, therefore, remain on the lessor's balance sheet. In a contract *purchase* transaction there is generally a balloon rental at the end of the lease term (as illustrated in the graph below) and a nominal sum is paid to acquire the title to the asset (in a similar way to a hire purchase agreement). In addition, the lessee has a put option to sell the vehicle on to another party for a pre-agreed price, which is often a subsidiary of the lessor. Therefore, the transaction is a full pay-out lease, but it can be argued that as the option mechanism puts the residual risk back to the lessor the asset should not be recognised on the hirer's balance sheet.

3.230 If the lessee exercises his put option, and puts the asset back to the subsidiary of the lessor, the commercial effect of the balloon payment and the option taken together is similar in cash flow terms to a contract hire arrangement, in that the residual risks are in practice being taken by the lessor's group. However, the lessee's liability to the lessor is for the full amount of the asset purchased and the related finance costs — often the contract will be non-cancellable — and the title will pass at the end of the lease term. The right to sell the asset to a subsidiary of the lessor in the future does not remove or limit the obligation in any way. Therefore, a liability exits in FRS 5 terms and should be recognised in the lessee's financial statements.

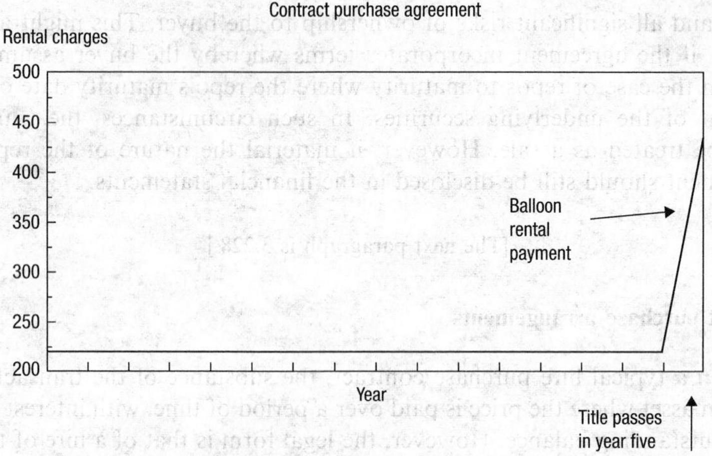

3.231 Consequently, also in accordance with SSAP 21, the asset and liability should appear on the lessee's balance sheet and the transaction should be treated as a finance lease. The partial derecognition rules of FRS 5 may also be relevant to such transactions. These rules state that, in special cases, an asset can be derecognised and another recognised in its place where significant risks and rewards relating to the original asset have been transferred to another party. It could be argued that because of the option's existence, the lessee has in substance transferred significant risks and rewards with regard to the residual to the other party. However, generally in such transactions this will not be so, because the sale will be contingent until it takes place. Normally there are important conditions that the lessee will have to comply with before the option can be exercised and these will often affect the price. Therefore, it is unlikely that the partial derecognition rules can be applied to contract purchase arrangements, because the risks and rewards of ownership reside with the lessee until the conditions to exercise the option have been complied with.

Stock lending

3.232 Another type of arrangement that can be affected by FRS 5 is stock lending. Stock lending is a growing activity within the investment management industry, affecting the assets of insurance companies, investment and unit trusts and the pension fund sector. Stock lending involves three parties: the lender (such as pension funds, insurance companies or building societies); a money broker (who acts as an intermediary); and a market maker (the borrower). Stock lending is a method used to help the liquidity of the stock market, by allowing a market maker who is short of a particular stock to borrow that stock from another party (the lender). Such arrangements are, therefore, generally only entered into for a short period of time. The borrowing is made through a money broker in order to ensure that the identity of the borrower and lender remain confidential. On receipt of the stock the market maker provides collateral to the money broker for the loan. If dividends are paid during the lending period on the stock transferred, the holder of the stock receives the dividends and the market maker pays an equivalent amount to the lender with relevant tax deducted and accounted for by the market maker as manufactured dividends. Although the process is called stock lending, the title to the stock actually passes to the market maker. Most of the business risks associated with stock lending can be managed by the provision of a legally binding agreement. There are basically three types of arrangement that can arise as outlined below.

3.233 In the first example, the market maker gives cash collateral for the loan to the money broker who in turn passes it on to the lender as illustrated in the diagram below:

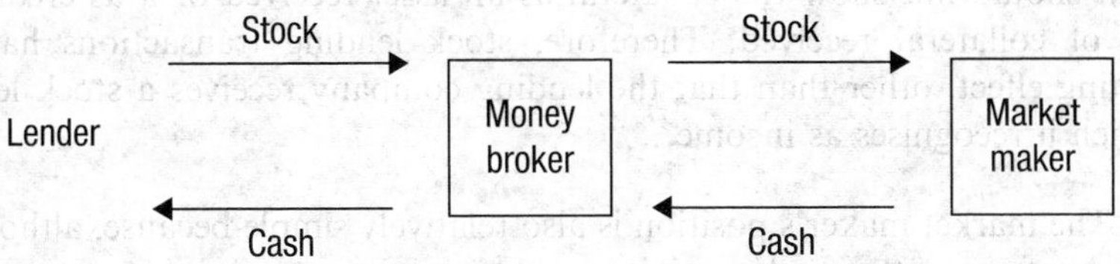

Although this is the simplest example of stock lending it is not the most frequent method used. In the situation described, the market maker deposits the cash collateral with the money broker and the money broker passes it on to the stock lender. Interest earned on the cash is passed to the market maker, but after the money broker and lender have deducted their fee.

3.234 In the next example illustrated below, the market maker borrows back the cash given to the money broker as collateral and deposits gilts with the money broker, who in turn passes these on to the lender.

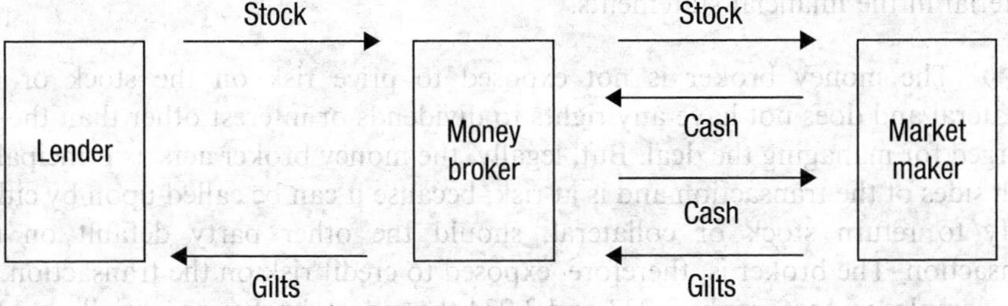

The market maker will pay a higher rate of interest on the cash it borrows back from the money broker than the rate it receives on the initial cash deposit. The difference is partly kept by the money broker and partly paid to the lender as his fee under the arrangement. If an interest payment is due on the gilts during the term of the loan, the market maker has to take the gilts back (and receive the income), but also has to substitute equivalent collateral for the gilts returned. This is the most common form of stock lending.

3.235 In some situations, the market maker will not borrow back the cash and the money broker will invest it in short-term paper (for example, certificates of deposit) and this investment is then passed to the lender as collateral. The interest earned on the collateral is passed to the market maker after deducting the lender and money broker's fees.

3.236 The position of the entity lending the stock is relatively simple in that it is exposed to normal market risks on the price of the stock and receives the equivalent of dividends on the stocks lent. Therefore, under FRS 5 the lender should retain the investment on its balance sheet and this was the practice adopted prior to FRS 5. In the event of default there is a legal right of offset of the amounts owed to and by the lender and the borrower. The practical effect of this for the lender is that he should show on his balance sheet the original securities lent, but should not show the collateral as an asset received or a as creditor in respect of collateral received. Therefore, stock lending transactions have no accounting effect, other than that the lending company receives a stock lending fee, which it recognises as income.

3.237 The market maker's position is also relatively simple because, although it is the legal owner of the stock (until it is sold to another party), it is not exposed to the risk of changes in the stock's market value. In addition, any dividends received on the stock are paid to the lender. Therefore, under FRS 5 the market maker does not retain any of the risks or rewards of ownership and hence should not recognise the stock on its balance sheet, but will reflect any cash collateral deposited with the money broker as a debtor in its balance sheet.

3.238 Both the lender and the market maker should disclose the arrangements and any contingencies or commitments in their financial statements. This might include the aggregate value of the securities on loan (or borrowed) at the balance sheet date, together with the value of collateral held (or given) in respect of those securities. The 'margin' should be accounted for separately and noted where material in the financial statements.

3.239 The money broker is not exposed to price risk on the stock or the collateral and does not have any rights to dividends or interest other than the fee charged for managing the deal. But, legally, the money broker acts as principal in both sides of the transaction and is at risk, because it can be called upon by either party to return stock or collateral, should the other party default on the transaction. The broker is, therefore, exposed to credit risk on the transaction. In the examples in paragraphs 3.233 and 3.234 the money broker potentially has the following assets and liabilities:

- Right to receive stock from the borrower.
- Obligation to give stock to the lender.
- Right to receive stock collateral from the lender.
- Obligation to give stock collateral to the borrower.

3.240 Some might argue that under FRS 5's requirements the money broker should recognise the rights and obligations as assets and liabilities in its financial statements. However, it can also be argued that in substance the conditions for offset are met and, as a consequence, the rights and obligations should remain off balance sheet. One of the offset conditions is that the company and the other party must owe each other determinable monetary amounts. For this condition, it can be argued that the amounts owed are determinable, because the money brokers attribute values to stock loans and associated collateral on a daily basis to ensure that the stock loans are adequately collateralised. The collateral is revalued each day and, if insufficient, additional collateral is obtained from the borrower. Furthermore, under many stock lending agreements, the broker has the right to settle net at any time if it is not satisfied that the other party can deliver the stock or the collateral. Whether the argument for netting can be sustained in practice depends on the particular stock lending agreement and care needs to be taken in analysing its terms in accordance with the standard, but certainly it appears that an argument can be made to justify not including them on the balance sheet.

3.241 Even where no assets or liabilities are recognised in the money broker's financial statements, FRS 5 requires that there should be sufficient disclosure in the financial statements to enable the user to understand the commercial effect of the transaction. Furthermore, any contingent obligations under the transaction should be disclosed, because of the general requirement in FRS 12 to disclosure all financial commitments and contingencies that are relevant to assessing the company's state of affairs.

3.242 An example of a group that has taken stock lending assets and liabilities off balance sheet following FRS 5 is given in Table 3.13.

Table 3.13 — B.A.T Industries p.l.c. — Directors' Report and Accounts — 31 December 1994

Directors' Report (extract)

Accounting policies (extract)

The group has adopted three new accounting standards. FRS 5 'Reporting the Substance of Transactions', FRS 6 'Mergers and Acquisitions' and FRS 7 'Fair Values in Acquisition Accounting'.

FRS5 has required reclassification of certain comparative figures, although there is no effect on the Group's equity or profit...

...Thirdly, stock lending arrangements with financial institutions, previously shown as separate assets and liabilities on the balance sheet, are now deemed not to result in the creation of an additional asset or liability. As a result, the comparative figures for life business 'other assets' and 'other liabilities' have each been reduced by £113 million.

3.242.1 Entities within the scope of FRS 26 should apply the derecognition requirements in FRS 26 to financial assets and liabilities (see further chapter 6) and the derecognition principles of FRS 5 to non-financial assets and liabilities. [FRS 5 para 13B]. Entities that are not within the scope of FRS 26 should continue to apply FRS 5 to the recognition and derecognition of both *financial and non-financial* assets and liabilities.

Bed and breakfast transactions

3.243 Bed and breakfast transactions are examples of sale and repurchase transactions to which the provisions of Application Note B apply. In such transactions, a company agrees to sell certain assets (such as securities) to a third party (normally a broker) and arranges to repurchase them, or identical assets, shortly thereafter, usually over night, for the same price. The essence of the agreement is that the entity takes no risk of loss, other than the extremely remote risk that the counterparty will default and similarly has no reward apart from any tax effect and potentially an effect on realised profits. Transactions of this nature are sometimes used in an attempt to turn unrealised revaluation gains on investments into realised gains so that they can be used for distribution by way of dividends to shareholders.

3.244 Under FRS 5, it is necessary to determine whether an actual sale has taken place in a bed and breakfast transaction. Although the legal title to the asset may have passed, generally the benefits and risks associated with it will not have. Normally, a transaction of this nature should be treated as a financing arrangement rather than a sale, leaving the asset and a corresponding liability on the balance sheet of the original owner. Furthermore, any profit or loss would not be reflected in the company's financial statements. The information required by Application Note B would also have to be given in the notes to the financial statements (see para 3.131).

3.245 There may be a few situations in practice where the substance of the transaction is a disposal of the asset and a reacquisition, which should be accounted for as such. In such transactions a realised gain may arise. In general in order to recognise a realised gain on such a transaction it is necessary to show that the risks and rewards of ownership have passed to the party buying the asset and the proceeds of the disposal are in the form of qualifying consideration (see further chapter 9).

[The next paragraph is 3.248.]

3.248 In practice, a bed and breakfast transaction involves contracting to sell to a broker with no express contract to buy back the following day. However, it is clearly understood that the shares will be repurchased at an agreed price. If the seller does not repurchase, the broker will be unlikely to deal for him again. Thus there is a moral contract. Consequently, it can be strongly argued that the sale and repurchase are linked and that the transaction is not 'arm's length', because there is an obligation, moral if not legal, for the sale to be reversed the next day. It seems reasonable to conclude that if the substance is not to dispose of the asset, but merely to change the tax base then no sale has occurred in substance and, in addition, no gain should be recognised. This conclusion is further reinforced by the probability that, because the sale and repurchase are generally between the same parties, no cash will actually pass.

3.249 For those entities applying FRS 26 and where the transaction falls within the scope of paragraphs 14 to 42 of FRS 26, FRS 5 Application Note B is not relevant, and the recognition and derecognition principles in FRS 26 should be applied (see further chapter 6). For those entities not within the scope of FRS 26, FRS 5's provisions should be applied to sale and repurchase agreements and the guidance in FRS 5 Application Note B is relevant.

Purchase commitments

3.250 One of the types of transaction that falls outside the scope of FRS 5 is a purchase commitment. In certain transactions it might not be as straightforward as it seems to spot a purchase commitment, for example::

Example

A vehicle manufacturer sells a vehicle to a dealer (an outright sale). At the same time a subsidiary of the manufacturer grants the dealer an option to sell the vehicle to the subsidiary after three years for 40% of the original sales price charged by the manufacturer (40% is the estimated residual value). In the subsidiary's financial statements the residual value and corresponding liability would not be recorded unless and until the dealer exercises his option and delivery takes place. This is because, even if the subsidiary were committed from day one to purchase the residual, it would not record the asset and liability until delivery takes place. In the manufacturer's consolidated financial statements, it would be necessary to determine whether or not it was likely that the option would be exercised. If it was likely then the sale of the vehicle would still be recognised, but the residual value and corresponding liability might need to be recorded in the consolidated financial statements under the partial derecognition provisions of FRS 5 (see further para 3.74). This would mean that any probable loss if the residual value is expected to be less than 40% should be provided for and a similar provision would be required in the subsidiary company.

Linked presentation and the cash flow statement

3.251 There is no guidance in FRS 5 concerning how to account for transactions in the cash flow statement where the linked presentation is used for the balance sheet and profit and loss account. For example, where a company uses the linked presentation for a factoring arrangement where the conditions in FRS 5 are met, there are two possible ways that the arrangement can be reflected in the cash flow statement: either treat the movement in the net debtors as an operating cash flow; or treat the proceeds from factoring as a source of finance under 'financing'. FRS 5 states that a scheme that qualifies for the linked presentation is in substance a financing, but the non-returnable proceeds are not a liability, nor is the original gross amount of the debtor an asset. These two statements may seem contradictory, but since the net amount is regarded as the asset, it is logical to show the non-returnable proceeds in the cash flow statement as an operating cash flow, that is, to treat the non-returnable proceeds as a partial collection of the debtors.

Take-or-pay contracts

3.252 In 'take-or-pay' contracts an entity enters into a long-term contract with a supplier at a pre-determined price for the supply of either goods or services and undertakes to pay for a minimum quantity whether or not the quantity is actually required. The advantage for the purchaser is that he is guaranteed delivery of a certain quantity of goods and will be able to negotiate a competitive price. Throughput contracts are very similar in nature to take-or-pay contracts. They are common in the oil industry, where more than one company might share, for example, an oil pipe line. The parties to the contract enter into an agreement to share the use of the facility and each party will pay a certain amount that will not necessarily depend on the amount of their oil that they transport through the pipe line.

3.253 Take-or-pay contracts and throughput contracts have not been specifically dealt with in FRS 5, but an argument can be made that they fall under the heading of expenditure commitments and as such are exempted from the standard's provisions. Essentially under such a contract the purchaser has a contractual commitment to pay a minimum amount to the supplier. The purchaser may or may not receive goods or services to the value of the amount committed, but he has the right to.

3.254 The guidance notes on SSAP 21 refer to take or pay contracts in a discussion of whether certain arrangements should, in exceptional cases, be treated as being in substance leases, although different terms might be used to describe them. They give the example of a company (company A) that builds a plant on the basis that company B is obliged to buy sufficient of the plant's output in order to give company A a full payout on the cost of the assets involved, together with a normal profit margin. They state that such arrangements will in many cases be in substance more in the nature of long-term purchase and supply contracts than contracts which are in substance leases of assets.

3.255 Therefore, if such a contract is a lease it will have to be accounted for in accordance with the requirements of SSAP 21 and, if it is a finance lease, recorded on the lessee's balance sheet. Alternatively, such an arrangement might purely be a long-term purchase or supply contract that is exempted form the requirements of FRS 5 because its is an expenditure commitment, in which case the purchaser has a contingent obligation which should be treated in accordance with the provisions of FRS 12. [FRS 5 para 58]. If it is necessary to make a provision for the purchase commitment in accordance with FRS 12, then this should be charged to the profit and loss account rather than recognised as an asset. Where it is determined that no provision should be made for the contract after considering FRS 12, the notes to the financial statements still have to give particulars of the financial commitment to comply with the Act.

3.256 Table 4.14 below illustrates the treatment and disclosure of a typical take-or-pay contract.

Table 3.14 — Imperial Chemical Industries PLC — Annual report and accounts — 31 December 1997

Notes relating to the accounts

41 Commitments and contingent liabilities (extract)

Significant take-or-pay contracts entered into by subsidiaries are as follows:

(i) the purchase of electric power which commenced April 1993 for 15 years. The present value of the remaining commitment is estimated at £688m.

(ii) the purchase of electric power, which will commence in the second quarter of 1998, for 15 years. The present value of this commitment is estimated at £141m.

3.256.1 For entities reporting in accordance with FRS 26, 'Financial instruments: Measurement', take-or-pay contracts will need assessing as to whether they contain an embedded derivative. This is because the price per unit paid varies in response to changes in the volume purchased. Embedded derivatives are considered in detail in chapter 6.

Chapter 4

Format of financial statements

Chapter 4

Format of financial statements

4.1 The general provisions that relate to the format and content of company financial statements prepared in accordance with UK GAAP are detailed in Schedule 1 to SI 2008/410, 'The Large and Medium-sized Companies and Groups (Accounts and Reports) Regulations 2008'. Schedule 6 to SI 2008/410 deals with the format of consolidated financial statements prepared in accordance with UK GAAP. These provisions are supplemented by specific requirements of accounting standards. The formats set out in SI 2008/410 apply both to the financial statements of those companies that are limited by either shares or guarantee and to the UK GAAP financial statements of unlimited companies. Special accounting and disclosure provisions apply to the UK GAAP financial statements of banks and insurance companies and are included in Schedules 2 and 3 respectively to SI 2008/410. These special provisions are not considered in this chapter.

4.2 Four primary statements are included within a company's financial statements:

- Balance sheet. [CA06 Sec 396(1)(2)]
- Profit and loss account. [CA06 Sec 396(1)(2)].
- Statement of total recognised gains and losses. [FRS 3 para 27].
- Cash flow statement. [FRS 1 para 4].

4.3 Schedule 1 to SI 2008/410 sets out two alternative formats for the balance sheet and four alternative formats for the profit and loss account. It also lays down certain general guidelines to be followed. In addition, the Schedule requires companies to disclose considerable detail both in the notes to the balance sheet and in the notes to the profit and loss account. These formats, guidelines and notes are discussed in this chapter.

4.4 Company law does not require companies to include in their financial statements a statement of total recognised gains and losses or a cash flow statement. These primary statements are required by FRS 3, 'Reporting financial performance', and FRS 1, 'Cash flow statements (revised 1996)', respectively, for all reporting entities' financial statements that are intended to give a true and fair view. The only exceptions to these requirements are that a cash flow statement is not required for most small companies and for subsidiaries, 90 per cent or more of whose voting rights are controlled within the group, provided the consolidated financial statements in which the subsidiary undertaking is included are publicly available.

4.5 The formats of UK GAAP consolidated financial statements are substantially similar to those of financial statements prepared by individual companies. Consolidated financial statements have to comply as far as practicable with the provisions of Schedule 1 to SI 2008/410 as if the undertakings included in the consolidation were a single company. [SI 2008/410 6 Sch 1(1)]. In addition, the consolidated financial statements have to comply with the provisions of Schedule 6 to SI 2008/410 as to their form and content. [CA06 Sec 404(3)]. A group's consolidated financial statements will include the following primary statements and related notes:

- The consolidated balance sheet and related notes of the parent company and its subsidiary undertakings. [CA06 Sec 404(1)(a),(3)].
- The consolidated profit and loss account and related notes of the parent company and its subsidiary undertakings. [CA06 Sec 404(1)(b),(3)].
- The group's cash flow statement and related notes. [FRS 1 para 4].
- The group's statement of total recognised gains and losses. [FRS 3 para 27].
- The parent company's individual balance sheet and related notes. [CA06 Sec 396(1)(a),(3)].

The parent company's individual profit and loss account should be published, unless advantage is taken of the exemption given by section 408 of the 2006 Act (see para 4.122 below). In practice, the exemption (which was also available under the 1985 Act) is usually taken and the parent's own profit and loss account is omitted from the published financial statements.

4.5.1 In addition to the required primary statements, FRS 3 also requires the reporting entity (that is, the company or, for consolidated financial statements, the group) to produce:

- A note of historical cost profits and losses, appearing immediately after the profit and loss account or the statement of total recognised gains and losses. [FRS 3 para 26].
- A reconciliation of the movement in shareholders' funds. [FRS 3 para 28].

4.6 The contents of the financial statements required by FRS 1 (cash flow) and FRS 3 (financial performance) are considered in chapter 30 and 8 respectively. The other statements mentioned above — balance sheet, profit and loss account and related notes — whose form and content is governed by SI 2008/410, are considered in this chapter, together with a summary of the rules that apply to the formats.

General rules

Choice of formats

4.7 Schedule 1 to SI 2008/410 leaves the choice of particular formats to the company's directors. Once the directors have selected the particular formats for the balance sheet and the profit and loss account, they should not subsequently change them, unless in their opinion there are special reasons for a change. [SI 2008/410 1 Sch 2(1)]. An example of such a reason might occur if a company changes both its operations and its accounting methods significantly and considers that, following the changes, its financial statements fit more naturally into a different format.

4.8 In most situations, however, few companies will have good reason to change their formats, and so they must select carefully the formats that they wish to adopt when they prepare their first set of financial statements after incorporation. If a company does eventually change its formats, it may incur a considerable amount of extra work, because it will have to restate the corresponding amounts for the previous year in accordance with the new formats. In addition, where the formats are changed, the notes to the financial statements must disclose:

- Particulars of the change – that is, the fact that the company has adopted a different format.
- The directors' reasons for the change.

[SI 2008/410 1 Sch 2(2)].

4.9 Table 4.1 illustrates the disclosure relating to a change of profit and loss account format. This disclosure was given under the Companies Act 1985, but the requirements are similar, in this respect, under SI 2008/410.

Table 4.1 — Change of profit and loss account format

British Gas plc — Annual Report and Accounts — 31 December 1993

Notes to the accounts (extract)

2 Operating costs — continuing operations

The Group profit and loss account in the 1992 Annual Report and Accounts was prepared on the basis of Format 1 of the Companies Act 1985, under which non-exceptional operating costs were divided into cost of sales, distribution costs and administrative expenses. In the opinion of the Directors such a division has become increasingly less appropriate for the Group for the reasons set out below.

There has always been a substantial degree of subjectivity and discretion in the allocation and apportionment of costs over these categories. More recently the Group has diversified and grown in areas outside the traditional gas business, for which the cost structures are different and the division of operating costs under Format 1 is less appropriate. Further, the major restructuring of the UK Gas Business into five units will result in an organisation where, for the Transportation and Storage Unit, Format 1 would be inappropriate. Finally FRS 3 requires exceptional charges before operating profit to be allocated over the statutory format headings to which they relate. The allocation of such charges over cost of sales, distribution costs and administrative expenses (Format 1) would be subject to the same reservations as for the allocation and apportionment of operating costs for non-exceptional charges.

Accordingly, at the same time as implementing the changes to the Group profit and loss account required by FRS 3, the Directors have decided that the Company should adopt for the Group profit and loss account another format, referred to in the Companies Act 1985* as Format 2, under which the operating costs are allocated according to type of expense. They consider that this will enable the operating costs, including the exceptional charges, to be divided in a less subjective and more helpful way and will enable readers of the Group's accounts to more easily compare and follow trends in particular operating costs.

* Editorial note: the profit and loss account formats in Schedule 4 to the Companies Act 1985 have been superseded by the formats in Schedule 1 to SI 2008/410.

Headings and sub-headings

4.10 The formats give a list of items either as main headings or as sub-headings. In the balance sheet, main headings are designated either by letters or by Roman numerals, and sub-headings are designated by Arabic numerals. The object of this notation is for identification purposes only, so that SI 2008/410 can refer to items by their prefix. There is no requirement for financial statements to show these letters or numbers. [SI 2008/410 1 Sch 1(3)(b)]. In the profit and loss account Formats 1 and 2, all items are designated by Arabic numerals.

4.11 Whichever of the balance sheet formats and profit and loss account formats a company chooses, the company must show the items in the fixed order and under the headings and the sub-headings set out in the particular formats it has used. [SI 2008/410 1 Sch 3]. There are, however, certain exceptions to this rule, which are explained in paragraphs 4.12 to 4.17 below.

4.12 An item may be shown in greater detail than the particular format used requires. [SI 2008/410 1 Sch 3(1)]. For example, most companies include motor vehicles under the sub-heading 'Fixtures, fittings, tools and equipment'. But where such motor vehicles are significant in value, additional details may be disclosed as follows:

Fixtures, fittings, tools and equipment:

Fixtures, fittings, tools and equipment:		
Motor vehicles	X	
Other	X	X

4.13 An item representing an asset or a liability, or an item of income or expenditure that is not covered in any of the prescribed formats may be shown separately .[SI 2008/410 1 Sch 3(2)]. An example is where a company holds stocks that do not fall easily within the sub-headings of raw materials and consumables, work in progress, finished goods and goods for resale, and payments on account. Tables 4.2 and 4.3 give two examples where companies provided additional headings: Bellway p.l.c included showhomes and part exchange properties as a separate category of stocks; Carlton Communications Plc included programme and film rights as a separate category of current assets.

Table 4.2 — Additional category used in stocks note

Bellway p.l.c. — Annual Report — 31 July 1997

NOTES TO THE ACCOUNTS (extract)

10 Stocks	**1997**	1996
	£000	£000
Group		
Work in progress and stocks	**317,440**	281,793
Grants	**(13,061)**	(13,231)
Payments on account	**(4,986)**	(3,129)
	299,393	265,433
Showhomes	**14,560**	14,926
Part exchange properties	**5,760**	7,569
	319,713	287,928

Table 4.3 — Additional heading used in balance sheet

Carlton Communications Plc — Annual Report and Accounts — 30 September 2001

Consolidated balance sheet (extract)

		2001	2000 (as restated)
	Notes	£m	£m
Current assets			
Stocks	15	**7.1**	47.7
Programme and film rights	16	**187.4**	171.6
Debtors	17	**216.6**	670.5
Investments		**214.8**	8.4
Cash and other liquid funds	19	**458.5**	341.8
		1,084.4	1,240.0

4.14 Items that are preceded by Arabic numerals in SI 2008/410 may be combined in the company's financial statements where either of the following circumstances apply:

- Their individual amounts are not material to assessing the company's state of affairs or profit or loss for the financial year in question. [SI 2008/410 1 Sch 4(2)(a)].
- The combination facilitates the assessment of the company's state of affairs or profit or loss (that is, it results in greater clarity). Where this applies,

however, the detailed breakdown of the combined items must be given in the notes to the financial statements. [SI 2008/410 1 Sch 4(2)(b),(3)].

4.15 A heading or a sub-heading should not be shown where there is no amount to be included for both the financial year in question and the immediately preceding financial year. However, where there is an amount for the item in question for the immediately preceding financial year, that amount is shown under the heading or sub-heading required by the format for that item. [SI 2008/410 1 Sch 5(1),(2)]. See also paragraph 4.20.1.

4.16 The arrangement, the headings and the sub-headings of items set out in the formats and preceded by Arabic numerals must be adapted if the special nature of the company's business requires this. [SI 2008/410 1 Sch 4(1)]. Table 4.4 shows an example where a company has adapted the format prescribed by the law. This disclosure was given under the Companies Act 1985, but the requirements are similar, in this respect, under SI 2008/410.

Table 4.4 — Adaptation of note to the profit and loss account

British Telecommunications plc — Report and Accounts — 31 March 1994

Notes to the financial statements (extract)

2 Operating costs	**1994 £m**	1993 £m
Staff costs		
Wages and salaries	**3,486**	3,625
Social Security costs	**294**	276
Pension costs (note 23)	**272**	161
Total staff costs	**4,052**	4,062
Own work capitalised	**(465)**	(473)
Depreciation (note 12)	**2,156**	2,116
Payments to telecommunication operators	**1,174**	1,020
Redundancy charges (a)	**517**	1,034
Other operating costs	**3,279**	3,120
Other operating income	**(53)**	(73)
Total operating costs	**10,660**	10,806
Operating costs included the following:		
Research and development	**265**	233
Rental costs relating to operating leases, including plant and equipment hire £21m (1993 — £27m)	**277**	234
Costs relating to HM Government sale of BT shares under combined offers	**3**	

(a) Redundancy charges for the year ended 31 March 1994 included £305m (1993 — £550m) being the cost of providing incremental pension benefits for employees taking early retirement in the year.

In prior years' accounts, the group's share of results of associated undertakings, which have been immaterial, was included within operating costs. In this year's accounts, these results are shown

> on the face of the group profit and loss account. Prior year comparative figures have been restated for this reclassification.
>
> The directors believe that the nature of the group's business is such that the analysis of operating costs required by the Companies Act 1985* is not appropriate. As required by the Act, the directors have therefore adapted the prescribed format so that operating costs are disclosed in a manner appropriate to the group's principal activity.
>
> * Editorial note: the requirement in Schedule 4 to the Companies Act 1985 has been superseded by Schedule 1 to SI 2008/410.

4.17 SI 2008/410 requires that companies should use the headings and sub-headings detailed in the formats [SI 2008/410 1 Sch 1(1)] and this was certainly the intention of the 4th Directive. Nevertheless, some companies in practice depart from this requirement, for example, describing 'land and buildings' as 'property', or 'stocks' as 'inventories' or 'turnover' as 'sales'. This practice is considered allowable, provided that the revised wording is not likely to mislead users of the financial statements and provided that the item remains the same.

4.18 A company should consider the presentation of its financial statements in three stages.

- First, it should consider which of the formats are most suitable for its purposes.
- Secondly, if the special nature of its business requires it, it must adapt the arrangement and headings and sub-headings of any items designated by Arabic numerals in the selected formats as set out in Schedule 1 to SI 2008/410.
- Thirdly, it should consider whether it needs to show any item listed in the formats in greater detail, and, if so, it may do so. (Unlike the adaptation of the formats, which is compulsory if the special nature of a company's business requires it, company law gives the reporting company the option to include greater detail under any heading if it wishes to do so. However, FRS 3 may require such additional disclosure – see further chapter 8.)

4.19 After having considered the presentation of the financial statements, the company must next consider whether compliance with the requirements of SI 2008/410 as regards the format of the financial statements, and compliance with other statutory requirements as to the information to be included in the notes to the financial statements, enable the financial statements to give a true and fair view of the state of the company's affairs as at the end of the financial year and of its profit or loss for the year. If the company decides that compliance with SI 2008/410 would not give a true and fair view, it should examine whether the solution to this problem might be to provide additional information in the financial statements. If in special circumstances, compliance with the provisions of the 2006 Act and its supporting regulations would be inconsistent with the requirement to give a true and fair view, the directors must depart from those provisions. In such a situation, particulars of the departure, the reasons for it, and its effect must be given in the notes to the financial statements (see further chapter 2). [CA06 Sec 396(4)(5)].

Corresponding amounts

4.20 FRS 28, 'Corresponding amounts', sets out the requirements for the disclosure of corresponding amounts for amounts shown in an entity's primary statements and notes to the financial statements. 'Corresponding amounts' are sometimes described as 'comparative figures' or 'comparative information' in other accounting standards. FRS 28's requirements apply except where an accounting standard or a UITF Abstract requires or permits an alternative treatment. [FRS 28 para 3].

4.20.1 Corresponding amounts for the year immediately preceding the year in question must be shown in respect of every item in each of the reporting entity's primary statements. [FRS 28 para 6]. This applies even when no such item exists to be disclosed in respect of the current financial year (see also para 4.15). [FRS 28 para 8]. There is a similar requirement in company law, which refers to the need for corresponding amounts in the balance sheet and the profit and loss account. [SI 2008/410 1 Sch 7(1)].

4.20.2 For the purpose of the requirement in FRS 28, the primary statements specifically mentioned in FRS 28 that require comparatives are:

- Statements of financial performance (for example, a profit and loss account or a STRGL).
- A statement of financial position (for example, a balance sheet).
- A cash flow statement.
- A reconciliation of movements in shareholders' funds (if presented as a primary statement, as permitted by FRS 3).

[FRS 28 para 7].

4.20.3 Although FRS 28 does not specifically require the inclusion of corresponding amounts in respect of a statement of historical cost profits and losses, where one is required by FRS 3, we consider the requirement general enough that this falls within the scope of 'Statements of performance' and corresponding amounts are required.

4.21 In general, the corresponding amounts for the previous financial year must be given in respect of each item shown in the notes to the financial statements. [FRS 28 para 10(a)]. The only exceptions to this relate to:

- Information relating to acquisitions taking place in the financial year (required by paragraph 13 of Schedule 6 to SI 2008/410).

- Details of shareholdings in subsidiaries held by the reporting entity (required by paragraphs 11 and 17 of Schedule 4 to SI 2008/410).
- Details concerning the identity and class of shares held in undertakings (and the proportion of nominal value represented by those shares) where the investment is 20 per cent or more of any class of shares (required by paragraphs 5(3) of Schedule 4 to SI 2008/410).
- The proportion of the capital of joint ventures held by the reporting entity (required by paragraph 18(1)(d) of Schedule 4 to SI 2008/410).
- The identity and proportion of each class of shares held in associated undertakings (required by paragraph 19(4)(5) of Schedule 4 to SI 2008/410).
- Movements on fixed assets (required by paragraph 51 of Schedule 1 to SI 2008/410).
- Movements on reserves and provisions (required by paragraph 59 of Schedule 1 to SI 2008/410).

[FRS 28 para 11].

4.22 Where the amount for the previous year is not comparable with the amount to be shown in respect of the current year, the previous year's amount must be adjusted. Where this applies, particulars of the adjustment and the reasons for it must be disclosed in the notes to the financial statements. This requirement applies in respect of every item in a reporting entity's primary statements and in respect of each item shown in the notes to the financial statements. [FRS 28 paras 9, 10(b); SI 2008/410 1 Sch 7(2)]. An example is shown in Table 4.5.

Table 4.5 — Reclassification of comparative figures

Royal Doulton plc — Annual Report — 31 December 1994

Notes to the financial statements (extract)

2 COMPARATIVE FIGURES

The comparative figures for the cost of sales, distribution costs and administrative expenses have been adjusted to reflect a reclassification between the administrative and distribution activities of the group. The effect is as follows:

	As previously reported £000	*Transfer* £000	*1993 (as restated)* £000
Cost of sales	129,218	(1,370)	127,848
Distribution costs	8,060	51,967	60,027
Administrative expenses — ordinary	73,315	(50,597)	22,718
	210,593	—	210,593

4.23 This requirement accords with the treatment required by FRS 3 in respect of prior period adjustments. A prior period adjustment (that has arisen, for example, because there has been a change of accounting policy during the year) is accounted for by restating the previous year's figures in the primary statements and notes and, where it is affected, by adjusting the opening balance of reserves accordingly. Where practicable, the effect of the change on the results for the previous year should be disclosed. [FRS 3 para 29].

4.24 In addition, company law requires that accounting policies should be applied consistently within the same financial statements and from one financial year to the next. [SI 2008/410 1 Sch 12]. It allows the directors to depart from this principle (that is, to change an accounting policy) if there are special reasons for doing so, but the particulars, reasons and effect of the departure from the principle of consistency should be disclosed. [SI 2008/410 1 Sch 10(2)]. The accounting and disclosure implications of changes in accounting policies are considered in chapter 8.

Offsetting

4.25 Asset and liability items may not be set off against each other. Similarly, income and expenditure items may not be set off against each other. [SI 2008/410 1 Sch 8]. Consequently, companies cannot, for example, show hire-purchase or finance lease liabilities as a deduction from the related asset. (They may, however, deduct from stock the payments they have received on account of orders.) [SI 2008/410 1 Sch Balance sheet formats note 8]. It should be noted that the offset rules do not preclude netting, for example, depreciation of fixed assets against their cost or provisions for bad debts against debtors — they are simply adjustments to asset values.

4.25.1 The rule against offsetting assets and liabilities is also covered in FRS 5, 'Reporting the substance of transactions', which states that assets and liabilities should not be offset. Debit and credit balances should be aggregated into a single net item where, and only where, they do not constitute separate assets and liabilities. For offset of financial assets and financial liabilities, FRS 25, 'Financial instruments: Presentation', applies. [FRS 5 para 29]. FRS 25 sets out conditions that must be met before debit and credit balances relating to financial instruments can be aggregated into a single net asset or liability, that is, where they do not constitute separate assets and liabilities. This is discussed in chapter 6.

Substance

4.26 The company's directors must, in determining how amounts are presented within items in the profit and loss account and balance sheet, have regard to the substance of the reported transaction or arrangement, in accordance with generally accepted accounting principles or practice. [SI 2008/410 1 Sch 9]. Reporting the substance of transactions is dealt with in chapter 3.

The balance sheet

Individual company formats

4.27 Schedule 1 to SI 2008/410 sets out two alternative balance sheet formats.

Format 1

4.28 In the Format 1 balance sheet, net assets can be shown as equal in total to the aggregate of share capital and reserves. This method of presentation probably represents UK companies' most common practice. SI 2008/410 does not, however, prescribe the place where the totals should be struck. Consequently, in this format a company can, unless it has a defined benefit pension asset (see below), equate total assets less current liabilities, on the one hand, with the aggregate of creditors falling due after more than one year, provisions for liabilities, and capital and reserves, on the other hand. Format 1 is set out in paragraph 4.28.3 below and is also illustrated in Table 4.6 (where the company's balance sheet total is struck at the earlier position of total assets less current liabilities).

4.28.1 However, FRS 17,'Retirement benefits', requires that companies show the defined benefit asset or defined benefit liability on the face of the balance sheet and is specific as to the position of the pension balance in the balance sheet formats. FRS 17 requires that the defined benefit asset or liability should be presented separately on the face of the balance sheet as follows:

- in balance sheets of the type prescribed by the Companies Act 1985, Schedule 4, format 1: after item J Accruals and deferred income but before item K Capital and reserves (and now by format 1 in Schedule 1 to SI 2008/410); and
- in balance sheets of the type prescribed by the Companies Act 1985, Schedule 4, format 2: any asset after ASSETS item D Prepayments and accrued income and any liability after LIABILITIES item D Accruals and deferred income (and now by format 2 in Schedule 1 to SI 2008/410).

[FRS 17 para 47].

4.28.2 For Format 1 presentations, FRS 17 prescribes the same positioning in the balance sheet for the pension balance, regardless of whether it is a pension asset or pension liability. As discussed above, companies are permitted to strike their balance sheet totals to equate total assets less current liabilities with the sum of non-current liabilities, provisions, capital and reserves. However, where a company has a defined benefit asset, the requirements of FRS 17 and Format 1 in Schedule 1 to SI 2008/410 taken together would mean that this pension asset would be included in the 'non-current liabilities/provisions/capital and reserves section' of the balance sheet. Therefore, where there is a pension asset, companies should not strike their balance sheet totals in this way, but should instead strike a total at net assets before and after the pension asset, as illustrated in Appendix 1 of FRS 17. Under this approach, total assets less current liabilities will be reported excluding the pension asset which, at first glance, would seem an inappropriate presentation but, as described in paragraph 6 of Appendix II to FRS 17, the ASB received legal advice that the FRS 17 requirements did not contravene the Companies Act 1985 (which included the same balance sheet formats as those now in SI 2008/410). Where the company has a pension deficit, it will be acceptable to strike the total to equate total assets less current liabilities with the sum of non-current liabilities, provisions, capital and reserves, because the pension liability will appear in the 'non-current liabilities/provisions/capital and reserves section' of the balance sheet.

4.28.3 The Format 1 balance sheet is set out below and is also illustrated in Table 4.6 (where, as noted in paragraph 4.28 above, the company's balance sheet total is struck at the position of total assets less current liabilities).

Balance sheet — Format 1

A Called up share capital not paid

B Fixed assets

- I Intangible assets
  - 1 Development costs
  - 2 Concessions, patents, licences, trade marks and similar rights and assets
  - 3 Goodwill
  - 4 Payments on account
- II Tangible assets
  - 1 Land and buildings
  - 2 Plant and machinery
  - 3 Fixtures, fittings, tools and equipment
  - 4 Payments on account and assets in course of construction
- III Investments
  - 1 Shares in group undertakings
  - 2 Loans to group undertakings
  - 3 Participating interests
  - 4 Loans to undertakings in which the company has a participating interest
  - 5 Other investments other than loans
  - 6 Other loans
  - 7 Own shares

C Current assets

I Stocks

1 Raw materials and consumables

2 Work in progress

3 Finished goods and goods for resale

4 Payments on account

II Debtors

1 Trade debtors

2 Amounts owed by group undertakings

3 Amounts owed by undertakings in which the company has a participating interest

4 Other debtors

5 Called-up share capital not paid

6 Prepayments and accrued income

III Investments

1 Shares in group undertakings

2 Own shares

3 Other investments

IV Cash at bank and in hand

D Prepayments and accrued income

E Creditors: amounts falling due within one year

1 Debenture loans

2 Bank loans and overdrafts

3 Payments received on account

4 Trade creditors

5 Bills of exchange payable

6 Amounts owed to group undertakings

7 Amounts owed to undertakings in which the company has a participating interest

8 Other creditors including taxation and social security

9 Accruals and deferred income

F Net current assets (liabilities)

G Total assets less current liabilities

H Creditors: amounts falling due after more than one year

1 Debenture loans

2 Bank loans and overdrafts

3 Payments received on account

4 Trade creditors

5 Bills of exchange payable

6 Amounts owed to group undertakings

7 Amounts owed to undertakings in which the company has a participating interest

8 Other creditors including taxation and social security

9 Accruals and deferred income

I Provisions for liabilities

1 Pensions and similar obligations

2 Taxation, including deferred taxation

3 Other provisions

J Accruals and deferred income

K Capital and reserves

I Called up share capital

II Share premium account

III Revaluation reserve

IV Other reserves

1 Capital redemption reserve

2 Reserve for own shares

3 Reserves provided for by the articles of association

4 Other reserves

V Profit and loss account

Table 4.6 — Format 1 balance sheet

British Telecommunications plc — Report and Accounts — 31 March 1994

Balance sheet of the company

	Notes	**1994 £m**	1993 £m
Fixed assets			
Tangible assets	12	**13,603**	13,710
Investments	13	**3,518**	2,822
Total fixed assets		**17,121**	16,532
Current assets			
Stocks		**118**	139
Debtors	14	**2,908**	2,702
Investments	15	**2,311**	1,327
Cash at bank and in hand		**2**	1
Total current assets		**5,339**	4,169
Creditors: amounts falling due within one year			
Loans and other borrowings	16	**1,269**	637
Other creditors	17	**5,472**	4,335
Total creditors: amounts falling due within one year		**6,741**	4,972
Net current liabilities		**(1,402)**	(803)
Total assets less current liabilities		**15,719**	15,729
Creditors: amounts falling due after more than one year			
Loans and other borrowings	16	**3,173**	3,323
Provisions for liabilities and charges*	18	**506**	929
Capital and reserves			
Called up share capital	19	**1,553**	1,546
Share premium account	20	**364**	314
Capital redemption reserve	20	**750**	750
Profit and loss account	20	**9,373**	8,867
Total capital and reserves	21	**12,040**	11,477
		15,719	15,729

Debtors include amounts receivable after more than one year of £297m (1993 — £354m).

* Editorial note: for periods beginning on or after 1 January 2005, the statutory line item was renamed 'provisions for liabilities' in company legislation.

Format 2

4.29 In the Format 2 balance sheet, assets are shown as equal in total to liabilities (which include capital and reserves). Because the information disclosed in Format 2 is identical in all respects (apart from one) to the information disclosed in Format 1, Format 2 has not been reproduced here, but an example is given in Table 4.7. The only difference between Format 1 and Format 2 is that Format 2 aggregates, on the face of the balance sheet, creditors due within one year and those due after more than one year. However, in respect of each item included in creditors the split between the amount due within one year and the amount due after more than one year, together with the aggregate, must still be disclosed either on the face of the balance sheet or in the notes. [SI 2008/410 1 Sch Balance sheet formats note 13]. This method of presentation is more common in some other EU countries (for example, France and Germany) than in the UK.

Table 4.7 — Format 2 balance sheet

The Peninsular and Oriental Steam Navigation Company — Annual Report and Accounts — 31 December 1998

Company balance sheet
at 31 December 1998

			Company
	Note	**1998 £m**	**1997 £m**
Assets			
Fixed assets			
Intangible assets: Goodwill	9	—	—
Tangible assets			
Ships	10	393.2	486.8
Properties	11	12.8	6.3
Other fixed assets	12	13.1	8.6
Investments			
Subsidiaries	13	3,286.3	3,213.7
Joint ventures		812.4	535.6
Associates			1.2
Other investments		0.2	0.2
	14	812.6	537.0
		4,518.0	4,252.4
Current assets			
Development and dealing properties	15	—	—
Stocks	16	4.6	4.9
Debtors	17	237.1	297.0
Investments		—	—
Cash at bank and in hand		10.7	4.9
		252.4	306.8
		4,770.4	4,559.2

	Note		
Liabilities			
Capital and reserves			
Called up share capital	18	769.3	751.3
Share premium account	19	595.8	562.7
Revaluation reserve	19	1.5	0.9
Other reserves	19	—	—
Profit and loss account	19	410.8	352.3
Equity stockholders' funds		1,627.6	1,516.9
Non-equity stockholders' funds	19	149.8	150.3
Stockholders' funds		1,777.7	1,667.2
Other liabilities			
Provisions for liabilities and charges*	21	30.8	44.8
Loans: convertible	22	164.8	189.8
non-convertible	22	983.7	1,093.5
Other creditors	23	1,813.7	1,563.9
		2,993.0	2,892.0
		4,770.4	4,559.2

* Editorial note: for periods beginning on or after 1 January 2005, the statutory line item was renamed 'provisions for liabilities' in company legislation.

Rules concerning particular items

Alternative positions in the balance sheet

4.30 The following items may be shown in alternative positions in a company's individual balance sheet (references given are for Format 1):

- Called up share capital not paid (A and C.II.5).
- Prepayments and accrued income (C.II.6 and D) – see paragraph 4.46.
- Accruals and deferred income (E.9, H.9 and J) – see paragraph 4.93.

Transfers from current assets to fixed assets

4.31 SI 2008/410 defines a fixed asset as one intended for use on a continuing basis in the company's activities and any assets that are not intended for such use are current assets. [SI 2008/410 10 Sch 4]. Where, at a date subsequent to its original acquisition, a current asset is retained for use on a continuing basis in the company's activities, it becomes a fixed asset and the question arises as to the appropriate transfer value.

4.32 An issue arises as a result of the different accounting rules for measuring fixed and current assets. Under the historical cost accounting rules, fixed assets are carried at depreciated cost less any provision for permanent diminution in value, whereas current assets are carried at the lower of cost and net realisable value (that is, after writing down for both temporary and permanent diminutions in value). The different rules gave rise to concerns that companies could avoid charging the profit and loss account with write downs to net realisable value arising on unsold trading assets. This could be done by transferring the relevant assets from current assets to fixed assets at above their net realisable value, as a result of which any later downward revaluation might be debited to the revaluation reserve.

[The next paragraph is 4.34.]

4.34 To address this issue, in July 1992, UITF Abstract 5, 'Transfers from current assets to fixed assets', was published. This states that where assets are transferred from current to fixed, the current asset accounting rules should be applied up to the effective date of transfer, which is the date of management's change of intent. Consequently, the transfer should be made at the lower of cost and net realisable value and, accordingly, an assessment should be made of the net realisable value at the date of transfer and if this is less than its previous carrying value the diminution should be charged in the profit and loss account, reflecting the loss to the company while the asset was held as a current asset. [UITF 5 para 5].

4.35 The timing of the transfer of current assets to fixed assets should reflect the timing of management's change of intent and should not be backdated (for example, to the start of the financial year). This change of intent will need to be evidenced, for instance in board minutes. Since the date of the management's decision is unlikely to correspond with the balance sheet date, at which a full review of carrying values would be made, consideration must be given to the appropriate amounts at which such assets should be transferred at the time of transfer.

4.36 Whether assets are transferred at cost or at net realisable value in accordance with UITF Abstract 5, the fixed asset accounting rules will apply to the assets subsequent to the date of transfer. In cases where the transfer is at net realisable value, the asset should be accounted for as a fixed asset at a valuation (under SI 2008/410's alternative accounting rules) as at the date of the transfer. At subsequent balance sheet dates it may or may not be revalued depending on the company's policy under FRS 15, but in either event the disclosure requirements appropriate to a valuation should be given. These disclosure requirements are discussed in chapter 16.

4.37 The abstract deals only with situations where current assets are included in the balance sheet at the lower of cost and net realisable value under paragraphs 23 and 24 of Schedule 1 to SI 2008/410. Therefore, it does not apply to current assets that are accounted for under the alternative accounting rules, for example, investments.

[The next paragraph is 4.39.]

Participating interests

4.39 'Participating interest' means an interest held by an undertaking in the shares of another undertaking that it holds on a long-term basis for the purpose of securing a contribution to its activities by the exercise of control or influence arising from or related to that interest. [SI 2008/410 10 Sch 11(1)]. A holding of 20 per cent or more of the shares of an undertaking is presumed to be a participating interest unless the contrary is shown. [SI 2008/410 10 Sch 11(2)]. In this context, a participating interest does not include an interest in a subsidiary undertaking. [SI 2008/410 10 Sch 11(5)]. It will however include associated companies as defined in FRS 9, 'Associates and joint ventures'. (see further chapter 27).

Own shares

4.40 The balance sheet formats in Schedule 1 to SI 2008/410 include a line item within investments (fixed and current) for 'Own shares'. However, in October 2003, the UITF issued Abstract 37, 'Purchases and sales of own shares', which requires a company's holdings of its own shares to be accounted for as a deduction in arriving at shareholders' funds, rather than as an asset. This was superseded by FRS 25 (applicable for accounting periods beginning on or after 1 January 2005) but the requirement to recognise 'treasury' shares (that is, own shares) as a deduction in arriving at shareholders' funds remains. The accounting treatment of 'own shares' is dealt with in chapter 23 for treasury shares and in chapter 12 for shares held by an ESOP trust.

Payments on account

4.41 'Payments on account' relate, as appropriate, to payments that a company makes in advance in respect of the acquisition of intangible assets, tangible assets or stocks (see further chapters 15, 16 and 20).

Presentation of debtors

4.42 The amount of each item to be shown under the heading 'Debtors' must be split between those receivable within one year of the balance sheet date and those receivable later than that. [SI 2008/410 1 Sch Balance sheet formats note 5]. For this purpose, a debtor is considered to be receivable on the earliest date on which payment is due, rather than on the earliest date on which payment is expected.

4.43 SI 2008/410 does not require this disclosure to be given on the face of the balance sheet. However, this means that there is an imbalance between the treatment of long-term debtors and long-term creditors where the latter are disclosed as long-term on the face of the balance sheet and not included in net current assets. There will be some instances where the absence of disclosure of long-term debtors on the face of the balance sheet may mean that users misinterpret the financial statements.

4.44 As a result of this imbalance, UITF Abstract 4, 'Presentation of long-term debtors in current assets', requires disclosure of debtors due after more than one year on the face of the balance sheet if the amount is material in the context of net current assets. [UITF 4 para 3]. The Abstract gives long-term trade debtors of lessors and deferred consideration on the sale of assets as examples where this additional disclosure may be appropriate. The debtor will still be included in current assets, but will be shown separately on the face of the balance sheet, normally as an additional line item 'Debtors: amounts falling due after more than one year' in the current assets section of the balance sheet.

4.45 Prior to the issue of UITF 4, some companies chose to show long-term debtors of this type as a separate category between fixed and current assets on the grounds that compliance with the company law formats, that is, including the long-term debtors within current assets, did not give a true and fair view. We consider that, following UITF Abstract 4, the inclusion of such an additional asset category on the balance sheet could only be achieved by using the true and fair override and that in most situations a true and fair view will be given by following the disclosure requirements of UITF Abstract 4. Therefore, long-term debtors should not normally be shown in a separate category between fixed and current assets. If a company wished to depart from SI 2008/410's formats it would have to justify this and give the disclosures required by FRS 18 (see chapter 2).

Pre-payments and accrued income

4.46 Pre-payments and accrued income may be disclosed in one of two alternative positions. [SI 2008/410 1 Sch Balance sheet formats note 6]. They may be disclosed either as a category of debtors (within current assets) or as a separate category in their own right. Where pre-payments and accrued income are disclosed within debtors, SI 2008/410 requires disclosure of the amount due in more than one year. If, however, they are included as a separate category, then strictly under SI 2008/410 no such analysis is required. However, UITF Abstract 4, requires separate disclosure of debtors due after more than one year where the amount is material in the context of the total net current assets. We consider that this applies to pre-payments and accrued income regardless of whether the total is included in debtors or shown as a separate category.

4.47 An example of disclosure of long-term pre-payments within debtors can be seen in the accounts of Seton Healthcare Group plc (see Table 4.8).

Table 4.8 — Disclosure of long-term pre-payments within debtors

Seton Healthcare Group plc — Annual Report — 28 February 1994

NOTES TO THE FINANCIAL STATEMENTS

16 DEBTORS: AMOUNTS FALLING DUE AFTER MORE THAN ONE YEAR

	Group		Company	
	1994	1993	**1994**	1993
	£'000	£'000	**£'000**	£'000
Other debtors	**1,779**	1,913	–	–
Prepayment	**453**	753	**453**	753
	2,232	2,666	**453**	753

Included within other debtors are £153,000 of deferred tax recoverable on the exceptional losses in 1992 and a £1,626,000 debt arising from the disposal of the USA businesses repayable over 5 years.

The prepayment of £453,000 is an advance payment relating to products to be supplied under a 5 year manufacturing agreement ending September 1996.

4.48 Pre-payments are not defined in company law, the Statement of Principles or any accounting standard. However, simply put, a pre-payment is expenditure incurred before the balance sheet that relates to activities and benefits arising after the balance sheet date. In addition, where costs are deferred as a pre-payment, the resultant asset must meet the definition of an asset in FRS 5. Therefore, the pre-payment should give rise to rights or other access to future economic benefits that are controlled by the entity, where control is the ability to obtain the future economic benefits relating to that asset and to restrict the access of others to those benefits. [FRS 5 paras 2, 3].

4.49 Pre-payments do not include expenditure that meets the criteria for recognition as a different category of asset under another accounting standard, such as FRS 10 'Goodwill and intangible assets', SSAP 13 'Accounting for research and development', FRS 15 'Tangible fixed assets', or SSAP 9 'Stocks and long-term contracts'.

4.50 Furthermore, applying the recognition criteria in FRS 5, a pre-payment should only be recognised in the balance sheet if:

- There is sufficient evidence of the existence of the item, including evidence that a future inflow of benefit will occur.
- The item can be measured at a monetary amount with sufficient reliability.

[FRS 5 para 20].

4.51 In order to determine whether costs relating to activities of future periods can be deferred as pre-payments therefore, the key issues are:

- Whether the entity *controls* those future benefits (that is, has the ability to obtain future economic benefits and can restrict others rights to those benefits).

- Whether there is sufficient evidence as to the *certainty* of those future economic benefits.

4.52 This is consistent with the approach adopted by the UITF in Abstract 24, 'Start up costs', (see chapter 16) and Abstract 34, 'Pre-contract costs', (see chapter 3), which both require a high level of certainty before the recognition of such costs as assets. There would generally need to be a strong connection between the cost and the expected future benefit.

4.53 In addition, consideration needs to be given as to the period in which the deferred cost should be recognised in the profit and loss account. This would generally be a defined period over which the expected benefits are to be received. However, if there is uncertainty over the amount of the expected benefits and timing of such a period, then the circumstances are more likely to lead to earlier recognition of the cost.

4.54 The following examples illustrate the principles described above.

Example 1 – Advance payment for producing advertisement

A company with a December year end makes a payment in December 20X1 to a film production crew to make a television advertisement in 20X2.

This is a 'traditional' pre-payment and under the accruals basis in most cases it will appropriate to defer such expenditure as a pre-payment. The benefit is the future services to be received, which the company controls by means of its contract and payment to the film production crew. Unless there are indications to the contrary, such as the film production crew being insolvent, there is certainty that the future benefit will be received.

Example 2 – Treatment of cost of advertisement that has not yet aired

The same company has paid a different production crew for another television advertisement that has been produced before the year end, but it is not to be aired on television until after the year end.

This is similar to the treatment of 'stock', but in respect of non-stock items. Again, in such a case in most instances it would be appropriate to defer the production cost as an asset at the balance sheet date, rather than expense it as soon as the production of the advertisement has finished. The supplier has carried out its contractual duties, so that the entity has received the goods or services, but the entity has not yet made use of them.

To defer such costs, however, it is necessary to demonstrate that the entity still controls the benefits. In this example, the entity owns the rights to the advertisement and can control when and where it is aired on television. There would also need to be evidence to support the certainty that the entity will benefit from those rights and some assurance that the amount is 'recoverable', that is that future inflows are reasonably expected. Clearly, there may be evidence after the year end of such inflows and past experience of similar events will also help to support such a case.

Example 3 – Treatment of cost of advertisement that has aired

By March 20X2, both of the advertisements described above have been aired.

In this scenario it is more difficult to make a case supporting continued deferral of the costs in a balance sheet produced at the end of March 20X2. Once the advertisement has been aired, the company no longer has direct control over the benefits it may receive as a result. Increased sales may be expected but the absolute amount and the period over which these sales are generated would generally be uncertain.

However, in some cases there may be a strong direct link between the future benefit (that is, new sales) and the asset on the balance sheet. For example, where a holiday company can clearly track specific sales generated from a brochure that has been sent to targeted potential customers, it may be appropriate to defer the costs of that brochure and release them to the profit and loss account over the period expected to benefit, that is the period in which those sales are recognised in the profit and loss account. Factors to consider in such circumstances would include whether:

- There is sufficient and strong evidence of a direct link between the expenditure being deferred and the future income or other benefit generated from that specific item. Where sales could be generated by more than one source, is there a way of tracking sales primarily to that source.
- There is a high expectation of sales or contracts for future services or goods that have not been generated by the time the financial statements are signed, but are expected from the item being deferred, for example by reference to past experience and current circumstances, market share etc.
- Deferring such costs is in line with industry practice.
- There is a defined period to which those costs relate.
- The costs to be deferred are limited to incremental external costs.
- The deferred cost is recoverable.

Cash at bank and in hand

Definition of cash

4.55 Schedule 1 to SI 2008/410 requires cash at bank and in hand to be included as a separate line item within current assets. The statutory instrument does not define cash and this has resulted in inconsistencies in practice.

4.56 FRS 1, 'Cash flow statements', defines cash as *"Cash in hand and deposits repayable on demand with any qualifying financial institution, less overdrafts from any qualifying financial institution repayable on demand. Deposits are repayable on demand if they can be withdrawn at any time without notice and without penalty or if* *a maturity or period of notice of not more than 24 hours or one working day has been agreed. Cash includes cash in hand and deposits denominated in foreign currencies*".

4.57 Therefore, the FRS 1 definition of cash includes deposits repayable on demand with any bank or other financial institution and so would include, for example, accounts with Building Societies. The definition excludes any term deposits with banks or other financial institutions. See further chapter 30.

4.58 Some companies follow this narrow interpretation of cash by including only cash held in current accounts and short-term deposits repayable on demand under the balance sheet heading for 'cash at bank and in hand'. This would include cash held on deposit with a bank or with another financial institution, such as a building society.

4.59 In contrast, another interpretation used in practice for the balance sheet heading 'cash at bank and in hand' is the total amount of money on deposit with a bank or other financial institution. This includes amounts on current account that can be withdrawn on demand and amounts in a deposit account, available after due notice has been given. This is a wide definition and does not restrict cash at bank to those deposits that are available on demand.

[The next paragraph is 4.62.]

Right of set-off of bank balances

4.62 Assets and liabilities are only allowed to be offset against one another in financial statements where there is a legally enforceable right of set-off between the balances. This stems from the requirement in paragraph 8 of Schedule 1 to SI 2008/410, which states that amounts in respect of items that represent assets or income may not be offset against amounts in respect of items that represent liabilities or expenditure, or *vice versa*.

4.63 FRS 25, 'Financial instruments: Presentation', expands upon this and sets out conditions that have to be met in order for offset to apply for financial assets and financial liabilities. The standard's rules require offset where, and only where, both the following conditions are met:

- The company has a legally enforceable right to set off the recognised amounts.
- The company intends either to settle on a net basis, or to realise the asset and settle the liability simultaneously.

[FRS 25 para 42].

4.64 These conditions are more restrictive than those contained in FRS 5 for other assets and liabilities, which do not require any intention to net settle, focussing entirely on an ability to do so.

4.65 Extreme care needs to be taken in consolidated financial statements, where it may be difficult to arrange for an amount that one group company owes to another party (such as a bank) to be offset against the amount of a deposit that another member of the group has lodged with that party. However, where a bank funds members of a group of companies this situation would be different if all of the following conditions applied:

- Each individual depositing company in the group has a joint and several liability to pay the same debts as the borrowing companies (that is, each is deemed to be a principal debtor for the same debts).
- The bank has a liability to each individual depositing company in respect of its deposit.
- The group has a demonstrable intention to net settle these balances.

4.66 In these circumstances such assets and liabilities may be offset against each other if all the criteria are met, although the restrictions imposed by FRS 25 make this relatively rare.

[The next paragraph is 4.71.]

Restricted cash balances

4.71 Cash at bank and in hand will sometimes include balances that can only be used for a specific purpose or where access is restricted. If these amounts are material then they should be disclosed, normally in the notes to the financial statements. Examples of such disclosure are found in the accounts of John Mowlem & Company PLC (cash balances subject to legal charges, see Table 4.9), Cable and Wireless plc (cash balances subject to exchange regulation, see Table 4.10) and Imperial Chemical Industries PLC (short-term deposits and cash held by insurance subsidiaries, see Table 4.11).

Table 4.9 — Cash balances subject to legal charges

John Mowlem & Company PLC — Annual Report and Accounts — 31 December 1994

NOTES TO THE ACCOUNTS

18 Cash

At 31 December 1994, cash balances with banks include £6.4 million (1993 £4.4 million) of cash deposits which are subject to either a legal assignment or a charge in favour of a third party. It is expected that they will be released in 1995.

Table 4.10 — Cash balances subject to exchange regulation

Cable and Wireless plc — Annual report and Accounts — 31 March 2003

Notes to the Accounts

20. SHORT-TERM DEPOSITS AND CASH AT BANK AND IN HAND (extract)

Of the total amounts shown, £49 million (2002–£45 million) is held in countries subject to exchange regulations which may delay repatriation.

Table 4.11 — Short-term deposits and cash held by insurance subsidiaries

Imperial Chemical Industries PLC — Annual Report and Accounts and Form 20-F — 31 December 2001

Notes relating to the accounts

18 Current asset investments and short-term deposits (extract)

Included in unlisted investments and short-term deposits and cash are amounts totalling £104m (2000 £224m) held by the Group's insurance subsidiaries. In 2001 £38m (2000 £24m) was readily available for the general purposes of the Group.

Net current assets and liabilities

4.72 In determining the amount to be shown under 'Net current assets (liabilities)' in Format 1, a company must take into account any amount that is shown separately under the heading 'Prepayments and accrued income'. [SI 2008/410 1 Sch Balance sheet formats note 11]. This applies whether the amount in question is shown as a sub-heading of debtors (C.II.6) or as a main heading (D). But as the alternative positions of this heading within Format 1 both automatically fall within net current assets (liabilities), this seems to be a self-evident requirement. In practice, it is fairly rare for prepayments to be disclosed as a main heading.

Liabilities

Disclosure

4.73 All items included under creditors must be analysed between amounts that will fall due within one year of the balance sheet date and amounts that will fall due after more than one year. [SI 2008/410 1 Sch balance sheet formats note 13]. SI 2008/410 requires that creditors should be analysed into the following categories:

- Debenture loans.
- Bank loans and overdrafts.
- Payments received on account.
- Trade creditors.
- Bills of exchange payable.
- Amounts owed to group undertakings.
- Amounts owed to undertakings in which the company has a participating interest.
- Other creditors including taxation and social security.
- Accruals and deferred income.

[SI 2008/410 1 Sch formats].

4.74 An item representing a liability that is not covered by the prescribed format may be shown separately. [SI 2008/410 1 Sch 3(2)]. Examples of creditors that are sometimes shown as separate categories within total creditors are amounts due in respect of factored debts or bills of exchange discounted with recourse, finance lease payables and deferred consideration in respect of acquisitions.

4.75 Both company law and FRS 29 specify a considerable amount of detail that a company should disclose in its financial statements in respect of its indebtedness. These disclosure requirements are considered in detail in chapter 6.

4.76 Where any item that is shown under the heading 'Creditors' includes liabilities for which the company has given security, these liabilities must be disclosed in aggregate. Also, the notes must give an indication of the nature of the securities given. [SI 2008/410 1 Sch 61(4)]. For this requirement to be meaningful, the financial statements should show some disaggregation of the relevant liabilities. This is because it could be misleading merely to disclose the aggregate of securities compared with the aggregate of liabilities.

Classification as short-term or long-term

4.77 For the purpose of SI 2008/410, a loan or advance (including a liability comprising a loan or advance) falls due for repayment (or an instalment falls due for payment) on the earliest date on which the lender could require repayment (or payment) if the lender were to exercise all options and rights available to him. [SI 2008/410 10 Sch 9].

4.78 FRS 25 clarifies that liabilities should be regarded (and classified) as falling due within one year even if:

- The original term was for a period longer than a year.
- An agreement to refinance, or to reschedule payments, on a long-term basis is completed after the balance sheet date and before the financial statements are authorised for issue.

[FRS 25 para 50A].

4.78.1 An entity classifies a liability as current if it does not have the unconditional right to defer its settlement for at least 12 months after the balance sheet date. [FRS 25 para 50C].

4.78.2 Many loan agreements include a change of control clause under which a borrowing becomes repayable if there is a change of control event. This raises the question as to whether the borrowing is required to be classified as a current liability under FRS 25 if an entity is unable to prevent a controlling shareholder selling its shares to a third party, even if there is no expectation that a change of control might happen within 12 months. Our view is that a change of control clause does not result in classification as a current liability if there has been no change of control event at the balance sheet date. In this respect, we consider that a change of control clause is similar in substance to a covenant (see para 4.80 below). FRS 25 requires classification as a current liability if there is an actual breach at the balance sheet date, but not if there is only a potential breach. Therefore, a borrowing is not classified as current if the counter-party does not have a right as of the balance sheet date to demand repayment within 12 months of that date.

4.79 A rescheduling or refinancing of debt that is at the lender's discretion and occurs after the balance sheet date does not alter the liability's condition at the balance sheet date. Such rescheduling or refinancing is regarded as a non-adjusting post balance sheet event and it is not taken into account in determining the current/long-term classification of the debt. If, however, the entity has the right, at the balance sheet date, to defer payments for more than one year, a liability should be classified as falling due in more than one year. [FRS 25 para 50B]. The entity must have full discretion to roll the obligation over; the potential for a refinancing alone is sufficient to classify an obligation as non-current.

Example – Right to defer repayment of loan

A company entered into a loan agreement with a bank on 15 January 20X5. The loan is due for repayment in five equal instalments payable at the end of each quarter until 31 March 20X6. The company's directors intend to keep to this payment schedule and cash flow forecasts indicate that the company will be able to do so. The loan agreement contains a clause permitting the company to defer all payments until 31 March 20X6 (the disadvantage of doing so being a higher total interest cost). The full amount of the debt should be classified as falling due in more than one year, because the company has the right to defer payments until after 31 December 20X5.

4.80 It is common practice for financial institutions to include borrowing covenants in the terms of loans. Under some borrowing covenants a loan, which would otherwise be long-term in nature, becomes immediately repayable if certain items related to the borrower's financial condition or performance are breached. Typically, these items are measures of liquidity or solvency based on ratios derived from the entity's financial statements. Where these types of breaches occur prior to the balance sheet date, the borrowings should be classified as a current liability unless a sufficient waiver of the covenant is granted by the lender, such that the borrowing does not become immediately repayable. Where the borrower has breached a covenant of this nature by the balance sheet date and the lender agrees, after the balance sheet date but before authorisation of the financial statements, not to require immediate repayment of the loan, the agreement of the lender is generally regarded as a non-adjusting post balance sheet event. This is because at the balance sheet date, the lender's agreement had not been obtained and the condition of the borrowing at that time was that it was immediately repayable. [FRS 25 para 50C].

4.80.1 Some borrowings may include 'cross default' clauses, such that the terms of the borrowing are assessed, at least in part, against compliance with covenants of another borrowing. Once the related borrowing covenant is breached, the borrowing with the 'cross default' clause, and any similarly linked borrowings, may become immediately repayable and, hence, should be classified as a current liability.

4.80.2 There may be a period between the measurement date of the covenants and the date at which the borrower needs to report any breach to the bank. If the covenant test date is at or before the balance sheet date, the fact that the borrower need not report the breach until after the period end does not indicate that the covenant has not been breached. Classification of the borrowing as a current liability would be required.

Example – Covenant breach reported after period end

A company has a long-term loan with a bank. The terms of the loan require quarterly testing of certain covenant ratios. The bank requires the company to file covenant compliance certificates within 60 days of the measurement date of the covenants. The company's year end is 31 December 20X8. The company was within the acceptable parameters based on the calculation of the ratios for the third quarter – that is, 30 September 20X8. The covenant testing date in the fourth quarter is 31 December 20X8. The financial results were finalised in January 20X9. Based on these, the company was in breach of its covenants at 31 December 20X8. The company is due to file the covenant compliance certificates on 2 March 20X9, which will show the breach. The company believes that the breach in covenant does not occur until the filing date, as this is the date at which the bank would call the loan in the absence of any remedy. How should the loan balance be classified at the year end?

Although reporting of the breach was not required until after the balance sheet date, the company was in effect in breach of its covenants at 31 December 20X8. This is the case even though the reported financial figures were not finalised until January. The company did not have the unconditional right to defer settlement of the loan for at least 12 months after the balance sheet date: the loan balance should, therefore, be re-classified as current.

4.80.3 Following a breach of a borrowing covenant, lenders often agree to a period of grace during which the borrower may rectify the breach. The lender agrees not to demand repayment during this time, but if the breach is not rectified, the debt becomes immediately repayable at the end of the period of grace. If, before the balance sheet date, the lender has agreed to such a period of grace and that period ends at least 12 months after the balance sheet date, the liability should be shown as long-term. [FRS 25 para 50D]. If the breach of the borrowing covenant occurs after the balance sheet date, the liability is still shown as long-term, unless the breach was so serious that the financial statements could no longer be prepared on a going concern basis. The presentation of the loan is dictated by the condition of the loan as at the balance sheet date. Events after the balance sheet date may give evidence of that condition, but they do not change it. This is consistent with FRS 21, 'Events after the balance sheet date'.

4.80.4 In contrast, some borrowing agreements include a period of grace, the effect of which is that the borrower does not lose the unconditional right to defer payment of the liability until the period of grace has expired. In this case, where the breach does not occur until this later date, the entity continues to present the borrowings as non-current.

Example – Borrowing agreement includes a period of grace

A term loan agreement includes a provision that the borrower must sell a foreign branch of its operations by 31 December 20X9. However, the agreement states that the borrower is permitted an additional 2 months to complete the sale if it is not able to sell the branch by that date. The borrower has not been able to find a buyer by 31 December 20X9. In its financial statements for the period ended 31 December 20X9, how will the borrowings be classified?

The entity should continue to classify the loan balance as non-current, as the agreement allows for a period of grace such that the actual breach of the loan conditions does not occur until 2 months after the end of the reporting period. The entity should consider the impact of the potential breach and the appropriateness of including disclosure on this item in the financial statements.

4.80.4.1 Where an entity experiences a downturn in trading results, in addition to the impact of these results on banking covenants, management should also consider if there is an impact on the entity's borrowing powers. For example, a company's Articles of Association may contain a borrowing restriction that requires the directors to restrict borrowings to a multiple of capital and reserves (as defined in the Articles). A significant loss might, therefore, affect the amount of any new borrowing that the company can take out or affect the roll-over of existing borrowings. If management considers that the company may breach (or has breached) the borrowing powers in its Articles it should discuss remedies (for example, ratification by shareholders) with its legal advisors.

4.80.5 Although events after the balance sheet date may not alter the classification of a liability, they may require disclosure as a non-adjusting event. Paragraph 50E of FRS 25 states that, in respect of loans classified as current liabilities, the following events should be disclosed as non-adjusting events in accordance with FRS 21, if they occur between the balance sheet date and the date of authorisation of the financial statements:

- Refinancing on a long-term basis.
- Rectification of a breach of a long-term loan agreement.
- The receipt from the lender of a period of grace to rectify a breach of a long-term loan agreement ending at least 12 months after the balance sheet date.

4.80.6 In the case of long-term liabilities, non-adjusting post balance sheet events requiring disclosure would also include breaches of loan agreements occurring between the balance sheet date and the date of authorisation of the financial statements. See chapter 22.

Debentures

4.81 There is no precise definition of a debenture, either in law or in practice. In legal terms it is generally construed as formal acknowledgment of a debt. However, section 738 of the Companies Act 2006 refers to debentures as including *"debenture stock, bonds and any other securities of a company, whether or not constituting a charge on the assets of the company"*. This definition does not distinguish clearly between a debenture loan and any other loan. Whether a particular loan is a debenture or not will depend on the documentation. A formal loan agreement, whether containing security or not, will often constitute a debenture. Although a bank loan may be a debenture loan, the balance sheet formats distinguish between bank loans and other debenture loans.

4.82 For accounting measurement and disclosure purposes, there is no difference between debentures, loans and other debt instruments. They are all financial instruments issued for raising finance and are dealt with in detail in chapter 6.

Amounts received on account

4.83 Unless a company shows the payments it has received on account of orders as a deduction from stocks, it must show them under creditors. [SI 2008/410 1 Sch Balance sheet formats note 8].

Trade creditors

4.84 Trade creditors normally represents amounts owed to suppliers of goods and services. It could comprise either all items included in the creditors ledger or simply those items that relate to the cost of sales. If companies classify all creditors ledger items as trade creditors, such treatment could distort the cost of sales/trade creditors ratio. A company should ensure that, whatever treatment it adopts, it is consistent from year to year.

[The next paragraph is 4.91.]

Other creditors including taxation and social security

4.91 The line 'other creditors including taxation and social security' must be analysed between other creditors, and taxation and social security. [SI 2008/410 1 Sch Balance sheet formats note 9]. The 'taxation and social security' headings should include the following items:

- Corporation tax.
- VAT.
- Social security and other amounts (such as PAYE owed in respect of wages and salaries).

- Excise duty.

The heading 'Other creditors' should include items that cannot be appropriately analysed elsewhere.

4.92 'Other creditors including taxation and social security' contrasts with the line under provisions for 'taxation, including deferred taxation'. The latter item will comprise all deferred tax liabilities.

Accruals and deferred income

4.93 In the same way that 'prepayments and accrued income' may be shown in either of two positions in the formats, the item 'accruals and deferred income' may be disclosed either as a category of creditors or as a separate category in its own right. [SI 2008/410 1 Sch Balance sheet formats note 10]. Where 'accruals and deferred income' is disclosed under creditors, it must be analysed between those amounts that will fall due within one year and those amounts that will fall due after more than one year. [SI 2008/410 1 Sch Balance sheet formats note 13]. No such analysis is required if 'accruals and deferred income' is included as a separate category.

4.94 'Accruals and deferred income' could include government grants of a capital or revenue nature that are accounted for as deferred credits. These are discussed in chapters 9 and 16.

Other liabilities

4.95 SI 2008/410 requires the amount of any convertible loans included in the caption of debenture loans to be shown separately. [SI 2008/410 1 Sch Balance sheet formats note 7]. FRS 25, 'Financial instruments: Presentation', requires the debt component of convertible debt (which is treated as a compound financial instrument) to be reported within liabilities. We consider that, in order to comply with the company law requirements, the liability element of convertible loans should be separately disclosed as part of debentures. FRS 25 is considered in detail in chapter 6.

[The next paragraph is 4.97.]

Consolidated formats

4.97 SI 2008/410 requires consolidated financial statements to comply as far as practicable with the provisions of Schedule 1 to SI 2008/410 as if the undertakings included in the consolidation were a single company. [SI 2008/410 6 Sch 1(1)]. In addition, the consolidated financial statements have to comply with the provisions of Schedule 6 to SI 2008/410 as to their form and content. [CA06 Sec 404(3)].

4.98 Schedule 6 to SI 2008/410 includes provisions that modify the formats detailed in Schedule 1 to SI 2008/410 , to include certain additional items that require disclosure in the consolidated balance sheet. [SI 2008/410 6 Sch 17(2), 20(2)]. The Format 1 balance sheet set out below includes the requirements of both Schedules 1 and 6 to SI 2008/410 (the additional requirements of Schedule 6 are shown in bold and modifications to the numbering and lettering have been made for illustrative purposes). The Format 2 balance sheet is not given as it is identical in all respects (apart from one) to the information disclosed in Format 1 (see para 4.29).

4.99 The format chosen by the group's parent for its individual balance sheet would normally also be used to present the consolidated balance sheet. However, there is nothing in the legislation to prevent the parent from adopting a different format for its consolidated balance sheet, although this is unlikely to happen in practice, unless the group has banking or insurance activities and the parent does not.

Consolidated balance sheet — Format 1

A Called up share capital not paid

B Fixed assets

- I Intangible assets
  - 1 Development costs
  - 2 Concessions, patents, licences, trade marks and similar rights and assets
  - 3 Goodwill
  - 4 Payments on account
- II Tangible assets
  - 1 Land and buildings
  - 2 Plant and machinery
  - 3 Fixtures, fittings, tools and equipment
  - 4 Payments on account and assets in course of construction
- III Investments
  - 1 Shares in group undertakings
  - 2 Loans to group undertakings
  - **3 Interests in associated undertakings**
  - **4 Other participating interests**
  - 5 Loans to undertakings in which the company has a participating interest
  - 6 Other investments other than loans

- 7 Other loans
- 8 Own shares

C Current assets

I Stocks

- 1 Raw materials and consumables
- 2 Work in progress
- 3 Finished goods and goods for resale
- 4 Payments on account

II Debtors

- 1 Trade debtors
- 2 Amounts owed by group undertakings
- 3 Amounts owed by undertakings in which the company has a participating interest
- 4 Other debtors
- 5 Called-up share capital not paid
- 6 Prepayments and accrued income

III Investments

- 1 Shares in group undertakings
- 2 Own shares
- 3 Other investments

IV Cash at bank and in hand

D Prepayments and accrued income

E Creditors: amounts falling due within one year

- 1 Debenture loans
- 2 Bank loans and overdrafts
- 3 Payments received on account
- 4 Trade creditors
- 5 Bills of exchange payable
- 6 Amounts owed to group undertakings
- 7 Amounts owed to undertakings in which the company has a participating interest
- 8 Other creditors including taxation and social security

9 Accruals and deferred income

F Net current assets (liabilities)

G Total assets less current liabilities

H Creditors: amounts falling due after more than one year

1 Debenture loans

2 Bank loans and overdrafts

3 Payments received on account

4 Trade creditors

5 Bills of exchange payable

6 Amounts owed to group undertakings

7 Amounts owed to undertakings in which the company has a participating interest

8 Other creditors including taxation and social security

9 Accruals and deferred income

I Provisions for liabilities

1 Pensions and similar obligations

2 Taxation, including deferred taxation

3 Other provisions

J Accruals and deferred income

K Capital and reserves

I Called up share capital

II Share premium account

III Revaluation reserve

IV Other reserves

1 Capital redemption reserve

2 Reserve for own shares

3 Reserves provided for by the articles of association

4 Other reserves

V Profit and loss account

4.99.1 In addition, Schedule 6 to SI 2008/410 requires that in the balance sheet formats there should be shown, as a separate item and under an appropriate heading, the amount of capital and reserves attributable to shares in subsidiary undertakings included in the consolidation held by minority interests. [SI 2008/

410 6 Sch 17(2)]. The position of the line item for minority interests is not specified in the statutory instrument. The presentation of minority interests is considered further in chapter 24.

Rules concerning particular items in consolidated formats

4.100 The following items may be shown in alternative positions in the balance sheet (references given are for Format 1):

- Called up share capital not paid (A and C.II.5).
- Pre-payments and accrued income (C.II.6 and D) – see paragraph 4.46.
- Accruals and deferred income (E.9, H.9 and J) – see paragraph 4.93.

4.100.1 In addition, as noted in paragraph 4.99.1 above, the position of the line item for minority interests in the balance sheet formats is not specified in SI 2008/410. See further chapter 24.

4.101 An example of a Format 1 consolidated balance sheet is given in Table 4.12.

Table 4.12 – Format 1 consolidated balance sheet

Glaxo Holdings p.l.c. – Annual Report and Accounts – 30 June 1994

Consolidated Balance Sheet

At 30th June	Notes	**1994 £m**	1993 £m
FIXED ASSETS			
Tangible assets	11	**3,184**	2,959
Investments	12	**55**	61
		3,239	3,020
CURRENT ASSETS			
Stocks	13	**575**	595
Debtors	14	**1,310**	1,346
Investments	15/17	**2,708**	2,434
Cash at bank	17	**55**	63
		4,648	4,438
CREDITORS: Amounts falling due within one year	16	**2,130**	2,200
NET CURRENT ASSETS		**2,518**	2,238
TOTAL ASSETS LESS CURRENT LIABILITIES		**5,757**	5,258
CREDITORS: Amounts falling due after more than one year	16	**169**	120
CONVERTIBLE BONDS	18	**129**	123
PROVISIONS FOR LIABILITIES AND CHARGES*	19	**293**	358
NET ASSETS	4	**5,166**	4,657

CAPITAL AND RESERVES			
Called up share capital	22	**762**	758
Share premium account	23	**229**	151
Other reserves	23	**4,052**	3,637
EQUITY SHAREHOLDERS' FUNDS	24	**5,043**	4,546
MINORITY INTERESTS		**123**	111
CAPITAL EMPLOYED		**5,166**	4,657

* Editorial note: for periods beginning on or after 1 January 2005, the statutory line item was renamed 'provisions for liabilities' in company legislation.

4.102 As explained in paragraph 4.29, in Format 2 assets are shown as equal in total to liabilities. An example is given in Table 4.13.

Table 4.13 – Format 2 consolidated balance sheet

The Peninsular and Oriental Steam Navigation Company – Annual Report and Accounts – 31 December 1998

Group balance sheet
at 31 December 1998

	Note	Group 1998 £m	1997 £m
Assets			
Fixed assets			
Intangible assets: Goodwill	9	6.8	–
Tangible assets			
Ships	10	1,877.8	1,885.4
Properties	11	1,351.7	1,396.6
Other fixed assets	12	567.7	567.4
Investments			
Subsidiaries	13	–	–
Joint ventures:			
Share of gross assets		1,731.3	1,315.4
Share of gross liabilities		(971.4)	(763.9)
Share of net assets		759.9	551.5
Associates		109.1	61.4
Other investments		31.5	17.0
	14	900.5	629.9
		4,704.5	4,479.3
Current assets			
Development and dealing properties	15	359.9	330.9
Stocks	16	125.0	124.0
Debtors	17	1,106.4	1,368.0
Investments		12.7	11.3
Cash at bank and in hand		134.1	122.6
		1,738.1	1,956.8
		6,442.6	6,436.1

Liabilities			
Capital and reserves			
Called up share capital	18	769.3	751.3
Share premium account	19	595.8	562.7
Revaluation reserve	19	46.6	8.6
Other reserves	19	527.5	522.8
Profit and loss account	19	1,048.5	972.9
Equity stockholders' funds		2,837.9	2,668.0
Non-equity stockholders' funds**	19	149.8	150.3
Stockholders' funds		2,987.7	2,818.3
Other liabilities			
Equity minority interests	20	39.7	32.9
Provisions for liabilities and charges*	21	103.0	138.9
Loans: convertible	22	164.8	189.8
non-convertible	22	1,309.0	1,618.6
Other creditors	23	1,838.4	1,637.6
		3,454.9	3,617.8
		6,442.6	6,436.1

Editorial notes:
* For periods beginning on or after 1 January 2005, the statutory line item was renamed 'provisions for liabilities' in company legislation.
** For periods beginning on or after 1 January 2005, the presentation of non-equity shareholders' funds in FRS 4, was superseded by FRS 25.

Interests in and amounts due to and from group undertakings

4.103 The Format 1 balance sheet specifies the place where the aggregate amounts should be shown of any amounts owed to and from, and any interests in, group undertakings. These items can be summarised as follows:

B Fixed assets

III Investments

1 Shares in group undertakings

2 Loans to group undertakings

C Current assets

II Debtors

2 Amounts owed by group undertakings

III Investments

1 Shares in group undertakings

E Creditors: amounts falling due within one year

6 Amounts owed to group undertakings

H Creditors: amounts falling due after more than one year

6 Amounts owed to group undertakings

4.104 Because amounts owed by and to group undertakings have to be shown in specific positions in the formats, these balances should not be netted off into a single balance disclosed in the balance sheet as 'Investment in subsidiaries'. This applies even where a note to the financial statements gives additional information that explains the net balance. Although shares in and loans to subsidiaries may, if they qualify as fixed asset investments and paragraph 4(2) of Schedule 1 to SI 2008/410 applies, be aggregated on the face of the balance sheet, the disclosure that follows is not permitted (because it does not comply with 1 Sch 4(2)).

Investment in subsidiaries — presentation *not* permitted

Shares in subsidiaries	X
Amounts owed by subsidiaries	X
Amounts owed to subsidiaries	(X)
	X

4.105 Moreover, the amounts owed and owing have to be ascertained on an undertaking by undertaking basis. [SI 2008/410 1 Sch 8]. Consequently, for accounting disclosure purposes in the parent's financial statements, amounts that one subsidiary owes to the parent cannot be offset against amounts the parent owes to another subsidiary. Set-off can be allowed only in circumstances where there is a legal right of set-off and the company has an intention to net settle (see further chapter 6).

4.106 Undertakings have to analyse 'amounts owed by (and to) group undertakings' between amounts that will fall due within one year and amounts that will fall due after more than one year. [SI 2008/410 1 Sch Balance sheet formats notes 5 and 13]. The results of this analysis will largely depend both on the way in which group undertakings are financed and on the terms of any formal or informal agreements between the undertakings.

The profit and loss account

Individual company formats

4.107 SI 2008/410 permits companies to use any one of the four alternative formats of the profit and loss account and it leaves the choice between these formats to the company's directors.

4.108 Unlike the choice between the balance sheet formats, the choice between the profit and loss account formats is significant. A company can choose not only between a vertical presentation (Formats 1 and 2) and a presentation in which it shows charges separately from income (Formats 3 and 4), but also between classifying expenses by function or by type (also referred to as 'by nature'). Thus, depending on which format a company chooses, its financial statements will contain certain additional information, for example, own work capitalised, as well as certain different information.

Classification of expenses by function

4.109 In Formats 1 and 3, expenses are classified by function (for example, cost of sales, distribution costs, administrative expenses). These formats, both of which require identical information, have much in common with the management accounts that many UK companies prepare on a regular basis. It should be noted that there is no line item for 'operating profit' in the statutory profit and loss account formats — the disclosure of operating profit derives from FRS 3 (see para 4.65). Format 1, which is the vertical presentation, is set out below, and illustrated in Table 4.14.

Profit and loss account — Format 1

1 Turnover

2 Cost of sales

3 Gross profit or loss

4 Distribution costs

5 Administrative expenses

6 Other operating income

7 Income from shares in group undertakings

8 Income from participating interests

9 Income from other fixed asset investments

10 Other interest receivable and similar income

11 Amounts written off investments

12 Interest payable and similar charges

13 Tax on profit or loss on ordinary activities

14 Profit or loss on ordinary activities after taxation

15 Extraordinary income

16 Extraordinary charges

17 Extraordinary profit or loss

18 Tax on extraordinary profit or loss

19 Other taxes not shown under the above items

20 Profit or loss for the financial year

4.109.1 These headings, which require the classification of expenses by function, give rise to questions concerning the allocation of costs. Chapter 5 includes guidance on the types of costs included under the line items for cost of sales, distribution costs and administrative expenses.

Classification of expenses by type

4.110 In Formats 2 and 4, expenses are classified by type (for example, raw materials and consumables, staff costs, and depreciation). Format 2, which is the vertical presentation, is set out below, and also illustrated in Table 4.15.

Profit and loss account — Format 2

1 Turnover

2 Change in stocks of finished goods and in work in progress

3 Own work capitalised

4 Other operating income

5 (a) Raw materials and consumables

(b) Other external charges

6 Staff costs:

(a) Wages and salaries

(b) Social security costs

(c) Other pension costs

7 (a) Depreciation and other amounts written off tangible and intangible fixed assets

(b) Exceptional amounts written off current assets

8 Other operating charges

9 Income from shares in group undertakings

10 Income from participating interests

11 Income from other fixed asset investments

12 Other interest receivable and similar income

13 Amounts written off investments

14 Interest payable and similar charges

15 Tax on profit or loss on ordinary activities

16 Profit or loss on ordinary activities after taxation

17 Extraordinary income

18 Extraordinary charges

19 Extraordinary profit or loss

20 Tax on extraordinary profit or loss

21 Other taxes not shown under the above items

22 Profit or loss for the financial year

Consolidated formats

4.111 For a consolidated profit and loss account, Schedule 6 to SI 2008/410 details the items that should be added to the formats prescribed in Schedule 1 to SI 2008/410. [SI 2008/410 6 Sch 17(3), 20(3)]. The formats illustrated below include the requirements of both Schedule 1 and 6 to SI 2008/410 (the additional requirements of Schedule 6 are shown in bold and modifications to the numbering have also been made for illustrative purposes). Formats 3 and 4 are not given as they are rarely used and they replicate the information in Formats 1 and 2.

Consolidated profit and loss account — Format 1

1 Turnover

2 Cost of sales

3 Gross profit or loss

4 Distribution costs

5 Administrative expenses

6 Other operating income

7 Income from shares in group undertakings

8 Income from interests in associated undertakings

9 Income from other participating interests

10 Income from other fixed asset investments

11 Other interest receivable and similar income

12 Amounts written off investments

13 Interest payable and similar charges

14 Tax on profit or loss on ordinary activities

15 Profit or loss on ordinary activities after taxation

16 Extraordinary income

17 Extraordinary charges

18 Extraordinary profit or loss

19 Tax on extraordinary profit or loss

20 Other taxes not shown under the above items

21 Profit or loss for the financial year

Consolidated profit and loss account — Format 2

1 Turnover

2 Change in stocks of finished goods and in work in progress

3 Own work capitalised

4 Other operating income

5 (a) Raw materials and consumables

(b) Other external charges

6 Staff costs:

(a) Wages and salaries

(b) Social security costs

(c) Other pension costs

7 (a) Depreciation and other amounts written off tangible and intangible fixed assets

(b) Exceptional amounts written off current assets

8 Other operating charges

9 Income from shares in group undertakings

10 Income from interests in associated undertakings

11 Income from other participating interests

12 Income from other fixed asset investments

13 Other interest receivable and similar income

14 Amounts written off investments

15 Interest payable and similar charges

16 Tax on profit or loss on ordinary activities

17 Profit or loss on ordinary activities after taxation

18 Extraordinary income

19 Extraordinary charges

20 Extraordinary profit or loss

21 Tax on extraordinary profit or loss

22 Other taxes not shown under the above items

23 Profit or loss for the financial year

4.111.1 In addition, Schedule 6 to SI 2008/410 requires that in the profit and loss account formats there should be shown, as a separate item and under an appropriate heading, the amount of any profit or loss on ordinary activities and the amount of any profit or loss on extraordinary activities, attributable to shares in subsidiary undertakings included in the consolidation held by minority interests. [SI 2008/410 6 Sch 17(3)]. The position of the line item for minority interests is not specified in the statutory instrument. The presentation of minority interests is considered further in chapter 24.

Rules concerning particular items

4.112 All items in the profit and loss account are preceded by an Arabic numeral and so they may be combined on the face of the profit and loss account and disclosed individually in the notes, if that treatment is considered to make a company's results more understandable. [SI 2008/410 1 Sch 4(2)]. However, FRS 3 requires that certain items (including turnover and operating profit) are shown on the face of the profit and loss account (see para 4.120). Also, whichever format of profit and loss account a company adopts, the account must, however, show separately on its face the amount of the company's or group's profit or loss on ordinary activities before taxation. [SI 2008/410 1 Sch 6].

[The next paragraph is 4.115.]

4.115 SI 2008/410 attaches to the formats certain notes and comments on specific profit and loss account items.

4.116 Where expenses are classified by function (Formats 1 and 3), the amounts to be shown under cost of sales, distribution costs and administrative expenses are to be stated after taking into account any necessary provisions for depreciation and for diminution in the value of assets. [SI 2008/410 1 Sch Profit and loss account formats note 14]. The amounts of the provisions for depreciation, or for the diminution in the value of tangible and intangible fixed assets, must be disclosed separately in the notes to the financial statements. [SI 2008/410 1 Sch Profit and loss account formats note 17].

4.117 Income or interest derived from group undertakings must be shown separately from income and interest derived from other sources. [SI 2008/410 1 Sch Profit and loss account formats note 15]. Similarly, any interest or similar charges payable to group undertakings must be shown separately. [SI 2008/410 1 Sch Profit and loss account formats note 16].

4.118 In the light of present practice in the UK, it is unlikely that any amount would fall to be disclosed under the heading 'Other taxes not shown under the above items'.

[The next paragraph is 4.120.]

The effect of FRS 3 on the profit and loss account formats

4.120 FRS 3 contains supplementary provisions relating to the format of the profit and loss account. These do not alter the legal requirements, but include standards for minimum disclosure that should be given on the face of the profit and loss account, together with certain additional disclosures. The detailed requirements of FRS 3 are considered in chapter 8. The following requirements are relevant to the formats.

- The face of the profit and loss account should include, as a minimum, an analysis of turnover and operating profit showing separately amounts attributable to continuing operations, acquisitions as a component of continuing operations, and discontinued operations. (There is no format heading for 'operating profit' in the company law formats; FRS 3 defines it as being normally, for non-financial entities, the profit before 'income from shares in group undertakings'.) [FRS 3 para 14].
- Exceptional items (apart from those items listed below) should be included under the statutory format headings to which they relate and should be disclosed on the face of the profit and loss account if that is necessary to give a true and fair view. [FRS 3 para 19].
- The following items, including provisions in respect of such items, should be disclosed separately on the face of the profit and loss account after operating profit and before interest, classified under continuing or discontinued operations as appropriate:
  - Profits or losses on the sale or termination of an operation.
  - Costs of a fundamental reorganisation or restructuring having a material effect on the nature and focus of the reporting entity's operations.
  - Profits or losses on the disposal of fixed assets.

[FRS 3 para 20].

- A company's ordinary activities have been defined so broadly that extraordinary items have all but disappeared from the profit and loss accounts of UK companies. Consequently, the line items in the company law formats for extraordinary income and charges, tax on and minority interests in extraordinary items, are practically redundant.

4.121 Tables 4.14 and 4.15 are examples of published profit and loss accounts that follow Formats 1 and 2 respectively.

Table 4.14 — Format 1 profit and loss account

BPB plc — annual report — 31 March 1999

Group profit and loss account

Year to 31 March	Note	**1999 £m**	1998 £m
Turnover			
Group and share of joint ventures and associates		**1,417.4**	1,401.1
Less: share of joint ventures' turnover		**(24.6)**	(24.3)
share of associates' turnover		**(77.5)**	(76.6)
Group turnover	3	**1,315.3**	1,300.2
Cost of sales		**(837.0)**	(838.5)
Gross profit		**478.3**	461.7
Net operating expenses	4	**(304.4)**	(298.1)
Operating profit	3	**173.9**	163.6
Share of operating profit in:			
Joint ventures		**0.8**	(0.8)
Associates		**12.2**	12.4
Exceptional items: continuing operations			
Disposals of fixed assets	7	**2.3**	2.7
Sale and termination of operations	7	**(20.1)**	(26.3)
Profit on ordinary activities before interest		**169.1**	151.6
Exceptional interest charge on bond buy-back	8	**(2.1)**	(14.9)
Other net interest payable	8	**(4.7)**	(2.1)
Profit on ordinary activities before tax		**162.3**	134.6
Tax on profit on ordinary activities	9	**(59.1)**	(50.1)
Profit on ordinary activities after tax		**103.2**	84.5
Minority interests		**0.5**	(0.8)
Profit attributable to BPB plc		**103.7**	83.7
Dividends*	10	**(56.8)**	(56.9)
Retained profit for the year		**46.9**	26.8
Basic earnings per share	11	**20.5p**	16.3p
Diluted earnings per share	11	**20.4p**	16.1p

Underlying results

Before net exceptional charge of £19.9 million *(1998 £38.5 million)*:

Profit on ordinary activities before tax (£m)		**182.2**	173.1
Earnings per share	11	**23.9p**	22.3p

4 Net operating expenses

Distribution costs	**187.6**	179.7
Administrative expenses	**125.6**	132.2
Other operating expenses	**(8.8)**	(13.8)
	304.4	298.1

The following are included within operating expenses:

Redundancy costs — Building materials	**6.8**	5.7
— Paperboard	**—**	2.1
	6.8	7.8
Research and development costs	**4.4**	6.4

* Editorial note: Prior to accounting periods beginning on or after 1 January 2005, company law required dividends to be shown within the profit and loss account as a deduction from profit for the period, but this requirement was deleted for later accounting periods. Therefore, the legal imperative for adopting such a treatment no longer exists. The presentation of dividends is covered in chapter 23.

Table 4.15 — Format 2 profit and loss account

English China Clays plc 1994 — Annual Report and Accounts — 31 December 1994

Group Profit and Loss Account (extract)
for the year ended 31st December 1994

	Note	1994 £M	1993 £M (Re-stated-see Accounting policies)
Turnover			
Continuing operations		**877.6**	766.0
Discontinued operations		**163.2**	364.7
	1(a)	**1,040.8**	1,130.7
Operating costs	2(a)	**(927.5)**	(1,025.5)
Operating profit			
Continuing operations		**109.6**	89.7
Discontinued operations		**3.7**	15.5
		113.3	105.2
Non operating items			
Continuing operations			
Profit on sale of properties		**–**	0.8
(Loss)/Profit on disposal of operations		**(1.6)**	0.1
Discontinued operations			
Profit on sale of properties		**–**	0.9
Costs of fundamental restructuring		**(4.4)**	(1.7)
Profit on ordinary activities before interest and taxation		**107.3**	105.3
Net interest expense	2(b)	**(14.3)**	(17.4)

Profit on ordinary activities before taxation	1(b)	**93.0**	87.9
Tax on profit on ordinary activities	3(a)	**(31.6)**	(27.3)
Profit on ordinary activities after taxation		**61.4**	60.6
Minority interests		**(0.4)**	(0.3)
Profit for the year		**61.0**	60.3
Dividends paid and proposed*	4		
Equity shareholders			
— ordinary shares		**(49.7)**	(60.5)
— demerger		**(224.0)**	–
Non-equity shareholders		–	(1.6)
Retained deficit		**(212.7)**	(1.8)

Movements in reserves are set out in Note 16.

Notes to the Accounts (extract)

2 PROFIT AND LOSS ACCOUNT (extract)

	Continuing £M	**Dis-continued £M**	**1994 Total £M**	Continuing £M	Dis-continued £M	1993 Total £M
(a) Operating costs						
Change in stocks of finished goods and work in progress	**17.6**	**5.8**	**23.4**	24.5	1.0	25.5
Own work capitalised	**(1.8)**	**(0.2)**	**(2.0)**	(1.6)	(0.8)	(2.4)
Other operating income	**(10.3)**	**(0.7)**	**(11.0)**	(5.1)	(1.6)	(6.7)
Raw materials and consumables	**163.0**	**54.7**	**217.7**	139.9	116.6	256.5
Other external charges	**317.1**	**42.1**	**359.2**	275.8	100.5	376.3
Employment costs (Note 6(b))	**210.3**	**41.6**	**251.9**	175.1	95.1	270.2
Depreciation of tangible fixed assets	**50.0**	**6.3**	**56.3**	46.5	16.3	62.8
Net income from interests in associated undertakings	**(0.7)**	**(0.4)**	**(1.1)**	(0.6)	(0.5)	(1.1)
Income from loan to unlisted undertakings	–	–	–	–	(0.1)	(0.1)
Operating lease rentals — property	**3.6**	**0.6**	**4.2**	4.2	1.2	5.4
plant and machinery	**8.4**	**3.4**	**11.8**	7.5	8.2	15.7

Hire of plant and machinery	**10.1**	**6.3**	**16.4**	9.3	13.1	22.4
Auditors' remuneration	**0.7**	–	**0.7**	0.8	0.2	1.0
	768.0	**159.5**	**927.5**	676.3	349.2	1,025.5

* Editorial note: for periods beginning on or after 1 January 2005, FRS 21 prohibits the recognition of proposed final dividends until they have been approved by shareholders at an AGM. Also, the legal requirement to show dividends in the profit and loss account no longer exists. The presentation of dividends is covered in chapter 23.

Parent's profit and loss account

4.122 When a parent company prepares consolidated financial statements in accordance with the Companies Act 2006, it is not required to include its own profit and loss account and related notes if the financial statements satisfy the following requirements:

- The notes to the parent company's individual balance sheet show the company's profit or loss for the financial year determined in accordance with the provisions of the Act. [CA06 Sec 408(1)(b)].
- The parent company's board of directors must approve the company's individual profit and loss account in accordance with the rules concerning approval of the company's financial statements. [CA06 Sec 408(3)].
- The notes to the financial statements disclose the fact that the parent company has taken advantage of this exemption. [CA06 Sec 408(4)].

4.123 Where the consolidated financial statements do not include the company's profit and loss account, it need not include certain supplementary information when presented to the Board for their approval. [CA06 Sec 408(2); SI 2008/410 Reg 3(2)]. The information that can be excluded is specified in section 411 of the Companies Act 2006 and in paragraphs 65 to 69 of Schedule 1 to SI 2008/410 and includes the following:

- Employee numbers and employee costs. [CA06 Sec 411].
- Interest and similar charges. [SI 2008/410 1 Sch 66].
- Detailed particulars concerning tax. [SI 2008/410 1 Sch 67].
- Disaggregated information concerning turnover. [SI 2008/410 1 Sch 68].
- Certain miscellaneous matters including:
  - The effect of including any preceding year items in the current year's profit and loss account.
  - Particulars of extraordinary income or extraordinary charges.
  - The effect of any exceptional items.

[SI 2008/410 1 Sch 69].

4.124 Suitable wording for a note to be included in the consolidated financial statements when the parent's profit and loss account is not reproduced would be:

Example

As permitted by section 408(3) of the Companies Act 2006, the parent company's individual profit and loss account has not been included in these financial statements. The parent company's profit for the financial year was £x (20XX: £y).

The notes to the balance sheet and the profit and loss account

General requirements of company law

4.125 Schedule 1 to SI 2008/410 requires companies to disclose considerable detail in the notes to their financial statements. The objects of the requirements are:

- To supplement the information given in the financial statements in respect of any particular items that are shown in either the balance sheet or the profit and loss account.
- To give details of anything else that is relevant, in the light of the information so given, to the assessment of the state of the company's affairs.
- To explain any particular circumstances that affect items shown in the profit and loss account.

[SI 2008/410 1 Sch 46, 65].

4.126 Any information that SI 2008/410 requires to be shown by way of a note to the financial statements may, alternatively, be shown in the company's profit or loss account or balance sheet. [SI 2008/410 1 Sch 42]. However, SI 2008/410 does not permit a company to use the directors' report as an alternative method of disclosure.

4.127 Schedule 4 to SI 2008/410 requires companies to disclose considerable detail about their investments in subsidiaries and other related undertakings. The Schedule sets out disclosures applying to all companies and then has separate sections for companies not required to prepare group accounts; companies required to prepare group accounts; and additional disclosures for banking companies and groups. The disclosures are grouped in the following categories:

- Subsidiaries included in consolidated financial statements (considered in chapter 24).
- Subsidiaries that are excluded from consolidation (considered in chapter 24).

- Disclosures about subsidiaries where the parent does not prepare consolidated financial statements (considered in chapter 24).

- Joint ventures, associated undertakings and other significant holdings (considered in chapter 27).

- Membership of certain undertakings, such as qualifying partnerships (considered in chapter 24).

4.128 Schedule 4 to SI 2008/410 also requires a subsidiary to disclose the name of its ultimate parent company and, if that company is incorporated outside the UK, the country in which it is incorporated should be stated (if known to the directors). This is considered in chapter 24.

4.129 Schedule 5 to SI 2008/410 sets out the disclosure requirements concerning directors' remuneration applying to all companies. In addition, Schedule 8 to SI 2008/410 sets out the disclosure requirements for a directors' remuneration report by quoted companies. These disclosures are considered in chapter 5 of the Manual of Accounting – Management reports and governance.

4.129.1 In addition, Schedule 1 to SI 2008/410 requires disclosure of particulars of material transactions that the company has entered into with related parties that have not been concluded under normal market conditions. The definition of related parties and the disclosure requirements in company law and in accounting standards (FRS 8) are dealt with in chapter 29.

4.130 The company law disclosure requirements for formats are supplemented by the requirements contained in individual accounting standards considered in the paragraphs that follow.

Additional statements required by FRS 3

4.131 FRS 3 requires two statements of a memorandum nature:

- A note of historical profits and losses should appear immediately after the profit and loss account or the statement of total recognised gains and losses. This note is required where assets have been revalued in the financial statements and there is a material difference between the results as disclosed in the profit and loss account and the results as they would have been reported on a pure historical cost basis. [FRS 3 para 26].

- A reconciliation of movements in shareholders' funds, providing a statement of all changes in shareholders' funds in the period, should be disclosed in a note or as a primary statement. This statement brings together the gains and losses for the period as reported in the primary financial statements, with other changes including dividends, new share capital issued and share capital redeemed. [FRS 3 para 28].

Where consolidated financial statements are presented, the note of historical profits and losses and the reconciliation of movements in shareholders' funds need only deal with the consolidated results, and not those of the parent company. These statements are considered in greater detail in chapter 8.

Compliance with accounting standards

4.132 Schedule 1 to SI 2008/410 requires companies to state whether the financial statements have been prepared in accordance with applicable accounting standards. In addition, if there are any material departures from these standards, the particulars and the reasons for the departure must be given. [SI 2008/410 1 Sch 45]. These requirements are dealt with in chapter 2.

True and fair override disclosures

4.133 Where a company departs from any of the accounting provisions of the Companies Act 2006 (or its supporting accounting regulations) in order to give a true and fair view, the Act requires that *"particulars of any such departure, the reasons for it and its effect must be given in a note to the accounts."* [CA06 Sec 396(5), 404(5)]. These requirements are dealt with in chapter 2.

Accounting policies

4.134 The notes to the financial statements must set out the accounting policies adopted by a company in determining the amounts to be included in the financial statements. [SI 2008/410 1 Sch 44]. In particular, this disclosure must include:

- The method of determining the provision both for depreciation and for diminution in the value of assets. [SI 2008/410 1 Sch 44].
- The method of translating foreign currency amounts into sterling. [SI 2008/410 1 Sch 70].

4.134.1 FRS 18, 'Accounting policies', requires disclosure of each material accounting policy, to enable users to understand the accounting policies adopted and how they have been applied. The disclosure of accounting policies is considered in chapter 2.

4.135 Many companies disclose their accounting policies as a separate statement that they locate before the remainder of the notes. This is generally accepted accounting practice and it has the advantage that the accounting policies are given more prominence and are not lost within the individual notes to the financial statements. Where this treatment is adopted, to ensure that the accounting policies are shown in compliance with company law, the page numbers that identify the financial statements for the purpose of the directors' adoption of the financial statements, and for the purpose of the auditors' opinion, should include the statement of accounting policies.

4.136 Where a company's financial statements have been drawn up under the alternative accounting rules in Schedule 1 to SI 2008/410, the accounting convention used should be stated in those financial statements. The company should also refer to the specific policy for each item that it has accounted for under the alternative rules and this disclosure would normally be made as part of the company's accounting policies. [SI 2008/410 1 Sch 34(2)].

Financial instruments

4.137 Schedule 1 to SI 2008/410 imposes additional disclosure requirements in respect of financial instruments. The nature of the disclosure requirements varies depending on whether the company has adopted fair value accounting; these disclosure requirements are considered in detail in chapter 6.

Reserves and dividends

4.138 Disclosure is required in the notes to the financial statements of:

- Any amount set aside or proposed to be set aside to, or withdrawn or proposed to be withdrawn from, reserves.
- The aggregate amount of dividends paid in the financial year (other than those for which a liability existed at the immediately preceding balance sheet date).
- The aggregate amount of dividends that the company is liable to pay at the balance sheet date.
- The aggregate amount of dividends that are proposed before the date of approval of the accounts, and not otherwise required to be disclosed.

[SI 2008/410 1 Sch 43].

Off-balance sheet arrangements

4.139 Following the transposition into UK law of the requirements of the EU Corporate Reporting Directive (2006/46/EC)('the Directive'), the Companies Act 2006 requires the disclosure of 'off-balance sheet arrangements' for financial years beginning on or after 6 April 2008. The premise underlying the new disclosure requirement is that certain arrangements a company undertakes may have a material impact on the company, but may not be included in the company's balance sheet. Consequently, if a company is or has been party to arrangements that are not reflected in its balance sheet, and the risks or benefits are material, the company should disclose:

- the nature and business purpose of the arrangements; and
- the financial impact of the arrangements on the company, to the extent necessary for enabling the company's financial position to be assessed.

[CA06 Sec 410A].

4.139.1 When the company belongs to a group, the group's financial position as a whole may also be affected. Consequently, aggregated disclosures have to be made in the notes to the consolidated financial statements.

4.139.2 Application guidance from the BIS (formerly BERR) draws attention to Recital (9) to the Directive which states:

> *"Such off-balance-sheet arrangements could be any transactions or agreements which companies may have with entities, even unincorporated ones, that are not included in the balance sheet. Such off-balance sheet arrangements may be associated with the creation or use of one or more Special Purpose Entities (SPEs) and offshore activities designed to address, inter alia, economic, legal, tax or accounting objectives. Examples of such off-balance-sheet arrangements include risk and benefit-sharing arrangements or obligations arising from a contract such as debt factoring, combined sale and repurchase agreements, consignment stock arrangements, take or pay arrangements, securitisation arranged through separate companies and unincorporated entities, pledged assets, operating leasing arrangements, outsourcing and the like. Appropriate disclosure of the material risks and benefits of such arrangements that are not included in the balance sheet should be set out in the notes to the accounts or the consolidated accounts."*

4.139.3 The term 'arrangements' is undefined, although Recital (9) to the Directive gives some examples of 'arrangements', the first sentence is very broad and could capture all executory contracts. The examples are not an exclusive list. Consequently, there is a danger that some companies may innocently provide unstructured disclosures covering large volumes of information (for example, purchase orders), that are really intended to be outside the scope (if that were made clear) of the legislation. Such a company would nevertheless appear to be compliant with the legislation.

4.139.4 The issue was raised with the UITF, which recognised the concern regarding the lack of clarity in the disclosure requirement, but stated in July 2008 that it could not issue an Abstract in absence of a definition of 'arrangement'. The UITF stated:

> *"(i) when a company provides disclosures, it should consider the types of transactions envisaged by the EC (as quoted above) and the aim of the legislation;*
>
> *(ii) the disclosure requirement applies only where, at the balance sheet date, the risks or benefits arising from arrangements are material;*
>
> *(iii) disclosure need only be given to the extent necessary for enabling the financial position of the company to be assessed; and*
>
> *(iv) some accounting standards already require some disclosures that address items not necessarily included in the balance sheet but*

companies will need to consider whether arrangements outside the scope of those standards will require disclosure."

4.139.5 We consider that, in the main, UK GAAP goes well beyond the minimum requirements of the law in ensuring that assets and liabilities are not inappropriately excluded from the balance sheet. It also imposes disclosure requirements on some types of arrangements, which are not included in the balance sheet, such as operating leases and contingent liabilities. Therefore, in most cases, compliance with UK GAAP should be sufficient to ensure compliance with the law. However, accounting standards do not necessarily provide for all circumstances and, as such, entities should consider making disclosures where, for example, they have had discussions with their auditors about off-balance sheet implications of transactions that their companies undertake or whether entities should be consolidated. In this respect, compliance with the requirements of FRS 5, 'Reporting the substance of transactions', (dealt with in chapter 3) should assist in formulating an appropriate disclosure that meets the legal requirement. In particular, paragraph 30 of FRS 5 requires that disclosure of a transaction in the financial statements, whether or not it has resulted in assets or liabilities being recognised, should be sufficient to enable the user of the financial statements to understand its commercial effect.

4.139.6 Furthermore, the experience from the 'credit crunch' of recent years and the ensuing problems with liquidity in the markets has highlighted concerns about latent risks and exposures that had not previously been considered an issue. Concerns have focused on, amongst others, unconsolidated special purpose entities, liquidity facilities, loan commitments, guarantees and derivatives. In meeting the disclosure requirement on off-balance sheet arrangements, entities may need to consider a broader concept of financial impact of its off-balance sheet arrangements, in terms of, for example, liquidity, capital resources and credit risk.

Summary financial statements

4.140 The Companies Act 2006 permits companies, subject to certain conditions, to send summary financial statements to members in place of full financial statements. [CA06 Secs 426 to 429]. The 2006 Act contains little of the detailed requirements surrounding summary financial statements: instead this is the subject of SI 2008/374, 'The Companies (Summary Financial Statement) Regulations 2008'. The conditions that must be complied with, together with the form and content of the statements, are considered in chapter 8 of the Manual of Accounting – Management reports and governance.

Format for small companies

4.141 A separate regime applies for companies and groups that qualify as small under the Companies Act 2006. SI 2008/409, 'The Small Companies and Groups (Accounts and Directors' Report) Regulations 2008', sets out the requirements on the detailed format and content of the accounts and directors' report of small companies. Where a small company is also the parent company of a small group, the parent company is not required to prepare consolidated financial statements, but can opt to do so. [CA06 Sec 398]. The form and content of small company financial statements are considered in chapter 32.

[The next paragraph is 4.143.]

Listed companies' historical summaries

4.143 Although company law does not require a company to include a historical summary of information in its financial statements, many companies do so. This practice arose because the chairman of the Stock Exchange wrote to all listed companies in 1964 recommending that they should include a ten-year historical summary in their annual financial statements. Disclosure of a historical summary has never become a requirement, but it has become well established practice, although most companies give a historical summary for a shorter period such as five years.

4.144 There is no set format for historical summaries, but the type of information that listed companies normally give in them is as follows:

Balance sheet

- Tangible assets.
- Other assets.
- Net borrowings.
- Capital and reserves.
- Minority interests.

Profit and loss account

- Turnover.
- Operating profit.
- Interest.
- Profit on ordinary activities before taxation.
- Taxation.
- Profit after taxation.
- Minority interests.
- Ordinary dividends and retained earnings.

Statistical information

- Earnings per share.
- Dividends per ordinary share.
- Dividend cover.
- Return on capital employed.

4.145 The historical summary will normally show the actual figures that were reported for each year. However, in certain situations, the reported figures for earlier years may need to be adjusted. The circumstances where adjustments may be necessary are as follows:

- Where there is a change in accounting policy, FRS 3 requires the comparative figures for the preceding period to be restated if this is necessary to ensure that the reported figures for each year are stated on a consistent basis. In historical summaries, the figures for each year would usually be restated if it is practical to do so; it should also be made clear which figures have been restated. If the figures have not been restated, then this fact should be disclosed.
- Where the results of operations are shown separately as discontinued in a financial year, FRS 3 requires the comparative profit and loss account figures to be adjusted to show those discontinued operations separately. In historical summaries, the figures for each previous year would usually also be adjusted where it is practical to do so; thus the results attributable to continuing operations would relate to operations that are currently continuing.
- Where fundamental errors have been corrected by a prior year adjustment, then the historical summary should be changed and again it should be made clear which figures have been restated.
- Earnings per share figures that are reported should be amended to reflect any:
  - New equity shares that have been issued by capitalising reserves.
  - Equity shares that have been split into shares of a lower nominal value.
  - New equity shares that have been issued by way of rights issues.
- Dividends per share should also be adjusted where there have been changes in the number of equity shares in issue due to capitalisation of reserves, a rights issue, or a split in the nominal value of shares in issue.

4.146 Because an historical summary is not a requirement of company law or of accounting standards, and it is not required in order for the financial statements to show a true and fair view, the auditors do not need to report on it. They should, however, read such information and, if they identify any apparent misstatements or inconsistencies with the audited financial statements, should take appropriate action. [ISA (UK & Ire) 720].

Pro forma financial statements

4.147 Some companies include, as additional information, *pro forma* balance sheet or profit and loss information where this assists disclosure about the financial effect of certain significant post balance sheet events. Such events are those classified as non-adjusting events under FRS 21, 'Events after the balance sheet date', that is, they do not result in changes to the amounts recognised in financial statements but they are so significant to the company that disclosure of their financial effect may be required. Examples include:

- Material business disposals occurring after the year end.
- Material business acquisitions.
- Financial reconstructions.

4.148 In some cases. *pro forma* summarised balance sheets or profit and loss accounts are presented as part of the notes to the financial statements disclosing the effect of a post balance sheet event. In other cases, the *pro forma* information is presented in the financial review in the front half of the annual report, to supplement the FRS 21 disclosure given in the notes to the financial statements.

4.149 *Pro forma* financial statements are not used exclusively in connection with post balance sheet events. Other reasons may include: presenting a continuous track record where a group reorganisation has occurred; presenting annualised figures where a company has changed its accounting reference period; and presenting financial statements that show the effect of eliminating from comparative figures the results and balance sheets of operations that have been demerged during the period.

Chapter 5

Other profit and loss account items

Chapter 5

Other profit and loss account items

Introduction

5.1 The profit and loss account is one of the primary statements that a company must include in its financial statements. Under company law, the profit and loss account has to comply with one of four alternative formats set out in Schedule 1 to SI 2008/410, 'The Large and Medium-sized Companies and Groups (Accounts and Reports) Regulations 2008': Formats 1 and 2 are vertical presentations; and Formats 3 and 4 show charges separately from income. These formats are set out and discussed in chapter 4. The format a company chooses can be significant because, depending on the format, some of the information the company discloses in its profit and loss account will be different. Some of the items that are discussed below may relate only to one pair of formats.

5.2 Chapter 9 deals with the measurement and disclosure of items included under the main revenue headings in the profit and loss account. This chapter considers other categories of income and expenditure that are recognised in the profit and loss account, insofar as they are not dealt with separately in other chapters, together with supplementary disclosure requirements.

5.3 Of the items included in the company law formats, only 'turnover' (see chapter 9) and 'staff costs' (see para 5.15 below) are actually defined in the legislation. The allocation to statutory captions of certain other items of income and expenditure requires companies to reach internal definitions and interpretations in order to achieve reasonable and consistent classifications.

Cost of sales, distribution costs and administrative expenses

5.4 These headings from Formats 1 and 3, which require the classification of expenditure by its function, give rise to many questions concerning the allocation of costs and overheads. The following lists are intended to provide guidance as to the items that may be included under each heading.

5.5 *Cost of sales* will normally include:

- Opening (less closing) stocks.
- Direct materials.
- Other external charges (such as the hire of plant and machinery or the cost of casual labour used in the productive process).
- Direct labour.

- All direct production overheads, including depreciation, and indirect overheads that can reasonably be allocated to the production function.
- Product development expenditure.
- Cash discounts received on 'cost of sales' expenditure (this is not an offsetting, but an effective reduction in the purchase price of an item).
- Stock write-downs.

5.6 *Distribution costs* are generally interpreted more widely than the name suggests and often include selling and marketing costs. Items normally included in this caption comprise:

- Payroll costs of the sales, marketing and distribution functions.
- Advertising.
- Salesperson's travel and entertaining.
- Warehouse costs for finished goods.
- Transport costs concerning the distribution of finished goods.
- All costs of maintaining sales outlets.
- Agents' commission payable.

5.7 *Administrative expenses* will normally include:

- The costs of general management.
- All costs of maintaining the administration buildings.
- Professional costs.
- Research and development expenditure that is not allocated to cost of sales (sometimes this is shown as a separate item).

5.8 If Format 1 or 3 is adopted, charges for depreciation or the diminution in value of assets have to be analysed under the above headings. [SI 2008/410 1 Sch Profit and loss account formats note 14]. The type of analysis will depend on the function of the related assets (see also para 5.29).

5.9 In some specific instances, the allocation of costs between the headings proposed above may not be appropriate. For example, in the context of a mail-order company, agents' commission payable may be regarded as a cost of sale rather than as a distribution cost.

5.10 The way in which a company analyses its costs will depend very much on the nature of its business. Where a company incurs significant operating expenses that it considers do not fall under any one of the headings 'cost of sales', 'distribution costs' and 'administrative expenses', there is nothing to prevent the company including an additional item for these expenses in Formats 1 or 3. The overriding consideration is that a company should analyse its operating expenses consistently from year to year. Exceptional items included in operating profit should be included within the statutory line item to which they relate. [FRS 3 para 19].

5.11 Some companies have adapted the statutory line items or shown additional items. However, these companies are in a minority. This is probably because the items are general enough to apply to most companies' expenditure. Examples of adaptations and additional items that companies have used in their financial statements are shown below.

Examples of adaptation of items:

- Selling and distribution costs.
- Marketing, selling and distribution costs.
- Distribution costs, including marketing.
- Administrative and selling expenses.
- Selling and general administration expenses.

Examples of additional items:

- Sales commission (shown in addition to distribution costs).
- Research and development.

5.12 Table 5.1 shows an extract from the profit and loss account of Rolls-Royce plc, where the analysis of operating expenses has been adapted (based on Format 1).

Table 5.1 — Adaptation of analysis of operating expenses

Rolls-Royce plc — Annual Report — 31 December 1994

Group Profit and Loss Account (extract)
for the year ended December 31, 1994

	Notes	1994 £m	1993 £m
Turnover	2	3,163	3,518
Cost of sales	3	(2,646)	(2,995)
Gross profit		517	523
Commercial, marketing and product support costs		(117)	(105)
General and administrative costs		(91)	(89)
Research and development (net)		(218)	(253)
Operating profit		91	76

Gross profit

5.13 The gross profit or loss has to be shown as a separate item in Format 1, and it can be readily ascertained from the items that are disclosed in Format 3. Formats 2 and 4 analyse expenditure in a different manner, that is, by its nature rather than its function and, as a result, gross profit is not disclosed.

Own work capitalised

5.14 Where a company has constructed some of its own tangible fixed assets, and it adopts either Format 2 or Format 4 (which classify expenses by nature) for its profit and loss account, it should include the costs of direct materials, direct labour and overheads it has capitalised as a credit under the heading 'own work capitalised'. The costs of direct materials, direct labour and overheads are charged in the profit and loss account, by including these amounts under the relevant expenditure headings. The amount capitalised is then credited in the profit and loss account as own work capitalised and it is debited to tangible fixed assets. Thus, items such as raw material costs in the profit and loss account will include the costs connected with such work.

Staff costs and numbers

Employee costs

5.15 Disclosure is required in the financial statements of the costs a company incurs in respect of the persons it employs under contracts of service. [CA06 Sec 411]. A contract *of service* (or a contract of employment as it is also called) is an agreement under which the employer agrees to employ the employee for a wage or a salary in return for the employee's labour. This agreement must be made in writing. However, self-employed persons are not employed by the company, but merely have contracts to perform specific services for that company. The costs of self-employed people should normally be excluded from staff costs, because their contracts will be contracts *for services*. Examples of such persons are consultants and contractors. Their costs should normally be included under 'other external charges' in Formats 2 and 4, and under an appropriate functional expense heading in Formats 1 and 3.

5.16 The item 'staff costs' does not appear in the profit and loss account Formats 1 and 3. This is because expenses are classified in these formats by function, rather than by type. However, where a company prepares its profit and loss account in the style of either Format 1 or Format 3, it has to disclose, in the notes to the profit and loss account, the equivalent information to that given when Formats 2 and 4 are used.

5.17 In summary, the legal requirement in section 411 of the Companies Act 2006 is that either the profit and loss account format or the notes should disclose, in aggregate, each of the following amounts:

- The wages and salaries that were either paid to employees or are payable to them, in respect of the financial year in question.
- Social security costs that the company has incurred on behalf of its employees. For this purpose, social security costs are any contributions the company makes to any social security or pension scheme, or fund or arrangement that the State runs. These costs will include the employer's national insurance contributions.
- Other pension costs the company has incurred on behalf of employees. For this purpose, pension costs include:
  - Any costs incurred by the company in respect of any non-State occupational pension scheme that is established to provide pensions for employees or past employees.
  - Any sums the company has set aside for the future payment of pensions directly to current or former employees.
  - Any amounts the company has paid in respect of pensions, without those amounts having first been so set aside.

Pension costs will, therefore, include the cost in respect of the company's participation in any pension scheme other than the State scheme. [CA06 Sec 411; SI 2008/410 10 Sch 14].

5.17.1 Schedule 10 to SI 2008/410 says that wages and salaries should be determined by reference to either the payments the company makes or the costs it incurs in respect of all persons it employs. [SI 2008/410 10 Sch 14(3)].

5.18 An illustration of the company law disclosure requirements for employee costs and numbers is given in Table 5.2. This disclosure was given under the Companies Act 1985, but the requirements are similar, in this respect, under SI 2008/410.

Table 5.2 — Company law disclosure requirements for employee costs and numbers

Scottish & Newcastle plc — Annual Report and Accounts — 2 May 1999

Notes to the Accounts (extract)

5 EMPLOYEE COSTS AND NUMBERS

(i) Employee costs	**1999 £m**	**1998 £m**
Wages and salaries	**463.4**	463.3
Social security costs	**47.3**	44.9
Other pension costs	**31.3**	30.0
Employee profit sharing scheme	**–**	8.5
	542.0	546.7

(ii) Number of employees	1999	1998
The average numbers of employees during the year were:		
Retail	**27,290**	26,851
Beer	**7,080**	7,103
Leisure	**12,468**	11,964
Group central functions	**283**	281
	47,121	46,199

[The next paragraph is 5.21.]

Average number of employees

5.21 In addition to requiring that the notes to the profit and loss account should disclose employee costs, the legislation requires that those notes should include information in respect of the number of employees.

5.22 The two disclosures that the notes must contain in connection with the number of employees are:

- The average number of employees in the financial year. The number should be calculated by:
  - Ascertaining the number of persons employed under contract of service, whether full-time or part-time, for each month in the year.
  - Adding together all the monthly numbers.
  - Dividing the resulting total by the number of months in the financial year.

  The average number of employees includes persons who work wholly or mainly overseas, as well as persons who work in the UK.
- The average number of employees by category. This number should be calculated by applying the same method of calculation as outlined above to each category of employees. For this purpose, the categories of persons employed are to be such categories as the directors select, having regard to the way in which the company's activities are organised.

[CA06 Sec 411].

5.23 Because the guidance on how to select categories is rather vague, directors of companies have chosen a variety of different categories. Methods have included splitting between part-time employees and full-time employees; between hourly-paid, weekly-paid and salaried staff; between production, sales and administration staff; and between staff employed in different geographical areas. If the company presents segmental information in accordance with SSAP 25, 'Segmental reporting', it may be appropriate to give the employee numbers on the basis of the segments presented.

These disclosure requirements are illustrated in Table 5.2.

5.24 There is no exemption from disclosure where (for example) a company is a wholly-owned subsidiary.

Directors

5.25 Directors who have a contract of service (that is, an employment contract) with the company are to be regarded as employees. Therefore, their salaries, their social security costs and their other pension costs must be included in the required analysis under staff costs, even if a note is included stating that directors' emoluments are shown elsewhere. In addition, directors' emoluments have also to be disclosed separately in accordance with the requirements of Schedule 5 to SI 2008/410. In that disclosure, their emoluments will exclude those social security costs that the company bears, because such amounts are neither paid to the director nor paid in respect of a pension scheme.

5.26 In contrast to payments under a contract *of service* (where the director is employed), amounts paid to directors under contracts *for services* (equivalent to the director being self-employed) should not be disclosed under staff costs. But, under Schedule 5 to SI 2008/410, they should be disclosed as directors' emoluments in the notes to the financial statements. Whether a director's contract with the company is a *contract of service* or a contract *for services* is a question of fact in each circumstance. Usually, however, executive directors will have contracts *of service*, whereas non-executive directors will have contracts *for services*. Contracts *for services* might include, for example, consultancy arrangements.

5.26.1 Directors' emoluments are dealt with further in chapter 5 of the Manual of Accounting — Management reports and governance.

Disclosures by groups

5.26.2 Where a parent company prepares group financial statements, the disclosure of staff costs and numbers is required to be presented for the consolidated group.

5.26.3 For financial years beginning on or after 6 April 2008, under Part 15 of the Companies Act 2006, where a parent company prepares group financial statements, a parent company is no longer required to present particulars of employee numbers and costs for the company. This is the case regardless of whether the parent company takes the exemption from presenting its own profit and loss account. [CA06 Sec 408].

Practical problems relating to employee costs

5.27 In practice, there may be problems in deciding on the employees to include in staff costs and in identifying the average number of employees. One of the most frequent problems arises where employees clearly work for one company, but their contracts of service are with another company (for example, the holding company). Also, further complications arise when that other company pays the wages and salaries of these employees. If section 411 of the Companies Act 2006 was strictly interpreted in these situations, it could lead to the disclosure of misleading information in the financial statements. Accordingly, as well as giving the statutory disclosures, a company may need to give additional information to enable its financial statements to give a true and fair view.

5.28 Some of the more common problems that arise in this respect are considered in the examples that follow:

Example 1 – Contracts of service with another group company

Employees work full time for, and are paid by, a subsidiary company, but their contracts of service are with the parent company.

It would be misleading if there were no disclosure of staff costs or numbers in the subsidiary company's financial statements. Consequently, the wages and salaries the subsidiary company pays to those employees should be disclosed as 'staff costs' in its financial statements and those employees should be included in the calculation of the average number of staff employed.

The notes to the subsidiary company's financial statements should explain that those staff have contracts of service with another group company. They should also explain why their remuneration and average number are disclosed in the financial statements.

The parent company's consolidated financial statements normally will not be affected (unless the subsidiary is not included in the consolidated financial statements), because they will show the average number of employees and staff costs of the group as a whole, as well as those of the parent company separately. Consequently, no explanatory note should be necessary in the parent company's financial statements.

(However, if the contracts of service are with a fellow subsidiary company, then that fellow subsidiary company's financial statements should include those employees in the calculation of staff costs and average number of employees and explain that certain employees having service contracts with the company work for and are paid for wholly by a fellow subsidiary company.)

Example 2 – Subsidiary company incurs management charge

Employees work full time for the subsidiary company, but they are not paid by the subsidiary company and they do not have service contracts with it. However, the subsidiary company bears a management charge for their services from the company that pays the employees and it can ascertain the proportion of the management charge that relates to staff costs.

Again, in this situation it could be misleading if the subsidiary company's financial statements disclosed no information about staff costs or numbers. Accordingly, the proportion of the management charge that relates to staff costs should be disclosed in the subsidiary company's financial statements as 'staff costs'. The employees concerned should be included in the calculation of the average number of employees. The notes to the financial statements should explain that the employees do not have contracts of service with the company, and they should also explain why their costs and average number are disclosed in the financial statements.

(If the contracts of service are with, and the employees are paid by, a fellow subsidiary company then that fellow subsidiary's financial statements should disclose the staff costs and average number in respect of all its employees and give details regarding the staff costs that are recharged to the fellow subsidiary.)

Example 3 – Subsidiary company incurs non-specific management charge

The facts are the same as in example 2 except that the subsidiary company is unable to break down the management charge and ascertain the part of it that relates to staff costs.

The notes to the subsidiary company's financial statements should explain that the employees' contracts of service are with the parent company and that their remuneration is included in the parent company's financial statements. The notes should also explain that the management charge that the parent company makes includes the cost of these employees, but that it is impossible to ascertain separately the element of the management charge that relates to staff costs.

(If the employees' contracts of service are with a fellow subsidiary, rather than with the parent company, and that fellow subsidiary also pays the employees, the fellow subsidiary's financial statements should disclose the employees' remuneration in its staff costs and should also include the employees in the calculation of average number employed. The notes should explain that these employees work for a fellow subsidiary company and that the company recharges the cost of their employment to that fellow subsidiary as part of a management charge.)

Example 4 – Subsidiary company does not incur management charge

The facts are the same as in example 2 above, except that no management charge is made for the employees' services. This will often apply where staff work either full-time or part-time for small companies.

In this situation, the notes to the subsidiary company's financial statements should explain that the company is not charged for the services provided by the employees that work for it. If appropriate, the notes should also indicate that the cost of these employees and their average number are included in the parent company's consolidated financial statements.

(Once again, if it is a fellow subsidiary that employs and pays the employees, its financial statements should include the cost of these employees in its staff costs and should include these employees in the average number employed. If appropriate, the notes to the financial statements should explain that these employees work for a fellow subsidiary company, but that no management charge is made for their services to that company.)

Depreciation (including other amounts written off assets)

5.29 Where the company prepares its profit and loss account in accordance with either Format 1 or Format 3, expenses are classified by function. Consequently, any provisions for either depreciation or the diminution in value of tangible and intangible fixed assets will not be disclosed in the profit and loss account format. Accordingly, SI 2008/410 requires that this information must be disclosed separately in the notes to the financial statements. [SI 2008/410 1 Sch Profit and loss account formats note 17].

5.30 In addition, company law requires separate disclosure of the aggregate amount of:

- Any provision against a fixed asset investment for diminution in value.
- Any provision against a fixed asset for permanent diminution in value.
- Any write back of such provisions which are no longer necessary.

[SI 2008/410 1 Sch 19, 20].

5.31 Accounting for depreciation and diminutions in value of fixed assets (under both the historical cost and alternative accounting rules) is considered fully in chapters 16 and 18.

Other operating charges (including other external charges)

5.32 The relevant formats (Formats 2 and 4) place 'other external charges' next to 'raw materials and consumables' under a single item number. Therefore, such charges are likely to include any production costs from external sources that are not included under other headings (for example, equipment rentals and the costs of subcontractors).

5.33 'Other operating charges' is a separate line item which tends to be a residual class of all charges relating to the trading activities of a business that do not fall into any other category. Losses on exchange may also be included under this heading (except for losses that are required by SSAP 20, 'Foreign currency translation', or FRS 23, 'The effects of changes in foreign exchange rates', to be taken directly to reserves).

5.34 In practice, the distinction between 'other external charges' and 'other operating charges' is blurred. Some companies do not attempt to make a distinction, and include only one heading to cover all residual operating costs. Table 5.3 gives an example in which a company discloses no 'other external charges', but analyses residual operating expenses under the heading 'other operating charges'.

Table 5.3 — Analysis of other operating charges

British Gas plc — Annual Report and Accounts — 31 December 1994

Notes to the accounts (extract)
4 Operating costs (extract)

	1994			
	Continuing operations £m	Other Discontinued operations £m	Exceptional charges £m	Total £m
Other operating charges:				
Other exploration expenditure	88	–	–	88
Monetary working capital adjustment	24			24
Lease rentals:				
Plant, machinery and equipment	24	–	–	24
Other assets	38	–	–	38
Research and development	74	1	–	75
Environmental costs	–	–	90	90
Other expenses	1,550	31	105	1,686

Income from investments

5.35 Each of the four profit and loss account formats for individual companies contain the same four investment income captions.

- Income from shares in group undertakings.
- Income from participating interests.
- Income from other fixed asset investments.
- Other interest receivable and similar income.

5.36 SI 2008/410 also requires the last two items referred to above, that is income from other fixed asset investments and other interest, to be split between that derived from group undertakings and that derived from other sources. [Note 15 to the profit and loss account formats].

[The next paragraph is 5.39.]

5.39 Dividends received and receivable from both subsidiary and fellow subsidiary companies will be included in 'income from shares in group undertakings'. In a group's consolidated financial statements, this line will appear only if dividends are received or receivable from subsidiaries that have not been consolidated. The accounting for dividend income is dealt with in chapter 9.

5.40 In an investing company's individual profit and loss account 'Income from participating interests' will include, for example, income from the following undertakings in which the investing company holds 20 per cent or more of the shares:

- Income from bodies corporate (including dividends received from associated undertakings).
- Share of profits from partnerships.
- Share of profits from unincorporated associations carrying on a trade or business, with or without a profit.

5.41 Chapter 27 explains the meaning of participating interests and associated undertakings and describes the accounting treatment of income from interests in associated undertakings in consolidated financial statements.

Interest payable and similar charges

5.42 'Interest payable and similar charges' appears as a separate item in all the profit and loss account formats. Apart from interest, the caption may include other finance costs such as:

- Accrued discounts in respect of zero coupon and deep discount bonds.
- Accrual of the premium payable on the redemption of debt.
- Dividends on preference shares that are classified as liabilities under FRS 25, 'Financial instruments: Presentation'.

5.43 Company law requires certain additional disclosures in respect of interest. Note 16 to the profit and loss account formats requires that interest payable to group undertakings must be disclosed separately. In addition, disclosure is required of the amount of the interest on or any similar charges in respect of:

- Bank loans and overdrafts.
- Loans of any other kind made to the company.

[SI 2008/410 1 Sch 66(1)].

5.44 The requirement to give the above analyses does not apply to either interest or charges on loans from group undertakings. But it does apply to interest or charges on all other loans, whether or not these are made on the security of a debenture. [SI 2008/410 1 Sch 66(2)].

Auditors' remuneration

5.45 The Companies Act 2006 requires separate disclosure of the amounts of remuneration receivable by a company's auditors, in their capacity as auditors and also in respect of services other than audit. The legal requirements are set out in The Companies (Disclosure of Auditor Remuneration and Liability Limitation Agreements) Regulations 2008 (SI 2008/489).

5.46 The 2008 Regulations have been revised by The Companies (Disclosure of Auditor Remuneration and Liability Limitation Agreements) (Amendment) Regulations 2011 (SI 2011/2198). The amendments apply for financial years beginning on or after 1st October 2011(with early adoption permitted from 1 October 2011 for financial years beginning before that date).

5.47 The analysis of fees receivable by auditors should be given in the notes to the financial statements. Disclosure is required of the amount of:

- Fees payable to the company's auditor for the statutory audit of the company's annual financial statements. Under the 2011 revised regulations, this disclosure also includes fees payable to associates of the company's auditors (as defined in the regulations).
- Fees payable to the company's auditor and its associates for the audits of the company's 'associates' (which includes its subsidiaries in this context) and for other services provided to the company and its associates (analysed between specified types of service). The types of other services required to be disclosed have been amended in the 2011 revised regulations.
- Fees payable to the company's auditor and its associates for audit and other services (analysed by specified type of services) supplied to the company's associated pension schemes. In respect of other services, this is irrespective of whether or not the company's auditor or any of its associates are the auditors of the pension schemes.

[SI 2008/489 Reg 5].

5.48 Remuneration includes payments in respect of expenses and benefits in kind. The nature and estimated money value of benefits in kind should be disclosed. [SI 2008/489 Reg 5].

5.49 The disclosure requirements apply irrespective of the accounting framework (IFRS or UK GAAP) used in preparing the financial statements and apply to all financial statements (individual and consolidated), except that the disclosures in respect of fees for 'other services' are not required to be given by:

- A small or medium-sized company as defined by the Companies Act 2006.
- A small or medium-sized group.
- A subsidiary company in its individual financial statements, whose parent is required to, and does, prepare consolidated financial statements in accordance with the Companies Act 2006 and the subsidiary company is included in the consolidation.

- A parent company in its individual financial statements, where the company to required to, and does, prepare consolidated financial statements in accordance with the Companies Act 2006.

[SI 2008/489 Regs 4,5,6].

5.50 Guidance on the 2008 Regulations is given in Tech 06/06 (revised), 'Disclosure of auditor remuneration', published by the ICAEW. The requirements for the disclosure of auditor remuneration are dealt with in a separate electronic chapter on PwCinform.com.

Chapter 6

Financial instruments including derivatives

Chapter 6

Financial instruments including derivatives

Introduction

6.1 Over the past ten years or so, the use of financial instruments by companies and the complexity of those instruments have increased remarkably. Many large companies now actively manage their risk using swaps, forward contracts and other such derivatives, but until recently the financial statements of such companies often gave very limited disclosure of the use of these techniques.

6.2 There have been a number of examples of what were perceived to be conservatively-managed organisations incurring substantial losses because they failed to appreciate, monitor and control the risks created by the use of financial instruments. Such problems gave financial instruments, and in particular derivatives, a reputation for increasing risk when in fact many are designed specifically to reduce or eliminate exposure to risk and achieve this when used properly.

6.3 At the heart of these well-publicised losses were internal control failures. One of the responses of this has been a call for tighter accounting rules to be set for financial instruments, in particular, accounting for derivative instruments.

6.4 Prior to 2004, there has been no recognition and measurement standard for financial instruments under UK GAAP. UK GAAP simply consisted of FRS 4, 'Capital instruments', which was published in December 1993 and FRS 13, 'Derivatives and other financial instruments: disclosures', which was published in September 1998. FRS 4 regulated how capital instruments (a sub-set of financial instruments) should be classified and presented in the financial statements of the issuing entity. FRS 13, the disclosure standard, requires entities within its scope (primarily listed companies and banks) to provide both narrative and numerical disclosures relating to financial instruments.

6.5 It was not until December 2004 that the ASB, as part of its convergence agenda to bring international standards into the UK reporting framework, published FRS 25, 'Financial instruments: Disclosure and presentation', and FRS 26, 'Financial instruments: Measurement'. These standards brought most of the requirements of the equivalent international standards IAS 32 and IAS 39, respectively, into UK GAAP. A year later, in December 2005, FRS 29, 'Financial instruments: Disclosures', was published. FRS 29 replicates the requirements of the equivalent international standard IFRS 7 and locates in one place all of the disclosures relating to financial instruments. As a result, the title of FRS 25 was amended to FRS 25, 'Financial instruments: Presentation'. Subsequently, in April 2006, the ASB amended FRS 26 to include all of IAS 39's recognition and derecognition requirements. At that time the title of the standard changed to FRS 26, 'Financial instruments: Recognition and measurement'.

6.6 After a period of transition, the three standards, FRS 25, FRS 26 and FRS 29 now represent a suite of new accounting standards on financial instruments. The old standards, FRS 4 was amended (see para 6.268) and FRS 13 is virtually abolished in all cases, except for a small number of companies.

6.7 FRS 26 requires some financial instruments (including derivatives) to be measured at fair value with movements reported in the profit and loss account. However, the Companies Act did not permit companies, other than banking and insurance companies, to measure financial instruments at fair value, except by using a true and fair override. Hence, for UK companies, particularly listed companies that are required by EU Regulation to prepare their consolidated financial statements from 2005 using IFRS, rather than national GAAP, changes to the Companies Act were required. The amendment was made in November 2004 with the publication of SI 2004/2947, 'The Companies Act 1985 (International Accounting Standards and Other Accounting Amendments) Regulations 2004', that added a new Section D to Schedule 4 of the Companies Act 1985. Section D came into effect for accounting periods commencing on or after 1 January 2005. Amongst other changes, the amendment *permits* companies to apply fair value accounting to some of their financial instruments, provided that fair value can be determined reliably. Following changes to the Companies Act 1985, the fair value accounting rules are now dealt with in SI 2008/410, 'The Large and Medium-sized Companies and Groups (Accounts and Reports) Regulations 2008'.

6.8 Due to the extent of the changes to UK GAAP in the area of financial instruments, there is now the old world of FRS 4 that generally applies to entities that do not fair value their financial instruments and FRS 13 that continues to apply to a small number of entities; and the new world of FRS 25, FRS 26 and FRS 29. This chapter deals with the provisions of FRS 13, FRS 4 and the requirements under the Companies Act that apply to all companies in respect of financial instruments and investments. The chapter also covers FRS 25, FRS 26 and FRS 29. However, as these standards are replicas of the international standards on financial instruments (IAS 32, IAS 39 and IFRS 7), the guidance is primarily dealt with in Manual of accounting – Financial instruments. Annex 1 to this chapter includes examples of the disclosures required by FRS 13. Accordingly, this chapter is divided into three main sections as noted below:

- Requirements that apply to all entities.
- Requirements for entities not applying FRS 26.
- Requirements for entities applying FRS 26.

What is a financial instrument?

6.9 As highlighted in the introduction to this chapter there are now a number of UK standards covering the accounting for financial instruments. This presents a problem, as each of the standards has its own scope, definitions and exclusions. Fortunately, the basic definition of a financial instrument is similar in FRS 13 and FRS 25.

6.10 The FRS 25 definition of a financial instrument is identical to the IAS 32 definition, which is explained in Manual of accounting – Financial instruments. The FRS 13 definition of a financial instrument is explained below.

6.11 FRS 13 defines a financial instrument as "*... any contract that gives rise to both a financial asset of one entity and a financial liability or equity instrument of another entity* ". [FRS 13 para 2]. Definitions are also given for a financial asset, financial liability and an equity instrument:

- A financial asset is cash, or any asset that is a contractual right to receive cash or another financial asset from another entity, or a contractual right to exchange financial instruments with another entity under conditions that are potentially favourable, or an equity instrument of another entity.
- A financial liability is any liability that is a contractual obligation to deliver cash or another financial asset to another entity, or to exchange financial instruments with another entity under conditions that are potentially unfavourable.
- An equity instrument is an instrument that evidences an ownership interest in an entity after deducting all of its liabilities. This has a wider meaning than equity shares, because it includes some non-equity shares, as well as warrants and options to subscribe for or purchase equity shares in the issuing entity.

[FRS 13 para 2].

6.12 Examples of financial instruments, financial assets and financial liabilities include:

- Cash, including foreign currency.
- Deposits, debtors, creditors, notes, loans, bonds and debentures.
- Finance lease obligations.
- Shares, options and warrants.
- Derivatives that are to be settled in cash or by another financial instrument (that is, commodity contracts are generally excluded, but see para 6.176).
- Contingent liabilities that arise from contracts and, if they crystallise, are to be settled in cash (for example, a financial guarantee).

- Certain provisions, for example, for onerous leasehold commitments or warranties that involve a contractual obligation to pay compensation. [FRS 13, App II para 15].

6.13 Non-equity minority interests should be treated as financial liabilities for the purposes of FRS 13's disclosures (see para 6.162).

Contracts and contractual rights

6.14 The references to 'contract', 'contractual right' and 'contractual obligation' are fundamental to the definition of a financial instrument, financial asset and financial liability. Consequently, assets and liabilities that are not contractual in nature are not financial assets or financial liabilities. Hence, tax liabilities that arise from statutory requirements imposed by governments, and not from contracts, are not financial liabilities. Although a contract must have clear economic consequences that the parties have little, if any, discretion to avoid and is usually enforceable in law, it does not necessarily need to be in writing and may take a variety of forms. Thus financial assets and financial liabilities may take a variety of forms.

6.15 It is important to consider the different rights and obligations that arise under contracts and how these may change, or be added to, as the contract is performed, because some of these rights and obligations may fall within the definition of a financial instrument. For example, a purchase order for a piece of plant and machinery is not a financial instrument as the right and obligations are for the exchange of a financial asset (cash) for a physical asset (the piece of plant and machinery). However, under the same contract, once the physical asset has been delivered, the purchaser will owe the vendor the purchase price. This creditor will be a financial liability.

6.16 'Contractual rights' and 'contractual obligations' encompass rights and obligations that are contingent upon future events. An example of contingent rights and obligations are those arising under a financial guarantee since the guarantor has a liability (the contractual obligation to pay the lender if the borrower defaults) and the lender has an asset (the contractual right to receive cash from the guarantor if the borrower defaults).

6.17 Trade debtors and creditors and bonds and debentures held or issued are common examples of financial assets representing a contractual right to receive cash in the future and corresponding financial liabilities representing a contractual obligation to deliver cash in the future. Each of the examples is a financial instrument, because one party's contractual right to receive (or obligation to pay) cash is matched by the other party's equal and opposite obligation to pay (or right to receive) cash.

FRS 13 exclusions and scope

6.18 FRS 13 includes a number of exclusions for particular items that appear to fit the definition of a financial instrument but are outside the scope of the standard. In addition, the standard does not apply to all UK GAAP reporting entities. These exclusions are explained in detail in from paragraph 6.137.

How the standards apply under UK GAAP

6.19 This section provides guidance on determining which elements of UK GAAP should be applied to which type of entity.

6.20 There are currently six principal elements of UK GAAP for financial instruments:

- The Companies Act 1985 dealing with the fair value accounting rules. These rules are now found in SI 2008/410, 'The Large and Medium-sized Companies and Groups (Accounts and Reports) Regulations 2008'.
- FRS 4, 'Capital instruments' (see para 6.268).
- FRS 13, 'Derivatives and other financial instruments: disclosures'.
- FRS 25, 'Financial instruments: Presentation' (equivalent to IAS 32).
- FRS 26, 'Financial instruments: Recognition and measurement' (equivalent to IAS 39).
- FRS 29, 'Financial instruments: Disclosure' (equivalent to IFRS 7).

6.21 All entities must apply the Companies Act disclosure requirements and FRS 25's presentation requirements. Companies must then determine whether they should apply old UK GAAP, (FRS 4 combined with FRS 13 (where applicable) and certain disclosure requirements of FRS 29 voluntarily) or new GAAP (FRS 26 and FRS 29).

6.22 The application of old or new GAAP will depend on the entity's status, in particular whether it is:

- listed on a regulated market;
- listed on a non-regulated market;
- unlisted entities applying the Companies Act fair value accounting rules; or
- unlisted entities not applying the Companies Act fair value accounting rules.

Listed on a regulated market

6.23 Listed groups are required to prepare their consolidated financial statements in accordance with IFRS by the EU Regulation. However, listed entities that are not part of a group can prepare their financial statements in accordance with UK GAAP. This includes listed parent companies preparing individual financial statements. These companies are required to apply the entire package of new financial instruments standards.

6.24 A listed entity is defined in paragraph 9A of FRS 26 as an entity that has in issue one or more securities (for example, debt, shares, or other financial or similar instruments) that are admitted to trading on a regulated market of any Member State by Council Directive 2004/39/EC. In the UK, the regulated markets are those that are regulated by the FSA and comprise the Main Market of the London Stock Exchange (LSE) and the Plus-listed market.

6.25 When FRS 26 refers to a listed entity it is by reference to the status of the individual entity that has any of its securities traded on a regulated market of any Member State. FRS 26 does not refer to a reporting entity. Consequently, FRS 26 only applies to the single entity financial statements of the listed entity and to that entity's consolidated financial statements. The listed status of other constituent parts of an entity's group is irrelevant in determining whether the entity's consolidated financial statements have to comply with FRS 26.

6.26 Note that it is an entity's status at the balance sheet date that is critical for determining which standards will apply. Hence, a company that de-lists during an accounting period will be treated as unlisted for the purpose of determining whether or not FRS 26 will apply.

Listed on a non-regulated market

6.27 Entities whose securities are admitted to listing on a non-regulated market, such as the AIM (a market regulated by the LSE), NASDAQ or EASDAQ, are not required to apply FRS 26 and FRS 29, unless they are applying the Companies Act fair value measurement rules (see below). Where such entities are not applying the fair value accounting rules, they fall within the scope of FRS 4 and FRS 13, unless they decide to voluntarily adopt FRS 26 and FRS 29 (see para 6.30.1 below).

6.28 Companies whose securities are traded on the AIM are required by the LSE's own rules to publish annual and half-yearly consolidated financial statements using IFRS. Therefore, the scope exemption is of little practical relevance to such entities. However, if an AIM company is not a parent company, it may prepare and present its financial statements either in accordance with IFRS or in accordance with UK GAAP as stated above. [AIM Rules 18 and 19].

Unlisted entities applying the Companies Act fair value accounting rules

6.29 Unlisted entities that are applying the Companies Act fair value accounting rules have to apply the entire suite of new financial instrument standards. There are no exemptions. This applies to AIM companies or companies whose securities are traded in an overseas exchange that prepare their financial statements in accordance with UK GAAP and the Companies Act fair value accounting rules.

The rules for banking and insurance companies are dealt with in paragraphs 6.34 and 6.35 below.

Unlisted entities not applying the Companies Act fair value accounting rules

6.30 Entities that are not applying the Companies Act fair value accounting rules must apply FRS 4 and the presentation requirements of FRS 25. Although not mandatory, such entities are encouraged to comply with certain disclosure requirements of FRS 29, adapting them in line with the entity's accounting policies (see para 6.371).

6.30.1 However, despite not being in the scope of the standard such entities may voluntarily adopt FRS 26, instead of FRS 4, as indicated in the ASB's preface to FRS 26. Adopting a policy of voluntarily applying FRS 26 and its related standards would need to be the most appropriate to an entity's particular circumstances for the purpose of giving a true and fair view. [FRS 18 para 17]. Further guidance on selection of accounting policies is given in chapter 2.

Summary of the above requirements

6.31 The above requirements are summarised in the table below.

Entities applying UK GAAP	Old GAAP – FRS 4, FRS 13 and FRS 25	New GAAP – FRS 25, FRS 26 and FRS 29
Listed		✓
Listed on a non-regulated market and applying the CA fair value accounting rules[1]		✓
Listed on a non-regulated market and not applying the CA fair value accounting rules[1]	✓	
Unlisted and applying the CA fair value accounting rules		✓
Unlisted and not applying the CA fair value accounting rules[2]	✓	

[1] AIM companies have to prepare their consolidated financial statements under IFRS. Their separate financial statements can be prepared under IFRS or UK GAAP. They may or may not apply the CA fair value accounting rules.

[2] FRS 13 is not applicable. Instead, such entities are encouraged to apply certain disclosure requirements of FRS 29.

Banks and insurance companies

6.32 There may be circumstances where an unlisted UK bank or insurance company is using a form of fair value accounting, but does not fall within FRS 26's scope. Schedule 2 to SI 2008/410 (formerly Schedule 9A to the

Companies Act 1985) permits banks to measure transferable securities at market value or current cost under the alternative accounting rules in that schedule. Similarly Schedule 3 to SI 2008/410 (formerly Schedule 9A to the Companies Act 1985) permits insurance companies to record their debt securities at current value under the current value accounting rules in that schedule. An entity applying these provisions within the Act does not, therefore, need to apply the new fair value accounting rules to continue to fair value these instruments. Accordingly, they fall outside FRS 26's scope.

6.33 However, banking and insurance companies that use fair value accounting rules set out in Schedules 2 and 3 respectively fall within the FRS 26's scope where they use fair value accounting for derivatives or financial instruments for which this is not specifically permitted under the historical cost accounting rules in Schedule 2 or under the current value accounting rules in Schedule 3 respectively. [FRS 26 para 1B].

Practical examples

6.34 The following examples illustrate circumstances where a company would apply old and new GAAP relating to financial instruments.

> **Example 1**
>
> Entity E is a parent of a listed group that is preparing its consolidated financial statements in accordance with IFRS under the EU Regulations. The parent company wishes to continue to use UK GAAP in its individual accounts. In this situation, the parent can continue to use UK GAAP and, as it is listed, it will need to apply the complete suit of financial instruments standards.

> **Example 2**
>
> Company A is an unlisted parent of a group of companies and is registered in the UK. Company A does not apply the Companies Act fair value accounting rules. Company A has a UK subsidiary B, which has issued debt on the London Stock Exchange. The consolidated financial statements of company A do not fall within FRS 26's scope (and neither do company A's individual financial statements) as company A is not listed and does not apply the fair value accounting rules. However, subsidiary B is required to apply the entire suite of financial instruments standards, FRS 25, FRS 26 and IFRS 7, within its own financial statements as it has listed debt in issue.

> **Example 3**
>
> Entity A is an investment management company that is listed on the London Stock Exchange. It has no subsidiaries. As entity A is not producing consolidated financial statements in accordance with IFRS under the EU Regulations, it is required to produce financial statements in accordance with UK GAAP. [DTR 4.1.6(2)].
>
> Consequently, as entity A is listed, it applies the entire suite of financial instruments standards (FRS 25, FRS 26 and FRS 29).

Example 4

Entity C is a medium-sized unlisted manufacturing company. The majority of business is transacted with UK suppliers and customers. However, there are a small number of overseas suppliers with which entity C trades. On occasion, entity C enters into forward foreign exchange contracts to reduce the risk of adverse movements in exchange rates on future purchases. Entity C has no fair value accounting policies and the forward exchange contracts are 'off-balance sheet'.

Entity A could continue to apply its accounting policy of not fair valuing derivatives, in which case FRS 4, FRS 25 and the disclosure requirements of the Companies Act apply. In addition, entity A may voluntarily apply certain disclosure requirements of FRS 29.

Alternatively, the company could also consider changing its accounting policy for the forward foreign exchange contracts to one of fair value accounting. This would require the use of the Companies Act fair value accounting rules and would automatically bring the entity within FRS 26's and FRS 29's scope.

Example 5

Company D is a bank that prepares its financial statements under Schedule 2 of SI 2008/410 of the Companies Act 2006. Company D trades in equity securities on behalf of itself and its clients and has always applied a mark-to-market accounting policy for these investments. Management wishes to avoid the complexities of the new UK accounting standards for financial instruments.

Company D is permitted to fair value these particular transferable securities under the alternative accounting rules in Schedule 2 and, hence, does not need to apply the Companies Act fair value accounting rules. As a result, company D does not need to apply FRS 26 or FRS 29. It continues to apply the FRS 25 presentation requirements and Part II of the disclosure requirements of FRS 13 applying to banks and other financial institutions.

Requirements that apply to all entities

Introduction

6.35 There are two sources of UK GAAP relating to financial instruments that are relevant to all entities, whether they are applying FRS 4 and FRS 13 or FRS 25 and FRS 26. The requirements of the Companies Act are explained below. In addition, the presentation requirements of FRS 25 are applicable to all UK reporting entities, whether they apply old GAAP or new GAAP for financial instruments. The presentation requirements of FRS 25 are the same as those of IAS 32 and are explained in Manual of Accounting – Financial instruments.

6.36 There are extensive requirements relating to the accounting for investments in the Companies Act. In particular, a significant amount of disclosure is required. Not all financial instruments are investments and not all investments are within the financial instruments standards' scope, but there is a significant overlap of items that are both financial instruments and investments. These items are within the scope of the financial instruments guidance, and also have to comply with the Companies Act requirements for investments.

Definition of investments

6.37 The Act does not provide a formal definition of investments although the model formats for the balance sheet include a heading for 'investments' under the general heading of both 'fixed assets' and 'current assets'. Moreover, there are separate sub-headings for investments under both the fixed and the current categories:

- The sub-headings identified for fixed asset investments are:
  - Shares in group undertakings.
  - Loans to group undertakings.
  - Participating interests.
  - Loans to undertakings in which the company has a participating interest.
  - Other investments other than loans.
  - Other loans.
  - Own shares.
- The sub-headings identified for current asset investments are:
  - Shares in group undertakings.
  - Own shares.
  - Other investments.

6.38 There is no specific UK accounting standard in place dealing with investments. In 1990, the ASC issued ED 55, 'Accounting for investments', that was never published as a standard. However, the ED defined an investment in general terms as "*...an asset that is characterised by its ability to generate economic benefits in the form of distributions and/or appreciation in value*". This definition is relatively broad and should cover all types of investments, such as:

- Shares.
- Debentures.
- Interest-bearing securities.
- Loan stock.
- Bonds and other debt instruments.
- Warrants and options.

- Commodities (other than those to be used in the enterprise's activities).
- Futures contracts.
- Rights to subscribe for any of these.

6.39 It should be noted that a number of items that meet the definition of financial instrument such as interests in subsidiaries, associates and joint ventures are outside of the scope of the financial instruments standards. However, much of the Companies Act guidance covered in this section is applicable to all investments including those that are scoped out of the financial instruments standards.

Classification

6.40 Under the Act, a company can treat investments in its balance sheet as either fixed asset investments or current asset investments depending on how it intends to use them. A company's investments that are "*...intended for use on a continuing basis in the company's activities*" should be classified as fixed assets in the company's financial statements. Generally, investments should be classified as fixed where the company intends to hold them for the long-term and this intention can clearly be demonstrated. Furthermore, such a situation might arise where the company's ability to dispose of an investment is restricted for a particular reason. If a company's investments do not fall within the category described above and are, therefore, not considered to be fixed asset investments, they will fall to be classified as current asset investments.

6.41 Whether a company intends to use an investment on a continuing basis (that is, hold it for the long-term) will often be obvious from the nature of the investment. Treatment as a fixed asset might also arise where there are practical restrictions on an investor's ability to dispose of the investment. Fixed asset investments will, therefore, comprise:

- Equity shareholdings in, or loan to, subsidiaries and associates.
- Investments arising from other trading relationships.
- Investments that either cannot be disposed of or cannot be disposed of without a significant effect on the operations of the investing company.
- Investments that are intended to be held for use on a continuing basis by investing companies whose objective is to hold a portfolio of investments to provide income and/or capital growth for their members.

6.42 It should be remembered, however, that the mere fact that an investment has been held for a long time does not necessarily make it a long-term asset, unless it also falls within one of the categories indicated in the above paragraph.

Measurement rules

6.43 The paragraphs below consider the Act's measurement rules that apply to investments and, hence, apply to financial instruments that meet the definition of investments. Historically, such investments could either be recorded in the financial statements in accordance with the Act's historical cost accounting rules or its alternative accounting rules, which allow such assets to be recognised in the financial statements at a valuation. As stated earlier, the Companies Act 2006 added a third possibility of measuring financial instruments at fair values.

6.44 How these rules apply to all assets (including investments) is considered in detail in chapter 16 and is summarised in the paragraphs that follow. When determining the amount at which an investment should be recognised in the financial statements, each individual investment should be considered separately. [SI 2008/410 1 Sch 15]. This means that a 'portfolio' basis of valuation (that is, treating a number of investments as a single asset) cannot be used for an investment portfolio; each investment has to be considered separately.

Fixed asset investments

Historical cost accounting rules

6.45 Under the Act's historical cost accounting rules, fixed asset investments, like other fixed assets, are required to be recognised in the financial statements at their purchase price or production cost. [SI 2008/410 1 Sch 17] Clearly, production cost is not relevant for fixed asset investments and hence they should be recorded at their purchase price. Where a fixed asset investment has diminished in value the diminution may be provided for in the profit and loss account, thereby reducing the investment to its recoverable amount. [SI 2008/410 1 Sch 19(1)]. Where the diminution in value is expected to be permanent, it must be recognised. [SI 2008/410 1 Sch 19(2)]. Therefore, in a similar way for other fixed assets, permanent diminutions in value must be taken to the profit and loss account, but also temporary diminutions in value of fixed asset investments (which would include market value fluctuations) can also be charged to the profit and loss account.

6.46 Where a diminution in value of a fixed asset investment has been charged to the profit and loss account, but the circumstances giving rise to the diminution have reversed to any extent (for example, the investment's market value has increased) the provision should be written back to the extent that it is no longer necessary. Any amounts of this nature written back should be shown in the profit and loss account or disclosed, either separately or in aggregate, in the notes. [SI 2008/410 1 Sch 19(3)].

6.47 FRS 11, 'Impairment of fixed assets and goodwill', scopes out investments that fall within FRS 13's scope. [FRS 11 para 6]. Investments other than subsidiaries, associates and joint ventures are within FRS 13's scope and so FRS 11's impairment provisions do not apply to these. [FRS 13 para 5].

However, FRS 11 does apply to investments in subsidiaries, associates and joint ventures. FRS 11's requirements are considered in chapter 18.

Alternative accounting rules

6.48 Under the Act's alternative accounting rules, fixed asset investments can be included in the balance sheet at either:

- their market value determined as at the date of their last valuation; or
- at a value determined on any basis that appears to the directors to be appropriate in the company's circumstances.

[SI 2008/410 1 Sch 32(3)].

Where a directors' valuation is used, the particulars of the method of valuation adopted and the reasons for adopting it must be disclosed in the notes to the financial statements.

6.49 Where the alternative accounting rules have been applied, the amount of any profit (or loss) arising on the revaluation must be credited to (or debited to) the revaluation reserve. Then the normal rules regarding the use of that reserve apply. Slightly different rules apply to investment companies (as defined in section 833 of the Companies Act 2006) who are allowed to take revaluation gains and losses to another reserve other than the revaluation reserve. In addition, they are allowed to take permanent diminutions in the value of fixed asset investments to that same reserve, whereas other companies have to take such losses to the profit and loss account.

6.50 The market value to be used where there is a quoted price for the investment would normally be the middle market price (that is the average of the bid and offer prices). But, where a company holds marketable securities of another company and the size and nature of the holding is such that the market is not capable of absorbing a sale of the investment without a material effect on its quoted price, the current market price may not be indicative of the true market value of the investment. In this type of situation, the market price should generally be adjusted to reflect the proceeds that the enterprise could realistically expect to raise by disposing of the holding in the ordinary course of business.

6.51 In certain situations, a holding of a size sufficient to affect market price, if sold, may not always be indicated by a large percentage ownership of shares. For example, where only a portion of the total is actively traded, a much smaller percentage holding could affect the market price significantly. Where this is so, the investment should normally be valued at the amount that could be raised if it was disposed of in smaller tranches, taking into account, for example, the higher transaction costs.

6.52 There may, however, be situations where an investor controls, say, five per cent of a very large enterprise. In this situation, the market price may be higher than the quoted price, because the quoted price usually reflects the trading of much smaller tranches of shares. Indeed, there may be a premium attached to such an influential stake. In this case, the quoted price would be lower than 'market' and should normally be used for valuation purposes. This would be required because any 'premium' price would not be attainable on short notice.

6.53 It should be noted that the above methods for valuing investments at mid market prices or adjusting an available market price for premium or discount based on the relative size of the investment held are not permissible under FRS 26. However, as the Act does not define how market values should be determined, the above methods of arriving at market values remain applicable under the Act's alternative accounting rules.

6.54 Where an investment is not quoted, the directors may still wish to record the investment at a value in the financial statements. As mentioned above, it is acceptable under the Act for them to carry out their own valuation as long as the disclosures set out in paragraph 6.50 are complied with. There are a number of valuation techniques that can be applied in these circumstances. One of the common approaches is to find a similar listed company to the unquoted company to be valued and apply the listed company's PE ratio to the unquoted company's earnings to arrive at a price. The valuation of unquoted investment is of great importance to certain industries, particularly the investment trust industry. Some investment trusts specialise in making high risk venture capital investments (often in management buyouts) and the British Venture Capital Association issued some guidelines in November 1993 for the valuation and disclosure of venture capital portfolios.

6.55 The rules and techniques for valuing investments that apply under the Act's alternative accounting rules are the same as those that apply when an investment is acquired as part of the acquisition of a subsidiary. The rules for fair valuing investments on such an acquisition are considered in chapter 25.

Current asset investments

Historical cost accounting rules

6.56 Current asset investments are required under the Act to be recorded at the lower of cost and net realisable value. [SI 2008/410 1 Sch 23, 24(1)]. Therefore, where a current asset investment's net realisable value is lower that its cost an amount should be provided in the profit and loss account for the diminution in value. Where the reason for making the provision has ceased to apply to any extent, the provision should be written back through the profit and loss account to that extent. [SI 2008/410 1 Sch 24(2)].

Alternative accounting rules

6.57 Under the Act's alternative accounting rules, current asset investments may be included in the balance sheet at their current cost. Current cost is, in effect, the value to the business of the asset and for current asset investments will often be the investment's market value, unless the investment is unquoted, when the directors can determine its value. In the same way as the rule applies for fixed asset investments, any profit or loss arising from the valuation of current asset investments must be credited or debited to the revaluation reserve. [SI 2008/410 1 Sch 32(4)].

6.58 The rules concerning the market value to be attributed to current asset investments are the same as the rules discussed for fixed asset investments in paragraphs 6.50 and 6.52 above.

Fair value accounting rules

6.59 Schedule 4 to the Companies Act has not previously permitted the 'marking to market' or fair valuing of investments with any resulting gains or losses being recognised in the profit and loss account. Entities that report under IFRS for accounting periods beginning on or after 1 January 2005 need to apply IAS 39 and one of the fundamental requirements of that standard is that certain financial instruments are measured at fair value with movements being taken to the income statement. In addition, UK GAAP reporters that are within FRS 26's scope will need to apply the same guidance to certain financial instruments. Hence, there was an urgent requirement to amend the Companies Act to permit the fair valuing of certain specific financial instruments. This need was addressed in November 2004 with the publication of The Companies Act 1985 (International Accounting Standards and Other Accounting Amendments) Regulations 2004 (SI 2004/2947). Following changes to the Companies Act, the fair value accounting rules are now set out in Regulations 36 to 41 of SI 2008/410.

6.60 Under the Regulations:

- All sizes and types of company are permitted (but not required) to apply fair value accounting to some of their financial instruments.
- Fair value accounting may be adopted in both individual and consolidated financial statements.
- Additional disclosure requirements are introduced, regardless of whether fair value accounting is adopted.

Measuring financial instruments at fair value

6.61 The Act now permits certain financial instruments, including derivative financial instruments, to be included at fair value, provided that fair value can be determined reliably. [SI 2008/410 1 Sch 36(1)]. 'Fair value' is determined as follows:

- If a reliable market can readily be identified for the financial instrument, its fair value is determined by reference to its market value.

- If a reliable market cannot readily be identified for the financial instrument but can be identified for its components or for a similar instrument, its fair value is determined by reference to the market value of its components or of the similar instrument.
- If neither of the above apply, the financial instrument's fair value is a value resulting from generally accepted valuation models and techniques. Any valuation models and techniques used must ensure a reasonable approximation to the market value.

[SI 2008/410 1 Sch 37].

6.62 The following financial instruments may not be fair valued:

- Financial instruments (other than derivatives) held to maturity.
- Loans and receivables originated by the company and not held for trading purposes.
- Interests in subsidiary undertakings, associated undertakings and joint ventures.
- Equity instruments issued by the company.
- Contracts for contingent consideration in a business combination.
- Other financial instruments with such special characteristics that the instruments, according to generally accepted accounting principles or practice, should be accounted for differently from other financial instruments.

[SI 2008/410 1 Sch 36(3)].

6.63 Notwithstanding the above exception, a financial instrument that is permitted to be fair valued under IASs adopted by the EU on or before September 2006 may be included at fair value provided the disclosure required by such accounting standards.

6.64 'Hedge accounting' is permitted in-so-far as, *"a company may include any assets and liabilities that qualify as hedged items under a fair value hedge accounting system, or identified portions of such assets and liabilities, at the amount required under that system"*. [SI 2008/410 1 Sch 38]. However, neither 'financial instruments' nor 'hedge accounting' are defined by the Act. This is deliberate as these terms are defined in accounting standards where the definitions can be kept up to date. However, 'derivative financial instruments' are stated to include *"commodity-based contracts that give either contracting party the right to settle in cash or some other financial instrument, except when such contracts—*

(a) were entered into for the purpose of, and continue to meet, the company's expected purchase, sale or usage requirements;

(b) were designated for such purpose at their inception; and

(c) are expected to be settled by delivery of the commodity."

[SI 2008/410 10 Sch 2].

Changes in fair value

6.65 Where fair value accounting is adopted, changes in fair value must be included in the profit and loss account. [SI 2008/410 1 Sch 40(2)]. This is subject to the following exceptions:

- Any change in value *must* be included in a separate fair value reserve:
- where the financial instrument accounted for is a hedging instrument under a hedge accounting system that allows some or all of the change in value not to be shown in the profit and loss account; or
- where the change in value relates to an exchange difference arising on a monetary item that forms part of the company's net investment in a foreign entity.
- Any change in value *may* be included in a separate fair value reserve where the financial instrument accounted for is an available-for-sale financial asset and is not a derivative.

[SI 2008/410 1 Sch 40(3)(4)].

Marking to market

6.66 Historically, businesses in a number of segments, have applied a policy of 'marking to market' their current asset investments. This approach, commonly used by market makers and other dealers in investments and commodities, results in such investments being carried at market value with changes in that market value being included in the profit or loss for the period.

6.67 Whilst the alternative accounting rules do permit this balance sheet treatment, they would require any movement in the market value to be treated as a revaluation surplus or deficit and taken to the revaluation reserve, rather than being dealt with in the profit and loss account. Hence, in the past, marking to market has involved a departure from the Companies Act requirements and so it was necessary to invoke a true and fair override under section 226(5) in order to take movements in market value to the profit and loss account.

6.68 With the change to the Companies Act now permitting certain financial instruments to be measured at fair value with movements being taken to the profit and loss account, many of these entities will no longer need to invoke a true and fair override.

Presentation

6.69 A further change to the Companies Act was required to enable entities to comply with FRS 25's presentation requirements. Paragraph 9 of Schedule 1 to SI 2008/410 states:

> *"The company's directors must, in determining how amounts are presented within items in the profit and loss account and balance sheet, have regard to the substance of the reported transaction or arrangement, in accordance with generally accepted accounting principles or practice."*

6.70 This is intended to enable convergence of UK accounting standards with EU-adopted IFRS. IAS 32 and FRS 25 require that certain preference shares are shown as liabilities and related preference dividends are shown as interest. Similarly, the debt and equity components of financial instruments must be separated and each element shown as liabilities or equity, as appropriate. Without this change in company law, such a presentation would not be legal in the UK. Determining whether preference shares should be treated as equity or as a liability in accordance with FRS 25 and IAS 32 is considered further in Manual of accounting – Financial instruments.

Disclosure requirements

Introduction

6.71 The Act contains extensive disclosure requirements for financial instruments. Any entity that has investments that are caught by the definition of a financial instrument will need to make these disclosures. These disclosure requirements are in addition to those that may be required by FRS 13 or FRS 29 (if appropriate).

6.72 The extent of the disclosures differs depending on whether or not the entity is applying fair value accounting to any of its financial instruments. Where fair value accounting is applied, it is important that the reader understands, at a high level, how the fair values are determined. Hence, there is a requirement to disclose, for example, the assumptions underlying the valuation models. Where no financial instruments are fair valued (typically for an entity that has not adopted FRS 26), there are requirements for certain fair values to be disclosed.

6.73 Set out below are the disclosure requirements for all investments under the Companies Act for entities not required to prepare group accounts. The disclosure requirements for entities preparing group accounts are given in chapter 24. The disclosures required by SI 2008/410 under the fair value accounting rules in relation to financial instruments are described from paragraph 6.82.

All investments

6.74 As mentioned above, a company can treat its investments in its balance sheet as either fixed asset investments or current asset investments depending on how it intends to use them. The model formats for the balance sheet include a heading for 'Investments' under the general heading of both 'Fixed assets' and 'Current assets'. Moreover, there are separate sub-headings for investments under both the fixed and the current categories.

6.75 For each of the sub-headings of fixed asset investments, a company has to disclose the information required for other fixed assets under Schedule 1 paragraphs 51(1)(2) of SI 2008/410. These include disclosure of the aggregate amount of that item at both the beginning and the end of the financial year and certain other information about the purchase and sale of those investments.

6.76 In addition, Schedule 1 paragraph 51(3) of SI 2008/410 requires details to be disclosed about any provision for diminution in value made in respect of each fixed asset investment category.

6.77 Furthermore, the Act requires the notes to the financial statements to include certain information about any listed investments a company holds (irrespective of whether these are shown as fixed assets or as current assets). In particular, the notes must disclose:

- The total amount that relates to all listed investments.
- The aggregate market value of listed investments where it differs from the amount at which they are stated in the balance sheet.
- Both the market value and the stock exchange value of any listed investments must be disclosed, where the former value is taken as being higher than their stock exchange value. This disclosure is required because the market value and the stock exchange value may differ according to the size of the investment and its marketability. For example, a controlling stake could be worth proportionately more than a minority interest in a company, because stock exchange prices traditionally reflect the values of small parcels of shares.

[SI 2008/410 4 1 Sch 54(1)(2)].

6.78 For this purpose, a 'listed investment' means any investment that is listed either on a 'recognised investment exchange' other than an overseas investment exchange within the meaning of the Financial Services and Markets Act 2000 or on any stock exchange of repute outside Great Britain. [SI 2008/410 10 Sch 8]. All other investments are to be regarded as unlisted and no additional information is required to be disclosed for these investments. A 'recognised investment exchange' is defined in section 285 of the Financial Services and Markets Act 2000 as an investment exchange in relation to which a recognition order is in force. Currently, the only bodies designated in Great Britain as recognised investment exchanges are:

- London Stock Exchange (the Stock Exchange).
- London International Financial Futures and Options Exchange (LIFFE).

- ICE Futures.
- EDX London.
- London Metal Exchange (LME).
- PLUS Markets Plc.
- VIRT-X Exchange.

6.79 There is no definition of 'stock exchange of repute' in the Act. In practice, whether a stock exchange outside Great Britain is reputable or not will depend both on its status in its own country and on the circumstances surrounding its operation.

6.80 The disclosure requirements for *listed* investments outlined above are best illustrated by an example:

Example

Details of investments held:

	Co	Balance sheet value £'000	Market value £'000	Stock exchange value £'000
Listed on the London Stock	A	100	250	300
Exchange (a recognised	B	150	110	110
investment exchange)	C	130	150	125
	D	75	25	20
		455	535	555
Listed on the New York Stock	E	190	200	225
Exchange (a stock exchange of	F	65	110	100
repute outside Great Britain)	G	15	25	25
		270	335	350
Traded on AIM		30	70	75
Total of investments		755	940	980

This disclosure may be summarised in the notes to the financial statements as follows:

Listed investments	**£'000**
Balance sheet value	725
Market value	870

The amounts shown above include certain investments for which the market value is considered to be higher than the stock exchange value. The market value of these investments is £285,000 and their stock exchange value is £245,000.

Listed investments include certain investments for which the market value is considered to be higher than the stock exchange value. The market value of these investments is £285,000 (that is £150,000 + £25,000 + £110,000) and their stock exchange value is £245,000 (that is £215,000 + £20,000 + £100,000). The investment in the company traded on AIM has been excluded from this disclosure as companies traded in this way are not listed investments.

6.81 In Table 6.1, Lonrho Plc provides an analysis for 'other' fixed asset investments.

Table 6.1 — Lonrho Plc — Annual Report and Accounts — 30 September 1994

Notes to the Accounts (extract)

20. Other investments — fixed assets

	Investments	Loans	Provisions	Total
Group	**£m**	**£m**	**£m**	**£m**
At 30 September 1993	26	3	(12)	17
Additions/advances	1	2		3
Disposals/repayments	(1)	(1)		(2)
Provisions			(3)	(3)
Transfers		(1)		(1)
At 30 September 1994	**26**	**3**	**(15)**	**14**

Net book value of investments shown above:	1994	1993
	£m	£m
Listed — on the London Stock Exchange	1	1
— on overseas stock exchanges	2	2
Unlisted	8	11
	11	14
Value at 30 September:		
Listed (market value)	11	8
Unlisted (Directors' valuation)	28	28

	Investments	Provisions	Total
Company	**£m**	**£m**	**£m**
Cost:			
At 30 September 1993 and 1994	10	(8)	2

	1994	1993
	£m	£m
Net book value of investments shown above:		
Listed — on the London Stock Exchange	1	1
Unlisted	1	1
	2	2
Value at 30 September:		
Listed (market value)	1	1
Unlisted (Directors' valuation)	1	1

Companies Act disclosure requirements

Companies adopting fair value accounting

6.82 In accounting periods beginning on or after 1 January 2005, companies have the option to adopt the fair value accounting rules in the Companies Act. Companies adopting fair value accounting must disclose:

- The significant assumptions underlying the valuation models and techniques used.
- For each category of financial instrument, the fair value of the instruments in that category and the amounts:
  - included in the profit and loss account; or
  - credited to or debited from the fair value reserve,

  in respect of instruments in that category.
- For each class of derivative financial instruments, the extent and nature of the instruments, including significant terms and conditions that may affect the amount, timing and certainty of future cash flows.
- Where any amount is transferred to or from the fair value reserve during the financial year, there shall be stated in tabular form:
  - the amount of the reserve as at the beginning of the financial year and as at the balance sheet date;
  - the amount transferred to or from the reserve during that year; and
  - the source and application respectively of the amounts so transferred.

[SI 2008/410 1 Sch 55(2)(3)].

Companies not adopting fair value accounting

6.83 Companies that elect not to adopt fair value accounting for certain financial instruments must give additional disclosures relating to their derivative financial instruments. The following disclosure is required for each class of derivative financial instrument:

- the fair value of the derivatives in that class, if such a value can be determined as described in paragraph 6.81; and
- the extent and nature of the derivatives.

[SI 2008/410 1 Sch 56].

6.84 In addition, where:

- a company has financial fixed assets that could be included at fair value;

- the amount at which those assets are included in the financial statements is in excess of their fair value; and
- the company has not made provision for diminution in value of those assets.

The following disclosure must be made:

- The amount at which either the individual assets or appropriate groupings of those individual assets is stated in the company's financial statements.
- The fair value of those assets or groupings.
- The reasons for not making a provision for diminution in value of those assets, including the nature of the evidence that provides the basis for the belief that the amount at which they are stated in the financial statements will be recovered.

[SI 2008/410 1 Sch 57].

6.85 The above disclosures apply to all companies including banking and insurance companies irrespective of whether the company applies FRS 26 or the fair value accounting rules.

Directors' report

6.86 Regardless of whether a company adopts fair value accounting, it must give the following information in the directors' report (unless such information is not material):

- The financial risk management objectives and policies of the company and its consolidated subsidiaries, including the policy for hedging each major type of forecasted transaction for which hedge accounting is used.
- The exposure of the company and its consolidated subsidiaries to price risk, credit risk, liquidity risk and cash flow risk.

[SI 2008/410 7 Sch 6].

6.87 It is likely that there will be some degree of duplication between the required Companies Act financial instrument disclosures and those required by either FRS 13 or FRS 29. Management will need to consider how the information is to be presented clearly, while ensuring that all the required disclosures are made.

Comparatives

6.88 The Act is silent on the subject of comparatives for the fair value disclosures. The normal rules should therefore be applied, so companies will be required to give comparative information for all items. [FRS 28 para 10(a)].

6.89 An example of the Companies Act disclosures under the fair value accounting rules is given below.

Example

XYZ is a limited company incorporated in the UK with a year end of 31 December 2006. The company sells computers in the UK and overseas and generates some of its revenue in US dollars. It hedges its exposure to foreign currency fluctuations by entering into forward contracts to buy sterling and sell dollars at a future date.

What disclosures does the company need to make in the financial statements if:

(a) the company does not adopt fair value accounting for these forward contracts; and

(b) the company adopts fair value accounting as permitted by the Companies Act?

(The company for the purposes of part (b) also has an available for sale (AFS) investment of 5% in G plc which was bought in December 2000 for £500,000.)

Note that the Companies Act also requires the directors' report to include certain information in relation to financial instruments as noted in paragraph 6.86 above.

Additionally any disclosures relating to FRS 29 have not been considered here.

A – Company does not adopt fair value accounting

Notes to the financial statements

The company's local currency is pounds sterling, but approximately one quarter of its sales are to customers in the United States. These sales are denominated in US dollars. As a result, the company is subject to foreign currency exchange risk due to exchange rate movements between pounds sterling and US dollars. The company seeks to reduce this risk by entering into forward contracts.

The company has forward contracts with the following fair values at the end of the year.

	2006 £'000	2005 £'000
Fair value of forward contracts	5,000	6,000

B – Company adopts fair value accounting

Notes to the financial statements

Fair value gains and losses

The company's local currency is pounds sterling, but approximately one quarter of its sales are to customers in the United States. These sales are denominated in US dollars. As a result, the company is subject to foreign currency exchange risk due to exchange rate movements between pounds sterling and US dollars. The company seeks to reduce this risk by entering into forward contracts that are fair valued with gains and losses recorded in the income statement.

Included in profit for the year are the following gains/ (losses) relating to changes in fair values of the forward contracts

	2006	2005
	£'000	£'000
Forward contracts	100	(250)

Debtors

	2006	2005
	£'000	£'000
Trade debtors	1,500	1,400
Other debtors	600	900
Derivatives – forward contracts	50	–

Available for sale investments

	2006	2005
	£'000	£'000
Investment in G plc	1,000	1,200

Fair value reserve

	2006	2005
	£'000	£'000
At 1 January	700	1,000
Fair value loss in the period	(200)	(300)
At 31 December	500	700

Significant holdings greater than twenty per cent

6.90 Where a company at the end of its financial year has a 'significant holding' of shares of any class in another undertaking, other than a subsidiary undertaking, a joint venture, or an associated undertaking, the Act requires the company to disclose certain information. [SI 2008/410 4 Sch 4].

6.91 For this purpose, a significant holding is a holding of 20 per cent or more of the nominal value of any class of shares in an undertaking, or a holding the carrying amount of which exceeds one fifth of the company's assets as stated in its balance sheet. [SI 2008/410 4 Sch 4(2)]. Reference to 'shares' means:

- The allotted shares in relation to an undertaking that has a share capital.
- The rights to share in the capital of an undertaking which has capital, but has no share capital. This would apply to partnerships.
- Interests that confer any right to share in the profits, or liability to contribute to the losses, of the undertaking, or that give rise to an obligation to contribute to the debts or expenses of the undertaking in the event of it

being wound up. This includes most other undertakings that are not bodies corporate or partnerships.

[CA06 Sec 1161(2)].

6.92 In interpreting the Act's disclosure requirements, shares held on behalf of the company by any other person should be attributed to the company and shares held by the company on behalf of another person should not be attributed to the company. Furthermore, shares held by a company (company A) by way of security should be treated as held by the company providing them as security (company B), where both of the following conditions apply:

- The rights attached to the shares (other than the right to exercise them for the purpose of preserving the security or of realising it) are exercisable only in accordance with the instructions of company B.
- Where the shares are held in connection with the granting of loans as part of normal business activities, those rights (other than the right to exercise them for the purpose of preserving the security or of realising it) are exercisable only in the interests of company B.

[SI 2008/410 4 Sch 14(3)(4), 22].

6.93 Where a company has significant holdings, the notes to the financial statements must disclose in respect of each such undertaking:

- Its name.
- Its country of incorporation, where it is incorporated outside Great Britain.
- If it is unincorporated, the address of its principal place of business.
- The identity of each class of shares the investing company holds.
- The proportion of the nominal value of the shares of each class that the investing company holds.

[SI 2008/410 4 Sch 5].

6.94 In addition, the following information should be given:

- The aggregate amount of the capital and reserves of the undertaking at the end of its relevant financial year (see below).
- The profit or the loss of that undertaking as disclosed by those financial statements.

[SI 2008/410 4 Sch 6].

6.95 The 'relevant financial year' is the financial year ending on or before the investing company's balance sheet date. [SI 2008/410 4 Sch 6(4)].

Exemptions from disclosure

6.96 Except as described below, where any of the information required by Schedule 5 relates to either an undertaking that is established under the law of a country outside the UK or an undertaking that carries on its business outside the UK, and the directors believe that disclosure would be seriously prejudicial to the business of that undertaking or to the business of the company or any of its subsidiary undertakings, and the company has obtained the Secretary of State's agreement, that information need not be disclosed. [CA06 Sec 409(3)(4)]. Where advantage is taken of this exemption, this must be stated in the notes to the financial statements. [CA06 Sec 409(5)]. Exemption is not available in respect of disclosures regarding shares in a company held by its subsidiary undertakings (see para 6.130) or membership of a qualifying undertaking (see from para 6.120).

6.97 Where a company has a significant number of investments such that, in the directors' opinion, compliance with the requirements of Schedule 5 would result in disclosure of excessive length, information need only be given in respect of those undertakings whose results or financial position principally affect the figures shown in the company's financial statements. [CA06 Sec 410(1)(2)]. Where advantage is taken of this exemption, this must be stated in the notes to the financial statements. [CA06 Sec 410(3)]. In addition, the full information (including both the information that is disclosed in the notes to the financial statements and the information that is not) must be annexed to the company's next annual return. [CA06 Sec 410(3)]. Failure to do so will result in the company and any officer of it who is in default being liable to a fine. [CA06 Sec 410(4)(5)].

6.98 The section 409(5) statement that the 'seriously prejudicial' exemption has been taken is required to be given irrespective of whether the group has taken advantage of the exemption in section 410(1) described above. Under section 410(1) the full information for all subsidiaries must be annexed to the company's next annual return, but where the secretary of state has granted exemption under section 409(3), this need not include the information regarding the subsidiary excluded on seriously prejudicial grounds.

6.99 The information described in paragraph 6.94 need not be given if it is immaterial. Furthermore, it need not be given in either of the following two situations where:

- The company is exempt by virtue of section 400 or 401 of the 2006 Act from the requirement to prepare consolidated financial statements (see chapter 24). But for this exemption to apply, the company's investment in all such undertakings must be shown, in aggregate, in the notes to the company's financial statements by way of the equity method of valuation (that is, by stating the company's share of the undertaking's net assets). [SI 2008/410 4 Sch 13(1)].
- The company's investment is in an undertaking that is not required by any of the Act's provisions to deliver a copy of its balance sheet to the Registrar of Companies and it does not otherwise publish that balance sheet in Great

Britain or elsewhere. Where this situation exists, the information need not be given, provided the company's holding is less than 50 per cent of the nominal value of the shares in the undertaking. [SI 2008/410 4 Sch 6(2)].

Participating interests

6.100 SI 2008/410 defines 'Participating interest' as "*...an interest held by an undertaking in the shares of another undertaking which it holds on a long-term basis for the purpose of securing a contribution to its activities by the exercise of control or influence arising from or related to that interest*". [SI 2008/410 10 Sch 11(1)].

6.101 A holding of 20 per cent or more of the shares of an undertaking is presumed to be a participating interest, unless the contrary is shown. [SI 2008/410 10 Sch 11(2)]. With regard to the presentation specified in paragraph 6.103 below, a participating interest does not include an interest in a subsidiary undertaking. It will, however, include associates and joint ventures as defined in both the Act and FRS 9.

6.102 The term 'associated undertaking' is defined in the Act for consolidated financial statements purposes. Consequently, this term does not appear in any of the balance sheet formats of an individual company. Therefore, where an investing company that is not required to prepare consolidated financial statements holds 20 per cent or more of the shares, whether voting or non-voting, in another undertaking, that investment will generally be shown as a 'participating interest' in the company's balance sheet. Participating interests will include associates and joint ventures as defined in FRS 9. If, however, the company is included in the consolidated financial statements of a larger group, in the group's consolidated balance sheet, any holding of 20 per cent or more of the voting shares in an undertaking (that is, in an associate or a joint venture) will be shown under the sub-headings 'interests in associated undertakings' or 'interests in joint ventures' as appropriate, and any holding of 20 per cent or more of the non-voting shares in an undertaking will be shown under the sub-heading 'other participating interests'.

6.103 'Participating interests' and 'loans to undertakings in which the company has a participating interest' appear as separate sub-headings under the fixed asset main heading of 'investments' in both balance sheet formats. Also, both balance sheet formats require the presentation of 'amounts owed by undertakings in which the company has a participating interest' under 'debtors' and the 'amounts owed to undertakings in which the company has a participating interest' under 'creditors'. In addition, 'amounts owed by and to undertakings in which the company has a participating interest' that are due for payment within one year must be shown separately from amounts due after one year. [SI 2008/410 1 Sch Notes 5 and 13 to the balance sheet formats]. Paragraph 55 of FRS 9 additionally requires that these balances are analysed into amounts relating to loans and amounts relating to trading balances. These format requirements effectively prohibit companies from showing participating interests and investments in associates and joint ventures as a single net figure including the cost of the shares in the undertakings, loans to them and after deducting loans from them.

Associates, joint ventures and other joint arrangements

6.104 As stated in paragraph 6.101 above, participating interests include investments in associates and joint ventures. Investments in associates and joint ventures should be shown in the investing company's own financial statements as follows:

- Income from associates and joint ventures should be shown as dividends received and receivable.
- Unless it is shown at a valuation, the amount at which the investing company's interests in associates and joint ventures should be shown is the cost of the investment less any amounts written off. [FRS 9 paras 20, 26].

The treatment of an investing group's interests in associates and joint ventures is covered in chapter 27.

6.105 If the investing company does not prepare consolidated financial statements then it will only report its own profit and loss account and balance sheet. The only income that can properly be included in that profit and loss account will be dividends received from the associate or joint venture. Inclusion of dividends rather than share of earnings is necessary because of the Act's requirement that only realised profits can be included in a company's profit and loss account. For this reason FRS 9 requires that a company should show its share of its associate's or joint venture's results and net assets by presenting a separate proforma profit and loss account in addition to its own profit and loss account. Alternatively, the company could add the information in supplementary form to its own profit and loss account in such a way that its share of the associate's or joint venture's profits is not treated as realised for the purposes of the Act, as illustrated below. [FRS 9 para 48].

Example

The supplementary information could be included on the face of the profit and loss account or in the notes to the company's financial statements.

Company profit and loss account

		Proforma information	
(All figures relate to continuing activities)		**Joint ventures**	
	Company	**& Associates**	**Total**
	£'000	**£'000**	**£'000**
Turnover	200	120	320
Cost of sales	120		
Gross profit	80		
Administrative expenses	40		

Operating profit	40	54	94
Interest	(20)	(22)	(42)
Profit on ordinary activities before tax	20	32	52
Tax on profit on ordinary activities	5	7	12
Profit for the financial year	15	25	30
Equity dividends	4		4
Retained profit for the year	11		26

6.106 Similarly, as the company's balance sheet will carry the investment at cost less amounts written off, FRS 9 requires that a separate proforma balance sheet should be given in which the associate or joint venture is presented on the equity method of accounting. Alternatively, the information could be added in supplementary form to the company's own balance sheet as illustrated below. [FRS 9 para 48].

Example

Company balance sheet

	Company £'000	*Proforma information* Company including associates & joint ventures £'000
Fixed assets		
Tangible assets	898	898
Investments:		
Company		
Joint ventures:	238	
Share or gross assets		2,359
Share of gross liabilities		1,448
		911
Associates		67
Other investments		82
		1,060
	1,136	1,958
Current assets		
Stocks	321	321
Debtors: amounts falling due after one year	10	10
Debtors: amounts falling due within one year	229	229
Cash at bank and in hand	43	43
	603	603
Creditors: amounts falling due within one year	520	520
Net current assets	83	83

Total assets less current liabilities	1,219	2,041
Creditors: amounts falling due after more than one year	647	647
Borrowings and other creditors	35	35
Provisions for liabilities and charges	204	204
	886	886
Net assets	333	1,155
Capital and reserves		
Called up share capital	200	
Share premium account	500	
Profit and loss account	(367)	
Total shareholders' funds—all equity	333	

6.107 In order to comply with FRS 9, it would also be necessary for the proforma information concerning joint ventures and associates to be further analysed in the notes between amounts relating to joint ventures and amounts relating to associates. It is also necessary to give additional information concerning the company's share of items appearing in the joint venture's or associate's statement of total recognised gains and losses and cash flow statement. Furthermore, FRS 9 requires more detailed information to be given for associates and joint ventures in aggregate and individually where they are particularly material to the company. These issues are considered further in chapter 27.

6.108 The disclosures described in paragraphs 6.105 to 6.107 above need not be given where the investing company is exempt from preparing consolidated financial statements, or would be exempt, if it had subsidiaries. [FRS 9 para 48]. However, the information described in paragraph 6.94 must still be given, unless advantage is taken of the exemptions described from paragraph 6.96.

6.109 FRS 9 also deals with the accounting requirements that apply to joint arrangements that are not entities and to structures with the form, but not the substance of, a joint venture. For both of these types of joint arrangements, the standard requires that the investing company should account in its individual financial statements for its share or part of the assets, liabilities and cash flows stemming from the arrangement. [FRS 9 paras 18, 24]. The accounting requirements explained above for associates and joint ventures do not apply to these types of joint arrangements. Such joint arrangements and their accounting requirements are considered in detail in chapter 27.

Subsidiary undertakings

6.110 Where, at the end of a financial year, a company does not prepare consolidated financial statements, but has subsidiary undertakings, the investing company's financial statements have to disclose the information outlined in paragraph 6.105 above for each of its subsidiary undertakings. [SI 2008/410 4 Sch 1, 2(1)].

6.111 In presenting this information, interests include not only those held by the company itself, but also those held by its subsidiaries. Consequently, the identity and proportion of the shares in each class that the investing company and its subsidiaries hold in a subsidiary undertaking has to be shown, distinguishing between those held by the company itself and those held by any of its subsidiaries. [SI 2008/410 4 Sch 11].

6.112 The Act also requires the company to state the reasons for not preparing consolidated financial statements. [SI 2008/410 4 Sch 10(1)]. If the reason why the company is not required to prepare consolidated financial statements is that its subsidiary undertakings fall within the exclusions from consolidation provided for in section 405 the reason for exclusion should be stated for each subsidiary undertaking. [SI 2008/410 4 Sch 10(2)]. Section 405 exclusions are covered in detail in chapter 24.

6.113 Except where one of the conditions below is satisfied, the information outlined in paragraph 6.106 above must also be given for each subsidiary. [SI 2008/410 4 Sch 2(1)].

- The company is exempt by virtue of section 400 or 401 of the 2006 Act from the requirement to prepare consolidated financial statements (see chapter 24). [SI 2008/410 4 Sch 2(2)].
- The company's investment is included in its financial statements using the equity method of valuation. [SI 2008/410 4 Sch 2(3)].
- The company's investment is in a subsidiary undertaking that is not required by any of the Act's provisions to deliver a copy of its balance sheet to the Registrar of Companies and it does not otherwise publish that balance sheet in Great Britain or elsewhere. Where this situation exists, the information need not be given, provided the company's holding is less than 50 per cent of the nominal value of the shares in the undertaking. [SI 2008/410 4 Sch 2(4)].
- The information to be disclosed is not material. [SI 2008/410 4 Sch 2(5)].

6.114 Directors are under an obligation to ensure that the financial years of the group's subsidiaries coincide with that of the parent, unless there are good reasons for a subsidiary's year end to be different. But where the financial year of a subsidiary undertaking does not coincide with that of the company and the company is not exempt from the giving the information set out in paragraph 6.106 above the notes to the company's financial statements must disclose the date on which the subsidiary's last financial year ended. [SI 2008/410 4 Sch 12].

6.115 The company need not give any of the above information required by Schedule 4 where either of the exemptions described in paragraphs 6.96 and 6.97 are taken. The exemption described in paragraph 6.99 is not available as it is replaced in the case of investments in subsidiaries by the exemption described in paragraph 6.113.

6.116 The balance sheet formats specify locations for amounts owed by and to and interests in group undertakings. Hence, it is not acceptable for companies to net these balances off and to disclose the net balance, together with the cost of the investments, in the balance sheet as 'Investments in subsidiaries'. Such offset is also precluded by FRS 5 paragraph 29 and FRS 25 paragraph 42. This applies even where a note to the financial statements gives additional information that explains the net balance.

6.117 Moreover, the amounts owed and owing have to be ascertained on an undertaking by undertaking basis. [SI 2008/410 1 Sch 8]. Consequently, for accounting presentation purposes, amounts that one subsidiary owes to the parent cannot be offset against amounts the parent owes to another subsidiary. Set-off can be allowed only where the offset criteria in FRS 5 and FRS 25 are met (see further chapter 3).

6.118 Furthermore, undertakings have to analyse 'amounts owed by (and to) group undertakings' between amounts that will fall due within one year and amounts that will fall due after more than one year. [SI 2008/410 1 Sch Notes 5 and 13 on the balance sheet formats]. The results of this analysis will largely depend both on the way in which group undertakings are financed and on the terms of any agreements between the undertakings.

Parent company information

6.119 Where, at the end of a financial year, a company is a subsidiary of another undertaking, certain information concerning the name and country of incorporation if incorporated outside the UK, etc, should be disclosed with respect to the company (if any) regarded by the directors as the company's ultimate parent company. [SI 2008/410 4 Sch 9]. In addition, similar information relating to potentially two further parent undertakings in the same group may have to be disclosed, where the parent undertaking draws up accounts for larger group. [SI 2008/410 4 Sch 8]. The rules concerning these disclosures are complex and are considered in detail in chapter 24 in relation to companies that are required to prepare consolidated financial statements.

Membership of a qualifying undertaking

6.120 For the purpose of these rules, 'qualifying undertakings', can either be companies or partnerships. A qualifying company (or qualifying partnership) is an unlimited company (or partnership) incorporated in (or governed by the laws of any part of) Great Britain if each of its members is:

- a limited company; or
- another unlimited company, or a Scottish firm, each of whose members is a limited company.

The references to limited company, another unlimited company and Scottish firm also encompasses any comparable undertakings incorporated in, or formed under the law of, any country or territory outside Great Britain. [SI 2008/410 4 Sch 7(6)].

6.121 Where at the year end the company is a member of a qualifying undertaking, it has to give the following information in its financial statements if material:

- The name and legal form of the undertaking.
- The address of the undertaking's registered office or, if it does not have such an office, its head office.

[SI 2008/410 4 Sch 7(1)(2)].

6.122 In addition, where the qualifying undertaking is a qualifying partnership one of the following must also be stated:

- That a copy of the latest financial statements of the undertaking has been, or is to be, appended to the copy of the company's financial statements sent to the Registrar under section 242 of the Act.
- The name of at least one body corporate (which may be the company) in whose consolidated financial statements the undertaking has been, or is to be, dealt with by the method of full consolidation, proportional consolidation or the equity method of accounting.

[SI 2008/410 4 Sch 7(3)].

6.123 The information required to be disclosed in the second bullet point of the previous paragraph need not be given if the partnership is dealt with on a consolidated basis in the consolidated financial statements prepared by:

- a member of the partnership that is established under the law of a member State; or
- a parent undertaking of such a member established in the same way.

[SI 2008/569 Reg 7(1)].

6.124 The exemption can only be taken, however, where the following two conditions are complied with:

- The consolidated financial statements are prepared and audited under the law of the Member State in accordance with the provisions of the 7th Directive.
- The notes to those consolidated financial statements disclose that advantage has been taken of the exemption.

[SI 2008/569 Reg 7(2)].

Own shares and shares in own parent

6.125 The Act permit companies with *'qualifying shares'* to purchase such shares out of distributable profits and hold them in treasury for resale, transfer or cancellation at a later date. 'Qualifying shares' are defined as shares that:

- are included in the official list (that is, listed on the London Stock Exchange);
- are traded on AIM;
- are officially listed in another EEA State; or
- are traded on a market established in an EEA State, which is a regulated securities market.

[CA06 Sec 724(2)].

6.126 The balance sheet format set out in Schedule 1 to SI 2008/410 has a sub-heading 'own shares'. However, shares held in treasury are not classified as investments, but are instead deducted in arriving at shareholders' funds. The rules relating to treasury shares, including disclosures, are dealt with in more detail in chapter 23.

6.127 A subsidiary company cannot normally hold own shares in its parent company. [CA06 Sec 136(1)]. However, this prohibition does not apply where the subsidiary is acting as a personal representative for a third party, or as trustee and the holding company or a subsidiary of it has no beneficial interest under the trust. [CA06 Sec 138(1)(2)]. This provision also does not extend to market makers. [CA06 Sec 141(1)(2)]. However, the prohibition does include those shares that might be held on behalf of the subsidiary by another person as its nominee. [CA06 Sec 144].

6.128 Where a body corporate becomes a subsidiary company because of the changes in the definition of subsidiaries included in section 1159 of the 2006 Act, it may retain any shares that it already held in its parent. However, where shares are held in this way, they will carry no right to vote at company meetings. [CA06 Sec 137(1)(2)].

6.129 In certain situations, a subsidiary may find that it does hold shares in its parent. This may arise, for example, where the parent has recently acquired the subsidiary which owned shares in the parent before it became a group member. Before the introduction of the Companies Act 1989, such holdings may have been in breach of section 23(1) of the Companies Act 1985. Now, however, where a company acquires shares in its parent after the commencement of section 23(1), but before it becomes a subsidiary of the parent, it may retain those shares. Also in this circumstance, those shares will carry no right to vote at company meetings. [CA06 Sec 137(1)(2)].

6.130 In the past, such shares have been classified as an asset, 'own shares', in the parent's consolidated financial statements. FRS 25 requires that where shares in a holding company are purchased or held by a subsidiary, the consideration paid should be deducted in arriving at shareholders' funds in the holding company's consolidated financial statements. [FRS 25 para 33]. However, in the individual financial statements of a subsidiary that holds shares in its parent, such shares are treated as an asset, rather than deducted in arriving at shareholders' funds, as these are not 'own shares' for the subsidiary itself.

6.131 The notes to the parent's financial statements must disclose the number, description and the amount of the shares that subsidiaries or their nominees hold. [SI 2008/410 4 Sch 3(1)]. This information is not required, however, where the subsidiary holds the shares as personal representative or as trustee. [SI 2008/410 4 Sch 3(2)]. However, the exemption for a subsidiary acting as a trustee will not be available if the company or any of its subsidiaries is beneficially interested under the trust, unless the beneficial interest is by way of security for the purpose of a transaction entered into by it in the ordinary course of business, which includes the lending of money. [SI 2008/410 4 Sch 3(3)]. Additionally, FRS 25 requires separate disclosure, either on the face of the balance sheet or in the notes, of the amount of treasury shares held. [FRS 25 para 34].

6.132 In recent years, many companies have established employee share ownership plans (ESOP), because of the tax advantages that they afford employees. The accounting treatment of shares held by an ESOP trust is considered in more detail in chapter 12.

Loans for acquisition of own shares

6.133 Where any outstanding loans made in respect of the acquisition of the company's shares under either section 682(2)(b), (c) or (d) of the 2006 Act (various situations of financial assistance by a company for purchase of its own shares) are included under any item in the balance sheet, these must be disclosed in aggregate for each item. [S1 2008/410 1 Sch 64(2)]. The acquisition by a company of its own shares is considered in chapter 7 of the Manual of Accounting – Management reports and governance.

Other investments

6.134 The category 'other investments' will normally include the following items (other than investments in subsidiaries and companies in which the investing company has a participating interest):

- Listed and unlisted securities.
- Life assurance policies.
- Joint ventures and partnerships, if they are not subsidiaries or participating interests.

6.135 Building society deposits and bank deposits could be included either as 'other investments' (either under fixed assets or under current assets – depending on the nature of the deposits) or as 'cash at bank and in hand'. If the amount is material, the accounting policies should disclose where such items are included. This is considered in more detail in chapter 4.

Requirements for entities not applying FRS 26

Introduction

6.136 As explained above, entities that do not fall within the scope of FRS 26 may be within the scope of the disclosure standard, FRS 13, and will need to apply FRS 4 for any capital instrument they issue. This section covers the FRS 13 disclosure requirements and explains the amended requirements of FRS 4. Furthermore, they may voluntarily adopt certain disclosure requirements of FRS 29, which is discussed in paragraph 6.371.

FRS 13

Scope of FRS 13

6.137 FRS 13 applies to entities that have any of their capital instruments (generally shares and debt, including minority interests) listed or publicly traded on a stock exchange or market (domestic or foreign). [FRS 13 paras 2, 119]. IAS 32 and IAS 39 apply under the EU Regulations to listed entities' consolidated financial statements. Hence, FRS 13 continues to apply to some listed entities that do not have subsidiaries and are not required to prepare IFRS consolidated financial statements and to those entities whose securities are not listed or traded on a regulated market. For example, FRS 13's requirements will apply to a company whose only listed capital instrument is a Eurobond quoted on a non regulated overseas stock exchange and a company whose shares are traded on OFEX or similar markets. Companies registered on the AIM have to prepare consolidated financial statements under EU adopted IFRS. However, for the parent entity financial statements they have a choice of adopting IFRS or continuing to use UK GAAP.

6.138 In addition, all banks and similar financial institutions (for example, building societies), whether quoted or not, must make the required disclosures unless they fall within the requirements of the EU directive to prepare IFRS financial statements. [FRS 13 para 82].

6.139 The FRS sets different rules for non-financial entities, for banks and for other financial institutions that are not banks. The last category includes leasing companies, investment and unit trusts, money brokers and 'in-store' credit card companies. [FRS 13 para 119]. Although the required narrative disclosures are common to all entities the reporting entity's classification determines the type of numerical disclosures that should be given. Accordingly, the standard is split into three parts:

- Part A deals with disclosures for quoted reporting entities other than banks and other financial institutions.
- Part B deals with disclosures for all banks and similar institutions.
- Part C deals with disclosures for quoted non-bank financial institutions.

6.140 The FRS does not apply to insurance companies or groups. Furthermore, as the Manual of Accounting – UK GAAP does not deal with banks and similar institutions or non-bank financial institutions, this chapter considers only the disclosures required for other reporting entities as set out in Part A of the standard.

6.141 Reporting entities and subsidiaries that themselves have no listed or traded capital instruments, unless they are banks or similar institutions, need not comply. Moreover, a quoted parent company to which the standard applies is not required to give the disclosures in its own financial statements if they are given on a group basis in its accompanying consolidated financial statements. [FRS 13 para 3(b)].

6.142 In the context of FRS 13, group refers solely to the parent entity and its subsidiaries and quasi-subsidiaries. Hence, details of an associate's or joint venture's own financial instruments should not be included in the FRS 13 disclosures for the investing group as the individual amounts are not included in the consolidation. However, if an associate's or joint venture's use of financial instruments is material to an understanding of the effect of the investments on the investing group, separate disclosures about their financial instruments would need to be considered in the light of the requirement in FRS 9 to make disclosure of such material matters. [FRS 9 para 53].

6.143 The exemption from giving entity-own disclosures needs to be considered carefully as illustrated in the following group structures as either the group or some subsidiaries will have to provide FRS 13 disclosures in circumstances where the fact that the FRS requires disclosure may not be readily apparent.

Example 1

An unquoted non-financial institution UK holding company H has an unquoted non-financial institution UK subsidiary S and another non-financial institution UK subsidiary L, which has a eurobond quoted on an unregulated overseas stock exchange. Which reporting entities must comply with FRS 13?

Subsidiary L has a quoted capital instrument, its eurobond, and thus must comply with FRS 13 and give the required disclosures in respect of all of its financial instruments, including inter-company balances (unless they fall within short-term 'trade' debtors and creditors (see para 6.166 below)).

As H group has quoted debt, namely subsidiary L's eurobond, its group financial statements must comply with FRS 13 and deal with all of H group's financial instruments including those in subsidiary S. In its individual financial statements, H group will be entitled to the 'entity-own' exemption from providing separate disclosures about its financial instruments, because they are given on a group basis in its accompanying consolidated financial statements.

Subsidiary S does not have to comply itself with FRS 13 since it is an unquoted non-financial institution. However, as noted it will, nevertheless, have to provide H with information on all its financial instruments.

Excluded financial instruments

6.144 The FRS 13 definition of a financial instrument (see para 6.11) is deliberately wide in order to capture instruments that may be devised in the future without the need for continual updating of the accounting standard. However, the following items, which appear to satisfy the definition, are specifically excluded:

- Interests in subsidiaries, quasi-subsidiaries, associates, partnerships and joint ventures, other than those held exclusively with a view to resale. This exclusion does not cover loans to or from subsidiaries, quasi-subsidiaries, associates and joint ventures and they should be dealt with in the disclosures.
- Equity minority interests. [FRS 13 para 5(a) footnote].
- Employer's obligations under employee option and share schemes and any shares held in order to fulfil such obligations (for example, shares held in an ESOP trust).
- Pensions and other post-retirement benefits.
- Obligations under operating leases (unless they become onerous and provision has to be made under FRS 12).
- Equity shares issued by the reporting entity and warrants or options on them, other than those held exclusively with a view to resale. But all non-equity shares (for example, preference shares) fall to be dealt with in the disclosures as a separate category of financial liabilities. [FRS 13 para 8].
- Financial assets, financial liabilities and cash-settled commodity contracts of an insurance company or group.

[FRS 13 para 5].

6.145 There is no exclusion for 'intra-group financial instruments' in FRS 13. This is important because in some situations, although intra-group financial instruments in FRS 13 eliminate on consolidation they will still feature in some of FRS 13's disclosures (see para 6.236). In addition, it is also relevant in situations where perhaps an intermediate parent has listed securities and thus has to prepare consolidated financial statements that have to comply with FRS 13. Inter-company balances with its parent and fellow subsidiaries will not eliminate on consolidation and thus have to be dealt with in the FRS 13 disclosures.

6.146 Appendix II to the standard makes clear that the following are not financial instruments:

- Physical assets, such as stock, property, plant and equipment.
- Intangible assets, such as patents and trademarks.
- Prepayments for goods or services, since these will not be settled in cash or another financial instrument, similarly deferred costs and expenses.
- Obligations to be settled by the delivery of goods or rendering of services, such as most executory contracts or most warranty obligations.
- Forwards, swaps and options to be settled by the delivery of goods or the rendering of services.
- Income taxes (including deferred tax), since these are statutory rather than contractual obligations, although this seems a very fine distinction.
- Contingent items that do not arise from contracts, for example, a contingent liability for a tort judgement.
- Equity minority interests that arise on consolidating a subsidiary that is not wholly-owned.

[FRS 13 App II para 4].

Short-term debtors and creditors

6.147 Although debtors and creditors fall within the definition of a financial instrument an entity can opt either to exclude certain short-term debtors and creditors from all the disclosures (other than the currency disclosures (see para 6.230)) required by the standard or to include them. Whatever it does, the reporting entity must state how such items have been dealt with. [FRS 13 para 6].

6.148 Short-term debtors and creditors that may be excluded are those financial assets and liabilities that meet all of the following criteria.

- They would be included under one of the following balance sheet headings if the entity was preparing its financial statements in accordance with Schedule 1 to SI 2008/410.
  - Debtors.
  - Pre-payments and accrued income.
  - Creditors: amounts falling due within one year, other than items that would be included under the 'debenture loans' and 'bank loans and overdrafts' sub-headings.
  - Provisions for liabilities and charges.

  - Accruals and deferred income.
- They mature or become payable within 12 months of the balance sheet date.
- They are not a derivative financial instrument.

[FRS 13 para 2].

6.149 Items that fall within the criteria are trade debtors and creditors, 'trade' balances due from or to associates and joint ventures, bills of exchange payable and payments received on account, perhaps in respect of a short-term contract, that have a maturity of less than 12 months. Short-term bank loans and overdrafts do not meet the criteria and cannot be excluded.

6.150 SI 2008/410 Schedule 1 balance sheet headings and sub-headings, however, do not specifically include a home for 'obligations under finance leases'. Indeed, SSAP 21 paragraph 51 states that such amounts "*should be disclosed separately from other obligations and liabilities, either on the face of the balance sheet or in the notes to the accounts* ". This is interpreted as creating new sub-headings within the two creditors captions (under one year and over one year) rather than totally different headings. For the purposes of FRS 13, any finance lease obligations falling within creditors under one year should not be excluded from the disclosures under the provision of paragraph 6 of the standard because they are of a financing nature. Similarly, short-term finance lease receivables should also be dealt with in the disclosures.

Identification of on balance sheet financial instruments

6.151 The first step when preparing FRS 13 disclosures is to identify all on balance sheet financial instruments. It is important, when performing this exercise, to drill down through each balance sheet caption in some detail to determine whether there is a financial instrument. When a list of all on balance sheet financial instruments has been compiled it is then necessary to go through the list and establish whether the instruments identified should be excluded from disclosure, either because they are specifically excluded by FRS 13 or because they fall under the short-term debtors and creditors exclusion, as discussed above.

6.152 The list below is an *aide-mémoire* to help the identification of on balance sheet financial instruments.

FRS 13 – Financial instruments

The following is a non-exhaustive list of common balance sheet items

	Financial instrument	Excluded from disclosure[1]	Can be excluded[2]
Tangible fixed assets	×		
Intangible fixed assets	×		
Investment in subsidiary – not held for resale	✓	✓	–
Investment in subsidiary – held for resale	✓	–	–
Investment in associate/joint venture – not held for resale	✓	✓	–
Other investments	✓	–	–
Stocks	×		
Trade debtors (short-term)	✓	–	✓
Trade debtors (long-term)	✓	–	–
Prepayments – goods and services	×		
Accrued income (short-term)	✓	–	✓
Dividends receivable (short-term)	✓	–	✓
Cash	✓	–	–
Bank loans and overdrafts (short-term)	✓	–	–
Bank loans and overdrafts (long-term)	✓	–	–
Convertible debt	✓	–	–
Debentures – current portion	✓	–	–
Debentures – long term portion	✓	–	–
Trade creditors (short-term)	✓	–	✓
Trade creditors (long-term)	✓	–	–
Accruals – goods and services	✓	–	✓
Deferred income	×		
Pensions and similar obligations	✓	✓	–
Provisions under 1 year (contractual obligation for cash or other financial asset)	✓	–	✓
Provisions over 1 year (contractual obligation for cash or other financial asset)	✓	–	–
Warranty obligations (settled by delivery of goods)	×		
Warranty obligations (settled by delivery of cash or other financial asset)	✓	–	–
Finance lease obligations	✓	–	–
Operating lease creditor	✓	✓	–
Taxation and social security	×		
Equity shares	✓	✓	–
Non-equity shares	✓	–	–
Investment in own shares	✓	✓	–
Equity minority interests	×		
Non-equity minority interests	✓	–	–
Final dividends proposed	×		
Interim dividend payable	✓	–	✓

[1] Financial assets and liabilities that are excluded from the disclosures (other than the currency disclosures) by FRS 13 paragraph 5.

[2] Financial assets and liabilities that may be excluded from all disclosures (other than the currency disclosure) by the short-term debtors and creditors exclusion per FRS 13 paragraphs 6-7.

Note also that inter-company balances and balances with associates and joint ventures are financial instruments. Short-term trade type balances may be excluded from disclosures by the short-term debtors and creditors exclusion noted in footnote 2 above.

Derivative financial instruments

6.153 A derivative is specifically defined in FRS 13 as: *"A financial instrument that derives its value from the price or rate of some underlying item"*. [FRS 13 para 2]. Such underlying items could include equities, bonds, commodities, interest rates, stock market and other indices. Hence, the term 'derivative' would apply to the following instruments, although the range and complexity of other derivatives, which are effectively hybrids of these, are not only substantial but increasing:

- Forward contracts — contracts for the purchase or sale of a specified amount of a commodity or financial instrument (such as foreign currency) at a fixed price with delivery and settlement at a specified future date.
- Futures contracts — similar to forward contracts except that the purchase or sale is of standardised amounts that are traded on an exchange.
- Options and warrants — give the purchaser the right, but not the obligation, to purchase (call) or sell (put) a fixed amount of a commodity or financial instrument at a fixed price with delivery and settlement at either a specified future date or over a fixed future period.
- Swaps — parties to the contract exchange cash flows in order to access a particular market as if they had entered it directly. For example, interest paid at a fixed rate may be exchanged for interest paid at a floating rate (an interest rate swap) or borrowings denominated in different currencies may be exchanged (a cross-currency swap).
- Caps — an interest rate cap is an agreement whereby the seller reimburses the purchaser with the excess of interest costs over and above a specified rate. Hence, interest costs for the purchaser are capped.
- Collars — an interest rate collar is a combination of a cap and its natural opposite, referred to as a floor. Hence, the purchaser locks into a specified range of interest rates.

6.154 Although worded differently to the FRS 26/IAS 39 definition of a financial instrument (see Annex 3), the meaning is essentially the same. An FRS 13 derivative would in most cases be an FRS 26/IAS 39 derivative, and *vice versa*.

6.155 On inception, derivative financial instruments give one party a contractual right to exchange financial assets with another party under conditions that are potentially favourable, or conversely a contractual obligation to make such an exchange under potentially unfavourable conditions. Some instruments include both a right and an obligation to make an exchange (for example, a forward foreign exchange contract). It is important to monitor the instrument, since the terms that were set at inception may become either favourable or unfavourable as prices in financial markets change.

6.156 But not all derivatives are financial instruments. Any derivative whose terms do not include the receipt or delivery of financial assets or exchange of financial instruments is not a financial instrument. For example, an option to buy or sell land is not a financial instrument. Similarly, commodity contracts that require settlement by physical delivery are not financial instruments.

Cash-settled commodity contracts

6.157 Cash-settled commodity contracts, such as commodities futures contracts, are to be treated as if they are financial assets and liabilities for the purposes of the following disclosures:

- Objectives, policies and strategies (see from para 6.170).
- Fair values (see from para 6.222).
- Financial assets and liabilities issued for trading purposes (see from para 6.238).
- Hedges (see from para 6.241).

[FRS 13 para 64].

6.158 They are not included in the interest rate risk and currency profile disclosures of financial liabilities and financial assets (see from paras 6.190 and 6.211 respectively), as this is not required by paragraph 64 of the standard. Cash and government securities should not be treated as commodities, but for this purpose commodity contracts include hard commodities (such as metals including gold) and soft commodities (such as oils, grains, cocoa, cotton, soya beans and sugar). But contracts for the purchase of commodities for actual delivery and use by an entity in its business, such as raw materials in the manufacture of its products, are not cash-settled commodity contracts and so are outside the scope of the standard. [FRS 13 para 2].

6.159 An example of a company, other than a commodity trader, providing information of this nature is British Airways plc.

Table 6.2 – Cash-settled comodity contract

British Airways Plc – Report & Accounts – 31 March 2000

Operating and financial review (extract)

Derivative financial instruments (extract)

British Airways uses derivative financial instruments (derivatives) with off-balance sheet risk selectively for treasury and fuel risk management purposes.

The risk management strategy for both treasury and fuel operations is implemented by the respective departments within the guidelines and parameters laid down by the board of Directors, and reflects a risk averse policy. The company's policy is not to trade in derivatives but to use these instruments to hedge anticipated expenses.

The company's fuel risk management strategy aims to provide the airline with protection against sudden and significant increases in oil prices while ensuring that the airline is not competitively disadvantaged in a serious way in the event of a substantial fall in the price of fuel. The strategy operates within limits set by the Board and agreed in detail by the Fuel Hedging Committee, which is made up of representatives from fuel, finance, treasury and strategy.

In meeting these objectives, the fuel risk management programme allows for the judicious use of a number of derivatives traded on regulated exchanges in London (the Institute of Petroleum Exchange) and New York (the New York Mercantile Exchange) as well as on the Over The Counter (OTC) markets with approved counterparties and within approved limits. The instruments used include futures and forward contracts, options, collars, caps and swaps. The hedging committee reviews the use of these instruments on a regular basis.

Notes to the accounts (extract)

43 Fair values of financial instruments (extract)

b Derivative financial instruments held to manage the interest rate and currency profile

	2000	1999
£ million	Fair value	*Fair value*
Interest rate swaps	(4)	*(15)*
Forward currency transactions	10	*14*
Fuel derivatives	55	*10*

Included within forward currency transactions are derivative financial instruments held to hedge the currency exposure on expected future sales.

c Hedges

The instruments used to hedge future exposures are interest rate swaps, forward currency contracts and fuel derivatives.

At March 31, 2000 there were unrecognised gains of £65 million and unrecognised losses of £4 million relating to hedges of future exposures. Of the unrecognised gains, £63 million are expected to occur within one year and £2 million after one year, and of the unrecognised losses, £1 million are expected to occur within one year and £3 million after one year.

At March 31, 1999 there were unrecognised gains of £26 million and unrecognised losses of £17 million. Of the unrecognised gains £24 million related to the period to 31 March, 2000 and £2 million related to periods over one year and of the unrecognised losses, £9 million related to the year to March 31, 2000 and £8 million related to periods in excess of one year.

6.160 A reporting entity might participate in an illiquid commodity market dominated by very few participants. Where this is the case, disclosure of some of the information on fair values and financial assets and liabilities held or issued for trading or hedging purposes required by the FRS in respect of its commodity positions could move the market significantly and prejudice the entity's interests. In order to avoid this happening, the standard allows disclosures that would be prejudicial in these circumstances to be omitted. [FRS 13 para 65]. The fact that the information has not been disclosed and the reasons for the omission must be stated.

6.161 References in this chapter to financial instruments include commodity contracts with similar characteristics as defined above, notwithstanding the commercial confidentiality exemption discussed in the previous paragraph.

Non-equity shares and non-equity minority interests

6.162 FRS 13 defines non-equity shares as those shares that have any of the following characteristics:

- Any of the rights of the shares to receive payments (whether in respect of dividends, in respect of redemption or otherwise) are for a limited amount that is not calculated by reference to the company's assets or profits or the dividends on any class of equity share.
- Any of their rights to participate in a surplus in a winding up are limited to a specific amount that is not calculated by reference to the company's assets or profits and such limitation had a commercial effect in practice at the time the shares were issued or, if later, at the time the limitation was introduced.
- The shares are redeemable either according to their terms, or because the holder, or any party other than the issuer, can require their redemption.

[FRS 13 para 2].

6.163 This definition is identical to the definition previously contained within FRS 4. The concept of non-equity shares has been removed from FRS 4 following the introduction of FRS 25 and all shares are now categorised and accounted for as either a financial liability or as equity. However, it is interesting to note that FRS 13 has not been amended. For clarity an entity could provide details alongside the FRS 13 disclosures of how the non-equity shares have been classified within the financial statements.

6.164 Under FRS 13, all non-equity shares issued by the reporting entity should be dealt with in the disclosures, both narrative and numerical, as if they are financial liabilities. However, they should be distinguished separately from financial liabilities in the disclosures. [FRS 13 para 8]. This is described as a pragmatic solution by the ASB to avoid introducing a complexity into the standard. A strict interpretation of the definitions would otherwise require all shares to be categorised as either equity or liabilities.

6.165 By extension, non-equity minority interests should be dealt with as financial liabilities and should be separately disclosed.

FRS 13 disclosures

6.166 For conventional instruments, such as shares and loans, other disclosure requirements give some indication of the risks to which a reporting entity is exposed. For example, the following disclosures are required by the Companies Act:

- Details of redeemable shares including the period for redemption and whether any premium is payable. [SI 2008/410 1 Sch 47(2)].
- Details of any options to subscribe for shares in the company including the number in issue, the period during which they may be exercised and the price to be paid. [SI 2008/410 1 Sch 49].
- Repayment terms and interest rates applicable to long-term liabilities. [SI 2008/410 1 Sch 61(2)].
- Market values of listed investments if different to the book value. [SI 2008/410 1 Sch 54].

6.167 Until FRS 13, neither company law nor accounting standards included detailed disclosure requirements in respect of derivatives. The Act does, however, require disclosure of financial commitments to the extent that they are relevant to a proper understanding of the company's state of affairs. [SI 2008/410 1 Sch 63(5)]. Therefore, where a company has outstanding forward contracts, the amounts outstanding under the forward contracts have had to be disclosed under this requirement. An example where a company discloses outstanding forward contracts, is given in Table 6.3 below.

Table 6.3 – Disclosure of outstanding forward contracts

British Airways Plc – Report & Accounts – 31 March 1999

Notes to the accounts (extract)

35 Forward Transactions

The Group had outstanding forward transactions to hedge foreign currencies and fuel purchases as follows:

	in currency		Sterling equivalents	
	1999	*1998*	**1999**	*1998*
Maturing within one year:				
– to cover future capital commitments in US Dollars	**US$774m**	*US$485m*	**£473m**	*£289m*
– to hedge future currency revenues in US Dollars	**US$27m**	*US$127m*		
– to hedge future currency revenues against sterling			**£62m**	*£65m*
– to hedge future operating payments against US Dollars	**US$66m**	*US$130m*		*£78m*
– to hedge future fuel costs in US Dollars	**US$319m**	*US$415*	**£194m**	*£247m*

– to hedge future operating payments against sterling				*£82m*
– to hedge debt in a foreign currency	**US$225m**	*US$150m*	**£138m**	*£90m*
Maturing after one year:				
– to cover future capital commitments in US Dollars	**US$90m**	*US$170m*	**£54m**	*£101m*
– to hedge future currency revenues against sterling			**£2m**	*£1m*
– to hedge future operating payments against US Dollars				*£16m*

6.168 FRS 13 requires a range of disclosures that are, in most areas, consistent with those required by FRS 25. Broadly, these disclosures may be divided into narrative and numerical information. The former is intended as an explanation of why the entity uses financial instruments, what it hopes to achieve and whether this is demonstrated by the latter period-end numerical disclosures. [FRS 13 paras 13, 20]. All of the required disclosures are outlined below, as are other disclosures that are made by certain companies, but that are not specifically required by the FRS.

6.169 Annex 1 to this chapter contains examples of narrative and numerical disclosures for some typical financial instruments (provided on an individual basis) and which comply with the disclosure requirements explained below and the numerical disclosures that are explained from paragraph 6.188.

Disclosure of objectives, policies and strategies

6.170 FRS 13 requires that an entity should provide an explanation of the role that financial instruments have had during the period in creating or changing the risks it faces in its activities. This should include an explanation of the objectives and policies for holding or issuing financial instruments (including derivatives) and similar contracts, such as cash-settled commodity contracts, and the strategies that have been followed in the period for achieving those objectives as agreed by the directors. [FRS 13 para 13]. For example, a company might have an objective of having 70 per cent of its borrowings at fixed rates. Its strategy to achieve this might be to borrow directly in this ratio or alternatively to use derivatives such as swaps, caps and collars to convert floating rate borrowings to fixed in the desired ratio.

6.171 The narrative should involve describing management's attitude to risk, in particular whether it is averse to cash flow risk or market price risk (steps taken to mitigate one often increases exposure to the other). For example, where an entity holds ten per cent gilts, changes in interest rates will cause their value to fluctuate (market price risk), but such changes do not alter future income (that is, no cash flow risk). If management is market price risk adverse, it will act to protect the gilts' value by, say, swapping the fixed rate interest for floating rate; but in doing so it creates cash flow risk, because net income from the gilts and the swap will fluctuate with changes in interest rates. The disclosure of its accounting (including hedging), treasury and risk management policies should be clear and concise.

6.172 The nature and extent of the discussion will vary depending on the circumstances of the organisation, but the ASB expects it to be at a high level and not commercially sensitive. Basically, it should set the scene for the numerical disclosures and should contain sufficient information to enable a reader to understand the reporting entity's objectives and policies and the strategies for achieving those objectives.

6.173 The discussion should focus only on the major financial risks faced during the period. Typically the major financial risks faced by entities include interest rate risk, liquidity risk and currency risk. Any other significant risks the entity might face should also be considered when considering the financial risks of the entity as a whole. The narrative on each of the financial risks faced by the entity should be structured to cover the requirements described below.

6.174 An explanation should be given of the role that financial instruments have had during the period in creating or changing the risks faced by the reporting entity. This should include an explanation of its objectives and policies for holding or issuing financial instruments and similar contracts and its strategies for achieving those objectives. [FRS 13 para 13].

- This disclosure would usually include a discussion of the nature of and purposes for which the main types of financial instruments and similar contracts are held or issued. This should cover separately instruments used for financing, risk management or hedging and for trading or speculation. [FRS 13 para 14].
- This disclosure would also typically include a discussion of the reporting entity's main risk management and treasury policies, quantified where appropriate, on:
  - The fixed/floating split, maturity profile and currency profile of financial liabilities (including borrowings) and financial assets.
  - The extent to which foreign currency financial assets and financial liabilities are hedged to the functional currency of the business unit concerned.
  - The extent to which foreign currency borrowings and other financial instruments (that is, derivatives) are used to hedge foreign currency net investments.
  - Any other hedging.

[FRS 13 para 15].

6.175 If the explanations given above reflect a significant change from the explanations given in the previous accounting period this should be explained and the reasons for the change given. [FRS 13 para 16].

6.176 If the directors have agreed before the date of approval of the financial statements to change significantly the role that financial instruments will have in the next accounting period, this should be explained. [FRS 13 para 18].

6.177 An explanation of how the period-end figures shown in the financial statements represent the objectives, policies and strategies of the reporting entity, or, if the period-end position shown by the financial statements is considered to be materially unrepresentative of the entity's use of financial instruments and thus its exposure to risks, an explanation of the extent to which it is considered unrepresentative. [FRS 13 para 20].

6.178 Where a reporting entity uses financial instruments as hedges it should describe:

- The transactions and risks that are hedged, including the time until they are expected to occur.
- The instruments used for hedging, disclosing those that have been accounted for using hedge accounting and those that have not. [FRS 13 para 21].

Note that the term 'hedge' here is with reference to original UK GAAP hedge accounting (see para 6.403) and is not the same as the hedge accounting that may be permitted under the provisions of FRS 26/IAS 39.

6.179 The reference to the period end figures in paragraph 6.196 above relates to the interest rate risk disclosures for financial assets and liabilities, the currency risk disclosures for the net amount of monetary assets and liabilities and the maturity profile of financial liabilities. The narrative disclosures should be consistent with each of these balance sheet orientated numerical disclosures. The narrative disclosures should be specific to the reporting entity concerned, explaining its year end position and any material movements from the previous year end position. An example of a company clearly explaining its year end position relative to its objectives, policies and strategies for assessing interest rate risk is given in Table 6.4 below.

Table 6.4 – Interest rate risk

South African Breweries Plc – Annual Report and Accounts – 31 March 2000

Notes to the Consolidated Financial Statements (extract)

Interest rate risk

The group finances its operations through a mixture of retained reserves and bank borrowings. The group borrows principally in rand, and increasingly in US dollars at both fixed and floating rates of interest. The interest rate characteristics of new borrowings and the refinancing of existing borrowings are positioned according to expected movements in interest rates. In order to hedge specific exposures in the interest rate repricing profile of existing borrowings and anticipated peak additional borrowings the group makes use of interest rate swaps and forward rate agreements to generate the desired interest profile and to manage the group's exposure to interest rate fluctuations. The group's policy is to keep between 25%, and 75%, of its borrowings (measured on a rolling basis) at a fixed rate of interest — intended to limit the impact, of a 1% change in interest rates, to 1% of group operating profit excluding exceptional items. As at 31 March 2000 – 8% (31 March 1999 – 29%) of the group's borrowings were at fixed rates after taking account of any interest rate swaps and forward rate agreements. The relatively low fixed rate percentage at 31 March 2000 is analysed further (in this note) under the interest rate risk profile of financial liabilities and financial assets.

6.180 The disclosures referred to above should be included within the financial statements, the directors' report or the non-mandatory OFR. If the disclosures are included in the directors' report or the OFR they should be incorporated within the financial statements by a clear reference in the notes to the statement in which they are located. (It should also be remembered that these disclosures, as they form part of the financial statements, are required to be audited.) In any event it will aid users of financial statements to include in one place the structured discussion on the financial risks faced by the entity as required by the standard.

6.181 Carlton Communications plc, provides an example (Table 6.5 below) of the type of narrative disclosure required by the standard.

Table 6.5 – Disclosure of objectives, policies and strategies

Carlton Communications Plc – Annual report and accounts – 30 September 2001

Finance Director's review (extract)

FINANCING

Carlton 's policy is to finance itself long-term using debt instruments with a range of maturities. Carlton has traditionally raised fixed rate debt from the US and European Capital Markets, as well as obtaining bank facilities from the UK Syndicated Market.

In March 2001 Carlton established a £1,000m Euro Medium Term Note programme which provides standard documentation for both public bond issues and private placement loan notes. By the year end Carlton had issued loan notes under the programme in a variety of currencies (swapped back to sterling) totalling about £168m. In April 2001 Carlton arranged a £300m 5 year Syndicated bank facility which has not been drawn at the date of writing. The purpose of the facility is to provide financial flexibility through short-term liquidity pending longer-term refinancing.

In November 2001 Carlton announced the issue of €638.6m (£397.6m) exchangeable bonds which will mature in 2007, will carry a coupon of 2.25 per cent per annum, and have a fixed exchange price of €41.2. The bonds will be exchangeable into 15.5m ordinary shares in Thomson representing Carlton 's underlying total equity interest in the company. Carlton also announced that it has reached agreement in principle for the sale of US$175m nominal amount of loan notes issued by Thomson which are unguaranteed. Both transactions are expected to complete early in the New Year.

OBJECTIVES, POLICIES AND STRATEGIES

The most significant treasury exposures faced by Carlton are raising finance, managing interest rate and currency positions and investing surplus cash in high quality assets. Clear parameters have been established, including levels of authority, on the type and use of financial instruments to manage these exposures. Transactions are only undertaken if they relate to underlying exposures. Regular reports are provided to senior management and treasury operations are subject to periodic independent reviews and internal audit.

INTEREST RATE MANAGEMENT

Carlton uses interest rate swaps, options and forward rate agreements to manage its interest rate exposures on its debt and cash positions with the objective of minimising its net interest cost.

The interest rate profile of Carlton 's interest bearing assets and liabilities at the year end are detailed in notes 18, 19, 21 and 25(a) respectively.

Net interest payable was £35.6m (2000 – £28.4m). A 1 per cent decrease in short-term sterling and dollar interest rates based on the year-end position would increase profits before tax by about £2.0m.

Borrowings are denominated in currencies that match Carlton 's net assets as described below. The fair values of borrowings and cash at the year-end are compared to their book values in Note 25(b).

CURRENCY MANAGEMENT

Carlton faces currency exposure on trading transactions undertaken by its subsidiaries in foreign currencies. In addition, Carlton is also subject to currency exposures resulting from the Technicolor sale consideration.

Carlton hedges a proportion of its transactional exposures by taking out forward foreign exchange contracts of up to four years forward against its anticipated and known sales and purchases. The decision to hedge is influenced by the size of exposure, the certainty of it arising, the trading and market position of the company in which the exposure arises and the current exchange rate.

At the year-end Carlton estimated that its net purchases of foreign currency in 2002 relating to trading transactions would total less than £50m after taking into account foreign currency hedging in place. The year-end fair value of hedging maturing in 2002 was £3.1m below book value, due to forward purchases of Swiss Francs to match Champion's League payments undertaken in previous years when sterling was weaker.

Carlton 's balance sheet translation exposure is managed by partially matching currency assets with a combination of currency borrowings and forward foreign exchange contracts. Post completion of the sale of Technicolor, exposure to the economic interest in 15.5m shares of Thomson has been Carlton 's largest single currency exposure. In November 2001 Carlton entered into a foreign exchange option contract to protect up to half of the anticipated currency translation exposure. A one per cent movement in the Sterling/Euro exchange rate should not impact the value of this investment by more than £3m.

INVESTMENT OF CASH

Carlton operates strict investment guidelines with respect to surplus cash and the emphasis is on preservation of capital. Consequently, discretionary investments with maturity greater than one year must be rated AA or better and discretionary investments of less than one year must be rated A1 or P1 by the major credit rating agencies. There are also conservative limits for individual counter-parties. The maturity profile of investments is managed according to the forecast cash needs of the Group.

Disclosure of accounting policies

6.182 FRS 18 requires financial statements to include a clear, fair and concise explanation of all material or critical accounting policies. Clearly, the disclosure of accounting policies for financial instruments and hedging will be necessary for all companies that are required to comply with FRS 13 as financial instruments and hedging practices are likely to be material for all listed companies. Furthermore, for other companies that use financial instruments, it will be necessary to explain material accounting policies to accord with FRS 18. FRS 18, reinforced by FRS 13, requires that such disclosure should include:

- The methods used to account for derivatives, the types of derivatives accounted for under each method and the criteria that determine the method used.
- The basis for recognising, measuring (both on initial recognition and subsequently) and ceasing to recognise financial instruments.
- How income and expenses (and other gains and losses) are recognised and measured.
- The treatment of financial instruments not recognised, including an explanation of how provisions for losses are recognised on financial instruments that have not been recognised.
- Policies on offsetting.

[FRS 13 para 74].

6.183 Where a company carries its financial instruments at historical cost, the accounting policies would typically cover the treatment of:

- Premiums and discounts on financial assets.
- Changes in the estimated amount of determinable future cash flows associated with a financial instrument, such as a debenture indexed to a commodity price.
- A fall in the fair value of a financial asset to below the asset's carrying value.
- Restructured financial liabilities.

[FRS 13 para 75].

6.184 Where a company accounts for its hedges using hedge accounting, the accounting policies should include a description of:

- The circumstances when a financial instrument is accounted for as a hedge.
- The recognition and measurement principles applied to a hedge instrument.
- The method used to account for an instrument that ceases to be accounted for as a hedge.

- The method used to account for a hedge when the underlying item or position matures, is sold, extinguished, or terminated.
- The method used to account for a hedge of a future transaction when that transaction is no longer likely to occur.

[FRS 13 para 76].

6.185 Again, note that the term 'hedge' here is with reference to original UK GAAP hedge accounting (see para 6.403) and is not the same as the hedge accounting that may be permitted under the provisions of FRS 26/IAS 39.

6.186 It might be expected that these requirements would mean companies producing at least one common disclosure in respect of the use of forward currency and similar contracts. This disclosure would explain whether the company follows the predominant practice as permitted by SSAP 20 paragraph 46 and translates its foreign currency assets and liabilities that it is hedging using, say, forward currency contracts, at the contracted rate. Alternatively, a company's accounting policy might be to amortise the forward premium in the forward currency contract to profit and loss account over the life of the contract and the hedged item would be recorded at the spot rate at inception of the forward contract. Whatever policy a company adopts, it will have an impact on the numerical disclosures on hedging (see from para 6.241).

6.187 Examples of accounting policies from the financial statements of BAE SYSTEMS plc, BP p.l.c. and BG plc are shown in Tables 6.6 to 6.8 below.

Table 6.6 – Accounting policies

BAE SYSTEMS plc – Annual Report – 31 December 2002

Notes to the accounts (extract)

Accounting policies (extract)

Foreign currencies

Transactions in overseas currencies are translated at the exchange rate ruling at the date of the transaction or, where forward cover contracts have been arranged, at the contracted rates. Monetary assets and liabilities denominated in foreign currencies are retranslated at the exchange rates ruling at the balance sheet date or at a contracted rate if applicable and any exchange differences arising are taken to the profit and loss account.

For consolidation purposes the assets and liabilities of overseas subsidiary undertakings and joint ventures are translated at the closing exchange rates. Profit and loss accounts of such undertakings are consolidated at the average rates of exchange during the year. Exchange differences arising on foreign currency net investments are taken to reserves.

Financial instruments

The Group uses derivative financial instruments to hedge its exposures to fluctuations in interest and foreign exchange rates. Instruments accounted for as hedges are designated as a hedge at the inception of contracts. Receipts and payments on interest rate instruments are recognised on an accruals basis, over the life of the instrument. Gains and losses on foreign currency hedges are recognised on maturity of the underlying transaction, other than translational hedges of foreign currency investments which are taken to reserves. Gains and losses arising from retiming of foreign exchange transactional cover are deferred to match the maturity of the underlying exposure. Gains or losses arising on hedging instruments which are cancelled due to the termination of underlying exposure are taken to the profit and loss account immediately. Finance costs associated with debt issuances are charged to the profit and loss account over the life of the instruments.

Table 6.7 – Accounting policies

BP p.l.c. – Annual accounts 31 December 2001

Accounting policies (extract)

Derivative financial instruments

The group uses derivative financial instruments (derivatives) to manage certain exposures to fluctuations in foreign currency exchange rates and interest rates, and to manage some of its margin exposure from changes in oil and natural gas prices. Derivatives are also traded in conjunction with these risk management activities.

The purpose for which a derivative contract is used is identified at inception. To qualify as a derivative for risk management, the contract must be in accordance with established guidelines which ensure that it is effective in achieving its objective. All contracts not identified at inception as being for the purpose of risk management are designated as being held for trading purposes, as are all oil price derivatives, and accounted for using the fair value method, as are all oil price derivatives.

The group accounts for derivatives using the following methods:

Fair value method: derivatives are carried on the balance sheet at fair value ('marked to market') with changes in that value recognized in earnings of the period. This method is used for all derivatives which are held for trading purposes. Interest rate contracts traded by the group include futures, swaps, options and swaptions. Foreign exchange contracts traded include forwards and options. Oil and natural gas price contracts traded include swaps, options and futures.

Accrual method: amounts payable or receivable in respect of derivatives are recognized ratably in earnings over the period of the contracts. This method is used for derivatives held to manage interest rate risk. These are principally swap agreements used to manage the balance between fixed and floating interest rates on long-term finance debt. Other derivatives held for this purpose may include swaptions and futures contracts. Amounts payable or receivable in respect of these derivatives are recognized as adjustments to interest expense over the period of the contracts. Changes in the derivative's fair value are not recognized.

Deferral method: gains and losses from derivatives are deferred and recognized in earnings or as adjustments to carrying amounts, as appropriate, when the underlying debt matures or the hedged transaction occurs. This method is used for derivatives used to convert non-US dollar borrowings into US dollars, to hedge significant non-US dollar firm commitments or anticipated transactions, and to manage some of the group's exposure to natural gas price fluctuations. Derivatives used to convert non-US dollar borrowings into US dollars include foreign currency swap agreements and forward contracts. Gains and losses on these derivatives are deferred and recognized on maturity of the underlying debt, together with the matching loss or gain on the debt. Derivatives used to hedge significant non-US dollar transactions include foreign currency forward contracts and options and to hedge natural gas price exposures include swaps, futures and options. Gains and losses on these contracts and option premia paid are also deferred and recognized in the income statement or as adjustments to carrying amounts, as appropriate, when the hedged transaction occurs.

Where derivatives used to manage interest rate risk or to convert non-US dollar debt or to hedge other anticipated cash flows are terminated before the underlying debt matures or the hedged transaction occurs, the resulting gain or loss is recognized on a basis that matches the timing and accounting treatment of the underlying debt or hedged transaction. When an anticipated transaction is no longer likely to occur or finance debt is terminated before maturity, any deferred gain or loss that has arisen on the related derivative is recognized in the income statement together with any gain or loss on the terminated item.

Table 6.8 – Accounting policies

BG plc – Annual Report and Accounts – 31 December 1999

Principal accounting policies (extract)

Financial instruments

Derivative instruments utilised by the Group are interest rate swaps, foreign currency swaps, forward rate agreements, interest rate swaptions, tax equalisation swaps and forward exchange contracts.

A derivative instrument is considered to be used for hedging purposes when it alters the risk profile of an existing underlying exposure of the Group in line with the Group's risk management policies. Derivatives used for hedging are accounted for on an accruals basis. During the year there were no derivatives used for trading purposes.

Termination payments made or received in respect of derivatives are spread over the shorter of the life of the original instrument or the life of the underlying exposure in cases where the underlying exposure continues to exist. Where the underlying exposure ceases to exist, any termination payments are taken to the profit and loss account.

Interest differentials on derivative instruments are recognised by adjusting the net interest charge. Premiums or discounts on derivative instruments are amortised over the shorter of the life of the instrument or the underlying exposure.

Currency swap agreements and forward exchange contracts are retranslated at the rates ruling in the agreements and contracts. Resulting gains or losses are offset against foreign exchange gains or losses on the related borrowings or, where the instrument is used to hedge a committed future transaction, are deferred until the transaction occurs.

Detailed numerical disclosures

6.188 The aim of the numerical disclosures required in FRS 13 is to show how the entity's objectives and policies were implemented under its strategies in the period and provide supplementary information for evaluating significant or potentially significant exposures. For example, the disclosures include information relevant to an assessment of interest rate and currency risk together with an analysis of fair values and information on the impact of using hedge accounting.

6.189 The disclosures required by the FRS are intended to be highly summarised and the FRS prescribes in some detail the offsetting and aggregation to be used for particular disclosures. However, this does not mean that the offsetting permitted in the disclosures is appropriate for recognition and measurement purposes in the primary financial statements. [FRS 13 para 24]. One effect of the high degree of aggregation and offsetting required, or encouraged, by the FRS is that it may not be possible to trace components of the disclosures back to their respective balance sheet captions. Where this is the case, the FRS encourages additional detail to be provided to facilitate such a reconciliation, unless it would unduly complicate the disclosure. [FRS 13 para 25].

Interest rate risk and currency profiles of financial liabilities

6.190 The standard requires extensive disclosure in respect of interest rate risks by currency related to the company's financial liabilities and where material, its financial assets (see para 6.205 below). An entity's financial liabilities are its contractual obligations to deliver cash or other financial assets to another entity or to exchange financial instruments with another entity under conditions that are potentially unfavourable. [FRS 13 para 2]. Consequently, this disclosure will embrace an entity's borrowings, finance lease obligations, trade creditors, certain provisions (such as those for onerous leasehold commitments) and, for the reasons explained in paragraphs 6.163 and 6.164, its non-equity shares and non-equity minority interests. A company may exclude from these disclosures those items that fall within the definition of short-term 'trade' creditors. [FRS 13 para 6].

6.191 For each major currency, financial liabilities should be analysed to show those at fixed rates, those at floating rates and those on which no interest is paid. Finance lease obligations, deep discounted bonds and other liabilities where the finance cost is allocated in accordance with FRS 4 or SSAP 21 are interest-bearing liabilities and should not be included as 'financial liabilities on which no interest is paid'. [FRS 13 para 27]. Non-interest bearing financial liabilities would include long-term trade creditors or qualifying provisions that are not discounted. Floating rate financial liabilities are defined as those that have their interest rate reset at least once a year. [FRS 13 para 2]. Those that reset less frequently are to be treated as fixed rate financial liabilities. However, the standard is silent on items such as deferred consideration or long-term monetary provisions where these are discounted. It can be argued that such discounted items are floating rate financial liabilities as the discount rate will have to be re-appraised, and changed if necessary, at least once a year to ensure that the financial liability reflects current market assessments of the time value of money and the risks specific to the liability, as required by FRS 12, 'Provisions, contingent liabilities and contingent assets'.

6.192 The standard requires the interest rate risk disclosures to be shown on a gross basis, that is without netting off cash, other liquid resources or similar items. [FRS 13 para 31]. Where a company wishes to show the interest rate risk disclosures on a net basis, for example where it manages its interest rate risk on a net basis, it can do so by giving additional information showing the net position as long as the gross position is also disclosed.

6.193 For each of the major currencies, the following details of interest rates should be disclosed:

- The weighted average interest rate for fixed rate financial liabilities.
- The weighted average period for which interest rates are fixed.
- The weighted average period until maturity of non-interest bearing financial liabilities.
- The benchmark rate for determining interest rate payments for floating rate financial instruments. This could, for example, result in disclosure that floating rate borrowings bear interest based on LIBOR. Although the standard has no requirement for disclosure of the interest differential this may well be caught by the disclosure requirement in the Companies Act (see para 6.166), as suggested by the footnote to the illustrative disclosures in appendix III to the standard.

[FRS 13 para 30].

6.194 The analysis should take account of instruments such as swaps and other derivatives, the effect of which is to alter the interest basis or currency of the financial liability (described as 'non-optional derivatives'). For example, if the company has a floating rate borrowing and has taken out an interest rate swap to swap its interest obligation to fixed rate, the borrowing would be disclosed in the table as a fixed rate borrowing. Other instruments, such as caps and collars, that are associated with these financial liabilities and which convert those liabilities over only a limited range of interest rates (described as 'optional derivatives') and cannot be adequately reflected in the analysis should be excluded and explained separately, as should any financial liabilities and non-optional derivatives with unusual terms. [FRS 13 para 26]. Convertible debt is an example of a financial liability that may be more appropriately dealt with separately outside the analysis.

6.195 For those instruments excluded from the analysis, there should be disclosure of the main terms and conditions sufficient to enable the reader to understand their significance. This could include a summary of the following:

- Notional principal amounts involved.
- Rates of interest.
- Periods for which contracts are operative.
- Terms of any options contained within the instrument.

[FRS 13 para 29].

6.196 Examples of the disclosures outlined above are shown in Tables 6.9 and 6.10 below by companies that have included FRS 13 disclosures in their financial statements. Table 6.10 illustrates an occasion when provisions that meet the definition of a financial liability are included in the disclosure.

Table 6.9 – Interest rate risk and currency profiles of financial liabilities

BG plc – Annual Report and Accounts – 31 December 1999

Notes to the accounts (extract)

19 Currency and Interest Rate Composition of The Group's Financial Liabilities and Borrowings (extract)

The following table analyses the currency and interest rate composition of the Group's financial liabilities after the effect of swaps.

	Fixed rate weighted average period	Fixed rate weighted average interest rate %	Fixed borrowings	Floating borrowings	Gross borrowings	Other financial liabilities (a)	**1999 Total**	1998 Total
	years		£m	£m	£m	£m	**£m**	£m
Currency:								
Sterling	6.7	6.2	3 246	3 407	6 653	217	**6 870**	4 120
US dollars	3.7	8.4	311	378	689	–	**689**	683
Brazilian reals	1.9	11.4	46	12	58	–	**58**	–
Indian rupees	4.1	14.0	24	–	24	–	**24**	26
			3 627	3 797	7 424	217	**7 641**	4 829

For the purposes of the above tables, debt with a maturity within one year, such as commercial paper, bills of exchange and other money market borrowings, has been treated as fixed. Index-inked bonds have been treated as floating. Borrowings falling due after more than one year of £5 333m (1998 £3 199m) (after currency and interest rate swaps) can be analysed as fixed interest rate 33% (1998 68%) and floating interest rate 67% (1998 32%).

(a) The weighted average period of other financial liabilities, which relate to provisions for long-term gas sales contracts (see Note 23), was 7 years as at 31 December 1999. These provisions have been discounted at around 10%.

Table 6.10 – Interest rate risk profile of financial liabilities and financial assets

South African Breweries Plc – Annual Report – 31 March 1999

Notes to the Consolidated Financial Statements (extract)

30 Financial instruments

Interest rate risk profile of financial liabilities and financial assets

After taking into account the Group's interest rate and currency swaps and forward rate agreements the currency and interest rate exposures of the gross borrowings of the Group for the year ended 31 March 1999 were:

	Total	Floating rate financial liabilities	Fixed rate financial liabilities	Financial liabilities where no interest is paid
Currency	**US$m**	**US$m**	**US$m**	**US$m**
Rand	488	325	163	–
US dollars	186	88	98	114
Central European currencies	41	41	–	–
EU currencies	86	83	3	–
Other currencies	152	141	11	–
At 31 March 1999	**953**	**678**	**275**	**114**
Rand	640	439	201	–
US dollars	341	257	84	139
Central European currencies	50	49	1	–
EU currencies	11	11	–	–
Other currencies	10	10	–	–
At 31 March 1998	1,052	766	286	139

Based on the above floating rate borrowings at 31 March 1999, a 1 per cent change in interest rates would impact Group pre-tax profits, over a twelve month period, by approximately US$7 million (R41 million)

	Fixed rate financial liabilities		Financial liabilities on which no interest is paid
Currency	**Weighted average interest rate %**	**Weighted average period for which rate is fixed (years)**	**Weighted average term to maturity years**
Rand	15	2	–
US dollars	8	2	1
EU currencies	5	4	–
Other currencies	6	4	–
At 31 March 1999	**12**	**2**	**1**
Rand	15	2	–
US dollars	9	3	2
Other currencies	16	2	–
At 31 March 1998	13	3	2

Floating rate borrowings are mainly bank sourced and bear interest at various money market rates which include overnight call, 90 day bankers' acceptance, and up to the 12 month term rates in respect of SA rand activities. US dollar floating rate borrowings are fixed in advance for periods ranging from 90 to 180 days and are mainly priced by references to LIBOR. Central European borrowing rates vary significantly between the various functional currency areas comprising this region, but are priced by reference to a combination of local market rates or LIBOR depending on the sophistication of the various markets.

The Group held the following financial assets, as part of the financing arrangements of the Group, during the year ended 31 March 1999.

	1999 **US$m**	1998 US$m	**1999** **Rm**	1998 £m
US dollar listed equity investments	–	177	–	891
Rand short-term deposits	–	–	**3**	–
US dollar short-term deposits	**587**	–	**3,638**	–
Other short-term deposits	**25**	10	**152**	49
Rand cash	**28**	327	**168**	1,650
US dollar cash	**57**	13	**357**	64
Other cash	**52**	75	**322**	377
	749	602	**4,640**	3,031

The above financial assets are all priced at floating rates with interest rates reset and/or maturity dates within one year. Rand assets attract interest rates at the overnight money market call rate, and US dollar assets attract LIBOR related interest rates at various margins. Other currencies include those of central European countries, the African continent and Australasia. No other currency represents a significant amount.

Rand cash and short-term deposits are subject to South African exchange control regulations. South Africa's exchange control regulations provide for restrictions on exporting capital from South Africa.

Maturity analysis of financial liabilities

6.197 A maturity profile of the carrying amount of financial liabilities (that is, those recognised on the balance sheet) is also required. This would show the total amounts falling due within the following time bands:

- In one year or less, or on demand.
- In more than one year, but not more than two years.
- In more than two years, but not more than five years.
- In more than five years.

[FRS 13 para 38].

6.198 This profile, which is, to a large extent, an aggregation of the analyses of debt and finance leases already required by the original FRS 4 and SSAP 21, is based on the carrying amounts determined by reference to the earliest date on which payment can be required or on which the liability falls due. The standard requires the maturity analysis to include all financial liabilities, other than short-term 'trade' creditors (if the exemption is utilised), and thus embraces the same liabilities that are analysed in the interest risk disclosure. Financial liabilities will also include, for example, swaps and non-optional derivatives, if they are recognised on balance sheet.

6.199 An amount that is due exactly five years after the balance sheet date falls within the third band 'in more than two years, but not more than five years', rather than the fourth one 'in more than five years'. Similarly an amount due exactly two years after the balance sheet date falls within the second band, 'in more than one year, but not more than two years'.

6.200 Where the original FRS 4 analysis of debt and the SSAP 21 analysis of finance lease obligations are disclosed in the same table as the FRS 13 maturity analysis, the analysis of debt and finance lease obligations will need to be based on the carrying amounts. They should not, for example, be based on the amounts to be paid on maturity or, in the case of finance lease obligations, on the gross obligations before deducting finance charges. Also the maturity analysis specified in SSAP 21 for finance leases only requires disclosure of the amounts payable in the second to fifth years inclusive, hence, this amount would have to be further analysed to satisfy FRS 13's requirements into amounts that are payable in more than one year, but not more than two years and those that are payable in more than two years, but not more than five years. [FRS 13 para 39]. In addition, an analysis of other financial liabilities would need to be given. An illustration of a combined disclosure using a columnar approach is given below.

Illustration of the maturity analysis

The maturity profile of the carrying amount of the group's financial liabilities, other than short-term trade creditors and accruals and the non-redeemable non-equity minority interests, at 31 December was as follows:

	Debt	Finance leases	Other financial liabilities	20X1 Total	Debt	Other financial liabilities	20X0 Total
	£m	£m	£m	£m	£m	£m	£m
In one year or less, or on demand	88.9	3.5	51.7	144.1	41.7	4.1	45.8
In more than one year but not more than two years	0.5	3.5	16.8	20.8	0.9	1.0	1.9
In more than two years but not more than five years	284.1	6.1	13.8	304.0	–	1.0	1.0
In more than five years	4.1	–	29.4	33.5	3.0	3.8	6.8
	377.6	13.1	111.7	502.4	45.6	9.9	55.5

Debt due after five years includes £2.0m (20X0: £2.0m) in respect of the company's preference shares. Other financial liabilities include the provisions for vacant leasehold properties £68.4m (20X0: £6.3m).

The company's £224.7m bank loan (gross of unamortised issue costs of £4.2m) is repayable within twelve months of the balance sheet date, but as the amount is drawn under a five year committed multi-option facility it is classified in the table above as repayable between two and five years on the basis of the expiry date of the facility in May 20X5.

6.201 Table 6.11 illustrates another method of disclosure by presenting a maturity analysis of total financial liabilities (including relevant provisions), gross borrowings and net borrowings. The latter is not required by the standard, but is an interesting interpretation of the suggestion in paragraph 43 of the standard that it might be helpful to provide a maturity analysis of financial assets in order to put the maturity analysis of financial liabilities and borrowing facilities in their proper context.

Table 6.11 – Maturity analysis of financial liabilities

BG plc — Annual Report and Accounts — 31 December 1999

Notes to the Accounts (extract)

18 Borrowings and financial instruments (extract)

Maturity profile of the Group's financial liabilities

The following table analyses the Group's financial liabilities comprising gross borrowings plus any long-term contractual obligations to deliver cash or other financial assets to another entity, after taking account of currency and interest rate swaps. These are repayable as follows:

	Total financial liabilities		Gross borrowings		Net borrowings (i)	
	1999	1998	**1999**	1998	**1999**	1998
	£m	£m	**£m**	£m	**£m**	£m
Within one year	**2 082**	1 403	**2 091**	1 394	**1 539**	850
Between one and two years	**613**	357	**613**	357	**613**	357
Between two and three years	**357**	755	**354**	755	**354**	755
Between three and four years	**778**	152	**762**	149	**762**	149
Between four and five years	**486**	759	**464**	743	**464**	743
After five years	**3 325**	1 403	**3 140**	1 195	**3 140**	1 195
	7 641	4 829	**7 424**	4 593	**6 872**	4 049

Further information on total financial liabilities is given in Note 19.

Net borrowings comprise gross borrowings less current asset investments and cash at bank and in hand.

Maturity analysis of undrawn committed borrowing facilities

6.202 FRS 13 also requires an analysis to be given of the maturity of material undrawn committed borrowing facilities, showing separately amounts expiring:

- In one year or less.
- In more than one year, but not more than two years.
- In more than two years.

[FRS 13 para 40].

If there are conditions that attach to a particular facility, then it should only be included in the above analysis if all the conditions are satisfied at the balance sheet date.

6.203 The maturity analysis of financial liabilities outlined in paragraph 6.216 above will include the drawn element of certain committed borrowing facilities. For example, a company might have an overdraft facility of £50 million, and by the year end it might have drawn on this facility and have an overdraft balance of £20 million, which would be included in the financial liabilities maturity analysis as an amount falling due for repayment 'in one year or less, or on demand'. To avoid double-counting, any amounts drawn down under borrowing facilities should not also be disclosed in the maturity analysis of undrawn committed borrowing facilities. [FRS 13 para 41]. Consequently, in this example only £30 million, which is the undrawn element of the committed facility, would be included in the undrawn committed facilities table. Furthermore, its inclusion in a particular banding in the analysis would depend on the date on which the facility expires. For example, if it were to expire in 18 months time, then the £30 million would appear in the line for amounts expiring 'in more than one year but not more than two years' even though the overdraft balance itself is categorised in the financial liabilities maturity analysis as 'in one year or less, or on demand'.

6.204 In order to enable the reader to assess the significance of these facilities, the FRS recommends that disclosure is given of the purpose and the period for which these facilities are committed and the extent to which they are subject to annual review by the provider of finance. This additional information is not mandatory. [FRS 13 para 42]. In any case, listed companies that continue to prepare an OFR should, and when preparing a business review may, already include a comment on liquidity and this may include details such as those suggested in the FRS (see further chapter 2 of the Manual of Accounting – IFRS and UK supplement).

Details of financial assets

6.205 f the reporting entity has significant holdings of financial assets, interest rate risk and currency profile analyses similar to those required for financial liabilities and described from paragraph 6.196 above should be provided (see Table 6.9 in para 6.196). [FRS 13 para 32]. A maturity profile similar to that described in paragraph 6.197 is not required, but may be presented if this would show the maturity analyses of financial liabilities and borrowing facilities in their proper context. [FRS 13 para 43].

6.206 Financial assets, those on-balance sheet and any derivative or other financial assets that are off-balance sheet, will have to be dealt with in the fair value disclosures (see from para 6.222). In the case of derivative financial assets used as hedging instruments these will also feature in the hedge disclosures (see from para 6.241).

6.207 Financial assets include holdings of cash, short-term deposits with banks, buildings societies or other financial institutions, money market investments, certificates of deposit, another company's commercial paper or loan stock, gilts and any other instruments that are classified as current asset investments or cash at bank and in hand in the balance sheet. Consequently, they include those assets regarded as liquid resources for cash flow classification purposes under FRS 1. Financial assets also include trade debtors, finance lease receivables, investments in equity shares (for example, trade investments) and other instruments that neither pay interest nor have a maturity date.

6.208 In determining the necessity for making the disclosures, the following points should be borne in mind. Short-term trading receivables due from associates and joint ventures can be excluded from the interest rate analysis under the exemption in paragraph 6 of the standard (with appropriate disclosure). However, long-term trading receivables due from, and all loans to or other financing type balances with, associates and joint ventures have to be dealt with in the interest rate disclosure. Such items also feature in the fair value disclosure.

6.209 In certain situations inter-company balances with parents, subsidiaries and fellow subsidiaries have to be included in the interest rate and currency profile and fair value disclosures. A particular example is the situation where an intermediate parent company has listed securities and has to prepare consolidated financial statements that comply with FRS 13. Although inter-company balances with subsidiaries should eliminate on consolidation, those with parents and fellow subsidiaries do not and are thus caught. The disclosures of the fair value of intra-group balances go beyond those required by FRS 8, 'Related party disclosures', and they may well have implications for tax purposes, particularly where the loan or other arrangement is not on an arm's length basis.

6.210 For equity shares and similar instruments, the disclosures will be typically limited to a footnote stating that they had been excluded from the interest rate risk and currency profile, as they have no maturity date and would thus distort the weighted average period information and the provision of pertinent information about any currency exposures involved. [FRS 13 para 33]. Financial assets on which no interest is earned include undiscounted long-term trade debtors, but do not include, for example, investments in deep discounted bonds for which an interest income can be imputed or holdings of another company's preference shares. [FRS 13 para 27]. In the latter case, the coupon is regarded as interest.

Currency risk disclosures

6.211 FRS 13 requires an analysis of the net amount of monetary assets and monetary liabilities at the balance sheet date, by reference to the principal functional currency of the reporting entity's operations, showing the amount denominated in each principal currency. [FRS 13 para 34]. Functional currency is defined in an identical manner to SSAP 20's definition of local currency, namely, "*the currency of the primary economic environment in which an entity operates and generates net cash flows*". [FRS 13 para 2]. The purpose of this analysis is to explain the currency exposures that give rise to those exchange gains and losses that are taken to the profit and loss account. [FRS 13 para 35]. The analysis will, therefore, need to be constructed to reflect the entity's application of SSAP 20. [FRS 13 para 36].

6.212 The term 'monetary assets and liabilities' refers to money held and amounts to be received or paid in money. [SSAP 20 para 44]. Consequently, whether or not short-term 'trade' debtors and creditors have been included within the other disclosures required by FRS 13, they are required to be included in the table of currency risk exposures (see further para 6.147). [FRS 13 para 6]. The amounts disclosed should be after taking account of currency swaps, forward contracts and other derivatives that contribute to the matching of the foreign currency exposures. [FRS 13 para 34(d)]. Thus, for example, if a UK company has taken out a forward exchange contract in respect of euro debtors to effectively convert the amounts receivable into sterling, then for the purpose of this analysis these debtors should be treated as a sterling asset. Therefore, in extreme circumstances where all currency exposures are hedged with counterparties external to the reporting entity there will be nothing to report, as demonstrated in Table 6.13 below (see para 6.621). In addition, a summary of the main effect should be given of any derivative financial instruments that have not been taken into account.

6.213 Only the principal functional currencies and the principal currencies in which the monetary items are denominated need be given. Monetary assets and liabilities denominated in the same functional currency as the particular operation should be excluded from the analysis. Similarly, where a company has foreign currency borrowings that provide a hedge against foreign net investments, under SSAP 20 gains and losses arising on translation would be taken to the statement of total recognised gains and losses not to the profit and loss account; consequently, such borrowings are 'matched' and are excluded from the analysis. [FRS 13 para 34]. As the analysis is prepared at the year end, it is somewhat forward looking as an indicator of those currency exposures that might give rise to gains and losses in the following year's profit and loss account, as well as representing the currency exposures that existed throughout the year. If the period end position is regarded as materially unrepresentative of the entity's position during the period then an explanation is required. [FRS 13 para 20]. The fact that the net position for the group as a whole may be zero due to compensating exposures in different parts of the group does not remove the necessity to provide the disclosure.

6.214 To illustrate the requirement consider the following example.

Example

Group A plc consists of the parent company in the UK, two subsidiaries in North America, one in the USA and the other in Canada, a subsidiary in Japan, a subsidiary in France and a number of small subsidiaries in other countries. The principal functional currencies of group A's operations are thus sterling, US dollar, the Yen and the euro. Since the Canadian dollar is aligned with the US dollar, it is considered to have the same currency risk and is thus not separately identified. To compile the required currency risk disclosure, each of the companies' operations has to analyse its year end balance sheet to identify those monetary assets and monetary liabilities that are in currencies other than its own functional currency (excluding those that it has hedged into its functional currency). This process determines that: the UK parent has US dollar, Yen and euro exposures; the French subsidiary has sterling, US dollar and Yen exposures; the North American operations are exposed to sterling only; the Japanese subsidiary has exposures in sterling, US dollar and the euro; and the other subsidiaries, collectively, have sterling, US dollar and euro exposures as well as some smaller exposures to other currencies. Consequently, group A constructs the following grid to make the required disclosure.

Illustration of the disclosure of currency exposures

Functional currency of group operation	Net foreign currency monetary assets/(liabilities)					
	Sterling	**US dollar**	**Yen**	**Euro**	**Other**	**Total**
	£m	**£m**	**£m**	**£m**	**£m**	**£m**
Sterling	–	20	10	–	–	30
US dollar	15	–	–	–	–	15
Yen	(30)	30	–	(90)	–	(90)
Euro	25	(300)	40	–	–	(235)
Other	(10)	(30)	–	40	10	10
Total	–	(280)	50	(50)	10	(270)

The amounts in the table take into account the effect of currency swaps, forward contracts and other derivatives entered into to manage currency exposures.

6.215 In this example, group A has US dollar monetary assets of £20 million in the UK and £30 million in Japan and US dollar liabilities of £300 million in France and £30 million in other countries. Hence, at the balance sheet date the group has £280 million of aggregate US dollar net liabilities, which result in gains or losses being recognised in the profit and loss account.

6.216 If the £300 million US dollar liabilities in France was a borrowing and was treated as a hedge of US dollar assets on consolidation, group A's US dollar position would be reduced to an asset of only £20 million and the total net foreign currency exposure would be only £30 million. Hence, it is easy to see how the picture portrayed by this analysis can be changed significantly. For groups with sophisticated treasury functions and diverse geographic operations the collation of the information from subsidiaries is not an easy task and the preparation and interpretation of this disclosure can be complex.

6.217 In preparing the required analysis, the interaction of foreign currency inter-company balances should not be overlooked. For example, if, in the above illustration, company A has sold goods or services to its US subsidiary and invoiced for these in sterling, the inter-company balance so created will cause a sterling exposure for the US operation. The exchange gains or losses on retranslation into US dollars at each balance sheet date until the balance is settled will go to the US profit and loss account and hence flow through into group A's consolidated profit and loss account. Although the inter company balances eliminate on consolidation, there is no elimination of the exchange differences in the profit and loss account. Consequently, in the above example, the sterling/US dollar inter-company exposure would be included in the £15 million sterling net monetary assets in the US.

6.218 Alternatively, assume that company A has made a US dollar loan to its US subsidiary to finance its activities and that, for all practical purposes, this is as permanent as equity and thus treated under SSAP 20 paragraph 20 as part of its net investment in the US. The US dollar/sterling exposure arising in company A would not feature in the required analysis since the exchange gains and losses would be taken to the statement of total recognised gains and losses under the provisions of SSAP 20.

6.219 Another feature that should not be overlooked when preparing the currency risk disclosure is the consequence of hedging transactions where the counterparty is another group company, perhaps one acting as a group treasury function. Any hedging transaction that removes the currency risk from one area of the group's operations to another merely shifts the place that the exposure is reported. Only in circumstances where the risk is on-hedged with counterparties external to the group or the internal counterparty has an existing, and opposite, currency risk, is the exposure reduced or removed and thus reported as such in the analysis required by FRS 13.

6.220 For example, a UK parent company has €10 million of creditors due for payment in three months from the balance sheet date. Its French subsidiary has £6.5 million of debtors due to be received in three months from the balance sheet date. If neither company hedges its exposures to foreign currencies, the group's currency risk disclosure would show the UK parent with a euro exposure of £6.5 million (assuming €1 = £0.65) and the French subsidiary with a sterling exposure of £6.5 million. However, if the parent company and its French subsidiary enter into a three month forward currency contract with each other at the balance date to buy euro and sell sterling, the French subsidiary removes its exposure to sterling and thus regards the sterling debtors as euro for the purposes of the currency risk analysis. For UK parent the forward contract eliminates the euro exposure on its creditors. Hence, there is nothing to show for either group operation under the currency risk disclosures. However, in the absence of the euro creditors in the UK parent company, the forward currency contract removes the reportable sterling exposure from France and creates a reportable euro exposure in the UK within the group's currency risk disclosure.

6.221 An example of the required disclosure is provided by South African Breweries Plc in Table 6.12 in its March 1999 financial statements. However, in the case where a company's policy is to hedge all currency exposures the disclosure becomes a 'nil report' as shown in example 2 of annex 1 to this chapter and by Imperial Chemical Industries PLC in Table 6.14.

Table 6.12 – Disclosure of currency exposures

South African Breweries Plc – Annual Report & Accounts – 31 March 1999

Notes to the accounts (extract)

30 Financial instruments (extract)

Currency exposures
The Group seeks to mitigate the effect of the currency exposures arising from its net investments overseas by borrowing as far as possible in the same currencies as the operating currencies of its main operating units. Gains and losses arising on net investments overseas and the financial instruments used to hedge the currency exposures are recognised in the statement of total recognised gains and losses.

The table adjacent shows the extent to which group companies have monetary assets and liabilities in currencies other than their local currency. Foreign exchange differences on translation of earnings are taken to the profit and loss account of the Group.

Net foreign currency monetary assets/(liabilities)

Functional currency of Group operation	Rand US$m	US dollar US$m	Central European currencies US$m	EU currencies US$m	Other African currencies US$m	Other currencies US$m	Total US$m
Rand	–	6	–	(2)	–	–	4
US dollars	–	–	1	–	–	–	1
Central European currencies	–	(13)	–	(8)	–	–	(21)
Other African currencies	(3)	(22)	–	(1)	–	–	(26)
Other currencies	–	–	–	5	–	–	5
31 March 1999	(3)	**(29)**	1	(6)	–	–	(37)
Rand	–	20	–	–	–	–	20
US dollars	–	–	–	–	19	(2)	17
Central European currencies	–	(4)	–	(11)	–	–	(15)
Other African currencies	(13)	(16)	–	(2)	–	–	(31)
Other currencies	–	(3)	–	–	–	–	(3)
31 March 1998	(13)	(3)	–	(13)	19	(2)	(12)

Table 6.13 – Currency exposures on monetary assets and liabilities

Imperial Chemical Industries PLC – Annual report and accounts and Form 20-F-31 December 1999

Notes relating to the accounts (extract)

40 Financial risk management (extract)

(b) Currency exposures on monetary assets and liabilities
As explained in the Operating and financial review, on page 22, the Group's policy is, where practicable, to hedge all exposures on monetary assets and liabilities.

Fair value disclosures

6.222 Disclosure is required of the fair values of all financial assets and liabilities, whether recognised (on-balance sheet) or not (off-balance sheet), compared to their book value, other than those exempted under paragraph 5 of the FRS (see para 6.144). [FRS 13 para 44]. In addition, disclosure of the fair value of short-term 'trade' debtors and creditors is not required if the exemption in paragraph 6 of the FRS is used (see para 6.147). The fair value should be given regardless of whether or not the instrument is used for hedging purposes. Such instruments are, like other instruments, to be disclosed by category and the standard suggests that it might be useful to indicate the link between the hedging instrument and the item that it is hedging and explain whether the fair value of the hedged item is also disclosed. [FRS 13 para 47].

6.223 It should be remembered that in producing the disclosure, unlike other FRS 13 disclosures, fair values should be given without taking into account related derivatives. For example, a fixed rate debt that has been swapped into floating rate debt by an interest rate swap will not appear as a floating rate debt in the fair value disclosure, as it does in the interest rate risk disclosure. It will be included as fixed rate debt within the fair value disclosure and the fair value of the interest rate swap will be included within, say, a category of 'derivative financial instruments used to manage interest rate risk'. The fair value of the synthetic floating rate debt is thus shown by the separate fair values of its constituent elements.

Determination of fair values

6.224 For the purpose of the required disclosures, fair value is defined as *"...the amount at which an asset or liability could be exchanged in an arm's length transaction between informed and willing parties, other than in a forced or liquidation sale"*. [FRS 13 para 2]. Often, quoted market prices will provide the best evidence of fair value. However, where there is little or no activity in a particular market, or there is no market at all, the FRS requires that estimation techniques are used (such as prices of similar instruments, discounted cash flows or option-pricing models) that will usually give a sufficiently reliable measure of fair value. If measurement of fair value proves particularly difficult, a range of values could be disclosed. [FRS 13 para 54(a); App IV paras 7-9]. In certain circumstances although a fair value might not be available for an individual financial instrument, it might be possible to value a portfolio of such instruments. Where this is so the standard requires the portfolio value to be used and disclosed. [FRS 13 para 54(b)]. The methods used and any significant assumptions used to determine fair value should be disclosed. [FRS 13 para 51]. Further guidance on fair valuing is given in appendix IV to the standard.

6.225 In extreme cases, where it is not practicable to estimate fair values with sufficient reliability, no fair value need be disclosed, but the following must be disclosed instead:

- A description of the financial asset or liability and its carrying amount.
- The reasons why it is not practicable to estimate fair value with sufficient reliability.
- Information about the principal characteristics of the instrument that are pertinent to estimating its fair value (for example, the factors that determine or affect the instrument's cash flows and the market for such instruments). But such information need not be disclosed if in the directors' opinion its disclosure at the level of aggregation and date of disclosure would be seriously prejudicial to the company's interests. The fact that such information has not been disclosed and the reason for non-disclosure should then be given.

[FRS 13 para 53].

6.226 The ASB expects that this exemption should be used only as a last resort, after all viable alternatives have been exhausted and it suggests that the following factors should generally be present if the exemption is to be invoked:

- The instrument is unique and no comparable instruments exist.
- The future cash flows associated with the instrument are difficult to predict with any degree of reliability.
- A reliable valuation model is not available from either internal or external sources.

[FRS 13 para 55].

6.227 It might only be possible for the fair value to be ascertained for some of the financial instruments included within a category. Where this is so, the standard requires the fair value of that sub-set to be disclosed and the disclosures set out in paragraph 6.244 above to be given for the rest of that category. [FRS 13 para 54(c)].

Disclosure by category

6.228 Unless a reporting entity has very few financial instruments or the differences between book value and fair value are immaterial, a table is the best means of disclosure. For this purpose instruments should be grouped into appropriate categories. The illustrative examples given in the appendices to FRS 13 group financial instruments into the following categories:

- Primary financial instruments held or issued to finance the group's operations.
- Derivative financial instruments held to manage the interest rate and currency profile.
- Derivative financial instruments held or issued to hedge the currency exposure on expected future sales.
- Financial instruments held or issued for trading.

As a result of grouping, a loan and a cross-currency swap will appear in different categories, for example, the loan in 'primary instruments' and the swap in 'derivative financial instruments used to manage interest rate and currency profile'.

6.229 In the illustrative example given in the appendices to the standard, fair values are given for each of the groups of financial instruments within the categories noted above. The standard's wording requires that for each category there should be disclosure of the aggregate fair value together with the aggregate carrying amount. Taken together with the illustration in appendix II, we interpret this to mean that each of the group's of financial instruments should be aggregated together and shown below each of the categories specified in the bullet points in paragraph 6.228.

6.230 When grouping financial instruments into categories, it is important to group like with like. Typically, the categories will follow the same structure as, but be in more detail than, that used in discussing the objectives, policies and strategies for holding or issuing financial instruments. Therefore, although financial assets and financial liabilities would not usually be included in the same category, an exception might be made to group together similar derivatives held or issued for the same purpose, regardless of whether their fair value was positive or negative. For example, interest rate and currency derivatives used for hedging would usually be grouped separately from those that are traded. However, the standard suggests that these categories should be analysed in more detail, for example, interest rate swaps shown separately from currency swaps and there should be separate disclosure of optional derivatives, such as currency options and interests caps and collars. [FRS 13 para 46].

6.231 The standard allows disclosure for a particular category of financial instrument of either the aggregate fair values (that is, a net figure) at the balance sheet date or the aggregate fair value of items with a positive fair value and the aggregate of items with a negative fair value. [FRS 13 para 44(a)(b)]. For example, some forward contracts will be in the money and have a positive fair value, whereas others will be out of the money and have a negative fair value. At any one time, an entity could have a portfolio of forward contracts, each issued for the same purposes, having both positive and negative fair values. A single forward contract could change from being a financial asset to a financial liability over time as it moves in and out of the money. Although the standard allows disclosure of either a single net fair value or the gross fair values (both negative and positive), it points out that for companies that may be developing systems to capture information for disclosure, a subsequent FRS on recognition and measurement of financial instruments might require that most or all financial assets and financial liabilities should be carried on the balance sheet at fair values. In this case, gross figures would be required.

Book value versus fair value

6.232 In preparing the fair value disclosure, it is important to remember that the standard requires the disclosure of the fair value of the separate instruments used by the reporting entity, albeit grouped together in appropriate categories as discussed above. It is less clear what should be shown alongside each of the fair values, because the standard refers only to the aggregate carrying amount in paragraph 44(a). This issue is considered further in paragraph 6.258.

6.233 All derivative financial instruments will have a fair value; whether they have a book value will depend on how much cash has been paid or received and will also depend on the accounting policy for such items. A 'book value' can arise because the accounting policy might be to mark-to-market the derivatives and recognise them on-balance sheet.

6.234 For some short-term financial instruments such as cash, and for floating rate debt, the difference between carrying amount and fair value will generally be immaterial. In such cases, the carrying amount may be used in place of fair value. However, both the carrying amount and fair value, which in this case will be the same figure, should still be disclosed; in some cases, it may be possible to state that the numbers are the same. [FRS 13 para 48]. Clearly, certain longer-term debtors, creditors and provisions if they are undisclosed might have market values that differ from their carrying values. This will be the case for long-term fixed rate debt and also for long-term debtors where the delay in settlement is not compensated by interest at current market rates.

6.235 In preparing the disclosure a practical problem arises if the book amount of a borrowing includes unamortised issue costs in accordance with FRS 4. Should the fair value of that borrowing be adjusted for an equivalent amount of unamortised issue costs? A solution would be to show the 'book value' of the borrowing gross of the unamortised issue costs as a comparison to the borrowing's 'clean' fair value. A footnote to the fair value disclosure should explain the adjustment made to the book amount of the borrowing thus providing the ability to trace the item back to its balance sheet caption. [FRS 13 para 25].

6.236 When obtaining fair values of borrowings, either internally or by asking the company's bankers or broker to do so, care should be taken to request a valuation that is clean of any interest accrual. The book amount of borrowings will not include the interest accrual, so neither should the fair value.

6.237 Examples of the fair value disclosures are shown below in Tables 6.14, South African Breweries Plc and 6.15, British Telecommunications plc. Whereas South African Breweries Plc analyses its derivatives by function, that is, their use to manage interest and currency profile or as anticipatory hedges. British Telecommunications plc shows their association with assets and liabilities.

Table 6.14 – Fair value disclosure

South African Breweries Plc – Annual Report and Accounts – 31 March 2000

Notes to the Consolidated Financial Statements (extract)

30 Financial instruments (extract)

Fair values of financial assets and financial liabilities

The following table presents the carrying amounts and the fair values of the group's financial instruments as at 31 March 2000. Fair value is the amount at which a financial instrument could be exchanged in an arm's length transaction between informed and willing parties, other than in a forced or liquidation sale and excludes accrued interest. Where available, market values have been used to determine fair values. Where market values are not available, fair values have been calculated by discounting expected cash flows at prevailing interest and exchange rates. The estimated net fair values, have been determined using available market information and appropriate valuation methodologies, as detailed below, but are not necessarily indicative of the amounts that the group could realise in the normal course of business.

	2000		1999	
	Book value US$m	**Fair value US$m**	Book value US$m	Fair value US$m
Primary financial instruments held or issued to finance the Group's operations				
Short-term borrowings and current portion of long-term borrowings	**308**	**308**	278	278
Long-term borrowings	**294**	**294**	675	682
Financial assets	**651**	**651**	1,320	1,320
Other financial liabilities	**1,085**	**1,085**	1,044	1,044
Derivative financial instruments held to manage the interest rate and currency profile				
Interest rate swaps and forward rate agreements	–	–	–	1
Forward foreign exchange contracts	–	**2**	–	1
Derivative financial instruments held or issued to hedge the currency exposure on expected future transactions				
Interest rate swaps and forward rate agreements	–	–	–	–
Forward foreign exchange contracts	–	**1**	–	–

Table 6.15 – Fair value disclosure

British Telecommunications plc – Annual Report and Form 20-F – 31 March 2001

Notes to the Financial Statements (extract)

33. Financial instruments and risk management (extract)

(d) Fair value of financial instruments

The following table shows the carrying amounts and fair values of the group's financial instruments at 31 March 2001 and 2000. The carrying amounts are included in the group balance sheet under the indicated headings, with the exception of derivative amounts, which are included in debtors or other creditors or as part of net debt as appropriate. The fair values of the financial instruments are the amount at which the instruments could be exchanged in a current transaction between willing parties, other than in a forced or liquidation sale.

	Carrying amount		Fair value	
	2001 £m	2000 £m	**2001 £m**	2000 £m
Non-derivatives				
Assets				
Cash at bank and in hand	**412**	253	**412**	253
Short-term investments (a)	**2,557**	2,051	**2,562**	2,052
Fixed asset investments – loans to joint ventures (b)	**737**	1,073	**737**	1,073
Liabilities				
Short-term borrowings (c)	**10,220**	5,121	**10,219**	5,121
Long-term borrowings, excluding finance leases (d)	**20,592**	5,874	**20,852**	6,085
Derivatives relating to investments and borrowings (net) (e)				
Assets	**259**	44	–	–
Liabilities	–	–	–	100

(a) The fair values of listed short-term investments were estimated based on quoted market prices for those investments. The carrying amount of the other short-term deposits and investments approximated to their fair values due to the short maturity of the instruments held.

(b) The fair value of loans to joint ventures approximated to carrying value due to loans bearing commercial rates of interest.

(c) The fair value of the short-term borrowings approximated to carrying value due to the short maturity of the instruments.

(d) The fair value of the group's bonds, debentures, notes and other long-term borrowings has been estimated on the basis of quoted market prices for the same or similar issues with the same maturities where they existed, and on calculations of the present value of future cash flows using the appropriate discount rates in effect at the balance sheet dates, where market prices of similar issues did not exist.

(e) The fair value of the group's outstanding foreign currency and interest rate swap agreements was estimated by calculating the present value, using appropriate discount rates in effect at the balance sheet dates, of affected future cash flows translated, where appropriate, into pounds sterling at the market rates in effect at the balance sheet dates.

Disclosure on financial assets and liabilities held for trading

6.238 The standard defines trading in financial assets and financial liabilities as "*buying, selling, issuing or holding financial assets and financial liabilities in order to take advantage of short-term changes in market prices or rates*". [FRS 13 para 2]. A financial asset or liability that is classified as a trading instrument under FRS 13, will meet the definition of 'held for trading' under FRS 26 paragraph 9. Consequently, if a reporting entity holds or issues financial instruments and meets this definition of trading the following disclosures have to be made:

- The net gain or loss from trading such instruments during the period included in the profit and loss account, analysed by type of financial instrument, business activity, risk or in such other way that is consistent with the entity's management of the activity.
- If the analysis above is given other than by type of financial instrument, a description for each line of that analysis of the types of financial instruments involved.
- The period-end fair values of financial assets and separately, of financial liabilities held or issued for trading.

[FRS 13 para 57].

6.239 An example of a company that has disclosed the required information in respect of its trading activities is BT Group plc in its 31 March 2002 financial statements.

Table 6.16 – Disclosure of financial assets and liabilities held for trading

BT Group plc – Annual report and Form 20-F – 31 March 2003

Notes to the accounts (extract)

36. Financial instruments and risk management (extract)

Fair value of financial assets held for trading	2003 £m	2002 £m
Net gain included in profit and loss account	**34**	50
Fair value of financial assets held for trading at 31 March	**2,610**	1,510

The net gain was derived from government bonds, commercial paper and similar debt instruments. The average fair value of financial assets held during the year ended 31 March 2003 did not differ materially from the year end position.

6.240 If the period-end position is considered to be materially unrepresentative of the reporting entity's use of financial instruments for trading purposes during the period, the average fair value of instruments held in the period should be disclosed. The average should be calculated using daily figures, or where these are not available, the most frequent interval, generated for management, regulatory or other reasons, should be used. An example of this disclosure is given in Table 6.19 (see para 6.266).

Disclosures about hedges

6.241 Companies use financial instruments for hedging purposes to reduce the risk associated with the hedged item. Depending on the accounting policy the company adopts, gains and losses on hedging instruments are often not recognised in the financial statements until the hedged transaction takes place. Companies that do recognise losses and gains on hedging instruments carry them forward in their balance sheets to match the gains and losses on the hedged items in the next or later financial year. In the past in the UK, hedge accounting has been permitted simply where it was believed that the resulting presentation in the primary statements better represented the economics of the situation. It is important to note that these FRS 13 hedging disclosure requirements apply to all such hedge relationships and not just to the hedging relationships that would qualify as FRS 26/IAS 39 hedges.

Hedging table

6.242 Where financial assets and financial liabilities are used by a company for hedging purposes, FRS 13 requires the following information about gains and losses to be disclosed.

- The cumulative aggregate gains and aggregate losses that are 'unrecognised' at the balance sheet date. Where, however, the item's fair value has not been disclosed, which is allowed for unique financial instruments where reliable estimates of fair value cannot be obtained (see para 6.224 and 6.225) or for cash-settled commodity contracts in the situation described in paragraph 6.160, any gain or loss on that item need not be dealt with in this disclosure.
- The cumulative aggregate gains and aggregate losses carried forward in the balance sheet at the balance sheet date (that is, 'deferred') pending their recognition in the profit and loss account.
- The extent to which the gains and losses disclosed in the above two points are expected to be recognised in the profit and loss account in the next accounting period.
- The amount of gains and losses included in the reporting period's profit and loss account that arose in previous years and were either unrecognised or carried forward in the balance sheet at the start of the reporting period.

[FRS 13 para 59].

6.243 It should generally be possible to tie in the figures for the fair values of derivatives disclosed in the fair value table to the figures given in the hedging table. This is also illustrated in examples 3 and 4 included in annex 1 to this chapter.

6.244 Read in isolation, the disclosure requirements set out above are, perhaps, not as clearly expressed by the standard as they might be. For example, it is not clear what is regarded as hedge accounting for this purpose (since the standard deals with disclosure and not accounting treatment). The standard avoids defining hedge accounting, because it seeks the reporting entity to explain what it means by hedging and thus set the numerical disclosures in context. An example of such an explanation is given by Imperial Chemical Industries Plc, which helpfully sets out in its accounting policies what it considers to be hedge accounting. This is reproduced in Table 6.17 below.

Table 6.17 – Definition of hedge accounting

Imperial Chemical Industries PLC – Annual Report and Accounts and Form 20-F – 31 December 1999

Notes to the accounts (extract)

Accounting policies (extract)

Financial derivatives

Hedge accounting
The Group uses various derivative financial instruments to reduce exposure to foreign exchange risks. These include currency swaps, forward currency contracts and currency options. The Group also uses interest rate swaps, forward rate agreements and interest rate caps derivatives to adjust interest rate exposures. The Group considers its derivative financial instruments to be "hedges" (i.e. an offset of foreign exchange and interest rate risks) when certain criteria are met. Under hedge accounting for currency options, the Group defers the instrument's impact on profit until it recognises the underlying hedged item in profit. Other material instruments do not involve deferral since the profit impact they offset occurs during the terms of the contracts.

Foreign currency derivative instruments:

The Group's criteria to qualify for hedge accounting are:

- The instrument must be related to a foreign currency asset or liability that is probable and whose characteristics have been identified;
- It must involve the same currency as the hedged item; and
- It must reduce the risk of foreign currency exchange movements on the Group's operations.

Interest rate derivative instruments:

The Group's criteria to qualify for hedge accounting are:

- The instrument must be related to an asset or a liability, and
- It must change the character of the interest rate by converting a variable rate to a fixed rate or vice versa.

Derivative financial instruments reported in the financial statements:

- The unamortised premium paid on purchased currency options is included in debtors in the balance sheet.

Cash flows related to foreign currency derivative transactions are reported along with related transactions in net cash inflow from operating activities or returns on investment and servicing of finance, as appropriate, in the Statement of Group cash flow.

Currency swaps
Principal amounts are revalued at exchange rates ruling at the date of the Group balance sheet and included in the sterling value of loans; exchange gains/losses are included in the Statement of Group total recognised gains and losses in accordance with SSAP 20.

Interest rate swaps and forward rate agreements
Interest payments/receipts are accrued with net interest payable. They are not revalued to fair value or shown on the Group balance sheet at period end. If they are terminated early, the gain/loss is spread over the remaining maturity of the original instrument.

Interest rate caps
The option premia are recognised on the Group balance sheet as 'other receivables'. The option premia, net of any realised gains or individual caplets, are taken to net interest payable spread evenly over the lifetime of the cap.

Forward currency contracts
Those forward currency contracts hedging transaction exposures (purchases and sales held in the books of account) are revalued to balance sheet rates with net unrealised gains/losses being shown as trade receivables/payables. Both realised gains and losses on purchases/sales and unrealised gains/losses on forward contracts are recognised in trading profit.

Those contracts used to change the currency mix of net debt are revalued to balance sheet rates with net unrealised gain/losses being shown as part of the debt they are hedging. The difference between spot and forward rate for these contracts is recognised as part of net interest payable over the period of the contract. Realised and unrealised exchange gains/losses are shown in the financial statements in the same place as the underlying borrowing/deposit.

Currency options
Option premia are recognised at their historic cost in the Group balance sheet as 'other receivables'. At maturity, the option premia net of any realised gains on exercise, are taken to the financial statements as trading profit.

Disclosure related to item being hedged

6.245 Another issue is whether the disclosures for hedging required by FRS 13 are concerned with the hedging instrument or with the underlying item which is being hedged (or with both). The UITF in its information sheet IS 33 indicated that it had confirmed with the ASB that the illustration in appendix III to FRS 13 reflects the ASB's intentions that paragraph 59 requires disclosure only of the gross gains or losses arising on the hedging instrument itself and not on the instrument being hedged. Hence, a one-sided disclosure is given that could suggest there are incremental profits to be taken or exposures exist when this is not the case. To counter such an impression, some explanation could be given adjacent to the disclosure to put it in context. The UITF added that its conclusion did not discourage disclosure also of the gain or loss on the instrument being hedged, for example, as part of the hedging strategy followed in the period.

6.246 To illustrate this point, consider the following example:

Example

Company A enters into a three year fixed rate loan of £20m at 7%. At the same time it enters into an interest rate swap for the same period to switch the loan to floating rate. Company A now has a synthetic floating rate loan of £20m and under the swap it will receive £1.4m a year and pay a variable rate on £20m. The amount received under the swap will cover its interest obligations on the original loan. Shortly afterwards the Bank of England's Monetary Policy Committee cuts Minimum Lending Rate by 0.5% and interest rates fall commensurately. Consequently Company A's interest rate swap acquires a positive value of, say £350,000. Another result of the interest rate cut is the fair value of the original 7% fixed rate loan will increase to, say, £20.35m.

The interest rate swap is hedging the interest cash flows on the fixed rate loan and, therefore, the swap is the hedging instrument. Consequently, the unrecognised gain on the swap of £350,000 will be included in the hedging disclosure required by paragraph 59. The unrecognised loss in the fair value of the hedged item, that is, the increase in the fair value of the fixed rate loan, is not included in the hedging disclosure.

6.247 As can be seen from Table 6.18, BG plc has only included the net unrecognised losses on the derivative financial instruments it has used for hedging purposes in its hedging disclosures. In addition, BG has indicated in a footnote that substantially all of the losses shown by the table will in fact be offset by corresponding gains on the hedged items; this is what would be expected where there is a proper hedging relationship.

Hedging using instruments other than derivatives

6.248 A further nuance that emerges from an analysis of FRS 13's requirements is that the disclosure is solely about gains and losses on *derivatives* that have been used as the hedging instruments. Hedging which is achieved through the use of primary financial instruments – that is, those that are on-balance sheet non-derivatives – do not produce unrecognised or deferred gains or losses that are the feature of paragraph 59's requirements. This is clearly illustrated by BG plc in Table 6.18, where the net losses on the derivative instruments shown in the fair value table are signposted to the hedging disclosure in the table below.

Table 6.18 – Hedging using instruments other than derivatives

BG plc — Annual Report and Accounts – 31 December 1999

Notes to the accounts (extract)

21 Financial instruments (extract)

Fair values of financial instruments	**1998**		1998	
	Book value £m	**Fair value £m**	Book value £m	Fair value £m
Primary financial instruments held or issued to finance the Group's operations:				
Short-term borrowings	**(2 091)**	**(2 091)**	(1 394)	(1 394)
Long-term borrowings	**(5 333)**	**(5 369)**	(3 199)	(3 477)
Current asset investments	**508**	**508**	504	504
Cash at bank and in hand	**44**	**44**	40	40
Other financial liabilities	**(217)**	**(217)**	236	236
Derivative financial instruments held to manage the interest rate and currency profile:				
Interest rate-related derivatives	–	**48**	–	3
Currency rate-related derivatives	–	**(102)**	–	(81)
Unrecognised total net losses (see Gains and losses on hedges below)	–	**(150)**	–	(78)
Other financial liabilities	**(217)**	**(217)**	236	236
Derivative financial instruments held to manage the interest rate and currency profile:				
Interest rate-related derivatives	–	**48**	–	3
Currency rate-related derivatives	–	**(102)**	–	(81)
Unrecognised total net losses (see Gains and losses on hedges below)	–	**(150)**	–	(78)

For the purpose of the above table, the fair value of short-term borrowings, related derivative instruments, current asset investments and cash at bank and in hand approximate to book value due to the short maturity of these instruments.

Hedges of future transactions

As at 31 December 1998 the value of future transactions hedged was £145m (1998 £nil).

Gains and losses on hedges

The table below shows the extent to which the Group has off-balance sheet (unrecognised) and on-balance sheet (deferred) gains and losses in respect of hedges at the beginning and end of the year.

	Unrecognised			Deferred	
	Gains £m	Losses £m	Net total £m	Gains £m	Losses £m
Gains/(losses) on hedges at 1 January 1999	131	(209)	(78)	27	(24)
Transfer from gains to losses	(62)	62	–	–	–
Transfer from losses to gains	(7)	7	–	–	–

(Gains)/losses arising in previous years that were recognised in 1999	(33)	128	95	4	(4)
Gains/(losses) not recognised in 1999					
Arising before 1 January 1999	29	(12)	17	19	(20)
Arising in 1999	107	(274)	(167)	12	(54)
Gains/(losses) on hedges as at 31 December 1999	**136**	**(286)**	(150)	**31**	**(74)**
Of which:					
Gains (losses) expected to be included in 2000 income	–	–	–	7	(15)
Gains (losses) expected to be included in 2001 income or later	136	(286)	(150)	24	(59)

£102m (1998 £81m), of the unrecognised total net losses above of £150m (1998 £78m), are offset by foreign exchange gains on the related foreign currency denominated borrowings.

Disclosures gross or net

6.249 In Table 6.18, BG Plc discloses the aggregate unrecognised gains and losses in line with the standard. The standard is ambiguous as to whether gains and losses should be shown net or gross. However in the illustrative example given in the appendices to the standard, the gains and losses are shown gross. Furthermore, the illustrative example presents the unrecognised gains and losses information in the form of a reconciliation of the opening to closing balances, which is not a requirement of the standard, but which we believe to be best practice (as illustrated by the hedging table given in appendix III to FRS 13). An example of how this hedging table might look is given below.

Illustration of the disclosure of unrecognised and deferred gains and losses

	Unrecognised			Deferred		
	Gains	Losses	Total net gains/losses	Gains	Losses	Total net gains/losses
	£m	£m	£m	£m	£m	£m
Gains and losses on hedges at 1 January 20X0	3.2	–	3.2	2.5	–	2.5
Arising in previous years included in 20X0 income	(3.2)	–	(3.2)	(2.5)	–	(2.5)
Gains and losses not included in 20X0 income						
Arising before 1 January 20X0	–	–	–	–	–	–
Arising in 20X0	6.4	(4.3)	2.1	–	–	–

Gains and losses on hedges at 31 December 20x0	**6.4**	**(4.3)**	**2.1**	–	–	–
of which:						
Gains and losses expected to be included in 20X1 income	6.4	(2.1)	4.3	–	–	–
Gains and losses expected to be included in 20X2 income or later	–	(2.2)	(2.2)	–	–	–

£8.5m of the net gain of £7.2m on the euro currency swaps has been recognised in 20X0 in the statement of total recognised gains and losses where it offsets the loss on retranslation of the net investments in the French and Dutch subsidiaries. The balance of £1.2m is an unrecognised loss in respect of the interest differential on the cross-currency swaps and is reflected in the above table.

Gains and losses included in fixed assets

6.250 The standard includes an exemption from the disclosures required in the last three bullet points in paragraph 6.242 on pragmatic grounds in respect of gains and losses on hedges that are included in the carrying amount of a fixed asset. This is because of the problems that can arise in trying to keep records of such gains and losses over a long period of time. Such amounts need not be included in the analysis of hedging gains and losses; they are of course included in the carrying value of the fixed asset amortised to the profit and loss account. [FRS 13 paras 60, 61].

Hedging a current asset, liability or non-equity share

6.251 The exemption in the above paragraph, however, does not extend to situations where the hedged item is a current asset, a liability or non-equity shares and the gain or loss on the hedging instrument has been accounted for by adjusting the carrying amount of the current asset, liability or shares. Common examples include foreign currency debtors and foreign currency borrowings that are translated into sterling in accordance with the company's accounting policy at the contracted exchange rate in the forward foreign exchange contracts or cross-currency swaps that have been used to hedge them.

6.252 The effect of adopting such an accounting policy is that the carrying value of the debtors or borrowings has been initially recorded at the forward rate, and has remained recorded at the forward rate at the year end. As a result, the exchange gain or loss, that would have arisen on translating the currency carrying amount at the closing rate, and the offsetting gain or loss on the forward contract, have not been recorded at all. Consequently, under such an accounting policy, for a forward contract open over the year end there will be an unrecognised gain or loss that would fall to be disclosed in the hedging table. A reporting entity that applies such an accounting policy must have adequate accounting systems to track the movement in value of the hedging instruments and the proportion of the unrecognised gains or losses that are taken to the profit and loss account in each accounting period. The gain or loss will become recognised at the forward transaction date, where there will also be an equal and opposite gain or loss arising on the hedged item. These, in effect, net out in the profit and loss account.

6.253 An illustration of the treatment of a forward currency contract taken out in anticipation of a future purchase is given in paragraph 6.254 below.

Hedging a forward purchase of stock

6.254 The example below, which deals with the purchase of raw materials, illustrates how a forward purchase of stock would be dealt with under FRS 13, it also illustrates the extent of data collection and compilation that the hedging disclosure entails.

Example

Company B has a 31 March 20X0 year end. It decides in March 20X0 to place an order for materials with its supplier in France for €100,000. At the same time it takes out a forward foreign exchange contract to purchase €100,000 for £67,000. The materials are delivered in September, paid for, turned into finished products and sold in May 20X1. Assuming that, at 31 March 20X0 the company could take out an equivalent forward contract to purchase €100,000 for the remaining five months of the contract for £65,500, the fair value of the forward contract is (£1,500). When the goods are delivered and paid for, the euros could be bought for £69,000, what disclosures are required by FRS 13?

At 31 March 20X0

Company B has an unrecognised loss of £1,500 on the forward contract. Hence in the fair value disclosure, the forward contract will be shown under the heading 'Derivatives used to hedge anticipated transactions' with a book value of £nil and a fair value of £(1,500). The hedging disclosure will show the unrecognised loss of £1,500 arising in the year but not included in 20X0 profit and loss account and thus carried forward. This amount will also be shown as an amount expected to be included in income for the year ending 31 March 20X2.

At 31 March 20X1

Company B will have to disclose a gain of £2,000 (the difference between the spot rate price of £69,000 at date of delivery and the forward rate in the contract of £67,000) carried forward in the balance sheet (within stocks). This will pose a number of presentational issues. There will be nothing to disclose in the fair value disclosure as there is no financial instrument involved any longer; the forward contract was settled in the year and stocks are not financial instruments. In the hedging disclosure £1,500 will be shown as the opening loss under unrecognised gains and losses. However, it will be necessary to show the change in value of the contract (£3,500) and to transfer the net gain of £2,000 to the deferred gains and losses section of the disclosure to reconcile to the carried forward deferred gain of £2,000. This amount will also be shown as an amount expected to be included in income for the year ending 31 March 20X2.

At 31 March 20X2

Company B will have to disclose that a gain of £2,000 has been included in the profit and loss account for the year. The hedging disclosure will show £2,000 as a deferred gain brought forward which is reduced to £nil carried forward at 31 March 20X2 by the amount recognised in the profit and loss account for the year.

The hedging disclosure for the three years to March 20X2 may be summarised in the tabular format likely to be used by most companies:

	March 20X2	March 20X1		March 20X0
	Deferred	Unrecognised	Deferred	Unrecognised
	£	£	£	£
Gain/(loss) at 1 April	2,000	(1,500)	–	–
Change in value from 1 April to settlement	–	3,500	–	–
Arising before 1 April not included in current year income and now deferred	–	(2,000)	2,000	–
(Gain)/loss arising in previous year(s) included in current year income	(2,000)	–	–	–
Arising in current year not included in current year income	–	–	–	(1,500)
Gain/(loss) on hedges at 31 March	–	–	**2,000**	**(1,500)**
Of which:				
Loss expected to be included in 20X1 income	–	–	–	–
(Loss)/gain expected to be included in 20X2 income	–	–	2,000	(1,500)

6.255 Note that example 4 included in annex 1 to this chapter contains example narrative and numerical disclosures for a forward contract taken out to hedge a purchase of raw materials.

Hedging the purchase of a fixed asset using an option

6.256 Some companies' hedging strategies involve the use of options. The question thus arises as to how option contracts should be dealt with in the fair value and hedging table required by the standard, particularly as the option may not have to be exercised at the balance sheet date.

Example

Company C purchases a foreign currency call option for a premium of £100,000 that gives it the right, but not the obligation, to buy US$5m at a pre-determined rate if the $/£ exchange rate is below $1.63 on 28 February 20X1. This is the date that the company expects to pay $5m for the purchase of a fixed asset. If the exchange rate at the end of February 20X1 has fallen below $1.63, company C will exercise the option. Company C has a 31 December year end.

Inception

At inception, company C paid the premium of £100,000. Its accounting policy (which should be disclosed) is to defer the premium in respect of anticipated commitments until they occur and thus the premium is included in the balance sheet as 'other debtors'.

At 31 December 20X0

The exchange rate is $1.55: £1 and, consequently, the option is 'in the money'. Company C determines from its broker that the mark to market value of the option is £165,000. In its fair value disclosure, it will show a 'book value' of the option of £100,000 with a £165,000 comparable fair value. In the hedging disclosure, the gain of £65,000 (the fair value of the option contract less the unamortised premium) will be included in the 'unrecognised' gains section of the disclosure. However, as the option is a hedge of an anticipated fixed asset purchase, the gain will not feature in the disclosure of the "*extent to which the gains and losses....are expected to be recognised in the next accounting period*". This is because of the exemption in paragraph 60 of the standard relating to gains and losses that adjust the carrying value of a fixed asset. However, it would be helpful to provide an explanation of this effect in the disclosure.

At 31 December 20X1

The purchase of the fixed asset took place as expected on 28 February 20X1, when the exchange rate was $1.60: £1. At this rate company C chose to exercise the option as it was cheaper than purchasing the US$5m at the spot rate. Company C wrote off the premium of £100,000 for the option. In our view the premium is not a directly attributable cost under FRS 15, 'Tangible fixed assets', as it relates to financing the purchase. The fixed asset is recorded at the option rate of $1.63: £1. This is a synthetic rate in that it incorporates the fixed asset recorded at the spot rate of $1.60: £1 and a deferred gain on the option, being the difference between recording the fixed asset at the option rate and recording it at the spot rate. In respect of this option contract, there are no FRS 13 fair value or hedging disclosures to be made. In the former case this is because the option contract is no longer outstanding and in the latter because of the exemption in paragraph 60. In this case the 'deferred' gain included in the book value of the fixed asset is the exchange difference between recording the fixed asset at the spot rate and recording it at the option rate.

Hedging a net investment using a cross-currency swap

6.257 Further complications arise where, say, a sterling borrowing is swapped into a foreign currency and this synthetic foreign currency borrowing is used to hedge a net investment in a foreign subsidiary. For example, a £100 million borrowing is swapped into US$150 million in order to provide a hedge of the US$150 million net investment in the group's US subsidiaries. At the balance sheet date, the $/£ exchange rate is $2: £1. The forward leg of the swap (to sell US$150 million) is revalued at the spot rate at £75 million, rather than the forward rate of exchange, since the interest rate differential between the spot and forward rates is reflected in the periodic payments made between the parties. The gain of £25 million (£100 million — £75 million) is netted against the £100 million carrying value of the sterling loan to adjust it to £75 million. The other side of the entry is recognised in the statement of total recognised gains and losses where it matches with the foreign exchange loss taken on the US investment.

6.258 As already stated in paragraph 6.222, the fair value of the separate instruments should be grouped together in appropriate categories. Therefore, the loan and the cross-currency swap will appear in different categories, for example, the loan in 'primary instruments' and swap in 'derivative financial instruments used to manage interest rate and currency profile'. However, there is also the question of what are the comparable 'book values' to be shown alongside these fair values?

6.259 There are two approaches that can be adopted.

- It is possible to separate the two instruments in the 'fair value' part of the disclosure, the loan could be shown as having an aggregate carrying amount of, say, £100 million and the gain (recognised on balance sheet and in the STRGL) of, say, £25 million shown as the aggregate carrying amount of the swap. The fair value of the swap will be different from the gain already recognised since the on-balance sheet amount merely measures the currency element of the swap, whereas the fair value of the swap includes the measure of the interest differential. The difference between the two is thus 'unrecognised' as it is not reflected on-balance sheet. If this approach is adopted, there should be a footnote to explain that the book values of the loan and swap need to be recombined to trace the amount to the borrowings shown in the balance sheet.

- Alternatively, the aggregate carrying amount of the loan could be shown as £75 million and a nil amount shown as the 'book value' of the swap. In this case, it would be appropriate to recognise the fair value of the interest differential only as the equivalent amount to be recognised next to the nil book value of the swap. This value would then be treated as unrecognised in the hedging table.

6.260 The first approach has an advantage in that, by highlighting the gain already recognised, it is not forgotten when constructing the required hedging disclosure considered from paragraph 6.241.

6.261 Paragraph 59 of FRS 13 requires disclosure of the cumulative aggregate gains and aggregate losses, both 'deferred' and 'unrecognised', at the balance sheet date together with the amount of such gains and losses recognised in the reporting period's profit and loss account or expected to be recognised in the profit and loss account in the next accounting period. To construct the disclosure requires, therefore, that those hedging gains and losses that have been recognised, or are expected to be recognised, in the profit and loss account to be separately identified. Assuming the fair value of the cross-currency swap is, say, £20 million the hedging disclosure starting with the year end position would be constructed to show the following:

	Unrecognised		
	Gains £m	**Losses £m**	**Total £m**
At balance sheet date	–	(5)	(5)
Of which:			
Expected to be recognised in 20X0 income	–	(1)	(1)
Expected to be recognised in 20X1 income	–	(4)	(4)

Market price risk

6.262 Disclosure of some measure of market price risk is an evolving area of financial reporting, both in the UK and internationally. Various techniques have been developed, but there is as yet no consensus as to which is the best method of providing adequate and meaningful information in a cost effective manner. Hence, the ASB encourages, rather than requires, entities other than banks to give some measure of the market price risk of all the financial instruments they hold or have issued (including cash settled commodity contracts and, if significant, all other items carrying market price risk). [FRS 13 para 66]. Banks must give market price risk information in respect of their trading book. [FRS 13 para 104]. Market price risk is the risk of loss arising from changes in market prices, such as interest rates or exchange rates. It is necessary to appreciate that any disclosures concerning market price risk can only give an estimate of the risks to a company and can never be precise or accurate.

6.263 Entities providing market price risk information should include:

- A discussion of market price risk where necessary to set the numerical information in context and to assist in its interpretation.
- Additional numerical disclosures that facilitate an assessment of the magnitude of market price risk over the period. These disclosures should include:
  - An explanation of the method used and the key parameters and assumptions underlying the data provided.
  - An explanation of the objective of the method used and of the limitations that may cause the information not to reflect fully the overall market price risk of the assets and liabilities involved.

- The reasons for material changes in the amount of reported risk compared to the previous accounting period.

[FRS 13 paras 67, 69].

6.264 The method chosen to measure market price risk should reflect how management manages the risk. If different approaches are used to manage market price risk in different parts of a business, separate disclosure for each part of the business is encouraged. [FRS 13 para 66]. In its simplest form, the information could be presented as a sensitivity analysis showing the impact on profit of, say, a one per cent change in interest rates. However, other methods such as 'value at risk' – that is, the expected loss from an adverse market movement with a specified probability over a specified period of time – may be more appropriate. Five possible approaches for reporting market price risk are discussed in paragraph 68 of the FRS, but it is acknowledged that this list is not exhaustive and other methods may be more appropriate.

6.265 Where material changes are made to the method or key assumptions and parameters used to calculate market price risk from one period to the next, the reasons for the change should be given and the previous period's information should be restated onto the new basis. [FRS 13 para 71].

6.266 An example of disclosure of market price risk based on the sensitivity of market values is shown in Table 6.19 below, which also includes disclosure of fair values, instruments held for trading and information on credit risk.

Table 6.19 – Disclosure of market price risk

BP p.l.c. – annual accounts – 31 December 2001

Notes on accounts (extract)

28 Derivatives and other financial instruments

In the normal course of business the group is a party to derivative financial instruments (derivatives) with off balance sheet risk, primarily to manage its exposure to fluctuations in foreign currency exchange rates and interest rates, including management of the balance between floating rate and fixed rate debt. The group also manages certain of its exposures to movements in oil and natural gas prices. The underlying economic currency of the group's cash flows is mainly the US dollar. Accordingly, most of our borrowings are in US dollars, are hedged with respect to the US dollar or swapped into US dollars. Significant non-dollar cash flow exposures are hedged. Gains and losses arising on these hedges are deferred and recognized in the income statement or as adjustments to carrying amounts, as appropriate, only when the hedged item occurs. In addition, we trade derivatives in conjunction with these risk management activities. The results of trading are recognized in income in the current period.

The group co-ordinates certain key activities on a global basis in order to optimize its financial position and performance. These include the management of the currency, maturity and interest rate profile of borrowing, cash, other significant financial risks and relationships with banks and other financial institutions. International oil and natural gas trading and risk management relating to business operations are carried out by the group's oil and natural gas trading units.

BP is exposed to financial risks, including market risk, credit risk and liquidity risk, arising from the group's normal business activities. These risks and the group's approach to dealing with them are discussed below.

Market risk
Market risks include the possibility that changes in currency exchange rates, interest rates or oil and natural gas prices will adversely affect the value of the group's financial assets, liabilities or expected future cash flows. Market risks are managed using a range of financial and commodity instruments, including derivatives. We also trade derivatives in conjunction with these risk management activities.

Currency exchange rates Fluctuations in exchange rates can have significant effects on the group's reported profit. The effects of most exchange rate fluctuations are absorbed in business operating results through changing cost competitiveness, lags in market adjustment to movements in rates, and conversion differences accounted for on specific transactions. For this reason the total effect of exchange rate fluctuations is not identifiable separately in the group's reported profit.

The main underlying economic currency of the group's cash flows is the US dollar and the group's borrowings are predominantly in US dollars. Our foreign exchange management policy is to minimize economic and material transactional exposures arising from currency movements against the US dollar. The group co-ordinates the handling of foreign exchange risks centrally, by netting off naturally occurring opposite exposures wherever possible, to reduce the risks, and then dealing with any material residual foreign exchange risks. Significant residual non-dollar exposures are managed using a range of derivatives.

Interest rates The group is exposed to interest rate risk on short- and long-term floating rate instruments and as a result of the refinancing of fixed rate finance debt. Consequently, as well as managing the currency and the maturity of debt, the group manages interest expense through the balance between generally lower-cost floating rate debt, which has inherently higher risk, and generally more expensive, but lower-risk, fixed rate debt. The group is exposed predominantly to US dollar LIBOR (London Inter-Bank Offer Rate) interest rates as borrowings are mainly denominated in, or are swapped into, US dollars.

The group uses derivatives to manage the balance between fixed and floating rate debt. During 2001, the proportion of floating rate debt was in the range 32-43% of total net debt outstanding.

Oil and natural gas prices BP's trading units use financial and commodity derivatives as part of the overall optimization of the value of the group's equity oil production and as part of the associated trading of crude oil, products and related instruments. They also use financial and commodity derivatives to manage certain of the group's exposures to price fluctuations on natural gas transactions.

Market risk management and trading In market risk management and trading, conventional exchange-traded derivative instruments such as futures and options are used as well as non-exchange-traded instruments such as swaps, 'over-the-counter' options and forward contracts.

Where derivatives constitute a hedge, the group's exposure to market risk created by the derivative is offset by the opposite exposure arising from the asset, liability, cash flow or transaction being hedged. By contrast, where derivatives are held for trading purposes, changes in market risk factors give rise to realized and unrealized gains and losses, which are recognized in the current period.

All financial instrument and derivative activity, whether for risk management or trading, is carried out by specialist teams which have the appropriate skills, experience and supervision. These teams are subject to close financial and management control, meeting generally accepted industry practice and reflecting the principles of the Group of Thirty Global Derivatives Study recommendations. A Trading Risk Management Committee has oversight of the quality of internal control in the group's trading units. Independent control functions monitor compliance with BP's policies. The control framework includes prescribed trading limits that are reviewed regularly by senior management, daily monitoring of risk exposure using value-at-risk principles, marking trading exposures to market and stress testing to assess the exposure to potentially extreme market situations. As part of its approach to ensuring that control over trading is maintained to a high and consistent standard, the group's business units dealing in the oil, natural gas and financial markets were brought together within a single integrated supply and trading organization during 2001.

Credit risk

Credit risk is the potential exposure of the group to loss in the event of non-performance by a counterparty. The credit risk arising from the group's normal commercial operations is controlled by individual operating units within guidelines. In addition, as a result of its use of financial and commodity instruments, including derivatives, to manage market risk, the group has credit exposures through its dealings in the financial and specialized oil and natural gas markets. The group controls the related credit risk by entering into contracts only with highly credit-rated counterparties and through credit approvals, limits and monitoring procedures, and does not usually require collateral or other security. Counterparty credit validation, independent of the dealers, is undertaken before contractual commitment.

Liquidity risk

Liquidity risk is the risk that suitable sources of funding for the group's business activities may not be available. The group has long-term debt ratings of Aa1 and AA+ assigned respectively by Moody's and Standard and Poor's. The group has access to a wide range of funding at competitive rates through the capital markets and banks. It co-ordinates relationships with banks, borrowing requirements, foreign exchange requirements and cash management centrally. The group believes it has access to sufficient funding and also has undrawn committed borrowing facilities to meet currently foreseeable borrowing requirements. At 31 December 2001, the group had available undrawn committed facilities of $3,400 million ($3,450 million). These committed facilities, which are mainly with a number of international banks, expire in 2002. The group expects to renew the facilities on an annual basis.

Trading activities

The group maintains active trading positions in a variety of derivatives. This activity is undertaken in conjunction with risk management activities. Derivatives held for trading purposes are marked to market and any gain or loss recognized in the income statement. For traded derivatives, many positions have been neutralized, with trading initiatives being concluded by taking opposite positions to fix a gain or loss, thereby achieving a zero net market risk.

The following table shows the fair value at 31 December of derivatives and other financial instruments held for trading purposes. The fair values at the year end are not materially unrepresentative of the position throughout the year.

				$ million
	2001		2000	
	Fair value asset	**Fair value liability**	Fair value asset	Fair value liability
Interest rate contracts	**–**	**–**	–	–
Foreign exchange contracts	**14**	**(17)**	10	(10)
Oil price contracts	**248**	**(222)**	159	(123)
Natural gas price contracts	**799**	**(787)**	1,288	(1,264)
	1,061	**(1,026)**	1,457	(1,397)

The group measures its market risk exposure, i.e. potential gain or loss in fair values, on its trading activity using value-at-risk techniques. These techniques are based on a variance/covariance model or a Monte Carlo simulation and make a statistical assessment of the market risk arising from possible future changes in market values over a 24-hour period. The calculation of the range of potential changes in fair value takes into account a snapshot of the end-of-day exposures, and the history of one-day price movements over the previous 12 months, together with the correlation of these price movements. The potential movement in fair values is expressed to three standard deviations which is equivalent to a 99.7% confidence level. This means that, in broad terms, one would expect to see an increase or a decrease in fair values greater than the value at risk on only one occasion per year if the portfolio were left unchanged.

The group calculates value at risk on all instruments that are held for trading purposes and that therefore give an exposure to market risk. The value-at-risk model takes account of derivative financial instruments such as interest rate forward and futures contracts, swap agreements, options and swaptions, foreign exchange forward and futures contracts, swap agreements and options and oil price futures, swap agreements and options. Financial assets and liabilities and physical crude oil and refined products that are treated as trading positions are also included in these calculations. The value-at-risk calculation for oil and natural gas price exposure also includes derivative commodity instruments (commodity contracts that permit settlement either by delivery of the underlying commodity or in cash) such as forward contracts.

The following table shows values at risk for trading activities.

								$ million
				2001				2000
	High	**Low**	**Average**	**Year end**	High	Low	Average	Year end
Interest rate trading	**1**	**–**	**–**	**–**	2	–	1	–
Foreign exchange trading	**3**	**–**	**1**	**–**	15	–	1	1
Oil price trading	**29**	**10**	**18**	**17**	23	4	13	13
Natural gas price trading	**21**	**4**	**10**	**9**	16	1	6	13

The presentation of trading results shown in the table below includes certain activities of BP's trading units which involve the use of derivative financial instruments in conjunction with physical and paper trading of oil and natural gas. It is considered that a more comprehensive representation of the group's oil and natural gas price trading activities is given by the classification of the gain or loss on such derivatives along with the gain or loss arising from the physical and paper trades to which they relate, representing the net result of the trading portfolio.

				$million
			2001	2000
	Oil	**Natural gas**	**Net gain (loss)**	Net gain (loss)
Derivative financial and commodity instruments	**419**	**(129)**	**290**	94
Physical trades	**265**	**405**	**670**	549
Total trading	**684**	**276**	**960**	643
Interest rate trading			**1**	1
Foreign exchange trading			**81**	52
			1,042	696

6.267 While the practice of disclosing a measure of market price risk is evolving, it should be recognised that this may not be the most significant risk faced by the reporting entity. For example, wage inflation or sales volumes may be far more significant. Clearly, therefore, any disclosed measure of market price risk should not be portrayed as comprehensive.

FRS 4 — Capital instruments

Background

6.268 During the 1980s there was considerable growth in the range of capital instruments available for raising finance. The development of such instruments had a sound economic purpose and provided issuers and investors with significant benefits. However, as investors and issuers became more sophisticated, the instruments became more complex with the result that accounting failed to keep pace with their development. The central issue that required resolution was the criteria to be used to determine whether a capital instrument represents debt or equity.

6.269 In December 1993, the ASB issued FRS 4, 'Capital instruments', with the aim of bringing much needed consistency to the treatment of the many different forms of capital instrument available. The standard took a rather legalistic approach towards accounting for capital instruments by ignoring the economic substance of the instruments and merely reflecting their legal form. Many argued that FRS 4's provisions were inconsistent with FRS 5, 'Reporting the substance of transactions'. Nevertheless, the standard provided guidance on many aspects of accounting for share capital, debt and minority interests that were the subject of differing treatments and interpretations prior to its publication. The standard prescribed methods that should be used to determine the amounts to be attributed to capital instruments and their associated costs and specifies how the instruments should be disclosed.

6.270 However, FRS 4's classification and presentation requirements have been withdrawn following the introduction of the presentation requirements of FRS 25 for all entities for accounting periods beginning on or after 1 January 2005. The remaining paragraphs of FRS 4 apply to all entities not applying FRS 26. The provisions of FRS 4 concern the allocation of the costs of capital instruments that are classified as liabilities.

FRS 4's objectives

6.271 Following its revision in December 2004, FRS 4's objective is to ensure that costs associated with capital instruments that are classified as liabilities are allocated to accounting periods on a fair basis over the period of the instrument. [FRS 4 para 1].

6.272 Ensuring appropriate classification, presentation and disclosure of capital instruments is no longer an objective of the standard, as this is now achieved by the application of those sections of FRS 25 that are mandatory for all entities for accounting periods commencing on or after 1 January 2005.

Scope

6.273 The scope of the revised standard is unchanged from the original 1993 version. FRS 4 applies to all financial statements intended to give a true and fair view of a reporting entity's financial position and profit or loss (or income and expenditure) for the period. Although the standard was written primarily for companies, its provisions apply to other entities, which should adapt the terminology used in the statement as appropriate. [FRS 4 para 18].

6.274 The standard's requirements apply to issuers of capital instruments and not to investments in capital instruments issued by other entities. [FRS 4 para 19]. Furthermore, its requirements apply to all capital instruments as defined in the standard (see para 6.296 below) apart from:

- Warrants issued to employees under employee share schemes.
- Leases, which should be accounted for in accordance with SSAP 21.
- Equity shares issued as part of a business combination that is accounted for as a merger.

[FRS 4 para 21].

6.275 Capital instruments that are issued at the same time in a composite transaction should be considered together. They should be accounted for as a single instrument, unless they can be transferred, cancelled or redeemed independently of each other. [FRS 4 para 22]. In accounting periods beginning on or after 1 January 2005 all entities are required to comply with the presentation requirements of FRS 25. These requirements deal with the accounting for capital instruments including compound instruments. For example, debt is sometimes issued with a warrant attached. Where the debt and the warrants are capable of being transferred independently, they should be accounted for separately under FRS 25.

Definition of capital instrument

6.276 FRS 4's definition of capital instruments is not as wide as the definition of financial instruments, which is discussed from paragraph 6.16, but is restricted to primary instruments like shares and debt as well as options and warrants to obtain such instruments. Consequently, derivative instruments that are issued for managing foreign exchange and interest rate risks rather than for raising finance are outside of FRS 4's scope. Capital instruments are defined in of FRS 4 to mean:

> *"All instruments that are issued by reporting entities as a means of raising finance, including shares, debentures, loans and debt instruments, options and warrants that give the holder the right to subscribe for or obtain capital instruments. In the case of consolidated financial statements the term includes capital instruments issued by subsidiaries except those that are held*

> *by another member of the group included in the consolidation."* [FRS 4 para 2].

6.277 It follows from the above definition that the instrument's principal purpose must be for raising finance. An instrument may come within the above definition whether or not the consideration given for its issue takes the form of cash. For example, the consideration may be a specified amount of commodity (commodity linked instruments) or other capital instruments. Furthermore, a capital instrument may take the form of contracts between two parties (for example, a borrower and its bank). [FRS 4 para 68].

6.278 Capital instruments that are either fully or in part classified as liabilities come in various forms. They may be: straightforward debentures and loan capital; convertible into shares; subordinated to other borrowings; perpetual in nature; or sometimes issued on terms that the lender's recourse is limited.

Finance costs

6.279 Following its amendment in 2004, FRS 4's primary focus is to ensure that finance costs (as defined) associated with a capital instrument are charged to the profit and loss account over the instrument's term. (The term of a capital instrument is considered from para 6.305.) This basic principle applies to the finance costs of capital instruments that are classified as liabilities. Finance costs are defined in the standard as:

> *"The difference between the net proceeds of an instrument and the total amount of the payments (or other transfers of economic benefits) that the issuer may be required to make in respect of the instrument."* [FRS 4 para 8].

6.280 For shares classified as liabilities, the finance costs include issue costs, the total dividend payments to be made on the shares over the term and the difference between any premium on issue and any redemption premium (see for example Table 6.20). Similarly for debt, the finance costs include issue costs, interest payments over the term, any redemption premium and any discount on issue. The implications of FRS 4 on the calculation of minority interests is considered in chapter 24.

Table 6.20 – Shares classified as liabilities

Pearson plc – Annual Report – 31 December 1997

Notes to the Accounts (extract)

1 Accounting policies (extract)

m) Capital instruments

Capital instruments are included at cost, adjusted for discount accretion or premium amortisation where the intention is to hold them to maturity. Interest receivable thereon and the premium or discount where relevant is taken to the profit and loss account so as to produce a constant rate of return over the period to the date of expected redemption.

Forward foreign exchange contracts and other off-balance sheet instruments are valued at the market prices prevailing at the balance sheet date. Borrowing is classified according to the maturity date of the respective individual holdings.

Elements making up finance cost

6.281 Finance costs can be split into three separate elements:

- Dividends or interest.
- The difference between any premium received on the issue of an instrument and any redemption premium; or the discount on issue added to any redemption premium.
- Issue costs.

Dividends or interest

6.282 Where the dividend or interest is floating rather than fixed, it will not be possible to determine it in advance. Therefore, it will not be possible to calculate the total finance cost, but that should not cause a difficulty, because the floating rate interest charge or dividend appropriation made each year will be the correct amount to be shown in the profit and loss account for that year. Contingent payments of this nature are dealt with further in paragraph 6.333.

Issue and redemption premiums

6.283 There may be circumstances where it is difficult to establish what the final redemption value of a capital instrument will be. For example, it may be linked in some way to future profits or to the market price of the company's shares, or it might be difficult to determine when the redemption might occur. These issues are considered further from paragraph 6.333.

Issue costs

6.284 The ASB considers that issue costs are incurred to provide funds over a period of time and to charge those costs in full to the profit and loss account in the year of issue is not in accordance with the matching concept. However, deferral of such costs as some form of prepayment is not appropriate because the Act does not allow these costs to be carried forward (see para 3(2)(b) of Schedule 1 to SI 2008/410) nor does the prepayment qualify as an asset as defined in the ASB's Statement of principles. Accordingly, issue costs are accounted for as a deduction from the amount of the consideration received. This will result in issue costs for non-equity shares and debt being written off over the instrument's life. If it became clear that the instrument would be redeemed early, the amortisation of the issue costs and any discount on issue would need to be accelerated. Where the instrument does not have a term, for example, perpetual debt, costs incurred in their issue would not be amortised (see para 6.321).

6.285 Issue costs are defined in the standard as:

> *"The costs that are incurred directly in connection with the issue of a capital instrument, that is, those costs that would not have been incurred had the specific instrument in question not been issued."* [FRS 4 para 10].

6.286 Clearly this definition is intended to be restrictive and the first point to note is that it excludes indirect costs. Consequently, the costs have to be directly related to the issue of the capital instrument before they fall to be treated as issue costs. This is rather obvious, otherwise inclusion of other indirect costs incurred on the issue as part of the cost of the instrument would only serve to defer those costs to future periods by overstating the finance cost charged in each period. Therefore, care needs to be taken in determining which costs fall to be treated as part of the cost of issuing the instrument.

6.287 In particular, the standard explains that the definition of issue costs does not allow the inclusion of costs incurred in:

- Researching sources of finance.
- Negotiating sources of finance.
- Ascertaining the suitability or feasibility of particular instruments.

[FRS 4 para 96].

6.288 Furthermore, the standard does not allow a company to allocate a proportion of its internal costs that would have been incurred had the instrument not been issued. This exemption would preclude, for example, management remuneration to cover their time involved with the issue from being treated as issue costs. [FRS 4 para 96]. Prudence should be exercised to ensure that only those costs that can be demonstrated to relate directly to the issue of the financial instrument are treated as issue costs.

6.289 The rules mentioned above relating to the types of costs that should be treated as issue costs are very similar to the rules concerning the costs that can be written off to the share premium account on the issue of shares or debentures. And for all practical purposes, issue costs can be regarded as the same as the costs that can be charged to the share premium account. Use of the share premium account is governed by the Act and it can only be used for specific purposes. Prior to the amendment to the Companies Act 1985, companies were able to write off expenses of any issue of shares or debentures to the share premium account. However, with effect from 1 October 2009, the Companies Act 2006 reduces the application of the share premium account by providing that it may only be used for the following purposes:

- Write off expenses ofi ssue of shares that gave rise to the premium.
- Write off commission paid on issue of shares that gave rise to the premium.
- Pay up new shares to be allotted as fully paid bonus shares.

[CA06 Sec 610(2)(3)].

6.290 There are certain direct costs of issuing shares that are clearly able to be written off against share premium that arise on the issue of those shares and should be treated under FRS 4 as issue costs. These costs include underwriting fees, registration fees and certain legal, merchant bank and accounting fees where these are incurred solely in the production of a prospectus offering shares to the public. In a straightforward issue of new shares to the public where a company already has a listing it is quite possible that all the costs incurred will be issue costs.

6.291 Lawyers fees in a complex financing (such as a management buyout) could cover general corporate finance work and tax advice, but will also inevitably include fees to cover drafting of legal documentation in relation to the issue of capital instruments. These latter costs are issue costs, but the former are less likely to be unless they are incurred directly in relation to the issue of shares or debt. Accountants' fees will also cover a wide variety of work and unless specifically related to the issue of the capital instruments will not be issue costs. However, where a company can make a reasonable allocation of such fees, as between those attributable to the issue of shares (for instance, costs of preparing and advising on a rights issue document), those attributable to the issue of the debt and those attributable to the other aspects of the financing, only the last of these will not fall to be treated as issue costs.

6.292 As to how a reasonable allocation can be made in practice, it may be possible for the company to ask its advisors to indicate on their invoices the amount of costs that are attributable to each area of the advisors' work. However, the invoices may not be definitive. If no such allocation is possible, but there is a list of the work which the professional advisors have done, then an analysis of the invoices would have to be made to segregate costs associated with the issue from other costs. If there is neither an allocation nor an analysis of professional advisors' costs, an estimate of the extent to which advisors' costs have been incurred on the issue, on some reasonable basis, would have to be made.

6.293 The fees charged by banks and other financial institutions for finance will be charged in two ways. First there is an arrangement fee, which is normally a fixed percentage of the finance raised, and secondly, the finance interest coupon.

The arrangement fee, as it relates to the specific instrument, should normally be treated as an issue cost as it can be regarded as part of the overall finance cost, having the effect of increasing the coupon. Syndication fees are charged by banks and financial institutions to arrange for other banks and financial institutions to participate in funding capital instruments (sub-participation). Again, these costs seem clearly to fall within the definition of issue costs.

6.294 Where several classes of equity, non-equity shares or debt are issued at once, it would be reasonable to make an apportionment of the total issue costs to each category on the basis of gross proceeds.

6.295 With regard, however, to costs incurred in connection with a financial restructuring or renegotiation, paragraph 96 of FRS 4 states that they do not qualify as issue costs. These costs are regarded under the FRS as relating to previous sources of finance even where a new instrument is issued following the restructuring or renegotiation. So costs incurred in negotiating with a financial institution to extend the term or change the interest rate on debt would be disallowed, even where a new debt instrument is issued. This also follows from paragraph 32 of the FRS which requires that gains and losses arising on the repurchase of early settlement of debt should be recognised in the profit and loss account in the period during which the repurchase or early settlement is made. But where an offer document is issued in relation to raising new debt or shares, the relevant costs of the offer should be regarded as issue costs, even though the debt so raised might be used to pay off previous borrowings.

6.296 It is not generally possible to write off issue costs to the profit and loss account in the year an instrument is issued. The only exceptions will be:

- Where issue costs are immaterial, the provisions of FRS 4 do not apply and, therefore, they can be charged to the profit and loss account immediately.
- If the term is only one year or less.
- Where the costs associated with an issue do not fall within the strict definition of issue costs.
- Where the costs, if spread, would give rise to an excessively high finance cost on the instrument, which is out of line with that expected to be charged.

The last two points are considered in the paragraphs that follow.

6.297 FRS 4 states in paragraph 96 that costs that do not qualify as issue costs should be written off to the profit and loss account. However, this statement is made as part of the explanatory section rather than in the FRS standard section and seems to be dealing with the basic situation where a company is simply raising finance for its continuing operations or organic growth. It does not seem to be intended to preclude a company that has issued capital instruments to fund an acquisition of another company from capitalising as part of its cost of investment external costs it has incurred in connection with the acquisition, which do not fall within the strict definition of 'issue costs' (see chapter 25). FRS 25 contains requirements in relation to transaction costs that are applicable to all entities and which supports this view. Under FRS 25, transaction costs of an equity transaction are deducted from equity, unless the costs were incurred in relation to the acquisition of a business, in which case FRS 6 is applied. [FRS 25 para 35]. Transaction costs are defined in FRS 26 as *"incremental costs that are directly attributable to the acquisition, issue or disposal of a financial asset or financial liability"*. [FRS 26 para 9]. Capitalisation of such costs can be made even where merger relief is taken, but where merger accounting is used for the acquisition, FRS 6, 'Acquisitions and mergers', requires such costs to be expensed (see further chapter 28).

6.298 Finance costs might be overstated where a company is in financial difficulties and in order to raise finance to continue trading it incurs material costs related to the issue. It may be imprudent for such a company to spread these excessive issue costs forward. In this type of situation, it would be prudent for the company to recognise some or all of the issue costs an exceptional finance cost in the year that they are incurred.

Facility fees

6.299 Where a company negotiates with a bank or other financial institution for a loan facility, the institution will charge a facility fee at the time of putting the loan facility in place. For example, such an arrangement might provide for the total facility to be £20 million which can be drawn down in specified or unspecified tranches over the life of the facility. The facility gives the company financial flexibility to draw down a range of finance from the full amount of the facility to nothing at all. Facility fees are very similar in nature to issue costs. The facility fee is a cost of negotiating a source of finance, which represents the cost the company is prepared to incur in order to obtain the necessary financial flexibility. Prior to the issue of the original FRS 4, facility fees of this nature were generally written off to the profit and loss account as incurred. The treatment of facility fees will be determined by the type of instrument to which they relate.

Shares and debenture stock

6.300 Paragarph 3(2)(b) of SI 2008/410 Sch 1 does not allow issue costs, which would include facility fees, in relation to shares and debenture stock to be held on balance sheet as an asset. Section 738 of the Companies Act 2006 refers to debentures as including *"debenture stock, bonds and any other securities of a company, whether or not constituting a charge on the assets of the company"*. 'Other securities' is open to wide interpretation. However, we believe that this refers to instruments which could be listed or traded in an active market. Pre-issuance costs in relation to such instruments cannot be deferred as an asset on the balance sheet.

Bank loans

6.301 We do not believe that the requirements in paragraph 3(2)(b) of SI 2008/410 Sch 1 apply to bank borrowings or committed facilities agreed between a borrower and lender on a bi-lateral basis or committed facilities between a borrower and a syndicate of banks which are not capable of being traded in an active market.

6.302 As noted in paragraph 6.293 above, paragraph 96 of FRS 4 requires issue costs to be accounted for as a reduction in the proceeds of a capital instrument. Such costs are not assets as defined in the Board's draft Statement of Principles because they do not provide access to any future economic benefits. Facility fees paid for access to liquidity *via* a committed facility; do provide the entity with access to future benefits. In our view, access to such liquidity does meet the definition of an asset in accordance with the statement of principles. The availability of finance on pre-arranged terms provides benefit to an entity in a similar way to an insurance policy. If finance is needed in the future due to unforeseen events, the facility in place ensures that an entity can obtain this finance on known terms regardless of the economic environment in the future.

6.302.1 To the extent there is evidence that it is probable that some or all of the facility will be drawn down, the facility fee is deferred and treated as an issue cost when draw-down occurs; it is not amortised prior to the draw-down. For example, draw-down might be probable if there is a specific project for which there is an agreed business plan. If a facility is for £20 million and it is probable that only £5 million of the facility will be drawn down, a quarter of the facility fee represents a transaction cost of the £5 million loan and is deferred until draw-down occurs.

6.302.2 To the extent there is no evidence that it is probable that some or all of the facility will be drawn down, the facility fee represents a payment for liquidity services — that is, to secure the availability of finance on pre-arranged terms over the facility period. As such, to the extent draw down is not probable, the facility fee is capitalised as a prepayment for services and amortised over the period of the facility to which it relates.

6.302.3 It should be noted that there are no specific requirements in IAS 39 for a borrower to write off facility fees and so such fees are often carried forward as assets. The treatment of facility fees under IAS 39 is discussed in chapter 9 Manual of accounting – Financial instruments and is consistent with the analysis above. Since FRS 26 replicates IAS 39, the question arises as to whether a similar treatment can be adopted under FRS 26. Consequently, the treatment set out above under FRS 4 remains applicable under FRS 26. This includes the requirements relating to expenses related to, and commissions paid on, any issue of shares or debentures which may not be treated as assets in any balance sheet in accordance with SI 2008/410 1 Sch 3(2)(b).

Term of capital instruments

6.303 Capital instruments come with various terms, which might be fixed, varying or indeterminate. A capital instrument's term is not necessarily the same period as its life. A capital instrument might have a number of different dates during its life when it can be redeemed or converted. These rights of redemption or conversion can be at the behest of the holder or the issuer of the instrument and are often granted by the use of options. The life of the instrument might extend for (say) ten years, but the impact of the options, if they are exercised, might be to shorten or lengthen the term considerably.

6.304 Under FRS 4 it is necessary to determine the term of an instrument for two reasons. First, the calculation of finance costs may depend on the term. For example a ten year bond might have an option to redeem after (say) five years at a premium of 20 per cent, but if not redeemed until year ten, the premium might reduce to (say) ten per cent. One of these premiums should be treated as part of the finance costs of the instrument, but the question is which one and this will depend on the instrument's term. Therefore, it is important to establish whether the term is five or ten years. Secondly, once determined, the finance costs are required by FRS 4 to be amortised over the instrument's term.

Definition of term

6.305 The term of capital instruments is defined in FRS 4 in the following way:

> *"The period from the date of issue of the capital instrument to the date at which it will expire, be redeemed, or be cancelled .*
>
> *If either party has the option to require the instrument to be redeemed or cancelled and, under the terms of the instrument, it is uncertain whether such an option will be exercised, the term should be taken to end on the earliest date at which the instrument would be redeemed or cancelled on exercise of such an option .*
>
> *If either party has the right to extend the period of an instrument, the term should not include the period of the extension if there is a genuine commercial possibility that the period will not be extended."* [FRS 4 para 16].

Implications of options

6.306 In many situations it will be obvious what the instrument's term is and this will in the majority of cases be the life of the instrument. However, where there are options built into the instrument the term becomes complicated. As can be seen from the second paragraph of the definition, where there is an option to redeem or cancel, the term is taken to end on the earliest date on which the option can be exercised. Paragraph 73 of FRS 4 goes on to comment that if there is an option for early redemption, the term should be taken to end on the earliest date the option could be exercised, unless there is *no* genuine commercial possibility that the option will be exercised. This requirement might at first sight seem a little odd, but it is based on the premise that options are normally granted for a purpose, for instance to allow a borrower to repay the debt early if the borrower either no longer needs debt or finds its interest rate unattractive. Therefore, because most options will have a genuine commercial reason, instruments' terms will often be determined to end on the earliest date on which an option can be exercised.

6.307 For example, a company might have a ten year £100,000 redeemable fixed rate five per cent bond which is redeemable at a premium of ten per cent and on which its costs of issue amounted to £2,000. In addition as part of the terms of the instrument, the company might hold an option to redeem the bond after year five and incur a premium of 15 per cent if early redemption is taken. If interest rates move down sufficiently, then it might pay the company to redeem the instrument early and this is a decision that the company will take in year five. The option, therefore, does have an economic purpose and under the provisions of the amended FRS 4 it appears that the option should be taken into account when determining the instrument's term, because it cannot be said that there is *no* genuine commercial possibility that the option will not be exercised.

6.308 Companies believed that this rule was too harsh, because they argued that in this circumstance the option is merely a right of the issuer (but not the investor) to redeem the instrument early on the payment of the premium (known as an issuer call option). In the example, the company will make the decision to refinance the debt in year five and any additional costs (such as the premium) should rightly be borne in the year the decision is taken. This issue was taken up with the UITF who agreed that the amount of premium payable under an issuer call option is not a payment *"that the issuer may be required to make in respect of the instrument"* and, consequently, does not fall within the definition of 'finance costs'.

6.309 The UITF, as a consequence, issued Abstract 11, 'Capital instruments: issuer call options', in September 1994 which concluded that where an instrument includes a call option that can be exercised only by the issuer, the payment required on exercise of that option does not form part of the instrument's finance costs. [UITF 11 para 6]. UITF 11 still applies for those entities that are not yet applying FRS 26. Therefore in the example given above, the premium of 15 per cent that could be payable in year five does not form part of the instrument's finance costs although it might seem to under a strict interpretation of FRS 4. But the Abstract's consensus can only be applied to genuine options and, as a consequence, does not apply to situations where it is clear that the issuer would be commercially obliged to exercise the call option. The UITF cites an example of such a case where the instrument's terms and conditions give the issuer the option of early redemption, but it is clear from the outset that in all conceivable circumstances it would be advantageous for the issuer to exercise the option rather than to allow the debt to remain in issue. [UITF 11 para 8].

6.310 Furthermore, the UITF also commented that where an instrument has an issuer call option the exercise of which is uncertain, the instrument's term will end on the date on which the option is exercisable. [UITF 11 para 7]. This statement is somewhat anomalous, because although the Abstract allows in the example above the 15 per cent premium to be excluded from finance costs, the instrument's term is still determined as five years. This means in practice that the costs of issuing the instrument have to be written off over the period to the option date (in the example five years and not the full ten years). It has been argued that the requirement that the term should end on the date the option is exercisable implies that all of the instrument's finance costs should be written off to the profit and loss account over this period, including any premium payable on the instrument's eventual redemption (a premium of ten per cent in the example payable in year ten). We do not believe that the UITF intended this outcome as it seems totally wrong to accrue ten years' interest and the £10,000 premium in the example over the first five years of the instrument and, therefore, not to accrue any finance cost over the last five years of the instrument's term. We, therefore, consider in this type of situation that issue costs should be charged to the profit and loss account over the shorter term, but interest cost and any redemption premium payable on the instrument's eventual redemption should be accrued over its full term.

6.311 Continuing with the example in paragraph 6.330, under UITF Abstract 11's provisions and our interpretation given above, the finance costs to be allocated to the first five years would be £32,000, comprising the fixed interest cost of £25,000 plus half of the premium arising on the eventual redemption of £10,000 plus the whole of the issue costs of £2,000. The example assumes that interest is paid semi-annually in arrears. The finance cost is allocated to accounting periods at a constant rate on the outstanding balance and for the first five years this rate is calculated to be 6.3385 per cent.

Interest rate compound semi-annually. Overall finance cost 6.3385%

Year	Balance b/f	Finance cost 6 months	Interest 6 months	Balance	Finance cost 6 months	Interest 6 months	Balance c/f
1	98,000	3,106	(2,500)	98,606	3,125	(2,500)	99,231
2	99,231	3,145	(2,500)	99,876	3,165	(2,500)	100,541
3	100,541	3,180	(2,500)	101,228	3,208	(2,500)	101,936
4	101,936	3,231	(2,500)	102,666	3,254	(2,500)	103,420
5	103,420	3,278	(2,500)	104,198	3,302	(2,500)	105,000
		15,945	(12,500)		16,055	(12,500)	
					15,945	(12,500)	
Total finance and interest costs					32,000	(25,000)	

6.312 For the second five years of the term, the interest rate reduces slightly to 5.6 per cent because all of the issue costs have been amortised over the first five year term. The total finance costs over the ten years come to £62,000, which is made up of interest of £50,000, redemption premium of £10,000 and issue costs of £2,000.

Interest rate compounded semi-annually. Overall finance cost 5.6%

Year	Balance b/f	Finance cost 6 months	Interest 6 months	Balance	Finance cost 6 months	Interest 6 months	Balance c/f
6	105,000	2,940	(2,500)	105,440	2,953	(2,500)	105,893
7	105,893	2,965	(2,500)	106,358	2,978	(2,500)	106,836
8	106,836	2,992	(2,500)	107,328	3,005	(2,500)	107,833
9	107,833	3,020	(2,500)	108,353	3,034	(2,500)	108,887
10	108,887	3,049	(2,500)	109,436	3,064	(2,500)	110,000
		14,966	(12,500)		15,035	(12,500)	
					14,966	(12,500)	
Total finance and interest costs					30,000	(25,000)	

6.313 The UITF made one exception to the general rule concerning issuer call options where the effective rate of interest increases after the date on which the option is exercisable. [UITF 11 para 9]. This type of circumstance arises where the economics of the instrument are such that the premium payable on exercising the option compensates the investor for forgoing the increase in interest due after the option date. In this circumstance, the finance costs calculation must include the redemption premium payable on exercising the option; and the term would remain, in the example, five years.

6.314 Where in the example in paragraph 6.307, the option is a put option, the instrument's term should be taken to be five years. In this case, the finance cost over the first five years is £42,000 comprising the fixed interest cost of £25,000 plus the early redemption premium of £15,000 and issue costs of £2,000. The example assumes that interest is paid semi-annually in arrears. The finance cost is allocated to accounting periods at a constant rate of 7.9923 per cent on the outstanding balance.

Interest rate compounded semi-annually. Overall finance cost 7.9923%

Year	Balance b/f	Finance cost 6 months	Interest 6 months	Balance	Finance cost 6 months	Interest 6 months	Balance c/f
1	98,000	3,916	(2,500)	99,416	3,973	(2,500)	100,889
2	100,889	4,032	(2,500)	102,421	4,093	(2,500)	104,014
3	104,014	4,157	(2,500)	105,670	4,223	(2,500)	107,393
4	107,393	4,292	(2,500)	109,184	4,363	(2,500)	111,048
5	111,048	4,438	(2,500)	112,985	4,515	(2,500)	115,000
		20,834	(12,500)		21,167	(12,500)	
					20,834	(12,500)	
Total finance and interest costs					42,000	(25,000)	

6.315 If, however, the option is not taken up in year five, then depending upon the terms of the instrument the finance cost for the next period of five years until the instrument is ultimately redeemed will be less than for the first five years. This is because a higher redemption premium has been accrued over the first five year period. This is illustrated in the table below which shows the allocation of the finance costs of £20,000 for the latter five year term. The finance cost is made up of £25,000 of interest plus £10,000 premium payable on redemption less £15,000 of premium already accrued.

Interest rate 5% compounded semi-annually. Overall finance cost 3.5454%

Year	Balance b/f	Finance cost 6 months	Interest 6 months	Balance	Finance costs 6 months	Interest 6 months	Balance c/f
6	115,000	2,039	(2,500)	114,539	2,030	(2,500)	114,069
7	114,069	2,022	(2,500)	113,591	2,014	(2,500)	113,105
8	113,105	2,005	(2,500)	112,610	1,996	(2,500)	112,106
9	112,106	1,987	(2,500)	111,593	1,978	(2,500)	111,071
10	111,071	1,969	(2,500)	110,540	1,960	(2,500)	110,000
		10,022	(12,500)		9,978	(12,500)	
					10,022	(12,500)	
Total finance and interest costs					20,000	(25,000)	

6.316 The requirement to take the term of the instrument, where an option (apart from an issuer call option) to redeem or cancel exists, to be up to the earliest date the option can be exercised has some odd consequences in practice. For example, in a typical management buyout (MBO), options for early repayment of redeemable shares and debt will often feature in the terms of those instruments. These may well operate to allow repayment of the finance at any time after the instrument has been issued. Where this is the case, unless it can be shown that there will be *no* genuine commercial possibility that the option will be exercised, the term will be less than one year (in effect it will be the notice period required). Thus, the whole of the finance costs should be written off to the profit and loss account in the year the instrument is issued and treated as an exceptional interest cost separately disclosed where material. The finance cost so written off will include the interest cost for the period and any issue costs. Finance costs should also include the difference between any premium on issue and any redemption premium. In the next year, if the instrument continues to be outstanding, the finance costs charged to the profit and loss account will merely be the interest cost for the period.

Term extended

6.317 As indicated in the definition, the term should not include any period for which the instrument might be extended, unless at the time the instrument is issued it is virtually certain that the term will be extended. [FRS 4 para 73]. Consequently, the economic interests of the parties to the instrument are important in determining its term. The FRS cites as an example the situation where a zero coupon bond is issued. If the terms of the bond are such that on early redemption the lender receives merely the original issue price, then the lender is unlikely to require early redemption unless there is a severe deterioration in the creditworthiness of the borrower. Therefore, at the outset, the bond's term should be taken to extend to its final maturity. [FRS 4 para 74].

6.318 These principles are illustrated in the two examples that follow:

Example 1

A company issues £1m 10% preference shares that are classified as liabilities. The terms are that £500,000 is redeemable in 20X2 and the balance is redeemable at the company's option in any year up to 20X9, when the balance must be redeemed. If the £500,000 is not redeemed in 20X2 additional dividends of 5% will accrue on that amount. The company is in financial difficulties and is unlikely to be able to redeem the shares in 20X2.

If there is no genuine possibility that redemption of the £500,000 will occur in 20X2, the term should be taken to be to the year 20X9 for the whole of the £1m preference shares. This means that the finance costs should include the additional dividends on the £500,000 that will not be redeemed in 20X2. The additional dividends should be accrued for over the whole of the instrument's term.

Example 2

A company has issued a bond to raise money from a securities house pending a flotation. The bond is convertible into shares when the company is floated. It has a low coupon at first, but if the company is not floated, it is repayable at a fixed date in the future at a premium. The term of the liability component of the instrument should be taken to be up to the date that is fixed for repayment in the event that the company is not floated. The total finance costs, including the premium should be amortised over this period to give a constant periodic rate of charge.

Term shortened

6.319 During an instrument's life, it is possible that its term could be shortened, for example, if for some reason the instrument is to be redeemed early in a way that was not foreseen. In this situation, the amortisation of issue costs and any discount on issue, or premium on redemption, should be accelerated over the remaining period of the shortened term from the point where it becomes clear that the instrument will be redeemed early. [FRS 4 para 94].

Example

A company has issued £10m of debt and has written off £0.5m of issue costs against the debt. The debt is redeemable in 5 years time and carries interest at 5% per annum. An effective interest rate (EIR) of 6.19% is applied to amortise the issue costs to the profit and loss account over the 5 years. (See para 6.323 onwards for details on EIR.)

At the end of the first year, it becomes clear that the company will redeem the debt at the end of year 3. The company has amortised 1 years worth of issue costs to date. In year 2, the company should revise the EIR (now 7.29%) to record the un-amortised issue costs in the profit and loss account over the remaining term of the debt of 2 years.

6.320 The point at which it *becomes clear* that an instrument will be redeemed early is debatable. A tentative board decision alone is unlikely to be sufficient and there would need to be a clear strategic reason for the early redemption, a timescale and sufficient funds to complete the transaction.

Indeterminate term

6.321 If the life of an instrument is indeterminate (for example, a perpetual bond) then FRS 4 comments that the benefit of the issue costs is reflected in the terms of the financing indefinitely. [FRS 4 para 95]. Where, for example, a perpetual bond of £100,000 is issued by a company and it incurs £2,000 of issue costs, the issue costs should reduce the carrying amount of the debt shown in the company's balance sheet. They would only be charged to the profit and loss account if and when the instrument is repurchased from the lender and would form part of the eventual profit or loss arising on the repurchase.

Measurement

Initial recognition

6.322 FRS 4 requires that immediately after issue, debt should be stated at the amount of the net proceeds (for example, see Table 6.21). [FRS 4 para 27]. The net proceeds are defined as the fair value of the consideration received on the issue of a capital instrument after deducting issue costs. [FRS 4 para 11]. Where debt is issued at a discount, the discount cannot be treated as an asset, rather the debt should be recorded at the fair value of the consideration received net of any discounts given.

Table 6.21 – Borrowings stated at fair value

Bass PLC – Annual Report –30 September 1994

Borrowings

All borrowings are initially stated at the fair value of the consideration received after deduction of issue costs. Issue costs together with finance costs are charged to the profit and loss account over the term of the borrowings and represents a constant proportion of the balance of capital repayments outstanding. Accrued finance costs attributable to borrowings where the maturity at the date of issue is less than 12 months are included in accrued charges within current liabilities. For all other borrowings, accrued finance charges and issue costs are added to the carrying value of those borrowings.

Treatment of finance costs

6.323 Having established that debt should be recognised initially at the amount of the net proceeds, the next question to consider is the value at which the debt should be stated in balance sheets drawn up at dates between the original issue of the debt and its redemption. The answer lies essentially in how payments are accounted for between the date of issue and redemption and the recognition of finance costs.

6.324 Finance costs are considered from paragraph 6.281 and comprise the issue costs, the interest payable over the instrument's life, the difference between any premium received on issue and any premium payable on redemption and any discount allowed on the instrument's issue.

6.325 Finance costs should be recognised as an expense over an instrument's life. The simplest method of accounting would be to recognise finance costs on a straight line basis. However, although this method of allocation is simple, it fails to reflect the true cost of finance. This is because the amount charged each year does not necessarily bear any relationship to the outstanding obligation; that is, the method ignores the time value of money which is clearly relevant for financial decisions. For this reason, the ASB rejected the straight line method of allocation and opted instead for a more sophisticated method.

6.326 Under the method adopted by FRS 4, finance costs are charged to the profit and loss account at a constant rate on the carrying amount of the instrument. [FRS 4 para 28]. The constant rate is the discount rate that equates the present value of the net proceeds of the instrument with the present value of the total amount repaid on the instrument. It is better known as 'the internal rate of return' or sometimes referred to as 'the effective periodic rate' or 'the effective yield'; and it is equivalent to 'the rate implicit in the lease' under SSAP 21. It may be found by mathematical techniques involving an iterative process or by using a financial calculator or computer. Various examples are included in this chapter that illustrate the allocation of finance costs to accounting periods using this method.

6.327 Therefore, generally, it will not be acceptable to use the straight line method to allocate finance costs, unless this produces a similar result to a basis which achieves a constant rate. In this respect the standard adds that in certain instances the nominal interest rate on debt will not be materially different from the amount required by the FRS to achieve a constant rate and in those circumstances the nominal interest rate can be charged in the profit and loss account instead. [FRS 4 para 75]. This will often be so where the issue costs on a debt instrument are immaterial and there is no redemption premium to be accrued over its term. Consequently, for simple debt, such as straightforward bank loans and overdrafts where issue costs are immaterial or do not feature, the actual interest charged on the debt should be the amount recorded in the profit and loss account. Otherwise a basis similar to that illustrated in the example in paragraph 6.348 should be used.

6.328 Clearly, the finance cost is not necessarily equal to the amount of interest payable. The following example illustrates the issues that arise.

Example

A company issues 5% debentures having a nominal value £100,000 at a discount of 10% repayable in five years' time at a premium of 20%. Debt issue costs amounted to £5,000 and interest is payable annually in arrears.

	£	£
Net proceeds received:		
Nominal value		100,000
Discount on issue @ 10%		(10,000)
Issue costs		(5,000)
		85,000
Total amount payable:		
Interest @ 5% for 5 years		25,000
Redemption premium		20,000
Nominal value		100,000
		145,000
Finance cost:		
Interest	25,000	
Issue costs	5,000	
Discount on issue	10,000	
Redemption premium	20,000	
		60,000

6.329 As explained in paragraph 6.301, the finance cost should be recognised over the term of the loan, that is, five years at a constant rate on the outstanding obligation. In the example used above, the rate can be found to be 12.323 per cent. If the finance costs are allocated to accounting periods using this rate, the movements on the loan would be as follows:

Interest rate 5% compounded annually. Overall finance cost 12.323%

Year	Balance b/f	Finance cost @ 12.323%	Interest paid	Balance c/f
1	85,000	10,474	(5,000)	90,474
2	90,474	11,149	(5,000)	96,623
3	96,623	11,906	(5,000)	103,529
4	103,529	12,757	(5,000)	111,286
5	111,286	13,714	(5,000)	120,000
Total finance costs and interest		60,000	(25,000)	

6.330 The effective interest rate of 12.323 per cent is higher than the nominal interest rate of 5 per cent because of the incidence of issue costs, the discount on issue and the premium payable on redemption. As explained in paragraph 6.301, in some circumstances the nominal interest rate may not be materially different from the effective interest rate, in which case the nominal interest rate may be used.

6.331 Although the FRS requires that the finance cost should be charged to the profit and loss account over the instrument's term, it does not preclude capitalising those costs. Where it is appropriate to capitalise finance costs as part of the cost of an asset, the costs should still initially be written off to the profit and loss account as part of the interest cost, but should also be credited simultaneously to the profit and loss account and debited to the asset in order to record the capitalisation. [FRS 4 para 76]. As a result, the interest charge shown on the face of the profit and loss account would be the net amount and in the notes this would be expanded to show the gross amount and the amount capitalised deducted. However, for assets of the company being constructed, only the finance costs incurred during the period of construction of the asset can be capitalised (see further chapter 16).

Subsequent recognition and measurement

6.332 Once the effective interest rate on the debt has been calculated by reference to the initial carrying value and the future cash outflows, it is a relatively simple matter to arrive at the carrying value of debt at each period end. As evident from the table above, the carrying value at the end of each period is obtained by adding to the carrying value at the beginning of the period the finance cost in respect of the reporting period (calculated by applying the effective interest rate to the carrying value at the beginning) and deducting any payments made in respect of the debt in that period. [FRS 4 para 29]. In fact, the carrying value at each balance sheet date is the discounted amount of the future payments specified in the debt instrument using the effective interest rate inherent in the amount at which the debt was initially recognised.

Contingent payments

6.333 The effective interest rate and, hence, the carrying value of debt is relatively easy to calculate where the cash outflows specified in the instrument are known or fixed at the outset. However, where the future cash outflows are not known in advance, but are variable, an effective interest rate cannot be calculated. For example, in the case of floating rate notes where the amount of periodic payments of interest is calculated by reference to a particular formula or by reference to LIBOR, say LIBOR plus two per cent, the interest payments over the instruments' life are not known in advance. Another example is that of index linked loans, which may be redeemable at the principal amount multiplied by an index. The effect of each is that the effective interest rate of the instrument over its life is not only unknown, but also changes every time there is a change in circumstance. The most practical way of accounting for such instruments is not to try to anticipate the change in circumstance, but to take account of it in the period in which the change occurs.

6.334 Therefore, the standard requires that where the amount of payments required by a debt instrument is contingent on uncertain future events such as changes in an index, those events should be taken into account in calculating finance costs and the carrying amount once they have occurred. [FRS 4 para 31]. In other words, the initial accounting for the instrument should take no account of those events, but the carrying value of the instrument at each subsequent balance sheet date should be recalculated to take account of the changes that have occurred in the period. The resulting change in carrying amount should be accounted for as an adjustment to the finance cost for the period. The treatment specified in the standard is illustrated by reference to a floating rate instrument below.

Example

A company borrows £1m from a bank repayable in five years' time. Interest is paid annually in arrears at a rate equal to the bank's prime rate plus 1%. Due to arrangement fees and bank commission, the company receives a net amount of £980,000. The bank's prime rate in years 1 and 2 remains at 5%. At the beginning of year 3, the prime rate rises to 6%.

As an effective interest rate cannot be calculated at inception without advanced knowledge of the change in future rates, the finance cost in each period would need to be calculated by reference to the actual rate prevailing in that period. The example is slightly complicated because of the incidence of issue costs of £20,000. The amortisation of the issue costs over the five year period can either be carried out if immaterial on a straight line basis (or written off to the profit and loss account immediately), or when they are material, on a constant interest rate basis by regarding them as being similar to a discount on issue. On the latter basis, the interest rate for amortising the issue costs over the five year period is 0.4049%. The additional finance cost which is the interest element would be charged in the period at the actual rate incurred.

Year	Balance b/f	Issue cost 0.4049%	Finance cost Interest for period	Total charge	Interest paid	Balance c/f
1	980,000	3,968	60,000	63,968	(60,000)	983,968
2	983,968	3.984	60.000	63.984	(60,000)	987,952
3	987,952	4,000	70.000	74,000	(70,000)	991,952
4	991,952	4.016	70,000	74,016	(70,000)	995,968
5	995,968	4,032	70,000	74,032	(70.000)	1,000,000
Total costs		20,000	330,000	350,000		

6.335 It is doubtful whether the above treatment can be applied to all situations where the amount of cash outflows on the instrument is not known in advance. Consider a situation, where a shareholder makes a non-interest bearing loan to his company which is redeemable at the end of three years at a premium determined by applying a known percentage to the aggregate profits for a three year period in excess of a benchmark amount. In this situation, the premium payable on redemption is contingent on the company achieving profits in excess of the benchmark amount and this amount will only be known at the end of the third year. If the wording of the standard is read literally, no amount of the premium payable will fall to be accrued in the first two years, but the whole amount will be charged in the profit and loss account in the third year, thus distorting the results for that year. Clearly this treatment does not accord with the spirit of FRS 4. Therefore, a 'best estimate' of the likely premium payable on redemption should be made at the outset and a proportion provided for every year. The provision would require adjustments in years two and three when the outcome becomes clearer and eventually known.

6.336 If, in the situation explained above, the company had incurred some issue costs and the loan was interest bearing, these components of finance costs should be charged to the profit and loss account at a constant rate, thus leaving the unknown element to be dealt with in the manner specified above.

Repurchase of debt

6.337 Companies sometimes have the opportunity to repurchase their own debt or settle debt early at an amount that differs from the amount at which the debt is stated in their balance sheet at the time. For example, a company may decide to take advantage of falling interest rates by repurchasing its existing long-term fixed interest debt, even though this may involve payment of a premium. The question arises as to how the difference on the repurchase or early settlement should be accounted for. Accounting for repurchase of debt was first addressed by UITF Abstract 8, which was superseded by FRS 4.

6.338 Some accountants supported the view that the difference on repurchase should be deferred on the grounds that the opportunity to repurchase the debt at a gain or loss is created principally by movements in interest rates. In effect, the economic decision to repurchase the debt is neutral, because the gain or loss is effectively counter balanced by a corresponding increase or decrease in interest costs in the future. Therefore, they argued that the accounting for the effect of the repurchase should also be neutral and, accordingly, the gain or loss should be deferred. The UITF, however, reached the conclusion that the gain or loss on repurchase should be taken to the profit and loss account in the period in which the repurchase occurs. The UITF reached this conclusion on the grounds that the finance cost reported by an entity should normally reflect only its current borrowing arrangements and should not be influenced by any arrangement that previously existed, but that had now been terminated.

6.339 FRS 4 follows the UITF's ruling, and accordingly, requires that gains or losses should be recognised in the profit and loss account in the period during which the repurchase or early settlement is made. [FRS 4 para 32].

6.340 The only time that it might be possible to argue that no profit or loss has arisen in the period is (following the principles of FRS 5) where in substance there is no repurchase and the old debt being repurchased has been replaced by new debt, which in effect gives the same economic result as the old debt. This was the argument followed in UITF Abstract 8 (see below), but it rests on the foundation that the new debt must give the same economic result as the old debt. In the majority of situations in practice this is unlikely to be the case, because there will always be a commercial reason compelling the change; otherwise why would the company repurchase? Consider the following example:

Example

A company repays £150,000 debt early and incurs a penalty of £5,000 which is specified in the agreement, but replaces it with a new loan of £150,000 from the same party. The terms of the loan and the loan covenants are very similar. The company is willing to pay this penalty, because the new loan is a variable rate loan, whereas the old loan is fixed rate. Therefore, although the loan is very similar in nature, the cash flows related to interest payments are different and because the penalty is pre-determined it does not reflect accurately the difference between the fixed rate of interest and the current and expected future variable interest rates. It seems clear in this situation that there has been a change in substance in relation to these loans and that as a result the £5,000 penalty should be charged in the profit and loss account in the year of repurchase.

6.341 UITF Abstract 8 was developed at the time that certain major utility companies were repurchasing their government debt to help reduce the government's public sector borrowing requirement. Some of these repurchases were special in nature and required different rules to normal repurchases. The Abstract was withdrawn on FRS 4's issue, but remains a good source of guidance to help determine those exceptional cases where in substance there has been no repurchase. UITF Abstract 8 made two exceptions to the requirement for immediate recognition of a gain or loss arising on the repurchase of debt. The exceptions, which are considered below are referred to in appendix III of FRS 4 which deals with the standard's development. The two exceptions are where:

- The agreement to repurchase the debt is also connected with its refinancing on substantially the same terms (other than interest costs). This would apply where the original debt is fully replaced by new debt which gives the same economic result as the original debt, that is, there has been no change of substance in the debt. For this to be the case, as a minimum the following conditions must be satisfied:
  - The replacement debt and the original debt are both fixed rate.
  - The replacement debt is of a comparable amount to the original debt.
  - The maturity of the replacement debt is not materially different from the remaining maturity of the original debt.
  - The covenants of the replacement debt are not materially different from those of the original debt.

A refinancing may fall within this exception whether or not the lender of the replacement debt is the same as the lender of the original debt.

- The agreement to repurchase the debt is not carried out on a fair value basis because the overall finance costs of the replacement debt are significantly different from market rates. This condition has been introduced to prevent recognition of an artificial profit, compensated by higher costs in the future.

6.342 Where either of the above exceptions apply, the gain or loss should be spread forward either over the remaining maturity of the original debt or, if not significantly different, over the maturity of the replacement debt. In addition, the circumstances should be disclosed, together with the method of accounting adopted and the principal terms of the original and replacement borrowing.

Renegotiation of debt

6.343 A company that is experiencing financial difficulties and is unable to meet its scheduled debt repayments may seek to renegotiate the terms of its debt obligations with its lenders. As a result of the negotiations, the lender may agree to a reduction or a deferral of the payments due to him. Since the company's obligations are significantly reduced, a gain may arise. The recognition and measurement of this gain are central to the accounting for renegotiation of debt.

6.344 The accounting for renegotiation of debt is not included in the standard, but the ASB's initial proposals, first published for public comment in a bulletin issued in July 1993 are examined here.

6.345 Accounting for the effects of the renegotiation (the concession granted by the lender) involves two particular issues, namely:

- The way in which the concession should be recognised. That is, whether the finance costs should be reduced over the remaining period in which the debt is in issue or whether the gain should be recognised at the time of the renegotiation.

- If it is considered that a gain arises, the way in which the gain should be determined. That is, whether market interest rates prevailing at the time of renegotiation should be used or whether the revised payments should be discounted at the rate inherent in the original debt.

6.346 With respect to the first point above, some support deferral of the gain on the grounds that they consider it paradoxical to recognise a gain that relates primarily to a deterioration of the company's financial condition. They believe that no gain should be recognised, but the benefit of the reduction should be recognised over the term of the replacement loan by way of a reduced interest burden. Others argue that the recognition of the gain at the time of renegotiation reflects the economic consequences of the concession granted by the lender. It also ensures that both liabilities and finance costs for subsequent periods are shown at amounts that properly represent the agreement then in force. The ASB supported the latter view and proposed that in principle the gain should be recognised in the period in which the renegotiation was concluded.

6.347 The ASB argued that the renegotiation was a transaction that effectively resulted in the original loan being replaced by a new loan giving rise to revised payments and, therefore, the amount relating to the old, superseded, debt was no longer relevant. Accordingly, the ASB proposed that the debt should be stated at its market value at the time of renegotiation, because this treatment best reflected the economic circumstances prevailing at that time. As the debt would generally not be traded, its market value would often be determined by discounting the revised payments by reference to the rate of interest which the company would have expected to pay on a loan of similar characteristics to that resulting from the renegotiation. Any change in the company's credit rating since the original loan was made, as well as changes in the general level of interests rates, would be reflected in that rate. Several respondents objected to this aspect of the ASB's proposal. Their objections can best be illustrated by an example.

Example

A company took out a long-term bank loan of £1m on 1 January 20X0 at a fixed rate of 8% per annum for 10 years. Interest on the loan is paid yearly in arrears. As a result of deteriorating financial condition, the company successfully agreed with its bankers to reduce the yearly interest payments from £80,000 to £20,000 per annum with effect from 1 January 20X4, but the loan is still repayable at the original amount on 31 December 20X9. At 1 January 20X4, the company would have paid 15% per annum on a loan of similar characteristics to that resulting from the renegotiation. Had the company's credit rating not declined, the interest rate on similar borrowings would have been 10% per annum.

	Original rate	Market rate excluding decline in credit rating	Market rate including decline in credit rating
Rate (%)	8.00%	10.00%	15.00%
	£'000	£'000	£'000
Original loan	1,000	1,000	1,000
PV of revised repayments	723	652	508
Gain on renegotiation	277	348	492
Future finance costs			
31 December 20X4	57	65	76
31 December 20X5	61	70	85
31 December 20X6	64	75	94
31 December 20X7	68	80	106
31 December 20X8	71	86	118
31 December 20X9	76	92	133
Total finance costs	397	468	612
Less: interest payments	120	120	120
Gain	277	348	492
Carrying value			
31 December 20X4	761	697	564
31 December 20X5	802	747	629
31 December 20X6	846	802	703
31 December 20X7	894	862	788
31 December 20X8	944	928	887
31 December 20X9	1.000	1,000	1.000

6.348 Under the ASB's proposal, the carrying value of the loan of £1,000,000 immediately after renegotiation, calculated by discounting the revised payments by reference to the market rate for new borrowings that takes account of the decline in the company's credit standing, would be restated at £508,000 giving rise to a gain of £492,000 that would be recognised immediately. This gain would reverse as finance costs are recognised at a higher amount of £612,000 over the subsequent six years compared with the actual interest payments of £120,000 over the same period, as indicated above. However, as is evident from the table above, the gain of £492,000 under the ASB's proposals is made up of three components:

- A gain of £277,000 (that is, £1,000,000 — £723,000) which is equal to the present value of the actual reduction in financing costs from £80,000 to £20,000, that is, £60,000 per annum for six years discounted at eight per cent.
- A gain of £71,000 (that is, £723,000 — £652,000) attributable to the change in market rate of interest from eight per cent to ten per cent.
- A gain of £144,000 (that is, £652,000 — £508,000) attributable to the decline in the credit standing of the company.

6.349 Many argue that in most cases the combined effect of the above components will mean that the more distressed the company's financial condition is, the greater will be the gain on renegotiation as a consequence of using a higher discount rate as the ASB proposed. This is highly imprudent and rather anomalous. Also, the second element of the gain is not considered to be suitable under existing accounting framework. Furthermore, the ASB's own draft Statement of principles recognised this anomaly when considering how to deal with changes in the market value of liabilities that result from changes in market interest rates. A footnote to paragraph 26 of chapter 5 of the ASB's original draft Statement of principles issued in 1995 stated:

> "*Some would wish to take account only of changes in the general rates of interest rather than in the rate applicable to the entity, since otherwise an entity will report gains and losses relating to changes in its own perceived creditworthiness. It is particularly questionable whether it is appropriate to reflect a gain relating to a decrease in creditworthiness, because the compensating loss is usually a change in future earning power, or the value of assets, some of which are not reflected in the financial statements.*"

6.350 Accordingly, opponents of the ASB's proposals believe that if a gain is recognised, it should be calculated by reference to the future expected cash flows as modified by the renegotiation, but discounted at the effective rate of interest inherent in the original loan.

6.351 Because of the above concerns, the ASB decided not to address the accounting for renegotiation of debt in FRS 4. With the introduction of FRS 26, it will no longer need to consider this issue. In the absence of adequate current UK guidance for those entities not yet applying FRS 26, it is regarded as preferable not to recognise the gain, but the effects of the renegotiation should be treated as an interest subsidy. It may be necessary to disclose the nature and amount of the renegotiation to give a true and fair view of the company's financing arrangements. This means that the debt would remain in the balance sheet at £1,000,000 and the new finance cost of £20,000 would be charged each year giving an effective interest rate of two per cent from the date of renegotiation to date of maturity.

6.352 Some would argue that a gain should be recognised, but based only on discounting the revised payments at the original interest rate of eight per cent (that is, the gain of £277,000 in the above example). The effect would be to restate the carrying value of the loan at £723,000 at the time of the renegotiation. In subsequent periods, the effective rate of interest charged in the profit and loss account is eight per cent on the new carrying value of the loan (which is increased in each period by the difference between the interest charged at eight per cent and the actual interest paid of £20,000). Furthermore, they argue that as a reduction in a liability is considered to be a realised profit, the gain of £277,000 should be reported in the profit and loss account. However, although this method is acceptable, it is less prudent because it leads to recognising a future gain arising from the reduction of future interest charges when the company is in financial distress.

6.352.1 There may be situations in which a change in the terms of a capital instrument such as a loan is so significant that it is, in substance, clearly an early settlement of one loan and simultaneous recognition of a new loan. FRS 5, 'Reporting the substance of transactions', requires transactions to be recognised in accordance with their economic substance and not necessarily their legal form. In these situations, it may be appropriate to recognise a gain on the renegotiation of the loan, as if it was an early settlement.

Example

A company has a £10m loan on which it pays interest at a margin over LIBOR. The carrying amount of the debt is £10m. The company in severe financial difficulty and the fair value of the debt is £1m. The company renegotiates the loan with its lender such that principal of the loan is reduced to £1m, since this is the maximum the company is likely to be able to pay. The loan is no longer subject to a margin over LIBOR, however, contingent payments are required if the company disposes of assets at a profit during the remaining period of the loan.

The difference between the original and revised principal on the loan cannot solely be addressed through adjusting the interest rate on the loan prospectively, since this would result in the recognition of large negative interest charges. This would not reflect the substance of the arrangement. The changes in interest and principal on the loan are such that, in substance, the previous loan has been settled early and a new loan issued. The previous loan is derecognised and the new loan is recognised at its net proceeds, which, in this case is £1m. This results in the recognition of a £9m gain.

Debt for equity swaps

6.352.2 A company experiencing financial difficulty may renegotiate its debt and issue equity instruments in order to reduce all or part of its debt obligations. For example, a lender may agree to reduce or cancel a loan in exchange for shares or warrants in an entity.

6.352.3 FRS 4 does not specify how these transactions should be accounted for. Our view is that there is an accounting policy choice. One argument is that the accounting treatment should be the same as when convertible debt is converted into shares. Alternatively, the part of the debt that has been extinguished may be viewed as having been repurchased, with the equity instruments being the consideration for the repurchased. This choice should be applied consistently.

Option 1 – Treat like a conversion of convertible debt under paragraph AG32 of FRS 25

Under this approach, the new equity is recognised at the carrying value of the existing financial liability. No gain or loss is recognised.

Option 2 – Treat as repurchase of debt and issue of new equity instruments

This approach will result in a gain or loss for the difference between the carrying value of the debt and the initial value of the new equity. Assuming that the liability's release meets the definition of qualifying consideration the gain or loss will be recognised in the profit and loss account. [Tech 02/10 paras 3.11(c), 3.5].

There are different views on how the new equity instruments should be valued when option 2 is applied.

Entities applying FRS 26 will also apply UITF 47 (IFRIC 19), 'Extinguishing financial liabilities with equity instruments'. Although UITF 47 does not apply to companies applying FRS 4, its concepts are not inconsistent with FRS 4 and can be applied in this situation. UITF 47 requires equity instruments issued for the extinguishment of debt to be recognised at their fair value.

Alternatively, FRS 4 requires new debt instruments to be recognised at the net proceeds, that is, the fair value of the consideration received. [FRS 4 paras 11, 27]. There is no guidance in FRS 4 for the recognition of equity instruments but this may be applied by analogy. The consideration for the equity instruments is relief from the debt cancelled in exchange for the equity issued. The equity instruments issued could, therefore, be recognised at the fair value of the debt cancelled.

There may be no difference between these two valuation methodologies in practice. This is an accounting policy choice which should be applied consistently.

Example

An entity owes £500 to a lender, but is unable to pay this liability. The carrying amount of the debt, including accrued interest, is £500. The lender agrees to waive this liability in exchange for ordinary shares in the entity. The liability has a fair value of only £100 because of the entity's inability to repay the loan in full, so the lender is willing to accept shares with a fair value of £100 in exchange for cancelling the liability. The accounting under the two options is:

Option 1	Dr £	Cr £
Dr Liability	500	
Cr Equity		500
The equity is recognised at carrying value of the loan		
Option 2		
Dr Liability	500	
Cr Equity	100	
Cr Profit and loss account	400	

A gain is recognised on extinguishment of the loan.

6.352.4 When shares are issued, share premium is recognised for the difference between the nominal value of the shares and the fair value of the consideration received. (See chapter 23.) When a company extinguishes its own debt in exchange for issuing shares the consideration for the shares is considered to be the 'face value' of the debt extinguished. This is the claim that a lender would have on the resources of an entity in the event of a liquidation, which is also known as the liquidated sum. The face value of the debt will include the principal, plus any redemption premium and accrued interest and may approximate the carrying value of the debt. Where there is a difference between the amount initially recognised in equity and the share capital and share premium to be recognised a reserves transfer is required.

Example

Consider further the example in paragraph 6.352.3. The ordinary shares issued have a nominal value of £10. The face value of the debt extinguished is £500. The journal entries including recognition of share capital and premium are given below.

Option 1	Dr £	Cr £
Dr Liability	500	
Cr Share capital		10
Cr Share premium		490
Option 2		
Dr Liability	500	
Dr Profit and loss reserve	400	
Cr Profit and loss account		400
Cr Share capital		10
Cr Share premium		490

A reserve transfer is required to recognise the appropriate share capital and premium

Disclosure

6.353 Both the Act and the original standard specify a considerable amount of detail that a company's financial statements must give in respect of its borrowings. In addition, companies listed on the Stock Exchange are required to give further information.

6.354 However, one of the most significant changes to FRS 4 as a result of the publication of FRS 25 is the deletion of all the disclosure requirements. As previously stated, entities that are applying FRS 4 will apply the presentation requirements of FRS 25.

6.355 An entity that is applying FRS 4 is required to comply with the Companies Act disclosure requirements discussed below. Such entities are also encouraged to comply with certain disclosure requirements of FRS 29. These disclosure requirements are discussed in paragraph 6.371.

Companies Act requirements

6.356 Under the Act, capital instruments in the form of debentures, loans and debt instruments fall to be included under the general heading of 'Creditors'. All items included under creditors must be analysed between amounts that will fall due within one year of the balance sheet date and amounts that will fall due after more than one year. [Note 13 on the balance sheet formats].

6.357 In distinguishing between the above two categories, a loan is regarded as falling due for repayment (or an instalment is regarded as falling due for payment) on the earliest date on which the lender could require repayment (or payment) if he were to exercise all options and rights available to him. [SI 2008/410 10 Sch 9].

6.358 For each item shown under creditors (whichever balance sheet format is adopted) there must be disclosed separately the aggregate amounts of debts falling into the two categories below:

- Debts that are payable or repayable otherwise than by instalments and falling due for payment or repayment after the end of the five year period beginning with the day after the end of the financial year.
- Debts that are payable or repayable by instalments, any of which will fall due for payment after the end of that five year period.

[SI 2008/410 1 Sch 61(1)].

6.359 The requirement is to disclose one figure showing the aggregate of the above two items, but the aggregation of instalment and non-instalment debts results in a figure that is rather meaningless. The Act's intention seems to have been to require disclosure of the amount of debts and instalments which are payable in over five years, to bring the disclosure in line with that required by Article 43(1)(6) of the 4th Directive. In practice, it seems sensible to give the intended disclosure as this is more meaningful.

6.360 The terms of payment or repayment and the applicable rate of interest for each debt covered by the disclosure under the preceding paragraph must also be given. [SI 2008/410 1 Sch 61(2)]. Where the number of debt instruments is such that, in the directors' opinion, this requirement would result in a statement of excessive length, this information need be given only in general terms. [SI 2008/410 1 Sch 61(3)].

6.361 Where any item that is shown under the heading 'Creditors' includes debts for which the company has given security, these debts must be disclosed in aggregate. Also, the notes must give an indication of the nature of the securities given. [SI 2008/410 1 Sch 61(4)]. For this requirement to be meaningful, the financial statements should show some disaggregation of the relevant liabilities. This is because it could be misleading merely to disclose the aggregate of a basket of securities compared with the aggregate of a basket of liabilities. However, in practice, companies often describe the charge in general terms, referring, for example, to 'mortgages on freehold land and buildings' rather than specifying the particular properties involved.

6.362 If a company has issued any debentures during the financial year, the notes to the financial statements must disclose:

- The classes of debentures issued.
- The amount issued and the consideration the company received in respect of each class of debentures issued.

[SI 2008/410 1 Sch 50(1)].

Requirements for entities applying FRS 25, FRS 26 and FRS 29

Introduction

6.363 FRS 25, FRS 26 and FRS 29 are the UK equivalents of the international standards IAS 32, IAS 39 and IFRS 7. With a small number of exceptions as noted below, the text of the UK standards is an exact replica of that of the international standards. Hence, the Manual of Accounting – Financial instruments is relevant to entities applying these standards.

Differences between the UK standards and their international equivalents

FRS 25

6.364 As explained in paragraph 6.21, FRS 25 applies to all entities preparing their financial statements in accordance with UK GAAP, whether or not the entity prepares its financial statements under old UK GAAP or new UK GAAP for financial instruments. FRS 25 scopes out entities that apply the FRSSE.

6.365 Certain paragraphs of IAS 1, 'Presentation of financial statements', have been included in FRS 25 (paras 50A-50E) to provide guidance in respect of the classification of current and non-current liabilities, particularly in relation to breaches of long-term loan covenants and refinancing arrangements. Refer to chapter 4 of the Manual of Accounting – Financial instruments.

6.366 In August 2008, the ASB amended FRS 25 to incorporate amendments made to IAS 32 by the IASB in relation to the classification as equity of certain puttable financial instruments and instruments that impose an obligation on the entity to deliver a *pro rata* share of the net assets of the entity on liquidation to another entity. The ASB also amended FRS 25 for certain consequential amendments made to the disclosure requirements of IAS 1 as a result of changes to IAS 32. For UK GAAP preparers these amendments are applicable for accounting periods beginning on or after 1 January 2010. Earlier adoption is applicable for accounting periods beginning on or after 1 January 2009 (see Manual of Accounting – Financial instruments).

FRS 26

6.367 The requirements and scope of FRS 26 are identical to IAS 39 except for the following:

- Entities applying the FRSSE are exempt from the FRS.
- Only those entities that are listed entities (securities listed on a regulated market) or whose financial statements are prepared in accordance with the fair value accounting rules set out in the Companies Act are required to adopt the standard.
- Changes in fair value that are recognised directly in equity under IAS 39 are required by FRS 26 to be recognised in the STRGL.
- The scope of IAS 39 includes a reference to the definition of an insurance contract as set out in IFRS 4. This definition and supporting material from IFRS 4 are included in an appendix that forms an integral part of FRS 26.

EU carve-out of IAS 39

6.368 In addition to the differences highlighted above, certain words and paragraphs, relating solely to the use of the fair value option for financial liabilities and certain aspects of hedge accounting that troubled the banks or the regulators, did not find favour with the EU and were removed from IAS 39. This 'carve out' version was endorsed by the EU in November 2004. A year later the curve out relating to the fair value option was removed, but the one relating to hedge accounting remains with the result that there is still a difference between full IAS39/FRS 26 and the EU endorsed IAS 39 that is applied in the UK by entities and groups that report under IFRS.

6.369 Hence, for the time being, UK entities applying IFRS are using a modified version of IAS 39. In publishing FRS 26, the ASB used the full, unamended version of IAS 39. The EU carve out, therefore, has no impact on those entities that continue to report under UK GAAP.

FRS 29

6.370 FRS 29, which replicates the requirements of IFRS 7, came into effect for accounting periods beginning on or after 1 January 2007. However, the following differences in scope and requirements exist between FRS 29 and IFRS 7:

- Entities applying the FRSEE are exempt from FRS 29. [FRS 29 para 2A].
- Entities that are not applying FRS 26 are exempt from FRS 29. [FRS 29 para 2B].
- Subsidiary undertakings, other than banks and insurance companies, where 90 per cent or more of the voting rights are controlled within the group, provided the entity is included in publicly available consolidated financial

statements that include disclosures that comply with FRS 29. [FRS 29 para 2D].

- Parent companies in their single entity financial statements, provided the entity is included in publicly available consolidated financial statements that include disclosures that comply with FRS 29. [FRS 29 para 2D].

6.371 Although not mandatory, entities that are not applying FRS 26 are encouraged to comply with the disclosure requirements of FRS 29, adapting them in line with the entity's accounting policies for the relevant transactions, and describing those accounting policies as required by paragraphs 21, 21A and 21B. In particular:

- Interest rate disclosures should be based on the rates at which interest is accounted for under the entity's accounting policies if this is different from the effective interest rate defined in FRS 26.

- Disclosures on hedge accounting set out in paragraphs 22 to 24 should be applied to the entity's own hedge accounting policies.

- Instruments should be treated as insurance contracts for the purposes of disclosure if they are accounted for as such under the entity's accounting policies, even if they meet the definition of a financial instrument in FRS 26.

[FRS 29 para 2E].

Annex — Example FRS 13 disclosures

Set out in this Annex are examples of the narrative and numerical disclosures required by part A of FRS 13 for the following four instruments:

- Example 1 – Fixed rate borrowing.
- Example 2 – SSAP 20 hedge.
- Example 3 – Fixed rate borrowings with interest rate swap.
- Example 4 – Purchases covered by foreign currency contract.

The example disclosures relate only to those required for each individual instrument in isolation. The narrative disclosures have been written based on assumed group objectives, policies and strategies and would have to be tailored for each entities individual situation.

Example 1

Description

It is very common for companies to take out fixed rate loans, that is, those having specified interest rates and maturity dates.

Borrowing information

GAAP UK plc has a ten year fixed rate sterling borrowing with the following terms:

- Original principal of £110 million.
- Annual repayments of £11 million on each anniversary of the borrowing.
- Final maturity on 31 December 2010.
- Fixed rate of 7.65 per cent.
- At 31 December 2005 there are five years remaining to maturity.
- The market rate at the year end for the same maturity period was 7.4 per cent (2000 – 7.8 per cent).

The disclosures required by FRS 13, solely in relation to this liability, should look similar to the following.

Accounting policies

Fixed rate bank borrowings are initially stated at the amount of the consideration received after deduction of issue costs. Issue costs together with finance costs are charged to the profit and loss account over the term of the borrowings and represent a constant proportion of the balance of capital repayments outstanding.

Objectives, policies and strategies

The financial risks faced by the group include interest rate risk and liquidity risk. The board reviews and agrees policies for managing each of these risks.

The group's financial instruments comprise fixed rate borrowings, the main purpose of which is to raise finance for the group's operations.

The group seeks to ensure stability in its cash flows and thus interest rate risk is managed through borrowing at fixed rates. The group's policy is to maintain 100 per cent (2000 – 100 per cent) of its borrowings at fixed rates, which is consistent with the year end position.

The group seeks to minimise the risk of uncertain funding in its operations by borrowing with a spread of maturity periods and by having committed facilities available. The group's policy is for current borrowings to be repayable in broadly equal instalments over no less than three years and for projected net borrowing needs to be covered by committed facilities. At the year end the group's borrowings were repayable in instalments over the next five years (2004 – six years) and the group had sufficient undrawn committed facilities available to cover its projected net borrowing needs as at each year end.

Note: It would be good practice to state whether these objectives, policies and strategies are consistent with those in the previous year. Also it would be helpful to indicate whether the balance sheet positions at 31 December 2005 are representative of the positions throughout the year.

Interest rate risk profile of financial liabilities

The interest rate profile of the group's financial liabilities at 31 December was:

Currency	Total £m	Floating rate financial liabilities £m	Fixed rate financial liabilities £m	Financial liabilities on which no interest is paid £m
2005				
Sterling	55	–	55	–
2004				
Sterling	66	–	66	–

Currency	Fixed rate financial liabilities Weighted average fixed interest rate %	Weighted average period for which rate is fixed* Years	Financial liabilities upon which no interest is paid Weighted average period until maturity Years
2005			
Sterling	7.65	3.0	–
2004			
Sterling	7.65	3.5	–

Note — Given the loan is a reducing balance loan the period for which the rate is fixed is calculated on a weighted average basis. Note that where there is one amortising loan the weighted average period for which the rate is fixed is calculated by treating each repayment as if it were a separate loan. (For example, the 2005 weighted average period above has been calculated treating each of the 5 repayment periods as different loans. The weighted average period is 1 + 2 + 3 + 4 + 5 = 15 years divided by 5 loans = 3.)

Currency exposures

Not applicable

Maturity of financial liabilities

The maturity profile of the group's financial liabilities at 31 December was as follows:

	2004 £m	2004 £m
In one year or less, or on demand	11	11
In more than one year but not more than two years	11	11
In more than two years but not more than five years	33	33
In more than five years	–	11
Total	55	66

Borrowing facilities

The group has an undrawn committed facility of £100 million which is negotiated on an annual basis with its bank.

Fair values of financial assets and financial liabilities

A comparison by category of fair values and book values of the group's financial liabilities at 31 December was as follows:

	Book value 2005 £m	Fair value 2005 £m	Book value 2004 £m	Fair value 2004 £m
Primary financial instruments held or issued to finance the group's operations:				
Short-term borrowings and current portion of long-term borrowings	11.0	11.0	11.0	11.0
Long-term borrowing	44.0	44.4	55.0	54;.7

The fair value of the fixed rate borrowing has been calculated by discounting cash flows at prevailing market interest rates.

Gains and losses on hedges

Not applicable.

Example 2

Description

It is common for companies to hedge their exposure to foreign currency exchange fluctuations arising from their overseas investments by borrowing in the same currencies. The resulting translation gains and losses may be taken to reserves (STRGL) in accordance with SSAP 20. In the example below the group has adopted this policy.

Borrowing information

GAAP UK plc has two ten year foreign currency borrowings as follows:

- US$ loan — original principal.
- US$ 180 million.
- Fixed rate of 5.65 per cent.
- Bullet repayment of US$ 180 million on 31 December 2011.
- At 31 December 2005 there are six years remaining to maturity.

- € loan — original principal.
- € 1,000 million.
- Floating rate.
- Bullet repayment of € 1,000 million on 31 July 2009.
- At 31 December 2005 there are three year and seven months remaining to maturity.

The year end exchange rates were as follows:

2005		2004	
£/US$	– 1.641	£/US$	– 1.500
£/€	– 10.452	£/€	– 10.00

The US$ market interest rate at year end for the 2011 maturity was 5.5 per cent (2004 – 5.8 per cent)

The disclosures required by FRS 13, solely in relation to these instruments, should look similar to the following.

Accounting policies

Assets and liabilities of subsidiaries in foreign currencies are translated into sterling at rates of exchange ruling at the end of the financial year and the results of foreign subsidiaries are translated at the average rate of exchange for the year. Differences on exchange arising from the retranslation of the opening net investment in subsidiary companies, and from the translation of the results of those companies at average rate, are taken to reserves and are reported in the statement of total recognised gains and losses. All other foreign exchange differences are taken to the profit and loss account in the year in which they arise.

Objectives, policies and strategies

The financial risks faced by the group comprise interest rate risk, liquidity risk and currency risk. The board reviews and agrees policies for managing each of these risks.

The group's financial instruments comprise fixed and floating rate borrowings, the main purposes of which are to raise finance for the group's operations.

The group seeks to minimise its exposure to an upward change in interest rates while enabling the group to benefit from a fall in interest rates by borrowing at a mix of fixed and floating rates. The group's current policy is to maintain 50 per cent to 65 per cent (2004 – 50 per cent to 65 per cent) of its borrowings at fixed rates with the remaining at floating rates. At the year end 53 per cent (2004 – 55 per cent) of the group's borrowings were at fixed rates.

The group seeks to minimise the risk of uncertain funding in its operations by borrowing within a spread of maturity periods and by having committed facilities available. The group's policy is for current borrowings to be repayable beyond at least three years and for undrawn committed facilities to be available to supplement the currency borrowings which provide a hedge against the group's net investments in its overseas subsidiaries. At the year end 53 per cent (2000 – 55 per cent) of the group's borrowings were repayable in six years (2004 – seven years) with the remaining 47 per cent (2004 – 45 per cent) repayable in four years (2004 – five years). The group had sufficient undrawn committed facilities available as at each year end.

The group seeks to minimise the currency risk arising from translation of the its net investments in its overseas subsidiaries in the United States and France by taking out borrowings in the denominated currencies. The group's policy is to operate with 80 per cent to 100 per cent (2000 – 80 per cent to 100 per cent) of its net investments to be covered by these foreign currency borrowings. At the year end 100 per cent (2000 – 100 per cent) of the total currency exposure was covered by currency borrowings.

Note: It would be good practice to state whether these objectives, policies and strategies are consistent with those in the previous year. Also it would be helpful to indicate whether the balance sheet position at 31 December 2005 are representative of the positions throughout the year.

Interest rate risk profile of financial liabilities

The interest rate profile of the group's financial liabilities at 31 December was:

Currency	Total £m	Floating rate financial liabilities £m	Fixed rate financial liabilities £m	Financial liabilities on which no interest is paid £m
2001				
US$	110	–	110	–
FFr	98	98	–	–
Total	208	98	110	–
2000				
US$	120	–	120	–
FFr	100	100	–	–
Total	220	100	120	–

Currency	Fixed rate financial liabilities: Weighted average fixed interest rate %	Fixed rate financial liabilities: Weighted average period for which rate is fixed Years	Financial liabilities upon which no interest is paid: Weighted average period until maturity Years
2001			
US$	5.65	6.0	–
2000			
US$	5.65	7.0	–

The floating rate financial liabilities comprise € denominated bank borrowings that bear interest rates based on 3 month Euribor (European Inter-Bank Offer Rate).

Currency exposures

Not applicable. The group uses its foreign borrowings to provide a hedge against its foreign net investments and the exchange gains or losses on its borrowings are included in the STRGL as permitted by SSAP 20. In accordance with paragraph 34c of FRS 13, these borrowings are not included in the currency analysis as the exchange gains and losses on the borrowings do not flow through the profit and loss account.

Maturity of financial liabilities

The maturity profile of the group's financial liabilities at 31 December was as follows:

	2005 £m	2004 £m
In one year or less, or on demand	–	–
In more than one year but not more than two years	–	–
In more than two years but not more than five years	98	100
In more than five years	110	120
Total	208	220

Borrowing facilities

The group has undrawn committed facilities of US$180 million and €30 million which are negotiated on an annual basis with its bank.

Fair values of financial assets and financial liabilities

A comparison by category of fair values and book values of the group's financial liabilities at 31 December was as follows:

	Book value 2005 £m	Fair value 2005 £m	Book value 2004 £m	Fair value 2004 £m
Primary financial instruments held or issued to finance the group's operations:				
Long-term borrowings	208.0	208.2	220.0	219.0

The fair value of the fixed rate borrowing has been calculated by discounting the cash flows at prevailing market interest rates.

Gains and losses on hedges

Not applicable

Example 3

Description

It is very common for companies to take out fixed rate loans, that is, having specified interest rates and maturity dates. Interest rate swaps enable a company to convert its fixed interest rate borrowings to floating rate and *vice versa* and commit a company to exchange interest cash flows on specified settlement dates. The notional principal of the swap is used to calculate the expected interest amounts.

Borrowing and interest rate swap information

GAAP UK plc has a ten year fixed rate sterling borrowing with the following terms:

- Original principal of £110 million.
- Fixed rate of 7.65 per cent.
- Two bullet payments of £55 million each on 31 December 2003 (that is, part paid) and 31 December 2008.
- At 31 December 2005 the loan had three years remaining to maturity.

  The group also has the following interest rate swap:

  - Receive fixed of 7.65 per cent.
  - Pay LIBOR.

- Notional principal of £55 million to 31 December 2008.

- The market rate for the interest rate swap at the year end was 7.4 per cent (2004 – 7.9 per cent).

The disclosures required by FRS 13, solely in relation to these instruments, should look similar to the following.

Accounting policies

Fixed rate bank borrowings are initially stated at the amount of the consideration received after deduction of issue costs. Issue costs together with finance costs are charged to the profit and loss account over the term of the borrowings and represent a constant proportion of the balance of capital repayments outstanding.

The interest differential amounts due to/from on interest rate swaps are accrued until settlement date and are recognised as an adjustment to interest expense.

Objectives, policies and strategies

The financial risks faced by the group include interest rate risk and liquidity risk. The board reviews and agrees policies for managing each of these risks.

The group's financial instruments comprise fixed rate borrowings, the main purpose of which is to raise finance for the group's operations. The group also enters into interest rate swaps, the purpose of which is to manage the interest rate risk arising from the group's borrowings.

The group seeks to minimise its exposure to an upward change in interest rates while enabling the group to benefit from a fall in interest rates by borrowing at fixed rates and, where overall borrowing costs can be reduced, by using interest rate swaps to convert such borrowings from fixed to floating rates. The group's policy is, while interest rates are declining, to maintain between 80 per cent and 100 per cent (2004 – 80 per cent and 100 per cent) of its borrowings at floating rates. At the year end all (2004 — all) of the group's fixed rate borrowings were at floating rates after taking account of interest rate swaps. The group hedges its exposure to interest rate fluctuations over five year periods.

The group seeks to minimise the risk of uncertain funding in its operations by borrowing within a spread of maturity periods and by having committed facilities available. The group's policy is for at least 80 per cent (2004 – 80 per cent) of borrowings to be repayable after two years and for projected net borrowing needs to be covered by committed facilities. At the year end the group's borrowings were repayable beyond three years (200 – four years) and the group had sufficient undrawn committed facilities available to cover its projected net borrowing needs as at each year end.

Note: It would be good practice to state whether these objectives, policies and strategies are consistent with those in the previous year. Also, it would be helpful to indicate whether the balance sheet position at 31 December 2005 are representative of the positions throughout the year.

Interest rate risk profile of financial liabilities

Paragraph 26 (a) of FRS 13 requires that this interest rate risk analysis be shown after taking into account the effect of interest rate swaps. The group's underlying borrowings are all on fixed rate terms, but these are all covered by interest rate swaps. Thus the borrowings are included in the table as floating rate borrowings.

After taking into account the interest rate swaps entered into by the group, the interest rate profile of the group's financial liabilities at 31 December was:

Currency	Total £m	Floating rate financial liabilities £m	Fixed rate financial liabilities £m	Financial liabilities on which no interest is paid £m
2005				
Sterling	55	–	55	–
2004				
Sterling	66	–	66	–

Currency	Fixed rate financial liabilities: Weighted average fixed interest rate %	Fixed rate financial liabilities: Weighted average period for which rate is fixed Years	Financial liabilities on which no interest is paid: Weighted average period until maturity Years
2005			
Sterling	–	–	–
2004			
Sterling	–	–	–

After taking into account the interest rate swaps, the floating rate financial liabilities comprise sterling denominated bank borrowings that bear interest at rates based on the six-month LIBOR.

Currency exposures

Not applicable.

The maturity profile of the group's financial liabilities at 31 December was as follows:

	2005	2004
	£m	£m
In one year or less, or on demand	–	–
In more than one year but not more than two years	–	–
In more than two years but not more than five years	55	55
In more than five years	–	–
Total	55	55

Borrowing facilities

The group has an undrawn committed facility of £100 million, which is negotiated on an annual basis with its bank.

Fair values of financial assets and financial liabilities

Note: The fair value of the fixed rate borrowing and that of the related interest rate swap must be shown separately in the fair value table.

A comparison by category of fair values and book values of the group's financial liabilities at 31 December was as follows:

	Book value	Fair value	Book value	Fair value
	2005	2005	2004	2004
	£m	£m	£m	£m
Primary financial instruments held or issued to finance the group's operations:				
Long-term borrowing	55.0	55.4	55.0	54.5
Derivative financial instruments held to manage the interest rate profile:				
Interest rate swap	–	(0.4)	–	0.5

The fair values of the fixed rate borrowing and the interest rate swap have been calculated by discounting the fixed cash flows at the prevailing interest rates at the year end.

Gains/losses on hedges

The fair value adjustments in relation to interest rate swaps represent unrecognised gains and losses that should be reported in the hedge effects table, as well as in the fair value table.

Note that a comparative table may be required but is not included in this example.

An analysis of the unrecognised gains and losses on the interest rate swap is as follows:

	Gains	(Losses)	Total net gains/(losses)
	£m	£m	£m
Unrecognised gains and losses on hedges at 1 January 2005		**(0.5)**	**(0.5)**
Gains and losses arising in previous years that were recognised in 2005		0.1*	0.1
Changes in value arising in 2005 and unrecognised during 2005		0.8	0.8
Gains and losses arising before 1 January 2005 and during 2005 that were not recognised in 2005	**–**	**0.4**	**0.4**
Transfer of gain position at the end of the year. †	0.4	(0.4)	–
Unrecognised gains and losses on hedges at 31 December 2005	**0.4**	**–**	**0.4**
Of which			
Gains and losses expected to be recognised in 2006	0.1*	–	0.1
Gains and losses expected to be recognised in 2007 or later	0.3	–	0.3

Notes:

* *These movements represent the interest rate swap differential payments that are made on a six monthly basis each year. For the purpose of this example these amounts have been estimated.*

† *As a result of the movement of £0.8 million, the balance is now a gain and hence it has been moved to the gain column.*

As the interest rate swaps are unrecognised on the balance sheet there are no deferred gains and losses shown on this table.

Example 4

Description

It is common for companies to use forward currency contracts to hedge against foreign currency exposure arising from product sales and stock purchases denominated in foreign currencies.

In this example the company uses a forward currency contract to hedge against committed purchases denominated in US dollars. The forward currency purchased under the forward contract is used to limit the group's exposure to US dollar fluctuations by fixing the purchase exchange rate at the forward currency contract rate.

Purchase commitment and forward currency contract information:

On 1 December 2004 GAAP UK plc entered into a purchase commitment with the following details:

- Purchase of 100,000 units of widgets – Price – $900,000.
- Delivery and payment date – 31 May 2005.
- On 1 December 2004 the group took out a forward currency contract to cover the purchase commitment. The terms of the contract are as follows:
  - Purchase of $900,000.
  - Forward rate – £1 = $1.50.
  - Settlement date – 31 May 2005.
- Other details:
  - Year end date – 31 December 2004, £1 = $1.47.
  - Settlement date – 31 May 2005, £1 = $1.43.
  - At 31 December 2005 GAAP UK plc had 60,000 units remaining in stock. The other 40,000 units were used in products sold in the year.

The disclosures required by FRS 13, solely in relation to these instruments, should look similar to the following.

Accounting policies

Transactions in foreign currencies are translated at the exchange rate ruling at the date of the transaction or, where forward foreign currency contracts have been taken out, at contractual rates. Monetary assets and liabilities are retranslated at the rates of exchange ruling at the balance sheet date or at a forward contractual rate if applicable. Exchange gains and losses are taken to the profit and loss account.

Forward currency contracts, entered into as hedges of committed purchases denominated in foreign currencies, are not recognised until they mature. At maturity gains and losses are included in the carrying value of the related stocks and work in progress.

Objectives, policies and strategies

The financial risks faced by the group include foreign currency risk. The board reviews and agrees policies for managing this risk.

The group's financial instruments, other than derivatives, comprise short-term monetary assets and liabilities that arise directly from the group's operations. The group also enters into forward currency contracts to manage the currency risk arising from foreign currency denominated purchase commitments, entered into by the group.

The group seeks to minimise its exposure to fluctuations in exchange rates by taking out forward currency contracts to hedge against foreign currency denominated purchase commitments. The group's policy is to enter into forward currency contracts for all such commitments immediately those purchase commitments are made. At the year end 100 per cent (2004 – 100 per cent) of purchase commitments were hedged by foreign currency contracts.

Note: It would be good practice to state whether these objectives, policies and strategies are consistent with those in the previous year. Also, it would be helpful to indicate whether the balance sheet positions at 31 December 2005 are representative of the positions throughout the year.

Interest rate risk profile of financial liabilities

Not applicable.

Currency exposures

Note: The amounts disclosed in this table should be after taking account of forward contracts. [FRS 13, para 34(d)]. In this case the forward contract converts the US dollar amount payable to a sterling liability. Monetary liabilities denominated in the same currency as the functional currency of the operations, in this case sterling, are not be included in this analysis. Although the analysis is not applicable in this case a note such as the following may be appropriate:

As explained in the objectives, policies and strategies note the group's policy is, where practicable, to hedge its currency exposure to monetary liabilities fully.

Maturity of financial liabilities

Not applicable.

Borrowing facilities

Not applicable.

Fair values of financial assets and financial liabilities

The fair value of the forward contract must be shown separately in the fair value table throughout the period from its inception until its maturity.

Note: The accounting policy for the group is to recognise the gain and loss on its forward contracts at maturity in the carrying value of the related stocks and work in progress. Consequently, no book value for forward contracts is included in the table below. In this example the forward contract is open over the 31 December 2004 year end so its fair value at that date is included in the table. By 31 December 2005 the contract has matured so no fair value is shown.

If, for instance, the stock had been delivered prior to the year end and payment to the supplier was outstanding, then the fair value of the creditor would need to be taken into account separately from the forward contract. The creditor would be recorded at the contract rate applicable to the forward contract, giving rise to a book/fair value difference.

A comparison by category of fair values and book values of the group's financial liabilities at 31 December was as follows:

	Book value 2005 £'000	Fair value 2005 £'000	Book value 2004 £'000	Fair value 2004 £'000
Primary financial instruments held or issued to finance the group's operations:				
Short term financial liabilities	–	–	–	–
Derivative financial instruments held to manage the interest rate profile:				
Forward foreign currency contract	–	–	–	12.2

The fair value of the forward currency contract has been determined by reference to prices available from the markets on which the instrument involved is traded.

Gains/losses on hedges

Note: The fair value of the forward foreign currency contract is an unrecognised gain at 31 December 2004 that should be reported in the hedge effects table, as well as in the fair value table. As per its accounting policy, GAAP UK plc does not recognise gains and losses on its forward contracts until the contracts mature. The fair value recognised in the table above is equal to the unrecognised gain at 31 December 2004.

When the contract is settled, in May 2005, the resulting gain is recognised in the balance sheet but the gain is not recognised in the profit and loss account until the stock purchased, covered by the forward contract, is sold. In between the gain being recognised and stock being sold the gain is deferred in the balance sheet carrying value of the stock. FRS 13 paragraph 59 requires detailed disclosure of deferred gains and losses of, inter alia, this nature other than gains and losses deferred in the carrying value of fixed assets. [FRS 13 para 60].

The calculations of the amounts included are explained in the notes immediately following the table. A comparative table is required but is not included in this example.

An analysis of the unrecognised/deferred gains and losses on the forward currency contract is as follows:

		Unrecognised:				**Deferred:**		
		Gains £'000	**Losses £'000**	**Total net gains/ (losses) £'000**		**Gains £'000**	**Losses £'000**	**Total net gains/ (losses) £'000**
Gains and losses on hedges at 1 January 2005	**(i)**	**12.2**	–	**12.2**		–	–	–
Change in value from 1 January 2004 to settlement	(ii)	17.2	–	17.2		–	–	–
Gains and losses arising before 1 January 2005 and during the period from 1 January 2005 to settlement that were recognised in 2005 and deferred	(ii)	(29.4)	–	(29.4)		29.4	–	29.4
Deferred gains and losses that were recognised in current year income.					(iii)	(11.7)	–	(11.7)
Gains and losses on hedges at 31 December 2005		–	–	–	**(iv)**	17.6	–	**17.6**
Of which: Gains and losses expected to be included in 2006 income		–	–	–		17.6	–	17.6
Gains and losses expected to be included in 2007 income or later		–	–	–		–	–	–

Notes:

(i) *At 31 December 2004 the contract was outstanding and no gain or loss in respect of the contract was recognised in the balance sheet. The unrecognised gain brought forward also represents the fair value of the contract at 31 December 2004*

For this exercise it has been assumed that the fair value of the forward contract is £12,245. The most accurate method to derive the fair value of a forward contract outstanding at the balance sheet date is to obtain a forward rate at the balance sheet date for the remaining maturity of the contract. The gain or loss is then calculated by taking the difference between the foreign currency amount of the forward contract translated at the balance sheet forward rate and the contracted forward rate (or the forward rate last used to measure an earlier gain or loss on the contract). As this gain/loss strictly arises on the maturity of the contract, it should be discounted by reference to the remaining maturity of the contract. In practice, however, the effect of discounting is immaterial given the short duration periods for forwards and is normally ignored. Where a company is unable to get a forward rate at the balance sheet date, then, as proxy, the fair value can be calculated by adding the 'deemed' unamortised premium (where it has been fully written off) to the gain/loss calculated as the difference between translating the currency amount at the spot rate on inception of the contract and translating it at the year end rate.

(ii) *During 2005 the contract was settled. On settlement of the contract the gain on the contract is recognised and is calculated as the difference between translating the currency amount at the contract rate and translating it at the spot rate on the settlement date.*

($900,000/1.43) – ($900,000/1.50) = £29,371.

The gain of £29,371 is deferred until the stock is sold when the resulting gain would be included in income for the year.

The change in value between 1 January 2005 and settlement in May is £17,200 (£29,371 – £12,245).

(iii) *At 31 December 2005, 40 per cent (£11,748) of the full gain (of £29,371) arising on settlement of the contract in May was initially deferred in stock and was subsequently realised in current year income when the stock was sold.*

(iv) *The remaining 60 per cent (£17,623) of the full gain of £29,371 arising on settlement of the contract in May remained deferred in stock, which was unsold at the year end. This stock is expected to be sold next year.*

Chapter 7

Foreign currencies

Chapter 7

Foreign currencies

Introduction

7.1 Businesses conducted by UK companies are not simply confined within national boundaries. The globalisation of markets for goods and services as well as capital makes it imperative for companies to engage in international trade, cross-border alliances and joint ventures if they are to survive and grow in today's competitive business environment. The ways in which companies enter the international market place are varied. First, companies directly undertake transactions of buying goods and services from overseas suppliers and selling goods and services to overseas customers. Secondly, they may extend their international business by conducting their affairs through overseas subsidiaries, branches and associates.

7.2 In the first situation, transactions undertaken by the UK company will often be expressed in foreign currencies and the results of these transactions will need to be translated into sterling for financial reporting purposes. In the second situation, it is usual for the foreign enterprise to maintain its accounting records in its local currency. In order to prepare consolidated financial statements, the complete financial statements of the foreign enterprise will need to be translated into sterling.

7.3 Accounting for foreign currencies is primarily concerned with the translation process whereby financial data denominated in one currency is expressed in terms of another currency. It is important to note that the translation process in no way changes the essential characteristics of the assets and liabilities measured. It merely restates assets and liabilities, initially valued in a foreign currency unit, to a common currency unit by applying a rate of exchange factor, a translation rate. It does not restate historical cost.

7.4 There are different translation rates that may be used depending on circumstances. These are:

- The historical rate — the rate of exchange ruling at the date the transaction occurred.
- The closing rate — the rate ruling at the balance sheet date.
- The average rate ruling during the year.

7.5 The average rate is generally confined to income and expenditure items. The rates used for balance sheet items will depend on the types of assets and liabilities being translated in individual company financial statements and upon the method of translation used for branches or consolidation of subsidiaries, namely the closing rate/net investment method or the temporal method. These methods are discussed in detail later in this chapter.

7.6 In addition to the difficulties in choosing an appropriate translation method, the treatment of exchange differences that arise on translation raises a number of questions, such as: the extent to which exchange gains and losses from different sources can be offset; whether some exchange differences should be recognised immediately whilst others should be deferred; and whether the recognition should be through the profit and loss account or through reserves. These and other vexing issues, such as the extent to which inflation in overseas countries should be taken into account in the translation process, are considered in this chapter.

7.7 Since its publication in 1983, SSAP 20, 'Foreign currency translation', has been successful in narrowing the range of permissible alternatives by stipulating that the closing rate/net investment method or, in some situations, the temporal method should be used for translating the financial statements of foreign enterprises. In spite of this, the standard is flexible and offers a range of choices both in the selection of exchange rates and in the treatment of the exchange differences in individual and consolidated financial statements.

7.8 SSAP 20 does not cover all the problem areas in accounting for foreign currencies. For example, it fails to provide adequate guidance on accounting for forward contracts and the treatment of hyper-inflation, both of which are adequately covered in IAS 21 and IAS 29. The latter shortcoming has, to some extent, been rectified by the publication of UITF Abstract 9, 'Accounting for operations in hyper-inflationary economies'.

7.9 The international equivalent to SSAP 20 is IAS 21, 'The effects of changes in foreign exchange rates' and the international equivalent to UITF Abstract 9 is IAS 29, 'Financial reporting in hyperinflationary economies'. As part of its convergence with IFRS, in 2004 the ASB issued FRS 23, 'The effects of changes in foreign exchange rates' and FRS 24, 'Financial reporting in hyperinflationary economies'. FRS 23 and FRS 24 are identical to IAS 21 and IAS 29 respectively. FRS 23 and FRS 24 must be applied by UK companies from the same date that FRS 26, 'Financial instruments: Measurement', is applied. SSAP 20 and UITF 9 are superseded by FRS 23 and FRS 24. For those entities not applying FRS 26, SSAP 20 and UITF 9 remain applicable, un-amended.

7.10 This chapter deals with the provisions of SSAP 20 and UITF Abstract 9. It covers many of the problem areas that are not adequately dealt with in SSAP 20, in particular, accounting for hedged transactions with forward contracts and currency options. This is an important area as many companies now manage their exposure to foreign exchange risks by adopting hedging strategies. However, this chapter does not deal with other currency instruments and derivative products which are discussed in chapter 6.

7.11 Accounting under FRS 23 is considered in the Annex to this chapter and companies that have adopted FRS 26 should refer to this.

SSAP 20

Scope

7.12 SSAP 20 sets out the standard accounting practice for foreign currency translation and applies to any entity that comes within the scope of statements of standard accounting practice and engages in foreign currency operations. The standard does not deal with the method of calculating profits or losses arising from a company's normal currency dealing operations. Consequently, all currency forward contracts, currency buying and selling activities, and cash balances that are associated with those activities are excluded from the standard's scope. However, when accounting for its currency dealing operations, a company should comply with the spirit of SSAP 20. The standard does not deal with how to determine distributable profits, although applying its provisions could give rise to problems with respect to distributability. This is considered further from paragraph 7.149.

Objectives

7.12.1 The translation objectives of SSAP 20 are as follows:

- To produce results that are generally compatible with the effects of rate changes on a company's cash flows and its equity.
- To reflect in consolidated financial statements the financial results and relationships as measured in the foreign currency financial statements prior to translation.
- To ensure that the financial statements present a true and fair view of the management's actions.

[SSAP 20 para 2].

The above objectives may appear to be relatively simple, but their achievement, in practice, is fraught with difficulties. In some situations, these objectives may well conflict as will be apparent later in this chapter.

[The next paragraph is 7.13.]

Procedures

7.13 SSAP 20 deals with the procedures that should be adopted when accounting for foreign currency operations in two stages, namely:

- The translation of foreign currency transactions by individual companies.
- The translation of foreign currency financial statements for consolidation purposes.

[SSAP 20 para 3].

The individual company stage

Reporting in local currency

7.13.1 SSAP 20 defines 'local currency' as the currency of the primary economic environment in which the entity operates and generates cash flows. [SSAP 20 para 39]. In order to meet this definition, a company that adopts (say) the euro as its local currency will be expected to have the majority of its income, expenses, assets and liabilities denominated in euro. In certain cases, however, it is likely that companies may invoice in euro and be invoiced by suppliers in euro, while most of their other expenses, particularly wages, salaries and rent, remain in sterling.

7.13.2.1 FRS 23 uses the term 'functional currency' rather than 'local currency', but the definition is very similar. FRS 23 provides more guidance than SSAP 20 in the form of indicators that are required to be considered in determining the functional currency and is prescriptive in how those indicators should be applied. The primary indicators are given more weight whilst the secondary indicators provide additional supporting evidence of the functional currency. There are additional indicators to consider when an entity is a foreign operation. FRS 23 goes on to state that, where the facts in a given situation do not clearly identify the functional currency, the determination rests on the judgement of management.

7.13.2.2 An entity has an accounting policy choice as to whether it applies the indicators described in FRS 23 in interpreting SSAP 20, in our view. This choice may have few practical implications for assessing the local currency of an operating company (such as the company with euro sales in para 7.13.1 above). This is because the indicators in FRS 23 support a definition of functional currency that is very similar to the definition of local currency.

7.13.2.3 For some entities such as intermediate holding companies, however, applying the indicators for foreign operations in FRS 23 may result in different conclusions on local currency than if the indicators are not applied. For example, if a foreign operation such as an intermediate holding company does not operate autonomously, that is, its operations are an extension of its parent, then FRS 23 considers this an indicator that its functional currency is the same as its parent. An assessment of local currency under SSAP 20 may put more focus on the cash flows of the entity, as these are the flows of its revenues, purchases and financing. The assessment may conclude that an intermediate holding company has a different local currency to its parent.

7.13.2.4 FRS 23 and the functional currency indicators are considered further in the Annex to this chapter.

7.13.2.5 Where an entity is applying the FRS 23 indicators the following lists some of the primary and secondary indicators to consider in deciding the functional currency:

- Cash flow indicators – the currency of the company's principal cash flows.
- Sales price indicators – whether sales prices are determined principally by local competition or by exchange rate changes. For instance, if price changes are determined not by exchange differences between sterling and the euro, but by competition between companies pricing in euro, this might indicate that the functional currency is the euro.
- Sales market indicators – the entity may have a significant market in those countries where the euro is the principal currency, rather than having its principal market in a non-euro economy.
- Expense indicators – the denomination of the entity's costs of production (labour and materials etc).
- Financing indicators – whether financing is in euro or in domestic currency.

7.13.3 Application of the above indicators may mean that companies with extensive European operations will determine that the euro is their local currency. In some cases the decision might depend on the weighting given to one indicator relative to another. For instance, a company that makes most of its sales in euro, but incurs the majority of its costs in sterling, may give more weight to the sales price and sales market indicators in order to determine that the functional/local currency is the euro. In cases where a reporting entity is merely a holding company for major operating companies with a euro local currency, the holding company may have a local currency of euro. Indicators would include that the holding company may, for example receive dividend income in euros and will manage its investments in the subsidiaries as euro denominated investments as well as borrowings in euros.

7.13.3.1 FRS 23 introduces the concept of a 'presentation currency', which may be different from the local currency of an operation. SSAP 20 does not have the concept of a presentation currency. The currency used to present financial statements prepared under SSAP 20 is considered further in paragraph 7.172.

Change in local currency

7.13.4 Once the local currency is determined, it is not changed unless there is a change in the underlying transactions, events and circumstances that are relevant to the entity.

7.13.5 Where a company changes its local currency, the change should be accounted for *prospectively* from the date of change. This means that all balance sheet items must be translated into the new local currency using the exchange rate at the date of the change. The resulting translated amounts for non-monetary items, even where they were originally purchased in the former local currency, are treated as their historical cost (or valuation for revalued assets). In relation to the current year profit and loss account, any transactions not in the 'new' local currency will be translated at the exchange rate that applies at the date of the transaction. For comparative figures in the profit and loss account, the company will have an accounting policy choice as SSAP 20 is silent on the matter. The comparatives in the profit and loss account may be translated using the relevant closing rate at the end of the previous year or by using the prior year average rate or actual rates as appropriate. This accounting policy choice must be applied consistently to all changes in local currency.

7.13.6 It may not be practicable to determine the date of change precisely at a point during the year. It is also possible that the change may have occurred gradually during the year. If so, it may be appropriate to account for the change as of the beginning or end of the period in which the change takes place,

Example – Change in local currency

A UK company previously reported its financial statements in US$ as the US dollar was its local currency. During the year, there has been a significant change in the nature of the company's operations and its local currency is now sterling. The company will now report its financial statements in sterling. How should the company account for the change in local currency?

The closing balance sheet for the previous period, prepared in US$, should be retranslated into sterling by applying the US$/£ closing rate at the end of the previous year to preserve the relationship of the numbers.

Assume that on 1 January 20X0 the UK subsidiary purchased an asset for £50,000 with a useful life of 10 years when the exchange rate was £1 = US$2.00. Therefore, the US dollar equivalent cost was $100,000. On 31 December 20X4, the equipment has a net book value of US$50,000 and a historical sterling book value of £25,000. As a result of the change in functional currency from US dollars to sterling on 1 January 20X5 (exchange rate at 31 December 20X4 is £1 = US$1.6), the functional currency amount of the asset should be carried at £31,250 (US$50,000 @1.6), which becomes its new historical cost rather than the previous historical value of £25,000. However, in this situation an impairment review should be carried out if the indications are that the recoverable amount is less than £31,250.

In relation to the current year profit and loss account, any US$ transactions will be translated at the US$/£ rate that applies at the date of the transaction. For comparative figures in the profit and loss account, the entity will have an accounting policy choice as SSAP 20 is silent on the matter. The comparatives in the profit and loss account may be translated using the US$/£ closing rate at the end of the previous year or by using the prior year average rate or actual rates as appropriate. This accounting policy choice must be applied consistently to all changes in local currency.

General rules for translation

7.14 The general rules that a company should follow in recording foreign currency transactions undertaken during an accounting period are as follows:

- Each asset, liability, revenue or cost arising from a transaction denominated in a foreign currency should be translated into the company's local currency at the exchange rate in operation on the date on which the transaction occurred.

- If rates do not fluctuate significantly, an average rate for a period *may* be used as an approximation.
- Where the transaction is to be settled at a contracted rate, that rate should be used.
- Where a trading transaction is covered by a related or matching forward contract, the rate of exchange specified in the contract *may* be used.

[SSAP 20 para 46].

The above rules appear to be relatively straightforward, but their application in practice may create a number of problems, for instance: determining the date of transaction may not always be that obvious; determining an average rate as an approximation to the actual rate; and the selection of an appropriate rate for translating foreign currency transactions where there is more than one rate in operation.

Date of transaction

7.15 There is no specific guidance in SSAP 20 as to whether the transaction date should be taken as the date on which the contract for the purchase or sale was signed, or the date of delivery, or the date when the invoice is received, or the date of payment. However, the standard does state that a difference may arise if a transaction is settled at a rate that is different from that used when the transaction was initially recorded. [SSAP 20 para 7]. It seems reasonable to assume, therefore, that the date on which a transaction is recorded under normal accounting rules should be taken as the transaction date. FRS 23 supports this, as it defines the transaction date as *"the date on which the transaction first qualifies for recognition in accordance with Financial Reporting Standards"*.

Determining the average rate

7.16 The standard permits the use of an average rate for a period for recording foreign currency transactions as a proxy to the actual rate prevailing at the date of each transaction, provided that there is no significant change in rates during that period. An average rate is unlikely to be used by companies undertaking few transactions in a foreign currency. It is also unlikely to be used for translating large, one-off transactions which would be recorded at the actual rate as illustrated in Table 7.1 below. The flexibility allowed in the standard is likely to be most beneficial to companies that enter into a large number of transactions in different currencies, or that maintain multi-currency ledgers. However, no guidance is provided in the standard as to how such a rate should be determined.

Table 7.1 — Trafalgar House Public Limited Company — Report and Accounts — 30 September 1994

Principal accounting policies (extract)

c) Foreign currencies

Trading results denominated in foreign currencies are translated into sterling at average rates of exchange during the year except for material exceptional items which are translated at the rate on the date of the transaction.

Assets and liabilities are translated at the rates of exchange ruling at the year end except where rates of exchange are fixed under contractual arrangements.

Differences on exchange arising from the translation of the opening net assets of foreign subsidiaries and branches and ships denominated in foreign currency and of any related loans are taken to reserves together with the differences between profit and loss accounts translated at average rates and rates ruling at the year end. Other exchange differences are taken to the profit and loss account when they arise.

7.17 The determination of an average rate and its use in practice will depend on a number of factors, such as: the nature of the company's accounting systems; the frequency and value of transactions undertaken; the period over which the rate will apply; and the acceptable level of materiality. The choice of the period to be used for calculating the average rate will depend on the extent to which daily exchange rates fluctuate in the period selected. If exchange rates are relatively stable over a period of say, one month, then the average exchange rate for that month can be used as an approximation to the daily rate. If, however, there is volatility of exchange rates, it may be appropriate to calculate an average rate for a shorter period such as a week. Whatever period is chosen, materiality is likely to be an important consideration.

7.18 Depending on the circumstances, a company may use an actual average rate or an estimated average rate. An actual average rate is likely to be used where there is some delay between the date when the transactions occurred and the date when they are recorded. In other situations, it may be necessary for a company to use an estimated average rate for a period rather than wait for the period to end in order to calculate an actual average rate. This estimate may be based on the average of daily exchange rates for the previous period or the closing rate of the previous period. Whichever basis is used, it will be necessary to ensure than the estimated average rate is a close approximation of the actual rates prevailing during the period. If it is not, the rate should be revised accordingly.

Dual rates or suspension of rates

7.19 Some countries may operate more than one exchange rate. In that situation, the question arises as to which rate should be used to translate and record the transaction. SSAP 20 provides no guidance. Obviously, where there is a marginal difference between the two rates, it does not matter which rate is used. But where the difference is considered to be significant, we suggest that companies should consider following the relevant provision in FRS 23. This states that *"when several exchange rates are available, the rate used is that at which the future cash flows represented by the transaction or balance could have been settled if those cash flows had occurred at the measurement date"*. In some situations, it may be prudent to use the less favourable rate.

Example – Use of an autonomous rate

The Nigerian budget in January 1995 made changes to the foreign exchange market. From that date all commercial foreign exchange transactions take place at the autonomous rate of exchange (say Niara 65 to US$1) rather than at the official rate of exchange (say Niara 22 to US$ 1). This means that all imports and exports and remittances of profits, dividends and technical services and other fees will take place at the autonomous rate of exchange.

Therefore, when retranslating foreign exchange transactions and monetary amounts receivable and payable in the financial statements of an individual company, the autonomous rate rather than the official rate of exchange should be used. This would also apply to the translation of the results and net assets of Nigerian subsidiary companies in consolidated financial statements.

7.20 From time to time, countries may experience economic conditions that affect the free-market convertibility of the local currency. As a result, the exchangeability between two currencies may be temporarily lacking at the transaction date or a subsequent balance sheet date. SSAP 20 is silent on this point, but FRS 23 requires companies to use the rate on the first subsequent date at which exchanges could be made.

[The next paragraph is 7.23.]

Treatment of monetary items

7.23 Monetary items, as the name implies, include money held and amounts to be received or paid in money. [SSAP 20 para 44]. Obvious examples include cash and bank balances, loans, debtors and creditors. FRS 23 considers whether an item is settled in *"fixed or determinable units of currency"* in determing whether it is monetary. [FRS23 para 16]. This concept can also be applied under SSAP 20 when considering whether an item is monetary. Monetary items would, therefore, also include contracts to receive (or deliver) a variable number of an entity's own equity instruments or a variable amount of assets in which the fair value to be received (or delivered) equals a fixed or determinable number of units of currency. In other words, an entity's own financial instruments can be used 'as currency' in a contract that can be settled at a value equal to a fixed or a determinable amount. Such a contract is not an equity instrument, but a monetary asset or liability. Not all financial assets should be treated as monetary items. For example, an investment in an equity instrument is not a monetary item – there is no right to receive a fixed or determinable amount of cash.

7.23.1 Monetary items can be categorised as short term or long term. Short-term monetary items are those that fall due within one year of the balance sheet date and long-term monetary items are those that fall due more than one year after the balance sheet date.

7.24 SSAP 20 requires that a company should translate its monetary assets and liabilities denominated in foreign currencies outstanding at the end of the year using the closing rate. [SSAP 20 para 48]. An example is given in Table 7.1. The closing rate is the exchange rate for spot transactions ruling at the balance sheet date and is the mean of the buying rate and the selling rate at the close of business on the day for which the rate is to be ascertained. [SSAP 20 para 41]. Where, however, the rate of exchange is fixed under the terms of the relevant contract, the company should use that rate. Where an outstanding trading transaction is covered by a related or matching forward contract, the rate specified in that contract may be used. [SSAP 20 para 48]. An example of a company that uses forward contracted rates is given in Table 7.2 below.

Table 7.2 — BAE SYSTEMS plc — Annual Report — 31 December 2002

Notes to the accounts

1 Accounting Policies (extract)

Foreign currencies

Transactions in overseas currencies are translated at the exchange rate ruling at the date of the transaction or, where forward cover contracts have been arranged, at the contracted rates. Monetary assets and liabilities denominated in foreign currencies are retranslated at the exchange rates ruling at the balance sheet date or at a contracted rate if applicable and any exchange differences arising are taken to the profit and loss account.

For consolidation purposes the assets and liabilities of overseas subsidiary undertakings and joint ventures are translated at the closing exchange rates. Profit and loss accounts of such undertakings are consolidated at the average rates of exchange during the year. Exchange differences arising on foreign currency net investments are taken to reserves.

Treatment of non-monetary items

7.24.1 Non-monetary items are all items other than monetary items. Non-monetary items are generally physical in nature, such as properties, plant and equipment, stocks and equity investments. In some instances, however, it may not be readily apparent whether an item should be regarded as a monetary item or a non-monetary item. The ambiguity can usually be resolved if it is considered whether the item represents an amount to be received or paid in money, in which case it would fall to be treated as a monetary item. Otherwise, it should be treated as a non-monetary item.

7.24.2 Advances paid and received (including pre-payments) can be difficult to classifiy as monetary or non-monetary. An example of a non-monetary item is an advance payment for goods, that, absent a default by the counterparty, must be settled by the counterparty delivering the goods. However, if an advance is refundable in circumstances other than default by either party, this may indicate that it is a monetary item as the item is receivable in units of currency.

7.24.3 SSAP 20 requires that where a non-monetary item has been translated at the rate ruling when it was originally recorded, no subsequent translation of the asset is normally required [SSAP 20 para 47]. This effectively means that such assets are recorded at historical cost. However, in certain circumstances, this treatment will not apply to foreign equity investments. These special circumstances are considered from paragraph 7.80 below.

Example – Foreign exchange gains and losses on investment in preference shares

A UK company, which prepares its financial statements in sterling, has purchased 6% preference shares in an unrelated company for US$5 million. It has financed the investment from cash, converted to US$ at the spot rate. It intends to hold the investment for the long-term, but is unsure whether it should retranslate the preference shares at each year end.

The accounting treatment would depend on whether the preference share investment should be classified as a monetary or a non-monetary asset. This will depend on the nature and terms of the preference shares. The two scenarios are considered below.

(a) Preference shares treated as a monetary asset

SSAP 20, 'Foreign currency translation', defines monetary items as 'money held and amounts to be received or paid in money'. To determine this, the terms of the preference shares and the individual facts and circumstances should be considered. If the terms indicate that the preferences shares rank for a fixed amount of dividends and are redeemable, then clearly they meet the definition of a monetary asset. Such investments should initially be recorded at the spot rate at the date of purchase and retranslated at each balance sheet date, with the exchange gains and losses recognised in the profit and loss account.

(b) Preference shares treated as a non-monetary asset

However, if the terms indicate that the shares are non-redeemable then clearly they cannot be classed as 'amounts to be received in money' and, therefore, should be treated as non-monetary assets. These should not be retranslated if the company applies the historical cost convention. However, if the company adopts a policy of regular revaluation of its foreign currency non-monetary investments under the alternative accounting rules, then the revaluation movements are recognised in the statement of total recognised gains and losses.

Treatment of exchange gains and losses

7.25 An exchange gain or loss will arise if a currency transaction is settled during an accounting period at an exchange rate which differs from the rate used when the transaction was initially recorded, or, where appropriate, the rate that was used at the last balance sheet date. An exchange gain or loss will also arise on unsettled transactions if the rate of exchange used at the balance sheet date differs from that used previously. All exchange gains and losses, whether arising on settled transactions or on unsettled transactions, should be reported as part of the profit or loss for the year from ordinary activities. There are two exceptions to this rule. An exchange difference on a currency transaction that is itself treated as an extraordinary item should be included as part of that item, but such items will be very rare following the issue of FRS 3 'Reporting financial performance'. The other exception is that, in the special circumstances considered further from paragraph 7.79, exchange gains and losses arising, where a foreign currency borrowing is used to hedge a foreign equity investment, may be taken to the STRGL. The classification of exchange differences in the profit and loss account formats is dealt with in paragraph 7.147.

Settled transactions

7.26 Where a transaction is *settled* at an exchange rate that differs from the rate used when the transaction was initially recorded, the exchange difference will be recognised in the profit and loss account of the period in which the settlement takes place. The rationale for this treatment is that, as the exchange difference will have been reflected in the cash flow at the time of the settlement, it is appropriate to recognise such exchange differences as part of the profit or loss for that year.

Example 1 – Purchase of plant in a foreign currency with settlement after transaction date

In March 20X4, a UK company purchases plant for use in the UK from a Danish company for DK 425,000. At the date the company purchases the plant, the exchange rate is £1 = DK 8.50. The purchase price is to be settled in three months time, although delivery is made immediately. The UK company should record the plant in its accounting records at £50,000. The company will not need to translate the plant again. At the settlement date, the exchange rate is £1 = DK 8.75 so the actual amount the UK company pays is £48,571. The company should include the gain on exchange of £1,429 (that is, £50,000 — £48,571) in arriving at its profit or loss on ordinary activities.

Example 2 – Purchase of plant at a contracted foreign currency rate

In March 20X4, a UK company purchases plant for use in the UK from a Canadian company for C$ 750,000. The transaction is contracted to be settled at £1 = C$ 2.50. The UK company should record the plant in its accounting records at £300,000. The company will not need to translate the plant again, and no exchange differences will arise.

Example 3 – Sales transaction in foreign currency with a specific related forward cover contract

In January 20X5, a UK company sells goods to an Australian company for A$ 405,000. The Australian company pays for the goods in March 20X5. At the time of the sale, the exchange rate is £1 = A$ 2.7, and at the time of the payment, the exchange rate is £1 = A$ 2.9. The UK company, however, covers the transaction by a matching forward contract to sell Australian Dollars. The exchange rate specified in the forward contract is £1 = A$ 2.75. The relevant translations are as follows:

A$ 405,000 at A$ 2.7 (transaction rate) =	£150,000
A$ 405,000 at A$ 2.9 (settlement rate) =	£139,655
A$ 405,000 at A$ 2.75 (forward contract rate) =	£147,273

The UK company could record the sale in one of the following ways:

- It could record the sale and the debtor at £150,000, that is, at the exchange rate ruling at the date of the sale. Because the company has entered into a matching forward contract, the amount received from the debtor is A$ 405,000 which is sold for £147,273. Consequently, the company would have a loss on exchange on the transaction of £2,727 (that is, £150,000 — £147,273) to include in its profit or loss on ordinary activities.

- It could record the sale and the debtor at £147,273, that is, at the exchange rate specified in the matching forward contract. Because the company has entered into a matching forward contract, the amount receivable and ultimately received from the debtor is £147,273. Consequently, the company would not recognise a loss on exchange on the transaction.

Whichever method the company chooses to record the sale (that has been settled in the same period), its profit or loss on ordinary activities will be the same.

It should be noted that under FRS 23 neither of the above treatments are permitted. Under FRS 23, the sale and receivable would be recorded at the transaction rate. The settlement of the debtor would be accounted for separately from the forward contract. Consequently, the company would have an exchange loss on the transaction of £10,345 (that is £150,000 — £139,655). FRS 26 would govern the accounting for the forward contract. FRS 26 would require that the contract is initially measured at cost (usually zero) and subsequently at its fair value immediately before settlement. Assuming the transaction was entered into and settled in the same period the movement in carrying value of the forward contract would be recorded in the profit and loss account where it would offset the exchange loss on the transaction. The detailed requirements of FRS 23 are considered in the Annex to this chapter while those of FRS 26 are considered in chapter 6.

Forward contracts are dealt with in more detail from paragraph 7.125.

Example 4 – Translation of foreign currency convertible loan stock

A company has a convertible loan stock in issue, which is denominated in dollars. Each year it is retranslated at closing rate and exchange differences are charged to the profit and loss account. On conversion the price of the shares to be issued is fixed and so is the rate of exchange (which is the rate prevailing when the loan stock was originally issued). The rate of exchange for conversion is different from the rate of exchange used for the translation of the loan stock in the balance sheet immediately prior to conversion. The difference is equal to the net exchange gains and losses charged over the period in which the loan stock has been in issue. Should these differences be written back to profit and loss account on conversion?

We consider that the consideration for the issue of the shares is the amount at which the loan stock is stated in the balance sheet immediately prior to conversion. This is despite the fact that there is a fixed rate of exchange stipulated in the conversion terms.

The net exchange gains or losses that have been charged to profit and loss in the past are properly to be regarded as part of the cost of financing the loan stock. Together with the interest paid they constitute the total cost of finance.

Even if legally the exchange gains or losses are not required to be taken to share premium they should be taken to an undistributable reserve as, in economic terms, the current sterling carrying value (that is, dollars at closing rate) is the equity's opportunity cost. The pre-determined rate specified in the contract is not relevant. (We consider that this is also consistent with FRS 4, 'Capital instruments').

Unsettled transactions

7.27 Where the transaction remains *outstanding* at the balance sheet date, an exchange difference arises as a consequence of recording the foreign currency transaction at the rate ruling at the date of the transaction (or when it was translated at a previous balance sheet date) and the subsequent retranslation to the rate ruling at the balance sheet date. Such exchange differences arise on monetary items (for example, foreign currency loans, debtors and creditors). To the extent that exchange differences relate to short-term monetary items, they will soon be reflected in cash flows and, therefore, they should be reported as part of the profit or loss for the year from ordinary activities.

Example –Treatment of an unsettled foreign creditor at balance sheet date

In January 20X4, a UK company purchases equipment from an overseas company for FC 11,250,000 (FC being a fictional currency). At the date the company takes delivery of the equipment, the exchange rate is £1 = FC 225. Therefore, the company initially records both the equipment and the creditor at £50,000 (FC 11,250,000 @ 225). At 31 March 20X4, the balance sheet date, the creditor is still outstanding. No further translation of the equipment is necessary, but the creditor should be retranslated using the rate of exchange at the balance sheet date, which is £1 = FC 240. The company should include the gain on exchange of £3,125 (that is, £50,000 — £46,875) in its profit or loss on ordinary activities.

7.28 Where exchange differences arise on the retranslation of unsettled long-term monetary items, SSAP 20 requires that these exchange differences should be reported as part of the profit or loss for the year on ordinary activities, even though they may not be reflected in cash flows for a considerable time. SSAP 20 argues that the treatment of these long-term items on a simple cash movements basis would be inconsistent with the accruals concept and goes on to state:

> *"Exchange gains on unsettled transactions can be determined at the balance sheet date no less objectively than exchange losses; deferring the gains whilst recognising the losses would not only be illogical by denying in effect that any favourable movement in exchange rates had occurred but would also inhibit fair measurement of the performance of the enterprise in the year. In particular, this symmetry of treatment recognises that there will probably be some interaction between currency movements and interest rates and reflects more accurately in the profit and loss account the true results of currency involvement."* [SSAP 20 para 10].

7.29 Paragraph 13(a) of Schedule 1 to SI 2008/410 states that *"only profits realised at the balance sheet date shall be included in the profit and loss account"*.

Paragraph 65 of SSAP 20 implies that exchange gains that arise on long-term monetary items are not realised profits, but SSAP 20 still requires them to be recognised in the profit and loss account, which would involve a departure from paragraph 12 of Schedule 4. However, as discussed in paragraph 7.151, the ICAEW and ICAS have issued guidance in Tech 02/10, 'Guidance on the determination of realised profits and losses in the context of distributions under the Companies Act 2006'. This states that a profit is realised where it arises from the translation of a monetary asset which comprises qualifying consideration, or a liability denominated in a foreign currency. [Tech 02/10 para 3.9]. Consequently, unless there are doubts as to the convertibility or marketability of the currency in question (see below), foreign exchange profits arising on the retranslation of monetary items are realised, irrespective of the maturity date of the monetary item. [Tech 02/10 para 3.21]. The impact of foreign currency translation on distributable profits is dealt with from paragraph 7.149.

7.30 In certain exceptional situations, however, a company may have doubts as to either the convertibility or the marketability of the currency of a long-term monetary item outstanding at the end of the year. Where this is so, on the grounds of prudence such a company should restrict the amount of any gain (or the amount by which any gain exceeds past exchange losses on the same item) that it recognises in its profit and loss account. [SSAP 20 para 50].

7.31 Doubts as to convertibility may arise if, for example, a UK company makes a long-term currency loan to, say, an overseas supplier, but restrictions on the remittance of funds are imposed by the overseas country sometime prior to the maturity of the loan. Such restrictions would probably arise if there is political upheaval or severe exchange control regulations in the overseas country. In that situation, the company should consider the loan's realisable value in the light of such restrictions and limit any exchange gains arising on the retranslation that is taken to the profit and loss account. The following example illustrates this type of situation.

Example – Impact of convertibility of foreign currency on recognition of foreign exchange gains or losses

In April 20X4, company A, which is incorporated in the UK, used surplus currency to make a long-term loan of FC 20m to its overseas supplier. The loan was made when the exchange rate was £1 = FC 5.00. Initially, the loan would be translated and recorded in company A's books at £4m. The amount that company A will ultimately receive will depend on the rate of exchange ruling on the date when the loan is repaid.

At 31 March 20X5, company A's year end, the exchange rate is £1 = FC 4.00. If the loan of FC 20m was translated at this rate it would give an asset of £5m and an exchange gain of £1m. There are, however, doubts as to the convertibility of FC. Therefore, company A considers that, on the grounds of prudence, it should limit the gain so that the sterling value of the loan is shown at its present estimated realisable value of £4,500,000. Accordingly, company A restricts the exchange gain that it includes in its profit and loss account for the year ended 31 March 20X5 to £500,000.

Transactions between group companies

7.32 Where transactions take place between companies in a group, exchange differences are likely to arise in one or other company since the transaction is likely to be carried out in the local currency of one of the companies in question. SSAP 20 requires that exchange gains and losses arising on such transactions should normally be reported in the individual company's financial statements as part of the profit or loss for the year in the same way as gains and losses arising from transactions with third parties. [SSAP 20 para 12].

The consolidation stage

Introduction

7.33 Translation of foreign currency financial statements is necessary so that the financial statements of overseas subsidiaries may be consolidated with the holding company's sterling financial statements. The method of translation in consolidated financial statements should be such as to reflect the financial and other operational relationships that exist between the investing company and its foreign enterprises. In this context, a foreign enterprise includes not only a foreign subsidiary, but also an associated company or branch whose operations are based in a currency other than that of the investing company or whose assets and liabilities are denominated mainly in a foreign currency. [SSAP 20 para 36].

7.34 The standard requires that, normally, a company should use the 'closing rate/net investment' method for translating the financial statements of its foreign enterprises. However, where the operations of the foreign enterprises are direct extensions of the investing company's trade, the temporal method should be used. [SSAP 20 para 14].

Closing rate/net investment method

7.35 The closing rate/net investment method is based on the premise that a foreign enterprise generally operates as a separate or quasi-independent entity. Such an entity normally conducts its day to day affairs in its local currency, is likely to be financed wholly or partly by local currency borrowings, and is not normally dependent on the investing company's reporting currency. If a foreign enterprise is relatively independent then what is at risk from the investing company's perspective is the net worth of the investment rather than the individual assets and liabilities of that enterprise. The investing company may or may not receive regular dividend income, but the net investment remains until the business is liquidated or the investment is sold.

7.36 Accordingly, it is important to retain the financial and operational relationships existing in the foreign entity's financial statements prior to translation in order to produce results that are meaningful at the consolidation stage. Use of a constant rate of exchange for all items maintains such a relationship in the retranslated financial statements of the reporting currency as existed in the foreign currency financial statements. Therefore, for example, fixed assets would be the same proportion of long-term liabilities.

7.37 This method is widely supported both in the UK and internationally.

7.38 Proponents of the closing rate/net investment method claim that the method acknowledges the fact that operations which are conducted in currencies and in economic environments other than those of the parent are essentially different from the parent's own operations. Accordingly, it clearly reflects the true economic facts, because stating all items at the closing rate presents the foreign enterprise's true earnings at that time, particularly since from the investor's point of view the only real earnings are those that can actually be distributed. The translation of the historical cost financial statements at closing rates is merely a restatement of assets and liabilities for the purposes of consolidation and does not constitute a revaluation.

7.39 Under the closing rate/net investment method:

- All items in a foreign subsidiary's balance sheet at the year end should be translated at the closing rate of exchange into the parent's reporting currency.
- On consolidation, the exchange differences that arise when the parent retranslates its opening net investments in the foreign subsidiary to the closing rate should be treated as a movement on consolidated reserves. Exchange differences may also arise where the closing rate differs from that ruling on the date of a subsequent capital injection (or reduction). Such exchange differences should also be dealt with as a movement in reserves. The rationale for taking such exchange differences to reserves is explained in paragraph 19 of SSAP 20, which states:

  "If exchange differences arising from the retranslation of a company's net investment in its foreign enterprise were introduced into the profit and loss account, the results from trading operations, as shown in the local currency financial statements, would be distorted. Such differences may result from many factors unrelated to the trading performance or financial operations of the foreign enterprise; in particular, they do not represent or measure changes in actual or prospective cash flows. It is therefore inappropriate to regard them as profits or losses and they should be dealt with as adjustments to reserves."

  SSAP 20, unlike FRS 23, does not require companies to maintain a separate reserve for exchange differences, but some companies do so.

- The profit and loss account of a foreign subsidiary may be translated either at the closing rate or at an average rate for the period. Although the use of a closing rate is more likely to achieve the objective of translation, stated in paragraph 7.12.1 above, of reflecting the financial results and relationships as measured in the foreign currency financial statements prior to translation, the use of an average rate reflects more fairly the profits or losses and cash flows as they accrue to the group throughout the period. Therefore, the standard permits the use of either method, provided that the one selected is applied consistently from period to period. [SSAP 20 para 17]. It should be noted that FRS 23 does not permit the use of closing rate. SSAP 20 requires that where the average rate is used, the company should record, as a movement on consolidated reserves, the difference between translating the profit and loss account at the average rate and translating it at the closing rate. [SSAP 20 para 54].

An example of a company that uses the closing rate/net investment method is given in Table 7.4 below.

Table 7.4 — The Peninsular and Oriental Steam Navigation Company — Annual Report and Accounts — 31 December 2000

Accounting Policies (extract)

Foreign currencies

Transactions in foreign currencies are recorded at the rate of exchange ruling at the date of the transaction. Profits and losses of subsidiaries, branches joint ventures and associates which have currencies of operation other than sterling are translated into sterling at average rates of exchange except for material exceptional items which are translated at the rate ruling on the date of transaction. Assets and liabilities denominated in foreign currencies are translated at the year end exchange rates.

Exchange differences arising from the retranslation of the opening net assets of subsidiaries, branches joint ventures and associates which have currencies of operation other than sterling and any related loans are taken to reserves together with the differences arising when the profit and loss accounts are translated at average rates and compared with rates ruling at the year end. Other exchange differences are taken to the profit and loss account.

7.40 The net investment which a company has in a foreign enterprise is its effective equity stake and comprises its proportion of such foreign enterprise's net assets; in appropriate circumstances, intra-group loans and other deferred trading balances may be regarded as part of the effective equity stake. [SSAP 20 para 43]. It follows from the above definition that the net investment is the amount at which the group states the net assets of the subsidiary in the consolidated balance sheet. It is not (for example) the amount at which the net assets are recorded in the subsidiary's financial statements which may be different if the group has restated the assets at fair value at the time of acquisition. Nor is it the market value of the foreign subsidiary.

Illustration of the closing rate/net investment method

7.41 The closing rate/net investment method is illustrated by the following example.

Example – Use of the closing rate/net investment method

Company A, a UK company, whose accounting period ended on 30 September 20X4, has a wholly-owned US subsidiary, S Corporation, which was acquired for US$ 500,000 on 30 September 20X3. The fair value of the net assets at the date of acquisition was US$ 400,000. The exchange rate at 30 September 20X3 and 20X4 was £1 = US$ 2.0 and £1 = US$ 1.5 respectively. The weighted average rate for the year ended 30 September 20X4 was £1 = US$ 1.65.

The summarised profit and loss account of S Corporation for the year ended 30 September 20X4 and the summarised balance sheets at 30 September 20X3 and 20X4 in dollars and sterling equivalents, are as follows:

S Corporation: Profit and loss account for the year ended 30 September 20X4

		Closing rate	Average rate
	$'000	£'000	£'000
Exchange rate £1 =		$1.50	$1.65
Operating profit	135	90.0	81.8
Interest paid	(15)	(10.0)	(9.0)
Profit before taxation	120	80.0	72.8
Taxation	(30)	(20.0)	(18.2)
Profit after taxation	90	60.0	54.6
Dividends paid in the year	(14)	(9.3)	(8.5)
Retained profit	76	50.7	46.1

Balance sheets of S Corporation

	20X4	20X3	20X4	20X4	20X3
	$'000	$'000	£'000	£'000	£'000
			P&L closing	P&L average	
Closing exchange rate £1 =			$1.50	$1.50	$2.00
Fixed assets:					
Cost (20X4 additions: $30)	255	225	170.0	170.0	112.5
Depreciation (20X4 charge: $53)	98	45	65.3	65.3	22.5
Net book value	157	180	104.7	104.7	90.0
Current assets:					
Stocks	174	126	116.0	116.0	63.0
Debtors	210	145	140.0	140.0	72.5
Cash at bank	240	210	160.0	160.0	105.0
	624	481	416.0	416.0	240.5
Current liabilities:					
Trade creditors	125	113	83.3	83.3	56.5
Taxation	30	18	20.0	20.0	9.0
	155	131	103.3	103.3	65.5
Net current assets	469	350	312.7	312.7	175.0
Loan stock	150	130	100.0	100.0	65.0
Net assets	476	400	317.4	317.4	200.0
Share capital	200	200	100.0	100.0	100.0
Retained profits	276	200	217.4	217.4	100.0
	476	400	317.4	317.4	200.0

The analysis of retained profits under the closing rate and the average rate method is as follows:

		Closing rate	Average rate
	$'000	£'000	£'000
Exchange rate £1 =		$1.50	$1.65
Pre-acquisition profit brought forward	200	100.0	100.0
Profit for the year	76	50.7	46.1
Exchange difference	–	66.7	71.3
Retained profits	276	217.4	217.4
Analysis of exchange difference:			
Arising on retranslation of opening net investments:			
at opening rate — $400,000 @ $2 = £1		200.0	200.0
at closing rate — $400,000 @ $1.5 = £1		266.7	266.7
Exchange gain on net investment		66.7	66.7
Exchange gain arising from translating profit and loss account at average rate (£46.1) rather than closing rate (£50.7)		–	4.6
Total exchange difference		66.7	71.3

Note: On consolidation, the above exchange differences will be included in consolidated reserves and shown in the statement of total recognised gains and losses (STRGL). This requirement is the same as that in FRS 23. However, unlike SSAP 20, FRS 23 requires that on disposal of the foreign entity the cumulative amount of exchange differences, which have been recognised in the STRGL in relation to that entity, should be 'recycled' through the profit and loss account. [FRS 23 para 48].

It is further assumed that parent company A does not trade on its own and its only income is dividends received from S Corporation. The summarised balance sheets of company A at 30 September 20X3 and 20X4 are as follows:

Company A — Balance Sheets	20X4	20X3
	£'000	£'000
Investments in subsidiary ($500,000 @ 2.0)	250	250
Cash	208	200
Net assets	458	450
Share capital	450	450
P&L account (dividend received: $14,000 @ 1.75*)	8	–
	458	450

* actual rate on date dividend received

Where company A uses the closing rate/net investment method, it may use either the closing rate or the average rate for translating the results of S Corporation. The summarised consolidated profit and loss account for the year ended 30 September 20X4 drawn up on the two bases and the summarised consolidated balance sheet at that date are as follows:

Consolidated profit and loss account for the year ended 30 September 20X4

	Closing rate	Average rate
	£'000	£'000
Operating profit of S Corporation	90.0	81.8
Operating profit of company A	8.0	8.0
	98.0	89.8
Elimination of inter company dividend*	(9.3)	(8.5)
Net operating profit	88.7	81.3
Interest paid	(10.0)	(9.0)
Profit before taxation	78.7	72.3
Taxation	(20.0)	(18.2)
Retained profit	58.7	54.1

* The exchange difference arising on the inter-company dividend, being the difference between the dividend calculated at the date of receipt and at the closing rate or at the average rate, is included in the profit and loss account.

Consolidated balance sheet at 30 September 20X4

	Closing rate £'000	Average rate £'000
Fixed assets	104.7	104.7
Current assets:		
Stocks	116.0	116.0
Debtors	140.0	140.0
Cash (S Corporation £160; company A £208)	368.0	368.0
	624.0	624.0
Current liabilities:		
Trade creditors	83.3	83.3
Taxation	20.0	20.0
	103.3	103.3
Net current assets	520.7	520.7
Loan stock	100.0	100.0
Net assets	525.4	525.4
Share capital	450.0	450.0
Reserves:		
Retained profit	58.7	54.1
Exchange difference on opening net assets	66.7	66.7
Exchange difference on P&L account	–	4.6
Goodwill written off (pre - FRS 10) ($100,000 @ 2.0)	(50.0)	(50.0)
	525.4	525.4

In the above illustration goodwill has been translated at the rate ruling on the date of acquisition on the grounds that it arises only on consolidation and is not part of the net assets of the foreign enterprise. An alternative treatment is to regard the goodwill as a currency asset which is retranslated at the closing rate. In this situation, an exchange difference would arise on the opening net investment including the goodwill. The alternative treatment, regarding goodwill as a currency asset, is consistent with FRS 10 which no longer permits goodwill to be written off directly to reserves as it has been in the above illustration (see further para 7.78). Furthermore, the alternative treatment is the method required by FRS 23, 'The effects of changes in foreign exchange rates'.

7.41.1 The above illustration included a wholly-owned subsidiary. Where the parent holds less than 100 per cent of the issued share capital, the minority's share of the assets and liabilities should also be included at year end rate. FRS 2, 'Accounting for subsidiary undertakings', states in paragraph 80 that the effect of the existence of minority interests on the returns to investors in the parent undertaking is best reflected by presenting the net identifiable assets attributable to minority interests on the same basis as those attributable to group interests. Accordingly, the minority's share of the exchange difference should be allocated to them in the balance sheet and only the amount of the exchange difference attributable to the group should be shown in the statement of total recognised gains and losses.

7.41.2 If a foreign subsidiary holds monetary assets such as cash in the currency of the parent, for example, sterling, such balances will be translated to the subsidiary's local currency under SSAP 20 at the year end. This will result in an exchange difference in the overseas subsidiary's financial statements, which will be taken to the profit and loss account of the overseas subsidiary. If this subsidiary is consolidated using the closing rate method, the exchange difference reported in the subsidiary's profit and loss account will be translated into sterling and remain in the consolidated profit and loss account. In addition, an equal and opposite exchange difference attributable to the sterling cash balance arising as part of the retranslation of the opening net assets (which includes the sterling cash balance) of the overseas subsidiary will also be included in reserves.

The temporal method

7.42 As stated in paragraph 7.34 above, SSAP 20 acknowledges that the use of the closing rate/net investment method may not be appropriate in certain circumstances. The circumstances relate to situations where the foreign enterprise's operations are so closely interlinked with those of the investing company that it no longer seems appropriate to regard the foreign currency as being that on which the foreign enterprise is dependent. In such a situation, the foreign enterprise's local currency is deemed to be that of the investing company and the temporal method should be used for translating the foreign enterprise's financial statements. Under the temporal method all of the foreign enterprise's transactions are treated as if they had been entered into by the investing company itself and all of the foreign enterprise's assets and liabilities are treated as though they belong directly to the investing company.

7.43 SSAP 20 acknowledges that it is not possible to select one factor which would indicate the temporal method should be used. All available evidence must be considered in determining which currency is the local currency (referred to in FRS 23 as the 'functional currency') of each foreign enterprise respectively.

7.44 The standard specifies a number of factors that need to be taken into consideration in determining the dominant currency. The factors, which are listed below, should be considered both individually and collectively before deciding on the appropriate method of translation. In those situations, where the indicators are mixed and the dominant currency is not obvious, considerable management judgment will be required.

- The extent to which the cash flows of the enterprise have a direct impact upon those of the investing company, for example, whether there is regular and frequent transfer of funds between the two companies or whether there are only occasional remittances of dividends.
- The extent to which the functioning of the enterprise is dependent directly upon the investing company, for example, whether major decisions are taken by the parent company, whether pricing decisions are based on local competition and costs or are part of a worldwide decision process.

- The currency in which the majority of the trading transactions are completed, for example, the sales market is mostly in the parent's country of origin or sales invoices are denominated in the parent's currency.
- The major currency to which the operation is exposed in its financing structure, for example whether the operation is dependent on finance raised locally or from the parent.

[SSAP 20 para 23].

7.45 Examples of situations where the temporal method may be appropriate are where the foreign enterprise:

- Acts as a selling agency receiving stocks of goods from the receiving company and remitting the proceeds back to the company.
- Produces a raw material or manufactures parts or sub-assemblies which are then shipped to the investing company for inclusion in its own products.
- Is located overseas for tax, exchange control or similar reasons to act as a means of raising finance for other companies in the group.

[SSAP 20 para 24].

It should be noted that the above are extreme situations where the use of the temporal method is rather obvious. In practice, this will rarely be so and determining the local currency will need to be made in the light of the above factors and the management's judgement.

Example – Subsidiary used for depositing surplus cash

A group has surplus cash and is investing it by way of subscription for shares denominated in Yen, in a newly formed subsidiary, in say, the Channel Islands. The subsidiary will place the money on deposit (in Yen) and will have no other business, nor does the group have any Yen denominated activities. When preparing consolidated financial statements should the group account for the subsidiary's net assets using the temporal method or the closing rate method under SSAP 20? At first sight it would appear that the subsidiary would qualify under SSAP 20 as a foreign enterprise, as the definition in SSAP 20 implies that a subsidiary whose assets and liabilities are in a foreign currency is a foreign enterprise. However, on closer inspection it appears that the subsidiary's only business is to hold the deposit. Indeed, the parent entity itself could have made the investment directly in Yen. Therefore, the temporal method should be used.

7.46 SSAP 20 states that the mechanics of the temporal method are identical to those used in preparing the financial statements of an individual company. [SSAP 20 para 22]. This is probably true to a degree, but applying this method in practice requires detailed and additional record keeping that is not required under the closing rate method and is far more complicated as illustrated in the example below. The similarity of the temporal method with the method used in individual financial statements implies that under the temporal method:

- All transactions should be translated at the rate ruling at the transaction date or at an average rate for the period if this is not materially different.
- Non-monetary items, such as fixed assets and stocks measured at historical cost or valuation, are translated at the exchange rate in effect at the date to which the historical cost or valuation pertains. They are not retranslated at each balance sheet date.
- Monetary items, whether short-term or long-term, are translated using the closing rate at the balance sheet date.
- All items in the profit and loss account are translated at the historical rate. An average rate may be used where it is not materially different from the rate ruling at the transaction date, except for depreciation and stocks which must be included at historical rate.
- All exchange gains and losses including those arising on the retranslation of opening monetary items should be taken to the profit and loss account for the year as part of the profit or loss from ordinary operations.

[The next paragraph is 7.48.]

Illustration of the temporal method

7.48 The way in which the temporal method is used in practice is illustrated by the following example.

Example – Use of the temporal method

The facts and the data are the same as that used in the closing rate method in paragraph 7.41 above, except that further details on exchange rates at the dates of acquisition of fixed assets and stocks are given, together with an analysis of operating profit.

Company A, a UK company, whose accounting period ended on 30 September 20X4, has a wholly-owned US subsidiary, S corporation, that was acquired for US$ 500,000 on 30 September 20X3. The fair value of the net assets at the date of acquisition was US$ 400,000. The exchange rate at 30 September 20X3 and 20X4 was £1 = US$ 2.0 and £1 = US$ 1.5 respectively. The weighted average rate for the year ended 30 September 20X4 was £1 = US$ 1.65.

S Corporation: Profit and loss account for the year ended 30 September 20X4

	$'000	Exchange rate	£'000
Sales	3,760	Average — $1.65	2,278.8
Opening stock	126	Historical — $2.0	63.0
Purchases	3,620	Average —$1.65	2,193.9
Closing stock	(174)	Historical — $1.6	(108.8)
Cost of sales	3,572		2,148.1
Gross profit	188		130.7
Depreciation	53	Historical — $2.0/ 1.85*	26.8
Operating profit	135		103.9
Interest paid	(15)	Average —$1.65	(9.1)
Exchange gain	–	Balance	16.8
Profit before taxation	120		111.6
Taxation	(30)	Average — $1.65	(18.2)
Profit after taxation	90		93.4
Dividends paid in the year	(14)	Actual	(8.5)
Retained profit	76		84.9

* The charge for depreciation is translated as follows; on original assets ($45,000 @ 2 = £22,500) and on additions ($8,000 @ 1.85 = £4,300) = £26,800.

Balance sheets of S Corporation

	20X4	Exchange Rate	20X4	20X3	Exchange Rate	20X3
	$'000		£'000	$'000		£'000
Fixed assets:						
Cost (i)	255	$2.0/1.85	128.7	225	$2.0	112.5
Depreciation (ii)	98	$2.0/1.85	49.3	45	$2.0	22.5
Net book value	157		79.4	180		90.0
Current assets:						
Stocks	174	$1.6	108.8	126	$2.0	63.0
Debtors	210	$1.5	140.0	145	$2.0	72.5
Cash at bank	240	$1.5	160.0	210	$2.0	105.0
	624		408.8	481		240.5
Current liabilities:						
Trade creditors	125	$1.5	83.3	113	$2.0	56.5
Taxation	30	$1.5	20.0	18	$2.0	9.0
	155		103.3	131		65.5
Net current assets	469		305.5	350		175.0
	626		384.9	530		265.0
Loan stock	150	$1.5	100.0	130	$2.0	65.0
Net assets	476		284.9	400		200.0
Share capital	200	$2.0	100.0	200	$2.0	100.0
Retained profits	276	Balance	184.9	200	Balance	100.0
	476		284.9	400		200.0

(i) Fixed assets are translated at the historical rate which, in this example, will be the exchange rate at the date of acquisition (£1 = $2.0) or, for subsequent additions, the actual rate at the transaction date (say £1 = $1.85). The translated amount at 30 September 20X4 is ($225,000 @ 2.0 = £112,500) + ($30,000 @ 1.85 = £16,200) = £128,700.

(ii) Cumulative depreciation is translated as follows; on original assets ($90,000 @ 2.0 = £45,000) and on additions ($8,000 @ 1.85 = £4,300) = £49,300.

Analysis of exchange difference included in the profit and loss account

	Opening monetary items	Closing monetary items
	$'000	$'000
Debtors	145	210
Cash at bank	210	240
Trade creditors	(113)	(125)
Taxation	(18)	(30)
Loan stock	(130)	(150)
	(94)	(145)
Opening monetary items at opening rate — $94 @ $2	47.0	
Opening monetary item at closing rate — $94 @ $1.5	62.7	15.7
Increase in monetary items at closing rate — $51 @ $1.5	34.0	
Increase in monetary items at average rate — $51 @ $1.65	30.9	3.1
Exchange gain		18.8
Exchange difference arising on acquisition of fixed asset:		
Cash outflow on non-monetary items at actual rate $30 @ 1.85	16.2	
Cash outflow on non-monetary items at average rate $30 @ 1.65	18.2	
Exchange loss		(2.0)
Total exchange difference included in profit and loss account		16.8

It is further assumed that parent company A does not trade on its own and its only income is dividends received from S Corporation. The summarised balance sheets of company A at 30 September 20X3 and 20X4 are as follows:

Company A — Balance Sheets	20X4	20X3
	£'000	£'000
Investments in subsidiary ($500,000 @ 2.0)	250	250
Cash	208	200
Net assets	458	450
Share capital	450	450
P&L account (dividend received: $14,000 @ 1.75*)	8	–
	458	450

* actual rate on date dividend received

The summarised consolidated profit and loss account for the year ended 30 September 20X4 drawn up on the temporal method and the summarised consolidated balance sheet at that date are as follows:

Consolidated profit and loss account for the year ended 30 September 20X4

	£'000
Profit before taxation of S Corporation	111.6
Profit before taxation of company A	8.0
	119.6
Elimination of inter company dividend	(8.5)
Net operating profit	111.1
Taxation	(18.2)
Retained profit	92.9

Consolidated balance sheet at 30 September 20X4

	Average rate £'000
Fixed assets	79.4
Current assets:	
Stocks	108.8
Debtors	140.0
Cash (S Corporation: £160; company A £208)	368.0
	616.8
Current liabilities:	
Trade creditors	83.3
Taxation	20.0
	103.3
Net current assets	513.5
Total assets less current liabilities	592.9
Loan stock	100.0
Net assets	492.9
Share capital	450.0
Reserves:	
Retained profit	92.9
Goodwill written off ($ 100,000 @ 2.0)	(50.0)
	492.9

Calculation of Goodwill	£'000
Consideration £500,000 @ 2.0	250.0
Net assets per balance sheet at date of acquisition	200.0
Goodwill written off (pre-FRS 10)	50.0

Foreign branches

7.49 Where a UK company conducts its foreign operations through a foreign branch, the translation method adopted would depend on the nature of the branch operations. A foreign branch may be a legally constituted enterprise located overseas or a group of assets and liabilities which are accounted for in foreign currencies. [SSAP 20 para 37]. Where the foreign branch operates as an extension of the company's trade and its cash flows have a direct impact upon those of the company, the temporal method described in paragraphs 7.42 to 7.48 above should be used. Where the foreign branch operates as a separate business possibly with local finance it should be accounted for under the closing rate/net investment method. [SSAP 20 para 25]. This applies in the individual entity financial statements in addition to the consolidated financial statements.

7.50 The following are examples of situations where a foreign branch consists of a group of assets and liabilities that should be accounted for under the closing rate/net investment method:

- A hotel in France financed by borrowings in French francs (now euros).
- A ship or aircraft purchased in US dollars — with an associated loan in US dollars — which earns revenue and incurs expenses in US dollars.
- A foreign currency insurance operation where the liabilities are substantially covered by the holding of foreign currency assets.

7.51 In each of the above situations the local operation's currency is not the investing company's currency, since the branch operates as a separate business with local finance. Therefore, it is not appropriate to use the temporal method and the closing rate/net investment method should be used. The net investment is likely to be represented by a Head Office Account with the branch which should be translated using the closing rate. Any exchange differences arising from this retranslation process will be taken to reserves. An example of the accounting treatment followed by British Airways, which treats aircraft financed by foreign currency borrowings as a separate group of assets and liabilities is given in Table 7.5 below.

Table 7.5 — British Airways Plc — Report & Accounts — 31 March 2001

ACCOUNTING POLICIES

Tangible fixed assets (extract)

Aircraft which are financed in US dollars, either by loans, finance leases or hire purchase arrangements, are regarded together with the related assets and liabilities as a separate group of assets and liabilities and accounted for in US dollars. The amounts in US dollars are translated into sterling at rates ruling at the balance sheet date and the net differences arising from the translation of aircraft costs and related US dollar loans are taken to reserves.

7.51.1 This treatment would not be appropriate in cases where the income is earned in sterling. In such cases, the aircraft fails to qualify as a foreign branch and no corresponding gain or loss on the 'value' of the asset will be recognised. Therefore, the exchange movements on the foreign currency borrowings should be taken to the profit and loss account as they arise.

Other matters

7.52 This section deals with a number of important practical matters that arise at the consolidation stage, but which are not adequately dealt with in SSAP 20. Where UK GAAP is silent on a topic, practice has developed with reference to IFRS or US GAAP.

Determining the average rate

7.53 As stated in paragraph 7.39 above, SSAP 20 permits the profit and loss account of a foreign enterprise to be translated at an average rate for the period. SSAP 20 intentionally does not prescribe any definitive method of calculating the average rate on the grounds that the appropriate method may justifiably vary as between individual companies. However, the standard suggests that the determination of an appropriate average rate will include such matters as the company's internal accounting system, the extent of any seasonal trade variation and the desirability of using a weighting procedure. [SSAP 20 para 18].

7.54 There are a large number of methods under which an average rate can be calculated, ranging from simple monthly or quarterly averages to more sophisticated methods using appropriate weighting that reflects changes both in exchange rates and in the volume of business. Where the results of an overseas subsidiary are affected by seasonal factors, it may be necessary to weight the average exchange rate used in the calculation by applying an average rate for a shorter period than the whole year. But whatever method a company uses, it should calculate it by the method it considers is most appropriate to the foreign undertaking's circumstances. [SSAP 20 para 54]. An example of an averaging method employed in practice is given in Table 7.6 below.

Table 7.6 — The Boots Company PLC — Report and Accounts — 31 March 2001

Accounting Policies (extract)

Foreign currencies (extract)

The results and cash flows of overseas subsidiaries and the results of joint ventures are translated into sterling on an average exchange rate basis, weighted by the actual results of each month. Assets and liabilities including currency swaps are translated into sterling at the rates of exchange ruling at the balance sheet date.

7.55 In recent years many companies have moved away from using the closing rate to using an average rate for translating the profit and loss accounts of foreign enterprises. In fact, a large majority of companies now use the average rate method. The fact that the use of an average rate reflects more fairly the results and cash flows as they arise throughout the accounting period and permits aggregation of interim results appears to outweigh the relative simplicity of the closing rate method. Where a company decides to change from the closing rate method to the average rate method, the change in method represents a change of accounting policy and not a refinement of accounting policy in view of the conceptual difference between the two methods. As a consequence, a prior year adjustment is required in accordance with FRS 3 if the amounts involved are material. It may be reasonably easy for a company to justify changing its accounting policy to move to an average rate of exchange on the grounds that it is using a more appropriate method, particularly given that FRS 23 does not permit the use of the closing rate for translating the profit and loss accounts of foreign entities. However, it would generally be much harder for such a company to justify a move back to year end rates, especially where the move to an average rate has only occurred recently. An example of a company that changed from the closing rate method to the average rate method is given in Table 7.7 below.

Table 7.7 — The Peninsular and Oriental Steam Navigation Company —

Annual report and accounts — 31 December 1994

Notes to the accounts

2 Change in accounting policy for foreign currencies

Profits and losses of subsidiaries, branches and associates which have currencies of operation other than sterling are translated into sterling at average rates of exchange except for material exceptional items which are translated at rates ruling on the date of transaction. Previously such profits and losses were translated at the exchange rates ruling at the year end. The accounting policy has been changed because the directors consider the new policy gives a fairer presentation of the Group's results and cash flows as they arise during the course of an accounting period. The effect of this change in accounting policy on the results for the year ended 31 December 1994 is to increase operating profit by £2.0m (1993 £1.5m decrease), increase the interest charge by £1.1m (1993 £0.3m decrease) and increase profit before tax by £0.9m (1993 £1.3m decrease).

Dual rates or suspension of rates

7.56 The problems of dealing with dual rates or suspension of rates in the context of individual financial statements have already been discussed in paragraph 7.19 above. The same principles also apply to consolidated financial statements when determining which rate should be used to translate results of foreign enterprises using the closing rate/net investment method. There is no guidance on this subject in SSAP 20. FRS 23, however, states that where several exchange rates are available, the rate used is that at which the future cash flows represented by the transaction or balance could have been settled if those cash flows had occurred at the measurement date. [FRS 23 para 26]. The rate applicable to dividend remittances is considered more meaningful than any other rate, because this is the rate indicative of ultimate cash flows from the entity to the investing company.

Local currency

7.57 The definition of local currency as discussed in paragraph 7.13.1, is also relevant at the consolidation stage. Where the closing rate/net investment method is used, the currency of the country in which the foreign enterprise operates will usually be its local currency. Similarly, where the temporal method is used, the investing company's currency will usually be the local currency. However, this will not always be the case.

7.58 In some circumstances, a foreign entity's local currency might not be the currency of that country. For example, a UK company may have a subsidiary in Amsterdam that deals in oil. Since the international oil market is conducted in US dollars, it is likely that the US dollar is the currency in which the subsidiary operates and generates net cash flows. If the majority of the transactions are recorded locally in US dollars rather than the euro or pound sterling, no particular problem arises as the US dollar financial statements can be translated into sterling using the closing rate/net investment method. However, where the transactions are recorded in euros, it would be necessary to first restate the financial statements in US dollars using the temporal method and then retranslate the US dollar financial statements to pounds sterling using the closing/rate net investment method.

7.58.1 Many entities reporting under SSAP 20 are studying previous decisions regarding local currency and are considering the impact of FRS 23, since it is more recent and its considerations are not in conflict with SSAP 20.

Example – Local currency of an integral entity

A UK company has US$ denominated share capital and an inter-company receivable also denominated in US$. It currently has a US$ local currency under SSAP 20. However, as it is an integral part of its parent's sterling operations, it is included in the consolidated financial statements using the temporal method under SSAP 20. If the UK company had been applying the guidance on functional currency in FRS 23, it would have the same functional currency as its parent, that is, sterling. Given that the definitions of local currency in SSAP 20 and functional currency in FRS 23 are so similar, could the UK company change its local currency under SSAP 20 to sterling in its entity financial statements before it was required to adopt FRS 23?

The FRS 23 approach to determining local currency could be used as guidance while still applying SSAP 20. It does not mean adopting the whole of FRS 23 early, or even that the entity has to be in the scope of FRS 26. However, such a change in the way in which SSAP 20 is interpreted would need to result in the most appropriate accounting taking into account an entity's particular circumstances for the purpose of giving a true and fair view. [FRS 18 para 17]. Further guidance on selecting accounting policies is given in chapter 2. A change of local currency under SSAP 20 in such circumstances would be treated as a change in accounting policy and applied retrospectively. This differs from a change in local currency due to a change in the entity's underlying transactions, events and conditions, which should be applied prospectively as noted in paragraph 7.13.4.

Change from the temporal method to the closing rate method or vice-versa

7.59 A company can change the basis of translating the financial statements of a foreign enterprise from the temporal method to the closing rate method or vice versa if the financial and other operational relationships that exist between the investing company and its foreign enterprises change so as to render the method currently used inappropriate. However, as the change is brought about by changed circumstances, it does not represent a change in accounting policy and, therefore, a prior year adjustment under FRS 3 is not necessary. It follows that the effect of the change should be accounted for prospectively from the date of change. Our view is that if this date is difficult to determine, the change may be accounted for generally as from the beginning of the period as an approximation of the date of change.

7.60 A practical solution would be that where a company changes from the temporal method to the closing rate method, the adjustment attributable to translating non-monetary items, previously included at historical rate, to the closing rate should be dealt with as a reserve movement.

Example – Change from the temporal method to the closing rate method

A foreign subsidiary of a UK parent purchases an equipment having an useful life of 10 years for FC 100,000 in 1 January 20X0 when the rate of exchange was FC 8 = £1. Under the temporal method, the asset would be recorded in the consolidated financial statements at £12,500. At 31 December 20X4, the equipment has a net book value of FC 50,000 in the subsidiary's books and £6,250 in the parent's consolidated financial statements.

On 1 January 20X5 the subsidiary acquires a significant local operation financed by borrowings raised locally. Under these circumstances, the parent considers that the temporal method is no longer appropriate and changes to the closing rate method. The fixed asset remains in the subsidiary's financial statements at FC 50,000, but on consolidation the asset will have to be retranslated at the closing rate of say FC 10 = £1, which is £5,000. The difference in the carrying value using the historical exchange rate and the closing rate, that is an exchange loss of £1,250, should be debited to consolidated reserves.

7.61 Where a company changes from the closing rate method to the temporal method, because the operations of the foreign subsidiary has become significantly dependent on the parent's reporting currency, the translated amounts for non-monetary assets at the end of the prior period become the accounting basis for those assets in the period of the change and in subsequent periods. This means that there is no need to restate non-monetary assets at rates ruling when those assets were originally acquired by the foreign enterprise. Any cumulative exchange adjustments for prior periods that have been taken to reserves remain in reserves and need not be reflected in the profit and loss account of the period of change.

Inter-company dividends

7.62 Where a foreign subsidiary pays a dividend to its parent company, the dividend income should be recorded by the parent company at the rate of exchange ruling at the date when the dividend is payable. An exchange gain or loss will arise if the rate of exchange moves between the date on which the dividend becomes payable and the payment date. This exchange difference will be reported in the parent's profit and loss account as a normal inter-company transaction exchange gain or loss.

7.63 Where the temporal method is used in the group financial statements, the dividend payment should be translated at the same rate, that is, the rate of exchange ruling at the date of declaration (or proposal at the year end). This means that both the dividend payment and receipt and the related exchange differences will be eliminated on consolidation.

7.64 Under the closing rate method, it is likely that the dividend, particularly an interim dividend that is a liability of the subsidiary under its local law and is recorded in the financial statements of the foreign subsidiary will be translated either at the closing rate or at an average rate. On consolidation, the translated amount recorded in the subsidiary's profit and loss account will not cancel with the amount at which the dividend is recorded in the parent's profit and loss account because of the exchange difference. Consider the following example:

Example – Payment of inter-company dividends

A foreign subsidiary declared an interim dividend of FC 100,000 on 30 June 20X4. At that date, under local law, it was a legal liability of the subsidiary. The interim dividend was paid on 15 July 20X4. The parent prepares consolidated financial statements for the year ended 31 December 20X4 and uses the average rate for translating the results of the foreign subsidiary. The relevant exchange rates are as follows:

30 June 20X4	FC 1.50 = £1
15 July 20X4	FC 1.60 = £1
31 December 20X4	FC 1.75 = £1
Average for the year	FC 1.55 = £1

The interim dividend will be recorded in the translated profit and loss account of the foreign subsidiary and in the parent as follows:

Subsidiary's translated financial statements	£
Profit and loss account	
Interim paid FC 100,000 at average rate — FC 1.55	64,516
In parent's profit and loss account	
Initially recorded at rate when dividend is declared — FC 1.5	66,667
Exchange loss in the profit and loss account	(4,167)
Amount recorded at rate when interim dividend paid — FC 1.6	62,500

On consolidation

Parent's P&L — dividend received	66,667
Subsidiary's P&L — dividend paid	64,516
Exchange gain on consolidation	2,151

The overall exchange difference in the consolidated financial statements is a loss of £2,016 comprising the loss of £4,167 in the parent's financial statements and the gain of £2,151 arising on cancellation of the inter-company dividends.

As can be seen from the above example, the cancellation of the inter-company dividends on consolidation gives rise to a further exchange difference, in this example, a gain of £2,151. Some argue that in order for the consolidated financial statements to retain the same financial relationships shown in the subsidiary's own financial statements, the results of the subsidiary should be translated at an average rate and the exchange gain arising on cancellation of the dividends should be taken to reserves. However, we prefer the argument that the exchange difference should be taken to the consolidated profit and loss account. This means that the consolidated profit and loss account reflects the economic effect, namely:

- Profits distributed by the subsidiary are included at the sterling amount remitted. The net exchange loss of £2,016 in the consolidated profit and loss account reflects the difference between the amount remitted translated at an average rate (£64,516) and the actual rate (£62,500).
- Profits retained by the subsidiary are translated at an average exchange rate.

[The next paragraph is 7.66.]

7.66 Given that exchange differences can arise on any transaction where the settlement date is different from the date when the transaction is recorded, it may be appropriate, particularly where there is a likelihood of an exchange loss arising, to ensure that inter-company dividends are paid on the same date as they become a legal liability. In practice, this may not always be possible, so it is not uncommon for a parent company to mitigate exchange differences arising by taking out appropriate forward contracts.

Example – Treatment of forward cover of inter-company dividends

A company has an overseas subsidiary that declares a dividend that is a legal liability under its local law at the year end. At that date the parent takes out a forward contract to sell foreign currency equal in amount to the dividend that will be remitted, thereby hedging the remittance. The forward sale will be deliverable at the same date as the remittance. Considering the treatment in the parent's financial statements:

- The parent could record the dividend receivable both in the profit and loss account and in the balance sheet at the contracted rate in which case no exchange difference will arise when the cash is received, which is clearly the reason for taking out the forward contract.

- The parent could record the dividend receivable at the year end rate in the profit and loss account, but the debtor at the contracted rate. The exchange difference arising is then taken to profit and loss account.

Although the dividend recorded in the profit and loss account is not the same under the above methods, the overall effect on the profit and loss account is the same. Since the purpose of taking out the forward contract is to eliminate the effect of exchange fluctuations on the overall profit for the year, both methods achieve this objective and are, therefore, acceptable.

In the consolidated financial statements there may still be an exchange difference when the dividends are eliminated on consolidation, depending upon the translation policy. If the parent records the dividend receivable at the contracted rate and translates the results of its subsidiaries at an average rate then there will be a difference on consolidation which, as explained in the example in paragraph 7.64, we believe should be included in the consolidated profit and loss account.

Intra-group trading transactions

7.67 Where normal trading transactions take place between group companies located in different countries, exchange differences will arise which will not be eliminated on consolidation. As the transactions will probably be recorded in the local currency of one of the companies in question, exchange differences will arise, which should be reported in the profit and loss account of the enterprise in the same way as gains or losses on transactions arising with third parties. On consolidation, the net exchange gain or loss will have affected group cash flows and, therefore, it is proper that it should be included in consolidated results for the year. The exchange difference arising simply reflects the risk of doing business with a foreign party, even though that party happens to be a group member.

Example – Elimination of intra-group trading transaction where the inventory is no longer owned by the group

A UK parent company has a wholly-owned subsidiary in the US. During the year ended 31 December 20X4, the US company purchased plant and raw materials to be used in its manufacturing process from the UK parent. Details of the transactions are as follows:

	Exchange rate
Purchased plant costing £500,000 on 30 April 20X4	£1 = US$ 1.48
Paid for plant on 30 September 20X4	£1 = US$ 1.54
Purchased raw materials costing £300,000 on 31 October 20X4	£1 = US$ 1.56
Balance of £300,000 outstanding at 31 December 20X4	£1 = US$ 1.52
Average rate for the year	£1 = US$ 1.55

The following exchange gains/losses will be recorded in the profit and loss account of the US subsidiary for the year ended 31 December 20X4.

	US$	US$
Plant costing £500,000 @1.48	740,000	
Paid £500,000 @ 1.54	770,000	
Exchange loss	(30,000)	(30,000)
Raw materials costing £300,000 @1.56	468,000	
Outstanding £300,000 @1.52	456,000	
Exchange gain	12,000	12,000
Net exchange loss recorded in P&L account		(18,000)

The inter-company creditor of US$ 456,000 in the US subsidiary's balance sheet will be translated into sterling at the closing rate to £300,000 and will be eliminated against the debtor recorded in the UK parent's inter-company account. The net exchange loss of US$ 18,000 will either be translated at the average rate or the closing rate depending on whether the UK parent uses the average rate or the closing rate to translate the profit and loss account of the US subsidiary. The resulting sterling figure for exchange losses will not be eliminated on consolidation and will be reported as part of the consolidated results of the group.

Unrealised profit on stocks

7.68 It is generally accepted that intra-group profit arising from the transfer of assets between companies in the group should be eliminated in full where such assets are still held in the undertakings included in the consolidation at the balance sheet date, because it does not represent profit to the group. No specific guidance is given in SSAP 20 or in FRS 23 as to the exchange rate at which the profit should be eliminated. US GAAP is more specific in that it requires elimination at the actual rate ruling at the date of the transaction or at a weighted average rate.

Example – Elimination of intra-group transactions where the inventory is still owned by the group

The facts are the same as in the previous example except that the raw materials purchased for £300,000 by the US subsidiary are still in stock at 31 December 20X4. These goods cost the UK parent £270,000.

Therefore, unrealised profit of £30,000 would need to be eliminated on consolidation. However, elimination of this unrealised profit of £30,000 will not necessarily result in the stocks being included in the consolidated balance sheet at cost to the group where the closing rate method is used as illustrated below.

The amount for raw materials included in stock in the balance sheet of the US company at the transaction date is US$ 468,000. Under the closing rate method, the stock would be retranslated at the year end rate of 1.52 to £307,895. Therefore, the stock will be recorded in the consolidated balance sheet as follows:

	£
Cost of stock US$ 468,000 @ 1.52	307,895
Unrealised profit	(30,000)
Stock carried in consolidated balance sheet	277,895

The difference of £7,895 represents the exchange difference arising on the retranslation of the stock in the subsidiary's financial statements to the year end rate under the closing rate/net investment method, that is, £307,895 less the cost to the subsidiary of £300,000.

If, on the other hand, the parent has purchased the raw materials from the US subsidiary for US$ 468,000 at 31 October 20X4, which cost the US subsidiary US$ 421,200, and these items were still in the parent's stock at the year end, a problem arises as to what rate the unrealised profit of US$ 46,800 should be eliminated.

As stated above, if the guidance in US GAAP is followed, the profit will be eliminated at the actual rate and the stock will be recorded in the consolidated balance sheet as follows:

	£
Cost of stock US$ 468,000 @ 1.56	300,000
Unrealised profit US$ 46,800 @ 1.56	(30,000)
Stock carried in consolidated balance sheet	270,000

The amount of stock recorded in the balance sheet represents the original cost to the group of US$ 421,200 translated at the rate ruling at the date of the intra-group transaction. This is the method required by US GAAP, which can be applied under FRS 23, but it will only be appropriate for a company applying US GAAP if the results of the subsidiary are translated at weighted average rates (that is, approximating to actual rates).

This method will not be appropriate for a company applying SSAP 20 if the results of the subsidiary are translated at closing rate. In this situation the amount of profit to be eliminated is that attributable to the subsidiary in the group profit and loss account, that is, US$ 46,800 @ 1.52 = £30,789.

	£
Cost of stock US$ 468,000 @ 1.56	300,000
Unrealised profit US$ 46,800 @ 1.52	(30,789)
Stock carried in consolidated balance sheet	269,211

In practice, a majority of companies use an average rate for translating the results of foreign operations under the closing rate/net investment method. In this situation, the amount of profit to be eliminated should be calculated using that average rate.

	£
Cost of stock US$ 468,000 @ 1.56	300,000
Unrealised profit US$ 46,800 @ 1.55	(30,194)
Stock carried in consolidated balance sheet	269,806

In any event, the amount of stock recorded in the consolidated balance sheet under the closing rate/net investment method will not be the same as the actual cost to the group.

Under the temporal method, the transaction would be recorded at actual rates and, therefore, any intra-group profit eliminated will automatically bring the amount of the stock back to its cost to the group.

7.69 Even if intra-group transactions do not give rise to intra-group profit, there could still be an effect on asset values as the following example illustrates.

Example – Intra-group trading transaction at cost

A UK parent has a wholly-owned subsidiary in Pololand where the currency is Pols. The net assets of the group at 31 March 20X4 are £54,000; consisting of cash £24,000, held in the UK parent and stock held in the Pololand subsidiary costing Pols 3m, which was included in the consolidated balance sheet at the closing rate of £1 = Pols 100. On 30 September 20X4, the subsidiary transfers the goods to its UK parent at cost price when the rate of exchange is £1 = Pols 125. The transaction is settled in cash and the goods are included in parent's stock at £24,000. At 31 March 20X5, the goods are still in stock. The Polos has weakened further against sterling and the exchange rate at the balance sheet date is £1 = Pols 150.

No gain or loss is recorded by either company on the transfer, hence there are no inter-company profits to be eliminated.

	31 March 20X4
	£
Net assets:	
Stock 3m @ 100 (held by sub)	30,000
Cash (held by parent)	24,000
	54,000

		31 March 20X5
		£
Net assets:		
Stock (held by parent)		24,000
Cash 3m @ 150 (held by sub)		20,000
		44,000
Exchange difference on retranslation of opening net assets of foreign subsidiary:		
3m @ 100 =	30,000	
3m @ 150 =	20,000	10,000
		54,000

In this example, no exchange difference falls to be included in the consolidated profit and loss account as there is no trading gain or loss, but the effect of switching stock round the group affects the carrying value of the assets. If the stock had not been transferred the net assets would still have to be decreased by £10,000 but the reduction would have been entirely in the stock value with the cash balance unchanged. However, the result of moving the stock around the group is that there is a decrease of £6,000 in the stock value and a decrease of £4,000 in the group's cash position. This reflects the fact that the group's foreign currency exposure is centred on different assets.

Intra-group long-term loans and deferred trading balances

7.70 The recording of intra-group loans made by one group member to another in a currency which is different from the local currency of the borrower is no different from the recording of any other foreign currency monetary items. The borrower will initially record the foreign currency loan at the rate of exchange ruling at the date the loan is made. At each balance sheet date thereafter, until it is repaid, the loan will be translated at the closing rate and any exchange difference will be reported in the profit and loss account. On consolidation, the intra-group loan account will cancel out, but the exchange difference reported in the borrower's profit and loss account will flow through in the consolidated profit and loss account. The same principles apply to an unsettled inter-company account that arises from trading transactions, for example, where a parent finances the acquisition of a fixed asset by the foreign subsidiary through the inter-company account.

7.71 In certain circumstances, however, the parent may decide, because of tax or other benefits, to finance a foreign subsidiary with long-term loans and deferred trading balances rather than wholly with equity. In those situations, it may not be appropriate to treat such financing as an ordinary monetary item and to include the resulting exchange differences in the consolidated profit and loss account when exchange difference arising on equivalent financing with equity capital would be taken to consolidated reserves. SSAP 20 recognises this situation and states:

> *"Although equity investments in foreign enterprises will normally be made by the purchase of shares, investments may also be made by means of long-term loans and inter-company deferred trading balances. Where financing by such means is intended to be, for all practical purposes, as permanent as equity, such loans and inter-company balances should be treated as part of the investing company's net investment in the foreign enterprise; hence exchange differences arising on such loans and inter-company balances should be dealt with as adjustments to reserves."* [SSAP 20 para 20].

The definition of net investment is stated in paragraph 7.40 and includes long-term loans and deferred trading balances.

7.72 The inclusion of long-term loans and deferred trading balances as part of net investment is only permitted where the parent regards them as being as permanent as equity. The parent will effectively regard them as permanent if there is no intention that such balances will be repayable in the foreseeable future. In practice it is likely that a long-term loan of say, 15 to 20 years, would be designated by the parent as being part of the effective equity stake in the foreign enterprise. It is also likely that a short-term loan that is allowed to be continuously rolled over and not intended to be repaid, whether or not the subsidiary is able to repay it, would be regarded for all practical purposes as permanent as equity. The same principle applies to inter-company balances arising from normal trading transactions. Where it is not intended that such balances will be settled in cash for the foreseeable future, they could be regarded as part of the effective equity stake.

7.73 Where exchange differences on long-term loans and deferred trading balances which are regarded as permanent are taken to reserves on consolidation, the question arises as to whether a similar treatment can be adopted in the financial statement of the individual company. Consider the following example:

Example — Currency loan made by parent to overseas subsidiary

A UK parent is preparing its financial statements to 30 June 20X5. It has a loan receivable from its overseas subsidiary of FC 1m which has been outstanding for some time. The parent notified the overseas subsidiary at the previous year end that no repayment of the amount will be requested for the foreseeable future.

The relevant exchange rates are as follows:

		30 June 20X4	30 June 20X5
£1	=	FC 2.45	FC 2.20

In the financial statements of the parent company, the following exchange difference will arise if the loan is retranslated at the closing rate:

UK parent:	£
Exchange difference on long-term loan	
FC 1m @ 2.45	408,163
FC 1m @ 2.20	454,545
Exchange gain	46,382

On consolidation, the retranslated long-term loan will be regarded as part of the net investment in the foreign subsidiary and, therefore, the related exchange gains will be taken to reserves under the closing rate/net investment method. It should be noted that there will also be a corresponding exchange loss included in reserves, arising as part of the retranslation of the net assets (which include the FC loan creditor) of the overseas subsidiary.

The question arises as to how the long-term loan should be treated in the financial statements of the parent company. Some take the view that the loan should be regarded as a monetary item and any exchange difference taken to the profit and loss account. This is because the definition of net investment in SSAP 20 applies to consolidated and not entity accounts. However, we consider that this is a restrictive interpretation.

The parent is exposed to foreign currency risk on the FC loan but, as it does not expect any repayment for the foreseeable future or until the investment is sold, the exchange risk is potentially eliminated. If the long-term loan can be regarded as a permanent investment on consolidation then it is reasonable to treat it in a similar manner in the parent's financial statements. This means that the long-term loan will not be retranslated in the books of the parent, but will be carried at the historical rate of exchange such that no exchange difference arises in the parent's financial statements.

This reflects the substance of the loan. Note that this approach of retaining the long-term loan at historical rates is not permitted by FRS 23.

The situation is more complicated if the long-term loan is financed by foreign borrowings in the parent company in which case the long-term loan would be retranslated to offset currency differences on the borrowings. This is dealt with in detail from paragraph 7.79.

Another problem that might arise is the appropriate treatment that should be adopted in the year in which the parent decides to designate any long-term loans or deferred trading balances as effective equity stakes. In the above example, the long-term FC loan was designated as being part of the parent's net investment in the overseas subsidiary from the beginning of the accounting period. If the parent did this part way during the year, say, at 31 December 20X4, it would be appropriate for the parent to treat the long-term loan as a monetary item up to that date and take any exchange difference arising to its profit and loss account. The exchange rate at the date that the loan is designated as permanent equity will be regarded as the historical rate for the purpose of translating the non-monetary asset and so no further exchange differences on the long-term loan will arise in the parent's financial statements.

7.74 In the above example, where the foreign currency loan is regarded as being as permanent as equity, there is no exchange difference in the profit and loss account of the parent company or in the group profit and loss account. However, the situation will differ where the loan is denominated in sterling such that it is the subsidiary that is exposed to the currency risk as there will be an exchange difference in the subsidiary's profit and loss account. Consider the following example:

Example — Sterling loan made by parent to overseas subsidiary

A UK parent is preparing its financial statements to 30 June 20X5. It has a deferred trading balance of £200,000 owed by its overseas subsidiary.

The relevant exchange rates are as follows:

		30 June 20X4	30 June 20X5
£1	=	FC 8.14	FC 7.71

In the financial statements of the individual companies, the following exchange differences will arise if the deferred trading balance is retranslated at the closing rate.

UK parent
There is no exchange difference in the parent's financial statements in respect of the deferred trading balance as this is denominated in sterling.

Overseas subsidiary
Exchange difference on deferred trading balance

£200,000 @ 8.14	FC	1,628,000
£200,000 @ 7.71	FC	1,542,000
Exchange gain	FC	86,000
Exchange gain translated at closing rate (@ 7.71)		£11,154

The exchange gain of FC 86,000 on the deferred trading account should be taken to the profit and loss account of the overseas subsidiary. This is because the trading transactions were originally carried out in the parent's currency and the subsidiary was exposed to the foreign currency risk. Therefore, it is appropriate to take the exchange difference to the subsidiary's profit and loss account.

On consolidation, the exchange gain in the subsidiary's profit and loss account will be translated into sterling (£11,154 assuming that the group uses the closing rate to translate its subsidiaries' results). The normal treatment would be to include this exchange gain in the consolidated profit and loss account. However, as the long-term loan is regarded as part of the net investment in the subsidiary, the exchange gain of £11,154 should be taken to reserves in the consolidated financial statements. There will be a corresponding exchange loss included in reserves arising as part of the retranslation of the net assets of the overseas subsidiary. The effect is that the consolidated profit and loss account will not reflect any exchange difference on the deferred trading balance, which is consistent with the fact that the deferred trading balance has no impact on group cash flows.

7.75 The two examples above consider the accounting implications when a loan is made by the parent company to an overseas subsidiary. In the case of a foreign currency upstream loan, that is, a borrowing by a UK parent company from the subsidiary in the subsidiary's local currency, the treatment of exchange differences in the consolidated financial statements will depend on the treatment in the parent company's own financial statements. Such loans are often regarded as hedging transactions because they reduce the net foreign currency investment in the subsidiary (see further para 7.90). If the borrowing is accounted for in the parent's financial statements as a hedge under the SSAP 20 offset procedure (see para 7.81 for details of the SSAP 20 offset procedure) then exchange differences on the borrowing are taken to reserves (insofar as they offset exchange differences on the investment being hedged) and do not appear in the parent company's profit and loss account. A similar treatment will apply in the consolidated financial statements.

Translation of subsidiary's non-coterminous accounts

7.75.1 The question may arise as to what exchange rate should be used when a foreign subsidiary's results are prepared up to a different date than that of the parent. FRS 2, 'Accounting for subsidiary undertakings', permits the use of financial statements for a period ending not more than three months before the parent's year end, where it is impracticable to prepare interim financial statements to the parent's year end. Therefore, the rate should be the year end date at which the subsidiary's financial statements are prepared. However, FRS 2 also requires that any changes that have taken place in the intervening period that materially affect the view given by the group's financial statements should be taken into account by adjustments in the preparation of the consolidated financial statements. In such cases, if the foreign exchange movements in the intervening period materially affect the consolidated financial statements, the rate as at the group's year-end should be used as a consolidation adjustment.

Goodwill arising on consolidation

7.76 Goodwill may arise on consolidation where a company acquires the equity share capital of a foreign subsidiary. Under SSAP 22, this goodwill may have been either written off to reserves or capitalised as an intangible asset and amortised through the profit and loss account over its useful economic life. Where the foreign investment is accounted for under the closing rate/net investment method, the question arises as to whether or not the goodwill, once calculated at acquisition, should be retranslated each year at closing rate.

7.77 In the example illustrating the application of the closing rate method in paragraph 7.41 above, goodwill is translated at the rate ruling on the date of acquisition and written off to reserves. It is not included in the retranslation of the opening net assets on the grounds that it arises only on consolidation and is not part of the net assets of the foreign enterprise. Under this view the goodwill is regarded as a sterling asset whose carrying amount does not fluctuate when the rate of exchange changes.

7.78 However, following the publication of FRS 10, which requires goodwill to be capitalised as an intangible asset and amortised through the profit and loss account over its useful economic life, most companies would regard goodwill as a foreign currency asset and include it in the retranslation of the opening net investment. Furthermore, the view that goodwill is a sterling asset that is not part of the net assets of the foreign enterprise was probably justified when goodwill was allowed to be written off to reserves, but does not appear to be credible any longer because FRS 11 requires capitalised goodwill to be attributed or apportioned to income generating units for the purposes of carrying out impairment reviews. The combination of FRS 10 and FRS 11 provides strong support for regarding goodwill as a currency asset that is very much a part of the net assets of the foreign investment. Accordingly, the exchange difference arising on foreign currency borrowings used to finance or provide a hedge against the foreign investment, that otherwise would have been taken to the profit and loss account had goodwill not been retranslated, will be available for offset against the exchange difference arising on the retranslated goodwill.

7.78.1 Furthermore, treating goodwill as a currency asset and retranslating it at the closing rate is the method required by FRS 23, 'The effects of changes in foreign exchange rates'.

7.78.2 An example of a company that has treated goodwill as a currency asset for hedging purposes is given in the Table 7.8 below.

Table 7.8 — Automated Security (Holdings) PLC — Report and Financial Statements — 30 November 1994

Accounting Policies (extract)

10. FOREIGN EXCHANGE

Foreign currency assets and liabilities of Group companies are translated into sterling at the rates of exchange ruling at the balance sheet date. The trading results of overseas subsidiaries and associated undertakings are translated at the average exchange rate ruling during the year, with the adjustment between average rates and the rates ruling at the balance sheet date being taken to reserves. The difference arising on the restatement of the opening net investment, including goodwill, to overseas subsidiary and associated undertakings, and of matching foreign currency loans and foreign currency swap facilities, are dealt with as adjustments to other reserves. All other exchange differences are dealt with in the profit and loss account.

NOTES TO THE FINANCIAL STATEMENTS

21. RESERVES (extract)	Group £'000	Company £'000
(d) OTHER RESERVES		
At 1st December 1993	(87,560)	80
Goodwill in the year written off (note 24)	(20,193)	–
Goodwill of associated undertakings transferred to profit and loss account	17,365	–
Exchange adjustments on:		
Net investments including goodwill	(6,945)	–
Hedging arrangements	2,136	–
Goodwill	4,516	–
At 30th November 1994	(90,681)	80

24 GOODWILL	Cost of goodwill eliminated £'000	Exchange adjustments £'000	Total £'000
Eliminated to 30th November 1993	196,496	7,482	203,978
Acquisitions in the year			
– Associated undertakings	17,466	–	17,466
– Other businesses acquired	1,769	–	1,769
Adjustments to previous year's acquisitions	535	–	535
Share of goodwill movements of associated undertakings	423	–	423
	20,193		20,193
Transferred to profit and loss account	(17,365)	–	(17,365)
Exchange adjustments (note 21 (d))	–	(4,516)	(4,516)
Eliminated to 30th November 1994	199,324	2,966	202,290

7.78.3 Further complexities arise where goodwill was written off to reserves (pre FRS 10).

Example – Treatment of retranslated goodwill on disposal of foreign subsidiary

A company treats goodwill written off to reserves as a currency item and re-translates it each year at the closing rate. (The goodwill all related to overseas acquisitions). As a result the disclosed figure for goodwill written off changes each year. The company has disposed of a subsidiary. Should it take the previously written off goodwill through the profit and loss account at the historical amount or at the most recently retranslated amount?

If the company has consistently retranslated goodwill, and the annual disclosure of cumulative goodwill is on the retranslated basis, then goodwill passed through profit and loss account on disposal should also be on this retranslated basis.

[The next paragraph is 7.79.]

Foreign equity investments financed by foreign borrowings

Treatment in individual company

7.79 As stated in paragraph 7.24.2, in certain circumstances the normal rule that non-monetary items should be carried in the balance sheet at their historical cost at the exchange rate ruling when they were originally acquired without further retranslation, does not apply to foreign equity investments. The exception arises in circumstances where a company or a group has used foreign currency borrowings to finance foreign equity investments, or to provide a hedge against the exchange risk associated with existing foreign equity investments.

7.80 If the normal rules of translation of monetary and non-monetary items are applied to the circumstances mentioned above, any exchange gain or loss on the borrowings would be taken to the profit and loss account, while no exchange gain or loss would arise on the equity investments. SSAP 20 recognises that in such circumstances, as no economic gain or loss would in fact arise where there is a movement in exchange rates, it would be inappropriate to recognise any accounting profit or loss. [SSAP 20 para 28].

7.81 Therefore, provided the conditions set out in paragraph 7.82 below apply, the company *may* denominate its equity investments in the appropriate foreign currency. This means that the investment will be regarded as a currency investment and the company will need to translate the carrying amount at the closing rate each year for inclusion in its financial statements. Where a company treats investments in this way, it should take direct to reserves any exchange differences that arise when the investments are retranslated. It should also take the exchange differences on the related foreign currency borrowings to reserves and not to the profit and loss account to be offset against those exchange differences. [SSAP 20 para 51]. This is known as the 'cover' method or 'offset' procedure.

7.81.1 In some cases a parent may elect to carry investments in subsidiaries at a valuation equal to net asset value (i.e under the alternative accounting rules, please refer to Chapter 6.77). Therefore, in the parent company's individual financial statements, the net asset value at the end of the year retranslated at the year end rate will be the new carrying value of the investment. The difference between this amount and the carrying value at the beginning of the year will be the increase in value. There will be an element of exchange difference included in this revaluation increase for the year, and it is appropriate for the holding company to split the revaluation between the element that relates to a genuine revaluation and an element that is an exchange difference, being the exchange difference arising on retranslating the opening carrying value at the closing rate. This latter element can be taken to profit and loss reserve or foreign currency translation reserve instead of a revaluation reserve and offset against the exchange difference arising on the loan. Any excess exchange difference on the loan is taken to the profit and loss account.

7.82 The conditions for offset under SSAP 20, all of which must apply, are as follows:

- In any accounting period, exchange gains or losses arising on the borrowings may be offset only to the extent of exchange differences arising on the equity investments.
- The foreign currency borrowings, whose exchange gains or losses are used in the offset process, should not exceed, in the aggregate, the total amount of cash that the investments are expected to be able to generate, whether from profits or otherwise.
- The accounting treatment adopted should be applied consistently from period to period.

[SSAP 20 para 51].

Offset restriction

7.83 The first condition deals with situations where there is not an exact match between the borrowings and the investments (either in amount or currency or both) and greater exchange gains or losses arise on the loans than are available for offset against the investments. Since the excess gains or losses are deemed to be speculative in nature they are not allowed to be used for offset in reserves and must be taken to the profit and loss account. Therefore, only that portion of the total gains or losses on the loans which is matched by an opposite exchange movement on the investments falls to be taken to reserves for offset purposes.

7.84 Whilst it is to be expected that for the cover to operate, exchange gains or losses on the borrowings would be matched by opposite exchange losses or gains arising on the investments, it is possible, particularly where investments are managed on a pool basis and financed by a basket of loans in different currencies, for both the borrowings and the investments to show either exchange gains or losses. In this context, it should be noted that the cover method need not be restricted to individual investments and borrowings. It can also be applied to a group of investments financed by a variety of different currencies. However, where an investment or a number of investments has been financed by a specific borrowing the offset should be applied on an individual matched basis, rather than putting them in a general pool.

Example – Illustration of the offset restriction when foreign equity investments are denominated in the relevant foreign currency

A UK company is preparing its financial statements for the year ended 30 June 20X5. On 31 December 20X4 it raised a loan of US$ 2m in order to finance two equity investments, one in Denmark costing DK 1,500,000 and the other in Canada costing C$ 2,500,000. The relevant exchange rates are:

31 December 20X4	£1 = US$ 1.48 = DK 8.89 = C$ 2.45
30 June 20X5	£1 = US$ 1.55 = DK 8.39 = C$ 2.54

	Exchange difference	P&L account	Reserves
	£	£	£
Exchange difference on investment in Danish company			
31/12/X4 — DK 1,500,000 @ 8.89	168,729		
30/06/X5 — DK 1,500,000 @ 8.39	178,784		
Exchange gain	10,055		
Exchange difference on investment in Canadian company			
31/12/X4 — C$ 2,500,000 @ 2.45	1,020,408		
30/06/X5 — C$ 2,500,000 @ 2.54	984,252		
Exchange loss	(36,156)		
Net exchange loss on equity investments	(26,101)		(26,101)
Exchange difference on US$ loan			
31/12/X4 — US$ 2m @ $1.48	1,351,351		
30/06/X5 — US$ 2m @ $1.55	1,290,323		
Exchange gain	61,028	34,927	26,101

In this example, the amount of the exchange gain on the loan that the company can offset as a reserve movement against the exchange loss on the investments is limited to £26,101. The excess gain of £34,927 is deemed to be speculative and, therefore, is taken to the profit and loss account.

7.85 If, in the example, there had been a loss on exchange on the loan for the year ended 30 June 20X5 of, say, £65,000 and a net gain on exchange on the investments of, say, £35,000, the amount of the exchange loss on the loan that the company could have offset as a reserve movement against the exchange gain on the investment would have been limited to £35,000. The company would have had to include the balance of the exchange loss on the loan (that is, £30,000) in its profit or loss on ordinary activities for the year.

7.86 On the other hand, if in the example there had been either a net gain on exchange on the retranslation of the equity investments as well as an exchange gain on the loan (or a net loss on exchange on the retranslation of the equity investments as well as an exchange loss on the loan) the company would have had to take the whole of the gain or loss on exchange on the equity investments to reserves and the whole of the gain or loss on the loan to its profit or loss on ordinary activities for the year. This is because the offset conditions place no limit on the amount of gain or loss on investments that may be taken to reserves, but limit the amount of the gain or loss on borrowings that may be taken to reserves to the amount of the loss or gain on the investments.

Borrowing restriction

7.87 The second condition is designed to ensure that the hedge is genuine by requiring that the borrowing is not greater than the total amount of cash generated from the investment. However, no guidance is given as to how the cash generation is to be measured or how long the foreign undertaking is given to generate profits. The condition should not cause any undue problem where a borrowing that is invested in a profitable company is sufficiently long-term to enable that company to generate sufficient profits to cover the borrowing. However, where the foreign enterprise is unprofitable or earns negligible profits not sufficient to cover the cash outflows on the borrowings, the expected cash generated will be represented by the net realisable value of the investment at the balance sheet date. To the extent that the net realisable value is less than the book value of the investment, the borrowing used for offset should be restricted accordingly. Restriction might also apply where the foreign enterprise is subject to severe exchange control restrictions such that the expected cash generated from the investment is considered to be insufficient to cover the borrowing. The next example illustrates this provision.

Example – Illustration of the borrowing restriction when foreign equity investments are denominated in the relevant foreign currency

Some years ago, a UK company raised a foreign currency loan in Argentina to finance the acquisition of a company in that country. Both at 31 March 20X4 and at 31 March 20X5, the loan amounted to Peso 5m, and the equity investment amounted to Peso 7m. The company is preparing its financial statements to 31 March 20X5 and considers that the total amount of cash that the investment is able to generate will be 4m Argentinean Pesos. The exchange rates are as follows:

31 March 20X4 £1 = Peso 1.6
31 March 20X5 £1 = Peso 1.4

In this example, the maximum amount of borrowings that can be used for offset purposes is limited to the net realisable value of the investment.

	Exchange difference	P&L account	Reserves
	£	£	£
Exchange difference on loan			
31/03/X4 — Peso 5m @ 1.6	3,125,000		
31/03/X5 — Peso 5m @ 1.4	3,571,429		
Exchange loss	(446,429)	(89,286)	(357,143)
But restricted to net realisable value of investment			
31/03/X4 — Peso 4m @ 1.6	2,500,000		
31/03/X5 — Peso 4m @ 1.4	2,857,143		
Exchange gain			357,143

In this example, the amount of the exchange loss arising on the loan that can be offset in reserves against the exchange gain arising on the investment is £357,143. The remaining exchange loss on the loan of £89,286 must be taken to the profit and loss account.

In addition, the company will also have to write down the investment for permanent diminution in value of Peso 3m as illustrated below.

		P&L account
	£	£
Equity investment		
Opening carrying value Peso 7m @ 1.6	4,375,000	
Permanent diminution Peso 3m @ 1.6	(1,875,000)	1,875,000
	2,500,000	
Retranslation gain (taken to reserves)	357,143	
Realisable value Peso 4m @ 1.4	2,857,143	

Therefore, the total charge in the profit and loss account for the year is £1,964,286 comprising permanent diminution of £1,875,000 and excess exchange loss on retranslation of the loan of £89,286.

7.88 Although, in the above example, it has been assumed that the company is able to determine the amount of the cash which the investment is expected to generate, in practice, it may be difficult or impractical to forecast the total cash to be generated from the investment, both from profits and from its ultimate realisation because of the speculative nature of long-term cash flow projections. It may also be that the investment cash flows are never converted into the currency of the borrowing because they are expected to be reinvested. In that situation, as a practical expediency the alternative would be to consider the amount that would be raised if the investment were sold immediately. If this amount is at least equal to the book value of the investment, then the whole of the book value is available for use in the offset calculation.

Consistent accounting treatment

7.89 Given that the application of the cover method is fairly flexible the third condition outlined in paragraph 7.82 above is simply designed to ensure that a company does not change its accounting treatment depending on the way in which exchange rates move, but adopts a consistent policy as laid down in FRS 18. For example, where exchange rate movements give rise to exchange losses on borrowings, and the first two conditions apply, it is obviously advantageous for a company to be able to use the offset procedure. If, however, in a subsequent year, exchange rate movements give rise to exchange gains on those borrowings, and the first two conditions still apply, the company must still use the offset procedure. It cannot include the exchange gains in its profit on ordinary activities.

Hedging by means of upstream loans

7.90 It is sometimes appropriate for a UK direct or indirect parent company to borrow from its overseas subsidiary. If the borrowing is in the subsidiary's local currency and the borrowed funds are converted into sterling or invested elsewhere in the business, this reduces the group's net assets in the foreign currency and, therefore, has the same effect that an external borrowing in the currency, used in the same way, would have had. This means that in the parent's individual accounts, the intra-group borrowing can be treated as a hedge against the equity investment under the provisions of paragraph 51 of SSAP 20, that is, exchange differences on the loan can be offset (subject to the criteria in the standard) against exchange differences on the investment which is treated as a currency asset and retranslated. Companies entering into such transactions with their overseas subsidiaries should seek specialist taxation advice as the rules in this area are complex.

Termination of hedging during the year

7.91 The application of the consistency principle becomes particularly relevant where hedging is terminated during the year following either the repayment of the foreign currency borrowing or the sale of the foreign equity investment. In those situations, the offset procedure should be applied up to the date of repayment of the loan or the date of sale of the investment and not stopped at the previous year end. Termination of a hedge is considered in the example below.

Example – Termination of hedging during the year and the impact of the consistency principle

A UK company, which prepares its financial statements to 30 June each year, borrowed US$ 2m to finance the acquisition of a company in Hong Kong costing HK$ 12m (£1,049,869) some years ago. The company's accounting policy is to take unrealised exchange differences on long-term borrowings that are matched with currency equity investments, direct to reserves. On 31 December 20X4, the company repaid the borrowing which resulted in an exchange gain. How should the gain arising on the repayment be treated in its financial statements for the year ended 30 June 20X5 and at what value should the equity investment be recorded in the balance sheet at 30 June 20X5?

The relevant exchange rates are as follows:

30 June 20X4	£1 = US$ 1.54	£1 = HK$ 11.93
31 December 20X4	£1 = US$ 1.56	£1 = HK$ 12.10
30 June 20X5	£1 = US$ 1.59	£1 = HK$ 12.31

	Exchange difference	P&L account	Reserves
	£	£	£
Equity investments			
30/06/X4 — HK$ 12m @ 11.93	1,005,868		
31/12/X4 — HK$ 12m @ 12.10	991,736		
Exchange loss	(14,132)		(14,132)
Loan			
30/06/X4 — US$ 2m @ 1.54	1,298,701		
31/12/X4 — US$ 2m @ 1.56	1,282,051		
Exchange gain	16,650	2,518	14,132

Given that the hedging continues up to the date of repayment of the borrowing and ceases thereafter, the company should continue with its consistent policy of taking the exchange gain on the loan to reserves to be matched with the exchange loss on the equity investment until 31 December 20X4. Since the amount of the exchange gain to be offset in reserves is limited to £14,132, the balance of £2,518 should be included in the profit and loss account for the year.

As far as the carrying value of the investment at 30 June 20X5 is concerned, the investment should be recorded at £991,736, its carrying value at the date when cover ceased (that is, 31 December 20X4). The rationale is that after the cover has been removed the investment ceases to be a currency asset and should thereafter be treated as a non-monetary asset without any further retranslation until such time as another loan is taken out to provide a hedge.

Some would argue that the investment should be recorded at the carrying value at the previous balance sheet date, that is, £1,005,868 on the grounds that, as there are no borrowings at the year end, the cover is deemed to have ceased at the beginning of the period. But this treatment fails to recognise the fact that the hedging continued until the date of repayment of the loan. Others might opt to record the investment at its historical cost of £1,049,869. The effect of this would be to reverse cumulative exchange differences of £58,133 (£1,049,869 – £991,736) on the investment that had been taken to reserves. This treatment ignores the fact that hedging on the investment ever took place.

7.92 If the foreign currency investment is sold, but the borrowing is retained, no particular problem arises. The company should apply the offset procedure up to the date of sale of the investment and not stop at the previous year end. At the date of sale, the borrowing changes its nature and becomes a borrowing that is not a hedge. Therefore, any movement from that date to the balance sheet date should be taken to the profit and loss account. Even if that were to show a loss while a hedge, and a profit while not a hedge, that would still be the proper treatment.

Borrowings taken out before or after the investment

7.93 The standard permits the cover method to apply to borrowings that have been taken out before or after the investment is made, because they can be designated as hedges against a new investment or an existing equity investment. In these situations, the period during which the borrowings are in place is different from the period during which the investments are held. Although no guidance is provided in the standard as to how the cover method should operate in these circumstances, it would appear that for the cover method to operate sensibly, the exchange differences on the borrowings that may be offset against the investments should be those that arise during the period when the hedge is effective.

Example – Borrowings taken out after the foreign equity investment in a subsidiary

Some years ago, a UK company acquired all the share capital of an overseas company for FC 10m when the rate of exchange was £1 = FC 10. The investment was carried at historical cost of £1m. On 30 June 20X4, the directors considered the investment to be worth FC 12m and took out a long-term loan of FC 12m to provide a hedge against the investment. The proceeds of the loan were used to reduce an existing sterling borrowing. The relevant exchange rates at 30 June 20X4 and 31 December 20X4 are £1 = FC 8.4 and £1 = FC 8.00 respectively. How should the company apply the cover method for the year ended 31 December 20X4?

The company can apply the cover method in the following ways:

The most straightforward method and the one which recognises the economic rationale of taking out the hedge is to record the investment at directors' valuation of FC 12m (£1,428,571) at 30 June 20X4. The difference between this value and the historical cost, that is, £428,571 is taken to the revaluation reserve. Since the investment and the borrowing are now perfectly matched after 30 June 20X4, the exchange differences arising on the retranslation of both the investment and the loan will cancel out in reserves and no exchange difference on the loan will fall to be taken to the profit and loss account. Note that in order to record the investment at the directors' valuation, the alternative accounting rules in Schedule 4 to the Companies Act must be applied. The implications of this are considered in chapter 6.

Alternatively, if the company does not wish to record the investment at the directors' valuation of FC 12m then, under the approach set out in paragraph 7.93 above, the exchange difference on the investment that arises during the period in which it is hedged is regarded as being available for offset against the exchange differences arising on the loan during the same period. To achieve this, the investment is first treated as a currency asset at 30 June 20X4, the date the loan was taken out, and recorded at £1,190,476 (FC 10m @ 8.4), the exchange gain of £190,476 being taken directly to reserves as it represents a revaluation surplus. Once the investment has been established as a currency asset and its value determined for offset purposes, no further problem arises and the normal rules apply as indicated below.

	Exchange difference	P&L account	Reserves
Equity investment	£	£	£
30/06/X4 — FC 10m @ 8.4	1,190,476		
31/12/X4 — FC 10m @ 8.0	1,250,000		
Exchange gain	59,524		59,524
Loan			
30/06/X4 — FC 12m @ 8.4	1,428,571		
31/12/X4 — FC 12m @ 8.0	1,500,000		
Exchange loss	(71,429)	(11,905)	(59,524)

It can be seen that a proportion of the exchange loss on the loan remains unutilised and is taken to the profit and loss account. If the directors had revalued the investment to FC 12m and followed the first approach outlined above, all of the exchange difference would have been taken to reserves. The first approach is considered to be superior as it better reflects the transaction's underlying purpose.

7.94 The situation where a borrowing is taken out before the investment is made is relatively straightforward. The cover should only apply for the period when the hedge is effective. This means that any exchange difference arising on the borrowing prior to the date that the investment is made should be taken to the profit and loss account. Thereafter, the normal rules of offset apply.

Carrying value of foreign equity investment

7.95 Paragraph 51(a) of SSAP 20 allows exchange gains and losses on foreign currency borrowings to be offset in reserves only to the extent of exchange differences arising on the foreign equity investments. Therefore, where companies use foreign currency borrowings to finance or provide a hedge against foreign equity investments, it may be necessary to consider the accounting policy for the carrying value of those investments. Furthermore, as this is likely to have taxation implications and the rules are complex in this area, specialist tax advice may be necessary.

7.96 The appropriate accounting policy is likely to be influenced by the treasury policy, for instance whether the company chooses to hedge against the investment's cost, the subsidiary's underlying net assets or the underlying fair value. A company applying SSAP 20 as opposed to FRS 26 has a number of choices of policy for the carrying value include the following:

- Cost (reduced to recoverable amount in the event of impairment).
- Net asset value (annual revaluation). It should be noted that if this policy is adopted, the carrying amount of the investment immediately after an acquisition will be reduced by any amount relating to goodwill. It may, however, be an appropriate policy if the subsidiaries were acquired a number of years ago or were set up by the parent, such that the net asset values being hedged are significantly in excess of original cost.

- Directors' valuation (periodic as required). This could be based on cost plus retained post-acquisition profits, or an estimate of the realisable value in the market place.

7.97 Whichever policy is adopted, it must be applied consistently from year to year. Any change in policy would have to be justified on the grounds that the new policy is preferable to the one it replaces, because it will give a fairer presentation of the reporting entity's results and financial position. [FRS 3 para 62; FRS 18 paras 30 to 49].

7.98 Where an investment is designated as a foreign currency asset and is carried at a valuation, it will be necessary to analyse separately the effect of exchange rate movements on the opening value of the investment and the effect of a revaluation of the foreign currency carrying value.

Example – Analysis of the impact in changes in foreign exchange rates on the opening value and the impact of revaluation of the investment

A UK company has an investment in a US subsidiary which is financed by US$ borrowings. It continues to apply SSAP 20 as opposed to FRS 26 and adopts a policy of net asset value for the carrying value of the investment.

	31 December 20X0	31 December 20X1
Net asset value of subsidiary	$100m	$110m
Exchange rate	2.0	1.67
Net asset value in sterling	£50m	£66m

The increase in value of £16m is analysed as follows:

	£m
Exchange gain on retranslation of opening net assets ($100m @ 1.67 — $100m @ 2.0) — taken to reserves for offset with exchange loss on borrowings	10
Gain on revaluation at the year end ($110m — $100m = $10m @ 1.67) — taken to revaluation reserves	6
	16

In the above example, it has been assumed that the whole of the increase in net assets of $10m arising from the increase in profits arose at the end of the year. In practice, however the profits will arise throughout the year. Therefore, it may be possible to split the $10m increase between a real revaluation gain that is taken to the revaluation reserve and a further exchange difference that recognises the fact that the increase in net assets occurs not on the last day of the year, but over the course of the year. For example, if the average exchange rate is £1 = $1.85, the increase in the value of £16m could be analysed as follows:

	£m
Exchange gain on retranslation of opening net assets ($100m @ 1.67 — $100m @ 2.0) — taken to profit and loss reserves for offset with exchange loss on borrowings	10.0
Exchange gain arising on the increase in net assets from use of average rate ($10m @ 1.67 — $10m @ 1.85) — taken to profit and loss reserves for offset with exchange loss on borrowings	0.6
Gain on revaluation = increase in net assets at average rate ($10m @ 1.85) — taken to revaluation reserves	5.4
	16.0

Although the effect of the above calculation is to squeeze out a further amount of exchange difference from the overall revaluation increase that may properly be taken to profit and loss account reserve for offset against the exchange loss on the borrowings, there is nothing in the standard to suggest that this treatment is inappropriate. Indeed, it makes good sense and is consistent with what actually happens in practice, that is, the company is hedging its net investments at the end of each year, provided of course the offset and the borrowing restrictions discussed above are not breached.

Partial hedges

7.99 Paragraph 51 of SSAP 20 refers to a company using foreign currency borrowings to finance its foreign equity investments, but it is not specific as to the extent to which an asset has to be financed in this way. We consider that the general interpretation should be that the investment is entirely or mostly financed by foreign currency borrowings as it would be contrary to the spirit of the standard if a low level of borrowings, say five per cent of the asset amount, could result in the asset being regarded as a foreign currency asset and, consequently, the exchange differences on the borrowings being taken to reserves rather than to the profit and loss account.

7.100 However, there may be circumstances where a less restrictive interpretation is appropriate. For instance, if a group has an overall balance sheet gearing of say 30 per cent and as a matter of policy wants to borrow, for all major subsidiaries, 30 per cent of the asset's carrying value in the relevant currency, then it would seem reasonable to regard the investment as a foreign currency asset. The question then arises as to the appropriate treatment for translation of the partially hedged investment.

7.101 One view is that the whole amount of the partially hedged investment is regarded as a foreign currency asset even though the borrowing in the relevant currency is only, say, 30 per cent of the carrying value of the investment. The effect of regarding such investments as foreign currency assets is that differences on the retranslation of the whole investment go to reserves, but they are only partially matched by differences on a smaller amount of borrowings. Some take the view that this is preferable to the alternative of regarding 30 per cent of the investment as a foreign currency asset and 70 per cent as a sterling asset.

7.102 However, there is also an argument in favour of this alternative treatment which is that the purpose under the offset procedures of retranslating the investment is solely to allow the exchange difference on the borrowings to be relieved, to reflect the fact that there is no economic risk. Taking this view, it would, therefore, make sense to limit the exchange difference recognised on the investment to that on the borrowing. We believe that either method is acceptable provided that it is consistently applied to all investments that are partially hedged.

Intermediate holding companies

7.103 A UK parent company may hold shares in an overseas intermediate holding company that holds investments in further overseas subsidiaries in various countries. A common example is for an intermediate holding company to be based in the Netherlands. If the UK parent company has taken out foreign currency borrowings to finance or hedge its investment then the SSAP 20 offset procedures will apply. At first sight, the UK parent would have a euro investment. However, economically, the investment is a multi-currency asset, that is, its value depends on fluctuations of the currencies in which the underlying subsidiaries operate. In this situation, the investment in the overseas intermediate holding company can be accounted for as a multi-currency asset such that exchange differences on foreign currency borrowings used as hedges can be offset against the exchange differences on each component of the multi-currency asset.

Example – Hedging of intermediate holding companies

A UK company holds subsidiaries in Canada, Hong Kong and Australia through an intermediate Dutch Holding company. The original cost of the investment in the Dutch company was €135m (equivalent to £90m). The Dutch company has no assets other than shares in the three subsidiaries. The UK company borrows C$ 150m to hedge the Canadian subsidiary and HK$ 360m to hedge the Hong Kong subsidiary, but does not hedge the investment in the Australian subsidiary. The relevant figures are as follows:

	Canadian Co	Australian Co	Hong Kong Co
	C$ m	A$ m	HK$ m
Cost	100	80	400
Net asset value			
– on acquisition	70	40	350
– post acquisition retained profits	100	10	(30)
– total	170	50	320
Financed by borrowings	150	–	360

All the assets of the Dutch company are shares in the overseas subsidiaries and, therefore, the investment in the Dutch company can be regarded as a multi-currency asset. In order to offset the exchange differences on the borrowings, it will be necessary for the UK company to establish a multi-currency carrying value in the relevant currencies by looking through the Dutch company and building up the carrying value by reference to the appropriate carrying value of the subsidiaries. Possible choices include the following:

- Cost — this would be C$ 100m + A$ 80m + HK$ 400m (reduced to a lower value if the reduction in reserves is regarded as representing a permanent diminution in value). However, a carrying value of cost is insufficient to allow the exchange differences on the whole of the C$150m borrowing to be taken to reserves.

- Net asset value — this would be C$ 170m + A$ 50m + HK$ 320m. However, this policy does not allow exchange differences on the whole of the HK$ 360m borrowing to be taken to reserves.

- Directors' valuation — a number of different bases could be adopted as a policy, for example, a valuation based on net asset value, cost plus retained post-acquisition reserves or a valuation based on the earnings stream.

In this example, the Australian investment is not hedged, and the implications of this need to be considered. If the UK company directly held the three subsidiaries then the C$ and HK$ investments that are hedged could be regarded as foreign currency assets whereas the A$ investment would remain a sterling investment. Where there is a Dutch intermediate holding company that has no other assets then it is possible to look through this company and split the investment into its component parts so that the same result is obtained as if the subsidiaries were directly held.

If the UK company's policy is to record investments at cost, the C$ and HK$ investments would retain a fixed cost in C$ and HK$ but this would be retranslated each year into varying sterling amounts and exchange differences would be taken to reserves (offset against exchange differences on the related borrowings). The A$ investment would retain a fixed sterling cost.

If the UK company's policy is to record investments at a valuation, say, net asset value, the above distinction between currency and sterling investments does not seem to apply. For the C$ and HK$ investments, the net assets figure would be a C$ or HK figure and this would be retranslated into sterling for the purpose of the UK company's entity financial statements. For the (unhedged) A$ investment, the objective would be to establish an up to date sterling figure for net asset value. But this could only sensibly be done by considering the net assets in A$ and translating them into sterling at the closing rate. The process seems to be the same. This is odd given that two are regarded as foreign currency investments and one regarded as a sterling investment, but appears not to matter.

If we assume that the UK company adopts a policy of cost plus retained post-acquisition profits for the carrying value of its investments and that during the year the retained profits are C$ 20m, A$ 10m and HK$ 15m, the opening and closing positions will be as follows:

	C$	A$	HK$	Total £m
Opening exchange rate	2.2	2.4	11.0	
Closing exchange rate	2.4	2.0	12.0	
Opening carrying value in currency	200	90	370	
Closing carrying value in currency	220	100	385	
Opening carrying value in £	90.9	37.5	33.6	162.0
Closing carrying value in £	91.7	50.0	32.1	173.8
Increase/(decrease) in carrying value	0.8	12.5	(1.5)	11.8

As the A$ investment is a sterling asset, the whole increase in value is regarded as a revaluation gain and taken to revaluation reserve. However, it will be necessary to split the changes in value of the currency assets between revaluation gains and exchange differences in order to offset the exchange differences on the borrowings.

		C$ £m	HK$ £m
Revaluation gains (increase in currency value @ closing rate)		8.3	1.3
Exchange losses on investments (opening net assets retranslated at closing rates)	[A]	(7.5)	(2.8)
		0.8	(1.5)
Currency borrowing		C$ 150.0	HK$ 360.0
Opening value in £		68.2	32.7
Closing value in £		62.5	30.0
Exchange gains on borrowings	[B]	5.7	2.7
Net exchange loss taken to reserves [A — B]		1.8	0.1

7.104 The above example uses the illustration of an overseas intermediate holding company. This is a foreign equity investment that is regarded as being denominated in different currencies than the actual currency of the shares in which the investment is made. However, where the intermediate holding company is a UK company, it is not itself a foreign equity investment. The question then arises as to whether the SSAP 20 offset procedures can be applied where the ultimate parent has currency borrowings taken out to finance the overseas subsidiaries held by the UK intermediate holding company. Our view is that where the UK intermediate holding company has no other assets and liabilities other than the investments in the overseas subsidiaries, it can be regarded as a foreign equity investment and valued by reference to its multi-currency component parts.

Treatment in consolidated financial statements

7.105 The offset procedure described above is available also in consolidated financial statements. Within a group, foreign currency borrowings are often used either to finance, or to provide a hedge against, equity investments in foreign undertakings. Where this is so and also the conditions set out below have been complied with exchange differences on the borrowings *may* be offset, as a movement on consolidated reserves, against exchange differences that arise when the opening net investment in the foreign subsidiary is retranslated for consolidation purposes. But the offset procedure is optional and, if it is not used, the effect is that exchange differences on the net investment are taken to reserves, whilst those arising on the borrowings used to finance the investment are taken to the profit and loss account. Our view is that where a group is covered in economic terms and not exposed to any exchange risk, it is preferable to adopt the offset procedure and, indeed, arguably inappropriate to record an accounting profit or loss when exchange rates change.

7.106 The conditions for offset under SSAP 20, all of which must apply, are as follows:

- The relationships between the investing company and the foreign undertakings concerned should justify the use of the closing rate/net investment method of translation for consolidation purposes.
- In any accounting period, exchange differences on the borrowings may be offset only to the extent of the exchange differences arising on the net investments in foreign enterprises.
- The foreign currency borrowings, whose exchange gains or losses are used in the offset process, should not exceed, in aggregate, the total amount of cash that the net investments are expected to be able to generate from profits or otherwise.
- The accounting treatment adopted should be applied consistently from period to period.

[SSAP 20 para 57].

7.107 The last three conditions stated above are similar to those relating to the offset conditions for individual companies as set out in paragraph 7.82 above. These conditions are explained above and the explanations apply equally to consolidated financial statements. The first condition is necessary because the offset applies to any foreign equity investments at the entity level, but applies only to those foreign enterprises that fall to be accounted for under the closing rate/net investment method at the consolidation level. It is for this reason that where a foreign investment is accounted for under the temporal method, the offset rules cannot be applied to that investment on consolidation and all exchange gains and losses on the foreign borrowings must be taken to the profit and loss account.

7.108 Despite the similarities between the offset conditions that apply in the individual company's financial statements and that apply on consolidation, it will usually be necessary to reverse the entries made at an entity level and recompute the adjustments on a consolidated level for the following reasons:

- At the entity level, the offset applies to *all* foreign equity investments, whereas on consolidation foreign enterprises accounted for under the temporal method are excluded. For these investments, exchange differences on foreign borrowings that have been taken to reserves in the individual company's financial statements must be reversed and reflected in the consolidated results for the year.
- At the entity level, only borrowings of the investing company may be used for offset purposes, whereas on consolidation borrowings of any group company may be included.
- At the entity level, the exchange difference arising each year on the carrying value of the investment translated at the closing rate is used for offset, whereas on consolidation the exchange difference used is that arising through retranslation of the opening net investment.

7.109 There is one situation in which there is no need to reverse the entry. The standard states that in the case of a foreign enterprise that is neither a subsidiary nor an associated company the same offset procedure that has been applied in the individual company's financial statements may be applied in the consolidated financial statements. [SSAP 20 para 58]. This is logical, as it merely acknowledges that where there is a genuine hedge of a simple equity investment at the entity level the hedge does not cease to exist at the consolidation level. Despite this, there may nonetheless be occasions where there is a different treatment on consolidation. An example would be where there was a relevant borrowing in the group, but not one in the investing entity.

7.110 As the next example shows, even where offset procedures are used, it does not always follow that the whole of the exchange difference on the borrowing can be offset in reserves against an exchange difference on the net investment.

Example – Recognition of some exchange differences in profit or loss when applying the offset procedures

A UK company is preparing its consolidated financial statements for the year ended 30 June 20X5. On 31 December 20X4 it raised a loan of US$ 2m in order to finance two wholly-owned subsidiaries, one in Denmark costing DK 1,500,000 and the other in Canada costing C$ 2,500,000. The net assets of the two subsidiaries at the date of acquisition are DK 2m and C$ 2,750,000. The relevant exchange rates are:

31 December 20X4	£1 = US$ 1.48 = DK 8.89 = C$ 2.45
30 June 20X5	£1 = US$ 1.55 = DK 8.39 = C$ 2.54

	Exchange difference £	P&L account £	Reserves £
Exchange difference on net assets in Danish company at acquisition			
31/12/X4 — DK 2m @ 8.89	224,972		
30/06/X5 — DK 2m @ 8.39	238,379		
Exchange gain	13,407		
Exchange difference on net assets in Canadian company at acquisition			
31/12/X4 — C$ 2,750,000 @ 2.45	1,122,449		
30/06/X5 — C$ 2,750,000 @ 2.54	1,082,677		
Exchange loss	(39,772)		
Net exchange loss on net investments	(26,365)		(26,365)
Exchange difference on US$ loan			
31/12/X4 — US$ 2m @ 1.48	1,351,351		
30/06/X5 — US$ 2m @ 1.55	1,290,323		
Exchange gain	61,028	34,663	26,365

In this example, the amount of the exchange gain on the loan that the company can offset as a reserve movement against the exchange loss on the net investments is limited to £26,365. The excess gain of £34,663 is deemed to be speculative and, therefore, is taken to the consolidated profit and loss on ordinary activities for the year.

Goodwill on consolidation

7.111 As stated in paragraph 7.78 above, there is some support among UK companies for regarding goodwill arising on consolidation as a currency asset residing in the foreign enterprise, so that any exchange difference arising on its retranslation is included with those arising on the retranslation of the opening net investment and taken to consolidated reserves. In the context of the cover method, the question arises as to whether the exchange difference arising on the goodwill is available for offset against exchange differences on group borrowings. The question is relevant because the availability of any exchange gain arising on the goodwill element may reduce or even eliminate exchange losses on borrowings not fully covered by exchange gains on the opening net investment, which would otherwise have been taken to the profit and loss account.

7.112 If goodwill is regarded as a currency asset, there is no reason why the exchange difference arising on the goodwill cannot be used in applying the cover method. This is consistent with economic reality that the group is covered in economic terms against any movements in exchange rates. The cover method can be applied even if goodwill on acquisition has been written off to reserves (pre-FRS 10), insofar as it would not have been amortised had a policy of capitalisation and amortisation been adopted, as the write off is a consequence of following an accounting policy not because of the fact that the goodwill has lost its value.

UITF Abstract 19

7.113 Under current tax legislation, exchange gains and losses on foreign currency borrowings and derivatives that are used by a company to finance or hedge its investment in a foreign enterprise are generally not taxable. This is based on the requirements of SI 2004/3256, 'The Loan Relationships and Derivative Contracts (Disregard and bringing into account of profits and losses) Regulations 2004', and subsequent amendments, which are intended to preserve the tax treatment, and restore mandatory matching, as it exists under current UK GAAP even where a company accounts under modified UK GAAP (for example, FRSs 23, 25 and 26) or IFRS.

7.113.1 However, some examples of circumstances where tax may be payable are as follows:

- The hedging is structured such that foreign exchange gains and losses are *not* 'matched' with shares and are therefore *not* disregarded. For example, the foreign investment and the borrowings may be located in different companies in a group and, although an economic hedge may exist for consolidated financial statements, the Disregard Regulations conditions are not met. Similarly, if the investment is financed using debt and not shares, the disregard conditions may not be met.
- The liability exceeds the carrying value of the foreign investment. Under the current tax regulations, a liability or derivative hedging shares is matched by the shares at any time only to the extent that the carrying value of the liability or the value of the currency obligation under the derivative does not exceed the carrying value of the asset at the time the liability is entered into or, if later, the asset is acquired.

7.114 The question then arises as to how the tax effects of any such exchange gains and losses on the borrowings should be recognised. The borrowings may have been offset in reserves (to an extent) under the SSAP 20 offset procedure and reported in the statement of total recognised gains and losses. Alternatively, if the company or group is using modified UK GAAP or IFRS then any exchange gains or losses will only be offset in reserves in the consolidated financial statements not in the entity's financial statements, but any amounts taxable in the entity accounts will still need to be reflected in the consolidated financial statements.

7.115 It was already current practice to account for the tax effects of transactions recognised directly in reserves also in reserves when the UITF adopted this principle in Abstract 19, 'Tax on gains and losses on foreign currency borrowings that hedge an investment in a foreign enterprise', which was issued on 20 February 1998. The Abstract states that where exchange differences on foreign currency borrowings that have been used to finance, or provide a hedge against, equity investments in foreign enterprises are taken to reserves and reported in the STRGL, in accordance with paragraphs 51, 57 and 58 of SSAP 20 and paragraph 27 of FRS 3, tax charges and credits that are directly and solely attributable to such exchange differences should also be taken to reserves and reported in that statement. This treatment was incorporated into FRS 16, 'Current tax'. [FRS 16 para 6] and is also in line with the treatment in IAS 12, 'Income taxes' [IAS 12 para 61].

7.116 The UITF also considered how such tax effects reported in the statement of total recognised gains and losses and in reserves would impact on the restriction on the amount of exchange differences on foreign currency borrowings that can be offset in reserves in accordance with paragraphs 51(a) and 57(b) of SSAP 20. The Abstract concludes that the restriction should be applied after taking account of any tax attributable to those exchange differences — that is, the net-of-tax exchange difference on borrowings should be offset only to the extent of exchange difference arising on the equity investment. The offset restriction is considered in detail from paragraph 7.83. Similarly, the comparison with the total amount of cash that the investments are expected to be able to generate and the exposure created by the borrowings (paragraphs 51(b) and 57(c) of SSAP 20) should be considered in after-tax terms.

7.117 Consistent with SSAP 20's requirement to disclose the amount of exchange gains or losses on borrowings that are taken to the statement of total recognised gains and losses, the abstract requires disclosure of any related tax charges and credits accounted for as described above, in addition to the gross amount of the exchange differences.

7.118 The way in which UITF Abstract 19 is likely to apply in practice is illustrated in the following example.

Example – Tax on foreign exchange differences of borrowings hedging an investment in a foreign enterprise

A UK company's financial year ends on 31 March.

Option A) On 31 March 20X5 it raised a loan of C$ 840,000 to finance an equity investment in Canada costing C$ 840,000.

Option B) The loan of C$ 840,000 was taken out by a Treasury company elsewhere in the group but is still intended to be a hedge at a consolidated level.

Option C) Instead of raising a loan of C$ 840,000 the company raised a loan of C$ 1,000,000 to finance the equity investment and to ensure that it had sufficient C$ liquidity for other Canadian trading activities. The additional loan funding is not used for any other hedging purposes.

Assume UK tax rate is 30%. The relevant exchange rates are as follows:

31 March 20X5 £1 = C$ 2.80
31 March 20X6 £1 = C$ 2.90

The company is still on old UK GAAP and adopts the offset procedure in SSAP 20 in its financial statements for the year ended 31 March 20X6. Therefore the exchange difference on the C$ borrowing that is offset in reserves before considering any tax consequences is as follows:

31 March 20X5 — C$ 840,000 @ 2.80	= £300,000
31 March 20X6 — C$ 840,000 @ 2.90	= £289,655
Gain on borrowing	£10,345

Under option A, there will be no further exchange difference on the loan to be accounted for.

The Disregard regulations apply as the company has used the borrowing to hedge its investment in the Canadian subsidiary. Therefore, under option A, there are no tax consequences. This is because the sterling carrying value of the liability is fully matched by the sterling carrying value of the asset and the exchange gain on the loan is fully matched with the exchange loss in reserves.

Under option B, the Treasury company will record the exchange movement on the borrowing in its profit and loss account and the equity investment will be held at historic cost in the investing company. On consolidation the group will use the offset procedure in SSAP 20 and therefore the exchange movements on the borrowing can be transferred to reserves.

The Disregard regulations do not apply even though hedging is available in the consolidated accounts as the borrowing is not intended to be a hedge in the Treasury or Investing company. Therefore the company would have to pay tax of £3,104 at 30% on the exchange gain of £10,345. Applying UITF Abstract 19, the group would offset £10,345 — £3,104 = £7,241 of net exchange gain on the borrowing against the exchange loss of £10,345 in reserves in the consolidated accounts. Both the exchange difference of £10,345 and the attributable tax of £3,104 would be disclosed.

Under option C, the exchange gain on the excess borrowing of £1,970 (C$160,000 × 2.8 — C$160,000 × 2.9) will be reported in the profit and loss account at an entity and consolidated level. The Disregard regulations will not apply to this excess borrowing and therefore the exchange gain will be taxed. The tax of £591 will be recorded in the profit and loss account.

7.119 The above example is fairly simple and does not demonstrate the complications that can arise in the tax treatment of exchange gains and losses. The tax rules on financial instruments and matching are complex and specialist taxation advice should be sought.

Hedging transactions

Identification of a hedge

7.120 Companies enter into hedging transactions primarily to reduce risks, including those associated with exchange rate movements that can have an adverse effect on their financial position and results. A diverse range of financial instruments, such as forward exchange contracts, futures contracts, currency swaps and currency options, are available for reducing foreign exchange risk. These instruments are often referred to as 'derivative products' because their values are derived from an underlying security, an index, an interest rate, or another financial instrument.

7.121 The word *hedge* is used in a variety of ways by derivatives traders, accountants and regulators and there appears to be no single accepted definition. However, most definitions are based on the notion of reducing exposure to price risk, interest rate risk or currency risk.

7.122 Hedging in an economic sense concerns the reduction or elimination of the effects of market risk, interest rate risk or currency risk, each of which may be present to some extent in a financial instrument. It involves entering into a transaction in the expectation that it will reduce an enterprise's exposure to loss from price risk, often with the additional consequence of reducing the potential for profit. A financial instrument is generally viewed as a hedge when an enterprise has a specifically identified position that is exposed to the risk of loss as a result of adverse price changes in financial markets and the effect of holding the instrument is to mitigate that risk of loss. A hedge is achieved by taking a position exposed to effects of price changes that move inversely and with a high degree of correlation with the effects of price changes on an existing or expected position.

7.123 A position to be hedged can be interpreted fairly broadly. A financial instrument may be accounted for as a hedge when it has an exposure to price risk that is equal but opposite to that of a group of financial instruments or a portion of one instrument. Furthermore, it is not necessary for hedges to be specifically matched with individual items being hedged. However, because different types of assets and liabilities have substantially different exposures to potential gain or loss, the items constituting a group of financial instruments must be similar at least to the extent of the common price risk being hedged.

7.124 Until recently, there was no measurement standard in the UK that dealt with the recognition and measurement of derivatives, nor was there a UK standard that dealt specifically with hedge accounting. In December 2004, the ASB issued FRS 25 and FRS 26, which deal with the accounting for financial instruments and hedge accounting. The requirements are almost identical to IAS 32 and IAS 39 and are covered in detail in the Manual of accounting – Financial instruments. For a company that is not applying those standards (and hence, is applying SSAP 20) there is no mandatory UK guidance in this area. In the context of foreign exchange transactions, the paragraphs that follow consider the appropriate accounting treatment, under the current UK historical cost accounting framework, for two hedging tools that are commonly in use that are not dealt with in SSAP 20. These are forward exchange contracts and currency options.

Forward exchange contracts

7.125 A forward exchange contract is a legal agreement under which a company contracts to buy or sell a specified amount of foreign currency at a specified exchange rate (which is the forward rate), but with delivery and settlement at a specified future date. One of the parties to a forward contract assumes a long position and agrees to buy the underlying currency on a specified future date at the forward rate. The other party assumes a short position and agrees to sell the currency on the same date for the same forward rate.

7.126 The duration of the contract is usually fixed, for example, one month, three months or six months. The forward rate specified in the contract is stated at a premium or discount to the spot rate based upon current market conditions and expectations, but it is not an estimate of what the spot rate will be at the end of the contract. Since the alternative to a forward contract is to buy (or sell) the required currency now, the amount of the premium or discount to the spot rate is principally based on:

- The interest rate differentials between the relevant currencies.
- The duration of the contract.

The following example (simplified) illustrates how forward exchange rates are calculated:

Assumptions	
UK interest rate	9%
US interest rate	6%
Spot rate at beginning of year	£1 = US$1.55
One year forward rate	To determine

Company borrows £1m for one year	£
Amount payable	
Principal	1,000,000
Interest @ 9% for one year	90,000
Total payable	1,090,000

Company converts £1m to US dollars at the spot rate, invests the dollars for one year and takes out a one year forward contract to sell the original dollars and interest for sterling.

Amount payable	US$
Principal £1m @1.55	1,550,000
Interest @ 6%	93,000
Total payable	1,643,000

Ignoring any transaction costs, the one year forward rate at inception of the contract would be calculated on the basis that the company is indifferent between choosing the above two strategies. For this to occur, the one year forward rate must be US$ 1,643,000/£1,090,000 = 1.50734. In fact, the forward rate can be determined arithmetically by applying the interest rate differential ruling between the two currencies in question to the spot rate.

$$\text{Forward rate} = 1.55 \times \frac{1.06}{1.09} = 1.50734$$

A further factor would need to be built into the calculation if the period was other than one year.

Forward rates are usually quoted as being either at a discount or premium to the spot rate. To arrive at the forward rate for US dollars the discount is added to the spot rate and a premium is deducted from the spot rate.

7.127 Forward exchange contracts are frequently used by companies to protect them from experiencing exchange gains or losses from existing positions and on anticipated transactions. They offer the advantage that they can be specifically tailored in terms of amount, currency and maturity date to any hedging situation. There is no initial deposit or margin to pay and settlement is made at maturity. The disadvantage is that there is no benefit from favourable exchange rate movements.

7.128 Accounting for forward contracts is dealt with only briefly in SSAP 20. Two viewpoints have been advanced to account for foreign exchange contracts under the current UK historical cost framework:

- All aspects are viewed as part of a single transaction (the 'one transaction' view). That is, the commitment to buy or sell currency necessary to settle a foreign currency payable or receivable is viewed as part of the purchase or sale transaction and the forward contract rate is used to record that transaction. This is the approach specifically adopted in SSAP 20.
- The transaction to settle a foreign currency payable or receivable is treated separately from the forward contract (the 'two transaction' view). In addition, the premium or discount on the forward contract is accounted for separately and spread over the life of the contract. The carrying value of the forward contract is adjusted each period as the contract progresses (for example, at the balance sheet date its carrying value is recalculated using the spot rate effective on that day).

The above viewpoints are illustrated below in some of the typical situations where a company enters into a forward contract for hedging purposes.

Forward exchange contracts taken out at the transaction date

7.129 This is the only situation that is dealt with in SSAP 20. The standard states that the rate specified in the forward contract *may* be the appropriate rate to use for the translation of trading transactions denominated in a foreign currency (or the monetary assets or liabilities arising from such transactions) where these are covered by a related or matching forward contract. This treatment recognises that the purpose of such a transaction is to hedge any exchange risk involved in foreign currency operations and that no economic gain or loss will therefore arise.

Therefore, under this approach, the premium or discount on a forward contract is immediately recognised in the profit and loss account.

Example – Accounting for forward cover entered into at transaction date

A company is preparing its financial statements to 31 December 20X5. In October 20X5, the company sells goods to an overseas company for FC 405,000. The overseas company pays for the goods in March 20X6. At the time of the sale, the exchange rate is £1 = FC 2.7, and at the balance sheet date the exchange rate is £1 = FC 2.9. The UK company, however, covers the transaction by a matching forward contract to sell FC. The exchange rate specified in the six month forward contract is £1 = FC 2.6. The relevant translations are as follows:

10/X5 — FC 405,000 @ 2.7 (transaction rate) =	£150,000
12/X5 — FC 405,000 @ 2.9 (balance sheet rate) =	£139,655
03/X6 — FC 405,000 @ 2.6 (forward contract rate) =	£155,769

The UK company could record the sale in one of the following ways:

- It could record the sale and the debtor at £155,769, that is, at the exchange rate specified in the matching forward contract. Because the company has entered into a matching forward contract, the amount receivable and ultimately received from the debtor is FC 405,000 which is sold for £155,769. Consequently, the company would not recognise a loss on exchange on the transaction and no further accounting entries are required. This approach is permitted by SSAP 20.

- A second method is to view the sale and the debtor separately from the commitment to sell foreign currency under the six month forward contract. Therefore, the sale and the debtor would be initially recorded at £150,000. At 31 December 20X5, the debtor would be translated at the exchange rate ruling at that date, that is £139,655. The loss on exchange of £10,345 would be taken to the profit and loss account. This would be matched by an equivalent gain on the forward contract, which is computed by taking the difference between the foreign currency amount of the forward contract translated at the spot rate at the date of inception of the forward contract (FC 405,000 @ 2.7 = £150,000) and the amount translated at the balance sheet date (FC 405,000 @ 2.9 = £139,655).

  In addition, the premium or discount on the contract should be accounted for separately. This will give rise to a profit or loss on the forward contract, calculated by taking the difference between the foreign currency amount of the forward contract translated at the spot rate at the date of inception of the forward contract (FC 405,000 @ 2.7 — £150,000) and the contracted forward rate (FC 405,000 @ 2.6 = £155,769). In this situation, there is a profit of £5,769 which should be amortised over that period. Accordingly, £2,885 should be taken to the profit and loss account for the year ended 31 December 20X5 and the balance should be recognised in the following year.

The effect of the two methods can be summarised as follows:

	Method 1	Method 2
	£	£
Balance sheet at 31 December 20X5		
Debtor	155,769	139,655
Forward contract	–	13,230
Profit and loss account for year ended 31 December 20X5		
Included in profit on sale of goods	5,769	–
Exchange loss on retranslation of debtor	–	(10,345)
Exchange gain on forward contract	–	10,345
Amortisation of profit on forward contract	–	2,885
	5,769	2,885
Profit and loss account for year ended 31 December 20X6		
Amortisation of profit on forward contract	–	2,884

7.130 Although SSAP 20 allows the first method, it does not rule out the use of the alternative method discussed above. The advantage of the first method is its simplicity, whilst the second method takes a completely different approach and is perhaps theoretically correct. It treats the forward contract as a separate instrument and attributes a value to it. The rationale for this treatment is that the revenue is determined by the original sale transaction and not by any subsequent agreement to exchange currencies.

Hedging an existing asset or liability with forward exchange contract

7.131 Companies may sometimes enter into a forward exchange contract to hedge an existing monetary asset or a liability.

Example – Forward cover of an existing loan and interest payments

A company is preparing its financial statements to 31 December 20X4. It took out a foreign currency loan of FC 1m at fixed interest rate of 10% on 1 July 20X4 with a maturity date of one year. Interest is payable on 31 December and 30 June. The company immediately enters into two forward contracts as follows

Contract No 1, to purchase FC 50,000 (half-yearly interest on FC 1m) for payment on 31 December 20X4 at a fixed contract price of £1 = FC 1.50.

Contract No 2, to purchase FC 1,050,000 (principal of FC 1m + half-yearly interest of FC 50,000) for payment on 30 June 20X5 at a fixed contract price of £1 = FC 1.46.

The relevant spot rates are as follows:

1 July 20X4 £1 = FC 1.54
31 December 20X4 £1 = FC 1.47

The illustration that follows views the loan and the commitment to purchase foreign currency under the forward contracts separately.

		P&L account	Balance sheet
		£	£
Loan	£		
Exchange difference on loan			
1/7/X4 — FC 1m @ 1.54 (transaction rate)	649,351		
31/12/X4 — FC 1m @ 1.47 (balance sheet rate)	680,272		(680,272)
Exchange loss	(30,921)	(30,921)	
Forward contracts			
Exchange gain on forward contract No 1			
31/12/X4 — Value at settlement FC 50K @ 1.47	34,014		
1/7/X4 — Value at inception date FC 50K @1.54	32,467		
Exchange gain on settled contract*	1,547	1,547	
Premium payable on contract No 1			
1/7/X4 — FC 50,000 @ 1.54 (spot rate)	32,467		
1/7/X4 — FC 50,000 @ 1.50 (forward rate)	33,333		
Premium payable*	(866)	(866)	
Interest FC 50,000 @ 1.47 paid on 31/12/X4		(34,014)	
		(33,333)	
Forward contract No 2			
Exchange gain on forward contract (principal amount only)			
31/12/X4 — Value at year end FC 1m @ 1.47	680,272		
1/7/X4 — Value at inception date FC 1m @ 1.54	649,351		
Exchange gain on outstanding contract	30,921	30,921	30,921
Premium payable on contract No 2			
1/7/X4 — FC 1.05m at @ 1.54 (spot)	681,818		
1/7/X4 — FC 1.05m at @ 1.46 (forward)	719,178		
Premium payable (half deferred)	(37,360)	(18,680)	(18,680)
Cash			
Loan proceeds	649,351		
Interest paid	(34,014)		
Net settlement on contract No 1 (gain — premium)*	681		
Cash balance	616,018		616,018
Net charge to P&L account		(52,013)	52,013
			—

* The net settlement on contract No 1 amounting to £681 can also be calculated as the difference between the forward contract amount at the spot rate at the date of settlement, being £34,014 (FC 50,000 @ 1.47) and the contracted rate, being £33,333 (FC 50,000 @ 1.50).

As can be seen from the above table, the exchange loss on the loan is matched by an equivalent gain on the outstanding forward contract No 2. This gain is calculated on the principal amount of FC 1m. The gain on the forward contract (FC 50,000) is not included in the profit and loss account because it is hedging a future commitment. It would, however, be recognised as a deferred gain on the balance sheet. An asset for the same amount would be recognised for the value of the hedge. This amount would be calculated as (FC 50,000 @ 1.47) – (FC 50,000 @ 1.54), which is £1,546. The accounting for deferred gains on hedges for future commitments is dealt with in detail from paragraph 7.132.

As contract No 1 matured during the year, the premium payable is taken to the profit and loss account. The premium payable on contract No 2 is amortised over its life, half the amount being charged during the year ended 31 December 20X4. This methodology does not differentiate between the premium paid on the portion of the forward contract relating to the principal and the premium paid on the portion relating to the future commitment. An alternative treatment would be to defer the portion of the premium relating to the future commitment and recognise it on the transaction date, when the deferred gain is recognised. The accounting for the premium or discount on hedges for future commitments is also dealt with in detail from paragraph 7.132.

If the treatment permitted by SSAP 20 is followed, the half-yearly interest charged to the profit and loss account is translated at the forward rate being £33,333 (FC 50,000 @ 1.5). The loan is translated at the forward rate at the balance sheet date, being £684,932 (FC 1m @ 1.46) and the difference between this amount and the amount at which it was initially recorded (£649,351), being an exchange loss of £35,581 is taken to the profit and loss account. This exchange loss represents the total premium on the portion of the forward contract relating to the loan principal, that is FC 1m @ 1.46 (contract rate) less FC 1m @ 1.54 (inception). Under this method no part of this premium is deferred.

Hedging a foreign currency commitment

7.132 Companies may also use forward exchange contracts to hedge anticipated future transactions, such as a foreign currency payable or receivable, or to a hedge a foreign currency commitment, such as an agreement to buy goods from or sell goods to a foreign entity at some time in the future. In these situations, the gain or loss arising on the forward contract is deferred until the actual date the commitment is fulfilled. This can be achieved by using either the 'one transaction' or 'two transaction' approach considered in 7.128. The example illustrated below deals with a future commitment. An anticipated future foreign currency payable or receivable, such as the anticipated interest payment in example 7.131, would be treated in a similar manner.

Example – Forward cover of a financial commitment

A company's financial year ends on 31 December 20X1. It intends to renovate part of its plant and enters into an agreement with a foreign supplier on 30 September 20X1 to purchase an improved version of the equipment for FC 1m. The equipment is to be delivered on 31 March 20X2 and the price is payable on 30 June 20X2. In order to hedge the commitment to pay FC 1m, the company enters into a forward contract on 30 September 20X1 to purchase FC 1m on 30 June 20X2 at a fixed exchange rate of £1 = FC 1.51.

The relevant spot rates are as follows:

Inception date	30 September 20X1	£1 = FC 1.54
Year end date	31 December 20X1	£1 = FC 1.47
Transaction date	31 March 20X2	£1 = FC 1.45
Settlement date	30 June 20X2	£1 = FC 1.43

As before, there are two possible treatments:

Method 1

If the treatment permitted by SSAP 20 is followed, then no accounting entries are required at the year end and the company will simply disclose the financial commitment in its balance sheet. On 31 March 20X2, both the equipment and the liability to pay the supplier will be recorded at the forward contract rate, being £662,252 (FC 1m @ 1.51).

Method 2

Method 2 is based on the two transaction approach. No entries are made in respect of the equipment at 31 December 20X1. At 31 March 20X2, the equipment and the liability to the supplier would be initially recorded at £689,655 (FC 1m @ 1.45 — transaction rate). The amount payable to the supplier at 30 June 20X2 is £699,301 (FC 1m @ 1.43 — spot rate at settlement). The exchange loss of £9,646 arising on the settlement will be charged in the profit and loss account for the year ended 31 December 20X2, but will be offset by a corresponding gain on the forward contract (see below).

The forward contract would be accounted for as a separate transaction as follows:

Exchange gain on forward contract	£
Gain up to balance sheet date	
30/09/X1 — FC 1m @ 1.54 (spot — inception date)	649,351
31/12/X1 — FC 1m @ 1.47 (spot — balance sheet date)	680,272
Gain on forward contract	30,921

The value of the forward contract relating to the change in spot rates is recognised on the balance sheet. The associated gain is not recognised in the profit and loss account at this stage, but instead is deferred on the balance sheet.

Dr Derivative asset	£30,921	
Cr Deferred gain		£30,921

Gain from balance sheet date to transaction date	
31/12/X1 — FC 1m @ 1.47 (spot — balance sheet date)	680,272
31/03/X2 — FC 1m @ 1.45 (spot — transaction date)	689,655
Gain on forward contract	9,383

The movement in the value of the derivative asset due to the change in spot rates is, again, deferred prior to the transaction date.

Dr Derivative asset	£9,383	
Cr Deferred gain		£9,383

Total gain to transaction date (deferred)	40,304

At the transaction date the purchase of supplies would be recognised at the spot rate and the cumulative deferred gain would be recognised as an adjustment to the cost of those supplies.

Dr Stock	£689,655	
Cr Payable		£689,655
Dr Deferred gain	£40,304	
Cr Stock		£40,304

Gain from transaction date to settlement date	
31/03/X2 — FC 1m @ 1.45 (spot — transaction date)	689,655
30/06/X2 — FC 1m @ 1.43 (spot — settlement date)	699,301
Gain on forward contract	9,646
Total exchange gain on forward contract	49,950

The asset purchased (stock) is a non-monetary asset and is, therefore, not retranslated for movements in foreign exchange rates. The payable balance, however, would be retranslated, using the movement in the spot rate between the transaction date and the settlement date. In addition, the value of the forward contract is also retranslated for foreign exchange movements. The associated foreign exchange gains and losses offset in the profit and loss account in the period up to the settlement of the payable.

Dr Derivative asset	£9,646	
Cr Foreign exchange gain		£9,646

Dr Foreign exchange loss	£9,646	
Cr Payable		£9,646

At the settlement date the payable is settled in cash and the forward contract is closed out. There is no profit and loss account effect.

Dr Payable	£699,300	
Cr Derivative asset		£37,048
Cr Cash		£662,252

The carrying amount of the derivative asset at this point is equal to the gains of (£30,921 + £9,383 + £9,646) = £49,950, less the forward premium of £12,902, which equals £37,048

Premium payable on forward contract	
30/09/X1 — FC 1m @ 1.54 (spot rate at inception)	649,351
30/09/X1 — FC 1m @ 1.51 (forward rate)	662,253
Premium payable	12,902

During the hedging period, between the transaction date and the settlement date, the exchange gain arising on the contract matches the exchange loss arising on the liability to the supplier, reflecting that the position is hedged. These exchange differences are offset in the profit and loss account.

As far as the premium on the contract is concerned, there are two possible treatments that will have an effect on asset values. The first treatment is to amortise the premium payable over the life of the contract. Therefore, half the premium, that is £6,451, would be charged to the profit and loss account for the year ended 31 December 20X1 and the remainder charged in the following year. If this treatment is followed, only the gain on the forward contract will have an effect on the asset value. The effect is that the asset will be recorded in 20X2 at the spot rate ruling at the date the forward contract was taken out as indicated below.

Asset	£
Initially recorded at transaction date — FC 1m @1.45	689,655
Less deferred gain on forward contract	(40,304)
Value — FC 1m @ 1.54 (spot rate at inception of contract)	649,351

Following this approach the journal below would be recorded at 31 December 20X1:

Dr Profit and loss account	£6,451	
Cr Derivative asset		£6,451

The remainder of the expense would be recognised the following year:

Dr Profit and loss account	£6,451	
Cr Derivative asset		£6,451

Alternatively, the premium that relates to the commitment period may be deferred and included in the related foreign currency transaction. The effect is that the asset will be recorded at the forward rate as indicated below.

Asset	£
Initially recorded at transaction date — FC 1m @1.45	689,655
Less deferred gain on forward contract	(40,304)
Plus deferred premium	12,902
Value — FC 1m @ 1.51 (forward rate)	662,253

Following this approach, an additional journal would be required to recognise the premium on the forward contract as a component of the cost of the stock. The premium would have been initially recorded as a component of the value of the derivative asset.

Dr	Stock	£12,902	
	Cr Derivative asset		£12,902

Although both treatments are acceptable, it is preferable to use the second alternative as the company 'locked in' the cost of the equipment at £662,552 by entering into the forward contract.

Hedging a net investment

7.133 A company may decide to hedge against the effects of changes in exchange rates in the company's net investment in a subsidiary. This may be done by taking out a foreign currency borrowing to hedge a foreign equity investment, which is recognised by SSAP 20 and discussed from paragraph 7.105. However, SSAP 20 does not deal with the situation of using forward exchange contracts to hedge foreign equity investments. The question then arises as to how the forward contract should be dealt with in the consolidated financial statements.

7.134 To be consistent with the treatment of the exchange differences on borrowings that are taken out as a hedge, we consider that any gain or loss arising on a forward contract from movements in the spot rate of exchange may be taken to reserves to match the movement in the net investment being hedged. This treatment is sensible as it recognises the economic rationale of taking out the forward contract. The forward points may be taken to the profit and loss account, because it represents the interest rate differential between the currencies being exchanged. However, as SSAP 20 is not clear, there are good arguments to take these changes to reserves.

Hedging future results of foreign investments

7.135 A company can also take out a forward contract as a hedge against the future results of a foreign subsidiary. Where this is done, the gain or loss on the contract should be included in the profit and loss account for the period being hedged. If the results are translated at the closing rate and the contract is for the whole year, the inclusion of the gain or loss on the contract will ensure that the results are stated at the contracted rate. Where the contract is not for a full year, the results up to the date of contract will effectively be hedged and reflected at the contracted rate. If the contract remains outstanding at the end of the year, the gain or loss on the contract from the date of inception up to the balance sheet date should be recognised in the profit and loss account and the related value of the contract included in the balance sheet. If the results are translated at an average rate and the contract is for less than a year, it may be appropriate to translate the results of that part of the year covered by the contract at the contracted rate and the balance at the average rate.

7.136 Where a company takes out a forward contract to hedge the future results of a foreign subsidiary (for example, the results of the following year) or where there is a rolling hedge so that at the year end there are contracts outstanding to hedge future results, a considerable degree of prudence should be observed in assessing whether or not the future results will be sufficient to ensure that the contract is not an excessive hedge. If projections of the results of the foreign subsidiary are too optimistic or the subsidiary suffers deterioration in its performance, some of the contract could become speculative with the result that any potential loss should be provided for immediately. Consider the following example:

Example – Forward cover of future trading results

A company has forward contracts outstanding at the year end for the sale of FC 20m at a contract rate of FC 1.60. The future trading results of the subsidiary for next year were originally estimated at FC 21m but at the year end have been revised to FC 15m. The relevant spot rate at the year end is FC 1.40.

The revised forecasts indicate that the company will have to purchase FC 5m in order to meet its commitment under the sales contract. At the exchange rates current at the year end, this will result in a loss of £446,429 (FC 5m @ 1.40 less FC 5m @ 1.60) which should be provided for in accordance with FRS 12. The part of the contract that is not considered speculative would be accounted for under either the 'one transaction' or the 'two transaction' approach considered in 7.128 onwards.

7.137 Some take the view that hedge accounting may not be appropriate for forward contracts that are taken out to hedge future results and that such contracts are in fact speculative. In fact FRS 26 does not permit hedge accounting for this type of hedging relationship.

Speculative forward contracts

7.138 A speculative forward contract is a contract that does not hedge an exposure. Because of the risks involved, companies do not normally enter into such speculative contracts and it is inadvisable for them to do so. However, where a company does enter into a forward contract as a speculative transaction, a gain or loss will arise during the period from inception to maturity. If this period straddles the company's year end it is necessary to deal with the gain or loss that arises for the year. Again SSAP 20 does not deal with this situation. For companies not applying FRS 26, such gains or losses can be regarded as contingent and, consequently, provision should be made for losses, whereas gains would normally be deferred until they crystallise. Companies wishing to apply mark to market accounting to such contracts have the option of adopting FRS 26 and the corresponding recognition and measurement requirements. If they adopt FRS 26 they would also be required to adopt FRS 23 and would, therefore, no longer apply the requirements of SSAP 20.

Foreign currency options as a hedge

7.139 An option is a contract conveying the right, but not the obligation, to buy (call) or the right to sell (put) a specified item at a fixed price (known as the strike or exercise price). A foreign currency option, therefore, is a right to buy or sell a foreign currency. A company acquiring an option will have to a pay a non-refundable premium to the option seller in exchange for the right to buy or sell a fixed amount of currency. The option premium represents the market's perception of the value of the option, which essentially consists of two parts:

- Intrinsic value — which for a call option is the excess of the market price of the underlying item over the option's strike price.
- Time value — which is the difference between the price paid for the option (the premium) and the intrinsic value.

The intrinsic value represents the benefit to the holder if the option was exercised immediately. The time value is associated with the remaining term to maturity of the option and reflects the income foregone from not holding the underlying item, the cost avoided by not having to finance the underlying item and the value placed on the possibility that the option's intrinsic value will increase prior to its maturity due to future volatility in the fair value of the underlying item.

7.140 If the spot exchange rate is lower than the strike rate, a foreign exchange call will not be exercised and the option is said to be 'out-of-the-money'. If it is advantageous to exercise the option, it is said to be 'in-the-money'. Where the strike rate is equal to the spot rate, the option is said to be 'at-the-money'. Therefore, unlike a forward foreign exchange contract, an option buyer will be able to gain from favourable exchange rate movements.

7.141 Accounting for currency options is not dealt with in SSAP 20. The general principle is that losses in the underlying item being hedged are offset by gains in the option position. It should be noted, however, that the maximum loss that the company can incur on an option is the premium as it will not exercise the option if the exchange rate movements are unfavourable. Due to the nature of a currency option, it would not be appropriate to record the item being hedged at the rate in the related currency option as it may never be exercised. Therefore, the asset or liability being hedged should be treated separately from the premium. The premium should initially be recorded as an asset. At the balance sheet date, the underlying currency amount under the option should be translated at the current rate and compared with the amount translated at the option rate. The resulting gain or loss should be treated as follows:

- If there is a gain, the gain less the cost of the option may be recognised provided that the loss on the item being hedged is also recognised. If a corresponding loss is not recognised, for instance, because the option is hedging a future transaction, then the gain should be carried forward to be matched with the loss when this is recognised.

If the option is speculative, that is, it is not taken out as a hedge, the gain would normally be deferred unless the company adopts a policy of marking to market. However, it is generally accepted that entering into speculative option contracts is inadvisable as companies have suffered losses in the past where they have taken out such contracts.

- If there is a net loss, the whole of the premium should be written off. If the loss is less than the premium paid then the premium should be written off to the extent of the loss.

7.142 Alternatively, the premium on the hedging option could be 'marked to market' to the current premium at the balance sheet date. If the premium has increased in value there is a gain on the contract indicating that the option is in the money. On the other hand if the premium has fallen in value such that the option is unlikely to be exercised, there will be a loss on the contract.

Disclosures

Requirements of the Act

7.143 The Act does not include any provisions that deal with either the translation of foreign currency transactions or the translation of foreign currency financial statements, other than to require the basis on which sums are translated into sterling (or the currency in which the accounts are drawn up) to be stated. [SI 2008/410 1 Sch 70]. The Act does require disclosure of financial commitments to the extent that they are relevant to a proper understanding of the company's state of affairs. [SI 2008/410 1 Sch 63(5)]. Therefore, where a company has outstanding forward contracts the amounts outstanding under the forward contracts should be disclosed.

Requirements of the standard

7.144 In addition to the above disclosure, SSAP 20 requires a number of other disclosures which are considered below. Furthermore, following the guidance on publication of the 'Operating and financial review', the disclosure requirements of FRS 13, 'Derivatives and other financial instruments; disclosures' and the requirement to comment in the Directors' report on the principal risks and uncertainties facing the company, companies now tend to give much more information on their foreign currency operations. Guidance on the preparation of an OFR and a directors' report is contained in chapters 2 and 3 of the Manual of Accounting – Management reports and governance respectively. The following paragraphs deal with the disclosures required by SSAP 20 and FRS 13 to be made both in individual financial statements and in consolidated financial statements.

7.145 The methods used in translation of the financial statements of foreign enterprises and the treatment accorded to exchange differences should be disclosed in the financial statements. [SSAP 20 para 59]. These disclosure requirements are illustrated in Table 7.10 below.

Table 7.10 — Reuters Group plc — Annual Report and Accounts — 31 December 2001

Accounting Policies (extract)

Foreign currency translation

Where it is considered that the functional currency of an operation is sterling the financial statements are expressed in sterling on the following basis:

a. Fixed assets are translated into sterling at the rates ruling on the date of acquisition as adjusted for any profits or losses from related financial instruments.

b. Monetary assets and liabilities denominated in a foreign currency are translated into sterling at the foreign exchange rates ruling at the balance sheet date.

c. Revenue and expenses in foreign currencies are recorded in sterling at the rates ruling for the month of the transactions.

d. Any gains or losses arising on translation are reported as part of profit.

For other operations, associated undertakings and joint ventures, assets and liabilities are translated into sterling at the rates ruling at the balance sheet date. Revenue and expenses in foreign currencies are recorded in sterling at the rates ruling for the month of the transactions and gains or losses arising on translation are dealt with through reserves.

Treasury

Reuters receives revenue and incurs expenses in more than 60 currencies and uses financial instruments to hedge a portion of its net cash flow and operating profit. Profits and losses from hedging activities are matched with the underlying cash flows and profits being hedged. Those relating to trading cash flows are reported as part of profit and those relating to capital expenditure programmes are adjusted against the cost of the assets to which they relate.

Reuters uses financial instruments to hedge a portion of its interest exposure. Profits and losses on financial instruments are reported as part of profit for the period to which they relate.

Financial instruments hedging the risk on foreign currency assets are revalued at the balance sheet date and the resulting gain or loss offset against that arising from the translation of the underlying asset into sterling.

7.146 The standard requires disclosure of the net amount of exchange gains and losses on foreign currency borrowings less deposits, identifying separately:

- The amount offset in reserves under the provisions of paragraphs 51, 57 and 58 of SSAP 20. This applies to exchange differences included in the offset process. Examples of this disclosure are included in Table 7.11 and Table 7.12 below.

- The net amount charged/credited to the profit and loss account.

In addition, disclosure is required of the net movement on reserves arising from exchange differences. [SSAP 20 para 60].

Table 7.11 — Reckitt & Colman plc — Report & Accounts — 31 December 1994

Notes to the accounts

32 OTHER RESERVES

	Group	Subsidiary undertakings	Parent
	£m	£m	£m
At beginning of year as previously reported	**542.32**	**395.74**	**146.58**
Prior year adjustment for post-retirement benefits other than pensions	(35.38)	(35.38)	–
At beginning of year restated	**506.94**	**360.36**	**146.58**
Movements during the year:			
Profit for the financial year	81.89	27.54	54.35
Ordinary dividends	(75.99)	–	(75.99)
Net exchange loss on foreign currency loans	(0.35)	–	(0.35)
Exchange differences arising on translation of net investments in overseas subsidiary undertakings	(22.58)	(13.83)	(8.75)
Dividend adjustment (Note 8)	3.09	–	3.09
Goodwill and acquisition costs written off	(206.41)	(206.41)	–
Goodwill reinstated	6.54	6.54	–
	293.13	**174.20**	***118.93**

As permitted by s.230 of the Companies Act 1985, no profit and loss account is presented for Reckitt & Colman plc.

The cumulative amount of goodwill written off to reserves since 1984 in respect of the acquisition of continuing businesses is £536m (1993, £336m).

* The reserves of subsidiary undertakings have generally been retained to finance their businesses. There were statutory or other restrictions on the distribution of £109m (1993, £81m) of the reserves of subsidiary undertakings at 31 December 1994.

Table 7.12 — Imperial Chemical Industries PLC — Annual report and accounts — 31 December 1994

notes relating to the accounts

23 Reserves (extract)

	Share premium account £m	Revaluation £m	Associated undertakings £m	Profit and loss account £m	**1994 Total £m**	1993 Total £m
GROUP						
Reserves attributable to parent company						
At beginning of year as previously stated						3,572
Prior year adjustment (note 2)						(89)
At beginning of year as restated	561	46	66	2,493	**3,166**	3,483
Profit/(loss) retained for year			(63)	52	**(11)**	(433)
Amounts taken direct to reserves						
Share premiums	8				**8**	59
Goodwill				(48)	**(48)**	80
Exchange adjustments		(6)	(11)	(79)	**(96)**	(23)
Share of other reserve movements of associated undertakings and other items			(9)	2	**(7)**	–
	8	(6)	(20)	(125)	**(143)**	116
Other movements between reserves		(3)	77	(74)		
At end of year	569	37	60	2,346	**3,012**	3,166

In the Group accounts, £33m of net exchange gains (1993 losses £26m) on foreign currency loans have been offset in reserves against exchange losses (1993 gains) on the net investment in overseas subsidiaries and associated undertakings.

7.147 Apart from the item mentioned in paragraph 7.146, there is no requirement to disclose the amount of exchange gains and losses taken to the profit and loss account. Nonetheless, the profit and loss account formats in Schedule 1 to SI 2008/410 distinguish between operating income and expenses and other income and expenses. Therefore, a company will need to consider the nature of each exchange difference. A company should normally show gains and losses that arise from trading transactions as 'other operating income/charges'. Where arrangements that can be considered as financing give rise to exchange gains and losses, a company should disclose these separately as part of 'other interest receivable and similar income' or as part of 'interest payable and similar charges'. Exchange gains and losses that arise from events that are disclosed as exceptional items should be included as part of such items. Similarly, exchange gains and losses that arise from events that fall to be treated as extraordinary items should be included as part of such items (though, in practice these will be rare following the introduction of FRS 3).

7.148 FRS 13 introduced narrative disclosure requirements relating to identification of the financial risks arising in the entity and discussion relating to how these risks have been managed. For companies reporting under FRS 29's disclosure requirements, FRS 13 is superseded by FRS 29. Financial risk includes currency risk. [FRS 13 para 11; FRS 29 paras B23, 24]. A number of the numerical disclosure requirements in each standard relate to currency exposure. Further consideration of the narrative and numerical disclosure requirements contained in FRS 13 and in FRS 29 are given in chapter 6.

Effect that foreign currency translation has on distributable profits

7.149 Companies can only make a distribution to their shareholders out of profits that are available for that purpose. The amount of distributable profits is calculated by reference to the financial statements of an individual company and the rules differ for private and public companies. The rules relating to calculating distributable profits are considered in detail in chapter 23. In order to determine distributable profits, it is necessary to distinguish between realised and unrealised profits and losses.

7.150 In an individual company, the exchange gains and losses that arise both on the currency transactions that the company completes during the year and on its outstanding short-term monetary items (as defined in para 7.23), are taken to the profit and loss account. Paragraph13(a) of Schedule 1 to SI 2008/410 states that *"...only profits realised at the balance sheet date shall be included in the profit and loss account"*. Where exchange gains and losses arise on short-term monetary items, their ultimate cash realisation can normally be assessed with reasonable certainty. For companies that prepare financial statements in accordance with Schedule 4, monetary items should be categorised as either short-term or long-term items. Short-term monetary items are those that fall due within one year of the balance sheet date. Therefore, gains and losses on such items are considered to be realised gains and losses in accordance with FRS 18 paragraph 28. Accordingly, the inclusion of these gains in the profit and loss account does not conflict with paragraph 13(a) of Schedule 1 to SI 2008/410.

7.151 Paragraph 65 of SSAP 20 implies that exchange gains that arise on outstanding long-term monetary items are not realised profits, but as discussed in paragraph 7.28, SSAP 20 requires these gains to be included in the profit and loss account. If the gains were unrealised, this would involve a departure from paragraph 12 of Schedule 4. However, since SSAP 20 was issued in 1983, the currency markets have become more sophisticated and companies have a greater ability to crystallise exchange profits on long-term monetary items. The ICAEW and ICAS have issued guidance in Tech 02/10, 'Guidance on the determination of realised profits and losses in the context of distributions under the Companies Act 2006'. This states that a profit is realised where it arises from the translation of a monetary asset which comprises qualifying consideration, or a liability denominated in a foreign currency. [Tech 02/10 para 3.9]. Qualifying consideration includes cash, or an asset that is readily convertible to cash and an amount receivable in cash where the debtor is capable of settling the receivable within a reasonable period of time, there is a reasonable certainty that the debtor will be capable of settling when called upon to do so and there is an expectation that the receivable will be settled. [Tech 02/10 para 3.9]. Consequently, unless there are doubts as to the convertibility or marketability of the currency in question (see para 7.30), foreign exchange profits arising on the retranslation of monetary items are realised, irrespective of the maturity date of the monetary item. [Tech 02/10 para 3.21].

[The next paragraph is 7.154.]

7.154 Where the exchange difference on a long-term monetary item such as a borrowing is a loss, SSAP 20 requires this to be included in the profit and loss account, unless the foreign currency borrowing is being used to finance or provide a hedge against a foreign equity investment (and the conditions in paragraph 51 of SSAP 20 are met). This means that a loss charged to the profit and loss account should be treated as a realised loss. This is because it is the current best estimate of the probable loss that will be incurred when the borrowing is repaid.

7.155 Where an individual company has a foreign currency borrowing that is being used to finance or provide a hedge against a foreign equity investment held by that same company then SSAP 20 permits the exchange gain/loss on the borrowing to be offset in reserves against the exchange loss/gain on the investment (subject to the conditions in paragraph 51 of SSAP 20 being met). Tech 02/10 includes guidance in respect of hedging. It states:

> *"Where hedge accounting is obtained in accordance with the relevant accounting standards, it is necessary to consider the combined effect of both sides of the hedging relationship to determine whether there is a realised profit or loss in accordance with the criteria in the guidance."*
> [Tech 02/10 para 3.19].

7.156 The guidance in Tech 02/10 takes the line that where a hedged asset or liability and a hedging instrument are accounted for as a hedge, it is the net exposure on the hedged asset or liability that determines whether any profit or loss arising is realised or unrealised. Therefore, it is not necessary to consider whether the gain/loss on the borrowing and the loss/gain on the investment are themselves realised or unrealised. Instead, the net position is considered as illustrated in the example below.

Example – Impact of hedged investment in foreign subsidiary on distributable profits

If Company A has an investment in a US subsidiary of $100 million and the investment is partially hedged by a US dollar borrowing of $80 million, the relevant amount for the purpose of determining the impact on realised profits is the foreign currency gain or loss on the $20 million net exposure on the investment in the US subsidiary.

If there is a foreign currency gain on the $20 million net exposure on the investment in the US subsidiary, this will be an unrealised profit. Paragraph 3.9(d) of Tech 02/10 states that a profit is realised where it arises from the translation of a monetary asset that comprises qualifying consideration. As the investment is a non-monetary item, the profit is regarded as unrealised.

If there is a foreign currency loss on the $20 million net exposure on the investment in the US subsidiary, this will generally be regarded as an unrealised loss. Paragraph 2.36 of Tech 02/10states that if an asset is revalued downwards below its recoverable amount, as defined in FRS 11, then the difference between that revalued amount and recoverable amount is treated as an unrealised loss as it reflects a revaluation adjustment rather than a provision under paragraph 9 of Schedule 1(1) of SI 2008/410. A similar principle applies to the retranslation of a non-monetary item. If the investment is not impaired and if the foreign currency loss is only recognised as a result of the accounting policy for the SSAP 20 offset (SSAP 20 para 51), then the foreign currency loss would be regarded as unrealised. This is consistent with paragraph 66 of SSAP 20.

[The next paragraph is 7.160.]

7.160 In practice, the financing and hedging of foreign equity investments can be complicated and may involve a number of group companies. For instance, the external borrowing may be held by the ultimate parent company, which then makes loans to an intermediate parent company that holds the foreign investments. It is necessary to consider the impact of the treasury arrangements on the distributable profits of each entity.

Hyper-inflation

7.161 Where a foreign subsidiary or an associate operates in a country in which a very high rate of inflation exists, the closing rate/net investment method is not considered to be suitable for translating the financial statements of the foreign enterprise for inclusion in the consolidated financial statements. This is because an asset acquired in foreign currency is worth very little in sterling terms at a time of high inflation when the foreign currency has weakened considerably against sterling, leading to a large debit to group reserves. At the same time, the results of the foreign enterprise are included at an inflated amount in the group's profit and loss account (whether from high interest income on deposits in a rapidly depreciating foreign currency or from trading operations which could be considered to reflect unrealistically high profitability).

7.162 The above problems were recognised by SSAP 20 which states:

"Where a foreign enterprise operates in a country in which a very high rate of inflation exists it may not be possible to present fairly in historical cost accounts the financial position of a foreign enterprise simply by a translation process. In such circumstances the local currency financial statements should be adjusted where possible to reflect current price levels before the translation process is undertaken." [SSAP 20 para 26].

7.163 SSAP 20 does not provide guidance on what is meant by a high rate of inflation and when or how this guidance should be applied in practice. As a result, the UITF considered this matter and issued Abstract 9, 'Accounting for operations in hyper-inflationary economies', in June 1993. The question of what constitutes hyper-inflation is judgemental. There is some guidance in FRS 24 which describes a number of characteristics of the economic environment of a country that indicate hyper-inflation. These are as follows:

- The general population prefers to keep its wealth in non-monetary assets or in a relatively stable foreign currency. Amounts of local currency held are immediately invested to maintain purchasing power.
- The general population regards monetary amounts not in terms of the local currency but in terms of a relatively stable foreign currency. Prices may be quoted in that currency.
- Sales and purchases on credit take place at prices that compensate for the expected loss of purchasing power during the credit period, even if the period is short.
- Interest rates, wages and prices are linked to a price index.
- The cumulative inflation rate over three years is approaching, or exceeds, 100 per cent.

7.164 The UITF reached a consensus that adjustments are required where the distortions caused by hyper-inflation are such as to affect the true and fair view given by the group financial statements. In any event adjustments must be made where the cumulative inflation rate over three years is approaching, or exceeds, 100 per cent and the operations in the hyper-inflationary economies are material. [UITF 9 para 5].

7.165 The Abstract is not clear whether the word 'cumulative' is intended to mean that the three-year inflation rate should be calculated by simply adding up the inflation rates for each of the three years or by computing the compound inflation rate over the three years. Consider the following example:

Example – Assessment of an economy as hyper-inflationary or not

The following data are relevant to a country operating in a hyper-inflationary economy:

	20X1	20X2	20X3	20X4
Inflation rate		30%	28%	34%
General price level	120	156	200	268

Based on simple addition the cumulative inflation rate for the years 20X2 to 20X4 is 92% (30 + 28 + 34).

Compounded annually (using the index at the end of 20X1 as the base), the cumulative inflation for 20X2 to 20X4 is (268 — 120) ÷ 120 = 123%.

In our view, the cumulative three-year inflation rate should be compounded, because it provides a measure of inflation for the three years taken as a whole.

7.166 The determination of whether a country has experienced cumulative three-year inflation of approximately 100 per cent or more should be based on an internationally or locally recognised general price-level index for that country. Information on inflation rates in various countries is available in International Financial Statistics, issued monthly by the Bureau of Statistics of the International Monetary Fund.

7.167 Although SSAP 20 suggested the use of a local price-level index for adjusting the financial statements of a local enterprise before translation, it may not always be possible to obtain a reliable local index. UITF Abstract 9, therefore, allows an alternative method, of using a relatively stable currency as the functional currency of the relevant hyperinflationary economy, which is similar to the method required by US GAAP although not permitted by FRS 24. The two methods specified in UITF 9, that are now considered to be acceptable and, therefore, consistent with SSAP 20 are as follows:

- Adjust the local currency financial statements to reflect current price levels before the translation process is undertaken as suggested in paragraph 26 of SSAP 20. This includes taking any gain or loss on the net monetary position through the profit and loss account.
- Using a relatively stable currency (which would not necessarily be sterling) as the functional currency (that is, the currency of measurement) for the relevant foreign operations. For example in certain businesses operating in Eastern Europe the US dollar or the euro acts effectively as the functional currency for business operations. The functional currency would in effect be the 'local currency' as defined in paragraph 39 of SSAP 20. In such circumstances, if the translations are not recorded initially in that stable currency, they must first be remeasured into that currency by applying the temporal method described in SSAP 20 (but based on the dollar or other stable currency rather than sterling). The effect is that the movement between the original currency of record and the stable currency is used as a proxy for an inflation index.

[UITF 9 para 6].

Example – Date from which translation into stable currency should begin

A company has a subsidiary that operates in a hyper-inflationary economy, because cumulative inflation over a 3 year period is over 100%. Using the same criterion, last year was also hyper-inflationary, but the previous year was not. Under the group's accounting policy under UITF Abstract 9 the subsidiary's financial statements should be translated, using the temporal method, into a stable currency, before being translated using the closing rate method into sterling. Should the translation into stable currency (US dollars) be done on the basis of the figures at the beginning of last year, and for that year and the current year only, or should it be done for all years previously as well?

UITF Abstract 9 states that the exchange differences arising on the translation into the stable currency, which are taken to profit and loss account, are a proxy for inflation adjustments. As there was no hyper-inflation in the years before last year the translation process set out in UITF Abstract 9 is not necessary for the earlier years. We, therefore, consider that the process should be based on the figures at the beginning of the previous year and should be done for the last year and the current year only. This means for instance that in the translation process non monetary assets will be recorded at the rate in force at the beginning of last year, rather than at the rate when they were originally acquired.

7.168 If neither of the above methods is considered appropriate for material operations, then the reasons should be stated and alternative methods to eliminate the distortions should be adopted. [UITF 9 para 7]. In practice, companies tend to follow one or the other method described above as illustrated in the examples below.

7.169 Where group operations in areas of hyper-inflation are material in the context of group results or net assets, the accounting policy adopted to eliminate the distortions of such inflation should be disclosed. [UITF 9 para 8].

Table 7.14 — Courtaulds plc — Report and Accounts — 31 March 1995

Statement of accounting policies (extract)

Foreign currencies

The accounts of overseas subsidiaries are translated into sterling at the rates at which the currencies could have been sold at the date of the Group balance sheet. Gains or losses arising on these transactions are dealt with in reserves. Other assets and liabilities denominated in foreign currencies are translated into sterling at year end rates and differences arising are dealt with in the profit and loss account. The results of subsidiaries in hyper-inflationary economies are dealt with in accordance with UITF 9 using the US$ as the functional currency.

Table 7.15 — Reckitt Benckiser plc — Annual Report & Accounts — 31 January 2001

Accounting policies (extract)

Foreign currency translation

Transactions denominated in foreign currencies are translated at the rate of exchange on the day the transaction occurs or at the contracted rate if the transaction is covered by a forward exchange contract.

Assets and liabilities denominated in a foreign currency are translated at the exchange rate ruling on the balance sheet date or, if appropriate, at a forward contract rate. Exchange differences arising in the accounts of individual undertakings are included in the profit and loss account except that, where foreign currency borrowing has been used to finance equity investments in foreign currencies. Exchange differences arising on the borrowing are dealt with through reserves to the extent that they are covered by exchange differences arising on the net assets represented by the equity investments.

The accounts of overseas subsidiary undertakings are translated into Sterling on the following basis:

Assets and liabilities at the rate of exchange ruling at the year end date.

Profit and loss account items at the average rate of exchange for the year.

Exchange differences arising on the translation of accounts into Sterling are recorded as movements on reserves.

The accounts of subsidiaries operating in hyper-inflationary environments are adjusted where possible to reflect current price levels before being translated into Sterling.

The currencies that most influence these translations and the relevant exchange rates are:

	2001	2000
Average rates:		
£/Euro	**1.6074**	1.6417
£/US Dollar	**1.4404**	1.5260
Closing rates.		
£/Euro	**1.6353**	1.5843
£/US Dollar	**1.4546**	1.4935

7.169.1 Determining whether a subsidiary operates in a hyperinflationary economy per UITF 9 is not a policy choice but rather a change in circumstances (inflation rising or falling). Therefore, the revised accounting method should be applied prospectively and comparatives should not be adjusted. However, the accounting policy note should indicate whether UITF 9 has been applied or no longer applies to the relevant subsidiaries.

Multi-currency share capital

7.170 It is not uncommon for a UK company to issue shares in a currency other than sterling. The legal aspects are dealt with in chapter 23. The question arises as to how such foreign currency share capital should be translated for reporting purposes at the company's year end. This is not dealt with either in SSAP 20 or in FRS 25, 'Financial instruments: Presentation'. There are two possible treatments:

- The shares could be maintained at the historical rate at the date the shares were issued.
- The shares could be retranslated at each year end at the closing rate of exchange.

In the latter case, exchange differences would normally be taken directly to reserves (but see example below). Overall, both methods have the same effect on shareholders' funds.

7.171 For equity shares either method is acceptable. For non-equity shares the substance of the instrument should be considered. For accounting periods beginning on or after 1 January 2005, the amendments to the Companies Act effected by SI 2004/2947 require the substance of these instruments to be considered. This is also required by FRS 25. Non-equity shares such as redeemable preference shares are in substance long-term debt and are accounted for as such. Long-term debt is retranslated at the closing rate at each year end under SSAP 20. This is considered further in the following example:

Example — US Dollar preference shares issued by a UK company

A company has issued preference shares denominated in dollars. These are redeemable at par in 20X9. How should the shares be recorded in the company's sterling financial statements and how should the exchange differences, if any, be dealt with under the Companies Act 1985 and also FRS 25?

The redeemable preference shares are economically similar to debt. Long-term debt is normally retranslated by using the closing rate of exchange at each year end, with exchange gains and losses taken into the profit and loss account. The most appropriate treatment, therefore, is to retranslate the preference shares at each year end at the closing rate.

FRS 4 requires the finance costs for non-equity shares to be calculated on the same basis as the finance costs for debt. Exchange gains or losses on debt or non-equity shares would fall within the definition of finance costs in FRS 4. In addition, paragraph 68 of SSAP 20 indicates that exchange differences on debt should be disclosed separately as part of interest payable and similar charges.

Since these shares are accounted for as debt under the Companies Act amendments and under FRS 25, the exchange gains or losses are taken to the profit and loss account and are charged or credited in arriving at the profit for the year.

An exception to the treatment described above is where the preference shares were issued to finance or provide a hedge against, for example, an equity investment in the US. In those circumstances it would be acceptable to use the offset method in SSAP 20. Under this method the investment would be designated as a dollar asset. Both the investment and the preference shares would then be retranslated at each year end at the closing rate. The exchange differences on the preference shares would then be offset, as a reserve movement, against the exchange differences on the investment. Application of the conditions for offset in paragraphs 51 and 57 of SSAP 20 would result in exchange gains or losses on the preference shares being offset only to the extent of exchange differences arising on the foreign equity investments. Any surplus exchange differences on the preference shares would then be shown as a charge or credit in the profit and loss account as described above.

Financial statements in foreign currencies

7.172 Financial statements may be prepared in a foreign currency if that currency is the 'local currency' of that company. SSAP 20 implicitly requires a company to prepare its financial statements in its local currency. Therefore, if the local currency is the dollar, the financial statements should be prepared in dollars. It is generally not appropriate for a company to publish its annual financial statements in a currency different to its local currency

7.173 Although not specifically dealt with in the Companies Act, the Registrar of Companies accepts annual financial statements prepared in a foreign currency, provided that the currency exists legally and the exchange rate to sterling at the balance sheet date is disclosed in the notes to the financial statements.

[The next paragraph is 7.188.]

Annex

7.188 The annex to this chapter reproduces the chapter from the Manual of Accounting – IFRS for the UK that deals with accounting for foreign currencies under IAS 21. As the requirements of FRS 23 and FRS 24 are almost identical to the requirements of IAS 21 and IAS 29, respectively, the accounting for foreign currencies will be the same under UK GAAP as under IFRS.

7.189 The text in the annex contains references to IFRSs. For these to be applied in the UK context, the following should be noted:

- The references to paragraphs in IAS 21 and IAS 29 are identical to the paragraph numbers in FRS 23 and FRS 24, respectively.
- References to other international standards should be read as referring to the equivalent UK standards, as issued by the ASB.
- The transitional provisions for first time adopters of IFRS insofar as they relate to the first time adoption of IAS 21 have been incorporated by the ASB into FRS 23.

Annex

Foreign currencies

Introduction

A7.1 Entities conduct businesses that are not confined within national boundaries. The globalisation of markets for goods and services as well as capital means entities have to engage in international trade, cross-border alliances and joint ventures if they are to survive and grow in today's competitive business environment. Entities conduct business in the international market place in a number of ways. First, entities may buy goods and services from overseas suppliers and sell goods and services to overseas customers. Secondly, they may extend their international reach by conducting business through overseas subsidiaries, branches and associates.

A7.2 In the first situation, transactions are often expressed in foreign currencies. The results of these transactions are translated into the entity's functional currency for financial reporting purposes. In the second situation, it is usual for the foreign operation to maintain its accounting records in the currency of the primary economic environment in which it operates. It is not possible to combine, add or subtract measurements expressed in different currencies, so management translates the foreign operation's results and financial position into the currency in which the reporting entity presents its consolidated financial statements.

A7.3 Accounting for foreign currencies is, therefore, primarily concerned with the translation process whereby financial data denominated in one currency is expressed in terms of another currency. The translation process does not change the essential characteristics of the assets and liabilities measured. It merely restates assets and liabilities, initially expressed in a foreign currency unit, to a common currency unit by applying a rate of exchange factor — a translation rate.

A7.4 Different translation rates may be used depending on the circumstances. These are:

- The historical rate — the rate of exchange ruling at the date the transaction or revaluation occurred.
- The closing rate — the rate ruling at the balance sheet date.
- The average rate ruling during the year.

The average rate is generally confined to income and expenditure items. The rates used for balance sheet items (historical or closing) depend on the types of assets and liabilities – monetary or non-monetary. These methods are addressed later in this chapter.

A7.5 The treatment of exchange differences that arise on foreign currency transactions is different from those that arise on foreign currency translation. Foreign currency translation also raises a number of questions, such as: the extent to which exchange gains and losses from different sources can be offset; whether some exchange differences should be recognised immediately whilst others should be deferred; and whether the recognition should be through the income statement or in other comprehensive income.

[The next paragraph is A7.23.]

Objectives

A7.23 IAS 21 prescribes how to:

- Include foreign currency transactions and foreign operations in an entity's financial statements.
- Specify which exchange rates to use and how to report the effects of changes in exchange rates in the financial statements.
- Translate the financial statements into a presentation currency.

[IAS 21 paras 1, 2].

Applying these requirements in practice can be complex. This chapter provides guidance on the issues commonly encountered.

Scope

A7.24 IAS 21 sets out the requirements for foreign currency translation. It applies to any entity that comes within its scope and engages in foreign currency operations. The standard is applied in:

- Accounting for transactions and balances in foreign currencies, except for those derivative transactions and balances that are within the scope of IAS 39, 'Financial instruments: Recognition and measurement'.
- Translating the results and financial position of foreign operations that are included in the entity's financial statements by consolidation, proportionate consolidation or equity accounting.
- Translating an entity's results and financial position into a presentation currency.

[IAS 21 para 3].

A7.25 Accounting for foreign currency derivatives is included in IAS 39; it is scoped out of this standard. Foreign currency derivatives that may be embedded in various contracts and that require separate accounting under IAS 39 are scoped out of IAS 21; embedded foreign currency derivatives that do not require separate accounting under IAS 39 are included in IAS 21. However, IAS 21 applies to translation of foreign currency derivatives from a functional currency to a presentation currency. [IAS 21 para 4].

A7.26 The standard does not apply to hedge accounting for foreign currency items, including the hedging of a net investment in a foreign operation. These issues are addressed in IAS 39. [IAS 21 para 5]. See chapter 6.

The functional currency approach

Introduction

A7.27 IAS 21 requires each individual entity to determine its functional currency and measure its results and financial position in that currency. Each individual entity included in the consolidation therefore has its own functional currency. There is no such thing as a group functional currency.

A7.28 The requirement to identify each entity's functional currency is the key feature of IAS 21. The functional currency serves as the basis for determining whether the entity is engaging in foreign currency transactions. This is because IAS 21 defines foreign currency as a currency other than the functional currency. [IAS 21 para 8]. Additionally, identifying the functional currency has a direct impact on the treatment of exchange gains and losses arising from the translation process and, thereby, the reported results, as will be evident later. IAS 21 provides guidance on determining the functional currency, which is considered from paragraph A7.31 below.

Example – Identification of foreign currency transactions

An entity trades in crude oil and has a US dollar functional currency per the assessment required under IAS 21, because substantially all of its sales and purchases are in US dollars. The entity is located in London and has significant transactions in sterling. It has issued euro-denominated share capital to its Dutch parent. Transactions with the parent are denominated in euros.

The sterling transactions and euro transactions are foreign currency transactions. The entity's physical location and the denomination of its share capital do not change the treatment of sterling- and euro-denominated transactions. This is because the entity has a US dollar functional currency; all transactions in other currencies are therefore foreign currency transactions.

[The next paragraph is A7.31.]

Determining the functional currency

A7.31 An entity's functional currency is a matter of fact. In some cases, the facts will clearly identify the functional currency, in other cases they will not. IAS 21 provides guidance on how to determine an entity's functional currency.

A7.31.1 An entity's functional currency is the currency of the primary economic environment in which it operates. [IAS 21 para 8]. It should, therefore, be determined at the entity level. An entity includes a foreign operation, that is, a subsidiary, associate, branch or joint venture whose activities are based or conducted in a country or currency other than that of the reporting entity.

A7.31.2 An individual entity (including a foreign operation) for these purposes may not correspond to a legal entity (for example, a company). For example, a branch that is part of a single legal entity may be a foreign operation. Judgement is required in determining an entity's functional currency based on individual facts and circumstances.

A7.31.3 A group comprised of multiple entities identifies the functional currency of each entity for the purpose of defining that entity's foreign currency exposure. Different entities within a multinational group, therefore, often have different functional currencies. The group as a whole does not have a functional currency.

A7.32 The primary economic environment in which an entity operates is normally the economic environment in which it primarily generates and expends cash. [IAS 21 para 9].The functional currency is normally the currency of the country in which the entity is located. It may, however, be a different currency. In addition, circumstances might indicate that the foreign operation's functional currency is the same as the reporting entity's functional currency. For this purpose, a foreign operation is defined as an entity that is a subsidiary, associate, joint venture or a branch of the reporting entity, the activities of which are based or conducted in a country or currency other than that of the reporting entity. [IAS 21 para 8].

A7.33 IAS 21 requires entities to consider primary and secondary indicators when determining the functional currency. Primary indicators are closely linked to the primary economic environment in which the entity operates and are given more weight. Secondary indicators provide supporting evidence to determine an entity's functional currency. Both of these indicators and the factors needing consideration are shown in the table below.

Primary indicators of functional currency [IAS 21 para 9]

Indicators		**Factors to be considered by the entity in determining the functional currency**
Sales and cash inflows	(a)	The currency that *mainly influences* sales prices for its goods and services. This will often be the currency in which sales prices for goods and services are denominated and settled. [IAS 21 para 9(a)(i)]. In other words, where an active local sales market exists for the entity's products that are also priced in the local currency, and revenues are collected primarily in that local currency, the local currency is the functional currency. However, the standard gives greater emphasis to the currency of the economy that determines the

	pricing of transactions than the currency in which transactions are denominated.
	(b) The currency of the country whose competitive forces and regulations *mainly determine* the sales prices of its goods and services. [IAS 21 para 9(a)(ii)].Where sales prices of the entity's products are determined by local competition and local government regulations rather than worldwide competition or by international prices, the local currency is the functional currency. For example, aircraft manufacturers often price aircraft in US dollars or in euros, but the legal and regulatory environment of the country in which the manufacturer is located may inhibit the entity's ability to pass hard currency costs to its customers. Therefore, while the business is influenced by the hard currency, its ability to generate revenue is determined by the local environment, which may indicate that the local currency is the functional currency.
Expenses and cash outflows	The currency that *mainly influences* labour, material and other costs of providing goods and services. This is often the currency in which such costs are denominated and settled. [IAS 21 para 9(b)]. For example, where labour, material and other operating costs are primarily sourced and incurred locally, the local currency is likely to be the functional currency, even though there also might be imports from other countries.

Secondary indicators of functional currency [IAS 21 para 10]

Indicators	**Factors to be considered by the entity in determining the functional currency**
Financing activities	The currency in which funds from financing activities (for example, issuing debt and equity instruments) are generated. [IAS 21 para 10(a)]. For example, where financing is raised in and serviced by funds primarily generated by the entity's local operation, this may indicate that the local currency is the functional currency, in the absence of other indicators to the contrary.
Retention of operating income	The currency in which receipts from operating activities are usually retained. [IAS 21 para 10(b)]. This is the currency in which the entity maintains its excess working capital balance, which would generally be the local currency.

A7.34 The above primary and secondary indicators for determining of the functional currency must be considered by all entities. If the entity is a foreign operation, the standard specifies four additional factors that should be considered in determining the functional currency and whether it is the same as that of the reporting entity. These additional factors are shown in the table below. They set out the conditions that point to whether the foreign operation's functional currency is the same as, or different from, the reporting entity (the reporting entity, in this context, being the entity that has the foreign operation as its subsidiary, branch, associate or joint venture).

Additional indicators for foreign operations [IAS 21 para 11]

Indicators	**Conditions pointing to functional currency being *different from* that of the reporting entity**	**Conditions pointing to functional currency being the *same as* that of the reporting entity**
Degree of autonomy	Activities are carried out with a significant degree of autonomy. An example is when the operation accumulates cash and other monetary items, incurs expenses, generates income and arranges borrowings, all substantially in its local currency.	No significant degree of autonomy – activities are carried out as an extension of the reporting entity. An example is when the foreign operation only sells goods imported from the reporting entity and remits the proceeds to it. It follows that such an entity (which would be considered an integral foreign operation in the previous version of IAS 21) must have the same currency as the reporting entity. This is because it would be contradictory for an integral foreign operation that *"carries on business as if it were an extension of the reporting entity's operations"* to operate in a primary economic environment different from its parent. [IAS 21 para BC6].
Frequency of transactions with reporting entity	Few inter-company transactions with the reporting entity.	Frequent and extensive inter-company transactions with the reporting entity.
Cash flow impact on reporting entity	Mainly in local currency and do not affect reporting entity's cash flows	Directly impact the reporting entity's cash flows and are readily available for remittance to the reporting entity.
Financing	Primarily in the local currency and serviced by funds generated by the entity's operation.	Significant financing from or reliance on the reporting entity to service existing and normally expected debt obligations.

A7.35 The relative importance of the various indicators will vary from entity to entity. For example, the primary and secondary indicators apply to the generality of entities that provide goods and services, but they may not be directly relevant in certain other situations. Examples of situations in which the primary and secondary indicators may be less relevant include treasury entities, special purpose entities and holding (including intermediate holding) entities. In those situations, management may need to consider the additional indicators stated in paragraph A7.34 above when determining the functional currency. When considering the autonomy indicator in paragraph 11 of IAS 21, our view is that it is not limited to situations where a subsidiary or a branch derives its functional currency from its parent. It may also be applicable to situations where an intermediate holding company is acting as an extension of its subsidiary or group of subsidiaries and, therefore, has the same functional currency as its subsidiary or group of subsidiaries. Associates and joint ventures are likely to be autonomous from an individual investor given the lack of control in the relationship and the paragraph 11 additional indicators are not likely to be relevant.

A7.35.1 The IFRS IC has considered the functional currency of a parent entity whose only activity is to hold investments in subsidiaries. In its March 2010 update, it noted that the primary indicators in IAS 21 should not be considered in isolation and that judgement is required when the functional currency is determined. In our view, a policy choice exists as to how such an entity determines its functional currency. The entity may determine that the parent entity is acting as an extension of its subsidiaries and, therefore, has the same functional currency as those subsidiaries. Alternatively, the entity may consider that IAS 21's 'foreign operation' indicators allow an entity to 'look up' to the entity from which it determines its functional currency, but that guidance does not require an entity to 'look down' and be a foreign operation of its subsidiaries. Under such a view, an entity looks at all of the primary and secondary indicators and will likely conclude that its functional currency is determined by the currency of its dividend revenue, its expenses and the currency of its financing. See further example 3 in paragraph A7.39 below.

A7.36 In assessing the indicators' relative importance, management may find it useful to consider the following aspects of each indicator:

- The significance of that indicator to the entity's operation. For example, the existence of sterling denominated debt in a foreign entity of a UK parent may not be significant if the foreign entity is primarily self-financing through retained earnings.
- How clearly the indicator identifies a particular currency as the functional currency. For example, if the same entity purchases raw materials both from the UK and locally, the 'expenses' indicator may be inconclusive.

In contrast, if the majority of sales occur in the host country at prices determined by local conditions, the 'sales' indicator might be regarded as the key determinant in concluding that the local currency is the functional currency.

A7.37 After considering all the factors, the functional currency may still not be obvious. The operation may be diverse, with cash flows, financing and transactions occurring in more than a single currency. In these situations, judgement is required in determining the functional currency that most faithfully represents the economic effects of the underlying transactions, events and conditions. In exercising that judgement, management should give priority to the primary indicators before considering the secondary indicators and the additional factors set out above. [IAS 21 para 12].

A7.38 The standard gives greater emphasis to the primary indicators because, as stated above, these indicators are closely linked to the primary economic environment in which the entity operates. The currency of the economy in which the entity operates generally determines the pricing of transactions; this is considered to be more influential than the currency in which the transactions are denominated and settled. This is because transactions can be denominated and settled in any currency management chooses, but as the pricing of the transaction is normally done by reference to the economy of the country whose competitive forces and regulations affect the transaction, the currency of that economy becomes the functional currency by definition. In other words, the currency of the country whose economy drives the business and which determines the gains and losses to be recognised in the financial statements most faithfully reflects the economic effects of the underlying transactions, events and conditions.

A7.39 The standard's intention that the primary and secondary indicators should be looked at as a hierarchy is intended to avoid practical difficulties in determining an entity's functional currency. For example, if all the primary indicators, which should be considered together, identify a particular currency as the functional currency, there is no need to consider the secondary indicators. Secondary indicators serve to provide additional supporting evidence in determining an entity's functional currency. [IAS 21 para BC9].

Illustrative examples

A7.40 Determining an entity's functional currency depends on the facts and circumstances. The following examples are for illustrative purposes only and should not be used as solutions for specific situations.

Example 1 – Functional currency of an entity with transactions denominated in a stable currency.
Example 2 – Functional currency of an entity with products normally traded in a non-local currency (such as oil and gold).
Example 3 – Functional currency of an offshore holding company.
Example 4 – Functional currency of an intermediate parent with some operating activities.
Example 5 – Functional currency of an intermediate parent with no operating or financing activities of its own.
Example 6 – Functional currency of an entity raising finance for the group in a foreign currency compared to the other entities in the group.

Example 7 – Functional currency of separate treasury centres in different geographical areas.
Example 8 – Functional currency of a treasury centre that pools resources in the group.
Example 9 – Functional currency of a foreign subsidiary importing products from parent for local distribution.
Example 10 – Functional currency of a special purpose entity ('SPE').
Example 11 – Different functional currencies for stand-alone accounts and for group reporting purposes?
Example 12 – Functional currency after a group restructuring.

Example 1 – Functional currency of an entity with transactions denominated in a stable currency

A real estate entity operates in Russia. It owns several office buildings in Moscow and St Petersburg that are rented to Russian and foreign entities. All lease contracts are denominated in US dollars, but payments can be made in either US dollars or in Russian roubles. However, almost all of the lease payments are settled in roubles. This has also been the historical pattern of payment.

On first analysis, the 'sales and cash inflows' indicators appear to produce a mixed response, because the currency that mainly influences the pricing of the lease contracts is the US dollar, whereas the cash inflows are in roubles. Also, cash outflows such as the principal operating costs, management of properties, insurance, taxes and staff costs are likely to be incurred and settled in roubles, which would indicate that the functional currency is the Russian rouble.

The lease payments are denominated in US dollars, but the US dollar is not considered to be significant to the entity's operation because: (a) most of the collection is in roubles, which is subject to short-term changes in US dollar/rouble exchange rate; and (b) it is the local conditions and circumstances in Russia, not the US, that determine the rental yields of properties in Moscow and St Petersburg that mainly influence the pricing of the lease contracts, which are merely denominated in US dollar.

It is, therefore, the currency of the Russian economy, rather than the currency in which the lease contracts are denominated, that most faithfully represents the economic effects of the real estate activity in Russia. Since the transactions are denominated in a different currency to the entity's functional currency, there is an embedded foreign exchange derivative in the contract that may have to be separated in as explained in paragraph AG33(d) of IAS 39. For further guidance on embedded derivatives refer to the Manual of Accounting – Financial instruments.

Example 2 – Functional currency of an entity with products normally traded in a non-local currency (such as oil and gold)

Entity A operates an oil refinery in Saudi Arabia. All of the entity's income is denominated and settled in US dollars. The oil price is subject to the worldwide supply and demand, and crude oil is routinely traded in US dollars around the world. Around 45% of entity A's cash costs are imports or expatriate salaries denominated in US dollars. The remaining 55% of cash expenses are incurred in Saudi Arabia and denominated and settled in riyal. The non-cash costs (depreciation) are US dollar denominated, as the initial investment was in US dollars.

The functional currency of entity A is the US dollar. The crude oil sales prices are influenced by global demand and supply. Crude oil is globally traded in US dollars around the world. The revenue analysis points to the US dollar. The cost analysis is mixed. Depreciation (or any other non-cash expenses) is not considered, as the primary economic environment is where the entity generates and expends cash. Operating cash expenses are influenced by the riyal (55%) and the US dollar (45%). Management is able to determine the functional currency as the US dollar, as the revenue is clearly influenced by the US dollar and expenses are mixed.

Example 3 – Functional currency of an offshore holding company

A group of companies is organised as follows:

Entity A is a reporting entity with three operating subsidiaries (entities B, C and D) that are incorporated in Russia. Management has concluded that the functional currency of each subsidiary should be the local currency.

Entity A is the holding entity and has been set up by institutional investors in Cyprus (a eurozone country). Entity A has obtained equity and loan financing and has invested in Russian entities B, C and D. It pools cash from all group entities, invests excess cash and obtains external financing, according to the group's needs. The financing is drawn in US dollars, and all of its monetary assets are denominated in US dollars. The entity retains cash in US dollars, its expenses that are not associated with financing are insignificant compared to the investments in the Russian investees or the funding costs and it has no employees. The entity's activities are carried out by employees of its operating subsidiaries. Its shares are denominated in US dollars and it pays dividends to its investors in US dollars.

In January 2010, the IFRS IC received a request for guidance on determining the functional currency of an investment holding company. The IFRS IC was asked whether the underlying economic environment of its subsidiaries should be considered in determining the functional currency of an investment holding company. The IFRS IC has decided not to issue guidance on this matter, but noted that assessing functional currency requires the exercise of judgement and that the paragraph 9 indicators (sales and expenses) should not be considered in isolation. Our view is that there is an accounting policy choice for determining the functional currency of a holding company in this situation:

Option 1: The holding entity is viewed as having the same functional currency as its operating subsidiaries. Entity A's functional currency is the Russian rouble.

Management is required to use its judgement to determine the functional currency that most faithfully represents the economic effects of the underlying transactions, events and conditions. [IAS 21 para 12]. Entity A has no activity of its own. The currency that reflects the economic substance of the underlying economic events that affect the holding entity is the Russian rouble, as all of the holding entity's subsidiaries operate in Russia and entity A's primary source of income will be dividends obtained from the subsidiaries in Russia. Entity A's ability to service debts and pay dividends to shareholders is dependent on the Russian economy. Although paragraph 11 of IAS 21 explicitly defines a foreign operation as a reporting entity's subsidiary, branch, associate or joint venture, paragraph 11 may be applied by analogy, and viewing an investment holding company as an extension of its subsidiaries is appropriate.

Option 2: The holding company's functional currency is not viewed as being dependent on its foreign operations. Entity A's functional currency is the US dollar.

Entity A has no sales or purchases, nor does it incur significant expenses other than in respect of its financing activities. The economic source of dividend revenues is not a key factor in determining the functional currency of a non-operating parent company. The primary indicators in paragraph 9 are not directly relevant. It is the currency denomination of the financing activities that drives the functional currency determination (the secondary indicators in paragraph 10). The functional currency is determined based on the primary economic environment in which the entity generates and expends cash, consistent with the secondary indicators. All cash flows associated with financing and dividends are US dollar. Paragraph 11 of IAS 21 explicitly defines a foreign operation as a reporting entity's subsidiary, branch, associate or joint venture. While a foreign operation may be viewed as an extension of its parent, paragraph 11 is not required to be applied by analogy to view an investment holding company as an extension of its subsidiary, because the parent controls the subsidiary and not *vice versa.*

Example 4– Functional currency of an intermediate parent with some operating activities

Parent (entity P) is a manufacturing business located in the UK with sterling as the functional currency. Entity P invests US dollars in an intermediate parent (entity IP), which then invests in three separate US dollar operating subsidiaries (entity S1, S2 and S3). Entity IP undertakes no 'operating' activities of its own; however, it acts as the holding entity of the US subsidiaries – heading up the US group. It has a dedicated management team and staff that carry out the head office functions, including the US group's payroll, cash management and preparation of a sub-consolidation package. The management team takes finance decisions related to the sub-group and controls the activities of the sub-group. Its management team reports monthly to entity P's board on the results of the US group. Its key cash inflows are the dividends from its subsidiaries (which it remits up directly to entity P), and inter-company balances from its subsidiaries (that are used to settle both entity IP's own administration costs and those costs incurred directly by entity IP on behalf of its subsidiaries — that is payroll costs, computer services, maintenance, etc). All cash inflows and outflows are denominated in US dollar. Entity IP is a US-registered company.

Entity IP does have operating activities in that it provides local management services to its subsidiaries. It incurs local costs and then either recharges these to its subsidiaries or retains dividend income from its subsidiaries to pay for these costs. All the costs incurred are incurred in US dollar and will be reimbursed in US dollar.

Entity IP does not raise finance; consideration of the currency in which funds from financing activities are generated is not directly applicable. However, the funding of its costs through dividends and inter-company balances is in US dollars. The currency in which receipts from operating activities is usually retained indicates a US dollar functional currency.

Looking to the additional factors in paragraph 11 of IAS 21 revised:

- Entity IP has a significant degree of autonomy: it has its own management team and staff; a budget for which it is responsible; and discretion over its head office functions.
- It has a number of transactions with parties outside the group.
- The cash flows of entity IP do not directly affect the parent; entity IP is not merely acting as a conduit.

Consideration of paragraph 11(d), *"whether cash flows from activities of the foreign operation are sufficient to service existing and normally expected debt obligations without funds being made available by the reporting entity"* is not applicable.

Unlike example 5, entity IP is carrying out operating activities of its own, albeit not in the traditional trading sense. These activities consist of holding and managing the subsidiaries of the sub-group. Under paragraphs 9 and 10 of IAS 21 revised, the costs entity IP incurs and any receipts retained from operating activities are in US dollar. IP in this example is not merely acting as a conduit/'cash box' for entity P. It is carrying out management activities and has a significant degree of autonomy. It has an active management team and exercises discretion over the US group's operations. The US group has been structured in this way for operational as well as tax reasons. This suggests that entity IP's functional currency is not necessarily that of entity P. The functional currency of entity IP would be US dollar.

Example 5 – Functional currency of an intermediate parent with no operating or financing activities of its own

Parent (entity P) is a manufacturing business located in the UK with sterling as the functional currency. P invests US dollar in an intermediate parent (entity IP), which then invests in a US-dollar operating subsidiary (entity S) on behalf of entity P. Entity IP is a shell company that undertakes no operating or financing activities as it only holds investments. Its key cash inflows are dividends from entity S, which it remits directly to parent entity P. Entity IP is a US-registered company.

Entity IP undertakes no operating or financing activities. Any investing activity that entity IP undertakes is not carried out as a separate stand-alone activity, but at the behest of its parent. It is not, therefore, relevant to consider the 'sales and cash inflow' indicator. The'expenses and cash outflow' indicator may be relevant, as it is more likely than not that entity IP will incur some local costs. But that indicator by itself is not considered significant to entity IP's operations, nor does it clearly identify the US dollar as the functional currency.

The secondary indicators do not clearly identify the US dollar as the functional currency, as entity IP does not raise any finance from external local sources – any finance raised is primarily from its parent or from sterling sources. Nor does entity IP retain any funds for own use, which are all remitted to the parent. All the additional factors also point to the US dollar not being the currency that most faithfully represents entity IP's activities of receiving dividend income from entity S in US dollar and remitting these to its parent.

Entity IP is, therefore, simply a device or a shell corporation for holding investments that could have been done by entity P itself. The functional currency of entity IP is the same as its parent: sterling.

Alternatively, the analysis could focus on the fact that the results of entity IP are dependent on the economic activities of its subsidiary whose functional currency is the US dollar. The cash inflow indicator, therefore, suggests that the US dollar is significant to its investing activity.

Where the indicators are mixed, management should exercise judgement in determining the currency that most faithfully represents entity IP's activities. Entity IP is a shell intermediate holding entity that merely holds the investment and receives occasional dividends, passing them on to the parent. It is, therefore, appropriate to regard it as carrying out a function that the parent could equally carry out. Our view is that sterling is entity IP's functional currency.

Example 6 – Functional currency of a company raising finance for the group in a foreign currency compared to the other entities in the group

A French-listed parent has significant French, UK and US operating subsidiaries, but no Japanese operations. The French parent creates a new subsidiary, Newco SA, incorporated and resident in France. Newco issues in yen 1bn of equity capital to French parent, receiving yen 1bn of cash. Newco also raises yen 100m of external financing and places the yen 1.1bn total cash on deposit with a bank in Japan, earning 0.1% interest per annum. The cash will be reinvested in yen-denominated financial instruments such as bonds and commercial paper. Newco has few staff that manages the entity's investing activities. It incurs sterling operational costs that are insignificant compared to the interest paid on its yen borrowing. Like any wholly-owned subsidiary, the retained profits are under the parent's control.

Newco does not undertake any key operating activities on its own. Consideration of the currency that mainly influences sales and costs is not directly relevant. Newco incurs expenses in euro, but these are not significant enough to suggest that the euro is the functional currency. It is necessary to look at the secondary indicators.

Newco does raise finance by issuing its own equity instruments to the parent in a currency that is different from the parent, but the proceeds are invested in yen-denominated assets at the behest of the parent. The external funds raised through the issue of debt instruments are insignificant compared to the issue of equity shares to the parent. The question is silent as to whether the income generated from the investments is reinvested in other yen denominated assets or whether it is wholly passed on to the parent. Whatever that may be, the decision to reinvest or distribute is under the parent's control.

Consideration of the other additional factors suggests that Newco is a 'cash box' type company with no independent management/activity. Newco is simply a conduit for the parent entity that could invest the yen directly. It may be that the only reason the parent entity has invested the yen through Newco is in the hope that its exposure to changes in the euro/yen exchange rate is reported in other comprehensive income through the translation of its net investment in Newco, rather than in the income statement, which would be the case if the yen deposits were treated as belonging to the parent. The 'autonomy factor' points to the euro as the functional currency, as Newco appears to be merely an extension of the activities of the parent. This would point to the functional currency being the same as that of its parent — the euro. This would be the answer if Newco carried out only the activities described.

The investing activity could have been done by the parent rather than the subsidiary and, therefore, the parent's functional currency should determine the foreign entity's functional currency.

Example 7 – Functional currency of separate treasury centres in different geographical areas

A Swiss multi-national entity with Swiss franc as its functional currency has operating subsidiaries in the US and Europe whose functional currencies are the US dollar and the euro respectively. It has established a treasury centre (TC) in each of these geographical regions. The activities of the two TCs are identical in that each provides financial and risk management services to its relevant operating subsidiaries. All transactions (for example, management of liquid funds, borrowings and hedging activities) between a TC and its respective operating subsidiaries are carried out either in US dollars or euros.

Each TC earns dividends and income from cash management activities in US dollars and euros respectively. Each TC charges a monthly fee for providing such financial services to its operating subsidiaries that is denominated either in US dollars or euros, depending on its area of operation. All operating costs — such as staff costs payable to treasury and financial management specialists and other administrative and running costs — are incurred and settled by each TC in US dollars or euros. The TCs' short and long-term financing are provided by the Swiss parent in the form of Swiss franc loans. The TCs do not retain any US dollars or euros generated from their operation for their own use. After meeting local expenses, management either uses US dollars or euros to settle the inter-entity payables to the operating subsidiaries or distributes any surplus to the parent as dividends.

This response addresses only the US dollar TC; the considerations for the euro TC are the same.

The primary factors (currency that influences sales price and the costs of providing goods and services) are arguably irrelevant because TC does not have any third-party sales and purchases. However, the determination of the functional currency is an entity-by-entity question and it is not relevant to whether an entity's fee income comes from inside or outside the group. What is relevant is the nature of the fee income and the manner in which it is earned. In this example, the TC provides financial services to the US operating subsidiaries for which it charges a fee. The fees are invoiced and settled in US dollar. TC also earns investment income in US dollars. As TC earns its revenue and income in US dollar and the underlying US economy determines the pricing of TC's fee income to the US operating subsidiaries, the 'sales and cash inflow' indicator identifies the US dollar as the functional currency of TC. As all administrative and local expenses are incurred and settled in US dollar, the 'expenses and cash outflow' indicator also provides strong evidence that the US dollars is the TC's functional currency. The primary economic environment in which the TC generates and expends cash is the US and, therefore, its functional currency is the US dollar.

The primary indicators are clear, so there is no need to consider the secondary indicators, even if these seem to provide evidence that the Swiss franc is the functional currency (for example, TC's short and long-term financing is primarily in the form of Swiss franc loans from the parent).

Example 8 – Functional currency of a treasury centre that pools resources in the group

A UK multi-national entity with sterling as its functional currency has set up a treasury centre (TC) in Switzerland. TC borrows US dollars, euros and sterling in the euro-market and lends the proceeds to its parent and other operating subsidiaries with the loans denominated in the borrowing entity's functional currency. As part of its cash management operations, it pools the liquid resources of the parent and the operational units and invests them temporarily in the euro-market. It also manages foreign exchange and interest rate risks of operating units by executing derivative contracts with third parties and/or with operating units.

TC earns dividends and income from cash management activities in US dollar, euros and sterling. It charges a monthly fee for providing such financial services to its parent and operating subsidiaries that is denominated in the relevant entity's functional currencies. All operating costs, such as staff costs payable to treasury and financial management specialists and other administrative and running costs are incurred and settled in Swiss francs. TC's short and long-term financing needs are provided by its parent in the form of sterling loans.

TC provides financial services to group companies for which it charges a fee. However, the fees are invoiced in the functional currencies of the group companies and settled in those currencies. This ensures that the risk of non-functional currency transaction gains and losses on all inter-company transactions with the TC are passed on from the operating units to the TC for centralised management and control. TC also earns investment income in US dollar, euro and sterling. As TC earns its revenue and income in different currencies, the 'sales and cash inflow' indicator fails to identify a particular currency that is significant in its own right as the functional currency of TC. Furthermore, there is no explicit or implicit evidence to suggest that the underlying Swiss economy determines the pricing of TC's fee income to the group companies.

On the other hand, as all administrative and local expenses are incurred and settled in Swiss francs, the 'expenses and cash outflow' indicator provides strong evidence that Swiss franc is the functional currency.

Therefore, as the primary indicators are not sufficiently conclusive in identifying the functional currency, it is necessary to consider the secondary indicators.

The secondary indicators provide evidence that sterling is the functional currency. This is because TC does not raise any finance from external local sources for meeting the cost of its operations in excess of its operating income but relies on short- and long-term financing from its parent. Furthermore, since cash inflows from operations occur in various currencies that are used to meet local expenses, retention of cash indicator is not significant in determining TC's functional currency.

The additional factors also support sterling as the functional currency. For example, the 'autonomy indicator' suggests that the UK parent has set up the TC to achieve overall financial efficiency of its international operations through centralised control and effective management of cash and financial risk. The volume of inter-company transactions is large due to the regular transfer of foreign currency cash balances from and to the parent. The cash flows of the TC, therefore, impact the parent's cash flows on a regular basis. The financing indicator also identifies sterling as the functional currency.

This analysis suggests that the primary indicators do not provide conclusive evidence that the local currency of the country in which TC operates is its functional currency. However, the secondary indicators support sterling as the functional currency. Overall, the evidence is mixed. Management should exercise judgement in determining the currency that most faithfully represents the economic effects of TC's activities. There are a number of possible solutions. One indicator may be that TC has been set up primarily as a conduit to undertake the treasury operations of the entire multi-national group headed by the UK parent. The currency of the country that most faithfully represents TC's operations is, therefore, the functional currency of the UK parent: sterling. Another factor to consider is whether any of the three major currencies (dollars, euros, sterling) is dominant. If no clear currency is suggested by the previous factors, and if the TC's operating expenses are significant, the Swiss franc may be the TC's functional currency.

Example 9 – Functional currency of a foreign subsidiary importing products from parent for local distribution

A subsidiary located in Spain imports a product manufactured by its US parent at a price denominated in US dollars. The product is sold throughout Spain at prices denominated in euros, which are determined primarily by competition with similar locally produced products. All selling and operating expenses are incurred locally and paid in euros. The operation's long-term financing is primarily in the form of US dollar loans from the parent. The distribution of profits is under the parent's control.

The 'sales and cash inflows' indicators suggest that the foreign subsidiary's functional currency is the euro, as that is the currency in which the sales prices are denominated and settled. Furthermore, the sales prices for the foreign entity's products do not respond on a short-term basis to changes in exchange rates, but are determined by local competition and local government regulation. This is a strong indicator that the functional currency is the euro.

The 'expenses and cash outflows' indicators provide a mixed response. This is because cost of sales is primarily denominated and settled in US dollars, whereas local expenses, including selling expenses, are denominated and settled in euros. Given that a significant part of the expenses are settled in US dollars, this indicator does not provide conclusive evidence that the euro is the functional currency.

The primary indicators produce a mixed response, although overall they favour the euro. It is, therefore, necessary to look at the secondary indicators.

The secondary indicators provide supporting evidence that US dollar is the functional currency. This is because the foreign subsidiary's long-term financing is primarily in the form of US dollar loans from the parent, and the subsidiary does not raise any finance from external local sources. Furthermore, the foreign subsidiary does not retain any euros generated from its operations for its own use. After meeting local expenses, management either uses the euros to settle the inter-entity payables to the parent, or distributes any surplus to the parent as dividends.

If the 'autonomy' indicator suggests that the foreign subsidiary is simply acting as an agent for its US parent by selling parent-produced goods to customers in Spain, collecting the proceeds and remitting the same to the US parent, the functional currency would be US dollar. The volume of inter-company transactions is large, as the foreign subsidiary imports goods from its US parent and settles the proceeds on a regular basis. The subsidiary's cash flows, therefore, regularly impact the parent's cash flows.

However, if the foreign subsidiary's operations were carried out with a significant degree of autonomy (that is, local management has a significant degree of authority and responsibility, such as to borrow loans, invest excess cash, modify prices or grant discounts and hire and fire staff), the functional currency would be determined independently from the parent. Management would conclude that the functional currency is the euro, as the primary indicators of paragraph 9 of IAS 21 are overall in favour of the euro.

Example 10 – Functional currency of a special purpose entity ('SPE')

Entity A is a US bank with a US dollar functional currency. Entity A establishes an SPE in a European country in order to invest in a European bond portfolio. Entity A has funded the SPE with equity and inter-company debt denominated in euros. The SPE uses the financing to purchase a portfolio of euro government bonds. There is no intention for the SPE to perform any activities other than holding the bond portfolio. The directors are all employees of the US parent, and the SPE has no active management of its own.

The functional currency of the SPE is the US dollar, as the entity has no operations and does not provide any services. The primary indicators, therefore, do not apply. The 'financing' indicator supports the euro, as all financing is in euros. However, all the financing is inter-company and entity A could denominate the financing in any currency it wanted. Considering the 'autonomy' indicator, it is clear the SPE is not autonomous. It is a shell company, has no independent activities and no active management of its own.

Example 11 – Different functional currencies for stand-alone accounts and for group reporting purposes?

Entity A is an autonomous foreign operation of reporting entity Z. Entity A operates in a country where the US dollar is frequently used because the local currency has been inflationary in the past.

Entity A primarily operates in the local market and is requested to prepare statutory standalone financial statements in accordance with IFRS. Local regulations require entity A to use the local currency as presentation currency for the statutory accounts. Management has determined that the local currency should be the functional currency for the standalone financial statements. Entity A is also required to prepare an IFRS reporting package for entity Z. Management believes that entity A should use the US dollar as the functional currency for group reporting purposes, because the US dollar is frequently used in the local economy and because the group presentation currency is the US dollar.

An entity can have only one functional currency. The functional currency is the currency of the primary economic environment. This is the same for standalone financial statements and group reporting purposes. Entity A should use the local currency as its functional currency for both statutory and group reporting purposes.

Example 12 – functional currency after a group restructuring

Group X is a complex multinational group with numerous intermediate parent companies. As part of a group restructuring, intermediate parent company A sold some of its subsidiaries to intermediate parent company B. Should the functional currency of both companies, A and B, be re-assessed after the group restructuring?

Yes. The functional currency of both companies should be re-assessed to determine whether the previous IAS 21 functional currency determination is impacted by the group restructuring. For example, if the subsidiaries sold to company B are substantial operating companies and company B has limited or no other activities, IAS 21 may require company B to have the same functional currency as that of the newly acquired subsidiaries. On the other hand, company B may be acting as an extension of its ultimate parent company X, in which case the functional currency will be the same as that of company X both before and after the group restructuring. The group restructuring by itself does not trigger a reassessment of the functional currency of the ultimate holding company X, because nothing has changed as regards to the primary economic environment in which the holding company operates. The functional currency of X would have been determined before by X's management according to the policy choice in example 3, and the ultimate holding company X may or may not have independent activities. The existence or not of such activities does not determine whether an intermediate holding company is an extension of its parent.

Entity with multiple operations

A7.41 The definition of a foreign operation indicates that an operation should have activities. [IAS 21 para 8]. An entity might have more than one distinct and separable operation, such as a division or a branch. In determining whether each operation may be considered a separate entity for the purposes of this standard, the definition of a 'business' per IFRS 3 could be useful. For example, a foreign entity might have one operation that acts as a selling agent, receiving inventories of goods from the parent entity and remitting the proceeds back to the entity, and another operation that manufactures and sells products locally. If those two operations are conducted in different economic environments, they may have different functional currencies.

A7.42 Once the number of operations has been determined, each foreign entity should determine its functional currency and measure its results and financial position in that currency before it can be included in the reporting entity when it prepares its financial statements. Once the foreign entity's functional currency is determined, the results and financial position of its branches having different functional currencies will be included in the foreign entity using the translation method set out in paragraph A7.83 below.

Different functional currencies for entities in the same country

A7.43 It is also possible for an entity to have two or more foreign operations in one country and determine different functional currencies for those entities. For example, a UK entity could have a sales branch and an operating subsidiary in the same country, which justifies different functional currencies. Another example is where the UK entity has a subsidiary in a foreign country that manufactures and sells goods locally, and another subsidiary in that same country whose operations are fundamentally different. Management should determine for each of these entities the appropriate functional currency using the guidance addressed in paragraph A7.31 above.

Accounting records not maintained in functional currency

A7.44 If a foreign operation's books or records are not maintained in its functional currency, management should remeasure into the functional currency. That remeasurement is required at the time the foreign operation prepares its financial statements before they are translated into the presentation currency of the reporting entity. The remeasurement into the functional currency, which should be carried out using the translation method set out in paragraph A7.48 onwards below, would produce the same amounts in the functional currency as would have occurred had all the items been recorded in the functional currency in the first place. For example, monetary items are translated into the functional currency using the closing rate, and non-monetary items that are measured on a historical cost basis are translated using the exchange rate at the date of the transaction that resulted in their recognition. [IAS 21 para 34].

Financial statements in foreign currencies

UK.A7.44.1 Although not specifically dealt with in the Companies Act, the Registrar of Companies accepts annual financial statements prepared in a foreign currency (that is, a currency other than sterling), provided that the currency exists legally and the exchange rate to sterling at the balance sheet date is disclosed in the notes to the financial statements.

Change in functional currency

A7.45 Once the functional currency of an entity is determined, it should be used consistently, unless significant changes in economic facts, events and conditions indicate that the functional currency has changed. For example, a branch that carried out its operations as an extension of the reporting entity's business may become independent and primarily regional in nature as a result of changed circumstances.

A7.46 A change in functional currency should be accounted for *prospectively* from the date of change. In other words, management should translate all items (including balance sheet, income statement and statement of comprehensive income items) into the new functional currency using the exchange rate at the date of change. [IAS 21 para 37]. Because the change was brought about by changed circumstances, it does not represent a change in accounting policy and, therefore, a retrospective adjustment under IAS 8, 'Accounting policies, changes in accounting estimates and correction of errors', is not relevant. As all items are translated using the exchange rate at the date of change, the resulting translated amounts for non-monetary items are treated as their historical cost. There is no specific guidance in IAS 21 on what should be done with equity items, but it would be consistent that these are also translated using the exchange rate at the date of the change of functional currency. This means that no additional exchange differences arise on the date of the change.

A7.46.1 Entities should also consider presentation currency (see further para A7.76) when there is a change in functional currency. It may be that the presentation currency does not change. For example, a standalone Irish entity previously presented its financial statements in its euro functional currency and its functional currency changes to US dollar. It is based in Ireland and has Irish shareholders. It does not wish to change its presentation currency and so continues to present its financial statements in euros. Alternatively, the entity is part of a group and the presentation currency of the group does not change following the change in functional currency of a foreign operation. In such a case the numbers in the entity's own financial statements for the period up to the change in functional currency do not change in presentational currency terms. From the point that the functional currency changes new foreign exchange differences will arise in the entity's own financial statements when items expressed in the new functional currency are translated into the presentation currency.

A7.46.2 An example follows of an entity changing its functional but not its presentation currency.

Example 1 – Change in functional currency

Using the Irish entity example from paragraph A7.46.1, assume that its functional currency changes to US dollars on 1 January 20X8. The entity presented its financial statements for the year to 31 December 20X7 in euros. It will continue to present its 20X8 financial statements in euros. In its 20X8 financial statements, its 20X7 comparatives will be exactly as they were in the 20X7 financial statements. A US dollar loan, for example, will be transalated into euro at the closing rate, with exchange differences between opening and closing rates recorded in the income statement. An item of property, plant and equipment (PP&E) that was purchased in euro will be stated at its euro historical cost less depreciation.

On 1 January 2008 all financial statement items are translated into US dollars at the rate ruling at that date.

In its 20X8 financial statements, no foreign exchange will arise on the US dollar loan in the entity's 20X8 income statement, as it is now an item expressed in the entity's functional currency. Any monetary items that are not denominated in US dollars will be translated at the closing rate with exchange differences recorded in the income statement.

Any items of PPE will have been retranslated into US dollars at 1 January 20X8 and these retranslated amounts become their US dollar historical cost and accumulated depreciation (see further para A7.46.3). The PPE is depreciated in US dollars throughout 20X8.

For the 20X8 financial statements, the US dollar (functional currency) balance sheet amounts are translated into euros (presentation currency) at the closing rate and income statement items are translated into euros at the actual or average rates for the period. Any exchange differences arising from opening to closing rates, and average to closing rates, is recorded in other comprehensive income (following the accounting set out from para A7.76 below).

In the entity's separate financial statements, CTA will be recognised in other comprehensive income and recorded in a separate component of equity. CTA is reclassified to profit or loss on disposal of a foreign operation (see further para A7.106). In the context of the entity's separate financial statements where there is one functional currency and a different presentation currency, the 'foreign operation' is the entire business of the entity. CTA would, therefore, only ever be reclassified if the entire business of the entity were to be sold, leaving a shell.

A7.46.3 In the case where a foreign entity such as a subsidiary is translated into a different presentation currency, cumulative translation adjustment (CTA) will arise in the presentation currency consolidated financial statements. When the functional currency of that foreign entity changes, to one that may be the same or different from the group's presentation currency, any CTA previously recorded in equity remains in equity and is only adjusted on disposal or part-disposal of the foreign entity. [IAS 21 para 37]. For disposals and partial disposals see paragraph A7.106.

A7.46.4 A change in functional currency may be accompanied by a change in presentation currency, as many entities prefer to present financial statements in their functional currency. Accounting for a change in presentation currency is dealt with from paragraph A7.82 below. A change in presentation currency is accounted for as a change in accounting policy and is applied retrospectively, as if the new presentation currency had always been the presentation currency.

Example 1 – Change in functional currency: impact on a depreciated asset

A UK entity has a branch in France with a sterling functional currency. The UK entity presents its financial statements in sterling. A significant change in trading operations and circumstances occurred during the first quarter of the financial year ended 30 June 20X6. This meant that sterling no longer faithfully represents the underlying transactions, events and conditions of the foreign branch. UK management decided that the euro should be the functional currency of its foreign operation and that all transactions undertaken from the beginning of the financial year 30 June 20X6 (that is, from 1 July 20X5) should be recorded in euros.

The branch purchased, on 1 January 20X0, an asset for €164,000 with a useful life of 10 years; the rate of exchange was £1 = €1.64. Since the branch's functional currency was sterling, the asset is recorded at the sterling equivalent cost of £100,000. At 1 July 20X5, the equipment has a net book value of £50,000.

As a result of the change in functional currency from sterling to euros on 1 July 20X5 (exchange rate at 30 June 20X5 is £1 = €1.45), the functional currency amount of the asset is carried at is €72,500 (£50,000 @ 1.45, presented as cost of €145,000 and accumulated depreciation of €72,500). This becomes its new historical net book value.

If the asset had been expressed in euro since its purchase it would have had a net book value of €82,000 (€164,000 × 5/10). This number is only relevant if, as a result of exchange movements, the new historical net book value exceeded the previous historical euro value at the date of change. In such a case an impairment review could be necessary if the indications are that the recoverable amount is less than €82,000 and the asset is carried at more than €82,000. [IAS 21 para 25].

The financial statements of the euro branch will be retranslated into sterling from the date that its functional currency changed to euro, and CTA will arise from this point on the difference between opening net assets at opening versus closing rates, and profit or loss at average to closing rates, where the UK entity presented, and continues to present, its financial statements in sterling.

If the UK entity decided to change its presentation currency to euro for its 30 June 20X6 financial statements, it would need to go through the process described in paragraph A7.82 below in order to present its sterling functional currency branch in euro for prior periods. This involves translating the assets and liabilities at the closing rate at 30 June 20X4 and translating the income statement at actual or average rates for year to 30 June 20X5. Equity items should be translated at historic or closing rates, and retained earnings and CTA should be restated if practicable to do so. From 1 July 20X5 no retranslation will be required in relation to the euro branch, since the euro branch has the same functional currency as the UK entity's presentation currency. The sterling to euro CTA that is calculated up to 30 June 20X5 will remain in equity until the branch is disposed of or subject to partial disposal.

A7.47 It may not be practicable to determine the date of change precisely at a point during the year. It is also likely that the change may have occurred gradually during the year. If so, it may be acceptable to account for the change as of the beginning or end of the accounting period in which the change occurs, whichever more closely approximates the date of change.

Example 1 – Change in functional currency

The facts are the same as in the previous example; a UK entity has a branch in France with sterling as its functional currency. A significant change in trading operations and circumstances occurred during the first quarter of the financial year ended 30 June 20X6. This meant that sterling no longer faithfully represented the underlying transactions, events and conditions of the foreign branch. The UK management decided that the euro should be the functional currency of its foreign operation and that all transactions undertaken from the beginning of the financial year 30 June 20X6 should be recorded in euros.

The foreign branch's financial statements at 30 June 20X5, previously prepared in sterling, are translated to euros at the rate of exchange ruling at the date of change — in this situation, 1 July 20X5, the first day of the current financial year. All items in the balance sheet are translated at the rate of exchange ruling at 30 June 20X5, which approximates to the date of change. Retrospective application is not permitted, as the change in functional currency is accounted for prospectively.

Foreign currency transactions

Introduction

A7.48 Foreign currency transactions are transactions denominated in a currency other than the entity's functional currency. Foreign currency transactions may produce receivables or payables that are fixed in terms of the amount of foreign currency that will be received or paid. For example, an entity may buy or sell goods or services in a foreign currency; borrow or lend money in a foreign currency; acquire or dispose of assets; or incur and settle liabilities in a foreign currency.

Initial recognition

A7.49 A foreign currency transaction is recorded, on initial recognition in the functional currency, by applying to the foreign currency amount the spot exchange rate between the functional currency and the foreign currency at the date of the transaction. [IAS 21 para 21]. This process is known as 'translation — financial data denominated in one currency is expressed in terms of another currency. Translation includes not only the expression of individual transactions in terms of another currency, but also the expression of a complete set of financial statements prepared in one currency in terms of another currency (see para A7.76).

A7.50 The date of transaction is the date on which the transaction first qualifies for recognition in accordance with IFRS. [IAS 21 para 22]. The spot exchange rate is the exchange rate for immediate delivery. [IAS 21 para 8]. For revenues, expenses, gains and losses, the spot exchange rate at the dates on which those elements are recognised is used. Translation at the actual exchange rate at the dates the numerous revenues, expenses, gains and losses are recognised is generally impractical; management may, therefore, use a rate that approximates to the actual rate — for example, an average rate.

A7.51 The above requirements appear straightforward, but their application may create problems. They include: determining the date of transaction, which may not always be obvious; determining an average rate as an approximation to the actual rate; and the selection of an appropriate rate for translating foreign currency transactions where there is more than one rate in operation.

Determining the average rate

A7.52 Management may use an average rate for a period for recording foreign currency transactions as a proxy to the actual rate prevailing at the date of each transaction, provided that there is no significant change in rates during that period. An average rate is unlikely to be used by entities undertaking few transactions in a foreign currency. It is also unlikely to be used for translating large, one-off transactions that would be recorded at the actual rate. The flexibility allowed in IAS 21 is likely to be most beneficial to entities that enter into a large number of transactions in different currencies, or that maintain multi-currency ledgers. However, no guidance is provided in the standard as to how such a rate is determined.

A7.53 Determining an average rate and its use in practice depends on a number of factors, such as: the frequency and value of transactions undertaken; the period over which the rate will apply; the extent of any seasonal trade variation and the desirability of using a weighting procedure as well as the acceptable level of materiality and the nature of the entity's accounting systems. There are a large number of methods under which an average rate can be calculated. These range from simple monthly or quarterly averages to more sophisticated methods using appropriate weighting that reflects changes both in exchange rates and in the volume of business. The choice of the period to be used for calculating the average rate will depend on the extent to which daily exchange rates fluctuate in the period selected. If exchange rates are relatively stable over a period of one month for example, the average exchange rate for that month can be used as an approximation to the daily rate. If, however, there is volatility of exchange rates, it may be appropriate to calculate an average rate for a shorter period such as a week. Whatever period is chosen, materiality is likely to be an important consideration.

A7.54 An entity may use an actual average rate or an estimated average rate, depending on the circumstances. An actual average rate is likely to be used where there is some delay between the date when the transactions occurred and the date when they are recorded. In other situations, it may be necessary for an entity to use an estimated average rate for a period rather than wait for the period to end in order to calculate an actual average rate. This estimate may be based on the average of daily exchange rates for the previous period or the closing rate of the previous period. Whichever basis is used, it will be necessary to ensure than the estimated average rate is a close approximation of the actual rates prevailing during the period. If it is not, the rate should be revised accordingly.

Multiple exchange rates

A7.55 Some countries may operate more than one exchange rate. When several exchange rates are available, the rate used to translate and record the foreign currency transactions and balances is that at which the future cash flows represented by the transaction or balance could have been settled if those cash flows had occurred at the measurement date. [IAS 21 para 26]. Chapter 6 contains an example of an entity disclosing the exchange rate it used when several are available (Table 6.2.1). When translating a net investment under IAS 21, the rate used would often be the dividend remittance rate, but another rate may be more appropriate if the proceeds would in practice be remitted in another way. Where a country has multiple exchange rates, judgement is often required to determine which exchange rate qualifies as a spot rate that can be used for translation under IAS 21. In determining whether a rate is a spot rate, an entity should consider whether currency is obtainable at a quoted rate and whether the quoted rate is available for immediate delivery. In practice, a normal administrative delay in obtaining funds would be acceptable.

Suspension of rates

A7.56 Countries may experience economic conditions from time to time that affect the free-market convertibility of the local currency. As a result, the exchangeability between two currencies may be temporarily unavailable at the transaction date or a subsequent balance sheet date. IAS 21 requires entities to use the rate on the first subsequent date at which exchanges could be made. [IAS 21 para 26].

A7.57 Doubts as to convertibility may arise if, for example, a Canadian entity makes a long-term currency loan to an overseas supplier but restrictions on the remittance of funds are imposed by the overseas country sometime before the balance sheet date. Such restrictions may arise as a result of currency devaluation, political upheaval or severe exchange control regulations in the overseas country. Management should use the rate on the first subsequent date at which exchanges could be made following restoration of normal conditions.

Example – Suspension of foreign exchange rates

In October 20X3, entity A, which is incorporated in the UK, used surplus currency to make a long-term loan of FC 15m to its overseas supplier. The loan was made when the exchange rate was £1 = FC 5.00 and is repayable on 30 September 20X5, entity A's year-end. Initially, the loan is translated and recorded in entity A's books at £3m. The amount that entity A ultimately receives depends on the rate of exchange ruling on the date when the loan is repaid.

On 28 September 20X5, a few days before the due date of the loan's repayment, the exchange rate was £1= FC 6. On the same date the local government announced that a devaluation would occur on 2 October 20X5 and all foreign exchange transactions would be suspended until 3 October 20X5. On 2 October 20X5, foreign exchange transactions were executed but left unsettled until the following day when a new rate was established. On 3 October 20X5 a new rate of £1 = FC 7.5 was established and was effective for transactions left unsettled the previous day.

An official exchange rate at 30 September 20X5 is temporarily unavailable. In this situation, the exchange rate was temporarily lacking and the rate established on 3 October 20X5, the first subsequent date, is the appropriate rate to use for translating the monetary asset at the balance sheet date of 30 September 20X5. Therefore, entity A would record the loan receivable at £2m and recognise a foreign exchange loss of £1m in profit or loss.

Subsequent measurement

A7.58 A foreign currency transaction may give rise to assets and liabilities that are denominated in a foreign currency. The procedure for translating such assets and liabilities into the entity's functional currency at each balance sheet date will depend on whether they are monetary or non-monetary.

Translation of monetary items

A7.59 Monetary items are units of currency held and assets and liabilities to be received or paid in fixed or determinable number of units of currency. [IAS 21 para 8]. The essential feature of a monetary item is a right to receive (or an obligation to deliver) a fixed or determinable number of units of currency. Examples are

- Financial assets such as cash, bank balances and receivables.
- Financial liabilities such as debt.
- Provisions that are settled in cash.
- Pensions and other employee benefits to be paid in cash, deferred taxes and cash dividends that are recognised as a liability.
- Derivative financial instruments, such as forward exchange contracts, foreign currency swaps and options are also monetary items as they are settled at a future date.

Short-term monetary items are those that fall due within one year of the balance sheet date; long-term monetary items are those that fall due more than one year after the balance sheet date.

A7.60 In some instances, it may not be readily apparent whether an item should be regarded as a monetary or a non-monetary item. Management should consider whether the item represents an amount to be received or paid in money, in which case it would fall to be treated as a monetary item.

A7.61 For an item to qualify as a monetary item, it does not need to be recovered or settled in cash. A contract to receive (or deliver) a variable number of an entity's own equity instruments or a variable amount of assets in which the fair value to be received (or delivered) equals a fixed or determinable number of units of currency is also a monetary item. [IAS 21 para 16]. In other words, an entity's own equity instruments can be used 'as currency' in a contract that can be settled at a value equal to a fixed or a determinable amount. Such a contract is not an equity instrument, but a monetary financial asset or a liability. Not all financial assets should be treated as monetary items. For example, an investment in an equity instrument is not a monetary item – there is no right to receive a fixed or determinable amount of cash. [IAS 39 para AG83].

A7.62 IAS 21 requires entities to translate foreign currency monetary items outstanding at the end of balance sheet date using the closing rate. [IAS 21 para 23(a)]. The closing rate is the spot exchange rate at the balance sheet date. [IAS 21 para 8]. A rate of exchange that is fixed under the terms of the relevant contract cannot be used to translate monetary assets and liabilities. Translating a monetary item at the contracted rate under the terms of a relevant contract is a form of hedge accounting that is not permitted under IAS 39. IAS 39 details strict criteria that must be fulfilled before hedge accounting can be applied and specifies the appropriate accounting treatment for foreign currency hedged items and hedging instruments where hedge accounting is permitted. The treatment of the exchange differences that arise on translating a monetary item at the balance sheet date is considered from paragraphs A7.67 below.

Translation of non-monetary items

A7.63 Non-monetary items are all items other than monetary items. In other words, the right to receive (or an obligation to deliver) a fixed or determinable number of units of currency is absent in a non-monetary item. Typical examples are:

- Intangible assets.
- Goodwill.
- Property, plant and equipment.
- Inventories.
- Amounts pre-paid for goods and services (pre-paid rent).
- Equity investments.
- Provisions that are to be settled by the delivery of a non-monetary asset.

[IAS 21 para 16].

A7.63.1 Advances paid and received (including pre-payments) can be difficult to classify as monetary or non-monetary. An example of a non-monetary item is an advance payment for goods that, absent a default by the counterparty, must be settled by the counterparty delivering the goods. However, if an advance is refundable in circumstances other than a default by either party, this may indicate that it is a monetary item as the item is receivable in units of currency.

A7.64 Translation of non-monetary items depends on whether they are recognised at historical cost or at fair value. For example, property, plant and equipment may be measured in terms of historical cost or revalued amounts in accordance with IAS 16, 'Property, plant and equipment'.

A7.65 Non-monetary items that are measured in terms of historical cost in a foreign currency are translated using the exchange rate at the date of the transaction. [IAS 21 para 23(b)]. This means that such assets are recorded at historical cost, and no retranslation of the asset is required at subsequent balance sheet dates. However, if the asset is impaired, the recoverable amount is translated at the exchange rate ruling at the date when that value was determined (for example, the closing rate at the balance sheet date). Comparing the previously recorded historical cost with the recoverable amount may or may not result in recognising an impairment loss in the functional currency. For example, an entity's functional currency is sterling. A foreign currency asset costing FC 925,000 is recorded at the date of purchase at £500,000 when £1 = FC 1.85. At a subsequent balance sheet date, the asset's recoverable amount in foreign currency is FC 787,500 when £1 = FC 1.5. Although there is impairment loss in foreign currency, no impairment loss is recognised, because the recoverable amount at the balance sheet date of £525,000 is higher than the carrying value.

A7.66 Non-monetary assets that are measured at fair value in a foreign currency are translated using the exchange rates at the date when the fair value was determined. [IAS 21 para 23(c)]. For example, a UK entity has a euro-denominated investment property located in France that is carried at fair value with gains and losses from changes in fair value recognised in profit or loss for the period in which they arise, in accordance with IAS 40. The fair values measured initially in euros due to the property's appreciation in value are translated to sterling at the exchange rate ruling at the relevant measurement dates. The resulting change in fair value in sterling includes foreign exchange differences arising on the retranslation of the opening euro carrying value. This exchange difference is recognised as part of the change in fair value in profit or loss for the period.

Recognition of exchange differences

Monetary items

A7.67 Exchange differences arising on the settlement of monetary items, or on translating monetary items at rates different from those at which they were translated on initial recognition during the period or in previous financial statements, are recognised in profit or loss in the period in which they arise, except as described in paragraph A7.70 below. [IAS 21 para 28].

A7.68 When monetary items arise from a foreign currency transaction and there is a change in exchange rate between the transaction date and the date of settlement, an exchange difference results. Where a transaction is *settled* within the same accounting period at an exchange rate that differs from the rate used when the transaction was initially recorded, the exchange difference is recognised in the income statement of the period in which the settlement takes place. [IAS 21 para 29]. This is because it is appropriate to recognise such exchange differences as part of the profit or loss for that year, as the exchange difference will have been reflected in the cash flow at the time of the settlement.

Example – Treatment of a foreign currency denominated purchase of plant

In March 20X5, a UK company purchases plant for use in the UK from an overseas company for FC 1,980,000. At the date the company purchases the plant, the exchange rate is £1 = FC 1.65. The purchase price is to be settled in three months, although delivery is made immediately. The UK company records both the plant and the monetary liability at £1,200,000 (FC 1,980,000/£1.65). The company will not need to translate the plant again. At the settlement date, the exchange rate is £1 = FC 1.75. The actual amount the UK company will pay to settle the liability is therefore £1,131,429. The company should include the gain on exchange of £68,751 (that is, £1,200,000 — £1,131,429) in arriving at its profit or loss.

A7.69 However, where a monetary item arising from a foreign currency transaction remains *outstanding* at the balance sheet date, an exchange difference arises as a consequence of recording the foreign currency transaction at the rate ruling at the date of the transaction (or when it was translated at a previous balance sheet date) and the subsequent retranslation of the monetary item to the rate ruling at the balance sheet date. Such exchange differences are reported as part of the profit or loss for the year.

A7.69.1 Monetary assets classified as available-for-sale in accordance with IAS 39 are carried at fair value but are treated for the purpose of calculating foreign exchange differences as if they were carried at amortised cost. The exchange differences resulting from changes in amortised cost are recognised in the income statement. [IAS 39 AG 83]. Other fair value gains and losses on available-for-sale monetary financial assets are required to be recognised in other comprehensive income. [IAS 39 para 55(b), IG E 3.2]. See 'Manual of Accounting – Financial instruments' for an example of the treatment of foreign exchange gains and losses on monetary available-for-sale assets.

A7.70 Not all exchange differences on monetary items are reported in the income statement. There are number of exceptions. These are:

- A monetary item that is designated as a hedging instrument in a cash flow hedge. Any exchange difference that forms part of the gain or loss on the hedging instrument is recognised in other comprehensive income. [IAS 39 para 95].
- A monetary item that is designated as a hedge of a net investment *in consolidated financial statements*. The exchange difference on the hedging instrument that is considered to be an effective hedge is recognised in other comprehensive income. [IAS 39 para 102]. See from paragraph A7.108 onwards below.
- A monetary item that forms part of the net investment in a foreign operation in the consolidated financial statement. See from paragraph A7.93 onwards below.

Non-monetary items

A7.71 When a gain or loss on a non-monetary item is recognised directly in other comprehensive income, any exchange component of that gain or loss is recognised directly in other comprehensive income. [IAS 39 para 30]. For example, an entity purchases equity securities denominated in a foreign currency that are classified as available for sale. Under IAS 39, the equity securities are carried at fair value. Any changes in fair value that are recognised directly in other comprehensive income also include any related foreign exchange element. [IAS 39 paras 55(b), AG83]. Another example is where a property denominated in a foreign currency is revalued. Any exchange difference arising when the property is translated at the rate of exchange ruling at the valuation date is reported directly in other comprehensive income along with other changes in value.

Example – Translation of a revalued foreign asset

A UK entity with a sterling functional currency has a property located in the US, which it acquired at a cost of US$1.8m when the exchange rate was £1 = US$1.6. The property was revalued to US$2.16m at the balance sheet date. The exchange rate at the balance sheet date was £1 = US$1.8.

Ignoring depreciation, the amount that would be reported directly to equity is:

	£
Value at balance sheet date = US$2,160,000m @ 1.8 =	1,200,000
Value at acquisition date = US$1,800,000 @1.6 =	1,125,000
Revaluation surplus recognised in other comprehensive income	75,000
The revaluation surplus may be analysed as follows:	
Change in fair value = US$360,000 @ 1.8 =	200,000
Exchange component of change = US$1,800,000 @ 1.8 – US$1,800,000 @ 1.6	(125,000)
Revaluation surplus recognised in other comprehensive income	75,000

A7.72 On the other hand, when a gain or loss on a non-monetary item is recognised in profit or loss, any exchange component of that gain or loss is also recognised in profit or loss. [IAS 21 para 38].

Example – Translation of an impaired foreign asset

A UK entity with a sterling functional currency has a property located in the US, which was acquired at a cost of US$1.8m when the exchange rate was £1 = US$1.6. The property is carried at cost. At the balance sheet date the recoverable amount of the property as a result of an impairment review amounted to US$1.62m. The exchange rate at the balance sheet date was £1 = US$1.8.

Ignoring depreciation, the impairment loss that would be reported in the income statement as a result of the impairment is:

	£
Carrying value at balance sheet date – US$1,620,000m @ 1.8 =	900,000
Historical cost – US$1,800,000 @ 1.6 =	1,125,000
Impairment loss recognised in profit or loss	(225,000)
The impairment loss may be analysed as follows:	
Change in value due to impairment = US$180,000 @ 1.8 =	(100,000)
Exchange component of change = US$1,800,000 @ 1.8 – US$1,800,000 @ 1.6	(125,000)
Impairment loss recognised in profit or loss	(225,000)

Foreign currency translation of financial statements

Introduction

A7.73 Accounting for transactions in foreign currencies that are directly undertaken by an entity and that are measured and expressed in the entity's functional currency is addressed earlier in this chapter. However, where foreign activities are undertaken through foreign operations, the financial statements of those foreign operations are translated so that they can be included in the reporting entity's financial statements by consolidation, proportional consolidation or the equity method. The process of translation addresses the appropriate exchange rates to use for translating the income statement and the balance sheet of the foreign operation and how the financial effects of changes in exchange rates are recognised in the reporting entity's financial statements.

A7.74 The standard permits an entity to present its financial statements in a currency other than its functional currency. The currency in which the financial statements are presented is referred to as the 'presentation currency'. [IAS 21 para 8]. There is no requirement in the standard for an entity to present its financial statements in its functional currency, which most faithfully portrays the economic effect of transactions and events on the entity. The IASB explains why entities are permitted to present their financial statements in any currency in paragraphs BC10 to BC14 of the Basis for Conclusions of IAS 21.

A7.75 Although entities have a free choice in the selection of the presentation currency, they are likely to use the functional currency, the currency used for measurement, as the presentation currency. If management uses an alternative currency, disclosure of the reasons for selecting a different currency is required. There must, therefore, be substantive and valid reasons for choosing an alternative presentation currency. For example, in some countries, an entity may be required by local and legal regulations to present its financial statements in the local currency even if this is not its functional currency.

Translation to the presentation currency

A7.76 Selecting a presentation currency that is different from the functional currency requires a translation from the functional currency into the presentation currency. For example, when a group contains individual entities with different functional currencies, the results and financial position of each entity is expressed in a common currency so that consolidated financial statements may be presented. IAS 21 has prescribed a translation methodology for translating from the functional currency to a different presentation currency. This translation methodology seeks to ensure that the financial and operational relationships between underlying amounts established in the entity's primary economic environment and measured in its functional currency are preserved when translated into a different measurement currency. The translation method is described in the next paragraph. A different translation methodology applies to an entity whose functional currency is the currency of a hyper-inflationary economy. This method is described in chapter 6.

A7.77 The translation methodology referred to above requires an entity's results and financial position whose functional currency is not the currency of a hyper-inflationary economy to be translated into a different presentation currency using the following procedures:

- Assets and liabilities for each balance sheet presented (including comparatives) are translated at the closing rate at the date of that balance sheet.

  Use of a constant rate of exchange for all items on the balance sheet maintains the relationship in the retranslated financial statements as existed in the foreign operation's financial statements. Therefore, for example, fixed assets are the same proportion of long-term liabilities.

- Income and expenses for each income statement (including comparatives) is translated at exchange rates at the dates of the transactions. For practical reasons, a rate that approximates the exchange rates at the dates of the transactions — for example, an average rate for the period — is often used to translate income and expense items. However, if exchange rates fluctuate significantly, the use of the average rate for a period is inappropriate (see para A7.81 below).

  The use of a closing rate is more likely to preserve the financial results and relationships that existed prior to translation, but the use of an actual or average rate reflects more fairly the profits or losses and cash flows as they accrue to the group throughout the period.

- All resulting exchange differences are recognised in other comprehensive income and accumulated as a separate component of equity.

[IAS 21 paras 39, 40].

Equity items

A7.77.1 The standard is silent on how to translate items that are recognised directly in equity, that is, items that have not been recognised through the performance statements. These will generally be recognised as a result of a transaction with a shareholder, such as share capital, share premium or treasury shares. Management has a choice of using either the historical rate or the closing rate for these items. The chosen policy should be applied consistently. If the historical rate is used, these equity items are not retranslated and the CTA will, therefore, only include the cumulative differences between opening and closing rates on total net assets, and average to closing rates on retained earnings and other performance statement items, such as AFS or hedging reserves. If the closing rate is used, the resulting exchange differences are recognised directly in equity as part of the CTA reserve. This effectively reduces the CTA that arises on retranslating the net assets. Any exchange differences arising on translating equity items are not recognised in the performance statements. They are instead recognised directly in equity, with the result that the CTA movement in equity will not equal the CTA recognised in total comprehensive income. The policy choice has no impact on the amount of total equity. The regulatory framework in some jurisdictions may mandate one treatment.

A7.78 The exchange differences referred to in the last bullet point in paragraph A7.77 above comprises:

- Differences arising from translating the income statement at exchange rates at the dates of the transactions or at average rates, and assets and liabilities at the closing rate. Such exchange differences arise on items recognised in the income statement as well as in other comprehensive income.
- Differences arising on the opening net assets' retranslation at a closing rate that differs from the previous closing rate.

[IAS 21 para 41].

CTA may also include differences on retranslation of equity items, depending on the policy choice made, as described in paragraph A7.77 above.

A7.79 The above exchange differences are not recognised in the income statement. This would distort the results from trading operations shown in the functional currency financial statements. Such differences, which primarily result from a translation process, are unrelated to the foreign operation's trading performance or financial operations; in particular, they do not represent or measure changes in actual or prospective cash flows. They do have an impact on the net investment that may be realised upon sale or liquidation, but that effect is related to the net investment and not to the investee's operations. It is, therefore, inappropriate to regard them as profits or losses. Hence, they are recognised in a separate component of other comprehensive income.

A7.80 The IASB chose the translation method described in paragraph A7.77 because, for a multi-national group comprising operations with a number of functional currencies, it means that the operations can be translated into the presentation currency directly without having to determine a 'functional currency' for the group first. The method also results in the same amounts in the presentation currency regardless of whether the financial statements of a foreign operation are first translated into the functional currency of the parent and then into the presentation currency or translated directly into the presentation currency. [IAS 21 para BC18].

Determining the average rate for translating the income statement

A7.81 The standard permits a foreign operation's income statement to be translated at an average rate for the period. IAS 21 does not prescribe any definitive method of calculating the average rate, probably because the appropriate method may justifiably vary between individual entities. For further information refer to paragraphs A7.52 and A7.53 above.

Change in presentation currency

A7.82 IAS 21 allows entities a free choice of the currency in which they present their financial statements. [IAS 21 para 38]. The question, therefore, arises how a change in presentation currency should be treated. An entity may choose to change its presentation currency when there is a change in its functional currency, although this is not required (see para A7.46.1). The choice of presentation currency represents an accounting policy and any change should be applied fully retrospectively in accordance with IAS 8, unless impracticable. This means that the change should be treated as if the new presentation currency had always been the entity's presentation currency, with comparative amounts being restated into the new presentation currency. Since using a presentation currency is purely applying a translation method, and does not affect the underlying functional currency of the entity or any entities within a group, it is straightforward to apply a change in presentation currency to assets, liabilities and income statement items. All assets and liabilities are translated from their functional currency into the new presentation currency at the beginning of the comparative period using the opening exchange rate and retranslated at the closing rate. Income statement items are translated at an actual rate or at an average rate approximating the actual rate.

A7.82.1 However, for the individual items within equity, the process can be more complex. Management has a choice of translating these equity items from an entity's functional currency into its presentation currency at either the closing rate or at the historical rate, with the balancing amount being reported in CTA (see para A7.77.1). Retained earnings, CTA and similar reserves should be expressed in the new presentation currency as if it had always been the presentation currency, unless it is impracticable to do so (see further para A7.82.4).

A7.82.2 A change in presentation currency is less problematic where a stand-alone entity (or a group with no foreign operations) reports equity at the closing rate, as it means that some of the CTA that would have arisen on retranslation of net assets will be offset by CTA on retranslation of equity items. CTA will, however, arise as a result of differences between the historical average and closing exchange rates when applied to profit or loss and other performance statement items.

A7.82.3 Where equity items are translated at the historical rate and/or where a group has foreign operations, the individual equity items should also be re-expressed in the new presentation currency on a change of presentation currency as if it had always been the presentation currency. [IAS 8 para 19]. This requires determining the amount of each individual equity balance on each earlier reporting date. For unvarying items of equity such as share capital and premium, this may not be too difficult, although even this may be complicated by share issues and buy-backs in different reporting periods.

A7.82.4 However, for retained earnings and other similar reserves, the amounts in functional currencies must be translated at the transaction dates with a resulting impact on the amount recognised in CTA. Calculating the split between retained earnings and CTA may be onerous in practice. How difficult will be influenced by whether average rates can be used as an approximation for actual rates, the period over which these changes are to be calculated as well as the number of transactions. It will usually be relatively straightforward to go back as far as the opening balance sheet of the first period presented. The effect of going back further (which will affect only the relative amounts reported in CTA and retained earnings), may not be material, although this will depend on factors such as:

- The size of assets and liabilities.
- The stability of the relevant exchange rates.
- Legal requirements around distributability of profits.
- The reclassification of the deferred foreign exchange gains and losses on the ultimate disposal of a foreign operation.

A7.82.5 Where an entity, on adopting IFRS, took the exemption to reset the CTA to zero, we believe that it would not be necessary to restate beyond its transition date (see chapter 3).

A7.82.6 In the case where an entity changes its presentation currency it should present a balance sheet as at the beginning of its earliest comparative period in accordance with paragraph 10(f) of IAS 1.

Consolidated financial statements

Translation of a foreign operation

A7.83 Translating foreign currency financial statements into the presentation currency is necessary so that the foreign operation's financial statements may be included in the reporting entity's financial statements by consolidation, proportional consolidation or the equity method. The method of translation in consolidated financial statements reflects the financial and other operational relationships that exist between the reporting entity and its foreign enterprises. This objective is achieved by following the closing rate/net investment method described in paragraph A7.77. This translation method is illustrated by the example below. Once the foreign operation's financial statements have been translated into the reporting entity's presentation currency, its incorporation into the reporting entity's consolidated financial statement follows normal consolidation procedures.

Example 1 – Translation of a foreign subsidiary

Company A, a UK company, whose accounting period ended on 30 September 20X5, has a wholly-owned US subsidiary, S corporation, which was acquired for US$500,000 on 30 September 20X4. The fair value of the net assets at the date of acquisition was US$400,000 giving rise to goodwill of US$100,000. The exchange rate at 30 September 20X4 and 20X5 was £1 = US$2.0 and £1 = US$1.5 respectively. The weighted average rate for the year ended 30 September 20X5 was £1 = US$1.65. During the year, S corporation paid a dividend of US$14,000 when the rate of exchange was £1 = US$1.75.

The foreign currency movements in this example have been exaggerated. In reality, if exchange rates were this volatile, an entity would not be permitted to use average rates for translating the income statement. [IAS 21 para 40].

The summarised income statement of S corporation for the year ended 30 September 20X4, and the summarised balance sheets at 30 September 20X3 and 20X4 in dollars and sterling equivalents, are as follows:

S corporation: Income statement for the year ended 30 September 20X5

	$'000	**Exchange rate**	**£'000**
Operating profit	135	1.65	81.8
Interest paid	(15)	1.65	(9.0)
Profit before taxation	120		72.8
Taxation	(30)	1.65	(18.2)
Profit after taxation	90		54.6

Balance sheets of S corporation

	20X5 $'000	**20X4 $'000**	**20X5 £'000**	**20X4 £'000**
Closing exchange rate £1 =			$1.50	$2.00
Property, plant and equipment				
Cost (20X5 additions: $30)	255	225	170.0	112.5
Depreciation (20X5 charge: $53)	98	45	65.3	22.5
Net book value	157	180	104.7	90.0
Current assets:				
Inventories	174	126	116.0	63.0
Debtors	210	145	140.0	72.5
Cash at bank	240	210	160.0	105.0
	624	481	416.0	240.5

Current liabilities:				
Trade creditors	125	113	83.3	57.5
Taxation	30	18	20.0	9.0
	155	131	103.3	65.5
Net current assets	469	350	312.7	175.0
Loan stock	150	130	100.0	65.0
Net assets	476	400	317.4	200.0
Share capital	200	200	100.0	100.0
Retained profits	276	200	217.4	100.0
	476	400	317.4	200.0

Analysis of retained profits

	$'000	£'000
Pre-acquisition profit brought forward	200	100.0
Profit for the year	90	54.6
Dividends paid in the year *	(14)	(8.0)
Exchange difference	–	70.8
Retained profits	276	217.4

* Dividend paid during the year is translated at the actual rate $1 = $1.75

Analysis of exchange difference:

Arising on retranslation of opening net assets (excluding goodwill – see below)	
at opening rate — $400,000 @ $2 = £1	200.0
at closing rate — $400,000 @ $1.5 = £1	266.7
Exchange gain on net assets	66.7
Exchange gain arising from translating retained profits from average to closing rate – $90,000 @1.5 – £54.6	5.4
Exchange loss arising from translating dividend from actual to closing rate – $14,000 @1.5 – £8.0	(1.3)
Total exchange difference arising on translation of S corporation	70.8
Exchange difference on goodwill of US$100,000 treated as a currency asset (see para A7.86 below)	
at opening rate — US$100,000 @ $2 = £1	50.0
at closing rate — US$100,000 @ $1.5 = £1	66.7
Exchange gain on goodwill included in consolidation	16.7
Total exchange difference included in consolidated balance sheet as a separate component of equity (see below)	87.5

It is assumed that parent company A's functional currency is the pound sterling. It has received a dividend from S corporation during the year. The summarised balance sheets of company A at 30 September 20X4 and 20X5 are as follows:

Company A — Balance sheets	**20X5**	**20X4**
	£'000	**£'000**
Investments in subsidiary S ($500,000 @ 2.0)	250	250
Cash	208	200
Net assets	458	450
Share capital	450	450
Retained profits (dividend received: $14,000 @ 1.75*)	8	–
	458	450

*actual rate on date dividend received

The summarised consolidated income statement for the year ended 30 September 20X5 and the consolidated balance sheet as at date prepared under the closing rate/net investment method are as follows:

Consolidated income statement for the year ended 30 September 20X5	
	£'000
Operating profit of S corporation	81.8
Operating profit of company A	8.0
	89.8
Elimination of inter-company dividend*	(8.0)
Net operating profit	81.8
Interest paid	(9.0)
Profit before taxation	72.8
Taxation	(18.2)
Retained profit	54.6

Consolidated balance sheet as at 30 September 20X5		
		£'000
Goodwill		66.7
Property, plant and equipment		104.7
		171.4
Current assets:		
Inventories		116.0
Debtors		140.0
Cash (S corporation: £160; company A £208)		368.0
		624.0
Current liabilities:		
Trade creditors		83.3
Taxation		20.0
		103.3
Net current assets		520.7
Loan stock		100.0
Net assets		592.1

Capital and reserves	
Share capital	450.0
Retained profit	54.6
Cumulative translation adjustment	87.5
	592.1

Different reporting dates

A7.84 Where a foreign subsidiary's financial statements are drawn up to a date that is different from that of the parent, the foreign subsidiary often prepares additional financial statements as of the same date as the parent for inclusion in the parent's financial statements. Therefore, the foreign subsidiary's financial statements are translated at the exchange rate at the parent's balance sheet date. Where additional financial statements are not prepared, IAS 27, 'Consolidated and separate financial statements', allows the use of a different reporting date that is not more than three months before or three months after the reporting entity's balance sheet date. The foreign subsidiary's financial statements are translated at the exchange rate ruling at the foreign operation's balance sheet date. However, if significant transactions or events occur between the date of the subsidiary's financial statements and the date of the parent's financial statements, adjustments are made. [IAS 27 para 23]. This may include changes to the exchange rate, as shown in the example below.

Example – Translation of a foreign subsidiary with a different reporting date to that of the parent

Entity A prepares its annual financial statements at 31 January. However, local regulations require one of its subsidiaries, entity B, to prepare its financial statements at 31 December. Entity A uses entity B's results for the 12 months to 31 December for consolidation purposes, rather than have a second set of results audited to 31 January.

The exchange rate between the US dollar (used for group reporting) and entity B's local currency was US$1: LC15,000 at 31 December 20X2 and US$1: LC18,000 at 31 January 20X3. There were no significant transactions or other events at entity B during January 20X3. Entity B's net assets at 31 December 20X2 were LC234 million.

The net assets of entity B at 31 December 20X2 using the exchange rate of 31 December 20X2 are US$15,600.

The change in exchange rates between 31 December 20X2 and 31 January 20X3 is significant. Therefore, entity A uses the exchange rate of 31 January 20X3 for consolidation purposes.

Accordingly, management should translate entity B's balance sheet as at 31 December 20X2 using the 31 January 20X3 exchange rate. This results in the consolidation of a balance sheet with net assets of US$13,000.

The same approach is used for foreign associates and joint ventures. [IAS 21 para 46].

Equity Items

A7.84.1 The standard is silent on how to translate equity items. Management, therefore, has a choice of using either the historical rate or the closing rate. The chosen policy should be applied consistently. If the closing rate is used, the resulting exchange differences are recognised in equity; the policy choice, therefore, has no impact on the amount of total equity. The regulatory framework in some jurisdictions may mandate one treatment. In this case, the policy choice does not apply.

Non-controlling interest

A7.85 Exchange differences arising on the retranslation of a foreign subsidiary's financial statements are recognised in other comprehensive income and accumulated as a separate component of equity. Where the foreign subsidiary is not wholly-owned, the exchange differences that are attributable to the non-controlling interest are allocated to, and reported as part of, the non-controlling interest in the consolidated balance sheet. [IAS 21 para 41].

Goodwill and fair value adjustments arising on an acquisition

A7.86 Goodwill arising in a business combination is measured as the excess of the cost of combination over the acquirer's interest in the net fair value of the acquiree's identifiable assets, liabilities and contingent liabilities.

A7.87 Goodwill and fair value adjustments form part of the acquired entity's assets and liabilities.

- Any goodwill arising on the acquisition of a foreign operation and any fair value adjustments to the carrying amounts of assets and liabilities arising on a foreign operation's acquisition are treated as the foreign operation's assets and liabilities.
- They are expressed in the foreign operation's functional currency and are translated at the closing rate in accordance with paragraphs A7.77 above, where the functional currency is not the currency of a hyper-inflationary economy, and in accordance with paragraph A7.109 below, where the functional currency is the currency of a hyper-inflationary economy.

[IAS 21 para 47].

A7.88 Therefore, where a parent entity acquires a multinational operation comprising businesses with many different functional currencies, the goodwill arising on acquisition is allocated to the level of each functional currency of the acquired foreign operation. This means that the level at which goodwill is allocated for foreign currency translation purposes may be different from the level at which goodwill is tested for impairment in accordance with IAS 36, 'Impairment of assets'. [IAS 36 para 83].

Example – Translation of goodwill and fair value adjustments

On 30 June 20X5, a UK parent entity with sterling as the functional currency acquired a multinational group with operations in Canada, the US and Europe. All foreign operations are highly profitable. The functional currencies of the foreign operations are their respective local currencies. The total purchase consideration amounted to £3,000m. The UK parent financial year ends on 31 December 20X5.

The fair values of the net assets of the acquired businesses, including fair value adjustments and the relevant exchange rates at the date of acquisition and at the balance sheet date, are given below. The UK parent allocates the purchased goodwill to the acquired businesses on the basis of their relative adjusted fair values of the net assets acquired.

Business acquired	**Canada**	**US**	**Europe**	**Total**
Exchange rate at acquisition £1 =	2.19	1.66	1.42	
Exchange rate at balance sheet date £1 =	2.29	1.80	1.45	
	C$000	**$'000**	**€'000**	**£'000**
Net assets — book value	1,200	1,500	2,000	
Fair value adjustments	150	50	(100)	
Adjusted fair values	1,350	1,550	1,900	
Allocation of goodwill				
Translated at exchange rate at date of acquisition	£616	£934	£1,338	2,888
Purchase consideration				3,000
Goodwill allocated on the basis of adjusted fair values	£24	£36	£52	112
	C$'000	**$'000**	**€'000**	
Adjusted net assets as above	1,350	1,550	1,900	
Goodwill treated as currency asset	53	60	74	
Adjusted fair value + goodwill	1,403	1,610	1,974	
Translation adjustment on opening net assets	**£'000**	**£'000**	**£'000**	**£'000**
Adjusted net assets + goodwill @ closing rate	613	894	1,361	2,868
Adjusted net assets + goodwill @ opening rate	640	970	1,390	3,000
Exchange loss taken to other comprehensive income on consolidation	(27)	(76)	(29)	(132)

Consolidated balance sheet at 31 December 20X5				
Goodwill at closing rate	23	33	51	107
Net assets at closing rate	590	861	1,310	2,761
Cash outlay				(3,000)
Consolidated net assets				(132)
Translation adjustments in equity	(27)	(76)	(29)	(132)

Intra-group trading transactions

A7.89 Where normal trading transactions take place between group companies located in different countries, the transactions give rise to monetary assets (liabilities) that may either have been settled during the year or remain unsettled at the balance sheet date. As the transactions will probably be recorded in the functional currency of one of the companies in question, exchange differences will arise. These are reported in the entity's income statement in the same way as gains or losses on transactions arising with third parties, as explained from paragraph A7.67 above. Where the monetary asset or liability is settled during the year, the exchange gain or loss will have affected group cash flows. It is, therefore, included in consolidated results for the year. The exchange difference arising simply reflects the risk of doing business with a foreign party, even though that party happens to be a group member. Even where the transaction remains unsettled at the balance sheet date and the monetary asset (liability) in one group company is eliminated against the corresponding liability (asset) in another group company, the exchange difference reported in the group company's own income statement continues to be recognised in consolidated profit or loss. This is because the monetary item represents a commitment to convert one currency into another and exposes the reporting entity to gain or loss through currency fluctuations. [IAS 21 para 45].

Example – Elimination of intra-group trading transactions where the inventory is still owned by the group

A UK parent company has a wholly-owned subsidiary in the US. During the year ended 31 December 20X5, the US company purchased plant and raw materials to be used in its manufacturing process from the UK parent. Details of the transactions are as follows:

	Exchange rate
Purchased plant costing £500,000 on 30 April 20X5	£1 = US$1.48
Paid for plant on 30 September 20X5	£1 = US$1.54
Purchased raw materials costing £300,000 on 31 October 20X5	£1 = US$1.56
Balance of £300,000 outstanding at 31 December 20X5	£1 = US$1.52
Average rate for the year	£1 = US$1.55

The following exchange gains/losses will be recorded in the US subsidiary's income statement for the year ended 31 December 20X5.

	US$	US$
Plant costing £500,000 @ 1.48	740,000	
Paid £500,000 @ 1.54	770,000	
Exchange loss – settled transaction		(30,000)
Raw materials costing £300,000 @ 1.56	468,000	
Outstanding £300,000 @ 1.52	456,000	
Exchange gain – unsettled transaction		12,000
Net exchange loss recorded in income statement		(18,000)

The exchange loss of US$30,000 that arises as the inter-company creditor for plant purchase is settled during the year will flow through on consolidation when the US subsidiary's results are incorporated in the consolidated accounts. The inter-company creditor of US$456,000 in the US subsidiary's balance sheet that remains outstanding will be translated into sterling at the closing rate to £300,000 and will be eliminated against the debtor recorded in the UK parent's inter-company account. However, the exchange gain of US$12,000 will not be eliminated on consolidation and will be reported as part of the consolidated results of the group. The rationale of keeping this gain in the group's result is that to repay the creditor balance, the US subsidiary will some day have to expend the amount of its local currency necessary to acquire the required amount of the reporting currency. This exposes the group to a gain or loss on reconversion.

A7.90 The same treatment that applies to an unsettled inter-company monetary item arising from trading transactions also applies to intra-group loans made by one group member to another in a currency that is different from the borrower's functional currency. That is, the borrower will initially record the foreign currency loan at the rate of exchange ruling at the date the loan is made. At each balance sheet date thereafter, until it is repaid, the loan will be translated at the closing rate and any exchange difference will be reported in the borrower's income statement. On consolidation, the intra-group loan account will cancel out, but the exchange difference reported in the borrower's income statement continues to be recognised in profit or loss.

Unrealised profit on inventories

A7.91 IAS 27, 'Consolidated and separate financial statements', requires intra-group profit arising from the transfer of assets between entities in the group to be eliminated in full in the group accounts where such assets are still held in the undertakings included in the consolidation at the balance sheet date. This is because it does not represent profit to the group (see further chapter 24). No specific guidance is given in IAS 21 as to the exchange rate at which the profit should be eliminated. However, SFAS 52 requires elimination at the actual rate ruling at the transaction date or at a weighted average rate.

Example – Elimination of intra-group trading transactions where the inventory had been sold outside the group

The facts are the same as in the example in paragraph A7.89 except that the raw materials purchased for £300,000 by the US subsidiary are still in inventory at 31 December 20X5. These goods cost the UK parent £270,000.

Unrealised profit of £30,000 (£300,000 — £270,000) that the parent entity made on the inter-company sale would, therefore, need to be eliminated on consolidation. However, elimination of this unrealised profit of £30,000 will not necessarily result in the inventories being included in the consolidated balance sheet at cost to the group where the closing rate method is used, as illustrated below.

The amount for raw materials included in inventory in the US company's balance sheet at the transaction date is US$468,000. Under the closing rate method, the inventory would be retranslated at the year end rate of 1.52 to £307,895. Therefore, the inventory will be recorded in the consolidated balance sheet as follows:

	£
Cost of inventory US$468,000 @ 1.52	307,895
Unrealised profit	(30,000)
Inventory carried in consolidated balance sheet	277,895

The difference of £7,895 represents the exchange difference arising on the retranslation of the inventory in the subsidiary's financial statements to the year end rate under the closing rate/net investment method — that is, £307,895 less the cost to the subsidiary of £300,000.

If the parent has purchased the raw materials from the US subsidiary for US 468,000 at 31 October 20X5, which cost the US subsidiary US$421,200, and these items were still in the parent's inventory at the year end, a problem arises as to what rate the unrealised profit of US$46,800 is eliminated.

As stated above, if the guidance in SFAS 52 is followed, the profit will be eliminated at the actual rate ruling at the transaction date. The inventory will be recorded in the consolidated balance sheet as follows:

	£
Cost of inventory US$468,000 @ 1.56	300,000
Unrealised profit US$46,800 @ 1.56	(30,000)
Inventory carried in consolidated balance sheet	270,000

The amount of inventory recorded in the balance sheet represents the original cost to the group of US$421,200 translated at the rate ruling at the date of the intra-group transaction – that is, US$421,200 @ 1.56 = £270,000. This is the method required by SFAS 52, which can be applied under IAS 21.

In practice, it is likely that the UK parent will use an average rate for translating the results of foreign operations. The amount of profit to be eliminated is calculated using that average rate. Use of an average rate is permissible where it approximates the exchange rate at the date of the transaction.

	£
Cost of inventory US$468,000 @ 1.56	300,000
Unrealised profit US$46,800 @ 1.55	(30,194)
	269,806

The amount of inventory recorded in the consolidated balance sheet under the closing rate/net investment method will not be the same as the actual cost to the group.

A7.92 Even if intra-group transactions do not give rise to intra-group profit, there could still be an effect on asset values, as the following example illustrates.

Example – Intra-group trading transaction at cost

A UK parent has a wholly-owned subsidiary in Pololand. The currency is Pol. The net assets of the group at 31 March 20X5 are £54,000, consisting of cash £24,000, held in the UK parent and inventory held in the Pololand subsidiary costing Pol 3m. This was included in the consolidated balance sheet at the closing rate of £1 = Pol 100. On 30 September 20X5, the subsidiary transfers the goods to its UK parent at cost price when the rate of exchange is £1 = Pol 125. The transaction is settled in cash, and the goods are included in the parent's inventory at £24,000. At 31 March 20X6, the goods are still in inventory. The Pol has weakened further against sterling and the exchange rate at the balance sheet date is £1 = Pol 150.

No gain or loss is recorded by either company on the transfer; there are therefore no inter-company profits to be eliminated.

		31 March 20X5
		£
Net assets:		
Inventory 3m @ 100 (held by subsidiary)		30,000
Cash (held by parent)		24,000
		54,000
		31 March 20X6
		£
Net assets:		
Inventory (held by parent)		24,000
Cash 3m @ 150 (held by subsidiary)		20,000
		44,000
Exchange difference on retranslation of opening net assets of foreign subsidiary:		
3m @ 100 =	30,000	
3m @ 150 =	20,000	10,000
		54,000

No exchange difference is included in the consolidated income statement, as there is no trading gain or loss. However the effect of switching inventory around the group affects the asset's carrying value. If the inventory had not been transferred, the net assets would still have decreased by £10,000, but the reduction would have been entirely in the inventory value with the cash balance unchanged. However, the result of moving the inventory and cash around the group is that there is a decrease of £6,000 in the inventory value and a decrease of £4,000 in the group's cash position. This reflects the fact that the group's foreign currency exposure is centred on different assets.

Monetary items forming part of net investment in a foreign operation

A7.93 The net investment that a reporting entity has in a foreign operation is its interest in the net assets of that operation. [IAS 21 para 8]. In circumstances described in paragraph A7.95 below, a monetary item that is receivable from or payable to a foreign operation, such as long-term loans and receivables and long-term payables, may be regarded as an extension of, or reduction, in the reporting entity's net investment in that foreign operation. In those situations, it may not be appropriate to include the resulting exchange differences arising on the retranslation of such monetary items in consolidated profit or loss when exchange difference arising on equivalent financing with equity capital would be taken to other comprehensive income on consolidation.

A7.94 IAS 21 recognises the above situation and requires exchange differences arising on a monetary item that forms part of a reporting entity's net investment in a foreign operation that is a subsidiary, associate or joint venture to be treated as follows:

- In the separate financial statements of the reporting entity or the individual financial statements of the foreign operation as appropriate, such exchange differences are recognised in the income statement.
- In the financial statements that include the foreign operation and the reporting entity (for example, consolidated financial statements when the foreign operation is a subsidiary), such exchange differences are recognised initially in a separate component of other comprehensive income and recognised in the profit or loss on disposal of the net investment (see further para A7.106).

[IAS 21 para 32].

A7.95 The inclusion of long-term loans and receivables as part of the net investment in the foreign operation is only permitted where settlement is neither planned nor likely to occur in the foreseeable future. [IAS 21 para 15]. In other words, the parent must regard them as permanent as equity. For example, a loan to a foreign entity that is repayable on demand may seem to be a short-term item, rather than part of capital. However, if there is demonstrably no intent or expectation to demand repayment (for example, the short-term loan is allowed to be continuously rolled over, whether or not the subsidiary is able to repay it), the loan has the same economic effect as a capital contribution. On the other hand, a long-term loan with a specified maturity (say 10 to 15 years) does not automatically qualify to be treated as being part of the net investment simply because it is of a long duration, unless management has expressed its intention to renew the note at maturity. The burden is on management to document its intention to renew by auditable evidence, such as board minutes. Otherwise, absent management's intention to renew, the note's maturity date implies that its settlement is planned in the foreseeable future.

A7.96 Some may argue that inter-company accounts of a trading nature should qualify for the same treatment as above because, although individual transactions are settled, the account's aggregate balance never drops below a specified minimum. In other words, as a minimum amount is permanently deferred, an appropriate amount of the resulting exchange difference should also be deferred in equity. This treatment is not permitted; the standard prohibits its application to trade receivables and payables. [IAS 21 para 15]. The rationale is that as each individual transaction included in the overall inter-company balance is settled and replaced by a new transaction; settlement is always contemplated and, therefore, exchange gains and losses arising on such active accounts as described above would not qualify for deferral treatment.

A7.97 The example below illustrates a number of scenarios setting out the treatment that management is required to follow on consolidation when inter-company loans are made between various members of a group.

Parent A is the reporting entity that has two subsidiaries B and C, which themselves have subsidiaries D and E. The functional currencies of each of the entities are as noted next to the letters designating the entities.

In all the scenarios that follow, loans made between group entities are permanent in nature (that is, settlement is neither planned nor likely to occur).

Scenario 1

Parent A has a loan receivable from or payable to its foreign subsidiary C that is denominated in either sterling or the dollar.

The loan would be regarded as an extension to or a reduction of entity A's net investment in entity C as appropriate. An exchange difference is recognised in entity A's income statement if the loan receivable or payable is denominated in dollars. An exchange difference will be recognised in entity C's income statement if the loan receivable or payable is denominated in sterling. Any exchange difference recognised in either entity's profit or loss is recognised in other comprehensive income on consolidation. The above situation is dealt with in the numerical examples below.

Example — currency loan made by parent A to foreign subsidiary C

Parent A with sterling as its functional currency is preparing its financial statements to 30 September 20X5. It has a loan receivable of US$1m from its foreign subsidiary C that has been outstanding for some time. The parent notified the overseas subsidiary at the beginning of the financial year that no repayment of the amount will be requested for the foreseeable future.

The relevant exchange rates are as follows:

	30 September 20X5	30 September 20X4
£1 =	US$1.82	US $ 1.45

The following exchange differences will arise in the financial statements of the individual entities if the loan is retranslated at the closing rate:

Foreign subsidiary C

No exchange difference arises in the foreign subsidiary as the loan payable is denominated in its functional currency.

UK parent A

Exchange difference on long-term loan receivable	£
On closing rate – US$1m @ 1.82	549,450
On opening rate – US$1m @ 1.45	689,655
Exchange loss	140,205

In the parent entity's separate financial statement, the loan is regarded as a monetary item and any exchange difference is taken to the profit or loss in accordance with paragraph A7.94 above. [IAS 21 para 32].

On consolidation, the retranslated long-term loan is regarded as part of the net investment in the foreign subsidiary and, therefore, the related exchange loss is recognised in other comprehensive income and accumulated as a separate component of equity in accordance with paragraph A7.94 above. [IAS 21 para 32]. There would also be a corresponding exchange gain included in other comprehensive income, arising as part of the retranslation of the net assets (which include the US dollar loan creditor) of the overseas subsidiary under the closing rate/net investment method.

Example — sterling loan made by parent A to overseas subsidiary C

The facts are the same as the above example, except that parent A has a loan receivable from its overseas subsidiary of £200,000 that has been outstanding for some time. The loan is treated by the parent entity as forming part of its net investment in the overseas subsidiary.

In the financial statements of the individual entities, the following exchange differences will arise if the loan is retranslated at the closing rate.

UK parent A

There is no exchange difference in the parent's financial statements in respect of the loan as it is denominated in sterling.

Subsidiary C

Exchange difference on long-term loan payable	US$
On closing rate – £200,000 @ 1.82	364,000
On opening rate – £200,000 @ 1.45	290,000
Exchange loss	74,000
Exchange loss translated at the closing rate @ 1.82	£40,659

The exchange loss of US$74,000 on the sterling loan is recognised in the foreign subsidiary C's income statement, because the subsidiary is exposed to the foreign currency risk.

On consolidation, the inter-company loan will cancel out. However, as the long-term loan is regarded as part of the net investment in the subsidiary, the exchange loss of £40,659 is recognised in other comprehensive income and accumulated as a separate component of equity in the consolidated financial statements. There is a corresponding exchange gain included in other comprehensive income arising as part of the retranslation of the net assets of the overseas subsidiary. The effect is that the consolidated income statement will not reflect any exchange difference on the loan, which is consistent with the fact that the loan has no impact on group cash flows, unless the investment is sold.

The two examples above consider the accounting implications when a loan is made by the parent entity to an overseas subsidiary. In the case of a foreign currency upstream loan, for example, a borrowing by a parent entity from its subsidiary in the subsidiary's local currency, the treatment of exchange differences in the consolidated financial statements will depend on whether the loan is regarded as part of the net investment in the subsidiary. If that is the case, the treatment will be the same as identified above. That is, the exchange difference arising on the currency loan's retranslation in the parent's income statement is classified to a separate component of equity in the consolidated financial statements. On the other hand, if the loan is not regarded as part of the net investment, the exchange difference will continue to be recognised in consolidated profit or loss.

Scenario 2

Subsidiary B makes a loan denominated in sterling to subsidiary C ('sister-company loans')

Subsidiary C recognises an exchange difference in its own income statement. The question is whether the exchange difference can be recognised in other comprehensive income and accumulated as a separate component of equity on consolidation.

IAS 21 has been amended to clarify in paragraph 15A that it is not necessary for the lender or the borrower to have the net investment in the foreign operation for the exchange differences on translation of the monetary item to be classified within entity. The entity that has the monetary item receivable from or payable to a foreign operation may be any member of group

A7.98 The above examples deal with situations where a monetary item forming part of the net investment was denominated in the functional currency of either the reporting entity or the foreign operation. The question then arises as to whether a similar treatment is permissible in circumstances where a monetary item forming part of the net investment in a foreign operation is denominated in a currency that is different from the functional currency of either the reporting entity or the foreign operation.

A7.99 Under IAS 21, a monetary item that meets the criteria to be part of an entity's net investment in a foreign operation is similar to an equity investment in a foreign operation. Hence, the accounting treatment in the consolidated financial statements does not depend on the currency in which the monetary item is denominated. Paragraph 33 of IAS 21 requires exchange differences on translation of such a monetary item to be recognised in other comprehensive income in the consolidated financial statements, irrespective of the currency of the monetary item.

A7.99.1 Consider the situation in the group structure set out in paragraph A7.97 above where parent A, whose functional currency is the pound sterling, makes a loan denominated in euros to subsidiary C, whose functional currency is the US dollar. If the euro loan meets the criteria to be regarded by entity A as part of its net investment in entity C, the exchange differences that arise from retranslating the loan receivable in sterling in entity A's income statement and the loan payable in dollars in entity C's income statement are recognised in other comprehensive income in the financial statements that include the foreign operation and the reporting entity (that is, entity A's consolidated financial statements). [IAS 21 para 33].

A7.100 Another issue that might arise is the appropriate treatment to be adopted in the year in which the parent decides to designate any long-term loans and receivables as part of its net investment in the foreign operation. Consider the first example in scenario 1 above where the long-term US dollar loan made by parent A was designated as being part of its net investment in the foreign subsidiary C from the beginning of the accounting period. If the parent did this part way through the financial year ended 30 September 20X5, say, at 31 March 20X5, the parent recognises any exchange difference arising in profit or loss up to that date and reclassifies any exchange difference that arises subsequently following the designation to the separate component in other comprehensive income in the consolidated financial statements.

A7.101 Although not dealt with in the standard, the designation of an inter-company loan as part of the net investment in a foreign operation is periodically reassessed. This is because management's expectations and intent may change due to a change in circumstances. Such changes in circumstances are carefully evaluated to determine that management's previous assertions for not requiring repayment remain valid. For example, the change in circumstances may be such that it could not have been anticipated at the time of initial designation or the change in circumstances could be outside management's control.

A7.102 Where, as a result of a change in circumstance, a previously designated 'net investment' loan is intended to be settled, the loan is de-designated. As the loan is no longer regarded as part of the net investment, a partial disposal of the net investment may have occurred and reclassification of cumulative translation adjustment may be required. See from paragraph A7.106 onwards for discussion of partial disposals.

A7.102.1 There is no explicit guidance in IAS 21 about the timing of reclassification in the circumstances described in the previous paragraph. Does it occur when the loan is no longer considered to form part of the net investment in the foreign operation, or when the loan is actually repaid? Either approach may be adopted as an accounting policy choice. The selected policy should be applied consistently to all of the entity's 'net investment' loans and all to of its investments in foreign operations.

Inter-company dividends

A7.103 Where a foreign subsidiary pays a dividend to its parent company, the dividend is charged directly to equity in its financial statements, and as the dividend is paid in the functional currency of the foreign subsidiary no exchange difference arises. However, if the dividends are payable in a currency that is different from the subsidiary's functional currency, exchange rate fluctuations between the dividend being recognised as an asset and being paid will produce foreign exchange gains or losses impacting profit or loss.

A7.104 In the parent entity's financial statements, the dividend is translated at the rate in effect upon declaration (that is, the transaction date). An exchange gain or loss will arise if the rate of exchange moves between the date of declaration and the payment date. This exchange difference is reported in the parent's income statement as a normal inter-company transaction exchange gain or loss that is also reported in the consolidated financial statements. Consider the following example:

Example – Treatment of foreign exchange gains or losses on inter-company dividends

A subsidiary with a dollar functional currency declared a dividend of $100,000 to its euro functional currency parent on 31 August 20X5 for the year ended 31 December 20X5. The dividend was appropriately authorised and recognised by the subsidiary as a liability at 31 August 20X5. The parent prepares consolidated financial statements for the year ended 31 December 20X5 in its presentation currency of euros. The following exchange rates are relevant:

31 August 20X5	$1.50 = €1
31 December 20X5	$1.75 = €1
15 January 20X6	$1.80 = €1

Dividend paid on 15 January 20X6

The dividend remains outstanding at the balance sheet date. The dividend is recorded in the subsidiary's and parent's separate and consolidated financial statements as follows:

In subsidiary's balance sheet (as translated for consolidation)

	€
Dividend payable – $100,000 @ 1.75	57,142

In parent's income statement

Initially recorded at rate when dividend is declared – $100,000 @ 1.5 (transaction date)	66,667
Exchange loss on receivable recognised in the income statement	(9,525)
In parent's balance sheet – Dividend receivable at year end rate – $100,000 @ 1.75	57,142

In consolidated income statement

In the consolidated financial statements the dividend receivable of €66,667 is reclassified to consolidated retained earnings and offsets the dividend payable in the subsidiary's retained earnings that is translated at the year end rate @ 1.75 = €57,142. The difference of €9,525 (€66,667 – €57,142) comprises a loss recorded in the parent's income statement and no further exchange difference arises. The inter-entity receivable and payable cancel out.

Some may argue that the exchange difference of €9,525 included in the parent's income statement should be removed from consolidated income and reclassified to equity as it relates to dividends that are initially charged to equity. We believe that this treatment is not appropriate, as the exchange difference arises on a monetary asset and would affect group cash flows when it is settled. Such an exchange difference should, therefore, remain in consolidated income.

A7.105 Given that exchange differences can arise on any transaction where the settlement date is different from the date when the transaction is recorded, it may be appropriate to ensure that inter-company dividends are paid on the same date as they are declared as liabilities, particularly where it is likely that an exchange loss will arise. This may not always be possible, so it is not uncommon for a parent company to mitigate exchange differences arising by taking out appropriate forward contracts so as to hedge the future remittance. Hedge accounting for foreign currency items is dealt with in IAS 39, 'Financial instruments: Recognition and measurement'. Hedge accounting is considered in chapter 6.

Disposal or partial disposal of a foreign operation

A7.106 As discussed in paragraph A7.77, the cumulative amount of exchange differences recognised in other comprehensive income is carried forward as a separate component of equity until there is a disposal of the foreign operation. On the foreign operation's disposal, such exchange differences are recognised in profit or loss (that is, reclassified) when the gain or loss on disposal is recognised. [IAS 21 para 48]. Disposal may occur either through sale, liquidation, repayment of share capital or a quasi-equity loan, or abandonment of all, or part of, the entity.

A7.106.1 Amendments were made to IAS 21 in January 2008 when IFRS 3, 'Business combinations', and IAS 27, 'Consolidated and separate financial statements', were revised. These amendments are applicable for annual periods beginning on or after 1 July 2009. The amendments state that when an entity loses control of a subsidiary that includes a foreign operation this is a disposal that triggers reclassification of the entire amount of CTA that has been recorded in equity attributable to the parent entity, even if the entity retains an interest in that former subsidiary. [IAS 21 para 48, 48A]. This applies, for example, when 80 per cent of a 100 per cent subsidiary is sold and a 20 per cent interest in an associate is retained. The entire amount of CTA in relation to that subsidiary is reclassified to profit or loss. In the case where a foreign operation is partially owned (that is, where a non-controlling interest exists) the amount of the CTA that has been allocated to the non-controlling interest is derecognised, but is not transferred to profit or loss. [IAS 21 para 48B]. Derecognition of the non-controlling interest that includes the non-controlling interest's share of CTA will form part of the journal to calculate the gain or loss on disposal of the foreign operation. The Annual Improvements 2010 clarified that the amendment to IAS 21 arising from IAS 27 should be applied *prospectively*. Entities, therefore, do not restate their CTA as if the amendment has always applied.

A7.106.2 The principle of full reclassification also applies to the loss of joint control or significant influence over a jointly controlled entity or an associate. All CTA that has been accumulated in equity in relation to that jointly controlled entity or associate is reclassified to profit or loss when joint control or significant influence is lost. [IAS 21 para 48A].

A7.107 On a partial disposal that does not involve loss of control of a subsidiary that includes a foreign operation, the entity re-attributes the proportionate share of the CTA to the non-controlling interests in that foreign operation. [IAS 21 para 48C].

A7.107.1 On the partial disposal of an interest in a jointly controlled entity or an associate, where joint control or significant influence are not lost, a proportionate amount of CTA is reclassified to profit or loss. [IAS 21 para 48C].

A7.107.2 A write-down of the carrying amount of a foreign operation does not constitute a partial disposal. No part of the deferred foreign exchange gain or loss is recognised in profit or loss at the time of a write-down. [IAS 21 para 49]. Where the write-down arises from an impairment assessment as a result of a planned sale or liquidation (for example, where the foreign subsidiary is treated as a disposal group in accordance with IFRS 5, 'Non-current assets held for sale and discontinued operations'), the write-down is also not treated as a partial disposal. [IFRS 5 BC 37, 38]. Therefore, any exchange difference attributable to that write down is not recognised in profit or loss. Reclassification will occur when the foreign operation is sold.

A7.107.3 The cessation of hedge accounting of a net investment as the hedge no longer meets the criteria for the hedge accounting in IAS 39 is not a disposal.

Therefore, the effective portion of the hedge as well as the related CTA previously recognised in other comprehensive income remain in other comprehensive income until the disposal, or partial disposal, of the foreign operation.

A7.107.4 The conversion of a 'net investment' loan to an equity instrument as defined in IAS 32 does not result in reclassification. The reason for this is that the conversion of the loan is the swapping of the legal form of an investment from a debt instrument to an equity instrument so no disposal has occurred. No further exchange differences will arise on the equity investment in the parent's separate financial statements, as it is now a non-monetary item. (However, exchange differences would continue to arise on the net assets of the foreign operation.) The re-denomination of a 'net investment' loan into a different currency also does not constitute a disposal or partial disposal of the foreign operation. It does not change the parent's net investment in the foreign operation, there is no cash movement therefore in substance there has been no disposal. Therefore, no gains or losses are reclassified from equity to profit or loss.

A7.107.5 Where a subsidiary that is a foreign operation repays a quasi-equity loan or share capital but there is no change in the parent's percentage shareholding there is an accounting policy choice regarding whether CTA should be reclassified.

Option 1 – No disposal of interest in subsidiary

Since the parent continues to own the same percentage of the subsidiary, and continues to control the foreign operation, there has been no change in its proportionate 'ownership interest' and hence no disposal or partial disposal under paragraphs 48D and 49 of IAS 21. CTA should not, therefore, be reclassified.

Option 2 – Disposal of interest in subsidiary

The transaction is a partial disposal under paragraph 49 of IAS 21, as there has been a reduction in the parent's absolute ownership interest. Under this view 'ownership interest' refers to either the percentage or the absolute interest held in a net investment. A *pro rata* share of CTA should be reclassified.

Entities should make an accounting policy choice between these two methods and apply this policy consistently.

A7.107.6 In 2008, the IASB made an amendment to IFRS 1, 'First-time adoption of IFRS', and IAS 27 with a consequential amendment to IAS 21. Under the amendment to IAS 27, an entity does not distinguish between dividends paid out of pre-acquisition profits or post-acquisition profits when accounting for an investment in a subsidiary in its separate financial statements. A parent recognises any dividend received as income and separately considers whether its investment in a subsidiary has been impaired. IAS 21, therefore, was changed and an entity receiving a dividend from a foreign operation no longer regards a dividend from pre-acquisition profits as always being a disposal or a partial disposal. It may only be considered a disposal or partial disposal when it is in substance a partial liquidation of the subsidiary and the parent entity applies the policy of treating such events as partial disposals (see example 3 in para A7.107.6 below).

A7.107.7 The rules on disposals and partial disposals and their effect on CTA can be summarised in the following table:

Event	Effect on CTA	Disposal or partial disposal
Subsidiary to Subsidiary (change in non-controlling interest)	Reattribute proportionate share of CTA to NCI	Partial disposal
Subsidiary to JV or Associate (loss of control)	All CTA reclassified to profit or loss	Disposal
Subsidiary to Investment (loss of control)	All CTA reclassified to profit or loss	Disposal
Associate to Associate (reduction in ownership percentage)	Proportionate share of CTA reclassified to profit or loss	Partial disposal
Associate or JV to Investment	All CTA reclassified to profit or loss	Disposal
Write down of carrying amount of foreign operation	None	Neither
Cessation of hedge accounting for a net investment	None	Neither
Conversion of 'net investment' loan to equity instrument	None	Neither
Partial liquidation of a subsidiary	Depends on policy choice	Accounting policy choice
Dividend from pre-acquisition profit	Proportionate share of CTA to profit or loss only if liquidation	Only if it is a partial liquidation

Example 1 – Partial disposal of an associate

An investor owns 40% of the share capital of an entity. It has significant influence over the entity and accounts for the investment as an associate using equity accounting. The associate is a foreign operation. The investor sells half of its total shareholding, retaining a 20% investment. It continues to have significant influence and to account for the investment as an associate.

How much, if any, CTA is reclassified to profit or loss?

The reduction in the investor's ownership interest is a partial disposal per IAS 21 para 48D. Half of the investment in associate has been disposed of, therefore 50% of the CTA relating to the foreign associate is reclassified to profit or loss [IAS 21 para 48C].

Example 2 – Partial disposal of a subsidiary while control is retained

A parent owns 100% of a subsidiary. The subsidiary is a foreign operation. The parent sells 30% of its shareholding, retaining a 70% shareholding and control.

How much, if any, CTA should be reattributed to the non-controlling interest?

The reduction in the parent's ownership interest is a partial disposal per IAS 21 para 48D. 30% of the subsidiary has been disposed of, therefore 30% of CTA should be re-attributed to the new non-controlling interest. This transfer is accounted for in the statement of changes in equity and is not presented in the performance statements. None of the CTA is reclassified to the income statement. [IAS 21 para 48C].

Example 3 – Partial liquidation of a subsidiary

A parent owns 100% of a subsidiary. The subsidiary is a foreign operation. The subsidiary repays a quasi-equity loan by paying cash equal to 10% of its net assets to its parent. Prior to the transaction there had been no intention of repaying the quasi-equity loan. After the transaction the parent continues to own 100% of the subsidiary.

How much, if any, CTA is reclassified to profit or loss?

There are two ways that this transaction might be analysed (para A7.107.6).

Option 1 – No disposal of interest in subsidiary

Since there has been no change in the parent's proportionate "ownership interest" there is no disposal or partial disposal under IAS 21 paras 48D and 49. CTA should not, therefore, be reclassified.

Option 2 – Disposal of interest in subsidiary

The transaction is a partial disposal under IAS 21 para 49, as there has been a 10% reduction in the parent's absolute ownership interest. A pro rata share (10%) of CTA should be reclassified.

The above options would equally apply to a repayment of share capital in similar circumstances.

Entities should make an accounting policy choice between these views and apply this policy consistently.

Example 4 – Reclassification of cumulative exchange differences due to a group restructuring

In a group restructuring, a foreign operation is transferred from one intermediate holding entity to another. The group continues to hold a 100% interest in that foreign operation. No third parties are involved with the group restructuring.

Are the cumulative exchange differences reclassified in the group's consolidated financial statements?

The key question is whether the restructuring results in an economic change from the group's perspective that constitutes a partial or full disposal. The foreign operation continues to be part of the consolidated group and the restructuring is not a disposal event from the group's perspective.

However, if the intermediate holding entity that disposes of the foreign operation prepares consolidated financial statements under IFRS, the cumulative translation adjustments deferred in equity (if any) that arise at that intermediate reporting level are reclassified to profit or loss.

A7.107.8 The tracking of cumulative exchange differences can be onerous. For a parent with more than one foreign operation, it could be tempting to aggregate these exchange differences related to all the net investments in one currency together, with the reclassification of these exchange differences on the disposal (or partial disposal) of some of those foreign operations being calculated proportionately based on the whole investments portfolio. However, IAS 21 requires reclassification whenever there is a disposal, or partial disposal, of a foreign operation, so the cumulative translation adjustments are required to be tracked on an individual net investment basis.

Hedging a net investment

A7.108 A net investment in a foreign operation is defined as *"the amount of the reporting entity's interest in the net assets of that operation"*. [IAS 21 para 8]. Management may decide to hedge against the effects of changes in exchange rates in the entity's net investment in a foreign operation. This may be done by taking out a foreign currency borrowing or a forward contract to hedge the net investment. Hedging a net investment in a foreign operation can only be carried out at the consolidation level, because the net assets of the foreign operation are reported in the reporting entity's consolidated financial statements. However, IAS 21 does not apply to hedge accounting for foreign currency items including the hedging of a net investment in a foreign operation. IAS 39, 'Financial instruments: Recognition and measurement', and IFRIC 16, 'Hedges of a net investment in a foreign operation', apply to hedge accounting. Under IAS 39, the hedging documentation and criteria set out in paragraph 88 of IAS 39 must be met, and any exchange differences recognised in equity through other comprehensive income relating to the foreign operation and the related borrowing are recognised in profit or loss on disposal of the foreign operation. IFRIC 16 gives further detailed guidance on hedges of net investments. Hedging of net investments is addressed in greater detail in chapter 6.

A7.108.1 Where a reporting entity has a foreign currency borrowing that is designated as a hedge of its net investment in a foreign operation and all the conditions in IAS 39 and IFRIC 16 are met, the exchange gain or loss on the foreign currency borrowing reported in the reporting entity's separate income statement is reclassified to other comprehensive income in the reporting entity's consolidated financial statements.

A7.108.2 IAS 27, 'Consolidated and separate financial statements', states that in a parent's separate financial statements, investments in subsidiaries, jointly controlled entities and associates that are included in the consolidated financial statements are carried at cost or accounted for in accordance with IAS 39. This means that the equity investment can either be carried at cost less impairment, designated as 'available for sale' or designated as 'at fair value through profit or loss' (if permitted by IAS 39). IAS 27 requires the same accounting to be applied for each category of investment. A question arises as to whether a foreign currency borrowing can be designated as a hedge of the entity's foreign equity investment in its separate financial statements where the foreign equity investment is recorded at cost. IAS 39's rules on net investment hedging apply only to consolidated financial statements. However, we believe that the reporting entity can designate the foreign currency borrowing as a fair value hedge of foreign currency risk attributable to its foreign equity investment. In those circumstances, the foreign equity investment is retranslated at each balance sheet date and exchange difference arising on the retranslation is recognised in profit or loss to offset the exchange difference arising on the retranslation of the foreign currency borrowings. However, the hedging criteria set out in paragraph 88 of IAS 39 must still be met in order to achieve fair value hedge accounting in the reporting entity's separate financial statements. Whether, in practice, such a parent entity would apply hedge accounting in its separate financial statements may well depend on the tax treatment of undertaking such hedging activities.

Foreign operations in hyper-inflationary economies

A7.109 Where a foreign entity operates in a country in which a very high rate of inflation exists and its functional currency is the local currency, the closing rate/net investment method is not suitable for translating the foreign entity's financial statements for inclusion in the consolidated financial statements. This is because an asset acquired in a currency that is the currency of a hyper-inflationary economy may be worth very little at a time of high inflation, when the foreign currency has weakened considerably against the reporting entity's functional currency, leading to a large debit to consolidated reserves. At the same time, the results of the foreign entity are included at an inflated amount in the consolidated income statement (whether from high interest income on deposits in a rapidly depreciating foreign currency or from trading operations that could be considered to reflect unrealistically high profitability). Therefore, as money loses purchasing power in a hyper-inflationary economy, the reporting of operating results and financial position in the local currency without adjustment to reflect current price levels is misleading.

A7.110 When an entity's functional currency is the currency of the hyper-inflationary economy, the entity applies IAS 29, 'Financial reporting in hyper-inflationary economies'. For information on the accounting treatment for entities operating in hyper-inflationary economies, refer to chapter 6.

[The next paragraph is A7.115.]

Presentation and disclosure

General

A7.115 The paragraphs that follow deal with IAS 21's disclosure requirements that apply to both individual financial statements and consolidated financial statements. IFRS 7, 'Financial instruments: Disclosures', require significant additional disclosures about foreign currency transactions and activities. The requirements of IFRS 7 are dealt with in Manual of Accounting – Financial instruments.

Accounting policies

A7.116 There is no specific requirement in IAS 21 to disclose accounting policies in respect of foreign currency transactions. This is because IAS 1, 'Presentation of financial statements', requires disclosure of significant policies that are relevant to an entity's financial statements. [IAS 1 para 108]. In respect of foreign currency transactions, the accounting policy note should state, as a minimum, the methods used in translating foreign currency transactions and the financial statements of foreign operations including those operating in hyper-inflationary economies, and the treatment accorded to exchange differences. The following is an example of a foreign currency accounting policy.

Table A7.1 – Accounting policy for foreign currency

Heineken N.V. – Report and accounts – 31 December 2010

2. Basis of preparation (extract)

(c) Functional and presentation currency

These consolidated financial statements are presented in euro, which is the Company's functional currency. All financial information presented in euro has been rounded to the nearest million unless stated otherwise.

3. Significant accounting policies (extract)

(b) Foreign currency

(i) Foreign currency transactions

Transactions in foreign currencies are translated to the respective functional currencies of Heineken entities at the exchange rates at the dates of the transactions. Monetary assets and liabilities denominated in foreign currencies at the reporting date are retranslated to the functional currency at the exchange rate at that date. The foreign currency gain or loss arising on monetary items is the difference between amortised cost in the functional currency at the beginning of the period, adjusted for effective interest and payments during the period, and the amortised cost in foreign currency translated at the exchange rate at the end of the reporting period.

Non-monetary assets and liabilities denominated in foreign currencies that are measured at fair value are retranslated to the functional currency at the exchange rate at the date that the fair value was determined.

Non-monetary items in a foreign currency that are measured in terms of historical cost are translated using the exchange rate at the date of the transaction. Foreign currency differences arising on retranslation are recognised in profit or loss, except for differences arising on the retranslation of available-for-sale (equity) investments and foreign currency differences arising on the retranslation of a financial liability designated as a hedge of a net investment, which are recognised in other comprehensive income.

Non-monetary assets and liabilities denominated in foreign currencies that are measured at cost remain translated into the functional currency at historical exchange rates.

(ii) Foreign operations

The assets and liabilities of foreign operations, including goodwill and fair value adjustments arising on acquisition, are translated to euro at exchange rates at the reporting date. The income and expenses of foreign operations, excluding foreign operations in hyperinflationary economies, are translated to euro at exchange rates approximating the exchange rates ruling at the dates of the transactions.

Foreign currency differences are recognised in other comprehensive income and are presented within equity in the translation reserve. However, if the operation is a non-wholly-owned subsidiary, then the relevant proportionate share of the translation difference is allocated to the non-controlling interests. When a foreign operation is disposed of such that control, significant influence or joint control is lost, the cumulative amount in the translation reserve related to that foreign operation is reclassified to profit or loss as part of the gain or loss on disposal. When Heineken disposes of only part of its interest in a subsidiary that includes a foreign operation while retaining control, the relevant proportion of the cumulative amount is reattributed to non-controlling interests. When Heineken disposes of only part of its investment in an associate or joint venture that includes a foreign operation while retaining significant influence or joint control, the relevant proportion of the cumulative amount is reclassified to profit or loss.

Foreign exchange gains and losses arising from a monetary item receivable from or payable to a foreign operation, the settlement of which is neither planned nor likely in the foreseeable future, are considered to form part of a net investment in a foreign operation and are recognised in other comprehensive income, and are presented within equity in the translation reserve.

The following exchange rates, for the most important countries in which Heineken has operations, were used while preparing these consolidated financial statements:

	Year-end		Average	
In EUR	2010	2009	2010	2009
GBP	1.1618	1.1260	1.1657	1.1224
EGP	0.1287	0.1273	0.1339	0.1292
NGN	0.0050	0.0047	0.0051	0.0048
PLN	0.2516	0.2436	0.2503	0.2311
BRL	0.4509	0,4001	0.4289	0,3610
MXN	0.0604	0.0533	0.0598	0.0532
RUB	0.0245	0.0232	0.0248	0.0227
USD	0.7484	0.6942	0.7543	0.7170

(iii) Hedge of net investments in foreign operations

Foreign currency differences arising on the retranslation of a financial liability designated as a hedge of a net investment in a foreign operation are recognised in other comprehensive income to the extent that the hedge is effective and regardless of whether the net investment is held directly or through an intermediate parent. These differences are presented within equity in the translation reserve. To the extent that the hedge is ineffective, such differences are recognised in profit or loss. When the hedged part of a net investment is disposed of, the relevant amount in the translation reserve is transferred to profit or loss as part of the profit or loss on disposal.

Disclosure

A7.117 In respect of exchange differences, IAS 21 requires disclosure of:

- The amount of exchange differences recognised in profit or loss except for those arising on financial instruments measured at 'fair value through profit or loss' in accordance with IAS 39.
- Net exchange differences recognised in other comprehensive income and classified in a separate component of equity and a reconciliation of the amount of such exchange differences at the beginning and end of the period.

[IAS 21 para 52].

A7.118 The disclosure required above is on an aggregate net basis. The total amount of exchange differences recognised in profit or loss include exchange differences recognised on subsequent settlement and restatement to closing rate on balances arising on foreign currency transactions. However, the standard is silent as to where in profit or loss they should be included. A cue can be taken from IAS 12, 'Income taxes', which states that exchange differences arising on foreign deferred tax assets and liabilities may be included as part of the deferred tax expense (income) if that presentation is considered to be the most useful to financial statement users. Therefore:

- Foreign exchange differences arising from trading transactions may be included in the results of operating activities.
- Foreign exchange differences arising from financing may be included as a component of finance cost/income.

A7.118.1 The following examples illustrate the disclosure of the recognition of exchange differences in profit or loss and as a separate component in equity.

Table A7.2 – Disclosure of exchange differences recognised in profit or loss

Associated British Foods plc – Report and accounts – 18 September 2010

2. Operating costs and gross profit (extract)

	Note	2010 £m	2009 £m
OPERATING COSTS ARE STATED AFTER CHARGING/(CREDITING):			
Employee benefits expense	3	**1,497**	1,295
Amortisation of non-operating intangibles	8	**81**	82
Amortisation of operating intangibles	8	**8**	3
Profits less losses on disposal of non-current assets		**9**	1
Depreciation of owned property, plant & equipment	9	**324**	290
Operating lease payments under property leases		**95**	81
Operating lease payments for hire of plant & equipment		**11**	10
Other operating income		**(14)**	(18)
Research and development expenditure		**22**	23
Fair value gains on financial assets and liabilities held for trading		**(27)**	(97)
Fair value losses on financial assets and liabilities held for trading		**31**	95
Foreign exchange gains on operating activities		**(40)**	(93)
Foreign exchange losses on operating activities		**38**	90

4. Interest and other finance income and expense

	Note	2010 £m	2009 £m
FINANCE INCOME			
Interest income on financial assets not at fair value through profit or loss			
– cash and cash equivalents		**11**	13
– unwinding of discount on receivables		–	3
– finance leases		**1**	1
Total finance income		**12**	17
FINANCE EXPENSE			
Interest expense on financial liabilities not at fair value through profit or loss:			
- bank loans and overdrafts		**(34)**	(55)
- all other borrowings		**(46)**	(31)
- finance leases		**(1)**	(1)
- other payables		**(3)**	(2)
- unwinding of discount on provisions		**(4)**	(5)
Fair value loss on current asset investments		–	(1)
Total finance expense		**(88)**	(95)
OTHER FINANCIAL INCOME			
Expected return on employee benefit scheme assets	12	**138**	154
Interest charge on employee benefit scheme liabilities	12	**(143)**	(142)
Net financial income in respect of employee benefit schemes		**(5)**	12
Net foreign exchange gains/(losses) on financing activities		**(3)**	1
Total other financial income		**(8)**	13

Table A7.3 – Disclosure of exchange differences recognised in a separate component of equity

Xstrata plc – Report and accounts – 31 December 2010

26. Capital and Reserves (extract)
Other reserves

US$m	Revaluation reserves	Other reserves	Net unrealised gains (losses)	Foreign currency translation	Total
At 31 December 2008	1,440	1,229	(107)	(1,108)	1,454
Gains on available-for-sale financial assets	–	–	209)	–	209
Realised losses on available-for-sale financial assets	–	–	1	–	1
Gains on cash flow hedges	–	–	456	–	456
Realised losses on cash flow hedges*	–	–	(312)	–	(312)
Foreign currency translation differences	–	–	–	3,930	3,930
Deferred tax	–	–	((59)	(73)	(132)
At 31 December 2009	1,440	1,229	188	2,749	5,606
Gains on available-for-sale financial assets	–	–	118	–	118
Realised gains on available-for-sale financial assets	–	–	(73)	–	(73)
Gains on cash flow hedges	–	–	117	–	117
Realised gains on cash flow hedges*	–	–	(131)	–	(131)
Foreign currency translation differences	–	–	–	2,459	2,459
Deferred tax	–	–	(9)	(48)	(57)
At 31 December 2010	**1,440**	**1,229**	**210**	**5,160**	**8,039**

* Recycled gains of US$115 million (2009 US$312 million) are included in Revenue in the income statement, including non-controlling interests.

Revaluation reserves

This reserve principally records the remeasurement from cost of the 19.9% interest held in Falconbridge Limited (Falconbridge) to the fair value of 19.9% of the identifiable net assets of Falconbridge on 15 August 2006, the date the Group obtained control of Falconbridge.

Other reserves

This reserve principally originated during 2002 from the merger of Xstrata AG into Xstrata plc of US$279 million and the issue of shares from the acquisition of the Duiker and Enex Groups of US$935 million.

Net unrealised gains/(losses) reserve

This reserve records the remeasurement of available-for-sale financial assets to fair value (refer to note 22) and the effective portion of the gain or loss on cash flow hedging contracts (refer to notes 23, 30 and 37). Deferred tax is provided on the remeasurement at tax rates enacted or substantively enacted.

Foreign currency translation reserve

This is used to record exchange differences arising from the translation of the financial statements of foreign subsidiaries. It is also used to record the exchange differences from the translation of quasi equity inter-company loans in foreign operations. On disposal or partial disposal of a foreign entity, the deferred accumulated amount recognised in this reserve is transferred to the income statement.

A7.119 The standard permits a reporting entity to present its financial statements in a currency that is different from its functional currency. In this situation, the following should be disclosed:

- The fact that the presentation currency is different from the functional currency.
- The disclosure of the functional currency.
- The reasons for using a different presentation currency.

[IAS 21 para 53].

In these cases the entity provides the foreign currency risk disclosures required by IFRS 7 in reference to its functional currency rather than its presentation currency. The entity's exposure to currencies other than the functional currency will affect its future performance, and the details of these exposures are provided in the financial statements.

Table A7.4 – Presentation currency differs from functional currency

DP World Limited – Report and accounts – 31 December 2010

2 Basis of preparation (extract)

(d) Functional and presentation currency

The functional currency of the Company is UAE Dirhams. Each entity in the Group determines its own functional currency and items included in the financial statements of each entity are measured using that functional currency.

These consolidated financial statements are presented in United States Dollars ("USD"), which in the opinion of management is the most appropriate presentation currency in view of the global presence of the Group. All financial information presented in USD is rounded to the nearest thousand.

UAE Dirham is currently pegged to USD and there are no differences on translation from functional to presentation currency.

A7.120 When there is a change in the functional currency of either the reporting entity or a significant foreign operation, that fact and the reason for the change in functional currency is disclosed. [IAS 21 para 54]. As changes in functional currency may be due to a number of reasons, it is not possible to say what disclosure might be required in a particular case. However, it will certainly require a more substantial disclosure than, for example, 'this currency was chosen because it gives the most appropriate presentation'. Table A7.5 below is an example where the company's functional currency is changed, but the presentation currency has remained the same as the latter was already in dollars. Table A7.5.1 is a situation where both the functional currency of the parent (see para A7.46) and the parent and group's presentation currency (see para A7.82) are changed. The parent accounts under UK GAAP, but the relevant standard, FRS 23, is the same as IAS 21 in all material respects.

Table A7.5 – Change of functional currency

Royal Dutch Shell plc – Report and accounts – 31 December 2005

3 Accounting policies (extract)

Change in functional currency

Following Royal Dutch Shell becoming the parent company of Royal Dutch and Shell Transport on July 20, 2005 and through Royal Dutch and Shell Transport, of the rest of the Shell Group, the Directors have concluded that the most appropriate functional currency of the Company is dollars. This reflects the fact that the majority of the Shell Group's business is influenced by pricing in international commodity markets, with a dollar economic environment. The previous functional currency of the Company was the euro.

On the date of the change of functional currency all assets, liabilities, issued capital and other components of equity and income statement items were translated into dollars at the exchange rate on that date. As a result the cumulative currency translation differences which had arisen up to the date of the change of functional currency were reallocated to other components within equity (refer to Note 13).

As a result of the change in functional currency the Company's functional and presentation currency are now the same.

13 Other reserves (extract)

Cumulative currency translation differences

Cumulative currency translation differences represent the currency differences which arose as a result of translating the financial statements from the Company's previous functional currency of euro to the reporting currency of dollars.

The impact of the change in functional currency was the reallocation at that date of the cumulative currency translation differences of $15 million to issued capital.

Table A7.5.1 – Change of functional and presentation currencies

Smith & Nephew plc – Annual report – 31 December 2006

NOTES TO THE PARENT COMPANY ACCOUNTS (extract)

A. General Information (extract)

Presentation of Financial Information

The Company redenominated its share capital into US Dollars on 23 January 2006 and will retain distributable reserves and declare dividends in US Dollars. Consequently its functional currency became the US Dollar. Financial information for prior periods has been restated from Sterling into US Dollars in accordance with FRS 23. As a result the presentational currency of the Company (i.e. US Dollars) in the restated 2005 accounts is different from the functional currency of the Company.

Share capital and share premium in comparative periods was translated at the rate of exchange on the date of redenomination.

NOTES TO THE GROUP ACCOUNTS (extract)

Presentation of financial information

As the Group's principal assets and operations are in the US and the majority of its operations are conducted in US Dollars, the Group changed its presentational currency from Pounds Sterling to US Dollars with effect from 1 January 2006. The Company redenominated its share capital into US Dollars on 23 January 2006 and will retain distributable reserves and declare dividends in US Dollars. Consequently its functional currency became the US Dollar. This lowers the Group's exposure to currency translation risk on its revenue, profits and equity. Financial information for prior periods has been restated from Pounds Sterling into US Dollars in accordance with IAS 21.

The cumulative translation reserve was set to nil at 1 January 2003 (i.e. the transition date to IFRS). All subsequent movements comprising differences on the retranslation of the opening net assets of non US Dollar subsidiaries and hedging instruments have been charged to the cumulative translation reserve included in "Other Reserves". Share capital and share premium was translated at the rate of exchange on the date of redenomination.

As a result of the above the presentational currency of the Group (i.e. US Dollars) in the restated years of 2005 and 2004 is different from the functional currency of the Company (i.e. Pounds sterling).

In previous years the Group protected its equity, as measured in Sterling, by matching non-Sterling assets with non-Sterling liabilities principally by the use of currency swaps. Exchange movements on both the non-Sterling net assets and the hedging instruments were recorded as movements in "Other Reserves". As hedging was effective up to the date of the change in functional currency, the Group has continued to present these as movements in "Other Reserves" as this hedging is regarded as valid in the comparator years. When presenting comparative periods in US Dollars the retranslation of the net Sterling assets results in the large exchange differences shown in the Statement of Recognised Income and Expense.

Table A7.5.2 – Change of functional and presentation currencies

Sibir Energy plc – Annual report – 31 December 2007

NOTES TO THE COMPANY FINANCIAL STATEMENTS (extract)

1 SIGNIFICANT ACCOUNTING POLICIES (extract)

Foreign currencies

Local currency

Sibir Energy plc is domiciled in the UK, although the Group's operations are based in the Russian Federation. The local currency of the Company was changed on 1 July 2007 from Pound Sterling to US Dollar as a result of significant changes in circumstances.

The significant circumstances that resulted in the necessary change of the local currency of the company to US dollars were an increase in US Dollar funding for the MOGC purchase, repayment by SPD of previous US Dollar lendings and the distributable funds used to pay a dividend originating in US Dollars.

On 1 July 2007 all assets and liabilities items were translated at exchange rate ruling for that day ($/£ 2.0064), and the profit and loss account was translated at an average rate ($/£ 1.9703) for the first six months of 2007. The Equity items were recalculated from 1 January 2005 at the rate ruling at that date (see table below), with any subsequent movements being translated at an appropriate rate for the period. All the currency translation changes are made in accordance with the UK GAAP accounting standard SSAP 20 'Foreign currency translation'.

Presentational currency

Given that the functional currency of the Company is now US Dollars, management have elected to present for the first time Company financial statements in US Dollars.

This is a change from prior years when the financial statements were presented in pound sterling in line with the previous functional currency of the Company.

Change in presentational currency

For the 2006 comparative period, assets and liabilities were translated into US Dollars using the closing rate ruling at the 2006 balance sheet date ($/£ 1.9572).

Equity and Share capital items were translated using the historic closing rate applicable on 1 January 2005 and were not re translated at each subsequent balance sheet date. All share capital transactions which were effected after 1 January 2005 were recorded using an exchange rate which prevailed at the date of those transactions.

Resulting exchange differences were reflected as currency translation adjustments and included in the cumulative currency translation reserve.

The applicable exchange rates used for 2005 and 2006 were:

	US Dollar to Pound Sterling Exchange Rate ($/£)		
Date	01/01/2005	31/12/2005	31/12/2006
Av Rate	–	1.8188	1.8369
Closing Rate	1.9212	1.7167	1.9572

NOTES TO THE CONSOLIDATED FINANCIAL STATEMENTS (extract)

2 SUMMARY OF SIGNIFICANT ACCOUNTING POLICIES (extract)

Presentational currency

In the 2006 financial statements, the functional currency of Sibir Energy plc (the Company) was Pound Sterling. Although the Company is domiciled in the UK the Group's operations are based in the Russian Federation. The functional currency of the Group's various entities is either the Russian Rouble or US Dollar. This is due to the direct or indirect linkage of oil and oil product prices to the US Dollar, even when some trades are priced and settled in Roubles. As a result the 2006 financial comparatives together with the 2007 financial statements have been presented in US Dollars ($).

This is a change from prior years and the Group's last published interims when the financial statements were presented in Pound Sterling.

Assets and liabilities were translated into US Dollars using the closing rate at the 2006 balance sheet date. Income, expenses and cashflows recognised in the period were translated at an average US Dollar exchange rate for the period. Resulting exchange differences were reflected as currency translation adjustments and included in the cumulative currency translation reserve.

Equity and share capital items were translated using the historic closing rate applicable on 1 January 2005 and were not re translated at each subsequent balance sheet date. All share capital transactions which were effected after 1 January 2005 were recorded using an exchange rate which prevailed at the date of those transactions.

The applicable exchange rates used for 2006 were:

Period Ended	1 January 2006	31 December 2006
Average	0.5498	0.5444
Closing Rate	0.5825	0.5109

A7.121 When an entity presents its financial statements in a currency that is different from its functional currency, it describes the financial statements as complying with International Financial Reporting Standards only if they comply with all the requirements of each applicable standard and each applicable interpretation of those standards including the translation method set out in paragraphs A7.77 and A7.109 above.

Convenience translation

A7.122 IAS 21 does not prohibit an entity from providing, as supplementary information, a 'convenience translation'. Such a convenience translation may display financial statements or other financial information (such as five year summaries) in a currency that is not its functional currency or its presentation currency, as convenience to some users. Convenience translations are normally prepared by applying a single exchange rate to all amounts appearing in financial statements presented in the entity's functional or presentation currency. The relationships among amounts in the financial statements do not change. Thus, convenience translation fails to account for the effects of changes in foreign exchange rates and, therefore, does not comply with the translation procedures set out in paragraphs A7.77 above. Therefore, where an entity displays its financial statements or other financial information in a currency that is different from either its functional currency or its presentation currency and the requirements of paragraph A7.121 above are not met, it should:

- Clearly identify the information as supplementary information to distinguish it from the information that complies with International Financial Reporting Standards.
- Disclose the currency in which the supplementary information is displayed.
- Disclose the entity's functional currency and the method of translation used to determine the supplementary information.

[IAS 21 para 57].

Table A7.6 – Disclosure for convenience translation

OJSC RBC Information Systems – Report and accounts – 31 December 2009

2 Basis of preparation (extract)

(c) Functional and presentation currency

The national currency of the Russian Federation is the Russian Rouble ("RUR") which is the Group's functional currency and the currency in which these consolidated financial statements are presented. All financial information presented in RUR has been rounded to the nearest thousand.

(d) Convenience translation

In addition to presenting the consolidated financial statements in RUR, supplementary information in USD has been prepared for the convenience of users of the consolidated financial statements.

All amounts in the consolidated financial statements, including comparatives, are translated from RUR to USD at the closing exchange rate at 31 December 2009 of RUR 30.2442 to USD 1.

Other matters

Tax effects of all exchange differences

A7.123 Gains and losses on foreign currency transactions and exchange differences arising on the translating the results and financial position of an entity (including a foreign operation) into a different currency may have tax effects. IAS 12, 'Income taxes', applies to these tax effects, and the issues are considered in chapter 13.

Cash flow statements

A7.124 Cash flows arising from transactions in foreign currency and cash flows of a foreign subsidiary are translated at the exchange rates between the functional currency and the foreign currency at the dates of the cash flows. IAS 7, 'Cash flow statements', applies to foreign currency cash flows, which is addressed in chapter 30.

Chapter 8

Reporting financial performance

Chapter 8

Reporting financial performance

Introduction

8.1 FRS 3 requires statements of performance that, taken together, give an information set that depicts the major elements of a company's performance, including all gains and losses of the period whether accounted for in the profit and loss account or in reserves. The aim of this approach is to give analysts and other users sufficient information to enable them to make judgements about a company's past performance and to assist them in forming a basis for predicting future trends in performance. The main features of FRS 3 are as follows:

- Two primary statements of financial performance are required. These are the profit and loss account and the statement of total recognised gains and losses. These formats are intended to provide an 'information set' that captures all recognised changes in shareholders' funds arising from a company's activities, except for capital contributed by shareholders, distributions and capital repaid to shareholders.
- The profit and loss account should disclose separately the results of a company's operations attributable to continuing operations, acquisitions as a component of continuing operations and discontinued operations.
- The definition of ordinary activities was drawn so widely that extraordinary items have all but disappeared from UK companies' profit and loss accounts.
- A framework for disclosing exceptional items, with rules to control their positioning in the profit and loss account formats.
- Guidance permitting alternative earnings per share figures to be disclosed in the notes to the financial statements provided that a reconciliation of the alternative measures to basic and diluted earnings per share is provided.
- The statement of total recognised gains and losses includes in one place all the gains and losses of the year, whether recognised in the profit and loss account or taken directly to reserves. Its purpose is to show the year's total financial performance. In addition to the profit for the financial year, the statement includes unrealised revaluation surpluses, exchange gains and losses on translation of net assets of overseas subsidiaries and other gains and losses recognised in the year.

[The next paragraph is 8.9.]

Profit and loss account formats — an overview

8.9 FRS 3 requires that the profit and loss account should include all gains and losses recognised in the financial statements for the period, except those that are specifically permitted or required by the FRS or by other accounting standards to be taken directly to reserves, or (in the absence of a relevant accounting standard) specifically permitted or required by law to be taken directly to reserves. [FRS 3 para 13]. Gains and losses that go directly to reserves must be included in the statement of total recognised gains and losses, together with the profit or loss for the year.

Layered format

8.10 FRS 3 sets out a layered format for the profit and loss account that is designed to highlight a number of important components of financial performance. These are:

- Results of continuing operations, including separate disclosure of the results of acquisitions, where material.
- Results of discontinued operations.
- Certain types of income or expense that are required to be shown on the face of the profit and loss account after operating profit, but before interest. These include:
  - Profits or losses on the sale or termination of an operation.
  - Costs of a fundamental reorganisation or restructuring having a material effect on the nature and focus of the reporting entity's operations.
  - Profits or losses on the disposal of fixed assets.

  Provisions made in respect of these items should also be included.

8.11 Exceptional items, other than those that fall into the category of post-operating profit items listed above, should be shown under the statutory format headings to which they relate, either in the notes or on the face of the profit and loss account if this is necessary in order to give a true and fair view. [FRS 3 para 19].

8.12 FRS 3 supplements the requirements of company law as to the form and content of the profit and loss account. The law provides a choice of four formats — of the two formats most commonly used by UK companies, Format 1 analyses operating expenses by function, Format 2 by type. These formats are fully described in chapter 4 and can be found in Schedule 1 to SI 2008/410 for large and medium sized companies and Schedule 1 to SI 2008/409 for small companies.

Operating profit

8.13 The standard requires that turnover and operating profit should be shown separately on the face of the profit and loss account split between: continuing operations; acquisitions as a component of continuing operations; and discontinued operations. [FRS 3 para 14]. As standards deal only with material items, the requirement to disclose results of acquisitions applies if those results are material in aggregate and the requirement to disclose results of discontinued operations similarly depends on those results being material in aggregate. FRS 6 added the requirement that the results of each material acquisition should be shown separately. When all of the entity's operations are 'continuing' in both the current and comparative periods, the entity is still required to indicate that fact in its profit and loss presentation. This could be achieved by showing 'continuing operations' against each of the statutory headings (for example, turnover, cost of sales etc). Alternative presentations would be the use of a header above the figures for each year or a footnote to the profit and loss account. [FRS 6 paras 23, 28].

8.14 Where operations that have been sold or terminated are classified as discontinued in the profit and loss account, the comparative profit and loss account figures are restated in order to show the previous year's results attributable to those operations as discontinued. Consequently, the results shown under the heading of continuing operations for both the current year and the previous year are attributable to the operations that are continuing at the end of the current year. This presents something of a track record of the operations that are continuing.

8.15 Analysis of other format headings between turnover and operating profit (under Format 1 these are: cost of sales; gross profit or loss; distribution costs; administrative expenses; and other operating income) should also be given, but this analysis may be by way of note, rather than on the face of the profit and loss account. [FRS 3 para 14].

8.16 The standard uses the term 'operating profit' as an important element of performance although there is no such heading in the statutory profit and loss account formats of Schedule 1 to SI 2008/410, 'Large and Medium-sized Companies and Groups (Accounts and Reports) Regulations 2008'. The term is described, however, in the standard as being normally the profit before income from shares in group undertakings. In consolidated financial statements, this would mean profit before income from interests in associated undertakings, although the standard acknowledges that, in certain situations, income from associated undertakings or from other participating interests may be considered to be part of the operating profit. In fact, FRS 9, 'Associates and joint ventures', introduced a new requirement that the group's share of operating results of associates and joint ventures should be included immediately after the group's operating result (see further chapter 27). [FRS 9 paras 21, 27].

8.17 A comparison of the two formats is given below, showing where operating profit is typically presented.

	Format 1		**Format 2**
1	Turnover	1	Turnover
2	Cost of sales	2	Change in stocks of finished goods and in work in progress
3	Gross profit or loss	3	Own work capitalised
4	Distribution costs	4	Other operating income
5	Administrative expenses	5a	Raw materials and consumables
6	Other operating income	5b	Other external charges
	Operating profit or loss	6	Staff costs
			(a) wages and salaries
			(b) social security costs
			(c) other pension costs
		7a	Depreciation and other amounts written off tangible and intangible fixed assets
		7b	Exceptional amounts written off current assets
		8	Other operating charges
			Operating profit or loss

As explained above 'Operating profit or loss' is not an item in either of the formats, but has been included to show where the requirement for analysis ends.

8.18 The illustrative examples in the FRS are prepared using Format 1, but the examples section explains that *equivalent information* should be shown if any of the other statutory formats are used. Irrespective of the format adopted, turnover and operating profit or loss must be analysed on the face of the profit and loss account, with the remainder of the analysis being permitted to be given in the notes.

8.18.1 The only three items required to be presented on the face of the profit and loss account are turnover, operating profit and profit before tax (the latter being required by Schedule 1 to SI 2008/410). All other format headings may be disclosed in the notes.

8.19 Two basic styles of profit and loss account analysis are envisaged in the illustrative examples in FRS 3. A multi-column approach isolates figures relating to continuing operations, acquisitions and discontinued operations into separate columns. A single-column approach lists such figures in a vertical analysis, with sub-totals providing further analysis. Table 8.1 shows an example of a multi-column analysis; Table 8.2 shows a single-column analysis. The multi-column approach has also been used increasingly to isolate exceptional items included in operating results (see para 8.128 below).

8.19.1 The examples below do not give a sub-total of acquisitions and other continuing operations, which arguably FRS 3 would require, but this point is unclear as the multi-column example given at the end of FRS 3 itself does not include such a sub-total. We would recommend that such a sub-total be given.

Table 8.1 – Coats Viyella Plc – Annual report and accounts – 31 December 1994

CONSOLIDATED PROFIT AND LOSS ACCOUNT (extract)

				Discontinued		
		Continuing operations		**operations**		
	Notes		**Acquisitions**		**Total**	Total
		1994	**1994**	**1994**	**1994**	1993
		£m	**£m**	**£m**	**£m**	£m
For the year ended 31 December 1994						
Turnover	1&2	**2,154.2**	**29.7**	**404.6**	**2,588.5**	2,443.8
Cost of sales	1	**(1,464.0)**	**(22.2)**	**(323.3)**	**(1,809.5)**	(1,702.6)
Gross profit		**690.2**	**7.5**	**81.3**	**779.0**	741.2
Distribution costs	1	**(362.2)**	**(3.9)**	**(50.8)**	**(416.9)**	(398.0)
Administrative expenses	1	**(168.7)**	**(1.8)**	**(19.9)**	**(190.4)**	(179.8)
Other operating income	1&3	**8.2**	–	**0.2**	**8.4**	8.3
Operating profit	1,2&3	**167.5**	**1.8**	**10.8**	**180.1**	171.7
Profit on sale of fixed assets	1	**1.3**	–	–	**1.3**	14.8
Provision for loss on sale or termination of operations	1	–	–	**(51.0)**	**(51.0)**	–
Gains/(losses) on sale or termination of operations	1	**2.3**	–	**0.1**	**2.4**	6.4
Profit/(loss) on ordinary activities before interest	2	**171.1**	**1.8**	**(40.1)**	**132.8**	192.9
Share of profits of associated companies					**0.8**	1.3
Interest receivable and similar income	6				**15.6**	21.5
Interest payable and similar charges	7				**(44.1)**	(65.4)
Profit on ordinary activities before taxation					**105.1**	150.3

Table 8.2 – Pearson plc – Directors' Report and Accounts – 31 December 1994

Consolidated Profit and Loss Account (extract)
for the year ended 31 December 1994

		Notes	1994 £m	1993 £m
Sales turnover				
Continuing operations			**1,469.9**	1,319.6
Acquisitions			**80.2**	
Discontinued operations			–	550.5
		2	**1,550.1**	1,870.1
Cost of sales		3	**(775.8)**	(1,005.6)
Gross profit			**774.3**	864.5
Net operating expenses	– normal	3	**(533.2)**	(628.4)
	– exceptional	3	**31.3**	(20.0)
Operating profit				
Continuing operations			**265.1**	190.3
Acquisitions			**7.3**	
Discontinued operations			–	25.8
		2	**272.4**	216.1
Continuing operations				
Profit on sale of fixed assets		3	**26.4**	4.4
Discontinued operations				
Profit/(loss) on sale of businesses		3	**15.2**	(68.4)
Write back of provision on investment in BSkyB			–	71.4
Profit before interest			**314.0**	223.5
Net interest payable		4	**(16.2)**	(14.9)
Profit before taxation		7	**297.8**	208.6

Allocation of interest and taxation

8.20 The standard explains that the analysis of results is only required down to the operating profit line, because an analysis of the interest cost and taxation charge between continuing, discontinued and acquired operations would normally be too subjective to be reliable. However, analysis of interest and taxation may also be given provided that the method and assumptions used in making the analysis are disclosed. In practice, such further analysis is rarely given. One example is shown in Table 8.3.

Table 8.3 – Glynwed International plc – Report & Accounts – 31 December 1994
notes to the accounts (extract)

1. Accounting Policies (extract)

Discontinued activities

The principle used in allocating interest is that the interest cost or credit on discontinued activities is the additional interest cost or credit arising during the period as a result of retaining the discontinued activity up to the date of discontinuance. The taxation charge or credit on discontinued activities is that which directly arises as a result of their trading operations and discontinuance.

8.21 Some of the issues that arise in respect of the allocation of interest to discontinued operations and acquisitions are:

- Allocating group interest costs where operations acquired or discontinued are funded by intra-group borrowings rather than external borrowings. One method has been to allocate interest to intra-group funding at a rate of interest that represents an average cost of group borrowings.

- Allocating interest costs in respect of new borrowings raised to finance acquisitions. The issue is whether the incremental borrowing costs should be allocated to the group's continuing operations (excluding acquisitions) or to the results of acquisitions. Either method would probably be acceptable. Allocating to the group's continuing operations excluding acquisitions emphasises the *actual results* of the acquired operations, whilst allocating to the acquisitions column emphasises the *effect* of the acquisition.

Exceptional items

8.22 Exceptional items charged or credited in arriving at operating profit should be analysed between continuing or discontinued operations as appropriate. [FRS 3 para 19]. Furthermore, the three categories of exceptional items that are required to be presented after operating profit (disposals of operations, fundamental reorganisations and disposals of fixed assets) should also be attributed to continuing and discontinued operations. [FRS 3 para 20]. The latter analysis is illustrated in Tables 8.1 and 8.2 above.

8.23 The treatment of exceptional items is considered from para 8.79 below.

Discontinued operations

Definition

8.24 Discontinued operations are defined as those operations that satisfy all of the following conditions:

- The sale or termination is completed either in the period or before the earlier of three months after the commencement of the subsequent period and the date on which the financial statements are approved.
- If a termination, the former activities have ceased permanently.
- The sale or termination has a material effect on the nature and focus of the reporting entity's operations and represents a material reduction in its operating facilities resulting either from its withdrawal from a particular market (whether class of business or geographical) or from a material reduction in turnover in the reporting entity's continuing markets.
- The assets, liabilities, results of operations and activities are clearly distinguishable, physically, operationally and for financial reporting purposes.

[FRS 3 para 4].

Discontinued compared to discontinuing

8.25 The ASB deliberately chose the term 'discontinued' rather than 'discontinuing' because it considered that there must be a cut off point to avoid manipulation. If it had chosen 'discontinuing' it would have left the way open for a company to declare that it intended to discontinue a loss making activity in the future and thus to separate out the results of that activity. The company would thereby be able to focus attention on the remaining profitable activities.

8.26 The explanatory note to the standard emphasises that any income and costs relating to a sale or termination that has not been completed within the prescribed period after the financial year end should be included in the continuing category. However, it then states that it may be appropriate in some cases to disclose separately in a note to the profit and loss account the results of operations which, although not 'discontinued', are in the process of discontinuing. They should not be classed as discontinued, but might be a subdivision of continuing operations. Such analysis would enable a company to enhance the predictive value of its financial statements by giving additional disclosure of its results exclusive of those activities that are not expected to be there at the next year end. An example of such a note is given in Table 8.4.

Table 8.4 – BM Group PLC – Annual Report – 30 June 1993

Notes to the financial statements (extract)

2 Continuing operations

As detailed in the Financial Review and Note 28, the Group has disposed of various subsidiary undertakings after the year end. The requirements of Financial Reporting Standard No. 3 (FRS 3) only permit those companies disposed of prior to 30th September 1993 to be classified for the purposes of these financial statements as a discontinued operation. The analysis below provides additional information regarding those companies which have been sold prior to the approval of these financial statements but after 30th September 1993 or are proposed to be disposed of as part of the Group's reorganisation plan. Continuing operations can be further analysed as follows:

	Turnover		Trading profit	
	1993	1992	**1993**	1992
	£000	£000	**£000**	£000
Businesses to be retained	**153,959**	111,812	**11,703**	16,593
Businesses to be sold	**301,831**	293,246	**6,088**	23,134
	455,790	405,058	**17,791**	39,727

Businesses to be retained for the year to 30th June 1992 include four months turnover and trading profit in respect of Thomas Robinson Group companies.

Meaning of 'ceased permanently'

8.27 For an operation that is closed down to qualify as discontinued, its former activities must have 'ceased permanently' within the prescribed time limit. In many situations this is clear-cut because all sources of revenues and costs have been terminated and all assets disposed of. In other situations, it is less clear-cut whether activities have ceased permanently. For example, whilst all revenue earning activities may have ceased, there may be run-off costs still to be incurred and assets still to be sold or scrapped. In those situations it is necessary to consider the nature of the costs still to be incurred (and, if applicable, the credits still to be received) and to form a judgement as to whether they comprise an activity.

Example 1

A company carried out a pharmaceutical wholesaling business which it operated from several leasehold premises throughout the country. The business has been closed, all stocks have been disposed of and employees made redundant before the end of three months into the next financial year. At that time some debtors remain to be collected and costs will continue to be incurred in respect of the vacated premises until the leases are disposed of.

In this example the former activity of pharmaceutical wholesaling has ceased permanently. The outstanding future transactions do not constitute the continuation of the activity and, consequently, the operation has been discontinued.

Example 2

A group is closing its household insurance underwriting business. No new policies are being written. A few staff have been retained to handle claims made on the existing policies. Has the activity ceased permanently when the revenue earning activity ceased or will it be when the last claim is paid?

In our view the complete cessation of carrying on the revenue earning activity is the most meaningful criterion. This is notwithstanding the possibility that the financial effect of settling as yet unknown liabilities may be significant to the results of future periods.

Example 3

A group has announced it is closing an engineering contracting segment. Although no new contracts are being undertaken, all existing contracts will be completed and the business will be run down accordingly.

In our view the operation will have ceased permanently when the contracting activity has been completed, that is, at the end of the last contract. In the period during which existing contracts are completed, the group is continuing to carry out a revenue earning activity, albeit that the activity is being wound down.

Materiality and separability of activities

8.28 The standard's definition of discontinued operations (see para 8.24) requires business disposals and closures to satisfy a high threshold of materiality if they are to be classified as discontinued in the profit and loss account. In addition, the operations discontinued must be clearly separable from the rest of the reporting entity's operations.

8.29 However, this does not mean that the discontinued activity has to constitute a complete business segment for the purposes of SSAP 25, 'Segmental reporting'. This is because the definition of discontinued operations also includes a material reduction in operating facilities resulting from a material reduction in turnover in the entity's *continuing* markets. This means that, although the activity should be *separate* from the rest of the entity's operations, it does not necessarily have to be *different*.

Example

A group had two subsidiaries of equal size, each operating in the field of car leasing. The sale of one of the subsidiaries would not be the disposal of the whole car leasing segment as defined for the purposes of SSAP 25. However, if it materially affected the nature and focus of the entity's operations (for example, if the disposal were made to release funds for investing in a different business such as a road haulage business, that materially changed the nature and focus of the group's operations) it would constitute a discontinued operation for the purposes of FRS 3, because it is a material reduction in operating facilities and causes a material reduction in turnover in the group's continuing markets. In addition, the assets, liabilities, results and activities can be distinguished physically, operationally and for financial reporting purposes. The nature of the operations disposed of is *not* different from that of the rest of the group, but that is not a test that has to be satisfied under the standard in order for the disposal of the subsidiary to qualify as a discontinued operation.

8.30 The nature and focus of a reporting entity's operations refers to the positioning of its products or services in their markets including the aspects of both quality and location. The example of a material change in the nature and focus of operations given in the standard is a hotel group which disposes of all its hotels in the US and buys instead hotels in Europe. Another example relating to products rather than geographical markets might be a property company, involved in development and investment properties, that decided to withdraw from the development activity and to hold only investment properties.

8.31 The standard makes it clear that unless there is a material effect on the nature and focus of operations any disposals should be treated as continuing operations. For example, a sale or termination that is undertaken primarily to achieve productivity improvements or other cost savings is part of an entity's continuing operations. In the example in paragraph 8.29 of a company with two car leasing subsidiaries, the disposal of one subsidiary might be regarded as part of continuing operations if it were not sold, but instead was closed primarily to achieve cost savings to the group, with its business and markets being transferred to the other subsidiary.

8.32 The following example combines several elements of the treatment of discontinued operations.

Example

The facts in this example are:

(a) The company's year end is 31 December 20X1.

(b) The directors approve the financial statements for the year to 31 December 20X1 in May 20X2.

(c) In the year to 31 December 20X1 the company sold subsidiary A and closed a surplus warehouse.

(d) The company achieved a reduction in its workforce of 5% through voluntary and compulsory redundancies.

(e) Before the year end the company decided to close subsidiary B and this was completed on 31 March 20X2. It also announced the decision to close subsidiary C, but this was not completed until April 20X2. It also announced, before the year end, a strategic withdrawal from one of its business segments that was to take place over the next two years.

(f) After the year end it decided to sell subsidiary D and found a buyer for a quick sale that was completed by February 20X2.

The various items would be treated under FRS 3 as follows:

- Sale of subsidiary A — assuming the disposal materially affected the nature and focus of the group's operations and represented a material reduction in its operating facilities, it should be shown as discontinued operations, because the sale was completed in the year.

- Closure of warehouse — if the assets, liabilities, results of operations and activities cannot be clearly distinguished, physically, operationally and for financial reporting purposes, then this would be classed as continuing operations. If they could be clearly distinguished, but the closure has neither a material effect on the nature and focus of the company's operations nor represents a material reduction in its operating facilities resulting from a withdrawal from a particular market or from a material reduction in turnover of continuing markets, then again it would be disclosed as continuing operations. It is most probable that as the warehouse was surplus it would not satisfy the latter condition and the costs would be shown as continuing operations.

- Reduction in workforce of 5% — assuming that no sale or closure was involved this would be shown as continuing, but exceptional if material.

- Closure of subsidiary B — assuming that this could be clearly distinguished and materially affected the nature and focus of operations and represented a material reduction in operating facilities, it should be classed as discontinued. This is because it also satisfies the condition of having been completed by the earlier of three months after the year end or the date of approval of the financial statements.

- Closure of subsidiary C — whether or not this satisfies all the other conditions it does not satisfy the condition of being completed by the earlier of three months after the year end or the date of approval of the financial statements. Therefore, it should be classed as continuing. As the announcement of the closure was made before the year end a provision for loss on closure of C should be made. The provision would be disclosed as a non-operating exceptional item, under continuing operations.

- Strategic withdrawal — this must be classed as continuing, but FRS 3's requirements for disclosing any provisions should be followed, and the company could analyse continuing operations between continuing and discontinuing in a note.

- Sale of subsidiary D — this would be treated as discontinued (assuming the materiality conditions are satisfied), irrespective of the decision date, because the sale has been completed by the earlier of three months after the year end or the date of approval of the financial statements.

8.33 FRS 3 only requires the analysis of results down to the 'operating profit' level. One of the criteria for qualifying as a discontinued operation is that the operating results of the operation that has been sold or terminated must be clearly distinguishable for financial reporting purposes from the rest of the group's activities. This implies that its turnover and operating costs must be readily identifiable from the accounting records. Nevertheless, there are still allocation issues to be dealt with in practice, in particular, in respect of central overheads. For example, the parent company of a group may allocate its head office overheads to all its subsidiaries on some *pro rata* basis. If an operation is disposed of, the relevant central overheads may not decrease, at least in the short term. In these circumstances, it seems logical to attribute the whole of the central overheads to continuing operations in the group's profit and loss account, because the costs are not being taken out of the group by the disposal.

Disposal of subsidiary with retained interest

8.34 A company may dispose of a controlling interest in a subsidiary and retain an interest that is treated either as a trade investment or as an associate. The question arises as to whether the turnover and operating profit of the subsidiary up to the date of disposal should be included as continuing operations or discontinued operations in the consolidated profit and loss account (assuming the subsidiary is material to the group). Where the retained interest is accounted for as an associate the group's share of associate's results will in future be brought into the consolidated profit and loss account on an equity accounting basis, but the full amount of turnover and operating profit of the associate will not be shown in the group profit and loss account because it is no longer a subsidiary.

8.35 We consider that the results of the subsidiary should be classified as discontinued if the retained interest is not regarded as being subject to significant influence by the group. This would be if the retained interest is accounted for as a trade investment rather than as an associate.

8.36 If, however, the remaining interest qualifies as an associate then we consider that it would be appropriate to show the subsidiary's results as continuing operations up to the date of disposal. The group's share of the associate's operating results would then be included on the equity basis in the group's profit and loss account from the date it ceases to be a subsidiary. A note giving details of the subsidiary's results that are included in the profit and loss account in these circumstances would be appropriate. An example of such disclosure is given in Table 8.5. (As mentioned in paragraph 8.19.1 above it is arguable that a total column for continuing operations should also be given.)

Table 8.5 – Dobson Park Industries plc – Annual Report – 2 October 1993

Consolidated Profit and Loss Account (extract)

For the 52 weeks ended 2 October 1993	Note	Continuing operations 1993 £000	Acquisitions 1993 £000	Discontinued operations 1993 £000	Total 1993 £000
Turnover	2	98,628	9,359	15,451	123,438
Cost of sales		(62,265)	(4,765)	(10,790)	(77,820)
Gross profit		36,363	4,594	4,661	45,618
Distribution costs		(15,797)	(1,429)	(1,217)	(18,443)
Administration expenses		(14,664)	(2,410)	(3,526)	(20,600)
Operating profit		5,902	755	(82)	6,575
Share of profits of associated companies		2,945	–	–	2,945
Net operating income	2	8,847	755	(82)	9,520

Notes on the Accounts (extract)

1 Mining Equipment (extract)

With effect from 18 January 1993, Dobson Park's Mining Equipment Division was merged with Meco International Limited to form Longwall International Limited (LIL).

As a result of this transaction, the Company acquired a 50% interest in the ordinary share capital of LIL together with certain preference shares having a redemption value of £2m.

Prior to the formation of LIL, the turnover and trading results of the Mining Equipment Division have been included in the consolidated profit and loss account within continuing operations. After that date, Dobson Park's interest in LIL's trading results has also been included within continuing operations although LIL's turnover has been excluded from the consolidated profit and loss account thus adopting the accounting convention for associated companies.

In the 9 month period to 2 October 1993, LIL's turnover and pre-tax profits were £169.3m and £4.4m respectively. LIL's net assets at 2 October 1993 were £31.6m comprising fixed assets £28.3m, other net assets £35.1m and borrowings £31.8m.

The profit before tax of the Mining Equipment Division for the 52 weeks ended 2 October 1993 comprises:

	£000
Trading profits for the period to 18 January 1993	1,153
Share of profits of LIL for the period from 19 January to 2 October 1993	2,723
Other fees and rents, after depreciation, received from LIL	606
	4,482

Operations discontinued by sale

8.37 Where an operation that qualifies as discontinued is sold, its results up to the date of sale should be disclosed as part of the normal profit and loss account captions under the heading 'discontinued operations'. The profit or loss on sale should be shown as an exceptional item after operating profit and before interest and should also be disclosed as 'discontinued operations'. Any reorganisation or restructuring of continuing operations resulting from the sale should be treated as part of continuing operations.

8.38 Where the operation is sold after the financial year end, that is, by the earlier of three months after the year end and the date of approval of the financial statements, only the operating results up to the year end should be included in the profit and loss account for that year as discontinued operations. In the subsequent year when the operation is actually sold, the operating results up to the date of sale will be shown as discontinued operations in that year.

Example

A group sells a subsidiary which had turnover and operating profits in 20X1 of £30,000 and £6,000 respectively in the previous year. Up to the date of sale in 20X2 it had turnover and operating profit of £8,000 and £2,000 respectively. It is sold for £15,000. Goodwill previously written off directly to reserves on acquisition (prior to FRS 10) was £4,000. Net assets at the date of sale were £5,000. The borrowings of the subsidiary were £7,000 on which it paid interest of £700 in the previous year and £200 in the current year up to the date of sale. The tax rate is 30%.

The sale would be accounted for as follows:

Profit and loss account (extract)

		20X2	20X1
	£	£	£
Turnover			
Discontinued operations		8,000	30,000
Cost of sales (say)		(5,000)	(20,000)
Gross profit		3,000	10,000
Net operating expenses		(1,000)	(4,000)
Operating profit – discontinued operations		2,000	6,000
Profit on disposal of discontinued operations –			
surplus over net assets	10,000		
less: goodwill previously written off directly to reserves	(4,000)	6,000	–
Interest payable		(200)	(700)
Profit on ordinary activities before tax		7,800	5,300
Tax on profit on ordinary activities		(2,340)	(1,590)
Profit on ordinary activities after taxation		5,460	3,710

Note: the further analysis of net operating expenses and tax required by the standard would be given in a note.

Profits and losses on sale

8.39 In the above example, the re-classification of operating results as discontinued and the profit on disposal of the operation are recognised in the same period. Under FRS 2, 'Accounting for subsidiary undertakings', the date on which an undertaking ceases to be another undertaking's subsidiary is the date on which control passes (see further chapter 24). Where control is transferred by public offer, the relevant date is usually when an offer becomes unconditional. Where it is transferred by private treaty, the date is usually when an unconditional offer is accepted. Therefore, if the date on which the company ceases to be a subsidiary is after the year end, the operating results up to the disposal date and the profit on disposal would be recognised in the profit and loss account in the following year, classified as discontinued.

8.40 Where an operation in the process of being sold is trading profitably and is expected to be sold at a profit, those profits will be recognised as they arise. Where the operation is loss-making or a loss on sale is expected, the rules are somewhat different. Provision for such expected losses may sometimes be recognised earlier than they arise. FRS 3 introduced rules aimed at controlling the recognition of provisions for future losses.

Provisions for losses on sale of operations

8.41 Where a decision has been taken to dispose of an operation, whether by sale or closure, the standard requires provision to be made for expected future losses if, but not before, the company is *"demonstrably committed to the sale or termination"*. In the case of a sale, the standard requires evidence of the commitment by the existence of a *"binding sale agreement"* that obliges the company to complete the sale. [FRS 3 para 18]. This requirement conflicts with the requirement in FRS 12 that provision should not be made for future losses unless they result from an onerous contract. Although FRS 12 is the later standard, we consider that the FRS 3 requirement was intended to be retained because the amendments to paragraph 18 of FRS 3 were made consequential upon the introduction of FRS 12 but this requirement was retained.

8.42 For most practical purposes, the date of a binding agreement as envisaged in FRS 3 would be the same as the date on which control passes, as defined in FRS 2 (see para 8.39 above), when a subsidiary ceases to be consolidated.

8.43 FRS 3 states that any provision should cover the following:

- The direct costs of the sale.
- Any operating losses of the operation up to the date of the sale.

In both cases, the provision should take account of the aggregate profit, if any, to be recognised in the profit and loss account from the future profits of the operation. [FRS 3 para 18]. It should be noted that FRS 3 was amended by FRS 12, 'Provisions, contingent liabilities and contingent assets', to preclude profits on disposals of assets from being taken into account in measuring such provisions.

8.44 The explanatory section of the standard deals with the situation where a decision to sell an operation has been made, but no legally binding sale agreement exists. In such circumstances, the standard says that no obligation has been entered into by the reporting entity and so provision for the direct costs of the decision to sell and for future operating losses should not be made.

8.45 Although it may not be appropriate to provide for a loss on sale, any impairments in asset values, including any capitalised goodwill, should be recognised regardless of whether a binding sale agreement has been entered into for the sale of the operation. Such impairments should be calculated in accordance with FRS 11, 'Impairment of fixed assets and goodwill'. If the carrying values of the net assets and capitalised goodwill of a business for sale exceed in aggregate their recoverable amount (which would usually be based on the expected sale proceeds), the assets are impaired. FRS 11 requires that, unless specific assets can be identified as having been impaired, the impairment loss should be allocated first to any capitalised goodwill, thereafter to any capitalised intangible assets and finally to tangible assets on a *pro rata* or more appropriate basis. [FRS 11 para 48].

8.46 If, say, a subsidiary was acquired several years ago and goodwill was written off to reserves, it would also be appropriate, if the goodwill is now worth little or nothing, to make a provision in the profit and loss account in respect of that goodwill in advance of any binding agreement, as the goodwill would in any event have to be included in the loss on sale when the disposal is accounted for (see para 8.54 below).

Example

A parent company carries its investments in subsidiaries at net asset value in its individual financial statements. It has decided to sell a subsidiary, but has no legally binding agreement for sale. The price it expects is below the net asset value of the subsidiary.

The parent company should provide for the impairment of the investment in the subsidiary. In the consolidated profit and loss account, no provision for loss on sale is made per se. However, the subsidiary's assets are impaired, because the carrying value of its net assets exceeds their recoverable amount (which would be based on the subsidiary's expected selling price). The impairment loss should, in accordance with FRS 11, be allocated to write down the consolidated carrying values of the subsidiary's assets in the following order: first, any attributable goodwill; secondly, any capitalised intangible assets; and finally, other assets on a *pro rata* or more appropriate basis.

[The next paragraph is 8.48.]

8.48 FRS 3 also allows some degree of hindsight because it states that a binding contract entered into after the balance sheet date may provide additional evidence of asset values and commitments at the balance sheet date. [FRS 3 para 45].

8.49 The following example illustrates the accounting for the sale of an operation that takes place after the year end.

Example

A group decides before the year end to sell a subsidiary. The sale will take place after the year end and after the financial statements of the group are signed. The subsidiary's net assets at the year end are £300,000 and the book value of the attributable purchased goodwill is £100,000. The subsidiary makes a loss of £110,000 from the year end to the date the financial statements are signed. The group expects the company to make further losses up to the possible date of sale estimated to be £20,000. The group is negotiating the sale at the time of signing the financial statements and expects the proceeds on sale will be £150,000.

As mentioned above, where there is no binding sale agreement, no provision for loss on sale should be made, but the value of the subsidiary's net assets consolidated will still have to be considered to determine whether an impairment loss needs to be recognised. If no impairment losses were recognised in respect of the net assets and goodwill amounting to £400,000, the group would expect to incur losses of £250,000 in the subsequent year, comprising the subsidiary's expected future losses of £130,000 and an estimated loss on sale of £120,000, as illustrated below:

	£'000	£'000
Net assets		300
Goodwill		100
Assets to be reviewed for impairment		400
Loss up to date of sale	(110)	
	(20)	(130)
Estimated net assets at date of sale		270
Expected proceeds on sale		150
Estimated loss on sale		(120)

It is clear in this example that the subsidiary's net assets plus attributable goodwill are impaired, because their carrying value is not recoverable. The recoverable amount (being the higher of net realisable value and value in use) at the balance sheet date should be determined for the subsidiary in accordance with the methods specified in FRS 11. The calculation would be based on the present value of the estimated future cash flows of the subsidiary, including the net proceeds expected from its ultimate disposal. These cash flows would include the net cash outflows in respect of the expected future losses. The impairment loss would be calculated as the amount of the shortfall between the estimated recoverable amount and the carrying value of the subsidiary's net assets, and would be allocated first to write off the goodwill of £100,000 and secondly among the subsidiary's assets.

The impairment loss would be included in the results of the group's continuing operations; the loss would not be categorised as a discontinued operation because in the example the sale is not completed before the earlier of three months after the year end and the date on which the financial statements are approved.

8.50 The above example demonstrates that, whereas FRS 3 restricts the circumstances where provisions for losses on sale can be recognised, FRS 11 has increased the emphasis on recognising impairments of assets at an earlier point in time.

8.51 Paragraph 18 of FRS 3 specifies, and illustrates, how any future loss provisions set up in one year in advance of a sale of an operation should be disclosed in the next year when they are utilised, that is, when the sale is completed (but note that this does not apply to any impairment losses recognised before a disposal). The results of the operation in the subsequent period should be presented under the normal profit and loss account headings and should be described as 'discontinued operations' if they qualify as such. Any part of the preceding year's provision that related to trading losses should be credited and separately disclosed under the actual operating loss incurred. Although the standard actually states that the provision should be separately highlighted under the operating loss, the examples in the appendices show it as being deducted from the heading 'net operating expenses'. Therefore, it seems reasonable to interpret the requirement as being to match the provision with the costs with which it is associated under the appropriate format heading, although either presentation is acceptable. The actual loss on sale should be disclosed after operating profit and before interest, again under the 'discontinued' heading if applicable. The balance of the provision relating to the loss on sale should be credited and separately disclosed under the actual loss on sale.

8.51.1 As set out in the example below, sometimes the provision set up in one year exceeds the actual loss suffered.

Example

A company provided for a loss on closure of operations last year as a post-operating profit exceptional item under FRS 3, 'Reporting financial performance'. The provision included £2 million for operating losses to the date of closure. Normally the reversal of the provision would be shown in the current year against the operating losses of the discontinued operation in the profit and loss account. However, as it turns out the operating losses to the date of closure have only been £500,000 and so £1.5 million of the provision is surplus. Should the £1.5 million release be shown against the operating losses of the discontinued operation in arriving at group operating profit, or should it be reversed as a post operating profit exceptional item, on the grounds that that is how the original provision was presented?

The operating losses in respect of the closure of an operation were previously provided in accordance with FRS 3.
We consider that the FRS 3 requirement to show the utilisation of the provision in the following period is satisfied by showing the £500,000 against the actual operating losses incurred of the same amount. The remaining £1.5 million is a material figure, therefore, we consider that it should be released as an over provision in the same profit and loss account line as was used for the creation of the original provision, that is the £1.5 million should be released as a post operating profit exceptional item. An explanation should be given of the reasons why the estimate of the losses has proved inaccurate.

8.52 The standard could be interpreted as implying that the accounting described above is only required for operations that qualify as 'discontinued'. That is because paragraph 18 uses the words "*...when the operation does qualify as discontinued, the provisions should be used to offset the results of the operation in the discontinued category*". However, we consider that it was not intended to restrict the treatment only to discontinued operations and that such treatment should also be used where the results of operations sold in the subsequent year are shown as part of the group's continuing operations, because they do not meet all the conditions described in para 8.24 above.

8.53 An example showing loss provisions created in one year and utilised the next is given in Table 8.6.

Table 8.6 – The Davis Service Group Plc – Annual Report and Accounts – 31 December 1993
Consolidated profit and loss account (extract)

	Note	*1993* *£000*	*1992* *£000*
Turnover			
Continuing operations		**225,325**	213,291
Acquisition		**46,681**	
		272,006	
Discontinued operations		**7,987**	34,155
	2	**279,993**	247,446
Cost of sales	3	**177,597**	172,627
Gross profit		**102,396**	74,819
Other operating expenses		**(82,089)**	(55,404)
Other operating income		**2,483**	2,359
Operating profit			
Continuing operations		**19,050**	19,221
Acquisition		**3,740**	
		22,790	
Discontinued operations		**(611)**	2,553
Less utilisation of 1992 provision	2	**611**	
		22,790	21,774
(Loss)/profit on disposal of discontinued operations	4	**(889)**	72
Less utilisation of 1992 provision	4	**889**	
Provision for loss on operations to be discontinued	4	**–**	(1,500)
Profit on sale of properties in continuing operations	4	**50**	73
Profit on sale of properties in discontinued operations	4	**291**	–
Profit on ordinary activities before interest		**23,131**	20,419

Treatment of goodwill on disposals

8.54 The previous section referred to provisions for losses on operations being sold and to impairments in asset values. Where goodwill relating to a previously acquired operation has been capitalised (shown separately among intangible fixed assets) on the balance sheet, the goodwill is subject to the same impairment rules as apply to other fixed assets. When the operation is disposed of, the unamortised carrying value of attributable goodwill is eliminated from the balance sheet and forms part of the calculation of the profit or loss on disposal.

8.54.1 Where goodwill relating to a previously acquired operation remains eliminated against reserves, special rules apply to disposals. FRS 10, 'Goodwill and intangible assets', requires any acquisition goodwill that has previously been eliminated against reserves and has not been charged in the profit and loss account to be credited in reserves and debited in the profit and loss account as part of the profit and loss on disposal. This requirement has the effect of treating purchased goodwill as an asset with continuing value, even though it is debited to reserves during the period of ownership of the acquired operation.

8.55 Where provision is made in accordance with paragraph 18 of FRS 3 for a loss on disposal that occurs after the year end, the question arises whether a provision should be made for impairment of the attributable goodwill that has been eliminated against reserves. This question can be extended further to the situation where the write-off of such goodwill turns an expected profit on disposal into a loss — should provision be made for part of the goodwill that has been lost? FRS 10, 'Goodwill and intangible assets', does not deal with the issue of whether provisions should be made in respect of purchased goodwill eliminated against reserves that has lost its value, that is, before the actual disposal occurs. In addition, FRS 11's rules for recognising and measuring impairments of fixed assets and goodwill do not apply to pre-FRS 10 goodwill that remains eliminated against reserves. [FRS 11 para 7]. We believe that, in both situations, the attributable goodwill should be written off. This also has the desirable effect that the whole of the write-down relating to the impending disposal is recognised in the same period.

8.56 The same principle could be applied where a decision has been made to dispose of a business, but there is no binding contract at the date the financial statements are approved. If the directors consider that the value of attributable goodwill that remains eliminated against reserves has been lost, It is common practice for the write-off to be recognised in such circumstances as an impairment loss before the disposal occurs. Table 8.7 shows an example where a company has written off goodwill in anticipation of a loss on disposal. The write-off of attributable goodwill would be shown under the relevant FRS 3 paragraph 20 heading (after operating profit) if there was evidence of a commitment to sell. For example, the business would probably be being actively marketed and it would be reasonable to expect that the disposal would be completed before the next interim accounts and in any event before the end of the next financial year (see para 8.115). If a company has a policy of recognising a loss in the value of goodwill in the profit and loss account in other circumstances (that is, where a disposal is not involved), the loss would be charged in arriving at operating profit.

Table 8.7 – Cable and Wireless plc – Report and accounts – 31 March 1995

Consolidated profit and loss account (extract)

for the year ended 31 March	Note	1995 £m	1994 £m
Operating profit	4	1,133.7	1,091.2
Other exceptional items			
Profits less losses on sale and termination of operations	9	(17.7)	–
Losses on disposal of fixed assets	9	(43.7)	–
Provision for goodwill charge on impending sale of a business	9	(178.0)	–
Profit on ordinary activities before associated undertakings and minorities		894.3	1,091.2

Note 9 Exceptional items (extract)

The exceptional charge of £178m relates to goodwill associated with the acquisition of Telephone Rentals plc (TR) in 1988. This acquisition was made in order to achieve rapid growth in Mercury's business customer base which continues to be reflected in the overall business. The Group has now decided to focus Mercury's activities on service provision and is seeking purchasers for the non-strategic elements of the former TR activities in the UK. The provision reflects the expected outcome of the disposal at the current time and is in accordance with accepted accounting practice.

8.57 Where goodwill that has been eliminated against reserves is written off in the profit and loss account in the period before the disposal occurs, a further question is whether the profit and loss account of the next period in which the disposal occurs should show the actual loss on sale including the goodwill, with the utilisation of the provision set against it, or whether, once written off in the profit and loss account, the goodwill does not re-enter the calculation of the loss on sale (or the provision set against it). The net effect on profit is the same in both cases. We believe that either treatment is acceptable. The latter treatment would be automatic where the goodwill had been capitalised.

Operations discontinued by closure

8.58 Where an operation that qualifies as discontinued is closed, its results up to the date of closure should be shown as part of the normal profit and loss account captions, under the 'discontinued operations' heading. The profit or loss on closure should be shown as an exceptional item after operating profit and before interest and should also be described as 'discontinued operations'. Any reorganisation or restructuring of continuing operations resulting from the closure should be treated as part of continuing operations.

8.59 FRS 3 states that the profit or loss on termination should only include revenue and costs that are directly related to the termination. [FRS 3 para 20]. Whilst this is not explained in more detail in the standard, the exposure draft (FRED 1) stated that such items should be limited to redundancy costs and profits or losses arising from the disposal of fixed assets. Certainly these items may be included, but it may also be appropriate to include other items (see para 8.65 for examples). Trading losses and profits from the date of the decision should, however, not be included in the loss on closure. They should be included as stated above under the appropriate format headings under the discontinued heading.

Provisions for losses on termination

8.60 Where a closure of an operation is completed within an accounting period there will be no need to consider the question of provisioning for losses on closure at the year end. However, where a decision has been made by the year end to close, but the closure is not made until the following period, a provision will be necessary for future losses to be incurred if the company is committed to the closure at the balance sheet date.

[The next paragraph is 8.62.]

8.62 FRS 3 requires a provision to be made if, but only if, a decision to close has been made *and* the decision is evidenced by a detailed formal plan for termination from which the reporting entity cannot realistically withdraw. [FRS 3 para 18]. Where a business termination is contemplated but no demonstrable commitment has been made by the company, no obligation has been incurred and, therefore, there is no liability to be provided for. This is echoed by FRS 21, 'Events after the balance sheet date'. [FRS 21 para 22(b)]. This rule applies in respect of all terminations and not just those that are so significant to the reporting entity that they will qualify as discontinued operations.

8.63 FRS 3 gives two examples of what might be regarded as sufficient evidence of a demonstrable commitment, that is, they would effectively oblige the company to complete the termination. These are:

- Public announcement of specific plans.
- Commencement of implementation.

[FRS 3 para 45].

In practice, the point at which a management decision to close an operation becomes a demonstrable commitment is less objectively determinable than where a sale is involved.

8.64 The provision required by the standard should include:

- Direct costs of the termination.
- Operating losses to be incurred by the operation between the year end and the date of termination.

In both cases, the provision should take into account the aggregate profit, if any, to be recognised in the profit and loss account from the future profits of the operation. [FRS 3 para 18]. FRS 3 was amended by FRS 12 to preclude profits on disposals of assets from being taken into account in measuring such provisions. Any such profits from disposal of assets should be accounted for separately when they arise. This may, in some cases, mean that a provision is made in one period (say for redundancies), but profits from the disposal of assets are not recognised until future periods when a binding contract for their sale is entered into. Where there are assets that will be sold at a large profit in future periods the effect may be that a provision that would have been relatively small before the amendment introduced by FRS 12 (because the potential gain on the assets was taken into account) is now much larger in the earlier period (because the potential sale is not taken into account) with the gain of the sale of the assets falling into a future period.

8.65 The standard does not give details of the costs that are intended to be included as direct costs of the termination. It would appear reasonable for the following items to be included:

- Redundancy costs (net of government contributions).
- Costs of retaining key personnel during the run-down period.
- Losses arising from the disposal of fixed assets and stocks.
- Ongoing costs relating to facilities being closed, such as rent, rates and security.
- Pension costs attributable to the termination.
- Bad and doubtful debts arising from the decision to close.
- Any losses due to penalty clauses in contracts relating to early termination.

8.66 The provision for loss on closure should be included as an exceptional item in the profit and loss account after operating profit. This applies whether the operation to be closed falls to be treated as discontinued in the current period, in the following period when it is closed (although it could be described in the notes to the financial statements as 'discontinuing' within the category of continuing operations), or whether it remains within continuing operations because it does not satisfy the threshold to be categorised as a discontinued operation.

8.67 It should be noted that where the closure commitment is made in one financial year, but the closure is completed in the following year, the items that may be included in the provision for loss on closure are different from those that may be included in the actual loss on closure where the whole closure process is completed within one financial year. Where a closure is completed within a period the trading results *up to the date of closure* should be shown under each of the profit and loss account headings used in arriving at operating profit. This means that trading losses between the commitment date and the date of closure would *not* be included in the profit or loss on sale, nor would on-going normal costs, such as rent and rates. They would form part of the operating profits or losses included as discontinued, but under the normal format headings up to the date of closure. In contrast, trading losses included in a provision for a closure that spans the year end do not reduce operating profits, because the element of the provision for such losses charged in one period (a non-operating charge) is credited back in the next period as an operating item to offset the operating loss in that period.

8.68 The disclosure requirements relating to the utilisation in a subsequent year of provisions for operations to be terminated are the same as for provisions for losses on sales (see para 8.51 above). The treatment described applies irrespective of whether the operation being terminated qualifies as a 'discontinued operation' or whether its results are included under continuing operations (see para 8.52 above which applies to terminated operations as well as sales).

8.69 The following example illustrates the accounting for provisions for losses on termination.

Example

In 20X1 a company announced a decision to close a subsidiary. The announcement was made three months before the year end, but the closure is not expected to take place until six months into the following year. The subsidiary had turnover and operating losses of £15,000 and £4,000 respectively up to the date of the announcement and had turnover of £3,000 and operating losses of £2,000 between the date of the announcement and the year end. It is expected to have turnover of £6,000 and operating losses of £3,000 in the first six months of next year up to the date of disposal. In addition, there will be stock write downs of £2,000 and fixed asset write downs of £4,000 resulting from the decision to close.

Strictly speaking, under the standard a provision should be established at the date of the announcement. However, if the operating losses were provided from the date of the announcement to the year end, the financial statements to the year end would still have to show the subsidiary's turnover and operating profit up to the year end under the appropriate headings and the reversal of the provision alongside them, which would be pointless. It is, therefore, more appropriate to make the provision as at the year end. The provision will contain the expected operating loss from the year end to the subsidiary's date of closure together with the write downs of stocks and fixed assets amounting in total to £9,000. In this example it is assumed that there was no goodwill written off to reserves on the subsidiary's acquisition. If there had been, it would be included in the provision.

The relevant extract from the profit and loss account will be as follows:

Profit and loss account – year 1

	20X1
	£
Turnover	
Continuing operations	18,000
Cost of sales (say)	(22,000)
Gross loss	(4,000)
Net operating expenses	(2,000)
Operating loss – continuing operations	(6,000)
Provision for loss on operations to be discontinued	(9,000)
Loss on ordinary activities before taxation	(15,000)

In the notes the analysis may be given of continuing operations between 'continuing' and 'discontinuing' as the standard permits this where an operation, although not qualifying as 'discontinued' is, nevertheless, 'discontinuing'.

In the following year the losses prove to have been underestimated and turnover and operating losses from the balance sheet date to the date of closure are £12,000 and £7,000 respectively. However, stock and plant write downs only amount to £5,000 in total. The figures in the profit and loss account in year two are:

Profit and loss account – year 2		20X2	20X1
	£	£	£
Turnover			
Discontinued operations		12,000	18,000
Cost of sales (say)		(15,000)	(22,000)
Gross loss		(3,000)	(4,000)
Net operating expenses		(4,000)	(2,000)
Less: release of provision made in 20X1		3,000	–
Operating loss			
Discontinued operations		(4,000)	(6,000)
Provision for loss on operations to be discontinued		–	(9,000)
Loss on disposal of discontinued operations	(5,000)		
Less: release of provision made in 20X1	6,000	1,000	–
Loss on ordinary activities before taxation		(3,000)	(15,000)

Although the provision is wholly included after operating profit in 20X1 it has to be allocated in 20X2 between operating profit and loss on disposal in 20X2. The total loss provided for in 20X1 was £9,000, but the actual loss incurred was £7,000 operating loss plus £5,000 loss on closure, which gives rise to the additional overall loss of £3,000 before taxation in 20X2. Note that 20X1 turnover and operating profit, which in the 20X1 financial statements were classified as continuing, are classified as discontinued in 20X2. Details of taxation on the loss on disposal would be given in the notes. In 20X2 the provision made for losses up to the date of termination of £3,000 has been released against net operating expenses as it is considered that this is the appropriate statutory format heading. Had the provision been in respect of increased cost of sales it would have been released against that heading. Alternatively, the provision could have been released against the total operating loss which would then be shown as an operating loss of £7,000 less provision released of £3,000.

Acquisitions

8.70 Acquisitions are defined in FRS 3 as those operations of the reporting entity that are acquired in the period. [FRS 3 para 3]. The results of acquisitions, excluding those that are also discontinued in the period, should, if material, be disclosed separately in aggregate as a component of continuing operations. As with the other continuing operations the minimum analysis given on the face of the profit and loss account should be turnover and operating profit. The analysis of each of the other profit and loss account headings between turnover and operating profit may be given in a note, instead of on the face of the profit and loss account. [FRS 3 para 14].

8.70.1 The 'acquisitions' disclosure in the post-acquisition profit and loss account should include 100 per cent of the acquired entity's turnover and operating profit from the date of acquisition. This applies even if the group has previously held a stake in the acquired entity. For example, where an entity held a 20 per cent holding in an associate at the end of the previous period and it acquires the remaining 80 per cent interest during the current period, it should still show, in the 'acquisitions' disclosure, 100 per cent of the acquired entity's turnover and operating profit from the date of acquisition of the additional 80 per cent interest. This is the case even if the entity accounted for the associate under the equity method in the previous period's financial statements. In that case, t he acquired entity should be included in the financial statements under the equity method up to the date it becomes a subsidiary.

8.71 The standard recognises that sometimes it may not be possible to determine an operation's post-acquisition results to the end of the period. This might occur, for instance, where the business of an acquired subsidiary is transferred to another group company and merged with the existing business of that company shortly after the acquisition. If the results of the acquisition cannot be obtained, the standard requires an indication to be given of the acquisition's contribution to turnover and operating profit of the continuing operations in addition to the information required by Schedule 6 to SI 2008/410. [FRS 3 para 16]. The indication might take the form of a general statement, such as that shown below:

Example

The effect of the acquisition is that the plastics division, into which it has been integrated, has been able to reduce costs relative to turnover. In addition, the acquisition has enabled the group to lift turnover in the division by 25% and the division's operating profit has increased by 15%.

8.72 Where an indication of the contribution of an acquisition cannot be given, that fact and the reason should be explained as illustrated below. [FRS 3 para 16].

Example

No indication can be given of the contribution to turnover and operating profit of XYZ Limited, which was acquired in the year. This is because the business and assets of XYZ Limited were divided up between and integrated into the group's existing subsidiaries immediately after acquisition and it is not now possible to identify the separate results or turnover of each of the separate parts of the business.

8.73 The requirements of FRS 3 concerning the reporting of the results of acquisitions are repeated in FRS 6, 'Acquisitions and mergers'. However, FRS 6 has added an important new interpretation of the requirements as summarised above. It requires the post-acquisition results of businesses acquired in the financial year to be disclosed separately for each material acquisition and for other acquisitions in aggregate. [FRS 6 para 23]. FRS 3 only requires such disclosures in aggregate. An example of the enhanced disclosure required by FRS 6 is given in Table 8.8.

Table 8.8 — Allied Domecq PLC — Report & Accounts — 31 August 1995

	Note	18 months to 31 August 1995 £m	Year to 5 March 1994* £m
Turnover	2		
Continuing operations		**6,954**	4,627
Acquired operations			
— Domecq		**998**	–
— Other		**40**	–
		7,992	4,627
Discontinued operations		**933**	899
		8,925	5,526
Operating costs	4	**(7,878)**	(4,796)
Operating profit	2		
Continuing operations		**950**	682
Restructuring and other costs in continuing operations	7	**(90)**	–
Acquired operations			
— Domecq		**146**	–
— Other		**1**	–
		1,007	682
Discontinued operations		**40**	48
		1,047	730

[The next paragraph is 8.75.]

8.75 FRS 6 incorporates and extends the disclosures required by SI 2008/410 in respect of companies acquired. It also requires disclosures about post-acquisition performance that are intended to make the post-acquisition profit and loss account of a group that has made a substantial acquisition more transparent. These disclosures cover exceptional profits and losses that arise from acquisition accounting and, in particular, post-acquisition reorganisation and integration costs. Disclosures for acquisition accounting are considered fully in chapter 25.

8.76 The information required by FRS 3 and FRS 6 in respect of the post-acquisition operating results of acquisitions may be of limited practical use where the acquisition has taken place late in the financial year. That is, because the standards only require the results to be shown separately in the financial year in which the acquisition occurs. FRS 3 suggests that, in some circumstances, it would be useful for the company to disclose voluntarily in the notes the operating results for the first full financial year for which the acquisition is included. [FRS 3 para 38]. Such disclosure would provide a more useful track record of recent acquisitions and would complement the disclosure of pre-acquisition results required by FRS 6. Table 8.9 provides an example of such additional disclosure; in fact, the company has shown the results of acquisitions made in both the current year and the previous year on the face of the profit and loss account.

Table 8.9 – Arjo Wiggins Appleton p.l.c. – Directors' Report and Financial Statements – 31 December 1992

Consolidated profit and loss account (extract)

Note			**1992**		1991
		£m	**£m**	£m	£m
	Turnover				
	Continuing operations (excluding acquisitions in 1991 and 1992)	**2,476.4**		2,456.8	
	Acquisition in 1991	**79.1**		29.9	
	Acquisitions in 1992	**67.1**		–	
2			**2,622.6**		2,486.7
3	Operating expenses		**(2,429.6)**		(2,239.9)
	Operating profit				
	Continuing operations (excluding acquisitions in 1991 and 1992)	**196.8**		245.9	
	Acquisition in 1991	**(4.8)**		0.9	
	Acquisitions in 1992	**1.0**			
			193.0		246.8

Mergers

8.77 Where a business combination is accounted for as a merger in the consolidated financial statements of the parent company that heads the new group, those financial statements are prepared as if the acquiring group and the new subsidiary had been combined throughout the current period, the previous period and at the previous balance sheet date. The reporting entity is, therefore, restated as an enlarged group that includes the new subsidiary throughout. FRS 3 defines acquisitions as operations of the reporting entity that are acquired in the period. Under merger accounting principles there is deemed for reporting purposes to be no acquisition in the period. Consequently, the results of the combined operations of the enlarged group would be shown as continuing without any separate analysis of acquisitions relating to the results of the new subsidiary.

8.78 FRS 6 requires extensive analysis of the results of the enlarged group that is formed by a merger. These disclosures are considered in chapter 28.

Exceptional items

Definition

8.79 Prior to FRS 3, companies occasionally reported the effects of certain isolated events as 'extraordinary'. FRS 3, however, defines ordinary activities so widely that extraordinary items have all but disappeared and one-off or unusual items are now presented as 'exceptional'. Exceptional items are defined in FRS 3 as:

> *"Material items which derive from events or transactions that fall within the ordinary activities of the reporting entity and which individually or, if of a similar type, in aggregate, need to be disclosed by virtue of their size or incidence if the financial statements are to give a true and fair view."* [FRS 3 para 5].

[The next paragraph is 8.81.]

8.81 The definition of ordinary activities is:

> *"Any activities which are undertaken by a reporting entity as part of its business and such related activities in which the reporting entity engages in furtherance of, incidental to, or arising from, these activities. Ordinary activities include the effects on the reporting entity of any event in the various environments in which it operates, including the political, regulatory, economic and geographical environments, irrespective of the frequency or unusual nature of the events."* [FRS 3 para 2].

8.82 The last sentence of the definition appears to be all embracing and, therefore, even the effects of events such as a war (political environment), a natural disaster (geographical environment), a devaluation (economic environment) or a fundamental change in the basis of taxation (regulatory environment) would be exceptional items arising from ordinary activities rather than extraordinary items.

8.83 In relation to the last of these examples, a fundamental change in the basis of taxation, the standard specifically covers this situation and states that such a change should be included in the tax charge or credit for the period and separately disclosed on the face of the profit and loss account. [FRS 3 para 23].

Non-operating exceptional items

8.84 The standard sets down rules for presenting exceptional items. Three types of profit or loss must, where material, be shown on the face of the profit and loss account *after* operating profit and before interest and described as continuing or discontinued, as appropriate. It is important that companies comply with the standard's requirements on the positioning of these profits or losses in the profit and loss account; in the past, incorrect positioning has been challenged by the

FRRP. These profits and losses will normally be exceptional items, but need not always be so, as they may not always meet the definition of exceptional items given in the standard. However, for convenience they are referred to as non-operating exceptional items in this text (they are sometimes also referred to as 'super-exceptional'). The three are:

- Profits or losses on the sale or termination of an operation.
- Costs of a fundamental reorganisation or restructuring having a material effect on the nature and focus of the reporting entity's operations.
- Profits or losses on the disposal of fixed assets.

Only revenues and costs directly related to the items in question should be included in calculating the profit or loss in respect of these items. The recognition of provisions in respect of these items are considered to be direct costs and should be included. When the net amount of the first or third bullet points above is not material, but the gross profits or losses are material, the relevant heading should still appear on the face of the profit and loss account with a reference to a related note analysing the profits and losses. [FRS 3 para 20].

8.85 The reason for requiring these items to be disclosed *after* operating profit is probably because they would distort the operating profit line if included above it. Disposals of operations and certain fixed assets are in a sense capital transactions that involve either dealing in the operations themselves or in the assets that support them. Often the figures involved are very material — all the more so as profits or losses on the disposal of operations have to take account of goodwill previously written off direct to reserves. Furthermore, the operations or assets may have been held for a long time. Consequently, such transactions can be distinguished from profits and losses generated by the underlying operating activities and so it is reasonable to exclude them from operating profit.

8.86 The rationale for including costs of a fundamental reorganisation or restructuring in the non-operating exceptional item category is less obvious. It is probable that they are given such prominence in FRS 3 because a fundamental restructuring should occur only very infrequently and the costs are so material that a separate classification is necessary to give a true and fair view.

8.87 Table 8.1 and Table 8.2 above show extracts from published profit and loss accounts containing non-operating exceptional items.

[The next paragraph is 8.90.]

Profits or losses on the sale or termination of an operation

8.90 The accounting and presentation issues relating to the sale of an operation are considered from paragraph 8.39 above; those relating to terminated operations are considered from paragraph 8.58. The standard requires profits or losses on the sale or termination of an operation to be included under the appropriate heading of continuing or discontinued operations.

8.91 FRS 10 requires disclosure of the profit or loss on each material disposal of a previously acquired business or business segment. [FRS 10 para 54]. In respect of goodwill on past acquisitions that remains eliminated against reserves under FRS 10's transitional arrangements, FRS 10 requires the amount of such goodwill attributable to an operation sold or terminated and included in the calculation of the profit or loss on disposal to be separately identified as a component of the profit or loss on disposal, either on the face of the profit and loss account or in the notes. [FRS 10 para 71(c)]. Where goodwill attributable to the disposed operation has been capitalised, there is no requirement in FRS 10 to disclose the amount separately as part of the profit or loss on disposal (although the figures can be worked out in aggregate from the note reconciling the balance sheet movements, including disposals, of goodwill).

[The next paragraph is 8.93.]

8.93 Table 8.10 illustrates one method of disclosing a loss on disposal, including the goodwill write-off.

Table 8.10 – Dixons Group plc – Annual Report – 30 April 1994

Consolidated Profit and Loss Account (extract)
for the 52 weeks ended 30 April 1994

				1993/94	1992/93
	Note	**Before exceptional charges £million**	**Exceptional charges £million**	**Total £million**	Total £million
Discontinued operations – exceptional charges (extract)					
(Loss)/surplus on disposal of operations		–	**(19.4)**	**(19.4)**	1.9
Goodwill previously written off to reserves		–	**(191.1)**	**(191.1)**	(2.9)
Net loss on disposal	6	–	**(210.5)**	**(210.5)**	(1.0)

Notes to the Financial Statements (extract)

	1993/4 £million	1992/93 £million
6 Disposal of operations		
Loss on disposal of Dixons US Holdings, Inc.	**(19.4)**	–
Surplus on disposal of Supasnaps Limited	–	1.9
Goodwill previously written off to reserves	**(191.1)**	(2.9)
	(210.5)	(1.0)

The sale of Dixons US Holdings, Inc., the parent company of Silo Holdings, Inc., to Fretter, Inc. in exchange for common and preferred stock in the enlarged Fretter group was completed on 3 December 1993. The loss on disposal represents the difference between the book value of assets disposed of and the directors' valuation of the investment in Fretter, Inc. at that date.

8.93.1 A company may 'dispose' of a subsidiary by demerger effected through a distribution in kind ('dividend in specie'). The costs of such demergers can be significant and we consider that, if material, they can be recorded as a super-exceptional (that is, non-operating) item relating to the disposal of an operation, which is one of the three non-operating exceptional items under paragraph 20 of FRS 3. The demerger costs should only include the direct costs of the demerger (for example, professional fees). Restructuring costs of either the continuing operations or the discontinuing operations prior to disposal should not be included in this non-operating exceptional item, although, if material, they may be an operating exceptional item (or a separate non-operating item if they relate to a fundamental restructuring (as per FRS 3 para 20)). Where the subsidiary itself incurs demerger costs, any costs incurred by the demerged entity should normally be treated as operating costs (exceptional if material) as they do not relate to a termination of an operation and there has not normally been a fundamental reorganisation in the demerged entity's operations.

Fundamental reorganisation or restructuring

8.94 Apart from indicating that it should have *"a material effect on the nature and focus of the reporting entity's operations"*, FRS 3 does not give any further guidance on how to identify a fundamental reorganisation. Some companies may feel under pressure to describe costs as part of a fundamental reorganisation in order to exclude them from operating profit.

8.95 From the dictionary definition of 'fundamental' it could be assumed that the ASB intends that to qualify as fundamental, a reorganisation must go to the root of the company's or group's operations and must involve a change in the basic operations. The 'nature and focus' test is discussed in FRS 3 in the context of discontinued operations. The standard states: *"the nature and focus of a reporting entity's operations refers to the positioning of its products or services in their markets including the aspects of both quality and location"*. [FRS 3 para 42]. An example is given of a hotel company which traditionally served the lower end of the hotel market selling its existing chain and buying luxury hotels. While remaining in the business of managing hotels the group would be changing the nature and focus of its operations.

8.96 We consider that a fundamental reorganisation is likely to be restricted to one that satisfies the following conditions:

- The reorganisation costs must be material.
- The reorganisation should go to the root of and should encompass the whole or a substantial part of the company's or group's total operations (and not be a reorganisation of only one among many different operations).
- The reorganisation, to affect materially the nature and focus of operations, must achieve more than cost savings which leave the existing operations intact.

- The reorganisation must involve a material change in the nature and focus of the group's operations, resulting in the repositioning of its products or services.

[The next paragraph is 8.98.]

8.98 Tables 8.11 and 8.12 give two examples of disclosures relating to group reorganisations that have been treated as fundamental.

Table 8.11 – TSB Group plc – Report to Shareholders and Accounts – 31 October 1993

CONSOLIDATED PROFIT AND LOSS ACCOUNT (extract)

Note		1993 £m	1992 restated (note 1) £m
	Operating profit	**366**	40
7	Reorganisation costs	**(70)**	2
	Profit before sale or termination of activities	**296**	42
8	Profit/(loss) on sale or termination of activities, including goodwill written off	**5**	(37)
4	Profit before taxation	**301**	5

Notes to the Accounts (extract)

Note 7 Reorganisation costs

Reorganisation costs of £70m (the major part being redundancy costs) relate to the implementation of the Group's announced policy of fundamentally reorganising TSB Retail Banking and Insurance and Hill Samuel Bank. In TSB the management, sales force and administration of TSB Retail Banking and TSB Insurance are being integrated to create a "bancassurance" business. Hill Samuel Bank has withdrawn from a number of areas of business, including branch banking, in order to focus on its merchant banking activities. This involves a reduction in its balance sheet and capital employed together with the consequent reduction in support operations.

In the year ended 31 October 1992, as a result of the decision to integrate the TSB Retail Banking and Insurance businesses, the value of long-term life assurance and pension businesses no longer required a provision for commission payable to TSB Retail Banking. As a result £30m (before taxation) was released to the profit and loss account and included as an offset against reorganisation costs (£28m).

Table 8.12 – Unigate PLC – Report and Accounts — 31 March 1995

Group Profit and Loss Account
for the year ended 31 March (extract)

	1995		
	Before exceptional items	**Exceptional items (note 7)**	**Total**
	£m	**£m**	**£m**
Total operating profit	**108.2**	–	**108.2**
Income from associated undertakings	**20.9**	**(2.5)**	**18.4**
Continuing operations			
– Fundamental restructuring of dairy businesses	–	**(55.1)**	**(55.1)**
– Profit on sale of fixed assets	–	–	–
Discontinued operations			
– Loss on disposal of businesses	–	**(0.7)**	**(0.7)**
– Release of 1991 provision	–	–	–
Profit on ordinary activities before interest	**129.1**	**(58.3)**	**70.8**

Notes to the Financial Statements (extract)

7 Exceptional items (extract)

a The costs of the fundamental restructuring of the dairy-related businesses comprise

	Cash spend	Asset write-off	Total
	£m	**£m**	**£m**
Dairies	**15.4**	**16.6**	**32.0**
Fresh Foods	**9.6**	**10.6**	**20.2**
Wincanton	**2.8**	**0.1**	**2.9**
	27.8	**27.3**	**55.1**

The background to, and basis of, the fundamental restructuring costs are set out in the Financial Review on page 19.

Financial Review (extract)

Exceptional Items Exceptional items principally comprise a charge for the fundamental restructuring of the Group's dairy-related activities in response to the upheaval in milk procurement in the UK, and our share of the extraordinary items reflected in the accounts of our associate, Nutricia.

As discussed in the Chief Executive's Review on page 7, the change in milk procurement arrangements and resultant milk cost increases, together with the changing pattern of milk sales away from doorstep to supermarket customers, which has been exacerbated by the milk cost increases, has necessitated a radical review and restructuring of the Group's dairy-related activities. The cost of this restructuring is £55.1 million before tax (£40.1 million after tax), and is separately identified as an exceptional cost as required by FRS 3. The provision comprises £27.8 million of cash costs and £27.3 million of asset write-off allocated across the Group's businesses as shown in Note 7 to the financial statements.

The restructuring plans envisage a 40 per cent reduction in liquid milk bottling capacity over the next three years, as well as rationalisation of our dairy products' activities. Also included are the costs of restructuring Wincanton's milk haulage operations. The cash costs analysed by year of expected implementation and the planned benefits are as follows:

Year ended 31 March	Cash spend	Planned cost reductions (cumulative)
	£m	£m
1995	3.1	–
1996	14.5	7.9
1997	7.3	16.6
1998	2.9	24.7
	27.8	

£18.6 million of the £24.7 million total planned cost reductions arise in the Group's liquid milk operations and will mitigate the impact on profitability of the switch from doorstep to wholesale and supermarket customers.

8.99 When a reorganisation is related to an acquisition, FRS 6 makes it clear that the reorganisation is not fundamental unless it is fundamental to the enlarged group. This issue is considered in chapter 25.

[The next paragraph is 8.103.]

Profits or losses on disposals of fixed assets

8.103 The third type of item that must be disclosed after operating profit is profits or losses on the disposal of fixed assets. This is intended to include profits or losses on sales of major assets, such as properties. It is not intended to include profits or losses on disposal that are in effect no more than normal adjustments to depreciation previously charged. Those adjustments would be included in operating profit as part of the normal depreciation charge.

Example

A company is in the business of hiring plant. Because its plant is subject to significant wear and tear, it has a high turnover of assets, making regular sales of ex-hire plant to third parties. Does the company have to report all gains and losses below operating profit, under FRS 3, 'Reporting financial performance', as a 'super-exceptional' item, every year? As well as being a regular feature in the profit and loss account, the directors believe it would look rather strange given that the company's business, while not being primarily trading in plant, does involve frequent buying and selling.

Paragraph 46 of FRS 3, clarifies that 'super-exceptional' gains and losses below operating profit are 'not intended to include profits or losses that are in effect no more than marginal adjustments to depreciation previously charged'. In such a business we would expect this to be the nature of any gains and losses on sale. If there are significant gains or losses, these should be rare. If they occur regularly then it would suggest that the company might wish to revisit its estimates of useful economic lives ('UEL's) and residual values in accordance with FRS 15, 'Tangible fixed assets', which requires annual reviews of estimates to UELs and residual values 'where expectations are significantly different from previous estimates'. [FRS 15 para 93]. This should ensure that the cost of the plant's economic benefits is correctly charged over the plant's life.

Following paragraphs 93 and 95 of FRS 15, changes to either the UEL or the residual value should be accounted for prospectively. The standard does not allow a backlog depreciation charge to be made.

If depreciation is appropriately charged, then we would not expect gains and losses on the sale of ex hire plant to be exceptional either by virtue of their size or incidence. Hence, it will generally be correct to record them above operating profit.

If the gains and losses are disclosed separately, it may be advisable to add an explanatory note stating that they are marginal depreciation adjustments, to ensure that readers do not gain the mistaken impression that they have been treated incorrectly under FRS 3.

8.104 The standard requires that the profit or loss on disposal of an asset should be accounted for in the profit and loss account for the period in which the disposal occurs as the difference between the net sale proceeds and the net carrying amount, whether carried at historical cost or at a valuation. [FRS 3 para 21].

[The next paragraph is 8.106.]

8.106 It should be noted that the requirement introduced by FRS 3 applies to all assets and not just to fixed assets.

8.107 The ASB considers that performance should be viewed by reference to the profit and loss account *taken together with* the statement of total recognised gains and losses. A valuation surplus in one year is a recognised gain of that year and is part of the performance of that year. It is shown as an unrealised gain in the statement of total recognised gains and losses. Under the ASB's view of performance, when that gain is realised in a future period it would be illogical to recognise it again in the profit and loss account, because it is not part of the performance of that year; rather it related to the performance of earlier years.

8.107.1 However, the prohibition on 'recycling' gains and losses from the statement of total recognised gains and losses (STRGL) to the profit and loss account was relaxed by a limited amendment to FRS 3 in 2007. This amendment permits gains and losses originally recognised through the STRGL in accordance with FRS 26, 'Financial instruments: Recognition and measurement', and FRS 23, 'The effects of changes in foreign exchange rates', to be recycled to the profit and loss account on disposal of the related financial asset or foreign operation. Such recycling is a requirement of those standards and the rule in paragraph 21 of FRS 3 requiring the profit or loss on disposal to be calculated on the carrying amount of the asset created a contradiction between the standards. The ASB remains against recycling as a principle for the reasons stated above and does not wish to promote the concept. The amendment applies only to entities within FRS 26's scope, and for those entities, only to the limited cases of disposals of financial instruments and to disposals of foreign operations under FRS 23. Entities that are outside FRS 26's scope are not affected by the amendment;

neither are FRS 26-compliant entities that have disposals of non-financial assets or disposals of domestic operations. When an item is recycled to the profit and loss account from the STRGL, a corresponding adjustment is made in the STRGL for the period (see para 8.148).

8.108 When first introduced, the FRS 3 prohibition on recycling was controversial because many people did not accept the ASB concept of 'performance' as measured by both principal statements referred to above. They considered that the profit and loss account was *the* primary statement which should include all gains *realised* in the year, whether or not they have previously been recognised as unrealised. To some extent this view stemmed from a more prudent view of performance, because it took no account of unrealised profits, but on the other hand it still allowed for the recognition of revaluation gains in the balance sheet before they were realised.

8.109 The ASB acknowledged the difference of view and, therefore, also required a note of historical cost profits or losses for the period to be presented immediately following the profit or loss account or the statement of total recognised gains and losses, where there is a material difference between the result as disclosed in the profit and loss account and the result on an unmodified historical cost basis (see para 8.169).

8.110 The following example illustrates the treatment of revaluation surpluses on the sale of an asset.

Example

A company has a property which cost £100,000. In year one it revalued it to £150,000. In year three it sells the property for £170,000. Taxation and depreciation are ignored.

In year one the asset is written up to £150,000 and the surplus of £50,000 is credited to revaluation reserve and appears in the statement of total recognised gains and losses. In year three the profit is calculated by reference to the carrying amount of £150,000 and is recorded as £20,000 in the profit and loss account (as an exceptional item after operating profit and before interest). Before FRS 3 the company could have calculated the profit by reference to historical cost of £100,000 and recorded a profit of £70,000 in the profit and loss account by transferring the revaluation reserve to profit and loss account. Under FRS 3, the previous revaluation surplus of £50,000 is taken to profit and loss account *reserve* and only the £20,000 is shown in the profit and loss account for the year.

In this example, if the taxation is calculated on the full surplus of £70,000 then the taxation attributable to the previous revaluation surplus of £50,000 would be charged in the statement of total recognised gains and losses.

8.111 The standard states that profits *and* losses are to be calculated by reference to carrying amount. Where fixed assets have been revalued downwards below cost, and the diminution in value is not considered to be an impairment (because, say, their value in use at the date of the revaluation is considered to be greater than their current market value), this could have the following effect:

Example

A company revalues all its fixed assets and there is a net surplus of £100,000 which is transferred to the revaluation reserve and shown in the statement of total recognised gains and losses. However, the net surplus is made up of a surplus of £150,000 above cost on one property and a diminution in value below cost on another property of £50,000. (If the diminution was an impairment it would have to be charged to profit and loss account.) There is no intention to sell the property with the diminution at the year end.

Three years later the company receives an offer for the second property and sells it for the revalued amount, that is, cost less the diminution of £50,000. As the profit or loss is calculated on the carrying value there is no profit or loss on sale. Thus the loss calculated by reference to historical cost never passes through the profit and loss account. Instead there is a transfer from the revaluation reserve to the profit and loss account *reserve* in the reserves note. This is consistent with the ASB's view of performance, as the loss was recognised in the year of revaluation in the statement of total recognised gains and losses. It emphasises the need, however, to make a clear distinction between diminutions that are impairments and diminutions that are downward revaluations.

A similar result would be obtained if, instead of the asset being sold in year three, the board decided that the asset was now impaired (that is, its recoverable amount had fallen to its carrying value). Under the law the impairment (as a permanent diminution in value) should be charged to the profit and loss account. However, as it has already been recognised (albeit as a downward revaluation) in one of the primary statements of performance (the STRGL), it is not shown in the profit and loss account for that year. Instead, under FRS 3 it would be charged to profit and loss account reserve by means of a reserve transfer in the reserves note.

8.112 A loss that arises on sale of a previously revalued asset must be recorded in the profit and loss account even if the loss arises wholly from the reversal of a previous revaluation surplus.

Example

A company revalues an asset costing £100,000 in year one to £150,000. The surplus of £50,000 is shown in the statement of total recognised gains and losses. The revaluation reserve is credited with £50,000 and the asset written up by that amount. In year five the asset is sold for £130,000. The loss on sale should be accounted for in the profit and loss account for the period as the difference between the net sale proceeds and the net carrying amount. This means that there will be a loss on sale of £20,000 recorded in the profit and loss account. The fact that the profit and loss account never recorded a *surplus* of £50,000 in the past is not relevant under the ASB approach, which looks at the profit and loss account and the statement of total recognised gains and losses *together* in assessing performance.

There will, of course, be a transfer from the revaluation reserve to profit and loss account reserve of £50,000 as the previous revaluation surplus is now realised. In the profit and loss account *reserve* the result will be a net gain of £30,000, but the profit and loss account will, in the year of disposal, record only the loss of £20,000, because the unrealised gain of £50,000 was recognised in the statement of total recognised gains and losses in year one.

[The next paragraph is 8.114.]

Impairments

8.114 FRS 3 requires losses on disposals of fixed assets or operations (including provisions in respect of them) to be charged after operating profit and before interest.[FRS 3 para 20]. FRS 11 requires impairment losses recognised in the profit and loss account to be charged in operating profit under the appropriate statutory heading. [FRS 11 para 67]. For example, Format 2 has a heading 'Depreciation and other amounts written off tangible and intangible fixed assets'. Impairment losses would be separately disclosed as exceptional items, if material. If FRS 11 was interpreted in isolation, most losses recognised in connection with asset disposals would be impairments (charged against operating profit) rather than losses on disposals (non-operating exceptional items). That is because in most cases any previously unidentified shortfall between an asset's carrying value and its recoverable amount that is identified as a result of a decision to sell or terminate would be an impairment, not a loss on disposal.

8.115 We consider that the requirements of FRS 3 and FRS 11 taken together should be interpreted as follows. Impairment losses in respect of fixed assets and businesses that are to be retained must be charged in arriving at operating profit. Impairment losses that, in FRS 3 terms, are provisions for losses on disposals (that is, they are recognised as a result of a decision to dispose of the assets or business concerned) should be shown under the relevant one of the three headings in paragraph 20 of FRS 3. In the latter case, if the disposal has not occurred before the balance sheet date, the company would be expected to be able to provide evidence that the asset or operation would not be retained. For example, the asset or business would probably be being actively marketed and it would be reasonable to expect that the disposal would be completed before the next interim accounts and in any event before the end of the next financial year.

8.116 This apparent inconsistency between FRS 3 and FRS 11 gives rise to some anomalies. If an asset is put up for sale and has not previously been reviewed for impairment, the loss on sale is presented in accordance with paragraph 20 of FRS 3. If, however, an impairment loss is identified earlier as a result of carrying out an impairment review in circumstances required by FRS 11, the loss would be presented as part of operating profit in accordance with FRS 11. An exception is for investment properties (which are outside the scope of FRS 11), where impairment losses recognised in the profit and loss account would usually be charged after operating profit under a caption that corresponds to 'amounts written off investments' in the Formats (that is, after operating profit and before interest payable).

[The next paragraph is 8.121.]

Other exceptional items

8.121 All exceptional items, other than the three described above, should be shown within the statutory format headings to which they relate. In practice, this means that almost all other exceptional items (except any exceptional item relating to finance costs, investment income, amounts written off investments or the tax charge) would be shown in arriving at operating profit. The amount of each exceptional item, either individually or in aggregate (if they are of a similar type), should be disclosed separately by way of a note or on the face of the profit and loss account if that is necessary in order to give a true and fair view. [FRS 3 para 19].

8.122 The format 1 headings used in arriving at operating profit are:

- Turnover.
- Cost of sales.
- Gross profit.
- Distribution costs.
- Administrative expenses.
- Other operating income.

8.123 This is a relatively small number of headings to absorb every single type and description of exceptional item that may occur. Some types of exceptional items are relatively straightforward, for instance, a provision for loss on a contract in a construction company might well be exceptional and would be shown under the 'cost of sales' heading. The proceeds of an insurance claim for loss of profits could be accommodated under the 'other operating income' heading. Provisions for redundancy and reorganisation costs might have to be allocated among several headings however. If, for instance, the reorganisation involved a relocation, the costs of that might be put under administrative costs, but any redundancy costs might have to be allocated to several headings (according to where the salary costs of those made redundant were charged). Costs of disposing of delivery vans and sub-contracting the distribution of goods to outside hauliers would be an exceptional distribution cost.

8.124 Some items may, at first, not appear to have an appropriate statutory format heading. One example would be the expropriation of assets by a foreign government. If this is the case, then it may well fit within one of the three categories of exceptional item that must be shown after operating profit. If the expropriation results in a loss on disposal of assets, or of a business, it should be shown separately after operating profit.

8.125 Costs incurred in connection with acquisition activities, such as abortive bid costs incurred by a company that launched a failed takeover bid would be shown as exceptional administrative costs, that is, charged in arriving at operating profit, because they relate to the company's attempt to expand its operations by acquisition (see, for example, Table 8.14). Listing costs or abortive listing costs are also shown as operating exceptionals under the appropriate format heading.

8.126 The following example illustrates the treatment of exceptional items.

Example

A group disposed of a subsidiary during the year making a profit on disposal (after goodwill) of £500,000. A leakage of toxic chemicals from one of its factories caused damage to nearby farmland which cost £1m to clean up. The group was fined £300,000. As part of a reorganisation programme 5% of the employees in the administrative function were made redundant at a cost of £250,000 and plant and machinery with a carrying value of £200,000 was scrapped. The group sold certain patents which were not reflected in its financial statements at a profit of £100,000 in order to raise working capital. The group also obtained a listing for its shares in Luxembourg and the costs of the listing were £150,000. The operating profit of the group prior to these items was £1m as follows:

	£'000
Turnover	8,000
Cost of sales	(5,000)
Gross profit	3,000
Net operating expenses	(2,000)
Operating profit	1,000

After accounting for the exceptional items the figures would be as follows:

	£'000	£'000
Turnover		8,000
Cost of sales	5,000	
Exceptional items:		
Plant write down	200	
Cost of environmental damage	1,300	(6,500)
Gross profit		1,500
Net operating expenses	2,000	
Exceptional operating expenses	400	2,400
Operating loss		(900)
Profit on sale of discontinued operations		500
Profit on sale of patents		100
Interest		–
Loss on ordinary activities before taxation		(300)

Clearly each company will have to decide which heading is appropriate for each exceptional item and the above is only a guide to illustrate how the disclosure might appear.

In the notes the net operating expenses and exceptional net operating expenses would be analysed to show the split between distribution costs and administrative expenses and other operating income.

The costs of listing would be administrative expenses and the costs of redundancy of the employees in the administrative function would also be under the administrative expenses heading.

The profit on sale of patents would be a post operating profit exceptional item on the basis that whilst the patents were not reflected in the balance sheet, they are in the nature of fixed assets and would have been shown as such, had they been recognised.

All of the above exceptional items would be shown under the heading of continuing activities except for the profit on disposal of the subsidiary.

The exceptional item in respect of the costs of environmental damage would need to be shown on the face of the profit and loss account in order to give a true and fair view. Because the balance of the exceptional cost of sales has to be shown separately, it has also been described on the face of the profit and loss account, but it could be relegated to a note.

In practice, the total of exceptional items in respect of net operating expenses might not be shown on the face of the profit and loss account. Instead net operating expenses might be shown as £2,400,000 and the exceptional element would be analysed only in the notes. This is because it may not be considered necessary to the true and fair view to show the amount separately on the face of the profit and loss account.

The tax effect of the profit on disposal of the subsidiary and the profit on disposal of patents would be shown in a note as required by the standard.

[The next paragraph is 8.128.]

8.128 Since FRS 3 was introduced, practice has developed regarding the presentation of operating exceptional items on the face of the profit and loss account. Various approaches have been adopted as some companies have sought to highlight operating profit before exceptional items as a key performance indicator and a measure of underlying operating performance excluding the distortive and volatile effect of significant one-off charges or credits. The approaches include:

- Multi-column analysis to segregate operating exceptionals as well as discontinued operations (see example in Table 8.13).
- Single-column analysis with imaginative use of boxes or sub-totals to highlight operating profit before and after operating exceptionals (see example in Table 8.14).
- Separate column to segregate operating exceptionals, whilst all other continuing operations, acquisitions and discontinued operations are analysed under a single column (see example in Table 8.15).
- Straightforward disclosure of operating exceptionals under the statutory caption on the face of the profit and loss account, perhaps with additional commentary or analysis in the operating and financial review (see example in Table 8.16).

Table 8.13 – Manweb plc – Annual Report & Accounts – 31 March 1995

Consolidated Profit and Loss Account (extract)

FOR THE YEAR ENDED 31 MARCH 1995

		Continuing Businesses				
		Before Exceptional Items 1995	Exceptional Items 1995	Total 1995	Discontinued Businesses 1995	1995
	Note	£ million	£ million	£ million	£ million	£ million
Turnover	1	**850.1**	–	**850.1**	**28.5**	**878.6**
Operating costs		**(719.9)**	–	**(719.9)**	**(30.8)**	**(750.7)**
Reorganisation and restructuring costs		–	**(26.9)**	**(26.9)**	–	**(26.9)**
Total operating costs		**(719.9)**	**(26.9)**	**(746.8)**	**(30.8)**	**(777.6)**
Operating profit	2	**130.2**	**(26.9)**	**103.3**	**(2.3)**	**101.0**

Table 8.14 – Anglo United plc – Annual Report – 31 March 1993

Consolidated Profit and Loss Account (extract)

For the year ended 31 March 1993

Notes		1993	(Restated) 1992
		£000	£000
1	Turnover from continuing operations	544,742	555,959
	Cost of sales (including exceptional items) from continuing operations	(463,224)	(458,291)
	Gross profit	81,518	97,668
2	Net operating expenses (including exceptional items)	(80,009)	(63,943)
	Operating profit before exceptional items	20,313	34,345
3	Exceptional items	(18,804)	(620)
	Operating profit from continuing operations	1,509	33,725

Notes to the Accounts (extract)
3 Exceptional items

	Cost of Sales	Distribution Costs	Administrative Expenses	**1993 Total**	1992 Total
	£000	**£000**	**£000**	**£000**	£000
Legal, professional and banking fees in respect of debt restructuring	–	–	**8,894**	**8,894**	–
Costs in connection with aborted disposals and acquisitions	–	–	**2,360**	**2,360**	–
Future discounted rents receivable	–	–	**(1,370)**	**(1,370)**	–
Reorganisation and restructuring costs of ongoing businesses	**1,450**	**720**	**4,853**	**7,023**	–
Write-off of loan to Employees' Share Ownership Plan Trust*	–	–	**1,367**	**1,367**	–
Professional costs in respect of environmental matters	–	–	**530**	**530**	620
	1,450	**720**	**16,634**	**18,804**	620

The comparative cost for 1992 relates wholly to administrative expenses.

In order to assist in understanding the Group's results for the year, and in view of the unusual materiality of exceptional items to the current year's results, the directors believe that it is appropriate to show separately the operating profit of the Group before exceptional items on the face of the profit and loss account as additional information.

* Note: For periods ended on or after 22 June 1995, the assets and liabilities of the Employee Share Ownership Plan are required to have been reflected in the financial statements as assets and liabilities of the sponsoring company, hence a write-off of a loan to an Employee Share Ownership Plan would not occur. This example does, however, demonstrate the disclosures of exceptional items.

Table 8.15 – Booker plc – Annual Report and Financial Statements – 31 December 1994

Consolidated Profit and Loss Account (extract)

for the fifty-two weeks ended 31 December 1994

	note	Before exceptional items £m	Exceptional items (Note 3) £m	1994 £m
Turnover:				
Continuing operations		3,688.7		3,688.7
Acquisitions		10.5		10.5
		3,699.2		3,699.2
Discontinued operations		23.1		23.1
Total turnover		3,722.3	–	3,722.3
Operating costs	2	(3,620.1)	(20.8)	(3,640.9)
Operating profit				
Continuing operations		98.1	(18.3)	79.8
Acquisitions		1.6	(2.5)	(0.9)
		99.7	(20.8)	78.9
Discontinued operations		2.5	–	2.5
Total operating profit		102.2	(20.8)	81.4

Notes to the Financial Statements (extract)

2. OPERATING COSTS (extract)

	Continuing operations £m	Acquisitions £m	Discontinued operations £m	Pre-exceptional items £m	Exceptional items £m	Total 1994 £m
Cost of sales	3,459.0	7.4	18.9	3,485.3	14.8	3,500.1
Distribution costs	63.3	0.8	1.9	66.0	0.5	66.5
Administrative expenses	66.4	0.7	1.7	68.8	5.5	74.3
Total operating costs	3,588.7	8.9	22.5	3,620.1	20.8	3,640.9
Income from investments	–	–	–	–	–	–
Total operating costs *less* other income	3,588.7	8.9	22.5	3,620.1	20.8	3,640.9
Gross profit as defined by the Companies Act 1985	229.7	3.1	4.2	237.0	(14.8)	222.2

Table 8.16 – Cable and Wireless plc – Report and accounts – 31 March 1995

Consolidated profit and loss account (extract)

for the year ended 31 March	Note	**1995** £m	1994 £m
Turnover	3,4	**5,132.8**	4,699.2
Operating costs before exceptional items	5	**(3,938.6)**	(3,608.0)
Exceptional items: charged against operating costs	5,9	**(60.5)**	–
Total operating costs		**(3,999.1)**	(3.608.0)
Operating profit	4	**1,133.7**	1,091.2

Note 5. Operating costs (extract)

	1995 After Exceptional items £m	**1995** Exceptional items therein £m	1994 £m
Outpayments to other telecommunications administrations and carriers	**1,564.6**	–	1,459.9
Employee costs	**799.2**	**30.3**	686.6
Pension costs* (Note 8) – principal schemes	**51.1**	–	48.6
– other schemes	**8.9**	–	11.2
Rental of transmission facilities	**71.5**	–	58.9
Hire of plant and machinery	**19.9**	–	20.7
Other operating lease rentals	**23.0**	–	21.3
Other operating costs	**942.1**	**30.2**	833.6
Depreciation of owned tangible fixed assets	**510.9**	–	461.1
Depreciation of tangible fixed assets held under finance leases	**6.3**	–	4.5
Auditors' remuneration – for audit services	**1.6**	–	1.6
	3,999.1	**60.5**	3,608.0

Having regard to the special nature of the Group's business an analysis of operating costs in the manner prescribed by the Companies Act 1985 is not meaningful. In the circumstances therefore the Directors have, as required by paragraph 3(3) of schedule 4 to the Companies Act 1985, adapted the prescribed format to the requirements of the Group's business.

Note 9. Exceptional items (extract)

Exceptional items are as follows:	**1995** £m	1994 £m
Mercury reorganisation costs		
Shown as:		
Charge to operating profit	**60.5**	–
Profit less losses on sale and termination of operations	**17.7**	–
Losses on disposal of fixed assets	**43.7**	–
	121.9	–

The exceptional pre-tax charge of £121.9m relates to the Mercury reorganisation announced in December 1994 to streamline its operations and strengthen its competitive position in the UK telecommunications market. Applicable to this exceptional charge is a tax credit of £13.2m relating to the operating cost element of the charge, and a minority interest share of £21.7m.

* Note: Cable and Wireless plc, in its 1995 financial statements applied SSAP 24, 'Pension costs', which has been superseded by FRS 17, 'Retirement benefits'.

[The next paragraph is 8.130.]

8.130 There are different schools of thought on segregation of exceptional items in the profit and loss account.

8.131 One view is that such treatment is consistent with the 'information set' approach that FRS 3 promulgates, because each component of performance is presented fully in the way management believes is most useful for and understandable to shareholders. Investors are particularly interested in analysing the quality of maintainable underlying profits and, hence, growth and dividend prospects. Prominent disclosure of exceptional items is sometimes argued to be an essential part of the overall picture.

8.132 A different view is that excessive emphasis on underlying or maintainable earnings after stripping out unusual items is a flawed concept. Focus on operating profit before exceptionals can encourage the over-use of the exceptional items category, presenting them in a way that leads them to be discounted by the market.

8.133 We believe that such treatment remains within the spirit of the standard if the exceptionals warrant that degree of prominence and provided that the overall position, including relevant commentary, is presented in an unbiased way and is not misleading.

8.134 Although the above examples illustrate that there is considerable room for experimentation with formats, companies should take great care that they comply with the standard's requirement for exceptional items to be shown on the profit and loss account under the statutory format headings to which they relate. The FRRP published a statement on this issue in May 1994. Following an investigation by the FRRP of the financial statements of BET plc for the year ended 27 March 1993, in which FRS 3 was adopted early, the company restated within its 1994 financial statements the presentation of the 1993 comparative exceptional items. The FRRP had concluded that the 1993 presentation *"did not fulfil the requirement of the standard that these items should be shown on the profit and loss account under the statutory format headings to which they relate"*.

8.135 Relevant extracts from the 1993 financial statements are shown in Table 8.17. The problem was that, although the operating exceptional items totalling £76 million were analysed between cost of sales, distribution costs and administrative expenses in the notes, they were not included in the totals shown under the format headings. The FRRP's quibble on this point seemed to many commentators to be rather pedantic, but showed that it was determined to enforce the new standards rigorously.

Table 8.17 – BET Public Limited Company – Annual Report – 27 March 1993

Consolidated profit and loss account (extract)

for the year ended 27th March 1993	Notes	Continuing Operations £m	Discontinued operations £m	1993 Total £m
TURNOVER	1	2,003.2	173.0	2,176.2
Cost of sales		(1,533.2)	(125.8)	(1,659.0)
Gross profit		470.0	47.2	517.2
Distribution costs		(187.5)	(32.2)	(219.7)
Administrative expenses		(231.0)	(20.9)	(251.9)
Other operating income		19.3	1.2	20.5
Income from interests in associated undertakings	4	8.1	–	8.1
OPERATING PROFIT/(LOSS) BEFORE EXCEPTIONAL ITEMS	1&2	78.9	(4.7)	74.2
Permanent diminution in asset values		(42.0)	–	(42.0)
Reorganisation costs		(34.0)	–	(34.0)
Deferred costs		–	–	–
OPERATING EXCEPTIONAL ITEMS	3	(76.0)	–	(76.0)
OPERATING PROFIT/(LOSS)		2.9	(4.7)	(1.8)

Note 3 Exceptional items (extract)

The operating exceptional items referred to above can be categorised as follows:

1993	Cost of sales £m	Distribution costs £m	Administrative expenses £m	Total £m
Permanent diminution in asset values	35.7	–	6.3	42.0
Reorganisation costs	24.5	–	9.5	34.0
	60.2	–	15.8	76.0

8.136 Extracts from the restated comparatives in the 1994 financial statements are shown in Table 8.18.

Table 8.18 – BET Public Limited Company – Annual Report – 2 April 1994

Consolidated profit and loss account (extract)

For the year ended 2nd April 1994	Notes	**Continuing operations**	**Discontinued operations**	**1994 Total**	1993 Restated (see page 36)
		£m	**£m**	**£m**	£m
TURNOVER	1	**1,785.1**	**188.9**	**1,974.0**	2,176.2
Cost of sales		**(1,318.7)**	**(154.7)**	**(1,473.4)**	(1,719.2)
Gross profit		**466.4**	**34.2**	**500.6**	457.0
Distribution costs		**(170.1)**	**(14.5)**	**(184.6)**	(219.7)
Administrative expenses		**(202.6)**	**(23.2)**	**(225.8)**	(267.7)
Other operating income / (expense)		**(0.5)**	**1.1**	**0.6**	20.5
Income from interests in associated undertakings	4	**5.6**	**0.2**	**5.8**	8.1
OPERATING PROFIT/(LOSS)	1	**98.8**	**(2.2)**	**96.6**	(1.8)

Note 3 Exceptional items (extract)

The following operating exceptional items are included within the statutory format headings on the face of the profit and loss account. In 1993 they were disclosed as separate line items on the face of the profit and loss account.

	1994	1993
	£m	£m
OPERATING EXCEPTIONAL ITEMS		
Permanent diminution in asset values	–	(42.0)
Reorganisation costs	–	(34.0)
	–	(76.0)

In the previous year a provision was made for reorganisation costs of £34.0 million. This has been fully utilised in the current year (see note 19). The £42.0 million operating exceptional item in 1993 provided for a permanent diminution in the value of land and buildings of £10.5 million, other fixed assets of £21.2 million and current assets of £10.3 million.
The operating exceptional items referred to above are categorised as follows:

	1994			1993		
	Cost of sales	**Administrative expenses**	**Total**	Cost of sales	Administrative expenses	Total
	£m	**£m**	**£m**	£m	£m	£m
Permanent diminution in asset values	–	–	–	35.7	6.3	42.0
Reorganisation costs	–	–	–	24.5	9.5	34.0
	–	–	–	60.2	15.8	76.0

8.150 The 'total recognised gains and losses' are the gains and losses arising from a company's activities as distinct from capital introduced or withdrawn by shareholders. Consequently, they do not include payments to shareholders in respect of capital redeemed or inflows of new capital from shareholders, nor do they include dividends to shareholders. These items are not elements of a company's performance, and so instead are recorded in the reconciliation of movements in shareholders' funds.

[The next paragraph is 8.153.]

8.153 An example of a statement of total recognised gains and losses is given in Table 8.19.

Table 8.19 – Grand Metropolitan Public Limited Company – Annual Report – 30 September 1994

Statement of Total Recognised Gains and Losses

For the year ended 30th September 1994

	1994 £m	*1993 £m*
Profit for the financial year	450	4[illegible]
Deficit on revaluation of properties in associate	(10)	*(80)*
Exchange adjustments	(47)	*(39)*
Total recognised gains and losses for the financial year	393	*291*
Prior year adjustment (note 1)	(21)	
Total gains and losses recognised since last annual report	372	

8.154 Where a reporting entity has no recognised gains and losses in a period, other than the profit or loss for the period, it should state this fact immediately below the profit and loss account. [FRS 3 para 57].

8.154.1 FRS 9 requires that the investor's share of total recognised gains and losses of its associates and (separately) joint ventures should be shown separately under each heading, if material, either in the statement or in a note that is referred to in the statement. The above example highlights a share of a deficit on revaluation in an associate that is material (this assumes that all other amounts attributable to associates are not material for the purpose of this example).

Purchased goodwill

8.155 Goodwill that was written off directly to reserves on acquisition before the adoption of FRS 10 was not permitted to be included in the STRGL in the year when it was written off. There is a footnote in FRS 3 to this effect. [FRS 3 para 27].

[The next paragraph is 8.157.]

8.161 The legal requirements in relation to reserves are that where any amounts are transferred to or from reserves that are required to be shown separately in the balance sheet the following information has to be given:

- The amount of the reserves at the beginning and end of the year.
- The amounts transferred to or from the reserves during the year.
- The source and application of any amounts so transferred.

[SI 2008/410 1 Sch 59].

8.162 This means, for example, that the reserves note is required to show movements between the revaluation reserve and the profit and loss account reserve in respect of previous revaluation surpluses realised in the year. Although the standard does not require the note to be given the same prominence as, for instance, the statement of total recognised gains and losses, it remains an important note to the financial statements.

8.163 Because the reserves note is required by law to show movements in each reserve and movements between reserves, it is not possible to substitute for such movements in the reserves note a figure, such as, the total recognised gains and losses figure for the year from the statement of total recognised gains and losses. That figure, which summarises several different types of reserve movements must be broken down into its component parts in the reserves note and transfers between reserves must also be shown in the note.

8.164 Many of the respondents to the exposure draft, FRED 1, considered that the statement of total recognised gains and losses should be extended to include other reserve movements and to provide a reconciliation between opening and closing shareholders' equity. The ASB did not amend its proposals, but instead introduced in FRS 3 the requirement for an additional statement or note reconciling movements in shareholders' funds (see para 8.183).

[The next paragraph is 8.169.]

Note of historical cost profits and losses

8.169 FRS 3 requires that a note of historical cost profits and losses for the period should be presented immediately following the profit and loss account or the statement of total recognised gains and losses, in those instances where there is a material difference between the result as disclosed in the profit and loss account and the result on an unmodified historical cost basis. Although it is not a requirement, where there is no material difference between the result as disclosed in the profit and loss account and the result on an unmodified historical cost basis, entities usually include a statement of that fact.

8.170 The standard gives the reasons for requiring this note. First, it is argued that for so long as discretion exists on the scale and timing of revaluations included in financial statements, the unmodified historical cost basis will give the reported profits or losses of different enterprises on a more comparable basis. Secondly, certain users wish to assess the profit or loss on sale of fixed assets based on their historical cost rather than, as the standard requires, on their revalued carrying amount.

8.171 The lack of comparability referred to occurs, for instance, where two companies have similar assets costing £100,000 each. The second company revalues the asset to £150,000 and the gain is shown in the statement of total recognised gains and losses in year one. In year two the companies sell the assets for £150,000. The first company will record a profit of £50,000 in the profit and loss account whilst the second will record neither gain nor loss.

8.172 Under the ASB's view of performance, the second company's gain occurs in year one and is recognised in the picture of performance given by the profit and loss account taken together with the statement of total recognised gains and losses. Nonetheless, the two companies' results in year one are not comparable because the first company has not revalued and, therefore, shows no gain. The same lack of comparability occurs in the second year, because the first company reports a profit and the second does not.

8.173 The note of historical cost profits remedies this. In the second company in year two adjustments are made in the note to show the profit on an unmodified historical cost basis and these results can then be fairly compared with those of the first company.

[The next paragraph is 8.178.]

8.178 The note also includes adjustments to the reported profit to remove depreciation charged on the revalued element of fixed assets and to restate profits and losses on sale of assets onto the historical cost basis.

8.179 Investment and dealing companies that apply FRS 26, 'Financial instruments: Recognition and measurement', and carry certain financial assets at fair value, taking the movements to the profit and loss account are not required by the standard to make adjustments in the note of historical cost profits and losses to eliminate gains taken to profit and loss account as a result. This is because the standard's explanation section states that where marking to market is an established industry practice it is not considered to be a departure from the historical cost convention for the purposes of the note of historical cost profits and losses. FRS 3 has now been amended, to extend this principle to the effects of fair value accounting under FRS 26, 'Financial instruments: Recognition and measurement', to hyperinflation adjustments under FRS 24, 'Financial reporting in hyperinflationary economies', and to UITF 9, 'Accounting for operations in hyper-inflationary economies', so that the effects of these items on historical cost profit or loss are not required to be included in the reconciliation. But this omission should be noted. This amendment is effective for accounting periods beginning on or after 1 January 2007 with early adoption permitted.

8.180 Companies holding investment properties, which are required by SSAP 19 to be revalued annually in the financial statements, generally do not include a depreciation adjustment in the note of historical profits and losses. That is because it is probable that either no depreciation would have been charged on a revalued or historical cost basis, so there is no difference to record or it is not possible to quantify depreciation on a revalued or historical cost basis.

8.181 Other companies that do not maintain records of historical costs may instead use the earliest available values. The standard specifically states that where full historical cost information cannot be obtained without unreasonable expense or delay, the earliest available values should be used.

8.182 An example of a note of historical cost profits and losses is given in Table 8.20.

Table 8.20 – Grand Metropolitan Public Limited Company – Annual Report – 30 September 1994

NOTE OF HISTORICAL COST

PROFITS AND LOSSES

for the year ended 30th September 1994

	1994	*1993*
	£m	*£m*
Profit on ordinary activities before taxation	654	*625*
Realisation of property revaluation gains of prior years	429	*6*
Difference between the historical cost depreciation charge and the actual depreciation charge for the year calculated on the revalued amount	1	*2*
Asset provisions created/(utilised) not required on an historical cost basis	26	*(7)*
Historical cost profit on ordinary activities before taxation	1,110	*626*
Historical cost profit for the year retained after taxation, minority interests and dividends	614	*142*

Reconciliation of movements in shareholders' funds

8.183 When the FRS was being developed, some commentators were concerned that the statement of total recognised gains and losses would not achieve the desired effect of bringing into a primary statement all the important movements in shareholders' funds that have hitherto been included only in the notes to the financial statements.

8.184 The ASB's reaction to this concern was to keep the statement of total recognised gains and losses as a primary statement containing only gains and losses — that is, as a statement of performance — but to introduce a new note or primary statement that reconciles the opening and closing totals of shareholders' funds. The reconciliation is not a statement of performance, but just brings together all items that affect shareholders' funds as reported in the financial statements, that is:

- Profit for the year.
- Other recognised gains and losses relating to the year (included in the statement of total recognised gains and losses).
- Other items that are not part of performance such as: dividends; the net proceeds of new share issues; payments for the redemption or repurchase of shares; and reversal on disposal of purchased goodwill previously eliminated against reserves.

8.185 As the reconciliation may be either in the form of a note or in the form of a primary statement, considerable flexibility is given as to where the reconciliation appears in financial statements and thus to the prominence or lack of prominence given to it. If included as a primary statement, however, it must be shown separately from the statement of total recognised gains and losses.

8.186 The reconciliation should include the components of the total recognised gains and losses of the year. The example in the standard shows dividends deducted from profit for the financial year rather than from total recognised gains and losses. This must be correct as dividends cannot be paid out of unrealised profits. The reconciliation should also include share capital subscribed or repaid. Other items could include amounts written off against the share premium account where permitted by law.

8.187 An example is shown in Table 8.21.

Table 8.21 — Marks and Spencer Group p.l.c. — Annual Report and Financial Statements — 30 March 2002

26. Reconciliation of movements in Group shareholders' funds	Group	
	2002	2001 As restated
	£m	£m
Profit/(loss) attributable to shareholders	153.0	(5.5)
Dividends	(238.9)	(258.3)
	(85.9)	(263.8)
Other recognised gains and losses relating to the year	0.6	11.6
New share capital subscribed	8.9	7.1
Issue/redemption expenses	(9.3)	–
Amounts added to profit and loss account reserve in respect of shares issued to the QUEST	2.5	–
Redemption of B shares	(1,717.9)	–
Purchase of own shares	(52.0)	(20.3)
Goodwill transferred to profit and loss account on sale/ closure of businesses	368.2	(1.3)
Net reduction in shareholders' funds	(1,484.9)	(266.7)
Opening shareholders' funds as previously stated	4,645.4	4,905.3
Prior year adjustment (see note 7)	(79.6)	(72.8)
Opening shareholders' funds as restated	4,565.8	4,832.5
Closing shareholders' funds	3,080.9	4,565.8

Prior period adjustments

Introduction

8.188 FRS 3 requires that prior period adjustments should be accounted for by restating the corresponding primary statements and notes for the preceding period and adjusting the opening balance of reserves accordingly. In the statement of total recognised gains and losses the cumulative effect of the adjustments should also be noted at the foot of the current year column, as shown in Tables 8.19 above and Table 8.22 below. [FRS 3 para 29].

Table 8.22 – Trafalgar House Public Limited Company – Report and Accounts – 30 September 1994

Statement of total recognised gains and losses

for the year ended 30 September 1994

	1994	1993
	£m	£m
		(restated)
Profit for the year	30.0	(366.6)
Surplus on revaluation	6.3	(38.9)
Exchange translation differences	(3.3)	(5.2)
Total recognised gains and losses relating to the year	33.0	(410.7)
Prior year adjustment (as explained in note 1)	(2.7)	
Total gains and losses recognised since last annual report	30.3	

Notes to the accounts (extract)

1 Changes in accounting policy and in presentation (extract)

(a) Changes in accounting policy

Comparative figures have been restated to reflect two changes of accounting policy:

(i) Trading results denominated in foreign currencies are translated into sterling at average rates of exchange. Previously trading results were translated at the rates of exchange ruling at the year end. The accounting policy has been changed because the directors consider the new policy gives a fairer presentation of group's results and cash flows as they arise during course of accounting period.

(ii) Sales of UK residential property are recognised on legal completion. Previously, sales were recognised when contracts were exchanged. The accounting policy has been changed because the new policy is adopted by most other UK housebuilders.

As a result, comparative figures for the year ended 30 September 1993 have been adjusted as follows:

	Loss for the year after dividends	Net assets
	£m	£m
As previously reported	(402.1)	290.2
Effect of the change from year end average rates	1.5	–
Effect of the change in the timing of recognition of UK residential property sales	(1.3)	(2.7)
As restated	(401.9)	(287.5)

Current year profit before is reduced by £0.9 million following the changes in the foreign exchange policy and reduced by £0.6 million following the change in policy for the recognition of UK residential property sales.

8.189 Normally, items relating to prior periods arise from the corrections and adjustments that are the natural result of estimates inherent in accounting and in the periodic preparation of financial statements. Therefore, they should be dealt with in the profit and loss account of the period in which they are identified. The only types of prior period items that should be adjusted against opening reserves are those that arise from a change of accounting policy or from the correction of fundamental error. The tax effect of a prior year adjustment, whether it arises from a change in accounting policy or from a fundamental error, should be dealt with as part of the prior year adjustment against opening reserves, rather than as part of the current year tax charge.

Changes in accounting policies

8.190 FRS 18, 'Accounting policies', defines accounting policies as the principles, bases, conventions, rules and practices for recognising, selecting measurement bases for, and presenting assets, liabilities, gains, losses and changes to shareholders' funds. [FRS 18 para 4]. FRS 18 distinguishes accounting policies from estimation techniques, which are methods used to estimate monetary amounts corresponding to selected measurement bases. A change of accounting policy requires a prior year adjustment. A change to an estimation technique should not give rise to a prior year adjustment, unless it reflects the correction of a fundamental error. Accounting policies and estimation techniques are discussed in chapter 2.

8.191 FRS 18 gives several examples of items that should be treated as changes of accounting policies or changes of estimation techniques. They are analysed according to the components of the definition of accounting policies, namely recognition, measurement bases and presentation.

8.192 The following would be changes to accounting policies as a result of different recognition policies:

- Changing from writing-off to capitalising interest relating to the construction of fixed assets.
- Changing from writing-off to capitalising development expenditure.
- Changing revenue recognition practices regarding the sale of goods and services.

8.192.1 The following would be changes to accounting policies as a result of different measurement bases:

- Changing from measuring a class of fixed assets at depreciated historical cost to a policy of regular revaluation.
- Changing from measuring deferred tax liabilities on an undiscounted basis to measuring them on a discounted basis.
- Changing from translating the results of foreign subsidiaries at closing rates to translating them at average rates for the year.

8.192.2 FRS 18 also regards as a change of accounting policy a change in the way an item is presented in the balance sheet or profit and loss account, such as classifying depreciation charges within cost of sales instead of administrative expenses. However, the only effect is to restate comparative amounts on a comparable basis.

8.192.3 A change in the basis of absorbing overheads into a stock or work-in-progress valuation is not a change of accounting policy. SSAP 9 requires overheads that are attributable to bringing a product to its present location and condition to be included in cost. In a historical cost setting, SSAP 9 does not allow a choice of accounting policies relating to the recognition and measurement of attributable overheads. Consequently, the change must be a change of estimation technique (the method of estimating the cost of stocks). Similarly, a change of depreciation methods for a class of fixed assets is not a change of accounting policy. The change of depreciation methods is regarded as a change of estimation technique used to measure the unexpired portion of the assets' economic benefits – there is no change to the historical cost or current value measurement basis being used.

8.193 A significant proportion of accounting policy changes are brought about by the introduction of new accounting standards. Others are changes voluntarily adopted by the directors. FRS 18 requires accounting policies to be reviewed regularly to ensure that they remain the most appropriate. [FRS 18 para 45]. It follows from the general requirement to adopt the most appropriate policies that a change in accounting policy can only be justified if the new policy is judged more appropriate than the one it replaces. [FRS 3 para 62].

8.194 FRS 3 notes that, where an accounting policy is introduced to account for transactions or events that are clearly different in substance from those previously occurring (that is, where no policy previously existed), that is not a change of accounting policy. For example, a subsidiary might operate in an economy that becomes hyper-inflationary as defined in UITF 9, 'Accounting for operations in hyper-inflationary economies' (or FRS 24, 'Financial reporting in hyper-inflationary economies'). The subsidiary's financial statements would then have to be adjusted for hyper-inflation before the closing rate/net investment method of translation in SSAP 20, 'Foreign currency translation', (or FRS 23, 'The effects of changes in foreign exchange rates') is applied. Similarly, inflation adjustments will no longer be required when the economy ceases to be hyper-inflationary. No change of accounting policy is involved in either situation.

Disclosures

8.195 A change of policy must be adequately explained and justified in the financial statements. The Act requires that where there is a change of accounting policy (that is, a departure from the consistency principle) the financial statements must disclose *"particulars of the departure, the reasons for it and its effect"*. [SI 2008/410 1 Sch 10].

8.196 Changes in accounting policies have interested the Financial Reporting Review Panel. Three of its published findings have referred to policy changes. In the first of these, Associated Nursing Services PLC, the Panel examined the adequacy of the explanation provided in respect of a change of policy. Although the Panel concluded that it was satisfied with the explanations provided, it stated that it *"welcomes the intention of the directors to ensure that future notes of changes in accounting policy will include reiteration of the former policy as well as a description of the new policy"*.

8.197 In the second case, Ptarmigan Holdings PLC, the Panel investigated a change of policy in respect of purchased goodwill from immediate write-off to reserves to capitalisation and amortisation. The Panel concluded that, although it was satisfied that the company had special reasons for making the change, it considered the reasons for the change had not been adequately disclosed in the financial statements.

8.197.1 More recently, in 2006 the FRRP investigated a change of policy made by Sanctuary plc in their financial statements for the year ended 30 September 2005. The Panel concluded that policies applied previously had been inappropriate and that the revisions made had been to correct fundamental errors (see para 8.203) and not changes in accounting policy.

8.197.2 Where accounting policy changes are brought about by new accounting standards, the reason is self-evident if the old policy is no longer permitted. Consequently, only a simple statement to this effect should normally be necessary. However, where a company voluntarily changes an accounting policy, the reasons for the change need to be clearly and fully disclosed.

8.198 The Large and Medium-sized Companies and Groups (Accounts and Reports) Regulations (SI 2008/410) require disclosure of the *effect* of a change of policy (see para 8.195 above). FRS 3 requires the effect of the change on the results for the preceding period to be disclosed where practicable. [FRS 3 para 29]. The FRS 3 requirement is satisfied by quantifying the adjustment to the comparative figures as a result of changing from the old policy to the new policy.

[The next paragraph is 8.200.]

8.200 The disclosure requirements of FRS 18 go further than either FRS 3 or the Companies Act 1985. It requires details of any changes to accounting policies including:

- A brief explanation of why each new accounting policy is thought more appropriate.
- Where practicable, the effect of a prior period adjustment on the results of the preceding period (as in FRS 3).

- Where practicable, an indication of the effect of a change in accounting policy on the results for the current period (formerly in UITF 14, see para 8.199).

[FRS 18 para 55(c)].

The last bullet point is particularly relevant because users may be interested to know how much more or less profit the company has made this year as a result of changing its accounting policies.

8.200.1 Where it is not practicable to disclose the effect on the previous year's or the current year's results, FRS 18 requires that fact, together with the reasons, to be disclosed. Non-disclosure of the effect on the previous year's results is rare, since the comparatives have to be restated as part of the prior period adjustment. Sometimes when new accounting standards are adopted it is impracticable to give the effect of changes on the current period's results, especially where the policies use different measurement bases.

8.201 Table 8.22 above shows the financial statement disclosures in respect of two voluntary changes of accounting policy: a change from the closing rate method to the average rate method for translating the results of foreign subsidiaries; and a change relating to revenue recognition on property sales. This example discloses the effect of the change on both the current and previous year.

8.202 Table 8.23 shows the disclosures relating to a change in accounting policy stemming from a new accounting pronouncement, in this case a change from a cash basis to an accruals basis of accounting for post-retirement medical benefits. This example also shows the effect of adopting the new policy on the results of both years.

Table 8.23 – Imperial Chemical Industries PLC – Annual Report and Accounts – 31 December 1994

statement of group total recognised gains and losses
for the year ended 31 December 1994

	Notes	1994 £m	1993† £m
Net profit for the financial year		**188**	129
Currency translation differences on foreign currency net investments and related loans		**(96)**	(23)
Share of other reserve movements of associated undertakings and other items		**(7)**	–
Total recognised gains and losses relating to the year		**85**	106
Prior year adjustment	2	**(95)**	
Total gains and losses recognised since last annual report		**10**	

†restated (note 2)

notes relating to the accounts (extract)

2 Basis of presentation of financial information (extract)

The results reflect the initial adoption of the accounting requirements of pronouncement UITF 6 "Accounting for Post-retirement Benefits other than Pensions". The cumulative cost of the benefits relating to previous years has been recognised in the accounts as a prior year adjustment and comparative figures for 1993 have been restated. The effect on continuing operations of implementing this new accounting policy was to reduce trading profit for the year by £12m (1993 £10m), to reduce the tax charge by £4m (1993 £4m) and to reduce the value of Group reserves at 1 January 1994 by £95m (1993 £89m) (Company £3m, 1993 £3m).

23 Reserves (extract)

	Share premium account	Revaluation	Associated undertakings	Profit and loss account	**1994 Total**	1993 Total
	£m	£m	£m	£m	**£m**	£m
GROUP						
Reserves attributable to parent company						
At beginning of year as previously stated						3,572
Prior year adjustment (note 2)						(89)
At beginning of year as restated	561	46	66	2,493	**3,166**	3,483

Fundamental errors

8.203 Under UK GAAP, corrections of errors are accounted for as a prior year adjustment only if they are considered to be fundamental. Otherwise, they are accounted for in the current period's results. Fundamental errors are those that are of such significance as to destroy the true and fair view and hence the validity of financial statements. [FRS 3 para 63]. The correction of such fundamental errors should not be included in the current year's profit and loss account. Instead, they should be adjusted by restating previous years' results and adjusting the opening balance of retained profits. The cumulative adjustment should also be noted at the foot of the current period's statement of total recognised gains and losses.

8.204 In practice, if the error came to light between the approval of the prior year's financial statements and the date of preparation of the current year's financial statements, the directors could have withdrawn the previous financial statements and revised them voluntarily under the Act (but this does not mean that every such revision is necessarily a fundamental error).

8.204.1 A fundamental error goes beyond a material error in that a fundamental error is such that it destroys the true and fair view and gives rise to financial statements that are misleading. This is relatively rare is practice. If an error is not fundamental, it should be corrected in the current period's results. This is consistent with paragraph 60 of FRS 3, which notes that corrections of items relating to prior periods are generally dealt with in the profit and loss account in the period in which they are identified, and their effect is stated where material. In addition, company law requires disclosure of any amounts relating to a prior year that are included in the current year profit and loss account. [SI 2008/410 69(1)].

Changes to estimation techniques

8.205 Where the effect is material, FRS 18 requires a change to an estimation technique to be described and its effect on the current period's results to be disclosed. [FRS 18 para 55(d)]. This does not necessarily mean that the effect of changes in assumptions underlying the estimation techniques need to be disclosed if there is no change in the estimation technique. Yet other standards may require it. For example, FRS 15 requires disclosure of the effect of changing from one depreciation method to another (change to estimation technique) and of the effect of revising assets' useful economic lives or residual values (change to the underlying assumptions). Estimation techniques are discussed in chapter 2.

Chapter 9

Revenue recognition

Chapter 9

Revenue recognition

Introduction

9.1 The issue of revenue recognition is fundamental to the reporting of performance. The ASB's Application Note G to FRS 5 sets out basic principles of revenue recognition relating to the supply of goods or services. It sets out basic principles for revenue recognition that should be applied in all cases and gives specific guidance on five types of transactions that give rise to turnover and that have been subject to different interpretations in practice. The five types of transactions are dealt with in the application note under the following headings:

- Long-term contractual performance.
- Separation and linking of contractual arrangements.
- Bill and hold arrangements.
- Sales with rights of return.
- Presentation of turnover as principal or as agent.

[FRS 5 App G para G1].

9.2 The application note does not apply to arrangements:

- Resulting from transactions in financial instruments.
- Arising from insurance contracts.
- Dealt with more specifically elsewhere in FRS 5 or in other accounting standards.

[FRS 5 App G para G2].

9.3 The application note is not a full accounting standard and focuses principally on turnover as a subset of revenue. Nonetheless, it sets out important principles and guidance that now provide the primary authority in UK GAAP for revenue recognition. These principles and guidance are discussed and explained in this chapter together with guidance from IAS 18, which remains useful supplementary guidance for UK preparers and users, where it covers areas not dealt with by the application note.

9.4 Even after Application note G was issued, there remained controversy surrounding its practical application to service contracts, particularly contracts for professional services. To clarify the situation, the UITF issued Abstract 40, 'Revenue recognition and service contracts'.

9.5 The scope of revenue recognition and its relationship to other areas is illustrated by the following example.

Company D is a diverse business and has four projects at various stages of progress at the year end. How should these projects be accounted for?

The projects are:

(a) A contract for the construction of a hospital for £10m (expected costs are £8m).

(b) The development of a bespoke computer system, in accordance with contractual specifications for a hospital for £200,000 (expected costs are £180,000 and it is expected to take two years to develop).

(c) The manufacture of a new type of hand disinfectant that has been developed and received all necessary regulatory approval.

(d) Monthly servicing of the hospital's X-ray machines for five years.

(a) Under UK GAAP, this falls within the scope of SSAP 9, 'Stocks and long-term contracts'. The accounting for the contract will require both contract revenue and expenses to be recognised by reference to the stage of completion of the contract at the balance sheet date. This results in the profit being recognised as the contract progresses. To the extent that costs incurred on the contract are not recognised in profit or loss, they should be recognised on the balance sheet as contract work-in-progress. See chapter 20.

(b) The accounting for the development of bespoke IT software, which will fall into two or more accounting periods, falls within the scope of SSAP 9 and the accounting uses the same principles as in (a).

(c) Company D is manufacturing the disinfecting handwash for general stock. The stock falls within the scope of SSAP 9 and is recognised on the balance sheet, measured at the lower of cost and net realisable value and sales revenue is recognised when the handwash has been delivered to customers in return for valuable consideration, in accordance with FRS 5 Application note G, 'Revenue recognition'.

(d) UITF Abstract 40, 'Revenue recognition and service contracts', clarifies that a contract for the monthly servicing of a hospital's X-ray machines does not meet the definition of a long-term contract in SSAP 9; instead it should be accounted for using the principles of FRS 5 Application note G. In substance, the contract is for the performance of a separate service each month and not for one long-term service. Because the contract is for 60 separate services, 1/60th of the contractual revenue should be recognised each month once the X-ray machines have been serviced. FRS 5 does not deal with the recognition of the costs associated with the contract. So entity D will recognise expenses as they are incurred.

9.6 This chapter deals mainly with the issues relating to the recognition of revenue. It considers:

- The basic principles of revenue recognition.
- The recognition of revenue from sales of goods.
- The recognition of revenue from sales of services.
- Multiple element transactions.
- Specific measurement issues.
- Vouchers and coupons.
- Dividends, royalties and other practical applications.
- Financial services fees.
- Presentation and disclosure issues.

[The next paragraph is 9.13.]

Basic principles

Definition of revenue

9.13 FRS 5 Application Note G does not explicitly define revenue, although in paragraph 4 it states that, *"A seller recognises revenue under an exchange transaction with a customer, when, and to the extent that, it obtains the right to consideration in exchange for its performance"*. However, under UK GAAP revenue and turnover are not interchangeable, because Application Note G goes on to define turnover as follows: *"Turnover (which may be described as 'sales' in a seller's financial statements) is the revenue resulting from exchange transactions under which a seller supplies to customers the goods or services that it is in business to provide"*. [FRS 5 App Note G para 11]. Company law also defines turnover in a manner consistent with Application Note G, *"The amounts derived from the provision of goods and services falling within the company's ordinary activities, after deduction of: (a) trade discounts; (b) value added tax; and (c) any other taxes based on the amounts so derived"*. [CA06 Sec 474]. Turnover is, therefore, a sub-set of revenue under UK GAAP.

9.14 The distinction between turnover and other gains is not always clear. Determining whether a transaction should result in recording turnover will depend on the facts surrounding the business and the transaction itself. Consider the following examples:

Example 1 – Sale of ex-demonstrator cars

A car dealership has demonstration cars available that can be used by potential customers for test drives. The cars are used for more than one year and then sold as used. The dealership sells both new and used cars. Does the sale represent the sale of a fixed asset, as the car was used by the dealership for the purpose of securing sales, or is the sale of the car the sale of an item of inventory, as the dealership is in the business of selling new and used cars, which would result in the recording of turnover?

The car dealership is in the business of selling new and used cars. As selling used cars is part of the dealership's normal business, the sale of the cars would represent turnover.

Example 2 – Turnover or other operating income?

A company has received a £1 million payment from a developer for an 18 month option to purchase its premises at a price of £40 million. The option payment has been received by the company at the year-end and is non-refundable. Can it be taken to income in the year?

Application Note G to FRS 5, paragraphs G11 and G12 (see para 9.13) make it clear that the sale of the company's premises would not give rise to revenue to be included in turnover. Instead, under paragraph 20 of FRS 3, 'Reporting financial performance', the gain or loss on sale of fixed assets is shown after operating profit.

The option payment is similar to a non-refundable deposit and should not be recognised in the profit and loss account until performance has occurred, that is, until either the option is exercised or lapses. It is not considered appropriate to recognise this amount rateably over the year since the right to consideration is not earned until the option period lapses. Furthermore, in circumstances where a breach of contract occurred, a full refund could be pursued through the courts. If the developer purchases the property the £1m will form part of the proceeds on disposal. If the developer does not purchase the property the option fee would be recorded as other operating income when the option period ends.

9.15 Similarly, interest receivable may constitute turnover for some entities, but not for others. The interest charged by banks on loans made to customers is turnover. The interest represents a gross inflow of economic benefits arising from the bank's ordinary course of business. Conversely, interest charged by a manufacturing company on delinquent customer receivables is not turnover. Deriving interest income is not part of a manufacturing company's ordinary activities.

9.15.1 Another area that requires consideration is the distinction between capital and revenue transactions. The Statement of principles excludes from its definition of gains (and, hence, revenue) changes in shareholders' funds that relate to contributions from or distributions to owners.

9.15.2 Contributions from owners are defined in the statement of principles as "*...increases in ownership interest resulting from transfers from owners in their capacity as owners*". [SoP chapter 4]. Such contributions are usually in the form of cash, but may also occur when other assets are transferred into the business or when equity is accepted in satisfaction of a liability. Such gifts of a capital amount are often made by parent companies to their subsidiaries. What constitutes a capital contribution might be difficult to determine in practice. A genuine gift without condition from a third party unconnected with the receiving company and, therefore, not in the capacity of an owner, should generally be treated as a gift and reported as a profit in the year of receipt. However, this is unlikely to occur in practice. A company may receive an amount that is to be repaid shortly thereafter other than by way of distribution and this repayment may be envisaged at the time the contribution was made. Such a payment would be a loan, if, in effect, there is an obligation to transfer economic benefits as the contribution is made on the basis that it will be repaid. This can be contrasted with a contribution that is made without conditions, but is subsequently repaid by a distribution at the discretion of the receiving company, which would be a capital contribution rather than a loan. The accounting treatment for capital transactions is considered from paragraph 9.277.

Identifying the transaction

9.16 Revenue has a variety of names: sales, turnover, fees, interest, dividends, royalties and rents. Many transactions are straightforward, but some can be highly complex. Outsourcing contracts, barter transactions, service contracts, contracts with multiple elements and contracts with milestone payments often provide challenges in understanding what the transaction entails, how much revenue should be recognised and when it should be recorded.

9.17 Revenue should be recognised in accordance with the substance, not the form, of a transaction. Application note G to FRS 5 sets out factors to consider in assessing a transaction's substance, for example in accounting for bill and hold arrangements or in presenting turnover as a principal or as an agent.

9.18 The substance will be determined based on the contractual terms, or the combination of the contractual terms of linked transactions, not only on the transaction's immediately visible effects. Contracts, while inherently form-driven, often provide strong evidence of the intent of the parties involved, as the contract is generally how the parties to the transaction protect their interests. Other factors, such as local legal frameworks and business practices, will also need to be taken into consideration, as well as any side agreements to the contract or other agreements between the parties.

9.19 Understanding a transaction's substance requires more than a high-level knowledge of the business deal. It is often a lack of understanding of the details of contracts or the existence of items such as side letters or verbal agreements that leads to difficulties in properly understanding the transaction. Only once the transaction has been properly understood, can the questions of when and how much revenue to recognise be addressed.

Timing of recognition

9.20 FRS 5 Application note G states that a seller should recognise revenue under an exchange transaction with a customer, when, and to the extent that, it obtains the right to consideration in exchange for its performance. At the same time, it normally recognises a new asset, usually a debtor. [FRS 5 App G para G4].

9.21 This principle incorporates the basic elements of performance and rights to consideration, which are both necessary for revenue recognition. Performance on its own is insufficient for revenue recognition, because no asset is created by performance alone. A right to consideration is not sufficient on its own because, although the right creates an asset, there is a corresponding liability for future performance and no revenue is recognised until such performance takes place.

9.22 Performance is defined in the application note as *"the fulfilment of the seller's contractual obligations to a customer through the supply of goods and services"*. The right to consideration is defined as *"a seller's right to the amount received or receivable in exchange for its performance"*. [FRS 5 App G para G3]. The application note continues *"This right does not necessarily correspond to amounts falling due in accordance with a schedule of stage payments which may be specified in a contractual arrangement. Whilst stage payments will often be timed to coincide with performance, they may not correspond exactly. Stage payments reflect only the agreed timing of payment, whereas a right to consideration arises through the seller's performance"*. [FRS 5 App G para G3].

9.23 When a seller receives payment from a customer in advance of performance, it recognises a liability equal to the amount received (often referred to as deferred revenue), representing its obligations under the contract. When the seller performs its obligations and, thereby obtains the right to consideration, it reduces the liability and recognises that reduction as revenue. [FRS 5 App G para G5].

9.24 This principle again demonstrates the link between performance and right to consideration. Both are essential before revenue can be recognised. It also establishes the principles for measuring the obligation for future performance. Revenue is not recognised in advance of performance, but rather the consideration received is deferred as a liability and the amount of the deferral is the full amount received in respect of future performance, not the cost of providing the goods or services.

9.25 A seller may obtain the right to consideration when it has fulfilled some, but not all, of its contractual obligations. Where the seller has only partly fulfilled its contractual obligations, it recognises revenue to the extent that it has obtained the right to consideration through its performance. [FRS 5 App G para G6].

9.26 This principle again links the elements of performance and rights to consideration. However, it establishes a hierarchy that places rights to consideration above performance. This is because in a situation where a seller may have performed ninety per cent of its obligations, but has obtained rights to only fifty per cent of the total consideration, revenue recognition would be limited to that fifty per cent. It is the right to consideration that determines the amount of revenue that can be recognised not the degree of performance. In practice, partial performance of contractual obligations will normally earn the same proportion of the total right to consideration in a contract. However, there may, for instance, be contracts with trigger clauses where no rights to consideration are obtained until performance is substantially complete (see further para 9.133).

9.26.1 In the majority of situations, the criteria for recognition of revenue will only be met once a signed contract is in place between the seller and the customer. This is because the contract drives key issues such as measurement of consideration, costs and the probability of economic benefits flowing to the vendor. However, in rare cases it may be possible to recognise revenue before the sales contract has been signed if all key terms and conditions are agreed upon by both parties. For example where a master agreement is in place, the seller has earned the right to consideration by satisfying relevant performance conditions. Before recognising revenue in such a situation, the entity should consider the likelihood of the contract being amended before it is signed. If the content of any possible or potential amendments is unknown, it becomes impossible to establish whether the seller has performed or earned the right to consideration. This may be the case even if certain elements of the contract appear to have already been delivered as, without knowing all obligations under the contract, it will not be possible to allocate the appropriate amount of revenue to the elements already performed.

What activities constitute performance?

9.27 Given that revenue may be recognised as performance takes place under a contract (provided there are no trigger events) the question arises as to what constitutes performance.

9.28 Consider two contrasting scenarios. A manufacturer may make standard items of stock that are not specific to any customer or items that are customer-specific. For example, contrast a stationery supplier who contracts with a stationery manufacturer for a lorry load of plain white photocopier paper (which is one of the manufacturer's main lines) with a customer who contracts with a stationery supplier for delivery of 50 reams of paper headed with its address and logo (the stationery supplier does the printing in house).

9.29 In the first of these two cases, it is likely that if the stationery supplier cancelled its order for white paper the manufacturer could claim only nominal damages, because it can easily sell the paper elsewhere. However, in the second case, if the customer cancels the order for printed stationery, the stationery supplier will be unable to sell the paper elsewhere and will seek damages from the customer for the full value of the order.

9.30 The difference between the two examples is that the stationery manufacturer would have manufactured the photocopier paper irrespective of the order from the paper supplier. The stationery supplier, however, would not have printed the 50 reams of paper for its customer without the customer's specific order.

9.31 The general principle drawn from this example is that an activity will constitute part of a contract's performance only if it is a necessary part of the contract, in that it is specific to the customer and would not have taken place had the contract not existed. This means that manufacturing a generic product for general sale is not 'performance' in respect of a contract, but manufacturing is part of the performance of a contract where, and to the extent that, it is a necessary part of the contract, because it is specific to the customer.

9.32 Thus, a manufacturing activity that is specific to a customer should be distinguished from one that is merely specified by a customer from a range of alternatives that are standard. For example, when purchasing a new car a customer may specify certain choices, for example, colour, optional extras and accessories. Because these are not specific to the customer, but are merely selections from a standard range, they are not treated as part of performance of the contract. However, if a customer were to order a house built to the customer's own specification, that activity would be specific to a customer.

9.33 Administrative, indirect and pre-contract activities and expenditure do not form part of the contract's performance. They are not, therefore, taken into account in determining the extent to which revenue should be recognised. This is not to imply, however, that associated costs must be written off as expenses as they are incurred. They may be recognised as assets if they satisfy the necessary recognition criteria. The most obvious example is the manufacture of generic stocks. That manufacture is not part of a specific contracted performance, but the assets are recognised until such time as they are sold or otherwise appropriated to a contract. See further chapter 20.

9.34 Just as revenue should not be recognised where performance has not occurred, revenue should only be deferred where there remains an obligation to perform in respect of the deferred element. Consider two examples:

- Sale of right to use software for £10,000. There is no time limit on the use of software and no obligation on the part of the vendor to upgrade the software or to provide any further services or support whatsoever.

- Sale of the right to use the same software for £9,900 but only for five years. Again, there is no obligation on the vendor to upgrade the software or provide further services or support whatsoever.

9.35 The reason for the difference in price being very small is that the value of the software is expected to be very low after five years. Looked at another way the customer who pays £10,000 is only paying £100 for the right to use the software from year five onwards.

9.36 In neither case does the vendor have any obligation to the customer for any performance after the software is delivered. Application note G requires revenue to be recognised when the seller performs. In the second of the above examples, a time period is stipulated over which the customer can use the software, but the income should not be spread over that five year period because, after delivery, there is no requirement for the seller to perform.

9.37 This illustrates the fact that the presence in a contract of a time element does not necessarily change the contract's substance.

9.38 It is possible to use variants of the examples above to illustrate that two questions need to be asked when evaluating when a supplier's performance occurs and when consideration should be recognised.

9.39 The first of these is *"what is the subject of the contract, that is, what is the customer obliged to pay for?"* In the second example above the contract was for the customer to use the software for five years and the customer was obliged to pay for this, whether it used the software or not. If instead the contract had been that the customer had to pay £6,000 for two years but could cancel after two years or renew for a further three years for £3,900, then the revenue to be recognised initially would have been £6,000 only and the £3,900 could not be recognised until the end of the second year and then only if the customer renewed.

9.40 Having identified the economic benefits that are the subject of the contract the second question is *"to what extent have they been transferred to the customer"*, and conversely, *"to what extent does the customer's access to them depend on the supplier's future performance?"* In both of the original examples above control has passed to the customer and performance has occurred. This is contrasted, however, with the situation where a customer pays for one year's hire of a bank safety deposit box, but where the customer remains dependent on the bank for access. Control, therefore, remains with the bank and full performance has not occurred at the outset. Performance occurs over the 12 month period and revenue is, therefore, recognised over that period. Another way of looking at this is that the bank still has unfulfilled promises under the agreement that it will breach if it fails to give the customer access at the times and for the period specified in the contract.

[The next paragraph is 9.42.]

Measurement of revenue

9.42 Revenue should be measured at the fair value of the right to consideration. Normally this will be the price specified in the contract, net of discounts, value added tax and similar sales taxes. [FRS 5 App G para G7].

9.43 Fair value is defined as the amount at which goods or services could be exchanged in an arm's length transaction between informed and willing parties, other than in a forced or liquidation sale. [FRS 5 App G para G3]. As noted above, the fair value of consideration is normally the price specified in the contract. However, there are situations where the amount of the contract price will need to be adjusted to arrive at the fair value and thus the amount to be recognised as revenue. These situations are described below.

9.44 Where the effect of the time value of money is material to reported revenue, the amount of revenue recognised should be the present value of the cash inflows expected to be received from the customer in settlement. The unwinding of the discount should be included in finance income, because it represents a gain from a financing transaction. [FRS 5 App G para G8].

9.45 Discounting may be necessary if goods are sold on extended credit. Normal terms of settlement (say, 30 days) are unlikely to give rise to a material difference if the consideration is discounted over that normal credit period. However, if the period of credit is unusually long, the effect of discounting may be material and this principle then requires the consideration to be split between the fair value of the consideration for the goods sold (recognised as revenue) and the consideration for the grant of extended credit (recognised as finance income).

Example – Sale on extended credit

A company sells goods on extended credit. The goods are sold for £1,200 on 1 January 20X1, receivable on 1 January 20X3. The customer can borrow at 4.5 % a year.

Management should determine the fair value of the revenue by calculating the present value of the cash flows receivable. On the transaction date, revenue of £1,099 is recorded, being £1,200 discounted for two years. The discounted receivable should be updated at each balance sheet date to reflect the passage of time. The resulting increase in the receivable represents finance income and should be recognised as such over the period from the date of sale to the expected date of receipt of cash.

9.46 If, when entering into a transaction, there is significant risk that there will be default on the amount of consideration due and the effect is material to reported revenue, an adjustment to the price specified in the contract is necessary to arrive at the amount to be recognised as revenue. [FRS 5 App G para G9].

9.47 In practice, we consider that the application note should be interpreted in the same way as IAS 18. That is, revenue should be recognised to the extent that it is probable that the transaction's economic benefits will flow to the entity. This treatment rests on the fact that the approach in the application note is based on the 'assets and liabilities' concept. This concept would not permit revenue to be recognised, unless at the same time an asset was created or a liability reduced. Under FRS 5, assets are defined as *"rights or other access to future economic benefits controlled by an entity as a result of past transactions or events"*. [FRS 5 para 2]. Control is *"the ability to obtain the future economic benefits relating to an asset and to restrict the access of others to those benefits"*. [FRS 5 para 3]. Assets should be recognised if there is sufficient evidence of the existence of the item (including, where appropriate, evidence that a future inflow of benefit will occur) and the item can be measured at a monetary amount with sufficient reliability. [FRS 5 para 20]. Where there is significant risk of default the adjustment required by the application note could often be such as to reduce the revenue recognised to nil.

9.48 In practice we expect adjustments of this nature to be extremely rare. It is hard to envisage circumstances where an entity would enter into a transaction with another party and at the time of the transaction be aware of a significant risk of default. However, the following example illustrates the point.

Example – Transaction with significant risk of default

A water company supplies water to domestic customers. A number of customers are unable to pay their bills and have not paid them for some time. However, the water company is barred by statute from cutting off their supply. As the water company continues to supply these known customers, it is aware at the time of entering into the transaction that there is a significant risk of default. Therefore, paragraph G9 of Application note G requires that the revenue should be adjusted to reflect the risk of default. In this circumstance, the adjustment is likely to bring the revenue to nil or, where a specially discounted rate has been negotiated, that rate should be used.

9.49 A feature of the above example is that the supplier can identify the individual customers that carry a significant risk of default in advance of entering into the transaction. This is distinct from the situation where a company knowingly transacts with a portfolio of customers with a relatively high credit risk and expects to suffer bad debts of approximately ten per cent of revenue but does not know which customers will default. In this circumstance, no adjustment would be made to revenue, instead the bad debt expense would be recorded as an operating expense. Paragraph G9 of Application note G deals only with the rare circumstances when a company knows at the time of entering into a particular transaction with a known customer that there is a significant risk of default. The following example illustrates the distinction between uncertainty at the time of sale and uncertainty arising subsequent to the sale.

Example – Timing of an uncertainty arising

Company A has an existing manufacturing customer, company B, who has recently announced that it expects to have to restructure its debts with current creditors, including company A, in order to ensure sufficient operating liquidity to avoid bankruptcy. Subsequent to the announcement, company A ships an order of replacement parts to company B based on a purchase order received from company B prior to the announcement.

Company A should not recognise revenue for the latest shipment to company B, as there is a significant risk that company B will default on the consideration due on the products shipped. Company A may record revenue only when company B pays for the shipment of replacement parts, which is when it becomes clear that consideration will flow to company A.

In contrast, any allowance recorded against any existing receivable balance as a result of company B's announcement of its need to restructure debts should be recorded as an expense, not as a reversal of revenue.

9.50 There may also be circumstances where the risk of default is less clear-cut. The transaction may involve future cash flows that are uncertain because of the time period over which they are expected to be received and the customer's credit profile. In these circumstances, the risk of default may be accounted for by adjusting the likely cash flows or by adjusting the discount rate applied to the deferred consideration for risk. IAS 18 envisages situations where there is doubt about the customer's credit standing. It requires that the discount rate used to arrive at the present value of deferred consideration should be the more clearly determinable of:

- the prevailing rate for a similar instrument of an issuer *with a similar credit rating*; or
- a rate of interest that discounts the instrument's nominal amount to the current cash sales price of the goods or services.

[IAS 18 para 11].

9.51 The principles of the application note could be applied using the same approach as in the first bullet point above, that is, the discount rate could be adjusted for credit risk applicable to the customer. Alternatively, the cash flows could be adjusted to reflect the risk and discounted using the risk free rate. This is the most common approach in practice.

9.52 Subsequent adjustments to a debtor as a result of changes in the time value of money and credit risk should not be included within revenue. [FRS 5 App G para G10].

9.53 This principle is consistent with the reversal of the discount being presented in finance income. Whilst the application note does not specifically say so, we consider that changes in the adjustment for credit risk that have been built into the discount rate should be reflected in finance income in the same way as the unwinding of the discount related to the time value of money. In substance, this reflects a gain or loss from providing extended credit, rather than from the sale of goods or services.

9.54 In summary, we consider that the principles of the application note as regards discounting above should be interpreted in the same way as the corresponding provisions of IAS 18. IAS 18 summarises succinctly the treatment of uncertainties about collection of consideration as follows:

> *"Revenue is recognised only when it is probable that the economic benefits associated with the transaction will flow to the entity. In some cases, this may not be probable until the consideration is received or until an uncertainty is removed. For example, it may be uncertain that a foreign*

governmental authority will grant permission to remit the consideration from a sale in a foreign country. When the permission is granted, the uncertainty is removed and revenue is recognised. However, when an uncertainty arises about the collectability of an amount already included in revenue, the uncollectable amount or the amount in respect of which recovery has ceased to be probable is recognised as an expense, rather than as an adjustment of the amount of revenue originally recognised."

[IAS 18 para 18].

9.55 Note that removal of an uncertainty in respect of revenue that has not previously been recognised because of that uncertainty, results in revenue recognition. This contrasts with the situation where revenue has been recognised, but an adjustment has been made for credit risk. As explained above changes in the adjustment for credit risk are not treated as revenue.

Contingent consideration

9.56 The measurement of revenue can be more complex if contractual terms introduce a variable or contingent element of consideration.

9.57 In some cases, the contingent element is within the seller's control. Generally, the only situation when the consideration is within the seller's control is where the seller is paid according to his performance or an aspect of his performance. An example might be a construction contract where completion of the contract by a certain date may give rise to a bonus payment, or where non-completion by a certain date gives rise to a penalty or deduction from an agreed consideration. Where performance is incomplete, such that it is not known whether bonuses or penalties (or neither) will arise, a fair estimate of the outcome should be made. This method involves predicting the actual outcome and adjusting it for risk.

9.58 Some contracts may contain elements of contingent consideration where the contingent event is outside the seller's control but within the control of the customer, for example where a customer of an estate agent agrees to pay a contingent variable fee, dependent on the property being sold and on the price at which it will be sold. The sale and sale price can only be confirmed once the customer has agreed a sale price with a purchaser. The variable contingent fee would normally be recognised only when the property has been sold. Ordinarily, once the seller has performed the contractual services, it should recognise the amount that the customer is obliged to pay. However, in this case the estate agent has no right to the variable consideration until the property has been sold. The variable amount should not be recognised until the sale has occurred and the estate agent has a right to it as the contingent event is outside the agent's control. [UITF 40 para 19]. The estate agent would need to consider whether it has a contingent asset, which should be disclosed under FRS 12, 'Provisions, contingent liabilities and contingent assets'.

9.59 In other situations, there may be a contingent element of consideration where the contingent event is in the control of neither the customer nor the seller. For example, a company sells land to a developer for £100,000. The company has no continuing involvement or obligation under the contract when the transfer of land is complete. However, it is entitled to receive five per cent of any future onward sales price in excess of £150,000.

9.60 Application note G of FRS 5 is clear that revenue should be recognised when the seller has obtained the right to consideration as a result of its performance. In this example, performance is complete at the time of sale, however, the seller does not have the right to all the future consideration as it only obtains this right after the occurrence of a contingent future event. The additional consideration should, therefore, only be recognised as the right to consideration arises, that is, upon onward sale of the land. Revenue should only be recognised when the contingent event is no longer contingent, that is, it has occurred or become virtually certain. However, the seller would need to consider whether it has a contingent asset, which should be disclosed under FRS 12, 'Provisions, contingent liabilities and contingent assets'.

9.61 When accounting for contingent revenue, it is also important to consider the recognition of any related receivable on the balance sheet. Under UK GAAP, debtors are accounted for following either Schedule 1 to SI 2008/410 or FRS 26, 'Financial instruments: recognition and measurement' (see further chapter 6).

9.62 For entities not applying FRS 26, the application of the guidance above is relatively simple. No receivable relating to the contingent consideration is recognised until such time as the revenue is recognised, that is, when the contingent event occurs.

9.63 For entities applying FRS 26, the situation is more complex. FRS 26 requires receivables to be recognised at their fair value when there is a contractual right to receive cash. In a contract with contingent consideration, the contractual right to receive cash exists from the contract's inception (albeit that the fair value of the receivable may be lower than its face value due to the risks associated with the contingency). This creates an apparent conflict between FRS 5 Application Note G, which prohibits the recognition of revenue until the contingent event occurs, and FRS 26, which requires a receivable to be booked. In this situation, we consider that it is the revenue recognition guidance in Application Note G that determines whether an asset exists and, therefore, no financial asset should be recorded for contingent consideration until the conditions for revenue recognition are met. At that time both Application Note G and FRS 26 require measurement at fair value.

Sale of goods

9.64 A contract for the sale of goods will normally give rise to revenue when all the criteria for revenue recognition have been satisfied. That is, usually when delivery of the goods to the customer takes place.

Transfer of significant risks and rewards of ownership

Bill and hold sales

9.65 Bill and hold sales are those where a customer obtains title to goods, but physical delivery is deferred until the customer requests delivery or collects the goods. [FRS 5 App G para G43].

9.66 Normally, revenue on sale of goods is only recognised when the performance conditions have been satisfied and the right to consideration has been obtained. One such performance condition is usually delivery of the goods to the buyer.

9.67 The issue, therefore, arises as to whether in the absence of delivery, the seller should recognise revenue and a right to consideration or whether it should continue to recognise the stock. [FRS 5 App G para G44].

9.68 The response would appear to depend on whether or not there has been substantive performance of the contractual obligations and whether the seller has obtained the right to consideration. Normally, for example, a customer might place an order for goods and then take delivery. Revenue would be recognised at the point of delivery. However, if the supplier agreed to offer a discount to the customer to accept title to the goods before delivery and to request a delay in delivery, the substance of the arrangement has not changed, but it could be argued that the arrangement is now a 'bill and hold' sale.

9.69 Clearly it would be wrong to advance revenue recognition as the result of an artificial arrangement such as that described above. Therefore, some specific conditions are needed to distinguish bill and hold sales from mere executory contracts. Goods cease to be assets of a seller and become assets of a customer when the seller transfers to the customer access to the significant risks and benefits of the asset and in exchange receives the rights to consideration. The principal benefits and risks for the customer are:

Benefits

- The right to take possession of the goods as and when required.
- The sole right to the goods for their sale to a third party and the right to the future cash flows from such a sale.
- No exposure to changes in prices made by the seller subsequent to the date of the bill and hold arrangement. (For example, changes to the seller's standard price list).

Risks

- Slow movement, resulting in increased costs of financing and holding the stock and obsolescence risk.

- Risk of being obliged to take delivery of the goods even if they have become obsolete or not readily saleable, with the consequence that there may be no onward sale or that such onward sale can only be made at a reduced price.

[FRS 5 App G para G45].

9.70 The application note states that, in order for the seller to have the right to recognise changes in its assets or liabilities and turnover, arising from its right to consideration in respect of a bill and hold arrangement, the contract should have all of the following elements:

- The goods should be complete and ready for delivery.
- The seller should not have retained any significant performance obligations other than storing the goods safely and arranging for their despatch when the customer requests it.
- Subject to any rights of return, the seller should have the right to consideration whether or not the goods are delivered in due course to the customer. Where there are rights of return, the arrangement's commercial substance, particularly in respect of transfer of risk, must be carefully considered to determine whether revenue may be recognised. Rights of return are considered from paragraph 9.75 below.
- The goods must be separately identified from the seller's other stock and should not be capable of being used to fill other orders that are received between the date of the bill and hold sale and delivery of the goods to the customer.
- The terms of the bill and hold sale should be in accordance with the customer's commercial objectives and not those of the seller (although, in many cases, the commercial objectives of the seller and customer will be mutually compatible). An example where the arrangement will be in line with the customer's commercial objectives is where the delay in delivery is to meet the customer's need for flexibility in the timing and location of delivery.

[FRS 5 App G para G46].

9.71 In relation to the fourth bullet point above, the reason for the requirement for the goods to be separately identified from the seller's other stocks is as follows. In a normal sales contract the passing of economic benefits and risks occurs on delivery, when specific goods are appropriated to the contract and passed to the customer. Until then, if the goods are of a general sort manufactured by the seller, the goods are not specific. The seller can still sell stocks that are earmarked for the customer and substitute similar stocks when it comes to delivery. Only if the goods are separately identified and unable to be used to fill other orders should the customer be deemed to have secured the stock's economic benefits on passing of title. 'Separately identified' would include (but would not be confined to) stocks that are so specific to the customer that they are unable to be replaced from the other general stocks of the seller. Examples of such stock might be stationery that is printed with the customer's name or goods manufactured to a customer's specification and not otherwise made by the seller or obtainable by the seller from other sources.

9.72 Where the conditions listed above are satisfied and the stock is considered to be the customer's asset, the seller should recognise the changes in its assets and liabilities and revenue. Where any of the conditions are not satisfied, the stock will continue to be the seller's asset and retained on its balance sheet. Any amounts received from the customer should be included in creditors as they represent the seller's liability to fulfil its contractual obligations. [FRS 5 App G paras G47, G48].

Payments in advance

9.73 Payments received in advance of performance do not represent revenue, because they have not been earned. Until the seller performs, the increase in cash is matched by an increase in liabilities, representing an obligation to supply goods or services or to make a refund.

Example – Non-refundable deposits

A company manufactures and supplies reproduction furniture. Since the choice of the final colouring and polishing of the furniture is left to the customer, the company takes a large non-refundable deposit from the customer at the time of the initial order. In some situations, the piece ordered is in stock and only needs finishing before it can be despatched to the customer, in other cases the item needs to be completely manufactured.

At first sight, it might appear as though there are many points along the production process at which revenue could be recognised: when the deposit is received provided the item only needs finishing; or when the goods have been despatched to the customer.

However, revenue must not be recognised until the company has the right to consideration regardless of whether payment has been received. Revenue cannot be considered to be earned until the manufacturing process is complete, including the finishing, and the goods have been delivered (if not bill and hold) and all risks and rewards have been transferred.

Example – Payment in advance

A distiller has obtained a contract to supply whisky at a later date for which the purchaser has made part payment at the time the contract was signed. The contract is for the sale of 600,000 gallons, but the distiller only has a stock of 200,000 gallons. The contract contains specific instructions with regard to the timing and location of the delivery.

For the 400,000 gallons that are not in stock, there can be no recognition of a sale; revenue cannot be recognised when there is merely an intention to acquire goods in time for delivery. The 200,000 gallons that are in stock may fall under the provisions outlined in paragraphs 9.65 to 9.72 above with regard to 'bill and hold' sales, in which delivery is delayed at the buyer's request, but the buyer takes title and accepts billing.

9.74 When an event such as an exhibition, conference or course is held at a particular time, income and costs may be received and incurred in advance. Such events may involve delegates paying in advance of attending and certain of the costs, such as advertising, may also be incurred in advance. Since performance does not occur and revenue is thus not earned until the exhibition is held or the course is given, the payments in advance represent a liability, which can be released to the profit and loss account when the event takes place. A stringent review of the costs incurred before the event is necessary because such costs should only be carried forward if they are directly related costs and they qualify for recognition as an asset under FRS 5.

Goods despatched subject to conditions (sale or return; consignment)

9.75 Some contracts may give the customer the right to return goods that they have purchased and obtain a refund or release from the obligation to pay. [FRS 5 App G para G49]. This occurs more often than in the obvious example where goods are held by a customer on a sale or return basis. For example, retailers often have a policy of giving refunds on returned goods, whether or not the goods are defective, provided only that the goods (for example, clothes) have not been used. Rights of return can be explicit or implicit in contractual arrangements and can also arise through statutory requirements. [FRS 5 App G para G50].

9.76 Application note G provides an analysis to determine the effect of rights of return on the recognition by a seller of changes in its assets and liabilities and turnover. It notes that rights of return in a contractual arrangement may affect the quantification of the seller's right to consideration compared to an arrangement that does not include any rights of return, but which is otherwise identical. The existence of rights of return may also affect the timing of revenue recognition. The reason for this is that the right of return imposes an obligation on the seller to transfer economic benefits to the customer should the customer return the item. Such a transfer of economic resources would normally be in the form of a refund or credit note. In some cases, the existence of the right of return would oblige the seller to defer recognition of the sales transaction for as long as the seller retains substantially all the risks associated with the goods. [FRS 5 App G paras G51, G52].

9.77 The sales transaction and the right of return that creates an obligation to transfer economic benefits to the customer in the event that the goods are returned are linked transactions. The seller should, therefore, account for changes in its assets and liabilities and turnover so as to reflect both the sale and any loss expected to arise from the rights of return. Thus, turnover should exclude the sales value of expected returns. [FRS 5 App G para G53].

9.78 A seller will normally be able to estimate reliably the sales value of returns. In doing so, it should consider the risk that returns will be made, which will in normal situations be less, and probably considerably less, than the seller's maximum potential obligation. The estimates of the risk of returns may be derived from the seller's historical experience of the amount of similar goods that have been returned in the past as a proportion of total sales of the product that have been made on a sale or return basis. [FRS 5 App G para G54].

9.79 Where the seller is unable to estimate reliably the sales value of future returns, it should calculate the maximum possible amount that it could be required to repay to the customer, in accordance with its contractual arrangement. This amount should then be excluded from turnover. [FRS 5 App G para G55]. To the extent that cash or other consideration has been received from the customer, a liability would be recorded up to the maximum amount that could be refundable. Conceivably, the maximum possible amount could be the whole, or substantially all, of the consideration for the original sale and, hence, the seller would have retained substantially all the risks associated with the goods.

9.80 Where the risk of return is so significant that the seller retains substantially all of the risks associated with the goods, the seller would not be able to recognise changes in its assets and liabilities or turnover, because it would not have earned the right to consideration. Hence, the seller should retain the goods on its balance sheet and recognise any amounts received from the customer as payments in advance (that is, as a liability). [FRS 5 App G para G56].

9.81 The application note sets out the appropriate accounting treatment. It states that:

- A seller should record changes in its assets and liabilities and turnover to the extent that its performance has earned it the right to consideration, taking account of the expected loss from returns. The amount of turnover recognised should exclude the sales value of expected returns.

- At each reporting date, the seller should re-estimate the amount of expected returns, taking account of changes in expectations and the expiry of rights of return. Adjustments to the estimate of returns should be recorded as revenue.

- Where a seller has been unable to recognise changes in its assets and liabilities and turnover, because substantially all the risks associated with the goods have not been transferred to the customer, the seller should recognise such changes and turnover on the earlier of:

  - The date when it is able to estimate reliably the level of returns.
  - The date when the right of return expires or is given up.

[FRS 5 App G paras G57 to G59].

9.82 In relation to rights of return, a contrast may be drawn between the example of a clothing retailer, which would expect customers to exercise the option to return clothing only in a minority of cases, and a wine merchant, which might supply glasses for functions, but expect the majority of the glasses to be returned with only those that are broken or lost resulting in actual sales.

9.83 In the former case, based on the analysis above, the most appropriate treatment would be to recognise revenue less an appropriate allowance for returns, whereas in the second case it would be more appropriate not to recognise revenue until the right of return expires (by which time most of the glasses would be returned with the result that little revenue is recognised).

Example – Sales with a right of return

A clothing retailer sells T-shirts. Customers have the right to return T-shirts within 28 days of purchase, provided that the T-shirts are unworn and undamaged. Based on past experience, the retailer is able to reliably estimate the level of T-shirts that will be returned.

Because the retailer can reliably measure the level of returns, revenue can be recognised when the sale is made, adjusted for the expected level of returns. Thus, for each T-shirt sold, an element of the consideration will be recognised as revenue, with the remaining element of the consideration being recognised as a provision. It would also be appropriate to adjust cost of sales recognised on each sale to reflect the impact of returned goods with the reduction in stock partially offsetting the provision for returns. This adjustment reflects the impact of the returned goods in measuring the provision in accordance with FRS 12, 'Provisions, contingent liabilities and assets'.

9.84 Table 9.2 illustrates a policy for returns in respect of book sales.

Table 9.2 – Pearson plc – Annual Report– 31 December 2004

Accounting policies (extract)

d. Sales (extract)

Sales represent the amount of goods and services, net of value added tax and other sales taxes, and excluding trade discounts and anticipated returns, provided to external customers and associates. Revenue from the sale of books is recognised when title passes. Anticipated returns are based primarily on historical return rates.

9.85 Consignment sales or items despatched on a sale or return basis are also covered by the principle of ensuring that performance must have taken place and the right to consideration obtained, before recognising revenue. In order to recognise revenue and derecognise the stock, the seller must have transferred the significant benefits and risks of the stock. The principal benefits and risks of the stock and the relevant considerations are explained in detail in Application Note A to FRS 5, while paragraphs G49-G59 of Application Note G provides further revenue guidance on the subject of sales with rights of return.

Example – Consignment sales

A company imports sports clothing and has a number of distributors. It gives its distributors an extended credit deal whereby it supplies new fashion items to each distributor for sale to third parties in order to encourage a market in these new items. The distributor does not have to pay for the goods until the goods have been sold to a third party. If they are not sold within six months of receipt, the distributor can either return them to the company or pay for them and keep them. The price the distributor pays for the goods is the importer's list price on the date of onward sale, or the date 6 months after transfer if the distributor decides to purchase them.

Revenue should not be recognised by the importing company until the earlier of the distributor receiving payment for the sale of the goods to a third party or 6 months after the distributor receives them, provided that they are not returned. It is only at this point that the importer has transferred the significant benefits and risks of the stock. The significant benefits and risks have not transferred before this time for the following reasons:

(a) the distributor has the right to return the goods without payment of a penalty and, therefore, does not bear obsolescence risk; and

(b) the importer retains the right to change the sale price right up to the date that the distributor has to pay for the goods and, therefore, the importer retains the benefits and risks associated with changing market prices.

Continuing managerial involvement

9.86 Application note G does not specifically consider the concept of continuing management involvement, however, the definition of an asset in the ASB's Statement of principles is *"rights or other access to future economic benefits controlled by an entity as a result of past transactions or events"*. [Statement of principles para 4.6]. It, therefore, follows that if an entity retains significant control over the asset, the transaction is not a sale and revenue is not recognised. This is similar to the guidance in IAS 18, which lists *"continuing managerial involvement to the degree usually associated with ownership or retention of control"* as one of the criteria to be considered in determining whether revenue should be recognised. [IAS 18 para 14].

9.87 Continued managerial involvement to the degree usually associated with ownership is less straightforward than control, but it is highly unlikely that an entity would retain such involvement without retaining also the asset's economic benefits. Nor is it likely that a buyer would allow such involvement if it had given fair consideration for the asset. Therefore, commercially, continuing involvement to the degree envisaged should not normally occur if a genuine sale has taken place. If it does, it is likely that there are other features of the arrangement that would need to be considered.

9.88 Examples in which a seller has retained continuing managerial involvement or effective control include:

- The seller can control the future onward sale price of the item.
- The seller is responsible for the management of the goods subsequent to the sale (outside of any other separable contract for management services).
- The economics of the transaction make it likely that the buyer will return the goods to the seller.
- The seller guarantees the return of the buyer's investment or a return on that investment for a limited or extended period.
- The transaction's substance is merely an option to purchase the item.

Example – Ongoing involvement

Entity A sold a racehorse to entity B, but continued to house and train the horse, determine which races to enter and set stud fees for the horse. Should entity A recognise revenue on the sale of the horse to entity B?

If a proper training agreement was in place that provided a commercial fee for the services entity A provides and any winnings or fees achieved by the horse going to the buyer, it may be appropriate to recognise revenue on the sale. However, it would also be necessary to consider whether entity A had given any guarantees or incurred other obligations that would indicate it had not disposed of the significant risks and rewards of ownership of the horse.

Significant risks and rewards

9.89 As indicated in the example above, if the significant risks and rewards associated with an asset have not been transferred from the seller to the customer, this may indicate that a sale has not occurred.

9.89.1 In some situations, the timing of transfer of the risks and rewards of ownership can be affected if the vendor enters into insurance arrangements during delivery. This will impact when revenue is recognised as is illustrated by the following example.

Example – Goods insured during delivery

Company A manufactures and sells transformers. The transformers are shipped to the buyer by sea, but in order to transfer risk related to the shipment of the transformers, company A purchases insurance coverage for the goods while they are in transit from the factory to the buyer's premises. The insurance policy reimburses the seller for the full market value of the goods in the event of loss or damage from the point when the goods depart from the factory to the point when the goods arrive at the buyer's premises. The legal title passes when the goods arrive at the buyer's premises one month later.

The seller should recognise revenue for the sale when the goods arrive at the buyer's premises. At the point when the goods depart from the factory, the seller has not transferred the transformers' significant risks and rewards of ownership to the buyer as evidenced by the fact that any insurance proceeds received from the goods' damage or destruction will be repaid to the seller. Also, legal title does not pass until the goods arrive at the buyer's location.

9.89.2 If, however, an entity retains only insignificant risks and rewards of ownership, a sale has occurred and revenue is recognised. In some situations, a seller may retain legal title solely to protect the collectability of the amount due. In fact, retention of legal title is no guarantee of collectability and the retention of title in such circumstances is normally only to ensure that the seller has a claim in the – usually unlikely – event that the buyer becomes insolvent. Where such a clause has been inserted in a contract this does not normally affect revenue recognition by the seller as the significant risks and rewards of ownership have been transferred to the buyer.

Example – Retention of legal title

Company A operates in a country where it is commonplace to retain title to goods sold as protection against non-payment by a buyer. The retention of the title will enable company A to recover the goods if the buyer defaults on payment.

Subsequent to the delivery of the goods to the buyer (company B), company A does not have any control over the goods. Company B makes payments in accordance with the normal credit terms provided by company A. Product liability is assumed by company B. Settlement is due 14 days after delivery.

Company A has sold the goods to company B. The buyer controls the goods following the delivery and is free to use or dispose of them as it wishes. The most significant risk of ownership, the product risk, has been transferred to company B. Company A's retention of legal title does not affect the substance of the transaction, which is the sale of goods from company A to company B. Company A should, therefore, derecognise the inventory and recognise the revenue from the sale.

9.89.3 Other potential indicators that the risks and rewards of ownership have not passed are:

- The seller retains the risk of physical damage to the product.
- The buyer lacks economic substance apart from that provided by the seller.
- There is significant doubt as to the buyer's intention or ability to take delivery of goods.
- The seller shares in the future revenue of the goods' onward sale.
- The seller has a repurchase option at a fixed price.

9.89.4 The inclusion of any of the above conditions in a sale agreement may indicate that the risks and rewards of ownership have not passed and, hence, preclude revenue recognition.

Warranties

Initial warranty

9.90 A warranty is often provided in conjunction with the sale of goods. Warranties represent guarantees made by the seller that a product will perform as specified for a period of time. Warranties should not be confused with general rights of return. A warranty only permits a customer to return or exchange a product if the product does not meet the specified performance criteria. Warranty costs represent additional costs that the seller may have to incur in relation to the product it has sold.

9.91 When a company sells a product subject to warranty, it must first determine whether the warranty represents a separable component of the transaction. (Multiple element arrangements are considered further from para 9.145.) When a warranty is not a separate element, the seller has completed substantially all the required performance and can recognise the full consideration received as revenue, on the sale of the product. The expected future costs to be incurred related to the warranty should not be recorded as a reduction of revenue but rather should be recorded as a cost of sale, as the warranty does not represent a return of a portion of the sales price. The costs of warranties should be determined at the time of the sale, and a corresponding provision for warranty costs recognised. Warranties and similar costs can normally be measured reliably because entities have historical evidence of the costs associated with various products.

Example – Sale with a standard warranty

A manufacturer of televisions sells them to retailers for £300 with a one year manufacturer's warranty. The manufacturer does not sell the televisions without this warranty, nor does any manufacturer of a similar product. The manufacturer expects claims to be made on one in every 100 televisions sold, with repairs costing an average of £100.

The warranty is not separable from the sale of the television. As a result, the revenue recognition criteria must be applied to the transaction as a whole. On making the sale to the retailer, the manufacturer has completed substantially all of its required performance, retaining only an insignificant interest in the risks of holding the stock. Thus, on the sale of the television the manufacturer should recognise revenue of £300 and make a provision of £1 against cost of sales for the expected cost of repair.

Extended warranty

9.92 An extended warranty is an agreement to provide warranty protection in addition to the scope of coverage of a manufacturer's original warranty, or to extend the period of coverage provided by the manufacturer's warranty. They are often sold separately from the original product but, where warranties included in the price of a product provide protection in excess of that provided by the normal terms and conditions of sale for the relevant product, the transaction's substance is that the entity has sold two products. This might be the case if similar warranties are sold separately by the entity or by competitors of the entity, or if the customer is able to purchase the same product with no equivalent warranty. See further from paragraph 9.145.

9.93 If a company sells an extended warranty, the revenue from the sale of the extended warranty should be deferred and recognised over the period covered by the warranty, as an extended warranty is similar in nature to a short-duration insurance contract. No costs should be accrued at the inception of the extended warranty agreement.

Example 1 – Extended warranty sold separately

Company A sells electrical goods. The goods come with a manufacturer's 1 year warranty. Company A also offers customers the option of purchasing an extended warranty to cover years 2 to 5.

The sales price of the extended warranty is £100 and company A typically receives valid warranty claims from 4% of customers during the extended warranty period. The average cost of repairing or replacing the goods under the warranty is £600 per valid claim.

As this is an extended warranty, management should defer the revenue and recognise it on a straight-line basis over years 2 to 5, which is the period over which the extended warranty is provided.

The costs incurred under the warranty should be charged to cost of sales as incurred and management should not recognise a provision for the expected costs of the warranty, but should monitor the arrangements to ensure that the expected future cost of the warranty does not exceed the amount of unamortised deferred revenue. The warranty contract will be onerous if, at any time, the expected future costs of meeting the warranty obligations exceed the unamortised warranty revenue. Management should recognise a provision to the extent that the future warranty costs are estimated to exceed the unamortised warranty revenue (see chapter 21).

Example 2 – Extended warranties sold as part of a package

X plc is a retailer of domestic appliances and sells washing machines. Each of a particular model of washing machine is sold with a one-year initial warranty and a three-year extended warranty at no extra cost to the customer. X plc sells this washing machine for £399 in its stores, while its competitor, Y plc, sells an identical washing machine with the initial warranty but without an extended warranty for £379 and an unrelated insurer offers an equivalent extended warranty for £60.

How should X plc account for its income from the sale of the washing machine, the initial warranty and the extended warranty?

Assuming that the initial one-year warranty cannot be separated (as the circumstances are similar to those discussed above), the substance of this transaction is that X plc has sold two products: the washing machine (inclusive of initial warranty) and the extended warranty. Where two or more components of a contractual arrangement operate independently from each other, they should be 'unbundled' and the revenue earned on the sale of each product recognised separately in accordance with the principles of Application note G. See further from paragraph 9.145.

X plc will need to attribute a fair value to each component of the bundle. Where the bundle of goods is sold at less than the aggregate of the fair values of each component, the discount should be allocated to the components on a reasonable basis.

For X plc, the relative fair value of the washing machine is £344 (being £399 x £379/ (£379 + £60)). It will be appropriate to recognise this revenue because X plc has fulfilled its contractual performance obligation relating to the supply of the washing machine in full.

The calculated fair value of the extended warranty is £55. This should be recognised over the three years over which it is earned by X plc.

Installation fees and conditions

9.94 Application note G requires that *"A seller recognises revenue under an arrangement with a customer, when and to the extent that, it obtains the right to consideration in exchange for its performance"*. [FRS 5 App G para G4]. Consideration received for the sale of a product may include amounts attributable to the product's installation. Where installation is incidental to the product's sale, installation fees are recognised when the goods are sold as the entity's remaining performance obligations are negligible. If installation is not incidental to the product's sale, and represents a separate component of the transaction (see further from para 9.145), the installation fees should be recognised as performance occurs. This applies the same principles as are applied to accounting for warranties.

9.95 Determining whether installation is incidental to the sale of a product or not is often difficult. In the case of a telephone line, for example, it can be argued that the installation is usually straightforward.

9.96 Where installation is more complicated, for example, in a contract to supply a computer system, the contract may be broken down into separate components one of which would be the installation. However, this approach would only be possible where a reliable fair value could be ascertained for the installation component (see para 9.145 onwards for further consideration of multiple element transactions).

Shipping and handling charges

9.97 Where a company sells items either FOB (free on board) or CIF (cost, insurance, freight), this may affect the timing of revenue recognition. If the seller is responsible for carriage, insurance and freight until the goods are delivered, these form part of the company's performance and result in retention of the risks and rewards of the item sold until delivery to the client site has occurred. As a result, the timing of revenue recognition will be different depending upon the terms of

Application note G of FRS 5 requires that revenue should be recognised when performance has occurred and a right to consideration is obtained. It further requires that revenue is recognised at fair value and that where at the time revenue is recognised there is a significant risk of default, on the amount of consideration due, an adjustment is made to the reported revenue.

The fact that there is a delay in completion may mean that there is an increased risk of default. In determining the amount of revenue that should be reported, risk factors such as the financial standing of the developer, the likelihood that it will still be in existence in two years time and whether there are any financial guarantees in place should be considered. If the company believes that the risk of default is not significant, it is appropriate to recognise the revenue, discounted for the time value of money if this is considered material. Alternatively, the decision may be reached that the risk of default is so great that in substance no sale has yet taken place and that revenue should only be recognised on completion when the cash is received.

9.102 Property is often sold subject to planning consent being obtained. In these situations, the vendor may be involved in obtaining the required planning consent and may incur costs in submitting planning applications and attending planning hearings. Obtaining the required planning permission is a material contract condition. Therefore, even if the vendor has performed all the tasks necessary to obtain consent before the year end, the sale cannot be recognised until the condition is satisfied and the consent has been granted. If such consent is received after the year end, then the sale should be recognised in the following year when the material condition is fulfilled.

9.103 Therefore, revenue should only be recognised on sales of property in a year if a binding and unconditional contract has been entered into before the year end or if the last material condition on a conditional contract has been satisfied before the year end. If the contract is entered into after the year end or if a condition is only fulfilled after the year end, then that sale represents the next year's revenue since it is only in the following year that it has been earned.

9.104 Many companies do not take credit for sales, commonly of private houses, until legal completion has taken place, as is illustrated in Table 9.4. This policy is, therefore, more conservative than recognising revenue on the exchange of unconditional contracts. The property industry has historically taken a more prudent approach to the sale of homes to individual buyers. However, the choice of either of these methods will usually depend on the circumstances of the sale.

Table 9.4 – Tarmac PLC – Annual Report – 31 December 2000

Principal Accounting Policies (extract)

Turnover

Turnover represents the net amount receivable, excluding value added tax, for goods and services supplied to external customers and, in respect of long term contracting activities, the value of work executed during the year. Sales of newly constructed private houses are included in turnover on legal completion.

9.105 Some property companies enter into transactions in which they build properties for particular customers (following the customer's detailed plans) rather than building speculative developments. The properties built may be effectively pre-sold so that the contract has been entered into before construction begins and all the terms and conditions of the sale are known. In such situations, the transaction may be a long-term contract which should be accounted for in accordance with SSAP 9, with profit being recognised according to the percentage of completion of the development, provided that the outcome can be assessed with reasonable certainty. However, selling 'off plan' does not mean it needs to be accounted for under SSAP 9. The accounting policy of Slough Estates plc in Table 9.5 is an example of pre-sold properties being accounted for as long-term contracts.

Table 9.5 – Slough Estates plc – Annual Report – 31 December 2001

ACCOUNTING POLICIES (extract)

Trading properties

Unless pre-sold, properties are held at the lower of cost, including finance costs, and market value. Pre-sold properties are stated at cost plus attributable profits less losses, where the outcome can be assessed with reasonable certainty, less progress payments receivable. Attributable profit consists of the relevant proportion of the total estimated profit appropriate to the progress made in construction and letting. Cost includes direct expenditure and interest, less any relevant income.

Sale of software

9.106 In the software industry, revenue recognition poses a number of problems which combine elements of sale of goods and sale of services. Software houses normally earn their revenue from three principal sources:

- Sale of off-the-shelf or ready made software where the licensing arrangement gives the customer the right to use the software for a specified period.
- Sale of customised software developed for specific application by the customer.
- Sale of software support services related to either own software or customised software.

9.107 Selling software is different from selling a tangible product, since the product being sold is the right to use a piece of intellectual property, rather than the actual computer disk or other media on which the programme is held. The physical delivery of the product in the form of the computer disk may, therefore, appear to be less important than it is where other types of goods are sold. If there is any risk that the customer may reject the software and the product is sold subject to customer satisfaction, then revenue recognition may need to be delayed until after delivery and acceptance by the customer. For example, an off-the-shelf package may require tailoring to meet the customer's specifications. In this situation, if the supply does not qualify as a long-term contract, revenue may not be earned until after delivery, set up and the subsequent testing of the software by the customer.

9.108 The sale of a completely standard package such as a word processing or spreadsheet package may, therefore, need to be treated differently from software that needs to be individually tailored for each customer. Companies that sell standard off-the-shelf packages generally treat their sales no differently than the sale of a physical product and recognise revenue on delivery. For example, Merant's accounting policy adopts this approach (see Table 9.6).

Table 9.6 – Merant plc – Annual Report – 30 April 2002

NOTES TO THE FINANCIAL STATEMENTS (extract)

Licence fees: the Company's standard end user licence agreement for the Company's products provides for an initial fee to use the product in perpetuity up to a maximum number of users. The Company also enters into other types of licence agreement, typically with major end user customers, which allow for the use of the Company's products, usually restricted by the number of employees, the number of users, or the licence term. Licence fees are recognised as revenue upon product shipment, provided a signed agreement is in place, fees are fixed or determinable, no significant vendor obligations remain and collection of the resulting debt is deemed probable. Fees from licences sold together with consulting services are generally recognised upon shipment provided that the above criteria have been met and payment of the licence fees is not dependent upon the performance of the consulting services. Where these criteria have not been met, both the licence and consulting fees are recognised under the percentage of completion method of contract accounting.

Maintenance subscriptions: maintenance agreements generally call for the Company to provide technical support and software updates to customers. Revenue on technical support and software update rights is recognised over the term of the support agreement on a pro-rata basis. Payments for maintenance fees are generally made in advance and are non refundable
Training and consulting: the Company recognises revenues from consulting and education as the services are performed.

9.109 Where a product is sold subject to continuing obligations under the agreement or the provision of updates free of charge, it will be necessary to determine whether the contract can be broken down into separable components. If it can, revenue will be recognised as the separable components are performed – see discussion on multiple element transactions from paragraph 9.145. Where the product's acceptance is in doubt, revenue should be delayed until acceptance.

Example – Software subject to acceptance

A company sells software packages that may be modified to meet the customer's exact requirements. The sequence of the transaction is: order; invoice and delivery; and acceptance by the customer. The order, invoice and delivery may be before the year end, but the acceptance may be after the year end.

Where acceptance is subject to installation and inspection the following principles may be relevant. If the installation process is simple in nature – for example, requiring unpacking and connecting only – then it is acceptable to recognise revenue immediately upon delivery. In general, however, where the installation process is more substantial, recognition should be delayed until the installation and inspection processes are complete and customer acceptance has occurred. For many types of software packages, it is acceptable to recognise revenue when delivery has taken place by the year end. However, when there is a risk that the customer may not accept the package, sufficient evidence must be obtained of the acceptance before revenue can be recognised.

9.110 The creation of software specifically developed for use by a customer usually meets the definition of a long-term contract in SSAP 9 and revenue should normally be recognised in accordance with the principles outlined in that standard. Consequently, the software house should recognise revenue in a manner appropriate to the contract's stage of completion, provided that the outcome can be assessed with reasonable certainty. The requirements of SSAP 9 are discussed in detail in chapter 20.

9.111 The procedure to recognise profit is to include an appropriate proportion of total contract value as turnover in the profit and loss account as the contract activity progresses. The costs incurred in reaching that stage of completion should be matched with this turnover, resulting in the reporting of results that can be attributed to the proportion of work completed. Where, however, the outcome cannot be assessed with reasonable certainty before the contract's conclusion, or where the contract is of a relatively short duration, the completed contracts method should be applied and, accordingly, revenue should be recognised when final completion takes place. Table 9.7 gives an example of accounting policies in this area.

Table 9.7 – MISYS plc – Annual Report – 31 May 2005

Accounting Policies (extract)

REVENUE RECOGNITION

Turnover represents amounts invoiced to customers for goods and services, net of sales taxes.

Revenue on certain larger composite contracts is recognised on a percentage of completion basis over the period from delivery of the product to customer acceptance. The degree of completion of a contract is measured using the costs incurred to date or milestones reached, depending upon the nature of the individual contract and the most appropriate measure of the percentage of completion. Losses on contracts are recognised as soon as a loss is foreseen by reference to the estimated costs of completion.

For all other contracts, revenue from system sales is recognised when a signed contract exists, delivery to a customer has occurred with no significant vendor obligations remaining and where the collection of the resulting receivable is considered probable. In instances where a significant vendor obligation exists, revenue recognition is delayed until the obligation has been satisfied. No revenue is recognised for multiple deliveries or multiple element products if an element of the contract remains undelivered and is essential to the functionality of the elements already delivered.

Maintenance fees are recognised rateably over the period of the contract. EDI and remote processing services (transaction processing) are recognised as the services are performed.

Revenue from professional services, such as implementation, training and consultancy, is recognised as the services are performed.

Within Sesame, commission revenue received from insurers based on gross premiums written is presented gross of commission payable to Independent Financial Advisers (IFAs) and is recognised when earned. Annual fees received from certain IFAs for industry training, compliance support and access to the Misys network's listing of insurance providers and products are recognised over the relevant subscription period.

9.112 When the project involves the provision of hardware as well as software, the contract will need to be carefully reviewed to ensure that income is not recognised before it is earned, that is, before performance has occurred and a right to consideration obtained.

Example – Sale of hardware and software

A company is developing a computer system for a customer. It has sold the hardware to the customer for a profit and this has been installed on the site where it will be eventually used, but the company is still working on developing the necessary software. The customer has the right to return the hardware if the software does not work. The company does not anticipate any problems with the software development which should take 12 months.

In this case, the two components of the contract do not operate independently of one another. Therefore, it seems that there is one contract for the supply of both hardware and software. If this is the case then the treatment in SSAP 9 should be followed. The contract is a long-term contract, revenue and profit would be recognised as the contract progresses, provided that the outcome can be assessed with reasonable certainty. The extent of profit recognition will depend on the degree of certainty over the contract's outcome rather than the margin on the hardware in isolation. If the outcome of the project or the costs of creating software of the required standard cannot be assessed with reasonable certainty, then no profit should be reflected in the profit and loss account.

Even if the contract for the supply of the hardware could be separated from the supply of the software as the two transactions operated independently there would still be an argument for delaying recognition of the sale of the hardware. If there is uncertainty about the possibility of return, revenue should only be recognised when the goods have been formally accepted by the customer or the goods have been delivered and the time allowed for their possible rejection has passed. Therefore, until the software has been installed and tested to the customer's satisfaction, revenue should not be recognised and any payments received for the hardware should be included in the financial statements as a liability.

9.113 Where a software house provides maintenance services or other after sales support it is necessary to determine if this can be regarded as a separable component. If it can, (see from para 9.145) then revenue under the separable component method is recognised as performance occurs. For example, maintenance revenue will be recognised as the service is provided. See Table 9.9.

Table 9.9 – Total Systems plc – Annual Report & Accounts – 31 March 2005
Accounting Policies (extract)

Software maintenance (extract)

For own software covered by maintenance contracts, income is credited to the profit and loss account over the period to which the contract relates. Costs associated with these contracts are expensed as incurred.

9.114 FRS 5 Application note G includes guidance on separation and linking of contractual arrangements (see from para 9.145) and illustrates the guidance with two examples relating to sales of software and related maintenance services. In the first example a customer purchases 'off the shelf' software from a seller who also offers a support service comprising helpline assistance and advice about the operation of the software package. Analysis of the arrangement shows that the customer has no obligation to purchase the support service and that the support service is not needed to enable the software to operate satisfactorily. In this case, there are two components of the contract and the seller should recognise turnover separately for each. [FRS 5 App G para G33]. The example is simplistic and should also consider two important criteria: (i) the seller must be able to determine fair values for each component; and (ii) the two components should operate independently of each other. For the meaning of 'operate independently', see paragraph 9.147.

9.115 The second example in the application note concerns the sale and maintenance of bespoke software and the customer's right to future upgrades for a period of three years. Analysis of the arrangement shows that the maintenance and upgrades are required to ensure that the software continues to operate satisfactorily throughout the three year period. These upgrade and maintenance services are offered only by the seller of the (bespoke) software. The application note concludes that the commercial substance is that the customer is paying for a three year service agreement and that the seller should treat all three components of the transaction (software, upgrades and maintenance) as linked and recognise turnover on a long-term contract basis. [FRS 5 App G para 34]. This conclusion was reached because the components do not operate independently of one another (that is, they cannot be sold separately and none of the components is available from another supplier) and fair values are not available for the individual components. It is key that this transaction involved the sale of 'bespoke' software. In other situations, the sale of ancillary services (and particularly maintenance) would normally be available for sale separately and/or as optional extras from the same or other suppliers.

Sale of services

Performance over time

Accounting for incomplete contractual performance

9.116 Full performance, that is fulfilment of contractual obligations, may not always occur immediately. Two examples where performance is not immediate are where performance of a single contract with only one component occurs over a period of time, and where performance of separate components of a contract are completed at different times (see further guidance on multiple element transactions from para 9.145 onwards).

9.117 Where performance of a single contractual obligation takes place over time and the right to consideration is obtained over that period, then revenue should be recognised as performance takes place. For example, under a maintenance contract for 12 months, revenue should be recognised over the 12 months as the service is provided over that period. It is not acceptable to record all the revenue upfront and provide for the costs expected to be incurred in providing the services, this is because to do so would be to recognise revenue before the seller had performed any part of the contract and before the seller has obtained the right to consideration.

9.118 Application note G of FRS 5 deals specifically with revenue recognition in relation to long-term contractual performance. It notes particularly that the seller should recognise changes in its assets and liabilities, and turnover, in accordance with the stage of completion of its contractual obligations, which reflects the extent to which it has obtained the rights to consideration. [FRS 5 App G para G6].

9.119 Following controversy surrounding the interpretation of Application note G, the UITF issued Abstract 40, 'Revenue recognition and service contracts'. UITF Abstract 40 applies to all contracts for services.

9.120 The Abstract concludes that:

- Where a contract is for the provision of a single service or a number of services that constitute one project and the performance of that service or those services falls into more than one accounting period, the contract should be accounted for as a long-term contract in accordance with SSAP 9. [UITF 40 paras 24, 25].
- Where a contract is not a long-term contract, but the seller's contractual obligations are performed over time, revenue should be recognised as the contract progresses to reflect the seller's partial performance. The amount of revenue recognised should reflect the seller's right to consideration by reference to the value of the work performed. [UITF 40 para 26].
- Where the right to consideration does not arise until the occurrence of a critical event (a trigger event), the revenue should be recognised when that trigger event occurs. [UITF 40 para 27].

9.120.1 The principles of UITF 40 are illustrated in the following example.

Example – Professional services

Mr A is an accountant who is half way through completing his client's tax return at the end of June (Mr A's year end). The client has agreed to pay Mr A £500 for the completion of the return. The contract specifies that Mr A has the right to receive payment for any work performed and should be paid for services rendered even if the contract is broken before completion. On the basis of this, Mr A has accounted for £250 of the revenue.

> In this case, the criteria for revenue recognition will be met over the period that Mr A works on his client's tax return. Although it might seem that a half-completed tax return is of little practical use to the client by agreeing to those terms, the client has agreed that Mr A is performing under the contract as he completes his work. On this basis, the revenue would be recognised by reference to the Mr A's partial performance and right to consideration and, as such, it would be appropriate to recognise £250 of the revenue at the end of June.
>
> If the contract specified that Mr A had no right to receive payment until the tax return was completed and accepted by the relevant authorities, revenue recognition would be postponed until that had occurred. This is because, under the agreed contractual terms, Mr A has no right to consideration under the contract until this significant act is fulfilled. As such, the criteria for revenue recognition are not met until this point.

9.121 Although Application note G considers accounting for long-term contracts, it does not change SSAP 9, but does suggest an important and overriding principle in how that standard is applied. Prior to the issue of Application note G the 'costs incurred as a proportion of total costs' method of determining the stage of completion was probably the most common method in use. The application note does not prevent use of this method, but it points out that this method will not always be appropriate. The application note states that the amount of turnover should be derived from the proportion of costs incurred only where these provide evidence of the seller's performance and hence of the extent to which it has obtained the right to consideration. [FRS 5 App G para G21]. To use the proportion of costs incurred as a basis for recognising turnover requires the seller to be able to demonstrate that costs incurred provide reliable evidence of performance of the contract terms and the right to consideration.

9.122 SSAP 9, 'Stocks and long-term contracts', contains principles for the recognition of revenues and costs on long-term contracts. These principles and the guidance in the application note that relates to long-term contracts are more fully described and discussed in chapter 20.

9.123 Where revenue from a contract is spread evenly over the period of a contract, because the service is provided evenly over that period, there is sometimes a problem if the up-front costs of securing the contract are written off as they are incurred. This is because the recognition of such costs may mean that the contract is loss making in the early stages and profitable later.

9.124 Because the approach in the Statement of principles, FRS 18 and Application note G to FRS 5 on revenue recognition is to apply the 'assets and liabilities' approach, it is not acceptable either to advance revenue recognition or to defer expense recognition (unless they meet the definition of an asset). The requirement in the application note that the right to consideration must be obtained before revenue may be recognised clarifies this, because such rights would not normally be obtained from incurring such up-front costs. Revenue should, therefore, not be advanced, but should be spread evenly if the service is performed and rights to consideration are obtained on that basis. Instead of advancing revenue it is necessary to look at whether any of the up-front costs would qualify for recognition as an asset, so that they could be carried forward and expensed as the future economic benefits that relate to that asset are recognised (as revenue).

9.125 The most common assets recognised as a result of expenditure in the early stages of a contract are stocks and tangible fixed assets. The criteria for recognition of such assets are considered in chapters 20 and 16 respectively.

9.126 In addition, Private Finance Initiative (PFI) contracts may raise specific issues and problems relating to asset recognition and, to some extent, revenue recognition. Accounting for PFI contracts is dealt with in chapter 3.

Determining the stage of completion of performance

9.127 SSAP 9 requires that turnover should be ascertained in a manner appropriate to the contract's stage of completion, the business and the industry in which it operates. [SSAP 9 para 28]. Paragraph 18 of UITF 40 applies this same principle to other contracts for services. It suggests that in some circumstances it might be appropriate to recognise revenue based on time spent, or on some other basis to reflect the fair value of work performed as a proportion of the total work contracted. With regard to recognising revenue based on the stage of completion of performance, IAS 18 is not dissimilar from SSAP 9 and UITF 40 and contains additional guidance that can assist in application of the principle.

9.128 According to IAS 18, the stage of completion of performance may be determined by a variety of ways depending on the nature of the service being provided. If the service consists of an indeterminate number of acts over a specified period of time, for example, the provision of a maintenance contract, then the revenue should be recognised on a straight line basis over the contract's duration, unless there is evidence that another basis more accurately reflects the stage of completion. If, however, one particular act in the contract's performance has a much greater significance than any of the other acts (or a particular act is outside the entity's control), then IAS 18 and UITF 40 are consistent in requiring that the revenue recognition should be postponed until the significant act is completed (see also para 9.58).

9.129 In general, the methods that might be used to determine the stage of completion would include those recommended by IAS 18:

- Surveys of work performed.
- Services performed to date as a percentage of total services to be performed.
- The proportion that costs incurred to date bear to the estimated total costs of the transaction. Only costs that reflect services performed to date are included in costs incurred to date. Only costs that reflect services performed or to be performed are included in the estimated total costs of the transaction.

[IAS 18 para 24].

9.129.1 Application of these methods is considered in the the following example:

Example – Measuring the stage of completion: contact with contingent and non-contingent consideration

A company provides consultation services, for example maintenance, IT support, marketing and general advice to a number of service providers. The service providers bring together buyers and sellers of agricultural produce and earn revenue from this. The company earns a non-refundable flat fee of £8,000 annually, receivable in advance, from each service provider, plus an additional 50 per cent of the revenue that each service provider earns from its transactions above a cumulative £10,000.

As the £8,000 fee is for a service during a year, it should be recognised evenly over the year. The remaining incremental fees should only be recognised as they are earned. This is because until they are earned, there is no guarantee that a further amount will be receivable and the company has no right to consideration. That is, the incremental revenue is only recognised when the service provider has earned revenue in excess of £10,000 and then only to the extent of 50 per cent of the excess over £10,000.

9.130 The application of the 'percentage of completion' basis where the provision of services straddles a year end is considered in the following examples.

Example – Service contract straddles the year end

A company has entered into fixed rate contracts with local authorities to inspect and report on local property values. Valuation reports were completed after the year end.

Since the work has been completed as evidenced by the submission of the valuation reports and since the contracts are fixed rate, it is acceptable to recognise the revenue and profits on the work performed before the year end.

UITF Abstract 40 clarifies that this is a long-term contract that falls to be accounted for in accordance with SSAP 9. UITF Abstract 40 states that a contract for services should be accounted for as a long term contract where contract activity falls into different periods and it is concluded that the aggregate effect is material for all such contracts. [UITF Abstract 40 para 25]. It will, therefore, be appropriate to recognise revenue to the extent to which the contract is completed, provided the outcome can be assessed with reasonable certainty.

On the other hand, if writing and submitting the reports formed the majority of the work required to complete the contracts, then it would be appropriate to delay recognition until the reports were completed.

9.131 Until the outcome of a transaction can be estimated reliably, revenue should only be recognised to the extent of the costs incurred that are expected to be recoverable. If it is not probable that the costs can be recovered, then they should be written off immediately.

[The next paragraph is 9.133.1.]

Contracts containing significant acts

9.133.1 In some contracts, one specific act may be significant. This may be the case even if the contract is not structured such that this significant event triggers the seller's right to consideration. When a contract contains a specific act that is much more significant than any other acts to be performed under the contract, the recognition of revenue is postponed until the significant act is executed. The existence of a specific act that is much more significant than any other act may indicate that the other acts do not substantively advance the transaction's stage of completion.

9.133.2 Examples of contracts containing significant acts are: commissions on the allotment of shares to a client, placement fees for arranging a loan between a borrower and an investor, and loan syndication fees that an entity receives for arranging a loan for which it retains no portion of the loan package for itself.

9.133.3 There are a number of factors that an entity needs to consider to determine whether an arrangement contains a specific act that is much more significant than any other acts. For example, tasks undertaken by a supplier that do not build on one another toward completion of the service, may indicate that there is a single significant act since each act is not integral to providing the service. This may be the case when the service is the bringing together of parties in an arrangement or an agreement, as indicated in the examples described above or, for example, with transactions undertaken by a travel agent or an estate agent. When the service provider determines the level of work performed and controls whether the service is ultimately delivered, this may indicate there is not a single significant act and the service is performed over the contract period.

9.133.4 The timing of cash payments should not, by themselves, determine whether a single act is more significant than any other in an arrangement. However, the terms of an arrangement that involve payment only upon completion of a single act should be assessed to determine whether the deferred payment suggests that one act is more significant than the others. Judgement will be required in many circumstances to determine whether a specific act is much more significant than any others.

Contracts with milestone payments

9.134 Contracts in certain industries, particularly pharmaceutical and biotechnology, are often structured to provide for the payment of cash upon the achievement of certain 'milestones' identified in the contract. Such contracts often relate to research and development of new product offerings and contract terms often include significant up-front payments or payments early on in the contract that in substance represent a form of financing, as opposed to compensation for services provided. Accounting for such contracts can be complex and the appropriate revenue recognition will vary depending on the substance of the arrangements.

9.135 Consideration should be given to a number of factors when determining the appropriate accounting for revenue in a milestone arrangement, including:

- The reasonableness of the payments compared to the effort, time and cost to achieve the milestones. If payments bear no relation to performance under the contracts, then revenue recognition in accordance with the payment profile would not be appropriate.
- The nature of royalty or licence agreements relating to the product being developed. Where a contract includes within it royalty or licence agreements, some of the payments under the contract will often relate to the royalty or licence element in the contract and not to the provision of services and should be accounted for accordingly (see further para 9.255 onwards).
- The existence of any cancellation clauses that require the repayment of amounts received under the contract upon cancellation by either party. Such cancellation clauses may indicate that recognition of amounts received as revenue is not appropriate as the amounts may be linked to future performance or a reduction in the contractual consideration to which the entity is entitled.
- The risks associated with achievement of milestones. If payments are dependent upon the achievement of certain milestones, and there is doubt as regards the achievement of the milestones, then revenue should not be recognised until the relevant milestone has been achieved (see further para 9.133 which deals with accounting for contracts containing significant acts).
- Any obligations that must be completed to receive payment or the existence of penalties for failure to deliver. Again, all obligations under a contract must be considered in assessing the extent to which an entity has performed under a contract. The existence of penalty clauses for failure to deliver may reduce the revenue that can be recognised as performance occurs if delivery is not probable or in the control of the entity.

Factors such as the above will impact the timing and recognition of revenue where milestone payments are included in customer contracts. The certainty and substance of related contract provisions should be carefully analysed to determine when recognition is appropriate.

Example – Milestone payments and measuring the stage of completion

Company A, a small pharmaceutical company, contracts with the much larger company B to develop a new medical treatment for cancer, which is expected to take five years. Company A will periodically have to update company B with the results of its work. Company B has exclusive rights over any development results. Company B will make an up-front payment of £1m on contract signature and five equal annual payments of £500,000 provided company A demonstrates compliance with the development programme. In addition, upon the successful testing of the treatment in clinical trials, company B will pay a further £1.5m. Company A's management estimates the total cost of the contract will be £3m.

Company A incurs costs of £600,000 in year one, in line with its original estimate. Company A is in compliance with the research agreement, including the provision of updates from the results of its work.

How should company A recognise the payments it receives from company B to conduct development?

The contract involves the rendering of pharmaceutical development services. As such, the principles in UITF Abstract 40 should be applied. Company A should recognise the revenue for the payments in accordance with the percentage of completion model, based on an estimate of total costs or on a straight-line basis, whichever provides the most appropriate recognition of revenue. A percentage of completion model based on the estimate of total costs appears to be the most appropriate in the circumstances.

In applying the percentage of completion model, the £1.5m payment upon the successful testing of the treatment in clinical trials will be excluded from any calculation. This is because the payment depends upon a significant act which is not in the control of company A, as successful testing cannot be assured. Until the test has been successful, Company A has no right to the £1.5m of consideration.

In year one, company A has met its obligations, the project is developing in line with the estimates and is forecast to be profitable, so company A should recognise revenue of £700,000 ((1m + 2.5m) ÷ 5) , costs of £600,000 (3m ÷ 5)and profit of £100,000. The consideration received in excess of the revenue recognised of £800,000 (1.5m — 700,000) will be recognised as a liability on company A's balance sheet, representing a liability for future performance.

Inception fees

9.136 Application note G describes inception fees as arising from contractual arrangements that require the payment of a fee at inception that permits the customer to purchase goods or services over a period of time. [FRS 5 App G para G35]. The application note's development section notes that such fees may or may not be refundable. However, the principle concerning when the seller should recognise the inception fee as revenue does not necessarily depend on whether or not it is refundable. Although the fact that a fee is non-refundable may suggest that the seller has no further performance obligations in respect of the fee, in some cases an obligation to provide goods or services may remain. [FRS 5 App G Dev para 39].

9.137 In determining whether or not the fee should be recognised as revenue at inception, it is necessary to determine whether or not the fee and the charges for subsequent goods or services operate independently of each other. [FRS 5 App G para G35]. This involves determining whether the components of the contractual arrangement (that is, the inception fee and the subsequent supply of goods or services) should to be treated as linked or as separable components for the purpose of revenue recognition (see further from para 9.145).

9.138 The application note states that often the inception fee together with the charges for subsequent goods or services will provide the seller's return on the contract as a whole. This may be so where the inception fee's payment entitles the customer to purchase subsequent goods or services at a discount to the prices that would otherwise be payable. Where this is the case, the inception fee is not separable from the subsequent supply of goods and services and should be recognised over the period during which the discounted goods or services are expected to be provided to the customer. The inception fee should be recorded as a liability to the extent that it has not been included in revenue. The liability would then be released to revenue on a systematic basis over the period during which the discounted goods or services are provided. [FRS 5 App G para G36].

9.139 Where, however, it can be demonstrated that the seller has no further obligations in respect of the fee once it has been received, the seller should recognise the fee on the date that it becomes entitled to receive it. The seller may have no further obligations in respect of the fee if the customer has to pay the full commercial price for all future goods or services. [FRS 5 App G para G37].

Subscriptions

9.140 The concept that performance must have occurred and the right to consideration obtained before revenue can be recognised in the profit and loss account is also relevant to other types of sales, where payment is received in advance of supply, such as subscriptions. If the subscription consists of the provision of items of a similar value over its duration, such as a typical magazine subscription, then the income should be recognised over the life of the subscription on a straight line basis. If the items provided vary in value, such as a wine of the month club, then the income should be recognised on the basis of the sales value despatched in relation to the total estimated sales value of all the items covered by the subscription. Table 9.11 illustrates an accounting policy where subscription income is recognised on a straight line basis.

Table 9.11 – Pearson plc – Annual Report – 31 December 2004

Accounting policies (extract)

d. Sales (extract)

Subscription revenue is recognised on a straight-line basis over the life of the subscription.

Admission fees

9.141 Admission fees from, for example, artistic performances, banquets and other special events are recognised when the event takes place. IAS 18 contains specific guidance in relation to such fees and states that when a subscription to a number of events is sold, the fee is allocated to each event on a basis that reflects the extent to which services are performed at each event. [IAS 18 App para 15]. The treatment would be the same applying the principles of Application note G, recognising revenue as performance occurs.

9.142 When an event is held at a particular time, income and costs may be received and incurred in advance. For example, exhibitions, conferences and courses may involve delegates paying in advance of attending and certain costs, such as advertising, may also be incurred in advance. Since performance does not occur and revenue is not earned until the exhibition is held or the course is given, the payments received in advance represent a liability, which can be released to the profit and loss account when the event takes place. A stringent review of the costs incurred before the event is necessary, since such costs should only be carried forward if they directly relate to the event being held and qualify for recognition as an asset.

Tuition fees

9.143 Tuition fees should usually be recognised as revenue over the period of instruction, that is, as performance occurs.

9.144 Whilst this deals with the straightforward situation where a single session of tuition is given over a fixed time period, some instruction courses are structured differently. For example, a course may be structured as a number of modules, each of which having repeated tuition sessions staged at regular intervals, with the student able to choose to attend and complete a module at any time within, say, a two-year period. In such a situation it would be more appropriate to recognise revenue as the modules are attended and completed by the student, that is, as the service is provided to the student.

Multiple element transactions

Separation of components

9.145 In some cases a single contractual arrangement may require a seller to provide a number of different goods or services ('components'). These components may be unrelated and capable of being sold individually. [FRS 5 App G para G22].

9.146 Application note G analyses the circumstances where a seller should (or should not) recognise changes in its assets and liabilities and turnover for each component separately. [FRS 5 App G para G24].

9.147 The application note states that a contractual arrangement with two or more components should be accounted for as two or more separate transactions only where the commercial substance is that the individual components operate independently of one another. In this context, components operate independently where each component represents a separable good or service that the seller also provides to customers on a standalone basis or as an optional extra. Alternatively, components operate independently where one or more component can be provided by another supplier. This separation of components of a contract is known as 'unbundling'. [FRS 5 App G para G25].

9.147.1 When considering the separation of components in a contract, if the vendor sells the different components separately (or has done so in the past), this is a strong indicator that separation is necessary for the purposes of revenue recognition: however, it is not a requirement. For example, even if the entity in question does not sell them separately, it may be that the transaction's components are sold separately by other vendors in the market. In such a situation, separation of the components may still be appropriate.

9.147.2 Certain contracts may include elements that the vendor has no legal obligation to deliver. An example is in the software industry where the contract may specify that the vendor will provide upgrades and enhancements to the customers on a 'when and if available' basis. As the vendor has no obligation to develop upgrades, the question arises as to whether the future upgrades to which the customer may become entitled are a separable component of the contract for the purposes of revenue recognition.

9.147.3 UK GAAP does not define identifiable components of a single transaction. Elements that have no legal obligation to deliver and immaterial costs to execute might not immediately be considered as separate elements. However, management should also consider the value of each element to the customer. The assessment of components and future obligations is a matter of judgement (regardless of whether the obligation is specifically stated in the contract or to some extent implied). If there is a history of delivering upgrades to clients every six months and the customers, therefore, consider the upgrades to have significant value, these upgrades may be regarded as separate elements. In some situations, it may be considered that much of the contract's value lies in the upgrades (for example, if the goods supplied are anti-virus software, which becomes rapidly obsolete if not upgraded regularly). Alternatively, a commitment to supply upgrades 'when and if available' may not be considered a separate element where the seller has not created an expectation in the mind of the purchaser that such upgrades will definitely be forthcoming. This will ultimately be a matter of judgement based upon the facts and circumstances of the specific transaction being considered.

9.147.4 Another situation where the separation of components may not be immediately clear is where goods or services are supplied based on a prepaid amount with a 'ceiling' for the amount that the customer can use within a specified period of time. Examples of such arrangements include the prepayment of monthly fees for mobile phone services (for X minutes per month), gift vouchers sold by a vendor for its services and goods that can be utilised for a specified period of time or take-or-pay arrangements. In such cases, the customer may not end up demanding full performance from the vendor. The question then arises as to when revenue associated with 'undemanded' or 'breakage' services can be recognised.

9.147.5 It could be argued that the revenue associated with the breakage should not be recognised until the possibility of redemption becomes remote or expires. This would be on the basis that, until such a time, the vendor still has an obligation to perform. However, when a reliable, supportable estimate can be made for the expected breakage, revenue recognition can take into account the expected forfeitures prior to the actual expiry date based on when forfeitures are expected to occur. Such a treatment would be dependent on a reliable and evidenced history of breakages. In such a situation, any consideration for the transaction would be allocated amongst the items expected to be redeemed on a consistent basis.

Allocation of consideration

9.148 For unbundling to be possible the seller should normally be able to attribute a fair value to each component by reference to individual transactions, that is, transactions in which the components are sold separately. [FRS 5 App G para G27]. However, in some situations fair value will only be available for some of the components. Where that happens unbundling of the components is still possible and is discussed further below.

9.149 The application note considers this situation in the context of a contract where there are completed and uncompleted components. As explained in paragraph 9.147 above, it must be demonstrated that these components are capable of operating independently if they are to be unbundled. In determining whether or not the contract can be successfully unbundled, the application note states that where a seller cannot attribute fair values to all components it may be possible to unbundle the arrangement where a fair value can be attributed to either the completed or to the uncompleted components. Where a fair value can be obtained only for the uncompleted components, the seller may be able to calculate a fair value for the completed components by deducting from the total consideration the fair value of the uncompleted components. The same applies in reverse where a fair value can only be obtained for the completed components. However, in that case the application note warns that care should be taken to ensure that turnover is not overstated for the completed components. [FRS 5 App G paras G28, G30]. This is because the total contract price may be at a discount to the sum of the individual fair values of the completed and uncompleted components when sold separately (see para 9.155 below). Some worked examples illustrating acceptable methods for allocating consideration are given from paragraph 9.226 below.

9.150 If a contract comprises more than two components and fair values can be attributed only to groups of completed or uncompleted components, those groups should be accounted for as separate components. For example, if a contract consists of three components A, B and C and a fair value can be attributed only to components B and C combined, those components should be treated as a single composite component. Component A may be treated as a separate component because a fair value can be attributed to it by deducting the combined fair value of B and C from the total contract consideration. [FRS 5 App G para G31].

9.151 The application note also deals with contracts that have multiple components, where the components do not operate independently of one another. In such a situation, the seller should account for them as a single contract. Where the contract meets the definition of a long-term contract under SSAP 9 it should be accounted for in accordance with that standard and the guidance in the application note relating to long-term contractual performance. [FRS 5 App G para G32]. Whilst the application note does not say so specifically, components should also be accounted for as one contract where fair values cannot be attributed to any one component or group of components.

9.152 A simple example of a contract with two components might be where a mobile phone company packages within a single sales contract a handset and pre-paid calls. If these two elements are also available for sale separately, their standalone prices may be a good guide as to how the contract price could be allocated between the two components. At the start of the contract, the handset will have been delivered, but provision of the calls will be outstanding. Thus, the revenue from the calls will be deferred and recognised on a usage basis.

9.153 Sometimes, when a contract has been broken down into separate components, some of those components are immaterial. In such a case it may be reasonable to recognise all the revenue when the contract has been substantially performed, that is, ignoring whether the immaterial element has been completed or not.

9.154 In some cases a measurement issue may arise. If the contract value exceeds the sum of the fair value of the separable components it may be that the additional contract value is attributable to some other factor, such as the activity of managing the two contract components. In that case, the management activity will only be performed when the separable components, and thus the full contract, are substantially complete. Therefore, it is at this point that the additional revenue attributable to the management element is recognised.

9.155 The contract value, on the other hand, may be less than the fair value of the separable components. This may indicate some double-counting of components, for example there may be set up time that would be incurred were the components to be performed separately, but which is only needed once when the components are part of the same contract. Another example might be where the seller gives a discount because the customer buys several goods or services (components) together rather than individually. Such double-counting or discounting should be eliminated by apportioning it between the separable components pro rata to their fair values. [FRS 5 App G paras G23, G27]. (Any loss on the overall contract should be recognised at the outset).

Example 1 – Contract value is lower than the fair value of the separable elements

A company supplies equipment and in addition provides a maintenance service for a year. The price of the equipment and the maintenance package is £100,000. The company also provides maintenance services and equipment sales separately. The price of maintenance contracts is £10,000 per annum, and the cost of the equipment when sold separately is £95,000. Therefore, the equipment and maintenance, if purchased separately, would cost £105,000. How should the sale of the equipment and maintenance package be accounted for?

It is possible to purchase the equipment and the maintenance separately, therefore, the contract has two separable components, the equipment sale and the maintenance contract. The 'discount' of £5,000 should be applied rateably to the fair values of the components so that the equipment should be attributed a value of £100,000 × £95,000 ÷ £105,000 or £90,476 and the maintenance contract would be attributed a value of £100,000 × £10,000 ÷ £105,000 or £9,524 totalling £100,000. The £90,476 of revenue for the sale of equipment would be taken to the profit and loss account on delivery, whilst the £9,524 would be taken to the profit and loss account over the 12 month period of the maintenance contract.

Note: In this example the 'discount' has been allocated between the elements in proportion to the fair value of the revenue estimated for each component. Other methods may be appropriate given different facts and circumstances.

Example 2 – Contract value exceeds fair value of the separable components

A company normally carries out site clearance activities as its sole activity. However, it agrees to clear a site and then order and install two prefabricated buildings for use as temporary offices.

It charges £50,000 for the whole contract. This can be broken down into £10,000, which is the charge it would normally make for the site clearance, and £38,000 for the two prefabricated buildings (cost of £30,000 to the company plus a normal mark-up on such buildings based on its normal profit margins). The balance of £2,000 is attributable to the management of the contract and is a fair price for such services.

The revenue recognition pattern will allow the revenue from the site clearance to be recognised when the work has been performed and right to consideration for that component has been earned. The revenue for the installation of buildings and for management of the contract would then be recognised when the buildings are delivered and installed and the contract is, therefore, complete.

Example 3 – Initial allocation of consideration indicates that one component is onerous

Company A sells a copy machine in December 20X7 and will provide maintenance services for one year; the total consideration received for both the sale and the maintenance activity is £1,200. Costs expected to be incurred in order to meet the requirements of the sale contract are £700 for the machine and £200 for the maintenance activity; the relative fair values are £1,050 and £150, respectively.

If the entity were to apply a relative fair value approach, this would result in a loss on the maintenance component of the contract. However this would not be appropriate since the contract as a whole is profitable. An alternative policy would be to apply a 'cost plus a reasonable margin' approach.

Having agreed on the overall profit of £300 (for example, for £250 on the machine and for £50 on the maintenance service), this amount is allocated between the two elements of the agreement:

December 20X7	Dr	Cr
Cash	£1,200	
Deferred revenue		£250
Revenue		£950
Cost of sales	£700	
Inventory		£700

9.156 Table 9.12 illustrates an accounting policy for transactions where there are separable components.

Table 9.12 – ARM Holdings PLC – Annual Report – 31 December 2001

1/Principal accounting policies (extract)

Turnover. Turnover (excluding VAT) comprises the value of sales of licences, royalties arising from the resulting sale of licensed products, revenues from support, maintenance and training, and consulting contracts and the sale of boards and software tool kits.

Each licence is designed to meet the specific requirements of each customer. Delivery generally occurs within a short time period after signing. Licence fees are invoiced according to an agreed set of milestone payments. Typically the first milestone is on signing of the contract, the second is on delivery of the customised technology and the third is related to acceptance of the technology by the licensee. Where agreements involve multiple elements, the entire fee from such arrangements has been allocated to each of the individual elements based on each element's fair value.

[The next paragraph is 9.158.]

Linked transactions

9.158 Application note G also deals with the situation where the commercial substance of two or more separate contracts may require them to be accounted for as a single transaction. This is referred to as the 'bundling' of a contractual arrangement. [FRS 5 App G para G26].

9.159 The application note does not elaborate further on this. However, the issue is dealt with in the main body of FRS 5, paragraph 14 of which states:

> *"A reporting entity's financial statements should report the substance of the transactions into which it has entered. In determining the substance of a transaction, all its aspects and implications should be identified and greater weight given to those more likely to have a commercial effect in practice. A group or series of transactions that achieves or is designed to achieve an overall commercial effect should be viewed as a whole."*

9.160 The main principles of FRS 5, including the above principle from paragraph 14 of the standard, are dealt with in chapter 3. An example of where separate contracts may need to be combined is given below.

Example – Linked transactions

A retailer has signed a contract lasting 12 months to purchase certain stocks from a supplier on an exclusive basis (that is, it will not purchase from any other supplier). On signing the contract the company has received from the supplier a 'marketing support' payment. The contract requires that the retailer displays the products prominently in the stores and must make purchases at the same level as in the previous year. If the conditions are not met for the full 12 months, the amount is refundable to the supplier.

The income should not be treated as revenue, rather in substance, the income is a discount on purchase (cost of stock), which will be recognised within cost of sales once the stock is sold. These two elements should be accounted for as part of one overall arrangement. The reduction in the cost of stock in respect of the agreement is earned over the period and is subject to significant performance conditions being satisfied, for example, the company must display the supplier's products etc. It could be argued that until all of these conditions have been satisfied none of the payment has been earned and that it ought, therefore, to be deferred in total until the conditions have been satisfied. However, the satisfaction of the conditions is within the company's control and so it is reasonable that it should spread the income over the period so long as it intends to abide by the conditions for the full period. It would not be acceptable, however, to recognise the full reduction in the cost of stock on day one as the transaction extends over the period of one year and on day one no part of it has been completed.

9.160.1 When such a sale and repurchase agreement is entered into, the agreement's terms need to be analysed to ascertain whether, in substance, the seller has transferred some or all of the benefits of the original asset to the buyer, the exposure to the risks inherent in those benefits and whether revenue should, therefore, be recognised. When the seller has retained the more commercially significant benefits and inherent risks associated with the asset, even though legal title has been transferred, the transaction is a financing arrangement and does not give rise to revenue. Paragraph B7 of FRS 5 Application Note B provides examples of the sorts of benefits and risks that a company should consider in determining whether a revenue generating transaction has occurred.

Example – Legal sale linked to a financing arrangement

The management of company A is considering the following two alternative transactions:

(a) sale of stock to a bank for £500,000 with an obligation to repurchase the stock at a later stage; or

(b) sale of stock to a bank for £500,000 with an option to repurchase the stock any time up to 12 months from the date of sale.

The repurchase price in both alternatives is £500,000 plus an imputed financing cost. The bank is required to provide substantially the same quality and quantity of stock as was sold to it (that is, the bank is not required to return precisely the same physical stock as was originally sold to it). The fair value of the stock sold to the bank is £1,000,000.

How should management record the transactions?

Management should recognise the transactions as follows:

(a) Sale with repurchase obligation: management should not recognise revenue on the transfer of the stock to the bank. The stock should remain on company A's balance sheet and the proceeds from the bank should be recognised as a collateralised borrowing.

Even though the stock repurchased from the bank may not be the stock sold, it is in substance the same asset. The substance of the transaction is that the sale and repurchase are linked transactions and company A does not transfer the more commercially significant benefits and risks associated with the stock to the bank.

(b) Sale with repurchase option: management should not recognise revenue unless and until the repurchase option is allowed to lapse. The stock should remain on company A's balance sheet and the proceeds recognised as a collateralised borrowing until company A's right to repurchase the stock lapses. (Company A is unlikely to let the repurchase option lapse as the enforced 'sale' was at significantly below fair value.)

9.160.2 Sometimes an issue can arise where one company sells one product to another company and that other company sells a different product to the first company. The Application note G guidance on separation and linking of contractual arrangements (see para 9.145 above), whilst principally concerned with segregation of components of sales contracts or linking of two or more sales contracts, is relevant to this situation and is taken into account in the following paragraphs. Provided the two transactions are not connected and operate independently of each other no problem arises. However, if the commercial substance is that the two contracts do not operate independently of each other, they should be considered together. 'Operate independently' is defined in paragraph 9.147 above.

[The next paragraph is 9.160.4.]

9.160.4 The issue to decide is whether or not the two transactions should be regarded as two separate contracts or together as one larger contract. The latter will be the case if the contracts are legally or economically conditional or dependent on each other, for example this might be the case where company A sells an item to company B, which company B uses to manufacture a product that company A is obliged to purchase (especially if the repurchase price is determined other than by reference to the fair value of the item). However, if the contracts are genuinely independent of each other they will be treated as two contracts and company A will recognise profit on the first sale to company B and record the price paid for the product purchased from company B as the cost of that purchase. Generally, the arrangement's individual circumstances will need to be analysed, but signs that the contracts are independent would include:

- Company B selling the product manufactured from products supplied by company A to other third parties.
- Company A having no obligation to purchase the product from company B.

- Arm's length market prices for each transaction with price risk resting with company B between the first transaction and the second.

[The next paragraph is 9.160.7.]

9.160.7 Application note G requires that: *"Where a contractual arrangement consists of various components that do not operate independently of each other, the seller should account for them together to reflect the seller's performance of its obligations as a whole in obtaining the right to consideration. ...".* [FRS 5 App G para G32]. However, as illustrated by the example below, where two transactions with the same counterparty do operate independently they should be accounted for as such.

Example 1 – Two way transactions that are not linked

Company A sells materials for making door frames to a manufacturer who assembles the frames and puts glass in the door. Company A then repurchases the doors and sells them to a house builder for installation in homes. It is argued that the sale of the frames and the purchase of the doors are not linked because:

- The manufacturer buys material for the frames regardless of whether the doors can be sold to company A, as the manufacturer has other markets to which it can and does sell assembled doors.
- Company A is not committed to buy doors from this manufacturer as it could and does use other suppliers.
- The price of the door is not fixed at the time the frame is sold and so the manufacturer takes risk on whether or not and at what price it can sell the door.

Should the sale of the materials for the door frames to the manufacturer be accounted for separately from the purchase of doors from the same manufacturer, or should the transactions be regarded as linked and conditional on each other for accounting purposes?

In this case, the details indicate that the transactions are not conditional on each other, because the manufacturer takes the risk on the manufactured doors, both in terms of price and because company A does not have to buy any doors from that manufacturer. Therefore, the sales and purchases should be accounted for as separate, distinct transactions.

Example 2 – Two way trading transactions that are linked

The facts are the same as in example 1 except that company A sold the materials (which cost it £5) for £10 per frame and at that time agreed to buy back the materials made up into a finished door with glass fitted for £100.

In this case, the two transactions might be linked. This is because the sale carries a corresponding commitment to repurchase the materials in the future at a fixed price. If after considering price risk and the circumstances of the arrangement, company A believes that a sale did not occur, it should not record a sale of the £10 materials (or a profit on that sale). Instead the cost of the materials should be retained in stock and the £10 received from the manufacturer should be recorded as a liability. When the door is repurchased the additional net £90 paid by company A will be recorded as stock, giving a stock value for the completed door of £95.

9.160.8 Transactions whereby cash is paid by company A to company B are sometimes related to transactions that require company B to pay cash to company A. These transactions have to be carefully analysed to determine if they should be viewed as separate transactions or a single transaction accounted for on a net basis. Factors to consider (in addition to those outlined above) that might lead to a net presentation include:

- The arrangements are entered into in close time proximity to each other and/or their mutual existence is acknowledged in the separate agreements.
- Sufficient verifiable objective evidence does not exist to support the assertion that the amount being charged for the product or service in each transaction is its fair value.
- The party to the transactions that receives the greater amount of cash inflows does not have a clear immediate business need for the product or service it is purchasing.

9.160.9 The latter point is even more problematic if the party had received cash before it had to pay cash. These types of transactions can be particularly troublesome if they involve what is, in reality, a barter transaction, such as advertising for advertising which is discussed under 'Barter transactions' below (see from para 9.187).

9.160.10 The UITF considered this subject further when it issued Abstract 36, 'Contracts for sales of capacity', in March 2003. Although aimed principally at transactions involving capacity in the telecommunications and electricity industries, the effect is to allow a gross presentation of two-way trading arrangements only where the assets or services in question have a readily ascertainable market value as defined in FRS 10, 'Goodwill and intangible assets'. The requirements of Abstract 36 are discussed further under 'Capacity transactions' below (see from para 9.201).

Measurement of revenue — specific issues

Agency arrangements

9.161 This issue concerns whether the company is functioning as:

- An agent acting as an intermediary, earning a fee or commission in return for arranging the provision of goods or services on behalf of a principal.
- A principal acting on its own account when contracting with customers for the supply of goods or services in return for consideration.

[FRS 5 App G paras G60, G61].

9.162 Application note G analyses the factors that determine whether a seller is acting as a principal in an exchange transaction or as an agent in relation to a transaction between its principal and the principal's customer. [FRS 5 App G para G62]. In order for a seller to account for a transaction as a principal it should normally have exposure to all the significant benefits and risks associated with at least one of the following:

- The selling price – that is, the ability, within economic constraints, to set the selling price with the customer. The price may be established directly or, where the selling price is fixed, indirectly by providing additional goods or services or adjusting the terms of a linked transaction.
- Stock – that is, exposure to the risks of damage, slow movement and obsolescence, and changes in suppliers' prices.

[FRS 5 App G para G63].

9.163 Other factors that indicate that a seller may be acting as a principal would include:

- Where the seller performs part of the services provided or modifies the goods supplied.
- Where the seller has or assumes the credit risk.
- Where the seller has discretion in selecting suppliers.

[FRS 5 App G para G65].

9.163.1 The following example illustrates some of these principles.

Example – Determining whether a company is acting as principal or agent

A retailer sells a number of products whose prices are determined by the supplier. The products can be split into two broad categories: electronic (including mobile phone e-top up) and tangible (including mobile phone top up cards, stamps and newspapers). As the retailer has no influence over the price, should the retailer account for sales of these products as principal or agent?

In the transactions being considered, the retailer has no influence over the price, does not modify the goods, bears minimal credit risk (because transactions are routinely for cash, credit card or guaranteed cheque) and has no discretion over supplier selection (as each product is sold by only one supplier, the mobile phone top ups being specific to a mobile phone network). The only exposure that the retailer may have relates to the stock. Where the product sold is electronic and there is no stock of any worth, the retailer is acting as an agent and will recognise its sales commission as turnover.

Where the product sold is tangible and the retailer bears the significant stock risks of obsolescence, damage or theft, then it will be acting as principal and should recognise the sale price as turnover and the associated costs as a cost of sale. However, where the retailer does not bear the significant stock risks, then it will be acting as an agent and will recognise its sales commission as turnover.

9.164 Where a seller acts as an agent it will usually not be exposed to the significant risks and benefits associated with the exchange transaction. Normally, where the seller acts as an agent the agency arrangements will include the following features:

- The seller discloses the fact that it is acting as an agent.
- When the seller has confirmed the customer's order with a third party (usually the supplier who may be the principal), the seller will have no further involvement in the performance of the supplier's contractual obligations.
- The amount that the seller earns is fixed in advance and is either a fixed fee per transaction or a stated percentage of the amount invoiced to the customer.
- The seller bears no stock or credit risk, except where it receives additional consideration from the ultimate supplier (who may be the principal) in return for assuming the risk.

[FRS 5 App G para G66].

9.164.1 The example below illustrates the application of revenue recognition to an agency arrangement involving the distribution of goods.

Example – Agent v principal – distribution agreement

Company A distributes company B's products under a distribution agreement. The terms and conditions of the contract are such that company A:

- Obtains title to the goods and sells them to third party retailers.
- Stores, repackages, transports and invoices the goods sold to third party retailers.
- Earns a fixed margin on the products sold to the retailers, but has no flexibility in establishing the sales price.
- Has the right to return the goods to company B without penalty.
- Is responsible for the goods while the goods are stored in company A's warehouse, but company B bears the risk of obsolete goods.

Company B retains product liability. Company B is, therefore, responsible for manufacturing defects. Also, the credit risk rests with company B.

Should company B recognise revenue on the transfer of the goods to company A?

No, company B should not recognise revenue on the transfer of the goods to company A. Company A is acting as agent for the principal, company B. Company B does not transfer the significant benefits and risks of ownership of the goods to company A. Company A has the option to return the goods so does not bear the risk of stock obsolescence, and also cannot set the selling price. For Company A to act as principal it would normally be expected that it would be exposed to either stock risk or be able to set the selling price. [FRS 5 App G para G63]. Therefore, company B should continue to recognise the stock on its balance sheet and it should only recognise revenue when company A sells the goods to a third party.

9.165 The application note states that where the seller has not disclosed that it is acting as agent there is a rebuttable presumption that it is acting as a principal. [FRS 5 App G para G64].

9.166 When the substance of a transaction is that a seller is acting as a principal it should recognise revenue based on the gross amount received or receivable in respect of its performance under the sales contract with the customer. [FRS 5 App G para G67].

9.167 When the substance is that the seller is acting as agent it should recognise as revenue only the commission or other amounts received or receivable in return for its performance under the contract. In this case the contract in question is usually the agency agreement with its principal rather than the sales contract with the customer. Any amounts received from the customer that have to be paid to the principal should not be included in the agent's turnover. [FRS 5 App G para G68].

9.168 The application note encourages disclosure by agents, where practicable, of the gross value of sales throughput as additional, non-statutory information. Where an agent gives such disclosure it should give a brief explanation of the relationship between recognised turnover and the gross value of sales throughput. [FRS 5 App G para G72].

9.169 The application note includes three examples illustrating how these principles should be applied in particular situations. In the first example, a building contractor has a contract with a customer. Analysis of the contract shows that the contractor negotiates the price, bears any credit risk of customer default and has primary responsibility for the work carried out, including work done by subcontractors. The contractor is, therefore, acting as principal in this transaction. The second example is of a travel agent that acts as an intermediary between holiday companies and customers. The travel agent does not set the price of the holidays and its terms of business exclude any liability to customers after it has put them in touch with a holiday company. The agent receives a fee for each customer that it puts in touch with a holiday company, but has no further involvement after that point. In this situation the travel agent is acting as an agent and should only record the fees as turnover. [FRS 5 App G paras G69, G70].

9.170 In the third example the application note deals with trading concessions operated in department stores. The application note's development section explains that there is a wide variety of potential arrangements between department stores and concessionaires, but that where the department store is not acting as principal in an exchange transaction with the concessionaire's customers it should not include the value of the concessionaire's sales in its own revenues. In the example in the application note, the department store provides space for concessionaires and receives a fixed rental income in return. Analysis of the arrangement shows that the concessionaires are acting as principals in their dealings with customers. In these circumstances, the concessionaires should include as revenue the amounts receivable from sales to customers. The department store should not include in its revenue the value of sales made by the concessionaire. [FRS 5 App G paras G71, Development para 51].

9.171 Another, more complicated example relating to concessions is as follows.

Example – Concession arrangements – transactions involving a lease

A department store contains concession outlets. Under the terms of a concession agreement, the department store provides the concessionaire with serviced space in the store, sales staff, point of sale equipment and stock-room space. The concessionaire pays the department store a fixed contractual amount of £100,000 each month plus five per cent of the outlet's revenue. The concessionaire determines the stock lines sold and the prices charged to customers and has the right to move stock between its concessions in different stores. At the end of a season, the concessionaire must take back any unsold stock. The agreement between the concessionaire and the department store is not for a fixed term, but is cancellable by the concessionaire at three months' notice and by the department store at six months' notice. How should the department store account for this arrangement?

SSAP 21, 'Leases and hire purchase contracts', defines a lease as *"a contract between a lessor and a lessee for the hire of a specific asset. The lessor retains ownership of the asset but conveys the right to the use of the asset to the lessee for an agreed period of time in return for the payment of specified rentals. The term "lease" as used in this statement also applies to other arrangements in which one party retains ownership of an asset but conveys the right to the use of the asset to another party for an agreed period of time in return for specified payments"*. [SSAP 21 para 14].

The arrangement between the department store and the concessionaire has the substance of a lease. The store retains ownership, but conveys the right to use a specified area of serviced, staffed and networked space to the concessionaire.

The lease is likely to be classified as an operating lease: it is unlikely that substantially all the risks and rewards of ownership of that area of the department store have been transferred to the concessionaire. Furthermore, the minimum contractual lease payments to which the department store is entitled are only for three months' rent, which is unlikely to amount to substantially all of the fair value of the leased space.

SSAP 21 requires that operating lease income is recognised on a straight-line basis over the period of the lease, unless another basis is more appropriate. We consider it most appropriate for the flat monthly rent of £100,000 to be recognised on a straight-line basis.

The revenue-based rent is contingent rent. SSAP 21 contains no guidance on the recognition of contingent rent in operating leases. Thus, the revenue-based rent should be recognised by the department store when the store is unconditionally entitled to it.

The guidance contained in Application note G to FRS 5 requires that the seller recognises the gross revenue. The seller is the entity that is the principal in the sales transaction, having exposure to all significant benefits and risks associated with the selling price and/or the stock. In this example, the concessionaire is able to determine the selling price of each item and bears the significant stock risks of damage and obsolescence. Consequently, the concessionaire will recognise the gross revenue and recognise the rent paid to the department store as a cost.

The department store is, in substance, acting as agent in selling to the customer and is receiving 'commission' (the substance of which is rent) in consideration for the service that it is performing for the concessionaire (making available space in the department store). It should not recognise the gross revenue of the concession. Instead it should report the 'commission' receivable as revenue.

As noted in paragraph 9.168 above, the application note does, however, encourage disclosure in the agent's financial statements of the gross value of sales throughput where the seller is acting as agent. Where such non-statutory information is given a brief explanation of the relationship of recognised turnover to the gross value of sales throughput should be given.

Sales taxes

9.171.1 Sales taxes are a common example of an agency relationship. When an entity sells a product, sales taxes that are collected on behalf of a government body should be excluded from the revenue recognised. These taxes are remitted to the government in full and do not increase equity. Revenue should, therefore, be presented net of sales taxes. [FRS 5 App note para G7; SSAP 5 para 8].

9.171.2 The treatment of sales taxes differs from that of production taxes, which are treated as a cost of sales. It may be necessary to analyse, for each jurisdiction in which the entity operates, whether certain taxes are sales taxes or production taxes to determine the accounting treatment for the tax in each jurisdiction. For example, excise duty payable by manufacturers of tobacco and alcoholic products, is a sales tax in some jurisdictions and a production tax in others. In some jurisdictions it may be difficult to determine the exact nature of the tax. The treatment of excise duty in one jurisdiction may, therefore, be different from that in another.

9.171.3 When determining whether revenue should be presented gross or net of excise tax, the key consideration is whether the entity is acting as agent or principal for the tax authority. There are several indicators that could help in this determination as outlined in paragraph 9.164. Indicators that the entity is acting as principal (and should recognise the excise taxes gross) include but are not limited to:

- Risks and rewards of the transaction – the entity holds the inventory and credit risk and the entity will not be refunded for the tax even if the inventory is not sold or receivables are not collected.
- Ability to choose the selling price – the entity has no legal or constructive obligation to change prices in order to reflect excise taxes. The entity bears the taxes and makes the decision whether to pass the tax on to the customer.

- Basis of calculation – the tax is based on the number of units or on the physical quantity (for example, number of cigarettes, or alcoholic content) produced by the entity.

- Point of payment – the entity must pay tax to the government when the unit is produced or relatively close to that date.

As circumstances are likely to differ between jurisdictions, this evaluation should be performed for each different jurisdiction as necessary.

Advertising agency commissions

9.172 Revenue should only be recognised on transactions, including advertising commissions, when the service is completed. Advertising agencies' income may consist of media commissions, which relate to the advertisement appearing before the public and production commissions, which relate to production of the advertisement. Recognition should occur for media commissions when the advertisement appears before the public and for production commissions when the project is completed, for example as in Table 9.13.

Table 9.13 – WPP Group plc – Annual Report – 31 December 2004

Accounting policies (extract)

Turnover, cost of sales and revenue recognition (extract)

Advertising and Media investment management

Revenue is typically derived from commissions on media placements and fees for advertising services. Traditionally, the Group's advertising clients were charged a standard commission on their total media and production expenditure. In recent years, however, this has tended to become a matter of individual negotiation. Revenue may therefore consist of various arrangements involving commissions, fees, incentive-based revenue or a combination of the three, as agreed upon with each client.

Revenue is recognised when the service is performed, in accordance with the terms of the contractual arrangement. Incentive-based revenue typically comprises both quantitative and qualitative elements; on the element related to quantitative targets, revenue is recognised when the quantitative targets have been achieved; on the element related to qualitative targets, revenue is recognised when the incentive is received/receivable.

[The next paragraph is 9.185.]

Volume or settlement discounts

9.185 Suppliers may offer customers discounts for either achieving a minimum threshold of purchases (volume discounts) or for prompt settlement of outstanding receivables (settlement discounts). In either case, Application note G requires that the amount of revenue recognised under the transaction is reduced by the amount of the discount at the time of sale.

9.186 In order to calculate the appropriate revenue to be recognised, it may be necessary for an entity to estimate the volume of sales or the expected settlement discounts to be taken. The revenue recognised would then be reduced by this estimate, such that the revenue recognised represents the fair value of the right to consideration. The need to estimate the amounts of discounts expected to be taken does not preclude the reduction of revenue for these discounts. However, if no reliable estimate can be made then the revenue recognised on the transaction should not exceed the amount of consideration that would be received if the maximum discounts were taken.

Example – Estimating cash volume discounts

A paint manufacturer with a 31 December year end offers several large customers stepped rebates on sales based on the following volumes:

Up to 100,000 litres – no discount

Between 100,000 litres and 250,000 litres – 5% discount on all sales

Over 250,000 litres – 10% discount on all sales

Rebates are paid to customers after the end of their contract year.

At 31 December 20X3, a particular customer has purchased 140,000 litres of paint. That customer has a past history of purchasing over 250,000 litres of paint each contract year (which runs from 1 July to 30 June), spread evenly during the year.

At 31 December 20X3, the manufacturer has a contractual liability to pay the customer a rebate of 5% on all sales to date, because the volume threshold of 100,000 litres has been exceeded. However, based on all the available evidence, it is probable that the customer will also exceed the 250,000 litre threshold and that the manufacturer will pay a rebate of 10% on all sales. Consequently, the adjustment to revenue (and the resultant provision made) would be based on 10% of the sales to date.

Example – Estimating settlement discounts

A food manufacturer sells canned food and has 100 customers. The delivery of the goods is made on the last day of each month. Standard payment terms require settlement within 45 days of delivery. The entity's policy is to grant a settlement discount of 2% to customers who pay within 15 days of delivery. Experience shows that 45% of customers normally pay within 15 days. How much should the food manufacturer recognise as revenue upon a month end delivery with an invoice value of £1,000?

The food manufacturer should recognise revenue of £991. This amount is calculated by deducting from the total invoiced value the expected amount of discounts to be taken of £9 (£1,000 × 45% × 2%).

Example – More complex discount arrangements

A manufacturer of cars pays various discounts, rebates and incentives to dealers and customers. There is a 2% trade discount on initial sale to the dealer, a further rebate of 5% if the dealer meets certain targets and other bonuses to fleet customers of 3% if certain targets are met. How should these be accounted for if it is considered likely that the dealers and customers will meet the targets?

These are all payments that relate to turnover (that is, to the number of vehicles sold) and should, therefore, be treated as a reduction of turnover. The company (manufacturer) would credit turnover with 90% of the sales value (total value less initial discount and best estimate of rebates/incentives), credit liabilities with the best estimate of the rebates (8%), and debit cash with 98% received initially. If the rebates and other bonuses are paid they will be charged to the liabilities. To the extent that they are not paid the liability is released (to turnover).

Barter transactions

9.187 Companies usually trade for cash or the right to receive cash. Sometimes, however, transactions are undertaken that involve the swapping of goods or services. These are known as barter transactions.

9.188 In terms of determining the point at which a sale should be recognised the accounting for barter transactions is no different from accounting for transactions that are settled in cash.

9.189 Measurement of the value of or consideration for barter transactions is, however, much more difficult than measurement of the consideration for transactions undertaken for cash or the right to receive cash.

9.190 In order to address these, the UITF issued Abstract 26, 'Barter transactions for advertising'. This concluded that, where advertising services are provided in exchange for advertising received, the arrangement provided little or no evidence of the value of the services provided. As the ASB Statement of Principles for financial reporting requires (a) sufficient evidence and (b) measurement at a monetary amount with sufficient reliability for recognition, the UITF concluded that turnover and costs in respect of advertising barter transactions should only be recognised if there was persuasive evidence of the value at which, if the advertising had not been exchanged, it would have been sold in a similar transaction. The Abstract lays down stringent conditions that need to be satisfied in order to conclude that there is evidence of the cash value of the advertising exchanged. In practice, in most cases the evidence will not be sufficient and the Abstract then requires that turnover and costs are not recognised in respect of the barter transaction.

9.191 When UITF Abstract 26 was issued, there was significant practice in barter advertising in one internet company's space for advertising in the counterparty internet company's space, that is, advertising for advertising barter. The Abstract provides guidance on the application of the Statement of

Principles to one specific type of transaction, but its principles may be applied to other barter transactions.

9.192 The Abstract states that it is appropriate to recognise revenue and costs in respect of barter transactions for advertising only if there is persuasive evidence of the value at which, if the advertising had not been exchanged, it would have been sold for cash in a similar transaction. The UITF believed that such circumstances would be rare.

[The next paragraph is 9.194.]

9.194 Persuasive evidence of the value of advertising exchanged will exist only where the entity has a history of selling similar advertising for cash and where substantially all of the revenue from advertising within the accounting period is represented by cash sales.

9.195 To provide evidence of the value of advertising exchanged, cash sales of advertising must be similar in all significant respects. This requires that the cash sales are of advertising space in the same vehicle (for example, the same web site or magazine) as that exchanged, and must have taken place within a reasonably short period of the exchange transaction (in no case more than six months before or after it). [UITF 26 paragraph 12]. There must also be no other factors that would be expected to make the value of the advertising sold for cash significantly different from that exchanged. Specific factors set out in the Abstract that should be considered include:

- Circulation, exposure, or saturation within an intended market.
- Timing (time of day, day of week, daily, weekly, 24 hours a day/seven days a week and season of the year).
- Prominence (page on web site, section of periodical, location on page and size of advertisement).
- Demographics of readers, viewers, or customers.
- Duration (length of time advertising will be displayed).

[UITF 26 para 12].

The above list is not meant to be exhaustive.

9.196 Even where similar advertising has been sold for cash, the Abstract states that it is necessary to consider whether, in the light of all available information, there is persuasive evidence of the value at which the advertising exchanged would have been sold if not exchanged. Specific factors that may be relevant include:

- The entity's practice in setting prices for the advertising it provides and the circumstances in which discounts are offered.

- The probability that, if the advertising were not exchanged, a cash sale would have taken place.
- The value to the entity of the advertising received in exchange, and the evidence that the entity would have been willing to buy that advertising for cash if it had not been able to obtain it through an exchange transaction.

[UITF 26 para 13].

9.197 Entities should disclose in the notes to the financial statements the total amount of barter transactions for advertising that is included in turnover. Entities are encouraged to disclose information on the volume and type of such transactions and other kinds of barter transaction (whether or not included in turnover).

9.198 The difficulty of ascertaining a reliable value for the consideration in advertising barter transactions is typical of most barter transactions.

9.199 Table 9.14 is an example of a company which states its policy on advertising barter transactions.

Table 9.14 – Freeserve plc – Report and accounts – 29 April 2002

1.2 Turnover (extract)

Advertising revenues are recognised rateably over the period in which the advertisement is displayed provided that no significant obligations remain at the end of the period and collection of the resulting debt is probable. Freeserve occasionally takes part in barter advertising deals whereby partners' banner advertisements are shown in unsold space on Freeserve sites, in exchange for Freeserve banners appearing in unsold space on their sites. Both the revenue and cost elements of these transactions are deemed to be nil.

[The next paragraph is 9.201.]

Capacity transactions

9.201 In some network-based industries, such as telecommunications and electricity, entities enter into transactions for the sale or purchase of network capacity. For example, a telecommunications company may sell excess capacity on its trans-Atlantic cables. The company would probably retain ownership of the network assets, but would convey an indefeasible right of use (usually referred to as an IRU) to the buyer for an agreed period of time.

9.202 Occasionally, an entity may sell capacity to another party in exchange for receiving capacity on that other party's network. Arrangements such as these have received significant media attention, it being argued that there is not always a valid commercial reason for the transaction. Where there is no valid commercial purpose, exchange transactions have come to be known as 'hollow swaps'. An example could be where the telecommunications company described above had exchanged its excess capacity for another company's excess capacity on the same route.

9.203 Transactions involving the sale of capacity bear some similarity to lease transactions accounted for under SSAP 21. However, varying interpretations of SSAP 21 and FRS 5, as well as adverse media comment concerning 'hollow swaps', led the UITF to issue Abstract 36, 'Contracts for sales of capacity'.

9.204 UITF Abstract 36 addresses three issues:

- Should a transaction be reported as an immediate sale of an asset or as the delivery of a service over time? (See para 9.206 onwards.)
- How should gains and losses be presented in the performance statements? (See para 9.208 onwards.)
- How should exchange or reciprocal transactions be accounted for? (See para 9.214 onwards.)

[UITF 36 para 3].

9.205 With regard to 'hollow swaps', the UITF stated that *"no accounting recognition should be given to transactions that are artificial or lacking in substance"*. [UITF 36 para 23].

Sale of an asset or a service?

9.206 Contracts that convey rights of use are, in many respects, akin to leases. The definition of a lease in SSAP 21 explains that the term *"also applies to other arrangements in which one party retains ownership of an asset but conveys the right to the use of the asset to another party for an agreed period of time in return for specified payments"*. [SSAP 21 para 14]. Hence, the principles of SSAP 21 are relevant when determining whether a transaction should be reported as a sale of an asset or as the delivery of a service over time. Further guidance on categorising leases is given in chapter 19.

9.207 UITF Abstract 36 concludes that contracts for rights of use cannot be treated as a sale, unless a specific asset component can be identified as having been 'sold' and substantially all the risks and rewards of ownership of that asset have been transferred from the seller to the buyer. In other words, the contract has the substance of a finance lease. In determining whether there has been a transfer of risks and rewards, the Abstract requires that the following criteria are satisfied:

- The purchaser's right of use is exclusive and irrevocable such that no other party, including the seller, would have the right to use the capacity that is the subject of the contract, even if the buyer is not using it.
- The asset component is specific and separable (such that the buyer's exclusivity is guaranteed and the seller has no right to substitute other assets). Where the capacity 'sold' is part of a larger infrastructure, it may be difficult to measure its cost or carrying value reliably, with the result that any gain or loss that would be recognised would be uncertain. Where the

cost or carrying value cannot be measured reliably, the Abstract concludes that a specific asset component cannot be identified. [UITF 36 para 8].

- The contract's term is for a major part of the asset's useful economic life.
- The attributable cost or carrying value can be measured reliably.
- No significant risks are retained by the seller. Such risks include:
  - Risk of changes in asset value.
  - Risk of obsolescence or changes in technology.
  - Risk of damage.
  - Risk of unsatisfactory performance (arising, for example, from performance guarantees).
  - Risks relating to the seller's obligations to provide continuing access by operating and maintaining the assets. For example, if the company described in paragraph 9.201 was contractually obliged to operate and maintain the cable, the transaction could not be treated as a sale.

[UITF 36 para 20].

Presentation in the performance statements

9.208 Where it has been determined that the transaction's substance is the delivery of a service, income is recognised over the life of the contract. If, on the other hand, the substance is the sale of an asset, the presentation in the profit and loss account will depend on whether the asset sold was a fixed asset or a current asset (that is, stock). Some entities acquire or build capacity both for use within their business and for resale. Accordingly, an entity may present its investment in capacity as both fixed assets and current assets.

9.209 Paragraph 20 of FRS 3 requires that profits or losses on the disposal of fixed assets are shown separately on the face of the profit and loss account after operating profit and before interest. Income and expenses arising on the sale of current assets are included within operating result, generally as turnover and cost of sales. However, UITF Abstract 36 contains a restriction regarding the latter treatment.

9.210 Where an entity intends to dispose of a fixed asset, that asset is no longer intended for use on a continuing basis in the entity's activities. Consequently, it may be inferred that the asset no longer satisfies the criteria for classification as a fixed asset. Accordingly, in such circumstances, it may at first appear appropriate to reclassify some fixed assets as current assets. However, this is not permitted by the Abstract, which provides that the proceeds of sale may be included within turnover only where *"the assets were designated as held for resale (and classified as stock) when they were acquired or on completion of construction"*. Furthermore, capacity may not be transferred from fixed assets to stock, even if it becomes surplus to requirements and is being actively marketed for sale. [UITF 36 paras 12, 21].

9.211 An example of an accounting policy that distinguishes sales of fixed assets from sales of current assets is shown in Table 9.15 below.

Table 9.15 – COLT Telecom Group plc – Annual Report – 31 December 2004

Accounting policies (extract)

Turnover (extract)

Turnover attributable to infrastructure sales in the form of indefeasible rights-of-use ("IRUs") with characteristics which qualify the transaction as an outright sale, or transfer of title agreements, are recognised at the time of delivery and acceptance by the customer. Proceeds from the sale of infrastructure qualify as turnover where the infrastructure was designated as built for resale at the outset and the associated costs of construction have been classified as inventory for future sale. Where the infrastructure was not designated for resale and was classified as tangible fixed assets, the proceeds from these infrastructure sales are recorded net of costs as a gain or loss on the disposals of a fixed asset.

9.212 Where transactions are reported as asset sales within operating results, the Abstract requires that there is separate disclosure of the amounts included in revenue and operating profit. [UITF 36 para 21].

9.213 The guidance in UITF Abstract 36 presumes that any profit arising on the sale of capacity will be realised. However, this may not be the case, for example in most exchange transactions (see from para 9.214). Where a profit is not realised, it should not be recognised in the profit and loss account. Instead it should be recorded in the STRGL. UITF Abstract 31, 'Exchanges of businesses or other non-monetary assets for an interest in a subsidiary, joint venture or associate', deals with this issue in the context of exchanges of business and other non-monetary assets. It requires that any unrealised profit arising on an exchange should be reported in the STRGL (see chapter 26). Although UITF Abstract 36 is silent on the subject, a similar treatment of unrealised profits on the sale of capacity is appropriate.

Exchange and reciprocal transactions

9.214 An entity may sell capacity on a network in exchange for receiving capacity on another entity's network. In some cases the two capacities are of a similar value and little or no cash is exchanged. In other cases, capacity is sold wholly or in part for cash (or the right to receive cash) and a separate agreement is entered into with the buyer at approximately the same time to purchase capacity of a similar value. Such cases are referred to in UITF Abstract 36 as 'reciprocal transactions' where this reflects the transaction's substance, even though the agreements may contain no reference to reciprocity.

9.215 The recognition criteria in the ASB's 'Statement of principles for financial reporting' require:

- sufficient evidence; and
- measurement at a monetary amount with sufficient reliability.

[SoP chapter 5].

9.216 In the case of reciprocal transactions, reliable measurement of the fair value of the asset or services exchanged may not be possible, even where there has been an exchange of cash between the transacting parties.

9.217 UITF Abstract 36 provides that revenue or gains in respect of reciprocal capacity transactions should be recognised only if the assets or services provided or received have a readily ascertainable market value as defined in FRS 10. This means that the value is established by reference to a market where:

- the asset belongs to a homogeneous population of assets that are equivalent in all material respects; and
- an active market, evidenced by frequent transactions, exists for that population of assets.

[FRS 10 para 2].

9.218 In practical terms, this means that revenue and gains in respect of reciprocal transactions will rarely, if ever, be recognised. In the case of a simple exchange of capacity, there will be no accounting entries in respect of the exchange itself. Revenues from the ongoing use of the capacity acquired will be recognised as earned. Where a reciprocal transaction involves an exchange of cash, the accounting will be similar if those cash amounts are equal. In substance, the movement of cash is ignored. However, the accounting is less straightforward where the cash amounts are not equal, as shown in the example below.

Example – Reciprocal transactions

Company A and company B have entered into a reciprocal transaction, the terms of which are as follows:

- Company A provides capacity for five years (with a book value of £300) and £1,000 cash.
- Company B provides capacity for the same period (with a book value of £400) and £800 cash.

There is no readily ascertainable market value for the capacity so, in accordance with UITF Abstract 36, revenue and gains are not recognised. However, company A has made a net payment of £200 while company B is a net recipient of the same amount. These net cash flows need to be accounted for. The accounting treatment will depend on the nature of the individual sale and purchase transactions.

If, for the reasons specified from paragraph 9.207 above, the transactions represent immediate sales and purchases of network assets, the net payment made by company A should be treated as an addition to the cost of its assets. The amount of the net payment should, therefore, be capitalised and, if the asset in question is a fixed asset, amortised over its useful life. As regards the net receipt by company B, this represents a part disposal of its network asset, which should be presumed to be at neither a gain (as this is not permitted by UITF Abstract 36) nor a loss (unless there are indicators that the network asset itself may be impaired).

If the transactions represent the delivery of a service over time, the net cash flows should be treated as payments and receipts in advance, which should be deferred and released to the profit and loss account over the periods of the contracts.

Vouchers and coupons

Vouchers or coupons granted for consideration

9.219 Vouchers or coupons for which separate consideration is received give a customer the right to enter into a future transaction on particular terms. One such example would be the purchase by a customer of a store voucher: the customer is paying to have the option of presenting the voucher to the store in order to receive goods at a later date.

9.220 FRS 5 Application note G does not deal specifically with vouchers for which consideration is received separately from the sale of goods or services. However, it does state that *"when a seller receives payment from a customer in advance of performance, it recognises a liability equal to the amount received, representing its obligation under the contract. When the seller obtains the right to consideration through its performance, that liability is reduced and the amount of the reduction is simultaneously reported as revenue"*. [FRS 5 App G para G5]. The application note does deal with other types of voucher and states in the context of recording the liability: *"Regard should also be paid to the proportion of vouchers that are expected to be redeemed"*. It also states: *"At each reporting date the seller should review its estimated liability for outstanding vouchers having regard to the experience of the proportion that are redeemed and expire. Adjustments to the estimate should be included within revenue"*. [FRS 5 App G paras G39, G41]. Thus, the revenue received on the sale of the voucher should be deferred and recognised when the seller performs.

9.221 Although the sale of a voucher or coupon is a contract with the customer, it needs to be considered together with the further contract that arises if and when the rights under that contract are exercised, because the two are inter-dependent. Application note G states that *"...the commercial substance of two or more separate contracts may require them to be accounted for as a single transaction. ..."*. [FRS 5 App G para G26]. The revenue from the sale of the voucher or coupon will generally be accounted for when the seller performs under the further contract – that is when the seller supplies the goods or services on exercise of the voucher or coupon.

9.222 Revenue from the sale of vouchers that were sold for cash should be recognised on the earlier of:

- The date of exercise (that is, the date on which the customer uses the voucher and the supplier completes its performance).
- The expiry of the voucher or coupon (that is, the date from which it is no longer legally valid and the supplier no longer has an obligation to supply 'contractual performance').

Where vouchers have no expiry date, the revenue should not be recognised if the supplier has not completed its contractual performance. Instead, the consideration received for the voucher should be deferred and recognised as a liability until it can be reliably demonstrated that it is unlikely the voucher will ever be presented. This determination must be made for each individual voucher (or group of vouchers in an ageing profile) and not to the whole portfolio of vouchers.

Example – Accounting for gift vouchers

A retailer has a 31 December year end. While in store, customers may purchase a gift voucher that entitles the holder to purchase goods from the store up to the amount spent on the voucher. The sale of gift vouchers greatly increases in December as customers purchase the vouchers to present as gifts to family and friends. In December, the retailer sold gift vouchers with a face value of £1,000. None of the gift vouchers were redeemed in December, but all of the gift vouchers were redeemed in the following year. The gift vouchers expire one year from the date of purchase.

The retailer should not recognise revenue from the sale of the gift vouchers until the voucher has been redeemed for merchandise, until the vouchers expire or until it can be reliably demonstrated that it is unlikely the voucher will ever be presented. Until this point, consideration received for the voucher should be deferred and recognised as a liability. This determination must be made for each individual voucher (or group of vouchers in an ageing profile) and not to the whole portfolio of vouchers. See also from paragraph 9.147.4.

Vouchers granted as part of sales transaction (vouchers)

9.223 Application note G provides specific guidance on vouchers, under the heading 'Separation and linking of contractual arrangements' (see also from para 9.145 above). In the application note the term 'vouchers' is intended to cover all types of arrangement where the seller is committed to perform in the future at a reduced price. [FRS 5 App G Dev para 37]. The term, therefore, includes a wide range of arrangements, including air miles and points schemes. The reason why vouchers are considered as part of the guidance relating to linking and separation of contractual arrangements is that often vouchers are issued as part of a single transaction that includes the sale of goods or services and the issue of the vouchers.

9.224 The application note deals only with situations where vouchers are redeemable against future purchases from the seller. The application note does not specifically mention situations where vouchers may be redeemable against purchases from other sellers, which is a feature of many points schemes, but this is also considered below from paragraph 9.240 in the light of the principles in the application note for vouchers.

9.225 The application note states that where vouchers are issued as part of a sales transaction and are redeemable against future purchases from the seller, the substance is that this is a 'bundled' transaction and the customer is buying both goods or services and a voucher at the same time. Thus, the principles of 'unbundling' which are discussed from paragraph 9.145 should be applied.

9.226 Using the principles of 'unbundling', it is necessary to allocate the consideration received from the customer across the transaction's components. Therefore, revenue should be reported at the amount of the consideration received or receivable less the voucher's fair value. The voucher's fair value represents a liability for future performance that is extinguished and recognised as revenue when the voucher is redeemed as part of the consideration for the future purchase by the customer. [FRS 5 App G para G38].

9.227 Where a voucher is accounted for separately, its fair value will often be less than its face value. Application note G sets out some of the factors that should be taken into consideration in determining the voucher's fair value including:

- The range of goods or services that the customer can obtain on the voucher's redemption.
- The discount the customer obtains when redeeming the voucher compared to the discount that could be obtained by customers who do not redeem vouchers.
- The length of time before the right to use the voucher expires.
- The extent to which the voucher is similar to other vouchers that are distributed to customers free of charge.
- Regard should also be paid to the proportion of vouchers that are expected to be redeemed.

[FRS 5 App G para G39].

Example 1 – Voucher for future money off (100% redemption expected)

A hotel company operates a loyalty scheme. A customer who stays in one of the company's hotels is given a voucher entitling them to a discount of £10 on a subsequent stay in any of the company's hotels. The price for one night's stay in a hotel is £100. The marginal cost to the hotel of one extra guest is negligible, because most of the hotel's costs are fixed costs.

The initial stay in the hotel is a multiple element arrangement, the components being the night's accommodation and the voucher. The total consideration (£100) is allocated to the components based on their fair values — £10 is allocated to the voucher, as that is its fair value to the customer. The remaining residual of £90 is allocated to the sale. The fact that the marginal cost of honouring this voucher is negligible is irrelevant.

Example 2 – Voucher for future money off (10% redemption expected)

The facts are the same as in example 1 except that the hotel company has reliable evidence that only 10% of vouchers are ever redeemed. No other factors affect the voucher's fair value. The fair value of the voucher, therefore, is £1.

The hotel has sold goods with a fair value (if sold individually) of £101 for consideration of £100.

Allocating the discount between the two components based on their fair values results in £99.01 being allocated to the initial stay in the hotel and £0.99 to the voucher.

9.228 An example of the accounting for a voucher issued as part of a sales transaction is as follows:

Example – Mechanics of accounting for vouchers

A retailer sells a toy for £10. A voucher entitling the bearer to a discount of £5 on a subsequent purchase of the same type of toy is issued with each sale. The retailer has historical experience that for every two vouchers issued, one is redeemed.

The customer is purchasing both the toy and a voucher. Therefore, part of the consideration received should be allocated to the 'money-off' coupon. Two of the ways in which the revenue could be allocated to the coupon are; by using a residual method or by using relative fair values. Under the residual method, the revenue allocated to the voucher is based on the fair value of those vouchers with the residual consideration being allocated to the sale of the toy. Under the relative fair value method, revenue is allocated to each component of a transaction on a relative fair value basis. Both approaches are illustrated below.

The residual method

In the absence of other factors, the fair value of the voucher would appear to be £2.50. This is calculated by comparing the nominal value of the voucher (£5) and adjusting that value for the proportion of vouchers expected to be redeemed (50%), arriving at a fair value of £2.50.

The consideration received is equal to the aggregate fair value of the toy and the voucher.

The accounting entry upon sale of, for instance, 10 toys and issue of the vouchers, would be:

Dr Cash	100	
Cr Revenue		75
Cr Deferred revenue		25

Given 50% of the vouchers are expected to be redeemed, out of the ten initial sales made, a further five sales will result in use of a voucher. The aggregate accounting entries for these five sales would be as follows:

Dr	Deferred revenue	25	
Dr	Cash	25	
	Cr Revenue		50

The amount of revenue recognised upon redemption of each voucher is based upon the number of vouchers redeemed relative to the total number expected to be redeemed. Given that only half of all vouchers are expected to be redeemed, amounting to 5 vouchers in this case, revenue of £5 (1/5 × 25) is released on the redemption of each voucher.

The relative fair value method

The facts are as in the example above whereby a retailer sells a toy for £10 along with a voucher entitling the bearer to a discount of £5 on a subsequent purchase.

As above, the fair value of the toy is £10 and the fair value of the voucher is £2.50. Hence, on a relative fair value basis, the revenue attributable to the toy is £8 ((£10/£12.50) × £10) and the revenue attributable to the voucher is £2 ((£2.50/£12.50) × £10). The accounting entries for the sale of 10 toys and issue of the vouchers would be:

Dr	Cash	100	
	Cr Revenue		80
	Cr Deferred revenue		20

Given 50% of the vouchers are expected to be redeemed, the aggregate accounting entries for these five sales would be as follows:

Dr	Deferred revenue	20	
Dr	Cash	25	
	Cr Revenue		45

As the amount of revenue recognised upon redemption of each voucher is based upon the number of vouchers redeemed relative to the total number expected to be redeemed, revenue of £4 (1/5 × 20) is released on the redemption of each voucher.

9.229 As noted above, the estimation of fair value of a voucher includes consideration of the proportion of vouchers expected to be redeemed. The expected rates of redemption may change over time as management update their estimates. Further to this, at any balance sheet date, the cumulative actual redemption rates may prove to be different from management's original expectations. This results in adjustments being made to revenue as illustrated below.

Example – Adjustments to revenue for changes in expected and actual redemption rates

Company A grants 100 award credits as part of sale transactions in year 1. The award points have a three year life. Initial expectations are that 80 credits will be redeemed. The fair value of the award credits is deemed to be £1.25 and hence, £100 (80 × £1.25) of the consideration received is deferred at the time of the transaction.

At the end of year 1, 40 points have been redeemed and hence £50 (being C100 × (40/80)) is recognised as revenue.

Scenario 1

At the end of year 2, 20 points have been redeemed. In addition, the redemption expectations have changed such that management now think that 75 points will ultimately be redeemed. Using the balance sheet approach, the total amount recognised as revenue at the end of year 2 should be:

(40 redeemed in year 1 + 20 redeemed in year 2) / (75 expected to be redeemed in total) × £100 = £80. As £50 was recognised in year 1, the amount to be recognised in year 2 is £30.

If the assumptions remain unchanged, the remaining £20 will be released in year 3.

Scenario 2

At the end of year 2, only 2 additional credits have been redeemed. In addition, the redemption expectations have changed such that management now think that 90 credits will ultimately be redeemed. The total amount recognised at the end of year 2 should be:

(40 redeemed in year 1 + 2 redeemed in year 2) / (90 expected to be redeemed in total) × £100 = £47. As £50 was recognised in year 1, the amount to be recognised in year 2 is a debit of £3.

If the assumptions remain unchanged, the remaining £43 will be recognised in year 3.

The illustration in scenario 2 is an extreme example and should not generally occur if redemption expectations are updated on a regular basis. However, it is included to illustrate how the adjustments made as a result of these revisions in expectations may cause credits or debits to the profit and loss account. We consider that it is appropriate to recognise any such adjustments (whether debits or credits) in the revenue line of the profit and loss account.

[The next paragraph is 9.232.]

9.232 Another possible outcome is that after considering the factors set out in paragraph 9.227 above, it may be determined that the fair value of a voucher is not significant, therefore no adjustment to revenue is required at the time the voucher is issued. In such circumstances the voucher may be an inducement to enter into a future transaction, rather than representing a separable component of the original transaction. [FRS 5 App G para G40].

9.233 Examples of how some of the factors in paragraph 9.227 above might be considered are as follows (in the same order as the bullet points):

- A seller includes with a popular line of goods a voucher giving money off a subsequent purchase of a line of goods that are not popular with customers or that are close to their sell-by date. The fair value of the vouchers will be relatively lower if the seller is likely to have to offer other similar discounts to all customers in order to dispose of the goods.
- A tour operator sells a holiday and offers £50 off the list price of a subsequent holiday taken with the tour operator between certain dates. If the operator has in the past offered or is likely to offer similar discounts on holidays between those dates to all customers, new or returning, the fair value of the £50 offer is most likely an amount below £50.
- A voucher for money off the next purchase of a certain item expires before it is likely that the first item will have been used by the customer. (For example, 50 per cent off the next purchase of anti-freeze included in sales made in August and expiring in December). In such cases the likelihood of exercise of the voucher is reduced and thus the value of the voucher may be insignificant.
- A supermarket sells a product with a voucher for money off the next purchase of that item, but at the same time regularly sends customers sheets of free coupons that they can use to purchase those and other goods at the same discounted price. In such a situation, the value of the voucher could again be lower than its face value.

9.234 The seller should review the estimated liability for outstanding vouchers, taking account of the proportion of vouchers that have been redeemed or have expired. The seller should make any adjustments necessary and include them in revenue. [FRS 5 App G para G41].

9.235 For companies applying FRS 26, 'Financial instruments: Recognition and measurement', vouchers that may be redeemed for cash meet the definition of a financial liability under that standard. As a result, any liability may not be derecognised until the derecognition criteria of FRS 26 are met. Furthermore, the liability may not be measured at an amount less than the cash redemption value. [FRS 26 para 49]. See further chapter 6 for recognition and measurement of financial liabilities.

9.236 Sometimes the provision of money-off coupons might result in a future sale appearing to be made at a loss. In such a case it is often unnecessary to provide for any future loss if, when the total consideration is apportioned between the linked transactions there is no loss. This is illustrated in the following example.

Example – Second transaction appears to be made at a loss

A company buys a particular product at £5 and normally sells it for £8. It gives an offer of 50% off a second item if a customer buys one at a later date. How should this be accounted for?

If, in the first sale, the voucher is not recognised, there is a gain on the first item of £3 (£8 — £5) and a loss on the second item of £1 (£4 — £5). However, if the fair value of the voucher is considered significant to the transaction, part of the consideration from the first sale, representing the fair value of the voucher, should be recorded as a liability. If this were to be done the fair value of the voucher may be £2. The proceeds of the first sale would be recorded as revenue of £6 and the revenue for the second sale plus the sale of the voucher would also be £6 (£4 + £2).

Note, however, that as the second transaction is made at a loss even once the voucher has been taken into consideration, management will have to consider whether the contract is onerous.

[The next paragraph is 9.240.]

Loyalty programmes (point schemes)

9.240 Some companies offer point schemes. Examples are airlines that offer 'free' air miles and supermarkets that offer loyalty cards that amass points that can then be used to reduce the cost of future purchases either from the same or a different supplier or may sometimes be redeemable for cash.

9.241 The rules in the application note described in the previous section apply equally to points schemes. Where points are awarded on sale of goods or services, revenue should be recorded at the amount of the consideration received or receivable less the fair value of the points awarded. Hence the fair value of the points awarded is deducted from the consideration received on the initial purchase and carried forward as a liability.

9.242 With points schemes it is also less likely that many of the factors listed in the application note for consideration when determining fair value (see para 9.227) will significantly reduce the fair value, with the exception of the proportion of points expected to be redeemed. This is because the range of goods or services that can be purchased with points is usually either very broad or not restricted. In addition, the discounts that points give rise to are usually over and above any discounts that are generally available to customers who do not have points, that is, the points are like cash. Nor is the length of time in which points may be redeemed usually restricted in such a way that their fair value is affected. Points are sometimes awarded as a 'bonus', but normally only to existing or new cardholders. They are not similar to other vouchers that are distributed to customers free of charge, but are incremental awards to cardholders or members.

Example – Determination of fair value for points

A company gives away 80 points with each purchase of goods valued at £100. These points can be exchanged for goods supplied either by the company or by a third party. For every 1,000 points, goods with an average fair value of £5 can be obtained. If the company provides these goods itself its cost is 80p. What is the 'exchange rate' of 100 points?

The exchange rate is 50p being the fair value of goods obtainable for 100 points. It is not 8p as that is the cost to the company of providing the goods. The total consideration received for the original purchase of goods should, therefore, be allocated as to £100 less eight-tenths of £5 (£4) making £96 for the goods and £4 for the points. The £4 should then be treated as a liability until the points are redeemed.

9.243 In some cases the points scheme may be run by a third party on behalf of the selling company, who makes a payment to the third party in respect of points granted by the third party. In principle this should not alter the way in which the company accounts for the points scheme, but in practice the payments to the third party may be close to the fair value of the points to the customer and it may be more practicable to use the payments to the third party (the operator) as a substitute for the fair value of the points.

9.244 If the agency relationship between the selling company and the operator is disclosed, the operator will normally be acting as principal and the customer will not have recourse to the selling company for unredeemed points. The selling company's only liability will be to make the necessary payment to the operator and the liability for this will be recorded when the goods that give rise to the points are sold. The selling company's income in respect of the points will not be the consideration received (which it has to pay over to the operator), but instead will be any commission it receives from the principal (the operator).

9.245 If the agency is undisclosed, the selling company will usually be acting as principal and the revenue from the sale of points will belong to the selling company. However, as noted above in that case the proceeds will be treated as a liability of the selling company until the points are redeemed. The selling company will also usually have to pay a fee to the operator for providing the service of operating the scheme.

Example – Loyalty card scheme

Company A runs a loyalty card scheme independently from any retailers. Company A has contracts with each retailer and the retailer can take any one of the following different roles:

- Be an issuer of points.
- Be a redeemer of points.
- Both issue and redeem points.

The customer holds a loyalty point card that is issued by company A and allows the customer to earn points at a given list of retailers and use points at other retailers. The face value of the point issued is £1 and for each point issued, the issuing retailers will pay £0.98 to company A and in doing so earn £0.02 of commission income. Once the issuing retailer has paid company A, it has no further obligation to the customer. When a retailer redeems points with a face value of £1, it will receive compensating cash from company A of £0.91. Company A's margin is the difference between the redemption price and the issue price. Where a retailer both issues and redeems points, there is no netting of cash flows: cash is paid to company A for points issued and cash is received from company A for points redeemed. The benefits for the participating retailers being:

- There is no need to administer the scheme.
- There is no obligation in respect of outstanding points and the retailer can exit the scheme.
- The fair value for the customer will be higher if the points are redeemable at a variety of stores.

The accounting for such as scheme is as follows. When the retailer makes a sale of £10, it issues points with face value of £1:

Dr	Cash		£10	
	Cr	Revenue		£9
	Cr	Commission income		£0.02
	Cr	Liability to A		£0.98

When the risks and rewards associated with the points are immediately passed to company A, the liability is offset:

Dr	Liability		£0.98	
	Cr	Cash		£0.98

When the points are redeemed, the redeeming retailers will recognise the revenue made by the points with a face value of £1 at £0.91:

Dr	Receivable from company A		£0.91	
	Cr	Revenue		£0.91

Vouchers granted without consideration

9.245.1 Some vouchers may be granted for no consideration separately from a sales transaction. An example of where a voucher is granted without consideration is where a supermarket, service provider or manufacturer issues money-off coupons or vouchers that can be redeemed in the future for goods or services. These are often included as part of marketing circulars or newspaper advertisements.

9.245.2 Application note G prescribes the treatment for this situation, where vouchers are distributed free of charge and independently of another transaction. It states that such vouchers do not give rise to a liability, except where redemption of the vouchers will result in products (or services) being sold at a loss. Where this is the case the seller has entered into an onerous contract and provision will need to be made in accordance with FRS 12, 'Provisions, contingent liabilities and contingent assets'. When the vouchers are redeemed, the seller should recognise revenue at the amount received for the product, after deducting the discount granted on exercise of the vouchers from the normal selling price. [FRS 5 App G para G42]. In essence, this type of voucher is no different from sales reductions in price made during an annual or seasonal sale.

Free products

9.245.3 Some sales promotions are described as 'buy one, get one free' or 'two for the price of one', or a vendor may price products below cost to attract volume. In the past, some have argued that the cost of the free product or the negative margin on a 'loss leader' is a marketing expense or that revenues, cost of sales and marketing expense should be grossed-up to reflect the normal selling price of the 'free' product. We do not consider that this argument is appropriate. The revenue is the actual sales proceeds and the purchase or production cost of the 'free' product and 'loss leader' is always a cost of sale. On the other hand, the cost of relatively insignificant promotional give-aways that are not part of the vendor's normal product offerings (for example, a 'free' bookmark with the purchase of a book, or a 'free' T-shirt bearing the logo of the vendor if you purchase £50 of merchandise) might be appropriately classified as a marketing expense. These principles are illustrated in the following examples.

Example 1 – Buy one get one half price

A retailer is offering a special 'buy one get one half price' deal whereby customers who purchase one box of chocolates are then entitled to purchase another box at the same time and obtain the second box for half the price. How should the retailer record the transaction?

The revenue recognised is the cash consideration received for the two boxes of chocolates. The additional cost of the second box being offered at a discount to the normal price is recorded as a cost of sales, not as a marketing expense.

Example 2 – First product sold for free

A company is a start-up, selling an electronic product. It is attracting a customer base by allowing the customer to have the first product free. The customer is under no obligation to take further products. The company has recorded the normal selling price for the free product as turnover and an equivalent amount together with the actual cost of the product to the company as a marketing expense. Is this acceptable?

No, this is not acceptable. No sale has been made and, therefore, no turnover should be recorded. The only amount to be charged is the cost of the product to the supplier, which may be charged as a marketing cost in this case, not cost of sales, as no sale has been made.

Other benefit schemes similar to point schemes

9.246 Other schemes that are similar to points schemes are where customers become entitled to benefits (such as free products) when they have satisfied certain criteria. Such criteria might be achieving a certain level of purchases or they might be time based, for example continuing to be a member of a scheme for a specified period.

9.247 Where benefits are based on achieving a level of purchases, the fair value of the benefit should be recognised by the supplier as the purchases occur. That is, part of the revenue equal to the fair value of the benefit to the customer should be deferred. This should be deferred until the free products are given (and matched against any costs thereof which are then charged).

Example – Other loyalty schemes

A DVD rental outlet stamps a card each time a customer hires a DVD. If the customer collects ten stamps and presents the completed card, this entitles the customer to one free DVD rental. In these circumstances, part of the consideration for each of the first ten rentals should be deferred and recognised as revenue when the customer presents the completed card and receives the free DVD rental.

9.248 Where a benefit is given in the form of a cash rebate the payment should be charged against the revenue that has been deferred, so that only the net revenue is recorded. This makes sense because reported revenue should not exceed amounts paid by the customer.

9.249 For those who receive rebates or free products on the attainment of certain targets the benefit should not be recognised until the targets are reached and receipt of the benefit is virtually certain.

9.250 Where criteria are based on a time factor, for instance on remaining a member for a specified period, consideration needs to be given as to whether the customer needs to complete any act of performance or whether the criteria are genuinely time based. Criteria that are time based with no act of performance are likely to be extremely rare. Generally, there will be some act of performance such as payment of a membership fee or subscription. In such cases, part of the fee or subscription should be treated as deferred revenue and recognised when the free products or other benefits are claimed (and any other associated costs are recognised). Where the benefits are genuinely time based only with no act of performance required, the obligation arises immediately and provision would need to be made (as there is no associated revenue there is no revenue to defer) and discounted if necessary to reflect the fact that the benefit may not be claimable until some later time.

Adjustments to revenue

9.250.1 In some situations, the adjustments made to revenue for discounts, returns and sale incentives can lead to entries being made that are debits to the revenue line of the profit and loss account. This will often be the result when the actual results differ significantly from estimates originally made. An example of when this may occur is given in the example below paragraph 9.83.

9.250.2 The recognition of a debit to the revenue line to recognise this adjustment may seem counter-intuitive. However, to the extent that the debit has been generated through the application of the requirements of FRS 5 Application Note G (to record revenue net of discounts and to make estimates in relation to the level of expected returns and expected redemption of sale incentives), we consider that it is appropriate to present such debits in the revenue line of the profit and loss account.

Dividends, royalties and other practical applications

Dividends

9.251 Treatment of dividends in a recipient's financial statements will follow that in the paying company, that is, dividends receivable will be recognised when the shareholder's right to receive payment is established. In the UK, the right to receive payment is established, for interim dividends, when they are paid and, for final dividends, when they are approved by shareholders at an Annual General Meeting. See further chapter 23.

Example – Recognition of dividend income

During the year ended 31 December 20X1 company A made the following investments in company B (a listed entity):

1 January 2,000 shares, registered on 28 February 20X1

15 June 5,000 shares, registered on 10 July 20X1

5 October 3,000 shares, registered on 20 December 20X1

29 December 1,000 shares, registration outstanding

The directors of company B declared an interim dividend on 31 July 20X1 of £0.05 per share, with a last registration date of 30 June 20X1. This dividend declaration does not require shareholder approval. The dividend was paid on 30 September 20X1.

At 31 December 20X1 the directors of company B proposed a final dividend of £0.15 per share, with a last registration date of 30 November 20X1. The proposed final dividend was approved by shareholders at the annual general meeting on 31 January 20X2 and the dividend was paid on 31 March 20X2.

Company A and company B both have December year ends. What should company A recognise as dividend income in the year ended 31 December 20X1?

Company A should recognise dividend income at 31 December 20X1 in respect of the interim dividend, but it should not recognise dividend income in respect of the final dividend.

The interim dividend is recognised as income by company A, as it was paid by company B in the period. However, company A is not entitled to receive the final dividend until the shareholders approve it.

Therefore, company A should recognise a dividend of £100 (2,000 × £0.05) in respect of the interim dividend on the 2,000 shares purchased in January 20X1.

9.252 A related issue concerning some dividends is whether the credit should be regarded as a revenue or capital item. One example of this is the treatment of dividends paid by a subsidiary to its parent. Under current UK company law, when a dividend is paid by a subsidiary (whether out of pre-acquisition or post-acquisition profits) it need not be applied in reducing the value of the investment in the subsidiary in the parent's books. It can be taken to the profit and loss account. Only if the underlying value of the subsidiary is impaired following the payment of the dividend, does the parent have to make a provision against its investment.

9.253 Bonus issues of shares by a subsidiary to its parent do not transfer any value from the subsidiary to the parent. There are more shares in issue, but there is no economic significance to the transaction. Therefore, a bonus issue does not give the parent a reason to recognise a gain, realised or unrealised, by increasing the carrying value of its investment in the subsidiary.

Shares for services

9.254 Other revenue recognition issues that create particular difficulties have arisen in respect of start-up companies where the practice of issuing shares for services or accepting equity stakes in exchange for services is particularly common. The following questions and suggested responses illustrate some of these difficulties.

Example – Consideration paid in shares

A company provides corporate finance services (for example, assistance in preparing for eventual flotation) to start-up companies and proposes to take equity stakes in the start-up companies instead of fees. In relation to revenue recognition, consider the outcome based on the following facts:

- In some cases securities received will be listed and in other cases they will be unlisted.
- Some securities will be marketable, whereas others may not be marketable.
- The company intends to hold the securities for the medium to long-term.
- There may be restrictions placed on the company's ability to dispose of the securities for a period.

The reason for the proposed arrangements is for the company to share in the success of the start-up companies it advises and to assist them by enabling them to obtain advice without having to pay substantial fees.

Application note G, states that revenue should be measured at the fair value of the right to consideration. However, compliance with company law is also necessary.

Company law (SI 2008/410 1 Sch 13) permits only realised profits to be included in the profit and loss account.

Listed or marketable shares

If the shares received are listed or marketable, there is a liquid market and the company was capable of readily disposing of the shares and it could do so without curtailing or disrupting its business, then the value of the shares can be regarded as revenue and, hence, as a realised profit and taken to the profit and loss account.

If, however, there are restrictions over the disposal of the shares, then this does not give rise to a realised profit (and no profit could be included in the profit and loss account) until the restrictions are lifted. This is because until the restrictions are removed the company could not have disposed of the shares. However, if the value of the shares can be reliably measured they should be recognised in the balance sheet and any gain taken to the STRGL.

Non-marketable shares

If the shares are not marketable, their receipt does not give rise to a realised profit and so no revenue is included in the profit and loss account. However, an unrealised gain could be recognised.

Whether the shares should be recorded at a value and an unrealised gain recognised will depend on whether the value (and the gain) can be measured reliably. If the investee company had a track record, then recognition at a value might be possible. The unrealised gain would be treated as a revaluation gain and shown in the STRGL. However, given that the company is a start-up, there is likely to be uncertainty as to the investment's value and it should not be included at a value (that is it should be treated as having nil cost, with disclosure of the facts). This is because in the absence of reliable measurement neither the value of the investment nor the gain can be recognised.

If subsequently a basis for reliable measurement of the value of the equity stake is established (such as where the investee company is floated or where other investors subscribe for shares) the company could revalue its investment and show the gain in the STRGL.

Cost of providing the services

The company will have incurred costs in providing the services in return for an equity stake. Where no value is able to be placed on the equity stake received for work done, any costs incurred to the date of billing the client should be written off to the profit and loss account.

Where the value of equity stake can be reliably measured and the stake is readily marketable the value can be recognised in the profit and loss account. The costs incurred should also be charged to the profit and loss account as soon as the work is billed.

Where the value of the equity stake can be reliably measured, but the value is recognised in the STRGL to the extent that the costs are 'covered' by the value of the equity that is recognised, the costs should be included in the carrying value of the investment. This is because the costs qualify for recognition as an asset from which future economic benefits are expected and which can be measured reliably. Here, only the net gain (value of equity stake less cost) is taken to the STRGL. To the extent that costs exceed the value attributable to the equity stake they should be written off to the profit and loss account. Comparison of costs to value of equity stakes for this purpose should be made on a case-by-case basis. Applying a portfolio of costs and matching it to a portfolio of investments is not appropriate.

It would also not be appropriate to capitalise the whole of the cash equivalent fee since it is includes an element of profit. Instead, only such costs as would be included in work in progress should be capitalised. By deciding to accept equity instead of fees, the company has effectively converted a revenue transaction into a capital transaction.

Licensing and royalties

Royalties

9.255 Royalties include other fees for the use of assets such as trademarks, patents, software, copyright, record masters, films and TV programmes. The terms of an agreement will normally indicate when the revenue has been earned. In general, revenue may be recognised on a straight line basis over the life of the agreement or another systematic basis such as in relation to sales to which the royalty relates (see Table 9.16).

9.255.1 For example, if an agreement provides for a five per cent royalty to be received on each sale by a third party it would be normal to recognise royalty income on the basis of five per cent of total sales made by the third party as notified to the entity.

9.255.2 On the other hand, in a similar situation, an up-front non-refundable payment might be made to the entity by the other party and then a royalty of one per cent of sales might be receivable thereafter. In that situation, it would be appropriate to reflect the agreement's substance rather than its form and spread the up-front receipt over the expected number of sales to be made in the future where, in substance, the receipt is an advance royalty.

Table 9.16 – Chrysalis Group PLC – Annual Report and Accounts – 31 August 2002
Notes to the Accounts (extract)

1 Accounting policies (extracts)

Record royalties (excluding music publishing royalties and record producer services)

Royalty income is included on a receivable basis calculated on sales of records arising during each accounting period as reported by licensees. Royalties payable are expensed on an accruals basis. Royalty advances payable are expensed on a paid basis except that they are carried forward and recognised as an asset where such advances relate to current unreleased products and where it is estimated that sufficient future royalties will be earned for recoupment from those products.

Advances received in respect of individual albums are carried forward and recognised as income over the expected life of each individual licence.

Music publishing royalties and record producer services

Music publishing royalties are accounted for on a notified earnings basis, with any unrecouped royalty advances carried forward until the end of the relevant contract period. This accounting policy was changed with effect from the year ended 31st August 2001, full details of which are set out in the Annual Report and Accounts for 2001. Royalties received for record producer services are accounted for on a cash basis. Royalties payable are expensed on an accruals basis except that music publishing royalty advances are carried forward and recognised as an asset where such advances relate to proven artists or songwriters and where it is estimated that sufficient future royalties will be earned for recoupment of these advances.

Film and broadcasting licensing and distribution income

Revenue from the licensing or distribution of film, broadcast or exhibition rights is recognised from the date of release for distribution or broadcast.

Television productions

Turnover and attributable profits on television programmes produced for commissioning broadcasters are recognised on television production contracts which are incomplete at the end of the year in the proportion that costs incurred to date bear to estimated ultimate costs after making provision for anticipated losses.

Investment in television rights

Investment in television rights is stated at cost and included in intangible assets in the Group balance sheet. They are amortised in the profit and loss account in the proportion that revenue bears to the estimated ultimate revenue after making provision for any anticipated shortfall.

Deferred television programme development expenditure

Pre-contract development expenditure is written off in the period in which it is incurred except where it relates to a clearly defined project, the outcome of which has been assessed with reasonable certainty as to its success and commercial viability. In such cases the expenditure is deferred to the extent that its recovery can be reasonably regarded as assured and the cost is written off against revenue over the period of the contract.

Licence income

9.256 In general, in line with the general principles in Application Note G, revenue should not be recognised under licensing agreements until performance under the contract has occurred and the seller has a right to consideration.

Example 1 – License fee with a continuing obligation

Company A grants a licence to a customer to use its website, which contains proprietary databases. The licence allows the customer to use the website for a two year period (1 January 20X1 to 31 December 20X2). The licence fee of £60,000 is payable on 1 January 20X1.

The agreement's substance is that the customer is paying for a service that is delivered over time. Although company A will not incur incremental costs in serving the customer, it will incur costs to maintain the website.

Hence, the revenue from the licence fees should be accrued over the period of the agreement that reflects the provision of the service. The entity has an obligation to provide services for the next two years, therefore, the fee of £60,000 received on 1 January 20X1 should be recognised as a liability. Each month for the period January 20X1 to December 20X2, an amount of £2,500 should be released from the liability and recognised as income to reflect the service that is delivered.

Example 2 – License fee with a trigger event

A film distributor grants a licence to a cinema operator. The licence entitles the operator to show the film once for consideration of the higher of a non-refundable guarantee or a percentage of the box office receipts.

The film distributor should recognise the revenue on the date the film is shown. It is only when the film is shown that the revenue has been earned.

9.257 In some situations, a licensing agreement may be recognised as an outright sale. For example, when an assignment of rights is granted for a non-refundable amount under a non-cancellable contract, this contract permits the licensee to use those rights freely and the license has no remaining obligations, it may be appropriate to recognise the income when the fee is received. Since the licensor has no control over any further use or distribution of the product and has no further action to perform under the contract he has effectively sold the rights detailed in the licensing agreement.

9.257.1 If a licence is granted for a limited period of time, the question arises as to whether revenue should be recognised at one point in time (for the sale of the license) or spread over the licence term. The appropriate treatment will depend on the facts and circumstances. A fixed license term is an indicator that the revenue should be recognised over the period; however, this is not definitive. The fixed period suggests that all the licence's risks and rewards have not been transferred to the customer. However, in some situations, there may be no clear performance obligation for the vendor subsequent to the transaction and the asset's risks and rewards may have been transferred for the asset's entire useful life. In such a case, it may be appropriate to recognise the revenue upfront even if the licence rights are sold for a fixed period only.

9.257.2 Whether it is appropriate to recognise revenue over the period of the license or as a sale of goods will be a matter of judgement. The following additional indicators should be considered when making that judgement (the presence of the indicator implying that treatment as a sale may be appropriate).

- Fixed fee or non-refundable guarantee. The fee is pre-determined in amount. It is non-refundable and is not contingent on the occurrence of a future event.
- The contract is non-cancellable. This will ensure that risks and rewards have been transferred and the inflow of economic benefit to the vendor is probable.
- The customer is able to exploit the rights freely. For this to be possible, the licence rights must be a separable component that can meet the sale of goods criteria on their own. The vendor should not have a significant involvement during the contractual period and should not have the right to control or influence the way the customer uses the rights (as long as the customer acts within the specified contractual terms). The ability to sub-licence the rights or even to stop using the licence at any time, may indicate that the customer is able to exploit the rights freely.
- Vendor has no remaining obligations to perform subsequent to delivery. Such obligations might include significant updating of the product (for example, software upgrades), marketing efforts and fulfilling specified substantive obligations to maintain the reputation of the vendors' business and promote the brand in question.

9.258 An example of policies for revenue recognition on sale and distribution of programmes is given in Table 9.17.

Table 9.17 – HIT Entertainment plc – Annual Report – 31 July 2004
Turnover

- **Consumer products**

The Group policy is to recognise licensing revenue by spreading the total guaranteed minimum value of a contract over the term, only recognising actual licensing income receivable once it exceeds the apportionment of the total guaranteed minimum contract value. In addition recognition of revenue and associated royalty expenses will only begin once the following criteria are met:

(a) a licence agreement has been executed by all parties; and

(b) the licence term has commenced.

Any licence fees received in advance which do not meet all of the above criteria, are included in deferred income until the above criteria are met.

Associated royalties on consumer products sales are recognised when the related turnover is recorded.

- **Home entertainment**

Revenues and associated costs of goods sold and royalty expenses from home entertainment revenues are recognised on the date that the products are made widely available for sale by the Group's retailer customers.

- **Television**

Income recognised on HIT-owned television programme series and from the distribution of other television programmes represents the invoiced value of licence fees including withholding tax but excluding value added tax. The Group's policy is to recognise the income and associated royalty payable when all of the following criteria are met:

(a) a licence agreement has been executed by both parties;

(b) the programme has substantially met all necessary technical quality requirements;

(c) delivery to the broadcaster has occurred;

(d) the licence term has commenced;

(e) the arrangement is fixed or determinable; and

(f) collection of the arrangement fee is reasonably assured.

Any licence fees received in advance, which do not meet all of the above criteria, are included in deferred income until the above criteria are met.

- **Stage show**

Turnover from stage shows is based on the invoiced value of the goods and services provided in the year excluding sales tax. Any licensing revenue related to stage show activity is accounted for in accordance with the consumer product policies above.

Franchise fees

9.259 Franchise agreements may provide for the supply of initial services such as training and assistance to help the franchisee set up and operate the franchise operation, subsequent services and the supply of equipment, stocks and other tangible assets and know-how. Therefore, these agreements may generate different types of revenue such as initial franchise fees, profits and losses from the sale of fixed assets and royalties as illustrated in Table 9.18.

Table 9.18 – Diageo plc – Annual Report and Accounts – 30 June 2001

Accounting policies (extract)

Franchising

Franchising generates initial franchise fees, as well as profits or losses arising from the franchising of developed or purchased outlets previously operated by the group, and ongoing royalty revenues based on sales made by franchisees. Income from franchising is included in operating profit, apart from any property element which is treated as a disposal of fixed assets.

9.260 In general, franchise fees should be recognised on a basis that reflects the purpose for which they were charged. For example, revenue from the supplies of assets should be recognised when the items are delivered or title passes, whereas fees charged for the use of continuing rights granted by a franchise agreement or for other continuing services provided during the period of the agreement should be recognised as the service is provided or the rights are used.

9.260.1 Where the agreement provides for the supply of more than one type of good or service, this will be a multiple element arrangement (see para 9.145). This means that the total consideration received under the agreement must be allocated to the components and recognised when goods or services are delivered.

9.261 Sometimes, franchise agreements require an upfront payment by the franchisee. Where the franchise agreement also provides for the franchiser to supply equipment, stocks or other assets at a price lower than that charged to others, or at a price that does not allow the franchiser to make a reasonable profit on the supplies, that part of the initial fee should be deferred. The amount of the initial fee deferred should be the difference between the fair value and the price actually charged for any assets and other goods supplied. This deferred income can then be recognised over the period the assets or goods are likely to be provided. The balance of the initial fee should be recognised when the initial services have been substantially accomplished. This approach is consistent with the accounting for inception fees (see from para 9.136) and based on the fact that the initial fee, in these circumstances, is unlikely to be capable of being treated as a separable component.

9.262 Similarly, if there is no separate fee for the supply of continuing services after the initial fee, then part of the initial fee should also be deferred and recognised as the subsequent services are provided.

Financial services fees

9.262.1 Financial services fees arise in many forms, including transaction such as loan origination fees, commitment fees and management and performance fees in relation to fund and unit trusts. The different types of fees are considered in the section below.

Fees that are an integral part of the effective interest rate

9.262.2 In many situations, the actual rate of interest charged by a lender will be the same as the effective rate (that is, the rate required to discount the expected future income streams over the life of the loan to its initial carrying amount). Other transactions may include elements both of interest and of other financial service fees. For these transactions it is necessary to differentiate between fees that are part of the transaction's effective yield and fees that are earned for performing a certain act.

> **Example – Loan origination fee**
>
> Company A grants a loan to company B for £100,000 on 1 January 20X1. The loan is repayable at 31 December 20X5. Interest of 8% that is equal to the market rate is payable annually. The loan origination fees amount to £2,000 and are paid by company B to company A on 1 January 20X1.
>
> Loan origination fees charged by company A are an integral part of establishing a loan. These fees are deferred and recognised as an adjustment to the effective yield. The effective yield is the interest needed to discount all the cash flows (£8,000 for 5 years and the principle amount of £100,000) to the present value of £98,000. In this case, the effective yield obtained by a discounted cash flow calculation is approximately 8.51% and, therefore, the entity recognises a finance cost at 8.51% on the carrying amount in each period.
>
> Table 9.20 gives The Royal Bank of Scotland's accounting policy for loan origination fees.

Table 9.20 – The Royal Bank of Scotland Group Plc – Annual Report and Accounts – 31 December 2004

Accounting policies (extract)

2 Revenue recognition (extract)

Loan origination fees: up-front lending fees are recognised as income when receivable except where they are charged in lieu of interest or charged to cover the cost of a continuing service to the borrower, in which case they are credited to income over the life of the advance.

9.262.3 The appendix to IAS 18 gives guidance on accounting for different types of financial service fees that can be applied in the UK. Reviewing the borrower's credit rating or registering charges, for example, are necessary and integral parts of the lending process. Fees for performing such services should be deferred and recognised as an adjustment to the effective interest rate. Commitment fees that are charged by the lender when it is probable that a specific transaction will take place should similarly be included in the effective interest rate (where the loan commitment is outside IAS 39's scope, which is the same as FRS 26), but if the commitment expires without the transaction taking place, then the fee may be recognised as revenue on expiration. For companies applying FRS 26 (see chapter

6), loan commitments that are within FRS 26's scope are accounted for as derivatives and measured at fair value.

Fees earned as a result of providing services

9.262.4 Other types of financial service fees are earned as the service is provided. For example, commitment fees that are charged by a lender when it is unlikely that a lending arrangement will be entered into should be recognised on a time apportioned basis over the commitment period (where the loan commitment is outside the scope of FRS 26). Fees for servicing a loan should also be recognised as the service is provided.

Fees earned upon the execution of a significant act

9.262.5 A third type of financial service fee relates to performing a particular significant act. Commissions received on the allotment of shares or placement fees for arranging a loan between a borrower and an investor are examples of such significant acts. Revenue should be recognised when the act has been performed, for example, when the shares have been allotted or the loan arranged. However, fees earned for the completion of a significant act must be distinguished from fees that relate to future performance or to any risk retained. A loan syndication fee, for example, may be earned when the transaction takes place, if the entity that arranges the loan either has no further involvement or retains part of the loan package at the same effective interest rate for comparable risk as the other participants. Such a fee is recognised as revenue when the syndication has been completed.

9.262.6 It is common within the investment management industry that a financial broker will receive an upfront payment from a fund manager for signing up a new customer. When the financial broker is also the fund manager, the question arises as to whether a non-refundable upfront fee can be recognised as revenue. The outcome has been debated at length under IFRS by IFRIC. The IFRIC provided limited guidance (in the form of a rejection) in determining whether an upfront fee could be recognised as revenue (details given below). In the absence of any other guidance in the UK, the limited guidance from IFRIC is the best that is available in helping to determine whether an upfront fee could be recognised as revenue:

- Fees may be recognised as revenue only to the extent that services have been provided.
- Whilst the proportion of costs incurred in delivering services may be used to estimate the transaction's stage of completion, incurring costs does not by itself imply that a service has been provided.
- The receipt of a non-refundable initial fee does not, in itself, give evidence that an upfront service has been provided or that the fair value of the consideration paid in respect of any upfront services is equal to the initial fee received.

- To the extent that:
  - an initial service can be shown to have been provided to a customer;
  - the fair value of the consideration received in respect of that service can be measured reliably; and
  - the conditions for the recognition of revenue in Application note G have been met,

  upfront and ongoing fees may be recognised as revenue in line with the provision of services to the customer.

9.262.7 To the extent that the fee is received upfront and the seller has no further obligations, the seller should recognise the fee on the date it has been received. Before this is possible, however, management should consider whether there is any indication that the fee is linked to other services or obligations. This could be indicated, for example, if the fee was not at fair value or the pricing of other services to be provided in the future could only be commercially understood with reference to the fee received upfront. In order to recognise upfront fees received as revenue upon receipt, management would need to demonstrate the existence of a separate service provided upfront; it would also be necessary to reliably estimate the fair value of the consideration received for that service.

9.262.8 If it is determined that the upfront fee is linked to future services to be provided, the revenue would be deferred on the balance sheet and recognition would occur over the period in which those future services were performed. In certain cases, the customer may have the option to extend their relationship with the seller such that they continue to receive services for a longer period than that covered by the original contract. In such a situation, we consider that it would be appropriate to spread the revenue over the period of the original contract. It would not be appropriate to look into the future to estimate whether the contract will be extended and to spread the revenue over a longer period.

Management and performance fees

9.262.9 An investment manager generally provides a number of services including investment advice, research services and certain administrative services under an investment advisory agreement to an investment fund in return for a fee. The fee is typically a fixed or a reducing percentage of the fund's average net assets. This type of fee is usually called a management fee. Recognition of revenue from management fees that are not dependent on fund's performance would be recognised when the criteria for sale of services are met.

9.262.10 In addition, fees could also be based on performance; these fees are known as incentive or performance fees. A performance fee is paid to the investment manager if it achieves a performance in excess of a specified minimum during a specified period (the performance period). The amount of the performance fee payable to the manager if this condition is met may be an absolute share of the fund's performance or a share of performance in excess of a specified benchmark, such as the FTSE 100 index or Standard and Poor's 500 index. There are numerous permutations of how these fees are calculated including the benchmark used and the performance period. Both the management and performance fees are deemed fees for the provision of services.

9.262.11 A performance period may not coincide with a reporting period, for example. an investment manager prepares interim financial statements for the 6 month period ended 30 June 20X7, and the performance period is for the 12 months ending 31 December 20X7. In this case, the performance fee will only be received if the investment manager achieves the performance condition at the end of the 12 month period, that is the fee is contingent upon a future event.

9.262.12 The recognition of revenue for a performance fee will depend on the facts and circumstances relating to the transaction in question. However, generally, we consider that revenue would not be recognised until the right to consideration has been earned. See further from paragraph 9.57 onwards.

Grants

9.263 Gifts in the form of grants may be given to a company to help finance a particular asset or specific profit and loss account expenditure. When these grants are given by government, including inter-governmental agencies and EU bodies, guidance on the accounting treatment is contained in SSAP 4, 'Accounting for government grants', which differentiates between the treatment for revenue and capital based grants. The treatment of monies received under grants is considered below. The treatment of assets acquired using capital grants is considered in chapter 16. Payments given to companies from sources other than government should be subject to similar analysis since SSAP 4 is indicative of best practice for accounting for grants and assistance from other sources. Thus, for example, a non-refundable payment by a third party franchiser to assist the franchisee with the purchase of specific assets would be more in the nature of a grant than a capital contribution.

9.264 The 'accruals' concept, which is the key principle underlying SSAP 4, implies that government grants should be recognised in the profit and loss account to match them with the expenditure towards which they are intended to contribute. The relationship between the grant and the related expenditure is, therefore, of paramount importance in establishing the accounting treatment to be adopted. Grants made as contributions to revenue expenditure should be credited to the profit and loss account of the period in which the related expenditure is incurred. For example, see Westland Group plc's accounting policy in Table 9.19.

Table 9.19 – Westland Group plc – Annual Report – 1 October 1993
Accounting policies (extract)
8 Research, development, launching costs and launch aid

To the extent that design, development and learning costs are not recoverable under specific contracts, including risk sharing contracts, they are written off as incurred, net of any launch aid recovered under the Civil Aviation Act 1982. Learning costs are the estimated excess cost of manufacturing initial production batches.

Launch aid from H.M. Government is credited in full against the initial research, development and learning costs in the year in which it is receivable. Additional research, development and learning costs required under launch aid agreements in excess of launch aid receivable are charged against revenue as incurred.

9.265 Government grants should not be recognised until the conditions for their receipt have been complied with and there is reasonable assurance that the grant will be received. In the event that a grant appears likely to have to be repaid, provision should be made for the estimated liability.

9.266 Difficulties of matching may arise where the terms of the grant do not specify precisely the expenditure towards which it is intended to contribute. For example, grants may be awarded to defray project costs comprising both revenue and capital expenditure. Project grants are normally awarded on this basis and may be related to the project's capital expenditure costs and the number of jobs created or safeguarded. In such circumstances, the expenditure eligible for grant aid may be all the costs incurred that are directly attributable to the project. The terms of the grant itself often need to be carefully examined to establish whether the intent is to defray costs or to establish a condition relating to the entire amount of the grant.

Example – Capital or revenue grant?

A company obtains a grant from an Industrial Development agency for an investment project in Scotland. The project is a building to house a manufacturing plant. The principal terms are that the grant payments relate to the level of capital expenditure and the intention of the grant is to help ensure that imports of the product can be replaced with products from sources in the UK to safeguard 500 jobs. The grant will have to be repaid if there is an underspend on capital or if the jobs are not safeguarded until 18 months after the date of the last fixed asset purchase.

This grant is related to capital expenditure. The employment condition should be seen as an additional condition to prevent replacement of labour by capital, rather than as the reason for the grant. If the grant was revenue it would be related to revenue expenditure such as a percentage of the payroll cost or a fixed amount per job safeguarded.

9.267 SSAP 4 states that where the terms of the grant do not specify precisely the expenditure it is intended to meet, the most appropriate accounting may be achieved by assuming that the grant is contributing towards the expenditure that forms the basis for its payment, that is, the expenditure included on the claim form. It will then be possible to account for the grant according to the different types of expenditure towards which it is intended to contribute. If the grant is paid when evidence is produced that certain expenditure has been incurred, then the grant should be recognised simultaneously with that expenditure.

Example – Treatment of a capital grant

Company A is awarded a government grant of £100,000 on 1 January 20X1 towards the construction of a manufacturing plant. The plant's useful life is estimated at 10 years. The entity took two years to construct the plant. At 1 January 20X3 the entity started to use the plant for manufacturing products. The entity has a December year end.

The £100,000 grant relates to the construction of an asset and should be initially recognised as a liability in the balance sheet. The liability should be recognised as income in line with the asset's depreciation.

The entity should recognise a liability on the balance sheet for the years ending 31 December 20X1 and 31 December 20X2. Once the plant starts being used in the manufacturing process, other operating income of £10,000 should be recognised in each year of the asset's 10 year useful life to match depreciation.

9.267.1 The treatment of a capital grant when the associated asset is impaired is considered in the example below.

Example — Treatment of a capital grant when the associated asset is written down for impairment

Some years ago a company constructed a factory with the assistance of a government grant. The grant is non-refundable and, following the construction of the factory, cannot be clawed back by the government. The grant received has been treated as deferred income and is being credited to the profit and loss account over the same period as the factory is being depreciated. Following an adverse change in the line of business the factory serves, the directors have concluded that the factory's carrying value is no longer recoverable in full and that a write-down for impairment is required. The write-down is more than covered by the unamortised deferred income balance relating to the grant.

Management would like to match the write-down of the asset to the corresponding release to deferred income.

Paragraph 12 of SSAP 4 states that government grants should be recognised as income over the periods in the same period as the related expenditure. In this case, the expenditure relating to the asset is being recognised in the profit and loss account through depreciation and impairment charges. We would therefore consider it reasonable to release an amount of deferred income to the income statement to match the impairment write-down.

9.268 In certain circumstances, however, the actual expenditure the grant is intended to contribute towards may differ from the expenditure that forms the basis of its payment. For example, the grant may relate to a total project expenditure that may include, in addition to capital expenditure, working capital costs, training costs and removal costs. However, the grant may become payable in instalments on incurring specific amounts of capital expenditure as the project progresses. In this situation, it would be wrong to treat the whole grant as a capital expenditure grant. The most appropriate treatment, therefore, would be to match the grant received rateably with the expenditure towards which the grant is assisting, that is, the grant would have to be spread rateably over the constituent parts of the project expenditure. This treatment is in accordance with SSAP 4 which provides that where such evidence exists and is sufficiently persuasive, then it is appropriate to match grants received with identified expenditure and this approach should always be preferred.

9.269 Sometimes grants may be payable on a different basis, for example on the achievement of a non-financial objective. In such situations, the grant should be recognised simultaneously with the identifiable costs of achieving that objective. Such costs must be identified or estimated on a reasonable basis. For example, if a grant is given on condition that jobs are created and maintained for a minimum period, the grant should be recognised in the same period as the cost of providing the jobs for that period. As a result, a greater proportion of the grant may fall to be recognised in the early stages of the project because of higher non-productive and set-up costs.

Example – Grant payable on the achievement of a non-financial goal

Company A is awarded a government grant of £60,000 receivable over three years (£40,000 in year 1 and £10,000 in each of years 2 and 3), contingent on creating 10 new jobs and maintaining them for three years. The employees are recruited at a cost of £30,000, and the wage bill for the first year is £100,000, rising by £10,000 in each of the subsequent years.

The income of £60,000 should be recognised over the three-year period to match the related costs.

In year 1, £21,667 of the £40,000 received from government will match the related costs of £130,000 incurred during the year, and should therefore be recognised as income. The amount of the grant that has not yet been credited to income (that is £18,333, being £40,000 of cash received less £21,667 credited to income) should be reflected in the balance sheet as such.

Year	Labour cost	Credit Grant	Grant calculations	Credit balance sheet Deferred income	Calculations
1	130 000	21 667	(130/360) x 60 000	18 333	(40 000 – 21 667)
2	110 000	18 333	(110/360) x 60 000	10 000	(50 000 – 40 000)
3	120 000	20 000	(120/360) x 60 000	–	
	360 000	60 000			

9.270 In certain circumstances, government grants may be awarded unconditionally without regard to the entity's future actions, or requirement to incur further costs. Such grants may be given for the immediate financial support, or assistance of an entity, or for the reimbursement of costs previously incurred. They may also be given to finance the general activities of an entity over a specified period, or to compensate for a loss of income. In some instances, the extent of these grants may constitute a major source of revenue for the entity. Where grants are awarded on such a basis, they should be recognised in the profit and loss account of the period in respect of which they are paid, or, if they are not stated to be paid in respect of a particular period, in the profit and loss account of the period in which they are receivable. The presentation and disclosure requirements of SSAP 4 are detailed from paragraph 9.293.

Example – Grant received unconditionally

Company A incurred expenses of £5,000 that related to training employees during the period May 20X1 to September 20X1. The employee training was a government requirement. Company A entered into negotiations with the government for compensation for the training expenses incurred in December 20X1. In February 20X2 the government agreed that it would compensate the entity for the expenses incurred for the year ended 31 December 20X1.

Although company A incurred the expenses for the year ended 31 December 20X1, it should recognise the income received from the government for the year ended 31 December 20X2. The grant of £5,000 will only become receivable for the year ended 31 December 20X2, that is the year in which the government agreed to compensate A for the training expenses.

[The next paragraph is 9.277.]

Treatment of capital transactions

9.277 In the year in which it is received, the capital contribution should be credited to reserves by the receiving company and reported in its reconciliation of movements in shareholders' funds because it is not a gain, but the receipt from a transaction with shareholders. Nevertheless, it appears that where the amount is received in cash, it is legally a realised profit and as such can be taken into account in determining whether a company has sufficient distributable reserves to pay a dividend. Where, however, a contribution is in the form of an asset (for example, shares in a subsidiary) that is not cash or readily convertible into cash the contribution is not a realised profit and may not, therefore, be taken into account in determining distributable profits. It is best recorded in a separate reserve to distinguish it from other reserves, because of its different nature.

9.278 It seems logical that in the paying company (in a group of companies) the opposite accounting treatment should be adopted. Therefore, the contribution should not be recorded as an expense in the profit and loss account, but should be added to the cost of the investment in the subsidiary. Only if there is an impairment in the underlying value of the investment in the subsidiary would the investing company need to make a provision against its carrying value.

Recognition of costs

9.279 Alongside considering when revenue can be recognised, companies must also consider the period in which costs should be recognised in the profit and loss account.

9.280 The Statement of Principles is based on a balance sheet approach. This balance sheet approach applies in considering how costs and revenues should be recognised. The balance sheet is a statement of financial position and the elements directly related to the measurement of financial position in the balance sheet are assets, liabilities and ownership interest. [Statement of Principles para 4.0]. Following this principle, balances should only be recognised on the balance sheet to the extent that they meet the Statement's definition of an asset or a liability.

9.281 The Statement of Principles specifies that the starting point for recognition is always the effect that a transaction has on the entity's assets and liabilities. It then goes on to specify that the notion of matching will often help in identifying these effects. [Statement of Principles paras 5.26 – 5.27].

9.282 In certain situations, the timing of costs can vary significantly from the profile of revenue recognition. This can happen, for example, in outsourcing contracts where the service provider may incur costs before revenue will be received. When this occurs, the question may arise as to whether it is appropriate to defer recognising these costs in the profit and loss account until revenue recognition begins.

9.282.1 Almost all expenditure is undertaken with a view to acquiring some form of benefit in exchange. Consequently, if matching were used in an unrestricted way, it would be possible to delay the recognition in the performance statement of most items of expenditure insofar as the hoped-for benefits still lay in the future. The Statement imposes a degree of discipline on this process, because only items that meet the definitions of, and relevant recognition criteria for, assets, liabilities or ownership interest (or residual interest for public benefit entities) are recognised in the balance sheet. This means that the Statement does not use the notion of matching as the main driver of the recognition process. [Statement of Principles para 5.24].

9.282.2 Generally speaking, this means that it may be appropriate to capitalise costs if the entity can recognise an asset in accordance with SSAP 9, 'Stocks and long-term contracts', FRS 15, 'Tangible fixed assets', or FRS 10, 'Goodwill and intangible assets'. The application of this principle to various contracts is considered in the examples below.

Example 1 – Contract for the performance of services to numerous customers

A shipping entity provides specialised transportation services to numerous customers. A ship travels (empty) to the load port where it picks up cargo. It then loads the cargo and transports it to the discharge port. Costs are incurred on the voyage to the load port. The question arises as to whether these costs can be deferred until the vessel reaches the load port so that they are recognised in the profit and loss account in the same period as the revenue?

Management should consider the nature of the costs incurred on a case by case basis. Only costs meeting the definition of stock, tangible fixed assets or intangible assets under SSAP 9, FRS 15 or FRS 10 respectively would be capitalised (in line with the relevant standard). In all other cases, costs should be expensed as incurred. To illustrate, the cost of fuel used to travel to the load port would be expensed, whereas fuel purchased but not yet utilised would be capitalised as stock. Other costs, such as staff costs, would be expensed as incurred.

Example 2 – Contract for the performance of a repetitive service to one customer

Company C offers outsourced travel booking services to corporate clients. A five-year contract is put in place whereby company C will undertake all travel bookings on behalf of one specific customer. Company C allocates separate space within its premises for the provision of services to that customer. Therefore, it is possible to obtain all direct costs for the contract, for example, rent, staff costs, computer and telephone links. Over the period of the contract, company C will make numerous individual bookings for this specific customer.

The revenue is on a transactional basis – that is, for each individual booking made a fee is charged. Often, transaction numbers are relatively low in the first year of the contract. In addition, certain non-recurring costs (such as training costs) are incurred in the early years of the contract. As such, income is expected to be below costs in the early years of the contract. However, the contract is very likely to be profitable overall as, in later years, the number of transactions will increase and fewer non-recurring costs will be incurred. The entity has good historical data when predicting future revenues and costs of the business under each contract based on experience with similar clients.

As above, costs incurred would be capitalised if they meet the definition of stock, tangible fixed assets or intangible assets. For example, the cost of acquiring equipment such as desks and computers would be capitalised under FRS 15. Other costs would be expensed as incurred.

Revenue associated with each booking would be recognised as each booking is made. If it is not appropriate to capitalise costs and they are expensed as incurred, then based upon the transaction pattern above, this may result in losses being made in the early years of the contract and profits being made in the later years.

9.282.3 Contracts may have initiation or pre-contract costs as well as costs incurred during the contract. Costs associated with long-term contracts are considered in chapter 20. For other types of contract, the question arises as to whether the costs of securing a service contract or a contract to deliver goods can be deferred and recognised over the contract period in a similar way. For such contracts, we consider that the principle in paragraph 9.282.2 above applies. Consequently, such costs may be capitalised only when they meet the definition of stock, tangible fixed assets or intangible assets.

Example 1 – Costs of acquiring a service contract

Telecoms operator A pays commissions of £175 to a third-party dealer for the acquisition of a subscriber that has passed the usual credit checks. The subscriber signs a 12 month contract with a minimum revenue guarantee. Operator A has estimated that the expected margin from the minimum contracted revenues will be £250. The subscriber acquisition costs are expected to be recovered in full within the initial contract term. Operator A tracks subscriber acquisition costs on an individual subscriber basis.

In this case, operator A should capitalise the cost of acquiring the service contract (the payment of £175) as these costs meet the definition of an intangible asset. Operator A has acquired an identifiable benefit – namely, the minimum contractual net cash flows from the subscriber – and has a legally enforceable contractual right to receive the minimum net cash flows. Additionally, it is probable that the contract's economic benefits will flow to operator A.

Example 2 – Pre-contract costs for a service contract

An event organiser runs exhibitions for its clients. Experience shows that each event makes a profit. In some cases, costs are incurred before the year end, but the exhibition takes place after the year end.

The timing of cost recognition in the profit and loss account depends on the types of costs that have been incurred (see from para 9.282.2). As above, costs may be capitalised if they fall to be stock, tangible fixed assets or intangible assets. Other costs should be expensed as incurred.

More specifically, it may be appropriate to capitalise costs relating to the advanced payment for space for the exhibition as a prepayment as the payment represents the right to use something in the future. It may also be possible to capitalise costs incurred in acquiring tables, chairs and other furnishings for the exhibition as these may meet the definition of tangible fixed assets under FRS 15.

However, costs such as staff costs are unlikely to meet the definition of an asset.

9.282.4 The same principle can be applied to situations outside of service arrangements. Consider the following examples:

Example 1 – Premium paid for the extension of a contract

A company has a contract with a supplier that expires in mid 20X8 (a three year contract at £4 million per annum). It has identified a new and cheaper supplier (five year contract at £3 million per annum). The new supplier will not be ready until January 20X9. The current supplier has stated that it will continue services beyond contract expiry until the end of the year, but will charge a premium rate over the rate they would have charged of £1 million, that is £5 million for the year.

It would not be appropriate to carry the premium forward and spread it over the contract term with the new supplier on the basis of the cost savings that will be made.

There are no economic benefits from the payment to the old supplier as this is not a prepayment for services to be received in the future from that old supplier, nor will the payment generate any cash inflow. Hence, the £5 million should be expensed in the year which it is incurred.

Example 2 – Payment for termination of a contract

Company X terminated a contract with a computer supplier that provided company X with production facilities. The termination payment was £250,000. It has entered into a contract with a new supplier and this will save the entity money in the future.

Company X may not carry forward the termination payment. There is no benefit from the old contract that has been terminated, so the costs do not meet the definition of an asset. The new contract is a separate agreement and the costs associated with it should be recognised as incurred.

9.282.5 As highlighted in the examples above, the key consideration with regards to the treatment of costs relating to sales contracts is whether they meet the definition of an asset at the balance sheet date in line with SSAP 9, FRS 15 or FRS 10 and are in line with the definition of an asset in the Statement of Principles.

Presentation and disclosure

9.283 Schedule 1 to SI 2008/410 requires the profit and loss account of a company or a group to comply with one of four formats. FRS 3 also affects the disclosure requirements of the profit and loss account. These requirements and the format requirements are set out in detail in chapter 4. The remainder of this chapter will deal with the different types of income that may be included in the turnover and other operating income lines of the profit and loss account and the disclosure requirements relating to grants.

Accounting policies

9.283.1 FRS 18 requires disclosure in the notes to the financial statements of "*a description of each of the accounting policies that is material in the context of the entity's financial statements*". [FRS 18 para 55(a)].

9.283.2 The purpose of the disclosure of accounting policies is to enable users to understand the financial statements. This is discussed further in chapter 2.

9.283.3 Application note G does not prescribe any specific accounting policies that must be followed, so a detailed description of those policies will be required. It is expected that an entity's revenue recognition accounting policy will address as a minimum, for each principal source of revenue:

- The timing of the recognition of revenue.
- The measurement of revenue.
- The treatment of discounts offered to customers.
- The method of allocation of revenue between different components of the same transaction (where different recognition policies are applied to the components).

Turnover

9.284 Company law specifies the amount a company must include in its profit and loss account under the heading of 'Turnover.' This comprises the amounts a company derives from providing goods and services that fall within its ordinary activities, after deducting trade discounts, VAT and any other taxes based on the amounts it so derives. [CA06 Sec 474(1)]. The definition accords with the requirement in SSAP 5 that turnover should exclude VAT on taxable outputs and is consistent with Application Note G that says in paragraph G11: *"Turnover is the revenue resulting from exchange transactions under which a seller supplies to customers the goods or services that it is in business to provide"*.

Trading activities

9.285 Since the income created by the ordinary trading activities of a company is by definition its turnover, the nature of the company's business will dictate what is included in turnover rather than the nature of the income. For most companies, other types of income or gains such as the profit on disposal of a subsidiary or interest receivable which is ancillary to the company's main business activities would be reported in the profit and loss account, but not in the turnover line. Other recognised gains, such as those relating to holding non-trading assets such as buildings which have increased in value may be reported as revaluation movements in the statement of total recognised gains and losses. Groups with diverse activities have turnover from different sources that may be subject to different recognition criteria.

Commissions and agency fees

9.286 Where a company acts as an agent or broker, such as a travel agent, insurance broker or stock broker, it should not include the gross value of the contracts in its turnover, but only the commission or margin that it charges on each deal. The exclusion of such amounts in turnover is consistent with Application note G, which excludes amounts collected on behalf of third parties from its definition of revenue. An estate agent, for example, should only recognise the commission that is earned on each property sold. This is illustrated in Table 9.21.

Table 9.21 – Debenham Tewson & Chinnocks Holdings plc – Report & Accounts – 30 April 1994

Notes to the accounts (extract)

1. Accounting policies (extract)

Turnover

Turnover comprises commissions and fees receivable exclusive of sales related taxes. Agency commissions are recognised on completion of the transaction.

9.287 Further discussion regarding criteria that may be relevant to determining whether companies are acting as agents or principals and accordingly whether they should report turnover gross or net are contained considered from paragraph 9.161.

9.288 As noted in paragraph 9.168 above, FRS 5 Application note G encourages disclosure by agents, where practicable, of the gross value of sales throughput as additional, non-statutory information. Where an agent gives such disclosure it should give a brief explanation of the relationship between recognised turnover and the gross value of sales throughput. [FRS 5 App G para G72].

Other operating income

9.289 'Other operating income' will include income that is associated with a company's normal activities, but that falls outside the definition of revenue. An item is not included in 'other operating income' just because it is small. For example, the revenue of the company's smallest division would nevertheless be included in turnover. Amounts shown in 'other operating income' are typically both incidental to the main activities of the company and are different in nature from amounts included in turnover.

9.290 For example, a manufacturing company that receives a small amount of royalty income may wish to include it in 'other operating income' rather than in turnover since in these circumstances the income is incidental because the provision of intellectual property in return for royalties is not within the definition of the company's main line of business.

9.291 In addition, 'other operating income' could include rents from land, unless the company involved were a property company that derived income from the renting of property.

[The next paragraph is 9.293.]

Government grants

9.293 Company law specifically does not allow income to be set off against expenditure [SI 2008/410 1 Sch 8]. In general, therefore, income that is received in compensation for expenditure incurred should not be netted off against the related expenditure. For example, a government grant that is received for employing a certain number of people for a certain length of time should be recognised on a basis that matches the costs of employing the people, but should not be used to reduce those employment costs. Such a grant is not revenue so, therefore, should be included in other operating income.

9.294 Where an enterprise receives government grants, the disclosures required by SSAP 4, 'Accounting for government grants', are as follows:

- The accounting policy adopted for government grants.
- The effects of government grants on the results and/or the financial position of the entity.
- Where an entity is in receipt of government assistance other than grants that have a material effect on its results, the nature of the assistance and, where possible, an estimate of the financial effects.
- Where applicable, the potential liabilities to repay grants.

[SSAP 4 para 28].

9.295 The accounting policy note should include the period or periods over which grants are credited to the profit and loss account. Where an entity is in receipt of various types of grants, it will normally be sufficient to give a broad indication of the period or periods over which they will be credited to the profit and loss account.

9.296 Where an entity is in receipt of a government grant that has a material effect on its results for the period and any future periods, the most practical way of identifying the effect of the grant on reported earnings may be to disclose the total amount credited in the profit and loss as an exceptional item.

9.297 Any unamortised deferred income relating to the grant will be included under the heading 'Accruals and deferred income'. Where the amount of unamortised deferred income is material, it may also be appropriate to identify this amount separately in a note to the balance sheet. It will provide readers of the financial statements with an indication of the extent to which future results may be expected to benefit from grants already received. Another way of showing the effect could be to include a statement of the changes during the period in the amount of the deferred income carried forward, showing: grants received; grants credited to the profit and loss account; and grants repaid, if any. For example, see Table 9.22.

Table 9.22 – Pilkington plc – Directors' Report and Accounts – 31 March 2002

Notes on the financial statements (extract)

	2002		**2001**	
30 Deferred Income	**Group £m**	**Company £m**	Group £m	Company £m
At beginning of year	19	6	**19**	**9**
Exchange rate adjustments	4	—	**3**	—
Investment grants receivable				
	23	6	**22**	**9**
Released to profit and loss account in the year:	(3)	(3)	**(3)**	**(3)**
At end of the year	20	3	**19**	**6**

9.298 Where government assistance is given in a form other than grants, SSAP 4 requires that the nature and, where measurable, the effects of the assistance should be disclosed. Similar disclosures should be given for significant assistance received from a source other than the government as discussed in paragraph 9.270.

9.299 Once a grant is recognised, any related contingency, such as the requirement to repay the grant in certain circumstances, should be treated in accordance with FRS 12, 'Provisions, contingent liabilities and contingent assets'. These requirements are detailed in chapter 21.

9.300 A question sometimes arises as to whether it is possible to analogise to SSAP 4 in the case of assets received free of charge from other parties that do not meet the definition of a government in paragraph 21 of SSAP 4. If an entity receives an asset from a service provider for no consideration and the asset is essential to other services received from the same provider, then it is clear from paragraphs 22–32 of FRS 5 Application Note G that the asset and services received are a linked transaction so it would not be appropriate to apply SSAP 4. However, if the asset was received from a charitable foundation for the reason that the company will use it for purposes that are consistent with the foundation's charitable objectives, then the substance of the transaction is similar to a government grant so applying SSAP 4 by analogy would be permissible.

Chapter 10

Segmental reporting

Page

Chapter 10

Segmental reporting

Introduction

10.1 For companies that operate in a variety of classes of business or in a number of different geographical locations, the availability of segmental information, (also called 'disaggregated information'), setting out meaningful analyses of turnover and profits, is essential for good management. Such information is essential if management is to be able to detect trends in performance and sales within its specific business and geographical regions. Armed with such information, management is better placed to devise strategies and focus actions towards countering adverse trends or exploiting opportunities in specific business lines or market places.

10.2 The form of segmental information that is of use in a business depends to a great extent on how the management of the business is organised. A business may be managed on a product basis, a geographical basis, or on a mixture of both. Where a business is managed on a geographical basis, the information that may be most useful is a geographical analysis of turnover and profits. An analysis by class of business may be difficult to obtain because, for instance, different classes of business within a geographical segment may be financed as one operation and may share resources. Where a business is managed on a product basis, an analysis of turnover and profits by product will be more important. The management structure of the majority of international companies, however, includes both geographical and product structures. Therefore, segmental information by product and by geographical region is relevant to most companies.

10.3 The value of segmental information is not limited to its application as an internal management tool. It also has an important role in external reporting, since by providing segmental information in financial statements, the management of a company can explain to readers many of the factors which have contributed to the result for the year. These factors might be developments instigated by management, such as the expansion of products or markets, or events outside management's control, such as political disturbances abroad.

[The next paragraph is 10.6.]

The regulatory framework

Statutory requirements and exemptions

10.6 SI 2008/410, 'The Large and Medium-sized Companies and Groups (Accounts and Reports) Regulations 2008' requires large and medium-sized companies to include certain information analysed by both class of business and geographical market in the notes to the profit and loss account. The specific disclosures are considered in detail in paragraphs 10.68 to 10.73. However, disaggregated information need not be disclosed where the directors have determined that such disclosure would be seriously prejudicial to the company's interests. Where this exemption is utilised, however, the financial statements must state that disaggregated information has not been disclosed.

10.7 An example of the circumstances that might result in the directors deciding to utilise the exemption is where a company or a group supplies customers in two countries only. If these companies are politically opposed to each other, to publish a geographical split of turnover could be considered to be prejudicial to the interests of the company or the group. Provided that the notes to the profit and loss account disclose the fact that this analysis has not been given, no further information is required to be published. In practice, the prejudicial exemption is applied by surprisingly few reporting entities. Further, where prejudice is claimed, it is frequently limited to specific segmental disclosures rather than the whole range.

10.8 The fact that SI 2008/410 gives the directors the responsibility for determining whether segmental information should be reported is a matter of note. This is because they alone determine:

- Whether two or more classes of substantially different business have been carried out by the company.
- Whether turnover has been generated in two or more substantially different geographical markets.
- Whether non-disclosure on the grounds of seriously prejudicing the company's interests is appropriate.

However, it is implicit that, in making their decisions on reportable segments, the directors should act in good faith.

10.9 Medium-sized companies filing abbreviated accounts are exempt from the requirement to provide the particulars of turnover. [SI 2008/410 Regulation 4(3)(b)]. Furthermore, SI 2008/409, 'Small Companies and Groups (Accounts and Directors' Reports) Regulations 2008' does not require small companies (and groups headed by a small company) to give details of segmental information by market. However, if the small company or group has supplied geographical markets outside the UK (turnover by destination), the notes must state the percentage of turnover (but not profit or loss) attributable to those markets. The analysis made for these purposes must still have regard to the manner in which the company's activities are organised. [SI 2008/409 Sch 1(60)]. The disclosure requirements applicable to small companies are considered in detail in chapter 32.

[The next paragraph is 10.13.]

SSAP 25

10.13 SSAP 25, 'Segment reporting', was issued in July 1990, since then the ASB has issued a number of subsequent standards that also have implications for segmental-type reporting. For entities applying IFRS, IFRS 8, 'Operating segments', has many different requirements from SSAP 25.

Scope and exemptions

10.14 Insofar as they repeat the requirements of paragraph 68 of Schedule 1 to SI 2008/410, the segmental disclosure requirements of SSAP 25 apply to all entities preparing Companies Act financial statements as defined by the Act.

10.15 SSAP 25, however, sets out additional requirements that apply to certain entities only. In effect, smaller companies are excluded from the standard's disclosure requirements, other than where those requirements are also prescribed by SI 2008/409. However, exempt entities can, and are encouraged to, adopt these additional disclosures on a voluntary basis.

10.16 The entities to which the additional disclosures apply on a mandatory basis are:

- All public companies or parent companies that have a public company as a subsidiary.
- Banking and insurance companies and groups.
- All other entities that exceed two of the three criteria for defining a medium-sized company under section 465 of the Companies Act 2006 multiplied in each case by ten.

It should be noted that a large number of the entities described above will be applying IFRS and, therefore, will not be required to apply SSAP 25.

10.17 The three criteria referred to in the paragraph above and as multiplied by ten result in the following cut-off points:

- Turnover in excess of £259 million.
- Balance sheet total in excess of £129 million.
- Number of employees in excess of 2,500.

10.18 The three criteria for turnover, balance sheet total and number of employees are amended from time to time by statutory instrument. However, their impact is intended to ensure that larger companies present the full segmental disclosures required by the standard. Conversely, all companies below that size are left with the freedom to choose what, if any, additional segmental disclosures they might make beyond those required by SI 2008/410.

10.19 In addition to the exemption available to smaller companies, there is a further exemption from complying with the non-statutory aspects of the standard. This exemption is intended to be a practical one, in that it seeks to avoid the need for voluminous disclosures by subsidiaries, where the group financial statements provide full segmental disclosures in accordance with the standard or in accordance with IFRS. 'Improvements to Financial Reporting Standards 2010' has extended the exemption previously available to companies whose parent provided segmental disclosures in accordance with UK GAAP. The amendment is applicable for accounting periods beginning on or after 1 January 2011, with earlier application permitted. Accordingly, where a subsidiary undertaking is neither a public company, nor a banking or insurance company, it need not comply with the provisions of the standard provided that its parent provides segmental information in compliance with SSAP 25 or IFRS 8.

10.20 It should be emphasised that, whether or not companies are exempt from the requirements of the standard, as a minimum, all companies still have to comply with the legal requirements contained in company law. Thus, a subsidiary undertaking that takes advantage of the exemptions described in paragraph 10.19 will still be required to disclose the segmental information required by company law, unless it can also take advantage of the exemptions in company law not to disclose segmental information.

10.21 It is not totally clear why subsidiary undertakings engaged in banking and insurance activities have been selected for special treatment, particularly given FRS 2, 'Accounting for subsidiary undertakings', prohibits the exclusion of a subsidiary from the consolidation on the basis of dissimilar activities. Thus, in most circumstances, segmental information will have been provided at a group level, presumably with financial service operations disclosed as a separate segment or segments. Consequently, there seems little benefit in requiring fuller segmental information in the subsidiaries' financial statements unless it is undertaking a wide spread of financial activities. For insurance groups this situation is compounded by UK insurers being required to submit annual returns to the BIS. The returns set out detailed revenue account analyses by insurance class in a prescribed format. The information contained therein seems likely to be of far greater benefit to analysts, than the more limited segmental information disclosed within statutory financial statements.

10.22 There is a further limitation on the scope and application of the standard in that the standard repeats the exemption contained in paragraph 68(5) of Schedule 1 to SI 2008/410 in the wider context of the standard. Thus, where, in the opinion of the directors, the disclosure of any information required by the standard would be seriously prejudicial to the interests of the company, that information need not be disclosed. However, like SI 2008/410, the standard requires the fact that any such information has not been disclosed to be stated. [SSAP 25 para 6]. Few companies now take advantage of this exemption in respect of all the segmental disclosures required by SI 2008/410 and the standard. Several, however, provide some segmental information, but apply the prejudicial override clause to limit certain types of segmental disclosures. For example,

Inspec Group plc, a chemicals manufacturer, provides segmental analysis of turnover by origin and destination, but does not provide a segmental analysis of net assets by class of business or geographical area of origin or an analysis of results by geographical origin, on the grounds that to disclose such information would be seriously prejudicial to the group's interests.

Table 10.1 — Inspec Group plc — Annual Report — 31 December 1997

Notes to the Accounts (extract)

2 SEGMENTAL INFORMATION (extract)

In the opinion of the directors the disclosure of segmental information relating to the business categories of net assets and the geographical origin of results and net assets would be seriously prejudicial to the interests of the Group and has not therefore been provided.

[The next paragraph is 10.24.]

Truth and fairness implications

10.24 Where an entity takes advantage of the exemption referred to in paragraph 10.22 above not to make segmental disclosures on the grounds that they would be seriously prejudicial, the question arises as to the impact of such non-disclosure on the truth and fairness of the financial statements as a whole.

10.25 The standard allows non-disclosure where the information, if disclosed, would be seriously prejudicial to the company. As noted above, this is based on an equivalent provision in the Statutory Instrument. The standard implies that, in such a situation, segmental information is not essential to the true and fair view.

10.26 The Foreword to Accounting Standards is helpful in this regard. It indicates that the prescription of information to be contained with financial statements does *"...not override exemptions from disclosure given by law to, and utilised by, certain types of entity"*. [Foreword to Accounting Standards para 15].

10.27 Auditors have to decide whether failure to provide segmental information should result in qualifying their opinion on financial statements on the grounds that the truth and fairness of those financial statements is affected. Clearly, if such information is not disclosed, but there are no grounds on which disclosure could be considered to be seriously prejudicial, then the auditor should state that the financial statements have not been properly prepared in accordance with company law. If the auditor considers that the non-disclosure is so material as to affect the truth and fairness of the financial statements, it will be necessary to qualify the opinion given on their truth and fairness.

10.28 However, if disclosure is not made and there is reason to believe that disclosure would be seriously prejudicial, then clearly the auditor could state that the financial statements had been properly prepared in accordance with company law. The omission of the information would also be in accordance with the standard and, therefore, qualification of the audit opinion on the truth and fairness of the financial statements would not be appropriate.

10.29 A similar issue potentially arises in the situation where small companies and medium-sized companies preparing abbreviated accounts take advantage of exemptions not to provide the same level of segmental information disclosures as are prescribed for large and public companies. In essence, if detailed segmental information is considered necessary for a true and fair view to be given by those types of entity, how can smaller entities be said to give a true and fair view, unless they mirror that level of segmental disclosure?

10.30 The matter of limited disclosure exemptions permitted to certain types of entity has been addressed in Counsel's opinion, reproduced in the Appendix to the Foreword to Accounting Standards. This indicates that, while it is a question of law as to whether financial statements give a true and fair view, the courts will look to the requirements of accounting standards in reaching their decision. It can be inferred from this that, if accounting standards permit exemptions to certain categories or sizes of company, the courts would not interpret these exemptions as detracting from the true and fair view.

Other accounting standards

10.31 Subsequent to the publication of SSAP 25 in 1990, the ASB has published a number of financial reporting standards that have an impact on segmental disclosures. The disclosure implications of these standards, in terms of segmental reporting, are considered in paragraphs 10.116 to 10.142 below.

General guidance

Determining segments

10.32 For financial statements that disclose segmental information to readers to have real value, a high level of consistency of approach across reporting entities is required. This is particularly important in terms of how directors determine what constitutes a reportable segment, so that different companies apply similar principles in determining what should be reported. This should enable readers of financial statements to make better comparisons of performance and prospects across reporting entities.

10.33 Both SI 2008/410 and the standard clearly view reportable segments in terms of either class of business segments or geographical segments and both conclude that the determination of a company's classes of business and geographical segments must depend on the judgement of the directors. Thus, it is the directors — and they alone — who decide whether the company operates in more than one class of business or geographical segment. However, as this could lead to inevitable inconsistencies across boards of companies, the standard sets out additional guidance on the matter.

10.34 The advice given by the standard emphasises how the directors should have regard to the overall purpose of presenting segmental information, in making their judgements about reportable segments. Of primary concern to the directors in their deliberations should be the question of whether the provision of segmental information is likely to be helpful and informative to users of financial statements.

10.35 The emphasis of the standard is that, for segmental reporting to be of real value to users of financial statements, the segmental information reported needs both to reflect the company's risk and reward profile and to inform users of the nature of that profile. This sentiment is reiterated in the explanatory note to the standard, which discusses the circumstances where the provision of segmental information may enhance a reader's understanding of the financial statements. Where an entity operates in more than one class of business or more than one geographical market, the circumstances described above arise where businesses:

- Earn a return on the investment that is out of line with the return earned by the remainder of the business.
- Are subject to different degrees of risk.
- Have experienced different degrees of growth.
- Have different potentials for future development.

[SSAP 25 para 8].

10.36 It follows from the above that in determining business or geographical segments, products or services (or a related group of products or services), with significantly differing risks, rewards and future prospects should not be combined together to create a reportable segment. Instead, they should be treated as separate segments and reported as such, provided that they are of sufficient materiality to justify separate disclosure.

10.37 The standard also emphasises the need for the directors to reconsider segment definitions periodically and re-define them where appropriate. [SSAP 25 para 10]. This means that the directors should reconsider the position on each occasion that financial statements are produced.

[The next paragraph is 10.42.]

Classes of business

10.42 When the directors of a reporting entity consider the provision of segmental analysis in that entity's financial statements, they are inevitably faced with the question of whether the entity has distinct business segments and, if so, how these are to be identified.

[The next paragraph is 10.44.]

10.44 SSAP 25 defines a 'class of business' in paragraph 30 of the standard, as *"...a distinguishable component of an entity that provides a separate product or service or a separate group of related products or services"*, it moves on to provide guidance on identification. In assessing whether the reporting entity has different classes of products or services, the standard suggests that directors should consider the following factors:

- The nature of the products or services.
- The nature of the production processes.
- The markets in which the products or services are sold.
- The distribution channels for the products.
- The manner in which the entity's activities are organised.
- Any separate legislative framework relating to part of the business, for example, a bank or an insurance company.

[SSAP 25 para 12].

10.45 Most of the criteria above are consistent with a risks and reward approach in that they look to the separability of products and services. However, the reference to the way in which activities are organised is more indicative of the management approach. In fact, for operating and management reporting purposes, directors often use the above criteria for organising corporate entities into divisions, branches or subsidiaries. In such situations, the management approach referred to in paragraph 10.43 also acknowledges risk and reward considerations. Consequently, in these instances class of business analysis based on risk and reward considerations will also reflect the organisation structure of the reporting entity.

10.46 Although the standard explains the criteria for identifying whether separate business segments exist, this explanation is merely guidance. The directors have to exercise their own judgement in this area based on the particular circumstances of their reporting entity. In effect, the standard recognises that no one set of characteristics can claim universal application, nor can any individual characteristic claim to be determinative in every situation. Consequently, although different boards might reach different decisions on identifiable and reportable segments, by providing guidance on types of segment and their characteristics, the standard should reduce the degree of difference, so long as boards act in good faith.

Geographical segments

10.47 When directors consider the reporting of segmental information, both SI 2008/410 and SSAP 25 require them to give such information by geographical segments. As for business segments, judgement is required by the directors, who have responsibility for determining whether distinct geographical segments exist and for identifying them.

10.48 The standard's definition of geographical segment indicates that it is "*...a geographical area comprising an individual country or group of countries in which an entity operates, or to which it supplies products or services*". [SSAP 25 para 31]. This is helpful insofar as it clearly envisages aggregations of groups of countries to form one geographical segment for reporting purposes. In addition, it emphasises that geographical analysis needs to consider two distinct aspects:

- Analysis by operating location (origin basis).
- Analysis by destination of sale or service (destination basis).

[SSAP 25 para 14].

10.49 The standard defines both origin of turnover and destination of turnover. The former term comprises "*...the geographical segment from which products or services are supplied to a third party or to another segment*". [SSAP 25 para 32]. The latter term is identified as "*...the geographical segment to which products or services are supplied*". [SSAP 25 para 33].

10.50 Beyond the above, the guidance given by the standard is very limited, insofar as criteria for determining the choice of geographical segments is concerned. In emphasising that the groupings selected should reflect the overriding purpose of presenting segmental information, the standard suggests that they should indicate to the reader the extent to which a company's operations are subject to factors such as:

- Expansionist or restrictive economic climates.
- Stable or unstable political regimes.
- Exchange control regulations.
- Exchange rate fluctuations.

[SSAP 25 para 15].

10.51 These suggestions indicate that the different risk environments in which a reporting entity operates are an important factor in determining segments. A multi-national operation might take account of its geographical risk profiles, for example, by treating Western Europe as a single geographical market, Eastern Europe as a second and the Far East as a third. On the other hand, an operation which trades out of, or sells into, four overseas countries only, may well treat each of those as a distinct geographical segment. This might be irrespective of whether all or the majority of them are, say, Western European, provided that each of them is significant to the results and future prospects of the reporting entity as a whole.

10.52 A number of examples of segmental disclosures are set out below. The General Electric Company p.l.c provides a wealth of geographical segmental analysis as Table 10.2 illustrates. Not only are turnover, profit and net assets analysed by territory of origin, but turnover is also analysed by territory of destination. The analysis provided enables the reader to understand that:

- The UK is the major originator of sales, but exports a significant proportion of its production. The company's UK-based operations are also responsible for approximately half of the group's worldwide profit.
- France is the other major European originator of sales and also exports a large proportion of its production. It appears to achieve this from a negative local asset base.
- While the rest of Europe represents a material element of The General Electric Company p.l.c's business, no individual European country, other than the UK and France, is considered to constitute a segment in its own right. However, the rest of Europe purchases more of its own products than it produces.
- The Americas constitutes another major originator of sales. However, in 1994, the segment was a net importer of The General Electric Company p.l.c products and services, since total sales within the segment slightly exceeded the value of sales originated therein. This is a reversal of the position that was reported for 1993.
- Although three other segments are identified, namely Australasia, Asia and Africa, they are relative immaterial in terms of their local production, asset levels and impact on profit. However, when considered from a destination perspective, they are clearly important to The General Electric Company p.l.c as notable importers of its products and services originating out of other geographical segments.

Table 10.2 — The General Electric Company p.l.c. — Annual Report and Accounts — 31 March 1994

Notes to the Accounts (Extract)

1 PRINCIPAL ACTIVITIES, PROFIT CONTRIBUTIONS, MARKETS AND NET ASSETS EMPLOYED (extract)

Analysis of turnover by classes of business

	To customers in the United Kingdom		To customers overseas	
	1994	1993	1994	1993
	£ million	£ million	£ million	£ million
Electronic Systems	930	943	1,819	1,774
Power Systems	535	596	2,568	2,539
Telecommunications	715	759	335	253
Consumer Goods	236	233	23	20
Electronic Metrology	139	132	350	281
Office Equipment & Printing	17	16	306	287
Medical Equipment	3	–	671	568
Electronic Components	94	107	197	195
Industrial Apparatus	207	236	126	106
Distribution & Trading	–	–	351	290
Other	59	77	13	20
Intra-Activity sales	(83)	(93)	(68)	(41)
	2,852	3,006	6,691	6,292

Analysis of turnover by territory of destination

	1994	1993
	£ million	£ million
United Kingdom	2,852	3,006
France	1,122	1,068
Rest of Europe	1,618	1,793
The Americas	2,044	1,886
Australasia	341	310
Asia	1,353	1,038
Africa	213	197
	9,543	9,298

Analysis of profit, turnover and net assets by territory of origin

			Turnover		Net assets	
	1994	1993	1994	1993	1994	1993
	£ million	£ million	£ million	£ million	£ million	£ million
United Kingdom	344	367	4,425	4,364	650	983
France	93	85	1,846	1,914	(180)	(104)
Rest of Europe	82	108	976	1,032	143	231
The Americas	142	116	1,884	1,620	506	473
Australasia	12	9	273	246	65	69
Asia	6	5	115	100	7	6
Africa	5	5	24	22	20	21
	684	695	9,543	9,298	1,211	1,679

10.53 The General Electric Company p.l.c extract is also notable for the analysis it provides of turnover by class of business. Where many companies provide such analysis on a total basis, The General Electric Company p.l.c sub-analyses such turnover between:

- Sales to UK customers.
- Sales to overseas customers.

[The next paragraph is 10.55.]

10.55 Although identifying geographical segments by risk and reward profile may be the preferred approach, multi-nationals that operate in a very large number of countries appear to find it either impractical to adopt or this is not their primary consideration. In practice, decisions may be influenced by the volume of disclosure that the basis chosen leads to. For example, consider a global entity that operates out of the majority of African countries. The directors will need to consider whether they should analyse these individually or in small risk groupings to reflect the different circumstances of each. Alternatively, they may decide that an aggregation as 'Africa' is the most sensible presentation. In any event, in making their judgements, the directors will need to take account of the significance of individual countries, aggregations of countries and the continent as a whole to the results and financial status of the reporting entity.

10.56 A further point of interest in this area is the way in which some companies redefine their chosen geographical segments for disclosing segmental information by origin, when they disclose turnover information on a destination basis. This is understandable where a reporting entity sells significant volumes of business into a geographical location where it has no production capacity or minimal physical representation, but this does not appear to be the only determining factor. Examples of this approach include Pilkington plc, which treats *"Europe (excluding United Kingdom)"*, as one segment in disclosing information by origin, but splits it into two segments, *"EEP"* and *"Non EEP"* for disclosure of turnover on a destination basis. Similarly, the *"Rest of the World"* segment on an origin basis becomes three segments for the destination basis: *"Australasia"*, *"South America"* and *"Rest of the World"* (see Table 10.4).

Table 10.4 — Pilkington plc — Directors' Report and Accounts — 31 March 1994

Notes on the Financial Statements (extract)

	1994			1993		
		Operating profit/	**Net operating**		Operating profit/	Net operating
	Turnover	**(loss)**	**assets**	Turnover	(loss)	assets
1 Segmental analysis of Continuing Operations	**£m**	**£m**	**£m**	£m	£m	£m
Flat and safety glass—						
Europe	**1,321.7**	**33.2**	**948.3**	1,196.7	42.8	975.6
North America	**691.6**	**26.8**	**372.1**	626.7	5.0	393.6
Rest of the World	**337.0**	**49.7**	**235.3**	304.6	39.0	227.2
Total	**2,350.3**	**109.7**	**1,555.7**	2,128.0	86.8	1,596.4
Other trading companies	**164.5**	**(0.5)**	**158.3**	171.4	(1.0)	153.4
Group technology management	**0.3**	**4.8**	**(16.3)**	1.1	7.0	9.0
Group operations	**–**	**(22.8)**	**(4.6)**	–	(16.3)	18.4
	2,515.1	**91.2**	**1,693.1**	2,300.5	76.5	1,777.2
United Kingdom	**453.8**	**17.4**	**293.3**	331.3	(1.7)	277.3
Europe (excluding United Kingdom)	**925.5**	**14.2**	**754.7**	936.1	37.8	791.2
North America	**780.3**	**25.1**	**427.7**	712.9	5.1	450.9
Rest of the World	**355.2**	**52.5**	**238.3**	319.1	44.6	230.4
Group operations/ technology management	**0.3**	**(18.0)**	**(20.9)**	1.1	(9.3)	27.4
	2,515.1	**91.2**	**1,693.1**	2,300.5	76.5	1,777.2

Comparative figures have been restated in accordance with FRS 3 and to take account of the repositioning of Pilkington Aerospace from other trading companies to flat and safety glass, and float process/product development costs from flat and safety glass to Group technology management.

The Companies Act 1985 requires the analysis of profit before tax but the analysis of operating profit is considered by the directors to be more meaningful.

Turnover derived from intra-segmental transactions is not material

Net operating assets are analysed in note 4.

2 Segmental Analysis of Discontinued Operations	1994 Turnover £m	1994 Operating profit/ (loss) £m	1994 Net operating assets £m	1993 Turnover £m	1993 Operating profit/ (loss) £m	1993 Net operating assets £m
Flat and safety glass						
Europe	–	–	–	4.0	(3.6)	–
North America	–	–	–	–	–	–
Rest of the World	–	–	–	–	–	–
Total	–	–	–	4.0	(3.6)	–
Other trading companies	**222.3**	**13.0**	**56.1**	268.0	15.1	191.4
	222.3	**13.0**	**56.1**	272.0	11.5	191.4
United Kingdom	**95.1**	**0.5**	**57.0**	92.2	2.3	76.1
Europe (excluding United Kingdom)	**29.8**	**2.4**	–	47.7	0.3	27.2
North America	**67.8**	**5.3**	**(0.9)**	93.4	3.1	52.1
Rest of the World	**29.6**	**4.8**	–	38.7	5.8	36.0
	222.3	**13.0**	**56.1**	272.0	11.5	191.4

Net operating assets are analysed in note 4.

3 Geographical Analysis of Turnover by Markets	1994 Group £m	%	1993 Group £m	%

This analysis of turnover shows the markets in which the Group's products are sold, whereas the regional analysis in notes 1 and 2 relate to the domicile of the Group undertakings making the sales.

	1994 Group £m	%	1993 Group £m	%
Continuing Operations				
United Kingdom	**376.6**	**15**	268.0	12
Europe (excluding United Kingdom)				
– EEP	**768.9**	**31**	792.3	34
– Non EEP	**179.6**	**7**	165.0	7
North America	**7702.2**	**31**	702.4	30
Australasia	**197.8**	**8**	180.4	8
South America	**156.7**	**6**	130.9	6
Rest of the World	**65.3**	**2**	61.5	3
	2,515.1	**100**	2300.5	100
Discontinued Operations				
United Kingdom	**92.9**	**42**	87.9	32
Europe (excluding United Kingdom)				
– EEP	**27.5**	**12**	44.1	16
– Non EEP	**3.2**	**1**	6.5	2
North America	**67.9**	**31**	93.5	34
Australasia	**8.6**	**4**	11.1	4
South America	**6.1**	**3**	9.7	4
Rest of the World	**16.1**	**7**	19.2	8
	222.3	**100**	272.0	100

4 Net Operating Assets	Continuing Operations 1994 £m	1993 £m	Discontinued Operations 1994 £m	1993 £m
The net operating assets referred to in notes 1 and 2 comprise the following:				
Tangible assets	**1,618.4**	1,634.0	**44.8**	97.9
Stocks	**382.5**	391.3	**13.2**	86.9
Debtors	**435.7**	424.9	**16.8**	61.8
Creditors – falling due within one year	**(430.1)**	(370.4)	**(13.7)**	(52.3)
– falling due after more than one year	**(16.8)**	(11.7)	**(0.7)**	(2.9)
Provisions	**(296.6)**	(290.9)	**(4.3)**	–
	1,693.1	1,777.2	**56.1**	191.4

Creditors exclude loans and overdrafts, taxation on profits, finance leases and dividends. Debtors exclude taxation recoverable. Provisions exclude deferred taxation.

10.57 Enterprise Oil plc's 1994 Report and Accounts provides a further illustration of this point, as Table 10.5 demonstrates. In terms of turnover, the analysis by production location reveals two significant geographical segments, the UK and Norway. A 'catch all' category, described as *"Rest of World"*, is introduced to produce an analysis of total entity turnover. However, this segment is responsible for generating less than two per cent of total turnover in the current or prior year. When the company analyses its turnover by geographical area of destination, it identifies its markets as *"UK"*, *"Europe, excluding UK"*, *"North America"* and *"Asia — Pacific"*. Unusually, the geographical destination disclosures are made on a percentage basis, rather than on a monetary value basis.

Table 10.5 — Enterprise Oil plc — Annual Report and Accounts — 31 December 1994

Notes to the financial statements (extract)
for the year ended 31 December 1994

1. TURNOVER AND GEOGRAPHICAL ANALYSIS

The group's activities predominantly comprise oil and gas exploration and production. The geographical analysis of the group's turnover (by location of production) and profit before tax and net assets is as follows:

	Turnover 1994 £m	1993 £m	Profit before tax 1994 £m	1993 £m	Net assets 1994 £m	1993 £m
UK	**528.0**	391.5	**180.4**	91.2	**1,058.0**	1,123.2
Norway	**118.5**	144.0	**32.8**	42.1	**121.6**	69.2
Rest of World	**4.8**	10.6	**(32.2)**	(43.5)	**93.1**	77.4
	651.3	546.1	**181.0**	89.8	**1,272.7**	1,269.8

Costs and expenses of the offer for LASMO plc	**(5.7)**	–	–	–
Equity in associated undertaking	**(19.6)**	2.1	**59.8**	74.3
Investment in LASMO plc	**(18.1)**	–	**141.9**	–
Net interest/net debt and loan to associate	**(43.7)**	7.9	**(538.1)**	(392.8)
	93.9	99.8	**936.3**	951.3

	1994	1993
Analysis of turnover by geographical area of destination:		
	%	%
UK	36.1	62.8
Europe, excluding UK	46.0	28.4
North America	17.7	7.6
Asia-Pacific	0.2	1.2
	100.0	100.0

Significant business segments

10.58 The problems that can arise when a reporting entity operates out of, or sells into, a large number of different countries have been referred to above. Similarly, when an entity is organised into a large number of relatively small business units or produces an extensive product range, the identification of reportable segments requires careful consideration and judgement. It is, in effect, a balancing act, between providing too little analysis and supplying so much that it obscures the reader's understanding.

10.59 The explanatory notes to the standard are of some assistance in this respect, in that they attempt to set out size criteria for determining whether a segment should be considered significant enough to justify separate identification and reporting. The standard suggests that a segment would normally be regarded as significant if:

- its third party turnover is ten per cent or more of the entity's total third party turnover; or
- its segment result, whether profit or loss, is ten per cent or more of the combined result of all segments in profit or of all segments in loss, whichever combined result is the greater; or
- its net assets are ten per cent or more of the entity's total net assets.

[SSAP 25 para 9].

10.60 The term 'net assets' is discussed later in this chapter in paragraphs 10.91 to 10.99. Although the second of the criteria set out above is tortuously worded, it means that, if a group makes an overall loss of £100, with some segments making losses amounting to £600 and others making profits amounting to £500, an individual segment that makes a profit or loss of £50 is not significant, whereas a segment that makes a profit or loss of £60 is significant.

[The next paragraph is 10.62.]

Allocation of costs

10.62 Reporting entities that provide detailed segmental information face further practical difficulties in dealing with cost allocation and attribution. These difficulties include dealing with costs that have been incurred on behalf of a number of reportable segments or that have been incurred on a segment's behalf by another party.

10.63 In principle, segment costs should be determined by their nature rather than by the location where they are incurred. For example, where costs are incurred at head office level solely on behalf of one specific business segment, it seems equitable in such circumstances to include them within that segment's results for segmental reporting purposes. This treatment will present a true picture of that segment's performance to the reader.

10.64 A similar situation arises where a head office or one segment incurs costs that relate to a number of segments. Such costs are normally referred to as common costs. The guidance given in the standard is that common costs should be treated in the way that the directors consider most appropriate. For example, where these costs are apportioned across different segments for the purposes of internal reporting, it may be appropriate to apportion them in a like manner for external segmental reporting purposes. However, the guidance acknowledges that some companies may not wish to apportion common costs, because any such apportionment might be done on an arbitrary basis and, therefore, could be misleading. Consequently in such circumstances, the common costs should be deducted from the total of the segment results.

10.65 In practical terms, the allocation of common costs is a particular area of difficulty, because the basis of allocation may significantly affect the reported segmental results. This is demonstrated by the following example:

Example

A company has three distinct business segments, A, B and C. Prior to the allocation of any common costs to these segments, the financial position of these segments is as follows:

	A	B	C
	£m	£m	£m
Net assets	2,000	300	800
Turnover	5,000	2,000	3,000
Profit before common costs	200	40	100

The common costs total £100m, the allocation of such costs on the basis of the turnover of each segment as a percentage of total turnover would lead to the following depiction of segment results:

	A	B	C
	£m	£m	£m
Profit before common costs	200	40	100
Allocation of common costs	50	20	30
Profit after common costs	150	20	70

This contrasts with the situation where common costs are allocated on the basis of the individual segment's proportion of total net assets. In this instance, the results would be as follows:

	A	B	C
	£m	£m	£m
Profit before common costs	200	40	100
Allocation of common costs	64	10	26
Profit after common costs	136	30	74

Thus, the basis of allocation chosen may have a material effect on the segment result that is reported. Despite this, the standard does not require disclosure of the basis of allocation, although voluntary disclosure is permissible.

10.66 If it is not possible to determine a reasonable basis for allocation, the standard allows common costs to be shown separately as a deduction from the total of segment results. [SSAP 25 para 23]. In practice it may be possible to allocate some of the common costs, but not others. For instance, if a group bears the costs of managing group properties centrally, it should be possible to allocate such costs reasonably fairly to each segment, on a basis that takes account of the type, age and value of properties used by each segment. Similarly, central administrative overheads in respect of personnel might be allocated on the basis of the number of employees in each segment. If more than one basis is appropriate for different types of common cost, it would be reasonable to apply each of these bases in allocating the respective costs. However, costs which cannot be allocated (except on an arbitrary basis), should be shown as a separate, unallocated, figure deducted from the total of segment results.

Disclosure requirements

10.67 The specific disclosure requirements of company law, SSAP 25 and other financial reporting standards are considered in detail below.

Legislative requirements

10.68 Although the disclosure requirements of SI 2008/410 in respect of segmental information are few in number, they apply to all large and medium-sized entities. Unless these entities adopt the prejudicial override clause, as referred to in paragraph 10.6, or meet the criteria of a small entity or medium-sized entity filing abbreviated accounts, the notes to the profit and loss account must include certain specified information, analysed by both class of business and geographical market.

10.69 Specifically, SI 2008/410 requires that, where a company has carried on two or more classes of business during the financial year in question, and these, in the directors' opinion, differ substantially from each other, the notes to the financial statements must give:

- A description of each class of business.
- The amount of turnover that is attributable to each class of business.

[SI 2008/410 1 Sch 68].

10.70 'Turnover' comprises the amounts a company derives from providing goods and services that fall within its ordinary activities, after deducting trade discounts, VAT and any other taxes based on the amounts it so derives. In this context, turnover will include that of both continuing and discontinued operations, as defined by FRS 3, 'Reporting financial performance'.

10.71 Under SI 2008/410, where a company has supplied goods or services to two or more markets during the financial year in question, the turnover must also be disaggregated between markets. This is necessary, however, only if the directors believe that the markets differ substantially. For this purpose, 'market' means a market delimited by geographical bounds. [SI 2008/410 1 Sch 68].

10.72 SI 2008/410 states that, in determining the turnover attributable to each class, the directors must have regard to the way in which the company's activities are organised. [SI 2008/410 1 Sch 68]. Where classes of business do not, in the directors' opinion, differ substantially, they are to be treated as one class. Similarly, where the directors believe that markets do not differ substantially, those markets are to be treated as one market. [SI 2008/410 1 Sch 68]. In interpreting these matters the directors should have regard to the practical issues discussed in paragraphs 10.32 to 10.66. They should also re-evaluate the position on each occasion that segmental information is published, to ensure that previous decisions on segmental determination remain valid.

10.73 Details of the exemptions available to small companies and medium-sized companies filing abbreviated accounts, in respect of the company law disclosure requirements, are set out in paragraph 10.9 above. In addition, details of exemptions available because segmental analysis would be prejudicial to the reporting entity, irrespective of its size, are set out in paragraph 10.6 above.

Additional disclosures required by the standard

10.74 SSAP 25 does not limit itself to a repetition of the requirements of company law. Instead it imposes additional, mandatory, segmental disclosure requirements on public and large companies and all banking and insurance companies reporting under UK GAAP, unless they avoid disclosure by taking advantage of the prejudicial override exemption. Thus, while smaller companies are never required to make disclosures beyond those specified in company law, public and large companies and all banking and insurance companies are required to provide the additional, wider disclosures specified by the standard.

10.75 Under the standard, where such companies have two or more classes of business, or operate in two or more geographical segments which differ substantially from each other, the following information should be disclosed in the financial statements in respect of each class of business or geographical segment:

- Turnover.
- Result, before accounting for taxation, minority interests and extraordinary items.
- Net assets.

[SSAP 25 para 34].

Note that extraordinary items have been all but eliminated by FRS 3 – see further chapter 24.

10.76 The directors of the entity are responsible for defining:

- Their identified classes of business.
- Their identified geographical segments.

[SSAP 25 para 34].

10.77 Furthermore, as indicated earlier, the standard requires the directors to *"...re-define the segments when appropriate"*. [SSAP 25 para 39]. Thus, as the classes of business or geographical segments of a reporting entity change over time, the financial statements are required to reflect those changes. In this event, the nature of and reason for the change(s) must be explained, as well as the effect of the change(s) being disclosed. Where this occurs, the standard states that the previous year's figures should be re-stated to reflect the change.

10.78 As an illustration of this in practice, in its 1994 financial statements, Lonrho Plc re-defined certain of its classes of business, to reflect the changing circumstances of the group. The segmental analysis, as set out in Table 10.6, highlights this.

Table 10.6 — Lonrho Plc— Annual Report and Accounts — 30 September 1994

Notes to the accounts (extract)

2 Turnover

Turnover represents sales of goods and services outside the Group net of discounts, and allowances and value added taxation and includes commission earned.

Due to the reduction in significance of the contribution from financial services this activity is now included in general trade whereas it was previously separately disclosed.

Turnover by origin is analysed by activity below:—

	1994			1993		
	Group	**Associates**	**Total**	Group *Restated*	Associates *Restated*	Total *Restated*
	£m	**£m**	**£m**	£m	£m	£m
Motor and equipment distribution	**578**	**8**	**586**	526	7	533
Mining and refining	**281**	**92**	**373**	249	95	344
Manufacturing	**346**	**6**	**352**	410	5	415
Hotels	**237**	**16**	**253**	227	15	242
General trade	**240**	**9**	**249**	224	14	238
Agriculture	**142**	**9**	**151**	112	8	120
Discontinued operations				258	572	830
	1,824	**140**	**1,964**	2,006	716	2,722

Turnover by origin is analysed by geographical area below:—

	1994			1993		
	Group	**Associates**	**Total**	Group *Restated*	Associates *Restated*	Total *Restated*
	£m	**£m**	**£m**	£m	£m	£m
United Kingdom	**781**	**2**	**783**	728	4	732
East, Central and West Africa	**346**	**112**	**458**	368	106	474
Southern Africa	**424**	**5**	**429**	406	15	421
The Americas	**160**	**16**	**176**	163	16	179
Europe and Other	**113**	**5**	**118**	83	3	86
Discontinued operations				258	572	830
	1,824	**140**	**1,964**	2,006	716	2,722

Turnover by destination is analysed below:—

United Kingdom	**679**	**1**	**680**	626		626
East, Central and West Africa	**333**	**23**	**356**	361	26	387
Southern Africa	**320**	**3**	**323**	293	15	308
The Americas	**220**	**16**	**236**	210	16	226
Europe and Other	**272**	**97**	**369**	258	87	345
Discontinued operations				258	572	830
	1,824	**140**	**1,964**	2,006	716	2,722

10.79 Similarly, Pilkington plc, which provided segmental analysis under continuing and discontinued operation categorisations in its 1994 financial statements, indicated that it had undertaken restatements not merely to meet FRS 3 requirements, but also to take account of the segmental *"repositioning"* of certain of its activities (see Table 10.4).

[The next paragraph is 10.81.]

Turnover and inter-segment sales

10.81 The financial statements must distinguish between:

- Turnover derived from external customers.
- Turnover derived from other segments.

[SSAP 25 para 34.]

10.82 In providing this analysis, geographical turnover should be disclosed on both an origin and a destination basis, unless there is no material difference between the two bases. In effect, therefore, where no material difference between the two bases exists, disclosure by origin will be sufficient. In making this distinction the standard recognises that the origin basis is generally considered to be more important than the destination basis of disclosure. This is logical, since disclosure of other segment information about results and net assets can often be provided only on the origin basis. As Table 10.4 indicates, Pilkington plc's 1994 financial statements provided geographical analyses on an origin basis for both continuing and discontinued businesses at turnover, operating profit and net operating assets levels. However, information on the geographical destination basis is given only for turnover.

10.83 By disclosing turnover on the origin basis, it is possible to assess turnover, results and net assets on a consistent basis and relate all three to the perceived risks and opportunities of the segments. Where turnover on the destination basis is not disclosed, because the amount is not materially different from turnover on an origin basis, the fact that there is no material difference must be stated. [SSAP 25 para 34]. In this context, the probability of origin and destination bases not being materially different is likely to be substantially influenced by the nature of the entity's operating activities. As an example, Johnson Group Cleaners PLC (see Table 10.7) is principally engaged in dry cleaning services and workwear and towel rental, operating nationwide in the UK and US. Identified business segments are dry cleaning and rental; while geographical markets are the UK and the US. The services the members of the group offer are not by nature exportable, so geographical markets are serviced by local operating units. In effect, therefore, the UK business segment sells into the UK and the US segment services the US. Accordingly, the financial statements note that *"...there is no material difference between turnover by origin and destination"*. On the other hand, where a company is structured with operations in a limited number of different countries, but these are export bases for servicing a large number of other locations, the origin and destination basis will be materially different and disclosure under both bases will be required.

Table 10.7— Johnson Group Cleaners PLC — Annual Report — 31 December 1993

SEGMENTAL INFORMATION RESULTS (EXTRACT)

	1993		1992	
	TURNOVER	PROFIT	TURNOVER	PROFIT
	£000	£000	£000	£000
GEOGRAPHICAL REGION				
United Kingdom	99,542	16,076	96,457	14,971
United States	65,623	2,871	54,376	2,572
Group	165,165	18,947	150,833	17,543
CLASS OF BUSINESS				
Drycleaning	120,036	8,873	109,839	8,818
Rental	45,129	10,074	40,994	8,725
Group	165,165	18,947	150,833	17,543
Profit on sales of property		77		(76)
Deficit on a property valuation		–		(689)
Profit before interest		19,024		16,778
Net interest payable		814		1,663
PROFIT ON ORDINARY ACTIVITIES BEFORE TAXATION		18,210		15,115

There is no material difference between turnover by origin and by destination.

	1993	1992
	£000	£000
NET ASSETS		
GEOGRAPHICAL REGION		
United Kingdom	69,199	66,561
United States	22,064	21,521
Group	91,263	88,082
CLASS OF BUSINESS		
Drycleaning	61,481	60,576
Rental	29,782	27,506
Group	91,263	88,082
Unallocated net liabilities	(23,315)	(25,170)
Group share of net assets of associated undertakings	482	438
Net assets	68,430	63,350

10.84 Inter-segmental turnover is only required to be shown in the segmental disclosure of turnover by origin. It is not required to be disclosed by destination. [SSAP 25 para 34]. In practice, where inter-segmental sales are not material in the context of the reporting entity as a whole, companies state that fact and avoid the need to provide further analysis. Pilkington plc adopt this approach in their 1994 financial statements (see Table 10.4).

[The next paragraph is 10.86.]

Segment result

10.86 The standard requires the financial statements to analyse the result by class of business and geographical segment. In this context, the result is defined as being before taxation, minority interests and extraordinary items. Normally, it will also be before accounting for interest. However, this will depend on the nature of the business. In effect, where the nature of the business is such that interest income and expense are central to the business, the segment result should be shown after interest. In the majority of companies, however, segments will be financed by a mixture of debt and equity. In such situations, interest earned or incurred will be the result of the company's overall financial policy rather than reflecting the result of individual segments. For this reason, segment result should normally be disclosed before interest, with interest shown separately. [SSAP 25 para 34].

10.87 Pilkington plc, as noted above, discloses operating profit or loss before investment income and interest. (See Table 10.4.)

10.88 As Table 10.8 demonstrates, British Aerospace Public Limited Company provides an interesting set of segmental disclosures in that it provides segmental analysis by class of business on the two following bases:

- Profit/(loss) before interest and exceptional items.
- Profit/(loss) before tax on ordinary activities.

Table 10.8 — British Aerospace Public Limited Company — Annual Report — 31 December 1993

2 Segmental Analysis (extract)

Following the implementation of FRS3, the comparative figures for 1992 have been restated to include exceptional items (note 7).

	Sales		Profit/(loss) before interest	
	1993	1992	1993	1992
Continuing operations	**£m**	£m	**£m**	£m
Defence	**3,963**	4,003	**345**	352
Commercial aircraft	**1,580**	1,485	**(162)**	(337)
Motor vehicles	**4,301**	3,684	**56**	(49)
Property development	**166**	88	**(17)**	(2)
Other businesses and headquarters	**347**	332	**(13)**	(38)
	10,357	9,592	**209**	(74)
Discontinued operations				
Construction	**947**	792	**28**	14
	11,304	10,384	**237**	(60)
Less: intra-group				
Continuing operations	**(211)**	(181)	–	–
Discontinued operations	**(333)**	(226)	–	–
Exceptional items	–	–	**(288)**	(1,015)
	10,760	9,977	**(51)**	(1,075)

Sales include rental income from operating leases of £46 million (1992 £93 million).

Included within loss before interest of Other businesses and headquarters in 1992 is a charge of £36 million in respect of full provision against the carrying value of the Group's investment in DAF NV. The Group disposed of all its investment in DAF NV during 1993.

	Profit and loss before tax on ordinary activities		Assets employed	
	1993	1992	1993	1992
	£m	£m	£m	£m
Continuing operations				
Defence	**513**	533	**1,731**	1,416
Commercial aircraft	**(224)**	(410)	**(248)**	(133)
Motor vehicles	**(9)**	(115)	**1,389**	1,444
Property development	**(31)**	(26)	**152**	130
Other businesses and headquarters	**(12)**	(40)	**282**	428
	237	(58)	**3,306**	3,285
Discontinued operations				
Construction	**31**	23	–	181
Exceptional items	**(308)**	(1,015)	–	–
Unallocated Interest and borrowings	**(197)**	(151)	**(1,575)**	(1,448)
	(237)	(1,201)	**1,731**	2,018

7 Exceptional Items

The **exceptional recourse provision** of £250 million represents an additional provision at net present value for the expected level of financial exposure arising over the lifetime of aircraft finance arranged by the Group or by third parties in respect of turboprop aircraft. A deferred tax asset of £30 million has been established in respect of this provision.

The **exceptional loss on sale or termination of operations** of £38 million arises in respect of the disposal of the Group's interest in Ballast Nedam.

The Ballast Nedam group of construction companies was disposed of on 30th December, 1993 for a cash consideration equivalent to £175 million. The proceeds net of disposal costs approximated to the net assets of the Ballast Nedam construction companies at the date of disposal. The disposal therefore had no impact upon shareholders' funds, however inclusion of £38 million of goodwill previously written off against capital reserves on acquisition has resulted in an accounting loss of £38 million being disclosed in the profit and loss account. There was no tax charge or credit arising in respect of this disposal.

Corporate Jets was disposed of with effect from 6th August, 1993. Completion accounts remain under discussion; no profit or loss has been recognised in these accounts in respect of this disposal.

The disposal of the Group's communications business in 1992 gave rise to a loss of £15 million. There was no tax charge or credit arising in respect of this disposal.

The **exceptional reorganisation provision** of £1,000 million in 1992 was in respect of the Group's Regional Aircraft activities. The provision was dealt with in the 1992 accounts as £830 million within provisions for liabilities and charges* and £170 million within stocks. A deferred tax asset of £250 million was established in respect of these costs. In view of the long term nature of these liabilities, the provision was calculated on a net present value basis, and accordingly, an **interest charge** of £20 million has been included in 1993.

* Note that for years beginning on or after 1 January 2005, the Companies Act 1985 (as amended by Companies Act (International Accounting Standards and Other Accounting Amendments) Regulations 2004) line item is 'provisions for liabilities' and not 'provisions for liabilities and charges'.

10.89 Amortisation of goodwill is included in operating profit and accordingly the segmental analysis of results should be given after taking account of goodwill amortisation. However, several companies have given additional disclosure of results before goodwill amortisation. An example is Table 10.9, United News & Media plc. A more simplified example is Pearson, which shows as additional information the result before exceptional items and goodwill amortisation, see Table 10.10.

Table 10.9 – United News & Media plc – Report & Accounts – 31 December 1998

Notes to the financial statements (extract)

	Group 1998 £m	Group share of joint ventures 1998 £m	Group share of associates 1998 £m	Subtotal 1998 £m	Exceptional items 1998 £m	Total 1998 £m
1. BUSINESS ANALYSIS (continued)						
*** Operating profit before amortisation of goodwill by division**						
Continuing operations						
Business services	**157.3**	**11.1**	**1.9**	**170.3**	**(12.2)**	**158.1**
Consumer publishing	**65.0**	**4.6**	**1.1**	**70.7**	**(4.2)**	**66.5**
Broadcasting and entertainment (excluding new ventures)	**67.4**	**1.0**	**12.2**	**80.6**	**(3.5)**	**77.1**
	289.7	**16.7**	**15.2**	**321.6**	**(19.9)**	**301.7**
Broadcasting and entertainment – new ventures		**(4.6)**	**(12.3)**	**(16.9)**	**–**	**(16.9)**
Continuing operations	**289.7**	**12.1**	**2.9**	**304.7**	**(19.9)**	**284.8**
Discontinued operations						
Consumer publishing	**5.6**	**–**	**–**	**5.6**	**–**	**5.6**
Garban business	**40.1**	**0.1**	**0.7**	**40.9**	**(0.8)**	**40.1**
Discontinued operations	**45.7**	**0.1**	**0.7**	**46.5**	**(0.8)**	**45.7**
Operating profit before amortisation of goodwill	**335.4**	**12.2**	**3.6**	**351.2**	**(20.7)**	**330.5**
Amortisation of goodwill	**(153.3)**	**(7.3)**	**(6.4)**	**(167.0)**	**–**	**(167.0)**
Operating profit						
Continuing operations						
Business services	**86.2**	**10.9**	**1.9**	**99.0**	**(12.2)**	**86.8**
Consumer publishing	**52.1**	**4.6**	**1.3**	**58.0**	**(4.2)**	**53.8**
Broadcasting and entertainment (excluding new ventures)	**(1.9)**	**1.0**	**5.6**	**4.7**	**(3.5)**	**1.2**
	136.4	**16.5**	**8.8**	**161.7**	**(19.9)**	**141.8**
Broadcasting and entertainment – new ventures	**–**	**(11.7)**	**(12.3)**	**(24.0)**	**–**	**(24.0)**
Continuing operations	**136.4**	**4.8**	**(3.5)**	**137.7**	**(19.9)**	**117.8**
Discontinued operations						
Consumer publishing	**5.6**	**–**	**–**	**5.6**	**–**	**5.6**
Garban businesses	**40.1**	**0.1**	**0.7**	**40.9**	**(0.8)**	**40.1**
Discontinued operations	**45.7**	**0.1**	**0.7**	**46.5**	**(0.8)**	**45.7**

Operating profit	**182.1**	**4.9**	**(2.8)**	**184.2**	**(20.7)**	**163.5**
Non-operating exceptional items						**277.9**
Net interest expense						**(40.6)**
Profit on ordinary activities before tax						**400.8**
by geographic market						
United Kingdom	**48.3**	**(5.9)**	**(9.6)**	**32.8**	**(12.8)**	**20.0**
North America	**105.3**	**1.8**	**–**	**107.1**	**(7.3)**	**99.8**
Europe and Middle East	**19.3**	**8.2**	**3.6**	**31.1**	**(0.5)**	**30.6**
Pacific	**9.2**	**0.8**	**3.2**	**13.2**	**(0.1)**	**13.1**
Operating profit	**182.1**	**4.9**	**(2.8)**	**184.2**	**(20.7)**	**163.5**
Non-operating exceptional items						**277.9**
Net interest expense						**(40.6)**
Profit on ordinary activities before tax						**400.8**

* Includes income from other participating interests.

Discontinued operations comprise United Provincial Newspapers, UPN España and United Southern Publications (all part of consumer publishing) and the demerged Garban businesses. Non-operating exceptional items of £277.9 million in 1998 comprise a profit of £298.1 million relating to consumer publishing and a loss of £20.2 million relating to the Garban businesses. Non-operating exceptional items of £50.6 million in 1997 comprise a profit of £57.3 million relating to broadcasting and entertainment and a loss of £6.7 million relating to business services. Operating exceptional items are described in note 5.

	As restated Group 1997 £m	As restated Group share of joint ventures 1997 £m	As restated Group share of associates 1997 £m	As restated subtotal 1997 £m	As restated Exceptional items 1997 Em	As restated Total 1997 Em
*** Operating profit before amortisation of goodwill by division**						
Continuing operations						
Business services	155.1	6.7	1.1	162.9	–	162.9
Consumer publishing	66.0	4.3	0.5	70.8	–	70.8
Broadcasting and entertainment (excluding new ventures)	58.8	0.3	15.4	74.5	7.5	82.0
	279.9	11.3	17.0	308.2	7.5	315.7
Broadcasting and entertainment – new ventures	–	–	(21.3)	(21.3)	–	(21.3)
Continuing operations	279.9	11.3	(4.3)	286.9	7.5	294.4
Discontinued operations						
Consumer publishing	36.3	–	–	36.3	–	36.3
Garban businesses	45.8	0.1	2.3	48.2	–	48.2
Discontinued operations	82.1	0.1	2.3	84.5	–	84.5

Discontinued profit before amortisation of goodwill	362.0	11.4	(2.0)	371.4	7.5	378.9
Amortisation of goodwill	(157.1)	(0.1)	(6.7)	(163.9)	–	(163.9)
Operating profit						
Continuing operations						
Business services	81.0	6.6	1.1	88.7	–	88.7
Consumer publishing	54.8	4.3	0.5	59.6	–	59.6
Broadcasting and entertainment (excluding new ventures)	(9.9)	0.3	8.7	(0.9)	7.5	6.6
	125.9	11.2	10.3	147.4	7.5	154.9
Broadcasting and entertainment new ventures	–	–	(21.3)	(21.3)		(21.3)
Continuing operations	125.9	11.2	(11.0)	126.1	7.5	133.6
Discontinued operations						
Consumer publishing	33.3	–	–	33.3	–	33.3
Garban businesses	45.7	0.1	2.3	48.1	–	48.1
Discontinued operations	79.0	0.1	2.3	81.4	–	81.4
Operating profit	204.9	11.3	(8.7)	207.5	7.5	215.0
Non-operating exceptional items						50.6
Net interest expense						(56.5)
Profit on ordinary activities before tax						209.1
By geographic market						
United Kingdom	53.2	4.0	(15.5)	41.7	7.5	49.2
North America	109.2	1.5	–	110.7	–	110.7
Europe and Middle East	28.8	4.9	3.2	36.9	–	36.9
Pacific	13.7	0.9	3.6	18.2	–	18.2
Operating profit	204.9	11.3	(8.7)	207.5	7.5	215.0
Non-operating exceptional items						50.6
Net interest expense						(56.5)
Profit on ordinary activities before tax						209.1

* Includes income from other participating interests

Table 10.10 — Pearson plc — Annual Report — 31 December 1998

Notes to the financial statements (extract)

2a) Analysis of sales and operating profit

ALL FIGURES IN £ MILLIONS	1998 SALES	1998 OPERATING PROFIT BEFORE GOODWILL & OTHER ITEMS	1998 OPERATING PROFIT AFTER GOODWILL & OTHER ITEMS	1997 SALES	1997 RESTATED OPERATING PROFIT
Business sectors					
FT Group	683	118	114	676	108
Pearson Education	702	99	(34)	563	60
The Penguin Group	523	48	46	525	58
Pearson Television	343	61	61	247	26
Lazard	–	42	42	–	43
Continuing operations	2,251	368	229	2,011	295
Discontinued operations	144	21	21	282	33
	2,395	389	250	2,293	328
Geographical markets supplied					
United Kingdom	497	51	48	487	54
Continental Europe	461	114	111	382	77
North America	1,078	181	54	916	134
Asia Pacific	161	16	11	179	23
Rest of World	54	6	5	47	7
Continuing operations	2,251	368	229	2,011	295
Discontinued operations	144	21	21	282	33
	2,395	389	250	2,293	328

NOTE: *In 1998 'other items' comprises exceptional items of £120m and Year 2000 costs of £7m.*

- *Exceptional items of £120m comprise integration costs following the acquisition of Simon & Schuster. These all relate to the Pearson Education business sector.*
- *1997 Operating profit is stated after restructuring costs of £34m which were classified as exceptional within operating activities. These related to FT Group, £14m, Pearson Education, £12m, Pearson Television, £4m, and discontinued businesses, £4m, and are shown mainly within United Kingdom, £16m, and North America, £17m. In 1998 operating restructuring costs of £11m were incurred of which £6m were in the FT Group and £5m in the Penguin Group.*
- *1997 has been re-analysed to reflect expanded business groups.*
- *Discontinued operations relate to the withdrawal of the Group from the consumer software business following its disposal of Mindscape Inc. in March 1998, the withdrawal of the Group from the consumer magazine business following its disposal of Pearson New Entertainment in April 1998 and the withdrawal of the Group from the visitor attractions business following its disposal of The Tussauds Group in October 1998.*
- *1997 has been restated to reflect the adoption of FRS 9 'Associates and Joint Ventures' (see note 1).*
- *Analyses of the profits of associates are shown in note 13.*

10.90 The standard suggests that in most cases the disclosure of results by segment should be based on the areas from which products or services are supplied (that is, the origin basis). [SSAP 25 para 21].

Segment net assets

10.91 Companies that have to comply with the segmental reporting disclosure requirements of the standard must disclose the net assets of each business segment and geographical segment. In this context, the standard explains that in most cases net assets will be the non-interest bearing operating assets less the non-interest bearing operating liabilities. This is consistent with the standard's general emphasis on looking at operational performance. However, where segment result has been disclosed after accounting for interest, because investment policy is a principal business activity of the segment and, therefore, a fair measure of the segment's performance, the corresponding interest bearing operating assets and liabilities should be included in net assets. [SSAP 25 para 34].

10.92 The standard provides further guidance on the allocation of assets and liabilities to segments. It indicates that a segment's assets and liabilities may include not only assets and liabilities relating exclusively to that segment, but also an allocated portion of assets and liabilities that are shared by it with other segments. The standard also states that assets and liabilities that are shared by segments should be allocated to those segments on a reasonable basis. [SSAP 25 para 25].

10.93 The words *"reasonable basis"* are not further explained in the standard. However, the guidance on the allocation of common costs, which is discussed from paragraphs 10.62 above, would seem equally relevant to the allocation of shared assets and liabilities. Accordingly, if the entity apportions such assets and liabilities for the purpose of internal reporting, it may be reasonable for such assets and liabilities to be similarly apportioned for external reporting purposes. If apportionment of such assets and liabilities would be misleading, however, it would seem sensible not to apportion them, but, instead, to show them separately. It would, however, be rare for an entity to be unable to find some reasonable basis for allocating shared assets and liabilities, and a preferable method of avoiding any possibility of the allocation being misleading would be to quantify the amount of such assets and liabilities and disclose the basis of allocation.

10.94 The standard also indicates that assets and liabilities that are not used in the operations of any segment should not be allocated to any segment. [SSAP 25 para 25]. These would be shown as a separate figure in reconciling the total of net assets to the balance sheet. Furthermore, operating assets of a segment should not normally include loans or advances to, or investments in, another segment, unless interest on them has been included in arriving at the results of the first segment. Operating assets should include capitalised goodwill, which should not be shown as a reconciling item, but should be allocated to the segments to which it relates. Table 10.11 includes £826.3 million of goodwill in the total of £1,563.3 million of net operating assets, which is analysed by segment.

Table 10.11 — United News & Media plc — Report & Accounts — 31 December 1998

Notes to the financial statements (extract)

	1998	As restated 1997
	£m	£m
Net operating assets by division		
Business services	**781.5**	850.7
Consumer publishing	**289.1**	411.4
Broadcasting and entertainment	**492.7**	558.5
Garban businesses	–	(3.6)
	1,563.3	1,817.0
by geographic market		
United Kingdom	**998.1**	1,131.6
North America	**382.2**	423.4
Europe and Middle East	**153.8**	224.2
Pacific	**29.2**	37.8
	1,563.3	1,817.0
Reconciliation of net operating assets to net assets		
Net operating assets	**1,563.3**	1,817.0
Investments	**147.9**	215.4
Corporation tax	**(72.1)**	(49.6)
Deferred tax	–	(0.4)
Net borrowings	**(703.2)**	(1,155.0)
Proposed dividend*	**(61.1)**	(66.2)
Net assets	**874.8**	761.2

The Garban businesses were previously reported as part of the financial services division, but have been shown separately and comparative amounts restated in order to be consistent with the demerger of those businesses. The financial services division also previously included certain properties, and the financial information business previously included within business services, has been demerged within the Garban businesses. The impact of redefining the segment on the group turnover, operating profit and net assets of the Garban businesses compared to financial services previously reported at 31 December 1997 is an increase of £6.3 million, an increase of £1.0 million and a reduction of £19.0 million respectively.

* Note that for years beginning on or after 1 January 2005, FRS 21 prohibits the recognition of proposed dividends as a liability.

10.95 Pilkington plc's 1994 financial statements include segmental information structured on an operating basis. For consistency, the segmental disclosures of net assets are given on an equivalent operating basis to that used in disclosing operating result. This means that not all of the assets employed by the group are included therein, so a helpful summary of net operating assets is provided in a separate note (see Table 10.4).

10.96 The Mersey Docks And Harbour Company's approach in its 1993 financial statements, as set out in Table 10.12, was to provide business segment information both gross and net of intra-segment sales. It also provided segmental analysis of profit on ordinary activities before interest and taxation, indicating by this treatment that interest could not be attributed on a fair basis to individual business segments. In disclosing segmental information on net assets, it excluded interest bearing assets and liabilities, which were then shown separately in the note, effectively reconciling the segmental net assets to the balance sheet.

Table 10.12 — The Mersey Docks and Harbour Company — Annual Report & Accounts — 31 December 1993

Notes to the Accounts
for the year ended 31 December 1993

2. SEGMENTAL ANALYSIS BY CLASS OF BUSINESS

The analysis by class of business of the Group's turnover, profit before taxation and net assets is set out below.

TURNOVER		**1993**			1992	
	Total sales	**Inter-segment sales**	**External sales**	Total sales	Inter-segment sales	External sales
	£000	**£000**	**£000**	£000	£000	£000
Port operations	**71,716**	**(3,685)**	**68,067**	64,867	(2,574)	62,293
Irish Sea subsidiaries	**35,113**	**(1,630)**	**23,482**	18,378	(1,621)	16,757
Property and property development	**2,674**	**(460)**	**2,314**	2,605	(500)	2,105
Non-port activities	**5,673**	**(980)**	**4,693**	6,189	(982)	5,207
	105,175	**(6,755)**	**98,430**	92,039	(5,677)	86,362

PROFIT ON ORDINARY ACTIVITIES BEFORE TAXATION

	1993	1992 as restated
	£000	£000
Port operations	**18,054**	12,496
Irish Sea subsidiaries	**1,321**	1,243
Property and property development	**1,698**	1,583
Non-port activities	**590**	287
	21,663	15,609
Net interest	**(798)**	(449)
	28,865	15,160
NET ASSETS (LIABILITIES)		
Port operations	**124,739**	102,690
Irish Sea subsidiaries	**1,372**	597
Property and property development	**20,005**	20,316
Non-port activities	**(693)**	(344)
	145,323	123,259
Interest bearing assets	**14,938**	9,478
Interest bearing liabilities	**(10,093)**	(8,656)
	150,161	124,081

Turnover and profit are predominantly derived from U.K. operations.

Turnover and profit before taxation for Liverpool Conservancy were £2,922,000 (1992: £2,837,000) and £8,000 (1992: loss £188,000) respectively.

Turnover for Liverpool Pllotage services was £3,859,000 (1992: £4,173,000). **The aggregate expenditure incurred in providing Liverpool Pllotage services was £3,827,000** (1992: £3,753,000).

10.97 In both of the above examples, the amount of net assets attributed to the identified segments is less than the sum of the total net assets in the balance sheet. However, the items excluded can be separately identified to facilitate a full reconciliation to the financial statements. This contrasts with the disclosure approach adopted by British Aerospace Public Limited Company (see Table 10.8) and Johnson Group Cleaners PLC (see Table 10.7) in their 1993 financial statements. These companies analyse total net assets between segments and then deduct unallocated net liabilities in total to reconcile back to the net assets stated in the balance sheet. This is less helpful to the reader in understanding the real level of net assets used in individual segments, but probably cannot be avoided.

10.98 In disclosing the net assets employed by individual segments, most reporting entities base the disclosures on the balance sheet at the accounting reference date. The standard is silent on this matter and it is possible to base disclosure on the average position for the year. This may be particularly appropriate in the context of evaluating the return on capital employed, in instances where the year end position is materially different from the average position. This may occur in an industry of a seasonal nature, where the balance sheet date may coincide with either a trading peak or trough and where stock, debtor and creditor levels are reflective of that situation. BTR plc is one company that has made disclosure on the basis of average net assets (see Table 10.13).

Table 10.13 – BTR plc – Annual Report and Accounts – 31 December 1997

Notes (extract)

1 Analysis of sales, profit before tax and average operating net assets (extract)

Average operating net assets represent, in the opinion of the Directors, the best estimate of net asset utilisation by the Business Groups, and exclude taxation, dividends*, net debt and provisions for liabilities and charges.†

* Note that for years beginning on or after 1 January 2005, recognition of dividends receivable as payable will be rare because FRS 21 prohibits the recognition of interim dividends until they are paid and final dividends until they are approved by shareholders. See further chapter 22.

† Note that for years beginning on or after 1 January 2005, the Companies Act 1985 (as amended by SI 04/2947, 'The Companies Act 1985 (International Accounting Standards and Other Accounting Amendments) Regulations 2004) line item is 'provisions for liabilities" and not 'provisions for liabilities and charges.

10.99 The segmental analysis of net assets will usually be based on the areas from which goods are supplied. This is a practical application, for in many instances the provision of such information on a destination basis would be difficult to obtain and its value dubious.

Associates and joint ventures

10.100 SSAP 25 and FRS 9 set out the segmental information to be disclosed in respect of associates and joint ventures. These requirements apply unless publication of such information would be prejudicial to the business of the associate or joint venture. Where disclosure is not made for this reason, the reason for non-disclosure should be stated in the notes, together with a brief description of the omitted business or businesses. [SSAP 25 para 36]. SSAP 25 also allows segmental information concerning associates or joint ventures not to be given if it is unobtainable. [SSAP 25 para 36]. But following the publication of FRS 9 and the increased emphasis on the investors in associates and joint ventures being able to exercise in practice significant influence or joint control (respectively), it seems unlikely that such information would be unobtainable, except in very unusual circumstances. In such circumstances the reason for non-disclosure and a brief description of the omitted business or businesses should also be given.

10.101 FRS 9 required that joint ventures are accounted for using the 'gross equity' method of accounting, which entails investors disclosing additionally their share of joint ventures' turnover and gross assets and liabilities. In addition, the standard requires that the share of the joint ventures' turnover should be included in the segmental analysis and should be clearly distinguished from the turnover of the group itself. [FRS 9 para 21]. Furthermore, an investor can, if it so wishes, disclose its share of its associates' turnover as a memorandum item in the profit and loss account where it considers that this is helpful in giving an indication of the group's size. But where this voluntary disclosure is made, the segmental analysis of turnover should, in addition, clearly distinguish between that of the group and that of associates. [FRS 9 para 27].

10.102 SSAP 25 also requires additional segmental information of results and net assets for associates and joint ventures but only where they form a significant part of a reporting entity's results or assets. In this regard, it notes that associate (including joint venture) undertakings are considered significant if, in total, they account for at least 20 per cent of the total result or 20 per cent of the total net assets of the reporting entity. There is nothing in SSAP 25 or FRS 9 which suggests this threshold should be applied separately for associates and joint ventures (although the additional disclosures in FRS 9 apply on this basis) and so it appears that it can be applied in aggregate. But it appears that the required disclosures should separate joint ventures from associates, following the general requirement to do so in FRS 9, which is also implied in paragraphs 21 and 27 of FRS 9.

10.103 The information required in respect of associates and joint ventures is a segmental analysis of both of the following:

- The reporting entity's share of profits or losses of associates and joint ventures before accounting for taxation, minority interests and extraordinary items (although the latter have been all but eliminated by FRS 3 – see further chapter 24).

- The reporting entity's share of the net assets of associates and joint ventures (including goodwill to the extent that it has not been amortised) stated, where possible, after attributing fair values to the net assets at the date of acquisition of the interest in each associate or joint venture.

[SSAP 25 para 36].

10.104 FRS 9 requires that, the share of associates' and joint ventures' operating results, interest, non-operating exceptional items and taxation is required to be disclosed for each of those line items. Consequently, if the reporting group analyses its segment result before charging interest, for the reasons discussed in paragraph 10.86, it will be able to disclose segment information for its associates and joint ventures on an equivalent basis.

10.105 The General Electric Company p.l.c also provides segmental analysis of its interests in joint ventures as Table 10.15 indicates. Again the analysis is provided on both a business and geographical segment basis.

Table 10.15 — The General Electric Company, p.l.c. — Annual Report and Accounts — 31 March 1998

Notes to the Accounts (extract)

11 Fixed asset investments — joint ventures, associates and other (extract)

	Profit		Turnover		Net assets at 31st March	
	1998	1997	**1998**	1997	**1998**	1997
	£ million	£ million	**£ million**	£ million	**£ million**	£ million
By classes of business						
Marconi Electronic Systems	**36**	38	**568**	646	**(16)**	(62)
Marconi Communications	**8**	8	**30**	22	**18**	13
Industrial Group — Rest of World	**25**	19	**298**	265	**44**	48
Alstom	**180**	169	**3,618**	3,505	**125**	(145)
Other	–	11	–	–	–	–
	249	245	**4,514**	4,438	**171**	(146)
Exceptional items in respect of continuing operations	**(21)**	(80)				
Non-operating exceptional items	**28**					
Interest bearing assets and liabilities	**36**	72			**572**	955
Unallocated net liabilities					**(4)**	(55)
	292	237	**4,514**	4,438	**739**	754

By territory of origin						
United Kingdom	**86**	58	**1,439**	1,202	**258**	126
France	**93**	126	**1,841**	2,111	**536**	294
Rest of Europe	**43**	52	**730**	772	**(572)**	(564)
The Americas	**14**	4	**275**	166	**(47)**	–
Africa, Asia and Australasia	**13**	5	**229**	187	**(4)**	(2)
	249	245	**4,514**	4,438	**171**	(146)

10.106 A further example of disclosure in respect of associates and joint ventures is Table 10.9 (United News & Media plc) above.

Joint arrangements

10.107 Joint arrangements are contractual arrangements under which the participants engage in joint activities that do not create an entity, because it would not be carrying on a trade or business of its own. [FRS 9 para 4]. FRS 9 requires that such arrangements should not be accounted for following the equity method of accounting, but participants should account for their own assets, liabilities and cash flows, measured according to the terms of the agreement governing the arrangement. Although SSAP 25 does not cover this type of entity, it seems appropriate that the amounts of the arrangement accounted for under FRS 9 should also be included within the segmental analysis. Joint arrangements are considered in more detail in chapter 27.

Reconciliation of figures

10.108 The standard requires the reporting entity to provide a reconciliation where the total of the amounts disclosed by segment does not agree with the related total in the financial statements. In this situation, the difference between the two figures should be identified and explained. [SSAP 25 para 37]. The issue of reconciling segmental net assets to total reported net assets has been discussed in paragraphs 10.91 to 10.99. Table 10.16 shows a helpful example of a company, The Rank Organisation Plc, reconciling the major areas of segmental disclosures to the figures reported in its primary statements.

Table 10.16 —The Rank Organisation Plc — Directors' Report and Accounts — 31 October 1994

Notes to the Accounts (extract)

1 SEGMENTAL INFORMATION
Analysis by division

	Turnover		Profit before tax		Year end net assets		Net cash flow	
	1994	1993	**1994**	1993	**1994**	1993	**1994**	1993
	£m	£m	**£m**	£m	**£m**	£m	**£m**	£m
Film and Television	**680.1**	571.7	**66.9**	49.4	**335.1**	357.1	**78.1**	29.2
Holidays	**459.9**	424.5	**57.0**	52.0	**485.6**	462.1	**39.5**	47.3
Recreation	**729.5**	692.1	**69.0**	64.0	**511.4**	493.5	**51.4**	54.7
Leisure	**281.7**	269.4	**47.7**	49.1	**334.7**	313.8	**3.5**	13.0
Other	**17.9**	17.1	**(10.8)**	(6.8)	**9.6**	8.6	**(13.2)**	(6.3)
Continuing operations	**2,169.1**	1,974.8	**229.8**	207.7	**1,676.4**	1,635.1	**159.3**	137.9
Discontinued operations	**30.3**	132.0	**(2.8)**	(7.3)	**31.7**	122.1	**58.8**	101.9
	2,199.4	**2,106.8**	**227.0**	200.4	**1,708.1**	1,757.2	**218.1**	239.8
Share of associated undertakings:								
Rank Xerox			**151.5**	151.2	**606.9**	586.5	**61.5**	72.1
Universal Studios Florida			**11.4**	13.0	**171.1**	199.9	**22.7**	24.4
Other			**(0.3)**	(1.5)	**31.8**	26.4	**(6.7)**	(19.7)
			162.6	162.7	**809.8**	812.8	**77.5**	76.8
			389.6	363.1	**2,517.9**	2,570.0	**295.6**	316.6
Non-operating items			**(30.6)**	2.0				
Interest			**(75.0)**	(88.5)			**(85.1)**	(57.3)
Profit before tax			**284.0**	276.6				
Tax and dividends*					**(102.3)**	(17.0)	**(83.0)**	(135.1)
Other non-operating liabilities (net)					**(50.0)**	(64.9)		
Net borrowings					**(759.0)**	(955.3)		
					1,606.6	1,532.8	**127.5**	124.2

* Note that for years beginning on or after 1 January 2005, FRS 21 prohibits the recognition of proposed final dividends until they have received shareholder approval (see further chapter 22).

[The next paragraph is 10.110.]

Comparative figures

10.110 The standard requires the provision of comparatives figures unless it is the first occasion on which an entity produces a segmental report. In that situation, if the necessary information to produce comparative figures is not readily available, then they need not be provided. [SSAP 25 para 38].

[The next paragraph is 10.116.]

Other disclosure requirements

10.116 Since SSAP 25's publication in 1990, the ASB has published many new standards. Although none of these standards and pronouncements relate specifically to segmental reporting, some of them have an impact upon the nature of segmental disclosures in financial statements. A number of these instances are considered below.

Cash flow statements

10.117 FRS 1, 'Cash flow statements', encourages, but does not require, entities to provide segmental breakdown of cash flows. [FRS 1 para 8]. While segmental cash flow information might be useful to readers of financial statements, by helping them to understand the relationship between the cash flows of the reporting entity as a whole and those of its constituent segments, the FRS is silent on how segmental cash flow information might be given. An example of a company giving a segmental breakdown of its operating cash flows is shown in chapter 30.

10.118 There are some examples of reporting entities providing segmental analysis of cash flows. While Pearson plc discloses operating cash flows for each of its main business lines (newspapers, books, television and visitor attractions) in its OFR, it does not provide segmental cash flow analysis in the main body of the audited financial statements. The Rank Organisation plc, which provides a segmental analysis of cash flow, appears to be the exception rather than the rule (see Table 10.16).

10.119 One situation where segmental reporting of cash flows has been disclosed is where consolidated financial statements include subsidiary undertakings with a wide variety of activities. The extracts from B.A.T. Industries plc financial statements, set out in Table 10.17, provide an illustration of this.

Table 10.17 — B.A.T Industries p.l.c. — Directors' Report and Accounts — 31 December 1993

Accounting Policies

1 The Group accounts have been prepared in accordance with applicable accounting standards and combine the accounts of Group undertakings at 31 December. As permitted by the Companies Act 1985 the accounts formats have been adapted, as necessary, to give a true and fair view of the state of affairs and profit of the commercial activities of the Group and to present the insurance activities in accordance with the provisions of that Act applicable to insurance companies. The accounts are on an historical cost basis as modified to include certain insurance assets at market value.

The accounts formats have been developed to reflect more appropriately the operations of the Group. All the assets and liabilities of the Group's businesses are included in the consolidated balance sheet. To equity account for either tobacco or financial services would not give a true and fair view of the total Group. However, given the differences between the two main businesses of the Group and the constraints of the regulatory environment within which insurance companies operate, the assets and liabilities are shown separately under headings covering commercial and corporate activities, financial services general business and financial service life business. This approach has been reflected in preparing separate cash flow statements for the three businesses as the regulatory environment in insurance limits the availability of cash flows between businesses. The Directors are of the opinion that this approach, where it differs from the Companies Act 1985 and applicable accounting standards as described further in the Directors' Report on page 1, is necessary to present a true and fair view of the Group.

Group Cash Flow Statements
for the year ended 31 December

			1993	1992
COMMERCIAL AND CORPORATE ACTIVITIES	NOTES		**£m**	£m
Net cash inflows from commercial operating activities	13		**977**	1,165
Dividends from—financial services subsidiary undertakings				
–general			**114**	137
–life			**119**	114
–associates			**59**	44
Net cash inflows from operating activities	13		**1,269**	1,460
Investment income		**113**		129
Interest paid		**(226)**		(239)
Dividends to B.A.T. Industries' shareholders		**(276)**		(528)
Dividends to minorities		**(46)**		(30)
Net cash outflows from returns on investments and servicing of finance			**(435)**	(668)
Taxation paid			**(288)**	(396)
Capital expenditure		**(338)**		(278)
Sale of fixed assets		**16**		26
Purchase of other investments	14	**(21)**		(8)
Sale of other investments	14		**42**	59
Subsidiary and associated undertakings				
–purchases	14	**(8)**		(42)
–sales	14			26
Investment in Farmers' insurance exchanges				(128)
Net cash outflows from Investing activities			**(309)**	(345)
Other cash outflows with financial services activities	15		**(15)**	(342)
Net cash inflow/(outflow) before external financing (from above items)			**222**	(291)
Proceeds from issue of shares		**5**		5
Commercial paper		**(1,296)**		76
Bank and other loans		**(38)**		58

Medium term debt issues		727		286
Eurobond issues		595		
Net cash (outflows)/inflows financing activities	16		(7)	425
Increase in cash and cash equivalents	16		215	134

Certain comparative figures have been restated as explained in accounting policy 1 on page 8 and details of these changes are given in the individual notes to which they relate.

		GENERAL		LIFE	
		1933	1992	**1993**	1992
FINANCIAL SERVICES	Notes	**£m**	£m	**£m**	£m
Net cash inflows from operating activities excluding investment gains	17	**558**	330	**495**	337
Dividend to					
–Group companies		**(114)**	(137)	**(119)**	(114)
–minority shareholders		**(2)**	(2)		
Interest paid		**(49)**	(28)		
Net cash outflows from servicing of Finance		**(165)**	(167)	**(119)**	(114)
Taxation paid		**(193)**	(56)		
Sale of investments		**2,886**	1,494	**667**	362
Less: purchase of investments		**(3,090)**	(1,884)	**(1,088)**	(567)
Sale proceeds less reinvestments	19	**(204)**	(390)	**(421)**	(205)
Capital expenditure		**(51)**	(42)	**(21)**	(21)
Sale of fixed assets		**7**	2	**9**	7
Proceeds on sale at subsidiary undertakings	18		119	**17**	
Investment in life fund					(102)
Investment in Farmers' insurance exchanges					100
Net cash outflows from investing activities		**(248)**	(311)	**(416)**	(421)
Other cash flows with the life funds			18		
Other cash flows between Group businesses	15	**(24)**	176	**39**	166
Other cash flows with commercial activities and financial services businesses		**(24)**	194	**39**	166
Net cash outflows before external financing (from above items)		**(72)**	(10)	**(1)**	(32)
Borrowings		**3**	59		
Issue of shares				**1**	4
Net cash Inflows from financing activities	19	**3**	59	**1**	4
(Decrease)/increase in cash and cash equivalents		**(69)**	49		(28)

The life business cash flows above exclude flows of the Allied Dunbar and Eagle Star life funds.

10.120 Cash flow statements are considered in more detail in chapter 30.

[The next paragraph is 10.122.]

Subsidiary undertakings

10.122 FRS 2, 'Accounting for subsidiary undertakings', indicates that parent undertakings should consider how best to provide segmental information for their group. It suggests that the ensuing disclosures should indicate the different risks and rewards, growth and prospects of the different parts of the group. In this regard, the requirements of SSAP 25 should be seen as the minimum disclosure level, rather than as the maximum. [FRS 2 para 94].

10.123 Although FRS 2 recognises the importance of segmental reporting in consolidated financial statements, it does not introduce any specific new requirements. However, it does suggest two situations where segmental information could supplement consolidated financial statements, namely:

- In respect of subsidiary undertakings whose activities differ from those of the rest of the group.
- In respect of disclosures relating to minority interests.

[FRS 2 para 94].

[The next paragraph is 10.126.]

10.126 It is likely that a subsidiary whose activities are dissimilar from those of the rest of the group will meet the definition of a reportable segment in its own right if it is material in the context of the group. Nonetheless, the suggestion that groups explain the impact of subsidiaries with dissimilar activities by way of segmental reporting remains.

Acquisitions and discontinued operations

10.127 FRS 3, 'Reporting financial performance', comments that an appreciation of the impact of changes on material components of the business is essential, if a reader is to obtain a thorough understanding of the results and financial position of a reporting entity. In this regard, the standard states that *"...if an acquisition, a sale or a termination has a material impact on a major business segment ... this impact should be disclosed and explained"*. [FRS 3 para 53]. To promote this understanding, FRS 3 requires reporting entities to analyse and disclose turnover, operating profit and exceptional items, as set out in the profit and loss account, between continuing and discontinued operations.

10.128 In making this distinction between continuing and discontinued operations, the standard requires that, for a component of a reporting entity's operations to be reported as discontinued, its *"...assets, liabilities, results of operations and activities of an operation must be clearly distinguishable, physically,* *operationally and for financial reporting purposes"*. In addition, *"…a sale or termination should have resulted from a strategic decision by the reporting entity either to withdraw from a particular market (whether class of business or geographical) or to curtail materially its presence in a continuing market (i.e. 'downsizing')"*. [FRS 3 paras 43, 44].

10.129 Since FRS 3 requires a detailed analysis of aggregate financial information, it is important to understand its relationship with SSAP 25. In this regard, for a business to be analysed and disclosed as discontinued in accordance with FRS 3, it does not necessarily have to constitute a complete business segment for the purposes of SSAP 25. This is because the definition of discontinued operations also includes a sale or termination that has a material effect on the nature and focus of a reporting entity's operations and represents a material reduction in operating facilities resulting either from its withdrawal from a particular market (whether class of business or geographical) or from a material reduction in turnover in the entity's continuing markets. In effect, therefore, what constitutes a discontinued operation for FRS 3 purposes may only be part of a segment for SSAP 25 reporting purposes.

10.130 An example of the above distinction between FRS 3 and SSAP 25 could be in the case of a group with two equally-sized subsidiaries, each operating in the field of car leasing. The sale of one of the subsidiaries would not be the disposal of the whole car leasing segment as defined for the purposes of SSAP 25. However, if it materially affected the nature and focus of the entity's operations (for example, if the disposal were made to release funds for investing in a different business, such as a road haulage business, that materially changed the nature and focus of the group's operations) it would constitute a discontinued operation for the purposes of FRS 3, because it is a material reduction in operating facilities and results from a material reduction in turnover in the group's continuing markets. In addition, the assets, liabilities, results and activities can be distinguished physically, operationally and for financial reporting purposes. The nature of the operations disposed of is not different from that of the rest of the group, but that is not a test that has to be satisfied under FRS 3 in order for the disposal of the subsidiary to qualify as a discontinued operation.

10.131 In practice, some entities, that have had material sales or terminations, have disclosed the impact of these in their financial statements by analysing continuing and discontinued operations by segment. Pilkington plc adopts this approach, providing detailed business segment and geographical segment analysis for both categories. Even its additional note analysing net operating assets by balance sheet category is disclosed on a continuing and discontinued basis (see Table 10.4).

10.132 In Table 10.18 Grand Metropolitan Public Limited Company also provides segmental information on this basis.

Table 10.18 — Grand Metropolitan Public Limited Company — Annual Report — 30 September 1994

Notes (extract)

2 SEGMENT ANALYSIS

	1994			1993		
	Turnover	Profit	Net assets	Turnover	Profit	Net assets
Class of business:	£m	£m	£m	£m	£m	£m
Continuing operations						
Food —branded	3,267	267	2,007	3,066	227	2,226
—retailing	1,104	230	1,353	1,153	175	1,378
Drinks	3,371	520	1,657	3,418	563	1,856
	7,742	1,017	5,017	7,637	965	5,460
Discontinued operations	38	6		483	77	658
	7,780		5,017	8,120		6,118
Operating profit before exceptional items		1,023			1.042	
Associates before exceptional items		45	729		24	620
Exceptional items		(291)			(286)	
Interest		(123)			(155)	
Profit before taxation		654			625	
Capital employed			5,746			6,738
Net borrowings			(2,159)			(3,025)
Net assets			3,587			3,713
Geographical area by country of operation						
United Kingdom	815	101	339	1,245	173	975
Rest of Europe	1,613	180	627	1,648	210	685
United States of America	4,644	677	3,714	4,499	582	4,140
Rest of North America	173	26	116	214	26	151
Africa and Middle East	183	315	32	182	15	31
Rest of World	352	24	189	332	36	136
	7,780		5,017	8,120		6,118
Operating profit before exceptional items		1,023			1,042	
Associates before exceptional items		45		729	24	620
Exceptional items		(291)			(286)	
Interest		(123)			(155)	
Profit before taxation		654			625	
Capital employed			5,746			6,738
Net borrowings			(2,159)			(3,025)
Net assets			3,587			3,713

Profit before interest relates to the following activities and geographical areas: Food — branded £214m, Food — retailing £183m, Drinks £351m, and discounted businesses £29m (1993 — £184m, £85m, £560m, and £23m respectively, and a £50m charge in respect of a write down of the group's UK properties); United Kingdom £71m, Rest of Europe £81m, United States of America £556m, Rest of World £69m (1993 — £117m, £136m, £458m and £91m respectively).

The group interest expense is arranged centrally and is not attributable to individual activities or geographical areas. The analysis of capital employed by activity and geographical area is calculated on net assets excluding associates, cash and borrowings.

Turnover between the above classes of business is not material.

Following the disposal of The Chef & Brewer Group, Burger King and Pearle are now disclosed as a separate segment of the Food sector and the loans to IEL are included in associates. Discontinued operations comprise The Chef & Brewer Group and, in the prior period, Express Foods; both businesses operated almost exclusively in the United Kingdom. On 19th September 1994, the group announced the sale, subject to regulatory approval, of ALPO Petfoods; the sale was not completed by 1st December 1994 and ALPO Petfoods has been classified as a continuing operation in these accounts.

The weighted average exchange rate used in translation of US dollar profit and loss accounts was £1 = $1.51 (1993 — £1 = $1.52). The exchange rate used to translate US dollar assets and liabilities at the balance sheet date was £1 = $1.58 (1993 — £1 = $1.50).

3 TURNOVER

			1994			1993
	Counting	**Discontinued**	**Total**	*Continuing*	*Discontinued*	*Total*
	£m	**£m**	**£m**	*£m*	*£m*	*£m*
Geographical area by destination:						
United Kingdom	**741**	**38**	**779**	*724*	*483*	*1,207*
Rest of Europe	**1,610**	–	**1,610**	*1,641*	–	*1,641*
United States of America	**4,546**	–	**4,546**	*4,389*	–	*4,389*
Rest of North America	**219**	–	**219**	*239*	–	*239*
Africa and Middle East	**210**	–	**210**	*221*	–	*221*
Rest of World	**416**	–	**416**	*423*	–	*423*
	7,742	**38**	**7,780**	*7,637*	*483*	*8,120*

Exports from the United Kingdom were £297m (1993 — £298m).

10.133 Although FRS 3 does not define a business segment, best practice would seem to be to disclose the effect of acquisitions and discontinued activities on both a business class and geographical location basis by segment. In the case of the geographical disclosures, these would be made on both a source and a destination basis. Comparative information would also be provided.

10.134 FRS 3 also requires that the results of acquisitions, excluding those that are also discontinued in the period, should be disclosed separately in aggregate as a component of continuing operations. As with the other continuing operations the minimum analysis given on the face of the profit and loss account should be turnover and operating profit. The analysis of each of the other profit and loss account headings between turnover and operating profit may be given in a note, instead of on the face of the profit and loss account.

[The next paragraph is 10.136.]

Exceptional items

10.136 FRS 3 identifies exceptional items as "*. . .material items which derive from events or transactions that fall within the ordinary activities of the reporting entity and which individually or, if of a similar type, in aggregate, need to be disclosed by virtue of their size or incidence if the financial statements are to give a true and fair view*".

[The next paragraph is 10.138.]

10.138 FRS 3 does not give specific guidance on the effect of the 'exceptional' items on segmental reporting, other than by stating that the effect of such items on segment results should be disclosed where material. We consider that the effect can be shown in one of several ways:

- Analyse 'profits after exceptional items but before interest', and then disclose the effect of the exceptionals in narrative form.
- Analyse operating profit (that is before super-exceptionals) and then show these exceptionals as one figure in the reconciliation to profit before tax, again with narrative explanation of their effect on individual segments.
- Analyse operating profit by segment and then give a separate column analysing the non-operating exceptionals by segment.

10.139 The important point is that the segmental analyses published must provide sufficient disclosure to enable the reader to understand the impact of exceptional items on business and geographical segments, and to be able to distinguish operating profit before exceptional items from operating profit after exceptional items.

10.140 Practical examples of companies providing segmental information in respect of exceptional items include Trafalgar House Public Limited Company, which, in addition to a detailed analysis of exceptional items in the notes to the financial statements, sets out a business segment analysis of their effect on operating (loss)/profit (see Table 10.19).

Table 10.19 — Trafalgar House Public Limited Company — Report and Accounts — 30 September 1994

Notes to the Accounts

3 Analysis by geographical area and class of business

Exceptional items charged to operating (loss)/profit analysed by class of business:

	Rationalisation costs 1994 £m	Rationalisation costs* 1993 £m (restated)	**Asset write downs and other items 1994 £m**	Asset write downs 1993 £m (restated)	**Total 1994 £m**	Total restated 1993 £m (restated)
Engineering	**(21.8)**	(45.8)	**(15.2)**	(21.1)	**(37.0)**	(66.9)
Construction	**(1.5)**	(10.1)	–	(6.2)	**(1.5)**	(16.3)
Residential Property	**(0.4)**	(6.3)	**5.7**	(17.4)	**5.3**	(23.7)
Commercial Property	**(0.7)**	(2.9)	**(6.6)**	(129.2)	**(7.3)**	(132.1)
Hotels	–	–	**1.9**	(12.5)	**1.9**	(12.5)
Shipping	–	(1.5)	–	(15.5)	–	(17.0)
Other activities	–	–	–	(57.2)	–	(57.2)
	(24.4)	(66.6)	**(14.2)**	(259.1)	**(38.6)**	(325.7)

* 1993 rationalisation costs include directors' compensation of £1.3 million.

10.141 AMEC p.l.c. analyses profit or loss by business and geographical segment gross of exceptional items, showing the gross amount of exceptional items as an aggregate one-line deduction. However, in a note analysing exceptional items, it provides various analyses including by class of business and by geographical area (see Table 10.20).

Table 10.20 — AMEC p.l.c. — Annual Report and Accounts — 31 December 1993

Notes to the accounts (extract)

2 Analysis by class of business and geographical origin

	Turnover 1993 £million	Turnover 1992 £million	Profit (loss) 1993 £million	Profit (loss) 1992 £million	Assets employed 1993 £million	Assets employed 1992 £million.
By class of business						
Building and civil engineering	704.8	674.7	9.6	22.7	30.4	11.0
Mechanical and electrical engineering	1,361.1	1,361.9	22.8	18.0	62.7	83.9
Housing and development	138.1	109.1	(7.6)	(17.1)	150.0	176.2
	2,204.0	2,145.7	24.8	23.6	243.1	271.1
Internal trading	(19.8)	(24.0)	–	–	–	–
Exceptional items (note 7)	–	–	–	(114.6)	–	–
Loss on disposals of operations	–	–	(2.2)	–	–	–
Net interest	–	–	(1.6)	2.8	–	–
Unallocated net liabilities	–	–	–	–	(2.7)	(28.9)
	2,184.2	2,121.7	21.0	(88.2)	240.4	242.2
By geographical origin						
United Kingdom	1,751.4	1,838.4	28.0	37.3	196.0	220.8
Europe	201.4	106.0	3.7	3.2	24.2	17.8
Americas	132.0	117.6	(6.1)	(2.6)	21.6	31.3
Middle East Asia and Australasia	119.2	83.7	(0.8)	(14.3)	1.3	1.2
	2,204.0	2,145.7	24.8	23.6	243.1	271.1
Internal trading	(19.8)	(24.0)	–	–	–	–
Exceptional items (note 7)	–	–	–	(114.6)	–	–
Loss on disposal of operations	–	–	(2.2)	–	–	–
Net interest	–	–	(1.6)	2.8	–	–
Unallocated net liabilities	–	–	–	–	(2.7)	(28.9)
	2,184.2	2,121.7	21.0	(88.2)	240.4	242.2

FRS 3 has been adopted in preparing the consolidated profit and loss account.

Certain businesses have been disposed of or terminated during the year none of which falls within the materiality definition of discontinued operations.

The results of businesses acquired during the year have not had a significant impact on the profit for the year.

Accordingly information disclosed in the consolidated profit and loss account includes the results of business disposals and acquisitions during the year.

The analysis of turnover by geographical market is not materially different from that by geographical origin.

7 Exceptional items

There were no exceptional items in 1993

	1992 £million
Exceptional items in 1992 are made up as follows	
Housing and development — write down of value of land and work in progress	63.0
Construction — Trafalgar Place Brighton — contract loss	15.9
Losses relating to investment in Power Corporation Plc	18.0
Closure and reorganisation costs	17.7
	114.6
Analysis by statutory profit and loss account format heading	
Cost of sales	85.1
Administrative expenses	11.5
Share of results of associated undertakings	18.0
	114.6
Analysis by class of business	
Building and civil engineering	20.7
Mechanical and electrical engineering	12.7
Housing and development	81.2
	114.6
Analysis by geographical area	
United Kingdom	88.3
Rest of Europe	20.0
Americas	0.8
Middle East, Asia and Australasia	5.5
	114.6

10.142 Table 10.9 above shows columnar analysis of operating exceptionals by segment and narrative explanation of non-operating exceptional items.

[The next paragraph is 10.144.]

Voluntary segmental disclosures

Introduction

10.144 There are many other types of segmental disclosure given by companies in practice. A number of examples are given below. While none of them are required by the standard, all are potentially useful and informative for the reader and analyst.

Employees

10.145 The Companies Act 2006 requires the average number of employees to be disclosed. This disclosure should be both in total and by category of employee, with the categories being determined by the directors, having regard to the manner in which the company's activities are organised. [CA06 sec 411]. Various types of disclosure have been adopted by companies, including by geographical region and by business segment. Lonrho Plc, for example, adopts the geographical basis approach, with further analysis between employees of the group and employees of associates (see Table 10.21).

Table 10.21 — Lonrho Plc — Annual Report and Accounts — 30 September 1994

Notes to the Accounts (extract)

5 Staff Numbers

The average number of persons employed during the year was as follows:—

	1994			1993		
	Group	**Associates**	**Total**	Group	Associates	Total
United Kingdom	**7,815**		**7,815**	8,246		8,246
East, Central and West Africa	**59,203**	**25,283**	**84,486**	56,710	26,708	83,418
Southern Africa	**22,637**	**35**	**22,672**	23,160	14	23,174
The Americas	**4,796**	**969**	**5,765**	4,881	949	5,830
Europe and Other	**5,662**	**1,050**	**6,712**	5,822	979	6,801
Discontinued operations				490	2,085	2,575
	100,113	**27,337**	**127,450**	99,309	30,735	130,044

10.146 Grand Metropolitan Public Limited Company, on the other hand, provides analysis by business segment. This analysis separates out full-time and part-time employees, distinguished between continuing and discontinued businesses (see Table 10.22).

Table 10.22 — Grand Metropolitan Public Limited Company — Annual Report — 30 September 1994

Notes (extract)

11 Employees

The average number of employees during the year was

		1994			*1993*		
		Full time	**Part time**	**Total**	*Full time*	*Part time*	*Total*
Continuing operations							
Food	– branded	**19,074**	**1,950**	**21,024**	20,293	2,047	22,340
	– retailing	**11,554**	**18,498**	**30,052**	13,422	22,083	35,505
Drinks		**11,464**	**335**	**11,799**	11,612	342	11,954
		42,092	**20,783**	**62,875**	45,327	24,472	69,799
Discontinued operations		**595**	**830**	**1,425**	7,391	9,973	17,364
		42,687	**21,613**	**64,300**	52,718	34,445	87,163

10.147 In contrast to the two above examples, The BOC Group plc provides segmental analysis on both a business and a territorial basis (see Table 10.23).

Table 10.23 — The BOC Group plc — Report and Accounts — 30 September 1994

Notes on Financial Statements (extract)

6 Employees

a) Number of employees by business	**1994 Year end**	**1994 Average**	1993 Year end	1993 Average
Gases & related products	**26,551**	**26,686**	27,615	26,037
Health Care	**5,754**	**6,002**	6,228	6,459
Vacuum Technology & Distribution Services	**6,880**	**6,470**	6,193	5,723
Corporate	**236**	**232**	230	215
	39,421	**39,390**	40,266	38,434

b) Number of employees by region	**1994 Year end**	**1994 Average**	1993 Year end	1993 Average
Europe	**13,849**	**13,601**	13,506	12,746
Africa	**8,427**	**7,944**	7,602	7,493
Americas	**8,858**	**9,201**	9,691	9,760
Asia/Pacific	**8,287**	**8,644**	9,467	8,435
	39,421	**39,390**	40,266	38,434

Fixed assets and capital expenditure

10.148 There is a view that segmental disclosure of expenditure on tangible fixed assets assists readers in assessing the growth potential and possible on-going capital needs of individual segments. While a number of reporting entities, including The BOC Group plc, as Table 10.24 shows, provide analyses of capital expenditure by either or both of business segment and/or geographical segment, few companies have extended this analysis so as to provide detailed segmental analyses of their tangible fixed assets. The British Petroleum Company p.l.c. is one of the exceptions, as it provides such an analysis by business segment (see Table 10.25).

Table 10.24 — The BOC Group plc — Report and Accounts — 30 September 1994

Notes on Financial Statements (extract)

b) Business analysis	Gases and Related Products £million	Health Care £million	Vacuum Technology and Distribution Services £million	Corporate £million	Total £million
1994					
Operating profit before exceptional items	**331.9**	**54.6**	**51.0**	**(2.1)**	**435.4**
Exceptional restructuring costs	**(25.0)**	**(60.0)**	–	–	**(85.0)**
Capital employed	**2,404.8**	**338.9**	**233.9**	**(12.1)**	**2,965.5**
Capital expenditure[4]	**341.6**	**22.3**	**49.9**	**1.8**	**415.6**
1993					
Operating profit	304.6	**86.2**	33.0	(3.0)	420.8
Capital employed	2,325.5	**381.0**	200.2	(0.5)	2,906.2
Capital expenditure[4]	331.0	**48.9**	28.8	2.2	410.9

c) Regional analysis	Europe £million	Africa £million	Americas £million	Asia/Pacific £million	Total £million
1994					
Operating profit before exceptional items	**151.9**	**56.0**	**95.2**	**132.3**	**435.4**
Exceptional restructuring costs	**(48.4)**	–	**(26.7)**	**(9.9)**	**(85.0)**
Capital employed	**1,035.3**	**191.4**	**823.9**	**914.9**	**2,965.5**
Capital expenditure[4]	**135.6**	**27.7**	**105.8**	**146.5**	**415.6**
1993					
Operating profit	130.6	52.3	128.0	109.9	420.8
Capital employed	980.3	158.9	901.7	865.3	2,906.2
Capital expenditure[4]	149.8	30.0	94.1	137.0	410.9

[4] includes capital expenditure of related undertakings of £59.3 million (1993: £51.1 million) mainly in Gases and Related Products and Asia/Pacific region.

Table 10.25 — The British Petroleum Company p.l.c. — Annual Report and Accounts — 31 December 1994

15 Tangible assets — property, plant and equipment [extract]

	Exploration and Production	Refining and Marketing	Chemicals	Other business and corporate	Total	**£million** of which: Assets under Construction
Cost						
At 1 January 1994	25,986	9,329	3,159	1,030	39,504	1,791
Exchange adjustments	(730)	124	–	6	(600)	(27)
Additions	1,157	655	110	32	1,954	1,409
Transfers	121	31	8	(38)	122	(801)
Deletions	(400)	(426)	(78)	(527)	(1,431)	(399)
At 31 December 1994	**26,134**	**9,713**	**3,199**	**503**	**39,549**	**1,973**
Depreciation						
At 1 January 1994	12,907	4,343	1,735	565	19,550	
Exchange adjustments	(421)	92	(4)	6	(327)	
Charge for the year	1,248	489	205	48	1,990	
Transfers	2	8	7	(15)	2	
Deletions	(341)	(262)	(61)	(395)	(1,059)	
At 31 December 1994	**13,395**	**4,670**	**1,882**	**209**	**20,156**	
Net book amount						
At 31 December 1994	**12,739**	**5,043**	**1,317**	**294**	**19,393**	**1,973**
At 31 December 1993	13,079	4,986	1,424	465	19,954	1,791
Principal rates of depreciation	*	2-25%	5-12%	3-25%		

* Mainly unit-of-production

Assets held under finance leases, capitalised interest and land at net book amount included above:

	Leased assets			Capitalised interest		
	Cost	Depreciation	Net	Cost	Depreciation	Net
At 31 December 1994	**1,420**	**506**	**914**	**1,518**	**814**	**704**
At 31 December 1993	1,442	448	994	1,519	746	773

	Freehold land	Leasehold land: Over 50 years unexpired	Leasehold land: Other
At 31 December 1994	**677**	**20**	**44**
At 31 December 1993	704	10	57

[The next paragraph is 10.150.]

Depreciation

10.150 In addition to the segmental disclosure of capital expenditure referred to above, a number of companies also give segmental disclosures for depreciation.

This enables readers to assess the impact of the employment of fixed assets during the period on the segment result and asset base. The British Petroleum Company p.l.c.'s full analysis of fixed assets by business segment *per se* means that it gives this segmental depreciation information.

[The next paragraph is 10.152.]

Research and development

10.152 This is another category of expenditure where companies can provide useful segmental information to readers of financial statements. Readers could, thereby, better understand the levels of investment in research and development made by different business and geographical segments. Indeed, in industries such as the pharmaceutical industry, many fledgling companies are likely to have a substantial proportion of their total assets invested in research and development activities, generating from this relatively little turnover and, in many instances, operating losses. In such circumstances, the directors may form the view that research and development is actually a separate business segment.

Annex — Comparison of segmental reporting requirements

	SI 2008/410	SSAP 25	
Description of segments	✓	✓	
Turnover			
Origin basis		✓	
Destination basis	✓	✓	
Class of business	✓	✓	
Inter-segment turnover		✓	
Profit before tax			
Class of business		✓	(1)
Geographical segment		✓	(1)
Net assets/capital employed			
Class of business		✓	(2)
Geographical segment		✓	(2)
Associated company profit before tax			
Class of business			✓
Geographical segment			✓
Associated company net assets			
Class of business			✓
Geographical segment			✓

Notes:

(1) Before or after interest.

(2) Including or excluding interest bearing assets and liabilities dependent or whether or not profit before tax is analysed before or after interest.

Chapter 11

Retirement benefits

Chapter 11

Retirement benefits

Introduction

11.1 Retirement benefits is one of the most difficult topics in accounting. For many years accountants across the world have struggled to reach a consensus on how defined benefit pension schemes should be reflected in the employers' financial statements.

11.2 The accounting model for defined benefit schemes in FRS 17, 'Retirement benefits', approaches pension cost accounting from a balance sheet perspective. It works from the premise that a surplus or deficit in a pension scheme (measured by reference to the fair values of the scheme assets and liabilities) should be shown on the employer's balance sheet. The overall figures in the performance statements reflect the changes in those fair values year on year.

11.3 Although the ASB, in conjunction with EFRAG, released a discussion paper reviewing the financial reporting of pensions from first principles in January 2008, any amendments to UK GAAP in this respect are not expected for several years to come, and are not considered further here.

[The next paragraph is 11.12.]

Types of pension scheme

11.12 There are three basic types of pension arrangement in the UK:

- The state scheme.
- Occupational pension schemes.
- Personal pension and stakeholder schemes.

11.13 The state scheme consists of two elements, the basic pension and the earnings related pension. All employers and employees make contributions towards the state scheme through their national insurance payments. The earnings related scheme is the State Second Pension (S2P), to which all employees pay, unless they choose to 'contract out'. Contracting out is possible if the employee is a member of an occupational pension scheme or contributes to a stakeholder or personal pension.

11.14 In a contracted out occupational scheme, both employer and employee pay a lower rate of national insurance contributions. The occupational scheme is then used to provide employees with benefits which replace part of their state earnings related benefits. The broad intention is that the pension provided by a contracted out scheme is at least as good as the pension that would have been available from S2P. On retirement, the employee receives a state basic pension and a pension from the occupational scheme.

11.15 Occupational pension schemes are not required to contract out of S2P and many do not. Where a scheme is 'contracted in' to S2P, employer and employee pay the full rate of national insurance contributions. The responsibility for payment of S2P remains with the state. On retirement, the employee receives a state basic and earnings related pension, together with a pension from the occupational scheme.

11.16 Personal pension and stakeholder schemes are pension arrangements available to the self-employed, employees with no company scheme, employees with non-pensionable earnings and those who wish to contract out of S2P or opt out of an occupational pension scheme. These are defined contribution schemes.

11.17 Accounting for the cost of providing pension benefits is particularly affected by the type of benefits that are promised by a scheme and by the way in which the employer's obligations in respect of such benefits are funded. The broad classifications used in pensions terminology are summarised in the following paragraphs. Each involves a cost to the employer insofar as it is obligated to contribute towards the cost of the benefits receivable by its employees or their dependants.

Defined contribution schemes

11.18 Defined contribution schemes (often referred to as money purchase schemes) are pension schemes where the benefits are determined directly by the value of contributions paid in respect of each member and the investment performance achieved on those contributions. Normally, the rate of contribution to be paid by the employer company will be specified in the scheme's rules. If the investments have performed well the individual will obtain a higher pension than if the investments have performed badly. In such schemes the risk of poor investment performance lies with the individual.

Defined benefit schemes

11.19 Defined benefit schemes are pension schemes where the rules specify the benefits to be paid, typically by reference to final salary levels, and such schemes are financed accordingly. The majority of these schemes define benefits in relation to an employee's final salary (typically the pension will be based on 1/60th of final salary for each year of pensionable service, up to a maximum of 40 years). In the UK, they are often referred to as final salary schemes. Another form of defined benefit scheme that is becoming increasingly common is the average salary scheme where the pension is calculated by reference to average pay over an extended period. In defined benefit schemes the risk of poor investment performance lies with the sponsoring company.

Funded schemes

11.20 Funded pension schemes are schemes where the future liabilities for pension benefits are provided for in advance by the accumulation of assets held externally to the employing company's business. The assets are usually placed under the control of trustees, who administer the scheme in accordance with the provisions of trust law and the terms of the trust deed governing the particular scheme. Employer and employee contributions paid to the trust are invested by the trustees; pensions are paid out of the accumulated funds of the trust.

11.21 Most funded schemes in the UK that are established under trusts enjoy considerable tax benefits through HMRC recognition as exempt approved schemes.

[The next paragraph is 11.23.]

Unfunded schemes

11.23 Unfunded pension schemes are schemes where pension benefits are paid directly by the employer. No assets are set aside in advance to provide for future liabilities; instead pension liabilities are met out of the employer's own resources. Such schemes are not common in the private sector in the UK but are found in the public sector.

Scope of FRS 17

11.24 FRS 17 applies to all types of benefits that an employer is committed to providing after employees have completed their service, including pensions and post-retirement healthcare benefits. The standard covers statutory and contractual commitments to provide retirement benefits in exchange for services rendered, together with commitments that are implicit in an employer's actions. The same accounting principles apply whether retirement benefits are funded or unfunded.

11.25 The standard does not apply to termination benefits that become payable because an employer decides to terminate an employee's employment before the normal retirement date or because an employee decides to accept voluntary redundancy. These are excluded from the definition of retirement benefits. [FRS 17 para 2].

11.26 There is no concession to multinational groups in respect of overseas schemes that have been accounted for under a different accounting standard. All schemes should be accounted for consistently in compliance with FRS 17 and so adjustments are required, where necessary, to convert retirement benefits accounting from local GAAP to a measurement and recognition basis that complies with the FRS.

11.27 FRS 17 includes within its scope other post-retirement benefits, including post-retirement private medical insurance benefits, which are commonly provided in the US by UK groups with US subsidiaries.

Accounting objective of FRS 17

11.28 FRS 17 approaches pensions accounting from a balance sheet perspective. The approach reflects the trend in accounting standards to base the accounting on the definitions of assets and liabilities and to make more use of fair value measurements for financial assets and liabilities. So the first stated objective of FRS 17 is to ensure that an employer's financial statements reflect at fair value the assets and liabilities arising from its retirement benefit obligations and any related funding. [FRS 17 para 1].

11.29 The next objective deals with recognising the cost of retirement benefits in the performance statements. It is to ensure:

- Operating costs are recognised in the accounting periods in which they are earned by the employees (not when they are due to be paid).
- Finance costs and any other changes in the value of the assets and liabilities are recognised in the accounting periods in which they arise.

[FRS 17 para 1].

This implies there is no scope for smoothing costs by spreading forward gains and losses into future accounting periods.

11.30 The third objective relates to disclosures, to ensure that adequate disclosure is provided about the cost of providing retirement benefits and the related gains, losses, assets and liabilities. [FRS 17 para 1]. Additionally, the ASB's reporting statement 'Retirement benefits – disclosures' aims to improve disclosure of retirement benefit schemes in UK financial statements, whether prepared under UK GAAP or IFRS (see para 11.148.13 onwards).

Defined contribution schemes

Definition

11.31 FRS 17 defines a defined contribution scheme as *"A pension or other retirement benefit scheme into which an employer pays regular contributions fixed as an amount or as a percentage of pay and will have no legal or constructive obligation to pay further contributions if the scheme does not have sufficient assets to pay all employee benefits relating to employee service in the current and prior periods".* [FRS 17 para 2]. In a defined contribution scheme, the employer's liability is limited to the contributions it has agreed to pay. The employee takes the investment risk because the value of the employee's retirement benefits is determined by the value of contributions paid into the scheme during the employee's service life and the investment return achieved on those contributions.

11.32 A defined contribution scheme may also provide death-in-service benefits, which do not relate to employee service in the current and prior periods. Therefore, the provision of death-in-service benefits does not change a defined contribution scheme into a defined benefit scheme.

11.33 With the exception of some multi-employer schemes, all other schemes are deemed to be defined benefit schemes and the defined benefit scheme accounting and disclosure rules apply.

Example – Overseas subsidiary without a formal pension scheme

Company E has a subsidiary overseas, entity F, in a territory where there is a legal requirement for an employer to provide a 'salary' to retired employees based on the duration of their service to the company and their salary during the period of employment. Entity F does not have a pension scheme but, in accordance with local GAAP, makes an accrual at each year end that is calculated by reference to the employees' service and salaries to date (that is, it represents an estimate of net present value of the amount that entity F would have to pay if all employees retired at the end of the year). Changes in the accrual are reflected in the income statement. Do such schemes fall within the scope of FRS 17, even though there is no pension scheme in place?

The FRS 17 definition of post-employment benefits includes any consideration given by an employer in exchange for employees' services that is payable after the completion of employment (other than termination benefits). There is no requirement for that consideration to be paid by a formal pension scheme arrangement. The 'salary' above falls within the scope of FRS 17 and is a defined benefit pension plan. There is no exemption for overseas subsidiaries, either at entity level (if entity F reports under IFRS) or consolidated level.

11.34 Some schemes contain features of both defined contribution and defined benefit schemes. For example, there are schemes that provide money purchase benefits, but with an underlying final salary guarantee. The FRS requires such schemes to be accounted for as defined benefit schemes if the employer has a potential liability to pay further contributions.

Accounting

11.35 Except for contributions outstanding or prepaid, an employer has no assets or liabilities in respect of a defined contribution scheme. FRS 17's accounting objective is met by charging to operating profit the contributions payable to the scheme for the accounting period. [FRS 17 para 7].

Disclosure

11.36 The following disclosures are required:

- The nature of the scheme (that is, defined contribution).
- The cost for the period.

■ Any outstanding or prepaid contributions at the balance sheet date.

[FRS 17 para 75].

Multi-employer and group schemes

11.37 FRS 17 addresses the accounting by individual entities that participate in multi-employer pension schemes, including group schemes. FRS 17 requires, *"Where more than one employer participates in a defined benefit scheme the employer should account for the scheme as a defined benefit scheme..."*. [FRS 17 para 9]. Therefore, an entity that participates in a defined benefit scheme should account for the scheme in the first instance as a defined benefit scheme in accordance with paragraphs 11.43 onwards. For defined benefit schemes, two situations are envisaged where individual participating employers would account as though the scheme was a defined contribution scheme rather than a defined benefit scheme.

11.38 The first situation is where the employer's contributions are set to cover the cost of the benefits earned in the current period only and are not affected by any surplus or deficit in the scheme relating to past service. So if a deficit arises, the employer has no obligation to increase its contributions to fund it. Similarly, if a surplus arises, the employer has no right to reduce its contributions. In this situation, the scheme is a defined contribution scheme from the individual employer's perspective. To qualify for defined contribution accounting, there must be clear evidence that a third party rather than the employer has an obligation to fund any deficit. [FRS 17 para 10]. Such schemes are likely to be rare – possibly non-existent – in the private sector.

11.39 The second situation is where an employer's contributions are affected by any surplus or deficit in the scheme, but *"the employer is unable to identify its share of the underlying assets and liabilities in the scheme on a consistent and reasonable basis"*. [FRS 17 para 9]. The standard gives as an example the situation where contributions are set at a common level for the scheme as a whole, rather than reflecting the characteristics of the workforces of individual employers. Each employer is, therefore, exposed to actuarial risks associated with other entities. In this situation, the employer should treat the scheme as a defined contribution scheme and recognise only the contributions payable each year. [FRS 17 para 11]. Additional disclosures are, however, necessary as set out in paragraph 11.42.

11.40 Some employers participate in industry-wide pension schemes, which provide centralised pension arrangements for identifiable groups of unrelated employers. Examples in the UK include the merchant navy pension funds for seafaring employees, the Electricity Supply Pension Scheme and schemes in the coal industry. Sometimes each employer has its own separate fund within the industry scheme. Where the arrangements are of the defined benefit type, each employer should follow the defined benefit accounting rules of FRS 17 if the assets and accrued pension liabilities in the scheme can be allocated to individual participating employers. Each employer would recognise an asset or liability relating to its share of the scheme assets less liabilities, and measure components of pension cost in the same manner as an entity that operates its own scheme. In other cases, each employer should treat the scheme as a defined contribution scheme, where the accounting is determined by the contributions payable for each period – no surplus or deficit, or actuarial gain or loss is recognised.

11.41 This part of the FRS is particularly relevant to group pension schemes. Group schemes often apply common contribution rates across the group as a whole. There are several scenarios where it may be difficult for a group company to determine its share of the pension scheme's underlying assets and liabilities on a reasonable basis. For example:

- The allocation of assets and liabilities relating to non-active members may be impossible, in particular for mature schemes where historical information is not readily available.
- Even if it were possible to allocate non-active members across subsidiaries based on last day of employment, members may have worked for more than one subsidiary. Therefore, it may not be possible to identify to whom the liability (and corresponding asset) for successive periods of employment belongs.
- Groups may have changed over the years, with various restructuring exercises, disposals and acquisitions to consider. This can make any allocation exercise extremely complex and perhaps meaningless. For example, a group scheme may have past service liabilities for pensioners and deferred pensioners of former subsidiaries that are no longer part of the group.

11.41.1 Where the structure of the scheme does not enable any of the individual group companies (that is, the parent or subsidiaries) to identify their share of the scheme's underlying assets and liabilities, the parent company as well as the participating subsidiaries should adopt the defined contribution treatment in their individual financial statements. [FRS 17 para 12]. The defined benefit accounting rules would be used only at the consolidation level. A consolidation adjustment will be required to replace the total of the pension costs in the companies' financial statements (based on contributions payable) with the specified components of pension cost for a defined benefit scheme. In addition, any surplus or deficit in the group scheme will be recognised as an asset or liability in the consolidated balance sheet only. In those circumstances the figures in the consolidated financial statements will not be the same as the total of the figures shown in the individual group companies' financial statements.

11.41.2 However, the requirements of the Pensions Act 2004 mean that, where a defined benefit scheme has insufficient assets to cover its liabilities, the trustees must establish a recovery plan setting out how the statutory funding objective (SFO) is to be met and over what period (see para 11.179). In detailing the steps to be taken in order to meet the SFO, the recovery plan will specify the contributions sought from each participating company. Although this deals with cash payments rather than each company's share of assets and liabilities, it is through adjustments to normal levels of contribution that the surplus or deficit (being determined as the net sum of the scheme's assets and liabilities) is often recovered or settled. So it is arguable that a contribution schedule as set out in the scheme's recovery plan provides evidence, on a reasonable and consistent basis, as to how the scheme surplus or deficit (and, hence, the relevant share of scheme assets and liabilities) should be allocated. It, therefore, follows that application of defined benefit accounting in each participating company is appropriate.

11.41.3 Further to this, for accounting periods ended on or after 6 April 2006 the rules for employers deducting pension contributions for tax purposes changed. The more general tax 'wholly and exclusively' test applies, so that deductions are allowed only for contributions made wholly and exclusively for the purposes of the employer's trade or profession. In the context of group schemes, where contributions to a group pension scheme are made by the holding company in the group with each employing subsidiary company in the group being recharged an appropriate amount relating to its employees, the intra-group recharge may be accepted as being a contribution paid by the employer to the registered scheme. More importantly, the contribution paid by the holding company on behalf of each subsidiary company must be recharged to each subsidiary company on a reasonable basis (so as to meet the 'wholly and exclusively' test) in order for a tax deduction to be available. This further increases the likelihood that group plans in the UK will have in place an agreement that allows participating companies to identify their share of assets and liabilities on a reasonable and consistent basis, such that defined benefit accounting is appropriate for each participating company.

11.41.4 A further consideration is where the ultimate parent of a group prepares its individual entity financial statements under IFRS. Whilst some differences do exist between the wording of IAS 19 and FRS 17 and differing treatments may be appropriate under the two standards, FRS 17 only requires an entity to be able to identify its share of the underlying assets and liabilities of the scheme on a consistent and reasonable basis. Therefore, if an entity can identify its share of assets and liabilities under IAS 19, it would seem likely that this allocation would form a consistent and reasonable basis for the purposes of FRS 17. We would, therefore, expect to see full defined benefit accounting in all participating companies in a group scheme under both FRS 17 and IAS 19 in these circumstances. Adoption of IFRS by individual companies within a group such as a parent company may result in a change in the treatment of a defined benefit scheme in the subsidiary companies still reporting under UK GAAP, as demonstrated in the following example.

Example 1 – Applicability of multi-employer exemption

A listed group has a number of subsidiaries and one defined benefit scheme, to which employees of all subsidiaries belong. The scheme is currently in deficit under both FRS 17 and IAS 19. In the past, under FRS 17, it has been determined that the scheme assets and liabilities cannot be identified on a 'consistent and reasonable basis'.

[FRS 17 para 9(b)]. The group prepares its consolidated financial statements and the parent entity financial statements in accordance with IFRS (applying IAS 19).

If there is a contractual agreement or stated policy for charging the net defined benefit cost for the plan as a whole to participating entities, the entity should, in its separate or individual financial statements, recognise the net defined benefit cost so charged (this would equate to the application of defined benefit accounting in each participating entity). Where a group has no contractual agreement or stated policy for charging the net defined benefit cost for the plan as a whole to individual group entities, IAS 19 requires that the entire scheme is recognised in the financial statements of the 'sponsoring employer'. [IAS 19 para 34A].

The group has considered IAS 19 and concluded that, in the absence of such a contractual agreement or policy, the parent entity would be the sponsoring employer. Given the resulting impact on distributable profits of the parent arising from recognising of the whole deficit in this company, the group forms a policy for charging the net defined benefit pension cost to the individual entities.

The formulation of this 'stated policy' means that, when considering the equivalent guidance under FRS 17 (see para 11.37), there is now a 'consistent and reasonable basis' for allocating the scheme assets and liabilities between the participating entities under FRS 17 and that the subsidiaries cease to qualify for the multi-employer exemption.

Example 2 – Non-trading service company

Company F, a trading company, has several trading subsidiaries, some of which are overseas. All employees in the 'company F group' are legally employed by a separate non-trading service company subsidiary, company G, for administrative reasons, but provide services to the trading entities within the group, not company G. Company G recharges staff costs, including pension costs, to company F and its trading subsidiaries. The existence of a recharge arrangement between the group companies is indicative of a consistent and reasonable basis for allocating costs. The net defined benefit cost (and the resultant asset or liability) should be recognised on the same basis as the costs are recharged in each of the participating trading companies' separate or individual financial statements.

11.41.5 The application of defined benefit accounting in the individual financial statements of subsidiary companies participating in a group defined benefit scheme may be appropriate where different contribution rates are applied to different members of the group.

11.41.6 If a high percentage of contributions to the scheme come from one company, then it may be that that company is most likely to benefit or suffer from any surplus or deficit in the scheme as a whole, including those generated by non-active members. This could be sufficient evidence to support a reasonable allocation, although this conclusion may not be reached if surpluses are applied to award benefit improvements to non-active members who are not attributable to that company.

11.41.7 Determining what constitutes a 'high percentage' is a matter of judgement. We consider that it should be presumed for anything above 90 per cent while there should be careful inspection of the directors' justification for non-allocation where one company contributes over 75 per cent.

11.41.8 Set out below are other examples of situations where it is considered more likely that a group's scheme assets and liabilities could be allocated on a consistent and reasonable basis.

- Where most of the scheme liabilities relate to active members, who can be identified with individual group entities, it is reasonable to allocate on the basis of this active membership.
- It is generally, although not always, easier to allocate unfunded schemes as there are no assets to be dealt with.
- Where the scheme's trust deed and rules specify what would happen on sale of a participating employer (for example, share of fund), these principles may be applied. The documentation might set out a rational manner in which to allocate the assets and liabilities.

11.41.9 Taking into account all the above factors, we believe it is becoming more difficult to defend the use of defined contribution accounting for group schemes. Defined benefit accounting should become increasingly common, and should be the expected default position. The following table summarises some common situations.

Over 90 per cent of the deficit relates to subsidiary A.	A reasonable allocation under FRS 17 might be to allocate the entire deficit to Company A.
There is an agreed allocation of contributions split between group companies for tax purposes.	Where tax deductions are allowed only for contributions made wholly and exclusively for the purposes of the employer's trade or profession, this increases the likelihood that group plans in the UK will have in place an agreement on how contributions are allocated. This agreement might present a reasonable basis for participating companies to allocate the assets and liabilities, such that defined benefit accounting would be applied. Therefore, arguments that the split for tax purposes does not provide a reasonable basis for accounting purposes would have to be justified.

The scheme's trust deed and rules specify what would happen on sale of a participating employer (for example, share of fund).	The documentation might set out a rational manner in which to allocate the assets and liabilities under FRS 17.
Acquisitive company, with large proportion of orphan members and it is difficult to trace to which company these orphan members relate.	DC accounting will be acceptable if reasonable arguments are provided.

In a few years time, we envisage that almost all groups will have to apply defined benefit accounting. Under UK GAAP, unless arising from a specific event such as a group reconstruction, the change from defined contribution to defined benefit accounting for group schemes will be a change in accounting policy and, therefore, result in an adjustment to opening reserves.

Disclosure of multi-employer and group schemes

11.42 In the situation covered by paragraph 11.39, the individual company financial statements should disclose:

- The fact that the scheme is a defined benefit scheme.
- That defined benefit accounting is not used and give the reason why sufficient information is not available to enable the employer to account for the scheme as a defined benefit scheme.
- Any available information about the surplus or deficit.
- The basis used to determine that surplus or deficit.
- The implications, if any, for the employer.

[FRS 17 para 9(b)].

11.42.1 The disclosure of information about the existence and implications of the surplus or deficit in the scheme has to be given in the subsidiary's financial statements. It cannot be dealt with by means of a cross-reference to the consolidated financial statements, as the subsidiary's financial statements have to comply with FRS 17 on a stand-alone basis.

11.42.2 Furthermore, in situations where the group is reporting under IFRS and the IAS 19 surplus or deficit is the only information available to a subsidiary company, then disclosure of the IAS 19 information would meet the requirements of paragraph 9(b) in respect of any available information about the existence of the surplus or deficit in the scheme. In these circumstances, the wording of the disclosure should explain that a valuation of surplus or deficit at a group level on an FRS 17 basis is not performed and, therefore, the surplus or deficit calculated in accordance with IAS 19 has been disclosed.

Example 1 – Additional payments to parent company

A subsidiary company is a member of a group defined benefit scheme, but is taking the multi-employer exemption, which, subject to certain conditions, permits the subsidiary to account for the scheme as if it were a defined contribution scheme. The subsidiary actually pays £10,000 per year directly into the scheme, but also makes an additional payment to the parent in respect of the scheme of £20,000 per annum. Which amount should it disclose as its pension cost?

We consider that if the subsidiary pays £10,000 to the scheme and £20,000 to its parent in respect of pension arrangements then the pension cost that it discloses should be £30,000. It would be too narrow an interpretation to disclose the cost as merely the actual contributions of £10,000 to the scheme.

However, there should be clear disclosure in the subsidiary's financial statements that £10,000 is payable to the scheme and £20,000 to the parent. It should be confirmed that the parent actually uses the £20,000 it receives from the subsidiary for the purpose of pensions and not for any other purpose. Amounts used for other purposes would not be pension costs in either the parent or the subsidiary and, if that were the case, (that is, if the £20,000 were not used for the purpose of pensions) it should not be disclosed as pension costs in the subsidiary.

Example 2 – Multi-employer exemption when UK parent does not prepare consolidated financial statements

A wholly-owned UK group has a German parent, which publishes consolidated financial statements. The UK employees belong to the UK group's multi-employer defined benefit pension scheme and wish to account for it as a defined contribution scheme in each of the UK companies, including the UK intermediate holding company. Must UK consolidated financial statements be prepared under FRS 17 in order to take this exemption?

The standard notes that, from the group's perspective, the pension scheme is not a multi-employer scheme and, therefore, should be accounted for as a defined benefit scheme in the consolidated financial statements in accordance with FRS 17. However, the availability of such consolidated financial statements is not a requirement for taking advantage of the multi-employer exemption.

Therefore, in this case, all the UK companies can use defined contribution scheme accounting, despite the fact that no set of consolidated or company financial statements will show the scheme being accounted for as a defined benefit scheme under FRS 17. The UK group can still take advantage of the exemption under section 400 of the Companies Act 2006 from preparing consolidated financial statements, by virtue of being a wholly-owned subsidiary of a German company that publishes consolidated financial statements.

Defined benefit schemes

Scheme assets and scheme liabilities

Scheme assets

11.43 FRS 17 does not provide a definition of 'scheme assets'. Identifying scheme assets is important because the accounting for them is quite different from the accounting for other investments that are not scheme assets. This applies to both the balance sheet and the performance statements. In the balance sheet, scheme assets less scheme liabilities are shown as a net item. In the performance statements, the profit and loss account is credited each period with the expected long-term rate of return (income plus capital growth) on the scheme assets; differences between the expected and actual return are recognised as actuarial gains or losses in the statement of total recognised gains and losses (STRGL).

11.44 There are several references in the FRS to scheme assets being assets held by the scheme. Furthermore, the ASB's rationale for the 'net' treatment of scheme assets and liabilities is that such assets are held in trust and are controlled by the scheme trustees rather than the employer. [FRS 17 App IV para 25]. In the UK, scheme assets should usually be apparent from the way funded pension schemes are constituted. The assets are usually placed under the control of trustees, who administer the scheme in accordance with the provisions of trust law and the terms of the trust deed governing the particular scheme. The FRS notes that for its purposes notional funding of a pension scheme does not give rise to assets in a scheme. [FRS 17 para 19].

11.45 In some other countries, the identification of scheme assets may not be so clear cut. IAS 19 provides the following definition, which is useful guidance for UK groups with overseas schemes:

> *"Assets held by a long-term employee benefit fund are assets (other than non-transferable financial instruments issued by the reporting entity) that:*
>
> *(a) are held by an entity (a fund) that is legally separate from the reporting entity and exists solely to pay or fund employee benefits; and*
>
> *(b) are available to be used only to pay or fund employee benefits, are not available to the reporting entity's own creditors (even in bankruptcy), and cannot be returned to the reporting entity, unless either:*
>
> > *(i) the remaining assets of the fund are sufficient to meet all the related employee benefit obligations of the plan or the reporting entity; or*
> >
> > *(ii) the assets are returned to the reporting entity to reimburse it for employee benefits already paid."*

[IAS 19 para 7].

Scheme liabilities

11.46 Scheme liabilities are defined as *"the liabilities of a defined benefit scheme for outgoings due after the valuation date"*. They reflect the benefits that the employer is committed to provide for employees' service up to the valuation date and comprise:

- Benefits promised under the formal terms of the scheme.
- Further benefits (if any) that the employer has a constructive obligation to provide as a result of a public statement or past practice that has created a valid expectation in the employees that such benefits will be granted.

[FRS 17 paras 2, 20].

11.47 The components of scheme liabilities specified above reflect the characteristics of a 'present obligation' in FRS 12. The recognition of a provision stems from the existence of a present obligation. A present obligation may be legal or constructive. A constructive obligation may be more difficult to discern in practice than a legal obligation as it derives from the employer's actions. FRS 12 defines a constructive obligation as:

> *"An obligation that derives from an entity's actions where:*
>
> *(a) by an established pattern of past practice, published policies or a sufficiently specific current statement, the entity has indicated to other parties that it will accept certain responsibilities; and*
>
> *(b) as a result, the entity has created a valid expectation on the part of those other parties that it will discharge those responsibilities."*

[FRS 12 para 2].

11.48 An example of a constructive obligation is a practice of granting annual increases to pensions in payment and deferred pensions (over and above any increases that may be required by law) that are on paper discretionary, but are in practice customarily granted as a measure of protection against inflation. The cost of such increases should be factored into both the annual current service cost (so that the operating cost is charged as it is earned through employees' service) and the measurement of the scheme liability at each year-end.

11.49 An employer may in the past have granted occasional discretionary increases to pensions without creating an expectation of similar increases in the future. The cost of such increases would have resulted in additional past service liabilities when they were granted (see para 11.93). If the employer's practice changes such that a valid expectation of future increases is created, the cost of future increases should also be provided for at the valuation date.

Example – Pensions deficit partly funded by members' contributions

A company's defined benefit pension scheme shows a deficit. Under the rules of the pension scheme, the employees are required to increase contributions in order to fund part of any deficit that arises. The company wants to know how this should be treated.

Paragraph 40 of FRS 17 deals with this situation. It states that, where both employees and employers make contributions, *"any deficit should be assumed to be borne by the employer unless the scheme rules require members' contributions to be increased to help fund a deficit"*. The key word here is 'require': only where the contribution from the employees is required would the employer not account for the full pension deficit. This accords with the company's situation.

Paragraph 40 of FRS 17 requires *"the present value of the required additional contributions [to] be treated as reducing the deficit to be recognised by the employer"*. Therefore, the net amount of the deficit that must be funded by the employer would be recognised on the balance sheet.

In some schemes, employees come to an agreement with the employer to fund part of a deficit. Although it might be argued that such funding creates a constructive obligation on the part of the employees for any future deficits, paragraph 40 of FRS 17 makes it clear that the employer cannot take account of the expected payments from employees. In such a case, the employer would be required to account for the full scheme deficit.

Death-in-service and incapacity benefits

11.50 Scheme liabilities may also include obligations to pay death-in-service and incapacity benefits. Such benefits are often calculated by reference to salary at the date of death or incapacity rather than the period of an employee's service. FRS 17 requires that:

> *"A charge should be made to operating profit to reflect the expected cost of providing any death-in-service or incapacity benefits for the period. Any difference between that expected cost and amounts actually incurred should be treated as an actuarial gain or loss.*
>
> *Where a scheme insures the death-in-service costs, the expected cost for the accounting period is simply the premium payable for the period. Where the costs are not insured, the expected cost reflects the probability of any employees dying in the period and the benefit that would then be paid out."*

[FRS 17 paras 73, 74].

11.51 Hence, by applying these paragraphs, the liability for death-in-service and incapacity benefits would include the estimated cost of paying benefits only in respect of employees that have died or become incapacitated by the reporting date.

11.52 However, the general principle of FRS 17 views the obligation to pay retirement benefits as arising over the entire period of employees' service. The scheme liability at the balance sheet date represents an accrual of a portion of those total benefits. If this principle was applied to accounting for death-in-service and incapacity benefits that are provided through a defined benefit pension scheme, the scheme liability would need to include a portion of the estimated cost of paying benefits in respect of employees who are expected to die or become incapacitated between the reporting date and the date of leaving service. This is inconsistent with paragraphs 73 and 74 of the Standard.

11.53 The UITF considered this issue and in May 2002 issued UITF 35, 'Death-in-service and incapacity benefits'. The UITF took the view that, unless there is insurance, death-in-service and incapacity benefits form part of the total pension promise, so where those benefits are provided through a defined benefit pension scheme and are uninsured they should be included in the calculation of scheme liabilities. In performing valuations, actuaries will make assumptions regarding mortality and will allow for a resultant reduction in future pension payments. The UITF concluded that it would be inconsistent for the benefits that would then become payable to be excluded from the valuation.

11.54 Hence, the provisions of paragraphs 73 and 74 will only apply where death-in-service and incapacity benefits are provided through a defined contribution scheme or through a defined benefit scheme but are wholly insured. Where benefits are provided through a defined benefit pension scheme and are not wholly insured, the uninsured scheme liability and the cost for the accounting period should be measured in the same way as other pension obligations, that is, by the projected unit method. Measurement of pension liabilities is considered further from paragraph 11.68.

Reflecting defined benefit schemes in the balance sheet

11.55 As noted earlier, FRS 17's first objective is to ensure that an employer's financial statements reflect at fair value the assets and liabilities arising from its retirement benefit obligations and any related funding. To achieve this, the scheme liabilities and (in the case of a funded scheme) the scheme assets are measured at each balance sheet date. The scheme assets are measured at fair value. The scheme liabilities are measured on an actuarial basis. The difference between the fair value of the scheme assets and the actuarial value of the scheme liabilities is a surplus or deficit that, subject to certain conditions, should be recognised as an asset or liability on the employer's balance sheet.

11.56 A surplus is regarded as an asset to the extent that the employer can benefit from it. A deficit is regarded as a liability to the extent that the employer has a legal or constructive obligation to make it good – this will nearly always be the case. In an unfunded scheme, the employer has a direct obligation to pay the retirement benefits and so the employer recognises as a liability the gross amount of the scheme liabilities. In a funded scheme, the employer does not have access to or control of the scheme assets, nor does it have a direct obligation to pay the retirement benefits, and so the employer recognises as an asset or liability the net surplus or deficit.

11.57 The FRS avoids implying that a surplus in a defined benefit pension scheme is 'owned' by the employer. But conceptually an employer does not have to own a surplus in order to recognise an asset. It is sufficient that the employer has access to future economic benefits that it controls via, for example, the ability to reduce future employer contributions. Consequently, a surplus should be recognised as an asset to the extent that the employer is able to recover it through reduced future contributions or refunds. Recoverability of a surplus is considered from paragraph 11.115.

11.58 With the exception of any outstanding contributions payable, assets and liabilities in respect of defined benefit schemes should be shown separately on the balance sheet after all other assets and liabilities. They should also be shown net of attributable deferred tax. The standard does not suggest that this adaptation of the Act's formats involves a true and fair override of those formats. The FRS's note on legal requirements states that the ASB has received legal advice that the requirement does not contravene the Act. [FRS 17 App II para 6]. Defined benefit assets and liabilities are sometimes significant in relation to other net assets and the method of calculating them will often lead to large variations in the balances year on year – but the figures are transparent and clearly visible as a separate category on the face of the balance sheet.

11.59 Where an entity operates more than one scheme, some schemes may be in surplus and some may be in deficit. Where this is the case, aggregate amounts of assets and aggregate amounts of liabilities (less attributable amounts of deferred tax in each case) should be shown separately on the face of the balance sheet. [FRS 17 paras 47, 49].

11.60 To illustrate the presentation, the consolidated balance sheet in Format 1 of Schedule 1 to SI 2008/410, 'Large and Medium-sized Companies and Groups (Accounts and Reports) Regulations 2008' would be adapted as follows.

Consolidated balance sheet – Format 1

A Called up share capital not paid

B Fixed assets

C Current assets

D Prepayments and accrued income

E Creditors: amounts falling due within one year

F Net current assets (liabilities)

G Total assets less current liabilities

H Creditors: amounts falling due after more than one year

I Provisions for liabilities

J Accruals and deferred income

Minority interests (alternative position after K)

Defined benefit assets

Defined benefit liabilities

K Capital and reserves

Minority interests (alternative position after J)

11.61 Any contributions owing to the scheme as at the employer's balance sheet date are reflected in the scheme assets (as a current asset receivable) and shown as a normal creditor in the employer's balance sheet.

11.61.1 Where a company has a pension asset, it will not be able to present its balance sheet by equating total assets less current liabilities, on the one hand, with the aggregate of creditors falling due after more than one year, provisions for liabilities, and capital and reserves, on the other, as this would include the pension asset within liabilities. Further guidance on sub-totalling in the balance sheet is included in chapter 4.

Measurement of scheme assets

11.62 Scheme assets should be measured at their fair value at the balance sheet date. Fair value is defined in other accounting standards as the amount at which an asset could be exchanged in an arm's length transaction between informed and willing parties, other than in a forced or liquidation sale. The FRS gives the following guidance for determining fair values of scheme assets:

- Quoted securities – use current bid price.
- Unquoted securities – make an estimate of fair value.
- Unitised securities – use current bid price.
- Property – use open market value or another appropriate basis of valuation sanctioned by the Royal Institution of Chartered Surveyors' Appraisal and Valuation Manual.
- Insurance policies that exactly match benefits payable – use the same value as the related obligations.
- Other insurance policies – use a valuation method that gives the best approximation to fair value.

[FRS 17 paras 14-18].

11.63 Current assets of the scheme (such as contributions receivable at the valuation date) should be included in the valuation of the scheme assets. Creditors and accruals of the scheme should be deducted from the valuation of the scheme assets. [FRS 17 para 15]. That is because the valuation of the scheme liabilities includes only liabilities to pay pensions and other retirement benefits in the future.

Other liabilities of the scheme will include current liabilities such as amounts owing to professional advisers and investment managers, and any borrowings of the scheme, and should be offset against scheme assets.

Example – Contribution to fund deficit

An entity has paid C1m to its defined benefit pension plan to help fund the deficit. This payment increases the plan assets, either as cash, or equities if the plan has invested the cash in equities, for example. This will reduce the overall net pension liability recorded on the balance sheet. The return on the scheme's assets will be higher and this will be reflected in the profit and loss account. In the cash flow statement the payment should be included as an operating cash flow, because the payment is in respect of employee costs rather than being a financial investment. The amount of the contribution should be disclosed. [FRS 17 para 76].

11.64 In the UK and the Republic of Ireland, the SORP, 'The financial reports of pension schemes (revised May 2007)', sets out recommended accounting practice for funded defined benefit pension schemes, including the form and content of their financial statements. The financial statements include a net assets statement that discloses the size and disposition of the scheme's net assets at the end of the scheme's financial year. The net assets statement comprises all the assets and liabilities of the scheme (other than liabilities to pay pensions and other retirement benefits in the future). As a general principle, the SORP requires a scheme's investments to be included in the net assets statement at their current market value. It gives more detailed guidance on valuing various types of investments. The composition and valuation of a scheme's net assets for the purpose of the SORP is, therefore, broadly comparable to that required by FRS 17.

11.65 The SORP gives some guidance on property valuation from the perspective of pension fund trustees. It notes that properties should be valued in accordance with the Royal Institution of Chartered Surveyors' Valuation Standards. These provide that the basis of valuation should be that:

- Properties in the occupation of the pension scheme should be valued at existing use value.
- All other properties, other than specialised properties should be valued at market value.
- Specialised properties should be valued at depreciated replacement cost.

11.66 SSAP 19, FRS 15 and the pension scheme SORP all have requirements for properties to be measured at their open market value. None of those statements requires all properties to be fully revalued each year by external valuers, but each sets out guidelines for ensuring valuations are kept up to date in the financial statements. That guidance is useful for establishing reliable valuation policies for the purpose of FRS 17. For example, the SORP recommends that where property comprises a significant proportion of total investments, valuations should be carried out by independent valuers at the same frequency as actuarial valuations of the fund, but in any case not less frequently than triennially. It recommends that in other cases, properties may be included on the basis either of an annual valuation by an internal or external valuer or, where the proportion of property assets within total investments justifies a less frequent valuation, on a rolling basis over one to three years by an internal or external valuer. The SORP notes that more frequent valuations may be necessary in the case of properties in the course of development, redevelopment or refurbishment.

11.67 FRS 17 differs from the SORP in the treatment of insurance policies that are purchased to match specifically the benefits of particular members – for example, pensions in payment. FRS 17 indicates that such polices should be included in the valuation of the scheme assets at the same value as the related liabilities, that is, the gross value of the related liabilities are included in both the scheme liabilities and scheme assets. [FRS 17 para 18]. For the pension scheme financial statements, the relevant legislation in the UK does not require insurance policies to be included at their market value (or an estimate) where the policies are specifically allocated to provide benefits for particular members and they provide all the benefits payable under the scheme to those members. The SORP recommends that in such cases, where the trustees have in effect discharged their full liability to the particular members or beneficiaries by purchasing matching policies, the policies should be included at nil value in the net assets statement.

Measurement of scheme liabilities

11.68 FRS 17 requires scheme liabilities to be measured on an actuarial basis using the projected unit method. [FRS 17 para 20]. This is the case for both open and closed schemes: no alternative method (for example 'attained age') is allowed. The projected unit method considers promised benefits for pensioners and deferred pensioners and accrued benefits for members in service taking into account projected earnings.

11.69 The objective of the valuation is to make the best estimate of the future cash outflows that will arise in respect of the benefits earned by employees at the valuation date. This normally requires the expertise of an actuary. The ground rules regarding the assumptions underlying the valuation of accrued liabilities are:

- The assumptions should be mutually compatible and provide the 'best estimate' of the future cash outflows.
- The directors, who are responsible for the assumptions used in preparing the financial statements, should take advice from an actuary.
- The financial assumptions that are affected by economic conditions should reflect market expectations at the balance sheet date.
- The assumptions should reflect expected future events that will affect the cost of the benefits to which the employer is committed at the balance sheet date.

[FRS 17 paras 23–27].

11.70 Demographic and financial assumptions underlying an actuarial valuation of pension scheme liabilities should take account of all existing legal and constructive obligations. Demographic assumptions include statistical matters such as:

- Mortality rates (before and after retirement).
- Age, sex and marital status of membership.
- Rates of leaving employment before retirement (employee turnover).
- Early retirements.
- Members' surviving spouses and dependants covered by the scheme.

11.71 The main financial assumptions relate to inflation, that is, general price inflation, salary inflation, inflation in pensions in payment and deferred pensions. The valuation of scheme assets and scheme liabilities needs to be internally consistent. Therefore, each of the inflation assumptions should reflect the same level of general price inflation that is reflected in the discount rate at the balance sheet date.

11.71.1 The choice of assumptions is a difficult area of judgement, because relatively small changes in certain key assumptions, such as mortality rates and the rate of growth in pensionable earnings, can have a material impact on the amount of the defined benefit obligation. It is not unusual for the assumptions that are made for a funding strategy to differ from an actuary's 'best estimates' that are applied for the purposes of FRS 17. For example, there may be a deliberate policy of funding very conservatively, so that the members' benefits are given a high degree of security.

11.72 Similar actuarial methodologies are followed to value the accrued liabilities of other types of retirement benefits, such as post-retirement medical plans. They consider claims experience for the population concerned and factor in assumptions about inflation in medical costs and future changes in medical practices.

11.73 To take account of the time value of money, the estimated accrued liabilities should be discounted to their present value at the current rate of return on a high quality corporate bond of a currency and term that matches the scheme liabilities. This should be taken to be an AA-rated bond.

11.73.1 In times of global market liquidity problems, AA rated corporate bond yields may increase significantly and there may be wide spreads of yields on AA rated bonds. This is likely to lead to both greater volatility and lower defined benefit liabilities as a result of the higher discount rate. At such times it becomes important to consider the following:

- Whether a robust methodology has been used to set the discount rate and whether this methodology has changed since the previous reporting date.

- What allowance has been made for plan specific factors such as age profile. For example, if the yield on an index has been used, how has the yield been adjusted to reflect differences between the term of bonds comprising the index and the term of the plan's liabilities.

- If the yield on an index has been used, what consideration has been given to whether the constituents of the index are appropriate? For instance, if an index contains a larger number of bonds issued by financial institutions which currently have high yields, it may not be appropriate to consider them 'high quality'.

Frequency of valuations

11.74 Full actuarial valuations are not required as at the employer's balance sheet date. The FRS stipulates that full actuarial valuations should be obtained at intervals of no more than three years. If the latest full valuation predates the employer's balance sheet date, that valuation should be updated to reflect current conditions. [FRS 17 para 35].

11.75 The employer's and the pension scheme's financial statements often have different accounting periods. In practice, it is likely that two full three-yearly actuarial valuations will be required for funded pension schemes: one for FRS 17 accounting and one (on a funding basis) for the pension scheme trustees. That is because the funding valuation may use different, possibly more conservative, assumptions in relation to the liabilities. The FRS 17 valuation need not necessarily be done as at the employer's balance sheet date. It could be done at an earlier date, or the same date as the valuation required by the trustees, as suits the employer's reporting timetable. In fact, the guidance for actuaries adopted by the FRC's Board for Actuarial Standards indicates that a triennial valuation as at an employer company's year end would not normally be available when the FRS 17 figures are required for the company's financial statements. For example, a company with a December year-end may have a pension scheme with a March year-end and obtain actuarial valuations as at 31 March. The full valuation would then have to be updated to each company year-end, including the one immediately following the date of the full valuation.

11.76 An update is in effect an estimate of a full valuation. The FRS indicates that some aspects of the valuation should be updated at each balance sheet date of the reporting employer. The scheme assets should in any case be revalued at market values at the balance sheet date. The financial assumptions underpinning the valuation of the scheme liabilities should also be updated to reflect changes in market conditions. Thus the discount rate should always be the current rate of return on the appropriate bond at the employer's balance sheet date. A change in the discount rate may also require other financial assumptions, such as the inflation assumption, to be updated. Other aspects of the valuation of the liabilities can be estimated from the previous full valuation by rolling the valuation forward and updating it for changes to the scheme, such as benefit improvements. Assumptions that are not directly affected by changes in market conditions (for example, mortality rates) need not be updated annually. The guidance for actuaries concerning liability updates under FRS 17 notes that reflecting changes in asset values and discount rates may dominate the calculation, but the actuary should also normally consider, as a minimum, the actual pension and salary increases awarded.

11.77 Individual circumstances will dictate whether a full valuation is required in between the normal triennial valuations or whether an update is sufficient. If the latest full valuation was a long time ago and many changes have occurred since, the actuary may not be confident that an update will produce a reliable current estimate of the scheme liabilities. The guidance for actuaries indicates that the actuary should advise the company how confident he or she is that the approximate figures fall within the materiality limits for the company's financial statements.

Example – Changes in actuarial assumptions during the period

A company has a financial year end of 31 December and it has recently published its interim statement for the period to 30 June 20X1. It has calculated the relevant profit and loss account items in respect of retirement benefits for the interim period on the basis of actuarial assumptions as at 1 January 20X1. Management has been advised by its pension scheme actuaries that appropriate discount rates for pensions scheme liabilities as at 30 June are lower than at the beginning of the year, while the expected return on scheme assets has increased. Should the profit and loss account for the second half of the year be updated for these changes in assumptions?

FRS 17 requires that periodic costs and income for recognition in the profit and loss account are based on assumptions at the beginning of the reporting period. Changes in the assets and liabilities of the scheme should be reflected in the calculation of costs and income, but the assumptions underlying those calculations will remain stable. If the service cost, interest cost or expected return on plan assets recognised in the STRGL were to be updated in each interim period, then the cumulative full year amounts in those primary statements would not be the same as if the opening assumptions had been used throughout the annual period. The difference would depend on how many interim periods there are.

The company's interim statement covers the six month period ended 30 June 20X1. There is no equivalent dealing with the second half of the year so the six months ending 31 December 20X1 will not represent a financial reporting period. Instead, the annual report will include a profit and loss account in respect of the full year. Accordingly, to comply with FRS 17, the amounts for inclusion within that profit and loss account should be based on actuarial assumptions as at the beginning of the period to which it relates, that is 1 January 20X1. To the extent that returns on assets differ from estimates at the beginning of the year, or liabilities are re-measured at the end of the year, amounts will be recognised as actuarial gains and losses in the STRGL.

Reporting performance

11.78 Since the scheme assets and liabilities are re-measured at each year end, the performance statements reflect the changes in the surplus or deficit except, that is, for contributions paid into the scheme. The FRS analyses the changes in the scheme assets and scheme liabilities into various components and specifies where they should be reported in the profit and loss account or STRGL, as follows:

Profit and loss account		STRGL
Operating	**Financing**	
Current service cost (capital cost of benefits earned in current period).	Interest cost (interest on the accrued pension liabilities).	Differences between the actual and expected return on scheme assets.
Past service costs (capital cost of benefit improvements).	Less: expected return on the assets held by the pension scheme.	Experience changes affecting scheme liabilities.
Gains and losses on curtailments and settlements (for example, early retirements, bulk transfers from scheme) – except for FRS 3 para 20 items.		Effect of changes in actuarial assumptions.

11.79 Under FRS 17, with very limited exceptions, no credit (debit) is reflected in the operating costs for any surplus (deficit) in the scheme and so the operating cost is unrelated to whether, or how, the scheme is funded. The exceptions arise in situations where part of a surplus has not previously been recognised, because it was not considered to be recoverable (see para 11.115).

11.80 The following example illustrates the double-entry for reporting the changes in a surplus or deficit in the performance statements.

Example – Double entry regarding changes in pension surplus or deficit

The actuarial valuation of a company's pension scheme at 31.12.20X1 showed a surplus of £39m. The profit and loss charge for 20X2 is £66m (that is, the aggregate of current service cost, interest cost and expected return on assets, which is not analysed here into different components). After consulting with its actuaries, the company decided to reduce its employer contributions for 20X2 to £50m. At 31.12.20X2 the surplus in the scheme was measured at £15m.

The double-entry for the year 20X2 would be as follows:

Dr Profit and loss account (net pension cost)	66	
Cr Defined benefit asset		66
Dr Defined benefit asset	50	
Cr Cash (contributions paid)		50
Dr Pension reserve – STRGL (actuarial loss)	8	
Cr Defined benefit asset		8

The movements in the pension asset are as follows:

Asset b/f	39
Pension cost (profit and loss account)	(66)
Contributions paid	50
Actuarial loss (STRGL)	(8)
Asset c/f	15

The asset of £39m at 31.12.20X1 is increased by contributions of £50m during 20X2 and reduced by the pension cost of £66m. At 31.12.X2 an asset of £15m is recognised reflecting the current surplus of £15m. This means there has been an actuarial loss of £8m. The surplus was expected to be reduced to £23m, not to £15m, but £15m is the right figure. This loss of £8m should be reported in the STRGL. It is important to note that the actuarial loss of £8m is not a balancing figure – it needs to be analysed into various components, as explained later (see para 11.110).

Current service cost

11.81 Current service cost is defined as *'the increase in the present value of the scheme liabilities expected to arise from employee service in the current period'.* [FRS 17 para 2]. It represents the actuarially calculated present value of the pension benefits earned by the active employees in each period and is supposed to reflect the true economic cost relating to each year based on current market conditions. This cost is determined independently of the funding of the scheme. In principle, therefore, for a given set of employees and benefit formula, the current service cost (shown as an operating cost) should be the same irrespective of whether the scheme is in surplus, in deficit or unfunded. The current service cost is not necessarily a stable percentage of pensionable pay year-on-year. For example, current service cost will vary if the discount rate changes. It will increase year-on-year as a proportion of pay if the average age of the workforce is increasing, as is likely where the scheme is closed to new entrants.

11.82 The valuation of the scheme liabilities and, hence, the calculation of current service cost for each year should be based on the scheme's benefit formula. An exception is where a disproportionate amount of total benefits relates to later years of service, in which case the benefit should be allocated on a straight-line basis over the period in which it is earned. [FRS 17 para 22]. Current service cost is reduced by employee contributions.

11.83 The following example illustrates the mechanics of the calculations. It should be noted that, for illustrative purposes, the example is extremely simplified to reflect the liability in respect of a single employee with a short service period.

Example – Calculation of current service cost

An employee will receive a retirement benefit of 5% of final salary for each year of service, payable as a lump sum on retirement. The scheme is non-contributory. Starting salary is £60,000 and is estimated to increase by 6% per year. The employee is expected to retire after 4 years service. The discount rate is 7%. Based on assumptions at the beginning of year 1, it is expected that a benefit of £14,292 will become payable at the end of year 4 (20% of expected final salary £71,461). That benefit is allocated on a straight-line basis to each year's service and discounted to its present value. Using a simple discounting model, the following table shows the estimated current service cost, scheme liability and interest cost attributable to each year.

Year	Estimated salary (6% growth)	Current service cost (not discounted)	Current service cost (discounted at 7%)	Liability B/f	Interest cost (7%)	Liability C/f
	£	£	£	£	£	£
1	60,000	3,573	2,917	0	0	2,917
2	63,600	3,573	3,121	2,917	204	6,242
3	67,416	3,573	3,339	6,242	437	10,018
4	71,461	3,573	3,573	10,018	701	14,292
		14,292	12,950		1,342	

11.84 The current service cost should be based on the most recent actuarial valuation at the beginning of the year. The financial assumptions underlying the calculation of the present value of the benefits earned (that is, the rate used to discount liabilities, rate of inflation, rate of salary increase, and rates of pension and deferred pension increases) should be current as at the beginning of the year. [FRS 17 para 51]. Although the current service cost for the year is based on the financial assumptions set at the beginning of the year, the financial assumptions should be updated at the end of the year for the purpose of re-measuring the scheme liabilities. The adoption of new assumptions at the end of the year does not affect the current service cost for the past year, but it sets the assumptions underlying the current service cost for the next year. Therefore, the financial assumptions on which the current service cost for 20X2 is based (that is, those at the beginning of 20X2) should already have been updated in the valuation of the scheme liabilities at the end of financial year 20X1 and will also have been disclosed in the financial statements for 20X1.

Interest cost and expected return on assets

Interest cost

11.85 Interest cost is defined as *'the expected increase during the period in the present value of the scheme liabilities because the benefits are one period closer to settlement'*. [FRS 17 para 2]. The interest cost represents the unwinding of the discount on the scheme liabilities. As for the current service cost, the interest cost is determined independently of the funding of the scheme. The discount rate applicable to any financial year, being the appropriate high quality corporate bond rate at the beginning of the year, is the same as the rate at which the scheme liabilities are measured at the end of the previous year.

11.86 The interest cost needs to reflect the liability at the beginning of the year and movements during the year. For example, the current service cost, past service costs relating to benefit improvements and transfers into the scheme will increase the liability during the year; benefits paid to pensioners and transfers out of the scheme will reduce the liability during the year. [FRS 17 para 53].

Expected return on assets

11.87 The expected return on assets component of the pension cost reflects the funding of a scheme. It is the actuarial forecast of total return (that is, income and gains) on the actual assets in the scheme. The profit and loss account is credited each period with the expected long-term rate of return on the scheme assets, based on their market values at the beginning of the year. Where applicable – for example, equities and properties – the rate of return will include expected capital growth as well as income from dividends and rents. The treatment in the employer company's profit and loss account is, therefore, unrelated to the realisation of income and capital gains in the pension scheme itself. The scheme assets are revalued to fair value at each balance sheet date. The difference between the fair value and the 'expected' value of the assets – that is, the value that has accrued by crediting the expected rate of return – is recognised as an actuarial gain or loss in the STRGL. Thus the amount credited each year in the profit and loss account should be a relatively stable long-term return, whereas short-term volatility in equity and other asset values is shown in the STRGL.

11.88 Users can be expected to pay considerable attention to the assumed rates of return; FRS 17 requires disclosure of the expected rates of return used as at the beginning of each period presented.

11.89 For each class of asset, the calculation needs to reflect the market value at the beginning of the year and movements during the year – for example, contributions received, pensions paid and transfers of assets in and out. Assumptions need to be made about where contributions are invested and from where benefit payments are sourced. The FRS does not require changes during the year in the portfolio mix or risk profile to be taken into account in the calculations, so the effect of such changes would in general be reflected as actuarial gains or losses reported in the STRGL rather than as adjustments to the expected long-term rate of return reported in the profit and loss account. However, if the pension scheme trustees significantly changed the risk profile of the portfolio mid-year (for example, making a significant switch from equities to bonds), it might be appropriate for the calculations to reflect this.

11.89.1 The definition of expected rate of return on assets in paragraph 2 of FRS 17 states that the rate of return is net of scheme expenses. Nevertheless, FRS 17 does not provide further guidance in this area. In our view, expenses will be included in the measurement of the defined benefit obligation where they reflect a present obligation (for example, to administer and pay pension benefits that have already been earned) and not where they reflect future obligations (for example, the production of annual financial statements). This raises the question as to which expenses should be included in the measurement of the obligation and which should be deducted from the return on scheme assets. In our view, expenses should be accounted for in accordance with their substance. Hence, investment management and similar expenses should be deducted from the return on scheme assets, while expenses in respect of commitments to administer the plan should be included in the measurement of the defined benefit obligation.

11.89.2 Sometimes administration expenses may be incurred by the sponsoring employer on behalf of a pension scheme, with or without a recharge to the scheme. The principles described in the previous paragraph will continue to apply, so:

- If the employer recharges pension administration costs, the scheme will be in the same position as where it makes payments to third parties. Hence, the measurement of the defined benefit obligation would take account of administration costs as described above.
- If the employer does not make a recharge, it should make a provision for future administration expenses and add this to the defined benefit obligation. In substance, the fact that the expenses are incurred by the employer rather than the scheme makes no difference to the accounting.

Profit and loss presentation

11.90 The net of the interest cost and the expected return on assets is shown as other finance costs (or income) adjacent to interest. [FRS 17 para 56]. The net figure in the profit and loss account is affected by how the scheme is funded. It will be a net credit if the expected return on the scheme assets exceeds the interest cost on the scheme liabilities. This is likely to occur if a scheme is in surplus on the accounting measurement basis and/or if a higher rate of return is applied to the scheme assets than the discount rate applied to the scheme liabilities. A higher rate of return on assets is inherent in the basis on which the respective rates are calculated – for example, any expected equity risk premium relating to an equity portfolio is reflected in the investment return, but is precluded from being recognised in the interest cost. As UK schemes hold a majority of scheme assets in equities, the profit and loss account will benefit from equities' expected long-term out-performance of bonds.

11.91 The note on legal requirements (paragraph 6 of Appendix II) makes it clear that FRS 17 has introduced a new format heading 'other finance costs (or income)' into the profit and loss account. The ASB received legal advice that this new heading was necessary and that it should be shown adjacent to, but separate from, the heading 'interest payable and similar charges'. FRS 17 requires that the total P&L expense recognised in respect of both interest cost and the expected return on scheme assets (among other P&L items) is disclosed, along with the line items on the face of the P&L account in which they are included. [FRS 17 para 77(f)].

[The next paragraph is 11.93.]

Past service costs

11.93 Past service costs are defined as *"the increase in the present value of the scheme liabilities related to employee service in prior periods arising in the current period as a result of the introduction of, or improvement to, retirement benefits"*. [FRS 17 para 2].

11.94 Benefit improvements may produce both an increase in the cost of future service relating to active members (reflected in a higher annual current service cost) and an increased liability for past service relating to current and ex-employees. The cost (that is, the capitalised present value) of the element of all benefit improvements that relates to past service and that have not previously been allowed for in the valuation of the scheme liabilities should be charged to the profit and loss account on a straight-line basis over the vesting period. [FRS 17 para 60]. Often the improvements will vest immediately they are granted and so the whole cost is charged immediately to operating profits. This treatment applies irrespective of whether the additional past service liability relates to pensioners, deferred pensioners or current employees, or whether the benefit improvements are funded by a surplus or give rise to a deficiency.

11.95 Where benefit improvements have been awarded but some have not yet vested, the FRS requires only the vested portion to be recognised in the reporting employer's financial statements. The unrecognised past service cost (that is, the cost that will be recognised in future periods when the benefits vest) should be deducted from the scheme liabilities in arriving at the asset or liability to be recognised in the balance sheet. [FRS 17 para 60]. The FRS implies, therefore, that the full past service cost (vested and unvested) will be included in the actuarial valuation of the scheme liabilities and that the existence of unrecognised past service costs will give rise to a difference between the surplus or deficit in the scheme and the asset or liability that is recognised in the reporting employer's balance sheet. The FRS also requires such a difference to be explained in the notes (see para 11.143). [FRS 17 para 77(e)(i)]. The difference will gradually be eliminated as the benefit improvements vest and the cost and liability are recognised in the financial statements.

11.96 It is important to distinguish between past service costs and experience losses. Past service costs are charged to operating profit; experience losses are charged in the STRGL. A larger than expected increase in pensionable salaries, for example, will increase the scheme liabilities relating to past service. The FRS indicates that this is an actuarial loss rather than a past service cost, since it is a re-measurement of the existing commitment to pay retirement benefits based on final salary. Similarly, the cost of a higher than anticipated increase to pensions in payment will generally be regarded as an experience loss, being a re-measurement of the employer's existing commitment to provide cost of living increases. On the other hand, the introduction of a new or additional commitment to protect pensions from inflation, where none previously existed, would give rise to a past service cost, because such pension increases would not previously have been allowed for in the valuation of the scheme liabilities.

11.97 Conceptually, the distinction between operating losses and STRGL losses is quite blurred in this area. Changes in estimates of other types of provisions generally are reflected in the profit and loss account rather than the STRGL. The rationale for the treatment of actuarial losses as explained in the development section of the FRS is that STRGL items reflect gains and losses that are caused by general changes in economic conditions. [FRS 17 App IV para 38]. Normal variations in assumed rates of salary inflation would fall into this category. On the other hand, if an employer gave large salary increases to certain employees shortly before retirement, this might well be regarded as a benefit improvement in substance. If so, the pension cost would be regarded as a past service cost rather than an actuarial loss.

11.98 Where the scheme rules or an established pattern of past practice requires the employer to share a surplus with the members, the amount that will be passed to members (probably as a benefit improvement) should be treated as increasing the scheme liabilities. [FRS 17 para 21]. Whether the members' share of the surplus is to be used up by increases in benefits or by reductions in future contributions is irrelevant. In these circumstances, any past service cost to which the employer is committed by virtue of a surplus would already have been anticipated in the recognition of a smaller surplus and a smaller actuarial gain – and no past service cost would arise.

11.98.1 On the other hand, where benefit improvements are awarded on an *ad hoc* basis as a result of a surplus arising in the scheme, the fact that they are funded out of a surplus does not result in there being no cost to the employer if the surplus was potentially recoverable by the employer – the use of the surplus for benefit improvements means that the employer cannot then benefit from it in other ways. [FRS 17 para 63].

11.99 FRS 17's definition of 'retirement benefits' specifically excludes benefits that become payable as a result of the early termination of an employee's employment. Therefore, where employees made redundant are granted enhanced pension benefits (say, for early retirement) in lieu of, or in addition to, redundancy payments, the cost of the enhanced pension benefits are in effect treated as redundancy payments rather than past service costs. Some such benefits might relate to the termination of an operation or fundamental reorganisation and be shown as FRS 3 paragraph 20 items outside operating profit.

Settlements and curtailments

11.100 Settlements and curtailments are events that materially change the liabilities relating to a scheme and that are not covered by the normal actuarial assumptions.

11.101 A settlement is defined as *"an irrevocable action that relieves the employer (or the defined benefit scheme) of the primary responsibility for a pension obligation and eliminates significant risks relating to the obligation and the assets used to effect the settlement"*. [FRS 17 para 2]. Settlements have the effect of extinguishing a portion of the scheme liabilities, usually by transferring scheme assets to or on behalf of scheme members – for example, when a subsidiary is sold or when assets and liabilities are transferred into a defined contribution scheme.

11.102 A curtailment is defined as *"an event that reduces the expected years of future service of present employees or reduces for a number of employees the accrual of defined benefits for some or all of their future service"*. [FRS 17 para 2]. Curtailments have the effect of reducing the obligations relating to future service, usually as a result of a significant reduction in the number of employees – for example, on the termination of an operation – or as a result of a reduction in future benefits – for example, following an amendment to the scheme rules such that employees only qualify for reduced benefits in future.

11.103 Calculating the gain or loss arising from a settlement or curtailment event requires a 'before' and 'after' measurement. The gain or loss is in principle the resulting change in the surplus or deficit (that is, the scheme assets less the scheme liabilities) attributable to the reporting employer.

11.104 The FRS specifies the date when the employer should measure and recognise the gain or loss arising:

- Losses – when the employer becomes demonstrably committed to the transaction.
- Gains – when all parties whose consent is required are irrevocably committed to the transaction.

[FRS 17 para 64].

11.104.1 Whether the entity is demonstrably committed is a matter of judgment but it should be noted that this is not as high a hurdle as being irrevocably committed. A management or Board decision alone is not sufficient to meet the definition of demonstrably committed. Communication or action outside of the entity is required. By analogy with FRS 12 paragraphs 80-81, which consider when a constructive obligation for restructuring exists, it is our view that to meet the demonstrably committed criterion, the entity would also have to:

(a) have communicated the decision to the employees affected by it (such that they would expect the settlement or curtailment transaction to go ahead);

(b) have commenced negotiations with any other third party involved, for example, with an insurer buying out a scheme liability as to the specific amounts to be settled bought out, or with an acquirer as to the terms of any transfer of benefits from the entity's scheme to the acquirer's scheme.

11.104.2 It is our view that an entity is only irrevocably committed to a transaction when the amended scheme terms become contractually binding. This is illustrated in the example below:

Example 1 – Timing of curtailment

Company A announced its intention to curtail a pension scheme. Under the current plan, employees earn a pension of 1% for each year worked. The plan will be amended so that the benefit is based on employee's average salary measured over the period from 1 January 20X4 to leaving.

Company A published amended terms of the pension scheme on its web site on 20 December 20X3. The entity's human resource department prepared amended employment contracts in early January 20X4 and sent them to employees for signature. All amended employment contracts were signed by the end of January 20X4. The amendment is not contractually binding under local legislation until signed by the employee.

The curtailment should not be recognised before the amended terms become contractually binding. The terms of a defined benefit scheme were amended in January 20X4 when the new terms became contractually binding through signature of the employees. Company A should account for the effects of the curtailment in January 20X4. The date from which arrangements are contractually binding will vary depending on local legislation.

Example 2 – Closure of pension scheme

A company is closing its defined benefit pension scheme. It proposes to make a one off payment that will end its involvement in the defined benefit pension scheme. The payment will have two elements:

- An amount to cover the deficit in the scheme.
- A 'risk premium' to an insurance company to take over the pensions liability and risk so that the scheme can be wound up as fully paid (a 'settlement' payment).

The company is to make a one-off payment to settle the deficit in the scheme and reward an insurance company for taking the risk regarding deferred pension entitlements. The company will have no further obligations in respect of the defined benefit scheme and contributions to the defined contribution scheme will not be related to the defined benefit scheme.

Under FRS 17 the cost of the settlement should be measured at the date on which the employer becomes demonstrably committed to the transaction and recognised in the profit and loss account covering that date (as an operating cost). [FRS 17 paras 64, 67].

11.104.3 It is possible that an entity might be demonstrably but not irrevocably committed to a course of action at a year-end. In this case, the settlement loss should be measured and recognised in the profit and loss at the date the entity becomes demonstrably committed. The settlement itself, that is, the derecognition of the pension liability, should not be accounted for in the balance sheet as the entity still has the obligation to settle.

Example – Demonstrably but not irrevocably committed at the year-end

Company B announced its intention to settle a pension scheme in deficit to the tune of 330 by giving a lump sum cash payment to scheme participants in exchange for their rights to receive benefits. In order to encourage the employees to take the cash payment, the lump sum represents an enhancement of 90 to the value of their accrued benefits. Any employee not accepting the offer remains as a deferred member in the scheme.

Company B published the terms of the proposed settlement on its web site on 20 November 20X4. The entity's human resource department prepared amended employment contracts and sent them to employees for signature in late December 20X4. All amended employment contracts were signed by the end of March 20X4. The amendment is not contractually binding under local legislation until signed by the employee.

At company B's December 20X4 year-end, the company is demonstrably committed to the settlement because it has communicated its terms to the employees affected and announced the decision publicly. It is not, however, irrevocably committed as the employees affected had not yet agreed the revised terms. Company B should record a settlement loss at the year-end as follows:

Dr	Profit and loss account – settlement loss	90	
	Cr Balance sheet – pension deficit		90

The pension deficit has, therefore, increased because company B is demonstrably committed to the settlement, but the deficit is not removed from the balance sheet until the cash is paid.

Once the employee contracts have been signed, and assuming that all employees accept the offer, the settlement is recognised and the pension deficit is eliminated as follows:

Dr Balance sheet – pension deficit	330	
Dr Balance sheet – provision for scheme settlement	90	
Cr Cash		410

11.105 The measurement of any settlement or curtailment gain or loss may not be straightforward. It is unfortunate, from a practical viewpoint, that the measurement dates are potentially different for gains and losses since, until the scheme is valued, it may not be certain whether a gain or a loss has arisen. Furthermore, the FRS does not specify whether the surplus or deficit at the measurement date should be measured using the actuarial assumptions at the beginning of the year (for example, the discount rate for liabilities) or at the later measurement date. Nor does not it indicate whether the value of the scheme assets should be updated to their fair values at the measurement date or based on their fair values at the beginning of the year. This issue is relevant because for both assets and liabilities, unrecorded actuarial gains or losses may have occurred between the beginning of the year and the measurement date. How the calculation is performed will affect the allocation of total gains and losses during the year between those relating to the settlement or curtailment event (reported in the profit and loss account) and other actuarial gains and losses (reported in the STRGL).

11.106 IAS 19 is more specific and requires the employer to re-measure the scheme liability and scheme assets using current actuarial assumptions. This means that a new discount rate should be used to measure the change in liabilities if the discount rate has changed since the beginning of the year and current market prices should be used to measure the change in assets. This approach makes sense, because the gain or loss attributed to the settlement or curtailment event is then based on fair values at the date of such event. In our view, under UK GAAP, we would expect the valuation to be updated using current information, consistent with the IAS 19 approach. Therefore, the company should update its actuarial assumptions in order to measure any settlement or curtailment gain or loss. Given that a measurement event has occurred, the company may (although it is not required to) use these updated assumptions to determine amounts that will be reported in the profit and loss account subsequent to any curtailment.

11.107 Where a subsidiary or other operation is sold, it should be remembered that any pre-existing surplus or deficit relating to that subsidiary will already have been recognised in the consolidated financial statements of the parent (although not in the subsidiary if it is using defined contribution accounting in respect of a group scheme). If the surplus or deficit is transferred to the purchaser, a corresponding settlement loss or gain will be reflected in the calculation of the profit or loss on disposal of the subsidiary, since it forms part of the attributable net assets disposed of.

Example – Disposal of subsidiary

A wholly-owned subsidiary is sold for £100m. The book value of the subsidiary's net assets on the date of the sale was £70m. The subsidiary participated in the group defined benefit pension scheme, but adopted defined contribution accounting in its own financial statements in accordance with FRS 17 paragraph 9. At the date of the sale, the scheme was in surplus by £35m. The surplus was recognised as an asset in the consolidated financial statements. As part of the sale agreement, a bulk transfer of scheme assets was made to the purchaser's pension scheme. The 'before' and 'after' measurements in the group scheme are as follows:

	Before disposal	After disposal	Settlement loss
	£m	£m	£m
Scheme assets	175	145	(30)
Scheme liabilities	(140)	(115)	25
Scheme surplus	35	30	(5)

The profit on sale is as follows:

	£m	£m
Sale proceeds	100	
Less:		
– subsidiary's net assets at date of sale	(70)	
– settlement loss	(5)	(75)
Profit on sale		25

11.107.1 Further complications can arise when a defined benefit plan is in surplus, but the surplus is not recognised because the entity cannot gain economic benefit from it (see further para 11.115). One question that arises is whether the unrecognised surplus should be adjusted through the STRGL and then included within the calculation of the settlement gain or loss recognised in the profit and loss account. The following example illustrates this.

Example – Settlement with an unrecognised surplus

Entity A has a defined benefit plan and at 31 December 20X1, the following amounts were attributable to the plan:

Fair value of plan assets	135
Defined benefit obligation	(100)
Surplus	35

This surplus cannot be recovered through reduced future contributions and a refund has not been agreed with the trustees; the surplus was, therefore, written off through the statement of recognised gains and losses.

Two years later, entity A settles its defined benefit plan. When the settlement occurs, all plan assets with their fair value of C135 are used to settle the defined benefit obligation of C100. What, if any, impact should this settlement have on the income statement?

A settlement loss of 35 should be recognised in the income statement. When the settlement takes place, the entity should re-assess its original irrecoverability assumption concerning the surplus. When the settlement occurs, the surplus is recoverable, in that the entity does not need to inject additional funds to settle the plan's obligation, which is an economic benefit. Therefore, the entity should first recognise the surplus adjustment through the STRGL and then calculate the settlement loss of C35.

11.108 Gains and losses on settlements and curtailments should be included in operating results, unless they attach to an FRS 3 paragraph 20 exceptional item shown after operating results, that is, the sale or termination of an operation or a fundamental reorganisation or restructuring. If the settlement or curtailment is attributable to one of those items, the gain or loss is reported as part of the profit or loss relating to that item, as in the previous example.

Actuarial gains and losses

11.109 FRS 17 defines actuarial gains and losses as:

'Changes in actuarial deficits or surpluses that arise because:

(a) events have not coincided with the actuarial assumptions made for the last valuation (experience gains and losses) or

(b) the actuarial assumptions have changed.'

[FRS 17 para 2].

11.110 Actuarial gains and losses arise when the values of scheme assets and scheme liabilities are re-measured at the balance sheet date. They result from unexpected increases or decreases in the fair value of the scheme assets or the present value of the scheme liabilities, including the effects of changes in actuarial assumptions. Actuarial gains and losses are recognised immediately in the STRGL, and are not recognised again in the profit and loss in subsequent periods. [FRS 17 paras 57 and 59]. The STRGL, therefore, picks up most of the short-term volatility in asset and liability values.

11.110.1 FRS 17 requires the following disclosures:

- The expected rates of return on scheme assets. [FRS 17 para 77 (m) (ii)].
- The actual return on scheme assets. [FRS 17 para 77 (l)].

- Actuarial gains and losses affecting the movement in scheme liabilities and scheme assets. [FRS 17 para 77 (b)(iv), (d)(ii)].

- The total and cumulative amounts of actuarial gains and losses recognised in the STRGL. [FRS 17 para 77 (g)(i), (h)].

11.111 The expected return on scheme assets is credited in the profit and loss account, based on the yield expected at the beginning of the year (see para 11.87). The difference between the expected and actual return, which is worked out when the assets are re-measured at market values at the end of the year, is treated as an actuarial gain or loss and is recognised in the STRGL.

11.112 Experience gains and losses relating to the scheme liabilities arise where actual events during the year differ from the actuarial assumptions in the previous valuation. They result from factors such as unexpectedly high or low rates of employee turnover, early retirements or mortality during the year and increases in pensionable salaries, pensions or medical costs that differ from previous assumptions. As described earlier, a full actuarial valuation is required at least every three years and the valuation should be updated at balance sheet dates between the full valuations (see para 11.74). Owing to the limitations of the interim updates, it is likely that experience gains and losses will be identified more fully in the years in which full actuarial valuations are performed.

11.113 The effects of changes in actuarial assumptions underlying the annual valuations of the scheme liabilities are also recognised in the STRGL. As noted earlier, the actuary's update at balance sheet dates between full valuations focuses mainly on financial assumptions reflecting current market conditions (see para 11.76). Thus the discount rate should always be updated to the current rate of return on the appropriate bond. Last year's discount rate will have been used to measure the scheme liabilities last year and the interest cost this year. Therefore, the effect of changes in the discount rate will feed into the STRGL each year. Demographic assumptions (such as leaving and mortality rates) are not necessarily updated between full valuations and so changes in those assumptions will tend to be identified only in the years in which full actuarial valuations are performed.

11.114 In addition to the items described above, the required accounting where the recoverability restriction on the recognition of defined benefit assets comes into effect will sometimes result in gains and losses that should be treated as actuarial gains and losses (see para 11.122). [FRS 17 paras 58(c), 67(d), 70].

Limit on pension asset

11.115 In some situations, a surplus in a scheme may be so large that the scheme is in effect 'self-financing', because the return on assets exceeds the total of the current service cost and the interest cost on the scheme liabilities. If the surplus was recognised in an unrestricted way, a potentially ever-increasing asset could result (and corresponding credits in the profit and loss account), some of which could never be realised. The FRS therefore caps the recognisable asset to the amount of the surplus that is recoverable. [FRS 17 para 37].

11.115.1 The amount of surplus recognised as an asset is limited to the amount that the employer can use to generate future economic benefits. The asset should not exceed the present value of the amounts that the employer can recover through reduced contributions, together with refunds that have been agreed by the trustees at the balance sheet date. [FRS 17 paras 38, 42].

11.115.2 The ASB believe that it is likely that an employer will be able to control the use of a surplus, as it is unlikely that the employer can be forced to make contributions when a surplus exists, and also because the employer is usually free to use the surplus to award benefit improvements to scheme members. [FRS 17 para 38].

11.115.3 FRS 17 has a harsher test for recognising surpluses compared to IAS 19. Under IAS 19 paragraph 58, and IFRIC 14 paragraph 11, a surplus may be recognised if economic benefits are available in the form of future contribution reductions or refunds to which the entity has an unconditional right. Under FRS 17, as well as being recoverable, refunds also have to have been *agreed* by the pension scheme trustees by the balance sheet date.

11.116 The calculation at each year end of the surplus that is recoverable through reduced contributions should assume a static (or, if applicable, declining) number of active scheme members. No increase in the number of active scheme members may be anticipated. [FRS 17 para 41]. It will be necessary to assume a declining active membership and, hence, a lower recoverable surplus, where a scheme is closed to new entrants. If the number of active members subsequently increases above what was assumed in the previous calculations, the value of the potential future contribution holiday and, hence, the recoverable surplus may increase. The FRS requires the increase to be credited to operating profit when it occurs (see para 11.124). [FRS 17 para 68].

11.117 The FRS makes it clear that the calculations of the recoverable accounting surplus should be based on the accounting assumptions rather than the funding assumptions, which may be more conservative. Even though reductions in contributions are typically agreed with trustees based on funding assumptions, over the life of any scheme, the accounting and funding contributions come together. [FRS 17 App IV para 27]. In addition, the same discount rate should be used to measure the present value of the reduction in future contributions as is used to measure the defined benefit liability. [FRS 17 para 41].

Benefit improvements

11.118 The required accounting for a surplus has an important effect on the treatment of the cost of benefit improvements in the profit and loss and STRGL. Where a surplus arises that is wholly recoverable, the cost of benefit improvements relating to past service (that is, past service cost) is charged as an operating cost over the period in which the increases in benefits vest. [FRS 17 para 60]. An actuarial gain that gives rise to the surplus is credited in the STRGL when it arises. The past service cost cannot be offset against the actuarial gain where the surplus is recoverable by the employer. Where a surplus arises, it may be used partly to fund the cost of benefit improvements, thereby reducing the amount that the employer can recover through reduced contributions. Such a use of a surplus should be treated as a past service cost when it occurs and not anticipated by reducing the amount recognised as an asset. This ensures that the employer recognises a cost to reflect the fact that it can no longer benefit from the surplus in other ways such as through reduced contributions. [FRS 17 paras 45 and 63].

11.119 An exception is where the scheme rules or an established pattern of past practice requires the employer to share a surplus with the members. In that situation, the amount that will be passed to members should be treated as increasing the scheme liabilities. [FRS 17 para 21]. When that occurs, any past service cost to which the employer is committed by virtue of a surplus to be shared with employees would be anticipated in the recognition of a smaller surplus and smaller actuarial gain – and no past service cost would arise.

11.120 A different treatment arises where the amount of surplus that is recognised as an asset has been restricted; the amounts recognised in the performance statements are adjusted. The operating cost of benefit improvements should be offset by the surplus to the extent that the cost is covered by an *unrecognised* surplus, as illustrated in the second example in para 11.123 below.

Required accounting

11.121 Where the recoverability restriction comes into effect, the opening and closing balance sheet figures are determined by calculating the maximum recoverable amount of surplus, using assumptions as described above. The rules for measuring the impact of restricting the asset on the components in the performance statements are complex. The existence of an unrecognised surplus may result in there being no net cost to the employer during the year, but the separate debit and credit components in the profit and loss account have to be measured and disclosed on a systematic basis.

11.122 The FRS specifies the following sequence for recognising amounts in the performance statements:

- Any refund from a previously unrecognised surplus should be credited to the profit and loss account under the heading ‘other finance income’ when the refund is agreed with the trustees. (Conversely, refunds from schemes where the whole surplus is regarded as recoverable do not give rise to gains. The cash received simply reduces the balance sheet asset.)

- Any past service costs or losses on settlements or curtailments arising during the year should be offset by recognition of any previously unrecognised surplus.
- The expected return on assets is restricted so that the recognised surplus does not exceed the amount that is deemed to be recoverable. Therefore, it is limited to the total of:
  - Current service cost.
  - Interest cost.
  - Any past service cost and losses on settlements and curtailments that have not been covered by the unrecognised surplus.
  - Any increase in the recoverable surplus.
- Any further adjustment necessary should be treated as an actuarial gain or loss.

[FRS 17 paras 58(c), 67].

11.123 Many different scenarios are possible, as illustrated in the following examples.

Example 1 – Recognition of surplus in a simple scenario

The following table illustrates the simple case where a recognised surplus is the same at the beginning and end of the year, no past service benefits are awarded, no curtailments or settlements occur, no actuarial gains or losses arise in the scheme and no employer contributions are paid during the year.

	Surplus in scheme	**Recoverable surplus and P&L account**
Surplus at beginning of year	350	180
Current service cost	(20)	(20)
Interest cost	(25)	(25)
Expected return on assets	60	45
Net finance income	35	20
Net pension credit	15	Nil
Surplus at end of year	365	180

The 'surplus in scheme' column shows the actual surplus in the scheme and the components of performance before any restriction on the asset. The surplus in the scheme has increased by 15 from 350 to 365, but the recognised surplus is restricted to 180 at the beginning and end of the year.

This example illustrates that the system set out in paragraph 11.122 works as follows.

- Current service cost (operating charge) is unaffected by the existence of the surplus. It cannot be offset under any circumstances.
- Interest cost is calculated as normal on the gross amount of the scheme liability.
- Expected return on scheme assets absorbs the effect of the irrecoverable surplus. In the example, the expected return on the gross assets in the scheme is 60. The credit recognised in the profit and loss account is restricted so that it does not exceed the current service cost and interest cost in aggregate, that is 45.
- The overall profit and loss charge is nil. No further adjustment is necessary in the STRGL. The actual surplus in the scheme has increased by 15, but that increases the irrecoverable (unrecognised) surplus.

Example 2 – Recognition of surplus in a more complex scenario

The following table adds some more features and becomes more complex. At the beginning of the year benefit improvements were granted out of the surplus, which vested immediately, giving a past service cost of 200. At the end of the year the recoverable surplus was estimated to have increased to 190 as a result of a reduced discount rate; the actual surplus in the scheme was valued at 210. The amounts recognised in the performance statements are shown below. The first column shows the amounts as if the surplus in the scheme was recognised in full. The second column shows the restricted amounts recognised in the employer's financial statements.

	Surplus in scheme	**Recoverable surplus and components of performance**
Surplus at beginning of year	350	180
Current service cost	(20)	(20)
Past service cost (gross)	(200)	(200)
Less: unrecognised surplus	–	170
Past service cost (net)	(200)	(30)
Operating cost	(220)	(50)
Interest cost	(25)	(25)
Expected return on assets	60	60
Net finance income	35	35
Net pension cost (P&L)	(185)	(15)
Actuarial gain (STRGL)	45	25
Surplus at end of year	210	190

First, in calculating the past service cost to the employer, credit is taken for the previously unrecognised surplus in the scheme. Therefore, the gross past service cost of 200 is reduced by 170 (that is, total scheme surplus 350 less surplus already recognised on the balance sheet 180). The separate components of the net past service cost of 30 do not have to be shown on the face of the profit and loss account. Paragraph 77(e)(i) of FRS 17 requires disclosure of any past service cost not recognised in the balance sheet. As noted earlier, the current service cost cannot be reduced in this way.

Secondly, the expected return on the scheme assets is 60. The amount credited in the profit and loss account cannot exceed the total of the current service cost (20), interest cost (25) and the net past service cost (30). As the total of these amounts exceeds the expected return on the actual scheme assets, no restriction is required.

Thirdly, any further adjustment necessary to increase the recoverable surplus should be credited in the STRGL as an actuarial gain. In this example, there is an actuarial gain of 45 in the valuation of the surplus in the scheme. In the company's financial statements an actuarial gain of 25 is recognised in the STRGL, bringing the recognised asset to 190.

11.124 As noted earlier, no increase in the number of active scheme members can be anticipated in the calculation of the recoverable surplus at each year end. Therefore, where a scheme has a surplus that is partly unrecognised by the employer, the recoverable amount of the surplus is likely to increase year on year if there is an increase in the number of active members. The FRS requires the portion of any increase in recoverable surplus that is attributable to an increase in the number of active members to be shown as an operating gain. [FRS 17 para 68].

11.125 An acquisition could give rise to an increase in the active membership of the acquirer's scheme. This might occur where employees of the acquired business are transferred to the acquirer's scheme and assets are transferred reflecting transfer values of their accrued pension benefits. In these circumstances, whilst there may be no increase in the surplus in the acquirer's scheme resulting from the transfer, the portion that is deemed to be recoverable may increase. A similar effect may occur where a scheme in an acquired group is merged with the acquirer's scheme. Consistent with FRS 7, the effect of such changes should be reflected in the acquirer's post-acquisition operating results rather than as adjustments in the fair value exercise. [FRS 17 para 69].

11.126 The amount of surplus previously regarded as recoverable may decrease year on year if there is a decrease in the number of active members compared with the number assumed in the previous calculation of recoverable surplus. If the decrease is related to a settlement or curtailment event (such as a disposal or closure of an operation), the loss should be reported in the profit and loss account as a loss arising on settlement or curtailment (as operating or post-operating, as applicable). In most other cases the decrease should be treated as an actuarial loss (reported in the STRGL), because it would be regarded as the effect of a change in the actuarial assumptions underlying the valuation of the surplus regarded as recoverable. [FRS 17 para 70].

Taxation

11.127 In the UK, tax relief on employers' pension contributions is usually given in the period in which they are paid rather than when the costs are recognised in the financial statements. In an unfunded scheme, and in the case of provisions for unfunded benefits such as post-retirement healthcare, the tax relief is given when the pensions or other benefits are paid. Where the total of the pension costs recognised under FRS 17 differs from the actual contributions (or unfunded benefits) paid, the resulting asset or liability recognised in the balance sheet is a timing difference for deferred tax purposes.

11.128 With some exceptions (none of which are applicable to pensions), FRS 19 requires deferred tax to be provided in full on all timing differences that have originated but not reversed by the balance sheet date. Deferred tax assets (which relate to defined benefit liabilities recognised under FRS 17) should be recognised to the extent that they are regarded as recoverable (see further chapter 13).

11.129 Under FRS 17, various components of pension cost are reported in the profit and loss account; actuarial gains and losses are reported in the STRGL. So in any period, pension cost accounting may give rise to current tax (tax relief on contributions) and deferred tax (on the timing differences between contributions and costs). FRS 16 requires current tax to be recognised in the profit and loss account, except where it is attributable to a gain or loss that has been recognised directly in the STRGL, in which case the attributable tax should also be recognised directly in the STRGL. Similarly, FRS 19 requires deferred tax to be recognised in the profit and loss account, except where it is attributable to a gain or loss that has been recognised directly in the STRGL. Normally, there is no direct relationship between the components of pension cost reported in the performance statements and the contributions and benefits paid in a period and so FRS 17 specifies a hierarchy for allocating current tax between the profit and loss account and the STRGL. This is dealt with in detail in chapter 13.

[The next paragraph is 11.135.]

Acquisitions

11.135 Arrangements for transferring defined benefit pensions obligations when an acquisition takes place are many, varied and often complex. They may include the acquisition of all schemes in an acquired group or, in the case of a business acquisition, the transfer of assets from the vendor's scheme to the purchaser's scheme reflecting transfer values of the accumulated pension rights of individual employees transferred. The value of the assets of an acquired scheme may differ from the value of the scheme's liabilities at the date of acquisition. In acquisition accounting, the surplus or deficit should generally be recognised as an asset or liability in the fair value exercise.

11.136 FRS 7 requires that a surplus or deficit as at the date of acquisition is measured consistently with how the acquirer would measure it under FRS 17. [FRS 7 para 71]. The accounting where an acquisition takes place is consistent with the normal (pre-acquisition) accounting for such pension schemes under FRS 17, as surpluses and deficits will be recognised on the balance sheet.

11.137 FRS 7 does not permit the valuation of a surplus or deficit at the date of acquisition to take into account the cost of any retrospective changes in benefits and membership that are decided on by the acquirer. Such costs should be reflected in the acquiring group's post-acquisition performance statements. [FRS 7 para 73]. Examples are:

- Costs of benefit improvements following the acquisition (treated as past service costs – charged in the profit and loss account over the period in which the benefits vest, which may be immediately).
- Pension effect of a significant reduction in the number of employees following a post-acquisition reorganisation (treated as a gain or loss on curtailment – recognised immediately in the profit and loss account).
- Cost of enhanced pensions initiated by the acquirer to induce early retirement (charged immediately in the profit and loss account).

[The next paragraph is 11.148.6]

Disclosures

11.148.6 The disclosures required by FRS 17 are set out in full below:

- Background information on the nature of the company's defined benefit schemes, including a general description of the type of schemes, as well as the financial effects of changes in those schemes during the period. [FRS 17 para 76-77(a)]. The description should distinguish, for example, flat salary pension schemes from final salary pension schemes and from retirement healthcare schemes, and should include informal practices that give rise to constructive obligations. [FRS 17 para 78].
- A reconciliation of opening and closing balances of the present value of scheme liabilities showing separately, if applicable, the effects during the period attributable to each of the following:
  - current service cost;
  - interest cost;
  - contributions by scheme participants;
  - actuarial gains and losses;

- foreign currency exchange rate changes on schemes measured in a currency different from the entity's presentation currency;
- benefits paid;
- past service cost;
- business combinations;
- curtailments; and
- settlements.

[FRS 17 para 77(b)].

- An analysis of scheme liabilities into amounts arising from schemes that are wholly unfunded and amounts arising from schemes that are wholly or partly funded. [FRS 17 para 77(c)].

- A reconciliation of the opening and closing balances of the fair value of scheme assets showing separately, if applicable, the effects during the period attributable to each of the following:
  - expected rate of return on scheme assets;
  - actuarial gains and losses;
  - foreign currency exchange rate changes on schemes measured in a currency different from the entity's presentation currency;
  - contributions by the employer;
  - contributions by scheme participants;
  - benefits paid;
  - business combinations; and
  - settlements.

[FRS 17 para 77(d)].

- A reconciliation of the present value of scheme liabilities and the fair value of the scheme assets in to the assets and liabilities recognised in the balance sheet, showing at least:
  - any past service cost not recognised in the balance sheet;
  - any amount not recognised as an asset, because of a limit to the recoverability of that asset through refunds or reductions in future contributions; and
  - any other amounts recognised in the balance sheet.

[FRS 17 para 77(e)].

- The total expense recognised in profit or loss for each of the following, and the line item(s) in which they are included: current service cost, interest cost, expected return on scheme assets, past service cost, the effect of any curtailment or settlement and the effect of the limit to the extent to which an asset can be recognised. [FRS 17 para 77(f)].
- The total amounts recognised in the statement of total recognised gains and losses for actuarial gains and losses and the effect of the limit to the extent to which an asset can be recognised. [FRS 17 para 77(g)].
- The cumulative amount of actuarial gains and losses recognised in the statement of total recognised gains and losses. [FRS 17 para 77(h)].
- For each major category of scheme assets, which shall include, but is not limited to, equity instruments, debt instruments, property, and all other assets, the percentage or amount that each major category constitutes of the fair value of the total scheme assets. [FRS 17 para 77(i)].
- The amounts included in the fair value of scheme assets for each category of the entity's own financial instruments and any property occupied by, or other assets used by, the entity. [FRS 17 para 77(j)].
- A narrative description of the basis used to determine the overall expected rate of return on assets, including the effect of the major categories of scheme assets. [FRS 17 para 77(k)].
- The actual return on scheme assets. [FRS 17 para 77(l)].
- The principal actuarial assumptions used as at the balance sheet date, including, when applicable:
  - the discount rates;
  - the expected rates of return on any assets of the scheme for the periods presented in the financial statements;
  - the expected rates of salary increases;
  - retirement healthcare cost trend rates; and
  - any other material actuarial assumptions used.

[FRS 17 para 77(m)].

- The effect of an increase of one percentage point and the effect of a decrease of one percentage point in the assumed retirement healthcare cost trend rates on the aggregate of the current service cost and interest cost components of net periodic retirement healthcare costs and the accumulated retirement healthcare obligation for healthcare costs. For the purposes of this disclosure, all other assumptions shall be held constant. [FRS 17 para 77(n)].
- The amounts for the current accounting period and previous four accounting periods of:

- the present value of the scheme liabilities, the fair value of the scheme assets and the surplus or deficit in the scheme; and
- the experience adjustments arising on the scheme liabilities and assets expressed either as (1) an amount or (2) a percentage of the scheme liabilities or assets respectively at the balance sheet date.

[FRS 17 para 77(o)].

- The employer's best estimate, as soon as it can reasonably be determined, of contributions expected to be paid to the scheme during the accounting period beginning after the balance sheet date. [FRS 17 para 77(p)].

11.148.7 Paragraph 77(o) requires a 5 year history of the fair value of scheme assets. Paragraph 95C clarifies that it is not necessary to restate corresponding amounts for the first two of those periods to take account of the requirement in the amended FRS 17 to value quoted securities at current bid price as opposed to mid market value.

11.148.7.1 There should be few sources of differences between the asset or liability recognised in the employer's balance sheet and the surplus or deficit in the scheme as measured under the FRS, because in most respects the surplus or deficit in the scheme should be recognised in full. Differences will occur as a result of:

- Attributable deferred tax balance netted off surplus or deficit in the balance sheet.
- Past service costs not yet recognised in the financial statements, because they have not yet vested.
- Part of a surplus is not recognised in the balance sheet, because it is not recoverable.
- Members being required to share the funding of a deficit, in which case the liability recognised by the employer is reduced by the present value of the additional contributions payable by the members.

An example reconciliation of the difference is set out below:

Fair value of scheme assets	350
Present value of scheme liabilities	(150)
Surplus in the scheme	200
Past service costs not yet vested	20
Irrecoverable surplus	(40)
Recognised pension asset	180
Related deferred tax liability	(54)
Net pension asset	126

Aggregation of schemes

11.148.8 Where an employer operates more than one scheme, the FRS permits the disclosures to be made in total for all schemes, separately for each scheme, or schemes may be grouped in the way that provides the most useful information. [FRS 17 para 79]. For multi-national groups that operate many pension schemes and other types of retirement benefit schemes in various parts of the world, some degree of aggregation is necessary to avoid disclosures of excessive length and detail. Where schemes are grouped, the groupings might be based on geographical operations (for example, distinguishing domestic schemes from overseas schemes), types of benefits with different risk profiles (for example, distinguishing flat salary pension schemes from final salary pension schemes and retirement medical healthcare schemes), or a combination of features as is considered to be most useful.

11.148.9 As noted earlier, the main assumptions underlying the valuation of schemes' liabilities and the expected rate of return on scheme assets have to be disclosed. Where schemes are aggregated, the FRS requires the assumptions to be stated as weighted averages for the schemes concerned or as relatively narrow ranges – any assumptions outside those narrow ranges should be disclosed separately.

11.148.10 Paragraph 82 of FRS 17 requires an entity to disclose information about contingent liabilities arising from retirement benefit obligations in accordance with FRS 12, 'Provisions, contingent liabilities and contingent assets'. Similarly, paragraph 94 of FRS 12 requires the nature of contingent assets, where an inflow of the economic benefits is probable, to be disclosed. In accordance with the provisions of FRS 12 an entity should therefore disclose contingent assets and contingent liabilities, including guarantees, arising from retirement benefit obligations.

11.148.11 Where required by FRS 8, 'Related party disclosures' information about related party transactions with retirement benefit schemes should be disclosed. See chapter 29 for further discussion on related party transactions.

11.148.12 The FRS does not permit surpluses and deficits to be netted off in arriving at the assets and liabilities that are disclosed on the face of the balance sheet. Where an entity operates more than one scheme, some schemes may be in surplus and some may be in deficit. Where this is the case, aggregate amounts of assets and aggregate amounts of liabilities (which include any unfunded benefits), less attributable amounts of deferred tax in each case, should be shown separately on the face of the balance sheet. [FRS 17 para 47]. A consequence of this requirement is that at least some of the footnote disclosures have to be disaggregated into schemes that have given rise to assets in the balance sheet and schemes that have given rise to liabilities. This is necessary, for example, in order to comply with the requirement to reconcile scheme surpluses or deficits to balance sheet assets and liabilities (see para 11.148.6). [FRS 17 para 77(e)]. To comply with that reconciliation requirement, say where deferred tax and irrecoverable surpluses arise, the following would have to be disclosed as a very minimum, but a further breakdown of the total assets and liabilities may also be necessary for a proper understanding of the net position.

Total schemes' assets	400			
Total schemes' liabilities	380			
Net surpluses	20			
Comprising:		**Surplus not recoverable**	**Related deferred tax**	**Net pension asset (liability)**
Surpluses	50	(10)	(12)	28
Deficits	(30)		9	(21)
	20	(10)	(3)	7

Best practice disclosures

11.148.13 The ASB considered that IAS 19 and FRS 17 address many, but not all, concerns about the adequacy of defined benefit pension scheme disclosures. Specifically, financial statements should contain sufficient information to allow users to obtain a clear view of the cost of providing retirement benefits, the related gains, losses, assets and liabilities, the risks and rewards arising from defined benefit schemes, and the entity's future funding obligations. The ASB therefore issued a best practice reporting statement, 'Retirement benefits – disclosures', which is intended to have persuasive rather than mandatory force. The reporting statement applies to both UK GAAP and IFRS reporters, and complements the disclosures required by FRS 17 and IAS 19.

11.148.14 The reporting statement sets out six principles (rather than requirements) to be considered when providing disclosures for defined benefit schemes, and these are considered below.

Relationship between the reporting entity and the trustees of defined benefit schemes

11.148.15 The relationship between the reporting entity and the trustees (managers) will determine how an entity manages and arranges its affairs with regard to the defined benefit scheme. This includes the investment strategy for the assets held by the scheme and the principles for funding the scheme, including how contribution levels to the scheme are agreed. The management and arrangement of affairs may be affected by the powers vested in the trustees.

11.148.16 In recognition of this, the reporting statement recommends that financial statements disclose the arrangements between the trustees of the scheme and the reporting entity, setting out any powers of the trustees that have a material financial effect on the reporting entity and that are both significant and unusual in relation to the legal and regulatory framework in which the entity operates.

Information about the principal assumptions

11.148.17 The reporting statement recommends that financial statements should include sufficient information about the principal assumptions used to measure scheme liabilities to allow users to understand the inherent uncertainties affecting the measurement of scheme liabilities. These assumptions should include mortality rates, even if not explicitly required by FRS 17. Disclosure should be given of the number of years post retirement it is anticipated pensions will be paid to members of the scheme, as this is often more useful than details of a mortality standard table or cohort factor. Where the number of years assumed alters depending on geographical, demographical or other significant reasons, the different mortality rates should be separately disclosed.

Sensitivity analysis for principal assumptions

11.148.18 Financial statements should disclose a sensitivity analysis for the principal assumptions used to measure the scheme liabilities, showing how the measurement of scheme liabilities would have been affected by changes in the relevant assumption that were reasonably possible at the balance sheet date. For the purposes of this disclosure, all other assumptions would be held constant. No further guidance is provided on how the sensitivity analysis would be undertaken other than an illustrative disclosure example in the appendix to the reporting statement.

How defined benefit liabilities are measured

11.148.19 There are alternative approaches to the projected unit credit method for measuring defined benefit scheme liabilities, as required by FRS 17. One such approach is measuring scheme liabilities on a buy-out basis, that is, the cost of buying out benefits at the balance sheet date with a suitable insurer. Where the cost of buying out benefits is made available to trustees and or members of a scheme, then the reporting statement recommends that it is disclosed.

Future funding obligations in relation to defined benefit schemes

11.148.20 FRS 17 requires the employer's best estimate, as soon as it can reasonably be determined, of contributions expected to be paid to the scheme during the annual period beginning after the balance sheet date. Scheme liabilities are, however, often of a long term nature and contributions expected to be paid in the next annual period may not provide sufficient information to allow the users of the financial statements to understand how the scheme liabilities affect the economic resources available to the entity, including its cash-flow.

11.148.21 Given this, the reporting statement recommends that the financial statements should disclose the following:

- The rates or amounts of contributions which have been agreed with the trustees (managers) of the scheme and are payable to the scheme by or on behalf of the reporting entity.
- The funding principles the entity has agreed or operates with regard to defined benefit schemes.
- Where a defined benefit scheme is in deficit and the entity has entered into an agreement with the trustees (managers) of the scheme to make additional contributions to reduce or recover the deficit, separate disclosure of such additional contributions, and the number of years over which it is anticipated the additional contributions will be paid.
- The duration of scheme liabilities allowing users to see the period of time over which the liabilities of the defined benefit scheme mature.
- Information that allows users to understand the projected cash flows of defined benefit schemes.

Nature and extent of the risks and rewards arising from financial instruments held by defined benefit schemes

11.148.22 Disclosures should be made to enable users to evaluate the nature and extent of the risks and rewards arising from the financial instruments held by defined benefit schemes. For each type of risk arising from financial instruments held by retirement benefits schemes, the reporting statement recommends the following disclosure:

(a) the exposures to risk and how they arise;

(b) the objectives, policies and processes undertaken by the defined benefits scheme or the entity for managing the risk and the methods used to measure the risk; and

(c) any changes in (a) or (b) from the previous period.

11.148.23 An entity may disclose a sensitivity analysis, such as value-at-risk, for types of risks to which the assets of the defined benefit scheme are exposed. Where an entity discloses such a sensitivity analysis it should also disclose the method and assumptions used in preparing this analysis and any changes from the previous period in the methods and assumptions used.

11.148.24 As well as disclosing the percentage or amount of the fair value of total scheme assets that each major category of assets constitutes, in accordance with FRS 17, the entity should also disclose the expected rate of return assumed for each category for the period presented.

Reserves relating to defined benefit schemes

11.149 Retirement benefit costs find their way into reserves via the profit and loss account and STRGL (actuarial gains and losses). The FRS does not specify to which reserves amounts passed through the STRGL should be debited or credited. The disclosure example in Appendix 1 to the FRS shows a pension asset that is reflected in its entirety in the profit and loss reserve (net of attributable deferred tax). Some may prefer to take the cumulative actuarial gains to a separate pension or retirement benefits reserve.

Distributable reserves

11.150 FRS 17 is silent on the question of whether pension assets and liabilities give rise to realised or unrealised gains and losses. The issue only arises in respect of assets and liabilities recognised in the financial statements of individual companies, not groups. Under sections 831 and 836 of the Companies Act 2006, the recognition of a deficit as a liability might affect the ability of a public company to make a distribution (because public companies must take into account unrealised losses).

11.151 Appendix IV to FRS 17 indicates that a distribution problem will arise only where individual company financial statements show a deficit so large that it reduces distributable reserves to below that needed to cover any intended distribution. [FRS 17 App IV para 58]. The possibilities of an unexpected decline in distributable profits are mitigated, however, by FRS 17's rules relating to group defined benefit schemes. Where a scheme that covers more than one company does not enable the individual companies to identify their share of the scheme's assets and liabilities, the FRS requires each company (including the parent) to treat the scheme as a defined contribution scheme. [FRS 17 paras 9, 12]. Each individual company should, therefore, recognise only the employer contributions payable to the scheme for each accounting period. The defined benefit accounting would be used only at the consolidation level (see further para 11.37 onwards). In these circumstances there is no impact on the distributable profits of the individual companies unless and until additional contributions become payable to fund the deficit. Nevertheless, note that the implications of the Pensions Act 2004, changes in tax rules and the use of IFRS at a group level may all effect the applicability of this exemption (see paras 11.41.2 to 11.41.4).

11.152 Tech 02/10, 'Guidance on the determination of realised profits and losses in the context of distributions under the Companies Act 2006' provides guidance on the effect of FRS 17 and IAS 19 on realised profits and losses. This guidance concludes that the existence of a pension surplus or deficit is not the sole factor relevant to determining distributable profits. This is because a pension asset or liability recognised in an entity's balance sheet will also be affected by net contributions paid to the scheme and any balances introduced as a result of a business combination. The Companies Act defines a company's distributable profits not in terms of its assets and liabilities, but as its accumulated, realised profits less its accumulated, realised losses. [CA06 Sec 830(2)]. Accordingly, it is the cumulative profit or loss credited or debited to reserves in respect of a pension surplus or deficit that is important. This is illustrated in the following example.

Example

Company A established a new defined benefit pension scheme at the beginning of 20X5. During 20X5 there is a net pension expense of £4m (encompassing items reflected in both the profit and loss account and the STRGL), but contributions to the scheme amount to £5m. Hence, at the end of 20X5 there is a surplus in the scheme, and an asset on the balance sheet of £1m (both taxation and questions over recoverability of the asset are ignored for the purpose of this example). However, the impact on distributable profits is not a credit of £1m, as represented by the surplus in the scheme, but a debit of £4m in respect of the net pension expense. Considered another way, the impact on reserves is derived by deducting the contributions to the scheme from the surplus.

11.153 As regards the question of whether cumulative profits or losses in reserves in respect of a pension surplus or deficit are realised (regardless of whether they were first recognised in the profit and loss account or the statement of total recognised gains and losses), the guidance concludes as follows:

- A cumulative net debit in reserves is a realised loss. Tech 02/10, 'Guidance on the determination of realised profits and losses in the context of distributions made under the Companies Act 2006', provides that all losses are realised losses except to the extent that the law, accounting standards or Tech 02/10 provide otherwise. Specifically, it goes on to say that provisions are treated as realised losses. Hence, the conclusion was reached in Tech 02/10 that a cumulative net debit in reserves in respect of a pension scheme is a realised loss.

- A cumulative net credit in reserves is a realised profit only to the extent that it is represented by an asset to be recovered by agreed refunds in the form of qualifying consideration (as defined in Tech 02/10 – see chapter 23). Any further cumulative net credit (in excess of agreed funds) is not covered by qualifying consideration so is treated as unrealised, although it will become realised in subsequent periods to the extent that it offsets subsequent net debits to reserves that are treated as realised losses.

11.154 Where an entity operates more than one defined benefit scheme, it should assess the impact of a surplus or deficit on its distributable profits separately for each scheme. In other words, schemes should not be aggregated or offset to reach a single net realised profit or loss.

11.155 As regards defined contribution schemes, the expense recognised in profit or loss is equal to the contributions payable to the scheme for the accounting period and is a realised loss. Some entities, however, account for their participation in a multi-employer defined benefit scheme as if it was a defined contribution scheme (see para 11.37). Where a scheme meets the criteria for this treatment in FRS 17, the position as regards realised profits and losses will be the same as for any other defined contribution scheme.

11.156 The guidance also considers the impact of deferred tax. It clarifies that the deferred tax impact of pension accounting generally relates to the pension asset or liability and not the cumulative net debit or credit in reserves. However, it also clarifies that the debit for deferred tax liability may be offset against an unrealised net credit in reserves in respect of the pension asset.

[The next paragraph is 11.170.]

Pensions Act 2004 implications

11.170 The Pensions Act 2004 became law in November 2004. It was followed by a web of supporting regulations, codes of practice and other guidance, much of which came into force from April 2005.

11.171 From an accounting perspective, the most significant provisions of the Pensions Act are in the following areas:

- The launch of the Pension Protection Fund (see para 11.173 onwards).
- Increased powers to the new Pension Regulator (see para 11.176 onwards).
- Revised rules for employers ceasing to participate in a pension scheme (see para 11.184 onwards).

11.172 The following paragraphs summarise only the main accounting implications of the new legislation and do not attempt to explore the rules in detail.

The Pension Protection Fund ('PPF')

11.173 The Pension Protection Fund (PPF), which came into force from April 2005, is designed to protect pension scheme members in the event that the sponsoring employer becomes insolvent. Broadly, the PPF will fund current pensions in payment as well as up to 90 per cent of the benefits of active and deferred scheme members when an 'insolvency event' occurs. The term 'insolvency event' encompasses the administration, administrative receivership or liquidation of the sponsoring employer.

Pensions Act 2004

11.174 The PPF is funded in part by the assets of the plans it takes over and in part by a levy on all plans covered by the PPF. The pension protection levy is charged annually; the levy year runs from 1 April to 31 March. Initially, the levy was based on factors related to plan size (number of members, value of liabilities, etc). From 2006/7 the PPF levy is divided into two parts: The scheme-based element, which makes up ca 20 per cent of the total levy, is based on a scheme's liabilities to members on a section 179 basis. The risk-based element, which makes up ca 80 per cent of the levy, takes into account funding levels (the worst funded plans pay a higher levy) and the likelihood of the employer's insolvency (the lower a company's Dun & Bradstreet rating, the higher the levy). From 2012/13 the way the PPF levy is calculated will change significantly. It is intended that the revised methodology and levy parameters will be fixed for three years until 2015. Under the new methodology, the funding levels will be assessed on smoothed assumptions (5 year average yields) so that sharp movements in financial markets will have less effect on the risk-based element. The risk-based element will take into account the investment risk of a scheme's portfolio of assets (the riskier the investment strategy the higher the levy). The method for allowing for insolvency risk of employers will change; the measure of insolvency risk will be averaged over 12 months (rather than at a single date) and employers will be divided into 10 rather than 100 risk bands.

11.175 The PPF levy can represent a signficantcost of maintaining a defined benefit pension scheme. Although not literally an administration cost, the levy's accounting treatment should mirror that of other costs incurred by the scheme.

The Pensions Regulator

11.176 The Pensions Regulator replaced the previous regulator (OPRA), inheriting all of its powers and functions along with several new powers. In our view, there are two areas in which the regulatory regime may influence the financial statements:

- The 'moral hazard' provisions (see para 11.177 onwards).
- The 'statutory funding objective' (see para 11.179 onwards).

The 'moral hazard' provisions

11.177 The 'moral hazard' provisions in the Pensions Act are designed to prevent employers from rearranging their affairs so as to avoid their pension obligations. The provisions permit the regulator to impose:

- Contribution notices on people that have been party to an act, or a deliberate failure to act, aimed at avoiding pension obligations.
- Financial support directions on associated or connected parties where the employer is either 'insufficiently resourced' or a service company (that is, a company the turnover of which is solely or principally derived from amounts charged for the provision of employee services to other group members). A financial support direction is a requirement to put financial support in place within a specified time period and to ensure that that support remains in place while the scheme is in existence.
- Restoration orders where the regulator is of the opinion that a transaction has been made at undervalue. Such orders require that a pension scheme's financial position is restored to its pre-transaction position.

11.178 The existence of these powers could influence the judgement of whether a scheme should be treated as defined contribution or defined benefit as they may indicate that an entity could have an obligation to provide funding where one was not thought to exist previously. It will also be necessary to determine whether the risk that the regulator may impose a notice represents a contingent liability (see further chapter 21).

The 'statutory funding objective'

11.179 With effect from September 2005, the previous minimum funding requirement ('MFR') was replaced by a statutory funding objective ('SFO'). This means that all defined benefit schemes have to have 'sufficient and appropriate assets' to cover their liabilities. Where a scheme has insufficient assets to cover its liabilities, the trustees must establish a recovery plan setting out how the SFO is to be met and over what period. Any failure to do this, or to reach agreement with the employer on a funding strategy for the scheme, must be reported to the regulator, who may take any of the following courses of action:

- Modify the scheme in relation to future accrual of benefits.
- Fix the period over which a shortfall is to be made up.
- Impose a schedule of contributions.

11.180 Under the SFO regulationsthe levels of contributions to defined benefit pension schemes have generally increased. However, of greater significance to the financial statements may be the valuation of a scheme in wind-up, which is based on the buyout of all accrued benefits. This makes it more expensive to wind up a pension scheme and, taken with the moral hazard provisions described above, almost impossible for a solvent company to walk away from its pension obligations. Employers can become liable to the trustees of a defined benefit scheme for a debt if there is a deficit in a defined benefit scheme. This can apply on:

- the winding-up of a scheme;
- the insolvency of an employer; or
- an employer ceasing participation in a multi-employer scheme (see para 11.184 onwards).

11.181 In situations where a buy-out valuation exceeds the defined benefit liability recognised under FRS 17, there should be consideration as to whether there ought to be disclosure in the financial statements. The ASB's best practice reporting statement on pension disclosures recommends that where the cost of buying out benefits is made available to trustees (managers) and/or members of defined benefit schemes, then the financial statements should also disclose the cost of buying out benefits. [ASB RS para 17].

11.182 Where there is a funding plan in place, FRS 17 requires disclosure of the contribution rate agreed for future years. [FRS 17 para 77(p)]. However, in the absence of an agreed funding plan, we consider that there should be disclosure of the potential implications of any action by the regulator. Furthermore, where a scheme is in wind-up, we consider that there should be disclosure of the fact that the buy-out obligation exceeds amounts recognised under FRS 17. In some circumstances, it may be appropriate to recognise these additional obligations.

11.183 Although not arising for the reasons described in paragraph 11.181 above, Table 11.18 shows an example of a company that made disclosure in its 2004 interim statement of a potential requirement to make additional contributions to its pension scheme following a failure to equalise properly the retirement ages of men and women. This extract shows the type of disclosure that may be appropriate in the context of obligations arising out of the Pensions Act.

Table 11.18 – Obligation to make further contributions

MFI Furniture Group plc – interim report – 12 June 2004

Notes to the financial statements (extract)

12 Pensions (extract)

On 6 May 2004 the Group announced that it had received actuarial and legal advice following a thorough review of an issue arising within its UK pension plans. This issue is liable to result in the Group recognising higher pension obligations than previously identified. The issue has its origins in a failure, back in 1994, effectively to properly equalise the pension age for men and women at age 65 for an employee's service from 17 November 1994. Although announcements to this effect were made at the time to plan members, the relevant trust documentation was not properly amended. This is liable to result in the part of the benefits earned by employee members over a period from 1994 to 2004 having to be calculated using a normal retirement date of age 60 rather than at age 65. Plan rules have now been amended to cap liability in relation to future service.

The Board has sought legal advice on the scope for correction and an independent actuarial assessment of the additional liabilities, which might arise, and of the contributions required to fund them. It appears far from certain that the situation can be corrected, in which case some £40 million of additional liabilities (before tax) will arise. This figure is assessed on the same actuarial assumptions as currently used for funding the UK pension plans and accounting for them under SSAP24 (see note 23 to the Group's 2003 financial statements). Under FRS 17, which the Group has not yet adopted, this figure would be approximately £50 million (before tax).

Under the pensions accounting standard SSAP24, the impact on future profits of the Group will depend on the period over which additional liabilities are recognised. At this stage the funding position has not yet been resolved and is uncertain. Given the current degree of uncertainty in the outcome of the discussions with the Trustees there is no recognition of any additional charge in these interim financial statements.

The Board and the Trustees will be reviewing the funding position in the light of further advice to be received and will then discuss how best to proceed. The Trustees will need to be satisfied both as to the period over which contributions are paid and the date from which contributions commence. The Board expects that the funding position will become clearer in the second half of the financial year and that this would be reflected in the year end accounts.

The Board continues to take advice from leading counsel as to the actions required to obtain recovery from the third parties on whose advice the Group and the Trustees of the plan relied in relation to this issue.

Employers ceasing to participate in a pension scheme

11.184 For a single-employer pension scheme, section 75 of the Pensions Act 1995 (as amended by the Pensions Act 2004) ensures that a debt can be placed on the pension scheme's sponsoring employer if the value of the scheme's assets is less than its liabilities. The debt is triggered if:

- the scheme winds-up; or
- on a relevant event (for example, the employer becomes insolvent).

11.185 Section 75A was inserted into the Pensions Act 1995 by the Pensions Act 2004 to modify the existing section 75 as it applies to multi-employer schemes (see para 11.187). For these schemes, the debt is triggered if:

- the scheme winds-up;
- on a relevant event (for example, insolvency) for any one or more companies; or
- on a withdrawal of an individual employer from a multi-employer scheme (referred to as an 'employment-cessation event').

11.186 When an employer ceases to participate in an under-funded defined benefit multi-employer scheme, whilst other employers continue to participate, the departing employer will normally be liable to pay their 'section 75' debt – their share of the pension scheme's liabilities calculated on a 'buy-out basis' (that is, the full cost of securing its liabilities with annuities, including an estimate of expenses) – see further paragraph 11.189 below. There are six prescribed ways in which an employer departing from a multi-employer scheme can have its section 75 debt reduced or removed (see paras 11.324.24 and 11.324.25 below).

11.187 A multi-employer scheme is a scheme in relation to which more than one employer is exposed to the scheme. 'Employer' in relation to an occupational pension scheme, means the employer of persons in the description or category of employment to which the scheme in question relates. Multi-employer schemes do not include, for the purposes of the section 75 rules, sectionalised schemes where:

- contributions payable by an employer are allocated to that employer's section;
- a specified part of the scheme's assets is attributable to each section and cannot be used for any other section; and
- there is only one employer in each section.

In such cases, section 75 will apply as if each section of the scheme were a separate scheme.

11.188 A liability is triggered when an 'employment-cessation event' occurs. In general, this event takes place when a participating employer ceases to have any employees who are members of the scheme and at least one participating employer remains. This could occur if:

- A company leaves the corporate group and, therefore, ceases to be a participating employer in the pension scheme.
- A company's business is sold, leaving it with no remaining employees.
- A company ceases to be employer of any individuals who are active members of the scheme (for example, a group restructuring).
- A company's employees cease employment through redundancy or resignation.
- Future accruals cease for that company.

This is a complex area and professional advice is likely to be needed.

11.189 When an 'employment-cessation event' occurs, part of the total deficit in a multi-employer scheme has to be attributed to the withdrawing employer. The attribution is by reference to the position at the date that the employer ceases to participate in the scheme. The total deficit is calculated on a buy-out basis (that is, based on the full cost of securing the scheme's liabilities with annuities, including an estimate of expenses). The total deficit is attributed to the participating employers according to the scheme's trust deed and rules, but if the rules are silent then the method for calculating the liability share for each employer is detailed in the Employer Debt Regulations.

11.190 Under the legislation, the amount of the employer's debt is:

- the proportion of the buy-out deficit that is attributable to employment with that employer; and
- the expenses attributable to the employer ceasing to participate.

11.191 Depending on what is set out in the scheme's own trust deed and rules, the withdrawing employer has to pay not only the buy-out deficit attributable to its own employees, but also a share of the orphan liabilities. 'Orphan liabilities' are material liabilities that are attributable to companies that have already left the scheme, including any liabilities that cannot be attributed specifically to any of the remaining employers. Unless the scheme rules state otherwise, the other employers share any exposure relating to these liabilities.

11.192 In simplified terms, the liability of the withdrawing employer is calculated as follows:

$$\frac{\text{buy-out liabilities for withdrawing employer}}{\text{buy-out liabilities for withdrawing employer + remaining employers}} \times \text{buy-out deficit for the scheme}$$

11.193 Under the amendments to the Employer Debt Regulations, from April 2010, there are two mechanisms which allow an employer to depart without becoming liable for the section 75 debt where there is a corporate restructuring event involving one departing and one receiving employer:

- *de minimis restructuring test* – where trustees are satisfied that the amount of the departing employer's liabilities is minimal; and
- *restructuring test* –where trustees are satisfied that there is no weakening of the employer covenant supporting the pension scheme.

11.194 There are four mechanisms which allow the employer to depart from the scheme having paid a modified section 75 debt (subject to agreement by the trustees and all the affected employers):

- *scheme apportionment arrangement* – where the departing employer pays a specified amount that is different from their section 75 debt and, if the amount is lower, the difference is apportioned to one or more of the remaining employers.
- *withdrawal arrangement* – where the departing employer pays an amount that is less than their section 75 debt (but more than their share of the deficit calculated on the technical provision basis and the difference is guaranteed by one or more guarantors.
- *approved withdrawal arrangement* – where the departing employer pays an amount that is less than their share of the deficit calculated on the technical provision basis and the difference is guaranteed by one or more guarantors. This type of arrangement must be approved by the Pension Regulator.
- *regulated apportionment arrangement* – this modifies the departing employer's section 75 debt so that it is greater or less than its liability share. If less, the difference is apportioned to one or more of the remaining employers. This type of arrangement is only available where the scheme is in a PPF assessment period.

[The next paragraph is 11.199.]

Accounting treatment

11.199 As noted in paragraph 11.185, a situation that will trigger measurement of the defined benefit obligation on a buy-out basis is where a participating employer ceases to participate in a multi-employer scheme. This may typically arise within group schemes where, for example, a subsidiary within a group is sold. Such an event will trigger a debt on the participating employer, being the amount of the employer's defined benefit pension obligation measured on a buy-out basis, under section 75 of the Pensions Act 1995. In the case where the employer ceases participation in the scheme, payment of the section 75 debt equates to a settlement event having the effect of extinguishing the participating employer's share of the scheme liabilities (see para 11.101). The examples below illustrate this further. For the purpose of these examples it is assumed that no withdrawal arrangements deferring payment of part of the debt (see para 11.193) are entered into.

Example 1 – section 75 payment made by withdrawing employer

Company B is wholly owned by company A. The employees of company B participate in the group A defined benefit pension scheme (other companies owned by company A, as well as company A itself also participate in this scheme). All companies that participate in the group A pension scheme are able to identify their share of the scheme's assets and liabilities on a consistent and reasonable basis such that defined benefit accounting is applied in each company's financial statements (see para 11.37). Company A subsequently sells company B to a third party purchaser.

Following the disposal of company B, the employees of company B remain in the group A pension scheme as deferred members. Company A now assumes responsibility for any liabilities arising in respect of these deferred members. Nevertheless, as company B itself is ceasing to participate in the group A pension scheme, this is determined to trigger a section 75 payment.

The group A pension scheme is in deficit at the time of the disposal and the share of the deficit relating to company B's employees (measured on an FRS 17 basis) amounts to £5m. On a buy-out basis, the share of the deficit relating to company B's employees is £9m (being the value of the section 75 payment). Following the section 75 payment, a surplus of £4m under FRS 17 arises on company B's share of the scheme. All companies in group A have a year end date of 31 December 20X6 and by this date, the disposal and section 75 payment have occurred.

In company B's individual financial statements, a settlement loss of £4m is recognised (see para 11.101) as company B has ceased to participate in the group A pension scheme and company B's liability in respect of the pension scheme has been extinguished (through the transfer of the obligation to company A). The settlement loss of £4m reflects the fact that company B had to make a payment of £9m (being the section 75 payment) in order to exit the group A pension scheme where the deficit attributable to company B's employees, previously recognised and measured on an FRS 17 basis, was £5m.

In company A's consolidated financial statements, no settlement loss is recognised as, whilst company B has ceased to participate in the scheme, company B's employees still remain in the scheme, albeit as deferred members. Hence, from the perspective of the group, the liabilities associated with company B's employees (£5m) have not been extinguished and the section 75 payment (£9m) will increase scheme assets, resulting in a surplus for this part of the scheme of £4m. In addition, a curtailment gain may arise as company B's employees are now deferred members resulting in a reduction in their future benefit entitlement (see para 11.102).

Furthermore, as defined benefit accounting is applied at an entity level, the surplus of £4m in respect of company B's employees needs to be allocated to the participating employers. As company A has assumed responsibility for any liabilities relating to the deferred members, it would appear reasonable for the £4m surplus to be allocated to company A. It will be recognised in company A's individual financial statements if it meets the criteria in paragraphs 37 to 42 of FRS 17 (see para 11.115 onwards). The basic rule is that the amount of surplus recognised as an asset should not exceed the present value of the amounts that the employer can recover through reduced contributions, together with refunds that have been agreed by the trustees at the balance sheet date. Recognition of the surplus in respect of company B's deferred members may depend on whether company A has active employees in the scheme for which it recognises a deficit and for which it can benefit from reduced contributions in the future. If the surplus is recognised in company A's individual financial statements, it will be included as part of the calculation of profit or loss on disposal of company B.

The table below summarises the position in respect of company B's employees (ignoring any curtailment gains):

	Company B (subsidiary)	Company A (parent)	Group
	£'m	£'m	£'m
Company B's deficit as at date of disposal	(5)	–	(5)
Section 75 payment *	9	–	9
Group transfer:			
Settlement loss in company B	(4)	–	–
Credit (included in profit or loss on disposal of company B) in company A	–	4	–
Surplus arising after section 75 payment to group A scheme **	–	4	4

* The section 75 payment forms part of the settlement loss calculation in company B's profit and loss account, but increases scheme assets in the group's consolidated financial statements.

** As company A now assumes responsibility for any liabilities arising in respect of the deferred members, it would recognise the surplus of £4m in its individual financial statements if it meets the recognition criteria in FRS 17 (see comments above).

11.200 The above example is based on the situation where the companies that participate in the group pension scheme have been able to identify their share of the scheme's assets and liabilities on a consistent and reasonable basis, such that defined benefit accounting is applied in each company's financial statements. In some cases, section 75 payments will become payable by companies that have not previously been able to identify their share of the scheme's assets and liabilities and which have, therefore, used defined contribution accounting in their individual financial statements as permitted by paragraph 9 of FRS 17 (see para 11.37 onwards). In such cases, the settlement loss in the withdrawing employer's individual financial statements will be the amount of the section 75 payment (that is, £9m in the example above). Under defined contribution accounting, there is no deficit previously recognised in the balance sheet and so the loss is recognised on the basis of contributions payable (in this case, the section 75 payment) in the period. Note that the consolidated financial statements of company A will always apply defined benefit accounting.

11.201 In the situation where the individual companies in the group have used defined contribution accounting on the grounds that it has not been possible to allocate the scheme's assets and liabilities, it will be necessary to consider if this is still applicable for the remaining companies where an allocation is made for the purposes of section 75 when one of the companies leaves the group. Depending on the specific circumstances, it may be that the remaining companies are now able to allocate the scheme's assets and liabilities on a consistent and reasonable basis, such that the exemption for group schemes is no longer applicable. See further paragraph 11.37 onwards.

11.202 The above example in paragraph 11.199 illustrates a relatively straightforward scenario. However, calculation of the section 75 payment often takes time and it may be the case that calculation of the payment is not completed until after the year end date. The following example illustrates this scenario.

Example 2 – section 75 payment made by withdrawing employer after the year end

The facts are as for example 1 in paragraph 11.199 and company A has taken over responsibility for the deferred members at the balance sheet date, but for administrative reasons company B has not made the payment at the balance sheet date, as the amount to be paid is only finalised after the balance sheet date (being £9m as in the previous example).

Similar to example 1, in company B's individual financial statements, a settlement loss of £4m is recognised as company B has ceased to participate in the group A pension scheme (through the transfer of the obligation to company A). This settlement loss of £4m represents the difference between the section 75 liability of £9m and the deficit, previously recognised and measured on an FRS 17 basis, of £5m. The unpaid section 75 settlement payment is included in creditors in company B's balance sheet replacing the previously recognised FRS 17 liability).

Again, similar to example 1, in company A's consolidated financial statements, no settlement loss is recognised as, whilst company B has ceased to participate in the scheme, company B's employees still remain in the scheme, albeit as deferred members. Hence, from the perspective of the group, the liabilities associated with company B's employees (£5m) have not been extinguished. At the balance sheet date, company B is no longer part of the group and so the creditor for the unpaid section 75 debt (£9m) will not be included in the group's consolidated balance sheet. However, it is taken into account in determining company B's net assets (which will be net assets excluding pensions less the section 75 creditor) in the calculation of the profit or loss on disposal of company B and so it has been recognised by the group. The unpaid section 75 contribution would be shown as part of scheme assets (as it is a current asset receivable by the scheme – FRS 17 para 15), resulting in a surplus of £4m. In addition, a curtailment gain may arise as company B's employees are now deferred members resulting in a reduction in their future benefit entitlement (see para 11.102).

Furthermore, as defined benefit accounting is applied at an entity level, the surplus of £4m in respect of company B's employees needs to be allocated to the participating employers. As company A has assumed responsibility for any liabilities relating to the deferred members, it would appear reasonable for the £4m surplus to be allocated to company A. It will be recognised in company A's individual financial statements if it meets the criteria in paragraphs 37 to 42 of FRS 17 (see further example 1). If the surplus is recognised, it will be included as part of the calculation of profit or loss on disposal of company B.

The table below summarises the position in respect of company B's employees (ignoring any curtailment gains):

	Company B (subsidiary) £'m	Company A (parent) £'m	Group £'m
Company B's deficit as at date of disposal	(5)	–	(5)
Unpaid section 75 payment *	9	–	9
Group transfer:			
Settlement loss in company B	(4)	–	–
Credit (included in profit or loss on disposal of company B) in company A	–	4	–
Surplus arising after section 75 amount payable to group A scheme **	–	4	4

* Note that the unpaid section 75 payment is recognised as a creditor and forms part of the settlement loss calculation in company B's individual financial statements. In the consolidated financial statements, the section 75 creditor is taken into account in determining company B's net assets in the calculation of the profit or loss on disposal of company B and the debit increases scheme assets in the group's consolidated financial statements as explained above.

** As company A now assumes responsibility for any liabilities arising in respect of the deferred members, it would recognise the surplus of £4m in its individual financial statements if it meets the recognition criteria in FRS 17 (see comments in example 1 above).

11.203 In the above example, the parent company has taken over responsibility for the deferred members at the balance sheet date, but the subsidiary has not made the section 75 payment at the balance sheet date for administrative reasons. The situation could be more complicated where the settlement itself has not been finalised at the year end, such that the subsidiary is still responsible for the employees. Losses arising on a settlement should be measured at the date on which the employer becomes demonstrably committed to the transaction and recognised in the profit and loss account covering that date. Gains arising on a settlement should be measured at the date on which all parties whose consent is required are irrevocably committed to the transaction and recognised in the profit and loss account covering that date. [FRS 17 para 64]. Therefore, the accounting treatment for settlements that straddle the balance sheet date will depend on the specific circumstances and whether there is a gain or a loss on settlement. See further paragraph 11.100 onwards.

11.204 The above two examples illustrate the appropriate accounting where the departing employer makes the section 75 payment. Nevertheless, it may be the case that the parent company agrees to pay the section 75 payment. The accounting impact is considered further in the following example.

Example 3 – section 75 payment made by the withdrawing employer's parent

The facts are as for example 1 in paragraph 11.199, but company A agrees to make the £9m section 75 payment. This amount is not repayable by company B.

In company B's individual financial statements, a settlement gain of £5m is recognised. As company B did not make payments in respect of the section 75 debt, but has ceased participation in the scheme, the settlement gain of £5m reflects the release of company B's share of the deficit (previously recognised and measured on an FRS 17 basis).

Similar to example 1, in company A's consolidated financial statements, no settlement loss is recognised (although a curtailment gain or loss may arise) as, whilst company B has ceased to participate in the scheme, company B's employees still remain in the scheme, albeit as deferred members. Hence, from the perspective of the group, the liabilities associated with company B's employees (£5m) have not been extinguished and the section 75 payment (£9m) will increase scheme assets, resulting in a surplus for this part of the scheme of £4m.

In company A's individual financial statements, the £5m deficit (measured on an FRS 17 basis) in respect of the liabilities that company A has taken over should be recognised, with a corresponding loss in respect of the transfer in the profit and loss account (as part of the calculation of profit or loss on disposal of company B). The payment of £9m into the scheme would be treated as a contribution to the pension scheme given that company A participates in the group A pension scheme and has taken over the responsibility for funding the obligation for these deferred members. As such, company A would increase the value of the scheme assets it recognises by £9m, resulting in a surplus of £4m (if the recognition criteria in paragraphs 37 to 42 of FRS 17 are met (see further example 1).

The table below summarises the position in respect of company B's employees (ignoring any curtailment gains):

	Company B (subsidiary)	Company A (parent)	Group
	£'m	£'m	£'m
Company B's deficit as at date of disposal	(5)	–	(5)
Section 75 payment *	–	9	9
Group transfer:			
Settlement gain in company B	5	–	–
Loss (included in profit or loss on disposal of company B) in respect of liabilities taken over	–	(5)	–
Surplus arising after section 75 payment to group A scheme **	–	4	4

* The section 75 payment increases scheme assets recognised in both company A and in the group's consolidated financial statements.

** As company A now assumes responsibility for any liabilities arising in respect of the deferred members, it would recognise the surplus of £4m in its individual financial statements if it meets the recognition criteria in FRS 17 (see comments in example 1 above).

11.205 A further situation that may arise is where there is also a bulk transfer of a subsidiary's share of the scheme into a new scheme. The accounting impact of this situation is considered further in the following examples.

Example 4 – section 75 payment made by withdrawing employer (+ bulk transfer out)

The facts are as for example 1 in paragraph 11.199 (that is, company B makes the section 75 payment), but in addition a bulk transfer is made of the assets and liabilities relating to company B's employees to the pension scheme of company B's new parent. Following the section 75 payment, a surplus of £4m arises on company B's share of the scheme. For the purposes of the bulk transfer of company B's share of the scheme, it is agreed that the value of the surplus to be transferred into the new parent's pension scheme will be £3m. It is decided that any surplus remaining after the bulk transfer will be allocated to company A.

In company B's individual financial statements, the section 75 payment of £9m (in respect of a recognised deficit of £5m measured on an FRS 17 basis) initially results in a surplus of £4m. Of this, £3m is transferred to a new pension scheme and remains on company B's balance sheet as an asset. The remaining £1m represents a settlement loss as company B has ceased to participate in the group A pension scheme and company B's liability in respect of that pension scheme has been extinguished.

In company A's consolidated financial statements, a settlement loss of £3m is recognised in respect of the bulk transfer to the new pension scheme (as part of the calculation of profit or loss on disposal of company B), leaving a surplus of £1m in the group A pension scheme.

Furthermore, as defined benefit accounting is applied at an entity level, the remaining surplus of £1m is recognised in company A's individual financial statements if it meets the criteria in paragraphs 37 to 42 of FRS 17 (see example 1). If the surplus is recognised, it will be included as part of the calculation of profit or loss on disposal of company B.

The table below summarises the position in respect of company B's employees:

	Company B (subsidiary)	Company A (parent)	Group
	£'m	£'m	£'m
Company B's deficit as at date of disposal	(5)	–	(5)
Section 75 payment *	9	–	9
	4	–	4
Bulk transfer to new scheme (settlement loss)	–	–	(3)
Group transfer:			
Settlement loss in company B	(1)	–	–
Credit (included in profit or loss on disposal of company B) in company A	–	1	–

Surplus arising after section 75 payment to group A scheme **	–	1	1
Surplus in new scheme	3	–	–

* The section 75 payment initially increases scheme assets recognised in both company B and in the group's consolidated financial statements (prior to the bulk transfer).

** In this example, any surplus remaining after the bulk transfer has been allocated to company A.

Example 5 – section 75 payment made by withdrawing employer's parent (+ bulk transfer out)

The facts are as for example 1 in paragraph 11.199, but company A agrees to make the £9m section 75 payment (and it is not repayable by company B). In addition, a bulk transfer is made of the assets and liabilities relating to company B's employees to the pension scheme of company B's new parent. Following the section 75 payment, a surplus of £4m arises on company B's share of the scheme. For the purposes of the bulk transfer of company B's share of the scheme, it is agreed that the value of the surplus to be transferred into the new parent's pension scheme will be £3m. It is decided that any surplus remaining after the bulk transfer will be allocated to company A.

In company B's individual financial statements, a total settlement gain of £8m arises. Company B did not make payments in respect of the section 75 debt, but has ceased to participate in the group A pension scheme and company B's liability in respect of that pension scheme has been extinguished. The gain of £8m comprises £5m in respect of the release of company B's share of the deficit (measured on an FRS 17 basis) and £3m in respect of the surplus (funded by company A) transferred to a new pension scheme (assuming that this is recognised on company B's balance sheet as an asset).

In company A's consolidated financial statements, a settlement loss of £3m is recognised in respect of the bulk transfer to the new pension scheme (as part of the calculation of profit or loss on disposal of company B), leaving a surplus of £1m in the group A pension scheme.

Similar to example 3 in paragraph 11.204, in company A's individual financial statements, the payment of £9m into the scheme is treated as a contribution to the pension scheme. However, as £8m of this contribution has been transferred out of the scheme as a result of the bulk transfer, it represents a loss in company A's books and it will be included in the profit or loss on disposal of company B reported in company A's profit and loss account. The remaining surplus of £1m is recognised in company A's balance sheet if it meets the criteria in paragraphs 37 to 42 of FRS 17 (see example 1).

The table below summarises the position in respect of company B's employees:

	Company B £'m	Company A £'m	Group £'m
Company B's deficit as at date of disposal	(5)	–	(5)
Section 75 payment *	–	9	9
			4
Bulk transfer to new scheme:			
Settlement gain/(loss)	8	–	(3)
Loss (included in profit or loss on disposal of company B) in company A	–	(8)	–
Surplus arising after section 75 payment to group A scheme **	–	1	1
Surplus in new scheme	3	–	–

* The section 75 payment initially increases scheme assets recognised in both company A and in the group's consolidated financial statements (prior to the bulk transfer).

** The surplus remaining after the bulk transfer is recognised in company A (if it meets the criteria in FRS 17) as this company made the section 75 payment.

11.206 As discussed in paragraph 11.203, the situation will be more complicated where the settlement and/or the bulk transfer straddle the balance sheet date.

Chapter 12

Share-based payment

Chapter 12

Share-based payment

National insurance contributions on share options gains

Background

12.1 UK employers are required to pay National Insurance Contributions (NIC) on the exercise of certain share options granted after 5 April 1999. The NIC charge applies to share options issued under unapproved share plans (that is, those not approved by the Inland Revenue) where the shares are 'readily convertible assets', that is, they can be sold on a stock exchange or there are arrangements in place that allow the employees to obtain cash for the shares acquired under the option plan.

12.2 The charge is based on the intrinsic value of the options at the date of exercise (intrinsic value is the excess of the market price of the shares over the exercise price). Previously, NIC was payable on the grant of an option not its exercise. The change in basis raised the question as to how to account for the NIC obligation between the date of grant and the date of exercise. This matter was addressed by the UITF in 2000 when it issued UITF Abstract 25, 'National insurance contributions on share option gains'. In this abstract, the UITF considered whether NIC on share option gains meet the recognition criteria under FRS 12, 'Provisions, contingent liabilities and contingent assets', and also the basis for calculating the estimated liability in advance of the exercise date. FRS 12 requires a provision to be recognised when:

- An entity has a present obligation (legal or constructive) as a result of a past event.
- It is probable that a transfer of economic benefits will be required to settle the obligation.
- A reliable estimate can be made of the amount of the obligation.

[FRS 12 para 14].

12.3 The UITF regards the granting of the option as the past event that gives rise to a present obligation to pay NIC at some point in the future (that is, when the option is exercised). [UITF 25 para 4]. The amount of the obligation is uncertain as it depends on future share prices, but FRS 12 requires that the amount recognised as a provision should be the best estimate of the present obligation at the balance sheet date. [FRS 12 para 36]. The market price of the shares at the balance sheet date provides a reliable basis for estimating the provision. [UITF 25 para 4].

12.4 The UITF concluded that provision should be made for NIC on outstanding share options that are expected to be exercised. [UITF 25 para 10]. Therefore, in assessing the potential charge, it is necessary in the case of performance related options to estimate the degree to which the performance conditions are likely to be met in the future.

12.5 The provision should be calculated by applying the latest enacted national insurance rate to the difference between the market value of the underlying shares at the balance sheet date and the option exercise price. The provision should be allocated over the period from the date of grant to the end of the performance period. This is illustrated in the example in paragraph 12.39 below. Where there is no performance period full provision should be made immediately. [UITF 25 para 10].

12.6 The performance period is the period during which the employee performs the services necessary to become unconditionally entitled to the options. [UITF 25 para 6]. This might involve satisfying performance criteria or service conditions and so in this respect, the term 'performance period' in UITF Abstract 25 is consistent with the term 'vesting period' in FRS 20, 'Share-based payment'.

12.7 From the end of the performance period to the date of actual exercise the provision should be adjusted by reference to the current market value of the shares. [UITF 25 para 10].

12.8 As noted in paragraph 12.3, the abstract requires the NIC provision to be determined on the basis of the period end share price. However, it is first necessary to determine the number of options expected to be exercised and, in order to do this, it might be necessary to take account of post balance sheet events. This is because FRS 12 requires that where the amount of a liability will be affected by future events, those events should be taken into account in estimating a provision if there is sufficient objective evidence that they will occur. In some cases the estimation necessarily involves a degree of hindsight.

12.9 For example, if a fall in share prices meant that it was clear that options would not be exercised and no NIC would be payable, a provision would not be made. This would be the case if the fall was so large that the options were 'out of the money' (that is, the exercise price is higher than market price) and the exercise period had expired prior to approval of the financial statements.

Example – National insurance contributions on share options — post year end fall in share price

An entity has outstanding employee share options that will attract a national insurance liability when exercised. The option exercise price is £10 and the market price of the entity's shares at the year end was £50. Since the year end there has been a significant fall in share prices in the sector and the entity's share price has dropped to £15. In addition, 30 per cent of the employees to whom options were granted have left and forfeited their options.

As described from paragraph 12.4 above, a liability is required for national insurance on outstanding share options expected to be exercised. The provision should be derived from the difference between the share price at the balance sheet date and the option exercise price, and the resulting amount should be spread over the period from the date the options were granted to the end of the performance period. It is clear, therefore, that where options are expected to be exercised, the provision recognised at the balance sheet date should not be adjusted for subsequent changes in the market price of the company's shares. The provision should be calculated at each balance sheet date to reflect the market price prevailing at that date. Although market prices may fluctuate widely after the year end, such fluctuations are disregarded, as with movements in foreign exchange rates that occur after the balance sheet date.

At each balance sheet date the entity needs to estimate the number of options that will ultimately be exercised. Where future events will affect the liability that will ultimately be payable, FRS 12 requires those events to be taken into account in estimating the provision where there is sufficient objective evidence that they will occur. In some cases the estimation necessarily involves a degree of hindsight. We believe the subsequent forfeiture of a substantial number of options should be taken into account when estimating the number of options expected to be exercised.

[The next paragraph is 12.36.]

Reimbursement or transfer of the liability

12.36 Since 2000, it has been permissible for employers and employees to agree that the employee can pay the employer's NIC on share options. The employee can bear the employer's NIC charge arising on share option gains in one of two ways:

- First, the employer and the employee can make an agreement that some or all of the employer's NIC liability can be recovered from the employee.
- Secondly, the employer and the employee may make a joint election to legally transfer the liability for the secondary NIC to the employee.

The agreements are only valid if made on or after 19 May 2000, but are not valid for gains made prior to 28 July 2000.

12.37 Where there is an agreement between the employer and employee under which the employee agrees to reimburse all or part of the employer's NIC, FRS 12 requires a provision for the full amount to be made and the expected reimbursement to be treated as a separate asset if receipt is virtually certain, with a net presentation permitted in the profit and loss account. [FRS 12 para 56-61].

12.38 Where there is a joint election by employer and employee under which the liability is formally transferred to the employee no liability appears in the employer's financial statements.

12.39 The following example illustrates the application of the requirements of UITF Abstract 25.

Example – Calculation of national insurance charge

The company's year end is 31 December. 20,000 share options are granted at 1 July 20X0, when the market value is £1, at an exercise price of £1, dependent upon performance from 1 July 20X0 to 30 June 20X2. The options are exercisable from 1 July 20X2 to 1 July 20X3.

Employer's national insurance contributions, currently at 12.8%, are payable on exercise of the options.

31 December 20X0

The market value of a share is £2.10. It is estimated that the maximum entitlement of options will be exercised.

National insurance charge for the year: One-quarter of 12.8% of 20,000 × (£2.10 – £1) = £704.

31 December 20X1

The market value of a share is £2.75. It is expected that 18,000 share options will be exercised.

National insurance cumulative charge: Three-quarters of 12.8% of 18,000 × (£2.75 – £1) = £3,024.

Charge for the year: £3,024 – £704 = £2,320.

31 December 20X2

The market value of a share is £2.50. Only 15,000 share options vested; none of these have been exercised.

National insurance cumulative charge: 12.8% × 15,000 × (£2.50 – £1) = £2,880.

Credit for the year: £3,024 – £2,880 = £144.

31 December 20X3

The 15,000 share options were exercised in May 20X3 when the market value of a share was £2.60.

The National insurance liability was, therefore: 12.8% × 15,000 × (£2.60 — £1) = £3,072.

Charge for the year: £3,072 – £2,880 = £192.

Disclosure

12.40 FRS 12 requires, for each class of provision, disclosure of an indication of the uncertainties about the amount or timing of the eventual transfer of economic benefits and, where necessary to provide adequate information, the major assumptions made concerning future events. [FRS 12 para 90]. In the case of a provision for national insurance on share options, disclosure of the share price and of the effect of a significant movement in that price may be necessary to provide a full understanding of these factors. [UITF 25 para 7].

12.41 An example of a company that has provided for NIC on share options and disclosed the unprovided amount based on year end share prices is Baltimore Technologies plc, in Table 12.1 below.

Table 12.1 — Provision for NIC on share options

Baltimore Technologies plc — Annual Report — 31 December 1999

Notes to the consolidated financial statements (extract)

23 CONTINGENT LIABILITIES (extract)

Share options granted subsequent to 5 April 1999 under unapproved schemes are subject to employers' and employees' national insurance on the gain made on exercise of such options by UK employees.

An accrual of £426,000 has been made at 31 December 1999 based on the year end share price of £51.25 and the elapsed portion of the relevant vesting periods.

Based on the year-end share price there is a further contingent liability of approximately £4.4 million arising by the end of the vesting period that has not been provided for in these Financial Statements.

Employee share ownership plans (ESOPs)

Background

12.42 Employee share ownership plans (ESOPs) are usually designed to enable employees to purchase shares in their employing company. The structures of ESOPs vary, but typically they are arrangements whereby a trust is set up by a sponsoring company to acquire shares in that company for the benefit of its employees, who generally acquire them at a later stage through share option plans, profit sharing arrangements or other share incentive plans. The commercial reasons for establishing an ESOP include the following:

- It allows a share plan to be extended to new participants without diluting existing shareholders' interests, because it can operate by acquiring and distributing shares that are already in issue rather than by requiring new shares to be issued.
- It can provide a private company with a market in its shares in order to operate an employee share plan, by buying shares from departing employees

and other shareholders, warehousing them and then distributing them to new and continuing employees.

- It can facilitate employee participation in connection with a management buyout, privatisation or listing of a private company.
- In cash flow terms, a company can hedge its obligations in respect of options issued under share option plans by avoiding exposure to increases in the market value of shares between the dates of granting the options and the dates of exercising those options.

ESOPs have to comply with a number of regulations including those of the Companies Act, the Financial Services and Markets Act and, where the company is listed, the Listing Rules.

12.43 The vehicle used to hold the shares in an ESOP is a discretionary employee benefit trust set up by the sponsoring company for the benefit of all, or most, of its employees. For capital gains tax purposes, the trustee will normally be resident outside the UK and a subsidiary of the sponsoring company will often act as a corporate trustee. The trust buys shares with funds provided by way of cash or loans from the sponsoring company or by a loan from a third party (which will be guaranteed by the company). The shares held by the trust are typically distributed to employees through an employee share plan. The trust's beneficiaries can only include the company's or group's employees or former employees and certain of their close relations. Generally the sponsoring company will have no beneficial interest in the trust's residual assets.

12.44 The detailed structures of individual ESOP trusts are many and varied. However, the main features are often as follows:

- The trust provides a warehouse for the sponsoring company's shares, for example, by acquiring and holding shares that are to be sold or transferred to employees in the future. The trust will normally purchase the shares with finance provided by the sponsoring company (by way of cash contributions or loans), or by a third party bank loan, or by a combination of the two. Loans from the company are usually interest free.
- Where the trust borrows from a third party, the sponsoring company will often guarantee the loan, that is, it will be responsible for any shortfall if the trust's assets are insufficient to meet its debt repayment obligations. The company will also generally make regular contributions to the trust to enable the trust to meet its interest payments (to make good the shortfall between the dividend income of the trust and the interest payable). As part of this arrangement, the trustees sometimes waive their right to dividends on the shares the trust holds.
- Shares held by the trust are distributed to employees through an employee share plan. There are many different arrangements, which include: the purchase of shares by employees when exercising their share options under an executive share option plan; the purchase of shares by the trustees of an

approved profit sharing plan for allocation to employees under the plan's rules; or the transfer of shares to employees under an incentive plan.

12.45 An example of the structure of an ESOP trust is given in Table 12.2.

Table 12.2 – SmithKline Beecham plc – Annual Report – 31 December 1994

NOTES TO THE FINANCIAL STATEMENTS (extract)

33 SHARE OPTION PLANS (extract)

Employee Share Ownership Trust. An Employee Share Ownership Trust (ESOT) was established on 9 March 1992. The ESOT has purchased the Company's A Shares in the open market, which are held on trust for employees participating in the 1991 share option plan. The ESOT has purchased 15.7 million A Shares at a cost of £86 million. The ESOT has borrowed £83 million from third party banks which is guaranteed by the Company and the Company has also lent £3 million to the ESOT. The Company gifts payments to the ESOT to pay the interest on the loans. These payments to third parties amounted to £4.7 million (1993 £1.5 million) and the Company also incurred further interest charges of £3.4 million in 1993. The ESOT has waived its rights to dividends. The external borrowings of the ESOT are now included on the balance sheet (see accounting policies page 48).

Accounting for ESOP trusts

12.46 FRS 20 does not deal with the accounting where an entity's shares are held by an ESOP trust. However, the UITF has considered ESOPs and related matters on a number of occasions. The current guidance is contained in UITF Abstract 38, 'Accounting for ESOP trusts'. This abstract draws on the principles of FRS 5, 'Reporting the substance of transactions', when it concludes that an entity should account for an ESOP trust that it sponsors in accordance with its substance and not merely its legal form. Vehicles other than an ESOP trust established to hold shares for employee remuneration purposes acting in a similar way to an ESOP may also be caught by UITF Abstract 38.

12.47 Although the trustees of an ESOP trust must act under the trust deed at all times in accordance with the beneficiaries' interests, most ESOP trusts (particularly those set up to remunerate employees) are specifically designed to serve an entity's purposes, (otherwise known as the sponsoring entity), and to ensure that there will be minimal risk of any conflict arising between the trustees' duties and the entity's interest. In substance, the sponsoring entity has *de facto* control of the ESOP trust and reaps the benefits or bears the risks associated with its assets and liabilities. For example:

- Where the ESOP trust has unallocated shares, the benefit of increases in value will accrue to the sponsoring entity because, for example, it can pass increased benefits to its employees without using its other resources. Conversely, if the shares fall in value, the sponsoring entity may have to use its other resources to make good the benefits promised to its employees.

- If the shares are under option, the employees' assets are the options rather than the shares themselves and the risks associated with any fall in value below the option price remains with the sponsoring entity.

- When shares are conditionally gifted to the employees, the sponsoring entity retains an interest in the shares, because the benefits and risks associated with them remain with the sponsoring entity until the conditions are fulfilled.

- In many ESOP trusts, dividends on the shares held by the trust are waived until they vest with employees. In other trusts dividends continue to be paid and these will accrue to the trust thereby benefiting the sponsoring entity by either defraying the trust's costs or by reducing the cost of future employee incentive arrangements, which are ultimately borne by the sponsoring entity.

[The next paragraph is 12.49.]

12.49 The consensus reached in UITF Abstract 38 is that FRS 5's principles require an ESOP trust's sponsoring company to recognise the trust's assets and liabilities as its own where the sponsoring company has *de facto* control of the assets and liabilities of the ESOP trust and reaps their benefits or bears their risks. This will generally be the case where the trust is established to hold shares for an employee remuneration plan. Where this type of trust exists, the shares held by the ESOP trust should be treated in a similar way to that if the sponsoring company had acquired the shares itself. FRS 25 (IAS 32), 'Financial instruments: disclosure and presentation' requires an entity to deduct the consideration paid in acquiring its own shares in arriving at shareholders' funds. [FRS 25 para 33]. Consistent with this, UITF Abstract 38 requires that, until such time as the share held by an ESOP trust vest unconditionally in employees, the consideration paid for those shares should be deducted in arriving at the sponsoring company's shareholders' funds. Other assets and liabilities of the ESOP trust should be recognised as assets and liabilities of the sponsoring company. [UITF 38 paras 10(a),(b)].

12.50 The treatment of own shares described in the previous paragraph appears to contradict the requirements of the balance sheet formats set out in Schedule 1 of SI 2008/410, the 'Large and Medium-sized Companies and Groups (Accounts and Reports) Regulations 2008'. These formats include sub-headings for 'own shares' in both fixed and current assets, which suggests that investments in own shares are to be presented as assets. This is unfortunate, as there are other requirements in both UK and international standards for own shares to be deducted in arriving at shareholders' funds. For example, as noted above paragraph 33 of FRS 25 requires that where shares are repurchased or redeemed, equity should be reduced by the value of the consideration given. The approach in UITF Abstract 38 is consistent with this other guidance, but it is hard to ignore the requirements of the formats. Any amount described on the face of the balance sheet as investment in own shares would need to be presented in accordance with those requirements. Accordingly, in our view, the amount deducted in arriving at shareholders' funds should not be presented separately on the face of the balance sheet, but should be deducted from reserves, usually the profit and loss reserve.

12.51 Consistent with the principle that an entity's purchase of its own shares is a transaction with owners in their capacity as such, no gain or loss should arise. Accordingly, UITF Abstract 38 requires that no gain or loss should be recognised in either the profit and loss account or statement of total recognised gains and losses on the purchase, sale, issue or cancellation of a company's own shares. Instead, consideration paid or received should be presented as separate amounts in the reconciliation of movements in shareholders' funds. [UITF 38 paras 10(c),(d)]. This means that the following items will not be recognised in either of the performance statements:

- Charges or credits reflecting the difference between the cost of the shares acquired by the ESOP trust and the amounts to be received from employees on the exercise of options.
- Provisions for permanent or temporary diminution in the value of the shares.

12.52 Finance costs and administrative expenses should be charged as they become due and not as funding payments are made to the ESOP trust. [UITF 38 para 10(e)]. Interest costs incurred on external funding should be shown as interest paid in the company's financial statements and not as staff costs.

12.53 Any dividend income arising on own shares held by the ESOP trust should be excluded in arriving at profit before tax and deducted from the aggregate of dividends declared and paid. The deduction should be disclosed if material. Under FRS 22, 'Earnings per share', the shares are treated as if they were cancelled when calculating earnings per share. [UITF 38 para 10(f)].

12.54 It must be remembered that the above principles relate to the accounting for shares (and other assets and liabilities) held by an ESOP trust. They have no impact on the recognition or measurement of the expense in respect of a share-based payment arrangement, which is dealt with in accordance with FRS 20.

Legal considerations

12.55 UITF Abstract 38 is based on the principles in FRS 5 and makes it clear that this is not intended to affect the legal characterisation of a transaction, or to change the situation at law achieved by the parties to it. Thus, shares acquired by an ESOP trust and deducted in arriving at shareholders' funds are not treasury shares as defined by section 724(5) of the Companies Act 2006. Neither does the accounting treatment imply that the shares have been purchased by the company as a matter of law nor that they are required to be cancelled, which would be the consequence of such a purchase except for treasury shares (under sections 706 and 688 of the Companies Act 2006).

Impact on distributable profits

12.56 The issue of the impact of the accounting required by UITF 38 on a company's profits available for distribution is addressed in Tech 02/10, 'Guidance on the determination of realised profits and losses in the context of distributions under the Companies Act 2006', issued by the ICAEW in November 2010. The guidance confirms, for public companies (where the top plc company is the sponsoring company), deduction of the shares held in an ESOP trust in arriving at shareholders' funds will restrict profits available for distribution by the amount of consideration paid for those shares. Therefore, we consider that own shares held through an ESOP trust should be deducted from the profit and loss reserve, thereby reflecting the reduced profits available for distribution.

12.57 Section 836 of the Companies Act 2006 requires that a company's 'relevant accounts' for the purposes of determining profits available for distribution are properly prepared under the Act. This means, for a company applying UK GAAP, that they comply with UK accounting standards and UITF Abstracts, so it follows that the financial statements of the combined sponsoring entity and ESOP trust are the relevant accounts for the purposes of determining profits available for distribution. Therefore, transactions entered into by an ESOP trust should be considered in the same way as if they had actually been entered into by the sponsoring entity itself.

12.58 UITF Abstract 38, states that, *'the acquisition of shares by an ESOP does not, of itself, affect the company's realised profits or realised losses. The accounting treatment required by this Abstract, which requires a deduction in arriving at shareholders' funds and that no gain or loss should be recognised in the profit and loss account, is consistent with this analysis'*. [UITF 38 Legal considerations]. This means that the acquisition of shares by an ESOP trust does not give rise to an immediate realised loss. However, if the shares are subsequently to be transferred to employees for less than their purchase price, the difference between the purchase price and the consideration to be received from the employees, if any, will be treated as a realised loss, recognised over the vesting period.

12.59 Similar principles were applied to goodwill written off against reserves prior to the introduction of FRS 10, 'Goodwill and intangible assets'. Appendix V to FRS 10 states that where goodwill is written off on acquisition as a matter of accounting policy, rather than because of an actual diminution in value, this does not represent a realised loss. However, goodwill should be treated as reducing distributable profits over its useful economic life so as to achieve the same result as if the goodwill had been amortised through the profit and loss account.

12.60 Sometimes an ESOP trust may hold shares that are not allocated to a specific share plan. Although under UITF 38 own shares held by an ESOP trust are not treated as assets, it will be necessary to apply the same principles to determine whether any notional diminution should be taken into account in determining distributable profits.

12.61 FRS 11, 'Impairment of fixed assets and goodwill', applies to investments in subsidiaries, associates and joint ventures, but investments in own shares are outside the scope of that standard. Nevertheless, the principles of FRS 11 (including the impairment indicators) and its methodology for determining impairment may be useful and relevant in measuring any diminution in value of shares held by an ESOP trust. Impairment of assets is considered further in chapter 18.

12.62 Where an ESOP trust has disposed of surplus shares, this may give rise to a profit to be recognised in the trust's own accounts. This profit will not be recognised in the profit and loss account of the sponsoring entity. Instead, the proceeds from sale will be credited directly to equity. Nevertheless, in the accounts of both the trust and the sponsoring entity there will be a net credit in equity, so it must be determined whether this credit is distributable by the sponsoring entity. Tech 02/10 concludes that the resultant profit from a disposal of surplus shares will be a realised profit from the perspective of the sponsoring entity. However, before making a distribution of such profits, the directors should have regard to their fiduciary duties, for example to ensure that the company is in a position to settle its debts as and when they fall due. Accordingly, Tech 02/10 suggests that it may not be prudent to distribute an amount represented by assets retained by an ESOP trust that are not available for the general purposes of the sponsoring entity. This reflects the fact the ESOP trusts are generally established to be for the benefit of the sponsoring entity's employees. However, if, in the future, the cash representing the gain is used to defray an expense of the sponsoring entity for which the trust is permitted to use its assets, an equivalent amount of the gain should at that time be treated as distributable. [Tech 02/10 paras 7.42 — 7.45].

12.63 Tech 02/10 also deals with the impact on distributable profits of any expenses recognised in accordance with FRS 20. All expenses and losses should be regarded as realised losses, except to the extent that the law or accounting standards provide otherwise. [Tech 02/10 para 7.48]. However, it is arguable that an expense recognised in respect of an equity-settled share-based payment transaction is not a loss at all because it does not result in a reduction in recorded net assets. Nevertheless, even if the expense is regarded as a realised loss, Tech 02/10 makes it clear in other contexts (such as revaluation reserves) that an unrealised reserve will be treated as having become realised by the amortisation or writing down of the related asset. Therefore, assuming that the expense has been included in the profit and loss account rather than capitalised as part of the cost of an asset, the credit entry to equity will be treated as a realised profit so there will be no impact on distributable reserves. [Tech 02/10 para 7.51].

Additional considerations for public companies

12.64 Public companies face additional restrictions on their ability to make distributions. Section 831 of the Companies Act 2006 requires that a public company may only make a distribution:

- if the amount of its net assets is not less than the aggregate of its called-up share capital and undistributable reserves; and
- to the extent that the distribution does not reduce the amount of those assets to less than that aggregate.

[CA06 Sec 831].

12.65 When a public company acquires its own shares through an ESOP trust, this will have the effect of reducing net assets. However, there will be no corresponding impact on undistributable reserves. This is because the deduction from equity in respect of an acquisition of shares by an ESOP trust is not, as a matter of law, a loss (see from para 12.58). Since the deduction is not a loss at all, it follows that it is neither a realised nor an unrealised loss. Accordingly, the deduction from equity for ESOP shares has no immediate effect on the balance of undistributable reserves. Hence, with net assets reduced, but share capital and undistributable reserves unaffected, the purchase of ESOP shares immediately restricts distributable profits under section 831 of the Companies Act 2006.

12.66 When the employees finally acquire their shares, the receipt of proceeds will increase net assets without a corresponding increase in share capital and undistributable reserves. Hence, distributable profits will be restored to the extent of those proceeds.

12.67 Where there is a new issue of shares to an ESOP trust, there will be no change in net assets, but there will be an increase in called-up share capital (and an increase in undistributable reserves if the shares are issued at a premium). Hence, the amount of a listed company's distributable profits will be restricted by the proceeds of the share issue. This means that, regardless of whether an ESOP trust acquires its shares in the market or through a new issue, the amount paid for the shares will immediately restrict distributable profits.

12.68 The financial assistance rules may also cause problems for public companies. Section 682 of the Companies Act 2006 provides that a public company may only give financial assistance for the acquisition of its own shares if the net assets of the company are not thereby reduced or, to the extent that net assets are reduced, the company has sufficient distributable profits to cover the full amount of the assistance. For this purpose, net assets are defined as: the amount by which the aggregate of the company's assets exceeds the aggregate of its liabilities (taking the amount of both assets and liabilities *'to be as stated in the company's accounting records immediately before the financial assistance is given')*. [CA06 Sec 682(4)(a)]. This is in contrast to section 831 of the Companies Act 2006 where, by reason of section 836, net assets are determined by reference to the company's relevant accounts. Although subtle, this is an important distinction. As noted in paragraph 12.57 above, relevant accounts are the financial statements of the combined sponsoring company and ESOP trust. However, there is no requirement for the company's accounting records to reflect the adjustments that would be necessary for these financial statements to be prepared in accordance with the requirements of UITF Abstract 38. Thus, in the absence of any such requirement, the company's assets and liabilities should be given their natural meaning, namely the assets and liabilities of the company as a separate legal entity, excluding the ESOP trust. Accordingly, for the purposes of section 682 of the Companies Act 2006, it is necessary to determine whether the manner in which a public company has funded an ESOP trust will reduce net assets. The assets of the trust itself and their treatment in the sponsoring company's financial statements have no relevance for a consideration of section 682 of the Companies Act 2006. The following example illustrates this point.

Example – ESOP acquires shares to satisfy requirements of employee share plan

A public company sponsors an ESOP trust. The trust does not currently hold any shares in the sponsoring company, but needs to acquire 100,000 shares in order to satisfy the requirements of an employee share plan. In order to enable the trust to make the purchase, the sponsoring company could provide funding by way of a gift, a loan or a combination of both.

As explained above, for the purposes of section 682 of the Companies Act 2006, the sponsoring company is considered in isolation (sometimes referred to as the 'narrow entity') and not in combination with the ESOP trust (the 'extended entity'). Hence, transactions between the company and the trust are considered in the same way as any other transactions involving the company and a third party. A gift to the trust is clearly an immediate realised loss (as it reduces the net assets of the narrow entity) and hence reduces the distributable profits of the sponsoring company. On the other hand a loan, provided it is considered recoverable (that is, sufficient cash is expected when employees exercise their rights to the shares), would not be a realised loss. However, any write down in the value of the loan (caused by a question over its recoverability) would be a realised loss.

12.69 Tech 02/10 makes it clear that where a company has reduced its distributable profits on the provision of financial assistance and shares have been acquired by an ESOP trust, section 831 of the Companies Act 2006 does not require a further reduction in distributable profits (referred to in the guidance as the maximum distribution permissible) equal to the amount of the reduction in net assets calculated under section 682 of the Companies Act 2006. [Tech 02/10 para 7.29]. This is because section 682 and section 831 are directed to different objectives. Section 682 determines the legality of the provision of financial assistance from the perspective of the company in isolation, whereas section 831 considers the combined company and ESOP trust as presented in the relevant accounts. On the latter basis, the assistance provided to the ESOP trust will be ignored as the assets and liabilities of the company and the trust are aggregated. Distributable profits for the purposes of section 831 are not diminished until the shares are purchased, at which point the net assets are restricted by the consideration paid. [Tech 02/10 para 7.30].

Illustrative examples

12.70 The examples that follow illustrate UITF Abstract 38's principles and include the examples in appendix II to the abstract.

Example 1 – Shares funded by bank loan

The ESOP trust holds unallocated shares costing £100,000, funded by a bank loan. The sponsoring company undertakes to make contributions to the trust whenever the loan-to-value ratio falls below a set figure. At the reporting date the market value is at least £100,000.

The company deducts the consideration paid for the shares of £100,000 in arriving at shareholders' funds. The company also recognises a liability of £100,000 in respect of the bank loan. Interest expense is accrued in the usual way. The amount of the reduction in shareholders' funds (£100,000) and the market value of the shares held should be disclosed.

Example 2 – Shares funded by bank loan and decline in value

The facts are the same as in example 1, except that the market value of the shares falls to £80,000 by the company's year end.

The fall in the market value of the shares does not give rise to a recognised loss. As in example 1, the amount of the reduction in shareholders' funds (£100,000) and the market value of the shares held should be disclosed.

Example 3 – Options granted over shares are below market value

The facts are the same as in example 1, but options are granted over the shares at £80,000 when the market value is £100,000.

The company recognises an expense over the option vesting period in accordance with FRS 20. The reduction to shareholders' funds of £100,000 in respect of the consideration paid for the shares, and the market value of the shares, are disclosed until the shares vest unconditionally in employees. When the options are exercised, the receipt of £80,000 is credited to shareholders' funds.

Example 4 – Co-operative

A company is a co-operative, owned by its employees. All of its shares are held in a trust for the employees' benefit collectively and the trust receives dividends from the company which are distributed to employees in accordance with the trust deed's provisions. The shares never vest in individual employees. The company does not have de facto control of the trust's shares.

The shares held by the trust are not in substance the company's own shares and are not accounted for as such.

Gains made by ESOPs

12.71 There are situations where ESOP trusts make gains, for instance on the sale of surplus shares (where previous awards have lapsed) or where the exercise price exceeds the cost of the shares. UITF Abstract 38 requires that no gain or loss should be recognised in the profit and loss account or statement of total recognised gains and losses on the purchase, sale, issue or cancellation of a company's own shares. [UITF 38 para 10(d)]. This means that the consideration received for the sale of own shares by an ESOP trust should be credited to shareholders' funds, but this raises the question as to whether a gain made by an ESOP trust is distributable by the sponsoring company. This is considered further in paragraph 12.62 above.

Trustee company

12.72 The above sections deal with the financial statements of the sponsoring company. In groups of companies, it is common for a non-trading subsidiary company to act as trustee to the ESOP. The accounting implications for the trustee company are considered in the example below.

> **Example – Subsidiary acts as corporate trustee**
>
> A group operates an employee share plan. A subsidiary of the group has been set up to act as a corporate trustee. What should the subsidiary include in its own entity financial statements?
>
> The corporate trustee for an ESOP trust normally holds legal title to the trust's assets, but if these are held on trust such that the trustee has no beneficial interest (that is, the trustee's interest is limited to its fiduciary or custodial interest) then under FRS 5 they are not its assets. Therefore, the trustee company itself does not account for the assets (and likewise, the liabilities and transactions) of the ESOP. These would be reported in the financial statements of the ESOP trust (and under UITF Abstract 38 in the financial statements of the sponsoring company and group).
>
> The trustee company may well be a dormant company with a nominal share capital. Even if the trustee company is not dormant (for instance, if it charges the trust a fee for its services), this does not change the fact that its financial statements do not normally include the transactions and balances of the trust.

Disclosures in respect of ESOP trusts

12.73 UITF Abstract 38 requires the following information to be disclosed concerning the ESOP trust:

- A description of the ESOP trust's main features, including the arrangements for distributing shares to employees.
- The amounts of reductions to shareholders' funds and the number and (for companies that have shares listed or publicly traded on a stock exchange or market) market value of shares held by the ESOP trust that have not yet vested unconditionally in employees.
- The extent to which the shares are under option to employees or have been conditionally gifted to them.

[UITF 38 para 11].

12.74 The objective of these disclosures is to enable the readers of the financial statements to understand the significance of the ESOP trust in the context of the sponsoring company. [UITF 38 para 11]. Where this is not achieved by disclosing the above information, the sponsoring company should give additional information to achieve this objective.

QUESTs and share symmetry arrangements

12.75 A QUEST (qualifying employee share ownership trust) is a trust that is often used to assume a company's obligation to deliver shares under an approved sharesave plan. Similar arrangements, often known as 'share symmetry arrangements' exist for other types of share plans (such as unapproved or discretionary plans).

12.76 Until 2003, the cost of shares issued cheaply to employees via a sharesave plan did not normally attract tax relief for a company. However, under the Finance Act 1989, a company that used a QUEST could obtain a statutory tax deduction for the difference between the market value of shares issued by the company and the option price paid by the employees of the company (or another company that it controls). Alternative structures, such as share symmetry arrangements, generally relied on case law to obtain the company's tax deduction.

12.77 The Finance Act 2003 introduced a statutory tax deduction for most employee share plans, thus reducing the attractiveness of QUESTs. Nevertheless, many companies do have such structures in place.

12.78 A QUEST may be either simultaneous or pre-funded. A simultaneous QUEST is one in which the company issues shares to the QUEST at the same time as the employees exercise their options. The QUEST immediately transfers the shares to employees to satisfy the exercised options. The company receives a tax deduction on the amount of the gift which tops up the option proceeds to the market value of the shares. The steps involved in a simultaneous QUEST are as follows:

- A UK company establishes the QUEST in accordance with the requirements of Finance Act 1989.
- The trustees of the QUEST agree to take over the UK company's liability to deliver shares under its existing sharesave options.
- The UK company grants a back-to-back option to the trustees of the QUEST to subscribe for the same number of shares, but with the exercise price being the market value at the date of exercise of the sharesave options.

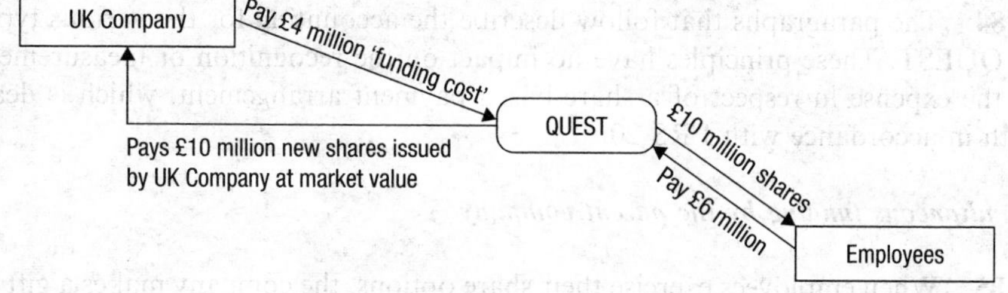

- When the employees exercise their options, they pay the exercise price to the QUEST rather than to the UK company.
- The UK company contributes the balance required to enable the QUEST to subscribe for newly issued shares at market value (the 'funding cost').
- The QUEST uses the aggregate sums to subscribe for shares at market value (that is, by exercising the back-to-back option) and immediately transfers those shares to employees.
- The UK company claims a statutory tax deduction for the funding cost.

12.79 The company should obtain a legal opinion as to whether the plan constitutes financial assistance as this can be an issue for some arrangements. This legal opinion should include advice as to whether the plan does not entail giving financial assistance, for instance, because it qualifies for exemption under section 682(2)(b) or (c) of the Companies Act 2006, as an 'employees' share scheme' (as defined in section 1166 of the Companies Act 2006).

12.80 In a pre-funded QUEST, the company provides finance to the QUEST by means of a loan to the value of the subscription monies receivable from employees when they exercise their options together with a contribution to the QUEST equal to the difference between the market price at the time of the funding and the exercise price of all outstanding sharesave options.

12.81 The QUEST would then subscribe for the shares within nine months subsequent to the year end (being the maximum period in which the QUEST must acquire the shares to allow the company to claim the tax deduction for that year).

12.82 Although this structure would result in an earlier tax cash flow advantage for the company, it may result in earlier and potentially greater share capital dilution than would have occurred in the absence of the QUEST.

12.83 Some companies use an alternative to the full pre-funding described above, where the amount of pre-funding is restricted to the difference between the market price at date of issue and the option exercise price. The QUEST then uses this funding to subscribe for shares at market price. The remaining shares are subscribed for at a later date using the proceeds from employees when the options are exercised.

12.84 The paragraphs that follow describe the accounting for the various types of QUEST. These principles have no impact on the recognition or measurement of the expense in respect of a share-based payment arrangement, which is dealt with in accordance with FRS 20.

Simultaneous funding by the parent company

12.85 When employees exercise their share options, the company makes a gift to the QUEST of an amount equal to the difference between the market value of the shares at the date of exercise and the amount receivable from the employees. The company then issues shares to the QUEST at market value at date of issue. Under UITF Abstract 38's principles, the company is regarded as the sponsoring company of the QUEST, that is, the QUEST is regarded as part of the company.

12.86 At the date the options are exercised, the company will account for the issue of shares at the amount subscribed by the QUEST, which will be their market price at that date. The company will credit share capital with the nominal value of the shares issued and credit share premium with the difference between the market value and the nominal value of the shares.

12.87 Although the transactions are initially recorded in the individual legal entity (that is, company and QUEST) books they are combined for the purpose of statutory reporting. As the QUEST is regarded as part of the company, there is no profit and loss account charge as a cost has not been incurred (that is, the gift made by the company and the gift received by the QUEST are eliminated). In accordance with UITF 38's principles, the consideration paid for the issue of the shares is deducted in arriving at shareholders' funds, namely the profit and loss reserve, while the consideration received on the exercise of the options should be credited to shareholders' funds. The net impact of these entries is that the part of the subscription price funded by the company is charged to profit and loss account reserve in the company's statutory accounts – in substance a capitalisation issue by the company reducing its distributable profits.

12.88 Consider the following example.

Example – Simultaneous QUEST funded by the company that issues shares

Number of shares under option	1,000,000
Nominal value of shares	10p
Market price of shares at date of grant	£6
Option exercise price	£6
Market price of shares at date of exercise	£10

Taxation is ignored for the purpose of this illustration.

- Employees exercise options and pay £6m to QUEST (£6 × 1m shares).
- The company pays £4m to the QUEST ((£10 – £6) × 1m shares).
- The QUEST subscribes for 1,000,000 newly issued shares in the company at the market price of £10.

The company will record share capital of £100,000 (1m shares × 10p) and share premium of £9.9m (1,000,000 shares × proceeds of £10 = £10m less nominal value of £0.1m).

The £10m consideration paid by the QUEST is deducted from equity and the £6m received from employees is credited to equity.

The overall effect is that the company's net assets are increased by the £6m cash received from employees. The effect on the company's balance sheet can be summarised as:

	£m
Net assets	
Cash	**6.0**
Capital and reserves	
Share capital	0.1
Share premium	9.9
Profit and loss account reserve	(4.0)
	6.0

If the company is the parent of a group then the treatment in the consolidated financial statements is the same as the treatment in the parent company's own financial statements.

Simultaneous funding by a subsidiary company

12.89 The above analysis deals with the situation where an individual company (or parent of a group) operates a QUEST. There are further complications in a group situation, for instance, if the payments are made by a subsidiary company. If a subsidiary company makes a payment to the QUEST for the difference between the issue price and the option price, it will be recognised as a deduction from the subsidiary's equity.

Pre-funding by the parent company

12.90 The accounting for a pre-funded QUEST follows the same principles as a simultaneous QUEST. That is, the amount paid by the QUEST on the issue of shares is deducted in arriving at the sponsoring company's shareholders' funds, while the amount received from employees on the exercise of options is credited to shareholders' funds.

12.91 An example where a QUEST is pre-funded by the company that issues the shares is considered below.

Example – QUEST fully pre-funded by company that issues the shares

Number of shares under option	1,000,000
Nominal value of shares	10p
Market price of shares at date of grant	£6
Option exercise price	£6
Market price of shares at date of issue	£10

Taxation is ignored for the purpose of this illustration.

- The company pays £10m to the QUEST comprising a loan of £6m and a gift of £4m ((£10 – £6) × 1m shares).
- The QUEST subscribes for 1,000,000 newly issued shares in the company at the market price of £10 (1m shares).
- The company will record share capital of £100,000 (1m shares × 10p) and share premium of £9.9m (1m shares × proceeds of £10 = £10m less nominal value of £0.1m).

As in the previous example, the QUEST is included in the company's financial statements and the loan from the company to the QUEST eliminates as it is intra-entity. The amount paid by the QUEST for the purchase of the shares is deducted from the sponsoring company's equity.

	Company (incorporating the QUEST)
	£m
Net assets	
Loan	–
	–
Capital and reserves	
Share capital	0.1
Share premium	9.9
Profit and loss account reserve	(10.0)
	–

When the options are exercised, the employees will pay £6m to the QUEST and the shares will be transferred in consideration. The £6m cash will be used by the QUEST to repay the loan to the company. In the sponsoring company's financial statements, £6m will be credited to equity. The overall effect is that the company's net assets are increased by the £6m cash received from employees.

If the company is the parent of a group then the treatment in the consolidated financial statements is the same as the treatment in the parent company's own financial statements.

Pre-funding by a subsidiary company

12.92 The above section deals with the situation where an individual company (or parent of a group) operates a QUEST. There are further complications in a group situation, for instance, if the payments are made by subsidiary companies. It will be necessary to determine which company is the sponsoring company of the QUEST. Normally, where the parent company sets up the QUEST and determines the arrangements then it will be regarded as the sponsoring company even if it requires its subsidiary companies to contribute funding in respect of their employees. However, there might be situations where it is considered appropriate for a subsidiary company to be regarded as the sponsoring company for the purpose of applying UITF Abstract 38 and determining which company should include the QUEST in its financial statements. This might be a situation where the QUEST is funded by a large trading subsidiary.

12.93 The treatment of payments by a subsidiary to a QUEST will depend on which company is the sponsoring company.

- Parent is the sponsoring company – where the parent is the sponsoring company, the treatment is similar to a simultaneous QUEST as described in paragraph 12.89.
- Subsidiary is the sponsoring company – the QUEST is included in the subsidiary's own financial statements. As the shares held by the QUEST are

not the subsidiary's own shares (they are its parent's shares), they should be treated as investments. This will have no impact on the recognition or measurement of the expense in respect of the share-based payment transaction, which will be accounted for in accordance with FRS 20.

Cash payments to employee trusts

12.94 Difficulties arise in regard to intermediate payment arrangements where an entity makes a payment to a trust for the benefit of the entity's employees. The trust then uses the assets accumulated from those payments to pay the entity's employees for some or all of the services rendered by the employee.

12.95 The main issue concerns where cash is paid into an employee benefit trust prior to the year end and the question arises as to whether the payment should be treated as an expense. Similar problems arise where an employee benefit trust is formed around the end of a company's accounting year. An amount is transferred into that trust after the year end and it may not be clear whether the amount should be accrued as a liability and an expense in the financial statements of the previous year. These types of arrangements did not fall precisely within FRS 17, 'Retirement benefits', so to clarify the UITF issued Abstract 32, 'Employee benefit trusts and other intermediate payment arrangement', in December 2001. This abstract applies to all intermediate payment arrangements other than those dealt with in UITF Abstract 38 or FRS 17. The abstract considers the issue of payments not only to trusts, but to other intermediaries with similar features, for example:

- Although such arrangements are most commonly used to pay employees, they are sometimes used to compensate suppliers of goods and services other than employees. Sometimes the sponsoring entity's employees and other suppliers are not the only beneficiaries of the arrangement. Other beneficiaries may include past employees and their dependants and the intermediary may be entitled to make charitable donations.
- Usually, the precise identity of the persons or entities that will receive payments from the intermediary, and the amounts that they will receive, are not agreed at the outset.
- The relationship between the sponsoring entity and the intermediary may take different forms. For example, when the intermediary is constituted as a trust, the sponsoring entity will not have a right to direct the intermediary's activities. However, in these and other cases the sponsoring entity may give advice to the intermediary or may be relied on by the intermediary to provide the information it needs to carry out its activities. Sometimes, the way the intermediary has been set up gives it little discretion in the broad nature of its activities.
- Often, the sponsoring entity has the right to appoint or veto the appointment of the intermediary's trustees (or its directors or the equivalent).

- The payments made to the intermediary and the payments made by the intermediary are often cash payments, but may involve other transfers of value.

[UITF 32 para 3].

12.96 The abstract focuses on two issues:

- Whether the sponsoring entity's payments to the trust represent an immediate expense.
- If the payments do not represent an immediate expense, what the nature and extent of the sponsoring entity's assets and liabilities are, after making the payments to the trust.

[UITF 32 para 4].

12.97 An immediate expense to the sponsoring entity will occur only if the payment neither results in the acquisition of another asset nor the settlement of a liability. As the settlement of a liability is a matter of fact, the abstract focuses on whether there is an acquisition of an asset. When determining whether an entity has an asset, FRS 5 requires that you should look beyond the transaction's structure and look at its substance. Based on this, the UITF has taken the view that when an entity transfers funds to a trust, there should be a rebuttable presumption that the sponsoring entity will obtain future economic benefit from the amounts transferred. The entity has control of the rights or other access to the future economic benefits of those amounts and hence has an asset. Consequently, the exchange of one asset for another does not lead to an immediate expense. [UITF 32 para 18].

12.98 In order to rebut the presumption, the abstract requires the sponsoring entity to demonstrate that either:

- the sponsoring entity will not obtain future economic benefit from the amounts transferred. For example, it may be that the only beneficiaries of the intermediary are registered charities or a benevolent fund that is in no way linked to amounts otherwise due from the entity; or
- the sponsoring entity does not have control of the rights or other access to the future economic benefits it is expected to receive. This will involve evidence that the payments made by the intermediary are not habitually made in a way that is in accordance with the sponsoring entity's wishes.

[UITF 32 para 10].

12.99 The abstract makes it clear that the presumption of future economic benefit would not be rebutted where payments are made by the intermediary that relieve the sponsoring entity from paying for items such as retirement benefits or benefits in kind. However, the presumption would be rebutted at the time the payment is made to the intermediary if at that time the assets transferred vest unconditionally in identified beneficiaries. [UITF 32 paras 11, 12].

12.100 In determining the nature and extent of the assets and liabilities, the UITF came to the same conclusion as it has under UITF Abstract 38, that the assets and liabilities of the trust are under *de facto* control of the sponsoring entity and hence the assets and liabilities should be accounted for as an extension of the sponsoring entity's business. When an entity recognises the assets and liabilities held by a trust on its balance sheet, it should disclose sufficient information in the notes to its financial statements to enable readers to understand any restrictions relating to those assets and liabilities. [UITF 32 para 19, 20].

12.101 Where a trust is included in the sponsoring company's financial statements, the issues as regards accruing a liability and expense are the same as if no transfer into the trust had been made.

- If, by the end of the year, the company or the trust has paid money to employees as, for example, bonuses, then those amounts would be properly charged as expenses.
- If at the end of the year, no cash has been paid (or cash has simply been transferred from the company to the trust) then in general, no liability or expense would be recorded. That is, the resources held in the company or transferred to the trust would be carried forward as an asset. This is so even though there may be restrictions as to the uses to which any assets transferred into a trust may be put. An exception arises and an expense should be recognised if:
  - an amount has been promised to employees in respect of the year in question, that is, the board has approved the amount and employees have been notified;
  - the obligation to pay employees in respect of the year in question can be inferred from an established pattern of paying bonuses (even if each one is *ex-gratia*); or
  - even if there is no established pattern, there is clear documentation that an amount is transferred after the year end, but relates to a bonus scheme for the previous year (evidence for this would be that the amounts would be paid, either directly from the company or *via* the trust, to employees, expressly as bonuses for the previous year, and paid during the first few months of the subsequent year).

12.102 The above rules are to some extent a reflection of long-standing practice, but were tightened following the introduction of FRS 12 on accounting for provisions. Some of the consequences are:

- If an amount is paid into a trust that is in practice much larger than could reasonably relate to bonuses for the first year and is likely to be used as a source for paying bonuses over a number of years or may be used in place of salary increases for the following year, then it should be treated as an expense over the years to which the service relates; not charged entirely in the first year.

- If an amount is paid into a trust and is not paid out to employees in the form of bonuses etc, but rather is loaned back to certain employees, then, subject to normal recoverability tests, the asset would remain an asset of the trust and, by virtue of UITF Abstract 38 an asset of the company/group. (If the amounts are loaned back to directors, then questions of legality under the Companies Act need to be considered).

Illustrative examples

12.103 The examples that follow illustrate UITF Abstract 32's principles in relation to payments to a trust for the benefit of the company's employees.

Example 1 – Entity pays cash into trust

The sponsoring company pays £60,000 into the trust, but no bonus is awarded at that stage to employees.

The sponsoring company has exchanged one type of asset (cash) for another asset (cash held in trust). As the trust has been set up for the benefit of the company's employees, the company has *de facto* control of the trust. Consequently, the trust's assets are included on the sponsoring company's balance sheet and there would be no charge at that stage to the profit and loss account. Disclosure of the fact that the cash is restricted would need to be given. Any subsequent bonus awarded will not be a share-based payment.

Example 2 – Entity pays cash into trust and awards bonus that vests after 3 years

The facts are the same as example 1, except that a bonus is awarded to the employees. This bonus vests unconditionally after three years provided that certain performance conditions have been met.

As for example 1, the sponsoring company will record the asset of cash paid to the trust on its balance sheet. A liability, however, will also be recorded as the sponsoring company has an obligation to transfer economic benefit in the future. The value of the liability should follow the normal FRS 12 rules and be based on the likely outcome of the performance conditions being met.

Example 3 – Entity pays cash into trust and awards bonus that vests (in part) immediately

The facts are the same as example 1, except that one third of the balance is awarded as a bonus to employees and vests immediately.

In this case, one third of the cash would be an immediate expense to the company as it relates to an award to the employees and has vested unconditionally with them. The remaining two thirds of the bonus would be treated as in example 1, that is no charge in the profit and loss account as the company has *de facto* control of the trust. Consequently, the assets of the trust are included in the sponsoring company's balance sheet.

[The next paragraph is 12.106.]

Developments

12.106 Amendments to FRS 20 (IFRS 2), 'Share-based payment — vesting conditions and cancellations' was issued by the Accounting Standards Board in December 2008 in order to maintain convergence between FRS 20 and IFRS 2. The amendment is effective for accounting periods beginning on or after 1 January 2009, with early adoption permitted. The amendment should be applied retrospectively. Application of the amendment is considered from paragraph A12.77.

12.107 Amendments to FRS 20 (IFRS 2), 'Share-based payment — Group cash-settled share-based payment transactions' was issued by the ASB in August 2009. The amendments are consistent with the IASB's amendments and, therefore, maintain the equivalence between FRS 20 and IFRS 2. Similar to IFRIC 8 and IFRIC 11, UITF 41, 'Scope of FRS 20', and UITF 44, 'Group and treasury share transactions', are withdrawn as they are incorporated into the amendments. The amendments apply retrospectively for annual periods beginning on or after 1 January 2010. Application of the amendments is considered from paragraph A12.169.

Annex

12.108 Attached is the chapter from the Manual of Accounting – IFRS for the UK that deals with accounting for share-based payment under IFRS 2. As the requirements of FRS 20 are almost identical to the requirements of IFRS 2, the accounting for share-based payment and related issues will be the same under UK GAAP as under IFRS. However, there are exceptions to this principle, particularly where the UITF has issued a consensus dealing with particular issues in a UK context. Hence, the following sections of the IFRS 2 chapter are not relevant to a consideration of UK GAAP.

- Social security (national insurance) contributions on share option gains. [Para 12.222].
- Employee share ownership plans. [Para 12.235].
- Impact on distributable profits. [Para 12.324].

Annex

Share-based payment

Introduction

A12.1 For some years, many companies have used share option plans for the purpose of employee remuneration, either as a management incentive or through employee share purchase plans that are available to all employees. A more recent development is the increasing use of share awards, either through annual bonuses or long-term incentive plans (LTIPs) as an alternative, or in addition to share option plans. In such plans the amount of the award is normally based on performance criteria; if these criteria are partially achieved, but not met in full, participants may be entitled to a proportion of the full award. Often, the shares are awarded to employees at nominal value or at nil cost (for instance, where an employee share ownership plan (ESOP) subscribes for shares at nominal value).

A12.2 In addition to the employee context, share-based payments are also used as a method by which entities procure other goods or services.

A12.3 IFRS 2, 'Share-based payment', applies to accounting periods beginning on or after 1 January 2005. The requirements for first-time adoption are considered in detail in chapter 3.

[The next paragraph is A12.7.]

Objective and scope

A12.7 The stated objective of IFRS 2 is *"to specify the financial reporting by an entity when it undertakes a share-based payment transaction. In particular, it requires an entity to reflect in its profit or loss and financial position the effects of share-based payment transactions, including expenses associated with transactions in which share options are granted to employees"*. [IFRS 2 para 1]. Behind this objective is the IASB's strongly held view that an entity should recognise all goods or services it obtains, regardless of the form of consideration. Where goods or services are obtained for cash or other financial assets, the accounting is generally straightforward. IFRS 2 starts from the premise that goods or services obtained in a share-based payment transaction should be recognised and measured in a similar way.

A12.8 IFRS 2 applies to all share-based payment arrangements. A share-based payment arrangement is defined as:

> *"an agreement between the entity (or another group entity or any shareholder of any group entity) and another party (including an employee) that entitles the other party to receive:*
>
> *(a) cash or other assets of the entity for amounts that are based on the price (or value) of equity instruments (including shares or share options) of the entity or another group entity, or*
>
> *(b) equity instruments (including shares or share options) of the entity or another group entity,*
>
> *provided the specified vesting conditions, if any, are met."* [IFRS 2 App A].

A12.9 Therefore, the requirements of IFRS 2 apply to any transaction in which an entity receives goods or services in exchange for a transfer of its own equity instruments, even if that transfer is made by an existing shareholder rather than by the entity itself. Only when a transfer is clearly for a purpose other than payment for goods or services would it be outside IFRS 2's scope. Furthermore as mentioned above, IFRS 2 will apply where goods or services are obtained by an entity in exchange for equity instruments of its parent or another member of the group. [IFRS 2 para 3A]. Group situations are considered further from paragraph A12.169.

A12.10 The standard applies to all share-based payment transactions whether or not the entity can identify specifically some or all of the goods or services received, including:

- *Equity-settled share-based payment transactions* – Share-based payment transactions in which the entity (a) receives goods or services as consideration for its own equity instruments (including shares or share options), or (b) receives goods or services but has no obligation to settle the transaction with the supplier. Such transactions include employee share option and share incentive plans.
- *Cash-settled share-based payment transactions* – Transactions in which the entity acquires goods or services by incurring a liability to transfer cash or other assets to the supplier of those goods or services for amounts that are based on the price (or value) of equity instruments (including shares or share options) of the entity or another group entity. Typical examples include 'phantom' options plans, share appreciation rights and certain long-term incentive awards.
- Transactions in which the entity receives or acquires goods or services and the terms of the arrangement provide either the entity or the supplier of those goods or services with a *choice* of whether the entity settles the transaction in cash (or other assets) or by issuing equity instruments.

[IFRS 2 para 2].

A12.11 There is no exemption from IFRS 2's scope for employee share purchase plans or similar broad-based employee share plans. In drafting IFRS 2, the IASB did consider including an exemption for plans similar to employee share purchase plans (such as save as you earn ('SAYE') plans in the UK and employee share ownership plans ('ESOPs') in the US) and other broad-based employee share plans. However, they concluded that the accounting for such plans should be no different from other employee share plans. The IASB also rejected the suggestion that plans should be exempted if the discount available to employees is small so that its impact is likely to be immaterial.

[The next paragraph is A12.18.]

A12.18 Associates and joint ventures are more complicated. For example, in situations where employees of a joint venture are granted the right to equity instruments over one or both joint venturer's equity instruments, such a transaction in the joint venture would be outside IFRS 2's scope. This is because the joint venture is not part of a group as defined by IAS 27, 'Consolidated and separate financial statements' (superseded by IFRS 10 'Consolidated financial statements'). Although the shareholders of the joint venture are transferring equity instruments in exchange for employee services to the joint venture, the fact that the equity instruments are not those of the joint venture or another entity in the same group as the joint venture means the awards are not in the scope of IFRS 2 in the financial statements of the joint venture. [IFRS 2 para 3A]. The position for associates is the same. Note that investors would be within IFRS 2's scope for their own financial statements as they are indeed issuing their own equity in return for services (see further para A12.61).

A12.19 In the situation described in the previous paragraph, the associate or joint venture entity would need to apply the hierarchy within IAS 8, 'Accounting policies, changes in accounting estimates and errors', to determine the appropriate accounting treatment, and apply the principles of IAS 8 paragraph 11. In such a situation, the entity is likely to determine that either IFRS 2 or IAS 19, 'Employee benefits', (refer to chapter 11) is the most appropriate standard. This would be a policy choice that the entity would make under IAS 8, and would have to be applied consistently. It is our view that the most appropriate treatment is to apply the principles of IFRS 2 to employee benefits that are settled in equity (our view is explained further in example 4, para A12.21 below). See from paragraph A12.169 for details of how to apply IFRS 2 in this situation.

A12.20 There are few exclusions from IFRS 2's scope, namely:

- Business combinations in the acquirer's financial statements to which IFRS 3, 'Business combinations', applies, notwithstanding the fact that such a transaction may be equity-settled. However, equity instruments granted to employees of the acquiree in their capacity as employees (for example, to encourage them to remain in the employment of the acquiree after the acquisition) do fall within the scope of IFRS 2. [IFRS 2 para 5]. Similarly, the cancellation, replacement or modification of existing share-based payment arrangements as result of a business combination should be accounted for in accordance with IFRS 2. See from paragraph A12.25 for further discussion of business combinations.

- Contributions of a business on formation of a joint venture and combinations of businesses or entities under common control. This is illustrated from paragraph A12.25.
- Contracts for the purchase of goods, such as commodities, other than to satisfy the reporting entity's expected purchase or usage requirements and to which IAS 32, 'Financial instruments: Presentation', and IAS 39, 'Financial instruments: Recognition and measurement', apply. [IFRS 2 para 6]. This is illustrated in example 1 of paragraph A12.22 below.

Transactions within the scope of IFRS 2

A12.21 Further examples of transactions within IFRS 2's scope are set out below.

Example 1 – Purchase of non-financial item expected to be used by the entity

Entity A enters into a contract to purchase silver for use in its jewellery manufacturing business, whereby it is required to pay cash to the supplier in an amount equal to the value of 1,000 shares of entity A at the date the silver is delivered. This meets the definition of a cash-settled share-based payment transaction (entity A has acquired goods in exchange for a payment the amount of which will be based on the value of its shares).

IAS 32, 'Financial instruments: presentation', and IAS 39, 'Financial instruments: recognition and measurement', apply to those contracts to buy or sell a non-financial item that can be settled net in cash or another financial instrument, or by exchanging financial instruments, as if the contracts were financial instruments, with the exception of contracts that were entered into and continue to be held for the purpose of the receipt or delivery of the non-financial item in accordance with the entity's expected purchase, sale or usage requirements. [IAS 32 para 8; IAS 39 para 5]. Regardless of whether this contract may be settled net, as it was entered into for the purpose of taking delivery of the silver for use in entity A's business and entity A has a history of doing this, it does not fall within the scope of IASs 32 and 39. Hence, it does fall within the scope of IFRS 2 as a cash-settled share-based payment transaction.

Example 2 – Definition of goods or services

Entity B is developing a new product and purchased a patent from entity C. The parties agreed a purchase price of 1,000 of entity B's shares. These will be issued to entity C within 60 days of finalising the legal documentation that transfers the patent from entity C to entity B.

This is an equity-settled share-based payment. IFRS 2 is applicable to a share-based payment for a patent. The goods to which IFRS 2 applies include inventories, consumables, property, plant and equipment, intangible assets and other non-financial assets.

Example 3 – Business combination and continued employee service

Entity D acquires 90% of the share capital of entity E. As part of the acquisition, entity D grants entity E's employees share options that vest after 2 years.

In this transaction, equity instruments are granted to employees of the acquiree in their capacity as employees and so fall within IFRS 2's scope. [IFRS 2 para 5].

Example 4 – Award of parent entity shares by a shareholder

An individual with a 40% shareholding in entity F awards 2% of his shareholding in entity F to a director of entity F's subsidiary, entity G.

The award is within IFRS 2's scope. A shareholder of entity F has transferred equity instruments of entity F (entity G's parent) to a party that has supplied services to the entity. [IFRS 2 para 3A]. The award will be reflected in both entity G's financial statements and entity F's consolidated financial statements.

Example 5 – Services paid for by issuing warrants

During the year, entity K's bank provided services to entity K; entity K agreed to issue warrants to the bank as consideration for this service. The warrants have a fixed subscription price and entity K will settle the warrants in equity – that is, if the bank chooses to exercise the warrants, it will receive one entity K share for each warrant held in return for paying the fixed subscription price.

Entity K has received services as consideration for issuing equity instruments of entity K. This is an equity settled share-based payment, which should be accounted for in accordance with IFRS 2.

Example 6 – Formation of a joint venture

Entities X and Y have formed an incorporated joint venture, entity Z. On formation, in exchange for their equity interests in Z, entity X contributed property, plant and equipment and entity Y contributed intangible assets that do not constitute a business.

The asset contributions by venturers X and Y upon entity Z's formation are equity-settled share-based payment transactions from Z's perspective and fall within IFRS 2's scope. The scope exclusion of paragraph 5 of IFRS 2 does not apply, as the formation of a joint venture does not meet the definition of a business combination and X and Y contributed assets not businesses. See further example 2 in paragraph A12.25 below, where the formation of a joint venture is determined to fall within the scope exclusion because two separate entities are being contributed to the formation of the joint venture. See further chapter 28.

Transactions outside the scope of IFRS 2

A12.22 The following are examples of transactions that are outside the scope of IFRS 2.

Example 1 – Commodity contracts

Entity H enters into a contract to purchase 100 tonnes of cocoa beans. The purchase price will be settled in cash at an amount equal to the value of 1,000 of entity H's shares. However, the entity may settle the contract at any time by paying an amount equal to the current market value of 1,000 of its shares less the market value of 100 tonnes of cocoa beans. The entity has entered into the contract as part of its hedging strategy and has no intention of taking physical delivery of the cocoa beans.

As in example 1 in paragraph A12.21 above, the transaction meets the definition of a cash-settled share-based payment transaction (entity H has acquired goods in exchange for a payment of which the amount will be based on the value of its shares). However, unlike example 1 in paragraph A12.21, the contract may be settled net and has not been entered into in order to satisfy entity H's expected purchase, sale or usage requirements. Accordingly, the transaction is outside IFRS 2's scope and is instead dealt with in accordance with the requirements of IASs 32 and 39. See further the Manual of Accounting – Financial instruments.

Example 2 – Cash payments dependent on earnings multiple

A non-quoted entity issued share appreciation rights (SARs) to its employees. The SARs entitle the employees to a payment equal to any increase in the entity's share price between the grant date and the vesting date. The arrangement's terms and conditions define the share price used to calculate payments to employees as five times EBITDA divided by the number of shares in issue.

IFRS 2 is unlikely to be applicable to this transaction because a fixed multiple of EBITDA is not likely to reflect the fair value of the entity's share price. If it does not, management should apply IAS 19 to this deferred compensation arrangement.

Example 3 – Plan investing in other entity shares

Entity I is implementing an unusual share option incentive plan. Entity I will lend C1m to an employee share trust, which will purchase shares in a number of publicly listed companies (but not in entity I). These companies may be suppliers, customers or competitors. Entity I's employees are granted options over 'units' held by the employee share trust. The units are an amalgam of the shares held by the trust. The options are granted at market value at the date of the grant and held over a three year period. When employees exercise their option over the units, they are paid the difference in cash between the market price of the units at the date of the grant (the exercise price) and the market value at the date of exercise. To fund the cash payment the trust sells the shares relating to the exercised units. It then repays the relevant portion of the loan from entity I and also pays the gain to employees (this assumes the price of the underlying investments has increased in value following the grant).

This transaction is outside IFRS 2's scope as the rights are over shares of companies other than the reporting entity, or companies within the entity's group.

Accounting for the changes in value of the assets in the trust will depend on how the assets are classified. If they fall into the definition of a plan asset under paragraph 7 of IAS 19 then they should be accounted for in line with IAS 19. Otherwise, the assets will be included in the consolidated accounts and should be treated as available-for-sale financial assets in line with IAS 39. The related liability will be within IAS 19's scope. See further chapter 11.

Accounting for employee share option plans (ESOPs) is considered in detail from paragraph A12.241.

Example 4 – Share options in a joint venture

Entity J is a 50:50 joint venture between entities K and L. Entity K grants senior employees of entity J options over its own shares without making any charge to entity J. Entity L does not provide any contribution to the joint venture to compensate entity K. Entity K applies the equity method to investments in joint ventures in its consolidated financial statements and the cost method in its separate financial statements.

Entity J's financial statements

IFRS 2 includes within its scope transfers of equity instruments of an entity's parent or of an entity in the same group in return for goods or services. [IFRS 2 para 3A]. However, entity K is a joint venture investor and is not entity J's parent, nor is it in the same group (defined in IAS 27 or superseded by IFRS 10 as being 'a parent and all its subsidiaries') as entity J. Therefore, on initial consideration, from entity J's perspective, the award in entity J of share options in entity K is not within IFRS 2's scope.

The arrangement also falls outside IAS 19's scope. IAS 19 applies to all employee benefits, but defines those as *"all forms of consideration given by an entity in exchange for service rendered by employees"*. Because no consideration is given by entity J, this does not meet the definition of an employee benefit.

However, IAS 8 requires entities to apply a hierarchy when determining their accounting policies. Where there is no IFRS governing a transaction, IAS 8 requires management to look first to any IFRS standard or interpretation dealing with similar or related issues. Paragraph 10 of IAS 8 states that in the absence of a standard or interpretation that specifically applies to a transaction, *"management shall use its judgment in developing and applying an accounting policy"*. Furthermore, paragraph 11 of the standard clarifies that in making such a judgement, management should consider "*the requirements and guidance in standards and interpretations dealing with similar and related issues*". While it is not a formal requirement, it is our view that the most appropriate treatment will be for entity J to apply the principles of IFRS 2 to this equity-settled share-based payment. This is further supported by the treatment where a parent entity grants options over its own shares to those of its subsidiary. In this case, while entity K does not meet the definition of a parent company, in the absence of any other guidance, this is an acceptable approach. (See further para A12.169.)

The disclosure requirements of IAS 24, 'Related party disclosures', should be applied by entity J if any of the employees are key management personnel. See further chapter 29.

Note that if compensation was, however, given by entity J for the share-based payment, perhaps in the form of a recharge payment required by entity K, then the transaction would be within IAS 19's scope.

Entity K's financial statements

Entity K has an equity-settled share-based payment arrangement and should measure the goods and services received in accordance with IFRS 2 as appropriate. Thus, in its separate financial statements, entity K would capitalise the IFRS 2 grant date fair value into its cost of the investment in the joint venture and consider whether there were any impairment indicators.

Entity K's consolidated financial statements should apply the principles of IAS 31 (or superseded by IAS 28 (revised)). To the extent that entity J has accounted for the share-based payment, 50% of this would be recorded by entity K when the equity method is applied. In addition, since entity L did not provide an equivalent contribution into the joint venture, entity K would record an additional cost resulting in its consolidated financial statements recording 100% of the share-based payment charge.

Entity L's financial statements

Other than the fact that entity L will need to account for its joint venture in entity J, there will be no impact on entity L's separate financial statements. To the extent that entity J has accounted for the share-based payment the proportional share (that is, 50%) of the charge that is recorded by entity L on consolidation would be eliminated against the gain recorded on application of paragraph 48 of IAS 31 (or paragraph 28 of IAS 28 (revised)), hence, there is no impact on consolidation.

A12.23 In some cases, the number of equity instruments to which a counterparty is entitled varies. For example, share appreciation rights may be settled in shares such that the number of shares issued to employees varies according to the appreciation of the employer's share price over a period of time. If the requirements of IAS 32 were applied to transactions such as these, an obligation to issue equity instruments would be classified as a liability (a variable number of shares issued for a fixed amount – see further Manual of Accounting – Financial instruments). This would have implications for the basis of measurement of the transaction as discussed later in this chapter. For example, equity-settled transactions involving employees are measured at the date on which awards are granted and are not re-measured, whereas liabilities in respect of cash-settled transactions are re-measured at each balance sheet date. The IASB concluded that different considerations applied in developing IFRS 2 and the standard inserts an amendment to IAS 32 that exempts from its scope any transactions to which IFRS 2 applies (except as discussed in para A12.20 above). [IAS 32 para 4(f)].

A12.24 The following examples consider some practical issues when determining whether a transaction is within the scope of IFRS 2.

Example 1 – Bonus with past history of cash settlement

An entity agrees to pay its employees a bonus. The entity has a choice of settlement, either cash or shares with a value equivalent to the value of cash payment. The entity has a past practice of settling in cash and is considering whether the transaction should be accounted for under IFRS 2.

It could be argued that by applying the principles of IAS 32, shares issued for a fixed amount would be accounted for as a liability and, hence, this type of award should be in the scope of IAS 19 and not IFRS 2. However, as the entity has a *choice* that allows it to settle the award using equity instruments or cash (and, therefore, could issue equity instruments), the transaction is a share-based payment with a settlement choice (see further from para A12.162). [IFRS 2 para 2c].

Example 2 – Variable number of shares for goods

Entity A signed a contract with a construction entity to acquire a new building for C1m with ownership transferring to entity A when the construction work is complete. The purchase price will be settled by entity A issuing a variable number of its own shares with a total market value of C1m.

As the purchase price is being settled in shares, the transaction is within IFRS 2's scope and is excluded from the scope of IAS 32.

Example 3 – Non-recourse loan enabling counterparty to purchase shares

An entity lends C100 to an employee to purchase the entity's shares from the market. The loan is interest free and only has recourse to the shares. Dividends paid on the shares must be used to reduce the loan. The employee must pay back the balance of the loan, or return the shares at the earlier of three years or resignation.

In November 2005, the IFRS IC confirmed that this transaction would fall within the scope of IFRS 2. The IFRS IC stated that the loan is considered to be part of a share-based payment transaction, which in substance is an option with a three year exercise window where the exercise price is reduced by any dividends. The employee is not exposed to any downside risk in the movement of the share price over the three year period as he/she can repay the loan or surrender the shares. The 'loan' is, therefore, recognised as a debit in equity. The option would be exercised on the date the loan is repaid. In this example the option would vest immediately as the employee could leave on day one, repay the loan and be fully entitled to the shares. Vesting conditions are considered in detail from paragraph A12.77.

Example 4 – Full recourse loan enabling counterparty to purchase shares

The facts are the same as example 3 above, except the entity has recourse to personal assets of the employee as well as the shares. This means that if the employee fails to repay the loan, the entity has the ability to take possession of the employees personal assets such as their car, house, etc.

The employee is unconditionally bound to repay the loan. The entity should record a receivable for the loan balance. Since the terms of the loan with the company are such that a preferential interest rate has been given to employees, a fair value adjustment to the loan balance should be recognised (under IAS 39, 'Financial instruments: Recognition and measurement') as an employee remuneration expense over an appropriate service period in accordance with IAS 19, 'Employee benefits'. This is because the fair value of the loan has been reduced through a preferential rate and a benefit has been provided to the employee.

Full recourse loans with employees are rare in practice. Before an entity determines that they have granted a full recourse loan to employees, the following factors should be considered to determine if the loan is, in substance, non-recourse:

- The employer has legal recourse to the employee's other assets but does not intend to seek repayment beyond the shares issued.
- The employer has a history of not demanding repayment of loan amounts in excess of the fair value of the shares.
- The employee does not have sufficient assets or other means (beyond the shares) to justify the recourse nature of the loan.
- The employer has accepted a recourse note upon exercise and subsequently converted the recourse note to a non-recourse note.

Business combinations, private equity deals and sweet equity

Business combinations

A12.25 The scope exclusion in respect of business combinations concerns those combinations as defined by IFRS 3 'Business combinations'. IFRS 3 defines a business combination as, *"A transaction or other event in which an acquirer obtains control of one or more businesses. Transactions sometimes referred to as 'true mergers' or 'mergers of equals' are also business combinations as that term is used in this IFRS."* [IFRS 3 App A]. In addition to business combinations as defined by IFRS 3, contributions of a business on formation of a joint venture and combinations of businesses or entities under common control are excluded from IFRS 2's scope, as explained in paragraph A12.20 above. This is illustrated in the examples below. Business combinations are considered further in chapter 25.

Example 1 – Common control transactions

A business combination occurs between two entities that are under common control. The transaction is outside IFRS 3's scope.

The primary purpose of the issue of shares in such a common control transaction is likely to be to reorganise the legal or managerial structure of a business or to transfer a business, rather than to acquire goods or services. The shares are issued in exchange for a business that is an integrated set of activities and assets that is capable of being conducted and managed for the purpose of providing a return to investors, or lower costs or other economic benefits directly to investors or other owners, members or participants. [IFRS 3 App A]. As such, the transaction is outside IFRS 2's scope. See further guidance on accounting for a business combination between entities under common control in chapter 25.

Example 2 – Formation of a joint venture

Entity A and entity B are brought together to form a joint venture.

The formation of a joint venture is outside the scope of IFRS 3 (see further example 6 in para A12.21 above). This transaction does not meet the definition of a business combination because two separate entities are being brought together into one reporting entity without either entity gaining control; therefore, the scope exclusion in paragraph 5 of IFRS 2 would apply.

The combination of separate businesses to form a joint venture involves the issue of shares for the purpose of forming a joint venture, not the acquisition of goods or services. As such, the transaction is outside IFRS 2's scope. See further guidance on accounting for joint ventures in chapter 28.

[The next paragraph is A12.30.]

A12.30 IFRS 3 states that if the accounting acquiree is not a business then it is not in the scope of IFRS 3. In some circumstances, for example for a reverse acquisition, it is not always clear whether a business has been acquired and, therefore, the substance of the arrangement should be considered. This is illustrated in the following example.

Example – Reverse acquisition into a shell company

Entity V, a listed entity that does not constitute a business at the time of the transaction, issues shares in exchange for shares in entity W. Although entity V becomes entity W's legal parent, the transaction is not a business combination under IFRS 3, because entity V is not a business and has not gained control over entity W in substance.

IFRS 2 scopes out transactions in which an entity acquires goods as part of the net assets acquired in a business combination as defined in IFRS 3.

We believe that the transaction is within IFRS 2's scope because the substance is that shareholders of private entity W have given shareholders of public entity V an interest in entity W in exchange for any assets sitting within entity V and entity V's listing. Accordingly, entity W should fair value the consideration that entity V's shareholders receive (the shares given out by entity W's shareholders) and the identifiable assets of entity V that entity W's shareholders acquired. Any resulting difference would be unidentifiable goods or services which should be expensed (unless it meets the definition of an asset under other standards). Appropriate disclosure to explain the accounting policy is necessary. See further chapter 25 for a more detailed example.

Transactions with employees and transactions with shareholders

A12.31 Transactions with employees in their capacity as holders of equity instruments are also outside IFRS 2's scope. [IFRS 2 para 4]. For example, if an entity makes a bonus issue of shares to all of its shareholders, and these include certain of the entity's employees, this will not represent a share-based payment transaction to be dealt with in accordance with IFRS 2. However, there could be a situation where an employee invests in an entity which is working towards a stock market listing or a trade sale. In these cases there could be a venture capital entity or similar investor involved in the transaction and the employee will subscribe for the shares at the same amount as the other investors. The issue is whether the employee is acting as a shareholder or an employee. Often the interested parties (including directors, management and other shareholders) have acquired shares for a 'fair' value, which may not equate to grant date fair value for the purposes of IFRS 2 and would typically be tax driven. It is important to note that a fair value determined for tax purposes often reflects factors which it would not be appropriate to allow for under IFRS 2 (that is, lack of marketability) and, therefore, may be lower than the IFRS 2 grant date fair value.

A12.32 It could be that there are no conditions or incentives attached to the acquired shares and, therefore, the employee is purely acting as a shareholder. However, in the majority of situations there are likely to be service conditions or leaver provisions such that the arrangement would be accounted for as a share-based payment transaction under IFRS 2. The shares in question are often referred to as 'sweet' or 'sweat' equity depending on whether they are offered at an advantageous price or in return for services rather than cash.

Example 1 – Employees acting in capacity as shareholders

Entity A made a rights issue to all of its shareholders, entitling them to purchase one new share for each five shares owned at a price of C10. The shareholders include 20 people who are also employees. No other conditions are attached to the rights issue.

In this example, shares are being issued to employees in their capacity as shareholders, and not in exchange for their services. Furthermore, the employees are not required to complete a period of service in exchange for the new shares. As such the transaction is outside IFRS 2's scope.

Example 2 – Capital contribution of a building in settlement of a rights issue

Entity B made a rights issue to all shareholders. Shareholders are entitled to acquire one new share for each share owned at a fixed price of C4 at the date of the rights issue. Entity C owns 1 million of entity B's shares, that is, 10% of the share capital. Entity C subscribed to 1 million of entity B's new shares. Following the subscription, entity C proposed to entity B to settle the purchase price of the new shares by transferring an office building it owns to entity B. Entity B agreed to accept the building as settlement for the new shares.

IFRS 2 is not applicable to this transaction because it is a rights issue to all shareholders. The method of payment is irrelevant as this is a transaction with shareholders in their capacity as shareholders; the transfer of the building is, therefore, outside IFRS 2's scope. The subscription established a right to receive a fixed payment of C4m from entity C. The transfer of the building was agreed after the receivable was established and is in settlement of the C4m receivable.

Example 3 – In-kind capital contribution by existing shareholder

Entity D needs a new office building and has arranged to acquire it from an existing shareholder. The purchase price will be settled by the entity issuing 1,000 new shares. For legal purposes, the transaction is considered an in-kind capital contribution of a building.

> The counterparty did not act in its capacity as shareholder, but as a supplier of the office building. As such, the in-kind capital contribution is within IFRS 2's scope. This would mean that the office building is recognised at its fair value with equity being credited by the same amount for the share issue.

A12.33 There are a number of issues that need to be considered before reaching a conclusion that transactions with employees are not within the IFRS 2's scope including:

- Whether the instrument that the employees are entitled to is an equity instrument or linked to an equity instrument, as defined by the standard. [IFRS 2 App A]. If the instrument is an equity instrument or linked to an equity instrument and the value varies depending on the extent to which the employee provides services the transaction would be within IFRS 2's scope as a share-based payment.
- Whether the rights/interests of employee shareholders differ from those of other investor shareholders (for example, venture capitalists). Employees may have the right to additional shares with other investor shareholders giving up their rights – a ratchet mechanism. This ratchet usually depends on the business' performance and hence employees get more shares if the business does well. This would qualify as a performance condition, as services from employees contribute towards the company meeting the performance targets and, hence, the transaction is within IFRS 2's scope.
- Whether holders have different rights following an exit event. Through the articles, employees may be given different rights (cash or shares) if an investor exits through an IPO rather than trade sale. This provides evidence of a performance condition (achieving different rights to cash or shares depending on the exit event that occurs) which could scope the arrangement into IFRS 2.
- Leaver conditions (the articles or terms and conditions may define good leavers and bad leavers). In this situation the employees may lose their right to shares by leaving the entity, either by the shares being repurchased or cancelled. Hence, employees may only earn their right to the shares if they stay with the company or, for example, in the event of an IPO. This would also be considered a service condition and, hence, the arrangement is in IFRS 2's scope.
- Whether additional services are being provided. As noted above, employees will often lose their rights to shares if they leave the company. There is often a service requirement, for example, to stay in employment for a number of years or until a change in control. However, this may not always be the case and some employees may have the right to shares whether they stay or leave. This does not automatically scope the arrangement out of IFRS 2, because the entity would still need to determine whether additional services (whether or not they are identifiable) are being provided by the shareholders in their capacity as employees, by reference to the fair value of the shares at the date of grant (refer to para A12.61 onwards). [IFRS 2 para 2].

- Whether a trust is involved in the arrangement. The existence of an employee benefit trust to buy back and warehouse shares for the benefit of other employees could well imply that shares are being issued as an incentive and, hence, the arrangement is in IFRS 2's scope.

The above list is not exhaustive. However, it highlights some of the areas that should be considered in order to determine if the transaction is within IFRS 2's scope.

Example – Purchase of shares at fair value, with service condition

A CEO is offered the opportunity to buy 100,000 shares in entity A at C1 each, the same price paid by the venture capital investor that holds 40% of entity A's shares. If the CEO resigns within two years he must give the shares back to the entity in return for a payment of the lower of his subscription price and the fair value of the shares.

This transaction is in IFRS 2's scope as in purchasing the shares the CEO accepts a service condition that must be satisfied before he is fully entitled to the risks and rewards of the shares (that is, there is a vesting period of two years).

The CEO might be paying IFRS 2 grant date fair value for the shares on grant date (C1), in which case, provided the award was equity-settled this would result in no IFRS 2 charge. However, since the arrangement is within the scope of IFRS 2, consideration should be given to disclosures prescribed in IFRS 2 (see further para A12.257) and IAS 24 (see further para A12.274).

Leaver provisions

A12.34 Some share-based payment arrangements include good and bad leaver provisions. A good leaver is often defined as an individual who leaves the entity due to injury, disability, death, redundancy or on reaching normal retirement age. A bad leaver is usually defined as any other leaver. The following example considers the scope implications in relation to typical leaver provisions.

Example – Exit event with good and bad leavers

Entity A's directors have been given an incentive in the form of share options that will vest when an exit event occurs (the entity is unlisted). Each director has paid an upfront exercise price of C10 per share and will become unconditionally entitled to shares in the entity if he or she is still in service when an exit event occurs.

'Exit event' is defined in the plan's terms and conditions as a trade sale, a listing or other change in control. An exit event is expected to occur in the form of a trade sale in three years' time.

The terms and conditions also set out provisions for good and bad leavers. For every share option held, a 'bad leaver' will receive cash equal to the lower of the amount paid (C10) and the market value of the share (market value will be determined by independent valuation consultants). A 'good leaver' will receive cash equal to the higher of the amount paid and the market value in respect of each share option held.

As any director can choose to leave the entity at any time triggering a contractual 'bad leaver' cash payment that the entity cannot avoid, entity A has a liability in respect of all directors as part of the share-based payment arrangement, that is, for the total number of share options granted. The liability will be measured at the lower of C10 per share and the market value of the share. The payments by the directors are in effect an advance payment of an exercise price due when the awards vest.

In addition to the bad leaver liability, the arrangement in respect of good leavers and directors who are still in service at the time of the trade sale falls within the scope of IFRS 2.

The fair value of share options (which will be incremental to the amount that has already been provided in case each individual becomes a bad leaver) awarded to any director expected to be a good leaver before the exit event occurs will be treated as a cash-settled share-based payment (see from para A12.98 in relation to non-market vesting conditions).

The fair value of share options that are expected to vest as a result of the trade sale will be treated as an equity-settled share-based payment (this will be incremental to the amount that has already been provided in case each individual becomes a bad leaver and will not include amounts in respect of any individual who is expected to become a good leaver before the exit event). Note that if the share options do vest as a result of the trade sale, the bad and good leaver liability in respect of each individual for whom the award vests will be transferred into equity.

Drag along and tag along clauses

A12.35 Some arrangements include 'drag along' and 'tag along' clauses. For example, if an existing majority shareholder chooses to sell his investment in an entity, a drag along clause in an arrangement's terms and conditions may state that the shareholder can force employee shareholders or share option holders to sell their holdings at the same price/date. Alternatively, in the event of a sale of an entity, a tag along clause may allow employees to force an acquirer to purchase their holdings at the same price/date.

Example – Settlement by an acquirer in cash

Entity A grants its employees restricted shares. The articles state that the shares will remain restricted until entity A is acquired. At the date that the entity is acquired, a drag along clause will be invoked such that the employees will be required to sell their shares to the acquirer.

In entity A's financial statements, the award of restricted shares is an equity-settled share-based payment under IFRS 2 because the entity will settle the award in shares. Although the employees can only receive cash for their shares, the cash will be paid by the acquirer to the employees as shareholders. Under no circumstances will entity A be required to settle in cash.

A12.36 In some situations, the acquirer may, in substance, initiate the cash payment by the acquiree or may reimburse the acquiree for any cash payment.

Further discussion of this and the interaction between IFRS 2 and IFRS 3, including in relation to the treatment of acquiree awards on an acquisition and the accounting in the acquirer's books, is provided in chapter 25.

[The next paragraph is A12.38.]

Recognition of share-based payment transactions

A12.38 The goods or services acquired in a share-based payment transaction should be recognised, either as an expense or as an increase in assets, when they are received. [IFRS 2 paras 7, 8].

A12.39 This is the aspect of IFRS 2 that has caused most controversy, primarily in respect of employee share and share option plans. Many respondents to ED 2, and the discussion paper before IFRS 2, argued that it was wrong to recognise an expense in respect of such plans, raising a number of conceptual and practical concerns. For example:

- The effect of an employee share transaction is that existing shareholders transfer some of their ownership interests to employees. Hence, the reporting entity is not involved in the transaction.
- Employees do not provide services in consideration for an award of shares or options. They are instead rewarded in cash.
- There is no cost to the entity in an equity-settled transaction as there is no transfer of cash or other assets. Furthermore, an expense recognised in respect of an equity-settled transaction would not be consistent with the IASB's 'Framework for the preparation and presentation of financial statements', which states in paragraph 70 that *"expenses are decreases in economic benefits during the accounting period in the form of outflows or depletions of assets or incurrences of liabilities that result in decreases in equity, other than those relating to distributions to equity participants"*. It is argued that as there is no outflow or depletion of assets, there can be no expense.
- By reducing earnings and increasing the number of shares (or potential shares) in issue, the impact of an equity-settled transaction is to 'hit' earnings per share twice.
- The expense in respect of an employee share or share option plan cannot be measured reliably.
- To require recognition (or greater recognition) of expenses in respect of employee share and share option plans could have adverse economic consequences as it might discourage entities from introducing or continuing with such plans.

A12.40 The basis for conclusions section of IFRS 2 discusses these concerns in detail. The rationale for recognising all types of equity-settled share-based payment transactions, irrespective of whether the equity instrument is a share or a share option, and irrespective of whether the equity instrument is granted to an employee or to some other party, is that the entity has engaged in a transaction that is in essence the same as any other issue of equity instruments. In other words, the entity has received resources (goods or services) as consideration for equity instruments. It should, therefore, account for the inflow of resources (goods or services) and the increase in equity. Subsequently, either at the time of receipt of the goods or services or at some later date, the entity should also account for the expense arising from the consumption of those resources. Hence, the issue of equity instruments and the consumption of resources are to be considered separately. The former results in an increase in equity while the latter is reflected as an expense.

Timing of recognition and vesting period

A12.41 As noted above, the goods or services acquired in a share-based payment transaction should be recognised when they are received. Typically it will be a question of fact as to when this occurs. However, sometimes, as in the case of employee services, this will be less obvious. For example, a company may grant share options to its employees. Certain performance conditions need to be satisfied over, say, the next three years for the options to be exercisable and even then they may only be exercised after a further year has elapsed and the employee forfeits the options if he leaves prior to exercise. Should an expense be recognised when the award is granted, over the three-year performance period or over the longer period until the options vest (that is, the employees become unconditionally entitled to exercise the options)?

A12.42 IFRS 2 concludes that where equity instruments, such as options awarded to employees, vest immediately, in the absence of evidence to the contrary, an entity should presume that they represent consideration for services already rendered. Accordingly, the entity should recognise the employee services received in full on the date on which the options are granted. [IFRS 2 para 14].

A12.43 On the other hand, if the options do not vest until the employees have completed a specified period of service, the entity should presume that services are to be rendered over that period. [IFRS 2 para 15]. This is referred to as the vesting period. IFRS 2 defines the vesting period as *"the period during which all the specified vesting conditions of a share-based payment arrangement are to be satisfied"*. [IFRS 2 App A].

A12.44 No distinction is drawn in IFRS 2 between vesting periods during which employees have to satisfy specific performance conditions and vesting periods during which there are no particular requirements other than to remain in the entity's employment. Hence, in the example in paragraph A12.41 above, the period over which employee services should be recognised is the four-year period until the options vest and employees become unconditionally entitled to them and not the shorter period during which the employees must satisfy specific performance conditions.

A12.45 The treatment of vesting conditions is considered in greater detail from paragraph A12.77.

A12.46 The following examples illustrate the period over which all specified vesting conditions are to be satisfied, which could be different for different employees in the same share award plan.

Example 1 – Award exercisable on chosen retirement date

An employee is currently 58 years old and is granted some options that vest over five years if he continues in employment. This employee, however, has the option to retire anytime between 60 and 65 (inclusive) without requiring the employer's consent. If the employee chooses to retire at the age of 60, the employee is able to keep the options, which become exercisable at that date. In this example the vesting period for this individual is two years as he becomes entitled to, and can walk away with, the options at the age of 60, whether he chooses to continue working beyond that date.

Example 2 – Options awarded instead of annual bonus

An entity normally awards options annually instead of an annual bonus. The entity grants options representing an annual bonus in 20X4, in respect of the year to December 20X3. The award is not exercisable for three years and the employee must remain with the entity throughout this period.

In this situation, there is an expectation on the part of the employees that they will receive a bonus each year. Consequently, employees are providing services in 20X3 to earn the right to equity instruments. However, there is an additional period of service that the employee is required to complete until the equity instrument vests unconditionally with them. Therefore, the expense should be over the performance period (20X3) and the service period (20X4 to 20X6). The vesting period is a total of four years.

It should be noted that if the employee was not required to remain with the entity for the three year period, the vesting period would be one year (20X3) and the three year delay until the award is exercisable would simply be a post-vesting restriction. See from paragraph A12.202.

Group situations and location of share-based payment charge

A12.47 In certain circumstances it may not be immediately clear which entity or entities within a group should bear the IFRS 2 charge. This may be, for example, where an award has been granted to employees who provide services to a number of entities within a group. It may be that employees are remunerated by a service company for services to a number of operating entities. Alternatively, individuals may be directors of both the parent company and an operating subsidiary. The charge should be borne by the entity that is in substance the employer.

A12.48 It will be necessary to assess the facts and circumstances surrounding each situation by considering a range of factors, including the following:

- Which entity obtains the benefits associated with the employee. For example, where an individual is a director of both the parent company and an operating subsidiary, consider whether the director is being rewarded for services to the group as a whole (contributing to strategic decisions for the group, or perhaps implementing a restructuring programme) or whether the director is being rewarded for services to the operating subsidiary's business. The latter would point towards the subsidiary being the employer.
- Whether there is a service company arrangement in place. For example, where an individual performs services for a large number of group operating entities and the time spent at each entity varies (or may change) from time to time, this may indicate that the service company is the employer.
- Which entity ultimately bears the employment cost. While one entity may physically pay the employee, the cost may be recharged to another group entity that receives services from the employee. The IFRS 2 charge would generally be expected to follow other employee costs.
- The nature of any management recharges. For example:
  - Whether management costs (such as wages and salaries, overheads and other administrative expenses) are charged back individually (such that the entity's income statement includes each cost as a separate line item) or as part of a larger 'block' management recharge. A larger 'block' of recharges may indicate that the entity receiving the management recharge for the employee is, in substance, the employer.
  - Whether the employee's costs are recharged to another entity at a margin. This may indicate that the entity receiving the management recharge is, in substance, the employer.
- Which entity sets the employee's salary, appraises the employee and determines any bonus. The IFRS 2 charge would generally sit with an entity performing such functions.
- Which entity has issued the employee's contract and which entity the employee considers to be their employer. As in the above bullet point, an entity performing such functions would generally be the employer.
- The nature of the employee's contract. For example, whether the employee's contract states that he/she may be required to work for a number of group entities or whether an employee is temporarily seconded to a specific operating entity. An entity to which an employee is temporarily seconded would be the employer for the period of the secondment.

The credit entry

A12.49 The treatment of the credit entry in respect of a share-based payment transaction will depend on whether it is accounted for as an equity-settled or as a cash-settled transaction. In the case of an equity-settled transaction, there is no obligation to transfer economic benefits so the credit entry should be recognised as an increase in equity. A cash-settled transaction, on the other hand, does give rise to an obligation so a liability should be recognised. [IFRS 2 para 7].

A12.50 As regards equity-settled transactions, IFRS 2 does not stipulate where in equity the credit entry should be recognised. In our view, subject to any statutory constraints, it would be permissible for the credit to be to the profit and loss reserve. This is a complicated area and companies may need to take legal advice to comply with local legislation.

> **UK.A12.50.1** In the UK it is acceptable to present the credit in the profit and loss reserve. Indeed, this is where it is commonly seen. The credit could be taken to a separate share-based payment reserve, but not the share premium account, which is determined by the amount of cash subscribed for the shares by the employees (or the ESOP trust as the case may be).

A12.51 The credit to equity will be presented in the statement of changes in equity. It will not be presented in a statement of other comprehensive income, as it reflects the issue of an equity instrument and does not represent a gain.

A12.52 How a subsidiary should disclose a recharge by its parent for a share-based payment is discussed in paragraph A12.182.

Equity-settled share-based payment transactions

A12.53 Equity-settled share-based payment transactions are transactions in which an entity receives goods or services as consideration for its own equity instruments or receives goods or services but has no obligation to settle the transaction with the supplier. Examples include the following:

- Employee share option plans.
- Employee share plans, including employee share purchase plans and share incentive plans.
- Transactions in which an entity obtains goods or services in exchange for its own equity instruments. For example, start-up companies may obtain consultancy and similar services in exchange for shares, thus preserving scarce cash resources and giving the supplier an opportunity to share in the company's success.

A12.54 In each case, IFRS 2 requires an entity to measure the goods or services received and the corresponding increase in equity at fair value. Fair value is defined as *"the amount for which an asset could be exchanged, a liability settled, or an equity instrument granted could be exchanged, between knowledgeable, willing parties in an arm's length transaction"*. [IFRS 2 App A].

Measurement of equity-settled share-based payment transactions

A12.55 Ideally, the fair value of the goods or services obtained by an entity will be measurable directly. However, if the fair value of the goods or services cannot be measured reliably, the standard requires that it should be measured by reference to the fair value of the equity instruments granted as consideration. [IFRS 2 para 10]. This is sometimes referred to as the 'indirect method'. In these circumstances, the fair value of the equity instruments represents the best surrogate for the price of the goods or services.

A12.56 The principle described in the previous paragraph is best illustrated in the context of employee services. Shares and share options are often granted to employees as part of their remuneration package, in addition to a cash salary and other employment benefits. Usually, it is not possible to measure directly the services received for particular components of an employee's remuneration package. Furthermore, options or shares are sometimes granted as part of a bonus arrangement, rather than as an element of basic remuneration. By granting options, in addition to other remuneration, the entity is paying additional remuneration to obtain additional benefits. Estimating the fair value of those additional benefits is likely to be difficult. Therefore, IFRS 2 requires an entity to measure the fair value of the employee services received by reference to the fair value of the equity instruments granted. [IFRS 2 para 11].

A12.57 Employees are individuals who:

- Render personal services to the entity and are regarded as employees for legal or tax purposes.
- Work for the entity under its direction in the same way as individuals considered employees for legal or tax purposes.
- Render services that are similar to those rendered by employees.

[IFRS 2 App A].

Example – Who are employees?

An oil company hired an external consultant to assess its oil reserves. The service was provided over a five month period and will be settled by the entity issuing 100 shares to the consultant, valued at C40,000 when the contract was awarded. The entity estimated the cash fair value of the service to be C38,000, based on bids from other consultants. The consultant was considered an employee for tax purposes.

The consultant is considered an employee or other providing similar services for the purpose of IFRS 2. Management should, therefore, recognise the service at the fair value of the equity instruments granted, that is, C40,000.

A12.58 In the case of transactions with parties other than employees including others providing similar services, it is presumed that it will be possible to measure the fair value of goods or services reliably. [IFRS 2 para 13]. However, this may not always be possible, in which case the presumption should be rebutted and the fair value should be measured indirectly by reference to the fair value of the equity instrument granted as consideration.

A12.59 Where the fair value of goods or services (other than those received from employees) is capable of direct measurement, it should be measured at the date on which the goods are received or the services are rendered. [IFRS 2 para 13]. An entity is required to consider if there are any unidentifiable goods or services received or to be received by the entity. This should be calculated as the fair value of the equity instruments granted, less the fair value of goods or services received. When the fair value of goods or services is measured by reference to the fair value of equity instruments granted, measurement should be at either:

- The date on which the equity instruments are granted, in the case of employee services or where the goods or services are unidentifiable.
- The date on which the goods are received or the services are rendered, in all other cases.

[IFRS 2 paras 11, 13, 13A].

A12.60 The measurement of fair value at grant date is considered further from paragraph A12.278. Measurement of fair value when the goods or services are received is illustrated in the following examples:

Example 1 – Measurement of fair value by the direct method

Entity A is a small start-up entity. To assist it in developing its business, it receives consultancy services from entity B. The entities have agreed that, as entity A has scarce cash resources, the consideration for the consultancy services will be in the form of entity A's ordinary shares. The agreed rate is one share for each hour of consultancy services. Entity B has a publicised schedule of scale rates and the amount charged for a project of this nature is normally C100 per hour. Therefore, subject to the guidance noted in paragraphs A12.61 to A12.64 below, an expense and an increase in equity of C100 should be recognised by entity A for each hour of consultancy services received.

Note that the counterparty is an entity that is providing services rather than an individual and, therefore, does not fall within the category of employees or others providing similar services.

Example 2 – Measurement of fair value by the indirect method

The facts are similar to example 1, except that further shares are issued to entity B as it assists entity A in respect of a particular project, with 100 shares being awarded if the project is successful.

In this case, it may not be possible to measure reliably the fair value of the consultancy services themselves. The value of the transaction and shares received may have little to do with the value derived from the time spent by the consultants. Instead, the fair value should be measured as the services are rendered by reference to the fair value of the shares offered as consideration.

Example 3 – Contribution of assets to a joint venture

Entities X and Y have formed an incorporated joint venture, entity Z. On formation, in exchange for their equity interests in Z, entity X contributed property, plant and equipment and entity Y contributed intangible assets that do not constitute a business.

As explained in example 6 of paragraph A12.21, the asset contribution by venturers X and Y upon entity Z's formation is an equity-settled share-based payment transaction within IFRS 2's scope. Since the fair value of the assets contributed can be estimated reliably, entity Z should measure the assets received and the corresponding increase in equity directly, at the fair value of the assets received. In addition, entity Z would have to consider whether or not the fair value of the shares issued exceeded the fair value of the assets contributed as that would indicate there are unidentifiable goods or services. See paragraph A12.61.

A12.61 The standard's scope has been expanded to include share-based payment transactions where it is difficult to identify that goods or services have been (or will be) received. For example, an entity may grant shares to a charitable organisation for nil consideration. It is usually not possible to identify the specific goods or services received in return for such a transaction. Additionally, there are some situations where the fair value of goods or services received (if any) appears to be less than the fair value of the equity instruments granted or liability incurred. In such situations, the standard requires the entity to measure the identifiable goods or services received at fair value and then the unidentifiable goods or services received will be measured as the difference between the fair value of the share-based payment and the fair value of any identifiable goods or services received. [IFRS 2 para 13A].

[The next paragraph is A12.64.]

A12.64 The standard seems to be an almost generic rebuttal of the presumption for non-employee goods or services that the fair value of the goods or services can be more reliably measured than the fair value of the equity instrument. The argument is that if the goods or services cannot be identified then clearly they cannot be reliably measured. As a result of the change to the standard, far more work is required to determine all aspects of the transaction (that is, the fair value of the equity instrument, the identifiable goods or services acquired and the unidentifiable element), and the appropriate accounting for each aspect. The following examples illustrate the principles above.

Example 1 – Measurement of fair value where services are unidentifiable

An entity granted shares with a total fair value of C100,000 to parties other than employees who are from a particular section of the community (historically disadvantaged individuals), as a means of enhancing its image as a good corporate citizen. The economic benefits derived from enhancing its corporate image could take a variety of forms, such as increasing its customer base, attracting or retaining employees (who may prefer to work for an entity that supports such 'good causes'), or improving or maintaining its ability to tender successfully for business contracts.

The entity cannot identify the specific consideration received. For example, no cash was received and no service conditions were imposed. Therefore, the identifiable consideration (nil) is less than the fair value of the equity instruments granted (C100,000). The circumstances indicate that unidentifiable goods or services have been (or will be) received and, therefore, IFRS 2 applies.

The rebuttable presumption in IFRS 2, that the fair value of the goods or services received can be estimated reliably, does not apply here. The entity should instead measure the goods or services received by reference to the fair value of the equity instruments granted. [IFRS 2 para 13, 13A].

Example 2 – Measurement of fair value where fair value of license cannot be reliably estimated

An entity grants 10% of its shares to the local government for nil consideration in exchange for an indefinite-lived license to operate in that country. The fair value of the license is not determinable.

The entity is expected to receive a benefit from the license and, thus, the transaction would fall within the scope of IFRS 2. As the license is an identifiable good, the share-based payment should be recognised at the date when the license is received. As the fair value of the license received cannot be estimated reliably, the entity should instead measure the license received by reference to the fair value of the equity instruments granted.

Note that if the fair value of the license is determinable and less than the fair value of the shares, there may be unidentifiable goods or services to be accounted for, as discussed above. The unidentifiable goods or services could be a premium paid by the company and, therefore, makes up a part of the license's cost. In this case, the company would need to consider if the carrying amount of the license is impaired and it may be able to support the carrying amount through a value-in-use model.

Example 3 – Services provided where equity value appears to be greater than the value of the services

The facts are the same as that in the example in paragraph A12.57, except the services are being provided by a large consulting firm.

In this case, although IFRS 2 requires the award to be measured directly, with reference to the value of the services received, the fact that the value of the shares given (C40,000) for the consultancy services are clearly worth more than the value for the services (C38,000) indicates that some unidentifiable goods or services will be received by the company. The oil company should, therefore, record a charge of C40,000.

Example 4 – Issue of shares to existing members and customers on listing

Entity A is a mutual entity and its shares are held by members. However, entity A plans to demutualise and list on the local stock exchange and it will convert the existing 'member' shares to ordinary equity capital in a listed entity. As part of the process, entity A will issue free shares to its customers (those customers that are not members).

The appropriate accounting for the share-based payment is determined by separately considering the shares issued to existing members and customers.

Existing members
This is not a share-based payment arrangement as it is with members in their capacity as existing equity holders.

Customers (that are not members)
The entity will issue shares for nil consideration and it is not possible to identify the specific goods and services received in return for the shares. Entity A will account for this arrangement under IFRS 2. Entity A measures the unidentifiable goods and services that are received in accordance with IFRS 2 by using the fair value of the equity instrument granted and recognises a related expense immediately.

A12.65 IFRS 2 envisages that it will normally be possible to estimate the fair value of equity instruments granted. However, it is acknowledged that there may be situations in which it is not possible to estimate fair value reliably. In these circumstances, IFRS 2 requires the following approach.

- The equity instruments granted should be measured at their intrinsic value, both initially and subsequently at each reporting date and at the date on which the award is finally settled. For a grant of share options, the award is finally settled when the options are exercised, forfeited or lapse. Any change in intrinsic value is recognised in the statement of comprehensive income.
- The amount recognised as an expense should be based on the number of equity instruments that ultimately vest or, in the case of options, are ultimately exercised.

[IFRS 2 para 24].

A12.66 We believe that it will rarely be the case that the fair value of equity instruments granted cannot be estimated reliably. If in a rare situation it is the case that the fair value cannot be measured, the entity would measure the transaction using an intrinsic value measurement method. However, specialist advice should be sought if this measurement method is to be followed.

Grant date

A12.67 Grant date is defined in IFRS 2 as *"the date at which the entity and another party (including an employee) agree to a share-based payment arrangement, being when the entity and the counterparty have a shared understanding of the terms and conditions of the arrangement. At grant date the entity confers on the counterparty the right to cash, other assets, or equity instruments of the entity, provided the specified vesting conditions, if any, are met. If that agreement is subject to an approval process (for example, by shareholders), grant date is the date when that approval is obtained"*. [IFRS 2 App A].

A12.68 Often it will be clear as to when the parties involved in a share-based payment arrangement have a shared understanding of the arrangement's terms and conditions. Sometimes, however, certain of the terms may need to be confirmed at a later date. For example, if a entity's board of directors agrees to issue share options to senior management, but the exercise price of those options will be set by the remuneration committee that meets in three months' time, grant date is when the exercise price is set by the remuneration committee even though the service period starts when the awards are offered to senior management.

A12.69 Similar questions are raised when equity instruments are granted subject to an approval process. This is considered in the following example.

Example – Grant subject to approval process

Directors of an entity customarily include in letters to new employees the offer of options to subscribe for shares in the entity. In February 20X5 the entity offered new employees options over 10,000 shares at the then market price of C10 per share. The letters stated that the board of directors supported the offer. The awards were approved by the shareholders in June 20X5, by which time the market price of the entity's shares had risen to C15 and the fair value of the options had also increased. What is the grant date for the purposes of IFRS 2? The possibilities are:

- The date on which the original offers were made – February 20X5.
- The date on which the awards were approved by shareholders – June 20X5.

The allotment of shares or rights to shares in general has to be authorised by shareholders in general meeting or by the entity's articles. In this case, the award of options was subject to shareholder approval so the grant date is the date on which that approval was obtained (that is, June 20X5).

In practice many companies have in place a pre-existing authorisation from shareholders to cover potential awards of equity instruments to employees before the next AGM. If such pre-authorisation were to exist, in this case, the grant date would generally be considered to have been February 20X5. The situation might differ where the board of directors, as majority shareholders, controls the entity. Where the directors' shareholding gives them the necessary power to authorise the award, for example if there is no shareholders' agreement or similar that requires the consent of the minority, the directors might be able to regard their meeting as being a properly constituted shareholders' meeting for this purpose and should, as a matter of good practice, record themselves as meeting in that form.

A12.70 In the previous example, if grant date is considered to be June 20X5, employees may have already begun to provide services to the entity before that date. As IFRS 2 requires the entity to recognise an expense as employee services are received, an expense will sometimes be recognised in respect of a share-based payment arrangement in advance of the grant date. [IFRS 2 IG 4]. In this situation, the grant date fair value of the equity instruments should be estimated, for example, by reference to the fair value of the equity instruments at the balance sheet date. An expense will then be based on an estimated amount until the date of grant has been established. At that point, the entity should revise the earlier estimates so that the amounts recognised for services received in respect of the grant are ultimately based on the grant date fair value of the equity instruments.

A12.71 The following examples provide further illustrations in determining the grant date when applying IFRS 2. It is vital that the grant date is correctly established as this is the point at which the fair value of the equity-settled share-based payment is measured.

Example 1 – Award subject to shareholder approval

An award is communicated to individual employees on 1 December 20X5, subject to shareholder approval. The award is then approved by shareholders on 1 February 20X6, with the same terms as had initially been communicated to employees. A letter to formalise the award is sent to individual employees on 1 March 20X6.

As the award is subject to an approval process (in this example, by shareholders), the grant date is the date when that approval is obtained. The letter to formalise the award is mainly administrative, both the employees and the employer have a shared understanding on 1 February 20X6 and, therefore, this is the grant date. The vesting period starts on 1 December 20X5 as this is when employees become aware of the nature of the award and begin providing services.

Example 2 – Individual notification of award

An award is approved by the board/shareholders on 1 December 20X5. The general terms and conditions of the award set out the relevant employee population that will participate in the award, but provide insufficient information to determine each employee's share. The general terms and conditions are posted to the website on 31 December 20X5. The employees are individually informed of their shares on 1 February 20X6.

The grant date is when both parties agree to a share-based payment arrangement. The word 'agree' is used in its usual sense, which means that there must be both an offer and acceptance of that offer. Hence, the date at which one party makes an offer to another party is not always the grant date. In some instances, the counterparty explicitly agrees to the arrangement, for example, by signing a contract. In other instances, agreement might be implicit for example, for many share-based payment arrangements with employees, the employees' agreement is evidenced by their commencing to render services. Therefore, in this example the grant date is 1 February 20X6. The vesting period begins on 31 December 20X5 as this is when employees become aware of the award's general terms and conditions and begin providing services.

Example 3 – Communication to employees following standard communication procedures

On 10 June 20X1, the key terms and conditions of an entity's share-based payment award were discussed with all employees concerned. Employees were also informed that the award was subject to board approval, which was expected to be obtained on 20 June 20X1.

As anticipated, the award was approved by the board on 20 June 20X1. Management subsequently followed the normal process for communications, sending the full terms and conditions of the award to the employees' home addresses, such that employees received them in the following few days.

We believe that the grant date in this example is 20 June 20X1 given the following:

- the key terms and conditions were communicated to employees;
- employees had no opportunity to further negotiate the terms and conditions following board approval;
- the entity followed its normal communication procedures to provide full terms and conditions to employees; and
- there is a very short period of time between board approval and employees receiving the full terms and conditions.

The vesting period starts on 10 June 20X1 as this is when employees become aware of the nature of the award and begin providing services. See next example for services received before the grant date.

Example 4 – Services received before grant date

A new compensation package for key employees is announced on 1 January 20X5. The plan covers the calendar year 20X5, incorporates the results of the year's annual appraisal process and includes a new share option plan. The option plan is subject to approval by shareholders. The shareholders approved the plan on 28 February 20X6.

The fair value of the share options is measured at the grant date, 28 February 20X6. If the agreement between the entity and its employees is subject to an approval process (for example, by shareholders), the grant date cannot be earlier than the date on which that approval is obtained. However, IFRS 2 requires the entity to recognise employee services as they are received and in this case the expense will be recognised in advance of the grant date from 1 January 20X5 when the employees begin rendering services. [IFRS 2 paras 7, IG 4]. The entity should estimate the grant date fair value for the purpose of recognising the expense during the period between the service commencement date and the grant date. Management should revise the estimate at each reporting period until the grant date has been established. Once the grant date has been established, the recognised expense is based on the actual grant date fair value of the equity instruments in the period of change.

Example 5 – Bonus plan with services received before grant date and settlement in both cash and shares

Note that this example also illustrates the impact of vesting conditions (see further from para A12.77).

On 1 January 20X5 an entity announced a bonus subject to exceeding the revenue target for 20X5.

C500 of the bonus will be paid in cash on 31 March 20X6 provided that the employee is in service at 31 December 20X5. The other part of the bonus will be settled in share options provided that the employee is still in service on 31 March 20X6. The exercise price and number of options will be approved by management on 31 March 20X6. Management expect that the revenue target will be met and that no employees will leave between 31 December 20X5 and 31 March 20X6. At 31 December 20X5 the estimated grant date fair value is C500.

The entity should accrue a liability of C500 for the cash part of the bonus at 31 December 20X5, because the revenue target was met and employees are entitled to the payment even if they leave by 31 March 20X6.

The entity should also recognise an estimated expense of C400 (12/15ths of C500) and a corresponding increase in equity for the part of the bonus that is to be settled in share options subject to the service vesting condition.

As for example 3 above, the share options did not have a grant date on 31 December 20X5, because the parties did not have a shared understanding of the arrangement's terms and conditions. However, IFRS 2 requires the entity to recognise the services when received and, therefore, the fair value at the grant date, 31 March 20X6, must be estimated.

Once the terms of the options are fixed on the grant date, 31 March 20X6, the actual fair value can be calculated and, if necessary, the cumulative charge should be revised.

Example 6 – Award at the discretion of remuneration committee

Employees have been awarded share options that will vest subject to achieving a total shareholder return (TSR) performance target over a three year period. However, at the end of the three year period, where the remuneration committee is not satisfied that the TSR position achieved is supported by the underlying performance of the business, the committee has discretion to refuse the award.

Where the remuneration committee has discretion to override an award, despite a performance condition being achieved, there is no shared understanding at the date the award is made. The grant date does not occur until the remuneration committee operates its overriding discretion at the end of the vesting period. The fair value of the award would, therefore, be estimated at each reporting date from the date that services are provided and final measurement would occur at the end of the vesting period. As a result, this may give rise to significantly greater charges in the income statement than where the grant date occurs when the award is made.

In certain circumstances it may be possible to conclude that grant date has been achieved when the award is made. For example, where a remuneration committee has discretion to alter the award but only where the value of each individual's award is not adversely affected, grant date may have been achieved for the guaranteed element of the award. Alternatively, where, in practice, the remuneration committee has never exercised its discretion to override and the entity can prove that it will not do so in the future (and employees share this understanding), it may be possible to conclude that grant date has occurred. It should be noted, however, that this is likely to be difficult to achieve where a discretion clause is set out in the articles.

The circumstances surrounding the award should be carefully assessed and the situation explained in the financial statements where it is concluded that the grant date has occurred when the award is made. Where material, it should be disclosed as a significant accounting policy judgement under IAS 1, 'Presentation of financial statements'. [IAS 1 para 113].

Example 7 – Market performance condition not met but remuneration committee agrees to continue with award

Employees were awarded share options in entity A subject to entity A's share price increasing by 10% between 1 July 20X0 and 30 June 20X3. The 10% target was not achieved. However, on 30 June 20X3 entity A's remuneration committee decided that all the share options should vest anyway.

Entity A modified the share option award at 30 June 20X3. There is likely to be a cumulative charge for the original award as the likelihood of meeting the share price target, a market performance condition, would have been factored into the original grant date fair value calculation. However, the fair value of the original share option award at the modification date is nil, because the performance condition has not been met. The modified award, therefore, has incremental fair value.

Note that if the vesting condition had been a non-market performance condition, such as achieving a net profit target, there would be no cumulative charge for the original award as this would have been reversed at the time it became clear that the net profit target would not be met. The full incremental fair value of the modified award would, however, be recognised.

In practice, the ability of a remuneration committee to make this kind of 'modification' may be set out in the award's terms and conditions as discussed in example 6 above and may mean that there is no grant date.

See from paragraph A12.96 below for definitions of market and non-market conditions. See also from paragraph A12.115 for guidance on modifications.

[The next paragraph is A12.77.]

Vesting conditions

A12.77 As explained in paragraph A12.43, where a counterparty to a share-based payment arrangement is required to complete a specified period of service before its equity instruments vest, the goods or services obtained by the reporting entity are recognised over that period. [IFRS 2 para 15]. For example, an entity grants options to its employees with a grant date fair value of C300,000. These options vest in three years' time with the only condition being that the employees remain in the entity's service for that period. Assuming that all of the options do vest (that is, none of the employees leave the entity), the amount charged as an expense each year will be C100,000. This will be the case regardless of any movements in the price of the entity's shares. So, even if the options have an intrinsic value of, say, C500,000 when they are exercised, the amount charged as an expense will be unchanged. Having determined the 'price' of employee services when the options were granted, this remains fixed.

A12.78 In reality, employee share option plans, indeed equity-settled share-based payment transactions generally, are seldom that simple. Typically, there will be performance conditions that must be satisfied before employees are absolutely entitled to the equity instruments. For example, the number of options to which employees are entitled under a bonus plan may depend on a certain increase in profit or growth in the entity's share price. Even in the simple example described in the previous paragraph, the amount charged as an expense in each period will vary depending on the latest estimate of the likely number of employees who will remain for three years and, hence, the number of options that will vest. Although the fair value of equity instruments granted is not re-measured, the estimate of the number of equity instruments that is likely to vest is revised, if necessary, until the instruments actually do vest.

A12.79 Conditions that must be satisfied before a counterparty becomes unconditionally entitled to the equity instruments it has been granted are referred to as vesting conditions. IFRS 2 defines vesting conditions as:

> *"the conditions that determine whether the entity receives the services that entitle the counterparty to receive cash, other assets or equity instruments of the entity, under a share-based payment arrangement. Vesting conditions are either service conditions or performance conditions. Service conditions require the counterparty to complete a specified period of service. Performance conditions, require the counterparty to complete a specified period of service and specified performance targets to be met (such as a specified increase in the entity's profit over a specified period of time). A performance condition might include a market condition."* [IFRS 2 App A].

It follows that the vesting period is the period during which all the specified vesting conditions are to be satisfied. Paragraph A12.41 above provides guidance on timing of recognition and the vesting period.

A12.80 Vesting conditions include the requirements to be satisfied for an employee to obtain the award. In some circumstances there may be, for example, a restriction on employees selling shares received from an award after they have become entitled to them. This is a post-vesting restriction and not a vesting condition. See further from paragraph A12.202.

A12.81 Share-based payment awards may include non-compete provisions either during or after the vesting period. This is a complex area where specialist advice should be sought in determining how to account for the non-compete provisions as the treatment is often based on facts and circumstances.

[The next paragraph is A12.83.]

A12.83 Any other conditions in a share-based payment transaction, such as a requirement to save or a requirement to hold shares, are 'non-vesting conditions'. Non-vesting conditions are taken into account when determining the award's fair value.

A12.84 There is a table summarising the implications of vesting and non-vesting conditions on accounting for share-based payment transactions in appendix 1 to this chapter.

A12.85 In summary, service vesting conditions (which are non-market conditions) and non-market performance conditions are not incorporated into the grant date fair value calculation. IFRS 2, however, requires that market performance conditions and non-vesting conditions be incorporated into the grant date fair value calculation. This is discussed in more detail in the following sections.

A12.86 The following diagram illustrates the principles discussed in this section.

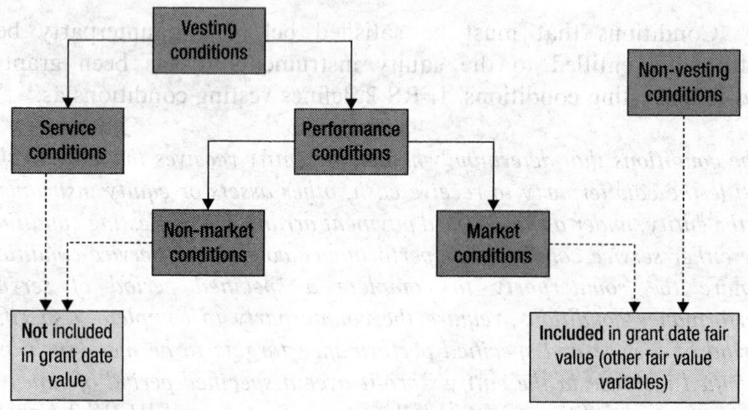

[The next paragraph is A12.88.]

Service conditions

A12.88 Identifying a service condition is more straightforward than identifying a performance condition. Service conditions are not explicitly defined by IFRS 2. However, the definition of 'vesting conditions' includes a statement that service conditions require the counterparty to complete a specified period of service.

A12.89 Service conditions are non-market conditions (see further from para A12.96 for discussion of market and non-market conditions) and this fact is important in relation to both the measurement and recognition of particular awards. Service conditions are not taken into consideration when determining the grant date fair value of an award. Instead, service conditions are taken into consideration when estimating the number of awards that will vest. On a cumulative basis, therefore, no amount is recognised for goods or services received where an award does not vest because a specified service condition has not been met. [IFRS 2 para 19]. As a result of this, during the vesting period, the IFRS 2 expense can change depending on changes in the service condition expectation.

Performance conditions

A12.90 Defining performance conditions is more difficult. As set out in paragraph A12.79 above, the definition of 'vesting conditions' includes a statement that performance conditions require the counterparty to complete a service period and meet specified performance targets.

A12.91 We believe that the following principles are appropriate for determining whether a condition is a performance vesting condition.

- The condition occurs during the service period. As explained in paragraph A12.79 above, IFRS 2 defines vesting conditions as the conditions that determine whether the entity receives the services that entitle the counterparty to receive the award. Conversely, if a condition's outcome will only be determined after any required service period, then the condition is not a vesting condition because it does not determine whether the entity receives services in exchange for the award granted. Examples would include where an employee has to work for three years but there is an EPS target based on a longer, say, five year period, or alternatively an employee has to work for three years and will become entitled to an award if the company has listed, whether or not the employee is still working for the company at the time of listing.
- The condition needs to be achieved. Achieving the condition, or target, may be partly within the employee's control, but cannot be wholly within their control (see next bullet point).
- The condition is not wholly within the control of either the employee or employer. Where the outcome of a condition (other than whether or not the employee carries on working) is wholly within the control of the employee then it is not a performance condition. If the employee can unilaterally decide whether or not the target is achieved, then services are not required. Examples include the requirement to hold a specified number of shares or to continue saving in the context of matching share awards and SAYE plans respectively.

A12.92 Performance conditions include performance targets such as revenue targets, EPS growth, total shareholder return (TSR) hurdles and share price growth.

A12.93 Performance conditions may be either market or non-market conditions. See further from paragraph A12.96 for discussion of market and non-market conditions.

A12.94 Performance conditions that include a market condition (often referred to as market performance conditions) are incorporated into the grant date fair value of an award. An expense will, therefore, be recorded, even if the market performance condition is not met (assuming all other service and non-market performance vesting conditions are met).

A12.95 The treatment of performance conditions that include a non-market condition is similar to that of service conditions, that is, they are not included in the grant date fair value. Instead, non-market performance conditions are taken into consideration when estimating the number of awards that will vest. Therefore, on a cumulative basis, no amount is recognised for goods or services received where an award does not vest, because a specified non-market performance condition has not been met. [IFRS 2 para 19]. As for service conditions, during the vesting period, the IFRS 2 expense can change as a result of a change in non-market performance vesting conditions expectation.

Market conditions

A12.96 The treatment of vesting conditions will vary depending on whether they relate to the market price of the entity's equity instruments. Such conditions, which IFRS 2 calls market conditions, are taken into account when determining the grant date fair value of the equity instruments granted. They are ignored for the purposes of estimating the number of equity instruments that will vest. [IFRS 2 para 21]. The full definition of 'market condition' is:

> *"A condition upon which the exercise price, vesting or exercisability of an equity instrument depends that is related to the market price of the entity's equity instruments, such as attaining a specified share price or a specified amount of intrinsic value of a share option, or achieving a specified target that is based on the market price of the entity's equity instruments relative to an index of market prices of equity instruments of other entities."* [IFRS 2 App A].

A12.97 Examples of market conditions include where an entity's share price must out perform the market, achieve a minimum price in a specified period, or achieve a total shareholder return target. Further examples are included in the table in paragraph A12.100. Such conditions are included in the estimate of the fair value of a share-based payment. They should not be taken into account for the purpose of estimating the number of equity instruments that will vest. Market conditions in the context of valuation are considered further from paragraph A12.288.

Non-market conditions

A12.98 Vesting conditions other than market conditions are non-market conditions. Examples of non-market conditions are earnings per share or profit targets.

A12.99 Unlike market conditions, non-market conditions are not considered when estimating the fair value of a share-based payment. For non-market conditions, an entity should recognise the goods or services it has acquired during the vesting period based on the best available estimate of the number of equity instruments expected to vest. It should revise that estimate, if necessary, when subsequent information indicates that the number of equity instruments expected to vest differs from previous estimates. Finally, on the vesting date, the entity should revise the estimate to equal the number of equity instruments that ultimately vest. [IFRS 2 paras 19-20].

A12.100 The following table illustrates some of the more common market and non-market conditions associated with share-based payment arrangements.

Market conditions	**Non-market conditions**
(Affecting the fair value of the award)	(Affecting the number of awards that vest)
Achieve a minimum share price by a specified date.	Remain in employment for a specified period of time.
Achieve a total shareholder return target.	Achieve earnings per share or profit targets.
Out perform a share price index.	Complete a particular project.
	Successful IPO (see para A12.113.1).

Non-vesting conditions

A12.101 Non-vesting conditions are conditions other than service and performance conditions. Non-vesting conditions include the requirement to save or the requirement to hold shares. Although such requirements occur during the vesting period, they are often wholly within the control of the employee and the conditions are not related to duties specified in an employee's employment contract. They, therefore, do not determine whether the entity receives the services linked to shares.

A12.102 A typical SAYE (save as you earn) plan, common in the UK, has terms requiring employees to contribute a maximum of £250 per month to an employee share trust. Employees are required to contribute to the SAYE plan for five years, after which they have the choice to either receive their cash back plus accrued interest or use the cash to acquire shares at a 20 per cent discount to the market price on the grant date. An employee that ceases saving receives a reimbursement of all amounts saved to date, plus interest, but must withdraw from the plan and forfeit their right to acquire shares.

A12.103 The requirement to hold shares is seen in matching share plans. For example, employees are part of a share award whereby they receive part of their bonus in shares. On becoming entitled to the bonus and shares employees can elect to hold their shares for three years, at which point the entity will give employees an additional share for every share that the employee has not sold, provided that the employees are still in service.

[The next paragraph is A12.105.]

A12.105 Non-vesting conditions should be incorporated into the grant date fair value of the award. As a result, the award's grant date fair value may well be lower than awards without such a requirement, because the probability of employees failing to save (and, hence, withdrawing from the plan) or selling their restricted shares (and, hence, losing the matching shares) will be taken into consideration.

A12.106 An employee's failure to save or failure to hold restricted shares is treated as a cancellation. This results in the acceleration of any unvested portion of the award on the date that the employee ceases to save or sells the restricted shares (see para A12.234).

A12.107 An example of a change of policy clarifying vesting and non-vesting conditions in accordance with IFRS 2 referred to above is in Table A12.2.

Table A12.2 – Non-vesting conditions – change of policy

F&C Asset Management plc – Annual report – 31 December 2009

Notes to the Consolidated Financial Statements (extract)

1. Prior period adjustment

With effect from 1 January 2009 the Group has adopted the revision to IFRS 2: Share-based Payment – vesting conditions and cancellations. The revision clarifies vesting conditions and the circumstances giving rise to cancellations. There are two categories of non-vesting conditions where the grant of equity instruments is considered cancelled: employees who elect to cease saving into the Group's Share Save Scheme or employees who are "good leavers" and have ceased saving for the Share Save Scheme. In both cases, the Group immediately recognises the amount of the expense that would otherwise have been recognised over the remainder of the vesting period. Previously these events were treated as forfeitures. The amendments are applied retrospectively and hence a prior period adjustment has been made at the transition date, 31 December 2007, and for the year ended 31 December 2008.

The effect of the Income Statement and Statement of Financial Position is as follows:

At 31 December 2007:	
*Statement of Financial Position impact**	**£m**
Retained earnings – share-based payment credit to equity	0.3
Retained earnings – share-based payment charged to operating expenses	(0.3)

Year ended 31 December 2008:	**£m**
Statement of Financial Position impact	
Retained earnings – share-based payment credit to equity	0.1
Income Statement impact	
Operating expenses – share-based payment expenses	(0.1)

* As the adjustment is within retained earnings there is no impact on the Statement of Financial Position at 31 December 2007 and accordingly a Statement of Financial Position has not been re-presented at that date.

There is no income tax effect on the above adjustments.

The impact of the prior period adjustment on the year ended 31 December 2008 loss per share is to increase the basic and diluted loss from 10.64p to 10.66p as disclosed in note 11.

A12.108 Share awards may have more than one vesting period, as illustrated in example 5 of paragraph A12.161.

Reload feature

A12.109 Some share options contain a reload feature. This provides for an automatic grant of additional options ('reload options') whenever the option holder exercises previously granted options using the entity's shares, rather than cash, to satisfy the exercise price. This is illustrated in the following simple example.

> **Example – Share options with a reload feature**
>
> An entity has issued 100 options to one of its directors. The total exercise price for the options is C100. However, there is a reload feature which means that the exercise price may be satisfied by the option holder surrendering shares in the entity to the value of C100 and, by doing so, becoming eligible for an additional option plan. Like vesting conditions, the existence of a reload feature may influence the value of the option to the holder, but it is not taken into account when estimating fair value. Instead, when a reload option is granted it is accounted for as a new option grant. [IFRS 2 para 22].

Revising estimates due to changes in service or non-market conditions

A12.110 Returning to the example set out in paragraph A12.77, management may have estimated at grant date that 10 per cent of employees will leave the entity before the end of three years. Hence, the expense in the first year would be reduced by 10 per cent to C90,000 (that is, C300,000 × 1/3 × 90%). If, during the second year it becomes apparent that fewer employees are leaving, management may revise their estimate of the number of leavers to only 5 per cent. Accordingly, an expense of C100,000 will be recognised in the second year such that the cumulative expense at the end of that second year is C190,000 (that is, C300,000 × 2/3 × 95%). At the end of the third year, 94 per cent of the options do vest. The cumulative expense over the vesting period is C282,000 (that is, C300,000 × 3/3 × 94%) so the expense in the third year is C92,000.

A12.111 In a more extreme example, management may estimate in the first year of an employee share option plan that a particular long-term profit target will be met. Accordingly an expense of, say, C100,000 is recognised. During the second year, following a serious downturn in the entity's fortunes, management may consider that there is little chance that targets will be met. If they estimate that no options will vest, the cumulative expense at the end of the second year will be adjusted to zero so the expense to date of C100,000 will be reversed in that second year. Of course, if the vesting condition had been a market condition rather than a profit target, no adjustment would be made. It is interesting to note that if management were to cancel the award in year two on the basis that it will never vest, we believe IFRS 2's cancellation requirements would result in accelerated recognition of an expense. See paragraph A12.138 for discussion on accounting for cancellations.

Post-vesting

A12.112 In each of the examples above, changes have been made to estimates during the vesting period. However, no further adjustments are made after the vesting date, regardless of whether the equity instruments are later forfeited or, in the case of share options, the options are not exercised. [IFRS 2 para 23]. In drafting IFRS 2, the IASB took the view that the lapse of a share option at the end of the exercise period does not change the fact that the original transaction occurred, that is, goods or services were received as consideration for the issue of an equity instrument. The share option lapsing does not represent a gain to the entity, because there is no change to the entity's net assets. In other words, although some might see such an event as being a benefit to the remaining shareholders, it has no effect on the entity's financial position. In effect, one type of equity interest (the option holders' interest) becomes part of another type of equity interest (the shareholders' interest). So, in the example described in paragraph A12.110 above, after vesting there will be no adjustment to the total expense of C282,000 even if none of the options are exercised, as a result of the market price of the shares falling below the exercise price.

A12.113 The method of revising estimates in each of the examples above is consistent with that applied in the Implementation Guidance to IFRS 2. [IFRS 2 paras IG4, IG12]. Where estimates are revised in a period, the cumulative expense to the end of that period is 'trued up' and the amount recognised in the period is simply the difference between that cumulative expense and the equivalent cumulative expense at the end of the previous period. However, despite the fact that this method is required by IFRS 2, it does not appear to comply with the requirements of IAS 8. A change to the estimate of, for example, the number of share awards that will vest will have an impact on the expense recognised in both the current and future accounting periods. In this scenario (which has some similarity to a change in the useful life or residual value of a fixed asset for the purposes of measuring depreciation) IAS 8 requires that the effect of the change should be recognised prospectively by including it in profit or loss in both the period of the change and future periods. [IAS 8 para 36]. This suggests that when an estimate of the number of share awards that will vest is changed, the revised expense ought to be recognised over the remainder of the vesting period rather than 'trued up' in the period of change. It can only be assumed that, in drafting the implementation guidance to IFRS 2, the IASB had in mind paragraph 37 of IAS 8, which requires that to the extent that a change in accounting estimate gives rise to changes in assets and liabilities, or relates to an item of equity, it shall be recognised by adjusting the carrying amount of the related asset, liability or equity item in the period of the change. This paragraph would appear to apply if the principle of IFRS 2 was to measure that fair value of the equity instruments granted, but it is less clear why it is invoked when the principle is to measure the fair value of the goods or services received.

Awards conditional on an IPO or change in control

A12.113.1 IFRS 2 does not deal explicitly with awards that are conditional on an initial public offering (IPO). As noted above, an expense in respect of an award of, say, options, is recognised immediately if the award vests immediately, or over the vesting period if one exists. [IFRS 2 paras 14, 15]. In the case of an IPO (or similar exit event), the award will generally not vest until the IPO occurs (and employees are still employed by the company at that time). It is, therefore, reasonable to conclude that the vesting period will commence no later than the grant date and end on the date of the IPO. However, this raises two questions:

- What will the grant date be?
- How can the date of a future IPO be estimated reliably?

A12.113.2 As regards grant date, the facts of individual awards will vary. Sometimes, an award will be subject to approval at the time of the IPO, in which case grant date would correspond with the date of the IPO. On other occasions, shareholder approval will have been obtained when the award is made or at some other time in advance of the IPO. Nevertheless, IFRS 2 requires that an expense is recognised as employee services are received, regardless of when grant date is determined to occur. Therefore, where the grant date falls after the employees have begun to provide services, the fair value of the award should be estimated at each reporting period until the grant date is established and then revised once the grant date has been established, as described in paragraph A12.70.

A12.113.3 Where an award vests on an IPO but employee service up to the IPO date is not required, or perhaps service is only required for part of the period, the IPO condition becomes a non-vesting condition. Non-vesting conditions are considered from paragraph A12.101.

A12.113.4 The more difficult question concerns how the date of a future IPO can be estimated reliably. Paragraph 15(b) of IFRS 2 requires that where the length of the vesting period varies, depending on when a performance condition is satisfied, an estimate is made on the basis of the most likely outcome. Some companies may find it extremely difficult in practice to estimate the date of an IPO. Nevertheless, a reasonable estimate should be made, although this may then be revised if necessary. This is illustrated in the following example.

Example – Estimating listing date

The directors of an entity with a June year end are contemplating a listing of the entity's shares. An award of unvested shares is made to employees on 31 March 20X5, but the shares vest only in the event of an IPO. The company will not pay dividends before an IPO. Furthermore, employees leaving the entity before this occurs will lose their entitlement to the shares.

When the award is made, the directors estimate that a stock market listing will be achieved in three years' time. However, during the remainder of 20X5 and the first half of 20X6, the entity performs well and, following discussions with the entity's bankers, the directors decide to seek a listing by the end of 20X6. Due to unforeseen circumstances, this target is not achieved, but the shares are finally listed on 31 August 20X7.

Assuming that the directors have the authority to make the award of shares to the employees, grant date will be 31 March 20X5 and the fair value of the award will be measured on that date. If the award is subject to shareholder approval at the date of the IPO, fair value will be estimated (for example, by reference to the fair value of the options at each balance sheet date) and revised at grant date when the shareholder approval is obtained.

When the award is made, the directors estimate that the listing may be achieved in three years' time. An expense in respect of employee services is therefore recognised over this period. By 30 June 20X6, the directors have revised their estimate of the date of listing to the end of 20X6, so the recognition of the expense is accelerated. By 30 June 20X7, the listing has not yet occurred, but the process has commenced, and the directors estimate that it will be achieved within two months. The expense for the year ending 30 June 20X7 will therefore be based on this estimate. So for the three financial years ending 30 June 20X7, the estimated vesting period for the award of shares for the purposes of recognising an expense in accordance with IFRS 2 will be as follows:

Year	Vesting period
30 June 20X5	Three years ending 31 March 20X8
30 June 20X6	One year and nine months ending 31 December 20X6
30 June 20X7	Two years and five months ending 31 August 20X7

The estimated length of the vesting period does not impact the award's grant date fair value as the IPO is a non-market condition. The accounting for changes in estimates such as these under IFRS 2 is illustrated in example 2 in paragraph A12.114.

A12.113.5 Where awards vest only on an exit event such as an IPO, and an exit event is not deemed to be probable, no expense is recognised. It may be determined that some of the awards will vest in another way. These points are illustrated in the following examples.

Example 1 – Vesting linked to a change in control requirement

An entity enters into an equity-settled share-based payment arrangement with employees whereby each employee is entitled to 1,000 free shares provided that:

- There is a change in control of the entity (that is, the majority of shareholders change); and
- The employee is employed by the entity on the date that the change in control occurs.

The change in control requirement is a non-market performance vesting condition. The accounting treatment is to estimate at the grant date and at each reporting date the number of awards that are expected to vest based on:

- the number of employees who are expected to achieve the service period; and

- whether the change in control is probable.

If the change in control condition assessment changes from probable to improbable, the cumulative charge recognised is reversed through the income statement.

Example 2 – Interaction with other vesting conditions

As in the example in paragraph A12.113.4, the directors of an entity are contemplating a listing of the entity's shares. The entity made an award of options to 10 employees on 31 March 20X5. The grant date was achieved on this date.

The award is exercisable in full on an IPO. Alternatively, where an employee who is leaving the entity is determined to be a good leaver before an IPO has occurred, he/she may exercise options on a *pro rata* basis (based on the length of time the employee has served since the award was granted as a proportion of the maximum five-year period that the award may be in existence). The arrangement's terms and conditions define a good leaver as someone who is made redundant, dies or retires on reaching normal retirement age.

There is a cut-off date such that unvested awards will lapse after five years, on 31 March 20Y0.

On 30 June 20X5, the directors estimate that a listing will be achieved on 31 March 20X8. One employee is expected to be a good leaver before 31 March 20X8, reaching normal retirement age on 31 December 20X6. All other employees are expected to remain with the entity beyond 31 March 20X8.

On 30 June 20X6, following a change in the entity's fortunes, the directors are of the view that the entity is unlikely to float before 31 March 20X0. A restructuring programme is underway; it is anticipated that three employees will be made redundant on 31 December 20X6.

For the entity's 30 June 20X5 year end, the award will be treated in two tranches. Awards are expected to vest on 31 March 20X8 for nine employees. The grant date fair value of their awards will be spread over the three-year vesting period — that is, three out of 36 months of the charge will be taken in the period to 30 June 20X5. The grant date fair value of the award for the good leaver will be spread over the 21-month vesting period to 31 December 20X6 — that is, three out of 21 months' charge will be taken in the period to 30 June 20X5. The calculation for the good leaver will also take into account the fact that vesting will be on a *pro rata* basis — that is, based on 21 out of 60 months' service.

At 30 June 20X6, a reversal of the charge in respect of the nine awards no longer expected to vest on an IPO will be necessary. However, this will only be a partial reversal in respect of the three employees who will be made redundant. The charge in respect of these good leavers will now be spread over the shorter 21-month period from the grant date to 31 December 20X6 and will be adjusted for the fact that it will vest on a *pro rata* basis. A charge will continue to be made for the employee expected to retire on 31 December 20X6.

Illustrative examples

A12.114 Having measured the fair value of the goods or services received (either directly or indirectly) and determined the period over which they should be recognised, it is necessary to calculate the amount that should be recognised in each reporting period. This is illustrated in the following examples, which have been categorised according to type of vesting conditions.

Service vesting conditions

Example 1 – Grant of equity instruments with a time-based vesting condition

On 1 January 20X5, entity A made an award of 1,000 options to each of its 60 employees. The only condition associated with the award is that recipients must remain in entity A's employment for three years. The grant date fair value of each option is C5.

At the date of the award, management estimated that 10% of employees (that is, 6 employees) would leave the entity before the end of three years. During 20X6 it became apparent that fewer employees than expected were leaving so management revised its estimate of the number of leavers to only 5% (that is, 3 employees). At the end of 20X7, awards to 55 employees actually vested.

The amount recognised as an expense in each year will be as follows:

Year	Expense for the year C	Cumulative expense C	Calculation of cumulative expense
31 December 20X5	90,000	90,000	54 (that is, 60 × 90%) × 1,000 × 5 × $^1/_3$
31 December 20X6	100,000	190,000	57 (that is, 60 × 95%) × 1,000 × 5 × $^2/_3$
31 December 20X7	85,000	275,000	55 × 1,000 × 5

Non-market performance conditions

Example 2 – Vesting subject to exit event

On 1 January 20X7, entity H granted share option awards to senior management. The awards vest when an exit event (defined in the articles as a listing or change in control) occurs and provided that the employees are still employed by the entity at that time. The number of option awards that vest depends upon the date that the exit event occurs. The time over which an option is outstanding will affect its value, hence there are multiple grant date fair values for the award depending on the date that the award vests, as follows:

Date of exit event	Number of awards that vest	Grant date fair value per award
		C
1 January 20X7 – 31 December 20X7	25%	11
1 January 20X8 – 31 December 20X8	50%	12
1 January 20X9 – 31 December 20X9	75%	13
1 January 20Y0 – 31 December 20Y0	100%	14

If the IPO is beyond 31 December 20Y0, the share option awards will not vest.

At the 31 December 20X7 reporting date, management concluded that a listing was probable and expected to occur on 30 June 20X9.

The IFRS 2 charge should, therefore, be taken over the period from 1 January 20X7 to 30 June 20X9 based upon the expectation that 75% of the awards will vest using a grant date fair value of C13 per award.

If at the 31 December 20X8 reporting date, the listing was still probable, but the expected date of the exit event changed to 31 December 20Y0, the cumulative charge recognised would be based on the expectation that 100% of the awards would vest using a grant date fair value of C14 per award.

Example 3 – Staged vesting (also known as tranched or graded vesting)

Entity I grants 1,000 share options to employees on 1 January 20X7. If an exit event (defined in the articles as a listing or change in control) occurs at any time during the period from 1 January 20X7 to 31 December 20Y0, and employees are still in service at the date of exit, the employees will be entitled to exercise all of their outstanding options. Additionally, until the date of exit, 25% of the options vest each year (provided that the employee is in service at that particular year end) as follows:

Tranche	Date	Number of awards that vest	Cumulative number of vested awards
a	31 December 20X7	250	250
b	31 December 20X8	250	500
c	31 December 20X9	250	750
d	31 December 20Y0	250	1,000

At the 31 December 20X7 reporting date, management concluded that a listing was probable and expected to occur after three and a half years, on 30 June 20Y0.

The expense will be calculated in award tranches, resulting in a front-loaded IFRS 2 charge. Assuming that no employees are expected to leave the entity and that the anticipated date of exit does not change, the charge for the first two years of the arrangement will be determined as follows:

Year end	Calculation of expense for year	Cumulative expense to date
31 December 20X7	FV tranche a option × 250 × 1	FV tranche a option × 250 × 1
	FV tranche b option × 250 × 1/2	FV tranche b option × 250 × 1/2
	FV tranche c option × 250 × 1/3	FV tranche c option × 250 × 1/3
	FV tranche d option × 250 × 1/3.5	FV tranche d option × 250 × 1/3.5
31 December 20X8	n/a	FV tranche a option × 250 × 1
	FV tranche b option × 250 × 1/2	FV tranche b option × 250 × 2/2
	FV tranche c option × 250 × 1/3	FV tranche c option × 250 × 2/3
	FV tranche d option × 250 × 1/3.5	FV tranche d option × 250 × 2/3.5

The following diagram illustrates 'front-loading' of the expense in similar circumstances. For simplicity, the grant date fair value of each option within each tranche has been taken as C10, thus the fair value of 250 options is C2,500. While employees would not be providing more service or be working harder in the first year when the charge is the highest, the reason for the higher charge indicates that the employees are working towards a number of different awards with different vesting periods.

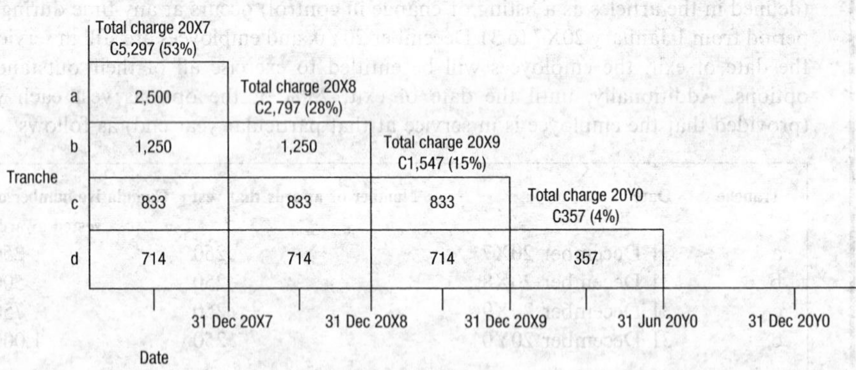

Example 4 – Grant of equity instruments with a specific performance condition (growth in earnings per share)

On 1 January 20X5, entity B made an award of shares to each of its 50 employees. The number of shares to which each employee will become entitled depends on growth in earnings per share (EPS). If EPS increases by an average of 10% over the next three years, each employee will receive 100 shares. If EPS increases by an average of 15%, each employee will receive 200 shares. If EPS increases by an average of 20%, each employee will receive 300 shares. No shares will be awarded if EPS increases by less than 10%. The recipients of the award must also remain in the employment of entity B for three years. The grant date fair value of each share at 1 January 20X5 is C12.

EPS is a non-market performance condition as it is not dependent upon share price. The condition is, therefore, relevant in determining the number of awards that will vest.

In the year ended 31 December 20X5, entity B's EPS increased by 16% and management forecast similar growth for the next two years. Hence, management predicted that each employee would receive 200 shares. However, 20X6 was a comparatively poor year and EPS increased by just 12% resulting in an average for the two-year period of 14%. Management cut back its forecast as a result, predicting growth of 14% for 20X7. On this basis, each employee would receive 100 shares. 20X7 was actually a much better year and EPS increased by 17% resulting in an average for the three-year period of 15% so each employee did, in fact, receive 200 shares.

During 20X5, five employees left the entity and management predicted a similar level of departures for the next two years, so 35 awards would vest. Six employees departed during 20X6, but management maintained its forecast of five departures in 20X7, so 34 awards would vest. However, only three employees left during 20X7, so 36 awards actually vested.

The amount recognised as an expense in each year will be as follows:

Year	Expense for the year C	Cumulative expense C	Calculation of cumulative expense
31 December 20X5	28,000	28,000	35 × 200 × 12 × 1/3
31 December 20X6	(800)	27,200	34 × 100 × 12 × 2/3
31 December 20X7	59,200	86,400	36 × 200 × 12

This example illustrates how the impact of 'truing up' the cumulative expense in each period may result in the reversal of amounts previously changed.

Example 5 – Grant of equity instruments in which the length of the vesting period varies

On 1 January 20X5, entity C granted 1,000 shares to each of its 500 employees, conditional upon the employees remaining in the employment of entity C throughout the vesting period. The shares will vest at the end of 20X5 if the entity's earnings increase by more than 20%; at the end of 20X6 if the entity's earnings increase by more than an average of 15% over the two-year period; and at the end of 20X7 if the entity's earnings increase by more than an average of 10% over the three-year period. The grant date fair value of each share at 1 January 20X5 is C6 (which in this case is assumed to be independent of the length of the vesting period).

During 20X5, earnings increased by 16% and 25 employees left the entity. Management forecast that earnings would grow at a similar rate in 20X6 so the share awards would vest at the end of 20X6. Management also estimated that a further 25 employees would leave the entity, so 450 awards would vest.

During 20X6, earnings increased by only 10% resulting in an average for the two-year period of 13% so the awards did not vest. However, management forecast that earnings growth for 20X7 would be at least 4%, thereby achieving the average of 10% per year. 30 employees left the entity during 20X6 and management estimated a similar level of departures for 20X7, so 415 awards would vest.

During 20X7, earnings increased by 10% (resulting in an average over the three-year period of 12%) and 27 employees left the entity.

The amount recognised as an expense in each year will be as follows:

Year	Expense for the year	Cumulative expense	Calculation of cumulative expense
	C	C	
31 December 20X5	1,350,000	1,350,000	450 × 1,000 × 6 × ½*
31 December 20X6	310,000	1,660,000	415 × 1,000 × 6 × 2/3
31 December 20X7	848,000	2,508,000	418 × 1,000 × 6

* ½ not 1/3 as at the end of 20X5 management expected the award to vest at the end of 20X6

Example 6 – Grant of equity instruments in which the exercise price varies

On 1 January 20X5, entity D made an award of 1,000 share options to each of its 50 senior employees. The recipients of the award must remain in entity D's employment for three years. The exercise price of each option is C10, but this will drop to C8 if EPS increases by an average of 10% over the next three years. If EPS increases by an average of 15% or more, the exercise price will drop to C6. The grant date fair value of each option 1 January 20X5 is C6 if the exercise price is C10; C9 if the exercise price is C8 and C12 if the exercise price is C6.

In the year ended 31 December 20X5, entity D's EPS increased by 16% and management forecast similar growth for the next two years. However, 20X6 was a comparatively poor year and EPS increased by just 12% resulting in an average for the two-year period of 14%. Management cut back its forecast as a result, predicting growth of 14% for 20X7. 20X7 was actually a much better year and EPS increased by 17% resulting in an average for the three-year period of 15%, so the options were exercisable at C6.

During 20X5, five employees left the entity and management predicted a similar level of departures for the next two years, so 35 awards would vest. Six employees departed during 20X6, but management maintained its forecast of five departures in 20X7, so 34 awards would vest. However, only three employees left during 20X7, so 36 awards actually vested.

Because the exercise price varies depending on the outcome of a performance condition that is not a market condition, the effect of that performance condition (that is, the possibility that the exercise price might be C10, C8 or C6) is not taken into account when estimating the fair value of the share options at grant date. Instead, the fair value of the options is estimated under each scenario and the accounting in each period reflects the most likely outcome. Hence, the amount recognised as an expense in the first year is based on the assumption that the exercise price will be C6 so the fair value of each option is C12. For 20X6, it is forecast that the exercise price will be C8, so the fair value of each option is C9. In both cases, the fair value is as measured at grant date.

The amount recognised as an expense in each year will be as follows:

Year	Expense for the year	Cumulative expense	Calculation of cumulative expense
	C	C	
31 December 20X5	140,000	140,000	35 × 1,000 × 12 × $^1/_3$
31 December 20X6	64,000	204,000	34 × 1,000 × 9 × $^2/_3$
31 December 20X7	228,000	432,000	36 × 1,000 × 12

Example 7 – Expected life of option depends on non-market vesting condition

On 1 January 20X5, entity E granted 1,000 share options to employees. Each option entitles the employee to purchase one share at a fixed price. The options are exercisable between 1 January 20X7 and 31 December 20X7 if the entity meets its EPS target for 20X5 and 20X6, or on 1 January 20X7 if any of the 20X5 and 20X6 EPS targets are not met. The options' grant date fair values are C1.20 if the options are exercisable on 1 January 20X7, and C2 if the options are exercisable between 1 January 20X7 and 31 December 20X7.

Management determined at 31 December 20X5 that the 20X5 EPS target was met and management expected to meet the 20X6 EPS target. However, the 20X6 EPS target was not met. No employees left the entity, and all 1,000 options ultimately vested.

Entity E should recognise an expense of C1,000 for 20X5 (1,000 options × C2 × 50% of the vesting period), because it met its 20X5 EPS target and at the balance sheet date expected to meet the 20X6 target. At 31 December 20X6, management should convert from the grant date fair value of C2 to C1.20 because the non-market EPS condition was not met. It should recognise an expense of C200 for 20X6 (1,000 options × C1.2 × 100% of the vesting period, less C1,000 expensed in 20X5), thus bringing the total expense recognised over the two years to C1,200.

Example 8 – Earnings per share hurdle

Entity G granted share options to employees on 1 January 20X5 in exchange for services through 20X6. The options become exercisable if entity G achieves its earnings per share (EPS) target of C0.23 per share for 20X5 and 20X6. The options' fair value on grant date, ignoring this condition, was C100,000.

Management assessed the probability of meeting the EPS target as 60%. The fair value of the options, including the EPS condition is C65,000. The EPS target was met for 20X5 and management also expects to meet the 20X6 target.

The EPS target is a non-market performance condition and, therefore, the fair value used should *not* include the EPS hurdle. As a result, management should recognise an expense of C50,000 (1/2 × 100,000) in 20X5 based on an expectation that 100% of the options will vest at the end of 20X6.

The outcome of the EPS condition can only be that either all options vest or that no options vest. Management's assessment that it is probable the EPS condition will be met means that management expect 100% of the options to vest.

If employees did not have to remain in service until the EPS target is met, in which case the award has vested, the EPS target is treated as a post-vesting restriction. Therefore, it would be appropriate to use the fair value that includes the EPS hurdle (C65,000) to recognise an expense.

Market performance conditions

Example 9 – Grant of equity instruments with a market condition

On 1 January 20X5, entity F made an award of 10,000 options to each of its 50 senior management employees, conditional upon the employees remaining in the entity's employment until the end of 20X7. However, the share options cannot be exercised unless the share price has increased from C10 at the beginning of 20X5 to at least C17.50 at the vesting date of 31 December 20X7; they can be exercised any time during the next two years.

At grant date, the fair value of each option (which takes into account the possibility that the share price will be at least C17.50 at 31 December 20X7) is C4.

At the date of the award, management estimated that 10% of employees would leave the entity before the end of three years. Hence, 45 awards would vest. During 20X6 it became apparent that more employees than expected were leaving so management revised its estimate of the number of awards that would vest to 42. At the end of 20X7, awards to 40 employees actually vested.

Where awards are granted with market conditions, paragraph 21 of IFRS 2 requires an entity to recognise the services received from a counterparty who satisfies all other vesting conditions, irrespective of whether the market conditions are satisfied. In other words, it makes no difference whether share price targets are achieved – the possibility that a share price target might not be achieved has already been taken into account when estimating the fair value of the options at grant date. Therefore, the amounts recognised as an expense in each year will be the same regardless of whether the share price has reached C17.50 by the end of 20X7.

The amount recognised as an expense in each year will be as follows:

Year	Expense for the year	Cumulative expense	Calculation of cumulative expense
	C	C	
31 December 20X5	C600,000	C600,000	45 × 10,000 × 4 × 1/3
31 December 20X6	C520,000	C1,120,000	42 × 10,000 × 4 × 2/3
31 December 20X7	C480,000	C1,600,000	40 × 10,000 × 4

Example 10 – Vesting conditions relate to share price growth

The facts are the same as in example 5, except that the vesting condition concerns the growth in entity C's share price rather than its earnings. Hence, the shares will vest at the end of 20X5 if the share price increases by more than 20%; at the end of 20X6 if the share price increases by more than an average of 15% over the two-year period; and at the end of 20X7 if the share price increases by more than an average of 10% over the three-year period.

As in example 5 the fair value of each share is C6, but this takes into account the possibility that the share price target will be achieved during the next three years as well as the possibility that it will not be achieved. At grant date, management estimated that the most likely outcome of the market condition was that the share price target would be reached by the end of 20X6. Management also estimated that 450 awards would vest. However, the target was actually reached in 20X7 and 418 awards vested at 31 December 20X7.

Paragraph 15(b) of IFRS 2 provides that where the length of the vesting period may vary, depending on when a performance condition is satisfied, an entity should base its accounting on an estimate of the expected length of the vesting period, based on the most likely outcome of the performance condition. This is illustrated in example 5. However, if the performance condition is a market condition, the estimate of the length of the expected vesting period should be consistent with the assumptions used in estimating the fair value of the options granted and should not be subsequently revised. Accordingly, in this example entity C should treat the award as if it did vest at the end of 20X6 (when 445 employees remained in employment). The fact that the award actually vested at the end of 20X7, after a further 27 employees had left the entity, is ignored.

The amount recognised as an expense in each year will be as follows:

Year	Expense for the year	Cumulative expense	Calculation of cumulative expense
31 December 20X5	C1,350,000	C1,350,000	450 × 1,000 × 6 × ½
31 December 20X6	C1,320,000	C2,670,000	445 × 1,000 × 6

Modifications, cancellations and settlements

Modifications and re-pricing

A12.115 An entity might modify the terms and conditions on which equity instruments were granted. For example, in recent years, during which equity markets have been somewhat volatile and with declining share prices as a result of the global economic crisis, many companies have reduced the exercise price of options to restore some of the perceived value of share option plans to their employees.

A12.116 The challenge for management in the current environment is how to modify share option awards where the share price is well below the exercise price ('underwater' options) in order to continue to motivate and reward employees, while managing the financial reporting consequences and shareholder and market expectations.

A12.117 There are a number of alternatives for reviving underwater options. For example, in addition to cancelling share option awards, which requires immediate recognition of an expense based on the grant date fair value of the original awards as discussed from paragraph A12.138 below, entities may reprice the options (lower the exercise price to the current market price) in order to increase the incentive to employees. To counter investor resistance to a straightforward repricing, management may do a combination of repricing share options and reducing the number of options, extending the service period or adding a performance or market condition. Alternatively, management may swap the share options originally awarded for actual shares (in order to avoid the risk of the options going underwater again) or for cash (which would require cash-settled treatment going forward).

A12.118 Whichever approach is taken, the decision taken by management will need to carefully balance factors including employee expectations, investor interests, market perception and the financial reporting impacts. Management will also need to be aware of any legal and contractual implications, for example, some option agreements may prohibit the employer from modifying the awards without approval of the option holders. Finally, management should consider the tax consequences, if any, of option repricing in the relevant jurisdiction.

A12.119 The accounting for modifications, along with a number of practical examples, is set out below.

A12.120 The approach taken in IFRS 2 to the accounting for modifications is to view the new/modified instruments as instruments in their own right. Where a modification increases the fair value of the equity instruments granted (for example, by reducing the exercise price of share options), an entity should include the incremental fair value granted in the measurement of the amount recognised for the services received over the remainder of the vesting period. The incremental fair value is the difference between the fair value of the modified equity instrument and that of the original equity instrument, both estimated as at the date of the modification. An expense based on the incremental fair value is recognised in addition to any amount in respect of the original instrument, which should continue to be recognised over the remainder of the original vesting period (unless there is a failure to satisfy vesting conditions – see from para A12.77). [IFRS 2 para 27].

A12.121 Guidance on how to apply the above requirements is given in Appendix B to the standard. In addition to modifications that increase the fair value of equity instruments granted (such as reductions in the exercise price of options), the principles of paragraph 27 of IFRS 2 also apply to other modifications that are otherwise beneficial to the employees. Examples include:

- An increase in the number of instruments granted.
- A reduction in the vesting period.
- The modification or elimination of a performance condition.

A12.122 If a modification increases the number of equity instruments granted, the entity should include the fair value of the additional equity instruments, measured at the date of the modification, in the measurement of the amount recognised for services received in a similar way to that described in paragraph A12.120. [IFRS 2 para B43(b)].

A12.123 If an entity modifies the vesting conditions associated with an award (for example, by reducing the vesting period or eliminating a performance condition, other than a market condition), this should be taken into account when considering the estimate of the number of equity instruments expected to vest. [IFRS 2 para B43(c)].

A12.124 The period over which the impact of a modification is recognised will depend on when it occurs and any vesting conditions it imposes. For example, if the modification described in paragraph A12.120 (reduction in option exercise price) occurs during the vesting period, the incremental fair value granted is included in the measurement of the amount recognised for services received over the period from the modification date until the date when the modified equity instruments vest. IFRS 2 does not, however, specify whether, in the case of a modification that reduces the vesting period, the change in vesting period should be accounted for prospectively or retrospectively. We believe that either approach is acceptable, for the reasons set out in example 4 of paragraph A12.127.

A12.125 Sometimes an entity may modify the terms and conditions of a grant of equity instruments in a manner that reduces the arrangement's total fair value or is not otherwise beneficial to the employee. The accounting treatment of such modifications is similar to that described above insofar as the entity should continue to account for the original grant as if the modification had not occurred. However:

- If the modification reduces the fair value of the equity instruments granted, this should be ignored. The entity should not recognise reduced expense as a consequence of the modification. This prevents an entity from modifying an award simply to reduce the overall income statement charge.
- If the modification reduces the number of equity instruments granted, this should be accounted for as a cancellation of that portion of the grant (see para A12.138).
- If an entity modifies the vesting conditions associated with an award (for example, by increasing the vesting period or adding a non-market performance condition), this should *not* be taken into account when considering the estimate of the number of equity instruments expected to vest.

[IFRS 2 para B44].

A12.126 Entities sometimes 'rebase' share-based payment awards by replacing existing tax inefficient awards with a new award that is more tax efficient. Where the total fair value of an award is the same immediately before and after modification (irrespective of whether there are tax benefits for the entity or employee as a result of the change), this is treated as a non-beneficial modification, that is, the entity should continue to account for the original award as if the modification had not occurred.

A12.127 The accounting treatment of modifications to terms and conditions is considered further in the following examples.

Example 1 – Existing options rolled into new award – reduction in exercise price

An entity has previously operated a share option award with an option exercise price of C15, which is equal to the market price of the shares at the date of grant. Management decide to roll the options into a new award. The entity, therefore, cancels the original option plan and issues share options under the new award. The new options are granted at a lower exercise price of C12 because the market price of the shares has fallen to C11 since the date of grant of the initial plan so that the original exercise price is now below the market price of the shares at the date of grant of the new options. The terms of the original options are otherwise the same (that is, they have the same exercise date).

This would not be treated as a cancellation and a new award, but instead as a modification. This is because the entity has indicated that the new award replaces a cancelled award and, therefore, under paragraph 28(c) of IFRS 2 it is treated as if the original award had been modified. Consequently, the entity would be required to account for the incremental fair value of the new award (compared with the existing award) at the date of modification and spread this over the vesting period of the new award. This would be in addition to the entity continuing to charge for the original award over the original vesting period. Note that replacement awards are sometimes structured with similar terms to those of the original award and it may, therefore, be possible that there is no incremental fair value.

It is also worth noting that if the entity had not identified the new award as a replacement award at the same date that the new options were granted, the cancellation and new award would be unrelated and there would be a requirement to accelerate the vesting of the original award and recognise immediately the amount that otherwise would have been recognised for services received over the remainder of the vesting period. (See also example 9 below.) Additionally, there would be a fair value charge for the new award over the new vesting period.

Example 2 – Reduction in option exercise price – worked example

On 1 January 20X5, entity A grants an award of 1,000 options to each of its 60 employees. The only condition associated with the award is that recipients must remain in the employment of entity A for three years. The grant date fair value of each option is C5.

Towards the end of 20X5, entity A's share price dropped so, on 1 January 20X6, management chose to reduce the exercise price of the options. At the date of the repricing, the fair value of each of the original share options granted was C1 and the fair value of each re-priced option was C3. Hence, the incremental fair value of each modified option was C2.

At the date of the award, management estimated that 10% of employees would leave the entity before the end of three years (that is, 54 awards would vest). During 20X6 it became apparent that fewer employees than expected were leaving so management revised its estimate of the number of leavers to only 5% (that is, 57 awards would vest). At the end of 20X7, awards to 55 employees actually vested.

The amount recognised as an expense in each year will be as follows:

Year	Expense for the year C	Cumulative expense C	Calculation of cumulative expense
31 December 20X5	90,000	90,000	54 × 1,000 × 5 × $^1/_3$
31 December 20X6	157,000	247,000	57 × 1,000 × ((5 × $^2/_3$) + (2 × ½))
31 December 20X7	138,000	385,000	55 × 1,000 × (5 + 2)

Example 3 – Increase in the number of options granted

The facts are similar to example 2, except that instead of reducing the option exercise price on 1 January 20X6, the number of options to which each employee was entitled was increased to 1,500. The fair value of each of these additional options was C1.

The amount recognised as an expense in each year will be as follows:

Year	Expense for the year C	Cumulative expense C	Calculation of cumulative expense
31 December 20X5	90,000	90,000	54 × 1,000 × 5 × $^1/_3$
31 December 20X6	114,250	204,250	57 × ((1,000 × $^2/_3$ × 5) + (500 × ½ × 1))
31 December 20X7	98,250	302,500	55 × ((1,000 × 5) + (500 × 1))

Example 4 – Reduction in the vesting period – prospective versus retrospective adjustment

On 1 January 20X6, entity B awarded an employee 100 shares (with no entitlement to dividends during the vesting period) subject only to the employee remaining in service for three years. At 1 January 20X6, the fair value of each share was C6.

On 1 December 20X6, entity B decided to reduce the service requirement from three years to two years, thereby reducing the vesting period to two years.

It is assumed that the employee remains in service beyond 31 December 20X6.

As no dividends are expected to be paid during the vesting period changing the vesting period has no impact on the fair value of the unvested shares.

We believe that entity A has a policy choice for accounting for modifications of equity-settled awards occurring part way through a reporting period that reduce the vesting period by either using a retrospective or a prospective treatment.

Retrospective treatment

The modification may be accounted for retrospectively to reflect the best estimate available as at that date of awards that are expected to vest. This is supported by paragraph 19 of IFRS 2 which states that "*...the amount recognised for goods or services received as consideration for the equity instruments granted shall be based on the number of equity instruments that eventually vest*". Where there is a change in estimate of the period over which the awards are expected to vest and that change occurs during the year, the cumulative expense may be 'trued up' at the balance sheet date to reflect the best estimate of awards expected to vest as of that date. On this basis, the expense each year as a result of the modification would be as follows:

Year	Expense for the year	Cumulative expense	Calculation of cumulative expense
	C	C	
31 December 20X6	300	300	100 × C6 × ½
31 December 20X7	300	600	100 × C6

Prospective treatment

Alternatively, the modification may be accounted for prospectively from the date of modification (1 December 20X6). While paragraph 19 of IFRS 2 states that the expense should be recognised based on the best estimate available, it does not specify the point at which changes in those estimates should be accounted for.

An analogy may be made to IAS 8 and the treatment of changes in estimates where a change in estimate is accounted for prospectively from the date of change. [IAS 8 para 36].

Furthermore, accounting for the change in vesting period prospectively would be consistent with the principle set out in paragraph B43 of IFRS 2, where other types of modifications are accounted for prospectively. In addition, paragraph 15 of IFRS 2 requires that where equity instruments do not vest until the counterparty completes a specified service period, the entity should account for those services as they are rendered by the counterparty over the specified vesting period. Prior to modification, employee services received as consideration were presumed to be received over a three year period and as such, the expense would be recognised on this basis. The presumption changes from three years to two years when the vesting period is modified, hence it would be appropriate to account for the modification prospectively and amend the recognition of expense from the modification date as follows:

Year	Expense for the year	Cumulative expense	Calculation of cumulative expense
31 December 20X6	C215	C215	Original charge, 11 months to 1 December 20X6: 100 × C6 × 1/3 × 11/12 = 183 Modification occurs 1 December 20X6. Expense over remaining 13 months to 31 December 20X7: 600 – 183 = 417 Expense for December 20X6: 417/13 = 32 Therefore, total expense for year to 31 December 20X6: 183 + 32 = 215
31 December 20X7	C385	C600	100 × C6

Whichever approach is followed, the policy should be clearly explained and consistently applied.

It should be noted that where vesting is conditional upon an exit event of some kind such as an IPO, the estimated time until the exit event should be reassessed at each reporting date with adjustments made retrospectively. Prospective treatment would not be appropriate, because any adjustment would be a change in estimate, not a modification.

Example 5 – Reduction in the vesting period before resignation

On 1 January 20X5, entity B granted an award of 1,000 options to its financial director. The only condition associated with the award is that the director must remain employed by entity B for four years. The grant date fair value of each option is C40. The entity expects the director to meet the service condition.

On 1 October of 20X6, the finance director informed the entity that he wished to take early retirement and that after serving his three month notice period, would resign from employment. The remuneration committee, in its ultimate discretion, made a decision in November 20X6 (before he actually failed to meet the service vesting condition by retiring) that entity B would still provide the finance director with his award on termination of his service. This would be accounted for as a beneficial modification, that is, a reduction in the vesting period. The amount recognised as an expense in each year will be as follows:

Year	Expense for the year	Cumulative expense	Calculation of cumulative expense
31 December 20X5	C10,000	C10,000	1,000 × 40 × 1/4
31 December 20X6	C30,000	C40,000	1,000 × 40

Example 6 – Modification that is not beneficial to employees

An entity granted 100 share options to employees at an exercise price of C10 per share. The grant date is 1 January 20X4 and the options are subject to a two-year vesting period. The grant date fair value of each option was C50. The entity modified the options at 31 December 20X4 by extending the vesting period to 30 June 20X6. At 31 December 20X4 management expected that the number of options outstanding at 31 December 20X5, the original vesting date, would be 90. The actual number of options outstanding at 31 December 20X5 was 85, of which only 80 vested on 30 June 20X6. The modification did not increase the options' fair value.

The extension of the vesting period should be ignored. Modification of vesting conditions in a manner that is not beneficial to employees should not be taken into account when determining amounts to be recognised.

The expense and corresponding increase in equity recognised for 20X4 is C2,250; C50 × 90 options × 50% of the original two-year vesting period. The expense for 20X5 is C2,000; C50 × 85 options × 100% of the original two-year vesting period less C2,250, the amount expensed in 20X4. No expense is recognised in 20X6 and no adjustment is made to reflect the fact that only 80 awards actually vest as this occurred after the original vesting date.

Example 7 – Modification or cancellation?

Due to an unexpected significant decline in entity C's share price, management reduced the exercise price of an award from C50 to C20. At the same time, the number of options awarded was also reduced from 100 to 17. The 17 remaining options had the same total fair value as the 100 options immediately before the repricing.

The accounting for this can be viewed in two different ways. One view is that for the options that remain, the treatment is the same as for a simple reduction in exercise price described in example 1 above, and the other options are cancelled, so the recognition of the grant date fair value is accelerated in accordance with paragraph B44 of IFRS 2. The alternative view, which we believe better reflects the economics of the situation, is that there is no change in the aggregate fair value of the award so there is neither an incremental fair value nor a cancellation. Therefore, any element of the grant date fair value of the original award will continue to be charged over the original vesting period.

The accounting treatment applied to a reduction in the number of awards and a corresponding, or greater, increase in the fair value of each award is a judgment that will depend on the specific facts of each case and should be applied consistently. Cancellations are discussed further from paragraph A12.138 below.

Example 8 – Re-priced options and extension of vesting period

Management granted 100 share options at an exercise price of C10 per share to employees in exchange for services. The grant date was 1 January 20X4 and the options were subject to a two-year vesting period. The grant date fair value of the options was C5,000 and all options were expected to vest at the end of the vesting period.

The options were modified on 1 January 20X5 by reducing the exercise price to C5 per share (the current market value) and extending the vesting period by six months to 30 June 20X6. The fair value of the options at 1 January 20X5 was C8,000 prior to the modification and C9,500 after the modification. At the modification date, all options were expected to vest.

The original grant date fair value is recognised over the original vesting period. The expense for the year to 31 December 20X4 is C2,500; C5,000 × 50%. The expense for the year to 31 December 20X5 is C3,500; C5,000 × 50% plus the recognised incremental fair value of the modification of C1,500 × 66.7%. The incremental fair value is recognised over the vesting period from 1 January 20X5 to 30 June 20X6; 66.7% of this period passed by the balance sheet date. The incremental fair value is the difference between the fair value of the re-priced options immediately before and after the modification, that is, C9,500 less C8,000. The expense for the six months to 30 June 20X6 is C500; C1,500 × 33.3%.

If an employee leaves during the six month period to 30 June 20X6 and thus fails to meet the revised vesting condition, it is only the repricing impact that is reversed; the original grant date fair value expense of C5,000 is unaffected because the employee satisfied the two-year service condition for the original award.

Example 9 – Impact of rights issue and modification of share schemes

Entity F is planning a rights issue to offer shares at a 30% discount. The entity operates numerous share schemes; it realises that employees in those share schemes will be worse off after the rights issue as the market value of the shares will be reduced. Entity F plans to modify the share schemes at a later date to ensure the awards granted to employees are uplifted to the equivalent value of the original award granted. Management believes that the rights issue and subsequent share-based payment modification are linked. It, therefore, wants to treat the impact of the rights issue and the modification as a single event.

A share-based payment modification occurs when the terms and conditions of the equity instruments change. The modification in this case would, therefore, be later than, not at the date of, the rights issue.

When a modification occurs, an entity will need to compare the fair value of the new and old awards at the modification date and consider whether there is an uplift in fair value. Any uplift will then be expensed, along with the charge for the original awards over the remaining vesting period. As this modification is happening at a later date than the rights issue, then it is likely there will be an increase in fair value as a of changes in volatility, market value and time value of money (since the date of the rights issue.) If entity F had structured the transaction differently, such that the modification of the awards occurred on the same day as the rights issue, then it is highly likely that the difference between the new and old awards would be nil resulting in no additional charge.

Reclassification — equity-settled to cash-settled

A12.128 Reclassification of a share-based payment award may occur because:

- An entity is de-listing. To provide greater liquidity to employees the entity might change the share-based payment from equity-settled to cash-settled.
- The entity has changed its settlement practice.

A12.129 Where an entity modifies a share-based payment award such that it will be settled in cash as opposed to shares, the entity measures the liability initially using the modification date fair value of the equity-settled award based on the elapsed portion of the vesting period. This amount is then recognised as a credit to liability and a debit to equity, by analogy to paragraph 29 of IFRS 2 which states that the repurchase of vested equity instruments is accounted for as a deduction from equity.

A12.130 The entity then re-measures the liability and does so at each subsequent reporting date and recognises any additional expense from increases in the liability. See further paragraph A12.164 below. The example below also illustrates this.

Example – Reclassification from equity-settled to cash-settled

Entity N has an equity-settled share-based payment that will vest when employees provide four years of continuous service. The grant date fair value is C10; the vesting period is four years. At the end of year two, a cumulative charge of C5 has been recognised in the income statement with a corresponding increase in equity.

At the end of year two, entity N decides to change the share-based payment award from equity-settled to cash-settled. The employees will now receive a cash payment based on the fair value of the shares at the end of year four.

When an award is modified to become a cash-settled award, this is accounted for as the repurchase of an equity interest (that is, a deduction from equity). Any excess over the grant date fair value should be treated as a deduction from equity (as opposed to an expense), provided that the deduction is not greater than the fair value of the equity instruments when measured at the modification date.

The accounting is illustrated by two scenarios, in which immediately before the change in classification, the fair value of the grant:

(a) Has increased:
Assume the fair value immediately before modification is C20. At the start of year three, a liability of C10 (20/2) is recognised with a corresponding debit to equity of C10. The subsequent measurement of the liability would follow the requirements for cash-settled share-based payment.

(b) Has decreased:
IFRS 2 requires an entity to recognise a charge in the income statement for services received of at least the grant date fair value, regardless of any modifications to or

cancellations of the grant. The only exception to this is where a non-market vesting condition is not satisfied. Assume that the fair value immediately before the modification has decreased to C5 and there are no further movements in the fair value in years three and four. The accounting would be:

- Years one and two: a total expense and increase in equity of C5, is recognised.
- At the start of year three: a liability of C2.5 (5 × 2/4) is recognised with a corresponding decrease to equity.
- Years three and four: an expense of C2.5 is recognised each year with a corresponding increase in the liability of C1.25 and equity of C1.25. The C1.25 expense and increase in equity recognised each year ensures that the income statement expense is at least equal to the grant date fair value.

At the end of the vesting period the total expense is C10 (of which C5 was a credit to equity and C5 a credit to liability). The total expense is equal to the grant date fair value of C10.

If the fair value was to change in years three and four, the entity would need to recalculate the amounts to expense in these years as follows:

- record the expense based on the grant date fair value and allocate this expense between debt and equity based on the ratio of debt to equity on the date of modification; and
- re-measure the value of the liability based on movements in the share price.

To illustrate, assume that at the end of year three, the fair value of the award had decreased to C4. The entity:

- records an expense, based on the grant date fair value, of C2.5 with a corresponding increase in the liability and equity of C1.25 (based on the ratio of equity to cash on the date of modification); and then
- re-measures the value of the liability through the income statement from C3.75 to C3 (representing three-quarters of the fair value of the liability of C4 as it is three years through the four-year vesting period).

A12.131 Reclassification from a cash-settled share-based payment to an equity-settled award is discussed in paragraph A12.154 below.

Modifications and business combinations

A12.132 IFRS 3, 'Business combinations', provides detailed guidance on when and how an acquirer should allocate equity instruments between the cost of the business combination and post-combination services for replacement awards granted to employees of the acquiree.

A12.133 For situations where the acquiree's employee awards may expire as a consequence of a business combination and the acquirer replaces those awards even though it is not obliged to do so, IFRS 3 requires the entire grant date fair value of the replacement awards to be recognised as remuneration cost in the post-combination financial statements. For all other situations, replacements of share-based payment awards are accounted for as modifications in accordance with IFRS 2. Depending on facts and circumstances, either all or a portion of the IFRS 2 measure of the replacement awards is allocated to the consideration transferred for the purposes of IFRS 3.

A12.134 The principle of IFRS 3 is to allocate a portion of a replacement award to the business combination based on the fair value of acquiree awards and the degree to which the acquiree awards have been earned at the date of acquisition. Any excess value in the replacement awards is accounted for as post-combination employee services incorporating any new or amended vesting conditions.

[The next paragraph is A12.136.]

A12.136 The requirements set out in IFRS 3 are covered further in chapter 25, along with a number of illustrative examples. Chapter 25 also discusses the employee compensation and contingent consideration guidance in Appendix B to IFRS 3.

An additional example illustrating the modification of a share-based payment award occurring at the same time as an acquisition is set out below.

Example – Modification as a result of acquisition

Entity C granted share options to its employees on 1 May 20X5. The options were exercisable subject to the completion of three years' service from that date. On 30 April 20X7, entity D acquired entity C. Entity D is obliged to replace entity C's share plans. The terms of the share options were modified on acquisition so that employees will be entitled to shares in entity D at the end of the original three year period as opposed to shares in entity C. The modified terms make clear that entity D, the acquirer, has granted, and has the obligation for, the replacement award. The terms of the plan are otherwise unchanged.

Entity C's financial statements

Entity C originally granted an equity-settled share-based payment award to its employees. Immediately upon the acquisition, the plan's terms were modified and the new parent, entity D, had the obligation to settle the award. In accordance with the guidance in IFRS 2 on group settled share-based payments, the award will continue to be treated as equity-settled in entity C's financial statements (see further from para A12.169).

The remainder of the original IFRS 2 charge (measured on 1 May 20X5) will continue to be spread over the vesting period to 30 April 20X8. In addition, if the modification has increased the award's fair value (measured as the difference between the award's fair value immediately before and after the modification), the incremental fair value will be spread over the remaining period to 30 April 20X8. [IFRS 2 para B43].

Entity D's separate and consolidated financial statements

From 30 April 20X7, entity D, as the acquirer, has granted an equity-settled award in its own shares to the employees of its subsidiary, entity C. This will be accounted for as a new award in both entity D's separate and consolidated financial statements. Say the award's fair value is C900, measured at the grant date, 30 April 20X7. The terms of the award require employees to provide three years service to entity C, from 1 May 20X5 to 30 April 20X8. Hence, part of the award's fair value relates to pre-combination services and will be taken as part of entity D's cost of investment in entity C.

Management will need to follow the guidance in IFRS 3 to determine the allocation between pre- and post-combination services and in this case, given that two thirds of the vesting period has passed and there is no incremental fair value or change in the vesting period, it would be appropriate to allocate two thirds (C600) of the fair value of entity C's award at the date of acquisition to pre-combination services (this would, therefore, be included as part of entity D's cost of investment in entity C). One third (C300) of the fair value of entity C's award at the date of acquisition, plus any incremental fair value between entity C's and entity D's award at the date of acquisition, would be treated as post-combination services (this would, therefore, be recognised as an expense over the period to 30 April 20X8).

For the year ended 30 April 20X8, the IFRS 2 entries in the consolidated financial statements will be:

Dr Income statement	C300 (being one third of the total fair value of the award measured at 30 April 20X7, grant date)
Cr Equity	C300

Further guidance on the treatment in entity D's separate financial statements is provided from paragraph A12.169. Based on this guidance, the entries in entity D's separate financial statements on 30 April 20X8 will be:

Dr Investment in subsidiary	C300 (being the fair value of award measured at 30 April 20X7)
Cr Equity	C300

[The next paragraph is A12.138.]

Cancellations and settlements

A12.138 All cancellations, whether by the entity or by other parties, are accounted for in the same way. If a grant of equity instruments is cancelled or settled during the vesting period, it should be treated as an acceleration of vesting and should recognise immediately the amount that otherwise would have been recognised for services received over the remainder of the vesting period. Opinions are divided as to the amount that should be recognised at the date of cancellation. Paragraph 28(a) of IFRS 2 states that:

"The entity shall account for the cancellation or settlement as an acceleration of vesting, and shall therefore recognise immediately the amount that otherwise would have been recognised for services received over the remainder of the vesting period."

We believe that the charge should reflect all awards that are outstanding at the date of cancellation, without adjusting for any estimate of the number of awards that are not expected to vest. This is because the cancellation results in early vesting (satisfaction of a non-market vesting condition) and thus accelerated recognition of the grant date fair value. There is an alternative interpretation that focuses on the words *"... the amount that otherwise would have been recognised for services received over the remainder of the vesting period". It* recognises a charge that reflects the number of awards that were expected to achieve the performance condition just prior to the award being cancelled. Either interpretation could be applied, but we believe that the first is more closely aligned with the principles of IFRS 2.

A12.139 Any payment made to a counterparty on the cancellation or settlement of a grant of equity instruments, even if this occurs after the vesting date, should be accounted for as a repurchase of an equity interest (that is, as a deduction from equity), except to the extent that the payment exceeds the fair value of the equity instruments repurchased, measured at the repurchase date. Any such excess should be recognised as an expense. [IFRS 2 paras 28(b), 29].

Example – Cancellation during vesting period

On 1 January 20X5 entity A made an award of 100 shares to an employee. The only condition associated with the award is that the employee must remain in entity A's employment for three years. The award's grant date fair value was C1,200. The employee is expected to remain with the entity for at least three years and, therefore, the award is expected to vest.

The award is cancelled on 1 January 20X6 and entity A settles in cash on a *pro rata* basis. The employee, therefore, receives C400 (C1,200 × 1/3 years). The award's fair value on this date is determined to have fallen from C1,200 to C300.

The amount recognised as an expense during 20X5 before taking account of the cancellation was C400 (C1,200 × 1/3 years). Paragraph 28(a) of IFRS 2 requires the entity to account for the cancellation or settlement as an acceleration of vesting and recognise immediately the amount that otherwise would have been recognised for services received over the remainder of the vesting period. Accordingly, on the basis of the number of awards outstanding at the cancellation date, the amount to be recognised immediately as an expense is C800 (that is, C1,200 – C400), with a credit to equity of C800. Note, if the above award was made to more than one employee, at the date of cancellation, we believe management should accelerate the share-based payment expense based on the actual number of awards on cancellation rather than on the basis of what management had previously expected to vest as discussed above.

However, as noted above, an alternative approach based on the number of awards expected to vest may also be considered.

Following the former interpretation, the C400 payment made to the employee on cancellation of the award exceeds the award's fair value of C300 on the date of repurchase. Paragraph 28(b) of IFRS 2 requires an amount equal to the fair value (C300) to be treated as the repurchase of an equity instrument. The excess is recognised as an expense. This means that C300 is deducted from equity while C100 (that is, C300 – C400) is recognised as an expense. In summary the entity would record the following:

Year ended 31 December 20X5

		Dr	Cr
		C	C
Dr	Employee benefits expense	400	
	Cr Equity		400
	Year ended 31 December 20X6		
Dr	Employee benefits expense – cancellation of the award	800	
	Cr Equity		800
Dr	Employee benefits expense – incremental fair value on settlement in cash	100	
Dr	Equity	300	
	Cr Cash		400

A12.140 Sometimes an entity may grant new equity instruments as consideration for the cancellation or settlement of an old grant. When this occurs and, on the date when those new equity instruments are granted, the entity identifies the new equity instruments as replacements for the cancelled equity instruments, the entity should treat this as a modification, as described from paragraph A12.115 above. Hence, the incremental fair value granted is the difference between the fair value of the replacement equity instruments and the net fair value of the cancelled equity instruments, at the date the replacement equity instruments are granted. For this purpose, the net fair value of the cancelled equity instruments is their fair value, immediately before the cancellation, less the amount of any payment made to the counterparty that is accounted for as a deduction from equity as described in paragraph A12.139 above. If the entity does not identify the new equity instruments as a replacement for the cancelled instruments, it should account for those new equity instruments as a new grant. [IFRS 2 para 28(c)].

A12.141 Where the cancellation of an award has been reported, an entity cannot subsequently identify a replacement award. We believe that the standard is clear that a replacement award should be identified at the same time as the original award is cancelled.

A12.142 It may not always be clear whether an award has been cancelled or modified. For example, where the number of share options awarded to an employee is reduced, the question arises as to whether part of the award has been cancelled. This point is illustrated in example 7 of paragraph A12.127.

Forfeitures

A12.143 A forfeiture occurs when either a service or a non-market performance condition is not met, as this affects the number of awards that vest. Failures to meet either market conditions or non-vesting conditions are not forfeitures as these are already taken into account when determining the grant date fair value.

A12.144 The accounting for forfeitures is different to that of cancellations described from paragraph A12.138 above. Forfeiture of a vested award has no accounting implications, unless it results from a post-vesting restriction, which will have been incorporated into the grant date fair value.

A12.145 Where a number of individual awards within a larger portfolio of awards are forfeited, the expense is revised to reflect the best available estimate of the number of equity instruments expected to vest. Hence, on a cumulative basis, no expense is recognised for goods or services received if the equity instruments do not vest as a result of a service or non-market performance condition (for example, if the employee or counterparty fails to complete a specified service period).

Example – Employee made redundant

Entity A granted share option awards to a number of its employees with a three year service requirement. The individuals were required to remain in service with the entity for three years from the date of grant. 18 months into the plan, one employee is made redundant.

Having been made redundant, the employee is unable to satisfy the three-year service condition and, therefore, this should be treated as a forfeiture rather than a cancellation. The expense recognised to date is reversed. If, however, the award was cancelled prior to the employee being made redundant, there would be an accelerated charge.

Cash-settled share-based payment transactions

A12.146 Some transactions are 'share-based', even though they do not involve the issue of shares, share options or any other form of equity instrument. Cash-settled share-based payment transactions are defined in IFRS 2 as transactions *"in which the entity acquires goods or services by incurring a liability to transfer cash or other assets to the supplier of those goods or services for amounts that are based on the price (or value) of equity instruments (including shares or share options) of the entity or another group entity"*. [IFRS 2 App A].

A12.147 The most common examples of cash-settled share-based payment transactions are employee incentive plans, such as share appreciation rights and 'phantom' share plans. These plans involve the payment of an amount based on the price of the employing entity's shares after a period of time.

A12.148 Sometimes, transactions that are actually settled in shares may be treated as cash-settled if this is more reflective of their substance. For example, an entity might grant to its employees a right to shares that are redeemable, either mandatorily (such as upon cessation of employment) or at the employee's option. As the entity has an obligation to make a cash payment, the transaction would be treated as cash-settled.

Example 1 – Repurchase of shares on termination of employment

Entity A is the sponsoring entity of a trust that administers an employee share-based compensation plan. Entity A issues new shares to the trust. The trust issues these shares to employees who satisfy the plan's vesting conditions. The shares are non-transferable while employees remain in entity A's employment and each employee has an obligation to sell the shares acquired through the plan back to the trust on termination of employment. The trust buys the shares back at fair value when returned.

Entity A prepares consolidated financial statements and, therefore, under SIC 12, 'Consolidation – special purpose entities', the trust should be consolidated. (SIC 12 is superseded by IFRS 10 'Consolidated financial statements'. See further para A12.246.1). When employment is terminated, the award is settled in cash based on entity A's share price and, therefore, the transaction should be accounted for as a cash-settled award under IFRS 2. [IFRS 2 para 31].

Example 2 – Funding of award – shares purchased by trust

Entity B awarded its employees rights to obtain its shares subject to a three year vesting period. Local legislation does not allow the entity either to issue new shares to employees or to buy its own shares. The entity will establish a trust that will purchase the entity's shares from third parties and transfer those shares to entitled employees. The entity will pay the trust the cash required to purchase those shares.

Entity B prepares consolidated financial statements and, therefore, as in example 1, the trust will be consolidated under SIC 12. (SIC 12 is superseded by IFRS 10. See further para A12.246.1.) The fact that the group, *via* the trust, must buy shares from third parties in order to satisfy the obligation to deliver shares does not change the nature of the award. Employee services will ultimately be settled in shares. As such, the transaction should be treated as an equity-settled transaction under IFRS 2 (and any share purchase would be treated as a treasury share transaction in the consolidation). [IFRS 2 paras B48, B49.]

Measurement of cash-settled share-based payment transactions

A12.149 Like share options and other equity instruments, the fair value of share appreciation rights and other cash-settled share-based payment transactions includes both their intrinsic value (the increase in the share price to date) and their time value (the value of the right to participate in future increases in the share price, if any, that may occur between the valuation date and the settlement date). Accordingly, many of the principles described previously for the measurement of equity-settled transactions apply equally to cash-settled transactions. So:

- The objective is to measure the goods or services acquired and the liability incurred at fair value.
- Fair value is determined using an option pricing model, taking into account the terms and conditions of the award.
- The goods or services are recognised as they are received by the entity.

[IFRS 2 paras 30, 32, 33].

A12.150 There is, however, an important difference. For cash-settled transactions, the fair value of the liability is re-measured at each reporting date and at the date of settlement. The measurement reflects the impact of all conditions and all possible outcomes on a weighted-average basis, unlike the measurement for an equity-settled award. Any changes in fair value are recognised in profit or loss for the period. [IFRS 2 para 30]. This is illustrated in the following example.

Example – Cash-settled award

On 1 January 20X5, an entity granted 1,000 share appreciation rights (SARs) to each of its 40 management employees. The SARs provide the employees with the right to receive, at the date the rights are exercised, cash equal to the appreciation in the entity's share price since the grant date. All of the rights vest on 31 December 20X6. They can be exercised during 20X7 and 20X8. Management estimates that, at grant date, the fair value of each SAR is C11, and that 10% of the employees will leave evenly during the two-year period. The fair values of the SARs at each year end are shown below.

Year	Fair value at year end
31 December 20X5	12
31 December 20X6	8
31 December 20X7	13
31 December 20X8	12

10% of employees did leave before the end of 20X6. On 31 December 20X7, when the intrinsic value of each SAR was C10, six employees exercise their options, while the remaining 30 employees exercise their options at the end of 20X8 (when the intrinsic value of each SAR was equal to the fair value of C12). The amount recognised as an expense in each year and as a liability at each year end will be as follows:

Year	Expense C	Liability C	Calculation of liability
31 December 20X5	216,000	216,000	36 × 1,000 × 12 × ½
31 December 20X6	72,000	288,000	36 × 1,000 × 8
31 December 20X7	162,000	390,000	30 × 1,000 × 13. Expense comprises an increase in the liability of C102,000 and cash paid to those exercising their SARs of C60,000 (6 × 1,000 × 10).
31 December 20X8	(30,000)	0	Liability extinguished. Previous cost reversed as cash paid to those exercising their SARs of C360,000 (30 × 1,000 × 12) was less than the opening liability of C390,000.

A12.151 For cash-settled transactions, it is perhaps more difficult to comprehend the difference between the fair value of a right and its intrinsic value. In the previous example, the fair value of each right at 31 December 20X7 was C13. However, the amount paid to each employee who exercised rights on that day was only C10 (that is, the intrinsic value). The reason for the higher fair value is the same for cash-settled transactions as for equity-settled transactions. The fair value of each SAR at 31 December 20X7 is made up of its intrinsic value (reflected by the current market price of the entity's shares) and its time value. The time value reflects the fact that the holders of the SARs have the right to participate in future gains. At 31 December 20X8, all of the outstanding SARs must be exercised so holders have no right to participate in future gains. Hence, the fair value (C12) at that date is made up entirely of the intrinsic value.

A12.152 Prior to applying IFRS 2, some territories may have measured the cash-settled share-based payment using the intrinsic value. Applying IFRS 2 requires measurement at fair value, so for some territories a change to IFRS will necessitate re-measurement of liabilities. Although the IASB did consider the use of intrinsic values to measure cash-settled share-based payment transactions, it concluded that such a method was not consistent with the overall fair value objective of its share-based payment standard.

A12.153 As mentioned in example 3 in paragraph A12.161, the fair value of a liability component is determined as the present value of the future cash outflow.

Change in classification — cash-settled to equity-settled

A12.154 Where an award is modified such that the classification changes from cash-settled to equity-settled, the entity immediately reclassifies the amount recognised as a liability, up to the modification date, to equity. The expense for the remainder of the vesting period is based on the award's fair value, measured at the modification date and not the original grant date.

A12.154.1 In some situations, an award is modified such that the fair value or other vesting conditions are changed in addition to the classification change from cash-settled to equity-settled (for example, additional fair value, extending the vesting period or adding a performance condition). There is no clear guidance in IFRS 2 whether an entity should account for the change in classification or the other modifications first; therefore, we believe either approach is acceptable. The following example illustrates this.

Example – Reclassification from cash-settled to equity-settled

Entity X has a cash-settled share-based payment in the form of share appreciation rights that will vest in three years. At the end of year one, the fair value of the award is estimated to be C300. Therefore, a charge of C100 has been recognised in the income statement with a corresponding liability. At the end of year two, the fair value of the award is C360. As such, a charge of C140 (C240 — C100) has been recognised in the income statement with a corresponding increase in the liability.

Additionally, at the end of year two entity X decides to modify the share-based payment award from cash-settled to equity-settled and extend the vesting period by a year. The employees will now receive equity instruments for the same value after four years. Entity X will provide shares based on the value of the share appreciation rights at the settlement date (that is, C360). However, employees will still need to provide services for two more years.

Under one approach, the entity could account for the change in classification from cash to equity-settled first and then apply modification accounting to the change in vesting period. Therefore, entity X would reclassify the total liability of C240 at the end of year two to equity. The expense for the remaining vesting period will be C120 which is based on the fair value of the award at the modification date of C360, less the amount already recognised in the income statement of C240. However, since the extension of vesting period is not beneficial to employees, it should not be taken into account when determining amounts to be recognised. (See further guidance on modifications in para A12.125.) Therefore, C120 should be expensed over the remaining vesting period of the original grant (that is, one year).

Under an alternative approach, the entity could apply modification accounting to the change in vesting period first and then account for the change in classification. Therefore, the entity would true-up the liability at the end of year two based on a change in vesting period. This would result in a credit of C60 to the income statement since a liability of C180 (C360 ÷ 4 years × 2 years less C240 already recognised) should be recorded at the end of year two. Then, entity X would reclassify the total liability of C180 to equity. An expense of C180, which is based on the fair value of the award at modification date of C360 less the amount already recognised in the income statement of C180, would then be recognised over the remaining vesting period of two years.

A12.154.2 Some awards may initially be an employee benefit under IAS 19, 'Employee benefits', and then be modified to a share-based payment arrangement in accordance with IFRS 2. See further guidance provided in chapter 11.

Transactions with settlement alternatives

A12.155 Some share-based payment transactions give either the entity or the counterparty the choice as to whether to settle in cash or equity instruments. IFRS 2 establishes a principle that an entity should account for such a transaction as cash-settled if, and to the extent that, it has incurred a liability to settle in cash or other assets, or otherwise as equity-settled. [IFRS 2 para 34]. In practice, the accounting is driven by determining which party appears to have the choice of settlement method.

The counterparty may choose the settlement method

A12.156 If the counterparty may choose the method of settlement, the entity is considered to have issued a compound financial instrument. This means that it has issued an instrument with a debt component (to the extent that the counterparty has a right to demand cash) and an equity component (to the extent that the counterparty has a right to demand settlement in equity instruments by giving up their right to cash). [IFRS 2 para 35].

A12.157 IAS 32, 'Financial instruments: Disclosure and presentation', requires that when valuing a compound financial instrument, an entity first establishes the value of the debt component. The equity component is then measured at the difference between that amount and the value of instrument as a whole. [IAS 32 para 31]. IFRS 2 applies similar measurement principles.

A12.158 For transactions in which the fair value of goods or services is measured directly, the fair value of the equity component is measured as the difference between the fair value of the goods or services received and the fair value of the debt component. [IFRS 2 para 35].

A12.159 For other transactions in which the fair value of goods or services is measured indirectly by reference to the fair value of the instruments granted, it is necessary to estimate the fair value of the compound instrument as a whole. [IFRS 2 para 36]. To do this, it will be necessary to value the debt and equity components separately, taking into account the fact that the counterparty must forfeit its right to receive cash in order to receive the equity instrument. Transactions are often structured such that the fair value of each settlement alternative is the same. For example, the counterparty might have the choice of receiving either share options or cash-settled share appreciation rights. In order to receive the options, the counterparty would have to 'give up' a cash award of equivalent fair value so, by deduction, the fair value of the equity component will be zero. However, where the fair value of the equity component is greater than zero, it will be necessary to account for each component separately. The debt component will be accounted for as a cash-settled share-based payment transaction as described from paragraph A12.146, while the equity component will be accounted for as an equity-settled share-based payment transaction as described from paragraph A12.53. [IFRS 2 para 38].

A12.160 At the date of settlement, the liability in respect of the debt component should be re-measured at fair value. The method of settlement actually chosen by the counterparty will then determine the accounting, as shown in the table below.

Method of settlement	Accounting implications
Cash	The payment is applied to settle the liability in full. Any equity component previously recognised in equity will remain there, although there may be a transfer from one component of equity to another. [IFRS 2 para 40].
Equity	The balance on the liability is transferred to equity as consideration for the equity instrument. [IFRS 2 para 39].

A12.161 The above requirements are illustrated in the following examples.

Example 1 – Compound instrument – mutually exclusive alternatives

An entity established a bonus plan on 1 January 20X5. The employees have a right to choose between a cash payment equal to the market value of 100 shares at 31 December 20X5 or to receive 100 shares on the same date. At the grant date, the fair value of the right to cash is C5,000 and the fair value of the right to shares is C5,000. The value of the two alternatives is the same at any point in time.

The equity component is determined as the difference between the fair value of the compound instrument as a whole and the fair value of the liability.

The fair value of the compound instrument as a whole is C5,000, as the cash and share alternatives are mutually exclusive and of equal value. The equity component is, therefore, zero, being the difference between the C5,000 fair value of the compound instrument and the C5,000 fair value of the debt component. This reflects the arrangement's economic substance where there is no benefit to the employee from choosing shares or cash.

Example 2 – Compound instrument – determining the equity component

On 1 January 20X5, an entity granted to its chief executive the right to choose either 10,000 phantom shares (that is, the right to receive a cash payment equal to the value of 10,000 shares) or 15,000 shares. The grant is conditional upon the completion of two years of service. If the chief executive chooses the share alternative, he must keep the shares for a period of five years. The entity's share price at grant date and at subsequent year end is as follows:

Year	Share price
1 January 20X5	7
31 December 20X5	9
31 December 20X6	15

After taking into account the effects of the post-vesting transfer restrictions (see further para A12.202), management estimates that the grant date fair value of the share alternative is C6.50 per share. Hence, the fair value of the share alternative at grant date is C97,500 (that is, 15,000 × C6.50). The fair value of the cash alternative at grant date is C70,000 (that is, 10,000 × C7) so, by deduction, the fair value of the equity component of the compound financial instrument awarded to the chief executive is C27,500. In simple terms, in order to obtain an equity instrument worth C97,500, the chief executive must surrender a right to C70,000 of cash. Thus, the fair value of the equity component is the difference between these amounts. The amount recognised as an expense in each year and as either an increase in equity or a liability at each year end will be as follows:

Year	Expense	Equity	Total liability	Expense calculation
	C	C	C	
31 December 20X5	13,750	13,750		C27,500 × ½
31 December 20X5	45,000		45,000	C10,000 × 9 × ½
31 December 20X6	13,750	27,500		C27,500 × ½
31 December 20X6	105,000		150,000	C10,000 × 15 less C45,000 recognised in 20X5

The chief executive exercises his rights on 1 January 20X7 (on which date the share price is the same as on 31 December 20X6).

If he chooses to receive cash, he will receive a payment of C150,000. This will settle the outstanding liability in full. The amount recognised within equity (C27,500) will remain there, although there may be a transfer from one component of equity to another.

If he chooses the share alternative, the balance on the liability of C150,000 is transferred to equity as consideration for the shares. Once again, the amount already recognised within equity (C27,500) will remain there, although there may be a transfer from one component of equity to another.

Example 3 – Compound instrument – determining the equity component

An entity granted a bonus to its employees on 1 January 20X5. The bonus is due in five years, when each employee will have a right to choose between a cash payment of C1,000 or obtaining 100 shares of the entity. The share price on 1 January 20X5 is C5 per share. There are no vesting conditions. The appropriate discount rate is 5% per year.

The entity should recognise the debt component on 1 January 20X5 at its fair value of C784. Fair value is determined as the present value of the future cash outflow, C1,000/1.05^5 (see further para A12.153 above). The entity should then measure the equity alternative, taking into consideration that the employee has to forfeit the right to C1,000 in cash to obtain the shares. The equity alternative is, in substance, a share option with an exercise price of C10 per share and a term of five years. The grant date fair value of the share options was determined as C25 at 1 January 20X5. A corresponding increase in equity should be recognised on 1 January 20X5.

The entity should re-measure the liability component to its fair value at each subsequent balance sheet date and recognise the changes in the fair value in the income statement. The amounts recognised for the equity component are not subject to subsequent re-measurement.

Example 4 – Compound instrument – settlement in shares

Consider the award granted in example 3 if the share price turned out to be C17 on 31 December 20X9.

A rational employee would select settlement in shares because this alternative has a higher fair value (1,700; 17 × 100 shares). The entity should accrete the liability to its fair value of C1,000 on the exercise date through the income statement. Total interest expense of C216 (1,000 – 784) on a cumulative basis is recognised between 1 January 20X5 and 31 December 20X9. The liability of C1,000 is transferred to equity as the shares are issued.

An employee may choose the cash alternative, despite the higher fair value of the settlement in shares. The entity first accretes the liability to its fair value of C1,000 on the exercise date through the income statement. Total interest expense of C216 on a cumulative basis is recognised between 1 January 20X5 and 31 December 20X9. It subsequently records the payment of C1,000 cash against the liability. The cumulative charge of C25 recognised in respect of the equity component is not adjusted.

Example 5 – Employee choice of settlement, with different length vesting periods

An entity agreed the details of an award with its employees on 1 January 20X6. Under the terms, employees can choose on 31 March 20X7 either:

- cash payment of 25%-50% of salary, depending on specified performance measures, at 31 March 20X7; or
- shares with value equivalent to 150% of the cash payment, but the employee must remain in service for a further three years.

The grant date would be 1 January 20X6, as this is the date both parties involved have a shared understanding of the terms and conditions including the formula that would be used to determine the amount of cash to be paid (or the number of shares to be delivered).

The entity has granted the employee the right to choose whether a share-based payment transaction is settled in cash or by the entity issuing equity instruments. The entity has granted a compound financial instrument, which includes a debt component (that is, the counterparty's right to demand cash payment) and an equity component (that is, the counterparty's right to demand settlement in equity instruments). (See paras A12.156 to A12.161.)

The entity should account separately for the goods or services received or acquired in respect of each of the compound instrument's components. [IFRS 2 para 38]. The vesting period of the equity component and that of the debt component should be determined separately and the vesting period of each component may be different. In the above example, the vesting period for the debt component is 1.25 years (1 January 20X6 – 31 March 20X7) and the vesting period for the equity component is 4.25 years (1 January 20X6 – 31 March 20Y0), because employees are entitled to shares only if they complete a 4.25-year service period.

The entity may choose the settlement method

A12.162 If the entity may choose the method of settlement, it should determine whether, in substance, it has created an obligation to settle in cash. This may be, for example, if:

- The choice of settlement in equity instruments has no commercial substance (for example, because the entity is legally prohibited from issuing shares).
- The entity has a past practice or stated policy of settling in cash.
- The entity generally settles in cash whenever the counterparty requests it.

[IFRS 2 para 41].

A12.163 If an obligation to settle in cash does exist, the entity should account for the transaction as a cash-settled share-based payment transaction as described from paragraph A12.146. Otherwise, the transaction should be treated as an equity-settled share-based payment transaction as described from paragraph A12.53. [IFRS 2 paras 42, 43].

Settlement choice changes from equity-settled to cash-settled

A12.164 In many cases, a company whose equity instruments are not publicly traded will enter into share-based payment arrangements with its employees where the entity has a choice of settlement. For example, the entity may have an option to allow an employee to keep shares when they leave or make a cash payment instead. In these cases, the entity is likely to determine that it will settle in cash for the reason that, in most cases, a private company would not allow employees who leave the company to continue to hold its shares. The entity may reach a different conclusion if it had an expectation of creating a market for the shares by, for example an IPO or sale of the company. Past practice can be the determining factor. The following examples explore this:

Example – Employer choice changes from equity- to cash-settled

Entity A is privately owned by a venture capitalist. The entity enters into a share-based payment arrangement with its senior employees whereby:

- Each employee will receive 1,000 shares if they remain employed for a period of five years.
- If the employee leaves the entity after the five year period, but before the entity is listed, the entity has an option to purchase the shares for fair value from the employee.
- The grant date fair value of the award is C2,000.
- No employees are expected to leave over the five year period.
- On grant date, the entity expects to list in the next three to five years. The entity has no past practice or stated policy of buying back shares from employees when the employees leave as this is the first such plan to be put in place. Furthermore, the entity does not expect or anticipate that it will settle the awards in cash.
- At the end of year two, the entity no longer expects to list and employees are informed of this fact. The entity states that, should it not be listed after five years and employees leave the company, it will repurchase the shares. The fair value of the shares is C3,000 on this date.
- At the end of year three, the fair value of the liability has increased to C4,000.

On grant date, the employer accounts for the arrangement as an equity-settled share-based payment as there is no present obligation to settle in cash. The entries recorded in the first year would be:

	Dr C	Cr C
Dr Employee expense	400	
Cr Equity		400
C2,000 to record the grant date fair value vesting over a period of five years		

At the end of year two, as the entity has stated its intentions the employees would assume that their award will be settled in cash if they work the five-year period. The award would be reclassified at the end of the second year, because the entity has created an obligation to settle in cash through a change in stated policy:

Dr Employee expense	400	
Cr Equity		400
To record the C2,000 vesting over a period of five years which was the expectation until year end		
Dr Equity		1,200
Cr Liability (C3,000 × 2/5)		1,200

Reclassification of the equity award to cash-settled. Although the cumulative credit to equity to date is C800, it is appropriate to debit equity by more than this amount in order to set up the liability, because IFRS 2 allows the fair value of the resulting liability to be accounted for as a deduction from equity similar to a repurchase of an equity instrument. [IFRS 2 para 43].

At the end of year three, the award is accounted for on a cash-settled basis as follows:

Dr Employee expense	1,200	
Cr Liability (C4,000 × 3/5 – C1,200)		1,200

A12.165 Where an entity has a choice of settlement and has classified an award as equity-settled, care should be taken when the entity actually settles the award. In the absence of other factors, an entity settling its first award in cash is a strong indication that a constructive obligation to pay cash has been established through past practice for the remaining awards and hence the other outstanding awards should be reclassified as cash-settled on a prospective basis.

Example – Employer choice of settlement where cash option taken

The facts are the same as in the example in paragraph A12.164, except that at the end of year two the entity does not make a statement to employees that it will repurchase the shares after a five-year period and a listing of the entity's shares is still seen as achievable. At the end of the year six the entity has not yet listed and one of the employees leaves the entity. The entity exercises its settlement choice and buys the leaving employees' shares for fair value.

In the absence of any other evidence, there might be a presumption that the settlement of this award with the employee creates a valid expectation that the remaining employees will also receive cash when they leave. However, judgement will be required in order to determine whether one transaction establishes 'past practice' for which the company has now created an obligation to settle in cash. If this is the case, the entity should treat the remaining awards as cash-settled, since the entity now has a past practice of settling in cash. The entity would also need to revisit the classification of any similar grants it has made and consider whether it should reclassify them to cash-settled.

A12.166 If the transaction is accounted for as equity-settled, the entity needs to consider if it has given away further value depending on which alternative has the greater fair value as at the settlement date, as shown in the table below. [IFRS 2 para 43].

Settlement method	Settlement method with the higher fair value	
	Cash	**Equity**
Cash	The amount of payment equal to the fair value of the equity instruments that would otherwise have been issued is accounted for as the repurchase of an equity interest and is deducted from equity. The excess over this amount is recognised as an expense.	The payment is accounted for as the repurchase of an equity interest and is deducted from equity.
Equity	No further accounting is required.	The excess of the fair value of the equity instruments issued over the amount of cash that would otherwise have been paid is recognised as an expense.

A12.167 The above requirements are illustrated in the following example, although in practice it is rare for the alternatives to have different values when the entity has the choice of settlement method.

Example 1 – Entity choice of settlement

An entity has granted to its chief executive the right to either 10,000 phantom shares (that is, the right to receive a cash payment equal to the value of 10,000 shares) or 15,000 shares. The entity may choose the settlement method. It has never made an award of this nature and it is free to select either settlement method (that is, there is no restriction over its ability to issue shares). Accordingly, management does not consider that the entity has established an obligation and the transaction is accounted for as equity-settled. An expense is measured on the basis of the fair value of the 15,000 shares at grant date is C80,000. The opposing credit is recognised in equity.

On the settlement date, the entity's share price is C10. Hence, the fair value of the phantom shares is C100,000 while the fair value of the shares themselves is C150,000. If the entity chooses to settle the transaction in cash, being the settlement method with the lower fair value, the payment of C100,000 is deducted from equity. Even though only C80,000 had been recognised as an expense in equity, the additional C20,000 should also be deducted from equity. In substance it represents the re-purchase by the entity of its own shares so no further expense is recognised. However, if the entity chooses to settle the transaction by issuing shares, the excess of the fair value of the shares over the amount of cash that would otherwise have been paid (that is, C50,000) is recognised as an expense.

If the facts were different, such that at settlement date the fair value of the phantom shares was C150,000 while the fair value of the shares was C100,000, the accounting would be as follows. If the entity chose to settle the transaction by issuing shares, being the settlement method with the lower fair value, no further accounting would be required. If the entity chose to settle the transaction in cash, C100,000 (being the fair value of the equity instruments that would otherwise have been issued) would be deducted from equity. The excess of the amount actually paid over the amount deducted from equity (that is, C50,000) is recognised as an expense.

In summary, if the award is treated as equity-settled it should be accounted for in the same way as any other equity-settled transaction until the point of settlement. On settlement, the accounting is straight forward provided the entity chooses the method of settlement with the lower fair value at that date. If, however, it chooses the settlement method with the higher fair value at that date, the excess is treated as an additional expense. In the first scenario described above (settlement in shares when cash settlement has a lower fair value) the double entry on settlement would be as follows:

	Dr C	Cr C
Dr Equity	100,000	
Dr Income statement	50,000	
Cr Share capital/equity		150,000

In the second scenario (settlement in cash when equity settlement has a lower fair value) the double entry on settlement would be as follows:

	C	C
Dr Equity	100,000	
Dr Income statement	50,000	
Cr Cash		150,000

Example 2 – Employer choice of settlement

An entity operates a share plan whereby employees are granted free shares in the company. The employee is, thereafter, entitled to the dividends and may vote. However, if an employee leaves within the first three years, the company may exercise a buy-back option at that time and repurchase all the shares. The price which the entity pays is dependent on when the employee leaves the entity:

- Before the end of year one – nil.
- After year one, but before the end of year two – 30% of the share's fair value.
- After year two, but before the end of year three – 50% of the share's fair value.

In the past, the entity has always exercised the buy back option as there is economic compulsion to do so (the repurchase right is below fair value and, furthermore, the entity does not want to form a non-controlling interest for employees that leave the entity). Although there is no legal obligation on the entity, there is a constructive obligation to buy the shares back on resignation (see para A12.162) through past practice and the fact that, in substance, the call option is a vesting mechanism.

In substance the award consists of three separate components: 30% vests over one year, 20% vests over two years (represented by 50% less the 30% that vests after year one) and 50% vests over three years. The entity has a choice of settlement for the 30% and 20% tranche although past practice indicates that the entity settles in cash. The remaining 50% can only be settled in equity (as the buy back option falls away after three years). Tranche vesting is discussed in more detail in example 3 in paragraph A12.114 above.

Settlement method contingent on an event outside the control of the entity or employee

A12.168 There may be occasions where the conditions of a share-based payment award provide the employee with either cash or equity, but the choice of which option occurs is outside the control of both the employee and the entity. We believe there are two acceptable approaches (covered in paras A12.168.1 and A12.168.2) to account for an award where the manner of settlement (that is, cash or equity) is contingent on an event that is outside the entity's control.

A12.168.1 One approach is to account for the award as two mutually exclusive awards, one equity-settled and one cash-settled:

- The cash-settled alternative is a liability. Although this is affected by the probability of being paid, it always has a fair value which is recognised over the vesting period. If the award is ultimately settled in equity the fair value of the liability falls to nil.
- The equity-settled alternative is only recognised if it is considered probable. If the award is ultimately settled in cash the equity alternative would have become improbable and so no cumulative expense would be recognised for this. The fair value of the liability will have increased to the cash amount ultimately paid.

As can be seen from the above, the settlement method is in effect treated as a vesting condition. Although the charge during the vesting period may appear to be in excess of the total value of the award granted, once the contingent settlement provision resolves, the cumulative charge will represent only the expense actually incurred under equity settlement option or the cash settlement option.

Example – Equity settlement contingent on a successful listing (IPO)

At 1 January 20X8 an entity enters into a share-based payment arrangement with its employees. The terms of the award are as follows:

- Employees are required to work for the entity for a period of five years after which time they will receive a cash payment equal to the value of the entity's shares.

- If the entity engages in a successful IPO before the five year period is met, however, the employees will receive free shares rather than a cash payment. Thus, employees might receive free shares or a cash payment, but not both.
- No employees are expected to leave the company over the next five years.
- At the date of the award and the first two year ends thereafter, it was not probable that a successful IPO would occur before year five.
- At the end of year three, a successful IPO becomes probable and management expect it to occur in year four.
- At the end of year four, a successful IPO occurs and employees receive free shares.
- The fair value of the equity-settled award alternative is C1,000 at grant date. The fair value of the cash alternative is C50 at the end of year one, C500 at the end of year two, C100 at the end of year three and C50 at the end of year four.

At the end of the first and second year ends, the entity would not record a charge for the equity-settled award as the vesting conditions are not expected to be met, as there has been no successful IPO. For the cash-settled award, the liability is measured at fair value at each reporting period, which includes the probability of settlement in cash. As such, the entity would record the following entries:

		Dr	Cr
Year end 31 December 20X8		C	C
Dr	Employee expense	10	
	Cr Liability		10
Fair value of cash-settled award recognised over the vesting period at the end of year one.			
Year end 31 December 20X9			
Dr	Employee expense	190	
	Cr Liability		190
Cash-settled award recognised over the vesting period ((500 × 2/5) – 10).			

At the end of the year three, the entity should start recording a charge for the equity-settled award as a successful IPO is now deemed probable. For the cash-settled award, the liability is measured at fair value at each reporting period, which includes the probability of settlement in cash. As such, the entity would record the following entries:

		Dr	Cr
Year end 31 December 20Y0			
Dr	Employee expense	750	
	Cr Equity		750
Equity-settled award recognised over the vesting period ((1,000 × 3/4) – 0) as management expect a successful IPO in year four.			
Dr	Liability	140	
	Cr Employee expense		140
Cash-settled award recognised over the vesting period ((100 × 3/5) – 200) which results in a reduction of the previous charge due to a change in fair value.			

		Dr	Cr
Year end 31 December 20Y1			
Dr	Employee expense	250	
	Cr Equity		250

A successful IPO occurs in year four and, therefore, the remaining charge for the equity-settled award is recognised (C1,000 – C750).

Dr	Liability	60	
	Cr Employee expense		60

The cash-settled share-based payment charge is reversed due to failure to meet the vesting conditions, that is, a successful IPO occurred before five years.

A12.168.2 The other approach is to look to the principles of IAS 37, 'Provisions, contingent liabilities, contingent assets', in determining whether or not an uncertain future event gives rise to a liability. Under this approach, only a contingent liability exists when the contingency that triggers cash settlement is not probable. The award should be treated as equity-settled, unless cash settlement becomes probable. The classification is an accounting estimate and any change in classification is treated as a change in estimate so that the cumulative expense (and related credit to equity or liability) should be the same as if the new classification had always been applied.

A12.168.3 While the cumulative expense over the life of the award will be the same under either approach, the 'IAS 37 approach' avoids the issue in the previous approach (see para A12.168.1) that during the vesting period there might be an expense for both the cash and equity-settled alternatives at the same time.

Example – Contingent settlement with IAS 37 approach

Using the same facts as in the example in paragraph A12.168.1 above, the amount charged to the income statement in each period will be different under the IAS 37 approach (refer to para A12.168.2).

At the end of the first and second year ends, the entity would not record a charge for the equity-settled award as the vesting conditions are not expected to be met, that is, no successful IPO. A liability is, therefore, recognised as cash settlement is probable until year three.

		Dr	Cr
Year end 31 December 20X8		C	C
Dr	Employee expense	10	
	Cr Liability		10
Cash-settled award recognised over the vesting period.			
Year end 31 December 20X9			
Dr	Employee expense	190	
	Cr Liability		190
Cash-settled award recognised over the vesting period.			

At the end of year three, a successful IPO becomes probable, therefore, the entity would record a charge for equity-settled award and there should be a reversal of the cash-settled award as it is now deemed not probable.

Year end 31 December 20Y0			
Dr	Liability	200	
	Cr Employee expense		200
Reversal of cash-settled share-based payment as IPO deemed probable.			
Dr	Employee expense	750	
	Cr Equity		750
Equity-settled award measured at grant date fair value of C1,000 (C1,000 × 3/4) as IPO is now deemed probable.			
Year end 31 December 20Y1			
Dr	Employee expense	250	
	Cr Equity		250
Equity-settled award measured at fair value of C1,000. Since all the vesting conditions for this award have been met in year four, the award has vested and the remaining charge of C250 (C1,000 – C750) is recognised in the income statement.			

Practical implications

Group share-based payment arrangements

A12.169 As described in paragraph A12.10, the scope of IFRS 2 is broad. Share-based payment transactions include not only transactions settled in an entity's own shares, but also transactions settled in equity instruments of the entity's parent or any other entity in the same group. [IFRS 2 para 3A]. This means that if the employees of a subsidiary are awarded options over the shares of the parent, the subsidiary will recognise an expense in respect of the employee services received.

A12.170 The question that arises is how to classify an award in the separate financial statements in the subsidiary and thus how the expense should be measured. IFRS 2 provides a clear basis to determine the classification of awards in both consolidated and separate financial statements by setting out the circumstances in which group share-based payment transactions are treated as equity-settled and cash-settled. The entity receiving goods or services should assess its own rights and obligations as well as the nature of awards granted in order to determine the accounting treatment. The amount recognised by the group entity receiving the goods or services will not necessarily be consistent with the amount recognised in the consolidated financial statements. [IFRS 2 para 43A].

A12.171 In group share-based payment transactions, the entity receiving the goods or services should account for awards as equity-settled when:

- the awards granted are the entity's own equity instruments; or
- the entity has no obligation to settle the share-based payment transaction.

[IFRS 2 para 43B].

In all other situations, the entity receiving the goods or services should account for the awards as cash-settled.

A12.172 For an entity settling a share-based payment transaction when another group entity has received the goods or services, the entity recognises the transaction as an equity-settled share-based payment transaction (and thus recorded in equity) only if it is settled in the entity's own equity instruments. In all other circumstances, the transaction is treated as cash-settled award and a liability is recognised. [IFRS 2 para 43C].

A12.173 The accounting treatment described above applies regardless of any intra-group repayment arrangements that may be in place. [IFRS 2 para 43D]. See further paragraph A12.180.

A12.174 The classification of both cash-settled and equity-settled share-based payment transactions in group situations is summarised in the flow chart in appendix 2 to this chapter.

A12.174.1 The following examples illustrate the principles.

Example 1 – Parent entity grants share awards to subsidiary employees

A parent grants its shares directly to subsidiary A and subsidiary B employees. The awards will vest immediately, and the parent will issue new shares directly to the employees. The parent will not charge subsidiaries A and B for the transaction.

In the consolidated financial statements, the transaction is treated as an equity-settled share-based payment, as the group has received services in consideration for the group's equity instruments. An expense is recognised in the group income statement for the grant date fair value of the share-based payment over the vesting period, with a credit recognised in equity.

In the subsidiaries' accounts, the award is treated as an equity-settled share-based payment, as the subsidiaries do not have an obligation to settle the award. An expense for the grant date fair value of the award is recognised over the vesting period with a credit recognised in equity. The credit to equity is treated as a capital contribution as the parent is compensating the subsidiaries' employees with no expense to the subsidiaries. In this example, the shares vest immediately, therefore, an expense is recognised in the subsidiaries' income statement in full based on the grant date fair value and a credit to equity.

In the parent's separate financial statements, there is no share-based payment charge as no employees are providing services to the parent. Therefore, the parent would record a debit, recognising an increase in the investment in the subsidiaries as a capital contribution from the parent and a credit to equity (see further para A12.181 below).

Example 2 – Subsidiary grants rights over equity instruments of its parent

Instead of granting rights over its own equity instruments, subsidiary A grants rights over the parent's shares to subsidiary A's employees. The shares vest over two years. When the shares vest, subsidiary A purchases shares from the market and passes them on to its employees. Subsidiary A only makes these purchases when it settles the award with its employees.

The transaction is treated as an equity-settled share-based payment in the consolidated financial statements, as the group has received services in consideration for the group's equity instruments. An expense is recognised in the income statement for the grant date fair value of the share-based payment over the vesting period, with a credit recognised in equity. The purchase of the shares from the market would be treated as a treasury transaction.

IFRS 2 requires the award to be treated in subsidiary A's financial statements as a cash-settled share-based payment, as subsidiary A has the obligation to settle the award (albeit in shares of the parent). An expense would be recognised in the income statement over the vesting period, with a liability being recorded as the other side of the entry. This liability is re-measured at each reporting date until settlement, in accordance with the accounting for cash-settled awards.

The above transaction has no impact on the parent's financial statements, as the parent is not a party to the transaction.

An arrangement that is similar in substance from an employee's point of view, but results in equity-settled accounting by the subsidiary is where the parent awards its own shares to employees of the subsidiary and makes a cash recharge to the subsidiary for the shares it acquires in the market. This is discussed further from paragraph A12.180.

Example 3 – Parent grants cash-settled awards to employees of its subsidiary

A parent grants share appreciation rights to subsidiary A's employees. At the end of two years, the parent will pay cash to the employees equivalent to the difference between the share price on vesting and the share price at grant date. No intra-group recharge is to be made.

In the consolidated financial statements, the transaction is treated as a cash-settled share-based payment as the group has received services in consideration for cash payments based on the price of the group's equity instruments. An expense is recognised in the group income statement for the fair value of the share-based payment over the vesting period, with a liability being recorded as the other side of the entry. This liability is re-measured at each reporting date until settlement.

In subsidiary A's financial statements, IFRS 2 requires the award to be treated as equity-settled, because the subsidiary does not have an obligation to settle the award. An expense would be recognised in the subsidiary's income statement over the vesting period, with a credit recognised in equity. The credit to equity is treated as a capital contribution from the parent, as the parent is compensating the subsidiary's employees at no expense to the subsidiary.

In the parent's financial statements, there is no share-based payment expense recorded as the employees are not providing services to the parent. Rather, the share-based payment transaction results in a debit to 'investment in subsidiary' with a corresponding liability recorded at fair value at each reporting period end.

Measurement could vary between the two sets of accounts.

A12.175 Where an employee receives shares in an unlisted entity, it is important to gain an understanding of how the employee will realise the value in that award. In order to provide an employee with an exit mechanism where there is no market for a subsidiary's shares, it is common for a parent entity to agree to exchange a vested equity award for either cash or for its own shares (where the parent is listed, for example). By providing an exit mechanism, the parent also ensures that its holding in the subsidiary will not be diluted when the shares vest.

A12.176 If the employees are provided with an option to convert their award in the subsidiary into the shares of a listed parent, the award would still be equity-settled on a consolidated basis, but the accounting in the individual entities may depend on which entity has the obligation to provide parent shares to the employees. See further the discussion on mandatorily redeemable shares in paragraph A12.148.

Example – Options over subsidiary's shares that are convertible into parent's shares

A group has a fast growing subsidiary and intends to incentivise the subsidiary's employees by granting them options over shares in the subsidiary. The options will be granted by the subsidiary. The grant date fair value of the options from the subsidiary's point of view is C1.

The parent is listed. In order to provide the employees with an 'exit mechanism' the parent has agreed to convert all the vested subsidiary shares into the parent's shares with the same fair value when the employee resigns.

From a consolidated financial statement point of view, this is an equity-settled share-based payment arrangement granted to the subsidiary's employees. The consolidated grant date fair value of C1 would be recorded as an expense in the group income statement over the vesting period.

In the subsidiary's separate financial statements, this would also be an equity-settled share-based payment, as the subsidiary has granted its employees equity instruments of the subsidiary.

In the parent's separate financial statements, there will be no IFRS 2 charge as the parent is only funding the award. The parent has not granted the awards nor have employees provided services to the parent. The parent would, therefore, record a debit, recognising an increase in their investment in subsidiary and a corresponding credit to equity.

A12.177 Further implications arise if the subsidiary's employees described in the example above are required to exchange their shares for cash from the parent entity upon vesting. The subsidiary is receiving services and has granted its own equity, but has no obligation to make any payment to its employees. The award would, therefore, be treated as equity-settled in the subsidiary's financial statements. [IFRS 2 para 43A]. The award would be treated as a liability in the parent entity's financial statements, with a corresponding amount recognised as an investment in the subsidiary (see further para A12.181).The award is cash-settled in the group's consolidated financial statements, as the group is obliged to provide employees with a cash payment based on the equity instrument of an entity within the group.

A12.177.1 Alternatively, the parent entity may agree to exchange the employees' shares in the subsidiary for its own shares — for example, because the parent entity is listed. In the same way as the situation described in the example above, the subsidiary would account for this as an equity-settled award in its own financial statements. The parent entity would recognise an increase in investment in the subsidiary, with the corresponding amount recognised in equity. [IFRS 2 para 43C]. Additionally, the award is treated as equity-settled in the group's consolidated financial statements.

A12.177.1.1 There may be some situations where the entity does not provide an exit mechanism for employees; rather the majority shareholder or other shareholders offers to buy the departing employees' interests. In these circumstances, an entity would still apply the principles of group arrangements as explained above to determine the accounting in the entity's accounts.

Example – Shareholders provide an exit mechanism

Entity T is an unlisted entity and grants restricted shares to key management that will vest in three years. The entity is not planning an exit event, so the terms of the award allow for key management to sell their shares for fair value after the three year vesting period, either to other shareholders or to an approved third party. In addition, there are leaver provisions, even after vesting, which require the employee to sell their shares when they leave the entity. However, in this example, the entity does not have an obligation to purchase the shares because the remaining shareholders are obligated to buy out their fellow shareholders.

The employees will ultimately receive cash as they cannot leave the company with shares and, therefore, do not have unconditional rights to the equity instruments. From their perspective, therefore, this is a group cash-settled arrangement. But in this example, it is the shareholders who have the obligation to settle the cash-settled share-based payment arrangement. Applying the principles in paragraph 43B of IFRS 2, the entity should account for the arrangement as equity-settled in its financial statements as the entity does not have an obligation to settle this arrangement. For equity-settled arrangements, IFRS 2 requires an entity to measure the services received and the corresponding increase in equity (debit expense, credit equity) at modified grant date fair value. The fair value will be measured at grant date and recognised over the vesting period (that is, 3 years).

A12.177.2 Another situation that might occur in group share-based payment arrangements is where shares in the parent entity are issued in another currency than the subsidiary's functional currency. The example below considers the interaction between foreign exchange and share-based payment accounting.

Example – Share awards granted in a different functional currency

Employees of a subsidiary are granted the rights to parent shares for services provided to the subsidiary. As the parent granted the award and the subsidiary has no obligation to settle the award, the award is treated as equity-settled by the subsidiary.

The shares in the parent are traded and reported in US dollars (both the presentation and functional currency is US dollars). The subsidiary reports (both functional and reportable) in pounds sterling.

At the grant date, the parent informs the subsidiary of the US dollar grant date fair value of the award for each new participant in the plan. Each year (based on leaver statistics supplied by the subsidiary), the parent informs the subsidiary of the charge to be reflected in the subsidiary's income statement (again in US dollars).

For share-based payment accounting, the fair value is fixed at the grant date for equity-settled awards (deemed to be the best estimate of the services provided where the entity and employee have a shared understanding) and spread over the vesting period to reflect services provided by the employee. This is initially evaluated in US dollars, being the parent's currency. IAS 21 identifies the date when foreign currency transactions should be translated. For an equity transaction that is non-monetary, the exchange difference would be calculated at transaction date (and not re-measured).

Therefore, the grant date fair value (US dollars) per share should be translated at the grant date to pounds sterling using the spot foreign exchange rate. It is then applied to the number of awards likely to vest over the period. The amount initially translated at grant date would be the amount used in local currency accounts over the vesting period.

Employees move between group entities

A12.178 IFRS 2 states that where an employee transfers employment from one subsidiary to another during the vesting period (the vesting period could be, for example, a service period), each subsidiary should measure the services received from the employee by reference to the fair value of the equity instrument at grant date, and not re-measure at the date of transfer. If, after transferring between group entities, the employee fails to meet a non-market vesting condition (for example, a service condition) each subsidiary should adjust the amount previously recognised in respect of the services received from the employee.

Intermediate holding companies

A12.179 Where a parent grants a share-based payment to a group entity and there are other intermediate subsidiaries within the group between the parent and the entity in which the goods and services are received, a question arises as to whether the intermediate subsidiaries should account for the share-based payment as IFRS 2 is silent in this respect. We believe it would be acceptable to account for the transaction only in the parent and subsidiary which receives the goods and services. The following example illustrates this view:

> **Example – Implications for intermediate holding companies**
>
> Parent entity P owns 100% of an intermediate holding company (entity H1). Entity H1 in turn owns 100% of another intermediate holding company (entity H2), entity H2 owns 100% of trading subsidiary entity S.
>
> Entity P grants, and has the obligation to settle, equity-settled options over P's shares to employees of entity S. The grant date fair value of the award, which has a two year vesting period, is C200,000. Should each intermediate holding company apply IFRS 2 or can entity P recognise an investment in its indirectly held subsidiary, entity S?
>
> The transaction is between entity P and the employees of entity S. Our view is that it is acceptable for entity P to recognise an investment in entity S. There will be no impact on the separate financial statements of entity H1 and entity H2. This is acceptable on the basis that it is possible for an indirectly-held subsidiary and its ultimate parent to transact directly without involving intermediate parent companies. The double entry in parent entity P's separate financial statements at the end of each year would be to recognise a capital contribution to entity S as follows:

		C	C
Dr	Investment in subsidiary entity S	100,000	
	Cr Equity		100,000

Trading subsidiary entity S will recognise the IFRS 2 charge in its separate financial statements:

		C	C
Dr	Income statement	100,000	
	Cr Equity		100,000

Funding arrangements between parent and its subsidiary

A12.180 The illustrative example attached to IFRS 2 clarifies that where the parent grants rights over its equity instruments to the employees of its subsidiary (accounted for as an equity-settled share-based payment), the debit would be recognised in the subsidiary's income statement and a credit to equity (as a capital contribution) recognised over the vesting period of the share-based payment arrangement. [IFRS 2 para IG 22A, Example 14].

A12.181 The accounting within the parent entity for the capital contribution is not addressed by IFRS 2. The IFRIC exposure draft (IFRIC draft interpretation D17) issued prior to the release of IFRIC 11 indicated that the parent entity would debit its investment in subsidiary and credit equity for the equity instruments it had granted (if the parent entity is satisfying the obligation). When the IFRS IC issued the final interpretation of IFRIC 11, it did not address this issue as the basis for conclusions notes that the IFRS IC *"did not wish to widen the scope of the Interpretation to an issue that relates to the accounting for intra-group* *payment arrangements"* generally. [IFRIC 11 BC12]. We believe that it was this wider issue that resulted in the deletion of the proposed guidance in the draft interpretation, as opposed to a flaw in the thinking. The only alternatives to the parent debiting its investment in subsidiary would seem to be recognising nothing or recognising an expense, neither of which are attractive. There is no indication in IFRS 2 that the accounting treatment set out in the draft interpretation would be inappropriate and, therefore, we believe it should continue to be applied. The accounting implications are considered in the examples in paragraph A12.187 below.

A12.182 Sometimes, a parent company makes a recharge to the subsidiary in respect of share options granted to the subsidiary's employees. IFRS 2 does not address how to account for such intra-group payment arrangements for share-based payment transactions. However, the illustrative example in the draft interpretation did consider the issue. It concluded that an inter-company charge payable by a subsidiary entity should be offset against the capital contribution in the individual or separate financial statements of the subsidiary entity and the parent entity. We believe that this is particularly appropriate where there is a clear link between the recharge and the share-based payment, for example where the recharge is based on the intrinsic value or market value of the shares when they vest. Consistent with the principle of shareholder distributions, if the amount of the inter-company charge exceeded the capital contribution, that excess should be treated as a distribution from the subsidiary to its parent. We consider this to be an appropriate treatment for such a recharge.

A12.183 The return of the capital contribution and any excess distribution payment are separate transactions to the credit to equity arising from the equity-settled share-based payment. Therefore, it is necessary to provide separate disclosure of the gross amounts.

UK.A12.183.1 If the recharge in excess of the IFRS 2 charge is treated as a distribution, a question arises on whether the distribution would be unlawful if a subsidiary does not have sufficient distributable profits. Tech 02/10, 'Guidance on the determination of realised profits and losses in the context of distributions under the Companies Act 2006', issued in November 2010, clarifies, "*...it will not be unlawful for the subsidiary to make the reimbursement payment, even in the absence of distributable profits, provided that the payment is not a distribution as a matter of law*". [Tech 02/10 para 7.54].

A12.184 We believe that it is important that management are able to justify a clear link between the recharge and the share-based payment charge in order to apply the principle of shareholder distributions described in paragraph A12.182. If there is no clear link between the recharge and the share-based payment we believe that the payment between the subsidiary and its parent should be treated in a manner consistent with management recharges. This would result in an expense recognised in the income statement for the amount recharged. Note that this would result in a 'double debit' to the income statement since the subsidiary would have already recorded the services received under IFRS 2.

A12.185 Where there is a clear link between the recharge and the share-based payment, the full amount of the recharge would be recorded within equity. It would *not* be acceptable for the subsidiary to split the recharge into two components:

- one equal to the share-based payment expense which is treated as a return of a capital contribution and recorded in equity; and
- the excess of the recharge over the amount above as an additional recharge expense in the income statement.

This would have the effect of creating the same result as if the subsidiary had applied cash-settled accounting. IFRS 2 is clear that this type of arrangement should be treated as an equity-settled award. [IFRS 2 paras 43B, 43D].

Timing of the recharge

A12.186 When a subsidiary is recharged by its parent for a share-based payment, the question arises as to when (if at all) a liability should be recorded for the amount that is expected to be recharged in the future, for example, when the award vests or the employees exercise their options. There are two acceptable approaches to account for the recharge. One approach is that when the arrangement can be linked to the IFRS 2 charge, recharges should not be accrued, but should be recognised when paid, for the following reasons:

- IASs 32 and 39 scope out financial instruments, contracts and obligations under share-based payment transactions, except for contracts that can be net settled and in relation to the disclosure of treasury shares. [IAS 32 para 4(f); IAS 39 para 2(i)]. Our view is that these scope exclusions should be read broadly and that recharges clearly related to a share-based payment can be considered outside of the scope of IASs 32 and 39.
- While there is no scope exclusion for share-based payment arrangements under IAS 37, under IAS 37, such recharge payments would not generally meet the recognition criteria to be recorded as liabilities until paid because:
  - The subsidiary does not have a present obligation as a result of a past event. In order for there to be a clear link between a share-based payment and a recharge, in most cases the recharge will generally be linked to employees exercising their options. Options cannot be exercised until they have vested and employees are likely to exercise their options once they are in the money. Therefore, there is unlikely to be a present obligation on the entity until all vesting conditions have been satisfied and until it is probable that employees will exercise their options (for example, where the options are in the money). This is further supported by the fact that distributions (such as dividends) are

only provided for when an entity has a present obligation and, as discussed above, an analogy may be drawn between such recharges and distributions to shareholders. There is no present obligation since the distribution is conditional upon an uncertain future event (such as employees providing services or choosing to exercise their options) that is not wholly within the control of the entity.

- It is not probable that an outflow of economic resources will be required. We consider that the point in time at which it becomes probable that there will be an outflow of economic resources would only be reliably known when the options are close to being exercised.

In most cases, we believe that a subsidiary entity would account for a recharge when the payment is made to the parent. The recharge would be disclosed as a contingent liability during the time that the recharge payment is not recognised as a liability. It may be appropriate to recognise a liability for a recharge before the payment is made — for example, once an award has vested and the options to be exercised are deeply in the money.

A12.186.1 There is, however, diversity in practice in this area, as there is no specific guidance on recharge arrangements in IFRS. There is an alternative approach in which the subsidiary entity would recognise the recharge over the vesting period as the recharge payment arises from the share-based payment arrangement in which employees are providing services. This approach may also be acceptable in practice.

A12.187 Where there is no link between the share-based payment and the future payment by the subsidiary (that is, the double debit treatment discussed in para A12.184), it would be necessary to consider whether the entity has a present obligation in a manner similar to that of a management recharge.

Example 1 – Recharge from parent company in respect of share options

The facts are the same as in example one under paragraph A12.174.1 above, except that the parent makes a recharge to the subsidiary on exercise of the options. The recharge is clearly linked to the share-based payment, being the difference between the option price and the market price of the shares at the date of exercise of the options.

From the subsidiary's perspective, this will still be an equity-settled share-based payment transaction. The requirement for the subsidiary to make a cash payment to the parent does not make this a cash-settled share-based-payment transaction. This is because the subsidiary's obligation is to its parent while the providers of goods or services (that is, the employees) receive equity instruments. Accordingly, the accounting for the share-based payment transaction will be the same as in the previous example. (The subsidiary will recognise an expense and an increase in equity of C100,000.)

Although a recharge such as in this example may be made for a number of reasons, it is often made to enable the parent to acquire shares in the market so as to satisfy the award. In substance, as discussed in paragraph A12.182, the payment by the subsidiary to the parent would be recorded directly in equity for a payment of up to C100,000. Any payment in excess of the amount of capital contribution initially recognised should be treated as a distribution from the subsidiary to its parent. Hence, if the amount of the recharge in this example is C150,000, the double entry in the individual financial statements of the subsidiary would be as follows:

		C	C
Dr	Equity – repurchase of equity instrument	100,000	
Dr	Equity – distribution	50,000	
	Cr Cash		150,000

Our view is that the subsidiary should not make a provision for the recharge during the vesting period, because it does not have a present obligation and it is not probable that there will be an outflow of economic resources until the options vest. The subsidiary will, however, disclose a contingent liability. However, as noted above, there are alternative views whereby the provision could be accrued over the vesting period.

It should be noted that certain entities may wish to show the recharge debit entry within the income statement as opposed to equity and we believe that this approach would also be acceptable, provided that it is applied consistently (this does lead to a 'double debit' in the income statement given that the IFRS 2 charge will also be recognised). In addition, where there is no clear link between the share-based payment and the recharge from the parent, we believe that it would be most appropriate to record a second debit through the income statement.

As regards the parent's separate financial statements, the double entry would be as follows:

		C	C
Dr	Cash	150,000	
	Cr Investment in subsidiary		100,000
	Cr Other income		50,000

Some entities may wish to take the full credit entry as other income rather than reducing the parent's investment in subsidiary and we believe that this approach would also be acceptable, provided that the payment is made from the subsidiary's post-acquisition reserves and the policy is applied consistently. Where a credit is taken to other income, the parent entity should ensure that it has considered whether its investment in subsidiary is impaired.

Note that, in certain jurisdictions, the impact of accounting for group share-based payment transactions could impact the ability for an entity to pay dividends. Therefore, legal advice may need to be sought.

Example 2 – Settlement in parent's shares with an advance recharge

Employees of a subsidiary are granted options to acquire 100 shares in the parent entity at a fixed price of C10 per share in exchange for services. The grant date is 1 January 20X6 when the fair value of the total award is C100. The award is subject to a two year vesting period and performance conditions. The options will vest if the total shareholder return exceeds 5% per annum during 20X6 and 20X7.

The parent entity agreed to issue new shares to entitled employees when the options are exercised. At the grant date the subsidiary paid the parent an option premium in exchange for the parent agreeing to satisfy the obligation to employees. The amount paid to the parent is the fair value of the options granted to employees as determined on 1 January 20X6, C100. The 'investment in subsidiary' in the parent entity balance sheet is in excess of C100.

As discussed in paragraph A12.171, the subsidiary should treat the transaction as an equity-settled share-based payment, as the subsidiary does not have an obligation to settle the award. [IFRS 2 para 43B]. The subsidiary should record the following:

		C	C
Year ended 31 December 20X6			
Dr	Employee benefits expense	50	
	Cr Equity		50
Dr	Equity	100	
	Cr Cash		100
Year ended 31 December 20X7		C	C
Dr	Employee benefits expense	50	
	Cr Equity		50

In its separate financial statements, the parent entity will record the following:

		C	C
Year ended 31 December 20X6			
Dr	Investment in subsidiary	50	
	Cr Equity		50
Dr	Cash	100	
	Cr Investment in subsidiary		100

In its separate financial statements, the parent entity records the exercise price received from employees when the options are exercised on 31 December 20X7 as follows:

Year ended 31 December 20X7			
		C	C
Dr	Investment in subsidiary	50	
	Cr Equity		50
Dr	Cash (100 shares at C10 each)	1,000	
	Cr Equity		1,000

The payment by the subsidiary is in substance an advance payment on the capital contribution the parent intends to make in the future. Whether the subsidiary makes a payment to its parent in advance or at a later date (such as when employees exercise their awards) does not affect the classification in the subsidiary or the parent accounts. If the upfront recharge is in excess of the 'investment in subsidiary' in the parent's accounts, the excess would be recognised in the income statement.

A subsidiary entity may wish to show the debit side of the cash payment as an additional expense, for example for tax purposes (again, this leads to a double debit). Similarly, a parent entity may wish to show the cash payment as income. We believe that these approaches would also be acceptable, provided that they are applied consistently. In addition, where there is no clear link between the share-based payment and the recharge from the parent, we believe that it would be most appropriate to record a second debit through the income statement in the subsidiary and as a credit through the income statement in the parent.

[The next paragraph is A12.200.]

IFRS 2 disclosures in group arrangements

A12.200 Where a subsidiary entity accounts for a share-based payment transaction in group situations such as those described between paragraphs A12.169 and A12.177 above, the disclosures prescribed by IFRS 2 are required in full (see further from para A12.257). The subsidiary entity's financial statements should be stand-alone; it is not possible, for example, to cross-refer to share-based payment disclosures given in the parent's (or group's) financial statements.

Classification issues

Entity purchases own shares from market

A12.201 The way in which an entity acquires the shares that will be used to satisfy a share-based payment award is a separate transaction that does not impact the classification of share-based payment awards under IFRS 2. For example, a share-based payment award would not be treated as cash-settled simply because an entity is forced to go to a third party to purchase its equity instruments in order to satisfy the award. If employees will always receive shares on meeting the vesting conditions, they would be treated as equity-settled, because the entity is providing its own equity to employees.

Example – Classification following purchase of own shares from the market

An entity granted employees rights to its shares subject to certain performance conditions. The entity purchases the shares on the market at the date that its employees satisfy those performance conditions.

The entity accounts for the arrangement as an equity-settled share-based payment transaction. When the performance conditions are met and the entity purchases the shares on the market, the transaction is recognised in equity as a treasury share transaction to reflect the purchase of the entity's own shares. This does not affect the share-based payment accounting.

Post-vesting restrictions

A12.202 Post-vesting restrictions may affect the classification of share-based payment transactions. IFRS 2 requires entities to consider the post-vesting terms and conditions of a share-based payment. The following example illustrates this point.

Example – Post-vesting restriction

A post-vesting restriction might be a pre-emption right. For example, an employee receives shares in the entity upon vesting, but he or she must offer them for sale to the entity if they resign or otherwise terminate their employment. Where the entity has an intention or established practice of exercising the pre-emption right it would indicate that the award is in fact cash-settled. See further discussion at paragraph A12.146.

A12.203 An entity may sometimes act as a broker for its employees by selling their shares to a third party on the employees' behalf. Where the entity is acting as a principal, for example where employees have no choice in the matter or where the employer is the purchaser, the entity having mandated the purchase of shares from the employees, the award would be treated as cash-settled.

A12.204 Alternatively, where the entity is acting as agent, for example, selling the shares on the market upon instruction by the employee, the award would be treated as equity-settled as the entity is settling in shares.

A12.205 Another situation arises where an entity settles a share option award net, that is, employees receive fewer shares, but pay no exercise price. For example, for an award of 100 shares an employee receives 70 shares. It is not relevant whether the company sells 30 shares on the market to satisfy the exercise price or continues to hold them, since there is no cash outflow or liability for the company. The award should be classified as equity-settled as the entity has settled the full value of the award in shares. See further from paragraph A12.222 for discussion of social security issues.

[The next paragraph is A12.211.]

Equity incentive plans

A12.211 Certain equity incentive plans offer organisations an opportunity to widen share ownership as part of their overall reward strategy. These incentive plans may include one or all of the following awards:

- *Free shares* – employers gift shares to employees.
- *Matching shares* – employers match shares which have already been purchased by employees provided the employee continues to provide services for a specified period of time.
- *Dividend shares* – employers offer dividend reinvestment in additional shares with shares held by employees in another plan.

Free shares

A12.212 When the award of free shares is not subject to a performance condition and the shares are not forfeitable, an expense will be recognised immediately. This expense will be based on the fair value of the shares at the date that the award is granted. Where the award is subject to vesting conditions, the expense will be recognised over the vesting period.

A12.213 In the situation where recipients of an award may retain their entitlements, even if they leave employment, the award would have vested at the point they retain entitlement. At this point, any remaining charge would be accelerated, because there is no further service period. This is considered in the example following paragraph A12.214.

Matching shares

A12.214 The accounting for matching shares should be similar to that of a free share award (see para A12.212 above), that is, the expense would be recognised over the vesting period. As discussed in paragraph A12.101, a requirement to hold shares in order to receive matching shares is a non-vesting condition. Failure to hold the required shares results in a cancellation. Where awards are part of an ongoing arrangement under which the employee can purchase shares and, consequently, receive matching shares, the charge should be made over the relevant vesting period. This is considered in example 1.

> **Example 1 – Matching shares with a service condition and good and bad leaver provisions**
>
> An entity operates an equity incentive plan for all of its employees. As part of the arrangement, employees have a right to matching shares when they apply for shares, although they must hold their purchased shares and remain with the entity for three years before the matching shares vest unconditionally. However, 'good' leavers (for example, those leaving due to death, injury, disability, transfer and retirement) will not forfeit their rights to the matching shares.

In the case of good leavers, it is assumed that the matching shares must have vested at the point they become a good leaver (as there are no service conditions to be satisfied for them to receive the shares). Hence, any remaining charge should be accelerated when a good leaver leaves. For an award that will vest on retirement, the vesting period, as anticipated at grant date, ends at the point where the employee is able to retire without requiring the agreement of the employer. For bad leavers, on the other hand, due to the fact they have forfeited their rights to the shares by failing to meet the service condition, there should be a reversal of the related charge to the extent they were not anticipated.

Therefore, at the date the matching shares are granted, it is necessary not only to assess the likely number of leavers and when they are going to leave, but also to split these into good and bad leavers. For those expected to be good leavers the estimated vesting period will be reduced to the likely date of their departure, for example, on retirement. However, it would be difficult to estimate vesting for death and/or disability events and these amounts may not be material. Where such events are unlikely to be material vesting for these conditions might not be adjusted until the event takes place.

What happens if an employee chooses to dispose of their purchased shares without leaving is considered in the next example.

Example 2 – Matching shares with a non-vesting condition (requirement to hold shares)

An entity enters into a share-based payment arrangement with employees whereby each employee is entitled to 1,000 free shares at the end of a three year period provided that:

- The employee completes a three year service period with the entity from the date of the grant of the award.
- The employee elects to take their cash bonus for the year in the form of 1,000 shares on the grant date and then holds them for the three year period ('restricted shares').

However, an employee that leaves the company prior to the end of the three year period or sells their restricted shares within this period will no longer be eligible to receive the matching shares.

IFRS 2 makes it clear that the requirement to hold restricted shares for three years is not a vesting condition. Although the requirement occurs during the service period, it is wholly within the employee's control and does not determine whether the entity receives the services linked to the matching shares. The probability of employees selling their restricted shares (and hence losing the matching shares) will need to be taken into account when calculating the grant date fair value.

An employee's failure to hold the restricted shares is treated as a cancellation. This would result in the acceleration of any unvested portion of the award on the date that the employee sells the restricted shares and receives the cash instead. See further paragraph A12.138.

Dividend shares

A12.215 Dividends paid on shares that have vested with employees (perhaps through another plan) accrue to the benefit of the employee. Clearly, these dividends will be included within dividends paid by the company.

A12.216 In some situations the shares have not vested (for example, where shares are subject to forfeiture) but dividends on those shares do vest (either by being paid to the employee or by reinvestment in dividend shares that are not forfeitable). This is a complex area and specialist advice may need to be obtained. Refer to paragraph A12.305 below for a discussion on cash dividends.

Deferred bonus plans

A12.217 A deferred bonus plan is a type of share incentive plan that is common in some territories. Terms are varied and often complex, but the following are typical features:

- A bonus is awarded to employees based on individual and company performance over one year.
- At the end of the year, employees may elect to receive a portion of their bonus in the form of shares rather than cash.
- If an employee elects to receive shares:
- the shares are restricted insofar as they cannot be sold for three years; and
- if the individual is still an employee at the end of the three year period, they receive an allocation of matching shares (see paras A12.211 and A12.214).

A12.218 The entitlement to matching shares introduces a degree of complexity as there are, in substance, two awards. The first, which may be settled in cash or shares, vests at the end of the first year. The second (the entitlement to matching shares) does not vest until the end of the fourth year and only then if the employee has chosen shares rather than cash at the end of the first year. This means that an expense should be recognised over one year for the first award and over four years for the second.

A12.219 As regards measurement, the grant date value of the cash alternative is the present value of the agreed amount of the bonus. The value of the equity alternative is made up of two components, namely the restricted shares (the value of which may be slightly less than the cash alternative if it is appropriate to reduce the value as a result of the sale restriction – see para A12.279) plus the matching shares.

A12.220 If at the end of the first year an employee chooses the cash alternative they will not receive the equity alternative or the matching shares. The accounting treatment is the same as that described in example 2 in paragraph A12.214. If the employee chooses the cash alternative, this would be a cancellation of the second tranche of the grant by the employee which would lead to accelerated expense recognition.

A12.221 On the other hand, if the employee chooses the equity alternative, the balance on the liability is transferred to equity and the entity will continue to recognise the balance of the expense in respect of the matching shares over the remaining three years. If, having taken the equity alternative, an employee leaves after, say, two years, this is a forfeiture as the employee has ceased to satisfy the service condition, so the expense will be reversed. The expense recognised in the first year in respect of the restricted shares will not be reversed, as the former employee will normally be entitled to retain the shares.

Social security contributions on share options gains

Background

UK.A12.221.1 UK employers are required to pay National Insurance Contributions (NIC) (social security contributions) on the exercise of certain share options granted after 5 April 1999. The NIC charge applies to share options issued under unapproved share plans (that is, those not approved by the Inland Revenue) where the shares are 'readily convertible assets', that is, they can be sold on a stock exchange or there are arrangements in place that allow the employees to obtain cash for the shares acquired under the option plan.

UK.A12.221.2 The charge is based on the intrinsic value of the options at the date of exercise (that is, the excess of the market price of the shares over the exercise price).

Treatment of social security contributions under IFRS

A12.222 There is no specific standard within IFRS that governs the accounting for social security contributions, as there is for income taxes. When considering under which standard social security costs should be accounted for, IAS 19 concludes that in the context of short-term employee benefits, social security contributions (such as NIC in the UK or FICA in the US) are employee benefits and should be considered in the same way as wages, salaries and so on. [IAS 19 para 8(a)]. For long-term benefits, non-investment related expenses that are an integral part of the entity's obligation should be included in actuarial assumptions used to measure the defined benefit obligation. Social security contributions are, therefore, considered a cost of providing the benefit. (See further chapter 11.) This suggests that the social security contributions payable in connection with a grant of share options should be considered as an integral part of the grant itself. Hence, the accounting for the social security contributions will be dictated by IFRS 2 and the charge will be treated as a cash-settled transaction. Cash-settled share-based payment transactions are discussed in detail from paragraph A12.146.

A12.223 The accounting for social security contributions as a cash-settled share-based payment transaction means:

- A liability should be recognised in respect of social security contributions payable in the future when options are exercised.
- The amount of the liability will depend on the number of options that are expected to be exercised (that is, vesting conditions are taken into account).
- The expense should be allocated over the period from the date of grant to the end of the vesting period. From the end of the vesting period to the date of actual exercise the liability should be adjusted by reference to the current market value of the shares (that is, fair value of the liability at the end of the reporting period).

A12.224 The important difference is that the liability will be based on an estimate of fair value, as if it represented an element of a cash-settled share-based payment transaction, rather than the market price of the shares at the balance sheet date. This is illustrated in the following example.

Example – Treatment of social security contributions

The facts are the same as example 1 in paragraph A12.114. On 1 January 20X5, entity A made an award of 1,000 options to each of its 60 employees. The only condition associated with the award was that recipients must remain in the employment of entity A for three years. At the date of the award, management estimated that 10% of employees (that is, six employees) would leave the entity before the end of three years. On 31 December 20X6, management revised their estimate of leavers to 5% (that is, three employees). However, awards to 55 employees actually vested on 31 December 20X7. All options must be exercised by the end of 20X9. On 31 December 20X8, when the intrinsic value of each option was C10, ten employees exercised their options. The remaining 45 employees exercised their options on 31 December 20X9 when the intrinsic value of each option was C14. The fair value of an option at each year end is shown below:

Year	Fair value at year end
31 December 20X5	6
31 December 20X6	8
31 December 20X7	9
31 December 20X8	12
31 December 20X9	14

Assuming the rate for employers' social security contributions throughout this period is 12.8%, the amount to be paid by entity A will be 12.8% of the intrinsic value of options exercised. For example, the amount payable at 31 December 20X8 is C12,800 (being 12.8% × C10 × 1,000 × 10). However, the amount recognised as a liability at each period end should be based on an estimate of the fair value of an option at that date. Hence, the amount recognised as an expense in each year and as a liability at each year end will be as follows:

Year	Expense	Liability	Calculation of liability
	C	C	
31 December 20X5	13,824	13,824	54 × 1,000 × 6 × 12.8% × $^1/_3$
31 December 20X6	25,088	38,912	57 × 1,000 × 8 × 12.8% × $^2/_3$
31 December 20X7	24,448	63,360	55 × 1,000 × 9 × 12.8%
31 December 20X8	18,560	69,120	45 × 1,000 × 12 × 12.8% Expense reflects extent to which social security contributions paid (C12,800) exceeds the liability at the previous year end in respect of the ten employees who exercised their options (C11,520) plus an adjustment to the liability of C17,280 (that is, 45 × 1,000 × (12-9) × 12.8%).
31 December 20X9	11,520	0	Liability extinguished. Expense reflects extent to which social security contributions paid exceeds the liability at the previous year end (45 × 1,000 × 14 × 12.8% = C80,640 less C69,120).

A12.225 The accounting treatment described above differs from that applied when accounting for the corporation tax effects of equity-settled share-based payments. IAS 12, 'Income taxes', specifies that if the amount allowed as a tax deduction in future periods is dependent upon an entity's share price at a future date, the measurement of the deductible temporary difference should be based on the entity's share price at the end of the period. [IAS 12 para 68B]. Hence, the accounting for deferred tax is based on the year end intrinsic value rather than an estimate of the fair value of the equity instrument. It is unclear from the basis of conclusions why the IASB concluded that an intrinsic value basis is appropriate for deferred tax accounting, although it is emphasised that an estimate of the fair value of an equity instrument is not intended to represent an estimate or forecast of a future share price. Nevertheless, in view of IAS 19's inclusion of social security contributions within the definition of employee benefits, in our opinion they should be considered an element of the share-based payment transaction and accounted for accordingly.

A12.226 A question arises as to how events after the balance sheet date affect the measurement of the liability in respect of social security contributions. This is illustrated in the following example.

Example – Social security contributions on share options — post year end fall in share price

An entity has outstanding employee share options that will attract a social security liability when exercised. The option exercise price is C10 and the market price of the entity's shares at the year end was C50. Since the year end there has been a large fall in share prices in the sector and the entity's share price has dropped to C15. In addition, 30 per cent of the employees to whom options were granted have left and forfeited their options.

Can the entity take those subsequent events into account when calculating the liability at the balance sheet date?

As described from paragraph A12.222 above, a liability is required for the social security contribution on outstanding option grants expected to vest. The liability is derived from the fair value of the equity instrument granted, re-measured at each reporting date and spread over the period from the date the options were granted to the end of the vesting period. It is clear, therefore, that where options are expected to be exercised, the provision recognised at the balance sheet date should not be adjusted for subsequent changes in the market price of the entity's shares. The liability should be calculated at each balance sheet date to reflect the fair value of the liability at that date. Although market prices may fluctuate widely after the year-end, such fluctuations are disregarded, as with movements in foreign exchange rates that occur after the balance sheet date.

At each balance sheet date the entity needs to estimate the number of options that will ultimately be exercised. Where future events will affect the liability that will ultimately be payable, IAS 37, 'Provisions, contingent liabilities and contingent assets', requires those events to be taken into account in estimating the provision where there is sufficient objective evidence that they will occur. In some cases the estimation necessarily involves a degree of hindsight. We believe the subsequent forfeiture of a substantial number of options should be taken into account when estimating the number of options expected to be exercised.

Reimbursement or transfer of the liability

A12.227 In some countries, such as the UK, it is permissible for employers and employees to agree that the employee can pay the employer's social security contributions on share options. The employee can bear the employer's social security charge arising on share option gains in one of two ways:

- First, the employer and the employee can make an agreement that some or all of the employer's social security liability can be recovered from the employee.
- Secondly, the employer and the employee may make a joint election to legally transfer the liability for the secondary social security contribution to the employee.

A12.228 Where there is an agreement between the employer and employee under which the employee agrees to reimburse all or part of the employer's social security contributions, a liability will be recognised by the employer as set out in paragraph A12.223. When considering the presentation of the reimbursement from the employee, IAS 19 would only permit recognition of the right to reimbursement as a separate asset if the receipt was virtually certain, with a net presentation permitted in the statement of comprehensive income. [IAS 19 para 104A]. Alternatively, as the reimbursement of the social charge by the employee is directly linked to the exercise of the stock option the employer will receive additional cash proceeds from the employee at the time of exercise. Thus, reimbursement from the employee could be treated as an adjustment of the exercise price of the options.

A12.229 Where there is a joint election by employer and employee under which the liability is formally transferred to the employee, no liability appears in the employer's financial statements unless the awards are settled net of this liability (see further guidance in para A12.230).

Awards settled net of tax

A12.230 Sometimes an entity may agree to pay employee tax on an employee's behalf at the time a share option award vests, giving the employee fewer shares in exchange for doing so. While the majority of the share option award will be treated as equity-settled, because the entity has agreed to settle in shares, the portion relating to tax will be treated as a cash-settled share-based payment transaction because the entity has agreed to pay cash to the tax authorities on its employee's behalf. Thus, the entity is acting as a principal in the settlement of the share-based payment using cash and as an agent in remitting that cash to the tax authority on behalf of the employee. In this case, the entity issues a reduced number of shares to the employee and uses its own cash reserves to settle the employee's tax obligation.

A12.231 If, instead of only paying cash to the tax authorities, the entity sells a portion of the award on the employee's behalf (thus settling the award using shares and acting as an agent to sell those shares and remit the proceeds) and uses the proceeds to pay the tax authorities, the award would be wholly equity-settled. In this case, all of the shares that are to be issued in accordance with the share-based payment transaction are issued, and the entity sells some of these shares to the market on behalf of the employee and pays the cash received to the tax authority to settle the employee's tax obligation.

Employee share purchase plans

A12.232 In some territories, sharesave plans are plans through which employees are given the opportunity to subscribe for shares often at a discount to the market price. This may be paid for from a reduction of payroll over a period rather than a lump sum payment.

> **UK.A12.232.1** In the UK, save as you earn (SAYE) plans are Inland Revenue approved plans through which employees are given the opportunity to subscribe for shares at a discount of up to 20 per cent of the market price. Typically the plans have a term of three, five or seven years. In the case of three or five year arrangements, employees must make regular savings throughout the term. In the case of a seven-year term, savings made under a five year agreement are left to increase in value for a further two years. The amount that

can be invested is up to £250 per month across all plans to which an employee belongs. If an employee ceases saving, they receive a reimbursement of all amounts saved to date, plus interest, but they must withdraw from the plan.

A12.233 As described in paragraph A12.11, employee share purchase plans (for instance SAYE plans in the UK) do fall within the scope of IFRS 2. Hence, they should be treated like any other equity-settled share-based payment arrangement. However, unlike many other arrangements, some employee share purchase plans, such as those in the UK, impose a condition on their members that requires regular saving. If an employee ceases saving, they forfeit their right to subscribe for shares.

A12.234 As discussed in paragraph A12.101 above, a requirement to save is a non-vesting condition; a failure to save should, therefore, be treated as a cancellation.

Example – Save as you earn (SAYE) plan cancellation

An entity enters into an SAYE plan with its employees. The terms of the plan are that:

- Employees will contribute C250 per month to an employee share trust.
- The employee is required to contribute to the SAYE plan for 5 years, after which the employee has a choice to either receive their cash back plus accrued interest or use this cash to acquire shares at a 20% discount to the market price on the grant date.
- An employee that ceases saving receives a reimbursement of all amounts saved to date, plus interest, but must withdraw from the plan and forfeit their right to acquire shares.

The entity should account for the employee's failure to save as a cancellation. The requirement to save does not meet the definition of a service or performance condition and, therefore, a failure to save cannot be interpreted as the failure to fulfil a service or performance condition.

This results in the acceleration of any unvested portion of the award on the date that the employee stops saving and receives their cash.

The probability of employees ceasing to save (and hence losing the equity option) will need to be taken into account when calculating the grant date fair value.

Employee share ownership plans (ESOPs) with trusts

Background

A12.235 Share plan trusts are often created by a sponsoring entity for employees. They are designed to facilitate employee shareholding and are often used as a vehicle for distributing shares to employees under remuneration plans.

A12.236 Entities usually engage in one of two methods to fund share-based payment arrangements – either they make a new issue of shares or buy their own shares on the market. The latter method is more common for commercial reasons, because it does not add to the share base and dilute the interests of existing shareholders.

A12.237 Employee share ownership plans (ESOPs) are usually designed to enable employees to purchase shares in their employing company. The structures of ESOPs vary, but typically they are arrangements whereby a trust is set up by a sponsoring company to acquire shares in that company for the benefit of its employees, who generally acquire them at a later stage through share option plans, profit sharing arrangements or other share incentive plans. The commercial reasons for establishing an ESOP include the following:

- It allows a share plan to be extended to new participants without diluting existing shareholders' interests, because it can operate by acquiring and distributing shares that are already in issue rather than by requiring new shares to be issued.
- It can provide a private company with a market in its shares in order to operate an employee share plan, by buying shares from departing employees and other shareholders, warehousing them and then distributing them to new and continuing employees.
- It can facilitate employee participation in connection with a management buyout, privatisation or listing of a private company.
- In cash flow terms, a company can hedge its obligations in respect of options issued under share option plans by avoiding exposure to increases in the market value of shares between the dates of granting the options and the dates of exercising those options.

A12.238 The vehicle used to hold the shares in an ESOP is a discretionary employee benefit trust set up by the sponsoring company for the benefit of all, or most, of its employees. For tax purposes, the trustee may be resident in a different country and a subsidiary of the company will often act as a corporate trustee. The trust buys shares with funds provided by way of cash or loans from the company or by a loan from a third party (which will be guaranteed by the company). The shares held by the trust are typically distributed to employees through an employee share plan. The trust's beneficiaries usually only include the company's or group's employees or former employees and certain of their close relations.

A12.239 The legal requirements in some jurisdictions state that entities are not allowed to hold their own shares. Therefore, many entities set up special purpose share plan trusts to hold entity shares on behalf of the plan participants.

A12.240 The detailed structures of individual ESOP trusts are many and varied. However, the main features are often as follows:

- The trust provides a warehouse for the sponsoring company's shares, for example, by acquiring and holding shares that are to be sold or transferred to employees in the future. The trust will normally purchase the shares with finance provided by the sponsoring company (by way of cash contributions or loans), or by a third party bank loan, or by a combination of the two. Loans from the company are usually interest free.
- Where the trust borrows from a third party, the sponsoring company will often guarantee the loan, that is, it will be responsible for any shortfall if the trust's assets are insufficient to meet its debt repayment obligations. The company will also generally make regular contributions to the trust to enable the trust to meet its interest payments (that is, to make good the shortfall between the dividend income of the trust and the interest payable). As part of this arrangement, the trustees sometimes waive their right to dividends on the shares the trust holds.
- Shares held by the trust are distributed to employees through an employee share plan. There are many different arrangements, which include: the purchase of shares by employees when exercising their share options under an executive share option plan; the purchase of shares by the trustees of plans approved by taxation authorities for allocation to employees under the plan's rules; or the transfer of shares to employees under an incentive plan.

A share nominee company could be used by an entity as opposed to an ESOP trust. A share nominee company is used by entities to hold shares and other securities on the entity's behalf to satisfy their obligation for employee share awards.

Accounting for ESOP trusts

A12.241 IFRS 2 does not deal with the accounting for an entity's shares held by an ESOP trust. IFRS 2 also does not deal with funding arrangements between group companies relating to share-based payments.

UK.A12.241.1 This is similar to the position in the UK, where there has never been an accounting standard on the subject of ESOP trusts. However, the UITF issued UITF Abstract 38, 'Accounting for ESOP trusts'. For further details, see the Manual of Accounting – UK GAAP.

A12.242 SIC 12, 'Consolidation – special purpose entities', concludes that an entity should consolidate a special purpose entity ('SPE') where the substance of the relationship between the parties indicates that the SPE is controlled by the entity. [SIC 12 para 8]. SIC 12 was amended by the IFRS IC in November 2004 to remove the exclusion from its scope of an equity compensation plan, such as an ESOP trust and consequentially ESOPs are now caught by this interpretation. (The amendment does not change the scope exclusion for employee benefit trusts, which continue to be accounted for under IAS 19.) The interpretation goes on to give examples of circumstances in which an SPE may be consolidated. These include the following:

- The activities of the SPE are being conducted on behalf of the entity according to its specific business needs so that the entity obtains benefits from the SPE's operation.
- The entity has rights to obtain the majority of the benefits of the SPE and, therefore, may be exposed to risks incident to the activities of the SPE.

[SIC 12 paras 10(a)(c)].

A12.243 Although the trustees of an ESOP trust must act under the trust deed at all times in accordance with the beneficiaries' interests, most ESOP trusts (particularly those set up to remunerate employees) are specifically designed to serve an entity's purposes, (otherwise known as the sponsoring entity), and to ensure that there will be minimal risk of any conflict arising between the trustees' duties and the entity's interest. In substance, the sponsoring entity has control of the ESOP trust and reaps the benefits or bears the risks associated with its assets and liabilities. In order to determine whether a sponsoring company does control the ESOP here follows a number of examples where control may occur:

- Where the ESOP trust has unallocated shares, the benefit of increases in value of those shares will accrue to the sponsoring entity because, for example, it can pass increased benefits to its employees without using its other resources. Conversely, if the shares fall in value, the sponsoring entity may have to use its other resources to make good the benefits promised to its employees. Therefore, the sponsoring entity benefits from the activities of the trust and will need to make decisions about how many shares, at any point in time, the ESOP should hold. It is also worth noting that shares in an ESOP that have been allocated to employees but have not vested unconditionally (for example, where the employee is still required to pay an exercise price), would result in the sponsoring entity retaining the benefits and risks associated with holding the shares. Therefore, the ESOP would still be controlled by the sponsoring entity and hence consolidated.
- At the point when shares are conditionally gifted to the employees, the sponsoring entity retains an interest in the shares, because the benefits and risks associated with them remain with the sponsoring entity until the conditions are fulfilled and the shares have been exercised by the employees. Therefore, again by taking the risks with respect to the number of shares the sponsoring company continues to control the ESOP. The benefits and risks associated with shares that have been allocated to employees that have conditionally vested with the employee could still remain with the sponsoring entity if the ESOP has ownership of the shares as it could have a liability to the employee to repurchase the shares.
- In many ESOP trusts, dividends on the shares held by the trust are waived until they vest with employees. In other trusts dividends continue to be paid and these will accrue to the trust thereby benefiting the sponsoring entity by

either defraying the trust's costs or by reducing the cost of future employee incentive arrangements, which are ultimately borne by the sponsoring entity. Hence, the sponsoring entity has power to govern the financial and operating decisions of the ESOP by determining how the additional dividend income should be allocated.

- In many ESOP trusts, the sponsoring entity will fund the ESOP to purchase shares in the market place. These loans are effectively a gift to the trust, which will then be used to satisfy the sponsoring company's employee share remuneration plans. Hence, financing decisions as well as how funds are used are controlled by the sponsoring company.

A12.244 Thus, an ESOP trust that is controlled by its sponsoring entity should be consolidated into the financial statements with the sponsoring company. If the shares held by the ESOP are those of the group's parent, then the requirements of IAS 32 relating to treasury shares should be used. [SIC 12 para BC15C].

Example – Treatment of ESOP trust

Parent entity P has a subsidiary entity S, which is the sponsoring company of an ESOP trust. Entity S does not prepare consolidated financial statements, but prepares separate financial statements.

The ESOP trust is required by SIC 12 to be included in the consolidated financial statements of entity P, but not in the separate financial statements of entity S.

A12.245 The impact on the consolidated financial statements, in which an ESOP trust should be accounted, is as follows:

- Until such time as shares in the sponsoring entity held by an ESOP trust vest unconditionally in employees, the consideration paid for those shares should be deducted from consolidated equity. This would be the case even if the shares vest unconditionally with the employee, but the shares are yet to transfer to the employee.
- No gain or loss is recognised in the income statement on the purchase, sale, issue or cancellation of those equity instruments. Instead, any consideration paid or received by the ESOP trust is recognised directly in equity.
- Other assets and liabilities, including borrowings, of the ESOP trust should be recognised as assets and liabilities of the group.
- External finance costs and administrative expenses should be charged as they become due and not as funding payments are made to the ESOP trust.
- Any dividend income arising on own shares held by the ESOP trust should be excluded from profit or loss and should not be reported as dividends paid or payable by the sponsoring entity.

- Shares held by the ESOP trust should be excluded from the calculation of earnings per share. The calculation of earnings per share is considered in detail in chapter 14.

A12.246 In the consolidated financial statements that include the trust, the shares are treated as treasury shares (that is, as a deduction from equity). If the trust prepares separate financial statements, the shares are accounted for as financial assets in accordance with IAS 32 and IAS 39. See the Manual of Accounting – Financial instruments.

A12.246.1 SIC 12, 'Consolidation-Special purpose entities', is superseded by IFRS 10, 'Consolidated financial statements', effective for annual periods beginning on or after 1 January 2013, with earlier application permitted. There will no longer be specific accounting guidance for special purpose entities because IFRS 10 applies to all types of entities. See chapter 24A for further guidance.

Separate financial statements of the sponsor

A12.247 There is no guidance in IFRS 2 concerning the accounting for an entity's interest in a trust in its separate financial statements. In our view, the appropriate accounting depends on whether:

- The entity has a beneficial interest in the trust's residual assets. If so, the entity would recognise an investment in the trust.
- The employees own the beneficial interest in the residual assets. If they do, and there is no formal loan agreement, the entity would record a debit in equity.
- A formal loan arrangement exists between the entity and the trust. The funding could be treated as a loan to the trust. Entities should be aware that this loan may become impaired.

A12.248 If the transfer of cash to the trust is treated as a 'loan and receivable' asset under IAS 39, an impairment charge may often be required, because the asset is not recoverable. The expectation is that the employees will ultimately receive the shares, at which time the trust would no longer have any assets to justify the receivable in the sponsoring entity's accounts and the asset would be impaired. If the transfer of cash to the trust is treated as a capital contribution, any 'investment in trust' balance generated would also be subject to impairment review.

A12.249 An impairment may result in a 'double debit', because the entity recognises both the share-based payment charge and an impairment charge. In our view, where it is clear that the sponsor retains the majority of the risks and rewards relating to the funding arrangement, the trust has, in substance, acted as an agent for the sponsor. We believe it would be acceptable in this case for the sponsor to account for the issue of the shares to the trust as the issue of treasury shares, thus eliminating the problem of the 'double debit'.

A12.250 Factors that may indicate that the trust has acted merely as an agent and the sponsor retains the risks relating to the funding include:

- the entity bears the ultimate risk of a fall in the price of the shares held by the trust;
- the trust has no other unencumbered assets on which the company could claim should the shares be issued to employees; and
- the entity has guaranteed any portion of a third-party loan the trust has obtained.

Example – Employee trust with loan funding

Entity A has made a decision to set up a trust in connection with its employee share option plan. The trust enters into the share-based payment arrangement on behalf of entity A with its employees. On the date that the terms of the plan are finalised, entity A makes a loan of C2,000 to the trust in order for the trust to purchase the same number of shares from entity A that have been offered to employees under the plan. The trust has no other assets and the trust deed states that the trust exists solely to provide remuneration incentives to employees of entity A.

In this case, it would be acceptable for entity A to account for the loan provided as the issue of treasury shares. The trust is clearly acting as an agent for entity A. Entity A retains the risks relating to the loan. Entity A would record the following entry on the date the loan was provided:

		C	C
Dr	Equity (treasury share reserve)	2,000	
	Cr Share capital and premium		2,000

[The next paragraph is A12.253.]

A12.253 The examples that follow illustrate the above principles.

Example 1 – Unallocated shares funded by a bank loan

An ESOP trust holds unallocated shares costing C100,000, funded by a bank loan. The trust's sponsoring entity undertakes to make contributions to the trust whenever the loan-to-value ratio falls below a set figure. At the reporting date the market value is at least C100,000. The entity deducts the consideration paid for the shares of C100,000 from equity in its consolidated financial statements. A liability of C100,000 in respect of the bank loan is also recognised. Interest expense is accrued in the usual way.

Example 2 – Reduction in the market value of shares

The facts are the same as in example 1, except that the market value of the shares falls to C80,000 by the entity's year end.

As in example 1, consideration paid for the shares of C100,000 is deducted from equity. The fall in the market value of the shares does not give rise to a recognised loss. Hence, there are no accounting entries to reflect the fall in the market value of the shares.

Example 3 – Market value of shares is in excess of exercise price

The facts are the same as in example 1, but options are granted over the shares at C80,000 when the market value is C100,000.

The entity recognises an expense over the option vesting period in accordance with IFRS 2. As in example 1, consideration paid for the shares of C100,000 is deducted from equity. When the options are exercised, the receipt of C80,000 is credited to equity.

Example 4 – Use of surplus shares for new award

An entity's ESOP trust purchased a number of its shares in the market some years ago when the share price was £1. The original share option awards have lapsed and the shares are to be used to satisfy new awards. The shares have been carried at cost. The share price has since risen to £4 and the entity proposes to grant options over those shares to employees at an exercise price of £1.

Under IFRS 2, the share-based payment charge is based on the fair value of the award at the date of grant and, therefore, awarding the options gives rise to an income statement charge. The award's grant date fair value would be charged over the vesting period of the award. In the consolidated financial statements, the own shares held through the trust would be deducted from equity at cost, in line with SIC 12 and, therefore, would not change with the new award. (SIC 12 is superseded by IFRS 10. See further para A12.246.1.)

A12.254 An entity could use a share nominee company as opposed to an ESOP trust. A share nominee company is used by entities to hold shares and other securities on the entities' behalf to satisfy their obligation for employee share awards. An ESOP would be acting on behalf of one entity, whereas a share nominee company would be providing a service to a number of entities. In such a situation, the shares are in the possession of the nominee company, but not under its control. Consideration would need to be given as to whether the entity consolidates part of the nominee company applying the principles of SIC 12, or accounts for the holding of shares that the entity has beneficial holding of and not the investment in the nominee company. (SIC 12 is superseded by IFRS 10. See further para A12.246.1.) This is a complex area that requires consideration on a case by case basis.

A12.255 It must be remembered that the above principles relate to the accounting for shares (and other assets and liabilities) held by an ESOP trust. They have no impact on the recognition or measurement of the expense in respect of a share-based payment arrangement, which is dealt with in accordance with IFRS 2.

UK.A12.255.1 Under UK GAAP, this credit arises in the sponsoring company's own equity so there is a question as to whether this is distributable. This is discussed further in paragraph A12.324 onwards.

UK.A12.255.2 Consolidation of an ESOP trust represents a difference to UK GAAP. Under UITF 38, individual assets and liabilities of such a trust are treated as if they were assets and liabilities of the sponsoring entity itself (that is, they are aggregated with the sponsoring company's own assets and liabilities in its separate financial statements). However, there is no GAAP divergence at a consolidated level: aggregation of a trust's assets and liabilities in consolidated financial statements under UK GAAP gives a similar effect to the consolidation of a trust under SIC 12 under IFRS. (SIC 12 is superseded by IFRS 10. See further para A12.246.1).

Example – Award investing in other entity shares

Entity I is implementing an unusual share option incentive plan. Entity I will lend C1m to an employee share trust, which will purchase shares in a number of publicly listed companies (but not in entity I). These companies may be suppliers, customers or competitors. Entity I's employees are granted options over 'units' held by the employee share trust. The units are an amalgam of the shares held by the trust. The options are granted at market value at the date of the grant and held over a three year period. When employees exercise their option over the units, they are paid the difference in cash between the market price of the units at the date of the grant (the exercise price) and the market value at the date of exercise. To fund the cash payment the trust sells the shares relating to the exercised units. It then repays the relevant portion of the loan from entity I and also pays the gain to employees.

Under UITF 38, 'Accounting for ESOP trusts', the trust would be considered part of entity I, because there will be an obligation on the trust (and, therefore, entity I) to pay the increase in the value of the units over the market price on the date of grant to the employees in cash. However, the trust will not be holding 'own shares' of the sponsoring entity, and so the shares will be presented as an asset of the entity, rather than as a deduction in arriving at shareholders' funds. [UITF 38 para 10(b)].

Therefore, entity I will be required to provide for the cost (the increase in value of the units) in line with FRS 12, 'Provisions, contingent liabilities and contingent assets'. The charge should be based on the difference between the market price of the units at the end of the year and the exercise price of the options.

However, when employees exercise their options and the trust sells the shares a corresponding gain will be recognised in the entity's profit and loss account. The charge under FRS 12 is made each year, but the shares may not be sold until later when the employee exercises the option. Therefore, the charge and the gain may not match in any one year. Assuming that the entity does not apply FRS 26, 'Financial instruments: recognition and measurement', the only way to achieve such a matching would be for the trust to sell the shares each year to realise a gain that matches the charge (taking market risk so that the gain can be regarded as realised) and then for the trust to repurchase the shares. This could achieve a matching each year in the profit and loss account, but the entity takes market risk.

Trustee company

A12.256 The above sections deal with the financial statements of the sponsoring company. In groups of companies, it is common for a non-trading subsidiary company to act as trustee to the ESOP. The accounting implications for the trustee company are considered in the example below.

> **Example – Treatment of ESOP by corporate trustee**
>
> A group operates an employee share plan. A subsidiary of the group has been set up to act as a corporate trustee. What should the subsidiary include in its own entity financial statements?
>
> The corporate trustee for an ESOP trust normally holds legal title to the trust's assets, but if these are held on trust such that the trustee has no beneficial interest (that is, the trustee's interest is limited to its fiduciary or custodial interest) then they are not, in substance, its assets. Therefore, the trustee company itself does not account for the assets (and likewise, the liabilities and transactions) of the ESOP. These would be reported in the financial statements of the ESOP trust and, as described from paragraph A12.241 above, in the financial statements of the group.
>
> The trustee company may well be a dormant company with a nominal share capital. Even if the trustee company is not dormant (for instance, if it charges the trust a fee for its services), this does not change the fact that its financial statements should not normally include the transactions and balances of the trust.

Disclosure

A12.257 IFRS 2 requires extensive disclosure under three broad headings:

- The nature and extent of share-based payment arrangements that existed during the period.
- How the fair value of the goods or services received or the fair value of the equity instruments granted during the period was determined.
- The effect of expenses arising from share-based payment transactions on the entity's profit or loss for the period.

[IFRS 2 paras 44, 46, 50].

A12.258 Furthermore, if the information that IFRS 2 requires to be disclosed is insufficient to enable users of the financial statements to understand each of these matters, further information should be provided. [IFRS 2 para 52].

Nature and extent of share-based payments

A12.259 Paragraph 44 of IFRS 2 requires disclosure of information that enables users of the financial statements to understand the nature and extent of share-based payment arrangements that existed during the period.

A12.260 To satisfy this objective, IFRS 2 requires disclosure of the following:

- A description of each type of share-based payment arrangement that existed at any time during the period, including the general terms and conditions of each arrangement, such as:
  - Vesting requirements.
  - The maximum term of options granted.
  - The method of settlement (for example, whether in cash or equity).
- An entity with substantially similar types of share-based payment arrangements may aggregate this information, unless separate disclosure of each arrangement is necessary for users to understand properly the nature and extent of share-based payment arrangements.
- The number and weighted average exercise prices of share options for each of the following groupings of options:
  - Outstanding at the beginning of the period.
  - Granted during the period.
  - Forfeited during the period.
  - Exercised during the period.
  - Outstanding at the end of the period.
  - Exercisable at the end of the period.
- For share options exercised during the period, the weighted average share price at the date of exercise. If options were exercised on a regular basis throughout the period, the entity may instead disclose the weighted average share price during the period.
- For share options outstanding at the end of the period, the range of exercise prices and weighted average remaining contractual life. If the range of exercise prices is wide, the outstanding options should be divided into ranges that are meaningful for assessing the number and timing of additional shares that may be issued and the cash that may be received upon exercising those options.

[IFRS 2 para 45].

A12.261 IFRS 2 requires the above disclosure to be given for share options. However, as share awards are equivalent to share options with a zero exercise price, it would be appropriate to give disclosure consistent with the above requirements for share awards as well as share options.

Disclosures for grants made before 7 November 2002

A12.262 IFRS 2 does not require a charge in respect of equity instruments granted before 7 November 2002. However, certain disclosures are required for such awards as set out in the following example.

Example – Disclosures for option award granted before 7 November 2002

An entity granted 100 share options at an exercise price of C10 per share to employees for services. The grant date was 1 January 2002 and the options were subject to a five year vesting period.

An IFRS 2 charge in respect of the share options is not required because they were granted before 7 November 2002. [IFRS 2 para 53]. However, the entity must disclose information that enables the reader to understand the nature and extent of the share-based payment arrangement. This includes disclosure of:

- A description of the share-based payment arrangement.
- The general terms and conditions.
- Vesting requirements.
- The maximum term of options granted.
- The number and weighted average exercise prices of share options:
- Outstanding at the beginning of the period.
- Granted during the period.
- Forfeited during the period.
- Exercised during the period.
- Expired during the period.
- Outstanding at the end of the period.
- Exercisable at the end of the period.
- The weighted average share price at the date of exercise.
- The range of exercise prices and weighted average remaining contractual life for share options outstanding at the end of the period.

[IFRS 2 paras 56, 44, 45].

Determination of fair values

A12.263 Paragraph 46 of IFRS 2 requires disclosure of information that enables users of the financial statements to understand how the fair value of the goods or services received, or the fair value of the equity instruments granted, during the period was determined. The level of disclosure will vary depending on whether the fair value of the goods or services was determined directly or indirectly (see from para A12.55).

A12.264 In the case of transactions with parties other than employees, there is a rebuttable presumption that the fair value of goods or services will be measured directly. [IFRS 2 para 13]. Where the presumption is rebutted, for example, where unidentifiable goods or services have been provided and the fair value of the goods or services is measured indirectly by reference to the fair value of the equity instruments granted as consideration, the entity should disclose that fact and explain why the presumption has been rebutted. [IFRS 2 para 49].

A12.265 Where the fair value of goods or services has been measured directly, the entity should disclose how this fair value was determined. [IFRS 2 para 48]. For example, the fair value may have been determined by reference to a published list of prices or scale rates.

A12.266 Where the fair value of goods or services has been measured indirectly by reference to the fair value of the equity instruments granted as consideration, the entity should disclose the number and weighted average fair value of those equity instruments at the relevant measurement date together with information on how the fair value was measured. [IFRS 2 para 45(b)(ii), 47(a)(b)].

A12.267 Information on how the fair value was measured will vary depending on the type of equity instruments granted. For share options granted during the period, the information will include the following:

- The option pricing model used and the inputs to that model. These will include, at least on a weighted average basis:
  - Price of the underlying share.
  - Price of the option.
  - Expected volatility of the share price.
  - Life of the option.
  - Dividends expected on the underlying shares.
  - Risk-free interest rate over the life of the option.
  - The method used and the assumptions made to incorporate the effects of early exercise.
- How expected volatility was determined, including an explanation of the extent to which expected volatility was based on historical volatility.
- Whether and how any other features of the option grant were incorporated into the measurement of fair value (for example, market conditions).

[IFRS 2 para 47(a)].

A12.268 For other equity instruments granted during the period, information on how fair value was measured will include the following:

- If fair value was not measured on the basis of an observable market price, how it was determined.
- Whether and how expected dividends were incorporated into the measurement of fair value.
- Whether and how any other features of the equity instruments granted were incorporated into the measurement of fair value.

[IFRS 2 para 47(b)].

A12.269 Where there has been a modification to a share-based payment arrangement during the period, the following should be disclosed:

- An explanation of the modification.
- The incremental fair value granted.
- Information on how the incremental fair value was measured, consistent with the requirements set out in paragraphs A12.267 or A12.268 as appropriate.

[IFRS 2 para 47(c)].

Impact on profit or loss

A12.270 Paragraph 50 of IFRS 2 requires disclosure of information that enables users of the financial statements to understand the effect of share-based payment transactions on the entity's profit or loss for the period and on its financial position.

A12.271 To satisfy this objective, IFRS 2 requires disclosure of the following:

- The total expense recognised in the period in respect of share-based payment transactions, with separate disclosure of the portion of the expense that relates to transactions accounted for as equity-settled. In satisfying this requirement, only expenses in respect of goods or services that did not qualify for recognition as an asset are considered. Therefore, depreciation of an asset acquired in a prior-year share-based payment transaction does not need to be disclosed.
- For liabilities arising from share-based payment transactions:
  - the total carrying amount at the end of the period; and
  - the total intrinsic value at the end of the period of liabilities for which the counterparty's right to cash or other assets has vested.

[IFRS 2 para 51].

A12.272 A question may arise as to whether the expense relating to a cash-settled award should be split between:

- the value of the services received based on the grant date fair value; and

- the movement as a result of changes in the liability's fair value.

Our view is that during the vesting period the full movements in the liability are employee related and the full movement should be employee compensation. Post vesting, since there is no longer a link to employee service, the movements would be either taken to finance costs or continue to be shown as employee costs. This policy choice should be applied consistently.

Example

A12.273 Table A12.3 is an example of IFRS 2 disclosures in respect of equity-settled share-based payments.

Table A12.3 – IFRS 2 share-based payment disclosures

British Sky Broadcasting Group plc – Annual Report – 30 June 2010

8. Employee benefits and key management compensation (extract)

a) Group employee benefits

	2010 £m	2009 £m
Wages and salaries	631	572
Social security costs	76	60
Costs of employee share option schemes(i)	32	50
Contributions to the Group's pension schemes(ii)	27	27
	766	709

(i) A £35 million charge relates to equity-settled share-based payments (2009: £48 million charge) and a credit of £3 million relates to cash-settled share-based payments (2009: £2 million charge). At 30 June 2010, the total expense relating to non-vested awards not yet recognised was £42 million which is expected to be recognised over a weighted average period of 1 year. At 30 June 2010, £5 million was recognised as liabilities arising from share-based payment transactions (2009: £8 million).

(ii) The Group operates defined contribution pension schemes. The pension charge for the year represents the cost of contributions payable by the Group to the schemes during the year. The amount payable to the schemes by the Group at 30 June 2010 was £3 million (2009: £4 million).

25. Share capital (extract)

Share option and contingent share award schemes

The Company operates various equity-settled share option schemes (the "Schemes") for certain employees.

The number of newly issued shares which may be allocated under the Schemes on any day shall not, when aggregated with the number of newly issued shares which have been allocated in the previous ten years under the Schemes and any other employee share scheme adopted by the Company, exceed such number as represents five percent of the ordinary share capital of the Company in issue immediately prior to that day. In determining this limit no account shall be taken of any newly issued shares where the right to acquire the newly issued shares was released, lapsed, cancelled or otherwise became incapable of exercise. Options and awards which will be satisfied by ESOP shares do not fall within these headroom limits.

The share awards outstanding can be summarised as follows:

	2010 Number of ordinary shares	2009 Number of ordinary shares
Executive Share Option Scheme options(i)	13,803,846	17,945,045
Sharesave Scheme options(ii)	6,175,446	6,514,732
All Employee awards(iii)	1,383,400	1,595,700
Management LTIP awards(iv)	13,447,526	19,276,851
LTIP awards(v)	5,869,560	9,293,347
Management Co-Investment LTIP awards(vi)	599,181	–
Co-Investment LTIP awards(vii)	728,736	–
	42,007,695	54,625,675

(i) Executive Share Option Scheme options

Included within the total Executive Share Option Scheme options outstanding at 30 June 2010 are 12,260,846 options (2009: 16,293,545) which may be exercised in the final year before their lapsing date, regardless of meeting performance criteria, provided that the employee remains in employment with the Group. Where performance criteria are achieved, the options may be exercised immediately following the end of the vesting period (being the term over which the performance criteria are required to be met). The remaining 1,543,000 options (2009: 1,651,500) have no performance criteria attached, other than the requirement that the employee remains in employment with the Group. The contractual life of all Executive Share Option Scheme options is ten years.

Grants under the Executive Share Option Scheme were made on an annual basis to selected employees, with the exercise price of options being equal to the Company's share price on the date of grant. For those options with performance conditions, growth in EPS had to exceed growth in the Retail Prices Index plus 3% per annum in order for awards to vest. Options vest on an accelerated basis over a period of up to four years from the date of grant.

(ii) Sharesave Scheme options

All Sharesave Scheme options outstanding at 30 June 2010 and 30 June 2009 have no performance criteria attached, other than the requirement that the employee remains in employment with the Group. Options granted under the Sharesave Scheme must be exercised within six months of the relevant award vesting date.

The Sharesave Scheme is open to all employees. Options are normally exercisable after either three, five or seven years from the date of grant. The price at which options are offered is not less than 80% of the middle-market price on the dealing day immediately preceding the date of invitation. It is the policy of the Group to make an invitation to employees to participate in the scheme following the announcement of the end of year results.

(iii) All Employee awards

The All Employee awards outstanding at 30 June 2010 and 30 June 2009 have no performance criteria attached, other than the requirement that the employee remains in employment with the Group. Awards granted under the All Employee award will be exercised upon the award vesting date.

The Company granted the All Employee award to all permanent employees on 5 February 2009. Awards under the scheme are granted in the form of a nil-priced option, and are satisfied using market-purchased shares.

(iv) Management LTIP awards

All Management LTIP awards outstanding at 30 June 2010 and 30 June 2009 vest only if performance conditions are met. Awards granted under the Management LTIP must be exercised within one year of the relevant award vesting date.

The Company grants awards to selected employees under the Management LTIP. Awards under this scheme mirror the LTIP, with the same performance conditions. Awards exercised under the Management LTIP can only be satisfied by the issue of market-purchased shares.

(v) LTIP awards

All LTIP awards outstanding at 30 June 2010 and 30 June 2009 vest only if performance conditions are met. Awards granted under the LTIP must be exercised within one year of the relevant award vesting date.

The Company operates the LTIP for Executive Directors and Senior Executives. Awards under the scheme are granted in the form of a nil-priced option, and are satisfied using market-purchased shares. The awards vest in full or in part dependent on the satisfaction of specified performance targets. 30% of the award vests dependent on TSR performance over a three year performance period, relative to the constituents of the FTSE 100 at the time of grant, and the remaining 70% vests dependent on performance against operational targets.

(vi) Management Co-Investment LTIP awards

All Management Co-Investment LTIP awards outstanding at 30 June 2010 vest only if performance conditions are met. Awards granted under the Management Co-Investment LTIP must be exercised within one year of the relevant award vesting date.

The Company grants awards to selected employees under the Management Co-Investment LTIP. Awards under this scheme mirror the Co-Investment LTIP, with the same performance conditions.

(vii) Co-Investment LTIP awards

All Co-Investment LTIP awards outstanding at 30 June 2010 vest only if performance conditions are met. Awards granted under the Co-Investment LTIP must be exercised within one year of the relevant award vesting date.

The Company operates the Co-Investment LTIP award for Executive Directors and Senior Executives. Employees who participate in the plan are granted a conditional award of shares based on the amount they have invested in the Group. The investment will be matched up to a maximum of 1.5 shares for every share invested, subject to a three-year EPS performance condition.

For the purposes of the disclosure below, the Sharesave Scheme options and All Employee awards ("Sharesave Schemes") and the Management LTIP, LTIP, Co-Investment Management LTIP and Co- Investment LTIP awards ("Senior Management Schemes") have been aggregated.

The movement in share awards outstanding is summarised in the following table:

	Executive Scheme		Sharesave Scheme		Senior Management Schemes		Total	
		Weighted average exercise price		Weighted average exercise price		Weighted average exercise price		Weighted average exercise price
	Number	£	Number	£	Number	£	Number	£
Outstanding at 1 July 2008	19,705,967	7.05	5,010,788	4.73	17,612,247	0.00	42,329,002	3.84
Granted during the year	–	–	4,911,084	2.49	12,533,050	0.00	17,444,134	0.70
Exercised during the year	–	–	(271,611)	4.26	(328,066)	0.00	(599,677)	1.97
Forfeited during the year	(1,463,143)	6.73	(1,448,515)	4.68	(1,245,746)	0.00	(4,157,404)	3.98
Expired during the year	(297,779)	5.01	(91,314)	4.33	(1,287)	0.00	(390,380)	4.84
Outstanding at 30 June 2009	17,945,045	7.11	8,110,432	3.40	28,570,198	0.00	54,625,675	2.84
Granted during the year	–	–	2,206,411	4.33	9,143,651	0.00	11,350,062	0.84
Exercised during the year	(2,067,227)	5.22	(1,307,893)	3.97	(12,449,270)	0.00	(15,824,390)	1.00
Forfeited during the year	(702,487)	7.23	(1,109,810)	3.80	(4,619,576)	0.00	(6,431,873)	1.47
Expired during the year	(1,371,485)	6.49	(340,294)	4.71	–	–	(1,711,779)	6.13
Outstanding at 30 June 2010	13,803,846	7.44	7,558,846	3.46	20,645,003	0.00	42,007,695	3.07

The weighted average market price of the Group's shares at the date of exercise for share options exercised during the year was £5.50 (2009: £4.59). For those exercised under the Executive Scheme it was £6.27 (2009: nil), for those exercised under the Sharesave Schemes it was £5.53 (2009: £4.67), and for those exercised under the Senior Management Schemes it was £5.37 (2009: £4.53).

The middle-market closing price of the Company's shares at 25 June 2010 was £7.01 (26 June 2009: £4.50).

The following table summarises information about share awards outstanding at 30 June 2010:

	Executive Scheme		Sharesave Scheme		Senior Management Schemes		Total	
		Weighted average remaining contractual life		Weighted average remaining contractual life		Weighted average remaining contractual life		Weighted average remaining contractual life
Range of exercise prices	Number	Years	Number	Years	Number	Years	Number	Years
£0.00 – £1.00	–	–	1,383,400	1.6	20,645,003	2.1	22,028,403	2.1
£3.00 – £4.00	–	–	2,720,290	2.5	–	–	2,720,290	2.5
£4.00 – £5.00	–	–	2,579,561	3.1	–	–	2,579,561	3.1
£5.00 – £6.00	3,383,932	3.5	875,595	1.6	–	–	4,259,527	3.1
£6.00 – £7.00	3,296,301	3.2	–	–	–	–	3,296,301	3.2
£7.00 – £8.00	3,574,429	1.3	–	–	–	–	3,574,429	1.3
£9.00 – £10.00	3,448,253	0.4			–	–	3,448,253	0.4
£12.00 – £13.00	100,931	–	–	–	–	–	100,931	–
	13,803,846	2.1	7,558,846	2.4	20,645,003	2.1	42,007,695	2.1

The following table summarises information about share awards outstanding at 30 June 2009:

	Executive Scheme		Sharesave Scheme		Senior Management Schemes		Total	
	Weighted average remaining contractual life		Weighted average remaining contractual life		Weighted average remaining contractual life		Weighted average remaining contractual life	
Range of exercise prices	Number	Years	Number	Years	Number	Years	Number	Years
£0.00 – £1.00	–	–	1,595,700	2.6	28,570,198	1.9	30,165,898	2.0
£2.00 – £3.00	–	–	43,868	0.8	–	–	43,868	0.8
£3.00 – £4.00	–	–	3,675,121	3.1	–	–	3,675,121	3.1
£4.00 – £5.00	–	–	1,598,744	1.3	–	–	1,598,744	1.3
£5.00 – £6.00	5,431,296	4.6	1,181,736	2.5	–	–	6,613,032	4.2
£6.00 – £7.00	5,050,304	3.1	15,263	0.0	–	–	5,065,567	3.1
£7.00 – £8.00	3,728,360	2.3	–	–	–	–	3,728,360	2.3
£9.00 – £10.00	3,609,581	1.4	–	–	–	–	3,609,581	1.4
£11.00 – £12.00	12,247	1.0	–	–	–	–	12,247	1.0
£12.00 – £13.00	113,257	1.0	–	–	–	–	113,257	1.0
	17,945,045	3.0	8,110,432	2.5	28,570,198	1.9	54,625,675	2.4

The range of exercise prices of the awards outstanding at 30 June 2010 was between nil and £12.88 (2009: nil and £12.98). For those awards outstanding under the Executive Scheme it was between £5.03 and £12.88 (2009: £5.03 and £12.98); for those outstanding under the Sharesave Schemes it was between nil and £5.38 (2009: nil and £6.11) and for all awards outstanding under the Senior Management Schemes the exercise price was nil (2009: nil).

The following table summarises additional information about the awards exercisable at 30 June 2010 and 30 June 2009:

	Options exercisable at 30 June	Average remaining contractual life of exercisable options	Weighted average exercise price	Options exercisable at 30 June	Average remaining contractual life of exercisable options	Weighted average exercise price
Executive Scheme	13,803,846	2.1	7.44	17,945,045	3.0	£7.11
Sharesave Schemes	204,427	0.1	4.35	453,217	0.1	£4.73
Senior Management Schemes	656,011	0.1	–	–	–	–
	14,664,284	2.0	7.06	18,398,262	3.0	£7.05

Information for awards granted during the year

The weighted average fair value of equity-settled share options granted during the year, as estimated at the date of grant, was £4.19 (2009: £3.06). This was calculated using the Black-Scholes share option pricing model, except for awards which have market-based performance conditions, where a Monte-Carlo simulation model was used, and for grants of nil-priced options, which were treated as the award of a free share. The fair value of nil-priced options granted during the year was measured on the basis of the market-price of the Company's shares on the date of grant, discounted for expected dividends which would not be received over the vesting period of the options.

The Monte-Carlo simulation model reflected the historical volatilities of the Company's share price and those of all other companies to which the Company's performance would be compared, over a period equal to the vesting period of the awards.

Expected volatility was determined by calculating the historical volatility of the Company's share price, over a period equal to the expected life of the options. Expected life was based on the contractual life of the awards and adjusted, based on management's best estimate, for the effects of exercise restrictions and behavioural considerations.

(i) Sharesave Schemes

The weighted average fair value of equity-settled share awards granted during the year under the Sharesave Schemes, as estimated at the date of grant, was £1.65 (2009: £1.98). This was calculated using the Black-Scholes share option pricing model.

The following weighted average assumptions were used in calculating these fair values:

	2010	2009
Share price	£5.73	£4.38
Exercise price	£4.33	£2.49
Expected volatility	28.3%	22.4%
Expected life	4.1 years	3.7 years
Expected dividends	3.1%	3.9%
Risk-free interest rate	2.3%	4.1%

(ii) Senior Management Schemes

The weighted average fair value of equity-settled share awards granted during the year under the Senior Management Schemes, as estimated at the date of grant, was £4.80 (2009: £3.49). The fair value of awards with market-based performance conditions was calculated using a Monte-Carlo simulation model. Awards granted as nil-priced options were treated as the award of a free share. For all other awards, fair value was calculated using the Black-Scholes share option pricing model.

The following weighted average assumptions were used in calculating these fair values:

	2010	2009
Share price	£5.47	£4.54
Exercise price	£0.00	£0.00
Expected volatility	34.8%	21.9%
Expected life	2.1 years	3.0 years
Expected dividends	3.2%	3.7%
Risk-free interest rate	2.1%	4.7%

Directors' emoluments disclosure

UK.A12.273.1 IFRS 2 does not deal with the disclosure of directors' emoluments. Disclosure requirements for long-term incentive awards and other share-based payment transactions involving directors are contained in sections 412 and 420 of the Companies Act 2006 and in the Listing Rules. Details of these requirements are covered in chapter 5 of the Manual of Accounting – Narrative Reporting.

Related party disclosures

A12.274 IAS 24, 'Related party disclosures', contains a requirement to disclose compensation payable to key management personnel, which includes share-based payment. [IAS 24 para 16]. This requirement is discussed further in chapter 29.

Voting rights

UK.A12.274.1 A UK company that has securities carrying voting rights admitted to trading on a regulated market at the end of its financial year is required to disclose, in its directors' report, details of how the rights regarding the company's control are exercisable where the company has an employees' share plan, but shares relating to that plan have rights regarding the control of the company that are not directly exercisable by the employees. Disclosures in respect of control over a company's shares are dealt with in chapter 3 of the Manual of Accounting – Narrative Reporting.

Cash flow statements

A12.275 IAS 7, 'Cash flow statements', requires an entity to report cash flows from operating activities. Employee share-based payment transactions that are equity-settled should be adjusted for in reporting the cash flows from operating activities as this represents a non-cash item that is operating in nature. [IAS 7 paras 19, 20]. Cash flow statements are covered in detail in chapter 30.

Materiality

A12.276 IAS 8 confirms that accounting policies set out in IFRSs do not need to be applied where the effect of applying them is immaterial. [IAS 8 para 8]. Both the quantitative and qualitative impact of an entity's share-based payment transactions should be assessed in order to determine the impact of applying IFRS 2. It will also be necessary to consider whether the impact of share-based payment transactions is likely to become material in the future. If the impact of applying IFRS 2 is determined to be either quantitatively or qualitatively material, the standard should be applied in full.

A12.277 Where IFRS 2 is not applied, certain disclosures in relation to share-based payment transactions may be required under local legislation or listings rules (such as gains on directors' share options or shares receivable under long-term incentive awards). It would be appropriate to explain, particularly in these circumstances, that the standard has not been applied in the financial statements, particularly where disclosures provided under local legislation indicate that the entity has share-based payment transactions in place.

Measuring the fair value of equity instruments

A12.278 Under IFRS 2, where the fair value of goods or services is measured by the indirect method (see para A12.55), the fair value of the equity instruments granted should be estimated at the relevant measurement date (see para A12.59). However, the standard also requires entities to measure the fair value of the equity instruments granted for goods or services received. If the fair value of the equity instruments granted is greater than the fair value of the goods or services received or to be received (measured using the direct method as at the grant date), the difference, being the unidentifiable goods or services received, must be recognised by the entity. As with the indirect method, the fair value of the equity instrument granted should be estimated at the relevant measurement date (see para A12.59).

A12.279 Fair value should be based on market prices, if available, taking into account any terms and conditions associated with the grant of the equity instruments. [IFRS 2 para 16]. For example, where employees have been granted an award of shares, but they are not entitled to receive dividends during the vesting period, this factor should be taken into account when estimating fair value. Similarly, if the shares are subject to restrictions on transfer after the vesting date, that factor shall be taken into account, but only to the extent that the post-vesting restrictions affect the price that a knowledgeable, willing market participant would pay for that share. If the shares are actively traded in a deep and liquid market, post-vesting transfer restrictions may have little, if any, effect on the price. [IFRS 2 para B3].

Example – Fair value implications for options that vest only on an IPO

An entity grants share options to employees that will vest only if the entity achieves a stock exchange listing within two years.

Management are aware that one of the inputs into the option pricing model to determine the award's grant date fair value is the current price of an entity's shares (see further para A12.284). When determining the current share price for an unlisted entity, a discount to the share price would normally be made to reflect the fact that there is not a market for the shares in the same way that there would be for a comparable entity with listed shares. Should the current share price of the entity's shares be discounted for illiquidity?

The standard requires that the estimated market price of an entity's shares is adjusted to take into account the terms and conditions upon which an award is granted. [IFRS 2 paras B2, B3]. In this case, the award vests only on listing and, therefore, employees will only ever be able to receive a listed share. Therefore, the input to the option pricing model would be the entity's current share price without a discount for lack of marketability which is the entity's current share price as if for a listed share.

Note that this logic would apply similarly if vesting occurred as a result of a trade sale or takeover, as the acquirer would be paying a control premium for the shares.

A12.280 Some shares and most share options are not traded on an active market so alternative valuation techniques must be considered. The objective is to derive an estimate of what the price of those equity instruments would have been at the relevant measurement date in an arm's length transaction between knowledgeable, willing parties. [IFRS 2 para 17]. Sometimes, it may be possible to make an estimate of market price based on prices of traded shares or options with similar terms and conditions, although this is unlikely in the case of executive options with specific performance criteria. It is more likely that an alternative valuation technique will need to be applied. Many pricing models are available and IFRS 2 does not specify which should be used. It does, however, describe the factors that should be taken into account when estimating fair value. It also requires the model used to be consistent with generally accepted valuation methodologies for pricing financial instruments.

A12.281 It should be remembered that the purpose of deriving a fair value for the equity instruments granted is to measure, indirectly, the fair value of the goods or services acquired by the entity. Accordingly, once the fair value of the equity instruments has been estimated at the relevant measurement date, so the 'price' of the goods or services has been determined, it is not re-measured.

Valuation techniques

A12.282 Option pricing models are based on the premise that it is possible to hedge an option exactly by buying (and continually adjusting) a portfolio of the shares over which the option has been granted. Setting up and adjusting the 'hedge portfolio' has a cost. In theory, this hedging cost will be the same, whatever happens to the share price. Given that the option can be hedged precisely at a fixed cost, it follows that this cost will be the market value of the option.

A12.283 In practice, real markets do not always follow the idealised behaviour of financial models and there are limits to how frequently a portfolio can be rebalanced. However, investment banks do, as a matter of fact, hedge option contracts using dynamically traded hedge portfolios. These portfolios are constructed in line with the theoretical models, which have proven robust in practice, despite their imperfections.

A12.284 All option pricing models take into account, as a minimum, the following factors:

- Exercise price of the option.
- Current price of the underlying share.
- Life of the option.
- Expected volatility of the share price.
- Dividends expected on the underlying shares.
- Risk-free interest rate over the life of the option.

A12.285 The first two items define the 'intrinsic value' of the option. The remaining four are relevant to its 'time value'. The time value of an option reflects the right of the holder to participate in future gains, if any. The valuation does not attempt to predict what the future gain will be, only the amount that a buyer would pay at the valuation date to obtain the right to participate in any future gains. In other words, option pricing models estimate the value of the share option at the measurement date, not the value of the underlying share at some future date.

A12.286 All other things being equal, a change in the expected volatility of the share price will have the greatest impact of the input assumptions listed in paragraph A12.284 on the option's fair value (an increase in volatility increases the fair value). A change to either the option's exercise price or its life has the next greatest impact on the option's fair value (an increase in the option's exercise price decreases the option's fair value and an increase in the option's expected life increases the option fair value). This will be the case irrespective of the option pricing model used.

A12.287 Other factors that knowledgeable, willing market participants would consider in setting the price should also be taken into account. Some of these are described in paragraph A12.279. In addition, many employee options have long lives, are exercisable during specified periods (usually between vesting date and the end of the life) and are often exercised early. Furthermore, the act of exercising the options at a price below the market price at that date might itself reduce the share price. However, vesting conditions (other than market conditions) and reload features are not taken into account in the valuation. Instead, these are dealt with as described from paragraph A12.77.

A12.288 Paragraph 21 of IFRS 2 requires that market conditions are taken into account when estimating fair value. Arguably, all conditions associated with a grant of equity instruments will influence the fair value of those instruments. This was the view taken by the IASB in developing ED 2. The exposure draft proposed that all conditions (market related or otherwise) should be taken into account when determining fair value. However, respondents to ED 2 raised a variety of concerns about the practicality and subjectivity of including non-market conditions in a valuation. In response, IFRS 2 draws a distinction between market and non-market conditions, with only the former being taken into account when estimating fair value. Broadly speaking a market condition is one that is dependent on share price.

A12.289 Market conditions include target share prices and requirements to achieve a certain level of total shareholder return (that is, the sum of dividends and increases in share price). There are various means by which they may be taken into account when estimating fair value, and some valuation models are better suited to dealing with their effects than others. This is a complex area and specialist advice may need to be obtained.

Inputs to an option pricing model

A12.290 The exercise price of the option and the current market price of the underlying share will usually be readily available. However, estimating the other inputs to an option pricing model can be a complex and time consuming exercise.

Life of the option

A12.291 Holders of traded options generally have a choice between exercising, keeping or selling their options at any point in time during the option's contractual life. As the sale of options realises both their intrinsic and time value, this will usually be a more attractive proposition than exercising, so the real choice becomes between keeping or selling (it is worthwhile to note that where options are traded in a liquid market, there is no need to use an option pricing model as the traded value of the option in the market is the fair value). A traded option would only be exercised (or lapse) at the end of its contractual term. The vast majority of employee options, on the other hand, cannot be traded, so employees only have the choice of either keeping or exercising their options. However, exercising is the only way in which an employee can realise value. In addition, it is common for the contractual life of the option to be cut short if the employee leaves the entity. This means that most employee share options are exercised much earlier than their contractual term. Accordingly, when estimating the fair value of an employee option, it is the expected life rather than the contractual life of the option that is considered.

A12.292 Appendix B to IFRS 2 describes a number of factors that should be taken into account when estimating the expected life of an option. These are:

- The length of the vesting period, because the share option typically cannot be exercised until the end of the vesting period. Hence, determining the valuation implications of expected early exercise is based on the assumption that the options will vest.
- The average length of time for which similar options have remained outstanding in the past.
- The price of the underlying shares. Experience may indicate that the employees tend to exercise options when the share price reaches a specified level above the exercise price.
- The employee's level within the organisation. For example, experience might indicate that higher-level employees tend to exercise options later than lower-level employees.
- Expected volatility of the underlying shares. On average, employees might tend to exercise options on highly volatile shares earlier than on shares with low volatility.

[IFRS 2 para B18].

A12.293 Other factors that could be considered include the following:

- The general state of the equity market, or the economy. Employees might be more inclined to hold on to their options where markets are climbing, or they might exercise their options once they see a gain if markets are performing poorly.
- The dividend yield on the underlying share. Where no dividend is paid, the option holder does not lose by not exercising. Where the dividend yield is high, the dividends lost by not exercising could outweigh the risk-free return available on the cash thus encouraging early exercise.
- The tax treatment of the benefits. In some jurisdictions, a tax charge may crystallise on vesting so employees may have to exercise their options to meet their tax liability.

A12.294 When estimating the expected life of share options granted to a group of employees, the entity could base that estimate on an appropriately weighted average expected life for the entire employee group, or on appropriately weighted average lives for subgroups of employees, based on more detailed data about employees' exercise behaviour. The distinction is likely to be important. Option value is not a linear function of option term – value increases at a decreasing rate as the term lengthens. For example, although a two-year option is worth more than a one-year option, it is not worth twice as much. That means that calculating estimated option value on the basis of a single weighted average life that includes widely differing individual lives would overstate the total fair value of the share options granted. Separating options granted into several groups, each of which has a relatively narrow range of lives included in its weighted average life, reduces that overstatement.

A12.295 For example, the experience of an entity that grants options broadly to all levels of employees might indicate that top-level executives tend to hold their options longer than middle-management employees hold theirs and that lower-level employees tend to exercise their options earlier than any other group. In addition, employees who are encouraged or required to hold a minimum amount of their employer's equity instruments, including options, might on average exercise options later than employees not subject to that provision. In those situations, separating options by groups of recipients with relatively homogeneous exercise behaviour will result in a more accurate estimate of the total fair value of the share options granted.

A12.295.1 An increase in an option's expected life will typically increase the option's fair value, as it gives the holder more time to participate in future gains.

Expected volatility

A12.296 Expected volatility is a measure of the amount by which the price of the underlying share is expected to fluctuate during the option's life. The measure of volatility used in option pricing models is the annualised standard deviation of the continuously compounded rates of return on the share. Volatility is typically expressed in annualised terms, regardless of the time period used in the calculation, for example, daily, weekly or monthly price observations.

A12.297 Standard deviation is a statistical measure of how tightly data are clustered around a mean – the more tightly clustered the data, the smaller the standard deviation. Standard deviation is measured as the square root of the variance, which in turn is measured as the average squared difference between each observation and the mean. This is shown in the following example.

Example – Calculation of standard deviation

Data	Difference between data and mean	Difference^2
53	(2.2)	4.84
58	2.8	7.84
52	(3.2)	10.24
56	0.8	0.64
57	1.8	3.24
Mean = 55.2		Mean = 5.36

The variance (that is, the average squared difference between each number and the mean) is 5.36 so the standard deviation is 2.32, being the square root of the variance.

A12.298 In the previous example, the data represents the entire population. However, the calculation of standard deviation will normally involve a sample of data from a population, in which case the calculation is amended slightly. The formula used in these situations is expressed in one of the ways shown below.

$$\sigma = \sqrt{\frac{n\Sigma x^2 - (\Sigma x)^2}{n(n-1)}} \qquad \sigma = \sqrt{\frac{\Sigma(x - \bar{x})^2}{n-1}}$$

Where: σ = standard deviation
x = an observation
$\bar{x}$ = the mean observation
n = the number of observations

Many spreadsheet packages and scientific calculators are able to calculate the standard deviation for a given series of data.

A12.299 An added complication when considering the volatility of rates of return is that the probability distribution of returns is considered to be lognormal rather than normal. This means that it is the logarithm of the returns that is normally distributed, rather than the returns themselves. This implies a smaller probability of significant deviations from the mean than is usually the case in practice. Consider now a more realistic example.

The market price of an entity's shares over a six week period fluctuated as follows:

Date	Share price
Week 1	C5.00
Week 2	C5.20
Week 3	C5.30
Week 4	C5.10
Week 5	C5.35
Week 6	C5.30

Hence, the return on the entity's shares each week, and the logarithm of those returns, is as shown below:

Date	Weekly return	Relative price change	Logarithm of relative price change
Week 1	–	–	–
Week 2	4.0%	1.040	0.03922
Week 3	1.9%	1.019	0.01882
Week 4	(3.8%)	0.962	(0.03874)
Week 5	4.9%	1.049	0.04784
Week 6	(0.9%)	0.991	(0.00904)

The standard deviation of the logarithm of the weekly return, and hence the weekly volatility, calculated using the formulae above, is 0.036. However, as noted above, the measure of volatility used in option pricing models is the annualised volatility. To derive this figure, it is necessary to multiply the weekly volatility by the square root of 52. This gives an annualised volatility of 0.258, normally expressed as 25.8%.

A12.300 So, what does this mean? Statistically, when data are distributed normally, one standard deviation lies within 68 per cent of the mean. Hence, the expected annualised volatility of a share is the range within which the continuously compounded annual rate of return is expected to fall 68 per cent (or approximately two-thirds) of the time. For example, if a share has an expected rate of return of 12 per cent and a volatility of 30 per cent, this means that the probability that the actual rate of return on the share will be between minus 18 per cent (12 per cent — 30 per cent) and 42 per cent (12 per cent + 30 per cent) is approximately two-thirds. This is illustrated in the diagram below.

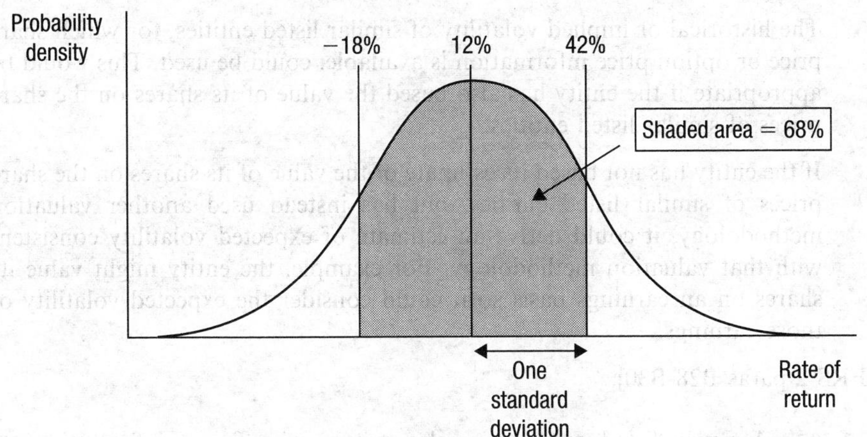

A12.301 Appendix B to IFRS 2 describes a number of factors that should be taken into account when estimating expected volatility. These are:

- The implied volatility from traded share options on the company's shares, or other traded instruments that include option features (such as convertible debt).
- The historical volatility of the share price over the most recent period that is generally commensurate with the expected term of the option.
- The length of time a company's shares have been publicly traded. Unlisted and recently listed companies are considered further below.
- The tendency of volatility to revert to its long-term average and other factors indicating that historical volatility may be an unreliable indicator of expected future volatility. For example, if a company's share price was extraordinarily volatile for a short period because of a failed takeover bid or a major restructuring, that period could be disregarded in computing historical average annual volatility.
- Appropriate and regular intervals for price observations. The price observations should be consistent from period to period. For example, a company might use the closing price for each week or the highest price for the week, but it should not use the closing price for some weeks and the highest price for other weeks.

[IFRS 2 para B25].

A12.302 An unlisted entity will not have historical data on which to base an estimate of expected future volatility. IFRS 2 suggests alternative methods by which an estimate may be made:

- If the entity regularly issues options or shares to employees (or other parties), it might have set up an internal market for its shares. The volatility of those share prices could be considered.

- The historical or implied volatility of similar listed entities, for which share price or option price information is available, could be used. This would be appropriate if the entity has also based the value of its shares on the share prices of similar listed entities.
- If the entity has not based its estimate of the value of its shares on the share prices of similar listed entities, but has instead used another valuation methodology, it could derive an estimate of expected volatility consistent with that valuation methodology. For example, the entity might value its shares on an earnings basis so it could consider the expected volatility of those earnings.

[IFRS 2 paras B28-B30].

A12.303 A newly listed entity may also not have sufficient information on historical volatility on which to base an estimate of expected future volatility. Nevertheless, it should compute historical volatility for the longest period for which trading activity is available. It could also consider the historical volatility of similar entities following a comparable period in their lives. For example, an entity that has been listed for only one year and grants options with an average expected life of five years might consider the pattern and level of historical volatility of entities in the same industry for the first six years in which the shares of those entities were publicly traded.

A12.303.1 Expected volatility has the most impact on the option's fair value. The higher the volatility is, the higher the potential gain for the holder, resulting in a higher option value.

Expected dividends

A12.304 Whether expected dividends should be taken into account when measuring the fair value of an option depends on whether the counterparty is entitled to dividends on the underlying shares. For example, if employees were granted options, but are not entitled to dividends on the underlying shares between grant date and exercise date, they will have effectively 'lost' those dividends. Hence, the grant date valuation of the options should take expected dividends into account. That is to say, the fair value of the option will be reduced.

A12.305 The concept is easier to understand in the case of grants of shares. When estimating the fair value of the shares, the fair value should be reduced by the present value of dividends expected to be paid, and hence 'lost' by the employees, during the vesting period. Conversely, no adjustment is required for expected dividends if the counterparty is entitled to receive dividends during the vesting period. The relatively greater value from receiving dividends during the vesting period is, therefore, included in the award's grant date fair value.

A12.306 An alternative method of accounting for dividends during the vesting period is to consider the grant as a compound instrument since the employee will receive both cash over the vesting period and an equity instrument if the award vests. The entity would, therefore, first calculate the value of the debt component (dividends expected to be paid over the vesting period) with the remainder being the equity component. As explained above, the equity component could be valued by estimating the value of the shares excluding the expected dividends to be paid. Once the award has been allocated between the cash and equity components, the entity should account for each element of the grant separately [IFRS 2 para 38].

Example – Shares with dividend rights during the vesting period

Employees of an entity are granted share options in the entity. The employees are required to provide three years service, after which time the options automatically convert into shares (the exercise price of the options is nil). As an added incentive and to align the employees' goals with those of the shareholders, the employees' options have the same rights to dividends as ordinary shares during the vesting period. A valuation shows that the expected value of the dividends over the three year vesting period is C600 and the grant date fair value of the options, excluding the dividends, is C3,000. At the end of the first year, a dividend of C200 is paid out and the entity expects to pay a further C550 in dividends over the remaining vesting period.

The entries required to account for the transaction at the end of the first year would be as follows:

		Dr C	Cr C
Dr	Employee expenses	1,000	
	Cr Equity		1,000
Equity component recognised straight line over the vesting period			
Dr	Employee expense	250	
	Cr Share-based payment liability		250
Cash-settled component recognised over the vesting period: 750 total expected liability × 1/3			
Dr	Share-based payment liability	200	
	Cr Cash		200
Partial settlement of the cash-settled portion of the share-based payment			

Once the options have vested and the employee holds the shares in the capacity as a shareholder, further dividend payments would be recorded as distributions through equity.

A12.307 The difference between the two treatments, where dividends are received during the vesting period, can be summarised as follows:

- Where the entity includes the expected dividends to be paid in the calculation of the grant date fair value, any dividends paid during the vesting period are recognised in equity and not in the statement of comprehensive income. Also, if the expected dividends included in the grant date fair value are not equal to the actual dividends paid, no adjustment is made for this, that is, the expected dividends are estimated only once.

- Where the entity treats the expected dividends to be paid as the debt portion of a compound instrument, any dividends paid during the vesting period are recognised in the statement of comprehensive income as an employee expense. In this way, the actual dividends paid are recognised as an expense.

A12.308 Option pricing models generally call for expected dividend yield, although they may be modified to use instead an expected dividend amount. If the latter is used, the historical pattern of increases in dividends must be taken into account. For example, if an entity's policy has generally been to increase dividends by around three per cent per year, its estimated option value should not assume a fixed dividend amount throughout the option's life, unless there is evidence to support that assumption.

A12.309 Generally, expected dividends should be based on publicly available information. An entity that does not pay dividends and has no plans to do so should assume an expected dividend yield of zero. However, an emerging entity with no history of paying dividends might expect to begin paying dividends in the near future. Such an entity could use an average of its past dividend yield (that is, zero) and the dividend yield of an appropriately comparable peer group.

A12.309.1 An increase in expected dividend yield will decrease the option's fair value. If the expected dividends are high, this will normally reduce the option's value, because a shareholder receives dividends and an option holder does not. Therefore, giving up the dividends is the opportunity cost of not exercising the option.

Risk-free rate

A12.310 Typically, the risk-free interest rate is the yield currently available on zero-coupon government bonds of the country in whose currency the exercise price is expressed, with a remaining term equal to the expected term of the option being valued. It may be necessary to use an appropriate substitute, if no such bonds exist or circumstances indicate that the yield on zero-coupon government bonds is not representative of the risk-free rate (for example, in high inflation economies). Also, an appropriate substitute should be used if market participants would typically determine the risk-free rate by using that substitute.

A12.311 All other things being equal, an increase in the risk-free rate would result in an increase in the option's fair value. We typically refer to the risk-free interest rate in terms of discounting future values whereby the higher the rate, the lower the present value. In fact when considering an option, the economics are that the option holder keeps their cash and is able to earn the risk-free interest rate until such time as the option is exercised. On this basis, an increase in the risk-free interest rate makes holding the option more valuable.

A12.311.1 The following diagram shows a summary of the impact on fair value when an input is increased (with all other inputs held constant). The more arrows shown, the greater the impact on fair value from changing the input assumptions.

Inputs and assumptions

Increase in: — Impact on fair value

- Current share price
- Exercise price
- Expected life
- Dividends
- Risk free rate of return
- Volatility

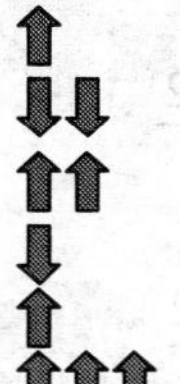

Selection of an option pricing model

A12.312 As noted above, IFRS 2 does not specify which model should be used to estimate the fair value of an equity instrument. Frequent reference is made to the Black-Scholes-Merton formula (more commonly known as the Black-Scholes formula) but other models such as the binomial model or Monte-Carlo simulation may sometimes be more suitable. Each of these models is described and considered in the following paragraphs.

The Black-Scholes formula

A12.313 The most widely used model for valuing straightforward options was published by Fischer Black and Myron Scholes in 1973 and is commonly known as the Black-Scholes formula. This model depends on several assumptions:

- Future returns are independent both of past returns and the current share price.
- Volatility and interest rates both remain constant throughout the option's life.
- The probability distribution of returns is lognormal.
- No transaction costs.

A12.314 Based on these assumptions, the price of a European call option (that is, an option that may only be exercised at the end of its life regardless of the country in which it is issued) is estimated by the following formula:

$$C = SN(d_1) - Xe^{(-rt)}N(d_2)$$

Where:

C = Price of an option (£)

S = Current share price (£)

X = Option exercise price (£)

D = Dividend yield on underlying share (%)

t = Time to expiry
s = Expected volatility (%)
r = Risk-free rate over the life of the option
$N(d_n)$ = Value of d found from standard normal distribution curve

And

$$d_1 = \frac{\text{Ln}(Se^{rt}/X) + \sigma^2 t/2}{\sigma\sqrt{t}}$$

$$d_2 = \frac{\text{Ln}(Se^{rt}/X) - \sigma^2 t/2}{\sigma\sqrt{t}}$$

A12.315 Although the Black-Scholes formula is widely used, it has several limitations in the context of employee options. For example:

- It does not allow for market conditions or non-vesting conditions or other terms and conditions that are relevant for determining fair value.
- The option is assumed to be exercised at the end of its life. Early exercise can only be taken into account by use of an expected life rather than a contractual life.
- Inputs (such as expected volatility) cannot be varied over the option's life.

A12.316 Nevertheless, for many of the simpler employee options, the Black-Scholes formula can give a reasonably reliable estimate of fair value.

The binomial model

A12.317 The binomial model applies the same principles as decision tree analysis to the pricing of an option. At each point, the possible outcomes are simplified to the possibility that prices may increase by a certain percentage or decrease by a certain percentage. On this basis, a 'tree' or 'lattice' is created. Depending on the relative probabilities of each path, an expected outcome may be estimated. This is illustrated in the following simple example.

Example – The binomial model

A entity has granted options that may be exercised in three year's time. The exercise price of the options is C5, which equates to the current market price of the entity's shares.

Management has estimated that there is a probability of p that the market price of the entity's shares will increase by 10% per year and a probability of (1 — p) that it will reduce by 10%. In order to estimate the value of p, management can equate the expected outcome of owning a share to the known outcome of earning a risk-free rate of interest on a cash deposit. If the risk free rate is assumed to be 6%, the value of a C5 investment after one year will be C5.30. Hence, as regards the share, the value of p may be calculated from the following:

$$p \times 5.50 + (1 - p) \times 4.50 = 5.30$$

Hence, p is 0.8, or 80%.

The current share price of C5 is assumed to be the correct fair value (a present value which already takes into account alternative future outcomes). The deviations from the value of C5.3 (which is expected for t + 1) deemed possible by management (that is, either C5.5 or C4.5) must be assigned probabilities, which average out at a value of C5.3, hence the above equation.

On this basis, the possible outcomes and their relative probabilities for each of the next three years may be estimated as shown below:

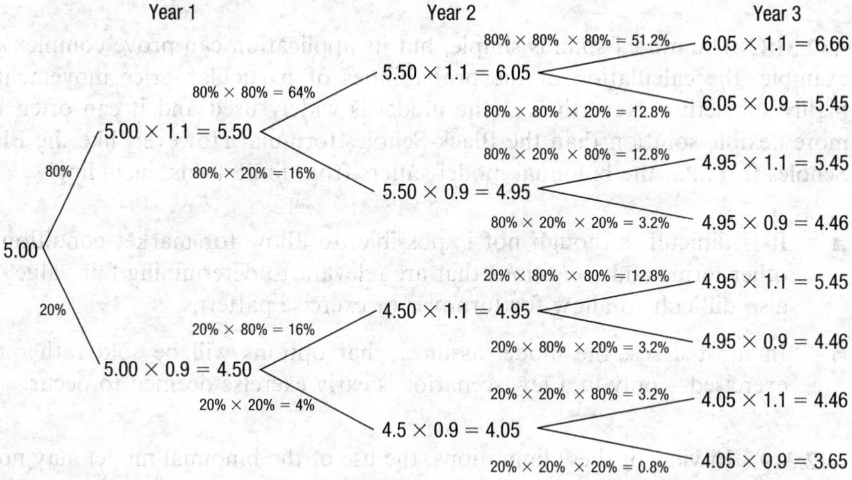

This means, for example, that there is a probability of 51.2% (that is, 80% × 80% × 80%) that the value of a share will be C6.66 in three year's time.

As the exercise price of an option is C5, it will only have value if the market price of the share exceeds C5 at the end of three years. Considering the top path of the tree, if a share is worth C6.66 then the option would be worth C1.66. This represents the intrinsic value of the option. However, considering the bottom path, if the share is worth C3.65 then an option with an exercise price of C5 will be worthless. On this basis, the expected value of the option in three years time may be derived.

Outcome	Option value (A)	Probability (B)	A × B
6.66	1.66 (6.66 – 5)	51.2% (80% × 80% × 80%)	0.85
5.45	0.45 (5.45 – 5)	12.8% (80% × 80% × 20%)	0.06
5.45	0.45 (5.45 – 5)	12.8% (80% × 20% × 80%)	0.06
4.46	0	3.2% (80% × 20% × 20%)	0
5.45	0.45 (5.45 – 5)	12.8% (20% × 80% × 80%)	0.06
4.46	0	3.2% (20% × 80% × 20%)	0
4.46	0	3.2% (20% × 20% × 80%)	0
3.65	0	0.8% (20% × 20% × 20%)	0
Expected value			1.03

If the expected value of an option in three year's time is C1.03, the current price will be the present value of this expected outcome. Hence, the estimated fair value at grant date is C0.865 (that is, $1.03/(1.06)^3$).

A12.318 The model sounds simple, but its application can prove complex. For example, the calculation of the probabilities of particular price movements is highly subjective. Nevertheless, the model is widely used and it can often be a more flexible solution than the Black-Scholes formula. However, like the Black-Scholes formula, the binomial model suffers from limitations, including:

- It is difficult, although not impossible, to allow for market conditions or other terms and conditions that are relevant to determining fair value. It is also difficult to allow for turnover or exercise patterns.
- In most cases, the model assumes that options will be sold rather than exercised – only in a few scenarios is early exercise deemed to occur.

A12.319 In view of these limitations, the use of the binomial model may not be appropriate for employee options where the probability of early exercise is significant.

Monte-Carlo simulation

A12.320 Monte-Carlo simulation takes the binomial model further by undertaking several thousand simulations of future outcomes for key assumptions and calculating the option value under each scenario. As for the binomial model, the expected outcome is then discounted to give an option value.

A12.321 Monte-Carlo models can incorporate even the most complex performance conditions, turnover and exercise patterns, such as those that are a function of gain or time since grant date. Consequently, they are generally the most reliable models for valuing employee options. The only drawback is their complexity, although this is rarely a problem with modern computing technology.

[The next paragraph is A12.324.]

Companies Act requirements

Impact on distributable profits

A12.324 International Financial Reporting Standards do not concern themselves with how to determine distributable profits. Such matters are dealt with in national law (and are considered in greater detail in chapter 24). In the case of share-based payment (and the related topic of ESOP trusts), several questions are raised:

- Does the expense in respect of an equity-settled share-based payment transaction represent a realised loss?
- Does the opposing credit entry to equity represent a realised profit?
- What is the impact on distributable profits of deducting the cost of acquiring shares through an ESOP trust from equity?
- If an ESOP trust makes a profit on the sale of surplus shares, is this distributable by the sponsoring entity?

A12.325 The answers to the above questions should be dealt with in accordance with national law.

UK.A12.326 In the UK, these questions are considered in Tech 02/10, 'Guidance on the determination of realised profits and losses in the context of distributions under the Companies Act 2006', issued by the ICAEW in November 2010. The implications for distributable profits will be similar for entities reporting under IFRS 2 and those reporting under UK GAAP (FRS 20).

Expenses in respect of equity-settled share-based payment transactions

UK.A12.327 All expenses and losses should be regarded as realised losses, except to the extent that the law or accounting standards provide otherwise. It is arguable that the expense in respect of an equity-settled share-based payment transaction is not a loss at all because it does not result in a reduction in recorded net assets. However, even if the expense is regarded as a realised loss, Tech 02/10, 'Guidance on the determination of realised profits and losses in the context of distributions under the Companies Act 2006' makes it clear in other contexts (such as revaluation reserves) that an unrealised reserve will be treated as having become realised by the amortisation or writing down of the related asset. Therefore, assuming that the expense has been included in the profit and loss account rather than capitalised as part of the cost of an asset, the credit entry will be treated as a realised profit so there will be no impact on distributable reserves.

ESOP trusts

UK.A12.328 Under UK GAAP, the accounting treatment of ESOP trusts results in a sponsoring entity including the assets, liabilities and transactions of an ESOP trust in its own financial statements as if the trust were an extension of the entity. These financial statements (that is, the combined entity and trust) are the relevant accounts for the purposes of determining profits available for distribution in accordance with section 836 of the Companies Act 2006. It follows, therefore, that transactions entered into by an ESOP trust will have an impact on the sponsoring entity's distributable profits in the same way as if they had actually been entered into by the sponsoring entity itself.

UK.A12.329 Under IFRS, as described from paragraph A12.241, an ESOP trust would be consolidated rather than aggregated with the sponsoring entity's individual assets and liabilities. Accordingly, for a sponsoring entity that has adopted IFRS within its individual financial statements, as the ESOP trust's individual transactions, assets and liabilities are not reflected in the sponsoring entity's relevant accounts, they do not affect that sponsoring entity's distributable profits.

UK.A12.330 In determining the impact of an ESOP trust on a sponsoring entity's distributable profits it will be necessary to consider the nature of transactions and balances between the two parties. An entity may fund an ESOP trust by making a gift, a loan or a combination of both. A gift to the trust is clearly an immediate realised loss (as it reduces the net assets of the sponsoring entity). On the other hand a loan, provided it is considered recoverable (that is, sufficient cash is expected when employees exercise their rights to the shares), would not be a realised loss. However, any impairment in the value of the loan (caused by a question over its recoverability) would be an immediate realised loss and, hence, would reduce the sponsoring entity's distributable profits.

UK.A12.331 Public companies may face additional problems in respect of the financial assistance rules. Section 682 of the Companies Act 2006 provides that a public company may only give financial assistance for the acquisition of its own shares if the company's net assets are not thereby reduced or, to the extent that net assets are reduced, the company has sufficient distributable profits to cover the full amount of the assistance.

Appendix 1 — Accounting treatment for vesting and non-vesting conditions

The following table, taken from the guidance in IFRS 2, summarises the implications of vesting and non-vesting conditions on accounting for share-based payment transactions.

Summary of conditions that determine whether a counterparty receives an equity instrument granted						
	Vesting conditions			**Non-vesting conditions**		
	Service conditions	**Performance conditions**				
		Performance conditions that are market conditions.	Other performance conditions.	Neither the entity nor the counterparty can choose whether the condition is met.	Counterparty can choose whether to meet the condition.	Entity can choose whether to meet the condition.
Example conditions	Requirement to remain in service for three years.	Target based on the market price of the entity's equity instruments.	Target based on a successful initial public offering with a specified service requirement.	Target based on a commodity index.	Paying contributions towards the exercise price of a share-based payment.	Continuation of the plan by the entity.
Include in grant-date fair value?	No	Yes	No	Yes	Yes	Yes[(a)]
Accounting treatment if the condition is not met after the grant date and during the vesting period	Forfeiture. The entity revises the expense to reflect the best available estimate of the number of equity instruments expected to vest (paragraph 19).	No change to accounting. The entity continues to recognise the expense over the remainder of the vesting period (paragraph 21).	Forfeiture. The entity revises the expense to reflect the best available estimate of the number of equity instruments expected to vest (paragraph 19).	No change to accounting. The entity continues to recognise the expense over the remainder of the vesting period (paragraph 21A).	Cancellation. The entity recognises immediately the amount of the expense that would otherwise have been recognised over the remainder of the vesting period (paragraph 28A).	Cancellation. The entity recognises immediately the amount of the expense that would otherwise have been recognised over the remainder of the vesting period (paragraph 28A).

(a) In the calculation of the fair value of the share-based payment, the probability of continuation of the plan by the entity is assumed to be 100 per cent.

Appendix 2 — Classification of share-based payment transactions in group arrangements

The flow chart summarises how to determine the classification of awards, in both consolidated and separate financial statements. This flow chart applies specifically to situations where there is either an equity- or cash-settled award in group situations and does not deal with awards where there is a choice of settlement (see further para A12.155).

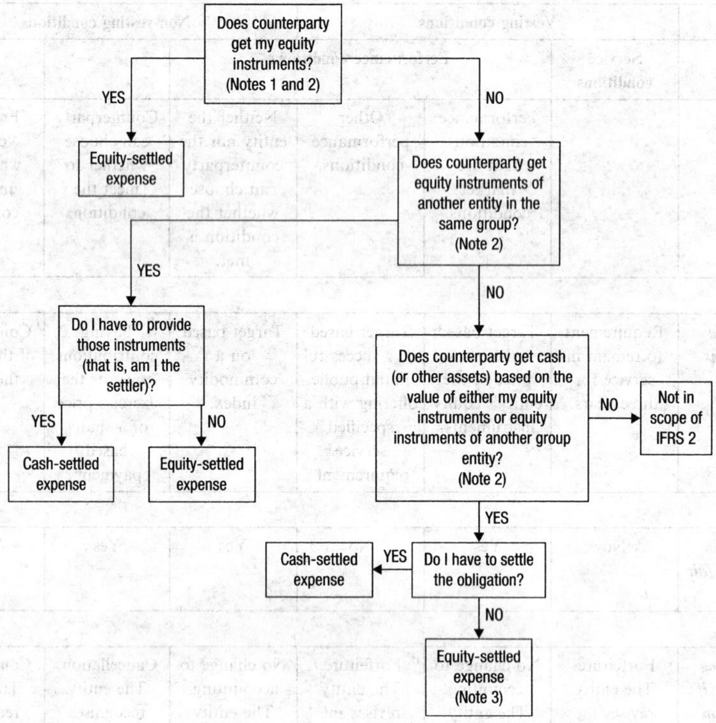

Notes:

1 'My equity instruments', include equity instruments of my subsidiaries (non-controlling interests) in consolidated financial statements, but not when equity instruments are accounted for as an investment in individual financial statements.

2 'Counterparty' includes employees and other suppliers of goods or services even where the goods or services are unidentifiable.

3 For the entity that settles the obligation, treatment will be as equity-settled only if the transaction is settled in equity instruments of that entity (including equity instruments of a subsidiary of that entity.) For the entity receiving the goods or services, treatment will be as equity-settled unless there is an obligation to settle in cash or other assets.

Chapter 13

Taxation

Chapter 13

Taxation

Introduction

13.1 The amount of tax payable on the taxable profits of a particular period often bears little relationship to the amount of income and expenditure appearing in the financial statements. This is because the computation of accounting profit is governed by the application of generally accepted accounting principles and company law, whereas the computation of taxable profit is governed by the application of tax law. For example, certain items of income appearing in the financial statements may be tax free, whilst others may be taxable in a different period. Similarly, certain items of expenditure may be disallowable for tax, whilst others may fall to be tax deductible in a period different from that in which they were recognised in the financial statements.

13.2 If the profit and loss account tax charge were based simply on the amount of tax payable on taxable profits, it would be inconsistent with the accruals concept, the basis on which all other expenses are stated in the financial statements. Therefore, it is generally accepted that the tax charge in the profit and loss account should include not only the current tax charge based on taxable profit that takes into account the effects of tax-free income and disallowable expenses, but also an amount that recognises the tax effects of transactions appearing in the financial statements in one period, but which fall to be taxed or tax deductible in a different period. This additional amount, comprising the tax effects of what are generally referred to as 'timing differences' resulting from the difference between fiscal and accounting rules, ensures that the correct tax expense is recognised in the financial statements in the same periods as the income and expenditure to which it relates. The recognition of this additional amount gives rise to deferred taxation either payable or recoverable in a subsequent accounting period. Therefore, the tax charge in the financial statements comprises deferred tax as well as current tax. Deferred tax was conceived and developed as a means of recognising the tax effects of the difference between accounting and taxable profit.

13.3 Although the concept of deferred taxation can be explained in the context of matching income and expenditure with their tax effects, it can also be viewed from the perspective of accounting for an asset or a liability and this has become a preferable way of understanding deferred tax. Given that an asset or a liability arises through the tax effects of timing differences, the principles of accounting require that these are recognised.

13.4 This chapter deals with accounting for current and deferred taxation in the light of the rules contained in the Companies Act 2006 and its supporting regulation SI 2008/410, 'The Large and Medium-sized Companies and Groups

(Accounts and Reports) Regulations 2008', FRS 16, 'Current tax', and FRS 19, 'Deferred tax'. There is also a further accounting standard SSAP 5, 'Accounting for value added tax', but as accounting for value added tax, although extremely complicated to administer in practice, poses few technical accounting problems, it is not dealt with in this chapter.

13.5 This chapter includes a number of worked examples. The tax rates used in these examples are illustrative only and are not intended to represent tax rates currently applicable to companies.

[The next paragraph is 13.8.]

Corporation tax

General principles

13.8 Corporation tax is assessed on a company's profits, whether distributed or retained, at the end of each accounting period. The tax charge is calculated by applying the current basic rate of corporation tax to the taxable profit for the period. The taxable profit is arrived at by applying relevant tax laws and rules and is rarely the same as the accounting profit disclosed in the financial statements. Differences between taxable and accounting profit form the basis of accounting for deferred taxation, which is considered later in this chapter.

13.9 Although the rate of corporation tax is set for a fiscal year, it should be noted that the assessments are made on the basis of the company's actual accounting period. If a company prepares financial statements for a year that straddles 31 March, and the rate of corporation tax is different for different fiscal years, an average rate has to be computed and applied in the tax computation, as illustrated in paragraph 13.49.1 below.

[The next paragraph is 13.18.]

FRS 16 — Current tax

13.18 FRS 16, 'Current tax', deals with the recognition and disclosure of current tax.

13.19 The objective of FRS 16 is *'to ensure that reporting entities recognise current taxes in a consistent and transparent manner'*. [FRS 16 para 1]. The standard is very wide in scope, covering all financial statements giving a true and fair view, except those prepared by smaller entities applying the FRSSE.

13.20 As stated above, FRS 16 specifies how current tax, in particular withholding tax and tax credits, should be reflected in financial statements. The standard defines current tax as *'the amount of tax estimated to be payable or recoverable in respect of the taxable profit or loss for a period, along with* *adjustments to estimates in respect of previous periods'*. [FRS 16 para 2]. The standard deals with the following matters:

- Recognition of current tax charge in the profit and loss account and the STRGL.
- The treatment of tax credits, withholding and underlying taxes in the context of dividends and other income payable and receivable.
- Income and expenses subject to non-standard rates of tax.
- Measurement of current tax charge.
- Recoverable ACT.
- Disclosure of current tax.

Apart from the last item which is considered from paragraph 13.236 below, the above matters are discussed in the paragraphs that follow. In addition, uncertain tax positions are dealt with from paragraph 13.50.10 onwards.

Recognition of current tax charge

13.21 FRS 16 requires that current tax should be recognised in the profit and loss account for the period, except to the extent that it is attributable to a gain or loss that is or has been recognised directly in the STRGL. [FRS 16 para 5]. Where a gain or loss is or has been recognised in the STRGL, the tax relating to that gain or loss should also be recognised in that statement. [FRS 16 para 6].

13.22 Because a UK company pays corporation tax on all its profits including those that may be reported in the STRGL, it may sometimes be difficult to determine the amount of current tax that is attributable to the amount of gain reported in the STRGL. In those circumstances, the standard permits the attributable tax to be calculated on a reasonable *pro rata* basis, or another basis that is more appropriate in the circumstances. [FRS 16 para 7]. Consider the following examples:

Example 1 – Allocation of tax on exchange loss

A parent company made a trading profit of £1,500,000 during the year. The parent has a foreign currency loan on which an exchange loss of £500,000 arose and on which tax relief is given in this instance. The corporation tax rate for the year is 30%. Therefore, the parent's tax liability for the year is £300,000 (profit before tax of £1,000,000 @ 30%). On consolidation, the loan held by the parent is treated as hedging the net assets of its foreign subsidiary so that the exchange loss of £500,000 is reported in the STRGL. The total tax charge of £300,000 that should be allocated between the profit and loss account and the STRGL is as follows:

	£'000
Tax on trading profit (£1.5m @ 30%)	450
Tax relief on exchange loss (£500,000 @ 30%)	(150)
Total tax charge	300

The profit and loss account would bear a tax charge of £450,000, with £150,000 of tax relief being credited to the STRGL.

Example 2 – Allocation of tax on land sale gain

A company sold a plot of land during the year for £10m. The land was acquired ten years ago for £4m and the carrying value prior to sale was £6m (following a revaluation three years ago). The tax value of the land after allowing for indexation relief is £5m. No deferred tax was provided on the earlier revaluation on the grounds that there was no commitment to sell the land at that time. Assuming that the corporation tax rate is 30% and rollover relief is not available, the tax payable on the gain of £5m is £1.5m (sale proceeds £10m less tax indexed cost of £5m @ 30%).

As the standard is not very specific as to how the tax of £1.5m on the total accounting gain of £6m (sale proceeds of £10m less cost of £4m) should be allocated between the gain of £4m (£10m — £6m) reported in the profit and loss account and the revaluation gain of £2m reported previously in the STRGL, one method would be to allocate the tax in proportion to the gain reported in the respective performance statement, that is, in the ratio 2:1. On this basis, the allocation would be as follows:

	Profit and loss account	STRGL	Total
	£'000	£'000	£'000
Total accounting gain	4,000	2,000	6,000
Total tax	1,000	500	1,500

An alternative method would be to reflect the fact that the purpose of indexation relief is to exclude from taxation purely inflationary gains. In principle, such gains form part of the holding gain dealt with in the STRGL. On this basis, the allocation would be as follows:

	Profit and loss account	STRGL	Total
	£'000	£'000	£'000
Total accounting gain	4,000	2,000	6,000
Indexation allowance	–	(1,000)	(1,000)
Taxable gain	4,000	1,000	5,000
Total tax	1,200	300	1,500

If the indexation allowance were sufficient to cover all the gain dealt with in the STRGL, any balance would be attributed to the profit and loss account. Furthermore, if the gain dealt with in the profit and loss account contained a significant holding gain, it may be appropriate to allocate part of the effect of the indexation allowance on an appropriate basis. For instance, in this example, it would be possible to attribute £300,000 (3/10 × £1m) of the indexation allowance of £1m to the profit and loss account on the grounds that this proportion of the inflationary gain arose subsequent to the revaluation that took place three years prior to sale. Although this method is arguably the most accurate method, it is also unnecessarily complex and in practice, companies are likely to choose between the first two approaches outlined above.

[The next paragraph is 13.24.]

Tax credits, withholding and underlying taxes

13.24 Under the relevant tax rules, dividend income may be a non-taxable item (for instance, if a dividend exemption applies). In other cases, if tax is payable on the dividend income, a credit system may apply whereby a tax credit is given to the dividend recipient to acknowledge that the income out of which the dividend has been paid has already been charged to tax in the dividend paying company (an imputed credit for underlying tax). FRS 16 defines tax credit as *'the tax credit given under UK tax legislation to the recipient of a dividend from a UK company'*. This situation can be distinguished from one where a withholding tax has been deducted at source and is paid to the tax authorities on behalf of the recipient by the dividend paying entity.

13.25 Withholding tax does not arise on UK dividends, but it may be relevant in the context of dividends received by a UK company from its investments located overseas. FRS 16 defines withholding tax as *'tax on dividends or other income that is deducted by the payer of the income and paid to the tax authorities wholly on behalf of the recipient'*. [FRS 16 para 2].

13.26 Apart from the fact that withholding tax is tax that is actually paid by (or at least on behalf) of the recipient of the dividends, there is often a fundamental difference in the way dividend and other income subject to withholding tax is treated for tax purposes from dividends and other income received with an imputed tax credit.

13.27 The different tax treatments are considered to be sufficiently significant for FRS 16 to require different accounting treatments for dividends and other income subject to tax credit (these are notional and should not be taken into account as income tax of the recipient entity) from those that are subject to withholding tax (real and should be taken into account as income tax of the recipient entity). In doing so, the standard harmonises the tax treatment of incoming and outgoing dividends and other income payable and receivable.

Outgoing dividends and other interest payable

13.28 Accordingly, FRS 16 requires that outgoing dividends, interest and other amounts payable should be recognised at an amount that:

- Includes any withholding taxes.
- Excludes any other taxes, such as attributable tax credits, not payable wholly on behalf of the recipient.

[FRS 16 para 8].

13.29 This is logical as the imputed tax credit is not part of the cost of the dividend. It is more concerned with the taxes paid by the payer of the dividend, rather than those paid by (or on behalf of) the recipient.

13.30 The requirement to include withholding tax in interest and other amounts payable by an UK company is not specifically relevant to the UK. However, if UK companies are required to deduct UK income tax on interest payable to third parties, as UK income tax deducted at source is very similar in substance to withholding tax, we believe that interest payable should be shown gross in the profit and loss account, that is, inclusive of the income tax deducted.

Incoming dividends and other interest receivable

13.31 Similarly, FRS 16 requires that incoming dividends, interest and other income receivable should be recognised at an amount that:

- Includes any withholding taxes.
- Excludes any other taxes, such as attributable tax credits, not payable wholly on behalf of the recipient.

[FRS 16 para 9].

13.32 The standard's requirement to show income at an amount inclusive of the withholding tax is consistent with its nature, which is tax actually suffered by the company as explained in paragraph 13.25 above. Withholding taxes normally arise on dividends received from investments located overseas. Where in accordance with paragraph 13.31 above, the income is reported gross of the foreign withholding tax, the standard requires the withholding tax suffered to be shown as part of the tax charge. [FRS 16 para 9].

13.33 Similarly, where tax has been deducted at source on interest income and paid by the payer of the interest to the tax authorities on behalf of the recipient, the interest income should be recorded gross of the tax deducted at source. The tax should be shown as part of the tax charge.

[The next paragraph is 13.35.]

Underlying tax

13.35 In some situations, relief is also available for foreign 'underlying tax' (that is, tax on the company's profits out of which the dividends are paid).

13.36 Notwithstanding the fact that a company can claim double tax relief for both withholding and underlying tax, the standard makes it clear that dividends or other income received should not be grossed up for the underlying rate of tax. [FRS 16 para 10]. This is because the underlying tax is the liability of another entity (the payer of the dividend) and is not tax that has been suffered by the recipient. The only tax that the recipient suffers is the withholding tax, which is a 'real tax', as opposed to the underlying tax which, from the perspective of the recipient, is a 'notional tax'.

13.37 If a UK company pays tax on its dividend income, it is normally able to obtain double tax relief on overseas tax paid against UK corporation tax but this depends on whether the overseas tax rate (withholding and underlying) is less than the UK corporation tax rate. Where, however, the rate of overseas tax exceeds the rate of UK corporation tax, a proportion of the overseas tax can remained unrelieved. The amount of overseas tax unrelieved cannot be carried forward and falls to be written off in the profit and loss account. This write off need not be disclosed separately as it is included within overseas taxation in the profit and loss account taxation charge. Consider the following example:

Example – Unrelieved overseas tax

A UK company has a US subsidiary that does not qualify for exemption from tax on dividends. The US subsidiary generated taxable profits of £100,000 on which it paid US income tax @ 35% amounting to £35,000. It distributed the remaining after tax profit of £65,000 to the UK parent after deducting 5% withholding tax amounting to £3,250. The UK parent received a cash dividend of £61,750. The rate of UK corporation tax is 30%.

UK corporation tax computation	£	£
Cash dividend of £61,750 grossed up for overseas taxes		100,000
Corporation tax @ 30%		30,000
Less double tax relief:		
Total overseas tax paid	38,250	
Relief restricted to UK tax payable	(30,000)	(30,000)
Unrelieved overseas tax	8,250	
UK corporation tax liability		Nil

Parent company's individual profit and loss account	£	£
Gross dividend received (grossed up for withholding tax)		65,000
Tax charge:		
UK corporation tax	–	
Overseas tax paid (withholding tax)	3,250	
Total tax charge		3,250
Profit after tax		61,750

Parent company's consolidated profit and loss account	£	£
Profit before tax		100,000
Tax charge:		
UK corporation tax	30,000	
Less: double tax relief	30,000	
	–	
Overseas tax paid*	38,250	
Total tax charge		38,250
Profit after tax		61,750

* Total tax charge is effectively UK tax of £30,000 and unrelieved overseas tax of £8,250 = £38,250

Income and expenses subject to non-standard rates of tax

13.38 It is necessary to distinguish income that is received after deduction of tax as discussed in paragraph 13.31 from income that is taxable at non-standard rates. It is not uncommon for companies to enter into transactions that give rise to income or expense that is not subject to the standard rate of corporation tax. Examples include some leasing transactions and advances and investments made by financial institutions. In some situations, the transaction may, after taking account of the financing cost, result in a pre-tax loss and a post-tax profit. Consider the following example:

Example – Income taxed at non-standard rate

A financial institution borrows £10m which bears interest at 9% per annum. The proceeds are immediately invested in an instrument that yields 8% per annum, but the income is taxable at 20%. The standard rate of corporation tax is 33%. The company makes a pre-tax loss of £100,000, but the transaction is profitable after tax effects are taken into account as shown below:

Profit and loss account	£'000	£'000
Investment income @ 8%		800
Less: interest expense		(900)
Pre-tax loss		(100)
Taxation:		
On income @ 20%	(160)	
Tax relief on interest @ 33%	297	
Tax credit		137
Post-tax profit		37

13.39 Banks and other institutions enter into such transactions precisely because it is profitable on an after tax basis. However, they may contend that the presentation shown above is misleading, because it makes it difficult to interpret the profit and loss account and inhibits comparison between different companies, especially as pre-tax profits are seen as an important measure of performance. They may advocate that income subject to the non-standard rate of tax should be presented on a grossed-up basis as shown below to eliminate the distortion between pre and post-tax profits by reporting tax at the standard rate.

Profit and loss account (grossed-up)	£'000
Investment income (grossed up): 640/(100%–33%)*	955
Less: interest expense	(900)
Pre-tax profit *	55
Tax charge @ 33% †	(18)
Post-tax profit	37

*Includes notional income of £155
†Includes notional tax charge of £155

13.40 However, grossing up, because it is notional, fails to report the true nature of the transaction. If a transaction results in a pre-tax loss and a tax benefit it is necessary that it is reported as such in order to achieve a faithful representation. Grossing up reports a false amount both as pre-tax profits and as the tax charge for the year. The tax treatment of the transaction should have no bearing on the way in which the transaction is reported for financial reporting purposes.

13.41 On this basis, income and expenses should be reported in the pre-tax results on the basis of the income or expenses actually receivable or payable. No adjustment should be made to reflect a notional amount of tax that would have been paid or relieved in respect of the transaction if it had been taxable, or allowable for tax purposes, on a different basis. [FRS 16 para 11].

13.42 Companies whose results are significantly affected by transactions that are subject to tax other than at a standard rate should disclose the full effects of such transactions in their financial statements. Indeed, both company law (SI 2008/410) and FRS 3 require disclosure of any special circumstances that affect the tax charge or credit during the period. These disclosure requirements are considered from paragraph 13.236.

13.43 FRS 16 makes it clear that the requirement applies only to notional tax. It is not intended to reverse the normal accounting treatment followed in some specialised industries, such as leasing and life insurance, of allocating profits to accounting periods on a post-tax basis and then grossing up those post-tax profits by the actual effective tax rate to arrive at the pre-tax profit and the tax charge. [FRS 16 para 13].

Measurement of the current tax charge

13.44 FRS 16 requires current tax to be measured at the amounts expected to be paid (or recovered) using the tax rates and laws that have been enacted or substantially enacted by the balance sheet date. [FRS 16 para 14].

13.45 A UK tax rate is taken as 'substantially enacted' if it is included in either:

- a Bill that has been passed by the House of Commons and is awaiting only passage through the House of Lords and Royal Assent; or
- a resolution having statutory effect that has been passed under the Provisional Collection of Taxes Act 1968 (PCTA 1968).

[FRS 16 para 15].

13.46 The parliamentary resolution under the PCTA 1968 is, in effect, a temporary enactment of tax changes relating to certain taxes that persists and has full statutory force for a limited period. During that period a permanent statutory provision is made with full parliamentary procedures and in the normal course of events the temporary statute falls away when the permanent one is enacted.

13.47 In the UK, changes in tax laws and rates are normally announced in a Finance Bill on Budget day. Therefore, where a company's accounting reference period ends on a date that straddles the Budget date and the date on which the process of enactment is regarded as substantively complete (for instance, when the Bill has been passed by the House of Commons), the substantively enacted rate would be the rate that is currently in force at the balance sheet date and current and deferred tax should be measured using that rate.

13.48 In practice, however, the above guidance is unlikely to make any difference since UK corporation tax rates are set by reference to a financial year and a year in advance. For instance, the main rate of corporation tax for the financial year 2008 (the year beginning 1 April 2008) was set at 28 per cent at the 2007 Budget on 21 March 2007. The Finance Bill 2007 was approved by the House of Commons on 26 June 2007 and after receiving Royal Assent became the Finance Act 2007. Therefore, this was the substantively enacted rate for accounting periods ending on or after 26 June 2007 where the tax arose on or after 1 April 2008 (until it was superseded by a change in rate in a later Finance Act).

13.49 The standard's requirement to use a tax rate that has been substantially enacted by the balance sheet date rather than the date of approval of the financial statements means that the subsequent receipt of information about rates of taxation is not an adjusting post balance sheet event (see further chapter 22).

13.49.1 Also of significance is the situation where a company prepares its financial statements for a period that straddles 31 March and the enacted tax rates or substantially enacted rates are different for different financial years. In that situation, the company may need to compute an effective tax rate. Under UK tax legislation, when a change in tax rate occurs, the tax law requires an entity to calculate a *pro-rated* tax rate for the transitional year, which applies to all profits for that accounting period. An example is given below:

Example – Change of tax rate during accounting period

A company has an accounting period ending on 30 October 20X8 and the rates of corporation tax for the financial years 20X7 and 20X8 are 30% and 28% respectively. The effective rate of tax that should be disclosed for the current tax in the financial statements is calculated as follows:

Period 1 November 20X7 to 31 March 20X8 (FY 20X7)	5/12 @ 30%	12.50%
Period 1 April 20X8 to 30 October 20X8 (FY 20X8)	7/12 @ 28%	16.33%
Effective rate of corporation tax		28.83%

Furthermore, the accounting period for corporation tax purposes can never exceed 12 months. If the financial statements cover a period longer than 12 months, the first 12 months constitute one accounting period and the remainder of the period constitutes the second accounting period for tax purposes.

Recoverability of ACT

13.50 Until April 1999, a company paid Advance Corporation Tax (ACT) when it paid a dividend. This tax could be set off, within a limit, against the corporation tax liability of the accounting period. The remaining tax liability was called 'mainstream' corporation tax. However, ACT was abolished as from 6 April 1999. This means companies paying a dividend (or other distribution of profits) after that date no longer have to pay any ACT.

13.50.1 Following the abolition of ACT , there has been no further build-up of unrelieved or surplus ACT. However, companies are able to recover past surplus ACT built up in the periods prior to the abolition of ACT. This is achieved through a system of 'shadow ACT'.

13.50.2 Although ACT can be carried forward indefinitely, if necessary, in each year there is an overriding restriction on the use of ACT for set-off imposed by the shadow ACT system. The shadow ACT system is designed to be no more generous than the old ACT system. Its effect is to ensure that ACT that was previously irrecoverable becomes recoverable only to the extent that it would have become recoverable under the old ACT system. [FRS 16 App II para 2].

13.50.3 The way in which shadow ACT works is illustrated by the following simple example.

Example – Shadow ACT

A company has surplus ACT of £100,000 as at 31 March 1999. During its accounting period to 31 March 2000, it expects to have taxable profits of £200,000 and pay a dividend of £60,000. In this situation:

- The limit on ACT set off is 20% of £200,000 = £40,000.
- If ACT was not abolished, the company would have to pay ACT on the dividend = say, 25% of £60,000 = £15,000. This ACT of £15,000 is referred to as shadow ACT.
- The effect of the shadow ACT is to restrict the set off of past surplus ACT to £25,000 (£40,000 — £15,000).
- As a result, the company's corporation tax liability will be reduced by £25,000, as is the figure for past surplus ACT carried forward to the next accounting period, which is £75,000.

The above is a simple example and ignores the effect of any carry back of shadow ACT of future periods. The actual rules on shadow ACT are extremely complex and tax advice should be sought in calculating the amount by which the corporation tax liability can be reduced.

13.50.4 The detailed accounting rules for ACT are contained in Appendix II to FRS 16, rather than in the main body of the standard.

13.50.5 Under FRS 16, ACT is regarded as recoverable where the amount of the ACT previously paid on outgoing dividends could either be:

- Set off against a corporation tax liability on the profits of the period under review or of previous periods.
- Properly set off against a credit balance on the deferred tax account.
- Expected to be recoverable taking into account expected profits and dividends – normally those of the next accounting period only.

13.50.6 ACT should be offset against a credit balance on the deferred tax account only if, in the period in which the underlying timing differences are expected to reverse, the reversal will create sufficient taxable profits to enable ACT to be recovered under the shadow ACT system. [FRS 16 App II para 4].

13.50.7 In the absence of a deferred tax liability against which it can be offset, ACT recoverable should be shown as a deferred tax asset. [FRS 16 App II para 5].

13.50.8 If ACT that was previously regarded as recoverable becomes irrecoverable, it should be charged in the profit and loss account as a separately disclosed component of the tax charge. [FRS 16 App II para 6].

13.50.9 Where ACT written off as irrecoverable in the past becomes recoverable under the shadow ACT system, the write back should be made in the year in which the ACT is actually recovered. Such ACT is required to be credited in the profit and loss account as a separately disclosed component of the tax charge. [FRS 16 App II para 8].

Uncertain tax positions

13.50.10 There may be situations when an entity's tax position is uncertain. Examples are where the tax treatment of an item of expense, or a structured transaction, may be challenged by the tax authorities. Uncertainties in current taxes are not addressed specifically in FRS 16. FRS 12, 'Provisions, contingent liabilities and assets', excludes taxes from its scope (as these are covered by another standard) and is not used to measure uncertain tax positions. The general measurement principles in paragraph 14 of FRS 16 should, therefore, be applied: *'Current tax should be measured at the amounts expected to be paid (or recovered) using tax rates and laws that have been enacted or substantively enacted by the balance sheet date'*. The unit of account and measurement method are not specified in FRS 16, so there is diversity in practice.

13.50.11 We believe the unit of account is an accounting policy. An entity may choose to consider uncertain tax positions at the level of the individual uncertainty or group of related uncertainties. Alternatively, it may choose to consider tax uncertainties at the level of its total tax liability to each relevant taxing authority.

13.50.12 When an entity elects to consider uncertain tax positions at the level of each uncertainty, it should first consider whether each position taken in the tax return is probable of being sustained on examination by the taxing authority. A liability should be recognised in connection with each item that is not probable of being sustained. The liability is measured using either an expected value (weighted average probability) approach or a single best estimate of the most likely outcome. The current tax liability would be the aggregate liability in connection with uncertain tax positions.

13.50.13 When an entity elects to consider uncertain tax positions at the level of its relationship with the taxing authority, the key issue is the measurement of the tax liability. It is usually probable that an entity will pay tax, so the recognition threshold has been met. The entity should determine the total amount of current tax it expects to pay, taking into account all the tax uncertainties, using either an expected value (weighted average probability) approach or a single best estimate of the most likely outcome.

13.50.14 The examples below are prepared on the assumption that the entity has elected to consider tax uncertainties at the level of each uncertainty. The examples illustrate that the liability determined using the two acceptable measurement methodologies referred to in paragraph 13.50.11 above may be materially different. In all cases, it is assumed that it is probable (more likely than not) that tax will be payable.

Example 1 – Measuring an uncertain tax position

Entity K has included deductions in a tax return that may be subject to challenge by the tax authorities resulting in an uncertain tax position. Entity K and its tax consultants estimate the probability of the potential outcomes for additional tax payable as follows:

Potential tax payable £	Individual probability	Cumulative probability	Probability-weighted calculation £
800	15%	15%	120
600	30%	45%	180
400	20%	65%	80
200	20%	85%	40
0	15%	100%	0
			420

- Most likely outcome £600.
- Probability weighted outcome £420.

Example 2 – Uncertain tax position with two possible outcomes

Entity K takes a deduction in a tax return that may be subject to challenge by the tax authorities. It is estimated that there is a 40% probability that additional tax of £120 will be payable and a 60% probability that additional tax of £80 will be payable.

- Most likely outcome £80.
- Probability weighted outcome £96 (£120 × 40% + £80 × 60%).

Example 3 – Use of probability weighted average method

A deduction of £100 may be subject to challenge. Entity K and its tax consultants estimate the probability of the potential outcomes for additional tax payable as follows:

Potential tax payable £	Individual probability	Cumulative probability	Probability-weighted calculation £
100	45%	45%	45.00
80	10%	55%	8.00
50	25%	80%	12.50
0	20%	100%	–
			65.50

- Probability weighted outcome £65.5.

- It would not be logical to use £100 as the most likely outcome in this case, as it is more likely than not that some of the deductions will be accepted by the tax authorities. Whilst there is a 45% chance that the full amount of £100 will be payable, there is a 55% change of reduced tax being payable on the basis of the information given above. In this scenario, measurement using the probability weighted average method would be appropriate.

13.50.14.1 Where an entity has made payments that are considered to be in excess of the amount payable under the relevant tax legislation, it will evaluate and estimate the recovery of a tax asset. On the other hand, where an entity has not remitted taxes related to an uncertain tax position, it will evaluate the uncertainty surrounding the potential liability. To the extent this evaluation relates to the recovery or payment of taxes (as opposed to interest and penalties, which are dealt with in para 13.50.15 below), we believe that the considerations are the same. FRS 16 requires uncertain tax positions (whether assets or liabilities) to be reflected at the amount expected to be recovered or paid. Consistent accounting policies should be applied to uncertain tax assets and uncertain tax liabilities.

13.50.14.2 Once an uncertain tax position is determined, the question arises as to when a change in estimate of the tax outcome is justified. We expect that a change in recognition and measurement would be justified where circumstances change or where new facts clarify the probability of estimates previously made. Such changes might be in the form of further judicial developments related to a specific case or to a similar case, substantive communications from the tax authorities, or a change in status of a tax year (for example, moving from open to closed in a particular jurisdiction).

Interest and penalties on uncertain tax positions

13.50.15 An entity may incur interest or penalties in relation to taxation, for example as a result of uncertain tax positions that have been successfully challenged by the tax authorities. FRS 16 does not specifically address the treatment of uncertain tax positions or associated interest and penalties. The liability for the uncertain tax position is for a tax based on taxable profits and is, therefore, a current tax liability. This liability is recognised and measured in accordance with FRS 16 (see further para 13.50.10 onwards above).

13.50.16 There is a strong argument that interest and penalties are different from tax liabilities. This is because these items are not measured and settled by the tax authorities on the basis of taxable profits. This suggests that interest and penalties should be recognised, measured and presented as provisions under FRS 12, 'Provisions, contingent liabilities and assets', and classified as finance or other operating expense, respectively, in the profit and loss account. This is because:

- such obligations are not based on taxable profit or loss and fall outside FRS 16's scope; and

- the economic substance of reducing or delaying a tax payment is not different from any other financing arrangement. Interest that increases with time and is in substance a financing cost of the liability is interest expense; other penalties represent operating costs.

13.50.17 There is, however, diversity in practice with regard to these items. In some cases, interest and penalties are accounted for as if they are within FRS 16's scope, either because the interest and penalties are rolled up into a lump sum settlement and cannot be separated from the taxes, or as a matter of accounting policy. In that case, any associated charge would normally be included within the tax line in the profit and loss account and the liability would be included within the tax liability on the balance sheet.

13.50.18 The accounting policy for interest and penalties applies to both interest payable (and any related penalties) and to interest recoverable (and any related damages). It should be noted that for interest and damages recoverable, FRS 12 prohibits the recognition of a contingent asset until it is 'virtually certain', whereas FRS 16 requires uncertain tax assets to be recorded on the basis of the amount expected to be recovered. As FRS 12 establishes a higher threshold for recognition than would be applied under FRS 16, the timing of the recognition of interest and damages recoverable will depend upon an entity's accounting policy.

13.50.19 Where the amounts involved are material, the accounting policy used to recognise, measure and classify interest and penalties/damages related to tax should be disclosed clearly in the financial statements and applied consistently.

Other expenses associated with taxation

Professional fees linked to tax expense

13.50.20 A company may incur expenses that are indirectly linked to the current tax expense, for example, fees payable to tax consultants that are based upon a percentage of savings made under a specific tax scheme. The fees paid to tax consultants are not 'tax on profit on ordinary activities', the format line in the profit and loss account formats in Schedule 1 to SI 2008/410. They should be charged in arriving at operating profit, probably under the administrative expenses heading.

Deferred tax

Introduction

13.51 Most transactions and events recorded in the financial statements have a tax consequence. A classic example is an acquisition of an asset that is deductible for tax purposes in the current and future periods.

13.52 The future tax consequences of transactions and events that have occurred by the balance sheet date cannot be avoided; whatever happens in the future, the entity will have to pay less or more tax than it would have done if those transactions and events did not happen. Therefore, it is necessary to recognise the tax effects of all income and expenditure, gains and losses, assets and liabilities in the same period in which they are recognised themselves and not in the period in which they form part of taxable profit. This matching of transactions and events with their tax effects gives rise, not only to current tax, but also to deferred tax balances that meet the definitions of, and recognition criteria for, assets and liabilities.

Method of computation

13.53 Notwithstanding its origin as a means of matching income and expenditure with their tax effects, deferred tax balances represent assets or liabilities. A deferred tax liability relating to an asset represents an obligation to refund a temporary cash flow advantage obtained by claiming capital allowances on that asset. Therefore, the tax effects of accelerated capital allowances should be reported as liabilities for taxes. Similarly, a deferred tax asset relating to a liability, for example pension costs, represents tax relief that is expected to be received when the pension liability is settled. Therefore, the tax effects of timing differences relating to pension costs should be reported as assets representing future tax recoverable.

13.54 The objective of the liability method is to recognise the expected tax effects of timing differences either as liabilities for taxes payable in the future or as assets recoverable in the future. Under this method, deferred tax on the timing differences originating in the period is provided using the rate of tax expected to apply when the asset is recovered or the liability is settled. Since the rate at which the timing difference will reverse is not normally known, the current rate of tax is taken as the best approximation to the rate that will apply in the future. This means that the deferred taxation account is always maintained at the current rate of tax and the movement in the balance sheet amounts is reflected as a deferred tax charge or credit, usually in the profit and loss account or STRGL. It follows that whenever there is a change in the rate of tax, the balance on the deferred taxation account is adjusted to that current rate with the result that the charge for deferred tax in the profit and loss account and STRGL (where applicable) will include the effects of any such change in rate, which is applied to the opening balance of cumulative timing differences. FRS 19 requires that deferred tax is determined using a method based on the 'income statement liability method' (see para 13.63).

Income statement liability method

13.55 In most countries, including the UK, profits disclosed in the company's financial statements form the basis for the computation of taxable profits on which the company's liability to tax is calculated. In practice, however, many governments introduce various incentives and disincentives in their fiscal policy for economic and social reasons. As a consequence, the taxable profits of a particular period often bear little relationship to the accounting profits disclosed in the financial statements.

13.56 The differences between accounting and taxable profits can be analysed into two categories: permanent differences and timing differences. Permanent differences arise because certain types of income appearing in the financial statements are not taxable, whilst certain types of expenditure are not tax deductible. Timing differences, on the other hand, arise from items that are either taxable or tax deductible, but in periods different from those in which they are dealt with in the financial statements. Therefore, such items are included in the measurement of both accounting and taxable profits, but in different periods. These differences are said to 'originate' in one period and are capable of 'reversal' in one or more subsequent periods.

13.57 It follows from the nature of permanent and timing differences that, over time, cumulative taxable and accounting profits are the same, except for permanent differences. Because permanent differences are the inevitable result of the differences between accounting and tax rules and do not give rise to any accounting entries, they do not represent an accounting problem. They merely give rise to effective tax charges that differ from the statutory rate. However, the question arises as to whether and to what extent the tax effects of timing differences between accounting and taxable profits should be recognised in the financial statements.

13.58 Since timing differences originating in one period reverse in a later period, the tax charged in the later periods is affected by transactions or events that have taken place in a previous period. As a result, future tax assessments (whatever their amount in absolute terms) will be lower or higher than they would have been if those timing differences had not arisen. These known increases or decreases in future tax liabilities, that is, the company's obligation to pay less or more tax in the future are recognised in the balance sheet as deferred tax assets and liabilities.

13.59 Therefore, the objective of the income statement liability method is to recognise the expected tax effects of timing differences either as liabilities for taxes payable in the future or as assets recoverable in the future. Under this method, deferred tax on the timing differences originating in the period is provided using the rate of tax expected to apply when the asset is recovered or the liability is settled. No deferred tax is provided on permanent differences.

13.60 The way in which deferred taxation is calculated under the income statement liability method is illustrated below.

Example – Income statement liability method

A company prepares its financial statements to 31 December each year. The company makes an annual profit of £100,000 and incurs the following capital expenditure.

Machine purchased on 1 January 20X1: Cost £100,000, residual value £nil, life 5 years.
Machine purchased on 1 January 20X3: Cost £230,000, residual value £20,000, life 7 years.

Depreciation is charged on a straight line basis and amounts to £20,000 per annum for the first machine and £30,000 per annum for the second machine. The rate of capital allowances is 25% per annum on a reducing balance basis. The rate of corporation tax for 20X1 and 20X2 is 50% and falls to 30% in 20X3 and remains at that level.

The calculation of the deferred tax charge and the balance arising are shown in the table below.

	20X1	20X2	20X3	20X4	20X5
Per financial statements	£	£	£	£	£
Carrying value b/f	–	80,000	60,000	240,000	190,000
Addition	100,000	–	230,000	–	–
Depreciation	(20,000)	(20,000)	(50,000)	(50,000)	(50,000)
Carrying value c/f	80,000	60,000	240,000	190,000	140,000
Per tax computation					
Pool b/f	–	75,000	56,250	214,687	161,015
Addition	100,000	–	230,000	–	–
Capital allowances	(25,000)	(18,750)	(71,563)	(53,672)	(40,254)
Pool c/f	75,000	56,250	214,687	161,015	120,761
Timing differences					
Capital allowances allowed	25,000	18,750	71,563	53,672	40,254
Depreciation charged	(20,000)	(20,000)	(50,000)	(50,000)	(50,000)
Originating (reversing)	5,000	(1,250)	21,563	3,672	(9,746)
Cumulative timing differences	5,000	3,750	25,313	28,985	19,239
Deferred tax balances					
Tax on opening cumulative difference	–	2,500	1,875	7,594	8,696
Tax on closing cumulative difference	2,500	1,875	7,594	8,696	5,772
Tax provided (released)	2,500	(625)	5,719*	1,102	(2,924)

* Includes impact of change in tax rate during year (see below)

In 20X3, when the tax rate changes from 50% to 30%, the deferred tax liability includes an adjustment of £750 under the liability method. The adjustment is simply due to the effect of the change in rate on the opening balance of cumulative timing difference of £3,750 × (50% — 30%) = £750, which is reflected in the tax charge under the liability method (but would be ignored under the deferral method referred to in para 13.55). The effect of this adjustment is to ensure that deferred tax liability or asset in the balance sheet is always maintained at the current rate as indicated in the table above.

13.61 It is also evident from the above table that the deferred tax liability at the end of 20X5 amounting to £5,772 comprises tax on the whole of the cumulative timing difference of £19,239 at 30 per cent that would crystallise when the timing difference reverses. This basis of providing in full for deferred tax on all timing differences is referred to as 'full provision' or 'comprehensive allocation'.

13.62 The profile of timing differences in the above example also indicates that in years 20X1, 20X3 and 20X4 originating timing differences exceed reversing timing differences, thus leading to an increase in the deferred tax liability for that year. It follows that whenever new timing differences originating in later periods more than offset the effect of timing differences reversing in those periods, the balance on the deferred tax account will keep on increasing. This may lead to the accumulation of large liabilities since their settlement is indefinitely postponed. This is particularly true in times of high inflation or under a tax system offering tax reliefs in the form of high capital investment allowances.

13.63 FRS 19 is based on the income statement liability method. However, it takes a different view on how an approach based on timing differences should be implemented. FRS 19 takes the view that deferred tax should be recognised only if it meets the strict criteria for recognition of a liability in its own right – 'obligations to transfer economic benefits as a result of past transactions or events'. Under this approach, the entity will provide deferred tax where the transaction and events giving rise to an obligation to pay tax in the future (the obligating events) are past events, that is, have occurred at the balance sheet date. Therefore, deferred tax would be provided for most types of timing differences where the obligating events have happened by the balance sheet date and the entity has no discretion to avoid the future reversal of a timing difference.

13.64 On the other hand, no deferred tax would be provided where the obligating events have not occurred by the balance sheet date or any of the events that have still to take place are under the entity's control and the entity retains discretion to avoid them. For example, an entity may revalue a property at the balance sheet date that has no tax consequence in the UK until the property is sold. Because the event that gives rise to the future tax payable – the sale of the asset – is under the entity's control and the entity retains a discretion to avoid the sale in order not to crystallise the liability, no deferred tax would be provided at the balance sheet date, unless an obligating event such as a binding agreement to sell the property exists at the balance sheet date. The ASB labelled this approach the 'incremental liability' approach and believes that it gives rise to deferred tax balances that are more meaningful and economically realistic. This method is conceptually different from the balance sheet liability approach that forms the basis of both IAS 12, 'Income taxes', and SFAS 109, 'Accounting for income taxes', and significant GAAP differences can arise.

[The next paragraph is 13.90.]

FRS 19 — Deferred tax

Objectives

13.90 The objectives of FRS 19 are to ensure that:

- Future tax consequences of past transactions and events are recognised as liabilities or assets in the financial statements.
- The financial statements disclose any other special circumstances that may have an effect on future tax charges.

[FRS 19 para 1].

13.91 The first objective is based on the definition of liabilities as 'obligations of an entity to transfer economic benefits as a result of past transactions or events' in the Statement of Principles. A liability for deferred tax should be recognised only for past transactions or events that give rise to an obligation to pay more tax in the future.

13.92 Past transactions and events will have future tax consequences only if they fall to be recognised as timing differences that have originated but not reversed at the balance sheet date. Since timing differences originating in one period reverse in a later period, the tax charged in the later period is affected by transactions or events that have taken place in a previous period. As a result, future tax assessments (whatever their amount in absolute terms) will be lower or higher than they would have been if those timing differences had not arisen. These known increases or decreases in future tax liabilities, that is, the company's obligation to pay more tax or the right to pay less in the future are recognised in the balance sheet as deferred tax assets and liabilities. This is the case whether or not future transactions occur that would reduce or increase the tax assessments in those periods.

13.93 In other words, an entity will have an obligation to pay more tax or a right to pay less tax where it has no discretion to avoid the future reversal of a timing difference, notwithstanding that it may have discretion to originate a new timing difference at the same time, which may have the effect of postponing the tax payable or recoverable. The reversal of an existing timing difference and the origination of a new timing difference at the same time are seen as two separate events. Only the first one is a consequence of a past event. The second originating timing difference does not prevent the first one from reversing.

13.94 Thus, a deferred tax asset or liability is recognised for the future tax consequences of past events. If the transactions or events have not occurred by the balance sheet date or any of the events that have still to take place are under the entity's control and the entity retains a discretion to avoid them, then no deferred tax asset or liability will fall to be recognised. For example, an entity may carry a property at the balance sheet date at a revalued amount in excess of cost. Because the event that gives rise to the future tax payable – the sale of the asset – is under the entity's control and the entity retains a discretion to avoid the sale in order not to crystallise the liability, no deferred tax would be provided at the balance sheet date.

13.95 The ASB labelled this approach the 'incremental liability' approach to deferred tax and believes that it is consistent with the Statement of principles. Although FRS 19 is based on full provision for deferred tax, it is significantly different (including conceptual differences) from both the International and US models.

General principles

13.96 FRS 19 states that deferred tax:

- Should be recognised in respect of all timing differences that have originated but not reversed by the balance sheet date.
- Should not be recognised on permanent differences.

[FRS 19 para 7].

13.97 The general rule is that deferred tax should be provided on timing differences that have originated but have not reversed by the balance sheet date where transactions or events that result in an obligation to pay more tax in the future or a right to pay less tax in the future have occurred at the balance sheet date. This is because, as stated above, the entity will not have the discretion to avoid the future reversal of a timing difference that has occurred by the balance sheet date. Permanent differences, on the other hand, are the opposite of timing differences. They simply affect current tax and not future taxes. So no deferred tax is recognised on permanent differences. The general rule is subject to certain exceptions that are considered in the paragraphs that follow.

13.97.1 Tax planning strategies cannot be taken into consideration in determining the amount of a deferred tax liability to be recognised. For instance, an entity cannot avoid recognising an existing deferred tax liability on the grounds that future tax losses will prevent the transfer of economic benefits. As explained from paragraph 13.149 below, tax planning strategies can only be considered in determining the extent to which an existing deferred tax *asset* will be recovered.

13.98 Under FRS 19, each individual timing difference should initially be considered in isolation to determine whether it gives rise to a deferred tax asset or a liability. The individual assets and liabilities can be offset in accordance with the rules considered from paragraph 13.258 below. This is consistent with the FRS 19's incremental liability approach that relies fundamentally on an item by item view of deferred tax. In other words, the reversal of a timing difference leads to a settlement or extinguishment of a liability even though it may be offset before it crystallises by a new originating timing difference.

13.98.1 Deferred tax should be measured at the average tax rates that are expected to apply in the period in which the timing differences are expected to reverse, based on the tax rates and laws that have been enacted or substantively enacted by the balance sheet date. [FRS 19 para 37]. See further paragraph 13.171 onwards.

Timing differences

13.99 Timing differences are defined in FRS 19 as differences between an entity's taxable profits and its results as stated in the financial statements that arise from the inclusion of gains and losses in tax assessments in periods different from those in which they are recognised in the financial statements. Timing differences originate in one period and are capable of reversal in one or more subsequent periods. [FRS 19 para 2].

13.100 It follows from the above definition that there are only two situations under which timing differences can arise, as illustrated below:

- An item of income or expenditure is included in accounting profit of the period, but recognised in taxable profit in later periods. For example, income receivable might be accrued in the financial statements in one year, but fall to be taxed in the subsequent year when received. Similarly, provisions might be made for restructuring costs in the financial statements in one period, but would qualify for tax deduction at some later period when the expenditure is incurred.
- An item of income or expenditure is included in taxable profit of the period, but recognised in accounting profit in later years. For example, development expenditure might be tax deductible in the year in which it is incurred, but capitalised and amortised over a period for financial reporting purposes. Similarly, income received in advance might be taxed in the period of receipt, but treated as earned in the financial statements in a later period.

13.101 A timing difference is said to 'originate' when a transaction is first reflected in the financial statements, but not yet in the tax computation (or vice versa). It is said to 'reverse' when in due course the transaction is reflected in the tax computation or the financial statements either wholly or partly as the case may be. It is not necessary for a timing difference to originate in the financial statements and reverse in the tax computation (or vice versa). A timing difference can also originate in the financial statements of one period and reverse in the financial statements of a subsequent period without ever having been reflected in the tax computations. An example is a general provision for bad debts made in one year, but written back as not required in the following year. Similarly, a transaction might be reflected in the tax computation of one period and reverse in the tax computation of a later period, without ever having been reflected in the financial statements, although such situations are rare.

13.102 FRS 19 provides the following list of timing differences:

- Tax deductions for the cost of a fixed asset (including deductions for expenditure on infrastructure assets capitalised and depreciated using renewals accounting) are accelerated or decelerated, that is, received before or after the cost of the fixed asset is recognised in the profit and loss account.
- Pension liabilities are accrued in the financial statements but are allowed for tax purposes only when paid or contributed at a later date.
- Interest charges or development costs are capitalised on the balance sheet but are treated as revenue expenditure and allowed as incurred for tax purposes.
- Intragroup profits in stock, unrealised at group level, are reversed on consolidation.
- An asset is revalued in the financial statements, but the revaluation gain becomes taxable only if and when the asset is sold.
- A tax loss is not relieved against past or present taxable profits, but can be carried forward to reduce future taxable profits.
- The unremitted earnings of subsidiary and associated undertakings and joint ventures are recognised in the group results but will be subject to further taxation only if and when remitted to the parent undertaking.

[FRS 19 para 2].

13.103 A number of the timing differences in the above list would be short-term timing differences, that is, those that usually reverse in the accounting period following the one in which they originate (hence the name). There are other timing differences that do not reverse within a year of their origination. A classic example is 'accelerated capital allowances'. Accounting for some specific timing differences are considered in the following paragraphs.

13.103.1 In some situations, it may not be clear whether a timing difference exists. This may occur if there is uncertainty with regards to the tax position. For example, the entity may have incurred certain costs that have been capitalised and will be recognised in the profit and loss account over time for accounting purposes. Management may have claimed these costs as tax deductions in a tax return and these claims could be subject to challenge by the tax authorities. In this case, it is not clear whether a timing difference exists. In such a scenario, we consider that management should judge what they expect the outcome of any uncertainty to be and determine the deferred tax on that basis. If it is more likely than not that the uncertain item will be accepted by the tax authorities, it is management's expectation that a timing difference exists and deferred tax should be recognised. If it is more likely than not that the tax authorities will disallow the deduction, the expectation is that the amounts recognised in the profit and loss account over time will be permanent differences and no deferred tax should be recognised.

Accounting for some specific timing differences

Accelerated capital allowances

13.104 In the UK, tax relief in respect of capital expenditure on plant and machinery is given by means of capital allowances that are a form of standardised tax depreciation. Since capital allowances are deducted from accounting profit to arrive at taxable profit, the amount of depreciation charged in the financial statements is always disallowed in the tax computation. Although depreciation for taxation and accounting purposes will be the same over the life of the asset, they will differ from year to year, thus giving rise to timing differences. In many cases, the capital allowances depreciate the asset at a faster rate for tax purposes than the rate of depreciation charged in the financial statements. For this reason, the timing differences created are often referred to as 'accelerated capital allowances'. The following example illustrates the creation of the timing differences:

Example – Origination and reversal of timing differences

A company purchases a machine in 20X1 for £100,000. The asset is expected to be sold at the end of its useful life of five years for £10,000. Depreciation is charged on a straight line basis for accounting purposes and amounts to £18,000 ((£100,000 — £10,000)/5) per annum. For the purpose of this example, the rate of capital allowances is assumed to be 25% per annum on a reducing balance basis.
The timing difference will arise as follows:

Per financial statements	20X1	20X2	20X3	20X4	20X5
	£'000	£'000	£'000	£'000	£'000
Carrying value of asset	100	82	64	46	28
Depreciation charge	18	18	18	18	18
Book written down value	82	64	46	28	10
Per tax computation					
Carrying value of asset	100	75	56	42	32
Capital allowance	25	19	14	10	8
Tax written down value	75	56	42	32	24
Timing difference					
Capital allowance allowed	25	19	14	10	8
Depreciation charged	18	18	18	18	18
Originating (reversing)	7	1	(4)	(8)	(10)
Cumulative	7	8	4	(4)	(14)

The table shows that a timing difference of £7,000 originates in the first year, but this gradually reverses from year three onwards. Over the useful life of the asset depreciation charged exceeds capital allowances by £14,000. For the first two years, capital allowances exceed depreciation and, hence, the tax assessed and provided in the profit and loss account as current tax payable is less than the tax that would eventually become payable on the profit reported in the financial statements. This early benefit of lower taxation gradually reverses from year three onwards when capital allowances have fallen below depreciation. In those years, the tax assessed and, hence, provided in the profit and loss account as current tax is higher than the amount due on the profit reported in the financial statements. The cumulative timing difference at the end of 20X5 of £14,000 will either gradually reverse from 20X6 onwards if the asset is included in the pool for capital allowance purposes, or it will give rise to a balancing allowance if the asset is sold in 20X6 for £10,000.

13.105 The description of accelerated tax deductions for the cost of fixed assets set out in the first bullet point in paragraph 13.102 above has been made more general by FRS 19 to clarify that it applies to tax deductions received before or after the *cost* of the fixed asset is recognised in the profit and loss account. The definition reflects the fact that the cost of a fixed asset is recognised in the profit and loss account either through depreciation or, if not depreciated, on sale of the asset. This means that the reversal of accelerated capital allowances occurs as the asset is consumed through use or on disposal.

13.106 The definition of accelerated capital allowances has wide implications in practice. For instance, many items of plant and machinery such as, standby electrical generators, air-conditioning plant and passenger and goods lifts that form part of investment properties are normally included in the overall valuation of the investment property and are not depreciated. Under FRS 19, if an asset is not depreciated (and has not otherwise been written down to a carrying value less than cost), a timing difference equal to the amount of the capital allowances claimed arises. [FRS 19 para 10]. This means that deferred tax should be provided on the timing difference. Therefore, in general, deferred tax should be provided on all tax deductible assets irrespective of whether or not they are depreciated. In the absence of depreciation or a write down for impairment, the timing difference will reverse on the asset's disposal, by way of a balancing charge.

13.106.1 The Finance Act 2008 introduced major changes to the capital allowances regime in the UK, including the following:

- The rate of writing down allowances (tax depreciation) on plant and machinery in the general pool is reduced from 25 per cent per annum to 20 per cent per annum from 1 April 2008.
- The rate of writing down allowances are further reduced for certain fixtures integral to buildings to 10 per cent per annum from 1 April 2008.
- The rate of writing down allowances on long-life assets is increased from 6 per cent per annum to 10 per cent per annum from 1 April 2008.
- There are also changes to the capital allowances rules for small enterprises.

13.106.2 Deferred tax is measured using the tax rates and laws that are enacted or substantively enacted (see para 13.45) at the balance sheet date. [FRS 19 para 37]. The above changes to the capital allowances regime were substantively enacted on 2 July 2008 following approval of the Finance Bill 2008 by the House of Commons; and so the effect of the changes should be recognised in accounting periods ending on or after that date (including interims). If an entity's recognition of deferred tax has taken into account the phasing of reversal of timing differences, these calculations will need to be refreshed to take into account changes in the timing of the capital allowances.

Industrial building allowances

13.107 As a general rule, in the UK capital allowances on fixed assets become repayable through a balancing charge if the asset is not consumed, but is instead sold for more than its tax written-down value at the time of sale. However, in the past, allowances on certain buildings have been subject to a different regime of Industrial Building Allowances (IBAs). Various amendments have been made to the regime, the impact of which is discussed in paragraph 13.109 onwards.

13.108 Under the original rules, IBAs on factories, warehouses, hotels and commercial buildings in enterprise zones did not need to be repaid if they were retained in the business for a qualifying holding period of 25 years following purchase. After 25 years, no balancing charge arose even if an industrial building was sold for more than its tax written-down value.

13.109 Deferred tax attributable to capital allowances of all types should be recognised until all the conditions for retaining those allowances have been met. Under the original IBA regime this meant that, in many cases, a deferred tax liability was held on balance sheet in relation to IBAs as accounting depreciation was booked at a slower rate than the IBAs (tax depreciation) were received. Once the conditions for retaining the allowances were met, that is, there was no longer any possibility that the allowances could be clawed back as a balancing charge on sale, the timing difference relating to the accelerated capital allowances became permanent and any deferred tax liability previously recognised was reversed. [FRS 19 para 9]. In practice, this meant that the deferred tax liabilities were released at the end of year 25.

13.109.1 Two key changes have been made to the IBA regime as follows:

- Balancing adjustment provisions and those that recalculate writing-down allowances for buyers were withdrawn for balancing events (such as disposals) occurring on or after 21 March 2007
- IBAs are phased-out gradually from 2008/2009 onwards. The rate will drop in successive years from 4 per cent to 3 per cent to 2 per cent to 1 per cent with the allowances being eliminated thereafter.

13.110 Deferred tax is measured using the tax rates and laws that are enacted or substantively enacted at the balance sheet date. [FRS 19 para 37]. Accounting for the changes to IBAs impacted on more than one accounting period. The removal of the IBAs balancing adjustment was included in the Finance Act 2007, which was substantively enacted on 26 June 2007. Therefore, this change was accounted for in periods ending on or after that date (including interims). The phased withdrawal of IBAs was included in the Finance Act 2008, which was substantively enacted on 2 July 2008; the effect of the withdrawal is recognised in accounting periods ending on or after that date (including interims).

13.110.1 The fact that balancing adjustments no longer arise means that any deferred tax liability will never be 'clawed back' by the tax authorities even if a balancing event occurs before the end of the 25 year time period. Under paragraph 9 of FRS 19, if and when all conditions for retaining IBAs have been met, any deferred tax liability previously recognised should be reversed. Therefore, the removal of the balancing adjustment (and with it, the removal of the qualifying period for retaining allowances) means that allowances received prior to the removal will become a permanent difference. This results in the release of any existing deferred tax liabilities. In the remaining years when reduced IBAs are available, the allowance is treated as a permanent difference as it arises.

13.110.2 The situation may differ if a company has a deferred tax asset with respect to industrial buildings. This will occur if the accumulated accounting depreciation at the balance sheet date is greater than the IBAs received. The general principle is to consider whether the deferred tax asset is recoverable under the applicable tax rules. If the expectation is that the building will continue to be used, it will be necessary to determine if sufficient IBAs will be received to cover the timing difference. In this situation, the elimination of the balancing adjustment by the Finance Act 2007 has no effect. The recoverability of the deferred tax asset could be impacted by the phasing out of IBAs, which was introduced by the Finance Act 2008. It could be the case that there will be insufficient IBAs in the future for the full timing difference to reverse. In this situation, all or part of the deferred tax asset should be written off, as appropriate. The write off is made in the first accounting period ending on or after the date of substantive enactment of the rules phasing out the IBAs (that is, 2 July 2008).

13.110.3 When recognising adjustments to deferred tax balances as a result of a change in tax laws, consideration must be given as to whether the adjustment should be recognised in the profit and loss account or in the STRGL (or a combination of the two). This is considered in more detail in paragraph 13.249 below.

Infrastructure assets

13.111 Infrastructure assets can be defined as groups of assets which together form an integrated system. Such a system could not be effectively operated if individual components were removed. Systems typically falling within this category include gas, water, railways, roads as well as electricity distribution systems.

13.112 Traditionally, depreciation accounting has been the method under which the consumption of service potential of fixed assets is recognised in financial statements. Renewals accounting emerged as an alternative method of recognising consumption of service potential of long-lived assets such as infrastructure assets. The renewals accounting approach is most applicable to that part of the networks or systems where the system as a whole is be maintained indefinitely at a particular level of service potential by the continuous replacement and refurbishment of its components. When renewals accounting is adopted, the level of annual expenditure required to maintain the operating capacity of the infrastructure asset is treated as the depreciation charged in the period. The actual expenditure incurred each year to maintain the asset is capitalised.

13.113 Under FRS 19, tax deductions for expenditure on infrastructure assets capitalised and depreciated using renewals accounting are included within the definition of accelerated capital allowances noted in paragraph 13.102 above. Therefore, deferred tax should be provided on the timing difference between the actual expenditure qualifying for tax relief and the assessed level of planned expenditure treated as depreciation. [FRS 19 App V para 62].

Provisions

13.114 Provisions, such as those made for refurbishment, or for plant closures following a reorganisation, or those arising on pensions and unfunded retirement benefits usually give rise to timing differences in that tax relief is obtained when the expenditure is actually incurred and not when it is recognised in the financial statements. It follows that such provisions will always give rise to a deferred tax asset, because taxable profits are higher than accounting profits in the year in which the provisions are made. The tax asset will be recovered in the year in which the actual expenditure is incurred, but for some provisions, like pensions and other post-retirement benefits, recoverability of the tax benefit may take many years (see further para 13.126 onwards).

[The next paragraph is 13.116.]

Deferred revenue expenditure

13.116 Deferred revenue expenditure, on the other hand, gives rise to deferred tax liabilities. In this situation, tax relief is typically obtained on the full amount of the expenditure in the year in which it is incurred, but only a proportion is recognised in the financial statements, the balance being carried forward as an asset to be charged to income over a period of time. The difference between book and tax treatment gives rise to a deferred tax liability to reflect the fact that the company has obtained full tax benefit on expenditure of which only a proportion has passed through the profit and loss account in the year.

13.117 Capitalisation of interest gives rise to similar tax considerations and is one of the examples of timing differences noted in FRS 19 (see para 13.102 above). The full interest incurred in the year is allowed for tax, but for accounting purposes the tax benefit is effectively recognised over the years in which the interest capitalised in the financial statements is charged through depreciation of the asset in the profit and account. Even where the asset is not depreciated, such as in the case of investment properties, deferred tax should be provided because the reversal of the timing difference (the interest charge in the performance statement) will arise when the asset is sold or the property is impaired. The deferred tax liabilities will be reversed when the costs are taken to the profit and loss account.

Government grants

13.118 The accounting treatment of government grants and their treatment for tax purposes may give rise to timing differences. SSAP 4, 'Accounting for government grants', requires grants to be treated as deferred income and amortised either over the periods in which the related revenue expenditure is recognised or, if the grant is made as a contribution towards capital expenditure, over the expected useful life of the related asset. In the latter situation, an alternative treatment of deducting the grant from the capital cost of the asset is permitted for entities not preparing their financial statements in accordance with the Companies Act 2006 (see further chapter 16). Grants given as a contribution towards the cost of acquisition of an asset may be non-taxable, although some are in effect taxed by reducing the cost of fixed assets for capital allowances purposes. Other grants, such as revenue-based grants, are usually taxable on a cash received basis.

13.119 If the grant is not taxable, it gives rise to a permanent difference between accounting and taxable profits. Non-taxable revenue-based grants do not have any deferred tax consequences, because the amortised credit to the profit and loss account is simply a permanent difference in arriving at taxable profits of each year. Similarly, receipts of non-taxable capital-based grants do not give rise to deferred tax adjustments, except that accelerated capital allowances will need to be calculated as the difference between the net book value of the asset (gross cost less accumulated depreciation calculated on the gross cost) and the tax written down value (gross cost less tax allowances claimed). This applies even if the asset is stated in the financial statements net of the grant since the balance sheet presentation permitted by SSAP 4 for entities that do not report under the Companies Act 2006 does not affect the deferred tax calculation.

13.120 If the grant is taxable, a timing difference will arise between the taxable profits and the accounting profits. Revenue-based grants that are taxed on receipt, but amortised over a period for financial reporting purposes, give rise to a timing difference on which a deferred tax asset may need to be set up on the unamortised balance carried forward in the financial statements. The deferred tax asset will fall to be recoverable in subsequent accounting periods as the deferred credit unwinds through amortisation. Where a grant that has been taxed on receipt becomes repayable, the repayment will qualify for tax relief in the year in which the repayment is made. In that situation, any deferred tax asset previously carried forward should be immediately written off as part of the tax charge.

13.121 Where a taxable grant is received as a contribution towards expenditure on a fixed asset, the nature of the deferred tax adjustment will depend on how the grant is treated for tax and accounting purposes. If the grant is deducted from the cost of fixed assets both for financial reporting and tax purposes, the deferred tax calculation is relatively straightforward as accelerated capital allowances are calculated on a reduced cost. On the other hand, if the grant is treated as a deferred credit for financial reporting purposes, but deducted against the cost of the asset for capital allowances purposes, the deferred tax calculation will consist of two components. A deferred tax debit balance will arise on the unamortised grant, which will be netted off against the deferred tax credit balance arising on the accelerated capital allowances. In practice, the balance on the deferred income account is netted off against the book value of the asset for the purposes of calculating the timing difference. Consider the following example:

Example – Capital allowances restricted by amount of grant

A company purchases a fixed asset for £120,000. The asset qualifies for a grant of £20,000 which is treated in the financial statements as a deferred credit. The asset has a useful economic life of five years. The company claims capital allowances, but these are restricted by the amount of the grant. The timing differences for deferred tax purposes are calculated as follows:

Per financial statements	20X1	20X2	20X3	20X4	20X5
	£	£	£	£	£
Cost of asset	120,000	96,000	72,000	48,000	24,000
Depreciation	(24,000)	(24,000)	(24,000)	(24,000)	(24,000)
Net book value	96,000	72,000	48,000	24,000	–
Unamortised deferred income	16,000	12,000	8,000	4,000	–

Per tax computation	20X1	20X2	20X3	20X4	20X5
	£	£	£	£	£
Cost of asset	120,000				
Less grant	(20,000)				
Cost net of grant/pool	100,000	75,000	56,250	42,187	31,640
Capital allowances @ 25%	(25,000)	(18,750)	(14,063)	(10,547)	(7,910)
Tax written down value	75,000	56,250	42,187	31,640	23,730
Timing difference					
Capital allowances	25,000	18,750	14,063	10,547	7,910
Depreciation	(24,000)	(24,000)	(24,000)	(24,000)	(24,000)
Accelerated capital allowances	1,000	(5,250)	(9,937)	(13,453)	(16,090)
Amortisation of grant	4,000	4,000	4,000	4,000	4,000
Net timing difference	5,000	(1,250)	(5,937)	(9,453)	(12,090)

Net book value of fixed asset	96,000	72,000	48,000	24,000	–
Unamortised grant	(16,000)	(12,000)	(8,000)	(4,000)	–
Tax written down value	80,000	60,000	40,000	20,000	–
	(75,000)	(56,250)	(42,187)	(31,640)	(23,730)
Cumulative timing difference	5,000	3,750	(2,187)	(11,640)	(23,730)

The timing difference profile will be the same if the grant is deducted directly from the cost of the asset and the net amount written off over the five year period.

Leases

13.122 Many companies enter into lease and hire purchase contracts under which they obtain the right to use or purchase assets. In the UK there is normally no provision in a lease contract for legal title to the leased asset to pass to the lessee. A hire purchase contract has similar features to a lease, except that the hirer may acquire legal title by exercising an option to purchase the asset upon fulfilment of certain conditions (normally the payment of a specified number of instalments).

13.123 Assets acquired under leases and hire purchase contracts give rise to timing differences between the amounts recorded in the profit and loss account and the amounts recorded in the tax computations. Where the asset is purchased under a hire purchase agreement, the hirer will normally account for the acquisition of the fixed asset in question and will be able to claim the capital allowances. Therefore, no particular deferred tax problems arise. Similarly, no deferred tax problems normally arise in accounting for an operating lease. This is because the amount that is charged to rentals in the profit and loss account for financial reporting purposes is likely to be the same as the amount charged in arriving at the taxable profit. The only exception to this will arise where there are accrued rentals that may give rise to a potential short-term timing difference.

13.124 A timing difference will arise in circumstances where the lessee enters into a finance lease that is accounted for under SSAP 21 and where the tax legislation provides that capital allowances are claimed by the lessor, rather than the lessee . In that situation, the asset acquired under a finance lease will be recorded as a fixed asset with a corresponding liability for the obligation to pay future rentals. The asset is then depreciated over the lease term or the useful life of the asset, whichever is shorter. Rents payable are apportioned between the finance charge and a reduction of the outstanding obligation for future amounts payable. The total finance charge is allocated to accounting periods during the lease term so as to produce a constant periodic rate of charge on the remaining balance of the obligation for each accounting period. A reasonable approximation is permitted (see further chapter 19).

13.125 If the finance lessee does not qualify for capital allowances, but is able to obtain a tax deduction for the whole of each rental payment, a timing difference arises if tax relief is given on the rentals paid, as a result of the differing treatment for accounting and tax purposes. In some situations, HMRC may accept the SSAP 21 treatment for tax purposes, in which case there are no deferred tax consequences. However, in principle, a timing difference arises and this is illustrated in the following example:

Example – Finance lease where lessee does not receive capital allowances

A company leases a fixed asset under a finance lease over a five year period. The annual lease payments amount to £12,000 per annum. The asset is recorded at the present value of the minimum lease payments of £48,000 and is depreciated at £9,600 per annum.

The timing difference arising is calculated as follows:

	Year 1	Year 2	Year 3	Year 4	Year 5
	£	£	£	£	£
Rentals	12,000	12,000	12,000	12,000	12,000
Finance cost @ 7.93%	(3,806)	(3,158)	(2,455)	(1,699)	(882)
Capital repayment	8,194	8,842	9,545	10,301	11,118
Timing difference					
Tax computations: rentals	12,000	12,000	12,000	12,000	12,000
Profit and loss account:					
Finance cost	3,806	3,158	2,455	1,699	882
Depreciation	9,600	9,600	9,600	9,600	9,600
	13,406	12,758	12,055	11,299	10,482
Timing difference	(1,406)	(758)	(55)	701	1,518
Net book value of fixed asset	38,400	28,800	19,200	9,600	–
Outstanding obligation (capital)	39,806	30,964	21,419	11,118	–
Cumulative timing difference	(1,406)	(2,164)	(2,219)	(1,518)	–

Finance leases capitalised under SSAP 21, therefore, tend to produce an originating negative timing difference (deferred tax asset) as greater finance charges are allocated to earlier years to reflect the reducing capital amount owed under the lease.

Post-retirement benefits

13.126 In the UK, tax relief on employers' pension contributions is often given in the period in which they are paid, rather than when the costs are recognised in the financial statements (with the exception of some large contributions, where tax relief is spread over a period). In an unfunded scheme, and in the case of provisions for unfunded benefits such as post-retirement healthcare, the tax relief is often given when the pensions or other benefits are paid. In the financial statements, on the other hand, pension costs and other post-retirement benefits are recognised as service is provided by the employee, in accordance with the principles set out in FRS 17, 'Retirement benefits'. Where the total of the pension costs recognised under FRS 17 differs from the actual contributions (or unfunded benefits) paid, the resulting asset or liability recognised in the balance sheet is a timing difference for deferred tax purposes. This is the case whether the defined benefit scheme is in a net deficit or a net surplus position.

13.126.1 In the UK, employer pension contributions are only deductible as an expense if they are incurred *'wholly and exclusively for the purposes of the employer's trade or profession'*. Tax relief is, therefore, not automatic and entities should consider this when accounting for tax in respect of pension schemes. In addition, where tax relief is obtained, tax deductions on any significant contributions may be subject to spreading rules. This will occur when 'relevant excess contributions' (RECs) are made. The implications of spreading of tax deductions on RECs are discussed in paragraph 13.126.12 below. This is a complex area and consultation with a tax specialist is advised.

13.126.2 FRS 19 defines timing differences as differences between an entity's taxable profits and its results as stated in the financial statements that arise from the inclusion of gains and losses in tax assessments in periods different from those in which they are recognised in financial statements. Timing differences originate in one period and are capable of reversal in one or more subsequent periods. Consider an actuarial gain. The actuarial gain is reflected in the entity's financial statements in the year it arises. If contributions are reduced in future years as a result of the surplus, the pension asset will be recovered because the pension cost accrued each year will exceed the contributions payable.

13.126.3 An actuarial gain does give rise to a timing difference. The gain is not taxed in the year it arises (when the timing difference originates), but in a sense it is taxed in future years as the surplus is recovered (when the timing difference reverses). In those future years, the accounting profits are adjusted to taxable profits by replacing the pension costs with the reduced contributions payable, the difference being the amount of surplus that is recovered in the year.

Example – Timing difference in respect of pension surplus

A company's defined benefit pension scheme is in surplus as a result of an actuarial gain and because contributions paid were greater than pension costs. In accordance with FRS 17, 'Retirement benefits', the surplus is recognised as an asset on the company's balance sheet. Management has queried whether it is appropriate to recognise a deferred tax liability as the pension surplus is not taxable. Should a deferred tax liability be recognised?

The key here is to determine whether the pension asset represents a timing difference.

Paragraph 37 of FRS 17 specifies that a pension asset should be recognised only to the extent that it is recoverable through reduced contributions in the future or through refunds from the scheme. This means that, for the pension asset to be recognised, there must be an expectation that it will be recovered.

Normally, contributions will be reduced in future years as a result of the surplus and the pension asset will thus be recovered.

The entity's taxable profits are arrived at after deducting the employer's pension contributions payable each period, rather than reflecting the pension gains and losses that are recognised in the financial statements.

In future years, the current tax deductions received will be lower as a result of the reduced contributions payable. Pension costs will be greater than the contributions and the surplus will be recovered. That difference in effect reflects the inclusion in the later period's tax assessment of a gain that has been recognised in an earlier period's financial statements. Hence it is necessary to build up a deferred tax liability as the surplus arises and to reverse that liability as the surplus is recovered.

13.126.4 With some exceptions (none of which are applicable to pensions), FRS 19 requires deferred tax to be provided in full on all timing differences that have originated but not reversed by the balance sheet date. In most cases, these timing differences will reverse, albeit over a long time scale. Deferred tax assets (which relate to defined benefit liabilities recognised under FRS 17) should be recognised to the extent that they are regarded as recoverable.

13.126.5 A deferred tax asset should be recognised to the extent that it can be regarded as more likely than not that there will be suitable taxable profits from which the future reversal of the underlying timing differences can be deducted. [FRS 19 para 23]. The question arises as to whether deferred tax liabilities resulting from taxable timing differences can be taken into account in determining the recoverability of the deferred tax asset relating to pensions. Recovery of deferred tax assets against existing deferred tax liabilities is dealt with in paragraph 13.156 onwards. A deferred tax asset in respect of a pension obligation cannot be recognised simply because there are sufficient taxable timing differences at the balance sheet date. The timing of reversal of the timing differences giving rise to liabilities also needs to be taken into account.

13.126.6 Therefore, some scheduling of the reversal of timing differences may be required to ensure that the reversal of the deductible timing differences would allow the company to carry the deferred tax asset against the profits arising on reversal of the taxable timing differences. The company must have plans in place to eliminate the pension deficit – simply paying the normal regular cost will not eliminate the deficit. Therefore, the recognition of a tax asset in respect of the pension obligations should take into account the expected timing of contributions necessary to eliminate the deficit.

13.126.7 Also, if the company has incurred losses in the past and has incurred losses in the current period as well, this will impact on the extent to which tax assets can be recognised. For example, if say the company continues to make losses in the next few years before a turnaround is anticipated, but the amount of the reversal of the existing taxable timing differences in those years is not enough to create taxable profits such that any pension contributions made in those years simply add to the tax loss, then the deferred tax asset may not be recoverable. The assessment of the likelihood that taxable profits will arise when there has been a history of trading losses is discussed in paragraph 13.158 onwards.

13.126.8 Under FRS 17, various components of pension cost are reported in the profit and loss account; actuarial gains and losses are reported in the STRGL. So in any period, pension cost accounting may give rise to current tax (tax relief on contributions) and deferred tax (on the timing differences between contributions and costs). FRS 16 requires current tax to be recognised in the profit and loss account, except where it is attributable to a gain or loss that has been recognised directly in the STRGL, in which case the attributable tax should also be recognised directly in the STRGL (see para 13.21). Similarly, FRS 19 requires deferred tax to be recognised in the profit and loss account, except where it is attributable to a gain or loss that has been recognised directly in the STRGL (see para 13.237). Normally, there is no direct relationship between the components of pension cost reported in the performance statements and the contributions and benefits paid in a period and so FRS 17 specifies a hierarchy for allocating current tax between the profit and loss account and the STRGL. Deferred tax will normally arise on the balance of costs and credits in each statement.

13.126.9 Tax relief on contributions should be allocated on the basis that the contributions cover profit and loss items first and actuarial losses (STRGL items) second, unless it is clear that some other allocation is more appropriate. If contributions exceed those items, tax relief relating to the excess should be credited in the profit and loss account, again unless it is clearly more appropriate to allocate it to the STRGL. The standard gives an example where an alternative method of allocation may be appropriate – when a special contribution is made to fund a deficit arising from an identifiable cause, say an actuarial loss, in which case the tax relief should be allocated to the STRGL. However, in the absence of a clear link between the contribution and the items recognised in the performance statements, the allocation above should be followed. [FRS 17 para 71].

13.126.10 The allocation of current and deferred tax is illustrated in the following simplified examples, which show the movements in the pension balance during the year. A tax rate of 30 per cent is assumed.

Example 1 – Defined benefit asset with an actuarial loss

	Change in defined benefit asset	Current tax relief (30%)	Deferred tax liability (30%)
	£	£	£
B/f	120		(36)
Contributions	70	(21)	
P&L – net pension cost	(60)	18	–
STRGL – actuarial loss	(20)	3	3
	(80)	21	3
C/f	110	–	(33)

Current tax relief arises on contributions paid of £70. This is allocated first to cover the pension cost of £60 reported in the profit and loss account (resulting in a credit of £18 in the tax charge in the profit and loss account). The balance of the contributions paid, £10, is allocated to the actuarial loss and hence current tax of £3 is credited in the STRGL. Deferred tax of £3 is attributable to the balance of the actuarial loss, £10 and is credited in the STRGL.

It should be noted that FRS 17 requires the deferred tax to be offset against the defined benefit asset in the balance sheet (see para 13.257).

Example 2 – Defined benefit liability with an actuarial loss

	Change in defined benefit liability	Current tax relief (30%)	Deferred tax asset (30%)
	£	£	£
B/f	(200)		60
Contributions paid	80	(24)	
P&L – net pension cost	(70)	21	–
STRGL – actuarial loss	(20)	3	3
	(90)	24	3
C/f	(210)	–	63

Current tax relief of £24 arises on contributions paid of £80. This is allocated first to cover the pension cost of £70 reported in the profit and loss account (resulting in a credit of £21 in the tax charge in the profit and loss account). The balance of the contributions paid of £10 is allocated to the actuarial loss and hence current tax of £3 is credited in the STRGL. Deferred tax of £3 is attributable to the balance of the actuarial loss of £10 and is credited in the STRGL.

Example 3 – Defined benefit liability with an actuarial gain

If, in the above example, there was an actuarial gain rather than an actuarial loss, the whole of the current tax relief of £24 would be credited in the profit and loss account. None of the current tax credit can be allocated to the STRGL as there is no debit to the STRGL. Thus the initial £21 (30% of £70) is allocated to the profit and loss account, nil is allocated to the STRGL and the excess of £3 is allocated to the profit and loss account. Deferred tax attributable to the actuarial gain would be charged in the STRGL. This is illustrated below.

	Change in defined benefit liability	Current tax relief (30%)	Deferred tax asset (30%)
	£	£	£
B/f	(200)		(60)
Contributions	80	(24)	
P&L – net pension cost	(70)	24	(3)
STRGL – actuarial gain	20	–	(6)
	(50)	24	(9)
C/f	(170)	–	51

13.126.11 The allocation is more complicated if a large contribution is made in the period, say to reduce an existing pension deficit. Assume that, in example 2 above, an additional contribution of £100 was paid and that tax deductions were received in the period.

Example – Receipt of tax relief on additional contribution

	Change in defined benefit liability	Current tax relief (30%)	Deferred tax asset (30%)
	£	£	£
B/f	(200)		60
'Normal' contributions paid	80	(24)	
Additional contribution paid	100	(30)	
P&L account – net pension cost	(70)	21	–
STRGL:			
Current year actuarial loss	(20)	3	3
Relating to previous actuarial losses	–	30	(30)
	(90)	54	(27)
C/f	(110)	–	33

Therefore, if tax deductions on the normal contribution of £80 and the additional contribution of £100 are all received in the period (that is, no spreading of deductions), then the current tax relief of £24 on the 'normal' contributions is allocated first against the pension cost in the profit and loss account and then the balance is allocated against the actuarial loss.

Further, current tax deductions of £30 are received on the additional contribution. There is, therefore, an excess deduction to be considered. Under the allocation hierarchy in paragraph 13.126.9, this excess would go to the profit and loss account, unless another method of allocation is more appropriate. The treatment of the deferred tax in relation to the additional contribution will depend on why that contribution was made. In this case, it is likely that the additional contribution is funding past actuarial losses, in which case it is necessary to backwards-trace the items in the performance statement to determine where the underlying items giving rise to the deficit that is being funded were originally recognised.

It will be necessary to backwards-trace further if the deductions received in the year exceed the current and prior year actuarial losses that had not been allocated current tax deductions. Assuming that it is possible to establish, using backwards-tracing, that the tax deductions relate to prior year actuarial losses, the excess tax deductions will be recognised in the STRGL, with a corresponding reversal of deferred tax, as shown above.

Alternatively, if the additional contribution was made to fund current year actuarial losses as well as previous actuarial losses, £3 would be allocated to the STRGL (to cover the £10 of actuarial loss made in the current year not yet tax effected). There is then an excess deduction of £27 after allocating to the net pension cost in the profit and loss account and any actuarial losses in the STRGL. Again, in this case, it would be appropriate to allocate this to the STRGL if the contribution was made to fund the accumulated actuarial losses. Notably, this has the same outcome as the allocation method illustrated in the table above. An element of judgement will be necessary when considering why the additional contribution was made.

Note that the fact that a pension liability recognised on transition to FRS 17 was charged to reserves does not necessarily mean that any current tax deductions or subsequent changes in any related deferred tax asset will also be recognised in reserves (see further para 13.249 below).

13.126.12 If tax deductions are spread across more than one accounting period then this will impact on the deferred tax calculation, as the deduction received in the current year will be lower. Assume that in the example in paragraph 13.126.11 above the additional contribution of £100 meets the definition of a REC (see para 13.126.1 above) and is thus spread over, say, three periods (that is only one-third of the relief on the additional contribution is received in the current period).

Example – Spreading of tax relief on additional contribution

	Change in defined benefit liability	Current tax relief (30%)	Deferred tax asset (30%)
	£	£	£
B/f	(200)		60
'Normal' contributions paid	80	(24)	
Additional contribution paid	100	(10)	
P&L account – net pension cost	(70)	21	–
STRGL:			
Current year actuarial loss	(20)	3	3
Relating to previous actuarial losses	–	10	(10)
	(90)	34	(7)
C/f	(110)	–	53

Note that in this example, the deferred tax balance at the period end is not 30% of the pension balance.

Assuming that a deferred tax asset has been recognised in relation to the pension liability at the beginning of the period, part of this deferred tax asset reverses as a result of the tax deductions received in the period. However, if the contributions paid do not receive tax relief in the period, then a corresponding portion of the deferred tax asset on the opening pension liability will continue to be carried forward (assuming the recognition criteria are met) and will reverse in the future when the tax deductions are received.

The deferred tax asset can be summarised as:

	£
On pension liability at year end (£110 × 30%)	33
Outstanding deductions on contributions made (£100 × 30% × 2/3)	20
Total deferred tax asset	53

A deferred tax asset should be recognised to the extent that it is regarded as more likely than not that the deferred tax asset will be recovered. Under FRS 17, it is presented as a deduction from the net pension deficit recorded in the balance sheet (see para 13.257). This applies even if part of the deferred tax asset relates to deductions to be received through spreading. In some cases, this may give an odd result, for example, where the deferred tax asset exceeds the pension deficit. Our view is that the deferred tax asset should still be shown with the related pension deficit. In this situation, it would be appropriate to make clear that there is not a pension asset, which may be achieved by expanding the disclosure to show both the pension deficit and the related deferred tax asset on the face of the balance sheet, with a sub-total.

13.126.13 FRS 16 requires the current tax charged or credited in the profit and loss account and the STRGL to be disclosed separately. In addition, FRS 19 requires the deferred tax charged or credited in the profit and loss account and the STRGL to be disclosed separately.

Share-based payment transactions

Equity-settled transactions

13.127 FRS 20, 'Share-based payment', requires companies to recognise the cost of equity-settled share-based awards (for example, share options) on the basis of the fair value of the award at the date of grant, spread over the vesting period (see further chapter 12). However, the amount of any deduction available for tax purposes in the case of equity-settled transactions does not often correspond to the amount charged to the profit and loss account in accordance with FRS 20.

13.127.1 Under current UK tax law a tax deduction in connection with an employee share option scheme is generally available at the date of exercise, measured on the basis of the share option's intrinsic value at that date (being the difference between the share's market price at the date of exercise and the option's exercise price).

13.127.2 When the FRS 20 charge (based on the share option's fair value at the date of grant) is recognised in the profit and loss account, there is a timing difference between the recognition of this cumulative charge and the related deduction for tax purposes that will be received in the future. This timing difference results in a deferred tax asset, which will be recognised if it meets FRS 19's criteria for recognition. On the basis of all available evidence it must be regarded as more likely than not that there will be suitable taxable profits against which the deferred tax asset can be utilised (see para 13.142 onwards), in order to meet these criteria.

13.127.3 It will also be necessary to consider whether the share options will be exercised and the implications of any changes in the market price. If the FRS 20 charge is revised as a result of a change in the number of options expected to vest, there will be a corresponding adjustment to the deferred tax asset. If it appears that the share options will not be exercised because they are out of the money, then it is likely that any deferred tax asset recognised should be written off. In addition, assuming the share options are likely to be exercised, if the option's intrinsic value falls below the option's fair value at the date of grant, then the carrying value of the deferred tax asset may not be recoverable in full and may need to be written down (see further para 13.127.8 below).

13.127.4 If the deduction for tax purposes that will be obtained (based on the share option's intrinsic value at the date of exercise) exceeds, or is expected to exceed, the total expected accounting charge based on the option's fair value at date of grant, the excess is regarded as a permanent difference under FRS 19. The excess of the option's intrinsic value over the fair value at date of grant is a permanent difference, because a share-based payment charge for this element is not recognised for accounting purposes so the difference will never reverse. The excess deduction is accounted for when it crystallises, that is, when the share options are exercised.

13.127.5 Both current and deferred tax should be recognised in the profit and loss account for the period, except to the extent that the tax is attributable to a gain or loss that is or has been recognised directly in the STRGL (in which case, the related tax is also recognised in the STRGL). [FRS 16 para 5; FRS 19 para 34]. If the tax deduction exceeds the cumulative amount of the FRS 20 charge, this indicates that the tax deduction relates not only to the FRS 20 charge recognised in the profit and loss account, but also to an unrecognised equity item. However, as this excess amount is not recognised in the STRGL, the related tax is required to be included in the profit and loss account and so, under UK GAAP, the full amount of tax relating to the deduction is recognised in the profit and loss account.

13.127.6 The accounting for deferred tax on an equity-settled share-based award is illustrated in the following example.

Example – Deferred tax on an equity-settled share-based award

On 1 January 20X3, 100,000 options are issued with a fair value of £360,000. The vesting period is 3 years and all the share options are expected to be exercised. All of the share options are exercised in year 4. The tax rate is 30%. The intrinsic value of the share options (being market value of the underlying shares less exercise price) at the end of years 1, 2, 3 and at the date of exercise in year 4 is £330,000, £300,000, £380,000 and £400,000, respectively.

The total share-based payment charge recognised in each year of the three year period is £120,000 (£360,000/3). Tax deductions are not received until the share options are exercised and so a timing difference arises.

Acceptable accounting policies for determining the timing difference for deferred tax purposes in respect of the share-based payment charge are:

(a) the timing difference is based on the cumulative share-based payment charge, which is based on the fair value at date of grant (£360,000/3 = £120,000 for year 1), capped, if necessary, at the total intrinsic value (£330,000 for year 1); or

(b) the timing difference is based on a *pro rata* share of the intrinsic value (£330,000/3 = £110,000 for year 1), capped at the cumulative share-based payment charge so that any permanent difference is not recognised (see para 13.126.4).

Approach (a) can be described as a first-in first-out basis for allocating the future tax deductions to the cumulative share-based payment charge. Approach (b) can be described as a weighted average allocation basis. These approaches are illustrated below.

(a) Deferred tax based on cumulative share-based payment charge

At the end of year 1, the cumulative share-based payment charge is £120,000, which is covered by the expected tax deduction of £330,000. It is considered acceptable for the timing difference for deferred tax purposes to be based on the cumulative share-based payment charge, up to the options' total intrinsic value. Therefore, at the end of year 1, the deferred tax asset is £36,000 (30% × £120,000).

At the end of year 2, the cumulative share-based payment charge is £240,000, which is covered by the expected tax deduction of £300,000. Therefore, at the end of year 2, the deferred tax asset is £72,000 (30% × £240,000).

At the end of year 3, the cumulative share-based payment charge is £360,000, which is covered by the expected tax deduction of £380,000. Therefore, at the end of year 3, the deferred tax asset is £108,000 (30% × £360,000). The cumulative position at the end of year 3 is shown in the table below.

	Profit and loss account Dr (Cr)			Balance sheet Dr (Cr)	
Year	**Expense**	**Current tax**	**Deferred tax**	**Current tax**	**Deferred tax**
	£	**£**	**£**	**£**	**£**
1	120,000		(36,000)		36,000
2	120,000		(36,000)		72,000
3	120,000		(36,000)		108,000
Cumulative position at the end of year 3	360,000		(108,000)		

(b) Deferred tax based on intrinsic value at balance sheet date

Under this policy, the cumulative timing difference (that is, the tax deductions relating to the cumulative share-based payment charge) is a *pro rata* share of the options' total intrinsic value at the balance sheet date, capped at the cumulative share-based payment charge. Therefore, at the end of year 1, the timing difference is £110,000 (£330,000 × $^1/_3$) and the related deferred tax asset is £33,000 (£110,000 × 30%).

At the end of year 2, the deferred tax asset is £60,000 (£300,000 × $^2/_3$ × 30%).

At the end of year 3, the deferred tax asset is £108,000 (£360,000 × 30%). A deferred tax asset is not recognised in respect of the excess of the option's intrinsic value (£380,000) over the cumulative share-based payment charge (£360,000). The cumulative position at the end of year 3 is shown in the table below.

Year	Expense	Profit and loss account Dr (Cr) Current tax	Deferred tax	Balance sheet Dr (Cr) Current tax	Deferred tax
	£	£	£	£	£
1	120,000		(33,000)		33,000
2	120,000		(27,000)		60,000
3	120,000		(48,000)		108,000
Cumulative position at end of year 3	360,000		(108,000)		

Exercise of share options

The actual current tax benefit obtained on exercise of the options in year 4 is £120,000 (30% of £400,000 intrinsic value at the date of exercise). The deferred tax asset of £108,000 at the end of year 3 is reversed through the profit and loss account in year 4, giving a net tax credit of £12,000 (120,000 – 108,000). The double entry is as follows:

	£	£
Dr Current tax claim (balance sheet)	120,000	
Cr Current tax (profit and loss account)		120,000
Dr Deferred tax (profit and loss account)	108,000	
Cr Deferred tax (balance sheet)		108,000

The overall position is shown in the table below:

	Expense	Profit and loss account Dr (Cr) Current tax	Deferred tax	Balance sheet Dr (Cr) Current tax	Deferred tax
	£	£	£	£	£
Cumulative position at end of year 3	360,000		108,000		108,000
Movement in year 4	–	(120,000)	108,000	120,000	(108,000)
Total	360,000	(120,000)	–	120,000	–

In years 1 to 3, since there is no current tax deduction in relation to the profit and loss account expense, this should be noted in the reconciliation of the current tax charge required by FRS 19.

In year 4, since there is no profit and loss account expense in relation to the current tax deduction of £120,000, the credit should be explained in the reconciliation of the current tax charge.

13.127.7 It should be noted that the accounting for deferred tax on equity-settled share-based payments under UK GAAP differs from the accounting under IFRS. Under IAS 12, a deductible temporary difference arises on the difference between the tax base of the employee services received to date (being the amount the tax authorities will permit as a deduction in future periods) and the carrying amount of nil in the balance sheet. As the future tax deduction depends on the share price at the date of exercise, the tax base of the employee services received is always remeasured at the end of each period (even if it exceeds the cumulative share-based payment charge), with a resulting adjustment to the deferred tax asset. Therefore, the tax on the deduction relating to the excess over the IFRS 2 charge is recognised over the period to exercise under IFRS. In addition, a further difference is that the tax relating to this excess amount is recognised in equity, rather than the profit and loss account.

13.127.8 Under UK GAAP, whether the deferred tax asset is remeasured in line with changes in the share options' intrinsic value (being market value of the underlying shares less exercise price) will depend on the entity's accounting policy for determining the timing difference (see the example in para 13.127.6). The impact of the options' intrinsic value on the deferred tax calculation is summarised below.

Intrinsic value is greater than fair value at date of grant

- If the share options' intrinsic value is greater than the fair value at date of grant, the tax deduction expected to be received exceeds the share-based payment charged to the profit and loss account at any given stage. There is a timing difference based on the cumulative share-based payment charge booked to date, resulting in a deferred tax asset. As explained in paragraph 13.127.4 above, the excess of the intrinsic value over the fair value at date of grant is a permanent difference, which is recognised as current tax when it crystallises.

Intrinsic value is less than fair value at date of grant

- The situation can be more complicated if the share options' intrinsic value is lower than the fair value at date of grant, because the tax-deductible amount based on the current intrinsic value may be lower than the cumulative share-based payment charged to the profit and loss account.

  If the entity's accounting policy for determining the timing difference is based on intrinsic value at the balance sheet date, the lower intrinsic value will be reflected in the calculation of deferred tax. This is illustrated in the example in paragraph 13.127.6, where the deferred tax asset under this policy at the end of year 1 is £33,000 (30% × $^{1}/_{3}$ × intrinsic value of £330,000).

  If the entity's accounting policy for determining the timing difference is based on the cumulative share-based payment charge and if the share options are expected to be exercised, there is no reason to 'cap' the deferred tax asset if the share-based payment charge does not exceed the total expected deduction. In the example in paragraph 13.127.6, the cumulative share-based payment charge is £120,000 and the expected future tax deduction of £330,000 covers this amount. Therefore, under this policy, at the end of year 1, the deferred tax asset is £36,000 (30% × £120,000).

However, there could be instances under this accounting policy where a low intrinsic value will result in a write down or a restriction on the deferred tax asset recognised. An example of such a situation is where the share options' total intrinsic value falls below the cumulative share-based payment charge. Therefore, in the example above, if at the end of year 1 the options' intrinsic value is less than £120,000, it may be considered appropriate to restrict the deferred tax asset to an amount based on the intrinsic value (assuming that the options are still expected to be exercised).

Intrinsic value is negative

- If the share options' intrinsic value is negative (that is, the options are out of the money) and is not expected to recover then, as noted in paragraph 13.127.3 above, this may mean that the options will not be exercised and a tax deduction will not be received. In this situation, a deferred tax asset is not recognised.

Cash-settled transactions

13.127.9 Cash-settled share based payment transactions, such as share appreciation rights issued to employees, give rise to a liability and not a credit to equity. The fair value of the liability is remeasured at each reporting date until the liability is settled. A timing difference arises on the cumulative difference between the share-based payment charge (remeasured to fair value) in the profit and loss account and the related deduction for tax purposes where that will be received in the future, resulting in a deferred tax asset (subject to FRS 19's recognition criteria). The tax effects of such transactions are recognised through the profit and loss account.

[The next paragraph is 13.128.]

Revaluation of non-monetary assets

General rule

13.128 Many companies revalue their non-monetary assets such as land and buildings. In the UK, revaluation of assets *per se* does not give rise to a timing difference, because taxable profits are not affected and no future tax liability arises as a result of the revaluation. However, to the extent that the valuation exceeds net book value, a potential timing difference arises, in that a balancing charge or tax on a chargeable gain may be payable if the asset is sold at its revalued amount.

13.128.1 Under FRS 19's incremental liability approach, an obligation for the deferred tax arises when the reporting entity enters into a binding sale agreement and not when the reporting entity decides, in principle, to sell the asset. An intention to sell, however compelling, is not sufficient for recognising deferred tax on a revaluation (under FRS 19). There must be a binding agreement that leaves the entity with no realistic chance of withdrawing from the sale and avoid paying tax. An asset that has been purchased with a view to resale such as stock does not create a binding sale agreement, even though the company in effect is committed to sell the stock. In other words, there must be an unconditional and irrevocable sales contract. Accordingly, FRS 19 requires that deferred tax should not be recognised on timing differences arising when non-monetary assets (other than those that are marked to market – see para 13.132 below) are revalued, unless, by the balance sheet date, the reporting entity has:

- entered into a binding agreement to sell the revalued assets; and
- recognised the gains and losses expected to arise on sale.

[FRS 19 para 14].

13.129 Where an unconditional and irrevocable contract has been entered into for the sale of a property before the year end, revenue and hence any profit arising on sale would also have been recognised at the time of exchange of contracts. It follows that any tax payable on the gain should similarly be recognised if the entity does not expect to claim rollover relief (see further para 13.137). Indeed, in practice, where an unconditional contract for the sale of a property has been exchanged before the year end but legal completion takes place after the year end, any tax payable on the gain would be provided as part of current tax, because under the tax rules a disposal for capital gains tax arises on the date when the contract is made. To the extent that the tax payable on the gain is not recognised as part of current tax, it should be recognised as part of deferred tax. On the other hand, if the contract is conditional, no profit on the sale and hence no tax payable would be recognised until all conditions have been satisfied.

13.130 It should be noted that to the extent that a revaluation gain that was previously recognised in the STRGL becomes realised as a result of the sale, any tax attributable to the gain should be charged to the STRGL as stated in paragraph 13.249 below.

Subsequent depreciation

13.130.1 When an asset has been revalued upwards, subsequent depreciation charges are based upon the revalued amount as opposed to original historical cost. Where there is no binding agreement to sell these revalued buildings no deferred tax is provided on the revaluation gains. However, a further question arises as to whether the deferred tax on the timing difference between capital allowances and accounting depreciation should be measured with reference to the historical cost depreciation or revalued depreciation.

13.130.2 Deferred tax should normally be provided on the difference between the capital allowances and the accounting depreciation charged to the profit and loss account. This is because a timing difference arises when tax deductions for the cost of a fixed asset are received before or after the cost of the fixed asset is recognised in the profit and loss account. In this case, however, the depreciation of the revaluation gain does not enter into the calculation of a timing difference, because there will never be a tax deduction for the revalued element of the building. The excess depreciation is an additional accounting cost and represents a permanent difference between the company's taxable and accounting profits. Consequently, deferred tax should be calculated using the 'historical' accounting depreciation, that is, in this case, the depreciation based on the building's original cost.

Subsequent devaluation and impairment

13.130.3 When a policy of revaluation is adopted, assets that have previously been subject to upward revaluation may subsequently be revalued downwards. If this devaluation takes the building below its original historical cost, management will need to judge whether this represents a clear consumption of economic benefit (an impairment) or whether the devaluation is temporary in nature. If there is a clear consumption of economic benefit an impairment loss will be recognised. FRS 19 does not appear to distinguish between revaluation gains and losses so it is not immediately clear how this impairment should be tax effected.

13.130.4 Paragraph 14 of FRS 19 applies equally to revaluation gains and losses. However, the standard does not define or clarify what it means by a 'revaluation'. We believe that the term revaluation should be interpreted in the normal way, that is, change in the carrying value of an asset as a result of value changes. Following the principles in FRS 11, 'Impairment of fixed assets and goodwill', and FRS 15, 'Tangible fixed assets', the tax effects of upward and downward changes in value that are reflected through the STRGL should not be tax effected, unless there is a binding agreement to sell the property and the gain or loss expected to arise on sale is recognised. All other changes in value (for example, impairments in the carrying value of assets that are dealt with through the profit and loss account) should be tax effected if the impairment represents a timing difference.

13.130.5 Where the revaluation loss is a clear consumption of economic benefits, it will be taken in full to the profit and loss account. The impairment will be treated as additional depreciation for accounting purposes, but the tax deductions will continue to be received on the cost of the building on a straight-line basis. Again it is necessary to go back to the principles set out above and to compare the extent to which the tax deductions on the cost of the building are received before or after the cost of the building is recognised in the profit and loss account. The amount of the impairment below depreciated historical cost will be treated as if it were depreciation on the historical cost; that is, it will reduce the difference between the tax written down value and the historical cost written down value and this will result in a partial reversal of deferred tax. To the extent that the reduction in value reverses a previous revaluation gain, this is a permanent difference, which is not tax effected.

Marked to market assets

13.131 Some companies have a policy of 'marking to market' current asset investments under which changes in fair values are reported in the profit and loss account, rather than in the revaluation reserve. This accounting policy ('fair valuing through profit or loss') is now included in FRS 26, 'Financial instruments: Recognition and measurement', and is required for certain types of financial assets and permitted for others if specified conditions are met. In many circumstances, the gains and losses are subject to current tax when they are recognised and no timing difference (and hence no deferred tax) arises. The question arises as to what would be the appropriate accounting treatment in circumstances where the gains and losses are not taxed until realised at a later date.

13.132 FRS 19 states that deferred tax *should* be recognised on timing differences arising when an asset is continuously revalued to fair value with changes in fair value being recognised in the profit and loss account. [FRS 19 para 12].

13.133 The above requirement is an exception to the general rule discussed in paragraph 13.128 above that deferred tax should be provided only when there is a binding agreement to sell the asset. The exception was introduced to address the concerns that it was wrong not to provide deferred tax on assets that are marked to market. To provide no deferred tax is considered to produce an incorrect answer in practice with the gain reported in the profit and loss account in one period and the tax on the gain reported in a subsequent period.

13.134 The limited exception ensures sensible results in the present tax and financial reporting regimes for those companies that adopt a policy of fair valuing through profit or loss account, without significantly altering the basic approach of the standard. As a corollary, the above requirement does not apply to other current asset investments that are revalued under the alternative accounting rules with gains and losses arising from the valuation reported in the revaluation reserve (see para 13.135.1 below). No deferred tax should be provided on them, unless they meet the criteria set out in paragraph 13.128 above.

13.135 The above requirement only applies when non-monetary assets are continuously fair valued with fluctuations being recognised in the profit and loss account. It would not apply, for instance, to situations where a one off downward revaluation of an asset, which is above historical cost but which is caused by a clear consumption of economic benefit, is recognised in the profit and loss account.

13.135.1 FRS 26 also introduced the concept of available-for-sale (AFS) financial assets. The accounting for these assets is dealt with in chapter 6. It results in fluctuations in the fair value of such assets being recognised in reserves, through the STRGL (although interest, foreign exchange and impairment losses are still taken directly to the profit and loss account). Similarly to those assets where the accounting policy is 'fair value through profit or loss', in many circumstances the fair value movements on AFS assets will be taxed immediately, so no deferred tax will arise. Where the fair value movements are not taxed as they arise (for example, certain overseas financial instruments), FRS 19's rules for revaluations apply and no deferred tax should be provided, unless the conditions in FRS 19 are met (see para 13.128 onwards).

13.135.2 In the UK, the tax rules with regards to gains and losses on financial instruments are complex. Depending on the elections made under the applicable tax rules, fair value gains and losses may either be taxable as they accrue for accounting purposes or may be taxable when realisation occurs at a later date. Consultation with a tax specialist is recommended in this area.

Rollover and holdover reliefs

13.136 On the disposal of certain assets used for trading purposes, such as properties, it may be possible to defer immediate payment of the tax arising on the chargeable gain provided the proceeds of the sale are reinvested within certain specified time limits in other qualifying assets. This relief, known as 'rollover relief', reduces the 'base cost' of the replacement asset by the chargeable gain 'rolled over' so that (subject to intervening period indexation) correspondingly higher tax may become payable when the replacement asset is sold. It is also possible to claim rollover relief on the gain arising on the sale of the replacement asset such that payment of the tax is further postponed. This situation can continue indefinitely.

13.137 FRS 19, therefore, states that deferred tax should not be recognised on timing differences arising when non-monetary assets (other than those referred to in para 13.132 above) are revalued or sold if, on the basis of all available evidence, it is more likely than not that the taxable gain will be rolled over, being charged to tax only if and when the assets into which the gain has been rolled over are sold. [FRS 19 para 15].

13.138 It is, therefore, important to take account of the possibility of obtaining rollover relief when assessing whether a tax liability will arise on the sale of an asset. This is because the relief has the effect of deferring the reversal of any timing differences arising on the revaluation of an asset beyond the sale date, or of creating a timing difference on the sale of an asset that has not been revalued, or a combination of the two. Consequently, where it is more likely than not that rollover relief will be claimed, then no deferred tax should be provided on the gain arising on disposal. However, there is a requirement in paragraph 13.286 to disclose the potential liability as rollover relief merely postpones, but does not extinguish the liability altogether. Even where an asset that has not been revalued is sold at a profit, there is no need to provide for the tax if the tax payable has been deferred by the operation of rollover relief, although again there is a need to disclose the potential liability.

13.139 Capital gains may also be 'held over' for a maximum of ten years with the result that tax payable on the gain is postponed for up to ten years. In that situation, as the tax is merely postponed and not permanently deferred, a timing difference arises and deferred tax on the gain should be provided in the normal way. Problems may arise, even in the tenth year, where under the tax rules the held-over gains are converted into rollover relief provided that qualifying assets are acquired in the 10-year hold over period. To the extent that the deferred tax liability remains unsettled, the company may need to review the position at each year end to determine whether any qualifying assets have been purchased against which the held-over gains can be rolled over. Where this is the case, any deferred tax previously recognised should be reversed by a credit to the profit and loss account.

13.140 Judgement is required to determine whether it is more likely than not that rollover relief would be available. However, no judgement is required and, therefore, no deferred tax would be provided if, in accordance with the tax rules, the company intends to roll the gain over onto a replacement asset that has been acquired or has entered into an unconditional contract to acquire the replacement asset within 12 months prior to the disposal of the existing asset. But judgement is required where the entity intends to invest the proceeds of sale in qualifying replacement assets within the period allowed under the tax rules. All available evidence, including the existence of approved budgets for capital expenditure, past pattern of claiming rollover relief, tax planning strategies and subsequent events should be considered to determine whether it is more likely than not that rollover relief would be claimed. If necessary, specialist tax advice should be sought to determine eligibility. If no deferred tax had been provided on sale and it subsequently transpires that no rollover relief would be claimed or that the terms of claiming the relief are unlikely to be met, any unprovided deferred tax should be provided immediately in the year as a change in estimate.

[The next paragraph is 13.142.]

Deferred tax assets

General rule

13.142 Timing differences may give rise to deferred tax assets. Common examples are tax losses carried forward and timing differences arising on provisions such as those made for refurbishment or those arising on pensions and retirement benefits where tax deductions are obtained only when the expenditure is actually incurred and not when the expense is recognised in the financial statements.

13.143 FRS 19 states that deferred tax assets should be recognised to the extent that they are regarded as recoverable. They should be regarded as recoverable to the extent that, on the basis of all available evidence, it can be regarded as more likely than not that there will be suitable taxable profits from which the future reversal of the underlying timing differences can be deducted. [FRS 19 para 23].

13.144 In order to recover a deferred tax asset, an entity would have to do more than simply *not make losses* in future: it would have to *make sufficient taxable profits*. Further, the need for prudence would suggest that more evidence of the likelihood of future profits was needed for recognition of a deferred tax asset than for recognition of a deferred tax liability. For these reasons, the FRS permits deferred tax assets to be recognised only when, on the basis of available evidence, it is more likely than not that there will be taxable profits in future against which the deferred tax asset can be offset. In other words, if it is more likely than not that either all or only a portion of the deferred tax asset will be recovered, a deferred tax asset should be recognised for the whole or the part that will be recovered.

13.145 The term 'more likely than not' is not defined in FRS 19, but paragraph 23 of FRS 12 suggests that it should be taken to mean that *'the probability that the event will occur is greater than the probability that it will not'*. In the US standard FAS 109, 'Income taxes', more likely than not is taken to mean a likelihood of more than 50 per cent. In IAS 12, a deferred tax asset is recognised if it is *probable* that the asset will be recovered. In IAS terminology, an event is regarded as probable if it is more likely than not to occur. Therefore, the more likely than not interpretation makes it clear that anything above 50 per cent qualifies for recognition.

13.146 However, paragraph 13.143 above also mentions that all available evidence has to be considered to justify recognition of deferred tax assets. This means both favourable and unfavourable evidence. If there is no unfavourable evidence, and the entity has historically been profitable and paid taxes, we believe FRS 19 permits an assumption that the situation will continue *in the absence of knowledge of facts to the contrary*. Reliance could be placed on expected future taxable profit in concluding that recording a deferred tax asset is appropriate. However, any unfavourable evidence must be considered carefully. Unfavourable evidence can usually be objectively verified, because it is a past event. However, estimates of future taxable profits can rarely be objectively verified; therefore, future taxable profits would be assigned lesser weight in assessing the appropriateness of recording a deferred tax asset when there is other unfavourable evidence.

Suitable taxable profits

13.147 As noted above, the future realisation of deferred tax assets ultimately depends on the expectation of sufficient taxable profit of the appropriate type (trading profit or capital gain). Sources of suitable taxable profit from which the future reversal of timing differences could be deducted are those that are:

- Generated in the same taxable entity (or in an entity whose taxable profits would be available for offset, for example under group relief rules) and assessed by the same taxation authority as the income or expenditure giving rise to the deferred tax asset.
- Generated in the same period as that in which the deferred tax asset is expected to reverse, or in a period to which a tax loss arising from the reversal of the deferred tax asset may be carried back or forward.
- Of a type (such as capital or trading) from which the taxation authority allows the reversal of the timing difference to be deducted.

[FRS 19 para 24].

13.148 In essence, the suitable taxable profits referred to above will be those against which the tax authority would permit the underlying timing difference in respect of the deferred tax asset to be offset.

Tax planning opportunities

13.149 The ASB acknowledges that entities sometimes take advantage of tax planning opportunities to reduce their future tax liabilities. FRS 19, therefore, permits an entity to create suitable taxable profits by undertaking tax planning opportunities. [FRS 19 para 25]. At first sight this may seem at odds with the general thrust of the standard that no account should be taken of future events. However, putting in place a tax scheme that may reduce future expenses or create additional income is, in substance, no different from procuring orders that will result in future sales. Both actions will create future taxable profits necessary for the recovery of the deferred tax asset.

13.150 A tax planning opportunity is an action that the entity would not normally take, but would do so to prevent, say, an unused tax loss from expiring. Such actions could include:

- Accelerating taxable amounts or deferring claims for writing down allowances to recover losses being carried forward (perhaps before they expire).
- Changing the character of taxable or deductible amounts from trading gains or losses to capital gains or losses or *vice versa*.
- Switching from tax-free to taxable investments.

[FRS 19 para 25].

13.151 Tax planning strategies should only be considered in determining the extent to which an existing deferred tax asset will be realised. They cannot be used to create a new deferred tax asset or to avoid recognition of, or reduce, a deferred tax liability (see para 13.154). The feasibility of the strategy would have to be assessed based on the individual facts and circumstances of each case. Whatever tax planning opportunities are considered, management must be capable of undertaking them and must have the ability to implement them.

13.152 A company may incur various expenses as a result of implementing a tax planning opportunity. A question arises as to whether the tax benefit of the expenses could be included in the carrying amount of any deferred tax asset recognised as a result of the plan's implementation, or included in current tax expense. We believe that any deferred tax asset recognised as a result of implementing a tax planning opportunity should be recorded net of the tax effects of any expenses or losses expected to be incurred as a result of the strategy, because that is the net amount by which future tax payments will be reduced as a result of implementing it. Consider the following example.

Example – Expenses of tax planning strategy

A company has gross timing differences of £1,000 in respect of a deferred tax asset which is not recognised in the balance sheet. The tax rate is 30% and the unrecognised deferred tax asset is, therefore, £300. As a result of implementing a tax planning strategy, the company expects to generate taxable profits of at least £1,000. However, the cost of implementing the strategy is expected to be £200. Therefore, only £800 of future taxable profits would be available against which the deferred tax asset can be offset. A maximum deferred tax asset of £240 (£800 @ 30%) would qualify for recognition. The remaining £60 will remain unrecognised. In other words, the deferred tax asset of £300 is reduced by £60, being the tax benefit of the expenses expected to be incurred as a result of implementing the tax planning strategy.

13.153 Similarly, where a tax planning opportunity is being used to support realisation of unused tax losses in a business combination that is an acquisition, the same principles apply, that is the benefit of any deferred tax asset recognised should also be reduced by the tax effects of any expenses or losses incurred to implement a tax planning opportunity.

13.154 Tax planning strategies cannot be taken into account to recognise a reduced deferred tax liability. For instance, a company cannot avoid recognising an existing deferred tax liability on the grounds that future tax losses will prevent the transfer of economic benefits.

13.155 Some examples of possible tax planning opportunities are considered below:

Example 1 – Sale of appreciated assets when operating losses are projected

A company has experienced a history of operating losses over the last five years with accumulated tax losses of £20m giving rise to a potential unrecognised deferred tax asset of £6m. Based on the introduction of a new product line, the company is currently projecting that for the next three years it will experience losses of approximately £5m in aggregate before it 'turns the corner' and becomes profitable. Due to appreciation in the real estate market, the company's investment in a shopping mall property is now valued at approximately £500,000 more than the carrying amount in the balance sheet. The company proposes to recognise a deferred tax asset of £150,000 (£500,000 × 30%) based on a tax planning opportunity to sell the investment. The shopping mall is not a 'core' asset of the entity, and management asserts that it would sell the shopping mall property, if necessary, before it would permit the unused tax losses to expire.

We believe that there is no case for recognising a deferred tax asset because of the above tax planning opportunity. A tax planning opportunity to sell appreciated assets constitutes a subset of the broader source of future taxable profit from operations. Thus, it would not be appropriate to recognise a deferred tax asset when it appears that the tax planning opportunity will merely reduce an expected future loss. In the above case, based on (1) the entity's history of losses, (2) an unproved new product line, and (3) the fact that the entity does not anticipate being profitable for at least three years, little weight can be assigned to the projection of profitability. Accordingly, there is no *incremental* tax benefit (at least for the foreseeable future), as the potential gain on the sale of the shopping mall property would only reduce what would otherwise be a larger operating loss.

Example 2 – Acquisition of a profitable company

A company that has incurred losses for many years proposes a tax planning opportunity to support its deferred tax asset related to unused tax losses. The company will use a portion of the cash balances it received from a recent public share offering to acquire a company that generates significant taxable profits. Could such a tax planning opportunity be considered for the recognition of the deferred tax asset?

No. We believe that a proposed business combination and, hence the availability of sufficient taxable profits, should not be anticipated for purposes of supporting a deferred tax asset. Until the acquisition of the company is irrevocable and there are no further statutory or regulatory impediments, the acquirer requires the co-operation of others to make the tax planning opportunity effective. That is, the acquirer does not control an essential part of the tax planning opportunity (the target company). Consequently, the tax effects of such an event (for example, the acquisition of a company) should not be recognised before the event has occurred. However, once the acquisition has taken place, the acquirer can recognise a deferred tax asset as a credit to the tax charge in the post-acquisition period in accordance with paragraph 22 of FRS 7 (as amended by paragraph 71 of FRS 19).

Example 3 – Unused tax losses in an acquiree

Company B has unrecognised deferred tax assets related to unused tax losses. Company C bought company B in December 20X3.

Company C's management intends to integrate company B's operations into company C in the first quarter of 20X4 in order to take advantage of the tax losses. Company C has a track record of generating taxable profits and management expects this to continue for the foreseeable future.

In this situation, management should recognise a deferred tax asset in respect of the unused tax losses in the consolidated financial statements for the period ended 31 December 20X3, provided that it is probable that management will carry out the integration and it is probable that company C will generate enough taxable profit to absorb company B's unused tax losses. This will impact the goodwill calculation in the consolidated financial statements.

This contrasts with the situation in example 2 above as both the newly-acquired entity holding the losses (company B) and the profitable entity (company C) are part of the same group at the balance sheet date.

Recovery of deferred tax assets against deferred tax liabilities

13.156 It can be assumed that the future reversal of any timing differences relating to deferred tax liabilities recognised at the balance sheet date will give rise to taxable profits. To the extent that those profits will be suitable for the deduction of the reversing deferred tax asset, the asset can always be regarded as recoverable. [FRS 19 para 26]. Therefore, where deferred tax liabilities exceed deferred tax assets and the reversal periods are consistent, recognition of the entire deferred tax asset is justified. The recoverability assessment becomes problematic, however, where there are insufficient deferred tax liabilities against which the deferred tax asset can be offset. In that situation, it is necessary to consider the likelihood of there being other suitable taxable profits as indicated in the following example.

Example – Recovery of deferred tax asset against deferred tax liabilities

A company has timing differences of £80,000 in respect of deferred tax liabilities that are expected to be included in taxable income at a rate of £20,000 a year in years one through four. The company also has a warranty provision of £40,000 that is expected to be deductible for tax purposes as follows: £30,000 and £10,000 in years two and three respectively. In addition to warranty provisions, the company has unused tax losses of £60,000. A schedule of the reversal of timing differences and the utilisation of tax losses carried forward is shown below:

	Year 1	Year 2	Year 3	Year 4
	£	£	£	£
Timing differences — deferred tax liabilities				
Opening balance	80,000	60,000	40,000	20,000
Recognised in taxable income	(20,000)	(20,000)	(20,000)	(20,000)
Closing balance	60,000	40,000	20,000	–
Timing differences — deferred tax assets				
Warranty provisions				
Opening balance	40,000	40,000	10,000	–
Deducted for tax purposes	–	(30,000)	(10,000)	–
Closing balance	40,000	10,000	–	–
Tax losses				
Opening balance	60,000	40,000	50,000	40,000
Increase (utilisation) in year	(20,000)	10,000	(10,000)	(20,000)
Closing balance	40,000	50,000	40,000	20,000
Total timing differences — deferred tax assets	80,000	60,000	40,000	20,000

At the end of year 1, the company would recognise a deferred tax asset in respect of at least £60,000 of timing differences at the appropriate tax rate. This is because there are timing differences in respect of deferred tax liabilities of the same amount that are expected to be included in taxable income and against which the expected reversal of the timing differences in respect of deferred tax assets can be utilised.

For similar reasons, a deferred tax asset in respect of at least £40,000 and £20,000 of timing differences would be recognised at the end of years 2 and 3 respectively, if circumstances remained the same at those dates.

However, in order to recognise a deferred tax asset in any of the years 1 to 4 with respect to the £20,000 of tax losses that remain unutilised, the company may have to look for other sources of taxable profit, other than reversals of timing differences, as indicated below.

Recovery of deferred tax assets against future taxable profits

13.157 As illustrated in the example in paragraph 13.156, to the extent that the deferred tax asset cannot be recovered against the reversal of deferred tax liabilities, it is necessary to consider other persuasive and reliable evidence suggesting that suitable taxable profits will be generated in future.

13.157.1 When projecting future taxable profits, the question arises as to whether such profits should take into account new originating timing differences (that is, timing differences arising on items first recognised after the current balance sheet date). FRS 19 does not specifically address this issue in the context of determining future taxable profits. Our preferred view is that new originating timing differences should not be taken into account in determining the future taxable profits available for the recovery of deferred tax assets at the balance sheet date. This is because the new originating timing differences will themselves reverse, so there is no overall impact on taxable profits.

13.157.2 To illustrate this, consider timing differences arising on new acquisitions of fixed assets in future periods.

- If the capital allowances exceed depreciation (the usual situation in the early years of a fixed asset's life), the excess deduction would reduce expected taxable profits if taken into account. However, as this timing difference relates to a future fixed asset, our preferred view is that the expected taxable profits are considered available to recover any existing deductible timing differences and losses, rather than covering the new timing difference. This is consistent with paragraph 25 of FRS 19, which states that an entity may take account of tax planning opportunities to create suitable taxable profits, such as deferring claims for writing down allowances to recover losses being carried forward before they expire – that is, future capital allowances do not have to be used to reduce expected taxable profits.
- If depreciation exceeds capital allowances, this would increase expected taxable profits if the timing difference is taken into account. However, the deferred tax asset arising from this timing difference will require future taxable profit in order to be recovered. Therefore, offset of the reversal of

the existing deducible timing differences against these new timing differences will not reduce the overall level of outstanding deductible timing differences. In effect, the new originating timing differences will themselves reverse, reducing future taxable profits so that there will be no net increase in future taxable profits when all future years are considered.

13.157.3 Therefore, our preferred view is that new originating timing differences should not normally be taken into account. Taxable profits in future periods that will be available for recovering deferred tax assets at the balance sheet date will include reversing/originating timing differences on assets and liabilities existing at the current balance sheet date, accounting profits adjusted for permanent differences and any expected tax planning opportunities that will generate taxable profits in future periods (see para 13.149 onwards).

13.157.4 Whilst this is our preferred view for the above reasons, we are aware that there is a more literal interpretation of FRS 19 that would not consider future taxable profits arising from new originating timing differences any differently than any other source of future taxable profits. If this more literal interpretation is adopted, it should be applied on a consistent basis to both new originating taxable timing differences and new originating deductible timing differences.

13.157.5 In any case, even if new originating timing differences are not normally taken into account in determining the sufficiency of taxable profits. careful analysis is needed where losses cannot be carried forward indefinitely. Under FRS 19, a deferred tax asset is recognised where tax planning opportunities are available to the entity that will create taxable profit in appropriate periods (see para 13.149 onwards). This can mean that unused losses are recoverable out of taxable profits made available by deferring claims for deductions (thus creating a deductible timing difference). A similar situation arises, without tax planning, where deductions are given under the relevant tax rules in later periods than the related accounting charge (again creating a deductible timing difference).

13.157.6 Particular issues arise where profit forecasts include the amounts relevant for tax purposes (rather than the accounting deductions) and losses that would otherwise expire are only recoverable against taxable profits arising as a result of future deductible timing differences. In such cases, those taxable profits can only be taken into account if the deferred tax assets relating to the future deductible timing differences can also be recovered subsequently. This is illustrated in the following example.

Example – Interaction of losses and deductible timing differences

An entity has unused losses of £300,000 and is assessing whether it can recognise a deferred tax asset. The losses expire in 5 years' time. In the next year (year 1) the entity is forecasting an accounting loss of £100,000, but this is after charging £400,000 for a loss on a loan. The tax deduction for the loan can be deferred, and the entity intends to claim this after year 5 (that is, in years 6 to 10).

Accounting profits in years 2 to 5 are forecast to be nil, and in years 6 to 10 to be £600,000 in total.

	Years 1 to 5 £'000	Years 6 to 10 £'000	Total £'000
Accounting result before loan loss	300	600	900
Loan loss	(400)	–	(400)
Accounting result	(100)	600	500
Taxable profit before loan loss deduction	300	600	900
Loan loss deduction	–	(400)	(400)
Loss carry-forwards utilised	(300)	–	(300)
Taxable profit	–	200	200

Overall, there are sufficient taxable profits (£900,000) to recover both the loss carry-forwards (£300,000) and the loan loss deduction (£400,000). Therefore, a deferred tax asset in respect of the loss carry-forwards is recognised in the current year.

13.157.7 The underlying principle in FRS 19 that deferred tax assets should be recognised to the extent they are regarded as recoverable means that recognition of a deferred tax asset is appropriate where an otherwise profitable entity has expiring unused losses that can be recovered by tax planning (or other deferral of deductions), which creates originating deductible timing differences that are themselves subsequently recoverable.

13.157.8 The projection of future taxable profits becomes difficult where the deferred tax asset arises from unrelieved trading losses, because the very existence of such losses may indicate significant uncertainty about the availability of future taxable profit. It is because of this uncertainty that the standard calls for the disclosure of the amount of deferred tax asset and the nature of the evidence supporting its recognition in the absence of profits arising from the reversals of existing timing differences (see para 13.272 below).

13.157.9 There are certain entities that, by their nature, would not ordinarily recognise deferred tax assets not supported through reversals of existing timing differences. Examples of such entities include development stage enterprises and start-up businesses. In these cases, the lack of a track record for profits means that it is unlikely that a deferred tax asset can be recognised. As noted in paragraph 13.146, evidence of future taxable profits may be assigned lesser weight in assessing the appropriateness of recording a deferred tax asset when there is other unfavourable evidence (such as actual trading losses). An exception might be where the entity has a contract in place that provides a future revenue stream (which exceeds expected costs).

13.157.10 The assessment of the likelihood that taxable profits will arise when there has been a history of trading losses is discussed in the paragraphs below.

Trading losses

13.158 Where a company incurs a trading loss for tax purposes, that loss, which is determined after the deduction of any capital allowances given in that trade, may be set off against other profits (including chargeable gains) made in the same accounting period. To the extent that it cannot be used against the current period's profits, it can be carried back against profits of the preceding year. Any trading losses of a company that are not relieved by offset against current profits or profits of the previous period can be carried forward to be set off against the first available profits of the same trade for subsequent accounting periods.

13.159 Therefore, where a company has tax losses that can be relieved against a tax liability for a previous year, it is appropriate to recognise those losses as an asset, because the tax relief is recoverable by refund of tax previously paid. This asset can be shown either separately in the financial statements as a debtor, or offset against an existing deferred tax balance.

13.160 Where tax losses can be relieved only by carry-forward against taxable profits of future periods, a timing difference arises. [FRS 19 para 2]. If the company is maintaining a deferred tax account that will result in future tax payable, then the tax losses will be recoverable by offset against taxable income that arises when those timing differences will reverse. Accordingly, losses carried forward can be set off against deferred tax liabilities carried in the balance sheet.

13.161 To the extent that the deferred tax liabilities are not sufficient to absorb all the tax losses, it is necessary to consider other 'persuasive and reliable evidence' suggesting that suitable taxable profits will be generated in future. [FRS 19 para 29]. In the case of unrelieved trading losses, such evidence may exist if both of the following conditions are satisfied:

- The loss resulted from an identifiable and non-recurring cause.
- The reporting entity has been consistently profitable over a long period, with any past losses being more than offset by income in later periods.

[FRS 19 para 30].

13.162 A strong earnings history will provide the most objective evidence in assuming future profitability when assessing the extent to which a deferred tax asset can be recognised. This justification becomes stronger if the tax loss arises from identifiable causes that are unlikely to recur as stated above. Hence, there would be less need for profitable companies to consider the pattern and timing of the reversals of existing timing differences.

13.163 The very existence of losses will often provide strong evidence that they may not be recovered. The ASB's reasons for setting a 'more likely than not' threshold for the recognition of all deferred tax assets are set out in Appendix V, paragraphs 78 and 79 of FRS 19.

13.164 For companies with no record of profit in recent years a more rigorous assessment is required of the probability that taxable profit will be available against which unrelieved tax losses can be utilised. If it is expected that it will take some time for tax losses to be relieved, the recoverability of the resulting deferred tax asset is likely to be relatively uncertain. In such circumstances, it may not be appropriate to recognise the deferred tax asset at all. [FRS 19 para 32]. See also paragraph 13.157.6 for start-up entities.

13.164.1 Where an entity is determining its future taxable profits to support recognising a deferred tax asset for trading losses, a tax planning opportunity that it could undertake to allow the deferred tax asset to be recovered would be considered (see para 13.149 onwards). On the other hand, a restructuring or exit plan would normally be regarded as an ordinary part of running a business and might be considered depending on the likelihood of implementing the plan and its expected success. This is illustrated in the following example.

Example – Strategy to implement an exit plan

A company has a history of recent losses. Management has developed an exit plan in which a loss-making activity will be discontinued. Management intends to implement the measures from March 20X4. The current date is January 20X4 and the plan has not yet been made public.

Management expects to reverse the losses over the two years following the implementation of the exit plan and proposes that a deferred tax asset in respect of the losses is recognised in the 31 December 20X3 financial statements, using the exit plan to justify the recognition of the deferred tax asset.

A deferred tax asset should be recognised in respect of the losses to the extent that it is probable that future taxable profit will be available against which the unused tax losses can be utilised.

The assessment of whether future taxable profits are probable should be undertaken based on circumstances as at the balance sheet date.

Consideration should be given to the following factors as at the balance sheet date:

- The probability that management will implement the plan.
- Management's ability to implement the plan (for example, obtaining concessions from labour unions or regulatory approval).
- The level of detailed analysis and sensitivity analysis that management has prepared.

Judgement will be required to establish whether it is probable that the exit plan will go ahead and that taxable profits will be earned. If, at the balance sheet date, management has not yet finalised its decision to sell, it may be difficult to argue that it is more likely than not that the exit plan will be implemented.

Capital losses

13.165 Whereas trading losses can be offset against chargeable gains, capital losses cannot be offset against trading profits. Where a company makes capital losses in an accounting period, those losses can generally be set off only against chargeable gains which it makes in the same period. If those capital losses are greater than the chargeable gains, they may be set off against gains of a later accounting period.

13.166 A capital loss that is available to relieve against chargeable gains creates a timing difference. However, as a deferred tax asset in respect of a capital loss cannot be offset against deferred tax liabilities arising from trading items, because of the offset rules in tax legislation, a deferred tax asset in respect of a capital loss will be recognised only if there is strong evidence that it will be recoverable against any available chargeable gains. Such evidence will exist only if:

- A potential chargeable gain not expected to be covered by rollover relief is present in assets, but has not been recognised as a deferred tax liability.
- Plans are in place for the sale of these assets.
- The carried-forward loss will be offset against the resulting chargeable gain for tax purposes.

[FRS 19 para 31].

In the context of the second point above, it is not necessary to have a binding sale agreement, only adequate evidence that it is more likely than not that a sale will take place.

Effect of a going concern uncertainty

13.167 FRS 18, 'Accounting policies', paragraph 61, requires disclosure when management concludes that uncertainty exists regarding an entity's ability to continue as a going concern for a reasonable period of time (usually understood to be at least one year from the date of approval of the financial statements). The inclusion of such disclosure would, in most situations, constitute significant unfavourable evidence under FRS 19 and recognition of all or a portion of a deferred tax asset would not be justified, unless realisation is assured by either (a) carry-back to prior tax years or (b) reversals of existing timing differences. However, there may be circumstances where the cause for the going concern uncertainty is not directly related to the entity's profitability. For example, the uncertainty may arise from concerns relating to liquidity or from other issues unrelated to profitability (for example, uncertainty relating to the renewal of an operating licence) while it is expected that the entity will continue to generate taxable profits. In these situations, recognising a deferred tax asset may be appropriate provided it is probable, although not certain, that future taxable profits will be available. The specific facts and circumstances giving rise to the going concern uncertainty should be considered in determining whether a deferred tax asset is recoverable. Additionally, the absence of significant uncertainty regarding an entity's ability to continue as a going concern, does not, by itself, constitute favourable evidence about the realisation of deferred tax assets.

13.168 In addition to going-concern considerations, there are certain entities that, by their nature, would not ordinarily recognise deferred tax assets not supported through either carry-back or reversals of existing timing differences. Examples of such entities include development stage enterprises, start-up businesses and entities emerging from a financial reorganisation or bankruptcy.

Reassessment of recoverability

13.169 The carrying amount of a deferred tax asset should be reviewed at each balance sheet date. This means that an entity would need to assess whether a net deferred tax asset recognised in the balance sheet is still recoverable and has not been impaired. For example, an entity may have recognised a deferred tax asset in respect of tax losses in a previous period based on information then available. A year later circumstances may have changed such that it is no longer probable that the entity would earn sufficient future taxable profits to absorb all the tax benefit. In that situation, the asset has suffered an impairment and should be written down. If circumstances giving rise to the previous write down no longer apply or it is probable that sufficient future taxable profit will be available, the reduction should be reversed.

13.170 Similarly, where an entity has been unable to recognise a deferred tax asset because of the unavailability of sufficient taxable profit, it should review the situation at each subsequent balance sheet date to ascertain whether some or all of the unrecognised balance should now be recognised. For example, an improvement in trading conditions or the acquisition of a new subsidiary might make it more likely that a previously unrecognised tax loss in the acquiring entity will be recovered. The recognition of a previously unrecognised deferred tax asset is a change in estimate that should be reflected in the results for the year as required by FRS 3, 'Reporting financial performance'. [FRS 19 para 33]. See further paragraph 13.252.1 onwards below.

Measurement issues

Introduction

13.171 FRS 19 requires deferred tax to be measured at the average tax rates that are expected to apply in the periods in which the timing differences are expected to reverse, based on tax rates and laws that have been enacted or substantively enacted by the balance sheet date. [FRS 19 para 37].

13.172 Timing differences may reverse over many years and, since the rate of tax will not normally be known in advance of those years, FRS 19 requires the use of a rate that has been enacted or substantively enacted by the balance sheet date.

Enacted means that the rate is part of tax law. The meaning of substantively enacted is considered in paragraph 13.45 above.

Average rates

13.173 It will normally be necessary to calculate an average tax rate only if the enacted or substantively enacted tax rates are graduated, that is, if different rates apply to different levels of taxable income. [FRS 19 para 38]. For instance, if the first five million of profit is taxed at the rate of 20 per cent and profit thereafter at 30 per cent, an average tax rate is used for measuring deferred tax liabilities and assets. This average rate is the rate that is expected to apply to taxable profit (or loss) in the years in which the liability or the asset is expected to be settled or recovered. To calculate the average tax rate it is necessary to estimate the levels of profits expected in the periods in which the timing differences reverse. [FRS 19 para 38]. In the above example, the estimated average rate will need to be calculated where the entity expects to earn annual taxable profit in excess of five million in the future. In order to determine a single average rate, which would be greater than 20 per cent but less than 30 per cent, it would be necessary to estimate future annual taxable profits, including reversing timing differences. Although a detailed analysis to determine the net reversals of timing differences in respect of deferred tax assets and liabilities is usually not warranted, consideration should be given to the effect of an abnormal level of taxable profit or any abnormally large timing difference that may reverse in a single future year and cause the average rate to be distorted.

13.174 The above situation may well arise in the UK for companies whose profits fall within the 'marginal bands' above the small companies rate (see para 13.8 above). These companies should generally provide deferred tax at the rate used in the past on the assumption that profits would continue at a comparable level. Where future profits are expected to be higher and there is reliable evidence to support this level of profit, it may be appropriate to use the rate applicable to that rate of profit. Where it is impossible to determine whether marginal relief will apply, it would be prudent to measure deferred tax at the standard corporation tax rate.

13.175 The requirement to calculate an average tax rate is not intended to lead to averaging of different rates expected to apply to different types of taxable profit or in different tax jurisdictions. If different rates of tax apply to different types of taxable profits (for example, trading profits and capital gains), the rate used will reflect the nature of the timing difference. The rates used for measuring deferred tax arising in a specific tax jurisdiction will be the rates expected to apply in that jurisdiction. [FRS 19 para 39].

Change in tax rates

13.175.1 The tax rate applicable to an entity may change as a result of changes in relevant legislation. The impact of such changes in tax rate will vary depending on the nature and timing of the legislative changes made. Any impact of the changes will be recognised in accounting periods ending on or after the date of substantive enactment (and may be disclosable prior to that date). In many cases, changes in tax rates will be prospective and thus there will be no impact on current tax assets and liabilities that have arisen prior to the effective date of the change. However, deferred tax balances are likely to be affected. Professional advice from tax advisors on how the changes impact on the company's tax position is likely to be necessary.

Example – Change in tax rates

A change in tax rate from 30% to 28% was substantively enacted on 26 June 20X7 with effect from 1 April 20X8. The change of tax rates will have no impact on current tax assets or liabilities arising prior to the effective date of the change. However, the measurement of deferred tax assets and liabilities will be impacted for accounting periods (including interim periods) ending on or after 26 June 20X7.

Deferred tax balances will need to be analysed to determine when they are expected to reverse and the tax rate that will be applicable in the period of reversal. The reduction in tax rate will not impact on deferred tax that is expected to reverse prior to 1 April 20X8. However, it will impact on subsequent reversals and will be further complicated for companies with a financial year that straddles 1 April 20X8 as, in that situation, the company will need to compute an effective tax rate for reversals in the financial year in which the change takes effect.

In accounting for the impact of this reduction in tax rate, it will be necessary to consider whether the impact will be reflected through the profit and loss account or the STRGL (see further para 13.249 below).

For accounting periods ending prior to 26 June 20X7, the change in tax rate would be disclosable as a non-adjusting post-balance sheet event in accordance with paragraph 22(h) of FRS 21, 'Events after the balance sheet date', to the extent that the impact is material.

Discounting

Introduction

13.176 Perhaps the most significant aspect of FRS 19 is the option for entities to adopt a policy of discounting deferred tax balances. FRS 19 states that reporting entities are permitted but not required to discount deferred tax assets and liabilities to reflect the time value of money. [FRS 19 para 42].

13.177 Discounting is also not permitted by any other major standard setters and specifically prohibited in IAS 12.

13.178 The arguments for and against discounting and the reasons why discounting has been made optional are set out in great detail from paragraph 85 in Appendix V of FRS 19. However, on closer inspection, the discounting methodology set out in the standard may not be so simple in its effect.

It could give rise to practical difficulties that make the discounted liability a more subjective figure.

13.179 Where it is necessary to choose between accounting policies, an entity should select whichever of those accounting policies is judged by the entity to be most appropriate to its particular circumstances for the purposes of giving a true and fair view. [FRS 18 para 17]. The FRS, therefore, provides the following list of factors that are likely to be especially relevant to the selection process:

- How material the impact of discounting would tend to be to the overall results and position reported in the entity's financial statements.
- Whether the benefits of discounting to users would outweigh the costs of collating the necessary information and performing discounting calculations.
- Whether there is an established industry practice, adherence to which would enhance comparability.

[FRS 19 para 43].

13.180 In practice, however, the effect of discounting accelerated capital allowances (arguably the most complex discounting calculation) is most likely to be material where:

- The reporting entity invests heavily in long-life fixed assets that are eligible for capital allowances early in their lives (for example, assets located in certain enterprise zones that qualify for 100 per cent first year allowances).
- The prevailing interest rate is high.
- The effect of discounting has been material to the financial statements as a whole in previous periods.

An example of a company that has considered the likely impact of discounting deferred tax liabilities in respect of accelerated capital allowances is given in the Table 13.2 below.

Table 13.2 – Severn Trent plc – Annual Report & Accounts – 31 March 2001

Notes to the financial statements (extract)

17 Provisions for liabilities and charges* (extract)

The accounting standard FRS 19, requiring full provision for deferred tax, will be adopted by the group in the year ended 31 March 2002. It is intended that, where material, the group will adopt a policy of discounting. If FRS 19 had been adopted for the year ended 31 March 2001, the tax charge would have been increased by £52.6 million, and a deferred tax liability of £324.1 million would have been reflected in the balance sheet as follows:

	2001
	£m
Origination and reversal of timing differences	65.1
Increase in discount	(12.5)
Total deferred tax charge	52.6

The provision for deferred tax would be disclosed as follows:

	2001	2000
	£m	£m
Accelerated capital allowances	750.0	685.3
Tax losses/other reliefs carried forward	(50.5)	(56.2)
Undiscounted provision for deferred tax	699.5	629.1
Discount	(375.4)	(362.9)
Discounted provision for deferred tax	324.1	266.2
Provision at start of period	266.2	
Deferred tax charge for period (above)	52.6	
Movements arising on acquisition of businesses	5.3	
Provision at end of period	324.1	

* *Note that, for years beginning on or after 1 January 2005, the statutory line item was renamed 'provisions for liabilities' in company legislation.*

13.181 All the above factors mentioned in paragraph 13.179 above and the way they interact with each other would need to be considered. It is impossible to single out one variable that would be significant enough to merit performing discounting calculations. Therefore, notwithstanding this guidance, the choice of whether to discount or not is unlikely to be an easy one. In practice, companies may well need to perform the calculations and consider the results before deciding whether to adopt a policy of discounting.

13.182 It should be noted that discounting would have the effect of making the effective tax rate (total tax charge as a percentage of profit before tax) volatile. This is because, as explained in paragraph 90 of Appendix V of FRS 19, under discounting, the benefit of receiving capital allowances on the acquisition of an asset will give rise to an instant credit in the profit and loss account. Undiscounted full provision, on the other hand, would produce a constant effective tax rate if permanent differences were ignored. Therefore, it would be necessary to carry out the trial calculation over a period and not just at a point in time to consider the implications that discounting would have on the stability of the effective tax rates.

It may well be that most companies conclude that the complexity of the calculation, the cost involved and the volatile result outweigh the benefit of recording a lower liability.

13.183 Where a reporting entity adopts a policy of discounting, FRS 19 requires that all deferred tax (and recoverable advance corporation tax) balances that have been measured by reference to undiscounted cash flows and for which the impact of discounting is material should be discounted. [FRS 19 para 44].

13.184 Discounting deferred tax assets and liabilities is only valid if the timing differences underlying those assets and liabilities give rise to future cash flows that are not already measured at their present value. This would apply, for example, to deferred tax arising on assets that are continuously marked to market and accelerated capital allowances. For some items, it would not be appropriate to discount the tax effects of the underlying timing differences that are already stated at their present values. Typical examples are long-term provisions measured on a discounted basis under FRS 12 and pension accruals.

Mechanics of the discounting calculation

13.185 In order to perform the discounting calculation, it is first necessary to schedule out or forecast the timing of the future tax cash flows that the deferred tax represents. For some items in the financial statements (for example, finance lease obligations) the dates and amounts of cash flows are known in advance. Where deferred tax is concerned, however, there is no equivalent pre-determined payment schedule and, therefore, it is necessary to determine what in principle are the future cash flows to which discounting should be applied.

13.186 Two approaches were considered by the ASB as noted in paragraph 106 of Appendix V of FRS 19. These are:

- *The full reversal method* under which the future cash flows are treated as occurring when the timing differences constituting the deferred tax balance at the year end are expected to reverse. In other words, as every individual reversing timing difference has the effect of increasing or decreasing the amount of tax cash flow in the year of reversal, the reversals of all timing differences at the balance sheet date are scheduled on a year-by-year basis. The tax effects on those reversals are calculated and discounted.

- *The net reversal method* under which the future cash flows are treated as occurring when the timing differences as a whole (that is, after taking account of new timing differences to replace those that reverse) are expected to reduce. In other words, the estimated payments of deferred tax (after taking account of the tax effects of likely future transactions) are discounted based on their expected year of payment.

13.187 The full reversal approach is appropriate to deferred tax calculated on a full provision basis as it does not take into account the tax effects of future transactions. It is, therefore, the approach adopted under the standard. The net reversal approach is rejected on the grounds that it can only be justified within a partial provision framework (see paras 107 and 108 in App V of FRS 19 for a fuller explanation).

Example

The company has estimated the following tax losses and profits:

Year 0	Year 1	Year 2	Year 3
(100)	(100)	100	100

The company is satisfied that it is 'more likely than not' that there will be suitable taxable profits. The losses are due to an identifiable and non-recurring cause and the reporting entity has otherwise been consistently profitable over a long period, with any past losses being more than offset by income in later periods. A deferred tax asset is, therefore, being recognised in year 0. Is the discount period for the asset to year 2 or to year 3?

Paragraph 47 of FRS 19 says that in scheduling the reversal of the timing differences no account should be taken of future tax losses, that is a full reversal rather than a net reversal basis should be used. Therefore, the tax losses in year 1 should be ignored and the reversal of the losses in year 0 should be taken to occur in year 2 from which date the asset should be discounted. This is also true of the asset to be recognised at the end of year 1, being discounted to year 3.

13.188 Once the cash flows have been scheduled out, the discounted amount is then calculated by applying an appropriate discount rate to the undiscounted cash flows. FRS 19 provides detailed guidance as to how the discounting calculations should be performed.

Scheduling the cash flows to be discounted

13.189 In scheduling the cash flows to be discounted, the following factors should be considered:

- The discount period(s) should be the number of years between the balance sheet date and the date(s) on which it is estimated that the underlying timing differences will reverse. [FRS 19 para 47].

  In practice, a round number of years should be used rather than the date on which the implicit tax cash flows occur. The assumption that timing differences would reverse at the end of each period is generally consistent with normal discounting calculation and is unlikely to introduce any material difference in the calculation.

- Assumptions made when estimating the date(s) of reversal should be consistent with those made elsewhere in the financial statements. [FRS 19 para 47].

Certain assumptions would have to be made when scheduling the reversals of the timing differences. For instance, the assumptions about future depreciation charges and residual values should be consistent with those used to account for the related fixed asset. Again, this is a simplification because in practice, residual values used in estimating depreciation rates are based on prices prevailing at the date of purchase (or revaluation) and these are unlikely to be the same as sales proceeds that may crystallise a balancing charge/allowance or reduce the capital allowance pool on which future capital allowances are received.

- The scheduling of the reversal(s) should take into account the remaining tax effects of transactions that have already been reflected in the financial statements. However, no account should be taken either of other timing differences expected to arise on future transactions or of future tax losses. [FRS 19 para 47].

  The requirement to schedule the reversals by taking account of the 'remaining tax effects' of transactions is crucial to the discounting calculation. The implication is that both reversing timing differences that have arisen at the balance sheet date and further originating timing differences that will arise in the future in respect of past transactions would have to be included in the scheduling. In the context of accelerated capital allowances, this means taking account of the remaining capital allowances to be received on assets 'held at the balance sheet date' on which timing differences have arisen, but without taking into consideration timing differences that might arise from future capital expenditure that is only appropriate under a partial provision model.

  It was suggested that the remaining capital allowances should be ignored on the grounds that they were future events that created further timing differences (rather than delaying the reversal of the existing timing differences). The existing timing differences would be viewed as reversing as soon as further depreciation occurred. However, the Board did not view the remaining capital allowances as arising from future events. Rather it regarded the allowances, like depreciation, as one of the expected consequences of a past event (the purchase of an asset) that had to be taken into account in measuring the tax liability arising from that event [FRS 19 App V para 109].

  The reversal of timing differences may occur in periods in which it is also expected that the entity will make tax losses. Any tax payments arising on the reversal of timing differences will, therefore, be postponed until the tax losses themselves are relieved. Since it would be difficult to forecast patterns of future losses reliably, especially those expected to arise in later years, (that is, those for which discounting would be most relevant), the scheduling of reversals should be carried out without taking account of the incidence of future tax losses. [FRS 19 para 49].

13.190 FRS 19 indicates that if a policy of discounting is chosen, all deferred tax balances that have been measured by reference to undiscounted cash flows and for which the impact of discounting is material, should be discounted. If a company has a very large fixed assets base, the question arises as to whether it is acceptable to group like assets together, and discount the deferred tax relating to the groups rather than to individual assets. Paragraph 48 of FRS 19 states (in relation to future depreciation charges and residual values of fixed assets) that *'it may be possible to use approximations or averages to simplify the calculations without introducing material errors'*. In addition, the example in Appendix 1 of FRS 19, which deals with discounting, uses an example that relates to a pool of plant and machinery. This implies that the FRS permits grouping of assets and use of approximations and averages where this does not produce material error. Clearly the selection of groups needs to avoid introducing material error into the calculations, but it would appear to be permitted by the standard.

Scheduling timing differences in respect of marked to market assets

13.191 The present value of any additional tax payable on the sale of an asset that is continuously revalued to fair values (through the profit and loss account) would depend on the timing of the tax cash flow. Since it would not be possible for an entity to identify when that tax would be payable, estimates would have to be made. It would be necessary for the company to examine the past pattern of sales, average portfolio churn etc to determine a reasonable estimate. [FRS 19 para 51]. It may be that in practice the portfolio is churned over a fairly short period, in which case the impact of discounting may not be material.

Discount rates

13.192 In determining a suitable discount rate, FRS 19 states that the discount rates should be the post-tax yields to maturity that could be obtained at the balance sheet date on government bonds with maturity dates and in currencies similar to those of the deferred tax assets or liabilities. [FRS 19 para 52]. (See further FRS 19 App V paras 113-119.)

13.193 Yields to maturity (redemption yields) of UK gilts are published daily. They are categorised under shorts (lives up to five years), five to ten years, ten to fifteen years and over fifteen years. The redemption yields quoted are gross redemption yields and, therefore, it would necessary to obtain the post-tax yield (quoted yield less tax at the enacted or substantially enacted rate) for discounting purposes. [FRS 19 para 53].

13.194 It should be possible to obtain a gilt yield with the same maturity as the period over which the underlying timing differences reverse. For instance, if the timing differences reverse before the earliest period for which a quote is available, it would be acceptable to use the earliest quoted rate. Where quoted yields are not available for particular maturity periods, it should be possible to derive an estimated rate by simple linear interpolation without introducing any significant error in the calculation. Where the rest of the discounting period is large, it would be acceptable to group the periods into short-term, medium-term and long-term and use a single discount rate for each period without introducing material differences in the discounting calculation. In the case of very long-lived assets (for example, infrastructure assets with lives of over 30 years), there may not be any UK gilt with maturity dates that correspond with the period over which the timing differences reverse. In that situation, the redemption yield for gilts with the longest maturity date available (likely to be 30 years) should be used. In other words, all timing differences reversing in years 30 onwards are treated as reversing in year 30. This is because the effect of estimating a rate for reversals beyond 30 years is unlikely to be material to the overall calculation.

13.195 For multinational groups adopting a policy of discounting, it would be necessary to match the discount rate with the maturity date and currency of the deferred tax asset or liability arising in each different tax jurisdiction. Therefore, the government bond rates should be those of the countries in which the timing difference arises. Bond yields of varying maturities for major economies are also found in the World bond prices section of the FT. In practice, for consolidation purposes, the group reporting packs would probably require foreign subsidiaries to provide data on their local government bond yield rates for various maturity dates for the discounting calculation to be performed at the group level.

Worked examples

13.196 The following example illustrates the principles of the discounting methodology discussed above.

Example 1 – Discounting deferred tax liabilities

A company has timing differences of £100,000 in respect of deferred tax liabilities at 31 December 20X0. These timing differences are expected to be included in taxable income at £40,000 in 20X3 and at £60,000 in 20X5. The tax rate is 30%. The three year and five year redemption yield on UK Treasury gilts are as follows:

Description of gilt	Years to maturity	Redemption yield %	Post-tax (yield less tax at 30%)
Tr 6½pc 'X3	3	5.21	3.65
Tr 8½pc 'X5	5	5.15	3.61

Without discounting

In the absence of discounting, the company would provide deferred tax of £30,000 (£100,000 @ 30%). This amount would reduce to £18,000 (£60,000 @ 30%) at 31 December 20X3 following reversal of £40,000 of timing differences. The liability would reduce to nil by 31 December 20X5 when the remaining timing difference of £60,000 reverses.

With discounting

The following table shows the discounted liability on the assumption that all future reversals occur at the end of the year:

Table 1 — Computation of discounted deferred tax liability as at 31 December 20X0

	31 December 20X3	31 December 20X5	Total
Reversing timing differences	£40,000	£60,000	£100,000
Undiscounted tax @ 30%	£12,000	£18,000	£30,000
Post-tax yield	3.65%	3.61%	
Discount factor	$1/(1+0.0365)_3$ = 0.8981	$1/(1+0.0361)_5$ = 0.8377	
Discounted deferred tax	£12,000 × 0.8981 = £10,777	£18,000 × 0.8377 = £15,078	= £25,855

As can be seen from the above table, the total discounted deferred tax liability is £25,855 which amounts to 86% of the total undiscounted liability. If a reduction of 14% is considered to be material to the financial statements as a whole, discounting would be necessary if the entity has adopted a policy of discounting deferred tax assets and liabilities. It should be noted that each reversing timing difference would need to be discounted separately by reference to the period in which it reverses. So the company would need to keep track of each reversal. This tracking becomes important since the unwinding effect of the discounting would need to be calculated for each reversal by reference to the same Treasury gilt yield for one year less as shown in the table below:

Table 2 — Computation of the unwinding of the discount for the year ended 31 December 20X1

	31 December 20X3	31 December 20X5	Total
Reversing timing differences	£40,000	£60,000	£100,000
Undiscounted tax @ 30%	£12,000	£18,000	£30,000
Post-tax yield	3.65%	3.61%	
Discount factor — one year less than maturity period	$1/(1+0.0365)_2$ = 0.9308	$1/(1+0.0361)_4$ = 0.8679	
Discounted deferred tax	£12,000 × 0.9308 = £11,170	£18,000 × 0.8679 = £15,622	= £26,792
Discounted deferred tax as previously calculated in Table 1	= £10,777	= £15,078	= £25,855
Unwinding of the discount	£393	£544	£937

The unwinding of the discount of £937 would be reported as part of the tax charge and not as part of the interest cost (see para 13.198 below). In practice, however, the unwinding effect could be calculated simply by applying the previous post-tax discount rate to the opening discounted deferred tax liability in respect of each reversal as shown below:

Opening discounted deferred tax for 20X3 reversal	£10,777 × 3.65% =	£393
Opening discounted deferred tax for 20X5 reversal	£15,078 × 3.61% =	£544
Total effect of unwinding of the discount for 20X1		£937

Obviously, the treasury gilt yield rates are unlikely to remain constant over the terms of the reversals. Therefore, the discounted deferred tax liability would change as the discount rate changes. In addition, for the year ended 31 December 20X1, the maturity periods of the reversals would reduce by one year. As a result, the appropriate discount rates would be the 2 year and 4 year post-tax Treasury gilt redemption yields as at 31 December 20X1.

Suppose the 2 year and the 4 year redemption yield on UK Treasury gilts are as follows:

Description of gilt	Years to maturity	Redemption yield %	Post-tax (yield less tax at 30%)
Tr 6½pc 'X3	2	5.24	3.67
Tr 8½pc 'X5	4	5.18	3.63

Table 3 shows the discounted liability at 31 December 20X1 calculated by reference to above gilt yields. It would be acceptable in practice to use a single discount rate where the rates applicable to each reversing period are close to each other (see also para 13.194).

Table 3 — Computation of discounted deferred tax liability as at 31 December 20X1

	31 December 20X3	31 December 20X5	Total
Reversing timing differences	£40,000	£60,000	£100,000
Undiscounted tax @ 30%	£12,000	£18,000	£30,000
Post-tax yield	3.67%	3.63%	
Discount factor — one year less than maturity period	$1/(1+0.0367)_2$ = 0.9305	$1/(1+0.0361)_4$ = 0.8677	
Discounted deferred tax	£12,000 × 0.9305 = £11,166	£18,000 × 0.8677 = £15,619	= £26,785

The movement of £26,785 — £25,855 (from Table 1) = £930 for the year ended 31 December 20X1 comprises:

Unwinding of the discount on opening timing differences (as these are now one year closer to reversal)	£937
Change in discount rate at which opening deferred tax is discounted	£ (7)
Total change in discounted liability reflected in the tax charge for 20X1	£930

The reduction in the opening discounted liability is due to the effect of an increase in the discount rates. In this example, the amount representing the change in the discount rate is small because only a small increase in the discount rate was assumed. The effect would be more pronounced had the discount rate changed by a bigger amount and a longer time period was involved.

13.197 It may so happen that, in addition to the change in discount rates, the company finds at 31 December 20X1 that the reversal of £100,000 is now likely to take place over 3 years — £25,000 in 20X3, £25,000 in 20X4 and the remaining £50,000 in 20X5. As the amount and timing of the reversals have changed, the company would need to discount the reversals of three separate timing differences by reference to three Treasury gilts redemption yields with maturity dates corresponding to the periods of reversals. A similar calculation as above would need to be performed and, in this case, the total movement would comprise three elements — (a) unwinding of the discount; (b) change in discount rate; and (c) change in timing and amount of reversing timing differences, not including the change that would arise if the tax rate itself changes.

13.198 Fortunately, it is not necessary to calculate the separate components. This is because the standard simply requires disclosure of the changes in the amounts of discounts deducted in arriving at the deferred tax balance (see further para 13.240 below). Therefore, only the net movement needs to be disclosed as part of the tax charge. This amount would be obtained simply by calculating the discounted deferred tax liability at the balance sheet date by reference to prevailing discount rates and future reversal of timing differences, which may have changed as to amount and timing compared with the previous estimate, and deducting the opening discounted deferred tax liability.

13.199 The discounting calculation becomes complicated for deferred tax arising from accelerated capital allowances and could, in certain circumstances, produce an odd result. As stated in paragraph 13.189 above, the discounting calculation is performed by scheduling out, by year, the future movements in accelerated capital allowances on assets — without regard to the effect of future asset purchases. It is important to appreciate that the scheduling of the future movements in accelerated capital allowances should include not only reversing timing differences, but also any further originating timing differences that would arise as a result of claiming the remaining capital allowances on the existing asset. In other words, the accelerated capital allowances build up to a maximum amount before starting to reverse. The way in which the scheduling and the discounting calculation should be performed is set out in great detail in the discounting example in Appendix 1 to FRS 19.

13.200 In certain circumstances, especially in the early years, an undiscounted deferred tax liability could, with discounting, turn into a deferred tax asset. The reason for this is relatively straightforward to understand. When an asset is purchased on which capital allowances are claimed, there are future originating and future reversing timing differences, which, over the life of the asset, will sum to zero or add up to a small net ouflow on an undiscounted basis. In the early years, however, the originating differences (proxies for cash inflows) dominate the reversing timing differences (proxies for cash outflows). As these early inflows are less affected by discounting than later outflows, it is possible that the net effect of discounting results in a net inflow, giving rise to a deferred tax asset. Consider the following example:

Example 2 – Deferred tax liability discounted into a deferred tax asset

On 1 January 20X0, a company acquires an asset costing £10,000, which has a life of 20 years. Depreciation is provided on a straight line basis and the asset qualifies for capital allowances of 25% on a reducing balance. The discount rate, for simplicity is assumed to be 6%, which remains constant over the life of the asset. At the end of the asset's life, the asset is scrapped and any capital allowances outstanding are claimed as a balancing allowance. The tax rate is 30%.

At 31 December 20X0:
Net book value of the asset = £9,500
Tax written-down value = £7,500
Timing difference at that date = £2,000

The timing difference of £2,000 is expected to reverse over the remaining 19 years as follows:

Year	Depreciation	Capital allowances	Reversal of timing difference/ (further originating timing difference)	Undiscounted deferred tax liability/ (asset) (being column 4 × 30%)	Discounted deferred tax liability/ (asset)
1	500	1,875	(1,375)	(413)	(389)
2	500	1,406	(906)	(272)	(242)
3	500	1,055	(555)	(166)	(140)
4	500	791	(291)	(87)	(69)
5	500	593	(93)	(28)	(21)
6	500	445	55	17	12
7	500	334	166	50	33
8	500	250	250	75	47
9	500	188	312	94	55
10	500	141	359	108	60
11	500	106	394	118	62
12	500	79	421	126	63
13	500	59	441	132	62
14	500	45	455	137	60
15	500	33	467	140	58
16	500	25	475	142	56
17	500	19	481	144	54
18	500	14	486	146	51
19	500	11	489	147	49
20	–	31	(31)	(10)	(3)
Total	9,500	7,500	2,000	600	(142)

13.201 As can be seen from the above table, an undiscounted deferred tax liability of £600 at the end of 31 December 20X0 becomes, on discounting, a deferred tax asset of £142. This is because the early years' amounts are less affected by discounting than the later years' amounts and so they predominate giving rise to a deferred asset. In accounting terms, this means that the discounted deferred tax asset of £142 is not simply the discounted equivalent of the undiscounted liability of £600 that represents the liability to pay back the upfront tax relief received to date. Rather, it also includes the right to receive further upfront tax relief before both the upfront tax relief received to date plus any upfront tax relief still to be received are paid back, again all discounted. In other words, if we view the accelerated capital allowances as an interest-free loan from the government, then the effect of discounting may be to value not just the interest free loan received upfront, but also the right to receive any further interest-free loans in the future. The profile for undiscounted and discounted liability over the life of the asset is shown below.

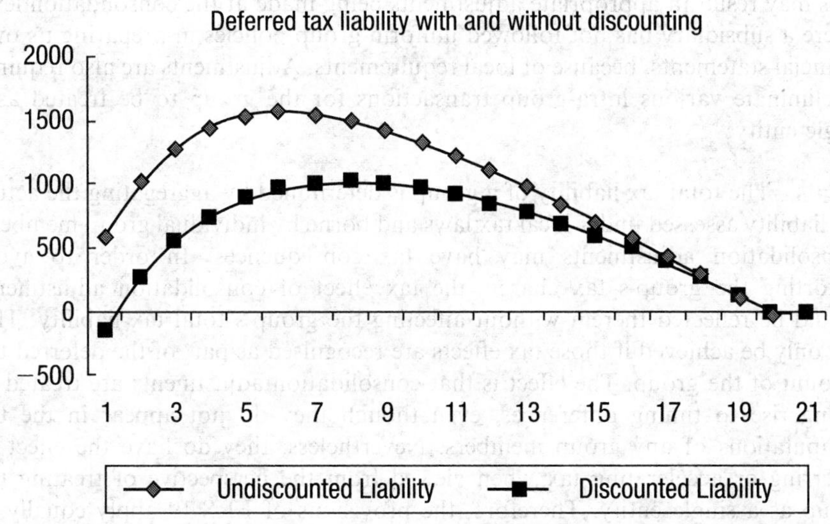

13.202 In practice, however, the above results are unlikely to show up in the generality of situations since most companies would have a portfolio of assets with different ages and the cumulative effect of the individual timing differences may prevent the liability/asset switch from occurring. It could, however, occur in start-up situations. If this were to happen in practice, a deferred tax asset should be recognised in the early years subject to meeting the recognition criteria. The apparent ambiguity would need to be explained in the financial statements.

Treatment of tax in consolidated financial statements

General principles

13.203 The treatment of taxation in the consolidated financial statements involves considerations that are different from those that apply to individual financial statements. In a group, the tax positions of the individual group members are unlikely to be similar. Some group members may be profitable, whilst others may be loss making, leading to different tax considerations. Some may operate in the same tax jurisdiction, whilst others may operate in different tax jurisdictions. Given that consolidated financial statements are prepared as if the parent company and its subsidiary undertakings were a single entity, it follows that the group's tax position has to be viewed as a whole.

13.204 It is a requirement of SI 2008/410 and of FRS 2 that a group should follow uniform accounting policies in preparing consolidated financial statements. This may result in appropriate adjustments being made at the consolidation level where a subsidiary has not followed uniform group policies in preparing its own financial statements, because of local requirements. Adjustments are also required to eliminate various intra-group transactions for the group to be treated as a single entity.

13.205 The total tax liability of a group is determined by aggregating the actual tax liability assessed under local tax laws and borne by individual group members. Consolidation adjustments may have tax consequences. In order to avoid distorting the group's tax charge, the tax effect of consolidation adjustments should be reflected therein without affecting the group's total tax liability. This can only be achieved if those tax effects are recognised as part of the deferred tax account of the group. The effect is that consolidation adjustments are treated as giving rise to timing differences, even though they do not appear in the tax computations of any group members. Nevertheless, they do have the effect of deferring or accelerating tax when viewed from the perspective of treating the group as a single entity. Therefore, the provisions of FRS 19 apply equally to consolidated financial statements.

Tax effects of consolidation adjustment

13.206 FRS 19 regards the reversal of intragroup profits in stock, unrealised at the group level, as a timing difference that should be tax effected. Assuming that a subsidiary sells goods costing £50,000 to its parent company for £60,000 and these goods are still held in stock at the balance sheet date, a consolidation adjustment is required to eliminate the profit of £10,000 from the consolidated profit and loss account. The subsidiary would have provided tax of £3,000 (£10,000 @ 30 per cent) as part of its current tax liability.

13.207 The tax provided by the subsidiary is eliminated on consolidation through recognition of a deferred tax asset at the group level. Under FRS 19, a deferred tax asset is recognised following elimination of any intragroup profits in stock held at the group level at the supplying company's tax rate. (This differs to IAS 12, which requires recognition of a deferred tax asset at the receiving company's tax rate.) The deferred tax asset would be recovered when the goods are sold to third parties.

13.208 Therefore, consolidation adjustments that have the effect of deferring or accelerating tax when viewed from the perspective of the group as a whole give rise to timing differences and should be accounted for as part of the deferred tax position of the group.

Example – Tax effect of a consolidation adjustment

A company is preparing consolidated financial statements. In one of its overseas sub-groups there was a transfer of assets from one subsidiary to another giving rise to a large profit in the transferor (which is taxable in the overseas country). The transferor company has paid the tax in the year. On consolidation the intra-group profit is eliminated but the tax charge remains. Can the group reverse this charge and set up a deferred tax asset on consolidation?

This is clearly a timing difference under FRS 19 so far as the consolidated financial statements are concerned. If the assets were sold outside the group there would be a different tax base for the value of assets sold compared to the value of the assets in the consolidated financial statements. Therefore, under FRS 19, provided the conditions in paragraph 23 of the standard are satisfied (that is, provided that the deferred tax asset is regarded as recoverable) the tax charge should be treated as a deferred tax asset on consolidation.

13.208.1 Another example is where borrowing costs incurred to finance the creation of a fixed asset for use by the group are expensed by a subsidiary, but capitalised on consolidation. As the subsidiary has already benefited from the tax deduction on the interest expense in the current period, but the group would recognise the interest expense as part of the subsequent depreciation or sale of the asset, a timing difference is created from the perspective of treating the group as a single entity. Consequently, a deferred tax liability should be set up to eliminate the benefit from the tax deduction arising as there is no associated interest charge in the consolidated financial statements.

Fair value adjustments

13.209 FRS 19 treats fair value adjustments as if they were timing differences in the acquired entity's own financial statements. For example, a non-monetary asset, such as a building of the acquired entity would be valued on acquisition at its market value. Any tax that would be payable if the asset were sold at that value would be provided for only if, before the acquisition, the acquired entity had itself entered into a binding agreement to sell the asset and rollover relief was not available. [FRS 7 para 74, as amended by FRS 19 para 71]. In general, if the acquired company's assets are fair valued upwards on acquisition, it is treated as being the same as revaluations and no deferred tax should be provided, unless the conditions in FRS 19 are met (see para 13.128).

13.210 Another way of looking at fair value adjustments on consolidation is to treat them as if they had been policy adjustments in the acquired entity. For instance, assume that the acquired entity has a number of outstanding forward currency contracts taken out to hedge committed transactions, which, at the date of acquisition, are sitting at a considerable loss. In accordance with FRS 7, the forward contracts would be fair valued on acquisition with a consequent adjustment to goodwill. However, if both the acquirer and the acquired entity apply SSAP 20 rather than FRS 23 and neither has a policy of fair valuing derivatives, any gains or losses arising are deferred until the contracts mature. The question arises as to whether it is appropriate to provide deferred tax on the fair value adjustments on consolidation under these circumstances. The answer will be impacted by the tax position of the entity. This will vary depending on the entity's elections under the applicable tax rules (see further paras 13.135.2 and 13.217). If the entity had a policy to fair value derivatives and fair value gains and losses are not taxable until their subsequent realisation, this would give rise to a timing difference on which deferred tax would have been provided in the entity's own financial statements. Consequently, as fair values are used in the consolidated financial statements, it is appropriate to recognise the tax effects of the adjustment on consolidation also.

13.210.1 If the acquirer is applying FRS 23 and FRS 26 (see further chapters 7 and 6 respectively), then its accounting policy must be that derivatives are marked to market with fair value movements being recognised in the profit and loss account. To the extent that the fair value movements are not taxed until their subsequent realisation, it is appropriate to recognise deferred tax on those fair value movements on consolidation.

13.211 A similar situation arises where the acquired entity has current asset investments and the group has an accounting policy of carrying these at cost, but which are fair valued at the date of acquisition. As stated above, we would treat the fair value adjustment as if it was a policy adjustment in the acquired entity. Unless the group applies FRS 26 (see below) a policy of revaluation for current asset investments would be effected through the STRGL and no deferred tax would be provided on the fair value adjustments, unless there was a binding commitment, see paragraph 13.209.

13.211.1 If the acquirer applies FRS 26 in its consolidated financial statements, it may account for equity investments (other than investments in subsidiaries, associates and joint ventures) either at cost or at fair value. The accounting treatment depends on the designation of the investment (see further chapter 6). The following table outlines for each category of investment held by the acquired entity, whether deferred tax should be recognised on acquisition or not.

Category of investment	Accounting for investment	Recognise deferred tax?
Held to maturity	Cost	No – the reasons given in paragraph 13.211 apply
Available for sale	Fair value, with movements recognised in STRGL	No – see paragraph 13.209
At fair value through profit or loss	Fair value with movements recognised in profit or loss	Yes – see paragraph 13.132

13.211.2 The examples below consider the deferred tax implications when assets are written down in a fair value exercise.

Example 1 – Write-down of stock in fair value exercise

A group made an acquisition during the year. The acquired company had stock stated in its books at cost (£l0 million). As part of the fair value exercise, the stock has been written down to its net realisable value of £8 million. This adjustment does not reflect the acquiring company's intentions, but rather reflects conditions at the date of acquisition. Should deferred tax be provided on the fair value adjustment?

Paragraph 18 of FRS 19 states that *'stock may be adjusted to its fair value on the acquisition of a business. However, even where such stock has been manufactured under the terms of a binding contract, that contract will generally be treated as an executory contract. The rights and obligations under that contract (and hence the gain on sale) will not have been recognised. In adjusting the value of the stock, the entity is merely recognising a movement in the replacement cost of the stock. In such circumstances the FRS does not allow a provision to be made for deferred tax on the adjustment'*. This would suggest that no adjustment should be made for deferred tax when a fair value adjustment is made to stock.

This part of the FRS deals with upward revaluations of stock for the purpose of fair valuing and is consistent with the principle that adjustments to record the acquired entity's assets and liabilities are treated in the same way as they would be if they were timing differences arising in the entity's own financial statements. [FRS 19, para 71]. Upward revaluations on the cost of stock would not be permitted in the acquired entity's own historical cost financial statements under SSAP 9, 'Stocks and long-term contracts', and even if they were allowed, deferred tax would not be provided under FRS 19. Paragraph 14 states that deferred tax should not be provided on timing differences arising when non-monetary assets are revalued, unless there is a binding commitment to sell and the entity has recognised the gains and losses expected on sale.

However, we consider that the provisions of paragraph 18 of FRS 19 do not apply in circumstances where a fair value adjustment is made to write an asset down to its net realisable value (where this write down has not been made in the acquired entity's own financial statements) and that in this case deferred tax should be provided on the difference between cost of £10m and fair value of £8m, as part of the fair value exercise. This is consistent with the principle described above: the acquired entity would have recognised a deferred tax asset in respect of the write-down if it had been made in the entity's own financial statements. It follows that FRS 7, as amended by FRS 19, requires deferred tax to be recorded on acquisition in this situation.

Example 2 – Write-down of fixed assets in fair value exercise

Should deferred tax be recognised on fair value adjustments to write down plant and machinery to its fair values?

Yes, FRS 19 amended FRS 7 and states that deferred tax on adjustments to fair values should be recognised in accordance with FRS 19. Where assets are revalued upwards to fair value in a fair value exercise there would normally be no deferred tax to provide, unless the company was committed to dispose of the assets. However, in this case the assets are being written down and this is like additional depreciation. As a result depreciation going forward will be reduced and this will affect the calculation of deferred tax relating to capital allowances resulting in a reduction of the deferred tax liability going forward.

13.212 Where a company with unrelieved tax losses is acquired, that company has a contingent asset in the form of future tax benefit attributable to the unrelieved tax losses. Under paragraph 37 of FRS 7, certain contingent assets and liabilities that crystallise as a result of the acquisition are recognised, provided that the underlying contingency was in existence before the acquisition. Future tax benefits attributable to the unrelieved tax losses should be recognised as a fair value adjustment provided the group has sufficient taxable profits. As a general rule, deferred tax assets of the acquired entity should be included in the fair value exercise, even if they had not been recognised before the acquisition, provided they meet the recognition criteria for deferred tax assets as set out in paragraph 13.143 above.

13.213 On the other hand, if the losses had arisen in the acquiring group and had remained unrelieved at the date of acquisition, FRS 19 would not permit recognition of a deferred tax asset in the fair value exercise even though the group is able to utilise the benefit of its unused tax losses against the future taxable profit of the acquired entity. This is because those losses are not the losses of the acquired entity and hence would not be recognised in the fair value exercise. [FRS 19 para 71; FRS 7 para 75]. Rather, as a result of the acquisition, the acquiring group is expected to be more profitable in future. FRS 19, therefore, requires unrecognised deferred tax assets of the acquirer or other entities existing at the date of acquisition that fall to be recoverable against the future taxable profits of the acquired entity to be recognised as a credit to the tax charge in the post acquisition period. [FRS 19 para 71; FRS 7 para 22].

Goodwill

13.213.1 In some jurisdictions outside the UK (and where goodwill arises in the UK on the acquisition of trade and assets), tax relief is available on goodwill (the goodwill being amortised for tax purposes over a pre-determined life or in accordance with any amortisation for accounting purposes). Where the goodwill is amortised over the same period for accounting purposes, then there is no timing difference. However, where a different period is used for tax purposes then deferred tax will arise. For example, it is common in the UK for companies to make an election to claim annual deductions at four per cent, thus deductions are received over a 25 year period whilst, for accounting purposes, the period over which amortisation is recognised is unlikely to be greater than 20 years (see further chapter 25). Additionally, a particular issue arises where goodwill that relates to acquisitions made before 1998 remains eliminated against reserves under the transitional arrangements in FRS 10, 'Goodwill and intangible assets'. Under FRS 19, the tax deductions for the goodwill's cost create timing differences in the consolidated financial statements as the tax relief is received before the cost is recognised in the profit and loss account. Whereas the tax deduction is obtained systematically over a pre-determined life, the goodwill is not charged in the profit and loss account until the business to which it relates is sold or closed (or earlier if the group's policy is to reinstate the goodwill when it is impaired and write it off through the profit and loss account). Under FRS 19, deferred tax should be provided on this timing difference.

13.213.2 For example, if goodwill costing £100 is being amortised for tax purposes over 20 years (that is, amortisation of £5 per annum), the tax written-down value at the end of, say, year eight would be £60 (£100 — £5 × 8). The goodwill was eliminated against reserves prior to 1998, but this was a matter of accounting policy rather than an accounting loss. A deferred tax liability should be provided on the timing difference of £40. The liability is increased each year up to 20 years as further timing differences of £5 originate, unless the goodwill is charged in the profit and loss account (for instance, on disposal of the business), when the timing difference would reverse and the provision would be released.

13.213.3 In the consolidated profit and loss account, the current tax charge reflects the benefit of the annual tax deductions. The tax-deductible goodwill is a reconciling item in FRS 19's reconciliation of the current tax charge to the charge that would result from applying the standard rate of tax to the profit on ordinary activities before tax (see further para 13.276 below).

Unremitted earnings of subsidiaries, associates and joint ventures

13.214 Earnings of subsidiaries, associates and joint ventures that are not remitted to the parent/investor do not normally suffer UK corporation tax. Similarly, if such profits are remitted by way of dividends, they may be exempt from UK corporation tax. However, if the profits would be subject to tax (UK or overseas) if remitted, then unremitted earnings of such entities that have been recognised in the consolidated financial statements are potentially timing differences which reverse when they are distributed or a commitment to distribute them exists. Accordingly, FRS 19 states that tax that could be payable (taking account of any double taxation relief) on any future remittance of the past earnings of a subsidiary, associate or joint venture should be provided for only to the extent that, at the balance sheet date:

- Dividends have been accrued as receivable; or
- A binding agreement to distribute the past earnings in future has been entered into by the subsidiary, associate or joint venture.

[FRS 19 para 21].

13.215 Therefore, there must be a binding agreement in place rather than simply an intention to remit profits, thus eliminating any degree of subjectivity. The standard acknowledges that, in practice, a binding agreement to remit profits is unlikely to arise. [FRS 19 para 22].

Foreign exchange differences

13.216 Gains or losses arising on the translation of the financial statements of overseas subsidiaries and associated companies are not regarded as creating a timing difference. However, gains or losses arising on the translation of an entity's own overseas assets (including investments in subsidiaries and associated companies) and liabilities may give rise to timing differences depending on whether or not the gains or losses have a tax effect. In addition, where gains and losses on foreign currency borrowings that have been used to hedge foreign equity investments are offset and reported in the STRGL, then, in accordance with UITF Abstract 19, any tax effects that are directly and solely attributable to the exchange gains or losses on the borrowings should also be reported in the STRGL (see also paragraph 13.239 below). See further chapter 7.

13.217 In the UK, the tax rules with regards to foreign exchange gains and losses are complex. Depending on the elections made under the applicable tax rules, exchange gains and losses may either be taxable as they accrue for accounting purposes or may be taxable when realisation occurs at a later date. Consultation with a tax specialist is recommended in this area.

Deemed disposals

13.218 When a profit or loss is made on a deemed disposal, the question arises as to whether deferred tax should be recognised.

Example – Deemed disposal

A company has a subsidiary that has issued shares for cash in a flotation. The shares were issued for a value that exceeds the share of net assets per share. Therefore, whilst the company's percentage holding has reduced, its attributable share of net assets has increased giving rise to a profit on the deemed disposal under FRS 2, 'Accounting for subsidiary undertakings'. Because this profit is represented by increased cash it is reflected in the group's profit and loss account. Should the company provide for deferred tax on this profit given that no actual tax arises at this stage, because the company has not actually sold any shares in the subsidiary?

If the parent were to sell the subsidiary at a later date there would be a gain based on the difference between the original cost to the parent and the proceeds. In the consolidated financial statements (ignoring goodwill) this gain would be represented by (a) retained profits since acquisition, (b) gain on deemed disposal and (c) actual gain between the proceeds and the carrying value of net assets at the date of sale. In the group only (c) would be recognised on disposal as (a) and (b) would already have been recognised. There is clearly a timing difference between the recognition in the consolidated financial statements of the retained profits and the gain on deemed disposal and their taxation on disposal of the shares in the subsidiary. However, FRS 19 does not permit deferred tax to be recognised on the sale of the subsidiary until there is a commitment to sell. This is implied because the recognition of retained profits and gain on deemed disposal of the subsidiary is like a revaluation and paragraph 14 of FRS 19 does not allow deferred tax on a revaluation to be provided, unless the entity has a binding agreement to sell and has recognised the gains expected to arise on sale. The conclusion, therefore, is that the gain on deemed disposal should be treated as a revaluation for FRS 19 purposes and no provision for tax made until there is a commitment to sell.

[The next paragraph is 13.234.]

Presentation and disclosures

General

13.234 It is generally accepted that, however they have been calculated, tax effects should be shown in the financial statements separately from the items or transactions to which they relate. It is not surprising, therefore, that a considerable number of disclosure requirements in respect of taxation are contained both in company law (SI 2008/410) and the relevant accounting standards, although there is significant overlap between the two. Most of the disclosure requirements apply to the financial statements of individual companies as well as to consolidated financial statements. The paragraphs that follow deal with the disclosure requirements of current tax as well as deferred tax.

Accounting policies

13.235 There is no specific requirement in FRS 16 and FRS 19 to disclose accounting policies in respect of current and deferred tax. This is because a description of each of the accounting policies that is material in the context of the entity's financial statements is required by FRS 18 and by SI 2008/410. [FRS 18 para 55(a); SI 2008/410 1 Sch 44]. In respect of deferred tax, the policy note should state the basis on which deferred tax has been recognised. It should also state whether deferred tax is measured on a discounted or undiscounted basis. Examples of accounting policy on deferred tax are given in Table 13.4 and 13.5 below.

Table 13.4 – Accounting policy for deferred tax

British Vita PLC – Annual Report & Accounts – 31 December 2000

NOTES ON THE ACCOUNTS

1 Accounting policies (extract)
Deferred taxation
Deferred tax is recognised in respect of all timing differences that have originated but not reversed at the balance sheet date where transactions or events that result in an obligation to pay more tax in the future or a right to pay less tax in the future have occurred at the balance sheet date. Timing differences are differences between the Group's taxable profits and its results as stated in the financial statements.

Deferred tax is recognised in respect of the retained earnings of overseas subsidiaries and associates only to the extent that, at the balance sheet date, dividends have been accrued as receivable or a binding agreement to distribute past earnings in future has been entered into by the subsidiary or associate.

Deferred tax is measured at the average tax rates that are expected to apply in the periods in which the timing differences are expected to reverse, based on tax rates and laws that have been enacted or substantially enacted by the balance sheet date. Deferred tax is measured on a non-discounted basis.

Table 13.5 – Accounting policy for deferred tax

Costain Group plc – Annual Report and Accounts – 31 December 2000

1 Accounting Policies (extract)
Taxation
Deferred taxation has been recognised as a liability or asset if transaction have occurred at the balance sheet date that give rise to an obligation to pay more taxation in future, or a right to pay less taxation in future. An asset is not recognised to the extent that the transfer of economic benefits in future is uncertain. Deferred tax assets and liabilities recognised have not been discounted.

No provision is made to cover any further liability to taxation that would arise in respect of the distribution of profits retained by overseas subsidiary undertakings and joint ventures.

Profit and loss account

Presentation and disclosures required by company law

13.236 The requirements in SI 2008/410 in relation to the presentation of taxation in the profit and loss account are as follows:

- There must be disclosed separately 'tax on profit or loss on ordinary activities' and 'tax on extraordinary profit or loss'. The latter is unlikely to arise under FRS 3. These are separate headings included in each of the four profit and loss account formats. In addition, all the profit and loss account formats include a further heading 'other taxes not shown under the above items'. As SI 2008/410 does not indicate the type of information that must be included under this heading and as no such 'other taxes' are presently collected in the UK, this heading in the format appears to be superfluous for the time being.

- The taxation charge in the profit and loss account should be analysed, distinguishing between:
- UK corporation tax, both before and after double tax relief.
- UK income tax.
- Overseas tax (that is, tax imposed outside the UK).

[SI 2008/410 1 Sch 67(2)].

- Particulars are required of any special circumstances that affect the liability in respect of tax for the period or that may affect those of future periods, whether in respect of profits, income or capital gains. [SI 2008/410 1 Sch 67(1)]. This requirement is also contained in FRS 3 which is discussed in paragraph 13.274.

Presentation required by the accounting standards

13.237 Both current and deferred tax should be recognised in the profit and loss account for the period, except to the extent that it is attributable to a gain or loss that is or has been recognised directly in the STRGL. [FRS 16 para 5, FRS 19 para 34]. All such amounts should be recognised as part of 'tax on profit and loss on ordinary activities'. This requirement is implicit within FRS 16, but explicitly stated in paragraph 59 of FRS 19 in respect of deferred tax.

Disclosures in the notes

13.238 A considerable amount of information relating to both current tax and deferred tax falls to be disclosed in the profit and loss account under the provisions contained in FRS 3, FRS 16 and FRS 19. These disclosure requirements have been grouped under appropriate headings for ease of reference and examples from published financial statements to illustrate the disclosure requirements of company law and accounting standards are included where relevant.

Analysis of current tax

13.239 FRS 16 requires that the current tax charge or (credit) reported in the profit and loss account should be analysed between UK tax and foreign tax. Each of these components should be further analysed to distinguish tax for the current period and adjustments recognised in respect of prior periods. The total UK tax should also be shown before and after double taxation relief. [FRS 16 para 17]. An example of a non-mandatory format, capturing all the disclosure requirements of paragraph 17 relating to the profit and loss account, is given in Appendix I to the standard and is reproduced below:

	£'000	£'000
UK corporation tax		
Current tax on income for the period	a	
Adjustments in respect of prior periods	b	
	c	
Double taxation relief	d	
		e
Foreign tax		
Current tax on income for the period	f	
Adjustments in respect of prior periods	g	
		h
Tax on profit on ordinary activities		i

Analysis of deferred tax

13.240 In addition to the disclosure of the major components of current tax considered above, the notes to the financial statements should disclose the amount of deferred tax charged or credited within tax on ordinary activities in the profit and loss account, separately disclosing material components, including those attributable to:

- Changes in deferred tax balances (before discounting, where applicable) arising from:
  - The origination and reversal of timing differences.
  - Changes in tax rates and laws.
  - Adjustments to the estimated recoverable amount of deferred tax assets arising in previous periods.
- Where applicable, changes in the amounts of discount deducted in arriving at the deferred tax balance.

[FRS 19 para 60(a)].

13.241 The above disclosure requirements are illustrated in the example in FRS 19 Appendix II. The single figure of the originating and reversing timing differences disclosed within the deferred tax charge in the profit and loss account is likely to include the tax effects of accelerated capital allowances, material provisions, utilisation of unrelieved tax losses, capitalised interest and other timing differences. It would appear from the requirement of the above paragraph that further analysis of the single figure for the originating and reversing timing is not required, although such an analysis could be computed from the available information in the tax note. Indeed, the example in Appendix II simply discloses a single figure for the origination and reversal of timing differences without providing further analysis. An example of a company that has followed the above disclosure requirements is given in Table 13.6 below.

Table 13.6 – Tax disclosures relating to the profit and loss account

Scottish Power plc – Annual Report & Accounts – 31 March 2001

Notes to the Group Profit and Loss Account (extract)
6 Tax on profit on ordinary activities (extract)

	Before exceptional item 2001 £m	Exceptional items 2001 £m	2001 £m	Before exceptional items 2000 £m	Exceptional items 2000 £m	2000 £m	1999 £m
Current tax:							
UK corporation tax at 30% (2000 30% and 1999 31%)	145.6	–	145.6	135.6	56.0	191.6	141.6
Double taxation relief	(61.2)	–	(61.2)	–	–	–	–
UK Corporation tax liability	84.4	–	84.4	135.6	56.0	191.6	141.6
Foreign taxation	5.7	(8.7)	(3.0)	26.1	–	26.1	–
Total current tax	90.1	(8.7)	81.4	161.7	56.0	217.7	141.6
Deferred tax:							
Origination and reversal of timing differences	51.0	(37.2)	13.8	45.2	–	45.2	33.5
Total deferred tax	51.0	(37.2)	13.8	45.2	–	45.2	33.5
Total tax on profit on ordinary activities	141.1	(45.9)	95.2	206.9	56.0	262.9	175.1

13.242 In addition to the disclosure of adjustments to deferred tax balances arising from changes in the tax rates and laws as stated above, the effect of a fundamental change in the basis of taxation, if applicable, should be included in the tax charge for the period and separately disclosed on the face of the profit and loss account. [FRS 3 para 23].

13.243 The standard simply calls for the disclosure of the total amount of discount that has been deducted in arriving at the deferred tax balance. As stated in paragraph 13.198 above, the total amount of discount charged in the profit and loss account would consist of the unwinding of discount, the effect of changes in discount rates and the effect of changes in timing and amount of reversing timing differences. It would have been consistent with FRS 12 if the unwinding of the discount was included as other finance costs adjacent to interest with the other components shown as part of the tax charge. The ASB believes this to be the correct approach in principle, but nevertheless requires the unwinding of the discount to be presented as part of the tax charge. The reason is that profit and loss account formats require all of the tax consequences of pre-tax profits to be shown separately, below the sub-total 'profits on ordinary activities before taxation'. The unwinding of a discount on a deferred tax balance, whether viewed conceptually as part of the tax expense or as a finance item, is not part of profits before tax. Hence, it is shown after the subtotal of profits before tax. [FRS 19 App V para 122]. Therefore, all the effects of discounting deferred taxes are recorded within the same tax line. On the other hand, interest charged on overdue tax or received in respect of overpayments are considered to be proper finance costs and should be included within interest in the profit and loss account (see para 13.50.15 onwards).

13.244 There is no requirement to disclose the discount rate. This is sensible since there is little subjectivity involved in determining gilt redemption rates as they are all obtained from published information and objectively verifiable. Furthermore, users are more interested in determining the impact that discounting has on the undiscounted deferred tax balance and such information is readily obtained from other disclosures.

Tax on non-operating exceptional items

13.245 The amount of tax attributable to the three non-operating exceptional items described in paragraph 20 of FRS 3 (sometimes referred to as 'super-exceptionals') should be disclosed in a note. The three items are: profits or losses on sale or termination of an operation; costs of a fundamental reorganisation or restructuring having a material effect on the nature and focus of the reporting entity's operations; and profits or losses on the disposal of fixed assets (and provisions in respect of each of these). The related tax is required to be shown only in aggregate and not for each individual item, unless the effect of the tax on each of the items differs, when further information should be given, where practicable. Although the FRS states that the tax attributable to the above types of exceptional item should be disclosed in a note, there could be no objection to disclosing the tax separately within the tax charge on the face of the profit and loss account, as the items are themselves disclosed there.

13.246 FRS 3 recognises that the above disclosure can be useful in understanding the period's charge or credit in respect of taxation. In support of this disclosure requirement, paragraph 50 of FRS 3 states:

> *'It is recognised that analysing an entity's total taxation charge between component parts of its result for a period can involve arbitrary allocations that tend to become less meaningful the more components there are. However, in respect of items such as disposal profits or losses the tax can often be identified with the exceptional item concerned and the relationship between the profit or loss and the attributable tax may be significantly different from that in respect of operating profits or losses. In such circumstances it is relevant to identify the tax charge or credit more specifically.'*

13.247 FRS 3 then goes on to stipulate the way in which tax attributable to exceptional items falling within any of the three categories set out above should be calculated for accounting disclosure purposes. The amount of tax attributable to the exceptional items should be calculated by computing the tax on the profit or loss on ordinary activities as if the items did not exist and comparing this notional tax charge with the tax charge on the profit or loss for the year (after extraordinary items if any). Any additional tax charge or credit (including deferred tax) that arises should be attributable to the items. If there are both non-operating exceptional items and extraordinary items in the same period, the tax attributable to the items combined should be calculated and then apportioned between the two groups in relation to their respective amounts. If a more appropriate basis is adopted the method of apportionment must be disclosed. [FRS 3 para 24]. In practice, it is unlikely that under FRS 3 there will be extraordinary items and so the apportionment of tax between the two categories should not arise.

13.248 The following examples illustrate some of the difficulties that may arise in calculating the taxation that relates to the non-operating exceptional items described above:

Example 1

Apportionment of tax where losses brought forward absorb a profit on ordinary activities

A group makes a profit on ordinary activities (excluding non-operating exceptionals) and there is an exceptional loss of the same amount. The group has sufficient tax losses brought forward which can be surrendered to relieve the tax charge on the profit on ordinary activities, or it can use the taxable loss arising from the exceptional item. It uses the former. The question arises as to whether or not the notes to the financial statements should assume a taxation charge on the profit on ordinary activities and show a taxation credit attributable to the exceptional item? The overall tax charge is nil.

In this situation, if the exceptional item were ignored, the tax charge on the profit on ordinary activities would still be nil, as the group would have used taxable losses to eliminate the tax charge. Therefore, the notes should not assume a tax charge on ordinary activities and should not show a tax credit on exceptional items. However, there will still be tax losses carried forward and the notes could disclose that part of the losses brought forward have been utilised to relieve the taxable profit of the group leaving other taxable losses attributable to the exceptional item to be carried forward.

Example 2

Apportionment of tax where goodwill previously written off is treated as non-operating exceptional item

A company makes a profit before non-operating exceptional items and then has an exceptional loss on disposal of a subsidiary. The exceptional loss arises wholly because of the inclusion, in the calculation of the loss, of goodwill previously written off to reserves on the acquisition of the subsidiary. After taking account of the exceptional loss the result before tax is neither a profit nor loss, but there is a substantial tax charge. This is wholly attributable to the profit excluding exceptional items and accordingly there is no taxation attributable to the exceptional item. In this case, however, there would need to be an explanation in the notes of the reasons for an apparently high tax charge relative to the profit on ordinary activities before tax.

Statement of total recognised gains and losses

13.249 Where a gain or loss is or has been recognised directly in the STRGL, both current and deferred tax attributable to that gain or loss should also be recognised directly in that statement [FRS 16 para 17, FRS 19 para 35].

13.250 Because a UK company pays corporation tax on all its profits including any that are reported in the STRGL, it may sometimes be difficult to determine the amount of deferred tax attributable to the amount of gain or loss reported in the STRGL. In those circumstances, both standards permits the attributable current and deferred tax to be calculated on a reasonable pro-rata basis, or another basis that is more appropriate in the circumstances. [FRS 16 para 7, FRS 19 para 36]. The practical implications of this are considered in paragraph 13.23.

Disclosure in the notes

13.251 Both FRS 16 and FRS 19 contain requirements for additional disclosures of the single line item disclosed in the STRGL.

13.252 FRS 16 requires that the current tax charge or (credit) reported in the STRGL should be analysed between UK tax and foreign tax. Each of these components should be further analysed to distinguish tax for the current period and adjustments recognised in respect of prior periods. The total UK tax should also be shown before and after double taxation relief. [FRS 16 para 17]. Similarly, FRS 19 requires separate disclosure of the material components of the tax charge or credit reported directly in the STRGL, including those listed in paragraph 13.240 above. [FRS 19 para 60].

Changes in the carrying amounts of deferred tax assets and liabilities

13.252.1 The carrying value of deferred tax assets and liabilities can change even though there is no change in the timing difference. Such changes may arise as a result of:

- a change in tax rates or laws; or
- a re-assessment of the recoverability of deferred tax assets (see para 13.169).

In such situations, the resulting change in deferred tax should be recognised in the profit and loss account, except to the extent that it relates to items that were previously recognised in the STRGL (see further para 13.249). [FRS 19 para 35].

Example

An entity has a defined benefit pension scheme that is in deficit at the period end. A deferred tax asset has been recognised in relation to the timing difference that exists in relation to the pension deficit.

The rate of corporation tax has been changed from 30% to 28% with an effective date of 1 April 20X8. This change has been substantively enacted at the balance sheet date and will impact the reversal of the timing difference from 1 April 20X8 onwards, reducing the deferred tax asset.

Management will need to consider what transactions gave rise to the timing difference and trace the impact of the change in tax rate to the same place. In this case, the pension deficit may have arisen as a result of service costs or other profit and loss account charges, actuarial losses recognised directly in the STRGL or, potentially, a combination of the two.

Depending on how the pension deficit arose, and thus how the deferred tax asset was originally booked, the reduction in the deferred tax asset will be recognised either solely in the profit and loss account, solely in STRGL or split between the two performance statements.

The backwards tracing for the change in tax rates should be consistent with the approach used for allocating tax deductions (see para 13.126.7). The deferred tax asset, which is impacted by the tax rate change, represents the amounts against which tax deductions have not yet been allocated. To the extent that amounts in the performance statements are covered by deductions received on contributions, no deferred tax arises. The deferred tax arises on any excess amounts in the performance statements and the backwards tracing should be carried out on that basis.

The fact that a pension liability recognised on transition to FRS 17, 'Retirement benefits', was charged to reserves does not necessarily mean that subsequent changes in the related deferred tax asset will also be recognised in reserves. Instead, it is necessary to determine where the items on which the original deferred tax arose would have been recognised if FRS 17 had been applied in the prior periods.

Where it is not possible to assess where the items on which the original deferred tax arose would have been recognised, the changes in the deferred tax should be taken, by default, to the profit and loss account.

Balance sheet

Presentation and disclosures required by company law

13.253 The requirements of SI 2008/410 that relate specifically to the presentation of taxation in the balance sheet are as follows:

- Liabilities, as opposed to provisions, for taxation must be included in the balance sheet heading 'other creditors including taxation and social security', with the liability for taxation and social security being shown separately from 'other creditors'. [Note 9 to the balance sheet formats].

'Other creditors including taxation and social security', like other categories of creditors, has to be split between amounts that will fall due within one year and amounts that will fall due after more than one year. [Note 13 to the balance sheet formats]. However, as all companies are due to pay corporation tax within nine months of the financial year end no corporation tax balances payable in over one year should arise.

- The provision for deferred taxation should be included under the balance sheet heading 'Provisions for liabilities' as part of the provision for 'Taxation, including deferred taxation', and stated separately from any other provision for other taxation. [Balance sheet formats 1 and 2, SI 2008/410 1 Sch 60].
- Where there has been a transfer to or from any provision in respect of tax other than a transfer from that provision for the purpose for which it was set up, the following information should be disclosed:
  - The aggregate amount of the provision at both the beginning and end of the financial year.
  - Any amounts transferred either to or from the provision during the financial year.
  - The source and the application of any amounts so transferred.

  [SI 2008/410 1 Sch 59(1),(2)].
- The tax treatment of amounts credited or debited to the revaluation reserve should be disclosed. [SI 2008/410 1 Sch 35(6)].

Presentation required by the accounting standards

13.254 FRS 16 does not contain any specific requirements for the presentation of current tax in the balance sheet, presumably because it is adequately covered by company law (SI 2008/410) as stated above. The paragraphs that follow deal with the presentation of deferred tax in the balance sheet in accordance with FRS 19.

13.255 With the exception of deferred tax relating to a defined benefit asset or liability recognised in accordance with FRS 17, 'Retirement benefits', which is considered in paragraph 13.257 below:

- Net deferred tax liabilities should be classified as provisions for liabilities.
- Net deferred tax assets should be classified as debtors, as a separate sub-heading of debtors where material.

[FRS 19 para 55].

13.256 The above requirement is consistent with SI 2008/410's requirement for including net deferred tax provisions under the balance sheet heading 'Provisions for liabilities' as stated in paragraph 13.253 above. However, there is no heading in the balance sheet formats for taxation recoverable, but the second point in paragraph 13.255 above clarifies that net deferred tax assets should be classified as debtors and shown as a separate sub-heading of debtors, where material. SI 2008/410 permits an item of asset or liability that is not covered by any of the prescribed formats to be shown separately. [SI 2008/410 1 Sch 3(2)]. See further paragraph 13.263 below.

13.257 FRS 19 specifically excludes deferred tax assets and liabilities in respect of defined benefit schemes from being included with other deferred tax assets or liabilities. Instead, deferred tax relating to a defined benefit asset or liability is offset against the related asset or liability in accordance with FRS 17. The resulting defined benefit asset or liability, net of the related deferred tax is then presented separately on the face of the balance sheet (see further chapter 11).

Offset of deferred tax assets and liabilities

13.258 An entity may have a large number of different timing differences, giving rise to deferred tax assets and liabilities, arising during a period. Although these deferred tax assets and liabilities are measured separately, the ability to offset assets against liabilities depends on the nature of the balances (for example, deferred tax relating to capital losses cannot be offset against deferred tax liabilities in respect of accelerated capital allowances) and whom they are due to or due from.

13.259 The ASB's Statement of principles states that:

> *'If a right to receive future economic benefits and an obligation to transfer future economic benefits exist and the reporting entity has the ability – which is assured – to insist on net settlement of the balances, the right and obligation together form a single net asset or liability regardless of how the parties intend to settle the balances.'*

13.260 The ASB acknowledges that if the above principle is applied, offset of deferred tax balances could take place only if the timing differences giving rise to a deferred tax asset reverse before or at the same time as those giving rise to a deferred tax liability. (If those giving rise to the liability reverse first, there will be a requirement to pay tax before any entitlement to recover tax.) The ASB felt that the need to schedule the timings of the reversals to measure the extent to which the balances should be offset would be impractical and unnecessarily costly. [FRS 19 App V para 124 to 127].

13.261 As a result the standard takes a pragmatic approach and requires offset of deferred tax debit and credit balances within the above headings set out in paragraph 13.255 to the extent, and only to the extent, that they:

- Relate to taxes levied by the same tax authority.
- Arise in the same taxable entity or in a group of taxable entities where the tax losses of one entity can reduce the taxable profits of another.

[FRS 19 para 56].

13.262 The above requirement effectively precludes offset of deferred tax assets and liabilities relating to different tax jurisdictions in consolidated financial statements. It also means that presenting a net group tax liability by offsetting group tax assets on the grounds of a group tax planning opportunity is not possible, unless the opportunity relates to taxes levied by the same tax authority on different group members and the entities are treated as a group for tax purposes.

13.262.1 The application of the rules of offset can be more complicated in consolidated financial statements when deferred tax arises as a result of a consolidation adjustment (see further para 13.208 above).

Example

Within a group, a UK subsidiary sells stock to a French fellow subsidiary. On consolidation, the elimination of unrealised profit in stock gives rise to a deferred tax asset, which meets the criteria for recognition. Should it be offset against other deferred tax liabilities in the balance sheet?

Paragraph 56 of FRS 19 states that deferred tax debit and credit balances should be offset to the extent that they relate to taxes levied by the same tax authority and arise in the same taxable entity, or in a group of them, where one entity's tax losses can reduce another's taxable profits.

In other words, provided that a group tax-pooling regime is in operation under each tax authority, deferred tax assets and liabilities should be offset if they arise within the same tax authority. However, deferred tax assets and liabilities arising in different tax jurisdictions cannot be offset.

It is, therefore, possible to have both deferred tax liabilities and deferred tax assets in the same group balance sheet. Deferred tax liabilities are included in provisions for liabilities, whereas deferred tax assets are recognised within debtors.

Here, the deferred tax asset arises on consolidation only. The UK subsidiary has a current tax charge in respect of the profit it made on the stock sold to the French subsidiary. However, the French subsidiary still holds the stock at the balance sheet date. Therefore, from a group perspective, the UK profit has not yet been recognised. This leads to the recognition of a deferred tax asset at the UK subsidiary's tax rate on consolidation, to eliminate the tax charge on the unrealised profit.

Although the deferred tax asset will reverse when the French subsidiary has sold the stock to a third party, it should not be offset against any of that company's deferred tax liabilities. This is because the deferred tax asset relates to tax already paid (or payable) to the UK tax authorities by the UK subsidiary. Hence it should properly be offset against any deferred tax liabilities that arise within the UK companies in the group that are part of the same tax group as the UK subsidiary.

Presentation of material balances

13.263 FRS 19 does not require separate presentation of all material deferred tax balances on the face of the balance sheet. In the ASB's view such a requirement would simply add clutter. Instead, the ASB has followed the consensus reached in UITF Abstract 4 in respect of any long-term debtor included within current assets. Accordingly, deferred tax liabilities and assets should be disclosed separately on the face of the balance sheet if the amounts are so material in the context of the total net current assets or net assets that, in the absence of such disclosure, readers may misinterpret the financial statements. [FRS 19 para 58].

13.264 It is not clear, however, whether the above requirement applies to the net deferred tax balance or to its gross components. We believe that the requirement applies to the net balance. For instance, a net deferred tax asset would normally fall to be disclosed within debtors with separate disclosure within that sub-heading in the notes as required by paragraph 13.255 above. However, where it is considered to be material in the context of total net assets or net assets it should, in accordance with the above requirement, be shown on the face of the balance sheet to avoid possible misinterpretation.

13.265 As a corollary, it is difficult to see how deferred tax liabilities could be material in the context of total net current assets or for that matter net current liabilities since they would normally be shown as a provision under long-term liabilities. A sensible interpretation would be to show deferred tax liabilities on the face of the balance sheet where they are material in the context of net assets and deferred tax assets on the face of the balance sheet under current assets where they are material in the context of total net current assets or net assets.

Disclosure required by accounting standards

13.266 FRS 16 contains no additional disclosure requirements in respect of current tax shown as a liability on the balance sheet. A significant amount of additional disclosures is required by FRS 19 in support of the deferred tax balances reported either net or as separate assets or liabilities in the balance sheet. As with disclosures in the profit and loss account, examples from published financial statements are given to illustrate the disclosure requirements of company law and accounting standards.

Analysis of deferred tax balance

13.267 FRS 19 requires the following disclosures to be given in the notes to the financial statements in respect of deferred tax included in the balance sheet:

- The total deferred tax balance (before discounting, where applicable), showing the amount recognised for each significant type of timing difference separately.

- The impact of discounting on, and the discounted amount of, the deferred tax balance.
- The movement between the opening and closing net deferred tax balance, analysing separately:
  - The amount charged or credited in the profit and loss account for the period.
  - The amount charged or credited directly in the STRGL for the period; and
  - Movements arising from the acquisition or disposal of businesses.

[FRS 19 para 61].

An example of a company giving the above disclosures is shown in Table 13.7 below:

Table 13.7 – Tax disclosures relating to the balance sheet

Scottish Power plc – Annual Report & Accounts – 31 March 2001

Notes to the Group Balance sheet (extract)
Deferred tax provided in the Accounts is as follows:

	Provided	
	2001	2000
	£m	£m
Accelerated capital allowances	**1,963.1**	1,999.7
Other timing differences	**(337.8)**	(387.6)
	1,625.3	1,612.1

	£m
At 1 April 1998 – as previously stated	–
Prior year adjustment for FRS 19	709.6
At 1 April 1998 – as restated	709.6
Charge to profit and loss account	33.5
Deferred tax provided at 1 April 1999	743.1
Charge to profit and loss account	45.2
Movements arising from acquisition	818.1
Exchange	5.7
Deferred tax provided at 1 April 2000	1,612.1
Charge to profit and loss account	13.8
Movements arising from revisions to fair values	(98.5)
Exchange	97.9
Deferred tax provided at 31 March 2001	**1,625.3**

13.268 The significant type of timing difference that will generally fall to be disclosed separately will include, amongst others, accelerated capital allowances, short-term timing differences, tax losses carried forward etc. These items should then be added to show a gross undiscounted amount from which the discount, if any, recognised on this total should be deducted to arrive at the discounted amount. There is no further requirement to analyse the discount or the discounted amount by significant type of timing difference. The standard supports this approach as is evident from the illustrative disclosure given in Appendix II to FRS 19.

13.269 In the case of multinational groups, it is likely that the balance sheet will show a net deferred tax asset of say £4 million (net of short-term liability of £6 million) as well as a net deferred tax liability of £10 million (net of short-term asset of £4 million). The same type of short-term timing difference, but of opposite signs, may be included in both the asset and the liability amounts because they arise in different tax jurisdictions and do not qualify for offset. However, for the purpose of the above analysis they would need to be included in the same category and offset (that is, a short-term liability of £2 million). Similar type of timing differences included in both assets and liabilities may need to be grouped together before they are all added to show a net deferred tax liability of £6 million before discounting.

13.270 The above disclosure may require modification where certain timing differences such as those arising on long-term liabilities or a lessor's investment in finance leases also exist. Since these timing differences are measured by reference to cash flows that have already been discounted, the deferred tax provisions to which they give rise already incorporate discounting. As a result, they should be presented after the discounted figure (if there is one).

[The next paragraph is 13.272.]

Disclosure of deferred tax asset

13.272 The amount of the deferred tax asset and the evidence supporting its recognition should be disclosed where an entity has incurred a tax loss in the current or preceding period and the recovery of the deferred tax asset is dependent on future taxable profits in excess of those arising from the reversals of deferred tax liabilities. [FRS 19 para 62].

13.273 The reasons for the disclosure requirements are noted in paragraph 13.157 above. The evidence supporting the recognition of the deferred tax asset is the specific circumstances that make it reasonable to forecast that there will be future profits against which the deferred tax assets can be recovered. [FRS 19 para 63]. Such circumstances are discussed from paragraph 13.157 above and are also likely to include tax planning strategies as explained from paragraph 13.149 above.

Circumstances affecting current and future tax charges

13.274 Paragraph 23 of FRS 3 requires disclosure of 'any special circumstances' affecting the overall tax charge or credit for the period, or that may affect those of future periods. As noted in paragraph 13.236, there is a similar requirement in company law. [SI 2008/410 1 Sch 67(1)]. FRS 3 requires quantification of the individual effects of any special circumstances. Such disclosures should include any special circumstances affecting the tax attributable to the exceptional items. [FRS 3 para 23]. Special circumstances could also include, for example, the effect of tax losses utilised, significant tax-free income and significant disallowables such as goodwill amortisation arising on consolidation.

13.275 The above requirements have been codified in FRS 19, which requires significant disclosures in respect of circumstances that affect the current and total tax charges or credits for the current period or may affect the current and total tax charges or credits in future periods. [FRS 19 para 64]. These requirements are considered in the paragraphs that follow.

Circumstances affecting current tax charge

13.276 A number of matters may have a significant effect on the current tax charge for the period. FRS 19 contains a standard treatment as to how these should be disclosed. The standard's requirements are as follows:

- A reconciliation of the current tax charge or credit on ordinary activities for the period reported in the profit and loss account to the current tax charge that would result from applying a relevant standard rate of tax to the profit on ordinary activities before tax.
- Either the monetary amounts or the rates (as a percentage of profits on ordinary activities before tax) may be reconciled.
- Where material, positive amounts should not be offset against negative amounts or *vice versa*: they should be shown as separate reconciling items.
- The basis on which the standard rate of tax has been determined should be disclosed.

[FRS 19 para 64(a)].

13.277 It should be noted that FRS 19 requires a reconciliation of the *current* tax charge or credit to the current tax charge or credit that would result from applying the standard rate of tax to the profit on ordinary activities before tax. Both of the International and US GAAP equivalent standards (IAS 12 and FAS 109) require a reconciliation of the total tax charge (current and deferred) for the period to a standard rate of tax charge.

13.278 The ASB, however, chose to focus the reconciliation on the *current* tax charge instead, because it believed that that was the element of the total tax charge that was of most importance to users. A reconciliation based on the current tax charge was the clearest and most direct way of providing information on the factors that might affect future current tax charges. [FRS 19 App V para 134].

13.279 Notwithstanding the ASB's reasons, a reconciliation of the current tax charge would obviously be more transparent, because it would provide users with a complete picture of the factors (both permanent and timing differences) that had influenced the current tax charge for the period. However, a lot of tax planning transactions are based upon delaying the payment of tax and so creating timing differences. These would all be highlighted in the reconciliation of the current tax charge required under FRS 19, notwithstanding that deferred tax would have been provided on these timing differences. It seems rather superfluous to provide further disclosure of timing differences that have already been tax effected thereby calling into question the reasons for providing deferred tax in the first place. This situation would not arise in a reconciliation of the total tax charge required by IAS 12 that would simply highlight permanent differences and other items such as adjustments related to prior year and unrecognised deferred tax.

13.280 The standard requires that material positive and negative reconciling items should not be offset, but shown separately in the reconciliation. This is rather obvious as aggregating material items into a single figure defeats the object of the reconciliation, which is to provide an explanation of the current tax charge. An analysis of the factors included in the reconciliation will serve as a final check on the tax computations made and will help management explain the effects of the tax provisions.

13.281 The standard provides significant guidance as to how the 'standard' rate of tax should be calculated. For a UK group, the relevant rate is the standard rate of corporation tax. This rate should be used even if some of the group's operations are conducted in other countries. In that situation, the impact of different rates of tax applied to profits earned in other countries would appear as a reconciling item. [FRS 19 para 65]. However, where a UK group carries out its operations mainly outside the UK, the standard rate of corporation tax is of limited relevance. For such a group, the standard recommends use of an average tax rate (weighted in proportion to accounting profits) as illustrated below:

Example – Determination of 'standard' rate for a group with significant overseas subsidiaries

Country	Profit	Tax rate		Weighted average
UK	100	30%	100/2030 × 30% =	1.48
US	600	40%	600/2030 × 40% =	11.82
France	500	35%	500/2030 × 35% =	8.62
Germany	450	38%	450/2030 × 38% =	8.42
Australia	380	33%	380/2030 × 33% =	6.18
Total	2,030		Average rate =	36.52

The above average rate of 36.52% should be used in the tax reconciliation. The basis on which the rate has been calculated should also be disclosed as stated in paragraph 13.276.

13.281.1 Use of a weighted average tax rate method may be appropriate when all the group entities are profit-making. However, when entities within a group have differing tax rates and some entities have profits while others have losses, calculation of an average tax rate might not provide a meaningful tax rate. For example, if the entity calculates the weighted average tax rate based on absolute values (that is, making all values positive), although the tax rate obtained may appear meaningful, there will be a reconciling item in the tax reconciliation. Alternatively, if the weighted average rate is calculated based on the actual values, although the theoretical tax expense will be the correct amount, the weighted average tax rate may not be as meaningful as it may be higher than any individual rate. Therefore, use of the weighted average tax rate method may not be appropriate in this situation.

13.282 Alternatively, multi-nationals may find it more meaningful to aggregate separate reconciliations prepared using the applicable tax rate in each individual jurisdiction, rather than provide a reconciliation to a single applicable tax rate for the whole group. Such information would normally be requested as part of the group reporting packs and would greatly simply the presentation of the tax reconciliation in the consolidated financial statements. Examples of companies that have presented the reconciliation using monetary amounts and tax rates are shown in Tables 13.8 and 13.9 below.

Table 13.8 – Tax reconciliation presented using monetary amounts

Costain Group plc – Annual Report – 31 December 2000

Notes to the Accounts (extract)

8 Taxation (extract)	**2000**	1999 (restated)
	£m	£m
On profit for the year:		
United Kingdom corporation tax at 30% (1999: 30.25%)	–	–
Overseas taxation	**(0.3)**	(0.2)
Adjustments in respect of prior years	**0.3**	–
	–	(0.2)
Deferred taxation	**(1.2)**	(1.3)
Adjustments in respect of prior years	**(0.2)**	–
	(1.4)	(1.5)

	2000 £m	1999 (restated) £m
Tax reconciliation:		
Profit before taxation	**6.5**	6.4
Tax at 30% (1999: 30.25%)	**(2.0)**	(1.9)
Rate adjustments relating to overseas profits	**0.5**	0.3
Profit relieved by capital losses and sundry disallowed expenses	**0.7**	0.3
Unrelieved overseas taxation	**(0.3)**	(0.1)
Timing differences relating to the pension asset	**1.0**	1.3
Other timing differences	**(0.1)**	–
Exchange differences	**(0.1)**	(0.1)
Adjustments in respect of prior years	**0.3**	–
Tax charge for current year	–	(0.2)

Table 13.9 – Tax reconciliation presented using tax rates

Scottish Power plc – Annual Report & Accounts – 31 March 2001

Notes to the Group Profit and Loss Account (extract)

6 Tax on profit on ordinary activities (extract)

The rate of current tax charge on profit on ordinary activities before exceptional items and goodwill amortisation varied from the standard rate of corporation tax in the UK due to the following factors:

	Before exceptional items 2001 %	Before exceptional items 2000 %	1999 %
UK corporation tax rate	**30.0**	30.0	31.0
Permanent differences	**(9.8)**	(2.6)	(1.9)
Net effect of different rates of tax in overseas businesses	**2.3**	0.7	–
Advance corporation tax written back	–	–	(2.0)
Effective tax rate on ordinary activities	**22.5**	28.1	27.1
Effect of deferred tax	**(8.1)**	(6.1)	(5.2)
Effective current tax rate on ordinary activities	**14.4**	22.0	21.9

Circumstances affecting future tax charge

13.283 FRS 19 requires a number of disclosures that provide information about the tax charge or credit that may arise in future periods. These requirements are considered below.

13.284 Where assets have been revalued in the financial statements without deferred tax having been recognised on the revaluation gain or loss or where the market values of assets that have not been revalued have been disclosed in a note, the following information should be disclosed:

- An estimate of tax that could be payable or recoverable if the assets were sold at the values shown.
- The circumstances in which the tax would be payable or recoverable.
- An indication of the amount that may become payable or recoverable in the foreseeable future.

[FRS 19 para 64(b)].

13.285 Although the above unprovided deferred tax represents neither a liability nor a contingent liability, users are entitled to know the possible tax effects of a sale at the revalued amounts either recognised or disclosed in the financial statements. The above disclosures would apply to fixed and current asset investments carried in the balance sheet at a valuation under the alternative accounting rules and where the year end market values have been disclosed in a note (or in the directors' report) because they differ materially from their book amounts. It would also apply to fixed assets whose values have been 'frozen' under the transitional provisions of FRS 15 and to investment properties carried in accordance with SSAP 19.

13.286 Where the reporting entity has sold (or entered into a binding agreement to sell) an asset but has not recognised deferred tax on a taxable gain because the gain has been or is expected to be rolled over into replacement assets, the following information should be disclosed:

- The conditions that will have to be met to obtain the rollover relief.
- An estimate of the tax that would become payable if those conditions were not met.

[FRS 19 para 64(c)].

13.287 The above disclosures apply in circumstances where deferred tax is not recognised, because it is regarded as no more than a contingent liability for as long as it appears more likely than not that the entity will be able to roll over the gain. In this respect, the above disclosures are consistent with those required by FRS 12 on contingent liabilities — its nature, an indication of the uncertainty affecting whether it will become payable and an estimate of the financial effect.

13.288 Where there is insufficient evidence that a deferred tax asset will be recoverable, the FRS does not permit that asset to be recognised. In those circumstances the following information should be disclosed:

- The amount that has not been recognised.
- The circumstances in which the asset would be recovered.

[FRS 19 para 64(d)].

13.289 If a deferred tax asset has not been recognised on the grounds of insufficient evidence of recoverability, it indicates that the entity is currently loss making and the recoverability of the asset is contingent on the entity improving its trading performance. In such circumstances, any statements made to explain the circumstances in which the asset would be recovered should be balanced, realistic and consistent with the other disclosures made in the financial statements, particularly in the financial review (if applicable). References to any profit forecasts etc should be avoided as far as possible.

13.290 The following disclosure should be given in respect of any other deferred tax that has not been recognised in the financial statements:

- The nature of the amounts not recognised.
- The circumstances in which the tax would become payable or recoverable.
- An indication of the amount that may become payable or recoverable in the foreseeable future.

[FRS 19 para 64(e)].

The above disclosure would apply to deferred tax not provided on the unremitted earnings of subsidiaries, associates and joint ventures, where applicable.

Example – Unrecognised deferred tax on fair value gains

A group made an acquisition and has fair valued fixed assets. The fair values are in excess of original cost to the acquired company. There is no binding agreement to sell these assets so no deferred tax has been provided. Is there a requirement in FRS 19 to disclose the potential tax payable if the asset is sold at the fair value?

Paragraph 64(e) of FRS 19 requires such disclosure as it states that if any other deferred tax has not been recognised, the circumstances and an estimate of the tax payable should be disclosed. It states that disclosure should include '*if any other deferred tax has not been recognised – the nature of the amounts not recognised, the circumstances in which the tax would become payable or recoverable and an indication of the amount that may become payable or recoverable in the foreseeable future*'. This means that where properties are stated in the group financial statements at fair value (that is, 'cost to the group') and sold at that value, tax would become payable if that value is above the tax base (that is, 'original cost'). Since the future tax payable is not recognised it falls to be disclosed under paragraph 64(e) of FRS 19.

Groups of companies

Group relief

13.291 Subject to meeting detailed provisions in the tax legislation, in the UK, trading profits and losses arising in the same accounting period may be offset for tax purposes between companies in the same group by way of group relief. For example, a subsidiary that incurred a loss during an accounting period may surrender that loss to another group member that made a profit during the same accounting period. The tax rules may allow the profitable subsidiary (the claimant company) to pay to the loss making subsidiary (the surrendering company) any amount up to the full amount of the loss surrendered by way of group relief, without giving rise to any tax impact in either company.

13.292 Whether payment should or should not be made is a matter for the group to decide and does not affect the granting of the relief. However, non-payment or underpayment for group relief received may be objectionable if there are minority interests in the company. The reason is that if a company that has minority shareholders surrenders its losses for group relief purposes without receiving an adequate compensation payment, the minority shareholders' interests will be impaired. Likewise, overpayment for group relief may be objectionable if there are minority interests in the receiving company. Therefore, it is advisable for a fair payment to be made where there are minority interests in either the surrendering company, or the receiving company.

13.293 Where a payment is made to the surrendering company, the payment may take one of the following forms:

- The payment may be of the amount of the tax saving by reason of group relief. In this situation, the claimant company pays as group relief what it would have paid as tax at the applicable rate in force; the surrendering company receives the benefit of losses relieved at the same time.
- The payment may be made of any other amount up to a maximum of the gross amount of the loss surrendered by way of group relief. For example, it could be for an amount that is less than the amount of tax savings, or it could be more than the amount of tax savings, but less than the gross amount of the losses surrendered. Any part of a payment in excess of the tax relief on the loss surrendered by way of group relief (for example, to finance the balance of the underlying loss) is not a payment in respect of group relief; it should not be dealt with as such in the financial statements.

13.294 Different accounting considerations arise in the financial statements of the claimant company and the surrendering company depending on whether payment is made for group relief or not. For the purposes of illustrating the impact of group relief made with or without payment, the tax computations of two wholly-owned fellow subsidiary undertakings, company X and company Y, for the year ended 31 December 20X4 are given in the table below. The tax rate for both companies is 30 per cent and is expected to remain constant for the foreseeable future.

Tax computations	Company X	Company Y
	31 December	31 December
	20X4	20X4
	£	£
Profit (loss) before tax	(90,000)	180,000
Timing differences	(10,000)	(30,000)
	(100,000)	150,000
Group relief	100,000	(100,000)
Taxable profit (loss) chargeable to tax	–	50,000
Tax @ 30%	–	15,000

No payments made for group relief

13.295 In surrendering company X's financial statements, no credit can be taken in the profit and loss account as losses surrendered without payment being received are of no value to the company. However, part of the losses surrendered may relate to timing differences, as indicated in the example. In that situation, a deferred tax liability should be set up with a corresponding debit to the profit and loss account tax charge even if there is no current tax charge. This is because the surrendering company has lost the benefit of the losses that could otherwise have been utilised against future trading profits created by the reversal of the timing difference. As a result, the losses cannot be taken into account in the deferred tax calculation.

13.296 Where the surrendering company has been advised by its parent to surrender losses without receiving payment, the taxation note to the profit and loss account should disclose this fact and the financial impact. An appropriate note is included in the profit and loss account presentation below.

Company X – The surrendering company		31 December 20X4
		£
Loss on ordinary activities before taxation		(90,000)
Taxation:		
Tax @ 30%	–	
Deferred tax	3,000	(3,000)
Loss for the financial year		(93,000)

Note on taxation:
The company has surrendered the benefit of tax losses amounting to £100,000 to a fellow subsidiary undertaking without receiving any payment. Therefore, no tax losses are available for carry-forward and the company has provided deferred tax amounting to £3,000 in respect of timing differences of £10,000 included in the losses surrendered.

13.297 In the claimant company's financial statements different considerations apply. Group relief received without payment is effectively a gift as far as the claimant is concerned. As the relief is included in arriving at the taxable profit of the claimant, it will reduce, or sometimes completely eliminate, the claimant's liability to current tax. As a result, there could be a significant difference between the actual effective tax rate (tax charge as a percentage of profit before tax) and the prevailing tax rate. In this situation, the difference will have to be explained and quantified as 'special circumstances affecting the tax liability for the current year' to comply with the requirements of SI 2008/410 and FRS 3 (see para 13.236 above).The presentation in the profit and loss account of the claimant company will be as follows:

Company Y – The claimant company	**31 December 20X4**	
	£	**£**
Profit on ordinary activities before taxation		180,000
Taxation:		
Tax @ 30%	15,000	
Deferred tax	9,000	24,000
Profit on ordinary activities after taxation		156,000
Effective current tax rate		8%

Note on taxation:
The tax charge for the year has been reduced by £30,000 because of losses surrendered by a fellow subsidiary undertaking. No payment for this surrender is to be made by the company.

The explanation can also be provided by way of a reconciliation between the actual rate of 30% and the effective current tax rate of 8% as follows:

Actual tax rate	30%
Group relief received without payment	(17)%
Deferred tax on timing difference	(5)
Effective current tax rate	8%

Workings:
Group relief received £30,000 ÷ £180,000 = 17%.

Deferred tax £9,000 ÷ £180,000 = 5%.

Payments made for group relief

13.298 Where a payment passes between the companies concerned, the accounting treatment in the financial statements of the claimant and the surrendering company will depend upon the nature of the payment as illustrated in the various situations discussed below.

Payment represents the amount of tax saving

13.299 In the financial statements of the surrendering company, the payment received or receivable may be credited as part of the tax charge with a corresponding debit to cash or amounts receivable from group companies. The treatment is similar to the repayment of tax by the taxation authority. In some situations, it may not be appropriate to take credit until the group's tax affairs have been finalised and the appropriate group election has been made. Alternatively, as the payment has been received from another group company rather than from the taxation authority, it can be viewed that the payment does not relate to taxation. If this view is taken, the benefit received is a contribution to the company from another group company on behalf of the parent and is reflected as a transaction in equity. This will be a matter of policy choice for the entity. In either case an appropriate note should be included in the tax note as illustrated below.

Example 1 – Payment included within equity

Company X – The surrendering company	**31 December 20X4**	
	£	**£**
Loss on ordinary activities before taxation		(90,000)
Taxation		
Deferred taxation	(3,000)	(3,000)
Loss for the financial year		(93,000)

Note on taxation:
The company has surrendered the benefit of tax losses to another group company for a consideration of £30,000, which will be receivable on 30 September 20X5. This contribution has been reflected within equity as a transaction with another group company on behalf of the parent. No tax losses are, therefore, available for carry-forward, and the company has provided deferred tax amounting to £3,000 in respect of timing differences of £10,000 included in the losses surrendered.

Example 2 – Payment included within taxation credit

	31 December 20X4	
	£	**£**
Loss on ordinary activities before taxation		(90,000)
Taxation:		
Amount receivable from a fellow subsidiary in respect of group relief	30,000	
Deferred taxation	(3,000)	27,000
Loss for the financial year		(63,000)

Note on taxation:
The company has surrendered the benefit of tax losses to another group company for a consideration of £30,000, which will be receivable on 30 September 20X5. No tax losses are, therefore, available for carry-forward and the company has provided deferred tax amounting to £3,000 in respect of timing differences of £10,000 included in the losses surrendered.

13.300 As far as the claimant company is concerned, the payment made should be dealt similarly to the treatment in the surrendering company: either as part of the tax charge to bring this into proper relationship with the profits – but suitably described as payment made for group relief; or in equity as a transaction with a group company as described above. The presentation is, therefore, similar to that included in the example above.

Example 1 – Receipt included within equity

Company Y – The claimant company

	31 December 20X4	
	£	**£**
Profit on ordinary activities before taxation		180,000
Taxation:	15,000	
Tax @ 30%		
Deferred tax	9,000	24,000
		156,000

Note on taxation:
The taxation payable for the year has been reduced by £30,000 because of group relief received from a fellow subsidiary for which a payment of £30,000 will be made on 30 September 20X5. This payment has been reflected within equity as a transaction with another group company on behalf of the parent.

Example 2 – Receipt included within taxation charge

	31 December 20X4	
	£	**£**
Profit on ordinary activities before taxation		180,000
Taxation:		
Tax @ 30%	15,000	
Amount payable to a fellow subsidiary in respect of tax saved by group relief	30,000	
Deferred tax	9,000	54,000
Profit on ordinary activities after taxation		126,000

Note on taxation:
The tax payable for the year has been reduced by £30,000, because of group relief received from a fellow subsidiary for which a payment of £30,000 will be made on 30 September 20X5.

Payment is an amount other than the amount of tax savings

13.301 In some circumstances where payment is made, the amount paid by the receiving company to the surrendering company may be an amount other than that of the tax saving obtained. Where the group relief payment is for an amount that is less than the amount of the tax saving, the payment may be treated in either of the ways noted above when payment is made for the full amount of the tax saving.

13.302 Where the amount paid is more than the amount of the tax savings, the excess amount is not a payment for tax and should not, therefore, be included in the taxation balance in the profit and loss account. The amount of the tax savings can be recognised either in the tax charge or equity as described above, as a policy choice of the entity. Any excess payment above the amount of the tax savings should be recognised in equity.

13.303 Where a payment for group relief is brought into account in a year subsequent to that to which it relates, because the group relief position and group election for the current year were not finalised by the time the financial statements were approved, it should be appropriately described (depending upon the nature of the payment) as set out in the examples above, with the addition of words indicating that it relates to previous years. If the tax relief relating to the payment is brought into account at the same time, that also should be described appropriately.

Chapter 14

Earnings per share

Chapter 14

Earnings per share

14.1 Earnings per share (EPS) is a ratio that is widely used by financial analysts, investors and others to gauge the profitability of a company and to value its shares. In December 2004, the ASB issued FRS 22, 'Earnings per share', on the measurement and presentation of EPS. This replaced the previous standard FRS 14, 'Earnings per share'. FRS 22 is almost identical to the 2003 revised version of IAS 33, 'Earnings per share', except that FRS 22 contains additional guidance on presenting EPS in business combinations presented as mergers. Such guidance is not included in IAS 33 (2003) because, under IFRS, it is not generally permitted for business combinations to be accounted for using merger accounting.

14.2 FRS 22 applies to either (a) the separate or individual financial statements of an entity, or (b) the consolidated financial statements of a group with a parent:

"*(i) whose ordinary shares or potential ordinary shares are traded in a public market (a domestic or foreign stock exchange or an over-the-counter market, including local or regional markets) or*

(ii) that files, or is in the process of filing, its financial statements with a securities commission or other regulatory organisation for the purposes of issuing shares in a public market".

[FRS 22 para 2].

UK groups whose parent's instruments are traded on either the London Stock Exchange or the Alternative Investments Market are required to prepare financial information under IFRS. FRS 22, therefore, no longer applies to most UK companies or groups. Hence, it only applies to listed companies with no subsidiaries (for example some investment companies).

14.3 The accounting and practical application issues arising under FRS 22 are the same as those arising under IAS 33. Guidance on the application of IAS 33 is included in the 'Manual of Accounting – IFRS for the UK'.

Annex

Earnings per share

Introduction

A14.1 Earnings per share (EPS) is a ratio that is widely used by financial analysts, investors and others to gauge a company's profitability and to value its shares. Its purpose is to indicate how effective a company has been in using the resources provided by the ordinary shareholders (described as ordinary equity holders in IAS 33). The allocation of earnings accruing to other providers of finance, such as preference shareholders is a prior charge and is often fixed. Therefore, the income remaining after making allocations to those parties is attributable to ordinary shareholders. This amount, when presented on the face of the profit and loss account on a pence per share basis, assists the ordinary shareholders to gauge the company's current net earnings and changes in its net earnings from period to period. It can, therefore, be relevant as a measure of company performance and in evaluating management's effectiveness. Another reason for the popularity of EPS is that it forms the basis for calculating the 'price-earnings ratio', which is a standard stock market indicator. Price-earnings ratios relating to both past and prospective profits are widely used by investors and analysts in valuing shares.

A14.2 EPS is simply a ratio of the numerator – earnings measured in terms of profits available to ordinary shareholders – to the denominator – the number of ordinary shares. Therefore, it is very simple in concept, but it is the determination of the numerator and, in particular, the denominator that can make the calculation of this ratio rather complex in practice. Also if the ratio is to be meaningful it must be calculated on a similar basis for every entity so as to facilitate comparisons between different accounting periods for the same entity and between different entities in the same period.

[The next paragraph is A14.5.]

A14.5 During 2008 the IASB issued, and received comments on, an exposure draft on EPS. The IASB considered comments on the exposure draft during 2009. The objective of the exposure draft was to simplify and converge the calculation of EPS according to IAS 33 and US GAAP SFAS 128. Many of the comment letters the IASB received recommended discontinuing the amendment project. At the time of writing, the IASB has deferred making a decision on how to proceed with the project indefinitely. The FASB had published a corresponding exposure draft to amend SFAS 128, 'Earnings per share', but has also put its project on hold pending the IASB re-deliberations.

A14.6 In May 2010, the IASB issued an exposure draft, 'Presentation of items of other comprehensive income', which (among other things) would require a single statement of 'profit or loss and other comprehensive income'. The IASB stated in the exposure draft that 'profit and loss' will remain the starting point for calculating earnings per share under its proposals despite the requirement to amalgamate other comprehensive income and profit or loss in a single statement.

[The next paragraph is A14.40.]

Objectives and scope of IAS 33

Objectives

A14.40 IAS 33 specifies the way in which earnings per share data should be calculated, presented and disclosed in the financial statements of entities. In doing so, it focuses primarily on determining the number of shares to be included in the denominator of the earnings per share calculation. [IAS 33 para 1].

A14.41 Although it is accepted that earnings per share data may have limitations because of the different accounting policies used for determining 'earnings', a consistently calculated denominator will improve the comparison of the performance of different entities in the same period and of the same entity in different accounting periods. Furthermore, a denominator calculated in accordance with international consensus will go a long way in enhancing global comparison of earnings per share data in spite of different national methods for determining 'earnings'.

Scope

A14.42 The standard applies to entities whose ordinary shares or potential ordinary shares (for example, convertible debt, warrants etc) are publicly traded. [IAS 33 para 2]. Therefore, entities whose securities are listed on a recognised stock exchange (for example, London Stock Exchange, Luxembourg Stock Exchange, NASDAQ) or are otherwise publicly traded, will have to calculate earnings per share data in accordance with the standard. Furthermore, entities that file or are in the process of filing financial statements with a securities commission or other regulatory body for purposes of issuing ordinary shares (that is, not private placements) are also required to comply with the standard. [IAS 33 para 2].

A14.43 When both the parent's separate and consolidated financial statements are presented, the disclosures are required only on the basis of consolidated information. Users of the financial statements of a parent are normally concerned with, and need information on, the results of operations of the group as a whole. Where an entity chooses voluntarily to present earnings per share based on its entity financial statements as well as earnings per share based on the consolidated financial statements, the entity earnings per share figures may be shown only on the face of the entity statement of comprehensive income (or income statement, if presented). They must not be shown in the consolidated financial statements. [IAS 33 para 4, 4A].

A14.44 Entities whose securities are not publicly traded are not required to disclose earnings per share data because, generally, they have a smaller number of ordinary shareholders. However, where such entities choose to disclose earnings per share data, to maintain comparability in financial reporting, they should comply with the standard's provisions. [IAS 33 para 3]. Such entities are likely to be those that intend to establish a track record before seeking entry to the public market at a future date.

[The next paragraph is A14.46.]

Basic earnings per share

Measurement

A14.46 Entities that fall within the standard's scope must calculate basic (and diluted) EPS for the profit or loss attributable to the parent entity's ordinary equity holders. Basic (and diluted) EPS should also be calculated for profit or loss from continuing operations if this is presented. [IAS 33 para 9]. Where an entity has no operations that qualify as discontinued under IFRS 5, 'Non-current assets held for sale and discontinued operations', the profit or loss for the year will all be attributable to continuing operations and so calculation of an additional EPS figure for continuing operations will be unnecessary. Where an entity has operations that qualify as discontinued under IFRS 5, however, it has to give separate disclosure of the results of such operations. IAS 33 then requires the basic (and diluted) EPS for profit or loss attributable to continuing operations to be calculated. The standard requires disclosure of basic and diluted EPS for profit or loss from continuing operations and profit or loss for the year, for each class of ordinary shares that has a different right to share in profit for the period – see 'Presentation and disclosure' from paragraph A14.173 below. The following paragraphs describe the EPS calculation for profit or loss for the period attributable to ordinary equity holders, but the principles are the same for calculating EPS for profit or loss from continuing and discontinued operations.

A14.47 Basic EPS should be calculated by dividing the profit or loss for the period attributable to the parent entity's ordinary equity holders by the weighted average number of ordinary shares outstanding during the period. [IAS 33 para 10].

A14.48 The term 'ordinary share' is defined as an equity instrument that is subordinate to all other classes of equity instrument. An equity instrument is any contract that evidences a residual interest in the assets of an entity after deducting all of its liabilities. [IAS 33 para 5; IAS 32 para 11].

A14.49 Ordinary shares participate in profit only after other types of shares such as preference shares have participated. [IAS 33 para 6]. Indeed preference shares that provide for mandatory redemption by the issuer for a fixed or determinable amount at a fixed or determinable future date or that give the holder the right to require such redemption are treated as liabilities under IAS 32, 'Financial instruments: Disclosure'. [IAS 32 para 18(a)]. An entity may have more than one class of ordinary share (see further para A14.59 below). Ordinary shares of the same class will have the same rights to receive dividends. [IAS 33 para 6].

A14.50 The computation of the EPS figure requires a calculation of the earnings as the numerator and the relevant number of ordinary shares as the denominator. If no adjustments are required to the numerator or the denominator, the profit or loss attributable to the ordinary equity holders and the relevant number of ordinary shares can be obtained directly from the financial statements and the figure computed. However, in practice the numerator or to the denominator or both may need to be adjusted for the reasons discussed in the paragraphs that follow. The circumstances in which such adjustments should be made are considered in the paragraphs that follow.

Computation of earnings

A14.51 For the purposes of calculating basic EPS, the profit or loss from continuing operations and the profit or loss for the period attributable to the parent entity's ordinary equity holders are the profit or loss after tax and minority interest and after adjusting for the after tax effects of preference dividends, differences arising on settlement of preference shares and other similar effects of preference shares classified as equity under IAS 32. [IAS 33 paras 12, A1]. In the absence of any preference shares, it is relatively simple to calculate the earnings figure for EPS purposes. However, where the entity has preference shares in issue, some further adjustments as stated above may be necessary. The ways in which such adjustments are likely to affect earnings for the purposes of calculating basic EPS are considered below. There is no requirement to compute 'Comprehensive earnings per share', but this information could be provided as supplementary information (see para A14.187).

Preference dividends

A14.52 Where an entity has preference shares in issue, those shares will be classified as financial liabilities or equity under IAS 32, depending on the terms of the shares. Where preference shares are classified as liabilities in accordance with IAS 32 (see para A14.49 above) any dividends or other appropriations in respect of such preference shares (for example, a premium payable on redemption) will be treated as finance costs in arriving at profit or loss for the period. [IAS 32 paras 35, 36]. However, where preference shares are classified as equity, any dividends and other appropriations would be debited directly to equity and an adjustment is, therefore, needed to deduct it from the profit for the period to arrive at the profit attributable to ordinary equity holders for the purpose of calculating EPS. [IAS 33 para 12]. Whether the preference shares are treated as liabilities or as equity, the calculation of amounts of dividend and other appropriations and adjustments attributable to such shares is the same, and in both cases the amounts are deducted to arrive at the profit attributable to ordinary equity holders for the purpose of calculating basic EPS.

A14.53 Where preference shares carry the right to a fixed dividend, then those dividends can either be cumulative or non-cumulative. If the preference dividends are cumulative, the dividend for the period should be taken into account, whether or not it has been declared. [IAS 33 para 14(b)]. Thus, in a year in which the company is unable to pay or declare a cumulative preference dividend, because of insufficient distributable profits (for example, the company has accumulated losses), the undeclared amount of the cumulative preference dividend (net of tax, if applicable) should still be deducted in arriving at earnings for the purposes of the EPS calculation. In the year in which these arrears of preference dividends are paid, they should be ignored in the EPS calculation for that year. [IAS 33 para 14(b)]. On the other hand, if the preference dividends are non-cumulative, only the amount of dividends declared in respect of the year should be deducted in arriving at the profit attributable to ordinary shareholders. [IAS 33 para 14(a)].

Other appropriations and adjustments in respect of preference shares

A14.54 Under IAS 32 (see para A14.49 above) and IAS 39, 'Financial instruments: Recognition and measurement', the charges made in the profit and loss account in respect of preference shares that are treated as financial liabilities will include not only the preference and/or participating dividends, but also other elements such as the amortisation of transaction costs and accrual for any premium payable on redemption. [IAS 39 paras 47, IAS 32 paras 35, 36]. It follows that these other elements should continue to be deducted in arriving at profit for the financial year and the earnings available to ordinary equity holders. In the year in which the preference shares are redeemed, any premium payable on redemption should be ignored in calculating EPS for that year to the extent that it has been accrued (and, therefore, already taken into account) in earlier years.

A14.55 In respect of preference shares classified as equity the following adjustments should also be made:

- Any original discount or premium that is amortised to retained earnings using the effective interest method is treated as a preference dividend for the purposes of calculating EPS. [IAS 33 para 15]. An example is non-convertible, non-redeemable preference shares that have been issued at a discount to compensate for non-payment of dividends in earlier years, the discount being amortised to retained earnings. Such shares are often referred to as 'increasing rate preference shares'. (See illustrative example 1 in IAS 33.)
- On the repurchase of preference shares, any excess of the fair value of consideration given over the carrying amount of the shares is a charge to retained earnings and is deducted in determining the profit, or added in determining the loss, available to ordinary equity holders for the purpose of calculating EPS. [IAS 33 para 16].

- Where preference shares are converted early on favourable terms, the excess of the fair value of ordinary shares or other consideration paid over the fair value of ordinary shares or other consideration payable under the original terms is deducted in determining the profit, or added in determining the loss, available to ordinary equity holders for the purpose of calculating EPS. [IAS 33 para 17].
- Any excess of the carrying amount of preference shares over the fair value of the consideration paid to settle them is added in determining the profit, or deducted in determining the loss, available to ordinary equity holders for the purpose of calculating EPS. [IAS 33 para 18].

A14.56 The treatment of preference shares in the EPS calculation is illustrated in the following example:

Example

An entity has the following preference shares in issue at the end of 20X4:

■ 5% Redeemable, non-cumulative preference shares, these shares are classified as liabilities under IAS 32. During the year a dividend was paid on the 5% preference shares.	C100,000
■ Increasing rate, cumulative, non-redeemable preference shares issued at a discount in 20X0 with a cumulative dividend rate from 20X5 of 10%. The shares were issued at a discount to compensate the holders, as dividend payments will not commence until 20X5. The accrual for the discount in the current year, calculated using the effective interest method amounted to, say, C18,000. These shares are classified as equity under IAS 32.	C200,000
■ 8% Non-redeemable, non-cumulative preference shares. At the beginning of the year the entity had C100,000 8% preference shares outstanding, but at 30 June 20X4, it repurchased C50,000 of these at a discount of C1,000.	C50,000
■ 7% Cumulative, convertible preference shares (converted in the year). These shares were classified as equity, until their conversion into ordinary shares at the beginning of the year. No dividend was accrued in respect of the year, although the previous year's dividend was paid immediately prior to conversion. To induce conversion, the terms of conversion of the 7% convertible preference shares were also amended and the revised terms entitled the preference shareholders to an additional 100 ordinary shares on conversion with a fair value of C300.	CNill

The profit attributable to ordinary equity holders for the year 20X4 is C150,000. Adjustments for the purpose of calculating EPS are made as follows:

	C	C
Profit for the year attributable to the ordinary equity holders		150,000
Amortisation of discount on issue of increasing rate preference shares	(18,000)[1]	
Discount on repurchase of 8% preference shares	1,000[2]	
		(17,000)
Profit attributable to ordinary equity holders for basic EPS		133,000

Notes

1 The original discount on issue of the increasing rate preference shares has been amortised to retained earnings, so must be treated as preference dividends for EPS purposes and adjusted against profit attributable to the ordinary equity holders. [IAS 33 para 15]. There is no adjustment in respect of dividends as these do not commence until 20X5. Instead, the finance cost is represented by the amortisation of the discount in the dividend-free period. In future years, the accrual for the dividend of C20,000 will be deducted from profits. [IAS 33 para 14(b)].

2 The discount on repurchase of the 8% preference shares has been credited to equity so must be added to profit. [IAS 33 para 18].

3 The dividend on the 5% preference shares has been charged to the income statement as the preference shares are treated as liabilities, so no adjustment is necessary to profit.

4 No accrual for the dividend on the 8% preference shares is required as they are non-cumulative. Had a dividend been declared for the year it would have been deducted from profit for the purpose of calculating basic EPS as the shares are treated as equity and the dividend would have been charged to equity in the financial statements. [IAS 33 para 14(a)].

5 As the 7% preference shares were converted at the beginning of the year, there is no adjustment in respect of the 7% preference shares as no dividend accrued in respect of the year. The payment of the previous year's cumulative dividend is ignored for EPS purposes as it will have been adjusted for in the prior year. [IAS 33 para 14(b)]. Similarly, the excess of the fair value of additional ordinary shares issued on conversion of the convertible preference shares over fair value of the ordinary shares to which they would have been entitled under the original conversion terms would already have been deducted from profit attributable to the ordinary shareholders and no further adjustment is required.

Participating securities and two-class ordinary shares

A14.57 Sometimes, preference shares may be given the right to participate in the profit with ordinary shares according to a predetermined formula, but with an upper limit or cap on the extent of participation by the preference shares. Such participation is usually in addition to a fixed dividend. Participating preference shares would be treated as either financial liabilities or equity instruments under IAS 32, dependent on their terms. Where participating preference shares are classified as liabilities, both the fixed and the participating element would have been charged in arriving at profit or loss attributable to the parent entity and no further adjustments are necessary. Where participating preference shares are classified as equity instruments, IAS 33 contains further guidance that is considered below.

A14.58 IAS 33 describes instruments that would include participating preference shares as 'participating equity instruments'. It notes that such instruments include instruments that participate in dividends with ordinary shares according to a predetermined formula (for example, two for one) with, sometimes an upper limit on participation (for example, up to a specified amount per share, but no more). [IAS 33 para A13(a)]. An example might be a participating preference share that receives a fixed dividend of 3 per cent and a variable participation of 20 per cent of the dividend on an ordinary share up to a maximum of 50 pence per participating preference share. Therefore, the total earnings would need to be calculated by reference to the fixed and the participating element in order to calculate the EPS attributable to the participating preference shares.

A14.59 In addition to participating equity instruments, an entity could have a class of ordinary shares with a different dividend rate from that of another class of ordinary shares, but without prior or senior rights. [IAS 33 para A13(b)]. IAS 33 describes such instruments as 'two-class ordinary shares'. Where this is the case, the earnings for the period should be apportioned over the different classes of equity shares in issue in accordance with their dividend rights or other rights to participate in undistributed earnings. [IAS 33 para A14]. This means that a company could disclose a number of EPS figures, each attributable to different classes of equity shares and participating equity instruments.

A14.60 The steps that should be followed in allocating earnings for the purposes of calculating basic EPS where an entity has different classes of ordinary shares and participating equity instruments that are not convertible into ordinary shares are as follows:

- Profit or loss attributable to ordinary equity holders is adjusted by the amount of dividends declared in the period for each class of shares and by the contractual amount of dividends that must be paid for the period (for example, unpaid cumulative dividends).
- The remaining profit or loss is allocated to ordinary shares and participating equity instruments to the extent that each instrument shares in earnings or losses. The allocation is made as if all the profit or loss has been distributed. The total profit or loss allocated to each class of equity instrument is determined by adding together the amount allocated for dividends and the amount allocated for the participation feature.
- The total amount of profit or loss allocated to each class of equity instrument is divided by the number of outstanding instruments to which the profits or losses are allocated (that is, the instruments in that class) to determine the EPS for that class of instrument.

[IAS 33 para A14].

A14.61 Where participating equity instruments (participating preference shares) are convertible into ordinary shares, conversion is assumed if the effect is dilutive. Where this is so, the conversion shares should be included in outstanding ordinary shares for the purposes of calculating diluted EPS (see below under 'Diluted earnings per share'). [IAS 33 para A14].

A14.62 The illustrative examples accompanying IAS 33 include a worked example illustrating how the allocation would be done. The following example is based on that example.

Example

An entity has two classes of shares in issue:

5,000 Non-convertible preference shares
10,000 Ordinary shares

The preference shares are entitled to a fixed dividend of C5 per share before any dividends are paid on the ordinary shares. Ordinary dividends are then paid in which the preference shareholders do not participate. Each preference share then participates in any additional ordinary dividend above C2 at a rate of 50% of any additional dividend payable on an ordinary share.

The entity's profit for the year is C100,000 and dividends of C2 per share are declared on the ordinary shares.

The calculation of basic EPS using the allocation method described in the previous paragraph is as follows:

	C	C
Profit		100,000
Less dividends payable for the period:		
Preference (5,000 × C5)	25,000	
Ordinary (10,000 × C2)	20,000	(45,000)
Undistributed earnings		55,000

Allocation of undistributed earnings:

Allocation per ordinary share = A
Allocation per preference share = B where B = 50% of A

(A × 10,000) + (50% × A × 5,000) = C55,000

A = 55,000 / (10,000 + 2,500) A = C4.4
B = 50% of A
B = C2.2

The basic per share amounts are:	Preference shares C per share	Ordinary shares C per share
Distributed earnings	5.00	2.00
Undistributed earnings	2.20	4.40
Totals	7.20	6.40

Proof: (5,000 × C7.2) + (10,000 × C6.4) = C100,000

A14.63 IAS 33 implies that the EPS attributable to the participating preference shares (participating equity instrument in IAS 33 terminology) should be disclosed even though only one of its two elements (the participating element) is subordinate to all other classes of equity instrument.

A14.64 Table A14.1 illustrates disclosure of EPS for different classes of shares – preferred shares and ordinary shares. The equity note describes the respective dividend rights of the shares.

Table A14.1 – EPS for different classes of shares

Volkswagen AG – annual report and accounts – 31 December 2010

Income statement of the Volkswagen Group

For the period January 1 to December 31, 2009 (extract)

	Note	2010	2009
Basic earnings per ordinary share in €	11	15.17	2.37
Diluted earnings per ordinary share in €	11	15.17	2.37
Basic earnings per preferred share in €*	11	15.23	2.43
Diluted earnings per preferred share in €*	11	15.23	2.43

11 Earnings per share
Basic earnings per share are calculated by dividing profit attributable to shareholders of Volkswagen AG by the weighted average number of ordinary and preferred shares outstanding during the reporting period. Earnings per share are diluted by potential shares. These include stock options, although these are only dilutive if they result in the issuance of shares at a value below the average market price of the shares.

A dilutive effect arose in fiscal year 2010 from the seventh and eighth tranches of the stock option plan. However, it was so insignificant that it did not affect the reported earnings per share.

As the new preferred shares issued in March/April 2010 carry retrospective dividend rights from January 1, 2009 and their subscription price was below their fair value, the number of shares in the previous year and therefore earnings per share for fiscal year 2009 were partially adjusted retrospectively by €0.01.

	Ordinary		Preferred	
	2010	2009	**2010**	2009
Weighted average number of shares outstanding – basic	295,024,566	294,963,231	154,905,434	107,652,546
Dilutive potential ordinary shares from the stock option plan	9,792	87,163	–	–
Weighted average number of shares outstanding – diluted	295,034,358	295,050,394	154,905,434	107,652,546

	€ million	
	2010	2009
Profit after tax	7,226	911
Non-controlling interests	392	49
Profit attributable to shareholders of Volkswagen AG	6,835	960
Basic earnings attributable to ordinary shares*	4,475	699
Diluted earnings attributable to ordinary shares*	4,476	699
Basic earnings attributable to preferred shares*	2,359	261
Diluted earnings attributable to preferred shares*	2,359	261

	€	
	2010	**2009**
Basic earnings per ordinary share*	15.17	2.37
Diluted earnings per ordinary share*	15.17	2.37
Basic earnings per preferred share*	15.23	2.43
Diluted earnings per preferred share*	15.23	2.43

* The prior-year figures were adjusted.

24 Equity (extract)

The subscribed capital of Volkswagen AG is denominated in euros. The shares are no-par value bearer shares. Each share has a notional value of €2.56. As well as ordinary shares, there are preferred shares that entitle the bearer to a €0.06 higher dividend than ordinary shares, but do not carry voting rights.

Based on the resolution by the annual general meeting on May 3, 2006, authorized capital of up to €90 million, expiring on May 2, 2011, was approved for the issue of new ordinary bearer shares.

There is also contingent capital of €7 million (originally €40 million) resulting from the resolution by the annual general meeting on April 16, 2002. This contingent capital increase will be implemented only to the extent that the holders of convertible bonds issued before April 15, 2007 exercise their conversion rights.

Based on the resolution by the extraordinary general meeting on December 3, 2009, there is authorized capital of up to €179.4 million (originally €345.6 million), expiring on December 2, 2014, for the issue of new preferred bearer shares.

Based on the resolution by the annual general meeting on April 22, 2010, there is contingent capital of up to €102.4 million, expiring on April 21, 2015, from the issue of up to €5 billion in bonds with warrants and/or convertible bonds.

Volkswagen AG issued 64,904,498 new preferred shares (with a notional value of €166 million) as part of a capital increase in the reporting period. Volkswagen AG recorded a cash inflow of approximately €4.1 billion from the capital increase. In addition, Volkswagen AG issued 40,170 new ordinary shares (with a notional value of €102,835) as a result of the exercise of convertible bonds from the seventh and eighth tranches of the stock option plan.

The subscribed capital is thus composed of 295,045,567 no-par value ordinary shares and 170,142,778 preferred shares, and amounts to €1,191 million (previous year: €1,025 million).

Change in ordinary and preferred shares and subscribed capital

	Shares		€	
	2010	2009	2010	2009
Balance at January 1	400,243,677	400,158,487	1,024,623,813	1,024,405,726
Capital increase	64,904,498	–	166,155,515	–
Stock option plan	40,170	85,190	102,835	218,086
Balance at December 31	465,188,345	400,243,677	1,190,882,163	1,024,623,813

Computation of number of ordinary shares

A14.65 The denominator of the basic EPS is calculated using the weighted average number of those ordinary shares that are outstanding during the period under review. [IAS 33 para 19].

A14.66 Where there have been no changes in capital structure during the year, the relevant denominator is the number of ordinary shares outstanding at the year end. However, if additional ordinary shares have been issued during the year, it would not give a fair presentation to apportion the earnings for the whole of the year over the larger equity base. This is because the capital invested through the issue of the additional shares was available to the entity to increase its earnings only for part of the year. Similar considerations apply where shares have been bought back during the year. In order to take these factors into account, and to permit comparison of EPS with the previous period when there may have been no such change in the issued equity capital, it is necessary to use an average of the number of shares weighted by the number of days outstanding (a 'weighted average ordinary share capital') in the calculation of the denominator. The time-weighting factor should generally be the number of days that the specific shares are outstanding as a proportion of the total number of days, although a reasonable approximation of the weighted average is adequate in most circumstances. [IAS 33 para 20].

A14.67 An example of how the weighted average number of shares should be calculated is given below. The example is derived from the illustrative example in IAS 33.

	Shares issued	Treasury shares	Shares outstanding
1 Jan 20X1 Balance at beginning of year	2,400	–	2,400
31 May 20X1 Issue of new shares for cash	800	–	3,200
1 Dec 20X1 Purchase of shares for cash	–	(200)	3,000
31 Dec 20X1 Balance at end of year	3,200	(200)	3,000

Computation of weighted average:
(2,400 × 5/12) + (3,200 × 6/12) + (3,000 × 1/12) = 2,850 shares
or
(2,400 × 12/12) + (800 × 7/12) — (200 × 1/12) = 2,850 shares

A14.68 The general principle under IAS 33 is that shares should be included in the weighted average calculation from the date the consideration is receivable (which is generally the date of their issue). [IAS 33 para 21]. Therefore, shares issued for cash are brought into the calculation from the date the cash is receivable. Where shares are issued as consideration for the acquisition of an asset or a satisfaction of a liability, the shares are included in the averaging calculation from the date the asset is recognised or the liability is settled. In other situations, the date of inclusion should be determined from the terms and conditions attaching to the issue. The substance of any contract associated with the issue should also be considered. The standard provides a number of examples illustrating the timing of inclusion of ordinary shares in the weighted average calculation. These examples are listed below:

- Ordinary shares issued in exchange for cash are included when cash is receivable.
- Ordinary shares issued on the voluntary reinvestment of dividends on ordinary or preference shares are included when dividends are reinvested.
- Ordinary shares issued as a result of the conversion of a debt instrument to ordinary shares are included as of the date when interest ceases accruing.
- Ordinary shares issued in place of interest or principal on other financial instruments are included as of the date when interest ceases accruing.
- Ordinary shares issued in exchange for the settlement of a liability of the entity are included as of the settlement date.
- Ordinary shares issued as consideration for the acquisition of an asset other than cash are included as of the date on which the acquisition is recognised.
- Ordinary shares issued for the rendering of services to the entity are included as the services are rendered.
- Ordinary shares issued as part of the cost of a business combination are included from the acquisition date (see para A14.76).

[IAS 33 paras 21, 22].

A14.69 The general rule that shares should be included in the basic EPS calculation from the date consideration is receivable does not apply to shares that are issued in partly paid form. Partly paid shares are treated as fractions of shares (payments received to date as a proportion of the total subscription price) and included in the averaging calculation only to the extent that they participate in dividends for the period. [IAS 33 para A15]. Partly paid shares that do not participate in dividends are excluded from the basic EPS calculation, but included in the calculation of diluted EPS (see further para A14.110).

Example

A company issues 100,000 ordinary shares of C1 each for a consideration of C2.50 per share. Calls amounting to C1.75 per share were received by the balance sheet date. The partly paid shares are entitled to participate in dividends for the period in proportion to the amount paid. The number of ordinary share equivalents that would be included in the basic EPS calculation on a weighted basis is as follows:

$$100{,}000 \times \frac{C1.75}{C2.50} = 70{,}000 \text{ shares}$$

A14.70 Whenever changes in ordinary shares occur during the accounting period, an amendment is necessary to the number of shares used in the EPS calculation. In some situations, the EPS in prior periods will also have to be adjusted. Some of the ways in which a company can change its ordinary share capital and the consequential effect on the number of shares used in the EPS calculation are considered below.

Purchase and holding of own shares and ESOPs

A14.71 Where a company has purchased its own ordinary shares during the year, there will be a lesser number outstanding after the repurchase. Such repurchases should be reflected in the weighted average number of shares outstanding during the period from the date shares are repurchased as illustrated in paragraph A14.67. Any premium payable on the purchase of a company's own ordinary shares will be charged against reserves and will not affect earnings for the year. No adjustments should be made to the prior year's EPS.

A14.72 A company may sometimes hold its own shares in treasury. This situation may arise where it has acquired them in the market, or by forfeiture, or by surrender in lieu of forfeiture, or by way of a gift. Shares held uncancelled in treasury are accounted for as a deduction from shareholders' funds. [IAS 32 para 33; IAS 33 para 20]. Another not uncommon group situation is where a subsidiary continues to hold the shares in the parent that were acquired before it became a group member. Since such shares are no longer available in the market, they are excluded from the weighted average number of ordinary shares for the purpose of calculating EPS. [IAS 33 para 20].

[The next paragraph is A14.75]

UK.A14.74.1 In the UK, a company may hold its own shares where the shares are held as treasury shares under Chapter 6 of Part 18 of the 2006 Companies Act (sections 724 to 732). Companies with *'qualifying shares'* may purchase such shares out of distributable profits and hold them in treasury for resale, transfer or cancellation at a later date. 'Qualifying shares' are defined as shares that:

- are included in the official list (that is, listed on the London Stock Exchange);
- are traded on AIM;
- are officially listed in another EEA State; or
- are traded on a regulated market.

[CA 2006 sec 724(2)].

A14.75 Another common situation where a company holds its own shares arises where it operates an Employee Share Ownership Plan (ESOP) for the benefit of its employees. For the purpose of calculating EPS these outstanding shares should also be excluded from the calculation to the extent that they have not vested unconditionally in the employees.

A14.76 An example where a company has excluded treasury shares for the purposes of determining the weighted average number of shares for calculating EPS is given in Table A14.2 below. In this example there were no other issues of shares in the year.

Table A14.2 – Treatment of treasury shares in EPS calculation

Telkom SA Limited – annual report and accounts – 31 March 2011

	Restated 2010	**2011**
12. EARNINGS PER SHARE (extract 1)	7,425.7	**239.9**
Total operations		
Basic and diluted earnings per share (cents)		
The calculation of earnings per share is based on profit attributable to equity holders of Telkom for the year of R1,222 million (2010: R37,458 million) and 509,311,296 (2010: 504,437,832) weighted average number of ordinary shares in issue. **		
12. EARNINGS PER SHARE (extract 2)		
Reconciliation of weighted average number of ordinary shares:		
Ordinary shares in issue (refer to note 24)	520,783,900	**520,783,900**
Weighted average number of treasury shares	(16,346,068)	**(11,472,604)**
Weighted average number of shares outstanding	504,437,832	**509,311,296**
Reconciliation of diluted weighted average number of ordinary shares		
Weighted average number of shares outstanding	504,437,832	**509,311,296**
Expected future vesting of shares	–	–
Diluted weighted average number of shares outstanding	504,437,832	**509,311,296**

** *The Telkom Conditional Share Plan was concluded with a final vesting in June 2010, therefore there is no adjustment in the weighted average number of shares as a result of the expected future vesting of shares allocated to employees under this plan. Due to the plan being concluded, there is no further dilutive effect on basic earnings per share.*

Contingently issuable shares

A14.77 Contingently issuable shares are ordinary shares that are issuable for little or no cash or other consideration if and when specified conditions in a contingent share agreement have been met. [IAS 33 para 5]. In other words, the consideration for the shares has effectively been received, but the shares remain to be issued – a typical example is contingent consideration on an acquisition payable in shares. Contingently issuable shares are considered to be outstanding and are included in the calculation of basic EPS from the date when all the necessary conditions have been satisfied, that is, the events have occurred. Shares that are issuable solely after the passage of time are not contingently issuable shares, because the passage of time is a certainty and should, therefore, be included in the calculation from inception of the contract. Outstanding ordinary shares that are contingently returnable (that is, subject to recall) are not treated as outstanding, that is they are excluded from the calculation of basic EPS until the date when the shares are no longer subject to recall. [IAS 33 para 24]. Contingently issuable shares are discussed further from paragraph A14.145.

Shares issued as consideration in a business combination

A14.78 Where ordinary shares are issued during the financial year as part of the cost of a business combination (for example, in exchange for a majority interest in the equity of another company) – that is, as non-cash consideration, the results of the new subsidiary are included in the consolidation from the acquisition date. Therefore, the shares issued as consideration to obtain those earnings should be included in the EPS calculation on a weighted average basis from the same date. [IAS 33 para 22].

Mandatorily convertible instruments

A14.79 An entity may issue a loan note or a preference share that is convertible into ordinary shares of the entity. The instrument may either be mandatorily convertible or convertible at the option of the issuer or holder into a fixed number of shares. Where an instrument is mandatorily convertible, the issue of ordinary shares is solely dependent on the passage of time. Consequently, ordinary shares that are issuable on conversion of a mandatorily convertible instrument should be included in basic EPS from the date that the contract is entered into. [IAS 33 para 23]. On the other hand, debt that is convertible at the option of the holder contains an obligation to issue a fixed number of shares *if* the conversion option is exercised. Such shares are treated as potential ordinary shares as they may never be issued if the conversion option is not exercised. Consequently, such potential shares are not considered outstanding for purposes of calculating basic EPS, but are included in the calculation of diluted EPS (see para A14.114 below).

Example

A company has issued debt that is mandatorily convertible into a fixed number of shares in five years time. Neither the issuer nor the holder has any option to require settlement in cash. Interest is payable (in cash) until conversion. How does it affect EPS?

For the purpose of EPS the potential ordinary shares that would be issued on conversion are included in the weighted average number of ordinary shares used in the calculation of basic EPS (and, therefore, also diluted EPS) from the date of issue of the instrument, since their issue is solely dependent on the passage of time. There is no adjustment to the profit or loss attributable to the ordinary equity holders for consequential interest savings, because the shares are treated as if had already been issued. The interest relates to a separate liability for the interest payments that remain payable.

A14.79.1 An entity may have preference shares that are mandatorily convertible when the entity's ordinary share price increases to a specified level. As the conversion is contingent on this uncertain event occuring, the issuable shares are treated in the same ways as an option that is convertible at the option of the issuer or holder. Hence, they are treated as outstanding and are included in the calculation of basic EPS only from the date when all necessary conditions are satisfied (that is, when the ordinary shares have reached the specified share price). [IAS 33 para 24]. Note, that it is still necessary to consider whether these preference shares are themselves participating equity instruments (see para A14.57).

Bonus issue (stock dividends), share split and share consolidation

A14.80 The weighted average number of ordinary shares outstanding during the period and for all periods presented should be adjusted for events, other than the conversion of potential ordinary shares, that have changed the number of ordinary shares outstanding, without a corresponding change in resources (see further para A14.169). [IAS 33 para 26]. Where an entity issues new shares by way of a bonus issue or stock dividend during the period, the effect is to increase only the number of shares outstanding after the issue. There is no effect on earnings as there is no flow of funds as a result of the issue. Consequently, the shares should be treated as outstanding as if the issue had occurred at the beginning of the earliest period reported. This means that the earnings for the year should be apportioned over the number of shares after the capitalisation. The EPS figure disclosed for the previous year should be recalculated using the new number of shares in issue. [IAS 33 para 28].

A14.81 Similar considerations apply where ordinary shares are split into shares of smaller nominal value (a share of C1 nominal value is divided into four shares of 25c each C1 = 100c) or consolidated into shares of a higher nominal amount (four shares of 25c each are consolidated into one share of C1). In both these situations, the number of shares outstanding before the event is adjusted for the proportionate change in the number of shares outstanding after the event. [IAS 33 para 27].

A14.82 The impact on the EPS figure of a bonus issue of shares is illustrated in the following example:

Example

On 31 December 20X7, the issued share capital of a company consisted of C1,000,000 in ordinary shares of 25c each and C500,000 in 10% cumulative preference shares of C1 each. On 1 October 20X8, the company issued 1,000,000 ordinary shares fully paid by way of capitalisation of reserves in the proportion of 1:4 for the year ended 31 December 20X8.

	20X8	20X7
	C'000	C'000
Calculation of earnings		
Profit for the year	550	450
Less: preference dividend	(50)	(50)
Earnings	500	400
Number of ordinary shares	No (000)	No (000)
Shares in issue for full year	4,000	4,000
Capitalisation issue at 1 October 20X8	1,000	1,000
Number of shares	5,000	5,000
Earnings per ordinary share of 25c	10.0c	8.0c

The comparative earnings per share for 20X7 can also be calculated by adjusting the previously disclosed EPS in 20X7, in this example 10c, by the following factor:

$$\frac{\text{Number of shares before the bonus issue}}{\text{Number of shares after the bonus issue}}$$

$$\text{Adjusted EPS for 20X7: } 10c \times \frac{4,000}{5,000} = 8.0c$$

The above ratio should also be used to restate previous years' EPS and other financial ratios (for example, dividend per share) disclosed in the historical summary.

Issue of shares at full market price

A14.83 Where new ordinary shares are issued during the year for cash at full market price, the earnings should be apportioned over the average number of shares outstanding during the period weighted on a time basis.

Example

On 31 December 20X7, the issued share capital of a company consisted of C1,000,000 in ordinary shares of 25c each and C500,000 in 10% cumulative preference shares of C1 each. On 1 October 20X8, the company issued 1,000,000 ordinary shares at full market price in cash for the year ended 31 December 20X8.

	20X8 C'000	20X7 C'000
Calculation of earnings		
Profit for the year	550	450
Less: preference dividend	(50)	(50)
Earnings	500	400
Weighted average number of ordinary shares	No (000)	No (000)
Shares in issue for full year	4,000	4,000
Issued on 1 October 20X8 (1,000,000 × 3/12)	250	–
Number of shares	4,250	4,000
Earnings per ordinary share of 25c	11.8c	10.0c

The calculation of earnings per share is based on earnings of C500,000 (20X7: C400,000) and on the weighted average of 4,250,000 ordinary shares in issue during the year (20X7: 4,000,000).

[The next paragraph is A14.85.]

Rights issue

A14.85 Companies sometimes raise additional capital during the year by issuing shares to existing shareholders on a *pro rata* basis to their existing holdings in the form of a rights issue. The rights shares may either be offered at the current market price or at a price that is below the current market price. Where shares are issued at full market price, the weighting is carried out on a time basis as discussed in paragraph A14.83 above. However, where ordinary shares are issued during the year by way of a rights issue at a discount to the market price, the weighting calculation must reflect the fact that the discount is effectively a bonus (stock dividend) given to the shareholders in the form of shares for no consideration and must, therefore, be taken into account in calculating the weighted average number of shares. [IAS 33 para A2]. In fact, it can be demonstrated (see example below) that a rights issue is equivalent to a capitalisation issue of part of the shares for no consideration and an issue of the remainder of the shares at full market price. The notional capitalisation issue reflects the bonus element inherent in the rights issue and is measured by the following fraction:

$$\frac{\text{Fair value per share immediately before the exercise of rights}}{\text{Theoretical ex-rights fair value per share}}$$

A14.86 The fair value per share immediately before the exercise of rights is the *actual* closing price at which the shares are quoted on the last date inclusive of the right to subscribe for the new shares. This is often referred to as the 'cum-rights price', being the price on the last day of quotation cum-rights. The 'ex-rights price', on the other hand, is the *theoretical* price at which, in a perfect market and without any external influences, the shares would trade after the exercise of the rights. Where the rights themselves are publicly traded separately from the shares themselves, as is the case in some countries, the fair value for the purpose of the above calculation is established at the close of the last day on which the shares are traded together with the rights. [IAS 33 para A2].

A14.87 The above factor should be used to adjust the number of shares in issue before the rights issue in order to correct for the bonus (stock dividend) element in the rights issue. This correction should be made both for the current period prior to the rights issue and the previous period. The way in which EPS should be calculated following a rights issue and the adjustment that should be made to the comparative EPS figure are considered in the example below.

Example

At 31 December 20X7, the issued capital of a company consisted of 1.8m ordinary shares of 10c each, fully paid. The profit for the year ended 31 December 20X7 and 20X8 amounted to C630,000 and C875,000 respectively. On 31 March 20X8, the company made a rights issue on a 1 for 4 basis at 30c. The market price of the shares immediately before the rights issue was 60c.

Calculation of theoretical ex rights price

	No		c
Initial holding	4	Market value	240
Rights taken up	1	Cost	30
New holding	5	Theoretical price	270
Theoretical ex rights price	$\frac{270}{5}$ = 54c		

The market price is the fair value of the shares immediately prior to the exercise of rights, that is, the actual cum-rights price of 60c.

Cost is the amount payable for each new share under the rights issue.

Calculation of bonus element

The bonus element of the rights issue is given by the fraction:

$$\frac{\text{Market price before rights issue}}{\text{Theoretical ex-rights price}} \quad \frac{60}{54} = \frac{10}{9}$$

This corresponds to a bonus issue of 1 for 9. The bonus ratio will usually be greater than 1, that is the market price of the shares immediately prior to the exercise of rights is greater than the theoretical ex-rights price. If the ratio is less than 1 it may indicate that the market price has fallen significantly during the rights period, which was not anticipated when the rights issue was announced. In this situation, the rights issue should be treated as an issue of shares for cash at full market price (see para A14.83 above).

As stated in paragraph A14.85 above, it can be demonstrated, using the figures in the example, that a rights issue of 1 for 4 at 30c is equivalent to a bonus issue of 1 for 9 combined with an issue of shares at full market price of 54c per share. Consider an individual shareholder holding 180 shares.

	No	Value	C
Original holding	180	Value at 60c per share	108.00
Rights shares (1:4)	45	Value at 30c per share	13.50
Holding after rights issue	225	Value at 54c per share	121.50

The additional 45 rights shares at 30p can be shown to be equivalent to a bonus issue of 1 for 9 on the original holding followed by an issue of 1:8 at full market price of 54c following the bonus issue as follows:

	No	Value	C
Original holding	180	Value at 60c per share	108.00
Bonus issue of 1 for 9	20	Value nil	nil
	200	Value at 54c per share	108.00
Issue of 1 for 8 at full price	25	Value at 54c per share	13.50
Total holding	225	Value at 54c per share	121.50

The shareholder is, therefore, indifferent as to whether the company makes a rights issue of 1 for 4 at 30c per share or a combination of a bonus issue of 1 for 9 followed by a rights issue of 1 for 8 at full market price of 54c per share.

Having calculated the bonus ratio, the ratio should be applied to adjust the number of shares in issue before the rights issue both for the current year and for the previous year. Therefore, the weighted average number of shares in issue for the current and the previous period, adjusted for the bonus element would be:

Weighted average number of shares

	20X8	20X7
Number of actual shares in issue before rights	1,800,000	1,800,000
Correction for bonus issue (1:9)	200,000	200,000
Deemed number of shares in issue before rights issue (1.8m × 10/9)	2,000,000	2,000,000
The number of shares after the rights issue would be: 1.8m × 5/4 = 2,250,000		
Therefore, the weighted average number of shares would be:		
2.0m for the whole year		2,000,000
2.0m × 3/12 (before rights issue)	500,000	–
2.25m × 9/12 (after rights issue)	1,687,500	–
Weighted average number	2,187,500	2,000,000

Calculation of EPS following a rights issue

	20X8	20X7 (as previously stated)
Basic EPS	C875,000	C630,000
	2,187,500	1,800,000
	40.0c	35.0c
Basic EPS for 20X7 (as restated)		C630,000
		2,000,000
		31.5c

The restated EPS for 20X7 can also be calculated by adjusting the earnings per share figure of the previous year by the *reciprocal* of the bonus element factor as shown below.

35c × 9/10 = 31.5c

In practice, the EPS for the corresponding period can be adjusted directly using the reciprocal of the bonus element factor above.

A14.88 A question arises as to whether the averaging calculation in a rights issue made during the year should be performed from the announcement date, or from the last date of acceptance of the subscription price, or from the share issue date following despatch of the share certificates. Depending on the circumstances of each case, there is often a delay of between 60 to 80 days between the date of announcement of the rights issue and the share issue date. Following the principle in paragraph 21 of IAS 33 that shares should generally be included from the date consideration is receivable, it follows that the averaging calculation should be performed from the day following the last date of acceptance of the subscription price, which is also the date when the rights are legally exercised. This is because the company begins to generate income from all the proceeds received from that date, which is often midway between the announcement date and the share issue date. Therefore, the new shares should be included in the EPS calculation from the day following the last date on which proceeds are received and not from the announcement date or from the date when the new shares are actually issued. An example of a rights issue (and a share consolidation – see para A14.81 above) is Table A14.2.A.

Table A14.2.A – Effect of rights issue on earnings per share

SEGRO plc – Annual report – 31 December 2009

14. EARNINGS AND NET ASSETS PER SHARE

The earnings per share calculations use the weighted average number of shares and the net assets per share calculations use the number of shares in issue at year end. Both earnings per share and net assets per share calculations exclude 1.3 million shares held on trust for employee share schemes (2008 1.5 million).

On 7 April 2009, the Company issued 5,240.7 million new ordinary shares (pre-share consolidation) through a rights issue. The rights issue was offered at 10 pence per share and represented a discount to the fair value of the existing shares. The number of shares used for prior year calculations of earnings per share and net assets per share shown below have been adjusted for the discounted rights issue in order to provide a comparable basis for the current year. An adjustment factor of 6.92 has been applied based on the Company's share price of 136.5 pence per share on 20 March 2009, the day before the new shares commenced trading on the London Stock Exchange and the theoretical ex-rights price at that date of 19.73 pence per share. In addition, the impact of the 10 for 1 share consolidation has also resulted in an adjustment to the prior period comparables. Note 25 provides further detail on the rights issue and the share consolidation. As discussed in note 1, these adjustments to comparative earnings per share and net assets per share calculations have not impacted the income statement or balance sheet and therefore, since it has not changed from the previously presented figures, a balance sheet at 31 December 2007 has not been shown.

14(i) – Earnings per ordinary share (extract)

	2008			2009		
	Earnings £m	Shares million	Pence per share	Earnings £m	Shares million	Pence per share
Basic EPS	(233.1)	563.8	(41.3)	(938.1)	300.5	(312.2)
Dilution adjustments:						
Share options and save as you earn schemes	–	0.2	–	–	–	–
Diluted EPS	(233.1)	564.0	(41.3)	(938.1)	300.5	(312.2)

25. SHARE CAPITAL AND SHARE-BASED PAYMENTS (extract 1)

On 7 April 2009, the Company issued 5,240.7 million new ordinary shares (pre share consolidation) at 10 pence per share on the basis of 12 new ordinary shares for every 1 existing ordinary share to raise £500 million (net of expenses).

25. SHARE CAPITAL AND SHARE-BASED PAYMENTS (extract 2)

At the General Meeting held on 28 July 2009;

(a) an ordinary resolution was passed to conduct a share consolidation, consolidating and re-classifying 10 of each existing authorised and existing issued shares of the Company of 1 pence each into 1 share of 10 pence each. The purpose of the share consolidation was to reduce the number of the Company's shares in issue so that the likely share price is appropriate for a Company of SEGRO's size. The share consolidation took effect on 31 July 2009.

Issue of shares at less than market price

A14.88.1 Sometimes shares may be issued at a discount to the market price, such as for the acquisition of an asset or the cancellation of a liability. Although the standard does not specifically deal with this situation, it would be appropriate to calculate the inherent bonus element in the issue for the purposes of adjusting the number of shares before the issue. This treatment is implicit in the wording in paragraph 27(b) of IAS 33, which makes reference to a bonus element in *any other issue*.

Dividends payable in shares or cash

A14.89 Where a company pays its dividends in the form of shares or gives the shareholder the option to receive a dividend in either cash or shares (sometimes referred to as scrip dividends or enhanced scrip dividends), the shares issued increase the weighted average number of shares used in the EPS calculation.

A14.90 Under IAS 33, paragraphs 5 and 7 and paragraphs 58 to 61 'Contracts that may be settled in ordinary shares or cash', scrip dividends may be regarded as potential ordinary shares (see para A14.98 below) that entitle the recipient to ordinary shares. These potential ordinary shares are converted into ordinary shares when the scrip shares are issued, which is after the balance sheet date. Since shares are included in the weighted average from the date consideration is receivable, ordinary shares issued on the voluntary reinvestment of dividends on ordinary or preference shares should be included on a weighted average basis at the date when the dividends are reinvested. [IAS 33 para 21(b)]. In practice, for scrip dividends, this is the dividend payment date.

A14.91 Furthermore, the cash dividend foregone by the shareholders electing to take a scrip dividend of shares is taken to be the consideration paid for those shares, which is normally equivalent to the current market value of the shares. The rationale for this is that the cash dividend foregone by the shareholders electing to take shares instead of cash is effectively reinvested in the company as fully paid up shares at market value. As a result, the earnings figure in the numerator already reflects the income generated by the additional cash retained from the dividend payment date. Consequently, for the purposes of the EPS calculation the issue of scrip shares should be treated as an issue at full market price and the relevant number of shares should be included in the denominator on a weighted basis from the dividend reinvestment date.

[The next paragraph is A14.93.]

Special dividend followed by share consolidation

A14.93 Companies sometimes return surplus cash to shareholders. This is normally effected by means of a share repurchase or by a synthetic share repurchase that is achieved by the payment of a special dividend to shareholders followed by a consolidation of share capital, for example, changing five 20c shares into four 25c shares.

A14.94 IAS 33 deals specifically with the effect on EPS of a special dividend accompanied by a share consolidation. Where a share consolidation is combined with a special dividend and the overall effect of the combined transaction is a share repurchase at fair value the reduction in the number of ordinary shares outstanding is the result of a corresponding reduction in resources. The weighted average number of ordinary shares outstanding for the period in which the combined transaction takes place is adjusted for the reduction in the number of ordinary shares from the date the special dividend is recognised. [IAS 33 para 29].

Example

A company has in issue 10,000 shares with a nominal value of 10c each. At the beginning of 20X8, it decides either to launch a share repurchase of 1,000 shares at the current market price of C1 per share or pay a special dividend of 10c per share (net) followed by a share consolidation of 9 new shares for 10 old shares. The profit after tax for 20X7 and 20X8 (before the effect of the share transactions) is C2,000. Interest rates are 8% per annum and the company pays corporation tax at 31%.

	Balance sheet before transactions	Repurchase of 1,000 shares at c1 per share	Special dividend of 10c per share followed by share consolidation of 10:9
	C	C	C
Net assets	5,000	4,000	4,000
Share capital 10,000 shares at 10c each	1,000		
9,000 shares at 10c each		900	
9,000 shares at 11.1c each			1,000
Capital redemption reserve		100	
Profit and loss account	4,000	3,000	3,000
	5,000	4,000	4,000
Net assets per share	C0.50	C0.44	C0.44

Effect on earnings per share — share repurchase

	20X8	20X7
	C	C
Profit for the year	2,000.00	2,000.00
Loss of interest on cash paid out (£1,000 × 0.08 × 0.69)	55.20	–
Earnings	1,944.80	2,000.00
Number of shares in issue	9,000	10,000
EPS	21.61c	20.00c

Effect on earnings per share – special dividend followed by share consolidation

The total nominal value of the shares remain unchanged, but whereas before there were 10,000 shares of 10p each there are now 9,000 shares of 11.1c each.

	20X8	20X7
	C	C
Profit for the year	2,000.00	2,000.00
Loss of interest on cash paid out (C1,000 × 0.08 × 0.69)	55.20	–
Earnings	1,944.48	2,000.00
Number of shares in issue (unadjusted)	9,000	10,000
EPS unadjusted (correct treatment)	21.61c	20.00c
Number of shares in issue (adjusted for consolidation)	9,000	9,000
EPS adjusted (incorrect treatment)	21.61c	22.22c

A14.95 As can be seen from the above example, the economic effect, in terms of net asset per share, of an actual share repurchase is identical to a synthetic share repurchase that is achieved by the combination of a special dividend with a share consolidation. It follows that the earnings per share figures for the two transactions should also be identical. If an adjustment were made to the previous year's EPS for the share consolidation as shown above, there would be an apparent dilution of 2.75 per cent ((22.22 — 21.61)/22.22) that would make the share repurchase look significantly more attractive than the special dividend route. But this would be misleading as the economic effect of the two transactions is identical. Therefore, no adjustment to prior year's EPS should be made for the share consolidation. [IAS 33 para 29].

A14.96 In the above example, it was assumed for simplicity that the combined transaction took place at the beginning of the year and so the new shares were treated as outstanding for a full year. If the combined transaction takes place part way through the year, the weighted average number of ordinary shares outstanding for the period in which the combined transaction takes place should be adjusted for the reduction in the number of shares from the date the special dividend is paid, that is, when resources leave the entity. [IAS 33 para 29]. An example of a company that has treated the payment of an exceptional dividend and a share consolidation carried out at the same time as equivalent to a share buy-back is given in the Table A14.3 below. The company is an investment company and also shows net assets per share (based on shares in issue at the period end).

Table A14.3 — Effect on EPS of special dividend and share consolidation

Mitchells & Butlers plc —Annual report — 29 September 2007

12. Dividends

	2007 52 weeks £m	2006 52 weeks £m
Amounts paid and recognised in equity		
In respect of the 53 weeks ended 1 October 2005:		
– Final dividend of 7.55p per share	–	38
In respect of the 52 weeks ended 30 September 2006:		
– Interim dividend of 3.65p per share	–	18
– Final dividend of 8.60p per share	35	–
In respect of the 52 weeks ended 29 September 2007:		
– Special interim dividend of 100.0p per share	486	–
– Interim dividend of 4.25p per share	17	–
	538	56
Proposed final dividend of 10.0p (2006 8.60p) per share	40	35

The payment of the special interim dividend amounting to £486m was made on 25 October 2006. The shareholders approved, at an Extraordinary General Meeting on 17 October 2006, the consolidation of the share capital of the Company by the issue of 34 new ordinary shares of 813/24p each for every 41 existing shares of 71/12p each.

The Board recommended on 28 November 2007 the proposed final dividend for the 52 weeks ended 29 September 2007. This did not qualify for recognition in the financial statements at 29 September 2007 as it had not been approved by the shareholders at that date.

13. Earnings per ordinary share

Basic earnings per share (EPS) has been calculated by dividing the profit or loss for the financial period by the weighted average number of ordinary shares in issue during the period, excluding own shares held in treasury and by employee share trusts.

For diluted earnings per share, the weighted average number of ordinary shares is adjusted to assume conversion of all dilutive potential ordinary shares.

Earnings per ordinary share amounts are presented before exceptional items (see note 9) in order to allow a better understanding of the underlying trading performance of the Group.

	Profit/(loss) £m	Basic EPS pence per ordinary share	Diluted EPS pence per ordinary share
52 weeks ended 29 September 2007			
Loss for the period	(10)	(2.5)p	(2.5)p*
Exceptional items, net of tax	155	38.0p	36.9p
Profit before exceptional items	145	35.5p	34.4p
52 weeks ended 30 September 2006			
Profit for the period	195	39.7p	38.8p
Exceptional items, net of tax	(51)	(10.4)p	(10.2)p
Profit before exceptional items	144	29.3p	28.6p

*The 2007 diluted EPS per ordinary share is unchanged from the basic EPS, as the inclusion of the dilutive potential ordinary shares would reduce the loss per share and is therefore not dilutive.

The weighted average number of ordinary shares used in the calculations above are as follows:

	2007 52 weeks millions	2006 52 weeks millions
For basic EPS calculations	408	491
Effect of dilutive potential ordinary shares:		
Contingently issuable shares	8	7
Other share options	5	5
For diluted EPS calculations	421	503

On 17 October 2006, shareholders approved a share capital consolidation together with a Special Dividend of 100.0p per ordinary share. The overall effect of the transaction was that of a share repurchase at fair value, therefore no adjustment has been made to comparative data.

At 29 September 2007, nil (2006 nil) contingently issuable shares and 1,034,538 (2006 965,822) other share options were outstanding that could potentially dilute basic EPS in the future but were not included in the calculation of diluted EPS as they are antidilutive for the periods presented.

24. Called up share capital

2007 2006	Number of shares	£m	Number of shares	£m
Authorised				
Ordinary shares of 813/24p each	1,181,130,148	101	–	–
Ordinary shares of 71/12p each	–	–	1,424,304,003	101
	1,181,130,148	101	1,424,304,003	101
Called up, allotted and fully paid				
Ordinary shares of 813/24p each:				
At start of the financial period	486,910,806	34	500,438,040	35
Share capital consolidation	(83,131,113)	–	–	–
Repurchase and cancellation	–	–	(13,527,234)	(1)
At end of the financial period	403,779,693	34	486,910,806	34

All of the ordinary shares rank equally with respect to voting rights and rights to receive ordinary and special dividends. There are no restrictions on the rights to transfer shares.

On 17 October 2006, shareholders approved a share capital consolidation on the basis of 34 new ordinary shares for every 41 existing ordinary shares. This provided for all of the authorised ordinary shares of 71/12p each (whether issued or unissued) to be consolidated into new ordinary shares of 813/24p each, which became effective on 18 October 2006.

Details of options granted under the Group's share schemes are contained in note 7.

Diluted earnings per share

Measurement

A14.97 As discussed from paragraph A14.65 above, the basic EPS is calculated on the number of ordinary shares outstanding in respect of the period. Sometimes companies may have 'potential ordinary shares' in issue. The standard defines a 'potential ordinary share' as a financial instrument or other contract that may entitle its holder to ordinary shares. [IAS 33 para 5]. Examples given in the standard are:

- Financial liabilities or equity instruments, including preference shares, that are convertible into ordinary shares.
- Options (including employee share options) and warrants.
- Shares that would be issued on satisfaction of certain conditions that result from contractual arrangements, such as the purchase of a business or other assets.

[IAS 33 para 7].

A14.98 In addition IAS 33, clarifies that contracts that may result in the issue of ordinary shares of the entity to the holder of the contract at the option of the issuer or the holder are potential ordinary shares. [IAS 33 paras 58 to 61]. Such contracts are dealt with from paragraph A14.159 below.

A14.99 In each of these situations, the effect of the conversion into ordinary shares may be to dilute future EPS. It should be noted that not all potential ordinary shares in issue will have a diluting effect (see further para A14.126). Any potential dilution, however, is of considerable interest to existing ordinary shareholders. This is because it indicates the possible reduction in current earnings that may be distributed to them by way of dividends in the future and the possible increase in the number of shares over which the total market value of the company may be divided.

A14.100 The standard, therefore, requires the calculation of diluted EPS, in addition to the basic EPS (see para A14.46), for profit or loss attributable to the parent entity's ordinary equity holders and separately for each of continuing and discontinued operations where these are presented in accordance with IFRS 5, 'Non-current assets held for sale and discontinued operations'. For the purpose of calculating diluted EPS, the profit or loss for the period attributable to ordinary equity holders adjusted for the effects of all dilutive potential ordinary shares should be divided by the sum of the weighted average number of ordinary shares used in the basic EPS calculation and the weighted average number of shares that would be issued on the conversion of all the dilutive potential ordinary shares into ordinary shares. [IAS 33 paras 30 to 32, 36].

A14.101 It should be noted that although existing ordinary shareholders are interested in future dilution, the diluted EPS figure calculated in accordance with the standard is not intended to be a predictor of dilution, or a forward-looking number. It is seen as an additional historical measure. The IASB and the FASB concluded that as the objective of basic EPS is to measure performance over the reporting period, the objective of diluted EPS should be consistent with that objective while giving effect to all dilutive potential ordinary shares that were outstanding during the period. A past performance method of computing diluted EPS will aid comparison between diluted EPS of different periods. In addition, presenting diluted EPS with undiluted EPS that are calculated on a consistent basis will enable users to view the spread between the two figures as representing a reasonable estimate of the potential dilution that exits in the entity's capital structure.

Computation of earnings

A14.102 For the purpose of calculating diluted EPS, the profit or loss attributable to the parent entity's ordinary equity holders should be adjusted for the after-tax effect of:

- Dividends or other items related to dilutive potential ordinary shares that have been deducted in arriving at profit attributable to ordinary equity holders for the purpose of calculating basic EPS, such as dividends on dilutive convertible preference shares.
- Interest recognised in the period on dilutive potential ordinary shares, such as interest on dilutive convertible debt.
- Any other changes in income or expense that would result from the conversion of the dilutive potential ordinary shares.

[IAS 33 paras 32(a), 33].

A14.103 Once potential ordinary shares are converted into ordinary shares during the period, the dividends, interest and other expense associated with those potential ordinary shares will no longer be incurred. The effect of the conversion, therefore, is to increase profit (or reduce losses) attributable to ordinary equity holders as well as the number of shares in issue. This is illustrated in paragraph A14.114 dealing with convertible securities. Adjustments to profit or loss attributable to ordinary equity holders also include any transaction costs, discounts or premiums on potential ordinary shares that are allocated to periods in accordance with the effective interest method in paragraph 9 of IAS 39, that is, the adjustment to earnings should add back the issue costs (or similar) amortised in the period, in addition to the interest/dividend cost.

A14.104 The adjustments to earnings include not only the direct savings in debt servicing cost or dividends and other appropriations and adjustments in respect of convertible preference shares and the related tax effects, but also any other consequential changes in other income or expense arising as a result of the conversion. A situation that often arises in practice is where the equity conversion option in a foreign currency convertible bond, which is treated as a liability, is marked to market through profit or loss. The marked-to-market adjustment needs to be removed from profit or loss for the purposes of calculating diluted EPS. IAS 33 also mentions, as an example, an increase in an employee non-discretionary profit sharing plan as a result of the savings in after-tax interest cost following conversion of convertible debt. [IAS 33 paras 34, 35]. The example given below illustrates such an adjustment. When calculating tax for the purposes of diluted EPS the standard tax rate rather than the entity's effective tax rate should be used. This is because the effective tax rate may be influenced by factors (such as group relief) that affect the entity's results other than the expenses associated with the potential ordinary shares.

Example

Entity A has in issue 25,000 4% debentures with a nominal value of C1. The debentures are convertible to ordinary shares at a rate of 1:1 at any time until 20X9. The entity's management receives a bonus based on 1% of profit before tax.

Entity A's results for 20X2 showed a profit before tax of C80,000 and a profit after tax of C64,000 (for simplicity a tax rate of 20% is assumed in this example).

For the purpose of calculating diluted EPS, the earnings should be adjusted for the reduction in the interest charge that would occur if the debentures were converted and for the increase in the bonus payment that would arise from the increased profit.

This is illustrated below:

	C
Profit after tax	64,000
Add: Reduction in interest cost[1]	
25,000 × 4%	1,000
Less tax expense 1,000 × 20%	(200)
Less: Increase in management bonus	
1,000 × 1%	(10)
Add tax benefit 10 × 20%	2
Earnings for the purposes of diluted EPS	64,792

[1] Note that for simplification, this example does not illustrate the classification of the components of the convertible debenture as liabilities and equity as required by IAS 32.

A14.105 It should be noted that the requirement in paragraph A14.102 above refers to adjusting the profit attributable to ordinary equity holders. This figure is after deducting dividends on convertible preference shares and is the figure used for the purpose of calculating basic EPS. In some cases those dividends will be charged as finance costs in arriving at profit for the year (preference shares treated as a financial liability under IAS 32) and no adjustment will be necessary to arrive at profit attributable to ordinary shareholders. In other cases they will be classified in equity (preference shares treated as equity instruments under IAS 32) and an adjustment will be made to profit for the year to arrive at profit attributable to ordinary equity holders. In either case, however, if the convertible preference shares are dilutive, the profit attributable to ordinary shareholders for the purpose of calculating diluted EPS is before deducting the preference dividend.

Computation of number of ordinary shares

A14.106 As noted in paragraph A14.100, the denominator of diluted EPS should be calculated as the sum of the weighted average number of ordinary shares used in the basic EPS calculation and the weighted average number of ordinary shares that would be issued on the conversion of all the dilutive potential ordinary shares into ordinary shares. [IAS 33 para 36].

A14.107 Entities may have more than one type of potential ordinary share in issue at the reporting date. Whether all these potential ordinary shares actually will be converted into ordinary shares in the future is usually not determinable at the reporting date. The standard requires the assumption that all potential ordinary shares have been converted into ordinary shares at the beginning of the period or, if not in existence at the beginning of the period, the date of the issue of the financial instrument or the granting of the rights by which they are generated. [IAS 33 para 36]. This is sometimes referred to as the 'if converted' method.

A14.108 The conversion into ordinary shares should be determined from the terms of the financial instrument or the rights granted and this determination should assume the most advantageous conversion rate or exercise price from the standpoint of the holder of the potential ordinary shares. [IAS 33 para 39]. The effect is to ensure that the diluted EPS is based on the maximum number of new shares that would be issuable under the instrument's terms. In practice, it may be that not all conversion rights or warrants are exercised, in which case the dilutive effect in reality would be less than the diluted figure suggests. Where an instrument has variable conversion terms such that it is convertible at reducing rates over its life (see the example in para A14.115 below), the effect is that the conversion rate at the end of the period is used to determine the number of shares that would be issued on conversion. This is because the maximum number of new shares would not take into consideration the higher conversion rates in previous periods, because the instrument could no longer be converted at those higher rates.

A14.109 Potential ordinary shares are included in the diluted EPS calculation on a weighted basis only for the period they were outstanding. Therefore, potential ordinary shares that are issued during the year are included on a weighted basis from the date of issue to the balance sheet date. Where potential ordinary shares that are outstanding at the beginning of the period are converted during the year, they are included on a weighted average basis from the beginning of the year to the date of conversion. This is illustrated in the examples in paragraph A14.115. The new ordinary shares that are issued on conversion are included from the date of conversion in both basic and diluted EPS on a weighted basis. The same principles apply where potential ordinary shares, instead of being converted, are cancelled or allowed to lapse during the reporting period. [IAS 33 para 38].

A14.110 In computing diluted EPS, only potential ordinary shares that are dilutive are considered in the calculation. Potential ordinary shares should be treated as dilutive when, and only when, their conversion to ordinary shares would decrease profit per share or increase loss per share from *continuing operations* attributable to ordinary equity holders. [IAS 33 para 41]. The effects of anti-dilutive potential ordinary shares are ignored in calculating diluted EPS. [IAS 33 para 43]. Where a company has a number of different types of potential ordinary shares in issue, each one would need to be considered separately rather than in aggregate. The way in which this should be done is considered further from paragraph A14.126 below.

[The next paragraph is A14.112.]

A14.112 As noted in paragraph A14.110, potential ordinary shares are either dilutive or anti-dilutive based on profit or loss from continuing operations attributable to ordinary equity holders. If the potential ordinary shares are dilutive at this level they must be treated as dilutive for all other EPS calculations (that is, total EPS, discontinued operations EPS and any additional EPS given) whether or not they are actually dilutive at the relevant level of profit (see further para A14.126). [IAS 33 para A3].

Partly paid shares

A14.113 As stated in paragraph A14.69, partly paid shares are included in the computation of basic EPS to the extent that they rank for dividends during the period. Partly paid shares that do not rank for dividends during the period — for example, they do not rank until they are fully paid — are regarded as the equivalent of share options and warrants. That is, the unpaid balance should be assumed to be the proceeds used to purchase shares under the treasury stock method (see further para A14.117). The number of shares included in diluted EPS is the difference between the number of partly paid shares already in issue and the number of shares assumed to be purchased at average market price during the period. [IAS 33 para A16].

Convertible securities

A14.114 Where a company has issued instruments in the form of debentures, loan stocks or preference shares that are convertible into ordinary shares of the entity, the instrument's terms will specify the dates, the number of shares and, in effect, the conversion price or prices at which the new shares will be issued. Convertible preference shares are dilutive when the amount of dividend on such shares declared or accrued in the period per ordinary share obtainable on conversion is below basic EPS for continuing operations (where it exceeds basic EPS, the convertible preference shares are anti-dilutive). Convertible debt is dilutive when the interest, net of tax and other changes in income or expense, per ordinary share obtainable on conversion is lower than basic EPS for continuing operations (where it exceeds basic EPS, the convertible debt is anti-dilutive). [IAS 33 para 50]. However, see paragraph A14.130 for situations where there is more than one class of potential ordinary share.

A14.115 A convertible security is a particularly good example to illustrate the application of the principles discussed from paragraphs A14.102 to A14.110 above for calculating diluted EPS.

Example 1

No conversion during the year

At 30 June 20X1, the issued share capital of a company consisted of 1,500,000 ordinary shares of C1 each. On 1 October 20X1 the company issued C1,250,000 of 8% convertible loan stock for cash at par. Each C100 nominal of the loan stock may be converted at any time during the years ended 20X6/X9 into the number of ordinary shares set out below:

30 June 20X6 135 ordinary shares
30 June 20X7 130 ordinary shares
30 June 20X8 125 ordinary shares
30 June 20X9 120 ordinary shares

If the loan stocks are not converted by 20X9, they would be redeemed at par. There are two different ways of assessing these instruments under IAS 32. The conversion option to convert to a number of shares which varies only with time may be viewed as either an option to convert to a variable or fixed number of shares and recognised as either a liability or equity respectively. See Manual of Accounting – Financial Instruments chapter 7 for more details. This example assumes the written equity conversion option is accounted for as a derivative liability and marked to market through profit or loss. The change in the options' fair value reported in 20X2 and 20X3 amounted to a loss of C2,500 and C2,650 respectively. It is assumed that there are no tax consequences arising from these losses.

The profit before interest and taxation for the year ended 30 June 20X2 and 20X3 amounted to C825,000 and C895,000 respectively and relate wholly to continuing operations. The rate of tax for both periods is 33%.

	20X3	20X2
Trading results	C	C
Profit before interest and tax	895,000	825,000
Interest on 8% convertible loan stock (20X2: 9/12 × C100,000)	(100,000)	(75,000)
Change in fair value of embedded option	(2,650)	(2,500)
Profit before tax	792,350	747,500
Taxation @ 33%	(262,350)	(247,500)
Profit after tax	530,000	500,000
Calculation of basic EPS		
Number of equity shares outstanding	1,500,000	1,500,000
Basic EPS	C530,000 / 1,500,000	C500,000 / 1,500,000
	35.3c	33.3c

Calculation of diluted EPS

Test whether convertibles are dilutive:
The saving in after-tax earnings resulting from the conversion of C100 nominal of loan stock amounts to C100 × 8% × 67% + C2,650/12,500 = C5.36 + C0.21 = C5.57. There will then be 135 extra shares in issue. Therefore, the incremental earnings per share = 4.12c (that is, C5.57/135). As this incremental earnings per share is less than the basic EPS at the continuing level, it this will have the effect of reducing the basic EPS of 35.3c. Hence the convertibles are dilutive (see further para A14.131).

	20X3	20X2
Adjusted earnings	C	C
Profit for basic EPS	530,000	500,000
Add: interest and other charges on earnings saved as a result of the conversion	102,650	77,500
Less: tax relief thereon	(33,000)	(24,750)
Adjusted earnings for equity	599,650	552,750

Adjusted number of shares
From the conversion terms, it is clear that the maximum number of shares issuable on conversion of C1,250,000 loan stock after the end of the financial year would be at the rate of 135 shares per C100 nominal, that is, 1,687,500 shares.

Number of equity shares for basic EPS	1,500,000	1,500,000
Maximum conversion at date of issue 1,687,500 × 9/12	–	1,265,625
Maximum conversion after balance sheet date	1,687,500	–
Adjusted capital	3,187,500	2,765,625
Diluted EPS	C599,650 / 3,187,500	C552,750 / 2,765,625
	18.8c	20.0c

Example 2

Partial conversion during the year

The facts are the same as set out in the previous example, but at 1 January 20X6, the holders of half the loan stock exercised their right of conversion.

	20X6	20X5
Trading results	C	C
Profit before interest and tax	1,220,000	1,000,000
Interest on 8% convertible loan stock	(75,000)*	(100,000)
Change in fair value of embedded option	(2,750)	(5,000)
Profit before tax	1,142,250	895,000
Taxation @ 33%	(377,850)	(297,000)
Profit after tax	764,400	598,000

*Interest = (C1,250,000 × 8% × ½) + (C625,000 × 8% × ½) = C75,000

Calculation of basic EPS		
Adjusted number of shares:		
Number outstanding before conversion	1,500,000	1,500,000
Weighted average shares issued on conversion at 1 January 20X6 = 843,750/2	421,875	–
Adjusted number of shares	1,921,875	1,500,000
Basic EPS	C764,400 / 1,921,875	C598,000 / 1,500,000
	39.8c	39.9c
Calculation of diluted EPS		
Adjusted earnings	C	C
Profit for basic EPS	764,400	598,000
Add: interest and other charges on earnings saved as a result of conversion	77,750	105,000
Less: tax relief thereon	(24,750)	(33,000)
Adjusted earnings	817,400	670,000

Adjusted number of shares		
Number of equity shares for basic EPS	1,921,875	1,500,000
Assumed conversion of C1,250,000 loan stock outstanding at the beginning of the year at the maximum rate of 135 shares per C100 of stock up to 1 January 20X6 (6 months)	843,750	–
Assumed conversion of C625,000 of remaining stock outstanding at 30 June 20X6 at the maximum rate of 135 shares per C100 of stock (6 months)	421,875	–
Maximum conversion after balance sheet date at the rate of 135 shares per £100 of stock	–	1,687,500
Adjusted number of shares	3,187,500	3,187,500
Diluted EPS	C817,400 / 3,187,500	C670,000 / 3,187,500
	25.6c	21.0c

Example 3

Final conversion during the year

The facts are the same as set out in the previous example, but the holders of half of the loan stock had exercised their right of conversion on 1 January 20X6 at 135 shares per C100 stock and the remaining stock was converted on 30 June 20X7 at 130 shares per C100 stock.

	20X7	20X6
Trading results	C	C
Profit before interest and tax	1,450,000	1,220,000
Interest on 8% convertible loan stock	(50,000)*	(75,000)
Change in fair value of embedded option	(3,500)	(2,750)
Profit before tax	1,396,500	1,142,250
Taxation @ 33%	(462,000)	(377,850)
Profit after tax	934,500	764,400

*Interest = C625,000 × 8% = C50,000

Calculation of basic EPS		
Adjusted number of shares:		
Number outstanding before conversion	1,500,000	1,500,000
Weighted average shares issued on conversion at 1 January 20X6	843,750	421,875
Weighted average shares issued on conversion at 30 June 20X7	–	–
Adjusted number of equity shares	2,343,750	1,921,875
	C934,500 / 2,343,750	C764,400 / 1,921,875

Basic EPS

	39.9c	39.8c
Calculation of diluted EPS		
Adjusted earnings	C	C
Profit for basic EPS	934,500	764,400
Add: interest and other charges on earnings saved as a result of conversion	53,500	77,750
Less: tax thereon	(16,500)	(24,750)
Adjusted earnings	971,500	817,400
Adjusted number of shares		
Number of equity shares for basic EPS	2,343,750	1,921,875
Assumed conversion of C1,250,000 loan stock outstanding at the beginning of the year at the maximum rate of 135 shares per C100 of stock up to 1 January 20X6 (6 months)	–	843,750
Assumed conversion of £625,000 of remaining stock outstanding at 30 June 20X6 at the maximum rate of 135 shares per C100 of stock (6 months)	–	421,875
Assumed conversion of C625,000 of stock outstanding at the maximum rate of 130 shares per C100 of stock†	812,500	–
Adjusted number of shares	3,156,250	3,187,500

† Deemed to be outstanding for the whole year because the remaining loan stock of C625,000 was redeemed on the last day of the financial year, that is, on 30 June 20X7.

Diluted EPS	C971,500	C817,400
	3,156,250	3,187,500
	30.8c	22.6c

A14.116 Table A14.4 shows the presentation of adjustments made for the purpose of diluted EPS that result from dilutive convertible debt. The extract also illustrates disclosure of continuing, total and discontinued EPS, the treatment of own shares held and the effect on diluted EPS of share options issued by a subsidiary, Genentech (see para A14.134).

Table A14.4 – Effect of potential ordinary shares on diluted EP

Roche Holding Ltd – Annual Report and Accounts – 31 December 2007

29. Earnings per share and non-voting equity security

Basic earnings per share and non-voting equity security

For the calculation of basic earnings per share and non-voting equity security, the number of shares and nonvoting equity securities is reduced by the weighted average number of its own non-voting equity securities held by the Group during the period.

Basic earnings per share and non-voting equity security

	Continuing businesses		Group	
	2007	2006	2007	2006
Net income attributable to Roche shareholders (millions of CHF)	9,761	7,860	9,761	7,880
Number of shares (millions)[28]	160	160	160	160
Number of non-voting equity securities (millions)[28]	703	703	703	703
Weighted average number of own non-voting equity securities held (millions)	(4)	(11)	(4)	(11)
Weighted average number of shares and non-voting equity securities in issue (millions)	859	852	859	852
Basic earnings per share and non-voting equity security (CHF)	11.36	9.22	11.36	9.24

Diluted earnings per share and non-voting equity security

For the calculation of diluted earnings per share and non-voting equity security, the net income and weighted average number of shares and non-voting equity securities outstanding are adjusted for the effects of all dilutive potential shares and non-voting equity securities.

Potential dilutive effects arise from the convertible debt instruments and the employee stock option plans. If the outstanding convertible debt instruments were to be converted then this would lead to a reduction in interest expense and an increase in the number of shares which may have a net dilutive effect on the earnings per share. The exercise of outstanding vested employee stock options would have a dilutive effect. The exercise of the outstanding vested Genentech employee stock options would have a dilutive effect if the net income of Genentech is positive. The diluted earnings per share and non-voting equity security reflects the potential impacts of these dilutive effects on the earnings per share figures.

Diluted earnings per share and non-voting equity security	Continuing businesses		Group	
	2007	2006	2007	2006
Net income attributable to Roche shareholders (millions of CHF)	9,761	7,860	9,761	7,880
Elimination of interest expense, net of tax, of convertible debt instruments, where dilutive (millions of CHF)	4	25	4	25
Increase in minority share of Group net income, net of tax, assuming all outstanding Genentech stock options exercised (millions of CHF)	(141)	(100)	(141)	(100)
Net income used to calculate diluted earnings per share (millions of CHF)	9,624	7,785	9,624	7,805
Weighted average number of shares and non-voting equity securities in issue (millions)	859	852	859	852
Adjustment for assumed conversion of convertible debt instruments, where dilutive (millions)	1	7	1	7
Adjustment for assumed exercise of equity compensation plans, where dilutive (millions)	2	3	2	3
Weighted average number of shares and non-voting equity securities in issue used to calculate diluted earnings per share (millions)	862	862	862	862
Diluted earnings per share and non-voting equity security (CHF)	11.16	9.03	11.16	9.05

28. Equity attributable to Roche shareholders (extract)

Share capital

As of 31 December 2007, the authorised and issued share capital of Roche Holding Ltd, which is the Group's parent company, consisted of 160,000,000 shares with a nominal value of 1.00 Swiss franc each, as in the preceding year. The shares are bearer shares and the Group does not maintain a register of shareholders. Based on information supplied to the Group, a shareholder group with pooled voting rights owns 50.0125% (2006: 50.0125%) of the issued shares. This is further described in Note 33. Based on information supplied to the Group, Novartis International Ltd, Basel, and its affiliates 33.3330% (participation below 331/3%) of the issued shares (2006: 33.3330%).

Non-voting equity securities *(Genussscheine)*

As of 31 December 2007, 702,562,700 non-voting equity securities have been authorised and were in issue as in the preceding year. Under Swiss company law these non-voting equity securities have no nominal value, are not part of the share capital and cannot be issued against a contribution which would be shown as an asset in the balance sheet of Roche Holding Ltd. Each non-voting equity security confers the same rights as any of the shares to participate in the net profit and any remaining proceeds from liquidation following repayment of the nominal value of the shares and, if any, participation certificates. In accordance with the law and the Articles of Incorporation of Roche Holding Ltd, the Company is entitled at all times to exchange all or some of the non-voting equity securities into shares or participation certificates.

Own equity instruments (extract)

Holdings of own equity instruments *in equivalent number of non-voting equity securities*

	31 December 2007 (millions)	31 December 2006 (millions)
Non-voting equity securities	0.4	0.2
Low Exercise Price Options	1.9	6.8
Derivative instruments	9.3	8.2
Total own equity instruments	11.6	15.2

Own equity instruments are recorded within equity at original cost of acquisition.

8. Discontinued businesses (extract)

The 2006 results include 20 million Swiss francs of profit from discontinued businesses. This consisted of income of 28 million Swiss francs relating to the release of certain accruals and provisions that were no longer required less 5 million Swiss francs of expenses for the unwinding of the discounted provisions and 3 million Swiss francs of income tax expenses. This had an impact of 0.02 CHF on earnings per share and non-voting equity security (basic and diluted).

Share warrants, options and other potential ordinary shares

A14.117 Where a company has issued warrants to subscribe for shares at fixed prices on specified dates in the future or granted share options to directors and employees, these and other potential ordinary shares should be taken into account in the calculation of diluted EPS if they are dilutive. [IAS 33 para 45]. Warrants or options are defined as financial instruments that give the holder the right to purchase ordinary shares. [IAS 33 para 5]. They are dilutive when they would result in the issue of ordinary shares for less than the average market price of ordinary shares during the period. Under IAS 33, the expected proceeds from the exercise of the dilutive share warrants and options are deemed to be used by the company in purchasing as many of its ordinary shares as possible in the open market, using an average market price for the period. Since these shares are fairly priced and are neither dilutive or anti-dilutive, they are ignored in the diluted EPS calculation. They are, therefore, deducted from the number of shares to be issued under the options or warrants to give the number of shares deemed to be issued at no consideration. As these shares are dilutive, they are added to the number of ordinary shares outstanding in the computation of diluted EPS. [IAS 33 paras 45 to 47].

A14.118 The method reflects more dilution as the value of options and warrants increases relative to the value of the underlying share. That is, as the average market price for the underlying share increases, the assumed proceeds from exercise will buy fewer shares, thus increasing the number of shares issued for nil consideration and, hence, the denominator. This method of accounting for share warrants and options and other share purchase agreements is often referred to as 'the treasury stock method'. However, although increases in the share price over a number of periods may increase the dilutive effect, the standard makes it clear that previously reported EPS figures are not retrospectively adjusted to reflect changes in share prices. [IAS 33 para 47].

A14.119 It should be noted that the fair value of share options and warrants under the treasury stock method should always be calculated on the basis of the average price of an ordinary share for the period rather than the period end market price. The use of the average stock price is consistent with the objective of diluted EPS to measure earnings per share for the period based on period in formation and that use of end-of-period data or estimates of the future is inconsistent with the objectives as discussed in paragraph A14.101 above. The standard indicates that a pragmatic basis of calculation, such as a simple average of weekly or monthly prices should be adequate for calculating the average price for the period. Also, closing market prices are adequate for calculating the average market price, but where prices fluctuate wildly an average of the high and low prices generally produces a more representative price. The method should be used consistently, unless it becomes unrepresentative due to changed market conditions. For example, an entity that had used closing market prices to calculate the average market price during several years of relatively stable prices might change to using an average of high and low prices, if prices began to fluctuate wildly and closing prices no longer produced a representative average price. [IAS 33 paras A4, A5].

A14.120 Paragraph 41 of IAS 33 says that potential shares are treated as dilutive when they decrease profit or increase loss per share from continuing operations attributable to ordinary equity holders. Where an entity is making profits from continuing operations, share options will always be additionally dilutive if the exercise price is below the average of the share price during the period (that is, the options are 'in the money'). However, where an entity has incurred a loss from continuing operations, options that are in the money would only be dilutive if they increased the loss per share from continuing operations, that is, made the loss per share more negative. But as the effect of bringing in more shares will be to increase the denominator and therefore reduce the loss per share, in the money options will be anti-dilutive and so are not included in the diluted EPS.

A14.121 An example that illustrates the mechanics of calculating diluted EPS where a company has granted options is given below.

Example

At 31 December 20X7 and 20X8, the issued share capital of a company consisted of 4,000,000 ordinary shares of 25c each. The company has granted options that give holders the right to subscribe for ordinary shares between 20Y6 and 20Y9 at 70c per share. Options outstanding at 31 December 20X7 and 20X8 were 630,000. There were no grants, exercises or lapses of options during the year. The profit after tax attributable to ordinary equity holders for the years ended 31 December 20X7 and 20X8 amounted to C500,000 and C600,000 respectively (wholly relating to continuing operations).

Average market price of share:
Year ended 31 December 20X7 = C1.20
Year ended 31 December 20X8 = C1.60

Calculation of basic EPS		
	20X8	20X7
Basic EPS	C600,000 / 4,000,000	C500,000 / 4,000,000
	15.0c	12.5c
Calculation of diluted EPS		
Adjusted number of shares		
Number of shares under option:		
Issued at full market price:		
(630,000 × 0.70) ÷ 1.20		367,500
(630,000 × 0.70) ÷ 1.60	275,625	
Issued at nil consideration — dilutive	354,375	262,500
Total number of shares under option	630,000	630,000
Number of equity shares for basic EPS	4,000,000	4,000,000
Number of dilutive shares under option	354,375	262,500
Adjusted number of shares	4,354,375	4,262,500
Diluted EPS	C600,000 / 4,354,375	C500,000 / 4,262,500
	13.8c	11.7c
Percentage dilution	8.00%	6.40%

Note – If options had been granted or exercised during the period, then the number of 'nil consideration' shares in respect of these options would be included in the diluted EPS calculation on a weighted average basis for the period prior to exercise.

A14.122 Table A14.5 illustrates the disclosure of the effect of options on diluted EPS.

Table A14.5 – Effect of share options on diluted EPS

Syngenta AG – Annual Report and Accounts – 31 December 2010

Consolidated Income Statement (extract)
(for the years ended December 31, 2010 and 2009)

(US$ million, except share and per share amounts)	**Notes**	**2010**	**2009**[a]
Earnings per share (US$):			
Basic earnings per share	8	**15.07**	15.11
Diluted earnings per share	8	**14.99**	15.01
Weighted average number of shares:			
Basic		**92,687,903**	93,154,537
Diluted		**93,225,303**	93,760,196

a After effect of accounting policy change for post-employment benefits described in Note 2 below

8. Earnings per share

Basic earnings per share amounts are calculated by dividing net income for the year attributable to ordinary shareholders of Syngenta AG by the weighted average number of ordinary shares outstanding during the year.

Diluted earnings per share amounts are calculated by dividing the net income attributable to ordinary shareholders of Syngenta AG by the sum of the weighted average number of ordinary shares outstanding during the year plus the weighted average number of ordinary shares that would be issued on the conversion of all the dilutive potential ordinary shares into ordinary shares.

Treasury shares are deducted from total shares in issue for the purposes of calculating earnings per share.

The calculation of diluted earnings per share for the year ended December 31, 2010 excluded 373,365 (2009: 226,897) of Syngenta AG shares and options granted to employees, as their inclusion would have been antidilutive.

(US$ million, except number of shares)	**2010**	2009[a]
Net income attributable to Syngenta AG shareholders	**1,397**	1,408
Weighted average number of shares		
Weighted average number of shares – basic		93,154,537
Adjustments for dilutive potential ordinary shares:		
Grants of options over Syngenta AG shares under employee share participation plans	**417,807**	478,964
Grants of Syngenta AG shares under employee share participation plans	**119,593**	126,695
Weighted average number of shares – diluted	**93,225,303**	93,760,196

a After effect of accounting policy change for post-employment benefits described in Note 2

A14.123 Although the standard does not specifically say so, it should be assumed that the average price for the period means the average price during the period covered by the financial statements. However, where options are issued during the period the average price should be taken to be the average price during the period for which the options were in issue. This may affect whether the options are dilutive or anti-dilutive.

Example

An entity issued share options on 1 January 20X3. The share options are exercisable upon issue. The exercise price of the share options is 20c. The average share price during the year was as follows:

Average share price 1 January 20X3 to 30 June 20X3	8c
Average share price 1 July 20X3 to 31 December 20X3	22c
Average share price for the year to 31 December 20X3	15c

Management is preparing the financial statements for the year ended 31 December 20X3 and is considering the effect on diluted EPS of the following two scenarios for year-end share prices:

(a) the share price is 18c at 31 December 20X3; or
(b) the share price is 23c at 31 December 20X3.

(a) The fact that the year end share price is less than the exercise price is not relevant because the standard requires the comparison to be made between the exercise price and the average market price of the shares for the period, not with the price at the year end. [IAS 33 para 45]. The share options should not be included in the diluted EPS calculation as they are out-of-the money, that is, the exercise price (20c) is higher than the average price of the ordinary shares for the period (15c).

(b) Similarly the fact that the year end share price is more than the exercise price is not relevant. There is no change in the answer from that given in (a) above, because the extent of dilution is calculated by reference to the exercise price and the average share price during the period. The exercise price is 20c and the average fair value of the shares is 15c and, therefore, the options are still out of the money for the purpose of the diluted EPS calculation.

The answer would change, however, if the options had been issued at 1 July 20X3. The average price of the shares during the second half of the year (22c) was above the exercise price of the options (20c), so that the share options would be included in the diluted EPS calculation.

A14.124 The basic method of including options or warrants in the EPS computation is the treasury stock method described in paragraph A14.117 above. However, the treasury stock method may not always be applicable for calculating the dilutive effects of options or warrants. Sometimes options or warrants may require or permit the tendering of debt or other securities of the entity in payment of all or part of the exercise price. In computing diluted EPS:

- Those options or warrants are assumed to be exercised and the debt or other securities are assumed to be tendered.
- Interest (net of tax) on any debt assumed to be tendered is added back as an adjustment to the numerator.
- If tendering cash would be more advantageous to the option holder or warrant holder and the contract permits tendering cash, the tendering of cash should be assumed.

[IAS 33 para A7].

Example

An entity issued 50,000 warrants at the beginning of the year. Each warrant may be exercised to purchase 10 ordinary shares by tendering either C100 cash or C100 nominal of outstanding 6% debentures of the entity. The market value of the debentures at the balance sheet date is C92 and the average market price of the entity's share for the period and at the balance sheet date is C9.50 and C9.60 respectively.

In the calculation of diluted EPS, it is first necessary to consider whether the warrants are dilutive. The warrants would be dilutive if either:

(a) The warrants are exercised for cash and the average market price of the related ordinary shares for the period exceeds the exercise price. This is not the case here as the average share price of C95 (10 shares @ C9.50) is less than the exercise price of C100.

(b) The warrants are exercised by tendering the entity's debentures and the selling price of the debenture to be tendered is below that at which the debenture may be tendered under the warrant agreement and the resulting discount establishes an effective exercise price below the market price of the ordinary shares obtained upon exercise. This is the case here as the market value of the debentures of C92 (nominal value C100) is less than the market price of the shares obtained of C96 at the balance sheet.

Therefore, the warrants are dilutive, and it is assumed that debentures will be tendered because it will be more advantageous to the warrant holder to surrender the entity's debentures that have a market value of C92 rather than pay cash of C100 to obtain 10 ordinary shares with a market value of C96.

For the purposes of calculating diluted EPS, the company will increase the numerator by the after-tax interest saved of C210,000 (C5m @ 6% less tax @ 30%) on effectively repurchasing C5m (C100 nominal for each 50,000 warrants) of the entity's outstanding debentures. In addition, the full amount of 500,000 shares to be issued following the exercise of warrants, (rather than the number computed under the treasury stock method using an effective exercise price equal to the market value of C92 for the debenture and an average share price of C9.50), is included in the denominator. This treatment reflects the fact that a repurchase of debt with the warrant/option proceeds followed by an issue of shares under the warrant/option agreement is in substance equivalent to a traditional or conventional debt instrument that is convertible into a fixed number of shares.

On the other hand, if the tendering of cash is considered to be more advantageous to the warrant holder, for instance, if cash tendered in the above example was C90 for each warrant, tendering of cash would be considered to be dilutive as the exercise price is less than the average share price. In that situation, the number of dilutive shares included in the denominator would be calculated under the treasury stock method in the normal way for options and warrants.

Furthermore, where both cash and debt instruments are tendered, the number of dilutive shares included in the denominator would be the sum of (a) the amount calculated using the treasury stock method to the cash proceeds and (b) the amount calculated by the treating the debt tendered as a conventional convertible debt.

A14.125 In some circumstances, the proceeds from the exercise of options or warrants may be required to be applied to redeem the entity's existing debt instruments. Upon the assumed exercise of such options or warrants, the proceeds are applied to purchase the debt at its market price rather than to purchase ordinary shares under the treasury stock method. The treasury stock method is applied, however, for the excess proceeds received from the assumed exercise of the options or warrants over the amount used for the assumed purchase of debt. Interest, net of income tax, on any debt assumed to be purchased is added back as an adjustment to the numerator. [IAS 33 para A9]

Example

An entity granted 500,000 new options at the beginning of the year to its debenture holders that also own all of the entity's 6% redeemable 20,000 nominal C100 debentures. The exercise price of the option is C6.50. The terms of the options require the company to use the proceeds received from the exercise of options to repurchase the company's outstanding debentures. The average market price of nominal C100 debenture and an ordinary share for the period are C105 and C8 respectively.

For the purposes of calculating diluted EPS, the above options are assumed to be exercised and the proceeds of C3,250,000 (500,000 @ 6.50) are applied to purchase all the outstanding 20,000 nominal debentures at the average price of C105 for C2,100,000. The excess proceeds of C1,150,000 are deemed to be applied to purchase shares in the market at C8 per share, that is, 143,750 shares. Therefore, the number of dilutive shares that are included in the denominator under the treasury stock method is 500,000 – 143,750 = 356,250.

In addition, the entity would increase the numerator by the after-tax interest saved on the assumed repurchase of the debentures, that is, C84,000 (C2m @ 6% less tax @ 30%).

The incremental earnings per share = C84,000 ÷ 356,250 = C0.24.

The options would be included in the diluted EPS calculation if the incremental earnings per share of C0.24 is less than the basic EPS at the continuing operations level.

Calculating diluted EPS

A14.126 As stated in paragraph A14.110 above, only potential ordinary shares that are dilutive are considered in the calculation of diluted EPS. Potential ordinary shares should be treated as dilutive when, and only when, their conversion to ordinary shares would decrease profit or increase loss per share from continuing operations attributable to ordinary equity holders. [IAS 33 paras 41, 43]. The profit from continuing operations is the profit for the period after deducting preference dividends (and other appropriations and adjustments in respect of preference shares) and excluding items relating to discontinued operations. This means that the entity would need to calculate a basic earnings per share from continuing operations. A potential ordinary share would be dilutive if its assumed conversion results in reducing this earnings per share from continuing operations below the basic level. On the other hand, if the effect is to increase this earnings per share above the basic level, the security is not dilutive and should be excluded from the diluted EPS calculation. [IAS 33 para 42].

A14.127 It follows from the above that on no account should the dilution be tested by reference to whether the conversion of a potential ordinary share reduces the standard basic EPS calculated on the total profit or loss for the period. The reason for choosing, as a control number, the 'profit from continuing operations' is because this level of profit, unaffected by discontinued operations, is likely to remain stable over time and reflect the earnings that will exist in the future when the dilution occurs. This is a sensible approach for the following reason. If there is a loss from discontinued operations and this turns the overall earnings per share attributable to ordinary equity holders into a loss per share, the exercise of, say, an option will increase the denominator and result in a lower overall loss per share. This is because the loss is 'shared' among a higher number of shares. In that situation, the option is anti-dilutive at this level, but may well be dilutive at the continuing operations level.

Example

A company has a profit from continuing activities, but a loss for the year overall because of losses on discontinued operations. Options are dilutive when considered at continuing operations profit level as the diluted EPS at that level decreases profit per share. However, at the overall loss for the year level, applying the dilution caused by the options decreases loss per share. Is it still correct to show the effect of the options in the diluted EPS?

Yes. If the options are dilutive at the profit from continuing operations level then they should be included in the diluted EPS calculation at the loss for the year level. If that reduces loss per share then so be it, but the company should explain the circumstances. A form of explanation might be *"Options are dilutive at the profit from continuing operations level and so, in accordance with IAS 33, have been treated as dilutive for the purpose of diluted earnings per share. The diluted loss per share is lower than basic loss per share because of the effect of losses on discontinued operations".*

In addition to disclosing basic and diluted EPS for the overall loss for the year, the entity would also be required to disclose basic and diluted EPS at the continuing operations level on the face of the income statement and the basic and diluted EPS for discontinued operations either on the face of the income statement or in the notes (see further para A14.173 onwards). [IAS 33 paras 66, 68].

[The next paragraph is A14.130.]

A14.130 In order to determine whether a particular convertible instrument, option or warrant will have a diluting effect, it is necessary to consider each of them separately rather than in aggregate. This consideration is complicated and involves the following steps:

- The entity first calculates the profit or loss from continuing operations attributable to ordinary equity holders.
- The entity next calculates the earnings per incremental share for each type of potential ordinary share. The earnings per incremental share is the increase in profit or loss (or less commonly the decrease) that would result from the exercise or conversion of the security divided by the weighted average increase in the number of ordinary shares that would result from the conversion.
- The entity next ranks all potential ordinary shares from the most dilutive (lowest earnings per incremental share) to the least dilutive (highest earnings per incremental share). Options and warrants are generally included first because they do not affect the numerator of the calculation and, hence, are most dilutive.
- The entity then calculates a basic EPS using profit or loss from continuing operations attributable to ordinary equity holders as the numerator.
- The most dilutive potential ordinary share with the lowest earnings per incremental share is then included and a new EPS as indicated above is calculated. If this new figure is lower than the previous one, the entity recalculates EPS including the potential shares with the next lowest earnings per incremental share.
- The above process of including increasingly less dilutive shares continues until the resulting EPS figure increases or there are no more potential ordinary shares to consider.
- Any potential ordinary share that has the effect of increasing the cumulative EPS from continuing operations is considered to be anti-dilutive and is excluded from the diluted per share calculation.
- All other potential ordinary shares with higher rankings are considered to be dilutive potential ordinary shares and are included in the diluted EPS calculation in the normal way.

[IAS 33 para 44].

In most instances, where there is a loss from continuing operations, there would be no difference between the basic and diluted EPS as potential ordinary shares would be anti-dilutive.

A14.131 The sequence of including each issue or series of potential ordinary shares from the most dilutive to the least dilutive guarantees that the final diluted EPS figure expresses maximum dilution of the basic EPS. A numerical example depicting the above steps is shown below.

Example

The issued share capital of C plc at 31 December 20X7 and 20X8 comprises 2,000,000 ordinary shares of 10c each. The company granted options over 100,000 ordinary shares in 20X6. The options can be exercised between 20X9 and 20Y1 at 60c per share. The average market price of C plc's shares during 20X8 was 75c.

In addition, C plc has 800,000 8% C1 convertible cumulative preference shares (treated as an equity instrument under IAS 32) and C1,000,000 5% convertible bonds in issue throughout 20X8. Each preference share and bond is convertible into 2 ordinary shares.

The company's results for the year ended 31 December 20X8 comprised operating profit from continuing operations of C300,000 and operating profit from discontinued operations of C100,000. Interest and tax at 30% amounted to C100,000 and C90,000 respectively. The profit for the year was C210,000.

The necessary steps to calculate C plc's diluted earnings per share for 20X8 are set out below. Comparative figures for 20X7 have not been included in this example.

1 Calculation of profit from continuing operations

1 Calculation of profit from continuing operations

	Total	Continuing operations	Discontinued operations
	C	C	C
Operating profit from continuing operations	300,000	300,000	
Operating profit from discontinued operations *	100,000		100,000
Profit before interest	400,000	300,000	100,000
Interest **	100,000	76,000	24,000
Profit after interest	300,000	224,000	76,000
Tax @ 30% **	90,000	67,200	22,800
Profit	210,000	156,800	53,200
Less: Preference dividend	64,000	64,000	–
Profit attributable to ordinary equity holders	146,000	92,800	53,200

* The above workings are for illustrative purposes and do not show the discontinued operations as they are required to be presented in the income statement by IAS 1, 'Presentation of financial statements' and IFRS 5, ' Non-current assets held for sale and discontinued operations'. The presentation of discontinued operations is dealt with in chapter 8.

** Interest has been allocated to the discontinued operation on the basis of the debt that has been attributed to the discontinued operation. Taxation has been attributed on the basis of the taxation actually payable by the discontinued operation.

2 Determine earnings per incremental share for each class of potential ordinary share and rank them from the most dilutive to least dilutive

	Increase in earnings C	Increase in number of ordinary shares	Earnings per incremental share c	Rank (note)
Options				
Increase in earnings	nil			
Incremental shares issued for nil consideration 100,000 × (75-60)/75		20,000	nil	1
8% Convertible preference shares				
Increase in earnings 8% × C800,000	64,000			
Incremental shares 2 × 800,000		1,600,000	4.00	3
5% Convertible bonds				
Increase in earnings after taxes 1,000,000 × 5% × 70%	35,000			
Incremental shares 1,000,000 × 2		2,000,000	1.75	2

Note: Ranking is in ascending order of earnings per incremental share.

Since the options, convertible preference shares and convertible bonds have been in issue throughout 20X8, the increase in number of ordinary shares is also their weighted average for the year. If options are granted during the year, they are brought into the averaging calculation from the date of grant.

If there were more than one series, say, of options these would have to be ranked by series.

3 Calculate the cumulative dilution effect on profit per share from continuing operations

	Profit from continuing operations C	Weighted average number of shares	Profit from continuing operations per share (c)	
Profit	92,800	2,000,000	4.64	
Options	–	20,000		
	92,800	2,020,000	4.59	Dilutive
5% Convertible bonds	35,000	2,000,000		
	127,800	4,020,000	3.18	Dilutive
8% Convertible preference shares	64,000	1,600,000		
	191,800	5,620,000	3.41	Anti-dilutive

Since diluted earnings per share from continuing operations is increased when taking the convertible preference shares into account (from 3.18 to 3.41), the convertible preference shares are anti-dilutive and are ignored in the calculation of diluted earnings per share.

4 Calculate diluted earnings per share including only dilutive potential ordinary shares

	Earnings C	Weighted average number of shares	Earnings per share (c)
Profit attributable to ordinary equity holders	146,000	2,000,000	7.30
Options		20,000	–
	146,000	2,020,000	–
5% Convertible bonds	35,000	2,000,000	–
Diluted earnings	181,000	4,020,000	4.50

The final diluted EPS is calculated by reference to profit attributable to ordinary equity holders, but the dilution test is carried out by using the profit from continuing operations as the 'control number' (see para A14.132 below) as set out in step three above.

The above example deals only with the calculation of the diluted EPS for the total profit attributable to ordinary equity holders. However, IAS 33 also requires disclosure of the basic and diluted EPS attributable to continuing and to discontinued operations. The figures to be disclosed would be as follows.

	Basic EPS (c)	Diluted EPS (c)
Profit attributable to ordinary equity holders	7.30	4.50
Profit from continuing operations	4.64[1]	3.18[1]
Profit from discontinued operations	2.66[2]	1.32[2]

Notes:

[1] As per step 3 above, Basic = 92,800/2,000,000 = 4.64 ; Diluted = 127,800/ 4,020,000 = 3.18

[2] Basic = 53,200/2,000,000 = 2.66; Diluted = 53,200/4,020,000 = 1.32

Note that the income statement effect of the convertible bonds is not adjusted against the discontinued operations results, because it relates to continuing operations. The additional shares are taken into account because the discontinued operation EPS is measured as one element of the EPS for the total entity result. Also, the sum of the continuing operations EPS and discontinued operations EPS (for both basic and diluted) equals the EPS calculated on the profit attributable to ordinary equity holders.

A14.132 Paragraph A3 of the standard illustrates the application of the 'control number' with a useful example. The following example is derived from that example.

Example

An entity has a profit from continuing operations of C4m, a loss from discontinued operations of C7m, a loss for the year attributable to equity holders of C3m and C4m ordinary shares and C1m potential ordinary shares outstanding.

The entity's basic EPS for continuing operations is C1 for continuing operations, a (C1.75) loss for discontinued operations and (C0.75) for the loss for the year.

The C1m potential ordinary shares are included in the diluted EPS calculation because (assuming no income statement effect for the potential ordinary shares) their effect on the EPS calculation for continuing operations is dilutive. On that assumption, the resulting diluted EPS for continuing operations is C0.8. Because the profit from continuing operations is the control number, the potential ordinary shares are also included in the calculation of the diluted EPS for loss from discontinued operations and for the total loss for the year attributable to equity holders. The resultant diluted EPS figures are respectively (C1.4) for discontinued operations and (C0.6) for the loss attributable to equity holders. This is despite the fact that these figures are anti-dilutive to their comparable basic EPS figures of (C1.75) and (C0.75).

EPS for interim periods

A14.133 IAS 33 states that dilutive potential ordinary shares should be determined independently for each period presented. The number of dilutive potential ordinary shares included in the year to date period should not be a weighted average of the dilutive potential ordinary shares included in each interim computation. [IAS 33 para 37]. In other words, the number of dilutive potential ordinary shares should be determined for each interim period based on the year to date position at the end of the interim period.

Example

An example of this principle might be where an entity made an acquisition in the previous year and entered into an agreement to issue 1,000 additional ordinary shares for each C50,000 of consolidated profit in excess of C1,000,000 in the following year, based on the entity's consolidated financial statements. The entity reports quarterly. The results for each quarter are as follows:

		Cumulative
	C	C
First quarter	600,000	600,000
Second quarter	700,000	1,300,000
Third quarter	(200,000)*	1,100,000
Fourth quarter	400,000	1,500,000

*includes a loss from discontinued operations of C300,000.

The company has 100,000 ordinary shares outstanding during the year.

The EPS and diluted EPS for each quarter are as follows:

	Quarter 1	Quarter 2	Quarter 3	Quarter 4	Year
Numerator C	600,000	700,000	(200,000)	400,000	1,500,000
Denominator:					
Ordinary shares	100,000	100,000	100,000	100,000	100,000
Basic EPS*	C6	C7	(C2)	C4	C15
Potential ordinary shares	–	6,000	2,000**	10,000	10,000
Total denominator for diluted EPS	100,000	106,000	102,000	110,000	110,000
Diluted EPS	C6	C6.6	(C1.96)	C3.64	CC13.64

* The potential ordinary shares are not included in the calculation of the basic EPS, because there is no certainty that the condition will be satisfied until the end of the period.

** In quarter 3 there is a profit from continuing operations of C100,000 and a loss from discontinued operations of C300,000 and as the potential ordinary shares are dilutive at the continuing operations level they are taken into account in the diluted EPS, even though they are anti-dilutive at the total loss level.

The above example demonstrates that the diluted EPS for the year differs from any average or weighted average of the diluted EPS figures reported in the individual quarterly accounts. This is simply because the denominator used in each of the first three quarters differs from the denominator at the year end. Under the rules in the standard the diluted EPS figure for the year should be based on the year to date figures, that is, at the year end the figure should be disclosed as C13.64.

Securities of subsidiaries, joint ventures and associates

A14.134 A subsidiary, joint venture or associate may issue potential ordinary shares to parties other than the parent, venturer or investor. These potential ordinary shares may be convertible into either ordinary shares of the subsidiary, joint venture or associate or they may be convertible into shares of the parent, venturer or investor (the reporting entity). If the potential ordinary shares have a dilutive effect on the reporting entity's basic EPS, they should be included in the calculation of the reporting entity's diluted EPS. [IAS 33 para 40].

A14.135 If the potential ordinary shares issued by a subsidiary enable their holders to obtain ordinary shares in the subsidiary, then those potential ordinary shares should be included in computing the subsidiary's EPS figures (if indeed the subsidiary is calculating an EPS figure). In any event, those earnings per share amounts would be included in the consolidated EPS based on the group's holdings of the subsidiary's securities. On the other hand, if the potential shares issued by the subsidiary enable their holders to obtain ordinary shares in the parent, then these potential ordinary shares should be considered along with the other potential ordinary shares issued by the parent in the computation of consolidated diluted EPS. The same considerations apply where potential ordinary shares issued by an associate or a joint venture are exchangeable into ordinary shares of the associate or joint venture, or into ordinary shares of the reporting entity. They should be included in the EPS computation of the reporting entity if they are considered to be dilutive. [IAS 33 para A11].

Example

A parent entity has profit attributable to ordinary shareholders of C100,000 (excluding any earnings of the subsidiary). There are 10,000 ordinary shares outstanding. The parent owns 800 ordinary shares in the subsidiary representing 80% of the subsidiary's ordinary share capital. It also owns 200 convertible preference shares in the subsidiary representing 50% of the subsidiary's preference share capital (which is treated as an equity instrument under IAS 32). The parent also has 20 warrants exercisable to purchase ordinary shares in the subsidiary.

The subsidiary has profit attributable to ordinary shareholders of C6,000. Its ordinary share capital consists of 1,000 ordinary shares and it has 400 convertible (one for one) preference shares in issue. It has also issued 150 warrants exercisable to subscribe for ordinary shares of the subsidiary, with an exercise price of C5 per warrant. The average market price of one ordinary share of the subsidiary was C10. Dividends on the preference shares are C1 per share. There were no inter-company transactions or eliminations other than dividends. Tax has been ignored for the purposes of this example.

Subsidiary's earnings per share

Basic EPS $\frac{6,000 - 400}{1,000}$ = C5.6

This is calculated as the subsidiary's profit from which is deducted the preference dividend that had been charged to retained earnings. The result is divided by the number of the subsidiary's ordinary shares.

Diluted EPS $\frac{6,000}{1,000 + 75 + 400}$ = C4.07

This is the subsidiary's profit (preference dividends are not deducted as they would be saved on conversion of the preference shares) divided by the number of ordinary shares plus the ordinary shares that would be issued on conversion of the preference shares on the basis of one for one and the number of ordinary shares that would be issued for nil consideration on exercise of the warrants calculated as follows:

Proceeds of warrants 150 × C5 = C750.
Number of ordinary shares that could be issued at fair value C750 ÷ C10 = 75
Number of ordinary shares that would be issued at nil consideration 150 — 75 = 75

Consolidated earnings per share

Basic EPS $\frac{100,000 + 4,680}{10,000}$ = C10.47

The earnings are calculated as the profit attributable to ordinary shareholders, before taking account of the subsidiary's results that are included in the consolidated financial statements, of C100,000, plus the share of the subsidiary's profits calculated as:

6,000 — 400 = 5,600 x 800 ÷ 1000 = 4,480 + 200 (share of preference dividend) = 4,680

Diluted EPS $\frac{100,000 + 3,256 + 41 + 814}{10,000}$ = C10.41

The earnings figure comprises:

(a) The profit of parent entity attributable to ordinary shares (excluding dividends from subsidiary) of C100,000.

(b) The share of subsidiary's profit calculated as (800 shares × 4.07) = C3,256. (C4.07 being the diluted EPS of the subsidiary).

(c) The parent's proportionate interest in the subsidiary's earnings attributable to the warrants calculated as (75 shares × 4.07) × 20 ÷ 150 = C40.7.

(d) The parent's proportionate interest in the subsidiary's earnings attributable to the convertible preference shares calculated as (200 shares × 4.07) = C814.

A14.136 Table A14.4 above discloses the effect on the group diluted EPS of options in a subsidiary that are convertible into shares of the subsidiary.

A14.137 The standard also covers the situation where securities of the reporting entity are issued that are convertible into ordinary shares of a subsidiary, joint venture or associate. In such a situation, the securities are assumed to be converted and the profit or loss attributable to ordinary equity holders of the reporting entity is adjusted, in the normal way, for any changes in dividends, interest or other changes that would result from conversion. The profit or loss is also adjusted for any changes in the reporting entity's share of results of the subsidiary, joint venture or associate that would result from the change in the number of shares in the subsidiary, joint venture or associate held by the reporting entity as a result of conversion. The denominator (number of shares and potential ordinary shares) of the diluted EPS calculation is not adjusted because the number of shares of the reporting entity itself would not change following conversion. [IAS 33 para A12].

Employee share and incentive plans

A14.138 Many companies have in place share options and other share award schemes to remunerate officers and other employees. Under some schemes, share options or share purchase rights are granted solely on the basis that the employees continue to render service for a specified period of time, that is, the award does not specify a performance condition for vesting. In other schemes, vesting of the shares depends on both the employee's rendering service to the employer for a specified period of time and the achievement of a specified performance target, for example, attaining a specified growth rate in return on assets or a specified earnings target.

A14.139 IAS 33 states that employee share options with fixed or determinable terms and non-vested ordinary shares are treated as options in calculating diluted EPS, even though they may be contingent on vesting. They are treated as outstanding on the grant date. Performance-related employee share options are treated as contingently issuable shares (see para A14.145 below) because their issue is contingent on satisfying specified conditions in addition to the passage of time. [IAS 33 para 48].

A14.140 As noted above, performance-related share options are treated as contingently issuable shares and these are dealt with from paragraph A14.145 below. All other awards that do not specify a performance criteria should be regarded as options for the purposes of computing diluted EPS. They should be considered to be outstanding as of the grant date for purposes of computing diluted EPS even though their exercise may be contingent upon vesting. They should be included in the diluted EPS computation even if the employee may not receive (or be able to sell) the stock until some future date. Accordingly, all shares to be issued should be included in computing diluted EPS if the effect is dilutive. The dilutive effect should be computed using the treasury stock method described in paragraph A14.117 above. If the share awards were granted during the period, the shares issuable must be weighted to reflect the portion of the period during which the awards were outstanding. [IAS 33 para 38].

A14.141 For share options and other share-based payment arrangements to which IFRS 2, 'Share-based payment', applies, the assumed exercise price should include the fair value (as calculated on the date the options were granted) of any goods or services to be supplied to the entity in the future under the share option or other share-based payment arrangement. [IAS 33 para 47A]. Therefore, in applying the treasury stock method described in paragraph A14.117 above, the assumed exercise price, for the purpose of determining the incremental number of shares issued for nil consideration, would comprise the amount, if any, the employee must pay upon exercise and the balance of any amounts calculated under IFRS 2 that has not yet been charged to the income statement. The assumed proceeds should not include cost attributable to past service. Neither should any adjustments be made to the numerator in respect of the IFRS 2 charge to the income statement as the charge represents the cost of issuing potential ordinary shares that would not be saved on conversion. The treatment of employee share options that are not related to performance is illustrated in the following example (ignoring tax).

Example

Share option scheme not related to performance
Company A has in place an employee share option scheme that awards share options to employees on the basis of period of service with the company.

The provisions of the scheme are as follows at the 20X0 year end.

Date of grant	1 January 20X0
Market price of option at grant date	C2.10
Exercise price of option	C2.50
Date of vesting	31 December 20X2
Number of shares under option	1 million

Applying IFRS 2, the income statement is charged with 70c per option in each of the three years 20X0-20X2 (that is, C2.10/3).

Profit for year 20X0 (after compensation expense)	C1,200,000
Weighted average number of ordinary shares outstanding	5 million
Average market price of an ordinary share during the year	C5.00
Assumed proceeds per option	C3.90 (being the exercise price of C2.50 and IFRS 2 expense attributable to future service, not yet recognised, of C1.40). Next year C3.20 (being C2.50 + 70c).

Computation of earnings per share	per share	earnings	shares
Profit for year 20X0		C1,200,000	

Weighted average shares outstanding for 20X0			5,000,000
Basic earnings per share	24.0c		
Number of shares under option			1,000,000
Number of shares that would have been issued at fair value: (1 million × C3.90)/ C5.00			(780,000)
Diluted earnings per share	23.0c	C1,200,000	5,220,000

[The next paragraph is A14.143.]

A14.143 Sometimes shares to satisfy the company's obligations under share award schemes have already been purchased by an ESOP trust and are held by the trust as pre-funding for options or other performance-related shares. The trust's holding in the company's shares is treated as treasury shares and deducted from equity. [IAS 32 para 33]. Accordingly, the rules relating to treasury shares would apply and those non-vesting shares should be excluded from both basic and diluted EPS as discussed in paragraph A14.75 above. Instead, the calculation of diluted EPS should include non-performance-related shares in the same way as options as set out from paragraph A14.140 above and performance-related shares in the same way as contingently issuable shares as discussed from paragraph A14.145 below.

A14.144 If share based awards are payable in ordinary shares or in cash at the election of either the entity or the employee, the determination of whether such awards are potential ordinary shares should be made in the same way as discussed in paragraph A14.163.

Contingently issuable ordinary shares

A14.145 It is not uncommon for acquisition agreements to include a clause under which the purchaser of an acquired entity is required to make an additional consideration payment in the form of ordinary shares in future. The value of such shares may either be known precisely at the time of the acquisition, or may be contingent upon the future performance or future evaluation of the acquired entity. In the first instance, the acquirer has an obligation to issue ordinary shares in future, but the obligation is simply deferred (deferred consideration). In the second instance an obligation may or may not arise depending on whether or not certain earnings conditions are met (contingent consideration). In any event, the need to issue ordinary shares in future could lead to dilution of EPS. The standard refers to these as 'contingently issuable ordinary shares'. [IAS 33 para 52]. Contingently issuable ordinary shares are defined as *"ordinary shares issuable for little or no cash or other consideration upon the satisfaction of specified conditions in a contingent share agreement"* (see also para A14.77 above). [IAS 33 para 5].

A14.146 The way in which diluted EPS should be calculated to take account of contingently issuable shares is described below:

- Contingently issuable shares are considered outstanding and included in the calculation of diluted EPS as if the conditions of the contingency are deemed to have been met, based on the information available, at the end of reporting period. In effect this means that the diluted EPS computation includes those shares that would be issued under the terms of the contingency, based on the current status of conditions, as if the end of the reporting period was the end of the contingency period. An example would be an estimate of the number of shares that would have been issued under an earn-out if that agreement had terminated at the balance sheet date (see further para A14.148). Ordinary shares issuable under such contingent share agreements are included in the diluted EPS calculation as of the beginning of the period or as of the date of the contingent share agreement, if later. Restatement is not permitted if the conditions are not met when the actual contingency period expires. [IAS 33 para 52].

- Where the conditions relating to the issue have been met (the events occurred) by the end of the period, the relevant shares are included in the computation of both basic and diluted EPS. In effect, this will be when issuing the shares is no longer contingent and when there are no circumstances under which the shares would not be issued. [IAS 33 para 52].

A14.147 The criteria under which additional shares are issuable under contingent consideration agreements are many and varied, although in practice most involve either future levels of earnings or the future share price of the issuing company or a mixture of both. It should be noted, however, that such contingently issuable shares should be included in the diluted EPS calculation only if the effect is dilutive.

A14.148 Where the number of contingently issuable shares depends upon the level of earnings, the diluted EPS computation should include those shares to the extent that that they would be issuable under the agreement based on the current amount of earnings. However, earnings conditions in earn out agreements come in various forms. Sometimes the terms may specify that further shares will be issued if the average profit earned over a period is a specific amount. Sometimes the maintenance of current earnings levels, or the attainment of specified increased level of earnings of the acquired entity for a specified number of years may be the condition. Other earnings conditions may specify the issue of shares when a minimum earnings target is reached, increasing rateably until the maximum earnings target is reached, with a cap on the maximum number of shares that could be issued.

A14.149 IAS 33 deals specifically with one such type of arrangement, where the achievement or maintenance of a specified level of earnings is the condition and that amount has been achieved at the end of the period, but must be maintained for a further period. In such a case the additional ordinary shares are included if dilutive in the *diluted* EPS, because the end of the period is *assumed* to be the end of the contingency period for the purpose of diluted EPS and the level of profit has been achieved at the end of the period. However, the shares are not included in *basic* EPS until the end of the *actual* contingency period, that is, the end of the further period for which the level of earnings must be maintained. This is because there may be losses in that further period that could mean that the contingent condition will not be met at the end of the actual contingency period. [IAS 33 para 53].

A14.150 Whatever the earnings criteria, the guiding principle is that the current level of earnings should be used to determine the number of shares that could be issued under the terms, assuming that the contingency period ended on the balance sheet date. They should be included in the diluted EPS calculation only if dilution results. If in the subsequent period, or until the end of the agreement, there is a decline in earnings such that the contingent shares no longer need to be issued, previous period's diluted EPS should not be restated. Hence, basic EPS should not include any contingently issuable shares, because all the necessary conditions have not been satisfied, but the shares would be included in calculating the diluted figure. The following examples illustrate the application of the above principle.

Example 1

Average earnings condition

On 1 January 20X4, company A acquired the whole of the issued share capital of company B. The total consideration payable in respect of the acquisition comprises initial consideration and deferred contingent consideration. Under the terms of the deferred contingent consideration, company A is required to issue 100,000 shares if company B's profit for the year averages C100,000 over a three year period. Any additional shares will be issued on 1 January 20X7 after the end of the three year contingency period. Company B's profit for the year ended 31 December 20X4 amounted to C120,000.

Given that the terms stipulate the achievement of C100,000 of average profit for the three year period, it would appear at first sight that the contingency condition at the balance sheet date has been met as the profit for the year ended 31 December 20X4 exceeds C100,000. This is not the case as it assumes that the company will earn at least C90,000 for each of the next two years ended 31 December 20X6. Projecting future earnings levels in this way is not permitted under the standard because as stated in paragraph A14.101 above, the standard takes a historical approach and not a predictive or forward-looking approach in measuring dilution. The provisions relating to contingently issuable shares in the standard are quite specific and do not allow an entity to consider the probability of a contingent issue occurring.

The correct analysis is to measure whether performance achieved in the current period is deemed to be that achieved over the whole of the contingency period as if the end of the reporting period was the end of the contingency period. On this basis, an average over a period has the same effect as if it were expressed as a cumulative amount over the period. So in this situation, the contingency condition should be expressed in terms of a cumulative target of C300,000 over the three year period. Since the profit for the year ended 31 December 20X4 is only C120,000, which is less than C300,000, the contingency condition is not met at the balance sheet and no additional shares would be brought into the diluted EPS computation.

Similarly, if the profit for the year ended 31 December 20X5 were to increase to C150,000 again the contingency condition is not met in that year, because the cumulative earnings to date amounts to C270,000. So no additional shares would be included in that year. In the final year ended 31 December 20X6 when the contingency period comes to an end, the company will know for certain whether the contingency conditions have been met or not. If the condition is met in that year, the company will include 100,000 shares in both basic and diluted EPS.

Example 2

Attainment of a specified increased level of earnings

The facts are the same as in the previous example except that the deferred contingent consideration agreement provides for the issue of 1,000 shares for each C1,000 of total profit in excess of C250,000 over the three years ending 20X6.

Using the above principles, the company did not earn C250,000 for the year ended 31 December 20X4. Again projecting future earnings levels (C120,000 for 3 years = C360,000) and including 110,000 ((C360,000 — C250,000)/C1,000 × 1,000) contingent shares in the diluted EPS calculation is not permitted by the standard.

For the year ended 31 December 20X5, the cumulative amount earned to that date is C270,000. As this amount exceeds C250,000, the contingency condition is met in that year and the company will include 20,000 contingently issuable shares in the diluted EPS calculation for that year. For the year ended 31 December 20X6, the cumulative amount earned to that date would be known and the actual number of shares issued would be included in both basic and diluted EPS. If the actual number of shares amounts to say 50,000 shares, prior year's diluted EPS, which was based on 20,000 contingent shares, should not be restated.

A14.151 Similar considerations apply when computing diluted EPS for interim reports. If at 30 June 20X5, the cumulative amount earned to that date was C245,000 (C120,000 to 31 December 20X4 + C125,000 to 30 June 20X5), the contingency provision is not met. Therefore, no contingently issuable shares would be included in calculating the diluted EPS for the half year, even though at the time of preparing the interim report it is apparent that 20,000 shares will be included in the year end diluted EPS calculation.

A14.152 IAS 33 also gives specific guidance for the situation where the number of shares issuable in the future depends on the market price of the shares at the future date. It states that the computation of diluted EPS should reflect the number of shares that would be issued based on the current market price at the end of the reporting period if the effect is dilutive. If the condition is based on an average of market prices over some period of time that extends beyond the end of the reporting period, the average for the period that has elapsed at the period end should be used. Because the market price may change in a future period, basic EPS should not include such contingently issuable shares, because all necessary conditions have not been satisfied. [IAS 33 para 54].

A14.153 Where the number of contingently issuable ordinary shares depends on both future earnings and the future market price of ordinary shares, the number of ordinary shares included in the diluted EPS calculation is based on both conditions. Unless both conditions are deemed to be met (using the guidance in the previous paragraphs) the contingently issuable shares are not included in the diluted EPS. [IAS 33 para 55].

A14.154 In some deferred consideration agreements, the value of the deferred consideration is known, but the number of shares to be issued when the deferred consideration falls due is not known. IAS 33 does not specifically consider this situation. However, we consider that the number of shares to be included in the calculation should be based on the market price at the balance sheet date as if it were the end of the contingency period.

A14.155 IAS 33 also gives guidance for the situation where the contingency is based on a condition other than earnings or market price (for example, opening a certain number of retail stores). It states that the contingent shares should be included in the computation of diluted EPS based on the assumption that the current status (at the period end) of the condition will remain unchanged until the end of the contingency period. So, if during the period only half the required number of new stores that would result in the issue of shares were opened, no contingently issuable shares are included in the diluted EPS computation. [IAS 33 para 56].

A14.156 If the contingency is based on a number of different conditions, we consider that the determination of the number of shares included in diluted EPS should be based on the status of all relevant conditions as they exist at the end of each reporting period. If one of the conditions is not met at the end of the reporting period, no contingently issuable shares should be included in diluted EPS. Though not specifically mentioned in IAS 33 it is implicit in the guidance described in paragraph A14.153 above.

A14.157 Contingently issuable potential ordinary shares that are not covered by a contingent share agreement, such as contingently issuable convertible instruments, should be included in diluted EPS on the following basis:

- It is first necessary to determine whether the potential ordinary shares may be assumed to be issued on the basis of the conditions specified for their issue under the contingently issuable share provisions discussed from paragraph A14.145.
- Depending on the type of those potential ordinary shares, they should be reflected in diluted EPS by following the provisions for convertible securities discussed from paragraph A14.114, the provisions for share options and warrants discussed from paragraph A14.117, and the provisions for contracts that may be settled in ordinary shares or cash discussed from paragraph A14.159.

However, exercise or conversion should not be assumed for purposes of computing diluted EPS, unless exercise or conversion of similar outstanding potential ordinary shares that are not contingently issuable is also assumed. [IAS 33 para 57].

A14.158 An example of contingently issuable potential ordinary shares is given in Table A14.6. This relates to contingent consideration for an acquisition that is subject to a lawsuit.

Table A14.6 – Diluted EPS and contingent consideration payable in shares
Altana AG – Annual Report and Accounts – 31 December 2002

Earnings per share

Basic earnings per share are computed by dividing net income by the weighted average number of shares outstanding for the year. Diluted EPS reflects the potential dilution that could occur if securities or other contracts to issue common stock were exercised or converted into common stock. Diluted earnings per share are calculated by adjusting the weighted average number of shares for the effect of the stock option plans as well as the impact of the DAT lawsuit which is payable in the Company's shares (Note 31). No adjustments to net income were necessary for the computation of diluted earnings per share.

The diluted earnings per share were calculated under the assumption that all potential diluting options are exercised.

	2002	2001
Basic earnings per share:		
Net income	**324,408**	327,937
Weighted average common shares outstanding	**136,622,766**	137,533,720
Basic earnings per share in €	**2.37**	**2.38**
Diluted weighted average shares:		
Net income	**324,408**	327,937
Weighted average shares outstanding	**136,622,766**	137,533,720
Dilution from stock options	**604,546**	607,434
Dilution from DAT lawsuit	**306,391**	306,391
Diluted weighted average shares outstanding	**137,533,703**	138,447,545
Diluted earnings per share in €	**2.36**	**2.37**

31 Litigation
Deutsch-Atlantische Telegraphen AG
In 1988, a group of minority shareholders of DAT brought a legal action against the Company in connection with an exchange offer made to these minority shareholders.

After consideration of the case, both the Landesgericht Köln and the Oberlandesgericht Düsseldorf stated that the 1.3 or 1.4 shares offered to the former shareholders was fair consideration. However, in 1999 the Federal Supreme Court of Germany overturned this ruling stating that the fair value should be determined based on a higher market value for DAT shares.

On March 12, 2001, the German Federal Court of Justice (Bundesgerichtshof, BGH) ruled that the exchange ratio must be based on the average market price of the shares to be exchanged during the three months preceding the approval by majority shareholders of DAT to sell its shares to the Company. The BGH referred the appeal back to a lower court (Landgericht Köln).

The expected settlement is recorded as contingent consideration based on the Company's best estimate of the exchange of 3.45 ALTANA shares for one DAT share. However, since all of the assets of DAT were either sold or written off in connection with the Company's restructuring plan in 1995, the additional consideration was expensed immediately as an impairment expense. As of December 31, 2002, consideration expected to be settled by the Company by issuance of shares has been measured at €13.8 million based on the Company's share price at December 31,

2002. The portion of the settlement expected to be paid in cash is €2.3 million. The estimated total settlement of €16.1 million is recorded as an accrual. The final settlement is subject to change based on the final exchange ratio and the market value of ALTANA's stock on the date of the settlement (Note 32).

In 2001, the addition of the accrual was recorded in other operating expenses. In 2002 the reduction of the accrual (€3.4 million) due to the decrease in the ALTANA's share price at the balance sheet date was recorded in other operating income.

32 Subsequent events (extract)
The management board and the supervisory board of ALTANA AG authorized the issuance of the financial statements as of March 17, 2003.

On January 15, 2003, the federal court decided that the consideration of the former DAT shareholders (Note 31) should be based on a conversion ratio of 3.45 shares of ALTANA for one share of DAT. The Company has appealed against that ruling.

Contracts that may be settled in ordinary shares or cash

A14.159 IAS 33 deals specifically with contracts that may be settled in ordinary shares or cash. The rules differ depending on whether the option is held by the entity (the issuer) or by the holder of the contract, as set out in the following paragraphs.

A14.160 If an entity has issued a contract that may be settled in ordinary shares or in cash at the *entity's option* (but not at the holder's option), IAS 33 lays down the following rules:

- The entity should presume that the contract will be settled in shares, and the resulting potential ordinary shares should be included in diluted EPS if the effect is dilutive.
- When such a contract is presented for accounting purposes as an asset or a liability, or when it has both an equity and a liability component under IAS 32, the entity should adjust the numerator (profit or loss attributable to ordinary equity holders) for any changes in the profit or loss that would have resulted during the period if the contract had been classified wholly as an equity instrument. This is similar to the adjustments required in paragraph 33 of IAS 33 (see para A14.102 above).

[IAS 33 paras 58, 59].

A14.161 An example of such a contract is a deferred or contingent consideration agreement where the entity has the unrestricted right to settle the consideration in the form of ordinary shares or cash. At the date of acquisition it may not be possible for the entity to determine how the deferred consideration will be settled. It should, therefore, be presumed that the contract will be settled in shares, the more dilutive method, and the resulting potential ordinary shares included in diluted EPS in accordance with the standard's relevant provisions. An example is given in Table A14.7. Another example given in the standard is a debt instrument that, on maturity gives the entity the unrestricted right to settle the liability in cash or in ordinary shares. [IAS 33 para 61].

Table A14.7 – Diluted EPS, contract that can be settled in shares or cash at entity's option

Informa PLC – Interim report – 30 June 2005

9 Earnings per share

Basic

The basic earnings per share calculation is based on a profit on ordinary activities after taxation of £48,769,000 (2004 profit: £15,115,000 six months and £69,836,000 twelve months). This profit (2004: six months profit and twelve months profit) on ordinary activities after taxation is divided by the weighted average number of shares in issue (less those non-vested shares held by employee share ownership trusts) which is 299,335,000 (2004: 193,647,000 six months and 244,928,000 twelve months).

Diluted

The diluted earnings per share calculation is based on the basic earnings per share calculation above except that the weighted average number of shares includes all potentially dilutive options granted by the Balance Sheet date as if those options had been exercised on the first day of the accounting period or the date of the grant, if later, giving a weighted average of 300,900,000 (2004: 195,557,000 six months and 246,713,000. twelve months). In accordance with IAS 33 the weighted average number of shares includes the estimated maximum number of shares payable to the vendors of Routledge Publishing Holdings Limited assuming that there are no claims for compensation by the Group that will reduce this deferred consideration and assuming that the Company does not exercise its option to pay the balance of deferred consideration in cash. The deferred consideration shares are also assumed for the purposes of this calculation to have been issued on 1 January 2005 at the closing mid-market share price on 30 June 2005 of 379p making 335,000 (2004: 314,000 six months and 336,000 twelve months) ordinary shares potentially issued.

The table below sets out the adjustment in respect of diluted potential ordinary shares:

6 months 2005	6 months 2004	12 months 2004	
Weighted average number of shares used in basic earnings per share calculation	299,334,804	193,646,662	244,927,883
Effect of dilutive share options	1,230,032	1,597,198	1,449,594
Shares potentially to be issued or allotted	334,734	313,624	335,629
Weighted average number of shares used in diluted earnings per share calculation	300,899,570	195,557,484	246,713,106

A14.161.1 The standard includes an example of the calculation of diluted EPS where the entity has in issue a convertible bond that may be settled in ordinary shares or cash at the issuer's option. The example illustrates also the adjustments that may have to be made to the numerator under the second bullet point in paragraph A14.160 above. The example below is based on the example in the standard.

Example

An entity issues 1,000 convertible bonds at the beginning of 20X5. The bonds have a three-year term and are issued at par with a face value of C1,000 per bond, giving total proceeds of C1,000,000. Interest is payable annually in arrears at a nominal annual interest rate of 4%. Each bond is convertible at any time up to maturity into 150 common shares. The entity has an option to settle the principal amount of the convertible bonds in ordinary shares or in cash.

When the bonds are issued, the prevailing market interest rate for similar debt without a conversion option is 9%. At the issue date, the market price of one common share is C3. Income tax is ignored.

	C
Profit 20X5	
Ordinary shares outstanding	1,000,000
Convertible bonds outstanding	1,200,000
Liability component	873,434[1]
Equity component	126,566
Proceeds of the bond issue	1,000,000

Note 1: Present value of the principal and interest discounted at 9% – C1,000,000 payable at the end of three years; C40,000 payable annually in arrears for three years.

The liability and equity components would be determined in accordance with IAS 32, 'Financial instruments: Disclosure and presentation'. These amounts would be recognised as the initial carrying amounts of the liability and equity components presented on the balance sheet. The amount assigned to the issuer conversion option equity element is a permanent addition to equity and is not adjusted.

Basic earnings per share 20X5:

$$\frac{C1{,}000{,}000}{1{,}200{,}000} = C0.83 \text{ per ordinary share}$$

Diluted earnings per share 20X5:

It is presumed that the issuer will settle the contract by the issue of ordinary shares; the dilutive effect is calculated in accordance with paragraph A14.158.

$$\frac{C1{,}000{,}000 + C78{,}609(a)}{1{,}200{,}000 + 150{,}000(b)} = C0.80 \text{ per ordinary share}$$

(a) The initial carrying amount is adjusted for the accretion of the liability using the effective interest rate – that is, C78,609 (C873,434 × 9%).

(b) 150,000 ordinary shares = 150 ordinary shares × 1,000 convertible bonds

[IAS 33 Example 8].

A14.162 For contracts that may be settled in ordinary shares or cash at the *holder's option*, the more dilutive of cash settlement and share settlement should be used in calculating diluted EPS. [IAS 33 para 60]. An example might be an incentive scheme where annual bonuses may be payable in either shares or cash at the election of the employee. In that situation it should be presumed that the contract will be settled by the more dilutive method. Another example given in the standard is a written put option that gives the holder the choice of settling in ordinary shares or cash. [IAS 33 para 61].

A14.163 Whilst the standard does not specifically cover the point if a contract may be settled in cash or shares at either the issuer's or the holder's option, the more restrictive of the above rules, that is those where only the issuer has an option should be applied. In practice the rules in the standard recognise that it is likely that only one party will have the option as otherwise there could be a conflict.

[The next paragraph is A14.166.]

Purchased options

A14.166 The standard notes that contracts such as purchased put options and purchased call options held by an entity over its own ordinary shares are not included in the calculation of diluted EPS. This is because their inclusion would be anti-dilutive. A put option (defined by IAS 33 as a contract that gives the holder the right to sell ordinary shares at a specified price for a given period) would be exercised only if the option exercise price were higher than the market price and a call option would be exercised only if the option exercise price were lower than the market price. [IAS 33 para 62]. In both instances, the options' effect would be anti-dilutive under the treasury stock method (see para A14.118 above) and the reverse treasury stock method (see para A14.167 below).

Written put options

A14.167 The standard also deals with written put options. Contracts that require the entity to repurchase its own shares, such as written put options and forward purchase contracts are reflected in diluted EPS if their effect is dilutive. If the contracts are 'in the money' during the period, that is, if the exercise or settlement price is above the average market price for the period, their dilutive effects should be calculated using the 'reverse treasury stock' method. Under that method:

- It should be assumed that at the beginning of the accounting period sufficient ordinary shares will be issued at the average market price for the period to raise the necessary proceeds to satisfy the contracts.
- It should be assumed that the proceeds from this issue are used to satisfy the contract to buy back ordinary shares.
- The incremental ordinary shares, that is, the difference between the number of shares assumed to be issued and the number of shares received (bought back) on satisfying the contract will be included in the calculation of diluted EPS.

[IAS 33 para 63].

Example

Assume an entity has outstanding 160 written put options on 160 of its ordinary shares with an exercise price of C10 per option. The put obligation is, therefore, C1,600. The average market price of the entity's ordinary shares is C8 for the period. In calculating diluted EPS the entity assumes that it issues 200 ordinary shares at C8 per share to raise the proceeds necessary to satisfy the put option. The difference between the 200 ordinary shares assumed to be issued and the 160 ordinary shares that would have been received on exercise of the option, that is 40 shares is added to the denominator (number of shares) in calculating the diluted EPS. No adjustments are made to the numerator (profit attributable to ordinary shareholders) as the shares are deemed issued for nil proceeds. [IAS 33 para A10].

Restatement of EPS data

A14.168 Diluted EPS of any prior period presented should not be restated for changes in the assumptions used (such as for contingently issuable shares) or for the conversion of potential ordinary shares (such as convertible debt) outstanding at the end of the previous period. [IAS 33 para 65]. This is because these factors are already taken into account in calculating the basic and, where applicable, the diluted EPS for the current period. However, in some circumstances, prior period's EPS data should be restated. These circumstances include certain post balance sheet changes in capital (see para A14.169) and prior period adjustments (see para A14.171).

Post balance sheet changes in capital

A14.169 As noted in paragraph A14.80 above, the weighted average number of ordinary shares outstanding for all periods presented (and, therefore, both basic and diluted EPS for all periods presented) should be restated for bonus issues, share splits, share consolidations and other similar events occurring during the period that change the number of shares in issue without a corresponding change in the resources of the entity. [IAS 33 para 26]. In addition, if such events occur after the balance sheet date, but before the financial statements are approved for issue, the basic and diluted EPS figures for the current period and for prior periods should be presented on the basis of the new number of shares. [IAS 33 para 64]. Where the EPS figures reflect such post balance sheet date changes, this fact should be disclosed (see further para A14.181 below).

A14.170 Other post balance sheet changes in capital should not be adjusted for, but disclosure is required of ordinary share transactions or potential ordinary share transactions that would have changed significantly the number of ordinary shares or potential ordinary shares outstanding at the end of the period if they had occurred before the end of the period (see further para A14.182).

Prior period adjustments

A14.171 EPS for all periods presented should be adjusted for the effects of errors and adjustments resulting from changes in accounting policies accounted for retrospectively in accordance with IAS 8, 'Accounting policies, changes in accounting estimates and errors'. [IAS 33 para 64]. That is, the EPS figure for the prior period should be restated as if the restated profit or loss had been reported originally in the prior period or periods.

A14.172 When a change in accounting policy: has an effect on the current period or any prior period; would have such an effect except that it is impracticable to determine the amount of the adjustment; or might have an effect on future periods, an entity should disclose for the current period and each prior period presented, to the extent practicable, the amount of the adjustment for basic and diluted earnings per share. Similarly, for the retrospective correction of material prior period errors, an entity should disclose for each prior period presented, to the extent practicable, the amount of the correction for basic and diluted earnings per share. [IAS 8 paras 28(f)(ii), 29(c)(ii), 49(b)(ii)]. Table A14.8 is an example of disclosure.

Table A14.8 – Effect of changes in accounting policy on EPS

China Mobile Limited – Annual Report and Accounts – 31 December 2009

2 Changes in accounting policies (extract)

(ii) IFRIC/HK(IFRIC) Interpretation 13, *Customer loyalty programmes*

The Group has launched a Reward Program to its customers, which provides customers the option of electing to receive free telecommunications services or other gifts. The level of point reward earned by customers under the Reward Program varies depending on the customers' services consumption, years in services and payment history.

In prior years, the Group accounted for the obligation to provide free or discounted services or goods offered to the customers under the Reward Program using the incremental costs method. The estimated incremental cost to provide free or discounted services or goods was recognized as expenses and accrued as a current liability when customers were entitled to bonus points. When customers redeemed awards or their entitlements expired, the incremental cost liability was reduced accordingly to reflect the outstanding obligations.

With effect from 1 January 2009, as a result of adoption of IFRIC/HK(IFRIC) Interpretation 13, the point reward is accounted for as a separately identifiable component of the sales transactions in which the points are granted. The consideration received in relation to the sales transactions is allocated to points reward by reference to the estimated fair value of the points as revenue and is deferred until such reward is redeemed by the customers or the points expired.

The new accounting policy has been adopted retrospectively and the comparative amounts have been restated.

The effect on the consolidated balance sheet as at 1 January 2008 is an increase in deferred tax assets, an increase in deferred revenue, a decrease in accrued expenses and other payables and a decrease in net assets of RMB676,000,000, RMB6,308,000,000, RMB3,542,000,000 and RMB2,090,000,000, respectively.

The effect on the consolidated balance sheet as at 31 December 2008 is an increase in deferred tax assets, an increase in deferred revenue, a decrease in accrued expenses and other payables and a decrease in net assets of RMB730,000,000, RMB6,841,000,000, RMB3,855,000,000 and RMB2,256,000,000, respectively.

The effect on the Group's consolidated statement of comprehensive income for the year ended 31 December 2008 is an decrease in operating revenue, operating expenses, taxation and profit for the year of RMB533,000,000, RMB313,000,000, RMB54,000,000 and RMB166,000,000, respectively. The effect on the basic earnings per share and diluted earnings per share for the year ended 31 December 2008 is a decrease of RMB0.01 and RMB0.01, respectively.

Presentation and disclosure

Presentation of basic and diluted EPS

A14.173 An entity should present both basic and diluted EPS on the face of the statement of comprehensive income or if an entity presents the components of profit or loss in a separate statement, it presents the basic and diluted EPS in that separate statement. The basic and diluted EPS should be presented for profit or loss from continuing operations attributable to the entity's ordinary equity holders and for profit or loss for the period (that is, including both continuing and discontinued operations) attributable to the entity's ordinary equity holders. The basic and diluted EPS should be presented with equal prominence for all periods presented. [IAS 33 paras 66, 67A]. This applies even if the basic and diluted EPS are the same. If they are the same the entity can disclose just one line described as 'Basic and diluted EPS'. [IAS 33 para 67].

A14.174 In practice, unless an entity has discontinued operations that it must disclose in accordance with IFRS 5, 'Non-current assets held for sale and discontinued operations', the EPS from continuing operations is likely to be identical to total EPS. Accordingly, if the basic EPS for continuing and total EPS is the same and the diluted EPS is the same, the entity could disclose the figures as follows:

Basic EPS for profit from continuing operations and for profit for the year	x
Diluted EPS for profit from continuing operations and for profit for the year	y
If the basic and diluted figures are the same the disclosure could be:	
Basic and diluted EPS for profit from continuing operations and for profit for the year	x

A14.175 The standard also requires disclosure either on the face of the statement of comprehensive income (or the income statement, if presented separately) or in the notes of basic and diluted EPS for discontinued operations, where an entity has such operations and is required to disclose them in accordance with IFRS 5. [IAS 33 para 68]. Where an entity has such operations, its EPS from continuing operations will not be the same as its total EPS and so disclosure of three basic and three diluted EPS figures will be required. Assuming that the EPS figures for profit or loss on discontinued operations are disclosed on the face of the statement of comprehensive income the disclosure might be as follows:

	20X5	20X4
Earnings per ordinary share:		
Profit from continuing operations	x	x
Profit from discontinued operations	x	x
Profit for the period	x	x
Diluted earnings per share:		
Profit from continuing operations	x	x
Profit from discontinued operations	x	x
Profit for the period	x	x

An example is also given in Table A14.5 above.

A14.176 Where there is more than one class of ordinary shares in issue with different rights to share in the profit for the period, basic and diluted EPS figures must be calculated and disclosed for each such class of ordinary shares. [IAS 33 para 66]. The way in which such calculations should be performed is considered from paragraph A14.57 above.

A14.177 If a company incurs a loss or the amount it earns for the ordinary equity holders is a negative figure, basic and diluted EPS should be determined in accordance with the rules set out in the standard and shown as a loss per share. [IAS 33 para 69]. Where the diluted loss per share is the same as the basic loss per share, because the company has incurred a loss from continuing operations and all the company's existing potential ordinary shares are not dilutive as they decrease the loss from continuing operations, the entity can disclose these in one line. An example is given in Table A14.9 below. The example illustrates the basic and diluted EPS figures for the loss attributable to ordinary equity holders only and does not illustrate the disclosure for continuing or discontinued operations.

Table A14.9 – Basic and diluted loss per share

Elan Corporation plc – Annual Report and Accounts – 31 December 2010

Consolidated Income Statement

For the Year Ended 31 December 2010 (extract)

	Notes	2010	2009
Basic and diluted net loss per Ordinary Share	14	$ (0.55)	$ (0.32)
Weighted-average shares outstanding (in millions)	14	584.9	506.8

14. Net Loss Per Share

Basic loss per share is computed by dividing the net loss for the period attributable to ordinary shareholders by the weighted-average number of Ordinary Shares outstanding during the period. Diluted net loss per share is computed by dividing the net loss for the period, by the weighted-average number of Ordinary Shares outstanding and, when dilutive, adjusted for the effect of all potentially dilutive shares, including share options and RSUs.

The following table sets forth the computation for basic and diluted net loss per share for the years ended 31 December:

	2010	2009
Numerator (amounts in $m):		
Basic and diluted net loss	(322.6)	(162.3)
Denominator (amounts in millions):		
Denominator for basic and diluted-weighted-average number of Ordinary Shares outstanding	584.9	506.8
Basic and diluted earnings per share:		
Basic and diluted net loss per share	$ (0.55)	$ (0.32)

For the years ended 31 December 2010 and 2009, there were no differences in the weighted-average number of Ordinary Shares used for basic and diluted net loss per Ordinary Share as the effect of all potentially dilutive Ordinary Shares outstanding was anti-dilutive. As at 31 December 2010, there were 22.9 million (2009: 21.3 million) share options and RSUs outstanding that could potentially have a dilutive impact in the future but were anti-dilutive in 2010 and 2009.

Additional disclosures

A14.178 The following additional information should be given for both basic and diluted EPS:

- The amounts used as the numerators in calculating the basic and diluted EPS figures. These amounts should also be reconciled with the profit or loss for the period. The reconciliation should include the individual effect of each class of instrument that affects EPS, that is, it should describe and list the adjustments arising from each of the types of potential ordinary share that has affected the basic earnings figure.

- The weighted average number of ordinary shares used as the denominator in calculating the basic and diluted EPS figures. The denominators used in the basic and diluted EPS should also be reconciled to each other. This reconciliation should include the individual effect of each class of instrument that affects EPS, that is, it should list and describe the effects of each of the types of dilutive potential ordinary shares that has affected the basic weighted average number.

[IAS 33 para 70(a)(b)].

A14.179 An example of how a company can give the above information in a concise manner is shown in the table below. The example illustrates the basic and diluted EPS figures for the profit attributable to ordinary equity holders only and does not illustrate the disclosure for continuing or discontinued operations.

Example

	Year ended 31 December 20X5		
	Earnings	Number of shares	Per-share amount
Profit for the year	6,525,000		
Less: preference dividends	75,000		
Basic EPS:			
Earnings available to ordinary shareholders	6,450,000	2,500,000	C2.58
Effect of dilutive securities:			
Options		45,000	
Convertible preferred stock	35,000	255,000	
6% convertible debentures	60,000	60,000	
Diluted EPS:			
Adjusted earnings	6,545,000	2,860,000	C2.29

A further example is given in Table A14.4 above.

A14.180 The standard also requires disclosure of instruments, including contingently issuable shares, that could dilute EPS in the future, but that were not included in the computation of diluted EPS in the period (or periods) presented, because they were anti-dilutive in that period (or those periods). [IAS 33 para 70(c)].

A14.181 As stated in paragraph A14.80, basic and diluted EPS for all periods presented should be restated for bonus issues, share splits, share consolidations and similar events occurring during the period that change the number of shares in issue without a corresponding change in the resources of the entity. If these events occur after the balance sheet date, but before the financial statements are approved for issue, the EPS figures for the current period, and those of any prior periods, should be based on the new number of shares issued (see para A14.169). As a result, the number of shares used in the EPS calculation will not be consistent with that shown in the balance sheet. Therefore, disclosure should be made to that effect. [IAS 33 para 64]. An example of a share split that occurred in the year is Table A14.10 (only the figures for basic EPS are reproduced in the table).

Table A14.10 – EPS adjusted for share split in the year

STADA Arzneimittel AG – Report and Accounts – 31 December 2004

2.18. Earnings per share (extract)	2004	Previous year
Earnings per share		
Net income distributable to shareholders of STADA Arzneimittel AG in € 000s	48,484	43,869
Average number of shares	53,348,910[1,2]	43,327,286[1,2]
Earnings per share in €	0.91[2]	1.01[2]

Basic earnings per share are calculated according to IAS 33.10 by dividing net income distributable to the shareholders of STADA Arzneimittel AG by the average number of shares outstanding, less treasury stock.

[1] Please refer to the notes on shareholders' equity (see note 3.12) regarding the change in the number of shares.

[2] Pursuant to IAS 33.20 in conjunction with IAS 33.22, a capital increase from existing funds changes the average number of shares without any concomitant change in the level of resources. The number of common shares in issue prior to the capital increase is adjusted in accordance with the proportional change in the number of outstanding common shares after the share issue as if the event (the de facto 1:1 stock split) had occurred at the beginning of the period under review. For the purposes of historical comparison, the historical figure for the average number of shares in each fiscal year ending prior to the conversion date will be doubled to adjust for the stock split when calculating the earnings per share.

3.12. Share capital (extract)

As of the balance sheet date, share capital consisted of 53,390,820 common shares, each with an arithmetical par value of € 2.60 (prior year: 26,695,290).

The increase in the number of shares in 2004 is almost entirely due to the de facto 1:1 stock split that took place in the year under review and only to a very small extent due to the increase in shares resulting from the initial exercise of options from STADA warrants 2000/2015. STADA executed the de facto 1:1 stock split resolved by the Annual Shareholders' Meeting on June 15, 2004 after close of trading on Friday, July 30, 2004, once the capital measure had been entered into the commercial register.

STADA shareholders received one bonus share for every registered bearer share of restricted transferability they already held (ISIN DE0007251803, WKN 725180). The Company's share capital thereby increased to €138,816,132.00. As a total of 26,695,410 bonus shares were issued, the number of STADA shares also doubled, arithmetically reducing its share price by half. This capital measure therefore constitutes a de facto 1:1 stock split. The bonus shares created by this capital increase from the Company's own funds were automatically credited to STADA shareholders' custody accounts with a value date of August 2, 2004. Shareholders holding their own shares were requested to effect the credit of the bonus shares to which they were entitled via a bank by submitting profit participation certificate no. 11 as proof of entitlement. The text of the official notification to shareholders was also published on STADA's website, www.stada.de.

A14.182 Entities are required to disclose details of all material ordinary share transactions or potential ordinary share transactions entered into after the reporting period, other than those described in the preceding paragraph. Such transactions should be disclosed where they would have significantly changed the number of ordinary or potential ordinary shares outstanding at the end of the reporting period if the transactions had occurred before the end of the reporting period. [IAS 33 para 70(d)]. EPS for the period is not adjusted for such post balance sheet transactions, because they do not affect the amount of capital used to produce the profit or loss for the period. Such transactions include:

- Issue of shares for cash.
- Issue of shares where the proceeds are used to repay debt or preference shares outstanding at the balance sheet date.
- Redemption of ordinary shares.
- Conversion of potential ordinary shares outstanding at the balance sheet date into ordinary shares.
- Issue of warrants, options or convertible securities.
- Achievement of conditions that would result in the issue of contingently issuable shares.

[IAS 33 para 71].

A14.183 Most of these transactions would fall to be disclosed anyway as material non-adjusting post balance sheet events under IAS 10, 'Events after the balance sheet date'. An example of disclosure is Table A14.11.

Table A14.11 – Disclosure of post balance sheet changes in capital

Swisscom AG – Annual Report and Accounts – 31 December 2004

41 Post balance sheet events (extract)

Approval by the Board of Directors

Swisscom Board of Directors approved these consolidated financial statements on March 7, 2005.

Dividend

At the General Meeting of Shareholders on April 26, 2005, a dividend of CHF 14 per share, amounting to a total income distribution of CHF 861 million, is to be proposed for 2004. In these financial this dividend payable is not disclosed as a liability. It is accounted for as a dividend contribution against shareholders' equity in 2005. The dividends declared at the 2004 General Meeting of Shareholders in respect of 2003 was CHF 861 million (previous year: CHF 794 million).

Share buy-back

In 2005 the Board of Directors decided to launch a share buy-back scheme in the amount of around CHF 2 billion in order to distribute the entire equity free cash flow.

Convertible bond of the Swiss Confederation on Swisscom shares

About one third of the convertible bonds of the Swiss Confederation related to Swisscom shares, which mature at the end of February 2005, were exercised by the maturity date. According to the Swiss Confederation authorities, of the 2.67 million shares included in the convertible bond, around 915,000 shares were converted. As a result of the conversion the share of the Confederation in Swisscom fell from 62.7% to 61.4%. On April 26, 2005 the Board of Directors applied to the Shareholders' Meeting for a capital reduction. Taking this into account the share of Confederation in Swisscom is now 66.1%.

A14.184 The standard also encourages companies to disclose the terms and conditions of financial instruments and other contracts generating potential ordinary shares if disclosure is not already required by IAS 32 or IFRS 7. Such disclosure may help users to understand the extent to which these instruments are dilutive and, if so, the effect they have on the disclosed diluted EPS data. Disclosure of the terms and conditions are particularly relevant for those anti-dilutive securities that are not included in the computation of diluted EPS. [IAS 33 para 72].

Volatility of published EPS

A14.185 The EPS figure, which is based on the profits available to ordinary equity holders, is an 'all inclusive' figure and may be volatile. This is because profits or losses of a period may be affected by certain unusual (exceptional) items, such as: profits or losses on the sale or termination of an operation; reorganisation costs; and profits and losses on the disposal of fixed assets. As a result, the presence or absence of such items will affect the EPS figure from one period to another. The requirement to disclose EPS figures for continuing and discontinued operations goes some way to explaining the volatility caused by disposing of operations. However, many companies prefer also to report an adjusted EPS that removes profits and losses of an unusual nature that do not relate to the entity's trading activities. An adjusted EPS is also popular with analysts.

[The next paragraph is A14.187.]

Additional earnings per share

A14.187 IAS 33 recognises that there may be instances where a company would wish to disclose additional EPS figures calculated on a level of earnings other than one required by the standard. It, therefore, permits companies to disclose an additional EPS using a reported component of the statement of comprehensive income other than profit or loss for the period, profit or loss for continuing operations and profit or loss for discontinued operations attributable to ordinary equity holders. Such EPS data should, however, be calculated using the weighted average number of ordinary shares determined in accordance with the standard. This means that the weighted average number of ordinary shares used in the calculation of this additional EPS should be the same as the number used in the basic and diluted EPS figures required by the standard. Entities should indicate the basis on which the numerator, that is, the income statement figure, is determined, including whether amounts per share are before or after tax. In addition, if a component of the income statement is used that is not reported as a line item in the statement of comprehensive income (or income statement if presented), a reconciliation should be provided between the component used and a line item that is reported in the statement of comprehensive income. Additional basic and diluted per share amounts should be disclosed with equal prominence and should be presented in the notes to the financial statements. The requirement that such figures should be presented in the notes means that they should not be shown on the face of the income statement as has often been the practice in the past, before the 2003 revision to IAS 33. [IAS 33 paras 73, 73A].

A14.188 In November 2005 the Committee of European Securities Regulators (CESR) issued a recommendation on disclosure of alternative performance measures (APMs), which were defined as including 'operating earnings', 'cash earnings', 'earnings before one-time charges', 'EBITDA – earnings before interest, taxes, depreciation, and amortisation' and similar terms denoting adjustments to line items of income statement, balance sheet or cash flow statement. Thus, for example, they would include additional EPS figures. The recommendation included the following points:

- Under the IAS Framework, there are four qualitative characteristics that make the information provided in financial statements useful to users: understandability, relevance, reliability and comparability. CESR believes that issuers should always follow these principles for preparation and presentation of financial information including the preparation of alternative performance measures.
- Issuers should define the terminology used and the basis of calculation adopted (that is, defining the components included in an alternative performance measure). Clear disclosure is key to the understandability of any alternative performance measure and its relevance. Where relevant, investors should be made aware of the fact that alternative performance measures are not prepared in accordance with the accounting standards applied to audited financial statements. Alternative performance measures should be given meaningful names reflecting their basis of preparation in order to avoid misleading messages.
- Where possible, issuers should present alternative performance measures only in combination with defined measures (for example GAAP measures). Furthermore, issuers should explain the differences between both measures. This might be through a reconciliation of figures to provide investors with enough information to fully understand the company's results and financial position.
- Comparatives should be provided for any alternative performance measure presented.
- Alternative performance measures should be presented consistently over time.
- To ensure that investors are not misled, alternative performance measures should not be presented with greater prominence than defined GAAP measures. Where alternative performance measures are derived from audited financial statements and resemble defined performance measures, but do not actually have the characteristics of the defined measures (such characteristics include being audited, based on an identified reporting framework, consistent and comparable with performance measures of other

enterprises), CESR recommends that defined measures should be given greater prominence than the alternative performance measures.

- Issuers may internally use alternative performance measures for measuring and controlling the company's profitability and financial position. Generally, issuers explain this as the reason for presenting alternative performance measures to investors. CESR expects issuers to give an explanation of the internal use of alternative performance measures in order to make investors understand the relevance of this information. This explanation is useful only when presented in direct relation to the alternative performance measures.

[CESR Recommendation on Alternative Performance Measures].

A14.189 In practice, most of these recommendations would normally be observed under IFRS in any case. For example, a requirement for consistency of presentation is contained in IAS 1 'Presentation of financial statements', and it would normally be logical to explain the reason for presenting additional EPS numbers. The recommendation for a reconciliation is to a large extent covered by the IAS 33 requirement that if components of profit are used that are not reported in the income statement there should be a reconciliation to a line item in the income statement.

A14.190 Where a company has disclosed an EPS that is additional to the ones required by IAS 33, the requirements stated in paragraph A14.187 above should be followed. An example where a company has followed the standard's requirements where an additional EPS is presented (as explained in para A14.187) is shown in Table A14.12 below. In this example there are no discontinued operations and basic and diluted continuing and total EPS figures are the same.

Table A14.12 – Disclosure of additional EPS figures

Sappi Limited – Annual Report and Accounts – 26 September 2010

7. Basic Earnings (loss) per share and headline earnings (loss) per share

Basic earnings (loss) per share (EPS)

EPS is based on the group's profit (loss) for the year divided by the weighted average number of shares in issue during the year under review.

			2010			2009[1]			2008
	Profit US$ million	**Shares millions**	**Earnings per share US cents**	Loss US$ million	Shares millions	Loss per share US cents	Profit US$ million	Shares millions	Earnings per share US cents
Basic EPS calculation	**66**	**516.7**	**13**	(177)	482.6	(37)	102	362.2	28
Share options and performance shares under Sappi Limited Share Trust	**–**	**3.9**	**–**	–	–	–	–	3.6	–
Share options granted under the Broad-based Black Economic Empowerment transaction	**–**	**0.2**	**–**	–	–	–	–	–	–
Diluted EPS calculation	**66**	**520.8**	**13**	(177)	482.6	(37)	102	365.8	28

(1) *In the 2009 financial year, Sappi conducted a renounceable rights offer of 286,886,270 new ordinary shares of ZAR1.00 each to qualifying Sappi shareholders. In accordance with IAS 33, the fiscal 2008 basic, headline and diluted earnings per share have been restated to take into account the bonus element of the rights offer. As such, the 2008 weighted average number of shares has been adjusted by a factor of 1.58 (the adjustment factor). The adjustment factor was calculated using the pre-announcement share price divided by the theoretical ex-rights price (TERP). TERP is the [(Number of new shares multiplied by the Subscription price) plus the (Number of shares held multiplied by the Ex-dividend share price)] all divided by the (Number of new shares plus the number of shares held prior to the rights offer).*

The diluted EPS calculations are based on Sappi Limited's daily average share price of ZAR31.86 (2009: ZAR30.12; 2008: ZAR94.08) and exclude the effect of certain share options granted under the Sappi Share Incentive Scheme as well as share options granted under the Broad-based Black Economic Empowerment transaction as they would be anti-dilutive.

There are 10.6 million (September 2009: 15.6 million; September 2008: 2.3 million) share options that could potentially dilute EPS in the future that are not included in the diluted weighted average number of shares calculation as they are anti-dilutive.

Headline earnings per share[1]

Headline earnings per share is based on the group's headline earnings divided by the weighted average number of shares in issue during the year. This is a JSE Limited listings required measure.

Reconciliation between attributable earnings (loss) to ordinary shareholders and headline earnings (loss):

	2010 Gross	2010 Tax	2010 Net	2009 Gross	2009 Tax	2009 Net	2008 Gross	2008 Tax	2008 Net
Attributable earnings (loss) to ordinary shareholders	**86**	**20**	**66**	(218)	(41)	(177)	188	86	102
Profit on sale and write-off of property, plant and equipment	**(4)**	–	**(4)**	(1)	–	(1)	(5)	–	(5)
(Impairment reversals) impairment of plant and equipment	**(10)**	–	**(10)**	79	–	79	119	–	119
Headline earnings (loss)	**72**	**20**	**52**	(140)	(41)	(99)	302	86	216
Basic weighted average number of ordinary shares in issue (millions)			**516.7**			482.6			362.2
Headline earnings (loss) per share (US cents)			**10**			(21)			60
Diluted weighted average number of shares (millions)			**520.8**			482.6			365.8
Diluted headline earnings (loss) per share (US cents)			**10**			(21)			59

(1) Headline earnings – as defined in circular 3/2009 issued by the South African Institute of Chartered Accountants, separates from earnings all separately identifiable remeasurements. It is not necessarily a measure of sustainable earnings.

A14.190.1 Under the IAS 32 amendments, certain puttable financial instruments that would otherwise be presented as liabilities are presented as equity (see Manual of Accounting – Financial instruments chapter 7 for further details). The IAS 32 amendment does not extend to IAS 33, so these puttable financial instruments do not meet the definition of ordinary shares for EPS purposes. Entities can, however, elect to provide EPS figures for these instruments, similar to the disclosures for other participating instruments as explained in A14.57 onwards.

A14.191 Directors should carefully consider what profit measure to choose when calculating additional EPS figures and what information they would wish those figures to convey. This is because whatever profit measure is chosen it must be used consistently (see para A14.189 above). It is not possible to choose a profit measure to present a particular aspect of a company's performance in one year, because performance at that level is good, and then to ignore that measure in the following year when performance at that level is not so good.

[The next paragraph is A14.200.]

Financial statistics in the historical summary

A14.200 Entities often publish a historical summary, usually covering at least five years. IAS 33 does not deal specifically with adjustments to historical summaries, but the following guidance is relevant in such situations. In order to present a fair comparison of EPS figures published in such a summary, the basic EPS figure will need to be adjusted for subsequent changes in capital as set out below:

- Where a capitalisation issue or share split has taken place during a financial year, all previously published EPS figures should be adjusted by the bonus factor as explained in paragraph A14.80 above.

- Where a rights issue at less than full market has taken place during a financial year, all previously published EPS figures should be adjusted by the reciprocal of the bonus element inherent in the rights issue as explained from paragraph A14.85 above.

Where there is more than one capitalisation or rights issue during the year, both these factors will operate cumulatively. The cumulative effect of all the above events should be taken into account. The resultant figures should be described as restated EPS and should be set out separately from the other financial data that is not so adjusted.

A14.201 Where there has been a bonus or rights issue in the period covered by the summary, the ordinary dividend actually paid in those periods should be set out in the form of pence per share and similarly adjusted by the same factors used in restating EPS. This adjustment is necessary to ensure that the ordinary dividends and EPS data are comparable. The adjusted dividend per share should be described as restated. In practice, the adjusted EPS and the adjusted dividend per share are normally presented next to each other.

A14.202 Sometimes companies also disclose a dividend cover, which is the number of times a dividend is covered by current earnings. Some companies even disclose price/earnings ratios, high and low share prices or market capitalisation.

A14.203 An example of disclosure in a historical summary is Table A14.13. This example includes adjustment of earlier years for a bonus issue (see para A14.200 above).

A14.204 IFRS 1 requires at least one year of comparative information prepared under IFRS in an entity's first IFRS financial statements. [IFRS 1 para 36]. The IFRS does not require earlier years in a historical summary (that is, the years before the current and previous year) to comply with IFRS. However, those earlier years, if not presented in compliance with IFRS, must be clearly labelled as not being prepared under IFRS. In addition the nature of the main adjustments that would make those earlier years comply with IFRS should be disclosed. An entity need not quantify those adjustments. [IFRS 1 para 37]. IFRS 1's requirements are considered in detail in chapter 3.

A14.205 In Table A14.13, Huhtamaki Oyj, presents the latest two years of the historical summary in accordance with IFRS and earlier years in accordance with Finnish GAAP, but gives the 2002 figures for the year of transition to IFRS under both Finnish GAAP and IFRS. Elsewhere in the financial statements it includes a detailed description of the differences between accounting policies applied under Finnish GAAP and IFRS (not reproduced in Table A14.13).

Table A14.13 – EPS in historical summaries

Huhtamaki Oyj – Annual Report and Accounts – 31 December 2003

Per share data

Comparison figures (1999-2001) adjusted for the 3:1 bonus issue in August 2002

			FAS			**IFRS**	
		1999	**2000**	**2001**	**2002**	**2002**	**2003**
Earnings per share	EUR	0.60	0.65	0.74	0.88	0.86	0.38
Earnings per share (diluted)	0.86	0.38					
Dividend, nominal	EUR	0.26	0.28	0.31	0.38	0.38	0.38[1]
Dividend/earnings per share	%	43.3	43.1	41.9	43.2	44.2	100.0[1]
Dividend yield	%	3.1	3.9	3.5	4.0	4.0	4.1[1]
Shareholders' equity per share	EUR	7.61	8.20	8.64	8.79	8.26	7.85
Share price at December 31	EUR	8.40	7.10	8.88	9.55	9.55	9.35
Average number of shares adjusted for share issue		111,856,128	125,903,852	117,117,696	100,769,970	100,769,970	96,292,220
Number of shares adjusted for share issue at year end		125,903,852	125,903,852	101,215,792	97,547,792	97,547,792	96,161,703
P/E ratio		14.0	10.9	12.0	10.9	11.1	24.6
Market capitalization at December 31 EUR million		1,057.6	893.9	898.3	931.6	931.6	899.1

[1] 2003: Board's proposal.

Chapter 15

Intangible fixed assets

Page

Chapter 15

Intangible fixed assets

Intangible fixed assets

Introduction

15.1 Accounting for intangible fixed assets, and in particular brands, has been one of the major issues facing the accounting profession for many years. The issue is closely related to the problems of accounting for goodwill. This is because, for many people, brands and certain other intangibles, irrespective of whether purchased or generated internally, are merely a part of goodwill. For others, however, brands are distinct from goodwill and their value can be independently measured.

15.2 The problem of accounting for intangibles was settled with the publication of FRS 10, 'Goodwill and intangible assets'. The ASB found it convenient to deal with both goodwill and intangibles in a single standard, because they are so closely related. The ASB also decided the same accounting rules should apply to both in order to avoid the sort of accounting arbitrage that would otherwise arise from labelling similar items differently on the balance sheet.

The Act's requirements

15.3 Recognition of intangible assets in company balance sheets is specifically permitted by Schedule 1 to the SI 2008/410, 'The Large and Medium-sized Companies and Groups (Accounts and Reports) Regulations 2008'. The model formats for the balance sheet include a heading for 'Intangible assets'. Under that heading there are separate sub-headings for:

- Concessions, patents, licences, trademarks, and similar rights and assets.
- Development costs.
- Goodwill.
- Payments on account.

15.4 The balance sheet may include amounts for concessions, patents, licences, trademarks and other similar rights and assets only where either of the following conditions is satisfied:

- They were acquired for valuable consideration in circumstances that do not qualify them to be shown as goodwill.

- They were created by the company itself. (FRS 10, however, restricts the circumstances where costs of self-developed intangibles may be capitalised.)

[Note 2 to the balance sheet formats].

15.5 The SI 2008/410 also permits intangible assets, other than goodwill, to be included in financial statements at their current cost (but FRS 10 is much more restrictive). Goodwill on the other hand may not be revalued. [SI 2008/410 1 Sch 32(1)].

15.6 Where capitalised intangible assets (including brands) are acquired or internally generated, they must be amortised over their estimated useful economic lives. [SI 2008/410 1 Sch 18]. If the lives are finite, the assets should be depreciated to their residual values. There is, however, an important distinction between the rule that applies to the depreciation of assets generally, and as a consequence to intangible assets, and the specific rule that applies to the amortisation of goodwill. For assets generally, it is acceptable to estimate the asset's residual value and to amortise the asset's cost or valuation down to its residual value over its useful life. However, the equivalent rule for goodwill requires that it is reduced by provisions for depreciation calculated to write it off completely on a systematic basis over a period chosen by the company's directors, which cannot exceed its useful economic life. [SI 2008/410 1 Sch 22]. This legal distinction has had important consequences for the development of the amortisation and impairment rules in FRS 10. In effect it is easier to justify carrying certain intangible assets permanently on the balance sheet without amortisation than it is for goodwill.

15.7 The disclosure requirements for intangible fixed assets are governed by paragraph 51 of Schedule 1 to the SI 2008/410. These requirements are identical to those for tangible fixed assets. The Act requires the information to be given in respect of each of the sub-headings that are preceded in the formats by Arabic numerals. FRS 10 requires detail of the movements to be disclosed for each class of intangible assets.

15.8 Where a company has applied one of the alternative accounting rules (see further chapter 16) to any intangible fixed asset, the notes must disclose the years in which the assets were separately valued (so far as the directors know these) and also the separate values. If any assets are valued during the financial year in question, the notes must also disclose the valuers' names or particulars of their qualifications and the basis of valuation used by them. [SI 2008/410 1 Sch 52]. FRS 10, however, limits the circumstances where intangible assets may be revalued.

Scope of FRS 10

15.9 In addition to goodwill, FRS 10 applies to all intangible assets except for oil and gas exploration and development costs, research and development costs (covered by SSAP 13) and any other intangible assets that are specifically addressed by another accounting standard.

15.10 The definition of intangible assets (see below) also scopes out items that are financial assets and items included as current assets (including prepaid expenditure).

15.11 FRS 10 deals with the following issues in respect of intangible assets:

- Recognition rules.
  - Intangible assets developed internally.
  - Intangible assets purchased separately.
  - Intangible assets acquired as part of the acquisition of a business.
- Valuation rules.
- Amortisation and impairment rules.
- Financial statement disclosures.

Definition of intangible assets

15.12 FRS 10 defines intangible assets as: *"non-financial fixed assets that do not have physical substance but are identifiable and are controlled by the entity through custody or legal rights"*. [FRS 10 para 2].

15.13 Application of the definition is important, first, to distinguish intangible from tangible assets and, secondly, to distinguish intangible assets from goodwill. These distinctions are important, because different accounting rules apply to each category. In particular, the rules for capitalising and revaluing intangible assets are much more conservative than those for tangible assets.

15.14 In some respects, it is arguable that the distinction between tangible and intangible assets, based on physical or non-physical substance, no longer has much relevance in the modern business world. For example, assets associated with electronic systems do not fit neatly into either category. FRS 10 recognises that software development costs present a problem within this framework and provides a convenient response. It explains that such costs should be treated as part of the cost of the related hardware (and, hence, as a tangible, rather than intangible, asset) where they are *"directly attributable to bringing a computer system or other computer-operated machinery into working condition for its intended use within the business"*. [FRS 10 para 2]. Costs that might fall to be treated as tangible assets in this way include the costs of developing electronic dealing systems and web sites.

15.15 There are other examples in practice where the benefit of intangible rights, such as the right to operate a licensed trading activity from specific premises (such as casinos), is treated as an integral part of the physical property rather than as a separate intangible asset (see, for example, Stakis plc in Table 15.1).

Table 15.1 – Stakis plc – Annual Report and Accounts – 28 September 1997

Accounting policies (extract)

Fixed Assets and Valuations
A professional valuation of approximately one-third of the Group's freehold and leasehold properties, excluding health clubs, is carried out annually on a rolling basis and the valuations incorporated in the accounts. In the year of acquisition, properties acquired are included at cost or fair value. Valuation or cost includes the benefit of licences where applicable. All other fixed assets are stated at cost.

Depreciation (extract)
(iii) The element of the carrying value of casino properties attributable to the casino licence is written down only if the trend in maintainable casino profits indicates that such value has reduced.

Separability from goodwill

15.16 Separability is a key component of the definition of an identifiable asset. The Act includes the requirement for separability in the definition of identifiable assets and liabilities that relates to acquisition accounting. [SI 2008/410 6 Sch 9(2)]. FRS 10 basically repeats the legal position without adding much to clarify the longstanding issue of whether certain intangibles that have characteristics that make them similar to goodwill are separable or not. FRS 10 states:

> *"An identifiable asset is defined by companies legislation as one that can be disposed of separately without disposing of a business of the entity. If an asset can be disposed of only as part of the revenue-earning activity to which it contributes, it is regarded as indistinguishable from the goodwill relating to that activity and is accounted for as such."* [FRS 10 para 2].

15.17 Some intangibles are more clearly separable than others, but defining the cut remains subjective. The ASB considered that, because intangibles such as brand names are, in any case, very similar to goodwill whether they are separable or not, the most important consideration was that the accounting treatment should be the same. Separability is less of an issue under FRS 10 than it was before, because in general neither intangible assets nor goodwill may be capitalised if they have been developed internally, whereas both purchased intangible assets and purchased goodwill must be capitalised. But there are still differences between the rules for purchased intangible assets and purchased goodwill – for example, non-amortisation of goodwill requires a 'true and fair override' of the Act's specific requirement that goodwill should be amortised to zero over a period that does not exceed its useful economic life, whereas non-amortisation of separable intangible assets does not require a true and fair override.

15.18 Some would consider that many brands and publishing titles do not meet the separability criteria, because they cannot be disposed of without at least reducing the revenue-earning activity that they are part of. However, FRS 10 refers to brands and publishing titles as examples of intangible assets that are unique, and so there is an expectation that they are regarded as identifiable assets at least in some circumstances.

15.19 Many brand names are identified with single products that form only part of a company's business. For example, a particular detergent may have a well known brand name, but the name could be sold and the company would still carry on making the product, even though that product might generate lower profits, because it was no longer 'branded'. Diageo plc provides an example where brands have been recognised separately from goodwill in acquisition accounting. It refers to the fact that the recognised brands could be sold separately from the rest of the business acquired (see Table 15.2).

Table 15.2 – Diageo plc — Annual Report and Accounts – 30 June 2001

Accounting policies (extract)

Brands, goodwill and other intangible assets
When the cost of an acquisition exceeds the fair values attributable to the group's share of the net assets acquired, the difference is treated as purchased goodwill. Goodwill arising from 1 July 1998 is capitalised; prior to that date it was eliminated against reserves, and this goodwill has not been restated.

Acquired brands and other intangible assets which are controlled through custody or legal rights and could be sold separately from the rest of the business are capitalised, where fair value can be reliably measured.

Where capitalised goodwill and intangible assets are regarded as having limited useful economic lives, their cost is amortised on a straight-line basis over those lives – up to 20 years. Where goodwill and intangible assets are regarded as having indefinite useful economic lives, they are not amortised*. Impairment reviews are carried out to ensure that goodwill and intangible assets are not carried at above their recoverable amounts. Any amortisation or impairment write downs are charged to the profit and loss account.

* Note – non-amortisation of goodwill requires a 'true and fair override' of the Companies Act 1985 and disclosure should be made of the override.

15.20 Other brand names cover a range of products or services. Where a product brand name is the same as that of the company itself, it is much less likely that the name could be sold without disposing of a business. It is sometimes argued that names can be exploited by granting licences or franchises to third parties and, hence, that they are identifiable assets not goodwill. For example, a name associated with a particular type of footwear may be exploited by granting a licence for a third party manufacturer of sports clothes to use the name. Another example is where a fast food chain grants franchises to third parties to use the name for their restaurants. In these situations, however, it is difficult to see how the separability criteria are met, because licensing the use of the name does not necessarily imply that it can be disposed of separately from the business; indeed, licensing and franchising may not involve disposals at all.

15.21 The separability test is relevant in the context of distinguishing intangible assets from goodwill when accounting for a business combination. An issue considered by the UITF was whether the definition precluded recognition of certain intangible assets that had been purchased separately from a business (such as mobile telephone licences) but could not be disposed of separately because, for example, they are non-transferable. The UITF clarified in Information Sheet 34 that licences and similar assets that are purchased separately meet FRS 10's definition of intangible assets – it is presumed that if an intangible asset is purchased separately, then in theory it can also be disposed of separately. The implication is that any intangible asset that is purchased separately from a business (that is, without goodwill) is to be regarded as identifiable for the purpose of the definition.

15.22 Interestingly, separability is not a necessary condition for identifying an intangible asset under the equivalent international standard, IAS 38, 'Intangible assets' (revised 2004) , if the intangible asset arises from contractual or other legal rights. Under the international standard, an intangible asset is identifiable when it is separable *or* when it arises from contractual of other legal rights, regardless of whether those rights are transferable or separable from the entity or from other rights and obligations. [IAS 38 para 12].

Control

15.23 Another key component of the definition of intangible assets is control. More generally, FRS 5 defines control in the context of an asset as: *'the ability to obtain the future economic benefits relating to an asset and to restrict the access of others to those benefits'*. [FRS 5 para 3]. In the context of intangible assets, FRS 10 says control must be exercised through custody or legal rights.

15.24 In respect of items such as trademarks, patents, copyrights, licences and franchises, control is secured by legal rights that restrict the access of others. The standard also recognises that control could be evidenced without legal rights, but this would be more difficult – for example, the benefits of know-how could be controlled by secrecy.

15.25 According to FRS 10, a company's workforce and clients cannot be recognised as intangible assets. Although they may be extremely valuable to a business, the business does not control them and, hence, their value is part of its goodwill.

[The next paragraph is 15.27.]

Readily ascertainable market value

15.27 FRS 10 identifies a special type of intangible assets — ones that have a readily ascertainable market value — where the accounting rules differ from the rules that apply to all other intangible assets.

15.28 FRS 10 defines readily ascertainable market value as a value that derives from:

- an asset belonging to a homogeneous population of assets that are equivalent in all material respects; and
- an active market in those assets, evidenced by frequent transactions.

[FRS 10 para 2].

[The next paragraph is 15.30.]

15.30 The differences between the accounting rules are summarised in the table below. In effect, intangible assets with readily ascertainable market values are accounted for in the same way as tangible fixed assets, whereas more restrictions are placed on the recognition and valuation of unique intangible assets. The ASB's rationale for the distinction is twofold: first, it considers that many unique intangible assets are similar to goodwill and should be treated similarly; secondly, it considers that the valuation of unique intangible assets is too subjective to allow them to be recognised (other than where they have actually been purchased) or revalued.

	Intangibles with readily ascertainable market value	**Unique intangibles**
Initial recognition (cost or fair value)		
Internally generated	Yes	No
Purchased separately	Yes	Yes
Business acquisition	Yes	Yes; but only if it can be measured reliably and does not create or increase negative goodwill
Subsequent revaluation	Yes, to market value	No
Impairment loss allocation	Not written down below net realisable value	Written down fully before any tangible assets
Impairment loss reversal	Yes, if net realisable value increases above impaired carrying value	Yes, but only if an external event is reversed in a way that was not originally foreseen

Internally developed intangible assets

15.31 An internally developed intangible asset may be capitalised only if it has a readily ascertainable market value. [FRS 10 para 14]. In all other cases, the costs of developing intangible assets must (as for internally developed goodwill) be written off as incurred.

15.32 As noted above, in practice hardly any intangible assets have a readily ascertainable market value. Those that do are in any case unlikely to have been developed internally.

15.33 Capitalisation of internal costs of obtaining copyrights, patents, licences and similar rights is not, therefore, permitted even though they may satisfy the conditions of identifiability embodied in the definition of intangible assets. Here the ASB has taken a very restrictive approach and thus avoided addressing issues that would be associated with a more permissive approach, such as defining which costs should and should not be capitalised.

[The next paragraph is 15.37.]

Purchased intangible assets

15.37 An intangible asset purchased separately from a business should be capitalised at its cost. [FRS 10 para 9].

15.38 One issue that is not altogether clear in the standard is whether external costs of patent applications and external costs of securing other legal rights in respect of products that a company has developed itself should be capitalised or expensed as incurred.

15.39 One view is that these are internally developed, not purchased, intangibles. The costs are incurred to secure legal protection for and, hence, control of intangible assets that the company has developed itself. Under this view, neither internal costs (for example, the salaries of in-house legal people involved in registering legal rights), nor external costs attributable to generating the intangible asset, would be capitalised.

15.40 However, FRS 10 can be interpreted as making a different cut, that is, between internal and external costs. The emphasis is on preventing internally created value from being recognised. Thus internally generated value and internal costs cannot be capitalised. But external costs of securing legal rights may be objectively determined and fall within the category of purchased intangible assets.

Acquisition accounting

15.41 An intangible asset acquired as part of the acquisition of a business should be capitalised separately from goodwill if its value can be measured reliably on initial recognition. [FRS 10 para 10].

15.42 The normal principles for fair valuing the identifiable assets in acquisition accounting (in FRS 7) apply to intangible as well as tangible assets. FRS 7 merely states that where an intangible asset is recognised, its fair value should be based on its replacement cost, which is normally its estimated market value. [FRS 7 para 10]. FRS 10 introduces a third criterion – reliable measurement – over and above the separability and control issues considered earlier.

15.43 The standard makes another accounting distinction between those rare types of intangible assets that have a readily ascertainable market value and those that are unique. Whereas the former should be included at their market value at the date of acquisition, the fair value of the latter should be limited to an amount that does not create or increase any negative goodwill arising on the acquisition (see chapter 25 for further discussion of the interaction between fair valued assets and negative goodwill).

15.44 During the development of FRS 10, the ASB was sceptical about the reliability of valuations of unique intangible assets, such as brands and publishing titles, where there is no market value as such. FRS 10, however, accepts that certain entities that regularly buy and sell them have developed reliable valuation techniques that would allow them to be capitalised separately from purchased goodwill as a result of an acquisition. The price paid for the acquisition of a business as a whole in effect forms a ceiling on the value that may be ascribed to such intangible assets and goodwill in aggregate.

15.45 The wording in FRS 10 on the reliability of measurement issue implies a degree of flexibility as regards the separate recognition of intangibles in acquisition accounting. Those entities that are not in a position that they have developed valuation techniques from their regular involvement in the purchase and sale of unique intangibles may legitimately subsume the value of intangibles within goodwill. [FRS 10 para 13]. The onus is on those entities that wish to capitalise intangibles separately from goodwill to demonstrate that they can measure them reliably.

[The next paragraph is 15.48.]

Valuation methods

15.48 FRS 10 refers briefly to valuation techniques that may be used to estimate fair values of intangible assets at the date of acquisition. It mentions techniques based on''indicators of value', such as multiples of turnover or present value of royalties that would be payable to license the asset from a third party. [FRS 10 para 12].

15.49 There are a number of methods commonly used by specialist valuers to value intangibles. These are not mutually exclusive – more than one method would normally be used in a valuation exercise and each would be used to cross-check the reasonableness of the valuation. Methods include:

- Relief from royalties.
- Premium profits.
- Capitalisation of earnings.
- Comparison with market transactions.

15.50 FRS 10 requires the method used to value intangible assets to be disclosed in the financial statements. [FRS 10 para 52]. The methods noted above are described briefly below.

Relief from royalties

15.51 Under the royalty method, an attempt is made to determine the value that could be obtained by licensing out the right to exploit the intangible asset to a third party or, alternatively, to determine the royalties that the owner of the intangible asset is relieved from paying by virtue of being the owner rather than the licensee.

15.52 A notional royalty rate is estimated as a percentage of revenue. This is applied to an estimate of the revenue to be generated by the intangible asset. This estimated royalty stream is capitalised, for example, by discounting at a risk-adjusted market rate, to arrive at an estimated market value.

15.53 The methodology is relatively simple, especially if the intangible asset is already subject to licensing agreements. Where this is not the case, the valuer may research licensing arrangements for comparable intangible assets or, where such information is not available, estimate a theoretical royalty rate that would give an acceptable return both to the owner and the licensee.

Premium profits

15.54 The premium profits approach attempts to determine a value that is based on capitalising the additional profits generated by the intangible asset (for example, a brand) over and above the profits achieved by similar businesses that do not benefit from the intangible asset (for example, similar unbranded products).

15.55 This approach is often used for brands. There are various methods of estimating the premium profits contributed by brands. These include calculating a margin differential, identifying the premium price compared with the price of generic equivalents and comparing the rate of return on capital employed of the business that owns the intangible asset with the normal rate of return of a comparable business that does not benefit from the asset.

15.56 The estimated premium profits attributable to the intangible asset are capitalised, for example, by discounting at a risk-adjusted market rate, to arrive at an estimated market value.

15.57 It is important that the premium profits identified are specifically attributable to the brand or other intangible asset and not some other factor, such as an efficient production facility or distribution network, that relates to the business as a whole.

15.58 In determining the value of a brand under this or similar methods, various specific factors may need to be taken into account, which include the following:

- The market sector.

  Brands that are established in a business sector that generates high sales, margins, or both, will clearly have a higher value than those in markets that are restricted in terms of total sales volume or profit margins. Expanding markets for a product will enhance the prospects for exploiting the brand name and will, therefore, increase its value.

- Durability.

  If a brand name has lasted for many years, it is likely to have considerable customer loyalty and will, therefore, support a higher valuation than a name that may be fashionable, but that is in a business sector where fashions change rapidly and brand names are less durable.

- Overseas markets.

  A brand name that is also known in overseas markets and which, therefore, has a larger potential customer base will usually be worth more than a brand that can be sold only in the domestic market.

- Market position.

  A brand that is a market leader will be worth more than one that is not recognised as a leader.

- Advertising support.

  This could be either a negative or a positive factor in valuing a brand. If a brand requires substantial advertising to maintain its place in the market, this could be a sign that the value of the brand is declining. If, however, advertising spend increases sales and/or margins significantly, so that the brand is better known, the value of the brand itself could be enhanced.

- Changes or prospective changes in legislation, or technological advances.

  Many brands are vulnerable to changes in legislation or environmental factors. However, if a brand name has survived such changes, the fact that it is able to adapt to new conditions may enhance its value.

- Competition.

  The introduction of alternatives to the branded product or indications that competitors are likely to increase spending on rival products could also affect the value of brands.

Capitalisation of earnings

15.59 The capitalised earnings method involves estimating the maintainable earnings that accrue to the intangible asset. A capitalisation factor, or earnings multiple, is then applied to the earnings. The multiple should take account of the expected risks and rewards, which include the prospects for future earnings growth and the risks involved.

15.60 This method is often used to value publishing titles and mastheads.

Comparison with market transactions

15.61 This approach considers actual market transactions in similar intangible assets. A multiple of turnover or earnings associated with an intangible asset would be derived from a market transaction and be applied to the asset being valued.

15.62 However, many intangible assets are unique and comparable market transactions may be infrequent. As a result, the scope for making direct comparisons with values actually achieved in the marketplace is limited. Nevertheless, acquisitions and disposals of businesses that include similar intangible assets can sometimes provide useful indicators of value that complement the other valuation methods.

Revaluation of intangible assets

15.63 With the following exception, no intangible assets may be revalued after their initial recognition at cost or fair value on acquisition. The exceptions are those rare intangible assets that have a readily ascertainable market value (see para 15.29 above). Such assets may be revalued to their market value, provided that all such intangible assets of the same class are revalued and that further revaluations are performed on a regular basis to ensure that the carrying value does not differ from the market value at the balance sheet date. [FRS 10 para 43].

15.64 It follows that for most recognised intangible assets, no value created after their acquisition may be recognised on the balance sheet. For example, if an ailing brand is purchased cheaply and relaunched by the new management, the carrying value must continue to be based on the historical cost or fair value. Furthermore, the brand development costs must be written off as incurred. This is consistent with the treatment of purchased goodwill.

[The next paragraph is 15.66.]

Amortisation and impairment

15.66 FRS 10's objective, in relation to capitalised intangible assets, is to ensure that they are charged in the profit and loss account in the periods in which they are depleted. [FRS 10 para 1]. The same amortisation and impairment rules apply whether intangible assets have been purchased separately or have been recognised as a result of fair valuing an acquisition.

15.67 Intangible assets should be amortised quickly, slowly or not at all according to the circumstances:

- Where an intangible asset has a limited useful economic life, it should be amortised systematically over that life.

- There is a rebuttable presumption that the useful economic life does not exceed 20 years.
- A longer life than 20 years, or an indefinite life, may be chosen where the asset can be demonstrated to be more durable.

15.68 Amortisation over more than 20 years or non-amortisation must be supported by annual impairment reviews to ensure that the carrying value of the intangible asset does not exceed its recoverable amount. If the review identifies an impairment, the asset should be written down to its recoverable amount.

15.69 Intangible assets that are amortised over 20 years or less should be reviewed for impairment at the end of the first full financial year following their acquisition. In other years an impairment review is required only if adverse events indicate the amortised carrying value of the asset may not be recoverable and an impairment write-down should be made if the review confirms this.

[The next paragraph is 15.71.]

Useful economic life

15.71 The useful economic life of an intangible asset is defined in FRS 10 as: *'the period over which the entity expects to derive economic benefits from that asset"*. [FRS 10 para 2].

15.72 A useful economic life of more than 20 years, or an indefinite life, may be chosen only if:

- the durability of the intangible asset for the longer (or indefinite) period can be demonstrated; and
- the intangible asset is capable of continued measurement (so that annual impairment reviews will be feasible).

[FRS 10 para 19].

15.73 FRS 10 requires that the useful economic lives should be reviewed at the end of each reporting period and revised if necessary. Where it is considered that previous estimates of useful economic lives need to be revised, the net book values at the date of revision should be amortised prospectively over the revised remaining useful economic lives. [FRS 10 para 33]. UITF Abstract 27, 'Revision to estimates of the useful economic life of goodwill and intangible assets', a change in an asset's useful economic life should be dealt with prospectively by amortising the carrying value over the revised remaining economic life (that is, it should not be dealt with as a prior year adjustment). This applies even if the change results from a decision to no longer rebut the 20 year life presumption.

15.74 One reason for having a presumed arbitrary upper limit on the useful economic life is that it would otherwise frequently be difficult to estimate it. A period of 20 years is a benchmark that has some significance internationally.

However, the uncertainty involved in estimating useful economic life does not allow 20 years to be automatically used by default, nor does it allow intangibles to be written off over an unrealistically short period. [FRS 10 paras 21, 22].

15.75 FRS 10 states that the 20 year upper limit *may* be rebutted if the conditions (that is, evidence of durability and continued measurability) are met. The assumptions used in forecasting become more vulnerable the longer the estimated life is. For example, in many industries the pace of developments means that consumer patterns cannot be predicted with much certainty over very long periods. The emphasis in the FRS is, therefore, on being prudent when choosing asset lives, without being unrealistically prudent.

15.76 The second condition for rebutting the 20 year upper limit, that the intangible asset must be capable of continued measurement, is also important. The annual impairment reviews, which must be carried out in accordance with FRS 11, 'Impairment of fixed assets and goodwill', have to be feasible. FRS 10 states that intangible assets will not be capable of continued measurement if the cost of such measurement is viewed as being unjustifiably high. This clearly invites directors to opt not to rebut the presumption of a 20 year life if they judge that the cost of carrying out annual impairment reviews outweighs the benefits. This may be so where, for example, an acquisition comprises a large number of publishing titles that individually are not material. [FRS 10 para 23].

15.77 FRS 10 gives examples of factors that contribute to the durability of intangible assets and goodwill. These factors refer to the nature of the business, the stability of the industry, the effects of future competition, the typical lifespan of the products involved and (in respect of business acquisitions) the extent to which the acquisition overcomes market entry barriers that will continue to exist.

15.78 These factors often combine to present an overall picture of durability. A long life (20 years plus) will generally require a business, industry and products with a long track record of stability and achievement and having high barriers to market entry. Added to this, of course, is the commitment of the new management to continue to invest for the long term to extend the period over which the intangible asset is expected to continue to provide economic benefits. Long or indefinite lives may be justified for certain long established brands and publishing titles that have demonstrated their ability to survive changes in the economic environment. Lives much shorter than 20 years may be appropriate for other brands and publishing titles that are relatively new and operate in more volatile sectors, where they are more likely to be affected by changes in fashions or technology.

15.79 In addition to the economic factors outlined above, for certain intangible assets useful economic lives are also restricted by the period for which legal rights are held. For some intangible assets, the legal rights either remain in force indefinitely or can be continually renewed (for example, trademarks that secure brand names). For others, the legal rights that protect a product's position in the market expire after a fixed period (that is, they are non-renewable), when competitors can introduce similar products (for example, drug patents). In other situations, a licence may give an entity the right to carry out a business activity for a fixed period and, although the entity can apply for renewal, there is no guarantee that it will be renewed (for example, broadcasting licences).

15.80 FRS 10 states that where legal rights are granted for a finite period, the useful economic life of the related intangible asset cannot extend beyond that period unless *"the legal rights are renewable and renewal is assured"*. [FRS 10 para 24]. In other cases, the useful economic life is restricted by the expiry date of the existing legal right. The FRS also limits the circumstances in which the renewal of a legal right may be regarded as assured to those where:

- The value of the intangible asset does not reduce as the expiry date approaches (or reduces only by the cost of renewal).
- There is evidence, possibly based on past experience, that the legal rights will be renewed.
- There is no evidence that any conditions that have to be complied with in respect of renewal have been or will be breached.

[FRS 10 para 26].

15.81 If the capitalised cost of an intangible asset includes costs that will recur each time the legal right is renewed, the amortisation period for that element of the cost should not extend past the renewal date. [FRS 10 para 24].

Residual values

15.82 Before FRS 10, two arguments were sometimes advanced to demonstrate that, in certain circumstances, no amortisation was required. Some companies stated that the lives of brands and publishing titles were indefinite and, therefore, no amortisation charge was necessary. Others considered that expenditure on advertising and other brand support costs meant that the brand's or publishing title's residual value was always equal to or greater than its cost and this was put forward as an alternative reason for not amortising.

15.83 Under FRS 10, a residual value at the end of the asset's useful economic life may be assumed only if it can be measured reliably. [FRS 10 para 28]. In practice, an intangible asset is only likely to have a significant residual value that can be measured reliably where a company has a legal or contractual right to receive an amount of cash when its right to use the asset expires, or in those rare cases where there is a readily ascertainable market value for the residual asset. [FRS 10 para 29]. This was confirmed by the FRRP Ruling in respect of Equator Group Plc for the year ended 31 December 1999, which held that the group's firm libraries should be amortised without regard to any estimate of residual value. This means that in practice a low or nil amortisation charge must generally be justified in terms of a long or indefinite useful economic life rather than the maintenance of a high residual value, although in many respects they amount to the same thing.

Methods of amortising intangible assets

15.84 FRS 10 states that the method of amortising an intangible asset should reflect the expected pattern of its depletion. However, a straight-line method should be chosen, unless another method can be demonstrated to be more appropriate. [FRS 10 para 30]. An example of an alternative amortisation method is a unit of production method in respect of a licence to produce a fixed quantity of output. [FRS 10 para 31]. The FRS also requires disclosure of the methods used. [FRS 10 para 55]. Although arbitrary, specifying straight-line as a benchmark method is a practical means of dealing with the difficulty of measuring depletion and it does promote comparability. The FRS also explains that it is unlikely that methods that are less conservative than the straight-line method could be justified with sufficient evidence. Furthermore, FRS 10 specifically prohibits amortisation methods that aim to produce a constant rate of return on the carrying value on an intangible asset, such as the 'reverse sum of digits' method and the annuity method. [FRS 10 para 32].

15.85 A company may conceivably wish to change its method of amortising intangible assets, say, to revert to the straight-line method from some other method. Where this occurs, FRS 10 requires the reason and the effect, if material, to be disclosed in the year of change. [FRS 10 para 57]. The effect of a change is the difference between the amortisation charge that results from applying the previous and the revised amortisation methods (that is, how much more or less profit a company records as a result of changing amortisation methods).

Impairment reviews

15.86 The requirements for impairment reviews on intangible assets are integrated with those for capitalised goodwill, which are explained in more detail in chapter 18. The details of impairment reviews for tangible and intangible fixed assets and goodwill are contained in a separate standard FRS 11, 'Impairment of fixed assets and goodwill'. The requirements for impairment reviews differ according to whether an intangible asset is attributed a useful live of more or less than 20 years, as illustrated below.

Useful life 20 years or less	**Useful life more than 20 years**
End of first full year (simplified review)	Every year (detailed review)
Other years – high level check for impairment indicators detailed review only if impairment indicators are present	

15.87 Where intangible assets or goodwill are carried permanently as assets or amortised over very long periods, there is a greater risk of impairment in the future. Where they are written off over shorter periods, there is less risk of impairment, because their net book value in any case diminishes more quickly. A threshold of 20 years has been chosen, below which the impairment reviews are less onerous than for longer periods.

Useful life 20 years or less — first year review

15.88 Intangible assets should be reviewed for impairment at the end of the first full year after their acquisition. Most recognised intangible assets are acquired through business acquisitions and the timing of this review corresponds with the end of the investigation period in FRS 7, when the fair value exercise on the assets and liabilities of the acquired business should be completed.

15.89 The first year review has two stages. The first stage in effect requires management formally to consider whether the acquisition has lived up to expectations. This is done by comparing post-acquisition performance with the forecasts used in the acquisition appraisal and by considering whether there have been any other unexpected adverse events or changes in circumstances that throw doubt on the recoverability of the intangible asset or capitalised goodwill. If the acquisition passes this test, there is no need to go on to the second stage.

15.90 The second stage, which is a full impairment review, is only necessary if the first stage indicates that there may be an impairment problem. [FRS 10 para 40].

Useful life 20 years or less — reviews in other years

15.91 After the first full year, management has to consider whether events or changes in circumstances indicate that the amortised carrying value of intangible assets or goodwill may not be recoverable. If there are no such indicators, no further work is required. FRS 11 and the impairment indicators are discussed in chapter 18.

[The next paragraph is 15.94.]

Detailed impairment review

15.94 A detailed impairment review is required in the following situations:

- Where intangible assets or goodwill are amortised over more than 20 years or carried permanently without amortisation: at each year end automatically (including the end of the year in which the acquisition took place).
- Where intangible assets or goodwill are amortised over 20 years or less:
  - At the end of the first full year following the acquisition, *only* if there is an indicator of impairment or if the first year review indicates that the post-acquisition performance has failed to meet pre-acquisition expectations.
  - In other years, *only* if there is an indicator of impairment.

15.95 The details of the impairment review are contained in FRS 11. An impairment review is a recoverable amount check on individual assets or groups of assets that may comprise tangible and intangible assets and capitalised goodwill. It follows the long-established principle that an asset's balance sheet carrying value should not exceed its recoverable amount, which is measured by reference to the future cash flows that can be generated from its continued use (value in use) or disposal (net realisable value), whichever is higher. To the extent that an asset's carrying value exceeds its recoverable amount, it is impaired and should be written down to the higher of its net realisable value or value in use. The requirements of FRS 11 are considered in chapter 18.

Disclosures

15.96 FRS 10 requires the following disclosures in respect of intangible assets:

- The method of valuation. [FRS 10 para 52].
- For each class of intangible asset:
  - The cost or revalued amount at the beginning and end of the period.
  - The cumulative provisions for amortisation or impairment at the beginning and end of the period.
  - A reconciliation of the movements, showing additions, disposals, revaluations, transfers, amortisation, impairment losses and reversals of past impairment losses.
  - The net carrying amount at the balance sheet date. [FRS 10 para 53].
- The methods and periods of amortisation and the reasons for choosing those periods. [FRS 10 para 55].
- The reason for, and effect of, changing useful economic lives. [FRS 10 para 56].
- The reason for, and the effect of, changing amortisation methods. [FRS 10 para 57].
- Where an intangible asset is amortised over more than 20 years or is not amortised, the reasons for rebutting the 20 year presumption. (This should be a reasoned explanation based on the specific factors contributing to its durability). [FRS 10 para 58].
- The following details where a class of assets has been revalued:
  - The year in which the assets were valued, the values and the bases of valuation.
  - The original cost or fair value of the assets and the amount of any provision for amortisation that would have been recognised if the assets had been valued at their original cost or fair value. [FRS 10 para 61].
- The name and qualifications of the person who valued any intangible asset that has been revalued during the year. [FRS 10 para 62].

15.97 In respect of the last two bullet points above concerning revaluations, it should be noted that FRS 10 only permits revaluation (to their market value) of those intangible assets that have a readily ascertainable market value.

15.98 Two of the above disclosure points refer to a 'class of intangible assets'. The most commonly encountered will be the second bullet point, which requires the analysis and movements on intangible assets to be shown separately for each class. A class of intangible assets is defined in FRS 10 as: *"a category of intangible assets having a similar nature, function or use in the business of the entity"*. The explanatory paragraph to the definition indicates that items such as licences, quotas, patents, copyrights, franchises and trademarks may be treated as separate classes, as may intangible assets that are used within different business segments. Further sub-division may be appropriate where there are different types of licences, etc, which have different functions within the business. [FRS 10 para 2]. For entities that recognise several types of intangible assets, the analysis has, therefore, to be given under several headings.

[The next paragraph is 15.100.]

Intangible assets — other information

15.100 In practice, given the lack of authoritative guidance on intangibles before FRS 10, the range of intangibles in addition to brands and publishing titles capitalised in financial statements has been relatively extensive and includes:

- Copyrights.
- Know-how.
- Licences.
- Patents and trademarks.

Copyrights

15.101 Copyrights are designed to provide the holder with the exclusive right to produce copies of, and control over, an original musical, artistic or literary work. They are granted by law for a specified number of years, which in the UK was, until 1 January 1996, 50 years from the date of the author's or composer's death. A statutory instrument, the Duration of Copyright and Rights in Performances Regulations 1995 (SI 1995/3297), enacting an EC Directive to harmonise the term of protection of copyright and related rights, has altered the period of copyright. For literary (including compilations and computer programs), dramatic, musical and artistic works, copyright expires 70 years from the end of the calendar year in which the author died. Where such a work is computer generated, the period of copyright is 50 years from the end of the calendar year in which the work was made. Copyright in films will generally expire 70 years from the last to die of the director, authors of the screenplay and dialogue and composer of any specially created music. Copyright in sound recordings expires 50 years from the end of the calendar year in which it is made or is released, although there are European proposals to extend this to 70 years.

15.102 There are complex transitional provisions of which the following is a very brief summary. The new provisions apply to new works and existing copyright works. However, the period of copyright existing before 1 January 1996 will continue to apply to an existing work if this period would expire later than the new period. The provisions may also apply to existing works in which copyright expired before 31 December 1995 where the authors died between 1925 and 1945. Consequently, some copyright which had expired may be revived under these provisions. As such, where companies acquire a copyright for exclusive rights to publish an author's or composer's work, it is done in the expectation of receiving future income streams. The copyright is an intangible asset which will result in potential financial benefits to a company over a considerable number of years.

15.103 In practice, a number of different accounting policies have been adopted, varying from those companies that amortise the asset over a few years, to those that do not amortise unless a permanent fall in value occurs.

Know-how

15.104 Know-how is, in effect, a technical aptitude or skill. As such, it may be people-reliant or process-reliant; it may be purchased by acquisition of, say, a specialist service unit; or it may be internally generated. Its nature and characteristics suggest that it is more nebulous than say a copyright and, therefore, more difficult to measure or prone to greater subjectivity in terms of both identification and valuation.

15.105 As an example, a company that acquires a specialist testing unit is likely to acquire few tangible assets and, therefore, the difference between the price it pays and the fair value of the tangible assets acquired could be significant. Many commentators would argue that what the company is buying is: the tangible assets; the know-how in terms of methodologies and personnel; and future trading opportunities. While the third of these equates to goodwill, the second does not. In effect, a prime element of the difference between the purchase price and the fair value of tangible fixed assets would be the bespoke testing procedures acquired and the specialist personnel taken on, or, put another way, know-how.

15.106 Under FRS 10, any value attributed to purchased know-how could not be recognised separately as an intangible asset, unless it is controlled through custody or legal rights. This is unlikely to be the case where, for example, the know-how is essentially related to specific people who have freedom of movement in the labour market, but it could be the case if the know-how relates to a secret process.

Licences

15.107 Licences are agreements that a reporting company enters into with a third party which enable it to carry out certain trading functions. Examples may be brewing concerns, which operate out of licensed premises, or bookmakers, who are required to obtain a gaming licence. Similarly, companies may purchase licences allowing them to use software and technology developed by third parties.

15.108 As with copyrights, licences are generally acquired to obtain access to benefits that may continue for many years. Under FRS 10, the cost of licences should be capitalised if they have been purchased separately from a business. If they have been acquired through the acquisition of a business, they should be capitalised separately from goodwill if their fair value can be measured reliably. They should generally be amortised over the life of the licences.

15.109 Some companies have included the benefit of licences within tangible fixed assets where they operate from licensed premises, that is, as part of the valuation of the properties that carry on the licensed activity.

Patents and trademarks

15.110 A patent is in effect a document granted by the government assuring an inventor of the sole right to make, use and sell his invention for a determined period. Registering a trademark provides legal protection to the name or symbol used to differentiate the products supplied by a manufacturer or authorised distributor from those of competing manufacturers and dealers. Brands are likely to be secured by trademarks. Such protection is clearly of vital importance to entities that invest in product development (such as pharmaceutical companies), to ensure that their competitors do not merely copy their commercially successful inventions. The legal rights may be granted for long periods (17 or 18 years for drug patents) or may be renewable indefinitely (some trademarks).

15.111 Under FRS 10, the cost of patents and trademarks should be capitalised if they have been purchased separately from a business. If they have been acquired through the acquisition of a business, they should be capitalised separately from goodwill if their fair value can be measured reliably. They should generally be amortised over the period covered by the legal rights or the period for which the owner expects to derive economic benefits, if shorter.

Research and development

15.112 The Act permits development costs to be capitalised in certain circumstances. [SI 2008/410 1 Sch 21(1)]. In contrast, however, research costs, whether pure or applied, must be written off to the profit and loss account as they are incurred. [SI 2008/410 1 Sch 3(2)(c)].

SSAP 13

15.113 The Act does not define development. However, SSAP 13, 'Accounting for research and development', defines development as *"use of scientific or technical knowledge in order to produce new or substantially improved materials, devices, products or services, to install new processes or systems prior to the commencement of commercial production or commercial applications, or to improving substantially those already produced or installed"*. [SSAP 13 para 21]. Therefore, development is the work a company performs after it has planned or designed a new or substantially improved product or service until the time that this is ready either to be manufactured or to be put into operation commercially.

15.114 In making this definition of development, the standard distinguishes it from pure and applied research, which are defined as follows:

- Pure or basic research is *"experimental or theoretical work undertaken primarily to acquire new scientific or technical knowledge for its own sake rather than directed towards any specific aim or application"*.
- Applied research is *"original or critical investigation undertaken in order to gain new scientific or technical knowledge and directed towards a specific practical aim or objective"*.

[SSAP 13 para 21(a),(b)].

15.115 The standard also specifically indicates that where companies enter into firm contracts to carry out development work on behalf of third parties, on terms such that the related expenditure will be fully reimbursed, then expenditure that has not been reimbursed at any period end is contract work-in-progress and not development expenditure. A similar situation occurs where companies contract to develop and manufacture at an agreed price calculated to reimburse expenditure on development as well as on manufacture. [SSAP 13 para 17].

15.116 Racal Electronics Plc and Oxford Instruments plc disclose accounting policies that show examples of this, as Tables 15.3 and 15.4 indicate.

Table 15.3 – Racal Electronics Plc – Annual Report and Accounts – 31 March 1995

Statement of Accounting Policies (extract)

7 RESEARCH AND DEVELOPMENT

Private venture research and development expenditure is written off in the year in which it is incurred. Uninvoiced research and development fully funded by customers is carried forward as work in progress.

Table 15.4 – Oxford Instruments plc – Report and Accounts – 31 March 2004

Notes on the Financial Statements (extract)

1 Accounting policies (extract)

Research and development

Research and development expenditure, net of the relevant proportion of grants receivable, is charged to the profit and loss account in the year in which it is incurred, unless it is recoverable under a customer contract when it is carried forward as work in progress at the lower of cost and net realisable value.

15.117 SSAP 13 also provides examples of activities that would normally be *included* in research and development. The examples are:

- Experimental, theoretical or other work aimed at the discovery of new knowledge, or the advancement of existing knowledge.
- Searching for applications of that knowledge.
- Formulation and design of possible applications for such work.
- Testing in search for, or evaluation of, product, service or process alternatives.
- Design, construction and testing of pre-production prototypes and models and development batches.
- Design of products, services, processes or systems involving new technology or substantially improving those already produced or installed.
- Construction and operation of pilot plants.

[SSAP 13 para 6].

15.118 The standard also gives examples of activities typically *excluded* from research and development activities:

- Testing and analysis either of equipment or product for purposes of quality or quantity control.
- Periodic alterations to existing products, services or processes even though these may represent some improvement.
- Operational research not tied to a specific research and development activity.
- Cost of corrective action in connection with breakdowns during commercial production.
- Legal and administrative work in connection with patent applications, records and litigation and the sale or licensing of patents.

- Activity, including design and construction engineering, relating to the construction, relocation, rearrangement or start-up of facilities or equipment other than facilities or equipment whose sole use is for a particular research and development project.
- Market research.

[SSAP 13 para 7].

15.119 The original standard, prior to revision in 1989, specifically permitted market research to be capitalised, if it was incurred in order to determine whether a product under development was commercially viable in terms of market conditions, public opinion and consumer and environmental legislation. Its exclusion from expenditure that can be carried forward under the revised version, represents a tightening of the rules.

Development costs

15.120 The types of development costs that may be capitalised are not defined either in the Act or in the revised standard. However, IAS 38 does give some guidance on the type of costs that may be capitalised. It indicates that development costs may include:

- The costs of materials and services used or consumed in generating the intangible asset.
- The cost of employee benefits (as defined in IAS 19, 'Employee benefits') arising from the generation of the intangible asset.
- Fees to register a legal right.
- The amortisation of patents and licences.
- Interest, in accordance with the criteria of IAS 23 (revised), 'Borrowing costs'.

[IAS 38 para 66].

Capitalisation of development costs

15.121 The Act permits development costs to be capitalised, but only in 'special circumstances'. However, as it does not define the term 'special circumstances', it is necessary to look to SSAP 13 for guidance. We interpret this to imply that, if all the conditions set out in paragraph 25 of SSAP 13 are met, special circumstances exist and so development costs may be capitalised. However, if any one of the conditions is not met, then development costs must be written off as they are incurred.

15.122 Paragraph 25 of SSAP 13 lays down the following conditions, all of which must all be satisfied if development expenditure is to be capitalised:

- There is a clearly defined project.
- The related expenditure is separately identifiable.
- The outcome of the project has been assessed with reasonable certainty as to both its technical feasibility and its ultimate commercial viability, considered in the light of factors such as likely market conditions (including competing products), public opinion, and consumer and environmental legislation.
- The aggregate of the deferred development costs, any further development costs, and related production, selling and administration costs, is reasonably expected to be exceeded by related future sales or other revenues.
- Adequate resources exist, or are reasonably expected to be available, to enable the project to be completed, and to provide any consequential increases in working capital.

15.123 Where these conditions are satisfied, a company can defer development expenditure, but only until commercial production begins. SSAP 13 requires a company to amortise the expenditure it has capitalised from the time that commercial production of the product or service begins. Where a company is developing a product, commercial production begins when the company is manufacturing the product with a view to selling it commercially. [SSAP 13 para 28].

[The next paragraph is 15.125.]

Amortisation

15.125 Amortisation of development expenditure must be allocated to each accounting period on a systematic basis. This can be done by reference to the sales or the use of the product or the service, or by reference to the period over which the product or service is expected to be sold or used. However, the period of amortisation may be difficult to determine. In determining this period, the directors must establish a realistic and prudent number of years over which they expect the development expenditure to produce a benefit. They must decide also whether they expect the benefit to occur evenly over these years.

Disclosure

15.126 SSAP 13 requires the following disclosures to be made in the financial statements where development costs are deferred and are shown as an asset in the balance sheet:

- The accounting policy should be stated, as required by FRS 18, and explained.
- The total amount of research and development expenditure written off to the profit and loss account in the period should be disclosed, analysed

between the current year's expenditure and amounts amortised from deferred expenditure.

- Movements on deferred development expenditure and the amount carried forward at the beginning and the end of the period should be disclosed. Deferred development expenditure should be disclosed under the heading of 'intangible assets' in the balance sheet.

[SSAP 13 paras 30-32].

15.127 In addition, the Act requires that further disclosure should also be made of the period over which the amount of those costs that were originally capitalised is being, or is to be, written off, together with the reasons for capitalising the development costs in question. [SI 2008/410 1 Sch 21(2)].

15.128 Capitalising development cost is an option and, in practice, many companies write off all research and development expenditure as it is incurred, rather than attempt to justify capitalising development expenditure under the SSAP 13 rules. However, in Table 15.5, the 1994 financial statements of Dobson Park Industries plc provide an example of a company that does capitalise development expenditure. The charge to the profit and loss account is analysed between amortisation of the capitalised development costs and the immediate write-off of other non-capitalised research and development expenditure.

Table 15.5 – Dobson Park Industries plc – Annual Report & Accounts – 1 October 1994

Accounting Policies (extract)

Research and Development Expenditure

Expenditure on research and development is charged to the profit and loss account in the year in which it is incurred with the exception of expenditure on the development of certain major new product projects where the outcome of those projects is assessed as being reasonably certain as regards viability and technical feasibility. Such expenditure is capitalised and amortised over a period not longer than five years commencing in the year sales of the product are first made.

Notes on the accounts (extract)

	1994	1993
	£000	£000
5. Profit on Ordinary Activities Before Taxation		
Stated after Charging:		
Depreciation of tangible fixed assets	**3,385**	4,431
Amortisation of intangible fixed assets	**370**	–
Research and development expenditure	**5,172**	5,594
Auditors' remuneration (including expenses)	**205**	252
Other fees paid to the auditors in the UK	**243**	295
Operating lease rentals – plant and machinery	**479**	630
Operating lease rentals – other assets	**1,857**	1,792

11. Intangible Fixed Assets	The Group £000
Development Expenditure:	
Cost	
At 2 October 1993	1,488
Incurred during the year	363
At 1 October 1994	1851
Amortised in year	370
Net Book Value	
At 1 October 1994	1481
At 2 October 1993	1488

Development expenditure is the amount incurred by IRD Mechanalysis in respect of 'IQ 2000', a major new product launched in the latter part of 1993. These costs are being amortised over a period of five years from 3 October 1993.

Exemptions from disclosure

15.129 SSAP 13 has exempted some smaller companies from certain of its disclosure requirements. Thus, a company that satisfies two of the three criteria for defining a medium-sized company under section 465 of the Companies Act 2006, *multiplied by ten* need not disclose the total amounts of research and development charged in the profit and loss account, unless it is:

- A public limited company.
- A banking company or an insurance company.
- A parent company that has either a public limited company or a banking or an insurance company as a subsidiary.

Guidance on determining small and medium-sized companies and groups is given in chapter 31.

15.130 As a result, most private companies will not have to disclose the research and development expenditure charged in the profit and loss account. However, they will still have to disclose their accounting policy for research and development and any amounts of deferred development expenditure carried forward in intangible assets.

Provisions for diminution in value

15.131 A company should review at the end of each accounting period the development expenditure it has capitalised. Where the circumstances that justified the original deferral of the expenditure no longer apply, or are considered doubtful, the company should write off immediately the expenditure to the extent that the company considers it to be irrecoverable. [SSAP 13 para 29]. Consequently, a company will have to consider the conditions outlined in paragraph 25 of the standard at each year end in order to establish whether it should write off all or some of the previously capitalised development expenditure.

15.132 Where the directors expect the diminution in value of the development expenditure to be permanent, the Act, SSAP 13 and FRS 11 require that provision should be made for the asset's diminution in value or impairment. However, the directors may consider that a diminution in value of development expenditure is only temporary. For example, when the financial statements are prepared, the directors may no longer be able to show that the development project is technically feasible, but they may believe that the company will find a solution to the feasibility problem in the future. However, they would need to provide for the diminution in value of the development expenditure in accordance with SSAP 13 and FRS 11, even though such a provision may not generally be required to be made under the Act.

15.133 Once development costs have been written off, the question arises whether they can be reinstated if the uncertainties which led to their write off no longer apply. SSAP 13 does not deal with this issue. However, development costs that are capitalised as intangible fixed assets are within the scope of FRS 11's rules regarding the recognition and reversal of impairment losses. FRS 11 does not permit impairment losses to be reversed unless (a) an external event caused the original impairment loss, and (b) subsequent external events clearly and demonstrably reverse the effects of that event in a way that was not foreseen in the original impairment calculations. [FRS 11 para 60]. Situations where development costs could be reinstated within those criteria are likely to be rare. In the situation described above, for example, the problem that led to the write-off is an internal one. If the company subsequently finds a solution to the technical problem, the expenditure written off cannot be reinstated even though it may once more be considered to be recoverable.

Effect on realised reserves

15.134 Where development expenditure is deferred by capitalising it, and the unamortised development expenditure is not treated as a realised loss, the notes to the financial statements must also state:

- The fact that the amount of unamortised development expenditure is not to be treated as a realised loss for the purposes of calculating distributable profits.
- The circumstances that the directors relied upon to justify their decision not to treat the unamortised development expenditure as a realised loss.

[CA06 Sec 844 (2)(3)].

Computer software

15.135 There is considerable diversity in practice in respect of accounting for the costs of computer software, both as regards software for internal use and software that is incorporated into products under development. In the past, many companies wrote off the cost of their computer software immediately to the profit and loss account. However, an increasing number of companies have capitalised their computer software costs as either tangible fixed assets or intangible fixed assets.

15.136 FRS 10 has an important bearing on the treatment of the costs of internal-use software. The FRS does not permit internally developed intangible assets to be capitalised (except for those that have a readily ascertainable market value, which in practice is few, if any). Therefore, the FRS would not permit any internal costs of developing computer software for internal use to be capitalised as an intangible fixed asset. FRS 10 recognises that the rules restricting the recognition of internally developed intangible assets potentially create a problem for computer software costs. It explains that such costs should be treated as part of the cost of the related hardware (and, hence, as a tangible, rather than intangible, asset (see chapter 16) where they are *"directly attributable to bringing a computer system or other computer-operated machinery into working condition for its intended use within the business"*. [FRS 10 para 2].

15.137 Computer software development costs may arise in several ways. Consider the following four situations:

- A company purchases computer software externally (including, for example, packages for applications such as payroll, or general ledger or other similar packages to be used on the company's own computer). The company should capitalise the cost of such software as a tangible fixed asset. This is because the software complies with the Act's definition of a fixed asset, as the company will generally purchase it to use on a continuing basis in the company's activities.

  The company should depreciate this software, in common with its other fixed assets, over its estimated useful life. Where a company purchases a software package specifically to run on a particular computer, the software's estimated useful life should generally not exceed the computer's remaining useful life.

  Where a company incurs subsequent expenditure to upgrade or enhance the software (so that its service potential is increased), it must decide if this additional expenditure gives rise to an asset. If so, then the costs should be capitalised, otherwise they should be expensed as incurred. If this expenditure is capitalised it should be written off over the remaining useful life of the software package. However, where the improvement costs lead to an extension of the software's useful life, the company will need to revise the depreciation charge, because the asset's life has been extended.

- A company employs programmers to develop software for the company's own use. In this situation, two problems exist, namely that:
  - The company will need to analyse the programmers' time and other expenses in order to identify the costs of developing the software.
  - If the software is not operational at the time the financial statements are prepared, the company will have to provide evidence to demonstrate that the software will be completed successfully and have a value to the business.

  Provided that it can overcome both of these problems, a company should capitalise this type of computer software cost as a tangible fixed asset if it meets the criteria in FRS 15 (see chapter 16). If the software is to be capitalised, but is not fully developed, it may be included under the balance sheet heading of 'Payments on account and assets in the course of construction'.

  SSAP 13 criteria are not relevant in assessing whether this expenditure should be capitalised, because the expenditure is not part of a commercial project. The company is merely producing its own fixed assets. However, it will be necessary to ensure that the definition of an asset is met, namely that the expenditure provides access to future economic benefits – which means that the development must be capable of being assessed as viable. Costs that might fall to be treated as tangible assets in this way include the costs of developing electronic dealing systems and web sites, where ongoing activities are associated with those assets. Web site costs are dealt with in UITF Abstract 29, 'Website development costs', (see chapter 16).

- A company buys computer software to incorporate into a product that it is developing. This could include software that an external software house writes and that the company will include in computer-controlled equipment it will produce and sell.

  This expenditure is a form of development expenditure and so the question of whether this can be capitalised is covered by the criteria included in SSAP 13. Provided that these criteria are satisfied, the company may capitalise the expenditure and amortise it over the product's estimated useful life.

- A company's own programmers write software that the company will include in its products. The question of capitalisation will again depend on whether the criteria set out in SSAP 13 are satisfied.

15.138 An example of a company that capitalises major software purchases is The Automobile Association (Table 15.6).

Table 15.6 – The Automobile Association – Annual Report and Accounts – 31 December 1996

Accounting policies (extract)

Software

Software costs are written off as incurred, except for purchases from third parties in respect of major systems. In such cases, the costs are written off over a maximum of five years from the date of implementation.

Table 22.6 — [illegible] — Annual Report and Accounts — 31 December 1998

Accounting policies (extract)

Software

Software costs are written off as incurred except for purchases from third parties in respect of major systems [illegible] which are written off over a maximum of five years from the date of implementation.

Chapter 16

Tangible fixed assets

Chapter 16

Tangible fixed assets

Introduction

16.1 This chapter considers the accounting treatment and disclosure of the standard categories of tangible fixed assets (as governed by FRS 15, 'Tangible fixed assets') and of capital grants. With the exception of impairments, which are dealt with in detail in chapter 18, this chapter covers the following matters:

- Initial measurement, based on historical cost.
- The concept and methods of depreciation.
- The alternative accounting rules, including bases of valuation.

Background — fixed assets generally

16.2 The key accounting issues relating to fixed assets are, first, what assets should be treated as fixed assets and, secondly, how should they be measured. The first question is largely answered by the legal definition, as set out in paragraph 16.9.

16.3 As regards to the second issue–measurement–various options are available. Companies can present financial statements which are:

- prepared under the historical cost convention;
- prepared under the historical cost convention as modified by the revaluation of certain assets; or
- prepared under the current cost convention.

16.4 There has long been controversy about the basis on which financial statements are drawn up in the UK and much of this has surrounded the valuation issue. The question of whether a balance sheet should present costs or values is a very fundamental one and the present position is an unhappy compromise between these two approaches. However, the point at issue is not restricted to the balance sheet, but also fundamentally affects the measurement of income.

16.5 Chapter 6 of the ASB's Statement of principles, 'Measurement in financial statements', discusses in detail the 'larger' questions surrounding the basis on which financial statements may be prepared. The Statement discusses the various bases of valuation used and the capital maintenance concepts that may be applied in preparing financial statements. It envisages that the present system based on a mixture of historical costs and current values will continue to be used. The Statement of principles is discussed in chapter 2.

16.6 The UK accounting model is based on historical cost. SI 2008/410, 'The Large and Medium-sized Companies and Groups (Accounts and Reports) Regulations 2008' sets out the 'historical cost accounting rules' as the principal framework, but also includes the 'alternative accounting rules', which are optional. The use of the alternative accounting rules has been patchy. Many companies stick to historical cost accounting, but many have also revalued at least some assets. The extent of this is very varied. Despite intense debate in the late 1970s and early 1980s about various forms of accounting for the effects of changing prices, very few companies now use a comprehensive system of inflation accounting. Companies often revalue assets selectively. It has been quite common, for example, for companies to revalue properties held as fixed assets, but fairly uncommon to revalue plant and vehicles.

16.7 This mixture of approaches made the balance sheets of many UK companies hard to interpret and, in particular, hard to compare with each other. FRS 15, 'Tangible fixed assets' addresses some of the concerns relating to previous revaluation practice. One of these concerns was that there had been no requirement for valuations to be kept up to date. Another was that previously an entity could 'cherry-pick' those assets which it revalued, that is, it could have revalued only some out of a class of fixed assets. FRS 15 requires that, where a tangible fixed asset is revalued, the whole of that class of asset should be revalued as well.

[The next paragraph is 16.9.]

Defining fixed assets

16.9 In terms of definition, the Act gives only limited assistance, because its guidance is of a general nature. The Schedule 1 formats in SI 2008/410 indicate that all assets are either fixed or current. The Act says that assets are fixed assets where they *"...are intended for use on a continuing basis in the company's activities"*. Consequently, current assets are *"...assets not intended for such use"*. [CA06 Sec 835(6)].

Categories of fixed asset under the Act

16.10 Schedule 1 to the SI 2008/410 provides further guidance, in that it sets out standard presentation formats. These formats are to be adopted, in respect of fixed assets, so far as is relevant to their individual circumstances, by reporting entities governed by the SI 2008/410. The balance sheet formats identify the following sub-classifications of fixed assets and their constituent parts:

- Intangible assets:
  - Development costs.

  - Concessions, patents, licences, trademarks and similar rights and assets.
  - Goodwill.
  - Payments on account.
- Tangible assets:
  - Land and buildings.
  - Plant and machinery.
  - Fixtures, fittings, tools and equipment.
  - Payments on account and assets in course of construction.
- Investments:
  - Shares in group undertakings.
  - Loans to group undertakings.
  - Participating interests.
  - Loans to undertakings in which the company has a participating interest.
  - Other investments other than loans.
  - Other loans.

16.11 The SI 2008/410 requires companies to use the headings and sub-headings prescribed in the formats other than in certain instances where the special nature of the company's business requires their adaptation. Some companies have changed the headings used on the face of the balance sheet. Examples of this are given in Tables 16.1 and 16.2.

Specifically excluded items

16.12 In addition to the guidance on asset recognition referred to in paragraphs 16.9 and 16.10 the SI 2008/410 specifically states that the following three items cannot be treated as assets – either fixed or current – in any company's balance sheet:

- Preliminary expenses.
- Expenses of, and commission on, any issue of shares or debentures.
- Costs of research.

[SI 2008/410 Sch 3(2)].

16.13 In view of the Act's prohibition, the above items should not be capitalised. Historically, they have been written off to the profit and loss account, except where a company had a share premium account, in which case, the first two items could be written off to that account. [CA06 Sec 610(2)(3)]. However, this treatment has been amended by FRS 4, 'Capital instruments', insofar as issue costs connected with such instruments are concerned. [FRS 4 para 76]. This is considered further in chapter 6.

Tangible fixed assets

Introduction

Pre-FRS 15

16.14 Before the publication of FRS 15, 'Tangible fixed assets', in February 1999, there had never been an accounting standard in the UK that specifically dealt with the measurement and valuation of tangible fixed assets.

16.15 In addition, there were, and still are, rules for accounting for tangible fixed assets and, more generally, fixed assets, within the Act. These rules, however, permit a fair degree of flexibility which has led to inconsistencies on application, as well as opportunities for abuse.

'Cherry-picking' revaluations

16.16 The alternative accounting rules in SI 2008/410 permit a company to use either a current value or a historical cost accounting system for its statutory financial statements. These rules, however, can be applied selectively and as such the law has been used by some companies in the past to enable particular assets to be revalued and determine when those revaluations are reflected in the financial statements (commonly called 'cherry-picking').

16.17 In particular, in the late 1980s, when the property market was at its peak, many companies chose to revalue some of their properties, so boosting net asset values. However, because there was no requirement for valuations to be updated in subsequent accounting periods. When the property market fell so spectacularly at the beginning of the 1990s, the fall in value was often not reflected in the financial statements on the grounds that it was believed to be only temporary.

16.18 The ASB first tackled these issues with a discussion paper, 'The role of valuation in financial reporting', issued in March 1993. This paper considered the wider question of whether the present hybrid modified historical cost system should be developed into one more clearly founded on principles embracing current values or alternatively whether the system should be pruned back to one rigorously based on principles of historical cost. The ASB concluded that although the present modified historical cost system involving both the retention of historical costs and irregular revaluation was clearly unsatisfactory, the approach should be evolutionary rather than revolutionary. Accordingly, it was proposed that the present modified historical cost system should continue, but an attempt should be made to remove some of the existing anomalies by requiring revaluations of certain assets on a more consistent basis.

16.19 The ASB subsequently published another discussion paper, 'Measurement of tangible fixed assets', in October 1996, which covered the initial measurement, valuation and depreciation of tangible fixed assets. Rather than impose mandatory valuation requirements, at least for large or listed companies with significant property portfolios, the discussion paper proposed to continue the present practice of optional revaluations, but with consistent rules that should be applied by those entities that decide to revalue their assets.

16.20 The discussion paper noted that replacing the cost of a tangible fixed asset with a valuation provided more relevant information to the user of the financial statements. However, the relevance of that information diminished over time as it no longer reflected the current value of the asset. Furthermore for current values to be meaningful and comparable from year to year, similar assets should be treated consistently. Therefore, it was proposed that if a policy of revaluation is adopted, it should be applied to all assets of the same class and those valuations should be kept up to date. These proposals were designed to reduce the scope for 'cherry-picking' and to increase the relevancy of valuations. They formed the basis for the eventual valuation requirements in FRS 15.

Start-up costs

16.21 In some industries, for example hotel and retail industries, it had become fairly common practice to capitalise start-up costs associated with new or expanding businesses, as part of the cost of the related tangible fixed asset, such as a new hotel or store.

16.22 The ASB's view was that whilst essential commissioning costs to prepare an asset for use were valid costs of a tangible fixed asset, other start-up costs were not costs of the physical asset, but rather operating costs associated with the setting up of a new business. Such start-up costs include marketing and advertising costs, staff recruitment and training costs and operating costs associated with initial slack periods because demand for the product or service has not yet built up. This issue was, therefore, tackled in FRS 15, which prohibits such costs from being capitalised as part of a tangible fixed asset. This was subsequently followed by UITF Abstract 24 in June 2000, which clarified the treatment of start-up costs that cannot be capitalised under FRS 15.

16.23 As well as addressing start-up costs, FRS 15 also tightened up the regime for the capitalisation of costs generally, providing a definition of directly attributable costs, and the period of production over which costs should be capitalised.

Capitalisation of interest

16.24 The capitalisation of interest has caused some debate in the past. As mentioned in the ASB's discussion paper, 'Measurement of tangible fixed assets', ideally the capitalisation of interest should be either mandatory or prohibited on the grounds of consistency. In the end, it was acknowledged that the arguments for each approach were finely balanced and, therefore, the compromise of allowing the optional adoption of a policy of interest capitalisation prevailed in the FRS. This accounting policy choice was removed from IFRS in the revised version of IAS 23, 'Borrowing costs', where capitalisation of borrowing costs that relates to qualifying assets is mandatory. There is currently no intention to bring this restriction into UK GAAP.

16.25 To avoid introducing different terminology, FRS 15 uses the term 'finance costs', as defined in FRS 4, 'Capital instruments' paragraph 8, rather than 'interest' or 'borrowing costs'.

FRS 15 and FRS 12 — component depreciation

16.26 FRS 12, 'Provisions, contingent assets and contingent liabilities', introduced strict rules about the costs it is appropriate to provide for. One of the consequences of FRS 12 is that entities are, in the main, no longer permitted to provide for the cost of major capital maintenance expenditure over the period that the related asset is in use. This is because the entity has no obligation to a third party in relation to the expenditure until it has been carried out. Despite this, the entity clearly benefits from that expenditure over a period of time that the related asset is in use and not just in the period that the maintenance takes place.

16.27 Therefore, in conjunction with the development of FRS 12, proposals were developed for inclusion in FRS 15 introducing the concept of 'component depreciation'. Rather than provide for the cost of major capital maintenance, part of the tangible fixed asset (a component) that will be replaced, restored or overhauled by the major capital maintenance expenditure is depreciated over the period until the expenditure is needed. In this way the depreciation of the asset more accurately reflects the consumption of the economic benefits of the asset as it is being used. When the capital maintenance expenditure takes place, it is capitalised as part of the cost of the asset, since it restores or replaces the previously depreciated component.

Non-depreciation

16.28 Although FRS 15 superseded SSAP 12, the key principles of SSAP 12 remained largely unchanged in the new standard. However, as highlighted by the ICAEW review of SSAP 12 in 1992 (FRAG 2/92, 'Review, for major practical problems, of SSAP 12'), an increasing number of entities were not depreciating their buildings, often for reasons that were inconsistent with SSAP 12. It was noted that this possibly stemmed from a misunderstanding of the nature and purpose of depreciation.

16.29 Consequently, FRED 17 proposed that subsequent expenditure on a tangible fixed asset did not negate the need for depreciation. In addition, it proposed that there should be an assumption that residual values were materially different from the carrying amount of the asset, hence forcing depreciation charges. This proposal was not generally supported by respondents to FRED 17 on the grounds that in certain circumstances it did not reflect the economic reality of the situation.

16.30 In FRS 15, therefore, the ASB acknowledged that there may be exceptional circumstances where depreciation is genuinely immaterial (because of either long useful economic lives or high residual values). However, to prevent the abuse of non-depreciation, FRS 15 contains a requirement for annual impairment reviews whenever depreciation is not charged (with the exception of land), or where the remaining useful economic life of an asset is expected to be greater than 50 years.

Objective of FRS 15

16.31 The objectives of FRS 15 reflect many of the concerns outlined above. They are to ensure that:

- Consistent principles are applied to the initial measurement of tangible fixed assets.
- If an entity adopts a policy of revaluation, the valuation is performed, and revaluation gains and losses are recognised, on a consistent basis, and valuations are kept up-to-date.
- Depreciation is calculated in a consistent manner and recognised as the economic benefits of the assets are consumed over their useful economic lives.
- Adequate disclosures are given concerning the impact of the entity's policies for the treatment of tangible fixed assets on the entity's financial position and performance.

[FRS 15 para 1].

Scope of FRS 15

16.32 FRS 15 applies to all tangible fixed assets, with the notable exception of investment properties, whose accounting treatment continues to be governed by SSAP 19. [FRS 15 paras 3, 4]. However, properties in the course of construction and development, including development properties, are not covered by SSAP 19 and, therefore, fall within the scope of FRS 15.

16.33 Whilst the standard deals with the initial measurement, valuation and depreciation of tangible fixed assets, it does not deal with their impairment, because this falls within the scope of FRS 11 'Impairment of fixed assets and goodwill'.

16.34 Accordingly, this section does not cover the accounting treatment of either investment properties (see further chapter 17), nor the impairment of tangible fixed assets (see further chapter 18).

Initial recognition

Definition of tangible fixed assets

16.35 The Act distinguishes between current and fixed assets, as noted in paragraph 16.9, but does not define tangible fixed assets. FRS 15 defines tangible fixed assets as:

> *"Assets that have physical substance and are held for use in the production or supply of goods or services, for rental to others, or for administrative purposes on a continuing basis in the reporting entity's activities."* [FRS 15 para 2].

16.36 Note that, as well as having physical substance and being used on a continuing basis in the business, a tangible fixed asset must also be an *asset*. This means that it must also satisfy the general definition of an asset, which is given in FRS 5, 'Reporting the substance of transactions', as *"rights or other access to future economic benefits controlled by an entity as a result of past transactions or events"*.

16.37 The definition of a tangible fixed asset is important in distinguishing tangible from intangible fixed assets, because the accounting treatments for tangible and intangible fixed assets differ quite significantly. Intangible fixed assets are discussed in chapter 15.

Classification of tangible fixed assets

16.38 The Act sub-analyses tangible fixed assets into the following four categories:

- Land and buildings.
- Plant and machinery.
- Fixtures, fittings, tools and equipment.
- Payments on account and assets in course of construction.

16.39 However, many companies face practical problems when categorising their tangible fixed assets into these four fairly restrictive headings. In particular, some companies find it difficult to decide whether certain assets should be described as 'plant and machinery' or 'fixtures, fittings, tools and equipment'. Some companies also have difficulty in deciding the category in which to include motor vehicles.

16.40 In practice, companies categorise their assets according to the nature of their particular business. As a general rule, companies treat major manufacturing assets (including motor vehicles involved in the manufacturing process – for example, fork-lift trucks and cranes) as plant and machinery. They include other assets not involved in the manufacturing process in 'fixtures, fittings, tools and equipment'.

16.41 Because the Act allows a company to show any item in greater detail than the formats require, a company may, for example, disclose the amount for motor vehicles as a subdivision of either plant and machinery or fixtures, fittings, tools and equipment. [SI 2008/410 1 Sch 3(1)]. However, where an asset does not fall under any of the headings given in the formats, paragraph 3(2) of Schedule 4 allows a company to include the amount of it under a separate heading. Consequently, motor vehicles could be included in the balance sheet as a separate item, a presentation format adopted by Caradon plc in Table 16.1.

Table 16.1 – Caradon plc – Annual Report & Accounts – 31 December 1998

Notes to the accounts (extract)

10 Tangible fixed assets (extract)

	Land and buildings						
	Freehold	Long leasehold	Short leasehold	Motor vehicles	Fixtures and fittings and tools	Plant machinery	Group total
	£m	£m	£m	£m	£m	£m	£m
Cost or valuation							
At 1 January 1998	179.6	20.3	7.1	46.0	105.9	663.7	1,022.6
Currency translation	2.4	(0.1)	(0.3)	(0.1)	1.1	0.3	3.3
Reclassification	0.8	(0.8)	–	0.1	1.2	(1.3)	–
Additions	5.1	0.2	0.9	4.8	9.6	50.1	70.7
Disposals	(7.0)	–	(0.6)	(7.3)	(6.8)	(38.7)	(60.4)
Divestments	(6.2)	–	–	(0.9)	(2.8)	(34.0)	(43.9)
At 31 December 1998	**174.7**	**19.6**	**7.1**	**42.6**	**108.2**	**640.1**	**992.3**

16.42 Furthermore, FRS 15 requires disclosures to be given for each class of assets, which may be narrower than the Act's categories of assets. As discussed from paragraph 16.158 below, a class of assets is defined as *"a category of tangible fixed assets having a similar nature, function or use in the business of the entity"*. [FRS 15 para 2].

Payments on account and assets under construction

16.43 The category of payments on account and assets in course of construction is in effect a suspense categorisation, pending the transfer of the assets to one of the other categories.

16.44 'Payments on account' represent payments a company has made in respect of tangible assets for which it has not yet taken delivery. As the assets are not yet being employed by the entity, it would seem inappropriate in most circumstances to depreciate them until they are received and utilised. However, in exceptional circumstances where their value is perceived to have been impaired, FRS 11 would require a provision to be made to reduce their carrying amount. This situation could occur, for example, where a company has contracted and paid for specialised machinery with a lead-time for delivery and where adverse changes in the company's circumstances or in technology during the lead-time mean that the intended use either disappears or is seriously reduced.

16.45 'Assets in course of construction' represent the cost of purchasing, constructing and installing tangible fixed assets ahead of their productive use. As a category of asset, it seems more prevalent in published financial reports than 'payments on account'. It is a category of a temporary nature, pending completion of the asset and its transfer to the appropriate and permanent category of tangible fixed assets. The timing of the transfer of an asset from this category to the appropriate heading will vary. Unless the exceptional circumstance described in paragraph 16.44 occurs, a company will not normally charge depreciation on, or impair, an asset that is in the course of construction until it is completed and it is transferred to an asset heading that is appropriate.

16.46 In Table 16.2, the BOC Group plc provides an illustration of a company with assets under construction and clearly sets out the nature of the assets reclassified during the reporting period. In addition, its accounting policies state that *"no depreciation is charged on … construction in progress"*.

Table 16.2 – The BOC Group plc – Report and Accounts – 30 September 1998

Notes to the financial statements (extract)

7. Fixed assets – tangible assets

a) Group summary	Land and buildings[1] £ million	Plant machinery and vehicles £ million	Cylinders £ million	Construction in progress £ million	Total £ million
Gross book value					
At 1 October 1997	703.0	3,545.0	550.2	406.2	5,204.4
Exchange adjustment	(69.2)	(290.3)	(47.8)	(41.8)	(449.1)
Capital expenditure[2]	32.4	311.2	25.9	226.7	596.2
Revaluations	1.6	–	–	–	1.6
Disposals	(10.2)	(106.4)	(5.9)	–	(122.5)
Transfers	8.2	145.7	7.0	(160.9)	–
Acquisitions and disposals of businesses	(61.4)	(198.0)	5.8	(22.7)	(276.3)
At 30 September 1998	**604.4**	**3,407.2**	**535.2**	**407.5**	**4,954.3**

Depreciation					
At 1 October 1997	191.3	1,860.9	198.5	–	2,250.7
Exchange adjustment	(13.5)	(143.4)	(16.9)	–	(173.8)
Provided during the year	19.3	224.1	24.5	–	267.9
Impairment	5.4	44.7	–	–	50.1
Revaluations	(0.4)	–	–	–	(0.4)
Disposals	(2.4)	(76.2)	(4.1)	–	(82.7)
Transfers	(2.1)	2.1	–	–	–
Acquisitions and disposals of businesses	(21.2)	(138.1)	–	–	(159.3)
At 30 September 1998	**176.4**	**1,774.1**	**202.0**	–	**2,152.5**
Net book value at 30 September 1998[3]					
Owned assets	389.3	1628.8	328.8	407.5	2,754.4
Leased assets	38.7	4.3	4.4	–	47.4
	428.0	**1,633.1**	**333.2**	**407.5**	**2,801.8**

1. Net book value of land and buildings at cost was £356.8 million (1997: £242.9 million).

2. Capital expenditure of joint ventures and associates is given in note 1.

3. Net book value includes net interest capitalised of £59.0 million (1997: £52.1 million).

Transfers to fixed assets

16.47 Most of the time, an item initially recognised as a tangible fixed asset will not have been previously recognised elsewhere in the balance sheet. However, occasionally an event may occur such that an item previously recognised as a current asset is transferred to tangible fixed assets. For example, a car dealer may decide to redeploy some of its stock as company cars for its employees. Those cars would then be transferred from current assets (stock) to tangible fixed assets, as they are now being used in the business on a continuing basis.

16.48 This issue is addressed in UITF Abstract 5, 'Transfers from current assets to fixed assets'. The abstract states that the transfer from current to fixed assets should be recognised in the financial statements at the date of management's change of intent. [UITF 5 para 4].

16.49 Furthermore, the UITF took the view that any diminution in value (or impairment) of a current asset that had taken place before the effective date of transfer of that asset to fixed assets should be charged in the profit and loss account, reflecting the loss to the entity while the asset was held as a current asset. In other words the asset should be transferred at the lower of cost and net realisable value. [UITF 5 para 5].

[The next paragraph is 16.51.]

Initial measurement

Introduction

16.51 The basic principle in FRS 15 that tangible fixed assets should be initially measured at cost is consistent with the requirement in the Act that fixed assets should be shown at either purchase price or production cost.

16.52 Experience has shown that, in particular for self-constructed assets, different practices have arisen on application of this principle. For example, one company may only capitalise external costs incurred on the construction of a building, whereas another company may also capitalise the direct and indirect costs of its own employees working on the asset. Both are acceptable under the Act's requirements. FRS 15, however, tightens the general rules in the Act, by requiring that directly attributable costs (but only those costs) be capitalised and defines what is meant by directly attributable costs.

16.53 Furthermore, FRS 15 gives detailed requirements about the period over which costs related to the constructed asset should be capitalised. It aims to prevent the capitalisation of costs relating to periods where no construction activity is taking place, in particular in the period after the asset is physically complete but before it has been put to full use.

16.54 FRS 15, therefore, ensures greater consistency over which costs, should be capitalised on the initial recognition of an asset and for what period capitalisation is allowed.

Cost

16.55 FRS 15 requires that a tangible fixed asset should initially be measured at cost, which should include only those costs directly attributable to bringing the asset into working condition for its intended use. [FRS 15 paras 6, 7]. This is based on the historical accounting rules in S1 2008/410, which require fixed assets to be shown at either their purchase price or their production cost, less any provision for depreciation or diminution in value. [S1 2008/410 1 Sch 17].

16.56 The FRS states that cost is purchase price (less trade discounts and rebates) plus directly attributable costs. [FRS 15 para 8].

16.57 This is the case even if assets were acquired at a bargain and, therefore, the purchase cost does not reflect the full value of the asset. However, except in exceptional circumstances, donated assets received by charities should be recognised at their current value, see from paragraph 16.90.

16.58 The Act also defines purchase price, in relation to an asset of a company or any raw materials or consumables used in the production of such an asset, as including any consideration (whether in cash or otherwise) given by the company in respect of that asset or those materials or consumables, as the case may be. [SI 2008/410 10 Sch (12)]. It is ascertained by adding to the actual price the company paid for the asset any expenses that were incidental to its acquisition. [SI 2008/410 1 Sch 27(1)]. These incidental expenses include, for example, the expenses that the company had to incur in order to get the asset to its present location and into its present condition.

16.59 The amount to be shown as the production cost of an asset is ascertained by adding the following amounts:

- The purchase price of the raw materials and consumables the company used in producing the asset.
- The direct costs of production the company incurred (excluding distribution costs in the case of current assets).

[SI 2008/410 1 Sch 27(2)].

16.60 The Act also *permits* the following costs to be included, although FRS 15 further stipulates when and in what circumstances these permitted costs should be included in the cost of tangible fixed assets if at all, as discussed in greater detail below.

- A reasonable proportion of indirect overheads, to the extent that they relate to the period of production.
- Interest on any capital the company borrowed in order to finance the production of that asset, to the extent that it relates to the period of production. Where such interest has been included in the production cost, the fact that it has been included and its amount must be stated in the notes to the financial statements.

[SI 2008/410 1 Sch 27(3)].

Directly attributable costs

16.61 Directly attributable costs are:

- Labour costs of the entity's own employees (for example, construction workers, architects and surveyors employed by the entity) arising directly from the construction or acquisition of the specific tangible fixed asset.
- Incremental costs to the entity that would have been avoided only if the tangible asset had not been constructed or acquired.

[FRS 15 para 9].

16.62 The standard gives some examples of directly attributable costs which include:

- Acquisition costs (such as stamp duty, import duties and non-refundable purchase taxes).
- The cost of site preparation and clearance.

- Initial delivery and handling costs.
- Installation costs.
- Professional fees (such as legal, architects' and engineers' fees).
- The estimated cost of dismantling and removing the asset and restoring the site, to the extent that it is recognised as a provision under FRS 12 (see para 16.75 below).

[FRS 15 para 10].

16.63 The FRS also identifies expenditure that should not be included. For example:

- Administrative and other general overheads.
- Employee costs not related to the specific asset (such as site selection activities).
- Abnormal costs arising from inefficiencies (such as costs relating to design errors, industrial disputes, idle capacity, wasted materials, labour or other resources and production delays).
- Other costs such as operating losses that occur because a revenue activity has been suspended during the construction of a tangible fixed asset.

[FRS 15 paras 9,11].

16.64 In addition, intra-group profits or losses should be excluded from cost in the consolidated financial statements of a group.

16.65 It is worth mentioning here that the standard does not allow entities to be selective about which directly attributable costs should be capitalised. All those costs (subject to materiality) that meet the FRS 15 definition of a directly attributable cost must be capitalised, whilst those costs that fall outside the definition cannot be capitalised. The capitalisation of all directly attributable costs could result in an initial cost of an asset that is greater than its recoverable amount. In that case the asset should be immediately written down to recoverable amount, in accordance with FRS 11.

Example 1 – Costs capitalised as part of refurbishment

A company has a number of retail stores. It has been refurbishing two of the stores and they were shut for 3 months whilst the refurbishment took place. However, the company has still incurred staff salaries, paid staff a retention bonus and paid to bus them to other stores to work. Can any of these costs be capitalised as part of the refurbishment?

None of these costs can be capitalised as they relate to retaining staff during the refurbishment and, consequently, must be expensed. FRS 15 specifically states that a tangible fixed asset should be measured at cost, but only those costs that are directly attributable to bringing the asset into working condition for its intended use can be capitalised. Therefore, the standard does not permit such costs to be capitalised. [FRS 15 paras 6-7].

Example 2 – Capitalisation of cash associated with a loyalty scheme

A company is introducing a loyalty card scheme in a number of its stores. It has a policy of capitalising software costs of the scheme, but can it also capitalise other costs such as call centre costs, consultants' costs and printing costs?

Software development and fixed asset costs can be capitalised under FRS 15. However, UITF 24 on start-up costs needs to be considered to determine whether these other costs can be capitalised. As they are not costs that the business usually incurs, also FRS 15, FRS 10 or SSAP 13 need to be considered to determine if they can be capitalised. As they do not satisfy the criteria of any of these standards, the company cannot capitalise the other costs referred to above, hence they should be written off.

Labour costs

16.66 The standard clarifies that only those labour costs that relate to the time spent by employees on constructing or acquiring the specific asset should be capitalised. Therefore, time spent on other potential acquisitions or developments cannot be included. For example, an internal surveyor may carry out surveys on five different properties as part of the process to determine which one of those properties the company will buy. However, only the surveyor's time in respect of the survey on the successful property should be capitalised as part of the tangible fixed asset.

16.67 Furthermore, if a site engineer spends 30 per cent of his time on a particular development project, then only 30 per cent of his employee costs should be capitalised as part of the cost of the asset. Other overhead costs should not be capitalised unless they are incremental costs to the company that would have been avoided only if the tangible fixed asset had not been constructed. Therefore, it is not permitted to capitalise in tangible fixed assets 30 per cent of the indirect overheads that could be apportioned to the engineer (for example, an allocation of the office rent or secretarial costs). (This contrasts with the position under SSAP 9 when certain indirect overhead costs may be allocated to stock, as discussed in chapter 20.) However, the costs of a temporary office on the site of the development, that would not have been incurred but for the project, should be capitalised.

Example – Capitalisation of staff costs

A company is capitalising software development costs. The software is for own use and so is classified as a tangible fixed asset to which FRS 15 applies. Directly attributable staff costs will be capitalised in accordance with paragraph 9 of FRS 15. Do such costs include national insurance and pension costs of the staff who are developing the software?

FRS 15 paragraph 7 states that costs that are directly attributable to bringing the asset into working condition for its intended use should be included in its measurement. Paragraph 9 states that directly attributable costs include the labour costs of own employees (for example site workers, in-house architects and surveyors) arising directly from the construction or acquisition of the specific tangible fixed asset. Employers' national insurance and pension costs are both part of staff costs and so fall within the meaning of labour costs in this context. Therefore, they should be included in the amount capitalised under FRS 15.

Pension costs are governed by FRS 17, 'Retirement benefits'. This standard makes specific reference to this situation in paragraph 51 which says that the current service cost should be included within operating profit in the profit and loss account (except insofar as the related remuneration is capitalised in accordance with another standard). The pension costs capitalised will require disclosure under paragraph 82 of FRS 17. On 7 December 2006, the ASB published an amendment to FRS 17, 'Retirement benefits', which removes this disclosure requirement.

Note that only the current service cost which is normally included in operating profit may be considered as a staff cost eligible for capitalisation (as per FRS 17 paragraph 51). Other elements of the pension cost included after operating profit, for example the finance cost, are costs of financing the pension scheme and are not eligible for capitalisation.

Incremental costs

16.68 External professional fees incurred in finding a suitable asset, which is then acquired or constructed, may be capitalised, as they are incremental costs to the entity that would have been avoided only if the tangible fixed asset had not been constructed or acquired. This contrasts with the treatment of labour costs of own employees in searching for suitable sites or assets, which cannot be included within the costs to be capitalised. However, costs such as external professional fees should only be capitalised as part of the cost of an asset when they relate directly to the acquisition or construction of the asset. Therefore, costs on speculative projects and costs of aborted plans should not be capitalised.

16.69 The definition of directly attributable costs in FRS 15 (see para 16.61) should be used in conjunction with the black letter requirement in FRS 15 that only costs directly attributable to bringing the tangible fixed asset into working condition for its intended use should be included in the cost of the asset. [FRS 15 para 7]. Therefore, although constructing or acquiring a new asset may result in other incremental costs that would have been avoided only if the asset had not been constructed or acquired, these should not be included in the cost of the asset if they do not bring the asset into working condition for its intended use.

16.70 For example, a mobile phone operator may be setting up a new network in a new territory, involving the construction of the network system (new transmitter towers etc). There will be incremental costs that would have been avoided only if the physical network system had not been constructed, as without the physical infrastructure in place there can be no business, but not all of these fall to be capitalised, because some are not directly attributable to bringing the physical asset into working condition. Costs that do not relate to the construction of the physical asset, but rather relate to setting up the new business as a whole, even though they are incurred during the construction phase of the new network (for example, market research, accounts staff, advertising, head office costs during the construction phase) do not qualify to be capitalised as part of the cost of the tangible fixed asset.

16.71 Another type of cost not specifically mentioned in the FRS, but sometimes put forward as a candidate for capitalisation, is the cost of training operatives for new machinery or computer equipment. Such costs should not be capitalised as they are operating costs rather than directly attributable to the tangible fixed asset. As operatives may leave at short notice, their training costs would not meet the definition of an asset and, therefore, may not be capitalised, since the access to future economic benefits is not controlled by the entity.

Example – Capitalisation of incremental costs in a new building

The company has an existing freehold factory property that it intends to knock down and redevelop. During the redevelopment period the company will move its production facilities to another (temporary) site. As a result the following incremental costs will be incurred, set up costs £50,000, rent £150,000 and removal costs £30,000. Can these costs be capitalised into the cost of the new building under FRS 15?

Although constructing or acquiring a new asset may result in incremental costs that would have been avoided only if the asset had not been constructed or acquired, they should not be included in the cost of the asset if they do not bring the asset into working condition for its intended use. This is because the black letter standard in paragraph 7 of FRS 15 specifically says that only costs directly attributable to bringing the asset into such working condition may be capitalised. Although paragraph 9 of FRS 15 then includes incremental costs as 'directly attributable', this is subject to the overriding condition for capitalisation set out in paragraph 7, which states that such costs must be attributable to bringing the asset into working condition. The costs to be incurred by the company do not meet that requirement of FRS 15 and cannot, therefore, be capitalised.

Software development costs

16.72 Computer software development costs may arise in several ways as discussed in more detail in chapter 15. However, only those directly attributable software development costs that are associated with computer hardware for the entity's own use that has been capitalised should be capitalised as a tangible fixed asset.

16.73 This is consistent with FRS 10, 'Goodwill and intangible assets', which does not allow any internal costs of developing computer software for internal use to be capitalised as an intangible fixed asset. Instead, FRS 10 prescribes that such costs should be capitalised as part of the cost of the related hardware (and, hence, as a tangible, rather than intangible, asset), where they are *"directly attributable to bringing a computer system or other computer-operated machinery into working condition for its intended use within the business"*. [FRS 10 para 2]. Table 16.3 gives an example.

Table 16.3 – Laura Ashley Holdings plc – Annual Report – 31 January 2004

Accounting policies (extract)

Fixed assets

Depreciation of property, plant and equipment and vehicles is calculated at rates estimated to write off the cost of the relevant assets, less any estimated residual value, by equal amounts over their expected useful lives.

The principle lives used are:

Freehold buildings and long leasehold property:	50 years
Short leasehold property:	Period of lease
Leasehold improvements:	Period of lease
Plant and machinery:	10 years
Vehicles:	5 years
Fixtures, fittings and equipment:	
Computer systems:	5 years
Shop fixtures and fittings:	5 years
Other equipments, fixtures and fittings:	5 to 10 years

Key money on properties which is paid in certain European countries is written down by 25% over 10 years to its estimated recoverable amount. Software development costs are capitalised as computer system expenditure.

16.74 One issue that caused considerable debate in the past was whether costs of developing a web site may be capitalised. In response to this the UITF issued an Abstract, UITF Abstract 29, 'Website development costs', in February 2001, which was effective for accounting periods ended on or after 23 March 2001. The Abstract details the factors that should be taken into account.

16.74.1 The Abstract divides the costs into four types:

(a) *Planning costs* – including, for example, the costs of feasibility studies, determining the objectives and functionalities of the web site, exploring how to achieve the desired functionalities, identifying appropriate hardware and Web applications and selecting suppliers and consultants.

(b) *Application and infrastructure development costs* – including the costs of registering a domain name and of buying or developing hardware and operating software for the site (for example, updateable content management systems and e-commerce systems, including encryption software, and interfaces with other IT systems used by the entity).

(c) *Design costs* – expenditure on the design and appearance of individual web site pages.

(d) *Content costs* – expenditure incurred on preparing, accumulating and posting the web site content, including graphics.

16.74.2 The Abstract states that planning costs do not give rise to future economic benefits that are controlled by the entity. Such costs should not, therefore, be capitalised as an asset, but should be charged to the profit and loss account as incurred. However, the other types of cost referred to above in paragraphs (b), (c) and (d) could give rise to an asset, which should be capitalised if the relationship between the expenditure and the future economic benefits is sufficiently certain.

16.74.3 But, there is often substantial uncertainty regarding the viability, useful economic life and value of a web site. The UITF took the view that amounts spent on the design and content of a web site should be capitalised only to the extent that they created an enduring asset and there were reasonable grounds for supposing that future economic benefits in excess of the amounts capitalised would be generated by the web site. This would be the case only if the web site was capable of generating revenues directly, for example by enabling orders to be placed.

16.74.4 The UITF considered that web site development costs were of the type that FRS 10 envisaged should be treated as tangible fixed assets. The UITF consensus was accordingly that:

- Web site planning costs should be charged to the profit and loss account as incurred.
- Other web site development costs should be capitalised as tangible fixed assets, in accordance with the requirements of FRS 15, 'Tangible fixed assets', subject to the *proviso* on design and content costs set out in the next paragraph below.
- Expenditure to maintain or operate a web site once it has been developed should be charged to the profit and loss account as incurred, in accordance with the requirements of FRS 15.

[UITF 29 para 11].

16.74.5 The *proviso* on design and content development costs is that they should be capitalised only to the extent that they lead to the creation of an enduring asset delivering benefits at least as great as the amount capitalised. This will be the case only to the extent that:

- The expenditure is separately identifiable.
- The technical feasibility and commercial viability of the web site have been assessed with reasonable certainty in the light of factors such as likely market conditions (including competing products), public opinion, and possible legislation.
- The web site will generate sales or other revenues directly* and the expenditure makes an enduring contribution to the development of the revenue-generating capabilities of the web site,
- There is a reasonable expectation that the present value of the future cash flows (that is, future revenues less attributable costs) to be generated by the

web site will be no less than the amounts capitalised in respect of that revenue-generating activity.

- Adequate resources exist, or are reasonably expected to be available, to enable the web site project to be completed and to meet any consequential need for increased working capital.

[UITF 29 para 12].

* For not-for-profit entities, the Abstract should be interpreted as permitting capitalisation only to the extent that the primary purpose of the web site is to provide a means of delivery of the specific services offered by the entity in fulfilment of its principal objectives.

16.74.6 If there is not sufficient evidence on which to base reasonable estimates of the economic benefits that will be generated in the period until the design and content are next updated, the costs of developing the design and content should be charged to the profit and loss account as incurred. [UITF 29 para 13].

16.74.7 Revenues that may be treated as arising directly from the website could include those attributable to orders placed *via* the website, amounts paid by subscribers for access to information contained on the website or advertising revenues obtained by selling advertising space on the web site. If a web site is used only for advertising or promotion of the entity's own products or services, it is unlikely to be possible to provide sufficient evidence to demonstrate that future sales or revenue will be generated directly by the web site. [UITF 29 para 14].

16.74.8 Revenues expected to arise directly from the web site might include some that would have been achieved by other means in the absence of the web site. Where this happens, it will be necessary to consider whether other fixed assets have become impaired as a result of the development of the web site. [UITF 29 para 15].

16.74.9 Capitalised web site development costs should be reviewed for impairment in accordance with FRS 11 if events or changes in circumstances indicate that the carrying amount may not be recoverable. [UITF 29 para 16].

16.74.10 Capitalised web site development costs should be depreciated over their estimated useful economic life, which should be reviewed each period in accordance with the requirements of FRS 15. Because of the rapid rate of technological innovation, the useful economic life of a web site is likely to be short. Also, where the design or content of a web site has to be replaced more frequently than the web site as a whole, it may be appropriate to select a depreciation period for the cost of the design or content that is shorter than the depreciation period selected for the remainder of the asset. [UITF 29 para 17].

[The next paragraph is 16.75.]

Decommissioning costs

16.75 As mentioned in paragraph 16.62 above, an example given in the FRS of a directly attributable cost for capitalisation as part of a tangible fixed asset is the estimated cost of dismantling and removing the asset and restoring the site ('decommissioning costs'), to the extent recognised as a provision under FRS 12, 'Provisions, contingent liabilities and contingent assets'. [FRS 15 para 10]. This is consistent with the requirement in FRS 12 that when a provision or a change in a provision is recognised, an asset should also be recognised when (but only when) the obligation incurred gives access to future economic benefits. [FRS 12 para 66].

16.76 At first glance it seems odd to capitalise decommissioning costs that are not going to emerge until later in the asset's life. However, where a provision is recognised in accordance with FRS 12 as a direct consequence of acquiring or constructing a tangible fixed asset, the entity has an obligation at that point to incur further costs in the future that it cannot avoid in connection with the acquisition or construction of the asset. Therefore, it is argued that the decommissioning costs at the end of the asset's life are just as much a cost of acquiring or constructing the asset as the costs incurred at the start of the asset's life.

16.77 Decommissioning or similar costs such as dilapidation expenditure can often arise in connection with operating leases and leasehold improvements. For example, the terms of an operating lease may allow the tenant to tailor the property to meet their specific needs by building an additional internal wall, say, but on condition that the tenant returns the property at the end of the lease in its original state. This will entail dismantling the internal wall. On building the internal wall, the tenant creates an obligation to remove the wall, which it cannot avoid, and, therefore, must recognise a provision for that obligation in accordance with FRS 12. The cost to the tenant, therefore, of the leasehold improvement is not only the cost of building the wall, but also the cost of restoring the property at the end of the lease. As such, both costs are capitalised when the internal wall is built and will be recognised in the profit and loss account over the useful economic life of the asset (generally the lease term) as part of the depreciation charge.

16.78 Other examples of decommissioning costs that may be capitalised as part of the cost of the asset typically arise in oil and gas and electricity industries where environmental damage is caused by, say the construction and commissioning of the facility (for example, the oil platform or nuclear plant). Similar costs are incurred in other industries such as: abandonment costs in the mining and extractive industries; clean up and restoration costs of landfill sites; and environmental clean up costs in a number of industries. Decommissioning and abandonment are considered in more detail in chapter 21.

Decommissioning costs arising later in the asset's life

16.79 Sometimes the obligation in respect of such decommissioning costs does not arise until, or only becomes apparent, later in the asset's life, due, for example, to a change in legislation in respect of environmental damage. If these costs meet the recognition criteria under FRS 12 for a provision, then FRS 15 says that these costs should still be capitalised as part of the cost of the asset to the extent that they related to the installation, construction or acquisition of the asset. [FRS 15 para 10].

16.80 In contrast, provisions that arise during an asset's life as a result of damage incurred through the use of the asset are production costs and should not be capitalised as part of the cost of the asset. For example, provisions arising in respect of the wear and tear of a leasehold property, which must be rectified at the end of the lease under the lease terms, are costs of using the property and, therefore, the related debit is a revenue, rather than a capital item and accordingly should be recognised in the profit and loss account.

16.81 Where such a provision is a cost related to the construction, acquisition or addition of a tangible fixed asset, there are two ways of determining the amount of the provision to be capitalised as an asset. Suppose an asset has a life of 30 years and, due to a change in legislation, after ten years an obligation arises in respect of decommissioning costs relating to the installation of the asset for which a provision of £900,000 has been recognised. Either:

- the whole £900,000 is capitalised as part of the cost of the asset and depreciated over the remaining useful economic life of 20 years (subject to recoverability); or
- only £600,000 of the provision is capitalised and depreciated over the remaining useful economic life of 20 years. The remainder of the provision of £300,000, which is the amount that would have been recognised as depreciation in the first ten years of the asset's life had the obligation been in existence then, is recognised immediately in the current year's profit and loss account.

16.82 The standard does not tell us which of these two approaches to use. However, the first approach is more appropriate, because the change arises from new information and developments and does not relate to past periods. In addition, it is consistent with the requirements for revisions to useful economic lives and residual values (see from para 16.302).

Changes in estimate

16.83 Inevitably, there are likely to be significant changes in the initial (and subsequent) estimates of decommissioning costs of an asset, particularly where asset lives are long. These changes in estimate may be due to changes in legislation, technology, timing of the decommissioning, management's assumptions etc. The question is how should these changes in estimates be reflected when such obligations had previously been recognised as a provision and the cost capitalised as part of the cost of the asset. These issues together with the problems associated with discounting are considered further in chapter 21.

Period of capitalisation of directly attributable costs

16.84 Consistent with paragraph 27(2) of Schedule 1 to SI 2008/410, the FRS allows capitalisation of costs to take place only in respect of the period in which the activities necessary to bring the asset into use are in progress. Thus, capitalisation should cease when substantially all the activities necessary to get the tangible fixed asset ready for use are complete, even if the asset has not yet been brought into use. [FRS 15 para 12]. 'Ready for use' means when *"physical construction is complete"*. [FRS 15 para 13].

Start-up costs

16.85 FRS 15 states that costs associated with a start-up or commissioning period should be included in the cost of a tangible fixed asset only where the asset is available for use, but incapable of operating at normal levels without such a start-up or commissioning period. [FRS 15 para 14].

16.86 A distinction is drawn between a commissioning period for plant, where the plant cannot yet physically operate at normal levels, and a start-up period, where plant can operate at normal levels, but it is not doing so because demand has not yet built up. The costs of an essential commissioning period, as in the former case, are capitalised, whilst the machinery is run in and equipment is tested. In the latter case, where the asset is ready for use, but demand has not yet built up, costs should not be capitalised. [FRS 15 paras 15, 16].

16.87 An example of where costs should not be capitalised is given in the FRS. This is a new hotel or bookshop, which could operate at normal levels almost as soon as it has been constructed or opened, but where demand usually builds up slowly and full use or sales levels will be reached only after several months. In such a case initial operating losses in the start-up period are not costs that may be capitalised.

16.88 Similarly marketing and similar costs associated with generating demand for the services of the tangible fixed asset may not be capitalised as part of the tangible fixed asset.

16.89 FRS 15 does not, however, specify how costs that cannot be included in the cost of a tangible fixed asset should be accounted for. In response to this, the UITF issued Abstract 24 on accounting for start-up costs in June 2000.

16.89.1 Abstract 24 does not attempt to give a precise definition of costs, but instead takes a takes a broad view, indicating that it covers costs (that is, expenses and losses incurred both before and after opening) arising from those one-time activities related to:

- Opening a new facility.
- Introducing a new product or service.
- Conducting business in a new territory.
- Conducting business with a new class of customer.
- Initiating a new process in an existing facility.
- Starting a new operation.
- Relocating or reorganising all or part of an entity.
- Establishing and organising a new entity.

16.89.2 The Abstract concludes that start-up costs should be accounted for on a basis consistent with the accounting treatment of similar costs incurred as part of the entity's on-going activities. However, where there are no such similar costs, start-up costs that do not meet the criteria for recognition as assets under a relevant accounting standard should be recognised as an expense as they are incurred.

16.89.3 Therefore, costs associated with a start-up situation should not be deferred as a current asset, unless they meet the conditions for recognition as an asset and it is the company's policy to defer similar costs that are incurred on an ongoing basis. Further discussion on prepayments and cost deferral is contained in chapter 21.

Example – Costs incurred in a staff-up period

A new store is being developed on a rented site. Can the rentals incurred before the store is opened be capitalised and then be amortised over the period of the lease?

Under SSAP 21, 'Leases and hire purchase contracts', operating lease rentals payable are normally charged as period expenses over the lease term (that is, from lease inception) rather than over the period the leased asset is actually in use. The rule in UITF Abstract 24 is that costs incurred in a start-up period should be treated consistently with the treatment of similar costs incurred at any other time in the business cycle. UITF Abstract 24 states that start-up costs include expenses incurred both before and after opening a new facility. Therefore, under UITF Abstract 24, there is no basis for capitalising operating lease rentals, despite the fact that the store has not yet been opened.

16.89.4 All other costs associated with an activity should be expensed as incurred, except where they can be capitalised as part of another asset as permitted by FRS 15, 'Tangible fixed assets', FRS 10, 'Goodwill and intangible assets', SSAP 13, 'Accounting for research and development', SSAP 9, 'Stocks and long-term contracts', and SSAP 21, 'Accounting for leases and hire purchase contracts'.

16.89.5 Where such costs have been expensed, they may fall within the definition of an exceptional item under FRS 3, 'Reporting financial performance', by virtue of their size or incidence. If so, the disclosures required by FRS 3 should be given, as set out in chapter 8, including an adequate description in the notes to the accounts to enable the nature of the item to be understood. In addition, the Abstract encourages companies to discuss the impact of activities and costs incurred in the operating and financial review, as recommended in paragraphs 16-18 of the ASB's statement (paragraph 23 of the revised statement – see chapter 2 of the Manual of Accounting – Management Reports and Governance).

[The next paragraph is 16.90.]

Donated assets

16.90 The FRS deals briefly with the receipt of donated assets by charities. Donated assets effectively have a nil cost to the recipient. However, rather than record the asset at nil cost, the FRS states that the initial carrying amount of tangible fixed assets received as gifts and donations by charities should be the current value of the assets at the date on which they are received. [FRS 15 para 17]. Unless the asset is impaired, the current value of the asset is its replacement cost for existing use (see from para 16.177).

16.91 Whilst the FRS lays down this general rule it acknowledges that there may be measurement difficulties and even where the value of a donated asset can be measured the cost of measurement may outweigh the benefits. The standard, therefore, permits alternative approaches to the measurement of assets in such circumstances provided that disclosure of the reason for the different treatment, and of the age, nature and scale of the assets is given in the notes to the financial statements. The FRS notes that this also applies where the FRS is first applied to tangible fixed assets that were not previously capitalised and reliable estimates of cost or value are not available. It refers to the industry specific guidance that is in the Statement of recommended practice (SORP) for charities. [FRS 15 para 18]. A revised SORP, 'Accounting and reporting by charities: Statement of recommended practice', was issued in 2005 and applies for all accounting periods beginning on or after 1 April 2005, with earlier adoption encouraged. The SORP recommends that the amount at which gifts in kind (including donated tangible fixed assets) are included in the Statement of Financial Activities should be either a reasonable estimate of their gross value to the charity or the amount actually realised as in the case of second-hand goods donated for resale. [SORP para 130].

16.92 Although donated assets should be recorded at their current value the FRS makes clear that this does not constitute a 'revaluation' for the purposes of the standard. Therefore, there is no need for further revaluations of the asset, or for other assets of the same class to be revalued as well. The revised SORP also makes this clear. [SORP para 263].

16.93 The standard does not state where the gain on recognition of the donated asset should be recognised in the financial statements. For charities preparing a statement of financial activities, the credit would be recognised in that statement, in the same way that a cash donation would be recognised, that is as incoming resources. Where a charity is an incorporated entity, it may then need to produce a separate income and expenditure account which would exclude the unrealised gain on the donation, as such unrealised gains may not be included in the profit and loss account under the Companies Act 2006. [SORP paras 423-425].

Unknown purchase price or production cost

16.94 The Act deals with circumstances where purchase price and production cost are unknown. In certain circumstances, an asset's purchase price or production cost is to be taken as the value the company ascribed to the asset in the earliest available record of its value that the company made on or after it either acquired or produced the asset. These circumstances are where there is no record of either of the following:

- The actual purchase price or the actual production cost.
- Any price, any expenses or any costs that are relevant for determining the purchase price or the production cost.

16.95 This exemption applies also where the relevant record is available, but it could be obtained only with unreasonable expense or delay. [SI 2008/410 1 Sch 29].

16.96 Where a company has determined, for the first time, an asset's purchase price or production cost according to its earliest known value, the company must disclose this fact in the notes to its financial statements. [SI 2008/410 1Sch 64(1)].

Recoverable amount and impairments

16.97 The general rule that an asset should be held at no more than its recoverable amount (see chapter 18) also applies on the initial recognition and measurement of a tangible fixed asset. [FRS 15 para 32].

16.98 In all cases, all directly attributable costs that fall to be capitalised as part of the cost of the asset (including finance costs, where the entity has a policy of capitalising finance costs) should be capitalised before considering whether the asset is impaired. Generally an asset is unlikely to be impaired on initial recognition, as this indicates that, from an economic perspective, the entity should not have acquired or constructed the asset in the first place. It is only necessary, therefore, to consider impairment if there is an indication of impairment, as set out in FRS 11, 'Impairment of fixed assets and goodwill'. [FRS 15 para 33].

16.99 Where an impairment has been identified on initial measurement, the carrying amount of the asset should be immediately written down to recoverable amount (that is, the higher of value in use and net realisable value). The impairment loss should be recognised in the profit and loss account.

Capitalisation of finance costs

Introduction

16.100 Views differ on whether finance costs should be included in the production cost of an asset or whether they should be expensed as incurred. Some regard such costs as forming part of the cost of the particular asset with which they can be either directly or indirectly identified. Others regard them as essentially period costs that should be charged to income regardless of how the borrowing is applied.

16.101 Both FRS 15 and the Act (as mentioned in para 16.60 above) permit either treatment. FRS 15 introduces further new requirements where a policy of capitalisation of finance costs is adopted. A description of the main features of these requirements is given below.

Definition of finance costs

16.102 Finance costs are defined in FRS 15 as:

> *"The difference between the net proceeds of an instrument and the total amount of payments (or other transfers of economic benefits) that the issuer may be required to make in respect of the instrument".* [FRS 15 para 2].

16.103 This definition is the same as that in FRS 4, 'Capital instruments'. As noted in FRS 15, finance costs include:

- Interest on bank overdrafts and short and long-term debt.
- Amortisation of discounts and premiums relating to debt.
- Amortisation of ancillary costs incurred in connection with the arrangement of debt.

16.104 The presentation requirements of FRS 25, which deal predominantly with the classification of financial liabilities and equity instruments, must be applied by all UK GAAP reporting entities (except those applying the current version of the FRSSE) in any accounting period commencing on or after 1 January 2005. Subsequent to the amendment of FRS 4 in January 2005, on the adoption of the presentation requirements of FRS 25, the treatment of interest, dividends, losses and gains in the profit and loss account follows the classification of the related instrument as debt or equity. To comply with paragraph 27 of Schedule 1 to S1 2008/410, only items that would otherwise be charged to the profit and loss account (and are not appropriations of profit) are eligible for capitalisation as part of the cost of a tangible fixed asset. Therefore, the actual or implied costs (including issue costs) of equity instruments are not eligible for capitalisation. Dividends on equity instruments are not finance costs since their payment is up to the discretion of the issuer.

16.105 The FRS is silent on whether or not foreign currency exchange differences on funds borrowed to finance construction of a fixed asset are included in finance costs. The international accounting standard IAS 23 (Revised), 'Borrowing costs', states that such exchange differences are included in borrowing costs to the extent that they are regarded as an adjustment to interest costs. In addition, SSAP 20, 'Foreign currency translation', suggests that, to ensure the format of the profit and loss account complies with Schedule 1 to SI 2008/410, exchange gains or losses from financing should be disclosed as part of interest payable and similar charges. Because UK companies applying FRS 23, 'The effects of changes in foreign exchange rates', are also required to comply with Schedule 4, the same principle applies. Exchange differences that are in effect an adjustment to interest costs would, in general, be included in finance costs, as defined by FRS 4.

16.105.1 However, in the preface to FRED 29, 'Property, plant and equipment and borrowing costs', which the ASB issued in May 2002, the ASB stated, *"FRS 15's definition of finance costs does not include exchange differences. The ASB does not believe that capitalisation of exchange differences is appropriate and proposes to omit exchange differences from the UK standard's definition of borrowing costs"*. FRED 29 is an exposure draft that was designed to replace FRS 15 with the international accounting standards IAS 16 and IAS 23 with minor modifications, such as the one referred to above. However, its implementation has been delayed as there is a separate revaluations project that is likely to result in further changes to international standards and the ASB does not intend to replace FRS 15 until the basis of valuation to be used under IFRS is clear. Until then, however, we consider that, in the absence of specific prohibition in FRS 15, exchange differences, to the extent that they are regarded as an adjustment to interest costs, may be regarded as finance costs under FRS 15.

Accounting treatment

16.106 The arguments for and against capitalisation of finance costs are set out in the 'The development of the FRS' section of FRS 15. The conclusion reached is that the arguments for and against are evenly balanced and that entities should be permitted to choose whether or not to capitalise finance costs on fixed assets that take a substantial period of time to bring into service.

16.107 Once a policy has been selected it should be applied consistently to all relevant assets, whether financed by specific or general borrowings. [FRS 15 para 20]. Relevant assets are assets that are constructed by the entity itself, or by third parties for the entity, to whom the entity is paying progress or stage payments. It also includes additions to existing fixed assets (for example, store refurbishment costs incurred by retailers), where material. However, only finance costs relating to the expenditure on the additions should be capitalised. Finance costs should not be capitalised on the carrying amount of the underlying asset, even if it is suspended from use during the period of the addition.

16.108 FRS 15 states that only directly attributable finance costs should be capitalised. 'Directly attributable' means those finance costs that would have been avoided (for example, by avoiding additional borrowings or by using the funds paid out for the asset to repay existing borrowings) if there had been no expenditure on the asset. [FRS 15 paras 19, 21].

16.109 A limit is placed on the amount of finance costs that may be capitalised. The amount should not exceed the total amount of finance costs incurred by the entity in that period. [FRS 15 para 19]. Therefore, 'notional' finance costs (that is, 'lost' interest on cash deposits used to finance the asset) may not be capitalised. This treatment is consistent with FRS 4, which requires all finance costs to be charged in the profit and loss account, but states that where appropriate, such costs may be capitalised as part of the cost of an asset by way of simultaneous transfer from the profit and loss account. [FRS 4 para 76].

16.110 The standard does not state whether this limit is in respect of gross or net finance costs that would otherwise be recognised in the profit and loss account. However, it would be consistent with the treatment of finance costs on borrowings specific to the asset, if the limit was based on gross finance costs payable, without offsetting interest receivable.

Example – Capitalisation of gross or net finance costs

A company with a policy of capitalising finance costs, constructs an asset. The actual physical construction takes a month to complete and the weighted average carrying amount of the asset (before finance costs) is £1m. The company has general borrowings during the period of £750,000, on which the company pays an average interest rate of 10% per annum. The notional finance costs incurred on the asset is, therefore, £8,333 (10% on £1m for one month). However, the company has only actually incurred finance costs of £6,250 (10% on £750,000 for one month) during the period of construction and, therefore, the company can only capitalise finance costs of £6,250 as part of the cost of the asset.

Period of capitalisation of finance costs

16.111 FRS 15 gives quite specific rules regarding which period should be used to determine the finance costs to be capitalised. It states:

"Where finance costs are capitalised, capitalisation should begin when:

(a) finance costs are being incurred; and

(b) expenditures for the asset are being incurred; and

(c) activities that are necessary to get the asset ready for use are in progress."

[FRS 15 para 25].

16.112 Therefore, where borrowings have been incurred specifically to fund the construction of an asset, finance costs on those borrowings cannot be capitalised in the period before activities necessary to get the asset ready for use are in progress. These activities would often coincide with the commencement of the physical construction of the asset. However, activities that are necessary to get the asset ready for use also includes other activities before construction starts such as drawing up site plans and obtaining planning permission.

16.113 FRS 15 also states that *"capitalisation of finance costs should be suspended during extended periods in which active development is interrupted"*. [FRS 15 para 27]. This means, for example, that finance costs should not be capitalised while land acquired for building purposes is held without any development activity taking place.

16.114 FRS 15 also determines when capitalisation should stop:

> *"Capitalisation of finance costs should cease when substantially all the activities that are necessary to get the tangible fixed asset ready for use are complete. When construction of a tangible fixed asset is completed in parts and each part is capable of being used while construction continues on other parts, capitalisation of finance costs relating to a part should cease when substantially all the activities that are necessary to get that part ready for use are completed."* [FRS 15 para 29].

16.115 This is consistent with the requirements for the cessation of capitalisation of other directly attributable costs.

16.116 Where assets are capable of being completed in parts, then finance costs associated with each part should cease being capitalised when each part is capable of being used, even if it has not yet been put into use. However, this does not apply to a part of an asset that is not capable of being put into use without the completion of another part. For example, an out of town store may be constructed in three phases: the first phase is the construction of the core building and the main car park closest to the store; the second phase is the construction of the internal fixtures and fittings; and the final phase is the completion of the overflow car park. The first phase, the basic building and initial car park, is not capable of being used as a store until the internal store fixtures and fittings are complete and, therefore, capitalisation of finance costs in respect of phases one and two should cease when both phases are complete, but before phase three is complete. In addition, where the development activities necessary to get an asset ready for its use are interrupted, costs of holding partially completed assets do not qualify for capitalisation during the interruption. [FRS 15 paras 26, 28].

16.117 These requirements in FRS 15 are also consistent with the requirement in the SI 2008/410 that *"...there may be included in the production cost of an asset ...interest on capital borrowed to finance the production of that asset, to the extent that it accrues in respect of the period of production"*. [SI 2008/410 1 Sch 27(3)].

Specific borrowings

16.118 FRS 15 gives guidance on how finance costs to be capitalised should be determined. If a particular borrowing can be specifically associated with expenditure on constructing or producing the asset, the amount of finance costs capitalised is limited to the actual finance costs incurred on that borrowing during the period in respect of expenditure to date on the asset. This means, for example, that if the borrowings are temporarily invested before being expended on the fixed asset, neither the finance cost during that investment period nor the investment income are taken into account in determining the amount of finance costs that may be capitalised.

Example

A company has borrowed £1m specifically to finance the cost of constructing a new head office and has a policy of capitalising finance costs. The loan is drawn on 1 February and during the year the company pays interest on that loan at a rate of 12% until 1 November when the interest rate is increased to 13% due to a rise in LIBOR. Construction on the building does not begin until 1 September and continues without interruption until after the year end on 31 December. During the period of construction the company incurs directly attributable costs of £100,000 in September and £250,000 in each month from October to December (for simplicity it is assumed that these costs are incurred on the first of each month). The borrowings that have not been used to pay for the building works are reinvested and earn interest at a rate of 5% per annum.

During the year ended 31 December, the company, therefore, incurs interest on the £1m loan totalling £111,667 and earns interest on the reinvested portion of the loan of £37,917.

However, only the interest paid on the borrowings actually used to finance the expenditures on the construction of the asset can be capitalised as part of the cost of the asset. Therefore, the total amount of finance costs capitalised is calculated as follows:

	£
Interest on expenditures of £100,000 at 12% for September	1,000
Interest on total expenditures of £350,000 (100,000 + 250,000) at 12% for October	3,500
Interest on £600,000 (350,000 + 250,000) at 13% for November	6,500
Interest on £850,000 (600,000 + 250,000) at 13% for December	9,208
Total interest to be capitalised	20,208

Therefore, £91,459 of the total interest payable on the loan of £111,667 is reported in the profit and loss account and £20,208 is capitalised and depreciated in future years as part of the cost of the asset. The total interest receivable of £37,917 on the funds that were temporarily reinvested is recognised in the profit and loss account.

IFRS difference

Under IAS 23 (revised), the amount of borrowing costs that should be capitalised on specific borrowings is slightly different. To the extent that borrowings are raised specifically for obtaining a qualifying asset, the amount of borrowing costs that are capitalised is the actual costs during the period less any investment income on the temporary investment of the borrowings. [IAS 23 para 12]. Under IAS 23 (revised), therefore, £32,917 would be capitalised, being interest paid of £41,667 from 1 September to 31 December less interest received of £8,750 from 1 September to 31 December.

16.119 Where construction of the asset spans more than one financial period, in subsequent periods the finance costs capitalised in respect of the construction of the asset in earlier periods should be included in the total expenditure on the asset upon which the current period's finance costs available for capitalisation are to be calculated. (Whilst this principle may be applied on a monthly basis, in practice this is often not done (as in the above example) on grounds of expediency and materiality.) This is the case regardless of whether the related borrowings are specific or general.

16.120 FRS 15 states that finance costs in respect of leased tangible fixed assets should continue to be accounted for in accordance with SSAP 21, 'Accounting for leases and hire purchase contracts'. [FRS 15 para 22]. Finance costs in respect of leased tangible fixed assets under construction should be capitalised in accordance with the above rules, where a policy of capitalisation of finance costs is adopted.

General borrowings

16.121 Where funds are borrowed generally and used for financing the construction or production of the asset, the amount of finance costs eligible for capitalisation should be determined by applying a capitalisation rate to the expenditure on that asset. The capitalisation rate should be the weighted average of the rates applicable to the borrowings of the entity that are outstanding during the period, other than borrowings made specifically for the purpose of constructing or acquiring other tangible fixed assets (such as lease liabilities) or for other specific purposes (such as loans used to hedge foreign investments). The 'expenditure' on the asset is the weighted average carrying amount of the asset during the period including finance costs previously capitalised. [FRS 15 paras 22, 23].

Example

As in the previous example, a company constructs a new head office building commencing on 1 September, which continues without interruption until after the year end on 31 December. Directly attributable expenditure on this asset is £100,000 in September and £250,000 in each of the months of October to December. Therefore, the weighted average carrying amount of the asset during the period is £475,000 ((100,000 + 350,000 + 600,000 + 850,000)/4).

The company has not taken out any specific borrowings to finance the construction of the asset, but has incurred finance costs on its general borrowings during the period of construction. During the year the company had 10% debentures in issue with a face value of £2m and an overdraft of £500,000, which increased to £750,000 in December on which interest was paid at 15% until 1 October, when the rate was increased to 16%. The capitalisation rate of the general borrowings of the company during the period of construction is calculated as follows:

	£
Finance cost on £2m 10% debentures during September – December	66,667
Interest at 15% on overdraft of £500,000 in September	6,250
Interest at 16% on overdraft of £500,000 in October and November	13,333
Interest at 16% on overdraft of £750,000 in December	10,000
Total finance costs in September – December	96,250

$$\text{Weighted average borrowings during period} = \frac{(2\text{ million} \times 4) + (500{,}000 \times 3) + (750{,}000 \times 1)}{4}$$

= £2,562,500

Capitalisation rate = total finance costs in period/weighted average borrowings during period

= 96,250/2,562,500

= 3.756%

The capitalisation rate, therefore, reflects the weighted average cost of borrowings for the four month period that the asset was under construction. On an annualised basis 3.756% gives a capitalisation rate of 11.268% per annum, which is what would be expected based on the borrowings profile.

Therefore, the total amount of finance costs to be capitalised

= weighted average carrying amount of asset × capitalisation rate

= £475,000 × 3.756%

= £17,841

Group situations

16.122 In calculating which general borrowings to include in the weighted average, judgement is needed in a group situation. It may be appropriate in some cases to include all borrowings of a parent and its subsidiaries when calculating the weighted average of finance costs, particularly where the treasury function is managed centrally within the group. In other cases, for example where each subsidiary is responsible for managing its own treasury function, it may be appropriate for each subsidiary to calculate the weighted average applicable to its own borrowings. [FRS 15 para 24].

16.123 In consolidated financial statements the limitation applied is the consolidated amount of finance costs, because the Act requires consolidated financial statements to be prepared so far as possible as if they were the financial statements of a single company. The limitation on capitalisation of finance costs, described above, is sometimes objected to by companies that have little borrowing, but which are using cash resources to finance the construction of fixed assets. The argument put forward is that cash being used to finance the construction could otherwise have been used to earn interest and it is, therefore, fair to attribute a notional finance cost representing the deprival cost of the cash employed in financing the construction of the asset. FRS 15 does not accept this argument and acknowledges in the 'Development of the FRS' section that the inability to capitalise notional interest was one of the reasons for not requiring compulsory capitalisation of interest. A further reason for rejecting the argument is that SI 2008/410 refers to 'interest' and not to 'notional interest' and, therefore, capitalisation of notional interest would be contrary to the law. [SI 2008/410 1 Sch 27 (3)(b)].

16.124 Some groups of companies with little or no borrowing have subsidiaries that are engaged in constructing assets. In such circumstances, it is possible for the subsidiary to capitalise interest in its own financial statements on finance provided by another group company, even though at the consolidated financial statements level such intra-group interest must be eliminated, because the group as a whole has not incurred interest on those borrowings. But where another group member borrows externally and on lends to the construction subsidiary, any interest capitalised will remain on consolidation.

Tax on capitalised finance costs

16.125 FRS 15 requires that finance costs should be capitalised gross of tax. [FRS 15 para 21]. Whilst the argument for capitalising net of tax relief is based on the matching concept which suggests that the tax relief should be treated in the same way as the interest, the reason for gross capitalisation is that all other costs are capitalised gross, so there is no reason for interest capitalisation to be any different. As the costs are capitalised on a gross basis, a deferred tax liability should be set up where it fulfils the conditions in FRS 19, 'Deferred tax', in the particular circumstances of the entity and is released to the profit and loss account

16.131 Often it is easy to tell whether expenditure is capital or revenue in nature and, therefore, whether it should be capitalised or expensed. For example, the cost of adding a new wing to a hotel should be capitalised as the additional rooms increase the revenue earning capacity of the hotel. Similarly the cost of cleaning the hotel should be expensed as incurred, since it merely maintains the standard of the hotel.

16.132 However, sometimes it is difficult to distinguish whether expenditure on improvements and repairs should be capitalised or expensed, for example hotel room refurbishment. FRS 15 provides more guidance and rules in this area and introduces the concept of 'component depreciation' as explained below.

Accounting treatment

16.133 FRS 15 requires that, as a general rule, subsequent expenditure on a tangible fixed asset should be written off to the profit and loss account as incurred. Such expenditure is generally of a repairs and maintenance nature and does not improve the asset beyond the standard of performance previously expected of it. [FRS 15 para 34].

16.134 There are three exceptions to this general rule. In each of the following circumstances subsequent expenditure should be capitalised:

- Where the subsequent expenditure provides an enhancement of the economic benefits of the asset in excess of the previously assessed standard of performance.
- Where a component of a tangible asset that has been treated separately for depreciation purposes (see para 16.143 below), and depreciated over its individual useful economic life, is replaced or restored.
- Where the subsequent expenditure relates to a major inspection or overhaul of the tangible fixed asset that restores the economic benefits of the asset that have been used up by the entity and that have already been reflected in the depreciation charge.

[FRS 15 para 36].

Previously assessed standard of performance

16.135 The treatment of subsequent expenditure depends upon the previously assessed standard of performance expected from an asset and how that has been reflected in the depreciation of that asset.

16.136 Consider a new tangible fixed asset. Before the asset is depreciated, an assessment must be made of the standard of performance expected from it, in order to determine the appropriate useful economic life, residual value and depreciation method to use. In doing so, it will be expected that there will be certain costs associated with the asset in order to keep the asset in a good enough condition to achieve that expected level of performance, such as routine maintenance and repairs. Expenditure that merely maintains the expected performance levels expected from the asset is written off to the profit and loss account as it is incurred. For example, a head office may have a useful economic life of 25 years. However, in order to provide the level of performance expected from it, the company must repaint the property every five years. Such expenditure is expensed as incurred, since it maintains the expected condition of the property.

16.137 Other expenditure may enhance the economic benefits of an asset in excess of its expected standard of performance by:

- Increasing the capacity or capability of the asset.
- Extending the useful economic life of the asset.
- Improving the quality of the asset's output.
- Significantly reducing the operating costs of the asset.

16.138 Examples of subsequent expenditure that results in the enhancement of economic benefits given in FRS 15 are:

- Modification of an item of plant to extend its useful economic life or to increase its capacity.
- Upgrading machine parts to achieve a substantial improvement in the quality of output.

[FRS 15 para 37].

16.139 Subsequent expenditure that enhances the economic benefits of an asset beyond that previously expected of it should be capitalised as an addition to the cost of the asset. Sometimes expenditure will both maintain and enhance the asset. Only that element that enhances the asset should be capitalised.

16.140 Subsequent expenditure that enhances the economic benefits of an asset may also result in a revision to the useful economic life, residual value or depreciation method of the asset. For example, increasing the size of the memory of a PC may allow it to be used for a year longer than previously expected, in which case the cost of increasing the memory bank is capitalised and the useful economic life of the whole asset is extended by a year. Another example is the conversion of a store room at the back of a shop into more retail space. This increases the sales capacity of the shop and, therefore, the cost of the conversion is capitalised. It does not increase the useful economic life of the shop, but may increase its residual value. Other expenditure may enhance the economic benefits expected from the asset, but may not result in a revision to its useful economic life, residual value or depreciation method.

16.141 Other developments and new information, as well as subsequent expenditure, may give rise to a revision of the originally assessed standard of performance of an asset. This reassessment may result in a revision to the useful economic life, residual value or depreciation method of the asset, or an impairment of the asset's carrying amount. In such cases, the capitalisation of further expenditure should depend upon the revised assessment of the standard of performance of the asset.

16.142 For example, a company estimated that an automated plant would have a useful economic life of ten years when it was acquired. However, due to falling market demand for the product produced by the plant, its useful economic life and residual value were revised downwards, resulting in increased depreciation charges. A year later, the company paid for the plant to be reconfigured, so that it could be used to produce an alternative product with a longer useful economic life. As this expenditure enhanced the previously assessed useful economic life of the asset, it should be capitalised and the useful economic life of the asset revised. If, however, the plant was modified at the point at which it was realised that the existing product had a shorter life than previously expected and, therefore, the useful economic life and residual value of the plant was not revised, then the costs of modifying the machine would be expensed as incurred as they merely maintained the standard of performance expected from the asset.

Replacing components

16.143 An asset may consist of several different physical components. FRS 15 states that, if a tangible fixed asset comprises two or more major components, with substantially different useful economic lives, then each component should be treated separately for depreciation purposes (that is, as if each component was a separate asset in its own right) and depreciated over its individual useful economic life. [FRS 15 para 83]. It follows, therefore, that when a component is replaced or restored, the old component is written off, to avoid double counting, and the new component capitalised.

16.144 An example of a component of an asset that might have a different life from the rest of the asset, and thus might be depreciated separately, is the lift or escalator within a head office. Another example is given in Table 16.5 below.

Table 16.5 – James Fisher and Sons PUBLIC LIMITED COMPANY – Annual Report and Financial Statements – 31 December 1998

1. Accounting policies (extract)

A summary of the more important accounting policies which have been applied consistently, throughout the year and the preceding year, with the exception explained in note 28, is set out below.

Tangible fixed assets
Tangible fixed assets are stated at cost, net of depreciation and any provision for impairment.

The inherent refit element in cost of ships is shown separately and is amortised over 30 months. Subsequent refit costs are capitalised and amortised over the 30 month period.

Depreciation is provided to write-off the cost of tangible fixed assets in annual instalments over their estimated useful lives. The principal rates used are:

Ships:	
owned	4% to 10%
under period charter	Over life of charter
Freehold property	2.5%
Leasehold property	
long term	2.5%
short term	Over the period of lease
Plant and equipment	5% to 20%

No depreciation is charged on assets under construction.

The calculation of depreciation on owned ships takes into account their estimated residual value.

Refit costs

For vessels held by the group under operating leases, where there is a contractual obligation to maintain the ships, provision is made on a straight line basis as the vessels are used, towards the future cost of refits to the end of the lease. The provision is utilised as expenditure is incurred.

For vessels owned by the group, and for which the group is responsible for maintenance, the accounting policy is detailed within the tangible fixed assets accounting policy earlier.

16. Tangible fixed assets

	Analysis of ships		Total Ships	Assets under construction	Freehold & leasehold property	Plant & equipment	Total
	ships	Refit					
	£000	£000	£000	£000	£000	£000	£000
GROUP							
Cost:							
At 1 January 1998	79,956	–	79,956	26,991	3,364	4,533	114,844
Prior year adjustment (note 28)	(2,224)	2,911	687	–	–	–	687
At 1 January 1998 as restated	77,732	2,911	80,643	26,991	3,364	4,533	115,531
Additions	6,336	1,947	8,283	5,009	3	290	13,585
Acquisition of subsidiary undertaking	–	–	–	–	336	580	916
Transfer	31,421	460	31,881	(31,881)	–	–	–
Disposals	(27)	–	(27)	–	(1,289)	(1,159)	(2,475)
At 31 December 1998	**115,462**	**5,318**	**120,780**	**119**	**2,414**	**4,244**	**127,557**
Depreciation:							
At 1 January 1998	16,780	–	16,780	–	2,567	2,839	22,186
Prior year adjustment (note 28)	(234)	1,219	985	–	–	–	985
At 1 January 1998 as restated	16,546	1,219	17,765	–	2,567	2,839	23,171
Provided during the year	5,551	1,307	6,858	–	34	475	7,367
Disposals	(27)	–	(27)	–	(745)	(1,011)	(1,783)
At 31 December 1998	**22,070**	**2,526**	**24,596**	–	**1,856**	**2,303**	**28,755**

Net book value:							
At 31 December 1997 as restated	61,186	1,692	62,878	26,991	797	1,694	92,360
At 31 December 1998	**93,392**	**2,792**	**96,184**	**119**	**558**	**1,941**	**98,802**

Included in ships are assets with a cost of £567,000 (1997 £554,000) and accumulated depreciation of £189,000 (1997 £94,000) which are held for use in operating leases. Included in tangible fixed assets is aggregate interest capitalised of £2,612,000 (1997 £1,924,000).

16.145 This approach was primarily adopted in response to FRS 12, 'Provisions, contingent liabilities and contingent assets'. The argument in that FRS revolved around the question of whether future maintenance constitutes a liability of the entity. The FRS concluded that even where there will in due course be a legal or constructive obligation the appropriate accounting treatment is to recognise depreciation to take account of the actual consumption of the asset's economic benefits. Thus, for example, where a separate component of an asset wears out more quickly than the rest, it is depreciated over a shorter period and subsequent expenditure on restoring the component is then capitalised. This replaces the previous general practice of depreciating such components over the same period as the rest of the asset, but providing in advance for the maintenance/replacement of the component.

16.146 Where the depreciation of an asset does not allow for the wearing out of a component of the asset, subsequent expenditure that restores or replaces a component is recognised in the profit and loss account as incurred. This approach, however, results in a lumpy charge to the profit and loss account and does not match the expense of replacing a component with the benefit of the use of that component.

Example – Depreciating components of an asset

A small manufacturing company has recently acquired a new factory, which cost £1m for the freehold and has a residual value of £100,000. This factory has a flat roof which needs replacing every ten years at a cost of £100,000. Before FRS 12, the company would have depreciated the whole factory over its estimated useful economic life of 30 years on a straight line basis, charging the profit and loss account £30,000 depreciation per annum. In addition, for the first 20 years it would have provided for £10,000 every year, which would be utilised in years 10 and 20 for the cost of the replacement roof.

However, in accordance with FRS 12, the company may not provide for the cost of replacing the roof. The company, therefore, has two choices:

- To depreciate the whole factory over its useful economic life of 30 years, charging £30,000 per annum and to write off the £100,000 cost of replacing the roof to the profit and loss account as incurred, in years 10 and 20.
- To depreciate the cost of the roof of £100,000 over 10 years, giving a depreciation charge of £10,000 per annum and to depreciate the remainder of the factory of £900,000 down to its residual value of £100,000 over 30 years, giving a depreciation charge of £26,667. In year 10, when the roof is replaced,

the original, fully written down roof is written off and the cost of the new roof is capitalised and depreciated over its useful economic life of 10 years.

The second approach more accurately reflects the company's consumption of economic benefits of the factory, resulting in an even charge to the profit and loss account of £36,667 per annum, over the 30 years of the useful economic life of the factory.

16.147 Whether to identify separate components of an asset in this way will be a matter of judgement and will depend on:

- The degree of irregularity in the replacement expenditure required.
- The materiality of the component.
- The materiality of the effect of separately depreciating the component.
- Whether the useful economic life of the component is substantially different from that of the rest of the asset.

16.148 In practice, a commonsense approach should be applied, so that separate components will only be identified where there is a material impact on the profit and loss account. For example, it is unlikely that an entity with a large number of properties would separately depreciate the roofs of each property, since the cost of replacing the roofs results in a similar size charge to the profit and loss account each year. However, an entity with just one major property may depreciate the roof of that property separately, as otherwise the cost of replacing the roof would distort the profit and loss account when it was incurred.

16.149 Where components of an asset have been separately identified, the components need not be disclosed separately in the fixed asset table in the notes to the financial statements as they do not constitute separate classes of assets.

Major inspections and overhauls

16.150 Sometimes a tangible fixed asset may require periodic major inspections or overhauls. The FRS applies a similar 'component' approach to major inspection and overhaul costs, even though the cost of a major inspection or overhaul is not a physical component of an asset.

16.151 An aircraft, for example, may be required by law to be overhauled every three years. In such a case the FRS permits a proportion of the cost of the asset equivalent to the expected overhaul cost to be depreciated over the period to the next overhaul. If this is done the actual cost of the overhaul or inspection is then capitalised (because it restores the economic benefits, usage of which has been reflected in depreciation). This overhaul cost is then depreciated over the period to the next overhaul. The cost and depreciation attributed to the overhaul originally is removed from the balance sheet once the cost of the new overhaul has been capitalised to avoid double counting. [FRS 15 para 39]. The remainder of the asset is depreciated over the full useful economic life of the asset, on the basis that the appropriate overhauls will be carried out as they are due. As shown in Table 16.6 PowerGen plc adopted this approach in their 1998 financial statements.

Table 16.6 – PowerGen plc – Report – Nine months ended 31 December 1998

Principal Accounting Policies (extract)

Overhaul of generation plant

Prior to the adoption of Financial Reporting Standard 12 'Provisions, Contingent Liabilities and Contingent Assets' from 30 March 1998, charges were made annually against profits to provide for the accrued proportion of the estimated costs of the cyclical programme for the major overhaul and maintenance of generation plant. Since that date overhaul costs have been capitalised as part of generating assets and depreciated on a straight-line basis over their estimated useful life, typically the period until the next major overhaul. That period is usually between four and six years. As a result of this change in accounting policy, prior year figures have been restated (see note 4).

Notes to the Accounts (extract)
for the financial period ended 3 January 1999

4 Prior year adjustment

Financial Reporting Standard 12 'Provisions, Contingent Liabilities and Contingent Assets' (FRS 12) was adopted from 30 March 1998. This has necessitated adjustment to provisions made in prior periods, principally relating to major overhaul and decommissioning of generation plant.

Prior to the adoption of FRS 12 charges were made annually against profits to provide for the accrued proportion of the estimated costs of the cyclical programme for the major overhaul and maintenance of generation plant. Since that date overhaul costs have been capitalised as part of generating assets and depreciated on a straight-line basis over the period until the next major overhaul. That period is usually between four and six years. As a result of this change in accounting policy, prior year figures have been restated.

In addition, a fixed asset has been recognised in respect of the estimated total discounted cost of decommissioning which is being depreciated over the remaining useful economic life of the associated power stations. The provision for decommissioning has also been increased to reflect the estimated total discounted cost. Prior year figures have been restated.

16.152 The decision to adopt this approach to overhaul expenditure may depend on:

- Whether the period until the next overhaul is substantially different from the useful economic life of the rest of the asset.
- The degree of irregularity in the level of expenditure on overhauls.
- The materiality of the expenditure in the context of the financial statements.

16.153 Where the 'separate components' method has not been adopted or part of the asset is not depreciated over a shorter timescale to allow for major overhaul expenditure as described above, the cost of replacements or overhauls should be charged to the profit and loss account as incurred. [FRS 15 para 41]. This is the approach adopted by BAA plc, as shown in Table 16.7.

Table 16.7 – BAA plc – Annual report – 31 March 1999

Accounting policies (extract)

3 Depreciation

Depreciation is provided on operational assets, other than land, to write off the cost of the assets by equal instalments over their expected useful lives as set out in the table below.

Fixed asset lives	
Terminal building, pier and satellite structures	50 years
Terminal fixtures and fittings	5 – 20 years
Airport plant and equipment:	
Baggage systems	15 years
Screening equipment	7 years
Other plant and equipment including runway lighting and building plant	5 – 20 years
Tunnels, bridges and subways	100 years
Runways, taxiways and aprons	up to 100 years
Airport transit systems:	
Rolling stock	20 years
Track	50 years
Railways:	
Rolling stock	30 years
Tunnels	100 years
Track	10 – 50 years
Signals and electrification work	40 years
Motor vehicles	4 – 8 years
Office equipment	5 – 10 years
Computer equipment	4 – 5 years
Computer software	3 – 7 years
Short leasehold properties	Over period of lease

Major periodic maintenance expenditure on runways, taxiways and aprons is charged to the profit and loss account as incurred except where the expenditure represents an asset improvement when the cost is capitalised and written off over the asset's estimated useful economic life.

Revaluing tangible fixed assets

Introduction

16.154 Having acquired or constructed a tangible fixed asset and recorded it in the books at cost, an entity can choose whether to subsequently revalue that asset.

16.155 The alternative accounting rules in Schedule 1 to the SI 2008/410 permit replacing the historical cost of a tangible fixed asset with a market value (as at the date of its last valuation) or its current cost. [SI 2008/410 1 Sch 32(2)]. Legally, companies may adopt all or any or none of the alternative accounting rules. So, for example, a company could include some of its plant and machinery in its balance sheet at current cost and include every other item on an historical cost basis. However, although it might appear reasonable for a company to include certain assets at a valuation, if it mixed the historical cost rules and the alternative accounting rules indiscriminately it might produce meaningless financial statements.

16.156 Whilst FRS 15 continues to permit the optional adoption of a policy of revaluation, it tightens up the application of the alternative accounting rules to tangible fixed assets by setting out the conditions that apply when determining:

- Which tangible fixed assets (if any) should be revalued.
- When those assets should be revalued.
- The valuation basis to be used.

16.157 To prevent 'cherry picking' of which assets are revalued and when, the FRS requires that, if a policy of revaluation is adopted, it must be applied to all assets within an individual class of assets, and the valuations must be kept up-to-date at current values. [FRS 15 paras 42, 43]. These aspects are considered in more detail below.

Class of assets

16.158 When an entity values its assets in accordance with the alternative accounting rules in SI 2008/410 it must value each asset separately, in order to comply with the separate valuation principle contained in paragraph 15 of Schedule 1. However, FRS 15 requires that if a single tangible fixed asset is revalued, then all the fixed assets of the same class should also be revalued, although the policy need not be applied to all classes of tangible fixed assets. [FRS 15 para 42]. This reduces the scope for picking out individual assets for revaluation, just because they happen to have significantly increased in value. However, this requirement means that adopting a policy of revaluation may be more onerous and involve more complex record keeping than before.

16.159 There is an exception to this general rule, however, which is that where an asset held outside the UK or Republic of Ireland cannot be revalued, it may be excluded from the class of assets to be revalued. This is expected to be rare in practice, although in certain parts of the world, assets (in particular properties) cannot be valued for a variety of reasons. For example, there may not be any suitably qualified valuers in a particular location, or there may be government controls over property ownership so that it is impossible to put a value on an asset. The existence of such a constraint does not prevent all the other assets in its class from being revalued. However, in such cases the carrying amount of the tangible fixed asset that has not been revalued and the fact that it has not been revalued must be disclosed. [FRS 15 para 61].

16.160 SI 2008/410 already defines quite broad categories or classes of assets, as follows:

- Land and buildings.
- Plant and machinery.
- Fixtures, fittings, tools and equipment.
- Payments on account and assets in the course of construction.

[SI 2008/410 1 Sch Part 1 Sec B].

16.161 However, for valuation purposes, an entity may adopt other, narrower, classes of assets, provided that they meet the following definition:

> *"A category of tangible fixed assets having a similar nature, function or use in the business of the entity."* [FRS 15 para 2].

16.162 Other than ruling out classes of assets determined on a geographical basis, this definition is reasonably flexible, so that an entity can adopt meaningful classes that are appropriate to the type of business and assets held by an entity. However, when determining which classes of assets to adopt, it is worth bearing in mind that separate disclosures must be made for each class of assets. For example, as noted from paragraph 16.309, each class of assets must be presented as a separate category in the table of movements in tangible fixed assets in the notes to the financial statements. [FRS 15 para 100]. In practice, this effectively prevents the adoption of many narrowly defined classes of assets.

16.163 Although property is often revalued, a class of assets for revaluation need not be confined to property. For example, Associated British Ports Holdings PLC revalues operational land, but holds other operating tangible fixed assets, such as buildings, dock structures and plant and equipment at historical cost, as can be seen in Table 16.8. Other examples of classes of assets include:

- All retail properties.
- Specialised or non-specialised properties.
- Short or long leasehold, or freehold properties.
- Art and antiques

Table 16.8 – Associated British Ports Holdings PLC – Annual Report & accounts – 31 December 2001

1 Accounting policies (extract)

Basis of preparation (extract)

The financial statements have been prepared on a going concern basis in accordance with applicable accounting standards and under the historical cost convention as modified by the revaluation of operational land, investment properties, land at ports held for development and investments in subsidiary and associated companies.

Frequency of revaluations

16.164 One of the requirements of FRS 15 is that valuations should remain up-to-date, as old valuations that do not reflect current values are meaningless. However, FRS 15 does not require valuations to be performed every year. Indeed to do so would be rather onerous, particularly if values have not materially changed from one year to the next. The specific requirements in respect of properties and other tangible fixed assets are set out from paragraph 16.169 below, although the FRS acknowledges that for cost-benefit reasons, charities and other not-for-profit organisations may adopt alternative approaches. Of course, other entities may undertake more rigorous valuation procedures than recommended in the standard, should they believe it appropriate to do so.

Qualified valuers

16.165 The guidance in FRS 15 is also concerned with the reliability of the valuations and, therefore, specifies the involvement of qualified valuers and whether and when they should be external to the entity.

16.166 A qualified valuer is a person who:

- Holds a recognised and relevant professional qualification.
- Has recent relevant post-qualification experience.
- Has sufficient knowledge of the state of the market in the location and category of the tangible fixed asset being valued.

[FRS 15 para 2].

16.167 In the UK a qualified valuer would usually be a member of the Royal Institution of Chartered Surveyors (RICS). As well as valuing properties, some members specialise in the valuation of plant and machinery and fine art and antiques. However, the above definition of a qualified valuer does not preclude non-RICS members from carrying out valuations where appropriate.

16.168 An internal valuer is defined as being a director, officer or employee of the entity. In contrast, an external valuer cannot be a director, officer or an employee of the entity, nor have a significant financial interest in the entity. [FRS 15 para 2].

Properties

16.169 The guidance in FRS 15 states that for each property subject to a policy of revaluation:

- A full valuation should be performed at least every five years.
- An interim valuation should be carried out in the third year after the full valuation.
- Interim valuations should be carried out in the intervening years only where it is likely that there has been a material change in value.

[FRS 15 para 45].

16.170 However, for portfolios of non-specialised properties, the need for an interim valuation in the third year after the full valuation, regardless of whether it is likely that there has been a material change in value, is dispensed with, provided that:

- A full valuation is performed on a rolling basis designed to cover all the properties over a five-year (or more frequent) cycle.
- An interim valuation is carried out on the remaining four-fifths of the portfolio where it is likely that there is a material change in value.
- The portfolio either consists of a broadly similar range of properties, which are likely to be affected by the same market factors, or can be divided on a continuing basis into five groups of a broadly similar spread.

[FRS 15 para 46].

16.171 FRS 15 summarises the main requirements of the RICS's Appraisal and Valuation Standards regarding the basic procedures to be carried out in respect of full and interim valuations, although ultimately the exact work needed will depend upon the individual circumstances and be down to the professional judgement of the valuer. [FRS 15 paras 47, 49].

16.172 FRS 15 states that for all properties being revalued:

- The five yearly full valuation should be performed by either:
  - a qualified external valuer, or
  - a qualified internal valuer, provided that the valuation performed by the internal valuer has been appropriately reviewed by a qualified external valuer. In the case of properties, such a review should involve the valuation of a sample of the properties, so that the external valuer

can give an opinion on the overall accuracy of the valuations performed.

- Interim valuations should be performed by a qualified valuer, who may be either internal or external to the entity.

[FRS 15 paras 48, 49].

Other tangible fixed assets

16.173 For tangible fixed assets other than properties (for example, plant and machinery, vehicles, art and antiques), where a policy of valuation is adopted, a qualified internal or external valuer is required to perform:

- A valuation at least every five years, which should be subject to review by a qualified external valuer if performed by an internal valuer.
- An update of the valuation three years after the original valuation.
- Further updates of the valuation in intervening years if it is likely that there has been a material change in value.

[FRS 15 para 50].

16.174 There is an exception to this general rule, however. In particular circumstances, the FRS acknowledges that the directors may be able to establish an asset's value with reasonable reliability, without going to the length of using a qualified valuer. Therefore, where there is an active market or appropriate indices for the assets concerned (such as in second hand cars), the valuation may instead be performed by the directors. In such cases, the directors should revalue the asset on an annual basis. [FRS 15 para 50]. Where the directors use an index it should be appropriate to the class of asset, to its location and condition and should take account of technological change. The index should have a proven record of regular publication and be expected to continue to be available in the foreseeable future. [FRS 15 para 51].

Material changes in value

16.175 The need for interim valuations in intervening years often relies upon an assessment of whether it is likely that there has been a material change in value. This is to avoid the need for unnecessary valuations each year when it is obvious that there has been no material change in value, but should ensure that material changes, when they occur, are reflected in the balance sheet.

16.176 FRS 15 states that a material change in value is one that *"would reasonably influence the decisions of a user of the accounts"*. [FRS 15 para 52]. It is a matter of judgement, which is ultimately the responsibility of the directors. However, in making that judgement, the directors would probably consult their valuers and consider, amongst other things, factors such as changes in the general market, the condition of the asset, changes to the asset and its location. In coming to their decision, the directors should consider the combined effect of all the relevant factors, as it is possible that the effect of one factor may be offset by other factors.

Bases of valuation

16.177 The Act specifies that tangible fixed assets may be included in the balance sheet at a market value determined as at the date of their last valuation or at current cost. However, it does not define current cost, nor does it give further details about the bases to be used to determine market value. FRS 15, however, gives more definitive requirements in respect of the valuation bases to be used.

16.178 The general requirement in FRS 15 is that tangible fixed assets subject to a policy of revaluation should be carried at current value. [FRS 15 para 43]. Current value is defined in FRS 15 as the lower of replacement cost and recoverable amount, where, as set out in FRS 11 'Impairment of fixed assets and goodwill', recoverable amount is the higher of net realisable value and value in use. [FRS 15 para 2; FRS 11 para 2]. This is illustrated diagrammatically below.

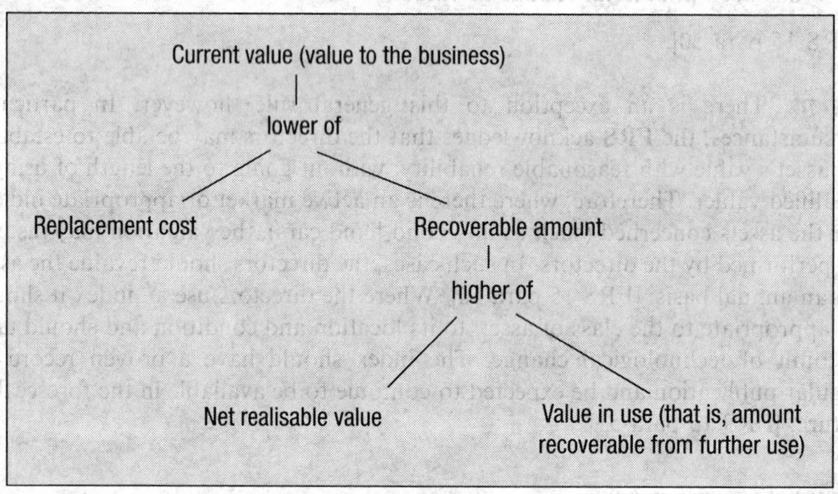

16.179 This definition of current value is based on the value to the business model. Under this model, the value of an asset to a business is the most relevant value when making economic decisions, that is, it is the loss that the entity would suffer if it were deprived of that asset.

16.179.1 The value to the business model is not used under IFRS, which also permits an entity to adopt a policy of revaluation. Under IAS 16, if a policy of revaluation is adopted, the basis of valuation used is 'fair value'. Fair value under IFRS is much the same as 'open market value' and is defined in IAS 16 as "*...the amount for which an asset could be exchanged between knowledgeable, willing parties in an arm's length transaction*". The effect of this difference in approach is that properties used in the business would be valued under IFRS at fair value (that is, open market value), whereas under FRS 15 existing use value would be used (see para 16.185 below). An important practical effect of the difference is where OMV is higher than EUV because, for example, it reflects the possibility of the property being developed for an alternative use. FRS 15 would not permit the higher value for alternative use to be reflected in an entity's balance sheet if the property were being used in the business, although it would require information about the higher OMV to be disclosed in the notes.

[The next paragraph is 16.180.]

16.180 A profit-making entity would only invest in an asset (or project) if it expected that the asset (or project) would generate profitable returns – in other words, if the asset's recoverable amount exceeded its cost of investment. If deprived of the asset in such circumstances then, from an economic view point, the entity would choose to replace it as this generates the most profitable return. Hence, the current value of the asset is its current replacement cost.

16.181 If, on the other hand, the cost of replacing the asset exceeds its recoverable amount (that is, the value of the asset in its most profitable use), then the entity would not replace that asset if deprived of it. Instead the asset's current value to the entity is its recoverable amount (that is, the greatest value obtainable from either continuing to use the asset or selling it).

16.182 Most of the time tangible fixed assets are used in profitable businesses and, therefore, replacement cost is usually the relevant measure of value to the business. In any event, FRS 11, 'Impairment of fixed assets and goodwill', requires an asset to be written down to its recoverable amount where the asset is impaired and recoverable amount falls below replacement cost. FRS 15, therefore, directs entities to use replacement cost when revaluing a tangible fixed asset, except where the asset is impaired, in which case FRS 11 should be followed.

16.183 As noted in FRS 15, a revalued asset should be recorded at the lower of its revalued amount (determined as set out in paras 16.185 and 16.189 below) and recoverable amount. Because recoverable amount is the higher of net realisable value and value in use, where the revalued amount of the asset is not materially different from its net realisable value, any further consideration of impairment is not generally necessary. [FRS 15 para 54].

16.184 FRS 15 specifies the valuation bases that provide the best approximation to replacement cost in the different circumstances. These valuation bases are defined by the Royal Institution of Chartered Surveyors (RICS) and are described in greater detail below from paragraph 16.190 onwards. The RICS publishes the RICS Appraisal and Valuation Standards, which include Practice Statements (PSs) and Guidance Notes that apply to valuations for incorporation in company financial statements and other financial statements that are subject to audit which should be applied. It should be noted that since the publication of FRS 15, The RICS definition of 'open market value' has been discarded and replaced by 'market value'. Appendix 1 of FRS 15 contains the RICS definition of open market value extant at the date of publication of the standard and we consider this should be applied.

Tangible fixed assets used in the business

16.185 For tangible fixed assets that are not surplus to an entity's requirements, FRS 15 requires that:

- Non-specialised properties are valued on the existing use value basis with the addition of notional directly attributable acquisition costs where material. Where the open market value differs materially from existing use value, the open market value and the reasons for the difference should be disclosed.
- Specialised properties are valued on the depreciated replacement cost basis.
- Tangible fixed assets other than properties are valued using market value, where possible. Material notional directly attributable acquisition costs should be added. If market value is not obtainable, assets should be valued on the basis of depreciated replacement cost, with the assistance of a qualified valuer.

[FRS 15 paras 53, 59, 60].

16.186 Specialised properties are defined in the RICS Appraisal and Valuation Standards as those properties that, because of their specialised nature, are rarely, if ever, sold in the market, except by way of a sale of the business or entity of which it is part, due to uniqueness arising from its specialised nature and design, its configuration, size, location or otherwise. See from paragraph 16.197 for greater detail. All other properties (that is, the majority of properties) are, therefore, non-specialised properties.

16.187 Notionally directly attributable acquisition costs are not included in market value or existing use value as defined by the RICS. However, they are added to the valuation where material, because they form part of the cost to the entity of replacing the asset. Notionally directly attributable acquisition costs include normal dealing costs such as professional fees, non-recoverable taxes and duties. They do not include costs incurred to enhance site value, such as site improvements, costs of obtaining planning permission, site clearance and preparation or other costs already included in the existing use value. [FRS 15 para 55]. In practice, notionally directly attributable acquisition costs are often not material and are, therefore, ignored. However, where they are included in the carrying amount of a revalued asset, their total amount must be separately disclosed. [FRS 15 para 74].

16.188 Some entities make structural changes to their properties or include special fittings within the properties (for example, shop or bank facias). These changes are referred to as adaptation works, which may have a low market value, because they are particular to the present owner. In such cases, the adaptation works and the shell of the building may be treated as separate components with only the shell of the building being revalued on the existing use basis. The adaptation works are then held at depreciated replacement cost (if revalued) or at depreciated historical cost, if not revalued. [FRS 15 para 57].

Tangible fixed assets surplus to requirements

16.189 Tangible fixed assets surplus to requirements would not be replaced by an entity and, therefore, replacement cost is irrelevant in these circumstances. Instead the current value of such assets to the business is their net realisable value. This is determined as follows:

- Properties surplus to an entity's requirements are valued on the open market value basis, with expected directly attributable selling costs deducted where material.

- Tangible fixed assets other than properties that are surplus to requirements are valued using market value, or depreciated replacement cost if market value is not available, with expected selling costs deducted if material.

[FRS 15 paras 53, 60].

Open market value

16.190 Open market value, not qualified by any reference to existing use or alternative use, implies the value for *any* use to the extent to which that value is reflected in the price obtainable in the open market.

16.191 Open market value means the best price at which the sale of an interest in property would have been completed unconditionally for cash at the valuation date assuming:

- A willing seller.
- A reasonable period, prior to the date of valuation, for the proper marketing of the interest, for agreement of price and terms and for the completion of the sale.
- That the state of the market, level of values and other circumstances were, on any earlier assumed date of exchange of contracts, the same as on the date of valuation.
- That no account is taken of any additional bid by a prospective purchaser with a special interest.
- That both parties to the transaction had acted knowledgeably, prudently and without compulsion.

[FRS 15, App I].

16.192 Open market value is the only basis of valuation that is appropriate for investment properties and properties that are surplus to a company's requirements.

Existing use value

16.193 The existing use value has a similar definition to that in paragraph 16.191, but additionally reflects the use of the property for the same or similar purposes as hitherto and assumes vacant possession on completion. It ignores any alternative use for the property, any 'hope value' for an alternative use, any value attributable to goodwill and any other possible increase in value due to special transactions, such as a sale and leaseback. This basis should be used for all non-specialised owner occupied properties (except those that are surplus to requirements), as it reflects the cost that the entity would suffer if it were to replace the tangible fixed asset with another, equivalent asset for the same use. An example of its use is given in Table 16.9.

Table 16.9 – Kingfisher plc – Annual Report and Accounts – 29 January 2000

Notes to the accounts (extract)

Tangible fixed assets (extract)

During each of the last five years a representative sample of the freehold and long leasehold properties owned by Chartwell Land plc, the Group's property subsidiary, have been valued by external qualified valuers. CB Hillier Parker, has carried out a valuation of a representative sample as at 31 December 1999 and based upon the results of these valuations there have been internal valuations by qualified valuers employed by the Group of the remainder of Chartwell Land's portfolio.

Properties with any element of Group occupancy are valued on an existing use basis which does not take account of formal lease arrangements with Group companies or the Group's occupation of the premises. Properties without Group occupancy are valued on the basis of open market value. These valuation bases comply with the RICS Appraisal and Valuation Manual.

16.194 An example of the distinction between the open market value (unqualified) basis and the existing use value basis is where a company operates a factory on the outskirts of a town. The site on which it operates might have a considerably increased value if it were to be sold for redevelopment. In such a case, the financial statements of the company should reflect any valuation on an existing use value basis, because it is intending to continue to operate the site as a factory and the additional value that could be obtained from closing the factory and selling the site for redevelopment should not be reflected in the valuation. However, as mentioned in paragraph 16.185, the company must disclose the open market value in the notes to the financial statements and explain the reasons for the difference. (See also para 16.179.1 above regarding the difference between FRS 15 and IAS 16 in this situation.)

16.195 Certain types of non-specialised property that are equipped as operational entities in their own right are valued with regard to trading potential. Existing use value that is determined on this basis includes the value of the trading potential that runs with the property, but should not include any goodwill that has been created by the owner, which would not remain with the property should it be sold. This basis applies to land and buildings that invariably change hands in the open market at prices based directly on trading potential for a strictly limited use. [FRS 15 para 56].

16.196 Examples of such properties include hotels, private hospitals and nursing homes, public houses, cinemas, theatres, bingo clubs, gaming clubs, petrol filling stations, licensed betting offices and specialised leisure and sporting facilities.

Depreciated replacement cost

16.197 The depreciated replacement cost (DRC) basis of valuation is used for specialised properties, as there is no means of ascertaining a market value for such properties. As noted in paragraph 16.186, such properties are rarely, if ever sold in the market, except by way of a sale of the business or entity of which it is part.

16.198 Such specialised properties might include:

- Oil refineries and chemical works where, usually, the buildings are no more than housings or claddings for highly specialised plant.
- Power stations and dock installations.
- Properties of such construction, arrangement, size or specification that there would be no market (for sale to a single owner occupier for continuation of existing use) for the properties.
- Standard properties of abnormal size in particular geographic areas that are isolated or remote from main business centres and which are located there for business or operational reasons, such that there is no market there for the properties.
- Schools, colleges and research establishments where there is no market for such properties from other competing organisations in the area.
- Hospitals, health centres and leisure centres where there is no competing market demand in the area.
- Museums, libraries and other similar public sector properties.

16.199 For a property, calculating DRC involves estimating the value of land in its existing use and the gross replacement cost of buildings and other site works. From this appropriate deductions ('depreciation') are made to allow for age, condition and economic or functional obsolescence and other factors which might result in the existing property being worth less than a new replacement. DRC is often calculated by applying relevant indices to both cost and depreciation.

16.200 Because of the nature of DRC valuations a valuer will qualify all valuations on this basis as being subject to the adequate potential profitability of the business compared with the value of the total assets employed. However, for properties in public ownership, or not occupied primarily for profit, where the test of adequate potential profitability is not available, DRC is expressed as subject to the prospect and viability of the continuance of the occupation and use.

Value of plant and machinery to the business

16.201 Where plant and machinery is valued the valuation is the price at which the plant and machinery could have been transferred at the valuation date assuming:

- Continuation of the present uses in the business.
- Adequate potential profitability of the business, or continued viability of the undertaking, having regard to the value of total assets employed and to the nature of the operation.
- Transfer of the plant and machinery is part of an arm's length sale of the business wherein both parties acted knowledgeably, prudently and without compulsion.

[FRS 15, App I].

16.202 Where suitable market evidence is not available, plant and machinery and other non-property tangible fixed assets are normally valued on a DRC basis. Therefore, the cost of replacing an existing asset with an identical or substantially similar new asset having similar production or service capacity is depreciated to reflect the value attributable to the remaining portion of the total useful economic life of the asset. In assessing the DRC of an asset, account should be taken of the age, condition, economic and functional obsolescence and environmental and other factors, including residual value at the end of the asset's useful economic life.

16.203 In practice, the actual determination of value will depend upon the individual circumstances and evidence available. Table 16.10 shows the valuation methods used by BG plc.

Table 16.10– BG plc – Annual Report and Accounts – 31 December 1998

Principal accounting policies (extract)

Accounting principles (extract)
These accounts have been prepared in accordance with applicable accounting standards, under modified historical cost principles. Under these principles the Group values regulatory assets at depreciated replacement cost (see Tangible fixed assets below) or, where lower, the estimated value in use (see Impairment of regulatory fixed assets below). Regulatory assets are those assets which are included in that part of the asset base which is subject to a regulatory regime. Revalued assets include operational land and buildings, mains, services, meters, storage and other plant and machinery in Great Britain.

Tangible fixed assets (extract)
Regulatory tangible fixed assets in Great Britain are included in the balance sheet at depreciated replacement cost or, where lower, the estimated value in use (see Impairment of regulatory fixed assets below). Investment properties are carried at valuation. All other categories of tangible fixed assets are carried at depreciated historical cost.

a) Modified historical cost
i) land and buildings – Great Britain regulatory assets – based upon periodic valuation by chartered surveyors employed by the Group, determined on the basis of open market value for existing use; land and buildings – investment properties – based upon periodic valuation by chartered surveyors employed by the Group, determined on the basis of open market value. Valuations take into account estimated non-statutory decontamination costs;
land and buildings – other – based upon historical cost;
ii) distribution mains, services and meters – Great Britain regulatory assets – based upon application of calculated average unit replacement costs to the physical lengths or quantities in use; distribution mains, services and meters – other – based upon historical cost;
iii) transmission mains, plant and machinery, and gas storage – Great Britain regulatory assets – based upon engineering assessments of the cost of replacing existing assets; transmission mains, plant and machinery and gas storage – other – based on historical cost;
iv) exploration and production tangible fixed assets – based upon historical cost; and
v) other tangible fixed assets – Great Britain regulatory assets – based upon indexation of historical cost using appropriate indices;
other tangible fixed assets – other – based upon historical cost.

Disclosures

16.204 The RICS Appraisal and Standards set out in Practise Statement 5 (PS 5) minimum disclosures that should be made in a published document, such as a company's financial statements that make reference to a valuers report. The disclosure requirements of FRS 15 broadly encompass and expand on those laid down by the RICS and those of SI 2008/410, but should be given for each class of revalued assets. In addition to the disclosure requirements mentioned in paragraphs 16.159 and 16.185 above, the disclosure requirements in respect of valuations are:

- The name and qualification of the valuer or the valuer's organisation and a description of its nature. [FRS 15 para 74; SI 2008/410 1 Sch 52; PS 5.11].
- Whether the valuer is internal or external. [FRS 15 para 74; PS 5.11].
- The date of the valuation. [FRS 15 para 74; SI 2008/410 1 Sch 52; PS 5.11].
- The amounts of the valuation. [FRS 15 para 74; SI 2008/410 1 Sch 52].
- The basis or bases of valuation (including whether notional acquisition costs have been included or expected selling costs deducted). [FRS 15 para 74; SI 2008/410 1 Sch 34, 52]. The RICS Appraisal and Valuation Standards require the valuation basis together with any special assumptions made. [PS 5.11].
- For revalued properties, the total amount of notional directly attributable acquisition costs included (or the total amount of expected selling costs deducted), where material. [FRS 15 para 74].

- Where properties have been valued as fully equipped operational entities and having regard to their trading potential, a statement to that effect and the carrying amount of the properties (see para 16.195 above). [FRS 15 para 74].

- Comment on the extent to which the values were determined directly by reference to market evidence or were estimated using other valuation techniques. [PS 5.11].

- Where appropriate, confirmation that the valuation has been made in accordance with the RICS Appraisal and Valuation Standards, or the extent of and reasons for departure from those standards. [PS 5.11].

- Where the directors are not aware of any material change in value and, therefore, the valuation has not been updated by an interim valuation as specified from paragraph 16.164 above, a statement to that effect. [FRS 15 para 74].

- Where the valuation has not been updated, or is not a full valuation, the date of the last full valuation. [FRS 15 para 74].

- Where historical cost records are available, the net carrying amount that would have been shown under the historical cost method less depreciation (see also from para 16.206 below). [FRS 15 para 74; SI 2008/410 1 Sch 34(3)].

16.205 The RICS Appraisal and Valuation Standards include useful examples of disclosures in Appendix 5.2 to the Practice Statements. One example is as follows:

"The company's freehold and leasehold properties were valued on 31 December 2004 by an External Valuer, Joe Smith, FRICS of Alpha, Chartered Surveyors. The valuations were in accordance with the requirements of the RICS Appraisal and Valuation Standards and FRS 15. The valuation of each property was on the following bases and assumptions:

(i) For owner occupied property: Valued to Existing Use Value (EUV) assuming that the property would be sold as part of the continuing business.

(ii) For investment property: Valued to Market Value assuming that the property would be sold subject to any existing leases.

(iii) For surplus property and property held for development: Valued to Market Value assuming that the property would be sold with vacant possession in its existing condition."

Actual examples of disclosure are given above in Tables 16.10 and 16.11.

16.206 SI 2008/410 requires either the balance sheet or the notes to disclose, in respect of every item affected by the alternative accounting rules (except stocks), one or other of the following amounts:

- The comparable amounts determined according to the historical cost convention.
- The differences between those comparable amounts and the actual amounts shown in the balance sheet.

[SI 2008/410 1 Sch 34(3)].

16.207 For this purpose, 'comparable amounts' means the aggregate amount the company would have shown if it had applied the historical cost convention and the aggregate amount of the cumulative provisions for depreciation or diminution in value that would have been permitted or required in determining those amounts according to that convention. [SI 2008/410 1 Sch 34(4)].

16.208 As noted in paragraph 16.204, FRS 15 requires the net amounts required by the first bullet point in paragraph 16.206 above but in greater detail, because it requires it for each class of revalued assets. [FRS 15 para 74].

16.209 To illustrate the requirement in paragraph 16.206, consider the following example:

Example

Details of a company's fixed assets are as follows:

	Cost	Valuation
	£	£
Fixed assets	10,000	15,000
Accumulated depreciation	6,000	4,000
	4,000	11,000

If the company records the fixed assets in the balance sheet at valuation, the effect of the Act's provisions is to require the balance sheet or the notes to the financial statements to state either the comparable amounts (namely, cost £10,000 and depreciation £6,000) or the difference between the comparable amounts and the amounts at which they are actually stated (namely, £5,000 and £2,000 respectively).

The historical cost net book amount (namely, £4,000) or the difference between the comparable net book amounts (namely, £7,000) is another interpretation of the amounts that are required to be disclosed. This latter disclosure is arguable because the Act refers to the amounts stated in the balance sheet and the amounts so stated will be the net book amounts of the assets.

16.210 As a result of this requirement, a company that has revalued its fixed assets has to maintain records of both the historical cost and the valuation of those fixed assets. In addition, the company has to calculate depreciation on the historical cost as well as on the valuation.

16.211 Table 16.11 shows how a company complied with these disclosure requirements.

Table 16.11 – Lonrho plc – Annual Report and Accounts – 30 September 1998

Notes to the Accounts (extract)

11. Tangible assets (extract)

Assets shown below at valuation were valued by independent professional valuers or by the Directors after advice from independent professional advisers in the year shown, on the basis of open market value for existing use.

	Land and buildings	Leasehold					
						Fixtures	
		Long	Short	Mining	Plant and	fittings and	
	Freehold	term	term	assets	machinery	equipment	Total
Group	£m	£m	£m	£m	£m	£m	£m
Up to 1994				67			67
1998				6			6
Valuation				73			73
Cost	19		1	548	8	39	615
	19		1	621	8	39	688
Capital work in progress							5
At 30 September 1998							**693**
Depreciation:							
Valuation				14			14
Cost				68	4	32	104
At 30 September 1998				**82**	**4**	**32**	**118**
Historical cost of revalued assets							
Cost				14			14
Depreciation				5			5
Net historical cost at 30 September 1998				**9**			**9**
Cost	70	12	2	19	2	4	109
Depreciation	1			6	1	1	9
Net historical cost at 30 September 1997	69	12	2	13	1	3	100

The Directors have valued the following asset after taking account of the advice of the independent professional adviser listed below:

Property valued	Independent professional adviser	Qualification
Corsyn Consolidated Mines	Northland Mining services 1991 Ltd	Chartered Engineers

16.212 In addition, the FRS highlights that paragraph 2(1) of Schedule 7 to SI 2008/410 also requires disclosure in the directors' report of any substantial differences between the market value of properties and their carrying value, if the directors think the difference is of such significance that members should be made aware of it. [FRS 15 para 76]. This difference is likely to be significant where, for example:

- Land and buildings are held at historical cost (or frozen at their pre-FRS 15 valuations, see para 16.212.1) and market values have significantly increased or decreased since the date of acquisition (or last valuation).
- Owner-occupied property is valued at existing use value, but the property has a more valuable alternative use, such that open market value is significantly greater than the carrying value.
- The open market value of a property is significantly less than existing use value, for example, where restrictive alienation clauses in the headlease, planning consents that are personal to the present occupier, or known contamination do not affect the existing use of a property, but would result in a significantly lower market value.

Frozen valuations

16.212.1 Where an entity decided not to adopt a policy of revaluation on the implementation of FRS 15, but had tangible fixed assets that had previously been recorded at valuation, it could either:

- Retain the assets at their book amounts (subject to the requirement to test them for impairment if an indication exists that impairment may have occurred). In such circumstances the entity should disclose that it has taken advantage of the transitional provisions of the FRS and that the valuation has not been updated. It should also disclose the date of the last valuation; or
- Restate the assets to historical cost (less depreciation), as a change of accounting policy.

[FRS 15 para 104].

16.212.2 An entity could adopt the transitional arrangement in the first bullet point above only on first application of the FRS and not thereafter. [FRS 15 para 105].

16.212.3 If advantage was taken of this transitional arrangement, for the purposes of FRS 15 the 'frozen' book values are treated as though they were historical cost. However, in terms of the Act, the company still has revalued assets and so the disclosure requirements for the alternative accounting rules under the Act must be complied with on an ongoing basis. The Act's disclosure requirements are:

- The amounts of fixed assets held at valuation, the years of valuation, and the basis adopted.

- The historical cost equivalents for revalued assets.
- The amount of a revaluation reserve and any transfers from that reserve to realised reserves.

[SI 2008/410 1 Sch 34,35,52].

In addition, a note of historical cost profits and losses should be given as required by FRS 3.

[The next paragraph is 16.213.]

Revaluation gains and losses

Introduction

16.213 A revaluation gain or loss arises on the revaluation of a tangible fixed asset. It is the difference between the revalued amount and the carrying amount of the asset (net of cumulative depreciation) immediately before the revaluation.

16.214 Part or all of a revaluation gain or loss may be an impairment or a reversal of an impairment. Both of these fall to be recognised in the profit and loss account. The remaining gain or loss on revaluation is required by FRS 3 and the Act to be transferred to the revaluation reserve *via* the statement of total recognised gains and losses.

16.215 The tricky part is determining the split between the profit and loss account and the statement of total recognised gains and losses in practice and FRS 15 provides specific rules to ensure consistency of application.

Gains on revaluation

16.216 FRS 15 requires that revaluation gains should be recognised in the statement of total recognised gains and losses (that is, treated as a transfer to revaluation reserve). The only exception is where a gain reverses a revaluation loss (which may have been an impairment) on the same asset that was previously recognised in the profit and loss account. In such a case the gain (to the extent that it reverses the loss after adjusting for subsequent depreciation) is recognised in the profit and loss account. [FRS 15 para 63]. Therefore, the net charge to the profit and loss account over time would be the same as if the downward revaluation had not been recognised in the profit and loss account in the first place. The mechanics of this are best illustrated by means of an example.

Example – Treatment of revaluation gains and losses

A company has a policy of revaluing its tangible fixed assets. An asset cost £1,000 at the start of year one. It has a useful economic life of ten years and is being depreciated on a straight line basis to nil residual value. It was revalued downwards at the end of year one to £850, which was assumed to be the asset's recoverable amount. The loss on revaluation in year one is recognised in the profit and loss account, because it is a fall in value below depreciated historical cost.

At the end of the following year (year two) market values had risen to £1,050. The revaluation gain and loss are recognised as follows:

	Year 1	Year 2
Cost/valuation brought forward	1,000	850
Depreciation charge (opening balance divided by remaining useful economic life)	(100)	(94)
	900	756
(Loss)/gain on revaluation – profit and loss	(50)	44
Gain on revaluation – STRGL	–	250
Carrying amount carried forward	850	1,050

Of the £294 gain on revaluation in year two, £44 is recognised in the profit and loss account. This reverses the £50 loss previously recognised in the profit and loss account, adjusted for depreciation of £6 (that is, £50 divided by 9), which is the additional depreciation charge that would have been recognised in year two had the opening balance been £900, that is, if the £50 loss had not been recognised in year one.

Note that the adjustment to depreciation of £6 is also the difference between depreciation that would have been charged of £100 (that is, 1,000 divided by 10) on the original cost of £1,000, and the depreciation actually charged for the year of £94.

Revaluation losses

16.217 FRS 15 requires revaluation losses caused by a clear consumption of economic benefits to be recognised in the profit and loss account in their entirety. Where there is no clear consumption of economic benefits, revaluation losses should be recognised as follows:

- In the statement of total recognised gains and losses until the carrying amount falls to depreciated historical cost.
- In the profit and loss account for falls in value below depreciated historical cost, except where it can be demonstrated that the recoverable amount is greater than the revalued amount, in which case the fall in value below recoverable amount is recognised in the statement of total recognised gains and losses.

[FRS 15 para 65].

16.218 The above rules seem rather complex. This is because the FRS is trying to differentiate between downward revaluations that are due to a consumption of economic benefits and those that are due to other factors such as a general change in prices. The general principle is that downward revaluations due a consumption of economic benefits are akin to depreciation and should be recognised in the profit and loss account. However, downward revaluations due to general price changes are not losses from operations and so should be recognised in the statement of total recognised gains and losses and ultimately in the revaluation reserve.

16.219 This approach is consistent with that taken in FRS 11 for impaired assets that have been revalued, as set out in chapter 18. Given that an impairment is defined as a reduction in the recoverable amount of a fixed asset below its carrying amount, it is possible that a downward revaluation of a tangible fixed asset may comprise, at least in part, an impairment loss. [FRS 11 para 2; FRS 15 para 2].

16.220 Where there is a clear consumption of economic benefits, for example due to physical damage to, or contamination or obsolescence of, the asset or a deterioration in the quality of service provided by the asset, then both FRS 11 and FRS 15 require the fall in value to be taken to the profit and loss account in its entirety. No part of it should be taken to the statement of total recognised gains and losses. [FRS 11 para 63; FRS 15 para 65]. Whilst FRS 15 uses the term 'revaluation loss' rather than 'impairment', in this case the two terms refer to the same type of loss.

16.221 However, where there is no clear consumption of economic benefits, it may be difficult, in practice, to distinguish between these different types of losses. The approach taken by the standard, however, makes this less of an issue, because in such circumstances the standard requires downward revaluations of an asset to be recognised in the statement of total recognised gains and losses, until the carrying amount reaches depreciated historical cost. Thereafter, the balance of the downward revaluation is recognised in the profit and loss account. [FRS 11 para 63; FRS 15 para 65].

16.222 Note, however, that an asset cannot be impaired where its carrying amount is less than its recoverable amount. Since recoverable amount is the higher of net realisable value and value in use, it is possible that revaluing a tangible fixed asset may result in a revalued amount that is both less than the previous carrying amount and recoverable amount. In such circumstances, where recoverable amount is known, the difference between the recoverable amount and the (lower) revalued amount cannot be an impairment and, therefore, should be recognised in the statement of total recognised gains and losses, as illustrated in the example following paragraph 16.225. [FRS 15 para 65]. This would lead to a negative balance in the revaluation reserve for that asset.

16.223 FRS 15 does not require an impairment test and calculation of recoverable amount to be performed every time an asset is revalued downwards. As noted in paragraph 16.183, a newly revalued asset can only be impaired below its revalued amount if either net realisable value or value in use is materially less than the revalued amount (which would generally be replacement cost). If recoverable amount is not known then the full revaluation loss below depreciated historical cost should be recognised in the profit and loss account (that is, it is assumed that recoverable amount is the same as the revalued amount – see also the chart in para 16.178, which shows that current value is the lower of recoverable amount and replacement cost).

16.224 All impairments of tangible fixed assets that are charged to the profit and loss account under the rules of FRS 11 and FRS 15 represent permanent diminutions in value under the Act and should be charged in arriving at operating profit, generally under the same statutory format headings as depreciation. One exception is where the impairment is effectively a provision for a loss on disposal, as noted from paragraph 16.325.

16.225 For the purpose of determining in which performance statement gains and losses on revaluation should be recognised, material gains and losses on individual assets in a class of asset should not be aggregated. [FRS 15 para 67].

Example

A tangible fixed asset cost £100 and is depreciated over ten years on a straight-line basis, with nil residual value. At the end of year one the asset is revalued to £135. The revaluation gain of £45 (£135 less £90 (that is, £100 less £10 depreciation)) is recognised in the statement of total recognised gains and losses.

At the end of year two, the asset's value has fallen to £50, however an impairment review has revealed that the recoverable amount of the asset is £60. After depreciation for the year of £15 (£135 divided by 9), there is a revaluation loss of £70 (£120 — £50).

(a) If there is a clear consumption of economic benefits (for example, the asset was damaged by fire), then all the fall in value down to recoverable amount, that is, £60 (£120 — £60) in this example, is recognised in the profit and loss account as an impairment. The remaining revaluation loss of £10 being the fall in value from recoverable amount (£60) to the revalued amount (£50) is recognised in the statement of total recognised gains and losses.

(b) If, however, there is no obvious consumption of economic benefits, then only the fall in value below depreciated historical cost (£80) to recoverable amount (£60), that is, £20, is assumed to be an impairment loss to be recognised in the profit and loss account. The remaining revaluation loss of £50 is recognised in the statement of total recognised gains and losses. This revaluation loss comprises the fall in value to depreciated historical cost of £40 (£120 — £80) and the fall in value below recoverable amount of £10 (£60 — £50), as follows:

	£
Carrying amount at beginning of year 2	135
Depreciation for year	(15)
Carrying amount at end of year 2 just before revaluation	120
Fall in value to depreciated historical cost – recognised in STRGL	(40)
Depreciated historical cost at end of year 2	80
Fall in value to recoverable amount – recognised in profit and loss	(20)
Recoverable amount at end of year 2	60
Fall in value to replacement cost (revalued amount) – recognised in STRGL	(10)
Carrying amount (revalued amount) at end of year 2	50

[The next paragraph is 16.227.]

Treatment of accumulated depreciation when assets are revalued

16.227 The only method allowed under FRS 15 for treating existing accumulated depreciation when revaluing fixed assets is the simple one of comparing the revalued amount with the net book amount immediately before revaluation. Any difference is taken to the profit and loss account or statement of total recognised gains and losses as discussed from paragraph 16.216 above. This method is illustrated by the following simple example:

Example

Details of a fixed asset before revaluation are as follows:	£
Fixed asset at cost	1,000
Accumulated depreciation	400
Net book amount	600
The asset is revalued to	1,500
Details of the fixed asset after revaluation are as follows:	£
Fixed asset at cost	1,000
Gain on revaluation	500
Fixed asset at revalued amount	1,500
Accumulated depreciation	400
Gain on revaluation	(400)
Nil depreciation after revaluation	–

The gain on revaluation, which is recognised in the statement of total recognised gains and losses and transferred to the revaluation reserve, is £900 (namely, £1,500 – £600). This includes £400 of accumulated depreciation.

16.228 For assets revalued using depreciated replacement cost, rather than market value, the gain or loss on revaluation is calculated in the same way (that is, as the difference between the net book amount immediately before revaluation and the revalued amount). However, the cost and accumulated depreciation carried forward after the revaluation may, alternatively, reflect the gross cost and accumulated depreciation used to determine depreciated replacement cost. [FRS 15 para 101].

Example

As previously, but the fixed asset is revalued to £1,500 on a depreciated replacement cost (DRC) basis, consisting of £3,000 gross cost and £1,500 depreciation.

Details of the fixed asset after revaluation on a DRC basis are as follows:

	£
Fixed asset at cost	1,000
Gain on revaluation	2,000
Fixed asset at revalued gross replacement cost	3,000
Accumulated depreciation	400
Loss (that is, additional depreciation) on revaluation	1,100
Accumulated depreciation after revaluation	1,500

The gain on revaluation, which is recognised in the statement of total recognised gains and losses and transferred to the revaluation reserve, is again £900 (namely, £2,000 – £1,100).

[The next paragraph is 16.230.]

16.230 Although the FRS makes clear that the reversal of accumulated depreciation should be credited to the revaluation reserve (and to the statement of total recognised gains and losses), it is unclear as to whether or not the amount thus credited in respect of the depreciation represents a realised profit or not. In our view the amount should not be assumed to be a realised profit and if a company wished to treat it as such it should seek legal advice.

Revaluation reserve

16.231 The Act specifies that any difference between the amount of any item that a company has determined according to one of the alternative accounting rules, and the amount that the company would have disclosed if it had adhered to the historical cost convention, must be credited or debited (as applicable) to a 'revaluation reserve'. [SI 2008/410 1 Sch 35(1)].

16.232 In determining the amount of this difference, a company should take account, where appropriate, of any provisions for depreciation or diminution in value that it made otherwise than by reference to the value it determined under the alternative accounting rules. It should also take account of any adjustments of any such provisions that it made in the light of that determination. [SI 2008/410 1 Sch 35(1)]. This wording seems simply to mean that the figures on the historical cost basis and the figures on the basis of the alternative accounting rules should be compared net of any depreciation. For example, if an asset shown under the historical cost rules at cost of £100 less depreciation of £40 (net carrying amount £60) were revalued to a gross figure of £150 less cumulative depreciation £60 (net revalued amount under the alternative accounting rules £90), the credit to the revaluation reserve should be £30 (that is, £90 – £60).

16.233 As required by FRS 3, 'Reporting financial performance', this transfer to the revaluation reserve should be recognised in the statement of total recognised gains and losses. Compliance with the requirements of FRS 15, as explained above from paragraph 16.216, will ensure that the Act's requirements are met.

16.234 The Act restricts the circumstances in which a company can transfer an amount from the revaluation reserve. It can do this only where one of the following circumstances exists.

- An amount may be transferred to the profit and loss account if the amount in question was previously charged to that account or represents a realised profit. [SI 2008/410 1 Sch 35(3)(a)].
- An amount may be transferred to capital on capitalisation. Capitalisation means applying the amount standing to the credit of the revaluation reserve wholly or partly to paying up unissued shares in the company to be allotted to the company's members as fully or partly paid shares, thereby allowing bonus and scrip issues to be made out of the revaluation reserve. [SI 2008/410 1 Sch 35(3)(a)].
- Furthermore, it is possible to transfer from the revaluation reserve an amount in respect of the taxation relating to any profit or loss credited or debited to that reserve. [SI 2008/410 1 Sch 35(3)(b)]. This applies for example to the tax relating to a previously recognised revaluation gain.

16.235 The implications of the first bullet point above are that when an entity charges the whole of the depreciation based on the revalued assets to the profit and loss account, it may also transfer an amount equal to the excess depreciation from the revaluation reserve to the profit and loss account reserve. However, such a transfer is not compulsory.

16.236 The transfer should be made between reserves in the notes. Where such an adjustment is made, the revaluation reserve is systematically reduced over the asset's life and, consequently, if the asset is sold any net profit on the sale that is credited to the profit and loss account reserve will ultimately be the same whether the asset has been revalued or not.

16.237 In addition, the revaluation reserve must be reduced to the extent that the amounts transferred to it are no longer necessary for the purpose of the valuation method that the company has adopted. [SI 2008/410 1 Sch 35(3)]. An example of this would be where an asset with a previous revaluation surplus, which has not already been transferred to the profit and loss account reserve, has been sold. On realisation, the revaluation gain held in the revaluation reserve should be transferred from the revaluation reserve to the profit and loss account reserve. This gain should not be recognised in the profit and loss account, because it has already been recognised in the statement of total recognised gains and losses on revaluation.

16.238 Schedule 4 paragraph 34(3), which was introduced by the Companies Act 1989 (now paragraph 5(3) of Schedule 1 to SI 2008/410), states that the revaluation reserve shall not be reduced except as mentioned above. This means that it is no longer available, for example, to write off goodwill, which companies had sometimes done prior to the 1989 Act. This prohibition does not, however, affect goodwill write offs made before the introduction of the Companies Act 1989. However, for companies that became subsidiaries because of the changes in the definitions in the Companies Act 1989, the provisions of that Act apply and consolidated goodwill is prohibited from being written off to the revaluation reserve. Following the introduction of FRS 10, which is effective for periods ending on or after 23 December 1998, it is no longer permissible to write goodwill off immediately to reserves.

16.239 The revaluation reserve must be shown on the face of the balance sheet as a separate amount, although it need not be shown under that name. [SI 2008/410 1 Sch 35(2)]. This concession is necessary for several reasons. For example, where current cost financial statements are being prepared the revaluation reserve may be described as the unrealised current cost reserve.

16.240 It should also be noted that sometimes a company's articles of association will govern the way in which the company operates its revaluation reserve and these articles may stipulate also the name of the reserve. Consequently, the company should use that name in its financial statements. Articles of this nature are commonly found in investment companies and pension funds.

16.241 The question of whether a revaluation surplus or deficit is realised or unrealised is considered in chapter 23.

Taxation consequences

16.242 The Act requires the taxation implications of a revaluation to be noted in the financial statements. [SI 2008/410 1 Sch 35(4)].

16.243 This does not mean that there must be a statement of whether the amount is taxable or allowable under tax legislation. It means that there must be an explanation of the tax effect of the revaluation.

16.244 The tax effect will often be deferred until a later period. FRS 19 says that a timing difference will arise when an asset is revalued in the financial statements, but the revaluation gain becomes taxable only if and when the asset is sold. However, deferred tax should not be recognised unless, by the balance sheet date, the reporting entity has entered into a binding agreement to sell the revalued asset and has recognised the gain or loss expected to arise on sale. Deferred tax should not be recognised when the asset is revalued or sold if, on the basis of all available evidence, it is more likely than not that the taxable gain will be rolled over, being charged to tax only if and when the asset into which the gain has been rolled is sold. [FRS 19 paras 2, 14, 15].

16.245 Where, in accordance with FRS 19, provision has not been made on revalued assets because the conditions for providing, as described above, have not been met, a company should disclose an estimate of the tax that could be payable or recoverable if the assets were sold at the values shown, the circumstances in which the tax would be payable or recoverable and an indication of the amount that might be payable or recoverable in the foreseeable future. Where deferred tax has not been provided, because rollover relief is expected to be available, this disclosure is replaced by disclosure of the conditions that will have to be met to obtain the rollover relief and an estimate of the tax that would become payable if those conditions were not met. [FRS 19 para 64].

16.246 Compliance with the disclosure requirements of FRS 19 will ensure compliance with paragraph 35(4) of Schedule 1 to SI 2008/410.

Depreciation

Introduction

16.247 Both FRS 15 and the Act require the depreciation of tangible fixed assets. The objective is to reflect in operating profit the cost of use of the tangible fixed assets in the period.

16.248 Depreciation applies to all tangible fixed assets, whether held at historical cost or current value, with two exceptions:

- Investment properties, which are not depreciated in accordance with SSAP 19, 'Accounting for investment properties', by invoking the true and fair override of the Act's requirements.
- Tangible fixed assets where it can be demonstrated that depreciation is immaterial.

Definition of depreciation

16.249 Although depreciation is not defined in the Act, it is defined in FRS 15 as:

> *"The measure of the cost or revalued amount of the economic benefits of the tangible fixed asset that have been consumed during the period."*

As explained in FRS 15:

> *"Consumption includes the wearing out, using up or other reduction in the useful economic life of a tangible fixed asset whether arising from use, effluxion of time or obsolescence through either changes in technology or demand for the goods and services produced by the asset."* [FRS 15 para 2].

16.250 Further guidance is given in FRS 15 about the factors to be taken into account when determining the depreciation of a tangible fixed asset, as follows:

- The expected use of the asset by the entity. This is the principal factor and is generally assessed by reference to the asset's expected capacity or physical output.
- The expected physical deterioration of the asset through use or the passing of time (that is, 'wear and tear'), when the asset is both in use and idle. This will depend upon how well the asset is maintained and repaired throughout its life.
- Economic and technological obsolescence. The asset itself or the product or service generated by the asset may become economically or technologically obsolete by being superseded by new or more advanced products. Similarly, changes in market demand may render an asset economically obsolete, for example changes in fads and trends or competitor actions.
- Legal or similar limits on the use of the asset, for example the expiry of a patent, licence or lease.

[FRS 15 para 80].

16.251 Notably, FRS 15 does not mention the financing of an asset as a factor that should be taken into account when determining its depreciation.

Determination of useful economic life and residual value

16.252 Depreciation is calculated by allocating the cost or revalued amount of a tangible fixed asset less its estimated residual value (that is, its 'depreciable amount') on a systematic basis over its useful economic life. [SI 2008/410 1 Sch 18; FRS 15 paras 2, 77].

16.253 The allocation of depreciation to a period is recognised in the profit and loss account, as part of operating profit, unless it is permitted to be included in the carrying amount of another asset. This will only occur when depreciation is included in stock or work-in-progress as part of an allocation of overheads, in accordance with SSAP 9, 'Accounting for stock and long-term contracts', or when it forms part of the cost of a tangible fixed asset. For example, a mining company may purchase earth moving equipment for the purpose of excavating a new mine. It is, therefore, a directly attributable cost of the mine and the depreciation charge of the equipment should be capitalised as part of the cost of the mine.

16.254 Useful economic life is defined in FRS 15 as *"...the period over which the entity expects to derive economic benefit from that asset"*. [FRS 15 para 2]. Note that if an entity intends to hold a tangible fixed asset for the asset's whole economic life, then the asset would only be good for scrap, that is, it will have nil or a residual scrap value. However, the useful economic life of a tangible fixed asset to an entity may be less than the asset's total economic life, in which case the value of the asset at the end of that life will reflect the remaining economic life of the asset. This may occur because the asset has an alternative use at the end of the useful economic life to the entity, or because it is the entity's policy to dispose of its assets before they reach the end of their economic lives.

16.254.1 The requirement to allocate depreciation over the useful economic life was underlined by the FRRP in 2001 when it criticised the accounts of Wyevale Garden Centres plc. The FRRP press notice stated: *"The company's stated accounting policy in respect of short leasehold properties was not to provide any depreciation until the last ten years of the lease from which point the depreciable amount was written off over the remainder of the useful life of the lease. In respect of plant and equipment it was the company's policy not to commence depreciation until the accounting year following that in which the assets were acquired. In the Panel's view, neither of these policies complied with the requirements of FRS 15 as they did not result in depreciation charges throughout the economic lives of the assets"*.

Example

A company has a policy of not providing for depreciation on tangible assets capitalised in the year until the following year, but provides for a full year's depreciation in the year of disposal of an asset. Is this acceptable?

This is not acceptable as the requirement of FRS 15 is to allocate the depreciable amount of a tangible fixed asset on a systematic basis over its useful economic life. The depreciation method should reflect as fairly as possible the pattern in which the asset's economic benefits are consumed by the entity. This means that depreciation should commence as soon as the asset is brought into use. The same applies to amortisation of intangible fixed assets and goodwill. FRS 10 states *"Where goodwill and intangible assets are regarded as having limited useful lives, they should be amortised on a systematic basis over those lives"*. It goes on to say that the method of amortisation should be chosen to reflect the expected pattern of depletion of the goodwill or intangible asset.

[The next paragraph is 16.255.]

16.255 Residual value is defined in FRS 15 as *"...the net realisable value of an asset at the end of its useful economic life. Residual values are based on prices prevailing at the date of the acquisition (or revaluation) of the asset and do not take account of expected future price changes"*. [FRS 15 para 2].

16.256 The effect of this definition is that future inflation should not be taken into account when calculating an asset's residual value. Strictly, therefore, the value of the asset in question should be considered at the end of its useful economic life, but expressed in pounds of the date of acquisition or latest revaluation.

Example 1 – Residual value used in depreciation calculation

An asset is bought for £1,000. Its estimated useful economic life is six years and its estimated residual value, based on prices prevailing at the date of acquisition, is £100. However, if future inflation is taken into account, the estimated residual value would be £400. The rule in FRS 15 would lead to a company making annual provisions for depreciation of £150 (assuming the straight-line method is used). At the end of the useful economic life, the asset would be written down to £100 and, if estimates proved correct, it would be sold for £400, resulting in a profit on sale of £300. Under the alternative (but not permissible) method – taking inflation into account – depreciation would have been charged at the rate of £100 a year and there would have been no profit or loss reported on sale.

The effect of the rule in the standard is that, in an inflationary environment, assets should be depreciated at a rate which is higher than the rate necessary to produce no profit or loss in the year of disposal. This effect may seem strange, although in support of the method required by the standard, it must be acknowledged that there is considerable difficulty in estimating future inflation and its effect on residual values, particularly in the present economic environment where some industries are experiencing deflation. It can also be argued that the gain (or loss) on disposal is a holding gain (or loss) on a fixed asset that should not be recognised in historical cost accounts until it is realised.

Example 2 – Residual value used in depreciation calculation

The facts are the same as in the above example, except the company has a policy of revaluing its fixed assets. The asset is bought for £1,000 and its useful economic life is estimated at six years. The residual value is expected to be £100 based on prices prevailing at the date of acquisition, but if future inflation is taken into account the residual value is estimated to be £400. In this example, however, the asset is revalued in year three. The written down value at that point is £700 and the revalued amount is £900. Based on prices prevailing at the time of the revaluation the residual value is expected to be £150. Accordingly, depreciation for year three will be based on the revalued amount of £900 less the revised residual value of £150 divided by the remaining useful life. Depreciation for the year would, therefore, be £187. The increase in the depreciation charge of £37 is equal to the revaluation surplus of £200 less the increase in the residual value of £50 divided by the remaining life of four years, that is, £37.

Methods of depreciation

16.257 FRS 15 notes that there is a range of acceptable depreciation methods. Management should select the method regarded as most appropriate to the type of asset and its use in the business so as to allocate depreciation as fairly as possible over the useful economic life to reflect the pattern in which the economic benefits of the asset are consumed. [FRS 15 para 77]. This section describes some of the most common methods.

16.258 The FRS warns that the method chosen should result in a depreciation charge throughout the asset's useful economic life and not just towards the end of its useful economic life or when the asset is falling in value. [FRS 15 para 81]. Therefore, it is not acceptable (except where depreciation in the earlier years would be immaterial – see from para 16.279) just to depreciate a leasehold property, mine or landfill site in, say, the last 20 years of its useful economic life. This is because the asset is being used throughout the whole useful economic life and the allocation of depreciation should reflect that.

Straight line method

16.259 This is the most common method used in practice and should be used whenever the pattern of consumption of an asset's economic benefits is uncertain. The cost (or revalued amount – see para 16.268 below) less the estimated residual value is allocated over the useful economic life so as to charge each accounting period with the same amount.

Reducing balance method

16.260 This method is designed to charge higher amounts of depreciation in the earlier years of an asset's use, as follows:

Example

	£
Cost	125
Depreciation charge (20%)	25
Carrying amount at end of year 1	100
Depreciation charge (20% of 100)	20
Carrying amount at end of year 2	80
Depreciation charge (20% of 80)	16
Carrying amount at end of year 3	64
and so on	

16.261 This method is appropriate when the economic benefits of an asset decline as they become older, for example because the asset becomes less reliable and more likely to break-down, less capable of producing a high-quality product or less technologically advanced. Furthermore, where charges for repairs and maintenance of assets are higher in later years, the lower depreciation charge in the later years offsets the higher repair and maintenance costs.

Sum of the digits (or 'rule of 78')

16.262 This method is similar in its effect to the reducing balance method although the mechanics are different. If an asset is expected to last, say, 12 periods (years, months, etc), the digits 1 to 12 are added (total 78); the first period is charged with 12/78, the next period with 11/78 and so on – hence the name 'rule of 78'.

Unit-of-production method

16.263 This method relates depreciation to the estimated production capability of an asset. The rate of depreciation per hour of usage or unit of production is given by dividing the depreciable amount by the estimated total service capability of the asset, measured in terms of hours or units. This method is sometimes employed when the usage of an asset varies considerably from period to period because, in these circumstances, it matches cost against revenue more satisfactorily. Examples of the types of asset that are often depreciated in this way are: for hourly rates – airline engines; and for unit of production – mineral resources.

> **Example 1 – Unit-of-production calculation**
>
> A machine cost £100,000 and its expected residual value is £10,000. The total usage of the machine is expected to be 500,000 hours. The depreciation rate per hour's usage is, therefore, £0.18 (£100,000 — £10,000 divided by 500,000).

> **Example 2 – Unit-of-production calculation**
>
> Exploration costs amounting to £5m are incurred in finding mineral reserves. The reserves are expected to be 5m tonnes. The rate of depreciation to be applied to the exploration costs is worked out as £1 per tonne. In the first year of production 200,000 tonnes are extracted and depreciation charged at £1 per tonne is £200,000.

Annuity method

16.264 The annuity method is not a commonly used method of depreciation and is rarely appropriate. It results in a depreciation charge that increases over time. Whilst paragraph 32 of FRS 10 specifically prohibits such methods for the amortisation of goodwill at present, FRS 15 is silent in respect of the use of the annuity method for the depreciation of tangible fixed assets.

16.265 The annuity method may be appropriate where an entity's rate of consumption of the economic benefits of an asset increases over its life. An example is where production begins at a low level, but builds up over time. However, such cases are rare in practice. In any event, the unit-of-production method of depreciation is probably more appropriate in these circumstances, as it reflects the consumption of an asset's economic benefit, since each homogeneous unit produced by the asset has the same value to the entity.

16.266 In certain circumstances, for example where an asset is leased to a third party under an operating lease, the economic benefits consumed by the lessor are not related to the units of production (or services) obtained from the physical asset. Instead, the profile of economic benefits of such an asset to the lessor is akin to that of a financial asset, in which case the overall performance may be more usefully measured using a method of depreciation that treats the asset as a monetary, as opposed to non-monetary, asset. Using the annuity method of depreciation produces results that, economically, are closer to the net constant rate of return on capital invested. This approach, however, is only permitted under the Finance & Leasing Associations' SORP, 'Accounting issues in the asset finance and leasing industry', provided that:

- The asset is let on a lease that is for a significant portion of the total economic life of the asset.

- The terms of the lease adequately protect the lessor against early cancellation.
- Adequate income is retained in the lease to cover future uncertainties in respect of the realisation of residual values.

[FLA SORP para 5.3.34].

The restrictions placed on the use of this method by the SORP mean that generally the method would not be appropriate for, say, assets held for short-term rentals such as motor vehicles or plant on hire.

16.267 It is sometimes argued, in respect of a wider range of assets, that the depreciation profile of an asset should reflect the cost of capital or, alternatively put, the time value of money, as well as the consumption of economic benefits of the asset. Where the entity consumes the economic benefits of an asset evenly over its useful economic life (for example, produces the same units of production each year), then the annuity method achieves the aim of also reflecting the effect of the cost of capital or time value of money in the depreciation profile of that asset. However, the appropriateness of such an approach has been a matter of hot debate under existing GAAP. As a consequence, the ASB issued an exposure draft of an amendment to FRS 15 and FRS 10 in June 2000, proposing to prohibit the use of interest methods of depreciation, such as the annuity method, for both tangible and intangible fixed assets, except in the limited circumstances described in paragraphs 16.265 and 16.266 above. The responses to this exposure draft are being considered by the ASB as part of its project on lease accounting.

Depreciation of revalued assets

16.268 With the exception of investment properties (see chapter 17), depreciation is required, by both FRS 15 and the Act, to be charged on revalued tangible fixed assets. The rules relating to depreciation of fixed assets that have been valued under the alternative accounting rules are essentially the same as those described above with the revalued amount being substituted for historical cost. The application of the rules for revalued assets is described in the following paragraphs.

16.269 Where an entity has revalued a tangible fixed asset in accordance with the alternative accounting rules in SI 2008/410, that value (rather than the historical cost) is to be (or else is to be the starting point for determining) the amount at which it discloses that asset in its financial statements. Accordingly, any references to cost in SI 2008/410's depreciation rules must be substituted by a reference to the value determined by the alternative accounting rules the company applied. [SI 2008/410 1 Sch 33(1)]. This means that, in determining the amount to be written off systematically over a tangible fixed asset's useful economic life, an entity must have regard to the asset's value determined according to the latest application of the alternative accounting rules, rather than to its historical cost.

16.270 FRS 15 states that ideally the average value of the asset for the period should be used as the basis for calculating the year's depreciation charge, but that in practice either the opening or closing balance may be used instead, provided that it is used consistently in each period. [FRS 15 para 79]. It is common to use the opening balance, together with the cost of subsequent additions, for determining the year's depreciation charge, which avoids the need to recalculate depreciation charged in the earlier part of the year, used, for example in interim reports. On this basis some might argue that until the year end valuation *"the most recently determined value"* would be the valuation carried out at the last year end and if depreciation is deemed to accrue evenly over the life of an asset, depreciation should be charged on that opening value plus additions throughout the year until the next valuation at the year end.

16.271 But the Act says that where the value of any fixed asset has been determined according to the alternative accounting rules, the amount of any provision for depreciation to be charged in the profit and loss account may be either the amount based on the valuation of the asset, or the amount based on its historical cost. However, where the amount so charged is based on historical cost, the difference between that charge and the charge based on the asset's valuation must be disclosed separately. It must be so disclosed either on the face of the profit and loss account or in the notes. [SI 2008/410 1 Sch 332(2)(3)]. This might appear to allow a company to either debit or credit the difference (as appropriate) direct to the revaluation reserve. This is, however, prohibited by FRS 15. [FRS 15 para 77].

16.272 FRS 15 echoes the Act's rules in most respects, but it requires that where an entity revalues assets, and gives effect to the revaluation in its financial statements, it should base the profit and loss charge for depreciation on the revalued amount. [FRS 15 para 79]. No depreciation previously charged should be written back to the profit and loss account on revaluation of an asset. The FRS states also that an increase in the value of an asset does not remove the necessity for a company to charge depreciation even where the market value of an asset is greater than its carrying amount. [FRS 15 para 78].

16.273 Consequently, it is clear that FRS 15 requires an entity to charge depreciation on the carrying amount of the revalued asset in the balance sheet and to charge it in its entirety to the profit and loss account. Thus, it is appropriate where a company revalues its assets at its year end to base the depreciation charge for the period on that revised amount.

16.274 The practice of 'split depreciation' where depreciation on the historical cost is charged to the profit and loss account, and depreciation on the revaluation is charged to the revaluation reserve is prohibited under FRS 15. [FRS 15, 'The development of the FRS, paras 42 to 47].

16.275 Whilst chapter 23 considers realised reserves and distributable profits in detail, it should be noted that section 841(5) of the Companies Act 2006 has a bearing on the way in which companies should treat depreciation on revalued assets. This section says that if the revaluation of an asset produces an unrealised profit, then an amount equal to any excess depreciation charged as a result of the revaluation may be treated as a realised profit. This section is concerned only with the determination of distributable profits (and not with the accounting treatment of excess depreciation). Despite this, it means that where a company properly charges the whole of the depreciation based on the revalued assets to the profit and loss account, it may also transfer an amount equal to the excess depreciation from the revaluation reserve to the profit and loss account reserve, as noted in paragraph 16.235 above. Because the amount transferred from the revaluation reserve to the profit and loss account reserve represents a realised profit, this treatment does not contravene paragraph 35(3) of Schedule 1 to SI 2008/410.

Component depreciation

16.276 FRS 15 requires that where a tangible fixed asset comprises two or more major components with substantially different useful economic lives, each component should be accounted for separately for depreciation purposes and depreciated over its useful economic life. The FRS makes it clear that this is a requirement in the case of assets where the components are clearly distinguishable such as land and buildings. In that example it states that land, with certain exceptions, normally has an indefinite useful life and is not depreciated, whereas buildings have a finite life and are depreciated. In other cases, where it is not so clear that an asset has separable components, there appears to be more choice. For example, the FRS states that another example of separable components that may have substantially different lives is the structure of a building and items within the structure such as general fittings. There is, therefore, a need for entities to review whether or not an asset has such separable components. If it decides it has, then separable components should be depreciated individually over their useful lives. [FRS 15 para 84].

16.277 Another example of the separable components approach is described above under 'subsequent expenditure' (see from para 16.130), where an example is of the lining of a blast furnace or major overhaul expenditure. In cases such as these, however, there is discretion given to the entity's management to decide whether or not to adopt the separate components approach, based on an analysis of various factors such as the materiality of the component and the degree of irregularity of replacement or overhaul expenditure.

16.278 The FRS notes, however, that it would not be appropriate to treat the trading potential associated with a property valued as an operational entity, such as a public house or hotel, as a separable component, where the trading potential is inherently inseparable from the asset to which it attaches. [FRS 15 para 85].

Non-depreciation of certain assets

16.279 Investment properties other than short leaseholds (20 years or less) are not depreciated. This is a requirement of SSAP 19, 'Accounting for investment properties', and is discussed in chapter 17.

16.280 However, for other tangible fixed assets, one issue that has caused debate and variations in practice over many years is whether, in some circumstances, it is appropriate to omit annual charges for depreciation in respect of certain assets. The issue is generally discussed in the context of buildings.

16.281 SSAP 12 was silent on the question of non-depreciation. However, in the accompanying Technical Release, the ASC referred to the general principle of SSAP 12 – that where a fixed asset has a finite useful economic life, its cost (or revalued amount) less residual value should be depreciated over that life – and acknowledged that there might be circumstances where following the principle rendered any depreciation charge unnecessary.

Example – Non-depreciation of certain assets

A property costing £1m is bought in 19X6. Its estimated total useful economic life is 50 years. However, the company considers it likely that it will sell the property after 20 years. The estimated residual value in 20 years' time, based on 19X6 prices, is (a) £1m, (b) £900,000. A residual value that is the same as or close to original cost is likely to be rare, as it assumes that in 20 years' time potential purchasers would pay, for a 20 year old property, an amount similar to what they would pay for a new property.

In case (a), the company considers that the residual value will equal the cost. There is, therefore, no depreciable amount and depreciation is correctly zero.

In case (b) the company considers that the residual value will be £900,000 and the depreciable amount is, therefore, £100,000. Annual depreciation (on a straight line basis) will be £5,000 (1m — 900,000/20). Depending on the context, the annual depreciation charge of £5,000 may be immaterial and it may, therefore, be acceptable not to provide for depreciation of the property on those grounds. It is, however, necessary to consider the materiality of the cumulative depreciation as well as the depreciation in the year.

16.282 This example demonstrates two points mentioned in paragraphs 16.254 and 16.256 above.

- The useful economic life is defined in terms of the present owner; therefore, 20 years rather than 50 years is the relevant period.
- Residual value is defined as being based on prices prevailing at the date of acquisition (or revaluation), that is, excluding the effects of future inflation.

16.283 In this example, maintaining the asset to a high standard is not assumed. Maintenance is of course one of the factors that determines the estimated residual value and in practice is almost invariably quoted as the reason why the residual value of particular assets is expected to be at least as high, in terms of prices prevailing at the date of acquisition or revaluation, as the present carrying value. As explained in paragraph 16.288 below consideration should now also be given to whether the asset is likely to suffer from technological and economic obsolescence and whether, in practice, such assets have been sold in the past for at least the expected residual value, based on prices prevailing at the date of acquisition or revaluation.

Tangible fixed assets other than non-depreciable land

16.284 In the 'Development of the FRS' section of FRS 15, the ASB stated that it did not accept that the estimate of a tangible fixed asset's useful economic life could be extended without limit by maintenance. This is because the physical life of a tangible fixed asset other than non-depreciable land, cannot be infinite. At some point it will be more economic to scrap the physical asset and replace it with a new one. On the other hand, the standard acknowledges that for some, exceptional, assets the useful economic life may be extended to such a degree that any depreciation charge would be immaterial (for example, heritage properties and fine art). The FRS states that immateriality is the only permissible grounds for not charging depreciation.

16.285 For this reason the FRS contains two provisions. First, it states that subsequent expenditure (for example, maintenance) that maintains or enhances the previously assessed standard of performance does not remove the need to charge depreciation. [FRS 15 para 86]. Where subsequent expenditure extends the useful life or adds to the previously assessed economic benefits, the expenditure may be capitalised, but it is then depreciated over its useful economic life. [FRS 15 para 88]. The circumstances in which subsequent expenditure may be capitalised are described under 'Subsequent expenditure' above (see from para 16.130).

16.286 Secondly, the FRS introduces a requirement for impairment tests to be performed on a tangible fixed asset (other than non-depreciable land) in accordance with FRS 11 at the end of each reporting period where either:

- No depreciation charge is made, because it would be immaterial (either because of the length of the estimated remaining useful economic life or because the estimated residual value (as defined in para 16.255 above) of the tangible fixed asset is not materially different from the carrying amount of the tangible fixed asset); or
- The estimated remaining useful economic life of the tangible fixed asset exceeds 50 years.

[FRS 15 para 89].

[The next paragraph is 16.288.]

16.288 In order to justify that depreciation is immaterial, reasonable assumptions and estimates of useful economic lives and residual values need to be made. The FRS states that conditions that might give rise to immaterial depreciation include:

- When the entity has a policy of regular maintenance and repair (charges for which are made to the profit and loss account) such that the tangible fixed asset is retained at its previously assessed standard of performance.
- When the tangible fixed asset is unlikely to suffer from technological or economic obsolescence (due to changes in demand for its products or services).
- Where estimated residual values are material:
  - the entity has a policy and practises the policy of disposing of similar assets well before the end of their useful lives; and
  - the disposal proceeds of similar assets (excluding inflationary effects since acquisition or later revaluation) have not historically been materially less than their carrying values.

[FRS 15 para 91].

16.289 Furthermore, the FRS requires that where depreciation is judged to be immaterial the aggregate depreciation should be considered as well as the depreciation on individual assets. This would include considering the effect of cumulative uncharged depreciation on the balance sheet. [FRS 15 para 91]. The FRS states that the depreciation charge and the accumulated depreciation are only immaterial if they would not reasonably influence the decisions of a reader of the financial statements. [FRS 15 para 90].

16.290 The impairment reviews may be performed on groups of assets, forming income generating units, if it is impracticable to perform them on individual assets. After the first review, subsequent reviews need only be updated. [FRS 15 para 92]. It is only necessary to carry out enough work to justify that the assets are not impaired (that is, that recoverable amount is at least as much as the carrying amount). For example, if it is known that the net realisable value of an asset is greater than its carrying amount, then there is no need to perform value in use calculations.

16.291 On the introduction of FRS 15 many companies, which previously did not depreciate properties on the grounds of having maintained them to a high standard, began to depreciate their properties. The UITF in Abstract 23 clarified that a prior year adjustment to identify and separately depreciate components of an asset (on implementation of FRS 15) did not extend to the remainder of the asset. In respect of the remainder of the asset a change in useful economic life or residual value should be accounted for prospectively (see further paras 16.340 to 16.346 below).

Non-depreciable land

16.292 Land is normally considered to be a non-depreciable asset, because it does not generally have a limited useful economic life. Therefore, annual impairment reviews are not required. Mineral bearing land, however, comprises two elements: the mineral reserves and the land itself. Mineral reserves are depreciated as they are extracted, whilst the land itself is not depreciated.

Renewals accounting

16.293 A major problem which the ASB faced when developing FRS 12 and FRS 15 concerned the application of the principles in those standards to large infrastructure systems or networks, as typically found in the water industry. Traditionally such networks had not been depreciated and instead provisions for maintenance had been established, which were designed to ensure that the infrastructure or network's useful economic lives were extended indefinitely. The charge to this renewals provision was based on the planned level of annual expenditure required to maintain the operating capacity or service capability of the infrastructure system. The provision, therefore, indicated the actual under spend, compared to plan. A prepayment indicated an overspend compared with planned expenditure.

16.294 This caused the standard setters problems, because FRS 12 prohibits provisions for future maintenance and FRS 15 requires assets with finite lives to be depreciated. However, if such provisions were not made the results shown for entities with large infrastructure or network assets would reflect a pattern of expenditure that would not match the actual plans and assumptions that underlay their economic performance.

16.295 A pragmatic solution is set out in FRS 15, which lays down detailed rules for accounting for tangible fixed assets within an infrastructure system or network. It is based on the principle that in a steady state system, the average level of expenditure to maintain the system is the best means available for determining the cost of consumption of economic benefits of the system to the entity, that is, depreciation.

16.296 Where major tangible fixed assets or components of fixed assets within such an infrastructure system or network have determinable finite lives the assets should be accounted for separately and depreciated over their useful economic lives. [FRS 15 para 97].

16.297 For the remaining tangible fixed assets within the infrastructure system or network, renewals accounting may be used to estimate the depreciation to be charged. This treatment may, however, only be adopted where:

- The infrastructure system or network as a whole is intended to be maintained at a specified level of service potential by continuing replacement and refurbishment of its components.
- The level of annual expenditure required to maintain the operating capacity or service capability of the infrastructure system is calculated from an asset management plan, which is certified by a person who is appropriately qualified and independent.

- The system or network is in a mature or steady state.

[FRS 15 para 97].

16.298 Where renewals accounting is adopted the level of annual expenditure that is needed to maintain the operating capacity or service capability of the infrastructure system is treated as depreciation for the period and is charged to the profit and loss account. The amount is then deducted from the carrying amount of the system and shown in arriving at accumulated depreciation. Actual expenditure is capitalised as part of the cost of the system. [FRS 15 para 98].

16.299 The treatment described above would risk overstating both cost and accumulated depreciation in the long run, if the carrying amount of that part of the infrastructure that is replaced or restored by subsequent expenditure is not removed. The standard, therefore, requires that this should be done. [FRS 15 para 99]. This will generally be achieved by applying estimates based on the percentage of the system that is replaced each year.

16.300 Where the renewals method is not adopted expenditure on maintaining the system should be charged to profit and loss account or capitalised as appropriate under the other provisions in the FRS. [FRS 15 para 99].

[The next paragraph is 16.302.]

Change in estimate of useful economic life

16.302 FRS 15 requires that the useful economic lives of assets should be reviewed at the end of each reporting period and, when necessary, revised. The net book amount is then written off over the revised remaining useful life. [FRS 15 para 93]. FRS 15, therefore, prohibits the practice of taking an adjustment to accumulated depreciation (commonly called 'backlog' depreciation) to the profit and loss account in the current period, where future results would be materially distorted.

16.303 An example that illustrates this treatment is as follows:

> **Example – Change in estimated useful life**
>
> A company purchased an asset on 1 January 19X0 for £100,000, and the asset had an estimated useful life of ten years and a residual value of nil. The company has charged depreciation using the straight-line method at £10,000 per annum. On 1 January 19X4, when the asset's net book value is £60,000, the directors review the estimated life and decide that the asset will probably be useful for a further four years and, therefore, the total life is revised to eight years. The company should amend the annual provision for depreciation to charge the unamortised cost (namely, £60,000) over the revised remaining life of four years. Consequently, it should charge depreciation for the next four years at £15,000 per annum.

16.304 An example of a company that has changed the useful economic lives and is depreciating the balance of the assets over the remaining useful life is given in Table 16.12.

Table 16.12 – Cable & Wireless plc – Report and Accounts – 31 March 1993

Financial Overview (extract)

Depreciation

Our depreciation policies are reviewed on a regular basis against the background of rapidly changing technology and competitive developments. In recent years, there have been significant changes in submarine cable technology and markets. This is reflected in significantly lower unit costs and capacity availability. The Group has considerable investments in both analogue and digital cable systems which were being depreciated over a 25 year estimated useful economic life. In the case of analogue cables, revised lives have been established having regard to both known plans to lay digital cables over similar routings and the view that it would be prudent for all existing analogue cables to be fully depreciated by the year 2000. With regard to digital cables, depreciation will be based upon an estimated economic life of 15 years. This takes account of anticipated cost trends and the related cost benefit economics that will influence future cable replacement decisions.

14 Tangible fixed assets (extract)

During the year the Group revised the life of its cables and repeaters to take account of technological changes. The effect of this revision is an increase in the depreciation charge for the year of £11.6m.

16.305 If a tangible fixed asset is carried at valuation the FRS states that, particularly if it is valued at depreciated replacement cost, a reassessment of useful economic life may require that the asset be revalued. The revalued asset should then be depreciated over its revised useful economic life. [FRS 15 para 94].

Change in estimate of residual value

16.306 The FRS also requires that where residual value is material, it should be reviewed at the end of each reporting period to take account of reasonably expected technological changes, based on prices prevailing at the date of acquisition or subsequent revaluation. Any change in the estimate of residual value should be accounted for prospectively over the remaining useful life, unless, and to the extent that, the asset has been impaired at the balance sheet date (when the impairment should be charged to profit and loss account immediately). [FRS 15 para 95].

Change in method of providing depreciation

16.307 If there is a change from one *method* of providing depreciation to another, the remaining undepreciated cost (that is, the net carrying amount) of the asset should be written off over the remaining useful life on the new basis, commencing with the period in which the change is made. A change from one method of providing depreciation to another is permitted only if the new method will give a fairer presentation of the entity's results and financial position. A change of method does not constitute a change of accounting policy and, therefore, a prior period adjustment is not permissible. [FRS 15 para 82].

16.308 Consequently, in the example given above (but assuming that the life remains as ten years) the company may decide that, from 1 January 19X4, the sum-of-the-digits method of calculation would give a fairer presentation than the straight-line method. If so, the depreciation charge for 19X4 would be £17,143 (namely, £60,000 × 6/6+5+4+3+2+1), because the asset still has a remaining useful life of six years.

Disclosures

16.309 The disclosure requirements in FRS 15 incorporate the Act's disclosure requirements to give a table that explains the movements in cost, or revalued amount and depreciation. However, FRS 15 requires disclosures to be given for each class of tangible fixed assets adopted, which may result in a greater volume of disclosures particularly where a revaluation policy has been adopted.

16.310 FRS 15 requires the following disclosures for each class of assets:

- The depreciation methods used (for example, straight-line method or reducing balance method).
- The useful economic lives or the depreciation rates used.
- Total depreciation charged for the period.
- Where material the financial effect of a change during the period of either the estimate of useful economic lives or the estimate of residual values.
- Where there has been a change in the depreciation method used, the effect, if material, and the reason for change should be disclosed in the year of change.
- The cost or revalued amount at both the beginning and end of the financial year.
- The cumulative amount of provisions for depreciation or impairment at the beginning and end of the financial year.
- A reconciliation of the movements, separately disclosing additions, disposals, revaluations, transfers, depreciation, impairment losses, and reversals of past impairment losses written back in the period.
- The carrying amount (that is, net book amount) at the beginning and end of the financial year.

[FRS 15 paras 100, 102].

16.311 The Act also requires that disclosures in respect of land and buildings should include an analysis of freehold, long leasehold and short leasehold.

[SI 2008/410 1 Sch 53]. For this purpose, a lease includes an agreement for a lease. It will be a long lease if it still has 50 years or more to run at the end of the financial year in question. Otherwise, it will be a short lease. [SI 2008/410 10 Sch 7]. Table 16.13 also illustrates these disclosures.

16.312 Although FRS 28, 'Corresponding amounts', requires comparative figures to be provided for every item included in a note to the financial statements, this requirement does not apply in respect of the disclosures discussed in paragraph 16.310. [FRS 28 para 11].

16.313 In addition, disclosures are required in respect of impairment, as set out in chapter 18, finance costs (from para 16.126), valuations (from para 16.204).

16.314 An example of the accounting policy note explaining the depreciation methods, useful economic lives or depreciation rates used is given in Table 16.13.

Table 16.13 – Thorn Plc – Annual Report and Accounts – 31 March 1998

ACCOUNTING POLICIES (extract)

Depreciation (extract)

Depreciation of tangible fixed assets (other than rental equipment) is calculated on cost at rates estimated to write off the cost less the estimated residual value of the relevant assets by equal annual amounts over their expected useful lives; effect is given, where necessary, to commercial and technical obsolescence.

The annual rates used are:	2%
Freehold buildings and long-term leasehold property	
Short-term leasehold property	Period of lease
Plant, equipment and vehicles	10 — 33 1/3%

Rental equipment (other than that on rent-to-own agreements) is depreciated at rates estimated to write off the cost to nil residual value by equal annual amounts over its estimated useful life, from the month of installation. Once commenced, depreciation is not suspended during off-lease periods. The estimated useful lives of rental equipment (other than that on rent-to-own agreements) are:

Colour television sets	5 — 6 years
Video recorder equipment	5 years
Domestic appliances	5 years
Personal computers	3 years

Rental equipment placed on rent-to-own agreements is fully depreciated over the expected life of those agreements, which range from one to five years.

Disposals of tangible fixed assets

Introduction

16.315 The treatment of the disposal of tangible fixed assets is set out in FRS 3, 'Reporting financial performance', and repeated in FRS 15. As well as dealing with the disposal of tangible fixed assets, this section also considers the treatment of intended disposals of tangible fixed assets.

Reporting gains and losses on disposal

16.316 FRS 15 repeats the requirement in FRS 3 (which is discussed in greater detail in chapter 8) that the profit or loss on disposal of a tangible fixed asset is the difference between the net sale proceeds and the net carrying amount, whether carried at historical cost or at a valuation. The profit or loss on disposal should be recognised in the profit and loss account for the period in which the disposal occurs. [FRS 3 para 21; FRS 15 para 72].

16.317 Profits or losses on disposal should be recognised in the profit and loss account as an exceptional item after operating profit. When the net amount is not material, but the gross profits or losses are material, the relevant heading should still appear on the face of the profit and loss account with a reference to a related note analysing the profits and losses. [FRS 3 para 20]. However, profits or losses on disposal that are in effect no more than normal adjustments to depreciation previously charged should be included in operating profit as part of the normal depreciation charge. [FRS 3 para 46].

16.318 FRS 15 also gives an example that relates to an asset that is destroyed, but for which insurance proceeds are received, which are used to buy a new asset. In such a case the destroyed asset is removed from the balance sheet and the resulting gain or loss (the difference between carrying amount and insurance proceeds) is recognised. The replacement asset is capitalised at cost in the normal way. [FRS 15 para 73]. A further example is given below.

Example – Treatment of insured asset destroyed by fire

A company had plant and machinery in its books at £200,000. These were destroyed by fire. However, the assets were insured under a 'new for old' policy and were replaced by the insurance company with new machines that cost £2m. The machines were acquired directly by the insurance company and the company did not actually receive the £2m in cash.

This situation is, in substance, the same as if the company had received cash and invested it in new machinery, because the insurance company has merely acted as agent for the company, effectively buying the new assets on behalf of the company, with the company's cash. The company has earned the profit through paying premiums for the 'new for old' insurance policy. Therefore, the profit on disposal of the destroyed assets of £1.8m (that is, the difference between the £2m insurance proceeds and the carrying amount of the destroyed plant and machinery of £200,000) should be recognised in the profit and loss account as an exceptional item separately identified immediately after operating profit. The new machines are capitalised at £2m.

Revalued assets

16.319 As noted above, the treatment for revalued assets is the same as that for assets held at historical cost. Therefore, the profit and loss on disposal of a revalued asset (that is, the difference between sales proceeds and carrying amount) is recognised in the profit and loss account. Whilst being consistent with the treatment of assets held at historical cost, this leads to some peculiarities.

16.320 Consider, for example, an asset that is revalued each year based on current market values. Since acquisition the asset has only increased in value and, therefore, on each revaluation, a revaluation gain is recognised in the statement of total recognised gains and losses (in accordance with the requirements explained in para 16.216). In the year of disposal, the asset has increased in value even further, but rather than recognising this element of the gain in the statement of total recognised gains and losses, as in previous years, it is required to be recognised in the profit and loss account. This seems at odds with the fact that both the revaluation gains and the gain on disposal arose solely as a result of the entity holding onto the asset and price movements.

16.321 The proposals in FRED 17, 'Measurement of tangible fixed assets', that preceded FRS 15, attempted to resolve this peculiarity, by proposing that an asset should be revalued to the anticipated disposal proceeds just prior to its disposal. Accordingly, the resulting gain or loss from this 'deathbed' revaluation would be recognised in the profit and loss account or the statement of total recognised gains and losses as though it were simply a gain or loss on revaluation. However, this proposal did not survive in the final FRS, mainly because it led to further inconsistencies elsewhere.

16.322 Paragraph 35(3) of Schedule 1 to SI 2008/410 allows a company to make a transfer from the revaluation reserve to the profit and loss account where the amount transferred represents a realised profit. Consequently, when a company sells a revalued asset, the Act permits it to credit the profit on the sale (including the amount of the realised revaluation surplus) to the profit and loss account. This would have the effect that the profit or loss on disposal would be the same as that recognised had the asset not been revalued, but held at historical cost. However, this treatment is prohibited by FRS 3. This is because under FRS 3 performance is measured by reference to total recognised gains for the year, which includes the profit or loss for the year and the other gains and losses which have been taken direct to the statement of total recognised gains and losses. Therefore, if a gain has been recognised when an asset was initially revalued, that gain should not be recognised a second time in either the profit and loss account or the statement of total recognised gains and losses, when the asset is sold.

16.323 Any revaluation surplus in the revaluation reserve that is realised on sale should, therefore, be transferred directly to the profit and loss account reserve and not to the profit and loss account for the year. This is in accordance with the requirement to reduce the revaluation reserve where it is no longer necessary for the purpose of the valuation method that the company has adopted, as noted in paragraph 16.237 above. [SI 2008/410 1 Sch 35(3)].

16.324 In order to deal with the wishes of some users to see what profits or losses on disposals of revalued assets would be if measured by reference to historical cost, the ASB introduced a requirement in FRS 3 for a note of historical cost profits and losses, where the effect was material. The information provided in such a note enables users to see what profits and losses have been made measured against historical costs rather than revalued amounts.

Intended disposal of fixed assets

16.325 Where a company intends to dispose of a fixed asset, the asset is no longer intended for use on a continuing basis in the company's activities. Consequently, it may be inferred that the asset no longer satisfies the criteria for classification as a fixed asset. Accordingly, in such circumstances, some entities consider that the asset needs to be reclassified as a current asset.

16.326 Where assets are transferred from fixed to current assets, it is not appropriate to include the asset in the balance sheet at an amount that exceeds cost, unless it is disclosed as a current asset investment. This is because the alternative accounting rules can only be adopted for stocks and current asset investments and not other current asset items. [SI 2008/410 1 Sch 32(4)(5)]. However, SSAP 9 does not allow stocks to be stated at current cost in either historical cost financial statements or financial statements modified to include the revaluation of only certain assets.

16.327 Not all companies that intend to dispose of fixed assets follow the transfer to current assets approach. As an alternative treatment, some companies consider it more appropriate to retain the asset within fixed assets under a new sub-heading 'assets held for resale'. Moreover, in many situations assets that are disposed of quickly, rather than held for disposal for some time, are simply retired from the sub-heading in which they have been held during their life.

16.328 Deciding to dispose of an asset by itself, or as part of a larger reorganisation or disposal of a business, may trigger an impairment review. If the asset held for disposal is impaired then the question arises as to whether the resultant loss is treated as though it were a loss on disposal or simply as an impairment. As discussed in chapter 18, if an impairment loss is first identified when the asset is put up for sale and is attributable to that decision, then the loss is treated as a loss on disposal and presented as an exceptional item immediately after operating profit. However, if the impairment loss is identified earlier, that is before the asset was intended for disposal, then the loss would be presented as part of operating profit as an impairment loss.

Capital grants

16.329 The accounting options available in respect of grants are dealt with in detail in discussing revenue recognition in chapter 9. This chapter, therefore, considers only grants awarded to companies because of their investment in fixed assets.

SSAP 4

16.330 Grants received against capital investment are dealt with in SSAP 4, 'Accounting for government grants'. The original version of the standard, as published in 1974, was developed following the introduction of Regional Development Grants by the Industry Act 1972. As such, however, its scope was relatively limited, with its main requirement being that companies should credit the grant received to revenue over the useful life of the related asset. In effect, this could be achieved in one of two ways:

- The grant could be deducted from the cost of the asset thereby reducing the depreciation charged to revenue (but see discussion below on legal requirements now prohibiting this treatment for Schedule 1 companies).
- The grant could be treated as a deferred credit of which a proportion would be credited to revenue annually. In this situation, the amount of the deferred credit should be shown separately on the balance sheet if material.

16.331 SSAP 4 was revised in 1990, following the issue of ED 43 in 1988 whose proposals it broadly adopted. One of the main reasons for the revision was the proliferation of types of grant that had occurred since the standard's original publication. In particular, there had been a growth not only in the range of both capital and revenue grants, but also in hybrid varieties whereby a grant might be partly capital and partly revenue in nature. The revised standard, therefore, sought to provide broader guidance on the area of grant recognition and accounting.

16.332 When the ASC first published ED 43, it proposed to remove the option to account for capital grants by deducting them from the cost of the related asset. This was proposed partly to further the ASC's objective of narrowing the differences in accounting treatment and partly on an interpretation of company law.

16.333 Schedule 1 to SI 2008/410 requires that (subject to any provision for depreciation or diminution in value) fixed assets should be stated, under the historical cost accounting rules, at their purchase price or production cost. The statutory definitions of purchase price or production cost make no provision for any deduction from that amount in respect of a grant or subvention from a third party. The references are to paragraphs 17 and 27 of Schedule 1 respectively. These requirements could be read as prohibiting the deduction of capital-based grants from the cost of fixed assets, a treatment previously permitted by SSAP 4.

In addition, the general rule that amounts in respect of items representing assets or income may not be set off against amounts in respect of items representing liabilities or expenditure can be interpreted as specifically forbidding this practice.

16.334 The proposal in ED 43 had the DTI's support, which expressed the view that the deduction from the cost method is contrary to paragraph 17 of Schedule 1. The DTI also indicated that the 'true and fair override' could not be held to apply, since the deferred income method is capable of giving a true and fair view. In effect, the override could only be invoked in specific, exceptional circumstances where the deferred income method failed to give a true and fair view, rather than in a blanket fashion to circumvent a particular legal problem.

16.335 Reactions to ED 43 were generally unfavourable, with many commentators opposing the proposal to remove the option allowed in the original version of SSAP 4. Their rationale was that the deduction from cost method was both expedient and generally acceptable in practice, while the interpretation of company law was also considered to be questionable.

16.336 In the face of this opposition, the ASC decided that the proposal in ED 43 to remove the option in SSAP 4 should be withdrawn. Consequently, the existing provisions, whereby both the deferred income and deduction from cost methods were permitted, were retained. In adopting this stance, the ASC recognised that, from a practical perspective, not all reporting entities are governed by Schedule 1. Thus, there was no legal reason why those other entities should not retain the option. However, the ASC also recognised that most reporting entities are governed by Schedule 1 to the SI 2008/410, so Counsel's opinion on the legality of the deduction from cost method was sought to clarify the position for such entities.

16.337 Counsel reiterated the DTI's opposition to the deduction from cost method and concluded that this treatment is not justifiable for companies that follow Schedule 1, even as a permitted option. Nor would SI 2008/410's requirements be satisfied by the disclosure in the notes to the financial statements of the gross cost of the related asset before deduction of the grant, together with the amount of the grant deducted.

16.338 As a result, the revised standard was issued in a way that continues to allow both treatments as being acceptable in practice and capable of giving a true and fair view. However, the standard also warns that Counsel's opinion is that the deduction from cost method is unlawful and cannot be used by enterprises to which Schedule 1 to SI 2008/410 applies.

Disclosure requirements

16.339 Where an enterprise receives grants, SSAP 4 (revised) requires the following disclosures:

- The accounting policy adopted for government grants.

- The effect of government grants on the results and/or the enterprise's financial position.
- Where an enterprise is in receipt of government assistance other than grants that have a material effect on its results, the nature of the assistance and, where possible, an estimate of the financial effects.
- Where applicable, the potential liabilities to repay grants.

[SSAP 4 paras 28, 29].

16.340 In this context, 'government' is defined in the broader context to include government and inter-governmental agencies and similar bodies whether local, national or international. [SSAP 4 para 21]. Thus, the basic requirements of the standard are interpreted to encompass grants made by such organisations as the National Lottery, the Foundation for Sport and the Arts and the Football Trust.

Grants on non-depreciable fixed assets

16.341 While the general rule is that tangible fixed assets are depreciated over their estimated useful life to reduce them to their residual value, there are instances where assets are not depreciated on the grounds that they do not have a finite life. The commonest asset to which this applies is freehold land.

16.342 The essential difficulty facing such companies is that, should they receive grants on such assets, it would not make sense to employ the deferred income method of accounting. This is because such assets have an infinite life and, therefore, there is no appropriate method for releasing the grant. In effect, it would never be released. The deferred income figure on the balance sheet would simply get bigger and bigger and would become meaningless. Faced with this situation, recipients of grants appear to have no alternative to employing the deduction from cost method of accounting. In so doing they are, in effect, invoking the true and fair override.

16.343 A similar situation arises with certain large infrastructure assets (for example, utility networks). Where the depreciation charge on these assets is calculated using renewals accounting (see para 16.293 onwards) and the assets do not have determinable finite lives, then no basis exists on which to recognise the grants as deferred income. Consequently, grants relating to these infrastructure assets are deducted from the cost or valuation of those assets, with use of the true and fair override.

Chapter 17

Investment properties

Chapter 17

Investment properties

Introduction

17.1 The objective of SSAP 19 is to set out the requirements for the accounting treatment and disclosures for investment property and these are the areas this chapter covers.

[The next paragraph is 17.3.]

SSAP 19

17.3 SSAP 19 defines 'investment property' as an interest in land and/or buildings, where:

- the construction work and development have been completed; and
- the interest is held for its investment potential, with any rental income being negotiated at arm's length.

[SSAP 19 para 7].

17.4 In addition to this definition, the standard indicates that the following properties should not be treated as investment properties:

- A property that is owned and occupied by a company for its own purposes.
- A property that is let to, and occupied by, another group company.

[SSAP 19 para 8]

17.5 On the other hand, the standard is relatively generous in terms of its scope, since it does not limit its application to companies such as investment trusts and property investment companies, whose main or sole activity is the holding of investments. Rather it also brings into its scope any investment properties held by companies whose main activity is other than investment holding and management.

Accounting requirements

17.6 The key requirements of the standard are that:

- Investment properties should not be depreciated, but should be included in the balance sheet at their open market value. The exception to this occurs when the investment properties are held on leases that have less than twenty years to run. In such instances, they should be depreciated over the remaining term of the lease. [SSAP 19 paras 11, 12]. Note that FRS 15 excludes investment properties from its scope and, therefore, the exemption from depreciation in SSAP 19 is still applies.

- The carrying value of investment properties and the investment valuation reserve should be displayed prominently in the financial statements. [SSAP 19 para 15].
- Changes in the value of investment properties should not be taken to the profit and loss account, but should be taken to the investment revaluation reserve. This is subject to an exception which is discussed from paragraph 17.17. [SSAP 19 para 13].

17.7 SSAP 19's requirement to include investment properties in the balance sheet at their open market value has been modified by the publication of UITF Abstract 28, 'Operating lease incentives'. Operating lease incentives are sometimes given to a lessee by a lessor to encourage the lessee to enter into a rental agreement with the lessor. These incentives take a variety of forms including rent free periods and contributions towards fit-out costs. The abstract, which is discussed more fully in chapter 16, requires lessors to treat the aggregate cost of operating lease incentives as a reduction of rental income. Therefore, the cost of the incentives should be allocated over the lease term or a shorter period ending on a date from which it is expected that the prevailing market rental will be payable. [UITF 28 para 15]. Any accrued rent receivable would be recognised as a separate asset.

17.8 Also the open market valuation of an investment property may also take into account the benefit of any such incentives. To avoid double-counting the same benefit in the balance sheet, the abstract, therefore, requires that the value at which the investment property is stated in the balance sheet should be adjusted so that it excludes any amount that is reported as a separate asset under the abstract. [UITF 28 para 16]. The result of this is that an investment property would be recognised in the balance sheet at an amount equal to open market value less the accrued rent receivable debtor.

Example

An investment property is leased to a tenant for 10 years. A rent free period is granted for the first year of the lease, as an incentive, and the rent is fixed at £1.11m per annum for the remaining nine years of the lease. This is equivalent to a rent receivable of £1m per annum for 10 years. Therefore, at the end of the first year, the lessor would have recognised rental income of £1m and accrued a rent receivable debtor of £1m, in accordance with Abstract 28. The open market value of the property at the end of year one will reflect the income stream under the lease of £1.11m per annum for nine years and the residual value of the property at the end of the lease period. For simplicity ignoring the residual value of the property at the end of the lease and the effects of discounting, the open market value of the property at the end of year one would be £10m to reflect the future cash inflows from the lease. However, in the balance sheet the investment property would be revalued to £9m, to reflect the £1m that has already been recognised as a separate asset. If the open market value of the property at the beginning of the lease was £10m, this would represent a downward revaluation, which, unless it was regarded as a permanent diminution in value, would be recognised in the STRGL.

17.9 In practice arriving at the open market value of a property is a complex and judgmental exercise. It will, therefore, be necessary to understand how the valuation has been derived and how the effect of any incentive has been reflected in the valuation to determine whether, and for how much, the valuation needs adjusting to compensate for the separate accrued rent receivable asset.

17.10 In Table 17.1, Hammerson plc's 1997 financial statements provide an illustration of investment property accounting in practice (before the introduction of UITF Abstract 28).

Table 17.1 — Hammerson plc — Annual Report — 31 December 1997

Notes to the Accounts (extract)

12 LAND AND BUILDINGS (extract)

	Book value		**Cost**	
	1997	1996	**1997**	1996
	£m	£m	**£m**	£m
Investment properties				
Fully developed properties	**1,840.5**	1,776.9	**1,401.5**	1,518.7
Properties held for or in the course of development	**94.6**	63.3	**94.6**	63.3
	1,935.1	1,840.2	**1,496.1**	1,582.0

Fully developed properties are stated at market value as at 31 December 1997, valued in each region by professionally qualified external valuers, Jones Lang Wootton, Chartered Surveyors. In the United Kingdom the valuation was performed jointly with Donaldsons, Chartered Surveyors, who also acted in the capacity of external valuers. The valuations have been prepared in accordance with the Appraisal and Valuation Manual of The Royal Institution of Chartered Surveyors.

As at 31 December 1997 the market value of properties held for development was £121.3m (1996: £66.6m). The total amount of interest included in development properties at 31 December 1997 was £3.6m (1996: £2.3m). Included within properties held for development is the group's 50% share in The Oracle Limited Partnership, a joint arrangement with Abu Dhabi Investment Authority for the development of The Oracle Shopping Centre, Reading.

Should the group's properties be sold at their market value a tax liability of approximately £83m (1996: £78m) would arise. No provision for this contingent liability has been made as it is not expected that any liability will arise in the foreseeable future.

A geographical analysis of the group's properties is provided on page 59.

	Freeholds £m	Long leaseholds £m	Short leaseholds £m	Total £m
Movements in the year				
Balance 1 January 1997	1,084.4	750.9	4.9	1,840.2
Exchange adjustment	(41.2)	–	(0.2)	(41.4)
Additions at cost	63.7	38.7	–	102.4
Disposals at valuation	(87.6)	(24.8)	–	(112.4)
Development outgoings capitalised	1.9	0.5	–	2.4
Revaluation surplus	41.4	101.3	1.2	143.9
Balance 31 December 1997	**1,062.6**	**866.6**	**5.9**	**1,935.1**

20 RESERVES

	Share premium account £m	Revaluation reserve £m	Other reserves £m	Profit and loss account £m
Balance 1 January 1997	524.2	212.0	1.5	292.3
Exchange adjustment	–	4.8	–	(10.4)
Premium on issue of shares	2.0	–	–	–
Adjustment in respect of scrip dividends	(0.3)	–	–	5.4
Surplus arising on revaluation of properties	–	140.0	–	–
Revaluation of properties in associated undertaking	–	(1.2)	–	–
Transfer to profit and loss account on disposal	–	35.5	–	(35.5)
Retained profit for the year	–	–	–	11.1
Balance 31 December 1997	**525.9**	**391.1**	**1.5**	**262.9**

17.11 SSAP 19 requires the names of the persons making the valuation, or particulars of their qualifications, to be disclosed, accompanied by an explanation of the bases of valuation applied. [SSAP 19 para 12]. Where the impact of UITF Abstract 28 is material this should be reflected in the explanation of the bases of valuation applied. Furthermore, although not a specific requirement, entities may wish to consider disclosing the amount of the rent receivable debtor so that the full open market value of their investment property portfolio can be derived from the information given in the financial statements. [SSAP 19 para 12].

17.12 Moreover, in accordance with SSAP 19, where the valuer is an officer or employee of the company or group which owns the property, that fact should be disclosed. Hence, whilst the standard does not require the valuation to be made by qualified or independent valuers, there is an underlying assumption that the persons responsible for making the valuation are sufficiently knowledgeable about property valuation principles to enable them to undertake the valuation in a competent manner. The explanatory note to the standard indicates that where investment properties represent a substantial proportion of the total assets of a major company (for example, a listed company), the valuation should normally be carried out:

- Annually by persons holding a recognised professional qualification and having recent post-qualification experience in the location and category of properties concerned.

- At least every five years by an external valuer.

[SSAP 19 para 6].

Balance sheet presentation

17.13 A further issue that arises with investment properties is whether they should be treated as tangible fixed assets or as fixed asset investments. While the description of such properties as 'investment' and their non-depreciation for that reason might suggest that they should be included within the 'investments' category, neither the Act nor SSAP 19 gives any clear guidance on this question. Consequently, both practices are adopted in practice. In Table 17.2, Great Universal Stores P.L.C, for example, includes its investment properties with fixed assets as part of its property portfolio, specifying also the valuation of investment properties and the names of the valuers.

Table 17.2 — The Great Universal Stores P.L.C. — Annual Report — 31 March 1999

NOTES TO THE FINANCIAL STATEMENTS (extract)

15. TANGIBLE FIXED ASSETS	*Freehold properties*	*Leasehold properties Long leasehold*	*Short leasehold*	*Plant vehicles & equipment*	*Assets in course of construction*	*Total*
The Group	*£m*	*£m*	*£m*	*£m*	*£m*	*£m*
Cost or valuation						
At 31 March 1998	242.7	20.9	24.9	741.8	8.8	1,039.1
Movements in year:						
Difference on exchange	2.7	0.5	0.9	6.8	0.4	11.3
Acquisition of subsidiaries	24.6	53.6	0.9	275.6		354.7
Additions	19.2	5.8	5.0	204.0	23.3	257.3
Transfers	5.1		5.8	(4.2)	(6.7)	–
Sales	(6.6)	(0.3)	(0.9)	(98.0)		(105.8)
Transfer to revaluation reserve	(0.1)	0.3	(5.0)			(4.8)
At 31 March 1999	287.6	80.8	31.6	1,126.0	25.8	1,551.8
Cost	158.2	67.9	30.6	1,126.0	25.8	1,408.5
Valuation — trading properties (1996)	120.5	9.8	1.0			131.3
Valuation — trading properties (1998)	3.4					3.4
Valuation — investment properties (1999)	5.5	3.1				8.6
	287.6	80.8	31.6	1,126.0	25.8	1,551.8

Depreciation						
At 31 March 1998	43.5	2.1	10.3	433.6	–	489.5
Movements in year:						
Difference on exchange	1.2	0.1	0.4	5.1		6.8
Acquisition of subsidiaries	3.7	15.1		158.7		177.5
Transfers	0.2		3.0	(3.2)		–
Provided in year	5.1	2.9	3.0	141.5		152.5
Sales	(21)	(0.1)	(0.7)	(69.9)		(72.8)
Transfer to revaluation reserve			(0.7)			(0.7)
At 31 March 1999	51.6	20.1	15.3	665.8	–	752.8
Net Book Value at 31 March 1999	236.0	60.7	16.3	460.2	25.8	799.0
Net Book Value at 31 March 1998	199.2	18.8	14.6	308.2	8.8	549.6

Assets of £155.8m (1998 £135.9m) are held for hire under operating leases, comprising cost or valuation of £216.2m (1998 £181.6m) and related depreciation of £60.4m (1998 £45.7m).

The net book value of plant, vehicles and equipment at 31 March 1999 includes £40.1m (1998 £65.3m) acquired under finance leases.

Investment properties were revalued as at 31 March 1999, in accordance with the Group's accounting policy, by external valuers, Colliers Erdman Lewis Limited, Chartered Surveyors. This valuation was carried out in accordance with the Royal Institution of Chartered Surveyors Appraisal and Valuation Manual.

On the historical cost basis the net book value of properties carried at valuation is £80.6m (1998 £78.7m), comprising cost of £104.4m (1998 £102.6m) and related depreciation of £23.8m (1998 £23.9m).

17.14 A number of other companies account for such properties within investments. This seems to be the common practice of entities such as general insurers with large investment portfolios and relatively small levels of tangible fixed assets for consumption by the business.

Interaction with the Companies Act 1985

Measurement at market value

17.14.1 The Companies Act 2006 permits tangible fixed assets (which include investment properties) to be measured under the alternative accounting rules at *'a market value determined as at the date of their last valuation or at their current cost'*. [SI 2008/410 1 Sch 32(2)]. The Act requires that, where the alternative accounting rules are applied, gains and losses resulting from movements in the assets' value are recognised in the revaluation reserve. [SI 2008/410 1 Sch 35(1)]. This is consistent with the requirements of SSAP 19.

17.14.2 SI 2004/2947, 'The Companies Act 1985 (International Accounting Standards and Other Amendments) Regulations 2004', introduced provisions into

UK GAAP to allow investment properties to be measured at *fair value* with movements in fair value recognised in the profit and loss account. However, this accounting is not consistent with the requirements of SSAP 19 (it was introduced to facilitate the convergence of UK GAAP with IFRS) and so should not be applied. In June 2008 the BIS (formerly BERR) published guidance on the accounting and reporting requirements under the Companies Act 2006. This largely restates in terms of the 2006 Act guidance issued in 2004 in SI 2004/2947.

[The next paragraph is 17.15.]

True and fair override

17.15 Although non-depreciation of investment properties is required by SSAP 19, it may be a departure from the Act in certain circumstances. Such circumstances would include where the amount of depreciation would be material. FRS 18, 'Accounting policies', sets out the disclosure requirements in financial statements where the true and fair override has been applied. These are fully discussed in chapter 2. The key disclosures are:

- A clear statement that there has been a departure from the Act and that the departure is necessary to give a true and fair view.
- A statement of the treatment which the Act would normally require in the circumstances and a description of the treatment actually adopted.
- A statement as to why the treatment prescribed would not give a true and fair view.
- A description of how the position shown in the financial statements is different as a result of the departure, normally with quantification, except:
  - where quantification is already evident in the financial statements themselves (an example of which might be a presentation rather than a measurement matter, such as an adaptation of the headings in the Act's format requirements not covered by para 4(1) of Schedule 1 to SI 2008/410; or
  - whenever the effect cannot reasonably be quantified, in which case the directors should explain the circumstances.

[FRS 18 para 62].

17.16 In Table 17.3, Trafalgar House Public Limited Company's 1994 financial statements provide a clear example of such a disclosure, including a statement that the effect of non-depreciation cannot be quantified.

Table 17.3 – Trafalgar House Public Limited Company – Report and Accounts – 30 September 1994

Principal accounting policies (extract)

d) Fixed assets (extract)

Investment properties

Investment properties are included in the balance sheet at their open market value at the balance sheet date on the basis of an annual professional valuation.

e) Depreciation (extract)

Depreciation is not provided on investment properties. This treatment, as regards certain of the company's investment properties, may be a departure from the requirements of the Companies Act concerning depreciation of fixed assets. However, these properties are not held for consumption but for investment and the directors consider that systematic annual depreciation would be inappropriate. The accounting policy adopted is therefore necessary for the accounts to give a true and fair view. Depreciation or amortisation is only one of the many factors reflected in the annual valuation and the amount which might otherwise have been shown cannot be separately identified or quantified.

Investment revaluation reserve

17.17 The standard states that:

'Subject to paragraph 14 below, changes in the market value of investment properties should not be taken to the profit and loss account but should be taken to the statement of total recognised gains and losses (being a movement on an investment revaluation reserve), unless a deficit (or its reversal) on an individual investment property is expected to be permanent, in which case it should be charged (or credited) in the profit and loss account of the period. In the special circumstances of investment companies as defined in companies legislation (as mentioned in paragraphs 31 and 66 of FRS 3 'Reporting Financial Performance') and of property unit trusts it may not be appropriate to deal with such deficits in the profit and loss account. In such cases they should be shown only in the statement of total recognised gains and losses.' [SSAP 19 para 13].

17.18 Paragraph 14 of the standard confirms that:

'Paragraph 13 does not apply to the financial statements of:

(a) insurance companies and groups (and consolidated financial statements incorporating such entities) where changes in the market value of investment properties (including those comprising assets of the long-term business) are included in the profit and loss account;

(b) pension funds where changes in the market value of investment properties are dealt with in the relevant fund account.'

[The next paragraph is 17.20.]

Investment properties — diminutions in value

17.20 The rules in SSAP 19 relating to diminutions in value and described in paragraph 17.18 above differ from the rules relating to impairments in FRS 11 and FRS 15, which apply to other tangible fixed assets. The SSAP 19 rules retain the terminology of temporary and permanent diminutions used in the Act and follow the Act's requirements. The rules are described below.

Investment properties — temporary diminutions in value

17.21 When a company applies the alternative accounting rules of the Act, it *must* debit to the revaluation reserve those deficits that arise from a *temporary diminution* in value of a fixed asset (other than a fixed asset investment, see chapter 6). This is because it would seem that the Act does not permit such revaluation deficits to be charged to the profit and loss account (see chapter 16). The deficit would instead be disclosed in the statement of total recognised gains and losses.

17.22 On a revaluation that gives rise to deficits which are *temporary* (for example, the situation when a diminution arises as part of an annual revaluation exercise and there are no indications that any of the deficit is permanent), it is possible for these deficits to be taken to the revaluation reserve and, in effect, netted off against surpluses on other assets. If the net of surpluses and deficits results in an overall deficit on the revaluation reserve it used to be the case that this overall deficit was charged in the profit and loss account on the grounds of prudence. This is consistent with the treatment prescribed in SSAP 19, 'Accounting for investment properties'.

17.23 As noted above, SSAP 19 requires all changes in the market value of investment properties (including deficits) to be taken to the statement of total recognised gains and losses unless a deficit on an individual investment property was expected to be permanent, in which case it should be charged to the profit and loss account. As a result it is possible to have a negative investment revaluation reserve (see para 17.32).

Investment properties — permanent diminutions in value

17.24 The treatment of permanent diminutions in value of previously revalued assets is governed by paragraph 33 of Schedule 1 to SI 2008/410 which, as described in chapter 16, requires that the rules relating to permanent diminutions should be applied by substituting the revalued amount for the historical cost of the asset.

17.25 The effect of this is that the amount of the permanent diminution includes not only the diminution below cost, but also the diminution in value between cost and revalued amount. Thus, for example, if an asset costing £100 has subsequently been revalued to £150 and then suffers a permanent diminution to £70, the amount of the permanent diminution under paragraph 33 of Schedule 1 is £80 (that is, £150 — £70) and not £30.

17.26 One view which follows from this is that the whole of the permanent diminution in value should be charged to the profit and loss account. Any previous revaluation surplus relating to the asset would then be transferred through reserves from the revaluation reserve to the profit and loss account reserve up to the amount of the permanent diminution. Thus, in the above example, £80 would be charged to the profit and loss account and the previous revaluation surplus of £50 would be transferred from revaluation reserve to profit and loss account reserve.

17.27 There is an alternative treatment of provisions for permanent diminution in value of previously revalued assets. The effect is that only that element of the diminution that represents the loss below cost is charged to the profit and loss account. There are two different technical routes through which this alternative treatment can be rationalised.

17.28 One route is to argue that when a permanent diminution occurs, it can be seen as the result of a valuation process that is governed by the rules in Schedule 1 to SI 2008/410. Under this interpretation, the diminution in value from the previous revalued amount down to cost is seen as the result of a valuation which, in accordance with SI 2008/410 1 Sch 35(1), should be taken to the revaluation reserve. Once this is done the asset is stated at cost, but there is still a permanent diminution in value which, under the historical cost accounting rules, must be taken to profit and loss account. [SI 2008/410 1 Sch 19(2),(3)].

17.29 The second route is to argue as follows. The full amount of the permanent diminution in value is charged to the profit and loss account (that is, £80 in the example). [SI 2008/410 1 Sch (2)(3)]. As noted above, paragraph 19(2) of Schedule 1 to SI 2008/410 applies in the context of the historical cost rules, but it can be argued that it also applies in the context of the alternative accounting rules. However, when the alternative accounting rules are used, Schedule 1 also states that *'an amount may be transferred from the revaluation reserve . . . to the profit and loss account if the amount was previously charged to that account or represents realised profits'*. [SI 2008/410 1 Sch 35(3)]. In the example, the £50 has been charged to the profit and loss account (as part of the £80) and so paragraph 35(3) of Schedule 1 to SI 2008/410 allows the relevant amount of the revaluation (that is, £50) to be transferred to the profit and loss account.

17.30 Both of these ways of rationalising the alternative treatment have the same effect, namely that only the diminution below cost of £30 would be charged in the profit and loss account, with the diminution of £50 between original cost and the revalued carrying amount being debited to the revaluation reserve and shown in the statement of total recognised gains and losses.

17.31 We believe that this alternative treatment is acceptable. The first view (see para 17.26) has the disadvantage that the initial uplift in value is credited to reserves and shown in the statement of total recognised gains and losses, whilst the subsequent reversal of the uplift is charged to the profit and loss account. This asymmetrical treatment is avoided in the alternative treatment.

Negative revaluation reserves

17.32 Under SSAP 19, a net deficit on an investment revaluation reserve, provided that it is temporary, is not charged to the profit and loss account, but instead is shown in the STRGL. The standard is silent as to whether a net deficit should remain on the revaluation reserve or whether there should then be a transfer to the profit and loss reserve. The implication appears to be that temporary net deficits can remain on an investment revaluation reserve.

17.33 A further point of note is that, despite the standard referring specifically to the 'investment revaluation reserve', the term is rarely used in practice. In fact, the majority of companies refer simply to the 'revaluation reserve', although other terms are used such as 'property revaluation reserve' and 'unrealised capital account'. Furthermore, as the standard requires the investment revaluation reserve to be displayed prominently in the financial statements, this can be interpreted to mean that where companies with investment properties also revalue other properties, the standard requires the revaluation reserve to provide an analysis of the reserve between investment properties and other revalued assets. However, this is not done very often in practice.

Owner-occupied properties

17.34 Although the standard indicates that a property that is used and occupied by a company for its own purposes is not an investment property, there may be instances where a property is only partially owner occupied. [SSAP 19 para 8]. In such circumstances, where a property is held for its investment potential, but is either partly occupied by the company or partly let to and occupied by another group company, it would normally be appropriate to apportion the property between an 'investment' element and a 'non-investment' element. This apportionment could, for example, be done on the basis of arm's length rentals. However, before a company apportions properties in this way, it should consider materiality. For example, if a company has a number of investment properties and one small 'split' property, all the properties could reasonably be treated as investment properties.

Disclosures

17.35 SSAP 19 requires the carrying value of investment properties and the investment revaluation reserve to be displayed prominently in the financial statements. [SSAP 19 para 15]. In addition, SSAP 19 and the Act both require disclosures about the valuation of investment properties as follows:

- The names of the persons carrying out the valuation, or particulars of their qualifications. [SSAP 19 para 12; SI 2008/410 1 Sch 52(b)].
- The bases of valuation used. [SSAP 19 para 12; SI 2008/410 1 Sch 34(2), 52(b)].

- Whether the valuer is an employee or officer of the group. [SSAP 19 para 12].
- Comparable amounts determined under the historical cost accounting rules. [SI 2008/410 1 Sch 34(2)].
- The year in which the assets were valued. [SI 2008/410 1 Sch 52(a)].

17.36 In addition, if a valuation has been performed in accordance with the RICS Appraisal and Valuation Manual and reference is made to that valuation in the financial statements, then various disclosures must be made under Practice Statement 7 (see chapter 16).

17.37 Furthermore, as a fixed asset, the Act's disclosure requirements must also be met:

- The aggregate amount of that item at both the beginning and the end of the financial year in question.
- The effect of any application of the alternative accounting rules during that financial year.
- The amount of any acquisitions and the amount of any disposals, during that financial year.
- The amount of any transfers of assets to, or from, that item during that financial year.
- The cumulative amounts of provisions for depreciation or diminution in value of assets at both the beginning and the end of the financial year in question.
- The amount of any such provisions that have been made during the financial year.
- The amount of any such provisions that have been eliminated during that financial year on the disposal of the fixed asset to which they related.
- The amount of any other adjustments made in respect of any such provisions during that financial year.

[SI 2008/410 1 Sch 51].

17.38 The Act also requires that disclosures in respect of land and buildings should include an analysis of freehold, long leasehold and short leasehold. [SI 2008/410 1 Sch 53(a)(b)]. For this purpose, a lease includes an agreement for a lease. It will be a long lease if it still has 50 years or more to run at the end of the financial year in question. Otherwise, it will be a short lease. [SI 2008/410 10 Sch 7(1)].

17.39 Although FRS 28, 'Corresponding amounts', requires comparative figures to be provided for every item included in a note to the financial statements, this requirement does not apply in respect of the disclosures discussed in para 17.37. [FRS 28 para 11].

Chapter 18

Impairment of fixed assets and goodwill

Chapter 18

Impairment of fixed assets and goodwill

Introduction

18.1 FRS 11, 'Impairment of fixed assets and goodwill', was published in 1998. The principles underlying the standard were not new. Long-established rules in the Companies Act and previous accounting standards (SSAP 12 'Accounting for depreciation') had the effect that the balance sheet carrying values of fixed assets should not exceed their recoverable amounts, that is, the net cash inflows they are expected to generate for the business. There was, however, little detailed guidance on how to apply those rules – for example, how cash flows could be related to individual assets, whether the cash flows should be measured on a discounted or undiscounted basis or, more generally, when a diminution in value should be regarded as permanent.

18.2 FRS 11 evolved in conjunction with the development of the methods of accounting for goodwill and intangible assets that are found in FRS 10, 'Goodwill and intangible assets'. FRS 10 requires purchased goodwill to be treated as an asset and that both purchased goodwill and intangible assets should generally be amortised over a useful economic life not exceeding 20 years. However, FRS 10 also allows for the possibility that purchased goodwill and intangible assets can, in appropriate circumstances, be amortised over longer periods or be carried permanently on the balance sheet without amortisation (where the useful economic life is considered to be indefinite).

18.3 A key feature of FRS 10 is that impairment reviews must be performed in certain circumstances to check whether the carrying values of goodwill and intangibles are recoverable. If a company amortises goodwill or intangibles over more than 20 years or does not amortise them at all, it has to carry out an impairment review annually. An impairment review for long-life goodwill or intangible assets should be a rigorous exercise that would require an entity to demonstrate that, in respect of acquisitions, the present value of the incremental future cash flows was enough to justify the carrying value of the goodwill or intangible assets. Thus the detailed methodology relating to impairment reviews that is contained in FRS 11 evolved from the development of the goodwill standard.

18.4 FRS 11 requires entities to focus more attention on the carrying values of fixed assets than previously. Greater use is made of cash flow projections to support asset values. Less emphasis is placed on the distinction between permanent and temporary diminutions in value because, essentially, the standard is concerned with identifying diminutions in value that should be recognised immediately. The impairment tests are complex and assumptions about future cash flows are inherently subjective.

[The next paragraph is 18.9.]

Scope and objective of FRS 11

Scope of FRS 11

18.9 FRS 11 applies to purchased goodwill that is treated as an asset on the balance sheet and, with the following specific exceptions, to all tangible and intangible fixed assets. The exceptions, which are assets covered by other accounting pronouncements, are:

- Fixed assets within the scope of FRS 13, 'Derivatives and other financial instruments: disclosures', or FRS 25, 'Financial instruments: Disclosure and presentation', – these include investments that are financial assets, such as investments in equity and non-equity shares and debt instruments. Investments in subsidiaries, quasi-subsidiaries, associates and joint ventures are, however, excluded from the scope of FRS 13 and FRS 25 and thus in effect included in the scope of FRS 11.
- Investment properties within the scope of SSAP 19.
- Costs relating to oil and gas exploration that have been capitalised pending the determination of whether or not economically developable reserves exist, which continue to be accounted for under the Oil Industry Accounting Committee's SORP 2, 'Accounting for oil and gas exploration and development activities'.

[FRS 11 para 5].

18.10 FRS 11 does not apply to current assets; neither does it apply to purchased goodwill that was previously written off to reserves and that remains so under the transitional arrangements of FRS 10. [FRS 11 para 7].

Objective

18.11 FRS 11's objectives are to ensure that:

- The carrying values of fixed assets and goodwill do not exceed their recoverable amount.
- Impairment losses are recognised and measured on a consistent basis.
- Adequate disclosures are given concerning the impact of impairment on an entity's financial position and performance.

[FRS 11 para 1].

18.12 FRS 11 puts in place a detailed methodology for identifying impairments and measuring recoverable amount.

18.13 Although the methodology is complex and recoverable amount calculations may appear to be precise and detailed, it needs to be borne in mind when applying the standard that the calculations are based on best estimates of unknown future events. The forecasts that may be required are inherently judgemental and subjective.

Identifying assets that may be impaired

Definition of impairment

18.14 The basic principle is that a fixed asset may not be carried in the balance sheet at more than its recoverable amount. An impairment is defined in FRS 11 as *'a reduction in the recoverable amount of a fixed asset or goodwill below its carrying amount'*. [FRS 11 para 2].

18.15 An asset's recoverable amount represents its greatest value to the business in terms of the cash flows that it can generate. That is the higher of net realisable value (what the asset could be sold for, net of direct selling expenses) and value in use (the cash flows that are expected to be generated from its continued use in the business, including those from its ultimate disposal). Value in use is explicitly based on present value calculations.

18.16 The theory is that this measurement basis reflects the economic decisions that management makes when assets become impaired – is the business better off disposing of the asset or keeping it in use? An asset is impaired only if both net realisable value and value in use are lower than its carrying value.

18.17 An impairment review involves estimating an asset's recoverable amount and comparing it with its carrying value, as illustrated in the panel below. If net realisable value cannot be estimated reliably, recoverable amount is determined by estimating value in use alone. If the recoverable amount is lower than the carrying value, the asset is impaired and must be written down to the recoverable amount. A write-off cannot be avoided by arguing that the diminution in value is not permanent.

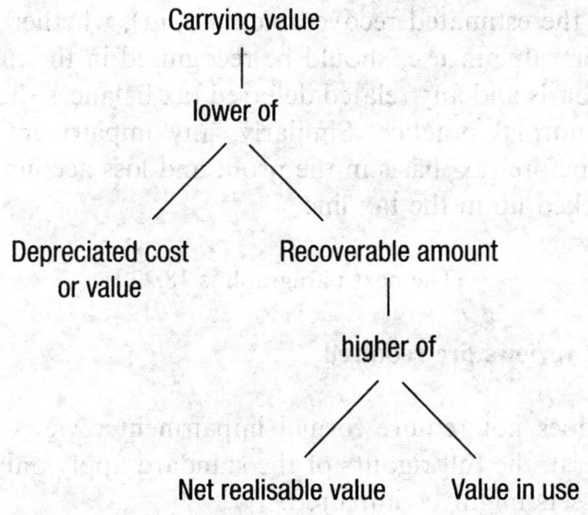

18.18 The standard is written from the perspective of commercial enterprises where fixed assets are employed to generate cash flows for the business. Where fixed assets are not held for the purpose of generating cash flows (such as certain assets held by non-profit making organisations), the value to such organisations of fixed assets acquired for the purpose of carrying out their activities cannot meaningfully be measured in terms of cash flow, because the benefits that derive from their use are not financial. Furthermore, such assets typically do not generate cash flows to cover financing costs or replacement. The normal accounting treatment for such assets is that they are depreciated systematically over their estimated useful lives, that is, as they wear out or as the benefits are otherwise consumed. The standard refers briefly to this issue and explains that it may not be appropriate to write down such assets to their recoverable amount and that *'an alternative measure of its service potential may be more relevant'*. [FRS 11 para 20]. In practice, an impairment of an asset employed in a non-cash generating activity is likely to arise only where the asset suffers impairment in a physical sense, for example, where the asset is physically damaged or where the quality of service that it provides has deteriorated. As long as such assets continue to provide the anticipated benefits to the organisation, the consumption of such benefits will be reflected in regular depreciation charges.

Deferred tax taken into account

18.19 FRS 11 explains that in determining whether recoverable amount (and, hence, the measurement of any impairment losses) should be based on net realisable value or value in use, any deferred tax balances that would arise in each case should be taken into account. [FRS 11 para 19].

18.20 The value of an asset to the business is affected by tax considerations, such as future tax reliefs or capital gains tax liabilities, which would typically be taken into account when deciding whether the business is better off disposing of the asset or keeping it in use. Thus, if a disposal at market value would give rise to a capital gains tax liability, this should be 'netted off' the calculation of net realisable value when comparing it with value in use. However, although the comparison should be made on a 'net of tax' basis, the impaired carrying value of the asset (that is the estimated recoverable amount), whether it is based on net realisable value or value in use, should be recognised in the financial statements on a 'before tax' basis and any related deferred tax balances should be recognised separately as is normal practice. Similarly, any impairment losses should be recognised on a 'before tax' basis in the profit and loss account and the deferred tax effects are picked up in the tax line.

[The next paragraph is 18.22.]

When impairment reviews are required

18.22 FRS 11 does not require formal impairment reviews to be carried out annually. In general, the full rigours of the standard apply only when there is an indication that assets might be impaired.

18.23 However, there are special rules in FRS 10 and in FRS 15, 'Tangible fixed assets'. FRS 10 requires purchased goodwill and intangible assets to be reviewed for impairment at the end of each reporting period where the amortisation period is more than 20 years; it also requires a special first year impairment review of goodwill and intangible assets relating to new acquisitions (at the end of the first full year following the acquisition). FRS 15 requires tangible fixed assets (other than non-depreciable land) to be reviewed for impairment at the end of each reporting period when either no depreciation is charged on the grounds that it would be immaterial or when the asset's estimated remaining useful economic life is greater than 50 years. Where annual impairment reviews are required, they should be carried out in accordance with FRS 11.

18.24 Where fixed assets or goodwill are being depreciated over relatively short periods, depreciation reduces the risk of impairment, but where assets or goodwill have very long economic lives, the greater is the risk that they may become impaired in the future. FRS 11 states that for tangible fixed assets impairments will be an infrequent addition to depreciation, which is likely to be the case provided that depreciation rates and useful economic lives of assets are determined realistically and reviewed frequently.

Impairment indicators

18.25 FRS 11 requires an impairment review of a fixed asset or goodwill if events or changes in circumstances indicate that the carrying amount of the fixed asset or goodwill may not be recoverable. [FRS 11 para 8].

18.26 FRS 11 includes a list of circumstances which may indicate that there has been an impairment. These are:

- A current period operating loss in the business in which the fixed asset or goodwill is involved or net cash outflow from the operating activities of that business, combined with either past operating losses or net cash outflows from such operating activities or an expectation of continuing operating losses or net cash outflows from such operating activities.
- A significant decline in a fixed asset's market value during the period.
- Evidence of obsolescence or physical damage to the fixed asset.
- A significant adverse change in:
  - Either the business or the market in which the fixed asset or goodwill is involved, such as the entrance of a major competitor.
  - The statutory or other regulatory environment in which the business operates.
  - Any 'indicator of value' (for example, turnover) used to measure the fair value of a fixed asset on acquisition.
- A commitment by management to undertake a significant reorganisation.

- A major loss of key employees.
- A significant increase in market interest rates or other market rates of return that are likely to affect materially the fixed asset's recoverable amount.

[FRS 11 para 10].

18.27 The above list is not exhaustive. Other indicators may be apparent that are relevant to the particular circumstances of a business. If there are any, an impairment review should be carried out. For example, changes in tax regulations or a significant devaluation of the currency in which the business derives its cash flows may require the recoverable amount of its assets to be investigated. Or management's own forecasts may show a significant decline from previous budgets and forecasts. A decision to sell an under-performing business would also give rise to a review of its asset values if impairment losses had not been identified and recognised earlier. Another indicator may be that the market capitalisation of the company is lower than the book value of its net assets.

18.28 Most of the examples of impairment indicators are self-explanatory. They reflect adverse events or conditions that affect either the assets directly or the business in which they are employed. They should normally trigger a review for impairment where they are relevant to the measurement of the fixed assets or goodwill. An impairment test should still be performed if there are any impairment indicators. This will be the case even where there are conflicting indicators of impairment.

18.29 Interest rates are identified as an indicator for entities to consider. The effect of calculating an asset's recoverable amount on the present value basis required by FRS 11 is that an asset will be deemed to be impaired unless it can earn sufficient to recover not only its carrying value but also its cost of capital. Therefore, if interest rates rise, the asset may need to earn more to recover a higher cost of capital. However, only significant movements in long-term rates would normally be relevant. FRS 11 emphasises that increases in short-term interest rates would not necessarily trigger an impairment review, because they may not affect the rate of return the market would require on long-term assets. [FRS 11 para 11].

[The next paragraph is 18.33.]

Special rules for goodwill and intangible assets

18.33 For goodwill and intangible fixed assets, the requirements for impairment reviews differ according to whether goodwill is amortised over more or less than 20 years, as illustrated below.

Impairment reviews

Useful life 20 years or less	**Useful life more than 20 years**
End of first full year (simplified review)	Every year (detailed review)
Other years – high level check for impairment indicators – detailed review only if impairment indicators are present	

18.34 The requirements for impairment reviews are set out in FRS 10. Apart from the first year review (see below), the methodology for performing the reviews set out in FRS 11 should be followed.

18.35 A threshold of 20 years is specified in FRS 10, below which the impairment reviews are less onerous than for longer periods. Where goodwill or an intangible asset is written off over a shorter period, there is less risk of impairment, because its net book value diminishes more quickly.

18.36 A detailed impairment review of goodwill and intangible assets is required in the following situations:

- Where they are treated as having a useful life of more than 20 years, at the end of each reporting period (including the one in which the acquisition took place).
- Where their useful life is 20 years or less:
  - At the end of the first full year following their acquisition, *only* if there is an indicator of impairment or if the first year review (see below) indicates that the post-acquisition performance has failed to meet pre-acquisition expectations.
  - In other years, *only* if there is an indicator of impairment (that is, following the normal procedures for identifying fixed assets that may be impaired).

[FRS 10 paras 34-37].

18.37 Where goodwill has to be reviewed annually for impairment, but is not actually expected to be impaired, the reviews in subsequent years after the first annual review can often be performed by updating the calculations performed for the first review. FRS 10 notes that if there have been no adverse changes since the first review, it may be possible to ascertain immediately that there has been no impairment. [FRS 10 para 38].

First year review

18.38 Where newly acquired goodwill or intangible assets are being amortised over 20 years or less, a first year impairment review is required. Purchased goodwill and most recognised intangible assets are acquired through business acquisitions. No equivalent review is required for newly acquired tangible fixed assets. This review should be carried out at the end of the first full financial year following their acquisition. It is intended to identify factors such as:

- Overpayment.
- Under-performance compared with expectations.
- Material adverse changes to the acquired business in the immediate post-acquisition period.

18.39 The first year review has two stages. The first stage in effect requires management formally to consider whether the acquisition has lived up to expectations. This is done by comparing post-acquisition performance with the forecasts used in the acquisition appraisal and by considering whether there have been any other unexpected adverse events or changes in circumstances that throw doubt on the recoverability of the capitalised goodwill or intangible assets. For all acquisitions that give rise to significant amounts of purchased goodwill or intangible assets, the requirement for the first year review means that management needs to document formally the projections used at the time of the acquisition.

18.40 If the acquisition passes the first stage, there is no need to go on to the second stage. The second stage is a full impairment review, which is only required if the first test is failed or if there is any other indicator of impairment. [FRS 10 para 40]. An example of the disclosures is shown in Table 18.1 below.

Table 18.1—Pearson plc—Annual Report & Accounts—31 December 2001

Financial Review (extract)

Goodwill Impairment

This £61m charge resulted from a review of the carrying value of goodwill on our balance sheet, required under FRS 10 (Goodwill and Intangible Assets) and FRS 11 (Impairment of Fixed Assets and Goodwill), which led to a decision to impair the value of Dorling Kindersley by £50m.

Dorling Kindersley was purchased in May 2000 for a price of £318m plus embedded debt of £49m. Although Dorling Kindersley adds value both to Penguin and our education businesses, and is expected to return to profit in 2002, the integration has taken longer to achieve than we initially envisaged and we have also reduced the revenue base in order to eliminate unprofitable publishing. Taken together with a difficult economic environment,which has affected Dorling Kindersley's travel guides in particular, we thought it prudent to write down the value of goodwill by just under 15%.

We also took a total of £11m in write-downs on various other businesses, the largest of these relating to a Latin American subsidiary. We undertook a detailed review of our 2000 acquisition of NCS but found no reason to reduce the goodwill we carry on our balance sheet as a result.

Companies Act's requirements

18.41 The Companies Act's rules on impairments are set out in SI 2008/410, 'The Large and Medium-sized Companies and Groups (Accounts and Reports) Regulations 2008' and are framed in terms of 'permanent diminutions in value' and 'temporary diminutions in value'. There has often been difficulty in determining what is permanent and what is temporary. The Companies Act requires that a company must make provision if *any* fixed asset (including a fixed asset investment) has diminished in value, and this reduction is expected to be *permanent*. In such a situation, the company must reduce the amount at which it recognises the asset in its financial statements by the amount of this diminution in value. This requirement applies whether or not the asset has a limited useful economic life. [SI 2008/410 1 Sch 19, 20].

18.42 FRS 11 does not specifically use the term 'permanent diminution' or contrast this with a temporary diminution. Where an impairment is identified in accordance with the methodology of the standard, the asset should be written down. In the case of fixed assets carried on the historical cost basis, the tests in the standard are designed to identify impairments that should be regarded as permanent. Where assets are carried at revaluation, any impairment identified using the tests in the standard will still be regarded as a loss that must be recognised, but FRS 11 specifies that the presentation of the loss will vary according to whether the impairment arises from:

- a clear consumption of economic benefits; or
- other impairments, for example impairments arising from general changes in prices.

These presentation issues are considered from paragraph 18.252.

18.43 FRS 11 also introduces the concept of the income-generating unit (IGU), which contrasts with the Act's requirements that *'…in determining the aggregate of any item the amount of each individual asset or liability that falls to be taken into account shall be determined separately'*. Whilst the Act, therefore, appears to require each asset or liability to be looked at separately, the standard requires assets and liabilities to be grouped together in some circumstances for the purpose of testing assets for impairment.

18.44 The standard, however, makes it clear that IGUs should be identified by dividing the total income of an entity into as many largely independent income steams as is reasonably practicable. Thus, it aims to ensure that the smallest possible grouping of income-earning assets and liabilities that is independent of the rest of the entity's income is chosen. This aims to come as close to the Act's requirements as is, in practice, possible, whilst at the same time being practical by recognising that assets that are inter-dependent can only be tested as one unit. Nonetheless, the standard emphasises that the value in use of a fixed asset should be estimated individually where reasonably practicable.

Measuring recoverable amount

General matters

18.45 FRS 11 defines recoverable amount as the higher of net realisable value and value in use. This reflects the greatest value of an asset in terms of the cash flows that can be derived from it, either by selling it or by continuing to use it in the business.

18.46 Both net realisable value and value in use can be difficult to determine in practice. It may be possible to determine net realisable value even if an asset is not traded in an active market. Sometimes it will not be possible to make an estimate of net realisable value as there is no basis for making a reliable estimate. In these circumstances, recoverable amount should be determined by estimating the asset's value in use. As explained later in this chapter, estimating value in use is a matter of judgement, requiring estimates of cash flows many years into the future and determining appropriate discount rates to bring them back to their present values. The objective is to make estimates as realistic as possible.

18.47 It is not always necessary to calculate both measures when performing an impairment review. If an asset's net realisable value or its value in use exceeds its carrying amount, there is no need to estimate the other amount. Similarly, if it is clear that net realisable value is lower than value in use, there is no need to estimate the other amount.

18.48 In some circumstances it may be apparent from a quick review of financial data that the value in use of an asset will either exceed its carrying value or be exceeded by its net realisable value, in which case a detailed calculation of value in use is not required. [FRS 11 para 18]. For example, where goodwill has to be reviewed for impairment each year (because its useful life is greater than 20 years) and there was previously substantial leeway between the value in use and the carrying value, a simple check on actual performance against previous estimates may be sufficient to demonstrate that value in use continues to exceed carrying value.

18.49 Where an asset is to be disposed of, its net realisable value and value in use will generally be approximately the same, because value in use then reflects mainly the net cash proceeds expected from the asset's disposal.

Income-generating units

Identifying income-generating units

18.50 In most practical situations, dividing the activities of an enterprise into IGUs is the first key step in carrying out impairment reviews. This establishes the level of aggregation at which impairment reviews should be carried out.

18.51 In general, the higher the level of aggregation the greater is the risk that impairment losses on unprofitable assets might be masked by unrecognised increases in value of profitable ones. Hence, impairment reviews should as a matter of principle be carried out at the lowest level that is practicable.

18.52 FRS 11 indicates that IGUs can be aggregated (that is, groups of similar IGUs can be considered as one IGU) for the purpose of determining value in use, provided that the level of aggregation is reasonable in the circumstances of the impairment review and that material impairments would not escape recognition by such aggregation. The rationale is that the standard is only concerned with identifying material impairments. [FRS 11 para 26]. Aggregation has important practical implications for businesses that trade through a large number of separate outlets, since it may be impracticable, or at least costly, for businesses to prepare separate cash flow forecasts for large numbers of individual outlets.

18.53 An income-generating unit is defined as:

> *'A group of assets, liabilities and associated goodwill that generates income that is largely independent of the reporting entity's other income streams. The assets and liabilities include those directly involved in generating the income and an appropriate portion of those used to generate more than one income stream'*. [FRS 11 para 2].

18.54 IGUs should be identified *"by dividing the total income of the business into as many largely independent income streams as is reasonably practicable in the light of the information available to management"*. [FRS 11 para 28].

18.55 An asset or business that is to be disposed of forms an IGU of its own and does not belong to any other IGU. [FRS 11 para 31]. Its recoverable amount consists mainly of the expected net proceeds from disposal and these are independent of the income streams of other assets or businesses.

18.56 For continuing operations, management has discretion to identify IGUs to fit their information systems within the following parameters set out in FRS 11:

- The groups of assets and liabilities should be as small as is reasonably practicable (consistent with the principle that assets should be valued separately).
- The income streams of each IGU should be largely independent of each other and should be capable of being monitored separately.
- IGUs are likely to be identified in a way that is consistent with the way in which management makes decisions about continuing or closing different lines of business.
- IGUs may be identified by reference to major products or services.

- Unique intangible assets (such as brands and mastheads) can often be used to identify IGUs, because they may generate income independently of each other and are usually monitored separately.

[FRS 11 paras 27 to 29].

18.56.1 Care is needed in respect of intangible assets as many do not generate independent cash flows and, hence, despite being 'unique intangible assets', they do not form an IGU. For example, a manufacturer that has previously acquired a branded competitor will use the brand to support the IGU that is the maintaining facility for the branded product.

18.57 There is subjectivity involved in identifying IGUs and considering when income streams are really independent. For example, in businesses that operate large numbers of retail outlets, such as stores, restaurants and financial services, different companies may take different views as to whether an IGU is an individual retail outlet or a group of outlets in a smaller or larger geographical region. Activities can also be cut in different ways – by geographical areas, product lines or in some other way. Much depends on how the operations are managed and how independent or interdependent they are.

18.58 In response to respondents' concerns about this issue, additional guidance was introduced into the FRS in the form of four mini-case studies. Although these are helpful, selection of IGUs remains a very judgmental area, particularly for vertically integrated operations and for businesses with multi-locations in retailing or manufacturing.

18.59 The first example in the FRS is a transport company operating a trunk route fed by supporting routes, which should be combined for the purposes of determining an IGU. The reasons given are that the cash flows of each route are not independent and that economic decisions about continuing or closing the supporting routes are not based on their returns in isolation.

18.60 An analogous situation is where a public transport operator runs a number of unprofitable routes in order to have access to profitable ones – it could not obtain the benefits of the latter without incurring the cost of the former where it may be under contract to provide a specified minimum level of service. Each route may or may not have its own dedicated assets and identifiable revenues and operating costs, but the income of each route is not independent in an economic sense, because management could not decide to discontinue any one route. The IGU for the assets of each route may be the whole franchise.

18.61 The second example in the FRS is a manufacturer that can allocate production across a number of facilities. One facility may be operating with surplus capacity and, hence, might be considered to be impaired if it were reviewed in isolation. However, there is not enough surplus capacity overall to enable any one manufacturing site to be closed. The FRS explains that, in this situation, the IGU should comprise all the sites at which the product can be made, because the cash inflows generated by any one site depend on the allocation of production across all sites. Therefore, the facilities are not reviewed separately, because impairment indicators affect them all together – at the larger IGU level, there may be no impairment.

Retail establishments

18.62 The third example in the FRS is a restaurant chain. The example concludes that each restaurant is a separate IGU, because its income is independent of the income of other restaurants – the cash inflows of each restaurant can be individually monitored and sensible allocations of costs to each restaurant can be made. However, since any impairment of individual restaurants is unlikely to be material, groups of restaurants that are affected by the same economic factors may be reviewed for impairment together for the purpose of identifying material impairments.

18.63 This example is relevant to a large spectrum of retail establishments but, in general, is of limited use in helping to reach a clear-cut view on whether an IGU is an individual site, a group of sites in a region, a country or the whole business. For the majority of modern multi-site retailers some level of aggregation of sites is normally appropriate, whether a larger grouping is treated as an IGU or whether each site is taken to be an IGU, but a pragmatic view of aggregation is taken on grounds of materiality, as in the restaurant example referred to above. Apart from other considerations, in some circumstances it may be impractical (or at least costly) to prepare detailed cash flow forecasts for each individual site – in any case, forecasts may to some extent be based on macro-assumptions about factors that affect larger groupings in a similar way. Some further examples are discussed below.

18.64 Judging which grouping of outlets produces largely independent income streams requires the characteristics of the way the business is managed to be assessed, for example, by considering whether:

- Performance is monitored at individual, regional or other levels – for example, considering the lowest level at which meaningful profitability statements are produced.
- Product offering and investment decisions are made at individual, regional or other grouping levels.
- Individual outlets generate custom for other parts of the network.
- Units are managed on a combined basis sharing systems, centralised purchasing and distribution functions.
- Product pricing is determined locally or on an area or national basis.
- Decisions to invest in or close outlets are taken on an individual basis.

18.65 Where regional or other groupings of establishments are taken as the normal basis for carrying out impairment reviews, any specific indicators of impairment affecting a smaller grouping would also need to be taken into account to ensure that material impairments are properly identified. Examples might include the entry of a major competitor into a local area, or the closure of a town's principal employer, both of which could have a long-term effect on the income of establishments in that area. A specific review of the smaller grouping or individual establishment affected by a local impairment indicator would then be necessary.

Banks and building society branches

18.66 Banking and building society branches generally sell a variety of products that are supported by central operations. In many ways the outlets represent a conduit for the central organisation which determines product pricing on a national basis. Whilst it may be possible to look at the income of each branch as being separate from the others, it is likely that very broad assumptions would need to be made to arrive at a measure of profitability, particularly in respect of recurring products such as life policies and savings schemes. In these circumstances it is unlikely that a branch is an IGU, unless for some reason management addresses profitability or contribution at a branch level. It is also unlikely that an individual branch would be material to the organisation.

Public houses

18.67 The income of individual public houses would usually be largely independent of others, and their performance would be capable of being monitored separately. Thus in the main they would be individual IGUs. However, as with the restaurants example in the FRS, where large numbers are operated it is unlikely that any one public house would be material and so it may be acceptable to consider them in groupings affected by the same economic factors.

Hotels

18.68 Individual hotels would usually generate income that is largely independent of others and their performance would be monitored closely by management on an individual basis. It is, therefore, probable that they form individual IGUs, even if there are central sales and marketing and finance functions. It is conceivable that a hotel chain that markets itself centrally to perhaps mainly commercial customers, might, as part of its business strategy, operate a loss making hotel in a particularly popular higher cost location in order, for example, to secure group wide contracts or a nationally advertised price pledge. On the other hand, a hotel may operate as part of a small cluster of similar quality hotels that are managed as a single operation and frequently refer guests to each other when one is full. In such circumstances, it might be argued that the hotel's income is not independent and, hence, an IGU is a larger grouping.

Petrol stations

18.69 The income of individual petrol stations is likely to be closely monitored by management, for example to determine the relative impact of local pricing differentials, and costs are likely to be able to be determined to arrive at a measure of profitability. If management would consider closing one station depending upon its individual performance, each petrol station may be an IGU – similar to the restaurant example in the FRS. However, it is unlikely that any one station owned by a major operator would be material. Therefore, where a large number of outlets is involved, impairment reviews would normally be carried out on the basis of groupings affected by the same economic conditions. Where establishments combine retail, catering, hotel and petrol outlets the interdependency of these income streams would also need to be taken into account.

Vertically integrated operations

18.70 The fourth example in the FRS illustrates vertical integration. When determining whether a group of assets involved in an intermediate stage in the production process should be treated as an IGU, the most important factor is to consider the extent to which there is an external market and source of supply for its products. This will help to determine whether the income of one facility is dependent on the income of another.

18.71 If there is a deep and liquid external market and source of supply for each stage of production, the income of each process is likely to be independent in the sense that management will monitor and make decisions about retaining or discontinuing it based on its own performance – for example, a line of production might be closed if its output could be sourced more cheaply externally. Similarly, the income generated at the retail end of the business may not be dependent on the fact that its input is supplied internally, if there are alternative sources. In such circumstances, there could be several IGU's within the vertically integrated operation.

18.72 On the other hand, if there is no external market for the output of a facility in the production chain, or the external market is not of sufficient depth to influence management decisions about the production facility itself, its income cannot be independent because the demand for its products depends entirely or substantially on the demand for the products of the facilities further up the line. In extreme cases, the whole enterprise could be a single IGU, because the income generated by each of its activities is entirely dependent on the demand for the end product.

Indefinite-lived intangible assets, for example, brands

18.72.1 Under US GAAP, indefinite-lived intangible assets are required to be tested for impairment separately by re-performing the fair value exercise on acquisition. Typically, the asset category that is most often impacted by this requirement is acquired brands. As noted in paragraph 18.53, an income generating unit is defined as a group of asset, liabilities and goodwill that generate income that is largely independent of other income streams. In many businesses, the brand is used to support production of a branded asset and the revenues from sales of the branded asset are not capable of being split between revenue for the brand and revenue for the costs of production. Hence, under FRS 11, brands are typically not an IGU and should not be tested alone, rather the brand should be tested with the associated manufacturing IGU.

18.72.2 It is, therefore, the case that it is possible for internally generated goodwill to shelter an impairment of a brand which would occur should it be considered in isolation. The principle in question is illustrated in the following example:

Example – Reviewing a brand for impairment as part of a larger IGU

Entity A is a manufacturer of consumer electronics. It has several identifiable divisions, including hi-fi, television and games consoles. In 20X1 it purchased the rights to a competitor's hi-fi brand for £300m. Production, development and marketing for the products sold under the new brand are undertaken in the same factories as the existing hi-fi operations. For the 20X2 year end, valuation specialists have been employed and have determined that the recoverable amount of the brand, in isolation, is £250m. This would, at first sight, suggest that an impairment of the brand is required of £50m. However, the recoverable amount of the overall hi-fi division at the end of 20X2 is £1,500m compared to carrying value of its assets (including the purchased brand) of £1,300m. As such, no impairment is required. The internally generated goodwill within the existing hi-fi business has sheltered any impairment on the brand, on the basis that it has been determined that the purchased brand does not generate cash inflows from continuing use that are largely independent to those from other assets.

Net realisable value

18.73 The definition of net realisable value is "*...the amount at which an asset could be disposed of, less any direct selling costs*". [FRS 11 para 2].

18.74 In calculating net realisable value, direct selling costs are deducted. Such costs include, for instance, legal costs and stamp duty or perhaps costs of removing a sitting tenant before selling a building.

18.75 However, costs associated with reducing or reorganising the business, such as costs of making staff redundant, that may be incurred before a factory building could be sold should not be deducted in arriving at net realisable value (nor should any incremental income from changes in capacity be assumed). Those costs are not regarded as part of the costs of selling the asset itself. [FRS 11 para 23]. Provisions for certain reorganisation costs are recognised (as liabilities) when the criteria of FRS 12, 'Provisions, contingent liabilities and contingent assets', are met, that is, when the company has a constructive obligation to carry out the reorganisation. If there is no such obligation at the time the asset is being reviewed for impairment, no provision is made. Either way, the question of whether provisions for reorganisation costs should be made does not affect the calculation of the asset's net realisable value.

18.76 Net realisable value is based on market value where there is an active market. Whilst active markets may exist, for example, in second-hand cars, commercial vehicles, computer equipment, certain plant and machinery and many types of property, they may not exist for specialised plant or buildings. For those assets it may also be difficult to find recent transactions for similar assets to provide reliable evidence of potential sales proceeds.

18.76.1 Where a business or an asset is being sold, the expected sale proceeds may provide reliable evidence of the net realisable value of its recognised net assets and goodwill. For example, a binding sale contract entered into after the balance sheet date would provide the best evidence, but an intended sale where negotiations are in progress may in some cases also provide reliable evidence of net realisable value.

18.77 Where there is an asset for which there is no active market, such as goodwill attaching to a business, then net realisable amount may still be derived using estimation techniques such as a discounted cash flow analysis. Discounted cash flow techniques may be used incorporating assumptions that market participants would use in estimating the asset's fair value. Any estimated net realisable value needs to be reliable in order for the net realisable value to be used. FRS 11 requires that a value in use basis should be used where no realisable estimate of net realisable value can be made. [FRS 11 para 16].

18.77.1 Some of the restrictions imposed by FRS 11 on assumptions inherent in the value in use calculations do not apply to a net realisable value and, hence, a valuation on a net realisable value basis might be higher.

18.77.2 In respect of assessing net realisable value, there are a number of valuation methodologies that are used to assess a businesses' value. More than one methodology is normally used to ensure that the valuations are cross-checked and considered in light of all appropriate market evidence.

18.77.3 In practice, a first assessment of the valuation is performed using cash flows from management. There must be, where appropriate, market evidence to support the key assumptions underpinning the cash flow analysis; for example, growth rates may be considered by benchmarking to industry/analyst reports. If certain of the assumptions used are not those that a market participant would use, those cash flows must be adjusted to take into account the assumptions that are supported by market evidence.

18.77.4 The cashflows to be used in a discounted cashflow prepared to determine net realisable value will also be different to those in a value in use calculation. Any differences in the assumptions in the cash flows used for the net realisable value compared to the cash flow forecasts used in the value in use analysis will also need to be considered for reasonableness. For example in a net realisable value cashflow working capital and tax cashflows would be included. The assumptions could also include restructurings, reorganisations or future investments. This is because all rational market participants would be expected to undertake these expenditures and reorganisations in order to extract the best value from the purchase and, hence, they would have been factored into the acquisition price.

18.77.5 If comparable transactions in similar assets or businesses are available, they should be used as market evidence. Consideration should be given to the comparability of the acquired asset/business to the asset/IGU being tested. For example, adjustments for factors such as size, growth expectations, profitability, risk will need to be considered. This evidence might arise in the implied multiple of earnings before interest, taxes, depreciation and amortisation ('EBITDA') or revenue that was paid in a comparable transaction which when applied to the current model (and adjusted for points of difference) provides support for the valuation. For example, if there are a number of recent transactions in comparable entities where the price paid is six times EBITDA and management has produced a valuation that is ten times EBITDA, then the external data would appear not to support the assumptions made in the valuation. Care is needed in selecting comparable entities; risk profile and size may well be more important than geography. Care is also needed to avoid selection bias, if one transaction in ten provides some support for the EBITDA multiple, but the same transaction is regarded in the financial press as an over-payment and an isolated example, then it should not be used.

18.77.6 As a cross-check, it is advised to benchmark the net realisable value of an IGU to multiples implied by quoted comparable companies, although consideration will need to be given to comparability in terms of size, growth expectations, profitability, risk etc. In the unlikely event that a benchmark or comparable transactions do not exist, any possible external evidence (growth rates, discount rates, etc) will be used to support the cash flow projections prepared by management.

18.77.7 Based upon the above, it is almost always possible to determine net realisable value. If net realisable value is used then the carrying value of the asset or IGU being tested for impairment must be determined on a consistent basis.

18.78 If net realisable value is found to be lower than the carrying amount of the asset, it should not automatically be written down to that value. For example, some assets could be sold only for their scrap value, because no market exists for the particular second-hand asset, and value in use may well be much higher. Before a write-down is booked, the asset's value in use also needs to be estimated in order to determine whether it is higher than its net realisable value. If it is, the impairment write-down, if any, is calculated by reference to value in use.

Value in use

18.79 The definition of value in use is *'the present value of the future cash flows obtainable as a result of an asset's continued use, including those resulting from its ultimate disposal'*. [FRS 11 para 2].

18.80 Where reasonably practicable, the value in use of a fixed asset should be estimated individually.

18.81 Investments that are within the scope of FRS 11 – subsidiaries, associates and joint ventures – generate cash flows as discrete assets and should normally be considered individually. To be consistent with the way such entities are accounted for, their value in use should normally be based on the future net cash flows of the underlying entities that are attributable to the group's interest, rather than on the basis of dividend flows. For associates and joint ventures, the carrying value of the group's interest reflects two elements – the group's share of net assets and any purchased goodwill. Any impairments in the underlying fixed assets should already be picked up in the financial statements of the associate or joint venture.

18.82 Measuring the value in use of most fixed assets (tangible and intangible) is not straightforward, because they do not generate cash flows by themselves. Cash flows are normally generated by groups of assets working together, usually by the whole range of assets used in a business. Goodwill by definition is not a separable asset and always has to be considered as part of a group of assets in a business unit. Therefore, in practice, a degree of aggregation is necessary in order to estimate value in use for complete groups of assets and associated goodwill.

18.83 If value in use cannot be estimated for individual assets, it should be estimated for groups of assets that generate income streams that are largely independent of each other. These are referred to as income-generating units (IGUs). Where an impairment review of an IGU is required, it is intended to cover all its tangible assets, intangible assets and attributable goodwill. The carrying value of each IGU containing the fixed asset or goodwill being reviewed should be compared with the higher of its value in use or net realisable value (if net realisable value can be measured reliably). If net realisable value cannot be measured reliably then the recoverable amount of an IGU is determined by estimating its value in use alone.

18.84 In summary, the key steps in calculating value in use for groups of assets are:

- Identifying separate IGUs.
- Establishing carrying values for the net assets of each IGU, comprising the assets and liabilities attributable to the IGU, plus allocated goodwill.
- Forecasting the future cash flows of the income-generating unit and discounting them to their present value.
- Comparing the present value of the cash flows with the carrying amounts of the net assets attributable to the income-generating unit and recognising any shortfall as an impairment loss.

The details of the methodology and calculations are considered in the paragraphs below.

18.85 When considering impairment issues, the separate valuation principles and the objective of FRS 11 (that fixed assets should be recorded in the financial statements at no more than their recoverable amount) should always be borne in mind. For example, if an individual asset is clearly no longer providing service potential (say, as a result of physical damage) it obviously has a recoverable amount of zero (or scrap value) and should be written off immediately, irrespective of whether the cash flows of the income-generating unit are sufficient to recover the carrying value of all its assets, including the one that has become redundant.

Calculating value in use

Composition of cash flow forecasts

18.86 Estimating value in use involves identifying the future cash flows that are expected to arise from the fixed asset or IGU (or group of IGUs) being tested for impairment. The cash flows consist of those expected to arise from the continued use of the asset or IGU and those, if any, expected to result from its ultimate disposal.

18.87 Relevant cash flow forecasts should be made on the basis of reasonable and supportable assumptions and should be consistent with the most up-to-date budgets and plans that have been formally approved by management. [FRS 11 para 36]. However, the detailed requirements include a number of exceptions to that principle, which have the effect of constraining the rate of growth and anticipated improvements that may be built into the assumptions. These are considered from paragraph 18.99 below.

18.88 The period covered by cash flow forecasts must obviously relate to the useful lives of the fixed assets or goodwill being reviewed for impairment. However, periods covered by detailed formal budgets and plans will vary in different companies and industries. In some, cash flows cannot be predicted with much certainty beyond short periods. The useful lives of the assets concerned may extend far beyond the period covered by formal budgets and plans. It is then necessary to extrapolate the formal cash flow projections into the future using reasonable and prudent broad assumptions about growth and future prospects. The standard places constraints on those assumptions that should be complied with in most circumstances and controls those assumptions by requirements for disclosure where higher growth rates are assumed.

18.89 Where the carrying value of an IGU includes goodwill or other fixed assets with an indefinite useful economic life, the calculation of value in use will include an estimated value of the IGU's cash flows relating to the indefinite period beyond that covered by detailed cash flow projections. This may be calculated by applying a terminal value multiple to, say, the cash flows expected in the last year ('CF') covered by the company's explicit forecasts, by using the formula $CF \times (1+g)/(r-g)$, where r is the discount rate and g is the estimated longer term annual rate of growth in the cash flows (constraints on long-term growth rates are considered from para 18.130). The terminal value calculated as at the end of the period covered by formal budgets and plans will, of course, have to be discounted to its present value.

18.90 The composition of the cash flows that are used to estimate value in use needs to be considered carefully. It is important, for example, to ensure that they are comparable with the basis on which the carrying amounts of the IGUs have been established, so that omissions or double-countings that would lead to errors in the calculations are avoided.

18.91 The cash flows will include:

- Cash inflows from the use of the asset or the activities of the IGU.
- Cash outflows directly attributable to the asset or IGU.
- Any allocation of cash flows attributable to central overheads.
- Net cash inflows expected from the disposal of assets or IGUs at the end of their useful lives.
- Cash outflows to maintain the operating capacity of existing fixed assets.

18.92 The cash flows should exclude cash flows relating to financing (which include interest payments), since financing items are also excluded from the liabilities attributed to IGUs and because the cost of capital is taken into account by discounting the cash flows. Tax cash flows should also be excluded, because the FRS requires value in use to be calculated on the basis of discounting pre-tax cash flows at a pre-tax discount rate (in practice, however, value in use if often likely to be derived from post-tax cash flows discounted at a post-tax discount rate, as discussed from para 18.131).

18.93 Cash inflows and outflows relating to working capital (that is, items such as trade debtors and creditors that are expected to generate cash flows equal to their carrying amounts) in the balance sheet at the time of the impairment review can be excluded from the calculations if that is easier than allocating the working capital components to individual IGUs. The assets and liabilities are then excluded from the carrying value of the IGU and the respective receipts and payments are also excluded from the value in use calculation. [FRS 11 para 33]. This exclusion of balances purely aids the preparation of the working capital forecasts, and should not make any difference to the impairment calculation. In practice, companies may find it easier to prepare an operating profit forecast for the IGU being tested for impairment and then to convert the operating profit forecast into a cash flow forecast by carrying out the same sort of reconciliation of operating profit to operating cash flow as specified in FRS 1, 'Cash flow statements'.

Transfer pricing between IGUs

18.94 Internal transfer pricing directly affects the cash inflows and operating cash outflows relating to separate IGUs in, say, vertically integrated groups. For example, consider a situation where one IGU transfers part of its output to another IGU in the same group at a price that is lower than the market price for its output. This issue is not addressed directly in FRS 11, however, the fourth mini-case study in the standard that discusses how IGUs are determined in vertically integrated groups (see para 18.70) indicates that the cash inflows of the transferor IGU and the cash outflows of the transferee IGU that are used in the value in use calculations should be adjusted to reflect market prices rather than internal transfer prices.

18.95 This principle of adjusting cash flows to reflect market prices, which is stated more explicitly in IAS 36, is logical if the cash inflows of both business units are properly to be regarded as independent. Otherwise, either the wrong assets (in terms of their true economic value to the business) could be identified as being impaired, or impairments might be avoided altogether purely by making adjustments to internal transfer prices. This is likely to be a subjective area in practice.

Central overheads

18.96 The inclusion in the cash flow forecasts of central overheads is mentioned only briefly in FRS 11, which notes that the cash flows include *'any allocation of central overheads'*. [FRS 11 para 36]. It is reasonable to assume that the cash outflows attributable to an IGU should include sensible allocations of central overheads, in the same way that the carrying values of IGUs should, where practicable, include apportionments of central assets. The assets of an IGU could be considered to be impaired if, for example, its own cash flows did not make a contribution to central overheads that are incurred to support its activities.

18.97 It is important to ensure that central overheads are not omitted altogether in the value in use calculations. It is also important to ensure that central assets and overheads are not double-counted in the impairment review. For example, if part of the carrying value of head office property is allocated to IGUs for the purpose of impairment reviews, any internal management charges that are rendered to IGUs relating to the use of that property should be excluded from their cash outflows – otherwise, the carrying value of the IGU would be increased and its value in use decreased by elements relating to the same item.

Inflation

18.98 Assumptions about inflation can be dealt with in one of two ways. One method is to forecast cash flows in current prices – that is, not to forecast future inflation. The cash flows are then discounted at a real discount rate (that is, a rate of return that excludes inflation). The second method is to forecast cash flows to include estimates of inflation in revenues and costs. The cash flows are then discounted at a nominal discount rate (that is, a rate of return that includes inflation). It is important that inflation is treated consistently in the cash flow projections and the choice of discount rate. [FRS 11 para 46]. It is arguable that the preferred method is to use nominal cash flows and a nominal discount rate. This is because the components of the discount rate are obtained from market data that reflect expectations of future inflation rates. It is difficult to remove the impact of inflation other than in a crude and thus unreliable fashion.

Constraints on forecasts

18.99 FRS 11 imposes several important limitations on the cash flows that may be recognised in the calculation of value in use, including restrictions on the growth assumptions that can be built into long-term cash flow forecasts.

Growth rates

18.100 In the period that is covered by formal budgets and plans, there are no restrictions as long as the period does not exceed five years. Therefore, in that initial period the cash flows will reflect the variability in growth rates that is included in the explicit forecasts.

18.101 However, the cash flows for periods beyond those covered by formal budgets and plans (whether they cover the full five years or a shorter period) should assume a steady or declining growth rate that does not exceed the long-term average growth rate for the country or countries in which the business operates. The UK's post-war average growth in gross domestic product, expressed in real terms (that is, assuming no inflation), is stated in the standard to be 2.25 per cent. Furthermore, the period before the steady or declining growth rate is assumed should not normally exceed five years. Only in exceptional circumstances may this growth constraint be overridden, with appropriate disclosure. [FRS 11 para 36].

18.102 Whilst this restriction is clearly aimed at preventing short-term difficulties from being overridden by over-optimistic long-term forecasts, the theory is that in the long run a business has no right to assume it can out-perform the economy as a whole. It is also prudent in the light of an uncertain future.

18.103 The FRS gives an example of a situation where a higher long-term growth rate may be justified. This is where the specific industry is expected to grow faster than the country's economy in the long-term and the business under review is expected to grow as rapidly as the industry as a whole, taking into account the prospects of increased competition. [FRS 11 para 37]. However, the ASB issues a caution in the development section of the FRS that, in its view, individual businesses in higher growth industries do not necessarily grow as quickly as the industry, because such industries may attract new businesses, reducing the opportunities for high growth rates in existing businesses.

18.104 Where the long-term growth rate assumed in the calculation of value in use for the period beyond that covered by explicit forecasts exceeds the long-term average for the country in which the business operates, the assumed growth rate and the circumstances justifying it must be disclosed. [FRS 11 para 73].

18.105 There may be situations where it would be unrealistic to cap the growth assumptions (that is, defaulting to a restricted steady or declining growth rate) after five years. This might be the case where hi-tech businesses are purchased at high multiples of current earnings, reflecting longer term growth prospects. For example, a recently acquired IGU with products under development may be expected to incur losses for two or three years and be followed by several years of significant growth as the new products reach the market – thus cash flow forecasts with explicit growth assumptions may exceed five years. But the circumstances for overriding the presumed five year cut-off must be clearly exceptional and must be disclosed.

18.106 Where, in the calculation of value in use, the period covered by explicit forecasts and before a steady or declining growth rate is assumed exceeds five years, FRS 11 requires the length of the longer period and the circumstances justifying it to be disclosed. [FRS 11 para 72].

'Look-back' tests

18.107 FRS 11 contains a safety net to safeguard against entities continually using over-optimistic forecasts to defer impairment losses. Where an impairment review has been carried out and recoverable amount has been based on value in use, the standard requires the results of the review to be monitored for the next five years, irrespective of whether or not an impairment loss was booked when the review was carried out. [FRS 11 para 54].

18.108 The actual cash flows should be compared with those forecast in the impairment review. If actual cash flows are significantly less than those previously forecast, the calculations should be re-performed by substituting the actual cash flows for those previously forecast. In this exercise, forecasts of future cash flows should remain as previously forecast in the original impairment review, except for where actual cash flows are lower than previously forecast, because certain cash inflows or outflows have occurred, or will occur, in an earlier or later period than was budgeted. If the reworked calculation identifies a previously unrecognised impairment (or increases a previously recognised impairment), an immediate impairment write-down should be made in the current period.

18.109 The under-performance in the years following the original impairment review might be an indicator of further impairment losses and, hence, a new impairment review will also be required, reflecting *current* budgets and plans. Any further impairment losses identified should be recognised immediately.

18.110 There is, however, an exception to the requirement for an immediate write-down when the exercise described above identifies an impairment. A new impairment review, reflecting *current* budgets and plans, might indicate that the impairment loss identified when the original impairment calculations were re-performed no longer exists. In this situation, an impairment loss is deemed to have arisen (based on the original calculations as reworked) and reversed (based on the new forecasts of value in use). If the reasons for the turnaround meet FRS 11's criteria for reversing previously recognised impairment losses, a write-down is not required. However, the impairment that would have been recognised and its subsequent reversal should be disclosed. [FRS 11 para 71].

18.111 The following example illustrates the calculations.

Example – Look back tests

At 31 December 20X1, an asset with a carrying value of £500,000 and a remaining useful economic life of 5 years was reviewed for impairment. Its recoverable amount was based on value in use of £506,000 and so no impairment loss was recognised.

In years 20X2 and 20X3 the actual net cash flows were significantly lower than forecast. In accordance with FRS 11 (para 54), the original value in use calculations are reworked using the actual net cash flows, as illustrated in the table below. The original value in use is recalculated as £450,000.

The future cash flows have been discounted at a rate of 5%. For simplicity, it has been assumed that the cash flows arise at the end of each year.

	Review at 20X1		**Review re-performed at 20X3**	
	Future net cash flows	Present value	Future net cash flows	Present value
Year	£000	£000	£000	£000
20X2	100	95	90*	85
20X3	110	100	60*	54
20X4	120	103	120	103
20X5	130	106	130	106
20X6	130	102	130	102
Value in use		506		450

*Actual cash flows

The revised calculation of value in use (£450,000) as at 31 December 20X1 indicates an impairment loss of £50,000 compared to the carrying value of £500,000. The impairment loss should be recognised in the year ended 31 December 20X3.

Part of the impairment loss of £50,000 would have been charged as depreciation in years 20X2 and 20X3. FRS 11 does not specify how such depreciation should be taken into account. A suggested method is shown in the table below, which indicates that an impairment loss of £30,000 is required at 31 December 20X3 after adjusting for depreciation, in order to write the asset down from its carrying value of £300,000 to the carrying value that would have been recognised if the impairment loss of £50,000 had been booked at 31 December 20X1.

	Carrying value before impairment	Carrying value after impairment
	£000	£000
31 December X1	500	500
Impairment loss	–	(50)
Depreciation 20X2 and 20X3	(200)	(180)
31 December X3	300	270

It should be noted that a further impairment review may be necessary at 31 December 20X3. Value in use would be calculated using management's latest forecasts of future cash flows. Any further impairment loss thus identified should be recognised immediately.

If the current estimate of value in use exceeds the impaired carrying value of £270,000, the impairment loss should not be reversed, unless the increase in value in use results from a forecast change in economic conditions or in the expected use of the asset. [FRS 11 para 56]. Thus in this example, if management's latest cash flow forecasts for the 3 years to 31 December 20X6 were in line with the previous estimates (£120,000, £130,000 and £130,000 respectively), their present value (that is, value in use) at 31 December 20X3 would be £345,000. Although value in use of £345,000 exceeds the impaired carrying value of £270,000, no reversal of the impairment loss is permitted, because the increase in value in use arises solely from the reduced net cash flows in years 20X2 and 20X3 now having past and from the discounted value of the future cash flows having increased (see further para 18.235).

Reorganisation and capital expenditure

18.112 A key – and controversial – constraint concerning the assumptions in the cash flow forecasts relates to future reorganisation and capital investment. Value in use is supposed to reflect the value of assets or goodwill in their current condition. Hence, the future costs and benefits of future reorganisations should not be recognised in the cash flow forecasts, unless related provisions have been made. Furthermore, the costs and benefits of future capital investment that is intended to improve or enhance the performance of the assets or business should not be taken into account in the cash flow forecasts. [FRS 11 para 38].

18.113 These are severe constraints on the calculations. Impairment reviews should be based on the most recent budgets and plans that have been formally approved by management. Where management has approved reorganisation and capital investment plans, however, the most recent formally approved budgets and plans would typically include both the costs and benefits (such as lower production costs or extra revenues from higher quality output) of the planned reorganisation and capital expenditure. Provisions for reorganisation costs might, however, be recognised in financial statements later than their inclusion in formal budgets and plans – say, after the balance sheet date at which assets are being reviewed for impairment.

18.114 FRS 12, 'Provisions, contingent liabilities and contingent assets', sets out in some detail the conditions that must be complied with before provisions for reorganisations may be recognised in financial statements. In particular, FRS 12 states that a management or board decision to restructure that is taken before the balance sheet date does not give rise to a constructive obligation (the trigger for recognising a provision) unless the entity has, before the balance sheet date (a) started to implement the restructuring, or (b) announced its main features to those affected by it in a sufficiently specific manner to raise a valid expectation in them that the entity will carry out the restructuring.

18.115 If those criteria are met by the balance sheet date and the costs have been provided for in the financial statements, the expenditure and the related benefits (such as savings from lower staff costs) of the reorganisation should also be included in the cash flow forecasts in the appropriate period for determining value in use.

18.116 If, however, those criteria are not met by the balance sheet date and, therefore, no provisions for reorganisation costs have been booked, the costs and benefits of the reorganisation should not be taken into account in the calculation of value in use either. To comply with FRS 11, it is necessary to strip out of the formally approved budgets and plans the planned expenditure on restructuring and the related benefits.

18.117 Stripping out the cash inflows and outflows relating to a planned reorganisation or improvement-type capital expenditure may not be straightforward. For example, it is hypothetical to forecast what future revenues would be if the business remained static rather than being developed in the way that is envisaged and so it may be difficult to adjust a budget to show what the cash flows would be estimated to be if a planned reorganisation or capital expenditure did not take place.

Future reorganisation

18.118 The following example illustrates the treatment of a future reorganisation and the interaction of the impairment calculations with the recognition of reorganisation provisions. The example contrasts the timing of impairment losses and reorganisation costs, which differ according to whether or not the reorganisation is sufficiently advanced in its execution for provisions to be recognised in the financial statements. It also shows how the rules may give rise to the recognition of impairment losses in earlier periods, even though management may expect to avoid impairment by reorganisation, and the reversal of such impairment losses in later periods when the reorganisation is implemented.

Example – future reorganisation planned

At 31 December 20X1, the assets and goodwill of an income-generating unit are being reviewed for impairment. The carrying value of the IGU's net assets is £6,500,000 (excluding any reorganisation provision) and the remaining useful economic life of the recognised assets is 8 years.

Management's approved budgets at 31 December 20X1 include reorganisation costs of £350,000 to be incurred in 20X2; the reorganisation is expected to generate cost savings of £100,000 per annum from 20X3 onwards. Formal budgets have been prepared for the three years to 31 December 20X4; thereafter, for the purpose of the impairment review, a zero growth rate is assumed, because market conditions are extremely competitive and this is expected to continue for the foreseeable future. The future cash flow estimates are set out below, along with figures that exclude from those estimates the cost and benefits of the planned reorganisation. Thus in 20X2 the net cash flows without reorganisation (£870,000) exceed the net cash flows with reorganisation (£520,000) by the amount of the reorganisation costs (£350,000).

The future cash flows (which exclude inflation) have been discounted at a rate of 4%. For simplicity, it has been assumed that the cash flows arise at the end of each year; therefore, the figures in the 'present value' columns for the cash flows (CF) in 'n' years time from 31 December 20X1 are derived from the formula $CF^n/(1+i)^n$, where i (the discount rate) is 0.04.

	With reorganisation		**Without reorganisation**	
	Future net cash flows	Present value	Future net cash flows	Present value
Year	£000	£000	£000	£000
20X2	520	500	870	836
20X3	1,000	925	900	832
20X4	1,050	933	950	845
20X5	1,050	898	950	812
20X6	1,050	863	950	781
20X7	1,050	830	950	751
20X8	1,050	798	950	722
20X9	1,050	767	950	694
Value in use		6,514		6,273

The impairment calculations at 31 December 20X1 differ according to whether or not provision for the reorganisation costs is recognised in the financial statements.

A – Provision for reorganisation costs recognised at 31 December 20X1

If provision has been made for reorganisation costs, the costs and benefits of the reorganisation are taken into account in determining the IGU's value in use. In this example, the post-reorganisation value in use (£6,514,000) exceeds the IGU's carrying value (£6,500,000 less reorganisation provision £350,000). Hence, there is no impairment of the IGU's assets.

In the year to 31 December 20X1, the financial statements reflect the following charges:

Reorganisation provision	£350,000
Impairment loss	Nil

B – No provision for reorganisation costs recognised at 31 December 20X1

If no provision for reorganisation costs is permitted by FRS 12, the costs and benefits of the reorganisation have to be stripped out of the projections in determining the IGU's value in use. In this example, the IGU's carrying value (£6,500,000) exceeds its pre-reorganisation value in use (£6,273,000). Therefore, there is an impairment loss of £227,000.

In the year to 31 December 20X1, the financial statements reflect the following charges:

Impairment loss	£227,000
Reorganisation provision	Nil

In the year to 31 December 20X2, the reorganisation is carried out. Assuming that the cash flow projections at 31 December 20X2 are the same as those previously estimated at 31 December 20X1 (including the benefits of the reorganisation), the calculation of the IGU's value in use at 31 December 20X2 is as follows. Note that the present values of each year's cash flows have increased from the previous table because they are one year closer.

Year	Future net cash flows £000	Present value £000
20X3	1,000	961
20X4	1,050	971
20X5	1,050	933
20X6	1,050	898
20X7	1,050	863
20X8	1,050	830
20X9	1,050	798
Value in use		6,254

As a result of the reorganisation, the IGU's value in use at 31 December 20X2 (£6,254,000) will exceed its impaired carrying value (£6,273,000 less depreciation charged in the year). For example, assume the carrying value of the IGU comprises fixed assets as follows, which are depreciated uniformly over their remaining useful life of eight years.

	Depreciated historical cost before impairment £000	Carrying value after impairment £000
31 December X1	6,500	6,273
Depreciation	812	784
31 December X2	5,688	5,489
Value in use		6,254

The IGU's value in use at 31 December 20X2 exceeds the impaired carrying value by £765,000, therefore the impairment loss of £227,000 should be reversed insofar as permitted by FRS 11. Impairment losses should be reversed in situations where the recoverable amount increases as a result of a reorganisation, the benefits of which had been excluded from the original measurement of value in use. [FRS 11 paras 56, 57]. In this case, the impairment loss should be reversed by increasing the carrying value of the fixed assets to what it would have been had no impairment loss been recognised in the previous year, that is, from £5,489,000 to £5,688,000 – a reversal of £199,000.

In the year to 31 December 20X2, the financial statements reflect the following charges and credits:

Reorganisation costs	£350,000
Reversal of impairment loss	£199,000 Cr

Future capital expenditure

18.119 Future capital expenditure and the related benefits should also be excluded from the calculation of value in use to the extent that the expenditure *'will improve or enhance the income-generating units or assets in excess of their originally assessed standard of performance'*. [FRS 11 para 38]. It should be noted that only improvement-type capital expenditure should be excluded; that which is necessary to maintain an asset or IGU at its originally assessed standard of performance should be included.

18.120 This treatment of capital expenditure needs to be considered carefully. For an individual fixed asset that is being reviewed for impairment, the treatment is relatively straightforward. The value in use takes into account the expenditure that is necessary to maintain the asset for its estimated useful economic life, but it does not anticipate the asset's enhancement or replacement. When those events occur, they result in new capital expenditure being recognised – until then, only the old asset exists.

18.121 FRS 15 codifies the accounting treatment of subsequent expenditure on fixed assets. FRS 15 sets out the circumstances where such expenditure should be capitalised or expensed in the profit and loss account. Repairs and maintenance-type expenditure (that is, expenditure necessary to ensure that an asset maintains its previously assessed standard of performance during its estimated useful life) should be recognised in the profit and loss account as incurred. Such expenditure should be included in the value in use calculations.

18.122 Capitalisation is required in three specific situations. The first is expenditure that enhances the fixed asset in excess of the previously assessed standard of performance. Under FRS 11, the costs and benefits of enhancing assets in excess of the previously assessed standard of performance should be excluded from the impairment calculations.

18.123 The second situation is expenditure that replaces or restores a separate component of the fixed asset (that is, depreciated separately from the rest of the asset). It is highly unlikely that the component would be tested individually for impairment, since it forms part of a larger asset or IGU.

Example – Restoration expenditure on a component of an IGU

The carrying value of a furnace is being reviewed for impairment. The furnace has a useful life of 20 years and requires relining every 5 years. The lining is treated as a separate asset component under FRS 15. Thus the cost of the lining is depreciated over 5 years; the remainder of the furnace is depreciated over 20 years.

For calculating the furnace's value in use, the net cash flows forecast for the remainder of the furnace's 20 year useful life would include the costs relating to relining the furnace every 5 years, because that expenditure is necessary to maintain the originally assessed standard of performance of the furnace.

18.124 The third situation is expenditure that relates to a major inspection or overhaul of a fixed asset that restores the economic benefits of the asset that have consumed and already reflected in depreciation charges.

Example – Overhaul expenditure

An aircraft with a useful life of 20 years requires a major overhaul every 3 years. The value in use of the aircraft would include the costs of each major overhaul (and revenues that assume that the overhauls are carried out and that the aircraft can continue to carry passengers for the whole of its useful economic life).

18.125 The following example illustrates the value in use calculations for an asset where future improvement-type capital expenditure is planned.

Example – Improvement-type capital expenditure

A cruise ship is being reviewed for impairment at 31 December 20X1. The ship forms an IGU of its own. Its carrying value is £72,000,000 and its estimated remaining useful life is 10 years, with a residual value estimated at £6,000,000.

Management has approved a major investment plan to increase the ship's passenger capacity and to replace its engines. The work will be carried out in 20X4 and is expected to result in a significant increase in passenger revenues and a decrease in running costs. The remaining useful life is expected to be extended by two years. The estimated cost of the new investment is £8,000,000.

It is assumed that recoverable amount is to be determined by reference to value in use alone. The future cash flow estimates are set out below, along with figures that exclude from those estimates the cost and benefits of the planned capital expenditure. The future cash flows (which exclude inflation) have been discounted at a rate of 6%. For simplicity, it has been assumed that the cash flows arise at the end of each year; therefore, the figures in the 'present value' columns for the cash flows (CF) in 'n' years time from 31 December 20X1 are derived from the formula $CF^n/(1+i)^n$, where i (the discount rate) is 0.06.

Year	Including new capex Future net cash flows	Including new capex Present value	Excluding new capex Future net cash flows	Excluding new capex Present value
	£000	£000	£000	£000
20X2	8,300	7,830	8,300	7,830
20X3	8,500	7,565	8,500	7,565
20X4	(4,000)	(3,358)	8,500	7,137
20X5	10,500	8,317	8,500	6,732
20X6	10,800	8,070	8,285	6,191
20X7	11,050	7,790	8,078	5,695
20X8	11,250	7,482	7,876	5,238
20X9	11,450	7,184	7,679	4,818
20Y0	10,990	6,505	7,487	4,431
20Y1	10,550	5,891	13,300	7,427
20Y2	10,130	5,336		
20Y3	15,725	7,815		
Value in use		76,427		63,064

For the purpose of the impairment review at 31 December 20X1, the future capital expenditure and the related benefits should be excluded from the calculation of value in use. On this basis, the estimated value in use of the ship in its existing state (£63,064,000) is lower than its carrying value (£72,000,000) and so an impairment loss of £8,936,000 should be recognised.

In the year to 31 December 20X4, the improvement work is carried out. Assuming that the cash flow projections at 31 December 20X4 are the same as those previously estimated at 31 December 20X1, the calculation of the ship's value in use at 31 December 20X4 is as follows.

Year	Future net cash flows	Present value
	£000	£000
20X5	10,500	9,906
20X6	10,800	9,612
20X7	11,050	9,278
20X8	11,250	8,911
20X9	11,450	8,556
20Y0	10,990	7,748
20Y1	10,550	7,016
20Y2	10,130	6,356
20Y3	15,725	9,307
Value in use		76,690

The ship's carrying value at 31 December 20X4 is as follows (straight-line depreciation at 10% per annum to the estimated residual value of £6,000,000 has been assumed).

	Carrying value £000
31 December 20X1	63,064
Depreciation 20X2 to 20X4	(17,119)
Capital expenditure	8,000
31 December 20X4	53,945

The ship's value in use following the improvement exceeds its impaired carrying value. In accordance with paragraph 57 of FRS 11, an increase in the recoverable amount as a result of further capital investment (the benefits of which had been excluded from the original measurement of value in use) should result in a reversal of the original impairment loss at 31 December 20X4. The amount of the reversal is restricted to the extent that the carrying value of the ship is increased to what it would have been had the original impairment not occurred, which is calculated as follows, resulting in a reversal of £6,255,000 (£60,200,000 — £53,945,000).

	Carrying value without impairment £000
31 December X1	72,000
Depreciation 20X2 to 20X4	(19,800)
Capital expenditure	8,000
31 December X4	60,200

18.126 Where all the fixed assets and goodwill of an IGU are being reviewed for impairment, the calculation of the IGU's value in use may need to include a level of fixed asset replacement expenditure in the period that is covered by the impairment review. For example, where the assets of an IGU include purchased goodwill with a long estimated useful economic life (in excess of the lives of many of the IGU's fixed assets), the cash flows of the IGU should include a normal level of fixed asset replacement expenditure that is necessary to maintain the operations of the IGU (and, hence, to support its originally assessed revenue-generating capability). However, the value in use of an IGU's existing assets and goodwill does not anticipate the costs of future improvement-type capital expenditure and the related benefits (such as additional revenues or cost savings from the use of more efficient technology). Those items would be factored into an impairment review when the capital expenditure has been incurred and new assets have been recognised, which need to be reviewed for impairment. In practice, the dividing line between maintenance-type and improvement-type capital expenditure is rarely clear-cut, since businesses are not static; the former often includes an element of the latter, especially as regards overhauls and regular refurbishments.

Newly acquired IGUs

18.127 The above rules relating to future reorganisation and capital expenditure are modified for newly acquired IGUs. FRS 11 allows the costs and benefits of planned reorganisation and capital investment relating to a newly acquired IGU to be taken into account for the purpose of impairment reviews in the initial years after the acquisition. In the case of a planned reorganisation, this is irrespective of whether provisions have yet been made in the post-acquisition financial statements (provision for such costs in determining the fair value of the net assets acquired is not permitted by FRS 7). However, the reorganisation or investment that is taken into account in those impairment reviews should be consistent with the budgets and plans that had been formulated by the end of the first full year after the acquisition. [FRS 11 para 39].

18.128 This is a somewhat pragmatic approach for the purpose of reviewing the value of goodwill on a recent acquisition. FRS 10 requires goodwill with a long (more than 20 years) or indefinite life to be reviewed for impairment at the end of each financial year, including the year immediately following the acquisition. Goodwill with a shorter life (20 years or less) should be reviewed for impairment at the end of the first full year following the acquisition. FRS 11's pragmatic approach recognises that purchasers generally share something of the perceived benefits from an acquisition with the vendors. It avoids the situation where goodwill on a new acquisition might be deemed to be impaired (and, hence, written down immediately) solely because the benefits of future reorganisation and investment, which were taken into account by the acquirer in framing its offer, could not be reflected in the impairment reviews over the initial years.

18.129 The FRS goes on to explain that the validity of this treatment would be called into question if the reorganisation or investment does not, in fact, proceed according to the acquisition plan. That situation would itself be an indicator that the assets and goodwill of the acquired business may be impaired and subsequent impairment reviews should then be carried out by excluding the costs and benefits of the originally planned reorganisation or capital investment from the value in use calculations. [FRS 11 para 40].

18.130 The formation of new IGUs in business start-up situations is not addressed in the FRS, but the principles described above from the perspective of acquisitions seem appropriate where, in order to obtain the benefits from initial investment, it is necessary to undertake further capital expenditure. For example, in the early stages of the development of a new project, an impairment loss might be identified if no account were taken of future capital expenditure required to complete the development plan, as it might be loss-making on a 'current condition' basis (that is, until successful completion). Applying the principles of paragraph 39 of FRS 11, if the projections in the development plan (taking account of future capital expenditure required to enable the IGU to reach its originally assessed standard of performance) showed an adequate expected rate of return on the new investment, there would be no impairment. However, if the business subsequently abandoned the development plan, it could no longer be used to support the avoidance of an impairment loss.

Discount rate

18.131 Investment decisions take account of the time value of money and the risks associated with expected future cash flows. These are also reflected in the measurement of an asset's value in use.

18.132 Expected future cash flows are discounted at a rate described as *'an estimate of the rate that the market would expect on an equally risky investment.'* [FRS 11 para 41]. This rate reflects both current assessments of the time value of money and the risks specific to the asset concerned. This means that (unless net realisable value is higher) an asset is regarded as impaired if it is not expected to earn a current market-related rate of return on its carrying value.

18.133 The rate of return expected by the market is independent of the way the asset is financed, although the entity's overall cost of capital will sometimes provide a good starting point for estimating a rate.

18.134 The choice of a discount rate is a subjective area. Furthermore, the value in use calculations are sensitive to variations in discount rates. Often there is no directly observable market rate. The FRS suggests the market rate can be estimated by a number of means:

- The rate implicit in market transactions of similar assets.
- The weighted average cost of capital (WACC) for a listed company with a similar risk profile.
- The WACC for the entity, adjusted up or down for the particular risks of the IGU being reviewed for impairment.

[FRS 11 para 42].

18.135 Rates applicable to different business units within a group may vary to reflect any risk factors that are specific to those units. Trading activities and investments in different countries are likely to have different risks, for example, currency and political risks. The rate should be appropriate to the country in which the IGU operates (or in whose currency it derives its major cash flows) rather than the country in which the finance is sourced. Different business sectors also attract different risks – for example, a biotechnology company will carry a greater market risk than a regulated utility. In general, the more uncertain the cash flows are, the more risky the investment is, and the greater the risk adjustment is to increase the discount rate.

18.136 For some companies, the WACC will be an observable rate that they are familiar with. IAS 36, the IFRS impairment standard, refers to using techniques such as the Capital Asset Pricing Model, which is commonly used in assessing the cost of equity. The FRS notes, however, that if the discount rates are derived from the entity's WACC, the weighted average of the rates applied to each IGU should equal the WACC of the entity as a whole. [FRS 11 para 43]. The FRS does not, however, indicate how this calculation might be performed; proving that the sum of the IGUs' WACCs equals the entity's WACC may be difficult and may not really be relevant if only one IGU is being reviewed for impairment.

18.137 If an impairment loss is recognised and is measured by reference to value in use of a fixed asset or IGU, the FRS also requires the discount rate to be disclosed in the financial statements. As an alternative to using a risk-adjusted discount rate, it may sometimes be more practicable to adjust the expected cash flows (downwards) for risk and to discount those risk-adjusted cash flows at a risk-free discount rate, such as a government bond rate. [FRS 11 para 45]. Where this is done, the FRS requires some indication of the risk-adjustments made to the cash flows to be disclosed. [FRS 11 para 69]. It is important that risk is not double-counted in the calculations; that is, the discount rate should not include a risk weighting if the underlying cash flows have already been adjusted for risk.

18.138 Inflation should also be treated consistently in the present value calculations. If the future cash flows are estimated at current values, the discount rate is a real rate, that is, inflation should be excluded. If the estimated future cash flows include inflation, the discount rate is a nominal rate, that is including inflation.

Pre-tax rate

18.139 FRS 11 requires the discount rate for value in use to be calculated on a pre-tax basis. [FRS 11 para 41]. Thus an IGU's pre-tax cash flows should be discounted at the determined pre-tax discount rate.

18.140 Where a pre-tax discount rate is available this presents no issues. FRS 11 recognises that in many cases the only observable market rate of return is a *post-tax* rate. This is the case, for example, where the discount rate is derived from an entity's WACC, which many companies would look to when estimating the appropriate discount rate. The FRS requires the post-tax rate to be adjusted to a pre-tax basis.

18.141 The use of pre-tax cash flows and a pre-tax discount rate means that the result is a pre-tax value in use, which will normally differ from the post-tax value in use. If an impairment loss arising from a pre-tax value in use, this creates a taxable temporary difference on which deferred tax should be recognised if required by FRS 19.

18.142 How to calculate the appropriate pre-tax rate from a post-tax starting point is a key practical issue. Unfortunately, it is not simply a matter of grossing up the required post-tax rate of return at the standard or effective rate of tax and discounting the pre-tax cash flows at that grossed up rate. This would only give the correct result if there is no growth in cash flows and no deferred tax. It is necessary to adjust the post-tax rate much more carefully, to reflect the specific amount and timing of the future cash flows.

18.143 Appendix 1 to the standard gives some guidance on how the adjustment to a pre-tax rate might be calculated. It states that the required pre-tax rate is *'the* *rate of return that will, after tax has been deducted, give the required post-tax rate of return*'. The example given in the standard is over-simplified, but some useful observations can be drawn from it.

18.143.1 The following example illustrates how the pre-tax rate could correctly be derived from the post-tax rate.

Example – Calculating a pre-tax discount rate (1)

An IGU is being tested for impairment at the end of 20X0. The IGU comprises a specific asset, which was purchased two years ago for £2,400. The asset has a ten year useful life for accounting purposes. Tax relief on the asset is available on a straight line basis over the first three years of the asset's life, hence there is a timing difference giving rise to a deferred tax liability. The tax rate is 35%.

Pre-tax profits from the asset are expected to be £125 at the end of 20X1, increasing by 5 for each of the following seven years. The appropriateness of such an increasing rate has been considered and determined reasonable. The results for the seven years in question are, therefore, as follows:

£	**20X1**	**20X2**	**20X3**	**20X4**	**20X5**	**20X6**	**20X7**	**20X8**
Pre-tax profit	125	130	135	140	145	150	155	160
Add back depreciation	240	240	240	240	240	240	240	240
Pre-tax cash flow	**365**	**370**	**375**	**380**	**385**	**390**	**395**	**400**
Tax on profit	(44)	(46)	(47)	(49)	(51)	(53)	(54)	(56)
Post-tax cash flow	**321**	**325**	**328**	**331**	**334**	**338**	**341**	**344**

The post-tax discount rate, determined from the WACC of the company, is 8%.

There are two potential misapplications of the requirements of FRS 11 that are commonly seen. Neither of these give the correct value in use per the requirements of FRS 11.

Misapplication 1: Discount post-tax cash flow at post-tax discount rate of 8%. This gives a value in use of £1,904.

Misapplication 2: Discount pre-tax cash flow at post-tax discount rate grossed up for the tax rate. This rate would be 8%/(1-0.35) = 12.3%. This gives a value in use of £1,866.

These misapplications fail to achieve the correct result, either by not accounting for varying period-on-period cash flows or by ignoring deferred tax. The correct value in use can be achieved by taking the value in use from Misapplication 1 and adjusting for the discounted cash outflows related to deferred tax. This is a complex iterative calculation as the discounted cash outflows in question relate to the pre-tax value in use – hence the result of the calculation feeds back into the calculation itself. The calculation is best solved with the aid of a computer, but the following summarises the final calculation for the above example once the iteration has been completed.

£	20X0	20X1	20X2	20X3	20X4	20X5	20X6	20X7	20X8
Pre-tax VIU (*a*)	1,729	1,513	1,296	1,080	864	648	432	216	0
Tax base (*ß*)	800								
a – *ß*	*929*	*1,513*	*1,296*	*1,080*	*864*	*648*	*432*	*216*	*0*
Change in *a* – *ß*		*584*	*(216)*	*(216)*	*(216)*	*(216)*	*(216)*	*(216)*	*(216)*
@ 35% (tax)		204	(76)	(76)	(76)	(76)	(76)	(76)	(76)
Discounted (8%)	(175)								
Post-tax VIU	1,904								
Pre-tax VIU	**1,729**								

The 'pre-tax VIU' number is as calculated in 'Misapplication 1' above. The iterative process will complete when a set of figures for the first line have been derived which, when discounted at 8%, produce the same number as in the bottom 'pre-tax VIU' line.

Having derived the correct pre-tax VIU, and having the correct pre-tax cash flows, it is possible to 'back-solve' to obtain pre-tax discount rate that discounts the latter to the former. In this case this figure is 14.5%.

18.143.2 Deriving a true pre-tax discount rate is a complex exercise. There are some practical methods to use to identify potential impairment losses and estimate the pre-tax impact.

18.143.3 One method is to calculate the post-tax cash flow discounted at the post-tax discount rate, as per Misapplication 1. This calculation should give a reasonable indication of whether there has been an impairment using readily available data. If no impairment is identified, a judgement can then be made with regard to the headroom above carrying value – if the headroom is considered sufficiently high, then it will be possible to infer that the likelihood of an impairment arising on a pre-tax calculation is remote. The pre-tax rate can be estimated for disclosure purposes.

18.143.4 If there is not significant headroom in the post-tax calculation then a pre-tax analysis will be required to identify the correct pre-tax value in use from which the pre-tax impairment loss and the related deferred tax effects can be derived (as can the pre-tax discount rate for disclosure purposes).

18.143.5 An alternative method would be to estimate the correct value in use of Misapplication 2 – estimating the pre-tax discount rate by grossing up the post-tax discount rate by an appropriate tax rate (for example, the estimated future cash tax rate). Care should be taken in this exercise. For instance the estimate made should be adjusted to reflect the effect of special factors that might materially distort the relationship between the post-tax rate and the pre-tax rate – for example, where the timing of the tax cash flows is very favourable to the entity because of accelerated capital allowances, as in our example. Applying this estimated rate to the the pre-tax cash flows would result in an estimated value in use (and an estimated impairment loss) of the asset or CGU. As above, judgement will be needed to assess the reasonableness of the estimate.

18.143.6 If neither of these approximations is deemed acceptable then a pre-tax analysis will be required. The required pre-tax rate is the rate of return that will, after tax has been deducted, give the required post-tax rate of return. The following simplified example illustrates further how the pre-tax rate may be derived from the post-tax rate.

Example – Calculating a pre-tax discount rate (2)

The post-tax market rate of return required from an asset is 14%. Profits are taxed at 30%; there is a capital allowance of 100% of the cost of the asset. All cash flows arise at the end of year 1.

For an asset costing £100, the required post-tax cash flows during year 1 are £114. Pre-tax cash flows of £120 must be earned in order to give the required post-tax return of £114. Pre-tax cash flows of £120 result in a tax charge of £6 – comprising tax on profit before depreciation of £36 (30% of £120) less tax relief on the cost of the asset of £30 (30% of £100). Thus the required pre-tax rate is 20%.

The value in use of £100 of an asset with the above cash flows can be derived either by discounting the post-tax cash flows of £114 at the post-tax rate of 14% or by discounting the pre-tax cash flows of £120 at the derived pre-tax rate of 20%. The same answer is obtained from both methods, because the cost of the asset is fully deductible for tax purposes as a result of the 100% capital allowances and, therefore, does not give rise to any timing differences.

18.144 The above examples demonstrate that the pre-tax rate has to be derived from the post-tax rate and the post-tax cash flows. Therefore, the starting point is a *post-tax* analysis, despite the value in use calculation being labelled as a pre-tax exercise.

18.145 Grossing up from a post-tax rate of 14 per cent to a pre-tax rate of 20 per cent reflects the assumed rate of corporation tax only because of its unrealistic simplicity. The relationship between the post-tax rate and the derived pre-tax rate will deviate from the standard rate as soon as real factors are introduced such as uneven multi-period cash flows, timing differences between pre-tax cash flows and the related tax cash flows and so on.

18.146 The pre-tax discount rate can be derived using the post-tax discount rates directly observable from capital markets by using a two-step iterative calculation process to convert the post-tax discount rate into an implicit pre-tax rate. This is based on: first, discounting the post-tax cash flows using a post-tax discount rate, then determining the implicit pre-tax rate that needs to be applied to pre-tax cash flows to arrive at the same result. Post-tax cash flows should reflect the specific amount and timing of the future tax cash flows.

18.146.1 In theory, discounting post-tax cash flows at a post-tax discount rate should lead to the same result as discounting pre-tax cash flows with a pre-tax discount rate, as long as the pre-tax discount rate is the post-tax discount rate adjusted to reflect the specific amount and timing of the future tax cash flows.

18.146.2 In practice, the following two-step approach can be applied to derive iteratively the implicit pre-tax discount rate from post-tax data. In Step 1, the expected actual tax cash payments are calculated to arrive at post-tax cash flows (after-tax cash flows) from pre-tax cash flow projections. These after-tax cash flows are discounted at an appropriate post-tax discount rate derived using information observable on the capital markets.

18.146.3 As a starting point for the derivation of the post-tax discount rate, the entity's weighted average cost of capital (WACC) could be taken into account (as opposed to entity's incremental borrowing rate or other market borrowing rates), as the WACC is usually a good reflection of the risk specific to the asset/IGU provided that it is similar to the rate a market participant would use. This WACC should be adjusted for specific risks associated with the asset/IGU's estimated cash flows (for example, country/currency/price risk). If such WACC for the entity is not available, it may be necessary to estimate a WACC using peer group data.

18.146.4 In Step 2, the pre-tax discount rate is derived by determining the rate required to be applied to the pre-tax cash flows to arrive at the result obtained in step 1. In practice, the rate is calculated using the same methodology as for the calculation of an internal rate of return.

Allocating assets and liabilities to IGUs

18.147 The carrying amount of each IGU being reviewed for impairment needs to be established. This is done by allocating assets and liabilities to individual IGUs. The carrying amount of an IGU consists of:

- Assets and liabilities that are directly and exclusively attributable to the IGU.
- An allocation of assets and liabilities that are indirectly attributable to more than one IGU (that is, central assets).
- Capitalised goodwill (or negative goodwill).

18.148 The assets and liabilities attributed to IGUs should be consistent with the cash flows that are identified for calculating value in use. Assets in the first category above will include all directly attributable tangible and intangible fixed assets and current assets such as stocks, trade debtors and prepayments. Liabilities will include trade creditors and directly attributable accruals and provisions. However, if it is easier in practice to exclude items of working capital in the IGU's balance sheet at the date of the impairment review (that is, items such as trade debtors and creditors that will generate cash flows equal to their carrying amounts), this is permitted provided, of course, that the receipts and payments are also excluded from the value in use calculation.

18.149 Liabilities that relate to financing the operations of IGUs (including interest-bearing debt, dividends and interest payable) are not allocated, because the related cash outflows are also excluded from the impairment calculations and such items are taken into account in the rate used to discount the future operating cash flows when calculating an IGU's value in use. Similarly, tax balances are not allocated for a value in use calculation, because the discounted cash flow forecasts are prepared on a pre-tax basis. In contrast in a net realisable value calculation current and deferred tax balances and their associated cash flows are taken into account.

18.150 The standard does not specify how leased assets should be treated. Under the standard's impairment review methodology, the approach would be as follows. For finance leases, the carrying value of the leased asset would be included in the carrying value of the IGU; the lease liability and the lease payments would be excluded from the impairment calculations because they relate to financing. For operating leases, no assets would be recognised in the carrying value of the IGU; the lease payments would be treated as operating cash outflows in the calculation of value in use.

Central assets

18.151 Where practicable, FRS 11 requires that assets that contribute indirectly to IGUs (such as corporate head offices, computer centres or research facilities) should be allocated to individual IGUs on a logical and systematic basis that reflects the extent to which those resources are applied to support each IGU. An example is given of pro-rating according to the carrying values of the net assets directly attributable to IGUs. The idea is that the carrying values of all IGUs in a group should add up to the carrying value of the group's net assets in aggregate (excluding tax and financing items) – thus no assets should escape attention in an impairment review.

18.152 The reason for including central assets (which may not generate any income) is that unless the operating assets or IGUs are expected to generate sufficient cash flows to recover the carrying amounts of all the entity's assets (that is, including the central assets which generate no external income themselves), there is an impairment.

18.153 This treatment of central assets may be problematical if companies' information systems do not readily provide such allocations. In addition, the basis for allocating central costs to operating units will need to be reviewed to ensure that the cash flows used for the impairment reviews are on a basis that is consistent with the basis on which the central assets have been allocated.

18.154 By including allocations of central assets within the IGU's carrying value, the impairment review checks whether or not the IGU's net cash flows (exclusive of any cash outflows relating to the IGU's use of those central assets) are expected to recover the carrying values of the IGU's own assets and the allocated portion of central assets. For example, if an IGU is allocated a portion of the book value of the group's head office, the impairment review compares the IGU's value in use with the carrying value as increased. Any internal charges that are payable relating to the use of the head office would need to be excluded from the IGU's cash flows; otherwise the consumption of head office resources would be double-counted, because the carrying value would be increased and the value in use decreased by the same item.

18.155 FRS 11 permits a simpler alternative approach to be used where central assets cannot readily be allocated on a meaningful basis. The alternative approach permits central assets to be reviewed for impairment on an aggregate basis where there is no reasonable basis for allocating them to individual IGUs. This would require a two-tier impairment review:

- A review at the individual IGU level, where only the assets and liabilities directly involved are reviewed for impairment.
- A review at a higher level, where any central assets that contribute to the relevant IGU are reviewed for impairment in aggregate with all other IGUs to which they contribute. This review compares the aggregate of the net assets of those IGUs and the central assets with their combined value in use.

18.156 A consequence of this approach is that impairment tests encompass certain IGUs irrespective of whether they are displaying characteristics which would trigger an impairment review.

18.157 The two methods described above of dealing with central assets are likely to result in different impairment calculations. The second method of not allocating central assets to IGUs reduces the prospect of impairment losses being identified. The reason is that impairment losses that may otherwise be attributed to individual IGUs (because their carrying values would reflect allocations of central assets) may to some extent be avoided if the carrying amounts of central assets can be recovered from other more profitable IGUs. At the IGU level, there is no impairment of the operating assets as long as they are earning a market-related return on their carrying values. At the combined level, there is no impairment of the central assets as long as the combined operations are in aggregate earning a market-related return on all the assets, including the central assets. An example in paragraph 18.199 illustrates the different calculations.

Purchased goodwill

18.158 For goodwill, the details of the impairment review differ according to whether:

- Goodwill *only* is being reviewed for impairment (for example, the mandatory annual review for goodwill with a useful life of more than 20 years, where there are no indicators of impairment).
- Goodwill *and* other fixed assets are being reviewed for impairment (for example, because there are indicators that an impairment may have occurred).

18.159 The differences relate to the level of aggregation at which groups of assets or businesses are reviewed for impairment. Although impairment reviews for fixed assets, including recognised intangibles, should be carried out at the level of each IGU that is being tested for impairment (subject to possible groupings on materiality grounds), FRS 11 allows a higher level of aggregation for impairment reviews on goodwill.

18.160 IGUs may be combined for testing the recoverability of the related goodwill if:

- they were acquired as part of the same investment; and
- they are involved in similar parts of the business.

[FRS 11 para 34].

18.161 This means that if goodwill relating to the acquisition of a group of companies has to be reviewed annually for impairment only because it is being carried permanently as an asset or is being amortised over more than 20 years, and there are no reasons to suggest that either the goodwill or other assets have actually been impaired, the whole acquisition could be treated as one IGU for the purpose of testing goodwill for impairment if the acquisition comprises similar activities. Thus, the overall goodwill on the acquisition would not have to be sub-divided for the purpose of this impairment review.

18.162 If, however, there are indicators that the carrying values of goodwill or fixed assets may not be recoverable, the normal rules of FRS 11 apply. Individual reviews of each relevant IGU must then be carried out to consider whether fixed assets (other than goodwill) have been impaired.

18.163 If IGUs are combined for testing goodwill, a two-tier impairment review is required, similar to the combined approach for dealing with central assets:

- A review at the individual IGU level, where the assets and liabilities (excluding any allocation of goodwill) are reviewed for impairment. Any impairment loss is attributed to the IGU's assets.
- A review at a higher level to test the recoverability of the goodwill, where all the IGUs to which the goodwill relates are reviewed in aggregate. This review compares the carrying amount of the net assets of those IGUs and the purchased goodwill in aggregate with their combined value in use. Any further impairment loss identified at this level relates to the goodwill.

An example illustrating the two different approaches to treating goodwill is given in paragraph 18.193.

Guidelines on allocating goodwill

18.164 The carrying amount of capitalised goodwill should be allocated either to individual IGUs or, if the alternative approach is taken, to groups of similar

IGUs that formed part of the same acquisition. An impairment of goodwill in one business could not be offset against an increase in value of another dissimilar business or one that was acquired at a different time.

18.165 Groups need to keep detailed records of the composition of the aggregate amount of purchased goodwill, that is, to which parts of the group it relates. Apart from the possibility of impairment reviews in the future, allocation of goodwill to business units is necessary to account for subsequent disposals (to determine how much goodwill should be written off when a business is sold) and to keep track of elements of goodwill with different useful economic lives.

18.166 It has always been recognised that there are practical difficulties with attributing goodwill to businesses closed or sold. Tracing purchased goodwill is an issue in complex group structures, particularly where an acquired business quickly loses its separate identity or when businesses undergo change and restructuring. Nevertheless, groups have generally managed to make reasonable allocations of goodwill to disposals.

18.167 As far as is practical and consistent with the requirements of the impairment review, the objective should be to allocate goodwill balances to business units on a basis consistent with the group's management reporting structure.

18.168 There is no real guidance in the accounting standards dealing with goodwill and impairment on how to allocate purchased goodwill to different business units. In principle, goodwill should be allocated based on information and factors existing at the date of acquisition.

18.169 If the acquirer, when framing its offer, had assessed individually the values of different businesses in an acquired group, such valuations should be a good starting point for the allocation of goodwill. Thereafter, various methods could be adopted to apportion goodwill to different IGUs or groups of similar IGUs. The choice should best reflect the basis on which the business would be valued by the market at the time of the acquisition. It should be noted, however, that FRS 10 does not permit purchased goodwill arising on a single acquisition transaction to be divided into components of positive and negative goodwill, because goodwill (positive or negative) is treated as a residual difference that arises from fair valuing the acquisition as a whole. Examples of possible allocation methods are:

- Using discounted cash flow forecasts where these are available at the time of the acquisition.
- Pro-rata on the basis of a price-earnings formula, using cash flows or income streams projected at the acquisition date.
- Pro-rata on net asset value at the acquisition date (probably excluding interest-bearing debt and other financing liabilities).
- Pro-rata using the fair values of the fixed assets at the acquisition date.

18.170 Earnings-based methods may give a very different goodwill allocation from asset-based methods. The choice would be determined by ascertaining how the market rates businesses similar to those acquired – on an earnings or net assets basis. Earnings-based methods are, in general, likely to be appropriate for most acquisitions, because asset-based methods do not generally reflect the relative profitability of different businesses. A cash flow/price-earnings (PE) approach is also consistent with the principles for calculating value in use and is therefore likely to be the most appropriate method to use. An asset value basis would be appropriate for some asset-based acquisitions, such as property companies.

18.171 The choice of a PE ratio could be influenced by considering PE ratios of similar businesses that are listed, although it would not be appropriate to look to PE ratios of those preparing their financial statements on a different basis, such as IFRS. For example, if an acquisition comprised a construction and a transport operation, the allocation would take account of the differing PE ratios relating to those sectors at the acquisition date.

18.172 Where an acquisition gives rise to positive goodwill overall, no goodwill (positive or negative) would be attributed to an IGU where management believe none existed when the group was acquired. For example, where a business is loss-making or operating at a low level of profitability that does not cover the cost of capital, no negative goodwill should be allocated; instead, the overall goodwill on the acquisition would be allocated to those IGUs where it is believed goodwill does exist.

18.173 An example of different allocation methods is illustrated below.

Example – allocation of purchased goodwill

An acquisition of a group comprises three business segments A, B and C. Total purchase consideration was £450m. The fair value of the net assets in aggregate was £350m (as allocated in the table below), leaving goodwill of £100m. Different allocation methods are illustrated in the table below.

Business acquired	**A**	**B**	**C**	**D**
–	–	–	–	–
Profit estimate	20	30	(5)	45
Net assets – fair value	200	100	50	350
Sector PE ratio	12	8		
Goodwill — earnings basis	22	78	Nil	100
Goodwill — net assets basis	67	33	Nil	100

Segment C (which is loss-making) receives a zero allocation of goodwill under both methods. Therefore, all of the goodwill has been allocated to segment A and segment B.

On an earnings basis, segment A and segment B are each valued at £240m (that is, 12 × £20m and 8 × £30m respectively), compared with fair valued net assets of £200m and £100m respectively. The purchased goodwill of £100m is allocated *pro rata* to the amount by which the values of segment A and segment B exceed the fair values of their net assets (£40m and £140m respectively) which results in £22m being allocated to segment A and £78m being allocated to segment B.

On a net assets basis, the purchased goodwill of £100m is allocated *pro rata* to the fair valued net assets of £200m in segment A and £100m in segment B, which results in £67m being allocated to segment A and £33m to segment B.

18.174 In the above example, no goodwill (positive or negative) has been allocated to segment C, which is loss-making. FRS 10 does not allow both positive and negative goodwill to be recognised in respect of a single acquisition. If the assets of that business are already impaired at the date of acquisition, FRS 7 requires the impairment to be reflected by reducing the fair values on acquisition. [FRS 7 paras 47].

[The next paragraph is 18.184.]

Recognition of impairment losses

Allocation of impairment losses to assets of income-generating units

18.184 Where the recoverable amounts of fixed assets can be estimated individually, the recognition of impairment losses is straightforward. The assets are written down to their individual recoverable amounts (that is, the higher of net realisable value and value in use).

18.185 Where the recoverable amounts of fixed assets or goodwill cannot be estimated individually and, hence, they need to be estimated in aggregate for the IGUs to which they belong, the question arises as to which assets in the IGU should be written down where the carrying value of an IGU's net assets in aggregate exceeds its recoverable amount.

18.186 FRS 11 requires that, unless an impairment is obviously attributable to a specific asset in an IGU, an impairment loss attributable to an IGU should be allocated to write down the assets in the following order:

- Purchased goodwill.
- Capitalised intangibles.
- Tangible assets, on a *pro rata* or more appropriate basis.

[FRS 11 para 48].

The reason for this hierarchy is to ensure that the assets with the most subjective valuations are written off first.

Example – Allocation of impairment losses

An IGU has attributed net assets of £500m, as set out in the table below. An impairment review estimates the present value of its future cash flows to be £300m. There is an impairment loss of £200m which is written off as shown.

		Write-off
	£m	£m
Purchased goodwill	150	(150)
Intangible assets	30	(30)
Net tangible assets	320	(20)
Net assets	500	(200)
Value in use	300	

18.187 However, within this allocation framework no intangible asset with a readily ascertainable market value or tangible asset with a net realisable value that can be measured reliably should be written down below those values. [FRS 11 para 49]. It should be noted that very few intangible assets have a readily ascertainable market value as defined in the FRS.

18.188 This rule accords with the general principle in the FRS that an asset should not be written down below the higher of its net realisable value or value in use. Whilst the value in use of individual assets in an IGU may not be determinable, their net realisable values may be. For example, individual properties occupied by branches of an integrated financial services operation that is treated as a single IGU for calculating value in use may have determinable market values. Any impairment losses that cannot be allocated on a *pro rata* basis to specific assets because they have higher net realisable values are allocated to other assets in the IGU.

18.189 The allocation process is important because it establishes new carrying values for individual assets that form the basis for subsequent depreciation charges and for accounting for subsequent disposals. However, it is necessarily arbitrary. The allocation between tangible fixed assets in an IGU would normally be made *pro rata* to their individual carrying values. However, management has discretion to adopt a different basis if that is considered to be more appropriate.

Example – Adopting an alternative basis for impairment allocation

The carrying value of an IGU's assets is £130 in aggregate, comprising tangible assets as analysed in the table below. The IGU's property has a market value of £70; the other assets do not have determinable net realisable values. The IGU's value in use is estimated to be £100, resulting in an impairment loss of £30 to be allocated.

The impairment loss is allocated to the assets of the IGU based on their relative carrying values, except that the property is not written down below its net realisable value of £70. Part of the loss that would otherwise be allocated to the property is reallocated to the other fixed assets, as illustrated below.

	Carrying value before impairment review	Impairment loss allocation		Impaired carrying value
		Pro-rata	Reallocated	
Property	80	18	10	70
Plant & equipment	30	7	12	18
Fixtures & fittings	20	5	8	12
	130	30	30	100

Different methods of treating goodwill

18.190 Paragraph 18.64 onwards explains the principles for allocating purchased goodwill to IGUs. Two methods are permitted and these are to some extent optional.

18.191 The first method is to fully allocate purchased goodwill to individual IGUs. Where relevant, the carrying values of IGUs reviewed for impairment then include a share of purchased goodwill.

18.192 The second method allows the purchased goodwill component to be reviewed for impairment at a higher level of aggregation than other assets. IGUs may be combined for testing the recoverability of the related goodwill if:

- they were acquired as part of the same investment; and
- they are involved in similar parts of the business.

[FRS 11 para 34]

18.193 If the second method is adopted, a two-tier impairment review is required, comprising:

- A review at the individual IGU level, where the assets and liabilities (excluding any allocation of goodwill) are reviewed for impairment. Any impairment loss is attributed to the IGU's assets.
- A review at a higher level to test the recoverability of the goodwill, where all the IGUs to which the goodwill relates are reviewed in aggregate. This review compares the carrying amount of the net assets of those IGUs and the purchased goodwill in aggregate with their combined value in use. Any further impairment loss identified at this level relates to the goodwill.

Example – Two tier impairment review

An acquisition made some years ago comprised two IGUs, A and B. There has been an indicator that the carrying value of A may be impaired.

A – Recognition of impairment where goodwill is allocated

The carrying values of the net assets and goodwill of IGUs A and B, and their value in use, are determined as follows:

Income-generating unit	**A**	**B**	**Total**
	£m	**£m**	**£m**
Net assets	220	110	330
Goodwill	40	40	80
Total net assets	260	150	410
Value in use	200	180	380
Impairment	60		

In this example, where purchased goodwill is allocated to the separate IGUs there is an impairment loss of £60m in A, reducing the carrying value of its net assets and goodwill to £200m. The impairment loss is attributed £40m to goodwill and £20m to other fixed assets.

The carrying values after recognising the impairment loss are as follows.

Carrying values after impairment	**A**	**B**	**Total**
	£m	**£m**	**£m**
Net assets	200	110	310
Goodwill	–	40	40
Total net assets	200	150	350

B – Recognition of impairment where goodwill is aggregated

If A and B, which were acquired together in one investment, were involved in similar parts of the business, the calculations could be done as follows:

Income-generating unit	**A**	**B**	**Goodwill**	**Total**
	£m	**£m**	**£m**	**£m**
Net assets	220	110	80	410
Value in use	200	180		380
Impairment	20		10	30

First, IGU A is reviewed for impairment without any allocation of goodwill. The value in use of £200m is compared with the carrying value of its net assets (excluding goodwill) of £220m. There is an impairment loss of £20m, reducing the carrying value of its net assets to £200m.

Secondly, A and B may be combined to assess the recoverability of the goodwill. The value in use of the combined units is now £380m, which is compared with the aggregate carrying value of the net assets and goodwill, which is £390m (that is, £410m less the £20m written off the net assets of unit A). Therefore, a further impairment loss of £10m is recognised to write down the goodwill to £70m.

The carrying values after recognising the impairment loss are as follows.

Carrying values after impairment	**A**	**B**	**Goodwill**	**Total**
	£m	**£m**	**£m**	**£m**
Net assets	200	110	70	380

18.194 The above example illustrates that significantly different accounting results can be achieved by adopting different approaches to aggregation and also serves to place impairment testing in its context – showing that impairment tests are not exact mathematical exercises. Under the first method, where no aggregation assumed, there is an impairment loss of £60 million. Under the second method, where goodwill is reviewed on an aggregate basis, there is an impairment loss of only £30 million. The second method in effect allows the impairment in the value of the goodwill of the impaired IGU to be partly offset against an increase in the value of the goodwill of the unimpaired IGU since its acquisition. It should be noted that this offset would not be allowed if A and B were involved in dissimilar activities or were acquired in different acquisitions.

18.195 It should also be noted that if A or B were subsequently sold separately, an allocation of the carrying value of goodwill would be necessary to eliminate it from the balance sheet (that is, to write it off as part of the profit or loss on disposal). Where the first method (allocating goodwill to separate IGUs) has been used to account for impairment, this is straightforward. Where the second method has been used, the allocation of goodwill between A and B that previously was not made would have to be made if there is a sale. In the above example, if A were sold, a loss of £30 million would have to be recognised on disposal in respect of purchased goodwill attributable to A that has not previously been written off. The figure of £30 million reflects the purchased goodwill of £40 million that would have originally been allocated to A less the previous impairment of £10 million that would have been attributable to A.

Central assets

18.196 Central assets that provide benefits to two or more IGUs in an enterprise (such as corporate head offices, computer centres or research facilities) should be dealt with in one of two ways.

- First, if possible, their carrying values should be apportioned across the IGUs that they support on a logical and systematic basis. The resulting carrying values of each IGU are then compared with their recoverable amounts.
- Secondly, if it is not possible to apportion central assets meaningfully, they are covered in a two-tier impairment review. The methodology for the two-tier review is similar to that relating to goodwill and permits the central assets to be reviewed in aggregate with all the IGUs that they support.

18.197 It should be noted that there is not a policy choice between the two methods as there may be in some circumstances for goodwill – if central assets can be allocated meaningfully across IGUs, they should be (see para 18.151 for further discussion of allocation methodology).

18.198 As with goodwill, the two methods of dealing with central assets may give different overall impairment results. The 'two-tier' approach could avoid some impairment losses that would be identified in the full allocation approach. The recoverable amount of one IGU might only just exceed the carrying value of its operating assets (without any allocation of central assets), whereas the recoverable amounts of the other IGUs might exceed the carrying values of both their operating assets and the central assets. In such circumstances, the 'two tier' review would not reveal any impairment, whereas the full allocation approach would reveal an impairment in the marginally profitable IGU. The 'two-tier' approach has the effect of allowing central assets to be allocated first to the more profitable IGUs, thus protecting less profitable IGUs from impairment losses. The view would presumably be that the central assets are not impaired as long as the more profitable parts of the business can support their carrying values.

18.199 The following examples illustrate the full allocation and two-tier approaches to dealing with central assets, coupled with the different approaches to the allocation of goodwill.

Example 1 – full allocation of central assets and goodwill to individual IGUs

An entity comprises two IGUs, A and B. The entity has a head office with a book value of £30m.

The following table illustrates the impairment review based on the calculation of value in use assuming that both the head office and purchased goodwill are allocated fully to the two IGUs. The head office is allocated *pro rata* to the other net assets; thus, £20m is allocated to A and £10m is allocated to B. (Note that any intra-group cash flows relating to the use of the head office should be excluded from the IGUs' value in use calculations in order to avoid double-counting).

Income-generating unit	**A**	**B**	**Total**
	£m	**£m**	**£m**
Directly attributable net assets	220	110	330
Head office	20	10	30
Goodwill	40	40	80
Total net assets	280	160	440
Value in use	200	180	380
Impairment	80		80
Net assets as written down	200	160	360

There is an impairment loss of £80m in A. This needs to be allocated between the assets of A – first to the allocated goodwill and thereafter to the tangible fixed assets. Possible methods are illustrated in the following table.

The first method allocates the balance of the impairment loss after goodwill write-off (£40m) *pro-rata* between all the tangible fixed assets attributable to the IGU, including the head office allocation. (The impairment attributable to the head office and the IGU's tangible fixed assets is calculated as 40 × 20/240 and 40 × 220/240 respectively.) The rationale would be that the part of the head office that is dedicated to the unprofitable IGU is impaired.

Some may find it curious to write down a proportion of the head office in this way and may prefer to charge the whole impairment loss against the IGU's operating assets, as in the second method. But it is still necessary (if possible) to allocate the head office asset for the purpose of the impairment calculations, even if impairment losses arising are allocated only to the IGU's assets.

Allocation of impairment loss	**1**	**2**
	£m	**£m**
Goodwill	40.0	40.0
Head office	3.3	–
Directly attributable tangible fixed assets of A	36.7	40.0
	80.0	80.0

A further complication that could arise is where the head office had a market value in excess of its impaired value as calculated on a value in use basis – say, its net realisable value were in excess of £30m. In that situation, because no asset can be written down below its net realisable value, the whole of the impairment loss would have to be allocated to the IGU's tangible fixed assets.

Example 2 – full allocation of central assets; goodwill reviewed in aggregate

The facts are as in example 1. The following table illustrates the impairment review assuming that the head office is allocated to the two IGUs, but goodwill is reviewed in aggregate, because it relates to a single acquisition and the two IGUs are involved in similar parts of the business.

The allocated net assets of A are impaired by £40m and the capitalised goodwill in aggregate is impaired by £20m, giving a total impairment loss of only £60m.

Income-generating unit	**A**	**B**	**Goodwill**	**Total**
	£m	**£m**	**£m**	**£m**
Directly attributable net assets	220	110	80	410
Head office	20	10	–	30
Total net assets	240	120	80	440
Value in use	200	180		380
Impairment	40		20	60
Net assets as written down	200	120	60	380

This method in effect allows the impairment of goodwill that was recognised in example 1 (£40m) to be offset by unrecognised internally generated goodwill of £20m in unit B. This offset would not be allowed if A and B were involved in dissimilar activities.

The impairment loss of £40m attributable to IGU A would be allocated on one of the bases described in example 1. Method 1 is a *pro rata* allocation between the IGU's tangible fixed assets and the allocated portion of the head office; method 2 allocates the whole of the impairment loss after goodwill write-off to the IGU's directly attributable fixed assets.

Allocation of impairment loss	**1**	**2**
	£m	£m
Goodwill	20.0	20.0
Head office	3.3	–
Directly attributable tangible fixed assets of A	36.7	40.0
	60.0	60.0

Example 3 – two-tier review of central assets and goodwill

The facts are the same as in examples 1 and 2. The following table illustrates the impairment review if neither the head office nor purchased goodwill is allocated to the individual IGUs. Instead, two impairment reviews are carried out. The first review is at the individual IGU level, comparing value in use with the carrying value of the net assets directly involved in the businesses (that is, excluding central assets and goodwill). The second review brings in the head office and goodwill at an aggregate level.

The first review shows an impairment loss of £20m in IGU A.

The second review compares the aggregate value in use (£380m) with the aggregate net asset value recognised after the first impairment review (£420m), comprising the impaired net assets of unit A (£200m), the net assets of unit B (£110m), the head office (£30m) and the capitalised goodwill (£80m). This results in a further impairment loss of £40m, which is allocated to the goodwill.

	A	**B**	**Head office**	**Goodwill**	**Total**
Income-generating unit	**£m**	**£m**	**£m**	**£m**	**£m**
Directly attributable net assets	220	110	30	80	440
Value in use	200	180			380
Impairment	20			40	60
Net assets as written down	200	110	30	40	380

The impairment loss of £20m attributable to IGU A would be allocated *pro rata* to its tangible fixed assets. The overall impairment loss would be allocated as follows.

Allocation of impairment loss	**1**	**2**
	£m	**£m**
Goodwill	40.0	40.0
Head office	1.7	–
Directly attributable tangible fixed assets of A	18.3	20.0
	60.0	60.0

18.200 The three examples above illustrate how different approaches to allocating central assets and goodwill can result in either different impairment losses or different allocations of impairment losses as between operating assets, central assets and goodwill. A further issue is to ensure that cash flows relating to central overheads are treated consistently in the calculation of value in use, that is, that they are neither omitted from nor double-counted in the impairment review. For example, in example 3 above, where no allocation of the head office carrying value was made to the IGUs, the inclusion of any compensating cash outflows relating to the head office property in the calculation of the IGUs' value in use would also affect the impairment calculations. Thus any rent payable to the parent company in relation to the head office would reduce the IGUs' value in use and, as a result, any impairment losses attributable to the IGUs would be correspondingly increased. The message is that the calculations can be significantly affected by subjective allocations of central assets or central costs.

Integration of acquired businesses with existing operations

18.201 FRS 11 addresses a specific issue relating to purchased goodwill. The situation is where an acquired business that resulted in the recognition of purchased goodwill is integrated with other operations of the acquiring group and, as a result, loses its separate identity. As the benefits from many acquisitions lie in the cost savings and other synergies that can be gained from merging the acquired operations with an existing unit, this is a common practice.

18.202 Where operations are merged in this way, the assets and purchased goodwill of the acquired business may then form part of the carrying value of a larger IGU that includes assets of pre-existing operations. If an impairment review of the larger IGU is required, its value in use would be compared with its carrying value. The IGU's carrying value comprises the carrying values of the recognised net assets of the acquired and pre-existing operations, together with the carrying value of the purchased goodwill relating to the acquired business. The IGU's value in use will reflect the value of any internally generated goodwill in the existing business, this internally generated goodwill is not permitted to be recognised as an asset. If impairment reviews were carried out on this basis, an impairment relating to the acquired business could be avoided to the extent that it was offset by unrecognised internally generated goodwill in the existing business with which the acquired business was merged.

18.203 FRS 11 sets out a method that should be applied to a combined IGU that contains both (capitalised) purchased goodwill relating to the acquired business and (unrecognised) internally generated goodwill that relates to the existing business. This method notionally preserves a distinction between the two types of goodwill in the IGU, and requires impairment losses to be allocated between them in order to prevent a potential impairment of the purchased goodwill from being avoided.

18.204 FRS 11 requires the internally generated goodwill of the existing business to be estimated at the date of merging the businesses. This exercise requires the existing business to be valued separately before the integration (that is, its value in use should be estimated). The internally generated goodwill should be calculated by deducting the fair value of the net assets (and any purchased goodwill) of the existing business from its estimated value in use before combining the businesses. [FRS 11 paras 50 to 52].

18.205 The internally generated goodwill as calculated should be added to the carrying value of the net assets of the combined IGU for the purpose of the impairment review as illustrated below (note that the internally generated goodwill is not actually recognised in the financial statements). The internally generated goodwill is assumed to be amortised on the same basis as the purchased goodwill.

Notional carrying value of integrated income-generating unit

	Net assets	**Goodwill**
New acquisition	Fair value	Purchased
Existing business	Carrying value*	Internally generated
		Purchased (re previous acquisitions by the existing business, if any)

* that is, existing book value, but note that fair values are used to calculate the internally generated goodwill when the businesses are integrated

18.206 FRS 11 states that this exercise should be carried out whenever an acquisition that gives rise to goodwill is merged with an existing business. [FRS 11 para 52]. Even if a full-scale impairment review is not required (say, because there is no indicator that the carrying amounts of fixed assets or goodwill may not be recoverable), the calculations are still necessary to create the records that would be required to carry out a full impairment review later if, say, an indicator of impairment arose some years after the integration of businesses. This is a requirement of FRS 11 that is easy to forget as it is not directly related to a current impairment. It is, however, very important to avoid significant difficulties in any impairment calculations required in the future.

18.207 At the time when the businesses are integrated, if the aggregate carrying value of the net assets and goodwill, including the notional internally generated goodwill as illustrated above, exceeds the recoverable amount of the combined IGU, the impairment should be allocated wholly to the capitalised purchased goodwill relating to the acquired business and, hence, recognised in full in the consolidated profit and loss account. This is because any impairment of the existing business will have been identified and recognised when the exercise to calculate the internally generated goodwill of the existing business (that is, when calculating fair values of the net assets) was carried out. By definition, therefore, if a further impairment arises when the review of the combined business is carried out, it must relate to the purchased goodwill of the acquired business. This should ensure that any overpayment for the acquisition is identified and written off and is not offset against the unrecognised goodwill of the existing business.

18.208 Any goodwill impairments identified in subsequent years should be apportioned on a *pro rata* basis between the carrying value of the purchased goodwill and the notional carrying value of the internally generated goodwill.

Only the impairment allocated to the capitalised purchased goodwill would be charged in the profit and loss account.

Example – Impairment test including notional goodwill (new business integrated with existing business)

The combined balance sheet of an IGU formed by integrating an acquired business with an existing business is set out in the following table. The figures in italics are those that include the notional value of (unrecognised) internally generated goodwill in the existing business. The actual recognised net assets and purchased goodwill of the combined IGU amounts to £400m. Added to this is unrecognised internally generated goodwill in the existing business of £500m (which derives from the value that was estimated when the businesses were merged, after deducting notional amortisation since that date), making a notional total of £900m.

Impairment review of combined IGU

	Acquisition	**Existing business**	**Combined**
Net assets	80	100	180
Goodwill	220	*500*	*720*
Total	300	*600*	*900*
Value in use			750
Impairment	46	*104*	*150*

An impairment review of the combined IGU compares its value in use of £750m with its aggregate (notional) net assets of £900m.

Assuming that this impairment review takes place some years after the integration of the acquired business, the impairment loss of £150m is allocated *pro rata* between the purchased goodwill (acquisition) and the internally generated goodwill (existing business). This allocates £46m to the former and £104m to the latter.

Only the impairment loss of £46m allocated to the capitalised purchased goodwill is written off in the consolidated profit and loss account.

If, however, the impairment was identified when the businesses were integrated, the whole loss of £150m would be allocated to the capitalised purchased goodwill relating to the acquisition and, hence, written off in the consolidated profit and loss account (see para 18.207).

It should be noted that if this *pro rata* exercise were not required, in the above example no impairment loss would be recognised in the profit and loss account. That is because there would be no impairment of the combined IGU's recognised net assets and purchased goodwill, which amount only to £400m. The impairment of the goodwill in the acquired business would in effect be offset against the unrecognised internally generated goodwill (£500m) in the existing business. Hence, the recoverable amount of the combined IGU would have to fall below £400m before any impairment loss were recognised in the consolidated profit and loss account.

18.209 This is a complicated approach and somewhat artificial. It was developed alongside the rules for capitalising and amortising purchased goodwill in FRS 10 and appears to be a consequence of the possibility of carrying goodwill permanently as an asset or amortising it over very long periods (more than 20 years). FRS 10 requires such long-life purchased goodwill balances to be reviewed annually for impairment in order to demonstrate formally that they are recoverable. The ability to perform annual impairment reviews on purchased goodwill balances is a pre-condition for rebutting FRS 10's presumption that goodwill should be amortised against profits over a period of no more than 20 years. Unless there was some standardised basis for measuring the recoverable amount of purchased goodwill in situations where the acquired business had lost its separate identity through the merging of operations, it might appear that it would not be possible to carry out an impairment review on the capitalised goodwill relating to the original acquisition. Groups that subsumed their acquisitions would then be less likely to be in a position to rebut FRS 10's presumption that the useful economic life does not exceed 20 years than those groups that ran their acquisitions as stand-alone businesses.

Goodwill previously written off to reserves

18.210 A further complication arises where the balance sheet of the existing business includes some purchased goodwill that was previously written off to reserves before capitalisation of purchased goodwill became mandatory and remains written off as permitted by the transitional provisions of FRS 10. Such goodwill is not internally generated goodwill of the existing business and so it should be treated in the impairment calculations as purchased goodwill within the existing business. This would mean that the notional balance sheet created for the purpose of allocating impairment losses would include three elements in respect of goodwill: purchased goodwill that has been capitalised; purchased goodwill that has been written off to reserves; and notional internally generated goodwill.

18.211 When it comes to allocating impairment losses to goodwill, it would seem logical to allocate the impairment *pro rata* to these three elements. The impairment relating to the element of goodwill remaining in reserves may or may not be recognised in the profit and loss account at that time (in addition to the impairment attributed to the capitalised purchased goodwill), depending on the group's policy for recognising such impairments. If the group's policy is not to account for goodwill written off to reserves until the business is disposed of, then no impairment relating to that goodwill would be recognised until disposal, when all the attributable goodwill that has not previously been written off in the profit and loss account would be written off as part of the profit or loss on disposal.

Impairment and depreciation

18.212 When a fixed asset or purchased goodwill has been impaired, the remaining carrying value (if any) should be amortised over the remaining useful economic life. The remaining useful economic life and, where applicable, estimated residual value, should also be reviewed and, if necessary, revised. [FRS 11 para 21]. (Note that FRS 10 does not permit any residual value to be assigned to goodwill.)

18.213 This requirement reiterates the normal principle in accounting for fixed assets that asset lives and residual values should be regularly reviewed to ensure they are realistic and be revised if this is not the case in the light of experience or changed circumstances. An impairment warrants particular attention, because it may indicate that previously estimated asset lives are unrealistically long and may need to be shortened.

Assets held for disposal

18.214 If a decision is made to sell an asset, a practical issue is when should the expected sale proceeds be factored into the value in use calculation in place of the cash flows from continued use. This may affect the timing and measurement of any impairment losses.

18.215 FRS 11 para 31 states: *'The income stream of a fixed asset to be disposed of will be largely independent of the income stream of other assets. Such an asset therefore forms an income-generating unit of its own and does not belong to any other income-generating unit.'* This suggests that the measurement of recoverable amount would normally anticipate the disposal when it is formally factored into management's cash flow projections. Value in use (which includes the estimated cash flows from the asset's ultimate disposal) would then be similar to net realisable value; hence, the future cash flows of the IGU to which the asset may have formerly belonged are no longer taken into account.

18.216 Similarly, where a decision is made to sell or terminate a business, the amounts expected to be recoverable from the sale or closure of the business would then provide the basis for measuring the recoverable amount of its fixed assets and goodwill. In the case of a business for sale, if the carrying values of the net assets and capitalised goodwill exceeded in aggregate their recoverable amount (which would be based on the expected sale proceeds), the assets are impaired.

18.217 It is also useful to consider how the requirements of FRS 11 interact with FRS 3 and FRS 12 where losses are expected to be incurred in respect of disposals of fixed assets or businesses. FRS 3 and FRS 12 prohibit recognition of provisions for liabilities in respect of sales or terminations of businesses until (a) in the case of a sale, there is a binding sale agreement, or (b) in the case of a termination, a constructive obligation has been incurred (requiring a detailed formal plan and evidence that implementation has started or that the plan has been communicated to those affected).

18.218 Provisions do not include amounts written off assets. The expression that is sometimes used 'provision for loss on disposal of fixed assets' is not a provision in the sense of FRS 12 and any such loss should not be shown as a provision or liability. Both FRS 3 (para 45) and FRS 12 (para 84) refer to the need for asset values to be reviewed for impairment before any provisions are recognised. For example, FRS 3 states that where a decision has been made to sell an operation, but there is no binding contract or other demonstrable commitment to the sale at the reporting date, no provisions for future costs or losses should be made but any impairments (formerly permanent diminutions) in asset values should be recorded.

18.219 Thus impairment losses should be recognised as soon as a disposal is envisaged, if they have not been identified and recognised earlier. The following example illustrates the accounting for the sale of an operation that takes place after the year end.

Example – Impairment losses and sale of an operation

A group decides before the year end to sell a subsidiary. The sale will take place after the year end and after the financial statements of the group are signed. The carrying values of the subsidiary's fixed assets and purchased goodwill at the year end are £300,000 and £100,000 respectively. Working capital is assumed to be zero.

The subsidiary makes a loss of £110,000 before depreciation from the year end to the date the financial statements are signed. Further losses up to the date of sale are estimated to be £20,000. The group is negotiating the sale at the time of signing the financial statements and expects the proceeds on sale will be £150,000. It is assumed that the group does not fund the subsidiary's losses after the balance sheet date.

As mentioned above, where there is no binding sale agreement, no provision for loss on sale should be made, but the value of the subsidiary's net assets consolidated will still have to be considered to determine whether an impairment loss needs to be recognised. If no impairment losses were recognised in respect of the fixed assets and goodwill amounting to £400,000, the group would expect to incur losses of £250,000 in the subsequent year, comprising the subsidiary's expected future losses of £130,000 and an estimated loss on sale of £120,000, as illustrated below:

	£'000	£'000
Fixed assets		300
Goodwill		100
Assets to be reviewed for impairment		400
Loss up to date of sale	(110)	
	(20)	(130)
Estimated net assets at date of sale		270
Expected proceeds on sale		150
Estimated loss on sale		(120)

It is clear in this example that the subsidiary's assets are impaired, because their carrying values are not recoverable. The subsidiary's net assets and goodwill would form a separate IGU, because the subsidiary is to be disposed of. The recoverable amount is £150,000, which is the cash inflow expected from ultimate disposal and represents the subsidiary's value in use to the group (discounting has been ignored for simplicity). It is assumed that net realisable value at the balance sheet date would be similar.

The impairment loss is, therefore, £250,000, which would be allocated first to write-off the goodwill of £100,000 and secondly to write down the subsidiary's fixed assets by the balance of £150,000. The impairment loss of £250,000 is the same amount that might have been provided for as a provision for loss on disposal had there been a binding sale agreement at the balance sheet date.

After the impairment loss of £250,000 has been recognised, the amounts to be included in the group's profit and loss account in the subsequent year in respect of the subsidiary would be:

	£'000
Operating losses	(130)
Profit on disposal	130
Net profit or loss	nil

The profit on disposal is calculated as follows:

	£'000
Fixed assets (as impaired)	150
Goodwill	nil
	150
Operating losses	(130)
Net assets at date of sale	20
Proceeds on sale	150
Profit on sale	130

18.220 The above example demonstrates that, whereas FRS 3 and FRS 12 restrict the circumstances where provisions for losses on sale can be recognised, FRS 11 has increased the emphasis on recognising impairments of assets at an earlier point in time. Issues concerning the presentation of such losses in the profit and loss account – whether the loss should be treated as an impairment (charged against operating profit) or as a loss on sale (charged as a non-operating exceptional item) are considered in paragraph 18.263.

Corporate structures — issues for parent companies and subsidiaries

Parent's investment in subsidiaries

18.221 Where capitalised goodwill on consolidation is written down as a result of impairment, the carrying value of the parent company's investment in the relevant subsidiary should also be reviewed for impairment. [FRS 10 para 42].

18.222 The recoverable amount (if determined by value in use) of an investment in a subsidiary would normally be based on the present value of the subsidiary's estimated cash flows.

18.223 The goodwill and other net assets in the consolidated financial statements that are attributable to an impaired subsidiary will usually differ from the subsidiary's carrying value in the parent's balance sheet as time goes by after the acquisition. The likelihood that the parent's investment has also been impaired will depend partly on its accounting policy, which may be:

- Cost less provision for impairment.
- Cost (excluding share premium qualifying for merger relief or group reconstruction relief) less provision for impairment.
- Net asset value (including unamortised goodwill).
- Directors' valuation

Subsidiaries that are part of larger IGUs

18.224 For groups, FRS 11 is principally targeted at identifying and recognising impairment losses from a group perspective. Thus the whole group as a reporting entity is divided into separate IGUs for the purpose of impairment reviews, such that the IGUs in aggregate cover the whole group and are non-overlapping.

18.225 Individual subsidiaries may also be separate reporting entities, but the allocation of a group's activities between separate companies within a group does not necessarily coincide with the way the group's IGUs are defined.

18.226 Issues arise where a subsidiary's activities form part of a larger IGU in the group. In particular, the cash flows of an individual subsidiary may appear not to support the carrying values of its fixed assets, yet from a group perspective there is no impairment, because the subsidiary is part of a profitable IGU.

18.227 Such situations may be numerous where wholly-owned subsidiaries are concerned and can be illustrated by reference to the examples in the standard that discuss how IGUs are identified. For example, a low-return supporting route operated by a transport group may reside in a separate subsidiary company, yet be part of an IGU that includes a profitable trunk route that is fed by the supporting route. Another example is where a factory owned by a subsidiary company is operating with surplus capacity, but the IGU comprises this and a number of other sites (owned by other subsidiary companies) at which the product can be made – overall there is no impairment, because demand is such that there is not enough surplus capacity to close any one site.

18.228 Transfer pricing also creates difficulties. A subsidiary may be only breaking even because it sells its output to a fellow subsidiary at cost, yet they are part of the same IGU from a group perspective. Where subsidiaries are separate IGUs, one subsidiary may be unprofitable, because it sells output to a fellow subsidiary at below-market prices. Conversely, the transferee subsidiary might be profitable, because it buys goods and services from its fellow subsidiary at below-market prices. The standard indicates (from a group's perspective) that the cash inflows of the transferor IGU and the cash outflows of the transferee IGU that are used in the value in use calculations should be adjusted to reflect market prices rather than internal transfer prices. Consequently, where there is an impairment in the consolidated financial statements the situation could arise where the assets of the 'profitable' subsidiary, rather than those of the 'unprofitable' subsidiary, might be impaired after such adjustments have been made to their respective cash flow forecasts.

18.229 In situations such as those outlined above, it cannot automatically be assumed that the allocation of impairment losses in subsidiaries' own financial statements would follow the way they are allocated in the consolidated financial statements. This is because FRS 11 has to be applied individually to all financial statements that are intended to give a true and fair view of a reporting entity's financial position and profit or loss. Therefore, in general, if the recoverable amount of an asset to a subsidiary (that is, the present value of the future cash flows obtainable by the subsidiary) does not support its carrying value, it should be treated as impaired in the subsidiary's financial statements. However, where wholly-owned subsidiaries enter into transactions at transfer prices that differ significantly from market prices (and such market prices are freely available), it does not make much sense to treat an asset as being impaired in a subsidiary if the carrying value in the subsidiary is supported when its cash flows are re-based to external market prices. In cases where a subsidiary is not earning an economic return on its assets in terms of its separate cash flows, the absence of any impairment loss should require explanation in the subsidiary's financial statements in order to give a true and fair view.

Reversals of impairment losses

General rules

18.230 FRS 11 requires impairment losses recognised in previous periods to be reversed in certain circumstances where the recoverable amount of the assets concerned subsequently increases. This corresponds to the requirement in SI 2008/410, 'The Large and Medium-sized Companies and Groups (Accounts and Reports) Regulations 2008'where a company has made provision for a diminution in value, but the factors that gave rise to it no longer apply to any extent, then the company must write back the provision to that extent. [SI 2008/410 1 Sch 19, 20].

18.231 For tangible fixed assets and investments in subsidiaries, associates and joint ventures, the reversal of an impairment loss should be recognised where the recoverable amount increases *'because of a change in economic conditions or in the expected use of the asset'*. [FRS 11 para 56]. This rule is based on the premise that the original impairment is caused by the inability of the asset to generate sufficient returns to recover its carrying amount. Once there is a change in economic conditions or in the expected use of the asset that enables the asset to recover its former carrying amount, the reason for the impairment ceases to apply. For intangible assets and goodwill the criteria for reversing impairment losses are stricter than for other assets (see para 18.242 below).

18.232 The amount of any reversal that can be recognised is restricted to increasing the carrying value of the relevant assets to the carrying value that would have been recognised had the original impairment not occurred (that is, after taking account of normal depreciation that would have been charged had no impairment occurred). [FRS 11 para 56]. In respect of depreciable assets, therefore, any reversals of impairment losses will tend not to be as large as the original impairment loss.

18.233 Indicators that impairment losses may have reversed are the reverse of those that indicated the impairment loss in the first place. Companies should consider whether there have been favourable events or changes in circumstances since the impairment loss was recognised that would indicate that the impairment loss no longer exists or may have decreased. If there are indicators, the recoverable amount of the relevant assets or IGUs should be estimated again. Such changes include situations where the recoverable amount increases as a result of further capital investment or a reorganisation, the benefits of which had been excluded from the original measurement of value in use (see paras 18.118 and 18.125 for examples showing how the recognition and reversal rules operate in respect of future reorganisation and capital investment).

18.234 It should be borne in mind that this exercise would only be undertaken if there is evidence of a significant improvement in actual performance or future prospects that would give rise to a material reversal of an impairment loss. As with the original impairment calculations, amounts recognised in respect of reversals are likely to be broad estimates; in fact, it could be positively misleading in terms of reporting performance to have regular impairment losses and reversals resulting from imputing spurious accuracy into the calculations.

18.235 The standard explains that increases in value in use should not be recognised as reversals of impairment losses if they arise simply from:

- The passage of time, resulting from the unwinding of the discount rate that was applied to arrive at the present value of expected future cash flows.
- The occurrence of forecast cash outflows – once the forecast cash outflows have happened they are no longer part of the value in use calculation and the value in use, therefore, increases.

[FRS 11 para 58].

18.236 The reason why the two events described in the previous paragraph do not give rise to the reversal of an impairment loss is because, whilst the value in use admittedly increases, the underlying reasons for the original impairment have not been removed. All that has happened is that time has passed and the expected cash flows have occurred – the service potential of the asset has not increased. The effect is illustrated in the following example:

Example – Reversal of impairment losses (1)

An asset cost £100 on 1 January 20X0. Its expected useful life is 5 years; depreciation is on a straight-line basis. An impairment review is carried out as at 31 December 20X0 when the carrying value is £80. The projected cash flows are as follows:

	20X1	20X2	20X3	20X4
Cash flows (nominal total 82; present value 64)	13	22	23	24

Using a discount rate of 10%, the present value of the cash flows (value in use) at 31 December 20X0 is £64. Thus an impairment loss of £16 is recognised.

The impaired carrying value of £64 is then depreciated on a straight-line basis over the remaining 4 years of its expected useful life. Assuming the cash flows materialise as projected in the impairment calculation, the carrying value and value in use (present value of remaining cash flows discounted at 10%) at each year end are as follows:

	20X0	20X1	20X2	20X3	20X4
Carrying value	64	48	32	16	–
Value in use	64	57	41	22	–

It can be seen that the value in use at 31 December 20X1, 20X2 and 20X3 exceeds the carrying amount. The reason is a combination of the unwinding of the discount (as the future cash flows get nearer, their present value increases) and the fact that the cash flows themselves increase during the life of the asset. But there is no reversal of the original impairment loss.

The profit and loss accounts for the remaining life of the asset are as follows (ignoring any timing differences between cash flows and profit):

	20X1	20X2	20X3	20X4
Profit before depreciation	13	22	23	24
Depreciation	(16)	(16)	(16)	(16)
Profit (loss) before interest	(3)	6	7	8

The effect of discounting is that a profit before interest of £18 emerges over the remaining 4 years' life of the asset. Discounting the cash flows in the first place reduced the value in use from the nominal amount of £82 to a present value of £64. The corollary of this is that the discount of £18 unwinds over those 4 years, in effect leaving an operating profit to cover the cost of capital. Of course, this profit does not accrue in any even pattern, because (a) the cash flows themselves are uneven and (b) depreciation is on an arbitrary straight-line basis.

18.237 It should be noted, however, that where a reversal of an impairment loss is recognised because economic conditions have changed, the FRS does not suggest that any increase in value in use that is due to 'the passage of time' should be estimated as a separate component and excluded from the reversal. In most practical situations this would be quite unrealistic.

18.238 To illustrate accounting for reversals, consider the following example:

Example – Reversal of impairment losses (2)

The history of a company's fixed assets is as follows:

	Investment in subsidiary £'000	Tangible fixed assets £'000
Cost at 1 January 20X1	10	6
Value at 31 December 20X1	8	5
Value at 31 December 20X2	*5	*3
Value at 31 December 20X3	9	4

* only these decreases in value are impairments. All other diminutions in value have arisen from a general fall in prices.

Ignoring the normal depreciation rules for the purposes of this example (and assuming historical cost rules apply), FRS 11 and the Companies Act apply as follows:

- At 31 December 20X1 both the investment and the fixed asset have fallen in value, but this is due solely to a general fall in prices. It is determined, following an impairment review that the recoverable amount of the investment and the fixed asset remain at £10,000 and £6,000 respectively. In these circumstances, the directors *could* (if they wish) write down the amount of the investment in subsidiary to £8,000. (This is because the Act permits, but does not require, provision to be made for the diminution in value of a fixed asset *investment* that the directors consider to be only temporary). However, the directors could not write down the value of the tangible fixed asset to £5,000 under the historical cost rules. (This is because the Act allows tangible fixed assets to be written down in value only in circumstances where the diminution in value is expected to be *permanent*. Also, in FRS 11 terms, there has been no impairment of the fixed asset.)

- At 31 December 20X2 a change in economic circumstances has occurred which leads the directors to believe that the recoverable amounts of the investment and the fixed asset have fallen to £5,000 and £3,000 respectively. Accordingly, the directors must write down the amount of the investment in subsidiary to £5,000 (whether or not they wrote it down to £8,000 at 31 December 20X1). In addition, they *must* write down the value of the tangible fixed asset to £3,000. This is because the fall in value of each of them is expected to be *permanent* and because in FRS 11 terms there has been an impairment loss.

- At 31 December 20X3, due to a further change in economic circumstances the recoverable amounts have been restored to £9,000 and £4,000 respectively and the reasons for the original impairment have disappeared. Therefore, the directors must write back £4,000 in respect of the investment in subsidiary and £1,000 in respect of the tangible fixed asset. This is because the reasons that gave rise to the provision for diminution in value/impairment loss on each of them have ceased to apply to that extent. Had the increase in the recoverable amount occurred only because of the passage of time (unwinding of discount) or because forecast cash outflows had occurred, the impairment losses could not be written back, because the reasons for the original impairment would not have ceased to apply.

18.239 Accounting for the reversal of an impairment loss should be consistent with the treatment adopted when the impairment was recognised. Where the asset is held at historical cost, the reversal should be recognised in the current year's profit and loss account, since the original loss would have been charged in the profit and loss account.

18.240 For a revalued asset, the reversal of an impairment loss should be recognised in the profit and loss account to the extent that the original impairment loss (adjusted for subsequent depreciation) was recognised in the profit and loss account. Any remaining balance of the reversal of an impairment loss should be recognised in the statement of total recognised gains and losses, since part of the original impairment loss would have been charged there. [FRS 11 para 66].

18.241 The reversal calculations for revalued assets can be rather complex, as illustrated in the following example.

Example – Recognition and reversal of impairment loss on revalued asset

At 31 December X1 an asset was purchased for £100. Its expected useful economic life is 20 years. Three years later it was revalued to £136.

At 31 December X6 the asset was reviewed for impairment and written down to its recoverable amount of £50.

The following table shows the movements in the asset's book value on a depreciated historical cost basis and as actually recognised in the financial statements.

	Depreciated historical cost	Revalued carrying value
	£	£
31 December X1 — cost	100	100
Depreciation (3 years)	(15)	(15)
Revaluation	–	51
31 December X4	85	136
Depreciation (2 years)	(10)	(16)
31 December X6	75	120
Impairment loss	(25)	(70)
31 December X6 after impairment loss	50	50

The impairment loss of £70 at 31 December X6 is not caused by a clear consumption of economic benefits, and so the loss is charged in the statement of total recognised gains and losses until the carrying amount reaches depreciated historical cost and thereafter in the profit and loss account, as follows:

	£
Statement of total recognised gains and losses	45
Profit and loss account	25
Impairment loss	70

At 31 December X8 economic conditions have improved and the asset's recoverable amount is estimated to be £90.

If no impairment loss had been recognised, the carrying value at 31 December 1998 would have been £104 (£120 at 31 December X6 less 2 years of further depreciation of £16), which is greater than the recoverable amount of £90. Therefore, the whole of the increase in the carrying value can be treated as a reversal of the previous impairment loss. It should be noted that if the carrying value had been increased to more than £104, the excess would be treated as a revaluation, not a reversal of the impairment. [FRS 11 para 59].

The impairment loss should be reversed, as indicated in the following table.

	Depreciated historical cost		
	Before impairment	After impairment	Carrying value
	£	£	£
31 December X6	75	50	50
Depreciation (2 years)	(10)	(7)	(7)
31 December X8	65	43	43
Reversal of impairment loss	–	22	47
31 December 98 after reversal	65	65	90

The reversal of the impairment loss of £47 is recognised as follows:

Profit and loss account	22
Statement of total recognised gains and losses	25

The profit and loss account figure of £22 represents the amount of the original impairment loss that was charged in the profit and loss account of £25 less an adjustment for the additional depreciation that would have been charged had the asset been carried at depreciated historical cost of £3. The balance of the reversal of £25 is credited in the statement of total recognised gains and losses.

Special rules for goodwill and intangible assets

18.242 Impairment losses relating to capitalised goodwill and intangible assets may be reversed only in limited circumstances. These are where (a) an external event caused the original impairment loss, and (b) subsequent external events clearly and demonstrably reverse the effects of that event in a way that was not foreseen in the original impairment calculations. [FRS 11 para 60]. FRS 11 makes an exception to this rule for intangible assets with a readily ascertainable market value, where impairment losses may be reversed to the extent that the net realisable value (based on market value) subsequently increases to above the impaired carrying value. [FRS 11 para 60]. However, there are very few intangible assets in that category.

18.243 For goodwill, the objective of restricting reversals of impairment losses is to prevent a goodwill write-off from being credited back to the profit and loss account if the credit is in effect attributable to the generation of new non-purchased goodwill. The accounting rules generally for goodwill and intangible assets are similar. Consequently, situations that justify reversals are likely to be rare and in most cases amounts written off goodwill or intangible assets will stay written off. The reason given for the different approaches to tangible and intangible assets is that tangible fixed assets can in any case be revalued, whereas goodwill and most intangible assets cannot.

18.244 An example of a situation that would meet the reversal criteria for an intangible asset is as follows.

Example – Reversal of impairment on an intangible asset

A brand name had previously been written off because a product had been withdrawn from the market as a result of a health scare that raised concerns about its safety. The safety concerns subsequently prove to be unfounded and the health authorities approved the product's reintroduction. The company's management had assumed that the product's withdrawal would be permanent when they recognised the impairment loss.

In this example, the impairment loss was caused by an external event (the health scare). An external event (the removal of the safety concerns and the permission to reintroduce the product to the market) clearly and demonstrably has reversed the effects of the external event that caused the impairment loss in a way that was not foreseen in the original impairment calculations. Consequently, the impairment loss should be reversed to the extent that the brand's recoverable amount has increased above its current written down value (assuming that the brand regains some value after the health scare).

18.245 An example of originating and reversing external events that would meet the reversal criteria for goodwill is the introduction of a new law that damages profitability (resulting in a goodwill write-off) and that is subsequently repealed by a new government. Another example is the confiscation of assets in an overseas territory (resulting in a goodwill write-off) that are subsequently released to allow the business to continue its operations. In both of these examples the original goodwill has been reclaimed.

18.246 The recoverable amount of an acquired business may increase in subsequent years after an impairment loss has been recognised, but the improvement will often be unrelated to the circumstances that gave rise to the original impairment. One example is where goodwill has been written off because a competitor has introduced a better product to the market; some years later, the company launches a new product of its own and develops a different market. Another example is where a business has been reorganised to curtail underperforming operations, resulting in a write-off of goodwill; in later years, the business may expand again as new market opportunities arise. In neither of these examples would the turnaround justify reversing the impairment loss relating to the goodwill even though the recoverable amount of the business has increased above the balance sheet value of its net assets and goodwill. This is because the higher value of goodwill that now exists includes goodwill that has been generated internally since the original impairment.

18.247 If, however, the reason for an impairment write-down was a competitor coming into the market and a reversal of the impairment was attributable to the competitor subsequently withdrawing from the market (or modifying its pricing policy in a way that was not foreseen), the criteria for recognising the reversal of the impairment loss in respect of goodwill would be met.

18.248 It should be noted that if the net assets of a business included impaired carrying values for both purchased goodwill and tangible fixed assets, the situation may occur where some impairment loss reversals are permitted (for tangible fixed assets) and others are not (for goodwill and most intangible fixed assets). This situation may occur with business restructurings. Goodwill and tangible fixed assets of businesses in need of reorganisation may have to be written down (there is a concession, though, for recent acquisitions – see para 18.127); if their values are restored as a result of reorganisation, only the impairment losses relating to the tangible fixed assets may be written back.

18.249 The amount that can be written back to reverse an impairment loss is restricted to an amount that increases the carrying value of the goodwill or intangible asset to the carrying value that would have been recognised had the original impairment not occurred (that is, after taking account of normal depreciation that would have been charged had the impairment not occurred). [FRS 11 para 61].

Presentation and disclosures

Presentation of impairment losses in performance statements

Assets carried at historical cost

18.250 FRS 11 requires impairment losses recognised in the profit and loss account to be included within operating profit under the appropriate statutory heading, and disclosed as an exceptional item if appropriate. [FRS 11 para 67]. This applies to goodwill as well as fixed assets.

18.251 The formats in Schedule 1 to SI 2008/410, 'The Large and Medium-sized Companies and Groups (Accounts and Reports) Regulations 2008', prescribe the headings under which depreciation and other amounts written off tangible and intangible fixed assets are to be included in the profit and loss account. Under Format 1, where expenses are classified by function, an impairment loss would generally be charged under the same format heading as depreciation of (or other amounts written off) the relevant assets. Under Format 2, where expenses are classified by type, there is a separate heading 'depreciation and amounts written off tangible and intangible fixed assets'.

Revalued assets

18.252 For revalued assets, FRS 11 introduces rules for recognition of impairment that are more conservative than the Act's requirements in respect of temporary diminutions in value.

18.253 Although FRS 11 does not use the term 'temporary diminutions in value' it distinguishes two types of impairments. These are impairments arising from:

- A clear consumption of economic benefits.
- Other impairments of revalued fixed assets.

18.254 The FRS requires that the former of these two types of impairment should be recognised in the profit and loss account in its entirety, because it is similar to depreciation. No part of it should be taken to the statement of total recognised gains and losses. [FRS 11 para 63]. Examples of clear consumption of economic benefits are physical damage, contamination, obsolescence, deterioration in quality of service – often something wrong with the asset itself.

18.255 Other impairments are accounted for by recognising them in the statement of total recognised gains and losses, until the carrying amount reaches depreciated historical cost. Thereafter, the balance of the impairment is recognised in the profit and loss account. [FRS 11 para 63].

18.256 This category is intended to cover impairments caused by a general fall in prices, for example a general slump in the property market. However, the FRS recognises that in many cases it will be unclear whether an impairment loss is the result of a consumption of economic benefits or some other cause – for example, when there is a fall in demand for an asset's output or services. The development appendix explains that where there is doubt whether the impairment is caused by a reduction in the quantum of an asset's service potential, it should be treated as falling into the other category, that is, the loss is recognised in the statement of total recognised gains and losses, until the carrying amount reaches depreciated historical cost. [FRS 11 App IV para 20].

18.257 An asset's recoverable amount may be reduced by specific factors that do not necessarily affect the general market, say, the establishment of a local competitor to a retail store. Whereas, there may be no physical impairment of the asset, there may be evidence that the impairment has not been caused by a general fall in prices and thus it could be argued that the impairment has been caused by a reduction in its service potential. But rarely will such situations be clear cut.

18.258 The FRS appears to acknowledge that a downward revaluation of a previously revalued asset may constitute partly an impairment due to consumption of economic benefits and partly an impairment due to general price changes. It may be difficult, in practice, to determine whether or not this is the case. The prudent approach taken by the standard, however, makes this less of an issue, because the standard requires all impairments of an asset below depreciated historical cost to be taken to the profit and loss account. (Note, however, that the standard does not apply to investment properties).

18.259 Impairment losses recognised in the profit and loss account should be included in operating profit under the appropriate statutory heading and disclosed as exceptional if appropriate. Impairment losses recognised in the statement of total recognised gains and losses should be disclosed separately on the face of that statement. [FRS 11 para 67].

18.260 It should be noted that if a company's policy is to carry assets at market value and market value is below recoverable amount, the shortfall is not an impairment under FRS 11. The additional write-down would be recognised in the statement of total recognised gains and losses as a revaluation deficit.

18.261 Where, therefore, the revaluation of a fixed asset results in a revalued amount that is below the previous carrying value and is below the value in use of that asset, FRS 11 only requires the asset to be written down, if necessary, to the value in use figure. The difference between the value in use figure and the (lower) revalued amount is simply a valuation adjustment which is then shown in the statement of total recognised gains and losses.

Example – Market value used for revaluation purposes is lower than value in use (1)

A tangible fixed asset cost £100 and is subject to a revaluation policy to reflect its current market value. Its previous revalued carrying amount was £150, with the surplus of £50 taken to the statement of total recognised gains and losses and the revaluation reserve.

In the current year the fixed asset is revalued and the revalued amount is £80 (in this example, for simplicity, depreciation has been ignored).

An impairment review is done on the asset and the recoverable amount (higher of net realisable value and value in use) is determined to be £90.

The following describes how the revaluation deficit of £70 (£150 — £80) should be accounted for:

(a) If the impairment of £60, that is, the difference between carrying value of £150 and recoverable amount of £90, is considered to have arisen due to a clear consumption of economic benefits, it should be charged in its entirety to the profit and loss account and shown under the appropriate statutory heading in arriving at operating profit.

The previous revaluation surplus of £50 in the revaluation reserve may then be transferred through reserves (but not through the statement of total recognised gains and losses) to profit and loss reserves.

(b) If the impairment of £60 is considered not to have arisen from a clear consumption of economic benefits, it should be charged as to £50 to the statement of total recognised gains and losses and £10 to the profit and loss account, again under the appropriate heading in arriving at operating profit. The charge of £50 to the statement of total recognised gains and losses should be shown on the face of that statement.

(c) In both cases, that is whether the impairment loss is due to a clear consumption of economic benefits or not, the remaining revaluation adjustment of £10 to reduce the asset from its recoverable amount of £90 to its revalued amount of £80 is shown in the statement of total recognised gains and losses. This is because it corresponds to a temporary diminution under the Companies Act rules and such diminutions should be taken, via the statement of total recognised gains and losses, to the revaluation reserve.

18.262 In the above example, a diminution in value of £10 below cost was charged in the statement of total recognised gains and losses rather than the profit and loss account, because that amount was purely a market value adjustment and not an impairment. Consider the presentation in the following year if a further impairment is identified.

Example – Market value used for revaluation purposes is lower than value in use (2)

The facts are as in the previous example. In the following year the fixed asset's market value has fallen from £80 to £50. A further impairment review is carried out and the recoverable amount is estimated also to be £50 (that is, it has fallen from £90 to £50).

The impairment loss in the following year is £40 (£90 less £50). However, the loss to be recognised in the year (in the profit and loss account) is only £30, because a loss of £10 was charged in the previous year (in the statement of total recognised gains and losses) as a revaluation deficit. In effect that revaluation deficit of £10 has become an impairment loss. But, in accordance with FRS 3, as the loss of £10 has already been recognised in the statement of total recognised gains and losses (albeit not as an impairment loss), it is not shown again in the profit and loss account. Instead, that part of the impairment loss would be charged to profit and loss account reserve by means of a reserve transfer in the reserves note (that is, crediting revaluation reserve and debiting profit and loss account reserve by £10).

Assets held for disposal

Loss on disposal or impairment loss?

18.263 FRS 3 requires losses on disposals of fixed assets or operations (including provisions in respect of them) to be charged after operating profit and before interest. [FRS 3 para 20]. FRS 11 requires impairment losses recognised in the profit and loss account to be charged in operating profit under the appropriate statutory heading. [FRS 11 para 67]. If FRS 11 was interpreted in isolation, most losses recognised in connection with asset disposals would be impairments (charged against operating profit) rather than losses on disposals (non-operating exceptional items). That is because in most cases any previously unidentified shortfall between an asset's carrying value and its recoverable amount that is identified as a result of a decision to sell or terminate would be an impairment, not a loss on disposal.

18.264 The apparent conflict may be interpreted as follows when the requirements of FRS 3 and FRS 11 are considered together. Impairment losses in respect of fixed assets and businesses that are to be retained must be charged in arriving at operating profit. Impairment losses that, in FRS 3 terms, are provisions for losses on disposals (that is, they are recognised as a result of a decision to dispose of the assets or business concerned) should be shown under the relevant one of the three headings in paragraph 20 of FRS 3. In the latter case, if the disposal has not occurred before the balance sheet date, the company would be expected to provide evidence that the asset or operation would not be retained. For example, the asset or business would probably be being actively marketed and it would be reasonable to expect that the disposal would be completed before the next interim accounts and in any event before the end of the next financial year.

18.265 This apparent inconsistency between FRS 3 and FRS 11 gives rise to some anomalies. If an asset is put up for sale and has not previously been reviewed for impairment, the loss on sale is presented in accordance with paragraph 20 of FRS 3. If, however, an impairment loss is identified earlier as a result of carrying out an impairment review in circumstances required by FRS 11, the loss would be presented as part of operating profit in accordance with FRS 11.

18.266 A similar issue arises where a company undertakes a fundamental reorganisation having a material effect on the nature and focus of its operations. FRS 3 requires the costs incurred to be shown after operating profit under a separate caption. Costs incurred often involve write-offs of assets and goodwill, which are regarded as impairments under FRS 11, as well as other reorganisation costs. In such circumstances, it is logical to present all the costs of the fundamental reorganisation, including the impairments, under the relevant FRS 3 caption.

Disposal of previously impaired asset

18.267 Where a previously impaired fixed asset is sold and the proceeds exceed the impaired carrying value, the gain should be recognised in the profit and loss account. A question arises whether the whole of the gain should be shown under the heading 'profits or losses on the disposal of fixed assets' (after operating profit) or whether at least part of the gain should be recognised as a reversal of the past impairment and be included in operating profit.

18.268 Paragraph 21 of FRS 3 requires the profit on disposal to be accounted for in the profit and loss account of the period in which the disposal occurs as the difference between the net sale proceeds and the net carrying amount, whether carried at historical cost (less any provisions made) or at a valuation. Therefore, the whole of the gain should be shown after operating profit (except where the gain is in effect no more than a marginal adjustment to depreciation previously charged).

18.269 However, where a previously impaired fixed asset has increased in value and has not been disposed of by the year end, paragraph 56 of FRS 11 requires the asset's carrying value to be increased if its recoverable amount has increased because of a change in economic conditions or in the expected use of the asset. The reversal of an impairment loss should be recognised in the profit and loss account to the extent that (a) the original impairment loss was charged in the profit and loss account and (b) the reversal increases the carrying amount up to the amount that it would have been had the original impairment not occurred. It is logical that the reversal of the impairment loss should be credited under the same statutory heading that the original impairment loss was charged, that is, included within operating profit.

Other financial statement disclosures

Fixed asset movements

18.270 In the notes showing fixed asset movements, impairment losses should be disclosed as follows:

- For assets held at historical cost, the impairment loss should be included within the cumulative depreciation. The cost of the asset should not be reduced.
- For revalued assets held at market value (that is, existing use value or open-market value) the impairment loss should be included within the revalued carrying amount and not shown within any cumulative depreciation.
- For revalued assets held at depreciated replacement cost, an impairment loss charged to the profit and loss account should be included within cumulative depreciation. The revalued carrying amount of the asset should not be reduced. An impairment loss charged to the statement of total recognised gains and losses should be deducted from the revalued carrying amount of the asset.

[FRS 11 para 68].

18.271 FRS 10, which applies to goodwill and intangible assets and FRS 15, which applies to tangible fixed assets, are rather more specific on detailing the movements. They require impairment losses, and reversals of past impairment losses, to be disclosed separately in the note that reconciles the movements between the opening and closing balances for goodwill and each class of intangible and tangible asset. [FRS 10 para 53; FRS 15 para 100].

Revalued assets held at market value

18.272 For revalued assets held at market value, revaluations are usually reflected in the reconciliation of fixed asset movements by adjusting the gross revalued carrying amount (that is, before depreciation) to the new market value. Accumulated depreciation charged up to the date of the new valuation is eliminated from the reconciliation. The disclosure of impairment losses in the reconciliation does not distinguish between impairments that are caused by a consumption of economic benefits (charged to the profit and loss account) and other impairments that are deemed to result from general changes in prices (charged to the statement of total recognised gains and losses). All impairments are deducted from the gross revalued carrying amount before depreciation and, hence, none are shown within accumulated depreciation.

18.273 The treatment of revalued assets held at market value is illustrated in the following example. It shows that all impairment losses are in effect treated as downward valuations in the reconciliation of fixed asset movements.

Example – Disclosure of revalued assets at market value; valuation adjustments and impairments

An asset cost £200 and has a useful life of 20 years; it is depreciated on a straight-line basis. At the end of year 3 it was revalued to £220 (compared with depreciated historical cost of £170).

At the end of year 5, the asset had a carrying value of £194 (comprising the revalued amount of £220 less accumulated depreciation of £26 relating to years 4 and 5). On a depreciated historical cost basis, the carrying value would have been £150 (comprising cost of £200 less accumulated depreciation of £50 relating to years 1 to 5).

At the end of year 5, as a result of an impairment review of the IGU to which the asset contributes, the recoverable amount of the IGU is found to be lower than its carrying value. The allocation of the impairment loss in accordance with paragraphs 48 and 49 of FRS 11 results in the asset being written down to its net realisable value (which is based on its current market value). The disclosure of the impairment loss in the reconciliation of fixed asset movements is illustrated in three different scenarios:

A Recoverable amount is £150. The impairment loss of £44 (which is equal to the surplus of the revalued carrying value of £194 over the depreciated historical cost of £150) is charged in the statement of total recognised gains and losses (that is, treated as a downward revaluation) because the loss is not considered to have been caused by a consumption of economic benefits.

B Recoverable amount is £150. The impairment loss of £44 is considered to have been caused by a consumption of economic benefits and is charged in the profit and loss account.

C Recoverable amount is £100. The impairment loss of £94 is charged £44 as in A above in the statement of total recognised gains and losses (that is, the surplus of the revalued carrying value of £194 over the depreciated historical cost of £150) and £50 (the balance) in the profit and loss account.

Impairment loss

	A	B	C
	£	£	£
Carrying value	194	194	194
Recoverable amount	150	150	100
Impairment loss	44	44	94
Charged:			
STRGL	44	–	44
Profit and loss account	–	44	50
Total	44	44	94

The impairment losses would be disclosed in the reconciliation of fixed asset movements as follows:

Note of fixed asset movements

	A	B	C
	£	£	£
Valuation			
At 1 January 05	220	220	220
Impairment	(44)	(44)	(94)
Valuation adjustment	(26)	(26)	(26)
At 31 December 05	150	150	100
Accumulated depreciation			
At 1 January 05	13	13	13
Charge for the year	13	13	13
Valuation adjustment	(26)	(26)	(26)
At 31 December 05	–	–	–
Net book value			
At 31 December 04	207	207	207
At 31 December 05	150	150	100

It should be noted that the valuation adjustment of £26 shown as movements under the 'valuation' and 'accumulated depreciation' headings is necessary to eliminate accumulated depreciation from the reconciliation; thus the recoverable amount at 31 December 05 is treated as a new valuation.

Revalued assets held at depreciated replacement cost

18.274 The treatment of revalued fixed assets carried at market value may be contrasted with the treatment of revalued fixed assets carried at depreciated replacement cost, where impairment losses charged in the profit and loss account should be included within accumulated depreciation. If the revalued asset in the previous example had been valued at depreciated replacement cost, the treatment in the reconciliation of fixed movements would be different, as illustrated in the following example.

Example – Disclosure of revalued assets at depreciated replacement cost; valuation adjustments and impairments

The facts are the same as in the previous example, except that the asset was revalued at depreciated replacement cost at the end of year 3. FRS 15 states that both the cost or revalued amount and the accumulated depreciation at the date of revaluation may be restated, so that the carrying amount of the asset after revaluation equals its revalued amount. [FRS 15 para 101]. If this approach was adopted, the valuation of £220 (net replacement cost) would be 'grossed up' to disclose a gross replacement cost and, separately, accumulated depreciation to reflect the portion of the asset's useful life already consumed, as follows:

	£
Cost or valuation	
Cost b/f	200
Revaluation	59
Gross replacement cost	259
Accumulated depreciation	
B/f	30
Revaluation	9
	39
Net replacement cost	220

The impairment at the end of year 5 would be shown as follows, under each of the three scenarios set out in the previous example.

Note of fixed asset movements

	A	B	C
	£	£	£
Gross replacement cost			
At 1 January 05	259	259	259
Impairment loss	(44)	–	(44)
At 31 December 05	215	259	215
Accumulated depreciation			
At 1 January 05	52	52	52
Charge for the year	13	13	13
Impairment loss	–	44	50
At 31 December 05	65	109	115
Net book value			
At 31 December 04	207	207	207
At 31 December 05	150	150	100

The impairment losses shown in the above reconciliation can be identified directly with the amounts charged in the profit and loss account (shown under accumulated depreciation) and in the statement of total recognised gains and losses (shown under gross replacement cost).

Value in use calculations

18.275 Where an impairment loss is recognised and has been measured by reference to value in use, the discount rate applied to the cash flows should be disclosed. If a risk-free discount rate is used, some indication of the risk adjustments made to the cash flows should be given. [FRS 11 para 69].

18.276 Where, in measuring value in use, the period before a steady or declining growth rate is assumed extends to more than five years, the financial statements should disclose the length of the longer period and the circumstances justifying it. [FRS 11 para 72].

18.277 Where, in measuring value in use, the long-term growth rate used has exceeded the long-term average growth rate for the country or countries in which the business operates, the financial statements should disclose the growth rate assumed and the circumstances justifying it. [FRS 11 para 73].

18.278 It should be noted that the disclosures referred to in the previous two paragraphs are not limited to circumstances where an impairment loss has actually been recognised. Thus, if a formal impairment review has been carried out and no impairment loss has been recognised, some disclosure of the facts appears to be necessary if the normal constraints on the growth assumptions relating to long-term cash flow forecasts have been exceeded when measuring value in use.

18.279 For the five years following each impairment review, where recoverable amount has been based on value in use, the cash flows achieved should be compared with those forecast. If the cash flows achieved show that an impairment loss should have been recognised in previous periods, that loss should be recognised in the current period, unless it has already reversed. Where an impairment loss would have been recognised in a previous period had forecasts of future cash flows been more accurate, but the impairment has since reversed and the reversal is permitted to be recognised by FRS 11, the impairment now identified and its subsequent reversal should be disclosed. [FRS 11 para 71].

Reversals

18.280 Where a previously recognised impairment loss has been reversed, the reasons for the reversal should be disclosed, including any changes in the assumptions upon which calculation of recoverable amount is based. [FRS 11 para 70].

Companies Act disclosures

18.281 The Companies Act in SI 2008/410, 'The Large and Medium-sized Companies and Groups (Accounts and Reports) Regulations 2008' requires that provisions for diminution in value are made in respect of any fixed asset that has diminished in value if the reduction in its value is expected to be permanent (whether its useful economic life is limited or not). Furthermore, the Act requires that any such provisions made that are not shown in the profit and loss account must be disclosed (either separately or in aggregate) in a note to the financial statements. [SI 2008/410 1 Sch 19, 20]. Specific disclosure requirements are also given in SI 2008/410. The amounts to be disclosed are:

- The cumulative amount of provisions for depreciation or diminution in value of assets included under that item at the beginning of the financial year and at the balance sheet date.
- The amount of any such provisions made in respect of the financial year.
- The amount of any adjustments made in respect of any such provisions during that year in consequence of the disposal of any assets.

- The amount of any other adjustments made in respect of any such provisions during that year.

[SI 2008/410 1 Sch (51)(3)].

Chapter 19

Leases and HP contracts

Page

Chapter 19

Leases and HP contracts

Introduction

19.1 This chapter considers the accounting treatment and disclosure of leased assets in a company's financial statements and discusses some of the practical issues concerning lease accounting. The UK accounting requirements for lease transactions for both lessees and lessors are set out in SSAP 21, 'Accounting for leases and hire purchase contracts'. Additionally, those lease transactions which form part of a complex arrangement or which contains options, conditional provisions and guarantees also fall under the scope of FRS 5. As explained in FRS 5, where a transaction falls under the scope of both FRS 5 and SSAP 21 the standard containing the more specific provision will apply. In general, SSAP 21 contains the more specific provisions, relating to stand-alone leases. The exception to this is in Application Note B of FRS 5, which deals specifically with sale and repurchase transactions including the treatment of options.

19.2 Under SSAP 21, a 'lease' is defined as a contract between the lessor and the lessee for the hire of a specific asset. The lessor retains ownership of the asset, but conveys to the lessee the right to use the asset in return for paying specific rentals. In addition, the definition of a lease in the standard includes other arrangements not described as leases, in which one party retains ownership but conveys to another the right to use the asset for an agreed period of time in return for specific rentals.

19.3 In broad terms, SSAP 21 requires that, where a company finances a significant amount of its capital investment through leasing, its financial statements should properly reflect the commercial effect of those transactions. Thus, where the substance of those transactions is akin to the lessee purchasing the asset, financed by borrowings drawn from the lessor (a 'finance lease'), the standard requires the lessee's balance sheet to show both an asset, reflecting the lessee's rights in the leased asset, and a liability, reflecting the future financial obligations under the lease. However, where the lease does not have the commercial effect of a financing arrangement for the acquisition of an asset (an 'operating lease') the lessee need only account for the rental expense through its profit and loss account.

19.4 Similarly, from the lessor's perspective, leases that have similar characteristics to other forms of lending ('finance leases') are classified in the balance sheet as receivables; whereas assets held for use in operating leases are treated in a similar way to other tangible fixed assets.

19.5 Thus, the accounting treatment of a lease depends on the commercial substance of the lease. The accounting distinction between a finance lease and an operating lease is, therefore, a crucial one.

19.6 The paragraphs below consider the factors to be taken into account when classifying leases. The following two sections consider the appropriate treatment from the perspective of the lessee and lessor, respectively, once the lease has been classified.

Classification of leases

19.7 Under SSAP 21, a finance lease is defined as *'...a lease that transfers substantially all the risks and rewards of ownership of an asset to the lessee'.* [SSAP 21 para 15]. Thus, a finance lease is an arrangement that has the substance of a financing transaction for the lessee to acquire effective economic ownership of an asset.

19.8 An operating lease, under SSAP 21, is simply *'...a lease other than a finance lease'*. [SSAP 21 para 17]. In practice, this means that an operating lease does not pass substantially all the risk and rewards of ownership to the lessee: a significant element of risk must, therefore, remain with the lessor or some party other than the lessee. Consequently, an operating lease is usually for a period substantially shorter than the asset's useful economic life and the lessor will be relying on recovering a significant proportion of his investment from either the proceeds from the asset's sale or the asset's further hire after the end of the lease term.

19.9 Whether or not a lease passes substantially all the risks and rewards of ownership to the lessee will normally be self-evident from the terms of the lease contract and an understanding of the commercial risks taken by each party. Where the lessor takes little or no asset-related risk, other than a credit risk on the lessee, the agreement will obviously be a finance lease. Similarly, where the lessor is exposed to significant levels of risks relating to movements in the asset's market value, utilisation, or performance, such as on a short-term hire agreement, the agreement will be easily classified as an operating lease. The difficulty, therefore, tends to emerge on classifying leases where the lessor recovers most of his investment through the terms of the lease, but retains some element of risk relating to the asset's residual value at the end of the lease term.

19.10 In order to provide guidance on when such risks and rewards could be reasonable presumed to have passed, SSAP 21 sets a simple test:

> *'It should be presumed that such a transfer of risks and rewards occurs if at the inception of a lease the present value of the minimum lease payments, including any initial payment, amounts to substantially all (normally 90 per cent or more) of the fair value of the leased asset'*. [SSAP 21 para 15].

19.11 In essence, the present value test is a measure of the risk that the lessor (or other third party) is taking in relation to the asset's residual value at the end of the lease term. Where the lessor (or other third party) is assuming a significant level of residual value risk (ten per cent or more in present value terms) then it is presumed that substantially all the risks of ownership could not have passed to the lessee. As a yardstick for measuring risk the present value test is somewhat crude, but it was seen as a reasonable test of risk at the time SSAP 21 was introduced. It was, however, never intended to provide a strict mathematical definition of a finance lease. Thus, SSAP 21 provides that the presumption can be overridden where there is demonstrable evidence to support doing so.

19.12 One of the principal criticisms of SSAP 21 is that it led to practices under which lessors would structure leases in a way that apparently gives a present value result below the 90 per cent threshold, often marginally so, in order to provide lessees with a source of off-balance sheet finance. In July 1987, the ICAEW took the unusual step of issuing a Technical Release, TR 664, to clarify the rules in SSAP 21. TR 664 seeks to dissuade preparers of financial statements from standing behind the present value test in determining whether a leased asset should be on- or off-balance sheet by emphasising that the leases should be classified according to an informed judgement as to what is the true substance of the leasing transaction. Thus, while the present value test sets a presumption, it should be overridden where the circumstances justify it.

19.13 The publication of FRS 5, 'Reporting the substance of transactions', in 1994 further reinforces the message of TR 664, because it requires emphasis to be placed on those aspects and implications of a transaction that are likely to have a commercial effect in practice. Moreover, FRS 5 is particularly relevant in interpreting leases containing options, guarantees and conditional provisions where it provides more specific guidance than SSAP 21.

19.14 Consequently, although the present value test may be a useful yardstick for measuring the lessor's risk in a lease, it is by no means conclusive of where the risks and rewards lie. A proper interpretation of the classification of a lease, therefore, requires the exercise of judgement to determine the agreement's true nature. In this matter, the terms dealing with: the contractual lease period, the cancellation provisions, the renewal options and the rights and obligations of each party in relation to the asset at the end of the lease term are particularly important.

Lease term

19.14.1 Under SSAP 21, the lease term includes both of the following:

- The period for which the lessee has a contractual obligation to lease the asset.
- Further periods for which the lessee has the option to continue to lease the asset, with or without further payments, and it is reasonably certain at the inception of the lease that the lessee will exercise that option.

[SSAP 21 para 19].

Those parts of the lease that deal with: the lease's minimum contractual period (sometimes referred to as the 'primary period'); cancellation (or 'break') clauses; exchange and upgrade conditions; and options to extend the lease must, therefore, be considered carefully.

[The next paragraph is 19.15.]

19.15 If a lease contains a clean break clause, that is, where the lessee is free to walk away from the lease agreement after a certain time without penalty, then the lease term for accounting purposes will normally be the period between the inception of the lease and the earliest point at which the break option is exercisable by the lessee. Thus, the inclusion of a break clause can significantly reduce the minimum lease payments for the purpose of the present value test with the effect that the present value of the minimum lease payments falls below the 90 per cent threshold and the lease is classified as an operating lease. This, however, is not an unreasonable result if there is a genuine commercial possibility that the lessee might exercise the option resulting in the realisation of the lessor's unrecovered investment in the leased asset being subject to market risk.

19.16 If a lease contains an early termination clause that requires the lessee to make a termination payment to compensate the lessor (sometimes referred to as the 'stipulated loss value') such that the recovery of the lessor's remaining investment in the lease was assured, then the termination clause would normally be disregarded in determining the lease term.

19.17 Where, however, there are break clauses that transfer some economic risk to the lessor, but at the same time give the lessor some protection from financial loss, the interpretation becomes more difficult. For example, certain computer lessors include right to exchange clauses in leases that would otherwise be classified as finance leases. These give lessees the right to return equipment, or a proportion of the equipment, at certain times during the primary lease term, but normally on condition that a replacement lease is entered into on the new and remaining equipment. These right to exchange clauses need to be considered very carefully.

19.18 On the one hand, the effect may be the replacement of one finance lease by another, analogous to an outright purchase of equipment with a right to trade in for new equipment at a future date. This will be particularly so where the commercial loss on early termination (the difference between market value and the lessor's book value) is effectively rolled into the new lease agreement either through higher rentals or through an extension of the term on the remaining pool of assets not subject to the exchange. On the other hand, if the lessor takes a genuine residual value risk under the exchange conditions and such losses are not passed on to the lessee in the way described, this may justify classification as an operating lease.

19.19 Renewal clauses can cause similar problems of interpretation as break clauses. Where the terms of renewal are set at what is anticipated to be significantly below a fair market rental then it is reasonable to assume that the lessee will act in his own commercial interests and extend the lease. In these situations, the lease term would include both the minimum period and the renewal period. Where, however, the rentals in the secondary period are based on a fair market basis, such that there is no compelling commercial reason why the lessee must extend the lease, then the lease term will normally exclude the secondary period.

19.20 Other factors that may need to be considered in determining whether secondary periods should be included in the lease term are other forms of commercial compulsion such as penalties. For example, if the lessee is subject to a penalty for failing to renew a lease or exercise a purchase option, or if the return conditions stipulated in the lease are unduly penal, it may be to the lessee's advantage to continue to lease the asset. Similarly, if the lessee's business is dependent on the asset such that the cost of its removal and disruption of business are disproportional to the costs of continuing the lease, the secondary period should be included in the lease term.

Minimum lease payments

19.21 Once the lease term is determined, the lessee's minimum lease payments can be calculated. These are the payments that the lessee is committed to make during the lease term, and include:

- Any initial payment the lessee makes.
- The minimum rentals over the lease term (excluding charges in respect of services, such as maintenance, and VAT).
- Any amounts guaranteed by the lessee, or by a party related to him, to the lessor in respect of the realisation of the asset at the end of the lease term.

[SSAP 21 para 20].

19.22 From the lessor's perspective, the minimum lease payments may be different from that defined above since the lessor's minimum lease payments includes all the above and further amounts that are guaranteed by third parties in relation to the asset's future realisation. Thus, if the manufacturer originally supplying the asset agreed to repurchase the asset from the lessor, or guaranteed the sales proceeds, at the end of the lease term, then this amount would be included in the lessor's minimum lease payments. Consequently, in these circumstances, the lessee and lessor may well classify the lease quite differently.

19.23 The inclusion of 'residual guarantees' in lease agreements and related documentation will have an important impact on the way leases are classified by both lessors and lessees.

19.24 Obviously, if the lessee guarantees the whole of the asset's expected residual value at the end of the lease term the lessor would not be taking any of the risks relating to the performance or market value of the asset and the transaction would be clearly a finance lease. It would also mean that, by definition, the present value of the minimum lease payments would be equal to 100 per cent of the asset's fair value.

19.25 However, it is not uncommon in certain leases for the lessee and lessor to share both the downside risks and potential upside benefits associated with the asset's market value at the end of the lease term such that the lessee is taking some, but not all, the residual risk. For example, in certain leases the terms of the agreement provide for the asset to be sold at the end of the lease term and any profit and loss arising against anticipated values is shared between the lessor and lessee. However, the profit and loss sharing arrangements are usually unevenly balanced between the parties, with the lessee often taking the first tranche of loss up to a stipulated amount, with the lessor (or other third parties) only taking losses beyond that sum. In these circumstances, the amount of losses the lessee guarantees is normally set at such an amount that the inclusion of the guaranteed amount in the minimum lease payments does not cause the 90 per cent test to be breached.

19.26 Interpreting these types of agreement can be particularly difficult. The lessor may have a residual risk of ten per cent in present value terms, but if this implies that residual values have to fall to a level substantially below that anticipated to occur in practice, even under the most pessimistic circumstances, then the lessor's risk is remote and all the real commercial risks must rest with the lessee. In these circumstances, there is a strong argument for overriding the results of the present value test and classifying the lease as a finance lease.

Example – Variation in residual risk

A lease of a car for two years has built into it an assumed residual value for the car of 45% of original cost. The market's perception is that the likely range of the residual value is 40-50% of cost. The terms of the lease provide that the lessee takes the risks and rewards regarding the residual down to a residual of 20% of cost. Below 20%, the lessor bears the loss.

It is clear under the combination of SSAP 21 and FRS 5 that the lessor's taking of risk below 20% of cost should not be taken into account in classifying the lease. The lessee takes the residual risk in all likely outcomes of residual value. Therefore, subject to any other terms in the lease, a finance lease is indicated.

19.27 However, in practice, the facts as illustrated above are rarely so simple. For example, under certain aircraft leases the lessee is offered a range of options under which it can terminate, or not renew, the leasing agreement. If it terminates the lease the residual sharing arrangements can be complex with the residual risk being shared by a number of parties including the lessor, lessee, supplier and residual insurer in a complex series of tranches. Interpreting these types of complex lease arrangements can be particularly difficult and the general principles and specific provisions of FRS 5 will need to be applied to determine the nature of transactions. For example, implementing FRS 5 had a dramatic impact on British Airways' Plc accounting for certain aircraft leases (see Table 19.1).

Table 19.1 – British Airways Plc – Report & Accounts – 31 March 1995

Notes to the accounts

1 CHANGES IN ACCOUNTING POLICIES (extract)

Adoption of new accounting standard (extract)

The Group has adopted the provisions of Financial Reporting Standard 5 'Reporting the Substance of Transactions' with effect from 1 April 1994 and corresponding amounts have been adjusted accordingly. As a consequence, the leases on twenty-four aircraft previously accounted for as operating leases are now accounted for as if they were finance leases and are aggregated with finance leases in the various disclosures in theses accounts. The effect of this change on the balance sheet at 31 March 1995 has been to increase tangible fixed assets by £870 million (1994: £1,006 million) and borrowings by £905 million (1994: £1,041 million) and to reduce opening reserves by £52 million (1994: £45 million). The effect on the results for the year ended 31 March 1995 has been to increase operating profit by £53 million (1994: £43 million) and to increase interest payable by £54 million (1994: £52 million), thereby reducing profit before taxation for the year by £1 million (1994: £9 million).

19.28 In some agreements relating to car fleets, the assessment of the commercial effects of these residual sharing arrangements can be further complicated by terms that mitigate a lessor's risk by providing for any residual losses on individual assets to be pooled against profits on others in the same portfolio. Again, these types of arrangement will need to be considered carefully to determine the nature of the risks borne by the lessor (and other third parties) and those transferred to the lessee. As a general rule, for instance, losses on some assets should not be set against profits on others.

The interest rate implicit in the lease

19.29 The rate of interest used for the present value test should be the interest rate implicit in the lease. This is the discount rate that, when applied at the inception of the lease to the amounts that the lessor expects to receive and retain from his investment in the lease, produces a present value equal to the leased asset's fair value. The amounts that the lessor expects to receive and retain comprise:

- The lessee's minimum lease payments.
- Any further amounts guaranteed by third parties in respect of the asset's residual value.
- The asset's expected residual value at the end of the lease, which is not guaranteed by the lessee or any other party.
- Less any amounts for which the lessor will be accountable to the lessee (for example, a rental rebate at the end of the lease based on the proceeds from the assets' sale).

[SSAP 21 para 24].

19.30 In more simple terms, the interest rate implicit in the lease is the lessor's internal rate of return from the lease taking into account the normal cash price of the leased asset, rentals and the amount he expects to recover from the residual value. In practice, the interest rate implicit in the lease is unlikely to be stipulated in the agreement and, unless the lessor volunteers the information to the lessee, the lessee will need either to derive an estimate of the rate from the information available to him or to use an approximation based on a similar lease.

19.31 A lessee can normally derive a reasonable estimate of the interest rate implicit in a lease where he either knows, or can make a reasonable estimate of, the cost of the asset and the anticipated residual value of the asset at the end of the lease term.

The present value calculation

19.32 The present value calculation is performed by discounting the minimum lease payments and comparing the resulting present value to the fair value of the leased asset. In most circumstances, the fair value will be the normal cash price at which the lessee could otherwise purchase the asset. A potentially misleading result can arise if the comparison is made against an amount that is not representative of the fair value, for example, a list price where substantial discounts are normally given to customers purchasing assets.

19.33 As indicated above, the present value test can also be misleading where the results of the present value test are engineered to provide a result marginally below the 90 per cent threshold. Such engineering can arise through the uses of break clauses, renewal clauses, and residual guarantees. Where there is evidence that the amount of residual risk taken by the lessor (or other unrelated parties) is insignificant or remote then there will be reasons to believe that substantially all the risks and rewards of ownership have passed to the lessee. In these circumstances, the results of the present value test should be overridden and the lease classified as a finance lease.

Property leases

19.34 Under the standard, leases of land and buildings are subject to the same accounting requirements as other leased assets. This means that they should either be classified as finance leases or as operating leases and should be accounted for accordingly. However, the present value test is difficult to apply to property leases and can sometimes be misleading. This is partly because of the practical difficulties of ascertaining the true interest rate implicit in the lease and partly because of the commercial nature of most UK institutional property leases.

19.35 Most UK institutional 'short' leases are for periods up to 25-30 years, and contain clauses that adjust lease payments to market rates at a regular interval (for example, five-yearly or three-yearly rent reviews). The lessor is often an institution that is seeking long-term rental and capital growth and is, therefore, taking most of the risks and rewards associated with changes in the property market. Although part of the investor's return may be protected by 'upward only' rental review clauses the overall return is dependent on market conditions, which may be substantially less or greater than originally anticipated. In this sense, the nature of the lessor's return is very different from a 'lender's return', which is based on the lender's cost of money plus margin.

19.36 However, it does not necessarily follow that all leases that look like institutional 'short' leases are operating leases. There are a number of hybrid leasing structures which, though in the legal form of a short lease, have many of the characteristics of financing arrangements.

19.37 Again the principles of FRS 5 and, in particular, whether the lender achieves a lenders' return, will help determine the true nature of the lease. An example could be a building with a relatively short life, perhaps built to a customer's specification or for a specific use, or certain types of sale and leaseback arrangements where the commercial objective is for the lessee to repurchase the property at an early option date.

19.38 Long leases (usually 99-999 years) are more likely to be finance leases. Such leases often involve the payment of a large lease premium with only a small annual ground rent. In these situations, the lease premium is normally capitalised and depreciated over the lease term. While, strictly, the present value of the ground rent should also be capitalised and an obligation set up, these amounts are often ignored as being immaterial.

Accounting by lessees

Accounting for finance leases

19.39 A finance lease should be recorded in a lessee's balance sheet both as an asset and as an obligation to pay future rentals. At the inception of the lease, the sum to be recorded both as an asset and as a liability should be the present value of the minimum lease payments, derived by discounting them at the interest rate implicit in the lease. [SSAP 21 para 32].

19.40 An asset leased under a finance lease should be depreciated over the shorter of the lease term and its useful life. [SSAP 21 para 36]. The lease term is the period for which the lessee has contracted to lease the asset plus any further optional periods, which are at the lessee's option and which are reasonably certain to be exercised. [SSAP 21 para 19]. With a hire purchase contract that has the characteristics of a finance lease, the asset should be depreciated over its useful life. [SSAP 21 para 36].

19.41 The lease is deemed to commence on the earlier of the date on which the asset is brought into use by the lessee and the date from which rentals first accrue. Therefore, if a lease provides for a rent-free period at the start of the lease, the lessee should treat the inception date as the date on which he started to use the asset.

19.42 Rentals payable should be apportioned between the finance charge and a reduction of the outstanding obligation for future amounts payable. The total finance charge under a finance lease should be allocated to accounting periods during the lease term, so as to produce either a constant periodic rate of charge on the remaining balance of the obligation for each accounting period or a reasonable approximation to it. [SSAP 21 para 35].

Example – Allocating rentals between finance charge and lease obligation

Cost of leased asset	£100,000
Lease term	5 years
Rental six-monthly in advance	£12,000
Expected residual on disposal at the end of the lease term	£10,000
Lessee's interest in residual proceeds	97%
Economic life	8 years
Inception date	1 January 20X4
Lessee's financial year end	31 December

In this example, the lease must obviously be a finance lease because the lessor has only a 3% interest in the residual value. There is, therefore, little point in performing the 90% test.

The amounts the lessor expects to receive and retain comprise the rentals, plus 3% of the residual at the end of the lease term. These amounts can be used to determine the interest rate implicit in the lease and the present value of the lessee's minimum lease payments as follows:

	Present value factor	Present value at 4.3535% £
Lessee's minimum lease payments (10 × £12,000)	8.3170	99,804
Lessor's residual (£10,000 – £9,700)	0.6533	196
Fair value		100,000

The interest rate that amortises these amounts is 4.3535%, compounded on a six-monthly basis.

The amount that is capitalised as both an asset and an obligation at the inception of the lease is, therefore, £99,804. Alternatively, it could be simply assumed that, because the lessor's residual was so immaterial, the fair value was a reasonable approximation of the present value of the lease payments and this would generally be allowed in such a case. If this approach was adopted, the amount that would be capitalised at the inception of the lease as an asset and an obligation would be £100,000.

The finance charge can now be allocated to each accounting period. In this example the actuarial method has been used:

Period commencing	Obligation at start of period	Rental paid	Obligation during period	Finance charge at 4.3535%	Obligation at end of period
	£	£	£	£	£
January 20X4	99,804	(12,000)	87,804	3,823	91,627
June 20X4	91,627	(12,000)	79,627	3,467	83,094
January 20X5	83,094	(12,000)	71,094	3,095	74,189
June 20X5	74,189	(12,000)	62,189	2,707	64,896
January 20X6	64,896	(12,000)	52,896	2,303	55,199
June 20X6	55,199	(12,000)	43,199	1,881	45,080
January 20X7	45,080	(12,000)	33,080	1,440	34,520
June 20X7	34,520	(12,000)	22,520	980	23,500
January 20X8	23,500	(12,000)	11,500	500	12,000
June 20X8	12,000	(12,000)	–	–	–
		(120,000)		20,196	

The finance charges for each year and, by deduction, the capital repayment element of the rental can now be summarised as follows:

	Rental	Finance charges	Capital repayment
	£	£	£
20X4	24,000	7,290	16,710
20X5	24,000	5,802	18,198
20X6	24,000	4,184	19,816
20X7	24,000	2,420	21,580
20X8	24,000	500	23,500
	120,000	20,196	99,804

In this example, the lessee's financial year end coincides with the end of a rental period and so no interest accrual is necessary.

Depreciation can now be calculated as follows:

Lease term = 5 years
Economic life = 8 years
Lessee's interest in the proceeds of the residual = £9,700

Therefore, the depreciation charge on a straight line basis is:

$$\frac{£99{,}804 - £9{,}700}{5 \text{ years}} = £18{,}021 \text{ per annum}$$

Where the lessee's interest in the anticipated proceeds of the residual is immaterial, the residual can be ignored for the purposes of calculating depreciation.

The effects on the lessee's balance sheet and profit and loss account for each year can now be summarised as follows:

	Obligations under finance leases	Net book value of leased assets	Depreciation	Finance charges	Total charges
	£	£	£	£	£
Start	99,804	99,804			
20X4	83,094	81,783	18,021	7,290	25,311
20X5	64,896	63,762	18,021	5,802	23,823
20X6	45,080	45,741	18,021	4,184	22,205
20X7	23,500	27,720	18,021	2,420	20,441
20X8	–	9,700	18,020	500	18,520
			90,104	20,196	110,300

The above example illustrates that, in addition to its impact on the lessee's balance sheet, lease capitalisation may also have a significant impact on the lessee's profit and loss account. For example, the lease rentals are £24,000 per annum, but the combined charge for depreciation and interest varies from £25,311 to £18,520 per annum. These differences between rental payments and profit and loss charges will be more pronounced on assets subject to long economic lives and leases with short primary lease periods, but which may have secondary periods at peppercorn rents.

Accounting for operating leases

19.43 Operating leases should not be capitalised and the lease rental should be charged on a straight-line basis over the lease term, unless another systematic and rational basis is more appropriate. This applies even if the payments are not made on such a basis. [SSAP 21 para 37].

Lease incentives

19.44 Prospective lessees are sometimes given incentives to sign operating leases for office or retail property. These incentives may include either rent-free or reduced-rent periods at the start of the lease or even contributions toward fitting out costs.

19.45 The UITF issued Abstract 28, 'Operating lease incentives', in February 2001. UITF Abstract 28 expands and clarifies the requirements of paragraph 37 of SSAP 21 with regard to incentives for lessees to sign leases from both the lessee's and the lessor's perspective.

19.46 Operating lease incentives may take many different forms. Examples of such incentives include: contributions to relocation or start-up costs; the assumption of liabilities, such as the rentals under the an old lease which would otherwise fall to be a vacant property; or the gift of an asset such as the lessor bearing directly all the costs of fitting out the property to the lessee's specifications or giving rent free or reduced rental periods for an initial period of the lease. However, both abstracts detail the same treatment for all incentives for the agreement of a new or renewed operating lease regardless of their form or cash flow effect. UITF Abstract 28 clarifies that a payment or other transfer of value from a lessor to a lessee (or for its benefit) should be regarded as a lease incentive when that fairly reflects the transaction's substance. Where it does not reflect the transaction's substance then it should not be regarded as an incentive. For example, a lessor may reimburse a lessee for expenditure that enhances the property generally (rather than for fixtures and fittings that are specific to the lessee) such that the lessor, rather than the lessee, will primarily benefit from that expenditure. The benefit to the lessor may be achieved through increases in the market rent of the property at the next rent review or on the termination of the existing lease. Such expenditure should be treated as a reimbursement of expenditure on the property, so that the lessee would simply record the amount owed by, and subsequently received from, the lessor in the balance sheet. [UITF 28 para 3]. An alternative scenario might be where the lessor pays the lessee compensation in respect of a delay in delivery of the leased asset, again provided that the compensation is genuine, it would not be treated as a lease incentive.

19.47 Benefits received and receivable by a lessee as an incentive to sign a lease in whatever form should be spread by the lessee on a straight-line basis over the lease term, or, if shorter than the full lease term, over the period to the review date on which the rent is first expected to be adjusted to the prevailing market rent. [UITF 12 para 8]. This requirement seeks to ensure that the profit and loss account reflects the true effective rental charge for the property irrespective of the particular cash flow arrangements agreed between the two parties. The lessor will seek to recover a market rental over the lease term. Therefore, the existence of an up-front incentive creates the presumption that the subsequent rental levels will be set at higher than the prevailing market level until either the end of the lease or until the review date when the rent is adjusted to the market level. In requiring that the incentive should be spread over the lease term or to the first rent review to market value if earlier, the abstract amended paragraph 16 of the guidance notes to SSAP 21, which had stated merely those incentives should be spread over the period in which the asset is in use.

19.48 UITF Abstract 28 similarly requires that a lessee should recognise the aggregate benefit of incentives as a reduction of rental expense. The benefit should be allocated on a straight-line basis over the shorter of the lease term and the period ending on the date from which it is expected that prevailing market rental will be payable. [UITF 28 para 14].

19.49 UITF Abstract 28 permits systematic bases other than a straight-line basis to be used to allocate the aggregate benefit of incentives, provided that they are more representative of the time pattern of the lessee's benefit from the use of the leased asset. [UITF 28 para 14]. No disclosure of this is required under UITF

Abstract 28, although if material it would require disclosure under the general requirements of FRS 18, as an estimation technique. In practice the use of bases other than straight-line is rare. In particular this is not a permission to recognise all the benefit of the incentive in a start up period with none recognised over the remaining lease period or until the next rent review to market rates, as this is not consistent with the requirement for a 'systematic' basis. For example, a retailer may lease a new store for a five year period, with no rent reviews. Although the retailer may not open the store for the first six months due to a fit-out period, the retailer still has the benefit of the use and enjoyment of the leased property during that initial period, as well as for the rest of the lease, and hence the incentive should be spread over the five years of the lease period from the start of the lease on a straight-line basis. There is no justification for not recognising lease costs for the initial period, as the lessee still has the benefit of use for this period.

19.49.1 The arguments in UITF Abstract 28 for deferring and spreading the recognition of lease incentives received also provide a good starting point for accounting for lease premiums paid. Therefore, where a substantial premium is paid with only nominal rents paid during the lease, the lease payments would never be adjusted to market rates and so the premium would be charged on a straight-line basis over the full lease term. Where there is a provision in the lease for the rents to be adjusted to market rates, it would be consistent with the reasoning in UITF Abstract 28 for the premium to be charged over the shorter period to the rent review date rather than the full lease term.

Lessee disclosure requirements

19.50 In respect of finance leases, SSAP 21 requires the following information to be disclosed in the lessee's financial statements:

- The gross amount, the related accumulated depreciation and the total depreciation allocated for the period, analysed by each major class of asset capitalised under finance leases. [SSAP 21 para 49].
- Alternatively, this information may be included within the totals disclosed by each major class of asset for owned assets. However, where this alternative is adopted, the total of the net amount of assets held under finance leases and the total amount of depreciation allocated for the period in respect of finance leases, need to be disclosed separately. [SSAP 21 para 50]. An example of this disclosure is in Table 19.2.
- The liability for net obligations under finance leases (net of finance charges allocated to future periods), shown separately from other liabilities. This liability should be disclosed either on the face of the balance sheet or in the notes to the financial statements (see Table 19.3). [SSAP 21 para 51].
- The liability for net obligations under finance leases, analysed between amounts payable in the next year, amounts payable in the second to fifth years inclusive from the balance sheet date and the aggregate amounts payable after the fifth year. [SSAP 21 para 52]. For example, Table 19.3

illustrates this disclosure. The detailed disclosure requirements for such creditors are also contained in chapter 6.

- Where the lessee discloses the analysis of obligations under finance leases separately, he may, as an alternative to analysing the net obligations, analyse the gross obligations and show future finance charges as a separate deduction from the total (see Table 19.5). [SSAP 21 para 52].
- The aggregate finance charge allocated to the period. [SSAP 21 para 53]. This disclosure is often made as part of the interest charge for the year as illustrated in Table 19.4.
- The commitments under finance leases existing at the year end that have been entered into, but whose inception occurs after the year end. [SSAP 21 para 54]. This requirement is analogous to the legal requirements in respect of commitments for capital expenditure (see chapter 21). Zeneca Group PLC, for example, includes such disclosure in the leases note (see Table 19.5).

Table 19.2 – British Airways Plc – Report & Accounts – 31 March 1995

Notes to the accounts (extract)

	Group	
£million	**1995**	1994
5 OPERATING PROFIT (extract)		
a Operating Profit is arrived at after charging:		
Depreciation of Group tangible fixed assets		
Owned assets	**263**	258
Finance leased aircraft	**109**	117
Hire purchased aircraft	**63**	48
Other leasehold interests	**23**	24
	458	447

15 TANGIBLE ASSETS (extract)

				Group total	
£million	Fleet	Property	Equipment	**1995**	1994
Net Book Amounts					
31 March 1995	5,155	801	207	**6,163**	
31 March 1994	5,127	484	200		5,811
Utilisation at 31 March					
Assets in current use					
Owned	1,883	734	165	**2,782**	2,631
Finance leased	1,436			**1,436**	1,623
Hire purchased arrangements	1,445			**1,445**	1,274
Progress payments	377	65	42	**484**	257
Assets held for resale	14	2		**16**	26
	5,155	801	207	**6,163**	5,811

Table 19.3 – Cable and Wireless plc – Report and Accounts – 31 March 1995

Balance sheets (extract)

		Group	
		1995	1994 Restated
at 31 March	Note	**£m**	£m
Creditors: amounts falling due within one year	21		
Loans and obligations under finance leases		**321.4**	359.5
Other creditors		**1,423.8**	1,318.8
		1,745.2	1,678.3
Creditors: amounts falling due after more than one year	22		
Convertible bonds		**149.5**	154.5
Other loans and obligations under finance leases		**1,190.2**	1,022.4
Other creditors		**33.4**	34.2
Provisions for liabilities and charges*			
Deferred taxation	23	**130.0**	126.8
Other provisions	24	**89.5**	28.8
		1,592.6	1,366.7

21. Creditors: amounts falling due within one year (extract)

	Group	
		Restated
	1995	1994
	£m	£m
Loans and obligations under finance leases		
Banks loans and overdrafts	**39.2**	32.6
Bills payable	**15.2**	31.1
Current instalments due on loans	**253.8**	287.4
Obligations under finance leases	**13.2**	8.4
	321.4	359.5

22. Creditors: amounts falling due after more than one year (extract)

	Group	
		Restated
	1995	1994
	£m	£m
Loans and obligations under finance leases		
Sterling repayable at various dates up to 2019	**353.2**	161.1
Hong Kong dollars repayable at various dates up to 1995	**200.9**	220.9
US dollars repayable at various dates up to 2041	**775.1**	838.8
Other currencies repayable at various dates up to 1997	**56.7**	63.6
	1,385.9	1,284.4
Less: Current instalments due	**253.8**	287.4
	1,132.1	997.0

Net obligations under finance leases	**71.3**	33.8
Less: Current instalments due	**13.2**	8.4
	58.1	25.4
Total loans and net obligations under finance leases	**1,190.2**	1,022.4
Total loans and net obligations under finance leases are payable as follows:		
Between one and two years	**130.7**	56.7
Between two and five years	**259.6**	289.3
In five or more years	**799.9**	676.4
	1,190.2	1,022.4

* Note that for years beginning on or after 1 January 2005, SI 2004/2947, 'The Companies Act 1985 (International Accounting Standards and Other Amendments) Regulations 2004', replaces the statutory line item 'provisions for liabilities and charges' with 'provisions for liabilities'. In June 2008 BIS published guidance on the accounting and reporting requirements under the Companies Act 2006, which largely restates in terms of the 2006 Act guidance issued in 2004 in SI 2004/2947.

Table 19.4 – Racal Electronics Plc – Annual Report & Accounts – 31 March 1994

Notes on the financial statements (extract)

5 NET INTEREST RECEIVABLE (extract)		**1994**
	£000	**£000**
Interest receivable:		
Interest receivable on loans and deposits		**12,283**
Interest receivable on finance leases		**3,499**
		15,782
Less interest payable:		
Bank overdrafts, loans and other borrowings repayable within five years	**(13,034)**	
Loans and other borrowings repayable wholly or in part after five years	**(405)**	
Finance charges on hire purchase contracts and finance leases	**(710)**	
		(14,149)
		1,633

Table 19.5 – Zeneca Group PLC – Annual Report and Accounts – 31 December 1994

Notes relating to the accounts (extract)

6 LEASES

The total rentals under operating leases, charged as an expense in the profit and loss account, are disclosed below.

	1994 £m	1993 £m
Hire of plant and machinery	8	6
Other	28	29
	36	35

Commitments under leases to pay rentals during the year following the year of these accounts are given in the table below, analysed to the period in which each lease expires.

	1994	1993
Obligations under operating leases comprise		
Land and buildings		
Expiring within 1 year	3	1
Expiring during years 2 to 5	3	3
Expiring thereafter	4	4
	10	8
Other assets		
Expiring within 1 year	7	4
Expiring during years 2 to 5	6	12
Expiring thereafter	–	–
	13	16
Obligations under finance leases comprise		
Rentals due within 1 year	2	4
Rentals due during years 2 to 5	6	5
Rentals due thereafter	2	2
Less interest element	(2)	(2)
	8	9

Obligations under finance leases are included in other creditors (Note 18).

The Group had commitments totalling £6m (1993 £nil) under finance leases at the balance sheet date which were due to commence thereafter.

19.51 In respect of operating leases, SSAP 21 requires the following information to be disclosed:

- The total of operating lease rentals charged as an expense in the profit and loss account, and analysed between amounts payable both in respect of hire of plant and machinery and in respect of other operating leases. [SSAP 21 para 55]. An example of this disclosure is included in Table 19.5 above.
- The payments that the lessee is committed to make during the next year, analysed between: those in which the commitment expires within that year;

those in which the commitment expires within the second to fifth years inclusive; and those in which the commitment expires more than five years after the balance sheet date. This analysis should show the commitments in respect of land and buildings separately from those of other operating leases. [SSAP 21 para 56]. This requirement is sometimes misunderstood; the intention is to show only the annual commitment not the total amount that will be payable until the end of the lease as illustrated in Table 19.5 above. If the amount to be paid in the next year is significantly different from the amount that will be charged to profit and loss, then details of the difference and the reasons should be given.

19.52 In respect of both finance leases and operating leases, the accounting policies that the lessee has adopted must be disclosed in the financial statements. [SSAP 21 para 57]. For example, Table 19.6 contains such an accounting policy.

Table 19.6 – Cable and Wireless plc – Annual report and Accounts – 31 March 2003

Statement of Accounting Policies (extract)

Leased assets

Where assets are financed by leasing agreements that give rights approximating to ownership, the assets are treated as if they had been purchased outright. The amount capitalised is the present value of the minimum lease payments payable during the lease term. The corresponding lease commitments are shown as obligations to the lessor. Lease payments are split between capital and interest elements using the annuity method. Depreciation on the relevant assets and interest are charged to the profit and loss account. All other leases are operating leases and the annual rentals are charged to operating profit on a straight line basis over the lease term.

19.53 In addition to the standard's disclosure requirements, the Guidance Notes to the standard indicate that other details about a company's leases may need to be disclosed in order to give a true and fair view of the company's state of affairs. These include for example: contingent rentals; profit participation arrangements; significant restrictions on future borrowing or leasing; and contingent liabilities. The information will depend on whether the user's appreciation of the company's state of affairs would be affected if he was aware of that information. The criteria to be applied to that information are no different from those to be applied to any other information about the company's financial affairs.

19.53.1 An up-front payment made under an operating lease would usually be regarded as prepaid rental (that is, presented as a prepayment, which is a current asset) rather than the acquisition of a fixed asset. Leases of property sometimes involve different considerations. Paragraph 144 of the guidance notes to the standard state that '*nothing in the standard precludes the recognition as a fixed asset of an amount paid in the form of a premium as consideration for a leasehold interest*'. The payment of a premium to purchase a leasehold interest in a property is traditionally reported as a fixed asset under UK GAAP rather than as prepaid rental, regardless of whether the lease would be classified as a finance lease or an operating lease. To be treated as a fixed asset, the lease term would normally be substantial, the premium paid would be material and would provide the lessee with continuing benefits during the lease term. For example, it is clear that a premium paid on a long lease that gives the lessee the benefit of a peppercorn rental for the lease term is appropriately shown as a fixed asset. On the other hand, if a lease provides for regular rent reviews, and the rent payable is brought up to fair market rates, any premium paid at inception has the characteristics of a prepayment. In such circumstances, the premium would normally be written off over the period until the rent is first expected to be adjusted to market levels.

Sale and leaseback transactions

19.54 A sale and leaseback transaction arises when a vendor sells an asset and immediately re-acquires the use of the asset by entering into a lease with the buyer. Such transactions are a popular method of releasing cash funds for new investment as an alternative to borrowing. Under SSAP 21, the accounting treatment depends on the type of lease entered into. It also depends on whether the sale and the subsequent leaseback are on a strictly arm's length basis.

Finance leasebacks

19.55 Where the seller enters into a finance leaseback, the transaction is essentially a financing operation. In essence, the seller/lessee never disposes of the risks and rewards of ownership of the asset and so he should not recognise a profit or loss on the sale. There are two ways of looking at this situation in accounting terms. SSAP 21's approach was that any apparent profit or loss on the transaction (that is, the difference between the sale price and the previous carrying value) should be deferred and amortised over the shorter of the lease term and the asset's useful life. [SSAP 21 para 46]. This treatment will have the effect of adjusting the overall charge to the profit and loss account for the depreciation of the asset to an amount consistent with the asset's carrying value before the leaseback.

19.56 Normally, a fixed asset's carrying value before a sale and finance leaseback will not be more than the leased asset's fair value. Indeed, if it were, it would need to be tested for impairment under FRS 11. Any such adjustments to the asset's carrying value should be made before determining the apparent profit or loss on the sale and leaseback transaction. The apparent profit or loss that is deferred and amortised over the lease term will then represent the difference between the sale price and the revised carrying value (the fair value). In these circumstances, such a difference would arise only if the sale proceeds and the subsequent rentals were determined other than on an arm's length basis.

[The next paragraph is 19.58.]

19.58 There is, however, a second, and now preferable, way of accounting for a sale and finance leaseback. This method views the transaction as being simply the raising of finance. Hence there is no change to the carrying value of the asset: it is regarded as being retained rather than disposed of and re-acquired. Hence, a sale and finance leaseback is treated not as a sale and repurchase, but simply as a source of finance, like raising a secured loan on an existing asset. Proceeds are then simply credited to a liability account (representing the present value of the obligation under the finance lease), and there is no need to show a disposal and a re-acquisition of an asset. It can be argued that this treatment better reflects the commercial substance of this transaction because it is only the legal form of the transaction that represents a disposal and re-acquisition of the underlying asset. This treatment is, therefore, consistent with the principles underlying FRS 5 (which are considered further in chapter 3).

19.59 A question arises as to whether the revaluation surplus on the asset becomes realised or not on a sale and finance leaseback. The accounting principles upon which SSAP 21 and FRS 5 are based argue that the seller/lessee does not dispose of the risks and rewards of ownership under a sale and finance leaseback arrangement. Section 853(4) of the Companies Act 2006 states that whether profits are realised or not depends on *"...principles generally accepted, at the time when the accounts are prepared, with respect to the determination for accounting purposes of realised profits or losses"*. Because in accounting terms there is no genuine disposal of the asset by the seller/lessee, it is considered that the revaluation surplus does not become realised immediately.

Operating leasebacks

19.60 Where the seller enters into a sale and operating leaseback, he effectively disposes of substantially all the risks and rewards of owning the asset in the sale transaction; and may re-acquire some of the risks and rewards of ownership in the leaseback, but does not re-acquire substantially all of them. Accordingly, the transaction should be treated as a disposal and any profit or loss on the transaction should be recognised. It is interesting to note that in this respect the specific requirements of SSAP 21 are different to the general principles of FRS 5. This is because SSAP 21 recognises assets and liabilities on an all or nothing basis. FRS 5, however, will only recognise a disposal of an asset in its entirety when all significant rights or other access to benefits and all exposures to risks have been transferred. However, in a sale and leaseback transaction rights and obligations are retained by the seller-lessee. In this case, however, as SSAP 21 contains the more specific requirements the SSAP 21 treatment would prevail. Under SSAP 21, the calculation of the profit or loss will depend on whether the sale proceeds and the rentals under the subsequent lease were determined on an arm's length basis.

19.61 Where the sale transaction is established at the fair value, any profit or loss on the sale should be recognised immediately. Consequently, no further adjustment is necessary. [SSAP 21 para 47].

19.62 Where the sale price is above the fair value, the excess of the sale price over the fair value does not represent a genuine profit. This is because the rentals payable in future years will almost certainly be inflated above the market value. Accordingly, the excess of the sale proceeds over the fair value should be deferred and amortised over the shorter of the remainder of the lease term and the period to the next rent review. [SSAP 21 para 47]. This treatment will have the effect of reducing the annual expense for rentals to a basis consistent with the fair value of the asset.

19.63 Where the sale price is below the fair value, the standard requires that any profit or loss should be recognised immediately. This requirement recognises the fact that the company, perhaps motivated by the need to raise cash quickly, may simply have negotiated a poor bargain. An exception is made, however, where a loss is compensated by future rentals that are below market levels. In such a circumstance, the standard requires the loss (to the extent that it is compensated by future rentals below market levels) be deferred and amortised over the remainder of the lease term (or, if it is shorter, the period during which the reduced rentals are chargeable). [SSAP 21 para 47]. This practice may seem to go against the prudence principle. In effect, however, it merely reverses the effect of an artificial loss created by establishing, in an artificial way, the sale price and the subsequent rental. Rather strangely perhaps, the standard does not require a similar adjustment where the profit that is made is lower than would be expected if the sale proceeds and the subsequent rentals were established on an arm's length basis.

Sale and leasebacks with repurchase options

19.64 The use of put and call options in sale and leaseback transactions involving properties is a popular method to enable a company to raise medium-term finance to the value of the property that it owns. Under such arrangements, the seller/lessee may have an option to repurchase the property (call option), or the buyer/lessor may have an option to require the seller/lessee to repurchase the property (put option), or there may be a combination of options.

19.65 The substance of the transaction needs to be considered very closely in order to classify the lease correctly as finance or operating lease. In essence, the objective is to determine whether the commercial effect of the transaction is that of a genuine sale or that of a secured loan.

19.66 If the repurchase price contained in an option to repurchase is the market value of the asset at the date of exercise, it is probable that the buyer/lessor acquires both the opportunity to benefit from any increase in the value of the asset and the risk of loss if there is a fall in its value. In this situation the option is a 'genuine' option and will not influence the way the lease is classified.

19.67 If, however, the repurchase price is predetermined so that, when exercised it assures the buyer/lessor of a return of his original purchase price together with his required rate of return, this may well be indicative of a finance lease. A key issue will be whether there is a genuine commercial possibility that the option will fail to be exercised and, in that event, what further conditions protect the buyer/lessor's return. For example, if the conditions of the leaseback were such that the rental rate increased to a rate substantially in excess of a commercial rate should the lessee fail to exercise his repurchase option, this could well have the effect of a penalty which would force the exercise of the option. Consequently, it is important to understand properly the commercial objectives for the inclusion of a repurchase option in the leaseback and the commercial effect it will have in practice.

Accounting by lessors

Finance & Leasing Association SORP

19.67.1 The guidance in SSAP 21 on matters such as income recognition and accounting for residual values is limited and does not relate specifically to the types of complex arrangements that may be entered into by, for example, specialist computer lessors.

19.67.2 In April 1994 the ASB approved the Finance & Leasing Association (FLA) for the development of a SORP on lessor accounting. The SORP, 'Accounting issues in the asset finance and leasing industry', was published in April 2000. The SORP supplements, but does not override, the basic accounting requirements of SSAP 21 and FRS 5 as they apply to lessors. It has been developed in order to improve comparability in the accounting practices of lessors and to provide more specific guidance on how SSAP 21 should be interpreted in certain problem areas.

19.67.3 The SORP endorses the requirements of SSAP 21 and FRS 5 that lease transactions should be accounted for and presented in accordance with their substance and not merely their legal form. In determining this substance, the SORP sets out a number of questions which, whilst not intended to be a comprehensive list, the lessor should consider. The SORP also emphasises prudent income recognition practices for lessors and recommends certain additional disclosures that are not required by SSAP 21 in order to make residual value risks more transparent.

19.67.4 The SORP applies to the financial statements of lessors that are members of the FLA and also encourages lessors that are not members of the FLA to follow its recommendations.

[The next paragraph is 19.68.]

Accounting for finance leases

19.68 The amount due from the lessee under a finance lease should be recorded in the lessor's balance sheet as a debtor at the amount of the net investment in the lease, after making provisions for items such as bad and doubtful rentals receivable. [SSAP 21 para 38].

19.69 At the inception of a finance lease, the lessor's net investment in the lease is the cost of the asset to the lessor. Over the lease term, rentals will be apportioned between a reduction in the net investment in the lease and gross earnings.

19.70 At any point in time during the lease term, the net investment in the lease will be represented by the remaining minimum lease payments (the amounts the lessor is guaranteed to receive under the lease from either the lessee or third parties), less that part of the minimum lease payments that is attributable to future gross earnings (namely, interest and the lessor's profit). The lessor's net investment in the lease may also include an unguaranteed residual value. The unguaranteed residual value, which will be small in a finance lease, represents the amount the lessor expects to recover from the value of the leased asset at the end of the lease term that is not guaranteed in any way by either the lessee or third parties.

19.71 SSAP 21 requires that the total gross earnings under a finance lease be allocated to each accounting period during the lease term in such a manner as to produce a constant rate of return (or a reasonable approximation to it) on each period's net *cash* investment. [SSAP 21 para 39]. The net cash investment in a lease represents the total cash invested after taking into account all of the cash flows associated with the lease. It differs, therefore, from the amount of the net investment in the lease that is shown in the balance sheet. This is because it takes account of other cash flows. The most important of these other cash flows relates to the tax effects of the lease.

19.72 One of the reasons why SSAP 21 requires that gross earnings should be allocated to accounting periods on the basis of the net cash investment is that the gross earnings will then be properly matched with the interest costs of funding the net cash investment in the lease. Consequently, SSAP 21 permits alternative methods of allocating gross earnings which allocate gross earnings so that net earnings (gross earnings less estimated interest costs) are recognised on a systematic basis. This means that an allocation of gross earnings is first made to each accounting period to cover the estimated costs of finance. The remaining balance of gross earnings is then allocated to accounting periods on a systematic basis. The FLA SORP, however, seeks to prohibit the general use of methods that allocate gross earnings after interest costs except where the normal treatment of allocating gross earnings before interest is imprudent given the risk profile of the lease. [FLA SORP para 5.3.4].

19.73 The SORP refers to SSAP 21's method of accounting as 'lease accounting incorporating tax cash flows'. It should be used where the tax consequences of the lease form a material and integral part of the overall return from the lease. This is the case where the lessor has the benefit of accelerated capital allowances that result in significant deferrals of tax payments. Where the tax consequences are not material, the SORP notes that a method that ignores the effect of tax may be used, because it will give a reasonable approximation to a constant return on the lessor's net cash investment in the lease. [FLA SORP 5.3.18]. Thus a finance company will normally allocate gross earnings from a hire purchase contract to give a constant periodic rate of return on its net investment (ignoring any tax effects). This is because the tax effects of a hire purchase contract are rarely significant as the lessee takes all of the benefit and so the company's net investment in a hire purchase contract will approximate to its net cash investment in that contract.

19.74 The most popular methods for allocating gross earnings to accounting periods that are used in practice in the leasing industry are the 'actuarial after-tax method' and the 'investment period method'. Below, we briefly describe the actuarial after-tax method and illustrate its application. The FLA SORP prefers this method, but allows the 'investment period method' or the 'sum of digits method' provided that the chosen method gives a reasonable approximation to the 'actuarial after-tax method' and does not result in gross earnings being recognised significantly earlier.

The actuarial after-tax method

19.75 The basis of the actuarial after-tax method is that rentals are allocated between interest (gross earnings) and capital (amortisation) in each accounting period in such a way that the anticipated after-tax profit (gross earnings less interest expense and tax) will emerge as a constant periodic rate of return on the lessor's average net cash investment in the lease. The accounting entries for 'amortisation' and 'gross earnings' for each period during the lease is, therefore, based on the forecast cash flows made at the start of the lease.

Example – Actuarial after-tax method

Lease term	Seven years from 31 March 20X4
Rental payments	£1,787.00 payable annually in advance
Asset cost	£10,000.00
Lessor's year end date	31 March
Lessor's tax payment date	Nine months after the year end (1 January)
Cost of money	8.5% per annum
Reinvestment rate	3.0% per annum
Interest assumptions	calculated daily in arrear (annual compounding)
Tax rate	33%
Capital allowances	25% writing down allowance
Balancing allowance (assumed)	31 March 20Y1

The first step, is to calculate the after-tax profit-take-out rate using the forecast lease cash flows. This is the rate at which the lessor could theoretically withdraw profit from the lease measured as a constant rate on the average daily net cash investment balance for each period. It is calculated by a computer program using an iterative process that involves a succession of trial-and-error estimates of the rate until the net cash investment balance becomes zero at the end of the cash flows. In this example the profit-take-out rate is calculated at 0.8458% per annum.

Date	Net cash investment start of period £	Rental £	Tax £	Interest paid/ (received) £	Profit taken out £	Net cash investment end of period £
31 March 20X4	10,000.00	(1,787.00)	–	–	–	8,213.00
1 January 20X5	8,213.00	–	(823.38)	–	–	7,389.62
31 March 20X5	7,389.62	(1,787.00)	–	681.04	67.76	6,351.42
1 January 20X6	6,351.42	–	(253.79)	–	–	6,097.63
31 March 20X6	6,097.63	(1,787.00)	–	536.03	53.34	4,900.00
1 January 20X7	4,900.00	–	(51.24)	–	–	4,848.76
31 March 20X7	4,848.76	(1,787.00)	–	415.44	41.34	3,518.54
1 January 20X8	3,518.54	–	104.57	–	–	3,623.10
31 March 20X8	3,623.11	(1,787.00)	–	301.24	29.97	2,167.32
1 January 20X9	2,167.32	–	229.26	–	–	2,396.58
31 March 20X9	2,396.58	(1,787.00)	–	188.97	18.80	817.35
1 January 20Y0	817.35	–	331.57	–	–	1,148.92
31 March 20Y0	1,148.92	(1,787.00)	–	76.62	7.62	(553.84)
1 January 20Y1	(553.84)	–	417.60	–	–	(136.24)
31 March 20Y1	(136.24)	–	–	(13.56)	–	(149.80)
1 January 20Y2	(149.80)	–	152.07	–	–	2.27
1 January 20Y2	2.27	–	1.12	(3.39)	–	–
		(12,509.00)	107.78	2,182.39	218.83	

The lessor's initial net cash investment in the lease is the cost of the leased asset (£10,000).

Interest paid is calculated at 8.5% per annum on the daily net cash investment balances. Similarly profit-taken-out is calculated at the profit-take-out rate of 0.8458% on the daily net cash investment balances. Thus interest of £681.04 and profit-take-out of £67.76 for the period to 31 March 20X5 is based on net cash investment balances of £8,213.00 for 276 days and £7,389.62 for 89 days.

Interest received is calculated at a conservative rate of 3.0% per annum on the daily cash surplus balances. No profit-take-out arises when the net cash investment is in surplus (after 31 March 20Y0).

Tax is payable/receivable on 1 January each year, based on rentals, interest paid, interest received, and capital allowances in the previous accounting year, as follows:

Year to 31 March	Accrued rental £	Capital allowances £	Interest £	Total £	Tax payable (receivable) £
20X4	4.90	(2,500.00)	–	(2,495.10)	(823.38)
20X5	1,786.99	(1,875.00)	(681.04)	(769.05)	(253.79)
20X6	1,787.01	(1,406.25)	(536.03)	(155.27)	(51.24)
20X7	1,787.00	(1,054.69)	(415.44)	316.87	104.57
20X8	1,787.00	(791.02)	(301.24)	694.74	229.26
20X9	1,786.99	(593.26)	(188.97)	1,004.76	331.57
20Y0	1,787.01	(444.95)	(76.62)	1,265.44	417.60
20Y1	1,782.10	(1,334.83)	13.56	460.83	152.07
20Y2	–		3.39	3.39	1.12
	12,509.00	(10,000.00)	(2,182.39)	326.61	107.78

In order to simplify the calculations of the tax cash flows, it has been assumed that the amount of expenditure unrelieved after five years' writing-down allowances is relieved in the computation for the year ending 31 March 20Y1. Where the lessor does not anticipate recovering the remaining unrelieved expenditure by the end of the lease term it may be appropriate for him to delay recognising some of his gross earnings.

A further simplification is that the cash flows are deemed to terminate at the last tax payment date relating to the above. Thus interest for the period 1 April 20Y1 to 1 January 20Y2 and tax thereon is deemed to be paid on 1 January 20Y2..

The apportionment of gross earnings to each period for accounting purposes is derived from the cash flows by working backwards from the anticipated after-tax profit as follows:

Year to 31 March	Anticipated after-tax profit £	Derived pre-tax profit £	Anticipated interest £	Derived apportionment of gross earnings £
20X4	–	–	–	–
20X5	67.76	101.14	681.04	782.18
20X6	53.34	79.60	536.03	615.63
20X7	41.34	61.70	415.44	477.14
20X8	29.97	44.73	301.24	345.97
20X9	18.80	28.06	188.97	217.03
20Y0	7.62	11.38	76.62	88.00
20Y1	–	–	(16.95)	(16.95)
	218.83	326.61	2,182.39	2,509.00

The anticipated after-tax profit is derived from the cash flows by time apportioning the profit-take-out. In this example, because the lease was written on 31 March and because it has been assumed interest is to be taken daily in arrear, the profit-take out on the cash flow matches the figures accrued for accounting purposes. An alternative basis would be to accrue one day's income and interest expense for the year to 31 March 20X4 and to adjust each year's figures by one day.

The pre-tax profit is derived by grossing-up the anticipated after-tax profit for each period by the appropriate tax rate. The tax rate is 33% and so the factor by which the after-tax profit is grossed up to arrive at the pre-tax profits is 1/(1 — 0.33).

The anticipated interest is derived from the cash flow summary in a similar way. In this example no interest accrual is necessary.

The derived apportionment of gross earnings is simply the sum of the derived pre-tax profit and anticipated interest.

For the purpose of calculating gross earnings for accounting purposes the small amount of interest receivable of £3.39 in the cash flows for the period to 31 March 20Y2 and tax thereon has been treated as arising in the year to 31 March 20Y1. This is a simplification for illustration purposes in order to limit the period over which gross earnings are spread. More sophisticated systems may well spread the gross earnings over a period extending beyond the lease term to take full account of the interest effects associated with tax cash flows arising beyond the end of the lease term.

The effect of allocating gross earnings in this way can be summarised as follows:

Profit & Loss Account								
	20X4	20X5	20X6	20X7	20X8	20X9	20Y0	20Y1
	£	£	£	£	£	£	£	£
Rent receivable	4.90	1,786.98	1,787.02	1,787,00	1,787.00	1,786.98	1,787.02	1,782.10
Amortisation	4.90	1,004.80	1,171.39	1,309.86	1,441.03	1,569.95	1,699.02	1,799.05
Gross earnings	–	782.18	615.63	477.14	345.97	217.03	88.00	(16.95)
Interest costs	–	681.04	536.03	415.44	301.24	188.97	76.62	(16.95)
Pre-tax profit	–	101.14	79.60	61.70	44.73	28.06	11.38	–
Tax:								
Current	(823.38)	(253.79)	(51.24)	104.57	229.26	331.57	417.60	153.19
Deferred	823.38	287.17	77.50	(84.21)	(214.50)	(322.31)	(413.84)	(153.19)
Post-tax profit	–	67.76	53.34	41.34	29.97	18.80	7.62	–
Balance sheet								
	20X4	20X5	20X6	20X7	20X8	20X9	20Y0	20Y1
	£	£	£	£	£	£	£	£
Assets								
Lease receivables	8,213.00	7,208.18	6,036.81	4,726.95	3,285.92	1,715.95	16.95	–
Group relief	823.38	253.79	51.24	–	–	–	–	–
Cash	–	–	–	–	–	–	553.84	153.19
	9,036.38	7,461.97	6,088.05	4,726.95	3,285.92	1,715.95	570.79	153.19
Liabilities								
Borrowings	8,213.00	6,351.42	4,900.00	3,518.54	2,167.32	817.35	–	–
Deferred tax	823.38	1,110.55	1,188.05	1,103.84	889.34	567.03	153.19	0.00
Current tax	–	–	–	104.57	229.26	331.57	417.60	153.19
	9,036.38	7,461.97	6,088.05	4,726.95	3,285.92	1,715.95	570.79	153.19

For the purpose of illustrating the profit and loss and balance sheet the actual interest charges have been assumed to match precisely those anticipated in the cash flows and the post-tax profit is assumed to be fully distributed. Consequently, in this example the net cash investment balances per the anticipated cash flows will match the borrowing/ cash position in the balance sheet. In practice, actual cash flows will almost certainly vary from those forecast, but this will not be sufficient reason by itself, to reassess the allocation of gross earnings.

Lease receivables at 31 March 20X5 of £7,208.18 represents future rentals of £8,935 less future gross earnings of £1,782.12. Alternatively, it can be proven as the cost of the leased asset of £10,000 less accumulated amortisation of £1,009.70 less prepaid rent of £1,782.12.

Accounting for operating leases

19.76 SSAP 21 requires that a lessor should record as fixed assets the assets held for leasing under operating leases. It also requires that the lessor should depreciate those assets over their useful economic lives. [SSAP 21 para 42]. This requirement was not followed by Brammer Plc in its financial statements for the year ended 31 December 1994. In these financial statements, the directors included rental assets, consisting of electronic instruments, in stock at the lower of amortised cost and net realisable value on the grounds that these assets were circulating capital. The FRRP rejected the directors' views and argued that SSAP 21 required such assets to be classified as fixed assets as they were held for use in operating leases. Accordingly, in the company's 1995 Annual Report the rental inventory was reclassified as fixed assets and the 1994 comparative figures were adjusted as indicated in Table 19.7 below.

19.77 Where assets held for use in operating leases are recorded as fixed assets, the lessor should recognise his rental income from operating leases (excluding charges for services such as insurance and maintenance) on a straight-line basis over the period of the lease, irrespective of when the payments are due. This requirement does not apply, however, if another systematic and rational basis is more representative of the time pattern in which the lessor receives the benefit from the leased asset (for example, the time pattern of the related depreciation charge). [SSAP 21 para 43]. UITF Abstract 28 requires a similar treatment for incentives, see paragraph 19.77.7 below.

Table 19.7 – Brammer plc – Annual Report – 31 December 1995

Accounting policies (extract)

Change of accounting policy – rental inventory

As explained in the financial review on page 14, the company has agreed with the Financial Reporting Review Panel that rental inventory, previously classified as current assets, should be reclassified as fixed assets. As a result of effecting this change:

- proceeds from the disposal of previously rented instruments are excluded from turnover and included in the profit on sale of fixed assets in the profit and loss account.
- rental inventory is classified as fixed assets and is valued at cost less depreciation on a straight line basis over the expected economic lives of the assets (generally 2 to 6 years) taking account of estimated residual values, less any necessary provision for permanent diminution in value.
- the depreciation charge for the year on rental inventory is added back to operating profit in arriving at net cash inflow from operating activities in the cash flow statement.

The accounts carrying value of rental inventory is unchanged and, accordingly, the change of classification does not affect the profit for the year in any year or the shareholders' equity at the end of the year. The figures in the 1994 consolidated profit and loss account, balance sheet and cash flow statement have been reclassified as a result of this change.

19.77.1 The FLA SORP gives additional guidance on the choice of depreciation methods. The principle is that the chosen method should best reflect the consumption of the benefits of the leased asset. The principal methods are:

- Straight-line method.
- After-tax methods.
- Annuity method.

19.77.2 The straight-line method is the benchmark method that is appropriate for all operating lease assets, particularly where the pattern of economic benefits is uncertain. This applies where assets are leased for periods that are considerably shorter than their useful economic lives, including all short-term hire agreements. This is consistent with the requirements of FRS 15 relating to depreciation of tangible fixed assets generally. [FLA SORP paras 5.3.27 to 5.3.30].

19.77.3 The SORP recognises, however, that lessors' interests in some operating lease assets have characteristics of financial assets rather than physical fixed assets and so it allows other depreciation methods that do not reflect the consumption of the physical asset but instead reflect the time value of money. These methods have the effect of 'back-loading' depreciation charges such that charges are lower in accounting periods near the beginning of the lease and increase in later accounting periods covered by the lease. These methods are in general only appropriate where the lease is similar to a finance lease.

19.77.4 After-tax methods are generally only suitable for finance leases. The SORP makes an exception, however, where a lessor has a portfolio of leases that comprise finance leases and similar leases that are classified as operating leases.

An after-tax method, such as the actuarial after-tax method described earlier, may be used to determine the pattern of profit that is recognised over the term of the relevant operating leases if that reflects more faithfully the substance of the lessor's investments and the similarity between the finance and operating leases in the lessor's portfolio. The annual depreciation charge is calculated so that the profit from the lease produces a constant periodic rate of return on the lessor's net cash investment.

19.77.5 The annuity method calculates the annual depreciation charge by taking into account the cost of financing the asset, such that the aggregate amount of depreciation and interest in each period is constant. Since rental income from operating leases is normally credited on a straight-line basis over the lease term, the effect of using annuity depreciation is that the amount of profit after interest recognised in each period is constant.

19.77.6 The SORP restricts the use of after-tax methods and the annuity method to the following circumstances where the lessor's asset is in substance a quasi-financial asset:

- the asset is let on a lease that is for a significant portion of the total economic life of the asset;
- the terms of the lease adequately protect the lessor against early cancellation; and
- adequate income is retained in the lease to cover future uncertainties in respect of the realisation of residual values.

[FLA SORP para 5.3.34].

Operating lease incentives

19.77.7 When negotiating a new or renewed operating lease, a lessor may provide incentives for the lessee to enter into the agreement. Such incentives may take various forms as discussed in paragraph 19.46. UITF Abstract 28 provides guidance for the treatment of such incentives.

19.77.8 The treatment of operating lease incentives by lessors in UITF Abstract 28 mirrors the accounting treatment by lessees. All incentives, regardless of their nature, form or timing, be it a payment, assumption of liabilities or a rent-free or reduced rent period, given by lessors for the benefit of lessees to sign a new or renewed operating lease should be recognised as an integral part of the net payment agreed for the use of the leased asset. [UITF 28 para 13]. Therefore, the aggregate cost of incentives should be treated as a reduction of rental income and allocated to the profit and loss account over the lease term or a shorter period ending on a date from which it is expected the prevailing market rental will be payable. The allocation should be on a straight-line basis, unless another more systematic basis is more representative of the time pattern in which the benefit from the leased asset is receivable. [UITF 28 para 15]. In practice the use of an allocation basis other than straight-line should be rare.

Example 1 — Spreading lease incentive

Under a ten year lease agreement, the lessor may give a one year rent free period followed by a fixed rent of £1.11m per annum for nine years. This is equivalent to ten years rent of £1m per annum. The benefit of the incentive should be spread over the period of the lease as there are no rent reviews. Therefore, each year £1m of rental income will be recognised in the profit and loss account. At the end of the first year, the lessor will recognise accrued rent receivable of £1m, which will be reduced by £0.11m each year for the next nine years.

Example 2 — How to treat an upfront payment from the lessor

Alternatively, the lessor may have agreed with the lessee to make an up front cash payment of £1m to contribute towards the lessee's own fit out costs, with a fixed annual rental of £1.1m per annum for the ten year lease. This is also equivalent to an annual rent of £1m per annum without the incentive. Therefore, £1m will be recognised as net rental income each year of the lease. The £1m incentive will initially be recognised as a debtor (accrued rent receivable), which will be amortised by £0.1m each year to the profit and loss account.

19.77.9 As with any asset, the amount recognised as a debtor in respect of an operating lease incentive should be written down to the extent that it is not recoverable. [UITF 28 para 17]. Furthermore, the debtor is likely to be long-term in nature, in which case UITF Abstract 4, 'Presentation of long-term debtors in current assets', may be relevant.

19.77.10 Investment properties are often leased to tenants under operating leases and incentives are common practice. The abstract states that to avoid double-counting on the revaluation of investment properties, the value recognised in the lessor's balance sheet should not include any amount that is reported as a separate asset, such as accrued rent receivable. [UITF 28 para 16]. This is discussed further in chapter 17.

[The next paragraph is 19.78]

Lessor disclosure requirements

19.78 In respect of finance leases (including hire purchase contracts that have similar characteristics) the following needs to be disclosed:

- The net investment in finance leases and hire purchase contracts at the balance sheet date. [SSAP 21 para 58].
- The costs of assets acquired in the period (whether by purchase, finance lease or hire purchase) for the purpose of letting under finance leases or hire purchase contracts. [SSAP 21 para 60(c)].

Table 19.7A contains an example of these disclosure requirements.

Table 19.7A – Inchcape plc – Annual report & accounts – 31 December 2000

notes to the accounts (extract)

9b Debtors (extract)

	Group	
	2000	**1999**
	£m	**£m**
Net investment in finance leases and hire purchase contracts comprises:		
Total amounts receivable	**90.6**	100.9
Less: Interest allocated to future periods	**(19.8)**	(23.0)
	70.8	77.9

Rentals receivable during the year under finance leases and hire purchase contracts amounted to £33.4m (1999 — £32.6m)

The cost of assets acquired during the year for onwards finance leasing was £18.1m (1999 — £22.1m).

[The next paragraph is 19.80.]

19.80 In respect of both finance leases and operating leases (including hire purchase contracts that have similar characteristics), the following need to be disclosed also:

- The policy adopted for accounting for operating leases and finance leases and, in detail, the accounting policy adopted for recognising finance lease income. [SSAP 21 para 60(a)]. Table 19.9 contains an example of such a policy.
- The aggregate rentals receivable in the accounting period, analysed between amounts receivable under finance leases and amounts receivable under operating leases. [SSAP 21 para 60(b)]. For example, Gestetner Holdings PLC includes this information in the analyses of trading profit (see Table 19.10).

Table 19.9 – Automated Security (Holdings) PLC – Report and Financial Statements – 30 November 1994

ACCOUNTING POLICIES (extract)

2. FIXED ASSETS

The cost of equipment on contract hire installed by Group companies is capitalised. Costs comprise materials, labour and attributable overheads relating to identifiable and recoverable equipment. All other costs are written off as they are incurred.

On the acquisition of installed systems from third parties, a fair value is placed on installed equipment acquired.

6. EQUIPMENT LEASED TO CUSTOMERS

Equipment leased to customers under finance leases is deemed to be sold at normal selling value which is taken to turnover at the inception of the lease. Debtors under finance leases represent outstanding amounts due under these agreements less finance charges allocated to future periods. Finance lease interest is recognised over the primary period of the lease so as to produce a constant rate of return on the net cash investments. Equipment leased to customers under operating leases is capitalised in accordance with 2 above. Operating lease income is accounted for on a straight line basis with any rental increases recognised during the period to which they relate.

Table 19.10 – Gestetner Holdings PLC – Report and Accounts – 31 December 1994

Notes to the accounts (extract)

Note 2 Trading profit (extract)	**1994** **£m**	1993 £m
Rental receivable under		
operating leases	**(21.7)**	(24.9)
finance leases	**(10.2)**	(12.3)
Equipment acquired for sale under finance leases	**73.4**	70.0

[The next paragraph is 19.83.]

19.83 The Guidance Notes to SSAP 21 indicate that the lessor may also need to disclose further information about leases and hire purchase contracts that is of particular significance to the users of the financial statements. This includes, for example, details of arrangements that could affect future profitability, such as contingent rentals or new-for-old guarantees.

19.83.1 The FLA SORP includes a number of disclosure recommendations that add to the limited disclosures required by SSAP 21. They are intended to improve users' understanding of the lessor's business and associated risks.

- General description of the lessor's leasing activities and related risks.
- Income recognition policies should be specified in detail.

- Maturity analysis of residual value exposures – for each type of leased asset, a table should be given setting out the carrying value of the lessor's unguaranteed residual interests and the years in which the residual value will be recovered.
- Details of contingent liabilities arising from lease transactions.
- Uncertainties relating to profits or losses arising from transactions that result in partial derecognition of leasing balances (for example, from the sale of a rental stream).
- Initial selling profits recognised by manufacturer or dealer lessors and the basis for determining them.
- State whether the SORP has been complied with and state the reasons for any non-compliance.

[FLA SORP para 5.9.1].

[The next paragraph is 19.84.]

Implications of the Act on the disclosure lessors make

19.84 Although some banks carry out leasing activities themselves, many banks prefer, for tax reasons, to carry out their leasing through separate subsidiaries. Consequently, many lessors, whether they are related to a bank or not, will not be a banking company within the meaning of the Banking Act 1987 and so they will have to comply with the requirements of Schedule 1 to SI 2008/410 for the purpose of their own statutory financial statements. However, at the same time those leasing companies with banking parents will need to provide information to their parent companies for consolidation purposes to comply with Schedule 2 to SI 2008/410.

19.85 The balance sheet formats set out in Schedule 1 to SI 2008/410 do not show any specific category for leased assets. Paragraph 3(2) of Schedule 1 to SI 2008/410, however, permits (with certain exceptions) a company's balance sheet or profit and loss account to include an item that is not otherwise covered in the formats. SSAP 21, however, requires that amounts due from lessees under finance leases be recorded as a debtor and assets held for use in operating leases as a fixed asset.

19.86 As a category of debtors, amounts due under finance leases will need to be analysed in the notes to the financial statements between amounts receivable within one year and those receivable after more than one year. However, where the amounts due over one year are particularly material in the context of net current assets such that a reader might misinterpret the financial statements, UITF abstract 4 requires the amounts over one year to be disclosed on the face of the balance sheet (see further chapter 4).

19.87 The turnover of a leasing company will consist of its 'gross earnings' from finance leases and rentals from operating leases.

19.88 Those leasing companies, or parents of leasing companies, that are banks will need to comply with the requirements relating to the form and content of financial statements of banking companies as set out in Parts 1 to 4 of Schedule 2 to SI 2008/410. Under these formats, finance leases would be shown either under 'Loans and advances to customers' or 'Loans and advances to banks' as appropriate and gross earnings from finance leases would be included under interest receivable. The treatment of operating leases and related income under the formats is less clear. A strict interpretation would be to classify: operating leases under 'Tangible fixed assets'; operating rentals under 'operating income'; and depreciation of operating leased assets under 'Depreciation and amortisation'.

19.89 However, where a bank has significant amounts of operating leases and a significant amount of the bank's interest costs relate to the financing of such activities it could be argued that this treatment gives a misleading picture of the true net interest income from banking activities. Some banks have, therefore, taken the view that operating lease rentals less related depreciation is in effect a form of 'interest receivable' and have treated it in this way. Thus, net interest income will reflect both net income from operating leasing and the related interest expense, while the bank's depreciation expense will reflect only those tangible fixed assets other than operating leases. While this form of presentation has considerable merit there is an element of doubt as to whether it strictly accords with the Act's requirements. The FLA SORP states that Schedule 9 to the Companies Act 1985 (note that the FLA SORP has not yet been updated to reflect the Companies Act 2006 reference which is Schedule 2 to SI 2008/410) requires depreciation to be shown under 'Depreciation and amortisation' and rental income under 'Other operating income' and that a different presentation may be used only where transactions relating to operating leases are immaterial. [FLA SORP para 5.10.2].

Direct costs

19.90 SSAP 21 states that initial direct costs may be apportioned over the period of the lease on a systematic and rational basis (or may alternatively be written off immediately). In allowing either of these treatments SSAP 21 draws no distinction between those initial direct costs from finance leases and those from operating leases.

19.91 SSAP 21 defines initial direct costs as:

> '*...those costs incurred by the lessor that are directly associated with negotiating and consummating leasing transactions, such as commissions, legal fees, costs of credit investigations and costs of preparing and processing documents for new leases acquired.*' [SSAP 21 para 30].

19.92 SSAP 21 gives no further guidance on the interpretation of the words 'directly associated' with these activities, although the Guidance Notes indicate that it is not intended to exclude salespersons' costs. The FLA SORP, however, takes a more restrictive view of the costs that may be deferred. The SORP defines initial direct costs as:

'…*costs incurred by the lessor that are:*

- *directly associated with negotiating and consummating a lease transaction;*
- *incremental to the lessor and would have been avoided had the transaction not taken place.*' [FLA SORP para 4.1].

19.93 ;Under the SORP's definition, only incremental costs may be deferred whereas internal costs that are not incremental (such as administration and selling expenses) should be written off as incurred. The SORP identifies the following types of initial direct costs:

- External costs such as commission, legal, arrangement and brokers' fees.
- Other commissions and bonuses paid to procure business that are based upon reaching sales volumes (such as dealer volume bonuses, salesman's incentive schemes).

[FLA SORP para 5.4.14]

19.94 The SORP recommends that initial direct costs should be deferred over the lease term (using the same pattern as used for income recognition) provided that the costs are recoverable (that is, the lease is expected to generate a normal commercial return commensurate with the risks involved after taking account of such costs). Otherwise the costs should be written off immediately. [FLA SORP paras 3.27, 5.4.15-16].

19.95 Generally, the most appropriate, systematic and rational basis for deferring initial direct costs will be the same pattern used for recognising income. For finance leases this can be achieved by either deducting initial direct costs from total gross earnings before the net amount is allocated to accounting periods, or recognising sufficient gross earnings in the first year to absorb the costs and allocating the balance of gross earnings over the lease term. For operating leases, a straight-line basis of deferral over the lease term will usually be the most appropriate method.

Rental variation

Tax variation clauses

19.96 Major changes in tax rates can create significant accounting issues for lessors. This is because many finance leases contain tax variation clauses that vary the rental the lessee pays in the event of a tax rate change in order to preserve the lessor's post-tax rate of return.

19.97 In simple terms, if tax rates are reduced lessors pay less future tax, but will instead receive reduced rentals under their existing leases. Under FRS 19, deferred tax is provided on timing differences that have originated, but not reversed by the balance sheet date. Thus, deferred tax is provided at the corporation tax rate at which it is expected to be paid based on tax rates and laws that have been enacted or substantively enacted at the balance sheet date. Consequently, the 'windfall' gain from a reduction in corporation tax rates will be reflected in the tax charge or credit in the profit and loss account in the year in which the tax changes are enacted. However, the related reductions in rentals will generally occur over the remaining periods of the leases and, therefore, reduce future pre-tax income. The reduction in future rental income means that the carrying value of the lease receivable has been impaired. This impairment should be recognised immediately as a charge to pre-tax income. Although the impairment loss may not be exactly offset by the tax credit arising from the reduction in corporation tax rate, the difference may not be significant in terms of preserving the lessor's post-tax rate of return. This treatment will ensure that the lessors do not report material future losses on their leases. The previous practice, widely used in the leasing industry, of 'grossing up' tax savings would not comply with the principles of FRS 16.

[The next paragraph is 19.101.]

Variations in interest rates

19.101 Normally, when a finance lessor apportions his gross earnings, he does this on the basis of the forecast he prepares, at the start of the lease, of his future cash flows under the lease. The amount of gross earnings he releases to the profit and loss account in subsequent periods will then follow the forecast, even though his actual cash flows may vary from those he initially anticipated.

19.102 Minor variations in interest costs from those expected in the original cash flows evaluation will almost certainly occur. The interest charged to the lessor's profit and loss account in the period will be the actual interest cost for the period, thus, any differences from that originally anticipated will be reflected in the profit and loss account in the period in which they occur.

19.103 To mitigate interest rate risk, the lease facility may provide for a specifically calculated periodic adjustment for the difference between the actual rate of interest incurred on the borrowings and the rate of interest initially used in the cash flow to determine the level of lease rentals. Such adjustments are made periodically in arrears by applying, for example, the difference in interest rates on the first day of each quarterly period to the amount of the lessor's cash investment in the lease.

Construction periods

19.104 Often, where a leased asset is constructed over a period of time, the terms of the lease provide for rentals to commence only when the lessee brings the asset into use. In effect, the lessor finances the asset during the period of construction and recovers his costs out of his rentals over the remaining lease term. In order to match his gross earnings from the lease with his interest costs, the lessor will need to spread his gross earnings over the whole lease term (including the construction period). Where he adopts this treatment, however, the lessor will need to consider carefully his potential risks of loss from cancellation or default.

Manufacturer/dealer lessors

19.105 SSAP 21 distinguishes manufacturer/dealer lessors from other lessors. Although the term is not defined in the standard, it is defined in the FLA SORP as:

'.....a lessor which either:

(a) manufactures particular equipment which it leases; or

(b) acquires the leased asset as part of its dealing activities where its leasing activities are ancillary to those of distribution and servicing.'

[FLA SORP para 4.1].

What makes the manufacturer/dealer lessor different from a normal lessor is the cost at which he acquires an asset for lease. Because he obtains the asset at his cost of manufacture or at a wholesale price his cost will be below a normal arm's length selling price. The accounting issue is whether he should recognise a normal sale profit and this will depend on the accounting classification of the lease.

19.106 Where the manufacturer/dealer enters into an operating lease, he should not recognise a selling profit when he leases the asset. [SSAP 21 para 45]. This is because the risks and rewards associated with the asset's ownership have not passed to the customer. Consequently, the manufacturer/dealer will account for the lease in the same way as any other operating lessor does. He will capitalise the asset at its cost and depreciate it over its remaining economic life. In addition, he will recognise rentals on a straight-line basis over the period of the lease.

19.107 Where a manufacturer/dealer enters into a finance lease with a customer, the manufacturer/dealer may be able to recognise a normal selling profit. This is because the risks and rewards associated with the ownership of the asset have passed to the customer. The gross earnings under the lease (namely, the difference between what the manufacturer/dealer expects to receive and retain and the normal selling price) would be allocated over the lease term in the normal way. For example, the accounting policy of Automated Security (Holdings) indicates that the company takes what it deems the 'normal selling value' to turnover at the inception of the lease (see Table 19.9).

19.108 In most circumstances, where the sales price is known, determining the split between selling profit (recognised immediately) and gross earnings from finance leasing (spread over the lease term) is relatively easy. The FLA SORP specifies that the selling profit should be quantified with reference to the fair market value of the asset, that is the normal sales price at which identical goods are sold for cash. The normal selling price of broadly similar products sold by competitors may be used if the lessor does not normally sell such goods for cash. [FLA SORP para 5.6.3]. Where, however, a manufacturer/dealer does not sell the asset separately he may have difficulty in determining a true arm's length sales price. In these circumstances, some lessors have sought to determine the sales profit by assuming a deemed selling price (of fair value) being the present value of the minimum lease rentals discounted at a commercial rate.

19.109 The practice of calculating the sales profit in this way does not contradict the spirit of the SSAP 21, but can be lead to abuse and excessive front-end profits unless the present values are calculated prudently. For example, understating the true commercial lease rate or including overly optimistic residual values in the present value calculation will overstate sales profit. For this reason, this method needs to be applied with care. The FLA SORP provides some additional guidance. It states that a fair value should be determined by discounting the minimum lease payments and any unguaranteed residual value '*at a rate sufficient to take account of the lessor's borrowing rate, overhead rate and commercial profit return requirements, provided that the payments/residual value are reasonably predictable and certain in amount*'. [FLA SORP para 5.6.5]. Unguaranteed residual values should be excluded if they are uncertain.

19.110 Even when the normal sales price is known, it does not necessarily follow that the full normal sales profit should be recognised at the lease's inception. In order to promote sales, a manufacturer/dealer lessor may offer finance leasing arrangements at concessionary rates. When it does this it should restrict its initial selling profit to an amount that will allow it to recognise its gross earnings at the normal commercial rate over the lease term.

Back-to-back and sub-leases

19.111 The term 'back-to-back' can be used to describe a variety of different agreements, each of which has different legal and tax implications. It is, therefore, difficult to prescribe specific accounting treatments for each variation. The Guidance Notes to SSAP 21, however, set out the broad principles that a lessor should follow when accounting for back-to-back leases and sub-leases. In addition, FRS 5 provides the more detailed rules on the treatment of non-recourse finance that can be applied to these types of arrangement (see further chapter 3).

19.112 For convenience, the Guidance Notes terms are used below. These refer to the three parties to a lease agreement as: the head lessor; the intermediate party (who may be either a lessor under a sub-lease to the lessee or merely an agent for the head lessor); and the lessee.

The head lessor

19.113 The head lessor's accounting is straightforward. Unless the original lease agreement between the head lessor and the intermediate party is replaced by a new agreement, the head lessor's accounting should not be affected if the intermediate party enters into a sub-lease.

The intermediate party

19.114 The intermediate party's accounting, however, is more complex. The form it takes will depend on the nature of the intermediate party's contract with the head lessor and the substance of the transaction.

19.115 If the intermediate party's role is genuinely in substance that of a broker or agent for the head lessor, such that the intermediate party has no significant commercial benefits or risks associated with the sub-leases, it should not include either the asset or the obligation on its balance sheet. Such a view would be consistent with the principles for recognising and ceasing to recognise assets set out in FRS 5 and the guidance given in the Guidance Notes to SSAP 21. [FRS 5 paras 20, 22; SSAP 21 para 165].

19.116 Where, however, the intermediate party enters into a lease with the head lessor, and that lease requires him to make payments to the head lessor regardless of whether he receives payments from the lessee under a sub-lease (a full 'recourse' arrangement) or he bears other significant risks such as 'slow payment' risk, he should account for the arrangement as two separate transactions. Such a view is supported by paragraph 21 of FRS 5 and paragraph 166 of the Guidance Notes to SSAP 21. This is because the intermediate party's liability under the head lease remains in effect and needs to be reflected in his accounting treatment. Where the intermediate party's lease with the head lessor is a finance lease, the intermediate party will need to record the obligation as a liability on his balance sheet. He will also need to record an asset on his balance sheet for the sub-lease to the ultimate lessee. Where the sub-lease is a finance lease the intermediate party should record the asset as a receivable. Where the sub-lease is an operating lease he should record the asset as a fixed asset.

19.117 The above explains the accounting treatment where the intermediate party acts purely as an agent or where the head lessor has full recourse to the intermediate party. Between these extremes, there are arrangements that might qualify under paragraphs 23 to 25 of FRS 5 as 'special cases' for partial de-recognition or which might qualify under paragraphs 26 and 27 of FRS 5 for 'linked presentation'. These are particularly difficult to interpret. The guidance in FRS 5 is discussed in detail in chapter 3.

19.118 Where the effect of the arrangement is to transfer all the risks and benefits relating to a separately identifiable benefit stream (for example, the rentals) to the head lessor, but retain others (for example, marketing rights); or to transfer a proportion of the benefit stream (for example, the sub-lease rentals less a margin, but no more) to the head lessor, it may be appropriate for the intermediate party to simply recognise a new asset, which reflects his remaining and distinctly separate parcel of rights in the arrangement. Such an approach would only be appropriate where the transaction met the 'special case' conditions of paragraphs 23 to 25 of FRS 5 concerning 'partial de-recognition'.

19.119 The way in which the intermediate party recognises his income will also depend on the nature of the agreement. Where the intermediate party accounts for a separate liability and asset, the treatment he applies both to his gross earnings from his sub-lease and to the finance charges that are due on the head lease, will follow the normal requirements of SSAP 21. Where the intermediate party uses the linked presentation, the 'net' earnings will be included in the profit and loss account with separate disclosures of the gross earnings and finance charges in the notes to the financial statements. Where the intermediate party acts an 'agent', the Guidance Notes state that he should recognise his income on a systematic and rational basis. For example, he could recognise a pure commission immediately, but he should spread a guarantee fee over the period at risk.

Residuals

19.120 Residual values will need to be recognised by lessors when they are a fundamental component to the profitability of the lease transaction. However, it is important that they are recognised prudently. This need for prudence is reflected in the FLA SORP, which states: *'the estimates of residual values should be the amounts that can be safely expected to be realised under anticipated business conditions, net of disposal costs and should reflect any uncertainty.'* [FLA SORP para 5.4.2].

19.121 The amount that the lessor 'can safely expect' is difficult to assess. If the lessor is too optimistic in his residual estimates he carries a risk of incurring a loss. If he is excessively conservative in his estimates his rental rates may prove uncompetitive. How he estimates residuals will depend on specific factors:

- The nature of the asset under consideration.
- The known volatility of second-hand values.
- The rate of technological change.
- Competitive conditions.
- The asset's economic life relative to the lease's primary period.
- The degree to which the lessor can spread his risks.

19.122 The accounting treatment of a residual will largely depend on the nature of the lease. This is because SSAP 21 recognises two different types of leases, finance and operating leases, and prescribes a very different accounting treatment for each.

Residuals under operating leases

19.123 Under an operating lease, the lessor's revenue (rental income) is normally allocated over the lease term on a straight-line basis to reflect the time pattern of the performance of the service he is providing. In the lessor's balance sheet, assets leased to customers are shown as fixed assets, which are depreciated over the assets' economic life to their expected residual values. Different estimates of residual value obviously give rise to different levels of depreciation and, therefore, different levels of profit being recognised over the lease term.

19.124 Where the lessor values his future residuals conservatively, an eventual profit is likely to emerge at the end of the lease term on the sale of the asset, which would be represented by the sales proceeds less residual value and related selling costs.

19.125 While depreciation methods can vary, the method most widely used by operating lessors is the straight-line method. Thus, under operating leases, gross profit (rentals less depreciation) is normally recognised on a straight-line basis.

Residuals under finance leases

19.126 While finance leases are treated for accounting purposes by the lessor as though they are financial products akin to lending, there can, of course, still be a small element of residual risk. This risk is often disregarded as it will represent, at most, less than ten per cent of the lessor's investment at the inception of the lease. However, even variations in a component as small as ten per cent of the original investment can have a significant effect on a lessor's profitability because, although the residual is a small part of the total investment, it may amount to a substantial proportion of the expected gross earnings from the lease.

Fluctuations in anticipated residual values

19.127 Where the amount of residual values is significant the lessor will need to monitor the second-hand market closely and continuously. He will need to do this both to ensure that he has based his current rental pricing structure on up-to-date estimates and to ensure that he is accounting for the residual values correctly. Where the lessor identifies market conditions that indicate that there has been a permanent fall in residual values, he will need to account for the deterioration.

19.128 If the lease is an operating lease the lessor should calculate new depreciation rates for his leased assets in order to ensure the remaining book value of the leased asset is amortised to its anticipated residual value over its remaining useful life. In some circumstances, however, the book value of the leased asset may not be recoverable (that is, the present value of the future cash flows expected from the leased asset, including the revised estimate of residual value, may be lower than the book value) Where such a situation arises, the lessor should write down his leased assets to their recoverable amounts immediately, by charging an additional impairment loss in the current period's profit and loss account in accordance with the principles of FRS 11.

19.129 Similarly, if the lease is a finance lease, the lessor may need to write down the future residual value and recalculate the remaining future earnings to be recognised over the lease term. Where the carrying value of the finance lease receivable asset becomes impaired, the loss should be recognised immediately in the profit and loss account.

19.130 Many lessors also adhere to the principle that residual values should not be revised upwards. While this is not a strict requirement of SSAP 21 or FRS 15, it is good practice. The FLA SORP in effect codifies this principle, because it requires that any profit arising through selling the asset, in excess of the residual value that was set at the inception of the lease, should not be recognised until the asset has been sold.

19.131 There are no specific disclosure requirements in SSAP 21 for lessors to provide additional information concerning the quantification of residual value exposures within the financial statements of leasing companies. However, the FLA SORP seeks to make residual value risks more transparent by requiring leasing companies to give additional information in their financial statements so that the users of such financial statements can properly assess the impact of residual exposures on the lessor's financial position. For each type of asset, lessors should provide a maturity analysis of unguaranteed residual values included in the carrying values of finance leases and operating leases. This analysis should indicate the years in which the residual value will be recovered (analysed as between amounts to be recovered within 1 year, between 1-2 years, between 2-5 years, and more than 5 years). The SORP also requires lessors to disclose their policy for monitoring residual value exposure and recognising related impairments. [FLA SORP para 5.9].

Tax-free grants

19.132 Grants are normally paid to the owner of the asset upon which the grant is claimed. When a lessor receives such a grant on an asset that is subject to a finance lease, it is usual for the lessor to pass the benefit of the grant to the lessee either in the form of a lump sum payment (a negative rental) or in lower rentals over the lease term. The benefit of the grant comprises not just the cash amount of the grant, but also the fact that it is non-taxable. The tax benefit arises because, although the grant reduces the net cost of the asset to the lessor, he can still claim capital allowances on the full gross cost of the asset. If the lessor passes the tax benefit of the grant back to the lessee in one of the two ways mentioned above, it could have the effect of reducing the total rentals payable by the lessee below the net cost of the leased asset. Thus the lessor shows an accounting loss in pre-tax terms, but a profit after tax.

19.133 Paragraph 41 of SSAP 21 requires that tax-free grants that are available to the lessor against the purchase-price of assets acquired for leasing should be spread over the period of the lease and dealt with by treating the grant as non-taxable income. [SSAP 21 para 14]. The practice of avoiding showing a pre-tax loss and an after-tax profit by recording the grant as a grossed-up amount as if the grant was a larger taxable amount that suffered a tax charge, and increasing the tax charge accordingly, is not permitted.

Chapter 20

Stocks and long-term contracts

Chapter 20

Stocks and long-term contracts

Introduction

20.1 This chapter deals with the accounting treatment and disclosure of stocks and long-term contracts. In particular, it deals with the carrying value of stocks and complex transactions involving stock, such as consignment stock and sale and repurchase of stocks. It also deals with the treatment of long-term contracts, including the carrying value of the contract and profit recognition and incorporates FRS 5, Application note G, 'Revenue recognition', but only insofar as the application note deals with revenue relating to long-term contracts. Other aspects of the application note are dealt with in chapter 9.

Stocks

20.2 Stocks include goods or other assets purchased for resale, consumable stores, raw materials and components purchased for incorporation into products for sale, products and services in intermediate stages of completion, long-term contract balances and finished goods. [SSAP 9 para 16].

20.3 The amount at which stocks are stated in the financial statements should be the total of the lower of cost and net realisable value of the separate items of stock or of groups of similar items. [SSAP 9 para 26]. These items should be considered individually, as to compare the total realisable value of stocks with the total cost would result in an unacceptable setting off of foreseeable losses against unrealised profits. [SI 2008/410 1 Sch 15].

[The next paragraph is 20.8.]

Definition of cost of stocks

20.8 Cost is defined as being that expenditure that has been incurred in the normal course of business in bringing the product or service to its present location and condition. This expenditure should include, in addition to cost of purchase, such costs of conversion as are appropriate to that location and condition. [SSAP 9 para 17]. Cost of purchase comprises purchase price including import duties, transport and handling costs and any other directly attributable costs, less trade discounts, rebates and subsidies. [SSAP 9 para 18].

Example 1 – Treatment of rebates

A car distributor values its items of inventory at the year end. Rebates are only received from the car manufacturers once a year and are only known after the year end, but relate to purchases in the current period.

Should the rebates be taken through the income statement as a deduction in the cost of sales without allocation to the items in inventory at the balance sheet date, or, should a proportion of the rebates be allocated to the inventory items at the year end?

Paragraph 18 of SSAP 9, 'Stocks and long-term contracts', states that the cost of purchase of stock comprises purchase price including import duties, transport and handling costs and any other directly attributable costs, less trade discounts, rebates and subsidies. A proportion of the rebates should be allocated to inventory items at the year end. For example, if purchases during the year are £100 and at the year end, inventory is £10, 10% of the rebate should be applied to the inventory items at the year end and 90% should be taken through the profit and loss account as a deduction in the cost of sales. The reasoning is that the rebates cannot be allocated to particular items in the year, therefore, they should be spread over all the items purchased during the year, sold or unsold.

Example 2 – Vehicle-related bonuses

A company is a motor dealer. It receives vehicle-related bonuses from manufacturers when it reaches certain sales targets. It credits the bonuses to income, but it is concerned about whether this is still allowed following the FRRP ruling on Northgate plc. In this case, the cars are initially held in inventory, rather than in fixed assets and the sales-related bonuses are received only after the cars have been sold (that is when they are no longer in inventory).

The bonus from the manufacturers is a contingent asset and should be recognised only when it becomes virtually certain. As it is a sales-related bonus in respect of inventory that has been sold and is not a rebate on the cost of a fixed asset, it is appropriate to take the credit to the profit and loss account. It should be shown as a reduction in cost of sales as it would not qualify as turnover.

Example 3 – Cost of building access road

A company has development land on which it intends to build houses for sale. It is to pay the local authority to build an access road from A to B, where A is on local authority land and B is on the edge of the land owned by the company. The company will not own the access road or have exclusive rights to use it. However, the company considers that there is an economic benefit from the cost of building the access road, because the homes that it builds on the development site will be more attractive to customers if there is a good road access. Can the cost of building the access road be capitalised? If so, is it an intangible asset, a separate asset, or is it added to the cost of the development?

Under SSAP 9, cost should include expenditure that has been incurred in the normal course of business in bringing the product or service to its present location and condition. [SSAP 9 para 17]. The cost of paying the local council to build an access road should be capitalised as part of the development (not as a separate asset), provided that it is clear that the company will gain economic benefits from the access road. This would be so, for example, if the company needs the access road built to obtain planning permission for the development, or if the company can sell the houses more easily or for a higher value.

If, however, the money paid to the local authority resulted in no future economic benefits to the company (for example, if the access road did not lead to the development site) and was more in the nature of a gift or goodwill gesture, then it should be written off to the profit and loss account.

20.9 Costs of conversion comprise:

- Costs that are specifically attributable to units of production, for example, direct labour, direct expenses and sub-contracted work.
- Production overheads, that is, those incurred in respect of materials, labour or services for production, based on the normal level of activity, taking one year with another.
- Other overheads, if any, attributable in the particular circumstances of the business to bringing the product or service to its present location and condition.

[SSAP 9 para 19].

20.10 The Companies Act 2006 also allows interest to be included in cost if it relates to capital borrowed to finance the production of the asset insofar as it arises in the period of production. [SI 2008/410 1 Sch 27(3)(b)]. This is discussed in more detail in chapter 16.

20.11 Paragraph 8 of Appendix 1 to SSAP 9 contains some guidance on the inclusion of overheads in cost of conversion noting that the allocation of overheads included in the valuation of stocks and long-term contracts needs to be based on the company's normal level of activity, taking one year with another. The governing factor is that the cost of unused capacity should be written off in the current year. In determining what constitutes 'normal' the following factors need to be considered:

- The volume of production that the production facilities are intended by their designers and by management to produce under the working conditions (for example, single or double shift) prevailing during the year.
- The budgeted level of activity for the year under review and for the ensuing year.
- The level of activity achieved both in the year under review and in previous years.

Although temporary changes in the load of activity may be ignored, persistent variation should lead to revision of the previous norm. The adoption of a prudent approach to the valuation of stocks has sometimes been used to argue against the inclusion of overheads. SSAP 9 states that prudence will be taken into account in determining net realisable value and is not a reason for excluding overheads from the cost of stock. Having said that, the overheads that should be included are those arising from normal activity. All abnormal conversion costs (such as exceptional spoilage, idle capacity and other losses), which are avoidable under normal operating conditions, should be excluded.

Example – Overhead absorption rates

Entity A's normal production is 10 units and normal overhead (fixed) is £10 so that £1 is allocated to each unit. If there are 3 units in inventory at the year end, then £3 of overhead is carried forward. If, however, 15 units are actually produced, to include a 'normal' level of overhead (£1 per unit) would be over valuing inventory.

The principle in SSAP 9 is that stock is carried at the lower of cost and net realisable value. We consider that allocating £1 to each unit in the case above, where 15 units are produced would mean stock is recorded above cost and so would be against SSAP 9. On the basis that 15 units were actually produced only £0.667 (that is £10/15 units) should be allocated to each unit, so if there are 3 units in inventory at the year end, £2.001 (£0.667 × 3 units) of overheads are carried forward.

20.12 The classification of overheads for the purpose of the allocation takes the function of the overhead as its distinguishing characteristic (for example, whether it is a function of production, marketing, selling or administration), rather than whether the overhead varies with time or with volume. The costs of general management, as distinct from functional management, are not directly related to current production and are, therefore, excluded from cost of conversion.

20.13 SI 2008/410 states that distribution costs may not be included in production cost. [SI 2008/410 Sch 27(4)]. This means that a company should not include external distribution costs such as those relating to the transfer of goods from a sales depot to an external customer. It may, however, include a proportion of the costs that a company incurs in distributing goods from its factory to its sales depot as these are costs incurred in bringing the product to its present location.

20.14 An example of a retail company disclosing its methods of determining cost of sales and distribution costs is illustrated in Table 20.1. Cost of sales includes costs of transfer to the point of sale. For retailers, costs of transfer to the point of sale will often include a proportion of normal warehouse costs. Distribution costs include holding costs at the point of sale and costs of transfer to the customer.

Table 20.1 – Costs of sales and distribution: Costs explained

Safeway plc – Annual Report and Accounts – 30 March 2002

Statement of Accounting Policies (extract)

Sales and profit

Cost of sales represents the purchase cost of goods for resale and includes the cost of transfer to the point of sale.

Net operating expenses

Distribution costs represent the cost of holding goods at the point of sale, selling costs and the costs of transferring goods to the customer and include store operating expenses.

Determination of cost

20.15 It is often not possible to relate expenditure to specific units of stock and so a near approximation has to be ascertained. This gives rise to two problems:

- The selection of an appropriate method for relating costs to stocks, for example:
- Job costing.
- Batch costing.
- Process costing.
- Standard costing.
- The selection of an appropriate method for calculating the related costs where a number of identical items have been purchased or made at different times.

20.16 SI 2008/410 allows companies to use certain methods for arriving at the purchase price or the production cost of stocks and other 'fungible items'. For this purpose, 'fungible items' are those items that are indistinguishable one from another (for example, identical nuts and bolts). [SI 2008/410 10 Sch 5].

20.17 Under the Act a company may adopt any of the following methods (but, in order to comply with the requirements of FRS 18, the method chosen must be the one which appears to the directors to be the most appropriate in the circumstances of the company and gives a true and fair view). [FRS 18 para 50]:

- First-in, first-out (FIFO).
- Last-in, first-out (LIFO) (but see para 20.21).
- Weighted average price.
- Any other similar method.

[SI 2008/410 1 Sch 18(1)(2)].

20.18 An example of a company using an average cost method is Cadbury Schweppes plc (see Table 20.2).

Table 20.2 – Stock valued on an average cost method

Cadbury Schweppes plc – Annual Report – 30 December 2001

Accounting Policies (extract)

(k) Stocks **Stocks are valued at the lower of average cost and estimated net realisable value. Cost comprises direct material and labour costs together with the relevant factory overheads (including depreciation) on the basis of normal activity levels.**

20.19 Under the FIFO method, the cost of stock is calculated on the basis that the quantities in hand represent the latest purchases or production. An example of a company using the FIFO method is Bass PLC (see Table 20.3).

Table 20.3 – Stock valued on a FIFO basis

Bass PLC – Annual Report – 30 September 1994

Accounting Policies (extract)

Stocks

The basis of valuation is as follows:

i) Raw materials, bought-in-goods and consumable stores at the lower of cost and net realisable value on a first in, first out basis.

ii) Work in progress and finished stocks at the lower of cost, which includes an appropriate element of production overhead costs, and net realisable value.

Cost includes all expenditure incurred in bringing each product to its present condition and location. Net realisable value is based on estimated selling prices less further costs expected to be incurred in bringing the stocks to completion and disposal.

20.20 The example below illustrates the calculation of the value of stocks on both a FIFO basis and a weighted average price basis.

Example – Valuing stock using the FIFO and weighted average cost methods

Assume that opening stock on 1 March 20X9 is nil. All stock is finished goods, and is of the same type. Details of the stock received and sent out are as shown below.

	Quantity unit	Unit cost
		£
Batch 1 received on 1 March 20X9	2	3.00
Batch 2 received on 15 March 20X9	4	4.50
On 25 March 20X9 the entity sold 5 units.		
Closing stock value on 31 March 20X9		

	Quantity unit(1)	Unit cost	Value
		£	£
(a) FIFO	1	4.50 (a)	4.50
(b) Weighted average	1	4.00 (b)	4.00

The quantity of goods remaining is one (2 + 4 — 5) for both of the measurement methods.

(a) FIFO: all units of batch 1 have been sent out first, then three units from batch 2 were sent out. One unit from batch 2 is remaining at £4.50.

(b) Weighted average: the average unit cost of all units received is £4.00 (2 × £3 + 4 × £4.50)/(2+4).

20.21 When choosing a method, the directors must ensure that the method they choose provides the fairest practicable approximation to 'actual cost'. SSAP 9 considers that the LIFO method (where the quantities in hand represent the earliest purchases or production) does not usually bear a reasonable relationship to actual cost and so LIFO is not an acceptable method of valuation in the UK.

20.22 Similarly, a base stock method is also not normally an acceptable method of stock valuation as it often results in stocks being stated in the balance sheet at amounts that bear little relationship to recent cost levels. Under this method, the cost of stocks is calculated on the basis that a fixed unit value is ascribed to a predetermined number of units of stock, any excess over this number being valued on the basis of some other method.

[The next paragraph is 22.24].

20.24 Costs are often allocated to stocks by the use of a standard costing method. The cost of stocks is calculated on the basis of periodically predetermined costs derived from management's estimates of expected levels of costs and operational efficiency. The standard costs should be based on normal levels of operations and any abnormal costs or costs arising from inefficiencies should be written off in the period. Where standard costs are used, they need to be reviewed frequently to ensure that they bear a reasonable relationship to actual costs arising during the period.

20.25 The method of arriving at cost by applying the latest purchase price to the total number of units in stock is unacceptable in principle because it is not necessarily the same as actual cost and, in times of rising prices, will result in the taking of profit that has not been realised.

20.26 One method of arriving at cost is the use of selling price less an estimated profit margin. This is acceptable only if it can be demonstrated that it gives a reasonable approximation of the actual cost. This method is often used by retailers with a large number of rapidly changing individual items in stores, for example, Tesco PLC (see Table 20.5).

Table 20.5 – Cost based on selling 'price' less as estimated profit margin

Tesco PLC – Annual report and financial statements – 22 February 2003

Accounting policies (extract)

Stocks

Stocks comprise goods held for resale and properties held for, or in the course of, development and are valued at the lower of cost and net realisable value. Stocks in stores are calculated at retail prices and reduced by appropriate margins to the lower of cost and net realisable value.

20.27 In industries where the production process results in minor by-products, the costs of the main products are calculated after deducting the net revenue from sales of the by-products. An example of this treatment is found in the accounts of Lonmin Plc (see Table 20.6).

Table 20.6 – Treatment of minor by-products

Lonmin Plc – Annual Report – 30 September 2001

Statement on accounting policies (extract)

Stocks (extract)

Platinum metal stock is valued by allocating costs to platinum, palladium and rhodium stock based on the annual cost of production, less revenue from by-products, apportioned according to the quantities of each of the three main metals produced.

Net realisable value of stocks

20.28 SSAP 9 requires that the figure of stocks disclosed in the financial statements should be the total of the lower of cost and net realisable value of the separate items of stock or of groups of similar items. [SSAP 9 para 26].

20.29 If there is no reasonable expectation of sufficient future revenue to cover cost incurred, the irrecoverable cost should be charged to revenue in the year under review. Net realisable value is the actual or estimated proceeds from the sale of items of stock (net of trade discounts, but before settlement discounts) less all further costs to completion and less all costs to be incurred in marketing, selling and distributing directly related to the items in question. [SSAP 9 para 5].

20.30 The principal situations in which net realisable value is likely to be less than cost are where there has been:

- An increase in costs or a fall in selling price.
- Physical deterioration of stocks.
- Obsolescence of products.
- A decision as part of a company's marketing strategy to manufacture and sell products at a loss.
- Errors in production or purchasing.

20.31 The initial calculation of write downs to reduce stocks from cost to net realisable value may often be made by the use of formulae based on predetermined criteria. The formulae normally take account of the age, movements in the past, expected future movements and estimated scrap values of the stock, as appropriate. Whilst the use of such formulae establishes a basis for making a write down that can be consistently applied, it is still necessary for the results to be reviewed in the light of any special circumstances that cannot be anticipated in the formulae, such as changes in external market information or in the state of the order book.

20.32 Where a write down is required to reduce the value of finished goods below cost, the stocks of the parts and sub-assemblies held for the purpose of the manufacture of such products, together with stocks on order, need to be reviewed to determine if a write down is also required against such items.

20.33 Events occurring between the balance sheet date and the date of completion of the financial statements need to be considered in arriving at the net realisable value at the balance sheet date (for example, a subsequent reduction in selling prices).

> **Example**
>
> A company supplies car parts to a major manufacturer. At the year end it had an inventory of parts and their carrying value was £1 million. However, after the year end the manufacturer changed the models of the cars and as a result the inventory became obsolete (the part is not interchangeable between models). Should the company provide against the inventory at the year end? It does not wish to provide on the grounds that the manufacturer did not make its decision to switch models until after the company's year end.
>
> The company should write down the inventory (to realisable value). SSAP 9's appendix states that events between the balance sheet date and the date of completion of the financial statements should be considered in determining net realisable value. In addition, FRS 21, 'Events after the balance sheet date', refers to the sale of inventories after the balance sheet date as giving evidence of the net realisable value at the balance sheet date.

20.33.1 However, a reduction is not necessary when the realisable value of material stocks is less than the purchase price, provided that the goods into which the materials are to be incorporated can still be sold at a profit after incorporating the materials at cost price.

Disclosure

20.34 The Companies Act 2006 requires that stocks should be analysed between the following four categories:

- Raw materials and consumables.
- Work in progress.

- Finished goods and goods for resale.
- Payments on account – this represents the payments a company makes on account of stocks and not the payments it receives from customers.

[SI 2008/410 Sch formats].

20.35 A company should follow this categorisation so long as it produces true and fair financial statements. However, in certain circumstances, the special nature of a company's business may mean that the company needs to adapt the formats. Table 20.7 shows a company that has included additional categories for show homes and part exchange properties within stocks.

Table 20.7 – Show homes and part exchange properties held as stocks

Bellway p.l.c. – Annual Report – 31 July 2001

Notes to the Accounts

9 Stocks (extract)	**2001**	2000
	£000	£000
Group		
Work in progress and stocks	**639,572**	506,437
Grants	**(8,483)**	(7,383)
Payments on account	**(9,387)**	(16,164)
	621,702	482,890
Showhomes	**14,483**	16,799
Part exchange properties	**8,236**	8,825
	644,421	508,514

20.36 The accounting policy that has been applied to stocks should be stated and applied consistently within the business and from year to year. [SSAP 9 para 32]. Although there is no requirement in SSAP 9 to state the methods used in calculating cost and net realisable value, these are estimation techniques and, if significant, should be disclosed as required by FRS 18, 'Accounting policies'. Examples of disclosure of these estimation techniques are illustrated above in Table 20.2 and Table 20.3.

Replacement value of stocks

20.37 Paragraph 28 of Schedule 1 says that, where the historical cost of stocks or fungible assets is calculated using a method permitted by the Act (for example, FIFO, weighted average or any similar method), and that valuation differs materially from the 'relevant alternative amount' of those items, then the difference should be disclosed in a note to the financial statements.

20.38 The 'relevant alternative amount' will normally be the amount at which the assets would have been disclosed if their value had been determined according to their replacement cost as at the balance sheet date. [SI 2008/410 1 Sch 28(4)]. The replacement cost of these types of assets will normally be their current cost. However, a company may instead determine the relevant alternative amount according to the most recent actual purchase price or the most recent actual production cost of assets of that class before that date. But it can do this only where this method gives a more appropriate standard of comparison for assets of the class in question. [SI 2008/410 1 Sch 28(5)]. The Act leaves it to the company's directors to form an opinion as to whether the method does this. An example of the disclosure of replacement cost is found in the accounts of BP p.l.c. (see Table 20.8).

Table 20.8 – Disclosure of replacement cost of stocks

BP p.l.c. Annual Accounts – 31 December 2001

Notes on accounts
22 Stocks

		$ million
	2001	**2000**
Petroleum	5,176	**6,933**
Chemicals	953	**1,046**
Other	568	**504**
	6,697	**8,483**
Stores	934	**751**
	7,631	**9,234**
Replacement cost	7,686	**9,392**

20.39 The example below considers the disclosure of the replacement cost of stocks. It uses the details from the previous example:

Example – Disclosure of replacement cost of stocks

Companies A and B have identical opening and closing stocks and purchases in a particular year, but company A chooses to determine the value of its closing stocks by the FIFO method, and company B does so by the 'weighted average price' method. In these circumstances, the amount to be included in the balance sheets would be calculated as follows:

Company A: £3,175 company B: £2,825 The value of the stocks at replacement cost is £3,300.

If the difference between the balance sheet value of stocks and their replacement cost is material in the context of their balance sheet value, it must be disclosed under the requirement outlined in paragraph 20.37. The difference for company A is £125 (£3,300 — £3,175), which is unlikely to be considered material. The difference for company B is £475 (£3,300 — £2,825), which is likely to be considered material. If it is, it must be disclosed.

20.40 Counsel has advised that a 'method' is not used when stocks are valued at either their actual purchase price or their production cost. It would appear, therefore, that where companies value their stocks at actual purchase price or production cost, they do not need to disclose, in their financial statements the difference between this value and the replacement value of those stocks.

20.41 In many situations, it is likely that some items of stocks will be valued by one of the methods mentioned above and that other items will be valued at actual purchase price or production cost. Where a company does this, the company will need to disclose not only the difference between the figure of stocks valued by a method and their replacement cost, but also the actual purchase price or production cost of the stocks it has valued by that method. Otherwise, it could be misleading for the company to disclose the figure that represents the difference, without also giving an indication of the proportion of the total stock value to which this difference relates.

Sale and repurchase of stocks

20.42 Sometimes stock is sold with an option (or obligation) to buy it back. The detailed terms of such options vary and, indeed, the options may sometimes be expressed at market value such that it is by no means certain that the options will be exercised. Perhaps more commonly, however, the option is constructed so that it is reasonably certain that it will be exercised. The arrangement may run for months, or even years, during which time the company that sold the stock will use the sale proceeds as a form of finance. The stock and the related purchase obligation (that is, the liability to repay the finance provided by the temporary holder of the stock) were often excluded from the balance sheet in the past.

20.43 Such arrangements are covered by FRS 5 and are considered in detail in chapter 3. In summary, the true commercial effect of a transaction is a sale if the seller genuinely relinquishes control of significant benefits and transfers the exposure to significant risks associated with the asset to the buyer (for example, if the repurchase price is market value at the date of repurchase). However, a transaction structured so that, in practice, the purchaser secures a lender's return on the purchase price without genuine exposure to, or benefit from, changes in value of the underlying assets (for example, if the repurchase price is pre-determined as original sale price plus an increment based on interest rates applied to the finance provided) should be treated as a financing arrangement.

Example – Stock repurchase arrangement

A company sells stock in year one for £100,000 and at the same time enters into an agreement to repurchase it a year later for £110,000. The £10,000 should not be treated as part of the cost of the stock, but represents interest, and should be charged to the profit and loss account.

If the company's year end fell halfway through the transaction, the company should initially show in its balance sheet stock of £100,000 and a financing liability of £100,000. Interest should be calculated at a constant rate on the carrying value of the liability although, if there was no significant difference, it could be assumed to accrue evenly throughout the period. In this case, interest of £5,000 should be accrued and charged to the profit and loss account.

Consideration would also need to be given as to whether the stock requires a write down to reduce it to net realisable value.

20.44 FRS 5 recognises that, in more complex situations, it may be determined that a sale and repurchase agreement is not, in substance, a financing transaction and that the seller only retains access to some of the benefits of the original asset. In this circumstance, the partial derecognition rules in paragraph 23 of the standard might apply. If, for example, the buyer receives more than merely a lender's return, as other benefits and risks associated with the asset have been transferred to the buyer, the seller will not have retained the original asset. In this situation, the original asset should be derecognised and the analysis should determine whether another asset should be recognised in its place. For example, the seller might have an interest in the asset's residual value at the end of its life, in which case the residual interest should be recognised as an asset and the repurchase obligation as a liability in the seller's balance sheet. An example of this can be found in the accounts of Inchcape plc, where equipment sold with repurchase obligations is included in stocks. (see Table 20.9).

Table 20.9 – Equipment sold with repurchase obligation included in stock

Inchcape plc – Annual Report – 31 December 2001

Stocks	**2001 £m**	2000 £m
Raw materials and work in progress	**2.3**	1.4
Finished goods and merchandise	**517.4**	528.7
	519.7	530.1

Certain subsidiaries have an obligation to repurchase, at a guaranteed residual value, certain vehicles which have been legally sold for leasing contracts. Although the credit risk is passed to the finance house, in substance these vehicles remain as assets of the Group. They have been included in stock at the guaranteed repurchase price less appropriate provisions where the anticipated realisable value is lower. The corresponding cross guaranteed repurchase price liability is included within trade creditors. Stock includes £93.8m (2000 – £110.1m) of such vehicles.

Vehicles held on consignment which are in substance assets of the Group amount to £37.0m (2000 – £29.0m). These have been included in finished goods stock with the corresponding liability included within trade creditors. Payment becomes due when title passes to the Group, which is generally the earlier of six months from delivery or date of sale.

20.45 The notes to the financial statements should include the following information concerning all sale and repurchase transactions:

- The transaction's principal features. [FRS 5 App B paras B19 and B21].
- The asset's status. [FRS 5 App B paras B19 and B21].

For example, disclosure that an asset has been legally sold to another party, but has been retained on balance sheet.

- The relationship between the asset and the liability. [FRS 5 App B paras B19 and B21].

Again, where an asset has been legally sold, but has been retained on balance sheet because the transaction is considered to be a financing arrangement, the notes should explain how the finance is connected with the asset (for example, whether it is non-recourse).

20.46 An example of stock retained on balance sheet where it has been legally sold is seen in Table 20.10.

Table 20.10 – Stock retained on balance sheet where it has been legally sold

Persimmon plc – Report & Accounts – 31 December 1997

NOTES TO THE FINANCIAL STATEMENTS

for the year ended 31 December 1997 (extract)

26 Contingent liabilities (extract)

The company has guaranteed the return to investors in the companies formed under the Business Expansion Scheme and has indemnified the company's bankers who have provided guarantees of up to £40,500,000 in support of these obligations.

27 Properties in Business Expansion Scheme (BES) companies

The group sold properties into BES companies set up under BES assured tenancy schemes from 1989 to 1993.

Persimmon plc has guaranteed the return to investors in the companies formed under the BES (see note 26). Because the company has guaranteed that the BES companies will have sufficient cash resources at scheme maturity to pay the guaranteed return to investors, the proceeds received for the properties are treated as loans under BES advances on the balance sheet. The finance cost implicit in the BES arrangements, calculated by reference to the difference between the sales proceeds received and the guaranteed distribution to investors, is being charged in the profit and loss account over the appropriate term. In addition, the net rental income arising in the BES companies is recognised in the profit and loss account in the appropriate period.

Turnover does not include properties sold to BES companies until the schemes mature, the properties being held at cost on the balance sheet as BES assets until the sale is recognised.

At 31 December 1997 only two schemes now remain, all obligations under the previous schemes having been fulfilled. The maturity dates of the two remaining schemes are 5 March 1998 and 24 January 1999. The company acts on behalf of the BES companies in the sale of the properties prior to the scheme maturity date in accordance with the original scheme rules. The company has the right to exercise its option to repurchase any properties that remain unsold at maturity date in fulfilling its obligations under the guarantees.

20.47 Where the substance of the transaction is that the seller has a different asset, then, in addition to the disclosure set out in paragraph 20.45, the terms of any provision for repurchase (including any options) and of any guarantees should be disclosed. [FRS 5 App B para B21]. Disclosure of repurchase obligations in respect of residual interests in equipment is shown in Table 20.9.

Consignment stock

20.48 Arrangements where goods are supplied from a manufacturer to a dealer on a consignment basis are common in certain industries, particularly in the motor vehicle trade. Application note A to FRS 5 shows how the principles of recognising assets and liabilities should be applied to these arrangements.

Objective of consigning stocks

20.49 The objective of both parties to a consignment stock arrangement is to enable the dealer to sell as many units of the product as possible. The dealer is often given some incentive by the manufacturer through various bonus schemes to ensure that the volume of items sold is as high as possible. The consignment arrangement serves to achieve this objective and benefit both parties.

20.50 However, under such arrangements the manufacturer (or a financier) generally retains title to the goods supplied to the dealer until some predetermined event occurs. This may be when the dealer sells the goods or has held them for a set period, or some other event triggers the dealer's adoption of the goods (that is, when he pays for them and acquires title). But the date that title transfers tends to be some time after the date that the stock item is physically transferred to the dealer. Title will generally pass on receipt of cleared funds (but not to the dealer if he has already sold the vehicle on).

20.51 Application note A to FRS 5 seeks to determine the point at which the dealer has in substance acquired an asset that should be recognised on its balance sheet (that is, whether it is when legal title passes or at some other time).

Principal sources of benefits and risks

20.52 In practice, the terms of consignment agreements vary considerably in important respects, for example: the right of return by the dealer; the determination of the sale price, known as the transfer price; and the terms under which deposits are required to be made by the dealer to the manufacturer or a requirement for the dealer to pay interest (which is in substance indicative of an advance of finance). These are normally the most important factors to be considered in the analysis. Other aspects of consignment transactions such as rights of inspection, responsibility for damage and loss or theft and related insurance are of less importance.

20.53 The standard analyses the principal benefits and risks associated with consignment stock arrangements from the point of view of the dealer to determine whether the stock should appear on the dealer's balance sheet. The application note identifies four principal sources of benefits and risks, which need to be considered in the analysis:

- Manufacturer's right of return.
- Dealer's right of return.
- Stock transfer price and deposits.
- Dealer's right to use stock.

20.54 These principal sources of benefits and risks are then considered in detail in the application note and the principles stemming from that discussion are summarised in a table. The summary table is reproduced below, but with the principal sources of benefits and risks added as headings; also included are references to the paragraphs of the application note that give the narrative explanation:

Indicates stock is not an asset of the dealer at delivery	**Indicates stock is an asset of the dealer at delivery**
Manufacturer's right of return [App A para A5].	
Manufacturer can require the dealer to return stock (or transfer stock to another dealer) without compensation, or	Manufacturer cannot require dealer to return or transfer stock, or
Penalty paid by the dealer to prevent returns/transfers of stock at the manufacturer's request.	Financial incentives given to persuade dealer to transfer stock at manufacturer's manufacturer's request.
Dealer's right of return [App A para A6].	
Dealer has unfettered right to return stock to the manufacturer without penalty and actually exercises the right in practice.	Dealer has no right to return stock or is commercially compelled not to exercise its right of return.
Manufacturer bears obsolescence risk, for example: — obsolete stock is returned to the manufacturer without penalty; or — financial incentives given by manufacturer to prevent stock being returned to it (for example, on a model change or if it becomes obsolete).	Dealer bears obsolescence risk, for example: — penalty charged if dealer returns stock to manufacturer; or — obsolete stock cannot be returned to the manufacturer and no compensation is paid by manufacturer for losses due to obsolescence.

Stock transfer price and deposits

Stock transfer price charged by manufacturer is based on manufacturer's list price at date of transfer of legal title. [App A para A7].	Stock transfer price charged by manufacturer is based on manufacturer's list price at date of delivery. [App A para A7].
Manufacturer bears slow movement risk; for example: — transfer price set independently of time for which dealer holds stock, and there is no deposit. [App A para A8].	Dealer bears slow movement risk, for example: — dealer is effectively charged interest as transfer price or other payments to manufacturer vary with time for which dealer holds stock. [App A para A8]; or — dealer makes a substantial interest-free deposit that varies with the levels of stock held. [App A para A9].

20.55 One of the principal sources of benefits and risks is not dealt with in the table above and concerns the dealer's right to use the stock. The existence of a right by the dealer to use consignment stock will not normally of itself require the stock to be recorded on the dealer's balance sheet. However, once that right is exercised and the dealer uses the stock (for example, as a demonstration model) and once he has paid for it this generally causes the legal title to be transferred to the dealer and thus the stock to be recognised on its balance sheet. [FRS 5 App A para A10].

20.56 The analysis of a consignment stock agreement will often give conflicting indications, as some aspects of the transaction might indicate that the stock should be put on the dealer's balance sheet while other aspects might indicate that it should remain off. In such a circumstance, one of the important factors will be to determine who pays the finance/interest cost of holding the stock. If the dealer pays an interest cost or another charge that varies with the time the stock is held (sometimes referred to by some other name, for example, display charge) then this strongly indicates that the dealer has an obligation and hence a liability that should be recognised in the dealer's financial statements. The related asset may only be an 'interest in consignment stock', but should be recorded as such until the dealer adopts the stock when that interest will convert to recognising the actual consignment stock on balance sheet. These principles are explained more fully in the example in paragraph 20.61.

Accounting treatment

20.57 The accounting treatment in the dealer's books specified in the standard is as follows. If the analysis shows that the asset should be recorded on the dealer's balance sheet then the double entry is:

Dr Stock or interest in stock	£10,000
Cr Liabilities – trade creditors	£10,000

To record the consignment stock brought onto the dealer's balance sheet.

20.58 Where the dealer has paid a deposit to the manufacturer for the consignment then this amount should be deducted from the liability to the manufacturer and the balance shown within trade creditors (assuming the asset and liability comply with the offset rules in FRS 5.

20.59 The notes to the financial statements should give the following information:

- An explanation of the nature of the arrangement.
- The amount of the consignment stock.
- The main terms under which the consignment is held.
- The terms of any related deposit.

[FRS 5 App A para A12].

20.60 Where the analysis of the transaction indicates that the stock should remain off the dealer's balance sheet, then the dealer should still give in the notes to the financial statements the information set out in paragraph 20.59. If the dealer has paid a deposit to the manufacturer, then this should be included within 'other debtors' on the balance sheet. [FRS 5 App A para A12].

Example of required analysis

20.61 Application Note A does not give any examples of how to apply the analysis, but the example that follows illustrates the types of feature that might underlie a typical consignment arrangement and how the analysis under FRS 5 would determine how to account for the arrangement.

Example – Consignment stock

A motor manufacturer enters into an arrangement with its dealers to consign stock to them. The agreement is the same for each dealer in the network. The basic principles of the consignment are as follows:

- The dealer orders and is allocated stock by the manufacturer under a consignment agreement and, in most cases, the stock is physically located at the dealer's premises. The manufacturer can reward or penalise dealers through the allocation of consignment stock.
- Title to the stock does not pass until the dealer has paid for the stock. The obligation to pay will arise on the earlier of:
  - The date of sale of the vehicle to the customer.
  - The date of adoption of stock (for example, as a demonstration model).
  - 180 days.
- A third party finance house has a separate agreement with the manufacturer and dealer, whereby the manufacturer receives a payment from the finance house, by way of a deposit, for all vehicles consigned to the dealer. The dealer has to pay a funding cost to the finance house based on the value of the vehicles consigned to it, which is set at 3% above LIBOR. There is a free stocking period of two months, where there is no finance charge to the dealer for the consignment stock (the finance cost being paid by the manufacturer).
- At any point, until the dealer adopts the stock or sells it or the 180 days has passed, the stock may be returned to the manufacturer, exchanged or transferred to another dealer in the manufacturer's network. This ensures that the dealer has access to the complete range of manufacturer's stock. In practice, stock is rarely returned to the manufacturer (only about 1% of vehicles consigned). In rare circumstances the manufacturer will request the return of a vehicle to fulfil a particular order elsewhere. In this situation no benefit accrues to the dealer. However, as much as 30% of stock is transferred between dealers generally by receiving a similar model in exchange.
- If a model is not selling well, then approaching its adoption date, the dealer can take one of the following actions:
  - Exchange it or transfer it to another dealer who may have a demand for that particular vehicle.
  - Negotiate an extension of the adoption date with the manufacturer.
  - Give an incentive to sell the stock, which might be supported by the manufacturer where the model is performing badly (for example, giving one year's free insurance).
- The transfer price is set at the adoption date by reference to the manufacturer's list price. However, prices on older models may be held to enable the dealer to discount his selling price.

It can be seen that such agreements can be very complex and very difficult to analyse in practice. Considering the principal benefits and risks the transaction can be analysed as follows:

	Off B/sheet	On B/sheet
Manufacturer's right to return Manufacturer can require dealer to return stock or transfer stock without compensation.	✓	
Dealer's right to return Dealer does have a right to return stock to the manufacturer without penalty, but because of the incidence of transfers between dealers, does not need to effect this right often.	✓	
Financial incentives are given by the manufacturer to prevent stock being returned in the event that a model becomes obsolete.	✓	
Regular exchanges or transfers between dealers.	✓	
Consignment period extended with agreement of the manufacturer.	✓	
Stock transfer price and deposits Stock transfer price is based on the manufacturer's list price at the date of adoption of the vehicle.	✓	
After the initial stocking period, which is interest free, the dealer pays the finance house a finance cost which varies with the level of stock held and as a consequence bears slow movement risk.		✓

It is necessary to consider the results of the analysis very carefully. It is not merely a matter of counting the ticks in the left hand column and those in the right hand column to determine which presentation wins. It is a matter of determining which of the parties bears the benefits and risks of ownership. It would appear that the manufacturer has retained the risk of obsolescence in this example, but the risk of slow movement falls to the dealer. This is a real risk as interest is paid following the period of free stocking. Therefore, after the free stocking period is complete (that is, after two months), the dealer has a risk which gives rise to an obligation that needs to be recognised by the dealer. Analysing this risk using the standard's definition of a liability, it is clear that the obligation should be recorded in the dealer's balance sheet as such at the end of the free stocking period and at an amount that equates to the deposit on which the interest is being paid. The corresponding asset could be disclosed as an 'interest in consignment stock' and would be recorded at the same amount. When the consignment stock is adopted it should then be recorded as stock of the dealer. Adoption will either take place for demonstration purposes or for onward sale.

20.62 As illustrated in the example, the interest payments in this particular transaction represent an obligation to transfer economic benefits and, as a consequence, a liability for them arises, which is in substance a loan. Under the standard, the loan should be recognised in the financial statements if it can be measured with sufficient reliability. The 'loan' would, therefore, be recorded in the dealer's balance sheet and an asset recognised which represents the dealer's interest in the consignment stock. In a study carried out for the motor industry on the impact of FRED 4, the exposure draft that preceded FRS 5, this test was seen as the primary test and has been termed the 'liability test'.

20.63 Alternatively, the analysis might have indicated that the dealer bore the risks and rewards of ownership of the stock and, as a consequence, the consignment stock itself (rather than just an interest in it) should be recorded on the dealer's balance sheet and the related finance recorded as a liability (known as the 'asset test'). Consequently, an asset (either the vehicle or an interest in it) and the corresponding liability should be accounted for on balance sheet at the earlier of: (a) the date the asset test is passed; and (b) the date the liability test is passed. However, the figure for the interest in stock recorded following the liability test will not necessarily be the same amount as the consignment stock recognised following the asset test.

Manufacturer's position

20.64 There is no discussion in the standard of the accounting treatment in the manufacturer's financial statements and its treatment cannot be assumed to be the reverse of that adopted in the dealer's books. For example, the manufacturer might recognise the physical stock in its financial statements while the dealer recognises an interest in that stock. Furthermore, there are no specific disclosures required to be given by the manufacturer in its financial statements other than the general requirement of paragraph 30 of FRS 5, which requires that the disclosure should be sufficient to enable the user of the financial statements to understand the transaction's commercial effect.

20.65 Revenue recognition by the manufacturer has to be decided on its own merits. The date that the dealer records the interest in the stock in its financial statements is not necessarily the date from which the manufacturer would recognise its revenue on sale of the stock. In the example in paragraph 20.61, the effect is that:

- In the period prior to the end of the free stocking period the manufacturer holds 'stock' whilst the dealer has no asset. The manufacturer will benefit from the deposit advanced by the finance company and pay interest to the finance company.
- In the period between the end of the free stocking period and the adoption date the manufacturer holds 'stock' whilst the dealer also holds an 'interest in consignment stock'. In this period the manufacturer will benefit from the

deposit advanced by the finance company and will not pay interest to the finance company as this is paid by the dealer.

- In the above example, the manufacturer recognises revenue at the date the consignment stock is adopted (which is when all the risks and rewards of ownership are transferred and the manufacturer has earned the right to the consideration).

Conclusion

20.66 Obviously, as mentioned above, the terms of consignment stock agreements differ significantly. It must be stressed, therefore, that the analysis of these transactions needs to be undertaken very carefully in conjunction with the detailed application note in FRS 5.

Goods with reservation of title

20.67 It is quite common for companies that sell goods to other companies to have reservation of title clauses included in their contracts. This enables the selling company to retain ownership of those goods until the purchaser has paid for them. Such clauses are often known as 'Romalpa clauses' following the Romalpa case (*Aluminium Industrie Vaassen B.V. v Romalpa Aluminium Limited* [1976] 1 WLR 676) in 1976, which was concerned with contractual relationships. The main effect of trading with reservation of title is that the position of the unpaid seller may be improved if the purchaser becomes insolvent. However, whether an effective reservation of title exists depends upon the construction of the particular contract.

20.68 Even if there is an effective reservation of title clause, on a going concern basis it is common practice for the purchaser to recognise such stocks in its balance sheet, although the supplier retains legal title to the goods. The liability to the supplier is also recognised. This was first recommended in guidance issued by ICAEW in 1976, 'Accounting for goods subject to reservation of title'. It is consistent with FRS 5 as it is the purchaser who bears the risks and benefits from the rewards of the asset.

20.69 The ICAEW guidance recommended that where the financial statements are materially affected by the accounting treatment adopted in relation to sales or purchases subject to reservation of title, the treatment should be disclosed and a note indicating the amount of liabilities that are subject to reservation of title clauses be given, where quantifiable. An example of such disclosure is given in Table 20.11.

Table 20.11 – Sales of stock subject to reservation of title

CHARNOS plc – Annual Report and Accounts – 31 December 1988

Notes on the accounts

16 Creditors – amounts falling due within one year (extract)

Part of the amount owing to trade creditors is or may be secured by the reservation by the supplier of legal title to the goods supplied and to the proceeds of their sale. The amount secured in this way depends on the legal interpretation of individual contracts and cannot readily be determined. In the opinion of the directors, the maximum amount likely to be involved is £1,150,000 (group) and £400,000 (company).

20.70 However, in practice, this note is often not given where the purchasing company is a going concern such that the likelihood of the reservation of title clause crystallising is remote. Whether or not disclosure is necessary in order to give a true and fair view will be a matter for judgement. FRS 5 requires sufficient details of a transaction to be given to enable the user to understand its commercial effect. [FRS 5, para 30]. It also requires an explanation where the nature of assets and liabilities differs from those items normally included under the relevant balance sheet headings. An example would be where the company did not have legal title to assets and disclosure of this fact was necessary for a true and fair view to be given.

Long-term contracts

20.71 Long-term contracts need to be considered separately, because of the length of time taken to complete such contracts. The main accounting issue is the allocation of turnover and costs to the accounting periods in which work is carried out. To defer recording turnover and not to take account of profit until completion of the contract may result in the profit and loss account reflecting not so much a fair view of the results of the activity of the company during the year, but rather a view of the results relating to contracts that have been completed in the year. It is, therefore, appropriate to take credit for ascertainable turnover and profit while contracts are in progress.

Definition of long-term contracts

20.72 A 'long-term contract' is defined in SSAP 9 as follows:

> *'A contract entered into for the design, manufacture or construction of a single substantial asset or the provision of a service (or of a combination of assets or services which together constitute a single project) where the time taken substantially to complete the contract is such that the contract activity falls into different accounting periods. A contract that is required to be accounted for as long-term by this accounting standard will usually extend for a period exceeding one year. However, a duration exceeding one*

year is not an essential feature of a long-term contract. Some contracts with a shorter duration than one year should be accounted for as long-term contracts if they are sufficiently material to the activity of the period that not to record turnover and attributable profit would lead to a distortion of the period's turnover and results such that the financial statements would not give a true and fair view, provided that the policy is applied consistently within the reporting entity and from year to year.' [SSAP 9 para 22].

20.73 A situation where a contract of duration of less than one year might be treated as long-term is, for example, when a company completes a material short-term contract just after the year end, but a substantial amount of work on the contract had been completed before the year end. If an element of turnover and profit is not attributed to the current period, this might distort that period's turnover and results to such an extent that they do not give a true and fair view.

20.73.1 In March 2005 the UITF issued Abstract 40, (see further chapter 9) which noted that contracts for the provision of single project professional services, the performance of which falls into two or more accounting periods, should be accounted for as a long-term contract in accordance with SSAP 9.

[The next paragraph is 20.74].

Accounting treatment of long-term contracts

20.74 Long-term contracts should be assessed on a contract by contract basis and reflected in the profit and loss account by recording turnover and related costs as the contract's activity progresses. Turnover is ascertained in a manner appropriate to the stage of completion of the contract, the business and the industry in which it operates. [SSAP 9 para 28]. Further guidance on the measurement of revenue (turnover) on long-term contracts is given in FRS 5 Application note G, 'Revenue recognition'.

20.75 Where it is considered that the outcome of a long-term contract can be assessed with reasonable certainty before its conclusion, the attributable profit should be recognised in the profit and loss account as the difference between the reported turnover and related costs for that contract. [SSAP 9 para 29]. This is illustrated in the following example.

Example – Pre-selling a development

A construction company has pre-sold a development to an institution. No work has yet been done on the construction. Profit will arise on proceeds less the cost of the land and the cost of the development, which it will sub-contract.

The contract should be accounted for, in accordance with SSAP 9, as a long-term contract, which means not taking profit until a stage of construction has been reached that enables the eventual outcome to be foreseen and then only taking profit attributable to the work performed at the balance sheet date.

Turnover

20.76 Application Note G to FRS 5 defines turnover as being, *'The revenue resulting from exchange transactions under which a seller supplies to customers the goods or services that it is in business to provide'*. SSAP 9 states that in the case of long-term contracts turnover is ascertained in a manner appropriate to the stage of completion of the contract, the business and the industry in which it operates thereby recognising revenue based on the company's right to consideration arising in exchange for performance under the contract. Appendix 1 to the standard states that turnover may sometimes be ascertained by reference to the valuation of work carried out to date. In other situations, there may be specific points during a contract where individual elements of work done will have separately ascertainable sales values, where costs can be identified and, therefore, turnover can be recorded as appropriate. This could be, for example, when delivery or when customer acceptance takes place.

20.76.1 FRS 5 Application note G, 'Revenue recognition', sets out basic principles for revenue recognition that should be applied to all transactions and deals with a number of specific areas. These are dealt with in chapter 9. It also includes guidance on long-term contractual performance and, specifically, on the recognition of turnover derived from such contracts. However, it does not amend the existing requirements of SSAP 9. [FRS 5 App G para G14].

20.76.2 The application note states in relation to long-term contracts that, in accordance with SSAP 9, the seller should recognise changes in its assets and liabilities, and related turnover that represent the accrual over the course of the contract of its right to consideration. This 'assets and liabilities' approach represented a shift in emphasis away from the 'matching concept' approach, which did, in the past, concentrate on matching revenue and expenses rather than measuring revenue by reference to changes in assets and liabilities. The difference in the approach can result in lower revenue being recognised at interim stages with correspondingly higher costs being carried forward. This does not necessarily give any different result from that which applying SSAP 9 would give, as SSAP 9 does not prescribe any particular method of determining revenue and merely requires that revenue is ascertained in a manner appropriate to the contract's stage of completion and to the business and industry in which the entity operates.

20.76.3 A seller should recognise turnover in respect of performance under a long-term contract when, and to the extent that, it obtains the right to consideration. [FRS 5 App G para G18]. The right to consideration is the right to receive amounts in exchange for its performance. The right does not necessarily correspond to amounts that fall due under a schedule of stage payments, as stage payments may not correspond to performance. Stage payments reflect only an agreed timing of payments whereas a right to consideration arises from a seller's performance. [FRS 5 App G para G3].

20.76.4 The right to consideration and, therefore, turnover under a long-term contract should be ascertained from assessing the fair value of the goods or services provided to the balance sheet date (that is, the stage of completion) as a proportion of the total fair value of the contract. [FRS 5 App G para G18]. Fair value means the amount at which goods or services could be exchanged in an arm's length transaction between informed and willing parties, other than in a forced or liquidation sale. [FRS 5 App G para G3].

20.76.5 In some contracts, the proportion of the total fair value will correspond to the costs to date compared to the total costs incurred and to be incurred on the contract. This is a commonly used basis, as it is the most straightforward method of arriving at a reasonable allocation of revenue. However, this method will not always be appropriate and the overriding principle is to consider the stage of completion of the contractual obligations, which reflects the extent to which the seller has obtained the right to consideration. To use the proportion of costs incurred as a basis for recognising turnover requires the seller to be able to demonstrate that costs incurred provide evidence of performance of the contract terms and the right to consideration. The emphasis on rights to consideration as the principal determining factor in revenue recognition means that as a result different stages of a contract may vary in their relative profitability. [FRS 5 App G para G18].

20.76.6 For example, a long-term contract might have a technical development stage and a construction stage. The technical development stage might have relatively low costs compared to the construction stage (because, for example, the seller has already developed the necessary technical expertise on other contracts). However, such development might represent a high proportion of the fair value of the contract and entitle the seller to a higher proportion of the total consideration under the contract than the construction stage. In such a case, as well as giving rise to higher turnover relative to the construction stage, the development phase may also give higher relative profits (subject of course to the overall contract remaining profitable).

20.76.7 The fair values used in determining the right to consideration should be based on the values applicable at the start of the contract. This applies unless the contract specifies that changes in prices will be passed on to the customer, in which case such amendments to the price are taken into account. The application note also contains guidance on separation and linking of contractual arrangements (see chapter 9 and below) and notes that that guidance may also be relevant in attributing fair values to the goods or services that have been provided up to the balance sheet date. [FRS 5 App G para G19, paras G22-G42].

20.76.8 An example of a situation where the application note provisions relating to separation and linking of contractual arrangements might affect attribution of fair values would be where two separate contracts need to be considered together under the provisions of the application note. If the two contracts had been priced artificially, with one contract having a much higher stated value than the other, adjustments would have to be made so that fair values were attributed to the rights to consideration earned under the respective contracts when they are accounted for as components of a single transaction.

20.76.9 Where payment is received in arrears then it may be necessary to discount the turnover. The application note states that *'where the effect of the time value of money is material to reported revenue, the amount of revenue recognised should be the present value of the cash inflows expected to be received from the customer in settlement. The unwinding of the discount should be credited to finance income as this represents a gain from a financing transaction'.* [FRS 5 App G para G8].

20.76.10 SSAP 9 requires that the means of ascertaining turnover should be disclosed as an accounting policy. [SSAP 9 para 32]. An example of such disclosure is found in the accounts of George Wimpey PLC (see Table 20.12).

Table 20.12 – Contracting turnover policy

George Wimpey PLC – Annual Report – 31 December 1994

ACCOUNTING POLICIES (extract)

Turnover

Contracting turnover comprises the value of work executed during the year including the settlement of claims arising from previous years, amounts received on management fee contracts funded by the client and the Group's share of unincorporated joint venture turnover. Other turnover is based on the invoiced value of goods and services supplied during the year and includes house and land sales completed, trading and investment property sales completed and rental income. Turnover excludes value added tax and intra-group turnover.

Profit

Operating profit comprises the results of contracting, the provision of goods and services, private housing development, land sales, property development and investment. It includes the results attributable to contracts completed and long-term contracts in progress where a profitable outcome can prudently be foreseen, after deducting amounts recognised in previous years and after making provision for foreseeable losses. Claims receivable are recognised as income when received or if certified for payment. Estate development profit is taken on the number of houses of an estate in respect of which legal completions have taken place.

Long-term contracts

The amount of long-term contracts, at costs incurred, net of amounts transferred to cost of sales, after deducting foreseeable losses and payments on account not matched with turnover, is included in work in progress and stock as long-term contract balances. The amount by which recorded turnover is in excess of payments on account is included in debtors as amounts recoverable on long-term contracts. Payments in excess of recorded turnover and long-term contract balances are included in creditors as payments received on account on long-term contracts. The amount by which provisions or accruals for foreseeable losses exceed costs incurred, after transfers to cost of sales, is included within either provisions for liabilities and charges or creditors, as appropriate.

[The next paragraph is 20.78.]

Recognition of profit

20.78 The profit and loss account should only include profit when the outcome of a particular contract can be ascertained with reasonable certainty (that is, where it is reasonable to foresee profits in advance of the completion of a contract). This is often a difficult exercise to undertake in practice. In addition, the standard comments that this judgement of future profitability should be exercised with prudence. [SSAP 9 para 29]. Such prudent judgements are not inconsistent with FRS 18, which requires the directors to achieve the balance between prudence and neutrality by making prudent judgements without systematic overstatements of liabilities and losses and understatement of assets and gains. [FRS 18 para 43].

20.79 In some businesses, long-term contracts for the supply of services or goods exist where the prices are determined and invoiced according to separate parts of the contract. FRS 5 Application note G, 'Revenue recognition', contains guidance on the separation and linking of contractual arrangements and states that a contractual arrangement should be accounted for as two or more separate transactions where the commercial substance is that the individual components operate independently of each other. Operating independently means that each component represents a good or service that the entity can supply separately to a customer either on a standalone basis or as an optional extra. Alternatively, one or more components may be capable of being provided by another supplier. [FRS 5 App G para G25]. This is discussed further in chapter 9.

20.80 Where a contract's individual components operate independently of each other, the most appropriate method of reflecting profits on each component is usually to record revenue and related costs as the right to consideration is earned by performance of the contract's separable parts, treating each such separable part as a separate contract. In such instances, however, future revenues from the total contract need to be compared with future estimated costs and provision made for any foreseeable loss. [SSAP 9 App 1 para 22]. More commonly, the separate stages of a long-term contract will fall to be treated as a single contract, as the separate stages are not independent of each other.

20.81 FRS 5 Application note G does not permit contracts to be 'unbundled' where the component parts do not operate independently of each other. Neither can this be done if reliable fair values cannot be attributed to any of the components individually. In addition, where there is more than one contract, the application note requires them to be treated as one contract where this best reflects the commercial substance. Typically, this would be where there was only one contract when the contracts do not operate independently of each other and reliable fair values cannot be attributed to each contract. [FRS 5 App G paras G26, G32]. This is discussed further in chapter 9. The following example considers how certain contracts should be valued.

Example

A company has a long-term contract for land reclamation. This involves clearing old collieries. As a by-product the company is entitled to sell off any coal that it recovers. On this site there are coal deposits that the company has sold to a third party for £500,000, although it has not yet recovered the coal.

The question is whether the company can take the £500,000 to the profit and loss account as it considers that there will be only minimal costs in recovering the coal. Our view is that the coal sale proceeds should be only one part of the assessment of profitability of the whole contract. It should not be accounted for separately. Therefore, the long-term contract should be accounted for including the coal sale recoveries in accordance with SSAP 9 and profit should only be taken on the contract when it has reached a stage of completion when the outcome can be foreseen and then only in proportion to the work completed.

20.82 The procedure to recognise profit is to include an appropriate proportion of total contract value as turnover in the profit and loss account as the contract activity progresses and entitlement to consideration is earned. An appropriate amount of contract costs are charged to cost of sales, such that the required amount of gross profit (or loss) is recorded based on the stage of completion of the contract, the contract's ultimate profitability and the degree of certainty of the outcome.

20.83 The turnover recognised on a particular contract will depend on the stage of completion of that contract and the entity's rights to consideration. When, in the contract's early stages, it is not possible to foresee its outcome with reasonable certainty, the related costs recorded in cost of sales will not be less than the recognised turnover (although they may be more if losses are expected on the contract as a whole or if there has been abortive or wasted expenditure). Therefore, no profit will be recognised in the profit and loss account. However, when in the later stages of a contract, the outcome can be assessed with reasonable certainty, it is appropriate to recognise profit and, therefore, turnover would exceed recorded costs.

[The next paragraph is 20.86.]

20.86 The figures to be included in the year's profit and loss account will be both the appropriate amount of turnover and the associated costs of achieving that turnover, to the extent that these exceed amounts recognised in previous years. The estimated outcome of a contract that extends over several accounting years will nearly always vary in the light of changes in circumstances and for this reason the result of the year will not necessarily represent the profit on the contract which is appropriate to the amount of work carried out in the period. It may also reflect the effect of changes in circumstances during the year that affect the total profit estimated to accrue on completion. This is illustrated in the following example.

Example – Calculating turnover, costs and profit recognised during the life of a contract

A construction contractor has a fixed price contract for £11,500. The initial estimate of costs is £7,500 and the contract is expected to take four years. In year two the contractor's estimate of total costs increases to £8,000. Of the £500 increase, £300 is to be incurred in year three and the remainder in year four.

The contractor determines the stage of completion of the contract by comparing the costs of work to date with the estimated total costs as this is a reliable method of determining the right to consideration earned through performance in the case of this particular contract.

	Year 1 £	Year 2 £	Year 3 £	Year 4 £
Turnover agreed in contract	11,500	11,500	11,500	11,500
Contract costs incurred to date	3,000	4,500	6,675	8,000
Contract costs to complete	4,500	3,500	1,325	–
Total estimated costs	7,500	8,000	8,000	8,000
Estimated profit	4,000	3,500	3,500	3,500
Stage of completion	40%	56.3%	83.4%	100%
	(3,000 ÷ 7,500)	(4,500 ÷ 8,000)	(6,675 ÷ 8,000)	

The amount of turnover, costs and profit recognised in the profit and loss account in the four years is as follows:

	To date	Prior years	Current year	Margin
Year 1				
Turnover (11,500 × 40%)	4,600		4,600	
Costs (7,500 × 40%)	3,000		3,000	
Profit	1,600		1,600	(35%)
Year 2				
Turnover (11,500 × 56.3%)	6,475	4,600	1,875	
Costs (8,000 × 56.3%)	4,504	3,000	1,504	
Profit	1,971	1,600	371	(20%)
Year 3				
Turnover (11,500 × 83.4%)	9,591	6,475	3,116	
Costs (8,000 × 83.4%)	6,672	4,504	2,168	
Profit	2,919	1,971	948	(30%)
Year 4				
Turnover	11,500	9,591	1,909	
Costs	8,000	6,672	1,328	
Profit	3,500	2,919	581	(30%)

The profit margin in year two (that is, 20%) is lower than in the subsequent years (that is, 30%) because it takes account of the fact that in the light of the revised estimates, too much profit has been taken in year one when the total estimated costs (and total expected performance) were lower.

If the initial cost estimates had been £8,000, then the percentage completion at the end of year one would have been 37.5% (that is, 3,000 divided by 8,000). This means that turnover of £4,313 (£11,500 × 37.5%) would have been attributed to the costs incurred to date of £3,000 giving a profit of £1,313 compared with the reported profit of £1,600. The turnover recognised in year two is that attributed to the total costs incurred to date, calculated on the basis of the revised estimates, less the turnover of £4,600 reported in year one. Therefore, the results in year two reflect the fact that an adjustment is necessary in respect of year one.

20.87 Contract costs are usually recognised as an expense in the period in which the work to which they relate is performed. However, where contract costs relate to future activity or, where contract completion is not derived from the proportion of costs incurred and recorded costs in the profit and loss are less than those actually incurred, they should be carried forward as work in progress. Where costs incurred to date are used to determine the percentage completion, then turnover attributed to work carried out should not be increased to offset additional costs incurred where these represent inefficiencies. SSAP 9 states that the profit accounted for needs to reflect the proportion of the work carried out at the accounting date and to take into account any known inequalities of profitability in the various stages of a contract. [SSAP 9 para 9]. This is illustrated by the following example.

Example – Determining the stage of completion of a contract

A construction contractor has a fixed price contract for £11,500. The initial estimate of costs is £7,500. The contract is expected to take four years. In year two the contractor's estimate of total costs increases to £8,000 as a result of inefficiencies in year two.

The contractor determines the stage of completion of the contract by comparing the costs of work to date with the estimated total costs – adjusted for inefficiencies.
Method one

	Year 1	Year 2	Year 3	Year 4
	£	£	£	£
Turnover agreed in contract	11,500	11,500	11,500	11,500
Contract costs incurred to date	3,000	5,000	6,875	8,000
Contract costs to complete	4,500	3,000	1,125	–
Total estimated costs	7,500	8,000	8,000	8,000
Estimated profit	4,000	3,500	3,500	3,500
Stage of completion	40% (3,000 ÷ 7,500)	62.5% (5,000 ÷ 8,000)	85.9% (6,875 ÷ 8,000)	100%

The amount of turnover, costs and profit recognised in the profit and loss account in the four years under this method would be as follows:

	To date	Prior years	Current year	Margin
Year 1				
Turnover (11,500 × 40%)	4,600		4,600	
Costs (7,500 × 40%)	3,000		3,000	
Profit	1,600		1,600	(35%)
Year 2				
Turnover (11,500 × 62.5%)	7,188	4,600	2,588	
Costs (8,000 × 62.5%)	5,000	3,000	2,000	
Profit	2,188	1,600	588	(23%)
Year 3				
Turnover (11,500 × 85.9%)	9,879	7,190	2,689	
Costs (8,000 × 85.9%)	6,872	5,000	1,872	
Profit	3,007	2,190	817	(30%)
Year 4				
Turnover	11,500	9,879	1,621	
Costs	8,000	6,872	1,128	
Profit	3,500	3,007	493	(30%)

Under this method the profit in year two is reduced as a result of the inefficiencies. However, part of this inefficiency is being spread forward into years three and four as is evident from the reduced profit margins of 30% compared with 35% in the initial estimates.

In view of the fact that the increased costs result from inefficiencies in year two, it is likely to be more appropriate to recognise the extra £500 inefficiency cost as incurred in year two as set out below.

	Year 1	Year 2	Year 3	Year 4
	£	£	£	£
Contract costs incurred to date	3,000	5,000	6,875	8,000
Total estimated costs	7,500	8,000	8,000	8,000
Stage of completion (Ignoring inefficiencies of £500)	40%	60%	85%	100%
	(3,000 ÷ 7,500)	(4,500 ÷ 7,500)	(6,375 ÷ 7,500)	

The amount of turnover, costs and profit recognised in the profit and loss account in the four years under this method would be as follows:

	To date	Prior years	Current year	Margin
Year 1				
Turnover (11,500 × 40%)	4,600		4,600	
Costs (7,500 × 40%)	3,000		3,000	
Profit	1,600		1,600	(35%)
Year 2				
Turnover (11,500 × 60%)	6,900	4,600	2,300	
Costs: normal (7,500 × 60%)	4,500	3,000	1,500	
inefficiencies	500	–	500	
	5,000	3,000	2,000	
Profit	1,900	1,600	300	(13%)
Year 3				
Turnover (11,500 × 85%)	9,775	6,900	2,875	
Costs: normal (7,500 × 85%)	6,375	4,500	1,875	
inefficiencies	500	500	–	
	6,875	5,000	1,875	
Profit	2,900	1,900	1,000	(35%)
Year 4				
Turnover	11,500	9,775	1,725	
Costs	8,000	6,875	1,125	
Profit	3,500	2,900	600	(35%)

This method is preferred because the inefficiencies are charged to the period in which they are incurred leaving a 'normal' contract profit margin in the subsequent periods.

20.88 No matter what method of determining attributable profit is adopted, it should be applied consistently and from year to year. Paragraph 32 of SSAP 9 requires that the method of ascertaining attributable profits should be stated in the accounting policies. This means that the basis of calculation should be disclosed. An example of a company with an accounting policy note giving details of the method of ascertaining attributable profit is Verson International Group plc which uses the percentage of completion method (see Table 20.13).

Table 20.13 – Method of assertaining attributable profit

Verson International Group plc – Annual Report – 31 January 1994

Accounting Policies (extract)

f) *Stocks and long-term contracts*

In the case of long-term contracts where the group's involvement is principally as a manufacturer, rather than contract manager, turnover represents the estimated contract revenues on work during the year. Contract revenues and profits are computed on the percentage of completion method, primarily by reference to labour hours, profits being determined after making reserves against all anticipated costs including possible warranty claims.

Where the group's involvement in a long-term contract is principally as a contract manager, turnover reflects costs incurred to date in establishing and managing the contract plus the directors' best estimate of profits attributable to the work performed to date. For this purpose the directors' estimate of attributable profits will include a proportion of the total profits anticipated to be made on the contract, to the extent that their realisation is reasonably foreseeable, and after making provision for all future costs including all possible warranty claims.

Long-term contract balances included in stocks comprise costs incurred on long-term contracts, net of amounts transferred to cost of sales, after deducting foreseeable losses and related payments on account. Costs include all direct material and labour costs incurred in bringing a contract to its state of completion at the year end, including an appropriate proportion of indirect expenses. Provisions for estimated losses on contracts are made in the period in which such losses are foreseen. Long-term contract balances do not include attributable profit.

The excess of payments received over amounts recorded as turnover is classified under creditors due within one year. Amounts recoverable on contracts, being the amount by which recorded turnover is in excess of payments on account, is classified under debtors.

Other stocks are stated at the lower of cost and net realisable value.

Provision is made for obsolete, slow-moving or defective items where appropriate.

Determination of future costs

20.89 When a company determines the amount of attributable profit to be recorded, it should take account of the company's type of business, the nature of the contract and the contractual relationship with its customer. Appendix 1 to SSAP 9 states that when estimating profit:

> '*It is necessary to take into account not only the total costs to date and the total estimated further costs to completion . . . but also the estimated future costs of rectification and guarantee work, and any other future work to be undertaken under the contract. These are then compared with the total sales value of the contract.*' [SSAP 9 App 1 para 25].

20.90 The definition of attributable profit requires that it should be calculated, specifically, after estimating 'remedial and maintenance costs'. [SSAP 9 para 23]. In practice, for example, these costs will include the usual snagging clause of a building contract (that is, the clauses covering completion of the finishing touches to a building).

20.91 In considering future costs, it is necessary to have regard to likely increases in wages and salaries, to likely increases in the price of raw materials and to rises in general overheads. Also, if interest on borrowings financing specific long-term contracts is capitalised (see chapter 16), then the calculation of total cost should include future interest costs.

Variations and claims

20.92 A variation is an instruction by the customer for a change in the scope of the work to be performed under the contract. Examples are changes in the specifications or designs of an asset and changes in the contract's duration.

20.93 Where approved variations have been made to a contract during its course and the amount to be received in respect of these variations has not yet been settled and is likely to be a material factor in the outcome, it is necessary to make a reasonable estimate of the amount likely to be received and this is then treated as part of the total sales value. On the other hand, allowance needs to be made for foreseeable penalties payable arising out of delays in completion or from other causes.

20.94 A claim is an amount that the contractor seeks to collect from the customer or another party as reimbursement for costs not included in the contract price. A claim may arise from, for example, errors in the initial specifications and delays caused by the customer.

20.95 The settlement of claims arising from circumstances not envisaged in the contract or arising as an indirect consequence of approved variations is subject to a high level of uncertainty relating to the outcome of future negotiations. In view of this, it is generally prudent to recognise receipts in respect of such claims only when negotiations have reached an advanced stage and there is sufficient evidence of the acceptability of the claim by the customer, with an indication of the amount involved also being available. Trafalgar House Plc provides an example of an accounting policy for claims on contracts (see Table 20.14). Another example is shown in Table 20.12.

Table 20.14 – Accounting policy concerning claims on contracts

Trafalgar House Plc – Report and Accounts – 30 September 1994

Principal accounting policies (extract)

g) Long-term contracts (extract)

Amounts recoverable on contracts (other than small works) are valued at anticipated net sales value of work done after provision for contingencies and anticipated future losses on contracts. Claims are included in the valuation of contracts and credited to the profit and loss account when entitlement has been established.

Losses on contracts

20.96 If it is expected that there will be a loss on a contract as a whole, all of the loss should be recognised as soon as it is foreseen. [SSAP 9 para 11].

20.97 Foreseeable losses are defined as losses which are currently estimated to arise over the duration of the contract (after allowing for estimated remedial and maintenance costs and increases in costs so far as not recoverable under the terms of the contract). This estimate is required irrespective of:

- Whether or not work has yet commenced on such contracts.
- The proportion of work carried out at the accounting date.
- The amount of profits expected to arise on other contracts.

[SSAP 9 para 24].

20.98 Where unprofitable contracts are of such magnitude that they can be expected to utilise a considerable part of the company's capacity for a substantial period, related administration overheads to be incurred during the period to the completion of those contracts should also be included in calculating the provision for losses. [SSAP 9 para 11].

Cost of sales

20.99 Turnover is always determined based on percentage of completion, while the profit recorded depends on the expected outcome of the contract, the degree of certainty surrounding this outcome and the percentage completion. As such, the costs to be recorded are the balancing figure between recorded turnover and profit. However, for a profitable contract where percentage of completion is determined by reference to costs incurred to date, costs are typically recorded as incurred.

20.100 Cost of sales will include costs that relate directly to the specific contract and also other costs that can be allocated to the contract. Costs that relate directly to the contract may include:

- Site labour costs.
- Costs of materials used in construction.
- Transport costs of plant and equipment to and from the site.
- Depreciation of plant and equipment used on the site.
- Design and technical costs related to the contract.
- The estimated costs of rectification and guarantee work.

20.101 Other costs that may be allocated to the contract include insurance, construction overheads and supervision costs.

20.102 Cost of sales will also normally include provisions made in respect of a loss making contract. An example of provisions for losses on contracts shown within cost of sales is shown in Table 20.15.

Table 20.15 – Treatment of provisions for losses on contracts

Trafalgar House Plc – Report and Accounts – 30 September 1993
Notes to the Accounts

2 Exceptional items (extract)

Total exceptional items included in continuing operations have been allocated to the following statutory headings:

	Note	1993 £m	1992 £m
Cost of sales			
Current asset write downs			
Commercial developments	*(f)*	**(87.2)**	(0.9)
Residential developments	*(g)*	**(16.7)**	(38.9)

(f) Commercial development properties have been valued by the directors at the lower of cost and net realisable value. The write downs of commercial developments relate principally to the following items:

- US business parks where, during the year, the directors have decided to accelerate the group's withdrawal from this activity and have therefore written down the developments to estimated disposal values expected to be achieved.
- The Paddington Basin developments where the directors believe there is now insufficient certainty that the development can be completed within the timescale previously envisaged and have therefore written down the development to the current value of the group's interests in the site, having regard to the group's obligations under the terms of its developments agreement with British Waterways Board.

(g) The write downs of residential developments reflect the effect of the decision, taken by the directors during the year, to withdraw from the group's activities in Portugal and a provision in respect of UK residential development.

20.102.1 Another issue that arises is in connection with costs incurred before a contract starts. The UITF addressed this matter in Abstract 34, 'Pre-contract costs'. This is discussed further in chapter 3. However, in summary, pre-contract costs may only be carried forward where it is virtually certain that the contract will be won. In such cases these costs will form part of the total contract cost.

Amounts recoverable on contracts

20.103 Amounts recorded as turnover in respect of a contract are treated as debtors to the extent that they are unpaid.

[The next paragraph is 20.105.]

20.105 A long-term contract bears the characteristics of any legally binding contract so that the contractor may sue for any monies rightfully owed by the customer. This implies that amounts receivable for work completed under a long-term contract can, correctly, be regarded as debtors. In addition, there is no necessity to disclose any further details, such as the profit element included in the debtor, in the notes to the financial statements.

Disclosure

20.106 Long-term contracts should be disclosed in the balance sheet as follows:

- The amount by which recorded turnover is in excess of payments on account should be classified as 'amounts recoverable on contracts' and separately disclosed within debtors.
- The balance of payments on account (in excess of amounts matched with turnover, and offset against long-term contract balances) should be classified as 'payments on account' and separately disclosed within creditors.
- The amount of long-term contracts, at costs incurred (net of amounts transferred to cost of sales) after deducting foreseeable losses and payments on account not matched with turnover, should be classified as 'long-term contract balances' and separately disclosed within the balance sheet heading 'stocks'. The balance sheet note should disclose separately the balances of:
- Net cost less foreseeable losses.
- Applicable payments on account.
- The amount by which the provision or accrual for foreseeable losses exceeds the costs incurred (after transfers to cost of sales) should be included within either 'provisions for liabilities and charges' or 'creditors' as appropriate.

[SSAP 9 para 30].

20.107 'Payments on account' are defined as all amounts received and receivable at the accounting date in respect of contracts in progress. [SSAP 9 para 25].

20.108 The accounting policies that have been applied to long-term contracts, in particular the method of ascertaining turnover and attributable profit, should be stated and applied consistently within the business and from year to year. [SSAP 9 para 32]. An example of typical disclosure for long-term contracts is George Wimpey PLC (see Table 20.12).

20.109 Each of the above balance sheet disclosure requirements is illustrated in the examples that follow:

Example – Turnover exceeds payments on account

	£'000
Turnover (value of work done and rights to consideration earned)	52
Cumulative payments on account	45
Excess – *included in debtors*	7
Balance of costs on this contract not transferred to cost of sales – *included in stocks*	10
Balance sheet (extract)	
Stocks	
Work in progress	
Net cost less foreseeable losses	10
Debtors	
Amounts recoverable on contracts	7

20.110 In the above example, the value of work included in turnover for the particular contract exceeds the progress payments received and receivable to date on that same contract. In accordance with SSAP 9, the excess amount is classified as 'amounts recoverable on contracts' and is shown separately under the heading 'debtors' in the balance sheet formats. The balance of costs not transferred to cost of sales is shown as work in progress.

Example – Payments on account exceed turnover

	£'000
Turnover (value of work done and rights to consideration earned)	52
Cumulative payments on account	60
Excess – *reduces stocks*	8
Balance of costs on this contract not transferred to cost of sales – *included in stocks*	10
Balance sheet (extract)	
Stocks	
Work in progress	
Net cost less foreseeable losses	10
Applicable payments on account	(8)
	2

20.111 In this example, there is nothing to be included as 'amounts recoverable on contracts', because all turnover has been invoiced as payments on account and so will either be included in trade debtors or will have been received.

20.112 The amount included in work in progress comprises the total costs incurred to date less:

- Amounts transferred to cost of sales in the profit and loss account in respect of work carried out to date.
- Any foreseeable losses.
- Any applicable payments on account, that is, those in excess of turnover.

The balance sheet note should disclose separately both the net cost less foreseeable losses and the applicable payments on account.

Example – Payments on account exceed turnover and balance of costs on contracts

	£'000
Turnover (value of work done and rights to consideration earned)	52
Cumulative payments on account	60
Excess – *part reduces stocks/and part included in creditors*	8
Balance of costs on this contract not transferred to cost of sales – *included in stocks*	5
Balance sheet (extract)	
Stocks	
Work in progress	
Net cost less foreseeable losses	5
Applicable payments on account	(5)
	–
Creditors	
Payments on account (£8,000 – £5,000)	3

20.113 In this example, payments on account exceed both the amount of recorded turnover and the balance of costs incurred to date included in stocks. The excess amount is classified as 'payments on account' and separately disclosed in 'creditors'.

20.114 An example of balance sheet disclosure for long-term contracts is provided by George Wimpey PLC (see Table 20.16). The accounting policy note is shown in Table 20.12.

Table 20.16 — Disclosure of long-term contracts

George Wimpey PLC — Annual Report — 31 December 1994

NOTES ON THE ACCOUNTS

15 Work in Progress and Stock

	Group	
	1994 **£m**	1993 £m
Long-term contract balances		
– net cost less foreseeable losses	**11.8**	11.6
– less applicable payments on account	**(11.2)**	(11.4)
Net valuation	**0.6**	0.2
Land development and construction	**504.8**	473.3
Other stock	**20.6**	20.0
	526.0	493.5

17 Debtors (extract)

	Group		**Parent**	
	1994 **£m**	1993 £m	**1994** **£m**	1993 £m
Receivable within one year:				
– trade debtors	**80.1**	78.7	–	–
– amounts recoverable on long-term contracts	**62.1**	56.0	–	–
– amounts owed by subsidiary undertakings	**–**	–	**140.4**	186.6
– amounts owed by associated undertakings	**2.1**	1.7	–	–
– prepayments and accrued income	**8.2**	5.9	**0.2**	–
– corporate taxation	**9.2**	12.2	**2.1**	–
– other	**15.7**	13.1	–	–
	177.4	167.6	**142.7**	186.6

18 Creditors Falling Due Within One Year

	Group		Parent	
	1994	1993	**1994**	1993
	£m	£m	**£m**	£m
Finance debt (Note 20)	**17.3**	14.2	**3.5**	0.3
Trade creditors	**313.5**	309.1	–	–
Payments received on account on long-term contracts	**53.2**	53.7	–	–
Amounts owed to subsidiary undertakings	–	–	**86.7**	173.0
Amounts owed to associated undertakings	**0.4**	0.1	–	–
National insurance, VAT and other taxes	**9.9**	0.1	–	–
Accruals and deferred income	**12.8**	10.6	–	–
Corporate taxation	**36.2**	30.3	**3.4**	5.0
Proposed dividend* (Note 6)	**12.6**	11.7	**12.6**	11.7
Other	**13.4**	11.1	**1.9**	1.6
	469.3	449.9	**108.1**	191.6

* Note that for years beginning on or after 1 January 2005, the recognition of proposed dividends as liabilities is prohibited by FRS 21.

Provision for foreseeable losses

20.115 Where a contact is expected to be loss-making, the expected loss must be provided for in full as soon as it is foreseen. [SSAP 9 para 11]. Turnover is still recognised based on the stage of completion, but recorded costs will significantly exceed those actually incurred to date in order that a cumulative gross loss equal to the expected contract loss is reported.

Example – Treatment of provisions for forseeable losses

	£'000
Turnover (value of work done and rights to consideration earned)	52
Cumulative payments on account	45
Excess – *included in debtors*	7
Total costs on this contract	50
Transferred to cost of sales	40
Balance – *included in stocks*	10
Provision/accrual for foreseeable losses – *included in cost of sales in the profit and loss account. In the balance sheet part reduces stocks and part is included in liabilities*	30

Profit and loss account (extract)

Turnover	52
Cost of sales (£40,000 + £30,000)	(70)
Loss	(18)

Balance sheet (extract)

Stocks	
Work in progress	
Net cost less foreseeable losses (£10,000 – £10,000)	–
Debtors	
Amounts recoverable on contracts	7
Liabilities	
Provision/accrual (£30,000 – £10,000 deducted from stocks)	20

20.116 In this example, foreseeable losses exceed the total costs incurred after transfers to cost of sales by £20,000 and the excess should be included in either accruals or provisions, as appropriate.

20.117 SSAP 9 provides no guidance on when these losses should be shown as an accrual and when they should be shown as a provision. The treatment used would appear to depend on the contract's state of completion at the time the financial statements are finalised. A provision is defined in FRS 12 as:

> '*A liability of uncertain timing or amount.*' [FRS 12 para 2].

20.118 Provisions can be distinguished from accruals in that the degree of uncertainty as to timing and amount is considerably lower in the case of an accrual. Typically where a contract is loss-making the degree of subjectivity over the loss, and hence the amount of costs provided for, can be significant and typically such liabilities would be reported as provisions on the balance sheet. For profitable contracts, where it is necessary to accrue for additional costs as a result of a mismatch between the stage of completion and costs actually incurred these amounts are typically far smaller and much easier to reliably estimate. Hence, they are typically presented as accruals within creditors.

	£'000
Profit and loss account (extract)	
Turnover	32
Cost of sales (£20,000 + £30,000)	(50)
Loss	(18)
Balance sheet (extract)	
Stocks	
Work in progress	
Net cost less foreseeable losses (£10,000 − £10,000)	–
Debtors	
Amounts recoverable on contracts	–
Liabilities	
Provision/accrual (£30,000 – £10,000 deducted from stocks)	20

20.116 In this example, foreseeable losses exceed the total costs incurred (after transfers to cost of sales) by £20,000 and the excess should be included in either accruals or provisions, as appropriate.

20.117 SSAP 9 provides no guidance on when these losses should be shown as an accrual and when they should be shown as a provision. The treatment used would appear to depend on the contract's state of completion at the time the financial statements are finalised. A provision is defined in FRS 12 as:

"A liability of uncertain timing or amount." [FRS 12 para 2]

20.118 Provisions can be distinguished from accruals in that the degree of uncertainty as to timing and amount is considerably lower in the case of an accrual. Typically where a contract is loss-making the degree of subjectivity over the loss, and hence the amount of loss provided for, can be significant and typically such liabilities would be reported as provisions on the balance sheet. For profitable contracts, where it is necessary to accrue for additional costs as a result of a mismatch between the stage of completion and costs actually incurred these amounts are typically far smaller and much easier to reliably estimate. Hence, they are typically presented as accruals within creditors.

Chapter 21

Provisions, contingencies and commitments

Chapter 21

Provisions, contingencies and commitments

Introduction

21.1 A liability is defined in FRS 12, 'Provisions, contingent liabilities and contingent assets', as *"obligations of an entity to transfer economic benefits as a result of past transactions or events"*. A provision falls within the category of liabilities and is defined as *"a liability of uncertain timing or amount"*. [FRS 12 para 2]. FRS 12 sets out rules on the recognition, measurement and disclosure of provisions. The standard also sets out rules for contingent liabilities and contingent assets.

Objective and scope

Scope of FRS 12

21.2 The objectives of FRS 12 are to ensure (i) that appropriate recognition criteria and measurement bases are applied to provisions, contingent liabilities and contingent assets and (ii) that sufficient information is disclosed in the notes to the financial statements to enable users to understand their nature, timing and amount.

21.3 The standard applies to all companies accounting for provisions, contingent liabilities and contingent assets, except:

- Those arising from executory contracts, where the contract is other than onerous. [FRS 12 para 3(b)].
- Financial instruments (including guarantees) that are carried at fair value (see para 21.5 onwards). [FRS 12 para 3(a)].
- Those covered by another standard dealing with a more specific type of provision, contingent liability or contingent asset, such as: long-term contracts (SSAP 9); deferred tax (FRS 19); leases (SSAP 21), except for onerous operating leases and retirement benefits (FRS 17), although FRS 12 does apply to provisions, contingent liabilities and contingent assets of an insurer other than those arising from its contractual obligations and rights under insurance contracts within IFRS 4's scope. [FRS 12 paras 3(d), 8].
- Those arising in insurance companies from contracts with policy-holders, although FRS 12 does apply to other provisions, contingent liabilities and contingent assets of insurance companies. [FRS 12 para 3(c), 7].

21.4 Additionally, FRS 12 does not address revenue recognition and does not, therefore, change the requirements of FRS 5 Application Note G, 'Revenue recognition'. Furthermore, FRS 12 does not specify whether expenditures are treated as expenses or assets when a provision is made.

21.5 Some provisions meet the definition of a financial instrument. FRS 25, 'Financial instruments: Presentation', defines a financial instrument as *"any contract that gives rise to a financial asset of one entity and a financial liability or equity instrument of another entity"*. [FRS 25 para 11]. FRS 12 states that it does not apply to provisions resulting from financial instruments that are within FRS 26's scope (for those companies applying this standard).

21.6 The list in paragraph 21.3 above of exclusions from FRS 12's scope refers to executory contracts, which are contracts under which neither party has performed any of its obligations or both parties have partially performed their obligations to an equal extent. Executory contracts encompass commitments to purchase goods or to deliver services where performance has not yet happened. In some situations these types of contracts might be onerous and where they are, the requirements in FRS 12 concerning onerous contracts should be applied (see further para 21.168 onwards).

21.7 The word 'provision' is often used to describe amounts that are deducted from assets to arrive at their balance sheet carrying amount. For example, provisions are made for depreciation or amortisation or impairment of assets and provisions are made for bad and doubtful debts. These types of provisions do not fall within FRS 12's scope, because they relate to the measurement of assets and are merely adjustments made to arrive at the asset's appropriate carrying value. [FRS 12 para 9].

21.8 In addition to FRS 12, company law also defines provisions as, *"any amount retained as reasonably necessary for the purpose of providing for any liability the nature of which is clearly defined and which is either likely to be incurred, or certain to be incurred but uncertain as to amount or as to the date on which it will arise."* [SI 2008/410 9 Sch 2]. Appendix V to FRS 12 states that taken in their respective contexts, this definition is consistent with that in FRS 12 as stated above in paragraph 21.1.

Provisions versus other liabilities

21.9 A provision is simply defined as *"a liability of uncertain timing or amount"*. [FRS 12 para 2]. Consequently, like other liabilities, for a provision to be necessary a company must have an obligation that is expected to result in an outflow of resources embodying economic benefits and that results from a past transaction or event.

21.10 The standard clearly makes a distinction between provisions and other categories of liabilities and sets detailed measurement and recognition rules that apply to particular types of provisions, although the basic definition of a liability applies to other categories of creditors as well as to provisions. The only difference between other liabilities and provisions is the degree of certainty about the amount of the payment or the timing of the payment. Hence, there is a clear distinction between provisions and other liabilities such as trade creditors and accruals.

21.11 Trade creditors form a separate line item in the balance sheet under Schedule 1 to SI 2008/410. This item should only include liabilities to pay for goods or services that have been received or supplied and that have been invoiced or formally agreed with the supplier. [FRS 12 para 11(a)]. Amounts arising from a contract are formally agreed. So, for example, an operating lease obligation would be a trade payable. Similarly, a contract to purchase a certain amount of a commodity per month would constitute a creditor at the month end even though an invoice might not have been raised.

21.12 Also, a distinction has to be made between accruals and provisions. Accruals are often reported within creditors, whereas provisions are reported separately. [SI 2008/410 1 Sch].

21.13 While there is little if any uncertainty relating to the amount of a creditor or the timing of when it becomes due, there is some uncertainty with an accrual, which primarily arises because an invoice has not yet been received at the balance sheet date. However, typically, a very good estimate can be made of the amount due at the period end and the timing of the payment is often certain (to within a short period of time). So accruals are a category of liability to pay for goods or services that have been supplied, but not yet paid for and where no invoice has been received or formally agreed with the supplier. [FRS 12 para 11(b)].

21.14 A familiar example is the supply of electricity. At the period end the company can make a very good estimate, or can measure the quantity, of electricity consumed within the business that has not been paid for and either by using current rates or previous bills can calculate the amount that is likely to be due. The amount of the liability is almost certain if the estimate is reliable and the timing of the payment is known to within a few days. Although an accrual is estimated and the timing of the payment is not known exactly, the degree of uncertainty is much less than that associated with a provision.

21.15 Goods and services supplied by utility companies such as electricity (see above), water and gas reflect common examples of accruals. In contrast, rent should be classified as a creditor, because the obligation arises under a contract and is formally agreed. Amounts due to employees relating to short-term holiday pay would usually be accounted for as an accrual. For example, a company with a factory that closes for three weeks in summer would accrue three weeks pay per worker over the year until the summer holiday.

21.16 The following table further identifies the types of liabilities that are usually presented as provisions and those that are presented as other liabilities.

Nature of the obligation	Provision	Other liabilities	Comments
Warranties given for goods or services sold (see para 21.206)	✓		
Refunds given for goods sold (see para 21.212)	✓		
Payments for damages connected with legal cases that are probable (see para 21.193 onwards)	✓		
Dilapidations payable at the end of an operating lease (see para 21.219)	✓		
Interest payments		✓	Accrual – the service has been received and the timing and amount of payment is known.
Holiday pay earned by employees		✓	Accrual – short-term compensated absences – see paragraph 21.15.
Property rentals		✓	Accrual – the service has been received and the timing and amount of payment is known.
Ordinary dividend declared and appropriately authorised before the period end		✓	Recognise as a current financial liability

Recognition

Definition of a provision

21.17 A provision is very simply defined in FRS 12 as *"a liability of uncertain timing or amount"*. [FRS 12 para 2].

21.18 As explained in the introduction (see para 21.1), a provision falls within the definition of a liability with the added feature that there is uncertainty over the amount to be paid or the timing of the payment. Liabilities are *"obligations of an entity to transfer economic benefits as a result of past transactions or events"*. [FRS 12 para 2].

21.19 It is clear from the definition of a liability given above, that it does not generally include expected future operating losses. Obviously, the reason future operating losses do not meet this definition is that they do not stem from a past event (see further para 21.36).

21.20 Where a company is expected to incur future operating losses, rather than indicating that a provision should be made, this might suggest that an impairment review should be carried out on the appropriate income generating unit (IGU) in accordance with the rules in FRS 11, 'Impairment of fixed assets and goodwill', or, where applicable, with the rules in other standards, for example, FRS 26, 'Financial instruments: Recognition and measurement' (if adopted). Such a review would then expose whether those assets have suffered an impairment and need to be written down.

21.21 Expected future trading losses might also indicate that a company has an onerous contract. In certain circumstances it is necessary to provide for the onerous element of a contract and the requirements in FRS 12 in this area are considered from paragraph 21.168.

Provision recognition criteria

21.22 Following from the definition of a provision above, the standard requires that a provision should only be recognised where all of the following conditions are met:

- An entity has a present obligation (legal or constructive) as a result of a past event.
- It is probable that an outflow of resources embodying economic benefits will be required to settle the obligation.
- A reliable estimate can be made of the amount of the obligation.

[FRS 12 para 14].

21.23 In order to comprehend the recognition criteria outlined above, it is first necessary to understand the meaning of the terms 'present obligation', 'past event' and 'reliable estimate'.

Present obligation

21.24 A present obligation can stem from a legal agreement (a 'legal obligation') or may be constructive in nature (a 'constructive obligation').

Legal obligations

21.25 Whether or not a legal obligation exists will usually be relatively easy to establish in practice as it derives either from a contract (through its explicit or implicit terms), or from legislation, or from the operation of the law.

21.26 A legal obligation can arise, for example, where a company operates an oilfield in the North Sea and its licensing agreement requires that the oil rig it constructs is removed and the seabed is restored at the end of the licence period. The licence forms the contract under which the obligation arises. An obligation can also arise where a government passes a new Act which requires, for example, certain environmental damage that has already been caused to be rectified. But it is important to realise that in such a circumstance the obligation will only arise once the law becomes operative or is virtually certain that it will become law (see further from para 21.39 below).

21.27 Manufacturers' standard warranties given at the time a sale is made are also examples of legal obligations even where the defect arises a number of years later (if the warranty is still effective), as they arise from the contract entered into with the customer at the time the original sale was made. The accounting for warranties is dealt with in more detail in paragraph 21.206 onwards. Obligations arising from onerous contracts (see from para 21.168) are also examples of legal obligations, because they arise from a contractual burden.

Constructive obligations

21.28 A constructive obligation will often be more difficult to discern in practice than a legal obligation as it derives from an entity's actions:

"(a) *by an established pattern of past practice, published policies or a sufficiently specific current statement, the entity has indicated to other parties that it will accept certain responsibilities; and*

(b) *as a result, the entity has created a valid expectation on the part of those other parties that it will discharge those responsibilities.*"

[FRS 12 para 2].

21.29 Some constructive obligations will be obvious, for example, many retailers have policies of giving cash refunds to dissatisfied customers whether or not the goods they bought are faulty. Such a policy is clearly over and above any legal obligation, but a constructive obligation arises from the retailer's established or published practice. In contrast, *ad hoc* refunds would be less clear in establishing any obligation. In some circumstances, for example where a company has published its environmental policies, this might also give rise to a constructive obligation, where no legal obligation exists, as there is no law compelling the company to carry out the environmental rectification. Clearly, the essence of a constructive obligation is the company's commitment to a third party. That commitment arises through the company's actions, that is, by establishing a pattern of practice or by publishing its policies or by making a statement setting out in detail its intended future actions.

Uncertainty as to whether a present obligation exists

21.30 The standard points out that in rare circumstances where there has been a past event it may not be clear whether there is a *present obligation*. In these situations, a past event is deemed by FRS 12 to give rise to a present obligation if, after taking account of all the available evidence, it is more likely than not that a present obligation exists at the balance sheet date. [FRS 12 para 15].

21.31 The issue here is not to determine whether the *outflow of resources embodying economic benefits* is probable (which is considered in para 21.47 below), but whether the *past event* gives rise to a *present obligation*. The principal difficulty in this area concerns litigation. Often in a legal case the events might be disputed by the parties. Because of the uncertainty concerning the past event it will be unclear whether a present obligation exists. In this type of situation, it may be necessary for a company to obtain an expert's opinion in order to determine, after taking into account all the available evidence, whether or not a present obligation arises for which provision is required. The standard requires that on the basis of such information:

- Where it is more likely than not that a present obligation exists at that balance sheet date, the company should recognise a provision (if the recognition criteria are met).

- Where it is more likely that no present obligation exists at the balance sheet date, the company should disclose a contingent liability, unless the possibility of an outflow of resources embodying economic benefit is remote, in which case no disclosure is required (see further para 21.61).

[FRS 12 para 16].

21.32 An example where there is uncertainty over whether a past event gives rise to a present obligation, is illustrated in the following example.

Example – Obligating events – regulatory notification

Company A has received notice from the governmental environment agency that official investigations will be made into claims of pollution caused by the company. Neighbours living near company A's factory claim that its operations have caused ground water contamination. The investigation will only consider whether company A has caused contamination and, if so, what penalties and fines should be levied on it.

Manufacturing operations have been conducted at the site for 150 years; however, company A acquired the factory only 50 years ago. Company A has used toxins at the plant, but only to an extent that is unlikely to cause pollution, according to available records. However, management is not sure whether it has all the information about the entire 50 years. Therefore, neither management nor external experts are able to assess company A's responsibility until the investigation is completed.

How should management account for a liability where it is not possible to reliably assess whether a present obligation exists?

FRS 12, paragraph 15, recognises that, in rare cases, it is not clear whether there is a present obligation. In these cases, a past event is deemed to give rise to a present obligation if, taking account of all available evidence, it is more likely than not that a present obligation exists at the balance sheet date. In this case, there is a limitation on the available evidence and management considers all the available evidence in assessing whether or not a present obligation exists. The available evidence does not support a conclusion that a present obligation exists. Therefore, management should disclose the contingent liability for potential penalties and fines that may be imposed if past contamination is proved, but should not recognise a liability for this at the balance sheet date.

The obligating event would be the contamination in the past by company A, not the future investigation. However, management cannot determine whether the obligating event has occurred until the investigation is complete. In accordance with FRS 21, any new evidence as to the existence of the obligating event, that becomes available after the balance sheet date up to the date of approval of the financial statements, is an adjusting event in assessing whether a present obligation existed at the balance sheet date.

If, and to the extent that, the company is obligated at the balance sheet date to meet any costs of the investigation, irrespective of the outcome of the investigation, the company recognises a liability for such costs at the balance sheet date.

21.33 This requirement introduces probability into assessing whether or not a liability exists. The term 'probable' is used extensively in international standards. Here, probable is often taken to mean that the chance of occurrence is 'likely'. 'More likely than not' would seem to suggest more than 50 per cent. In fact paragraph 23 of FRS 12 confirms this view as it indicates (in considering the term 'probable' as it applies to an outflow of economic benefits) that 'more likely than not' means that the *"...probability that the event will occur is greater than the probability that it will not"*.

21.34 Further information might become available between the balance sheet date and the date on which a company's financial statements are finalised. Where this is so, that information should be taken into account in determining whether or not a present obligation exists at the balance sheet date. [FRS 12 para 16]. For example, in a legal case evidence might come to light after the balance sheet date, which clearly indicates that a past event giving rise to an obligation arose before the balance sheet date. However, a provision should not be made at the period end where the obligating event occurs after the balance sheet date (see further para 21.80).

21.35 Another instance where post balance sheet evidence is taken into account in determining whether a provision should be recognised is where a company 'self insures' some of its risks for example, from potential damages resulting from use of its products. At the balance sheet date provision will be made for claims that have been incurred but are not yet reported (that is, IBNR claims – see further para 21.292). During the period between the company's balance sheet date and the date on which its financial statements are finalised, a number of previously unreported claims might have surfaced, in which case a more accurate estimate for these IBNR claims can be made. Of course it will still be necessary to estimate and provide for claims that have not yet been reported but that are likely to be, where these arise from events that occurred before the balance sheet date.

Past event

21.36 In order for there to be a liability and a need to make a provision, it is necessary for something to have happened in the past (a 'past event') to trigger a present obligation. The past event is known in FRS 12 as the 'obligating event'. An 'obligating event' is *"an event that creates a legal or constructive obligation that results in an entity having no realistic alternative to settling that obligation"*. [FRS 12 para 2]. Many obligating events are obvious; for example, the obligating event giving rise to the need to make a warranty provision is the original sale of the warrantied goods. Similarly, with the contamination of land, the obligating event is the original contamination. Some obligating events can occur over a period of time. For example, an obligating event might arise when an oil rig is first built relating to its eventual removal, but other obligating events might arise over time as oil and gas are extracted from the resulting well, where there is a need subsequently to make good any damage caused by that extraction.

21.37 Another example where past events give rise to obligating events over a period of time is open cast mining. Here, the environmental damage is done as the top soil is removed and coal is dug out. The obligating event occurs as the damage is caused and provision should be made progressively for the necessary rectification work that will need to be undertaken in the future to restore the site to its pre-agreed condition.

21.38 The notion of 'no realistic alternative' is at the heart of the definition of an obligating event. It means that if there is a realistic possibility that the company can avoid settlement, no obligation arises. A company has no realistic alternative to settling an obligation only where:

- The settlement of the obligation can be enforced by law.
- The event, in the case of a constructive obligation, creates a valid expectation in others that the company will discharge the obligation.

[FRS 12 para 17].

Legal enforcement

21.39 The first of the bullet points in paragraph 21.38 above is relatively straightforward. However, even with legal enforcement, problems can arise where legislation is in process but not yet on the statute book, or where the law has been passed but the enforcement date has not yet been reached. For example, where environmental damage has occurred prior to period end, if there is no current law to require clean-up, but it is virtually certain that one will be passed shortly after the period end, there will be a present obligation that results from a past event (because the law enforcement is virtually certain and the contamination has already taken place). Such an obligation is treated as a legal obligation, because the legislation is virtually certain to be enacted as drafted. [FRS 12 para 22]. On the other hand, where the environmental legislation is still in its infancy (for example, where only a preliminary paper has been issued) no obligation exists, because although the potentially obligating event has taken place (that is the contamination of the land) there is as yet no obligation that can be enforced by law.

21.40 In contrast, a company might need to operate in a particular way in the future, because of commercial pressure or legal requirements. [FRS 12 para 19]. For example, legislation might require a company to fit smoke filters to its chimneys by a fixed future date in order to continue operating. This requirement, although legal in nature, relates to the company's future operations. If legislation exists but the enforcement date has not yet been reached, no obligation arises to fit the smoke filters. Once the enforcement date has been reached, still no obligation arises to fit the filters as the factory could cease operating and avoid the cost, although an obligation might arise for any fines for non-compliance with the legislation.

21.41 It is clear from the examples above that although some circumstances result in potentially obligating events, a provision should not be made, because there is no legal or constructive obligation. However, over time the legal position could change and what was originally a potential obligation (see further para 21.61) might become an actual obligation for which provision is required.

21.42 Because of the different legal jurisdictions in which a company might trade, it is very difficult to set specific rules to identify when enactment of a law might be virtually certain. This will be a matter of judgement after considering the legal due process in each particular country. The standard comments that in many cases it will be impossible to be virtually certain of the enactment of a law until it is actually enacted. [FRS 12 para 22].

Third party expectation

21.43 In practice, companies may have more difficulty in determining exactly when a constructive obligation arises from which they cannot realistically withdraw. Here the expectation of other parties is the key. For example, a company's board might have taken a decision to undertake a major restructuring programme, but until its plans are actually being carried out or they have been communicated to others to the extent that the company cannot realistically withdraw from its course of action (that is, when it has no realistic alternative but to carry it through) no obligation exists and no provision for restructuring should be made.

21.44 Although the expectation of other parties is critical, the standard comments that it is not necessary to know the other party's identity for an obligation to arise. [FRS 12 para 20]. This is clearly the case with warranted goods, as a company cannot know which of its customers will claim under a standard warranty, but an obligation still arises from a general commitment to those who buy the product. Similarly, with a restructuring programme, there needs to be a valid expectation created in those affected by it in a *"sufficiently specific manner"* that the company has no alternative but to discharge its responsibilities. [FRS 12 para 20]. Consequently, it is not acceptable under FRS 12 to make a provision for restructuring where the company's board has merely decided on such a course of action before its year end, but its plan is not actioned or communicated sufficiently until the new year. Restructuring programmes are specifically dealt with in FRS 12 and are considered in more detail from paragraph 21.126.

21.45 Where a potentially obligating event has taken place (such as environmental damage), but where no legal obligation exists, a constructive obligation could arise, for example, where the company makes a public statement that in future it will rectify such damage. Again it is necessary that the public announcement carries such weight that it leaves the company no alternative but to carry out the rectification work.

21.46 In practice there will often be situations where it appears that a constructive obligation exists, but because it can be avoided, no obligating event has occurred. For example in the airline industry, the licensing authorities require aircraft to undergo major engine overhauls at regular intervals (say every five years). Without the overhaul, the aircraft cannot renew its licence and continue to fly. Prior to FRS 12, one way of accounting for the costs of an overhaul was to provide for them over the period to the next overhaul. Following the rules outlined above, it is no longer possible to provide for these costs, because no obligating event arises prior to the overhaul taking place. This is because the airline operator can avoid the costs by, for example, selling the aircraft or otherwise discontinuing its use. The proper accounting treatment now is either (i) to charge the maintenance as incurred or (ii) to identify the cost of the element of the aircraft which will wear out over the five-year period and amortise this to profit or loss. Then when the overhaul takes place, the relevant replacement costs can be capitalised to replace the fully-amortised original cost, the new cost again being amortised over the period to the next overhaul (see further para 21.215). Accounting for overhaul costs is dealt with in FRS 15, 'Tangible fixed assets' – see further chapter 16.

Probable outflow of economic benefits

21.47 Once it has been established that a present obligation exists (that is, it is at least more likely than not to exist) it is then necessary to determine whether this will result in the outflow of resources embodying economic benefits to settle the obligation. This judgement is similarly determined on the probability of the outcome. The standard says that also in this case *"an outflow of resources or other event is regarded as probable if the event is more likely than not to occur..."*. [FRS 12 para 23]. The same thresholds as discussed in paragraph 21.33 apply in this analysis, that is 'more likely than not' means a probability of more than 50 per cent that the transfer will occur. Where the probability of the outflow of economic benefits is below 50 per cent, no provision is necessary, but a contingent liability will exist, which will require disclosure in the financial statements unless the contingency is remote.

21.48 With litigation, not only will there be a need to assess whether or not the evidence supports the fact that a past event has occurred (that is, that there is a case to answer), but there will also be a need to consider whether or not it is probable that an outflow of economic benefits will result from the obligation. Again, it might be necessary to seek an expert's advice to determine the amount that might have to be settled and for which provision should be made.

Reliable estimate

21.49 In extremely rare cases, there will be situations where it will not be possible for even an expert to make a reliable estimate of the obligation such that a provision can be made. In this type of circumstance, because of the uncertainty in the measurement of the obligation, the liability is disclosed as a contingent liability. [FRS 12 para 26]. (See further the disclosure requirements concerning contingent liabilities from para 21.324.)

21.50 The standard emphasises that, in nearly all cases, a company will be able to determine a range of possible outcomes and will generally be competent to make an estimate of an obligation that will be sufficiently reliable to use in recognising a provision. [FRS 12 para 25]. The standard does not, however, elaborate further on the type of situations where a provision would not be made. Clearly, in circumstances where the amount is uncertain (as opposed to the timing being uncertain), it will be necessary to make a judgement about the appropriate amount to be provided. In many situations, this judgement will be relatively easy to make by using a variety of estimation techniques (see para 21.86).

Continued recognition and reversal

21.51 Creditors, provisions, disclosed contingencies and remote contingencies lie on a spectrum and an obligation might move between all four categories during its existence. At one extreme where an obligation arising is *remote*, no disclosure of the contingency is required in the financial statements. When the obligation becomes less remote, it might require disclosure as a contingent liability, until it becomes *probable* when it would be required to be recognised and provided for in the financial statements. When the liability becomes *certain* it would move away from being treated as a provision and become a creditor.

21.52 It is clear from the definition of a provision that it differs from other liabilities, because of the degree of uncertainty surrounding the amount of the settlement or the uncertainty of the timing of that settlement. Once the outcome becomes certain, then the provision will become a normal creditor. For example with litigation, the uncertainty remains until a judgement is made and accepted (that is, it is not subject to appeal). Once the judgement is made and accepted, uncertainty is removed and the provision should be reclassified as a creditor and disclosed as current or non-current as appropriate until it is paid. A transfer would have to be made out of the specific provision in order to reclassify the item as a creditor (see further FRS 12's disclosure requirements as discussed from para 21.305).

21.53 Where, however, a previously recognised provision is no longer expected to give rise to an outflow of economic benefits, the provision should be reversed. [FRS 12 para 62].

21.54 A provision should only be used for the expenditures for which it was originally set up and should be reversed when it is no longer required. [FRS 12 para 64]. Where the original provision was charged as an expense, any subsequent reversal should be credited to the same line in the profit and loss account. Changes in provisions that were originally recognised as part of the cost of an asset are dealt with in paragraph 21.118. The reversal of a provision is illustrated in the example below.

> **Example – Reversing provisions**
>
> During 20X1 15 customers of a food manufacturer suffered from severe food poisoning, allegedly from products the company sold. Management withdrew the product from supermarket shelves as a precaution. During the year a legal action was brought against the company. At 31 December 20X1, the company's lawyers advised management that the manufacturer was more likely than not to lose the court case. Management recognised a provision for damages in the 31 December 20X1 balance sheet.
>
> At 31 December 20X2, the company's lawyers advised management that the chances of losing the court case were now negligible as a result of a favourable decision made in a similar case. As lawyers now believe that it is no longer probable that the company will be found liable, management has questioned how this change in the assessment of the legal action should be reflected in the financial statements.
>
> Management should reverse the provision and recognise the reversal in the income statement within the same line item in which the original expenditure was charged. Management should also disclose the litigation as a contingent liability, unless the possibility of an outflow of economic benefits is regarded as remote.

Groups of similar obligations

21.55 Obligations arising from a group of similar transactions should be considered together. For example, with a warranted product, the chances of a particular customer making a claim that would result in an outflow of economic benefits might be very small (that is, not probable). Here, FRS 12 requires the probability that an outflow of resources will be required in settlement to be determined by considering the class of obligations as a whole. [FRS 12 para 24]. A provision would hence be made for the best estimate (see further para 21.77) of the costs of rectifying the goods sold under warranty.

Where does the debit go?

21.56 The recognition rules considered so far in this chapter all relate to determining whether or not a company can recognise a provision. What has not been considered in any great detail is what happens to the other side of the double entry. It cannot be assumed that the debit should be charged to the income statement, although this will often be the case. Recognition of a provision could also relate to the creation of an asset, in which case a charge to profit or loss would be inappropriate.

21.57 FRS 12 does not directly address the issue of how the debit should be treated. Therefore, the treatment of the debit will follow the requirements for recognition of assets and expenses as set out in the Statement of Principles and in other accounting standards. This means that when a provision or a change in a provision is recognised, an asset should also be recognised when (but only when) the obligation incurred gives access to future economic benefits. Where this is not so, the provision should be charged immediately to profit and loss.

21.58 An example where the debit relating to a provision is capitalised, is decommissioning obligations. If an energy generating company builds a nuclear reactor, it would estimate the obligation when the reactor was turned on and the obligation to decommission arose. This amount would be provided for at the outset and a matching asset would be capitalised. The company would recover the cost of the facility and the decommissioning cost over the life of the facility, both aspects of the asset being depreciated over that life.

21.59 This is illustrated in example 3 in Appendix III of FRS 12, which gives as an example an obligation for decommissioning costs incurred by commissioning an oil rig. Here, the commissioning of the rig gives access to oil reserves over the years of the oil rig's operation. Therefore, the decommissioning cost represents a further element of the cost of the asset that is supported by future access to oil reserves, and recognised concurrent with the provision for decommissioning. The issues stemming from this requirement are considered further from paragraph 21.116.

Provisions, contingent liabilities and contingent assets

21.60 FRS 12 makes the point that in a general sense, all provisions are contingent because they are uncertain in timing or amount. However, the standard uses the term 'contingent' for liabilities and assets that are not recognised because their existence will be confirmed only by the occurrence or non-occurrence of one or more uncertain future events not wholly within the company's control (see para 21.61). In addition, the term 'contingent liability' is used for liabilities that do not meet the recognition criteria in the standard. [FRS 12 para 12].

Contingent liabilities

21.61 A contingent liability should not be recognised, but should be disclosed, unless the possibility of an outflow of resources embodying economic benefits is remote. [FRS 12 paras 27, 28]. The definition in FRS 12 states that a contingent liability is:

"(a) *A possible obligation that arises from past events and whose existence will be confirmed only by the occurrence or non-occurrence of one or more uncertain future events not wholly within the entity's control; or*

(b) *a present obligation that arises from past events but is not recognised because:*

(i) *it is not probable that an outflow of resources embodying economic benefits will be required to settle the obligation; or*

> *(ii) the amount of the obligation cannot be measured with sufficient reliability."*

[FRS 12 para 2].

21.62 As explained in paragraph 21.60 above and following directly from the definition, contingent liabilities can arise in the following three situations where there is a:

- *Present obligation* as a result of a past event:
  - That *probably* requires an outflow of resources embodying economic benefits, but where the obligation *cannot be measured* reliably.
  - That *may, but will probably not,* require an outflow of resources embodying economic benefits.
- *Possible obligation* as a result of a past event, that may, but will *probably not*, require an outflow of resources embodying economic benefits.

21.63 This contrasts with the need to make a provision, which is only required where a *present obligation* exists that will *probably* require an outflow of economic benefits, which can be *measured reliably*. On the other hand where the likelihood of an outflow of economic benefits is remote, it is not necessary to refer to the contingency in the financial statements, even where there is no uncertainty over whether or not it exists.

21.64 In certain situations, companies are jointly and severally liable for an obligation. Joint and several obligations often arise in joint venture arrangements where two or more parties co-operate to build, develop or exploit a particular product. Where joint and several obligations arise, the part of the obligation that is expected to be met by other parties is required by FRS 12 to be treated as a contingent liability. [FRS 12 para 29]. The accounting for the part of the obligation that the company is obligated for in its own right will depend on the normal rules as outlined above. The company would recognise a provision for any part of the obligation for which an outflow of economic benefits is probable. If an outflow of economic benefits is not probable, a contingent liability is disclosed, unless the likelihood of this arising is remote.

Contingent assets

21.65 Under FRS 12, contingent assets are not recognised – just as contingent liabilities are not recognised. An asset remains contingent until such time as the inflow of economic benefits becomes virtually certain, as opposed to probable in case of liabilities. While contingent assets are required to be disclosed by FRS 12 in a similar way to contingent liabilities, this is only required to the extent that an inflow of economic benefits is probable. [FRS 12 para 34]. This can be contrasted with the standard's requirement for disclosure of contingent liabilities, as set out above, under which disclosure is given, unless an outflow of economic resources is remote.

21.66 Contingent assets generally only arise from unplanned or other unexpected events that give rise to the possibility of an inflow of resources embodying economic benefits to the company. Contingent assets are, consequently, defined in the standard in the following terms: *"A possible asset that arises from past events and whose existence will be confirmed only by the occurrence or non-occurrence of one or more uncertain future events not wholly within the control of the entity"*. [FRS 12 para 2]

21.67 If the existence of a possible asset is not (or is no longer) subject to confirmation by an uncertain future event not wholly within the company's control, the related asset is not (or is no longer) a contingent asset. It is recognised in accordance with the Statement of Principles if there will be an inflow of economic benefit and it can be measured reliably. If it is not expected that there will be an inflow of economic benefit or it cannot be reliably measured, it is an unrecognised asset, but does not fall within the definition of a contingent asset. This can be contrasted with the definition of a contingent liability, as set out in paragraph 21.61 above, under which, even if there is a present obligation whose existence does not depend on an uncertain future event, the item falls within the definition of a contingent liability if it is not probable that there will be an outflow or if the item cannot be reliably measured.

21.68 The reason for not recognising a contingent asset is that this may result in the recognition of income that may never be realised. [FRS 12 para 33]. It would be inappropriate to recognise an item as an asset where it is only probable that it exists and the confirmation of its existence is dependent on the occurrence of an uncertain future event. However, the standard notes that when it becomes virtually certain that an inflow of economic benefits will arise, the asset and the related income should be recognised in the financial statements in the period in which the change occurs (that is, when the future event occurs and confirms the asset's existence or, if earlier, when it becomes virtually certain that the future event will confirm the asset's existence and it is virtually certain the asset will be realised).

21.69 Therefore, the spectrum that exists around contingent assets is as follows:

- An inflow of economic benefits is not probable — do not mention in the financial statements.
- An inflow of economic benefits is probable — disclose as a contingent asset (see further para 21.327).
- An inflow of economic benefits is virtually certain — recognise an asset and the related income in the financial statements as the asset is no longer 'contingent'.

21.70 Like contingent liabilities, contingent assets may move through this spectrum during their existence. For example, where a company is pursuing a legal claim against another party through the courts, at the outset of the legal process the probability of winning the case or the other side settling out of court might be slim. In this circumstance, an inflow of economic benefits is not probable so a contingent asset should not be noted in the company's financial statements. Where the company has received a favourable judgement, but the case has been taken to appeal, it will still only be appropriate to note a contingent asset where success by the company in the court of appeal is probable. Until the final judgement is made, it would be rare for the outcome of the case to be virtually certain. Hence, only when the final judgement is received should the asset be recognised and the related profit be recorded in the financial statements of the period in which the change occurs. [FRS 12 para 35]. In effect, a judgement received after the balance sheet date up to the date of approval of the financial statements is normally a non-adjusting event. See chapter 22 on post balance sheet events.

Reimbursements

21.71 FRS 12 includes specific guidance on accounting for reimbursements. Under FRS 12, where some or all of the expenditure required to settle a provision is expected to be reimbursed by another party, the reimbursement should be recognised only when it is virtually certain that reimbursement will be received if the company settles the obligation. [FRS 12 para 56]. Reimbursements of this nature are required to be treated as separate assets and the amount recognised for reimbursement should not exceed the amount of the related provision. [FRS 12 para 56].

21.72 In some situations, it may not be clear at the balance sheet date as to whether there is an obligation (and a related reimbursement asset). However, where evidence arises after the balance sheet date that relates to conditions that existed at the balance sheet date, this is an adjusting event under FRS 21, 'Events after the balance sheet date', and would result in recognising a liability for the obligation. Provided that it is virtually certain at the year end that the reimbursement will be received if the company settles the obligation – that is, any post year end negotiation in respect of the asset relates to agreement of the final amount to be paid and not to whether the reimbursement will be paid if there is a related liability, then a reimbursement asset would be recognised at the balance sheet date. For the avoidance of doubt, however, a confirming post balance sheet event is not necessary if it is clear at the balance sheet date that an obligation (and a related reimbursement asset) exist.

Example – Recognising anticipated insurance recoveries

A company had a provision for a legal case that was in progress at the year end. Also at the year end the company was negotiating with its insurance company for reimbursement of the amount to be paid out in the legal case, although there was general agreement with the insurance company that reimbursement would be made if the company lost the legal case. While the final amount of the reimbursement from the insurer was not agreed at the year end, it is very likely that the amount to be paid in the legal case would be incurred after the year end and the reimbursement agreed with the insurer before the financial statements are approved. If this happens should the asset for the reimbursement be included in the financial statements for the year?

The asset should be recognised in the financial statements provided it is virtually certain at the balance sheet date that reimbursement will be received if the company settles the obligation. [FRS 12 para 56]. The post year end settlement of the court case confirms the amount of the liability that should be recognised at the balance sheet date. IAS 10 gives as an example of an adjusting event the settlement after the balance sheet date of a court case that confirms that the company had a present obligation at the balance sheet date. [FRS 21 para 9(a)]. In the same way as a liability would be recognised at the balance sheet date on the basis of post year end evidence that confirms its existence, the related reimbursement asset should be recognised if it is virtually certain to be received.

21.73 Although there is a general prohibition on netting recoveries against related obligations and contingent assets against contingent liabilities, this does not extend to their recognition in the profit and loss account. Here, expenses relating to a provision may be presented net of the amount recognised for a reimbursement. [FRS 12 para 57]. For example, a company might have identified during the year a *present obligation* that *probably* requires an outflow of economic benefits and makes a provision for that obligation. In addition, it might have an insurance contract under which it can claim when the obligation arises. The insurance company has accepted that it will pay-out under the policy. As in the example above, the company can recognise an asset representing the recovery as it is virtually certain that it will receive the amount due from the insurance company. Although the company has to recognise the provision for the obligation and a debtor for the expected recovery on a gross basis, it may net the related charge and recovery in the income statement. This presentation in the profit and loss account better reflects the substance of the transaction. In practice, this concession has little impact as both the provision and the recovery will often form part of operating profit and, therefore, may only affect the allocation between say administrative expenses and other income.

21.74 In most cases, a company will remain liable for the whole of an obligation even where it can recover some or all of the loss from another party. But the general prohibition on netting, does not extend to situations where, for example, the obligation has been extinguished because another party has agreed to assume the obligation and will settle it directly. The key here is that the company that has transferred the obligation cannot be left with any significant risks and rewards associated with it. In this case, the company no longer bears, for example, the credit risk associated with the recovery and this risk is passed to the party to whom the obligation is owed. In such cases, the company has no liability for those costs arising under the obligation and they should not be included in the provision. [FRS 12 para 60].

21.75 The practical implication of the different recognition criteria for provisions and related reimbursement rights is that a company may recognise an obligation (and an expense) before recognising a related insurance recovery. This is because companies must provide for insured risks if these become probable while, as explained above, the insurance recovery has to be separately assessed. However, if the recovery is virtually certain, the related asset and provision must be shown separately on the balance sheet, while netting is permitted in the income statement. Table 21.1 below illustrates the asset for reimbursement from insurance, in relation to asbestos claims and (separately) certain other environmental liabilities.

Table 21.1 – Reimbursement asset for insurance claims

Hanson PLC – Report and accounts – 31 December 2005

17 Receivables

Trade and other current receivables	Notes	**2005 £m**	2004 £m
Trade receivables		**629.0**	594.5
Amounts due from joint-ventures		**7.0**	5.3
Amounts due from associates		**0.7**	0.3
Prepayments		**31.3**	37.0
Amounts recoverable from insurers – Koppers	21	**39.3**	45.2
Amounts recoverable from insurers – asbestos	21	**7.1**	5.1
Derivatives		**6.2**	49.2
Other receivables		**54.2**	51.4
		774.8	788.0

Non-current receivables	Notes	**2005 £m**	2004 £m
Amounts recoverable from insurers – Koppers	21	**101.5**	117.0
Amounts recoverable from insurers – asbestos	21	–	7.4
Derivatives		**33.9**	–
Other receivables		**46.8**	34.7
		182.2	159.1

The Directors estimate that the carrying amount of trade and other receivables approximates their fair value.

21 Provisions (extract 1)
Insurance asset
The insurance asset of $26.1m at January 1, 2005 was reduced by insurance utilisation during the year of $11.5m, to give a closing insurance asset at December 31, 2005 of $14.6m, equivalent to £7.1m on a discounted basis.

Most of the US subsidiaries involved with asbestos claims have had agreements with their respective insurance carriers regarding the defence and settlement of asbestos claims, the terms of which varied for each such subsidiary. These insurance arrangements have resulted in the insurance companies having met substantially all of the amounts such subsidiaries have paid in the past in settlements and defence costs. More of these costs are now being borne by the relevant subsidiaries as these arrangements are assumed, for accounts purposes, to be exhausted.

In February 2006, one of the Company's US subsidiaries reached a settlement with its insurers covering approximately 20% of the group's present asbestos costs. Details are provided in note 31.

Certain other US subsidiaries, not party to the recent settlement, continue to pursue litigation and negotiation to maximise the insurance cover available. Litigation proceedings are progressing in the state of California with a view to establishing whether or not substantially all of the primary cover available to one of our US subsidiaries has been exhausted and, to the extent that such cover has been exhausted, the amount of excess cover that is available to it.

21 Provisions (extract 2)
Koppers' liabilities
Koppers' environmental obligations and related costs arise primarily from the US chemical and related operations formerly operated by Koppers Company Inc, a company acquired by Beazer PLC which itself was acquired by the Company in 1991. Members of the Beazer group remain contractually and statutorily liable for certain environmental costs relating to these discontinued operations. During 1998 an agreement was signed under which, for a one-off premium and related transaction costs totalling $275.0m, insurance cover of $800.0m in perpetuity (after payment by members of the Beazer group of the first $100.0m of remediation costs arising since January 1, 1998) was provided by subsidiaries of two reinsurance companies, Centre Solutions and Swiss Re.

At the end of 2005, $413.9m of the $800.0m insurance cover had been utilised. The estimate of future probable cost, discounted at 5.3% (5.1%), is shown as a provision of £140.8m at December 31, 2005. These costs are the responsibility of the insurers and hence a receivable of £140.8m is recorded at December 31, 2005 as shown in note 17.

Based upon existing known circumstances, the Company considers that the remaining $386.1m of insurance cover should meet the related future costs, recognising that the estimate of future probable costs could increase. Factors which could cause such remediation costs to increase include (i) unknown adverse conditions arising at sites; (ii) third party claims in excess of estimates; (iii) changes to regulatory requirements; (iv) changes in remediation techniques; and (v) any other significant variations to assumptions made in support of these estimates.

Provision recognition summary

21.76 The criteria for provision recognition as discussed above are illustrated in FRS 12 by the use of a flow chart, which is reproduced below.

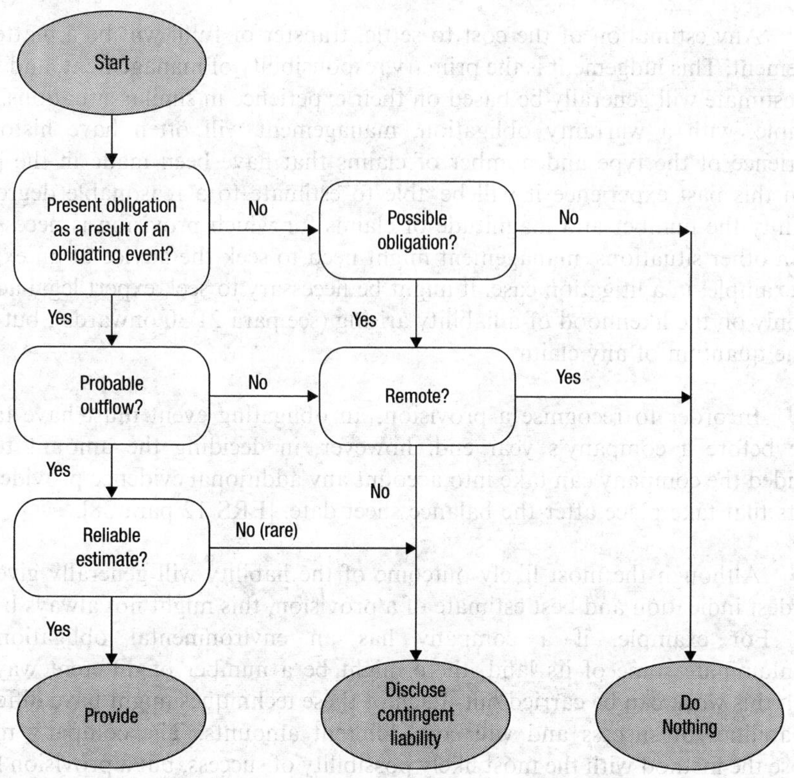

Measurement

Best estimate

21.77 The standard specifies that the amount to recognise as a provision should be the best estimate of the expenditure required to settle the present obligation at the balance sheet date. [FRS 12 para 36]. The best estimate of a provision represents the amount that a company would rationally pay to settle the obligation at the balance sheet date or to transfer it to a third party.

21.78 There is no guidance in the standard as to when a company should provide for the amount required to settle an obligation compared to when they should provide for the cost of transferring the obligation to a third party. Equally, in practice it will often be impossible to settle or transfer the obligation at the balance sheet date, and in these cases companies often provide for the cost of fulfilling the obligation. However, where an obligation can be settled, transferred or fulfilled, it appears logical that a company would take the least net cost route in satisfying its obligation so, therefore, a provision should be recorded at the lowest of the cost to settle, transfer and fulfil. In most cases it is expected that settlement and fulfilment will be cheaper than transfer because a third party would seek to cover its administrative expenses and apply a risk premium and profit margin in determining the price at which it would assume the liability.

21.79 Any estimation of the cost to settle, transfer or fulfil will be a matter of judgement. This judgement is the primary responsibility of management, and their best estimate will generally be based on their experience in similar situations. For example, with a warranty obligation, management will often have historical experience of the type and number of claims that have been made in the past. From this past experience it will be able to estimate to a reasonable degree of certainty the number and magnitude of claims for which provision is necessary. But in other situations, management might need to seek the advice of an expert. For example, in a litigation case, it might be necessary to seek expert legal advice not only on the likelihood of a liability arising (see para 21.30 onwards), but also on the quantum of any claim.

21.80 In order to recognise a provision, an obligating event must have taken place before a company's year end, however, in deciding the amount to be provided the company can take into account any additional evidence provided by events that take place after the balance sheet date. [FRS 12 para 38].

21.81 Although the most likely outcome of the liability will generally give the soundest indication and best estimate of a provision, this might not always be the case. For example, if a company has an environmental obligation to decontaminate some of its land, there might be a number of different ways in which this work can be carried out. Each of these techniques might have different probabilities of success and will cost different amounts. The company might choose the method with the most likely possibility of success, but a provision for a larger amount may be necessary if there is a significant chance that further work will be necessary before success is achieved. [FRS 12 para 40].

21.82 Inevitably, in establishing the amount of any provision, judgements have to be made concerning the risks and uncertainties that surround the particular events which give rise to the obligation. These all have an impact on the amount that is recognised.

21.83 While the measurement of provisions will usually require significant judgement, sometimes it may be difficult to predict how future developments in (say) technology should impact the amount to be provided. This will typically be so in situations where provision is being made for rectification work that will be incurred a significant number of years into the future. Clearly it would be wrong to assume, for example, in the case of contaminated land, that in 50 years time a clean-up solution will be found that will have minimal cost and, as a consequence, little if any provision is required now. The standard says in these situations that the amount recognised (for both the provision and the asset if one is recognised) should reflect *"a reasonable expectation of technically qualified, objective observers, taking account of all available evidence as to the technology that will be available at the time of the clean-up"*. [FRS 12 para 52]. The standard goes on to explain that it is appropriate to include, for example, *"expected cost reductions associated with increased experience in applying existing technology or the expected cost of applying existing technology to a larger or more complex clean-up operation than has previously been carried out"*. But the standard is also quite clear that it does not mean that the company can anticipate the development of a completely new technology, unless this is supported by sufficient objective evidence.

21.84 So undoubtedly great care needs to be taken in ascertaining that changes in technology that are taken into account are appropriate. It is reasonable to anticipate the use of existing methods with some refinement, adaptation and cost reduction, if there is sufficient evidence that such factors are likely to arise in practice. But it is not acceptable to assume there will be bright new ideas, which will reduce costs significantly.

21.85 Provisions are required under the standard to be measured before tax, as opposed to using an after tax method. Therefore, as a provision is required to be measured before taking into account the effects of tax, the standard says that the provision's tax consequences, should be dealt with in accordance with FRS 19, 'Deferred tax'. [FRS 12 para 41]. Accounting for deferred tax is considered in detail in chapter 13.

Estimation techniques

21.86 There are a number of different techniques that can be used to arrive at the best estimate of the amount of a provision, where the creditor does not wish to settle and where there is no market in obligations of the kind for which provision is being made. Generally though, companies will base their estimate either on:

- the single most likely outcome; or
- a weighted average of all the possible outcomes (the 'expected value' method).

21.87 The example below is based on the example in paragraph 39 of FRS 12, which uses a warranty claim to illustrate how to apply the 'expected value' method.

> **Example – Estimating using expected value**
>
> A company sells goods with a standard warranty under which customers are covered for the cost of repairs of any manufacturing defects that become apparent within the first six months after purchase. If minor defects were detected in all products sold, repair costs of £1m would result. If major defects were detected in all products sold, repair costs of £4m would result. The company's past experience and future expectations indicate that, for the coming year, 75% of the goods sold will have no defects, 20% of the goods sold will have minor defects and 5% of the goods sold will have major defects.
>
> The expected value of the cost of repairs under the standard warranty is calculated as follows:

	Expected value
	£
75% × nil	nil
20% × C1,000,000	200,000
5% × C4,000,000	200,000
Total	400,000

Note that in this example, the warranty is a standard manufacturing warranty and it is presumed that it is not a separate element and that it represents an insignificant part of the sales transaction. The accounting for warranties is dealt with in more detail in paragraph 21.206 onwards.

21.88 While the example above applies the expected value method to a large population of similar claims, it might equally be applied to a single obligation with variable outcomes in order to estimate a settlement, transfer or fulfilment value.

21.89 The weighted average approach builds risk into the estimated cash flows as it takes account of all potential outcomes whereas a single most likely outcome approach does not build in risk. The standard requires that the risks and uncertainties about the amounts and timing of cash flows required to meet a provision must be taken into account in reaching the best estimate of the expenditure required to settle the present obligation at the balance sheet date. [FRS 12 para 42]. To meet the requirements of the standard, cash flows estimated based on the single most likely outcome are typically risk adjusted through the discount rate applied (see further para 21.96).

21.89.1 Some take the view that a further risk adjustment to increase the value of the provision is necessary, even where a weighted average calculation is performed. Proponents of this view believe that this is required to take account of the spread of possible outcomes, and that the more diverse the possible outcomes the greater the value of the liability. In making further risk adjustments though, companies should remember that uncertainty does not justify the creation of excessive provisions, and that adjustments for risk should not be duplicated within the measurement methodology resulting in the overstatement of a provision. [FRS 12 para 43].

Discounting

21.90 Once the cash flows associated with an obligation have been estimated, it is then necessary to consider whether or not the time value of money has a material effect on the sums to be paid. The standard requires that where the effect of the time value of money is material the amount of a provision should be the present value of the expenditures expected to be required to settle the obligation. [FRS 12 para 45]. Clearly, provisions for cash outflows that arise soon after the balance sheet date are more onerous than those where cash outflows of the same amount arise some time later. But, in practice the standard makes it clear that it only requires cash flows to be discounted where this has a material effect. Therefore, for the majority of provisions that will reverse in the short-term, for example, within the next and perhaps in the following financial year, the effects of discounting may be immaterial and are not then required to be made.

Time value of money and discount rate

21.91 Paragraph 49 of FRS 12 states that where the cash flows have been adjusted for risk, the discount rate to be used should be a risk-free rate and, consequently, we believe that this risk-free rate represents the time value of money. Typically, a government bond 'yield' rate (not the coupon rate) should be used, as this is a nominal, risk-free pre-tax rate. The yield to redemption rates vary within a small range that depends upon the period of time to redemption. Government bond rates may typically be quoted in bands of: up to five years; five to 15 years; and over 15 years. Within these bands the rates remain fairly constant. Consequently, in practice it is logical to select a rate that matches the maturity of the liability being discounted. This is relatively straightforward where the amount being discounted is a single payment to be settled in the future, as a government bond will have a single capital repayment at the end of its term. But where the provision is made up of a string of cash flows arising in different periods, it might be necessary to adjust the discount rate to reflect the different timing of the cash flows.

21.92 As well as reflecting the time value of money, the standard requires that the discount rate should reflect the risks specific to the liability. The discount rate should not, however, reflect risks for which future cash flow estimates have been adjusted. [FRS 12 para 47]. Therefore, where risk has been built into the cash flows the discount rate should not be adjusted for the same risks.

Inflation

21.93 For the purposes of measuring provisions, cash flows are usually expressed in expected future prices (that is, including inflation) and should, therefore, be discounted using a 'nominal' (or 'money') rate that includes inflation. Alternatively, in certain circumstances where required cash flows have been estimated at current prices it would be appropriate to discount such cash flows using a 'real' discount rate that excludes the effects of inflation (for example a government bond rate adjusted to eliminate the effect of inflation). [FRS 12 para 50]. Note that a real discount rate will be lower than a nominal discount rate in a normal inflationary environment. However, theoretically discounting cash flows adjusted for price changes using a nominal rate should result in the same net present value as that derived by using a real rate to discount cash flows that have not been adjusted for inflation (assuming the inflation rate applying to the cash flows is the same as that inherent in the bond), as illustrated in the example that follows.

Example – Nominal rate versus real rate

A company has estimated that it needs to pay £1,000 (in current prices) at the end of each of the next three years to settle an obligation. If it takes into account inflation these cash flows will increase to the amounts shown in the table below. The company has established that the nominal discount rate (that is, including inflation) is 4.5%. By discounting the cash flows the net present value works out to be £2,887. By using an estimation process called iteration, it is possible to calculate the discount rate (that is, the real rate) that would have to be applied to the cash flows excluding inflation to arrive at the same present value.

	Net present value	Cash flows Year 1	Year 2	Year 3
	£	£	£	£
Cash flows reflecting inflation of 2.5% per annum				
NPV based on nominal discount rate of 4.5%	2,887	1,025	1,051	1,077
Cash flows excluding inflation				
NPV based on real discount rate of 1.95%	2,887	1,000	1,000	1,000

The example shows the equivalent real rate is 1.95%. Clearly it would be wrong to discount the cash flows that exclude inflation (that is, £1,000 per annum) using the nominal discount rate of 4.5% (that includes inflation) as this would give an understated net present value of £2,749.

21.94 Mathematically, the relationship between the nominal rate and the real rate is expressed by the following formula:

$$(1 + \text{real rate}) = \frac{(1 + \text{nominal rate})}{(1 + \text{inflation rate})}$$

Which in the case of the example above gives the following:

$$\text{Real rate} = \frac{(1 + 4.5\%)}{(1 + 2.5\%)} - 1$$

$$= \frac{(1.045)}{(1.025)} - 1$$

$$= 1.0195 - 1$$

$$= 1.95\%$$

21.95 While using either nominal or real cash flows and discount rates theoretically result in the same net present value, this is only the case if the rate of inflation reflected in the cash flow estimates equals the rate of inflation reflected in the nominal risk free rate used to discount such cash flows. In cases where the two inflation rates are expected to diverge significantly and the expected cash flows are expressed in real terms, typically a company should first convert real cash flows into nominal cash flows using the rate of inflation expected to apply to the costs in question before discounting using a nominal risk free rate.

Risk

21.96 As discussed above, paragraph 42 of FRS 12 requires risk to be taken into account in determining the value of the provision. Paragraph 47 requires that the discount rate should take account of the risks specific to the liability while also noting that the discount rate should not be adjusted for risks already accounted for in the cash flows (that is, no double counting).

21.96.1 FRS 12 does not explicitly state whether an entity's own credit risk should be taken into account in determining the value of the provision. Own credit risk is generally viewed in practice as a risk of the entity rather than a risk specific to the liability. Our view is that risk in the context of a provision reflects uncertainty about the resources that will be required to settle or fulfil the obligation, which does not include the entity's own credit risk.

21.97 Paragraph 21.89 above noted that applying the 'expected value' method to determine the cash flows takes account of the risk of variability in outcome. As such this risk should not also be built into the discount rate where the 'expected value' method is used. However, where a single most likely outcome approach is applied to determining the expected cash flows the risk of variability in outcome should typically be adjusted for in the discount rate.

21.98 In practice adjusting the discount rate to take account of risk is very difficult and generally we would expect companies to instead adjust the cash flows for risk and discount the result using a risk free rate (that itself appropriately reflects inflation consistent with the approach to the cash flows). The example below illustrates how the present value of the liability is the same whether risk is accounted for in the cash flows or the discount rate.

Example – Discount rates

Ignoring the impact of inflation, a company's best estimate of its liability in two years time on a single most likely outcome basis is £1,000. The actual liability could be anything between £950 and £1,050 with the 'expected value' method giving a liability in two years time of £1,020. So the company's best estimate is £1,000 (that is, excluding any risk adjustment) and the equivalent certain amount payable in two years time is £1,020 (that is, including an adjustment for risk of £20). The obligation that arises at the balance sheet date for which provision is required should typically be the same net present value amount whether the unadjusted best estimate or the risk-adjusted best estimate equivalent is used as the basis for the measurement. The risk-free rate for 2 year money is 4.5%.

	Net present value	Cash flows Year 1	Year 2
	£	£	£
Certain cash flow (adjusted for risk)			
Risk-free rate 4.5%	934[1]	0	1,020
Expected cash flow (unadjusted for risk)			
Risk-adjusted rate 3.5%[2]	934	0	1,000

[1] Using a risk-free rate of 4.5% on the certain cash flow of £1,020 gives a discounted net present value of £934.

[2] To arrive at the same net present value of 934, a risk-adjusted rate of 3.5% would need to be used to discount the expected cash flow of £1,000.

21.99 Often companies will find that a risk adjusted discount rate is lower than the risk free rate in cases where the single most likely outcome is lower than the risk adjusted 'expected value' estimate. However, in cases where the single most likely outcome is near the top of the range of possible outcomes the risk adjusted discount rate may be higher than the risk free rate.

21.100 As noted in paragraph 21.96 above, where a risk-adjusted discount rate is used (as opposed to adjusting cash flows for risk), the discount rate should reflect the risks specific to the liability. This is illustrated in the following example.

Example – Risk adjusted discount rate

A company sells a vacuum cleaner, model A, on which it provides a standard warranty of a three year guarantee for parts and labour.

At the beginning of the year, the company manufactures a new range of vacuum cleaner, model B. Model B is a high-end vacuum cleaner and uses the latest technology. The company also provides a standard warranty of a three year guarantee for parts and labour.

For the purpose of this example, it is presumed that the standard warranty represents an insignificant part of the sales transaction and is not a separate element.

How should the discount rate be determined for warranty provisions?

Management should not use the same rate in discounting the warranty provision for model A as that used to discount the warranty provision for model B. The provisions are for different products that display different kinds of risk and, therefore, unless otherwise reflected in the gross cash flow estimates, different discount rates should be used even though the nature of both provisions is for warranty repairs. As a starting point, the company may take into account the discount rate of model A and adjust it to reflect specific risks of model B and to exclude specific risks of model A.

Unwinding the discount

21.101 The unwinding of the discount due to the passage of time should be included as other finance costs (adjacent to interest) in arriving at profit or loss for the year. [FRS 12 paras 48, 63]. The unwinding of the discount is illustrated in the simplified example below.

Example – Measuring the unwinding of a discount

Company A has litigation pending. Legal advice is that company A will lose the case and costs of £1,200 in two years' time are estimated. The liability is recognised on a discounted basis. The discount rate at which the liability has been discounted is the nominal risk free rate which is 4.5% and, for the purposes of this example, it is assumed that the discount rate does not change.

How should management calculate the amount of borrowing costs recognised on the unwinding of a discount?

Management should initially recognise a provision for £1,099, being the present value of £1,200 discounted at 4.5% for two years.

	Discount factor at 4.5%	**NPV**	**Cash flows**	**Borrowing cost**
	0.9157	1,099		
Year 1	0.9569	1,148		49
Year 2	1.0000	1,200	1,200	52

At the end of year 1, the provision will increase to £1,148 as management discounts the cash outflow of £1,200 for one year instead of two. The increment of £49 should be recognised as a borrowing cost in the income statement. Similarly in year 2, the provision will increase by £52 to equal the amount due.

The situation is more complicated if the discount rate changes over the period – this is dealt with in paragraph 21.104 onwards.

21.102 In the above example the liability has been discounted using the nominal risk free rate and the discount was unwound using this rate. However, as described above the discount rate can be adjusted to remove inflation when discounting real cash flows and it can also be adjusted for risk when risk has not been taken into consideration in the cash flows. For provisions discounted to present value using adjusted discount rates, the question arises as to how the discount should be unwound.

21.103 In our opinion, irrespective of the discount rate used to calculate the present value of the provision, the finance cost should always be calculated based on the weighted average outstanding liability during the reporting period (before taking account of discounting – see para 21.112) unwound using the nominal risk free discount rate. This is because the time value of money corresponds to a nominal risk free rate and the standard only specifies that the increase in the value of a provision as a result of the passage of time to be taken to finance costs.

Changes in discount rate

21.104 The discount rate might change over time, particularly where the obligation is a number of years away. The rate to be applied in assessing the amount of the provision should be the rate which is current at the year end date (rather than a longer term average). This will mean that different rates might apply at different year ends.

21.105 The standard provides no guidance regarding how to address changes in the discount rates used to measure the provision. However, whether the discount rate increases or decreases, the resulting adjustment represents a re-assessment of the provision. As a consequence, the movement should be charged or credited as an operating item rather than as a borrowing cost.

21.106 Where the discount rate goes down in a period, the liability would increase as illustrated in the following example.

Example – Decrease in discount rate increases liability

A company has a £1,000 obligation which is due at the end of year 5. It provides now for the net present value of the obligation of £802, which has been arrived at by using a nominal risk-free pre-tax rate of 4.5%. At the end of year three the discount rate has changed to 4%. The obligation at the beginning of the year 3 (measured at a discount rate of 4.5%) is £876 and at the end of year 3 it would be stated at £916 if the rate were still 4.5%. However, based on a current rate of 4% the estimated net present value needs to be £925. The difference of £49 (£925 – £876) is made up of a finance cost (for the unwinding of the discount) and a change in estimate of the provision (due to the change in discount rate). If in the example the rate changed at the beginning of the year, it would be appropriate to charge £35 (that is, £876 × 4%) as a finance charge, representing the unwind of the discount for the year. This would increase the provision to £911. The additional amount of £14 to bring the provision to £925 would be charged as an operating expense.

		Net present value	Provision at end of				
			Year 1	Year 2	Year 3	Year 4	Year 5
		£	£	£	£	£	£
Original discount rate	4.50%	802	839	876	916	957	1,000
Revised discount rate	4.00%				925	962	1,000

21.107 The effect of a change in rates can be particularly significant where provision is for costs expected to be incurred a long time into the future, as is the case with decommissioning obligations.

21.108 The above example deals with a scenario where the present value of the provision is calculated by discounting estimated cash flows using a nominal risk-free rate. However, as mentioned in paragraph 21.102, companies may discount using a real rate or a rate adjusted for risk. In these cases the new real or risk adjusted discount rate should be used to arrive at the correct liability on the closing balance sheet date. The movement in the recorded provision over the course of the year should then be analysed between the amount of the provision used in the year, the unwind of the discount calculated as described in paragraph 21.103 and the adjustment to the provision, which is the balancing figure required to establish the provision at its estimated net present value as at the year end.

21.109 Consider an example where a company initially recorded a provision of 800 after discounting using a risk-adjusted discount rate (derived from a nominal risk-free discount rate of 4.5 per cent). Over the course of the next reporting period, 50 has been paid in relation to the provision decreasing it from 800 to 750, without taking into account the effects of discounting. Assume for the purposes of this example, that there is no change in the estimate of total future cash flows, other than in respect of repayments/settlements. If the repayment arose evenly throughout the period, the average provision outstanding during the year would be 775. The unwind of the discount, calculated using the nominal risk-free discount rate of 4.5 per cent on this amount, would be 35 and this amount would be charged as a finance cost in the income statement. Taking into account the settlement of 50 during the year and the 35 increase due to the unwind of the discount, the adjusted provision at the end of year 1 is 785 before re-assessment. The provision is then re-assessed at the end of year 1 using a revised risk-adjusted discount rate giving a present value of 850. In this case the difference of 65 between the adjusted provision of 785 and the re-estimated provision of 850 should be charged as an operating expense.

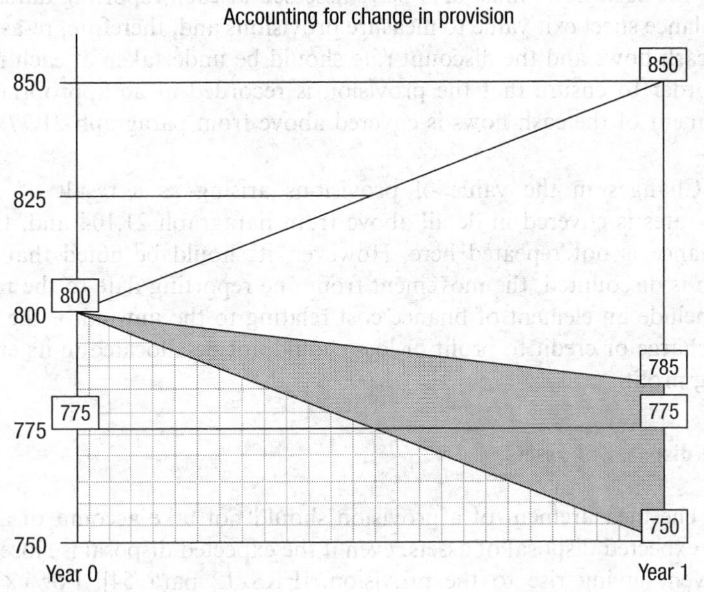

21.110 Even if the revised provision in the above example had fallen to say 700 at the end of year 1 the finance charge of 35 would still have been recorded but, instead of a charge of 65 to operating profit, there would have been a credit of 85.

21.111 Discount rates are likely to change gradually over time rather than move suddenly on a specific date and, therefore, it is necessary to consider how frequently a company should revisit its discount rates. The frequency with which discount rates are revisited will have an impact on how much of the provision movement is allocated to borrowing costs as the unwind of the discount (see para 21.103) and how much is determined to result from the change in the value of the provision taken to operating costs (see para 21.105).

21.112 Paragraph 62 of FRS 12 requires that provisions should be re-assessed at the end of each reporting period and adjusted to reflect current best estimates. This re-assessment should include the discount rate so, therefore, a re-assessment of the discount rate should be undertaken at least once every reporting period. A reporting period should be taken to mean quarterly or half-yearly reporting if the company makes such reports public. While re-assessment should be made at least at the end of each reporting period, there is no reason why a company should not re-assess more frequently. To the extent that the frequency of re-assessment has a material impact on the amount classified as borrowing costs, the company's policy should be disclosed under FRS 18.

Changes in estimate of provisions

21.113 As discussed above in paragraph 21.112 the discount rate should be revisited at the end of each reporting period and changes to the discount rate will give rise to changes in the value of the provision. As well as the discount rate, however, the cash flows must also be re-assessed at each reporting date. FRS 12 uses a balance sheet exit value to measure provisions and, therefore, re-assessment of both cash flows and the discount rate should be undertaken at each reporting date in order to ensure that the provision is recorded at an appropriate value. Measurement of the cash flows is covered above from paragraph 21.77.

21.114 Changes in the value of provisions arising as a result of changing discount rates is covered in detail above from paragraph 21.104 and, therefore, this guidance is not repeated here. However, it should be noted that where a provision is discounted, the movement from one reporting date to the next must always include an element of finance cost relating to the unwind of the discount and the charge or credit to profit or loss should not be allocated in its entirety to operating profit.

Expected disposal of assets

21.115 The measurement of a provision should not take account of any gains from the expected disposal of assets, even if the expected disposal is closely linked to the event giving rise to the provision. [FRS 12 para 54]. For example, a restructuring provision cannot be reduced by an expected gain on disposal of a factory that is being sold as part of the restructuring. Instead, the gain will be recognised when the factory is sold.

Measurement of related asset

21.116 In certain circumstances, where recognising the obligation gives access to future economic benefits, it might be appropriate to recognise an asset rather than charging the costs to be provided to profit or loss (see para 21.56). This typically arises in oil and gas and generating industries where environmental damage is caused by, say, the construction and commissioning of the facility (for example, the oil platform or nuclear plant). In the circumstances explained from paragraph 21.56 there is often a need to recognise an asset at the outset for an amount equivalent to the decommissioning obligation, which will be recovered from the benefits derived from the facility (for example, the future sale of oil or electricity).

21.117 Obviously, discounting has an important part to play in establishing both the obligation and the equivalent asset to be recognised where decommissioning is unlikely to take place for a number of years. In the case of decommissioning a nuclear facility, the work might not be expected to start for (say) 100 years. With an oil rig the time-frame is likely to be shorter, but could be anywhere between 25 and 50 years. Consequently, the impact of discounting can be significant as illustrated in the next example.

Example – Discounting long term liabilities

A company has constructed a nuclear facility for £100m. It expects that the plant will run for the next 30 years. It has estimated, using existing technology, that the cost of decommissioning the plant in 100 years time will be £1 billion in today's currency. It has been assumed that the obligation arises at the end of year 100.

Present value of obligation	**Discount rate**	**Net present value £m**	**Cash flows Year 100 £m**
	4.5%	12.26	1,000.00

Unwinding of discount	**Discount**	**Total discount in first 10 years £'m**
Year 1	0.55}	
Year 2	0.58}	
Year 3	0.60}	
Year 4	0.63}	
Year 5	0.66}	
Year 6	0.69} =	6.78
Year 7	0.72}	
Year 8	0.75}	
Year 9	0.78}	
Year 10	0.82}	
……	……	
Year 25	1.59	
……	……	
Year 50	4.76	
……	……	
Year 75	14.32	
……	……	
Year 100	43.06	
Total discount	987.74	

It can be seen that the net present value of the decommissioning obligation is only £12.26m at inception using a discount rate of 4.5%. Hence, the facility should be recorded at its original cost of £100m together with the initial cost of the obligation of £12.26m – giving a total cost of £112.26m. This amount should then be amortised over the 30 year operating life of the facility giving an annual amortisation charge using the straight line method of £3.74m (of which £0.41m per annum relates to the capitalised obligation).

The example also illustrates that the increase in the obligation arises solely from the addition of the discount. Although in the opening years the effect is relatively small (for example, at the end of year 1 £0.55m is added to the obligation to bring it to a figure of £12.81m), the discount effect is back-end loaded and in the final year the obligation increases by £43.06m. The effect is, however, that the unwinding of the discount appears as a borrowing cost whilst the benefits of the asset and the depreciation appear in operating profit.

Although there is a mismatch between the useful life of the facility and the length of time before the decommissioning will take place, in theory this should pose no problem, as long as the company has retained sufficient funds (that is, it has not over-distributed) to honour the obligation at the end of year 30. In the example, the obligation will be £45.91m at the end of year 30. These funds can then be invested in risk free investments to generate the required risk-free rate (in this case 4.5%) to build up the provision until the obligation crystallises at the end of year 100.

21.118 It should be noted that with such long-tail commitments, there are significant challenges in estimating the costs that will arise so far ahead, and very significant assumptions have to be made in practice to arrive at an initial estimation of such a decommissioning obligation. Accordingly, once the obligation is established, further amendments and re-assessment throughout its life are certain to be required. Because the standard prohibits management from postulating anything other than existing technology (unless the development of new technology is supported by sufficient objective evidence – see para 21.83), changes to the estimate of the amount or timing of the obligation and changes in management's assumptions are likely.

21.119 There is no guidance in the standard concerning how to treat these types of adjustments. The discussion paper on provisions that preceded FRED 14 proposed a simple method whereby, after the initial recognition of a decommissioning provision, if the estimate of its amount changed, the entire change of estimate should be capitalised and charged to the profit and loss account prospectively over the remaining life of the facility and indeed, it is a variation of this method that has become the generally accepted practice and that has been adopted for IFRS in IFRIC 1, 'Changes in existing decommissioning, restoration and similar liabilities' (see further para 21.125). However, after the proposal in the discussion paper was made, the ASB carried out some field testing which indicated that changes in the expected life of an oilfield and changes in the expected decommissioning cost could result in a reduction in the necessary provision, which could be significantly greater than the net book value of the decommissioning asset originally capitalised. Therefore, the ASB revised its proposal in FRED 14 and suggested that where subsequent changes are made to the provision, the carrying amount (net of accumulated depreciation) should be recalculated based on current knowledge; and the balance of the change in the provision should be recognised in the profit and loss account. Although this proposal was not included in FRS 12, it might still be appropriate in certain situations as illustrated below.

Example – Change in provision recognised in profit and loss

The facts are the same as in the previous example. At the end of year 10 the obligation stands in the books at £19.04m. The value of the asset is £74.84 (amortisation of £37.42m having been charged – £4.08m relating to the decommissioning element of the asset). Researchers have found a new way of decommissioning which has been tested satisfactorily in the laboratory. It is believed that this new method, which is far safer and less labour intensive, will cost £400m and can be undertaken in a further 75 years time.

Present value of obligation	**Discount rate**	**Net present value £'m**		**Cash flows Year 100 £m**
	4.5%	14.73		400.00
Unwinding of discount		**Discount**		**Total discount in first 10 years £'m**
Year 11		0.66}		
Year 12		0.69}		
Year 13		0.72}		
Year 14		0.76}		
Year 15		0.79}		
Year 16		0.83}	=	8.14
Year 17		0.86}		
Year 18		0.90}		
Year 19		0.94}		
Year 20		0.99}		
…..		…..		
Year 35		1.91		
…..		…..		
Year 60		5.73		
…..		…..		
Year 85		17.22		
Total discount		385.27		

The net present value of the obligation needs to be decreased from £19.04m to £14.73m as illustrated in the table below. This is easily done, but a problem then arises as to what to credit. Should the amount of £4.31m be deducted from the depreciated cost of the asset? If the new technology had been in existence when the original provision was made, the provision needed then would have been £9.49m compared to the actual provision made of £12.26m, a reduced amount of £2.77m. The asset capitalised would have been less by this amount and ten years amortisation would have been less by £0.92m.

	Original assessment £'m	Revised assessment £'m	Difference £'m
Provision year 1	12.26	9.49	2.77
Charged to P&L over 10 years	6.78	5.24	1.54
Provision year 10	19.04	14.73	4.31
Asset capitalised year 1	12.26	9.49	2.77
10 years depreciation	4.08	3.16	0.92
Net book value year 10	8.18	6.33	1.85

Therefore, it would be necessary to make the following adjustments in order to restate the provision and asset:

Dr balance sheet provision	£4.31m	
Cr fixed asset		£1.85m
Cr P&L depreciation		£0.92m
Cr P&L discount		£1.54m

As these adjustments are a revision of an estimate rather than a fundamental error, their effect would be recorded in the current year's profit and loss account rather than as a prior year adjustment.

21.120 Another way of calculating the adjustment is to consider the proportion of the adjustment that relates to past depreciation. Suppose that when an asset was built a provision for decommissioning costs was estimated to be £100. The £100 was capitalised as part of the cost of the asset and depreciated over the useful economic life of the asset of 20 years. After ten years the estimate of the decommissioning costs was revised and the provision reduced to £40. Ignoring the effects of discounting, the release of the provision of £60 should be recognised in the same place as the original debit associated with the initial provision. £100 was initially capitalised as a tangible fixed asset, but ten years later on, only half of this remains in the carrying amount of the asset in the balance sheet. Therefore, only half of the £60 now being reversed remains in the balance sheet, so £30 should be credited to tangible fixed assets. The remaining £30 was previously recognised in the profit and loss account (*via* depreciation) and, therefore, its reversal should also be reflected in the profit and loss account.

[The next paragraph is 21.122.]

21.122 We consider that it is also acceptable when the adjustment decreases the provision to reduce the corresponding asset by the same amount, until the asset's carrying value reaches nil, in which case any remaining credit would be taken to the profit an loss account.

21.123 The example in paragraph 21.119 considers the situation where the revision of the estimate leads to a reduced provision, but the need to increase the original provision will also arise in practice. Where this is the case, similar calculations can be performed to work out what effect the revised assessments would have had on the originally recognised provision and asset. The resulting adjustment would be to increase the provision and asset and charge the adjustment as additional depreciation and discount in the profit and loss account. But it could be argued following the introduction of FRS 15, that a backlog depreciation adjustment of this nature is no longer appropriate.

21.124 The better way of dealing with such adjustments to the provision is merely to add any increase in provision to the carrying value of the asset and depreciate the balance prospectively over its life. Any possible over-valuation caused by adding such adjustments to the carrying value of the asset would be taken care of by carrying out impairment tests to ensure that the asset's carrying value does not exceed its recoverable amount.

21.125 Our view is that, although any of the methods outlined above could be argued to be acceptable, we would normally expect companies to adopt the prospective method. This is the method specified in the SORP, 'Accounting for oil and gas exploration, development, production and decommissioning activities', issued by the UK Oil Industry Accounting Committee (OIAC). Furthermore, use of the prospective method is now required under IFRS. In May 2004, the IFRIC issued an interpretation, IFRIC 1, 'Changes in existing decommissioning, restoration and similar liabilities'. This requires that, where the related asset is accounted for under the cost method, changes in the liability that result from changes in the estimated timing or amount of economic benefits required to settle the obligation, or a change in the discount rate, should be accounted for as follows:

- Changes in the liability should be added to, or deducted from, the related asset's cost in the current period. However, the amount deducted from the asset's cost should not exceed its carrying amount. If a decrease in the liability exceeds the asset's carrying amount, the excess should be recognised immediately in profit or loss.
- If the adjustment results in an addition to the asset's cost, the company should consider whether this is an indication that the new carrying amount of the asset may not be fully recoverable and, if so, should test the asset for impairment.

IFRIC 1 also sets out requirements for where a policy of revaluation is used for the related asset. [IFRIC 1 paras 5, 6].

Restructuring

21.126 Provisions under FRS 12 are obligations to transfer resources embodying economic benefits as a result of past transactions or events (that is, liabilities) that are uncertain as to their timing or amount.

21.127 The key elements of the definition of a liability are considered in detail from paragraph 21.17. One of those relates to the need to have an obligating event, which evidences that a past event has taken place. For restructurings, FRS 12 sets down detailed rules that indicate when an obligating event has occurred and when an obligation to restructure arises. The impact of these rules means that it is still possible in certain defined circumstances to make restructuring provisions under FRS 12.

21.128 The paragraphs that follow explore the rules that apply when a company proposes to carry out a restructuring programme.

Restructuring rules in FRS 12

21.129 FRS 12 applies to provisions for restructuring, although provisions in respect of the termination of operations are covered instead by FRS 3, 'Reporting financial performance'. Discontinued operations are dealt with in chapter 8.

Definition

21.130 FRS 12 introduces the following definition of a 'restructuring':

> *"A programme that is planned and controlled by management, and materially changes either:*
>
> *(a) the scope of a business undertaken by an entity; or*
>
> *(b) the manner in which that business is conducted."*

[FRS 12 para 2].

21.131 The standard gives some helpful examples of situations that fall within the restructuring definition:

- The sale or termination of a line of business.
- The closure of business locations in a country or region or the relocation of business activities from one country or region to another.
- Changes in management structure, for example, eliminating a layer of management.
- Fundamental reorganisations that have a material effect on the nature and focus of the entity's operations.

[FRS 12 para 75].

Applying the recognition criteria

21.132 It is only acceptable to make a provision for restructuring when an obligating event has arisen. Without the existence of an obligating event no obligation can exist. For a restructuring programme, it is unlikely that a liability will arise from a legal obligation as the obligation is more likely to be constructive in nature. As explained in paragraph 21.28 it is often more difficult to discern when a constructive obligation originates, so the standard introduces specific conditions that have to exist before a constructive restructuring obligation can exist. The minimum evidence needed is:

- A detailed formal plan for the restructuring, which identifies at least:
  - The business or part of a business concerned.
  - The principal locations affected.
  - The location, function, and approximate number of employees who will be compensated for terminating their services.
  - The expenditures that will be undertaken.
  - When the plan will be implemented.
- A valid expectation in those affected that it will carry out the restructuring by starting to implement that plan or announcing its main features to those affected by it.

[FRS 12 para 75].

21.133 The standard indicates examples of the type of evidence needed to demonstrate that the company has started to implement a restructuring plan. This includes:

- Dismantling plant.
- Selling assets.
- Public announcement of the plan's main features.

[FRS 12 para 78].

Board decision

21.134 It is not possible to make a provision where only a management or board decision to restructure has been taken before the balance sheet date, as this does not in itself give rise to a constructive obligation. [FRS 12 para 80]. Furthermore, even if the management or board complete the detailed plan and announce the restructuring after the company's year end, but before its financial statements are approved by the board, provision for the restructuring should not be made. This is because the announcement does not represent an adjusting event after the balance sheet date as there is no commitment to restructure at the year end from which the company cannot withdraw. The company could, for instance, change its plans completely in the new year. Consequently, the 'obligating event' does not take place until after the year end and should be reported as a non-adjusting event after the balance sheet date if the restructuring is of such importance that its non-disclosure would affect the ability of the users of the financial statements to make proper evaluations and decisions. [FRS 12 para 80].

21.135 FRS 12 specifies precisely the requirement for a commitment at the year end and makes it clear that even for a sale or termination, the binding sale agreement or the formal plan (the 'obligating event') must exist at the balance sheet date for an obligation to arise. [FRS 12 paras 83, 77]. Examples of disclosure of post balance sheet events involving restructurings are given in chapter 22 'Events after the balance sheet date'.

Third party expectation

21.136 To be a constructive obligation, a public announcement has to be made in such a way and in sufficient detail (that is, setting out the main features of the plan) that it raises valid expectations in employees (or their representatives), customers, suppliers, and others that the company will carry out the restructuring. [FRS 12 para 78]. Practically, this means that in order to provide for a restructuring at the balance sheet date the company must have started to implement its restructuring plan or if it has not started to implement its plan it must have announced the main features of the restructuring plan to those affected by it in a sufficiently specific manner to raise a valid expectation in them that the company will carry out the restructuring. [FRS 12 para 80]. This is illustrated in the following example.

> **Example – Announcing intentions**
>
> Company A's management has prepared a plan for a reorganisation of its operations. The board has approved the plan, which involves the closure of ten of company A's fifty retail outlets. Management will conduct further analysis before deciding which outlets to close. Management has announced its intentions publicly and believes that this has given rise to an obligation that should be recognised as a liability. Should a provision for restructuring costs be recognised?
>
> No, a provision for restructuring should not be recognised. A constructive obligation arises only when a company has both a detailed formal plan for restructuring and makes an announcement of the plan to those affected by it. The plan to date does not provide sufficient detail that would permit recognition of a constructive obligation.

21.137 By 'starting to implement the plan', the standard means that something must have happened to make those affected expect that the plan will be carried out. Examples include dismantling plant, selling assets or making a detailed public announcement. Where only an announcement has been made, it must be to a level of detail that raises a valid expectation in customers, suppliers, employees or trade unions, that the company will actually carry out the restructuring and will not be able to change its mind.

Example – Announcing plans

A company is planning a head office restructuring. The year end is 31 March 20X1. The company will have made announcements before the year end (say in January 20X1). However, there is a 90 day consultation period and so individual employees will not have been notified by the year end. Can the company provide for the restructuring costs at 31 March 20X1?

At the balance sheet date there has to be a detailed plan and the company has to have raised a valid expectation in those affected that it will carry out the restructuring by starting to implement that plan or announcing its main features to those affected by it. Paragraph 78 of FRS 12 states that a public announcement of a detailed plan to restructure constitutes a constructive obligation to restructure only if it is made in such a way and in sufficient detail (that is, setting out the main features of the plan) that it gives rise to valid expectations in other parties such as customers, suppliers and employees (or their representatives) that the company will carry out the restructuring.

Our view is that it is not necessary for individual employees to have been notified at the year end, provided that employee representatives have been notified. It will be necessary to consider what is involved in the specific consultation, but if it is negotiation of terms rather than something that could change the company's plans (which have already been announced in detail), then provision would be made.

21.138 In some situations, however, a board decision might be all that remains to confirm that an obligation exists. For example, in the situation where employees have been consulted about the restructuring and the restructuring plan has been developed with their participation, board approval will crystallise an obligation when the decision has been made and it has been communicated to the company's employees. Similarly, where negotiations for the sale of part of the business have been agreed with a purchaser, but the terms of the sale are subject to board approval, once that approval has been gained and this has been communicated to the buyer (see further para 21.197) an obligation will arise, because the agreement will then be unconditional. [FRS 12 para 81].

21.139 Also in certain countries a board decision and a formal plan might be all that is necessary to give rise to an obligation. This might occur, for example, where the board includes worker representatives and management representatives. Or formal communication to management and worker representatives might be required by the local laws of the country concerned. [FRS 12 para 82]. In both these cases, a valid expectation that the company will carry out the restructuring will be instilled in the company's employees as soon as the board decision is taken.

Example – Committing to a re-organisation plan

A company has prepared a formal plan for a reorganisation involving site closures and redundancies. The plan has been approved by the board at the year end. However, the company does not wish to provide for the reorganisation this year as it is planning a rights issue and does not want to depress the results. Accordingly, it will not implement or announce the reorganisation until after the year end and until after the financial statements are approved and the rights issue document is published.

If the company has not committed itself to the reorganisation or begun to implement it, the company's proposed treatment is acceptable. However, disclosure should be made of the board's plans in the financial statements and the rights issue document in order to give users of those documents the ability to make proper evaluations and decisions. On the other hand if the board has actually begun to implement the reorganisation by the end of the year, for example by scrapping plant or informing employees and suppliers of the reorganisation, then there is an obligating event and provision should be made, despite the fact that no formal announcement has been made.

Restructuring time-frame

21.140 Many company reorganisations can take a number of years to complete. Typically a programme can run for two or three years and some might take up to five years. Where a restructuring will take a long time, it is unlikely that all of the re-organisation will represent an obligation at the first year end following the decision, as the company will inevitably be able to change its plans. [FRS 12 para 79].

21.141 If it is expected that there will be a long delay before the restructuring begins or that the restructuring will take an unreasonable length of time, it is unlikely that the plan will raise a sufficiently valid expectation on the part of others that the company is committed to restructuring.

21.142 For example, a company involved in a retailing business has a significant number of small retail outlets and it has decided to restructure to consolidate its retailing activities into a smaller number of larger outlets. This sort of decision could take a long time to implement in practice and so the company might decide to phase the work. The time-frame will depend on a number of factors some of which will be outside the company's control (for example, the availability of suitable retail outlets of the appropriate size and location). If the time-frame for the plan's implementation is over a number of years, it will be unlikely that the plan can be specific enough initially to make a provision for all of the costs associated with the proposed restructuring. Again the issue here comes back to whether there is a valid obligation from which the company cannot realistically withdraw. Certainly, the early part (say phase one) of a restructuring plan might create a valid expectation such that a provision can be made on commencement of the programme, but subsequent phases might not do so until later in the programme. In future years as the restructuring progresses it might become appropriate to make a provision for the next phase when there is a valid expectation that this will be carried through.

21.143 Clearly this is an area where there will be considerable debate concerning whether or not a plan is detailed enough and firm enough to create a valid expectation in others that it will be carried through. Any plan that is over one year in length is unlikely to be sufficiently detailed on initial announcement to permit provision in full for all costs, and for major restructuring programmes this is likely to lead to costs being charged to profit or loss over a number of accounting periods.

21.144 One of the consequences of the standard is that the costs of a single re-organisation programme could be charged in different accounting periods, because it may not be possible under the recognition criteria in FRS 12 to provide for these costs all at once. Consequently, where this happens it might be useful for the totality of such costs and any related capital expenditure to be disclosed. An example of a restructuring programme extending over a number of years is Table 21.3.

Table 21.3 – Restructuring costs charged over several years

GlaxoSmithKline plc – Report and accounts – 31 December 2008

29 Other provisions (extract)

	Legal and other disputes	Major restructuring programmes	Employee related provisions	Integration and manufacturing reorganisation	Other provisions	Total
	£m	£m	£m	£m	£m	£m
At 1 January 2008	1,152	246	234	116	179	**1,927**
Exchange adjustments	424	91	48	13	42	**618**
Charge for the year	719	740	55	9	2	**1,525**
Reversed unused	(149)	(7)	(16)	(14)	(30)	**(216)**
Unwinding of discount	8	5	–	–	3	**16**
Utilised	(251)	(215)	(67)	(34)	(14)	**(581)**
Transfer to pensions obligations	–	(208)	–	–	–	**(208)**
Reclassifications and other movements	–	–	14	–	4	**18**
At 31 December 2008	1,903	652	268	90	186	**3,099**
To be settled within one year	695	606	68	54	31	**1,454**
To be settled after one year	1,208	46	200	36	155	**1,645**
At 31 December 2008	1,903	652	268	90	186	**3,099**

Major restructuring programmes

In October 2007 GSK announced a significant new Operational Excellence programme to improve the effectiveness and productivity of its operations (see Note 7 'Major restructuring programmes'). A significant expansion of the Operational Excellence programme was approved by the Board and announced in February 2009. Total costs for the implementation of the expanded programme are now expected to be approximately £3.6 billion, to be incurred over the period from 2007 to 2011.

Provisions for staff severance payments are made when management has made a formal decision to eliminate certain positions and this has been communicated to the groups of employees affected. No provision is made for staff severance payments that are made immediately.

Approximately 40% of the costs were incurred by 31st December 2008, and approximately 35% are expected to be incurred in 2009, 20% in 2010 and the balance mostly in 2011. In total, approximately 75% of these costs are expected to be cash expenditures and 25% are expected to be accounting writedowns. Uncertainties exist over the exact amount and timing of cash outflows, as a result of potential future exchange rate fluctuations and as many elements of the restructuring programme are subject to employee consultation procedures, making it difficult to predict with precision when these procedures will be completed. However, the majority of the remaining cash payments are expected to be made in 2009 and 2010.

In addition, costs of £34 million were incurred during the year under the restructuring programme related to the integration of the Reliant Pharmaceuticals, Inc. business in the USA, following its acquisition in December 2007.

Pension augmentations arising from staff redundancies of £208 million have been charged during the year and then transferred to the pension obligations provision as shown in Note 28 'Pensions and other post-employment benefits'. Asset write-downs have been recognised as impairments of property, plant and equipment in Note 17 'Property, plant and equipment'.

Binding sale agreement

21.145 FRS 12 requires that a binding sale agreement evidencing a commitment to sell part of the business must exist before an obligation to sell can arise. [FRS 12 para 83]. A company needs to have found a purchaser and signed unconditional contracts before a legal obligation can arise under which a provision might become necessary. This means that an unconditional sale agreement must be signed before the year end for an obligation to arise at the year end. During the period between the board decision to sell and the date on which the sale becomes unconditional, there might be a need to consider the carrying value of the cash generating unit to which the operations relate. For example, if it is envisaged that a loss will arise on the sale of the operations or the operations are loss making, it would generally be necessary to carry out an impairment review in accordance with FRS 11 and this might necessitate a provision for impairment against the assets being sold. Impairment reviews are considered in more detail in chapter 18.

21.146 If a company has announced at its year end that it has put a subsidiary up for sale and if it cannot find a buyer it will close down the company, the question arises whether or not an obligation exists. In this type of situation it is hard to say that the company is committed to a course of action if it still has options open to it. Therefore, it is unlikely that the company can make provision for the re-organisation costs in this type of circumstance, although it may still have to carry out an impairment review.

21.147 In some situations, the sale of an operation might be a small part of a larger restructuring. Where this is the case, an obligation might arise for other aspects of the restructuring plan for which provision can be made before a formal sale agreement has been reached for the operation being sold. [FRS 12 para 84].

Sale or termination of operations

21.148 Restructurings that involve the termination of an operation are dealt with in FRS 3. In a similar way to FRS 12, that standard requires provision for any losses to be made if a decision to close has been made and the decision is evidenced by a detailed formal plan for termination from which the reporting entity cannot realistically withdraw. [FRS 3 para 18]. Evidence of the commitment might be the public announcement of specific plans, the commencement of implementation or other circumstances effectively obliging the reporting entity to complete the termination.

21.149 The provision required by the standard should include direct costs of the termination and any operating losses of the operation up to the date of termination, after taking account of any future profits of the operation, but not from the disposal of its assets. [FRS 3 para 18 as amended by FRS 12 para 100]. FRS 3 was amended by FRS 12 to preclude profits on disposals of assets from being taken into account in measuring such provisions. [FRS 12 para 100]. Although generally it is not possible under FRS 12's rules to provide for future operating losses, this is not the case for a provision made in accordance with FRS 3 on the termination of an operation. Future operating losses up to the date of termination of an operation should be included in a provision made under FRS 3's rules. Whereas for a sale of an operation, profits arising on its eventual sale cannot be taken into account, if the sale gives rise to a loss this should be provided for. There is no justification given in the standard for allowing provision to be made for future operation losses where an operation is being terminated, but it is possible to surmise that this situation is akin to an onerous contract where provision is required (see further para 21.168). However, often before there is a need to make provision for future losses in this way, assets should be written down for impairment as a result of FRS 11. Provisions for losses on termination of operations are discussed in detail in chapter 8.

Example – Provision for redundancies

A company is closing an operation and by the year end a formal plan has been approved by the board and an announcement has been made. The closure will involve redundancies, but there will be a corresponding gain when the factory is sold. The factory has been valued professionally at above its carrying value and is expected to be sold after the year end, but before the financial statements are approved. Can the provision for redundancies be reduced by the profit on sale of the factory assuming it is sold before the financial statements are approved?

The company has a constructive obligation in respect of the redundancies and should provide for them. The gain on disposal is, however, a contingent gain whose receipt is not virtually certain at the year end. Thus, the gain should not be recognised at the year end, although disclosure may be required.

Post balance sheet events

21.150 Post balance sheet events are dealt with in detail in chapter 22. However, in summary, FRS 21, 'Events after the balance sheet date', requires that a material event after the balance sheet date should be reflected in the prior year's financial statements only where it is an adjusting event. An adjusting event is an event that occurs after the balance sheet date that provides additional evidence of conditions that existed at the balance sheet date. [FRS 21 paras 3, 8].

21.151 Provision should not be made in the current year for non-adjusting post-balance sheet events. FRS 21 describes the type of events that are adjusting events and those that are non-adjusting events. [FRS 21 paras 9, 22]. The non-adjusting list includes:

- Announcing, or commencing the implementation of, a major restructuring.
- Announcing a plan to discontinue an operation.
- A major business combination after the balance sheet date or disposing of a major subsidiary.

21.152 FRS 21 also addresses going concern. Where management determine after the balance sheet date either that it intends to liquidate the company or to cease trading, or that it has no realistic alternative but to do so, the financial statements should not be prepared on a going concern basis. [FRS 21 para 14]. Therefore, where a decision to close down a company's operation is made after the balance sheet date, this may indicate that applying the going concern concept to the company is not appropriate. This is dealt with in chapter 4.

Costs of restructuring

21.153 FRS 12 specifies that a restructuring provision should include only the direct expenditures arising from the restructuring, which are those that are both:

- necessarily entailed by the restructuring; and
- not associated with the ongoing activities of the company.

[FRS 12 para 85]

21.154 Expenditure allowed in a restructuring provision includes the following:

- Expenditure necessarily entailed by the restructuring and not associated with the ongoing activities of the business.
- Costs of making employees redundant (see para 21.158).
- Costs of terminating certain leases and other contracts, the termination of which results directly from the reorganisation.
- Costs representing contractual obligations that would either continue after the restructuring with no economic benefit to the company, for example, where the company is not permitted to cancel the lease and is unable to use the property in its continuing operations. Onerous contracts are discussed in more detail from paragraph 21.168.

The following table distinguishes between costs that are generally included in, and those generally excluded from, a restructuring provision.

Description of costs	Included	Excluded	Reason for exclusion
Voluntary redundancies.	✓		
Compulsory redundancies, if the target for voluntary redundancies are not met.	✓		
Lease cancellation fees for a factory that will no longer be used.	✓		
Relocation of employees and related equipment from a factory (to be closed) to a factory that will continue to be used.		✓	Costs associated with ongoing activities.
Retraining of remaining employees.		✓	Costs associated with ongoing activities.
Recruitment costs for a new manager.		✓	Costs associated with ongoing activities.
Marketing costs to develop new corporate image.		✓	Costs associated with ongoing activities.
Investments in a new distribution network.		✓	Costs associated with ongoing activities.
Future identifiable operating losses up to the date of a restructuring.		✓	Costs associated with ongoing activities.
Impairment write-down of certain property, plant and equipment.		✓	The impairment provision should be assessed in accordance with IAS 36 and offset against the asset.
Costs of the remaining non-cancellable term of an operating lease after operations cease.	✓		
Rental costs under the lease contract for the period after the criteria in FRS 12 paragraph 77 were met (see para 21.132), but before the operation ceased.		✓	Operations continued to be used.
Consulting fees to identify future corporate strategies and organisational structures.		✓	Costs associated with ongoing activities.
Costs of relocating inventory and equipment that will be used at another location.		✓	Costs associated with ongoing activities.
Acquisition integration costs, for example, integrating the combining companies' computer systems.		✓	Costs associated with ongoing activities.

21.155 FRS 12 states that retraining or relocating continuing staff, marketing, or investment in new systems and distribution networks should not be included in the restructuring provision. [FRS 12 para 86]. This is because these costs relate to the future conduct of the business and, as a consequence, do not represent an obligation arising from a past event. Also, the restructuring provision does not include future operating losses (unless these relate to an onerous contract) as the losses do not result from a past event (see para 21.187). [FRS 12 para 87].

21.156 Where relocation has already occurred at the balance sheet date, such that a liability exists for these costs, for example, freight company charges, then clearly an accrual should be made. But where relocation costs have not yet been incurred at the balance sheet date, any provision would be for future expenditure, albeit committed at the balance sheet date. It is clear from FRS 12's rules that provisions for restructuring should include only those commitments for future expenditure that relate to past operations (that is, past events), not expenditure commitments that relate to future operations. Therefore, in order to recognise a provision, it is not sufficient to demonstrate that a commitment for future expenditure exists at the balance date, it is also necessary for that expenditure commitment to relate to past operations, not future operations (except in the case of onerous contracts).

Example 1 – Relocation and recruitment of employees

A company has drawn up a plan to restructure its management and has decided to make a number of its managers redundant. It is also going to bring in a new senior manager to take over responsibility for running the business as part of the overall plan. The new manager is to be recruited from outside the company and the company will pay for the relocation costs for its new employee. There will also be some retraining of the remaining employees in new systems to be introduced.

In this case, redundancy costs and other closure costs associated with terminating any of the company's operations will not yield any future economic benefits. These costs are, therefore, eligible under FRS 12 to be included in the company's restructuring provision. Staff retraining costs, on the other hand, are likely to generate future economic benefits to the company's future operations, so are excluded from the restructuring provision. Doubtless, the company would be unlikely to have committed to the appointment of the new manager unless it considered that the future economic benefits to be derived from that appointment exceeded the costs. Hence, no provision should be made to cover the recruitment and relocation costs relating to the new manager as part of the restructuring provision.

Example 2 – Relocation incentives

A company has announced before its year end that it will be closing its offices in London and will be relocating staff to Brussels after its year end. The company recognises that, normally under FRS 12, a relocation provision would be prohibited. However, in this case, all employees affected have been advised in writing before its year end that if they relocate they will be paid a one off incentive to do so. There is, therefore, either a legal or at least a constructive obligation at the balance sheet date, in that those asked to relocate now have a valid expectation that such payments will be made and that the company is not in a position to withdraw from this.

Should the company make a provision for the relocation incentive under FRS 12 based on the current best estimate of the number of employees expected to accept the incentive offer to relocate?

No it should not. Whilst it appears that the company is far enough down the track to enable provision to be made in principle, it could only make a provision for costs associated with past operations. An incentive to relocate is the same as a relocation cost and, therefore, cannot be provided prior to being incurred. In these circumstances no obligation would exist until the employee had rendered the service of moving to Brussels.

21.157 Gains on the expected disposal of assets are not taken into account in measuring a restructuring provision, even if the sale of assets is envisaged as part of the restructuring (see para 21.115). [FRS 12 para 88]. This is illustrated in the following example.

Example – Gain on disposal of assets

A company is closing an operation and by the year end a formal plan will have been approved by management and announced. The closure will involve redundancies, but there will be a related gain when the factory is sold. The factory has been valued professionally at above its carrying value and is expected to be sold after the year end, but before the financial statements are approved. Can the provision for redundancies be reduced by the profit on sale of the factory, assuming it is sold before the financial statements are approved?

No, it cannot. Paragraph 54 of FRS 12 states that gains from the expected disposal of assets should not be taken into account in measuring a provision. Paragraph 55 of FRS 12 states that:

"Gains on the expected disposal of assets are not taken into account in measuring a provision, even if the expected disposal is closely linked to the event giving rise to the provision. Instead, an entity assesses such gains for recognition under the principles of asset recognition, which include the requirements in FRS 11, 'Impairment of fixed assets and goodwill.'"

A specific application of this rule given in paragraph 88 of FRS 12 is a restructuring.

Redundancy provisions

21.158 An area that often results in significant provisions and is often associated with reorganisations concerns redundancies. The timing of such provisions is considered below by looking at the various stages involved in the redundancy process.

Compulsory redundancies

21.159 The process of making compulsory redundancies usually involves several stages:

- Initial board decision.
- Identifying the business or part of the business concerned and the principal locations affected.
- Identifying the location, function and approximate number of employees to be made redundant.

- Approval of the detailed formal plan by the board, which includes details of the expenditures to be incurred and the timing of implementation.
- Identifying employees to be made redundant in terms of individuals.
- Informing employees.
- Making the redundancy payments.

Situation 1 — redundancy payments made

21.160 Where all the above steps have been taken by the balance sheet date, the cost of the redundancy programme will be reflected in the financial statements of the year. This is because the liability has been incurred and settled.

Situation 2 — employees informed

21.161 Where the employees have been informed of their redundancies by the balance sheet date, provision should be made in the financial statements for the year, because the company's detailed formal plan is being actioned. A clear obligation has been incurred to specific employees. It is probable that there will be an outflow of resources and the cost can be measured with reliability.

21.162 It is sometimes argued that the liability represents only the amount that is legally payable to employees and that *ex-gratia* amounts, paid over and above the legal minimum, need not be provided. This may be an argument in some cases where it has not been the company's practice in the past to make such *ex-gratia* payments. However, if it is established practice in the company to make *ex-gratia* payments and the decision has been made as part of the detailed formal plan to pay such extra amounts in the particular case, then the additional payment forms part of the constructive obligation. Clearly this would also be the case if the employees had terms in their contracts that provided for the payment of extra amounts, or if the employees included directors who are entitled to such amounts under their service contracts. Generally, the full amount of redundancy payments should be provided and not just the legal minimum.

Situation 3 — employees identified but not informed

21.163 Where the employees have been identified both in terms of numbers and individuals no provision should be made, unless an obligating event has taken place. At this stage in the process, the board has formally approved the detailed formal plan, but it is also necessary for the company to have raised a valid expectation in those affected that it will carry out its proposals. Even where the company has identified the specific employees that it wishes to make redundant, no expectation will have been raised on the part of others that the company will carry out its plans, unless the company has made a formal announcement or has started to implement its plans. Only when such a commitment has been made does an obligating event arise and provision can be made. If, for example, the company has started to implement its plan and has announced its intention to 100 of 300 employees affected, provision will be allowed where this announcement makes it clear that more employees are to be made redundant as part of the plan. Where, however, the announcement only specifies that the 100 told will be made redundant, this does not raise a valid expectation that other redundancies will occur and, consequently, provision cannot be made for the further 200 redundancies still to be announced.

Situation 4 — numbers determined but not specific employees

21.164 In this situation the detailed formal plan has been approved by the board, the numbers to be made redundant have been identified, but not the specific employees. It is likely that no provision can be made for the redundancies at this stage, because it is possible that the board can still change its plans thereby avoiding the potential obligation. However, as the board has approved a detailed formal plan, if it raises a valid expectation in its staff that it will carry out the redundancy programme, by either starting to implement the plan or by announcing its main feature to those affected, it should make provision for the redundancies.

Voluntary redundancies

21.165 The same principles apply to voluntary redundancies. In general, provision should be made for the expected amount of the redundancy payment, but only where the conditions in FRS 12 have been complied with. That is, the company has a detailed formal plan and its main features have been announced to those affected or the plan has started to be implemented. Where a detailed formal plan has been approved, but it has not been communicated to employees, there is no obligating event and no provision can be made. What could happen in practice is that a detailed formal plan might be approved by the balance sheet date to reduce the workforce and this might have been announced, but the board does not know how much of the reduction will come from voluntary redundancies (giving rise to a higher payment), how much from natural wastage (no payment arising) and how much from compulsory redundancies (a lower amount being payable). Hence, it is possible that any liability that arises as a result of the detailed plan decision etc will not be capable of being reliably measured.

21.166 Although this uncertainty might suggest that no provision should be made for the full liability, there may be minimum amounts that can be estimated reliably. For instance, it may be possible to estimate the maximum number of people that could be lost through natural wastage and, therefore, to estimate the numbers who would be made redundant, whether voluntarily or compulsorily. If the latter numbers could be determined it might be possible to quantify the legal minimum that would have to be paid in redundancy pay and provide for that. If on the other hand it is not possible to determine the split between those taking voluntary or compulsory redundancy, then the company should probably, depending on the circumstances, make provision for the maximum amount that will become due under the terms of the voluntary scheme. It should be remembered that the standard says that it will only be in extremely rare circumstances that a company will not be able to make as estimate of the obligation. [FRS 12 para 25].

21.167 A further factor that may make it impossible to quantify a liability reliably is if the reduction in employees is to take place over an extended period. This could, for instance, affect the numbers of employees who would be lost through natural wastage and thus make more difficult the estimates of how many would be made redundant. In such a case, where the amounts cannot be reliably measured, no provision should be made and the obligation should be disclosed as a contingent liability (see further para 21.61). It may be necessary to make a provision in a subsequent period when the obligation becomes more certain and can be reliably estimated.

Onerous contracts

21.168 Under FRS 12, if a company has a contract that is onerous, the present obligation under the contract should be recognised and measured as a provision. [FRS 12 para 71]. An onerous contract is defined in the standard as a contract under which the unavoidable costs of meeting the obligations under the contract exceed the economic benefits expected to be received under it. [FRS 12 paras 2, 73].

21.169 A typical example of an onerous contract is an operating property lease which has been abandoned by a company and cannot be sub-let. While an operating lease would be regarded as an executory contract (a contract where either neither party has yet performed any obligations or where both parties have performed equally), and executory contracts are generally outside the scope of FRS 12, an exception exists where such contracts are onerous. In this example it can be seen that the contract is onerous as the company expects to receive no further benefit under the contract but it is still committed to pay the landlord the future rentals.

21.170 An onerous contract is no different to any other provision as explained above in paragraph 21.168 and must be recognised and measured in the same way as any other provision.

21.171 In considering the scope of FRS 12 in respect of onerous contracts it is important to note that the standard does not apply to other provisions where a more specific standard exists, for example SSAP 9, 'Stocks and long-term contracts'.

Unavoidable costs and expected benefits

21.172 To determine whether a contract is onerous in more complex cases than the simple example given in paragraph 21.169 above, it is necessary to understand what is meant by unavoidable costs and expected benefits. Without a clear understanding of these terms a company will not be able to ascertain whether unavoidable costs exceed expected benefits under any given contract.

21.173 Firstly, unavoidable costs under a contract are defined by the standard as being the least net cost of exiting the contract. This will be the lower of the cost to exit or breach the contract and the cost of fulfilling it. [FRS 12 para 73].

21.174 In terms of economic benefits expected to be received under the contract, it would be possible to define this either very narrowly as being only those benefits directly arising from the contract or more widely including other indirect benefits. In our opinion this term should be defined in its widest sense to include all benefits arising either directly or indirectly under the contract.

21.175 The reason for this is that no company is in business to lose money and as such 'day 1' onerous contracts should not exist (in the absence of manifest error on the part of a company). Nevertheless, a company may knowingly choose to enter into a contract with a customer to supply goods or services to them at a price lower than cost because the seller is obtaining some other indirect benefits as well as the cash consideration from the customer. Such benefits may for example be advertising or additional know-how about production of the goods or services being supplied. Looking only at direct benefits, this contract would appear to be onerous, but invariably when such contracts are considered in more detail it transpires that the commercial reason behind the contract supports apparent 'loss leader' pricing.

21.176 Following on from this issue, a question arises in practice as to whether the words *"benefits expected to be received under the contract"* mean only those monetary benefits that are contractually committed or whether they mean a potentially broader population of benefits that are expected, although no contract has been entered into that assures their receipt. We consider that the latter interpretation is appropriate, because quite often the benefits expected (direct and indirect) will not be contractual. Similarly, in the case of a property lease that has been abandoned, a company can usually have a reasonable expectation of sub-letting the premises at a market rent even if no tenant has yet been identified.

Assets dedicated to the contract

21.177 The standard requires that before a separate provision for an onerous contract can be made, a company should recognise any impairment that has occurred on assets *"dedicated to that contract"*. [FRS 12 para 74]. It is then necessary to consider what the words 'dedicated to that contract' mean. For instance, do they mean only assets used for the purpose of fulfilling the contract, or can they, or should they, include the other assets of the IGU that has the onerous contract?

21.178 An asset is only dedicated to a contract if there is a contractual requirement to use a specific asset and no other asset can be used. For the purposes of impairment testing, identifying the IGU is based on the facts and circumstances of the particular case. The IGU may be the contract and its dedicated assets, or it may include a wider group of assets. If an asset is dedicated to the contract, it is likely that the asset cannot be sold without the contract and thus any fair value less costs to sell calculation should reflect that fact.

Overhead costs

21.179 Where a company has an onerous contract to supply goods or services, a question sometimes arises as to whether it is possible to include an apportionment of overheads in the amount to be provided. This question might arise where a central pool of assets or resources representing fixed costs are required to service a number of contracts, but where only one contract is onerous. Provided the other profitable contracts cover central costs and support the carrying value of central assets, it is not appropriate to provide for a proportion of overheads.

21.180 The reason for this treatment is that the central fixed overhead costs represent future operating costs of a profitable business and would be incurred irrespective of the onerous contract. Therefore, companies should not provide for an apportionment of fixed overheads, but a provision would be appropriate for marginal overhead costs where such costs are clearly incremental and directly related to support of the contract.

Separation of a single contract

21.181 In general, contracts should be assessed in their entirety. An onerous contract provision should not be recognised for a period shorter than the remaining contract terms. For example, if a company rents a property for a retail business and temporarily closes the store for renovation, no onerous contract provision should be made for the closure period unless the lease contract is onerous as a whole for the remaining lease period (see example 3 in para 21.186 below).

21.182 Arguably, in certain limited situations, an operating lease contract could be split into several component contracts. However, it is worth noting that provision for the onerous part should be recognised if, and only if, both of the following criteria are met:

1 The onerous and non-onerous portions are clearly identifiable and separable under the operating lease contract. In determining whether the onerous portion is identifiable and separable, it is necessary to consider whether the one contract could reasonably at inception have been agreed as a number of separate contracts. Any interdependency between the elements of the contract would indicate that the contract is not separable.

2 The unavoidable costs and future economic benefits can be allocated on a reliable basis to the various elements of the contract.

Illustrative examples

21.183 The principles outlined above are examined further using examples of two types of contracts (long-term purchase contracts and property operating leases) to illustrate situations that might arise in practice.

Long-term purchase contracts

21.184 The examples that follow illustrate when a contract is onerous, whether or not dedicated assets need to be impaired and how payments to vary contract terms or terminate contracts should be dealt with in the financial statements.

Example 1 — Contract not onerous

A company has a contract to purchase one million units of gas at 23p per unit giving a contract price of £230,000 and the current market price for a similar contract is 16p per unit giving a price of £160,000. The gas will be used in generating electricity and the electricity will be sold at a profit.

In this case the economic benefits from the contract include the benefits to the company of using the gas in its business and because the electricity that is produced can be sold at a profit, the contract is not onerous.

Example 2 — Impairment of assets

The contract's terms are the same as in example 1, as is the market price. However, when the gas is used to generate electricity, the high cost of the gas means that the electricity is sold at a loss and the company makes an overall operating loss. (It is assumed that all the gas used by the company to generate electricity is purchased under the contract.)

In this case, as the company is making losses, it will be necessary to comply with paragraph 74 of the standard to carry out an impairment test (in accordance with FRS 11) on the assets dedicated to the contract and write down any assets that are impaired. To the extent that there is still a loss after the assets have been fully written down, a provision for an onerous contract should be recorded. The impairment test on the dedicated assets (or their IGU) should be carried out by reference to the normal time span for impairment testing of assets/IGUs set out in FRS 11 and not by reference to the contract's duration.

Example 3 — Sale to third party at below purchase price

The facts are the same as in example 1 with regard to the price of the gas subject to the contract and the market price. However, in this example there is a sales contract to sell the gas on to a third party as it is in excess of the company's requirements. The sales contract is priced at 18p per unit (5p below contract cost). The company would have to pay £55,000 to exit the purchase contract.

In this example the only economic benefits to be derived from the purchase contract costing £230,000 are the proceeds from the sales contract, which are £180,000. Therefore, a provision should be made for the onerous element of £50,000, being the lower of the cost of fulfilling the contract and the penalty cost of cancellation (£55,000).

21.185 In practice, a company may decide to terminate an existing contract and incur a penalty, in order to enter into a more beneficial contract. The example below considers the accounting for the termination cost in this situation.

Example – Contract termination costs

In the year ended 31 December 20X1, a company has an existing contract with a third party supplier. The company wishes to terminate this contract in 20X2 even though it will still have two years to run, because it can enter into a cheaper contract with a new supplier. It will incur a charge for terminating the contract.

(a) Does the company have to provide in 20X1 for the contract that it will be exiting in 20X2?

If the contract with the existing supplier is an onerous contract (that is, one in which the unavoidable costs of meeting the obligations under it exceed the economic benefits expected to be received under it) then provision should be made under FRS 12 for the least net cost of exiting from it. However, if the business in which the products supplied under the contract are used is profitable then the contract is not onerous and provision should not be made in 20X1 in advance of termination. Instead, the termination cost should be charged as incurred in 20X2.

(b) The company considers that as the old contract is being terminated in order to enter into the new one (at a lower cost), it should be permitted to spread the termination payment over the period of the new contract. Can it defer the termination charge to match this against the benefits of the new contract?

Although the decision to terminate the old contract is commercially linked to the decision to enter into the new contract, the cost does not form part of the cost of the new contract. The fact that there will be future benefits from entering into the new contract would not be sufficient to justify deferring recognition of the cost to terminate the old contract when it is incurred (comparable with treatment of redundancy costs). Such costs would not qualify for recognition as an asset as there are no future economic benefits specifically attributable to the cost.

Operating leases on property

21.186 Where leased property is abandoned and there is no prospect to sub-lease, determining the necessary provision for the contract is fairly straightforward. However, where companies continue to occupy leased property, or where sub-lease opportunities exist a number of complications can arise. The examples that follow illustrate for property leases where a contract becomes onerous, when assets need to be impaired, the treatment of sub-leases and the issues concerning groups of similar properties.

Example 1 — Above market rentals

A company has a 10 year lease on the head office property of one of its trading operations at a rental of £50,000 per annum. The market rent is £30,000 per annum. The property is used in the business and the business is profitable.

In this situation the lease is not onerous, because the economic benefits are assumed to include those that derive from the asset's use in the company's continuing business.

Example 2 — Head office of loss making business

The company has the same lease as in example 1 and the property is used in the business, but the business is loss making.

A lease can only be considered onerous to the extent that the unavoidable cost of fulfilling the lease exceeds the expected economic benefits to be received under it. In this case, the expected benefits associated with the lease are the profits or cash flows that the division will generate. These profits or cash flows need not occur over the period of the lease; in fact it is necessary to consider profits or cash flows arising after the term of the lease. The reason for this is that for the division to access future profits beyond the term of the lease, it is necessary to pay the costs of this lease now to enable the head office to function. As such the access to these future profits is considered to be a benefit derived from the current lease.

As a result of the conclusion about future profits in the previous paragraph, a lease in a loss making business may only be considered onerous if management conclude that there is no way of returning to profit. In practice this would likely be determined by preparing discounted cash flows (using a risk-free rate) modelling all of management's possible alternatives to turn the division around or sell it. The consequence of seeing no profitable future for the division under any alternative course of action would be that management have no alternative other than ultimately closing it down. This closure need not be imminent as the least net cost of exiting the head office lease may be to trade at a loss for the period up to the end date of the lease. Nevertheless, provision should only be made for leases and other similar committed future overhead payments where management see no way of returning to profit and have, therefore, concluded that closure is the only realistic course of action (although closure need not have been announced). To provide in other circumstances would be to provide for future operating losses, which is prohibited by paragraph 68 FRS 12.

Example 3 — Sub-lease to third party at below head lease cost

The company has an operating lease as in example 1. It no longer occupies the property and it is not used in the business. A sub-lease on the property has been arranged at a rent of £30,000 a year for 10 years. The company has established that the present value of the net cost of continuing with the lease is less than the penalty for exiting the lease.

In this example the maximum benefits to be derived from the contract are £30,000 for 10 years. The cash inflow of £30,000 should be deducted from the cash outflows of £50,000 and the balance of £20,000 each year should be discounted to give the amount that should be provided on the onerous element of the lease.

Example 4 — Sub-lease negotiation not complete

The facts are the same as in example 1 with regard to the lease. However, the company no longer uses the property and never will do so again. It is, therefore, going to make a provision for an onerous contract. It has not yet found a sub-lessee, but expects to do so soon. The question is whether or not it is acceptable for the company to anticipate the future sub-lease in determining the provision to be made.

FRS 12 clearly says in the definition of an onerous contract that the expected benefits to be received under the lease should be taken into account. [FRS 12 para 2]. Consequently, the company should take account of the expected rent to be received under a sub-lease in determining the provision, provided that the company is actively seeking to sublet the property, there is evidence (from estate agents or similar) that the property can be let and there is reasonable evidence as to the rent that may be obtained in an open market rental. Alternatively, the least cost could be determined as the cost of negotiating out of the lease with the landlord.

Example 5 — Multiple sub-leases

The facts are as in example 4 except that the company intends to sub-lease the remaining 10 year period in 4 periods of 2½ years each. While the market rent achieved in the first sub-lease is only £30,000, the property market is cyclical and the company expects that over the 10 year term it will more than recover the head lease costs. Should a provision be made for the first 2½ years given that the sub-lease rentals are expected to be at a discount to the head lease cost?

No, the sub-leases as a whole are expected to recover the cost of the head-lease and, therefore, the head lease is not onerous. The sub-lease should not be considered from an onerous contract perspective, because the sub-lease is a positive contribution to what is in effect a sunk cost. As stated in paragraph 21.175 above, a contract cannot be onerous at its inception.

Example 6 — Separable contract

The facts are the same as in example 1 except that the property is split across five floors, each of which has external access and could be used as a self-contained space. The company restructures its head office and consolidates the remaining staff onto just four floors leaving the fifth one vacant, which it seeks to sub-let. As the market rent is below the lease rentals payable, can the company record an onerous lease provision in respect of the abandoned fifth floor if sub-lease rentals are not expected to cover the head-lease cost?

A provision could be recorded for an onerous contract in respect of the abandoned fifth floor. Looking at the lease as a whole, the expected benefits are still likely to cover the costs of the lease provided the business is profitable. However, applying the guidance in paragraphs 21.181 and 21.182 it can be seen that the benefits of the fifth floor have been abandoned, and this abandoned floor is identifiable and separable. In substance, there is little reason why the five floors couldn't have been leased under five separate agreements. Equally it is possible to determine the cost of the fifth floor in isolation by reference to the floor space as a percentage of the property as a whole.

Example 7 — Temporary closure of retail store

A company has an operating lease on a retail store. The air-conditioning system is unreliable and the company proposes to replace it. The store will be closed while work is carried out. Can the company provide in advance for the rent that is payable during the closure period?

FRS 12 does not permit provisions to be made for future operating losses. A provision for future operating lease payments cannot be made unless the lease is an onerous contract. An onerous contract is defined as *"a contract in which the unavoidable costs of meeting the obligations under it exceed the economic benefits expected to be received under it"*. In the context of the store's lease, the economic benefits from it include the future cash flows that are expected to be earned from operating the store. The lease would be onerous only if the rentals for its full term could not be recovered (in present value terms) from the future cash flows.

A lease is not onerous merely because an operating loss is expected for a short period during the lease. If, as is probable, the rentals payable over the full lease term (including those relating to the closure period) were expected to be recovered, the lease as a whole is not an onerous contract and so no provision should be made. The company's reported earnings for each period would then show operating losses and profits for the store as they arise.

Future operating losses

21.187 There is a general rule in FRS 12 that provisions should not be recognised for future operating losses. FRS 12 specifically states that future operating losses do not meet the definition of a liability and the general recognition criteria set out for provisions in the standard (see para 21.22). [FRS 12 paras 68, 69]. The reason that future operating losses do not meet the definition of a liability is that they do not result from a past event (see para 21.36). This is similar to the prohibition on provisions for future operating costs where it is not acceptable under FRS 12 to make provision for costs that will be incurred in order to operate in the future, if those costs could be avoided by the company's future actions.

21.188 In certain cases the measurement of an onerous contract provision may be based upon the net cost of fulfilling a contract that would otherwise be abandoned, if doing so represents the cheapest exit route. As explained in the preceding paragraph, such costs are not future operating losses as a result of there being a past event – the signing of the (now onerous) contract, and the provision represents the least net avoidable cost of a contract that would otherwise be abandoned.

21.189 Where a company is expected to incur future operating losses, this is firstly an indication that an impairment review should be carried out on the appropriate income generating unit (IGU) in accordance with the rules in FRS 11, 'Impairment of fixed assets and goodwill'. Such a review would determine whether those assets have suffered an impairment and need to be written down. [FRS 12 para 70]. Alternatively, anticipated future operating losses might indicate that a company has an onerous contract. Onerous contracts are covered in detail from paragraph 21.168.

Other practical application of the rules

21.190 A number of examples have been used throughout the text to illustrate how each of the specific aspects of FRS 12 is likely to apply in practice. The paragraphs that follow consider how FRS 12 applies to different types of transactions in their entirety. Some of these transactions are also considered in Appendix III to FRS 12.

21.191 The rules in FRS 12 that specify when a provision can be made are summarised in the five bullet points below. The paragraphs that follow make reference to these points. In order for a company to make provision:

- It must have a present obligation (which can be legal or constructive in nature) that is more likely than not to arise.
- The obligation must arise from an obligating event (that is, a past event) that either can be legally enforced or is an undertaking given to third parties from which the company cannot realistically withdraw.
- The obligation must not relate to costs that will be incurred in the future as part of the company's future operations.
- It must be more likely than not that the obligation will result in an outflow of economic benefits.
- It must be possible to make a reliable estimate of the obligation.

21.192 When considering the examples below, it is also helpful to consider what would happen if the company were to stop trading as of its balance sheet date. Would it have an obligation to incur further expenditure? This simple test often gives a very good indication of whether or not an obligation exists that arises from a past event. This is referred to in the paragraphs below as the 'year end test'.

Litigation

21.193 Throughout the recognition section of this chapter, litigation has been used to illustrate how certain aspects of FRS 12 apply. These issues are brought together here.

21.194 A company might find that it is taking an action against another party or is defending an action. Whichever side of the fence a company finds itself on, there will be costs associated with the litigation process (that is, primarily lawyers' fees and perhaps fees for expert witnesses) and finally costs (or proceeds) from either settling the action out of court or arising from the court's decision. There may also be, for the party losing the action, an insurance claim and potential insurance recoveries if the action was covered by insurance.

21.195 During the stages of the litigation process, it will be necessary for the company to consider carefully whether or not an obligation arises for which provision is required. Initially, the likelihood of settlement might be remote and, as a consequence, there is no need even to note a contingent liability. However, once an action has been started a contingent liability might arise which initially requires disclosure but, as the litigation progresses, becomes more certain and may warrant a provision being made. The outcome will not be assured until the final judgement has been given. Even then, there may still be uncertainties concerning whether claims against insurers will be successful. The example and paragraphs that follow consider a number of these aspects.

Example – Product liability

A company sells an additive for leaded petrol engines, which allows them to comply with new emission requirements. The company has heard from the representatives of ten customers who claim that the canisters have burst open on use and the additive has burnt their hands. They contend that the canisters were faulty. The company is insured for such liabilities and does not expect to lose any money if the claims succeed.

The first stage in establishing whether a provision should be made is to determine whether there is a present obligation. The past event is the sale to the customer of the potentially faulty goods. A present obligation will arise if the company is found responsible for the canisters bursting. The prosecution will have to prove that a present obligation has arisen from the canisters bursting and that some compensation is then payable. Where it is unclear whether the company is liable, it will be necessary for the company defending the action to determine whether there is a present obligation arising from the past event and this might entail its seeking expert advice. In this example, the company might contend that there is nothing wrong with the canisters and the customers did not follow the company's instruction leaflet, which clearly shows how to avoid the reported problem. If it is more likely than not (that is, greater than a 50% chance) that the company is liable for the canisters bursting, there is a present obligation for which provision should be made.

21.196 Once it has been established that a present obligation exists, it is then necessary to establish whether an outflow of economic benefits will result from settling the claim. Again, this judgement is based on whether it is more likely than not that there will be an outflow of economic benefits. Often further information might become available between the balance sheet date and the date on which a company's financial statements are finalised. Where this is so, that information should be taken into account in determining whether or not a present obligation arose at the balance sheet date (see para 21.34).

21.197 Where it is established that an outflow is probable, the next step is to decide how much to provide. It is helpful here to consider the simple year end approach. If the company stopped trading at its year end, how much would it have to pay to settle the obligation? This will obviously depend on the outcome of the claim. For example, if the company decided that it was going to settle out of court, it would provide for the estimated cost of settlement. An example of disclosure of contingencies, provisions and expected reimbursement in respect of asbestos litigation is given in Table 21.1 above.

21.198 It is common practice for companies not to provide for future legal costs to defend against claims as the lawyers have not yet performed their service. This is the case even when such claims result in a probable liability for which a provision has been recorded. However, in certain circumstances (and with appropriate disclosure), some companies do provide for such costs.

21.199 Where it is established that an outflow of economic benefits is probable, it might be appropriate to include an estimate of future direct and incremental legal costs within the provision. This would meet the FRS 12 measurement criteria as the company would have to include future legal costs in any amount paid to a third-party to transfer the liability. However, if the company was able to reasonably settle with the claimant (for example, where a claim is settled shortly after the period end) and the provision was measured on this basis, provision for future legal costs would not be appropriate. Provision should always be made for the lowest amount at which the company can reasonably settle.

21.200 A provision for future legal costs might also be recorded when a company has a portfolio of similar claims (for example related to damages from a product's defects), some of which might be won but others lost. In this scenario, the recognition criteria have been met because there is an obligation and an outflow of economic benefits is probable at least in respect of a portion of the claims. It may, therefore, be appropriate to include all future legal costs required to defend the portfolio of claims in the provision's measurement. The rationale for this is the same as in paragragh 21.199, that an estimate of future legal costs would be included in any sum required to be paid to a third-party to transfer the claims portfolio. Paragraph 21.87 considers large populations of similar claims in more detail.

21.201 If it was more likely than not that no obligation exists and/or an outflow of economic benefits was not yet probable (for example, in the case of a single claim that a company does not expect to settle), no provision would be made for future legal costs. The reason for this is that the recognition criteria for a provision have not been met and the future legal costs simply represent future operating costs of the business.

21.202 Regardless of the approach adopted, it is necessary to consider the consistency in the methodology applied in respect of legal costs, and the accounting policy should be described in the financial statements where the effect is material.

21.203 Where a company does not believe that a present obligation exists (that is, in the example in para 21.195, if it is more likely than not that the bursting of the canisters does not create a present obligation), it would not recognise a provision, but would disclose a contingent liability (unless the possibility of an outflow of economic benefit is remote).

21.204 If, as in the example in paragraph 21.195, a present obligation arises, the company would need to make a provision. But the example also mentions that the company is insured for such claims. FRS 12 is clear that the obligation and the potential insurance recovery need to be considered separately. As explained above, a provision for the obligation will be made when it is more likely than not both that an obligation exists and that an outflow of economic benefits will be necessary and if a reliable estimate of the obligation can be established. However, the same rules do not apply to recognising an insurance recovery. A receivable can only be recognised as an asset where it is virtually certain that it will be received if the company settles the obligation. If the receipt is not virtually certain, then the notes to the financial statements should merely disclose the amount as a contingent asset. Such a claim would be virtually certain of receipt once it has been accepted by the insurance company or where previous experience indicates that settlement is virtually certain.

21.205 One of the issues that will be important in practice is the sensitivity associated with the disclosures that the standard requires. It might be appropriate for a company to provide for the settlement of a legal claim because it is more likely than not that the obligation will arise, but to give the full disclosures required by the standard could prejudice the case's outcome. In extremely rare cases, the standard allows companies an exemption from disclosure (see para 21.333) of all the information required as illustrated in the table below.

Table 21.4 – Use of seriously prejudicial exemption in FRS 12

Roche Holdings Ltd – Annual Report – 31 December 2006

7. Major legal cases (extract)

Income (expenses) from major legal cases *in millions of CHF*

	2006	**2005**
Roche Pharmaceuticals legal cases		(210)
Genentech legal cases	–	–
Diagnostics legal cases		(146)
Total income (expenses) from major legal cases – continuing businesses	–	(356)
Discontinued businesses – vitamin case	–	–
Group total	–	(356)

Income (expenses) from major legal cases (continuing businesses) is disclosed separately in the income statement due to the materiality of the amounts and in order to fairly present the Group's results. The total net cash outflow from major legal cases during the year was 31 million Swiss francs (2005: 180 million Swiss francs).

Roche Pharmaceuticals legal cases

Roche Diagnostics GmbH ('RDG') and SmithKline Beecham (Cork) Ltd ('SB') are party to arbitration concerning RDG's termination in 1998 of the Carvedilol License Agreement of 1987, as amended in 1995, relating to the licensing and co-marketing of carvedilol. RDG has submitted two claims for damages to two Arbitration Tribunals in Zurich and SB has submitted a counterclaim asserting the invalidity of RDG's termination and claiming damages. Based on the development of the current arbitration and settlement negotiations, the Group increased its existing provisions by 210 million Swiss francs in 2005. There have been no developments in 2006 that would require any further changes to the provisions already recorded by the Group. The total amount of provisions recorded by RDG is not disclosed as this may seriously prejudice RDG's position in this matter.

Warranties

21.206 A warranty is often provided in conjunction with the sale of goods. Warranty costs represent additional costs that the seller may have to incur to rectify defects in, or to replace, the product it has sold. The warranty obligation can arise either through the operation of the law (contract or statute) or through a company's stated policies or practices as explained from paragraph 21.24 onwards.

21.207 When a company sells a product subject to warranty, it must first determine whether the warranty represents a separable component of the transaction. If an item sold proves to have been defective at the time of sale (usually based on evidence coming to light within a standard period), the purchaser may have the right to require the seller to rectify the defect or replace the faulty item. Such a warranty is considered to be a 'standard warranty' that relates to the condition of the item sold at the date of sale. It is not usually considered separable from the sale of goods.

21.208 When the warranty is not a separate element and represents an insignificant part of the sale transaction, generally the full consideration received is recognised as revenue on the sale and a provision is recognised for the expected future cost to be incurred relating to the warranty. An example of such an arrangement is a standard manufacturing warranty given under the normal terms and conditions of sale. Warranties that are not separate elements are dealt with in FRS 12. The principles included in the example given in Appendix III to FRS 12 are explained below.

Example 1 – Product repairs or replacement

A company sells gardening merchandise. On some of its products it warrants at the time the sale is made that it will make good by repair or replacement manufacturing defects that become apparent within one year from the date of sale. Its past experience shows that it does receive warranty claims on these products.

A provision should be made for the best estimate of the obligation for the following reasons:

- A legal obligation exists which is more likely than not to arise.
- The obligating event is the sale of the product and the normal one-year warranty can be legally enforced.
- The related costs of repair do not relate to the company's future operations.
- From past experience, it is more likely than not that the obligation will result in an outflow of economic benefits.
- A reliable estimate of the obligation can be made from the company's previous claims experience.

Using the simple year end test, if the company stopped trading at its year end, it would still be liable for the obligations arising from warranties it has already given. Hence, provision is required. The company should use past experience to estimate reliably the amount of potential claims.

Example 2 – Insured warranty obligation

The facts are the same as those outlined in example 1, except that the company makes a payment to a third party insurer, which underwrites the risk. In the event of a claim by a customer, the company would claim a corresponding amount from the insurer.

Provision would be made for the warranty for the reasons given in example 1 above. The mere existence of the underwriting agreement does not mean that the company can ignore the warranty obligation. The customer has recourse directly to the company for the warranty. The company in turn has a claim on the insurance company, but this does not offset the company's obligation to its customer.

Hence, the company will have to provide for its best estimate of its warranty obligation. It will have to consider whether or not it can recognise its counter-claim on its insurer. It cannot recognise a separate debtor for such claims, unless it is virtually certain that it will recover the funds from the insurer in the event that claims are received. If it is not virtually certain but is probable, then it should disclose the existence of the contingent asset in the notes to its financial statements.

21.209 An example of how to measure a provision for warranty claims is given from paragraph 21.87.

21.210 Where the warranty goes further than a standard warranty, it may well be separable from the sale of goods. An extended warranty is an agreement to provide warranty protection in addition to the scope of coverage of a manufacturer's standard warranty, or to extend the period of coverage provided by the manufacturer's warranty. They are often sold separately from the original product but, where warranties included in the price of a product provide protection in excess of that provided by the normal terms and conditions of sale for the relevant product, the transaction's substance is that the company has sold two products. If a company sells a product with an extended warranty, it is treated as a multiple element arrangement and the revenue from the sale of the extended warranty should be deferred and recognised over the period covered by the warranty. No costs should be provided for at the inception of the extended warranty agreement, because the warranty is deemed to relate principally to rectification of defects, the risks relating to which were transferred to the buyer in the sales transaction. Therefore, the obligation to repair or replace only arises for the seller if and when a defect arises, rather than at the time of selling the goods. Provision is recognised for rectification and/or replacement only as defects arise through the warranty period, which differs from the situation with a standard warranty where provision is made at the time of selling the goods (see para 21.208).

21.211 Accounting for warranties (both standard and extended) is dealt with further in chapter 9.

Refunds

21.212 Many companies have refund policies which are over and above the customers' rights under consumer law. A number of retailers, for example, give cash refunds for products returned whether or not they are defective, whereas others make cash refunds even where the customer does not have the receipt showing when the goods were purchased. Yet these policies have been operated in such a way, and for so long, that the customer has come to expect that they will be honoured.

21.213 FRS 12 includes an example in Appendix III which considers how such refund policies should be dealt with under its rules:

> **Example – Refund obligations based on past practice**
>
> A retail company has a policy of refunding purchases by dissatisfied customers, even where it is under no legal obligation to do so. It has adopted this policy for a number of years and it is well known to its customers.
>
> The company should make a provision for the best estimate of its refund obligation for the following reasons:
>
> - It has a present obligation that is constructive in nature, which is more likely than not to arise.
> - The obligating event is the sale of the goods, which has raised a valid expectation on the part of its customers from which the company cannot realistically withdraw.
> - The obligation does not relate to costs of future operations.
> - Past experience shows that it is more likely than not that the obligation will result in an outflow of economic benefits.
> - A reliable estimate of the obligation can be made from past refunds.

21.214 A situation where a refund may have to be made is where faulty goods have to be recalled. The example below considers the implications where goods sold prior to the period end are recalled after the period end.

> **Example – Product recalls**
>
> A retailer has to make a product recall on goods sold before its year end, as it has subsequently been found that the goods are faulty. The recall notice was issued after the year end. Costs of the recall can be recovered from the supplier under the retailer's supply contract.
>
> (a) Does the retailer need to make a provision at the year end for the recall costs?
>
> Under FRS 12, provision for the costs of the recall should be made at the year end. The obligating event was the sale of the faulty goods, not the recall notice. At the balance sheet date the company has an obligation to recall the faulty goods.

(b) How should it account for the recovery from the supplier?

Recovery of the costs from the supplier can only be recorded if it is deemed to be virtually certain they will be recovered if the recall expenditure is incurred. If it is not virtually certain, but is probable, it is disclosed as a contingent asset under FRS 12.

Major repairs and maintenance

Owned assets

21.215 It is highly unlikely that provision would ever be made for repairs and maintenance on owned assets as it would not meet the FRS 12 paragraph 14 recognition criteria as set out in paragraph 21.191 because there is no past event. Rather, to the extent that a significant part of a fixed asset requires regular replacement or overhaul, this significant part should be capitalised separately and depreciated over the remaining period to the next replacement date. [FRS 15 paras 36, 83].

Example – Overhaul of PPE

A company has a blast furnace which requires its lining to be replaced every five years.

Prior to the company incurring the expenditure, no provision can be made for replacement of the furnace lining, because the company has no present obligation as it does not have to replace the lining. For example, it could avoid the obligation by shutting the blast furnace. This conclusion is confirmed by using the simple year end test, because if the company did not continue to trade beyond the end of (say) year three, there would be no need to incur the future expenditure. But although no provision can be built up over the five years before the expenditure is due to be incurred, the blast furnace lining should be separately identified and depreciated over that period. When the expenditure is incurred to replace the lining, this will be capitalised as part of the cost of the furnace and depreciated over the period until it is next replaced.

The cost and depreciation attributed to the blast furnace lining originally should be removed from the balance sheet once the cost of the new blast furnace lining has been capitalised as the asset has been replaced.

21.216 Maintenance expenditure in respect of owned assets cannot be provided for in advance of being incurred even if there is an external requirement for maintenance of those assets. This is illustrated in the following example:

Example – Covenants requiring maintenance

A company has purchased some assets outright and borrowed from a bank to do so. The bank covenants include conditions that the company should maintain the assets in good condition. Should the company provide for maintenance on the owned assets that are financed by borrowings that contain the maintenance covenant?

Where an owned fixed asset is used as a security for a loan, and the covenants require that the asset is maintained, there is no penalty as such in respect of non-maintenance.

Of course, should the covenant be broken in any way, the bank could call in its loan. If the company is unable to pay back the loan in cash the bank may repossess the asset and consider this as settlement of the outstanding balance. In extreme cases, the bank may sue the company for returning the asset in a state of disrepair. However, we do not consider that this would justify providing for maintenance on an ongoing basis. A failure to maintain an asset used for secured lending does no more than trigger a repayment of the lending, which, in any case, has already been recognised as a liability. It does not trigger a claim for compensation for the maintenance work the owner has to carry out.

This is in accordance with FRS 12, which requires that a provision should be made only when there is a present obligation arising from a past event and it is probable that a transfer of economic benefits will be required to settle the obligation. FRS 12 also confirms that maintenance of owned property, plant and equipment is not a liability. Accordingly, we do not believe that a provision for maintenance on owned assets should be made, even where they have been mortgaged and covenants that require their regular maintenance have been given.

The response would differ for leased assets, where the lease agreement can impose penalties for non-maintenance on the lessee. This is considered further in the following paragraphs.

Operating leases

21.217 As explained above, the owner of a fixed asset cannot provide for major inspection or overhaul costs, because it has discretion over whether to incur the expenditure and could avoid the expenditure, for example, by selling the asset. However, obligations that arise under an operating lease may give rise to the need to make provision at an earlier stage. In some operating leases the lessee is required to incur periodic charges for maintenance of the leased asset or to make good dilapidations (see para 21.219) or other damage (see para 21.220) occurring during the rental period. The general principle for fixed assets does not preclude the recognition of such liabilities arising under operating leases once the event giving rise to the obligation under the lease has occurred. The example that follows illustrates the type of situation that can arise in practice in respect of maintenance.

Example – Refit and maintenance required under lease

A company leases an aircraft on an operating lease, which includes options to cancel the lease at year four, eight and twelve. Every four years the aircraft has to undergo a major refit and maintenance programme in order to be able to continue to fly. The operating lease specifies that this work must be undertaken every four years and before the aircraft is returned to the operator. In addition, the aircraft has to have its engines serviced about once a year after a certain number of flying hours have been reached, but there is no mention in the operating lease of this obligation.

As the lease is an operating lease, the aircraft does not appear on the lessee's balance sheet. The lessee charges its lease rentals to its income statement as they arise. Furthermore, because it has no asset on its balance sheet, it cannot recognise the wearing out of the asset to be replaced in the major refit over the period before the refit takes place. The operating lease creates an obligation on the company to carry out the major refit. Therefore, it would be appropriate to provide for the costs of the major refit and maintenance over the four years to the refit (based on the value of the liability at each balance sheet date) for the following reasons:

- The lessee has a legal obligation arising under the lease, which will arise. If the company decided to mothball the aircraft and not to use it or to terminate the lease, the company's action would result in the operating lease becoming onerous and provision for future rental payments would need to be made instead or termination penalties would need to be provided for. (Onerous contracts are considered further from para 21.168.)
- The past event is the action of using and flying the aircraft.
- The costs to be incurred do not relate to the company's future operations, because it is clear from considering the final period (between years nine and twelve) that the aircraft has to be returned in a maintained state. Therefore, the obligation in the last period clearly arises over the four-year term. Some might argue that the costs incurred at the end of year four and year eight relate to the following four-year terms, but this ignores the underlying obligation created by the lease, which is in effect to put right the damage that is caused through the asset's usage.
- An obligation will result under the lease that will result in an outflow of economic benefits.
- It will be possible to make a reliable estimate of the obligation to be provided each year based on the extent of wear and tear over the period.

The engine service each year is not covered by the lease, although it is an integral part of operating the aircraft. But because the obligation does not arise from the lease agreement, the normal rules in FRS 12 apply and provision cannot be made. These costs would be charged to the company's profit and loss account as they are incurred.

Table 21.5 – Provision for maintenance on operating leased assets

Air France – KLM S.A. – Report and accounts – 31 March 2009

3 Accounting Policies (extract)

3.18. Provisions for restitution of aircraft under operating leases (extract)

For certain operating leases, the Group is contractually committed to restitute aircraft to a defined level of potential.
The Group accrues for restitution costs related to aircraft under operating leases as soon as the asset does not meet the return condition criteria.

Finance leases

21.218 Major maintenance programmes can also arise under a finance lease and may or may not be specified as part of the lease terms. Because the asset under a finance lease is accounted for as if it is owned by the lessee, it would generally account for major renewal and maintenance programmes in the same way as if it owned the asset outright.

Example – Overhaul costs under finance lease arrangements

A company leases a ship under a finance lease for 25 years. In order to be seaworthy it has to obtain a certificate of seaworthiness, which entails the company carrying out significant maintenance and overhaul work in a dry dock every five years. Without such a certificate the ship cannot operate. This matter is referred to in the finance lease agreement, which requires the ship to be maintained in a seaworthy condition.

Although the ship cannot continue to operate without a certificate of seaworthiness, this in itself does not obligate the company to carry out the required maintenance work. It could, instead decide to lay-up the ship and not continue its operation. The terms of the lease would have to be carefully scrutinised to ensure there were no clauses that could change this conclusion, for example termination clauses might create an obligation. Where no obligation is created by the lease, no provision can be made for these costs. However, if the element of the asset that wears out can be identified at the outset, this cost should be amortised over the five-year term in the same way as if the asset were an 'owned asset'. When the maintenance work is carried out, this may be capitalised if it restores the ship's economic benefits.

If the ship has to be returned fully reinstated and the company is obliged to do the reinstatement, then the finance leased asset is different from an owned equivalent asset. The company should make provision as the damage is done. This is in effect decommissioning expenditure (see para 21.222).

Lease dilapidations

21.219 Major repair and maintenance costs in respect of leases in general have been dealt with in paragraphs 21.217 and 21.218 above. Many property leases include tenant repairing clauses for dilapidations. They typically require the tenant to return the property to the landlord at the end of the tenancy in a specified condition. The question then arises as to whether or not it is acceptable to make a provision for the costs relating to dilapidations during the tenancy period or whether these costs have to be borne in the period the work is undertaken. The following example illustrates the type of issues that arise in practice.

Example – Repairs specified under property lease terms

The company is currently a tenant of a property and is due to vacate it in five years time. There is a clause in the tenancy relating to dilapidation work which must be undertaken before the property is vacated. In addition, there is also a clause which enables the landlord to recharge the tenant for costs related to repairing the fabric of the building. In this regard, the landlord is intending to replace the cladding on the building and is obtaining quotes for this work.

Provision should be made for the estimated costs of the dilapidation repairs spread over the period of the tenancy for the following reasons:

- The tenant has a present legal obligation, arising from the lease agreement.
- The obligating event is the wear and tear to the property, which arises over the period of the tenancy and its repair can be legally enforced.

- Because the obligation arises from the wear and tear to the property, it is not related to future operating costs.
- It is almost certain that the obligation will result in an outflow of economic benefits.
- It is possible to make a reliable estimate of the yearly obligation arising from the extent of the wear and tear taking place each year. This will not necessarily equate to one fifth of the estimated total.

With regard to repairing the fabric of the building, it should be clear from the lease whether or not an obligation arises. If the damage has already been done to the property, then a provision should be made for the whole of the rectification work when the damage is identified.

Operating leasehold improvements

21.220 Some operating leases allow the tenant to improve the property by adding, for example, additional partitioning, but include obligations on the lessee to return the property at the end of the lease in its original state. Often this will entail dismantling certain aspects of the asset. For example, consider the situation described below.

Example – Returning property to its condition at lease inception

A company has entered into an operating lease for a warehouse. The company wishes to use the warehouse for office accommodation. It has planning permission to build a mezzanine floor and partition the building for offices at a cost of £1.5m. The operating lease is for a period of 15 years and the property must be returned to the lessor in its original condition as this is clearly specified in the lease. The company estimates that it will cost £500,000 in today's currency to remove the improvements.

The company should capitalise leasehold improvements of £1.5m and amortise those over the term of the lease in accordance with FRS 15. The company has an obligation under the lease to remove the improvements at the end of the lease term. The obligation arises as the company completes the improvements and this represents a past event. Therefore, if the improvements have been made by the company's year end a provision for the present value of £500,000 in 15 years time should be made for their eventual removal. In addition, an asset of the same amount should be recognised for what is, in effect, decommissioning, which will be recovered from the benefits generated by the business over the term of the lease. The asset should then be amortised over the remaining lease term.

21.221 The rules applied to the example above are the same as apply to decommissioning an oil well or a nuclear facility and are considered further from paragraph 21.222 below.

Abandonment and decommissioning costs

21.222 Abandonment is the term used to describe: the plugging and abandonment of wells; the dismantlement of wellheads, production and transportation facilities; and restoration of producing areas in accordance with the licence requirements and the relevant legislation. It normally commences at the date when the facility ceases to produce, treat, transport or store saleable quantities of oil or gas.

21.223 Similar costs are incurred in other industries such as: decommissioning costs in the electricity and nuclear industries; abandonment costs in the mining and extractive industries; clean up and restoration costs of landfill sites; and environmental clean up costs in a number of industries.

21.224 The underlying issue is whether, on developing a facility (such as drilling an oil well, excavating a mine or commissioning a power station), the liability that will arise in the future to abandon or decommission should be recognised either in full as a liability on day one or gradually by spreading over a period.

21.225 Typically under FRS 12 decommissioning costs are provided for as a liability because, in the circumstances set out above, the creation of the asset gives rise to a present obligation (see para 21.58).

21.226 Appendix III to FRS 12 includes an example of how the rules apply in practice and this example is explained below.

Example – Decommissioning oil rigs and repairing environmental damage

A company operates an oil field in the North Sea. Its operating licence requires it to remove the oil rig at the end of its production life and to restore the seabed. 90% of the costs of undertaking this work relate to removing the rig and restoring the damage it has caused. A further 10% arise through the extraction of oil. At the balance sheet date the rig has been constructed, but no oil has been extracted.

A provision should be made at the balance sheet date for the discounted cost of removing the rig and restoring the seabed for the following reasons:

- A legal obligation exists that stems from the operating licence and it is more likely than not to arise.
- The obligating event is installing the rig, which has caused the damage.
- The costs to be incurred do not relate to the company's future operations, as when they are incurred the rig will no longer be operating.
- The obligation will result in an outflow of economic benefits as this is required under the licence.
- The difficult area is whether or not it is possible to make a reasonable estimate of the obligation. This will depend on a number of factors and the standard says that only in exceptional circumstances will it not be possible to make some estimate of the obligation.

> The costs provided will be treated as part of the cost of the oil rig to be depreciated over the production life of the rig (see para 21.58).
>
> However, there is no obligation to rectify the damage caused by the extraction of the oil, until that oil is extracted. Hence, the costs of making good this damage (the 10% referred to above) will be accrued as the damage is caused (that is, the oil is extracted).

21.227 The measurement issue of providing for such long-term obligations and how subsequent re-measurement should be accounted for are considered from paragraph 21.116 and from paragraph 21.118 respectively.

Environmental liabilities

21.228 Environmental damage covers a whole spectrum of problems, including: contamination of land; pollution of rivers and waterways; emission of harmful gases into the atmosphere (see para 21.268 onwards); excavating holes and drilling mines in the ground. Some sensitive areas of the environment are controlled by legislation whereas others are not. Often companies have a moral obligation to rectify environmental damage, but this alone is no longer enough to justify making a provision for the necessary work to be undertaken.

21.229 FRS 12's requirements mean that provisions for environmental liabilities can be recognised only at the time that the company becomes obliged, legally or constructively, to rectify the environmental damage or to perform restorative work on the environment. These rules have a significant impact on the timing of recognition of all environmental liabilities.

21.230 Environmental costs can typically be split into the following four categories:

- Costs incurred at the company's option.
- Costs required to be incurred because of existing or new legislation.
- Costs that have to be incurred because of environmental damage caused by the company.
- Fines relating to environmental damage.

21.231 Appendix III to the standard covers these issues in a number of examples, which are explored below:

> **Example 1 – Environmental legislation due to be enacted**
>
> An oil company causes contamination which it will clean-up only when compelled by law in the particular country in which it operates. No laws currently exist in a particular country where it has contaminated some land, but at its year end, it is virtually certain that a draft law requiring clean-up will be enacted shortly.

The company should provide for its best estimate of the clean-up costs because:

- It has a legal obligation that is virtually certain to arise, as it is virtually certain that the legislation will be enacted. [FRS 12 para 22].
- The obligating event is the contamination of the land. Once the law has been passed, clean-up can be legally enforced.
- The related costs do not form part of the company's future operations.
- It is more likely than not that the obligation will result in an outflow of economic benefits.
- It will be possible to make a reliable estimate of the obligation.

Example 2 – Published environmental policy

The facts are similar to example 1 with the exception that there is no planned environmental legislation. However, in this case the company has a widely published environmental policy under which it undertakes to clean up all contamination that it causes. The company has a record of honouring its published policy.

In this circumstance, the company should also provide for its best estimate of the clean-up costs as:

- It has a present constructive obligation that arises from its commitment to the public at large by the publication of its environmental policies. It has raised a valid expectation that it will carry them through from which it cannot realistically withdraw.
- The obligation arises from the contamination of the land, which is the obligating event. But the key here is that it must not be able to realistically withdraw from carrying out its stated policy (that is, it cannot be able to change its mind).
- The related costs do not form part of the company's future operations.
- It is more likely than not that the obligation will result in an outflow of economic benefits.
- It will be possible to make a reliable estimate of the obligation.

Example 3 – Legislation in respect of future activity

A new law has been passed that requires smoke filters to be fitted to factories by the middle of the company's next year. The company has not yet fitted the smoke filters.

As the legislation has still to come into operation, there is no present obligation of a legal nature for the company to fit the filters. Furthermore, the company's management have done nothing to suggest that a constructive obligation arises either. Consequently, no provision should be made. Using the year end test arrives at the same conclusion, because if the company stopped trading there would be no obligation to fit the filters, as their fitting relates to reducing future pollution.

Example 4 – Legislation in force

The facts are the same as in the previous example, except that the company is now in the subsequent year, and while the law is operational, the company still has not fitted the filters.

The company should not make a provision for the cost of fitting the filters. Even though at first sight it might appear that there is a present obligation, as the law compelling the filters to be fitted is now operational, no obligation arises for the cost of fitting the filters because no obligating event has taken place (that is, the filters have not yet been fitted). Again using the simple year end test, if the company stopped trading there would be no requirement to fit the filters. Nevertheless, a provision may still be necessary for the cost of paying fines as follows:

- An obligation might arise for any penalties that the company might incur for not complying with the legislation to the year end.
- The obligating event giving rise to the liability to pay fines is the fact that the factory does not comply with the law.
- The fines do not relate to costs of future operations, if they have to be paid whether or not the company continues to trade.
- Whether it is more likely than not that the obligation will result in an outflow of economic benefits will depend on an assessment of the probability of incurring the fines. This might depend, for example, on the stringency of the enforcement regime.
- Whether it is possible to make a reliable estimate of the fines, will depend on factors such as whether the rates have been published.

Example 5 – Legislation in force in respect of past contamination

Health and safety legislation has been introduced that requires asbestos to be removed from all buildings. Where its existence is known, asbestos removal is required whether the property is in use or operations have ceased. The legislation is effective from 31 December 20X2. Company A owns a 20 year old factory that it has confirmed includes asbestos. The estimated cost of removing the asbestos is £70,000, plus a further £30,000 in lost profits because the factory will not be able to operate at full capacity while the asbestos is being removed. At 31 December 20X2, the work has not commenced in respect of the asbestos removal; however, contracts have been signed with contractors for the work to be performed in the first few months of 20X3.

The Health and Safety legislation has been enacted and there is, therefore, a requirement for the asbestos to be removed. The obligating (past) event is the contamination caused by the presence of the asbestos and the existence of a legal requirement to remove it creates an obligation that should be provided for. Therefore, company A should recognise a provision for £70,000, being the direct cost of removing the asbestos.

No provision should be made for the operating losses that will be incurred during the period of asbestos removal, because there is no obligation to incur these losses. Management could attempt to reschedule or relocate operations to avoid or minimise the losses. The operating losses are an indirect result of the requirement to remove the asbestos.

The existence of signed contracts does not affect the conclusion of whether to provide for the costs. The contracts are executory contracts, so no liability to the contractor arises until the contractor performs work under the contract.

The introduction of the new law does not create the obligating event on its own. It is the combination of the past contamination and the new law that creates the obligation to remove the asbestos. This can be contrasted with the smoke filters in example 4 above where there is no past contamination and so the obligation created when the legislation comes into force is only for penalties and fines.

21.232 An example of a company's accounting policy for provisions, including environmental liabilities, is given in Table 21.6 below.

Table 21.6 – Accounting policy for provisions, including environmental liabilities

Syngenta AG – Report and accounts – 31 December 2008

2. Accounting policies (extract)

Provisions

A provision is recognized in the balance sheet when Syngenta has a legal or constructive obligation to third parties as a result of a past event and it is probable that an outflow of economic benefits will be required to settle the obligation. The amount recognized as a provision is the best estimate of the expenditure required to settle the obligation at the balance sheet date. If the effect of discounting is material, provisions are discounted to the expected present value of their future cash flows using a pre-tax rate that reflects current market assessments of the time value of money and, where appropriate, the risks specific to the liability. Where some or all of the expenditures required to settle a provision is expected to be reimbursed by another party, the reimbursement is recognized only when reimbursement is virtually certain. The amount to be reimbursed is recognized as a separate asset. Where Syngenta has a joint and several liability for a matter with one or more other parties, no provision is recognized by Syngenta for those parts of the obligation which are expected to be settled by another party. Syngenta self-insures or uses a combination of insurance and self-insurance for certain risks. Provisions for these risks are estimated in part by considering historical claims experience and other actuarial assumptions and, where necessary, counterparty risk.

Environmental provisions

Syngenta is exposed to environmental liabilities relating to its past operations, principally in respect of remediation costs. Provisions for remediation costs are made when there is a present obligation, it is probable that expense on remediation work will be required within ten years (or a longer period if specified by a legal obligation) and the cost can be estimated within a reasonable range of possible outcomes. The costs are based on currently available facts; technology expected to be available at the time of the clean up, laws and regulations presently or virtually certain to be enacted and prior experience in remediation of contaminated sites. Environmental liabilities are recorded at the estimated amount at which the liability could be settled at the balance sheet date. Environmental liabilities are discounted if the impact is material and if cost estimates and timing are considered reasonably certain. Environmental costs are capitalized as part of property, plant and equipment where they are expected to increase the economic benefits flowing from the use or eventual disposal of the asset, or when they represent an obligation to remediate at the end of the asset's life and are recoverable from future economic benefits of using the asset. In all other cases, they are expensed. Environmental costs, unless related to restructuring, are included in cost of goods sold.

Additional environmental remediation costs and provisions may be required were Syngenta to decide to close certain of its sites. Syngenta's restructuring programs have involved closure of several sites to date. Remediation liabilities are accounted for as restructuring provisions and recognized when the site closure has been announced. In the opinion of Syngenta, it is not possible to estimate reliably the costs that would be incurred upon eventual closure of its continuing sites that have no present obligation to remediate because it is neither possible to determine a time limit beyond which the sites will no longer be operated, nor what remediation costs may be required upon their eventual closure.

Restructuring provisions
A provision for restructuring is recognized when Syngenta has approved a detailed and formal restructuring plan and the restructuring has either commenced or been announced publicly.

Provisions for severance payments and related employment costs are made in full when employees are given details of the termination benefits which will apply to individual employees should their contracts be terminated as a direct result of the restructuring plan. Costs relating to ongoing activities, such as relocation, training and information systems, are recognized only when incurred.

Waste electrical and electronic equipment

21.233 The European Union's Directive on Waste Electrical and Electronic Equipment (2002/96/EC) (the 'WEEE Directive'), which regulates the collection, treatment, recovery and environmentally sound disposal of electronic and electrical equipment waste, gave rise to questions about when a liability for the decommissioning of WEEE should be recognised. As a result, the UITF issued an interpretation, UITF 45 (IFRIC 6), 'Liabilities arising from participating in a specific market – waste electrical and electronic equipment', to provide guidance regarding what constitutes an obligating event in certain circumstances under the WEEE Directive.

21.234 The WEEE Directive distinguishes between 'new' and 'historical' waste and between waste from private households and waste from sources other than private households. New waste relates to products sold on or after 13 August 2005. All equipment sold before that date is deemed to give rise to historical waste for the purposes of the Directive.

21.235 The WEEE Directive states that the cost of waste management for historical household equipment should be borne by producers of that type of equipment that are in the market during a specified period (the 'measurement period'). The WEEE Directive states that each Member State should establish a mechanism for producers to contribute to costs proportionately, for example, in proportion to their respective market share by type of equipment.

21.236 Member States within the EU will have their own interpretation of the WEEE Directive enacted into their law. The detailed requirements associated with the Directive will, therefore, vary from State to State.

21.237 UITF 45 provides guidance on the recognition, in the financial statements of producers, of liabilities for waste management of WEEE in respect of sales of historical household equipment.

21.238 The interpretation only addresses sales of historical household equipment; it does not address new waste or historical waste from sources other than private households. The UITF considers that the liability for such waste management is covered by FRS 12's general requirements. It notes, however, that if, in national legislation, new waste from private households is treated in a similar manner to historical waste from private households, UITF 45's principles apply. [UITF 45 para 7].

21.239 UITF 45 addresses what constitutes an obligating event in accordance with paragraph 14(a) of FRS 12 for the recognition of a provision for waste management costs.

21.240 The UITF concluded that participation in the market during the measurement period is the obligating event. For this reason, a liability for waste management costs for historical household equipment does not arise when the products are manufactured or sold. As the obligation for historical household equipment is linked to participation in the market during the measurement period, rather than to production or sale of the items to be disposed of, there is no obligation unless and until a market share exists during the measurement period. [UITF 45 para 9].

21.241 Paragraph BC 5 of UITF 45 illustrates the interpretation's requirements with the following example.

> **Example**
>
> A company selling electrical equipment in 20X4 has a market share of 4% for that calendar year. It subsequently discontinues operations and is thus no longer in the market when the waste management costs for its products are allocated to those companies with market share in 20X7. With a market share of 0% in 20X7, the company's obligation is nil. However, if another company enters the market for electronic products in 20X7 and achieves a market share of 3% in that period, then that company's obligation for the costs of waste management from earlier periods will be 3% of the total costs of waste management allocated to 20X7, even though the company was not in the market in those earlier periods and has not produced any of the products for which waste management costs are allocated to 20X7.

21.242 The timing of the obligating event may also be independent of the particular period in which the activities to perform the waste management are undertaken and the related costs incurred. Incurring costs in the performance of the waste management activities is a separate matter from incurring the obligation to share in the ultimate cost of those activities. [UITF 45 paras 9, BC 6].

21.243 As noted in paragraph 21.238, UITF 45 deals only with sales of historical household equipment under the WEEE Directive. Companies will need to determine appropriate accounting policies for other types of waste in accordance with FRS 18 (see para 21.238 above). The detailed rules for attributing cost in respect of other types of WEEE may vary between Member States (see para 21.236) and where a group operates in more than one location, it will need to consider the legal requirements in different jurisdictions.

21.244 The decision tree below provides a high-level overview of factors to be considered when reviewing specific disposal obligations for *new waste from private households*. It provides a starting point to begin considering the accounting implications of such waste. The considerations may be applied to new waste from commercial users if the fact patterns are similar. The decision tree is not meant to consider all possible situations or specific scenarios within a particular Member State and, in particular, the legal determinations.

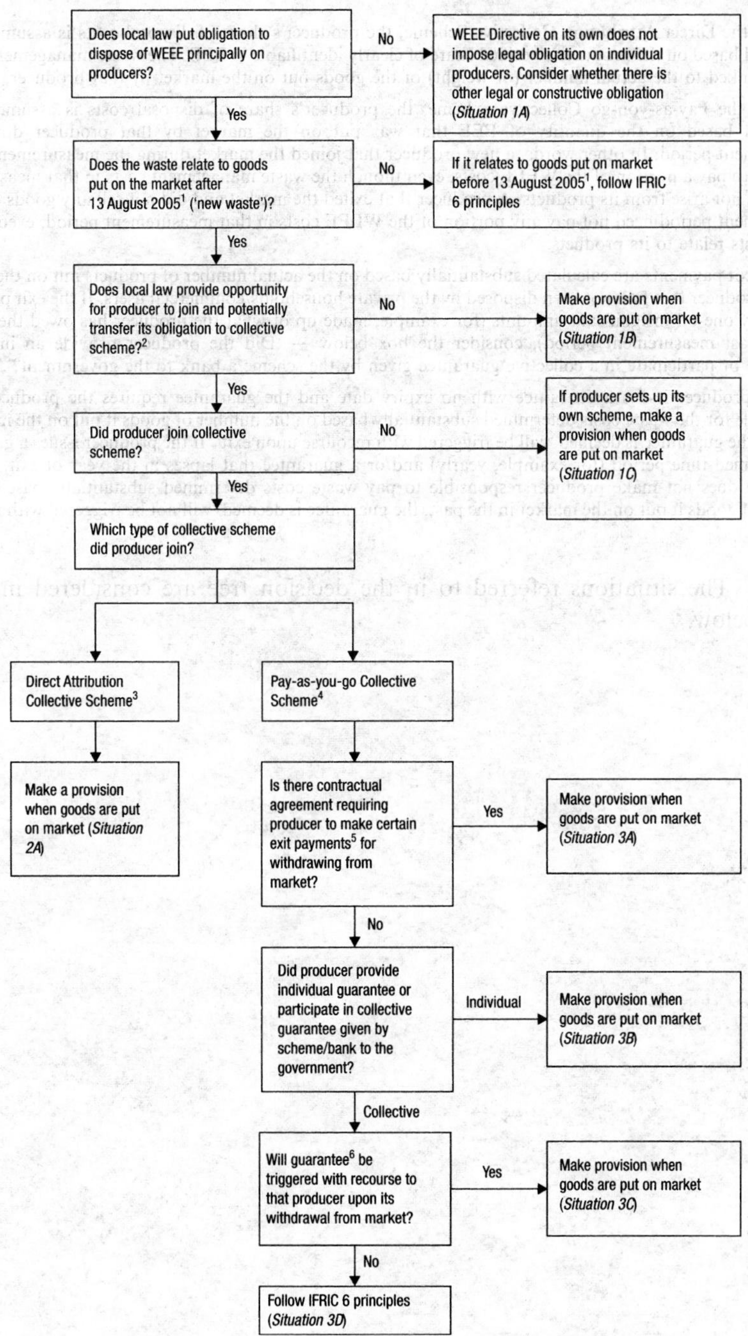

Footnotes to the decision tree:

[1] This date may be changed during the transposition to the local law; if changed, it is normally to a later date.

[2] Companies may wish to seek a legal opinion to determine whether the local law provides opportunity for the producer to join and transfer its obligation to a collective scheme.

3 Under the Direct Attribution Collective Scheme, the producer's share of disposal costs is assumed to be calculated based on the producer's verified share of clearly identifiable WEEE. The waste management cost is directly linked to the actual number (or weight) of the goods put on the market by that producer.

4 Under the Pay-as-you-go Collective Scheme, the producer's share of disposal costs is assumed to be calculated based on the quantity of EEE that was put on the market by that producer during the measurement period. In other words, a new producer that joined the market during the measurement period will need to pay a portion of the WEEE costs, even though the waste management costs in that measurement period do not arise from its products. A producer that exited the market and did not sell any goods during a measurement period need not pay any portion of the WEEE costs in that measurement period, even if some of the costs relate to its products.

5 These exit payments are calculated substantially based on the actual number of products put on the market by that producer that had not been disposed by the private households/commercial users. If the exit payments are merely one-off insignificant amounts (for example, made up of what the producer has owed the scheme for the past measurement period), consider the box below — 'Did the producer provide an individual guarantee or participate in a collective guarantee given by the scheme/a bank to the government?'.

6 If the producer issues a guarantee with no expiry date and the guarantee requires the producer to be responsible for the waste costs determined substantially based on the number of goods it put on the market in the past, the guarantee is deemed 'will be triggered with recourse upon exit'. If the producer issues a guarantee with specified time period (for example, yearly) and/or a guarantee that lapses in the year of exit, and the guarantee does not make producer responsible to pay waste costs determined substantially based on the number of goods it put on the market in the past, the guarantee is deemed 'will not be triggered with recourse upon exit'.

21.245 The situations referred to in the decision tree are considered in more detail below.

Situation 1 – Transposition of the WEEE Directive into local law

Situation	Accounting treatment	Basis of conclusion
1A The local law does not/has not put the obligation to dispose of the WEEE principally on the producers.	WEEE Directive on its own does not impose legal obligation on individual producers. Companies will need to consider whether there is any other legal/constructive obligation.	• The WEEE Directive on its own cannot impose any legal obligation on individual producers; legally, it imposes obligation only on the government/country to transpose it into local law. • Paragraph 22 of FRS 12 requires an obligation arising from a proposed new law that is virtually certain to be enacted to be treated as a legal obligation. Company should consider whether there is a legal obligation if the transposition is not yet complete.
1B The local law puts the obligation to dispose of the new waste principally on the producers. The local law does not, however, provide the opportunity for each producer to join and potentially transfer its obligation to a collective scheme; each producer must set up its own scheme to meet its obligation and provide an individual guarantee.	A provision should be made when goods are put on the market.	• Local law makes the producer responsible for financing the cost of waste management and does not provide the opportunity to join and potentially transfer its obligation to a collective scheme. • The producer cannot avoid the obligation as a result of the law as well as the individual guarantee.
1C The local law puts the obligation to dispose of the new waste principally on the producers. The local law provides the opportunity for the producer to join and potentially transfer its obligation to a collective scheme, but the producer chooses to set up its own scheme and provide an individual guarantee to the government.	A provision should be made when goods are put on the market.	• By choosing to set up its own scheme, the producer cannot avoid settling the obligation.

Situation 2 – Direct attribution collective scheme

Situation	Accounting treatment	Basis of conclusion
2A Direct attribution collective scheme, where disposal costs are allocated based on the producer's verified share of clearly identifiable WEEE and each producer provides an individual guarantee to the government.	A provision should be made when goods are put on the market (even when not yet billed by the scheme).	• Such a scheme is meant only to reap the benefits from the economies of scale in collecting waste together. • The measurement basis is closely related to the actual quantity/weight of products being put on the market by that producer (and not the relative market share during the measurement period when the costs incurred). • The producer is still obliged to bear the disposal costs of its product when withdrawing from the market. • The obligation has not been transferred to the scheme.

Situation 3 – Pay-as-you-go collective scheme

Situation	Accounting treatment	Basis of conclusion
3A Pay-as-you-go collective scheme with a contractual agreement requiring the producer to make certain exit payments to the scheme for withdrawing from the market. These exit payments are calculated substantially based on the actual number of products put on the market by that producer that had not yet been disposed.	A provision should be made when goods are put on the market (even if not yet billed by the scheme).	• The producer is obliged to bear disposal costs (closely related to the actual quantity/weight of products it puts in the market) when withdrawing from the market as a result of the contractual agreement; the obligation has not been transferred.
3B Pay-as-you-go collective scheme with no contractual agreement (requiring the producer to make certain exit payments to the scheme for withdrawing from the market, as situation 3A), but the producer provides an individual guarantee to the government.	A provision should be made when goods are put on the market (even when not yet billed by the scheme).	• The producer is obliged to bear disposal costs (closely related to the actual quantity/weight of products it puts in the market) when withdrawing from the market as a result of the individual guarantee given to the government; the obligation has not been transferred to the scheme.

3C Pay-as-you-go collective scheme with no contractual agreement (for exit payments), but the producer participates in the collective guarantee given by the scheme/a bank to the government and the guarantee is triggered *with recourse* to the producer upon its withdrawal from the market.	A provision should be made when goods are put on the market (even when not yet billed by the scheme).	• The producer is obliged to bear disposal costs (closely related to the actual quantity/weight of products it puts in the market) when withdrawing from the market as a result of participating in a collective guarantee that is triggered with recourse to the producer upon its withdrawal from the market; the obligation has not been transferred to the scheme.
3D Pay-as-you-go collective scheme with no contractual agreement requiring exit payments and the producer did not give an individual guarantee. The producer, however, participates in the collective guarantee given by the scheme/a bank to the government and the guarantee is *not* triggered with recourse to that producer upon its withdrawal from the market.	The principles of IFRIC 6 should be followed (see para 21.240).	• The producer can avoid disposal costs if it exits the market. The obligating event is the participation in the measurement period when the costs are incurred. • The producer is responsible for disposal costs substantially based on the producer's relative market share during the measurement period when the costs are incurred (and not based on the actual quantity/weight of products being placed in the market by that producer).

The WEEE Regulations in the UK

21.246 The UK legislation creates obligations for producers, distributors and, in certain circumstances, end-users of electrical and electronic equipment ('EEE') with respect to the collection, treatment, recovery and environmentally sound disposal ('processing') of waste arising from such equipment in any compliance period. Compliance periods run for 12 months from 1 January to 31 December each year.

Scope

21.247 The WEEE Regulations relate to electrical and electronic equipment and apply to the following groups:

- Producers (that is, any business that manufactures, imports or rebrands EEE.
- Retailers and distributors (that is, any business that sells EEE to end-users).
- Local authorities.

- Waste management industry.
- Exporters and reprocessors.
- Businesses and other non-household users of EEE (that is, the end users).

21.248 The WEEE Regulations recognise two categories of waste, being waste from:

- Private households (that is, consumer use by members of the public – 'household waste').
- Users other than private households (that is, professional, business or official use – 'non-household waste').

Household waste includes waste from other users if it is similar to that from private households by nature or quantity. Annex C to the WEEE Guidance Notes presents the suggested criteria for EEE to be considered as non-household. Companies may wish to seek legal advice in interpreting this in some cases.

21.249 As noted in paragraph 21.234, the WEEE Directive also distinguishes between 'new' and 'historical' waste. New waste relates to products sold on or after 13 August 2005 and historical waste relates to products sold before that date. Under the WEEE Regulations, the same model of attributing waste management costs is applicable to all WEEE from private households (that is, the Regulations do not distinguish historical waste and new waste for household EEE). However, a distinction is made for non-household WEEE.

[The next paragraph is 21.268.]

Emissions obligations

21.268 Many jurisdictions have introduced cap and trade schemes as a way to encourage a reduction in greenhouse gas emissions. The schemes generally involve the allocation of a limited number of allowances at the start of a compliance period and require companies to have sufficient allowances at the end of the compliance period to cover the volume of emissions made. Some schemes permit companies to purchase additional allowances (on top of their free allocation) or to sell any surplus allowances generated from reducing their emissions.

21.269 Under the schemes, the emission of greenhouse gases creates an obligation to deliver allowances. Companies must recognise a liability (and related expense) in respect of this obligation to the extent of emissions made as at the balance sheet date. There are a number of accounting models that can be used for accounting for participation in schemes aimed at reducing greenhouse gas emissions. The liability's measurement will depend on the accounting model used. These are discussed further below.

21.270 The EU ETS was introduced into the UK in 'The Greenhouse Gas Emissions Trading Scheme Regulations 2005' (SI 2005/925), which came into force on 21 April 2005. The EU ETS works on a 'cap and trade' basis. EU

Member State governments are required to set an emission cap for all installations covered by the scheme. These installations include those carrying out activities in the following areas:

- Energy activities (for example, electricity generation).
- Production and processing of ferrous metals.
- Mineral industries.
- Pulp and paper industries.

21.271 The significant elements of Phase I of the EU ETS can be summarised as follows:

- Each installation covered by the scheme is allocated allowances for a particular compliance period (calendar year). The number of allowances allocated to each installation for any given period, (that is, the number of free tradable allowances each installation receives), is set down in a document called the National Allocation Plan (which is approved by the EC).
- Companies have the flexibility to sell any surplus allowances expected to be generated from reducing their emissions below their allocation. This enables other companies to buy additional allowances (on top of their free allocation) to cover any expected shortfalls. The buying and selling of allowances takes place on an EU-wide market.
- After the end of each compliance period (calendar year), companies are required to ensure they have sufficient allowances to cover the actual emissions of their installations for that period. By a specified deadline, the operator of each installation has to surrender a number of allowances equal to the total emissions from that installation during the compliance period.
- If the company fails to deliver the requisite number of allowances at the end of the compliance period, it may be fined and may face other sanctions, but also remains liable to deliver the requisite number of allowances from later years' allowances supply.

21.272 Under cap and trade schemes (such as the EU ETS), the emission of greenhouse gases creates an obligation to deliver allowances. Companies must recognise a liability (and related expense) in respect of this obligation to the extent of emissions made as at the balance sheet date. There are a number of accounting models that can be used for accounting for participation in schemes aimed at reducing greenhouse gas emissions. The liability's measurement will depend on the accounting model used. These are discussed further below.

21.273 There is no specific accounting guidance in UK GAAP dealing with accounting for emissions. In December 2004, the IASB's interpretations committee, the IFRIC, published an Interpretation, IFRIC 3, 'Emission rights' which dealt with the accounting for a 'cap and trade' emission rights scheme. It required that companies should account for the emission allowances they receive from governments as intangible assets, recorded initially at fair value. Where allowances are issued for less than fair value, the difference between the amount paid and the fair value is treated as a government grant. The grant is initially recognised as deferred income in the balance sheet and subsequently taken to income on a systematic basis over the compliance period for which the allowances were issued, regardless of whether the allowances are held or sold. A liability is recognised for the obligation to deliver allowances equal to emissions that have been made. The liability is measured at the best estimate of the expenditure required to settle the present obligation at the balance sheet date (usually, the market price of the number of allowances required to cover emissions made up to the balance sheet date).

21.274 IFRIC 3 proved to be a controversial interpretation, as it resulted in a mismatch in performance reporting, due to the different rules on accounting for changes in value of the intangible asset and the related emissions obligation. The UITF issued proposals for emissions accounting similar to those in IFRIC 3, but decided not to proceed with an Abstract as it was considered likely that there would be further changes to accounting in this area. IFRIC 3 was withdrawn by the IASB in June 2005, but despite its withdrawal, it remains a valid accounting model for emissions accounting under UK GAAP. However, its withdrawal indicates that other accounting models are acceptable. Two acceptable accounting models for emission schemes are summarised in the table below (note: this summary does not deal with the accounting for emission allowances by broker/traders).

Acceptable accounting models for emissions accounting

	'Full market value approach' (similar to IFRIC 3)	**'Cost of settlement approach' ('Initial market value')**
Allowances (asset)		
When to recognise	Recognise when able to exercise control.	Recognise when able to exercise control.
How much to recognise	Measure initially based on the market value at the date of initial recognition. Measure subsequently based on either: (i) the amount initially recognised (cost model); or (ii) the revalued amount (revaluation model).	Measure initially based on the market value at the date of initial recognition. Measure subsequently based on either: (i) the amount initially recognised (cost model); or (ii) the revalued amount (revaluation model).
Government grant		
When to recognise	Recognise at the same time as allowances.	Recognise at the same time as allowances.
How to recognise	Measure initially based on the market value of the allowances at the date of initial recognition. Amortise over the compliance period on a systematic and rational basis.	Measure initially based on the market value of the allowances at the date of initial recognition. Amortise over the compliance period on a systematic and rational basis.

Emissions obligations (liability)

When to recognise	Recognise when the liability is incurred.	Recognise when the liability is incurred.
How to recognise	Re-measure the liability based on the market value of allowances at each period end (or a value based on a forward rate – see paras 21.281-283), whether they are to be settled using the allowances on hand or to be purchased from the market.	Re-measure the liability at each period end. The liability to be settled using allowances on hand is measured at the carrying amount of those allowances; any excess emission is measured at the market value of allowances at the period end (or a value based on a forward rate – see paras 21.281-283).

21.275 The first accounting model in the above table (the 'full market value' approach) is similar to the model set out in IFRIC 3, as summarised in paragraph 21.273 above. There are two variants under UK GAAP – the cost model and the revaluation model, depending on whether the intangible asset is revalued on an ongoing basis under FRS 10. The other accounting model is based on a 'cost of settlement approach', under which the liability is measured at the amounts expected to be incurred in settling it, but is otherwise similar to the IFRIC 3 approach. Under the cost of settlement approach, the liability is measured, to the extent allowances are held at the period end, at the carrying amount of those allowances and any excess obligation is measured at the market value of allowances at the period end.

21.276 Under both the accounting models in the above table, the emissions allowances held are intangible assets, accounted for in accordance with FRS 10, 'Goodwill and intangible assets', and should be recognised at cost if separately acquired. Allowances that are received free of charge from the government are accounted for in accordance with SSAP 4, 'Accounting for government grants'. Paragraph 16 of SSAP 4 states that where a government grant takes the form of a transfer of non-monetary assets, the amount of the grant is the fair value of the assets transferred. Therefore, allowances received free of charge are recognised at fair value with a corresponding deferred income.

21.277 It should be noted that, under UK GAAP, an accounting model that recognises allowances received free of charge at a nominal amount (for example, nil) cannot be used, as this is not consistent with paragraph 16 of SSAP 4, which requires the use of fair value. This differs from IFRS, where IAS 20, 'Accounting for government grants and disclosure of government assistance', permits a government grant received in the form of a non-monetary asset to be recorded at a nominal amount (as an alternative to fair value).

21.278 The intangible assets recognised should not be amortised if they have indefinite useful economic lives, but should be reviewed for impairment at the end of each reporting period. [FRS 10 paras 17, 37]. If the intangible assets have limited useful economic lives, they should be amortised on a systematic basis over those lives. In amortising an intangible asset, a residual value may be assigned to that asset if the residual value can be measured reliably. [FRS 10 paras 15, 28]. If residual values can be measured reliably, it is likely that these will be equal to the asset's carrying amount at initial recognition or subsequent revaluation and so there will be no amortisation. Emission allowances recognised as an asset should be tested for impairment, in accordance with the requirements of FRS 11,'Impairment of fixed assets and goodwill', which is dealt with in chapter 18.

21.279 Under the above two models in the table in paragraph 21.274, the company may choose to apply the revaluation model in FRS 10 for the subsequent measurement of the emissions allowances. [FRS 10 para 43]. The revaluation model requires that the carrying amount of the allowances is restated to market value at each balance sheet date with changes to market value recognised directly in equity, except for impairments which are recognised in the profit and loss account. Accounting for intangible assets is considered further in chapter 15.

21.280 The balance recognised as deferred income for the government grant is amortised to the income statement on a straight line basis over the compliance period. An alternative to the straight line bases should be used if this can be determined to provide a better reflection of the consumption of the economic benefits of the government grant; this could, for example, be based on the volume of emissions generated.

21.281 Where a company records some or all of its emissions obligations at market value, it should ordinarily calculate its provision by reference to the open market price of the relevant allowances it will need to purchase. However, to the extent that the company has entered into a forward contract to buy allowances at a fixed price on a future date, it is permissible to provide at the forward contracted rate (rather than the market rate) as this will represent the best estimate of the amount the company expects to pay to settle its obligation.

21.282 Using the forward rate would not be appropriate when the company trades in these derivatives. Once the company commences trading, we would expect the company to apply FRS 26, 'Financial instruments: measurement' as the most appropriate accounting policy for these instruments under FRS 18. Trading these instruments causes them to fall outside of the 'own use exemption' in paragraph 5 of FRS 26. The consequence of this is that once the forward contracts are within FRS 26's scope, they are required to be carried at fair value and, therefore, providing at the forward rate will result in double-counting the effect of the derivative.

21.283 Throughout this section, any provision required to be made based on the market rate may alternatively be based on a forward rate, provided the company meets the 'own use exemption' in FRS 26 with respect to its emissions allowances forward contracts.

21.284 The accounting policy chosen for emission obligations (which should be consistently applied) will depend on the overall accounting model that is being used for emissions (including allowances) and will impact on the liability's measurement as follows:

- The obligation may be measured at market price at the balance sheet date of the allowances required to cover the emissions made to date (the 'full market value' approach in the table above) – see further paragraph 21.285 below.
- The obligation may be measured at the amounts expected to be incurred in settling the liability (the 'cost of settlement' approach in the table above), as follows:
  - To the extent that the obligation can be met from allowances already held by the company – this is measured at the carrying amount of the allowances held (see para 21.275 above).
  - To the extent that the obligation cannot be met from allowances held, it must be met from allowances purchased in the market – this is measured at the market price of allowances at the balance sheet date.

Companies should make clear in their accounting policy note which approach they are following.

21.285 The 'full market value' approach (that is, similar to the method set out in IFRIC 3) is illustrated in the following example.

Example

A company participates in a 'cap and trade' scheme for emission rights and is allocated on 1 January 20X6, free of charge, allowances to emit 10,000 tonnes of carbon dioxide during the calendar year 20X6, which is also its financial accounting period. The market price of an allowance (equivalent to one tonne of carbon dioxide) at 1 January 20X6 is £10, giving a fair value of £100,000.

At the half year, 30 June 20X6, the company has emitted 6,000 tonnes of carbon dioxide and expects its emissions for the full year to be 12,500 tonnes. The market price for allowances has risen to £11 (per tonne).

At the year end the company has emitted the expected 12,500 tonnes and the market price of allowances is £12 (per tonne). How should the company account for the scheme under the method similar to that set out in IFRIC 3 (the 'full market value' approach), assuming that the company uses the revaluation model in FRS 10 to measure the intangible asset at fair value after its initial recognition?

The company would record the initial receipt of allowances at fair value of £100,000, setting up an intangible asset for this amount and recording a government grant as deferred income for the same amount. There would be no depreciable amount as the residual value (as defined in FRS 10) equals the carrying value (fair value) at acquisition.

At the half year stage the company would record a liability for the emissions to date of £66,000 (6000 tonnes at £11 per tonne). The asset of £100,000 is revalued to £110,000 (10,000 tonnes at £11 per tonne). The deferred income is released in the proportion that emissions to date bear to total emissions expected for the year, that is £100,000 x 6,000/12,500 = £48,000.

At the half year the profit and loss account, therefore, reflects deferred income released of £48,000 less the accrued emission liability expense of £66,000, giving a net charge to the profit and loss account for the period of £18,000. The revaluation surplus of £10,000 on the intangible asset is taken to the revaluation reserve *via* the STRGL.

At the full year (and ignoring the half year entries) the company records a liability for emissions of £150,000 (12,500 tonnes at £12 per tonne). The asset is revalued to £120,000 (10,000 tonnes at £12 per tonne). All of the deferred income of £100,000 is released.

The effect on the profit and loss account for the full year is to record a liability of £150,000 (based on the market price of allowances at the balance sheet date) in respect of the emission obligation and to release deferred income of £100,000. The revaluation surplus of £20,000 is taken to the revaluation reserve *via* the STRGL. There is a net charge to the profit and loss account of £50,000. Taken together with the revaluation surplus in the STRGL of £20,000 the net total recognised gains and losses of £30,000 (loss) represents the cost to the company of excess emissions of 2,500 tonnes (over the free allowances granted) multiplied by the market price at the year end of £12 per tonne.

If the cost model in FRS 10 had been used for the intangible asset and, accordingly, it had been measured after its initial recognition at cost less amortisation and/or impairment (cost being fair value on initial recognition for this purpose) there would be no revaluation surplus of £20,000 at the year end and the intangible asset would be stated at £100,000. Because part of the liability of £150,000 would be settled by using allowances stated at £100,000 (but worth £120,000), the company would need to pay only £30,000. There would remain a balance of the liability of £20,000 that would be released to the profit and loss account when settlement occurs. Thus the net charge in the profit and loss account would be £30,000. Again this represents the cost of the excess emissions of 2,500 tonnes multiplied by £12 per tonne. Therefore, the overall net effect on the performance statements would be the same (£30,000 loss) whether the cost model or the revaluation model in FRS 10 is adopted. However, there will be a timing difference, because, under the cost model, the gain (£20,000) on release of the liability will only be recognised when the liability is settled, which will be after the year end.

21.286 In contrast to the above example, companies using the 'cost of settlement' approach will only measure the obligation at the current (that is, balance sheet date) market price of allowances to the extent that emissions made to date exceed the volume of allowances held. If emissions do not exceed allowances held, there is no obligation to purchase additional allowances and, so, no basis to use the current market price under this approach. Therefore, in the example above, under the 'cost of settlement' approach, at the year end the liability would be measured at 10,000 x £10 (for allowances held by the company) + 2,500 x £12 (for allowances to be purchased on the market), that is, a total liability at the year end of £130,000 (rather than £150,000 under the 'full market value' approach).

21.287 There is an additional consideration for companies using the 'cost of settlement' approach, as the measurement of the obligation for which allowances are held will depend on whether the carrying amount of allowances is allocated to the obligation on a FIFO or on a weighted average basis. This is a particular issue, where a balance sheet date is not the end of a compliance period, for example, at an interim balance sheet date (where the financial year is the same as the compliance period), or at a financial year end (where the financial year is not the same as the compliance period).

21.288 Companies using the FIFO method should measure the obligation at the carrying amount per unit of emissions, up to the number of allowances (if any) held at the balance sheet date and at the expected cost (the market price at the balance sheet date) per unit for the shortfall (if any) at the balance sheet date (see further para 21.291).

21.289 Companies using the weighted average method should measure the obligation using the weighted average cost per unit of emission expected to be incurred for the compliance period as a whole. To do this, the company determines the expected total emissions for the compliance period and compares this with the number of allowance units granted by the government (and/or purchased) and still held by the company for that compliance period, to determine the expected shortfall (if any) in allowances held for the compliance period. The weighted average cost per unit of emission for the compliance period is the carrying amount of the allowances held plus the cost of meeting the expected shortfall (using the market price at the balance sheet date), divided by the expected total number of units of emission for the compliance period. In other words:

$$\frac{\text{Carrying amount of allowances held} + \text{Cost of meeting expected shortfall}}{\text{Expected total units of emission for the compliance period}} = \text{Weighted average cost per unit of emission for the compliance period}$$

21.290 The weighted average method is consistent with the approach to measuring items at an interim date, such as tax, bonuses and volume rebates. The general principle under this approach is that where a company has an obligation, the effective rateable measurement of which is determined by reference to a full period's activities, then measurement is made on the basis of the volume of activity giving rise to the obligation up to the interim date at the expected effective rate for the period (determined on the basis of expected activity for the full year). This principle can be rationalised on the basis that there is a presumption that the company will continue operating and that the best estimate of the amount the company expects to pay should recognise this as well as the fact that settlement can in fact only be for a specified period which straddles the interim period.

21.291 The following example (using the facts in the example in paragraph 21.285) illustrates the difference under the FIFO and weighted average methods of applying the 'cost of settlement' approach to the measurement of an obligation for emissions.

Example – FIFO method

A company participates in a 'cap and trade' scheme for emission rights and is allocated on 1 January 20X6, free of charge, 10,000 allowances (to cover emissions of 10,000 tonnes of carbon dioxide) during the calendar year 20X6, which is also its financial accounting period. It has recognised these allowances in its balance sheet at fair value (being £100,000 at a fair value of £10 per allowance).

The company is preparing its interim financial report for the 6 months to 30 June 20X6. At the interim balance sheet date, the company has generated emissions equivalent to 6,000 allowances. For the full year, the company expects to require 12,500 emission allowances and, hence, expects to purchase an additional 2,500 allowances from the market. The company allocates allowances to cover the obligation on a FIFO basis. How should the company's liability be measured in the interim financial report?

At the interim balance sheet date, the company has generated an obligation equal to 6,000 allowances. As the company allocates its allowances on a FIFO basis and has not yet allocated all the emission allowances it holds (10,000 allowances held at £100,000), there is no shortfall of allowances at the interim date. Therefore, the liability will be recognised at the interim date at the carrying amount per unit held at the balance sheet date (£10), that is, 6,000 x £10 = £60,000.

If in the second half of the year, the company generates the further expected emissions of 6,500 (giving a total of 12,500 for the year) and if the market price of allowances is £12 at the year end balance sheet date, the liability at the end of the year will be measured at 10,000 x £10 = £100,000 (for allowances held by the entity) + 2,500 x 12 = 30,000 (for allowances to be purchased on the market), that is, a total liability at the year end of £130,000, recognising a further cost of £70,000 in the results for the second half of the financial year.

Example – weighted average method

The facts are the same as above, except that the company allocates allowances on a weighted average basis. The market price of an allowance at the interim balance sheet date is £11 and at the year end is £12.

Again, at the interim balance sheet date, the company has generated an obligation equal to 6,000 allowances and expects to require 12,500 emission allowances for the full year. It is probable that a portion of the settlement of the obligation for the compliance year as a whole will involve the outflow of economic benefit. This outflow can be estimated by allocating the total expected cost of the additional 2,500 allowances that the company expects to purchase in the market (using the market price at the interim balance sheet date for estimation purposes) across all emissions expected to be generated during the year.

Carrying amount of allowances held + Cost of meeting expected shortfall / Expected total units of emission for the compliance period	= Weighted average cost per unit of emission for the compliance period
£100,000 + £27,500 (2,500 × £11) / 12,500	£10.2

Therefore, at the interim balance sheet date, the liability will be measured at 6,000 x £10.2 = £61,200.

If in the second half of the year, the company generates the further expected emissions of 6,500 (giving a total of 12,500 for the year), the liability at the end of the year will be measured at 10,000 x £10 = £100,000 (for allowances held by the company) + 2,500 x £12 = £30,000 (for allowances to be purchased on the market), that is, a total liability at the year end of £130,000 (that is, £10.4 per unit), recognising a further cost of £68,800 in the second half of the financial year.

Comparison of methods

The effect of using the different methods for allocating allowances to the obligation under the 'cost of settlement' approach is that the total expense for the year will be recognised in different periods as shown below. The corresponding figures under the full market value approach are shown below for comparison purposes.

	'Cost of settlement' approach (FIFO)			'Cost of settlement' approach (weighted average)		
	Emissions	**Grant[1]**	**Net**	**Emissions**	**Grant[1]**	**Net**
	£	**£**	**£**	**£**	**£**	**£**
Expense in first half-year	60,000	(48,000)	12,000	61,200	(48,000)	(13,200)
Expense in second half-year	70,000	(52,000)	18,000	68,800	(52,000)	(16,800)
Total	130,000	100,000	30,000	130,000	(100,000)	30,000

	'Full market value' approach			
	Emissions	Grant	Gain (STRGL)	Net
	£	£	£	£
Expense in first half-year	66,000[2]	(48,000)	(10,000)	8,000
Expense in second half-year	84,000	(52,000)	(10,000)	22,000
Total	150,000[3]	(100,000)	(20,000)	30,000

[1] The grant has been allocated *pro rata* to expected emissions as for the full market value approach (see para 21.284)

[2] 6,000 × £11 = £66,000

[3] 12,500 × £12 = £150,000

Under the FIFO method using the 'cost of settlement' approach, if the company holds sufficient allowances to cover the obligation at the interim period and if those allowances are recognised at a lower cost per unit than the market price prevailing at the period end, there will be a relatively lower expense in the first half year. This contrasts with the weighted average method for the 'cost of settlement' approach, where the cost of meeting the expected shortfall (measured at the market price at the interim balance sheet date) is taken into account in measuring the cost per unit applied to the obligation at the interim balance sheet date.

The emissions charge of £68,800 in the second half of the year under the weighted average approach comprises the cost (of £67,600) in respect of the obligation generated in the second half (6,500 x (£100,000 + (2,500 x £12))/12,500 = £10.4) and the uplift of the obligation for the first half year (cost of £1,200) for the change in market value (= 6,000 x (£10.4 – £10.2)).

The full market value approach is shown above for comparison purposes. Under this approach (with revaluation of the intangible allowances), the net charge in the first half year (including the recognised gain on revaluation) is lower than the cost of settlement (weighted average approach), because the whole of the revaluation gain is recognised in the STRGL (£10,000), rather than just the proportion relating to the allowance units attributable to emissions in the first half year (£10,000 x 6,000/12,500 = £4,800). The net charge in the first half year is, therefore, reduced by the excess interim revaluation of £5,200 (that is, a net charge of £13,200 – £5,200 = £8,000) and the net charge in the second half is correspondingly increased (that is, a net charge of £16,800 + £5,200 = £22,200).

The example above illustrates the accounting where financial statements are drawn up at a date part way through the compliance period (for example, an interim financial report). As noted in paragraph 21.287, the above accounting will also be applicable for a financial year end where the financial year is not coterminous with the compliance period.

Self-insurance

21.292 If a company takes out insurance to cover potential future losses, the cost is accounted for annually on the basis of the premium paid. However, if a company does not take out insurance cover, but instead decides to self-insure, often by means of a separate captive insurance subsidiary, the question arises as to how this should be accounted for.

21.293 FRS 12 only allows a provision to be recognised if there is an obligation at the balance sheet date and, therefore, no provision should be recorded until a relevant obligating event has occurred. However, in deciding the extent to which obligating events have occurred by the balance sheet date, the company can take into account any additional evidence provided by events that take place after the balance sheet date. [FRS 12 para 38]. For example, where a company self insures some of its risks, at the balance sheet date provision will be made for claims that are reported post year end but occurred before, and for an estimate of those that have been incurred but are still not yet reported (that is, IBNR claims).

Example – Self insurance

A company that operates a chain of retail outlets decides not to insure itself with a third party for the risk of minor accidents to customers. Instead it opts to self-insure. Its past experience suggests it will pay £200,000 in respect of such accidents.

An obligation to another party does not arise until such time as an accident occurs. This means that under FRS 12 rules a provision of a larger amount than the cost of the actual accidents is not permitted. Therefore, if no accidents have occurred as at the year end, there is no present obligation to another party and hence no provision should be made.

Clearly, where an accident has happened the retailer might not know of its occurrence, but this in itself does not preclude it from making a provision. As long as the company has a track record of claims experience from which it can estimate (probably actuarially) the level of accidents that have occurred but which have not yet been reported (that is, IBNR claims) it may make a provision for its estimate of the obligation.

Therefore, the company should make provision for the expected cost of all accidents that have occurred before the balance sheet date, including those for which the customer has yet to make a claim. During the period between the company's year end and the date on which its financial statements are finalised, a number of IBNRs might have surfaced which means that a firmer estimate for these claims can be made. However, it will still be necessary to estimate those that have not yet been reported but that are likely to be, where these arise from events that occurred before the year end date and hence qualify for provision.

21.294 In summary:

- The company has an obligation which is legal in nature and its past experience shows it is likely to have arisen by the balance sheet date.
- The obligating event is the occurrence of the accident and the obligation cannot be avoided (unless the risk is passed to a third party for a payment).
- The costs do not relate to future operations.

- From past experience it is probable that an outflow of economic benefits will arise (that is, the settlement of the future claim).
- A reliable estimate can be made by (say) an actuary from the past claims experience.

21.295 The year end test arrives at the same conclusion, because if the company stopped trading, it would still be liable for claims that had been incurred by the balance sheet date but that had not been reported.

21.296 This basis is clearly not the same as building up (say) a reserve for insurance claims and, in practice, will mean that the expenses of different periods will vary, depending upon the number of accidents that occur. This might contrast with the more constant expense that would arise if the company's policy had been to insure these risks with an insurance company. However, this variability in expense is a consequence of the company's exposure to risk. Furthermore, even where a company is insured, it would be necessary to recognise the gross amount of an obligation and may or may not be possible to recognise an amount recoverable from the insurer (see para 21.71 onwards). An example of an accounting policy for self-insurance is given in Table 21.7.

Table 21.7 – Self-insurance provisions

Severn Trent plc – Report and accounts – 31 March 2009

2 Accounting policies (extract)

t) Provisions (extract)

Insurance provisions are recognised for claims notified and for claims incurred but which have not yet been notified, based on advice from the group's independent insurance advisers.

30 Provisions (extract)

Derwent Insurance Limited, a captive insurance company, is a wholly owned subsidiary of the group. Provisions for claims are made as set out in note 2 t. The associated outflows are estimated to arise over a period of up to five years from the balance sheet date.

Regulatory fines, compensation and systems rectification

21.297 Many regulated industries have their business activities scrutinised and if they do not comply with their regulators' rules may be subject to fines and compensation payments. Regulators can look at company systems and operations to determine whether a company is acting in a fit and proper manner to continue its trade. Sometimes, regulators recommend system changes for the future, but can also levy fines for past breaches of their rules. In extreme cases, regulators can withdraw licences or close businesses.

21.298 There are different types of costs resulting from these rule breaches. These include: fines paid to the regulators; compensation payments made to customers; and the costs associated with improving systems to ensure compliance in the future. Whether or not a company can provide for these will depend on a number of factors as illustrated in the following example. Table 21.8 includes an example of disclosure of provisions including regulatory fines and reimbursements to customers.

Example

A company expects to be fined £250,000 for the time taken in settling an obligation imposed on it by its regulator for mis-selling personal pensions. At its year end, the company has not paid the fine, but it knows the amount it will have to pay from published rates. It anticipates that it has a pension mis-selling obligation of £5m, but it still needs to calculate how much to repay its customers and who those customers are. In addition, the regulator has requested that it make certain system changes to the way it sells pensions and this is expected to cost the company a further £500,000, £100,000 of which relates to training costs.

The pension mis-selling obligations clearly arise from a past event, which was the original sale of personal pensions to customers. If the simple year end test is applied as if the company discontinued trade at its year end, the company would be responsible for paying the fine of £250,000. In addition, it would have an obligation of £5m to compensate its customers for mis-selling them personal pensions.

Clearly the costs of £400,000 to rectify the company's systems and the £100,000 training costs relate to the company's future operations and are not eligible for provision.

Table 21.8 – Disclosure of regulatory fines

Roche Holdings Ltd – Report and accounts – 31 December 2002

8. Vitamins and Fine Chemicals Division in millions of CHF (extract)

Vitamin case

Following the settlement agreement with the US Department of Justice on 20 May 1999 regarding pricing practices in the vitamin market and the overall settlement agreement to a class action suit brought by the US buyers of bulk vitamins, the Group recorded provisions in respect of the vitamin case in 1999. These provisions were the Group's best estimate at that time of the total liability that may arise, taking into account currency movements and the time value of money. Provisions for legal fees were recorded separately. At 31 December 2001, based on the development of the litigation and recent settlement negotiations, the Group recorded additional provisions of 760 million Swiss francs.

At 31 December 2002 the Group reassessed the adequacy of its remaining provisions for the vitamin case. Based on the development of the litigation and recent settlement negotiations, mainly in the United States with direct customers who had previously opted out of the class action settlement, the Group has recorded additional provisions of 1,770 million Swiss francs. Total payments during the year were 3,266 million Swiss francs (2001: 330 million Swiss francs). Payments made in 2002 include fines imposed by the European Union totalling 525 million euros (778 million Swiss francs) and settlements with direct and indirect customers in the United States totalling 1,707 million US dollars (2,455 million Swiss francs).

The Group is seeking to resolve the remaining outstanding issues, however the timing and the final amounts involved are uncertain. The provisions recorded are based on current litigation and recent settlement agreements. As the litigation and negotiations progress, it is possible that the ultimate liability may be different from the amount of provisions currently recorded.

On 17 January 2003 the District of Columbia Circuit Court of Appeals ruled that non-US plaintiffs may bring claims in US courts under US anti-trust laws for alleged damages suffered from transactions outside the United States in connection with the vitamin case. The defendants,

> including Roche, will appeal against this decision. No provisions have been recorded in respect of this litigation as the eventual outcome is uncertain at this stage.
>
> As part of the demerger process, the liabilities in respect of the vitamin case will remain with the Roche Group. Roche and DSM have signed an Indemnity and Co-operation Agreement under which Roche may provide DSM with certain indemnities and guarantees in connection with the vitamin case.

Financial guarantee contracts

21.299 Appendix III to FRS 12 includes an example of a financial guarantee. The accounting treatment for such an item depends on whether the company is applying FRS 26, 'Financial instruments: Recognition and measurement'. If FRS 26 does not apply, then the normal rules in FRS 12 are applied. This is illustrated in the example in paragraph 21.303 below.

21.300 If the company applies FRS 26, then its scope specifically considers financial guarantee contracts that provide for payment to be made if the debtor fails to make payment when due. FRS 26 defines a financial guarantee contract as:

> '*... a contract that requires the issuer to make specified payments to reimburse the holder for a loss it incurs because a specified debtor fails to make payment when due in accordance with the original or modified terms of a debt instrument*'. [FRS 26 para 9].

21.301 This would, therefore, apply to financial guarantees given by or to financial institutions, but also certain guarantees given by parent companies to their subsidiaries and other intra-group guarantees. Financial guarantee contracts are dealt with in detail in chapter 6, but in summary, such contracts (other than certain specified exemptions – see chapter 6 for details) are required to be accounted for as follows under FRS 26:

- Initially at fair value. If the financial guarantee contract was issued in a stand-alone arm's length transaction to an unrelated party, its fair value at inception is likely to equal the premium received, unless there is evidence to the contrary. [FRS 26 paras 43, AG4(a)].
- Subsequently (unless they are designated as at fair value through profit or loss, if permitted) at the higher of:
  - the amount determined in accordance with FRS 12; and
  - the amount initially recognised less, when appropriate, cumulative amortisation.

[FRS 26 para 47(c)].

21.302 An exception to the above rules in FRS 26 for financial guarantee contracts is where an issuer has previously asserted explicitly that it regards a financial guarantee contract as an insurance contract and has used accounting applicable to insurance contracts. In that case, the issuer may elect to apply either FRS 26 or continue to use accounting applicable to insurance contracts. The issuer can make that election on a contract by contract basis, but the election for each contract is irrevocable. [FRS 26 para 2(e)].

21.303 As noted above, Appendix III to FRS 12 includes an example dealing with a financial guarantee. The example below, which is based on the example in FRS 12 considers this further, both for companies that are applying FRS 26 and those that are not.

Example

On 31 December 20X2, company A gives a guarantee of certain borrowings of company B, whose financial condition at that time is sound. Under the guarantee's terms, company A will make specified payments to reimburse the holder for any loss it incurs if company B fails to make payment when due. During 20X3, company B's financial condition deteriorates and at 30 June 20X3 entity B files for protection from its creditors.

At 31 December 20X2

- The obligating event is the giving of the guarantee, which gives rise to a legal obligation.
- At 31 December 20X2, the financial position of company B is sound. Therefore, an outflow of economic benefits is not probable at 31 December 20X2.

Companies not applying FRS 26 – No provision is recognised. [FRS 12 paras 14, 23]. The guarantee is disclosed as a contingent liability, unless the probability of any transfer is regarded as remote. [FRS 12 para 91].

Companies applying FRS 26 – The guarantee is initially recognised at fair value. [FRS 26 para 43].

At 31 December 20X3

- The obligating event is the giving of the guarantee, which gives rise to a legal obligation.
- At 31 December 20X3, the financial position of company B has deteriorated such that it is probable that an outflow of economic benefits will be required to settle the obligation.

Companies not applying FRS 26 – A provision is recognised for the best estimate of the obligation. [FRS 12 paras 14, 23]. Note that this example deals with a single guarantee. If an company has a portfolio of similar guarantees, it will assess that portfolio as a whole in determining whether a transfer of economic benefit is probable. [FRS 12 para 24].

Companies applying FRS 26 – The guarantee is subsequently measured at the higher of (a) the best estimate of the obligation determined in accordance with FRS 12 and (b) the amount initially recognised less cumulative amortisation. [FRS 26 para 47(c)].

Tariff over-recoveries

21.304 FRS 12 does not allow a provision to be made to transfer profits from one year to the next, where the results achieved in the current period may cause the pricing structure in the next period to be adjusted such that the higher the profits in the current year the lower the prices that will be permitted in the next year. In this situation there is no present obligation that requires the outflow of economic benefits and, therefore, there is nothing to justify recognition of a provision under present UK GAAP.

Disclosure requirements

21.305 FRS 12 has extensive disclosures that companies have to make when they recognise provisions and have contingent liabilities and assets, and also Schedule 1 to SI 2008/410 contains other disclosure requirements. For companies applying FRS 26, unless specifically exempted, FRS 29, 'Financial instruments: Disclosure', is applicable to those provisions that meet the definition of financial instruments, but which are accounted for under FRS 12 as they are exempt from FRS 26.

Provisions

21.306 SI 2008/410 requires 'Provisions for liabilities' to be analysed into the following categories:

- Pensions and similar obligations.
- Taxation, including deferred taxation.
- Other provisions.

[SI 2008/410 1 Sch formats].

21.307 The legislation goes on to say that apart from the categories of provision mentioned above, an item representing a provision that is not covered by the prescribed format may be shown separately. [SI 2008/410 1 Sch 3(2)]. FRS 12 ties in with this as it requires each class of provision to be disclosed separately. [FRS 12 para 89].

21.308 In order to determine which provisions can be aggregated together to form a class, it is necessary to consider whether the nature of the items is sufficiently similar for a single statement about them to fulfil FRS 12's disclosure requirements, which are set out below. [FRS 12 para 92]. Examples of different classes of provision include those set up in relation to restructurings, integration of acquisitions, self-insurance, warranties and environmental liabilities. It might, for example, be appropriate to treat warranties for different products as a single class, but the standard comments that it would not be appropriate to treat as a single class amounts relating to normal warranties and amounts that are subject to legal proceedings. Also the materiality of each class needs to be considered and some aggregation might be necessary where individually provisions are immaterial.

Tabular information

21.309 The Act's requirements concerning how to analyse the movements on provisions are set out in paragraph 59 of Schedule 1 to SI 2008/410. But these disclosures are only required where there has been a transfer to or from any provision for liabilities other than a transfer from that provision for the purpose for which that provision was originally established. FRS 12's requirements cover the same types of disclosure as the legislation, except that the standard's requirements are more prescriptive and apply whether or not the provision is being used for the purpose it was originally intended. Therefore, putting the two sets of disclosure requirements together, companies now have to give the following information for each class of provision:

- The carrying amount at the beginning and end of the period. [FRS 12 para 89(a); SI 2008/410 1 Sch 59(2)(a)].
- Additional provisions made in the period, including increases to existing provisions. [FRS 12 para 89(b); SI 2008/410 1 Sch 59(2)(b)].
- Amounts used (that is, incurred and charged against the provision) during the period. [FRS 12 para 89(c); SI 2008/410 1 Sch 59(2)(b)].
- Unused amounts reversed during the period. [FRS 12 para 89(d); SI 2008/410 1 Sch 59(2)(b)(c)].
- The increase during the period in the discounted amount arising from the passage of time and the effect of any change in the discount rate. [FRS 12 para 89(a); SI 2008/410 1 Sch 59(2)(a)].

21.310 One of the Act's requirements is not exactly mirrored by the disclosures required by FRS 12. Paragraph 59(2)(c) of Schedule 1 to SI 2008/410 requires that disclosure should be made of the source and the application of any amounts transferred to or from provisions. This disclosure, prior to the introduction of FRS 12, was aimed in particular at the situation where a provision was not used for its intended purpose. But following the prohibition in paragraph 64 of FRS 12, provisions can now only be used for their intended purpose. Still the Act requires the source and application of the provision to be disclosed and this can either be mentioned in the description in the table or is probably better dealt with in the narrative disclosures (see para 21.313 below).

21.311 Although comparative information is required for most items included in financial statements, FRS 28, 'Corresponding amounts', contains an exemption from the requirement to disclose an analysis showing the movement between the opening provision and the closing balance in the preceding period. [FRS 28 para 11].

21.312 Where a provision and a contingent liability arises from the same set of circumstances, the company should make the disclosures required by the standard's paragraphs 89 to 91 in such a way that clearly shows the link between the provision and the contingent liability.

Narrative information

21.313 In addition to the tabular information, the standard requires the following narrative disclosures to be given for each class of provision:

- A brief description of the nature of the obligation and the expected timing of any resulting transfers of economic benefits.
- An indication of the uncertainties about the amount or timing of those transfers of economic benefits. This might necessitate disclosure of the major assumptions made concerning those future events.
- The amount of any expected reimbursement, stating the amount of any asset that has been recognised for that expected reimbursement.

[FRS 12 para 90].

21.314 As mentioned above in paragraph 21.310 company law requires that the source and the application should be disclosed of any amounts transferred to or from provisions and this information could be given as part of the narrative disclosure.

Unwinding of discount

21.315 Where the measurement of a provision has been discounted the tabular disclosures described in paragraph 21.309 above require separate disclosure of the increase during the period in the discounted amount arising from the passage of time and the effect of any change in the discount rate. The unwinding of the discount will be charged to the profit and loss account. The standard says that this charge should be included as a financial item. However, in order to ensure that the relationship between a company's debt and its interest charge is visible, the standard requires that the charge should be shown adjacent to interest. [FRS 12 para 48].

21.316 Originally, companies could present the charge for unwinding of a discount either separately on the face of the profit and loss account or in a note to the financial statements. In practice, many companies chose to show one figure for interest payable and similar charges, including the discount, on the face of the profit and loss account whilst showing the split in the notes. However, FRS 17 introduced an amendment to FRS 12 requiring that the unwinding of a discount on provisions is shown as 'other finance costs adjacent to interest'. The legal requirements section of FRS 17 makes it clear that 'other finance costs (or income)' involves a new profit and loss account format heading and that the unwinding of a discount is not now part of the format heading for interest payable and similar charges. [FRS 17 App II para 6]. However, in practice, because all items in the profit and loss account can be aggregated and given in the notes to the financial statements, it is likely that companies will still aggregate 'interest receivable and similar income' and 'interest payable and similar changes' with 'other finance costs (income)' on the face of the profit and loss account, disclosing the three items separately in the notes.

Further rules included in other regulations

21.317 In addition to the requirements in accounting standards, SI 2008/410 requires certain additional information to be given with regard to pensions and similar obligations and for taxation including deferred tax, as explained in the paragraphs below.

Pensions and similar obligations

21.318 SI 2008/410 requires the following disclosure in respect of pensions provisions:

- Any pension commitments included under any provision shown in the company's balance sheet.
- Any such commitments for which no provision has been made.

[SI 2008/410 1 Sch 63(4)].

21.319 Such commitments in relation to pensions payable to the company's past directors must be separately disclosed. [SI 2008/410 1 Sch 63(4)]. This principally relates to unfunded pension arrangements.

21.320 In addition, FRS 17, contains extensive disclosure requirements in respect of pensions. These are considered in detail in chapter 11.

Taxation provisions

21.321 SI 2008/410 also specifies that if a provision for liabilities and charges includes any provision for taxation (excluding deferred taxation) it must be disclosed separately. [SI 2008/410 1 Sch 60].

21.322 In addition, deferred taxation should be included under the balance sheet heading 'Taxation, including deferred taxation' within provisions. Both SI 2008/410 and FRS 19 require any provision for deferred taxation to be shown separately. The deferred tax balance, its major components, and transfers to and from the deferred tax account are also required by FRS 19, to be disclosed in the notes to the financial statements. [FRS 19 paras 60, 61]. Taxation and deferred tax are considered further in chapter 13.

Acquisition provisions

21.323 FRS 6, 'Acquisitions and mergers', requires movements on provisions or accruals for costs related to an acquisition to be disclosed and analysed between the amounts used for the specific purpose for which they were created and the amounts released unused. [FRS 6 para 32]. Such disclosure should be given separately for each material acquisition and for other acquisitions in aggregate. [FRS 6 para 23]. These rules are consistent with the FRS 12's requirements and indicate that each material acquisition should be treated as a separate class for the purposes of the disclosures required by FRS 12. Acquisition provisions are discussed further in chapter 25.

Contingent liabilities

21.324 As explained in paragraph 21.91, under FRS 12 it is not appropriate to provide for contingent liabilities, but contingencies of this nature are required to be noted, because of the chance that they might turn into an obligation in the future. However, if the likelihood of an obligation arising is remote, no disclosure is required.

21.325 For each class of contingent liability that exists at the balance sheet date a company should disclose a brief description of the nature of the contingent liability and where practicable:

- An estimate of its financial effect (including the amount or estimated amount of the liabilities, measured under paragraphs 36 to 52 of FRS 12 – see para 21.107 onwards).
- An indication of the uncertainties relating to the amount or timing of any outflow.
- The possibility of any reimbursement.
- Its legal nature.
- Whether any valuable security has been provided by the company in connection with the liability and a description of that security.

[FRS 12 para 91; SI 2008/410 1 Sch 63(2)].

21.326 In order to meet the requirements in the first two bullet points above, a company should disclose both:

- an amount for the best estimate measured under paragraphs 36 to 52 of FRS 12, which may, for instance, be:
  - the most likely outcome; or
  - a probability weighted average depending on facts and circumstances; and

- an indication of uncertainties relating to the amount and timing; this may be achieved by disclosing:
  - a range of outcomes, for example, by giving maximum exposure accompanied by a narrative description of the uncertainties; or
  - probabilities used to determine the weighted average amount, which would allow the user to assess the uncertainties of the exposure, accompanied by a narrative description of the uncertainties.

The level of disclosure necessary will depend on the specific facts and circumstances.

Contingent assets

21.327 Contingent assets are required to be disclosed by FRS 12, but only where an inflow of economic benefits is probable. This can be contrasted with the standard's requirement for contingent liabilities, which is to require disclosure of them all, unless they are remote.

21.328 Hence, where an inflow of economic benefits is probable, a company must disclose a brief description of the nature of the contingent assets at the balance sheet date and, where practicable, an estimate of their financial effect. [FRS 12 para 94]. Because of the higher degree of certainty needed before a contingent asset is even disclosed, it is important that disclosures of contingent assets avoid giving a misleading indication of the likelihood of a profit arising. [FRS 12 para 95].

Guarantees

21.329 FRS 12's scope includes guarantees, other than those falling within the scope of FRS 26 for companies applying that standard – see further chapter 6. These may fall to be disclosed as contingent liabilities and, in certain circumstances, provision might be required where an obligation under the guarantee arises. In addition, SI 2008/410 requires the notes to the financial statements to give details of:

- Any charge on the company's assets that has been given in order to secure the liabilities of any other person.
- The amounts so secured (where practicable).

[SI 2008/410 1 Sch 63(1)].

21.330 In addition to the requirement to disclose details of any charge on the company's assets, paragraph 63(2) of Schedule 1 to SI 2008/410 (other contingent liabilities) requires the notes to disclose whether any valuable security has been provided.

Exemptions from disclosure

21.331 As can be seen from the explanation of the disclosures required to be given under FRS 12 outlined above, significant information is necessary for each class of provision. In certain situations some of this information might not be readily available or might be of a highly sensitive nature. The standard does include some relaxation in these circumstances as explained below.

21.332 Where any of the information required to be disclosed by the standard is not given because it is not practicable to do so, that fact must be stated. [FRS 12 para 96]. The standard does not elaborate on what is meant by 'not practicable' in this context. But it is possible to imagine situations where it might not be possible to ascertain what uncertainties might relate to the timing of a provision or perhaps difficulties with estimating the financial effect. There is no doubt, however, that the ASB's intention is that companies should use their best endeavours to ascertain all of the required information and only whether this is totally impracticable should the facts surrounding the problem be given instead.

21.333 Some information concerning provisions and contingent liabilities and assets, for example, litigation and litigation recoveries (particularly through insurance) might be very sensitive and disclosure could prejudice the outcome of a particular case. The ASB has acknowledged this and concedes in the standard that, in extremely rare cases, disclosure of some or all of the information required by FRS 12 might prejudice seriously the position of the company in a dispute with other parties on the subject matter of the provision, contingent liability or contingent asset. In such situations the standard accepts that a company need not comply with the standard's disclosure requirements, unless the particular disclosure is required by law. The disclosures required by law are primarily set out in paragraph 59 of Schedule 1 to SI 2008/410.

21.334 Where advantage is taken of this exemption, the standard requires instead disclosure of the general nature of the dispute, together with the fact that, and reason why, the information has not been disclosed. [FRS 12 para 97]. See the example below.

Example

Company A is in dispute with a competitor, which is alleging that company A has infringed patents. The competitor is seeking damages of £100 million. Management recognises a provision for its best estimate of the obligation, but does not disclose the information required by paragraphs 89 and 90 of FRS 12 on the grounds that this would be prejudicial to the outcome of the case.

Management should disclose the following in a note to the financial statements:

> Litigation is in process against the company relating to a dispute with a competitor, which alleges that the company has infringed patents and is seeking damages of £100 million. The information usually required by

FRS 12 is not disclosed, because the directors believe that to do so would seriously prejudice the outcome of the litigation.

21.335 As to what might fall into the category of 'extremely rare' is a matter of judgement. But it is clear that if, for example, disclosure of certain information is likely to change the course of a particular legal action, then this would justify non-disclosure. Whether this would extend to all of the required disclosures would depend on the particular circumstances.

Commitments

General

21.336 SI 2008/410 requires the notes to the financial statements to disclose details, where practicable, of:

- Capital commitments.
- Pension commitments.
- Other financial commitments.

[SI 2008/410 1 Sch 63(3)-(5)].

Capital commitments

21.337 Where practicable details must be disclosed of the aggregate amount or estimated amount of capital expenditure contracted for, but not provided for, at the balance sheet date. It is no longer necessary to disclose the aggregate amount or estimated amount of capital expenditure authorised by the directors, but not contracted for, at the balance sheet date. [SI 2008/410 1 Sch 63(3)].

21.338 In circumstances where a business is highly capital intensive and the capital commitments are of particular significance in the context of the financial statements as a whole, it may be considered appropriate to provide more information as to the extent and nature of the commitments. An example of the more detailed disclosures made by British Airways is illustrated below in Table 21.9.

Table 21.9 – British Airways Plc – Report & Accounts – 31 March 1997

Notes to the accounts (extract)

15 CAPITAL EXPENDITURE COMMITMENTS

Capital expenditure authorised and contracted for but not provided in the accounts amounts to £3,030 million for the Group (1996: £3,788 million) and £2,871 million for the Company (1996: £3,788 million).

The outstanding commitments include £2,539 million which relates to the acquisition of Boeing 747-400 and Boeing 777 aircraft scheduled for delivery during the next four years and £255 million which relates to the acquisition of Boeing 757-200 and Boeing 737-300 aircraft scheduled for delivery during the next year. It is intended that these aircraft will be financed partially by cash holdings and internal cash flow and partially through external financing, including committed facilities arranged prior to delivery.

At March 31, 1997 British Airways had an unused long term secured aircraft financing facility of US$2.31 billion and unused overdraft and revolving credit facilities of £40 million, and undrawn uncommitted money market lines of £229 million and US$45 million with a number of banks. In addition, British Airways had arranged a £150 million bank-guaranteed facility from the European Investment Bank to assist in funding the airline's ongoing longhaul fleet replacement programme.

The Group's holdings of cash and short-term loans and deposits, together with committed funding facilities and net cash flow, are sufficient to cover the full cost of all firm aircraft deliveries due in the next two years.

Pension commitments

21.339 Under SI 2008/410, the notes to the financial statements must give details of pension commitments. See further paragraph 21.318.

21.340 The law does not specify the basis a company should use to measure pension costs or pension commitments that it has not provided for. However extensive guidance is given by FRS 17 and, except in relation to disclosure of any commitments to pay pensions to past directors, compliance with FRS 17 is considered to be sufficient to meet the law's requirements. The provisions of FRS 17 are considered in chapter 11.

Other financial commitments

21.341 SI 2008/410 requires details to be disclosed of any other financial commitments that:

- Have not been provided for.
- Are relevant to assessing the company's state of affairs.

[SI 2008/410 Sch 63(5)].

21.342 However, the law does not define financial commitments nor does it give guidance as to the nature of the commitments that are required to be disclosed.

21.343 Part 4 of SSAP 21, 'Accounting for leases and hire purchase contracts', sets out the legal requirements that are relevant to that standard's application. The legal requirements referred to include paragraph 50(5) of Schedule 4 to the 1985 Act thereby implying that a commitment under a lease is an example of an 'other financial commitment' now covered by SI 2008/410 1 Sch 63(5).

21.344 Commitments that represent an unusual risk to the reporting entity, either because of their nature or their size or duration, are likely to be relevant to an assessment of the reporting entity's state of affairs and, consequently, should be disclosed. Examples of such contracts could include significant long-term purchase contracts and forward exchange or commodity contracts held by a company that is not applying FRS 26 (see further chapter 6) that do not hedge existing commitments. Examples of companies that disclose details of purchase commitments are shown in Tables 21.10 and 21.11 below.

Table 21.10 – Imperial Chemical Industries PLC – Annual Report and Accounts – 31 December 1997

Notes relating to the accounts (extract)

41 Commitments and contingent liabilities (extract)

Significant take-or-pay contracts entered into by subsidiaries are as follows:

(i) the purchase of electric power, which commended April 1993, for 15 years. The present value of the remaining commitment is estimated at £688m.

(ii) the purchase of electric power, which will commence in the second quarter of 1998, for 15 years. The present value of this commitment is estimated at £141m.

Table 21.11 – PowerGen plc – Report and Accounts – 31 December 2000

Notes to the Accounts (extract)

31 Commitments and contingent liabilities (extract)

c) The Group has in place a portfolio of fuel contracts of varying volume, duration and price, reflecting market conditions at the time of commitment. These contracts are with UK, US and other international suppliers of coal and are backed by transport contracts for rail, road, canal and sea movements. At 31 December 2000 the Group's future commitments for the supply of coal under all its contractual arrangements totalled £798 million.

The Group is also committed to purchase gas under various long-term gas supply contracts including the supply of gas to the Group's UK CCGT power stations. At 31 December 2000 the estimated minimum commitment for the supply of gas under all these contracts totalled £2.660 million.

Chapter 22

Post balance sheet events

Chapter 22

Post balance sheet events

22.1 Accounting for post balance sheet events is dealt with in FRS 21, 'Events after the balance sheet date', which is based on the international standard IAS 10, 'Events after the reporting period'.

22.2 The chapter from the Manual of Accounting – IFRS for the UK that deals with IAS 10 is included as an annex to this chapter. FRS 21 is identical to IAS 10 with the exception that the international standard refers to the 'balance sheet' as the 'statement of financial position' and 'events after the balance sheet date' as 'events after the reporting period'.

22.3 The text in the annex contains references to the international standard. For these to be applied in the UK context, references to paragraphs in IAS 10 should be read as references to FRS 21, whose paragraph numbers are identical.

22.4 In addition, the annex makes reference to other IASs and IFRSs which may, or may not, be relevant under UK GAAP. The table immediately below identifies those international standards quoted in the annex with a direct UK GAAP equivalent (although the specific paragraph references may differ):

International standard	UK standard	Title
IAS 32	FRS 25	Financial instruments: presentation
IAS 33	FRS 22	Earnings per share
IAS 37	FRS 12	Provisions, contingent liabilities and contingent assets
IAS 39	FRS 26*	Financial instruments: recognition and measurement

* Applicable only to those entities that fall within the scope of FRS 26 or those that choose to adopt it voluntarily

22.5 In addition to the above, other references are made to IASs and IFRSs in the annex where the international and UK standards cannot be considered equivalent. However, where for the purposes of the points being illustrated in the specific examples in this chapter, the international and UK standards require broadly consistent accounting, the table below shows the international standard quoted and the relevant UK standard which covers the same issue:

International standard	UK standard / Company law reference
IAS 1 (revised), 'Presentation of financial statements'	FRS 18, 'Accounting policies'
IAS 2, 'Inventories'	SSAP 9, 'Stocks and long-term contracts'
IAS 12, 'Income taxes'	FRS 19, 'Deferred tax'
IAS 18, 'Revenue'	FRS 5, 'Reporting the substance of transactions'
IAS 36, 'Impairment of assets'	FRS 11, 'Impairment of fixed assets and goodwill'
IAS 39, 'Financial instruments:' recognition and measurement*	SI 2008/410 Schedule 1

* For entities not applying FRS 26, the relevant guidance on measurement of financial assets is embodied in company law.

The disclosures required by these international standards as quoted in the text of the annex may differ to those required by UK GAAP, and the relevant UK GAAP standard should be consulted for the UK GAAP disclosures.

22.6 The following sections of the annex are not relevant to a consideration of UK GAAP as the requirements of IFRS depart from the UK requirements in these areas:

- Acquisitions and disposals: While FRS 21 requires significant acquisitions and disposals to be disclosed as non-adjusting post balance sheet events, the specific disclosure requirements of IFRS 3, 'Business combinations' and IFRS 5, 'Non-current assets held for sale and discontinued operations' do not apply under UK GAAP. [Paras 22.43 – 22.43.4].
- Commitments: Disclosure of commitments under UK GAAP is covered in chapter 21. [Paras 22.65 – 22.72].

22.7 All references to other chapters in the annex are references to chapters in the Manual of Accounting – IFRS for the UK.

Annex

Events after the reporting period and financial commitments

Introduction

A22.1 Almost invariably, it will not be practicable for preparers to finalise financial statements without a period of time elapsing between the balance sheet date and the date on which the financial statements are authorised for issue. The question, therefore, arises as to what extent events occurring between the balance sheet date and the date of approval (that is, 'events after the reporting period') should be reflected in the financial statements. Some of these issues are considered in chapter 21 in relation to provisions, whereas this chapter considers the requirements of IAS 10, 'Events after the reporting period'.

A22.2 While IAS 10 uses the terminology 'events after the reporting period', the terms 'events after the balance sheet date' and 'post balance sheet events' are also commonly understood. Accordingly, throughout this chapter 'events after the reporting period' are generally referred to as 'post balance sheet events'.

[The next paragraph is A22.16.]

Objectives and scope

A22.16 IAS 10 applies to the accounting and disclosure of events that happen after the balance sheet date. In addition, IAS 10 requires disclosure of the date that the financial statements are authorised for issue and who gave such authorisation. The standard also requires that the going concern basis of preparation should not be applied to financial statements if events after the balance sheet date indicate that the going concern assumption is no longer appropriate. [IAS 10 paras 1, 2].

A22.17 IAS 10 covers all post balance sheet events up to the date that the financial statements are authorised for issue and distinguishes between events that require changes in the amounts to be included in the financial statements ('adjusting events') and events that only require disclosure ('non-adjusting events'). The classification of an event depends on whether it presents additional information about conditions already existing at the balance sheet date or indicates conditions that arose after the balance sheet date.

Adjusting events

A22.18 A material post-balance-sheet event requires changes in the amounts to be included in financial statements where either of the following applies:

- It is an adjusting event (that is, it is an event that provides additional evidence relating to conditions that existed at the balance sheet date). [IAS 10 paras 3, 8].
- The event indicates that it is not appropriate to apply the going concern basis of accounting. [IAS 10 para 14].

A22.19 In some circumstances, a post balance sheet determination that an entity is no longer a going concern will require changes to amounts to be included in the financial statements.

A22.20 Going concern is dealt with separately below from paragraph A22.31, while examples of adjusting events are given in IAS 10 and include:

- The settlement of a court case after the balance sheet date that confirms that the entity had a present obligation at the balance sheet date. The entity adjusts any existing provision for the obligation or creates a new provision.
- The receipt of information after the balance sheet date indicating that an asset was impaired as at the balance sheet date; for example, the bankruptcy of a customer that occurs after the balance sheet date or the sale of inventories after the year end that gives evidence about their net realisable value at the balance sheet date.
- The determination after the balance sheet date of the consideration for assets sold or purchased before the balance sheet date.
- The determination after the balance sheet date of profit-sharing or bonus arrangements if the entity had an obligation to make such payments as a result of events before the balance sheet date.
- The discovery of fraud or errors that show that the financial statements are incorrect.

[IAS 10 para 9].

Settlement of a court case

A22.21 In relation to the first bullet point in paragraph A22.20 above, IAS 10 requires that an entity should remeasure the amount of a provision for an obligation if the result of a court case after the balance sheet date requires such remeasurement. However, in some cases the result of a court case may also affect the degree of probability of an outflow of economic benefits. For example, an entity may not have recognised a provision at the balance sheet date because it considered that it was not probable that an outflow of future economic benefits would occur. In such situations, the entity should create a new provision as at the balance sheet date if the outcome of a court case clarifies that such an outflow was probable at the balance sheet date. Thus, the standard requires that the result of a court case after the year end is taken into account, not only in determining whether changes in measurements are required, but also in determining, as at the balance sheet date, whether a provision should be recognised. [IAS 10 para 9(a)].

A22.22 This latter requirement is consistent with the requirement of IAS 37 for provisions. Paragraph 16 of IAS 37 notes that in rare cases, for example in a law suit, it may be disputed either whether certain events have occurred or whether those events result in a present obligation. In such a case, an entity determines whether a present obligation exists at the balance sheet date by taking account of all available evidence, including, for example, the opinion of experts. The settlement of a court case after the year end could also provide evidence of conditions existing at the balance sheet date.

A22.23 IAS 10 refers to a present *obligation* at the balance sheet date, but a court case in progress at the balance sheet date might also concern a matter in which the entity was claiming damages. In this situation, under IAS 37, an asset is not recognised unless an inflow of economic benefits is virtually certain at the balance sheet date. Until the final court judgement is made, it would be rare for the outcome of the court case to be virtually certain. Hence, only when the final judgement is received should the asset be recognised and the related profit be recorded in the financial statements of the period in which the change occurs. [IAS 37 para 35]. In effect, where an entity is claiming for damages, a judgement received after the balance sheet date up to the date of approval of the financial statements is normally a non-adjusting event. The receivable when recognised then becomes subject to normal credit risk evaluation.

Assets sold or purchased before the year end

A22.24 Consider the situation where a property is being sold at the balance sheet date and the sale is conditional on planning permission being granted. Planning permission is granted and the sale is completed, with both these events occurring after the balance sheet date, but before the financial statements are approved. In that situation receipt of planning permission does not permit the sale proceeds to be recognised at the year end, because there is no existing condition at the balance sheet date for which the grant of planning permission would provide additional evidence. This is because no sale had taken place at the balance sheet date and the conditional sale would not be recognised at that date. By contrast, in the example in paragraph A22.21, there is an ongoing court case in existence at the balance sheet date that relates to a transaction or event that occurred before the balance sheet date. The outcome of the court case confirms the existence of the liability and resolves the uncertainty about the amount. In the case of the property sale, the planning permission is critical to whether there is a sale – it is a new event that causes the sale.

A22.25 Now consider a different scenario where the property is *sold unconditionally* before the year end and only the amount of the consideration is dependent on whether or not planning permission is obtained. In such a situation, the potential for planning permission would be taken into account in determining the fair value of the receivable at the balance sheet date in accordance with IAS 39, 'Financial instruments: Recognition and measurement'. Any adjustment to the receivable's value resulting from the granting or refusal of planning permission after the balance sheet date would be a non-adjusting event.

Information that indicates impairment or provides evidence of net realisable value

A22.26 An entity should consider an impairment loss if it becomes aware of conditions after the balance sheet date that must have existed at the balance sheet date (adjusting events). Whilst a post balance sheet restructuring and discontinuance of operations by sale or closure are not in themselves adjusting events, as explained in paragraph A22.39 below, they may often provide evidence of impairment at the balance sheet date. Indeed, such impairment may be a cause rather than a consequence of those post balance sheet events. Therefore, it is common for entities to review carrying values of assets in the light of post balance sheet events of this type and make impairment write-downs as appropriate. The following examples illustrate the distinction between an impairment indicator regarded as adjusting and an impairment indicator regarded as non-adjusting.

Example 1 – Impairment of trade receivables

The insolvency of a customer after the year end normally provides evidence that at the balance sheet date, receivables due from that customer were impaired, because the customer was unable to pay. This type of event would typically be treated as an adjusting post balance sheet event, because it would be unusual (although not impossible) for a customer's business to fail only as a result of events occurring after the balance sheet date and before approval of the financial statements.

Example 2 – Destruction of an asset

Destruction or expropriation of an asset subsequent to the balance sheet date represents a new impairment indicator arising after the balance sheet date that is a non-adjusting event. The event was not indicative of a condition existing at the balance sheet date. However, management should disclose the nature of such an event and an estimate of its financial effect.

A22.26.1 In a recessionary environment, it may be the case that a goodwill impairment review conducted based on management approved budgets at the year end does not give rise to an impairment, but a few months later (before the financial statements are signed) budgets are revised downwards because of a decline in economic conditions leading to an impairment. The question that arises is whether the impairment that is now apparent should be recorded in the previous year's financial statements. Market deterioration is not defined by a specific event, but occurs gradually over time. Where such decline occurs after the balance sheet date it is not an adjusting event. Provided the budgets in existence at the year end truly represented management's best estimate of the future outlook at the year end date and were based on reasonable and supportable assumptions given market conditions, then no impairment would be recorded at the previous year end as a result of the subsequent decline.

A22.26.2 While a post balance sheet restructuring may provide evidence of impairment at the balance sheet date, in accordance with IAS 37, provision is not made for future restructuring costs until a legal or constructive obligation exists (see further para A22.44 onwards). The example in Table A22.1 below and the later example in Table A22.9 illustrate how post year end restructurings have been taken into account in determining the impairment of assets at the year end, consistent with IAS 10 and IAS 37.

Table A22.1 – Impairment loss related to post year end restructuring

Carphone Warehouse Group plc – Annual report and accounts – 31 March 2001

6(b) Profit and loss on disposal of fixed assets (extract)

In certain non-key markets where the prospects of achieving acceptable financial returns are not evident, the Group has announced its intention to either restructure its operations or to withdraw its involvement.

As such the Group has provided for the loss of £2.9m expected to arise on the disposal of specific fixed assets. The Group anticipates that further restructuring costs of £3.0m will be incurred in the period to 30 March 2002.

29 Post-balance sheet events

As detailed in note 6b, the Group is in the process of restructuring its involvement in certain non-key markets. Whilst provision has been made for the anticipated loss on disposal of certain fixed assets, the Directors expect additional exceptional restructuring costs of £3m to arise in the period ended 30 March 2002.

A22.27 The above example in Table A22.1 illustrates an impairment that applies to fixed assets, while the examples given in the second bullet point of paragraph A22.20 relate to debtors and inventory. Impairments of current assets that become evident as a result of post balance sheet events are usually fairly straightforward to identify and quantify, because they are usually the direct result of an insolvency of a debtor or the sale of inventory. Where either a current or fixed asset is sold at a loss or revalued downwards subsequent to the balance sheet date, this may also provide additional evidence of a diminution in value that existed at the balance sheet date and would indicate that an impairment review should be carried out in accordance with IAS 36, 'Impairment of assets', (see chapter 18).

Example 1 – Impairment of inventory

An entity supplies parts to a car manufacturer in respect of a particular model of car. At the balance sheet date the entity has a high level of inventory of parts due to low order levels. After the balance sheet date, the car manufacturer announces that the specific model will no longer be produced. There is no alternative market for the inventory. Does the subsequent event trigger a write-down of inventory to net realisable value?

Estimates of net realisable value are based on the most reliable evidence available at the time the estimates are made. These estimates consider fluctuations of price or cost directly relating to events occurring after the end of the period to the extent that such events confirm conditions existing at the end of the period. [IAS 2 para 30].

The inventory should be written down to net realisable value. The high inventory levels indicated slow demand from the manufacturer. The post balance sheet announcement confirmed the over-supply at year end.

Example 2 – Impairment of properties

Consider the situation where, prior to the approval of the financial statements but subsequent to the balance sheet date, a company in trading difficulties obtained a valuation of its properties for the purpose of providing additional security to its bankers. In view of its trading difficulties, the company is also considering selling certain properties to generate cash. The amount shown by the valuation is materially lower than the historical cost carrying amount attributed to the properties at the balance sheet date based on the last impairment review carried out three years ago. How should this be reflected in the financial statements?

We consider that the valuation provides evidence of an impairment in value that had occurred prior to the balance sheet date. An impairment review should be carried out in accordance with IAS 36 and a provision to write down the properties would be regarded as an 'adjusting event' with the values attributed to the properties in the balance sheet being adjusted accordingly.

[The next paragraph is A22.29.]

A22.29 An example of an adjustment reflected in interim accounts because of the insolvency of a debtor after the end of the interim period is given in Table A22.2 below. There are also instances where losses on current assets are incurred prior to the period end as a result of internal control failures, but are only discovered after the period end. These types of events are also adjusting events as the last bullet point in paragraph A22.20 indicates. Some examples are given in the following section.

Table A22.2 – Adjusting event, insolvency of debtor

Carclo plc – Interim report – 30 September 2005

Operating review (extract)

A significant customer in the USA, Delphi Corporation, filed for chapter 11 protection shortly after the period end and a provision of £0.1 million has been reflected in the half year accounts. This provision is lower than previously indicated in the statement made on 10 October due to the recent US court ruling which enabled Delphi to pay up to 75% of outstanding amounts, subject to certain conditions being met.

Fraud, error and other irregularities

A22.30 Fraud, error and other irregularities that occur in the entity's books and records prior to the balance sheet date but that are only identified after the balance sheet date are adjusting items. This type of adjusting event sometimes gives rise to uncertainties about the entity's ability to continue its operations (see further para A22.31 on going concern). Often the consequences of failures in internal controls extend back to earlier years, necessitating not only adjustments to the current year figures, but also a prior year adjustment (see chapter 5). An example which is consistent with IAS 10, is given in Table A22.3. In this example, the irregularities did not extend to earlier years.

Table A22.3 – Adjustment in respect of internal control failure

Azlan Group plc – Annual report and accounts – 5 April 1997

Chairman and chief executive's statement (extract)

Overview

The financial year to 5 April 1997 has been one of major disappointment.

On 28 April 1997, Azlan announced that the anticipated pre-tax profits for the financial year ended 5 April 1997 would be broadly in line with market expectations at around £14.8 million and that cash flow from operating activities in the second half had improved significantly and was positive for that period. This announcement was based on the unaudited management accounts for that financial year, which showed a pre-tax profit of £15.1 million.

As a result of initial audit work by Azlan's auditors, KPMG Audit Plc, and, inquiries by the new Group Finance Director, Peter Bertram, certain accounting issues were identified which required further investigation and which caused the Board to conclude that the results for the financial year ended 5 April 1997 would be materially lower than previously indicated. Accordingly, the Board requested the suspension of the listing of the Company's Ordinary Shares on 13 June 1997. To assist the audit work, Azlan's Audit Committee appointed a specialist Forensic team from KPMG to investigate certain specific matters. Your Board is now in a position to report on these matters and other issues which came to light during the course of the investigations carried out by the Company and KPMG.

Your Board regrets to inform you that, due principally to a serious failure of management and internal financial controls in the UK operations and at Group level during the financial year ended 5 April 1997, the management accounts which formed the basis of the 28 April 1997 announcement significantly overstated profits. The audited accounts for the financial year ended 5 April 1997, show a loss of £14.1 million before taxation. In addition, the audited accounts show a cash outflow from operating activities of £14.3 million during the financial year and a cash outflow, after financing, of £4.1 million. There has also been a significant cash outflow since 5 April 1997, when the Group had net cash of £7.7 million, the reasons for which are described in more detail below.

In view of the deterioration in your Company's financial position and in order to meet anticipated cash requirements, the Directors have had to seek revised bank facilities. The availability of the new bank facilities is conditional, *inter alia,* upon the receipt by the Company of the net proceeds of the Rights Issue. The Rights Issue has been fully underwritten by SBC Warburg Dillon Read, which is also broker to the Rights Issue.

The adjustments made as a result of the audit and forensic work are summarised below:

Financial year ended 5 April 1997	Turnover £million	Pre-tax profit/(loss) £million
Per unaudited management accounts	293.4	15.1
Adjustments		
Purchasing and inventory management		(16.6)
UK operations	(0.5)	(4.4)
Central costs		(3.6)
Overseas operations accounting adjustments		(1.7)
Consolidation adjustments		(1.1)
Additional costs and fees		(1.8)
Per audited financial statements	292.9	(14.1)

As the table above shows, the largest category of adjustments, totalling £16.6 million, relates to central purchasing and inventory management in the product business. These adjustments include balances which were incorrectly treated as recoverable from suppliers in respect of: returns of stock (£0.9 million); compensation for adverse product price movements (£2.7 million); and stock rotations, that is 'swapping' old stock for new (£3.4 million). Additional provisions of £3.3 million have been made for unreconciled balances on suppliers' statements, including £2.1 million in respect of one supplier alone. Further adjustments of £0.9 million were made to write off other unreconciled balances and £0.6 million to adjust for unrealised stock profits which had been incorrectly recognised in the profit and loss account. Finally, as a result of a thorough post year end review, the stock provision (previously £0.5 million) was increased by £4.8 million to cover slow-moving, excess and obsolete stock.

The table above also shows adverse adjustments of £4.4 million in respect of the management accounts of the UK operations. Of this amount, £2.0 million was to increase provisions in respect of debtors no longer considered to be recoverable, £0.6 million to defer profit from services and training courses which had not been delivered at the year end, and £1.8 million of sundry adjustments.

Central costs were increased by a total of £3.6 million, which includes accruals of £0.9 million for overhead for the extra five days in the financial year, £0.8 million for general under accrual of expenses and the balance of £1.9 million in relation to sundry smaller adjustments, principally in respect of irrecoverable stock and debtor balances. Profits from overseas operations were reduced by £1.1 million reflecting adjustments to inter-company transactions in relation to pace protection and rebates on stock supplied by the Group and a further £0.6 million in respect of other sundry adjustments. Adjustments totalling £1.1 million were necessary principally to remove items which had previously been incorrectly charged against goodwill created on acquisitions. Additional costs and professional fees of £1.6 million have been incurred in respect of the audit and investigations.

A22.30.1 The example above deals with fraud identified in the reporting entity's books and records, but not fraud external to the entity. Where entities invest in investment funds or other marketable securities that suffer a diminution in value due to fraud discovered by the underlying entity post year end, a question arises as to whether such a discovery is an adjusting or a non-adjusting event.

A22.30.2 In these circumstances, it is necessary to determine whether the underlying investment actually existed at the balance sheet date. To the extent that the underlying investment held at the balance sheet date existed and had a value on that date determined by reference to market activity, then the post year end loss as a result of the discovery of fraud by the underlying entity would be a non-adjusting event. The reason for this is that the reporting entity could have sold their underlying investment on the balance sheet date without suffering loss.

A22.30.3 However, if the underlying investment of the reporting entity never actually existed then the reporting entity would not have been able to avoid the loss at the balance sheet date and the post year end discovery of fraud would be an adjusting event. This is because it provides further evidence of conditions existent at the balance sheet date (that is, that the investment did not exist).

Going concern

A22.31 Under IAS 1, 'Presentation of financial statements', an entity's management is required to assess, at the time of preparing the financial statements, the entity's ability to continue as a going concern, and this assessment must cover the entity's prospects for at least 12 months from the balance sheet date. [IAS 1 paras 25, 26]. This is considered in more detail in chapter 4. IAS 10 makes it clear that an entity should not prepare its financial statements on the going concern basis if management determines *after the reporting period* either that it:

(a) intends to liquidate the entity or to cease trading; or

(b) that it has no realistic alternative to doing so (even if the liquidation or cessation will occur more than 12 months after the balance sheet date).

[IAS 10 para 14].

A22.32 When the economic condition of an entity deteriorates after the balance sheet date, management has to consider whether or not the going concern basis of accounting remains appropriate. [IAS 10 para 15]. Additionally, where a decision to close down an entity's operation is made after the balance sheet date, this may indicate that applying the going concern concept to the entity is not appropriate. If it is not appropriate, the financial statements should not be prepared on this basis but on a fundamentally different basis of accounting. This is dealt with further in chapter 4. IAS 1 requires disclosure of certain information where financial statements are not prepared on the going concern basis including:

- The fact that the financial statements are not prepared on a going concern basis.
- Details of the basis used in preparing the financial statements, for example, the realisable value basis.
- The reason why the entity is not regarded as a going concern.

[IAS 1 para 25; IAS 10 para 16(a)].

[The next paragraph is A22.34.]

A22.34 Examples of financial statements prepared on a non-going concern basis are uncommon, but they may occur where an entity's operating licence expires and is not renewed, for example in the television broadcasting or train operating sectors. Or they might arise where an entity's management has decided that shareholder value would be maximised by an orderly liquidation of assets.

A22.35 Whilst preparing financial statements on a non-going concern basis is uncommon, it is not uncommon for there to be significant uncertainty about whether the going concern basis of accounting is appropriate. Such uncertainty may arise because of post balance sheet events. Where material uncertainties cast doubt about an entity's ability to continue as a going concern, and its financial statements continue to be prepared on the going concern basis, full disclosure of the uncertainties is required. [IAS 1 para 25; IAS 10 para 16]. An example of disclosure, which is consistent with IAS 10's requirements, is given in Table A22.6. This also includes disclosure of the loss of a major customer.

Table A22.6 – Post year end going concern uncertainties

Cordiant Communications Group plc – Preliminary announcement – 31 December 2002

Preliminary statement (extract)

Introduction (extract)
Cordiant was notified on Friday 25 April 2003 by one of its major clients, Allied Domecq plc, of its intention to terminate its contract with Cordiant with effect from October 2003. In the current financial year Cordiant had budgeted for revenue from this global contract of approximately £18.0 million, some 3.4% of the Group's revenue in 2002. The direct impact of this client loss on revenue in 2003 is not expected to be material, although the Group will incur associated restructuring costs in the current year. However, there will be a substantial impact on operating profit from 2004 onwards.

Following Allied Domecq's decision, and particularly with the interests of the Group's clients in mind, the Board of Cordiant is actively investigating alternative strategic options for the Group, in addition to the disposal programme previously announced, which is progressing well.

The financial statements have been presented on a going concern basis. However until the outcome of the Group's evaluation of strategic options, and the implications of this for the Group's future funding structure are known, there is considerable uncertainty about the appropriateness of this basis of presentation. Attention is drawn to Note 1 of this statement which explains the basis of preparation of the financial information and the form of the auditor's report.

Notes (extract)

1. Accounting policies and presentation (extract)

Basis of preparation (extract)
In February 2003 the Group commenced negotiations with its principal lenders designed to reset the terms of its principal lending facilities consistent with current trading conditions and the planned disposal programme. Prior to the expected agreement of new financing terms on 29 April 2003 with its lenders, one of its major clients, Allied Domecq plc, notified Cordiant of its intention to terminate its contract with the Group with effect from October 2003. Whilst the direct impact of this client loss on revenue in 2003 is not expected to be material, the Group will

incur associated restructuring costs in the current year and there will be a substantial impact on operating profit from 2004 onwards.

Following Allied Domecq's decision, Cordiant is now working with its lenders to amend the financing terms and in addition, the Board is also actively investigating its strategic options for the Group which include, amongst other actions, the realisation of value through disposals, and alternative financing arrangements to reflect its revised circumstances.

Discussions with the lenders have progressed well and Cordiant has reached an agreement in principle, subject to contract, for continuing financing arrangements to 15 July 2003 whilst the Board concludes its review of strategic options and agrees new financing terms consistent with the outcome of that process. These financing arrangements incorporate a waiver of existing financial covenants and continued access to existing committed undrawn facilities. Cordiant expects to make a further announcement once documentation has been signed.

The financial information set out in this preliminary announcement has been presented on a going concern basis. However, until the outcome of the Group's evaluation of its strategic options and negotiations with its lenders, and the implications of this for the Group's future funding structure are known, there is considerable uncertainty about the appropriateness of this basis of presentation.

The financial information does not reflect any adjustments which would be required if the going concern assumption was not appropriate. Given the uncertainty described above it is not currently possible to determine the extent and quantification of such adjustments but these might include the reclassification of creditors due in more than one year to less than one year, the write down of the carrying value of goodwill in the balance sheet to the best estimate of its net realisable value on disposal, the write down of certain assets carried on a value in use basis to net realisable value, and the disclosure of or provision for additional liabilities.

Updating disclosures

A22.36 As described above, where information is received after the balance sheet date about conditions that existed at that date, adjustments may be required to the figures at the balance sheet date. However, even where no adjustments are required, disclosures that relate to conditions existing at the balance sheet date may need to be updated to reflect new information received after the balance sheet date. [IAS 10 para 19]. An example given in the standard is where information obtained subsequent to the balance sheet date gives evidence of a contingent liability that existed at the balance sheet date. [IAS 10 para 20]. An example of disclosure consistent with IAS 10, is given in Table A22.7. This includes additional post balance sheet information about a legal action in progress at the balance sheet date. Although no adjustments are required, the information is disclosed to inform shareholders of the progress of the case.

Table A22.7 – Post year end developments relating to legal action

Cable and Wireless plc – Annual report and accounts – 31 March 2003

34 Legal Proceedings (extract)

Class action litigation against Cable and Wireless plc
Between December 2002 and February 2003, ten shareholder class action lawsuits were filed in the United States District Court for the Eastern District of Virginia naming Cable and Wireless plc and several of its officers and directors as defendants.

In March 2003, the court consolidated all of the cases into one action, styled as In re Cable and Wireless plc Securities Litigation, Civil Action No. 02-1860-A. The Court has appointed Ontario Teachers' Pension Plan Board, an institutional investor located in Canada, and Alex Osinski, a U.S. citizen, as co-lead plaintiffs (collectively 'lead plaintiffs') to prosecute on behalf of all plaintiffs.

In May 2003, the lead plaintiffs filed a consolidated complaint that alleges violations of certain sections of the Securities and Exchange Act of 1934 and the rules promulgated thereunder. A central allegation is that the defendants made false and misleading statements about the Company's financial condition by failing to disclose on a timely basis the existence of a tax indemnity and a ratings trigger to place money in escrow until any liability which the Company may have had under the tax indemnity was finally determined. The indemnity and ratings trigger appear in an agreement between the Company and Deutsche Telekom for the sale of the Company's interest in the mobile telephone company that operated under the name One2One.

In addition to the allegations relating to the tax indemnity, the consolidated complaint also alleges that the defendants made false and misleading statements by: (1) failing to disclose certain lease liability commitments and (2) improperly recognising revenue received from sales of capacity to other carriers.

The plaintiffs seek unspecified money damages in their complaints.

Cable & Wireless believes that it has meritorious defences to these claims and intends to vigorously defend itself in this litigation.

Non-adjusting events

A22.37 Adjustments to amounts recognised in the financial statements are not made for material non-adjusting post balance sheet events, but they do require disclosure in the notes to the financial statements. [IAS 10 paras 10, 21]. A non-adjusting event is an event that arises after the balance sheet date concerning conditions that did not exist at that time and is material in that its non-disclosure could influence the users' economic decisions taken on the basis of the financial statements. [IAS 10 para 3].

A22.38 In such circumstances, the information to be disclosed in the financial statements is the nature of the event and an estimate of its financial effect. Where it is not possible to make an estimate of an event's financial effect, that fact must be disclosed. [IAS 10 para 21].

A22.38.1 No guidance exists in the standard as to what is meant by the term 'financial effect' as to whether it refers to the effect on profit or loss, other comprehensive income, equity, cash flows or the balance sheet. The purpose of disclosing non-adjusting events, however, is to inform the user of the financial statements of material events that have happened since the year end. The disclosure should, therefore, give sufficient numerical information to enable the reader to understand the event and its impact on the reporting entity. The exact figures given will depend on the precise facts and circumstances of each non-adjusting event and the information required to understand it and its impact.

A22.39 Examples of non-adjusting post balance sheet events are given in the standard as follows:

- A major business combination or disposal of a major subsidiary after the balance sheet date.
- The announcement of a plan to discontinue an operation.
- Major purchases of assets, classification of assets as held for sale in accordance with IFRS 5, 'Non-current assets held for sale and discontinued operations', other disposals of assets, or expropriation of major assets by government.
- The destruction of a major production plant by fire after the balance sheet date.
- Announcing or commencing a major restructuring.
- Major ordinary and potential ordinary share transactions after the balance sheet date. IAS 33, 'Earnings per share', requires an entity to give a brief description of such transactions, except when they involve capitalisation or bonus issues, share splits or share consolidations (which are all treated as adjusting events under IAS 33). IAS 33 is dealt with in chapter 14.
- Abnormally large changes after the balance sheet date in asset prices or foreign exchange rates.
- Changes in tax rates or tax laws enacted or announced after the balance sheet date that have a significant effect on current and deferred tax assets and liabilities.
- Entering into significant commitments or contingent liabilities for example by issuing significant guarantees. Commitments are dealt with from paragraph A22.65 below.
- Commencing major litigation arising solely out of events that occurred after the balance sheet date.

[IAS 10 para 22].

A22.40 Breaching a contract or bank covenant in the period after the balance sheet date is generally also a non-adjusting event that warrants disclosure consideration. However, breaches that become apparent after the year end often raise issues as to whether an entity's borrowings should be presented as current or non-current in the balance sheet being published (that is, whether the event is adjusting or non-adjusting). They may also give rise to going concern uncertainties. Breaches of covenants and waivers of such breaches are covered in detail in chapter 4 and this issue is, therefore, not considered here.

A22.41 In addition, as discussed above from paragraph A22.31, IAS 10 notes that IAS 1, 'Presentation of financial statements', requires disclosure of uncertainties about whether the going concern basis of accounting is appropriate, noting that such uncertainties may emerge after the balance sheet date.

A22.41.1 Another example of a post balance sheet event which is commonly non-adjusting is a post year end breach of law or regulation. It would be rare for a post year end breach to provide further evidence of a condition existent at the balance sheet date, but nevertheless such breaches are often relevant to a user's understanding of the position of the reporting entity going forward. Therefore, disclosure as a non-adjusting event should be made to the extent that the breach has had, or will have, a material impact on the entity.

A22.42 The appropriate accounting treatment for a post balance sheet event can normally be determined by reference to IAS 10's underlying principle – that is, that events arising after the balance sheet date need to be reflected in financial statements if they provide additional evidence of conditions that existed at the balance sheet date. This principle is illustrated in the following examples.

Acquisitions and disposals

A22.43 Acquisitions and disposals that are made subsequent to the balance sheet date are examples of non-adjusting post balance sheet events that require disclosure in financial statements. In addition, IFRS 3, 'Business combinations', requires specific disclosures in the case of acquisitions after the balance sheet date. [IFRS 3 para 60]. IFRS 5, 'Non-current assets held for sale and discontinued operations', requires specific disclosures in respect of assets classified as held for sale after the balance sheet date. [IFRS 5 para 12]. These requirements are considered below.

A22.43.1 IFRS 3 is dealt with in detail in chapter 25. The standard sets out specific disclosure requirements in respect of business combinations. It requires an acquirer to disclose information that enables users of its financial statements to evaluate the nature and financial effect of a business combination that occurs either:

(a) during the current reporting period; or

(b) after the end of the reporting period, but before the financial statements are authorised for issue.

[IFRS 3 para 59].

A22.43.2 Entities are often unable to complete the accounting for business combinations prior to issuing their financial statements where such business combinations occur after the balance sheet date but before the financial statements are finalised. In the event that the accounting is incomplete in such circumstances, the disclosures not given should be described along with the reasons for not providing them. [IFRS 3 para B66]. Otherwise, the information required to be disclosed is prescribed by paragraph B64 of IFRS 3 and includes the following:

- General information (the name and description of the acquiree; the acquisition date; the percentage of voting equity instruments acquired; the primary reasons for the combination; and the method by which control was obtained).
- A qualitative description of the factors that make up goodwill; the amount of goodwill that is expected to be deductible for tax purposes; and in the case of 'negative goodwill' the reason why the transaction resulted in a gain.
- Acquisition date fair value of each major class of consideration and an aggregate total.
- Details of contingent consideration.
- Identifiable assets, liabilities and contingent liabilities.
- Details of transactions with the acquiree that do not form part of the business combination.
- Fair value of the acquiror's interest in the acquiree prior to the combination and information about minority interests remaining after the combination.
- Post-acquisition activities.

A22.43.3 IFRS 5 has specific disclosure requirements for non-current assets or disposal groups classified as held for sale and is dealt with in detail in chapter 8. An example of disclosure in respect of a post balance sheet sale of a disposal group that is classified as held for sale (as a discontinued operation) is given in Table A22.8.1 below.

Table A22.8.1 – Post balance sheet disposal of asset group classified as held for sale

Cadbury Schweppes plc – Annual report and accounts – 01 January 2006

39. Events after the Balance Sheet date

On 1 September 2005, the Group announced its intention to sell Europe Beverages. On 21 November 2005, the Group received a binding offer to buy the business from a consortium acting on behalf of the funds managed by Blackstone Group International and Lion Capital LLP. The transaction was conditional upon receiving European Union regulatory approval.

The sale completed on 2 February 2006 for gross proceeds of €1.85 billion (£1.26 billion). Net proceeds after tax and expenses are expected to be £1.15 billion and we anticipate reporting a profit on disposal in 2006 of around £480 million. The proceeds from the disposal will be used to reduce the Group's borrowings and to increase the funding of our defined benefit pension schemes. In accordance with IFRS 5, Europe Beverages has been classified as a discontinued operation in these financial statements. The results of Europe Beverages are included as discontinued operations in the consolidated income statement and the assets and liabilities are classified as held for sale in the consolidated balance sheet as described in Note 32.

On 1 March 2006, the Group announced its intention to repurchase a proportion of the outstanding £400 million 4.875% Sterling Notes due 2010. It is expected that on 14 March 2006 a repurchase of £323 million will take place.

A22.43.4 Entities cannot classify a non-current asset or disposal group as held for sale if it only meets the criteria to be classified as held for sale *after* the balance sheet date. However, if the criteria are met between the balance sheet date and the date that the financial statements are authorised, the entity should give the disclosures described below:

- A description of the asset or disposal group.
- A description of the facts and circumstances of the sale or those leading to an expected disposal and the expected method and timing of the disposal.
- Where applicable, the segment that the non-current asset or disposal group is part of. This applies in all cases where an entity is required to present segmental information.

[IFRS 5 para 12].

Major restructuring

A22.44 As noted in paragraph A22.26, a post balance sheet restructuring may provide evidence of impairment at the balance sheet date, which is an adjusting event. However, in accordance with IAS 37, a provision is not made for future restructuring costs, until a legal or constructive obligation to restructure arises. Where an entity commences a restructuring after the balance sheet date but prior to the approval of the financial statements, and the significance of this event could influence the economic decisions of users of the financial statements, disclosure of the restructuring is required.

A22.45 Table A22.9 shows an example of disclosure of a restructuring announced after the year end. In this example disclosure is also made of uncertainties that cast doubt on the ability to continue as a going concern as mentioned in paragraph A22.35 above. In addition, the post year end announcement of restructuring has been taken into account in determining impairment, as mentioned in paragraph A22.26.

Table A22.9 – Post balance sheet restructuring and going concern uncertainty

Swiss International Airlines Ltd. – Report and accounts – 31 December 2004

39. Business risks and going concern

The restructuring programme announced in 2003 was implemented in full in 2004. The Group workforce comprised 6 625 full-time equivalents on December 31, 2004 (compared to 8 072 full-time equivalents on December 31, 2003).

In view of the still-difficult market environment, the high cost of aviation fuel and continuing declines in yields, the Board of Directors approved a further package of measures on January 17, 2005 under which the regional aircraft fleet will be reduced by at least 13 aircraft. This action, in association with the corresponding reduction in flying personnel numbers, the renegotiation of all collective labour agreements and supplier contracts and further efficiency enhancements in the administrative field, is intended to reduce net annual costs by a recurring CHF 300 million. These actions will be taken over the next 18 months. The Business Plan envisages a break-even result or better for 2006. Consequently these consolidated financial statements were prepared on a going concern basis.

In the event of unexpected negative developments caused by the impact of unplannable exceptional events which cannot be offset by appropriate corrective action, further restructuring measures may be required. In such an event, the Group's liquidity position and – in a worst case – its going concern ability might be seriously affected within the next 18 to 24 months.

40. Subsequent events

The Group announced restructuring measures on January 18, 2005 which are designed to provide a profitable and competitive basis for its future growth. Under these measures, the fleet will be downsized by at least 13 regional aircraft operating largely from Basel. A large part of the Group's current operations from Basel should be transferred to the operation of partner airlines in the course of 2006, with the Group retaining a presence on these routes as a codeshare partner. The restructuring envisages the elimination of 800 to 1 000 positions over the next 18 months. The Group expects to achieve further cost savings through renegotiations with its unions and suppliers.

These actions are intended to gradually achieve a recurring CHF 300 million improvement in net annual costs, the full effect of which should be effective from 2007 onwards. No restructuring provisions were made for this programme in 2004, but impairment as far as recognisable. The costs of the restructuring will depend on the outcome of the ongoing negotiations with the unions and suppliers, and cannot yet be estimated with any degree of accuracy.

19. Aircraft fleet (extract)

An impairment loss of CHF 154 million had to be recognised in respect of the aircraft fleet. The impairment, which is for part of the fleet, was based on negative results from point-to-point traffic not contributing to the long-haul network. The impairment was made on the estimated net realisable value of the aircraft fleet, based on market studies and comparable transactions. The supplementary depreciation for a further part of the aircraft fleet is based on the values established as a result of the planned use of manufacturers' repurchase guarantees in 2005 and 2006. All aircraft are traded in USD. Part of the impairment loss was based on the weakening of the USD over the past few years.

The results for 2004 include any impairments required in relation to the corporate restructuring communicated in January 2005 as far as they could be estimated. With associated negotiations still under way, the precise extent of such impairments is currently impossible to determine.

Changes in foreign exchange rates or asset prices

A22.46 Changes in currency exchange rates or in asset prices occurring after the balance sheet date do not normally reflect the conditions at the balance sheet date, as the recoverable value at the balance sheet date was defined by the market, that is, by knowledgeable and willing participants. The following two examples illustrate how changes in exchange rates or asset prices after the year end would be treated. Table A22.9.A shows the disclosure of a devaluation that takes place after the year end.

Example 1 – Movement in foreign exchange rates

Consider the situation where an adverse movement on the foreign exchange rate after year end has had the effect that the exchange differences arising on the retranslation of the bank overdraft since the balance sheet date exceed the profit for the period under review. How should this be reflected in the financial statements?

Exchange rate changes are included in the list of non-adjusting post balance sheet events set out in paragraph 22 of IAS 10. Although the bank overdraft existed at the balance sheet date, the conditions that gave rise to the loss did not. The exchange rate fluctuation occurred subsequent to the balance sheet date. Accordingly, in normal circumstances, the effect of the exchange rate fluctuations should not be adjusted for in the financial statements. However, the effect of the exchange rate fluctuations should be referred to in the financial statements as a post balance sheet event if the fluctuations are of such a materiality that knowledge thereof could influence the economic decisions of users taken on the basis of the financial statements. Where this is the case they should be quantified (as at the latest date before the financial statements are authorised for issue by the directors) and disclosed by way of note to the financial statements.

Example 2 – Decline in asset market values

A further example that often arises in practice is where the company has a holding of shares in a listed company and these are included in the balance sheet at market value at the balance sheet date. Subsequently, the listed company disclosed financial problems and, as a result, the holding is now worth less than at the balance sheet date. Such an event is regarded as non-adjusting because the loss has arisen subsequent to the balance sheet date and it would have been possible for the holding to be sold for its market value at the balance sheet date.

A major stock market movement after the balance sheet date would be a similar example of a decline in value that is considered to have occurred subsequent to the balance sheet date. Such a 'crash' would, therefore, generally be regarded as being a 'non-adjusting' event.

Table A22.9.A – Post balance sheet currency devaluation

Telefonica S.A. – Annual report – 31 December 2009

(24) EVENTS AFTER THE REPORTING PERIOD (extract)

Devaluation of the Venezuelan Bolivar fuerte

Regarding the devaluation of the Venezuelan Bolivar fuerte on January 8, 2010 (see Note 2), the two main factors to consider with respect to the Telefónica Group's 2010 financial statements will be:

- The decrease in the Telefónica Group's net assets in Venezuela as a result of the new exchange rate, with a balancing entry in equity of the Group. This effect is estimated at approximately 1,810 million euros.
- The translation of results and cash flows from Venezuela at the new devalued closing exchange rate.

Finally, on January 19, the Venezuelan Authorities announced that they would grant a preferential rate of 2.60 Bolivar fuerte per dollar for new items, among which payment of dividends is included, as long as the request for Authorization of Acquisition of Foreign Exchange was filed before January 8, 2010. To that date, the Company had in fact requested authorizations related to the distribution of dividends of prior years (see Note 16).

Changes in tax rates

A22.47 Proposed or expected changes in tax laws and rates are not reflected in the financial statements, unless they have been enacted or substantively enacted by the balance sheet date. [IAS 12 para 47]. However, IAS 10 requires disclosure of changes in the tax laws and rates enacted or announced after the balance sheet date that have a significant effect on current or deferred tax. This is illustrated in the following example.

Example – Announcement of change in tax rates

An entity has deferred tax assets recognised in the balance sheet at 31 December 20X1 in respect of unused tax losses that can be used to reduce taxable income in future years. The income tax rate used to calculate the deferred tax asset was 40%, which was the current rate of tax applicable at the balance sheet date. On 1 January 20X2 a new government came to power and passed legislation such that on 17 January 20X2 the income tax rate was reduced to 33% with immediate effect.

The change in the income tax rate was announced (and enacted) after the balance sheet date, therefore, it is a non-adjusting event. The change in the tax rate is an event that occurred after the year-end. Management should not adjust the amounts recognised in its financial statements because of this event.

If the effect of the new tax rate on the deferred tax asset will be material, management should disclose details of the change in the income tax rate and its related effects on the entity, in the notes to the financial statements. Where applicable, the disclosure should consider the impact on the different performance statements (see para A22.47.1 below).

A22.47.1 It will be necessary to consider whether the accounting impact of a change in tax rates will be reflected in profit or loss, other comprehensive income or in the statement of changes in equity. IAS 12 requires that deferred tax should be recognised in profit or loss for the period, except to the extent that it is attributable to a gain or loss that is or has been recognised outside of profit or loss. This applies to changes in deferred tax resulting from a change in tax rates. [IAS 12 para 60]. Therefore, where the impact is likely to be material for the purpose of the post balance sheet disclosure, companies will need to consider how the transactions that gave rise to deferred tax were accounted for and trace the impact of the change in tax rate to the same place. Backwards tracing of adjustments to deferred tax is considered further in chapter 13.

A22.47.2 Table A22.10 is an example where announced changes in tax rates have been disclosed and the effect has been quantified.

Table A22.10 — Proposed changes in tax rates

Verbund – Annual report and accounts – 31 December 2003

Income Tax (9) (extract)

The Austrian federal government has announced that the corporate tax rate will be reduced from 34 % to 25 % with effect from 2005. In accordance with the IFRS provisions, the rate of 34 % is still used as a basis for the calculation of the deferred taxes stated. Under utilization of the new corporate tax rate, deferred tax liabilities as of 31 December 2003 would drop by €18.3 million. The actual relief in fiscal year 2004 will depend on the final decision relating to the tax rate, the determination of taxable income and the tax result in 2004.

[The next paragraph is A22.52]

Dividends payable and receivable

A22.52 Dividends to holders of equity instruments are recognised when declared (that is, when the dividends are appropriately authorised and no longer at the entity's discretion). Dividends may be payable only with the approval of the entity's directors or may require other levels of approval, for instance by the holders of the equity instruments. Therefore, dividends on equity instruments can be considered under four categories:

- Dividends declared and paid in an accounting period (see para A22.52.2).
- Interim dividends announced by the directors, but unpaid at a balance sheet date (see para A22.52.3).
- Final dividends proposed by the directors, but not declared (see para A22.52.4).
- Final dividends declared (see para A22.53).

[The next paragraph is A22.52.2.]

A22.52.2 Dividends on equity instruments that are declared and paid in an accounting period are recognised in that accounting period and disclosed in accordance with IAS 1, 'Presentation of financial statements', as discussed in chapter 4. Dividends declared after the balance sheet date are not recognised as a liability at the balance sheet date. [IAS 10 para 12].

A22.52.3 Interim dividends announced by the directors but unpaid at a balance sheet date are a liability at that balance sheet date where, and only where, the directors do not retain an ability to cancel them. This is because the test for recognition in paragraph AG13 of IAS 32 is that a legal obligation exists to the shareholders to pay the dividend. In many jurisdictions, the directors retain the discretion to cancel interim dividends until such time as they are paid. Hence, they are not 'declared' (appropriately authorised and no longer at the discretion of the entity) and are, therefore, not recognised until paid. Where interim dividends are a liability prior to payment, and shareholders but not the directors, have a right to waive the interim dividend, they remain a liability of the company until waived by the shareholders or are otherwise paid.

A22.52.4 In many jurisdictions final dividends for a year are proposed by directors but are then subject to approval by shareholders in general meeting, at which point they become formally declared. In such a situation, final dividends proposed by directors are not a liability of the company until such time as they are declared by the company in general meeting. In practice, final dividends are usually proposed by the directors after the balance sheet date for declaration by the company at the annual general meeting at a date even further removed from the balance sheet date. Were directors to propose the final dividend prior to the balance sheet date, its declaration would not happen until the subsequent general meeting. Lastly, even where an entity has a history of paying dividends, this does not give rise to a liability at the balance sheet date because paragraph AG13 of IAS 32, 'Financial instruments: Presentation', is clear that there must be a legally binding obligation before a dividend is recognised. Therefore, no liability should ever be recognised at the balance sheet date for proposed final dividends that are subject to shareholders' approval. Disclosure is required in the notes to the financial statements by paragraph 137 of IAS 1. Table A22.12 is an example where a statutory minimum dividend is required to be declared by law and this element is treated as a liability with the remaining portion of the dividend accounted for when approved by shareholders.

Table A22.12 – Disclosure of proposed dividends

Coca-Cola Hellenic Bottling Company S.A. – Annual report and accounts – 31 December 2010

1. Basis of preparation and accounting policies (extract)

Dividends

Dividends are recorded in the Group's consolidated financial statements in the period in which they are approved by the Group's shareholders, with the exception of the statutory minimum dividend.

Under Greek corporate legislation, companies are required to declare dividends annually of at least 35% of unconsolidated adjusted after-tax IFRS profits. This statutory minimum dividend is recognised as a liability.

29. Dividends

The reported net results of the parent company's statutory accounts do not require a 2010 statutory minimum annual dividend payment. As a result the Group has not recorded a dividend liability in respect of 2010.

The statutory minimum dividend recognised for 2009 amounted to €41.6m and was recorded as liability under 'Other payables' in the consolidated balance sheet. The remaining dividend of €68.1m was recorded in shareholders' equity in the second quarter of 2010 as an appropriation of retained earnings.

During 2010, a dividend of €0.30 per share totalling €102.0m was paid. During 2009, a dividend of €0.28 per share totalling €102.3m was paid. During 2008, a dividend of €0.25 per share totalling €91.3m was paid.

[The next paragraph is A22.53.]

A22.53 Final dividends should be recognised as a liability in the period in which they are declared (that is, appropriately authorised and no longer at the discretion of the entity); in many jurisdictions, this binding declaration occurs through the passing of a resolution by the company. They remain as liabilities until such time as they are paid.

A22.54 In the same way that dividends declared after the year end are not recognised by the paying company at the balance sheet date as they do not meet the definition of a liability, the recipient of such dividends cannot recognise them as an asset and, consequently, as income at the balance sheet date. Treatment of dividends in a recipient's financial statements will mirror that in the paying company — that is, dividends receivable will be recognised when the shareholder's right to receive payment is established. [IAS 18 para 30]. This may have significant consequences for those companies that depend on dividends from subsidiaries to cover their dividends to shareholders. In jurisdictions where distributable profits are required to cover dividend payments, it will be vital to get the subsidiaries' dividends declared and properly approved prior to the year end so that the parent has the recognised income. Whether or not the recognised income can then be distributed by the parent will depend on the legal rules governing distributions by the parent.

UK.A22.54.1 The law relating to distributions and dividends made by companies governed by the Companies Act 2006 applies to all such companies irrespective of the accounting framework used in preparing their relevant accounts for the purposes of section 836 of the Companies Act 2006. Thus it applies to companies using IFRS in their individual financial statements.

UK.A22.54.1.1 The legal position under the Companies Act 2006 is set out in ICAEW Tech Release 02/10, 'Guidance on the determination of realised profits and losses in the context of distributions under the Companies Act 2006'. This guidance has been approved by English and Scots Counsel. In particular, paragraph 2.10 of Tech 02/10 states that:

> *"A distribution is made when it becomes a legally binding liability of the company, regardless of the date on which it is to be settled. In the case of a final dividend, this will be when it is declared by the company in general meeting or, for private companies, by the members passing a written resolution. In the case of an interim dividend authorised under common articles of association (e.g. 1985 Act Table A), normally no legally binding liability is established prior to payment being made of the dividend ..."*

UK.A22.54.2 In the UK, the standard articles of association (Table A) stipulate that, subject to the provisions of the Companies Act 2006, directors may declare and pay interim dividends without authorisation from shareholders at a general meeting. As stated in paragraph 2.10 of Tech 02/10, an interim dividend declared by directors only becomes a liability at the moment it is paid. This is because their resolution is not irrevocable. The directors have discretion over whether the interim dividend is paid; that is, the directors are able to reverse their resolution to pay an interim dividend at any time up to the date of payment. In *Potel v IRC 46 TC 658* it was determined that the directors, by resolution of the board, are authorised to pay 'interim dividends' (Table A, article 103), but that such a resolution of the board can be revoked prior to actual payment, as no debt is created. Under the law, shareholders cannot force the directors to pay a dividend they declare, but subsequently revoke. Hence, an interim dividend declared but unpaid at a balance sheet date should not be recognised, as there is no obligation at the end of the reporting period; neither does a past history of paying interim dividends give rise to an obligation. Dividends that are declared but unpaid at the balance sheet date should be disclosed in the notes to the financial statements in accordance with paragraph 137(a) of IAS 1.

UK.A22.54.3 Under their common law duties, directors in the UK have to be able to revoke their resolution as they must test for sufficient distributable profits at both the date of declaration and at the date of payment. They may be sufficient at the first date, but if by the latter those profits have been eroded by subsequent losses, the dividend must not be paid. [Tech 02/10 paras 2.1 to 2.3]. For example, in the UK, if an interim dividend is declared by the directors on

4 May and is payable on 4 July, but profits available for distribution are insufficient at the date of payment (4 July), the dividend will not be paid and will not be recognised as a liability at either date. Where, however, the dividend is a final dividend, declared by the company in general meeting on 4 May and payable on 4 July, but profits available for distribution are insufficient at the date of payment, the dividend will not be paid, but will remain as a liability of the company until there are sufficient profits available for distribution to allow it to be paid, or until it is waived by the shareholders.

UK.A22.54.4 There is specific guidance in Tech 02/10 for intra-group dividends. This refers to the implications of IAS 10 for dividends. Paragraph 9.7 of Tech 02/10 states:

> *"A dividend payable is accrued in accordance with IFRIC 17, IAS 10 or FRS 21 only when it is 'appropriately authorised and no longer at the discretion of the entity'. This test will be met when a legally binding liability is established as described at 2.10 above. A dividend will be accrued as receivable by a parent company only when the subsidiary has a legally binding obligation to make the distribution."*

UK.A22.54.5 It is clear from Tech 02/10, therefore, that interim dividends declared by UK companies are not to be recognised as liabilities. This is discussed further in chapter 23.

UK.A22.54.6 The position for UK parent companies that rely on dividends from UK subsidiaries to support their own distributions is also considered in chapter 23.

Date of authorisation of the financial statements for issue

A22.55 IAS 10 requires an entity to disclose the date on which the financial statements are authorised for issue and who gives that authorisation. [IAS 10 para 17]. If, for example, the board authorises the financial statements for issue, IAS 10 requires the financial statements to disclose that the board (or similar body for unincorporated entities) gave the authorisation. Also, the standard requires that if the entity's owners or other parties have the power to amend the financial statements after issue, that fact should be disclosed. [IAS 10 para 17].

UK.A22.55.1 In practice, in the UK, the financial statements are approved by the board of directors and, therefore, authorised for issue; hence, it will normally be the board that is identified as the body that gave authorisation for their issue. In the UK the entity's owners or other parties do not have the power to amend the financial statements so that requirement of paragraph 17 is unlikely to apply.

A22.56 The reason for requiring that the date of authorisation should be disclosed so users understand that the financial statements do not reflect events after this date. [IAS 10 para 18]. Table A22.12A shows an example of a company whose financial statements are authorised for issue by the board, but where the shareholders may require the financial statements to be amended at a later date. The standard devotes several paragraphs to situations that may arise in various jurisdictions. It notes that the process of authorisation of financial statements will vary according to the management structure and legal environment in which an entity operates. [IAS 10 para 4]. In some situations, an entity has to submit its financial statements to shareholders for approval after they have been authorised for issue by, for example, the board. In such situations, the date of authorisation for the issue of the financial statements is the date of the board's authorisation for issue not the date on which the shareholders approve them – see Table A22.12A. [IAS 10 para 5]. It is the former date that is disclosed under IAS 10.

UK.A22.56.1 In the UK, shareholders do not formally approve the financial statements, but instead the financial statements are 'laid' before the members. (Under the Companies Act 2006, only the financial statements of public companies are required to be laid before the members.) Table A22.12A shows an example of a company whose financial statements are authorised for issue by the board, but where the shareholders may require the financial statements to be amended at a later date.

Table A22.12A – Disclosure of date of authorisation of financial statements

Swiss Prime Site AG – Report and accounts – 31 December 2010

37 Events after the balance sheet date (extract)

The annual consolidated financial statements were approved for publication by the Board of Directors on 07.03.2011 and are subject to the approval of the Annual General Meeting of Swiss Prime Site AG of 19.04.2011.

A22.57 Table A22.12B below is an example from the UK where the financial statements are authorised for issue by the board. In the UK, once the board has authorised the financial statements for issue, they are usually not amended.

Table A22.12B – Disclosure of date of authorisation of financial statements

BP p.l.c. – Report and accounts – 31 December 2009

Authorization of financial statements and statement of compliance with International Financial Reporting Standards (extract)

The consolidated financial statements of the BP group for the year ended 31 December 2009 were approved and signed by the chairman and group chief executive on 26 February 2010 having been duly authorized to do so by the board of directors.

A22.57.1 Table A22.12C below shows a more complex scenario where the financial statements are authorised for issue by an executive board, but the financial statements are subject to potential amendment by a supervisory board at a later date. Effectively this means the financial statements require approval from two corporate bodies. In such cases, the financial statements are authorised for issue when management authorises them for issue to the supervisory board. [IAS 10 para 6]. However, in this example, no issues arise, as the authorisation by management is the same date as authorisation by the supervisory board, and the supervisory board did not suggest any changes to the financial statements.

Table A22.12C – Disclosure of date of authorisation of financial statements

Deutsche Börse AG – Report and accounts – 31 December 2010

52. Date of approval for publication

Deutsche Börse AG's Executive Board approved the consolidated financial statements for submission to the Supervisory Board on 3 March 2011. The Supervisory Board is responsible for examining the consolidated financial statements and stating whether it endorses them.

Report of the Supervisory Board (extract – report is dated 17 March 2011)

Based on its own examination of the annual financial statements, the consolidated financial statements, the management report and the Group management report, the Supervisory Board concurred with the results of the audit performed by the auditors. The final results of the auditors' examination did not lead to any objections. The Supervisory Board approved the annual financial statements prepared by the Executive Board and the consolidated financial statements at its meeting on 17 March 2011 in line with the Audit and Finance Committee's recommendation. The annual financial statements of Deutsche Börse AG are thereby adopted.

A22.58 Table A22.12D below is an unusual situation where notes to the financial statements have been changed after they were authorised for issue by the management board. Following review by the supervisory board, various changes were made before the revised financial statements were finally authorised for issue. Disclosure is given of the date of authorisation for issue of the financial statements and of the date of the subsequent changes. As amendments have been suggested by the supervisory board, the date of authorisation for issue of the financial statements is the date when management re-authorises them for issue.

Table A22.12D – Disclosure of date of authorisation of financial statements

Vivendi Universal SA – Report and accounts – 31 December 2005

Notes to the consolidated financial statements (extract)

On February 21, 2006, the Management Board approved the consolidated financial statements for the year ended December 31, 2005. On February 28, 2006, they were reviewed by the Supervisory Board, after their presentation to the Audit Committee on February 22, 2006.

On February 28, 2006 and March 21, 2006, the Management Board met again to modify the notes to the consolidated financial statements relating to the consolidation method used for Elektrim Telekomunikacja (Telco) and PTC (see Note 2.3), the total distribution of dividend for the year 2005 (see Note18.3) and Directors and Officers' compensation (see Note 28.1).

On April 20, 2006, the consolidated financial statements for the year ended December 31, 2005 will be submitted for adoption to Vivendi Universal shareholders at the Annual General Shareholders' meeting.

A22.58.1 Some local regulators require previously issued financial statements to be reissued for inclusion in public offering and similar documents. These regulators may require the financial statements to be updated for events that occur between the date of original authorisation and the issue date of the offering document, such as for discontinued operations or changes in segments. IAS 10 requires that a set of financial statements can have only one date of authorisation. In our view, therefore, the requirement to reissue financial statements for inclusion in a public offering document should be approached as follows:

- The date of authorisation can be moved to a later date. The financial statements are then updated to this later date to reflect any adjusting events to this later date, while non-adjusting events are disclosed in the notes, in accordance with IAS 10.
- If there are no significant adjusting or non-adjusting events, the original date of authorisation can be retained as no adjustment or additional disclosure will be necessary.

UK.A22.58.1.1 In the UK, where there is a unitary board system of executive and non-executive directors, non-executive directors play a major part in reviewing and monitoring financial information, for example, through audit committees. They also have equal responsibility with executive directors for the financial statements. As a result, financial statements are not authorised for issue before being seen by non-executive directors. Therefore, the circumstances where financial statements might be amended after being authorised for issue do not usually arise in the UK.

Preliminary announcements

UK.A22.59 IAS 10 notes that events after the balance sheet date include all events up to the date on which the financial statements are authorised for issue. This applies even if the events occur after the public announcement of profit or other selected financial information. [IAS 10 para 7]. This rather simple fact can sometimes be very significant. Following the implementation by the FSA of the EU Transparency Directive (see chapter 31), the publication of preliminary announcements by UK listed companies is voluntary, although any company choosing to publish one, for example, to ensure the timely release of price-sensitive information, must still follow FSA guidance on its preparation and publication. The preliminary announcement may contain figures taken from full financial statements that have been audited and approved for issue or from unaudited full financial statements that have not yet been authorised for issue.

UK.A22.60 In the former situation any events that occur after the issue of the preliminary statement based on audited full financial statements are not post balance sheet events in respect of the year, because they occur after the financial statements have been approved for issue. However, if the preliminary statement is based on figures from full financial statements that have not yet been authorised for issue by the board and on which the audit has not yet been completed, any events between the date of the preliminary announcement and the date of authorisation of the full financial statements for issue are post balance sheet events. Such events are accounted for in accordance with the standard, irrespective of the fact that the entity has already announced figures publicly by way of the preliminary statement.

UK.A22.61 Practical difficulties can sometimes arise if significant post balance sheet events occur after the preliminary publication of results for the year, but before the full financial statements have been authorised for issue. An example might be the announcement of the insolvency of a major debtor, which would require adjustments to the figures previously announced if a loss event, as defined in paragraph 59 of IAS 39 (see the Manual of Accounting – Financial instruments), occurred before the balance sheet date and the announcement merely confirms that the loss was incurred. Other non-adjusting events might only require additional disclosure. In such circumstances, the entity may have to release revised information with the adjusted figures and/or disclosures. An example of restatement of unaudited preliminary figures and reissue of the preliminary statement is given in Table A22.13. The example is from as long ago as 1990, but the incidence of revisions to preliminary announcements for subsequent events is not uncommon even today and the example has been used here because it illustrates the point well, rather than because of a lack of more recent examples. The example is consistent with IAS 10. Table A22.3 above is also an example of revising previously published figures.

Table UK.A22.13 – Revision of previously published figures

Brent Walker Group plc – Preliminary announcement – 31 December 1990

1990 RESULTS AND DIVIDENDS

On 20th May the Group announced its unaudited preliminary results for the year ended 31st December 1990. At that time the Group stated that the net worth of the Group had fallen by £690 million.

In addition, however, the Group indicated the material difference existing in the valuations adopted for the development properties of the Group compared to professional valuations which had been received. Further consideration of the values of these and certain other assets has persuaded the Board that it would be more appropriate to recognise the professional valuations and make other write downs in the accounts for the year ended 31st December 1990.

This has led to a significant restatement of the Group's results for the year, the principal features of which are set out below:

	1990 £million Revised	1990 £million As previously announced	1989 £million Revised
Turnover	1,763.4	1,778.4	572.0
Group Operating Profit	107.2	122.2	112.9
Interest	(116.2)	(116.2)	(44.1)
(Loss)/profit before exceptional items	(5.9)	9.1	72.7
(Loss)/profit for the financial year	(385.5)	(246.8)	119.9
Shareholders' funds	(56.1)	139.0	827.7

A summary of the movements in shareholders' funds is shown in the accounts.

The reduction in Group Operating Profit of £15 million from the figure of £122.2 million reported in the preliminary figures arises because we have not yet concluded the Walker Power transaction announced on 12th April 1991. The current position of this negotiation is referred to below.

In view of the reduction in net worth and the continuing losses, the Board considered it likely that a "serious loss of capital" as defined by S142 of the Companies Act 1985 had occurred. Consequently an extraordinary general meeting was called where the Board stated that the proposed restructuring was the appropriate action to be taken. At that meeting shareholders sanctioned the Group's borrowings exceeding the limit specified in the articles of association.

In the light of these results the Board are unable to recommend the payment of a final dividend on the Ordinary shares or the payment of the dividend on the Preference shares which fell due on 1st July 1991. Interest was due on the 13% Convertible Capital Bond on 23rd May 1991 and, after discussion with the principal holders of the bonds, arrangements were made to defer the payment of their interest subject to the implementation of the financial restructuring. These particular arrangements have since lapsed but are currently the subject of further negotiation.

Listing Rules disclosures for post balance sheet events

UK.A22.61.1 The Listing Rules for UK listed companies require disclosure of any change in directors' interests occurring between the end of the period under review and a date not more than one month prior to the date of the notice of the annual general meeting in the entity's annual financial report. Furthermore, if there has been no such change, that fact should be disclosed. [LR 9.8.6 R(1)]. See further chapter 29.

UK.A22.61.2 Similarly, details of certain interests in a company's share capital need to be disclosed as at a date not more than one month prior to the date of the notice of the annual general meeting. If there is no such interest that fact must be stated. [LR 9.8.6 R(2)]. The relevant interests in a company's share capital are those disclosed to the company in accordance with DTR 5 (in respect of notifiable shareholdings).

UK.A22.61.3 The Listing Rules also require disclosure of any purchases of own shares (including treasury shares), or options or contracts to make such purchases, entered into since the end of the period covered by the financial statements. The information to be disclosed is equivalent information to that required by sections 724 to 732 of the Companies Act 2006 and the relevant accounts regulation (SI 2008/410 7 Sch 9 — disclosure required by company acquiring its own shares, etc). [LR 9.8.6 R(4)].

[The next paragraph is A22.65.]

Financial commitments

A22.65 If an entity enters into any significant commitment or contingent liability after the year end, disclosure of this non-adjusting event is required. [IAS 10 para 22(i)]. This is the only specific disclosure requirement concerning commitments in IAS 10, however, other international standards require disclosure of commitments that exist at the balance sheet date that will affect future periods. These include:

- Capital commitments (see para A22.67).
- Operating lease commitments (see para A22.68).
- Commitments in respect of investment properties (see para A22.68.1).
- Other commitments (see para A22.69).

[The next paragraph is A22.67.]

A22.67 IAS 16, 'Property, plant and equipment', requires the disclosure of contractual commitments that exist at the balance sheet date to acquire fixed assets. [IAS 16 para 74(c)]. IAS 38, 'Intangible assets', requires disclosure of contractual commitments for the acquisition of intangible assets. [IAS 38 para 122(e)]. In addition, IAS 41, 'Agriculture', requires disclosure of the amount of commitments for the development or acquisition of biological assets. [IAS 41 para 49(b)]. IAS 16, IAS 38 and IAS 41 are dealt with in chapters 16, 15 and 32 respectively, which include examples of disclosure.

A22.68 IAS 17, 'Leases', requires the disclosure of future minimum lease payments for non-cancellable operating leases. These disclosures are required to be split between the periods in which the amounts fall due. [IAS 17 paras 35 and 56]. IAS 17 is dealt with in chapter 19.

A22.68.1 IAS 40, 'Investment property', requires disclosure by an entity that holds investment properties of contractual obligations to purchase, construct or develop investment property or for repairs, maintenance or enhancements. [IAS 40 para 75(h)].

A22.69 IFRS 7, 'Financial instruments: Disclosure', contains extensive disclosure requirements in respect of financial instruments. It applies to both recognised and unrecognised financial instruments within its scope, even if the financial instrument may not be recognised under IAS 39 (for example, some loan commitments). IFRS 7 is dealt with in the Manual of Accounting – Financial instruments.

A22.70 IAS 31, 'Interests in joint ventures', requires separate disclosure by the venturer of its capital commitments in respect of a joint venture and its share of capital commitments incurred jointly with the other venturers. It is also required to disclose its share of the joint venture's own capital commitments. IAS 31 is dealt with in chapter 28.

A22.70.1 In June 2011, the IASB issued IFRS 12, 'Disclosure of interest in other entities', which is effective for accounting periods beginning on or after 1 January 2013. The standard requires separate disclosure by an entity of its commitments in respect of a joint venture. The requirements of IFRS 12 in relation to a joint venture are dealt with in chapter 28A.

A22.71 IAS 34, 'Interim financial reporting', states that interim reports should include any events or transactions that are material to an understanding of the interim period. It gives as one example, commitments for the purchase of property, plant and equipment. [IAS 34 para 15B(e)]. Interim reports are dealt with in chapter 31.

A22.72 Commitments that represent an unusual risk to the reporting entity, either because of their nature or their size or duration, are likely to be relevant in assessing the reporting entity's financial position and, consequently, should be disclosed — for example, significant long-term purchase contracts. An example of disclosure of commitments is given in Table A22.14.This example illustrates disclosure of future capital expenditure and of long-term purchase commitments.

Table A22.14 – Disclosure of financial commitments

National Grid plc – Annual report and accounts – 31 March 2011

28. Commitments and contingencies (extract)

	2011 £m	2010 £m
Future capital expenditure		
Contracted for but not provided	**1,614**	1,738
Operating lease commitments		
Less than 1 year	**83**	91
In 1-2 years	**79**	84
In 2-3 years	**93**	79
In 3-4 years	**72**	96
In 4-5 years	**70**	76
More than 5 years	**398**	500
	795	926
Energy purchase commitments (i)*		
Less than 1 year	**1,081**	1,195
In 1-2 years	**480**	506
In 2-3 years	**328**	372
In 3-4 years	**272**	304
In 4-5 years	**241**	245
More than 5 years	**1,141**	1,326
	3,543	3,948
Guarantees and letters of credit		
Guarantee of sublease for US property (expires 2040)	**328**	377
Letter of credit and guarantee of certain obligations of BritNed Interconnector (expire 2011)	**36**	374
Guarantees of certain obligations of Grain LNG Import Terminal (expire up to 2028)	**139**	164
Other guarantees and letters of credit (various expiry dates)	**259**	274
	762	1,189

* Comparatives have been restated to present items on a basis consistent with the current year classification

(i) Energy commitments relate to contractual commitments to purchase electricity or gas that are used to satisfy physical delivery requirements to our customers or for energy that we use ourselves (ie normal purchase, sale or usage) and hence are accounted for as ordinary purchase contracts. Details of commodity contracts that do not meet the normal purchase, sale or usage criteria, and hence are accounted for as derivative contracts, are shown in note 33.

The total of future minimum sublease payments expected to be received under non-cancellable subleases is £20m (2010: £14m).

First-time adoption of IFRS in the UK

Companies Act 2006

UK.A22.72.1 The provisions of the Companies Act 2006 relating to post balance sheet events and the disclosure of commitments are mainly contained in Schedule 1 to SI 2008/410 and these do not apply to companies reporting under EU-adopted IFRS. However, the disclosure requirements in Schedule 7 to SI 2008/410, relating to the directors' report, do apply to companies reporting under EU-adopted IFRS. Schedule 7 requires material post balance sheet events to be disclosed in the directors' report, but does not specify to what extent such events should be adjusted for in preparing the financial statements. [SI 2008/410 7 Sch 7(a)]. The disclosures required in the directors' report are discussed in chapter 2 of the Manual of Accounting – Narrative Reporting.

Chapter 23

Share capital and reserves

Chapter 23

Share capital and reserves

Introduction

23.1 This chapter covers the general accounting and disclosure requirements for share capital and reserves and treasury shares. Classification and accounting for shares under FRS 25, 'Financial instruments: Presentation', UITF 39, 'Members' shares in co-operative entities and similar instruments', FRS 26, 'Financial instruments: Recognition and measurement', and FRS 4, 'Capital instruments' is addressed in detail in the 'Manual of Accounting – Financial instruments'. That chapter also addresses the initial recognition and subsequent measurement of financial instruments (including shares) that are classified as financial liabilities and those that contain embedded derivatives.

23.2 Different classes of share capital may be treated as debt or equity, or compound instruments with debt and equity components. This may differ from the instrument's legal form.

23.3 Assets, liabilities and equity are the three elements used to measure financial position. 'Equity' is the residual interest in the entity's assets after deducting its liabilities, equal to its net assets (an entity with net liabilities will have 'negative equity'). 'Equity' encompasses an entity's equity instruments and reserves. Corporate entities may refer to it as owners' equity, shareholders' equity, capital and reserves, shareholders' funds or proprietorship.

23.4 Equity instruments (for example, issued, non-redeemable ordinary shares) are recorded at the proceeds of issue net of transaction costs and are not subsequently remeasured. Equity instruments issued in consideration for goods and services are accounted for under FRS 20, 'Share-based payments'. Chapter 12 addresses share-based payments accounted for under FRS 20 and shares held by ESOP trusts.

23.5 Reserves include retained earnings, fair value reserves, hedging reserves, asset revaluation reserves, foreign currency translation reserves and other statutory reserves.

[The next paragraph is 23.7.]

Nature and characteristics of 'equity'

Types of shares

23.7 There are numerous types of shares including ordinary shares, preference shares, non-voting shares and redeemable shares. Accounting classification under FRS 25, 'Financial instruments: Presentation', depends on whether the issuer has discretion over transferring economic benefits. Where there is no discretion, the instrument is recorded, wholly or partly, as a liability. Voting rights do not affect the classification of shares.

23.8 For accounting purposes, ordinary shares are typically classified as equity (and referred to as 'equity' shares) because the issuer has discretion over future dividend payments and the shares are non-redeemable. Ordinary shares contain no contractual obligation to pay cash or other financial assets. Shares that are redeemable by the holder in cash or a variable number of equity shares are recorded as liabilities. [FRS 25 para 18(b)]. Non-redeemable shares with a mandatory fixed coupon are classified as liabilities at their net present value.

23.9 Under FRS 25 the classification of a financial instrument between liabilities and equity is based on the substance of the contractual arrangement. [FRS 25 para 15]. This is discussed in detail in the 'Manual of Accounting – Financial instruments'. The key issues are summarised below.

23.10 FRS 25 is based on IAS 32 and, accordingly, comments made by the IASB or the IFRIC are relevant to the interpretation of the requirements of FRS 25 when no equivalent interpretive comment has been provided by the ASB or the UITF. In the June 2006 edition of IASB Update (as set out under 'IFRIC activities'), the IASB confirmed the 'substance of contractual arrangement approach'. The IASB stressed that IAS 32 does not require or permit factors not within the contractual arrangement to be taken into consideration in classifying a financial instrument (for example, economic obligations). The same approach should, therefore, be taken in respect of FRS 25. As with IAS 32, under FRS 25, the critical test is whether the issuer has discretion over the transfer of benefits (being cash or another financial asset). If the issuer has no discretion over the payment, then the instrument (or a component part) is a liability. As a result there are certain instruments, such as redeemable preference shares, that are shown, in whole or in part, as liabilities. [FRS 25 paras AG25, AG26, AG37].

23.11 In its discussions in June 2006, the IASB considered whether economic compulsion should affect the classification of a financial instrument (or a component of a financial instrument) under IAS 32. The IASB noted that for a financial instrument (or a component of a financial instrument) to be classified as a financial liability under IAS 32, the issuer must have a contractual obligation either:

- to deliver cash or another financial asset to the holder of the instrument; or
- to exchange financial assets or financial liabilities with the holder under conditions that are potentially unfavourable to the issuer.

23.12 Different requirements apply to financial instruments that may or will be settled in the issuer's own equity instruments. The IASB confirmed that a contractual obligation can be established explicitly or indirectly, but it must be established through the instrument's terms and conditions. The IASB stressed that IAS 32 does not require or permit factors not within the contractual arrangement to be taken into consideration in classifying a financial instrument. Economic compulsion alone does not, therefore, result in a financial instrument being classified as a liability under IAS 32.

23.13 This clarifies, in relation to paragraphs 15 and AG26 of FRS 25 that a financial instrument that appears to be debt, and which an entity may be economically compelled to treat as cash, is nevertheless an equity instrument for accounting purposes. An example is a perpetual bond that carries a coupon that the issuer can defer indefinitely. If it defers payment, the issuer has to cease paying dividends on its ordinary shares. The issuer, therefore, has discretion over payment of the coupon. It may be economically compelled to pay the coupon so it can pay ordinary dividends, but it is not contractually obliged to pay it. As there is no contractual obligation to repay the bond's principal (it is perpetual) or to pay the coupon, the whole financial instrument is classified as equity and the coupons are treated as equity dividends.

23.14 A contract that may be settled in an entity's own shares may be a financial liability. A contract to be settled by a variable number of the entity's shares, whose value equates to a specified fixed amount or a value determined by reference to another item (for example, a commodity price), is a financial liability. The entity is using its own shares as a 'currency' to settle the contract. As the holder will always get 'shares equal to the value of', it is not exposed to a gain or loss from variation in the entity's share price. The contract does not evidence a residual interest in the entity's assets after deducting all of its liabilities. [FRS 25 para 21].

23.15 For example, a written option to buy gold that, if exercised, is settled net in the entity's own shares by the entity delivering shares equal to the value of the option contract is a financial liability. [FRS 25 para AG27(d)]. Similarly, a contract that will be settled in a fixed number of the entity's own shares, but the rights attaching to those shares will be varied so that the settlement value equals a fixed amount or an amount based on changes in an underlying variable, is a financial asset or liability. [FRS 25 para AG27(d)]. Equally, a contract that may be settled in a fixed number of the entity's equity shares for a variable amount of cash in the entity's functional currency is a financial liability. See further 'Manual of Accounting – Financial instruments'.

23.16 Puttable shares are generally classified as financial liabilities. If the holder's right to request redemption for cash or another financial asset is unconditionally prohibited by local law, regulation or the entity's governing charter (constitution), the puttable shares may be classified as equity. If redemption is only prohibited under certain conditions, such as liquidity constraints, the shares are liabilities. [UITF 39 para 8].

23.17 FRS 25 has been amended to change the classification of certain financial instruments from liabilities to equity. The amendment allows for certain puttable financial instruments and certain financial instruments that impose an obligation on the entity to deliver a *pro rata* share of its net assets to another party on liquidation to be classified as equity rather than liabilities. The amendment is mandatory for periods starting on or after 1 January 2010 with early adoption permitted for periods starting on or after 1 January 2009. This amendment is an exception to the ordinary requirements of FRS 25 and is narrowly defined. It is addressed in more detail in 'Manual of Accounting – Financial instruments'.

Legal form

23.18 Companies Act and common law rules apply to all shares irrespective of their accounting classification. Failure to comply with the statutory and common law rules relating to shares can result in legal sanctions against companies and their directors. The interaction of these rules and FRS 25 is often complex.

23.19 Legal classification depends on the rights given to the shares in the company's memorandum and articles of association. The Act defines equity share capital as a company's issued share capital except for any shares that, neither in regard to dividends nor in regard to capital, carry any right to participate beyond a specified amount in a distribution. [CA06 Sec 548]. Generally, ordinary shares are legally equity shares. It is possible to design preference shares that are legally equity share capital. Clearly FRS 25's definition of equity shares differs from this legal definition. There is another definition of equity shares for tax purposes.

23.20 Certain financial instruments may be accounted for as equity (and the coupons as equity dividends) but are legally debt. They impact distributable profits and capital maintenance as debt and not as shares with dividends. Legally, compound instruments are either wholly debt or wholly shares. The law does not contemplate that instruments will be broken into components. Determining the legal consequences can be complex, particularly for distributions and capital maintenance purposes. Section 6 of Tech 02/10, 'Guidance on the determination of realised profits and losses in the context of distributions under the Companies Act 2006', provides illustrative examples of the interaction of the accounting and legal rules.

23.21 Other instruments are classified as debt but are legally shares, such as mandatorily redeemable preference shares. The nominal value and share premium of such instruments should be shown as a liability. Shares and share premium presented as liabilities are subject to the capital maintenance requirements of the 2006 Act. Companies should maintain sufficient records to ensure that if legal shares presented as liabilities are repurchased, the company's capital base is preserved and appropriate amounts are transferred to the share premium account and capital redemption reserve in equity shareholders' funds.

23.22 The Act strictly governs the purchase of own shares by a company. The rules governing the redemption of redeemable shares are very similar. If authorised by its articles, a company may issue shares that are redeemable at the option of the company or the shareholder, provided that there are also non-redeemable shares in issue. [CA06 Sec 684]. Classifying redeemable shares under FRS 25 is considered in 'Manual of Accounting – Financial instruments'.

Reserves and their purposes

23.23 UK GAAP does not define reserves. Some result from accounting requirements (for example, fair value and foreign currency translation reserves) to reflect certain measurement changes in equity rather than in profit or loss. Others arise from jurisdictional requirements.

23.24 Typical reserves include:

- Share premium account.
- Capital redemption reserve.
- Revaluation reserve.
- Fair value or available-for-sale reserve.
- Hedging reserve.
- Foreign currency translation reserve.
- Capital reserve.
- Retained profits.
- Other reserves, including reserves arising from local statutory requirements.

23.25 The redenomination of share capital from one currency to another may create a 'redenomination reserve'. Companies may also create a 'merger reserve' when they obtain merger or group reconstruction relief.

23.26 'Other reserves' includes all reserves, realised and unrealised, that do not fit elsewhere. If material they are specifically described.

Equity arising from transactions with owners — recognition and measurement

Equity share capital

23.27 There are no requirements in FRS 25, 'Financial instruments: Presentation', on the initial recognition and measurement of equity shares. Equity shares are normally recorded as paid-in capital in the balance sheet at the net proceeds of issue, when the proceeds of issue are received or receivable. Net proceeds of issue are measured after deducting directly attributable transaction costs of the share issue. Any tax benefit obtained on such costs is taken to equity. [FRS 25 para 35].

23.28 If the equity shares have a par (nominal) value, paid-in capital is split between par value and any premium at the date of issue, less any directly attributable transaction costs. FRS 26, 'Financial instruments: Recognition and instrument', does not apply to equity instruments, although net proceeds of issue can be similar to the initial measurement of financial instruments not carried at fair value through profit or loss. [FRS 26 paras 2(d), 43, AG64].

23.29 A company can issue shares for any amount that the laws of the country in which it is established permit. Changes in the fair value (market value) of an equity share do not affect the amount at which it is stated in the financial statements.

23.30 Shares can be issued for consideration greater than their nominal value. The excess over the nominal amount is recognised in the share premium account (unless relief is available).

Non-equity share capital

23.31 Some share issues may not qualify as equity. Such shares and any associated premium are presented as financial liabilities under FRS 25. They are initially recognised and measured in accordance with FRS 26 (FRS 26 paras 43, AG64) usually at net proceeds of issue, after deducting directly attributable transaction costs. Subsequent measurement is generally at amortised cost. [FRS 26 para 47].

Compound instruments

23.32 Regardless of their legal form instruments consisting of equity and liability components (such as convertible debt) are split into those components and accounted for separately. The liability component is measured first and the residual is the equity component. [FRS 25 paras 28 — 32].

23.33 For example, on initial recognition the debt component of a mandatorily redeemable, non-cumulative preference share with discretionary dividends is the net present value of the principal redemption amount. [FRS 25 para AG37]. The equity component comprises the balance of the proceeds of issue before deducting transaction costs. Directly attributable transaction costs are allocated to the debt and equity components in proportion to the proceeds allocated to these components. [FRS 25 para 38]. The debt component is subsequently measured at amortised cost. The equity component is not re-measured.

Partly paid shares

23.34 Shares may be issued fully or partly paid. With fully paid equity shares, the amount recognised in equity as share capital and share premium (less any directly attributable transaction costs) is equal to the cash received by the issuer. The accounting treatment for partly paid shares depends on the terms and conditions of the share issue and possibly the company's constitution. The issuer of equity shares records at least the amount received in cash (which will be less directly attributable transaction costs) on the partly paid shares as an asset and as a credit to equity. The issuer will also need to consider whether to recognise the balance not yet paid on the shares as a receivable, with a corresponding credit to equity.

23.35 For example, a company issues partly paid shares. The share agreement sets out a fixed schedule of definite call dates when the shareholders must pay instalments of the outstanding amount on the shares. The shareholders have rights to full dividends (irrespective of the proportion paid up on the shares) and cannot avoid the calls. The company's constitution or national law determines whether the schedule of calls legally obliges the shareholders to make the scheduled payments.

23.36 If the shareholder is contractually obliged to pay, and they have full rights to dividends, the issuer recognises a receivable for the outstanding future receipts (discounted, if material) at the issue date of the shares, with a corresponding entry to paid-in capital (share capital/share premium).

23.37 The receivable is a financial asset, as the issuer has a contractual right to receive cash from the shareholder. It is measured at fair value on initial recognition and subsequently at amortised cost (unless designated at FVTPL). Amortised cost is calculated using the effective interest rate. The receivable is recorded at the net present value of the future payments. The unwinding of the discount on that receivable will be recognised through the profit and loss account over the expected payment period.

23.38 Under the model articles (Table A), dividends are paid according to the amounts paid up on shares, as defined by the Act. If there is a fixed payment schedule for calls or an undertaking to pay calls to the company at a future date, companies following the model articles recognise a receivable for the outstanding issue proceeds. The receivable is recorded at the next present value of the future payments and the discount is unwound through the profit and loss account. Share capital and share premium are recorded in aggregate at the amount of the receivable. Share capital must be stated at nominal value. The difference if positive is share premium, if negative, is a debit to reserves.

23.39 Depending on the legal terms of the share allotment, the discount recognised through the profit and loss account may be transferred to share premium in order to reflect the legal share premium. If the nominal value of the shares exceeds the receivable, the difference is taken as a debit to equity. The discount unwinds through the profit and loss account. The credits taken to retained earnings *via* the profit and loss account offset the initial debit to equity.

23.40 Although the discount unwind will be receivable in cash and is, in principle, realised, in some instances it may be deemed part of the company's legal share capital for capital maintenance purposes and should not be distributed.

23.41 In UK law, shares do not have to be fully paid at issue. For a private company, there are no rules to determine the minimum amount of consideration that must be paid or how the consideration paid should be divided between the nominal value of the share and the share premium. For example, a private company can issue a 20p nominal value share at £1 and have only 30p paid up. A public company must have at least a quarter of the nominal value plus the whole of any premium paid up. [CA06 Sec 586]. Using the same example, a public company must have at least 85p paid up (20p × ¼ + premium of 80p).

23.42 A company can make calls on partly paid shares at its discretion in the future. If shareholders can avoid these calls and do not have a right to full dividends until the shares are fully paid, this is a discretionary call and hence no receivable (or the corresponding share capital/share premium) is recognised until the call is made and the shareholder has agreed to meet the call.

23.43 To prevent undistributable profits being made distributable (indirectly), a company cannot apply an unrealised profit to pay up debentures or to pay any amounts that are unpaid on its issued shares. [CA06 Sec 849].

Called up share capital

23.44 Issued share capital and called up share capital may differ. Under UK law 'called up share capital' means:

- That proportion of a company's share capital as equals the aggregate amount of the calls made on its shares (whether or not those calls have been paid).
- Any share capital that has been paid up without being called.
- Any share capital that is to be paid on a specified future date under the Articles of Association, or under the terms of allotment, or any other arrangements for paying for those shares.

[CA06 Sec 547].

23.45 Called-up share capital is relevant for a number of purposes, including:

- Accounting for share capital.
- Serious loss of capital.
- The 'net asset test', restricting distributable profits of a public company

23.46 Under the Act, share capital is 'called up' or 'paid up' not just when the cash is received, but when there is a schedule of payments due on fixed future dates or there is an undertaking to pay cash to the company at a future date. 'Paid up' share capital may, therefore, surprisingly, be unpaid. [CA06 Sec 547]. Uncalled share capital is to be construed accordingly. [CA06 Sec 547]. A share in a company is deemed paid up in cash if one of five types of specified consideration has been received. [CA06 Sec 583(2)(3)].

Serious loss of capital

23.47 If the value of a public company's net assets falls to half or less than half of its called up share capital (as defined by the Act), the directors have a duty to convene a general meeting in order to consider what action, if any, to take to deal with the situation. Proper notice must be given and the directors must convene the meeting not later than 28 days from the earliest date the serious loss of capital was known to a director. The meeting must be held within 56 days of that earliest date. If the company fails to convene the meeting, each of the company's directors responsible is liable to a fine. [CA06 Sec 656].

23.48 For these purposes, called-up share capital is generally taken to exclude share premium. Under the Act, share premium is transferred to the share premium account. [CA06 Sec 610]. The balance sheet formats in Schedule 1 to SI 2008/410 show separate captions for called-up share capital and for share premium account. This implies that share premium is not part of paid-up share capital.

23.49 Where shares are recognised as liabilities under FRS 25, 'Financial instruments: Presentation', this affects the assessment of whether the value of the company's net assets is half or less than half of its called up share capital. It also affects the 'net asset test'. The DTI (now Department for Business, Innovation and Skills (BIS)) provided guidance that, for the purposes of the net assets test, *"where preference shares are classified as liabilities, they should be treated as such for the purposes of the net asset test, and should not be treated as part of called-up share capital and undistributable reserves for that purpose"*. ['Guidance for British companies on changes to the reporting and accounting provisions of the Companies Act 1985, para 6.5]. Similar guidance is included in the equivalent publication under the 2006 Act issued in June 2008. Although the net asset test rules appear in a different part of the Act to the serious loss of capital rules, we believe that the same approach should be applied to serious loss of capital. Therefore, where shares are classified as liabilities, we believe that they should not be included in called up share capital, but should be treated as liabilities for the purposes of the serious loss of capital test. However, as this requires legal interpretation, companies should take legal advice.

Allotment of shares

23.50 Part 17 of the 2006 Act sets out the law on allotment of shares. In essence, the previous law was restated in the 2006 Act. However, the main change is that private companies with only one class of share capital no longer need authority to allot shares unless their articles of association require it. [CA06 Sec 550].

23.51 Section 550 empowers the directors to allot shares (or to grant rights to subscribe for or convert any security into shares) where the company is a private company with only one class of shares, unless they are prohibited from doing so by the articles of association. This removes the previous requirement (contained in section 80 of the 1985 Act) for the directors to have prior authority from the company's members for such an allotment of shares. The members may, if they wish, restrict or prohibit this power through the articles of association. The definition of 'classes of shares' is contained in section 629 of the 2006 Act and provides that shares are of one class if the rights attached to them are in all respects uniform.

23.52 A company's memorandum must state the amount of the nominal share capital and the nominal value of each type of share. Under the 2006 Act, the memorandum is a simple document evidencing that the subscribers wish to form a company under that Act and that they agree to become members of the company and to take at least one share each if the company has share capital. All other matters relating to the company's constitution are addressed in the articles, which may be drawn up as the company sees fit. Any provision contrary to the 2006 Act is void.

23.53 For companies formed before the 2006 Act, provisions that are not designated for the memorandum in the 2006 Act are deemed transferred to the articles. Normally, the minimum requirement for a change in the articles is a special resolution. Provisions deemed transferred to the articles are regarded as entrenched (meaning they can only be changed if more restrictive conditions than a special resolution are met).

23.54 The 2006 Act introduces a requirement for a statement of capital and initial shareholdings to be delivered to the Registrar of Companies on registration. This provides, *inter alia*, the information that would have been contained in the memorandum for companies formed under previous legislation. The statement of capital and initial shareholdings must state:

- The total number of the company's shares to be taken on formation by the subscribers to the memorandum of association.
- The aggregate nominal value of those shares.
- For each class of shares:
  - Prescribed particulars of the rights attached to the shares.
  - The total number of shares of that class.
  - The aggregate nominal value of shares of that class.
- The amount to be paid up and the amount (if any) to be unpaid on each share (whether nominal value or premium).

[CA06 Sec 10(2)].

23.55 With very limited exceptions, whenever a company alters its share capital, it will be required under the 2006 Act to file a statement of capital. The requirement to file a statement of capital with the Registrar of Companies where a company has altered its share capital is contained in 'The Companies (Shares and Share Capital) Order 2009' (SI 2009/388).

Shares to be issued

23.56 Companies may receive consideration for shares before the shares are issued. Whether shares have been issued is a legal matter and does not depend on the date on the share certificate. If the company believes that a shareholder is legally entitled to the shares (for example, is entitled to dividends), the consideration received is credited to paid-in capital (share capital/share premium) regardless of whether the certificate has been issued. If the shares have not been legally issued, the consideration received is credited to 'shares to be issued'.

Allotment of shares for non-cash consideration

23.57 Companies may allot shares, including any premium, for money or for other items that can be valued in money, such as fixed assets or intellectual property. In these circumstances the non-cash consideration should be valued to determine the amount to be recognised as paid-in capital. This amount is split between the par value of the shares and share premium where this is required by law.

23.58 The Companies Act provides that a share's nominal value and any premium can be paid up in money or money's worth (including goodwill and know-how). [CA06 Sec 582]. Although shares need not be fully paid up at issue, they may not be issued at a discount to their nominal value. If shares are allotted at a discount by mistake, the allottee must pay the company the discount plus interest. [CA06 Sec 580].

23.59 Public companies may not accept an undertaking to work or perform services to the company as payment for shares. [CA06 Sec 585(1)]. If a public company treats the undertaking of work or services as payment for shares, the shareholder is liable to pay the company the nominal value of the shares and any share premium and pay interest on this. [CA06 Sec 585(2)]. Under FRS 20, 'Share-based payment', a share-based payment includes transactions in which the entity receives goods or services as consideration for the entity's equity instruments. In the vast majority of cases, this does not breach this legal requirement.

23.60 The UITF obtained legal advice on the application of section 99 of the 1985 Act in developing UITF 17, 'Employee share schemes', which FRS 20, 'Share-based payment', superseded. Although FRS 20 requires different accounting from UITF 17, in the 'Notes on the standard's application in the UK and in the Republic of Ireland' to FRS 20, the ASB state that this legal advice may still have relevance in the context of FRS 20. The legal advice is also relevant to section 585(2) of the 2006 Act. UITF 17 stated:

> *"The UITF has received legal advice as to the implications for share premium account when the accounting treatment required by this Abstract is followed. It has been advised that where new shares are issued in*

connection with an employee share scheme the share premium account will normally have to reflect only the cash subscribed for the shares (e.g. by the employee or by an ESOP). In such cases, any difference between the cash subscribed for the shares (which must be at least as much as the nominal value, as shares cannot be issued at a discount) and the fair value at the date of grant of rights should be credited to reserves other than the share premium account. This is on the basis that the services of the employee do not, as a matter of law, form part of the consideration received for the shares issued, and the Task Force has been advised that this would be the usual legal interpretation of such transactions. Exceptionally, however, the terms of a transaction might be such as to lead to the opposite interpretation, and companies may need to take legal advice on this point. In such a case, the operation of section 99(2) of the Companies Act 1985 [now section 581(1) of the Companies Act 2006][prohibition of public company accepting undertaking to perform services in payment up of its shares] and of section 103 of the Companies Act 1985 [now section 593 of the Companies Act 2006] [non-cash consideration to be valued before allotment of shares] would also have to be considered."

[FRS 20 para N28].

23.61 Section 7 of Tech 02/10, 'Guidance on the determination of realised profits and losses in the context of distributions under the Companies Act 2006', further considers the law relating to realised and distributable profits and its implications for the accounting for employee share schemes.

23.62 A public company that intends to accept non-cash consideration (other than for work or services) for the allotment of shares must have the consideration independently valued. [CA06 Sec 593]. The valuation report must be made for the company, during the six months before the allotment, by a person qualified to be the company's auditor who may seek assistance from any suitably qualified and independent valuer. [CA06 Secs 593, 1150]. The report should contain sufficient information to make the amount of the paid-up share capital and any premium readily apparent. The report must state in particular:

- The nominal value of the shares to be wholly or partly paid for by the consideration being valued.
- The amount of any premium payable on the shares.
- The description of the consideration.
- The extent to which the nominal value of the shares and any premium are to be treated as paid up either by the consideration that has been valued or by cash.

[CA06 Sec 596(2)].

The report must also state that, on the basis of the consideration's valuation, together with any cash paid, the nominal value of the share capital (plus the whole of any premium) that is to be treated as paid is not less than the valued consideration plus any cash paid. [CA06 Sec 596(3), 600(3)]. A copy of the report must be sent to the proposed allottee. [CA06 Sec 593(1)].

23.63 A valuation report is not necessary if shares are issued in consideration for the transfer or cancellation of shares in another company (an example being a business combination) provided that the arrangement is open to all the other company's shareholders or all the shareholders of the class of shares that is being transferred. [CA06 Sec 594(1) — (5)].

23.64 Shares issued in exchange for the issuing company taking over all the assets and liabilities of another company, with or without any cash payment, do not require a valuation report. [CA06 Sec 595(1)(2)].

Bonus shares

23.65 Companies may issue bonus shares using share premium account, capital redemption reserve, retained earnings or the revaluation reserve. The relevant reserve is debited with the nominal value of the shares issued. Paid-up share capital in equity is credited with an equivalent amount, if the bonus shares are equity shares under FRS 25. If the bonus shares are not equity shares under FRS 25, they are recognised as financial liabilities.

23.66 Companies may not make bonus issues unless their articles of association expressly permit them to do so. Companies that existed before 22 December 1980 need not alter their articles to do this if immediately before that date they had power under their articles to capitalise unrealised profits. For companies that existed at 22 December 1980, a power in the articles to make bonus issues out of profits available for dividend is deemed to include a power to make bonus issues out of unrealised profits. [CA06 Sec 848(1) (2)].

23.67 A valuation report is not required where a public company uses the credit balance on a reserve account, such as the profit and loss account reserve or a revaluation reserve to allot shares, including any premium on the shares, to any of the company members. [CA06 Sec 593(2)]. Amounts are transferred from the reserve to share capital and share premium in accordance with the articles and memorandum and the terms of the issue.

Multi-currency share capital

23.68 Companies may issue share capital denominated in a currency that is not their functional currency. When foreign currency share capital is presented as a financial liability in the balance sheet, the liability is initially stated at the spot rate prevailing at the date of issue. Subsequently, the financial liability will be retranslated, as a monetary item, at each balance sheet date in accordance with SSAP 20, 'Foreign currency translation', or, for FRS 26 users, FRS 23, 'The effects of changes in foreign exchange rates'. Equity share capital is initially stated at the spot rate prevailing at the date of issue, but is generally not retranslated under SSAP 20 or FRS 23. However, some companies do retranslate their foreign currency share capital and take the translation differences to reserves. This is not specifically precluded by SSAP 20 and while this may seem contrary to FRS 23, the overall effect on equity, taking the retranslated foreign share capital and the cumulative translation differences together, is as if the foreign currency share capital is carried at the original historical spot rate.

23.69 Historically, a number of companies have issued share capital denominated in foreign currencies. In 1986 the Scandinavian Bank Group plc petitioned the court for confirmation of a special resolution to cancel part of its existing sterling share capital in order to increase its share capital to £30m, $30m, SFr 30m and DM 30m (see *Re Scandinavian Bank Group plc, [1987] BCLC 220*).

23.70 The court confirmed that a company can have shares in more than one currency. Individual shares must be denominated in one particular currency, but different shares can be denominated in different currencies. This does not conflict with the Act's requirement, because section 5(a) states that *"... the memorandum must...state the amount of the share capital...and the division of the share capital into shares of a fixed amount"*. By fixed amount, the Act does not mean a fixed value in sterling terms. The 2006 Act places into statute the common law rule that shares may be denominated in different currencies and introduces provisions to enable all companies to redenominate shares in a fixed nominal value in one currency to a fixed nominal value in another currency. [CA06 Sec 542; CA06 Sec 622].

23.71 A public company is required to have an authorised minimum allotted share capital of £50,000. [CA06 Secs 761-763]. This stems from Article 6 of the EU 2nd Company Law Directive. In *Re Scandinavian Bank Group plc,the* court held (*obiter*) that this 'authorised minimum' must be in pounds sterling. A private company can have all of its share capital in foreign currency, but a public company must have at least £50,000 of its share capital in pounds sterling. The 2006 Act relaxes this rule, permitting public companies to meet the minimum share capital requirements in sterling or euros, but not a combination of the two. [CA06 Sec 765]. The 2006 Act does not expressly provide that the authorised minimum must continue to be denominated in sterling or euros once the initial minimum capital requirements have been satisfied (that is, it has obtained a trading certificate under section 761, or, where a private company is re-registering as a public company, it has complied with the requirements as to share capital set out in section 91). According to the Explanatory Notes to the 2006 Act, because the 2006 Act is silent on this point, this means that a public company will be free to re-denominate all of its share capital, including the authorised minimum, into euro's once the initial minimum capital requirements have been satisfied. 'The Companies (Authorised Minimum) Regulations 2008', SI 2008/729 came into force on 6 April 2008 and prescribes the amount in euros that is to be treated as equivalent to the sterling amount as EUR 65,600. 'The Companies (Authorised Minimum) Regulations 2009', SI 2009/2425 came into force on 1 October 2009. The regulations provide a euro figure and rules necessary for certain provisions of the Companies Act 2006, which refer to the 'authorised minimum' share capital requirement for public companies. The euro figure of €57,100 replaces the one currently fixed in 'The Companies (Authorised Minimum) Regulations 2008' (SI 2008/729).

23.72 Foreign currency share capital is generally redeemed or repurchased in the currency in which the shares are denominated. There will be a difference between the functional currency amount at redemption and the amount recorded at the issue of the shares. It seems logical that this difference should affect distributable profits. A debit difference will absorb distributable profits. A credit difference should also be taken to distributable profits, provided that the shares were originally issued for cash or near cash.

23.73 There are two legal views on the application of the Act's capital maintenance rules to the redemption or repurchase of foreign currency share capital (assuming that the shares are not redeemed or repurchased out of the proceeds of a fresh issue of shares made for this purpose). One is that the nominal value of the shares concerned translated at the original exchange rate should be transferred from distributable profits to the capital redemption reserve. The alternative view is that the nominal value transferred is translated at the exchange rate ruling on the date of the redemption or repurchase. Companies redeeming or repurchasing foreign currency share capital should take legal advice.

23.74 Under the 1985 Act it has not been easy for limited companies to 'convert' existing shares from one currency to another. Companies would instead have to go through the normal cancellation or buy back or redemption procedures, accompanied by a new issue of shares in the desired currency, or convert their paid-up shares into stock and re-convert that stock into paid-up shares of the required denomination (using section 121(2)(c) of the 1985 Act).

23.75 The 2006 Act simplifies the law to allow limited companies to redenominate their share capital easily. As before, unlimited companies with share capital are able to redenominate their shares if they wish. Redenomination is defined in the 2006 Act: *"To redenominate means to convert shares from having a fixed nominal value in one currency to having fixed nominal value in another currency"*. [CA06 Sec 622(1)].

23.76 Provided that the articles do not prohibit or restrict redenomination, a limited company may redenominate its share capital or any class of its share capital by resolution. The resolution may specify conditions that must be met before the redenomination takes effect and the exchange rate at which the conversion must be made. [CA06 Sec 622(4)].

23.77 The exchange rate must be either the rate prevailing on the resolution date or a rate determined by taking the average of rates prevailing on consecutive days of a period specified in the resolution. [CA06 Sec 622(3)]. The new nominal values of the shares is calculated as follows:

- Step one – Take the aggregate of the old nominal values of all the shares of that class.

- Step two – Translate that amount into the new currency at the rate of exchange specified in the resolution.

- Step three – Divide that amount by the amount of the number of shares in that class.

[CA06 Sec 623].

23.78 The resulting nominal value is inevitably not a round number. The 2006 Act anticipates this and provides for the reduction of capital and creation of a redenomination reserve to deal with this problem.

Example

Company A has 1,000,000 £1 class A shares in issue and wishes to re-denominate these shares as US dollar shares. It passes a resolution to re-denominate these shares at an exchange rate of £1 = $2.0132. The company also has 500,000 £1 class B shares in issue.

Step one: Take the aggregate of the old nominal values of all the shares of that class. This is £1,000,000.

Step two: Translate that amount into the new currency at the rate of exchange specified in the resolution. £1,000,000 at £1 = $2.0132 is $2,013,200.

Step three: Divide that amount by the amount of the number of shares in that class. $2,013,200/1,000,000 gives a new nominal value of $2.0132.

Company A believes that it would be more suitable if the new nominal value were $2 per share; this would mean that the nominal value of the new shares was in aggregate $2,000,000, $13,200 less than the US dollar equivalent of the sterling nominal value. Section 626 of the 2006 Act allows the company to reduce its share capital, provided that it passes a special resolution to that effect within three months of the resolution effecting the redenomination and provided that the amount of the capital reduction is not more than 10% of the entity's total allotted share capital immediately after the reduction.

The amount of the reduction in this example is $13,200, equivalent to £6,557 (translated at the rate £1 = $2.0132).

The nominal value of the class A shares after the reduction expressed in pounds sterling is £993,443. The total allotted share capital in pounds sterling is, therefore, £1,493,443 (£993,443 + £500,000). £6,557 is less than 10% of £1,493,443. The capital reduction is permitted.

Under section 628 of the 2006 Act, the amount of the capital reduction is transferred to the 'redenomination reserve'. Assuming that the company retains a sterling functional currency, the following entry will be made:

	Dr £	Cr £
Dr Nominal share capital – $2 Class A shares	£6,557	
Cr Redenomination reserve		£6,557

The financial statements of company A will, therefore, show:

Nominal share capital – $2 Class A shares	£993,443
Nominal share capital – £1 Class B shares	£500,000
Redenomination reserve	£6,557

In sterling terms, the share capital's nominal value before the redenomination is equal to the nominal value of the share capital plus the redenomination reserve after the redenomination.

23.79 The redenomination reserve may be used to allot fully paid bonus shares. [CA06 Sec 628(2)]. It is treated as paid up share capital of the entity for the purposes of a reduction in capital. [CA06 Sec 628(3)].

Sub-division or consolidation of share

23.80 Companies may sub-divide their shares into shares of a smaller nominal amount or consolidate their shares into shares of a larger nominal amount. [CA06 Sec 618]. The 1985 Act required express permission in the articles for such actions; the 2006 Act requires only a resolution of members (unless the company has prohibitions or restrictions in the articles). The resolution may give the company the power to sub-divide or consolidate the shares at any time in the future, or at certain times by reference to specified dates or circumstances. [CA06 Sec 618(4)].

23.81 From 1 October 2009, a company's shares may no longer be converted into stock (an archaic UK word generally meaning undenominated share; but also the US term for shares). Shares previously converted into stock may be reconverted in accordance with section 620 of the 2006 Act. [CA06 Sec 540(2)(3)]. Section 621 requires the company to give notice of any re-conversion of stock to the registrar. It also requires the company to file a statement of capital.

Share premium

23.82 Share premium is the amount by which the fair value of the consideration received exceeds the nominal value of shares issued.

23.83 The Act governs the creation of share premium on an issue of shares and how that premium may be used. The Act's rules apply to all shares, regardless of how they are classified for accounting purposes. Share premium associated with shares presented as liabilities is included as part of the liability and remains subject to the capital maintenance rules. For accounting purposes, legal share premium is analysed between amounts relating to shares presented as liabilities and as equity.

23.84 The basic rule for share premium is that, where a company issues shares at a premium to the nominal value (whether for cash or otherwise), the aggregate amount or value of the premium must be transferred to a share premium account. [CA06 Sec 610(1)]. For example, if a company issues 100,000 £1 shares at £1.50 each, it must credit £50,000 to a share premium account.

23.85 The 2006 Act restricts the use of the share premium account. Under the 2006 Act, the share premium account may be used to write off share issue expenses and commission paid on the issue of shares. Issue expenses can only be written off against the share premium from the same issue. [CA06 Sec 610(2)]. The 2006 Act continues to permit the use of the share premium account to fund the premium on an acquisition of own shares where those shares were initially issued at a premium and the redemption is made from the proceeds of a new issue of shares. [CA06 Sec 687(4) (5), 692(3) (4)].

[The next paragraph is 23.89.]

23.89 The share premium account is treated as part of the company's paid up share capital, except in the case of a serious loss of capital (see para 23.32.5). Consequently, the provisions of the Act that apply to the reduction of share capital apply to the share premium account (see further para 23.32.5). [CA06 Sec 610(4)].

23.90 Legal requirements in respect of share premium apply regardless of accounting classification.

Example

A company issues shares with a nominal value of £100 for £1,000. There is a share premium of £900. The shares are non-redeemable and carry a cumulative fixed non-discretionary dividend for the first five years. Dividends are payable at the company's discretion after that period.

The company determines that, under FRS 25, 'Financial instruments: Presentation', the five-year coupon on the share is debt and the principal is equity. It determines that the fair values of the two elements at the date of issue are £200 for the debt element and £800 for the equity element. Therefore, at the date of issues, the company records:

	Dr £	Cr £
Dr Cash	1,000	
Cr Equity		800
Cr Liability		200

The liability of £200 comprises £20 nominal value and £180 share premium. Share capital of £80 and share premium of £720 is included in equity. The share premium of £720 is calculated by taking 9/10ths of the equity element of £800, because the original share premium amount was 9/10ths of the original proceeds.

The notes to the financial statements should state that (legal) share capital is £100 and share premium £900. The company has to maintain sufficient records such that it can reconstruct a 'legal' balance sheet should it wish to repurchase shares, as share capital and share premium are still subject to capital maintenance requirements.

If the company repurchases the shares out of distributable profits for £1,000, the company records the following entries:

	Dr	Cr
	£	£
Dr Equity – share capital	80	
Dr Liability	200	
Dr Equity – Retained earnings	1,000	
Cr Capital redemption reserve (see para 23.142)		100
Cr Equity – share premium		180
Cr Cash		1,000

£180, the element of the share premium that was previously included in the carrying amount of the debt, is transferred to the share premium account in equity once the debt has been repaid, to maintain the company's legal capital.

If, say, the company had retained earnings of £11,000 before the repurchase, the company's balance sheets before and after the repurchase of shares would be:

	Balance sheet	
	Before repurchase	After repurchase
	£	£
Debt	(200)	–
Cash/assets	12,000	11,000
Net assets	11,800	11,000
Share capital	80	–
Share premium	720	900
Capital redemption reserve	–	100
Retained earnings	11,000	10,000
Total equity	11,800	11,000

A separate memorandum account maintained to record the legal position of the share capital and premium accounts shows:

	Memorandum account	
	Before repurchase	After repurchase
	£	£
Share capital	100	–
Share premium	900	900
Capital redemption reserve	–	100
Retained earnings	11,000	10,000
Total equity	12,000	11,000

23.91 The reliefs from recognising share premium in respect of mergers (acquisitions) and group reconstructions are set out in sections 611 to 615 of the 2006 Act.

23.92 Only the costs of a successful issue can be written off against the share premium account. For example, if an entity incurs costs in anticipation of a flotation that does not go ahead, these costs are taken to the profit and loss account. They cannot subsequently be resurrected and written off against the proceeds of a subsequent flotation.

23.93 Costs of issue do not include the costs of issuing warrants, as these are not a share but a right to a share. Therefore, the cost of issuing warrants cannot be taken to the share premium account. However, as warrants are typically an equity instrument under FRS 25, the costs are taken to equity. [FRS 25 para 22]. They may be taken to the profit and loss reserve.

Implications of Shearer v Bercain Ltd

23.94 The tax case of Shearer v Bercain Ltd. questioned the construction of section 56 of the Companies Act 1948, which is now section 610 of the Companies Act 2006). [*Shearer v Bercain Ltd.* [1980] 3 AER 295]. The court held that where shares were issued at a premium, whether for cash or otherwise, section 56 of the 1948 Act required the premium to be carried to a share premium account in the issuing company's books, and the premium could be distributed only if the procedure for reducing capital was carried through.

23.95 This judgement gave authority to the interpretation of section 56 of the 1948 Act that required a company to set up a share premium account in any transaction where it acquired another company's shares in return for the allotment of its own shares and the fair value of the shares it acquired exceeded the nominal value of the shares it issued. Following the court's decision, the government introduced legislation that relieved companies, in certain circumstances, from the obligation to carry some, or all, of this share premium to a share premium account. The provisions that give this relief appear in sections 611 to 615 of the 2006 Act.

Merger relief

23.96 Merger relief is a statutory relief from recognising share premium when acquiring the shares of another company where certain conditions are met. It affects accounting for capital and reserves in the issuing company's separate financial statements. It does not affect the accounting treatment of acquisitions in consolidated financial statements, which is addressed in chapter 25.

23.97 Where the conditions for merger relief are satisfied, applying the relief is compulsory. This is based on the wording of section 612(2) of the 2006 Act, which states that *"if the equity shares in the issuing company allotted in pursuance of an arrangement in consideration for the acquisition or cancellation of equity shares in the other company are issued at a premium, section 610 does not apply to the premium on these shares"*.

23.98 For a company to obtain merger relief, a transaction must satisfy all of these conditions:

- A company (known either as the issuing company or the acquiring company) secures at least 90 per cent of the nominal value of each class of the equity share capital of another company (the acquired company) as a result of an arrangement.
- The arrangement provides for the allotment of equity shares in the issuing company. (Such allotment will normally be made to the acquired company's shareholders.)
- The consideration for the shares so allotted is either: the issue or the transfer to the issuing company of equity shares in the acquired company; or the cancellation of those the equity shares in the acquired company that the issuing company does not already hold.

[CA06 Sec 612(1)].

In this connection the following points should be noted:

- For this purpose, equity share capital is as defined in law — a company's issued share capital, excluding any part that (as regards dividends and capital) does not carry a right to participate beyond a specified amount in a distribution. [CA06 Secs 548, 616(1)].
- Any shares in the acquired company that are held by other companies in the same group as the issuing company or their nominees (parent companies, subsidiaries and fellow subsidiaries) are treated as being held by the issuing company. [CA06 Sec 613(5)].
- An 'arrangement' means any agreement, scheme or arrangement, including a company compromise with creditors and members or one sanctioned under section 110 of the Insolvency Act 1986 (liquidator accepting shares, etc., as consideration for the sale of the company's property). [CA06 Sec 616(1)].

- A company is treated as having secured a 90 per cent holding in another company as part of an arrangement, irrespective of whether or not it actually acquired all these shares under that arrangement. [CA06 Sec 613(2)(3)]. In determining whether a company has obtained a 90 per cent holding in another company, prior holdings are taken into account.
- The issuing company is regarded as having secured at least a 90 per cent equity holding in another company if it holds equity shares in that company of an aggregate nominal value equal to 90 per cent or more of the nominal value of that company's equity share capital (excluding any shares in that company held as treasury shares). [CA06 Sec 613(2)(3)].
- 'Company' includes any body corporate, except where reference is made to the issuing company (the acquiring company). [CA06 Sec 616(1)].
- In any provisions that relate to a company's acquisition of shares in another company, shares that a nominee of a company acquired are to be treated as having been acquired by the company itself. Similarly, the issue, or the allotment or the transfer of any shares to or by a company's nominee is to be regarded as if the shares were issued, or allotted or transferred to or by the company itself. [CA06 Sec 616(2)].
- The transfer of a company's shares includes the transfer of a right to be included in the company's register of members in respect of those shares. [CA06 Sec 616(3)].

23.99 These examples illustrate how the provisions of the Act apply:

Example 1

Company A issues equity shares and acquires 90% of company B's equity shares in a share-for-share exchange. This is the most obvious application of the provisions. Company A is entitled to merger relief.

Example 2

Company C owns 60% of company D's equity shares. The members of company D agree to cancel the equity shares that company C does not hold, in return for equity shares in company C. In this situation, also, company C is entitled to merger relief. There are two factors in this:

- Cancelling the remaining shares increases company C's 60% holding to 100% (over the 90% threshold).
- The consideration for the allotment of company C's equity shares is the cancellation of those of company D's shares that it does not already hold.

It is irrelevant that company C did not acquire the original 60% holding as part of the arrangement. Prior holdings are taken into account in determining whether company C has secured 90% of company D's equity share capital. Company C is only entitled to relief on the shares it issues in consideration for the cancellation of the shares in company D that it does not hold. It cannot write back any share premium that it set up on any shares it issued when it acquired the 60% holding.

Example 3

Company E acquires all of company F's 'A' equity shares. Company F also has 'B' equity shares in issue, but company E holds none of these. Company E is not entitled to merger relief, because it has not secured a 90% holding of each class of equity shares in company F. This applies even if the total 'B' shares represent 10% or less of the nominal value of company F's equity share capital.

Example 4

Company G acquires 95% of company H's equity shares. The consideration for these shares is, in equal proportions, equity shares in company G and cash. Company G is entitled to merger relief. There is no 'cash limit' criterion in the conditions for obtaining the relief, and there is no minimum proportion of the consideration that should consist of shares for merger relief to apply.

Application of merger relief

23.100 Where a transaction satisfies the conditions for merger relief, the relief extends to shares issued in consideration for the acquisition or the cancellation of the non-equity shares. [CA06 Sec 612(3)].

23.101 Non-equity shares are defined by the Act and not by accounting standards (see para 23.98).

23.102 As part of the same arrangement when it issues equity shares for the equity shares of the target, the issuing company may also allot non-equity shares for the acquisition or cancellation of the target's non-equity shares not held by the issuing company. In this case, the issuing company also takes merger relief on the non-equity shares that it issues.

Group reconstruction relief

23.103 Under the basic rule in section 610 of the 2006 Act, the issuing company should transfer any premium on the issue of its shares to a share premium account, not only where a 'third party' acquisition occurs, but also where a group reconstruction occurs. The Act provides some relief from but does not altogether dispense with, the requirement to recognise share premium when a group reconstruction occurs. [CA06 Sec 611]. Merger relief provisions are not available for group reconstructions. [CA06 Sec 612(4)]. Group reconstruction relief does not affect the accounting for group reconstructions in consolidated financial statements.

23.104 Group reconstruction relief applies under the following conditions:

- A wholly-owned subsidiary (the issuing company) allots some of its shares either to its holding company or to another wholly-owned subsidiary of its holding company. [CA06 Sec 611(1)].

- The allotment is in consideration for the transfer to it of any assets (other than cash) of its holding company or of another wholly-owned subsidiary of its holding company. [CA06 Sec 611(1)].
- 'Company' includes any body corporate except where reference is made to the issuing company (that is, the acquiring company). [CA06 Sec 616(1)].

23.105 Use of the relief is not compulsory. This is based on the wording of section 611(2) of the 2006 Act, which states that *"Where the shares in the issuing company allotted in consideration for the transfer are issued at a premium, the issuing company is not required by section 610 to transfer any amount in excess of the minimum premium value to the share premium account"*.

23.106 Group reconstruction relief only applies to the transfer of 'non-cash' assets. [CA06 Sec 611(1)]. If the assets being transferred include cash, it must be determined how many of the shares the issuing company has allotted for that cash. Share premium must be recognised for those shares.

23.107 For example, the allotment may be in consideration for the transfer to the issuing company of shares in another of its parent's subsidiaries (which is not necessarily wholly-owned). Diagrammatically, the situation before and after the reconstruction would be:

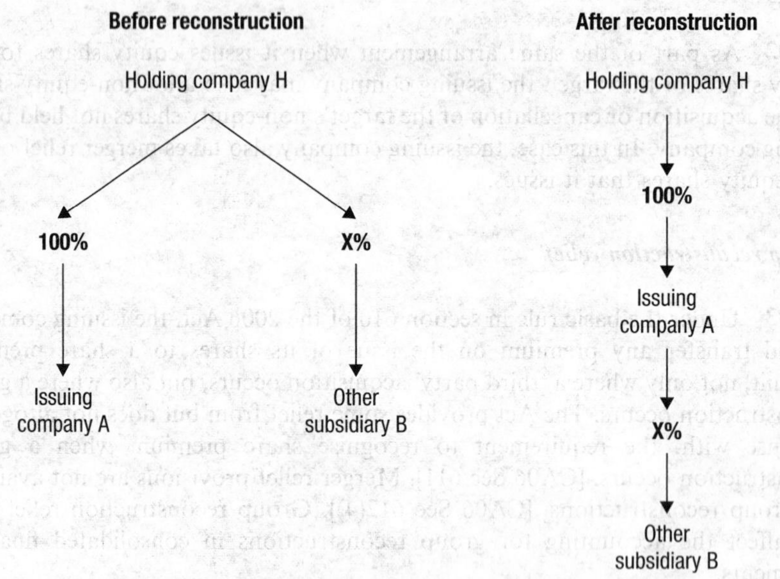

23.108 The issuing company need only transfer the 'minimum premium value' to the share premium account where the shares relating to the transfer are issued at a premium. [CA06 Sec 611(2)].

23.109 For this purpose, the following definitions apply:

- The 'minimum premium value' is the amount by which the base value of the consideration that the issuing company receives exceeds the aggregate nominal value of the shares that it allots in consideration for the transfer. [CA06 Sec 611(3)].
- The 'base value' of the consideration that the issuing company receives is the amount by which the base value of the assets transferred to it exceeds the base value of any liabilities that the issuing company assumes as part of that consideration. [CA06 Sec 611(4)].
- The 'base value of the assets transferred' is the lower of:
  - The cost to the transferor company of those assets.
  - The amount at which the assets are stated, immediately before the transfer, in the transferor company's accounting records.

  [CA06 Sec 611(5)].
- The 'base value of the liabilities' assumed is the amount at which those liabilities are stated, immediately before the transfer, in the transferor company's accounting records. [CA06 Sec 611(5)].

23.110 The following examples illustrate how the relief is calculated.

Example 1

Company Y allots 1,200 £1 ordinary shares to its holding company (company X). The consideration is valued at £5 per share. In consideration for this allotment, company X agrees to transfer to company Y its 75% holding in a fellow-subsidiary (company Z), which is considered to have a fair value of £6,000. Company X originally paid £3,000 for its 75% holding in company Z. Immediately before the reconstruction, the holding was stated in company X's accounting records at £2,000.

The base value of the shares in company Z is £2,000. This is the lower of the cost of the shares to company X (£3,000) and the amount at which the shares are stated in company X's accounting records (£2,000). The nominal value of the shares that company Y allots in respect of the transfer is £1,200. Therefore, the 'minimum premium value' is £800: the base value of the shares in company Z less the nominal value of the shares company Y allots.

Company Y must transfer £800 to the share premium account. Without the relief, the company would have had to transfer £4,800 to its share premium account: the difference between the value of £5 and the nominal value of £1 for each of the 1,200 shares.

Example 2

Company H has a wholly-owned subsidiary (company S). Company H owns land that originally cost £110,000 and is currently included in the company's accounting records at £175,000. The purchase of the land was partly financed by a loan of £40,000 that is secured on the land and is still outstanding. The land is currently valued at £200,000.

It is proposed that company S allots 25,000 of its ordinary £1 shares to company H in consideration for the transfer to it of the land that company H currently owns. Company S will also assume the liability for the loan of £40,000 secured on the land.

If the Act did not provide relief in respect of group reconstructions, company S would need to transfer £135,000 to a share premium account, calculated as follows:

	£	£
Nominal value of shares allotted		25,000
Fair value of consideration received:		
Current value of the land	200,000	
less: liability assumed	40,000	160,000
Premium on the shares allotted		135,000

If company S takes group reconstruction relief, it transfers £45,000 (which is the 'minimum premium value') to a share premium account calculated as follows:

	£
Base value of the land transferred (being the lower of the original cost of £110,000 and the amount at which it currently stands in company H's books, £175,000), less	110,000
Base value of the liability that company S assumes	40,000
Base value of the consideration that company S receives for the shares it allots	70,000
Nominal value of the shares that company S allots	25,000
Minimum premium value	45,00

Differences between merger and group reconstruction reliefs

23.111 With group reconstruction relief, the 'minimum premium' must be recognised in the share premium account. Merger relief is an absolute relief from recognising share premium. Furthermore, where it applies merger relief is compulsory, but group reconstruction relief is not.

23.112 In our view, crediting more to the share premium account than the 'minimum premium value' is unusual and potentially confusing to users of the financial statements. Users may infer that the excess over the 'minimum premium' is subject to the normal restrictions on the share premium account. [CA06 Sec 610]. We recommend that the excess premium over the 'minimum amount' in group reconstructions is credited to an 'other reserve', often called a 'merger reserve' or 'capital reserve', rather than to the statutory share premium account.

Carrying value of the investment

23.113 Legally, where a company acquires a subsidiary and qualifies for merger relief or group reconstruction relief, the cost of investment in the subsidiary can be recorded at either the nominal value plus any minimum premium or the fair value of the shares issued. [CA06 Sec 615].

23.114 The difference between the nominal value plus minimum premium amount and the fair value is credited to a merger reserve. The merger reserve should be treated as part of the company's equity. In the rare circumstances that the shares issued do not meet the definition of equity in FRS 25, the difference is included in the carrying amount of the financial liability and is not taken to equity. Accounting for investments is addressed in more detail in chapter 24.

Reduction of share capital

23.115 A company may wish to reduce its share capital for a variety of reasons, the most common ones being:

- Where the company has surplus capital in excess of its needs which it proposes to return to shareholders; this could be as part of reducing the scale of its trading operations.
- Where the company has a dividend block (that is, it is unable to pay a dividend or make other distributions, because it has negative or insufficient distributable reserves).
- Where the company needs to create distributable reserves to finance a redemption or purchase of its own shares or a dividend.
- Where the company wishes to render a non-distributable reserve distributable (for example, share premium or capital redemption reserve).
- Where the company wishes to release a liability to pay up capital. For example, it may have issued partly paid shares and wishes to cancel the unpaid amount.
- Where the company is undertaking a major reconstruction, such as a scheme of arrangement of which a court approved reduction forms part.

23.116 The circumstances listed above are not exhaustive. The majority of provisions dealing with the court approval procedure have been restated in the Companies Act 2006 (with minor amendments). The key changes under the Companies Act 2006 are, therefore, as follows:

- Private companies have the option of reducing their share capital either by applying to the court for approval or by issuing a solvency statement. [CA06 Sec 642].
- It is no longer necessary for a company to have express authority in its articles of association to reduce its share capital (unless there is a specific

prohibition or restriction in the articles). This is, however, expected to be subject to the transitional provisions that require public companies incorporated under the Companies Act 1985 and transitional companies incorporated under the transitional provisions of the Companies Act 2006 to have authority either (a) in the articles of association; or (b) granted by way of a special resolution before they can carry out a court approved reduction of share capital.

Public companies, however, still require court approval for a reduction of capital.

[The next paragraph is 23.118.]

23.118 A company may reduce its share capital under the Companies Act 2006 as follows:

- by extinguishing or reducing the liability on any unpaid share capital;
- by cancelling any paid-up share capital which is lost or not represented by available assets; or
- by repaying any surplus paid-up share capital.

[CA06 Sec 641(4)].

23.119 A company can, therefore, reduce its issued share capital, share premium account and capital redemption reserve as share premium and capital redemption reserves constitute share capital for the purpose of a reduction. However, other types of reserves such as a revaluation reserve cannot be reduced by way of a capital reduction, but could be capitalised into shares by a bonus issue of shares prior to the reduction.

23.120 A private company limited by shares can reduce its share capital using the new solvency statement procedure under the Companies Act 2006 from 1 October 2008, although it could also apply to the court as an alternative way of reducing its capital. The procedural requirements for a capital reduction by using the solvency statement procedure are as follows:

- all of the company's directors must make a 'solvency statement' in the prescribed form. If any directors are unable or unwilling to make this statement, the company will not be able to use the solvency statement procedure, unless the dissenting directors resign;
- a copy of the directors' solvency statement is circulated to all of the shareholders (where a written resolution is being proposed) or made available at the shareholders' meeting (where a shareholders' meeting is being convened to pass the special resolution referred to below); and
- within 15 days of the directors making the solvency statement, the company passes a special resolution to reduce its share capital.

[CA06 Sec 642].

23.121 The solvency statement must be in the prescribed form, stating the following:

- The date on which it is made.
- The name of each director (there is no requirement that the directors must all be in the same location for the purpose of making this statement).
- That the directors are of the opinion that:
  - as regards the company's situation at the date of the statement, there is no ground on which the company could then be found to be unable to pay or discharge its debts; and
  - if they intend to commence the winding-up of the company within 12 months of that date, that the company will be able to pay or discharge its debts in full within 12 months of the commencement of the winding-up, or, in any other cases, the company will be able to pay or discharge its debts as they fall due during the year immediately following that date.

23.122 In forming their opinions, the directors must take into account all of the company's liabilities, including contingent and prospective liabilities. [CA06 Sec 643(2)]. However, there is no requirement for the directors to prepare any statutory accounts for this purpose or to obtain an auditors' report.

23.123 Directors could face claims for breach of duty if a solvency statement is found to be incorrect and criminal penalties apply under the Companies Act 2006 if a statement is made without having reasonable grounds to do so. [CA06 Sec 643(4)]. Therefore, directors should seriously consider whether they need advice when carrying out their creditor review, particularly where the company has had a lengthy history or is an active trading company.

23.124 Under the new regime, private companies wishing to reduce their share capital may opt for the solvency statement procedure rather than applying to the court for the following reasons:

- The process will take less time to complete.
- It is likely to cost less as, for example, counsel will not need to represent the company at court.
- The company will have more flexibility concerning the levels of creditor protection it wishes to put in place and it is likely that this will be less costly than what might be imposed by the court.

23.125 However, there might be certain situations where the court approved procedure will be necessary or advisable for the following reasons:

- With the approval of the court it is possible to reduce a company's share capital to zero. In practice this is done as part of a scheme of arrangement where shares are immediately issued in replacement. Under the solvency statement procedure, a company must have at least one shareholder remaining after the proposed reduction holding at least one non-redeemable share.

- The court determines the appropriate level of creditor protection rather then the board. In complex creditor situations or where creditors are unknown, this will provide a greater level of protection for directors from actions for breach of duty.
- It may not be possible for all directors to sign the solvency statement or there may be directors who refuse to do so.
- Pursuant to the provisions of the Companies Act 1985, a court approved reduction always creates realised profits, while it is necessary to have qualifying consideration for the capital reduced by a company by other means (which, typically, involve a reduction of capital by an unlimited company by passing a special resolution). However, the Government has published regulations, 'The Companies (Reduction of Share Capital) Order 2008' SI 2008/1915, pursuant to the Companies Act 2006, which provides that a court approved reduction and a reduction by way of the solvency statement procedure both create realised profits. The advantage of a court approved procedure (over the other procedures) to reduce capital by creating distributable reserves from the capital reduction, therefore, no longer applies.

23.126 Shares presented as debt in accordance with FRS 25 are included in the financial statements at the carrying value of the liability. If the share capital or share premium is legally reduced, this does not affect the carrying value of the liability.

[The next paragraph is 23.129.]

23.129 It is important to note that if a distribution is contemplated after a reduction of capital, interim accounts of the company are likely to be required showing the company's financial position after the reduction to determine whether it is possible to make a distribution.

Capital redemption reserve

23.130 In the UK, private companies can acquire their own shares out of capital. Otherwise, under the Acts companies must maintain their capital after redeeming or acquiring their own shares or cancelling treasury shares. [CA06 Sec 733(1)]. Where a redemption or repurchase is wholly or partly funded specifically by a new or 'fresh' issue of shares and the proceeds of the fresh issue is less than the nominal value of the shares redeemed or purchased, the difference is transferred to the capital redemption reserve. [CA06 Sec 733(3)]. The capital of the company is still maintained. Some of the capital may then be represented by share premium and some by the capital redemption reserve.

[The next paragraph is 23.132.]

Capital contributions

23.132 Owner's contributions to an entity are usually made in cash, in consideration for shares. Contributions by a parent to a subsidiary may take other forms — for example, property, plant and equipment, equity shares in another entity, interest-free loans or the provision of services. Contributions from the owner that increase its investment in the entity are distinguished from transfers that arise from trading activities in the normal course of business.

23.133 Contributions are non-reciprocal in nature. In essence, they are a gift. They can be assets or services given or liabilities forgiven, without the transferee being obliged to give anything of benefit in exchange. Where a company receives consideration from one or more shareholders without a contractual obligation to repay it (a gift or a 'capital contribution'), this is an increase in equity. Typically, such amounts are recorded in a separate reserve, often known as the 'capital reserve'.

Distributions

23.134 Distributions by an entity to its equity instrument-holders are usually dividends or returns of capital such as share buybacks but may take other forms. Distributions are made at the entity's directors' discretion, often subject to shareholders' approval.

23.135 Distributions are non-reciprocal transfers, like contributions. For example, in substance the transfer of a subsidiary's trade and assets to a parent may be a distribution in kind (a dividend *in kind*).

23.136 The 2006 Act defines 'distribution' as any distribution of a company's assets to its shareholders (whether or not it is made in cash), other than a distribution that is made by way of any one of the following:

- The issue of either fully-paid or partly-paid bonus shares.
- The redemption or the purchase of any of the company's own shares, either out of capital, out of the proceeds of a fresh issue of shares, or out of unrealised profits in accordance with chapters 3, 4 or 5 of part 18 of the 2006 Act.
- The reduction of share capital by either of the following means:
  - Extinguishing or reducing the liability in respect of share capital that is not paid up.
  - Repaying paid-up share capital.
- The distribution of assets to shareholders on a winding-up.

[CA06 Sec 829(1)(2)].

Accounting for dividend

23.137 Distributions include dividends on equity shares and coupons on other instruments that are classified as equity. Distributions to holders of equity instruments are debited directly to equity, net of any related income tax benefit. [FRS 25 para 35]. The corresponding entry is made to cash if paid immediately, or recognised as a liability when settlement is to be made at a future date. Paragraph AG13 of FRS 25, 'Financial instruments: Presentation', states that *"an issuer of non-puttable ordinary shares assumes a liability when it formally acts to make a distribution and becomes legally obligated to the shareholders to do so"*. FRS 12, 'Provisions, contingent liabilities and contingent assets', states that where there is no obligation at the balance sheet date, a liability is not recorded. A history of paying dividends does not give rise to a contractual obligation nor a constructive obligation (see chapter 22).

23.138 If dividends are declared (that is, the dividends are appropriately authorised and no longer at the discretion of the entity) after the reporting period but before the financial statements are authorised for issue, the dividends are not recognised as a liability at the end of the reporting period because no obligation exists at that time. [FRS 21 para 13 (as amended)].

23.139 In the UK, directors can propose final dividends to be approved by members. Dividends become a legally binding liability when approved by members of a public company in general meeting or a private company's members' written resolution is passed, regardless of the date on which it is to be paid. A proposed unapproved final dividend is not a legal obligation to shareholders at the balance sheet date.

23.140 A company's articles may provide that directors can declare interim dividends. Such dividends are never a liability until their actual payment as the directors can revoke their resolution any time before paying it; no contractual obligation is created. For further discussion, see chapter 22.

23.141 Dividends on shares accounted for as financial liabilities are treated as interest expense and recognised on an accruals basis. Compound financial instruments that are divided into their liability and equity components, have a consequential effect on the amounts recognised as interest expense and distributions. For example, the net present value of the redemption amount of a mandatorily redeemable non-cumulative preference share whose dividends are payable at the discretion of the entity is recognised as a financial liability. The balance of the proceeds of issue of the shares is allocated to the equity component. The unwinding of the discount is recognised as an interest expense. The discretionary dividends on the shares relate to the equity component are recognised as distributions. [FRS 25 para AG37].

23.142 Many publicly-traded companies make arrangements for ordinary shareholders to elect to receive their dividends in additional ordinary shares rather than in cash – a scrip or stock dividend. A short-term advantage of this is that it improves the company's cash position. The shares are fully paid up out of the company's profits. Such dividends are recognised in the financial statements at the amount of the cash alternative. The notes to the financial statements should give a full explanation of the situation. Some scrip or stock dividends are offered without a cash alternative; the issue of such shares is accounted for as a capitalisation or bonus issue of shares and not a distribution.

Unlawful dividends

23.143 If dividends are paid unlawfully the accounting for such dividends and their repayments follows a liability and receivable approach.

23.144 If the recipient is obliged to repay a dividend, the entity recognises a receivable provided that receipt is sufficiently certain. The receivable is recognised in the period in which it arises, not by reversing the original transaction through opening reserves. If the recipient is not obliged to repay the dividend but has nevertheless agreed to do so, the repayment is accounted for in the period in which it occurs.

23.145 In either case, the entity discloses the dividend and the proposed remedy.

23.146 Shareholders who receive an unlawful distribution are liable to repay it to the company if, at the time it was received, they knew, or had reasonable grounds to believe, that it was made in contravention of the Act. [CA06 Sec 847(1)(2)]. This provision is without prejudice to any other liability of shareholders to repay distributions that have been unlawfully made to them. [CA06 Sec 847(3)(4)]. If the directors make an unlawful distribution they may be in breach of their fiduciary duties to the company and, therefore, may be personally liable to repay the company, even if the director is not a shareholder. In *Bairstow v Queens Moat Houses plc and Others ([2000] 1 BCLC 549)* it was held that a director who authorised the payment of an unlawful dividend in breach of his duty as *quasi* trustee would be liable to repay such dividend if he:

- knew the dividends were unlawful (whether or not that actual knowledge amounted to fraud);
- knew the facts that established the impropriety of the payments, even though he was unaware that such impropriety rendered the payment unlawful;
- in all the circumstances knew all the facts that rendered the payments unlawful; and
- ought to have known, as a reasonably competent and diligent director that the payments were unlawful.

23.147 More recently, in *HM Revenue & Customs v Holland and Another [2008] EWHC 2200 (Ch)*, the High Court held that, where a company paid dividends out of profits that would not have been available had the directors made proper provision for tax, and the directors were aware that such provision should have been made, the dividends are an unlawful distribution of profits for which the directors might be personally liable.

23.148 The 2006 Act does not impose criminal penalties on directors for making unlawful distributions.

23.149 Under common law, a company cannot make a distribution out of capital. Thus the directors should consider at the time of proposing a distribution and at the time it is made whether the company has incurred losses subsequent to the balance sheet date to which the last 'relevant accounts' were prepared that have eroded its profits available for distribution.

23.150 If a company goes into liquidation after making an unlawful distribution, the liquidator could apply to the court for an order to compel the directors to compensate the company for having misapplied its property.

Accounting for distributions in kind

23.151 A company may distribute non-cash assets. The company debits distributions to its equity instrument-holders to equity. [FRS 25 para 35]. FRS 25 doesn't specify the amount to be debited: should the paying company measure the distribution at the book value or fair value of the assets transferred? The book value and fair value of cash and short-term monetary assets are normally close and the distinction between book and fair value treatments, therefore, does not arise. Where the asset being distributed is carried at fair value, its book and fair value are the same. The position is less clear when the asset to be distributed is a non-monetary asset, such as an investment in a subsidiary or a property, carried at cost. Should the paying company use the historical cost amount or its fair value to measure the amount of the distribution?

23.152 Traditionally, book values of the assets being distributed have been used to measure the value of the dividend. For example, in a demerger of a subsidiary, the parent company may record a demerger dividend *in kind* at an amount equal to the investment's book value and the group may record the same dividend *in kind* at the amount of the net assets of the subsidiary at the date of the demerger.

23.153 Section 846 of the 2006 Act provides that where the non-cash asset to be distributed has been included in the relevant accounts, and part of the amount at which it is stated represents an unrealised profit, that profit is treated as realised for the purpose of the distribution. [CA06 Sec 846(1)(2)]. For example, this applies when the asset has been revalued and a revaluation surplus has been taken to the revaluation reserve. There is nothing in section 846 to require a company to revalue a non-cash asset prior to distributing it *in kind* or to require the distribution to be recorded at anything other than the asset's book value. Hence, if a company wishes to distribute *in kind* a non-cash asset with a historical cost of £100,000 that is carried in the relevant accounts at a revalued amount of £130,000, the surplus of £30,000 is treated as realised for the purpose and only £100,000 of other realised profits are required to make the distribution. If, however, the revaluation surplus has been capitalised and is no longer available, all of the £130,000 would have to be covered by other realised profits.

23.154 The company's articles must contain a power to make distributions *in kind* (non-cash distributions). For companies following Table A, article 105 contains this power. It requires the dividend to be approved at a general meeting. [SI 1985/805 as amended by SI 2007/2541, SI 2007/2826, SI 2008/739]. The dividend is declared as a cash amount. The Companies (Model Articles) Regulations 2008, made under the Companies Act 2006 set out model articles of association for the three main types of company – a private company limited by shares, a private company limited by guarantee and a public company. Such companies do not have to adopt the model articles, but they will automatically be the articles for those companies that are formed under the 2006 Act on or after 1 October 2009, unless the company chooses to adopt its own tailor-made articles in place of all or part of the model articles.

23.155 A dividend or distribution *in kind* from a subsidiary is an unrealised profit in the hands of the parent (even where there is a cash alternative) unless the asset distributed is qualifying consideration. If the parent distributes this non-cash asset, then provided that the unrealised profit was recorded in the parent's relevant accounts, the parent treats the distribution *in kind* as a realised profit for onward distribution purposes. [Tech 02/10 para 9.33; CA06 Sec 846].

Transfers at undervalue

23.156 Section 846 of the 2006 Act also applies where a company makes a distribution arising from the sale, transfer or other disposition by it of a non-cash asset. That is likely to be the case when the transaction involves a transfer at undervalue, which is where section 845 of the 2006 Act also applies.

23.157 Section 845 clarifies when a transfer of a non-cash asset to a member amounts to a distribution. Before the 2006 Act came into force, the legal position was as set out in *Aveling Barford v Perion Ltd and others [1989] BCLC 626*. The plaintiff company sold a property at considerably less than its fair value to a company controlled by the company's sole beneficial shareholder when it had no distributable reserves.

23.158 The *Aveling Barford* case confirmed that where a company undertakes a transaction for a consideration less than its fair value (an 'undervalue') when the company has no distributable reserves, this is an unauthorised return of capital. Shareholders cannot validate the transaction by approval or ratification.

23.159 The *Aveling Barford* case decided nothing about the situation where a company that has distributable profits makes an intra-group transfer of non-cash assets at book value. However, there was a concern that a transfer at book value may contain an element of undervalue and thus the transaction would constitute a distribution. This would require the company to have distributable profits sufficient to cover the difference between the asset's fair and book values. This often caused companies to abandon a transfer or to structure it in a more complex manner.

23.160 To assist companies in this predicament, section 845 of the 2006 Act has been written to facilitate such transactions by providing that the amount of any distribution consisting of, or arising from, the sale, transfer or other disposition by a company of a non-cash asset to a member of the company is measured by reference to that asset's book value and not its fair value. The company must have profits available for distribution at the time of the transaction and, the amount of the distribution must be determined in accordance with section 845. If these conditions are met, the company can make the distribution without contravention of Part 23 of the 2006 Act. [CA06 Sec 845(1)(a)(b)].

23.161 Accordingly, if an asset is transferred for a consideration not less than its book value, the amount of the distribution is zero. However, for a transfer at less than its book value, the amount of the distribution is equal to the shortfall and must be covered by profits available for distribution. [CA06 Sec 845(2)(a)(b)].

Example

Company A has an investment property that has a book value of £1,000,000, comprising cost of £800,000 and a revaluation surplus of £200,000. The directors of Company A decide to sell this property to its parent for £550,000 at a time when Company A has distributable profits of £400,000. Is this legal under the 2006 Act?

Yes. The shortfall between the sales price and the book value is £450,000; Company A has distributable profits of £400,000. However, £200,000 of the amount at which the asset is stated in the financial statements is an unrealised profit which, by virtue of section 846 of the 2006 Act, is regarded as realised. Total realised profits available for distribution are, therefore, £600,000. This covers the shortfall of £450,000.

Deficit on profits available for distribution

23.162 Section 845 of the 2006 Act does not disturb the position in the *Aveling Barford* case where the company has no profits available for distribution and makes a distribution by way of a transfer of assets at an undervalue. This is an unlawful distribution contrary to Part 23 of the 2006 Act.

23.163 However, careful consideration of section 845(3) of, and paragraph 1156 of the Explanatory Notes to, the 2006 Act leads to a conclusion that a transfer at an undervalue may be possible where a company has no profits available for distribution. It would seem that this is the case where the transfer is made for an amount that exceeds the book value of the asset to be transferred by at least the amount of the deficit on profits available for distribution plus £1. Directors wishing to use section 845(3) where of their company has zero, or a deficit of, profits available for distribution should take legal advice before committing to the transaction, as the above analysis and the illustrative example below are subject to debate as to the appropriate reading of the section.

Example

Company A has an investment property that has a book value of £1,000,000. The directors of company A decide to sell this property to its parent for £1,500,000 at a time when company A has a deficit of profits available for distributable of £499,000. Is this legal under the 2006 Act?

Based on the wording of section 845(3), Yes. The excess of the sales price over the book value is £500,000 and is added to Company A's profits available for the distribution, which creates a positive balance of £1,000. [CA06 Sec 845(3)]. Applying section 845(3) solely for the purpose of this transaction, the balance is treated as available for distribution. The sales price is in excess of the book value of the investment property and thus the amount of the distribution is deemed to be zero. [CA06 Sec 845(2)(a)]. Hence, the transfer can be made. The balance carried forward of £1,000 is not available for distribution unless Company A receives 'qualifying consideration' for the sale or the consideration received becomes qualifying in due course.

23.164 A transfer of an asset at undervalue will *prima facie* involve a breach of duty by the directors and the transferor company. This might not be so, if, for example, the transferor and transferee are UK companies wholly-owned within the same group, the transferor company is permitted to dispose of assets for such a consideration as is thought fit, the shareholders of the transferor company approve the transfer and the transaction does not place the solvency of any of the parties to it in any doubt.

23.165 Typical transactions not undertaken at market value include the following:

- The sale of an asset at an undervalue.
- The purchase of an asset at an overvalue — for example, the transfer of a subsidiary intra-group without warranties and indemnities normally given on third-party sales and purchases.
- Book/tax written down value transfers where these do not correspond to market value.
- Sale for debt in certain circumstances — for example, where the debt is not repayable on demand and does not bear interest, or where the purchaser does not have a realistic prospect of settling the debt.
- Capitalising or subordinating debt.
- Waivers of debt.
- Capital contributions — UK company law is silent about such contributions, but essentially these are gifts.
- Interest-free loans or loans with excessive rates of interest.
- Non-payment for the surrender of group relief.

- Assumption of an inherent tax liability under the Taxation of Capital Gains Act 1992, section 171 — when an asset is transferred by one member of a capital gains group to another member — the transferee inherits the transferor's base cost and, therefore, is liable to corporation tax on the increase in asset's value that accrued during the transferor's period of ownership.

23.166 A transaction not at market value may have one or more of these further company law consequences, as it may be:

- *Ultra vires.*
- In breach of the directors' fiduciary duties and their duty to act in the best interest of their company.
- A fraud on the minority.

23.167 The company law consequences depend on the transaction's circumstances. Section 678 of the 2006 Act prohibits public companies from giving financial assistance for the acquisition of their own shares. This prohibition does not apply to a lawful dividend. [CA06 Sec 681(2)(a)(i)].

23.168 Although the rules on financial assistance no longer apply to private companies from 1 October 2008, nevertheless, the following general company law principles still need to be taken into account:

- the transaction must be in the best interests of the company (*"likely to promote the success of the company for the benefit of its members"*); and
- the transaction must not breach the rules on distributions or otherwise constitute an illegal reduction in the company's capital.

23.169 For public and private companies, therefore, transactions not at market value may be questioned if they are carried out in connection with the acquisition of shares. Section 238 of the Insolvency Act 1986 applies if an administration order is made in relation to the company or the company goes into liquidation and permits the liquidator or administrator to apply to the court to have a transaction at undervalue (which would include the payment of a dividend) set aside.

Treasury shares

23.170 FRS 25 paragraph 33 defines treasury shares as re-acquired own equity instruments. This definition is wider than equity shares and includes share options. Law may determine whether entities may re-acquire their shares and hold them in treasury. Management should also consider the consequences of any statutory and common law rules on capital maintenance and distributions.

23.171 Sections 724 to 732 of the Companies Act 2006 set out the rules relating to treasury shares, which are effective from 1 October 2009.

23.172 Where a limited company purchases its own shares out of distributable profits it can, provided that the shares are 'qualifying shares', elect to hold the shares as treasury shares or dispose of them provided certain conditions are met. This means that the shares once purchased are not cancelled, but remain in existence.

23.173 The law in respect of treasury shares applies to all qualifying shares, irrespective of whether they are classified as liabilities or equity.

23.174 'Qualifying shares' are effectively quoted ordinary shares. They are defined as shares that:

- are included in the official list maintained by the FSA (that is, listed on the Main Market of the London Stock Exchange or on the PLUS-listed market);
- are traded on AIM (but not PLUS-quoted);
- are officially listed in another EEA State; or
- are traded on a regulated market established in an EEA State.

[CA06 Sec 724(2)].

23.175 For the purpose of the last bullet point above, regulated securities markets in the UK include:

- LIFFE.
- London Stock Exchange.
- ICE Futures Europe.
- EDX.
- The London Metal Exchange Limited.
- PLUS Stock Exchange.

23.176 Private companies that do not have traded shares cannot, therefore, take advantage of these provisions.

23.177 Once the shares have been purchased the company may: continue to hold all or some of them; or sell them or transfer them, to an employee share scheme. If the company holds the shares its name must be entered in the register of members as the holder of the shares. [CA06 Sec 724(4)].

23.178 Companies that acquire shares other than 'qualifying shares' (for example, shares that are not traded, such as unlisted redeemable preference shares) must cancel those shares, following the Acts' rules for the acquisition of own shares.

23.179 Where a company purchases qualifying shares out of distributable profits in accordance with section 724(1) of the 2006 Act, it may:

- hold some or all of the shares in treasury; or
- deal with any or all of them, at any time, as follows:
  - sell the shares for cash;
  - transfer the shares for the purposes of, or pursuant to, an employees' share scheme; or
  - cancel the shares.

[CA06 Secs 724(3), 727(1), 729(1)].

Conditions applying to treasury shares

23.180 In this section, 'treasury shares' mean those qualifying shares held by a company that were (or are treated as having been) purchased by it in circumstances in which section 724 of the 2006 Act applies and have been held by the company continuously since they were purchased. [CA06 Sec 724(5)].

23.181 Where a company has only one class of shares, the nominal value of treasury shares held must not exceed 10 per cent of the nominal value of the company's issued share capital. If the company has more than one class of shares, the nominal value of treasury shares of any class must not exceed 10 per cent of the nominal value of that class of shares. If the limit is exceeded, the excess shares must be disposed of or cancelled within 12 months. [CA06 Sec 725].

23.182 The company may not exercise any rights over the treasury shares, including voting rights. No dividend or any other distribution of the company's assets (including on winding up) may be paid to the company in respect of the treasury shares it holds. Rights over bonus issues and redemption rights (if the shares are redeemable) remain. [CA06 Sec 726].

23.183 A company may not purchase its shares if as a result of the purchase all of its shares would either be held in treasury or be redeemable. [CA06 Sec 690(2)].

Sale or cancellation of treasury shares

23.184 A company may at any time sell treasury shares for a cash consideration or transfer them into an employees' share scheme. [CA06 Sec 727]. Cash is defined as one of the following:

- Cash (including foreign currency) received by the company.
- A cheque received by the company in good faith that the directors have no reason for suspecting will not be paid.
- A release of a liability of the company for a liquidated sum.

- An undertaking to pay cash to the company within 90 days of the date on which the company agrees to sell the shares.
- A payment by any other means giving a present or future entitlement (of the company or a person acting on the company's behalf) to a payment, or credit equivalent to payment, in cash.

[CA06 Sec 727(2)(a)-(e)].

23.185 The Companies (Shares, Share Capital and Authorised Minimum) Regulations 2008 that came into force on 1 October 2009 contain a regulation that removes uncertainties surrounding other settlement methods, such as the CREST assured payment system. [CA06 Sec 727(3)]. It allows the definition to be updated automatically should other settlement systems be identified or developed in the future by linking it to SI 2001/3755, 'Uncertificated Securities Regulations 2001' (as amended).

23.186 Where treasury shares are sold, if the proceeds are equal to or less than the company's original purchase price, the proceeds are a realised profit. For example, if the original cost of the purchase was £100 and the treasury shares are sold for £60, all of the £60 is credited to distributable profits as a realised profit. If the proceeds exceed the purchase price, the excess over the purchase price is transferred to the share premium account. The realised profit arising on the sale of the shares cannot exceed the purchase cost. For example, if the original cost is £100 and the treasury shares are sold for £120, £100 is credited to distributable profits and £20 is credited to share premium account. Distributable reserves can be restored to their original amount, but cannot be increased overall.

23.187 The purchase price paid by the company for the shares is determined using a weighted average price. If the shares were allotted to the company as fully paid bonus shares, the purchase price is deemed to be nil. [CA06 Sec 731].

23.188 If a company cancels treasury shares, it reduces the amount of its issued share capital by the nominal value of the cancelled shares. [CA06 Sec 729(4)]. The nominal value of the cancelled treasury shares is transferred to a capital redemption reserve. [CA06 Sec 733(1)(2)(4)]. For a company that has an authorised share capital the cancellation does not reduce that amount. [CA06 Sec 729(4)]. Details must be filed with the Registrar of Companies within 28 days of the cancellation together with a statement of capital. [CA06 Sec 731(1)(5)].

23.189 If shares held as treasury shares cease to be 'qualifying shares' (for example, if the company delists completely), the company is required to cancel them immediately. This does not apply when shares are only suspended from listing or trading. [CA06 Sec 729].

23.190 Where a company purchases its own shares to be held as treasury shares and subsequently has transactions in those shares, it must meet certain formalities under the Companies Acts by making returns to the Registrar of Companies. These returns are made at the time of the purchase and the subsequent transactions. [CA06 Secs 707, 708, 728].

Listing Rule requirements

23.191 Listed companies are subject to further restrictions, set out in the UKLA Listing Rules. The principal requirements on treasury shares are:

- Sales and transfers of shares out of treasury cannot be made during a prohibited period, subject to the exemption in LR 12.2.1: *"The company has in place a buy back programme managed by an independent third party which makes its trading decisions in relation to the company's securities independently of, and uninfluenced by, the company"*.
- Capitalisation issues and sales, transfers and cancellations of treasury shares must be notified.
- The discount to market price at which shares can be sold for cash out of treasury is limited in certain situations.

These restrictions are discussed in the following paragraphs.

23.192 During a 'prohibited period' treasury shares cannot be sold for cash or transferred for the purposes of, or pursuant to, an employees' share scheme. A prohibited period is when a company is in a close period or any matter that constitutes inside information exists. [LR 12.6.1 R]. It does not apply to:

- Transfers of treasury shares arising from the operation of an employees' share scheme where the transfer facilitates dealings that do not fall within the provisions of the Model Code (section 2(h) to (k)) annexed to Listing Rule 9.
- Sales or transfers by the company of treasury shares (other than equity shares) of a class whose price or value would not be likely to be significantly affected by the publication of the information giving rise to the prohibited period. [LR 12.6.2 R – as amended by FSA 2007/40 40 – Listing, Prospectus and Disclosure Rules (Miscellaneous Amendments) Instrument 2007].
- A company that has a buy-back programme managed by an independent third party that makes its trading decisions in relation to the company's securities independently of, and uninfluenced by, the company. [LR 12.2.1R].

Buying back shares in prohibited (close) periods

23.193 The exemption in Listing Rule 12.2.1R from the general prohibition on buying back shares in close periods is very useful for companies that need a full 12-month period in order to complete an announced buy-back programme (although shorter periods are also common), or to gain maximum pricing flexibility for a buy-back. Listed companies can use this permission to buy back shares in their close period by giving the company's broker an authority, before a close period starts, to continue buying shares during the close period. The purchases should be made following the annual buy back authority passed at most companies' AGMs. No new authority is generally needed.

23.194 As companies cannot control these independent programmes, directors should be satisfied with the authority they invest in their broker. The accounting for these types of contracts with banks and brokers is governed by paragraph 23 of FRS 25.

Treasury shares and capitalisation issues

23.195 If a company is allotted shares as part of a capitalisation issue by virtue of holding treasury shares, it must notify a Regulatory Information Service as soon as possible (no later than 07:30 am on the following business day). The notification must include:

- The date of the allotment.
- The number of shares allotted.
- How many shares allotted have been cancelled and how many are held as treasury shares.
- Where shares allotted are being held as treasury shares:
  - The total number of treasury shares of each class held by the company following the allotment.
  - The number of shares of each class that the company has in issue, less the total number of treasury shares of each class held by the company following the allotment.

[LR 12.6.3 R].

23.196 Similar notification to a Regulatory Information Service is required where treasury shares are either sold for cash, cancelled or transferred for the purposes of (or pursuant to) an employees' share scheme. The highest and lowest sale or transfer price paid must be notified where relevant. [LR 12.6.4 R].

Other Listing Rules requirements on treasury shares

23.197 Where a company makes an issue out of treasury shares, any discount on the price of those shares is limited to 10 per cent of the middle market price of those shares. [LR 9.5.10 R].

23.198 This prohibition does not apply if the issue is made under a pre-existing general authority to disapply section 561 of the 2006 Act (Offers to shareholders on a pre-emptive basis). [LR 9.5.10 R(3)(b)].

[The next paragraph is 23.200.]

Accounting treatment for the purchase of own shares (including treasury shares)

23.200 If an entity re-acquires its own equity instruments, those instruments should be deducted from equity. [FRS 25 para 33].

23.201 FRS 25 requires that subject to paragraph 23 of the standard:

- No gain or loss should be recognised in profit or loss on the purchase, sale, issue or cancellation of an entity's own equity instruments.
- Consideration paid or received for the purchase or sale of an entity's own equity instruments should be recognised directly in equity.

[FRS 25 para 33].

23.202 Under the Act, a company is permitted to hold qualifying shares in treasury (subject to meeting the conditions described in para 23.180 onwards) where these have been purchased out of distributable profits. Therefore, when these shares are purchased there is a charge to distributable reserves, normally the profit and loss reserve. As a result, the company should not show a separate debit reserve on the face of the balance sheet as this would give a misleading view of distributable profits.

23.202.1 The treatment of treasury shares described in the previous paragraph appears to contradict the requirements of the balance sheet formats set out in Schedule 1 to SI 2008/410, 'The Large and Medium-sized Companies and Groups (Accounts and Reports) Regulations 2008'. These formats include subheadings for 'own shares' in both fixed and current assets, which suggests that investments in own shares are to be presented as assets. This is unfortunate, as FRS 25 requires treasury shares to be deducted in arriving at shareholders' funds. However, it is hard to ignore the requirements of the formats. Any amount shown separately on the face of the balance sheet as investment in own shares would need to be presented in accordance with those requirements. Accordingly, in our view, to comply with FRS 25 the amount deducted in arriving at shareholders' funds should not be presented as a separate item on the face of the balance sheet, but should be deducted from the profit and loss reserve.

23.202.2 Where a company uses an ESOP trust to purchase its shares, these shares are also reported as a deduction from shareholders' funds in accordance with UITF 38, although the distributable profits position is less straightforward (see Tech 02/10 para 7.1 onwards). However, in our view, own shares held in an ESOP trust should also be presented as a deduction from the profit and loss reserve rather than as a separate component of equity to avoid any inconsistency with the balance sheet formats as explained above.

23.202.3 Irrespective of whether own shares are held directly by the company as treasury shares, or in an ESOP trust, disclosure should be made of the amount of own shares held. [FRS 25 para 34].

23.203 Often entities place contracts with brokers or banks to acquire own shares on their behalf. Such contracts fall within paragraph 23 of FRS 25, which states that *"a contract that contains an obligation for an entity to purchase its own equity instruments for cash or another financial asset gives rise to a financial liability for the present value of the redemption amount (for example, for the present value of the forward repurchase price, option exercise price or other redemption amount). This is the case even if the contract itself is an equity instrument"*. The entity accounts for the acquisition of the 'treasury shares' at the inception of the contract, not when the shares are paid for. [FRS 26 para 14].

23.204 When paragraph 23 of FRS 25 applies to a contract containing an option or obligation, such as a forward contract, to re-acquire an entity's own shares for cancellation or to be held in treasury, there may well be gains or losses to be recognised in profit or loss.

23.205 The gains or losses arise because the financial liability is measured at the present value of the acquisition or repurchase price or redemption amount. The corresponding debit is to equity. The financial liability is subsequently measured in accordance with FRS 26. If the contract specifies the number rather than the value of the shares to be acquired, the financial liability is initially measured using an estimate of the share price it will have to pay. The best estimate of the share price is the price at inception of the contract. The financial liability is subsequently adjusted to reflect movements in the share price. There will, therefore, be gains or losses to be recognised in profit or loss, as paragraph AG8 of FRS 26 requires the carrying value of financial liabilities to be adjusted through the profit or loss account for changes to actual and estimated cash flows.

23.206 If the contract caps the amount that may be spent, the financial liability is measured at that maximum amount discounted for the time value of money for the period between the inception of the contract and the date of payment. In this case, the effect on profit or loss may be limited to unwinding the discount.

23.207 When the liability is recognised, the corresponding debit is to equity. If the contract expires without delivery or full delivery, the amount of the financial liability attributable to the undelivered shares is reclassified to equity, reversing the original entry. [FRS 25 para 23].

23.208 The entity has a contractual obligation to purchase its own equity instruments even if the obligation to purchase, re-acquire or redeem is conditional on the counterparty exercising its rights (for example, a written put option giving the counterparty the right to sell an entity's own equity instruments to the entity for a fixed price). The entity recognises a financial liability for the present value of the purchase, re-acquisition or redemption amount. [FRS 25 para 23].

23.209 The FRS 25 paragraph 23 accounting entries anticipate what happens when the shares are actually purchased. The question arises as to whether the debit to equity consumes distributable profits at inception of the contract. Tech 02/10, 'Guidance on the determination of realised profits and losses in the context of distributions under the Companies Act 2006', makes it clear that, from a legal perspective, the advance recognition of a capital transaction does not consume distributable profits as that only happens when it is paid. [Tech 02/10 paras 6.10 — 6.15]. However, the initial debit to equity restricts the ability of public companies to make distributions by the amount of the debit through the 'net asset test'. [CA06 Sec 831; Tech 02/10 para 6.31]. As there is no similar test for a private company, the debit to equity can be ignored until the shares are actually purchased, reacquired or redeemed by the company.

23.210 Directly attributable costs of an equity transaction are accounted for as a deduction from equity. [FRS 25 para 35]. Expenses directly relating to the purchase of treasury shares are treated as part of the overall cost of purchase and, like the purchase cost are deducted from equity. [FRS 25 para 37]. The treatment of transaction costs of equity instruments is addressed in 'Manual of Accounting – Financial instruments'.

23.211 Own equity instruments may be acquired and held in treasury by the entity or by other members of the consolidated group. In consolidated financial statements, subsidiaries' interests in the parent's equity instruments are deducted from equity. [FRS 25 para 33]. This applies to all such shareholdings, including those held by subsidiaries that carry on a business of dealing in securities (see chapter 24). In the individual financial statements of a subsidiary that holds shares in its parent, such shares are treated as an available-for-sale financial asset or a financial asset measured at fair value through profit and loss. 'Treasury shares' accounting does not apply, as these are not 'own shares' for the subsidiary.

23.212 Under UK law, a subsidiaries and subsidiary undertakings cannot become a member of its parent company. Any allotment or transfer of shares in a company to its subsidiary is void. [CA06 Sec 136(1)]. Subsidiaries for its purpose are those defined in section 1159 of the 2006 Act and subsidiary undertakings are those defined in section 1162(2) of the 2006 Act. There are exemptions for subsidiaries that carry on a business dealing in securities. [CA06 Sec 141(1)(2)].

23.213 A company that is a subsidiary undertaking by virtue of section 1162(4) of the 2006 Act (power to exercise, or actually exercises, dominant influence etc.) may hold its parent company shares. This is because such a subsidiary undertaking is not also a subsidiary for legal purposes. Consequently, companies captured as subsidiaries by SIC 12, 'Consolidation – special purpose entities' (including EBTs and ESOPs) may acquire and hold their parent undertaking's shares. These are 'treasury shares' in their parent undertaking's consolidated financial statements.

23.214 Paragraph 33 of FRS 25 also applies to 'treasury shares' sold, issued or cancelled in connection with employee share option plans, employee share purchase plans and all other share-based payment arrangements. [FRS 25 para 4(f)(ii)]. These are addressed in chapter 12.

23.215 As, under the Act, treasury shares are purchased out of distributable profits, the cost of their purchase is normally charged to the retained profits reserve. The company does not also show a separate debit reserve on the face of the balance sheet, as this would be double-counting. The amount of treasury shares held is disclosed separately.

23.216 A company can cancel treasury shares, sell them for cash or transfer them for the purposes of an employees' share scheme. The accounting treatment for these various scenarios is considered in the examples below. Examples 2 to 4 are based on the purchase of treasury shares in example 1.

Example 1 – purchase of treasury shares

Company A (a listed company) has 1,000,000 £1 ordinary shares originally issued at a premium of £9. It buys back 20,000 shares when their market value is £40 per share. The purchase is made out of distributable profits. The company holds the shares in treasury. The company does not reduce its issued share capital; instead it reduces its distributable profits by the consideration paid for the shares (that is, 20,000 × £40 = £800,000):

	Before purchase £'000	Purchase £'000	After purchase £'000
Net assets other than cash	20,000		20,000
Cash	5,000	(800)	4,200
	25,000	(800)	24,200
Share capital	1,000		1,000
Share premium	9,000		9,000
Capital	10,000		10,000
Distributable reserves	15,000	(800)	14,200
	25,000	(800)	24,200

In the notes to its financial statements, company A should explain that "*20,000 £1 ordinary shares with an aggregate nominal value of £20,000 were purchased during the period and are held in treasury. Distributable reserves have been reduced by £800,000, being the consideration paid for these shares*".

The debit to distributable reserves of £800,000 is a realised loss.

Example 2 – cancellation of treasury shares

Company A subsequently cancels all the shares held as treasury shares. It must reduce its issued share capital by the aggregate nominal value of the cancelled shares (£20,000) and, in accordance with the Act, transfer this amount to a capital redemption reserve (CRR). This is shown below:

	After purchase £'000	Maintain capital £'000	After cancellation £'000
Net assets other than cash	20,000		20,000
Cash	4,200		4,200
	24,200		24,200
Share capital	980	(20)	980
Share premium	9,000		9,000
Capital redemption reserve		20	20
Capital	10,000	–	10,000
Distributable reserves	14,200		14,200
	24,200	–	24,200

Example 3 – Sale of treasury shares

Following on from example 1, company A subsequently sells all the treasury shares for, say, £55 per share (total sales proceeds of £55 × 20,000 = £1,100,000). The sales proceeds are treated as a realised profit up to the amount of the purchase price of £40 per share, £800,000. As the sales proceeds exceed the purchase price, the excess over the purchase price ((£55-£40) × 20,000 = £300,000) is transferred to the share premium account (see para 23.54.14):

	After purchase £'000	Sale of shares £'000	After sale £'000
Net assets other than cash	20,000		20,000
Cash	4,200	1,100	5,300
	24,200	1,100	25,300
Share capital	1,000		1,000
Share premium	9,000	300	9,300
Capital	10,000	300	10,300
Distributable reserves	14,200	800	15,000
	24,200	1,100	25,300

Example 4 – Transfer for the purposes of an employees' share scheme

Following on from example 1, company A sells all the treasury shares to its ESOP trust for cash. The accounting for the sale in company A's individual financial statements follows that in example 3 above. However, in company A's consolidated financial statements they appear as a debit within consolidated equity. The ESOP trust is considered to be company A's subsidiary. Paragraph 33 of FRS 25 applies to the presentation of treasury shares held by members of the consolidated group.

Awards of the shares to employees are accounted for under FRS 20, 'Share-based payment'. If treasury shares are used to satisfy an employee share award (but without being transferred into an ESOP trust), the award is also accounted for under FRS 20. This is covered in chapter 12. Chapter 12 also addresses the treatment of any consideration received for shares transferred to an ESOP trust.

23.217 Where shares classified as financial liabilities are re-acquired the financial liability is removed provided the derecognition criteria are met (see 'Manual of Accounting – Financial instruments'). The accounting must also reflect any legal capital maintenance requirements of UK law.

Entities without shares

23.218 Entities such as partnerships and trusts do not have share capital. If they have instruments that meet the accounting definition of equity, the same accounting considerations apply for these instruments as for instruments that are legally shares and classified as equity.

Reserves arising from the presentation of gains and losses

23.219 Reserves, together with equity share capital and other own equity instruments, make up the shareholders' equity section of an entity's balance sheet. Reserves are frequently referred to as components of equity.

23.220 As well as retained earnings, reserves include fair value (or AFS) reserve, cash flow hedge reserve, asset revaluation reserve, foreign currency translation reserve and other statutory reserves. Most reserves result from accounting requirements to reflect certain measurement changes in equity rather than the profit or loss account.

Revaluation reserve

23.221 Schedule 1 to SI 2008/410 includes rules on the transfer of amounts to and from the revaluation reserve. [SI 2008/410 1 Sch 6].

23.222 Where a company has valued an item in accordance with one of the alternative accounting rules, the Act states that the revaluation surplus or deficit must be credited or debited to a revaluation reserve. [SI 2008/410 1 Sch 35(1)].

23.223 Furthermore, a company can transfer an amount from the revaluation reserve to the profit and loss account, if the amount was previously charged to that account or represents a realised profit. A company is also permitted to apply the whole or a part of the revaluation reserve in wholly or partly paying up unissued shares in the company to be allotted to the members as fully or partly paid shares. The revaluation reserve will also be reduced by any amounts transferred to it that are no longer necessary for the purpose of the valuation method that the company has adopted. Furthermore, it is possible to transfer from the revaluation reserve an amount in respect of the taxation relating to any profit or loss credited or debited to that reserve. This applies for example to the tax relating to a previously recognised revaluation gain.

23.224 The revaluation reserve must be disclosed on the face of the balance sheet. It may be described by a different name, although it is generally preferable for companies to keep to the terminology in the Act. [SI 2008/410 1 Sch 35(2)].

23.225 Where an amount has been credited or debited to the revaluation reserve, its treatment for taxation purposes must be disclosed in a note to the financial statements. [SI 2008/410 1 Sch 35(6)].

Fair value or available-for-sale reserve

23.226 FRS 26 requires that gains or losses on available for sale financial assets are recognised in equity, through the statement of total recognised gains and losses, except for impairment losses and foreign exchange gains and losses (when they relate to a monetary item), interest and dividends. [FRS 26 paras 55(b) AG83]. These gains and losses must, under the 2006 Act, be included in a separate reserve, (typically known as the fair value or available-for-sale reserve) and are recycled to the profit or loss account on derecognition (for example, when sold) or impairment. [FRS 26 para 55(b)]. FRS 3, 'Reporting financial performance', was amended for accounting periods commencing on or after 1 January 2007, to disapply the prohibition on recycling between the STRGL and profit and loss account for companies using FRSs 23 and 26. [FRS 3 para 12B]. The treatment of available-for-sale financial assets is considered further in Manual of Accounting – Financial instruments. Companies not using FRS 26 but that choose to carry investments at market value and take the changes in value to revaluation reserve do so under the 'Alternative accounting rules' of the Act, not the Act's 'Fair value accounting rules'. Companies that take the change in market value of their investments to profit and loss account put themselves within the 'Fair value accounting rules' and, therefore, within FRS 26's scope. [FRS 26 paras 1A and 1B].

23.227 The profits and losses arising on the remeasurement of available-for-sale (AFS) financial assets are realised or unrealised according to the same principles that apply if the same assets are accounted for at fair value through profit or loss (FVTPL). It would be illogical if the question of whether a profit is realised or unrealised depended on whether the directors designated the particular financial assets as FVTPL on initial recognition. Consequently, profits on remeasurement of AFS financial assets are realised or unrealised irrespective of whether they meet the requirements to be accounted for at FVTPL.

23.228 In respect of losses, cumulative net losses arising on fair value accounting (both for AFS and FVTPL purposes) are generally realised and can only be unrealised if:

- profits on remeasurement of the same financial asset would be unrealised; and
- the losses would not have been recorded otherwise than pursuant to fair value accounting.

23.229 With reference to the second condition above, absent fair value accounting, a loss may need to be recorded for a financial asset, for example, on the basis of amortised cost less impairment provisions.

23.230 If the fair value or AFS reserve is in an overall loss position (that is, it is a net debit), public companies will find that operation of the net assets test in section 831 of the 2006 Act will restrict the amount of profits available for distribution by the amount of the net debit balance.

Hedging reserve

23.231 FRS 26 requires that the effective portion of gains (profits) and losses (net of tax), arising from the remeasurement of a financial instrument designated as the hedging instrument in a cash flow hedge, be recognised in reserves, through the statement of total recognised gains and losses. [FRS 26 para 95]. The 'Fair value accounting rules' require that these profits and losses are taken to the fair value reserve. However, some companies designate a separate reserve as a hedging reserve. Legally, this is subject to the same rules as the fair value reserve, of which it is, in effect, a sub-set. These gains and losses are subsequently recycled to the profit and loss account in the period (or periods) when the hedged item affects the profit and loss account. [FRS 26 para 100]. FRS 3 was amended for accounting periods commencing on or after 1 January 2007 to allow recycling where the company uses FRSs 23 and 26. [FRS 3 para 12B]. If the hedged cash flows result in the recognition of a non-financial asset or liability on the balance sheet, the entity can choose to adjust the basis (that is, measurement on initial recognition) of the asset or liability by the amount of gains and losses recognised in reserves. [FRS 26 para 98]. However, this 'basis adjustment' is not permitted if the hedged cash flows result in the recognition of a financial asset or liability. In that case, the deferred amount remains in equity and is recycled to profit or loss according to the profile of the effect that the asset or liability has on profit or loss. If the hedging relationship ceases because one of the criteria for hedge accounting is no longer met, the hedge is revoked or the hedging instrument is expired, sold, terminated or exercised, the gains and losses accumulated in equity are either:

- released to the profit and loss account immediately if the hedged item is no longer expected to occur; or
- left in equity until the hedged cash flow occurs at which point they are released to the profit and loss account.

[FRS 26 para 101].

Companies not using FRS 26

23.232 Companies that do not use FRS 26 do not use the 'fair value accounting rules' under the Act and thus do not have a fair value or hedging reserve. Such companies account for their hedges on an 'accruals basis', that is, one where the gains and losses on the hedging instruments are generally not recognised until the gains and losses on the hedged items are recognised in the profit and loss account.

Where a company carries out net investment hedging under SSAP 20, profits and losses on the hedging instrument (for example, a foreign currency borrowing or a forward foreign exchange contract) are taken to the profit and loss account reserve *via* the STRGL as are the profits and losses on the retranslation of the cost of investment in the subsidiary (in the company's individual financial statements) or the subsidiary's net assets (in the company's consolidated financial statements), where they offset each other.

23.233 For companies that do not use FRS 26, the effect on the determination of realised and distributable profits of hedge accounting on an 'accruals basis', the principle in paragraph 5.1 in Tech 02/10 still applies *'Where hedge accounting is obtained in accordance with the relevant accounting standards, it is necessary to consider the combined effect of both sides of the hedging relationship to determine whether there is a realised profit or loss in accordance with the criteria in this guidance'*. [Tech 02/10 para 5.1]. Consequently, in a hedging model where profits and losses on the hedging instruments and the hedged items are not recognised until there is a cash realisation, there is normally an automatic set off for the purposes of determining the effect on realised and distributable profits. In circumstances where the strategy is to use a series of 'rolling' instruments the hedging principle above applies irrespective of whether profits or losses have been recognised from settled transactions. Such profits and losses should be treated as unrealised.

Foreign currency translation reserve

23.234 Exchange differences that arise on translation of a foreign operation must be recognised through the statement of recognised gains and losses; cumulative net exchange differences so recognised must be separately disclosed, together with a reconciliation of the amount of such differences as at the beginning and end of the period. [FRS 23 para 32, 52]. These differences may arise on the translation of a foreign branch to be included in the entity's separate financial statements or may arise on the translation of a foreign subsidiary to be included in the entity's consolidated accounts. Similarly, gains or losses that arise on hedging instruments that are effective hedges against the effect of exchange rates on the net assets of an operation (a 'net investment hedge') should be included in the consolidated foreign currency translation reserve. Entities need to track separately the translation differences contained within an entity's own equity and its consolidated equity because, on disposal of a foreign branch or operation, the cumulative translation difference relating to that operation must be transferred (recycled) to the profit and loss account and included in the gain or loss on disposal. [FRS 23 para 48]. FRS 3 was amended with effect for accounting periods commencing on or after 1 January 2007 to allow this type of recycling for entities using FRSs 23 and 26. [FRS 3 para 12B]. Such recycling also applies to the required portion of the cumulative translation difference on an actual or deemed partial disposal. [FRS 23 paras 48, 49]. Accounting for the effects of changes in foreign exchange rates is considered further in chapter 7.

23.235 Under FRS 26, net investment hedge accounting of foreign operations arises in consolidated financial statements. These financial statements are not relevant for the purposes of justifying distributions. However, in the case of a foreign branch, net investment hedge accounting can take place in the company's separate financial statements. A net investment hedge is accounted for similarly to a cash flow hedge. The extent to which the profit or loss on remeasurement of the hedging instrument is realised is determined by reference to the loss or profit on the hedged item. In the case of a foreign branch, determining whether the retranslation profits and losses of a branch's assets and liabilities are realised can be complex. Consequently, this has implications for the profits and losses on the hedging instrument. The issues in respect of the hedged item are considered in paragraphs 5.10 to 5.11 of Tech 02/10.

23.236 If the foreign currency translation reserve is in an overall loss position (that is, it is a net debit) on retranslation of foreign currency assets and liabilities, public companies will find that operation of the net assets test in section section 831 of the 2006 Act will restrict the amount of profits available for distribution by the amount of the net debit balance. Where foreign currency denominated shares have been classified as financial liabilities under FRS 25, careful consideration is needed of whether the retranslation gains and losses (whether recognised under FRS 23 (for companies using FRS 26) or SSAP 20 (for companies not using FRS 26)) are gains and losses in law, as it may be that the accounting is made in anticipation of the eventual distribution or capital repayment.

Companies not using FRSs 23 and 26

23.237 Companies that are not using FRS 26 are not permitted to use FRS 23 and, consequently, continue to use SSAP 20. This standard does not require the maintenance of a cumulative translation reserve nor does FRS 3 (absent the use of FRSs 23 and 26) permit any recycling from reserves through the STRGL to the profit and loss account. Hence, translation differences on the cost of investment (individual financial statements) or on net assets (consolidated financial statements) that have previously been taken to reserves are not recycled on disposal or partial disposal of the relevant foreign subsidiaries or other foreign equity investments and thus not included in the gain or loss on disposal reported in the profit and loss account.

23.238 Net investment hedge accounting for a branch under SSAP 20 is not dissimilar from that under FRS 23. Accordingly, the issues discussed in paragraph 23.235 are equally relevant when considering the impact on determining of realised and distributable profits for a branch.

Capital reserve

23.239 Where a company receives consideration from one or more shareholders without a contractual obligation to make any repayment (a gift or a 'capital contribution'), this will represent an increase in equity. Typically, such amounts are recorded in a separate reserve, often known as the 'capital reserve'.

23.240 If the gift or 'capital contribution' is received in cash or an asset that is readily convertible to cash, the amount included in the capital reserve will be realised. However, if it is not received in qualifying consideration the amount will be unrealised, although it may become realised if the consideration is converted into qualifying consideration, or the asset is depreciated or sold.

Disclosure

23.241 Under Schedule 1 to SI 2008/410, certain information must be included in the notes to the financial statements in respect of movements on each reserve that is shown either on the face of the balance sheet or in the notes to the financial statements. This information is as follows:

- The amount of the reserve at the beginning and end of the year.
- The amounts transferred to or from the reserve during the year.
- The source and application of any amounts so transferred.

[SI 2008/410 1 Sch 59].

23.242 Companies may either give the information for each reserve in a separate note or prepare a combined note. Combining reserves helps clarify reserves movements when there are transfers between different reserves.

Share capital

23.243 Although there is no requirement to disclose the total (legal) amount of share capital and share premium, it is a reasonable disclosure to make, as the capital maintenance rules under the Act apply irrespective of where share capital and share premium are shown in the balance sheet. Shares classified as financial liabilities are dependent on profits available for distribution before their dividends can be paid or the shares are redeemed or purchased.

23.244 The UKLA's Listing Rules require disclosure of certain information when a listed company (or its unlisted major subsidiary) has allotted any types of shares for cash and the allotment has neither been made to the company's shareholders in proportion to their shareholdings nor specifically authorised by the company's shareholders:

- The classes of shares allotted and for each class, the number allotted, their aggregate nominal value and the consideration received.
- The names of the allottees, if less than six in number; in the case of six or more allottees, a brief generic description of each new class of equity holder (for example, a holder of loan stock).
- The market price of the securities concerned on the date on which the terms of the issue were fixed, together with that date.

[LR 9.8.4 R (7)(8); SI 2008/410 1 Sch 47].

23.245 Disclosures about share capital in an entity's financial statements may also be required by national law, or by a regulator or under the terms of the market on which the shares may be traded. Management needs to be familiar with these requirements and ensure that the necessary disclosures are made.

Realised and distributable reserves

23.246 Tech 02/10, 'Guidance on determination of realised profits and losses in the context of distributions under the Companies Act 2006', makes it clear that there is no requirement under law or accounting standards for financial statements to distinguish between realised and unrealised profits. It may be helpful to users of financial statements if there is an indication of which reserves in a company's separate financial statements are realised. Generally, however, there is no need for directors to form a view on whether profits are realised, unless they intend to utilise them to make a distribution. [Tech 02/10 paras 2.25 — 2.27].

23.247 Companies should maintain sufficient records to enable them to distinguish between those profits that are available for distribution and those that are not.

23.248 Although distributions are made from the distributable reserves of individual companies, rather than groups, users of financial statements may nonetheless draw inferences from the amount shown on the consolidated profit and loss account reserve. It would be misleading if consolidated financial statements gave the impression that subsidiary companies' distributable profits were readily available for distribution outside the group through payments to the parent when there were significant restrictions on their distribution to the parent. Where there are significant restrictions (for example, resulting from borrowing arrangements or regulatory requirements) on the ability of subsidiaries to transfer funds to the parent in the form of cash dividends or to repay loans or advances, the nature and extent of the restrictions should be disclosed. [FRS 2 para 53]. There is a similar disclosure requirement in respect of associates and joint ventures. [FRS 9 para 54].

23.249 Indeed, users of consolidated financial statements may wish to know how much a parent could distribute if all the subsidiaries in the group were to pay up their realised profits by way of dividends to the parent. In the past, some groups have voluntarily disclosed this amount or state in their reserves note any amounts that are not available for distribution. For example, the financial statements of Coats Viyella include a note that clarifies the reserves that are, or are not, available for distribution by the company. Coats Viyella's note also details the distributable reserves of the group that is the reserves that would be available if all the subsidiaries paid up their reserves as dividends to the parent company (see Table 23.3).

Table 23.3 – Coats Viyella Plc – Annual Report and Accounts – 31 December 1999

Notes to the accounts (extract)

	Group		Company	
	1999	1998	**1999**	1998
25 Total reserves	**£m**	£m	**£m**	£m
Available for distribution	**223.1**	160.2	**426.0**	331.2
Not available for distribution	**330.5**	324.9	**242.1**	242.1
	553.6	485.1	**668.1**	573.3

23.250 Companies may also consider it necessary to give such disclosure when the size of a dividend paid or proposed is substantial, in the context of the total distributable reserves of the company, and there is the risk that the shareholders may be under the mistaken impression that the same level of dividends can be maintained in the future.

Statement of movement on reserves

23.251 A reserves note is required by the 2006 Act to show movements in each reserve and movements between reserves. Therefore, it is not possible to substitute for share capital and for the movements in the reserves note a figure such as the total recognised gains and losses for the year. That figure, which summarises several different types of reserve movements, must be broken down into its component parts in the reserves note, and transfers between reserves must also be shown in the note. For example, the reserves note is required to show movements between the revaluation reserve and the profit and loss account reserve in respect of previous revaluation surpluses that have been realised in the year. This movement would not be evident from either the profit and loss account or the statement of total recognised gains and losses.

23.252 FRS 3 requires an additional statement or note reconciling movements in shareholders' funds. This reconciliation between opening and closing shareholders' funds should include the components of the total recognised gains and losses of the year. The reconciliation will also include dividends as a deduction from the profit or loss for the year and other movements in shareholders' funds such as share capital issued or redeemed. Since the reconciliation can be provided in the form of a note or in the form of a primary statement, considerable flexibility is given to where this statement appears and thus to the prominence or lack of prominence given to it.

23.253 It may, however, be appropriate to combine the statement of movements on reserves with the reconciliation of movements in shareholders' funds. This can be done by including a column for the total shareholders' funds brought forward from the previous year and carried forward for the year in the reserves note. Siebe plc provides a reconciliation of movements in shareholders' funds that also serves as the reserves note (see Table 23.4).

Table 23.4 – Siebe plc – Report and Accounts – 1 April 1995

Consolidated Balance Sheet (extract)

		Group		Company	
			1994 Restated		
		1995	Note 1	**1995**	1994
	Notes	**£m**	£m	**£m**	£m
Capital and reserves					
Called up share capital	25	**107.1**	106.9	**107.1**	106.9
Share premium account	26	**393.4**	390.1	**393.4**	390.1
Other reserves	26	**(10.3)**	24.7	**217.3**	222.2
Revenue reserve	26	**476.0**	428.4	**64.1**	59.0
Shareholders' funds – equity		**966.2**	950.1	**781.9**	778.2
Minority interests – equity		**79.0**	63.3	**–**	–
		1,045.2	1,013.4	**781.9**	778.2

26 Reconciliation of movements in shareholders' funds (extract)

	Share capital £m	Share premium account £m	Merger reserve £m	Other reserves: Exchange variation reserve £m	Other reserves: Total other reserve £m	Revenue reserve £m	Total £m	1994 Total £m
Group								
At 3 April 1994	106.9	390.1	–	24.7	24.7	428.4	950.1	742.6
Profit attributes to the members of Siebe plc	–	–	–	(35.0)	(35.0)	160.3	125.3	127.0
Dividends	–	–	–	–	–	(51.9)	(51.9)	(47.1)
Rights issue	–	–	–	–	–	–	–	184.3
New Share capital subscribed	0.2	3.3	–	–	–	–	3.5	3.1
Goodwill written off	–	–	–	–	–	(60.8)	(60.8)	(59.8)
At 1 April 1995	107.1	393.4	–	(10.3)	(10.3)	476.0	966.2	950.1

The cumulative amount of goodwill resulting from acquisition which has been written off between 1 April 1984 and 2 April 1994 is £228.9 million, of which £218.6 million has been charged to Merger Reserve and £10.3 million to Revenue Reserve.

Treasury shares

23.254 Own shares held by the entity and its subsidiaries (including EBTs and ESOPs) are accounted for as treasury shares if those entities have a beneficial interest in the shares. If the shares are held on behalf of others (for example, a financial institution holding its own equity on behalf of a client), there is an agency arrangement. The shares are not, therefore, included in the entity balance sheet. [FRS 25 para AG36].

23.255 Chapter 29 of this manual addresses the UKLA Listing Rules' requirements regarding related-party transactions in the company's shares. Entities whose shares are publicly traded observe the rules of the market and/or the relevant regulator governing the purchase of shares for cancellation or to hold in treasury. Such rules may also dictate certain disclosures to be made in the entities' consolidated financial statements.

23.256 The UKLA's Listing Rules require listed companies incorporated in the UK that have a valid authority for the purchase of own shares and have either purchased their own shares or have sold treasury shares for cash in off-market transactions to make the following disclosures in their financial statements:

- Details of any shareholders' authority for the purchase by the company of its own shares still valid at the period end.
- For purchases and proposed purchases of own shares made otherwise than through the market or by tender or partial offer to all shareholders during the period under review, the names of the sellers.
- For purchases made other than through the market or by tender or partial offer to all shareholders, or options or contracts to make such purchases, entered into since the end of the period, equivalent information as required under Part II of Schedule 7 to SI 2008/410 (see 'Manual of Accounting – Narrative reporting').
- In the case of sales of treasury shares for cash made other than through the market, or in connection with an employees' share scheme, or other than pursuant to an opportunity that was made available to all holders of a relevant class of the company's securities on the same terms, the names of the purchasers of such shares sold, or proposed to be sold, by the company during the period under review.

[LR 9.8.6 R (4)].

These disclosures apply to qualifying shares that are classified as equity or as financial liabilities.

23.257 Entities whose shares are publicly traded observe the rules of the market and/or the relevant regulator governing the purchase of shares for cancellation or to hold in treasury. Such rules may also dictate certain disclosures to be made in the entities' consolidated financial statements.

Dividends

23.258 The following items should be disclosed in the notes to the financial statements:

- Any amount set aside or proposed to be set aside to, or withdrawn or proposed to be withdrawn from, reserves.

- The aggregate amount of dividends paid during the year (other than those for which a liability existed at the immediately preceding balance sheet date).
- The aggregate amount of dividends that the company is liable to pay at the balance sheet date.
- The aggregate amount of dividends that are proposed before the date of approval of the accounts, and not otherwise disclosed under the second or third bullet above.

[SI 2008/410 1 Sch 43].

23.259 Where equity dividends are shown on the face of the profit and loss account, they should preferably be shown as a footnote, separate from the profit and loss account itself. Although there is no legal prohibition on presenting equity dividends as a deduction from the profit for the period, such a presentation could be regarded as inconsistent with the accounting for equity dividends. In particular, FRS 25 states:

> *"Interest, dividends, losses and gains relating to a financial instrument or a component that is a financial liability shall be recognised as income or expense in profit or loss. Distributions to holders of an equity instrument shall be debited by the entity directly to equity, net of any related income tax benefit…."* [FRS 25 para 35].

Coupons on financial instruments that are classified as equity under FRS 25 are taken to reserves, not treated as an expense in the profit and loss account. As equity, dividends are a transaction with equity owners and they are not included within the statement of total recognised gains and losses. Instead, the aggregate amount of equity dividends is dealt with in the reconciliation of movements in shareholders' funds.

23.260 Prior to accounting periods beginning on or after 1 January 2005, Schedule 4 of the Companies Act 1985 required dividends to be shown within the profit and loss account as a deduction from profit for the period, but this requirement has been deleted for later accounting periods. Therefore, the legal imperative for adopting such a treatment no longer exists. However, it can be argued that the presentation of equity dividends after profit for the financial year as an appropriation, rather than as an expense, is acceptable under UK GAAP.

23.261 The question arises as to when a dividend should be recognised as a liability in a company's statutory accounts, with a consequential reduction of distributable profits. Directors have no discretion to pay final dividends. They can propose a final dividend but it does not become a legally binding liability until it is approved by members of a public company in general meeting (or a when a private company's members' written resolution is passed). Thus a proposed, but not approved, final dividend at the balance sheet date is not a legal obligation to shareholders. Therefore, a proposed final dividend is not booked in the financial statements of the year to which it relates, but is recognised in the following period when it is paid. Where a company's articles provide that interim dividends can be declared by directors, such dividends are never a liability until their actual payment as the directors' resolution to pay a dividend can be revoked by them prior to actual payment; no contractual obligation is created. A past history of paying dividends does not give rise to a contractual obligation nor a constructive obligation. (For further discussion, see chapter 22.) This is consistent with FRS 25 para AG13, which states that *'an issuer of non-puttable ordinary shares assumes a liability when it formally acts to make a distribution and becomes legally obligated to the shareholders to do so'*. Similarly, it is consistent with FRS 12, 'Provisions, contingent liabilities and contingent assets', where there is no obligation at the balance sheet date; a liability is not recorded.

23.262 Dividends on shares treated as liabilities are treated as interest expense and recognised on an accruals basis. Regardless of the accounting treatment, dividends can only be paid if the company has sufficient distributable profits; that is, even where a company has charged the dividend on a preference share as interest expense and therefore reduced its balance sheet profit and loss reserve accordingly, it is still prohibited from paying that dividend if there were insufficient distributable profits for that purpose before the accrual was made. Compound financial instruments are divided into their liability and equity components with a consequential effect on amounts recognised as interest expense and distributions. For example, a non-cumulative preference share that is mandatorily redeemable, but with dividends payable at the discretion of the entity is recognised as a liability in respect of the redemption amount (and the unwinding of the discount is classified as interest expense), whilst the dividends relate to the equity component and are recognised as distributions. [FRS 25 para AG37].

23.263 The treatment of shares as financial liabilities or compound instruments for accounting purposes has a complex interaction with the legal rules on distributions and capital repayments. Section 6 of Tech 02/10 and its appendix provide ten key principles, underlying statute and common law in respect of distributions and capital maintenance. These principles should be used for determining distributable profits when dealing with such contracts. They illustrate how the principles are applied in eight scenarios involving shares and compound instruments. The appendix provides the detail of the accounting and capital maintenance book-keeping entries. Principles 1, 2 and 3 are particularly relevant for distributions presented as interest expense. In essence, these principles say that dividends accounted for as interest expense are not losses, as a matter of law; that the accounting is an advanced recognition of a future distribution; and that distributable profits are only consumed by a dividend when it is paid or when it is approved by members and becomes a legal liability. Consequently, when directors assess whether their companies have sufficient distributable profits to make a distribution they will have to reverse the accounting for dividends that has been charged as interest expense.

23.264 Dividends per share excludes any attributable tax credit. A distinction is not required to be made between the dividends on different classes of equity share, but it is best practice to do so as it enables dividend per equity share to be compared with the relevant earnings per share. The denominator for the calculation of dividends per share would usually be the number of shares on which the dividends are actually paid. Where a dividend was paid in instalments, and the number of shares varied during the year, a weighted average number of shares should be used. The weighted average number of shares for this purpose should be calculated in the same way as the weighted average number of shares used in earnings per share calculations. The method of calculation is set out in paragraph 20 of FRS 22, 'Earnings per share' (see further chapter 14).

23.265 Many listed companies choose to make arrangements for ordinary shareholders to elect to receive their dividends in the form of additional ordinary shares rather than in cash. The share equivalent is sometimes referred to as a scrip dividend or a stock dividend and consists of shares fully paid up out of the company's profits. An advantage of issuing scrip dividends is that, in the short term, the company's cash position would be improved. Such dividends should be recognised in the financial statements at the amount of the cash alternative and the notes to the financial statements should give a full explanation of the situation.

23.266 The Listing Rules for listed companies require particulars to be disclosed of any arrangements under which a shareholder has either waived or agreed to waive any dividends. [LR 9.8.4 R (12)].

Distributable reserves

23.267 Profits available for distribution are addressed in Part 23 of the 2006 Act. Companies may only make a distribution out of *"profits available for the purpose"*. The Act's requirements in respect of distributions apply to all UK companies whether they report under EU-adopted IFRS or UK GAAP. The provisions of Part 23 of the 2006 Act apply to distributions made on or after 6 April 2008.

23.268 Distributions may also be subject to any enactment, any rule of common law or any provision in the memorandum or articles of association that may restrict either the amounts available for distribution or the circumstances in which a distribution may be made. [CA06 Sec 852]. Distributions must be paid in accordance with the company's memorandum and articles, which contain special provisions regarding dividends and other distributions. For example, investment companies are restricted by their constitutions from distributing realised 'capital' profits.

23.269 Under common law, dividends cannot be paid out of capital. The directors should also consider their fiduciary duties in the exercise of the powers conferred on them and act in their company's best interests. Examples of fiduciary duties include the obligation on directors to safeguard the company's assets and to ensure that the company is in a position to settle its debts as they fall due. Consequently, even if the company has profits available for distribution under Part 23 of the 2006 Act, its directors should consider the future cash needs of their company before making a distribution. It would probably be unlawful to pay a dividend if, as a result, the company became insolvent or had insufficient working capital to carry on its business.

23.270 The ICAEW and ICAS have in the past decade published guidance on realised profits and distributions under the 1985 Act (Techs 7/03, 50/04, 64/04 and 02/07). In February 2008, the Institutes published Technical Release 01/08, 'Guidance on the determination of realised profits and losses in the context of distributions under the Companies Act 1985'. This technical release consolidates the Institutes' previous guidance. The technical release covers the application of the statutory and common law rules and directors' fiduciary duties. [Tech 01/08, section 2]. It is *de facto* GAAP for distributable profits. As an interpretation of pre-existing law, its principles apply to transactions entered into before Tech 01/08 was published.

23.271 Due to changes resulting from the new provisions of the Companies Act 2006 that came into effect from 1 October 2008, on capital reductions and distributions in kind and the relaxation of the law on financial assistance for private companies, the Institute published Tech 01/09 in July 2009. The purpose of this guidance is to identify, interpret and apply the principles relating to the determination of realised profits and losses for the purposes of making distributions under the Companies Act. Tech 02/10 published in November 2010 supersedes Tech 01/09. Most of the guidance from Tech 01/09 has been carried forward. The changes are almost entirely concerned with addressing new issues or providing more detail in areas that were covered only briefly in Tech 01/09.

General principles

Defining distributable profits

23.272 Any company (whether public or private) may make a distribution only out of *"profits available for the purpose"*. [CA06 Sec 830(1)]. In this context, 'make' means 'pay'. A company must have sufficient profits when the dividend is paid not just when it is declared.

23.273 A company's available profits for distribution are *"... its accumulated, realised profits ... less its accumulated, realised losses"*. [CA06 Sec 831(2)]. The origin of these profits and losses may be either revenue or capital. [CA06 Sec 830(2)(3)]. 'Realised' is not exactly defined in the Act. Section 853(4) of the 2006 Act says that *"... references to realised profits and realised losses, in relation to a company's accounts, are to such profits or losses of the company as fall to be treated as realised in accordance with principles generally accepted, at the time when the accounts are prepared, with respect to the determination for accounting purposes of realised profits or losses"*.

23.274 Not only is this definition somewhat circular, there is little indication in case law of what is meant by 'realised'. The few cases that there have been mainly relate to tax rather than company law. All that can really be derived from the cases is that judges have interpreted 'realised' more widely than 'realised in cash', and that they, like the legislature, see realisation as an accounting concept rather than a strictly legal concept.

23.275 Tech 02/10 identifies interprets and applies the principles for determining realised profits and losses for the purposes of making distributions under the 2006 Act. It does not provide guidance on how transactions and arrangements should be accounted for in a company's financial statements.

23.276 Tech 02/10's guidance is based on the principle that realised profits are primarily those that are realised in the form of *"cash or of other assets the ultimate cash realisation of which can be assessed with reasonable certainty"*. [Tech 02/10 para 3.3].

23.277 In assessing whether a company has a realised profit, transactions and arrangements should not be looked at in isolation. A realised profit will arise only where the overall commercial effect on the company satisfies the definition of realised profit set out in the guidance. A group or series of transactions or arrangements should be viewed as a whole, particularly if they are artificial, linked (whether legally or otherwise) or circular or any combination of these. The principle in paragraph 3.5 is likely to be of particular relevance for, but not limited to, intra-group transactions. [Tech 02/10 para 3.5, 3.5A].

23.278 Part 23 of the Act came into effect on 6 April 2008 and applies to distributions made on or after that date. There are no substantive changes in the law on distributions made by the 2006 Act, although some changes of wording have been made. Section 845 of the Act is a new provision (not previously in the 1985 Act), which removes doubts arising from the decision in *Aveling Barford v Perion Ltd [1989] BCLC 626*.

23.279 Certain provisions of the Act relating to capital reductions, including those that permit a private company to reduce its capital by way of a solvency statement, came into effect on 1 October 2008. The Companies (Reduction of Share Capital) Order 2008 SI 2008/1915 came into effect at the same time and specifies the cases in which a reserve arising from a reduction of a company's share capital is to be treated as realised as a matter of law. The Order also disapplies the general prohibition in section 654 on distributing a reserve arising from a reduction of share capital. In accordance with the Companies Act 2006 (Commencement No.7, Transitional Provisions and Savings) Order 2008, the new provisions apply irrespective of when the reduction in capital occurred or when the reserve arose. The new requirements, therefore, apply to capital reductions made under the 1985 Act and those made by unlimited companies.

Additional conditions applying to public companies — the 'net asset test'

23.280 A public company must not make a distribution that reduces the amount of its net assets below the aggregate of its called-up share capital and its undistributable reserves; the 'net asset test'. [CA06 Sec 831(1)(6)].

Investment companies

23.281 Investment companies (as defined in section 833 of the 2006 Act) may make distributions either on the basis of the '*net asset test*' applicable to all public companies or the specific '*asset ratio test*' that is available only to investment companies.

Long-term insurance business

23.282 Insurance companies are subject to the normal distribution rules of the 2006 Act. That is the section 830 requirement for realised profits and the section 831 'net asset test'. However, the definition in section 853(4) of the 2006 Act of realised profits, as being determined by reference to generally accepted accounting principles, is replaced with special rules in section 843 of that Act.

Principles of realisation

Realised profits — 'qualifying consideration'

23.283 Paragraph 3.9 of Tech 02/10 sets out when a profit is realised. First, a profit is realised where it arises from a transaction where the consideration received by the company is 'qualifying consideration'. This is defined in paragraph 3.11 of Tech 02/10 as any of the following:

- Cash.
- An asset that is readily convertible to cash.
- The release, or the settlement or assumption by another party, of all or part of a liability of the company.
- An amount receivable in any of the above forms of consideration where:
  - (i) the debtor is capable of settling the receivable within a reasonable period of time;
  - (ii) there is a reasonable certainty that the debtor will be capable of settling when called upon to do so; and
  - (iii) there is an expectation that the receivable will be settled.
- An amount receivable from a shareholder where and to the extent that:
  - (i) the company intends to make a distribution to the shareholder of an amount equal to or less than its receivable from that shareholder;
  - (ii) the company intends to settle such distribution by off-setting against the amount receivable (in whole or in part); and
  - (iii) within the meaning of paragraphs 3.5 and 3.5A, of this guidance. That is, in assessing whether a company has a realised profit, transactions and arrangements should not be looked at in isolation. A realised profit will arise only where the overall commercial effect on the

company is such that the definition of realised profit set out is met, and (i) and (ii) are linked.

[Tech 02/10 para 3.11]

For the purpose of applying paragraph 3.11 above, references to settlement include settlement by way of set-off with a liability to the same party. [Tech 02/10 para 3.11A]

Example 1 – Sale of property to parent company

A subsidiary sells a property to its parent company, making a profit. The consideration for the sale is left outstanding in the inter-company account, although the parent is capable of settling the inter-company balance and would normally do so within a reasonable period of time. The subsidiary then pays a dividend from the profit on sale to the parent. It settles the payment by cancelling part of the inter-company balance. Is the profit made by the subsidiary realised? Is the dividend received by the parent a realised profit?

The profit is realised in the subsidiary's financial statements if the consideration is 'qualifying consideration'. This includes an amount receivable where the debtor is capable of settling the receivable within a reasonable period of time, there is reasonable certainty that the debtor will be capable of settling when called upon to do so and there is an expectation that the receivable will be settled. [Tech 02/10 para 3.11(d)].

The dividend paid by the subsidiary is not a realised profit to the parent. In substance, the transaction is a dividend *in kind* of the property to the parent. The property is not qualifying consideration, hence the dividend the parent receives is an unrealised profit.

Example 2 – Transfer of investment

A company has a fixed asset investment, which is recorded at cost at £250,000. The market value of the investment is £2.5 million. A supplier bills the company £2.5 million for research work (an arm's-length price that the company would normally settle in cash). The company settles the bill by transferring the investment to the supplier. Is the profit on transfer of the investment realised?

At first sight, it appears that as the company is exchanging its investment for non-cash consideration (the benefit arising from research work) and, therefore, the gain is unrealised. However, when the company initially charged the profit and loss account with the amount due to the supplier, this was a realised loss. The company settled its liability to the supplier by transferring assets worth £2.5 million. Qualifying consideration includes the release of a liability, unless the liability arose from the purchase of an asset that does not meet the definition of qualifying consideration and has not been disposed of for qualifying consideration. [Tech 02/10 para 3.11(c)(i)]. In this case, the liability arose from the purchase of the research work and the charge for research has been treated as a realised loss. The gain on the transfer of the investment of £2.25 million is realised.

Example 3 – Sale partly for qualifying consideration

An asset with a book value of £5m is sold for a mixed consideration of cash and a freehold property. The fair value of the consideration is £10m (£4m is cash and £6m is freehold property). The profit arising is realised to the extent of the fair value of the cash received (the qualifying consideration). The total gain is £5m, but the realised profit is limited to £4m. [Tech 02/10 para 3.18]. This approach is referred to as 'top-slicing'. Paragraph 4.9 of Tech 02/10 makes clear that 'top-slicing' into realised and unrealised elements is not relevant when considering profits and losses on remeasurement of assets and liabilities carried at fair value.

Examples of realised gains

23.284 Examples of realised gains are:

- The recognition in the financial statements of a change in fair value, where fair value has been determined in accordance with accounting standards, to the extent that the change recognised is readily convertible to cash.
- The translation of a monetary asset that comprises qualifying consideration or a liability denominated in a foreign currency (see chapter 7).
- The reversal of a loss previously regarded as realised (for example, writing back a charge for impairment or releasing a provision for a specific loss).
- A profit previously regarded as unrealised that has not been capitalised (for example, a revaluation reserve, merger reserve or other similar reserve) becoming realised as a result of:
  - Consideration previously received by the company becoming qualifying consideration.
  - The related asset being disposed of in a transaction where the company receives qualifying consideration.
  - A realised loss being recognised on the scrapping or disposal of the related asset.
  - A realised loss being recognised on the write-down for depreciation, amortisation, diminution in value or impairment of the related asset.
  - The distribution *in kind* of the asset to which the unrealised profit relates.
- The receipt of a dividend in the form of qualifying consideration when no profit is recognised because the dividend is deducted from the book value of the related investment. In such situations, an appropriate corresponding proportion of the related unrealised profit becomes a realised profit. [Tech 02/10 para 3.9].
- The remeasurement of a liability, to the extent that the change recognised is readily convertible to cash.

[The next paragraph is 23.286.]

23.286 The Companies (Reduction of Share Capital) Order 2008 (SI 2008/1915, Reg 3) specifies the cases from 1 October 2008 in which a reserve arising from a reduction in a company's share capital is to be treated as a realised profit as a matter of law. They are as follows:

- If an unlimited company reduces its share capital, a reserve arising from the reduction is treated a realised profit.
- If a private company limited by shares reduces its share capital and the reduction is supported by a solvency statement but has not been subject to an application to the court for an order confirming it, the reserve arising from the reduction is treated as a realised profit.
- If a limited company having a share capital reduces its share capital and the reduction is confirmed by order of court, the reserve arising from the reduction is treated as a realised profit, unless the court orders otherwise.

These provisions are without prejudice to any contrary provisions of an order or undertaking given to the court, the resolution for, or any other resolution relevant to, the reduction of capital, or the company's memorandum or articles of association.

23.287 The Companies Act 2006 (Commencement No.7, Transitional Provisions and Savings) Order 2008 (SI 2008/1886, Reg 7(2)), in effect, provides that reserves arising prior to 1 October 2008 from:

- a reduction of capital confirmed by the courts under Chapter IV of Part V of the Companies Act 1985;
- a reduction of capital confirmed by the courts under the provisions of the Companies Act 2006; or
- a reduction in the capital of an unlimited company not under those provisions,

are treated as a matter of law as realised profits irrespective of when the reduction occurred or the reserves arose.

Readily convertible to cash

23.288 For the purposes of 'qualifying consideration' an 'asset or change in the fair value of an asset or liability that is readily convertible to cash' means that:

- A value can be determined at which a transaction in the asset or liability could occur, at the date of determination, in its state at that date, without negotiation and/or marketing, to either convert the asset, liability or change in fair value into cash, or to close-out the asset, liability or change in fair value.
- In determining the value, information such as prices, rates or other factors that market participants would consider in setting a price is observable.

- The company's circumstances should not prevent immediate conversion to cash or close-out of the asset, liability or change in fair value; for example, the company should be able to dispose of, or close–out, the asset, liability or the change in fair value, without any intention or need to liquidate, to curtail materially the scale of its operations, or to undertake a transaction on adverse terms.

[Tech 02/10 para 3.12].

See further section 4 of Tech 02/10.

Other realised profits

23.289 In addition, the following are realised profits:

- The receipt or accrual of investment or other income receivable in the form of qualifying consideration.
- A gain arising on a return of capital on an investment where the return is in the form of qualifying consideration.
- A gift (such as a 'capital contribution') received in the form of qualifying consideration.
- The release of a provision for a liability or loss that was treated as a realised loss.
- The reversal of a write-down or provision for diminution in value or impairment of an asset that was treated as a realised loss.

[Tech 02/10 para 3.14].

Profits and losses made before 22 December 1980

23.290 The Companies Act 1980 introduced statutory distribution rules and the concept of realised and unrealised profits. Its commencement date was 22 December 1980.

23.291 Where, after making all reasonable enquiries, the directors are unable to determine whether a profit or a loss that was made before 22 December 1980 is realised or unrealised, they may treat a profit as realised and a loss as unrealised. [CA06 Sec 850(1) — (3)]. This prevents problems occurring if no record exists of the original cost of an asset or the amount of a liability.

Linked, circular and intragroup transactions

23.292 A profit is not realised if it arises from a circular transaction. That is, if a profit arises within a group from a transaction with a group entity that has directly or indirectly provided the funding for that transaction, that profit is not realised and is not distributable. If an intra-group transaction is funded by a company that then receives a dividend from the proceeds, there is a circular flow of cash. There is no incremental cash coming into the recipient group company or its sub-group. The company has effectively funded the dividend it receives.

23.293 Section 9 of Tech 02/10 considers a number of intra-group transactions, including:

- Cash-pooling arrangements and group treasury functions.
- Dividend received or receivable on an investment in a subsidiary.
- Dividend by a subsidiary to a parent that provides or reinvests the funds in the subsidiary.
- Dividends received out of pre-acquisition profits.
- Sale of an asset by a parent to its subsidiary.
- Sale of an asset by a subsidiary to a parent, followed by a dividend to the parent of the resulting profit.
- Sale of an asset by a subsidiary to a fellow subsidiary followed by a dividend to the parent of the resulting profit.
- Dividend *in kind*.
- Return of capital contribution.
- Transfer of an asset for consideration followed by waiver of the resulting inter-company debt.

Example – Intra-group sale of assets

A company has a scheme to generate realised profits. It has 10 subsidiaries with a carrying value of £1 million. The subsidiaries have a fair value of £10 million. The company borrows £10 million from a bank, which it then injects as share capital into a newly formed subsidiary, Newco. Newco buys the subsidiaries for £10 million. Has the company realised a profit of £9 million?

No realised profit has been created, because the parent has directly funded the purchase of the subsidiaries by injecting share capital of £10 million into Newco. [Tech 02/10 para 9.28(b)].

Linkage

23.293.1 The term 'realised profits' is generally accepted as meaning profits that are realised in the form of cash or other assets readily convertible into cash. In assessing whether profit is realised, transactions and arrangements must not be looked at in isolation. The overall commercial effect on the company of a group or series of transactions should be looked at, particularly if they are linked (legally or otherwise), artificial or circular [Tech 02/10 para 3.5A]. Issues typically occur in the case of intra-group transactions, where profits may arise from the transfer of cash and assets around a group, although linkage may also need to be considered when analysing some transactions with third parties.

Example: Transaction with a third party

A subsidiary is sold for cash to a third party on the condition that the cash is applied in subscribing for shares in the purchaser. The transaction's substance or overall commercial effect is a sale with consideration in shares of the purchaser. The profit will be unrealised unless the shares of the purchaser are readily convertible to cash, for example because they are quoted on an active market.

23.293.2 The above example illustrates a clear instance of linkage. In practice, it may be far less clear, for example if there is a period of time between the two transactions and perhaps no legal obligation to complete the second one. Judgement will often be required. Tech 02/10 aims to achieve greater consistency in those judgements by setting out a series of principles that should be followed. [Tech 02/10 paras 3.43 to 3.75].

Group treasury balances

23.293.3 Groups of companies often operate cash pooling arrangements and group treasury functions. An example of such an arrangement is where a group company acts akin to a banker to other group companies by accepting funds and settling debts on behalf of those group companies. Group companies sometimes do not have their own bank accounts or have accounts that are cleared to a central account, in the name of one group company, at the close of business each day. The guidance in Tech 02/10 confirms that the normal considerations apply when assessing whether a realised profit arises from a transaction that results in an increase in a balance due from a group treasury company. That is to say that the balance must represent qualifying consideration and the profit must not arise from artificial, linked or circular transactions. The nature of such arrangements varies widely in practice. It is always necessary to have regard to the practical facts and circumstances of each case.

23.293.4 A group company may have a 'current account' balance with another group company through which many transactions, both debits and credits, are processed. There may be a considerable 'churn' on the account even though a substantial balance remains outstanding. The fact that there is no expectation that the core balance will be settled does not preclude transactions processed through the account being realised profits when they arise from normal trading transactions in the ordinary course of business. This is because the debit entries on the account arising from these transactions are expected to be settled by offset with credit entries on the account. However, large or unusual transactions that result in a 'permanent' increase in the core balance will require careful consideration. [Tech 02/10 paras 9.4 to 9.4B].

Realised losses

23.294 Losses should be regarded as realised losses except to the extent that the law, accounting standards or the guidance in Tech 02/10 provide otherwise. [Tech 02/10 para 3.10]. Under the Act, provisions for depreciation or diminution in value (impairment) of assets and provisions for liabilities are realised losses. [CA06 Sec 841(1)(2)]. The exception is when fixed assets are found to be impaired when all the fixed assets (or all fixed assets other than goodwill) of a company are revalued. [CA06 Sec 841(3)].

According to Tech 02/10 realised losses include:

- A cost or expense (other than one charged to the share premium account) that results in a reduction in recorded net assets.
- A loss arising on the sale or other disposal or scrapping of an asset.
- The writing down or providing for the depreciation, amortisation, diminution in value or impairment, of an asset. If the asset has previously been revalued, the appropriate proportion of the unrealised profit on revaluation becomes a realised profit, mitigating the effect of the realised loss.
- The creation of, or increase in, a provision for a liability or loss that results in an overall reduction in recorded net assets. However, when assets are revalued to their fair value, with any unrealised gain being included in the profit and loss account, the deferred tax on that gain should be treated as a reduction in that unrealised gain rather than as a realised loss.
- A gift made by the company (or the release of all or part of a debt due to the company or the assumption of a liability by the company) to the extent that it results in an overall reduction in recorded net assets.
- A loss arising from fair value accounting where profits on remeasurement of the same asset or liability would be treated as realised profits.
- Cumulative net losses arising on fair value accounting, unless:
  - profits on remeasurement of the same asset or liability would be unrealised; and
  - the losses would not have been recorded otherwise than pursuant to fair value accounting.

[Tech 02/10 paras 3.15 — 3.17, 4.31].

Fair value accounting

23.295 Profits arising from the use of fair value accounting (where the change is readily convertible to cash) are realised irrespective of whether the profit is recognised in the profit and loss account (for financial instruments at fair value through profit or loss) or in the fair value reserve or available-for-sale reserve (for available-for-sale financial assets). [Tech 02/10 para 4.24]. Similarly, losses arising from fair value accounting are realised unless a cumulative net loss arises where both the profits on remeasurement of the same asset or liability would be unrealised; and the losses would not have been recorded otherwise than pursuant to fair value accounting. [Tech 02/10 para 4.31]. Other than under fair value accounting, losses on assets may arise due to impairment. Losses on liabilities may be recorded under amortised cost accounting for financial instruments or on onerous contracts. [Tech 02/10 para 4.32]. Special considerations apply to whether the profit or loss on remeasurement of a hedging instrument are realised. [Tech 02/10 section 5].

23.296 Fair value accounting profits that are 'readily convertible into cash' are realised. 'Readily convertible to cash' means that the entity has an unrestricted ability to convert the asset or the change in the fair value of an asset or liability to cash almost instantaneously at the balance sheet date — that is, without protracted negotiations. The changes in the fair value of many, though not all, financial instruments fulfil this definition. Some, such as unquoted equity instruments and investments held for strategic purposes, do not. [Tech 02/10 paras 4.10 — 4.11]. Changes in the fair value of non-financial assets, such as investment property and agricultural and biological assets, rarely, if ever, fulfil the definition. Although agricultural and biological assets (which are also held at fair value) are not specifically addressed in the guidance, the treatment of their fair value gains and losses should follow the same principles.

23.297 Paragraphs 4.14 to 4.22 of Tech 02/10 address profits and losses on remeasurement of financial instruments that may be affected by the company's own creditworthiness and block discounts for securities traded in an active market.

23.298 The statement in which gains or losses are recognised does not affect whether that gain or loss is realised for distribution purposes. For example, a company may hold one tranche of listed shares as an available-for-sale (AFS) financial asset and have a second tranche of those shares designated as 'at fair value through profit or loss' (FVTPL). Fair value gains/losses on the AFS tranche are deferred in equity until sale. Those in the FVTPL tranche are taken direct to the profit and loss account. The fair value of both tranches of shares is determined on the same basis from the quote on the relevant market. Both tranches are 'readily convertible to cash'. The movements in fair value of both tranches are treated as realised.

23.299 The fair value of financial instruments determined in accordance with FRS 26, 'Financial instruments: Recognition and measurement', may be volatile. Directors will need to consider, given their fiduciary duties, whether it is prudent to distribute fair value gains. [Tech 02/10 para 2.4].

'Relevant accounts'

23.300 To determine whether a company has profits available, and (if it is a public company) whether the net assets test has been met, reference is made to certain items in the company's 'relevant accounts':

- Profits, losses, assets and liabilities.
- Provisions of any kind.

- Share capital and reserves (including undistributable reserves). [CA06 Sec 836(1)].

23.301 The 'relevant accounts' are normally the company's last audited individual financial statements that have been circulated to members in accordance with section 423 of the 2006 Act. Where a company circulates to members a summary financial statement under section 426 of the 2006 Act, the relevant accounts are the full accounts that form the basis of the summary financial statement. [CA06 Sec 837(1)]. Distributions are made by individual companies, not groups. A parent company's consolidated financial statements are not relevant for determining the parent's distributable profits.

23.302 If a proposed distribution exceeds the amount distributable according to the company's latest audited individual financial statements, *'interim accounts'* should be prepared and used in addition to justify the payment. These additional financial statements are necessary to enable a proper judgement to be made of the items referred to in paragraph 23.118.87. [CA06 Sec 836(2), 838(1), 839(1)]. Interim accounts for distribution purposes are different to the half-yearly reports required under the UKLA's DTR.

23.303 *'Initial accounts'* are prepared and used where a company proposes to make a distribution during its first accounting reference period or before it circulates its first audited financial statements. [CA06 Sec 836(2), 838(1), 839(1)]. These initial accounts must be such as to enable a reasonable judgement to be made.

23.304 The company's directors can present the company's individual financial statements in a currency other than its functional currency, a 'presentation currency', as permitted by FRS 23, 'The effects of changes in foreign exchange rates'. Profits available for distribution are measured in that presentation currency.

23.305 The legislation regarding 'relevant accounts' is particularly important for investment trusts, because they must distribute the majority of their reserves each year. Consequently, an interim dividend is unlikely to be covered by the remaining profits available for distribution derived from their last audited annual financial statements. Therefore, such companies generally prepare interim accounts in order legally to pay an interim dividend.

23.306 The Act lays down strict requirements for relevant accounts. Failure to comply with these requirements means that the distribution is unlawful. [CA06 Sec 836(3)(4)]. The shareholders cannot agree to waive the requirements. [*Re Precision Dippings Ltd v Precision Dippings Marketing Ltd* [1985] *Ch 447*]. The requirements of sections 838 and 839 of the 2006 Act regarding the form and content of interim and initial accounts of public companies do not apply to private companies. Instead, private companies may use management accounts as interim or initial accounts to support a distribution provided that they enable the directors to make a reasonable judgement of distributable profits. [CA06 Sec 836].

However, management accounts may need to be adjusted, as they will often not deal with all relevant matters and for the sort of closing adjustments made when preparing annual financial statements.

23.307 The following requirements apply to the published annual financial statements of all companies and the interim and initial accounts of public companies.

- They must be 'properly prepared', or they must be so prepared at least to the extent that is necessary in order to decide whether or not a proposed distribution is legal. In particular, the items referred to in paragraph UK.23.118.33 above must be determined. [CA06 Secs 837(2), 838(3), 839(3)].
- For annual financial statements, 'properly prepared' means that they must fully comply with Part 15 of the 2006 Act and with section 837 of the 2006 Act. For a public company, they must not include any uncalled share capital as an asset. [CA06 Sec 831(5)].
- Interim and initial accounts must be 'properly prepared' or properly prepared subject only to matters that are not material for determining, by reference to those accounts, whether the proposed distribution would contravene sections 830 or 831 of the 2006 Act. 'Properly prepared' means they must comply with sections 395 to 397 of the 2006 Act, which includes the true and fair requirement for 'Companies Act accounts'. These requirements are to be applied with such modifications as necessary, because the accounts are prepared otherwise than in respect of an accounting reference period.
- They must include the company's individual balance sheet and profit and loss account (in the format required by Schedule 1 to SI 2008/410) and such notes as are relevant to determining whether a distribution would be lawful under the Act. Comparative figures are not required for *interim accounts*, as these are not relevant for determining the legality of a proposed distribution. A directors' report (required by section 415 of the 2006 Act) and a cash flow statement (which are required by accounting standards not the Act) need not be included.
- In the case of interim accounts, the balance sheet is signed by a director in accordance with section 414 of the 2006 Act. There is no equivalent statutory requirement for initial accounts but, in practice, the auditors will require the accounts to be approved and signed by the directors before the auditors' report is signed.
- With annual financial statements, the auditors must have given their opinion on them in accordance with sections 475 and 495 of the 2006 Act. [CA06 Sec 837(3)(4)]. For initial accounts the auditors must have reported whether, in their opinion, those accounts have been properly prepared. [CA06 Sec 839(5)(6)]. If their report is qualified, the auditors must make an additional statement which states whether, in their opinion, the matters in respect of

which their report is qualified is material for determining whether a distribution would contravene Part 23 of the 2006 Act. [CA06 Secs 837(4)(a), 839(6)(a)]. Interim accounts are not required to be audited.

- With initial accounts, a copy of those accounts, with a copy of the auditors' report and statement (where initial accounts have been qualified), must be delivered to the Registrar of Companies before the proposed distribution is made. [CA06 Sec 839(7)]. The auditors' statement must also have been laid before the members in general meeting before delivery to the Registrar of Companies. [CA06 Sec 839(6)(b)(ii)]. The copy of the balance sheet, auditors' report and statement must be physically signed in the manner required by section 839(8) of the 2006 Act.

- With interim accounts, a copy of the accounts must be delivered to the Registrar of Companies before the proposed distribution is made. [CA06 Sec 838(6)]. The copy of the balance sheet must be physically signed in the manner required by section 838(7) of the 2006 Act.

- If the company is listed on a regulated market (for example, the Main Market of the LSE or Plus Markets' 'PLUS-listed' market), the company should also release the interim or initial accounts to a Regulatory Information Service as soon as they are available, as they may contain price-sensitive information. This should be at the same time as they are sent to the Registrar of Companies. The UKLA's Listing Rules also require companies to notify a Regulatory Information Service of any decision to make a distribution on listed equity. [LR 9.7A.2 R (2)].

Sections 838 and 839 were amended by paragraphs 17 and 18 of Schedule 1 to SI 2007/3495 Companies Act 2006 (Commencement No.5, Transitional Provisions and Savings) Order 2007 to require the physical signature of the relevant documents filed with the Registrar of Companies. The requirement for signature was repealed from 1 October 2009 when regulation 6 of the Eighth Commencement Order, repealed the transitional amendments in Schedule 1 to SI 2007/3495).

23.308 A certified translation of any document in a foreign language that is in a set of accounts that must be delivered to the Registrar of Companies must also be delivered to the Registrar of Companies. [CA06 Secs 1072, 838(7), 839(8)].

23.309 It is relatively common for directors of public companies to fail to send the interim or initial accounts to the Registrar of Companies before the proposed distribution is made. This renders the distribution unlawful. Remedies have to be put in place to legitimise the dividend. Due to the legal implications for the directors (under section 847 of the 2006 Act), such remedies require legal advice. Repayment may be an option where the recipient is another group company or only a few individuals. This is impractical for a listed company and other solutions are necessary.

23.310 If directors propose to use a particular set of financial statements to determine whether a second distribution can be made, the total distributions made by reference to these accounts must be compared to the distributable profits contained in them. [CA06 Sec 840(1)]. This prevents a company avoiding the restrictions by making several small distributions that are permissible individually, but that exceed the amount available for distribution in aggregate.

23.311 Similarly, if financial assistance for the purchase of own shares from distributable profits has been given since the financial statements were prepared, the relevant accounts must be adjusted by the amount of financial assistance or certain payments in respect of, or in connection with, the purchase of own shares. [CA06 Sec 840(1)(2)].

Qualified audit reports and distribution

23.312 If the auditors have qualified their opinion on financial statements that the company is proposing to use to justify paying a dividend, the auditors must state in writing whether the subject matter of their qualification is material in determine the legality of the proposed distribution. [CA06 Secs 837(4), 839(6)]. This statement can be drafted to cover future distributions (including the one proposed) of the same description. [CA06 Sec 837(5)]. This statement must be circulated to members in accordance with section 423 of the 2006 Act (private companies). [CA06 Sec 837(4)].

23.313 There is no legal requirement for the auditors to make a statement regarding a proposed distribution if they gave an unqualified audit report that contains a matter of emphasis. However, if that matter was about, for example, going concern, it may be uncertain whether the directors would be acting in the best interests of the company if they pay a dividend. The directors would be wise to seek legal advice in such circumstances.

23.314 In the case of an interim dividend the previous year's audited annual financial statements will constitute the relevant accounts for that purpose. If the auditors are required to make a statement regarding the materiality of their qualification to proposed dividends, they should, whenever possible, word their statement to cover future distributions (for example, dividends to the value of £X). Otherwise the auditors would need to make a further statement in respect of any interim dividends. The company would have to hold another general meeting to lay that statement before the shareholders (public companies) or (in the case of private companies) circulate it to members in accordance with section 423 of the 2006 Act.

23.315 In audit qualification may be material for distribution purposes but on a 'favourable' sense: any adjustment made to eliminate the need for qualification could only increase the company's net assets or realised profits. An 'unfavourable' qualification means that distributable profits could be less than the amount than would be inferred from the 'relevant accounts'.

23.316 Where the effect of the auditors' qualification is favourable, the auditors could include the following additional statement in their request:

"In our opinion, the qualification is not material for the purpose of determining whether any distribution payable by reference to these financial statements is permitted under sections (830) (and 831 [for public companies only]) of the Companies Act 2006."

23.317 Where the auditors can quantify the effect of an unfavourable audit qualification that is not material for determining a distribution up to a certain amount, they could word the additional statement in their reports as follows:

"In our opinion, the qualification is not material for the purpose of determining whether distributions not exceeding £X in total payable by reference to these financial statements are permitted under sections 830 (and 831 [for public companies only]) of the Companies Act 2006."

Specific issues

Effect of revaluations of PPE on distributable profits

23.318 The revaluation of property, plant and equipment (PPE) can affect the amounts recorded in profit or loss and distributable profits in the following ways:

- Depreciation on revalued assets passes through the profit and loss account.
- The profit on revalued assets that are subsequently sold may not pass through the profit and loss account.
- The revaluation itself may involve writing off depreciation that has previously been charged to the profit and loss account.
- Diminutions in value of assets may need to be taken to the profit and loss account.

Depreciation of revalued assets

23.319 When property, plant and equipment (PPE) is revalued, depreciation is charged to the profit and loss account based on the asset's carrying value, not its original cost. If depreciation on the revalued amount of the asset exceeds the depreciation that would have been charged on the asset's original cost, for distributable profits purposes companies treat the excess depreciation on the revaluation surplus as a realised profit. [CA06 Sec 841(5)].

23.320 Consequently, when PPE is revalued, depreciation of the revaluation surplus does not normally affect the amount of a company's accumulated distributable profits.

Example – Depreciation adjustment for revalued PPE

Ignoring the effect of taxation, a revaluation would have the following effect on the profit and loss account:

	Cost	Valuation	Difference between cost and valuation
	£	£	£
Property, plant and equipment (PPE)	1,000	2,500	1,500
Profit before depreciation	5,000	5,000	n/a
Depreciation at 10% a year	100	250	150
Profit after depreciation	4,900	4,750	150

Therefore, without the requirement to treat the difference between the depreciation of the asset at cost and at valuation as a realised profit, the distributable profit would be £4,750. The profit per the financial statements is after charging depreciation on the revalued amount. Section 841(5) of the 2006 Act adds back the additional depreciation of £150 (that arises because the assets have been revalued) in determining the profits available for distribution.

Without this requirement of the Act, companies might be discouraged from revaluing their PPE, because the extra depreciation charged on the revalued amount would otherwise reduce their profits available for distribution. (Of course, companies might be discouraged from revaluing their assets despite this, because of the effect of the additional depreciation on their reported profits.)

Subsequent sale of revalued assets

23.321 Some items taken to equity need to be included in determining profits available for distribution. For example, an unrealised profit on a revaluation of an item of PPE is credited to a revaluation reserve. If that piece of PPE is disposed of, the gain or loss on the disposal reported in the profit or loss account is calculated by reference to its carrying value, rather than its original cost. Not all the profit on sale based on original cost necessarily passes through the profit or loss account. However, if the asset is sold for qualifying consideration, the whole profit compared to original cost is clearly realised. When an item of PPE carried at valuation is sold, the balance on the revaluation reserve relating to the asset is transferred *via* reserves to retained profits.

23.322 Where an asset's original cost is not known, or where it is not possible to ascertain it without unreasonable delay or expense, then for the purpose of determining whether the company has made a profit or loss in respect of that asset, its cost is taken to be the value shown in the company's earliest available record of its value. [CA06 Sec 842].

Treatment of revalued assets in relevant accounts

23.323 A provision for depreciation or impairment in value of an item of PPE normally is a realised loss if it does not offset a previous revaluation surplus on that asset. Section 841(1) of the 2006 Act permits an exception to this rule. These provisions are complex. A company seeking to rely on them in order to have sufficient distributable profits to pay a dividend is likely to have other difficulties and would be well advised to first seek legal advice.

23.324 Where a company revalues all of its 'fixed assets' even if the revaluation shows an overall deficit, the fall in value can be treated as an unrealised loss for distribution purposes if the company takes advantage of section 841 of the 2006 Act. This applies even if the fall in value is taken to the income statement. If the diminution in value creates a net deficit on the revaluation reserve this restricts a public company's profits available for distribution under section 831 of the 2006 Act's 'net asset test'.

23.325 For this purpose 'fixed assets' are defined as the assets of a company that are intended for use on a continuing basis in the company's activities. [CA06 Sec 853(6)]. These may include PPE, intangibles, investments in subsidiaries, joint ventures and associates and other items traditionally shown under the heading 'Fixed assets' in a Companies Act balance sheet..

23.326 The directors' consideration of the value at any particular time of any 'fixed asset' may be treated as a revaluation. [CA06 Sec 841(4)]. 'Consideration' does not necessarily mean each individual asset is actually valued. It simply means that the directors should have addressed themselves to the question of the asset's value for the purpose of determining the legitimacy of distributions.

23.327 A company may take advantage of the exception in sections 841(1) and (2) of the 2006 Act only if these conditions are satisfied:

- All the company's 'fixed assets' (or all those other than goodwill) have been revalued, either by an actual revaluation or by the directors' consideration of their value.
- The directors' consideration of the value of those fixed assets that have not actually been revalued must take place at the same time as, and must consider the value at the same date as, the revaluation that recognised the particular asset's diminution in value.
- Where there has been no actual valuation, the directors are satisfied that the aggregate value of the fixed assets that they have treated as having been revalued by virtue of their considering the assets' value at the time in question, is not less than the aggregate amount at which those assets are, for the time being, stated in the company's financial statements. [CA06 Sec 841(4)].

23.328 Where the directors are using their consideration of the value of some or all of the fixed assets to justify treating a loss as unrealised the notes to the relevant accounts must state that:

- The directors have considered the value of some of the company's fixed assets without actually revaluing those assets.
- The directors' consideration of the value of those assets that have not been revalued took place at the same time as, and considered the values at the same date as, the revaluation that recognised the particular asset's diminution in value.
- The directors are satisfied that the aggregate value of those assets whose value they have considered was not less than the aggregate amount at which those assets are or were stated in the company's accounts.
- The asset or assets that have diminished in value are recorded in the company's relevant accounts after providing for that diminution in value.

[CA06 Sec 841(4)].

23.329 The examples below illustrate the effect of section 841 of the 2006 Act in different situations.

Values of all of a company's fixed assets

	Book value	Market value	Deficit
	£000	**£000**	**£000**
Land and buildings	1,000	750	250
Plant and machinery	50	40	10
	1,050	790	260

Example 1 – All assets are professionally valued

The market value of all of the fixed assets has been determined by a professional valuation. The diminutions in value may, therefore, be treated as unrealised losses, even though there is an overall deficit of £260,000, because this deficit results from a revaluation of all the fixed assets. [CA06 Sec 841(1)(2)].

Example 2 – Some assets are professionally valued

The market value of the land and buildings has been determined by a professional valuation. The market value of the plant and machinery results from the directors' consideration of its value. The aggregate value of the assets that the directors have considered is £40,000, which is less than their book value of £50,000. The directors cannot claim to be satisfied that those assets' aggregate value is not less than their book value. The directors are, therefore, not able to rely on the exception from sections 841(1) and (2) of the 2006 Act. They must treat both the deficit on the revaluation of the land and buildings and the deficit on the plant and machinery as a realised loss. [CA06 Sec 841(4)].

If the directors had *valued* the plant and machinery assets rather than merely considering their value, both deficits would result from a revaluation of all the fixed assets and the diminutions in value would be treated as unrealised losses. [CA06 Sec 841(1)(2)].

Example 3 – Value of assets 'considered' is greater than the book value

If the directors considered that the plant and machinery's market value was £60,000 (not £40,000), they would be able to treat the deficit on the land and buildings of £250,000 as unrealised. This applies even though the fixed assets (see para 23.118.101) have an overall deficit of £240,000.

However, in both the first and the third examples, if the company were a public company, it might still be prevented from making a distribution even if it could treat the loss as unrealised. This is because a distribution must not reduce the amount of a public company's net assets below the aggregate of its called-up share capital plus its undistributable reserves. [CA06 Sec 831(1)(6)].

Interpreting section 841 of the 2006 Act using a previous interpretation of section 275 of the 1985 Act

23.330 The interpretation of section 841 may cause difficulties in certain circumstances. The responses to the questions discussed below are based on guidance given by Counsel on the application of section 275 of the 1985 Act, which it appears reasonable to read across to section 841 of the 2006 Act. The guidance given below should not be relied upon in isolation. Directors should take their own legal advice in the light of their company's particular circumstances and on the application of section 841 of the 2006 Act.

23.331 When the directors have some of the company's assets valued resulting in falls in value of those assets that affect the company's ability to pay a dividend, after taking legal advice the directors may wish to:

- Consider the value as at the same date of all other assets (excluding goodwill) themselves at the same time that the valuation of the assets that shows the deficit is made.
- Include section 841(4)(b) note in the financial statements for the year in which the valuation took place. The directors should do this even if they do not intend to rely on their consideration of the value to justify a distribution.
- Repeat that note in all subsequent financial statements, because they may become relevant accounts for the purpose of making a distribution in the future.

If the directors take these three steps, unless the value of the assets considered but not revalued by the directors is less than their book value, any falls in value that arise from a revaluation of the company's assets may be treated as unrealised for determining profits available for distribution.

Example 1 – Subsequent release of a provision

Where a provision has been charged to realised profits, and it is subsequently released, does this restore the realised profits in question?

Where an asset has been either written down or provided against and it is then written up again, the initial reaction is that the write-up constitutes a profit that *prima facie* appears to be unrealised. However, the write-up should be treated as a realised profit to the extent that the previous reduction was charged to realised profits. [Tech 02/10 para 3.9(e)]. (This view is supported by *Bishop v Smyrna and Cassaba Railway Co. [1895]* 2 Ch 596, in particular at 601, and by *Stapley v Read Bros. [1924]* 2 Ch 1.)

Example 2 – Which order to apply in releasing provisions

In what order should releases of provisions be applied where provisions have been made in previous years, and where some of these have been treated as realised losses and some as unrealised losses?

The principle expressed above is easy to apply when all provisions have been charged against the same reserve and where the whole of a particular provision is restored at the same time. It seems that there is no established authority or principle that lays down any rule where the position is less simple. The best solution would seem to be to apply common sense. This approach leads to the conclusion that the more recent parts of the provision should normally be regarded as being released before the earlier parts.

Example 3 – Meaning of 'value' and the 'company's accounts'

What is the meaning of the words 'value' and 'the company's accounts' in section 841(4) of the 2006 Act)?

It seems clear that the word 'value' in section 841(4) of the 2006 Act) means market value, not book value.

The question arises whether the 'company's accounts' that are referred to in section 841(4) of the 2006 Act are those financial statements (to, say, 30 September 20X5) that are in the course of preparation, and in which the directors have adjusted the assets' book values (for example, by taking into account depreciation), or the previous financial statements (that is, those to 30 September 20X4).

When section 841(4)(a) of the 2006 Act is relied on, section 841(4)(b) deals with the contents of the note to the financial statements where the directors have considered the value of any of the company's fixed assets, without actually revaluing those assets. Section 841(4)(b)(ii) requires the notes to state:

> *"That they (the directors) are satisfied that the aggregate value of those assets at the time of their consideration was not less than the aggregate amount at which they were then stated in the company's accounts."*

This note makes it clear that the company's accounts for the purpose of section 841(4) of the 2006 Act are those in which the revaluation is incorporated. Thus the directors must compare actual values with the values at which the relevant assets are to be incorporated in the accounts.

This view is supported by the fact that the section 841(4)(a) of the 2006 Act procedure, including the requirement for a section 841(4)(b) of the 2006 Act note, applies also to initial accounts being prepared. [CA06 Sec 841(1)].

Example 4 – Directors' consideration of the value of the company's assets

If no dividend is to be paid by reference to the relevant accounts but the directors have considered the value of the company's fixed assets in accordance with section 841(4) of the 2006 Act, should the note that is needed if a distribution is to be made be included in those accounts under section 841(4)(b) of the 2006 Act?

Relevant accounts are those financial statements that contain the entries that justify a particular distribution, either because they show adequate distributable profits or because they have been specially prepared in order to justify the distribution. (This interpretation seems clear from sections 837(2), 838(2) and 839(2) of the 2006 Act.)

It appears to follow that, if a company does not propose to justify a particular distribution by reference to a particular set of financial statements, section 841(4) does not require those financial statements to contain the special note, because those financial statements are not relevant accounts.

It seems that the note that section 841(4)(b) of the 2006 Act requires need not appear in the financial statements either for the year in which the section 841(4)(a) of the 2006 Act revaluation took place, or for a subsequent year, unless those financial statements are to be relied upon for the purpose of justifying a distribution.

However, if the note is excluded from the financial statements, the directors cannot use those financial statements to justify a distribution in the future. Although the directors may have no plans at that time to make a distribution, they may wish to do so at some time before the next audited financial statements are prepared. If they have not included the note required by section 841(4)(b) of the 2006 Act in their last set of financial statements, they will need to prepare interim accounts to justify the proposed distribution. Consequently, it will be sensible to include in the financial statements the note that section 841(4)(b) of the 2006 Act requires, even where the directors do not intend at that time to make a distribution.

For a private company, the note need not appear in the interim or the initial accounts that the directors rely upon to justify making a distribution. This is because sections 838 and 839 of the 2006 Act, which prescribe the format of interim and initial accounts, do not apply to private companies, which can use management accounts for these purposes.

Example 5 – Omission of the note required by section 841(4)(b) of the 2006 Act

Where the note that section 841(4)(b) of the 2006 Act requires is not included in a company's financial statements, does this omission convert a provision on a revaluation that is made in those financial statements into a realised loss for all future financial statements that are to be used as relevant accounts?

It appears that any financial statements used to justify a distribution are *relevant accounts*. They are also relevant accounts for the purposes of section 841(4)(b) of the 2006 Act, even if the directors do not need to rely on the particular section 841(4)(a) of the 2006 Act revaluation in order to justify a current distribution. Therefore, if a set of financial statements that does not contain a note relating to a section 841(4) of the 2006 Act revaluation that took place in either that year or a previous year become relevant accounts (because they are used to justify a distribution), it seems that the provision that is made on that revaluation becomes, and must remain, a realised loss. Where it becomes necessary to rely on 841(4)(a) of the 2006 Act to justify a subsequent distribution, it will be too late to include the section 841(4)(b) of the 2006 Act note in a subsequent set of financial statements.

This last point, however, is a difficult issue and remains the subject of debate. This is another reason why it is advisable to include the note that section 841(4)(b) of the 2006 Act requires in any financial statements, even where a distribution is not to be made by reference to those financial statements.

Summary of action relating to section 841 of the 2006 Act

23.332 When the directors have some of the company's assets valued resulting in falls in value of those assets that affect the company's ability to pay a dividend, after taking legal advice the directors may wish to:

- Consider the value as at the same date of all other assets (excluding goodwill) themselves at the same time that the valuation of the assets that shows the deficit is made.
- Include the note referred to in section 841(4)(b) in the financial statements for the year in which the valuation took place. The directors should do this even if they do not intend to rely on their consideration of the value to justify a distribution.
- Repeat that note in all subsequent financial statements, because they may become relevant accounts for the purpose of making a distribution in the future.

If the directors take these three steps, unless the value of the assets considered but not revalued by the directors is less than their book value, any falls in value that arise from a revaluation of the company's assets may be treated as unrealised for determining profits available for distribution.

Foreign currency translation

23.333 The accounting standard applied by companies preparing their financial statements in accordance with UK GAAP will depend on whether or not they have adopted FRS 26. Those that have adopted FRS 26 are required to apply FRS 23, 'The effects of changes in foreign exchange rate', while those that have not adopted FRS 26 are required to apply SSAP 20, 'Foreign currency translation'. These standards are considered in detail in chapter 7.

23.334 SSAP 20 and FRS 23 both require that a company should translate into its functional currency those of its currency transactions that are outstanding at the end of the year (for example, creditors for fixed assets purchased from overseas and currency loans) using the rate of exchange at the balance sheet date (that is, the closing rate). Where, however, the rate of exchange is fixed under the terms of the relevant transaction, SSAP 20 (but not FRS 23) requires the company to use that rate. [SSAP 20 para 48].

23.335 Exchange gains and losses arise both on completed foreign currency transactions during the year and on the retranslation of balance sheet foreign currency monetary items. Profits arising from the translation of a monetary asset that comprises qualifying consideration, or a liability denominated in a foreign currency, are realised. [Tech 02/10 para 3.9(d)].

23.336 Under SSAP 20 or FRS 23, where a company has a foreign branch with a functional currency that is different from that of its parent, the exchange differences arising on the translation of the branch's assets and liabilities into the functional currency of the parent are taken directly to reserves *via* the STRGL. The issue is to what extent are these exchange differences realised or unrealised. Gross profits and losses should be analysed separately according to the nature of the assets and liabilities on which they arise. A profit that arises on the retranslation of an asset that comprises qualifying consideration, or a liability, is a realised profit. A profit arising on the retranslation of assets such as property, plant and equipment that does not constitute qualifying consideration is an unrealised profit. Losses on retranslation are realised losses, unless they reverse an unrealised profit. There may be a realised loss to be taken into account when determining profits available for distribution even when the net amount on the reserve is a profit. [Tech 02/10 para 10.60].

23.337 This analysis applies only in straightforward situations where the composition of the foreign branch's assets has not changed significantly during a period. Tech 02/10 addresses more complex situations, noting that reasonable approximations can be made in analysing whether profits arising on exchange differences are realised. [Tech 02/10 paras 11.15, 17].

23.338 While a company measures its foreign currency assets, liabilities and transactions in its functional currency, FRS 23 permits (and SSAP 20 is generally understood not to allow) a company to present its individual financial statements in any currency, referred to as a presentation currency. The presentation currency financial statements include exchange differences arising from translation from functional currency. These exchange differences are similar to those that arise when dealing with a foreign branch with a different functional currency to the parent. Paragraph 11.17 of Tech 02/10 notes that the nature of these exchange differences is complex, but does not address whether they are realised or unrealised. We believe that directors should be conservative regarding such exchange differences bearing in mind their fiduciary duties.

Foreign currency share capital

23.338.1 Companies sometimes have shares denominated in a currency other than their functional currency. For example, a UK based company, with operations located in the UK and transactions mainly denominated in sterling, may have issued shares denominated in US dollars. Tech 02/10 provides useful clarification of the implications of such arrangements based on legal advice received by the Institutes.

23.338.2 Where a company's shares are denominated in a currency other than the company's functional currency, an adjustment arising on any retranslation for accounting purposes is not a profit or loss as a matter of law. The guidance in paragraph 11.20 of Tech 02/10 refers to it as "*an arithmetical difference which does not spring from any substance in law*". This applies irrespective of whether the shares are classified as equity or debt for accounting purposes, although in the former case it is unlikely that an exchange difference would be recognised. Any 'profit' on retranslation cannot enhance a company's distributable reserves. A 'loss' on retranslation of shares presented as debt can, however, reduce the distributable reserves of a public company, because of the additional requirement in law about net assets exceeding share capital and undistributable reserves.

23.338.3 The effect of exchange rate movements should be considered even if no retranslation is recorded for accounting purposes. The common law has the effect of restricting distributions where to do otherwise would result in the net assets falling below the functional currency worth of the share capital. There is a rule of law that where the share capital is denominated in another currency (other than the functional currency) the share capital is in fact fixed as that other currency amount. Thus the current worth of the share capital in functional currency terms must be compared with the net assets in functional currency. To the extent that a distribution would result in the net assets falling below the current functional currency worth of the share capital, the ability to make such a distribution is restricted. [Tech 02/10 paras 11.21 to 11.24].

Use of presentation currency

23.338.4 Realised profits and losses are measured by reference to the company's functional currency. The accounting gain or loss arising upon the retranslation of the whole of the accounts from the company's functional currency to a presentation currency is not a profit or loss as a matter of law. Such an amount cannot, therefore, be a realised profit or loss. The position is, hence, similar to exchange differences arising on foreign currency share capital as described above. [Tech 02/10 para 11.8].

23.338.5 The situation is, distinguished from that of a branch where the exchange difference arising on retranslation will be a realised profit or loss to the extent that the branch net assets were qualifying consideration when the profit or loss arose. [Tech 02/10 para 11.12].

23.338.6 Paragraphs 11.7 to 11.34 of Tech 02/10 set out seven principles to be applied in relation to foreign currency share capital and the use of presentation currencies. Examples of the application of the principles are set out in Appendix 5 to Tech 02/10.

Capitalisation of development costs

23.339 Where development costs are shown as an asset in the financial statements, any amount in respect of those costs should be treated as a realised loss, unless there are special circumstances justifying the directors' decision not to treat the costs as a realised loss and certain statements are made in the notes to the financial statements. [CA06 Sec 844]. Where development costs are capitalised in accordance with SSAP 13 (see chapter 15), these special circumstances generally exist. The note to the financial statements that states the special circumstances that permit the company to capitalise development costs must state also that the development costs have not been treated as a realised loss and the justification (the special circumstances contained in SSAP 13) the directors used for adopting this treatment. [CA06 Sec 844(2)(3)].

Goodwill

23.340 Goodwill arising on consolidation does not affect realised and distributable profits, because individual companies make distributions not groups. Goodwill can arise in a company — for example, where a company purchases an unincorporated business.

23.341 Where goodwill arises in a company's individual financial statements the goodwill will become a realised loss as the goodwill is amortised or written down for impairment in accordance with relevant accounting standards.

23.342 For periods ending before 23 December 1998, purchased goodwill may have been accounted for under SSAP 22 'Accounting for goodwill'. Such goodwill may have remained eliminated against reserves under UK GAAP under the transitional provisions of FRS 10. Such goodwill should be regarded as a realised loss to the extent that, had it always been recognised as an asset, it would have been amortised or impaired in accordance with FRS 10, 'Goodwill and intangible assets'.

23.342.1 If the business to which the acquired goodwill relates is disposed of or closed, FRS 10 requires the profit or loss on disposal to include the goodwill previously taken to reserves to the extent that it has not previously been charged to the profit and loss account. Notional amortisation or impairment for the purposes of calculating realised profits does not affect this financial reporting requirement. However, the effect of the disposal on realised profits, is therefore, net of any amount already treated as a realised loss.

23.343 Where negative goodwill pre-dating FRS 10 remains credited to reserves, a company should credit it initially to an unrealised reserve (see further chapter 25). Under the principles in Tech 02/10, negative goodwill up to the fair values of the non-monetary assets acquired should be treated as being realised in the periods in which the non-monetary assets are recovered, whether through depreciation or sale. Where the negative goodwill exceeds the value of the non-monetary assets, this excess should be treated as being realised in the periods expected to benefit. However, negative goodwill should not be treated as a realised profit in the case of a sale of the non-monetary asset where the consideration received is not qualifying consideration.

Hedge accounting

23.344 Where hedge accounting is obtained under FRS 26, 'Financial instruments: Recognition and measurement', management should consider the combined effect of both sides of the hedging relationship to determine whether there is a realised profit or loss. [Tech 02/10 para 3.19]. This applies both to changes in fair value of open contracts and settled transactions.

23.345 Under FRS 26, net investment hedge accounting of foreign operations arises in consolidated financial statements. Consolidated financial statements are not relevant for justifying distributions. A company may hedge account for a net investment in a foreign branch in its individual financial statements. As noted above, determining whether the retranslation profits and losses of a branch's assets and liabilities are realised can be complex, with a consequent effect on the profits and losses on the hedging instrument.

23.346 Where a company undertakes a fair value hedge of a foreign currency risk, the gross profits and losses on remeasuring the hedging instrument and the hedged item for the hedged risk are both recognised in the profit and loss account. Foreign currency markets are generally very liquid and active, thus both the profit on one side of the hedge relationship and the loss on the other are 'readily convertible to cash' and are, therefore, realised. In such cases, no special consideration of hedging aspects is required (including hedge effectiveness and ineffectiveness). [Tech 02/10 para 5.2]. However, if the currency being hedged is illiquid or inactive, further analysis is required. [Tech 02/10 paras 5.3-5.4].

23.347 Under a cash flow hedge, profits and losses deferred in the hedging reserve are unrealised and become realised only when the hedged item affects profit or loss. Whether the ineffective element of the profit or loss on remeasurement of the hedging instrument recognised in profit or loss is realised depends on whether it is 'readily convertible to cash'.

23.348 Amounts taken to the hedging reserve may, for example, include profits or losses on short-term derivative contracts that form part of a rolling-hedge strategy, but which have matured. Such profits and losses are unrealised, while FRS 26 requires them to remain deferred in equity as part of a cash flow hedge. [Tech 02/10 para 5.8].

23.349 Under a group's hedging strategy, different companies in the group may hold the hedging instrument and hedged item. In these cases, there is no hedge relationship within an individual company and thus the hedging principles in the distributable guidance do not apply. Accordingly, the general realisation principles apply to the hedged item and hedging instrument separately. [Tech 02/10 paras 5.20 to 5.21].

Treasury shares

23.350 Treasury shares are purchased out of distributable profits. When a company purchases the shares, it reduces its distributable profits by the consideration paid.

23.351 If the company cancels treasury shares, it reduces its issued share capital by the nominal value of the cancelled shares and transfers this amount to a capital redemption reserve. This does not impact distributable profits; the cost of the treasury shares has already been charged to distributable profits.

23.352 Where treasury shares are sold for cash, the proceeds are treated as a realised profit up to the original purchase price paid by the company for the shares. If the proceeds exceed the purchase price, the excess is transferred to the share premium account.

23.353 Sometimes an ESOP trust acquires its sponsor's treasury shares for cash for the purposes of the company's employee share scheme. This is a sale of treasury shares for cash, so the impact on distributable profits is as described above. The former treasury shares, now held by the ESOP trust, are accounted for and treated for distributable profit purposes as if they had been purchased by the ESOP trust from a third party. The impact on distributable profits of shares held within an ESOP trust is considered in section 7 of Tech 02/10 and in chapter 12.

Shares classified as financial liabilities and debt instruments classified as equity

23.354 The treatment of shares as financial liabilities, or debt instruments as equity or either as compound instruments for accounting purposes has a complex interaction with the legal rules on distributions and capital repayments. Section 6 of Tech 02/10 provides ten key principles, underlying statute and common law in respect of distributions and capital maintenance, for determining distributable profits when dealing with such contracts. The application of the principles to eight common scenarios involving shares and compound instruments is illustrated in the technical release.

23.355 Principles 1, 2 and 3 are particularly relevant for distributions presented as interest expense. Essentially, a dividend accounted for as interest expense is not a loss, as a matter of law; the accounting is an advanced recognition of a future distribution; and distributable profits are only consumed by a dividend when it is paid or when it is approved by members and becomes a legal liability. [Tech 02/10 paras 6.7 to 6.15]. Conversely, an interest expense presented as a dividend is a loss not a distribution. Consequently, when directors assess whether their companies have sufficient distributable profits to make a distribution, they will have to reverse the accounting for dividends that have been charged as interest expense and *vice versa* for interest expense treated as a distribution.

Capitalisation of reserves

23.356 Section 831(4) of the 2006 Act defines a company's undistributable reserves as including *"the amount by which the company's accumulated unrealised profits, so far as not previously utilised by capitalisation … exceed its accumulated, unrealised losses (so far as not previously written off in a reduction or reorganisation of capital duly made)"*. Capitalisation is defined as including every description of capitalisation except a transfer of the company's profits to its capital redemption reserve (on or after 22 December 1980). This definition implies that a company may utilise its undistributable reserves, such as a revaluation reserve, for bonus issues. The Act does not require the revaluation reserve to be reinstated if it has been used in a manner permitted by law.

23.357 Tech 02/10 concludes that the debit is an unrealised loss. Private companies do not take unrealised losses into account in determining profits available for distribution. The restatement of a revalued asset (whether investment property, other property plant and equipment or investment in subsidiaries) to a cost basis restricts a public company's profits available for distribution under section 831 of the 2006 Act's 'net asset test'. The effect of the unrealised loss on the net assets test may be mitigated by the existence of recognised unrealised profits. [Tech 02/10 para 10.35].

Transactions within the group

Capital contributions

23.358 'Capital contributions' or gifts are realised profits for the recipient company if they are received in cash or an asset that is readily convertible to cash. If they are not received in qualifying consideration, the amount is unrealised, although it may become realised if the consideration is converted into qualifying consideration, or the asset is depreciated or sold. [Tech 02/10 para 3.9(f)].

Proposed dividends

23.359 Proposed dividends and intra-group dividends from UK companies are addressed in paragraphs 9.6-9.18 of Tech 02/10. Following legal advice, the Institutes have determined that companies that rely on dividends from UK subsidiaries to support their own distributions have to require those subsidiaries to pay or approve those dividends before the year end.

23.360 Under FRS 21, dividends are recognised when a liability to pay the dividend is created. Receiving companies recognise dividends at the same time as the paying company recognises the liability to pay a dividend. In the UK, this means that:

- Interim dividends are booked when paid. As a matter of law, interim dividends do not become a legal liability until they are paid. This is because they are at the discretion of directors, who can reverse a decision to pay a dividend at any time up to the date of payment.
- Final dividends are booked when they legally become a liability. This is when they are approved, either by the members in general meeting or, for private companies, by the members passing a written resolution. Companies can 'convert' an interim dividend into a final approved dividend (by approval by members in general meeting or, for private companies, by written resolution);

[Tech 02/10 para 2.10].

23.361 In some jurisdictions, the declaration of a dividend by the board of directors creates a liability for the company, because it would require a members' resolution to cancel the payment of that dividend. In such cases, the receiving company recognises the dividend receivable when it is declared by the directors. Where a parent company relies on dividend income from UK subsidiaries to create distributable reserves from which it will pay its own dividend, the dividend must be paid or approved by members before the parent company's year end. Otherwise the parent must prepare 'interim accounts' that account for the dividends received after the year end to support its distribution.

23.362 Paragraphs 9.11 to 9.17 of Tech 02/10 address what constitutes 'payment' in a group context. The following items constitute payment; in other scenarios, the position is more complex and depends on the specific facts. Companies may wish to seek legal advice.

- Payment in cash or other assets. (To support a cash distribution by the parent, the 'other assets' received from the subsidiary must be 'qualifying consideration'.)
- Recording the dividend in an inter-company account if this reduces the amount previously owed to the subsidiary by the parent. (Recording a dividend on inter-company account does not necessarily constitute payment.)
- Effecting the dividend *via* a group treasury function, where the subsidiary company instructs the group treasury function to debit the subsidiary's account and credit the parent's account.

- If there is no doubt as to the paying subsidiary's ability to pay the dividend, individual dividends can be 'paid' by the execution as a Deed of an acknowledgment of liability to pay the amount entered in the accounting records as a payable by the subsidiary and a receivable by the parent company or the constitution of such liability pursuant to an enforceable contract under Scots law. The effect of this latter arrangement is that the subsidiary has paid the interim dividend and the parent has returned the same amount to its subsidiary by way of loan without the need for a cash transaction.

[Tech 02/10 paras 9.12 – 9.16].

23.363 If a parent company or a subsidiary has property, plant and equipment (PPE) that has been revalued in accordance with the alternative accounting rules, the surplus taken to the revaluation reserve is unrealised. If the company sells these revalued assets to another company within the same group for qualifying consideration, the revaluation surplus attaching to those assets in the company's revaluation reserve is realised. This amount is then *prima facie* available for distribution.

23.364 Similarly, a parent company could sell one of its subsidiaries to another subsidiary at more than its carrying amount for qualifying consideration and thus generate a gain on disposal that would, *prima facie*, be a realised profit available for distribution.

23.365 These transactions should be carried out at arm's length and supported by proper legal documentation. The fact that a transaction is undertaken between companies in the same group need not prevent the profit on the transaction being realised and, therefore, distributable. A profit arising on an intra-group transaction is unlikely to be realised if, for example, the transaction (and any related arrangements) results in an increase in the inter-company balance between the companies involved.

23.366 Directors have to take into account the effect of the accounting standards in force when the dividend is proposed and when it is paid. In determining a dividend proposed in respect of one financial year but paid in the following financial year, directors should consider the known impact of new accounting standards on the latter year. Similarly, in paying an interim dividend in the current financial year, directors should consider the effect on opening distributable reserves of new accounting standards adopted in the current year, even if the 'relevant accounts' used to justify the distribution were prepared prior to the implementation of the new standard. [Tech 02/10 paras 3.30 — 3.32].

Pre-acquisition profits

23.367 Pre-acquisition profits are those profits earned by a subsidiary company before it is acquired by a group. Following a change brought about by the Companies Act 1981, in certain circumstances, it is now possible for a parent company to distribute to its shareholders pre-combination profits arising in its subsidiaries (see the example below).

> **Example**
>
> Pre-acquisition reserves are a company's retained earnings at the date on which that company becomes a subsidiary of another company. Before the enactment of the Companies Act 1981, where a subsidiary paid a dividend to its parent company out of its pre-acquisition profits, the parent company would treat the dividend received as a reduction of the cost of its investment in that subsidiary. Consequently, dividends the subsidiary paid to the parent company out of pre-acquisition profits were not available for distribution to the parent company's shareholders.
>
> However, the Companies Act 1981 amended paragraph 15(5) of the then Schedule 8 to the Companies Act 1948. This change had the effect that where a subsidiary now pays a dividend to its parent company out of pre-acquisition profits, that dividend need not necessarily be applied as a reduction in the cost of the investment in the subsidiary. [FRS 6 App 1 para 16]. Such a dividend should be applied to reduce the carrying value of the investment to the extent that it is necessary to provide for a diminution in value of the investment in the subsidiary as stated in the parent company's financial statements. To the extent that this is not necessary, it appears that the amount received will be a realised profit in the hands of the parent company. However, in this example, on consolidation, any part of the dividend received by the parent company that has not been applied to reduce the cost of the investment, will need to be adjusted on consolidation by taking out of the parent company's realised reserves an amount that will cause the goodwill on consolidation to remain the same as in previous years.

Other transactions

23.368 A bed and breakfast transaction is one in which a company agrees to sell certain assets (such as securities) to a third party (normally a broker) and arranges to repurchase them, or identical assets, shortly thereafter, usually overnight, for the same price. Such transactions are normally undertaken to crystallise a capital gain or loss for tax purposes. They may also be undertaken in an attempt to turn an unrealised revaluation gain on investments into realised and therefore distributable profits. Bed and breakfast transactions are examples of sale and repurchase transactions to which the provisions of FRS 5 apply. In general, they are unlikely to create realised profits. Chapter 3 considers the implications of such transactions.

Other matters covered by Technical Release 02/10

'Cash box' structures

23.369 Cash box structures are used in a variety of ways by listed companies to raise cash. The most common use is in a cash placing where the cash box structure is used to raise cash, usually to finance an acquisition. However, cash box structures are also commonly used in convertible bond issues and also in conjunction with a rights issue. Cash box placings are typically structured in such a way that merger relief applies, so that the premium representing the difference between the issue price of the shares and their nominal value does not go to the share premium account. Instead this amount goes to a reserve, and Tech 02/10 provides guidance on whether this reserve is a realised profit. Applying the linkage principle, it is necessary to look beyond the initial cash box placing to the purpose for which the cash is raised and what is done with it. If the transaction taken as a whole results in an increase in qualifying consideration (that is, is readily convertible into cash as set out in paragraph 3.11 of Tech 02/10), the reserve will be realised. Tech 02/10 applies this analysis to assess whether realised profits are created in a number of scenarios linked to cash box placings. For example, if the capital had been raised to finance the acquisition of a subsidiary, the company is not free to retain the cash and the overall effect is an acquisition by way of share for share exchange. The resulting profit is, therefore, unrealised. [Tech 02/10 paras 12.20 to 23]. By contrast, if the cash box placing is to fund unspecified acquisitions in the future which are not yet identified, the reserve will be in the form of qualifying consideration and this will increase the distributable profits. [Tech 02/10 paras 12.29 to 31].

23.369.1 Applying the linkage principle, it is necessary to look beyond the initial cash box placing to the purpose for which the cash is raised and what is done with it. If the transaction taken as a whole results in an increase in qualifying consideration (that is, is readily convertible into cash as set out in paragraph 3.11 of Tech 02/10), the reserve will be realised. Tech 02/10 applies this analysis to assess whether realised profits are created in a number of scenarios linked to cash box placings. For example, if the capital had been raised to finance the acquisition of a subsidiary, the company is not free to retain the cash and the overall effect is an acquisition by way of share for share exchange. The resulting profit is, therefore, unrealised. [Tech 02/10 paras 12.20 to 23]. By contrast, if the cash box placing is to fund unspecified acquisitions in the future which are not yet identified, the reserve will be in the form of qualifying consideration and this will increase the distributable profits. [Tech 02/10 paras 12.29 to 31].

Other items

23.370 Tech 02/10 also considers the implications for distributable profits of the following:

- Business combinations involving businesses under common control carried out at fair value (see further chapter 25).
- Changes in circumstances including changes in accounting policies.

[Tech 02/10 para 3.28].

Public companies — impact of 'net asset test'

23.371 A public company cannot make distributions that reduce its net assets below the aggregate of its called-up share capital plus undistributable reserves (the 'net asset test'). Whereas a private company can make a distribution provided it has realised profits available, a public company must also take any net unrealised losses into account.

23.372 'Net assets' means the aggregate of the company's assets less the aggregate of its liabilities, which are shown in its 'relevant accounts'. [CA06 Sec 831(2)(3)].

23.373 'Undistributable reserves' include:

- The share premium account.
- The capital redemption reserve.
- The excess of accumulated unrealised profits that have not previously been capitalised over accumulated unrealised losses that have not previously been written off by a reduction or a re-organisation of capital. For this purpose, capitalisation includes the issuing of bonus shares, but it excludes transfers of profits to the capital redemption reserve that have been made after 22 December 1980.
- Any reserve that the company, for any other reason, is prohibited from distributing. For instance, a reserve that is subject to a restriction by the court in a reduction of capital approved by the court; or revaluation reserves in respect of property, plant and equipment, which are unrealised profits. Under the guidance in Tech 02/10, cash flow hedge reserves are unrealised profits or losses until the hedged transaction affects profit or loss. A fair value or available-for-sale reserve may, however, be wholly or partly realised, depending on whether the assets fair valued are 'readily convertible into cash'. If there is a net debit on the fair value or AFS reserve, the foreign currency translation reserve or the cash flow hedge reserve, this will restrict a public company's profits available for distribution.

[CA06 Sec 831(4)].

23.374 Although not specifically mentioned in section 831 of the 2006 Act, the redenomination reserve is also an undistributable reserve. It may be used to pay up fully paid bonus shares but is otherwise regarded as part of the company's paid up share capital. [CA06 Sec 628].

23.375 Under UK GAAP financial instruments are presented according to the substance of their contractual terms, determined by the principles in FRS 25inancial instruments: Presentation', (see 'Manual of Accounting – Financial instruments'). This accounting treatment can impact a company's net assets and may affect the application of the section 831 'net asset test'. For example, where preference shares are presented as a liability, that liability reduces net assets, from a pure accountancy point of view but as indicated below does not in itself affect the 'net asset test' in the Act.

23.376 Similarly, the presentation of some components of compound financial instruments that are legally debt within equity (shareholders' funds) creates debits and credits that are difficult to interpret in the net asset test. Debits in equity may restrict a public company's profits available for distribution. Credits in equity do not increase such profits, but they may be unavailable to absorb debits that restrict them.

23.377 The Institutes, in section 6 of Tech 02/10, developed and codified with English and Scottish Counsel some principles for dealing with these items, including these four principles (which remain valid under the 2006 Act; references to the 1985 Act have been changed to those in the 2006 Act):

- The treatment of certain shares wholly as liabilities does not in itself affect the application of the section 831 of the 2006 Act 'net asset test' for public companies and thus does not restrict distributable profits. [Tech 02/10 para 6.24].
- A debit to equity arising from an advance recognition of a future distribution or capital repayment does not form part of share capital and undistributable reserves (as defined) for the purposes of section 831 of the 2006 Act and thus restricts distributable profits for public companies under that section. [Tech 02/10 para 6.31]. Legally, when dividends are treated and accrued as interest expense, this is anadvance recognition of the distribution.
- On initial recognition, split accounting for compound financial instruments does not restrict distributable profits for public companies under section 831 of the 2006 Act. [Tech 02/10 para 6.35]. Split accounting a compound instrument that is legally a share is neutral to the net asset test. However, where the compound instrument is legally debt, any credit to equity reflects an increase in net assets, but not a corresponding increase in 'share capital and undistributable reserves'. This imbalance reduces any pre-existing restriction on distributable profits. It does not create distributable profits. (See para 6.37 of Tech 02/10.)
- The accretion of the liability component of compound financial instruments reduces distributable reserves for public companies under section 831 of the 2006 Act, unless the instrument is legally debt. [Tech 02/10 para 6.38]. Where a compound financial instrument is legally a share and has been split accounted into its debt and equity components, the 'interest charge' for the accretion of the debt component is not a loss as a matter of law and has no effect on share capital and undistributable reserves. Hence, under the net asset test, the amount that a public company can distribute is restricted by the accumulated amount of 'interest charge' debit. The initial credit to equity, which is legally share capital (and share premium) cannot absorb the accumulating 'interest charge' debited ultimately to retained earnings due to the accretion of the liability. Ultimately this debit will cumulatively equal the initial credit to equity. (See para 6.39 of Tech 02/10.) Where the compound instrument that has been split accounted is legally debt, the 'interest charge' can be offset by the initial credit to equity (as it is not legally share capital or share premium). The debit does not cause a restriction on a

public company's profits available for distribution. (See para 6.40 of Tech 02/10.)

23.378 Similar issues arise from some aspects of share-based payment accounting. Section 7 of Tech 02/10 provides guidance on the impact these have on companies in general and the 'net asset test' for public companies.

23.379 Legally, if share capital or share premium is shown as a liability, this does not reduce the total share capital and related share premium. However, for the net asset test, the amount of share capital and undistributable reserves is determined by reference to the amount in equity in the company's relevant accounts. Therefore, the amount of share capital and related share premium presented as a financial liability is excluded from the amount of share capital and undistributable reserves for the purpose of the net asset test. This was confirmed in BERR's (formerly the DTI and now known as BIS) guidance notes on applying Statutory Instrument 2004/2947. Similar guidance is included in the BIS's equivalent publication under the 2006 Act issued in June 2008.

23.380 Consequently, the presentation of preference shares as a liability does not result in an immediate restriction in the amount of profits available for distribution by a public company.

23.381 The table below, which sets out extracts from the balance sheets of four companies, gives examples of the method of calculating distributable profits.

Examples of distributable profits in private and public companies

	Company 1		Company 2		Company 3		Company 4	
	£	£	£	£	£	£	£	£
A share capital		1,000		1,000		1,000		1,000
B Unrealised profits	150		150		150		–	
C Unrealised losses	–		(200)		(200)		(200)	
D Net unrealised profits		150		–		–		–
E Net unrealised losses		–		(50)		(50)		(200)
F Realised profits	300		300		300		300	
G Realised losses	–		–		(120)		(120)	
H Net realised profits		300		300		180		180
I Share capital and Reserves		1,450		1,250		1,130		980
Maximum distributable profit:								
Private company (H)		300		300		180		180
Public company (H-E)		300		250		130		Nil

Investment companies

23.382 An investment company may make a distribution at any time out of those of its accumulated realised *revenue* profits that have not previously been either distributed or capitalised, less its accumulated revenue losses (realised and unrealised, and only insofar as they have not been previously written off in a reduction or re-organisation of capital). Capital profits and losses are ignored:

- if at the time the amount of its assets is at least equal to one and a half times the aggregate of its liabilities to creditors;
- if, and to the extent that, the distribution does not reduce that amount to less than one and a half times that aggregate; and
- if the conditions in section 832(5) of the 2006 Act are met.

23.383 An investment company is, therefore, able to satisfy the HM Revenue and Customs condition to be an investment company of non-retention of income, because it may make distributions even where the value of its investments has fallen.

23.384 The conditions in section 832(5) of the 2006 Act, which must be satisfied before an investment company may make a distribution on this basis, are:

- The company's shares must be listed on a recognised UK investment exchange (other than an overseas investment exchange) within the meaning of Part 18 of the Financial Services and Markets Act 2000.
- During the period beginning with the first day of the accounting reference period immediately preceding that in which the proposed distribution is to be made (or, where the distribution is proposed to be made during the company's first accounting reference period, the first day of that period) and ending with the date of that distribution, the company must not have:
  - Distributed any of its capital profits.
  - Applied any unrealised profits or capital profits (whether realised or unrealised) in paying up debentures or any amounts unpaid on any of its issued shares. This means that company may not distribute indirectly any amounts that are not available for distribution directly.

  [CA06 Sec 832(5)(6)].
- The company must have given the Registrar of Companies notice of its intention to carry on business as an investment company at one of the following times:
  - Before the beginning of the period referred to in the point immediately above.
  - As soon as reasonably practicable after the date on which the company was incorporated.

  [CA06 Sec 832(5)(c)].

  This condition prevents companies adopting investment company status merely for a particular distribution.
- The amount of the company's assets must be at least 50 per cent greater than the aggregate of its liabilities to creditors. [CA06 Sec 832(1)(3)]. The company must not include any uncalled share capital as an asset. [CA06 Sec 832(7)]. In this context, 'liabilities to creditors' includes any provision for liabilities to creditors. [CA06 Sec 832(4)]. However, although 'creditors' is not defined for this purpose in the Act, it is the clear intention of the legislators that this amount should exclude amounts in respect of shares. 'Liabilities to creditors', therefore, excludes share capital and share premium presented as financial liabilities. It also excludes other amounts due to shareholders in their capacity as such, including accruals for dividends and redemption premiums that have been presented as expenses in the profit and loss account/income statement and liabilities in the balance sheet. It does not exclude general accruals, deferred income or deferred tax. [Tech 02/10 para 2.47]. Ordinary dividends are rarely accrued in the balance sheet. Only once they become legally binding liabilities are they recognised in the

balance sheet. A shareholder's right to an unpaid dividend is as a creditor of the company rather than as a shareholder.

23.385 Section 832 of the 2006 Act is an alternative rather than an additional test for investment companies. An investment company may be able to make a distribution in accordance with section 831 of the 2006 Act even if cannot comply with section 832 of that Act.

23.386 The following example sets out extracts from the balance sheets of four investment companies. The example shows the difference if the four companies calculated their distributions in accordance with section 832 of the 2006 Act compared with section 831 of that Act:

Examples of distributable profits in investment companies under sections 832 and 831 of the 2006 Act

	Company 1		Company 2		Company 3		Company 4	
	£	£	£	£	£	£	£	£
A Share capital		1,000		1,000		1,000		1,000
B Share premium		100		100		100		100
C Unrealised capital profits	600		600		600		600	
D Unrealised revenue profits	–				100		100	
E Unrealised Capital losses	–		(700)		(700)		(700)	
F Unrealised revenue losses	–		(250)		(250)		(250)	
G Net unrealised reserves		600		(350)		(250)		(250)
H Realised revenue profits	1,200		1,200		1,200		1,200	
I Realised capital profits	–		–		100		100	
J Realised capital losses	–		–		–		(600)	
K Realised revenue losses	–		–		(150)		(150)	
L Net realised reserves		1,200		1,200		1,150		550

	Company 1 £	Company 2 £	Company 3 £	Company 4 £
M Share capital and reserves	2,900	1,950	2,000	1,400
N Total liabilities to creditors[3]	1,300	1,300	1,300	1,300
O Total assets	4,200	3,250	3,300	2,700
Maximum distributable profits—				
Special rules for an investment company				
(I) per section 832				
The lower of:				
(a) Realised revenue profits (H) less accumulated revenue losses (K + F)	1,200	950	800	800
(b) 150 per cent asset test, O–(1 ½ × N)	2,250	1,300	1,350	750
Amount distributable	1,200	950	800	750
Normal rules for a public company				
(ii) per section 831 (the lower of L and (L + G))	1,200	850	900	300

[3] It is presumed for the purpose of this example that all liabilities are to creditors and do not relate to shares classified as liabilities.

Long-term insurance business

23.387 The normal rules of section 830 of the 2006 Act (requirement for realised profits and the section 831 'net asset test') apply to insurance companies. However, for the purposes of determining whether there is a realised profit, the definition of realised profits in section 853(4) of the 2006 Act that refers to being determined by reference to generally accepted accounting principles is displaced in favour of special rules in section 843 of the 2006 Act.

23.388 These special rules apply to an authorised insurance company (as defined in section 1165 of the 2006 Act), other than an insurance special purpose vehicle (as defined in section 843(8) of that Act), carrying on long-term insurance business. An amount included in the relevant part of the company's balance sheet is treated as a realised profit if it:

- represents a surplus in the fund or funds maintained by it in respect of its long-term business (as defined in sub-section (7) and which includes both with-profits life business and other like business); and

- has not been allocated to policyholders or, as the case may be, carried forward unappropriated in accordance with asset identification rules made under section 142(2) of the Financial Services and Markets Act 2000.

23.389 For this purpose the relevant part of the balance sheet is that part of the balance sheet that represents accumulated profit or loss. A surplus in the fund or funds maintained by the company in respect of its long-term business means an excess of the assets representing that fund or those funds over the liabilities of the company attributable to its long-term business, as shown by an actuarial investigation.

23.390 A deficit in the fund or funds maintained by the company in respect of its long-term business is treated as a realised loss. For this purpose, a deficit in any such fund or funds means an excess of the liabilities of the company attributable to its long-term business over the assets representing that fund or those funds, as shown by an actuarial investigation.

23.391 Subject to this, any profit or loss arising in the company's long-term business is left out of account when determining realised profits and losses.

23.392 For the purpose of these requirements, an actuarial investigation means an investigation made into the financial condition of an authorised insurance company in respect of its long-term business, by an actuary appointed as actuary to the company:

- carried out once every period of twelve months in accordance with Rules made under Part 10 of the Financial Services and Markets Act 2000; or
- carried out in accordance with a requirement imposed by section 166 of that Act.

23.393 Much of the guidance (such as in Tech 02/10) on identifying generally accepted principles used in determining of realised profits and losses is in relation to section 853(4) of the 2006 Act. To that extent, it is inapplicable to authorised insurance companies (other than special purpose vehicles) to which the above mentioned special rule applies instead. That guidance, however, should not be overlooked, because, where such a company is a public company, it must also have regard to the section 831 'net asset test'.

Unlimited companies

23.394 An unlimited company can repay its share capital by passing a special resolution of members to reduce its share capital or share premium in any manner. The 2006 Act does not require a company to have the power to do so in its articles of association, as was the case under the 1985 Act. If the amount of the reduction is not repaid immediately or in an agreed schedule of staged repayments, it is credited to a reserve. Such a reserve in an unlimited company is still subject to the same rules on distribution of profit as a limited company. That is that the profit must be realised and available for distribution.

23.395 Under Regulation 7(2) of SI 2008/1886, any reserve created by a reduction of capital prior to 1 October 2008 is treated as a realised profit available for distribution in accordance with Part 23 of the 2006 Act. Similarly, for capital reductions on or after 1 October 2008 the reserve is also realised and available for distribution in accordance with Part 23 of the 2006 Act. [SI 2008/1915]. As such, if the company has a deficit on distributable profits the amount of any distribution from the reserve arising on the capital reduction must take this deficit into account. An unlimited company may have unrealised profits that it is not able to distribute. It can capitalise these profits as share capital then reduce its capital with immediate or staged repayment to shareholders.

Chapter 24

Consolidated financial statements

Chapter 24

Consolidated financial statements

Introduction

24.1 This chapter refers to the requirements of FRS 2, 'Accounting for subsidiary undertakings'. FRS 2 was amended in June 2009 to update references that were previously made to the Companies Act 1985 to the corresponding requirements which are now included in the Companies Act 2006. The amendments arise from the introduction of the Companies Act 2006, 'The Large and Medium-sized Companies and Groups (Accounts and Reports) Regulations 2008 and from 'The Small Companies and Groups (Accounts and Directors') Report Regulations 2008'. Section I of this chapter considers the purpose of consolidated financial statements. It also considers those entities that are required to prepare consolidated financial statements and those entities that are required to be consolidated as subsidiaries. Furthermore, it looks at the reasons parents must exclude certain subsidiary undertakings from their consolidated financial statements and the additional disclosures that then apply. It also sets out the disclosure required in the consolidated financial statements concerning all subsidiary undertakings. Section II deals with the practical aspects of performing a consolidation and section III deals with the measurement and disclosure of minority interests.

24.2 In this chapter the terms 'subsidiary' and 'subsidiary undertaking' are used interchangeably and unless otherwise stated, 'subsidiary' is used to mean 'subsidiary undertaking' as defined in section 1162 of the Companies Act 2006 with regard to preparing consolidated financial statements and not as defined in section 1159 of the Companies Act 2006. (See further para 24.172.)

[The next paragraph is 24.6.]

Section I — The group and its structure

Concept of the group

24.6 The 'group' is defined in the Act to mean *'a parent undertaking and its subsidiary undertakings'*. [CA06 Sec 474(1)]. However, three concepts have evolved since the first consolidations were made that concern how the group is established and how the financial statements of the companies forming the group are consolidated. The three concepts are the:

- Proprietary concept.
- Entity concept.
- Parent company concept.

24.7 Each of these concepts is explained in the paragraphs that follow.

Proprietary concept

24.8 The proprietary concept considers the group as if the parent's members are only concerned with the proportion of the assets and liabilities of the group that they own. Consequently, it takes a very narrow view of the group. The members are, therefore, not concerned with the control they might have over the proportion of assets (and liabilities) that are owned, in effect, by minorities.

24.9 Under this concept the consolidated balance sheet deals only with the proportion of assets and liabilities that the parent owns in a subsidiary. Similarly, the profit and loss account would deal with only an equivalent proportion of revenues and expenses of such a subsidiary. Consequently, no minority interests would be shown in the consolidated financial statements.

24.10 This concept of accounting is not generally used in the UK, although it may be seen as a foundation for the equity method and for proportional consolidation. Equity accounting and proportional consolidation are considered further in chapter 27.

Parent company concept

24.11 The parent company concept requires 100 per cent consolidation of all controlled subsidiaries as its base, even if the parent has less than 100 per cent of the shares in the subsidiary. However, it does recognise that the parent company's members' interest is limited to its shareholding in subsidiaries. Consequently, minority interests are not recognised as shareholders' funds, but are shown separately either before or after shareholders' funds.

24.12 This concept developed in the UK and stems from the early days of consolidation when the consolidated balance sheet was seen as a supplement to the parent company's balance sheet. It is the concept that still underlies UK GAAP. Traditionally, this concept has also been the one embodied within IFRS, but the issue of IAS 27 (revised) in January 2008 sees international accounting move to the entity concept (see further Manual of Accounting – IFRS for the UK).

Entity concept

24.13 The entity concept considers the group as a single entity. Consequently, any companies that are controlled by the parent would be consolidated. In a similar way to the parent company concept this concept requires 100 per cent consolidation of all subsidiaries.

24.14 Minority interests are sometimes recognised under this concept, but they are treated as part of shareholders' funds, thereby emphasising the control that the parent and its shareholders have over a subsidiary. The entity concept has not traditionally been used in the UK and minority interests have not been traditionally treated as part of shareholders' funds under UK GAAP. As mentioned above, this is now the concept that underlies IFRS since the publication of IAS 27 (revised).

[The next paragraph is 24.16.]

Statement of principles

24.16 The Statement of principles (see chapter 2) addresses how a reporting entity is defined and how interests in other entities are reported in consolidated financial statements. It notes that consolidated financial statements present a view of the group, from the perspective of the parent's shareholders, where the gains, losses, assets, liabilities and cash flows of all subsidiaries are reflected in full.

24.17 The boundary of a group (that is, the entities which form the group) which are the subject of a set of consolidated financial statements is set by the extent of control. The statement explains that control is the power to direct and that there are two aspects to control:

- The ability to deploy the economic resources, whether assets or entities.
- The ability to benefit by (or to suffer from) their deployment.

To have control an entity must have both these abilities. An entity has control of another entity where it has the ability to direct the operating and financial policies of that entity with a view to gaining economic benefits from its activities (or the power to do this). This is the essence of control and control of the operating and financial policies forms the basis of the definitions of subsidiaries found in FRS 2, 'Accounting for subsidiary undertakings', as explained below.

Accounting for investments

24.18 At present in the UK there are a number of ways a company may account in its consolidated financial statements for an investment in another undertaking, which depend upon the size of the investment and the control or influence the investing company has over the entity in which it is investing. These different situations are summarised below:

- Where the investing entity does not exercise significant influence over the operating and financial policies of the other undertaking (normally holdings of below 20 per cent), its investment is recorded at:
  - cost unless there is a permanent diminution in its value; or
  - market value.

  (see further chapter 6).

- Where the investing entity does exercise significant influence over the operating and financial policies of the other undertaking (normally holdings of over 20 per cent), its investment is accounted for using equity accounting, unless the entity is a joint arrangement in which case, another method of accounting should be used (see further chapter 27).
- Where the investing entity controls (or has the power to control) the operating and financial policies of the other undertaking (normally holdings of more than 50 per cent) its investment is consolidated in full and any minority interests are recognised.

24.19 There are, therefore, several ways in which an undertaking can be incorporated into the consolidated financial statements of its investor including:

- Equity accounting – the investing undertaking incorporates its share of the assets and liabilities of the entity in which it has invested on a one line basis in its consolidated balance sheet (netting assets and liabilities). In the consolidated profit and loss account, the investing group's share of operating profit, super-exceptional items, interest and taxation is shown. Only dividends received are recorded in the investing entity's cash flow statement. Where the investing undertaking does not prepare consolidated financial statements the equivalent information has to be given in the notes to the financial statements. Equity accounting is explained in chapter 27.
- Proportional consolidation – in this method, the investing undertaking consolidates into its financial statements its share of assets and liabilities, profits and losses and cash flows of the entity in which it has invested line by line in its consolidated balance sheet, its consolidated profit and loss account and its consolidated cash flow statement, respectively. As only the investing company's share of assets and liabilities are consolidated, this method does not result in recognising any minority interests. Proportional consolidation is mentioned in more detail in chapter 27 in relation to accounting for joint arrangements.
- Full consolidation – the investing undertaking consolidates in full 100 per cent of the assets and liabilities, profits and losses and cash flow of the entity in which it has invested on a line by line basis in its consolidated balance sheet, its consolidated profit and loss account and its consolidated cash flow statement, respectively. Where the investing undertaking's interests is less than 100 per cent, a minority interest is recognised representing the minority's share of assets and liabilities and profits and losses on a net basis. The rules that apply to preparing consolidated financial statements are considered in section II, paragraph 24.303.

Purpose of consolidated financial statements

24.20 The explanatory section of FRS 2 provides the following justification for requiring parents to prepare consolidated financial statements:

'For a variety of legal, tax and other reasons undertakings generally choose to conduct their activities not through a single legal entity but through several undertakings under the ultimate control of the parent undertaking of that group. For this reason the financial statements of a parent undertaking by itself do not present a full picture of its economic activities or financial position. Consolidated financial statements are required in order to reflect the extended business unit that conducts activities under the control of the parent undertaking.' [FRS 2 para 59].

Scope of the Act's and FRS 2's provisions

24.21 The Companies Act 2006 requires *parent companies,* subject to certain exemptions, to prepare consolidated financial statements and it sets out the form that those financial statements should take. [CA06 Secs 399, 403].

24.22 The provisions of FRS 2 go further and apply to *all parent undertakings*, not just parent companies. Subject to certain exemptions, FRS 2 requires *all parents* preparing financial statements that are intended to give a true and fair view of the financial position and profit or loss of the group to prepare them in the form of consolidated financial statements (see further para 24.37). [FRS 2 para 18].

24.23 FRS 2 also directs a parent that uses one of the exemptions from the requirement to prepare consolidated financial statements, but prepares individual financial statements intended to give a true and fair view, to include certain additional disclosure (see para 24.72). FRS 2 does not otherwise deal with the individual financial statements of a parent.

24.24 FRS 2 was drafted within the framework of the Act and, although it does not conflict with it, there are circumstances where the standard is more restrictive than the Act. Furthermore, the standard states that:

"Parent undertakings that do not report under the Act should comply with the requirements of the FRS, and of the Act where referred to in the FRS, except to the extent that these requirements are not permitted by any statutory framework under which such undertakings report". [FRS 2 para 19].

24.25 By referring to sections of the Act and applying them to parents that are not subject to the Act, the FRS achieves a single set of rules that apply to parents preparing consolidated financial statements, whether or not they are companies.

[The next paragraph is 24.27.]

Parent and subsidiary undertakings

24.27 The Companies Act refers throughout to 'parent undertaking' and 'subsidiary undertaking'. These terms stem directly from the EC 7th Directive. The term 'undertaking' is defined in the Act and FRS 2 as follows:

> '...*a body corporate or partnership, or an unincorporated association carrying on a trade or business, with or without a view to profit.*' [CA06 Sec 1161(1); FRS 2 para 16].

24.28 Consequently, a *parent undertaking* could be a partnership or an unincorporated business. However, under the Act consolidated financial statements have only to be prepared where, at the end of a financial year, an undertaking is a parent company. [CA06 Sec 399(2)]. Therefore, parent undertakings that are not companies are not required by the Act to prepare consolidated financial statements, but as explained above they are required to do so in certain circumstances by FRS 2 (see further para 24.37).

24.29 However, *subsidiary undertakings* (including both partnerships and unincorporated associations) are required to be consolidated into the group's consolidated financial statements. Such entities are normally required to be fully consolidated and any minority interests (see section III, paragraph 24.353) are shown separately in the consolidated balance sheet.

24.30 The Act and FRS 2 require as a starting point that all subsidiary undertakings should be included in UK GAAP consolidated financial statements. [CA06 Sec 405(1); FRS 2 para 23]. The FRRP commented in July 1993 that the Report and Accounts of Breverleigh Investments plc for the year ended 30 June 1992 did not include its subsidiary The Banyan Tree of Key West Inc. in its consolidated financial statements. Following discussions with the FRRP this subsidiary was consolidated in accordance with the Act and FRS 2 in the group's consolidated financial statements for the year to 30 June 1993 and comparatives were amended accordingly. There are, however, a number of situations where subsidiary undertakings may, or should, legitimately be excluded from consolidated financial statements and may be accounted for in some other way. These situations are covered in the provisions of both the Act and FRS 2.

24.31 The provisions of both the Act and FRS 2 that relate to the definitions of subsidiary undertakings and the exemptions from the requirement to consolidate certain subsidiary undertakings are considered in detail below (see paras 24.76 and 24.176 respectively).

Requirement to prepare consolidated financial statements

24.32 Whether or not there is a legal or regulatory obligation for a parent to prepare consolidated financial statements will depend on how the parent is constituted.

Parent companies

24.33 As mentioned above, where a *company* is a parent company at the end of a financial year the directors of the company are required by the Act, subject to certain exemptions, to prepare consolidated financial statements as well as individual company to certain financial statements for the financial year. [CA06 Sec 399(2)]. The consolidated financial statements must comply with the Act's requirements. [CA06 Sec 403(2)].

24.34 Such consolidated financial statements prepared by a parent company are also required by law to give a true and fair view. [CA06 Sec 404(2)]. In order to comply with the true and fair requirement, the parent should comply with the provisions of FRS 2.

Small groups

24.35 Under the Companies Act 2006 a parent company under the small companies regime has the option to prepare consolidated financial statements. Companies that are subject to the small companies regime are those that qualify as small and are not excluded from the regime. [CA06 Secs 398, 382 to 384]. Any other parent company must prepare consolidated financial statements unless subject to one of the exemptions noted below. [CA06 Sec 399(2)(3)].

24.36 The exemptions available to companies subject to the small companies regime and the conditions that need to be fulfilled are explained further in chapter 31.

Other parent undertakings

24.37 Whether or not an unincorporated parent undertaking is *required* to prepare consolidated financial statements will depend on the statutory framework under which that undertaking was established. If that framework requires the undertaking to prepare *consolidated* financial statements and to prepare financial statements that give a *true and fair view* (and, as a consequence, require it to comply with FRS 2), then that undertaking will be *required* to prepare consolidated financial statements (providing it is not entitled to an exemption). [FRS 2 para 18].

24.38 For example, a partnership that owns a subsidiary company is not required by the Act to prepare consolidated financial statements as it is not itself a parent *company*. However, if there is a requirement in the partnership deed for the partnership to prepare consolidated financial statements and for it to prepare financial statements that give a true and fair view (and, therefore, comply with FRS 2) the partnership would be required to prepare consolidated financial statements in accordance with FRS 2.

24.39 The basic rule is that any parent preparing consolidated financial statements purporting to give a true and fair view is required to comply with

FRS 2, unless it is specifically exempt from preparing such financial statements. [FRS 2 paras 18, 19].

[The next paragraph is 24.41.]

Form of consolidated financial statements

24.41 Both the Act and FRS 2 require the financial statements of a group to be in the form of consolidated financial statements, unless the parent is exempt.

24.42 FRS 2 defines consolidated financial statements as '*the financial statements of a group prepared by consolidation*' and it defines consolidation as '*the process of adjusting and combining financial information from the individual financial statements of a parent undertaking and its subsidiary undertaking to prepare consolidated financial statements that present financial information for the group as a single economic entity*'. [FRS 2 paras 4, 5].

24.43 The Act requires that for parent companies consolidated financial statements should include:

- A consolidated balance sheet dealing with the state of affairs of the parent and its subsidiary undertakings.
- A consolidated profit and loss account dealing with the profit or loss of the parent and its subsidiary undertakings.
- Notes to the consolidated financial statements dealing with additional disclosure requirements.

[CA06 Sec 404(1)(3)].

These provisions are explained further in chapter 4.

24.44 FRS 3 now also requires the consolidated financial statements to include a consolidated statement of total recognised gains and losses, a consolidated note of historical cost profits and losses and a consolidated reconciliation of movements in shareholders' funds. Entities preparing such consolidated financial statements are not required to publish equivalent statements for the parent entity itself. The provisions of FRS 3 concerning these statements are considered in detail in chapters 4 and 8.

24.45 In addition, subject to certain exemptions, FRS 1 requires all undertakings preparing financial statements that are intended to give a true and fair view to prepare a cash flow statement. Undertakings preparing consolidated financial statements should prepare a consolidated cash flow statement and related notes; they are not then required to prepare an entity cash flow statement. The detailed requirements of FRS 1 are dealt with in chapter 30.

24.46 Both the Act and FRS 2 state that the consolidated financial statements should include the parent and all its subsidiaries, except for those subsidiaries that are required to be excluded. The provisions relating to exclusion of subsidiaries are considered further in paragraph 24.176.

Parent's profit and loss account

24.47 When a parent company prepares consolidated financial statements in accordance with the Act, it is not required to include its own profit and loss account and related notes if the financial statements satisfy the following requirements:

- The notes to the parent company's individual balance sheet show the company's profit or loss for the financial year determined in accordance with the provisions of the Act. [CA06 Sec 408(1)(b)].
- The figure to be given is the profit or loss reported in the parent's profit and loss account format line item 'profit or loss for the financial year', which is before any consolidation adjustments or dividends.
- The parent company's board of directors must approve the company's individual profit and loss account in accordance with the rules concerning approval of the company's financial statements. [CA06 Sec 408(3)].
- The notes to the financial statements disclose the fact that the parent company has taken advantage of this exemption. [CA06 Sec 408(4)].

24.48 Where the consolidated financial statements do not include the company's profit and loss account, the consolidated financial statements need not include certain supplementary information when presented to the Board for their approval. [CA06 Sec 408(2)]. The information that can be excluded is specified in paragraphs 65 to 69 of Schedule 1 to SI 2008/410, 'The Large and Medium-sized Companies and Groups (Accounts and Reports) Regulations 2008', which includes the following:

- Interest and similar charges. [SI 2008/410 1 Sch 66].
- Detailed particulars concerning tax. [SI 2008/410 1 Sch 67].
- Disaggregated information concerning turnover. [SI 2008/410 1 Sch 68].
- Certain miscellaneous matters including:
  - The effect of including any preceding year's items in the current year's profit and loss account.
  - Particulars of extraordinary income or extraordinary charges.
  - The effect of any exceptional items.

  [SI 2008/410 1 Sch 66].

The information that can be excluded in financial statements prepared under the Companies Act 2006 is information regarding employee numbers and costs. [CA06 Sec 408(2)].

24.49 Suitable wording for a note to be included in the consolidated financial statements when the parent's profit and loss account is not reproduced would be:

> '*As permitted by section 408 of the Companies Act 2006, the parent company's profit and loss account has not been included in these financial statements and its profit/loss for the financial year amounted to £X.*'

24.50 In certain situations an intermediate parent, for example, might wish voluntarily to prepare consolidated financial statements even though it might comply with the conditions that would allow it not to prepare consolidated financial statements (see para 24.56). In this situation, it might not wish to include its individual company profit and loss account in those consolidated financial statements. However, the wording of section 408 of the Companies Act 2006 would only seem to allow the exemption where the company is *required* to prepare consolidated financial statements. The solution to this technical issue is for the intermediate parent deliberately not to comply with one of the conditions outlined in paragraph 24.62. For example, one of those conditions is that the company must disclose that it is exempt from the requirement to prepare consolidated financial statements in its financial statements. If it does not make this disclosure, then it is strictly required by the Act to prepare consolidated financial statements and, therefore, can take the exemption from presenting its own profit and loss account.

True and fair view

24.51 It is an overriding requirement of the Act that a company's consolidated financial statements must give a true and fair view of the state of affairs as at the end of the financial year and of the profit or loss for the financial year, of the undertakings included in the consolidation. [CA06 Sec 404(2)].

24.52 Where, however, compliance with the disclosure provisions of the Act (including Schedule 6 to the Companies Act 2006) would not be sufficient to give a true and fair view, then additional information should be given in the financial statements or in the notes to the financial statements. [CA06 Sec 404(4)]. This additional information needs to be of sufficient detail to ensure that its disclosure enables the financial statements to give a true and fair view.

24.53 There is a further provision concerning the true and fair view, which provides that if in 'special circumstances' compliance with the Act's provisions would be inconsistent with the requirement to give a true and fair view, the directors of the company must depart from the Act's provisions. [CA06 Sec 404(5)]. Where such a departure is necessary, the particulars of the departure, the reasons for it and its effect must be given in a note to the financial statements. [CA06 Sec 404(5)]. FRS 18 specifically requires the following disclosures, which give a more precise meaning to 'particulars, reasons and effect':

- A statement of the treatment which the Act would normally require in the circumstances and a description of the treatment actually adopted.

- A statement as to why the treatment prescribed would not give a true and fair view.
- 'Its effect' should be interpreted to mean a description of how the position shown in the financial statements is different as a result of the departure, normally with quantification, except where:
- quantification is already evident in the financial statements themselves; or
- the effect cannot reasonably be quantified, in which case the directors should explain the circumstances.

[FRS 18 para 62].

These provisions are considered further in chapter 2.

24.54 The true and fair override given by section 404(5) of the Companies Act 2006 cannot be used to justify not consolidating a subsidiary; it merely entitles the directors to depart from the other requirements of the Act with respect to the matters to be included in the consolidated financial statements. In interpreting the Act's provisions the court would be bound to give effect so far as possible to the provisions of the EC 7th Directive. In the EC 7th Directive the true and fair override in article 16(5) (included in section 404(5) of the Companies Act 2006 applies only to specific articles of the directive (that is, articles 17 to 35 and 39). It does not apply to the articles which set out the conditions for consolidation. Therefore, the override cannot be used to override provisions relating to the composition of consolidated financial statements so as to exclude a subsidiary undertaking from consolidation.

24.55 This requirement of the law has been reinforced by the ASB in FRS 2. The ASB consider that for consolidated financial statements to give a true and fair view they must present information about the group that is complete and, for this reason, the conditions set out in the Act for exclusion of subsidiaries from consolidation have been further restricted in the standard. These restrictions are considered from paragraph 24.176 onwards.

Exemptions from preparing consolidated financial statements

24.56 There are three situations where a parent may be exempt from the general requirement to prepare consolidated financial statements. The exemptions are for:

- Parents of small groups (see para 24.35).
- Certain parents that are also subsidiaries (that is, intermediate parents – see para 24.56.1).
- Parents, all of whose subsidiaries are permitted or required to be excluded from consolidation (see para 24.70).

[FRS 2 para 21].

The provisions concerning small and medium-sized groups are explained in chapter 31.

Intermediate parent exemption

24.56.1 Under certain circumstances an intermediate holding company is not required to prepare consolidated financial statements. There are two potential exemptions available. These are found in sections 400 and 401 of the Companies Act 2006. The two exemptions differ as their requirements vary depending on the group structure. The exemption under section 400 of the Companies Act 2006 is only available if the immediate parent is established under the law of an EEA state. The section 401 exemption is wider and is available to any company which has a non-EEA parent (not necessarily immediate parent). The section 401 exemption is, therefore, potentially available to any subsidiary included in the consolidated financial statements of a larger group regardless of political geography.

24.56.2 Depending on the group structure, it may be that a particular intermediate parent company can look to one or both of these sections for its potential exemption. The following flow chart summarises this principle and highlights which exemption might be available in the circumstances in question.

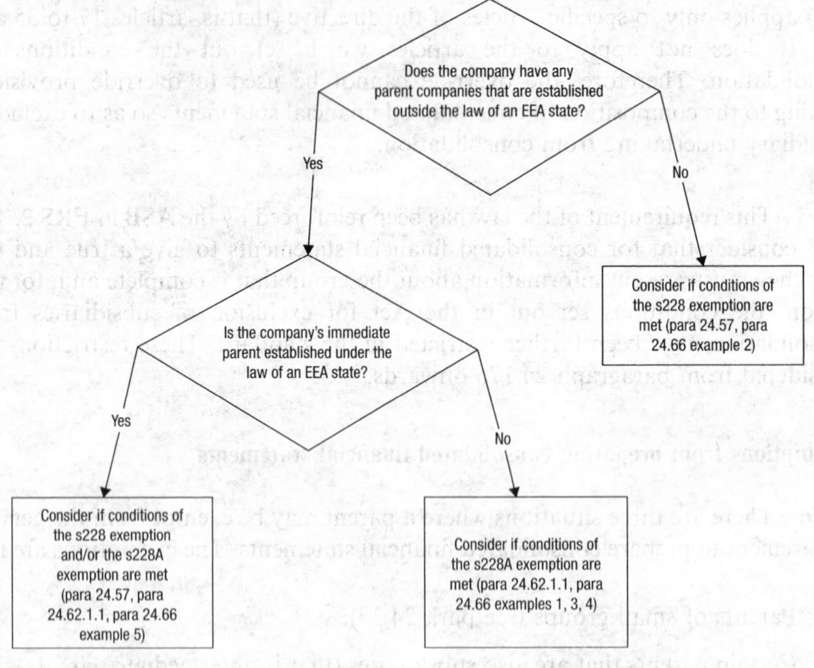

Immediate parent is an EEA company exemption

24.57 An intermediate holding company is not required to prepare consolidated financial statements where it is wholly owned by its immediate parent undertaking, and this immediate parent company is established under the law of an EEA state. [CA06 Sec 400(1)(a)]. However, there are a number of conditions that must apply before the exemption can be taken and these are summarised below in paragraph 24.62. The conditions stated in section 400 of the 2006 Act do not need to be satisfied at the intermediate holding company's financial year end date. The qualifying conditions can be satisfied during the period after the intermediate holding company's year end date and before the filing date of its immediate parent's consolidated financial statements. The consolidated financial statements must include the intermediate holding company and all of its subsidiaries, and to obtain the exemption all of the conditions must be met.

24.58 In addition to wholly-owned subsidiaries, this exemption extends to the situation where the immediate parent holds more than 50 per cent of the shares by number in the intermediate holding company and no notice has been served on the company to prepare consolidated financial statements. Such notice has to be made by either of the following:

- Shareholders holding in aggregate more than half of the remaining shares in the company.
- Shareholders holding in aggregate five per cent of the total shares in the company.

As with paragraph 24.57, the immediate parent company must be established under the law of an EEA state.

[CA06 Sec 400(1)(b)].

24.58.1 The EEA (European Economic Area) encompasses the member states of the EC and the EFTA countries of Iceland, Liechtenstein and Norway. The member states of the EC are Austria, Belgium, Denmark, Finland, France, Germany, Greece, Republic of Ireland, Italy, Luxemburg, Netherlands, Portugal, Spain, Sweden, United Kingdom, Cyprus, Czech Republic, Estonia, Latvia, Lithuania, Hungary, Malta, Poland, Slovakia, Slovenia, Romania and Bulgaria.

24.59 The notice has to be served within six months of the end of the previous financial period (that is, normally within the first six months of the financial year for which the consolidated financial statements are being prepared). [CA06 Sec 400(1)]. Consequently, the onus is clearly on the minority shareholders to serve such notice if they require consolidated financial statements to be prepared for a sub-group.

24.60 FRS 2 extends the scope of the relevant sections of the Act outlined above to apply also to unincorporated parents, hence reference to 'company' should be treated as applying to any undertaking where appropriate. [FRS 2 para 21].

24.61 For the purposes of determining whether the company is wholly owned or whether the parent holds more than 50 per cent of the company's shares, the rules below apply:

- Shares held by directors to comply with their share qualification requirements should be disregarded when determining whether a company is wholly owned in paragraph 24.57. [CA06 Sec 400(5)].
- In determining whether the parent holds more than 50 per cent of the shares of the company in paragraph 24.58, shares held by a parent's wholly owned subsidiary should be attributed to the parent undertaking. Also shares held on behalf of the parent, or by or on behalf of a wholly-owned subsidiary, should be attributed to the parent undertaking. [CA06 Sec 400(3)].

24.62 Both the exemptions outlined above in paragraphs 24.57 and 24.58 only apply, however, where the following conditions have been followed:

- The company is included in the consolidated financial statements of a larger group drawn up to the same date (or an earlier date in the same financial year – see para 24.63) by a parent undertaking established under the law of an EEA state. [CA06 Sec 400(2)(a)]. This parent does not have to be the EEA immediate parent referred to in 24.57, it could be an EEA parent further up the chain. This parent will be referred to henceforth as the 'reporting parent'.

  'Included in' for this purpose means by way of full consolidation. Equity accounting or proportional consolidation is not sufficient.
- The reporting parent's consolidated financial statements and annual report must be drawn up and audited in accordance the law of the EEA state under which it is established, in accordance either:
  - with the provisions of the EC 7th Directive (where applicable as modified by the provisions of the Bank Accounts Directive or the Insurance Accounts Directive); or
  - with IFRS.
- It must be noted in the company's individual financial statements that it is exempt from preparing and delivering to the Registrar of Companies consolidated financial statements. [CA06 Sec 400(2)(c)].
- The reporting parent's name must be noted in the company's individual financial statements stating:
  - The reporting parent's country of incorporation, if it is incorporated outside Great Britain.
  - The address of the reporting parent's principal place of business, where it is unincorporated.

  [CA06 Sec 400(2)(d)].
- The company must deliver to the Registrar of Companies, within the period allowed for delivering its individual financial statements, a copy of the reporting parent's consolidated financial statements and annual report, together with the audit report thereon. [CA06 Sec 400(2)(e)].

- Where any of the documents delivered to the Registrar of Companies in accordance with the previous requirement is not in English (or Welsh for a company registered in Wales), a copy of a translation must be annexed to those documents. The translation has to be certified in the prescribed manner to be a correct translation. [CA06 Sec 400(2)(f)].

- The company cannot have any securities listed on a regulated market in an EEA member state. [CA06 Sec 400(4)]. For this purpose, 'securities' include shares and stocks, debentures (including debenture stock, loan stock, bonds, certificates of deposit and other similar instruments), warrants and similar instruments and certain certificates and other instruments that confer rights in respect of securities. [CA06 Sec 400(6)].

24.62.1 With regard practical application of the requirement in the second bullet point of paragraph 24.62, the national GAAPs of the 27 countries that are members of the EC should have implemented the EC 7th Directive. If the reporting parent is established in another country in the EEA, in order for the exemption to be taken appropriate analysis will be needed to confirm that the GAAP under which the financial statements are prepared is either IFRS or a GAAP that is in accordance with the EC 7th Directive.

Parent companies included in non-EEA group accounts exemption

24.62.1.1 An intermediate holding company is not required to prepare consolidated financial statements where it is wholly owned by a parent undertaking not established under the law of an EEA state. [CA06 Sec 401(1)(a)]. However, there are a number of conditions that must apply before the exemption can be taken and these are summarised below in paragraph 24.62.6. The conditions stated in section 401 of the 2006 Act do not need to be satisfied on the intermediate holding company's financial year end date. The qualifying conditions can be satisfied during the period after the intermediate holding company's year end date and before the filing date of its parent's consolidated financial statements. The consolidated financial statements must include the intermediate holding company and all of its subsidiaries, and to obtain the exemption all of the conditions must be met. There is a key difference here to the section 400 exemption requirement, since the parent undertaking identified need not be the 'immediate parent' of the company, merely a 'parent'.

24.62.2 In addition to wholly-owned subsidiaries, this exemption extends to the situation where the parent holds more than 50 per cent of the shares by number in the company looking to claim the exemption and no notice has been served on the company to prepare consolidated financial statements. Such notice has to be made by either of the following:

- Shareholders holding in aggregate more than half of the remaining shares in the company.

- Shareholders holding in aggregate five per cent of the total shares in the company.

As with paragraph 24.62.1.1, the parent undertaking identified may not be established under the law of an EEA state, but may be any parent of the company, with no restriction to 'immediate parent'.

[CA06 Sec 401(1)(b)].

24.62.3 The notice has to be served within six months of the end of the previous financial period (that is, normally within the first six months of the financial year for which the consolidated financial statements are being prepared). [CA06 Sec 401(1)]. Consequently, the onus is clearly on the minority shareholders to serve such notice if they require consolidated financial statements to be prepared for a sub-group.

24.62.4 FRS 2 extends the scope of the relevant sections of the Act outlined above to apply also to unincorporated parents, hence reference to 'company' should be treated as applying to any undertaking where appropriate. [FRS 2 para 21].

24.62.5 For the purposes of determining whether the company is wholly owned or whether the parent holds more than 50 per cent of the company's shares, the rules below apply:

- Shares held by directors to comply with their share qualification requirements should be disregarded when determining whether a company is wholly owned in paragraph 24.62.1. [CA06 Sec 401(5)].
- In determining whether the parent holds more than 50 per cent of the shares of the company in paragraph 24.62.2, shares held by a parent's wholly-owned subsidiary should be attributed to the parent undertaking. Also shares held on behalf of the parent, or by or on behalf of a wholly-owned subsidiary, should be attributed to the parent undertaking. [CA06 Sec 401(3)].

24.62.6 Both the exemptions outlined above in paragraphs 24.62.1 and 24.62.2 only apply, however, where the following conditions have been followed:

- The company and all of its subsidiary undertakings are included in the consolidated financial statements of a larger group drawn up to the same date (or an earlier date in the same financial year – see para 24.63) by a parent undertaking. [CA06 Sec 401(2)(a)]. This group does not have to be the non-EEA parent referred to in paragraph 24.62.1, it could be an alternative parent in the group structure, referred to hence forth as the 'reporting parent'.

  Note that this is a stronger requirement than under section 400 of the Companies Act 2006, which does not include the requirement *"and all of its subsidiary undertakings"*.

  'Included in' for this purpose means by way of full consolidation. Equity accounting or proportional consolidation is not sufficient.

- The reporting parent's consolidated financial statements and annual report must be drawn up in accordance with the provisions of the EC 7th Directive (where applicable as modified by the provisions of the Bank Accounts Directive or the Insurance Accounts Directive) or otherwise in a manner equivalent to consolidated accounts and annual reports so drawn up. [CA06 Sec 401(2)(b)].

  The financial statements must also be audited by one or more persons authorised to audit accounts under the law under which the parent undertaking which draws them up is established. [CA06 Sec 401(2)(c)].

- It must be noted in the company's individual financial statements that it is exempt from preparing and delivering to the Registrar of Companies consolidated financial statements. [CA06 Sec 401(2)(d)].

- The name of the reporting parent must be noted in the company's individual financial statements stating:

  - The reporting parent's country of incorporation, if it is incorporated outside Great Britain.

  - The address of the reporting parent's principal place of business, where it is unincorporated.

  [CA06 Sec 401(2)(e)].

- The company must deliver to the Registrar of Companies within the period allowed for delivering its individual financial statements a copy of the parent's consolidated financial statements and a copy of the parent's annual report together with the audit report thereon. [CA06 Sec 401(2)(f)].

- Where any of the documents delivered to the Registrar of Companies in accordance with the previous requirement is not in English (or Welsh for a company registered in Wales), a copy of a translation must be annexed to those documents. The translation has to be certified in the prescribed manner to be a correct translation [CA06 Sec 401(2)(g)].

- The company cannot have any securities listed on a regulated market in an EEA member state. [CA06 Sec 401(4)]. For this purpose, 'securities' include shares and stocks, debentures (including debenture stock, loan stock, bonds, certificates of deposit and other similar instruments), warrants and similar instruments and certain certificates and other instruments that confer rights in respect of securities. [CA06 Sec 401(6)].

24.62.7 A problem that may occur in practice arises from the requirement for the reporting parent's consolidated financial statements and annual report to be drawn up in line with the EC 7th Directive or in a manner equivalent. Paragraph 62.1 above discusses which national GAAPs are 'in accordance with' the Directive. Further to this, the UITF Abstract 43, 'The Interpretation of equivalence for the purposes of Section 228A of the Companies Act 1985' (now section 401 of the Companies Act 2006), gives guidance for determining whether a particular GAAP is 'in a manner equivalent' for the purposes of the section 401 exemption. It is generally accepted by the UITF that the reference to equivalence in section 401 does not mean compliance with every detail of the 7th Directive. The UITF believes that a qualitative approach, being one with a focus on compliance with the basic requirements of the Directive and in particular the requirement to give a true and fair view, is more in keeping with the deregulatory nature of the exemption.

24.62.8 With respect IFRS-based financial statements, the UITF notes that there are various varieties of IFRS, each of which has a different treatment with regard equivalence:

- IFRS as adopted by the EU. This will meet the test of equivalence as the procedure for adoption of IFRS by the EU requires a standard to meet the basic requirements of the EU Directives.
- IFRS as issued by the IASB. This will currently meet the test of equivalence as there are currently no standards issued by the IASB which conflict with the basic requirements of the Directives. However if, in future, the European Commission fails to adopt a standard on the grounds that it does not meet the 7th Directive's basic requirements, it will be necessary to consider whether the reasons for the failure to adopt the standard suggest that compliance with that standard will fail to give a true and fair view and will, therefore, fail the test of equivalence.
- IFRS-based GAAPs. These include Australia, South Africa and Hong Kong. It is not practicable to give specific guidance on all of the increasing number of GAAPs that are based on, or are converging with, IFRS. In those cases where they are more restrictive than IFRS by eliminating choices (for example, Australian GAAP) they will currently meet the test of equivalence for the purposes of section 401. In other cases, it will be necessary to obtain an understanding of how they differ from IFRS and whether those differences might result in a departure from the basic requirements of the 7th Directive.

24.62.9 Furthermore the UITF has considered the specific cases of US, Canadian and Japanese GAAP. It notes that, in most cases, application of these GAAPs will result in financial statements that fulfil the basic principles of the 7th Directive. There are, however, three areas where there is potential for application of these GAAPs to result in financial statements that are not equivalent to the 7th Directive.

- Scope of consolidated accounts. The 7th Directive contains a definition of subsidiary undertakings that is based on a widely defined concept of control and is likely to ensure that many SPEs are included in consolidated financial statements. There may be cases where a country's GAAP does not require the consolidation of an entity in circumstances where the 7th Directive would do so. This could lead to a lack of equivalence where the effect on the consolidated financial statements is material.

- Consistent accounting policies. There are instances where these are not required by the GAAPs in question. To accept the conclusion of equivalence it will be necessary to ensure the consolidated financial statements are drawn up on the basis of consistent accounting policies.
- Any exemptions of modifications to the GAAPs allowed by specialised industry standards that have been applied. The effect of any such modifications would need to be specifically considered with respect to equivalence.

Provided the above points have been addressed, then the three GAAPs in question would be considered equivalent to the 7th Directive

24.62.10 Financial statements prepared using other GAAPs should be assessed for equivalence with the 7th Directive based on the particular facts and circumstances in question. This will include consideration of the similarities to, and differences from, the GAAPs considered specifically above.

Relevant dates

24.63 The relevant dates specified in the exemptions above can cause particular problems in practice as explained in the example that follows:

Example – Relevant dates where year ends differ

A parent company acquires the whole of the company S sub-group in June 19X1 during its current financial year and after the acquisition the group has the following structure.

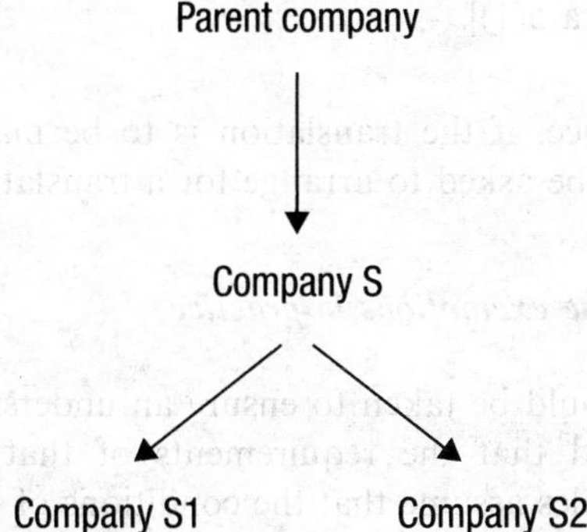

The parent company's year end is 31 December, but the year end of the company S sub-group is 30 September. The question then arises as to whether company S can take advantage from the exemption to prepare consolidated financial statements for its sub-group (that is including both company S1 and company S2). If it complies with the other conditions of the exemption it will fail on the first condition in the year of acquisition (that is, 19X1). This is because at its year end, 30 September 19X1, it will not have been included in the parent's consolidated financial statements drawn up to the same date (that is, 30 September 19X1) or to an earlier date in company S's financial year. The company S sub-group will only be included in the parent's consolidated financial statement as at 31 December 19X1. In 19X2, company S does comply with this condition, because its results will be consolidated into its parent's financial statements to an earlier date in its financial year to 30 September 19X2 (that is, its parent's consolidated financial statements for the financial year to 31 December 19X1). Therefore, in 19X1 company S will have to prepare consolidated financial statements, but in 19X2 if it complies with the other conditions it will not have to prepare them. The simple way round this problem is for company S to change its year end from 30 September to 31 December.

Certified translations

24.64 The term 'certified translation' used above means a translation made by any of the following:

- A notary public.
- A solicitor if the translation was made in the UK.
- A person authorised in the place where the translation was made to administer an oath or any of the British officials mentioned in section 6 of the Commissioners for Oaths Act 1889 for translations made overseas. This includes British Ambassadors, envoys, ministers, charges d'affaires and secretaries of embassies and every British consul-general, consul, vice-consul, acting consul, pro-consul, consular agent, acting consul-general, acting vice-consul, and acting consular agent exercising his functions in any foreign place, including anyone with the diplomatic rank of counsellor.
- Any person certified by any of the above to be known to him to be competent to translate the document into English.

[SI 1990/572 para 5(1)].

24.65 In practice, if the translation is to be made in the UK, a notary or a solicitor should be asked to arrange for a translation to be made and certified.

Application of the exemptions in practice

24.66 Care should be taken to ensure an understanding of which exemption is being taken and that the requirements of that exemption are fulfilled. The following examples assume that the conditions of the exemptions in question are met.

Example 1 – EU ultimate parent with non-EU intermediate parent

An ultimate parent company is incorporated in Germany and prepares its consolidated financial statements in accordance with EU-adopted IFRS. The German ultimate parent has a wholly-owned subsidiary in the US, which does not prepare consolidated financial statements. The US parent in turn wholly owns a UK company and its subsidiaries.

The section 400 exemption would not be available to the UK company in this circumstance due to the fact that the immediate parent is not incorporated under the law of an EEA state.

However, since the company has a non-EEA parent (the US company) the section 401 exemption is available. Since the UK group is included in the consolidated financial statements of its German parent that are prepared in accordance with a variant of IFRS that is consistent with the 7th Directive, it is able to take advantage of the exemption and need not prepare consolidated financial statements.

Example 2 – EU ultimate parent with EU intermediate parent

The facts are the same as in example 2, except that there is a Belgian company in the group structure instead of the US company.

In this example the immediate parent company and the reporting parent are both incorporated under the law of an EEA state. Hence, the section 400 exemption is available to the UK company. Since the UK company is included in the consolidated financial statements of its German parent that are prepared in accordance with the 7th Directive, it is able to take advantage of the exemption and need not prepare consolidated financial statements.

The section 401 exemption would not be available to the UK company in this circumstance due to the fact that all of the UK company's parent undertakings are incorporated under the law of an EEA state.

Example 3 – Non-EU ultimate parent with non-EU intermediate parent that prepares IFRS consolidated financial statements

The ultimate parent of a group is incorporated in the US and prepares its consolidated financial statements in accordance with US GAAP. The US ultimate parent has a wholly-owned subsidiary incorporated in Bermuda that prepares and has audited consolidated financial statements in accordance with 'pure' IFRS. The Bermudan subsidiary, in turn, owns a UK company and its subsidiaries.

The section 400 exemption would not be available to the UK company in this circumstance due to the fact that the immediate parent is not incorporated under the law of an EEA state.

However, since the company has a non-EEA parent the section 401 exemption is potentially available. As the UK group is included in the consolidated financial statements of its Bermudan parent that are prepared in accordance with IFRS (which per para 24.62.8 is consistent with the 7th Directive), it is able to take advantage of the exemption under section 401 and need not prepare consolidated financial statements.

Example 4 – Non-EU ultimate parent with non-EU intermediate parent that does not prepare IFRS consolidated financial statements

The facts are the same as in example 2, except that the Bermudan parent does not prepare consolidated financial statements.

The section 400 exemption would not be available to the UK company in this circumstance due to the fact that the immediate parent is not incorporated under the law of an EEA state.

However, since the company has a non-EEA parent the section 401 exemption is potentially available. In this case, the UK parent company is included in the consolidated financial statements of its US parent prepared in accordance with US GAAP. It will be necessary to determine whether the US GAAP consolidated financial statements are prepared *'in a manner equivalent to the 7th Directive'*. Such assessment should be made based on the principles in 24.62.9 above. If equivalence is agreed for the circumstances in question, then the UK group may take advantage of the exemption in section 401 and will not need to prepare consolidated financial statements. If equivalence cannot be agreed then the exemption will not be available.

Example 5 – Non-EU ultimate parent with EU intermediate parent

An ultimate parent company is incorporated in the US and prepares its consolidated financial statements in accordance with US GAAP. The US ultimate parent has a wholly-owned subsidiary in France. The French parent in turn wholly owns a UK company and its subsidiaries.

In this example the immediate parent company is incorporated under the law of an EEA state. Hence, the section 400 exemption is potentially available to the UK company. If the French company prepares consolidated financial statements in accordance with the 7th Directive, it is able to take advantage of the exemption and need not prepare consolidated financial statements.

Since the company has a non-EEA parent the section 401 exemption is also potentially available. In this case, the UK parent company is included in the consolidated financial statements of its US parent prepared in accordance with US GAAP. It will be necessary to determine whether the US GAAP consolidated financial statements are prepared *'in a manner equivalent to the 7th Directive'*. Such assessment should be made based on the principles in paragraph 24.62.9 above. If equivalence is agreed for the circumstances in question, then the UK group may take advantage of the exemption in section 401 and will not need to prepare consolidated financial statements. If equivalence cannot be agreed then the section 401 exemption will not be available.

[The next paragraph is 24.70.]

All subsidiaries excluded from consolidation

24.70 Where all of a parent's subsidiaries are permitted or required to be excluded from consolidation by sections 402 and 405 of the Companies Act 2006 (as restricted by FRS 2), that parent is exempt from the requirement to prepare consolidated financial statements. [FRS 2 para 21(f)]. The conditions for exclusion of subsidiaries from consolidation are considered in detail in paragraph 24.176.

Accounting treatment

24.71 Where a parent makes use of any of the above exemptions not to prepare consolidated financial statements, it should treat in its individual financial statements its interests in subsidiaries as fixed asset investments except for those held exclusively with a view to resale. Subsidiaries held exclusively with a view to resale should be recorded as current asset investments at the lower of cost and net realisable value (see further para 24.193).

Disclosure

24.72 Where a parent makes use of any of the exemptions and does not prepare consolidated financial statements, FRS 2 requires that parent to:

- Comply with the disclosure requirements of Parts 1 and 2 of Schedule 4 to SI 2008/410, 'The Large and Medium-sized Companies and Groups (Accounts and Reports) Regulations 2008' and also sections 409 and 410 of the Companies Act 2006 in respect of parent companies not required to prepare consolidated financial statements.
- State that its financial statements present information about it as an individual undertaking and not about its group. The statement should include or refer to the note giving the grounds on which the parent undertaking is exempt from preparing consolidated financial statements, as required by paragraph 10(1) of Schedule 4 to SI 2008/410.

[FRS 2 para 22].

24.73 The disclosure requirements set out in Parts 1 and 2 of Schedule 4 to SI 2008/410 are extensive. They cover the following subjects:

- Reason for not preparing consolidated financial statements.
- Details about subsidiaries including: name; country of incorporation or registration; proportion of shares held; profit/loss for the year; aggregate capital and reserves at the year end; details about non-coterminous year ends; and holdings in shares of the parent.
- Details about significant holdings of greater than 20 per cent in undertakings other than subsidiary undertakings including: name; country of incorporation; proportion of shares held.
- Additional information about significant holdings of greater than 20 per cent in undertakings other than subsidiary undertakings including: aggregate capital and reserves and profit or loss for the year.
- Details about parents including: name of ultimate parent; name of largest group of undertakings for which consolidated financial statements are drawn up of which the undertaking is a member; and the name of the smallest such group.

24.74 The disclosure requirements of Parts 1 and 2 to SI 2008/410 that relate to subsidiaries are explained in detail from paragraph 24.257.

Suggested wording for exempt parents

24.75 In practice, it is likely that many parent undertakings will be exempt from the requirement to prepare consolidated financial statements. Set out below are examples of wording that may be included in the accounting policies of parent undertakings that use one of the exemptions from preparing consolidated financial statements.

Example – Suggested wording for parents exempt from preparing consolidated financial statements

Intermediate parent undertaking

Accounting policy extract – company

The financial statements contain information about GAAP UK Limited as an individual company and do not contain consolidated financial information as the parent of a group. The Company is exempt under [section 400 (for EEA immediate parents), 401 (for non-EEA parents)] of the Companies Act 2006 from the requirement to prepare consolidated financial statements as it and its subsidiary undertakings are included by full consolidation in the consolidated financial statements of its parent, [GAAP (UK) plc/ FRGAAP SA], a company [registered in England and Wales/ registered in Scotland/incorporated in (for example) France].

Accounting policy extract – unincorporated undertaking

The financial statements contain information about GAAP & Co as an individual undertaking and do not contain consolidated financial information as the parent of a group. The [Partnership/Trust/ or other undertaking as applicable] is exempt under paragraph 21 [(b), (c), (d) or (e) as applicable] of FRS 2 from the requirement to prepare consolidated financial statements as it is included by full consolidation in the consolidated financial statements of its parent, [GAAP & Co/GAAP (UK) plc, a [partnership whose principal place of business is at [insert address]/company registered in England and Wales].

All subsidiaries excluded from consolidation

Accounting policy extract – company

The financial statements contain information about GAAP UK Limited as an individual company and do not contain consolidated financial information as the parent of a group. The Company is exempt under section 402 of the Companies Act 2006 from the requirement to prepare consolidated financial statements as the directors consider that all the company's subsidiaries [may/should] be excluded from consolidation for the reasons set out [below/in note x].

Accounting policy extract – unincorporated undertaking

The financial statements contain information about GAAP & Co as an individual undertaking and do not contain consolidated financial information as the parent of a group. The [Partnership/Trust/ or other undertaking as applicable] is exempt under paragraph 21(f) of FRS 2 from the requirement to prepare consolidated financial statements as the [directors/corresponding officers] consider that all its subsidiaries [may/should] be excluded from consolidation for the reasons set out [below/in note x].

Subsidiary undertakings

Introduction

24.76 Before the parent of a group of companies can start to prepare consolidated financial statements, it is important to decide exactly which undertakings form the group and should, therefore, be included in the consolidation. In addition, it is important to determine whether any subsidiaries should be excluded from the group under the exemptions allowed or required by the legislation and FRS 2.

24.77 Consequently, determining which undertakings are the parent's subsidiaries and should, therefore, be consolidated is fundamental to the preparation of consolidated financial statements and this section considers the rules that govern whether an undertaking is a subsidiary for this purpose.

[The next paragraph is 24.79]

Company Law

24.79 The Companies Act 1985 (International Accounting Standards and Other Amendments) Regulations (SI 2004/2947) introduced an updated EC 7th Directive definition of a subsidiary, removing the requirements for a participating interest to be held and introducing the notion of consolidation due to the 'power' to control. The Companies Act 2006 retains this definition of subsidiary. [CA06 sec 1162(4)]. This brings the UK GAAP definition of a subsidiary closer to IAS 27, 'Consolidated and separate financial statements', and may mean that some entities that were previously classified as quasi-subsidiaries and some special purpose entities become full legal subsidiaries (see further para 24.149.1 onwards).

Meaning of subsidiary undertaking

24.80 As mentioned above, a subsidiary undertaking can mean any of the following undertakings:

- A body corporate.
- A partnership.

- An unincorporated association carrying on a trade or business for profit.
- An unincorporated association not trading for profit.

[CA06 Sec 1161(1); FRS 2 para 16].

24.81 Consequently, any undertakings included in the above list may fall to be consolidated with the parent's financial statements if they are subsidiary undertakings.

24.82 It appears that the definition of 'undertaking' in section 1161 of the Companies Act 2006 is wide enough to include trusts. Case law refers to 'association' meaning a combination of persons or of firms carrying on a particular venture, which seems to encompass trusts. The distinction in case law between associations and undertakings is that undertakings carry on business for gain. However, the definition in section 1161 is not restricted to there being a profit or gain resulting from the association's activities. Therefore, it would seem that generally trusts are associations that fall within the definition of undertaking in section 1161.

24.83 The Act provides the definitions of parent and subsidiary. FRS 2 uses the same definitions as those given in the Act and builds on them by giving additional guidance on their interpretation. There are six situations where an undertaking may be a subsidiary of a parent undertaking and these are where the parent:

- Holds a majority of the voting rights in the undertaking (see further para 24.89 onwards).
- Is a member of the undertaking and has the right to appoint or remove directors holding a majority of the voting rights at meetings of the board on all, or substantially all, matters (see further para 24.96 onwards).
- Has a right to exercise dominant influence over the undertaking by virtue of provisions either in its memorandum or articles, or in a control contract (see further para 24.125 onwards). (Note that no shareholding is necessary.)
- Is a member of the undertaking and controls alone, pursuant to an agreement with other shareholders or members, a majority of the voting rights in the undertaking (see further para 24.155 onwards).
- Has the power to exercise, or actually exercises, dominant influence or control over the undertaking (see further para 24.130 onwards).
- Is managed on a unified basis with the undertaking (see further para 24.152 onwards).

[CA06 Sec 1162(2)(4), 7 Sch].

24.84 The common feature of these definitions is that of control, or power to exercise control, by the parent (or the parent and its subsidiaries) over the subsidiary. The definitions are considered in detail in the paragraphs that follow.

24.85 Where an undertaking is determined not to be a subsidiary undertaking under the Act and FRS 2 it may still be necessary for it to be consolidated if it is a quasi-subsidiary. A quasi-subsidiary is defined in FRS 5 as '*a company, trust, partnership or other vehicle that, though not fulfilling the definition of a subsidiary, is directly or indirectly controlled by the reporting entity and gives rise to benefits for that entity that are in substance no different from those that would arise were the vehicle a subsidiary*'. [FRS 5 para 7]. Where a quasi-subsidiary is identified, it is accounted for in the same way as other subsidiaries, that is, by way of full consolidation. Quasi-subsidiaries and how to account for them are considered in chapter 3.

Expressions used by unincorporated undertakings

24.86 Although subsidiaries can include unincorporated undertakings such as partnerships, various parts of the legislation use expressions that are common to companies only. Consequently, the Act provides the following provision:

> '*Other expressions appropriate to companies shall be construed, in relation to an undertaking which is not a company, as references to the corresponding persons, officers, documents or organs, as the case may be, appropriate to undertakings of that description.*' [CA06 Sec 1161(3)].

24.87 This provision will apply in a number of situations, but a good example of its effect concerns the expressions used by limited partnerships. A limited partnership is made up of a 'general partner' and a number of 'limited partners'. The general partner manages the business and the limited partners cannot be involved in the day to day business of the partnership. The partnership itself does not have a board of directors, but the equivalent to the board is the general partner himself. Consequently, if a company is a general partner in a limited partnership, then it will control the board of the limited partnership and the partnership will, therefore, be a subsidiary under section 1162(2)(b) of the Companies Act 2006. (See further para 24.212.1 onwards).

24.88 Section 1161(3) of the Companies Act 2006 is also important because various disclosure provisions concerning subsidiary undertakings detailed in Schedule 4 to SI 2008/410, 'The Large & Medium-sized Companies and Groups (Accounts and Reports) Regulations 2008', are expressed using terms that are only relevant to companies. These disclosure requirements are considered further in paragraph 24.213.

Majority of voting rights

24.89 An undertaking is a subsidiary where the parent undertaking holds a majority of its voting rights. [CA06 Sec 1162(2); FRS 2 para 14(a)].

24.90 This is the definition of a subsidiary that is applied most frequently in practice to identify subsidiaries. While ownership (equity) and voting rights are usually held in equal proportions, there are situations where an undertaking may own a majority of the equity in another undertaking and yet not hold a majority of the voting rights in it. In such a situation, the undertaking will not be a subsidiary (unless it is a subsidiary by virtue of one of the other definitions).

24.91 The example that follows illustrates how these provisions work in practice. Company A owns 100 ordinary shares in company B and company C owns 100 five per cent preference shares in company B. Company B has no other share capital.

Example – Parent hold a majority of the voting rights

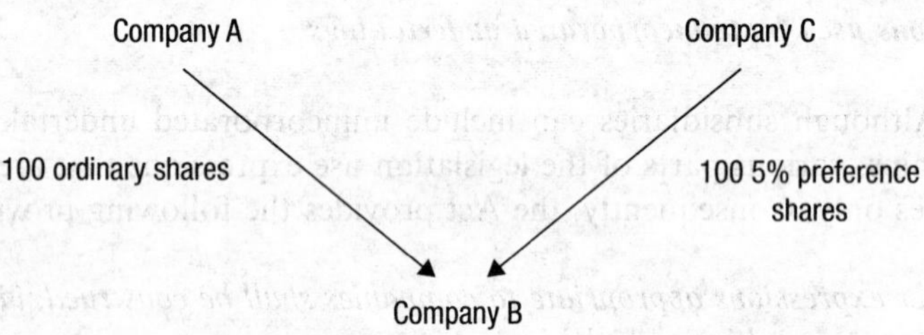

The rights attached to company B's shares are as follows:

- Ordinary shares:
  - 100 £1 ordinary shares.
  - All dividends after payment of preference dividends.
  - Right to all surplus assets on a winding up of the company after repayment of 5% preference shares.
  - Right to vote on all matters at any meetings of the company.
- Preference shares:
  - 100 £1 preference shares.
  - Fixed preference dividend.
  - Right on winding up to the repayment of par value and up to 25% of any sum standing to the credit of the share premium account.
  - No rights to vote at company meetings.

Under the Companies Act 2006 rules the distinction between equity share capital and other share capital is irrelevant in determining whether an undertaking is a subsidiary of another. The definition looks at who controls the 'voting rights' in the undertaking. The preference shares have no voting rights, while the ordinary shares do. Consequently, under the Act's rules, company B is a subsidiary of company A, but is not a subsidiary of company C. This of course ignores the other five tests for potential subsidiaries outlined in paragraph 24.83.

24.92 The Act and FRS 2 provide considerable guidance on the interpretation of the term 'voting rights', both in the context of companies and in the context of unincorporated undertakings.

24.93 'Voting rights' means the rights conferred on shareholders in respect of their shares to vote at the undertaking's general meetings on all, or substantially all, matters. [CA06 7 Sch 2(1); FRS 2 para 17]. Similarly, where an undertaking does not have share capital, voting rights also mean the rights conferred on members to vote at the undertaking's general meetings on all, or substantially all, matters. [CA06 7 Sch 2(1); FRS 2 para 17]. If the undertaking does not have general meetings where matters are decided by exercising voting rights, 'voting rights' will mean having the right under the undertaking's constitution to direct its overall policy, or to alter the terms of its constitution. [CA06 7 Sch 2(2)].

24.94 In determining whether an undertaking holds a majority of the voting rights, certain common rules apply and these are explained further in paragraph 24.165. In particular, options will generally only be taken into consideration, for the purposes of determining whether any party has a majority of voting rights or control of the board, when the option *has been exercised* (see further para 24.167). They may, however, be relevant for consideration of whether the parent has the power to exercise dominant influence over the other party (see further para 24.132).

24.95 In addition, the total voting rights in an undertaking have to be reduced where any rights are exercisable by the undertaking itself. [CA06 7 Sch 10]. This means, for example, that where an undertaking holds any of its own shares they should be excluded from the total voting rights taken into account in deciding whether the undertaking is a subsidiary.

Appointment or removal of majority of board

24.96 An undertaking is a subsidiary where the parent is a member of that undertaking and has the right to appoint or remove a majority of its board of directors. [CA06 Sec 1162(2)(b); FRS 2 para 14(b)]. The meaning of the term 'member' is discussed in paragraph 24.161.

24.97 In this circumstance, *"the right to appoint or remove the majority of the board of directors"* means the right to appoint or remove directors that have a majority of the voting rights at board meetings on all or substantially all matters (without the need for any other person's consent or concurrence, except in the case where no other person has the right to appoint or, as the case may be, remove in relation to that directorship). [CA06 7 Sch 3(1)(3)]. In these circumstances, an undertaking should be treated as having the right to appoint a person to a directorship where:

- The person's appointment follows directly from his appointment as a director of the investing undertaking.
- The directorship is held by the investing undertaking itself.

[CA06 7 Sch 3(2)].

24.98 Certain common rules apply to the expression 'rights' used in paragraph 24.96 above and these are explained further in paragraph 24.165.

24.99 The operation of this definition of subsidiary is illustrated by the example that follows. In this example, the structure is the same as that described in the example in paragraph 24.91 above and illustrated in the diagram. However, in this example the rights attaching to the two different types of share are as follows:

Example – Parent appoints or removes a majority of the board

- Ordinary shares:
  - 100 £1 ordinary shares.
  - All dividends after payment of preference dividends.
  - Right to all surplus assets on a winding up of the company after repayment of 5% preference shares.
  - Right to vote on all matters at any meetings of the company.
  - Power to appoint two directors of the company with one vote each.
- Preference shares:
  - 100 £1 preference shares.
  - Fixed preference dividend.
  - Right on winding up to the repayment of par value and up to 25% of any sum standing to the credit of the share premium account.
  - No rights to vote at company meetings.
  - No voting rights, but where the preference dividend payment is passed the shareholders have the power to appoint two directors with two votes each.

Initially, company A holds the majority of the voting rights of company B and by virtue of section 1162(2)(a) of the Companies Act 2006 (as explained in para 24.91 above) company B is a subsidiary of company A. However, if the preference dividend is in arrears and, as a consequence, the preference shareholders appoint their two directors, company B becomes a subsidiary of company C by virtue of section 1162(2)(b) of the Companies Act 2006, as company C then has the right to appoint or remove directors holding a majority of the voting rights at company B's board meetings.

24.100 The situation described in the example is unusual and it is likely that in this situation as soon as company C is able to control company B's board, company A will lose effective control and will have to exclude company B from its consolidated financial statements. In this regard, FRS 2 states that where more than one undertaking is identified as a parent in such a situation, only one of those parents can have control in practice. [FRS 2 para 62]. In practice, when the arrears of dividend are paid the directors appointed to company B by company C might cease to hold office, in which case control would again reside with company A.

24.101 Where severe long-term restrictions exist on the rights or the ability of one of the parents to exercise control the subsidiary is required under FRS 2 to be excluded from consolidation (see para 24.185). Alternatively, in a situation where there is effectively deadlock in voting rights there might be common control, in which case this might indicate the existence of a joint venture (see chapter 27). [FRS 2 para 63].

24.102 Where an undertaking has the right to appoint a director with a casting vote in the event of a board deadlock and that undertaking controls half of the voting rights on the board, it will effectively control the board as it holds the casting vote and can, therefore, control any board decision.

24.103 In practice a further complication can arise. Many 50/50 joint ventures are set up in the form of companies with each party owning 50 per cent of the equity, holding 50 per cent of the voting rights in general meeting and having the right to appoint directors with 50 per cent of the votes on the board. In order to avoid total deadlock in the event of a disagreement a 'rotating' chairman is appointed with a casting vote. The chairman, who is chosen from the directors, is appointed in alternate years by each party to the joint venture. Therefore, in theory, by virtue of the casting vote, in years one, three and five the undertaking is the subsidiary of one of the venturers while in years two, four and six it is a subsidiary of the other.

24.104 Clearly it does not make sense for each party to consolidate in alternate years. Consequently, using the provision in paragraph 63 of FRS 2 mentioned in paragraph 24.101, such problems can be resolved in practice by considering the substance of the arrangement. It is likely that the arrangement outlined above would be treated as a joint venture with shared control, that is, both parties equity account, their interests.

[The next paragraph is 24.121.]

Dominant influence

24.121 The Act uses the term dominant influence in two of its definitions of subsidiaries. These definitions are as follows; an undertaking is a subsidiary of a parent if the parent:

- Has a *right to exercise a dominant influence* over the undertaking by virtue of provisions either in its memorandum or articles, or in a control contract (see para 24.125).
- Has the *power to exercise, or actually exercises, dominant influence or control* over it (see para 24.130).

24.122 The Act defines the term 'right to exercise a dominant influence', but it does not define 'actually exercises dominant influence' or 'power to exercise dominant influence'. Furthermore, the Act specifically states that its definition of 'right to exercise a dominant influence' should *"not be read as affecting the construction of the expression 'actually exercises a dominant influence' "*. [CA06 7 Sch 4(3)]. The right sought in the first bullet point above is a contractual right, whereas with the latter definition, it is the control that the investing entity actually has in practice or the power to exercise dominant influence or control that is important. The contractual right to exercise a dominant influence was introduced into the EC 7th Directive to deal with situations that arose in another EC member state; although it was also included in the UK legislation, it may not be effective in the UK (see further para 24.129).

24.123 FRS 2 first defines 'dominant influence' and then provides definitions for *'right to exercise a dominant influence'*, *'actually exercises dominant influence'* and *'the power to exercise dominant influence'*.

Dominant influence is defined as:

> *'Influence that can be exercised to achieve the operating and financial policies desired by the holder of the influence, notwithstanding the rights or influence of any other party.'* [FRS 2 para 7].

24.124 By defining 'dominant influence', as well as the three longer expressions in the Act containing the term, FRS 2 is, in effect, linking the three expressions. The common thread is the implementation by the subsidiary of the operating and financial policies desired by the holder of the influence, that is, the parent.

Right to exercise a dominant influence

24.125 As stated above, an undertaking will be a subsidiary where the parent has the right to exercise a dominant influence in either of the following two ways:

- By provisions contained in the undertaking's memorandum or articles of association.
- By a 'control contract' with the undertaking.

[CA06 Sec 1162(2)(c)].

24.126 A 'control contract' is a contract in writing that confers such a right that is authorised by the memorandum or articles of the undertaking in relation to which the right is exercisable and is permitted by the law under which that undertaking is established. [CA06 7 Sch 4(2)].

24.127 It should be noted that for this definition of a subsidiary the parent need not have an interest in the subsidiary.

24.128 Both the Act and FRS 2 state that the right to exercise dominant influence over another undertaking shall not be regarded as exercisable unless:

'*...it has a right to give directions with respect to the operating and financial policies of that other undertaking which its directors are obliged to comply with whether or not they are for the benefit of that other undertaking*.' [CA06 7 Sch 4(1); FRS 2 para 7(a)].

24.129 It is thought that 'the right to exercise a dominant influence' is unlikely to apply to UK subsidiary companies as, in the UK, directors have a duty under common law to act in the company's best interests. There is some doubt whether the directors of a UK subsidiary could be obliged to comply with the directions of the holder of the influence if to do so would not be for the benefit of the subsidiary as this might leave them in breach of their duties as directors.

Power to, or actually exercise, dominant influence or control

24.130 An undertaking is a parent in relation to another undertaking, its subsidiary, if it has the *power to exercise, or actually exercises, dominant influence or control* over it. [CA06 Sec 1162(4)(a); FRS 2 para 14(e)].

24.131 This definition of subsidiary, like the others, has been taken from the amended EC 7th Directive. Although implementation of the Directive by Member States into their national laws was optional, it was incorporated initially into the UK legislation by the Companies Act 1989 deliberately to catch a number of off balance sheet schemes that used special purpose entities to avoid consolidation (see further chapter 3). The original definition was *'if it owns a participating interest in the undertaking and actually exercises a dominant influence over it'*. This definition was subsequently amended by the Modernisation Directive (2003/51/EC) to be closer to that used in IFRS. In the UK, SI 2004/2947, 'The Companies Act 1985 (International Accounting Standards and Other Amendments) Regulations 2004' updated the Act for this change and this was also incorporated as an amendment to FRS 2. The Companies Act 2006 retained this definition of a subsidiary.

24.131.1 As can be seen, a parent is no longer required to have a 'participating interest' in a subsidiary for section 1162(4) and FRS 2 to apply. (A participating interest is an interest in the shares of another undertaking held on a long-term basis for the purpose of securing a contribution to its activities by the exercise of control or influence arising from or related to that interest.) The second change is that under the new definition, the *power* to exercise dominant influence *or control* is enough for a company to qualify as a subsidiary. Previously, a company had to actually exercise dominant influence over the undertaking for it to be a subsidiary under this provision of the Act and FRS 2.

[The next paragraph is 24.132.]

Definition

24.132 The 'power to exercise dominant influence' is defined as *'a power that, if exercised, would give rise to the actual exercise of dominant influence'*. [FRS 2 para 7(c)].

24.133 FRS 2 defines 'actual exercise of dominant influence' as follows: *'The actual exercise of dominant influence is the exercise of an influence that achieves the result that the operating and financial policies of the undertaking influenced are set in accordance with the wishes of the holder of the influence and for the holder's benefit whether or not those wishes are explicit. The actual exercise of dominant influence is identified by its effect in practice rather than by the way in which it is exercised.'* [FRS 2 para 7(b)].

24.134 The definitions above hinge on the terms 'control' and 'dominant influence'. Control is the ability of an entity to direct the operating and financial properties of another undertaking with a view to gaining economic benefits from its activities. Whereas, dominant influence is defined in FRS 2 in terms of the influence that can be exercised to achieve the operating and financial policies desired by the holder of the influence (see para 24.123). [FRS 2 para 7].

24.135 The term 'power to, or actually exercises, dominant influence or control' can be difficult to interpret in practice, principally because of the degree of judgement involved. However, in many cases it should be relatively obvious where control arises.

Example

Company A owns 5% of company B, but in addition has call options exercisable at any time that would give it all the voting rights in company B. Although company A's management do not intend to exercise the call options, the existence of the options and company A's ability to exercise them at any time to gain control of company B gives company A the power to exercise dominant influence. The presence of the options means that the operating and financial policies are set in accordance with company A's wishes and for its benefit, as the other shareholders of company B are mindful of the options in voting on operating and financial policies, as should company B make a decision not in accordance with company A's wishes, company A has the power to exercise the call options and reverse the decision.

24.136 An illustration of a group that consolidates subsidiaries because of dominant influence is given in Table 24.1.

Table 24.1 – Subsidiary consolidated as a result of dominant influence

BET Public Limited Company – Annual Report – 2 April 1994
Accounting policies (extract)

(b) Basis of consolidation (extract)

SUBSIDIARY UNDERTAKINGS (extract)

All companies over which the group is able to exercise a dominant influence are consolidated as subsidiary undertakings. Dominant influence is defined as the right to give directions with respect to operating and financial policies.

Operating and financial policies

24.137 The operating and financial policies of an undertaking will normally be set by the board of directors (in the case of a company) or a similar body for unincorporated undertakings. Usually, a parent would have a *right* to control the board by having the power to appoint or remove a majority of the board and would, therefore, be a parent by virtue of section 1162(2)(b) of the Companies Act 2006.

24.138 The 'actual exercise of dominant influence' and 'power to exercise dominant influence' definitions of a subsidiary, discussed above, are intended to apply to those undertakings that, although effectively controlled by the parent, are not specifically caught by other definitions of the Act.

24.139 The operating and financial policies over which dominance would be needed in a typical entity would cover (but may not be limited to) the following subjects:

- Overall strategy.
- Financial (including most importantly the dividend policy).
- Marketing.
- Production.
- Personnel.

Practical ability and power to control

24.140 Heavy emphasis is placed on the effect of the influence in practice to ensure that undertakings genuinely controlled by the parent are defined as subsidiaries under this definition. But now powers that are unlikely to be exercised to change the decisions of those in day-to-day control of an entity's and financial policies do come into play. Their mere existence is likely to indicate that an entity has the ability to control (that is, the power to control). It is no longer just what happens in practice that is important, it is now also the ability to do something to gain control that is important as well.

Power of veto and other reserve powers

24.141 A power of veto (or other reserve power) that has the necessary effect in practice may give the holder a basis for actually exercising a dominant influence or the power to exercise dominant influence. However, the nature of the power of veto will be of critical importance.

24.142 For example, if an undertaking has shares carrying less than 50 per cent of the votes, but has over 75 per cent of the equity share capital of a company, it may only be able to block business that requires a special resolution. Such a power of veto is not, alone, sufficient to give the undertaking control, but would clearly have to be taken into account with other factors in determining whether the undertaking has the requisite control over the other party.

Commercial relationships

24.143 Certain undertakings can become very dependent on others by virtue of the commercial relationship between them. Examples include undertakings with:

- Only one customer.
- Only one possible supplier.
- Large borrowings from a bank.

24.144 In each of the above examples there may be situations where the undertaking concerned may be significantly influenced by the desires of the other party. With this in mind FRS 2 states that '*Commercial relationships such as that of supplier, customer or lender do not of themselves constitute dominant influence*'. [FRS 2 para 72].

24.145 These relationships will not, generally, give rise to dominant influence unless some other factors are involved. For example, in the situation where undertakings only have one customer or supplier, if the customer or supplier concerned has a substantial participating interest in the undertaking, but it is not quite sufficient to control the undertaking on the grounds of his/her interest alone, the participating interest and the customer/supplier relationship taken together could be sufficient to give the customer/supplier the required control.

Two parents

24.146 The definition of a parent may give rise to an anomaly in that in certain situations it may seem that there are two parents. For example, one company may appear to be exercising dominant influence, yet another may have the power to do so. This situation is likely to arise when the shareholder with the power to exercise dominant influence chooses to be passive and does not prevent the other shareholder from actually exercising dominant influence. Where more than one undertaking appears to be the parent, only one can have control [FRS 2 para 62]. Control is defined as the ability to direct the financial and operating policies of another with a view to gaining economic benefits from its activities. Under the revised definitions in the law and FRS 2 the shareholder with the power to exercise dominant influence has control, despite choosing to be passive.

Example 1 – Government has a controlling shareholding

A government has a controlling shareholding in a company, has board representation and is able to cast a majority vote, but in practice permits the other shareholder to govern the operating and financial policies of an entity. The government elects to be passive, voting consistently with the other shareholder appearing only to intervene where necessary to protect the national interest. In this situation, the government's ownership does constitute control as despite being passive and only intervening where necessary to protect the national interest it has the power to intervene. In effect, it has the power to exercise dominant influence as its presence on the board means that the operating and financial policies are set in accordance with the government's wishes and for its benefit.

Example 2 – Government has a golden share

A government does not have a controlling shareholding in a company, but has a golden share that enables it to replace the board of directors with its nominees should the government disagree with the operating and financial policies decisions taken by the other shareholder. Whilst the share exists to enable the government to protect its national interest, the power that this share gives the government extends beyond this as there are no restrictions on the circumstances on which it can intervene. The share gives the government a power to exercise dominant influence as the presence of the share means that the operating and financial policies are set in accordance with the government's wishes and for its benefit. However, if there were restrictions on when the government could intervene, for example only in preventing the issuance of additional shares or the sale of a material ownership interest to foreign shareholders, then this would indicate that the government does not control the company.

Ceasing to exercise a dominant influence

24.147 As interpretation of the terms 'actual exercise of dominant influence' and 'power to exercise dominant influence' is subjective it might be seen as an opportunity, by some, to manipulate profit or gearing. In theory, at least, a parent might consolidate the results of a subsidiary in some years and exclude them in others, on the grounds that the parent either does, or does not, exercise dominant influence in a particular year. FRS 2 recognises that this may cause problems and states that:

> *'Once there has been evidence that one undertaking has exercised a dominant influence over another, then the dominant undertaking should be assumed to continue to exercise its influence until there is evidence to the contrary. However, it is still necessary for the preparation of the consolidated financial statements to examine the relationship between the undertakings each year to assess any evidence of change in status that may have arisen.'* [FRS 2 para 73].

24.148 For example, if an undertaking has demonstrated that it actually exercises a dominant influence by vetoing a board decision or removing a chief executive then that undertaking will be presumed to continue to actually exercise dominant influence. This will continue to apply, even if the veto is not exercised again, unless there is some change in status of the relationship between the two undertakings.

24.149 Once an undertaking has been treated as a subsidiary of another, it should continue to be treated as a subsidiary until there is persuasive evidence that the relationship between the two undertakings has changed, such that the parent does not have dominant influence over the subsidiaries.

Special purpose entities

24.149.1 As a result of the introduction of 'power to exercise dominant influence' in 2005, certain entities that were previously considered to be quasi-subsidiaries under FRS 5 could now actually be full legal subsidiaries.

24.149.2 However, this might not always be the case. For example, where a parent gained the majority of the benefits arising from a special purpose entity (SPE) and its operating and financial policies were pre-determined, it would have fallen to be treated as a quasi-subsidiary under FRS 5 and not a full subsidiary under FRS 2. In this case, the changes to the definitions of subsidiaries under the Companies Act and FRS 2 do not impact the classification as a quasi-subsidiary, because the parent's control relationship has not changed. In relation to control FRS 5 says that where arrangements are made for allocating the benefits arising from the activities of an entity such active exercise of control is not necessary. It also says that in these situations no party has direct control and that control is exercised indirectly. Hence it can still be argued that the entity is not a full subsidiary, because the parent does not control or have the power to control (that is, cannot change) the SPE's financial and operating policies as these are predetermined and the SPE is a quasi-subsidiary as it is still caught by the provisions of FRS 5 (see further chapter 3).

24.149.3 Whilst this distinction may seem arbitrary, given that the entity in question is consolidated in both circumstances, there were previously potential advantages to designation as a quasi-subsidiary rather than as a full subsidiary. The key advantage was the availability of 'linked presentation' under FRS 5 for the consolidated assets and liabilities. This potential advantage has been removed for those companies applying FRS 26. The amendment to FRS 26 published by the ASB introducing the IAS 39 recognition and derecognition criteria into UK GAAP, removes 'linked presentation' from FRS 5.

[The next paragraph is 24.150.]

Summary

24.150 To decide whether or not, in practice, an undertaking has the power to exercise, or actually exercises, dominant influence or control over another, a number of different factors have to be considered. Therefore, it is important that the full circumstances of each situation are considered, including the effect of any formal or informal agreements between the undertakings. Any decision in this respect is likely to be judgemental and should take into account the following:

- The degree of board representation.
- The degree of day-to-day influence over the undertaking's financial and operating policies.
- The extent of any powers of veto (or other reserve powers) held by the investor.
- Evidence of intervention to ensure that the investor's preferred operational and financial policies are implemented by the undertaking.
- Powers held by other investors or third parties that affect the degree of influence of the investor over the undertaking.
- Evidence of decisions *not* being taken in accordance with the investor's wishes.
- Other contrary evidence that indicates that dominant influence is not held.

Disclosure

24.151 Where an undertaking is a subsidiary only because its parent undertaking has the power to exercise, or actually exercises, a dominant influence or control over it, the consolidated financial statements should disclose the basis of the parent's dominant influence or control. [FRS 2 para 34].

Managed on a unified basis

24.152 An undertaking is a parent in relation to another undertaking, a subsidiary, if it and the undertaking are managed on a unified basis. [CA06 Sec 1162(4)(b); FRS 2 para 14(e)].

24.153 The Act provides no definition of 'managed on a unified basis', however, FRS 2 defines it as follows:

> '*Two or more undertakings are managed on a unified basis if the whole of the operations of the undertakings are integrated and they are managed as a single unit. Unified management does not arise solely because one undertaking manages another.*' [FRS 2 para 12].

24.154 The application of this definition in practice will, as for dominant influence, require considerable judgement. The definition seems to suggest unified management at all levels in the undertakings. Characteristics of unified management could include:

- Adoption of an overall management strategy for the group which includes the undertaking in question.
- The group treating the undertaking as if it were a subsidiary, for example by determining its dividend policy.
- Common management teams, both at board level and operationally.
- Common employees.
- Common administrative functions, for example, accounting, personnel and marketing.
- Common premises.

Control governed by an agreement

24.155 An undertaking will be a subsidiary where the parent is a member of it and controls alone, following an agreement with other shareholders or members of the undertaking, a majority of its voting rights. [CA06 Sec 1162(2)(d); FRS 2 para 14(d)].

24.156 The term 'voting rights' in this context means the same as the term explained in paragraph 24.93 above.

[The next paragraph is 24.159.]

Control contrasted with shared control

24.159 There is an important distinction to be drawn between the control that identifies the parent/subsidiary relationship and shared control. Shared control is the principal feature of a joint venture. A parent that has sole control over its subsidiary's resources can exercise that control to use the subsidiary's resources in a similar way to its own. The ability of an undertaking that shares control of the operating and financial policies of an undertaking is limited by the need to take account of the wishes of the other parties that share control. Shared control may indicate the presence of a joint venture and such ventures are considered further in chapter 27.

Common expressions and interpretations

24.160 In the definitions of subsidiaries explained above there are a number of common expressions and interpretations and these are considered in the paragraphs below.

Parent and subsidiary undertakings

24.161 The subscribers of a company's memorandum are deemed to have agreed to become members of the company and are entered as such in the company's register of members. Every person who agrees to become a member of a company and whose name is entered in its register, is a member of the company. [CA06 Sec 112]. A person holding preference shares in a company is a member of that company for this reason.

24.162 In the definitions of subsidiaries a parent undertaking is treated as a member of another undertaking if any of the parent's subsidiaries are members of that other undertaking. [CA06 Sec 1162(3)(a); FRS 2 para 14]. Furthermore, this is also so if any shares in the other undertaking are held by a third party on behalf of the parent or its subsidiaries. [CA06 Sec 1162(3)(b); FRS 2 para 14]. These provisions, however, do not extend to the situation where an undertaking is consolidated for the reason that its parent has the power to exercise or actually exercises dominant influence or control over it, or manages it on a unified basis.

Example – Parent is treated as a member of another company where it is not itself a member

A parent's subsidiary company B may be a member of company C. In this circumstance, even where the parent is not a member of company C itself (for the purposes of determining whether company C is a subsidiary of the parent), the parent is treated as a member of company C by virtue of section 1162(3)) of the Companies Act 2006.

24.163 In addition, where a group has intermediate parent undertakings (which can either be companies or unincorporated undertakings), their subsidiaries will also be regarded as subsidiaries of any parent undertakings further up the group structure. [CA06 Sec 1162(5)]. Consequently, subsidiaries of all parent undertakings within a group are deemed by this provision to be subsidiaries of the ultimate parent company.

24.164 In the situation where an undertaking is not a company, the Act provides no specific guidance on what constitutes membership of that undertaking. The Act does, however, provide general guidance on interpreting expressions used by companies that are not used by unincorporated undertakings. These provisions are discussed in paragraph 24.86.

Provisions concerning rights

24.165 There are a number of common provisions that explain how to treat rights in different situations. These rules apply to voting rights (see para 24.89 and 24.155 above) and rights to appoint or remove the majority of the board of directors (see para 24.96 above).

24.166 In determining whether rights should be attributed to a parent, rights held by a subsidiary undertaking should be treated as if they are held by the parent. [CA06 7 Sch 9(1)].

24.167 Rights exercisable in certain circumstances should only be taken into account when those circumstances have arisen and only for as long as they continue. [CA06 7 Sch 5(1)(a)]. Furthermore, such rights should also be taken into account where the circumstances are in the control of the person having the rights. [CA06 7 Sch 5(1)(b)]. In this respect, it is obvious that where the option *has been exercised* the shares must be taken into account in determining whether any party has a majority of voting rights or control of the board. Where an option to acquire shares has not yet been exercised, but can be freely exercised by its holder (that is, the option is within its exercise period) the rights in the shares under option (such as the voting rights) do not vest with the holder until the option is actually exercised. However, the existence of such an option might indicate that the holder has the power to actually exercise a dominant influence (using FRS 2's definition of that term) and the entity would be a subsidiary under section 1162(4) of the Companies Act 2006.

24.168 In addition, rights that the undertaking can normally exercise, but that are temporarily incapable of being exercised, should continue to be taken into account. [CA06 7 Sch 5(2)].

24.169 Rights should not be treated as held by a person (which includes an undertaking) if they are held in a fiduciary capacity. [CA06 7 Sch 6]. Similarly, rights held by a person as nominee should not be treated as held by him. Such rights will be considered held 'as nominee' for another person if they can only be exercised on his instructions or with his consent or concurrence. [CA06 7 Sch 7]. However, this provision cannot be used to require rights held by a parent to be treated as held by any of its subsidiaries. [CA06 7 Sch 9(2)].

24.170 Rights that are attached to shares held as security shall be treated as held by the person providing the security where those rights (excluding any right to exercise them to preserve the value of the security, or to realise it) are only exercisable in accordance with his instructions. This rule applies where the shares are held in connection with granting loans in the normal course of business and, except where they are exercisable to preserve the value of the security or to realise it, the rights are exercised only in the interests of the person providing the security. [CA06 7 Sch 8]. This provision, however, cannot be used to require rights held by a parent to be treated as held by any of its subsidiaries. [CA06 7 Sch 9(2)]. Furthermore, rights should be treated as being exercisable in accordance with the instructions, or the interests of, an undertaking if they are exercisable in accordance with the instructions of, or in the interests of, any group undertaking. [CA067 Sch 9(3)].

Provisions concerning capital

24.171 References to shares in an undertaking with a share capital are to allotted shares. [CA06 Sec 1161(2)(a)]. In an undertaking that has capital, but no share capital, shares mean the rights to share in the capital of the undertaking. [CA06 Sec 1161(2)(b)]. For example, in the case of a partnership, this would mean the relevant partners' share in the capital of the partnership. For an undertaking that has no capital, shares mean an interest conferring any right to share in the profits, or to contribute to the losses, of the undertaking. In this situation, it could also mean an interest giving rise to an obligation to contribute to the debts or expenses on winding up the undertaking. [CA06 Sec 1161(2)(c)].

Meaning of subsidiary used elsewhere in the legislation

24.172 Whereas the paragraphs above explain the definitions of subsidiary undertaking used in the Act to determine which undertakings should be included in consolidated financial statements, section 1159 of the Companies Act 2006 explains the meaning of 'subsidiary', 'holding company' and 'wholly-owned subsidiary' used elsewhere in the legislation; and the definitions of subsidiary differ. Section 1159 is narrower than section 1162 (which defines the undertakings to be included in the consolidation) in that section 1159 only includes some of the definitions of subsidiaries discussed above. Section 1159 does not include the following definitions used for consolidation purposes:

- Rights to direct operating and financial policies (see para 24.125).
- Dominant influence or unified management (see paras 24.130 and 24.152).

24.173 The notion of 'equity share capital' as the main criterion in determining whether a company is a subsidiary of another, does not apply either when determining whether an undertaking is a subsidiary for the purposes of consolidation or as part of the section 1159 definitions of subsidiary for other purposes within the Act. However, the term remains in the Act as it is used elsewhere in the legislation.

24.174 Loan stock deeds often refer to the parent and its subsidiaries as defined by section 1159 in determining borrowing restrictions.

Examples of practical situations

24.175 The examples that follow illustrate the type of situations that might arise in practice.

Example 1 – Convertible shares and an option to acquire shares

A group takes an interest in a company that has £500,000 net liabilities in the hope that it can turn the company around. The group's interest is £100,000 preference shares and the preference shares are convertible at any time at the option of the group into 51% of the company's equity carrying 51% of the company's voting rights. The group also has an option to acquire the other 49% of the company's equity shares.

In this situation it is necessary to establish whether the company has the power to exercise, or actually exercises dominant influence or control over the company, or manages it on a unified basis, before it is deemed to be a subsidiary. The existence of the potential voting rights would *prima facie* give the required control. If it is determined that the undertaking is a subsidiary, the group will consolidate fully the assets and liabilities of the company and will show a significant minority interest. Such a situation could be very confusing for a reader of the financial statements and, as a consequence, some additional disclosure might be necessary.

In contrast, if the preference shares were convertible into the same number of ordinary shares at the option of the issuer, then the group would not have the power to exercise dominant influence or control over the company and, in the absence of any other factors, the company would not be a subsidiary.

Example 2 – Commercial arrangement indicate management on a unified basis

A UK group has a 50% interest in an overseas joint venture company and the other 50% is held by another overseas company incorporated in the same overseas country. Representation on the board and the share of income is spilt equally. Any disputes are referred to an arbitrator or to the High Court. The joint venture company manufactures goods only for the UK group and sells these goods at a price that is designed to provide a fixed return to the joint venture. The managing director of the joint venture is also an employee of the UK group.

Although the joint venture appears to have been set up as a 'deadlock' company the commercial arrangements suggest that it may be managed on a unified basis with the UK group and that the UK group might have dominant influence over the joint venture. In order to determine the extent of the influence, it would be necessary to establish if the joint venture's board is independent of the UK group. If, for example, the managing director reports to the board of the UK group and that board decides on, for instance, production levels and other management issues, then the joint venture may well be a subsidiary of the UK group.

Example 3 – Disposal and retention of convertible shares

A group decides to dispose of a subsidiary to its management. After the disposal the group retains 49% of ordinary shares, management has 30% and outsiders have 21%. The group, management and outsiders also have convertible shares, which are convertible into the same proportions of ordinary shares. Those of the group are convertible after five years without any conditions, but those of the management are convertible only if certain profit targets are met. If they are not met management's shares will not be converted and the conversion of the group's shares will result in the company becoming a subsidiary again.

It is necessary to decide whether in practice the group has the power to exercise, or actually exercises, dominant influence or manages the subsidiary on a unified basis. If that is so, the company would remain a subsidiary throughout. If the group does not have dominant influence over the company or manage it on a unified basis, a view has to be taken as to whether it is probable and there is reasonable evidence that the profit targets will be met. If it is considered probable that they will be met, the company would not be treated as the group's subsidiary and, consequently, would not be consolidated. However, full details of the conversion rights should be disclosed in the group's consolidated financial statements.

Subsidiaries excluded from consolidation

24.176 As mentioned in paragraph 24.29 above, the general rule under both the Act and FRS 2 requires that all subsidiary undertakings should be included in the consolidated financial statements. [CA06 Sec 405(1); FRS 2 para 23]. The Act *permits* exclusion of a subsidiary from consolidation where:

- Inclusion is not material for the purposes of giving a true and fair view. [CA06 Sec 405(2)].
- The information necessary for the preparation of consolidated financial statements cannot be obtained without disproportionate expense or undue delay. [CA06 Sec 405(3)(b)].
- There are severe long-term restrictions over a parent's rights in respect of a subsidiary. [CA06 Sec 405(3)(a)].
- The parent's interest is held exclusively with a view to resale. [CA06 Sec 405(3)(c)].

24.177 Paragraph 25 of FRS 2 restricts the fourth exemption to allow only when *'the subsidiary has not previously been consolidated in group accounts prepared by the parent undertaking'*.

[The next paragraph is 24.179.]

24.179 Within the constraints of the statutory framework set out in the Act, FRS 2 refines the conditions for exclusion so that they identify those undertakings that, though defined by the Act as subsidiaries, are not controlled by the parent in a way that would in principle justify consolidation. Having identified such subsidiaries, FRS 2 *requires* their exclusion from consolidation.

Inclusion not material

24.180 As mentioned above, a subsidiary undertaking need not be consolidated where its inclusion in the consolidation would have an immaterial effect. Two or more undertakings may only be excluded using this provision where taken together they are still not material to the consolidation. [CA06 Sec 405(2)]. As Financial Reporting Standards deal only with material items, this exemption is not found in the main body of FRS 2, but is dealt with and permitted by paragraph 78(a) of the explanatory section of FRS 2. However, materiality needs to be judged carefully, as Alliance Trust was commented on by the Financial Reporting Review Panel (FRRP) in April 1995 for not consolidating its banking subsidiary. In its financial statements for the year to 31 January 1994, Alliance Trust had excluded its subsidiary on the grounds of immateriality, but has consolidated it in the subsequent year following discussions with the Stock Exchange and the FRRP (see Tables 24.3 and 24.4).

Table 24.3 – Immaterial subsidiaries not consolidated

The Alliance Trust PLC – Report and Accounts – 31 January 1994

NOTES ON THE ACCOUNTS (extract)

1. ACCOUNTING POLICIES (extract)

f The accounts of Alliance Trust (Finance) Limited have not been consolidated with those of the Company as the directors consider that the amounts involved are not material and that their inclusion would detract from the clarity of the accounts in respect of the principal activity of the Company as an authorised investment trust. A separate statement of the affairs of Alliance Trust (Finance) Limited is on page 23.

Table 24.4 – Previously immaterial subsidiary now consolidated

The Alliance Trust PLC – Report and Accounts – 31 January 1995

REPORT OF THE DIRECTORS (extract)

The consolidated accounts, which are provided for the first time this year, include the results of our banking and savings subsidiary. Alliance Trust (Finance) Limited. These have been produced in the light of developing accounting standards, which will lead shortly to adoption of a Statement of Recommended Practice for investment trusts, and after discussion with the Financial Reporting Review Panel, the Company having raised the issue of consolidation with the Stock Exchange. Full information on the subsidiary has previously been included separately within the accounts. Relevant information continues to be given in note 12.

Disproportionate expense or undue delay

24.181 Although the Act allows a subsidiary that is material in the context of the group to be excluded on the grounds that the information necessary for the preparation of the consolidated financial statements cannot be obtained without disproportionate expense or undue delay, this is not permitted by FRS 2. [CA06 Sec 405(3)(b); FRS 2 para 24]. FRS 2 takes the view that mere expense or undue delay are not sufficient grounds to exclude a material subsidiary and, therefore, in practice this reason for exclusion cannot be used. The ASB's view is that if the subsidiary is material, it must be included and the consolidated financial statements cannot give a true and fair view without its inclusion.

Severe long-term restrictions

Basis of exclusion

24.182 Consolidation of a subsidiary undertaking is *not required* by the Act where severe long-term restrictions substantially hinder the exercise of the parent company's rights over the assets or over the management of the undertaking.

[CA06 Sec 405(3)(a)]. The rights that must be restricted for this exclusion to apply are those that would result in the undertaking being a subsidiary of the parent and without which it would not be a subsidiary (see para 24.165). [CA06 Sec 405(3); FRS 2 para 25(a)]. They include all such rights attributed to the parent undertaking under section 405(3). Table 24.5 illustrates a situation where certain subsidiaries are excluded from consolidation because of severe long-term restrictions.

Table 24.5 – Subsidiaries excluded because of severe long-term restrictions

BM Group PLC – Annual Report – 30 June 1993

NOTES TO THE FINANCIAL STATEMENTS (extract)

15. Investments (extract)

The net assets of certain African subsidiaries of the Group have been excluded from consolidation on the basis that severe long term restrictions are in place which hinder the exercise of the Group's rights over the assets employed. The subsidiaries concerned are Blackwood Hodge (Kenya) Ltd, Blackwood Hodge (Cote d'Ivoire) SarL. Blackwood Hodge (Tanzania) Ltd, Blackwood Hodge (Ghana) Ltd (60% owned) and Blackwood Hodge (Sierra Leone) Ltd.

24.183 The ASB considers, however, that where the parent's rights are restricted in this way the subsidiary concerned *should* be excluded from consolidation. The important difference is that the Act *permits* exclusion on these grounds whereas FRS 2 *requires* exclusion. However, FRS 2 states that in order to justify not consolidating a subsidiary the effect of the restrictions must be that the parent does not *control* its subsidiary.

24.184 Furthermore, severe long-term restrictions are identified by their effect in practice rather than by the way in which the restrictions are imposed. For example, a subsidiary should not be excluded because restrictions are threatened or because another party has the power to impose them unless such threats or the existence of such a power has a severe and restricting effect in practice in the long-term on the parent's rights. [FRS 2 para 78(c)].

24.185 There are a number of situations where a parent's control over its subsidiary *may* be subject to severe long-term restrictions. These include situations where the following exist:

- A power of veto is held by a third party.
- Severe restrictions exist over remittances.
- Insolvency or administration procedures are in progress.
- Two parent undertakings are identified under the definitions in the Act, but one does not control the subsidiary undertaking or they exercise joint control.

An example of a situation where a company holds a majority of the subsidiary's voting rights, but its ability to exercise those rights is restricted, is given in Table 24.6.

Table 24.6 – Ability to exercise voting rights restricted

British Steel plc – Report and Accounts – 2 April 1994

ACCOUNTING POLICIES (extract)

1. BASIS OF CONSOLIDATION (extract)

The Company holds a majority of the voting rights in UES Holdings Limited (UES), but is restricted in its ability to exercise those rights under an agreement with the other shareholder. Consequently, the investment has not been consolidated in these accounts but has been included based on the Group's share of its results and net assets.

24.186 In general, restrictions are better dealt with by disclosure rather than by exclusion. However, the overriding principle is that a parent *should not* consolidate a subsidiary that it does not control. Consider the following example, which deals with a power of veto and restrictions over remittances.

Example – Power of veto and restrictions over remittances

A parent has a subsidiary overseas. The subsidiary is owned and managed by the parent, but the host government has the power to:

- Veto the sale of the parent's interest in the subsidiary to an overseas investor.
- Veto any board decisions that are not in the interests of the local community.
- Restrict or prevent the remittance of funds from the subsidiary to the UK.

The parent company does not intend to sell the subsidiary and it has never experienced a veto of a board decision or restrictions of remittances by the host government. In practice, the parent's and the host government's objectives are the same and it is, therefore, extremely unlikely that the veto will be used or the restrictions over remittances imposed.

Although the host government has a power of veto over a sale and certain board decisions and can restrict remittance of funds to the UK, it has never used these powers and it is assumed, from the facts given, that it is unlikely to do so. Furthermore, as the parent's objectives and those of the local government are similar, it is unlikely that the threat of the veto or restrictions have any effect on the manner in which the subsidiary is managed by the parent. This would, therefore, appear to be a situation where the veto and restrictions have little effect in practice and consolidation would be required. The potential restrictions over distributions should then be disclosed in accordance with paragraph 53 of FRS 2.

24.187 FRS 2 specifically considers the situation where a subsidiary undertaking is subject to an insolvency procedure in the UK. Where control over that undertaking has passed to a designated official (for example, an administrator, an administrative receiver or a liquidator), the effect will be that severe long-term restrictions are in force. A company voluntary arrangement does not necessarily lead to loss of control and in some overseas jurisdictions formal insolvency procedures may not amount to loss of control. [FRS 2 para 78(c)].

Example – Parent is in administration

An intermediate holding company's parent is in administration and is unlikely to produce consolidated financial statements. It therefore appears that the intermediate holding company will have to prepare consolidated financial statements as it will not be able to avail itself of the exemption from preparing consolidated financial statements given in the Companies Act (see para 24.57). Most of the intermediate parent's subsidiaries have been sold since the year end because of the group's need to realise assets. There is also a problem in obtaining information from the purchasers of those companies.

If it can be demonstrated that there are significant restrictions imposed on the intermediate parent by the administrator such that the intermediate parent was unable to exercise its rights over the assets and management of the subsidiaries then that would be a justifiable reason for non-consolidation.

Accounting treatment

24.188 Where a parent's control over a subsidiary is subject to severe long-term restrictions, that subsidiary should be excluded from consolidation and treated as a fixed asset investment. If the subsidiary was acquired with the restrictions, the investment should be carried initially at cost. However, if the restrictions came into force at a later date, the investment should be carried at a fixed amount calculated using the equity method at the date on which the restrictions came into force. While the restrictions are in force the parent should make no further accruals for the profits or losses of the undertaking. But if it continues to exercise significant influence over the undertaking it should account for its investment as an associate using equity accounting (see chapter 27). [FRS 2 para 27].

24.189 A review of the value of subsidiary undertakings subject to severe long-term restrictions should be carried out to assess whether the carrying value of the investment has suffered an impairment. Where any impairment has occurred, this should be reflected by providing against the carrying amount of the relevant subsidiary and charging the provision to the consolidated profit and loss account. It may then be necessary also to make a provision against the carrying value of the investment in the undertaking holding the investment and charge that provision to that undertaking's profit and loss account. In assessing impairment, each subsidiary should be considered individually. The intra-group balances with subsidiary undertakings excluded on the grounds of severe long-term restrictions should also be reviewed and written down, if necessary. [FRS 2 para 27].

24.190 When the severe long-term restrictions cease and the parent undertaking's rights are restored, the amount of the profit or loss for that subsidiary that accrued during the period of restriction should be separately disclosed in the consolidated profit and loss account for the period in which the control is resumed. Any amount previously charged as an impairment that is written back as a result of restrictions ceasing, should be separately disclosed. [FRS 2 para 28]. An example of this situation is given in Table 24.7.

24.191 It should be remembered, however, that where a subsidiary is liquidated during or after the year end, it should still be consolidated up to the point that the restrictions come into force. Such a subsidiary should only be excluded from consolidation after the date on which it has gone into liquidation.

24.192 It is possible that restrictions may lift sufficiently for a subsidiary that has previously been treated as an investment to be equity accounted as an associated undertaking, because the parent now has significant influence over that undertaking, but does not exercise sufficient control to justify full consolidation. In practice this is likely to be rare, but should it occur, the *group's share* of the profit or loss that accrued during the period of the restriction should be dealt with in the consolidated profit and loss account of the period in which significant influence is resumed. The amount should be separately disclosed if it is material.

Interest held exclusively with a view to subsequent resale

Basis of exclusion

24.193 Consolidation of a subsidiary undertaking is *not required* where the interest of the parent company is held exclusively with a view to subsequent resale. [CA06 Sec 405(3)(c)]. In this situation, the 'interests' of the parent company are the interests attributed to it under the definition of 'parent undertaking' (see para 24.161). Again, this exemption is repeated in FRS 2, but with the important difference that the Act *permits* exclusion on these grounds whereas FRS 2 *requires exclusion*. [FRS 2 para 25(b)]. FRS 2 also restricts the circumstances in which a subsidiary held for resale is permitted (and required) to be excluded to those where *'the undertaking has not previously been consolidated in group accounts prepared by the parent undertaking'*. [FRS 2 para 25(b)].

24.194 The standard defines an interest held exclusively with a view to subsequent resale as:

> *'a An interest for which a purchaser has been identified or is being sought, and which is reasonably expected to be disposed of within approximately one year of its date of acquisition*; or
>
> *b An interest that was acquired as a result of the enforcement of a security, unless the interest has become part of the continuing activities of the group or the holder acts as if it intends the interest to become so.'* [FRS 2 para 11].

24.195 FRS 2 gives specific guidance on the interpretation of disposal 'within approximately one year'. An interest for which a sale is not completed within one year of its purchase may still meet the requirement if, at the time the financial statements are signed:

- The terms of sale have been agreed.
- The process of disposing of the subsidiary is substantially complete.

[FRS 2 para 78(d)].

24.196 FRS 2 includes only 'enforcement of a security' and excludes other methods of involuntary acquisition (unless they meet the first definition's requirements). Typically 'enforcement of a security' will apply to banks that have made secured loans to undertakings that have subsequently defaulted on their loans and which are, therefore, controlled by the banks. Provided such an undertaking has not become part of the continuing activities of the bank's group and the bank does not act as if it intends it to become so, the undertaking should not be consolidated.

24.197 FRS 2 draws attention to paragraph 8 of Schedule 7 to the Companies Act 2006 which provides that *rights* that are *'attached to shares held by way of security'* should be treated as held by the 'person providing the security' where those rights are only exercisable in accordance with his instructions. The right of the holder of the security to exercise the rights to preserve the value of the security or to realise it does not affect the above provision. This rule applies where the shares are held in connection with granting loans in the normal course of business and, apart from the purpose of preserving the value of the security or of realising it, the rights are exercisable only in the interests of the provider of the security.

Example – Interest held exclusively for resale

A bank has acquired over 50% of the voting rights of a company as a result of a reconstruction whereby it and other lenders converted debt into equity. The bank intends to dispose of the equity when it gets the opportunity.

The company is technically a subsidiary of the bank, but it would not require to be accounted for on a full consolidation basis in the bank's consolidated financial statements as it is held for resale. It should, therefore, be excluded from consolidation and accounted for in the way described below.

26.197.1 An illustration of a company excluding a subsidiary from consolidation on this ground is given in Table 24.7.

Table 24.7 – Subsidiary excluded from consolidation as held exclusively for resale

Barclays PLC – Report and Accounts – 31 December 1993

Notes to the accounts (extract)

54 Subsidiary and associated undertakings (extract)

Certain subsidiaries not consolidated in previous years are now included in these accounts because, in the opinion of the Directors, the long-term restrictions which hindered the exercise of the rights of the Group over their assets or management have ceased. After allowing for dividends received and foreign exchange adjustments, there were no unrecognised profits or losses accruing during the period of restriction.

During 1992, the Group acquired a 100% interest in Imry Holdings Limited (Imry), a company registered in England, as a result of enforcing security against a loan to Chester Holdings (UK) Limited, the parent company of Imry. The interest is held exclusively with a view to subsequent resale and therefore has not been consolidated. The Group holds all the issued shares of Imry and all of the £100m zero coupon preference shares in its subsidiary, Imry Jersey Limited. The shareholdings were valued at £56m at 31st December 1993 (1992 £56m). At 31st December 1993, the capital and reserves of Imry amounted to £79m (1992 £71m). The profit before taxation of Imry for the year ended 1993 was £8m. There were outstandings of £81m (1992 £85m) due to the Group, secured by a fixed and floating charge on the assets of Imry. During the year, Barclays Mercantile Limited paid £2,147,000 in rentals to Imry under a lease. Imry paid £675,000 to Barclays Bank PLC in exchange for the Bank providing a guarantee for the rental obligations of Barclays Mercantile Limited under its lease, and £385,000 to Barclays Property Holdings on behalf of Barclays Mercantile Limited to cover the cost of repair work required under the terms of the lease. There were no other material transactions between Imry and the Group during the year.

Accounting treatment

24.198 A subsidiary held exclusively with a view to resale and not previously consolidated, although controlled by its parent, does not form part of the group's continuing activities. The parent's control is temporary and is not used to deploy the underlying assets and liabilities of that subsidiary as part of the group's continuing activities and for the parent's benefit. The subsidiary should, therefore, be excluded from consolidation on these grounds and should be treated as a current asset investment, included in the group balance sheet at the lower of cost and net realisable value. [FRS 2 paras 29, 79(b)]. Where the subsidiary has still not been sold within approximately one year of the acquisition, it should be consolidated and fair values attributed to its individual assets and liabilities as at the date of acquisition (see further chapter 25). [FRS 7 para 18]. An example of a subsidiary excluded on these grounds is given in Table 24.8.

[The next paragraph is 24.200.]

Disclosure for subsidiaries excluded from consolidation

24.200 Schedule 4 to SI 2008/410 'The Large and Medium-sized Companies and Groups (Accounts and Reports) Regulations 2008' sets out certain information about subsidiaries that companies that prepare consolidated financial statements have to give; these general requirements are considered in paragraph 24.213 below. Also, companies that do not prepare consolidated financial statements have to give information about their subsidiaries and this information is similarly set out in Schedule 4. These provisions are considered in chapter 6.

24.201 The additional disclosure required by Schedule 4 to SI 2008/410 and FRS 2 concerning subsidiaries that have been excluded from consolidation where consolidated financial statements are prepared is extensive. Although, in general, the disclosures relate to individual subsidiaries excluded from consolidation, there are circumstances where it may be possible to provide the information on an aggregated basis for some or all of the subsidiaries concerned. FRS 2 extends the Act's disclosure requirements for subsidiaries excluded from consolidation (including those that are unincorporated subsidiaries).

The Act's requirements

24.202 Where a subsidiary is excluded from consolidation, the notes to the consolidated financial statements must disclose:

- The reasons why the subsidiary or the subsidiaries are not dealt with in the consolidated financial statements. [SI 2008/410 4 Sch 10(1)]. The reason disclosed would have to be one of those explained above.
- The aggregate amount of the subsidiary's capital and reserves at the end of its relevant financial year and its profit or loss for the period. [SI 2008/410 4 Sch 2(1)]. This information need not be given, however, where either of the following conditions is satisfied:
- The group's total investment in its subsidiaries' shares is included in the consolidated financial statements by the equity method of valuation (see chapter 27). [SI 2008/410 4 Sch 2(3)].
- The company is exempt by virtue of section 400 (see para 24.56.1) or section 401 (see para 24.62.1.1) of the Companies Act 2006 from the requirement to prepare consolidated financial statements. [SI 2008/410 4 Sch 2(2)].
- The undertaking is not required under the Act to file its balance sheet with the Registrar of Companies or publish it in Great Britain or elsewhere. Exemption is only allowed under this provision, however, if the group's holding in the undertaking is less than 50 per cent of the nominal value of that undertaking's shares. [SI 2008/410 4 Sch 2(4)].

An example of the type of disclosure required where a subsidiary has been excluded on the grounds of being held exclusively for resale is illustrated in Table 24.8.

Table 24.8 – Disclosure where a subsidiary is held exclusively for resale

Airtours plc – Annual report and accounts – 30 September 1993

Notes to the financial statements (extract)

10) Fixed asset investments (extract)

All of the subsidiary undertakings, with the exception of Moon Leasing Limited, have been consolidated in the Group financial statements. The financial statements of Moon Leasing Limited have not been consolidated as it is being held exclusively for resale.

The aggregate amount of the capital and reserves of Moon Leasing Limited was £149,808 at 30th September 1993. The profit for the year was £149,807.

26.202.1 References to 'relevant financial year' above are to the subsidiary's financial year ending with the parent's year end or the last financial year ending before that date. [SI 2008/410 4 Sch].

26.202.2 The information required by paragraph 2 of Schedule 4 to SI 2008/410 need not be given if it is not material. [SI 2008/410 4 Sch 2(5)].

Additional requirements of FRS 2

24.203 In addition to the disclosures required by Schedule 4 to SI 2008/410 'The Large and Medium-sized Companies and Groups (Accounts and Reports) Regulations 2008', the following information should be given in the consolidated financial statements for subsidiaries not included in the consolidation:

- Particulars of the balances between the excluded subsidiaries and the rest of the group.
- The nature and extent of transactions of the excluded subsidiaries with the rest of the group.
- For an excluded subsidiary carried other than by the equity method, any amounts included in the consolidated financial statements in respect of:
  - Dividends received and receivable from that subsidiary (although the adoption of FRS 21 all but prohibits the recognition of dividends receivable at the year end).
  - Any write-down in the period in respect of the investment in that subsidiary or amounts due from that subsidiary.

[FRS 2 para 31].

- Guarantees in respect of subsidiary undertakings excluded from consolidation have to be treated in the same way as guarantees given by members of the group to third parties. [FRS 2 para 79(d)]. The detailed disclosure in respect of commitments and guarantees is set out in paragraph 63 of Schedule 1 to SI 2008/410 and is discussed in detail in chapter 21.

Aggregation of disclosures

24.204 The general disclosure requirements listed above are required for individual excluded subsidiaries. However, if the information about excluded subsidiaries is more appropriately presented for a sub-unit of the group made up from more than one excluded subsidiary, the disclosures may be made on an aggregate basis. The sub-units for which these disclosures should be given are to be made up from subsidiary undertakings *'excluded under the same sub-section of section 229'*. [FRS 2 para 32]. The three permitted or required exclusions are dealt with in section 405 of the Companies Act 2006 as follows:

- Not material (see para 24.180 above).
- Severe long-term restrictions (see para 24.182 above).
- Held for subsequent resale (see para 24.193 above).

24.205 As FRS 2 does not deal with immaterial matters the disclosures are not required for subsidiaries excluded from consolidation on the grounds of immateriality.

24.206 A strict interpretation of paragraph 32 of FRS 2 suggests that aggregation of the information concerning subsidiaries excluded because of severe long-term restrictions and subsequent resale is permitted as they are both dealt with by the Companies Act 2006 in section 405 (3). However, as the subsidiaries concerned are excluded for different reasons this may lead to some confusion. To avoid such confusion, aggregation might be given under the following headings:

- Severe long-term restrictions.
- Held for subsequent resale.

24.207 However, individual disclosures should be made for any excluded subsidiary, including its sub-group where relevant, that alone accounts for more than 20 per cent of any one or more of the group's:

- Operating profits.
- Turnover.
- Net assets.

[FRS 2 para 32].

24.208 The group amounts in paragraph 24.207 should be measured by including all excluded subsidiaries. [FRS 2 para 32].

General exemptions from disclosure requirements

24.209 The information required to be disclosed under the Act concerning subsidiaries excluded from consolidation outlined above (except for that required by paragraphs 3 and 7 to SI 2008/410 'The Large and Medium-sized Companies and Groups (Accounts and Reports) Regulations 2008') need not be disclosed if, in the directors' opinion, its disclosure would be seriously prejudicial to the subsidiary's business or to the business of the parent or any of its subsidiaries. This exemption applies where the particulars relate to a subsidiary that is established under the law of a country outside the UK or where its business is carried on outside the UK. However, the Secretary of State has to agree that the disclosure need not be made and the fact that advantage is taken of this exemption has to be disclosed. [CA06 Sec 409(3)(4)(5)]. It is then questionable whether this exemption extends to disclosures required by FRS 2 and this is considered further in paragraph 24.233.

24.210 An example of an occasion when it would be allowable not to disclose this information would be when a company has trading subsidiaries in two countries and those two countries are either in conflict, or have trade embargoes between them. In these two situations where these subsidiaries are excluded from consolidation on one of the grounds considered above, the disclosure of the UK group's investment in each subsidiary might impair its trading ability in those countries.

24.211 The general exemption from the disclosure requirements of Schedule 4 to SI 2008/410 (where certain information is not required if the number of undertakings is such that the resulting disclosure is, in the opinion of the directors, excessively lengthy) does not apply to subsidiaries that are excluded from consolidation. [CA06 Sec 410(2)(b)].

24.212 Note that, where a subsidiary has been excluded from consolidation as outlined from paragraph 24.176 above, the Act requires that the information outlined below from paragraph 24.213 should still be given as there is no exemption in this respect.

Limited partnerships

24.212.1 As mentioned in paragraph 24.87 above a limited partnership is made up of one or more 'general partners' and one or more 'limited partners'. A limited partner that is registered under the Limited Partnership Act 1907 is prevented from taking any active role in the affairs of the entity. If a limited partner does involve itself in the entity's affairs, it will be liable for the debts and obligations of the entity whilst its participation continues. The partnership itself does not have a board of directors, but the nearest equivalent to the board is the general partner. Consequently, if a company is the general partner in a limited partnership, then it will control the equivalent of the board and *prima facie*, under both the Companies Act and FRS 2 the limited partnership should be consolidated in full.

24.212.2 Therefore, the starting point when a group is considering how to account for a limited partnership in which it is the general partner should be to consider whether full consolidation is appropriate. In determining whether full consolidation is necessary, it should be borne in mind that in certain situations the general partner might be liable for all of the debts of the limited partnership in excess of the capital contributed by the limited partners. Consequently, full consolidation might be appropriate, for example where:

- the limited partnership operates a business which could incur losses; or
- the limited partnership has external debt additional to partners' capital; or
- the limited partners have only contributed nominal capital.

A similar treatment might be applicable also where there are guarantees given by the limited partnership that might if called fall due to the general partner where the limited partners' capital would not cover the obligation.

Consolidation of limited partnerships by general partner — historical approach

24.212.3 Fully consolidating such limited partnerships can cause particular problems in practice, especially where a company's investment as the general partner in a limited partnership is only nominal in amount and the funding of the limited partnership comes mainly from its limited partners, external funding being minimal. This often arises in the case of venture capital or property asset management companies where the limited partnership route is seen as being the most tax efficient vehicle for some investors. For example, where a company's investment as a general partner is only (say) one per cent of the capital of the limited partnership, full consolidation of the assets and liabilities of the limited partnership would be required and there would be a large minority interest of 99 per cent. Consequently, prior to the publication of FRS 9 (referred to below), many companies in this situation (particularly in the venture capital industry) historically applied a true and fair override to avoid full consolidation. As the 'true and fair override' cannot be used to exclude a subsidiary from consolidation, some companies proportionately consolidated the company's share of the assets and liabilities and profits and losses of the limited partnership (see further chapter 27). This represents an override of the requirement in paragraph 1 of Schedule 6 to SI 2008/410, which requires consolidation in full of those results and assets and liabilities. This illustrates the point that a group cannot override those sections of the Act that specify the composition of the group; but it can override the detailed provisions of (in this case) Schedule 6 to SI 2008/410 as to how a subsidiary is to be consolidated. Where such an override is used, the particulars, reasons and effect should be given in the notes in accordance with the Act and FRS 18. (see para 24.51 and chapter 2).

24.212.4 Using the true and fair override in this way is no longer considered appropriate in most situations given the guidance available in FRS 9, which is explained in the paragraphs that follow.

Severe long-term restrictions over general partner's control — FRS 9 approach

24.212.5 FRS 9 paragraph 11, recognises that in certain situations an investor may qualify as the parent of an entity under the definition of a subsidiary in the Act and FRS 2, but that contractual arrangements between the parties mean that the other investors in practice control the investee. In such cases, 'severe long-term restrictions' exist over the parent's interests that *'substantially hinder the exercise of the rights of the parent undertaking over the assets or management of the subsidiary undertaking'*.

24.212.6 With a limited partnership, severe long-term restrictions might arise where the general partner's ability to control the partnership is restricted by the rights that the limited partners have. In this type of situation, where the limited partnership is funded mainly by its limited partners, the limited partnership should be excluded from consolidation by the general partner because FRS 2 requires, and the Act permits, exclusion of a subsidiary from consolidation if severe long-term restrictions exist. [CA06 Secs 405, 402; FRS 2 para 25(a)].

24.212.7 Depending upon the particular circumstances, severe long-term restrictions would probably exist where the limited partners (excluding any related party to the general partner) have the ability to dismiss the general partner within a short notice period. In addition, depending upon the particular circumstances, it might be possible to show that severe long-term restrictions exist over the general partner's ability to exert control where a combination of the following factors arise:

- The involvement of the limited partners in high level strategic decisions (these would have to be prescribed in the partnership deed as limited partners are not permitted to be involved in the day to day running of the partnership).
- Limited partner representation on the board of the general partner.
- Limited partners voting on key decisions (again this would need to be specified in the partnership deed).
- Pre-determined sharing of profits between the partners.
- Active participation by the limited partners in determining the limited partnership agreement.
- Very narrow investment guidelines.

24.212.8 If severe long-term restrictions do apply and the subsidiary is not consolidated, the accounting treatment will then depend on the nature of the investment in the partnership. If the interest is less than 20 per cent, then generally the investment in the partnership should be treated as a simple investment and recorded at cost or valuation (unless the investor exercises significant influence).

Associated undertakings and joint ventures

24.212.9 FRS 2 paragraph 79 highlights certain situations where significant influence may be retained even though severe long-term restrictions exist. For example, the general partner may be influential in the decision making process. In such circumstances, the limited partnership should be treated as an associated undertaking in accordance with FRS 9 and accounted for using the equity method of accounting (but see para 24.212.12 below). But this treatment might not be appropriate where the limited partners' have only contributed nominal capital or where there is a substantial amount of debt within the limited partnership. These circumstances indicate that full consolidation would be appropriate.

Interest more than 50 per cent

24.212.10 Where a group holds an interest in a limited partnership that comprises the general partner together with a limited partner interest, such that in aggregate it owns more than 50 per cent of the partnership, there is a presumption that the limited partnership should be consolidated, unless it can be clearly demonstrated that the partnership should be excluded from consolidation on the grounds of severe long-term restrictions. However, the circumstances of each case, including the terms of the partnership agreement or group structure, would need to be considered closely, before the appropriate accounting treatment can be decided.

Severe long-term restrictions do not apply

24.212.11 In cases where severe long-term restrictions do not apply, it will generally be appropriate to fully consolidate the limited partnership, because it will be under the control of the general partner. Where the substance of the arrangement is that there is no significant economic benefit or risk to the general partner group other than a management fee or priority profit share for managing the limited partnership it may, in exceptional circumstances, still be possible to avoid consolidation by using the true and fair override as explained in paragraph 24.212.3 above. However, this option is unlikely to be available if:

- the general partner group has a significant economic interest.
- the interests of the limited partners are nominal in value, or
- there is substantial external debt in the limited partnership, or
- the limited partnership has given significant third party guarantees.

Accounting for a limited partnership as part of a portfolio

24.212.12 A situation that often arises in the asset management industry is where an investor has an interest in a limited partnership (of less than 50 per cent) as part of a portfolio of investments. In this instance, paragraph 49 of FRS 9 requires that the interest is regarded for accounting purposes as being held as part of a basket of investments even when the investor has significant influence or joint control. This would mean accounting for the investment at cost or valuation rather than equity accounting. This conflicts with the Act's provisions which require 'associated undertakings' to be shown by the equity method of accounting when preparing consolidated financial statements. [SI 2008/410 6 Sch 21(1)]. The Act defines an 'associated undertaking' as an investment in which the investor has a participating interest and over whose operating and financial policies the investor exercises significant influence, excluding subsidiaries or joint ventures dealt with by proportional consolidation. [SI 2008/410 6 Sch 19(1)]. Therefore, where an investor has an investment in a limited partnership as part of a portfolio and accounts for it at cost or valuation in accordance with paragraph 49 of FRS 9 (as opposed to equity accounting), it will need to invoke the true and fair override. This is because compliance with paragraph 49 of FRS 9 requires departure from the accounting rules in the Companies Act. If a true and fair override is used, the particulars, reasons and effect should be given in the notes in accordance with the Act and FRS 18 (see para 24.51 and chapter 2).

Accounting for a limited partnership's interest in subsidiaries

24.212.13 An additional complication arises when the limited partnership itself holds interests in entities that qualify as its subsidiaries. The investor in a limited partnership may have to consolidate not only the partnership, but also that partnership's subsidiaries. For example, where a general partner (the investor) holds a one per cent interest in a limited partnership, which itself has (say) a 51 per cent interest in its subsidiary, then the general partner would have to consolidate 100 per cent of the limited partnership and 100 per cent of its subsidiary, in which it holds (indirectly) an interest of just over half a per cent. This would result in a large minority interest.

24.212.14 It will only be possible to avoid consolidating such a subsidiary where either:

- there are severe long-term restrictions over the ability of the investing company to control the limited partnership (as explained in para 24.212.11 above), in which case it would be appropriate to treat the investment in the limited partnership at cost or valuation if the exemption in paragraph 49 of FRS 9 applies (as explained in para 24.212.12 above); or
- where the limited partnership cannot exercise control over its subsidiary, because there are severe long-term restrictions over its ability to exercise such control.

24.212.15 In the latter situation, if severe long-term restrictions do exist, but the limited partnership still has significant influence, on the face of it equity accounting would be required. However, the exemption from equity accounting in paragraph 49 of FRS 9 would be available to the limited partnership itself if it regards such investments as part of its investment portfolio. These investments would then be recorded at cost or market value as explained in paragraph 24.212.12 above. This would effectively mean that on consolidation the general partner would also record in its investment portfolio its investment in the underlying subsidiary at cost or valuation, rather than by full consolidation.

Implications for the limited partnership's financial statements

24.212.16 The accounting method adopted by the general partner can have implications for the financial statements of the limited partnership itself. As discussed in chapter 8 of the 'Manual of Accounting – Management Reports and Governance', limited companies that are members of a qualifying partnership are required to prepare and append to their own financial statements a copy of the audited financial statements of the partnership. [SI 2008/410 4 Sch 7]. The partners are exempt from this requirement if the limited partnership *'is dealt with on a consolidated basis'* in one of the partners' consolidated financial statements either by consolidation, proportional consolidation or equity accounting. [SI 1993/1820 Reg 7(2); SI 2008/569 Reg 2,7]. For a limited partnership, these provisions apply to the general partner and not to the limited partners. In that case, to avail itself of the exemption from preparing full Companies Act style financial statements for the limited partnership, the general partner has to deal with the partnership on a consolidated basis in its financial statements (or those of its group) by consolidation, proportional consolidation or equity accounting. Clearly, if the partnership is included at cost or valuation, for example, as required by paragraph 49 of FRS 9 where the partnership is part of an investment portfolio, then this exemption is not available, because the partnership is not consolidated or equity accounted in the group's consolidated financial statements. This may cause some difficulty as the partnership's financial statements will then have to comply with all accounting standards and the Companies Act, whereas the accounting requirements (if any) specified in the partnership deed, which would otherwise apply, might be less onerous.

[The next paragraph is 24.213.]

Disclosure requirements concerning subsidiaries and investments

24.213 Certain additional information has to be given for all subsidiaries and this is detailed in Schedule 4 to SI 2008/410 'The Large and Medium-sized Companies and Groups (Accounts and Reports) Regulation 2008'. Considered below are the disclosure requirements concerning the information required for subsidiaries that are included in consolidation and these requirements are supplemented by FRS 2. The information required about subsidiaries when the parent does not prepare consolidated financial statements is considered in chapter 6.

Place of origin and reason for consolidation

24.214 The Act requires disclosure of the following information concerning subsidiary undertakings:

- Name of each subsidiary undertaking.
- The country of incorporation, if incorporated outside Great Britain.
- The address of the principal place of business if the undertaking is unincorporated.
- Whether the subsidiary is included in the consolidation, and if not, the reasons for excluding it.

[SI 2008/410 4 Sch 1(1) to (3), 16(2)].

These disclosures are illustrated in Tables 24.9 and 24.10.

Table 24.9 – Disclosure of principal subsidiaries

Whitbread PLC – Annual Report and Accounts – 27 February 1999

NOTES TO THE ACCOUNTS (extract)

14 INVESTMENT IN SUBSIDIARY UNDERTAKINGS (extract)

	PRINCIPAL ACTIVITY	COUNTRY OF INCORPORATION OR REGISTRATION	COUNTRY OF PRINCIPAL OPERATIONS	% OF EQUITY AND VOTES HELD
BrightReasons Group Ltd	Restaurants	England	England	100
Churrasco Steak-Restaurant GmbH.*	Restaurants	Germany	Germany	100
Country Club Hotels Ltd.	Hotels	England	England	100
David Lloyd Leisure Ltd	Leisure	England	England	100
The Pelican Group PLC	Restaurants	England	England	100
Whitbread Hotels Ltd	Hotels	England	England	100

Shares in the above are all held directly by Whitbread PLC unless marked with an asterisk. All subsidiary undertakings have the same year end as Whitbread PLC. All the above companies have been included in the group consolidation. The companies listed above include all those which materially affect the amount of profit and the assets of the Group. A full list of subsidiary undertakings, joint ventures and associates will be annexed to the next annual return of Whitbread PLC to be filed with the Registrar of Companies in August 1999.

Table 24.10 – Disclosure of principal subsidiaries

Guinness PLC – Report and accounts – 31 December 1994

Principal subsidiary and associated undertakings and joint ventures (extract)

6. The registered addresses of partnerships in which the group has an interest are:

Schieffelin & Somerset Co	2 Park Avenue, 17th Floor, New York, NY10016, USA.
Asbach GmbH & Co.	AM Rottland 2-10, 65385 Rudesheim am Rhein, Germany.
Bundaberg Rum Company	Whittred Street, Bundaberg, Queensland 4670, Australia.

24.215 Furthermore, it is necessary to disclose the particular definition of 'subsidiary undertaking' that makes an undertaking a subsidiary under the provisions of the Act. [SI 2008/410 4 Sch 16(2)]. However, there is an exemption where the undertaking is a subsidiary because the parent holds a majority of its voting rights and it holds the same proportion of shares in the subsidiary as it holds voting rights. This will obviously be the reason for consolidating most subsidiaries and, consequently, disclosure will only be required for other subsidiary undertakings, of which there will be relatively few.

24.216 FRS 2 supplements the above disclosures by requiring the following additional information to be given for subsidiaries:

- The proportion of voting rights held by the parent and its subsidiary undertakings.
- An indication of the nature of the subsidiary's business.

[FRS 2 para 33].

24.217 FRS 2 also requires that where an undertaking is a subsidiary because its parent has the power to exercise or actually exercises dominant influence or control over it (see para 24.130), the financial statements should indicate the basis of the parent's dominant influence or control (for example, see Table 24.1 in para 24.136). [FRS 2 para 34].

Holdings in subsidiary undertakings

24.217.1 The following information has to be given separately (where different) concerning the subsidiary's shares held by the parent and the group:

- The identity of each class of shares held.
- The percentage held of the nominal value of each of those classes of shares.

[SI 2008/410 4 Sch 17].

24.218 Shares that are held on the parent's or group's behalf by any other person should be treated for this purpose as if they are held by the parent. [SI 2008/410 4 Sch 22(1)(2)(a)(3)]. However, shares held on behalf of a third party other than the parent or the group should be disregarded for this purpose. [SI 2008/410 4 Sch 22(3)].

Financial years of subsidiaries

24.219 Where a subsidiary's financial year, for which financial statements are drawn up for consolidation purposes (that is, either statutory financials or management accounts), does not coincide with its parent's financial year, FRS 2 requires that the notes should disclose, for each principal subsidiary that has a different accounting date, its name, its accounting date and the reasons for using a different accounting date. If a principal subsidiary's accounting period is of a different length from that of its parent, this accounting period should also be stated. [FRS 2 para 44].

24.220 The requirements concerning non-coterminous year ends are considered further in paragraph 24.319.

Company shares held by subsidiaries

24.221 A subsidiary company cannot generally own shares in its parent company. [CA06 Sec 136(1)]. This prohibition also applies equally to subsidiaries incorporated overseas. This provision extends to sub-subsidiaries holding shares in their immediate parent companies and also their ultimate parent companies. It also includes any shares held on behalf of the subsidiary by another person as its nominee. [CA06 Sec 144]. However, the prohibition does not apply where the subsidiary is acting as a personal representative for a third party, or as a trustee. This exemption only applies, however, where the subsidiary or a parent company is not beneficially interested under the trust. [CA06 Sec 138(1)(2)]. An exemption is also given to market makers. [CA06 Sec 141(1)(2)].

24.222 For the purposes of sections 136 to 138 and 141 to 143 of the Companies Act 2006, the definitions of holding company and subsidiary given in section 1159 of the Companies Act 2006 are relevant and not those given in section 1162 (see further para 24.172).

24.223 Where a corporate body became a subsidiary company because of the changes to the definition of subsidiaries included in section 1159 of the Companies Act 2006, it may continue to retain any shares that it already held in its parent. However, where shares are held in this way, they will carry no right to vote at company meetings. [CA06 Sec 137(1)].

24.224 In certain situations a subsidiary may find that it does hold shares in its parent. This may arise, for example, where the parent has recently acquired a subsidiary which owned shares in the parent before it became a group member. Sections 136 to 138 and 141 to 143 of the Companies Act 2006 expressly provides that, where a company acquires shares in its parent, but before it becomes a subsidiary of the parent, it may retain those shares. In this circumstance also, those shares will carry no right to vote at company meetings. [CA06 Sec 137(2)].

24.225 The notes to a parent's consolidated financial statements must disclose the number, the description and the amount of any of its shares that subsidiaries or their nominees hold. [2008/410 4 Sch 3(1)]. This information is not required, however, where the subsidiary holds the shares as personal representative or as a trustee. [2008/410 4 Sch 3(2)]. However, the exemption for a subsidiary acting as a trustee will not be available if the company or any of its subsidiaries is beneficially interested under the trust, unless the beneficial interest is by way of security for the purpose of a transaction entered into by it in the ordinary course of a business which includes the lending of money. [2008/410 4 Sch 3(2)]. Additionally, FRS 25 requires separate disclosure, either on the face of the balance sheet or in the notes, of the amount of treasury shares held. [FRS 25 para 34]. See further chapter 6.

24.226 In the past, such shares held by subsidiaries may have been classified as an asset, 'own shares', in the parent's consolidated financial statements. However, UITF Abstract 37, 'Purchases and sales of own shares', effective for accounting periods ending on or after 23 December 2003, required that where shares in a holding company are purchased or held by a subsidiary, the consideration paid should be deducted in arriving at shareholders' funds in the holding company's consolidated financial statements. This was subsequently superseded by FRS 25, which followed the same principle. [FRS 25 para 33].

Significant investment holdings of the parent or group

24.227 Where the parent or any of its subsidiaries has *significant holdings* in undertakings, certain additional information has to be given in the consolidated financial statements. A 'significant holding' means one where the investment in the undertaking concerned amounts to twenty per cent or more of the nominal value of *any class* of shares in the undertaking. [SI 2008/410 4 Sch 4(2)(a), 20(2)(a)]. (Joint ventures and associated undertakings are considered separately in chapter 27.)

24.228 The disclosure is also required where the holding by the parent or its subsidiaries exceeds twenty per cent of the amount of the parent's, or the group's, assets. [SI 2008/410 4 Sch 4(2)(b), 20(2)(b)]. The information to be disclosed is as follows:

- The name of the undertaking.
- The country of incorporation of the undertaking, if it is incorporated outside Great Britain,
- The address of its principal place of business, if it is unincorporated.
- The identity of each class of shares held.
- The percentage held of the nominal value of each of those classes of shares.

[SI 2008/410 4 Sch 5].

24.229 Furthermore, additional information is required to be disclosed as follows:

- The aggregate amount of the capital and reserves of the undertaking at the end of its 'relevant year'. Relevant year means the year ending with, or last before, that of the company.
- Its profit or loss for the year.

[SI 2008/410 4 Sch 6(1)].

24.230 This additional information need not be disclosed if the undertaking is not required by the Act to deliver to the Registrar of Companies a copy of its balance sheet and does not otherwise publish it (for example, a partnership). However, this exemption only applies where the company's holding is less than 50 per cent of the nominal value of the undertaking's shares. [SI 2008/410 4 Sch 6(2)]. Consequently, this exemption is likely to apply to investments in partnerships where the interest in the partnership is less than 50 per cent. The information is also not required if it is immaterial.

24.231 For investments in unincorporated undertakings with capital, 'shares' for the purposes of the paragraphs above means the rights to share in the capital of the undertaking, by virtue of section 1161(2)(b) of the Companies Act 2006. In respect of an undertaking that does not have capital, the term 'shares' refers to any right to share in the profits or liability to contribute to losses of the undertaking, or an obligation to contribute to its debts or expenses on winding up. [CA06 Sec 1161(2)(c)].

Interpretation of 'shares held by the group'

24.232 In the paragraphs above, reference to shares held by the group are to shares held by the parent company or any of its subsidiaries, or to shares held on their behalf. However, such references do not include shares held on behalf of third parties. [SI 2008/410 4 Sch 22(3)]. Furthermore, shares held by way of security must be treated as held by the person providing the security where both the following apply:

- The rights attached to the shares are exercisable only in accordance with that person's instructions (apart from the right to exercise them for the purpose of preserving the value of the security or of realising it).
- The shares are held in connection with granting loans as part of normal business activities and the rights attached to the shares are exercisable only in that person's interest (apart from the right to exercise them for the purpose of preserving the value of the security, or of realising it).

[SI 2008/410 4 Sch 22(4)].

Disclosure 'seriously prejudicial'

24.233 In certain circumstances, the information required by Schedule 4 to SI 2008/410, 'The Large and Medium-sized Companies and Groups (Accounts and Reports) Regulations 2008', concerning subsidiaries and other significant holdings in undertakings (summarised above) need not be given where the undertaking is established under the law of a country outside the UK, or carries on business outside the UK. [CA06 Sec 409(3)(4)]. The situations where this exemption will apply are where, in the directors' opinion, disclosing information would be *seriously prejudicial* to the business of that undertaking, or to the business of the parent company, or to any of the parent's subsidiaries. Permission to exclude the information also needs to be obtained from the Secretary of State before advantage can be taken of this exemption. A group that takes advantage of this exemption is required under section 409(5) of the Companies Act 2006 to disclose this fact in its financial statements.

24.234 The section 409(5) statement that exemption has been taken is required to be given irrespective of whether the group has taken advantage of section 410(1)(2) (see para 24.236 below), which only requires information for subsidiaries that principally affect the group's reported figures to be given in its financial statements. Under section 410(1)(2) the full information for all subsidiaries must be annexed to the company's next annual return, but where the Secretary of State has granted exemption under section 409(3)(4), this need not include the information regarding the subsidiary excluded on seriously prejudicial grounds.

24.235 The exemption does not apply, however, to the information required by paragraph 3 of Schedule 4 to the 2008/410, which is summarised in paragraph 24.225 above.

Disclosure of excessive information

24.236 There is a further relaxation of the disclosure requirements of Schedule 4 that applies if, in the directors' opinion, the resulting disclosure would be excessively lengthy. This will often be the situation where the group has a significant number of subsidiaries. Where this is so, the directors need only give the required information concerning the undertakings whose results or financial position principally affect the figures shown in the company's annual accounts. [CA06 Sec 410(1)(2)]. However, the directors are required to give the necessary information that relates to undertakings excluded from consolidation, except where they are excluded on the ground of materiality (see para 24.180).

24.237 Where the directors take advantage of this exemption, they have to note in the financial statements that the information given is only in respect of principal subsidiaries and significant investments. [CA06 Sec 410(3)(a)]. In addition, the full information (including that disclosed in the financial statements) has to be annexed to the parent's next annual return. [CA06 Sec 410(3)(b)].

Disclosure of parent company

24.238 The Companies Act 2006 deals with the disclosures concerning a company's parent (or parents) in Schedule 4 to SI 2008/410, 'The Large and Medium-sized Companies and Groups (Accounts and Reports) Regulations 2008'. Part 1 of Schedule 4 sets out the disclosures to be made by all companies. Part 2 sets out the disclosures to be made by companies not required to prepare consolidated financial statements, whereas Part 3 deals with the disclosure requirements concerning those companies that are required to prepare consolidated financial statements. These requirements are identical. The paragraphs that follow summarise these disclosures and make reference to the paragraphs of Schedule 4 that are duplicated.

24.239 Where, at the end of a financial year, a company is a subsidiary, or where the company is a parent company and is itself a subsidiary, it should disclose concerning its *ultimate parent company* its name and if incorporated outside Great Britain the country of its incorporation (if known). 'Company' includes any corporate body in this context. [SI 2008/410 4 Sch 9].

24.240 An example of the disclosures required by the Act is given in Table 24.11.

Table 24.11 – Disclosure of ultimate parent company

Dunhill Holdings PLC – Report and Accounts – 31 March 1993

NOTES TO THE ACCOUNTS (extract)

28 ULTIMATE HOLDING COMPANY

The Company is a subsidiary of Rothmans International p.l.c., which is incorporated in England and Wales. Copies of the accounts of Rothmans International p.l.c. are available from 15 Hill Street, London, W1X 7FB.

The Directors consider the Company's ultimate holding company to be Compagnie Financière Richemont AG, which is incorporated in Switzerland. Copies of that company's accounts are available from its registered office at Rigistrasse 2, CH-6300 Zug, Switzerland.

24.241 Furthermore, where the parent company is itself a subsidiary, similar information has to be disclosed (whether or not it prepares consolidated financial statements) for the parent undertaking that heads the following:

- The largest group of undertakings that prepares consolidated financial statements and of which the company is a member.
- The smallest group of undertakings that prepares consolidated financial statements and of which the company is a member.

[SI 2008/410 4 Sch 8(1)].

24.242 The information to be disclosed in respect of both these undertakings is similar to that required by paragraph 24.239 above:

- The name of the parent undertaking.
- The country of incorporation of the undertaking, if it is incorporated outside Great Britain.
- The address of its principal place of business, if it is unincorporated.
- If copies of the undertaking's consolidated financial statements are available for the public, then the address where copies of the financial statements can be obtained.

[SI 2008/410 4 Sch 8(2)(3)(4)].

24.243 Where the ultimate parent company prepares consolidated financial statements, the information in paragraph 24.242 disclosed in the sub-group parent's financial statements need be given only for the ultimate parent and for the smallest group of undertakings that prepare consolidated financial statements which include the sub-group (if such an undertaking exists) (see for example Table 24.12). [SI 2008/410 4 Sch 8(1)].

Table 24.12 – Disclosure of ultimate parent company

The Telegraph plc – Annual Report and Accounts – 31 December 1994

Notes to the accounts (extract)

32. Ultimate parent company

Hollinger Inc., incorporated in Canada and listed on the Toronto, Montreal and Vancouver stock exchanges, is regarded by the directors of the company as the company's ultimate parent company.

The largest group in which the results of the company are consolidated is that of which Hollinger Inc. is the parent company. The consolidated accounts of Hollinger Inc. may be obtained from Montreal Trust Company of Canada, 151 Front Street West, 8th Floor, Toronto, Ontario, Canada M5J 2N1.

The smallest such group is that of which DT Holdings Limited is the parent company, whose consolidated accounts may be obtained from 21 Wilson Street, London EC2M 2TQ. DT Holdings Limited is registered in England and Wales.

24.244 However, where the ultimate parent does not prepare consolidated financial statements, the information in paragraph 24.239 above has to be disclosed in the sub-group parent's financial statements. In addition, the information set out in paragraph 24.242 may also be required to be disclosed concerning the largest and smallest groups that prepare consolidated financial statements which include the sub-group.

24.245 These provisions can be very confusing and are best illustrated by an example. Consider the group structure set out in the diagram below.

Example

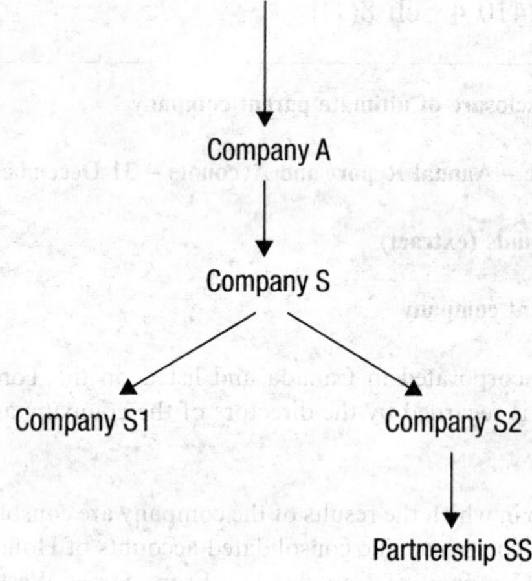

In the situation where the ultimate parent company *does prepare* consolidated financial statements, the following disclosure applies:

- Company A will have to disclose in respect of the ultimate parent company (being the largest group parent) the information set out in paragraphs 24.239 and 24.242 above by virtue of paragraphs 8 and 9 of Schedule 4 to SI 2008/410 'The Large and Medium-sized Companies and Groups (Accounts and Reports) Regulations 2008'.
- Company S will have to disclose in respect of company A the information set out in paragraph 24.242 above by virtue of paragraphs 8 of Schedule 4 to SI 2008/410 (if company A prepares consolidated financial statements as it is the parent of the smallest group that prepares consolidated financial statements). Company S will also have to give in respect of the ultimate parent company (being also the largest group parent) the information set out in paragraphs 24.239 and 24.242 above by virtue of paragraphs 8 and 9 of Schedule 4 to SI 2008/410 'The Large and Medium-sized Companies and Groups (Accounts and Reports) Regulations 2008'.
- Company S2 will have to disclose in respect of the ultimate parent company (being also the largest group parent) the information set out in paragraphs 24.239 and 24.242 above by virtue of paragraphs 8 and 9 of Schedule 4 to the SI 2008/410. If company S prepares consolidated financial statements, then company S2 will also have to disclose in respect of company S (being the parent of the smallest group that prepares consolidated financial statements) the information set out in paragraph 24.242 above by virtue of paragraph 8of Schedule 4 to SI 2008/410. Where company S does not prepare consolidated financial statements, then company S2 has to give the same information in respect of company A (if company A prepares consolidated financial statements as it is the parent of the smallest group that prepares consolidated financial statements).

In the situation where the ultimate parent company *does not* prepare consolidated financial statements, the following disclosure applies:

- Company A will have to disclose in respect of the ultimate parent company the information set out in paragraph 24.239 above by virtue of paragraph 9 of Schedule 4 to SI 2008/410.
- Company S will have to disclose in respect of company A the information set out in paragraph 24.242 above by virtue of paragraphs 8 of Schedule 4 to SI 2008/410 (if company A prepares consolidated financial statements as it is the parent of the largest group that prepares consolidated financial statements). Company S will also have to give in respect of the ultimate parent company the information set out in paragraph 24.239 above by virtue of paragraph 9 of Schedule 4 to SI 2008/410.
- Company S2 will have to disclose in respect of the ultimate parent company the information set out in paragraph 24.239 above by virtue of paragraphs 9 of Schedule 4 to SI 2008/410. If company A prepares consolidated financial statements it is the parent of the largest group that prepares consolidated financial statements and company S2 will have to disclose in respect of company A the information set out in paragraph 24.242 above by virtue of paragraphs 8 of Schedule 4 to SI 2008/410. In addition, the same information will have to be given in respect of company S (if company S prepares consolidated financial statements as it is the parent of the smallest group that prepares consolidated financial statements). This means that in the situation described, company S2 is required to disclose information concerning three parent companies. Furthermore the situation might arise, for example, where another intermediate parent undertaking exists in the group structure between company S and company A. Even where such an undertaking prepares consolidated financial statements company S2 is still only required to give information concerning company A, company S and its ultimate parent. This is because the legislation only requires the information concerned to be disclosed in respect of the largest and smallest groups preparing consolidated financial statements and is not concerned with other intermediate parents in between that prepare consolidated financial statements.

24.246 In practice in the majority of situations, these provisions will mean that the information required by paragraph 24.242 above will have to be given for the next parent undertaking in the group that prepares consolidated financial statements that included the sub-group, and will also have to be given for the ultimate parent company that prepares consolidated financial statements.

Membership of a qualifying undertaking

24.247 Where at the year end a parent company or group is a member of a qualifying undertaking, it has to give the following information in its financial statements:

- The name and legal form of the undertaking.
- The address of the undertaking's registered office or, if it does not have such an office, its head office.

[SI 2008/410 4 Sch 7(1)(2)].

24.248 In addition, where the qualifying undertaking is a qualifying partnership one of the following must also be stated:

- That a copy of the latest financial statements of the undertaking has been, or is to be, appended to the copy of the company's financial statements sent to the Registrar under section 444 of the Act.
- The name of at least one body corporate (which may be the company) in whose consolidated financial statements the undertaking has been, or is to be, dealt with by the method of full consolidation, proportional consolidation or the equity method of accounting.

[SI 2008/410 4 Sch 7(3)].

24.249 For the purpose of these rules, 'qualifying undertakings' can either be companies or partnerships. A qualifying company (or qualifying partnership) is an unlimited company (or partnership) incorporated in (or governed by the laws of any part of) Great Britain if each of its members is:

- a limited company, or
- another unlimited company, or a Scottish partnership, each of whose members is a limited company.

The references to limited company, another unlimited company and Scottish partnership also encompass any comparable undertakings incorporated in, or formed under the law of, any country or territory outside Great Britain. [SI 2008/410 4 Sch 7(6); SI 2008/569 Reg 3].

24.250 The information required to be disclosed in the second bullet point of paragraph 24.248 need not be given if the partnership is dealt with either by consolidation, proportional consolidation or equity accounting in the consolidated financial statements prepared by:

- a member of the partnership that is established under the law of a Member State; or
- a parent undertaking of such a member established in the same way.

[SI 2008/410 4 Sch 7(5); SI 2008/569 Reg 7(1)].

24.251 The exemption can only be taken, however, where the following two conditions are complied with:

- The consolidated financial statements are prepared and audited under the law of the member State in accordance with the provisions of the 7th Directive.
- The notes to those consolidated financial statements disclose that advantage has been taken of the exemption. An example of the disclosure is given in Table 24.13.

[SI 2008/410 4 Sch 7(5); SI 2008/569 Reg 7(2)].

Table 24.13 – Exemption from the requirement to deliver to the Registrar account of a qualifying partnership

BP p.l.c. – Annual Report – 31 December 2001

42 Subsidiary and associated undertakings and joint ventures (extract)

The more important subsidiary and associated undertakings and joint ventures of the group at 31 December 2001 and the group percentage of equity capital or joint venture interest (to nearest whole number) are set out below. The principal country of operation is generally indicated by the company's country of incorporation or by its name. Those held directly by the parent company are marked with an asterisk (*), the percentage owned being that of the group unless otherwise indicated. A complete list of investments in subsidiary and associated undertakings and joint ventures will be attached to the parent company's annual return made to the Register of Companies. Advantage has been taken of the exemption conferred by regulation 7 of The Partnerships and Unlimited Companies (Accounts) Regulations 1993 from the requirements to deliver to the Register of Companies and publish the annual accounts of the Ca To Finance V Limited Partnership.

Other disclosure issues

Realised and distributable reserves

24.252 The restrictions on distributions contained in the Act apply to individual companies and not to groups. This is because individual companies make distributions, whereas groups do not. However, users of consolidated financial statements may wish to know the amount the holding company could distribute if all the group's subsidiaries were to pay up their realised profits by way of dividends to the parent company. Some groups specifically disclose the amount of their distributable reserves and this issue is discussed in chapter 23.

24.253 Furthermore, FRS 2 requires that, where significant statutory, contractual or exchange control restrictions exist which materially limit the distributions a subsidiary undertaking can make and, therefore, the parent undertaking's access to distributable profits, the nature and extent of the restrictions should be disclosed. [FRS 2 para 53].

24.254 The parent company's ability to distribute pre-acquisition reserves of its subsidiaries is discussed in chapter 23.

Tax on the accumulated reserves of overseas subsidiaries

24.255 FRS 19, 'Deferred tax', provides some guidance on the treatment of overseas retained earnings. Its provisions require that deferred tax should be computed using the 'incremental liability' approach. The general principle is that deferred tax should be recognised as a liability or asset if the transactions or events that give the entity an obligation to pay more tax in the future or a right to pay less tax in the future have occurred by the balance sheet date. More specifically, FRS 19 paragraph 21 states that tax that could be payable on any future remittance of the past earnings of a subsidiary or joint venture should only be provided in certain situations; and FRS 2 adds to the disclosure requirements. These matters are considered in chapter 13.

[The next paragraph is 24.296.]

Section II — Consolidation rules

Introduction

24.296 Consolidated financial statements must give a true and fair view of the state of affairs and the profit or loss of the company and those of its subsidiaries included in the consolidated financial statements as a whole, so far as concerns the parent company's shareholders. [CA06 Sec 404(2)]. As with individual financial statements, this is an overriding requirement. This overriding requirement is explained in chapter 2.

24.297 In addition to the overriding requirement to give a true and fair view, the Act and FRS 2 include accounting rules that apply to consolidated financial statements. In general, the Act's provisions correspond to those that apply to an individual company's financial statements. Consequently, consolidated financial statements must comply with the requirements of Schedule 4 to SI 2008/410 'The Large and Medium-sized Companies and Groups (Accounts and Reports) Regulations 2008' both as to their form and content and as to the information they must disclose in the notes (to the extent that this Schedule applies to consolidated financial statements).

24.298 Furthermore, Schedule 6 to SI 2008/410 details the rules concerning the form and content of consolidated financial statements and introduced into UK company law the majority of the 7th Directive's provisions. One exception to these consolidation rules is that if any member of a group is a banking or an insurance company the Schedule 1 to SI 2008/410, formats are not appropriate. Banks have to comply with Schedule 2 to SI 2008/410. Insurance companies have to comply with Schedule 3 to SI 2008/410. The accounting requirements that apply to banking and insurance companies are not within the scope of this book.

24.299 If, at the end of the financial year, a company has one or more subsidiaries, consolidated financial statements must be prepared in addition to the parent company's individual financial statements. The consolidated financial statements should deal with the state of affairs and the profit or loss of the company and its subsidiaries. [CA06 Sec 399(2)].

24.300 FRS 2 extends the Act's provisions to require that consolidated financial statements should be prepared also where a parent undertaking is an entity other than a company and its financial statements are to give a true and fair view. [FRS 2 para 18].

24.301 The only exceptions to the general rules outlined in paragraph 24.299 above are considered in paragraph 24.176.

24.302 The particular provisions in Schedule 6 to SI 2008/410 and the provisions in FRS 2 that form the basic consolidation rules are explained below, together with other rules that have become generally accepted accounting principles through their general use in preparing consolidations.

Generally accepted accounting principles

24.303 Consolidated financial statements have to incorporate all of the information contained in the individual financial statements of the undertakings included in the consolidation. [SI 2008/410 6 Sch 2(1)]. However, this provision is subject to adjustments authorised by Schedule 6 to SI 2008/410 'The Large and Medium-sized Companies and Groups (Accounts and Reports) Regulations 2008' and to any adjustments that are necessary in order to accord with '*generally accepted accounting principles or practice*'. [SI 2008/410 6 Sch 2(1)]. Although the term in the Companies Act 2006 incorporates the word 'practice', the term is more often referred to by accountants as 'Generally Accepted Accounting Principles' (GAAP). The term UK GAAP is one that means generally accepted accounting principles that apply to UK companies and groups and that encompass UK law, accounting standards, UITF Abstracts, the FSA's accounting requirements included in the Listing Rules (if appropriate) and other generally accepted accounting practices (see further chapter 2).

24.304 The accounting principles that are used in the consolidation process should be disclosed in the accounting policies note to the consolidated financial statements. This note generally covers the following matters relating to consolidations:

- The methods of accounting used to consolidate new subsidiaries, that is either of the following:
  - Acquisition accounting (see chapter 25).
  - Merger accounting (see chapter 28).
- The treatment of any goodwill arising on consolidation, and the treatment of other differences arising on consolidation (see further chapter 25).
- The translation of overseas subsidiaries' financial statements (see chapter 7).
- How minority interests are dealt with (see para 24.344).
- How associated companies and joint ventures are dealt with (see chapter 27).
- How the trading between non-coterminous year ends of the parent and subsidiary are dealt with (see para 24.322).
- The treatment of intra-group transactions (see para 24.332 below).

Procedure for consolidation

24.305 As mentioned in paragraph 24.303 above, the Companies Act 2006 specifies that the consolidated balance sheet and the consolidated profit and loss account should incorporate in full the information contained in the individual financial statements of the undertakings included in the consolidation, subject to certain consolidation adjustments. [SI 2008/410 6 Sch 2(1)]. However, it does not specify how the aggregation of this information should be undertaken.

24.306 FRS 2 makes no comment on the process of consolidation and SSAP 14, its predecessor, only commented that the method for preparing consolidated financial statements on an item basis, eliminating intra-group balances and transactions and unrealised intra-group profit, was well understood and did not deal further with the matter. IAS 27, 'Consolidated and separate financial statements', mentions that, in preparing consolidated financial statements, the financial statements of the parent and its subsidiaries are combined on a line by line basis by adding together like items of assets, liabilities, income and expenses. [IAS 27 para 22]. IAS 27 then goes on to mention some of the steps in the consolidation process. These are very similar in nature to the matters mentioned in paragraph 24.304 above.

24.307 In practice, there are two methods of preparing consolidated financial statements. In the first method the individual financial statements of subsidiaries are aggregated centrally by adding together the profit and loss account and balance sheet figures on a line by line basis. These aggregate figures taken from the subsidiaries' statutory financial statements are then amended to deal with consolidation adjustments. Such adjustments would be necessary in order to:

- Adjust individual figures in the financial statements of subsidiaries to bring them onto common accounting policies (see para 24.310 below).
- Achieve the consolidation by, for example, dealing with goodwill and minority interests (see para 24.317 below).

24.308 A second method, more suitable for large groups, is for each subsidiary to prepare a consolidation return. The consolidation return is made up from the individual subsidiary's financial statements which are:

- Adjusted to common accounting policies.
- Edited into a format and analysis that makes the consolidated process easier.

These returns are then aggregated to form the group's consolidated financial statements. Even using this basis, there may still be a need to make consolidation adjustments. For example, company A would not know how much intra-group profit to eliminate on goods sold to its subsidiary company B, because it would not know how much of that stock company B had sold.

Consolidation adjustments

24.309 There are a number of reasons why a parent may have to make consolidation adjustments to its subsidiaries' financial statements in preparing the group's consolidated financial statements. Some of these reasons and the rules relating to such adjustments are considered in the paragraphs that follow.

Uniform accounting polices

24.310 Except in exceptional situations, which are explained below, uniform group accounting policies should be used to determine the amounts to be included in the consolidated financial statements. This may require adjustment, on consolidation, of the amounts that have been reported by subsidiaries in their individual financial statements. [SI 2008/410 6 Sch 3(1); FRS 2 para 40].

24.311 In practice, a group that operates wholly within the UK and prepares UK GAAP financial statements is unlikely to have to make such adjustments, because in situations where UK GAAP permits the use of different accounting policies, the parent is likely to impose the group policy on each of its subsidiaries. See also chapter 2, which deals with consistency of accounting policies in group situations.

24.312 The Companies Act 2006 specifically requires consolidation adjustments to be made where a subsidiary undertaking's assets and liabilities have been valued using accounting rules that differ from those used by the group. [SI 2008/410 6 Sch 3(1)]. For example, the need for such an adjustment would arise where a subsidiary values its stocks using a LIFO method of valuation. In the UK LIFO stock valuations are not allowed for UK corporation tax purposes and are considered in SSAP 9 to be likely to be incompatible with the requirement to give a true and fair view. Such valuations are, however, allowed for both tax and accounting purposes in other countries and, consequently, subsidiaries that operate in those countries may value their stocks on that basis. Clearly, when such subsidiaries are consolidated, an adjustment will be required to bring the stock valuations onto a basis acceptable in the UK (for example, FIFO or average cost).

24.313 However, in certain situations, the parent's directors might consider that there are special reasons for retaining the different accounting rules adopted by the subsidiary. Where this is so, the Companies Act 2006's and FRS 2's provisions require that particulars of the departure, the reasons for it and its effect should be disclosed in the notes to the consolidated financial statements. [SI 2008/410 6 Sch 3(2); FRS 2 para 41]. FRS 18 sets out the disclosure requirements in such a situation and its implications are considered further in chapter 2.

24.314 It may also be that the accounting policies used by the parent in its individual financial statements differ from those of the group. However, this is less common. While the law does not require the policies of the parent and the group to be the same, it requires disclosure of any differences in the notes to the consolidated financial statements and of the reason for the differences. [SI 2008/

410 6 Sch 4]. An example of where such a difference could arise is where the parent records its fixed asset land and buildings at historical cost, but the group carries them at revalued amounts, but in practice this is unlikely to happen.

24.315 Where a new subsidiary is acquired by a group and the two have different accounting policies, the new subsidiary has sufficient reason to change its accounting policy and make a prior-year adjustment in accordance with FRS 18. Alternatively, the new subsidiary may continue with its original accounting policy in its entity financial statements, in which case the group would need to make an adjustment on consolidation to reflect the subsidiary's results in accordance with the group's accounting policy.

24.316 Problems can arise with overseas subsidiaries in applying uniform accounting policies. Where the subsidiaries are subject to either company law or tax law that is different from that in the UK, it may not always be practicable for the parent to insist that the subsidiaries change their accounting policies to bring them into line with the group's accounting policies. For example, in many European countries depreciation is calculated in accordance with local tax regulations rather than by reference to the estimated useful life of the asset. However, in order to obtain the tax relief, the tax-based depreciation figure must be shown in the subsidiary's individual financial statements. In order to comply with FRS 2 and the Companies Act 2006 an adjustment must then be made on consolidation to both the depreciation charge for the year and the accumulated depreciation to bring them into line with UK (and the group's) practice. In this situation, an adjustment to deferred taxation may also be required. Table 24.16 illustrates a situation where local legislation prevents the subsidiaries adopting the group's accounting policies.

Table 24.16 – Uniform accounting policies not applied by subsidiaries

GKN plc – Report & Accounts – 31 December 2000

Notes on the accounts (extract)

1 Basis of Consolidation

Accounting policies

The Group's accounting policies are shown in the notes on pages 47 to 69. Local legislation prevents certain overseas subsidiaries from conforming with the accounting policies adopted by the Group. Adjustments are made on consolidation so that the group accounts are presented on a uniform basis.

Other consolidation adjustments

24.317 Consolidation adjustments are required for a variety of reasons and the group's accounting policies will often describe the areas where adjustments are made as detailed in paragraph 24.304 above. The elimination of pre-acquisition reserves, although it would not generally be dealt with specifically in the accounting policies note, is another adjustment that is fundamental to the consolidation process (see further chapter 25).

24.318 A consolidation adjustment may also be necessary where a material 'subsequent event' occurs in a subsidiary between the date when the subsidiary's directors sign the subsidiary's own financial statements and the date when the holding company's directors sign the consolidated financial statements. If the 'subsequent event' is material to the group and is an 'adjusting event' (which is a post balance sheet event that provides additional evidence of conditions that exist at the balance sheet date), a consolidation adjustment should be made for it in the consolidated financial statements.

Subsidiary year ends

24.319 The financial statements of all subsidiaries to be used in preparing the consolidated financial statements should, wherever practicable, be prepared to the same financial year end and for the same accounting period as those of the parent. [FRS 2 para 42]. The directors have an obligation under section 390(5) of the Companies Act 2006 to secure that the financial year of each of its subsidiary undertakings coincides with the parent company's own financial year, unless in their opinion there are good reasons for this not to be so.

24.320 The Act requires that the financial statements of a subsidiary may not be consolidated if its accounting period ends more than three months before that of its parent. [SI 2008/410 6 Sch 2(2)(a)]. If the subsidiary's financial year ends before this period, it has to prepare interim financial statements to coincide with the end of the parent company's financial year. [SI 2008/410 6 Sch 2(2)(b)].

Interim financial statements

24.321 However, FRS 2 takes a stricter approach and requires that where the financial year of a subsidiary undertaking differs from that of the parent, interim financial statements should be prepared to the same date as those of the parent for use in preparing consolidated financial statements (see for example Table 24.17). If it is *not practicable* to use such interim financial statements, the subsidiary's financial statements should be used, providing that its year ended not more than three months before the relevant year end of the parent. In this situation, any changes that have taken place in the intervening period that materially affect the view given by the financial statements should be taken into account by adjusting the consolidated financial statements. [FRS 2 para 43]. In certain circumstances, such adjustments might be considered to be immaterial as illustrated in Table 24.18.

Table 24.17 – Use of interim financial statements on consolidation

Abbey National plc – Directors' Report and Accounts – 31 December 2000

Accounting policies (extract)

Basis of consolidation

The Group financial statements comprise the financial statements of the Company and all its subsidiary undertakings. The accounting reference date of the Company and its subsidiary undertakings is 31 December, with the exception of those leasing, investment, insurance and funding companies which, because of commercial considerations, have various accounting reference dates. The financial statements of these subsidiaries have been consolidated on the basis of interim financial statements for the period to 31 December 2000.

Table 24.18 – Use of interim financial statements on consolidation

National Westminster Bank Plc – Annual Report and Accounts – 31 December 1997

Notes to the accounts (extract)

1 PRINCIPAL ACCOUNTING POLICIES (extract)

(ii) **Basis of consolidation (extract)**

To avoid undue delay in the presentation of the Group's accounts, the accounts of certain subsidiary undertaking have been made up to 30 November. There have been no changes in respect of these subsidiary undertakings, in the period from their balance sheet dates to 31 December, that materially affect the view given by the Group's accounts. Details of principal subsidiary undertakings are given in note 25.

24.322 Consolidation adjustments of this nature might be required for settlement of intra-group balances outstanding at the subsidiary's year end, which would obviously have to be dealt with as part of the consolidation process. Other transactions might not be so obvious, such as a post balance sheet event in the subsidiary. For example, an adjustment would have to be made for a substantial loss on a contract undertaken by a subsidiary that has occurred in between the subsidiary's year end and that of its parent. Another example, where the subsidiary is incorporated overseas, is where there has been a devaluation of the currency in which it trades between its year end date and that of its parent.

24.323 FRS 2 is, therefore, restricting the legislation by giving preference to the requirement to prepare interim financial statements and only permitting the use of the subsidiary's own financial statements if the preparation of interim financial statements is *not practicable*. One practical reason sometimes given for having different year ends is to avoid delays in presenting the consolidated financial statements (for example, see Table 24.18 and Table 24.19).

Table 24.19 – Practical reason for non-coterminous year end

Blue Circle Industries PLC – Annual Report & Accounts – 31 December 1999

Accounting Policies (extract)

2 Consolidation

The Group accounts incorporate the results of the Company and its subsidiary and joint venture and associated undertakings. To avoid delay in the presentation of the accounts the accounting period of one overseas subsidiary ends on 30 November. The results of joint ventures and associates are based upon statutory or management accounts for periods ending on either 30 November or 31 December. Where subsidiaries, joint ventures and associates are acquired or disposed of during the year, results are included from the date of acquisition or to the date of sale.

24.324 The example below illustrates the options that are available when consolidating a subsidiary with a non-coterminous year end.

Example – Subsidiary with non-coterminous year end

A parent company has a year end of 31 December 20X1. One of its subsidiaries has a year end of 30 June 20X1 and another has a year end of 30 September 20X1. What figures may the parent include in its consolidated financial statements in respect of these subsidiaries?

In the first situation the subsidiary must prepare interim financial statements covering the year ended 31 December 20X1 (that is, coinciding with that of its parent). It may not prepare interim financial statements to, for example 30 November, despite this date being within three months of the parent's year end. Under no circumstances (unless the subsidiary is immaterial) may the parent consolidate the subsidiary's own statutory financial statements as the subsidiary's year end is more than three months before that of the parent.

In the second situation the parent should consolidate interim financial statements prepared by the subsidiary for the year ended 31 December 20X1, but if this is not practicable it may consolidate the financial statements of the subsidiary for the year ended 30 September 20X1 (as it ends no more than three months prior to the parent's year end). If the financial statements for 30 September 20X1 are used, consideration should be given to the requirement to adjust for transactions between the subsidiary's year end and that of the parent.

24.325 The interim financial statements are not required by the Act to be audited. However, they would have to be audited at least to the group materiality to satisfy the requirement that the group's consolidated financial statements have to give a true and fair view.

Disclosure where year ends differ

24.326 The following information should be given for each material subsidiary that is included in the consolidated financial statements on the basis of information prepared to a different date or for a different accounting period from that of the parent:

- Its name.
- Its accounting date or period, including the date on which its last financial year ended.
- The reason for using a different accounting date or period, including why the directors consider that the subsidiary's financial year should not end with that of its parent.

[FRS 2 para 44].

These disclosures are illustrated in Table 24.20.

Table 24.20 – Disclosures where subsidiaries have different period ends

Imperial Chemical Industries PLC – Annual report and accounts –31 December 1994

notes relating to the accounts (extract)

Composition of the Group

The Group accounts consolidate the accounts of Imperial Chemical Industries PLC (the Company) and its subsidiary undertakings, of which there were 363 at 31 December 1994. Owing to local conditions and to avoid undue delay in the presentation of the Group accounts, 62 subsidiaries made up their accounts to dates earlier than 31 December, but not earlier than 30 September; one subsidiary makes up its accounts to 31 March but interim accounts to 31 December are drawn up for consolidation purposes.

principal subsidiary undertakings (extract)

OTHER COUNTRIES (extract)	**Class of capital**	**Held by ICI %**	**Principal activities**
AECI Explosives Ltd Republic of South Africa	Ordinary	51†	Manufacture of industrial explosives and initiating systems
ICI Australia Ltd Australia (Accounting and reporting date 30 September)	Ordinary*	62†	Manufacture and distribution of chemicals and other products including fertilisers and crop care, industrial and specialty chemicals, consumer and effect products, plastics and performance of related services
ICI China Hong Kong and China	Ordinary	100†	Merchanting of ICI and other products

ICI India Ltd India (Accounting date 31 March; reporting date 31 December)	Equity*	51	Manufacture of industrial explosives, paints, agrochemicals, pharmaceutical, polyurethanes, catalysts, rubber chemicals and surfactants

* Listed
† Held by subsidiaries
The country of principal operations and registration or incorporation is stated below each company. The accounting dates of principal subsidiary undertakings are 31 December unless otherwise stated.

Practical problems

24.327 Problems often arise in deciding what accounting periods to include in the consolidation when subsidiaries have different accounting year ends to their parent. The example below illustrates the type of situation that can arise in practice.

Example – Subsidiary with different year end to its parent

A parent whose year end is 31 March has for a number of years consolidated a subsidiary's financial statements drawn up to 31 December. It has now decided to use the subsidiary's management accounts to 31 March 20X2 for consolidation with the group's financial statements to 31 March 20X2. The situation can be illustrated as set out below:

The consolidated financial statements for the year to 31 March 20X2 would include 15 months of the subsidiary's trading. By comparison, the group's published financial statements for the year to 31 March 20X1 include 12 months of the subsidiary's trading ending on 31 December 20X0. Therefore, the consolidated financial statements prepared for the year to 31 March 20X2 include comparatives which are not truly comparable. Also, if the subsidiary was particularly material to the group, it might be misleading to describe the group's consolidated financial statements as representing the group's trading for merely 12 months.

Consequently, if the subsidiary's trading is particularly material to the group, the consolidated financial statements should indicate clearly that they include the financial statements of the parent (and other subsidiaries) for the year to 31 March 20X2, but the result of the material subsidiary for the 15 month period ending on the same date. Then it would be necessary to show the impact that the additional three months has on the reported results. This can be done in a variety of ways, the best approach would be to split the trading into three columns and show the subsidiary's trading for the 3 months to 31 March 20X1 in one column, the trading for the 12 months to March 20X2 (including the subsidiary) in the next column and a total column. The comparatives would remain unchanged. This method gives users clear disclosure of the group's most recent 12 months trading which may assist in their projections of future comparable trading periods. It also satisfies the Act's requirements concerning consolidations. Some would argue that this basis still does not solve the problem as the comparatives are not truly comparable. To resolve this issue it would also be necessary to disclose the subsidiary's trading for the 3 months to 31 March 20X2. The need for this additional disclosure will depend on the individual circumstances.

Parent's period differs from group

24.328 Similar difficulties to those explained above arise where the parent has recently been incorporated and acquires subsidiaries which have different reporting periods to that of the parent.

Example – Parent has a shorter reporting period than its subsidiary

A parent is incorporated on 1 September 20X1 and acquires a group of subsidiaries on 1 January 20X2. Acquisition accounting is adopted. The parent's first financial statements cover the 16 month period to 31 December 20X2. December is the year end of the group of subsidiaries.

The question then is should the group's financial statements be prepared to cover the same 16 month period. This is certainly one answer, but poses problems because the subsidiaries' financial years run from 1 January. The solution to this problem is to prepare the consolidated financial statements for the 16 month period to 31 December 20X2 including the parent's results for the 16 months (of which the first three months may well be immaterial, because the company will have been set up to acquire the subsidiaries and will not have traded in that period) and the results of the subsidiaries for 12 months, that is, from the date of acquisition. Appropriate disclosure of the basis adopted would be necessary. Pro forma comparatives comprising the subsidiaries' results for the 12 months to 31 December 20X1 may be given for information.

24.329 A similar type of situation arose in Chubb Security Plc, where a new parent was incorporated on 17 August 1992 and acquired Chubb International Holdings Limited (CIHL) on 5 October 1992. The group's financial statements ended 31 March 1993 show pro forma financial statements for 1993 and 1992 as if the group had existed independently for those two years. The statutory financial information is given as a separate column and includes the results of CIHL from the date of its acquisition in October 1992 to 31 March 1993. The balance sheet shows the statutory group balances for the year to 31 March 1993 and pro forma information as comparatives (see Table 24.21).

Table 24.21 – Parent has a short reporting period

Chubb Security Plc – Annual Report & Accounts – 31 March 1993

Notes to the Accounts

1 **BASIS OF REPORTING**

Chubb Security Plc was incorporated on 17 August 1992. During 1992 all companies within the Security Division of Racal Electronics Plc (Racal) which were not already owned by Chubb International Holdings Limited (CIHL), formerly Racal Security Limited, were transferred into its ownership and companies owned by CIHL which were not part of the Security Division were transferred out of its ownership. CIHL was then transferred into the ownership of Chubb Security Plc which was demerged from Racal on 5 October 1992.

The proforma financial statements include the results for the Group as currently constituted and show the results that would have been presented if Chubb Security Plc had been an independent company throughout the two years ended 31 March 1993. The results for the year ended 31 March 1992 are as previously presented in the Introduction to the Official List (Listing Particulars) circulated to Racal shareholders in September 1992.

The Statutory financial statements for the period ended 31 March include the results for the Group for the 21 weeks from 10 October 1992 (the closest date to the demerger up to which management accounts had been prepared) to 31 March 1993. It was not practical to adjust these management accounts by the results for the period 5 to 9 October 1992.

Consolidated Profit and Loss Account (extract) for the Period and Year Ended 31 March 1993

Note		1993 proforma £000	1992 proforma £000	1993 Statutory £000
2	Turnover	**674,402**	668,943	**330,880**
2 & 3	Operating profit before exceptional items	**75,602**	53,326	**40,078**
4	Exceptional items	**(7,822)**	(5,943)	**(2,248)**
	Trading profit	**67,780**	47,383	**37,830**
5	Group interest payable less investment income	**3,577**	8,311	**1,995**
	Profit on ordinary activities before taxation	**64,203**	39,072	**35,835**

Consolidated Balance Sheet (extract) at 31 March 1993

Note		1993 Statutory £000	1992 proforma £000
	FIXED ASSETS		
13	Tangible assets	**123,671**	121,935
14	Investments	**1,624**	4,154
		125,295	126,089

24.330 In the reorganisation of Rothmans International in 1993, a new parent company was incorporated to acquire the tobacco business of the group, but here the principles of merger accounting were applied (see Table 24.22). In this case, the parent company's accounting period (28 July 1993 to 31 March 1994) was shorter than that of the subsidiaries acquired and group accounts were prepared including the new parent's results for the period 28 July 1993 to 31 March 1994, but incorporating the results of the subsidiaries for their full financial year, that is, for the year to 31 March 1994 in accordance with the principles of merger accounting. Comparatives for the group were the results of the subsidiaries for the year to 31 March 1993.

Table 24.22 – Parent has a short reporting period-merger accounting

Rothmans International p.l.c. – Annual Report and Accounts – 31 March 1994

DIRECTORS' REPORT (extract)

INCORPORATION AND CHANGE OF NAME The Company was incorporated on 28th July 1993 as New Rothmans plc. On 25th October 1993 the Company changed its name to Rothmans International plc.

STATEMENT OF ACCOUNTING POLICIES (extract)

BASIS OF PREPARATION As part of the amalgamation and reconstruction of the tobacco and luxury goods interests of Rothmans International p.l.c. ('old Rothmans'), Compagnie Financière Richemont AG ('Richemont') and Dunhill Holdings PLC ('Dunhill') in October 1993, the tobacco businesses of old Rothmans and certain tobacco trade marks owned or controlled by Dunhill and by Richemont, were transferred to two new listed companies, Rothmans International plc (formerly New Rothmans plc) and Rothmans International N.V. (together, 'new Rothmans'). Rothmans International plc acquired the UK based tobacco business of old Rothmans and the Dunhill tobacco trade marks. Rothmans International N.V. acquired the non UK based tobacco business of old Rothmans and certain tobacco trade marks owned or controlled by Richemont. The luxury goods interests of old Rothmans, comprising its 58 per cent interest in Dunhill and its 47 per cent indirect interest in Cartier Monde S.A., were transferred to form part of a new separate listed group under the name Vendôme Luxury Group. Shareholders in old Rothmans received units in new Rothmans, each comprising one Rothmans International plc share and one Rothmans International N.V. share, in exchange for their shares in old Rothmans which were transferred to that group, and a payment of cash, representing funds not required by new Rothmans. Units in new Rothmans were also issued to the shareholders in Dunhill and to Richemont representing the tobacco trade marks transferred to new Rothmans. Pursuant to the reconstruction, old Rothmans is in voluntary liquidation.

The consolidated financial statements of the Rothmans International plc group have been prepared using the principles of merger accounting. As a result, although the reconstruction did not take effect until 23rd October 1993, the financial statements are presented as if the reconstruction had taken place on 1st April 1992, except for the exchange of shares, which took place on 23rd October 1993, the return of surplus cash on 1st November 1993 and certain other transactions connected with the reconstruction. The results of the UK based tobacco business of old Rothmans for the year ended 31st March 1993 and for the full year ended 31st March 1994 have been included in these consolidated financial statements except that net dividends received from companies which are now in the Rothmans International N.V. group and dividends received from Dunhill have been excluded from the profit and loss account and are shown as a movement in reserves.

> The consolidated accounts include the accounts of Rothmans International plc and its subsidiary undertakings together with the Group's share of the profits and retained post-acquisition reserves of associated undertakings.

24.331 Non-coterminous accounting periods are also considered in chapter 28 which looks at the problems that can arise in merger accounting.

Elimination of intra-group transactions

24.332 It has been accepted accounting practice to eliminate transactions between group members in the consolidated financial statements. SSAP 14 stated that such eliminations should be made, but did not detail how, apart from stating that the method was well understood. However, the Companies Act 2006 specifically requires '*debts and claims*' (that is, debtors and creditors) between group undertakings to be eliminated on consolidation. Also, income and expenditure relating to transactions between group undertakings should be eliminated on consolidation. [SI 2008/410 6 Sch 6(1)].

24.333 Similarly, profits and losses resulting from transactions between group undertakings included in the value of assets retained at the year end should be eliminated. [SI 2008/410 6 Sch 6(2)]. The Companies Act 1985, but not FRS 2 (see below), permits the elimination of such profits and losses to be made in proportion to the group's interest in the undertaking's shares. [SI 2008/410 6 Sch 6(3)].

24.334 The rules set out in FRS 2 are consistent with the Act except that they are further restricted as follows:

- Profits or losses on any intra-group transactions, to the extent that they are reflected in the book value of assets to be included in the consolidation, should be eliminated in full.
- Intra-group debtors and creditors should be eliminated.
- The elimination of profits or losses relating to intra-group transactions should be set against the interest held by the parent and its other subsidiaries and against the minority interest in proportion to their respective holdings in the undertaking whose individual financial statements recorded the eliminated profits or losses.

[FRS 2 para 39].

24.335 The rationale for full elimination of unrealised profits or losses even where the related transactions are between subsidiary undertakings with minority interests is set out below.

24.336 Transactions between subsidiaries included in the consolidation are wholly within the control of the parent company, whether or not the subsidiaries are wholly-owned. All the assets and liabilities of a subsidiary and transactions between subsidiaries are brought into the consolidation in full, again whether or not they are wholly-owned. Therefore, as the group includes 100 per cent of all the subsidiaries' assets and liabilities, intra-group transactions that give rise to profits or losses that are unrealised at the balance sheet date are wholly unrealised to the group and do not represent any increase or decrease in the group's net assets. They should, therefore, be eliminated in full, even where the transactions involve subsidiaries with minority interests.

Elimination calculations

24.337 The following examples deal with the elimination of intra-group profit on the sale of assets by a subsidiary to its parent and the elimination of intra-group profit on sale of assets by a parent to its subsidiary.

Example 1 – Elimination of intra-group profits – Subsidiary sells to its parent

A parent owns 60% of a subsidiary. The subsidiary sells some stock to the parent for £70,000 and makes a profit of £30,000 on the sale. The stock is in the parent's balance sheet at the year end.

The parent must eliminate 100% of the unrealised profit on consolidation. The stock will, therefore, be carried in the group's balance sheet at £40,000 (£70,000 — £30,000). The profit and loss account will show a corresponding reduction in profit of £30,000. The minority interest in the profit and loss account for the year will be credited with the minority's share of the unrealised profit, £12,000 (40% × £30,000).

The double entry on consolidation is as follows:

	£'000	£'000
Dr Sales	70	
Cr Cost of sales		40
Cr Stock		30

Being the elimination of 100% of the unrealised profit from the balance sheet.

Dr Balance sheet minority interest	12	
Cr Profit and loss account minority interest		12

Being the allocation to the minority of its 'share' of the elimination of the unrealised profit.

The effect on the profit and loss account and balance sheet is as follows:

Profit and loss account	Results of sub (say)	Adjustment	Results consolidated
	£'000	£'000	£'000
Profit before taxation	100	(30)	70
Minority interests	(40)	12	(28)
Profit for the financial year	60	(18)	42

Consolidated balance sheet	Before adjustment (say)	Adjustment	After adjustment
Stock	800	(30)	770
Other shareholders' funds	400	–	400
Profit and loss account	275	(18)	257
Minority interests	125	12	113
	800	(30)	770

In other words, from the group's point of view, no profit has been recognised. The stock is retained at cost to the group of £40,000. The profit before tax also does not include any of the profit of £30,000 on the stock in question. This reflects the fact that the group as an entity has not made a profit on selling stock to itself. Since in this method, the objective is to eliminate the entire profit, it is necessary to show the effect of the subsidiary in question earning £30,000 less profit. The effect of this is that the group has earned £18,000 less (60% × £30,000). Hence the adjustment of £12,000 shown above in the minority's line.

Example 2 – Elimination of intra-group profits – Parent sells to subsidiary

The situation is as above except that, on this occasion, it is the parent that makes the sale. The parent owns 60% of a subsidiary. The parent sells some stock to the subsidiary for £70,000 and makes a profit of £30,000 on the sale. The stock is in the subsidiary's balance sheet at the year end.

The parent must eliminate 100% of the unrealised profit on consolidation. The stock will, therefore, be carried in the group's balance sheet at £40,000 (£70,000 — £30,000). The profit and loss account will show a corresponding reduction in profit of £30,000. As the minority has no interest in the company that made the profit (the parent) there will be no element of the elimination attributed to the minority.

The double entry on consolidation is as follows:

	£'000	£'000
Dr Sales	70	
Cr Cost of sales		40
Cr Stock		30

Being the elimination of 100% of the unrealised profit from the balance sheet.

The effect on the profit and loss account and balance sheet is:

Consolidated profit and loss	Before adjustment (say) £'000	Adjustment £'000	After adjustment £'000
Profit before taxation	100	(30)	70
Minority interests	(40)	–	(40)
Profit for the financial year	60	(30)	30

Consolidated balance sheet	Before adjustment (say)	Adjustment	After adjustment
Stock	800	(30)	770
Other shareholders' funds	400	–	400
Profit and loss account	275	(30)	245
Minority interests	125	–	125
	800	(30)	770

Profit elimination from fixed assets

24.338 The rules explained above apply equally to any profit that might be included in the group's fixed assets (including investments) as a result of one group company selling assets to another group company at a profit. Before the introduction of FRS 2 many companies did not eliminate such profits immediately from their fixed assets, but eliminated them over the life of the asset *via* higher depreciation charges. This method is not acceptable under FRS 2 and such intra-group profits must be eliminated in full.

Losses

24.339 Where a company makes a loss selling assets (at fair value) to another group company, no consolidation adjustment should be necessary at the year end. This is because it would be wrong to reinstate the asset at a value above its recoverable amount.

Subsidiaries excluded from consolidation

24.340 Profits or losses arising on transactions with undertakings excluded from consolidation because they are held exclusively with a view to subsequent resale or because of severe long-term restrictions need not be eliminated, except to the extent appropriate where significant influence is retained and the subsidiary is treated as an associate (that is, equity accounted). However, it is important to consider whether it is prudent to record any profit arising from transactions with subsidiaries excluded on these grounds (see the examples in para 24.342 below). [FRS 2 para 83].

24.341 The adjustments required to eliminate the effects of intra-group trading between a group and an undertaking included in the consolidation by the equity method are straightforward. The elimination of intra-group profits or losses should be in proportion to the group's interest.

24.342 To eliminate the profits or losses of such undertakings in proportion to the group's share is logical as it ensures that only profits that are actually recorded in the profit and loss account are eliminated. It would clearly be wrong to eliminate a greater proportion of profit than was recorded originally. Two examples below deal with whether or not any adjustments are necessary when intra-group profits are made on sales of assets to subsidiaries that have been excluded from consolidation. In the first example, the two subsidiaries have been wholly excluded. In the second example, the subsidiary is equity accounted as significant influence is retained.

Example 1 – Intra-group transactions where subsidiaries has not been consolidated

A group has a subsidiary that manufactures office equipment. It also has two subsidiaries that are not included in the group's consolidated financial statements either by full consolidation or by equity accounting. The first of these subsidiaries is profitable and has not been consolidated as it is being held exclusively with a view to subsequent resale and the second has been excluded due to severe long-term restrictions (remittances to the UK are virtually impossible and are not expected to be in the future, representing a loss of control of financial and operating policy). At the year end the consolidated financial statements show substantial debtor balances due from each of the excluded subsidiaries. Are any consolidation adjustments necessary?

As neither of the debtor balances are with subsidiaries included in the consolidation the balances do not require elimination as intra-group transactions. However, consideration should be given to whether it would be prudent to recognise any element of profit included in those balances.

The first of the subsidiaries is profitable and provided there is no reason to believe that the debt will not be settled there is no reason to make an adjustment to eliminate the profit included in the debtor.

The second subsidiary has been excluded on the grounds that remittances to the UK are virtually impossible. It would clearly be imprudent for the group to recognise a profit on a sale to such a company until the debt was settled. Indeed, in this situation it may be necessary to provide for the whole debt in the group's profit and loss account.

Example 2 – Intra-group transaction where there are severe long-term restrictions

Company H prepares its consolidated financial statements to 31 December 20X1. It has a 60% holding in a subsidiary (company S) which has been excluded on the grounds of severe long-term restrictions, but it retains significant influence and accounts for the subsidiary under the equity method of accounting. During the year company H purchased stock amounting to £1 million on which company S made a profit of £500,000. At the year end half of this stock remained unsold to third parties. Company H's consolidated financial statements would initially record its share of this profit under the equity method at £300,000 (60% × £500,000) and the unrealised element of this should be eliminated. The unsold stock amounts to £500,000 on which there is £250,000 unrealised profits. The elimination journal in the consolidation would be to debit share of the subsidiary's profit £150,000 (60% × £250,000), and to credit stock £150,000.

24.343 Where an undertaking that is fully consolidated makes a sale to an undertaking that is included in the consolidation under the equity method, a profit may arise in the group. The undertaking's assets that are equity accounted will be overstated by the profit element if the asset is held at the year end. Consequently, an adjustment is required on consolidation to reduce the group's share of the associate's net assets by the same amount. But in this case, the group's profit will not be eliminated in full as the element of profit which is attributable to the minority's share is not recorded in the balance sheet. This is because under the equity method the group's balance sheet will only include its percentage share of the net assets of the subsidiary. Therefore, for a 60 per cent subsidiary that is equity accounted, 40 per cent of the group's profit on the transaction (that is, the element of the profit that is attributable to the third party shareholders) will be recorded in the consolidated profit and loss account and 60 per cent eliminated.

Example – Parent sells stock to a subsidiary excluded from consolidation

A parent company sells stock worth £100,000 to a 60% owned subsidiary which has been excluded from consolidation on the grounds of lack of control because of severe long-term restrictions. The profit on the transaction is £20,000 and the subsidiary retains the stock at the year end. The results of the subsidiary are equity accounted with those of the group. The profit to be eliminated is 60% of the £20,000, that is, £12,000. The stock included in the net assets that are equity accounted before the profit elimination would be £60,000 (that is, £100,000 × 60%). The stock would, therefore, be reduced to £48,000. The double entry on consolidation is as follows:

	£'000	£'000
Dr Profit before taxation	12	
Cr Net assets of equity accounted subsidiary		12

Being the elimination of the group's share of 60% of the unrealised profit included in the balance sheet by the equity method of accounting.

Section III — Minority interests

Introduction

24.344 Under the parent company concept of accounting for groups (explained in paragraph 24.6), which is the basis adopted for consolidations in the UK, minority interests are shown separately either before or after shareholders' funds and therefore, unlike under the entity concept, do not form part of shareholders' funds. Minority interests represent the share of net assets of subsidiaries consolidated into the group's consolidated financial statements that are financed by shareholders who are not members of the group and are outside third parties.

24.345 This chapter considers the general accounting and disclosure requirements that apply to minority interests now to be found in the Companies Act 2006 (as amended), FRS 2 and FRS 25. The latter half of this section concentrates on the problems associated with calculating minority interests and considers:

- Measurement of minority interests (see para 24.371).
- Indirect holdings (see para 24.375).
- Treatment of minority interests on acquisition (see para 24.377).
- Acquisition of minority interests (see para 24.380).
- Loss making subsidiaries (see para 24.383).

Definition

24.346 'Minority interests' is defined in the Companies Act 2006 to mean "*the amount of capital and reserves attributable to shares in subsidiary undertakings included in the consolidation held by or on behalf of persons other than the parent company and its subsidiary undertakings*". [SI 2008/410 6 Sch 17(2)]. The effect of the legislation is, for example, that where a parent owns 70 per cent of a subsidiary, it has to consolidate 100 per cent of the subsidiary's results and net assets and show minority interests of 30 per cent.

24.347 FRS 2 also defines minority interests based on the Companies Act 2006 definition, but the standard's definition recognises also that a parent need not be a company. It states that the minority interest in a subsidiary is:

> '*The interest in a subsidiary undertaking included in the consolidation that is attributable to the shares held by or on behalf of persons other than the parent undertaking and its subsidiary undertakings.*' [FRS 2 para 13].

24.348 The definition in FRS 2 and the Companies Act 2006 requirements can be seen reflected in companies' accounting policies. For example Table 24.23 below shows Marconi plc's policy for minority interests. Whilst the accounting extract is before the application of Companies Act 2006, the disclosure would be the same if the Companies Act 2006 had been applied.

Table 24.23 – Explanation of minority interests

Marconi plc – Annual Report and Accounts – 31 March 2001

Notes to the Accounts (extract)

7 Minority Interests

Equity minority interests represent the share of the profits less losses on ordinary activities attributable to the interests of equity shareholders in subsidiaries which are not wholly owned by the Group.

24.349 The term 'minority interests' was originally introduced into company law at a time when consolidation was based on equity ownership rather than control. Under the current provisions of the Companies Act 2006, where consolidation is based on control, it is possible, although fairly uncommon, for minority interests to be more than 50 per cent. Indeed there are situations where minority interests might be considerably higher than 50 per cent (see further para 24.351).

24.350 With regard to the disclosure of minority interests, paragraph 17 to schedule 6 of SI 2008/410, 'The Large and Medium-sized Companies and Groups (Accounts and Reports) Regulations 2008, on group accounts states that minority interests should be shown as a separate item (with an appropriate heading) in the company's capital, reserves and results brought forward. See further paragraph 24.357, which specifies where minority interests should be shown in both the consolidated balance sheet formats and the consolidated profit and loss account formats.

Minority or majority interests

24.351 A company has to be treated as a subsidiary where its parent has the power to exercise, or actually exercises, dominant influence or control over it or manages it on a unified basis (see further para 24.130). Consequently, it is quite possible for a parent to own only (say) 20 per cent of the undertaking's equity and exercise dominant influence over it, or manage it on a unified basis, or have the power to control it. Where this is so, it is also quite possible that the minority shareholders will hold (say) 80 per cent of the undertaking's equity. Accordingly, the minority interests shown in the consolidated financial statements will be calculated using this percentage. This could result, for example, in the group consolidating 100 per cent of the assets and liabilities of the subsidiary, but showing also minority interests of 80 per cent of those assets and liabilities. A similar situation could arise where the parent owns a majority of the voting rights, but owns (say) only 20 per cent of the total equity.

24.352 Where these types of situation arise, it is unlikely that this is a good enough reason for the term 'minority interests' to be amended to (say) 'majority interests'. Furthermore, we consider that it is unlikely that circumstances would exist where using the term 'minority interests' would affect the true and fair view and, therefore, justify using another term. In the situation described above, the minority although owning the majority of capital will be in a minority position with regard to controlling the company and, consequently, the term 'minority interests' still describes the outside interest fairly. However, we consider that in this type of situation it is necessary to explain the relationship with the subsidiary fully in the consolidated financial statements in order that they should give a true and fair view. In particular, FRS 2 requires that where the parent has the power to exercise, or actually exercises, a dominant influence or control over it, the consolidated financial statements should disclose this fact and should explain the basis of the parent's dominant influence. [SI 2008/410 4 Sch 16(3); FRS 2 para 34].

Basis of recognising minority interests

24.353 FRS 2 states that the effect of the existence of minority interests on the returns to investors in the parent is best reflected by presenting the net identifiable assets attributable to minority interests on the same basis as those attributable to group interests. The same general approach applies to the balance sheet where the group's assets and liabilities, whether they are attributable to minorities or to the parent, should be presented on a consistent basis. This is logical as the group includes 100 per cent of the assets and liabilities of a subsidiary in its consolidated balance sheet (after consolidation eliminations) whatever the parent's holding in the subsidiary. As explained briefly above, this basis is consistent with the parent company concept.

24.354 Although the basis for recognising minority interests under UK GAAP is consistent with the parent company concept, this consistency of approach does not extend to all of the goodwill of the subsidiary. When a parent purchases a controlling, but not 100 per cent, interest in a subsidiary, goodwill may arise (see chapter 25). The goodwill that arises on consolidation relates only to the parent's share of the subsidiary and not to the minority's share. Although it might be possible to estimate a goodwill figure for minority interests by extrapolation or valuation, it would be inappropriate under existing UK GAAP to include that amount in the balance sheet as the minority is not party to the group's transaction to acquire the subsidiary. To include an amount for goodwill would, from the group's point of view, represent the recognition of inherent goodwill, which is not permitted by the Act or FRS 10. The requirement that goodwill arising on acquisition should only be recognised with respect to the part of the subsidiary undertaking that is attributable to the interest held by the parent and its other subsidiaries is summarised in paragraph 38 of FRS 2. This would be the situation, for example, where company P acquires 70 per cent of sub-group A. The net assets of sub-group A would be fair valued on consolidation (ignoring any goodwill recognised in sub-group A) and the minority would be given their share of those net assets. However, where a subsidiary (company A) of parent (company P) has acquired a sub-subsidiary (company B), any goodwill arising on the acquisition of company B, which in company A's consolidated financial statements is capitalised and amortised, will have an effect on the calculation of any minority interests in company A recognised in the parent's consolidated financial statements (see further para 24.378).

Measurement of minority interests

24.355 As explained above, shares issued by subsidiaries to persons outside the group are normally accounted for as minority interests. But in situations where the minority interest has one or more features that would lead it to fall within the definition of a liability contained in FRS 25, 'Financial instruments: Disclosure and presentation', it should be recognised and measured in accordance with that standard (see further chapter 6). Examples of such features include preference shares with fixed dividends and situations where the group guarantees the payment of the minority's dividends or the repayment of its capital. Prior to FRS 25 classification of a minority interest as a liability was restricted to circumstances where a potential guarantee was in place.

Equity minority interests

24.356 Minority interests that meet the definition of equity under FRS 25, 'Financial instruments: Disclosure and presentation', are no less straightforward than those classified as liabilities. Such minority interests are merely represented by the net proceeds on issue of the shares (that is, net of issue costs) plus the equity minority shareholders' percentage interest in the other reserves of the company. Examples of such calculations follow from paragraph 24.371.

Presentation in financial statements of equity minority interests

Balance sheet

24.357 In the balance sheet Format 1 'minority interests' should be shown either directly above or below 'capital and reserves'. Because it is possible to total the format 1 balance sheet in different positions, it is possible to:

- Draw a total before capital and reserves which includes minority interests.
- Draw a total before capital and reserves and minority interests, showing minority interests either before or after capital and reserves.

Chapter 4 includes a summary of Format 1 which shows the positioning of 'minority interests'.

24.358 In Format 2 the disclosure of 'minority interests' should be made under 'liabilities' between the headings 'capital and reserves' and 'provisions for liabilities'. [SI 2008/410 6 Sch 17(1)(2); FRS 2 para 35].

24.359 In determining how the disclosure of minority interests can be changed or adapted in the consolidated balance sheet, the Act states that the item should be treated in the same way as if a letter were assigned to it. [SI 2008/410 6 Sch 17(5)(a)]. But in practice even under the Companies Act 2006 strict criteria there are a number of ways of presenting minority interests to emphasise different balance sheet totals as illustrated in the examples that follow. Most commonly the balance sheet shows minority interests after drawing a total for shareholders' interests. By contrast Table 24.25 shows ICI PLC's balance sheet which follows Format 1.

Table 24.25 – Presentation of minority interests

Imperial Chemical Industries PLC – Annual Report and Accounts and Form 20-F – 31 December 1999

Balance Sheets (extract) at 31 December 1999

		Group		Company	
	Notes	**1999 £m**	1998 £m	**1999 £m**	1998 £m
Total assets less current liabilities	4	**4,073**	4,647	**5,921**	5,376
Financed by					
Creditors due after more than one year					
Loans	21	**2,252**	2,954	**247**	360
Other creditors	20	**71**	55	**1,256**	2,784
		2,323	3,009	**1,503**	3,144
Provisions for liabilities and charges	22	**1,456**	1,440	**321**	210
Minority interests – equity		**50**	49	**–**	–
Shareholders' funds – equity					
Called-up share capital	24	**728**	728	**728**	728
Reserves					
Share premium accounts		**588**	587	**588**	587
Associates' reserves		**26**	15	**–**	–
Profit and loss account		**(1,098)**	(1,181)	**2,781**	707
Total reserves	25	**(484)**	(579)	**3,369**	1,294
Total shareholders' funds (page 51)		**244**	149	**4,097**	2,022
		4,073	4,647	**5,921**	5,376

Profit and loss account

24.360 For the profit and loss account formats the Companies Act 2006 requires two additional lines to be added for minority interests. The first line requires the disclosure of minority interests in the profit or loss excluding extraordinary items, and in Format 1 and Format 2 this item should be included after 'profit or loss on ordinary activities after taxation'. In addition, the Companies Act 2006 specifies that the item should be described 'minority interests'. For Format 3 and Format 4 minority interests should be included under 'charges' or 'income' as appropriate, in the same position after striking the 'profit or loss on ordinary activities after taxation'. [SI 2008/410 6 Sch 17(3); FRS 2 para 36]. This presentation can be seen in many of the extracts from the financial statements reproduced in this chapter, for example see Table 24.26.

Table 24.26 – Marks and Spencer p.l.c. – Annual Report and Financial Statements – 31 March 1995

Consolidated profit and loss account (extract)
FOR THE YEAR ENDED 31 MARCH 1995

	Notes	**1995** 52 weeks £m	1994 53 weeks Restated £m
PROFIT ON ORDINARY ACTIVITIES BEFORE TAXATION	2	**924.3**	851.5
Tax on ordinary activities	6	**(299.5)**	(272.2)
PROFIT ON ORDINARY ACTIVITIES AFTER TAXATION		**624.8**	579.3
Minority interests (all equity)		**(1.0)**	(1.1)
PROFIT FOR THE FINANCIAL YEAR	7	**623.8**	578.2

24.361 The second line required to be disclosed by the legislation is the minority's share of any extraordinary items. [SI 2008/410 6 Sch 17(4)]. However, the introduction of FRS 3 (see chapter 8) has, in effect, stopped the use of extraordinary items as a caption for presentation in the profit and loss account. Consequently, the position of the minority's share of extraordinary items is no longer relevant.

24.362 The consolidated profit and loss account disclosure for 'minority interests' under Format 1 is illustrated in chapter 4.

24.363 There is in principle more scope to adapt and combine the minority interests disclosure in the consolidated profit and loss account than there is in the balance sheet. This is because the Act states that minority interests shall be treated as if they have been assigned an Arabic number. [SI 2008/410 6 Sch 17(5)(6)]. This means that the minority interests disclosure in the profit and loss account can be adapted where the special nature of the group's business requires such adaptation. [SI 2008/410 6 Sch 3(3)]. It is, in practice, difficult to imagine when this particular provision would apply apart from perhaps in the circumstance of stapled stock (see para 24.368).

24.364 FRS 3, 'Reporting financial performance', requires that the notes to the financial statements should include information regarding the effect on any minority interests of the three non-operating exceptional items specified in that standard, which are:

- Profits or losses on the sale of termination of an operation.
- Costs of a fundamental reorganisation or restructuring having a material effect on the nature and focus of the reporting entity's operations.
- Profits or losses on the disposal of fixed assets.

[FRS 3 para 20].

24.365 Table 24.27 shows an extract from Unitech plc's annual report and accounts which has shown the minority's share of a non-operating exceptional.

Table 24.27 – Minority's share of a non-operating exceptional item

Unitech plc – Annual report and accounts – 31 May 1993

Notes (extract)

2 Segment information (extract)

The gains arising on the sale of buildings include a £1,225,000 gain, less tax of £55,000, on the disposal of buildings owned by Nemic-Lambda in Israel, of which the minority interest share is £578,000.

[The next paragraph is 24.368.]

Stapled shares

24.368 An example of where the minority interests in the balance sheet might need to be shown in another position in order to give a true and fair view is where shareholders in the parent have been issued with shares in a subsidiary that have been 'stapled' with their shares in the parent. This method of share issue is often used where the subsidiary is resident overseas for tax purposes to ensure that distributions from the subsidiary are still treated as distributions of the UK company. Therefore, depending upon the circumstances and the rights attaching to the subsidiary's shares, those shares might, in substance, be more akin to shareholders' funds than to minority interests.

Directors' interests

24.369 It is often a requirement of a company's articles of association for the company's directors to acquire nominee shareholdings in the company's shares. Generally these shareholdings are very small and the directors have no beneficial interest in them. Where such a situation arises in a subsidiary company, clearly the directors' shareholding from the group's perspective does not constitute a minority interest in the company as the shares are normally held on the parent company's behalf.

24.370 Other situations arise in practice where directors have beneficial interests in the company's shares. These situations need to be considered very carefully to determine whether the shareholding constitutes a minority interest or should be recognised for accounting purposes in some other way. For example, if a director is given shares in his/her company and the company's parent arranges to reacquire those shares at a future date, the substance of the transaction might be to remunerate the director. Where this is so, the cost to the company should be charged to the profit and loss account as staff costs over the term of the arrangement in accordance with FRS 20, 'Share-based payments' (see further chapter 12) and disclosed as directors' emoluments. Alternatively, the substance of the transaction could be quite different, for example, it might be a way of acquiring intellectual property rights or expert knowledge that the director has or has some right to. In such a situation it could be argued that the transaction relates to the acquisition of that right or knowledge and as such represents an intangible asset and should be accounted for as such. Clearly, transactions with directors of this nature need to be considered very carefully and inevitably where they are not accounted for as minority interests additional disclosure will be necessary, because the transaction is likely to be material to the director (see further chapter 6 of the Manual of Accounting – Management Reports and Governance) and it will be a transaction with a related party (see chapter 29).

Measurement of minority interests

24.371 Minority interests included in the consolidated balance sheet should represent the total amount of capital and reserves attributable to shares in the subsidiary held by or on behalf of persons other than the parent and its other subsidiaries. [SI 2008/410 6 Sch 17(2)]. Similar wording is also used to indicate how to calculate the minority's interest in the profit and loss for the period. [SI 2008/410 6 Sch 17(3)(4)]. In practice, the calculation of minority interests is fraught with complications. These complications can include changes in stake and the treatment of losses. The examples that follow illustrate each of these problems.

Profit and loss account calculation

24.372 The minority interests in a subsidiary's profit for the year is calculated by taking the profit after taxation and calculating the proportion of the profit that is attributable to the minority. Consider the following simple example.

Example – Calculation of minority interest

A parent owns 80% of a subsidiary's ordinary share capital (there are no other classes of capital) since the subsidiary's incorporation. The subsidiary's profit and loss account is as follows:

	£'000
Operating profit	1,000
Non-operating exceptional item	1,250
Profit on ordinary activities before taxation	2,250
Tax on profit on ordinary activities	(280)
Retained profit for the financial year	1,970

The figures that would be brought into the consolidated financial statements in respect of the subsidiary (ignoring any intra-group profit elimination) are:

	£'000
Operating profit	1,000
Non-operating exceptional item	1,250
Profit on ordinary activities before taxation	2,250
Tax on profit for the financial year	(280)
Profit on ordinary activities after taxation	1,970
Minority interests (20% × £1,970,000)	(394)
Retained profit for the year	1,576

Balance sheet calculation

24.373 The calculation of the balance sheet minority interests follows directly from the definition. In a simple situation involving only equity shares, the balance of the minority interests at the year end is the minority's interest in the capital and reserves of the subsidiary. An example of the calculation of the balance sheet minority interests is shown below:

Example

Following on from the example above, the subsidiary's balance sheet is as follows:

		£'000
Net assets		3,820
Equity share capital		250
Share premium		500
Revaluation reserve		300
Profit and loss account	800	
Retained profit for the year	1,970	2,770
Equity shareholders' funds		3,820

The minority interests in the capital and reserves of the subsidiary are calculated as follows, assuming that issue costs are immaterial (if they were material the relevant proportion should be deducted from the minorities' equity share capital):

		£'000	£'000
Equity share capital	20% × 250,000		50
Share premium	20% × 500,000		100
Revaluation reserve	20% × 300,000		60
Profit and loss account b/f	20% × 800,000	160	
Minority's interest in the profit after taxation		394	554
Minority interests			764

24.374 This is clearly a very straightforward example and would be made more complicated by, for example, a share structure involving different classes of shares (particularly if one or more of those classes is a share classified as a liability) or where there are intra-group transactions that require elimination.

Indirect holdings

24.375 Where a parent holds an indirect interest in a subsidiary the treatment of minorities becomes more complicated. Before the minority interests can be calculated it is first necessary to establish whether the entity is a subsidiary of the parent and, therefore, should be consolidated.

Example – Indirect holdings – Calculation of minority interest

Consider the following group structure:

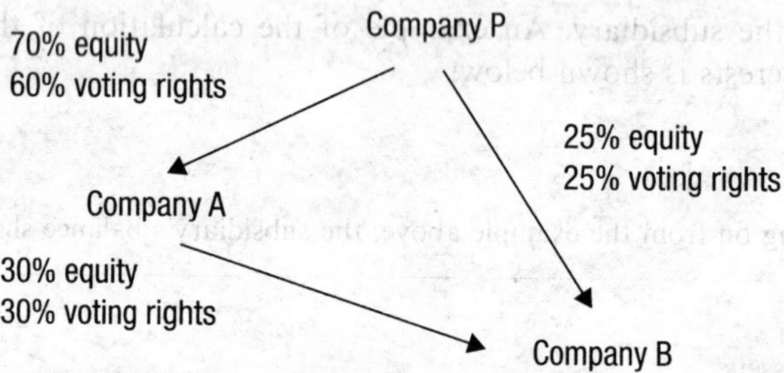

A number of factors have to be considered to determine whether company B is a subsidiary of company P. These matters are fully discussed from paragraph 24.76 onwards. However, in the example company P owns 70% of the equity of company A and 60% of the voting rights of company A. Company A is, therefore, a subsidiary of company P, because company P controls more than 50% of the voting rights of company A.

Company P owns 25% of the equity and voting rights in company B, while company A owns 30% of the equity and voting rights in company B. Company B is not a direct subsidiary of company A as company A only controls 30% of its votes (assuming company B is not a subsidiary of company A for other reasons, for example, dominant influence – see further in para 24.76 onwards). However, company P controls 25% of the votes in company B directly and, by virtue of its control of company A, 30% of the votes in company B indirectly. Company B is, therefore, a subsidiary of company P as company P controls in total 55% of the voting rights in company B. On the other hand, if company A had not been a subsidiary of company P, then company P would not have controlled company B and, as a consequence, company B would not have been a subsidiary of company P either.

The summarised balance sheets of each of the group companies is as follows:

Summarised balance sheets

	Company P	Company A	Company B
	£'000	£'000	£'000
Investment in subsidiaries	60*	30	–
Net assets	190	120	200
	250	150	200
Equity share capital	100	50	100
Profit and loss account	150	100	100
Equity shareholders' funds	250	150	200

* The investment in subsidiaries represents the investments in company A and company B, which were acquired for their nominal value at incorporation, being 35 for the investment in A (70% × 50) and 25 for the investment in B (25% × 100).

The balance sheet minority interests can be ascertained in two ways: either by considering the minority interest arising when company B is consolidated with company A; or by considering company P's indirect holding in its subsidiaries. Both methods will arrive at the same result unless goodwill has been capitalised (see para 24.378)

Indirect method

The indirect method involves calculating the total minority interests by considering the indirect minority interests from the parent's perspective. In this case there is an indirect minority interest in company B of 54% (100% — (30% x 70% + 25%)) and a direct minority interest of 30% in company A. The minority interests calculated under the indirect method is as follows:

Minority interest in group – indirect method	£'000
Minorities' share of net assets of company A net assets × direct minority interest (£120,000 × 30%)	36
Minorities' share of net assets of company B net assets × indirect minority interest (£200,000 × 54%)	108
	144

Direct method

The direct method of calculating the minority interests involves consolidation of the minority interests of company B with company A and then consolidating company A with company P. The calculation is as follows:

Minority interest in group – direct method	£'000
Company B consolidated into company A	
Equity share capital of company B (£100,000 × 70%)	70
Reserves of company B (£100,000 × 70%)	70
Minority interest in group A	140
Group A consolidated into company P	
Equity share capital of company A (£50,000 × 30%)	15
Reserves of company A (£100,000 × 30%)	30
Reserves of company B ((£100,000 – £70,000) × 30%)*	9
Adjustment to eliminate 25% of company B owned directly by company P†	
Equity share capital of B (£100,000 × 25%)	(25)
Reserves of B (£100,000 × 25%)	(25)
	144

* The minority in group A will take their proportion of the reserves of company B that have been consolidated with company A's reserves.

† The adjustment is necessary because the 70% minority interest in company B consolidated into company A includes the 25% held by company P.

24.376 The two methods arrive at the same result, a minority interest of £144,000. However, the use of the indirect and direct methods would not arrive at the same result when there is goodwill arising on the acquisition of company B by company A and, in such cases, the direct method should be used.

Treatment of minority on acquisition

Acquisition of direct subsidiary

24.377 When a subsidiary is acquired it is necessary to allocate to the minority its share of the net assets of the subsidiary. This is normally done in the consolidation process by allocating to the minority its share of the adjusted capital and reserves of the subsidiary (that is, after fair value adjustments). However, they are not allocated any goodwill (see para 24.354). The example that follows illustrates these principles.

Example – Calculation of minority interest on acquisition

At the end of year 1, company P acquires company S. Immediately before the acquisition the summarised balance sheets of both companies are as follows:

Summarised balance sheets	**Company P**	**Company S**
	£'000	**£'000**
Net assets	500	100
Equity share capital	200	20
Share premium account	100	–
Profit and loss reserve	200	80
Equity shareholders' funds	500	100

On the acquisition company P issues 10,000 £1 equity shares to the shareholders of company S to acquire 80% of its issued capital. The fair value of the consideration is valued at £150,000 and the fair value of the net assets of company S at the date of acquisition is determined to be £160,000. Consequently, the companies' balance sheets will look as follows after the acquisition:

Summarised balance sheets	**Company P**		**Company S**	
	£'000	**£'000**	**£'000**	**£'000**
Investment in subsidiary		150		–
Other net assets	500		100	
Fair value adjustment	–	500	60	160
		650		160
Equity share capital		210		20
Share premium		240		–
Profit and loss account		200		80
Revaluation reserve		–		60
Equity shareholders' funds		650		160

The goodwill arising on acquisition and the minority interests are calculated as follows:

Cost of control account/goodwill

	£'000		£'000
Investment	150	Equity share capital (£20,000 × 80%)	16
		P&L reserve (£80,000 × 80%)	64
		Revaluation reserve (£60,000 × 80%)	48
			128
		Goodwill	22
	150		150

Minority interests account

	£'000		£'000
Balance	32	Equity share capital (£20,000 × 20%)	4
		P&L reserve (£80,000 × 20%)	16
		Revaluation reserve (£60,000 × 20%)	12
	32		32

The consolidated balance sheet for the group immediately after the acquisition would be as follows:

Summarised consolidated balance sheet	**Group £'000**
Goodwill	22
Net assets (£500,000 + £160,000)	660
	682
Equity share capital	210
Share premium account	240
Profit and loss account reserve	200
Equity shareholders' funds	650
Minority interests	32
	682

24.378 When a subsidiary acquires another company and goodwill arises on that acquisition, that goodwill will affect the calculation of the minority interest and goodwill to be shown in the consolidated financial statements of the ultimate parent. Consider the following example:

Example – Calculation of minority interest where a company has acquired a subsidiary in which there is a minority shareholding

A parent company (company P) has an 80% owned subsidiary (company S). Company S makes an acquisition for cash of a third company (company A), which it then wholly owns. Goodwill of £100,000 arises on the acquisition of company A. How should that goodwill be reflected in the consolidated financial statements of company P. Should it be reflected as:

(a) 100% of the goodwill with 20% then being allocated to the minority; or

(b) 80% of the goodwill that arises?

Assuming that company S prepared consolidated financial statements, 100% of the goodwill would be recognised on the acquisition of company A in those financial statements.

In company P's consolidated financial statements, the argument for showing £100,000 as goodwill with a minority interest of £20,000 is that the Companies Act defines minority interest as the amount of capital and reserves attributable to shares in the subsidiary undertakings included in the consolidation held by or on behalf of persons other than the parent company and its subsidiary undertaking. [SI 2008/410 6 Sch 17(2)]. The capital and reserves attributable to the shares in the subsidiaries (or rather the net assets) would include £100,000 of the goodwill on the acquisition of company A by company S, and this would be included in company P's consolidated financial statements if no adjustment were made on consolidation. Therefore, if no adjustment is required, the consolidated financial statements of company P would include goodwill of £100,000 and a related minority interest of £20,000.

However, this raises the question of whether or not any adjustment is required. FRS 2 para 38 states:

> *'However, goodwill arising on acquisition should only be recognised with respect to the part of the subsidiary undertaking that is attributable to the interest held by the parent and its other subsidiary undertakings. No goodwill should be attributed to the minority interest.'* [FRS 2 para 38].

This might appear to mean that an adjustment is required to reduce goodwill in company P's consolidated financial statements to £80,000. However, paragraph 82 of FRS 2 explains further:

> *'The FRS requires that the goodwill arising on acquisition of a subsidiary undertaking that is not wholly owned should be recognised only in relation to the group's interest and that none should be attributed to the minority interest. Although it might be possible to estimate by extrapolation or valuation an amount of goodwill attributable to the minority when a subsidiary undertaking is acquired, this would in effect recognise an amount for goodwill that is hypothetical because the minority is not a party to the transaction by which the subsidiary undertaking is acquired.'* [FRS 2 para 82].

From this explanation, it is clear that FRS 2 is referring only to direct acquisitions by a parent of a part interest in a subsidiary. This is clear because in such a case the minority is not a party to the transaction. However, in the case of an acquisition of a third company by a partly owned subsidiary, as in the question above, the minority is a party to the transaction. Accordingly, it would appear that the requirement of FRS 2 not to attribute goodwill to the minority applies where the minority is not a party to the transaction, but does not apply where the minority is a party to the transaction. Therefore, company P should reflect 100% of the goodwill and allocate 20% to the minority.

Compulsory acquisition of minority

24.379 In certain situations it might appear that there is a minority to recognise at the year end, where one should not be recognised. Such a situation might arise, for example, where the investing company makes an offer before the year end and receives (say) 90 per cent of acceptances before the year end. If it has given notice to compulsorily acquire the minority and were to acquire the remaining 10 per cent soon after the year end, then it would be acceptable for the group not to record a minority interest in its consolidated financial statements, but explain in the notes the circumstances.

Acquisition of minority interests

24.380 Where a holding company acquires more shares in a subsidiary either by buying them from the minority or by subscribing for a fresh issue of shares in the subsidiary itself, the goodwill arising on the acquisition will need to be recalculated. The identifiable assets and liabilities of the subsidiary should be revalued to fair value and the goodwill arising on the increase in interest should be calculated by reference to those fair values. This revaluation is not required if the difference between net fair values and the carrying amounts is not material. [FRS 2 para 51]. An example of a group acquiring a minority interest is given in Table 24.28.

Table 24.28 – Acquisition of minority interests

Tesco PLC – Annual Report and Accounts – 25 February 1995

Notes to the financial statements (extract)

Note 29 Acquisitions

The company acquired a controlling interest in the Hungarian food retailer Global TH ('Global') on 28 June 1994.

On 2 September 1994 the company also acquired the UK food retailer Wm Low & Company PLC ('Wm Low'). Wm Low results from this date until 25 February 1995 have been consolidated within the group profit and loss account. In the year ended 2 September 1994 the Wm Low group made a profit after taxation of £15m (1993 – £17m).

During the year the group also acquired the remaining ordinary share capital of Ets. Catteau S.A. ('Catteau') for a consideration of £9m, increasing its holding from 95% to 100%.

All of the group's acquisitions have been accounted for using acquisition accounting.

The acquisitions of Global, Wm Low and the remaining share capital of Catteau have been consolidated into the Tesco group balance sheet as follows:

	Balance sheet at acquisition			
	Wm Low	Other	Fair value adjustments	Fair value balance sheet
	£m	£m	£m	£m
Fixed assets	240	5	27	272
Working capital	(13)	1	(2)	(14)
Taxation	(2)	–	–	(2)
Net short term borrowings	(51)	19	–	(32)
Minority interests	–	(8)	–	(8)
Shareholders' funds	174	17	25	216
Goodwill				65
Total purchase consideration				281

The purchase consideration for Wm Low includes £181m that was settled by the issue or ordinary shares in Tesco PLC. The remaining consideration for Wm Low and other acquisitions was settled by cash of £100m.

The net outflow of cash and cash equivalents for the purchase of subsidiary undertakings comprises:

	£m
Cash consideration	100
Cash at bank and in hand acquired	(26)
Bank overdrafts of acquired subsidiary undertakings	58
	132

Fair values at acquisition, total purchase consideration and goodwill are analysed as follows:

	Fair value balance sheet	Total purchase consideration	Goodwill
	£m	£m	£m
Wm Low	199	257	58
Global	14	15	1
Catteau	3	9	6
	216	281	65

Fair value adjustments

All fair value adjustments relate to the acquisition of Wm Low.	£m
Revaluation (a)	27
Accounting policy alignment	(1)
Other	(1)
	25

a) The principal adjustment relates to the revaluation of the property portfolio totalling £30m following advice from independent chartered surveyors.

There were no provisions for reorganisation or restructuring made in the accounts of Wm Low in the year ended 2 September 1994.

No fair value exercise

24.381 The example below is a continuation of the example in paragraph 24.377 and considers how to account for a reduction in the minority interests.

Example – Purchase of minority interest – no fair value exercise

On the first day of year 2 company P subscribes for a further 20,000 £1 equity shares in company S for cash amounting to £40,000. The minority interests in the subsidiary are, therefore, reduced from 20% to 10%. During the year company P makes a profit of £200,000. In the same period company S makes a loss of £30,000. Immediately prior to the share issue the fair value of company S's net assets was £180,000 compared with a book value of £170,000. As this difference is not material, company P does not intend to fair value the net assets attributable to company S included in the consolidation.

The balance sheets of company P and company S at the end of year 2 are as follows:

Summarised balance sheets	**Company P**		**Company S**	
	£'000	**£'000**	**£'000**	**£'000**
Investment in subsidiary		190		–
Other net assets				
Company P (500 — 40 + 200)		660		–
Company S (160 — 30 + 40)		–		170
		850		170
Equity share capital		210		40
Share premium		240		20
Profit and loss account	200		80	
Profit for the year	200	400	(30)	50
Revaluation reserve		–		60
Equity shareholders' funds		850		170

The goodwill arising on acquisition and the minority interests are calculated below:

Cost of control account/goodwill

	£'000			£'000
Investment (£150,000 + £40,000)	190	Equity share capital (£20,000 × 80%)		16
		Acquired in year		20
		Total capital (£40,000 × 90%)		36
		P&L reserve		
		(£80,000 × 80%)	64	
		(£80,000 × 10%)	*8	72
		Revaluation reserve		
		(£60,000 × 80%)	48	
		(£60,000 × 10%)	*6	54
		Share premium		
		(£20,000 × 90%)		18
				180
Negative goodwill	12	Initial goodwill		22
	202			202

* It is only necessary to bring into the cost of control account pre-acquisition reserves. Consequently, the additional percentage acquired need only be applied to the reserve balances at the date of acquisition, which in the example is the first day of the year. Therefore, the balances at the previous year end date have been used.

Minority interests account

	£'000		£'000
Balance	17	Equity share capital (£40,000 × 10%)	4
		Share premium (£20,000 × 10%)	2
		P&L reserve (£50,000 × 10%)	5
		Revaluation reserve (£60,000 × 10%)	6
	17		17

The consolidated profit and loss account would be arrived at in the following way:

Extract from profit and loss accounts	**Company P**	**Company S**	**Group**
	£'000	**£'000**	**£'000**
Trading profit/(loss)	200	(30)	170
Profit on ordinary activities	200	(30)	170
Minority interest (£30,000 × 10%)	–	–	3
Retained profit	200	(30)	173

The consolidated balance sheet for the group at the end of year 2 would be as follows:

Summarised consolidated balance sheet		**Group**
	£'000	**£'000**
Goodwill	22	
Negative goodwill	(12)	
		10
Net assets (£660,000 + £170,000)		830
		840
Equity share capital		210
Share premium account		240
Profit and loss account reserve	200	
Profit for the year	173	373
Equity shareholders' funds		823
Minority interests		17
		840

Consequences of fair valuing

24.382 The example that follows is exactly the same as the example above in paragraph 24.381, except that immediately prior to the share issue at the beginning of year 2 the fair value of company S's net assets is £330,000 compared with a book value of £170,000. As this difference is material to company P's consolidated financial statements it must fair value the net assets attributable to company S included in the consolidation.

Example – Purchase of minority interests – fair value exercise undertaken

The balance sheets of company P and company S at the end of year 2 are as follows:

Summarised balance sheets	**Company P**		**Company S**	
	£'000	**£'000**	**£'000**	**£'000**
Investment in subsidiary		190		–
Other net assets				
Company P (500 – 40 + 20)		660		–
Company S (160 + 40 – 30 + 160)		–		330
		850		330
Equity share capital		210		40
Share premium		240		20
Profit and loss account	200		80	
Profit for the year	200	400	(30)	50
Revaluation reserve		–		220
Equity shareholders' funds		850		330

The goodwill arising on acquisition and the minority interests are calculated below:

Cost of control account/goodwill

	£'000			£'000
Investment		Equity share capital		
(£150,000 + £40,000)	190	(£20,000 × 80%)		16
		Acquired in year		20
		Total capital (£40,000 × 90%)		36
		P&L reserve		
		(£80,000 × 80%)	64	
		(£80,000 × 10%)	*8	72
		Revaluation reserve		
		(£60,000 × 80%)	48	
		(£220,000 × 10%)	*22	70
		Share premium		
		(£20,000 × 90%)		18
				196
Negative goodwill	28	Initial goodwill		22
	218			218

* See the explanation in the previous example.

Minority interests account

	£'000		£'000
Balance	33	Equity share capital £40,000 × 10%)	4
		Share premium (20,000 × 10%)	2
		P&L reserve (£50,000 × 10%)	5
		Revaluation reserve (£220,000 × 10%)	22
	33		33

The consolidated profit and loss account is the same as that given in paragraph 24.381. The consolidated balance sheet for the group at the end of year 2 would be as follows:

Summarised consolidated balance sheet

	£'000	£'000
Goodwill	22	
Negative goodwill	(28)	
		(6)
Net assets (£660,000 + £330,000)		990
		984
Equity share capital		210
Share premium account		240
Profit and loss account reserve b/f	200	
Profit for the year	173	373
Revaluation reserve (80% × £160,000)		128
Equity shareholders' funds		951
Minority interests		33
		984

The effect of these entries is that not only is there a fair valuation of the 10% acquired, but also a revaluation of the 80% which represents the share of assets previously owned (credited to the group's revaluation reserve) and a revaluation of the share still attributable to minority interests of 10%.

An alternative approach is that the proportion of assets of the subsidiary held prior to the acquisition of part of the minority (that is, 80%) plus the proportion of assets of the subsidiary attributable to the remaining minority (that is, 10%) need not be revalued when part of the minority is acquired. If this approach is adopted, the result will be that only 10% of the assets will be subject to fair valuing at the date of the acquisition of the 10% minority. 90% of the assets will remain at their cost to the group.

Loss making subsidiaries

24.383 The treatment of minority interests requires special attention for subsidiaries that have made losses in the current year or in previous years. As seen above, minority interests for profitable subsidiaries are shown as a deduction in the profit and loss account and, consequently, reduce the group's profits transferred to shareholders' funds. Conversely, minority interests in a loss making subsidiary are, if recognised, added to the consolidated profit and account, thereby reducing the loss transferred to shareholders' funds.

24.384 The balance sheet minority interests in respect of a loss making subsidiary will be a credit if the subsidiary has net assets and will be a debit if it has net liabilities. Debit minority interests recognised in the balance sheet need careful consideration and FRS 2 requires the group to consider making a provision against such a balance where it arises. A provision should be made to the extent that the group has an obligation (whether formal or implied) to provide finance that may not be recoverable in respect of the accumulated losses attributable to the minority interests. [FRS 2 para 37]. For example, where a parent issues a letter of support to its subsidiary, the existence of the letter would indicate that there is a legal or commercial obligation on the parent to make good the losses of its subsidiary. Consequently, in these circumstances, a provision would need to be made against any debit minority interests arising on consolidation.

24.385 In situations where no provisioning is necessary it is argued that not recognising a debit minority interest balance in the consolidated balance sheet obscures the comparison between the assets and liabilities attributable to the minority interests and those attributable to group interests. This is particularly true where over a period of time accumulated losses accrue and are then made good by subsequent profits. Accumulated losses of this nature do not necessarily require funding by the parent, but, as mentioned above, a provision should be made in the consolidated balance sheet where funding is likely to be required. A debit balance does not represent an amount receivable from a minority, but rather the net liabilities attributable to the shares held by the minorities in that subsidiary.

24.386 FRS 2 makes it clear that the group should provide for any commercial or legal obligation, whether formal or implied, to provide finance that may not be recoverable in respect of the accumulated losses attributable to the minority interests. Any provision made with respect to minority debit balances should be set directly against the minority interests shown in the profit and loss account and in the balance sheet.

24.387 Provisions of this sort would go beyond merely providing against a debit balance and could include the minorities' share of any liability guaranteed by the group, or any liability that the group itself would be likely to settle for commercial or other reasons, if the subsidiary could not do so itself.

24.388 As losses are incurred by a subsidiary the minority's share of these losses will:

- First, be set against the minority's share of the subsidiary's reserves.
- Secondly, be set against the minority's share of the subsidiary's capital.
- Finally, be recognised as a debit balance in the consolidated balance sheet to the extent that the group does not have a commercial or legal obligation in respect of the losses attributable to the minority interests.

The above process should be reversed when profits attributable to the minority start to make good the losses incurred previously.

Puts and calls over minority interests

24.389 A parent may write a put option on shares in an existing subsidiary that are held by minority interests. The put option gives the minority shareholder the right to force the parent entity to purchase the shares subject to the put in accordance with the option's terms and conditions. The put might be created at the time that the parent acquires the controlling interest in the subsidiary or at some later date. The put's exercise price may be a fixed price, fair value or a formula, for example a multiple of EBITDA. A purchased call option might also accompany the written put. The call option gives the parent entity the right to force the minority shareholder to sell its shares to the parent in accordance with the option's terms and conditions. A common variation on this type of arrangement is a forward purchase contract for the shares in the subsidiary that are held by minority interests.

24.390 The terms of the put and any related call should be analysed in detail to assess whether in substance the minority interest has been acquired. It is necessary to consider whether the minority has retained the risks and rewards associated with the continued ownership of the shares or whether in substance the risks and rewards have been transferred to the parent.

24.391 Typically a put option with an exercise price at the fair value of the shares at the date of exercise will not result in a transfer of the risks and rewards until the put option is exercised. However, a put option with a fixed exercise price, that is accompanied by a similarly priced call option, exercisable at the same future date, will, in substance result in a transfer of risks and rewards of ownership of the shares to the parent from the date the options are written. In this situation, it is virtually certain that either the parent or the minority will exercise the option, as it will be in one of their economic interests to do so. If the share price falls below the fixed strike price the minority will exercise the put option and sell the shares (that is, the parent has retained access to the risks) and if the share price increases above the fixed strike price the parent will exercise the call option and buy the shares (that is, the parent has retained access to the benefits). Even if the minority retains the right to dividends during the put and call exercise period, the risks and rewards of ownership have transferred to the parent as the parent has full control over whether dividends are to be paid to the minority.

24.392 Judgement should be applied in assessing when the risks and rewards of ownership are transferred from the minority interest shareholder to the parent. A fixed price put and a call option with matching exercise prices and dates is economically the same as a forward purchase contract. The accounting for a matching put and call should, therefore, be the same as for a forward purchase contract.

24.393 If the risks and rewards of the shares subject to the put have transferred to the parent, the minority is treated as having been acquired. The minority interest is derecognised and goodwill is calculated on the additional interest acquired (see para 24.380). No amounts are allocated to the minority in respect of the shares subject to the put. A liability is recognised for management's best estimate of the present value of the put option's redemption amount.

24.394 The accretion of the discount on the put liability is recognised as a finance charge in the profit and loss account.

24.395 If the put was written over an existing subsidiary, any adjustments to the expected settlement amount included in the estimated amount of the liability are recognised in the income statement. If the put was written at the time the controlling interest in the subsidiary was acquired (that is, as part of a business combination) the put liability is treated as contingent consideration and, therefore, other than the accretion of discount, any adjustments to the estimated amount of the liability are recognised against goodwill. [FRS 7 para 81].

24.396 If the risks and rewards have not transferred to the parent, then the minority interest is not treated as having been acquired.

24.397 Companies applying FRS 26 are required to account for derivatives on an interest in a subsidiary in accordance with FRS 26, unless the derivative meets the definition of an equity instrument of the entity in FRS 25. [FRS 26 para 2(a)]. FRS 25 applies to all derivatives on interests in subsidiaries, associates and joint ventures and, therefore, this standard determines the debt/equity classification of such derivative interests.

24.398 However, the accounting that results is complex as FRS 2 requires that a minority interest is recognised in respect of the shares subject to the put and FRS 25 additionally requires that a liability is recognised for management's best estimate of present value of the put option's redemption amount. Paragraph 23 of FRS 25 states:

> *'A contract that contains an obligation for an entity to purchase its own equity instruments for cash or another financial asset gives rise to a financial liability for the present value of the redemption amount (for example, for the present value of the forward repurchase price, option*

exercise price or other redemption amount). This is the case even if the contract itself is an equity instrument.' [FRS 25 para 23].

24.399 Minority interests are presented in the consolidated balance sheet within equity. Therefore, if a parent enters into a contract to purchase the shares of a subsidiary, in the consolidated financial statements, this is a contract to purchase own equity. In addition, when classifying a financial instrument in consolidated financial statements it is necessary to consider whether the group as a whole has an obligation that results in liability classification. [FRS 25 para AG 29]. Shares that are puttable by the minority back to the group are more appropriately classified as a liability rather than equity as the group has no discretion to refuse redemption of the shares should the minority exercise the put option.

24.400 The minority interest continues to be recognised as normal. A liability is recognised in respect of the put, measured at management's best estimate of the redemption amount discounted back from the expected redemption date. [FRS 25 para AG27(b)]. The put liability is recognised by reclassification from parent equity (not minority interest). The accretion of the discount on the put liability is recognised as a finance charge in the income statement. The put liability is re-measured to the final redemption amount and any adjustments to the estimated amount of the liability are recognised in the income statement, also as a finance charge.

24.401 On exercise of the put, the liability is eliminated as paid. The minority interest is derecognised and goodwill is calculated on the additional interest acquired (see further para 24.380). The amounts charged to finance costs (accretion of discount and adjustments in re-measuring the liability) during the exercise period of the put are in effect re-categorised from retained earnings to goodwill (because goodwill is calculated based on the actual cash paid at the date risks and rewards transfer). If the put option lapses unexercised, the liability is derecognised against equity.

Section IV — Transferring business around a group

24.402 Chapter 25 considers in detail group reconstruction relief under section 611 of the Companies Act 2006. Group reconstruction relief can be taken in certain situations where assets are transferred around the group where the acquiring company issues shares and where the subsidiaries concerned are wholly-owned. However, many transfers of business are transacted for cash or are left outstanding on the inter-company account and often transactions of this type within a group are not transacted at fair value.

Transfer of a business from a subsidiary to its parent

24.403 An issue arises where a parent acquires a subsidiary and transfers the business of that subsidiary to its parent. This is often referred to as a 'hive-up'. These transfers are carried out at fair value, at book value or at some other amount. This transaction can happen at the same time as the original acquisition of the subsidiary or at a later date.

24.404 These transactions are commonly undertaken at book value (perhaps to achieve a certain tax result). Often the consideration is payable *via* an inter-company account. The issue is how to account for the transaction and in particular whether it is necessary to impair the investment in the subsidiary after the hive-up has taken place. From a group perspective, such a transaction does not result in any loss of value.

24.405 A hive up where the parent acquires a business from its wholly-owned subsidiary can be accounted for in two ways. An entity can account for such a transaction using merger accounting principles (that is, predecessor values) or account for the transaction using acquisition accounting in accordance with FRS 6. If an entity has undertaken such transactions before, then it should generally account for the transaction using the same accounting policy it has previously used.

Example – Hive up immediately after acquisition.

Company A acquires company B for fair value £100. Immediately after the acquisition, 100% of company B's business (net assets) is transferred to company A for £40, the carrying value of the business in company B's financial statements. The fair value of the net assets is £80 and the consideration is payable *via* the inter-company account.

This is the first transaction of this type company A has undertaken, hence it should select an appropriate accounting policy and apply this consistently to all future transactions of this type. The initial investment in company B would be recorded as follows:

Company A:		
	£	£
Dr Investment in company B	100	
Cr Cash		100

To recognise the initial purchase of the investment in company B.

If predecessor values are used, then generally it is necessary to look to the values in the highest level of the group.

If company A had prepared consolidated financial statements immediately after the acquisition but before the hive-up, it would have recorded net assets acquired of £80 and goodwill of £20 for company B.

Using predecessor values would give the following accounting entries:

	£	£
Dr Net assets acquired	80	
Dr Goodwill	20	
Cr Investment in company B		60
Cr Inter-company payable		40

To record the acquisition of the business of company B at its predecessor values that would have arisen in the consolidated financial statements of company A had those been prepared immediately after the acquisition.

The credit to the investment in company B is in substance part of the consideration for the acquisition (that is, part of the investment's value is given up as consideration).

(Note: that the same principles would apply if company A were a NewCo.)

Company B:		
	£	£
Cr Net assets transferred		40
Dr Inter-company receivable	40	

To record the transfer of assets to company A.

If acquisition accounting is used in accordance with the acquisition accounting rules in FRS 6, a full fair value exercise would need to be carried out on acquisition. Where a hive-up takes place immediately after an acquisition, applying acquisition accounting to the hive-up results in the same accounting entries as if predecessor values had been used.

The use of predecessor values or acquisition accounting is a policy choice for the company. Normally this choice would result in different accounting, but in the circumstance where the transfer of the business is made immediately after the acquisition, both policies result in the same accounting.

24.406 Where the transaction takes place some time after the original acquisition it can be argued that there has not been another business combination, because company A and its group acquired company B some time ago. If this argument is followed it is necessary to develop an accounting policy for this transaction and following this approach using merger accounting principles (that is, predecessor values) is an appropriate method. However, there might be other situations where the facts and circumstances could justify a different accounting approach.

Example – Hive up some time after original acquisition.

Using the same basic facts as in the example in paragraph 24,405, except that, the business is transferred to company A for £45, the net assets of company B in the consolidated financial statements are £90 and the goodwill recognised is £20 at the date of the transfer. Taking the values in the highest level of the group, using predecessor values this would give the following accounting entries.

Company A		
	£	£
Dr Net assets acquired	90	
Dr Goodwill	20	
Cr Investment in company B		55
Cr Inter-company payable		45
Cr Unrealised reserve		10

To record the reorganisation of the business of company B at its predecessor values in the consolidated financial statements of company A and to recognise an increase in shareholders' funds.

The credit to the investment in company B is in substance part of the consideration for the reorganisation (that is, part of the investment's value is given up as consideration).

Transfer of a subsidiary from one group member to another

24.407 Groups may reorganise themselves by transferring subsidiaries or businesses around the group for less than the carrying amount of the investment, for example, for the carrying amount of the subsidiary's net assets or for no consideration. This can appear to cause an impairment of the parent's investment in the transferor. Consider this example:

Example – Impairment in a group reorganisation

Company A has direct 100% subsidiaries B and C. Company C has a 100% subsidiary D.

```
      A
     / \
    B   C
        |
        D
```

Company A:	
Investment in company B	£100m
Investment in company C	£200m
Company C:	
Investment in company D	C150m
Other assets	C50m
Company D:	
Net assets	C120m

The recoverable amounts of company A's investments in company B and company C exceed their carrying amounts. Company A accounts for investments in subsidiaries at historical cost.

In this reorganisation company C transfers its investment in company D to company B for £120m cash, being the carrying amount of company D's net assets. Company C accounts for the transaction at transaction price and records a loss of £30m. Following the transaction, the recoverable amount of company A's investment in company C falls to £170m. Hence, company A's investment in company C appears to be impaired. However, company A has not suffered any loss of value and so it would not be appropriate to recognise an impairment.

Company A should account for a transfer of value from the investment in company C to the investment in company B. As this type of transaction is not covered by UK GAAP an accounting policy should be developed to support this treatment. This treatment is supported by FRS 5, 'Substance of transactions', as this requires transactions to be accounted for and presented in accordance with their substance and economic reality and not merely their legal form.

This method recognises that the cost to company A of this transaction is a reduction in the value of its investment in company C, so recognition of this value as part of the investment in company B is a cost method.

24.408 In many cases it is inappropriate to transfer the full carrying amount of the investment in company C to the investment in company B, because company C may retain other assets, and company D may be one of many subsidiaries of company C. The transfer should be done at a value that reflects the economic effect of the transaction. Therefore, one approach would be to measure the value transferred based on the relative values of the portion of company C's group that is transferred and the portion that is retained by company C.

24.409 Therefore, on the transfer of a subsidiary as in the example in paragraph 24.407, an entity may choose to transfer value from its investment in the transferor subsidiary to its investment in the transferee subsidiary. The value transferred is measured based on the relative values of the transferred subsidiary and the remainder of the transferor's group, unless it can be demonstrated that another method better reflects the value transferred.

Example – Transfer of investment value based on relative values

This example uses the same facts as the example in paragraph 24.407. If the fair value of company D is £170m and the fair value of company C's group after the transaction is £170m, company A transfers half of its investment in company C to the investment in company B, that is, £100m, because company A's investment in company C before the transfer was £200m.

Transfer of a subsidiary by dividend

24.410 Where the transfer of the subsidiary is achieved by means of a dividend between companies under common control, the transferee recognises the dividend at the fair value of the investment received. The transferor has an accounting policy choice as to whether to recognise the dividend at the book value or fair value of the investment that is being distributed.

Chapter 25

Acquisition accounting

Chapter 25

Acquisition accounting

Introduction

25.1 Under UK GAAP, there are two accounting methods that might be applicable in a business combination. Groups will generally have to use acquisition accounting, but in certain exceptional circumstances merger accounting *must* be used to account for the business combination. There are now strict conditions that must be satisfied before merger accounting may be adopted.

25.2 The Companies Act 2006 contains rules on acquisition accounting and merger accounting. Schedule 6 to SI 2008/410 states that an acquisition should be accounted for by the acquisition method of accounting, unless the conditions for accounting for it as a merger are met and the merger method of accounting is adopted. [SI 2008/410 6 Sch 8]. Merger accounting is optional under the Companies Act 2006, but must be used where the merger accounting conditions set out in FRS 6 are met (see further chapter 28).

25.3 Although the criteria for merger accounting in FRS 6 are strict, international standard-setters do not consider that they are sufficient to enable 'true mergers' to be distinguished from business combinations in which one entity obtains control of another entity (or entities). The IASB's IFRS 3 and IFRS 3 (revised, issued in 2008), 'Business combinations', and the business combination standard for US GAAP prohibit merger accounting. They require the use of acquisition accounting ('the purchase method') for all business combinations within their scope.

Comparison of acquisition accounting to merger accounting

25.4 Before considering the detailed accounting requirements that apply to business combinations, it is useful to understand the three main differences between acquisition accounting and merger accounting, which are explained in the paragraphs below.

25.5 In acquisition accounting, the consolidated financial statements reflect the acquired company's results from the date of acquisition only. However, in merger accounting, the consolidated financial statements incorporate the combined companies' results as if the companies had always been combined. Consequently, under merger accounting, the consolidated financial statements reflect both companies' full year's results, even though the business combination may have occurred part of the way through the year. Under merger accounting, the corresponding amounts in the consolidated financial statements for the previous year should reflect the results of the combined companies, even though the business combination did not occur until the current year.

25.6 In acquisition accounting, the acquiring group should attribute fair values to the identifiable assets and liabilities of the acquired business at the date of acquisition. These fair values are used as the initial carrying values (or 'cost') in the acquiring group's balance sheet. However, in merger accounting, the group does not restate any assets and liabilities to their fair values. Instead, the group incorporates the assets and liabilities at the amounts recorded in the books of the combined companies, adjusted only to achieve harmonisation of accounting policies.

25.7 Acquisition accounting may give rise to goodwill on consolidation. However, goodwill does not arise in merger accounting. Merger accounting may lead to differences on consolidation. For example, in merger accounting, there may be a difference between the nominal value of the shares issued together with the fair value of any additional consideration given and the nominal value of the other company's shares that have been acquired. However, such differences are not goodwill as defined in FRS 10 because they are not based on the fair values of both the consideration given and the identifiable assets and liabilities acquired.

25.8 An example that demonstrates the difference between acquisition accounting and merger accounting is given in chapter 28. It is somewhat artificial in that the two methods are not alternatives in accounting for the same transaction and hence it is merely illustrative.

25.9 The rules governing how to account for the acquisition of a subsidiary are now contained in FRS 2, FRS 6, FRS 7, FRS 10 and the Companies Act. This chapter considers the requirements that determine how a company should account for the acquisition of a subsidiary including the disclosure requirements (contained in section I), the fair valuing rules (contained in section II) and accounting for goodwill (contained in section III).

Section I — Accounting for acquisitions

25.10 This section considers primarily the accounting treatment that should be adopted when a subsidiary is acquired and also considers some of the problems that arise with piecemeal acquisitions. Many investments that end up as subsidiaries start out as much smaller interests in the undertakings concerned and may be treated in the group's financial statements in a variety of ways before they actually become subsidiaries. The most common way for an undertaking to become a subsidiary of another is by acquisition. It is also possible for a parent to gain a subsidiary other than by acquisition, for example:

- By gaining the power to control without acquiring a further interest in an undertaking, perhaps by virtue of an agreement with another shareholder.

- By enforcement of a security by a lender where a creditor defaults on a loan or breaches a covenant.
- By the company purchasing and cancelling its own shares held by third parties.
- By changes to the voting rights attached to shares.

25.11 These issues are fully explained in this section, which also outlines the disclosure that is required in the year that a company acquires a subsidiary. This section also considers the accounting for reverse acquisitions, where it is the acquired company's shareholders and board of directors who effectively control the combined group even though the other party is the legal acquirer.

Merger relief and group reconstruction relief

25.12 It is extremely important in any business combination to understand how merger relief might impact the accounting treatment. Merger relief is a relief given under section 612 of the Companies Act 2006 from the need to transfer to a share premium account the difference between the nominal value of any shares issued by the company to acquire shares in another company and the fair value of those issued shares. Merger relief does not only apply to business combinations accounted for as mergers, it also applies to those accounted for using acquisition accounting techniques. By obtaining merger relief a group may be able to distribute pre-acquisition profits which would otherwise be locked in the subsidiary it acquires. The rules as they apply to both acquisitions and mergers are considered in chapter 23.

25.13 Group reconstruction relief is a relief given under section 611 of the Companies Act 2006. Group reconstruction relief can be taken in certain situations where assets are transferred around the group and where the subsidiaries concerned are wholly owned. This relief applies to the transfer of both shares in wholly-owned group companies and other assets where the consideration is shares issued by the group company acquiring the assets. Chapter 23 explores this complex area and explains in detail how the minimum premium value is calculated on such transactions, being the amount that it is necessary to credit to the share premium.

Summary of accounting rules

25.14 As explained above, there are two methods that a parent company can use to account for a business combination in its consolidated financial statements. The vast majority of business combinations are accounted for using acquisition accounting and only a small minority are required to use merger accounting.

25.15 The rules concerning acquisition accounting are contained in FRS 2, FRS 6, FRS 7 and FRS 10, as well as the Act. These rules, which deal with the determination of the date of acquisition, the method of consolidating a new subsidiary and the accounting treatment for changes in stake, are dealt with in the following section of this chapter.

25.16 Acquisitions of subsidiaries can also arise where a parent sells a subsidiary for shares in another undertaking, which results in that other undertaking becoming a subsidiary of the vendor. Therefore, at the same time as the acquisition, there is a disposal. This is addressed by UITF Abstract 31, 'Exchanges of businesses or other non-monetary assets for an interest in a subsidiary, joint venture or associate'. The accounting for these transactions is dealt with in chapter 26.

25.17 Although FRS 6 primarily defines the situations where merger accounting must be used, it also brings together in one standard most of the disclosure requirements that must be followed for all business combinations, whether accounted for as acquisitions or mergers (including those required by the Act). However, most of the disclosure requirements concerning goodwill arising on an acquisition are set out in FRS 10.

Date of changes in group membership

Background

25.18 The date on which an undertaking becomes or ceases to be a subsidiary marks the point at which a new accounting treatment for that undertaking in the group's consolidated financial statements applies. The Act does not define the effective date of acquisition or disposal. However, the Act does state that undertakings that the group controls, or has the power to control, should be consolidated and that other undertakings should not be consolidated. FRS 2, therefore, contains a definition which is based entirely on the passing of control (or the power to control).

Definition

25.19 Both the Act and FRS 2 require consolidation of undertakings that the investing company has the power to control.

25.20 The date of change in group membership is the date on which control of that undertaking passes to its new parent undertaking. Furthermore, this date is said in FRS 2 to be the date of acquisition for the purposes of paragraph 9 of Schedule 6 to SI 2008/410 (which is the Act's requirement to account for the purchase of a subsidiary using acquisition accounting). [FRS 2 para 45]. The date, therefore, hinges on 'control' (or the power to control) passing and control is defined as:

> *"The ability of an undertaking to direct the financial and operating policies of another undertaking with a view to gaining economic benefits from its activities."* [FRS 2 para 6].

Gaining the power to control would equally mark a change in group membership. Use of 'control' in the following paragraphs should be taken to mean 'control, or the power to control'.

25.21 The definition of control refers to 'gaining economic benefits'. This is not intended to be interpreted restrictively, but covers a wide range of situations in practice, including gaining benefits:

- In the form of current or future profits.
- By preventing another competitor from buying the business.
- By preventing a key supplier or distributor from going out of business.
- By reducing losses of the acquiring group.

For undertakings that are not formed for the purpose of making profits, for example charities, the economic benefits will not necessarily be profit related.

25.22 The date of change in group membership under FRS 2 should also be taken as the date on which an undertaking becomes or ceases to be a subsidiary under section 1162 of the Companies Act 2006. In practice, although it may often be difficult to determine, the date on which control passes is a matter of fact and cannot be backdated or artificially altered. [FRS 2 para 84]. Consequently, the definition under FRS 2 applies even if the acquirer has a right to profits from a date earlier than the effective date of acquisition.

25.23 The following factors could, for example, indicate that the acquirer has gained control of an undertaking:

- The acquirer starts to direct the operating and financial policies of the acquired undertaking.
- The acquirer starts to benefit from the economic benefits arising from the undertaking. However, this does not cover the situation where a potential acquirer is given a right to profits from a date which is conditional on the completion of the purchase at some later date. Equally, it does not apply to an agreement giving the acquirer rights to past profits.
- The date the consideration is paid. The payment date for the consideration will often in simple acquisitions be the date on which control passes, however, this cannot be assumed because this date can easily be manipulated. Furthermore, payment of consideration is often made by instalments and, as a consequence, may have little relevance to when control passes.

25.24 In practice, control might pass in a number of ways, which will often depend on whether the offer for the entity is made to the public (a public offer) or is a private sale (a private treaty) or is effected by the issue or cancellation of shares.

25.25 Where control is transferred by a public offer, the date control is transferred is the date the offer becomes unconditional. This will usually be the date on which a sufficient number of acceptances are received to enable the new parent to exercise control over the undertaking. [FRS 2 para 85]. Under a private treaty, the date control is transferred is generally the date an unconditional offer is accepted. [FRS 2 para 85].

25.26 It can be seen that in both a public offer and a private treaty, the key to control passing is dependent on acceptance of *unconditional* terms. The negotiations to purchase or sell a subsidiary may take place over a considerable period and there may be considerable delays between the time when agreement is reached in principle and the time when the legal formalities are completed. Other conditions, such as third party or shareholder approval may also take time to be satisfied. Until such time as agreement is reached and all conditions are satisfied, the transaction cannot be regarded as unconditional.

25.27 Where an undertaking becomes a subsidiary through an issue of shares or by a cancellation of shares, the date that control will be transferred is the date on which those shares are issued or cancelled. [FRS 2 para 85].

Effective date post balance sheet

25.28 Where the effective date of acquisition of a subsidiary is after the parent's year end, but before the consolidated financial statements are approved and signed on behalf of the board, the transaction should be treated as a non-adjusting post balance sheet event in accordance with the requirements of paragraph 21 of FRS 21, 'Events after the balance sheet date'. If the group wishes to show the effect that this post balance sheet acquisition will have, it will be necessary for it to prepare proforma accounts in addition to its statutory financial statements.

Consolidation of a new subsidiary

25.29 The Companies Act 2006 sets out the basic requirements for consolidating a subsidiary when it is first acquired in SI 2008/410. It specifies that:

- The identifiable assets and liabilities of the undertaking acquired should be included in the consolidated balance sheet at their fair values as at the date of acquisition.
- The income and expenditure of the undertaking acquired should be brought into the consolidated financial statements from the date of the acquisition.
- The interest of the group in the adjusted capital and reserves of the undertaking acquired should be offset against the acquisition cost of the group's interest in the shares of the undertaking. The difference if positive represents goodwill and if negative represents a negative consolidation difference (that is, negative goodwill).

[SI 2008/410 6 Sch 9].

25.30 Consequently, on an acquisition it is necessary to ascertain the following elements in respect of the undertaking acquired in order to account for that undertaking as a subsidiary on consolidation:

- Acquisition cost.
- Adjusted capital and reserves.
- Identifiable assets and liabilities.
- Date for recognising profits or losses from operations.

Each of these elements of acquisition accounting is considered in the paragraphs that follow.

Acquisition cost

25.31 The Companies Act 1985 defined 'acquisition cost' incurred in acquiring a subsidiary to include the amount of any cash consideration paid and the fair value of any other consideration (such as shares and debentures), together with fees and other expenses of the acquisition. This definition was not carried forward into the Companies Act 2006. However, our view is that the previous definition would still apply. FRS 7 deals with the fair value issues that arise when determining the cost of acquisition and these issues are considered in detail in section II, paragraph 25.383.

25.32 When a company issues shares as part of the consideration to acquire a subsidiary, the difference between the fair value of the consideration and the nominal value of the shares issued has to be credited to the share premium account, unless the company is eligible for merger relief. Eligibility for merger relief is considered in detail in chapter 23. If the company can obtain merger relief on the issue, the difference between the fair value of the shares issued and their nominal value is credited to a merger reserve (as opposed to a share premium account) or need not be recorded in the parent company's own financial statements. Where a merger reserve is used, the parent's investment will be recorded in its financial statements at an amount equal to the fair value of the investment.

25.33 Where a merger reserve is not set up on an acquisition, the investment will be recorded in the parent's financial statements at the nominal value of shares issued plus the fair value of any other consideration given in the acquisition. This is discussed further in paragraph 25.49 onwards.

25.34 Where the parent company does not recognise the merger reserve in its own financial statements, the merger reserve will be brought into the consolidated financial statements as part of the consolidation adjustment for goodwill (that is, to include the consideration for the acquisition at fair value).

Fees and expenses of acquisition

25.35 The fees and expenses of an acquisition have to be analysed. Some may relate to the issue of any capital instruments (that is, shares or debt) given as part of the consideration. Issue costs are defined in FRS 4 as:

> *"The costs that are incurred directly in connection with the issue of a capital instrument, that is, those costs that would not have been incurred had the specific instrument in question not been issued."* [FRS 4 para 10].

25.36 However, FRS 4 has been superseded by FRS 26 and, for those companies applying FRS 26 (see further chapter 6), the equivalent term is 'transaction costs', which are defined as:

> *"...incremental costs that are directly applicable to the acquisition, issue or disposal of a financial asset or financial liability... An incremental cost is one that would not have been occurred if the entity had not acquired, issued or disposed of the financial instrument."* [FRS 26 para 9].

25.37 The definitions of issue costs are restrictive and their accounting treatment complex. Further guidance on issue costs is given in chapter 6.

25.38 Certain fees and expenses of acquisition that do not relate to the issue of capital instruments can be added to the cost of an investment. These fees and expenses are considered further in section II, paragraph 25.426. However, the UITF clarified in Information sheet 35 that costs such as arrangement fees for bridging finance facilities, participation fees and costs of researching alternative financing arrangements for a takeover, that do not qualify as issue costs under FRS 4, are not incremental costs incurred directly in making an acquisition. Such costs should not be included as part of the cost of the acquisition, but should be written off immediately. Similarly, FRS 26 notes that: *"transaction costs include fees and commissions paid to agents, advisers, brokers and dealers, levies by regulatory agencies and securities exchanges, and transfer taxes and duties. Transaction costs do not include debt premiums or discounts, financing costs or internal administrative or holding costs"*. [FRS 26 para AG13].

Adjusted capital and reserves acquired

25.39 The Companies Act 2006 requires that the adjusted capital and reserves is set off against the acquisition cost of the acquired subsidiary in order to ascertain the figure of goodwill (or negative goodwill) arising on the acquisition. In this context 'adjusted capital and reserves' means the subsidiary's capital and reserves at the date of acquisition after adjusting the undertaking's identifiable assets and liabilities to fair values. [SI 2008/410 6 Sch 9(4)]. This is equivalent to 'adjusted net assets'. Consequently, the subsidiary's adjusted capital and reserves will be made up of its capital and reserves disclosed in its books of account adjusted for any changes in the value of net assets determined in fair valuing its assets and liabilities. The following example illustrates this provision of the legislation.

Example — Adjusted capital reserves acquired

Company A acquires 80% of company B. The acquisition cost is £50m and at the date of acquisition, the reserves of the subsidiary are determined as follows:

Capital and reserves of company B

	£m
Share capital	2
Share premium account	1
Revaluation reserve	10
Profit and loss account	15
Total capital and reserves	28

Company A carries out a fair value exercise on Company B as at the date of acquisition and ascertains that its fixed assets and stocks have values in excess of their book values of £12m and £3.5m respectively.

Adjusted capital and reserves of company B

	£m
Capital and reserves (as above)	28.0
Fair value adjustment	15.5
Total capital and reserves	43.5

Consequently, the difference arising on consolidation (goodwill) would be calculated as follows:

Difference arising on consolidation

	£m
Acquisition cost	50.0
Adjusted capital and reserves (£43.5m × 80%)	(34.8)
Goodwill	15.2

Identifiable assets and liabilities

25.40 The Companies Act 2006 requires in SI 2008/410 that the subsidiary's identifiable assets and liabilities must be included in the consolidated balance sheet at their fair values, as at the date of acquisition. [SI 2008/410 6 Sch 9(2)]. For this purpose the Act defines 'identifiable assets and liabilities' to mean the:

> *"...assets or liabilities which are capable of being disposed of or discharged separately, without disposing of a business of the undertaking."* [SI 2008/410 6 Sch 9(2)].

FRS 7, which also applies to entities other than companies, contains an equivalent definition.

25.41 The test to establish whether an asset should be included in the category of identifiable assets, is whether the asset can be identified and sold separately without disposing of a business as a whole. In this context, goodwill is clearly not separable from a business as a whole. Such assets, however, may well include other intangible assets (including trade marks and publishing titles) and their valuation is considered in more detail in chapter 15.

25.41.1 There is no guidance in the Act on how to determine the fair values of assets and liabilities, but rules on fair valuing are detailed in FRS 7. Ascertaining the fair values of identifiable assets is very difficult in practice and substantial problems can arise. These issues are considered in detail in section II, paragraph 25.232.

Recording adjustments to fair values

25.42 Although an acquiring company has to carry out a fair value exercise as at the date of acquisition, there is no general requirement to record these values in the books of account of the subsidiary (unless, for example, they relate to impairments of assets). The adjustments would be made in the subsidiary's books of account if they were consistent with the subsidiary's accounting policies. Therefore, a write down of stock to its net realisable value (where this is lower than cost) would be recognised in the subsidiary's books. However, it is not normally possible for UK subsidiaries to record their stocks at a fair value that exceeds cost, because the Act and SSAP 9 require stocks to be valued at the lower of cost and net realisable value. [SI 2008/410 1 Sch 24; SSAP 9 para 26].

Treatment of goodwill

25.43 Any difference between the total of the subsidiary's acquisition cost (that is, the fair value of the purchase consideration plus expenses) and the group's share of the subsidiary's adjusted capital and reserves represents purchased goodwill arising on consolidation (or, if negative, negative goodwill, termed a negative consolidation difference in the Companies Act 2006). [SI 2008/410 6 Sch 9(5); FRS 10 para 2; FRS 6 para 20]. The treatment of both goodwill and negative goodwill arising on consolidation is considered in section III, paragraph 25.451.

Date for recognising trading

25.44 SI 2008/410 states that income and expenditure of the subsidiary should only be brought into the consolidated financial statements from the date of acquisition. [SI 2008/410 6 Sch 9(3)]. The date of acquisition is discussed under the heading of 'date of changes in group membership' above from paragraph 25.18 onwards. Similarly, FRS 6 requires that the results and cash flows of the acquired company should be brought into the consolidated financial statements only from the date of acquisition. [FRS 6 para 20].

25.45 It is, therefore, necessary on an acquisition to apportion the results between pre-acquisition and post-acquisition on a reasonably accurate basis. In practice, this is often achieved by using the subsidiary's management accounts or completion accounts, if any, prepared as at the date of acquisition. However, there may be rare situations where there is no alternative but to use a time apportionment method. Where such a method is used, however, it will be necessary to identify any profit and loss account items that do not arise evenly over the accounting period. For such items, a time apportionment would not be acceptable. For example, this may be the situation with exceptional items. Such items would, therefore, need to be analysed into the period in which they arose and treated as either pre-acquisition or post-acquisition.

25.46 Under FRS 3, the operating results of continuing operations have to be shown separately from those of discontinued operations. Furthermore, acquisitions in the period have to be shown separately as a component of continuing operations. As a minimum on the face of the profit and loss account, turnover and operating profit have to be analysed between continuing operations, acquisitions as a component of continuing operations and discontinued operations. In addition, this analysis has also to be given in the notes (if not given on the face of the profit and loss account) for each of the profit and loss account format line items between turnover and operating profit. The provisions of FRS 3 are dealt with in detail in chapter 8.

25.47 Although the method of consolidating the results in the profit and loss account outlined above has to be adopted, groups may still wish to give their members an idea of what the results of the new group would have looked like for a whole period's trading. Clearly, the shareholders will not be able to ascertain this picture entirely from the consolidated results as presented, although for 'substantial acquisitions' as defined in FRS 6 a summarised profit and loss account and statement of total recognised gains and losses has to be given for the subsidiary acquired from the beginning of its last accounting reference period to the date of acquisition (see further paragraph 25.109). [FRS 6 para 36]. There is no reason, however, why the group should not also include in its consolidated financial statements a *pro forma* consolidated profit and loss account in a note showing the combined results of all subsidiaries for the entire period of trading, regardless of when they were acquired. In addition, the group may wish to disclose a *pro forma* earnings per share in a note based on the *pro forma* consolidated profit and loss. In this way, it is possible for a group to account for its acquisition using acquisition accounting in its statutory financial statements, but retain some of the benefits of the merger accounting principles, namely of reporting the trends of the enlarged group as if the subsidiary has always been combined with the rest of the group.

25.48 Where the group decides to include this type of additional information in its consolidated financial statements, it should not give the *pro forma* accounts more prominence than its statutory accounts.

The parent company's financial statements

Carrying value of investment

25.49 The Companies Act 2006 clarifies the accounting treatment of an investment in an acquired company that should be used in an issuing company's balance sheet where there is:

- Merger relief under section 612 of the Companies Act 2006.
- Group reconstruction relief under section 611 of the Companies Act 2006.

25.50 In these circumstances, the amount at which the issuing company carries its investment in the acquired company does not need to include an amount corresponding to the premium (or the part of the premium) that the issuing company has not credited to its share premium account. [CA06 Sec 615]. That is, the issuing company has a choice. Disregarding other considerations such as cash, the issuing company can record both the shares it issues and the investment in the new subsidiary at either:

- the nominal value of the shares issued and any minimum premium under section 611 of the Companies Act 2006; or
- the fair value of the shares issued, with the premium in excess of any minimum premium under section 611 of the Companies Act 2006 credited to a merger reserve instead of to a share premium account.

25.51 Although the Act says that the value of the investment shown in the balance sheet need not include the premium, it appears that FRS 4 would require it to do so where merger relief or group reconstruction relief is taken, but acquisition accounting is adopted for the business combination. This is because FRS 4 requires that the net proceeds from the issue of equity shares should be credited to shareholders' funds. 'Net proceeds' are defined as *'the fair value of the consideration received on the issue of a capital instrument after deduction of issue costs'*. [FRS 4 para 11].

25.52 This issue does not arise for entities that are applying FRS 26, because FRS 26 (which supersedes FRS 4) excludes from its scope investments in subsidiaries. There is no applicable accounting standard and the permission within the Act is unrestricted.

25.53 Therefore, where acquisition accounting is adopted on consolidation for the business combination, FRS 4 would appear to require the shares issued by the acquiring company to be recorded at fair value. This does not mean that the difference between the nominal value and the fair value would be credited to share premium account. Only the minimum premium value, where group reconstruction relief is taken, would be credited to that account. The balance of the difference (all of it, if merger relief is taken) would be credited to a separate reserve, normally called a merger reserve.

25.54 As the shares issued would then be recorded at fair value, it follows that the investment would also have to be recorded at fair value in these circumstances.

25.55 However, where merger accounting is adopted for the business combination, on consolidation the requirements of FRS 4 do not apply to equity shares issued. There is an exception in FRS 4 for equity shares issued as part of a business combination that is accounted for as a merger. This exception appears only to apply to equity shares that are issued and not to non-equity shares that are issued.

25.56 Despite the apparent requirements of FRS 4 in this regard, it has become clear since the issue of FRS 4 that it was not the ASB's intention to restrict the reliefs available under section 615 of the Companies Act 2006 where either acquisition or merger accounting is adopted. As evidence of this the Appendix to FRS 6, 'Note on Legal Requirements', states:

> *"The FRS deals only with the method of accounting to be used in group accounts; it does not deal with the form of accounting to be used in the acquiring or issuing company's own accounts and in particular does not restrict the reliefs available under Sections 611, 612 and 615 of the Companies Act."*

In addition, in paragraph 6 to Appendix 1 to FRS 7, the ASB states:

> *"...where (if the merger relief provisions apply) the premiums are disregarded, the cost of investment in the parent company's books will be different from the cost of acquisition for the purposes of paragraph 9(4)."* [SI 2008/410 6 Sch 9(4)].

25.57 Therefore, the apparent requirements of FRS 4 may be disregarded both when acquisition accounting and merger accounting is adopted. This does not prevent a company from recording the shares issued and the investment acquired at fair value where acquisition accounting is adopted, if it wishes, but does leave a choice.

25.58 Where acquisition (or merger) accounting is adopted on consolidation and the investment shown in the holding company's balance sheet does not include the premium, it is debatable whether the investment should be described as being at cost, because the amount shown in the balance sheet may be quite different from the actual cost. It could be argued that the 'true' cost of the shares issued is their fair value and not their nominal value. Consequently, the company may need to use appropriate wording other than 'cost' to describe the investment (for example, 'at nominal value of shares issued').

Example

A company owns 40% of another company that it acquired for cash several years ago. It decides to acquire the remaining 60% in an exchange for shares. Merger accounting does not apply, but merger relief is available. The company is considering how it should record its investment in the parent company's financial statements.

Even though merger accounting is not available, the parent can record its investment at the nominal value of the shares it issues in exchange for the 60% interest, plus the existing cost of the investment. Alternatively, the fair value of the shares issued can be added to the previous investment cost. The difference between the fair values of the shares issued and their nominal value would then be shown as a merger reserve (as opposed to share premium).

25.59 Where one company acquires another company, the identifiable assets and liabilities acquired from the point of view of the acquiring company will be the shares in the acquired company, not the individual assets and liabilities of the acquired company. Consequently, when one company acquires another company, purchased goodwill will not arise in the parent's balance sheet.

25.60 However, goodwill will arise on consolidation because the fair value of the consideration given is not, in general, the same as the aggregate fair value of the acquired company's identifiable assets and liabilities.

25.61 FRS 10 does not require an adjustment to be made in the parent's financial statements to the carrying value of the shares in the subsidiary in respect of any goodwill written off either in the consolidated financial statements or in the subsidiary's own financial statements. An exception is that where consolidation goodwill is written off because it is impaired, FRS 10 requires the carrying value of the parent's investment also to be reviewed for impairment. [FRS 10 para 42]. The parent company will in normal circumstances only write down the investment's carrying value to reflect any impairment.

Pre-acquisition and post-acquisition reserves

25.62 In the past, an important element of consolidations was whether profits of a subsidiary should be treated as pre-acquisition or post-acquisition. In particular, this was important because it had a bearing on how dividends paid by the subsidiary were treated in the parent's financial statements. If, for example, a subsidiary paid a dividend out of pre-acquisition profits to a parent, the parent would reduce its investment in the subsidiary by this amount (assuming that the net worth of the subsidiary had decreased by a similar amount). The parent could not treat this amount as realised and could not distribute it.

25.63 The Companies Act requires that when a cash dividend is paid out of pre-acquisition profits by a subsidiary, it need not be applied in reducing the carrying value of the investment in the subsidiary in the parent's books. It should be taken to the profit and loss account. Only if the underlying value of the subsidiary does not support the amount at which the parent carries its investment in the subsidiary following the dividend does the parent have to make a provision against its investment. This accords with the legal requirements included in paragraph 19(2) of Schedule 1 to SI 2008/410 which requires a company to make provision for any permanent diminution in value of any fixed asset. Consider the following example.

Example – Pre-acquisition dividend

Company A has an investment in its subsidiary company B. Company A acquired the subsidiary for £22m. The net assets of the subsidiary at that time were £18m. In the following year, the subsidiary's net assets are £20m and it decides to pay a cash dividend to its parent of £1m. It is unclear whether this dividend is made out of pre-acquisition reserves or post-acquisition reserves. Company A should take the dividend it receives from company B to its profit and loss account. However, company A then has to consider whether it is necessary to make a provision against the carrying value of its investment in company B. This assessment will take into account not only the net asset value of company B (which after the dividend payment has reduced to £19m), but also any additional value that the shares in company B have. When it was acquired, this additional value was £4m, which equates to the goodwill arising on consolidation. If company A considers that the premium on the value of company B's shares has not diminished, the worth of company B is in excess of £23m. On this basis company A does not need to make a provision against its investment in company B and can treat the dividend received as realised and, consequently, distributable.

This provision as it applies to merger relief is considered in chapter 23.

Increases in stake

Introduction

25.64 Many accounting problems can arise on increasing a stake in an undertaking. Such acquisitions arise where the investing company acquires a small stake in an undertaking and gradually increases its investment. Initially the interest in the undertaking may be no more than an investment that will be either valued at cost (less any provisions for diminution in value of the investment) or at a valuation (under the alternative accounting rules).

25.65 Once the interest in the undertaking becomes 20 per cent or more of the equity voting rights of a company and the investor exercises significant influence, the investment is likely to be treated in the consolidated financial statements as an associate in accordance with the requirements of FRS 9 (see further chapter 27). In certain circumstances an interest in an undertaking can be treated as an associate where the investment is below 20 per cent and equally interests in excess of 20 per cent may, in certain circumstances, be treated as investments.

25.66 If the investor has joint control over an undertaking that has a business of its own, this would be accounted for in the consolidated financial statements as a joint venture in accordance with the requirements of FRS 9 (see further chapter 27).

25.67 Once an interest in the undertaking is over 50 per cent of the voting rights of a company, such that the investor controls the undertaking, the investment is treated in the consolidated financial statements as a subsidiary to accord with the Act and FRS 2. In certain circumstances an interest below 50 per cent might be regarded as a subsidiary, where control over the undertaking is exercised in some other way or the entity has the 'power to control' the undertaking (see chapter 24).

Accounting principles

25.68 The basic principles of accounting for acquisitions set out in the Act apply equally to increases in stake. FRS 2 provides specific guidance on interpreting the

Companies Act 2006 in the context of changes in stake. The principles that apply are as follows:

- The identifiable assets and liabilities of the subsidiary acquired should be included in the consolidated balance sheet at their fair values at the acquisition date, that is, the date it becomes a subsidiary. [SI 2008/410 6 Sch 9(2); FRS 2 para 50].
- The income and expenditure of the undertaking acquired should be fully consolidated into the consolidated financial statements from the date of acquisition. [SI 2008/410 6 Sch 9(3)].
- The interest of the group in the adjusted capital and reserves of the undertaking acquired should be offset against the acquisition cost of the group's interest in the shares of the undertaking. The difference if positive represents goodwill and if negative represents a negative consolidation difference (that is, negative goodwill). [SI 2008/410 6 Sch 9(4), 9(5)].

25.69 Paragraph 9 of Schedule 6 to SI 2008/410 requires goodwill to be calculated as the difference between the following two amounts:

- The fair value, at the date an undertaking becomes a subsidiary, of the group's share of its identifiable assets and liabilities.
- The total acquisition cost of the interests held by the group in that subsidiary.

25.70 This approach, a one-off exercise at the time the undertaking becomes a subsidiary, is required by the Companies Act 2006 even where the interests have been purchased at different dates. FRS 2 points out that that approach will provide a practical means of applying acquisition accounting in most cases, because it does not require retrospective fair value exercises to be performed. [FRS 2 para 89]. However, FRS 2 notes that, in special circumstances, not using fair values at the dates of earlier purchases, while using an acquisition cost part of which relates to earlier purchases, may result in accounting that is inconsistent with the way the investment has previously been treated in the group's consolidated financial statements. It suggests that the inconsistency may lead to the treatment required by the Companies Act 2006 failing to give a true and fair view. [FRS 2 para 89].

25.71 FRS 2 considers two examples of such inconsistency that might lead to failure to give a true and fair view:

- An acquisition of a further interest in an undertaking that has already been treated as an associate by the group is acquired so that the undertaking becomes a subsidiary. Using the method set out above to calculate goodwill will lead to the group's share of post acquisition profits, losses and reserve movements of its associated undertaking being reclassified as goodwill (usually negative goodwill). This situation is considered in detail in paragraph 25.83 below.

- A group has substantially restated an investment that subsequently becomes its subsidiary. For example, where a provision has been made against such an investment for an impairment, the effect of using the Act's method of calculating goodwill would be to increase reserves and create goodwill. This situation is considered in detail in paragraph 25.77 below.

[FRS 2 para 89].

25.72 In such situations, where the calculation of goodwill in accordance with the Act's provisions would be misleading, the FRS states that goodwill should be calculated as the sum of the goodwill arising from each purchase of an interest in the relevant undertaking adjusted as necessary for any subsequent impairment. [FRS 2 para 89]. The goodwill arising on each purchase should be calculated as the difference between the cost of that purchase and the fair value *at the date of that purchase* of the identifiable assets and liabilities attributable to the interest purchased. The difference between the goodwill calculated using the true and fair override and that calculated in accordance with paragraph 9 of Schedule 6 to SI 2008/410 is shown in reserves. [FRS 2 para 89].

25.73 Adopting this alternative treatment requires the use of the true and fair override under section 404 of the Companies Act 2006 as it does not comply strictly with the requirements of the Act. This section of the Act provides that in this type of situation:

> *"If in special circumstances compliance with any of those provisions is inconsistent with the requirement to give a true and fair view, the directors must depart from that provision to the extent necessary to give a true and fair view. Particulars of any such departure, the reasons for it and its effect must be given in a note to the accounts."*

The disclosures required when the true and fair override is used are set out in FRS 18. Table 25.1 gives an example of such disclosure in respect of accounting for an associated company that has become a subsidiary.

Table 25.1 – THORN EMI plc – Report and accounts – 31 March 1995

Notes to the accounts (extract)

30. Purchase of businesses (extract)

TOEMI – On 3 October 1994, THORN EMI plc increased its shareholding in TOEMI from 50 to 55 per cent. TOEMI became a consolidated subsidiary on this date, having previously been accounted for as an associated company.

The transaction was effected by a redemption of shares owned by the joint venture partner, Toshiba Corporation, and funded by TOEMI's cash reserves in which the Group already had a 50 per cent beneficial interest. The indirect cost to the Group was therefore Yen 3.75 billion (£24.1m).

The Companies Act 1985 normally requires goodwill arising on the acquisition of a subsidiary undertaking to be calculated as the difference between the total acquisition cost of the undertaking and the fair value of the Group's share of the identifiable assets and liabilities at the date it became a subsidiary undertaking.

FRS 2 recognises that, where an investment in an associated undertaking is increased and it becomes a subsidiary undertaking, in order to show a true and fair view goodwill should be calculated on each purchase as the difference between the cost of that purchase and the fair value at the date of that purchase.

If goodwill had been calculated in accordance with the basis set out in the Companies Act 1985, £61.2m of the Group's share of the retained earnings of TOEMI would have been reclassified as goodwill and in total negative goodwill of £63.9m would have been recognised.

Practical examples

25.74 There are three basic situations that might arise with a piecemeal acquisition, as follows:

- An undertaking has an investment in another undertaking and increases its stake in the undertaking so that it becomes a subsidiary.
- An undertaking has an investment in an associate (or a joint venture) and increases its stake in the undertaking so that it becomes a subsidiary.
- A parent has an investment in a subsidiary and acquires part or all of the minority's interest.

Each of these situations is explained in the paragraphs that follow.

An investment becomes a subsidiary

25.75 This is the simplest situation to account for. The rules that apply in determining the date upon which an undertaking becomes a subsidiary are considered from paragraph 25.18.

25.76 The initial investment will be recorded in the parent's accounting records at either its cost (less provisions) or at a valuation (in accordance with the alternative accounting rules). With piecemeal acquisitions, up to the date of acquisition the parent will only have accounted for dividend income received from the undertaking. On acquisition, the goodwill arising on the acquisition has to be ascertained and this will be the difference between the fair value of the consideration given for the subsidiary (including the cost of the investment to date, any revaluation being ignored) and the fair value (at the date the investment becomes a subsidiary) of the parent's share of net assets acquired. Consider the following example:

Example – Calculation of goodwill arising on acquisition

A group made an investment of 10% in a company in 20X2. The investment cost £2.5m and has subsequently been revalued to £5m. In 20X8 it makes a further investment in the company of 50% to bring its total investment to 60%. The fair value of the consideration given for the 50% is £25m. The net assets of the company acquired stand in its books at the date of acquisition at £20m (including share capital of £5m). The fair value exercise shows that the company's net assets are worth £35m, which is also the adjusted capital and reserves. The goodwill on acquisition and minority interest would be calculated in the following way:

Cost of acquisition

	£m
Original investment in company (at cost)	2.5
Fair value of consideration given	25.0
Total consideration	27.5
Consolidation goodwill	
Total consideration	27.5
Adjusted capital and reserves (being 60% of £35m)	21.0
Goodwill	6.5
Minority interests	
Share capital (40% of £5m)	2.0
Reserves (40% of £30m)	12.0
Minority interests	14.0

The only additional adjustment that is required in this example, in contrast to a straight acquisition of a subsidiary, is to reduce the value of the original investment from its revalued amount to cost. The entry on consolidation would be to debit the revaluation reserve with £2.5m and credit the investment £2.5m. Whether the parent decides to make this adjustment in its own balance sheet might depend on whether the total cost of the subsidiary, including the valuation adjustment, exceeds the parent's share of the subsidiary's worth (including goodwill). Consequently, in this example the total consideration paid for the subsidiary together with the book value of the original investments is £30m (that is, £25m + £5m). If 60% of the subsidiary (including goodwill) is worth more than £30m, then no provision will have to be made in the parent's books of account against the carrying value of its investment.

25.77 As already mentioned, a further complication can arise where a provision has been made against an investment for permanent diminution in value. Consider the following example:

Example – Treatment of a provision previously made against the investment

A parent acquired a 10% interest in a property company in 20X3 for £11m. At that time the fair value of the net assets of the property company was £100m. The parent has subsequently provided for a permanent diminution in value of its investment and written it down from £11m to £4m. In 20X8 the other shareholder sold its 90% holding to the parent for £40m. At that time the fair value of the net assets of the property company were £50m.

Calculation of goodwill — applying the provisions of paragraph 9 of Schedule 6 to SI 2008/410

Cost of acquisition	£m
Original investment 10% in 20X3	11
Final investment 90% in 20X8	40
Total consideration	51

Calculation of goodwill		£m
Total consideration		51
Less: adjusted capital and reserves at date property company became subsidiary		(50)
Goodwill arising on acquisition of subsidiary		1

The double entry on consolidation is as follows:

	£m	£m
Dr Investment	7	
Cr Profit and loss account reserve		7
Being the restatement of the original investment to original cost.		
Dr Capital and reserves of subsidiary	50	
Dr Goodwill	1	
Cr Investment		51
Being the capitalisation of goodwill		

In practice some of the provision for permanent diminution of £7m may be written back through the parent's profit and loss account, as the parent's cost of investment (after provision for permanent diminution in value) is £44m compared to underlying net assets of £50m. Let us suppose, for example, that £6m of the provision is written back through the parent's profit and loss account. The write-back of £6m should then be credited to the consolidated profit and loss account (as it was originally charged to the consolidated profit and loss account) and the remaining £1m credited to the consolidated profit and loss account reserve with the corresponding debit shown as goodwill arising on the acquisition.

25.78 The method just described gives a figure for positive goodwill by, in effect, reinstating the provision for permanent diminution in value and offsetting it against a substantial negative goodwill figure which arose on the second tranche. However, in substance the effects of the transactions are:

- A substantial holding loss on the original investment.
- A purchase at a discount.

25.79 The substance of the transaction is more closely represented by the following approach, which uses the true and fair override in calculating the goodwill arising on consolidation.

Example — Use of the true and fair override in calculating goodwill

Calculation of goodwill — using the true and fair override

Cost of acquisition	£m
Original investment 10% in 20X3	11
Final investment 90% in 20X8	40
Total consideration	51

Consolidation goodwill

Total consideration		51
Less: adjusted capital and reserves at dates of original investments		
10% × £100m	10	
90% × £50m	45	55
Negative goodwill		(4)

The double entry on consolidation is as follows:

	£m	£m
Dr Investment	7	
Cr Profit and loss account reserve		7

Being the restatement of the original investment to original cost.

Dr Capital and reserves of subsidiary	50	
Cr Cost of investment		51
Cr Negative goodwill		4
Dr Profit and loss account reserve	5	

Being the recognition of negative goodwill arising on consolidation and the reduction in the underlying net assets of £5m attributable to the original 10% investment between its acquisition date in 20X3 and the date the undertaking became a subsidiary (10% × (£100m – £50m)).

As above, in practice, some of the provision for permanent diminution may be written back through the parent's profit and loss account, as the parent's cost of investment (after provision for permanent diminution in value) is £44m compared to underlying net assets of £50m. Again let us suppose that £6m of the provision is written back through the parent's profit and loss account. Only £1m of the £6m provision also reported in the consolidated profit and loss account in previous years could be credited back through the consolidated profit and loss account, because in effect £5m of that provision has already been adjusted to reserves in the calculation to arrive at the goodwill arising on the acquisition of the 10% interest.

25.80 If the true and fair override is adopted, the particulars of the departure from the requirements of paragraph 9 of Schedule 6 to SI 2008/410, the reasons for it and its effect should be disclosed in a note to the financial statements. [CA06 Sec 404(5)]. In addition, the disclosure provisions of FRS 18 must be complied with (see chapter 2).

An associate becomes a subsidiary

25.81 When an associate becomes a subsidiary the accounting treatment is not as straightforward as in the previous example. The main difference lies in the fact that a proportion of the associate's results have already been dealt with in the consolidated profit and loss account and consolidated balance sheet. In addition, goodwill will have been calculated on the acquisition of the interest in the associate and will have been either written off to reserves or amortised over its useful economic life.

25.82 The method set out in the Act still applies and the goodwill arising on the acquisition of the subsidiary should be calculated as the difference between the following two amounts:

- The fair value, at the date an undertaking becomes a subsidiary, of the group's share of its identifiable assets and liabilities.
- The total acquisition cost of the interests held by the group in that subsidiary.

25.83 Using this method to calculate goodwill leads to the group's share of post acquisition profits, losses and reserve movements of its associated undertaking becoming reclassified as goodwill, thus reducing goodwill or creating negative goodwill on the acquisition. FRS 2 recognises that this accounting treatment is inconsistent with the way the investment has previously been treated and that this inconsistency could lead to a failure to give a true and fair view.

Example – Acquisition of an associate

A group made an investment of 20% in a company in 20X2. The investment cost £12m and the book value (also fair value) of the associate's net assets at that date was £50m. In 20X8 it makes a further investment in the company of 50% to bring its total investment to 70%. Goodwill on the acquisition of the associate was written off directly against reserves in the year of acquisition which was prior to the implementation of FRS 10. The net assets of the associate stand in its books at £68m on the date it becomes a subsidiary. The associate would be treated as follows up to the date of acquisition:

Acquisition of associate

	£m
Original investment in company	12.0
Fair value of net assets acquired (20% × £50m)	10.0
Goodwill arising	2.0

Consolidation of associate up to date of increased investment

Share of net assets	
Date of acquisition	10.0
Post acquisition profits	
(being (£68m – £50m) × 20%)	3.6
	13.6

The fair value of the consideration given for the additional 50% is £42m. The fair value exercise shows that the company's net assets are worth £75m, which is also the adjusted capital and reserves. The group must include the whole amount of the fair value of the subsidiary's net assets in the consolidated balance sheet. The goodwill on acquisition and minority interest would be calculated as follows:

Associate becomes a subsidiary — applying the provisions of the Act

Cost of acquisition as shown in the parent's books

	£m	£m
Original investment in company		12.0
Fair value of consideration given for new investment		42.0
Total investment in subsidiary		54.0

Consolidation goodwill

Total consideration		54.0
Adjusted capital and reserves		
being 20% of £75m	15	
being 50% of £75m	37.5	52.5
Total goodwill arising on the acquisition		1.5
Goodwill previously written off		2.0
Balance of goodwill (negative)		(0.5)

Minority interests

Share capital (30% of £5m)	1.5
Reserves (30% of £70m)	21.0
Minority interests	22.5

The problem with this method of calculating the goodwill is that it treats the post acquisition profits and reserve movements of the undertaking while it was an associate of the group as a deduction from goodwill. The amount of the undertaking's profits while it was an associate have to be 'removed' from the profit and loss account reserves as part of the double entry on consolidation, as follows:

	£m	£m
Dr Profit and loss account reserve	3.6	
Cr Investment		3.6

Being the restatement of the original investment to original cost.

This method gives a figure of negative goodwill of £0.5m, which is the difference between the goodwill arising on the acquisition of £1.5m less the goodwill of £2m previously written off on the initial acquisition of the associate interest. However, the goodwill of £1.5m is understated because the total interest of 70% has been applied to the fair value of the net assets at the date the undertaking becomes a subsidiary (in compliance with the Act) and does not take into account the fact that when the 20% interest was acquired the fair value of the net assets was less. Therefore, if the difference is material, it is necessary to adopt the Act's true and fair override in order to arrive at the correct amount of goodwill arising on the acquisition.

Associate becomes a subsidiary — adopting true and fair override

Cost of acquisition as shown in the parent's books	**£m**	**£m**
Original investment in company		12.0
Fair value of consideration given for new investment		42.0
Total investment in subsidiary		54.0

Consolidation goodwill

Total consideration		54.0
Adjusted capital and reserves		
being 20% × £50m	10.0	
being 50% × £75m	37.5	47.5
Goodwill		6.5
Goodwill previously written off		2.0
Balance of goodwill		4.5

Minority interests

Share capital (30% × £5m)	1.5
Reserves (30% × £70m)	21.0
Minority interests	22.5

In this case, the goodwill figure that emerges is instinctively correct as it reflects the fact that a premium of £4.5m arises on the acquisition of the additional 50% (that is, £42m – (£75m × 50%)). The results since the date of acquisition of the associate are attributable to the group and as such, are correctly treated as post-acquisition.

There is one further adjustment that is required to be made on consolidation in this example. There is a difference of £5m between the fair values of the net assets consolidated (that is, £75m) and the adjusted capital and reserves taken into account above (that is, £47.5m + £22.5m = £70m). The amount relates to two items. Part relates to the post acquisition profits of £3.6m taken into account since the acquisition of the associate (that is, 20% × (£68m — £50m)). The other part relates to the increase in net assets of £7m from their book value of £68m to their fair value of £75m. In the above example, 30% of that increase is reflected in the minority's interest and 50% is taken into account in calculating goodwill. The other 20% (that is, £1.4m) is the further adjustment that will need to be credited to the consolidated revaluation reserve. This represents a revaluation (not a fair value adjustment) of the assets that were already included in the consolidated balance sheet by virtue of the inclusion of the associate interest.

If the revaluation adjustment is made, the double entry on consolidation is as follows:

	£m	£m
Dr Profit and loss account reserve	3.6	
Cr Investment		3.6

Being the restatement of the original investment to original cost.

Dr Share capital and reserves	75.0	
Cr Minority interest		22.5
Cr Cost of investment		54.0
Cr Revaluation reserve		1.4
Cr Profit and loss account reserve		3.6
Dr Goodwill written off to reserves *	2.0	
Dr Goodwill capitalised *	4.5	

Being the adjustment necessary to reflect minority interests and goodwill

*Even though the goodwill arising on the original acquisition of the associate interest was written off to reserves, which was allowed prior to the introduction of FRS 10, the goodwill arising on the further transfer of shares acquired must be capitalised in accordance with FRS 10.

A parent acquires part or all of the minority

25.84 FRS 2 states that when a group increases its interest in an undertaking that is already its subsidiary, the identifiable assets and liabilities of that subsidiary should be revalued to their fair value and goodwill arising on the increase in interest should be calculated by reference to those fair values. This rule is additional to the general rule in FRS 2 that requires a fair value exercise to be carried out when an entity becomes a subsidiary. However, the standard goes on to say that such a revaluation is not required if the difference between net fair values and carrying amounts of the assets and liabilities attributable to the increase in stake is not material. [FRS 2 para 51].

25.85 When a group increases its stake in a subsidiary, the consideration it pays may not equal the fair value of the identifiable assets and liabilities acquired from its minority. If the net assets of the subsidiary, which are already included in the consolidation, were not revalued to up to date fair values before calculating the goodwill arising on the change in stake, the difference between the consideration paid and the relevant proportion of the carrying value of the net assets acquired would be made up in part of goodwill and in part of changes in value. For that reason FRS 2 requires that the assets and liabilities of the subsidiary be revalued to their fair value at the date of the increase in stake, unless the difference between the fair values and the carrying amounts of the share of net assets acquired is not material. [FRS 2 para 90].

Example – Acquisition of minority interest

A parent acquired a 60% interest in an undertaking in 20X2 for £50m. At that time the fair value of the net assets of the subsidiary was £60m. In 20X8 the parent purchased a further 30% interest in the subsidiary for £40m. At that time the fair value of the net assets of the subsidiary was £150m; the increase in fair value of net assets between the original investment date and 20X5 is due to revaluation increases of £70m and profits of £20m.

Assuming that the difference between the fair values and carrying values of the net assets acquired is material the acquisition will be dealt with as follows:

Cost of acquisition	£m	£m
Original investment 60% in 20X2		50
Additional investment 30% in 20X8		40
Total consideration		90

Consolidation goodwill		£m
Total consideration		90
Less: share of adjusted capital and reserves		
60% × £60m	36	
30% × £150m	45	81
Goodwill		9

The profits of the subsidiary company between 20X2 and 20X8 will have already been reflected in the assets and liabilities in the consolidated balance sheet. The treatment of the £70m revaluation element will depend on whether it has already been reflected in the consolidated balance sheet. If the revaluation had been booked prior to the purchase of the second tranche of shares, the entries would have been:

	£m	£m
Dr Net assets	70	
Cr Revaluation reserve		42
Cr Minority interests		28

On the acquisition of the additional 30%, the minority's share of the revaluation (£21m (30% × £70m)) would be transferred from minority interests to the cost of control account together with the other elements of minority interests that relate to the 30% interests (that is, share capital, profit and loss account and other reserves).

If, on the other hand, the revaluation had not been reflected in the consolidated balance sheet, the entries to reflect the revaluation would be:

	£m	£m
Dr Net assets	70	
Cr Revaluation reserve		42
Cr Minority interests		7
Cr Cost of control account †		21

† The entries in the cost of control account are shown below:

Cost of control account

Dr		Cr	
Original cost of investment	50	Share of adjusted capital and reserves in 20X2 (£60m × 60%)	36
		Goodwill on original acquisition	14
	50		50
Additional cost of investment	40	Share of adjusted capital and reserves in 20X8 (£60m + £20m × 30%)	24
		Share of revaluation reserve	21
Negative goodwill	5		
	95		95

The effect of these entries is that not only is there a fair valuation of the 30% acquired, but also a revaluation of the 60% which represents the share of assets previously owned (credited to the group's revaluation reserve) and a revaluation of the share still attributable to minority interests of 10%. It can also be seen that the goodwill of £9m is made up of £14m on the original acquisition and negative goodwill of £5m arising on the increase in stake.

An alternative view is that the proportion of assets of the subsidiary held prior to the acquisition of the minority (60% in this case) need not be revalued when the minority interest is acquired. If this approach is adopted, the result will be that only the additional 30% of assets acquired will be subject to fair value at the date of acquisition of the 30% minority, the bulk of the assets will be held at their original cost to the group.

Change in stake not material

If the difference between the carrying values of the assets of the subsidiary and their fair values was not deemed to be material and the change in stake was not considered significant, there would have been no requirement to revalue the assets of the subsidiary in the consolidation and the calculations would be as follows:

Cost of acquisition		£m
Original investment 60% in 20X2		50
Final investment 30% in 20X8		40
Total consideration		90
Consolidation goodwill		£m
Total consideration		90
Less: share of adjusted capital and reserves		
60% × £60m	36	
30% × (£60m + £20m) net assets in balance sheet prior to revaluation	24	60
Goodwill		30

The goodwill of £30m is made up of £14m on the original acquisition and £16m arising on the increase in stake (cost of £40m less net assets of £24m) attributable to the 30% purchased.

Becoming a subsidiary other than by a purchase or an exchange of shares

25.86 Some investments that end up as subsidiaries start out as much smaller interests in the undertakings concerned and may be treated in the group's financial statements in a variety of ways before they actually become subsidiaries. The most common way for an undertaking to become a subsidiary of another is by acquisition, but it is also possible for a parent to gain a subsidiary other than by acquisition, for example:

- By gaining control or the power to control without acquiring a further interest in an undertaking, perhaps by virtue of an agreement with another shareholder.

- By the default by a creditor on a loan, that gives the lender an option to convert the loan into a holding of shares that is sufficient to make the creditor a subsidiary.

- By the subsidiary company purchasing and cancelling its own shares held by third parties.

- By changes to the voting rights attached to shares.

25.87 Where an undertaking becomes a subsidiary other than as a result of a purchase or exchange of shares, not only should its name be disclosed as required by paragraph 21(a) of FRS 6, but also FRS 2 paragraph 49 requires the circumstances to be explained.

Disclosure for acquisition accounting

25.88 Schedule 6 to SI 2008/410 sets out various details that have to be disclosed in the consolidated financial statements in the year that a subsidiary is acquired. These disclosure requirements concern business combinations that are accounted for using either acquisition accounting or merger accounting. In addition, FRS 6 repeats these requirements and includes further disclosure requirements relating both to acquisitions and mergers. Those relating to merger accounting are dealt with in chapter 28. The disclosures related to fair valuing on an acquisition have been consolidated into FRS 6 and include disclosures of post-acquisition reorganisation costs which are discussed in section II, from paragraph 25.208. The disclosures relating to the treatment of goodwill that arises on an acquisition are detailed in section III, from paragraph 25.473. The disclosures required where the group has taken merger relief on the issue of its shares in an acquisition are given in chapter 23. The paragraphs that follow outline the general disclosure requirements that apply to business combinations that are accounted for as acquisitions.

25.89 With the exception of goodwill, the disclosures concerning acquisitions can now be found in one standard, FRS 6. This standard encompasses the disclosure requirements of the Companies Act 2006. FRS 6 also repeats some of the disclosure requirements contained in FRS 1 and FRS 3, and expands the latter in an important respect.

25.90 A group may make several acquisitions in an accounting period. There is no exemption from disclosure on the grounds of excessive information, although information relating to non-material acquisitions can be aggregated. For acquisitive groups the disclosure resulting from FRS 6 and the Companies Act 2006 is extensive.

General requirements

25.91 The acquiring company should disclose certain information in respect of all acquisitions. The parent must disclose in the consolidated financial statements that deal with the period in which the acquisition occurs:

- The names of undertakings acquired during the financial year, the names of the combining entities, or where a group of companies is acquired, the name of the group's parent. [SI 2008/410 6 Sch 13(2)(a); FRS 6 para 21(a)].

- Whether the combination is accounted for by the acquisition or merger method of accounting. [SI 2008/410 6 Sch 13(2)(b); FRS 6 para 21(b)].

- The date of the acquisition or combination (that is, the date on which control passes). [FRS 6 para 21(c)].

25.92 As described in the following paragraphs, FRS 6 requires certain additional disclosures to be given in respect of each *material acquisition*, and in aggregate for other acquisitions that are individually not material. Whilst the FRS 6 disclosures encompass those required by the Companies Act 2006, which are required *"in relation to an acquisition which significantly affects the figures shown in the group accounts"*, they go further than the Act. FRS 6 indicates that an acquisition should be judged to be material when *"the information relating to the acquisition might reasonably be expected to influence decisions made by the users of general purpose financial statements"*. [FRS 6 para 84]. However, FRS 6 also introduced a new class of *substantial acquisitions*, which are defined by reference to a size test and lead to certain enhanced disclosures.

25.93 If in the directors' opinion the disclosure of any of the information in paragraph 25.91 above and paragraphs 25.94 to 25.102 below that is required by the Companies Act 2006 (relating to an undertaking established under the law of a country, or one that carries on a business, outside the UK) would be seriously prejudicial to the business of the undertaking, its parent or its fellow subsidiaries, it need not be given if the Secretary of State's permission is obtained. [SI 2008/410 6 Sch 16].

Purchase consideration

25.94 The following information should be disclosed for each material acquisition and for other non-material acquisitions in aggregate:

- The composition and the fair value of the consideration for the acquisition given by the parent and its subsidiaries. [SI 2008/410 6 Sch 13(3); FRS 6 para 24].

- Where applicable, a statement that the attributed fair value of the purchase consideration has been determined on a provisional basis at the end of the accounting period in which the acquisition took place. Any material adjustments in subsequent periods should be disclosed and explained. [FRS 6 para 27].

- The nature of any purchase consideration where settlement is deferred or where the amount is contingent on future events. [FRS 6 para 24].

- The range of possible outcomes and the principal factors that might affect the amount of contingent purchase consideration that may become payable in the future. [FRS 6 para 24].

25.95 Fair valuing the purchase consideration, including deferred and contingent consideration, is considered in section II, paragraph 25.383.

Fair values of identifiable assets and liabilities

25.96 The following information should be disclosed for each material acquisition and for other non-material acquisitions in aggregate:

- A table of assets and liabilities acquired, including a statement of the amount of goodwill or negative goodwill arising on the acquisition (see para 25.97 below). [SI 2008/410 6 Sch 13(4); FRS 6 para 25].
- Where applicable, a statement that the attributed fair values at the end of the accounting period in which the acquisition took place are provisional, together with the reasons. Any material adjustments made to those provisional fair values in the next financial statements should also be disclosed and explained. [FRS 6 para 27]. (See section II, from para 25.243.)

Table of assets and liabilities acquired

25.97 The Companies Act 2006 and FRS 6 require the book values and fair values of each class of assets and liabilities of the undertaking or group acquired to be stated in tabular form. The book values to be shown in the table are those recorded in the books of the acquired entity immediately before the acquisition and are before any fair value adjustments. [FRS 6 para 25(a)]. The book values of assets and liabilities of a group acquired must include all the necessary consolidation adjustments within that group. [SI 2008/410 6 Sch 13(4)].

25.98 The table should also detail the fair value adjustments of those same categories of assets and liabilities at the date of acquisition. FRS 6 also requires the fair value adjustments to be analysed between the following:

- Revaluations.
- Adjustments to bring accounting polices of the subsidiary onto the same basis as those of the group.
- Any other significant adjustments, including reasons for the adjustments.

[FRS 6 para 25(b); SI 2008/410 6 Sch 13(4)].

[The next paragraph is 25.100.]

25.100 The table should also include a statement of the amount of goodwill or negative goodwill arising on acquisition. [FRS 6 para 25;SI 2008/410 6 Sch 13(4)].

Table 25.2 gives an example of a fair value table showing a material acquisition separately and other acquisitions in aggregate.

Table 25.2 – Hanson PLC – Annual Report – 30 September 1995

Notes to the accounts (extract)

20 Acquisitions, demerger and disposals (extract)

Acquisitions

Eastern was acquired on September 18, 1995 and included in the consolidated balance sheet at September 30, 1995. For the period since acquisition, sales of £74mn and operating profit of £7mn are included within the consolidated profit and loss account as continuing operations – acquisitions.

On September 18, 1995 the acquisition of Eastern was declared unconditional. The purchase consideration was £2.5bn. The operating assets and liabilities of Eastern, Carter Mining and other acquisitions during the year were as follows:

	Eastern Book value £ million	Others Book value £ million	Total Book value £ million	Total Adjustments £ million	Total Fair value £ million
Fixed assets	1,118	211	1,329	625	1,954
Stock	12	49	61	(1)	60
Debtors	364	16	380	(11)	369
Cash	264	1	265	–	265
Unlisted investments	251	–	251	295	546
Creditors	(411)	(15)	(426)	–	(426)
Loans and finance leases	(688)	(16)	(704)	–	(704)
Provision for liabilities	(113)	(49)	(162)	(497)	(659)
	797	197	994	411	1,405
Accrued purchase consideration					2,495
Cash consideration					299
Consideration (Eastern £2,496mn and others £298mn)					2,794
Goodwill (Eastern £1,377mn and others £12mn)					(1,389)
					1,405

Of the provisions for liabilities above, £88mn was provided by Eastern for reorganisation costs in the year up to acquisition.

The following fair value adjustments which relate principally to Eastern and Carter Mining were made to the book value of the assets and liabilities of the above acquisitions:

	Eastern £ million	Others £ million	Total £ million
Revaluations			
Tangible fixed assets	242	383	625
Unlisted investments	295	–	295
Alignment of accounting policies			
Liabilities in respect of mining reclamation	–	(94)	(94)
Black lung excise tax liability	–	(183)	(183)
Other			
Liabilities in respect of purchase contracts	(129)	–	(129)
Taxation	(86)	–	(86)
Other liabilities	–	(17)	(17)
	322	89	411

> The above figures reflect a preliminary allocation of the purchase consideration to the net assets and liabilities of Eastern and other acquisitions of the year. The preliminary allocation will be reviewed based on additional information up to September 30, 1996. The directors do not believe that any net adjustments resulting from such review would have a material adverse effect on Hanson.
>
> For the year ended March 31, 1995, Eastern reported an audited post-tax profit of £141mn. For the period ended September 18, 1995 the unaudited operating profit before exceptional items was £80mn and the unaudited post-tax loss after exceptional items was £19mn based on its then accounting policies.

25.101 Because of the intention of FRS 7 to curtail provisioning as part of the fair value exercise (as explained in section II, para 25.198), FRS 6 requires that any provisions for reorganisation and restructuring costs which have been included in the liabilities, or related asset write-downs, of the acquired entity to be identified separately in the table. This is, however, only required where the provisions were made in the twelve months up to the date of acquisition. [FRS 6 para 26]. The example in Table 25.2 discloses the existence of such provisions.

25.102 This disclosure is an anti-avoidance measure. To a very limited extent, some reorganisation provisions may be properly regarded as pre-acquisition liabilities of the acquired company where, for example, the acquired company was already committed to the expenditure before the acquisition was in prospect. By requiring separate disclosure of any such provisions in the fair value table, the ASB sought to ensure that the spirit of FRS 7 is observed. The disclosure of such provisions in the fair value table is likely to be a sensitive matter. Accordingly, the directors of the acquiring group may wish to include a statement explaining why the provision is valid.

Pre-acquisition activities of material acquisitions

25.103 For each *material acquisition* (but for *substantial acquisitions*, see para 25.106 below) the notes should disclose the following:

- The profit or loss after tax and minority interests of the acquired entity for the period from the beginning of its financial year up to the date of acquisition.
- The profit or loss after tax and minority interests of the acquired entity for its previous financial year.
- The date on which the acquired entity's financial year before the acquisition began.

[FRS 6 para 35].

25.104 FRS 6 is silent on the question of whether the disclosed profit or loss of the acquired undertaking should be adjusted to comply with the accounting policies of the acquiring group. It would be consistent with the disclosures for substantial acquisitions (see para 25.111 below) for this information to be reported on the basis of the acquired undertaking's accounting policies prior to the acquisition, although the directors of the acquiring group may wish to disclose additional adjusted figures.

25.105 The above disclosures are not required to be given in aggregate for non-material acquisitions.

Pre-acquisition activities of substantial acquisitions

25.106 The ASB was anxious to meet the concerns of users who were interested in assessing the performance of acquisitions in the acquiring group, by requiring a more detailed analysis of the pre-acquisition results of significant acquisitions than was previously required by the Act. The objective was to enable users to put together something of a track record for the acquisition before and after it enters the group, given that in most acquisitions it is continuing businesses that are acquired. Such information has the effect of complementing the layered format for the profit and loss account required by FRS 3, which provides separate disclosure of the post-acquisition results of acquisitions made during the year.

25.107 FRS 6 requires, for each acquisition that meets the following size tests, disclosure of additional information about the pre-acquisition results of the acquired entity for its financial year in which the acquisition takes place.

25.108 The size tests are:

- 'Class 1' acquisitions, where the acquirer is listed on the Stock Exchange. UITF 15 requires references to Class 1 transactions in FRS 6 to be interpreted as meaning those business combinations in which any of the ratios set out in the Listing Rules for the classification of transactions exceeds 15 per cent (it should be noted that a transaction is a Class 1 transaction under the Listing Rules where any of the ratios is 25 per cent or more). The ratios are specified in Annex 1 to Chapter 10 of the Listing Rules.
- For other acquiring entities, if either of the following conditions are met:
  - The net assets or operating profits of the acquired entity (as shown its last statutory financial statements before the date of acquisition) exceed 15 per cent of those of the acquiring entity. For this purpose, the amount of net assets is determined after adding any purchased goodwill that has been written off to reserves as a matter of accounting policy and not charged in the profit and loss account.
  - The fair value of the consideration given exceeds 15 per cent of the net assets of the acquiring entity.
- Other exceptional cases where an acquisition does not meet the above criteria, but is nevertheless of such significance that the disclosure is necessary in order to give a true and fair view.

[FRS 6 para 37].

25.109 For each substantial acquisition as defined above, the disclosures required in the financial statements of the acquirer for the financial year in which the acquisition took place are:

- For the period from the beginning of the acquired entity's latest financial year to the date of acquisition:
  - A summarised profit and loss account of the acquired entity, disclosing as a minimum the turnover, operating profit, any exceptional items falling within paragraph 20 of FRS 3, profit before taxation, taxation, minority interests, and extraordinary items.
  - A summarised statement of total recognised gains and losses of the acquired entity.
  - The date on which the period began.
- For the acquired entity's previous financial year, the profit or loss after tax and minority interests. This is the same as the disclosure required for each material acquisition (see para 25.103 above).

[FRS 6 para 36].

25.110 The principal components of the statement of total recognised gains and losses would usually be:

- Profit or loss for the period.
- Exchange gains or losses taken direct to reserves.
- Revaluation surpluses or deficits booked in respect of asset revaluations in the period.
- Total recognised gains or losses.

25.111 The information described above may in some situations be of limited practical use to analysts. Firstly, the period for which the more detailed summary of the results of the acquired entity is included will vary according to the timing of the acquisition in relation to the financial year end of the target and may be very short. Secondly, FRS 6 requires the results of the acquired entity to be shown on the basis of its own accounting policies prior to the acquisition. [FRS 6 para 36].

25.112 Where harmonisation of accounting policies on to the acquiring group's own policies gives rise to a material restatement of the results of the acquired company, their disclosure on the old basis may be misleading when compared to the disclosure of post-acquisition performance on the basis of the new policies. However, the standard explains that management may in those circumstances wish voluntarily to disclose, as additional notes, the same information restated on to the basis of the accounting policies of the acquiring group. [FRS 6 para 89]. Although this is sensible, it could give rise to excessive disclosure in the acquirer's consolidated financial statements.

25.113 There may be practical difficulties in complying with the disclosure requirements where a business (for example, the trade and assets of a division) rather than a subsidiary is acquired. Information about pre-acquisition results may not be readily available to the acquirer. Furthermore, profitability may have been distorted by intra-group charges under previous ownership, or matters such as taxation may not have been dealt with at a divisional level. In such circumstances, the acquirer should comply as far as is practically possible. The disclosure note may need to explain how the figures have been derived. Tables 25.3, 25.4 and 25.5 illustrate different solutions to the disclosure problem in practice. In Table 25.5, the acquirer disclosed that the information could not be given.

Table 25.3 – Reckitt & Colman plc – Report and Accounts – 31 December 1994

Notes to the accounts (extract)

27 ACQUISITION OF BUSINESSES

The 1994 full year trading result and statement of recognised gains and losses of L&F Household, as reported on the US accounting basis used by the business as part of Kodak, were as follows:

	1994 US$m
Net sales	**809.13**
Operating profit	**105.87**
Profit before tax	**101.62**
Taxation	**(40.65)**
Profit after tax	**60.97**
Foreign currency translation adjustments	**3.36**
Other	**4.88**
Total recognised gains and losses relating to the financial year	**69.21**

In 1993 profit after tax was $53.49m. The taxation affairs of L&F Household were treated integrally with those of Kodak, and the above figures include a charge of 40% of profit before taxation. There were no minority interests.

There is no material difference in the result when calculated using Reckitt & Colman's accounting policies.

Table 25.4 – SmithKline Beecham plc – Annual Report & Accounts – 31 December 1994

NOTES TO THE FINANCIAL STATEMENTS (extract)

Acquisitions (extract)

Acquisitions consist of Diversified Pharmaceutical Services, Inc., which was acquired from United HealthCare on 27 May 1994 and the worldwide consumer healthcare business of Sterling Winthrop Inc., which was acquired from Eastman Kodak on 31 October 1994.

From 1 January 1994 to 27 May 1994 Diversified had sales of £74 million and a trading profit of £31 million; profit before taxation was £16 million and taxation £6 million. The profit after tax for Diversified for the year to 31 December 1993 was £17 million. There is no difference between profit after tax and the recognised gains and losses for the period.

From 1 January 1994 to 31 October 1994 Sterling had sales of £379 million and a trading profit of £66 million. The trading profit for Sterling for the year to 31 December 1993 was £80 million. The trading profit is presented before corporate and other charges, interest and taxation, as all financing items and US taxation matters were dealt with on a group basis by Eastman Kodak, and no meaningful allocation of such items can be made.

Table 25.5 – Scottish & Newcastle plc – Annual Report & Accounts – 28 April 1996

NOTES TO THE ACCOUNTS (extract)

25 ACQUISITION OF THE COURAGE BUSINESS (extract)
The Courage business was acquired from the Foster's Brewing Group on 16 August 1995.

Prior to acquisition the Courage business was part of Courage Limited. However, only certain of the assets and liabilities of Courage Limited were acquired. In these circumstances, it is not practical to provide details of profits or recognised gains and losses for the Courage business for financial periods before acquisition. Since acquisition the operations of the Courage business have been integrated into the existing Beer Division. As a result it is impractical to isolate the cashflows of the Courage business.

Post-acquisition activities

FRS 3 layered formats

25.114 FRS 6 repeats the requirements of FRS 3 concerning the reporting of the results of acquisitions made during the financial year of the acquiring group. The results of acquisitions, excluding those that are also discontinued in the period, should be disclosed separately in aggregate as a component of the group's continuing operations. As with the other continuing operations, the minimum analysis given on the face of the profit and loss account should be turnover and operating profit. The analysis of each of the other profit and loss account headings between turnover and operating profit may be given in a note, instead of on the face of the profit and loss account. In addition, where an acquisition has a material impact on a major business segment, this should be disclosed and explained.

25.115 FRS 3 recognises that sometimes it may not be possible to determine post-acquisition results of an acquired operation to the end of the period. This might occur, for instance, where the business of an acquired subsidiary is transferred to another group company and merged with the existing business of that company shortly after the acquisition. If the results of the acquisition cannot be obtained, the standard requires an indication to be given of the contribution of the acquisition to turnover and operating profit of the continuing operations. If that is also not possible, this fact and the reason should be explained. An illustration of this latter situation is given in Table 25.6, where the operations of the continuing and acquired businesses were merged for the latter part of the reporting period.

25.116 FRS 6 has added an important new interpretation of the requirements of FRS 3 as summarised above. It requires the post-acquisition results of businesses acquired in the financial year to be disclosed separately for each material acquisition and for other acquisitions in aggregate. [FRS 6 para 23]. This new interpretation – FRS 3 only refers specifically to separate disclosure of the aggregate results of acquisitions – is explained, in the appendix to the standard that deals with its development, as a clarification of FRS 3.

25.117 The FRS 3 presentation is considered in more detail in chapter 8, together with examples from published financial statements.

Exceptional items

25.118 The results of acquired companies disclosed for the first period after acquisition may not be entirely indicative of the ongoing performance of such companies. This is because, for example, they may be distorted significantly by fair value adjustments made on acquisition. Alternatively, they may be affected by changes introduced by the acquirer soon after the acquisition. FRS 6 indicates that exceptional profits or losses that arise as a result of fair valuing the assets and liabilities of acquired companies should be disclosed in accordance with FRS 3 and should be identified as relating to the acquisition. Once again, such disclosure should be given separately for each material acquisition and for other acquisitions in aggregate. [FRS 6 para 30].

25.119 The standard gives examples of circumstances where such disclosures may be necessary:

- Abnormal trading margins resulting from the revaluation of stocks to fair values on acquisition.
- Material profits resulting from the acquirer turning a loss-making long-term contract into a profitable contract.
- Material profits or losses resulting from contingent assets or liabilities crystallising at amounts different from their attributed fair values.

[FRS 6 para 85].

25.120 The above examples are considered in the subsections in section II that deal with fair valuing stocks (para 25.295) and contingencies (para 25.350).

Post-acquisition reorganisation and integration

25.121 FRS 6 requires the profit and loss account or notes to the financial statements of periods following an acquisition to disclose the costs incurred in those periods in reorganising, restructuring and integrating the acquisition. [FRS 6 para 31]. Such disclosure should be given separately for each material acquisition, and for other acquisitions in aggregate. [FRS 6 para 23].

25.122 Such costs are restrictively defined in the standard. The practical implications of this requirement are considered in section II, paragraph 25.189.

Acquisition provisions

25.123 FRS 6 requires movements on provisions or accruals for costs related to an acquisition to be disclosed and analysed between the amounts used for the specific purpose for which they were created and the amounts released unused. [FRS 6 para 32]. Such disclosure should be given separately for each material acquisition and for other acquisitions in aggregate. [FRS 6 para 23]. This disclosure is considered in section II, paragraph 25.230.

25.124 Table 25.6 provides extracts from the accounts of Glaxo Wellcome plc and illustrates the extensive profit and loss account disclosure required where a group makes a material acquisition and other acquisitions during the financial year. In addition, the group changed its year end from 30 June to 31 December, thus presenting its results for an 18 month period.

Table 25.6 — Glaxo Wellcome plc — Annual Report and Accounts — 31 December 1995

Consolidated Profit and Loss Account

	Notes	12 months to 30.6.95		6 months to 31.12.95			18 months to 31.12.95	12 months to 30.6.94 (restated)
		Glaxo continuing business	Acquisitions	Merged business	Combined business	Integration	Total	
		£m	£m	£m	£m	£m	£m	£m
Turnover	26	5,834	638	4,018	10,490	–	10,490	5,656
Operating costs	5	3,863	438	2,592	6,893	1,215	8,108	3,839
Trading profit	26	1,971	200	1,426	3,597	(1,215)	2,382	1,817
Profit on disposal of business	7	35	–	–	35	–	35	–
Share of profits/(losses) of associated undertakings	8	(8)	26	39	57	–	57	(3)

Profit before interest		1,998	226	1,465	3,689	(1,215)	2,474	1,814
Net (interest payable)/ investment income	9	130	(96)	(121)	(87)	–	(87)	21
Profit on ordinary activities before taxation	26	2,128	130	1,344	3,602	(1,215)	2,387	1,835
Taxation	10	627	53	417	1,097	(230)	867	524
Profit on ordinary activities after taxation		1,501	77	927	2,505	(985)	1,520	1,311
Minority interests		39	5	18	62	–	62	12
Profit attributable to shareholders		1,462	72	909	2,443	(985)	1,458	1,299
Dividends	12	1,004	–	526	1,530	–	1,530	823
Retained(loss)/ profit	23	458	72	383	913	(985)	(72)	476
Earnings per Ordinary Share	11	47.8p			74.6p		44.5p	42.7p
Weighted average number of shares in issue (millions)		3,056			3,274		3,274	3,040
Dividends per Ordinary Share	12				45.0p		45.0p	27.0p

The basis of analysis between Glaxo continuing business, Acquisitions, Merged business and Integration is set out in Note 1 on the Accounts.

Notes to the Accounts (extract)

1 Presentation of Accounts (extract)

Presentation of Profit and Loss Account

The Company has presented the profit and loss account in columnar form to illustrate the respective effect on the results for the period of the acquisitions during the period and their subsequent integration. This analysis is consistent with the way the business was managed and reported during the period. The analysis by column is defined as follows:

Glaxo continuing business reflects the results of the Glaxo business for the 12 months to 30th June 1995. Net investment income is stated as if Glaxo's investment funds had been available for investment throughout the period.

Acquisitions reflects the trading results of the acquisitions from their respective dates of acquisition to 30th June 1995. Interest payable on acquisitions represents the interest costs on borrowings taken out to finance the acquisitions, as if none of the combined Group's investment funds had been utilised to reduce borrowings. Taxation is stated at the rates applicable to the acquired businesses and to the interest costs.

Merged business reflects the results for the six months from 1st July 1995, from which date the continuing and acquired businesses were effectively merged and managed on a unified basis. It is therefore not feasible to identify and report separately the acquired businesses from 1st July 1995.

Integration reflects the costs charged relating to the integration of the continuing and acquired businesses. Taxation is stated at the rates applicable to integration costs and internal restructuring.

5 Operating costs (extract)

	12 months to 30.6.95		6 months to 31.12.95			18 months to 31.12.95	12 months to 30.6.94 (restated)
	Glaxo continuing business	Acquisitions	Merged business	Combined business	Integration	Total	
	£m	£m	£m	£m	£m	£m	£m
Cost of sales	1,037	115	654	1,806	558	2,364	1,004
Selling, general and administrative expenditure	1,986	227	1,368	3,581	400	3,981	1,988
Research and development expenditure	852	103	585	1,540	257	1,797	858
Other operating income	(12)	(7)	(15)	(34)	–	(34)	(11)
	3,863	438	2,592	6,893	1,215	8,108	3,839

Costs expected to be incurred in integrating the businesses of Glaxo and Wellcome are estimated at £1,215 million, comprising severances and other cash costs of £763 million and losses on disposal of fixed assets of £452 million. Costs of £384 million had been incurred by 31st December 1995 and provision for further costs of £831 million has been made at that date.

Operating and Financial Review (extract)

Acquisitions

The results of Wellcome have been consolidated into the Group results from 16th March 1995. In the period to 30th June 1995 Wellcome sales added £628 million to Group turnover and £204 million to trading profit; this represents a trading margin of 32 per cent.

The consolidation of Glaxo Korea Limited added £10 million to sales in this period but made no contribution to trading profit. The consolidation of Affymax N.V. added £4 million to operating costs.

Integration

Plans and financial targets for integration, as developed by the integration task forces in the period to 30th June 1995, were referred to in the Second Interim Report sent to shareholders in September 1995. The plans and targets were updated in November and December 1995 and form the basis of the figures reflected in this Annual Report and Accounts. Compared with the separate forward plans of Glaxo and Wellcome prior to Glaxo's bid for Wellcome, the new plan for the combined Group envisaged the achievement of cost savings year by year amounting to £700 million per year by the end of 1998, and progress is being made towards this objective.

The costs expected to be incurred in achieving these savings are forecast at £1,215 million. Some £452 million of the costs relate to potential losses on asset disposals resulting from site closures.

Cumulative savings are expected to achieve payback of total costs by around the end of 1997. In terms of the cash costs of £763 million, payback will be achieved earlier. The proceeds of asset disposals will reduce the net cash costs of integration.

To recognise the impact of integration activities, the anticipated costs of £1,215 million have been charged in the Accounts at 31st December 1995. The charge comprises costs incurred by 31st December 1995 of £384 million, and a provision for a further £831 million of costs. Taxation relief on integration amounts to £230 million. In calculating the attributable taxation, no taxation relief has been assumed on asset write downs.

Cash flow statement

25.125 Where a group acquires a subsidiary, FRS 1 requires the cash flows relating to the purchase consideration to be reported under 'acquisitions and disposals' in the consolidated cash flow statement. The amounts of cash and overdraft acquired should be shown separately along with the gross consideration paid for the acquisition.

25.126 A group's consolidated cash flow statement should be consistent with the rest of its consolidated financial statements. That is, cash flows should be included from the date of acquisition. Recording the gross consideration separately along with the cash and overdraft balances acquired means that the assets and liabilities of the acquired subsidiary at the date of acquisition, excluding cash and overdraft, would need to be eliminated so as to avoid double counting. For example, stock, debtors and creditors acquired would need to be eliminated from the total balance sheet changes in stock, debtors and creditors in the reconciliation of operating profit to operating cash flows.

Disclosures

25.127 FRS 1 requires a significant amount of disclosure to be made in respect of the cash flow effects of subsidiaries acquired during the financial year. These disclosure requirements are also referred to in FRS 6. The information should be disclosed for each material acquisition and for other non-material acquisitions in aggregate. These disclosure requirements are considered in chapter 30.

Reverse acquisition accounting

25.128 Reverse acquisition accounting is a method of acquisition accounting that may, in certain circumstances, be required to give a true and fair view of a business combination. Normally, where one company acquires another, the shareholders of the acquiring company retain the majority holding in the combined group. However in certain circumstances, the positions may be reversed and it is the acquired company's shareholders who effectively control the combined group even though the other party is the legal acquirer. In such circumstances, the acquired company's board will normally dominate the combined group's board. There could be exceptions to this, for instance if as part of the reverse acquisition, there is a change in the acquired company's management.

25.129 Another example of a reverse acquisition is where a listed company with little or no business (sometimes called a cash shell) acquires a well-established unlisted trading company, which is much larger in size. The motive for such acquisitions is often that by combining with the cash shell, the unlisted trading company obtains a listing for itself. In such circumstances it may not give a true and fair view to account for the combination as the acquisition of the trading company by the cash shell. A true and fair view may require the combination to be accounted for as the acquisition of the cash shell by the trading company, in other words reverse acquisition accounting.

25.130 UK company law and accounting standards do not envisage reverse acquisition accounting and to adopt that approach is a departure from the law and accounting standards. However, such a departure is required by both the Companies Act and accounting standards where it is necessary to give a true and fair view. In such cases the particulars, reasons and effect of the departure have to be given.

25.131 The UITF considered reverse acquisition accounting in an information sheet that it issued in 1996. In this it stated:

> *"Reverse takeovers*
>
> *A reverse takeover occurs when a company that is being acquired issues sufficient voting shares, as consideration for a business combination, for control of it (and hence of the combined enterprise) to pass to the owners of the company whose shares it acquires. In these circumstances IAS 22 'Business Combinations' requires that the enterprise issuing the shares is deemed to be acquired by the other. FRS 6 'Acquisitions and Mergers' notes (in Appendix II) that this accounting, which is sometimes described as 'reverse acquisition accounting', is incompatible with companies legislation in the UK and the Republic of Ireland. It has been suggested that, in the light of the reference in FRS 6, it is not possible to invoke the true and fair override in such cases.*
>
> *The UITF discussed this point and concluded that, whilst each case should be considered on its merits, there are some instances where it would be right and proper to invoke the true and fair override and apply reverse acquisition accounting. It also agreed that, as this is simply an application of the general requirement that the true and fair override may be invoked in the circumstances prescribed by companies legislation, and the point could be clarified by this announcement, no useful purpose would be served by issuing an Abstract on this issue."*

25.132 The UITF referred to IAS 22. This has now been superseded by IFRS 3 (revised, issued in 2008), 'Business combinations', which states the following concerning reverse acquisitions:

> *"In a business combination effected primarily by exchanging equity interests, the acquirer is usually the entity that issues its equity interests. However, in some business combinations, commonly called 'reverse acquisitions', the issuing entity is the acquiree. Paragraphs B19–B27 provide guidance on accounting for reverse acquisitions. Other pertinent facts and circumstances shall also be considered in identifying the acquirer in a business combination effected by exchanging equity interests, including:*

(a) *the relative voting rights in the combined entity after the business combination —The acquirer is usually the combining entity whose owners as a group retain or receive the largest portion of the voting rights in the combined entity. In determining which group of owners retains or receives the largest portion of the voting rights, an entity shall consider the existence of any unusual or special voting arrangements and options, warrants or convertible securities.*

(b) *the existence of a large minority voting interest in the combined entity if no other owner or organised group of owners has a significant voting interest — The acquirer is usually the combining entity whose single owner or organised group of owners holds the largest minority voting interest in the combined entity.*

(c) *the composition of the governing body of the combined entity — The acquirer is usually the combining entity whose owners have the ability to elect or appoint or to remove a majority of the members of the governing body of the combined entity.*

(d) *the composition of the senior management of the combined entity — The acquirer is usually the combining entity whose (former) management dominates the management of the combined entity.*

(e) *the terms of the exchange of equity interests — The acquirer is usually the combining entity that pays a premium over the pre-combination fair value of the equity interests of the other combining entity or entities.*

The acquirer is usually the combining entity whose relative size (measured in, for example, assets, revenues or profit) is significantly greater than that of the other combining entity or entities."

[IFRS 3 (revised) para B15-B16].

25.133 Whilst the UITF acknowledges that reverse acquisition accounting may be required in certain circumstances, it does not set out in detail how the accounting should work in practice. However, some guidance is included in an appendix to IFRS 3 and IFRS 3 (revised, issued in 2008).

25.134 In practice, under UK GAAP, the accounting on consolidation for reverse acquisitions will normally follow the principles outlined below (the company issuing the shares – the legal acquirer – is referred to as the 'issuer' and the other party – the in substance acquirer – is referred to as the 'acquirer'):

- The assets and liabilities of the legal subsidiary (that is, the 'acquirer' for accounting purposes) will be recognised and measured in the consolidated financial statements at their pre-combination carrying amounts.
- The assets and liabilities of the legal parent (that is, the 'issuer' – the acquiree for accounting purpose) will be fair valued.

- The consideration for the reverse acquisition of the issuer will be taken to be the number of shares of the issuer in issue immediately prior to the reverse acquisition times the market price of those shares at the point in time when the offer goes unconditional. The premium on these shares which is thus derived will be taken to a reverse acquisition reserve.
- Where merger relief is available under section 612 of the Companies Act 2006 no share premium or merger reserve will be recorded on the shares issued by the issuer for the combination with the acquirer.
- The profit and loss reserve, revaluation reserve and 'other' reserves of the acquirer will be shown in place of those of the issuer.
- The share capital, share premium and capital redemption reserves of the issuer (being of a capital nature) will be shown, as these are legal capital reserves and may not be altered.

How this works in practice is illustrated in the following example.

Example 1 – Reverse acquisition accounting

Issuer with share capital of 1m 10p shares and net assets of £200,000 (fair value £250,000) combines with acquirer, which has share capital of 20,000 £1 shares and net assets of £5m (fair value £7m). The balance sheets before the reverse acquisition are:

	Issuer £'000	Acquirer £'000
Net assets	200	5,000
Share capital	100	20
Share premium	50	580
Capital redemption reserve	20	300
Revaluation reserve	20	600
Profit and loss	10	3,500
Shareholders' funds	200	5,000

The share price of the issuer at the date of acquisition is 30p per share and it issues 30m shares giving a consideration of £9m. However, a true and fair override is adopted and reverse acquisition accounting is used to account for the combination.

The £9m represents the value of acquirer (which legally has been acquired by issuer). However, if acquirer was buying issuer it would pay market value which at the date of acquisition is 1m x 30p per shares and equals £300,000. Therefore, the consideration is determined, not as £9m for the acquisition of acquirer by issuer, but rather as £300,000, being the share capital in issue immediately prior to the combination times the share price of issuer's shares at the date when the offer went unconditional. The £300,000 represents 1m shares at a price of 30p per share.

Immediately after the combination, the share capital of the combined group is shown as £3,100,000 (31m shares at their nominal value of 10p). The share premium is shown at £50,000 because merger relief under section 612 is available for the 30m shares that have been issued and thus, no premium need be recognised for those shares. The capital redemption reserve (CRR) is £20,000 as this, like the share premium account, is a statutory capital reserve of the legal parent, the issuer.

The reverse acquisition reserve is credited with the difference between the nominal value of the issuer's share capital immediately prior to the combination and the fair value of those shares based on the market price at the date the offer went unconditional – that is as if the shares had been issued as consideration for the acquisition of the issuer itself. This amount is £300,000 less nominal value of £100,000, that is £200,000.

Goodwill is calculated as the difference between the fair value of the consideration notionally given for the issuer (£300,000) and the fair value of the issuer's assets and liabilities, which is £250,000, giving goodwill of £50,000.

The consolidation, therefore, appears as follows:

	Issuer	Acquirer	Fair value adjustment	Consolidated
	£'000	£'000	£'000	£'000
Net assets (excluding goodwill)	200	5,000	50	5,250
Goodwill				50
Investment	3,000			
Net assets	3,200	5,000		5,300
Share capital	3,100	20		3,100
Share premium	50	580		50
Capital redemption reserve	20	300		20
Revaluation reserve	20	600		600
Profit and loss	10	3,500		3,500
	3,200	5,000		7,270
Difference — reverse acquisition reserve				(1,970)
Shareholders' funds				5,300

As explained above, one element of the reverse acquisition reserve is a credit of £200,000. The full amount of the difference can be explained as follows:

	£'000
Premium on issue of shares for issuer (1m shares @ 30p = £300,000 less nominal value £100,000)	200
Difference between reserves of acquirer and issuer included in consolidation (£600,000 + £3.5m – £20,000 – £10,000)	(4,070)
Excess of net assets of acquirer over nominal value of shares issued (£5m – £3m)	2,000
Less excess of net assets of issuer over share capital of issuer at date of acquisition (£200,000 – £100,000)	(100)
Reverse acquisition reserve	(1,970)

The figure of £1.97m is the extent to which the reserves of the acquirer have been capitalised as a result of the combination. Another method of reconciling the reverse acquisition reserve is given in paragraph 25.136 below.

25.135 In the above example if the nominal value of the issuer's 1 million shares was 1p instead of 10p, there would have been a different result as follows:

Example 2 — Reverse acquisition accounting

	Issuer £'000	Acquirer £'000
Net assets	200	5,000
Share capital	10	20
Share premium	140	580
Capital redemption reserve	20	300
Revaluation reserve	20	600
Profit and loss	10	3,500
Shareholders' funds	200	5,000

The only changes to the figures in the previous example are reducing the share capital of the issuer to £10,000 from £100,000 and increasing the share premium account by £90,000 (that is, assuming the shares were originally issued at a premium of £90,000).

The reverse acquisition is still made for a consideration of £9m, and 30m shares are issued at 30p per share. This gives a nominal value of £300,000 rather than £3,000,000 as in the previous example.

The consolidation is:

	Issuer £'000	Acquirer £'000	Fair value adjustment £'000	Consolidated £'000
Net assets (excluding goodwill)	200	5,000	50	5,250
Goodwill				50
Investment	300			
Net assets	500	5,000		5,300
Share capital	310	20		310
Share premium	140	580		140
Capital redemption reserve	20	300		20
Revaluation reserve	20	600		600
Profit and loss	10	3,500		3,500
	500	5,000		4,570
Difference – reverse acquisition reserve				730
Shareholders' funds				5,300

The reverse acquisition reserve is made up of:

	£'000
Premium on issue of shares for issuer (1m shares @ 30p = £300,000 less nominal value £10,000)	290
Difference between reserves of acquirer and issuer included in consolidation (£600,000 + £3.5m – £20,000 – £10,000)	(4,070)
Excess of net assets of acquirer over nominal value of shares issued (£5m – £300,000)	4,700
Less excess of net assets of issuer over share capital of issuer at date of acquisition (£200,000 – £10,000)	(190)
Reverse acquisition reserve	730

25.136 Another method of reconciling the reverse acquisition reserve in the two examples above is as follows:

		Example 1		Example 2
	£'000	£'000	£'000	£'000
Additional 'premium' recognised re issuer				
Premium on issue of shares for issuer		200		290
Statutory reserves of issuer		(70)		(160)
		130		130
Reverse acquisition difference re acquirer				
Shares issued (nominal value)		(3,000)		(300)
Share capital and statutory reserves:				
Share capital	20		20	
Share premium	580		580	
Capital redemption reserve	300		300	
		900		900
		(2,100)		600
Reverse acquisition reserve		(1,970)		730

25.137 Where reverse acquisition accounting is adopted, a true and fair override of the Companies Act and FRS 6 and FRS 7 is required. The particulars, reasons and effect must be disclosed in accordance with companies' legislation and FRS 18.

25.138 The reasons given will normally be that the acquisition results in control passing from the issuer to the acquirer and thus, the substance is an acquisition by the acquirer. Particulars will include the fact that the Act and accounting standards would normally require that an acquisition is accounted for as an acquisition by the issuer of the acquirer, but that to reflect the transaction's substance it has been accounted for as the acquisition of the issuer by the acquirer and reverse acquisition accounting has been adopted.

25.139 The effect will include disclosure of the fair value of assets and liabilities and of the goodwill that would have arisen had normal acquisition accounting in accordance with the Act and accounting standards been adopted, together with the effect on reserves of adopting reverse acquisition accounting.

25.140 In the former of the two examples above, the goodwill that would have arisen had normal acquisition accounting been adopted would be calculated as follows:

Example 1 — Goodwill arising had acquisition accounting been used

	£'000
Consideration at fair value (30m shares @ 30p)	9,000
Fair value of acquirer's net assets	(7,000)
Goodwill	2,000

Reserves under normal acquisition accounting would be:

	£'000
Share capital	3,100
Share premium	50
Merger reserve (30m shares @ 30p – 10p)	6,000
Capital redemption reserve	20
Revaluation reserve	20
Profit and loss	10
Shareholders' funds	9,200
Net assets on consolidation (£7m + £200,000) (excluding goodwill)	7,200
Goodwill	2,000
Net assets	9,200

The reconciliation of reserves between normal acquisition accounting and reverse acquisition accounting would be:

	Note	Normal acquisition accounting £'000	Adjustment £'000	Reverse acquisition accounting £'000
Share capital		3,100	–	3,100
Share premium		50	–	50
Merger reserve	1	6,000	(6,000)	–
Capital redemption reserve		20		20
Revaluation reserve	2	20	580	600
Profit and loss	3	10	3,490	3,500
Reverse acquisition reserve	4	–	(1,970)	(1,970)
Shareholders' funds		9,200	(3,900)	5,300

Notes:

1 Removes merger reserve arising on fair value of consideration for acquirer as acquirer is not treated as being acquired under reverse acquisition accounting.
2 Replaces revaluation reserve of issuer with that of acquirer.
3 Replaces profit and loss reserve of issuer with that of acquirer.
4 Includes notional merger reserve on fair valuing notional consideration for acquisition of issuer (credit of £130,000 – see para 25.136 above) and reflects the difference between the share capital issued as a result of the combination and the share capital and statutory reserves of the acquirer (debit of £2.1m – see para 25.136 above).

25.141 The reverse acquisition reserve, where it is negative, should be applied against the profit and loss reserve. Where it is positive, it should be carried as a separate reserve.

25.142 The reconciliation of reserves for the second example above is as follows:

Example 2 — Goodwill arising had acquisition accounting been used

	£'000
Goodwill is calculated as above	2,000

Reserves under normal acquisition accounting would be:

Share capital	310
Share premium	140
Merger reserve (30m shares @30p – 1p)	8,700
Capital redemption reserve	20
Revaluation reserve	20
Profit and loss account	10
Shareholders' funds	9,200
Net assets (excluding goodwill)	7,200
Goodwill	2,000
Net assets	9,200

The reconciliation of reserves would be:

	Normal acquisition accounting £'000	Adjustment £'000	Reverse acquisition accounting £'000
Share capital	310		310
Share premium	140		140
Merger reserve	8,700	(8,700)	–
Capital redemption reserve	20		20
Revaluation reserve	20	580	600
Profit and loss	10	3,490	3,500
Reverse acquisition reserve	–	730	730
Shareholders' funds	9,200		5,300

Cash alternative

25.143 In some cases a partial cash alternative might be offered by the issuer when making the bid for the acquirer. Such a cash alternative would not form part of the consideration for accounting purposes when adopting reverse acquisition accounting, because it would be paid to the acquirer's shareholders. Instead it would be treated as if it were the repurchase of shares. This can be illustrated as follows.

Example – Accounting for a cash alternative

In the second example above (in para 25.135) 30m shares were issued at 30p per share giving a value of £9m. Suppose there had been a cash alternative of 30p instead of one share and this was taken up such that only 29m shares were issued (value £8.7m) and £300,000 was paid in cash.

In such a case, the share capital in the consolidated financial statements would be £300,000 (that is, 29m shares × 1p = £290,000 + £10,000 of shares already in issue) rather than £310,000. Net assets would be £4.95m (that is, £5.25m less cash paid out of £300,000) and the reverse acquisition reserve would be £440,000 rather than £730,000 as follows:

	Issuer	Acquirer	Fair value adjustment	Consolidated
	£'000	£'000	£'000	£'000
Net assets (excluding goodwill)	(100)	5,000	50	4,950
Goodwill				
Investment	590			50
Net assets	490	5,000		5,000
Share capital	300	20		300
Share premium	140	580		140
Capital redemption reserve	20	300		20
Revaluation reserve	20	600		
Profit and loss	10	3,500		3,500
	490	5,000		4,560
Difference — reverse acquisition reserve				440
Shareholders' funds				5,000

Using the two reconciliation methods used in the previous examples, the reverse acquisition reserve can be reconciled as follows:

Method 1

	£'000
Premium on issue of shares for issuer (1m shares @ 30p = £300,000 less nominal value £10,000)	290
Difference between reserves of acquirer and issuer included in consolidation (£600,000 + £3.5m – £20,000 – £10,000)	(4,070)
Excess of net assets of acquirer over nominal value of shares issued and cash paid (£5m – £590,000)	4,410
Less excess of net assets of issuer over share capital of issuer at date of acquisition (£200,000 – £10,000)	(190)
Reverse acquisition reserve	440

Method 2

		£'000
Additional 'premium' recognised re issuer		
Premium on issue of shares for issuer		290
Statutory reserves of issuer		(160)
		130
Reverse acquisition difference re acquirer		
Shares issued (nominal value)		(290)
Share capital and statutory reserves:		
Share capital	20	
Share premium	580	
Capital redemption reserve	300	
		900
Cash paid out for 'repurchase of shares'		(300)
		310
Reverse acquisition reserve		440

Section II — Fair values

Introduction

25.144 Consolidated financial statements are prepared on the principle that the reporting entity and its subsidiary undertakings are a single economic entity. Thus, the activities, assets and liabilities of all the undertakings in a group are included within the consolidation.

25.145 When a group extends its activities through the purchase of a new business entity, the purchase price is seldom negotiated on the basis of the values of the individual assets and liabilities of the entity being acquired. Instead, it is more likely to be determined by reference to the purchase of a stream of future profits or cash flows, so that a value is arrived at for the entity as a whole. Nevertheless, for the purposes of the consolidated financial statements the transaction has to be 'looked through' in order to determine initial carrying values for the underlying assets and liabilities of the acquired entity. This is sometimes described as a process of allocating the purchase price to the underlying net tangible and intangible assets to arrive at a 'cost' to the group. Establishing initial carrying values for those assets and liabilities, as a proxy for their cost, also provides a basis for reporting the performance of the enlarged group from the date the new entity is acquired.

25.146 The elements of accounting for a typical business acquisition can be demonstrated as follows:

Purchase consideration
Add: Expenses of acquisition
=
Cost of acquisition
Less: Fair valued assets and liabilities
=
Goodwill on acquisition

25.146.1 Fair values are a key part of acquisition accounting because:

- The fair value of the purchase consideration determines the cost of acquisition of the investment to the acquiring company.
- The fair value of the identifiable net assets acquired will be used as the carrying amounts for the newly acquired assets and liabilities in consolidated financial statements.
- The difference between the cost of acquisition and the sum of the fair values of the identifiable assets less liabilities is goodwill.

25.147 The principle of fair valuing assets and liabilities in acquisition accounting has been recognised for many years, both in the UK and internationally. The principle is also recognised in the Companies Act 2006, which requires that a newly acquired subsidiary's identifiable assets and liabilities must be included in the consolidated balance sheet at their fair values, as at the date of acquisition. [SI 2008/410 6 Sch 9(2)].

25.148 While the principle is relatively simple, applying it in practice has proved a difficult matter. FRS 7, 'Fair values in acquisition accounting', was issued in 1994 and has brought rigour to the principles to be applied when acquisition accounting.

Scope and basic principles of FRS 7

Scope

25.149 FRS 7 deals with fair value in the context of the acquisition of subsidiary undertakings by a parent company that prepares consolidated financial statements. Acquired subsidiary undertakings can include unincorporated entities, such as partnerships. The principles of the FRS also apply where a group or an individual company acquires the trade and assets of an unincorporated business (including a division of a company). [FRS 7 para 4]. Whether the acquisition is of a subsidiary or a business, it is necessary for the acquirer to account for the cost of acquisition by recognising the underlying assets, liabilities and goodwill of the acquired subsidiary or business. A subsidiary's assets, liabilities and goodwill will be recognised at fair value in the acquiring company's consolidated financial statements. Where a business is acquired, the fair values will be reflected in the acquiring company's own financial statements.

25.150 Other transactions that require fair value accounting, and the calculation of goodwill, include:

- The purchase of an additional interest in an existing subsidiary from a minority shareholder. FRS 2 states that when a group increases its interest in an undertaking that is already its subsidiary, the identifiable assets and liabilities of that subsidiary should be revalued to their fair values and goodwill arising on the increase in interest should be calculated by reference to those fair values (except where the effect of changes in value is not material). [FRS 2 para 51]. (See section I, para 25.84.)
- The purchase of interests in associated undertakings and joint ventures which are accounted for under the equity method or gross equity method in accordance with FRS 9. [FRS 9 para 31].

The principles of FRS 7 are relevant to accounting for the above transactions in the acquirer's consolidated financial statements.

Purchase of business or assets

25.151 The definition of an 'acquisition' in FRS 7 derives from the definition of a 'business combination', which is framed as *"the bringing together of separate entities into one economic entity as a result of one entity uniting with, or obtaining control over the net assets and operations of, another"*. [FRS 7 para 2].

25.152 In some purchase transactions, it is necessary to determine whether the substance of the transaction is really the acquisition of a business or simply the purchase of assets or other payment. In the latter case, the transaction does not give rise to goodwill in the acquirer's financial statements, but results in the recording of any identified assets at their cost, as evidenced by the purchase price.

25.153 The above definitions imply that, for acquisition accounting to be applicable, the acquired entity must be more than a collection of assets and liabilities. It would normally be carrying out a continuing trade with an identifiable turnover, which means that the assets and liabilities of the acquired entity interact with each other and, importantly, with the people who operate the assets as a business.

Objective

25.154 The standard's overriding objective is twofold:

- All the assets and liabilities that existed in the acquired entity at the date of acquisition should be brought into the acquirer's financial statements at fair values reflecting their condition at that date.
- All changes to the acquired assets and liabilities, and the resulting gains or losses, that arise after control has passed to the acquirer are reported as part of the post-acquisition financial performance of the acquiring group.

[FRS 7 para 1].

25.155 By restricting the assets and liabilities recognised in the fair value exercise to those that already existed in the acquired entity, and by limiting the extent to which future events may be anticipated in arriving at fair values, the ASB has established a strict framework for determining whether revenues and costs should be treated as pre-acquisition (that is, reported within the pre-acquisition assets and liabilities of the target) or post-acquisition (that is, reported as profits or losses) in the acquirer's consolidated financial statements.

25.156 Consistent with its stated objective, the FRS precludes an acquirer from recognising any costs of planned post-acquisition reorganisation in the fair value exercise and, as a result, in the calculation of purchased goodwill. The rationale for this is that such costs were not liabilities of the acquired entity at the date of acquisition.

Fair value of identifiable assets and liabilities

Overriding principles

25.157 The objective of FRS 7 is reflected in the two stated principles that underpin the standard for determining initial fair values for the assets and liabilities of an acquired entity, which are:

- The identifiable assets and liabilities to be recognised should be those of the acquired entity that existed at the date of the acquisition. [FRS 7 para 5].
- The recognised assets and liabilities should be measured at fair values that reflect the conditions at the date of the acquisition. [FRS 7 para 6].

Identifying the assets and liabilities acquired

Definitions of assets and liabilities

25.158 Identifiable assets and liabilities are defined as:

> *"The assets and liabilities of the acquired entity that are capable of being disposed of or settled separately, without disposing of a business of the entity".* [FRS 7 para 2].

This definition is for all intents and purposes the same as the definition in the Act. [SI 2008/410 6 Sch 9(2)].

25.159 An acquiring company should review its acquisition and determine all the identifiable assets and liabilities as soon as possible after making the purchase. Goodwill is not an identifiable asset, because it cannot be sold separately from a business.

25.160 Definitions of assets and liabilities have been developed by the ASB in its Statement of Principles, and have been incorporated into FRS 5, 'Reporting the substance of transactions'. These definitions are implicitly embodied in the principles of FRS 7. Assets are defined as:

> *"Rights or other access to future economic benefits controlled by an entity as a result of past transactions or events."* [FRS 5 para 2].

Liabilities are defined as:

> *"An entity's obligations to transfer economic benefits as a result of past transactions or events."* [FRS 5 para 4].

25.161 When applied to acquisition accounting, the 'entity' is the acquired entity. The past transactions or events giving rise to the rights or obligations (including those that are contingent) of the acquired entity must have occurred before the date of acquisition if they are to be regarded as pre-acquisition.

25.162 Therefore, to qualify for recognition in the fair value exercise, FRS 7 requires that, in the case of assets, the rights to future benefits must have been obtained by the acquired entity before the date of acquisition. In the case of liabilities, there must have been a commitment by the acquired entity before the date of acquisition to transfer economic benefits.

25.163 The definitions of assets and liabilities quoted above are wide ranging and encompass most items that would usually be recognised in the balance sheet of an acquired entity under conventional accounting principles. For example, the definition of assets would generally include prepayments, where payments have been made which give the acquired entity rights to obtain future services or access to future benefits. Similarly, the definition of liabilities would generally include, in addition to creditors and accruals, items of deferred income, where the entity has still to incur costs in respect of future obligations relating to payments that have been received. These items, which would normally be recognised in the financial statements of the acquired entity, should also be taken into account in the fair value exercise.

Inclusion of additional assets and liabilities

25.164 Not all items that meet the above definitions of assets and liabilities are necessarily recorded in the financial statements as soon as they are identified. Consequently, some identifiable assets and liabilities may need to be recognised by the acquirer although they have not been recognised in the financial statements of the acquired entity.

25.165 An acquisition requires a fair value allocation to be made, so far as is practically possible, over all the existing assets and liabilities of the acquired entity. Ensuring that all pre-acquisition assets and liabilities are recognised at the acquisition date ensures that the post-acquisition profit and loss account will not include any items relating to the pre-acquisition period, giving more useful post-acquisition performance information.

25.166 Examples of liabilities that may not previously have been recognised in the acquired company's financial statements, but would be included as fair value adjustments, include provisions for the following:

- Onerous financial contracts entered into by the acquired company, such as forward, futures and options contracts, where the provision is calculated by reference to current market values of the relevant financial instruments.
- Contingent losses, provided that the contingency was in existence before the acquisition (see para 25.350 for further discussion of contingencies).
- Losses arising from pre-existing contractual arrangements, such as 'poison pill' clauses in shareholder agreements or compensation clauses in directors' service contracts, that crystallise as a result of the acquisition. An example is where the acquired entity had previously entered into a contract that triggers an obligation upon a change of ownership or change of control where the crystallisation of the liability is independent of any decision or action of the acquirer. This type of identifiable liability is referred to in the explanation section of the standard. [FRS 7 para 37].

25.167 Following the issue of FRS 12, UK entities should have recognised provisions for items such as environmental clean up obligations related to their past activities or provisions for onerous contracts. However, the principle in FRS 7 requiring recognition of liabilities of the entity at the date of acquisition means that even if such items have not been recognised by the acquired entity (for example, an overseas company), they will be identifiable liabilities for the fair value exercise.

25.168 In each of the above examples, the item meets the criteria for recognition in the fair value exercise because either the obligation had been incurred before the acquisition or the underlying contingency giving rise to the provision was in existence before the acquisition and, in the latter case, the outcome was not dependent on the acquirer's intentions. Various practical examples are considered in paragraph 25.177 below.

25.169 FRS 7 makes specific reference to onerous contracts and commitments:

> *"Identifiable liabilities include items such as onerous contracts and commitments that existed at the time of acquisition, whether or not the corresponding obligations were recognised as liabilities in the financial statements of the acquired entity."* [FRS 7 para 38].

Whilst the standard does not define what 'onerous' means, this should generally be interpreted with reference to its basic principles. Firstly, a contract must have been onerous to the acquired entity at the date of acquisition and not have become onerous as a result of the acquirer's actions. Secondly, whether or not a contract is onerous can often reasonably be interpreted as meaning whether or not the obligation exceeds the current (that is, at date of acquisition) market value.

25.170 Examples of potentially onerous contracts include long-term supply contracts for commodities such as oil, gas and electricity, where the price to which the acquired company is committed exceeds the current market price for such contracts. They should usually be capable of being bought and sold in an arm's length transaction. They would not be recognised on the acquired entity's balance sheet unless, unusually, it had a policy of marking such contracts to market or they qualified as onerous contracts under FRS 12. The 'losses' derived from fair valuing such commitments – the value at which a contract for a similar product, a similar amount and for a similar future delivery date could be entered into at the date of acquisition – would be recognised as identifiable liabilities in the fair value exercise.

25.171 Long-term purchase commitments that are onerous contracts under FRS 12 (that is, those that result in loss-making business – see chapter 21) clearly have to be recognised as liabilities in the fair value exercise. However, an important consideration in fair valuing other long-term purchase commitments is that there should be consistency of treatment. This means that where other long-term purchase commitments (that is, those that are unfavourable, but which are used in profitable business) are recognised as identifiable liabilities, all such commitments, whether unfavourable or favourable, should be recognised. Thus where commitments have been entered into at prices lower than current market prices for equivalent commitments, the 'gains' derived from valuing them at fair value should be recognised as assets in the fair value exercise.

25.172 Table 25.7 gives an example of onerous purchase contracts recognised as fair value adjustments.

Table 25.7 – United Utilities PLC – Annual Report & Accounts – 31 March 1996

Notes to the accounts (extract)

12 Purchase of subsidiary (extract)

The Group acquired NORWEB plc on 8 November 1995 and the acquisition method of accounting has been adopted. The analysis of net assets acquired and the fair value to the Group is as follows:

	Book value £m	Revaluation £m	Accounting policy alignment £m	Other £m	Fair value to Group £m
Tangible fixed assets	779.3	234.9	–	–	1,014.2
Investments	147.4	247.6	–	–	395.0
Stocks	68.4	–	(3.7)	–	64.7
Debtors	248.2	–	(14.7)	(21.1)	212.4
Cash and cash equivalents	254.9	–	–	–	254.9
Creditors falling due within one year	(281.0)	(48.0)	–	4.0	(325.0)
Creditors falling due after more than one year	(517.7)	(32.5)	–	–	(550.2)
Provisions for liabilities and charges*	(44.2)	(1.0)	(1.3)	(217.9)	(264.4)
Net assets before special dividend	655.3	401.0	(19.7)	(235.0)	801.6
Special dividend, including advance corporation tax	(195.6)	–	–	–	(195.6)
Net assets	459.7	401.0	(19.7)	(235.0)	606.0
Consideration:					
Cash					1,463.2
Shares allotted					197.0
Share option obligations					22.7
Total consideration					1,682.9
Goodwill arising					1,076.9

Explanations of the major fair value adjustments in the above table are given in the financial review on pages 12 and 13.

The fair value adjustment of £217.9 million relating to provisions for liabilities and charges includes £173.2 million in respect of onerous gas and electricity contracts.

The fair value adjustments are provisional and may be subject to revision in the 1996/97 accounts. Any adjustments made will be reflected in the goodwill calculation.

Financial review (extract)

Acquisition of Norweb (extract)

Norweb's net assets acquired, excluding the special dividend and associated advance corporation tax, amounted to £801.6 million. This was after a net increase of £146.3 million for provisional fair value adjustments.

The **distribution network** was revalued upward on the basis of the return being earned on those assets increasing the net book value by £248 million.

The **investments** in the National Grid and Pumped Storage Business were revalued upward by £199.6 million, net of £48.0 million tax provisions, reflecting the net proceeds received on disposal.

Provision was made for **gas and electricity contracts** of £173.2 million mainly in relation to long term power purchase agreements, where the recent collapse in gas prices and reduced capacity

> costs resulted in onerous conditions compared to prices available in November 1995, the date the fair valuation was made. The provisions are of a long term nature and, in any event, will not be utilised prior to 1998. Also included is a small element relating to short term take or pay gas purchase contracts.
>
> Other adjustments are given in note 12 to the accounts.
>
> The fair value adjustments will be reviewed again during the course of 1996/97 and amended as necessary in the light of subsequent knowledge or events.
>
> * Note that, for years beginning on or after 1 January 2005, SI 2004/2947, 'The Companies Act 1985 (International Accounting Standards and Other Amendments) Regulations 2004', changes this schedule 4 line item to 'provisions for liabilities'.

Exclusion of certain assets and liabilities

25.173 Conversely, certain items recognised by the acquired entity may not be recognised by the acquirer. An obvious example is where purchased goodwill is recognised as an asset in the acquired entity's balance sheet in respect of its previous acquisitions. That purchased goodwill is by definition not an identifiable asset and would be subsumed within the calculation of goodwill arising on the acquisition in the acquirer's consolidated financial statements. Another example is development expenditure capitalised in the accounts of the acquired entity. In the fair value exercise it may be impossible to arrive at a reliable fair value relating to the balance of unamortised deferred development expenditure; alternatively, deferral of development costs may be inconsistent with the accounting policies of the acquiring group (see 25.175 below). In those circumstances, it would be necessary to reflect the value of all past research and development expenditure in goodwill.

25.174 Where the acquired entity has recognised provisions for expenditure not yet incurred, the standard requires the circumstances to be considered very carefully in order to determine whether the provisions are proper pre-acquisition liabilities. It states that *"only if the acquired entity was demonstrably committed to the expenditure whether or not the acquisition was completed would it have a liability at the date of acquisition"*. [FRS 7 para 40]. Any provisions that fail this test do not meet the definition of identifiable liabilities and should be added back to the net assets of the acquired entity in the fair value exercise. This issue is considered further in paragraph 25.200.

Adjustments for different accounting policies

25.175 FRS 7 requires that, subject to the detailed rules that apply its principles to specific types of assets and liabilities of an acquired business, recognition and measurement should be determined in accordance with the acquirer's accounting policies for similar assets and liabilities. [FRS 7 para 8].

25.176 Examples where fair value adjustments may be necessary to achieve consistency with the acquirer's accounting policies include: current assets affected by different revenue recognition policies; and deferred tax liabilities where the acquirer has adopted a policy of discounting but the acquiree had not. The purpose of the requirement to base fair values on the acquirer's accounting policies is so that post-acquisition performance is not distorted purely by accounting policy differences.

Examples — identifiable liabilities or post-acquisition costs

25.177 Some examples of items that would be included in pre-acquisition liabilities and items that would be treated as post-acquisition costs are considered below:

Example 1 – Vacant leasehold property

An acquired company has a lease on a property that it no longer occupies. The acquirer decides to move out of one of its existing properties, which it also leases, and occupy the surplus property leased by the acquired company. The acquirer decides to incur the costs of early termination of its existing lease.

FRS 12 considers the general question of whether the rent payable and other expenses of vacant leasehold property should be provided for when such property ceases to be used. FRS 12 requires provision to be made where there is an onerous contract. An example of an onerous lease contract is one where the property is vacant and the company is unable to find a sub-lessee or can only sub-let at a rental less than it is paying under the head lease.

Following the principles of FRS 7 and FRS 12, the acquired company's obligations in respect of the lease on the vacant property is likely to be an identifiable liability that existed at the date of acquisition. If provision is appropriate in the circumstances of the acquired company at the date of acquisition, it should be recognised in the fair value exercise as a liability of the acquired company.

The reoccupation of the property leased by the acquired company and the abandonment of the property leased by the acquirer are part of the post-acquisition reorganisation of the combined group and, therefore, the financial effects of the relocation would be included in the consolidated profit and loss account. Thus any provision recognised as an identifiable liability at the date of acquisition would be reversed and the cost of terminating the acquirer's lease would be recognised, with both items being treated as post-acquisition.

Example 2 – Property vacated in rationalisation

An acquired company had occupied a rented warehouse. After the acquisition the acquiring group rationalised its distribution facilities and the warehouse occupied by the acquired company was vacated. The group is making provision for the rentals payable under the unexpired lease.

Under FRS 7 the abandonment of the property should be accounted for as a post-acquisition event. The provision for rent payable on the property being vacated should be charged in the profit and loss account as part of the cost of post-acquisition reorganisation.

Example 3 – Property lease at above market rent

An acquired company leases its head office on an operating lease. The rent for the next 15 years is fixed at a level that is in excess of the rents payable on leases of comparable buildings that are on the market at the time of the acquisition. This is not an onerous lease under FRS 12 as the company continues to occupy the property and the business of the acquired company makes adequate profits to absorb the lease costs. Can a provision be made in the fair value exercise for the lease, that is, the difference between the committed lease payments over the term of the lease and those that would reflect current market rents?

There are alternative approaches to this question. One view is that operating leases are not recognised as liabilities under standard accounting practice, and FRS 7 does not specifically indicate that they should be recognised in acquisition accounting. SSAP 21 requires rents payable under operating leases to be expensed on a straight-line basis over the term of the lease; the method of expensing is not accelerated (or decelerated) as market rentals fluctuate. Only timing differences between the amount of rentals expensed and rentals paid are normally recognised as accruals or prepayments. Under this view, the 'above-market' element of the lease is not regarded as an identifiable liability, and no provision is recognised in the fair value exercise. The actual lease payments would continue to be expensed in the acquirer's consolidated profit and loss account until the acquirer renegotiates the lease.

A different view is that recognising a provision for the 'above-market' element of the lease when accounting for the acquisition is consistent with FRS 7's principles with regard to identifying and measuring the fair value of the acquired company's existing obligations. A leasehold interest will have a negative value where the rent reserved under the lease exceeds the open market rental. By recognising a provision for this commitment's estimated market value, the acquiring group would be reflecting the fact that it would have received an incentive to take on such a lease, in the form of a reduction in the purchase consideration. Under the principles of UITF Abstract 28, 'Operating lease incentives', a cash incentive given to a lessee to take on a lease is recognised as a liability initially and is allocated to reduce the future rental expense over the shorter of the lease term and a period ending on a date from which it is expected the prevailing market rental will become payable.

In our view, it is acceptable for an acquirer to have an accounting policy of fair valuing an acquired company's leases. Of course, if this treatment is adopted, it should be applied consistently by valuing all leasehold interests acquired. Where applicable, any favourable operating leases (that is, where the rent under the lease is below the current open market rentals) should be included as assets in the fair value exercise. Whether or not the acquirer has a policy of fair valuing operating leases, the policy should also be applied consistently to all acquisitions.

An identifiable liability that is recognised in the fair value exercise in respect of the 'above-market' rentals is not a type of provision that is normally recognised under FRS 12 where no acquisition is involved. Instead, the liability established at the acquisition date would in effect be treated as a premium received for taking on the lease. The balance would not be re-measured in subsequent years if market rentals change, but would be amortised to reduce the future rental expense during the lease.

Example 4 – Relocation costs

Company A acquired a subsidiary of company B. The subsidiary occupied premises that it shared with other operations in company B's group. As part of the purchase agreement, the new subsidiary was required to vacate those premises. Company A is making a provision in the accounts of the subsidiary for the estimated costs of relocation.

Under FRS 7 the relocation costs were not an identifiable liability of the acquired subsidiary at the date of acquisition. The relocation is a post-acquisition event and is not an action that the subsidiary was committed to whether or not the acquisition was completed, nor the crystallisation of a pre-existing contingent liability. In addition, FRS 12 does not permit costs of relocation to be provided in advance. [FRS 12 paras 85, 86]. The costs of relocation should, therefore, be charged as incurred as a post-acquisition revenue cost in company A's consolidated financial statements.

Example 5 – Golden parachute

The directors of the target company have clauses in their contracts that entitle them to receive twice their basic salary, together with an amount in respect of loss of pension benefits, if they decide to terminate their contracts within 28 days of an offer for more than 50% of the company's share capital being declared unconditional. The company has been taken over and the directors have exercised their rights to terminate their contracts and claim compensation.

In this example, a so-called golden parachute, the acquirer has no control over the decision to terminate the service contracts of the acquired company's directors and incur the consequential costs. As the change of ownership clauses were already in existence before the acquisition took place, those directors had the right to claim compensation regardless of the acquirer's intentions towards the acquired company. It is, therefore, appropriate to treat the compensation costs as identifiable liabilities resulting from the crystallisation of a pre-acquisition contingency, that is, to include them as fair value adjustments under the principle in paragraph 37 of FRS 7.

In contrast, if the acquirer decided to fire the directors of an acquired company where those directors had no such rights to terminate their contracts as a result of an acquisition, it would not be appropriate to accrue for the ensuing compensation costs in the fair value exercise. That is because paragraph 7 of FRS 7 requires changes resulting from the acquirer's intentions or actions after the acquisition to be treated as post-acquisition costs. Similarly, the costs would be post-acquisition if artificial arrangements were made between acquirer and target to put in place such clauses during the negotiations for the acquisition.

Example 6 – Redundancy costs

Company A has acquired company B. Company A has the management capacity to integrate the operations of company B into its own operations without taking on the majority of company B's employees. The purchase price for B of £20m has been negotiated in contemplation of redundancy costs of £2m being incurred after the acquisition. The employees to be made redundant, and their costs, had been identified during the course of negotiations and a formal plan had been drawn up and agreed between the acquirer and vendor. The balance sheet in the completion accounts of company B included a provision of £2m in respect of the anticipated redundancy costs.

In accordance with paragraph 40 of FRS 7, the redundancy costs of £2m should be treated as post-acquisition costs in company A's consolidated financial statements. Despite the fact that provision was included in the completion accounts of company B, the provision was clearly made for the purposes of reaching an agreed purchase price with company A, and did not reflect expenditure that company B was committed to whether or not the acquisition was completed.

Example 7 – Redundancy costs and vendor refunds

Facts as in the previous example except that instead of a provision being included in the completion accounts, the purchase price payable on completion is £22m and the vendor has undertaken to refund up to £2m as and when the employees of company B are made redundant after the acquisition. In addition, company B is currently making losses and the agreement says that up to £1m should be refunded in respect of future operating losses of company B.

In accordance with paragraph 7 of FRS 7, both the future redundancy costs and the future operating losses should be treated as post-acquisition in the consolidated profit and loss account of company A because they are not identifiable liabilities of company B at the date of acquisition. Amounts up to £3m refunded by the vendor of company B would be applied by company A to reduce the purchase consideration, that is, the cost of investment in company B and goodwill.

While some may believe that the amounts refunded should be matched with the costs and losses to which they relate (that is, that they should be credited in the profit and loss account), the net purchase price of £19m payable to the vendor reflects the fact that the acquired business is loss-making and requires management action to turn it around. Such action involves incurring revenue costs. Following the principles in FRS 7, the short-term operating losses and the costs of reorganisation should all be shown as part of post-acquisition performance.

Intangible assets

25.178 FRS 7 makes only the briefest of references to identifiable intangibles. It merely states that *"where an intangible asset is recognised, its fair value should be based on its replacement cost, which is normally its estimated market value"*. [FRS 7 para 10].

25.179 A number of companies have included a variety of intangibles in their fair value exercises in recent years. Such intangibles have included brand names, publishing titles, the embedded value of life insurance, milk quotas and even company names. Intangibles can constitute very significant proportions of a company's consolidated balance sheet. For example, a substantial portion of the capital employed of Reed Elsevier comprises intangibles identified on past acquisitions, see Table 25.8.

Table 25.8 – Reed Elsevier plc – Annual Review – 31 December 1996

Accounting policies (extract)

Intangible fixed assets

Publishing rights and titles, databases, exhibition rights and other intangible assets are stated at fair value on acquisition and are not subsequently revalued. Having no finite economic life, no systematic amortisation is applied, but provision is made for any permanent impairment in value. Internally developed intangibles are not carried on the balance sheet. Intangible assets are only recognised on more significant acquisitions.

Combined Balance Sheet (extract)

£ million	1996
Fixed assets	
Intangible assets *note 13*	2,550
Tangible assets note 13	323
Investments note 14	180
	3,053
Current assets	
Stocks	139
Debtors: amounts falling due within 1 year *note 15*	667
Debtors: amounts falling due after more than 1 year *note 16*	147
Cash and short term investments *note 17*	1,141
	2,094
Creditors: amounts falling due within 1 year *note 18*	(2,146)
Net current (liabilities)/assets	(52)
Total assets less current liabilities	3,001

25.180 This treatment has reflected the increased commercial importance of brands and similar assets in the context of many acquisitions. This is because the most significant value is often in intangible benefits rather than in the tangible assets of the acquired entity. The practice has attracted much attention among preparers and users of financial statements, with the debate centred around two problem areas: first, the problem of establishing which intangibles are truly identifiable assets; and second the problem of how to value them.

25.181 The problem of accounting for intangibles was eventually settled with the publication of FRS 10. The ASB considered that, because some intangibles, such as brand names, are very similar to goodwill, the most important principle was that the accounting treatment should be the same irrespective of whether intangibles are labelled separately on the balance sheet or subsumed within goodwill.

25.182 Since FRS 10 requires purchased goodwill to be capitalised and accounted for alongside intangible assets, the separate recognition of intangibles has become less of an issue. Nevertheless, the standard sets three thresholds that must be passed before an intangible asset of an acquired business can be capitalised separately from goodwill:

- Separability.
- Control.
- Reliable measurement.

25.183 First, FRS 10's definition of an intangible asset requires it to be identifiable. Identifiability is a basic concept in both FRS 7 and the Act for recognising any asset and liability in an acquisition (see para 25.158). Separability is a key component of the definition of an identifiable asset. FRS 10 explains that an asset is not identifiable if it *"can be disposed of only as part of the revenue-earning activity to which it contributes"*. [FRS 10 para 2].

25.184 These words do little to clarify the issue – some intangibles are more clearly separable than others, but defining the cut remains subjective. In practice, the standard admits a wide range of intangibles such as those specifically mentioned in the balance sheet formats in the Act (concessions, patents, licences, trademarks and similar rights) as well as quotas, publishing titles, franchise rights and brands. But not all such items would necessarily be identifiable in all circumstances; to some extent this depends on how fundamental the intangible item is to the continuation of the acquired business. A business name is much less likely to qualify as identifiable.

25.185 Secondly, an identifiable intangible must be controlled through custody or legal rights that secure an entity's access (and restrict the access of others) to the benefits that are expected to derive from it. In practice, this rules out recognition of items such as a skilled workforce or a customer list because whilst they may be extremely valuable to a business, the business does not control them and, hence, their value is part of its goodwill.

25.186 Thirdly, an intangible should be recognised if (and only if) its initial fair value can be measured reliably. [FRS 10 para 10]. The FRS refers to two categories of intangibles:

- Intangibles with a readily ascertainable market value.
- Intangibles that are unique to the business.

25.187 In practice, hardly any intangibles fall into the first category. The FRS defines them as belonging to a homogeneous population of assets that are equivalent in all material respects and where there are frequent transactions in an active market. These are very strict conditions, because the FRS also allows intangibles of this type only to be revalued and to be recognised where they have been self-developed. The FRS suggests that some operating licences, franchises and quotas might meet these conditions (although many of these will in fact be unique).

25.188 The ASB has been sceptical about the reliability of valuations of unique intangibles such as brands and publishing titles where there is no market value as such. This is evident in FRS 10, because the standard specifically precludes intangibles (other than those with a readily ascertainable market value) from being recognised to the extent that their valuation would increase the net assets of the acquired business above the purchase price to give rise to negative goodwill. The standard accepts, however, that certain entities that regularly buy and sell them have developed reliable valuation techniques that would allow them to be capitalised separately from purchased goodwill as a result of an acquisition. This implies that those entities that are not in that position may legitimately choose not to attempt to value such intangibles and may subsume them within goodwill. The accounting treatment and valuation of intangibles is discussed in chapter 15.

Post-acquisition reorganisation and integration costs

25.189 FRS 7 specifically requires the following items to be *excluded* from the fair value exercise and treated as post-acquisition items in the acquirer's consolidated financial statements:

- The accounting effects of changes to the acquired entity resulting from the acquirer's intentions or future actions.
- Impairments in asset values, or other changes, resulting from events subsequent to the acquisition.
- Provisions for future operating losses.
- Provisions or accruals for reorganisation and integration costs expected to be incurred as a result of the acquisition, whether they relate to the acquired entity or to the acquirer.

[FRS 7 para 7].

Background

25.190 Prior to FRS 7 there had been much criticism of the use of provisions and excessive asset write-downs in fair valuing acquisitions. By establishing provisions in the fair value exercise, in the post-acquisition period companies could offset subsequent costs that would otherwise have to be charged in the profit and loss account against those provisions. On the other hand, if provisions are not set up as fair value adjustments, these costs will flow through to the profit and loss account in the subsequent periods and will, therefore, adversely affect the earnings per share of the combined group.

25.191 The principal objection that was raised by many companies to the treatment of reorganisation costs in the manner prescribed by FRS 7 was that, in their view, it does not reflect commercial reality. In their view, where an acquiring company has taken account of the costs of future reorganisation in arriving at a price it is prepared to pay, those costs should be reflected as capital costs. They argue that such costs should be included in the fair value exercise and should not be charged as revenue costs in the profit and loss account in subsequent periods. This view was supported by one ASB member in a 'dissenting view' published with the standard. However, the majority view in FRS 7 prevailed.

25.192 One of the ASB's main arguments for the approach taken in FRS 7 has been that financial statements should treat the costs and benefits of reorganisations related to acquisitions in the same manner as reorganisations of continuing operations. The benefits derived from realising synergy, and from implementing other post-acquisition restructuring and investment programmes, add post-acquisition value to the acquiring group by improving its profitability. Consequently, the costs of achieving such improvements should also be treated as post-acquisition. Those costs should be treated as revenue or capital according to normal accounting principles. The ASB has also stated that the approach adopted in FRS 7 is consistent with its Statement of Principles and with the profit and loss account formats introduced by FRS 3.

Post-acquisition activities

25.193 There are many reasons why companies seek to expand by acquisition. These might include:

- Gaining access to new markets.
- Diversification into a new business or a different product line.
- Expanding market share or protecting an existing market position.
- Acquiring production or distribution facilities, market skills or other expertise.
- Achieving economies of scale by rationalising facilities.
- Securing the supply of a key component or service.
- Financial reasons such as securing the utilisation of unrelieved tax losses and allowances.

25.194 A successful acquisition will normally involve:

- A thorough investigation of the target before the acquisition is completed.
- A detailed post-acquisition integration plan for maximising the value of the acquisition to the acquiring group.

25.195 In other words, few companies buy blind. They have commercial and strategic plans underlying their acquisitions, conduct a detailed evaluation and due diligence exercise and develop a strategy for getting the required or best return out of the enlarged operation. Frequently this means that the integration plans are already at an advanced stage of development, even before the acquisition contract is signed.

25.196 The post-acquisition plan would examine how the combining organisations are to be fitted together. It would identify opportunities to:

- Integrate activities, for example by harmonising systems and strategies. This would include activities such as consolidating marketing and advertising functions, financial control systems, data processing and other administrative systems.
- Achieve cost savings by reducing management and other overheads.
- Rationalise activities through closure of facilities that are surplus to the combined group.
- Invest in the development of the target company's business.

25.197 FRS 7 does not permit provisions to be made in the fair value exercise to cover the costs of such post-acquisition activities, even where these costs were taken into account by the acquirer when negotiating the acquisition price. This is because they were not liabilities of the acquired entity at the date of acquisition. The following are examples of items that should be treated as post-acquisition costs under FRS 7:

- Redundancy costs.
- Closure of head office and certain branches of acquired company.
- Costs of restructuring and strategically realigning operations to acceptable levels of efficiency.
- Cost of implementing strategic changes subsequent to acquisition.
- Costs of implementing the acquirer's quality standards, including training.
- Costs of converting and integrating acquired retail outlets into the acquirer's chain.
- Plant and other fixed assets written off as part of post-acquisition reorganisation.
- Rationalisation and reorganisation of existing business as a consequence of the acquisition.

Anti-avoidance measures

25.198 FRS 7 contains measures specifically addressed at a potential loophole concerning the timing of provisions for future reorganisation. Provisions for the type of expenditure to be incurred in reorganisation plans are generally recognised before the relevant expenditure is incurred. Most acquisitions do not involve hostile bids, but are agreed between willing buyers and willing sellers. The ASB has been concerned that, particularly in the case of 'friendly' takeovers, there could be scope for provisions for reorganisation planned by the acquirer to be recognised by the acquired company during the course of negotiations with the acquirer, and before the date of acquisition. Those provisions would then be entered as pre-acquisition liabilities when the newly acquired company is consolidated. An example is where reductions in excessive manpower in the acquired company are 'negotiated' during the course of the acquisition. Potentially a significant principle of the standard could relatively easily be circumvented.

25.199 The FRS (together with FRS 6, which contains the relevant disclosure provisions) deals in three ways with the problem of provisions made by the acquired company shortly before the acquisition. The explanation states that:

- Only if the acquired entity was demonstrably committed to the expenditure whether or not the acquisition was completed would it have a liability at the date of acquisition. [FRS 7 para 40].
- If obligations were incurred by the acquired entity as a result of the influence of the acquirer, it would be necessary to consider whether control (or the power to control) had been transferred at an earlier date and, consequently, whether the date of acquisition under FRS 2 should also be taken to be an earlier date. [FRS 7 para 40].
- *Disclosure* is required in the fair value table of any provisions for reorganisation and restructuring costs made within the 12 months preceding the date of acquisition that are included in the identifiable liabilities acquired, together with related asset write-downs. [FRS 7 para 40; FRS 6 para 26].

25.200 As mentioned in paragraph 25.174 above, a pre-condition for inclusion in the identifiable liabilities at the date of acquisition is that the acquired entity must have been *committed* to a particular course of action by the date of acquisition.

25.201 This approach to the recognition of certain liabilities is already embodied in FRS 3, where principles are set out in respect of setting up provisions for losses on businesses to be sold or terminated. That standard requires a provision to be made if, but not before, a decision has been made to close an operation *and* the commitment is evidenced by a detailed formal plan from which the reporting entity cannot realistically withdraw.

25.202 It follows from the above that, if a reorganisation provision set up by the acquired entity before the date of acquisition relates to a reorganisation that is only implemented because of the acquisition, the provision should not be treated as an identifiable liability of the acquired entity in the fair value exercise. This is because the acquired entity is not committed to the expenditure before the acquisition, as it is conditional on the acquisition taking place.

25.203 Similarly, if a reorganisation provision set up by the acquired entity before the date of acquisition relates to its plans as a stand-alone operation, but those plans are subsequently cancelled by the acquirer before they have been implemented, the provision should not be treated as an identifiable liability of the acquired entity. That is because the acquired entity could not have been demonstrably committed to the expenditure regardless of whether or not the acquisition was completed.

25.204 In practice, it may be unlikely that management of a company being acquired could commit the company irrevocably to a particular course of action at the request of an acquiring company unless the completion of the acquisition was a foregone conclusion. If they did bind the acquired company, this might suggest that the acquirer had *de facto* already obtained control.

25.205 If the acquirer has gained control, or has the power to control, the date of acquisition should be brought forward and the new subsidiary should be consolidated from the earlier date. Hence, the profits and losses (including the reorganisation provisions) would be brought into the acquirer's consolidated profit and loss account from that earlier date. Identifying the date of acquisition for the consolidated financial statements is dealt with in FRS 2 and is considered in section I, from paragraph 25.18. It should be stressed that all aspects of the relationship between the acquirer and the target would need to be considered before the date of acquisition is brought forward. Where, for example, completion of the acquisition is conditional on the approval of the shareholders of the acquirer, it is unlikely that, in practice, control could have passed at an earlier date. It is equally unlikely in such a case that the acquired company could, in fact, commit itself irrevocably to the reorganisation.

25.206 The effect of the above anti-avoidance measures is that any commitments entered into by the acquired company at the request of the acquirer may well be deemed to be post-acquisition in substance. However, it is not unusual for a vendor to reorganise a business that is to be put up for sale in order to make the business more attractive to a potential purchaser. The purchase price would then reflect the business in its reorganised or semi-reorganised state. Thus reorganisation costs may be incurred by a company shortly before it is sold and there may be some provisions related to the reorganisation that are properly regarded as pre-acquisition liabilities.

25.207 The ASB also seeks to ensure that the spirit of FRS 7 is observed in respect of reorganisation provisions by requiring disclosure, in the fair value table, of any reorganisation provisions that were made by the acquired company in the 12 months immediately preceding the date of acquisition and which are included in its pre-acquisition liabilities.

Disclosure of post-acquisition reorganisation costs

25.208 FRS 7 requires that all post-acquisition reorganisation costs should be charged in the profit and loss account of the acquiring group. The ASB believes that, where they are material, separate disclosure of such costs is important for a proper assessment of post-acquisition performance to be made, particularly in the context of the 'information set' style of the profit and loss account under FRS 3.

To some extent these disclosures may mitigate the adverse effect of the accounting requirements in the eyes of preparers.

25.209 All the disclosure requirements relating to acquisitions, including those stemming from FRS 7, are consolidated in FRS 6. FRS 6 *requires* the following disclosure regarding reorganisation costs to be made in the financial statements of an acquiring group for each material acquisition, and for other acquisitions in aggregate:

- The profit and loss account or notes to the financial statements of periods following the acquisition should show the costs incurred in those periods in reorganising, restructuring and integrating the acquisition. [FRS 6 para 31].
- If material, these costs should be shown as exceptional items, and disclosed separately from other exceptional items, whether they relate to a fundamental restructuring or not. [FRS 6 para 86].

25.210 FRS 6 explains that post-acquisition integration, reorganisation and restructuring costs, including provisions in respect of them, would, if material, be reported as exceptional items under FRS 3. Only if a reorganisation or restructuring is fundamental, having a material effect on the nature and focus of the *enlarged* group's operations, would the costs be included as one of the items required by paragraph 20 of FRS 3 to be shown separately on the face of the profit and loss account after operating profit and before interest. [FRS 6 para 86].

25.211 Tables 25.9, 25.10, and 25.11 show examples of different methods that have been used to present acquisition reorganisation costs in the profit and loss account.

Table 25.9 — SmithKline Beecham plc — Annual Report and Accounts — 31 December 1994

CONSOLIDATED PROFIT AND LOSS ACCOUNT (extract)

	Notes	Comparable business £m	Acquisitions (note 1) £m	Business performance £m	One-off items (note 1) £m	**1994 £m**
Sales						
Continuing operations		5,877	194	6,071	–	**6,071**
Discontinued operations		421	–	421	–	**421**
	1	6,298	194	6,492	–	**6,492**
Cost of goods sold		(2,109)	(95)	(2,204)	(243)	**(2,447)**
Gross profit		4,189	99	4,288	(243)	**4,045**
Selling, general and administrative expenses	2	(2,261)	(85)	(2,346)	(320)	**(2,666)**
Research and development expenditure	2	(620)	(1)	(621)	(17)	**(638)**

Trading profit						
Continuing operations	1&2	1,224	13	1,237	(580)	**657**
Discontinued operations	1&2	84	–	84	–	**84**

NOTES TO THE FINANCIAL STATEMENTS (extract)

One-off items

A restructuring provision, to be utilised over three years, of £580 million has been established and is included under a separate column headed 'one-off items' on the profit and loss account. This provision is to cover the cost of closing Sterling's New York headquarters; the integration of the Sterling and existing Consumer Healthcare operations; the establishment of an integrated Pharmaceutical and Consumer Healthcare International business; the creation of shared services across all of the business operations and the reorganisation of the Group's supply chain.

The 'one-off items' column also includes the tax charge arising on the reorganisation of Sterling in connection with the sale by SB of Sterling's North American business and a credit associated with the deferred tax asset arising on the creation of the restructuring provision. (see note 5).

Table 25.10 — Reckitt and Colman plc — Report & Accounts — 31 December 1994

Group profit and loss account (extract)

Notes		**1994** **£m**	1993 £m
3	**Sales to customers:**		
	Continuing operations	**2,070.78**	2,068.09
	Discontinued operations	**8.17**	27.56
	Total sales to customers	**2,078.95**	2,095.65
3	Cost of sales	**(1,073.22)**	(1,048.26)
	Gross profit	**1,005.73**	1,047.39
	Net operating expenses	**(834.67)**	(735.94)
3	**Operating profit:**		
	Continuing operations [1]	**169.35**	305.22
	Discontinued operations	**1.71**	6.23
4	**Total operating profit**	**171.06**	311.45

[1] In 1994 operating profit from continuing operations is stated after charging exceptional reorganisation costs of £56.00m in Europe and £83.10m in connection with the L&F Household integration in the USA.

Table 25.11 — Scottish Power plc — Annual Report & Accounts — 31 March 1996

Group Profit and Loss Account (extract)

	Before acquisitions 1996 £m	Acquisitions 1996 £m	Total before reorganisation costs 1996 £m	Reorganisation costs 1996 £m	Total 1996 £m	Total 1995 £m
Turnover from continuing operations	**1,832.1**	**439.4**	**2,271.5**	–	**2,271.5**	1,715.8
Cost of sales	**(1,091.3)**	**(283.7)**	**(1,375.0)**	–	**(1,375.0)**	(1,011.8)
Gross profit from continuing operations	**740.8**	**155.7**	**896.5**	–	**896.5**	704.0
Transmission and distribution costs	**(152.4)**	**(49.8)**	**(202.2)**	**(1.0)**	**(203.2)**	(141.9)
Administrative expenses	**(199.6)**	**(28.6)**	**(228.2)**	**(41.7)**	**(269.9)**	(188.0)
Other operating income	**7.8**	**3.1**	**10.9**	–	**10.9**	6.0
Operating profit from continuing operations	**396.6**	**80.4**	**477.0**	**(42.7)**	**434.3**	380.1

The group profit and loss account includes under Acquisitions the results of Manweb for the period 6 October 1995 to 31 March 1996.

[The next paragraph is 25.213.]

25.213 Where a post-acquisition reorganisation does not qualify as fundamental in the context of the operations of the enlarged group, the costs should be charged in arriving at the profit or loss on ordinary activities before tax and shown under the statutory format headings to which they relate. In practice, this means that reorganisation costs that qualify as exceptional items (but are not fundamental) would be shown in arriving at operating profit or loss. In accordance with FRS 3, the amount should be disclosed separately by way of note, or on the face of the profit and loss account if that is necessary to give a true and fair view.

25.214 FRS 6 *suggests* that, for major acquisitions where post-acquisition reorganisation is expected to extend over more than one period, management may wish to disclose in the notes the total expenditure expected to be incurred and the nature of the expenditure. This suggested disclosure analyses the total: between amounts charged in the profit and loss account and further amounts expected to be incurred; and between cash expenditure and asset write-offs. [FRS 6 para 87].

25.215 The above-mentioned suggested disclosures were in response to users who believed that it is important to be able to ascertain the total expected costs relating to an acquisition. They also enable management to present what they believe to be the true total acquisition cost, that is, the consideration given for the acquisition plus, for example, the planned costs of turning the acquisition around and integrating it into the acquiring group. Appendix IV to FRS 6 gives an example of the type of disclosure that the ASB had in mind.

25.216 Many companies already give significant disclosures about the progress of recent acquisitions, details of post-acquisition integration plans and their associated costs in the part of the annual report in which the Board reviews the group's activities for the year. Discussion of post-acquisition reorganisation plans and their likely future benefits, together with the subsequent monitoring of those costs and benefits, often forms an integral part of this disclosure. See further chapter 2 of the Manual of Accounting – Management reports and governance.

[The next paragraph is 25.218.]

25.218 There are two practical issues regarding the disclosure of exceptional post-acquisition reorganisation costs required by FRS 6:

- What is *fundamental* in the context of the enlarged group?
- Which costs should be included in the captions that are required to be separately disclosed as costs of *reorganising, restructuring and integrating the acquisition*?

Fundamental reorganisation or not

25.219 Identifying a fundamental reorganisation under FRS 3 is considered in chapter 8. FRS 6 makes it clear that whether a post-acquisition reorganisation is fundamental must be judged in relation to the enlarged group. It is not automatic that such costs would be shown as a non-operating exceptional item. Clearly, the use of judgement is required to determine whether a particular reorganisation is fundamental or not. However, by requiring the reorganisation to have a material effect on both the nature and focus of the enlarged group's operations, it is implicit that the reorganisation should encompass the whole or a substantial part of the enlarged group's total operations and should not be a reorganisation of only one among many different operations of the enlarged group.

25.220 At one end of the spectrum, a group may acquire a new subsidiary and run it as a stand alone operation. The acquired subsidiary may be reorganised to achieve cost savings, but the existing operations of the subsidiary and the group are essentially left intact. The reorganisation would not be fundamental to the enlarged group, nor even probably to the acquired subsidiary. In this situation, the reorganisation costs should be charged in arriving at operating profit and, if material, separately identified. FRS 3 already requires the profit and loss account of an acquiring group to disclose separately (in aggregate) the operating results attributable to acquisitions made in the year, as a component of the group's continuing operations.

25.221 At the other end of the spectrum, a group may make a substantial acquisition in its core business. Soon after the acquisition the business of the new subsidiary is subsumed into the existing operations of the acquiring group. The post-acquisition plan for the enlarged group involves material expenditure in respect of both integrating the combining operations and repositioning their market focus. This results in the enlarged group withdrawing from certain market sectors and investing in those that are core to the group's future strategy. The restructuring goes to the root of the enlarged group's operations and the repositioning process includes significant asset disposals from both the pre-existing and acquired operations. In these circumstances, the post-acquisition reorganisation is likely to be fundamental and the costs would be shown separately after operating profit.

25.222 However, in the majority of cases it is likely that post acquisition reorganisation costs will be included as part of the acquiring group's operating results and not as fundamental reorganisation or restructuring. Although the integration of combining operations may require significant reorganisation across the enlarged group, this fact alone does not make the reorganisation fundamental. A fundamental reorganisation must involve a material change in the nature and focus of the enlarged group's operations – that is, the combined operations of the acquirer and acquired business after the acquisition – and this would need to result in the repositioning of its products or services in their markets.

Nature of reorganisation costs

25.223 The nature of reorganisation costs is important because requiring post-acquisition reorganisation costs to be shown in the profit and loss account would not, of itself, remove the often publicised possibilities under previous practices for flattering the operating results following an acquisition. In practice, the headline reporting of performance tends to focus on a company's operating results. If the amount shown under exceptional reorganisation costs (in particular, fundamental costs) were inflated by items that should properly be shown as normal operating costs, the operating result would also be inflated.

25.224 FRS 6 gives a strict definition of which costs are permitted, as a matter of principle, to be included in the captions of costs relating to reorganising, restructuring and integrating an acquisition. It states that such costs are those that:

- Would not have been incurred had the acquisition not taken place.
- Relate to a project identified and controlled by management as part of a reorganisation or integration programme set up at the time of acquisition or as a direct consequence of an immediate post-acquisition review.

[FRS 6 para 31].

25.225 Subject to meeting the criteria in the above paragraph, examples of costs that might be included under this definition are:

- Employee redundancy and early retirement costs.
- Costs of relocating facilities as part of an integration plan.
- Contract cancellation costs.
- Plant closure costs, including costs of eliminating duplicate facilities.

- Write-off of fixed assets and stocks relating to the reorganisation.

  (The write-down of assets is mentioned in paragraph 87 of FRS 6 as a potential component of reorganisation costs, which suggests that the profit and loss charge is properly shown under reorganisation costs rather than as, for example, losses on the disposal of fixed assets.)

- Incremental costs incurred in converting branches of the acquired company into the format of the acquiring group.
- Incremental costs incurred in implementing the administrative and management information systems of the acquiring group into the acquired company.
- Costs of retraining the workforce of the acquired company.

25.226 FRS 6 refers to costs of integrating as well as reorganising and restructuring the acquisition. Consequently, it appears that some integration costs admitted under this caption could relate to the acquirer's own business, provided that the costs are incurred as a direct consequence of the acquisition and relate directly to the activities being integrated. Such costs might include the following:

- Costs of closing facilities in the acquiring group that are duplicated in the enlarged group in preference to closing those of the acquired company.
- Costs of redundancies in the acquiring group resulting from the merging of head office functions.

25.227 Where other activities of the acquiring group are reorganised following an acquisition, the costs would not be admitted into the FRS 6 definition.

25.228 The following items would not appear to qualify as costs of reorganising, restructuring and integrating the acquisition. They should be included in the relevant headings in normal operating costs:

- Ongoing salaries of staff to be made redundant, unless they have effectively been made redundant, that is they have ceased to provide services to the group.
- Operating costs of running facilities to be merged or closed pending the implementation of the reorganisation plan.
- Internal management costs relating to time spent on developing and implementing the reorganisation plan.

25.229 It might be argued that some of the above items, for example the 'additional' costs of running two departments rather than one, should be included as reorganisation costs because they are additional costs incurred from the time of the acquisition to the date of the implementation of the reorganisation. Arguments against this are: first, it does not reflect what happened after the acquisition because the fact is that two departments did exist and their operating costs were incurred; second, it is probable that each of the departments carried out a necessary task up to the date that the reorganisation was implemented and, therefore, until that time the costs incurred were not, in fact, 'additional' costs.

Disclosure of acquisition provisions

25.230 FRS 6 *requires* movements on provisions or accruals for costs related to an acquisition to be disclosed and analysed between the amounts used for the specific purpose for which they were created and the amounts released unused. [FRS 6 para 32]. The information should be disclosed separately for each material acquisition and for other non-material acquisitions in aggregate. Inclusion of the word 'accruals' is interpreted to mean that the information should be given in respect of all material costs accrued and shown in the profit and loss account as costs of reorganising, restructuring and integrating an acquisition and not just those that are shown in the balance sheet under the caption of provisions. An example of the disclosure is given in Table 25.12.

Table 25.12 — Glaxo Wellcome plc — Annual Report and Accounts — 31 December 1995

Notes on the Accounts (extract)

19 Provisions for liabilities and charges* (extract)	Integration costs	Pensions and other post-retirement benefits	Deferred taxation	Other provisions	Total
	£m	£m	£m	£m	£m
At 1st July 1994 as previously stated	–	90	139	64	293
Prior period adjustment	–	26	(9)	–	17
At 1st July 1994 restated	–	116	130	64	310
Exchange adjustments	–	3	(3)	2	2
Acquisition of subsidiary undertakings	–	92	187	75	354
Charge/(credit) for the period	1,215	138	(251)	67	1,169
Applied	(384)	(34)	(33)	(67)	(518)
At 31st December 1995	831	315	30	141	1,317

The provision for integration costs at 31st December 1995 represents the costs expected to be incurred in integrating the business of Glaxo and Wellcome.

* Note that, for years beginning on or after 1 January 2005, SI 2004/2947, 'The Companies Act 1985 (International Accounting Standards and other Amendments) Regulations 2004', changed the Companies Act line item to 'provisions for liabilities'.

25.231 FRS 6 and FRS 7 set out requirements for identifying and disclosing post-acquisition reorganisation costs. They do not provide any guidance on the principles for setting up provisions for such costs where they are expected to be incurred over more than one period. Recognition and measurement rules that apply to provisions for restructuring costs generally are contained in FRS 12. These rules affect the amount of 'one-off' acquisition reorganisation provisions that can be charged in the immediate post-acquisition period. Where costs relating to a post-acquisition reorganisation and integration programme are charged over more than one period, FRS 6 suggests that management may wish to disclose the total expected costs, indicating the extent to which they have been charged in the profit and loss account, in order to give a fuller picture of the progress of the post-acquisition plan. [FRS 6 para 87]. Appendix IV to the standard provides an illustration, in tabular form, of how this information might be presented by analysing details of amounts charged and amounts still to be charged.

Measuring fair values of identifiable assets and liabilities

Meaning of fair value

25.232 FRS 7 defines fair value as:

> *"The amount at which an asset or liability could be exchanged in an arm's length transaction between informed and willing parties, other than in a forced or liquidation sale".* [FRS 7 para 2].

25.233 This basic definition of fair value, or similar versions of it, is well recognised in accounting literature. The problem in accounting for business combinations is that many of the assets and liabilities to be recognised in an acquisition are not regularly exchanged in arm's length transactions. Consequently, the definition is of limited practical use in measuring fair values for this purpose.

25.234 Before FRS 7, it had been accepted practice for acquisitions to be fair valued from the perspective of the acquiring company. The perspective of the acquirer was favoured because it took into account the acquirer's plans for the future and its style of operation. It was also consistent with the concept of the acquirer's perspective that provisions for reorganisation costs included in those plans should be taken into account in the fair value exercise.

25.235 The ASB considered that the notion of a 'fair value to the acquiring company' seemed to contradict the basic definition of fair value, which is a market value concept reflecting both buyers and sellers. The ASB also argued that, as a general principle, management intent is not a sufficient basis for recognising changes to an entity's assets and liabilities; and in the context of acquisition accounting, the acquirer's intentions regarding the future use of acquired assets are not necessarily relevant to determining their cost.

25.236 Consequently, FRS 7 rejected the acquirer's perspective as a principle for determining fair values. Instead, the standard attempts to adhere to the definition of fair value by requiring that:

- Fair values should reflect the conditions at the date of acquisition.
- Fair values should *not* reflect:
  - Changes resulting from the acquirer's intentions or future actions.
  - Impairments, or other changes, resulting from events subsequent to the acquisition.

- Provisions or accruals for future operating losses or for reorganisation and integration costs expected to be incurred as a result of the acquisition.

[FRS 7 paras 6, 7].

25.237 The basic concept of fair value in FRS 7 is, therefore, free from any particular 'perspective'. It attempts to establish what the price paid for a whole business represented, taking into account the conditions of the acquired business, including its existing cost structures, that existed at the time of acquisition.

25.238 The last part of the definition of fair value in paragraph 25.232 indicates that fair values of individual assets and liabilities should generally be valued on a going concern basis, even if the business was acquired cheaply in a fire sale from, for example, a vendor who was in financial difficulty. In circumstances where the acquirer has obtained a bargain purchase as a result of a forced or liquidation sale, the fair values of the identifiable net assets may well exceed the cost of acquisition, with negative goodwill arising on consolidation.

25.239 The standard provides a detailed framework for establishing fair values for individual categories of assets and liabilities. Although the concept of fair value as described above is intended to prevail, there are several exceptions or modifications to the concept when applied in practice to certain assets and liabilities where market values do not exist. This framework draws heavily on the chapter of the ASB's Statement of Principles, 'Measurement in Financial Statements', that deals with valuations in financial statements generally. This describes the concept of deprival value or 'value to the business' that in many cases corresponds to fair value under FRS 7.

25.240 The overall framework can be summarised as follows:

- Fair values are indicated by market values where similar assets are bought and sold on a readily accessible market.
- Where market values are not available, or are inappropriate to the circumstances of the acquired company, fair values should be based on replacement cost, reflecting the acquired company's normal buying process and the sources of supply and prices available to it (but see below).
- The fair value of an asset should not exceed its recoverable amount. Therefore, where the fair value of an asset is based on its depreciated replacement cost, the recoverable amount will also need to be considered.

  The recoverable amount of an asset is in effect the maximum discounted cash flows that can be obtained from the asset, either by selling it or by continuing to use it (see para 25.280 below).
- A valuation of an asset at recoverable amount should reflect its condition on acquisition, but not any impairments or enhancements resulting from subsequent events or actions of the acquirer.

- The accounting policies of the acquiring group should be adopted where they affect fair values attributed to assets and liabilities.

25.241 The attribution of fair values is not determined from the 'acquirer's perspective', in the sense that the acquirer's intentions for the future use of assets do not affect the valuation of the business as it stood when it was acquired. However, fair values can only be arrived at under the system described in paragraph 25.240 after a detailed investigation of the acquisition by the acquirer. Therefore, in several cases fair values would represent the acquirer's judgement of the worth of the underlying assets in their existing state.

25.242 Examples of situations where considerable judgement needs to be exercised by the acquirer include:

- Review of useful lives of fixed assets, for determining depreciated replacement cost.
- Compilation of cash flow projections for the business being acquired, for determining the recoverable amount of assets where the business is unable to recover the depreciated replacement cost.
- Review of provisions against the value of slow-moving stock, for determining net realisable value.
- Review of the recoverability of debtors.

25.242.1 In carrying out the fair value exercise, it would be appropriate to work at a fairly detailed level and, therefore, to assign fair values to individual assets or small groups of assets. For example, if a property portfolio is being fair valued, it would usually be necessary to carry out the exercise on individual assets. Clearly, this may not be possible where stocks are concerned. Also, where a business of the acquired company is to be resold soon after acquisition, the standard requires the whole business unit to be valued as a single item (see further para 25.322).

Period for completing the fair value exercise

25.243 The standard requires that fair values of assets and liabilities should be based on conditions at the date of acquisition. They should not generally be affected by matters arising after this date. In practice, sufficient time is required to enable an acquirer to examine the acquisition in order to identify all the assets and liabilities existing at the date of acquisition and to perform a full and reliable fair value exercise.

25.244 As far as the assets and liabilities of the acquired company are concerned, the fair value exercise should, if possible, be completed by the date on which the board of the acquirer approves for publication the acquiring group's first annual financial statements following the acquisition. [FRS 7 para 23].

25.245 However, the standard recognises that some acquisitions need more time to be properly investigated. Situations where this is likely to arise include the following:

- The acquisition is complex and is completed late in the financial year of the acquirer.
- The acquired company has assets and liabilities where more evidence is required before they can be valued reliably – examples include evaluating environmental liabilities and contingent liabilities involving legal claims.

25.246 In circumstances where the fair value exercise cannot be completed in time for publication of the acquirer's first post-acquisition financial statements, FRS 7 requires *provisional* fair values to be included. These provisional fair values should be amended, if necessary, in the next financial statements with a corresponding adjustment to goodwill. [FRS 7 para 24].

25.247 The cut-off point for making fair value adjustments is, therefore, the date of approval of the acquirer's second annual financial statements after the acquisition. By basing the investigation period on the financial year of the acquirer rather than on an absolute time limit, there could in practice be significant differences in the time available for completing the fair value exercise in respect of different acquisitions. The time available depends on the timing of an acquisition in relation to the financial year end of the acquirer and could, in theory, extend for over two years.

Subsequent amendments to fair values

Amendments after investigation period has expired

25.248 Amendments may still be necessary to fair values after the investigation period, as described above, has expired. Because the standard does not allow any further goodwill adjustments to be made, the effect of such amendments should, where applicable, be dealt with in the profit and loss account for the year. If material, they may require separate disclosure as exceptional items.

25.249 The only exception to the above treatment is where amendments discovered outside the permitted investigation period result from fundamental errors in the fair value exercise rather than from the normal process of revising estimates that is inherent in financial reporting. An example is where hidden problems relating to past activities of the acquired company are only discovered later by the acquirer. In these circumstances, the fundamental errors would, in accordance with FRS 3, be treated as prior period adjustments, that is, by adjusting the goodwill arising on the acquisition.

25.250 An example of adjustments that have been treated as fundamental errors was contained in the accounts of Ferranti International Signal plc (see Table 25.13).

Table 25.13 – Ferranti International Signal plc – Annual report & accounts (revised) – 31 March 1989

Notes to the accounts (extracts)

1 Basis of accounting

For the reasons given in paragraphs 2 to 4 of the Report of the Directors the accounts of the group and the parent company for the year ended 31 March 1989, despatched to shareholders on 11 August 1989, have been withdrawn and revised to write off assets in respect of certain suspect contracts (as defined in the Report of the Directors) and incorporate a consequential adjustment to the fair value of the net tangible assets of International Signal & Control Group PLC ("ISC") at the date of acquisition by the company, 16 November 1987, and a restatement of the comparative amounts shown for the year ended 31 March 1988. No credit has been taken for any amounts which may be recoverable from third parties in respect of the suspect contracts. The Revised Accounts also reflect other adjustments for post balance sheet events occasioned by the extension of the date of approval of the Accounts from 13 July 1989 to 16 November 1989 and reflecting additional evidence relating to conditions in the group existing at 31 March 1989.

Note 20 Reserves (extract)

	Share premium £M	Merger £M	Revaluation £M	Profit & loss £M	Total £M
Group					
As previously reported at 31 March 1988	3.8	73.5	38.9	152.4	268.6
Adjustment in respect of acquisitions other than ISC		17.0		(17.0)	–
Adjustment to the fair value of the net tangible assets of ISC as at the date of acquisition		(90.5)		(50.9)	(141.4)
Adjustment to retained profit:					
Operating profit previously taken on suspect contracts				(13.5)	(13.5)
Consequential tax effects				4.7	4.7
Currency translation effects				12.1	12.1
As restated at 31 March 1988	3.8	–	38.9	87.8	130.5
Deficit for the year				(6.6)	(6.6)
Premium on allotments	1.0				1.0
Goodwill arising on acquisitions (note 21)				(4.0)	(4.0)
Currency translation				(5.0)	(5.0)
At 31 March 1989	4.8	–	38.5	72.2	115.5

Amendments within investigation period

25.251 Where fair values attributed to the assets and liabilities of an acquired company are considered provisional in the acquirer's first post-acquisition financial statements, FRS 6 requires this fact to be stated and the reasons to be given. It also requires any material adjustments made to those fair values in the next financial statements, with corresponding adjustments to goodwill, to be disclosed and explained. [FRS 6 para 27].

25.252 When a company adjusts its provisional values to the final fair values, a similar level of disclosure and explanation is required to comply with the requirements of paragraph 25 of FRS 6 and paragraph 13(5) of Schedule 6 to SI 2008/410. An analysis of the adjustments and an explanation of the reasons for them should be included.

25.253 An example of a provisional fair value allocation and subsequent goodwill adjustment is taken from the accounts of RJB Mining PLC (see Table 25.14).

Table 25.14 — RJB Mining PLC — Annual Report and Accounts — 31 December 1995

NOTES TO THE FINANCIAL STATEMENTS (extract)

23 Goodwill on acquisition of English Coal	Provisional fair value to the Group 1994 £'000	Completion and hindsight period adjustments 1995 £'000	Final fair value to the Group 1995 £'000
Fixed assets	643,818	(84,258)	559,560
Stock & WIP			
Coal stock	189,407	6,121	195,528
Stores	54,927	(8,278)	46,649
Work in progress	95,271	(11,781)	83,490
Debtors	2,395	(1,604)	791
Creditors	(28,264)	(1,568)	(29,832)
Provisions for liabilities and charges*			
Concessionary coal	(29,041)	–	(29,041)
Claims	(43,500)	1,673	(41,827)
Surface damage	(28,439)	–	(28,439)
Restoration and closure costs (opencast)	(41,580)	–	(41,580)
Restoration and closure costs (deep mines)	(8,832)	(1,380)	(10,212)
Draglines maintenance	(3,597)	2,508	(1,089)
Deferred taxation	(17,000)	38,441	21,441
	785,565	(60,126)	725,439
Purchase consideration	844,289	(1,074)	843,215
Goodwill written off	58,724	59,052	117,776

The principal adjustments to fair value to the group are in respect of the Asfordby colliery which has been written down to a nominal carrying value following a reassessment due to the difficult geological conditions and consequent operational problems associated with safe and economic extraction of coal from these reserves. The other adjustments to fair value in the hindsight period relate to agreement of the final acquisition cost and to asset and liability valuation and existence assessments in the period.

1. Asfordby	£77.8m
2. Revaluation of deferred opencast assets	£11.5m
3. Other	£8.2m
4. Deferred tax on adjustments	(£38.4m)

* Note that, for years beginning on or after 1 January 2005, SI 2004/2947, 'The Companies Act 1985 (International Accounting Standards and other Amendments) Regulations 2004', changed the Companies Act line item to 'provisions for liabilities'.

25.254 FRS 7 indicates that fair values should not be considered provisional in the first post-acquisition financial statements unless it has not been possible to complete the investigation of fair values by then and the fact is disclosed in those financial statements. This would suggest that no further adjustments should be made to fair values (and goodwill) in subsequent financial years if an acquirer has completed its investigation and obtained all the evidence considered necessary to arrive at reliable estimates of fair values by the date of approval of the financial statements for the year in which the acquisition took place.

25.255 Even if additional information is obtained in the next financial year which causes previous estimates to be changed, those changes would usually be dealt with in the profit and loss account of the period in which they are identified. This principle is consistent with normal practice in financial statements where items relating to prior periods, which arise from corrections and adjustments that are the natural result of estimates inherent in accounting and in the periodic preparation of financial statements, are dealt with as they arise and are not adjusted retrospectively.

25.256 However, there may be exceptional situations where fair values and goodwill would need to be adjusted retrospectively in the acquirer's second post-acquisition financial statements, even where the fair values attributed to the acquired company at the previous balance sheet date had not been declared provisional in the previous financial statements.

25.257 For example, paragraph 57 of FRS 7 discusses the treatment of exceptional stock profits arising after the date of acquisition. It states that, if exceptional profits appear to have been earned on the realisation of stocks after the date of acquisition, it will be necessary to re-examine the fair values determined on acquisition and, if necessary, to make an adjustment to these values and a corresponding adjustment to goodwill. It goes on to state that if, alternatively, the profit is attributable to post-acquisition events, it should be disclosed as an exceptional item in the post-acquisition profit and loss account.

25.258 Paragraph 57 is clearly addressing a potential source of abuse because errors made in calculating the fair value of stocks quickly feed through into the profit and loss account. If the fair value attributed to stocks is understated, post-acquisition profits are inflated by their realisation in the post-acquisition period.

Fair valuing fixed assets

25.259 If there are separately identifiable asset transactions in an acquisition, the bargained price would normally provide the initial fair value (that is, actual cost), assuming the price is a proper arm's length value. In other cases, fair values should be estimated using conventional measurement principles (that is, market value, replacement cost or recoverable amount). FRS 7 requires the choice of valuation basis to be determined by a structured analysis of the circumstances, as summarised in paragraph 25.240 above.

Market value

25.260 Where there is a ready market in the types of fixed assets held by the acquired company, market values should generally be used. Such assets would include properties in which an active market exists. Properties that are sometimes referred to as *non-specialised* properties may be included in this category – examples include shops, offices, and general purpose warehouses that could be occupied by a number of different users. Professional valuers would normally be required to value such assets.

25.261 Where assets are sold shortly after the acquisition, the price obtained will often provide the most reliable evidence of fair value at the date of acquisition.

25.262 There may be some confusion as to what market value means, because variants are used in practice when properties are included in accounts at valuations. The most commonly used bases are market value and existing use value. Until a consistent framework or guidelines are established for revaluing properties generally, it is not possible to be dogmatic about the question of market value in the fair value exercise.

25.263 Guidelines for the valuation of property assets for the purposes of financial statements are presently contained in the RICS Appraisal and Valuation Manual, published by the Royal Institution of Chartered Surveyors (RICS).

25.264 Market value, as defined in those statements, reflects the value for any use to the extent to which that value is reflected in the price obtainable in the open market between a willing buyer and a willing seller, assuming that a reasonable period of time is allowed for marketing and selling the asset. This definition corresponds closely to the definition of fair value in FRS 7 and is the basis generally used for valuing investment properties, properties held for future development and surplus properties.

25.265 Existing use value is the basis normally used for valuing properties that are occupied in the company's business and that have not been declared surplus. It is based on market value, but the valuation reflects an important assumption that the property can be used for the foreseeable future only for the existing use. It is intended to represent the cost of replacing the remaining service potential of a property.

25.266 Neither market value nor existing use value include any value attributable to the goodwill generated by the business that occupies the property with the following exception. A variation of existing use value is 'existing use as a fully operational business unit'. This basis applies to properties that invariably change hands in the open market at prices based directly on trading potential for a strictly limited use. Examples of such properties include hotels, private hospitals and nursing homes, public houses, cinemas, theatres, bingo clubs, gaming clubs, petrol filling stations, licensed betting offices and specialised leisure and sporting facilities. The valuation includes the value of the trading potential which runs with the property, but should not include any goodwill which has been created by the owner and which would not remain with the property should it be sold.

25.267 In acquisition accounting, properties that would normally be valued under the alternative accounting rules on an existing use value basis in the acquired company's financial statements (that is, those occupied for the purpose of its business) would also usually be valued on this basis in the fair value exercise. That is because FRS 7 requires fair values to reflect the conditions of the acquired company at the date of acquisition. If an acquirer determines to change the use of an acquired property, subsequently carrying out the necessary planning and redevelopment procedures, any resulting change in value is attributable to the acquirer's actions and, consequently, treated as post-acquisition as required by paragraph 7 of FRS 7.

25.268 FRS 7 discusses the use of market values in secondhand assets. It states that where a fair value is based on a market price, it is important to ensure that such price is appropriate to the circumstances of the acquired business. [FRS 7 para 44].

25.269 Fixed assets that can be traded in secondhand markets include cars, commercial vehicles, computer equipment and certain plant and machinery. Where, for example, a company operates a fleet of vehicles, the market price of a used vehicle that is not due for replacement may be irrelevant to the business if, as is usually the case, it would never consider replacing vehicles in the secondhand market. In this situation, the standard indicates that the fair value of a vehicle should be the current purchase price of a new vehicle, depreciated to reflect its age and condition. For certain used assets, the depreciated replacement cost could be significantly different from the value in the secondhand market owing to a different pattern of depreciation in value.

25.270 As a general rule, depreciated replacement cost should be used for such assets unless the acquired business is genuinely able to consider the purchase of secondhand equipment as a viable alternative to purchasing new replacement assets.

Depreciated replacement cost

25.271 Where market values are not applicable, FRS 7 explains that depreciated replacement cost should be used as a proxy for fair value, provided it does not exceed the recoverable amount.

25.272 Depreciated replacement cost should reflect the acquired business's normal buying process and the sources of supply and prices available to it. [FRS 7 para 9].

25.273 Depreciated replacement cost is normally used by professional valuers for valuing *specialised* properties. These are defined in the RICS valuation manual as those properties that, because of their specialised nature, are rarely sold in the market except by way of a sale of the business or entity of which it is part. This may be due to uniqueness arising from its specialised nature and design, its configuration, size, location or otherwise. Depreciated replacement cost would also generally be the appropriate basis of valuation of such properties in a fair value exercise. Examples of properties that might be valued on this basis include chemical installations, power stations, docks, breweries and other special purpose factories.

25.274 Depreciated replacement cost is the proper basis for fair valuing most items of plant and machinery. This may be viewed as the cost of replacing an asset with one having a similar service potential.

25.275 In principle, all fixed assets should be fair valued. The carrying value in the financial statements of an acquired company should not be used in the fair value exercise unless there is a reasonable basis for concluding that the current depreciated replacement cost is not materially different.

25.276 The gross replacement cost of an asset may be determined by reference to sources of information such as:

- Suppliers' quotations and current price lists.
- Recent purchases of the same or similar assets.
- Expert knowledge of the industry, which might include expert opinion.
- Relevant specific price indices for indexing historical cost.
- Cost of modern equivalent assets.

25.277 To arrive at the depreciated replacement cost, an appropriate amount of depreciation should be deducted to reflect the age and condition of the asset. FRS 7 explains that when the acquirer is assessing the remaining useful lives and, where applicable, residual values of fixed assets for the purposes of arriving at an estimate of their depreciated replacement cost, the *acquirer's* own policies for determining depreciation rates for similar assets should be used where these differ from the acquired company's. This is consistent with the general principle in FRS 7 that accounting policies should be harmonised by way of fair value adjustments, so that post-acquisition profit and loss accounts are not distorted by this type of non-performance adjustment.

25.278 Where government grants would be available to the acquired company for the replacement of fixed assets, it would be consistent with the principles of FRS 7 for allowance to be made for such grants in the calculation of a depreciated replacement cost to the acquired company. The fair value would be reduced by the notional grant; the amount of grant deducted would normally be calculated as an amortised amount that matches the amount of depreciation deducted from the gross replacement cost in order to reflect the acquired asset's age and condition. (Any deferred income in the books of the acquired company relating to grants previously received for the purchase of fixed assets would be eliminated on consolidation.)

25.279 Fair valuing by one of the techniques referred to above is inherently a process of estimation and as a practical measure, it seems acceptable to use an appropriate level of aggregation for valuing groups of similar assets rather than valuing each asset separately.

Recoverable amount

25.280 Although depreciated replacement cost places a cap on the fair values that a purchaser can ascribe, fair value should also not exceed the asset's recoverable amount.

25.281 'Recoverable amount' is defined in FRS 7 as *"the greater of the net realisable value of an asset and, where appropriate, the value in use"*. 'Value in use' is defined as *"the present value of the future cash flows obtainable as a result of an asset's continued use, including those resulting from the ultimate disposal of the asset"*. [FRS 7 para 2]. In other words the fair value attributed to a fixed asset should not exceed the net cash flows the business can recover from the asset, either by disposing of it or by continuing to use it. This is one of the most difficult and subjective areas of valuation in practice.

25.283 FRS 7 explains that an asset is impaired when its replacement cost is not recoverable in full. The recoverable amount should be assessed to reflect the condition of the asset on acquisition, but not any impairments resulting from subsequent events or actions of the acquirer. [FRS 7 para 47]. Thus, for example, if an acquirer decides to close a profitable factory occupied by the acquired company in order to rationalise the enlarged group's manufacturing facilities, any asset write-downs related to the closure (to reduce the assets' carrying values to net realisable value) should be charged in the post-acquisition profit and loss account and should not be included in the attributed fair values.

25.284 Recoverable amount needs to be considered in situations where it is unlikely that a fixed asset would be worth replacing at its current replacement cost because, even with the most efficient and profitable use of the asset, the business could not generate sufficient cash flows to earn an adequate return on the investment. Examples might include businesses owning major infrastructure assets whose replacement cost could not be recovered in full from the cash flows of the acquired business. In such situations, fair values reflecting lower recoverable amounts would need to be estimated.

25.285 The recoverable amount of fixed assets also needs to be reviewed in circumstances where the fair value exercise gives rise to negative goodwill, that is, where the fair values assigned to the identifiable assets and liabilities exceed, in aggregate, the cost of acquisition. FRS 10 requires the fair values of the acquired assets to be tested for impairment and the fair values of the acquired liabilities checked carefully to ensure that none has been omitted or understated. [FRS 10 para 48].

25.286 Where negative goodwill arising on an acquisition is material, after reviewing the assets' recoverable amounts, this may indicate that the acquirer has made a genuine bargain purchase, for example as a result of a distress sale. However, under FRS 7, negative goodwill may arise in other circumstances. For example, the purchase consideration for an acquisition may be lower than the fair value of the net assets acquired, because the acquired business is in need of reorganisation. The purchase price may reflect the fact that the acquirer has to incur reorganisation costs after the acquisition. FRS 7 does not allow the anticipated reorganisation costs to be recognised as an identifiable liability in the fair value exercise; it requires the reorganisation costs to be expensed in the profit and loss account of the acquiring group. The requirement to reassess the fair values of assets and check liabilities implies, however, that negative goodwill may be due to an error in the fair value exercise rather than being the result of a real bargain purchase.

25.287 Where the recoverable amount of an asset is estimated by reference to the 'value in use', that is *via* projected future cash flows, those cash flows should be discounted to their present value. Any valuation based on future cash flows is inherently very subjective.

25.288 One problem is that it is often very difficult to attribute cash flows to individual fixed assets. In estimating future cash flows for determining recoverable amount, FRS 7 allows assets to be considered as a group where they are used jointly. [FRS 7 para 49]. The grouping of assets by reference to cash flows is also inevitably subjective. One approach would be for such grouping to be taken as the smallest group of assets for which cash flows can be identified that are broadly independent of the cash flows of other assets or groups of assets. This approach has been adopted in FRS 11, 'Impairment of fixed assets and goodwill', which specifies methods for measuring value in use when fixed assets are reviewed for impairment. Such impairment reviews are usually carried out at the level of 'income-generating units' which comprise groups of assets, liabilities and associated goodwill that generate cash flows that are largely independent of an entity's other income streams.

25.289 FRS 7 gives no guidance on the choice of discount rate to be applied to the future cash flows in arriving at a value in use. The following two documents contain guidance on discounting and illustrate the emerging methodologies that may be useful for the purposes of estimating fair values of fixed assets by reference to recoverable amounts:

- A working paper entitled 'Discounting in financial reporting' issued by the ASB in April 1997.
- FRS 11 'Impairment of fixed assets and goodwill' published in July 1998.

25.290 The working paper explains the concepts involved in discounting where long-term assets and liabilities are measured by reference to future cash flows. The value of future cash flows is affected not only by the time value of money, but also by the variability (risk) associated with the cash flows. The paper specifically considers the value in use calculations that are required to estimate an asset's recoverable amount. The principle is that value in use represents the cash flows expected by the entity discounted at a market rate that takes account of the riskiness of the cash flows. The risk adjustment should be based on the market's price for risk. In effect, value in use is intended to simulate the market value of the cash flows expected by the entity.

25.291 Although it does not specifically deal with acquisition accounting, FRS 11 sets out in considerable detail the methodology for estimating cash flows and choosing a risk-adjusted discount rate for the purpose of calculating value in use when reviewing fixed assets for impairment. Some relevant points are summarised below.

- All relevant cash flows attributable to the group of assets or operation being valued should be taken into account, including an allocation of central overheads. Interest payments and other costs of capital are not included since these are taken into account in the discount rate.
- Cash flow forecasts should be based on reasonable and supportable assumptions and be consistent with budgets and plans that have been formally approved by management. Beyond the period covered by formal budgets and plans, the projections should generally assume a steady or declining growth rate.
- The cash flows used for estimating the value in use of income-generating units or individual fixed assets in their current condition should not include:
  - the costs or benefits that are expected to arise from a future reorganisation for which provision has not yet been made; or
  - the effects of future capital expenditure that is expected to enhance the assets from their current condition.
- The discount rate should be an estimate of the rate of return that the market would expect on an equally risky investment. Therefore, the riskiness of the cash flows, taking into account any significant uncertainties about their amount or timing, will affect the risk factor built into the discount rate. There may be a variety of means of estimating this rate including reference to:
  - The rate implicit in market transactions of similar assets.
  - The weighted average cost of capital of a listed company whose cash flows have a similar risk profile to those of the asset.
  - The weighted average cost of capital for the entity, but only if adjusted for the particular risks associated with the asset or the operation in which the asset is employed.
- FRS 11 requires that value is use is measured, for the purpose of impairment reviews, using cash flow forecasts that do not include tax cash flows. The pre-tax cash flows are discounted using a pre-tax discount rate.

25.292 The net present value that emerges from the discounted cash flow exercise will represent, in aggregate, the recoverable amount of all the identifiable assets less liabilities of the group of assets that generates the cash flows on which the calculation is based. If the recoverable amount is lower than their aggregate book value immediately before the acquisition, a fair value adjustment is required.

25.293 Any fair value adjustment to reduce aggregate book values to a lower recoverable amount will need to be allocated on a rational basis to the identifiable assets of the acquired business. FRS 11 could be used for guidance in the context of a fair value exercise. It proposes that, unless a specific asset is obviously impaired, assets with the most subjective valuations should be written down first. Any capitalised intangibles would thus be written down first; thereafter, tangible assets would be written down on a pro rata or more appropriate basis. However, no intangible asset that has a reliably ascertainable market value should be written down below its net realisable value; and no tangible asset with a net realisable value that can be measured reliably should be written down below its net realisable value.

25.294 Table 25.15 gives an example where assets acquired (on the acquisition by RJB Mining PLC of the principal coal mining activities of British Coal Corporation in England) have been fair valued at recoverable amounts.

Table 25.15 — RJB Mining PLC — Annual Report and Accounts — 31 December 1994

Notes to the Financial statements (extract)

13 Tangible fixed assets (extract)

	Land and buildings £'000	Mineral rights £'000	Mines and surface works £'000	Assets in course of construction £'000	Plant and machinery £'000	Total £'000
Group						
Cost or valuation						
At 1 January 1994	3,511	4,150	–	420	63,556	71,637
Additions	1,125	–	12,560	11,773	9,759	35,217
Acquired with Monckton	723	–	–	–	6,607	7,330
Acquired with English Coal	52,795	–	412,846	151,774	26,403	643,818
Disposals	(220)	(65)	–	(699)	(6,121)	(7,105)
Reclassification	–	(988)	485	988	(485)	–
At 31 December 1994	**57,934**	**3,097**	**425,891**	**164,256**	**99,719**	**750,897**

On acquisition, book values of collieries assets have been adjusted to net recoverable amounts. These amounts have been arrived at, following existing mining plans, by estimating future cash flows, net of all costs of running collieries, including capital expenditure, an allocation of central overheads and closure restoration costs and discounting these to their present values. The discount rate used has been based on the weighted cost of capital and taking into account appropriate risk. The methodology used to value fixed assets on acquisition is in accordance with Financial Reporting Standard 7 and Technical Release 773 issued by the Institute of Chartered Accountants in England and Wales.

Fair valuing stocks

25.295 Fair values of stocks and work-in-progress are determined using the same measurement principles as for fixed assets, that is by reference to market value, replacement cost or net realisable value, according to the circumstances. 'Value in use' is not relevant to the valuation of stocks, because stocks are held for resale and not for their continued use in the business.

25.296 The application of 'value to the business', or deprival value, principles to stocks mean that, in general, the valuation relates to the acquired company as a buyer rather than a seller. Consequently, FRS 7 does not require a profit element to be included in the fair value of finished and partly finished stocks. This means that, where stocks are revalued to market value or replacement cost, the consequent reduction in post-acquisition profits (assuming stock values move up rather than down) when the revalued amounts feed through into cost of sales is limited to the effect of market price or input price changes during the period the stocks were held by the acquired company. Often, where the turnover period is short, the effect of price changes will be immaterial and no revaluation will be necessary. Consequently, the post-acquisition operating profit of the acquired company will not be reduced in the acquirer's consolidated financial statements by the application of replacement cost principles.

25.297 If fair values are attributed to stocks and these values are in excess of historical cost to the acquired company, it would seem that the provisions of SSAP 9 would not allow the fair values to be incorporated in the financial statements of the acquired company. This is because the standard requires that stocks, other than long-term contracts, should be recorded at the lower of cost and net realisable value. [SSAP 9 para 26]. Fair values should be incorporated in the consolidated financial statements because they represent cost to the group, but not in the acquired company's financial statements if they are in excess of cost to that company.

25.298 It will again be necessary for the group to keep separate records of any stocks that are recorded at fair values in excess of cost to the acquired company. A consolidation adjustment will be necessary to adjust the profits and stocks of the acquired company for the effect of the fair value exercise, as long as the stocks remain unsold.

25.299 Whether market value, replacement cost or net realisable value is used, FRS 7 stresses that the basis of valuation must be consistent with the circumstances pertaining to the acquired company at the date of acquisition. Thus, for example:

- Market values are relevant where stocks are replaced by purchasing in a ready market to which the acquired entity has access. [FRS 7 para 52].

- Replacement cost should reflect the acquired company's normal buying process, the sources of supply available to it and its current cost of manufacture. [FRS 7 paras 12, 53].

- Estimates of net realisable value should be justified by the circumstances of the acquired entity before acquisition. [FRS 7 para 57]. However, the standard's definition of fair value does not permit stocks to be written down to values that would reflect a forced or liquidation sale.

Market value

25.300 Fair values would normally be based on market values in the following cases:

- Commodity and dealing stocks.
- Land and buildings held as trading stock.
- Land and buildings held for development.

Replacement cost

25.301 FRS 7 explains that for most manufactured stocks, fair value is represented by the current cost to the acquired company of reproducing the stocks. Account should be taken of the way the acquired company purchased or manufactured the stocks. [FRS 7 paras 52, 53].

25.302 The implications for the valuation of raw materials, work in progress and finished goods are as follows:

- Raw materials should be valued at replacement cost, reflecting the acquired company's normal sources of supply and current prices available to it.
- Manufactured work in progress and finished goods should be valued at the current cost of bringing the stocks to their present location and condition, reflecting the acquired company's own cost structures at the date of acquisition. Current standard costs would be used where these are available and reliable.
- Properties in the course of development would usually be valued at the replacement cost to the acquired company of the land and the development at its current stage of completion.
- Bought-in finished goods should be valued at replacement cost, reflecting the acquired company's normal sources of supply and current prices available to it.

25.303 In times of low inflation in manufacturing input prices, it is likely that the difference between historical cost and current replacement cost of most short-term manufactured stocks would not be material. In such circumstances no fair value adjustments would be necessary. There is an existing Companies Act requirement to disclose any material difference between the historical cost of stocks and their current replacement cost. [SI 2008/410 1 Sch 28(3)].

25.304 FRS 7 explains how these principles should be applied to determine the replacement cost of certain long-term maturing stocks, such as distillery products and growing timber. As an example, a whisky distiller holds stocks of whisky at different stages of maturity; there is also a market in semi-matured whisky. In a fair value exercise the question is whether such stocks should be valued at a market price or at the acquired company's own replacement cost.

25.305 FRS 7 indicates that market prices should be used if the acquired company normally purchases stocks in the market. If it does not replace stocks by purchasing in the market, market prices would not be used. Where, as is likely to be the case, there is market trading at the margin, but the market is very thin compared to the volumes of stocks held, the standard indicates that market prices would not be appropriate. Where replacement by manufacture would not be possible in the short term, the standard suggests that a surrogate for replacement cost may be found in the historical cost of the stocks, together with an interest cost in respect of holding the stock. [FRS 7 para 55].

25.306 An example of fair valuing long-term maturing stocks is taken from the financial statements of Guinness PLC when it accounted for the acquisition of Distillers. (Table 25.16.) The policy described appears to correspond to the method suggested by FRS 7.

Table 25.16 — Guinness PLC — Annual Report — 31 December 1986

Notes to the consolidated accounts (extracts)

15 Effect of the acquisition of Distillers on the Consolidated Balance Sheet (extract)

(ii) Stocks

Stocks have been included at fair value which has been determined by taking account of costs of production, including financing costs, and after writing off surplus stocks and providing for costs of realisation.

18 Stocks

	1986 £m	1985 £m
Raw materials and consumables	127	52
Work in progress	11	8
Stocks of maturing whisky	788	82
Finished goods	118	55
Goods purchased for resale	77	55
	1,121	**252**

The estimated replacement cost of all stocks is not materially different from the above figures.

In accordance with the Group's accounting policy, stocks of maturing whisky include an appropriate proportion of financing costs in determining production costs. At 31 December 1986 the total cost of £788m included £360m as a result of the application of this policy, of which £62m arose during the period. The balance of £298m represents the amount remaining of the accumulated financing costs taken into account in the Group's assessment of fair value at date of acquisition and is stated after a reduction of £46m in respect of sales during the period.

The net adjustment to stocks of £16m during the period, resulting from the increase of £62m and the reduction of £46m as set out above, has been credited to the profit and loss account as described in Note 7.

25.307 The emphasis on valuing stocks according to the existing cost structures of the acquired company means that one potential source of fair value adjustment is avoided. An acquiring company might consider that it could reduce the cost base of the acquired company and, accordingly, lower its cost of sales by reorganising its manufacturing operations and negotiating discounts with its suppliers. Under FRS 7 the acquirer is not allowed to reduce the fair value of the acquired company's stocks if it believes it could have produced those stocks more cheaply. Thus, the benefit of lower cost of sales would not feed into the acquirer's post-acquisition operating results until stocks produced after the post-acquisition reorganisation (that is, at a lower cost) are sold.

Net realisable value

25.308 The principles for determining net realisable value of stocks are set out in SSAP 9. The calculation of provisions to reduce stocks from cost to net realisable value is often subjective and involves the use of different criteria by different companies. Where an acquisition is involved, the acquirer should review the book values of slow-moving, excess or obsolescent stocks and, if necessary, make adjustments to those values to reflect the application of its own criteria as represented by its own accounting policies.

25.309 FRS 7 explains that any material write-down in the fair value exercise should be justified by the circumstances of the acquired company before acquisition. [FRS 7 para 57]. As with any other impaired assets, the fair value attributed to stocks should not reflect any impairments resulting from post-acquisition events, such as stock written off in a post-acquisition reorganisation.

Example 1 – Lower value attributed to stock on acquisition

The management of a company that is acquired may have certain stocks that are slow moving, but which they hope to sell after conducting an advertising campaign. They may, therefore, value these stocks at cost. The management of the acquirer may decide, on investigating the company, that an advertising campaign would not work and that, consequently, the stocks are unsaleable. The management of the acquirer would, therefore, attribute a lower fair value to the stocks, as the impairment in value existed at the date of acquisition.

Example 2 – Post acquisition reduction in the value of stuck

An acquired company has stock relating to a continuing product range, that has been turning over within a reasonable period. The management of the acquired company considered that the net realisable value exceeded cost. The management of the acquirer decides to discontinue that product range and reduces the selling price of the product in order to achieve a quick clearance of the remaining stocks. A provision is then necessary to reduce the cost of the stocks to their new net realisable value. Under FRS 7 the fall in net realisable value is attributable to the post-acquisition actions of the acquirer and, accordingly, the provision should be charged against post-acquisition profits and not as a fair value adjustment.

25.310 Although the above examples show a clear distinction between a stock provision that is allowed as a fair value adjustment and a stock provision that should be charged against post-acquisition profits, some situations will be less clear cut.

25.311 Paragraph 57 of the explanatory section of FRS 7 indicates that some hindsight should be applied in situations where exceptional margins appear to have been earned in the post-acquisition period, that is, within the period allowed for making fair value and goodwill adjustments. First, the attributed fair values would need to be re-examined in the light of actual experience and adjusted if they are found to have been materially understated. Secondly, if the profits are attributable to post-acquisition events, they may need to be disclosed as an exceptional item as required by paragraph 30 of FRS 6.

25.312 Although the standard discusses the implications of exceptional post-acquisition profits, there is no reason why the same logic should not be used where stocks are realised at a loss in the post-acquisition period. That is, fair values should be re-examined within the permitted hindsight period and adjusted if they are found to have been overstated.

Long-term contracts

25.313 The presentation of long-term contracts under SSAP 9 is convenient for FRS 7, because amounts recorded as turnover in respect of a contract are treated as debtors and not as work-in-progress. Amounts included as work-in-progress are generally very small. Consequently, the application of replacement cost principles is unlikely to be an important issue for long-term contracts in a fair value exercise.

25.314 A 'long-term contract' is defined in SSAP 9 as *"a contract entered into for the design, manufacture or construction of a single substantial asset or the provision of a service... where the time taken substantially to complete the contract is such that the contract activity falls into different accounting periods"*. [SSAP 9 para 22].

25.315 Although such contracts usually extend for more than one year, some contracts with a duration of less than one year should be accounted for as long-term contracts. This may be appropriate if the contracts are sufficiently material to the activity of the period and not recording turnover and the attributable profit would lead to distortion of the period's results such that the financial statements would not give a true and fair view. This policy should be applied consistently within the reporting entity and from year to year.

25.316 In acquisition accounting, the acquirer first needs to identify those contracts that fulfil the criteria in the definition described above. By applying the principles of accounting for long-term contracts in SSAP 9, the turnover and profit attributable to such contracts are allocated to the pre-acquisition and post-acquisition periods, as well as to discrete financial years, on a basis that matches the progress of the contracts.

25.317 As the guidance in SSAP 9 is very general, methods of calculating turnover and recognising attributable profit (or foreseeable losses) on long-term contracts vary between different companies and different industries and, of course, between different countries. Some companies in the UK take a more prudent approach to profit recognition than others.

25.318 The main source of fair value adjustments under FRS 7 is likely to be in the area of harmonising the methods of accounting in the acquired company with those of the acquirer. For example, if both the acquiring and acquired companies took a similar approach to identifying long-term contracts, calculating turnover and determining attributable profit, no fair value adjustments would be necessary to the balances shown as amounts recoverable on contracts.

25.319 Additionally, an acquirer would wish to make a critical review of the estimated outcome of each long-term contract, in order to ensure that adequate provisions have been made by the acquired company's management for any foreseeable losses as required by SSAP 9. Fair value adjustments would be made, as necessary, where the acquirer considered existing provisions to be inadequate or excessive, taking into account the circumstances of the acquired company before the acquisition.

25.320 Where exceptional margins or deficits appear to have been earned on acquired long-term contracts post acquisition, the principles described in paragraph 25.311 above should be applied. First, previously attributed fair values should be re-examined and, if necessary, adjusted. Secondly, if the profit or loss is attributed to post-acquisition activities, the acquirer should consider whether the profit or loss should be disclosed as an exceptional item in the profit and loss account. An example of a potential exceptional item given in paragraph 85 of FRS 6 is the release of a provision in respect of an acquired loss-making long-term contract that the acquirer makes profitable.

25.321 The following question sometimes arises in connection with fair valuing long-term contracts, where contracts are acquired that are similar in nature to contracts already being carried out by the acquirer. If the contracts undertaken by the acquired company are less profitable than those of the acquirer, the acquirer may consider that provisions should be made in the fair value exercise so that the contracts acquired will then give similar margins to those of the acquirer. Clearly such a practice would be contrary to the principles of FRS 7 because, even though the contracts may not be as valuable as the acquirer would like, they are not loss-making contracts. Whereas SSAP 9 requires provision to be made for contracts that are expected to result in a loss as soon as the loss is foreseen, it does not permit provision to be made for sub-normal future profits. Consequently, such contracts cannot be identifiable liabilities of the acquired company.

Disposals of business segments

25.322 There have been many examples of acquisitions where the acquirer has subsequently disposed of unwanted portions of the acquired business, sometimes recouping the major part of his initial outlay in the process.

25.323 FRS 2 had already dealt in a limited way with the treatment of interests in subsidiaries held exclusively with a view to subsequent resale. Such an interest is defined as *"an interest for which a purchaser has been identified or is being sought, and which is reasonably expected to be disposed of within approximately one year of its date of acquisition"*. [FRS 2 para 11]. FRS 2 requires such a subsidiary to be excluded from consolidation (provided it has not previously been consolidated) and to be shown in the acquirer's consolidated financial statements as a current asset at the lower of cost and net realisable value. [FRS 2 para 29].

25.324 FRS 7 has extended this treatment to any business operation acquired and held exclusively with a view to subsequent resale, whether a separate subsidiary or not, provided that its assets, liabilities, operating results and activities are clearly distinguishable, physically, operationally and for financial reporting purposes, from the other assets, liabilities, results of operations and activities of the acquired entity. [FRS 7 para 16]. In other words, the treatment only applies to a discrete business unit, including a business that operates as a division of an acquired company, which should be accounted for in the fair value exercise as a single identifiable asset instead of a collection of underlying assets, liabilities and goodwill. Additionally, the operation must be sold as a single unit.

25.325 The accounting treatment described in this section only applies to business operations sold. If an acquirer decides to *close* an operation of the acquired business, the assets, liabilities and results of that operation should be fully consolidated from the date of acquisition. Fair values should be attributed individually to identifiable assets and liabilities according to the normal rules of FRS 7. Closure costs and asset write-downs would have to be charged in the profit and loss account to the extent that they do not relate to identifiable liabilities that already existed or to assets that were already impaired at the date of acquisition. The treatment of disposals by means of sale is, therefore, inconsistent with the treatment of disposals by closure and with the general principles of FRS 7, which do not allow the acquirer's intentions regarding the acquired business to affect the fair valuing process.

25.326 FRS 7 requires the fair value of businesses sold or held exclusively with a view to subsequent resale to be determined as follows:

- Where the business has been sold by the time the first post-acquisition accounts are approved, fair value is based on the net proceeds of the sale, adjusted for the fair value of any assets or liabilities transferred into or out of the business. [FRS 7 para 16].

Such transfers would include items such as dividends from and capital contributions to the business between the date of acquisition and the date of disposal.

- Where the business has not been sold by the time the first post-acquisition financial statements are approved, fair value is based on the estimated net proceeds of sale. [FRS 7 para 17].

25.327 Where the business has not been sold by the time the first post-acquisition financial statements are approved, for it to be excluded from consolidation the acquirer must be able to demonstrate that:

- A purchaser has been identified or is being sought.
- Disposal is reasonably expected to occur within approximately one year of the date of acquisition. [FRS 7 para 17].

Otherwise, normal consolidation of the assets, liabilities and results of the business according to the general requirements of FRS 2 and FRS 7 is required.

25.328 The effect of the prescribed period for disposing of the business is that the disposal must have occurred within the period allowed in FRS 7 for completing the fair value exercise, because that period extends for more than one financial year. Any provisional fair value in the first post-acquisition financial statements (based on estimated net proceeds) should be adjusted in the subsequent period, with a corresponding adjustment to goodwill.

25.329 The FRS requires that if the business is not, in fact, sold within approximately one year of the acquisition, it should be fully consolidated with fair values attributed to the individual assets and liabilities as at the date of acquisition. [FRS 7 para 18]. This means that a prior period adjustment would be necessary (as a change of accounting policy) in order to 'backdate' the consolidation to the date of acquisition and to re-work the fair value exercise. The prior period adjustment would involve replacing the previously identified single asset. That is, the current asset investment in the subsidiary or business would be replaced by fair values of individual assets and liabilities (and goodwill). The profit and loss account of the previous period would be adjusted to include the results of that operation from the date of acquisition. These accounting adjustments would need to be accompanied by adequate management explanation.

25.330 It is interesting to consider what would happen in the opposite scenario – where an acquired business that was consolidated in the immediate post-acquisition period (because it was not then up for sale) is actually sold in the next financial year and within a year of its acquisition. In that situation, once consolidated, a business would continue to be consolidated right up to the date of disposal, as required by FRS 2, because the exclusion from consolidation of subsidiaries held exclusively for resale does not apply where the subsidiary has previously been consolidated. There is no question of altering the previous treatment and restating comparative figures.

25.331 The choice of net realisable value as fair value at the date of acquisition is justified by the ASB on the grounds that the resale value of a business in an arm's length transaction shortly after the valuation date would normally provide the most reliable evidence of its fair value at the date of acquisition. Otherwise, if a low fair value were placed on a business segment and it were subsequently sold at a profit, it would be tempting to try to present the profit, as entirely due to the expertise of the new management.

25.332 FRS 7 states that fair value should not be based on net realisable value in the following cases:

- Where the adjusted net proceeds are *demonstrably* different from the fair value at the date of acquisition *as a result of a post-acquisition event.*

- Where the acquirer has made a material change to the acquired business before disposal.

- The disposal is completed at a reduced price for a quick sale.

[FRS 7 paras 69].

25.333 In each of the above circumstances, the proceeds from disposal may be materially different from fair value at the date of acquisition as defined in the standard. It would then be necessary to estimate separately fair values at the date of acquisition and record a profit or loss on disposal in the post-acquisition profit and loss account. An example is where there is a collapse in the market for one of the subsidiary's products, which is attributable to an identifiable post-acquisition event.

Example 1 – Post acquisition increase in the value of a subsidiary held for sale

An acquisition of a group of companies included a coffee trading subsidiary that the acquirer intends to sell. Since the acquisition date, but before the first consolidated financial statements following the acquisition were completed, the price of coffee has risen by 100%, thus increasing the value of the subsidiary's stocks and the market value of the company.

If there is evidence of a post-acquisition increase in value which is reflected in the price obtained for the subsidiary, the increase should not be included in the fair value attributed to the subsidiary; it should be accounted for as a profit on the sale of an operation in the post-acquisition profit and loss account of the acquiring group.

Example 2 – Reorganisation of an acquired subsidiary prior to resale

An acquirer has carried out a reorganisation of an acquired subsidiary prior to its resale. In such a case the net realised value would in all likelihood be above the fair value of the subsidiary at the date of acquisition. The costs of reorganisation borne by the subsidiary, and the increase in value that could reasonably be attributed to the reorganisation would (because the subsidiary is excluded from consolidation) in effect be combined and shown as a post-acquisition profit on sale, which would be disclosed as a post-operating exceptional item.

25.334 An explanatory paragraph to FRS 7 also states that where the effect is material, the net proceeds from disposal would be discounted to obtain their present value at the date of acquisition. [FRS 7 para 65]. The effect of discounting is to shelter the post-acquisition profit and loss account from any notional or actual interest cost in respect of financing the purchase of the subsidiary or business operation during the period it is held by the group. It may, therefore, be appropriate to discount the net proceeds at a debt rate of interest.

25.335 An example of an acquisition including businesses held for resale is shown in Table 25.17.

Table 25.17 – De La Rue plc – Annual Report – 31 March 1995

Notes to the Accounts (extract)

23 **Acquisitions (extract)**

On 6 February 1995 the Group acquired the entire issued share capital of Portals Group plc (Portals) for a consideration, including expenses, of £716.7m. The acquisition has been accounted for using the acquisition method.

On 7 March 1995 the Group announced its intention to dispose of all the Portals non-security papermaking businesses. These businesses are held as assets for disposal and their results are excluded from the operating profit of the Group. The book values of the assets and liabilities of the retained Portals businesses immediately prior to the acquisition and the fair value adjustments required in recognition of the change of ownership are as follows:

	Book value prior to acquisition £m	**Revaluations £m**	**Accounting policy alignment £m**	**Assets for disposal £m**	**Fair value to the Group £m**
Tangible fixed assets	**48.8**	**2.7a**	–	–	**51.5**
Stocks	**11.1**	–	**(0.8)b**	–	**10.3**
Debtors	**8.3**	**0.6c**	–	–	**8.9**
Assets held for disposal	–	–	–	**158.0d**	**158.0**
Cash at bank and in hand	**23,1**	–	–	–	**23.1**
Bank loans and overdrafts	**(6.9)**	–	–	–	**(6.9)**
Creditors due within one year	**(8.4)**	–	–	–	**(8.4)**
Taxation	**(2.1)**	–	–	–	**(2.1)**
Deferred taxation	**0.8**	**(0.8)c**	**(8.5)e**	–	**(8.5)**
Provisions for liabilities and charges*	**(5.1)**	**2.5c**	–	–	**(2.6)**
Net assets acquired	**69.6**	**5.0**	**(9.3)**	**158.0**	**223.3**
Consideration					
Cash					**402.8**
Shares issued (at market value)					**295.4**
Loan notes					**18.5**
Total consideration					**716.7**
Fair value of net assets acquired (as above)					**223.3**
Goodwill					**493.4**

Notes:

a The revaluations of plant and machinery employed in the security papermaking businesses are based upon depreciated replacement cost.

b The value of maintenance stocks has been adjusted as a result of applying De La Rue's accounting policies.

c The Portals pension scheme was revalued on acquisition. The assumptions upon which this revaluation is based are stated in note 24.

d The assets for disposal represent the anticipated net sale proceeds, as estimated by the Directors of De La Rue plc, discounted to their present value at the date of acquisition (see note 13).

e Deferred taxation has been provided for timing differences in accordance with the tax provisioning policy of De La Rue.

13 **Assets Held for Disposal**

Assets held for disposal represents the Group's investment in those companies listed as "Businesses held for resale" on page 62. These companies, all of which were subsidiaries of Portals Group plc when the Group acquired Portals Group plc, are held exclusively with a view to resale. They are held at the Directors' valuation of anticipated net sales proceeds discounted to their present value at 31 March 1995.

Included within other creditors is £3.3m owing to these businesses by the rest of the Group as at 31 March 1995, representing £2.6m of cash received and £0.7m of trading items. Apart from these transactions, during the period from acquisition to 31 March 1995 there were no material transactions between these businesses and the rest of the Group, and there were no dividends received or receivable from them.

* Note that, for years beginning on or after 1 January 2005, SI 2004/2947, 'The Companies Act 1985 (International Accounting Standards and other Amendments) Regulations 2004', changed the Companies Act line item to 'provisions for liabilities'.

25.336 The principles set out in the FRS for attributing expenses to the cost of an acquisition would also apply to the costs of disposals. [FRS 7 para 65].

25.337 Where fair value is based on net realised value, it is arrived at after deducting costs incurred in disposing of the business. The rules on acquisition costs restrict expenses that can be capitalised to fees and similar incremental costs that would not have been incurred had the acquisition not taken place (see para 25.426). They do not permit any allocation and capitalisation of internal costs that would have been incurred anyway. In the same way that the FRS takes a restrictive view on acquisition costs to avoid overstating the cost of acquisition, it takes a similarly restrictive view on disposal costs. The FRS prevents internal costs from being taken out of the profit and loss account and deducted from the disposal proceeds and, as a result, from increasing goodwill.

Fair valuing monetary assets and liabilities

25.338 The fair value of most short-term receivables and payables is usually not significantly different from their book values, because they reflect amounts expected to be received or paid in the short term. Fair value adjustments would usually be limited to those arising from the acquirer's different estimates of amounts recoverable or payable.

Example – Debtors

A significant debtor of an acquired company has gone into liquidation between the date of acquisition and the completion of the group accounts. No provision was made against the debtor in the acquired company's books. Is the provision now required as a fair value adjustment in the consolidated financial statements?

Any new evidence that comes to light before the fair value exercise is completed and that concerns the condition of the acquired entity's assets at the acquisition date would be taken into account in arriving at fair values. The adequacy of bad debt provisions is one area where a certain amount of hindsight is usually necessary.

FRS 21 cites the insolvency of a customer in the post balance sheet period as an example of an adjusting post balance sheet event. An adjusting event is an event that provides additional evidence relating to conditions existing at the balance sheet date. This principle is consistent with FRS 7's principle of reflecting conditions at the date of acquisition. Although the debtor was not in liquidation at the date of acquisition, it is likely that it was in financial difficulties, even if those only became apparent after the date of acquisition. On this basis we consider that the provision is a fair value adjustment.

25.339 For long-term monetary items, the time value of money also needs to be taken into account. The fair value of most long-term receivables and payables is represented by their face values where a market rate of interest is paid during the term the item is outstanding. However, fair values of long-term receivables and payables may be materially different from their book or face values where they either carry no interest or carry interest at rates significantly different from prevailing market rates at the date of acquisition. Long-term monetary items would include finance lease receivables and payables.

25.340 For example, the fair value today of £1 million receivable in one year's time is obviously less than £1 million. Similarly, the fair value today of a five year loan of £1 million carrying a fixed rate of interest of 12 per cent is greater than £1 million if the current rate for similar borrowings is 6 per cent.

25.341 In these circumstances, FRS 7 requires the items to be recognised at fair values, which are deemed to be one of the following:

- Market prices, where these are available.
- Current prices at which the business could acquire similar assets or enter into similar obligations.
- Discounted present values.

[FRS 7 para 14].

25.342 The effect of making such fair value adjustments is that the post-acquisition profit and loss account of the acquiring group shows finance charges or interest receivable that equate to market rates of interest at the date of acquisition.

25.343 The standard gives the following guidance on the choice of discount rate to be used for discounting items to their present values:

- Long-term borrowings: based on current lending rates for an equivalent term, the credit standing of the issuer and the nature of any security given.
- Long-term debtors: based on current lending rates, after any necessary bad debt provisions have been made.

[FRS 7 para 61].

25.344 The fair value of assets would be measured by their market value if an active market for them exists. For example, if an acquired company has invested in long-term debt issued by an entity that the market perceives to be at risk of default, there may be a secondary market in which the debt is traded at a discount to its face value. This discounted value may be the best available evidence of fair value.

25.345 Similarly, the fair value of any quoted debt securities issued by the acquired entity would usually be measured by their market values at the date of acquisition. However, an explanatory paragraph to the standard makes an exception where the acquired company is perceived to be at risk of defaulting on its debt obligations and the pre-acquisition market value of issued securities is reduced from its face value to reflect this risk. The standard states that such a reduction in the value of debt would not be recognised in the fair value allocation if the debt was expected to be repaid at its full amount after the acquisition. [FRS 7 para 63].

25.346 By making this exception to its general principles of fair valuing, the standard is recognising that, in such circumstances, the acquired company still has a liability to repay the gross amount of its debt. The acquired company is not absolved from its debt obligations where the market value of its debt is discounted to reflect market concerns. Accordingly, when attributing fair values to such debt in the financial statements of the acquiring group, the acquirer should recognise either the gross amount or, if the rates of interest on such debt are significantly different from current market rates, a present value that reflects current market rates, but not distress rates. If this were not done, recognising such debt in the fair value exercise at its (discounted) market value would mean a pre-acquisition gain would be attributed to the acquired company, followed by a post-acquisition loss attributed to the acquiring group, whereas, in fact, no such gain or loss has arisen.

25.347 It could also be inferred from the exception described above that a similar approach should be adopted where the debt issued by an acquired company that is in financial difficulty is not quoted, notwithstanding the reference to *"the credit standing of the issuer"* as mentioned in paragraph 25.343 above. To be consistent, and for the same reasons, we consider that it would be inappropriate to fair value the debt at a deep discount to its face or book value if the total payments (capital and interest) the acquired company is required to make under the terms of the debt are expected to be made.

25.348 The market interest rate applicable to a particular loan may alter because of a change in the perceived risk of the specific business, rather than because of a general change in market rates. An increase in business risk will increase the interest rate applicable to the entity, thus reducing the market value of its loans. This applies in particular to long-term fixed rate debt. In fair value accounting, we consider that fair values of unquoted debt obligations should not, in general, be reduced to reflect any deterioration in the creditworthiness of the acquired company since the debt was issued, if the debt is expected to be repaid at its full amount.

25.349 FRS 7 also requires the fair values of accruals and provisions to be determined by taking into account the amounts expected to be paid and their timing. [FRS 7 para 14]. It gives discounting to present value as one of the options for determining the fair values of monetary assets and liabilities generally. Accounting practices relating to the measurement of long-term provisions have previously varied according to the nature of the liability. However, FRS 12 introduced rules that apply to measuring all provisions – they should be measured at present values of expected expenditures where the effect of the time value of money is material. The discount rate should be a pre-tax rate that reflects current market assessments of the time value of money and the risks specific to the liability. Alternatively, the expected future cash outflows may be adjusted (that is, increased) for risk and discounted by using a risk-free rate (such as a government bond rate). Care should be taken to ensure the effect of risk is not double-counted – that is, risk should be taken into account either in estimating the (undiscounted) future expenditures or by adjusting (that is, reducing) the discount rate, but not both. The measurement basis required by FRS 12 should generally be consistent with the principles for determining fair values of provisions in FRS 7.

Fair valuing contingencies

25.350 The treatment of contingent purchase consideration is considered later in paragraph 25.410. The paragraphs that follow consider contingencies that affect the value of identifiable net assets.

Identification of contingencies

25.351 Paragraph 2 of FRS 12 defines a contingent liability:

"(a) *a possible obligation that arises from past events and whose existence will be confirmed only by the occurrence of one or more uncertain future events not wholly within the entity's control; or*

(b) *a present obligation that arises from past events but is not recognised because:*

(i) *it is not probable that a transfer of economic benefits will be required to settle the obligation; or*

(ii) *the amount of the obligation cannot be measured with sufficient reliability.*"

The standard defines a contingent asset as *"a possible asset that arises from past events and whose existence will be confirmed only by the occurrence of one or more uncertain future events not wholly within the entity's control"*. [FRS 12 para 2].

25.352 In acquisition accounting, a pre-acquisition contingency would be a contingent asset or liability of the acquired company that existed at the date of acquisition. For fair value exercises, the identifiable assets and liabilities of an acquired company must include certain contingent assets that existed before the date of acquisition (see below).

Measurement of contingencies

25.353 The normal rules in FRS 12 for recognising and measuring contingencies in financial statements are as follows:

- Contingent liabilities should not be recognised as provisions, but should be disclosed, unless the possibility of a transfer of economic benefits is remote. If it becomes probable that a transfer of economic benefits will be required for an item previously dealt with as a contingent liability, a provision should be recognised in the period in which the change in probability occurs. [FRS 12 paras 27 to 30].
- Contingent assets should not be recognised as assets, but should be disclosed where an inflow of economic benefits is probable. If it becomes virtually certain that an inflow of economic benefits will arise, the asset and the related profit should be recognised in the period in which the change occurs. [FRS 12 paras 31 to 35].

25.354 Under FRS 12, where an item is expected to result in a transfer of economic benefits, a provision should be recognised. Where a transfer of economic benefits is not probable, the item is a contingent liability and no provision should be recognised. In acquisition accounting, it is unlikely that a contingent liability (as defined in FRS 12) would result in the recognition of an identifiable liability, because by definition it is not probable that a transfer of economic benefits will be required. An exception to this would in rare cases be where the contingent liability had a fair value that could be determined from a market in such items.

25.355 In acquisition accounting, the identifiable assets to be included in the fair value exercise include contingent assets that are expected to result in an inflow of economic benefits, as assets, even though they are not normally included in financial statements as gains until their realisation becomes virtually certain. Recognition of contingent assets in a fair value exercise has no immediate profit and loss account effect. Rather, it means all assets that have value are recognised, with only the residual difference between the purchase price and the identified net assets being reported as goodwill. In contrast, omitting a pre-acquisition contingent asset in the fair value exercise would mean that a pre-acquisition asset may be recognised as a post-acquisition gain in succeeding financial statements. The recognition of such contingent assets should follow the same process as that of contingent liabilities. That is, contingent assets should be recognised in the fair value exercise where an inflow of economic benefits is probable.

25.356 FRS 7 requires all identifiable assets and liabilities to be recognised in the fair value exercise, provided they can be reliably valued. Fair values, representing the price at which such an item might be exchanged in an arm's length transaction, would rarely be ascertainable unless the contingent asset or liability were of a kind that is normally exchanged. Consequently, the standard allows reasonable estimates of the expected outcome to be used as the best approximation to fair value. [FRS 7 para 15].

25.357 For this purpose, the standard explains that the acquiring company's management's best estimate of the likely outcome should be used in place of any previous estimate, assuming that no post-acquisition events or other changes in circumstances are reflected in the valuation. [FRS 7 para 64].

25.358 Many contingencies, such as legal claims, require a considerable amount of time to be investigated in order to make reliable predictions of the outcome. Often it may not be possible to incorporate reliable figures in the first set of consolidated financial statements following the acquisition. In such circumstances, the fair values would be declared provisional and adjustments would be made in the second post-acquisition group accounts if new information becomes available within the permitted hindsight period that enables the resolution of the contingency to be reliably predicted. In practice, such items are sometimes covered by warranties given by vendors or by insurance (see para 25.425).

25.359 In accounting periods that follow the period in which the fair value exercise is completed, there may be changes in the amount of any contingent assets or liabilities that have been recognised. Such changes would be reflected in the profit and loss account for the period in which they are recognised in the same way as changes in estimates of other assets and liabilities are dealt with.

25.360 FRS 6 gives, as an example of a post-acquisition profit or loss that would require separate disclosure as an exceptional item in the financial statements of the acquiring group, the *"realisation of contingent assets or liabilities at amounts materially different from their attributed fair values"*. [FRS 6 para 85].

25.361 Where contingent assets are recognised on acquisition, but subsequently they do not materialise, there will be an adverse effect on the profit and loss account. In this respect, where a contingent asset is set up on acquisition, it will be necessary to consider in future periods whether there is a reduction in its value. Where there is, the asset should be written down, by providing an amount against post-acquisition profits. On the other hand, where a contingent asset is subsequently expected to be realised at an amount in excess of its attributed fair value on acquisition, the normal rules of FRS 12 would preclude the recognition of any gain in the profit and loss account of the acquiring group until its realisation becomes virtually certain.

25.362 Similarly, where contingent liabilities are recognised in the fair value exercise, they will have to be reconsidered in future periods to ascertain whether the provisions are adequate. Where they are not, an additional provision will have to be made and charged to the post-acquisition profit and loss account. On the other hand, where the amount accrued in the fair value exercise is subsequently found to be excessive, the excess provision would be written back in the post-acquisition profit and loss account.

25.363 If the amount of the expected inflow or outflow relating to a contingency in the acquired company cannot be reliably estimated from information available at the end of the period allowed for completing the fair value exercise, contingent assets or liabilities would not be recognised, but would be disclosed in the acquirer's consolidated financial statements as required by FRS 12.

25.364 When evaluating pre-acquisition contingencies, in practice it is not always clear whether adjustments to the acquired company's financial statements should be reported as fair value adjustments or as post-acquisition events. The following examples illustrate the difficulties.

Example 1 – Difference between fair value adjustments and post-acquisition events

An acquired publishing company has a publishing subsidiary which has been sued for libel. The company's counsel has advised that, in his opinion, the case could be successfully defended. Accordingly, no provision has been included in the acquired company's financial statements, other than for estimated legal fees. The management of the acquiring company decide that the case should be settled out of court in order to avoid a protracted court case and the risk that the company could lose. The overall settlement cost exceeds the legal costs provision in the acquired company's financial statements.

It could be argued that the acquired company's financial statements reflected the best estimate of the likely outcome and that no further fair value adjustment is required. The financial effect of the acquirer's decision not to defend the case would then be reflected as a current, that is, post-acquisition, event.

However, a different view is that as the settlement related to a contingency that was already in existence and as there has been no new information or change in circumstances relating to the contingency, the cost of settlement is an event that confirms the outcome of the contingency. Therefore, the cost should be reflected as a fair value adjustment. This seems to be the more sensible interpretation and reflects the acquiring company's management's best estimate of the likely outcome as explained in paragraph 64 of FRS 7.

Example 2 – Difference between fair value adjustments and post-acquisition events

An acquired company was pursuing a claim for negligence against a firm of accountants who had provided investigation services in respect of a previous acquisition that failed. The claim amounted to £10m. The accountants strenuously denied acting negligently. However, they had made an offer of settlement of £2m, which the company had rejected. The case was, therefore, scheduled for a court hearing. The management of the acquiring company subsequently negotiated, and accepted, an out of court settlement of £3m.

In this example, it is likely to be impossible to arrive at any meaningful fair value without the benefit of hindsight, that is, unless the actual outcome of the claim is reflected. If the claim was settled within the period for completing the fair value exercise, the credit of £3m should probably be accounted for as a fair value adjustment, because it relates to a contingency that was already in existence. However, it would be tempting for the management to argue that the settlement was due to their own efforts and skills, or that changes in the litigious environment had favoured a higher settlement and that, accordingly, some or all of the credit should be reflected in the post-acquisition profit and loss account.

If the settlement is not reached by the time the period for completing the fair value exercise has expired, the treatment would depend on the information available at the end of that period. If the outcome of the claim could be reliably predicted at that time, a best estimate of the settlement amount would be included as a contingent asset, that is, as a fair value adjustment. Later, when a settlement is reached, any income would be credited in the profit and loss account in the period it is received. Of course, it would be reported as an exceptional item, if material.

25.365 Table 25.18 gives an example where the receipt after the acquisition date of a pre-existing claim by the acquired company has been partly recognised as a fair value adjustment (increasing the fair value of debtors) and partly as an exceptional post-acquisition profit.

Table 25.18 — GKN plc — Report & Accounts — 31 December 1994

NOTES ON THE ACCOUNTS (extract)

23 ACQUISITIONS

Westland (extract from fair value table)

	BOOK VALUE PRIOR TO ACQUISITION	ACCOUNTING POLICY ALIGNMENT	REVALUATIONS	OTHER	FAIR VALUE TO THE GKN GROUP
	£m	£m	£m	£m	£m
Debtors – joint venture termination	–	–	–	112.0	112.0
– other	120.2	–	–	–	120.2

The fair value adjustments made include:

(c) a debtor for the net cash received in June 1994 amounting to £112 million arising from an arbitration award against the Arab Organisation for Industrialisation (AOI) following the termination of a joint venture between AOI and Westland Helicopters Limited to manufacture Lynx helicopters under licence. This receipt was secured as a result of actions initiated by Westland prior to acquisition and has accordingly been referred back to 31st March 1994. A further final net receipt of £51 million was negotiated in August 1994 and has been treated as a post acquisition exceptional profit (see note 4). These items, taken together with the net £15 million received by Westland in December 1993, give a total net receipt of £178 million from the award.

4 EXCEPTIONAL ITEMS (extract)

	1994	
	CONTINUING OPERATIONS	**DISCONTINUED OPERATIONS**
	£m	**£m**
Subsidiaries		
Profits (£83.7 million) less losses (£109.1 million) on sale or closure of businesses:		
Westland joint venture termination (note 23c)	**50.9**	–
Reduction in shareholding in Chep UK	**22.2**	–
Sale of US and Australian rental businesses	–	**(34.0)**
Provision for loss on sale of UES Holdings	**(59.6)**	–
Other	**(7.4)**	**2.5**
	6.1	**(31.5)**

Pensions and other post-retirement benefits

Identification of assets and liabilities

25.366 Where an acquisition involves the assumption of pension schemes or other post-retirement benefit plans, FRS 7 requires the following to be recognised as identifiable assets or liabilities in the fair value exercise:

- A surplus in a funded scheme, to the extent that it can be recovered through reduced contributions or through refunds from the scheme.
- A deficiency in a funded scheme.
- Accrued obligations in respect of an unfunded scheme.

[FRS 7 para 19 as amended by FRS 17 para 101(a)].

25.367 FRS 7 does not permit companies to recognise, as adjustments in the fair value exercise, changes in pension or other post-retirement arrangements following the acquisition. The cost of such changes should be dealt with in the post-acquisition profit and loss account under the normal rules for pension costs (see chapter 11) [FRS 7 para 20].

25.368 Defined contribution schemes do not pose any problems in acquisition accounting, because the employer's obligation at any point in time is restricted to the amount of contributions payable to date, including to the date of acquisition. A liability will exist in the acquired company's financial statements if all contributions due by it have not been paid to the scheme and an asset will exist where excess contributions have been paid.

25.369 Defined benefit schemes, however, pose greater problems because the employer's liability for future benefits payable is not, in the case of funded schemes, restricted to the amount of contributions paid to the scheme.

25.370 Arrangements for transferring pension obligations when a change of ownership takes place are many, varied and often complex. They may include: the acquisition of all schemes in the acquired group, in the case of the takeover of a listed group of companies; the acquisition of part of the vendor's pension schemes, in the case of the purchase of a subsidiary from a parent company; or simply the transfer of assets from the vendor's scheme to the purchaser's scheme reflecting transfer values of the accumulated pension rights of individual employees.

25.371 The value of the assets of a scheme acquired may exceed the estimated liability for the benefits that have accrued to members at the date of acquisition and, therefore, there may be a surplus. Equally, if the assets are insufficient to cover future liabilities for pensions there would be a deficiency. The surplus (with exceptions – see para 25.377 below) or deficiency should generally be recognised as an identifiable asset or liability in the fair value exercise.

25.372 In the past, a problem faced by many companies, and particularly those that have acquired subsidiaries in the US, has been how to deal with post-retirement health care benefits, which were sometimes a substantial hidden liability of acquired subsidiaries. Both FRS 17 in the UK and the related standards in US GAAP have introduced guidance for such schemes. Companies need to review acquisitions to ensure that any material post-retirement benefits are identified and appropriate liabilities recognised in the fair value exercise.

25.373 The appointed actuary, or an actuary acting for the acquirer in the due diligence exercise, will play a key role in determining the surplus or deficit position for pension schemes and in determining the liability for other post-retirement benefits.

Measurement of assets and liabilities

25.374 FRS 7 does not prescribe any rules for measuring the amount of surplus or deficiency to be recognised. The standard merely explains that the actuarial valuation depends on several assumptions about the future; and the *acquirer* would apply its own judgement in determining these assumptions. [FRS 7 para 73].

25.375 Generally, therefore, an actuarial valuation should be carried out as at the date of acquisition using actuarial methods and assumptions that are consistent with those the acquirer normally uses for the purpose of accounting for defined benefit schemes. These may differ from those previously used by the acquired company. FRS 17 requires use of the projected unit method for measuring scheme liabilities. [FRS 17 para 20].

25.376 However, the valuation should not take into account the cost of any retrospective changes in benefits and membership that are decided upon by the acquirer. Such costs should be written off in the acquirer's consolidated profit and loss account over the vesting period under the principles of FRS 17. The following are examples of items that should be treated as post-acquisition:

- Costs of benefit improvements following the acquisition.
- Pension effect of a significant reduction in the number of employees following a post-acquisition reorganisation.
- Cost of enhanced pensions initiated by the acquirer to induce early retirement.

25.377 FRS 7 notes that the fair value of the surplus or deficit should be measured in accordance with the rules of FRS 17.

25.378 Many defined benefit schemes are designed such that the employees pay a fixed rate of contribution and the employer has an obligation to fund the balance. If a scheme is in surplus, the employer may be able to suspend or reduce the normal level of contributions until the surplus is eliminated. Where a surplus in an acquired company's scheme is to be run off by a contribution holiday after the acquisition, the surplus at the date of acquisition should clearly be recognised as an asset in the fair value exercise. The same goes for amounts subsequently refunded to the employer.

25.379 Situations where it would be either inappropriate or imprudent to recognise the full amount of a surplus as an asset might include the following:

- It is a condition of the scheme that part of the surplus belongs to the employees.
- The employees share in a contribution holiday.
- The trust deed prevents a refund of surplus to the employer company, and the surplus is so large that even an extended employer contribution holiday would not recover the whole amount of the surplus in the foreseeable future. Accordingly, it may be prudent to recognise a smaller surplus in the fair value exercise, for example the present value of a contribution holiday.

25.380 One means of utilising a surplus is to allow it to finance benefit improvements to employees that would otherwise be funded by increased contributions. Because the standard is quite specific that the cost of changes in pension arrangements such as benefit improvements following an acquisition should be accounted for in the profit and loss account as post-acquisition variations, it appears that such costs should not be deducted from the amount of surplus recognised on acquisition. The treatment of the costs (and corresponding reduction in surplus) is dealt with in chapter 11.

Deferred taxation

25.381 Fair value adjustments made to the identifiable assets and liabilities of the acquired entity may give rise to timing differences. Deferred tax should be provided on those timing differences in the fair value exercise in the same way as they would be if they were timing differences arising in the acquired entity's own accounts. [FRS 7 para 74 as amended by FRS 19 para 71]. Such deferred tax should be provided in accordance with requirements of FRS 19. [FRS 7 para 21 as amended by FRS 19 para 71]. For example, if the acquired entity's property was fair valued on acquisition, this would be treated as a revaluation on which no deferred tax would be provided in the fair value exercise unless the acquired entity had entered into a binding agreement to sell the asset prior to its acquisition and no rollover relief was available.

25.382 It is also possible that the acquired entity may not have recognised deferred tax assets, including those arising in respect of tax losses, because it was unable to satisfy the recognition criteria for deferred tax assets as specified in FRS 19. As a result of the acquisition, such deferred tax assets may need to be recognised because they now satisfy the recognition criteria. For example, a previously unrecognised tax loss may become recoverable because the acquiring group will have sufficient taxable profits to offset the tax losses acquired. In that situation, the unrecognised tax asset should be recognised in the fair value exercise. [FRS 7 para 22 as amended by FRS 19 para 71]. Deferred tax on fair value adjustments are considered further in chapter 13.

Fair valuing the purchase consideration

Cost of acquisition

25.383 SI 2008/410 and FRS 7 state that the acquisition cost of a subsidiary is made up of some or all of the following elements:

- Cash consideration.
- Fair value of other consideration.
- Expenses of acquisition.

[SI 2008/410 6 Sch 9(4); FRS 7 para 26].

25.384 Consequently, the objective of determining the fair value of the consideration given is to fix the acquisition cost of the investment. Where cash forms part of the consideration, the fair value will be the amount payable in respect of the item, unless settlement is deferred, where it may be necessary to discount it (see para 25.404 below).

25.385 Non-cash consideration may take the form of:

- The assumption of liabilities by the acquirer.
- Quoted securities issued.
- Unquoted securities issued.
- Consideration given in the form of non-monetary assets, including securities of another entity.

25.386 The assumption of liabilities by the acquirer may take the form of the repayment of borrowings in an acquired company owed to its former investors, including, in the case of the purchase of a subsidiary from its former parent, the repayment of an acquired company's intra-group debt.

25.387 The fair value would be the amount paid or payable, discounted to present value, if necessary, where settlement of the liabilities is due at a future date.

25.388 Securities issued by the acquirer may take the form of:

- Ordinary shares.
- Preference shares (convertible or non-convertible).
- Loan stock (convertible or non-convertible).
- Share warrants and other options relating to the securities of the acquiring company.

25.389 The various elements that make up the total consideration are considered further in the paragraphs that follow.

Quoted securities

25.390 The most common form of securities given as consideration is ordinary or equity shares. The standard states that the fair value would usually be taken to be the market price at the date of acquisition. For practical purposes, the mid-market price is normally used. There are two related issues:

- The point in time at which shares should be valued.
- The use of alternative valuations to a valuation based on the quoted market price.

25.391 Where control is transferred by a public offer, the fair value of securities given as consideration should be based on the market price of the security on the date on which the final successful offer becomes unconditional. This is in line with FRS 2 which defines this as the date on which an undertaking becomes a subsidiary. This price takes account of the market's reaction to a bid and movements in the share price of a bidder.

25.392 In order to avoid a major fluctuation in share price on a single day distorting the acquisition price, the standard states that market prices for a reasonable period before the date of acquisition, during which acceptances could be made, would need to be considered. It may then be appropriate to base the fair value on an average of market prices over a short period. Such method of valuation would, however, be the exception rather than the rule, because only in very unusual circumstances – for example, a market rumour causing a very temporary blip in the share price – would the actual market price on the date of acquisition fail to provide the most reliable measure of fair value.

25.393 Where the shares are quoted, but trade in them is infrequent, as in the case of some public companies with significant family shareholdings (close companies) and unprogressive dividend policies, market price could be an unreliable measure of fair value. In such circumstances, the approach applied for valuing unquoted securities, as set out below, may be more appropriate.

Unquoted securities

25.394 Where no market price is available for ordinary shares (or where the market price of quoted securities is inappropriate), the fair value should be estimated by traditional share valuation methods. For example, applying an appropriate capitalisation rate to earnings (P/E ratio), or discounting the cash flows of securities to their present value. The values of unquoted securities can sometimes be estimated by reference to securities with, and issued by enterprises with, similar characteristics.

25.395 In some cases it may not be possible to value the consideration given by any of the above methods. The cost of acquisition, in such circumstances, should be determined by valuing the business being acquired (that is, including its goodwill) rather than by valuing the securities issued.

Other securities

25.396 The general principles that apply to determining the fair value of ordinary shares can also be applied to other securities, such as preference shares, loan stock, share warrants and other options. Consequently, where there is a market price available, the market price on the date on which the successful offer finally becomes unconditional should be used. Where there is no market price, similar bases to those described above should be used. For convertible securities, such as convertible loan stock or preference shares, the fair value will include the value of the conversion rights and be related to the value of the security into which it can convert in the future.

Non-monetary consideration

25.397 FRS 7 states that where the purchase consideration takes the form of non-monetary assets, fair values would be determined by reference to market prices, estimated realisable values, independent valuations, or other available evidence. [FRS 7 para 80].

25.398 The purchase consideration may sometimes take the form of other assets, for example, where a company has an investment in a second company (which may be listed) and swaps that investment for a controlling interest in another company. In acquiring the holding in the new subsidiary, the consideration given will be the shares in the second company. Under FRS 7 it would be necessary to arrive at a current fair value of the holding in the second company and this would represent the cost of the holding in the new subsidiary.

25.399 If the fair value of the investment in the second company is greater than the carrying value, a difference will arise between the original carrying value of the second company and the cost of the investment in the new subsidiary. The question arises as to whether this difference represents a realised profit. The answer to this question would probably be that the profit should be treated as unrealised, because it will not be realised until the new subsidiary is disposed of.

Other consideration

25.400 There are certain forms of 'consideration' that for tax or other reasons are sometimes given. These include payments made for an agreement by a vendor not to compete with the acquirer for a number of years and bonus payments to vendors who continue to be directors of the acquired company after the acquisition. The standard mentions that in practice it will be necessary to look at the substance of the relevant transactions in order to determine the accounting treatment. If the payments represent compensation for post-acquisition services or profit sharing, they should be reported as post-acquisition revenue costs. If the payments are in substance consideration for the business acquired, they should be capitalised as part of the acquisition cost.

25.401 The accounting treatment should reflect the transaction's true commercial effect, both the initial purchase consideration and subsequent payments, in the eyes of the acquirer and vendor. UK GAAP does not give any detailed guidance on this point, however, factors that could indicate whether a contingent payment is in substance part of the purchase consideration or employee compensation are:

- Link between continuing employment and contingent consideration. If, for example, payments are conditional on the recipients remaining with, and providing continuing future services to, the acquired company, there would be a presumption that the post-acquisition payments should be charged as post-acquisition expenses in the acquiring group's profit and loss account. Arrangements that are not affected by employment ending may indicate that contingent payments are additional purchase consideration.
- Length of required employment period. If this coincides with, or is longer than, the contingent payment period, this would suggest that the payment is compensation for post-acquisition services.
- Remuneration of vendors compared to other key employees. If the vendor's employee compensation, excluding the contingent payment, is comparable to other key employee's compensation, this would suggest that the contingent payment is consideration for the acquisition rather than a payment for employee services.

- Level of contingent payment for the vendors who stay on as employees compared to those who do not. If the vendors who stay on as employees are paid more than those who do not become employees, this would indicate that the additional amount received by the vendors who become employees is payment for post-acquisition services.
- Value of the business compared to the consideration paid upfront. If it can be clearly demonstrated that the purchase consideration has been reduced in anticipation of additional payments, and such payments are not conditional on the recipient providing future services to the company, the payments are likely in substance to be additional purchase consideration.
- Formula used to determine the amount of the contingent payment may help ascertain the arrangement's substance. Where the formula is based on a percentage of profit, this may indicate a profit sharing arrangement. If the formula is based on a multiple of EBITDA, this suggests it is intended to verify the value of the business and, therefore, it is part of the acquisition cost.
- Other agreements between the vendor and acquirer should also be reviewed as they may provide some guidance to the arrangement's substance. If, for example, the vendor is also entering into an agreement to lease a property from the acquirer and they will be paying less than market rent, then this could be an indication that some or all of the contingent consideration is in substance lease payments.

The factors, listed above, should be considered in determining whether a contingent payment is part of the acquisition cost or compensation for post-acquisition employee services. The factors can be used to provide an indication of the substance of a payment. However, this is an area of judgement and the particular facts and circumstances should be considered in each case.

25.402 Purchase consideration can take the form of a special dividend paid by the acquirer after the date of acquisition. For example, as part of the offer a special dividend might be paid shortly after the acquisition to those members who became shareholders as a result of accepting the acquirer's offer for the shares of the acquired company, and the dividend may be equivalent to an interim or final dividend payable by the acquirer in respect of a period prior to the acquisition. This is not specifically mentioned in FRS 7, but in principle such dividends could be treated as part of the purchase consideration where it can be demonstrated that the payment was in substance part of the acquisition cost. An example of this treatment is shown in Table 25.19. Where a dividend is capitalised in this way, the acquirer would need to ensure that the cost of the dividend is not double-counted in arriving at the fair value of the total consideration. For example, the shares issued in consideration for the acquisition may need to be valued at an ex-div price.

Table 25.19 — Redland PLC — Report and Accounts — 31 December 1992

Notes to the accounts (extract)

6 Dividends	Year ended 31.12.92 £million	Year ended 31.12.91 £million
Ordinary shares:		
Interim paid: 8.25p per share net (1991: 8.25p)	39.5	27.9
Final proposed 1992: 16.75p per share net (1991: 16.75p)	80.3	57.0
Total dividends on Redland PLC ordinary shares: 25.0p per share net (1991: 25.0p)	119.8	84.9
Less: transfer to cost of investment to Steetley plc	(8.6)	–
	111.2	84.9

Scrip dividends to the value of £5.1 million in respect of the 1991 final dividend and £1.9 million in respect of the 1992 interim dividend were taken instead of a cash payment.

25.403 For tax reasons, payments that are in substance a form of purchase consideration are sometimes made by the acquired company itself (subject to financial assistance considerations), rather than by the acquirer. If the acquired company's financial statements include a provision in respect of such payments, on consolidation this provision should be regarded as part of the cost of acquisition rather than as a pre-acquisition liability of the acquired company. Accordingly, the obligation to make such payments should be treated in the fair value table as an element of the purchase consideration and not as a reduction in the net assets of the acquired company.

Deferred consideration

25.404 Part of the consideration for an acquisition may become payable at a date after the acquisition has been completed. Such deferred consideration could take the form of cash, shares or other consideration where the amounts are known with certainty. FRS 7 requires the fair value of all forms of consideration to be reflected in the cost of acquisition.

Deferred cash consideration

25.405 The fair value of deferred consideration payable in cash should be taken to be the amount of cash payable discounted to its present value. In addition, the present value of deferred cash consideration would be provided in the acquirer's financial statements as a liability. The standard states that the appropriate discount rate is the rate at which the acquirer could obtain a similar borrowing, taking into account its credit standing and any security given. [FRS 7 para 77].

25.406 The measurement of deferred consideration in FRS 7 is consistent with the treatment of the various forms of debt finance in FRS 4 (or for those entities applying FRS 26, the amortised cost valuation methodology of that standard).

The difference between the amount (fair value) at which the liability is stated at the acquisition date and the total amounts payable at future dates is a finance cost, analogous to the finance costs of debt where a liability is carried at amortised cost. This difference should be charged as an interest expense in the acquirer's post-acquisition profit and loss account over the period the liability is outstanding. The 1994 financial statements of Verson International Group plc disclose deferred cash consideration that has been discounted to present value. The relevant extract is reproduced in Table 25.20.

Table 25.20 — Verson International Group plc — Annual Report — 31 January 1994

Notes to the accounts (extract)

16. Creditors — amounts falling due after more than one year (extract)

		Group	
		1994	1993
		£000	£000
Bank loans	– U.K. (secured)	**2,250**	2,750
	– overseas (secured)	**10,529**	10,204
Other loans		**2,023**	2,483
Deferred consideration		**6,554**	6,454
Hire purchase and finance lease creditors		**646**	1,306
Other long term creditors		**2,122**	1,923
		24,124	25,120

Deferred consideration includes an amount of £5,334,000 (1993 — £5.024,000) relating to the agreement to repurchase, on or before 8 September 1996, 42,094 non-voting preference shares in Clearing-Niagara Inc. (formerly Niagara Machine and Tools Works) held by the former owners, for a total amount of $9,500,000. The balance reflects amounts outstanding on the acquisition of a freehold property in the USA also acquired during 1993.

The deferred consideration in respect of the acquisition of Clearing-Niagara Inc. has been discounted from the anticipated settlement date at a rate of 6.875%. The difference between this present value and the mandatory purchase amount has been accrued through a charge to interest payable of £343,000 (1993 — £128,000) during the year.

Deferred share consideration

25.407 Where the deferred consideration is in the form of shares, the classification in the balance sheet is governed by FRS 25, 'Financial instruments: Disclosure and presentation'. If the deferred consideration meets the definition of an equity instrument, the fair value should be credited directly to shareholders' funds. The most appropriate treatment is to disclose such deferred consideration under share capital as a separate caption with a heading such as 'shares to be issued'. The shares would qualify as an equity instrument if, for example, the number of shares to be issued is fixed and, as a consequence, the acquiree's shareholders bear the risk of falls in the value of the shares and the rewards if the shares rise in value.

25.408 However, often with shares, the amount of deferred consideration payable is fixed at the acquisition date and the number of shares issued to satisfy that consideration varies according to the market price of the shares at the date the consideration is issued. A contractual obligation is a financial liability if it is required to be settled by a variable number of the entity's own shares equal in value to the amount of the contractual obligation. [FRS 25 para 21]. Where this situation applies, the shares to be issued are shown, not as equity, but as a financial liability. Debt/equity classification is dealt with further in chapter 6.

25.409 FRS 7 makes no reference to the question of discounting deferred share consideration classified as an equity instrument. The ASB's discussion paper that preceded FRED 7 explained that deferred share consideration is analogous to the issue of warrants, and that theoretically its fair value at the date of acquisition is the value of the right conferred upon the vendor to receive shares at a future date.

Contingent consideration

25.410 FRS 7 deals specifically with the treatment of deferred consideration where the amount payable is uncertain because it is contingent on the outcome of future events. The most common form of contingent consideration arises where the acquirer agrees to pay additional consideration if the acquired company achieves a certain level of performance.

25.411 The standard requires *"a reasonable estimate of the fair value of amounts expected to be payable in the future"* to be included in the cost of acquisition when the fair value exercise is undertaken. [FRS 7 para 27].

25.412 This amount will have to be adjusted, if necessary, when the final amount payable is determined, or when revised estimates are made. Such adjustments should continue to be made to the cost of acquisition and, therefore, to goodwill, until the consideration is finally determined. In contrast to fair valuing assets and liabilities acquired, there is no limit on the period in which this aspect of the fair value exercise must be determined.

25.413 Once a reasonable estimate has been made of the future consideration payable, the same principles of valuing the components of the consideration (including discounting estimated amounts to their present values) that are discussed in the above section on deferred consideration would be applicable in order to record the initial cost of acquisition at its estimated fair value.

25.414 In practice, the acquirer may need to look at profit forecasts for the acquired company on expected, best case and worst case scenarios. Provision for future consideration would normally be made on the basis of the expected outcome.

25.415 A practical problem is that it may be very difficult to make reliable estimates of the future consideration in some cases. For example, such consideration might depend on an average of profits of the acquired company for three years into the future and might not be payable at all unless the average exceeded a certain amount. The acquired company may be in a development phase where any forecasts are extremely subjective and unreliable. When the acquirer's first post-acquisition financial statements are prepared, it could be very difficult to assess the probable amount, or indeed whether any amount will be payable. In those circumstances, the standard explains that at least those amounts that are reasonably expected to be payable would be recognised. [FRS 7 para 81].

25.416 If, for example, a minimum sum is guaranteed to be paid as part of contingent consideration, at least this minimum must be provided initially. Any further sums must be provided as soon as reasonable estimates can be made. It cannot be assumed that contingent consideration can adequately be dealt with by giving details of the contingency in a note to the financial statements, together with a range of possibilities. An example of a company that provided for contingent consideration is given in Table 25.21.

Table 25.21– Logica plc – Annual Report – 30 June 1994

Notes to the accounts (extract)

12 Acquisitions

On 2 May 1994 Logica North American Inc, acquired the business of Precision Software Corporation for an initial consideration of £2,340,000. The balance sheet of Precision Software Corporation on acquisition was as follows.

	Book value at 2 May £000	Fair value adjustments £000	Fair value at acquisition £000
Intangible assets	1,381	(1,381)	0
Tangible assets	296	68	364
Work in progress	66	0	66
Trade debtors	87	(45)	42
Creditors — amount falling due within one year	(217)	(198)	(415)
Net assets acquired	1,613	(1,556)	57
Goodwill			3,582
Consideration			3,639
Satisfied by:			
Cash			2,200
Related costs of acquisition			140
Deferred consideration			1,299
			3,639

The fair value adjustments relate to the revaluation of a freehold property, a debtor provision, and the alignment of accounting policies with those of the Group.

The deferred consideration is payable upon the achievement of certain minimum targets. This represents the minimum amount that is reasonably expected to be payable. Further performance related payments up to a maximum of £4,545,000 may become payable between the date of acquisition and June 1998.

Initial estimates of the deferred consideration will be revised as further and more certain information becomes available with corresponding adjustments to goodwill.

Discounting contingent cash consideration

25.417 Following the principle in paragraph 77 of FRS 7 (see para 25.405 above), the fair value of contingent consideration payable in cash should be taken to be the estimated amount of cash payable discounted to its present value.

25.418 A practical problem arises, because when the contingent consideration becomes more certain as the time gets nearer to its payment, the previously estimated amount may prove to be incorrect. Where this is so, the amount provided should be revised as the outcome becomes more certain until the ultimate amount is known. These amendments will also affect the amount of goodwill recognised on the acquisition and similar adjustments should be made to the goodwill figure until the consideration is finally determined. The problem is how to account for the interest effect in each accounting period if the estimate (undiscounted) of the future consideration is continually revised – in effect, how to discount a moving target. Consider the following example.

Example – Changes in the outcome of contingent cash consideration

An acquisition is made on 1 January 20X1. Part of the consideration for the acquisition, payable in cash on 1 January 20X4, is subject to the achievement of specified performance levels in the acquired company over the next three years. The maximum consideration payable is £20m, and the directors of the acquirer have estimated that the final figure will be £10m. This figure of £10m, subject to discounting, is to be added to the cost of acquisition and included as a provision in the acquirer's consolidated financial statements. A discount rate of 10%, reflecting the acquirer's cost of debt, is to be used.

The fair value (that is, net present value) at 1 January 20X1 of the estimated deferred liability of £10m is £7,513,000. This figure is included in the cost of acquisition and the calculation of goodwill. An interest cost of 10% should be charged on the deferred liability, giving an interest charge of £751,000 for 20X1, which is added to the deferred liability. At 31 December 20X1 the deferred liability will stand at £8,264,000.

During the year ending 31 December 20X2, interest of £826,000 is charged and added to the deferred liability, which then stands at £9,090,000 in the acquirer's books.

The acquired company performs better than expected during 20X2. When preparing the financial statements for the year ending 31 December 20X2, the directors revise their estimate of contingent consideration upwards to £12m.

The present value as at 31 December 20X2 of the revised estimate of £12m is £10,908,000; hence the provision in the acquirer's books needs to be increased from £9,090,000 to £10,908,000 (that is, by £1,818,000). The question arises as to what to debit. How much should be debited to cost of investment/goodwill and how much should be written off as additional interest? This is illustrated in the table below.

	Original estimate £'000	Revised estimate £'000	Difference £'000
Present value 1.1.X.1	7,513	9,015	1,502
Interest 20X1	751	901	150
Present value 31.12.X1	8,264	9,916	1,652
Interest 20X2	826	992	166
Present value 31.12.X2	9,090	10,908	1,818
Interest 20X3		1,092	
Present value 31.12.X3		12,000	

The most appropriate method is to recalculate the cost of investment and goodwill as at the date of acquisition, based on the present value of the revised estimate. The restated amounts are then the amounts that would have been recorded if the revised estimate had been available at the date of acquisition. The following adjustments would be necessary to restate the provision and goodwill as at 31 December 20X2.

	£'000	£'000
Dr Goodwill	1,502	
Dr P&L; backlog interest for 20X1	150	
Dr P&L; backlog interest for 20X2	166	
Cr Provision for deferred consideration		1,818
	1,818	1,818

As these adjustments arise from a change of estimate, the whole of the additional interest charge (including the backlog charge for 20X1 resulting from the increased estimate of the liability) would be recorded in the current year's profit and loss account. Thus the interest charge amounts to £1,142,000 (comprising £992,000 relating to 20X2 based on the increased estimate and £150,000 backlog adjustment relating to 20X1).

Interest would then be charged in 20X3 on the revised liability of £10,908,000, taking the book value of the liability to its nominal value of £12m at 31 December 20X3, assuming no further revisions of the consideration payable are made.

An alternative method is to account prospectively for the change in estimate, that is to discount the revised estimate back only to 31 December 20X1, and add the increase in the provision of £1,652,000 calculated as at 31 December 20X1 to cost of investment and goodwill. Under this method, the interest charged in 20X2 reflects the interest cost of £992,000 attributable to that year only (based on the revised estimate of the liability). The problem with this method is that, if the adjustment is material, the historical cost of investment and goodwill will be overstated.

A further question arises as to what effect the adjustment to goodwill has on the amortisation profile of the goodwill asset. This question is addressed in section III, paragraph 25.500.

Consideration involving settlement options

25.419 Whilst contingent consideration is notionally scoped out of FRS 25 by paragraph 4(c), FRS 7 paragraph 82 makes it clear that FRS 25 should be consulted for situations in which contingent consideration is to be settled by the issue of shares. As in paragraph 25.407, the classification will depend on whether the definition of 'equity instrument' is met. Where contingent consideration is payable by a pre-defined number of shares if certain conditions are met, this will meet the definition of equity. For example, an agreement may state that if post acquisition profit in the first year is £40 million, 400 shares will be issued and if profit is £30 million, 300 shares will be issued. Where the contingent consideration is based on a variable amount of shares, this will not meet the definition of equity, because the amount fluctuates in response to changes in a variable (for example, profits) rather than to the market value of the shares and, hence, will be a financial liability. [FRS 25 para 21]. The practical application of this is that previously under FRS 7 such consideration would have been classified within equity or shares to be issued, whereas under FRS 25 such consideration will be classified as a liability. An example of contingent share consideration meeting the definition of a liability would be when the earn-out agreement states that shares to the equivalent value of 10 per cent of profit in the first year post-acquisition will be issued. This is not a fixed number of shares and, therefore, will be shown as a liability.

25.420 Paragraph 26 of FRS 25 notes that where settlement options exist, the consideration will be treated as an equity instrument only if all of the settlement options would result in an equity instrument. Hence if there is a cash option, for instance, the instrument will be a liability.

25.421 However presented, the amounts earmarked for settlement of consideration (and held, as appropriate, within liabilities or shareholders' funds) will be adjusted during the period the consideration is outstanding, such that the settlement will be recorded at the amount of cash payable or the market value of the shares to be issued. The balance sheet treatment required by the standard also has a profit and loss effect over the period the consideration is outstanding. Whilst changes in estimates of the final value of contingent consideration will result in changes to the cost of acquisition and goodwill, the time value of the deferral of monetary consideration (not deferred share consideration) will also result in an interest cost in the profit and loss account.

25.422 If the vendor has the option to demand shares or cash and subsequently elects to receive shares rather than cash, the acquirer will suffer an interest cost during the period the consideration was outstanding, because the deferred consideration would have been reported as a liability.

Disclosure of contingent consideration

25.423 FRS 6 requires the following to be disclosed in respect of deferred or contingent purchase consideration:

- The nature of the consideration.
- The range of possible outcomes.

- The principal factors that affect the outcome.

[FRS 6 para 24].

25.424 This disclosure is required individually for each material acquisition, and in aggregate for other acquisitions. [FRS 6 para 23]. The example in Table 25.21 covers these requirements.

Consideration contingent on net assets

25.425 In some cases the amount of contingent consideration depends not on the future performance of the acquired company, but on the outcome of an uncertainty in the valuation of the net assets acquired, for example the settlement of a contingent liability. Purchase price contingencies not only relate to additional payments by the acquirer, but also to refunds by the vendor. Often in business combinations the acquired company may have various contingent liabilities (for example, tax risks, environmental problems or court cases) for which the acquirer may seek some form of indemnity or warranty from the vendor. By their nature these indemnities can be considered as negative contingent consideration as they are often repayments / reimbursements made by the vendor to the acquirer. Often the substance is that both the purchaser and vendor wish to 'set aside' these contingent obligations so that they do not have any economic impact on the acquisition.

25.425.1 Examples of compensation payments that may become payable by a vendor include:

- Redundancy costs.
- Reorganisation costs.
- Incentive payments to key employees.
- Contingent liabilities (for example, tax risks, environmental, legal, fines).
- General indemnity or warranty clauses.
- Contractual obligations in the event of a change of ownership.
- Accounting irregularities.

25.425.2 The outcome of the contingency may not be determined until after the hindsight period allowed for finalising the fair values of assets and liabilities has expired. FRS 7 does not deal with this situation. Although FRS 7 requires the cost of acquisition to be revised without time limit where any part of the purchase consideration is contingent, it does not normally permit any further fair value adjustments to the acquired subsidiary's assets and liabilities after the specified investigation period.

25.425.3 The consequences of FRS 7's requirements in relation to vendor compensation payments are that:

- Where the related cost that is being compensated is not an identifiable liability at the acquisition date, the cost is taken to the post acquisition profit and loss account, whereas the compensation from the vendor (that is, a reimbursement of the consideration) is taken to goodwill.
- Where the related cost that is being compensated is either an identifiable liability or contingent liability at the acquisition date and adjustments to the measurement of these liabilities occur after the hindsight period, those adjustments are taken to the post acquisition profit and loss account, whereas the compensation payment is taken to goodwill.

Therefore, asymmetric accounting results.

25.425.4 The accounting described in the second bullet point in paragraph 25.425.3 above may not reflect the underlying economics of the transaction, particularly when all of the following circumstances are present:

- There is an identifiable liability or contingent liability at the acquisition date that is not conditional on the entity being acquired.
- There is no burden of proof that the risk existed at the acquisition date and it is the explicit wish of both parties that the acquirer be compensated for these risks should they materialise.
- The vendor agrees to specifically indemnify the acquirer for all or a specified proportion of the costs to be incurred.
- The acquirer may have to provide evidence to substantiate the amount being claimed, but on delivery of that evidence there is no doubt that the amount will be reimbursed.
- There are no further negotiations to take place between the acquirer and vendor in relation to the subject matter of the claim or attached conditions. There are no clauses that allow for arbitration.
- The acquirer has not, in substance, economically assumed the liability as part of the business combination transaction. The liability has been 'set aside' in undertaking the purchase price negotiations.

In these circumstances, it might be possible to argue symmetrical accounting.

Fees and other expenses of acquisition

25.426 Costs incurred in carrying out an acquisition need to be analysed into two elements.

- Costs of raising capital for the acquisition and of issuing capital instruments in consideration for the acquisition. Where these fall within the restrictive definition of 'issue costs' contained in FRS 4 (or 'transaction costs' in FRS 26 for entities applying that standard), they should be accounted for as a deduction from the proceeds of those capital instruments.

- Fees and similar incremental costs, excluding costs of raising capital, incurred directly in making an acquisition. These should be added to the cost of acquisition.

25.427 Costs of raising capital that do not qualify to be treated as either of the above, and other expenses that cannot be treated as part of the cost of acquisition under FRS 7 (see para 25.430 below), should be written off to profit and loss account as incurred.

25.428 First, it is necessary to allocate the expenses between those that relate to issuing capital instruments and those that relate to other aspects of negotiating and transacting the acquisition. The treatment of issue/transaction costs required by FRS 4 (or FRS 26 for entities applying that standard – see further chapter 6) applies whether capital is raised to finance acquisitions or for any other purpose. Such costs might include underwriting, legal and other fees in connection with share issues, and arrangement fees payable to banks for providing loan finance. This will result in any issue costs associated with an acquisition being accounted for as follows:

- Issue costs relating to bank loans and other forms of debt (including shares classified as liabilities under FRS 25) should be initially deducted from the liability and subsequently written off in the profit and loss account over the term of the debt.
- Costs of issuing shares classed as equity instruments should be debited against reserves. The share premium account would be available for the write-off of such issue costs.

25.429 Secondly, it is necessary to consider which of those expenses that do not qualify for the above treatment should be capitalised by adding them to the cost of acquisition as required by FRS 7. By treating expenses as part of the cost of acquisition, they are included in the calculation of goodwill

25.430 FRS 7 also provides a narrow definition of costs that may be capitalised. They include *"fees and similar incremental costs incurred directly in making an acquisition"*, but must not include *"internal costs, and other expenses that cannot be directly attributed to the acquisition"*. [FRS 7 para 28].

25.431 The UITF took the view (Information Sheet No 35, issued in February 2000) that incidental financing costs that do not qualify to be treated as issue costs (such arrangement fees for bridging finance facilities, participation fees and costs of researching alternative financing arrangements) are not to be regarded as incremental costs incurred directly in making an acquisition. Consequently, such costs should not be included as part of the cost of acquisition, but should be expensed as incurred.

25.432 Therefore, costs eligible for capitalisation might include fees payable to merchant banks, lawyers, accountants and other advisors for:

- Investigating and valuing the target.
- Auditing the completion accounts.
- Negotiating the price and completing the transaction.
- Undertaking due diligence work.

25.433 The treatment of fees in respect of searching for and identifying the business that was subsequently acquired is marginal. A finders' fee resulting from work commissioned to identify a suitable target might qualify to be capitalised where it relates to the business that was acquired; however, in general, other search and investigation fees incurred before a specific target has been identified would need to be expensed as incurred.

25.434 Moreover, where such services are provided by in-house departments of the acquirer rather than by external advisors, FRS 7 does not allow the costs to be capitalised. Previously there was sometimes argument over whether allocations of costs such as time spent by a company's management on researching and negotiating an acquisition, or specific overtime payments related to work on the acquisition, could be capitalised. FRS 7 precludes capitalisation of *any* internal costs.

25.435 The ASB had exposed an alternative view in FRED 7 that would also have allowed costs to have been capitalised where they were incurred in respect of equivalent services provided by in-house departments, such as legal advice or acquisition search and investigation services. The ASB decided that the difficulty of satisfactorily defining eligible internal costs, and the consequent risk of allowing excessive costs to be capitalised, outweighed the anomalies in the restrictive approach taken in FRS 7.

25.436 In practice, the work carried out by advisors in respect of transacting the acquisition will overlap the work on raising capital. It may then be necessary to make reasonable allocations of advisors' expenses to determine which accounting treatment is appropriate.

Section III — Goodwill

Introduction

25.437 Goodwill has been one of the most hotly debated subjects in accounting. The most fundamental issue was whether purchased goodwill arising from acquisitions should or should not be treated as an asset in the balance sheet. During one of the longest running of accounting debates, deeply entrenched views were held on both sides. The publication of FRS 10 in December 1997 was a major event that would change the shape of the financial statements of acquisitive companies. For financial years from December 1998, purchased goodwill has had to be accounted for as an asset.

[The next paragraph is 25.441.]

25.441 The ASB settled on capitalisation of purchased goodwill, rather than elimination, for a number of reasons:

- Management accountability for the cost of goodwill on acquisitions is maintained (rather than lost) in the accounting treatment.
- Purchased goodwill and intangibles that are similar to goodwill are accounted for consistently.
- Capitalisation had become the accepted treatment internationally.

25.442 One of the key issues for the ASB was to develop an acceptable method of dealing with the amortisation problem. Just as there is a conceptual divide between treating the amount spent on goodwill as an asset and treating it as a reduction in shareholders' equity, so there is a divide between treating capitalised goodwill as a depreciable asset and treating it as an investment with continuing value. One view is that the original purchased goodwill is depleted over time and replaced by internally generated goodwill which cannot be recognised. Another view is that the cost of goodwill to the group should be treated consistently with the cost of investment by the parent, which is only written down if its carrying value is impaired, that is, not supported by the value of the future cash flows of the acquired business.

25.443 The ASB has been sympathetic to the investment argument and to the principle that goodwill should be written off in the profit and loss account only if, and when, its value is impaired and not gradually over an arbitrary period. But an important constraint is that the Act requires purchased goodwill to be fully amortised over a finite period if it is treated as an asset. It does not allow goodwill to be carried permanently as an asset. FRS 10's method of accounting for goodwill is, however, something of a hybrid between the automatic amortisation and impairment approaches. The constraints of law and practicality led the ASB to develop a method that would allow goodwill to be amortised quickly, slowly or not at all according to the circumstances. But the final standard steers companies firmly towards automatic amortisation over a maximum 20-year period, which is the same approach that had previously met such strong opposition from the corporate sector.

25.444 International standard-setters are not constrained by the UK's legal requirements. The IASB considers that the useful life of acquired goodwill and the pattern in which it diminishes are, generally, not possible to predict. Consequently, the amount of goodwill amortised in any given period is an arbitrary estimate of the consumption of acquired goodwill during that period. The IASB's view is that the amortisation of goodwill over an arbitrary period fails to provide useful information. Therefore, under IFRS 3 and IFRS 3 (revised, issued in 2008), goodwill is not amortised, but instead is subject to an annual impairment test (consistent with US GAAP). In July 2005 the ASB issued an exposure draft proposing convergence of UK GAAP with IFRS in this area, however no further action has been taken given the consideration of replacing UK GAAP with IFRS for small and medium-sized entities.

Scope of FRS 10

25.445 FRS 10 is really two standards rolled into one. It covers all goodwill (arising from business acquisitions and from acquisitions of equity accounted interests in associates and joint ventures) and, with a few exceptions, all intangible assets (including those identified in a business acquisition, those purchased separately and those developed internally). The ASB found it convenient to deal with both goodwill and intangibles in a single standard because they are closely related and the ASB decided the same accounting rules should apply to both.

25.446 Many intangibles and goodwill share similar characteristics. Accounting for intangibles is an important issue in acquisition accounting because any values ascribed to separate intangibles reduce the residual amount of goodwill.

25.447 The rules relating to identifying intangible assets in acquisition accounting are discussed in section II, paragraph 25.178. The recognition and measurement rules that apply to purchased and internally developed intangible assets are discussed in chapter 15. The discussion in this chapter primarily considers purchased goodwill arising from business combinations. FRS 10's application to associates and joint ventures is discussed in chapter 27.

Definition of purchased goodwill

25.448 Purchased goodwill is simply an accounting difference. It is the amount by which the cost of a business entity as a whole exceeds the aggregate fair values of its identifiable assets and liabilities at the date of acquisition. Those fair values are determined by applying the rules in FRS 7 and they are used as the carrying amounts (a proxy for cost) for the newly acquired assets and liabilities in the acquirer's financial statements. If the aggregate fair values of the acquired business' identifiable assets and liabilities exceed the cost of acquisition, the difference is referred to as negative goodwill.

25.449 Purchased goodwill may arise in the acquirer's consolidated financial statements only (where a parent company acquires a new subsidiary), or in the acquiring entity's individual financial statements (where it purchases an unincorporated undertaking or a business and assets of another company).

Accounting for goodwill — summary

Internally generated goodwill

25.450 Internally generated goodwill may be viewed as the difference between the market value of a business entity and the aggregate fair value of its net assets. Neither the Act nor FRS 10 allows internally generated goodwill to be recognised on the balance sheet. The Act states that goodwill may be shown as an asset only if it was acquired for valuable consideration. [Note 3 on the balance sheet formats; FRS 10 paras 7, 8].

Purchased goodwill

25.451 FRS 10 requires purchased goodwill to be treated as an asset on the balance sheet. Its objective, in relation to capitalised goodwill, is:

- To ensure that goodwill is charged in the profit and loss account in the periods in which it is depleted.
- To ensure that disclosure is sufficient to enable users to determine the goodwill's impact on financial position and performance.

[FRS 10 para 1]

25.452 Goodwill should be amortised quickly, slowly or not at all according to the circumstances:

- Where goodwill has a limited useful economic life, it should be amortised systematically over that life.
- There is a rebuttable presumption that the useful economic life does not exceed 20 years.
- A longer life than 20 years, or an indefinite life, may be chosen where the value can be demonstrated to be more durable.
- Non-amortisation of goodwill is a 'true and fair override' of company law (which requires goodwill to be amortised down to zero) and so can only be adopted in special circumstances when following the basic rule of amortisation would not give a true and fair view.

25.453 If a company either amortises goodwill over more than 20 years or does not amortise goodwill at all, it has to carry out an annual impairment test. This is a thorough exercise which is aimed at demonstrating whether the present value of the future cash flows that the acquisition will earn are, or are not, enough to justify the carrying value of the goodwill. If they are not, an impairment write-down should be made.

25.454 If a company amortises goodwill over no more than 20 years, a recoverable amount check is required at the end of the first full financial year following the acquisition. This 'first year review' is intended to capture any overpayment for the acquisition or failure of the acquired business to meet expectations at the time of the acquisition. If the impairment review confirms that the carrying value of the goodwill is not recoverable, it should be written down. In other years an impairment test is required only if adverse events indicate that the amortised carrying value of the goodwill may not be recoverable, and an impairment write-down should be made if the test confirms this.

25.455 The details of the impairment tests are found in FRS 11, 'Impairment of fixed assets and goodwill'. The tests are complex and subjective. This is particularly so in a situation where a group acquires a new subsidiary and integrates it into the group. In these situations it is not possible to isolate and track the cash flows attributable to the acquisition. Chapter 18 provides further guidance on impairment testing.

25.456 Goodwill cannot be revalued above original cost.

25.457 Amortisation or impairment charged in previous periods cannot be reversed in subsequent periods except in limited circumstances with respect to impairment.

Useful economic life

25.458 For each acquisition the useful economic life of the residual amount of purchased goodwill must be estimated.

Definition

25.459 The useful economic life of purchased goodwill is defined as *"the period over which the value of the underlying business acquired is expected to exceed the values of its identifiable net assets"*. [FRS 10 para 2].

25.460 Purchased goodwill is in effect treated as an element of the investment in the acquired business, that is, the premium over its net asset value. In theory, the useful economic life can be indefinite if management continues to invest in the acquired business so as to maintain the premium; furthermore, the above definition allows for goodwill to be continuously regenerated after the acquisition.

25.461 The definition of useful economic life was a contentious issue during the development of FRS 10. The ASB has described its approach to amortisation as one which seeks to charge goodwill to the profit and loss account only to the extent that the carrying value of the goodwill is not supported by the *current* value of the goodwill within the acquired business. This allows for purchased goodwill to be carried permanently without amortisation in some circumstances.

[The next paragraph is 25.463.]

Rebuttable presumption of 20 years or less

25.463 Despite the opportunity given by FRS 10's definition to regard goodwill as having a very long or indefinite useful economic life, the practical emphasis in the standard is rather different. The standard explains that *"the transient nature of many business opportunities makes it appropriate for there to be a presumption that the 'premium' that an acquired business has over its net asset value cannot be maintained indefinitely"*. [FRS 10 para 20]. The framework for determining goodwill's useful economic life is as follows:

- There is a rebuttable presumption that the useful economic life does not exceed 20 years.

- A useful economic life exceeding 20 years, or an indefinite life, may be chosen *only* if:
  - the durability of the acquired business for the longer (or indefinite) period can be demonstrated; and
  - the goodwill is capable of continued measurement (so that annual impairment reviews will be feasible).

[FRS 10 para 19].

25.464 One reason for having a presumed arbitrary upper limit on the useful economic life is that it would otherwise frequently be difficult to estimate it. A period of 20 years is a benchmark that has had some significance internationally. However, the uncertainty involved in estimating useful lives does not allow 20 years to be automatically used by default, nor does it allow goodwill to be written off over an unrealistically short period. A company could not, for example, simply expense all goodwill as a one-off hit to earnings in the year of acquisition in order to avoid future amortisation charges. [FRS 10 paras 21, 22].

25.465 On the other hand, the FRS states that the 20-year upper limit may be rebutted if the conditions (that is, evidence of durability and continued measurability) are met. Furthermore, the standard's interpretation of those conditions make it improbable that a company could be forced to adopt a useful economic life of more than 20 years if it chose not to, even if the value of the goodwill was expected to be more durable. The assumptions used in forecasting become more vulnerable the longer the estimated life is. For example, in many industries the pace of developments means that consumer patterns cannot be predicted with much certainty over very long periods. Clearly the emphasis is on being prudent, without being unrealistically prudent.

25.466 The second condition for rebutting the 20-year upper limit, that the goodwill is capable of continued measurement, is important. The annual impairment reviews specified by FRS 11 have to be feasible and be expected to remain so for the foreseeable future. FRS 10 states that goodwill will not be capable of continued measurement if the cost of such measurement is viewed as being unjustifiably high. This clearly invites directors to opt not to rebut the presumption of a 20-year life if they judge that the cost of carrying out annual impairment reviews outweighs the benefits. The standard gives as an example the situation where businesses are integrated after acquisition so that the goodwill relating to the acquired business can no longer be readily tracked. Even if there are no such integration plans, the directors may not wish to rule out future reorganisations that could lose the separate identity of the acquired business. Other examples given are where the company's management information systems are not compatible with the detail of the impairment reviews required by the standard, and where the amounts of goodwill involved are not sufficiently material to justify the cost of carrying out the impairment reviews. [FRS 10 para 23].

Factors determining useful economic life

25.467 Apart from explaining the conditions for rebutting the 20-year threshold, FRS 10 gives little guidance on how to estimate the useful economic life. It gives examples of factors that contribute to the durability of goodwill and, since these will limit useful economic lives, they are also relevant for estimating lives that are considered to be 20 years or less. These factors refer to the nature of the business, the stability of the industry, the effects of future competition, the typical life-spans of the products of the acquired business and the extent to which the acquisition overcomes market entry barriers that will continue to exist. [FRS 10 para 20].

25.468 These factors often combine to present an overall picture of durability. A long life (20 years plus) will generally require a business, industry and products to have a long past track record of stability and achievement and to have high barriers to market entry. Added to this, of course, is the commitment of the new management to continue to invest in the acquired business for the long-term to maintain and enhance its value. Other businesses, industries and products may be relatively new, potentially much more volatile and possibly requiring a payback for the acquirer over a much shorter period. An amortisation period much shorter than 20 years may then be appropriate. This may be so for products with expected short life cycles or where there are few barriers to prevent new competitors from entering the market. An example of a business acquisition with an estimated useful life substantially below 20 years is shown in Table 25.22.

Table 25.22 – 3i plc – Annual Report and Accounts – 31 March 2000

Notes to the accounts (extract)

Goodwill in the year arose on the acquisition of TH Technologieholding GmbH (see note 22). This purchased goodwill relates to TH Technologieholding GmbH's market position and the experience in early stage technology investment of its staff. It is being amortised over its estimated useful economic life of five years, the period over which the Group expects to benefit from TH Technologieholding GmbH's reputation, contacts and skills, using the straight line method.

25.469 A group should assess the factors at the time it makes an acquisition. Examples of issues to consider are:

- Expected changes in products, markets or technology. A high technology company that only has one main product might have considerable goodwill while that product is leading the market, but if a competitor produces a better product, then the company's goodwill can diminish rapidly.
- Expected future demand, competition or other economic factors that may affect current advantages.
- The expected period of future service of certain employees or the retention period of key clients. An advertising agency's goodwill may be very dependent on key employees/clients and the agency's goodwill may depend significantly on their retention period.

- The extent to which goodwill is linked to the economic lives of intangible assets.

25.470 The last of the above is an important factor that is attached to the definition of useful economic life itself. Where intangible assets have been subsumed into the residual amount of goodwill, because they cannot be measured reliably, the useful economic life of the goodwill is linked to the lives of those intangibles. [FRS 10 para 2]. For example, an acquired company may have a licence to carry on a particular business for a finite period. If the licence were recognised as a separate intangible, it would be amortised over the licence period, unless the licence rights were renewable and renewal were assured. If the value of the licence were subsumed within purchased goodwill, the amortisation period should be the same, that is, aligned with the life of the underlying rights.

25.471 This factor could also work to demonstrate a long or indefinite useful economic life. For example, much of the value of goodwill on an acquisition may be in a brand name that does not meet the recognition criteria for a separate intangible asset. Nevertheless, the brand may have been well established for decades and an indefinite future life may be justifiable by linking the goodwill to the brand that is fundamental to maintaining the current value of the premium in the acquired business.

Accounting implications of life above or below 20 years

25.472 The accounting implications of choosing a useful economic life above or below 20 years are summarised below:

20 years or less	**More than 20 years**
Amortisation charge against earnings 5% or more	Amortisation charge against earnings less than 5%
	Nil amortisation requires true and fair override
Impairment review at end of first full year, thereafter only on exception basis	Detailed annual impairment reviews
Less exposure to future (unpredictable) impairment losses	Greater exposure to future (unpredictable) impairment losses
	Additional disclosure

25.473 FRS 10 requires disclosure of the amortisation periods and the reasons for choosing those periods. [FRS 10 para 55].

25.474 The additional disclosures required where the useful economic life is more than 20 years are as follows:

- the grounds for rebutting the 20-year presumption, including

- a reasoned explanation based on the specific factors contributing to the durability of the acquired business.

[FRS 10 para 58]

25.475 In addition, where goodwill is not amortised, additional disclosures are required to support the true and fair override required by the standard in such circumstances to comply with the Companies Act 2006 (see para 25.480). [FRS 10 para 59].

25.476 In May 2004, the FRRP issued a general warning on the need to provide adequate disclosures when the presumption of a 20 year useful economic life for an intangible asset or goodwill is rebutted. The FRRP points out that, however well known a brand or other asset is, the directors must provide a 'reasoned explanation' for their decision, sufficient to satisfy paragraphs 58 and 59 of FRS 10 so that users of the financial statements can understand the rationale for the chosen accounting treatment.

Indefinite life — true and fair override

25.477 SI 2008/410 states that where goodwill is treated as an asset, it should be reduced by provisions for depreciation calculated to write it off in full (that is, to nil) systematically over a period chosen by the company's directors, which must not exceed its useful economic life. [SI 2008/410 1 Sch 22(2)(3)]. Therefore, whilst the Companies Act 2006 permits goodwill to be amortised over a shorter period than its useful economic life, it does not allow either an indefinite useful economic life or any residual value to be assumed. The Act in effect reflects the traditional view of the useful economic life where the value of purchased goodwill is depleted over time and replaced by non-purchased goodwill generated by the new owners.

25.478 So, non-amortisation can be adopted only by invoking the 'true and fair override' of the Act's requirement for amortisation. Moreover, the Act's true and fair override provisions can only be invoked in 'special circumstances' when following the basic rule of amortisation would not give a true and fair view. [CA06 Sec 404(5)].

25.479 In the appendix to FRS 10 that explains its development, the ASB states that it believes there may be circumstances where a true and fair view will be given only if goodwill or an intangible asset is not amortised, but is instead subject to annual reviews for impairment. [FRS 10, Appendix III para 35]. But FRS 10 in effect restricts non-amortisation to exceptional circumstances in order to avoid being in conflict with the Act, since the 'true and fair override' cannot be applied indiscriminately. Restricting non-amortisation of goodwill to such 'special circumstances' means that it raises a number of policy issues for companies making acquisitions:

- Non-amortisation must be considered on an acquisition-by-acquisition basis – it cannot be adopted as a general accounting policy.

- The circumstances specified in FRS 10 regarding the indefinite durability of the acquired business place a clear onus on a company's directors to demonstrate that they can maintain (or enhance) the value of the premium paid for the acquisition indefinitely.
- Non-amortisation would be restricted to material acquisitions where amortisation charges would not give a true and fair view.
- The directors must be confident that they will always in the future be able to measure the current value of such goodwill with sufficient reliability to carry out the annual impairment reviews; future business reorganisations may have an impact on this.
- The reaction of analysts and other users needs to be considered if a company claims it has demonstrated no need for amortisation, but other companies in similar sectors chose to amortise their goodwill (and *vice versa*). In this regard, the Society of Investment Professionals (formerly the Institute of Investment Management and Research) (IIMR) at present excludes goodwill amortisation from its definition of 'headline earnings'.

25.480 The required disclosures, which must also comply with FRS 18, give considerable prominence to the 'true and fair override'. The disclosures, which are intended to convey to users the circumstances justifying its use, are:

- A statement that the financial statements depart from the specific requirement of the Act to amortise goodwill over a finite period and that the departure is necessary to give a true and fair view.
- Particulars of the departure from the Act. This means a statement that the Act would normally require amortisation and a description of the treatment actually adopted.
- The reasons for the departure from the Act, which should include an explanation of the specific factors contributing to the durability of the acquired business. Also there should be a statement as to why amortisation would not give a true and fair view.
- The effect of the departure from the Act – however, this will not normally be possible to quantify, because where goodwill arising from a particular acquisition is assigned an indefinite life, there is no benchmark for calculating an amortisation charge required by the Act. The circumstances should, therefore, be explained.
- The disclosure above should either be included, or cross-referenced, in the note required by paragraph 45 of Schedule 1 to SI 2008/410 (regarding compliance with accounting standards).

[FRS 10 para 59; FRS 18 para 62].

25.481 An illustration of the disclosures required where the true and fair override has been invoked in shown in Table 25.23.

Table 25.23 – Kelda Group plc – Annual Report & Accounts – 31 March 2001

10 Intangible assets (extract)

The goodwill arising on the acquisition of Aquarion Company, which amounted to £164.3m, has, in the opinion of the directors, an indefinite life and, therefore, is not being amortised. The company operates in the stable US market of clean water supply in which barriers to entry are high due to significant infrastructure requirements. In addition, Aquarion Company has the rights to operate in its current territory in perpetuity. Consequently, the goodwill is demonstrated to be 'durable' and since it is not the Group's intention to merge the business with its existing businesses, is capable of 'continued measurement' as defined by FRS 10 'Goodwill and Intangible Assets' . In accordance with FRS 10 an impairment review was carried out on 31 March 2001, which showed that the company value of goodwill was not more than its recoverable amount. The accounting treatment is a departure from the requirements of Paragraph 21 of Schedule 4 to the Companies Act 1985 and is adopted in order to present a true and fair view of the Group's results. If the goodwill had been amortised over 20 years, the amortisation charge for the period ended 31 March 2001 would have been £8.2m and the net book amount of goodwill at 31 March 2001 would have been £154.0m (2000: £162.2m). Goodwill capitalised in respect of the Group's other acquisitions since 1 April 1998 has been assigned a useful economic life of 20 years.

Goodwill with more than one useful economic life

25.482 An acquisition of a group of companies may comprise two or more lines of business whose activities differ significantly from one another. The question arises whether the goodwill that arises overall on the acquisition should be allocated to the separate lines of business and, if applicable, those components attributed different useful economic lives. If that is done, the amortisation charge would reflect the different economic lives of the different components.

25.483 Some would argue that, since there is only one acquisition, there is only one composite goodwill amount and one life.

25.484 Allocation of purchased goodwill to different businesses is, however, necessary in order to properly account for future business disposals and to perform the impairment reviews which are specified by FRS 11, 'Impairment of fixed assets and goodwill'. FRS 11 requires capitalised goodwill to be allocated to income-generating units along with other assets and liabilities for the purpose of impairment reviews. It also requires goodwill on an acquisition comprising two dissimilar businesses to be reviewed separately for impairment. [FRS 11 para 34]. Therefore, an impairment loss is one business segment could not be offset against an increase in value of the other.

25.485 Although FRS 10 is silent as to whether goodwill can be divided into one or more elements for calculating amortisation periods, it would be consistent with FRS 11's impairment rules for goodwill attributable to dissimilar businesses to be amortised separately if they demonstrably have different useful economic lives. The resulting annual amortisation charge would also better reflect the estimated rate of depletion of the purchased goodwill than using, say, an average of the useful lives of different components.

Example – Treatment of goodwill allocated to different business segments

An acquisition comprises two different business segments. The total goodwill is £1m which is allocated £600,000 to segment A and £400,000 to segment B. The goodwill attaching to segment A is considered to have a useful life of 40 years, whereas the goodwill attaching to segment B has a useful life of 10 years.

One approach might be to estimate a weighted average of the useful economic life in aggregate, that is, 28 years. This may be shortened to 20 years if FRS 10's presumption of a maximum life of 20 years is not rebutted. A 20-year life would give an annual amortisation charge of £50,000; a 28-year life would give an annual amortisation charge of £35,714. However, this approach appears to be flawed, because averaging the short-life goodwill over a longer period means the amounts charged to the profit and loss account in the first 10 years (that is, the short life of segment B's goodwill) understates the amount by which the goodwill is in aggregate expected to be depleted. Therefore, this method may fail FRS 10's objective that goodwill is charged in the profit and loss account in the periods in which it is depleted. A preferable approach is to amortise the goodwill attributable to the two segments separately. This in turn could lead to two different amortisation patterns.

The first is to amortise £600,000 in segment A over 40 years (£15,000 per annum) and £400,000 in segment B over 10 years (£40,000 per annum). This produces an annual amortisation charge of £55,000 for 10 years and £15,000 for the subsequent 30 years. This pattern matches the actual expected rate of depletion of the goodwill. However, the goodwill in segment A would be subject to annual impairment reviews.

The second is to amortise £600,000 in segment A over 20 years (£30,000 per annum) and £400,000 in segment B over 10 years (£40,000 per annum), if the company decides not to rebut FRS 10's presumption of a maximum life of 20 years. This produces an annual amortisation charge of £70,000 for 10 years and £30,000 for the subsequent 10 years.

25.486 It should be noted that allocating goodwill to different segments could not result in negative goodwill being attributed to one segment and positive goodwill being attributed to another, because neither FRS 10 nor the Act permit purchased goodwill (positive or negative) arising on a single acquisition to be divided into positive and negative components.

Revisions of useful economic lives

25.487 Estimating useful economic lives of goodwill is very judgemental. FRS 10 requires that the useful economic lives should be reviewed at the end of each reporting period and revised if necessary. [FRS 10 para 33].

25.488 Useful lives may need to be revised to reflect previously unexpected events or changes in circumstances, such as a major technological change or a market being opened up to greater competition. Adverse factors that might lead to a write-off of goodwill (via the impairment review procedures) might similarly indicate that the remaining useful life of the balance has been shortened.

25.489 Where it is considered that previous estimates of useful economic lives need to be revised, the net book values at the date of revision should be amortised prospectively over the revised remaining useful economic lives. [FRS 10 para 33].

25.490 The requirement in paragraph 33 of FRS 10 means that if, for example, a company decided that the goodwill on an acquisition made in previous periods now had an indefinite life, whilst there would be no amortisation going forward, the goodwill amortisation already charged could not be written back.

25.491 UITF Abstract 27, 'Revision to estimates of the useful economic life of goodwill and intangible assets', confirmed that, other than on the initial implementation of FRS 10, a change from non-amortisation over a period should be dealt with prospectively by amortising the carrying value over the revised remaining economic life (that is, it should not be dealt with as a prior year adjustment). This applies even if the change results from a decision to no longer rebut the 20 year life presumption.

25.492 An estimated useful economic life may be shortened or increased. However, if it is increased from 20 years or less to more than 20 years from the date of acquisition, annual impairment reviews would be required thereafter in accordance with the normal rules for goodwill that is amortised over more than 20 years or not at all. Therefore, a 20-year life in effect remains a ceiling for those companies that are unable or unwilling to carry out annual impairment reviews.

25.493 Where a useful economic life is revised, the reason and the effect, if material, should be disclosed in the year of change. [FRS 10 para 56]. The effect of a change is the difference between the amortisation charge that results from applying the previous and the revised estimated useful lives (that is, how much more or less profit a company records as a result of changing useful economic lives).

Methods of amortising goodwill

25.494 Where goodwill is amortised, it must be amortised down to zero over its estimated useful economic life. No residual value is allowed to enter the calculation. [FRS 10 para 28; SI 2008/410 1 Sch 22(2)].

25.495 For example, it would not be permitted to identify a useful economic life of 20 years and yet charge little or no amortisation because a significant residual value was expected at the end of 20 years. In that situation, the goodwill is in effect expected to be more durable than 20 years. A low or nil annual amortisation charge can only be arrived at if the presumption of a maximum 20-year life is rebutted and a longer or indefinite life is chosen. Of course, the goodwill would then be subject to annual impairment reviews. If the 20-year presumption is not rebutted, the goodwill must be amortised to zero over 20 years.

25.496 FRS 10 states that the method of amortising goodwill should reflect the expected pattern of its depletion. However, a straight-line method should be chosen, unless another method can be demonstrated to be more appropriate.

[FRS 10 para 30]. Although arbitrary, specifying a benchmark method is a practical means of dealing with the difficulty of measuring depletion and it does promote comparability.

25.497 The FRS also explains that it is unlikely that methods that are less conservative that the straight-line method could be justified with sufficient evidence. It also states that interest methods, such as the 'reverse sum of digits' methods, which have the effect of backloading the amortisation charge to later periods, are not appropriate methods of amortising goodwill because they are not related to its depletion. [FRS 10 paras 31, 32].

25.498 FRS 10 requires the methods of amortising goodwill to be disclosed. [FRS 10 para 55].

25.499 A company may conceivably wish to change its method of amortising goodwill, say, to revert to the straight-line method from some other method. Where this occurs, FRS 10 requires the reason and the effect, if material, to be disclosed in the year of change. The effect of a change is the difference between the amortisation charge that results from applying the previous and the revised amortisation methods (that is, how much more or less profit a company records as a result of changing amortisation methods).

Acquisition with contingent consideration

25.500 An important practical effect of the goodwill amortisation requirements arises where the consideration for an acquisition is payable in the future and contingent on the acquired company achieving a specified level of performance in future years. FRS 7 requires a reasonable estimate of the fair value of amounts expected to be payable in the future to be included in the cost of acquisition when the fair value exercise is undertaken. Any such amounts recognised increase the purchased goodwill that is recognised when the acquisition is first accounted for.

25.501 Amortising the whole amount of the estimated purchased goodwill on a straight-line basis from the date of acquisition results in full charges against earnings in the immediate post-acquisition periods, before the future contingent payments have fallen due or been finally determined and possibly before the specified levels of post-acquisition earnings have been achieved. This situation can only be avoided if an amortisation pattern can be justified that increases in line with the actual consideration payments. But, although FRS 10 does not rule this out, as mentioned above, the standard suggests that it is unlikely that there will be circumstances justifying an amortisation pattern that is less conservative than straight-line.

25.502 When contingent consideration is finally determined any adjustments to the amounts estimated at the time of the acquisition would feed through as adjustments to purchased goodwill. The adjustments would have the effect of increasing or decreasing the annual amortisation charges over the goodwill's remaining useful economic life.

25.503 Where material adjustments are made to estimates of contingent consideration, a question arises as to what effect this has on the amortisation of goodwill. There are two possible ways of dealing with this:

- Amortise the revised carrying value prospectively.
- Restore the excess amortisation previously charged (crediting profit and loss account with the excess amount).

25.504 These methods are illustrated in the following example.

Example – Impact of changes in estimates of contingent consideration on the amortisation of goodwill

An acquisition was made at the beginning of year 1. Consideration of £40m was paid on completion and further consideration was payable based on an earn-out formula relating to the performance of the acquired business over the next three years. £60m of further consideration was provided for in the acquirer's first post-acquisition accounts, giving an estimated cost of acquisition of £100m. Net assets were fair valued at £20m, leaving purchased goodwill of £80m. The goodwill is being amortised over five years (straight-line basis) – an amortisation charge of £16m was recognised in year 1, leaving a carrying value of £64m at the end of year 1.

The acquisition does not perform as well as expected. At the end of year 2, the estimate of further consideration payable is revised downwards from £60m to £20m, resulting in an adjustment reducing the carrying value of goodwill by £40m.

The two methods are illustrated in the following tables (a zero discount rate is assumed).

Method (a) — prospective amortisation

Year	**1**	**2**	**3**	**4**	**5**
Goodwill b/f	80	64	18	12	6
Adjustment		(40)			
		24			
Amortisation	(16)	(6)	(6)	(6)	(6)
Goodwill c/f	64	18	12	6	–

Method (b) — reversal of excess amortisation charged in previous year

Year	**1**	**2**	**3**	**4**	**5**
Goodwill b/f	80	64	24	16	8
Adjustment		(40)			
Amortisation reversal (credit P&L)		8			
		32			
Amortisation	(16)	(8)	(8)	(8)	(8)
Goodwill c/f	64	24	16	8	–

FRS 10 does not deal with a situation where the amount of goodwill relating to an acquisition is adjusted as a result of a revision of the estimated cost of acquisition.

Apart from the reversal (in limited circumstances) of some impairment losses, FRS 10 states *"goodwill...should not be revalued, either to increase the carrying value above original cost or to reverse prior period losses arising from impairment of amortisation"*. [FRS 10 para 45]. Thus, for example, where the useful economic life is revised, the carrying value at the date of revision should be amortised (prospectively) over the revised remaining useful economic life. [FRS 10 para 33]. This corresponds with method (a) above.

However, the issue described above is not a revaluation in the sense of paragraph 45. The carrying value of goodwill has to be adjusted downwards as a result of the revised estimate of the cost of acquisition. The question in the example above is whether the carrying value at the beginning of year 2 should be adjusted to 24 (method (a)) or to 32 (method (b)).

One of the objectives of FRS 10 is *"to ensure that...capitalised goodwill and intangible assets are charged in the profit and loss account in the periods in which they are depleted..."*. Neither method properly achieves this.

Method (a) overstates the cumulative depletion of goodwill, because an amount has previously been charged in the profit and loss account which, with hindsight, will not be paid for. It also arguably understates the cost of goodwill consumed over the remaining estimated useful economic life.

Method (b) better reflects the cumulative depletion of goodwill, but the current year's amortisation charge does not properly reflect the goodwill consumed in that year, because it is credited with the excess charge of the previous year.

It should also be noted that if the purchased goodwill was being accounted for in the accounts of an individual company, the reversal or non-reversal of past amortisation would directly affect the company's distributable profits.

Our view is that either method is acceptable. Whilst we would normally expect the prospective treatment in method (a) to be adopted where estimates are revised, method (b) could be used where the effect of the adjustment to the cost of acquisition is material to the pattern of goodwill amortisation. Whichever method is chosen, material debits should be treated consistently with material credits in respect of different acquisitions.

Presentation of amortisation and impairment charges

25.505 FRS 11 requires impairment losses recognised in the profit and loss account to be included within operating profit under the appropriate statutory heading, and disclosed as an exceptional item if appropriate. [FRS 11 para 67].

25.506 FRS 10's note on legal requirements states that the formats in Schedule 1 to SI 2008/410 prescribe the headings under which depreciation and other amounts written off tangible and intangible fixed assets are to be included in the profit and loss account. [FRS 10 appendix 1 para 16]. Amortisation and other amounts written off goodwill fall within those headings. Under Format 1, where expenses are classified by function, goodwill would normally be treated as an administrative expense. Under Format 2, where expenses are classified by type, there is a separate heading 'depreciation and amounts written off tangible and intangible fixed assets', which is an operating expense. Both amortisation and impairment losses in respect of goodwill should, therefore, be charged in arriving at operating profit. The FRRP confirmed in a statement (published in January 2000) regarding the financial statements of PWS Holdings PLC that regular goodwill amortisation charges are not exceptional items.

25.507 In the financial year in which an acquisition is made, FRS 3 requires the operating results of the acquired business to be disclosed separately in the acquiring entity's profit and loss account. The amortisation or impairment of any goodwill related to the acquisition for that period should be attributed to the results of the acquisition rather than included with other goodwill amortisation charges that are attributable to the results of continuing operations excluding the acquisition.

25.508 Although goodwill write-offs should generally be included in arriving at operating profit or loss, companies that report earnings per share figures may wish to exclude goodwill write-offs in any additional EPS calculated on another level of earnings. The 'headline' earnings figure defined by the Society of Investment Professionals (formerly the Institute of Investment Management and Research) (IIMR) in its Statement of Investment Practice No 1, which seeks to produce a standardised measure of trading performance, states that *"goodwill should not affect earnings in any way"*. Consequently, the 'headline' earnings figure excludes any charges in respect of goodwill in its reconciliation of FRS 3 earnings to IIMR 'headline' earnings.

Reversals of past goodwill write-offs

25.509 The carrying value of purchased goodwill cannot be increased by revaluation or by reversing past amortisation charges. If goodwill is considered to have been amortised too quickly in the past, its useful economic life may be increased, but the carrying value should be amortised prospectively over the remaining revised useful life.

25.510 Impairment losses in respect of goodwill may be reversed (that is, credited back in the profit and loss account), but only in limited circumstances. These are where (a) an external event caused the original impairment loss, and (b) subsequent external events clearly and demonstrably reverse the effects of that event in a way that was not foreseen in the original impairment calculations. [FRS 10 para 44; FRS 11 para 60].

25.511 An impairment loss in FRS terminology is similar to provision for permanent diminution in value in the Act. Where there is a permanent diminution in the value of any goodwill held as an asset which is expected to be permanent, a provision should be made in the profit and loss account. [SI 2008/410 1 Sch 19(2)]. If the reasons for such a provision no longer apply, then the provision should be written back to the extent that it is no longer necessary. [SI 2008/410 1 Sch 20(1)].

For all practical intents and purposes the reversal criteria in FRS 10 and the Companies Act 2006 are deemed to be the same.

25.512 The objective of restricting reversals of impairment losses is to prevent a goodwill write-off from being credited back to the profit and loss account if the credit is in effect attributable to the generation of new non-purchased goodwill. Consequently, situations that justify reversals are likely to be rare and in most cases, amounts written off goodwill will stay written off. In this respect, the reversal criteria for goodwill (and most intangible assets) are stricter than those for tangible fixed assets, where impairment losses should be reversed in a much wider range of circumstances provided that subsequent increases in recoverable amount can be attributed to changed economic conditions. The reason given for the different approaches is that tangible fixed assets can in any case be revalued, whereas goodwill and most intangible assets cannot be.

25.513 One example of originating and reversing external events that would meet the reversal criteria for goodwill is the introduction of a new law that damages profitability (resulting in a goodwill write-off) and that is subsequently repealed by a new government. Another example is the confiscation of assets in an overseas territory (resulting in a goodwill write-off) that are subsequently released to allow the business to continue its operations. In both of these examples, the original goodwill has been reclaimed.

25.514 The recoverable amount of an acquired business may increase in subsequent years after an impairment loss has been recognised, but the improvement will often be unrelated to the circumstances that gave rise to the original impairment. One example is where goodwill has been written off because a competitor has introduced a better product to the market; some years later, the company launches a new product of its own and regains its lost market share. Another example is where a business has been reorganised to curtail underperforming operations, resulting in a write-off of goodwill; in later years, the business may expand again as new market opportunities arise. In neither of these examples would the turnaround justify reversing the impairment loss relating to the goodwill if the recoverable amount of the business has increased above the balance sheet value of its net assets and goodwill, because the higher value of goodwill that now exists includes goodwill that has been generated internally since the original impairment.

25.515 The amount that can be written back to reverse an impairment loss is restricted to an amount that increases the carrying value of the goodwill to the carrying value that would have been recognised had the original impairment not occurred. [FRS 11 para 61]. Accounting for reversals of impairment losses is discussed in more detail in chapter 18.

25.516 The following disclosures relate to reversals of past impairment losses:

- The Companies Act 2006 requires provisions for permanent diminutions in value that are written back because they are no longer necessary to be disclosed in the profit and loss account or in a note to the financial statements. [SI 2008/410 1 Sch 20(2)].

- FRS 10 requires reversals of past impairment losses to be disclosed separately in the note that reconciles the movements between the opening and closing goodwill balances. [FRS 10 para 53].
- FRS 11 requires that the reason for the reversal of impairment losses in respect of fixed assets or goodwill should be disclosed, together with any changes in the assumptions upon which the calculation of recoverable amount is based. [FRS 11 para 70].

Allocation of purchased goodwill

25.517 Groups need to keep detailed records of the composition of the aggregate amount of purchased goodwill, that is, to which parts of the group it relates. Allocation of goodwill to business units is necessary in order to:

- Account for subsequent disposals.
- Carry out impairment reviews.
- Keep track of elements of goodwill with different useful economic lives.

Disposals

25.518 Where businesses are disposed of, the net book value of any related goodwill has to be eliminated from the balance sheet and written off as part of the profit or loss on disposal.

25.519 Even where pre-FRS 10 goodwill was written off to reserves, profits or losses on disposals of businesses had to include any related goodwill that had not previously been written off in the profit and loss account. This continues to be a requirement in respect of pre-FRS 10 goodwill that remains written off to reserves under FRS 10's transitional arrangements.

25.520 It has always been recognised that there are practical difficulties with attributing goodwill to businesses disposed of. Traceability of purchased goodwill is an issue in complex group structures, particularly where an acquired business quickly loses its separate identity or when businesses undergo change and restructuring. The requirement in UITF 3 (since superseded by FRS 10) was that records should normally be sufficient to enable *"an appropriate estimate or apportionment"* of goodwill to be made. This implied that the amount of goodwill attributed to disposals is often likely to be a 'soft' number which is the product of a judgmental allocation exercise. Nevertheless, groups have generally managed to make reasonable allocations of goodwill to disposals.

Impairment reviews

25.521 Some allocation of purchased goodwill to separate businesses may also be necessary for carrying out the impairment reviews required by FRS 10. For example, impairment tests on goodwill relating to dissimilar businesses have to be performed separately on each dissimilar business.

25.522 Any goodwill that is amortised over more than 20 years (or not amortised at all) must be formally reviewed for impairment each year. Even where goodwill is amortised over 20 years or less and, as a result, no annual impairment reviews are required, there is still a possibility that an impairment review will be required in the future. This will be the case if evidence emerges that the net book value may not be recoverable.

25.523 Principles of allocating purchased goodwill to different business units are discussed in chapter 18.

Positive and negative goodwill

25.524 The acquisition of a group may give rise to positive goodwill overall. Where the acquisition includes a loss-making or marginally profitable business, the issue is whether negative goodwill can be attributed to that business, leaving a larger amount of positive goodwill attributable to the others. This could have a significant impact on disposal profits and losses.

25.525 Allowing both positive and negative goodwill to be recognised in respect of a single acquisition would introduce far more subjectivity into the allocation process than already exists. The ASB specifically prohibited such an approach in FRS 10, following the principle that goodwill (positive or negative) is a residual difference that arises from fair valuing the acquisition as a whole.

25.526 Businesses would, therefore, receive a zero allocation of goodwill where it is believed to be negative or nil at the date of acquisition. The overall goodwill on the acquisition would be allocated to those businesses where it is believed goodwill does exist.

25.527 Similarly, where an acquisition gave rise to negative goodwill overall, the negative goodwill would be allocated to those businesses where it is believed negative goodwill existed. No positive goodwill would be attributed to other businesses.

Integrated acquisitions

25.528 Tracing goodwill is more difficult, and allocations may become more arbitrary, where acquired businesses lose their separate identity as a result of post-acquisition integration with pre-existing operations and reorganisation.

25.529 However, it is usually possible to make such allocations on a reasonable basis, for example by tracking products, markets and key assets introduced by acquisitions. Subsequent business reorganisations would require a reallocation of goodwill balances.

25.530 Allocations can normally be readily achieved where branded activities were acquired, since these may be easily identifiable in current business units, especially if the products have not changed significantly over time. In other cases, more judgement is required. For example, where an established brand has been re-branded since its acquisition, the original purchased goodwill would (assuming the acquired operation is still continuing in some form) be attributed to the operation where the re-branded activity resides.

25.531 If a subsidiary is acquired and the business is subsequently transferred to another part of the group, leaving the subsidiary to be liquidated, no goodwill is transferred to the consolidated profit and loss account (as would happen if the business were sold). This is because the goodwill attaches to the retained business, not to the legal entity.

Impairment reviews

Purpose of impairment reviews

25.532 The impairment review is a recoverable amount check. It follows the long-established principle that an asset's balance sheet carrying value should not exceed its recoverable amount, which is measured by reference to the future cash flows that can be generated from its continued use or disposal. Impairment is defined in FRS 10 as *"a reduction in the recoverable amount of a fixed asset or goodwill below its carrying value"*.

25.533 Measuring the recoverable amount of purchased goodwill is complicated, because goodwill is by definition not a separable asset – it attaches to a business as a whole. The details of impairment reviews for fixed assets and goodwill are quite prescriptive and are contained in FRS 11, 'Impairment of fixed assets and goodwill'.

When impairment reviews are required

25.534 The requirements for impairment reviews differ according to whether goodwill is amortised over more or less than 20 years, as illustrated below.

Impairment reviews

Useful life 20 years or less	**Useful life more than 20 years**
End of first full year (simplified review)	Every year (detailed review)
Other years – high level check for impairment indicators with a detailed review only if impairment indicators are present	

25.535 Where goodwill is carried permanently as an asset or amortised over a very long period, there is a greater risk of impairment in the future. Where goodwill is written off over a shorter period, there is less risk of impairment, because its net book value in any case diminishes more quickly. A threshold of 20 years has been chosen, below which the impairment reviews are less onerous than for longer periods.

Useful life 20 years or less

First year review

25.536 A first year impairment review is required on all acquisitions where goodwill arises. This should be carried out at the end of the first full financial year following the acquisition. The timing of this review corresponds with the end of the investigation period in FRS 7, when the fair value exercise on the assets and liabilities of the acquired business should be completed and the final goodwill figure established. This review is intended to identify factors such as:

- Overpayment.
- Under performance compared with expectations.
- Material adverse changes to the acquired business in the immediate post-acquisition period.

25.537 The first year review has two stages. The first stage in effect requires management formally to consider whether the acquisition has lived up to expectations. This is done by comparing post-acquisition performance with the forecasts used in the acquisition appraisal and by considering whether there have been any other unexpected adverse events or changes in circumstances that throw doubt on the recoverability of the capitalised goodwill. If the acquisition passes this test, there is no need to go on to the second stage.

25.538 The second stage, which is a full impairment review (as described from para 25.540 below), is only necessary if the first stage indicates that there may be an impairment problem. [FRS 10 para 40].

Reviews in other years

25.539 After the first full year, management has to consider whether events or changes in circumstances indicate that the amortised carrying value of goodwill may not be recoverable. If there are no such indicators, no further work is required. In many situations it would be immediately apparent that there is no impairment. The goodwill will in any case be fully written off over 20 years at most. If there are factors that indicate that the carrying value of goodwill may not be recoverable, a full impairment review has to be carried out. If impairment is confirmed, the carrying value should be written down to the recoverable amount. Impairment reviews are considered in detail in chapter 18.

Detailed impairment review

25.540 A detailed impairment review is required in the following situations:

- Where goodwill is amortised over more than 20 years or carried permanently as an asset, an impairment review is automatically required at each year end (including the end of the year in which the acquisition took place).
- Where goodwill is amortised over 20 years or less:
  - At the end of the first full year following the acquisition, an impairment review is required *only* if there is an indicator of impairment or if the first year review indicates that the post-acquisition performance has failed to meet pre-acquisition expectations.
  - In other years, *only* if there is an indicator of impairment.

The requirements are considered in detail in chapter 18.

Negative goodwill

25.541 In some acquisitions, the fair value of the identifiable assets less liabilities may exceed the cost of acquisition, giving rise to negative goodwill.

25.542 Negative goodwill is the mirror image of positive goodwill. FRS 10 requires negative goodwill to be shown as a separate (negative) item on the asset side of the balance sheet immediately below positive goodwill, followed by a net sub-total, as illustrated below. [FRS 10 para 48]. If the amount of negative goodwill exceeds the amount of positive goodwill, there would be a net credit figure on the assets side. An example of the disclosure of positive and negative goodwill is shown in the extract from the Babcock International Group plc accounts below in Table 25.24.

Table 25.24 — Babcock International Group PLC — Annual Report & Accounts — 31 March 2001

Group balance sheet (Extract)

at 31 March 2001

	Notes	**2001 £'000**	**2001 £'000**	2000 £'000	2000 £'000
Fixed assets					
Intangible assets	12				
Development costs			**1,507**		1,771
Goodwill					
– Goodwill		**88,279**		27,801	
– Negative goodwill		**(14,916)**		(18,703)	
			73,363		9,098

Goodwill

When the fair value of the consideration for an acquired undertaking exceeds the fair value of its separable net assets the difference is treated as purchased goodwill and is capitalised and amortised through the profit and loss account over its estimated economic life. The estimated economic life of goodwill is between ten and twenty years.

Where the fair value of the separable net assets exceeds the fair value of the consideration for an acquired undertaking the difference is treated as negative goodwill and is capitalised and amortised through the profit and loss account in the period in which the non-monetary assets acquired are recovered. In the case of fixed assets this is the period over which they are depreciated, and in the case of current assets, the period over which they are sold or otherwise realised.

25.543 Negative goodwill is generally attributed to one of two causes:

- The first is where the acquirer has made a genuine bargain purchase. This might occur as a result of a distress sale, for example, where the vendor is forced to sell the business quickly and cheaply to relieve cash flow problems.
- The second is where the purchase price is reduced to take account of future costs or losses, for example, where it is recognised that the acquirer will have to incur significant reorganisation costs to turn the business around. Such costs or losses are not identifiable liabilities of the acquired business at the date of acquisition.

25.544 FRS 10 seeks to restrict situations where negative goodwill is recognised. The first requirement where a fair value exercise appears to give rise to negative goodwill is that the fair values of the identifiable assets should be tested for impairment and the fair values of the identifiable liabilities should be checked carefully to ensure none has been omitted or understated. [FRS 10 para 48]. Any further reductions to the acquired net assets that need to be made as fair value adjustments as a result of this exercise will reduce or eliminate the negative goodwill.

25.545 The recoverable amount of the assets should be considered particularly carefully in the second of the situations mentioned in paragraph 25.543 above. Where the acquired business is loss-making or under-performing and in need of reorganisation, it must be questionable whether the fair values of the net assets in aggregate, which (as required by FRS 7) should be measured to reflect the conditions at the date of acquisition, are actually worth more than the price paid for the business as a whole. It should be noted that FRS 7 requires a valuation at recoverable amount to reflect the condition of the asset on acquisition (reflecting, for example, lack of profitability, under-utilisation or obsolescence). [FRS 7 para 47]. The ASB considers that much of any negative goodwill that would otherwise be attributed to future costs or losses would be eliminated by reducing the fair value of the assets in this way. [FRS 10 Appendix III para 57]. It follows that negative goodwill will most commonly arise in genuine bargain purchase situations.

25.546 A further restriction is that FRS 10 does not allow both negative goodwill and intangible assets to be recognised in respect of a single acquisition. It does this by capping the fair values attributable to any identifiable intangibles at an amount that does not give rise to negative goodwill overall, as illustrated below. [FRS 10 para 10].

	Valuation	Restricted fair value
	£m	**£m**
Tangible net assets	200	200
Intangibles	400	300
	600	500
Cost of acquisition	500	500

25.547 The ASB's reason for this treatment is that valuations of intangibles are very subjective. Also, many intangibles are similar to goodwill and FRS 10 does not allow both positive and negative goodwill to be recognised on the same acquisition. This requirement was reinforced by the FRRP decision in relation to Equator Group plc published in July 2002, which held that the directors should not have created negative goodwill on the acquisition of a company whose principal asset was film libraries, an intangible asset without a readily ascertainable market value. The same ruling welcomed the director's decision to revise the indefinite life attributed to the film libraries down to 20 years, with a nil residual value.

25.548 Negative goodwill that remains after the fair values of the acquired assets and liabilities have been re-checked should be accounted for as follows.

- Negative goodwill up to the fair values of the non-monetary assets acquired should be amortised to the profit and loss account in the periods in which the non-monetary assets are recovered, whether through depreciation or sale. [FRS 10 para 49]. Non-monetary assets include stocks as well as fixed assets.

- Any negative goodwill in excess of the fair values of the non-monetary assets acquired should be recognised in the profit and loss account in the periods expected to be benefited. [FRS 10 para 50].

25.549 The standard does not specify where in the profit and loss account amounts of negative goodwill credited should be shown. It would be consistent with the treatment of positive goodwill to include negative goodwill as a negative component of goodwill amortisation charges that are treated as operating costs in arriving at operating profit or loss.

25.550 By matching the release of negative goodwill into the profit and loss account with the depreciation or cost of sales of the non-monetary assets acquired, a wide range of amortisation patterns is possible. No guidance on this is given in FRS 10. If the release of negative goodwill is matched first with the depreciation of the fixed assets, it will be credited, say, over the average useful life of the fixed assets acquired. Intuitively, this would seem to be a sensible treatment in most circumstances. It is also prudent, considering that fair valuing tangible fixed assets acquired can sometimes be as subjective as fair valuing intangible assets. If the release of negative goodwill is matched first with the cost of sales relating to the sale of the stocks acquired, it will be credited much more quickly. But, relative to fixed assets, stock is less likely to be subject to measurement uncertainty.

25.551 Situations where negative goodwill exceeds the fair values of the non-monetary assets acquired should be very rare indeed. If, for example, the only non-monetary assets were debtors, it would be logical to credit the excess negative goodwill in the profit and loss account over the period the debtors were collected.

25.552 The following disclosures are required in respect of negative goodwill:

- The aggregate movements on negative goodwill should be disclosed separately from those on positive goodwill, detailing additions, disposals, impairments, and amounts written back to profit and loss account in the period. [FRS 10 para 53].
- The period(s) in which negative goodwill is being written back in the profit and loss account. [FRS 10 para 63].
- Where negative goodwill exceeds the fair values of the non-monetary assets (which should be very rare), details of its amount and source and the period(s) in which it is being written back. [FRS 10 para 64].

Pre-FRS 10 goodwill that remains in reserves

25.553 SSAP 22's preferred method of accounting for goodwill was immediate elimination against reserves. FRS 10's transitional arrangements permitted, but did not require, previously eliminated goodwill to be reinstated on the balance sheet (see paragraph 25.598). Under the transitional options, unless all goodwill relating to pre-FRS 10 acquisitions is reinstated, one of the following amounts will remain eliminated against reserves:

- All goodwill written off before the adoption of FRS 10.
- All goodwill written off before the adoption of FRS 7 (which became effective in 1995).
- All goodwill written off before 23 December 1989 where its composition is not known.

Separate goodwill write-off reserve prohibited

25.554 Under the elimination method preferred by SSAP 22, there had been an increasing trend for groups to have a policy of writing goodwill off against a special reserve set up for the purpose. The reserve initially had a nil balance and so the reserve created would be negative and would equal the figure of goodwill written off. This was similar to a (prohibited) treatment known as a 'dangling debit' where goodwill would be carried on the balance sheet as a permanent debit deducted from shareholders' funds. One of the perceived advantages of this method was that the accounting treatment maintained some accountability for goodwill through its visibility in the financial statements, in contrast to writing goodwill off to, say, the profit and loss account reserve where it was 'lost'. The 'dissenting view' of one ASB member published with FRS 10 advocated an alternative approach to goodwill that was based on a separate goodwill reserve.

25.555 FRS 10 does not allow previously eliminated goodwill that is not reinstated on the balance sheet under the transitional arrangements to be carried forward in a separate goodwill write-off reserve. It requires such goodwill to be offset against the profit and loss account or another appropriate reserve. Furthermore, it does not allow such goodwill to be shown separately on the face of the balance sheet in any way, such as a separate component of the reserve to which it has been written off. [FRS 10 para 71(b)].

25.556 The ASB's justification for the decision to outlaw the goodwill write-off reserve is that, in the context of a new standard based on specific capitalisation, amortisation and impairment requirements, it could be misleading and confusing to have goodwill appearing in two different places on the balance sheet. Otherwise, some balance sheets would contain a permanent reminder of the transition. If continued accountability for the cost of past acquisitions is considered to be of overriding importance by companies, recapitalisation is the only method allowed to achieve this.

Reserves used for write-offs

25.557 The following reserves are the principal candidates for carrying goodwill that remains written off under FRS 10's transitional arrangements:

- Profit and loss account reserve.
- Merger reserve.
- Other non-distributable reserves (except those noted below).

25.558 The following reserves *cannot* be used to carry goodwill write-offs:

- Share premium account.
- Capital redemption reserve.
- Revaluation reserve.

Profit and loss account

25.559 Where more than one reserve is available to absorb the goodwill that is not recapitalised, no order of write-off is specified. Therefore, the profit and loss account can be used as a first choice or as a last choice to bear the goodwill write-off. In the latter case, the profit and loss account would absorb any balance of goodwill that cannot be offset against other reserves.

Merger reserve

25.560 A merger reserve arises on consolidation where a company issues shares as part of the consideration to acquire another company and it takes merger relief on the issue of those shares. The provisions of merger relief are explained fully in chapter 23. Where merger relief is available, the amount by which the fair value of the shares issued exceeds their nominal value results in a merger reserve on consolidation (rather than a share premium). Under the old rules for goodwill, a merger reserve could be used to write off goodwill that arose on the acquisition that gave rise to the reserve and it could also be used to write off any other goodwill. This was one of the key advantages of obtaining merger relief on the issue of shares to acquire another undertaking.

25.561 Where purchased goodwill is capitalised under FRS 10, the merger reserve can, of course, no longer be used to absorb goodwill write-offs on acquisition. But any old goodwill that is not recapitalised can continue to be offset against any existing merger reserve.

25.562 If a group wishes to use the merger reserve first to absorb any such goodwill, but the reserve is insufficient to offset all of the goodwill, the balance of goodwill would have to be offset against another reserve (that is, the profit and loss account reserve, if no other reserve is available). However, if the merger reserve subsequently increases as a result of a new share for share acquisition, there is nothing to prevent that balance of goodwill offset from being transferred from the other reserve to the increased merger reserve.

Other non-distributable reserves

25.563 Apart from the capital reserves that are governed by the Act (see below), neither the Act nor SSAP 22 restricted groups from writing off goodwill arising on consolidation against any other non-distributable reserves. Such reserves might include a special reserve created on a court-approved reduction of share premium which was carried out in the past specifically to enable goodwill to be written off against it on consolidation (see para 25.565 below).

Share premium account

25.564 The use of the share premium account is governed by the Companies Act 2006, which specifies that share premium arising on the issue of shares can be used to:

- Pay up fully paid bonus shares.
- Write off expenses of the issue of those shares.

- Write off commission paid on the issue of those shares.

[CA06 Sec 610(2)(3)].

25.565 Although the share premium account can only be used for specific purposes, and writing off goodwill is not one of them, it does form part of a company's capital and, as such, can be reduced under section 641 of the Companies Act 2006 by application to the court. Where groups fund acquisitions in part or in full by issuing shares, the parent, unless it is eligible for merger relief, has to credit the difference between the fair value of the shares issued and their nominal value to its share premium account. A share premium account may also exist from previous share issues. The parent company may take steps to reduce its share premium account by a specified amount. That amount would, in the consolidated financial statements, be redesignated as another reserve to be used specifically to write off consolidation goodwill that remains written off in reserves. The steps involved are determined by company law. Initially, a special resolution for the reduction is required and all of the relevant facts about the proposal must be set out in the documentation sent to shareholders.

25.566 Once the shareholders have passed the necessary special resolution, an application has to be made to the court to obtain its confirmation. Such confirmation is required by the Act and the court will be concerned in particular to ensure that the parent company's creditors are not prejudiced.

25.567 Share premium reductions of this nature were common when goodwill was eliminated against reserves. This route remains an option for groups that wish to write off all pre-FRS 10 goodwill against a reserve created by reducing share premium rather than against the profit and loss account reserve.

25.568 It should be remembered that the share premium account in such situations is that of the parent company. The reserve that is created from the share premium account is in most cases initially not available for distribution by the parent. It remains undistributable until certain conditions specified by the court have been satisfied, for instance, that the creditors that exist at the date of the reduction have been paid. Once these conditions have been fulfilled, the reserve becomes distributable. However, whether the reserve arising on the reduction is distributable is not relevant for consolidation purposes. Consolidation goodwill can be written off to the reserve created out of the parent's share premium account whether or not it is distributable by the parent.

Capital redemption reserve

25.569 Capital redemption reserves are set up for a specific purpose and will be utilised at some future date for that purpose. Therefore, their use is restricted. Furthermore, the normal provisions that apply to the reduction of share capital also apply to the capital redemption reserve. [CA06 Sec 733(5)(6)]. Consequently, except where there has been a reduction confirmed by the court, this reserve is not available to write off goodwill arising on consolidation.

Revaluation reserve

25.570 The use of the revaluation reserve is restricted by the Companies Act 2006 which states:

> *"An amount may be transferred*
>
> *(a) from the revaluation reserve*
>
> *(i) to the profit and loss account, if the amount was previously charged to that account or represents a realised profit, or*
>
> *(ii) on capitalisation*
>
> *(b) to or from the revaluation reserve in respect of the taxation relating to any profit or loss credited or debited to the reserve.*
>
> *The revaluation reserve must be reduced to the extent that the amounts transferred to it are no longer necessary for the purposes of the valuation method used.*
>
> *In sub-paragraph (a)(ii) 'capitalisation', in relation to an amount standing to the credit of the revaluation reserve, means applying it in wholly or partly paying up unissued shares in the company to be allotted to members of the company as fully or partly paid shares.*
>
> *The revaluation reserve must not be reduced except as mentioned in this paragraph."*

[SI 2008/410 1 Sch 35(3A)(3B)(4)(5)].

25.571 The wording of paragraph 34 was changed by the Companies Act 1989 specifically to ensure that goodwill arising on consolidation could no longer be written off against the consolidated revaluation reserve. Before that, the Act (by reference to the EC 4th Directive) prohibited goodwill arising in a company's individual financial statements from being written off against the company's revaluation reserve. However, this restriction did not extend to goodwill arising on consolidation.

25.572 The commencement order introducing part I of the Companies Act 1989 into the UK's legislation, however, included certain transitional provisions. One of these provisions concerned those groups that had in the past written off consolidation goodwill to their consolidated revaluation reserve. Where a group had previously written consolidation goodwill off against the revaluation reserve, it did not have to reverse this treatment. However, for any acquisitions that a group made following the change brought about by the Companies Act 1989, the treatment was no longer possible.

Effect on distributable profits — groups

25.573 Where, under the old rules, a group wrote off consolidation goodwill arising on the acquisition of subsidiaries immediately to reserves, the write-off did not affect the distributable profits of the parent or any individual group company. Since it is individual companies, not groups, that make distributions, the write-off of goodwill did not affect the amount of the total potential distributable profits of the group.

25.574 Consequently, whether pre-FRS 10 goodwill remains eliminated against the profit and loss account reserve or against unrealised reserves (such as a merger reserve) has no effect on distributable profits. Furthermore, a group does not need to transfer any amounts from unrealised reserves to realised reserves over the estimated useful economic life of such goodwill.

25.575 Although it is individual companies, not groups, that make distributions, users of consolidated financial statements may wish to know how much the parent could distribute if all the subsidiaries in the group were to pay up their realised profits by way of dividends to the parent. Some groups specifically disclose this amount. In the absence of such disclosure, users of the consolidated financial statements might mistakenly interpret the group's profit and loss account reserve as representing realised reserves.

Effect on distributable profits — companies

25.576 Where goodwill arises in a *company* as opposed to a group, questions arise as to whether, or how, any write-off affects realised and distributable profits. This situation would arise where a company purchased the trade and assets (including goodwill) of an unincorporated business. SSAP 22 provided guidance on this issue which is reproduced in Appendix V to FRS 10, because it is still relevant for pre-FRS 10 goodwill that remains eliminated against a company's reserves under the transitional options.

25.577 The appendix states that to the extent that goodwill is considered to have suffered an actual diminution in value, the write-off should be charged against realised reserves; but realised reserves should not be reduced immediately where goodwill is written off as a matter of accounting policy and there is no actual diminution in value. It goes on to explain that immediate depletion of realised reserves can be avoided by eliminating goodwill initially to a suitable unrealised reserve. The amount eliminated against the unrealised reserve should then be transferred to realised reserves over the goodwill's useful economic life so as to reduce realised reserves on a systematic basis in the same way as if the company had amortised goodwill. [FRS 10 appendix V para 2]. A transfer to realised reserves would also have to be made if the carrying value of goodwill deducted from the unrealised reserve was found to have been impaired because, for example, an adverse event damaged the profitability of the acquired business.

25.578 The availability of suitable unrealised reserves is, however, limited. Merger relief reserves (if recognised by the company), negative goodwill and other capital reserves (except for share premium, capital redemption and revaluation reserves) can be used. However, FRS 10's prohibition of carrying goodwill in a separate (negative) goodwill write-off reserve applies to companies as well as groups. The profit and loss account reserve can, therefore, no longer be protected from goodwill write-offs by carrying a separate negative reserve. If pre-FRS 10 goodwill remains eliminated against reserves, it has to be eliminated against the profit and loss account reserve to the extent that no other reserves are available. The appendix does not specifically address the question whether goodwill that is actually eliminated against the profit and loss account reserve has the effect of reducing a company's realised reserves.

25.579 We consider that the elimination of goodwill does not become a realised loss just because it is offset against the profit and loss account reserve. This is primarily a matter of presentation. The principle remains that goodwill only becomes a realised loss to the extent that it is amortised or considered to have suffered an actual diminution in value. Therefore, FRS 10's prohibition of a separate goodwill write-off reserve should make no difference to the basis on which a company had previously been allocating such goodwill from unrealised to realised reserves, that is, over its estimated useful economic life as determined under SSAP 22. It should be noted that SSAP 22 defined useful economic life differently from FRS 10 and did not allow goodwill to be carried in the balance sheet as a permanent item.

25.580 Where purchased goodwill has been offset against a company's profit and loss account reserve, it would be important to disclose in the notes the amount of goodwill offset that is an unrealised loss in order to give a clear picture of the company's distributable profits.

Goodwill on disposals

25.581 FRS 10 retains the rules previously set out in UITF Abstract 3. Where goodwill attributable to a past acquisition remains eliminated against reserves (and, hence, has not been previously charged in the profit and loss account), it must be transferred to the profit and loss account when the business is subsequently disposed of, by treating it as part of the profit or loss on disposal. The attributable goodwill is credited in reserves and debited in the profit and loss account. The amount of goodwill included as a component of the profit or loss on disposal should be separately disclosed. [FRS 10 para 71(c)]. The disclosure could be either on the face of the profit and loss account or in the notes.

25.582 An exemption from this treatment is given if the business disposed of was acquired before 1 January 1989 and it is impracticable or impossible to ascertain the attributable goodwill that was originally written off. In this situation the facts and the reasons should be stated. This exemption coincides with the transitional provisions of the Companies Act 1989, before which there was no necessity to keep detailed records of goodwill eliminated against reserves.

Impairment of goodwill

25.583 Where goodwill is capitalised, timely recognition of impairment losses is a key feature of FRS 10's rules. However, neither FRS 10 nor its predecessors have dealt with the issue of whether goodwill that is eliminated against reserves and has lost its value should be charged in the profit and loss account earlier than on disposal of the acquired business. FRS 11's rules for measuring and recognising impairments of capitalised goodwill specifically do not apply to old goodwill that remains written off to reserves. [FRS 11 para 7]. In some situations, either as a matter of accounting policy or as part of the accounting for an impending disposal, goodwill may be written off in the profit and loss account earlier to recognise an impairment. This issue is discussed in chapter 8. Any impairment that has been written off in the profit and loss account does not pass through the profit and loss account again on disposal of the business.

Disclosures

25.584 FRS 10's transitional provisions contain some specific disclosure requirements that relate to goodwill that remains eliminated against reserves.

Accounting policy

25.585 The accounting policy relating to that goodwill should be separately disclosed. [FRS 10 para 71(a)(i)]. It would be useful for companies to indicate what the balance eliminated against reserves comprises by reference to the transitional option they adopted: all goodwill eliminated before FRS 10 was adopted, or all goodwill eliminated before FRS 7 was adopted, or goodwill relating to acquisitions made before 23 December 1989.

25.586 Another policy issue that might be considered for disclosure is the basis on which such goodwill is charged in the profit and loss account, that is, on disposal or (if applicable) when an impairment is identified.

Cumulative amounts written off

25.587 The notes to the financial statements should disclose the cumulative amount of positive goodwill eliminated against reserves, net of any goodwill attributable to businesses disposed of before the balance sheet date. If both positive and negative goodwill have been taken to reserves, the cumulative amounts of each should be disclosed separately. [FRS 10 para 71(a)(ii)].

25.588 The notes should also state that this goodwill has been eliminated as a matter of accounting policy and would be charged or credited in the profit and loss account when the businesses to which it relates are subsequently disposed of. [FRS 10 para 71(a)(iii)]. Not all of the disclosable cumulative amount of goodwill may in fact be chargeable in the profit and loss account on disposal. For example, some of this goodwill may already have been written off in the profit and loss account, because the company has a policy of recognising impaired goodwill earlier. Another example is where the identity of goodwill relating to acquisitions made before 1 January 1989 is unknown and, hence, by virtue of the exemption in FRS 10, may never pass through the profit and loss account.

25.589 The Companies Act also requires the cumulative amount of goodwill written off that results from acquisitions in the current year and in earlier years to be disclosed. [SI 2008/410 6 Sch 14(1)]. The amount disclosed should also be stated net of any goodwill attributed to an undertaking that has subsequently been sold. [SI 2008/410 6 Sch 14(2)]. This requires disclosure of the aggregate of amounts written off directly to reserves, but not the amounts amortised through the profit and loss account.

25.590 The FRRP published a statement in December 1995 in connection with the financial statements of Ferguson International Holdings PLC confirming that, where advantage is taken of the merger relief provisions of the Act, the figures disclosed for goodwill arising on acquisitions in the year and the cumulative amount of goodwill written off should be the gross amounts before deducting merger relief.

25.591 The Companies Act 2006, however, does not require the gross amount of goodwill written off to be disclosed in certain circumstances where an undertaking that is established outside the UK or that carries on its business outside the UK has obtained the permission of the Secretary of State. [SI 2008/410 6 Sch 16]. Similarly the transitional provisions on the introduction of the Companies Act 1989 do not require the amount to be disclosed in certain situations where it is not possible to ascertain the figure for goodwill written off that has arisen on acquisitions made prior to the introduction of the Companies Act 1989 and to do so would cause unreasonable expense or delay. In these situations the financial statements must state that the gross figure disclosed does not include an amount on these grounds.

Pre-FRS 10 negative goodwill that remains in reserves

25.592 SSAP 22 required negative goodwill to be credited directly to reserves. Under FRS 10's transitional arrangements, some or all negative goodwill attributable to pre-FRS 10 acquisitions may remain credited to reserves.

25.593 SSAP 22 did not require a group to set up a separate reserve for negative goodwill, but some companies and groups did so. FRS 10 does not allow the amount by which any reserve has been increased by the addition of negative goodwill to be shown separately on the face of the balance sheet. [FRS 10 para 71(b)]. To be consistent with positive goodwill, this implies that negative goodwill should also not be carried as a separate reserve if it can be credited to another appropriate reserve. Therefore, negative goodwill arising on consolidation may either be credited to a capital reserve, if any is available (excluding the statutory share premium, capital redemption and revaluation reserves), or to the consolidated profit and loss account reserve. In the former case, it would normally be included under 'other reserves' in the balance sheet format.

25.594 The negative goodwill that remains credited to reserves should be transferred to the profit and loss account when the business to which it relates is sold or closed, by inclusion in the calculation of the profit or loss on disposal. The amount of negative goodwill transferred should be separately disclosed as a component of the profit or loss on disposal.

25.595 The cumulative amount of negative goodwill added to reserves, net of any attributable to businesses disposed of before the balance sheet date, should be disclosed in the notes, together with the fact that this would be credited in the profit and loss account on subsequent disposal of the business to which it related. If both positive and negative goodwill have been taken to reserves, the cumulative amounts of each should be disclosed separately. [FRS 10 para 71(a)].

Effect on distributable profits — companies

25.596 Where negative goodwill arises in a company, it should credit it initially to an unrealised reserve. The company may then transfer the negative goodwill from that unrealised reserve to realised reserves. This transfer should be in line with the depreciation or the realisation of the assets acquired in the business combination that gave rise to the goodwill in question. [FRS 10 App V para 3].

25.597 Unlike negative goodwill arising on consolidation, negative goodwill in an individual company should not be credited immediately to the profit and loss account reserve, because it is not a realised profit. It would have to be shown under the heading 'other reserves' in the company's balance sheet.

Implementing FRS 10 — transitional arrangements

Options for reinstating goodwill eliminated against reserves

25.598 FRS 10 had to be applied to goodwill relating to acquisitions first accounted for in financial years ending on or after 23 December 1998. Where goodwill relating to earlier acquisitions had been eliminated against reserves, the standard permitted, but did not require, the goodwill to be recapitalised as an asset on the balance sheet. There were effectively four options for dealing with old goodwill eliminated against reserves:

- Leave all goodwill eliminated against reserves.
- Reinstate all goodwill previously written off to reserves.
- Reinstate all goodwill relating to post-23 December 1989 acquisitions (where the information on earlier acquisitions cannot be obtained without unreasonable expense or delay), leaving the balance eliminated against reserves.
- Reinstate all goodwill eliminated since the adoption of FRS 7, leaving the balance eliminated against reserves.

[FRS 10 para 69].

25.599 Each of the reinstatement options required a prior period adjustment for a change of accounting policy from immediate write-off to capitalisation. The transitional arrangements were a once-only opportunity to establish the goodwill accounting going forward and hence, there should be no change to the policy previously adopted without providing compelling reasons for such a change. Any goodwill reinstated is subject to the normal requirements of FRS 10 and FRS 11 outlined earlier in the chapter, notably the requirement to review useful economic lives at the end of each accounting period and the need to monitor the carrying value of the goodwill for impairment.

Additions to goodwill in existing subsidiaries

Increases in stake

25.600 If a parent company increases its stake in an existing subsidiary by purchasing additional shares from the minority, goodwill may arise on the purchase. The new goodwill must be capitalised if the purchase is accounted for when FRS 10 is effective. The old goodwill (pre-dating FRS 10) may or may not be capitalised, depending on whether or not it was reinstated under the transitional options. Therefore, it is possible that goodwill relating to one subsidiary may appear in two different places. The more recent purchase will appear on the balance sheet and be subject to the amortisation and impairment rules, whereas the older purchase will remain eliminated against reserves.

Earnout consideration

25.601 Sometimes an acquirer agrees to pay additional consideration for an acquisition that depends on its future performance. The additional consideration may give rise to more goodwill. In this situation, however, the additional goodwill does not relate to a new acquisition or to the acquisition of a further tranche of shares. It is an adjustment to the goodwill on the previous acquisition. FRS 7 in fact requires estimates of future performance-related consideration to be provided for when the acquisition is first accounted for. Therefore, any additional goodwill should always be treated in the same way as the goodwill that was accounted for when the acquisition was made.

25.599 Each of the transitional options permitted a prior period adjustment for a change of accounting policy from immediate write-off to capitalisation. The transitional arrangements were a once-only opportunity to establish the goodwill accounting going forward and, hence, there should be no change to the policy previously adopted without pre-existing compelling reasons for such a change. Any goodwill reinstated is subject to the normal requirements of FRS 10 and FRS 11 outlined earlier in the chapter, notably the requirement to review useful economic lives at the end of each accounting period, and the need to monitor the carrying value of the goodwill for impairment.

Additions to goodwill on existing subsidiaries

Increases in stake

25.600 If a parent company increases its stake in an existing subsidiary by purchasing additional shares from the minority, goodwill may arise on the purchase. The new goodwill must be capitalised if the purchase is accounted for when FRS 10 is effective. The old goodwill (preceding FRS 10) may or may not be capitalised, depending on whether or not it was reinstated under the transitional options. Therefore, it is possible that goodwill relating to one subsidiary may appear in two different places. The more recent purchase will appear on the balance sheet and be subject to the amortisation and impairment rules, whereas the older purchase will remain eliminated against reserves.

Contingent consideration

25.601 Sometimes an acquirer agrees to pay additional consideration for an acquisition that depends on its future performance. The additional consideration may give rise to more goodwill. In this situation, however, the additional goodwill does not relate to a new acquisition or to the acquisition of a further tranche of shares. It is an adjustment to the goodwill on the previous acquisition. FRS 7 in fact requires estimates of future performance related consideration to be provided for when the acquisition is first accounted for. Therefore, any additional goodwill should always be treated in the same way as the goodwill that was accounted for when the acquisition was made.

Chapter 26

Disposals of subsidiaries

Chapter 26

Disposals of subsidiaries

Introduction

26.1 Typically, an undertaking will cease to be a subsidiary of another when the group sells it or reduces its percentage interest in the undertaking. Equally a parent may lose control over an undertaking because of changes in the rights it holds or in those held by another party in that undertaking or because there is a change in some other arrangement that gave the parent its control (see further chapter 24).

26.2 A reduction in percentage interest may arise from a direct disposal (for example, the sale of shares in a company) or from a deemed disposal (for example, the exercise of share options by another party). A gain or loss will normally arise on both a disposal and a deemed disposal (for example, see Table 26.1).

Table 26.1 – Forte Plc – Report and Accounts – 31 January 1994

Notes to the Accounts (extract)

7 Profit on disposal of discontinued operation
The profit on disposal of discontinued operations, amounting to £122m, relates to the flotation of the Group's interest in its Airport Services Division (now called ALPHA Airports Group Plc – "ALPHA") on 25 January 1994 and the sale of the Group's interest in Kentucky Fried Chicken (Great Britain) Ltd on 2 December 1993. Proceeds amounting to £155m from the ALPHA disposal were outstanding at the year end and were received on 10 February 1994. The Group has retained a 25% interest in ALPHA.

14 Fixed assets – investments (extract)
ALPHA
Following the flotation of the Group's Airport Services Division in January 1994, the Group retained 25% of the ordinary shares of the new holding company, ALPHA Airports Group Plc. In addition the Group holds 46,000 6.5% cumulative redeemable preference shares of £1 each. The Group's share of the net assets of ALPHA as at 31 January 1994, calculated using Forte's accounting policies, amounted to £12m. ALPHA shares were listed on 10 February 1994 at a price valuing this interest at £53m.

26.3 Where a parent loses control because of changes in its rights or the rights of other parties, or because of changes in some other arrangement, neither a gain nor a loss will arise in the consolidated profit and loss account, unless there is a payment for the transfer of the control. This is because there will be no change in the net assets attributable to the group's holding in the former subsidiary. [FRS 2 para 86]. See further paragraph 26.24. However, a gain or loss (albeit normally unrealised) can arise where, for example, a company (company P) disposes of shares it holds in its subsidiary (company S) in exchange for shares in another company (company A). The subsidiary (company S) will often then become a subsidiary of the acquiring company (company A). The acquiring company will also often become a subsidiary of the original parent (company P). An example of this type of arrangement is given in paragraph 26.23.8.

26.4 The disposal of a business has to be accounted for in much the same way as a disposal of a subsidiary. Therefore, many of the principles explained in this chapter apply equally to the disposals of businesses as they do to disposals of subsidiaries. Furthermore, the disclosures that have to be given are also similar. Disposals of businesses are not dealt with in the Companies Act, but the provisions in FRS 2, FRS 3 and FRS 10 are the same for disposals of businesses and subsidiaries.

The accounting rules

Rules in FRS 2

26.5 Accounting for an undertaking that ceases to be a subsidiary is often as complex as accounting for the acquisition of a subsidiary. The matters that need to be considered when an undertaking ceases to be a subsidiary include both how to account for trading in the period after the implementation of the decision to dispose of the subsidiary and how to account for the cessation itself.

26.6 Where an undertaking ceases to be a subsidiary during a period, the consolidated profit and loss account for that period should include, to the extent that they have not already been provided for in the consolidated financial statements:

- The results of the subsidiary up to the dāte it ceases to be a subsidiary.
- The gain or loss arising on the cessation.

[FRS 2 para 46].

26.7 The calculation of the gain or loss arising on cessation (whether it is the result of a direct disposal, a deemed disposal or another event) is the difference between the following two amounts:

- The carrying amount of the net assets of the subsidiary attributable to the group's interest before the cessation (including any attributable goodwill — see para 26.10).
- Any remaining carrying amount attributable to the group's interest after the cessation (including any attributable goodwill), together with any proceeds received.

[FRS 2 para 47].

26.8 In many sales an element of contingent performance-related consideration is included as part of the proceeds. This element would normally be treated as a contingent asset under FRS 12; consequently it would not be recognised in the profit and loss account until it became receivable and, until then, it would merely be disclosed in the notes to the financial statements. Where consideration is simply deferred (and, hence, not contingent on future performance), the amount receivable may need to be discounted to its present value at the disposal date depending on the length of time over which it has been deferred and whether or not it bears interest.

26.8.1 Any contribution by the vendor to the purchaser's costs should be treated as a reduction in the proceeds received and, therefore, should be taken into account in determining the profit or loss on disposal.

26.8.2 Such a contribution may be dependent on future profits of the business being sold, for example, an agreement to reimburse the acquirer for a percentage of management bonuses granted by the acquirer depending on performance. The reduction in proceeds should be recognised when it is more likely than not that the reimbursement will be required.

26.8.3 If as part of the disposal arrangements the group continues to provide services to the business being disposed of for a specified period, for example providing IT support for twelve months at nil cost, the appropriate treatment is to defer part of the sales proceeds and release the deferred income to profit and loss over the twelve month period.

26.9 There may be other losses or gains that arise as a result of an undertaking ceasing to be a subsidiary that need to be recognised (for example, provisions for guarantees). Such gains or losses are not directly part of the profit or loss on the disposal, but where they need to be provided for, if they are quantifiable, they should normally be included as part of the profit or loss on disposal. If for some reason they are not provided for, they might need to be disclosed to show the full effect of the cessation. [FRS 2 para 87].

26.9.1 If the group has adopted FRS 23, the cumulative exchange differences previously taken to equity on the translation of the net investment in that subsidiary should also be included in the gain or loss on disposal. [FRS 23 para 48]. The practical impact of this requirement is that groups will need to keep detailed records in order to analyse the exchange reserve by entity.

26.9.2 The group may use the proceeds of the sale to redeem existing debt used to finance the business being sold. Any loss on the redemption of this debt is not part of the profit on disposal of the business. It should be shown as an exceptional finance cost (if material) and included within the interest line, but separately disclosed.

FRS 10

26.10 The value of net assets used to calculate the profit or loss on disposal (see para 26.7) should include any related goodwill (including any negative goodwill) not previously written off through the profit and loss account. [FRS 2 para 47]. The effect of this requirement in practice is that goodwill (or negative goodwill), arising before the introduction of FRS 10, which has remained written off (or credited) directly to reserves on acquisition following FRS 10's transitional provisions [FRS 10 para 71(c)], and any goodwill that has been capitalised but not yet amortised, must be charged (or credited) to the profit and loss account on disposal. This treatment is considered necessary to ensure that purchased goodwill (or negative goodwill) having been written off (or credited) to reserves prior to the implementation of FRS 10 does not bypass the profit and loss account completely. The requirement applies whether the disposal is a direct disposal, a deemed disposal or another event. In contrast, the treatment of such goodwill will differ under IFRS as both IFRS 3, 'Business combinations', and IFRS 1, 'First-time adoption of international financial reporting standards', prohibit the transfer of goodwill previously written off to reserves to the income statement on disposal of the subsidiary.

26.11 The practical impact of the provisions of both FRS 2 and FRS 10 means that groups have to keep detailed records of how the aggregate amount of goodwill written off direct to reserves prior to the implementation of FRS 10 is made up and to which parts of the group it relates. Because of the difficulties this can cause, particularly where the acquisition took place many years ago, there is some relief given, but this is subject to disclosure. In such a situation, it is necessary to state that goodwill has not been included in the calculation of the profit or loss arising on the sale and to explain the reason why this is so (see also para 26.41). [FRS 10 para 71(c)]. The requirement to include the attributable goodwill when calculating the profit or loss on sale of a subsidiary does pose particular problems. Consider the following examples.

Example — Goodwill allocations pre and post adoption of FRS 10

A group acquired another group of companies some years ago before the introduction of FRS 10. The consideration was £100m and the fair value of the net assets acquired was £40m. The resultant goodwill of £60m was written off to reserves on acquisition. The acquired group consists of five companies and the goodwill was allocated between them on the basis of a price earnings formula. The allocation was positive goodwill of £70m relating to four of the companies and negative goodwill of £10m relating to the fifth. The group is now disposing of the company in respect of which the negative goodwill arose.

Prior to FRS 10, companies could apportion the goodwill arising on acquisition in this way and, therefore, on the sale of the part of the group that gave rise to the negative goodwill, the negative goodwill would have been taken into the calculation of the profit or loss on the sale. However, for acquisitions arising following FRS 10's introduction purchased goodwill on a single transaction should not be divided into positive and negative components. In this situation, using the same facts as in the example, the £60m of goodwill should still be allocated over the five companies. However, because of the new rules in FRS 10 the original allocation would need to be changed. This would mean allocating a figure of nil to the first company and £60m of goodwill over the other four companies. As a result, goodwill of nil would be attributed to the company being disposed of.

26.12 As explained in chapter 25, prior to the introduction of FRS 10 it was acceptable to write goodwill off against the merger reserve. This continues to be acceptable practice for goodwill arising prior to FRS 10's implementation. On the sale of a subsidiary, as explained above, it is necessary to include in the calculation of any profit or loss on sale any goodwill written off direct to reserves on the original acquisition. Where an amount was credited to a merger reserve on the acquisition, that reserve would at the time be unrealised. On disposal the merger reserve arising on the acquisition becomes realised. The question then arises as to whether it is acceptable to take that part of the merger reserve to the profit and loss account on the sale of the subsidiary to mitigate the goodwill charged there. This is not, however, an acceptable treatment, because the intention of FRS 2 and FRS 10 is to measure the profit or loss on the sale by reference to its cost. The original cost for this purpose is represented by the fair value of the consideration, that is the nominal value of the shares issued plus the merger reserve. To take the release of the merger reserve to the profit and loss account would mean that the loss on sale of the subsidiary was not calculated by reference to this amount. Therefore, any merger reserve that is realised should instead be transferred to the profit and loss account reserve as a reserve movement.

Implications of FRS 3

26.13 FRS 3 requires the profit or loss on the sale of an asset to be calculated by reference to the carrying value of that asset. [FRS 3 para 21]. This requirement might seem to conflict with the FRS 2 calculation explained in paragraph 26.10 above, which requires goodwill written off to reserves in the past prior to FRS 10's implementation to be brought back into the calculation of the profit or loss on the sale of a subsidiary. The explanation of this apparent inconsistency is that the write-off of goodwill direct to reserves was not regarded as a recognised loss and, therefore, when the write-off was initially made it did not appear in the statement of total recognised gains and losses. Because it has not been 'recognised' in the past it follows that it must be recognised on disposal of the subsidiary by inclusion in the profit or loss.

26.14 The treatment of profits and losses on disposals of operations, including the rules concerning loss provisions, is considered in detail in chapter 8.

Discontinued operations

26.15 Where an operation is sold, its results up to the date of sale should be disclosed as part of operating profit under either the heading 'discontinued operations' or, if it does not qualify as a discontinued operation (see para 26.16), as 'continuing operations'. The profit or loss on sale should be shown as an exceptional item after operating profit and before interest and should also be disclosed as relating to 'discontinued operations' or, if it does not qualify, it should be disclosed as relating to 'continuing operations'. [FRS 3 para 20]. It is quite possible for a business or a subsidiary that is being sold not to qualify as a discontinued operation under FRS 3 (see for example Table 26.2).

Table 26.2 – Grand Metropolitan Public Limited Company – Annual Report – 30 September 1996
Consolidated profit and loss account (extract)

for the year ended 30th September 1996

	Notes	1996 Before exceptional items £m	1996 Exceptional items £m	1996 Total £m	1995 Before exceptional items £m	1995 Exceptional items £m	1995 Total £m
Turnover							
Continuing operations		8,727		8,727	7,733		7,733
Discontinued operations		247		247	292		292
Total turnover	3	8,974		8,974	8,025		8,025
Operating costs	4	(7,866)		(7,866)	(6,993)	(122)	(7,115)
Operating profit							
Continuing operations		1,096		1,096	1,009	(122)	887
Discontinued operations		12		12	23	–	23
Total operating profit		1,108		1,108	1,032	(122)	910
Share of profits of associates	5	47	(24)	23	48	(15)	33
		1,155	(24)	1,131	1,080	(137)	943
Continuing operations							
Disposal of fixed assets			(3)	(3)		(9)	(9)
Sale of businesses	6		27	27		(44)	(44)
Provisions for losses on sale of businesses	6		(250)	(250)		–	–
Discontinued operations							
Sale of businesses	6		(327)	(327)		198	198
			(553)	(553)		145	145
Interest payable (net)	7	(190)	–	(190)	(168)	–	(168)
Profit on ordinary activities before taxation		965	(577)	388	912	8	920

Notes (extract)

6 Sale of businesses

	1996		1995
	Profit/(loss) on sale of businesses	Provisions set up for businesses to be sold	Profit/(loss) on sale of businesses
	£m	£m	£m
Continuing operations			
National food businesses in Europe (note (a))	35	(250)	–
Green Giant processing	–		(42)
Other	(8)	–	(2)
	27	(250)	(44)
Discontinued operations			
Pearle (note (b))	(291)	–	–
Betting and gaming (note (c))	(36)	–	–
Alpo Petfoods	–	–	198
	(327)	–	198

(a) The sale of the German food business, Erasco, was completed on 30th September for a consideration of £134m; provisions of £250m have been set up in respect of the remaining national food businesses in Europe. The profit on sale and the provisions are after charging goodwill previously written off attributable to the businesses of £222m.

(b) The sale of Pearle for a consideration of £138m was agreed on 25th September 1996 and was completed on 15th November 1996. The loss on sale was after charging goodwill previously written off attributable to Pearle of £270m.

(c) The £36m in respect of betting and gaming relates to a £118m downward adjustment to the consideration for the group's former retail betting operation, which was sold in December 1989 for £685m, offset by £82m which remained outstanding from The William Hill Group Ltd in relation to the sale. This disposes of the major aspect of a dispute with the purchaser, but there are other ongoing claims arising from the sale which have yet to be resolved.

26.16 FRS 3 defines discontinued operations as those operations that satisfy all of the following conditions:

- The sale or termination is completed either in the period or before the earlier of three months after the commencement of the subsequent period and the date on which the financial statements are approved.
- If a termination, the former activities have ceased permanently.
- The sale or termination has a material effect on the nature and focus of the reporting entity's operations and represents a material reduction in its operating facilities resulting either from its withdrawal from a particular market (whether class of business or geographical) or from a material reduction in turnover in the reporting entity's continuing markets.
- The assets, liabilities, results of operations and activities are clearly distinguishable, physically, operationally and for financial reporting purposes.

[FRS 3 para 4].

26.17 The very strict definition of 'discontinued operations' and the detailed disclosure requirements of both continuing and discontinued operations are considered in detail in chapter 8. Any reorganisation or restructuring of continuing operations resulting from a sale should be treated as part of the continuing operations. [FRS 3 para 17].

Date of sale

26.18 The date of sale is the date on which a binding legal agreement for the sale of an operation is entered into (see further chapter 8). The date on which an undertaking ceases to be another undertaking's subsidiary is the date on which control passes. [FRS 2 para 45]. Where control is transferred by public offer the relevant date is usually when an offer becomes unconditional. Where it is transferred by private treaty the date is usually where an unconditional offer is accepted. The signing of a binding legal agreement for the sale of an operation would, therefore, appear to be the date on which an offer becomes unconditional and is accepted and, therefore, should be the date from which the disposal is accounted for as having occurred. [FRS 2 para 85]. The effective date for accounting for changes in group membership is discussed in detail in chapter 25.

Impact of FRS 1

26.19 The provisions of FRS 1, 'Cash flow statements', require that where a group disposes of a subsidiary, the amounts of cash and overdrafts transferred as part of the disposal should be shown separately from the gross consideration received for the disposal. [FRS 1 para 23(a)]. Where a subsidiary is disposed of during the year, the cash flows of the group should include the cash flows of the subsidiary up to the date of sale. [FRS 1 para 43]. The provisions of FRS 1 are explained in detail in chapter 30 and the disclosure requirements relating to disposals are summarised in paragraph 26.39.

Accounting for the sale of a subsidiary

Full disposal

26.20 The most common transaction that results in an undertaking ceasing to be a subsidiary is a straight disposal. The consolidated profit and loss account should include the trading results of the undertaking up to the date of its ceasing to be a subsidiary, disclosed, where appropriate, as discontinued operations as explained above. Any gain or loss arising on disposal would be included in the profit and loss account on the basis explained above.

26.21 In effect, the profit or loss on disposal of all or part of a subsidiary will be the difference at the date of sale between the following amounts:

- The proceeds of the sale.
- The group's share of the subsidiary undertaking's net assets disposed of, together with any premium or discount on acquisition (apportioned if necessary to that element of the net assets sold) that has not been written off through the profit and loss account.

26.22 The calculation of the profit or loss on sale is illustrated by the following examples. The example below looks at the calculation of the gain on disposal of a subsidiary where the group capitalised goodwill arising on the initial acquisition and amortises that goodwill over its useful life.

Example – Sale of a subsidiary (goodwill amortised)

A parent purchased an 80% interest in a subsidiary for £80,000 during 19X1 when the fair value of the subsidiary's net assets was £87,500. Goodwill on consolidation that arose on the acquisition is being amortised over its estimated useful life of ten years and a full year's charge for amortisation was made in the consolidated financial statements to 31 December 19X1. The parent sold its investment in the subsidiary on 31 December 19X4 for £100,000. The book value of the subsidiary's net assets in the consolidated financial statements on the date of the sale was £112,500.

The parent's profit and loss account for 19X4 would show a gain on the sale of the investment of £20,000 calculated as follows:

	£'000
Sale proceeds	100
Less: cost of investment in subsidiary	(80)
Gain on sale in the parent's accounts	20

However, the group's profit and loss account for 19X4 would show a gain on the sale of the subsidiary of £4,000 calculated as follows:

	£'000	£'000
Sale proceeds		100
Less: share of net assets at date of disposal (£112,500 × 80%)	(90)	
goodwill on consolidation unamortised at date of sale*	(6)	(96)
Gain on sale in the group's accounts		4

*The unamortised goodwill on consolidation is calculated as follows:

	£'000
Fair value of consideration at date of acquisition	80
Less: fair value of net assets of subsidiary at date of acquisition (£87,500 × 80%)	70
Goodwill arising on consolidation	10
Amortisation (4 years × £1,000)	4
Unamortised goodwill at 31 December 19X4	6

The difference between the gain in the holding company's profit and loss account and the gain reported in the group's consolidated profit and loss account is £16,000 (that is, £20,000 — £4,000). This difference represents the share of post-acquisition profits retained in the subsidiary of £20,000 (that is, (£112,500 — £87,500) × 80%) that have been reported in the group's profit and loss account up to the date of sale, less goodwill of £4,000 that has been written off in the group's profit and loss account.

26.23 The next example looks at the calculation of the gain or loss on disposal where the group on acquisition, prior to the implementation of FRS 10, wrote off the goodwill arising on purchasing the subsidiary direct to reserves.

Example – Sale of subsidiary (goodwill recognised in reserves)

The facts are identical to those in the example in paragraph 26.22 except that the goodwill that arose on consolidation was written off direct to reserves in the year of acquisition.

As before, the parent's profit and loss account for 19X4 would show a gain on the sale of the investment of £20,000. The group's profit and loss account for 19X4 would show no gain or loss on the sale of the subsidiary calculated as follows:

		£'000	£'000
Sale proceeds			100
Less:	share of net assets at date of disposal (£112,500 × 80%)	(90)	
	goodwill written off directly to reserves*	(10)	(100)
			–

*The goodwill on consolidation is calculated as follows:

		£'000
Fair value of consideration at date of acquisition		80
Less:	fair value of net assets of subsidiary at date of acquisition (£87,500 × 80%)	70
Goodwill arising on consolidation		10

The difference between the gain in the parent's profit and loss account and the gain reported in the group's consolidated profit and loss account is £20,000. This difference represents the share of post-acquisition profits retained in the subsidiary of £20,000 (that is, (£112,500 – £87,500) × 80%) that have been reported in the group's profit and loss account up to the date of sale. The goodwill is required by FRS 2 and FRS 10 to be written back to reserves on sale of the subsidiary and charged as part of the overall profit or loss on the disposal (see further para 26.10).

Sale of a subsidiary for shares

26.23.1 Disposals often arise where a parent sells a subsidiary for shares in another undertaking, which results in that other undertaking becoming an associate, joint venture or subsidiary of the vendor. Therefore, at the same time as the disposal there is an acquisition. UITF Abstract 31 sets out the approach to be adopted.

[The next paragraph is 26.23.3.]

26.23.3 The abstract requires that where an entity (A) exchanges a business or other non-monetary asset for an interest in another entity (B), which thereby becomes A's subsidiary or which becomes A's joint venture or associate, the following accounting treatment is required in A's consolidated financial statements.

- To the extent that A retains an ownership interest, that retained interest, including any related goodwill, should be included at its pre-transaction carrying amount (that is, it should not be fair valued).
- A's share of net assets acquired through its new interest in B should be accounted for at fair value, with the difference between these fair values and the fair value of the consideration given being accounted for as goodwill.
- To the extent that the fair value of the consideration received by A exceeds the book value of the part of the business or non-monetary assets no longer owned by A (and any related goodwill) together with any cash given up, A should recognise a gain. Any gain arising on the exchange that is not realised should be reported in the STRGL.
- Where the fair value of the consideration received by A is less than the book value of the part of the business or non-monetary assets no longer owned by A (and any related goodwill) together with any cash given up, A should recognise a loss, either as an impairment in accordance with FRS 11 or, for any loss remaining after an impairment review of the relevant assets, in A's profit and loss account.

26.23.4 The abstract states that no gain or loss should be recognised where the artificiality or lack of substance of the transaction is such that any gain or loss on the exchange could not be justified. In such cases the circumstances should be disclosed.

26.23.5 The method required for calculating the gain or loss and goodwill under UITF 31 is as follows:

- The book value of assets and liabilities effectively disposed of plus attributable goodwill is compared to the fair value of the consideration received, that is the fair value of the part of the business that is acquired. This is not necessarily the same as the fair value of the net assets acquired as the fair value of the business includes the goodwill of that element of the business that is acquired. The result is either a gain or a loss arising on the exchange.
- The fair value of the consideration given, which is the fair value of the part of the business disposed of (which again may be different from the fair

values of the assets and liabilities given up as it will include a value for the unrecognised goodwill of the business) is compared with the fair values of the assets and liabilities acquired, with the result being recognised as goodwill (either positive or negative).

- The above calculations will be affected if cash settlements are made as part of the exchange.

26.23.6 To illustrate the first bullet above, if the book value of the net assets disposed of is £50 and the fair value of the net assets acquired is £60, but the fair value of the business acquired (which contains the net assets acquired) is £70, the comparison is between the £50 and the £70, not between the £50 and the £60.

26.23.7 Similarly to illustrate the second bullet point, if the book value of the net assets disposed of is £50 and their fair value is £55, but the fair value of the business given up is £70, it is £70 that is compared with the fair value of the net assets acquired in order to determine the goodwill arising.

26.23.8 The method prescribed by UITF 31 calculates the gain or loss only on the element that has been disposed of to a third party. Therefore, no intra-group profit or loss arises, which would otherwise need to be eliminated on consolidation.

In exchange for an interest in a subsidiary

Example – Disposal of subsidiary in exchange for shares in other subsidiary

Company A has a wholly-owned subsidiary company B. Company A sells its subsidiary company B to company C, a listed company, for shares in company C and ends up owning 75% of company C's shares (as illustrated in the diagram).

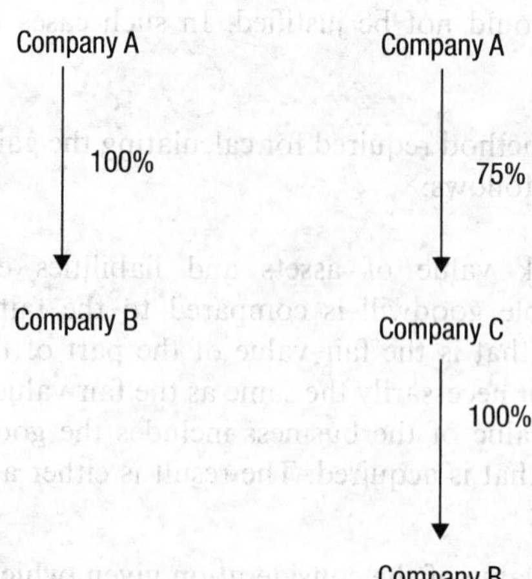

The net assets of company B prior to the disposal are £1 million (fair value £1.3 million) and goodwill previously capitalised is £600,000 (for simplicity, goodwill has not been amortised in this example); the carrying value of company B in company A's books is £1.5 million. At the date of its acquisition by company A, company B's profit and loss account reserve was £400,000 and B has since made £100,000 post acquisition profits. The position prior to the transaction was, therefore, as follows:

Consolidation of companies A and B before transaction	Co A	Co B	Consol
	£'000	£'000	£'000
Goodwill	–	–	600
Investment in subsidiary	1,500	–	–
Net assets	10,000	1,000	11,000
	11,500	1,000	11,600
Equity share capital	2,000	500	2,000
Profit and loss account reserve	9,500	100	9,600
– pre acquisition reserves	–	400	–
Equity shareholders' funds	11,500	1,000	11,600

The goodwill arising on the acquisition by company A of company B is calculated as follows:

Cost of control account/goodwill

	£000		£000
Investment	1,500	Equity share capital	500
		P&L reserve	400
			900
		Goodwill	600
	1,500		1,500

The net assets of company C prior to its acquisition of company B are £380,000 (fair value £500,000). Company C then issues shares worth £1.75 million (which is the fair value of the consideration given for the acquisition of 100% of B), being £600,000 nominal value and £1.15 million premium. The balance sheets of the three companies directly after the issue of shares by company C are as follows:

Summarised balance sheets

	Co A £'000	Co B £'000	Co C £'000
Investment in subsidiary	1,500	–	1,750
Net assets	10,000	1,000	380
	11,500	1,000	2,130
Equity share capital	2,000	500	800
Merger reserve	–	–	1,150
Profit and loss account reserve	9,500	500	180
Equity shareholders' funds	11,500	1,000	2,130

The parent, company A, had an interest in company B that cost £1.5 million, and has in effect swapped this for an interest in company C's group. The cost to company A remains £1.5 million, although this investment has a market value of £1.75 million.

With regard to company A's consolidated financial statements, it is necessary to calculate the gain or loss and the goodwill arising in accordance with UITF 31.

Gain or loss on disposal of 25% of B	£'000
Book value of assets and liabilities given up plus attributable goodwill ((£1m + £600,000) × 25%)	400.0
Fair value of business received in consideration (£1.75m × 25%) (note 1)	437.5
Gain on disposal (note 2)	37.5
Goodwill on acquisition of 75% of C	
Fair value of business given in consideration (note 3)	437.5
Fair value of assets and liabilities acquired (£500,000 × 75%)	375.0
Goodwill	62.5

Note 1: A receives consideration (that is, shares in C) with a fair value of £1.75 million. However, the amount included in the UITF 31 calculation is the amount attributable to the interest in B that has been disposed of, that is 25% of £1.75 million.

Note 2: The gain is regarded by A as unrealised because it is received in the form of shares which, though listed, are in a company which is treated as a subsidiary. Accordingly, the gain is credited to the STRGL.

Note 3: The fair value of the part of the subsidiary B that is effectively disposed of is derived from the price paid by C for the whole of B, that is £1.75m.

Consolidation of A, B and C after the transaction (note: Company C's net assets are adjusted to fair value for the purpose of the consolidation as C has been acquired by A).

Consolidation of companies A, B and C after the transaction	Co A	Co B	Co C	Consol	
	£'000	£'000	£'000	£'000	Notes
Goodwill	–	–	–	512.5	1
Investment in subsidiary	1,500.0	–	1,750.0	–	
Net assets	10,000.0	1,000.0	380.0	11,500.0	2
	11,500.0	1,000.0	2,130.0	12,012.5	
Equity share capital	2,000.0	500.0	800.0	2,000.0	
Merger reserve	–	–	1,150.0	–	
Other reserve	–	–	–	37.5	3
Profit and loss account reserve	9,500.0	500.0	180.0	9,600.0	4
Minority interest	–	–	–	375.0	5
	11,500.0	1,000.0	2,130.0	12,012.5	

Note 1: The goodwill balance of £512,500 represents the balance (75%) of the goodwill of £600,000 arising on the acquisition of B, being £450,000 plus the goodwill of £62,500 arising on the acquisition of C.

Note 2: On consolidation the net assets of C are increased from £380,000 to their fair value of £500,000.

Note 3: The other reserve represents the unrealised gain arising on disposal of 25% of B.

Note 4: The consolidated profit and loss account represents the profit and loss account of A (£9,500,000) plus the post-acquisition profits of B of £100,000.

Note 5: The minority interest represents 25% of C's net assets of £500,000 at fair value being £125,000 plus 25% of B's net assets of £1,000,000, being £250,000, making £375,000 in total.

One complication that could arise in this situation is if C were required to prepare consolidated financial statements. In that case C would have to acquisition account for B, which would involve fair valuing B's net assets and not fair valuing its own. This is precisely the opposite of what happens where A accounts for the acquisition of C. The accounting by C for its acquisition of B in the consolidated financial statements of C is not dealt with further here.

In exchange for an interest in a joint venture or associate

26.23.9 In recent times there has been a large number of transactions through which companies have formed joint ventures or associates, to which each party has contributed businesses.

26.23.10 The following examples illustrate the accounting where the resulting interest is a joint venture or associate. Also illustrated is a case where there is a cash element in the transaction.

Example 1 – Disposal of subsidiary in exchange for an interest in a joint venture

Company A owns 100% of company B. The book value of company B's net assets is £400,000 and their fair value is £600,000. Goodwill on the acquisition of company B was £150,000 which has been amortised and stands at a book value of £100,000. The fair value of company B's business is estimated at £800,000 for the purpose of the transaction. Company C owns 100% of company D. The book value of company D's assets is £300,000 and their fair value is £400,000. The value of company D's business is £800,000.

A new joint venture company, Newco, is formed into which companies A and C contribute the businesses of companies B and D respectively and each of company A and company C receives shares in Newco giving each a 50% share.

	£'000
Balance sheet of Newco immediately after the transaction	
Net assets (at fair value) (£600,000 + £400,000)	1,000
Goodwill	600
	1,600
Shareholders' funds	1,600

Shareholders' funds represents the fair value of the consideration given, which in this case is based on the fair values of the businesses acquired (£800,000 + £800,000)

Under UITF 31, company A accounts for the gain or loss arising and the goodwill arising on acquisition of its 50% share in Newco as follows:

	£'000
Calculation of gain/(loss) on disposal of 50% of B	
Share of net assets disposed of at book value (50% × £400,000)	200
Share of goodwill disposed of (50% × £100,000)	50
	250
Share of value of D received as consideration (fair value of consideration being half of fair value of D's business)	400
Gain on disposal	150
Calculation of goodwill on acquisition of 50% of D	
Value of half of business of B given up	400
Fair value of net assets acquired (50% × £400,000)	200
Goodwill arising	200

Under UITF 31, company C accounts for the gain or loss arising and the goodwill arising on the acquisition of a 50% share in Newco as follows:

	£'000
Calculation of gain/(loss) on disposal of 50% of D	
Share of net assets disposed of at book value	
(50% × £300,000, assuming no goodwill in books of C)	150
Share of value of B business received as consideration (fair value of consideration being half of fair value of B business)	400
Gain on sale	250
Calculation of goodwill on acquisition of 50% of B	
Value of half of business of D given up	400
Fair value of net assets acquired (50% × £600,000)	300
Goodwill	100

Example 2 – Disposal of subsidiary in exchange for share in a joint venture and cash

The facts are the same as in the above example except that the value of D is not £800,000 but £500,000. In order to make up the difference, company C pays £300,000 in cash into the joint venture.

The balance sheet of Newco immediately after the transaction is as follows:

	£'000
Net assets at fair value (excluding cash) (£600,000 + £400,000)	1,000
Cash	300
Goodwill	300
	1,600
Shareholders' funds	1,600

The calculations for company A are as follows:

	£'000
Calculation of gain/(loss) on disposal of 50% of B	
Share of net assets and goodwill disposed of (at book value)	250
Share of value of D received as consideration	250
Cash (50%)	150
Gain on disposal	150
Calculation of goodwill on acquisition of 50% of D	400
Share of businesses given up (half of B)	400
Fair value of net assets acquired (50% × £400,000)	200
Share of cash	150
	350
Goodwill	50

The calculations for company C are as follows:

Calculation of gain/(loss) on disposal of 50% of D	
	£'000
Share of net assets disposed of (50% × £300,000)	150
Cash (50%)	150
	300
Share of value of B received as consideration	400
Gain on disposal	100
Calculation of goodwill on acquisition of 50% of B	
Value of businesses and cash contributed	
((£500,000 + £300,000) × 50%)	400
Fair value of assets acquired (50% × £600,000)	300
Goodwill	100

A simple proof of the calculations can be done. For example, company A starts with net assets of £400,000 and goodwill of £100,000 in company B at book value. In example 2 it finishes with a share of assets of Newco of half of the book value of assets contributed by itself (50% x £400,000), half of the fair value of the assets contributed by company C (50% x £400,000) and half of the cash contributed by company C (50% x £300,000) making £550,000 in all. The difference (£550,000 less £500,000) is a net gain of £50,000, which when added to the £50,000 of goodwill which company A retains relating to company B, makes a net gain of £100,000. This is the same as the difference between the gain calculated as above of £150,000 and the goodwill of £50,000.

In company C's case it starts with net assets in company D at book value of £300,000 and cash of £300,000. It finishes with half of the original net assets at book value (£150,000), half of the cash (£150,000) and half of the fair value of the assets of company B contributed by company A (50% x £600,000). This gives £600,000 less £600,000, that is neither gain nor loss on a net basis. This is the same as the difference between the gain calculated as above on a UITF 31 basis of £100,000 and the goodwill of £100,000.

Ceasing to be a subsidiary other than by sale or exchange of shares

26.24 An undertaking may cease to be a subsidiary undertaking as a result of loss of control. Such loss of control could occur, for example, because of: changes in voting rights attaching to shares held; changes in the power to appoint or remove directors or their voting rights; or the parent no longer actually exercising or having the power to exercise dominant influence or control (see further chapter 24). In these situations no profit or loss will arise in the consolidated financial statements, unless there is a payment for loss of control, because there is no change in the net assets attributable to the group's holding in the former subsidiary undertaking.

26.25 Where loss of control arises in this way, the former subsidiary undertaking should not be consolidated, but should be shown instead at its net asset value as an associated undertaking (see chapter 27) or as an investment depending on the degree of influence retained. In addition, the circumstances that resulted in the undertaking ceasing to be a subsidiary should be explained in a note to the consolidated financial statements. [FRS 2 para 49].

[The next paragraph is 26.27].

Partial disposals

26.27 Partial disposals arise where a parent disposes of part of its interest in a subsidiary (for example see Table 26.4). The remaining interest of the parent in the undertaking might result in the undertaking continuing to be a subsidiary or it might become an associate or an investment.

Table 26.4 – Cable and Wireless plc – Report and Accounts – 31 March 1993

Notes to the Accounts (extract)

Exceptional items: profit on partial sale of subsidiaries		1993	1992
	£m	£m	£m
Consolidation adjustment arising as a result of the sale of 20% of Mercury Communications Limited to BCE Inc.	166.0		
Less: Goodwill previously written off to reserves (Note 25)	48.3		
		117.7	–
Profit arising on the sale of shares in Hong Kong Telecommunications Limited as a result of the exercise of warrants	63.6		
Less: Goodwill previously written off to reserves (Note 25)	3.5		
		60.1	–
		177.8	–

There was no taxation or minority interest charge or credit applicable to the exceptional items shown above.

26.28 The basic principles that apply to disposals also apply to partial disposals. Therefore, where a group reduces its stake in an undertaking any profit or loss should be calculated as the difference between the following:

- The carrying amount of the net assets of that subsidiary attributable to the group's interest before the reduction.
- The carrying amount attributable to the group's interest after the reduction together with any proceeds received.

The net assets compared should include any related goodwill not previously written off through the profit and loss account.

26.29 Where the undertaking continues to be a subsidiary after the disposal, the minority interests in that subsidiary should be increased by the carrying amount of the net identifiable assets that are now attributable to the minority interests because of the decrease in the group's interest. However, as explained in chapter 24, no amount for goodwill that arose on the acquisition of the group's interest in that subsidiary should be attributed to the minority interests.

26.30 Three examples follow that illustrate the consequences of a partial sale where the subsidiary undertaking after the sale:

- Remains a subsidiary, but with a reduced interest (see para 26.31).
- Becomes an associate (see para 26.32).
- Retains a small shareholders' interest (see para 26.33).

Remaining a subsidiary

26.31 The example that follows illustrates the calculation of the gain or loss arising on a partial disposal, where the undertaking remains a subsidiary.

Example – Partial disposal of a subsidiary (remaining a subsidiary)

A parent purchased a 100% subsidiary for £500,000 during 19X1 when the fair value of the subsidiary's net assets was £400,000. Goodwill arising on the acquisition prior to the implementation of FRS 10 was written off direct to reserves in the year of acquisition. The parent sold 40% of its investment in the subsidiary in December 19X4 for £450,000. The book value of the subsidiary's net assets included in the consolidated balance sheet on the date of the sale was £800,000. The parent's profit and loss account for 19X4 would show a gain on the sale of the investment of £250,000 calculated as follows:

	£'000
Sale proceeds	450
Less: cost of investment in subsidiary	
(£500,000 × 40%)	(200)
Gain on sale in the parent's accounts	250

However, the group's profit and loss account for 19X4 would only show a gain on the sale of the subsidiary of £90,000 calculated as follows:

	£'000	£'000
Net assets and proceeds after disposal:		
Share of net assets (£800,000 × 60%)	480	
Goodwill written off directly to reserves (£100,000 × 60%)	60	
Sale proceeds	450	990
Less: net assets before disposal		
Net assets	800	
Goodwill written off directly to reserves*	100	900
Gain on sale to the group		90

*The goodwill on consolidation is calculated as follows:

	£'000
Fair value of consideration at date of acquisition	500
Less: fair value of net assets of subsidiary at date of acquisition	400
Goodwill arising on consolidation	100

The difference between the gain in the parent's profit and loss account and the gain reported in the group's consolidated profit and loss account is £160,000. This difference represents the share of post-acquisition profits retained in the subsidiary of £160,000 (that is, (£800,000 – £400,000) × 40%) that have been reported in the group's profit and loss account up to the date of sale.

The minority interests immediately after the disposal will be 40% of the net carrying value of the subsidiary included in the consolidated balance sheet of £800,000, that is, £320,000.

Becoming an associate

26.32 The next example illustrates the calculation of the gain or loss on a partial disposal where the subsidiary becomes an associate.

Example – Partial disposal of a subsidiary (becoming an associate)

The facts of this example are the same as the example in paragraph 26.31 except the group disposes of a 60% interest for £675,000, leaving the parent with 40% and significant influence. The parent's profit and loss account for 19X4 would show a gain on the sale of the investment of £375,000 calculated as follows:

	£'000
Sale proceeds	675
Less: cost of investment in subsidiary (£500,000 × 60%)	(300)
Gain on sale in the parent's accounts	375

However, the group's profit and loss account for 19X4 would only show a gain on the sale of the subsidiary of £135,000 calculated as follows:

	£'000	£'000
Net assets and proceeds after disposal:		
Share of net assets (£800,000 × 40%)	320	
Goodwill written off directly to reserves (£100,000 × 40%)	40	
Sale proceeds	675	1,035
Less: net assets before disposal		
Net assets	800	
Goodwill written off directly to reserves	100	900
Gain on sale to the group		135

In this situation, after the sale the undertaking will no longer be treated as a subsidiary, but rather as an associate and equity accounted. It will be included in the consolidated balance sheet as an investment in an associated undertaking of £320,000 (40% × £800,000) using the equity method of accounting. Goodwill relating to the associate of £40,000 has already been written off to reserves and will remain there.

Becoming an investment

26.33 The example below considers the situation where a parent disposes of part of its interest in a subsidiary such that it merely has a small remaining investment in the undertaking.

Example – Partial disposal of a subsidiary (becoming an investment)

The facts of this example are the same as the previous two examples above, except that the group disposes of a 90% interest for £855,000, leaving the parent with a 10% investment.

The parent's profit and loss account for 19X4 would show a gain on the sale of the investment of £405,000 calculated as follows:

	£'000
Sale proceeds	885
Less: cost of investment in subsidiary (£500,000 × 90%)	(450)
Gain on sale in the parent's accounts	405

However, the group's profit and loss account for 19X4 would only show a gain on the sale of the subsidiary of £45,000 calculated as follows:

	£'000	£'000
Net assets and proceeds after disposal:		
Share of net assets (£800,000 × 10%)	80	
Goodwill written off directly to reserves (£100,000 × 10%)	10	
Sale proceeds	855	945
Less: net assets before disposal		
Net assets	800	
Goodwill written off directly to reserves	100	900
Gain on sale to the group		45

In this situation the undertaking will no longer be treated as a subsidiary, but rather as an investment. Unless the entity has adopted FRS 26, 'Financial instruments: Recognition and measurement', the undertaking will be included in the consolidated balance sheet at 'cost' determined on an equity basis as £80,000 (£800,000 × 10%). The investment, however, is only recorded in the parent at £50,000 (that is, £500,000 × 10%). The double entry needed to ensure that the consolidation reserves reconcile on consolidation would be as follows:

	£'000	£'000
Dr Investment	40	
Cr Reserves		40
To recognise the group's share of post-acquisition reserves previously recognised in the consolidated financial statements which relates to the 10% investment retained.		
Dr Reserves	10	
Cr Investment		10
To recognise the group's share of the goodwill arising on the acquisition of the original investment which relates to the 10% investment retained.		

The reserves of £40,000 have already been recognised in the consolidated reserves as they represent the share retained of the post-acquisition reserves that have arisen from the subsidiary's original acquisition up to the date of sale. It can be argued that this is the only adjustment required and that the investment should be recorded at £90,000 in the consolidated financial statements. However, it is more prudent to show the goodwill investment value reduced by the amount of goodwill that has previously been written off to reserves.

The parent could in this circumstance revalue the investment from its cost of £50,000 to £80,000 to show the same figure as that shown in the group. It is necessary, of course, to consider whether the £80,000 is substantiated by the group's remaining share of the underlying value of the undertaking. If it is not, a provision would be required to write it down to the investment's underlying value.

If the entity has adopted FRS 26, the investment should be classified and measured in accordance with that standard (see chapter 6).

Deemed disposals

26.34 An undertaking may also cease to be a subsidiary, or the group may reduce its percentage interest, as a result of a deemed disposal. A deemed disposal may arise, *inter alia*, where:

- The group does not take up its full allocation of rights in a rights issue.
- The group does not take up its full share of a scrip dividend.
- Another party exercises its options or warrants.
- The subsidiary issues shares to other non-group parties (for example, see Table 26.5).

[FRS 2 para 87].

Table 26.5 – Capital and Regional Properties plc – Report and Accounts – 25 December 1993

Notes to the Accounts (extract)

27. Deemed disposal on flotation of CenterPoint

The flotation of CenterPoint on the American Stock Exchange reduced the Group's effective interest in its operations (excluding the additional shares acquired directly by the Group at the flotation) from approximately 60% to 18.8%. The reduction in the Group's effective interest is a deemed disposal within the meaning of Financial Reporting Standard No. 2 and resulted in a loss of £90,000, which has been dealt with as an exceptional item in the profit and loss account:

	£000
Group share of CenterPoint net assets at the date of deemed disposal	12,360
Loss arising on deemed disposal	(90)
Market valuation of shares retained in CenterPoint following flotation (see note 15)	12,270

No goodwill has been dealt with previously in reserves. US operations contributed £652,000 to the Group profit before taxation up to the date of the deemed disposal. The reduction in value of £6,582,000 arising on the US properties up to the deemed disposal is explained in note 13.

26.35 Deemed disposals have the same effect as changes in ownership by disposal and should be accounted for in the same way. Such disposals fall into three categories for accounting purposes:

- Another party subscribes for shares in an undertaking and the parent does not increase its investment (see Table 26.6 and example below).

  This might arise, for example, where another party exercises options or warrants, or it subscribes for rights in a rights issue, but the parent does not. It may also arise where another party subscribes for new shares in the subsidiary.

- Another party subscribes for shares in an undertaking and a proportionally smaller number of shares are subscribed for by the parent (see example in para 26.37).

- Another party subscribes for shares in an undertaking and the parent sells its right to subscribe to a third party (see example in para 26.38).

Table 26.6 – Daily Mail and General Trust plc – Annual Report – 2 October 1994

Notes to the Accounts (extract)

7 Surplus on the Reduction of Interest in Subsidiary

	1994	1993
	£m	£m
	15.9	–

In May 1994, Euromoney Publications raised cash of £23.1 million through a market placing of shares in which the Group could not participate for technical reasons. The Group has reported its share of the increase arising in its net assets as exceptional profit, as required by FRS 2.

Example – Deemed disposal (minority subscribes to further shares)

In January 19X4 a group had a 60% interest in a subsidiary with share capital of 100,000 £1 ordinary shares. The goodwill arising on the acquisition of £40,000 was written off directly to reserves in the year of acquisition prior to FRS 10's introduction. On 31 December 19X4 the 40% minority shareholder exercised an option to subscribe for a further 50,000 £1 ordinary shares in the subsidiary at £12 per share, raising £600,000. The net assets of the subsidiary in the consolidated balance sheet prior to the exercise of the option were £900,000.

Shareholdings	Before		After	
	No	%	No	%
Group	60,000	60	60,000	40
Other party	40,000	40	90,000	60
	100,000	100	150,000	100
Net assets	£'000	%	£'000	%
Group's share	540	60	600	40
Other party's share	360	40	900	60
	900	100	1,500	100

Calculation of group loss on deemed disposal	£'000	£'000
Net assets and proceeds after deemed disposal		
Net assets	600	
Goodwill written off directly to reserves*	27	
Proceeds	–	627
Less: net assets before deemed disposal		
Net assets	540	
Goodwill written off directly to reserves*	40	580
Profit on deemed disposal		47

* A loss of goodwill has been attributed to the deemed disposal, because the minority has in effect bought part of the goodwill in the price it has paid for its

increased stake in the company. The group's interest is now 40% and, provided that the parent exercises significant influence over its former subsidiary, it will be treated as an associate and equity accounted. The goodwill attributable to the interest in the subsidiary was previously written off to reserves when the entity was originally acquired and consolidated. Part of this goodwill, £13,333 (that is £40,000 ÷ 60 × 20) is attributable to the deemed disposal and must be taken to the profit and loss account as part of the profit on sale of £47,000. The remaining goodwill of £26,667 is now attributable to the interest in the entity after the deemed disposal and under equity accounting the remaining goodwill would continue to be written off against reserves.

26.36 An illustration of such a deemed disposal is given in Table 26.1. In that situation, although the group's interest is diluted, a profit arises on the deemed disposal as the dilution took place by a public offer of shares.

26.37 The next example considers a deemed disposal that arises from the parent subscribing for proportionally fewer rights in a rights issue.

Example – Deemed disposal (parent subscriber to proportionately fewer shares)

At the beginning of the year a group had a 55% interest in a subsidiary company. The goodwill arising on the acquisition of £450,000 was written off directly to reserves in the year of acquisition, which was prior to the implementation of FRS 10. The subsidiary's share capital was £2 million (ordinary £1 shares) and its net assets were £10 million immediately prior to the rights issue. During the year the subsidiary made a 1 for 2 rights issue priced at £6 per share. The group exercised its rights to 100,000 shares and neither exercised nor sold its remaining rights. All the minority shareholders exercised their rights.

The group owned 55% of the share capital prior to the rights issue, that is, 1,100,000 shares. As it exercised rights to 100,000 shares it owns 1,200,000 shares after the rights issue.

Shareholdings

The number of shares of the subsidiary in issue following the rights issue was:

2,000,000 + 100,000 + (2,000,000 × 0.45 × ½) = 2,550,000 shares

	Before		After	
	No	%	No	%
Group	1,100,000	55	1,200,000	47
Other party	900,000	45	1,350,000	53
	2,000,000	100	2,550,000	100

Net assets

The net assets of the company post rights issue were:

£10,000,000 + (550,000 × £6) = £13,300,000

	£'000	%	£'000	%
Group's share	5,500	55	6,251	47
Other party's share	4,500	45	7,049	53
	10,000	100	13,300	100

Calculation of group profit on deemed disposal

	£'000	£'000
Net assets and proceeds after deemed disposal		
Net assets	6,251	
Goodwill written off directly to reserves*	385	
Cost of subscribing for rights	(600)	6,036
Less: net assets before deemed disposal		
Net assets	5,500	
Goodwill written off directly to reserves*	450	5,950
Profit on deemed disposal		86

* A loss of goodwill has been attributed to the deemed disposal as the minority have subscribed for their rights issue at full market price. Assuming the voting rights follow the share capital the company would no longer be a subsidiary of the group and would be treated as an associated company and, therefore, equity accounted. The goodwill attributable to the interest in the subsidiary was £450,000 and was previously written off to reserves when the entity was originally acquired and consolidated. Therefore, an adjustment needs to be made for that goodwill figure as a result of the deemed disposal. The group has disposed of an interest of 8% and this equates to goodwill of £65,455 (that is, £450,000 ÷ 55 × 8). This amount is written off to the profit and loss account and included in the net profit on disposal of £86,000. The residual £384,545 of goodwill will remain written off against reserves on equity accounting the retained associate interest of 47%.

26.38 The next example considers the situation where a deemed disposal arises from the sale by the parent of its rights in a rights issue.

Example – Deemed disposal (parent sells rights to rights issue to third party)

At the beginning of the year a group had a 55% interest in a subsidiary company. The goodwill arising on the acquisition of £450,000 was written off directly to reserves in the year of acquisition, which was prior to the implementation of FRS 10. During the year the subsidiary made a 1 for 2 rights issue priced at £6 per ordinary £1 share. The group did not exercise its rights, but sold them to a third party for £200,000. The third party then exercised those rights as did other minority shareholders owning 40% of the remaining 45% of the company's share capital. The rights issue was, therefore, taken up by 95% of the shareholders. The subsidiary's share capital was £2 million (ordinary £1 shares) and its net assets were £10 million immediately prior to the rights issue.

The group owned 55% of the share capital prior to the rights issue, that is, 1,100,000 shares. As it exercised no rights it also owned 1,100,000 shares following the issue.

Shareholdings

The number of shares of the subsidiary in issue following the rights issue was:

$$2{,}000{,}000 + (2{,}000{,}000 \times 0.95 \times \tfrac{1}{2}) = 2{,}950{,}000 \text{ shares}$$

	Before		After	
	No	%	No	%
Group	1,100,000	55	1,100,000	37
Other party	900,000	45	1,850,000	63
	2,000,000	100	2,950,000	100

Net assets

The net assets of the company post rights issue were:

$$£10{,}000{,}000 + (950{,}000 \times £6) = £15{,}700{,}000$$

	£'000	%	£'000	%
Group's share	5,500	55	5,809	37
Other party's share	4,500	45	9,891	63
	10,000	100	15,700	100

Calculation of group profit on deemed disposal

	£'000	£'000
Net assets and proceeds after deemed disposal		
Net assets	5,809	
Goodwill written off directly to reserves*	303	
Proceeds from sale of rights	200	6,312
Less: net assets before deemed disposal		
Net assets	5,500	
Goodwill written off directly to reserves*	450	5,950
Profit on deemed disposal		362

* A loss of goodwill has been attributed to the deemed disposal as the parent's percentage interest has reduced. As with the previous two examples, assuming the voting rights follow the share capital the company would no longer be a subsidiary of the group and would be treated as an associated company and, therefore, equity accounted. The goodwill attributable to the interest in the subsidiary previously written off to reserves was £450,000 when the entity was originally acquired and consolidated. Therefore, an adjustment needs to be made for that goodwill figure as a result of the deemed disposal and the group has in effect disposed of an 18% interest, which equates to goodwill of £147,272 (that is, £450,000 ÷ 55 × 18). This goodwill write off is charged to the profit and loss account as part of the net profit on the deemed disposal of £362,000. The balance of the goodwill will remain written off to reserves on equity accounting the associated interest.

Disclosure requirements

26.39 Where, during the period, an undertaking has ceased to be a subsidiary and this significantly affects the figures shown in the consolidated financial statements, the following should be disclosed in the notes to the financial statements:

- The name of the undertaking that has ceased to be a subsidiary. In the case of a group of undertakings ceasing to be subsidiaries, the name of the parent of that group. [SI 2008/410 6 Sch 15(a); FRS 2 para 48].
- The Act requires disclosure of the extent to which the profit or loss shown in the consolidated profit or loss account is attributable to the undertaking or group that has been disposed of. [SI 2008/410 6 Sch 15(b)]. In addition, FRS 3 requires that the results up to the date of sale should be disclosed as a discontinued operation assuming that the criteria are met. [FRS 3 para 14]. Therefore, if there is only one sale of an undertaking or group of undertakings during a period, the Act's requirement would be fulfilled by the FRS 3 disclosure of discontinued operations. However, if there is more than one undertaking or group disposed of during the year then the profit or loss attributable to each undertaking or group of undertakings disposed of would appear to require to be separately disclosed, as the Act refers to the profit or loss attributable to '*that undertaking or group*'.
- The profit or loss on disposal shown as a non-operating item below operating profit and described as 'Profit or loss on sale of an operation' (see for example para 26.15). [FRS 3 para 20].
- The amount of purchased goodwill (or negative goodwill) attributable to the business disposed of included in the profit or loss on disposal, separately disclosed as a component of the profit or loss on disposal. [FRS 10 para 71(c)(ii)]. Where the item is presented as two components there should be, in addition, a single subtotal showing the total profit or loss on disposal. This disclosure can either be given on the face of the profit and loss account or in a note to the financial statements.

- The amount of any ownership interest retained in any material undertaking that has ceased to be a subsidiary in the period. [FRS 2 para 48].
- Where any material undertaking has ceased to be a subsidiary other than by the disposal of at least part of the interest held by the group, the circumstances should be explained. [FRS 2 paras 48, 49].
- 'Acquisitions and disposals' in the cash flow statement should include receipts from sales of investments in subsidiary undertakings and any balances of cash and overdrafts transferred as part of the sale (shown separately), but this can be in a note. [FRS 1 para 23].
- A note to the cash flow statement should show a summary of the effects of disposals indicating how much of the consideration was made up of cash. [FRS 1 para 45].
- Where the disposal has had a material effect on the amounts reported under each of the standard headings in the cash flow statements (such as operating, capital expenditure and financial investments, financing, etc.), the effect should be disclosed as a note to the cash flow statement. This information can be given by segregating cash flows between continuing and discontinued operations. [FRS 1 para 45]. However, the information need only be given in the period the disposal is made. [FRS 1 para 48].
- Where part of the consideration for the disposal is other than cash (such as, shares), it should be disclosed in the notes to the cash flow statement where this is necessary to fully understand the transaction. [FRS 1 para 46].
- The profit or loss on each material disposal of a previously acquired business or business segment. [FRS 10 para 54].

26.40 The Act provides that where the directors consider that the disclosure required by paragraph 15 of Schedule 6 to SI 2008/410 (bullet points one and two above) would be seriously prejudicial to the business of any undertaking in the group and the subsidiary being sold is established, or carries on business, outside the UK, the information is not required to be given. However, the Secretary of State's permission is required. [SI 2008/410 6 Sch 16]. The Secretary of State's permission would only be given in certain extreme circumstances. For example, his permission might be given not to disclose the name of the subsidiary disposed of where it operates in a politically sensitive country. Although FRS 2 does not appear to extend this exemption to apply to its disclosure requirements, it would seem that it was not the ASB's intention to restrict this exemption and it should, therefore, be assumed that the exemption, if agreed by the Secretary of State for the Companies Act disclosures, also applies to the disclosures required by paragraph 48 of FRS 2 outlined above. It is probably best if the company's letter to the Secretary of State also covers the FRS 2 disclosures that the company proposes not to give.

26.41 In order to give the disclosure required in the third bullet point of paragraph 26.39 and to calculate the total profit or loss arising on a disposal, companies need to maintain detailed records of the cumulative amount of goodwill written off to reserves (net of disposals) and records of the parts of the group to which it relates. In practice, it may be necessary to estimate or apportion goodwill written off to the part of the business being disposed of. However, it is recognised in the Act and FRS 10 that there may be situations where it is not practicable to make a reasonable estimate of the purchased goodwill attributable to the business being disposed of. This situation might arise, for example, where the part of the group being disposed of was acquired many years ago prior to the implementation of FRS 10. In such a situation where it is not possible to ascertain the goodwill that was acquired before 1 January 1989 attributable to the disposal, or to make a reasonable apportionment of the goodwill arising on the acquisition of that part of the business, this fact and the reason should be explained in the financial statements. [FRS 10 para 71(c)].

Chapter 27

Associates, joint ventures and joint undertakings

Chapter 27

Associates, joint ventures and joint undertakings

Introduction

27.1 Equity accounting for associates has stood the test of time with only minor amendments over the years and it was further endorsed by its incorporation into international accounting in November 1988 by the issue of International Accounting Standard (IAS) 28, 'Investments in associates'. This basis of accounting recognises that through the investor's long-term 'significant influence' over its associate it has a measure of direct responsibility for the return on its investment. Furthermore, that basis also recognises that the investor has an interest in its share of the reserves of its associate and is not merely interested in a dividend stream.

27.2 There is a statutory requirement to equity account associated undertakings and most joint ventures. The term 'participating interest' was introduced by the Act and has become integral in determining whether or not an investment is an associated undertaking. A participating interest in an undertaking is necessary before it could be judged to be an associate, however, the legislation still envisages that there could be situations where a participating interest may be held in an undertaking that is not an associated undertaking, although in practice this is rare. Furthermore, it is presumed under the Act, unless otherwise shown, that a participating interest exists where the investing company holds more than 20 per cent of the voting rights in another undertaking.

27.3 FRS 9 was published by the ASB on 27 November 1997. The standard's objective is to reflect the effect on an investor's financial position and performance of its interests in two special kinds of investments – associates and joint ventures – for whose activities it is partly accountable, because of the closeness of its involvement:

- In associates, as a result of its participating interest and significant influence.
- In joint ventures, as a result of its long-term interest and joint control.

[FRS 9 para 1].

The FRS also deals with joint arrangements that do not qualify as associates or joint ventures, because they are not entities.

27.4 Under FRS 9 all associates and joint venture entities are required to be equity accounted. But the distinction between associates and joint ventures is important, because the standard requires a different type of presentation for joint ventures called the 'gross equity method' and separate disclosure for associates and joint ventures. Proportional consolidation does not feature at all in the standard even for shared facilities; instead a new category of investment – a joint arrangement that is not an entity – is introduced. Consequently, it is also necessary to identify these joint arrangements separately from associates and joint ventures, as a new set of accounting requirements apply to them.

27.5 The 'gross equity' method requires the investor's share of joint ventures' turnover to be disclosed (equivalent disclosure for associates is optional). In addition, under the gross equity method the investor's share of joint ventures' gross assets and gross liabilities must be shown on the face of the balance sheet before the investor's share of associates' net assets. Other than these two additional disclosures, the gross equity accounting requirements are identical to those for associates using the normal equity accounting method.

27.6 The investor's share of investees' operating results is required to be included immediately after the group operating result. In addition, the investor's share of super-exceptionals, interest and tax must be separately disclosed.

27.7 Additional disclosures arise where the investor's share in its associates in aggregate (or in its joint ventures in aggregate) exceeds 15 per cent, or individually 25 per cent, of the group's: gross assets; gross liabilities; turnover; or operating results (on a three-year average).

27.8 A new category of investment – joint arrangement that is not an entity – was introduced in FRS 9. An investor in such an entity should account for its own transactions in accordance with the terms of the agreement. Similarly, a participant in a joint venture structure used as a framework within which each participant carries on its own business should also account for its own transactions in accordance with the terms of the agreement.

27.9 This chapter considers in detail the distinction between associates and joint ventures and then from paragraph 27.68 looks at how to account for them. Other joint arrangements and their accounting requirements are considered from paragraph 27.177.

27.10 This chapter does not focus on the disclosure requirements required for these investments. Full details of the disclosure requirements for investments are found at the end of section I of chapter 24.

[The next paragraph is 27.25.]

Scope

27.25 FRS 9's requirements apply to all financial statements that are intended to give a true and fair view of the reporting entity's financial position and profit or loss (or income and expenditure) for the period. [FRS 9 para 2].

27.26 The FRS states that entities entitled to report under the Financial Reporting Standard for Smaller Entities (FRSSE) are exempt from the standard's requirements, unless they prepare consolidated financial statements. It then goes on to state that, where the entity does prepare consolidated financial statements, it should apply the accounting standard that is required to be used by the FRSSE currently in issue. [FRS 9 para 3].

Investment funds

27.27 For a number of years prior to FRS 9's introduction, problems had arisen in the venture capital industry, where companies often invest in high risk start-up ventures and look for capital growth rather than an income return. As a consequence, the industry views valuation information as relevant and equity accounting as irrelevant. This issue led to a number of companies in that sector adopting the Act's true and fair override in order not to equity account such investments, which was a requirement of both the Act and SSAP 1. Following consultation with the Association of Investment Trust Companies (AITC) and others, the ASB accepted that in such entities, whilst the interests held by the investor and the rights attaching to those interests vary according to particular circumstances, the investor's relationship to its investment tends to be that of a portfolio investor. [FRS 9 para 50]. The standard requires that, in these circumstances, the stake is properly accounted for as an investment using the same accounting policy as that applied to other investments in the entity's investment portfolio, rather than accounting for the interests as associates or joint ventures. This applies even where the investor has significant influence or joint control. [FRS 9 paras 49, 50].

27.28 The standard explains that:

> *"Investments are held as part of an investment portfolio if their value to the investor is through their marketable value as part of a basket of investments rather than as media through which the investor carries out its business".* [FRS 9 para 49].

Consequently, investments of this nature are specifically exempted from FRS 9's requirements to equity account associates and joint ventures. However, it does appear that such investments might still fall to be treated as associates under the Act. This will depend on whether or not the investor has significant influence. Significant influence is defined in FRS 9 and this definition applies also to associated undertakings under the Act. The investor will exercise significant influence if it is actively involved and influential in the direction of its investee. In those situations where a company adopts FRS 9's relaxation in respect of its associates and joint ventures included in its investment portfolio, if the investor still exercises significant influence over those undertakings, it should recognise a departure from the Act by giving the particulars, reasons and effect as required by the Act and FRS 18, 'Accounting policies'. The reason should include the fact that FRS 9 specifies the accounting treatment to be adopted.

27.29 Investment companies might also have investments that should be treated as joint ventures and associates that are held outside their investment portfolio.

Such joint ventures and associates often carry on businesses which are similar or complementary to those of the investor. In these circumstances, the provisions of FRS 9 should be applied and such joint ventures and associates should be equity accounted in accordance with the normal rules as explained below.

Classification as associates and joint ventures

27.30 As mentioned above, equity accounting applies to both associates and joint venture entities. However, under FRS 9 joint venture entities must give slightly more information using the 'gross equity method' of accounting than associates. Therefore, the distinctions between the two types of arrangement are important and the paragraphs below explain the definitions that apply in determining whether an investment is an associate or a joint venture entity.

Definition of associate

27.31 The term associate is defined in both the Companies Act and in FRS 9. The Act's definition hinges on the investing company having a participating interest and exercising significant influence. Under the legislation a participating interest is presumed to exist where the investing company holds more than 20 per cent of the voting rights in the other undertaking. This presumption is rebutted under FRS 9, which sets out a more stringent test to determine whether there is a participating interest. But where the Act's presumptions are rebutted the investor should explain the facts in the financial statements (see para 27.106 below).

27.32 An 'associated undertaking' is defined in the Act in the following terms:

> "... *an undertaking in which an undertaking included in the consolidation has a participating interest and over whose operating and financial policy it exercises a significant influence, and which is not—*
>
> *(a) a subsidiary undertaking of the parent company, or*
>
> *(b) a joint venture dealt with in accordance with paragraph 18.*"

[SI 2008/410 6 Sch 19(1)].

27.33 'Participating interest' is defined in paragraph 11 of Schedule 10 to SI 2008/410, 'The Large and Medium-sized Companies and Groups (Accounts and Reports) Regulations 2008 to mean "... *an interest held by an undertaking in the shares of another undertaking which it holds on a long-term basis for the purpose of securing a contribution to its activities by the exercise of control or influence arising from or related to that interest*".

27.34 The meaning of 'shares' in the definition is explained in section 1161(2) of the Act. For this purpose, references to shares in relation to:

- An undertaking with a share capital, are to allotted shares.
- An undertaking with capital in a form other than share capital, are to rights to share in the capital of the undertaking.
- An undertaking without capital, are to interests:
  - conferring any right to share in the profits or the liability to contribute to the losses of the undertaking; or
  - giving rise to an obligation to contribute to the debts or expenses of the undertaking in the event of a winding up.

[CA06 Sec 1161(2)].

27.35 In addition, it is quite clear under the Act that a participating interest includes an option to acquire shares or any interest that is convertible into shares. [SI 2008/410 10 Sch 11(3)]. For this purpose, it does not matter whether the options can be exercised now or in the future, their mere existence is taken into account whether or not they are currently exercisable. An interest or option in shares falls within this definition even if the share to which it relates, until conversion or the exercise of the option, is unissued. [SI 2008/410 10 Sch 11(3)]. In addition, interests held on behalf of an undertaking should be treated as held by it. [SI 2008/410 10 Sch 11(4)].

[The next paragraph is 27.37.]

27.37 The definition of 'associated undertakings' in the Act is consistent with that given in FRS 9 for an associate. The definition in FRS 9 is also expressed making reference to the need for both a participating interest and the exercise of significant influence as follows:

> *"An entity (other than a subsidiary) in which another entity (the investor) has a participating interest and over whose operating and financial policies the investor exercises a significant influence."* [FRS 9 para 4].

27.38 Therefore, it is essential to have both a participating interest and be able to exercise significant influence and these two terms are also defined in the standard. A participating interest is:

> *"An interest held in the shares of another entity on a long-term basis for the purpose of securing a contribution to the investor's activities by the exercise of control or influence arising from or related to that interest. The investor's interest must, therefore, be a beneficial one and the benefits expected to arise must be linked to the exercise of its significant influence over the investee's operating and financial policies. An interest in the shares of another entity includes an interest convertible into an interest in shares or an option to acquire shares."* [FRS 9 para 4].

The term 'shares' in the definition has the same meaning as explained in paragraph 27.34 above.

27.39 As mentioned above, the Act presumes there is a participating interest where the investor holds 20 per cent or more of the shares in the undertaking. However, whilst both the Act and FRS 9 require the interest to be for the long term, FRS 9 introduced a very restrictive interpretation of the meaning of 'long-term'. Under FRS 9, an interest held on a long-term basis is one that is *not* 'held exclusively with a view to subsequent resale' and the latter term is defined in the standard as: "*... (a) an interest for which a purchaser has been identified or is being sought, and which is reasonably expected to be disposed of within approximately one year of its date of acquisition; or (b) an interest that was acquired as a result of the enforcement of a security, unless the interest has become part of the continuing activities of the group or the holder acts as if it intends the interest to become so*". [FRS 9 para 4]. Table 27.1 includes an example of an associate which is held for resale. The standard comments that 'enforcement of a security' should be interpreted to include other arrangements that, in substance, have the same effect.

Table 27.1— Granada Group PLC — Annual Report & Accounts — 27 September 1997

Notes to the Accounts (extract)

12 Investments

The investment in Savoy comprises 69.7% of the 'A' shares and 12.6% of the 'B' shares, representing 68.4% of the equity of Savoy and 42.1% of the voting rights. During the period Savoy was accounted for as an investment as it is not the Group's intention to hold this investment for the long term. As at 31 December 1996, Savoy had share capital and reserves amounting to £372.1 million and the loss for the financial year then ended amounted to £26.8 million.

27.40 The effect of the requirement for the investment to be for the long term on short-term property development investments, which might run for (say) up to 18 months, is considered in paragraph 27.185.

27.41 The 20 per cent presumption in the Act is also rebutted where the interest is a non-beneficial one. In judging whether an interest is, or is not, a beneficial one, dividends are not the only way that a beneficial interest might be enjoyed. There may be other ways of extracting benefits, for example, through a management contract with a fee that is based on performance, which would make the receiver of the fee more than just a manager.

27.42 The other essential element to the definition of an associate is that the investor must exercise a 'significant influence' over the entity's financial and operating policies for there to be an associate relationship. The Act similarly presumes that the investor will have significant influence where the investor holds more than 20 per cent of the voting rights in the undertaking. [SI 2008/410 6 Sch 19(2)]. Whilst the Act does not define 'significant influence' FRS 9 does. The definition of 'significant influence' in FRS 9 is as follows:

> *'The investor is actively involved and is influential in the direction of its investee through its participation in policy decisions covering aspects of*

policy relevant to the investor, including decisions on strategic issues such as:

(a) the expansion or contraction of the business, participation in other entities or changes in products, markets and activities of its investee; and

(b) determining the balance between dividend and reinvestment.'

[FRS 9 para 4].

27.43 It is often difficult in practice to determine whether there is an associate relationship with an undertaking. FRS 9 indicates that significant influence over a company essentially involves participation in the financial and operating policy decisions of that company. It mentions that for significant influence to exist it must generally have a substantial basis of voting power and a holding of 20 per cent of more of the voting rights does not in itself ensure this level of influence. [FRS 9 para 16]. That is, even where the investing group holds more than 20 per cent of the voting rights it might not have significant influence. This situation could also arise where one or more other large shareholders could prevent the group exercising 'significant influence'. This might arise, for example, where the investor holds 25 per cent of the shares, but another entity holds the remaining 75 per cent (see for example Table 27.2). On the other hand, FRS 9 also confirms that it is not necessary to control those policies for an associate relationship to exist (otherwise the investment would be a subsidiary). In order to gain the level of influence necessary, representation on the board of directors (or its equivalent for unincorporated entities) is essential in most circumstances, unless it is clear that there are other arrangements in place that would allow the investor to participate effectively in policy-making decisions. [FRS 9 para 16].

Table 27.2 – Delancey Estates plc – Annual Report & Accounts – 31 March 1999

Notes to the Accounts (extract)

Participating interests

In accordance with the Companies Act 1985, Centrols Properties Limited (CPL) (a company in which Delancey Estates plc has a 37.5% interest) is described as a participating interest. As Delancey Estates plc does not participate in the commercial or financial policy decisions, and has no board representation, CPL is not regarded as an associated undertaking and is therefore included within the group balance sheet at cost and not equity value. The latest reported profit before tax of CPL was £219,721 and the net liabilities were £83,348. CPL is registered in England, which is also the main country of operation.

27.44 In order to obtain significant influence, the investor needs an agreement or understanding, formal or informal, with its associate to provide the basis for its significant influence. The investor must be actively involved in the operating and financial policy decisions – a passive role is clearly not sufficient. The type of relationship that is necessary is one whereby the investor uses its associate as a medium through which it conducts a part of its activities, although it is not envisaged that the associate need be in the same business as the investor. The associate's policies over time should accord with (and not be contrary to) the investor's strategy. Consequently, if an investee persistently implements policies that are inconsistent with its investor's strategy, no associate relationship exists. [FRS 9 para 14].

27.45 Significant influence means that the investor must be involved in strategic decisions, for example, determining the balance between dividend and reinvestment. Furthermore, the investor should not only be interested in maximising the payment of dividends, but should also be concerned that the entity's future cash flows are compatible with the investor's objective of reinvestment. The investor's participation in policy decisions should be with a view to gaining economic benefits from the entity's activities, but this involvement should also expose the investor to the risk that those activities might be loss-making. [FRS 9 para 15].

Example

A group has a 30% investment in a company at the beginning of the year. It has previously been treated as an associated company in the group's financial statements. Another shareholder increases his shareholding in the company during the year from 40% to 60%. The group no longer wishes to treat its investment in the undertaking as an associate.

As explained above, where the investment in another undertaking is greater than 20%, it will not be presumed that the undertaking is an associate. In this situation, if the group can demonstrate that it no longer has a significant influence over the undertaking then it may be necessary to treat the investment as a trade investment rather than as an associate.

27.46 A practical problem arises in judging the amount of influence the investor has over its investment where the investment has only just been made. In these circumstances the actual relationship usually becomes clear fairly soon after an investment is acquired. In the intervening period the number of board members the investor may nominate and the proposed decision-taking process may be used to evaluate the relationship before its record is established. [FRS 9 para 17]. If the actual relationship were to develop differently from that assumed from the arrangements on acquisition, it would be necessary subsequently to change the way in which the investment is accounted. For example, if it looked at the outset as if the entity were an associate, then it would have been equity accounted in the first financial statements produced post acquisition. If subsequently it was judged that this analysis did not prove to be correct in practice, then it would be necessary to treat the interest in the entity as an investment. This might, therefore, indicate that there was a fundamental error in accounting for the investment as an associate in the previous year and require a prior year adjustment. However, in practice, this is only likely to arise when the investment is made close to the investor's year end, in which case the profits brought in in error would be small.

27.47 Where an investing group ceases to exercise significant influence over an investment treated as an associate, it will be necessary to change the accounting treatment. In the case of British Telecommunications plc, a 20 per cent investment in MCI was treated as an associate from the date of acquisition in 1994. The subsequent proposed merger of MCI with WorldCom led British Telecommunications plc to change the treatment and to account for its interest in MCI as an investment (see Table 27.3 below).

Table 27.3 – British Telecommunications plc – Annual Report and Accounts – 31 March 1998

Notes to the accounts

Fixed asset investment (extract)

(b) MCI Communications Corporation

In September 1994, the company completed the acquisition of a 20% equity interest in MCI (the second largest carrier of long distance telecommunications services in the USA) represented by a holding of 136 million Class A common shares, whereupon MCI became the group's most significant associated undertaking. On 3 November 1996, the company entered into a merger agreement with MCI whereby the group would acquire the entire share capital of MCI, not already owned. On 21 August 1997, the terms of the merger agreement were modified. On 1 October 1997, WorldCom announced its intention to offer shares in its company to MCI shareholders as an alternative to the proposed merger and, following an improved offer from WorldCom on 9 November 1997, the company agreed that it would support the proposed merger with WorldCom to which the MCI board had agreed on the same day. On 11 March 1998, both MCI's and WorldCom's shareholders approved their merger.

The company has agreed with WorldCom and MCI to sell the group's holding of 136 million unlisted Class A common shares in MCI to WorldCom for US$51 per share in cash at the time the MCI/WorldCom merger is completed. The potential consideration of US$6,936m was equivalent to £4,137m, at the exchange rate ruling on 31 March 1998. The completion of the merger is subject to regulatory clearance. The group also holds 0.7 million listed common shares in MCI, most of which were purchased in November 1995. These shares will be exchanged for WorldCom common shares on completion of the merger. If fully listed, the market value of the MCI shares held by the group at 31 March 1998 would have been £4,048m.

As a consequence of the termination of the company's merger agreement with MCI and the company's agreement with WorldCom and MCI, the group ceased treating MCI as an associate from 1 November 1997. The group's share of its associates' results includes a loss before tax of £27m for its share of MCI's results up to that date (1997 — £175m profit, 1996 — £101m profit).

At 31 March 1998, the group's investment in MCI is stated at £813m (1997 — £834m). Goodwill amounting to £2,214m has been written off to group reserves in prior years in respect of this investment and this goodwill will be accounted for at the completion of the MCI/WorldCom merger in determining the profit on the sale of the shares which the group will recognise.

In the period 1 April 1997 to 31 October 1997, the group's turnover with MCI amounted to £108m (1997 — £134m, 1996 — £92m) and the group purchased £56m in the same period (1997 — £87m, 1996 — £77m) in services and products from MCI.

27.48 Furthermore, where an investing group treats an undertaking as an associate where it controls less than 20 per cent of the votes, it is important to ensure that it can clearly demonstrate that it has significant influence. But it is undoubtedly possible under FRS 9's definitions for significant influence to exist where the investing group controls less than 20 per cent of the voting shares.

27.49 An associate relationship can also arise where a company was initially legally a subsidiary of its investor, but the investor no longer controls or has the power to exercise dominant influence or control over the operating and financial policies of the undertaking. This could occur, for example, where the investor's interest is 40 per cent, but it previously had call options over a further 20 per cent that could be exercised at any time. The existence of the options gave the company the power to exercise control but, when the options lapsed, this power fell away and the company was no longer a subsidiary of the investor. Although there is no change in the shareholding, the investor's influence has reduced and it now exerts only significant influence and the investment is, therefore, an associate.

Treatment of voting rights

27.50 The Act gives a significant amount of guidance on when to take into account voting rights in order to determine whether an associate relationship exists between two undertakings. The paragraphs that follow summarise the guidance given in the Act.

27.51 For the purposes of the definition of an associated undertaking, 'voting rights in the undertaking' means the rights conferred on the shareholders in respect of their shares to vote at general meetings of the undertaking on all, or substantially all, matters. It can also mean, in a situation where the undertaking has no share capital, any other rights conferred on members to vote at the undertaking's general meetings on all, or substantially all, matters. [SI 2008/410 6 Sch 19(3)].

27.52 Voting rights should not be treated as held by a person (which includes an undertaking) if they are held in a fiduciary capacity. [SI 2008/410 6 Sch 19(4); CA06 7 Sch 6]. Similarly, voting rights held by a person as nominee should not be treated as held by him. Such voting rights will be considered held 'as nominee' if they can only be exercised on the instructions or with the consent of another person. [SI 2008/410 6 Sch 19(4); CA06 7 Sch 7(2)]. It is not possible to treat voting rights held by a parent undertaking as held by a subsidiary by using nominee holdings. [SI 2008/410 6 Sch 19(4); CA06 7 Sch 9(2)].

27.53 Voting rights that are attached to shares held as security shall be treated as held by the person providing the security where those voting rights (excluding any right to exercise them to preserve the value of the security, or to realise it) are only exercisable in accordance with his instructions. This rule applies where the shares are held in connection with granting loans in the normal course of business and the rights are exercised only in the interest of the person providing the security. [SI 2008/410 6 Sch 19(4); CA06 7 Sch 8]. This provision cannot be used to require voting rights held by a parent to be treated as held by any of its subsidiaries. [SI 2008/410 6 Sch 19(4); CA06 7 Sch 9(2)]. Furthermore, voting rights should be treated as being exercisable in accordance with the instructions of, or in the interests of, an undertaking if they are exercisable in accordance with the instructions of, or in the interests of, any group undertaking. [SI 2008/410 6 Sch 19(4); CA06 7 Sch 9(3)].

27.54 The voting rights in an undertaking have also to be reduced by any voting rights held by the undertaking itself. [SI 2008/410 6 Sch 19(4); CA06 7 Sch 10].

Definition of joint venture entities

27.55 Although joint ventures are required under FRS 9 to be equity accounted, the level of detail that investors in joint ventures are required to give in their consolidated financial statements is greater than for investments in associates. Therefore, it is important that investors categorise their investments correctly between those in associates and those in joint ventures. FRS 9 makes a distinction between joint venture entities and joint arrangements that are not entities. Joint arrangements that are not entities are not equity accounted and their accounting requirements and how to distinguish them from other forms of joint venture are considered from paragraph 27.177.

27.56 Particular care needs to be taken in assessing whether an undertaking is a joint venture entity or a joint arrangement (under FRS 9), or a subsidiary undertaking (under FRS 2), or a quasi-subsidiary (under FRS 5). An FRRP ruling in February 1995 concerned joint ventures which were determined to be quasi-subsidiaries. The implications of this case for joint ventures and joint arrangements are considered from paragraph 27.205. The paragraphs that follow look at the definitions found within both the Act and FRS 9 concerning joint ventures.

27.57 Under the Act, paragraph 18(1) to SI 2008/410 refers to a joint venture arising in a situation where an *undertaking* manages another undertaking jointly with one or more other undertakings that are not included in the consolidation. Consequently, the Act places emphasis on the undertaking's *joint management*. But the Act's provisions concerning joint ventures do not apply if the joint venture undertaking is a limited company, as proportional consolidation for joint ventures is only allowed for unincorporated undertakings under the Act. Also, the Act's provisions concerning joint ventures do not apply where the undertaking is a subsidiary for consolidation purposes under the definitions in the Act (see further chapter 24). [SI 2008/410 6 Sch 18(1)].

27.58 FRS 9 defines a joint venture in the following terms:

> *"An entity in which the reporting entity holds an interest on a long-term basis and is jointly controlled by the reporting entity and one or more other venturers under a contractual arrangement."* [FRS 9 para 4].

27.59 As can be seen from the definition, the interest must be held on a long-term basis and this is to be judged in the same way as for associates (see para 27.39 above). The definition also hinges on the term 'joint control' which is defined in FRS 9 as follows:

> *"A reporting entity jointly controls a venture with one or more other entities if none of the entities alone can control that entity but all together can do so and decisions on financial and operating policy essential to the activities, economic performance and financial position of that venture require each venturer's consent."* [FRS 9 para 4].

27.60 This definition can be contrasted with 'control', which was originally defined in FRS 2 and is repeated in FRS 9 as:

> *"The ability of an entity to direct the operating and financial policies of another entity with a view to gaining economic benefits from its activities."* [FRS 9 para 4].

27.61 Although to be treated as a joint venture partner the investor must have joint control with its other investors, the standard envisages the situation whereby *one* of the parties to a joint venture might not share control with the other joint venturers. In this type of situation, the investor that does not share control would account for its interest as an investment. [FRS 9 para 10]. The other venturers would gross equity account for their interests in accordance with the standard.

27.62 The standard explains that in a true joint venture the venturers exercise their joint control for their mutual benefit, each conducting its part of the contractual arrangement with a view to its own benefit. The venturers must play an active role in setting the operating and financial policies of the joint venture. However, their involvement can be at quite a high level, for example, setting the general strategy of the venture. [FRS 9 para 11]. But their interest should not necessarily only occur at the outset of a venture, for example, in setting the general policies to be included within a partnership agreement. If this were to be the case, then the financial and operating policies might be predetermined, in which case the entity could be a joint arrangement or a quasi-subsidiary (see further para 27.205).

27.63 It seems clear from the definition that it is quite possible to have a joint venture between investors where the venturers do not have equal shares in the entity, as long as they control the entity jointly together. For example, it would be possible to have an arrangement whereby the investors' interests were 30:35:35 or 25:35:40. But there must be joint control including the ability for one party to veto the wishes of the other parties. For example, the 25 per cent shareholder would have to have the ability to veto the financial and operating policies being advocated by the other two venturers owning 75 per cent of the shares. In this type of situation, one of the parties might manage the venture under a management agreement and, in this circumstance, it is important to establish clearly that the veto can be applied in practice.

27.63.1 An example of a joint venture where shareholdings are not equal is shown in Table 27.4.

Table 27.4 – Galliford Try plc – Annual Report & Accounts – 30 June 2003

Notes to the accounts (extract)

12 Investments (extract)

During the year the Group invested £120,000 in shares and loans in Oak Fire Protection Limited representing a 70% investment. Under the terms of the shareholders' agreement, the investment has been treated as a joint venture.

27.64 The standard also does not preclude a venturer from managing the joint venture provided that the venture's principal operating and financial policies are collectively agreed by the venturers and the venturers have the power to ensure that those policies are followed. [FRS 9 para 11]. This is often the case in the venture capital industry, where it is common for the venture capitalist investor to have an interest in the joint venture, but also to manage the venture *via* a separate management agreement.

27.65 The standard also points out that in some cases an investor may qualify as the parent of an entity under the definition of a subsidiary in the Act and FRS 2, but contractual arrangements with the other shareholder mean that in practice the shareholders have joint control over their investee. [FRS 9 para 11]. For example, a company might control over 50 per cent of the entity's voting rights, but the joint venture agreement might significantly restrict this control. It could, for example, require unanimous agreement between the venturers before it could: pay a dividend; change direction of the company's business; incur capital expenditure over a specified level; pay its directors and other employees; change other major operating and financial policies, etc. In this type of situation, the interests of the minority shareholder (the other joint venture partner) would amount to 'severe long-term restrictions' that would substantially hinder the exercise of the parent's rights over the assets or management of its legal subsidiary. In such cases, following from the requirements in FRS 2, the standard requires that the subsidiary should not be consolidated, but should instead be treated as a joint venture and be gross equity accounted. [FRS 9 para 11]. However, this type of situation is unlikely to arise frequently in practice, because even where there is such a shareholders' agreement, unless it does impose a significant restriction (which it will not if the agreement means the subsidiary follows the parent's wishes) it will remain a subsidiary.

27.66 Joint control of high-level strategic decisions will entail each venturer having a veto on those decisions. Such a veto distinguishes a joint venturer from a minority shareholder in a company, because the latter has no veto and, consequently, is subject to majority rule. [FRS 9 para 12]. It is the practical application of this which is important and, hence, it is not necessary that the consent to strategic decisions is set out in the joint venture agreement, although in many instances this will be the case in practice. One indication that the arrangement might be a joint venture is where the joint venture agreement sets out arbitration procedures in the event the parties to the venture cannot agree.

27.67 IAS 31, 'Interests in joint ventures', defines a joint venture in similar terms to those used in FRS 9: *"a contractual arrangement whereby two or more parties undertake an economic activity that is subject to joint control"* Joint control is *"the contractually agreed sharing of control over an economic activity, and exists only when the strategic financial and operating decisions relating to the activity require the unanimous consent of the parties sharing control (the venturers)"*. [IAS 31 para 3]. IAS 31 comments that it is this contractual arrangement that distinguishes a joint venture from an associate and without a contractual arrangement to establish joint control a joint venture does not exist. Such a contractual arrangement can be evidenced in a number of ways, for example, by: contract; minutes of discussions between the venturers; or incorporation in the joint venture's articles or other by-laws. The matters that such an agreement might deal with are:

- The joint venture's activity, duration and reporting obligations.
- The appointment of the joint venture's board of directors or equivalent governing body and the voting rights of the venturers.
- Capital contributions by the venturers.
- The sharing by the venturers of the joint venture's output, income, expenses and results.

[IAS 31 para 10].

Equity method of accounting

Introduction

27.68 FRS 9 specifies that equity accounting is the method that should be used to reflect investors' interests in both associates and joint ventures. The form of presentation under this method has been extended for joint ventures and this is referred to in FRS 9 as the 'gross equity method'. The requirements for equity accounting differ from the form of equity accounting required by IAS 28, 'Investments in associates'. The Act also stipulates that associated undertakings should be accounted for by the 'equity method' of accounting, but leaves it to the accounting standard to specify what this method entails. [SI 2008/410 6 Sch 21(1)].

27.69 There is now an extensive definition in FRS 9 which explains what the equity method of accounting involves. It describes the equity method as:

> *"A method of accounting that brings an investment into its investor's financial statements initially at its cost, identifying any goodwill arising. The carrying amount of the investment is adjusted in each period by the investor's share of the results of its investee less any amortisation or write-off for goodwill, the investor's share of any relevant gains or losses, and any other changes in the investee's net assets including distributions to its owners, for example by dividend. The investor's share of its investee's results is recognised in its profit and loss account. The investor's cash flow statement includes the cash flows between the investor and its investee, for example relating to dividends and loans."* [FRS 9 para 4].

27.70 The 'gross equity method' is identical in most respects with the normal equity method, but it requires in addition that the investor's share of the aggregate gross assets and liabilities underlying the net equity investment be shown on the face of the balance sheet [FRS 9 para 4]. Consequently, it is not adequate to disclose this information in the notes to the consolidated financial statements. In addition, in the profit and loss account, the investor's share of the investee's turnover has to be given. [FRS 9 para 4].

27.71 The disclosures required for both the equity method and the gross equity method have to be given separately. The information relating to the investor's share in its joint ventures must be given separately and before that relating to its share in its associates.

Profit and loss account

27.72 Under FRS 9's requirements, there are a number of line items in the profit and loss account for which the investor's share of its joint ventures' and its associates' results have to be included and disclosed. The requirements cover primarily:

- Turnover (but optional disclosure for associates).
- Operating profit.
- Super-exceptional items as specified in paragraph 20 of FRS 3.
- Interest.
- Taxation.

Turnover

27.73 As explained above, the gross equity method requires that the investor's share of turnover for joint ventures must be shown. [FRS 9 para 21]. Equivalent disclosure for associates is not required, but may be given where it is helpful to give an indication of the size of the business as a whole. [FRS 9 para 27]. The standard specifically states that joint ventures' and associates' turnover cannot be shown as part of group turnover, because the Act requires turnover to be disclosed excluding amounts attributable to associates and joint ventures. [CA06 Sec 539]. So it is important that the turnover is shown in such a way that the group turnover excluding joint ventures and associates is clearly disclosed. Table 27.5 shows how this can be done.

Table 27.5 — Tate & Lyle Public Limited Company — Annual Report — 25 March 2000

GROUP PROFIT AND LOSS ACCOUNT **(extract)**

For the 78 weeks to 25 March 2000

Profit and Loss Account (extract)	2000 £ million	1999 £ million
Sales	**6183**	4467
Less share of sales of		
— joint ventures	**(491)**	(310)
— associates	**(46)**	(40)
Group sales	**5646**	4117

27.74 In addition, in the segmental analysis required by SSAP 25, the joint ventures' turnover (and associates' turnover where disclosed voluntarily) should be distinguished clearly from that of the group. [FRS 9 para 21, 27]. Segmental reporting is dealt with in chapter 10.

Operating results

27.75 The share of operating results of joint ventures and associates must be included *immediately* after the group's operating result. [FRS 9 paras 21, 27].

27.76 Unlike goodwill arising on an acquisition of a subsidiary, there is nothing in the Companies Act that specifies where goodwill arising on the acquisition of an interest in a joint venture or an associate should be amortised in the profit and loss account. As a consequence, the ASB has determined in FRS 9 that any amortisation or write-down of goodwill (that arose on the acquisition of a joint venture or an associate) should be charged at the same point as the share of operating results of associates and joint ventures. [FRS 9 para 21, 27]. This would seem to allow any amortisation or write-down of goodwill to be aggregated with the share of operating results on the face of the profit and loss account as a single item. But where this is done, the goodwill amortised or written off must be separately disclosed in the notes to the financial statements.

Super-exceptional items

27.77 The investor's share of joint ventures' and associates' super-exceptional items appearing after operating profit must be shown with the group's super-exceptionals, but separately from them. [FRS 9 paras 21, 27]. The super-exceptional items specified in FRS 3 are known as 'paragraph 20 items' and cover:

- Profits or losses on the sale or termination of an operation.
- Costs of a fundamental reorganisation or restructuring having a material effect on the nature and focus of the reporting entity's operations.
- Profits or losses on the disposal of fixed assets.

Other line items

27.78 The standard also specifies that the investor's share of joint ventures' and associates' interest must be shown separately from the amounts of the group. [FRS 9 para 21, 27]. In addition, for the line items that appear in the Act's formats at and below the level of profit before tax, the standard specifies that the investor's share of its joint ventures' and associates' equivalent line items must be included within the amounts for the group. This would include, for example, the investor's share of its joint ventures' and associates' taxation. Although the standard says that these amounts should be included with those of the group, it still requires separate disclosure of the investor's share of each such item for its joint ventures and its associates.

How the Act's requirements are satisfied

27.79 In addition to FRS 9's requirements, the Act indicates the position in the profit and loss account formats where associated undertakings (which includes joint venture entities) should be dealt with. In the profit and loss account formats shown in Schedule 1 to SI 2008/410, for the purposes of consolidated financial statements, the item 'income from shares in related companies' is replaced by 'income from interests in associated undertakings' and 'income from other participating interests'. [SI 2008/410 6 Sch 20(3)]. Although the position is specified in the formats, companies can draw their operating profit line before 'income from interests in associated undertakings'. This is because the formats do not contain a line item for operating profit. However, as can be seen from the explanation above, FRS 9 requires the line item in the Act to be split between share of: operating result (which must be shown immediately after the group's operating profit or loss); three super-exceptional items; interest; taxation and any further line items below profit before tax. There is nothing in the standard that explains how this anomaly is overcome, but appendix IV example 1 explains that the amounts shown for associates and joint ventures are subdivisions of the item for which the statutory prescribed heading is 'Income from interests in associated undertakings'. Paragraph 3(1) of Schedule 1 to SI 2008/410 allows format line items to be shown in greater detail than required by the profit and loss account format adopted and there is nothing in the legislation that specifies that such additional analysis needs to be summed to show the total for the particular line item required by the formats.

Ability to aggregate and relegate to the notes

27.80 It is not at all clear from the standard which elements of the disclosures considered above have to be shown on the face of the profit and loss account and which can be relegated to the notes. The only help on this issue is again given in appendix IV example 1 which notes that subdivisions for which the statutory prescribed heading is 'Income from interests in associated undertakings' may be shown in a note rather than on the face of the profit and loss account. This seems to imply that all the disclosures specified above can be relegated to the notes and yet the example in FRS 9 that directly follows the note shows each of the required disclosures with the exception of taxation on the face of the profit and loss account (albeit the example does not include any super-exceptional items). In addition, all of these disclosures show the share of joint ventures' and associates' results separately on the face of the profit and loss account, which for many groups would be impracticable because of printing space constraints. To further compound the issue, the Act requires that 'Income from interests in associated undertakings' in the formats should be treated as if it is preceded by an Arabic numeral. Under the format rules, which are discussed in chapter 4, items preceded by an Arabic numeral can be relegated to the notes.

27.81 We, therefore, suggest the following practical solution to the issues raised above:

- The share of joint ventures' turnover should be shown separately from that of the group on the face of the profit and loss account in order to comply with the Act's requirements (as explained in para 27.73 above). It is also possible, however, to show a total figure for turnover including joint ventures, as long as joint ventures' turnover and the group's turnover excluding that of its joint ventures is clearly shown.
- Where the share of associates' turnover is disclosed voluntarily, it should be shown on the face of the profit and loss account, but may be combined with that of joint ventures, but must be separately analysed in the notes. It is also possible to give a total for the group's turnover including both joint ventures and associates as long as the group's turnover excluding that of its associates and joint ventures is clearly shown.
- Share of operating results of joint ventures and associates should be shown on the face of the profit and loss account, but may be combined in a single line item 'share of joint ventures and associates operating profit' as long as they are shown separately in the notes, with the share of joint ventures' operating results shown first.
- Amortisation or the write-down of goodwill arising on the acquisition of joint ventures or associates should be included within 'share of joint ventures and associates operating profit'. There should be separate disclosure of this item in the notes.
- Share of each super-exceptional item of joint ventures and associates should be shown separately on the face of the profit and loss account below any super-exceptional items of the group. (Immaterial amounts should be aggregated with the share of their operating results.) For each super-exceptional item, the investor's share of joint ventures' and associates' figures may be combined in a single line item suitably styled on the face of

the profit and loss account, but should be shown separately in the notes, with the joint ventures' share shown first.

- Share of interest and format line items below the level of profit before tax should be included within the amounts shown on the face of the profit and loss account for the group. The share should then be separately disclosed in the notes, with the share of joint ventures' items shown first.
- In addition, the share of results of associates and joint ventures has to be analysed between continuing activities (including acquisitions) and discontinued activities as required by FRS 3 (see further chapter 8).

Illustrative example

27.82 An illustration of this type of disclosure is given below:

Consolidated profit and loss account

	Notes	Continuing operations £m	Acquisitions £m	Total £m	Discontinued operations £m	Total £m
Turnover including share of joint ventures and associates		250	50	300	20	320
Less: Share of joint ventures and associates turnover	1	105	10	115	5	120
Group turnover		145	40	185	15	200
Cost of sales		89	23	112	8	120
Gross profit		56	17	73	7	80
Administrative expenses		28	4	32	8	40
Group operating profit (loss)		28	13	41	(1)	40
Share of operating profit of joint ventures and associates	2	52	3	55	(1)	54
Operating profit including joint ventures and associates		80	16	96	(2)	94
Sale of operations:						
Group					20	20
Joint ventures and associates	3				(15)	(15)
		–	–	–	5	5

Profit on ordinary activities before interest		80	16	96	3	99
Interest						(42)
Profit on ordinary activities before tax	5					57
Tax on profit on ordinary activities						12
Profit on ordinary activities after tax						45
Minority interests						6
Profit for the financial year						39
Equity dividends						10
Retained profit for the year						29

The notes to the financial statements would analyse the line items above to give the disclosures required by the standard as follows:

1 Turnover (extract)

	Continuing operations £m	Acquisitions £m	Total £m	Discontinued operations £m	Total £m
Share of joint ventures' turnover	30	10	40	–	40
Share of associates' turnover	75	–	75	5	80
	105	10	115	5	120

2 Operating profit(extract)

Share of joint ventures' operating profit	27	3	30	–	30
Share of associates' operating profit	25	–	25	(1)	24
	52	3	55	(1)	54

3 Profit/loss on sale of operations (extract)

Share of joint ventures' profit on sale of operations				21	21
Share of associates' loss on sale of operations				(36)	(36)
				(15)	(15)

4 Interest (extract)	£m	£m
Interest receivable (group)		6
Interest payable:		
Group	(26)	
Joint ventures	(10)	
Associates	(12)	(48)
		(42)

5 Taxation (extract)	3	£m
Group		(5)
Joint ventures		(5)
Associates		(2)
		(12)

Presenting an associate's or joint venture's minority interest in the group profit and loss account

27.83.1 A group's associate or joint venture may have a subsidiary which is partly owned by outside shareholders. The investing group, when equity or gross equity accounting, bases its share of the associate's or joint venture's results and net assets on the associate's or joint venture's consolidated financial statements.

27.83.2 As noted above, paragraph 27 of FRS 9 requires that for items at and below the level of profit before tax, the investor's share of the relevant amounts for associates should be included within the amounts for the group. Minority interest is presented below profit before tax and so the investing group's profit and loss account should include the group's share of the associate's minority interest in the normal minority interests' line. The amount should be disclosed separately.

27.83.3 If the group's investment was a joint venture, then the treatment of a joint venture's minority interest is the same as described above for an associate.

Segmental reporting

27.83.4 SSAP 25 and FRS 9 set out the segmental information to be disclosed in respect of associates and joint ventures and these are considered further in chapter 10.

Statement of total recognised gains and losses

27.84 The investors' share of its joint ventures' and associates' other gains and losses included in the statement of total recognised gains and losses (STRGL) must also be disclosed where they are material. The requirement would apply, for example, to the investor's share of any revaluation surpluses of its joint ventures and associates reported in their STRGLs. Here the standard is more helpful in that it states specifically that such amounts should be: *'shown separately under* *each heading, if the amounts are material, either in the statement or in a note that is referred to in the statement'*. [FRS 9 paras 21, 28]. The requirement is still to disclose separately the investor's share of joint ventures' relevant amounts from those of its associates and in that order, but this detail can be given in the notes to the financial statements.

Statement of total recognised gains and losses

	Notes	£m
Profit for the financial year		39
Unrealised surplus on revaluation of properties	6	25
Currency translation differences on foreign net investment		(8)
Other recognised gains and losses relating to the year		17
Total recognised gains and losses for the year		56

Notes to the financial statements

6 Fixed assets (extract)

The revaluation gains arising in the year are analysed as follows:

Group	19
Joint ventures	(8)
Associates	14
	25

Balance sheet

27.85 Unless it is shown at a valuation, the amount at which the investing company's interest in its joint ventures or its associates should be shown in the investing company's own financial statements is the cost of the investment less any amounts written off, as explained in chapter 6. [FRS 9 paras 20, 26].

27.86 The amount at which the investing group's interests in joint ventures and associates should be shown in the group's consolidated balance sheet is the value under the 'equity method' of accounting, being the total of:

- The investing group's share of the net assets (other than goodwill) of the joint ventures and associates, stated after attributing fair values to the net assets at the time the interests in the joint ventures and associates were acquired.
- The goodwill (or negative goodwill) arising on the acquisition of the interests in the joint ventures and associates, insofar as it has not already been written off or amortised.

[FRS 9 paras 21, 29].

27.87 It is not appropriate, once the balance sheet interest has been ascertained using the equity method of accounting as explained above, to then revalue the investment in the associate or joint venture to its market value, even where the entity is listed. This method was adopted by Foreign and Colonial Investment Trust plc before the introduction of FRS 9. The FRRP issued a press notice in April 1996 in respect of the company's December 1994 financial statements. At issue was the adequacy of the *explanation* given for a departure from equity method of accounting in the balance sheet treatment of an associate, which was carried at a directors' valuation. Following discussions with the FRRP, the directors gave a fuller explanation of the departure and its effect in their 1995 financial statements. The departure from SSAP 1 was explained in the 1995 group accounts as follows:

> *"Hypo Foreign and Colonial Management (Holdings) Limited ('HFCM'), the group's associated undertaking, is accounted for in the revenue account using the equity method prescribed in SSAP 1. The carrying value is restated in the consolidated balance sheet at directors' or market valuation, to be consistent with the group's accounting policy for investments.*
>
> *As the investment in HFCM forms part of the group's investment portfolio, the directors believe adoption of the equity method in the balance sheet would not show a true and fair view. The effect of this departure from SSAP 1 is set out in note 12 on the accounts."*

We considered at the time that this was an odd ruling, because whilst criticising the disclosure the FRRP appeared to be condoning adoption of a policy for the balance sheet (that is, valuation) that was inconsistent with the policy adopted for the revenue account (that is, equity accounting). We consider that such a treatment would be an unacceptable departure from FRS 9. In addition, FRS 9 has special rules that apply to investment funds. Investments included within their investment portfolio should be accounted for using the same policy that applies to other investments included in the portfolio, namely cost or market value and not equity accounted (see further para 27.27).

Goodwill

27.88 Any goodwill carried in the balance sheet of the joint venture or associate on acquisition is excluded from the calculation of goodwill arising on the acquisition and is, therefore, not recognised separately on consolidation. [FRS 9 para 31]. It is acceptable to aggregate the two disclosures in paragraph 27.86 on the face of the balance sheet, but where this is done the standard requires that the balance of goodwill after amortisation and any write-downs should be disclosed separately. [FRS 9 para 29]. Furthermore, it is necessary to show a reconciliation of movements in the year on the goodwill arising on joint ventures and associates in a table in order to accord with FRS 10, 'Goodwill and intangible assets'. [FRS 10 para 53]. Although it is necessary to disclose this reconciliation separately from the reconciliation relating to goodwill arising on the consolidation of the group's subsidiaries, it does not seem necessary to analyse the movements between goodwill attributable to joint ventures and goodwill attributable to associates. It is only necessary to analyse the closing balance of goodwill between joint ventures and associates.

27.89 Where a parent company acquires a subsidiary which has an investment in an associate or joint venture, it will be necessary to apportion the goodwill arising on acquisition between the subsidiary undertaking and the associate or joint venture. Although allocation of goodwill is not specifically dealt with in FRS 7, it would appear to be required by FRS 11. This is because under FRS 11, capitalised goodwill should be allocated to income generating units along with other assets and liabilities for the purpose of impairment reviews.

27.90 Paragraph 34 of FRS 11 requires goodwill on an acquisition comprising two dissimilar businesses to be reviewed separately for impairment so that any impairment loss arising, say, in the subsidiary undertaking does not fall to be offset against an increase in value of the joint venture.

27.91 If the acquired subsidiary has an investment in an associate, the element of the goodwill arising on the parent's acquisition of the subsidiary which relates to the associate should be included in the associate's carrying amount under the equity method and disclosed separately.

27.92 Paragraph 21 of FRS 9 requires that, under the gross equity method, a joint venture should receive the same treatment as set out for associates, except that in the consolidated balance sheet the parent company's share of the gross assets and liabilities underlying the net equity amount for the joint venture should be shown in 'amplification of that net amount'. It follows, therefore, that it is appropriate to include the element of the goodwill arising on the acquisition of the subsidiary which relates to the joint venture as part of the gross asset disclosure on the face of the balance sheet, and to show it as a separate item either there or in the notes. Alternatively, it could be included in the net amount by disclosing it as a separate item on the face of the balance sheet, after the sub-total comprising the share of gross assets less the share of gross liabilities.

27.93 In addition, the Act requires that any goodwill arising on the acquisition of the associated undertaking (including joint venture entities) should be dealt with in accordance with the rules in Schedule 1 to SI 2008/410, which require amortisation of capitalised goodwill to nil on a systematic basis over a period chosen by the directors. [SI 2008/410 6 Sch 21(1); 1 Sch 22(2)]. The rules in FRS 10 also apply to goodwill that arises on the acquisition of an associate. Under FRS 10 the required treatment is to capitalise goodwill and amortise it over its useful life, which would normally not exceed 20 years. There are special rules that apply where the goodwill life exceeds 20 years or is indeterminate. In certain special circumstances it is possible not to amortise goodwill, but this requires use of the true and fair override and specific impairment tests then apply. The rules in FRS 10 are considered in detail in chapter 25 and apply equally to goodwill arising on the acquisition of a joint venture or an associate. FRS 10 also included transitional provisions that allowed companies either to capitalise goodwill previously written off directly to reserves prior to the standard's introduction, or allowed it to remain written off against reserves. Where goodwill remains written off against reserves, the financial statements must state:

- The accounting policy followed in respect of that goodwill.
- The cumulative amounts of positive goodwill eliminated against reserves and negative goodwill added to reserves, net of any goodwill attributable to businesses disposed of before the balance sheet date.
- The fact that this goodwill had been eliminated as a matter of accounting policy and would be charged or credited in the profit and loss account on subsequent disposal of the business to which it related.

[FRS 10 para 71(a)].

Gross equity method

27.94 Investors have also to supplement the disclosure in paragraph 27.86 where they have interests in joint ventures. To accord with the gross equity method of accounting, the investor's share of both the aggregate gross assets and liabilities underlying the net amount included for the investment must be shown on the face of the balance sheet. [FRS 9 paras 4, 21]. In this situation, the standard is clear that this disclosure cannot be relegated to the notes to the financial statements and must appear on the face of the balance sheet.

Illustrative example

27.95 An illustration of the required disclosure is given below:

Consolidated balance sheet (extract)	Group £'000
Fixed assets	
Goodwill	130
Intangible assets	898
Tangible assets	31,082
Investments:	
Investments in joint ventures:	
Share of gross assets	1,273
Share of gross liabilities	(1,014)
	259
Investments in associates	148
Other investments	617
	1,024
	33,134

27.96 The share of gross liabilities of £1,014,000 shown in the example above includes the group's share of a loan from the group to the joint venture of £80,000 which is included in other investments (see following example). When there are intra-group transactions, it will normally be appropriate to eliminate a proportion of those transactions (see from para 27.145). In this case, however, the loan to the joint venture should not be eliminated with the element of that loan included in the share of joint ventures' gross liabilities, because the Companies Act formats require that loans to participating interests should be shown separately. This also applies to loans to and from associates.

27.97 The balance sheet formats in the Act require participating interests and loans to participating interests to be shown as separate line items. Separate disclosure of the loans to associates and the loans to joint ventures should, therefore, be given. In addition, paragraph 55 of FRS 9 requires disclosure of amounts owing and owed between an investor and its associates *or* joint ventures, that is, it distinguishes between the two. This is consistent with the general requirement for separate disclosure in respect of joint ventures and associates. One way of complying with this disclosure is to give a columnar presentation in the notes to the financial statements, where the column headings are the line items found in the formats, as illustrated in the example below:

Fixed asset investments (extract)

Group	Joint ventures	Associates	Subsidiary excluded from consolidation	Loans to joint ventures	Loans to associates	Other investments	Total
	£'000	£'000	£'000	£'000	£'000	£'000	£'000
Cost or valuation							
At 31 March 20X6							
Goodwill	66	43	—	—	—	—	109
Other	172	121	654	80	40	352	1,419
	238	164	654	80	40	352	1,528
Additions	—	—	—	—	—	151	151
Share of retained profit	33	7	—	—	—	—	40
At 31 March 20X7							
Goodwill	66	43	—	—	—	—	109
Other	205	128	654	80	40	503	1,610
	271	171	654	80	40	503	1,719
Amounts written off							
At 31 March 20X6							
Goodwill	10	15	—	—	—	—	25

Other	—	—	654	—	—	6	660
	10	15	654	—	—	6	685
Amortisation of goodwill	2	3	—	—	—	—	5
Impairment of goodwill	—	5	—	—	—	—	5
At 31 March 20X7							
Goodwill	12	23	—	—	—	—	35
Other	—	—	654	—	—	6	660
	12	23	654	—	—	6	695
Net book value At 31 March 20X7							
Goodwill	54	20	—	—	—	—	74
Other	205	128	—	80	40	497	950
	259	148	—	80	40	497	1,024
Net book value At 31 March 20X6							
Goodwill	56	28	—	—	—	—	84
Other	172	121	—	80	40	346	759
	228	149	—	80	40	346	843

Presenting an associate's or joint venture's minority interest in the investor's group balance sheet

27.98.1 An associate or joint venture may have a subsidiary, which is partly owned by outside shareholders. As noted in paragraph 27.83.1, the investing group, when equity or gross equity accounting, bases its share of the associate's or joint venture's results and net assets on the associate's or joint venture's consolidated financial statements.

27.98.2 Under the equity method, the investor's share of the net assets of its associate should be presented separately as a fixed asset investment. [FRS 9 para 29]. The amount is calculated after deducting the minority interest in the associate's consolidated balance sheet. There is no requirement to separately disclose the group's share of the minority interest in the group's balance sheet.

27.98.3 Under the gross equity method, the group's share of the joint venture's gross assets and gross liabilities should be presented separately under the heading of investment in joint ventures, as a fixed asset investment. [FRS 9 paras 21, 29]. Since the joint venture's minority interest is not an asset or a liability, the most appropriate presentation is to show the group's share of the minority interest as a separate item deducted from its share of gross assets and liabilities.

Investor's individual financial statements

27.98.4 For investments in both joint ventures and associates, in the investor's individual financial statements, the investments should be treated as fixed asset investments and shown either at cost, less amounts written off, or at valuation. [FRS 9 paras 20, 26].

Cash flow statement

27.99 FRS 9 also details how the results of associates and joint ventures should be dealt with in the cash flow statement and the standard makes a number of amendments to FRS 1, 'Cash flow statements'. The revised requirements are considered in chapter 30. Prior to FRS 9, dividends received from equity accounted entities were reported either within operating cash flows where their results were included as part of group operating profit or under returns of investments and servicing of finance where their results were reported outside group operating profit. Under FRS 9, the investor's share of the results of its equity accounted entities is included immediately *after* group operating profit rather than in group operating profit. Consistent with this treatment, the option of including dividends within operating cash flows is no longer available. The ASB also rejected the alternative of including dividends from equity accounted entities under returns on investments and servicing of finance, because it felt that such dividends have a different significance from the normal returns on investments. As a result, the cash flows relating to dividends received from joint ventures and associates are reported under a new heading 'Dividends from joint ventures and associates' between operating activities and returns on investment and servicing of finance. [FRS 1 para 12A].

Additional disclosure

General requirements

27.100 Schedule 4 to SI 2008/410 includes certain additional information that has to be disclosed in the consolidated financial statements about an undertaking's investments in its joint ventures and associates. Some of this information is also required to be given by FRS 9. Investors have to give the following information:

- The name of the principal joint ventures and associates.
- If the joint venture or associate is incorporated outside Great Britain, the country of its incorporation.
- Where the joint venture or associate is unincorporated, the address of its principal place of business.
- In respect of shares held by the parent company or by other members of the group:

- The identity of each class of shares.
- The proportion held of the nominal value of each class.
- Any special rights or constraints attaching to each class.

The disclosures in the first two bullet points have to be split between those held by the parent and those held by the group.

- The accounting period or date of the joint venture's or the associate's financial statements used if they differ from those of the investing group.
- An indication of the nature of the joint venture's or the associate's business.

[SI 2008/410 4 Sch 19; FRS 9 para 52].

This type of information is illustrated in Table 27.6.

Table 27.6 – Cable and Wireless plc – Annual report and accounts – 31 March 2000

Principal subsidiary undertakings, associates and joint ventures and trade investments at 31 March 2000 (extract)

Associates		Ownership					
		Issued share capital m	Direct	Via subsidiaries	Class of shares	Country of incorporation	Area of operation
Bahrain Telecommunications Company B.S.C.*	Dinar	1,000	20%	–	Ordinary	Bahrain	Bahrain
Eastern Telecommunications Philippines, Inc.†*	P.Peso	200	40%	–	Ordinary	Philippines	Philippines
Joint ventures							
Gemini Submarine Cable System Limited†	US$	–	50%	–	Ordinary	Bermuda	Worldwide
Telecommunication Services of Trinidad and Tobago Limited†	T$	283	–	49%	Ordinary	Trinidad and Tobago	Trinidad and Tobago
MobileOne (Asia) Pte Ltd	Singapore $	140	–	30%	Ordinary	Singapore	Singapore

Notes

Full details of all subsidiary undertakings, associates and joint ventures and trade investments will be attached to the Company's Annual Return, to be filed with the Registrar of Companies.

* These companies had a financial year end of 31 December 1999 due to the requirements of the shareholders' agreements.

† These companies are audited by firms other than KPMG International member firms.

27.101 The information required by Schedule 4 to SI 2008/410 'The Large and Medium-sized Companies and Groups (Accounts and Reports) Regulations 2008' above need not be disclosed where the joint venture or associate is established under the law of a country, or carries on a business, outside the UK, if in the directors' opinion the disclosure would be seriously prejudicial to the business of the joint venture or associate, or to the investor's business or any of its subsidiaries. But this information may only be withheld in this type of situation where the Secretary of State agrees that it need not be disclosed and this fact must be stated in the notes to the financial statements. [CA06 Sec 409(3)(4)].

27.102 Where the company's directors are of the opinion that the number of undertakings in respect of which the company is required to disclose the above information required by Schedule 4 to SI 2008/410 would result in excessive disclosure being given, the information need only be given in respect of joint ventures and of associates whose results or financial position, in the opinion of the directors, principally affected the figures shown in the financial statements. Where advantage is taken of this provision the notes to the financial statements should state that the information is given only with respect to principal joint ventures and associates and should state that the full information (both that disclosed in the notes and that which is not) will be annexed to the company's next annual return. [CA06 Sec 410(1)(2)(3)].

27.103 In addition, information is required to be disclosed concerning the trading balances with joint ventures and associates. The amount of loans owing and owed between an investor and its joint ventures or its associates must be disclosed (for example, see the illustration in para 27.97). [FRS 9 para 55]. Also, balances that arise from unsettled normal trading between joint ventures or associates and other group members should be included under current assets and current liabilities and disclosed separately if material. [FRS 9 para 55].

27.104 Furthermore, the standard requires other matters to be disclosed that are material in understanding the effect on the investor of its investments in its joint ventures and its associates. [FRS 9 para 53]. For example, this covers any notes of particular significance included in the joint venture's or associate's own financial statements. It also covers explanations of matters that should have been noted had the investor's accounting policies been applied. In addition, the investor's share in contingent liabilities incurred jointly with other venturers or investors should be given and its share of joint venture's, or associate's, capital commitments should be disclosed. It would seem to follow from the disclosure requirements given earlier in the standard that this information should be shown separately for joint ventures and associates.

27.105 If there are any significant statutory, contractual or exchange control restrictions on a joint venture's or an associate's ability to distribute its distributable reserves, the extent of the restrictions should be disclosed. [FRS 9 para 54]. This type of situation could arise where, for example, the associate is situated in a country where there are exchange control restrictions, which restrict the associate's ability to pay dividends out of that country.

27.106 A note of explanation is required in two situations where the Companies Act's presumptions concerning the definition of associates (including joint ventures) are rebutted. The first situation is where the presumption is rebutted that an investor holding 20 per cent or more of the voting rights of another entity exercises significant influence over its operating and financial policies. The second is where the presumption is rebutted that an investor holding 20 per cent or more of the shares of another entity has a participating interest. [FRS 9 para 56].

15 and 25 per cent threshold information

27.107 Additional disclosures arise where the investor's share in its associates in aggregate, or in its joint ventures in aggregate, exceeds 15 per cent of certain thresholds. In addition, where the investor's share in any of its individual joint ventures and associates exceeds 25 per cent of certain thresholds individually, then additional disclosures have to be given for that entity. The thresholds should be applied by comparing the investor's share for either its associates in aggregate or its joint ventures in aggregate (or its individual associates or joint ventures) of the following:

- gross assets;
- gross liabilities;
- turnover; or
- operating results (on a three-year average),

with the corresponding amounts for the group (excluding joint ventures and associates). If any of the thresholds are breached the additional disclosures detailed below have to be given. [FRS 9 para 57].

27.108 The intention is that additional disclosures should be given where associates or joint ventures have a significant impact on the group. It is possible for an associate or joint venture to make an insignificant profit over a three year period while still having a material impact on the group in each of the three years. Suppose an associate makes a profit of £300,000 in each of two years, but a loss of £600,000 in the third year. The total profit/loss for the three year period is £nil, but the group's share of the profit or loss in each of the three years may exceed the 15 per cent threshold. For this reason, we believe the operating results should, in calculating the three-year average, be included in absolute terms. In this case, the three year average would be (£300,000 + £300,000 + £600,000)/3 + £400,000. The investor's share of this average should then be compared with the average group's results (excluding results of associates and joint ventures) calculated on the same basis.

27.109 Where the 15 per cent threshold is exceeded for all associates the aggregate of the investor's share in its associates of the following must be given:

- Turnover (unless it is already included as a memorandum item).
- Fixed assets.
- Current assets.
- Liabilities due within one year.
- Liabilities due after one year or more.

[FRS 9 para 58(a)].

27.110 Similar information is required for joint ventures in aggregate where the 15 per cent threshold is exceeded for all joint ventures. But, in this case, the turnover will already have been given as one of the requirements of gross equity accounting. [FRS 9 para 58(b)].

27.111 Where the 25 per cent threshold is exceeded for an individual associate or joint venture, the associate or joint venture should be named and the investor's share of the following should be disclosed for that entity:

- Turnover.
- Profit before tax.
- Taxation.
- Profit after tax.
- Fixed assets.
- Current assets.
- Liabilities due within one year.
- Liabilities due after one year or more.

[FRS 9 para 58(c)].

27.112 However, where the individual joint venture or associate accounts for nearly all of the amounts included for that class of investment, only the aggregate, not the individual, information in paragraph 27.111 need be given, provided that this is explained and the associate or joint venture identified. [FRS 9 para 58(c)].

27.113 In addition to the disclosure requirements outlined above, the standard requires further analysis to be given where this is necessary to understand the nature of the amounts disclosed. The headings to be given under the disclosure requirements detailed above will not conform with those used by some joint ventures and associates. This might be because they are, for example, banks, insurance companies or investment companies. In this situation it is necessary to consider the nature of the joint venture's or associate's business in deciding the most relevant and descriptive balance sheet amounts to be disclosed. Furthermore, the standard says that it may be important to give an indication of the size and maturity profile of the liabilities held. [FRS 9 para 58].

Optional disclosure for joint ventures

27.114 For joint ventures, the ASB adopted equity accounting (albeit a slightly expanded version, the 'gross equity method') as it did not consider that proportional consolidation should be used for joint ventures. Its main reason for rejecting proportional consolidation was that it believed that it would be misleading to represent each venturer's joint control of a joint venture as being in substance equivalent to it having sole control of its share of each of that entity's assets, liabilities and cash flows. This becomes particularly apparent when considering the impact of proportional consolidation in the cash flow statement, which would lead to the venturer's share of the joint venture's cash flows being treated as direct cash flows of the investor.

27.115 However, the ASB believes that it is important to encourage experimentation concerning how best to report the results and operations of joint ventures, particularly where they are a significant part of a group's activities. The ASB is happy for groups to give additional information concerning their joint ventures provided that it is in a form that is consistent with the gross equity method of accounting. To this end, the ASB includes an illustration of an optional presentation in appendix IV to the standard. Two illustrative presentations are given below of the profit and loss account and the balance sheet showing memorandum information, which is based on the previous examples. One of the major constraints on this type of disclosure is purely a practical one and concerns how much information it is possible to get onto a printed page. Another issue concerns whether or not users will fully understand the implications of the additional information, which amounts to proportional consolidation.

The *pro forma* information given in the two right hand columns is of a memorandum nature only and is presented to give an indication of the effect of the group's share of the trading of its joint ventures on the results of the group.

Consolidated profit and loss account

						Pro forma information	
	Continuing operations	Acquisitions	Total	Discontinued operations	Group	Joint ventures	Total
	£m	£m	£m	£m	£m	£m	£m
Turnover including share of joint ventures and associates	250	50	300	20	320		
Less: Share of joint ventures and associates	105	10	115	5	120		
Group turnover	145	40	185	15	200	40	240
Cost of sales	89	23	112	8	120	8	128

Gross profit	56	17	73	7	80	32	112
Administrative expenses	28	4	32	8	40	2	42
Group operating profit (loss)	28	13	41	(1)	40	30	70
Share of operating profit of:							
Joint ventures	27	3	30	—	30		
Associates	25	—	25	(1)	24		24
Operating profit including joint ventures and associates	80	16	96	(2)	94		94
Sale of operations:							
Group	—	—	—	20	20		
Joint ventures and associates	—	—	—	(15)	(15)		
	—	—	—	5	5		
Profit on ordinary activities before interest	80	16	96	3	99		
Interest					(42)		
Profit on ordinary activities before tax					57		
Tax on profit on ordinary activities					12		
Profit on ordinary activities after tax					45		
Minority interests					6		
Profit for the financial year					39		
Equity dividends					10		
Retained profit for the year					29		

Consolidated balance sheet

		Pro forma information	
	Group	Joint ventures	Total
	£'000	£'000	£'000
Fixed assets			
Goodwill	130	—	130
Intangible assets	898	—	898
Tangible assets	31,082	835	31,917
Investments:			
Investments in joint ventures	259	(259)	—
Investments in associates	148	—	148
Other investments	617	23	640
	1,024		788
	33,134		33,733
Current assets			
Stocks	7,821	230	8,051
Debtors: amounts falling due after one year	510	22	532
Debtors: amounts falling due within one year	9,029	127	9,156
Investments	166	—	166
Cash at bank and in hand	843	36	879
	18,369	415	18,784
Creditors: amounts falling due within one year	8,520	530	9,050
Net current assets (liabilities)	9,849	(115)	9,734
Total assets less current liabilities	42,983	743	43,467
Creditors: amounts falling due after more than one year			
Borrowings and other creditors	7,851	8,231	8,231
Provisions for liabilities	10,035	104	10,139
	17,886	484	18,370
Net assets	25,097		25,097
Capital and reserves			
Called up share capital	11,161		
Share premium account	1,512		
Revaluation reserve	5,426		
Profit and loss account	5,503		
Total shareholders' funds	23,602		
Minority interests	1,495		
	25,097		

The *pro forma* information shows the group's share of the gross assets and liabilities of its joint ventures and the effect on the group's assets and liabilities if it were to be proportionally consolidated. The figure of £259,000 represents the elimination of the group's share of its joint ventures' net assets included within the group column.

Equity accounting principles

Introduction

27.116 The principles concerning how to equity account for joint ventures and associates mainly follow those that apply to the consolidation of subsidiaries. These principles concern, for example, the date from which to equity account an interest in a joint venture or associate, how to determine goodwill and the types of consolidation adjustments that are necessary. The primary difference between an associate interest, or a joint venture interest, and an interest in a subsidiary is the level of the investor's control. An investor controls its subsidiaries, and therefore has access to the information necessary for carrying out certain consolidation procedures, but it exercises only significant influence over its associates or jointly controls its joint ventures. Consequently, this might mean that access to information necessary to make the required consolidation adjustments is limited. Where this is so, the standard states that estimates may be used. But such a limitation in itself might call into question the investor's relationship with its associate or joint venture. Where the information available is extremely limited, the investor will need to reassess whether or not it actually has significant influence over, or whether or not it jointly controls, its investment. [FRS 9 para 35].

27.117 Furthermore, the standard mentions that regulations on the dissemination of information could possibly restrict the extent to which the financial statements of an investor might contain information about its joint ventures and its associates, unless such information is available to other interested parties at the same time. [FRS 9 para 37]. This is of particular importance where the associate is itself listed (as explained in para 27.137 below). Investors should, therefore, consider how to satisfy any regulations that apply concerning publishing price sensitive information about its joint ventures and its associates.

27.118 The paragraphs that follow consider the consolidation rules that apply to equity accounting both associates and joint ventures, starting with examining how the share to be equity accounted is ascertained.

Share

27.119 Before it is possible to equity account for joint ventures and associates, it is necessary to establish what share the group owns. There are a number of matters that need to be considered in determining what is the appropriate share, as in many situations the percentage will not be easily ascertained.

Paragraphs 27.33 to 27.35 above explain how to determine whether or not the investor has a participating interest in the joint venture or the associate and paragraphs 27.50 to 27.54 consider what voting rights should be taken into account. These rules also apply in determining what percentage share the group has in the joint venture or associate.

27.120 Where the investor is a group, its share of its associate or joint venture is the aggregate of the parent's interest and the interest of its subsidiaries in that entity. [FRS 9 para 32]. Therefore, it is the group's aggregate interest in the joint venture or associate which needs to be ascertained and this is the appropriate percentage which should be applied in equity accounting. But the holdings of any of the group's other associates or joint ventures should be ignored for this purpose. [FRS 9 para 32].

27.121 In a simple situation where the investor only has an interest in the equity share capital of the associate or joint venture it is easy to ascertain the share to be equity accounted: it will normally be the number of shares held divided by the total number of equity shares in issue. This amount will equate to the investor's entitlement to dividends and other distributions. Complications arise where the investee has different classes of shares or where the entitlement to dividends, or capital on winding up, vary. For example, the investor might have an interest in the non-equity capital as well as the equity capital. Clearly in this type of situation, the rights attaching to each class of share need to be considered carefully to determine the appropriate percentage to be brought into the equity interest calculation. It is a matter of looking at the substance of the respective rights to establish the appropriate accounting treatment.

Example – Interest in cumulative preference shares – associate

A group has an interest in the equity shares of its associate and owns all of the other class of the company's shares in issue, which are cumulative preference shares. The group owns 45% of the equity shares and 500,000 6% cumulative preference shares with a nominal value of £1 each. There were no issue costs relating to the preference shares. The preference shares are classified as debt of the associate (in accordance with FRS 25) and are accounted for in accordance with FRS 4 or FRS 26 (depending on which standard is being applied – see further chapter 6). The net assets of the associate are £1m, but it does not have sufficient distributable reserves in order to enable it to pay the cumulative dividend.

The liabilities of the associate include unpaid finance costs (dividends) of £60,000 which is solely attributable to the investor's interest in the cumulative preference shares. The investor's share of net assets is determined by adding together its entitlement to cumulative dividends and its interest in the preference shares before calculating its share of the remaining net assets. Ignoring fair values and goodwill, the investor's share of net assets would be £758,000 (that is, £60,000 + £500,000 + 45% (£1,000,000 – £500,000 – £60,000)).

27.122 In many situations the share to be taken into account will be derived from the percentage holding in shares, but in other situations the economic interest might differ from the shareholding, but will be the appropriate interest to take into account. For example, although the shareholding in a joint venture might be 50:50, the venturers might share profits in the ratio 40:60. Therefore, in this circumstance it will be appropriate to equity account for the economic share rather than the equity participation. Consequently, considerable care needs to be taken in establishing the appropriate share to be equity accounted.

27.122.1 A further complication arises when the group's interest is in a joint venture rather than an associate. This is because FRS 9 requires the investor to disclose, in addition to the amounts that would be included under the equity method if the investment was an associate, the investor's share of the gross assets and liabilities of its joint venture.

Example – Interest in cumulative preference shares – joint venture

Facts as in the example above except that the group's interest is in a joint venture, not an associate. The joint venture's balance sheet is as follows:

	£000
Gross assets	1,250
Gross liabilities (excluding preference shares)	(250)
	1,000
Preference shares (£500,000 capital plus £60,000 finance costs)	(560)
Net assets	440
Ordinary share capital	500
Profit and loss reserve	(60)
Share capital and reserves	440

The share of net assets of a joint venture is calculated in the same way as for associates and, accordingly, in this case, is £758,000 as per the previous example. That is, the group's share of net assets is 75.8% of the joint venture's net assets excluding preference shares. It follows, therefore, that the group's share of gross assets is 75.8% of the joint venture's gross assets, £947,500 (75.8% × £1,250,000), and similarly that its share of gross liabilities excluding preference shares is £189,500 (75.8% × £250,000).

It might be expected that the share of gross assets and liabilities would reflect the preferential treatment accorded to preference shareholders in the event of a winding up. Before the ordinary shareholders could be paid, the preference shareholders would be entitled to receive both the nominal value of their preference shares and any arrears of dividend. In this case, those two components amount to £560,000. If this approach was taken, the group's share of gross assets would be £870,500 (£560,000 + 45% × (£1,250,000-£560,000)) and its share of gross liabilities excluding preference shares would be £112,500 (45% × £250,000). However, this approach is conceptually flawed. In the event of a winding up, preference shareholders are, like ordinary shareholders, paid out of the proceeds of net assets, not gross assets. To allocate the share of gross assets by applying them first to the preference shareholder's interest, is to imply that the preference shareholders are paid out in advance, not just of the ordinary shareholders, but also of creditors.

Options, convertible shares and convertible debt

27.123 Where the investor holds options, convertibles or non-equity shares in its joint venture or its associate, the standard says that these should be taken into account in determining the investor's share where the conditions attaching to such holdings indicate that this is appropriate. The standard goes on to say that, in such cases, the costs of exercising the options or converting the convertibles, or future payments in relation to the non-equity shares, should also be taken into account. It also states that the necessary calculation depends on the relevant circumstances in any particular case, but notes that care should be taken not to count any interest twice. For example, such double counting would occur where an investor included a greater share of its associate under the equity method than that which would arise on the basis of the investor's existing equity holding, while simultaneously writing up the value of options held in the associate to reflect an increase in market value. [FRS 9 para 33]. It is not easy to see what these requirements mean in practice and these issues are explored in the paragraphs that follow.

27.124 The standard's section 'The development of the FRS' says that the basis of paragraph 33 outlined above is the requirement in FRS 5 that the substance of transactions should be reported. In particular, paragraph 14 of FRS 5 specifies that *'in determining the substance of a transaction, all its aspects and implications should be identified and greater weight should be given to those more likely to have a commercial effect in practice'*. FRS 9 goes on to say that the investor should, therefore, account for the substance of its interests in its joint ventures or its associates in cases where this is affected by its holdings of options, convertibles or non-equity shares. It gives one example where the existence of such a holding might affect the share. This is where the price of exercising or converting options or convertibles is so low that there is commercially near certainty that they will be exercised or converted. It is, therefore, quite clear from this explanation that the ASB considers that the share to be equity accounted should in certain special circumstances be adjusted to take account of the existence of options and convertibles.

27.125 As mentioned earlier, it is clear under the Act that a participating interest, which is defined in paragraph 11 to Schedule 10 to SI 2008/410 includes an option to acquire shares or any interest that is convertible into shares. [SI 2008/410 10 Sch 11(3)]. For this purpose, it does not matter whether the options or other interests can be exercised now or in the future; their mere existence is taken into account whether or not they are currently exercisable. An interest or option in shares falls within this definition even if the shares to which it relates, until conversion or the exercise of the option, are unissued. [SI 2008/410 10 Sch 11(3)].

In addition, interests held on behalf of an undertaking should be treated as held by it. [SI 2008/410 10 Sch 11(4)].

27.126 These rules apply in determining whether or not an investor has a participating interest in an entity and, as a consequence, are important in establishing whether or not the entity is a joint venture or an associate. But the question arises as to whether such interests should be taken into account in determining the share to be equity accounted. Clearly for this purpose, having an option interest or a convertible interest is very different from holding the shares to which they relate. For example, it seems clear that if the options or convertible interests are not within their exercise or conversion period, it is unlikely that they should be brought into account in determining the investor's interest in the associate, unless they are exercisable at a purely nominal figure and it appears in the circumstances that it would be in the investor's interest to exercise them. However, where they are within their option period and exercisable at a fair market price and the holder can exercise them at any time unconditionally then whether or not they fall to be treated as part of the investor's interest will depend on a number of factors. It would be highly unusual to take options and convertible interests into account in determining the share before they have been exercised, so the circumstances would have to be considered very carefully before adjusting the share to be equity accounted for such interests. One issue to consider is the distribution policy of the associate. If, for example, the associate was planning to pay an enhanced dividend this would need to be taken into account. The example that follows illustrates some of these issues.

Example – Interest in options – situation 1

A group has a 25% interest in its associate's equity share capital of £100,000. It also has options which it has held for a number of years to acquire a further 5,000 shares of £1 each from the company at £14 per share. The options, which cost £1 per share, are traded and have been valued in the group's financial statements at £2 per share. The net assets of the associate at the year end are £1m.

Ignoring fair values, the investor's equity interest in its associate's net assets is worth £250,000 which would normally be consolidated in the group's balance sheet. In addition, the group has shown the interest in the options at a value of £10,000. If the group had exercised its options at the year end and paid the £14 per share, the associate's net assets would increase by £70,000 (that is, 5,000 × £14) to £1,070,000 and the investor's interest would increase from 25% to 28.57% (that is, 30,000 ÷ 105,000 × 100). Therefore, the investor's share of the net assets and goodwill on the increase in stake would be £325,000. This is made up of the share of net assets of £305,700 (that is, £1,070,000 × 28.57%) and goodwill arising on the increase in stake of £19,300. The goodwill is the difference between the consideration of £75,000 (that is, the cost of the additional shares of £70,000 plus the initial cost of the options of £5,000) and the additional share of net assets of £55,700. Clearly, if this increased interest is booked in the consolidated balance sheet, then it would be necessary to eliminate the revaluation of the options of £5,000 in order to avoid double counting. In addition, it would be necessary to make a provision for the purchase of the additional shares, which would cost £70,000.

Consequently, in this example the net assets relating to the associate without taking into account the exercise of the options are £260,000 (that is, £250,000 + £10,000), but after taking into account the exercise of the options, the share of net assets of £325,000 (that is, share of net assets of £305,700 plus goodwill of £19,300) less a provision for consideration of £70,000 gives a total of £255,000; a net decrease of £5,000.

Following the introduction of FRS 10, because goodwill is capitalised the amount paid for an acquisition always equates to the increase in net assets plus goodwill recognised on consolidation (the fair value exercise only determining how the consideration figure is split between assets and goodwill). Consequently, anticipating an acquisition by providing for the consideration to be paid has a nil effect on the share of net assets plus goodwill shown on consolidation. In this example, the decrease in net assets of £5,000 is merely due to the reversal of the revaluation of £5,000 relating to the options recognised in the balance sheet.

27.127 Whether or not the investor would take into account an interest in options in ascertaining its share of its joint ventures and associates will depend on the facts of each case. The investor's intentions are, therefore, important. For example, if the options were exercisable at market value, the investor might intend to wait until the share price falls before it exercises its options or might intend to exercise them for other strategic business reasons. Where the investor does intend to exercise the options (say, shortly after the year end) then FRS 9 implies in paragraph 33 that it should take this into account in reflecting its interest in its joint venture or associate. But, as mentioned above, the circumstances that would justify adjusting the company's share for such options are not likely to arise very often in practice.

27.128 In certain situations the investor's intentions might be more obvious. This will be the case, in particular, where a fixed price put and call option exists. In this situation, either the investor or the investee is assured to exercise the option, as it will be in one of their economic interests to do so. However, care needs to be taken, because the effect of exercising options might not be obvious even where they are exercisable at below their market value. Consider the following example.

Example – Interest in options – situation 2

If in the previous example the investor's options were exercisable at £2 per share as opposed to £14 per share, then the effect on the group's net assets would be as follows.

The investor's share of the net assets and goodwill on the increase in stake would be £265,000. This is made up of the share of net assets of £288,557 (that is, £1,010,000 × 28.57%) less negative goodwill arising on the increase in stake of £23,557. The goodwill is the difference between the consideration of £15,000 (that is, the cost of the additional shares of £10,000 plus the initial cost of the options of £5,000) and the additional share of net assets of £38,557. Consequently, if the exercise of the options is taken into account, the share of net assets of £265,000 (that is, share of net assets of £288,557 less negative goodwill of £23,557) less a provision for consideration of £10,000 gives a total of £255,000; a net decrease of £5,000.

The net assets recognised is the same as in the previous example. This is no coincidence and is the effect of having to recognise purchased goodwill or negative goodwill on the balance sheet. As mentioned in the previous example, the increase in net assets recognised on consolidation always equates to the amount paid for the acquisition. Similarly in this example, anticipating an acquisition by providing for the consideration to be paid has a nil effect on the net assets on consolidation. Again in this example the decrease in net assets of £5,000 is due to the reversal of the revaluation of £5,000 relating to the options recognised in the balance sheet.

27.129 As can be seen from the previous two examples, the exercise price has no impact on the net assets recognised before or after acquisition, the net assets will remain the same. However, there would be an impact on the gross assets and liabilities recognised.

27.130 Another situation which arises in practice is where the investor has options over shares in the joint venture or associate which are held by third parties. Again the facts of the situation will have to be considered carefully. The intention of the investor might be influenced by the purchase price compared to the increased interest and possibly by the additional influence this gives the investor.

27.131 Problems can also arise at the margins, because the existence of options might tip the balance at the opposite extremes of the associate/joint venture spectrum. At one end an investment might become an associate by taking into account options (as discussed in para 27.125 above). At the other end of the spectrum the existence of options might turn a joint venture or an associate into a subsidiary. The issues concerning when such an interest becomes a subsidiary are considered in detail in chapter 25.

Convertible shares

27.132 The standard applies the same rules to convertible shares as it specifies for options as explained in paragraph 27.123 above. Therefore, it is necessary to establish whether or not the convertible shares are within their conversion period. If they are, the next step is to consider whether this gives the investor the power to exercise dominant influence or control. If the investor does not have such power, only if it is clear that the investor intends to convert and no significant distributions will be made before it does so should the conversion be taken into account in determining the share to be equity accounted. Also it will be necessary to take into account any costs of conversion to ensure that there is no double counting.

Example – Convertible shares

A group has a 25% interest in its associate's equity share capital of £100,000. It also holds 100,000 convertible redeemable preference shares of 25p. These are convertible into 10,000 £1 equity shares. The net assets of the associate at the year end are £1m. There is no cost of conversion, but if there was, then it would have to be provided for.

Ignoring fair values and goodwill, the investor's equity interest in its associate's net assets before conversion is £268,750 (that is, (£1,000,000 — £25,000) × 25% + £25,000), which would be consolidated in the group's balance sheet. If the group had exercised its options to convert at the year end, the investor's interest would increase from 25% to 31.82% (that is, 35,000 ÷ 110,000 × 100). Therefore, the investor's share of the net assets will increase to £318,200 (that is, £1,000,000 × 31.82%).

Convertible debt

27.133 Similar issues arise if the investor has invested in convertible debt of its joint venture or associate. It is necessary to consider the implications and substance of the transaction to determine whether the potential voting rights represent a present ownership interest. Also, anticipating conversion would have no impact on the net assets of the group as illustrated in the following example.

Example – Convertible debt – situation 1

A group has a 25% interest in its associate's equity share capital of £100,000. It also holds £100,000 of debt, convertible into a variable number of equity shares valued at £110,000. The net assets of the associate at the year end are £1m. There is no cost of conversion, but if there was, then it would have to be provided for.

Ignoring fair values, the investor's equity interest in its associate's net assets before conversion is £250,000 (that is, £1,000,000 × 25%) and it also has a loan to the associate of £100,000. Therefore, its total interest before conversion is £350,000. The share price is £10. If the group had converted its debt at the year end, the investor's interest would increase from 25% to 32.43% (that is, 36,000 ÷ 111,000 × 100). The associate's net assets increase by the £100,000 of debt which would be transferred to share capital and to share premium on conversion. Therefore, the investor's share of the net assets and goodwill after the conversion also comes to £350,000. This is made up of the share of net assets of £356,730 (that is, £1,100,000 × 32.43%) less negative goodwill arising on the increase in stake of £6,730. The negative goodwill is the difference between the consideration of £100,000 (that is, the value of the loan given up) and the additional share of net assets of £106,730.

As mentioned in the previous examples, the increase in net assets recognised on consolidation always equates to the amount paid for the acquisition. In this example, the group's net assets have remained the same, because the loan of £100,000 has been replaced by an increased share of net assets offset by negative goodwill.

27.134 Problems can also arise where other investors in the associate hold converting interests, which might have the effect of diluting the share of the associate to be equity accounted. Again it is necessary to consider carefully the implications and the substance of the transaction to determine whether or not the equity share should be adjusted.

Example – Convertible debt – situation 2

A group has a 38% interest in its associate's equity share capital. The associate has convertible debt in issue which is held by third parties. This debt will convert into equity shares of the associate in two years' time and it is almost certain that the debt-holders will opt for conversion. Once converted the investor's interest will decrease to 35%.

In this case, although it is almost certain that the debt will convert and conversion is not within the control of the investor, the investor should still equity account for its 38% interest until the conversion takes place. Only after conversion has taken place should the investor account using the 35%, because this is the actual date of the deemed disposal (see further para 27.170). However, because conversion is likely, the investor should provide for any losses (but not profits) in relation to the change in interest from 38% to 35%. It is, therefore, necessary to calculate the loss or gain on the deemed disposal. The gain or loss is calculated by comparing the share of net assets before the deemed disposal with the share of net assets after the deemed disposal (adjusted for any proceeds on the conversion of the debt). This calculation would also have to take into account a share of the goodwill given up on the deemed disposal, which would reduce any profit or increase any loss. If there is a resulting loss this would have to be provided for in the consolidated profit and loss account.

Crossholdings

27.135 One complicated issue that arises with equity accounting is how to deal with crossholdings of shares between the investor and its investee. This situation can arise whereby one company (the investor) issues shares to another company in exchange for shares in that other company. Obviously, without some adjustment there will be an element of double counting if the investor equity accounts for its share of the investee's net assets, which includes the holding of shares in the investor company. Therefore, this crossholding needs to be eliminated as explained in the following example.

Example – Equity swap

Company H takes a 25% stake in company A, which has net assets of £1m. The market value of the associate's shares is £1.5m. For simplicity, the net asset value and the fair value of the net assets is the same, that is, £1m. Company H issues shares with a value of £375,000 to acquire its interest.

In the simple situation where the investor issues its shares to the owners of the associate in exchange for the 25% interest, company H's share capital and share premium would increase by £375,000, being its investment in company A. On consolidation, the investment in company A of £375,000 is simply allocated between the group's share of the fair value of its net assets (that is, £250,000) and goodwill arising on the acquisition of £125,000 (that is, £375,000 — £250,000).

But now assume there is an equity swap, such that the investor issues shares worth £375,000 to the associate in consideration for the associate issuing the investor new shares. The associate's net assets increase by £375,000, the cost to it of the shares it holds in company H. Consequently, company A's worth has increased to £1,875,000 and it has net assets of £1,375,000. Company H's share of company A's increased net assets is £343,750 (that is, £1,375,000 × 25%), but this includes the value of the interest in its own shares of £93,750 (that is, 25% × £375,000). Company A's goodwill is still worth £500,000, of which company H's share is still £125,000. So it might appear that on consolidation the value of company H's interest in its associate should be £468,750 (that is, £1,875,000 × 25%), but company H's consolidated net assets (including goodwill) should not exceed £375,000, the value of the shares it has issued. If the group had recognised its share as £468,750 instead, it would have inflated its consolidated balance sheet by recognising some value for its own internally generated goodwill.

Therefore, to avoid double counting for the self-investment it is then necessary to split the interest in the associate of £375,000 between the share of the fair value of the net assets acquired and goodwill. It seems appropriate to reduce the value of company H's investment in company A's net assets by £93,750 to £250,000 and state goodwill at £125,000. The rationale is that the net assets are reduced to eliminate the crossholding and this also ensures that purchased goodwill in company A is recorded at the appropriate value. A problem arises if company A subsequently sells its interest in company H – an adjustment is required to bring company H's investment in its consolidated financial statements back up to the increased share of net assets of company A (that is, to £468,750). The double entry would be to credit the group's revaluation reserve with the increase in value of the associate interest.

In the consolidated profit and loss account, company H's share of company A's results should be included excluding any portion of those results attributable to company A's investment in company H. However, it should include a share of any dividends paid by company H to company A.

Financial statements used

27.136 The financial statements used for the purpose of including the results of joint ventures and associates should be either coterminous with those of the group (which for an associate with a different year end would involve preparing special financial statements to the same date as the investor's year end) or, where this is not practicable, made up to a date that is not more than three months before the investing group's period end. [FRS 9 para 31(d)].

[The next paragraph is 27.138.]

Consolidation adjustments

27.138 Adjustments similar to those required for the purposes of including subsidiaries in the consolidated financial statements should be made when the associates or joint ventures are incorporated into the group's consolidated financial statements. The type of adjustments that may be necessary cover the following matters:

- To achieve consistency of accounting policies.
- To set up goodwill arising on the associate's or joint venture's acquisition and to deal with fair value adjustments.
- To deal with abnormal transactions that arise between an associate's or joint venture's year end and its parent's year end.
- To eliminate the effects of intra-group trading.
- To translate the results of overseas associates or joint ventures.

27.139 These types of adjustments are similar to those made generally on the consolidation of subsidiaries. Some specific issues are considered in the paragraphs that follow.

Consistent accounting policies

27.140 The standard states that in arriving at the amounts to be included by the equity method of accounting, the same accounting policies as those of the investor should be applied. [FRS 9 para 31(c)]. This will entail making adjustments to the joint venture's or associate's results to harmonise accounting policies. However, in practice, such adjustments will not always be possible, because the information necessary to make them may not necessarily be available. Where this situation arises, the standard offers no guidance. However, this is also another area where the investor's relationship with its associate (that is, significant influence), or with its joint venture (that is, joint control), would be called into question, if the appropriate information is not available.

Goodwill and fair values

27.141 The standard requires that when an entity acquires a joint venture or an associate, fair values should be attributed to the investee's underlying assets and liabilities. [FRS 9 para 31(a)]. These fair values should be ascertained in accordance with the principles of FRS 7, 'Fair values in acquisition accounting', and adjustments should be made to conform with the investor's accounting policies. Again, as explained in the previous paragraph, where it is not possible to ascertain fair values on acquisition of a joint venture or an associate interest, this would call into question whether or not the entity fulfils the definitions of joint venture or associate, because it could suggest that the appropriate level of control or interest has not been achieved in practice.

27.142 For joint ventures and associates, it is unlikely that any necessary fair values adjustment would be booked in the joint venture's or associate's books of account, but nevertheless the fair value of assets should provide the basis for subsequent depreciation that is reflected in the investor's share of the results. The standard requires that both the consideration paid in the acquisition and the goodwill arising should be calculated in the same way as on the acquisition of a subsidiary. These issues are considered in detail in chapter 25. As explained in paragraph 27.88 above, the investee's assets used in calculating the goodwill arising on acquisition should not include any goodwill carried in the balance sheet of the joint venture or associate. Goodwill arising on the acquisition of joint ventures or associates has now to be accounted for in accordance with the provisions of FRS 10, 'Goodwill and intangible assets'. These requirements are fully explained in chapter 25.

27.143 Paragraph 31(a) in FRS 9, which specifies the above rules, deals with the measurement issues that arise when the equity accounting method is used, but it does not specify what disclosure requirements apply on acquisition. Therefore, for acquisitions of joint ventures and associates we do not consider that the disclosure requirements specified in FRS 6, 'Acquisitions and mergers', for acquisitions of subsidiaries apply. Consequently, there is no need to give the fair value table information required by that standard, although some companies do give this type of information — see Table 27.7. The disclosures required for joint ventures and associates are considered from paragraph 27.100 above.

Table 27.7 — British Telecommunications plc — Report & Accounts — 31 March 1998

Notes to the financial statements (extract)

15 Fixed asset investments (extract)

(c) Cegetel

On 24 September 1997, the group completed its acquisition of a 26% interest in Cegetel, a leading French telecommunications company. Of the cost of the investment in the associated undertaking of £1,029m, goodwill arising of £862m has been written off against reserves.

The acquisition of the interest in Cegetel comprised:

	£m
Group share of original book value of net assets	483
Fair value adjustment to achieve consistency of accounting policies	(316)
Fair value to the group	167
Goodwill	862
Total cost	1,029

Abnormal transactions between year ends

27.144 Care should be taken where the joint venture's or associate's year end does not coincide with that of the investing undertaking to ensure that there are no material events that have occurred since the joint venture's or associate's year end. Where such events have taken place, then if the effect is material it will be necessary to make adjustments to the results and net assets of the associate before they are consolidated with the group's financial statements. [FRS 9 para 31(d)].

For example, the associate might sell fixed assets to the group (or *vice versa*) during this period. Another example is where the group increases loans made to the joint venture or associate after the joint venture's or associate's year end.

Elimination of intra-group trading

Profits and losses included in assets

27.145 The method used to eliminate intra-group trading with joint ventures and associates may be different from that adopted for subsidiaries. The normal method of adjustment for a subsidiary company would be to eliminate profits and losses fully. However, the Act specifies that the elimination of profits and losses resulting from transactions between group undertakings, which have been included in the value of assets, may be eliminated in proportion to the group's interest in the shares of the undertaking. [CA85 4A Sch 6(3)]. The implication of this method of elimination as it applies to subsidiaries is restricted by FRS 2 and is considered further in chapter 24. Although only brought into the legislation by the introduction of the Companies Act 1989, this method of eliminating profits had been used for joint ventures and associates being equity accounted for some time before that date. This treatment is confirmed in FRS 9, which states that where profits and losses resulting from transactions between an investor and its associate, or its joint venture, are included in the carrying amount of assets in either entity, the part relating to the investor's share should be eliminated. [FRS 9 para 31(b)]. In addition, the standard notes that where the transaction provides evidence of the impairment of those assets or any similar assets, this should be taken into account. Blue Circle Industries PLC eliminates profits in this way as explained by their accounting policy (see Table 27.8).

Table 27.8 — Blue Circle Industries PLC — Annual Report & Accounts — 31 December 2000

1 Accounting Policies (extract)

13 Property (extract)

Sales of properties are recognised when a legally binding and unconditional contract for sale has been exchanged. Where properties are sold to joint ventures or associates, profits are only recognised in proportion to third parties' interests in these entities. The remaining profits are recognised when the properties are sold by joint venture or associate to unrelated parties.

27.146 The following example explains how the adjustment should be made.

Example – Elimination of intra-group trading

Company H prepares its consolidated financial statements to 31 December 20X7. It has a 25% investment in an associate. During the year company H purchased an investment from the associate for £120,000. The associate made £50,000 profit on the sale. On consolidation, using the equity method of accounting, that element of the associate's profit should be reduced to the extent of the group's investment in it (that is, reduced by 25%). Consequently, the share of the associate's profit consolidated with the group would be reduced by £12,500 (that is, 25% × £50,000), thereby, eliminating the group's share of that profit. In addition, to complete the double entry, the value of the investment shown in the group's consolidated balance sheet should be reduced by £12,500 to £107,500.

27.147 This type of adjustment is logical for joint ventures and associates, because the consolidated financial statements only include the group's share of the profits and losses of joint ventures and associates and, consequently, it would be wrong to eliminate a greater proportion of the profit. Furthermore, in the situation where a group member makes a sale to a joint venture or an associate, then a profit will arise in the group to the extent of the outside interest in the joint venture or associate. Similarly, the joint venture's or associate's assets will also, in this situation, be overstated by the profit element. Consequently, a similar adjustment will be required on consolidation to reduce the group's share of the joint venture's or associate's assets by the same amount.

Transfers of assets to a joint venture

27.148 The requirement to eliminate such profits applies equally to transfers of assets or liabilities to set up a joint venture or to acquire an initial stake in an associate as well as to all other transactions during the life of the associate or joint venture. [FRS 9 para 36].

Example – Transfer of assets to a joint venture

A group enters into a 50/50 joint venture with a third party. The joint venture is to be set up in a limited company and the group is to contribute assets worth £1,000,000 to the joint venture. The other party is to contribute cash for its 200,000 £1 shares. In consideration for the assets the group receives 200,000 £1 shares, long-term loan stock of £600,000 and cash of £200,000 (which the joint venture has received from its other shareholder).

The amount of the profit on the disposal of the group's property to the joint venture to be eliminated on consolidation depends upon the proportion of capital invested by the group and the other party to the venture. The proportions are as follows:

	Group £'000	Other JV partner £'000	Total capital £'000
Shares	200	200	400
Loan stock	600	—	600
	800	200	1,000
	80%	20%	100%

If the group made a gain on the disposal of the property to the joint venture, it should eliminate 80% of that gain, being the proportion of its interest it still retains in the asset (that is, share capital and long-term loan stock). Only 20% of the gain can be recognised in the consolidated financial statements. The elimination entry would be to debit the group's profit and loss account with the proportion of the gain being eliminated and credit the group's interest in the joint venture's assets shown on the face of the balance sheet following the gross equity method of accounting. Alternatively, the credit could be treated as deferred income, particularly where the assets will be realised subsequently. If the loan stock is subsequently repaid, the proportion to be eliminated would change to 50%.

In the individual entity making the disposal, the amount of the profit and any revaluation reserve being treated as realised will not depend on the capital invested in the joint venture, but will depend on the qualifying consideration (for instance, cash) received under the transaction.

	Proceeds £'000	Asset value £'000	Proportion
Cash received	200		20%
Loan Stock	600		60%
	800		80%
Shares	200		20%
Total	1,000	1,000	100%

Under Tech 01/09, 'Guidance on the determination of realised profits and losses in the context of distributions under the Companies Act 2006', paragraph 3.18 where an asset is sold partly for qualifying consideration and partly for other consideration, any profit arising will be realised to the extent of the fair value of the qualifying consideration. Therefore, in this case the amount of the profit that can be recognised in the profit and loss account is £200,000 (that is, the amount received in cash). Any remaining unrealised gain would be recognised in the STRGL.

Intra-company trading transactions

27.149 The standard also makes the point that because associates and joint ventures are not part of the group, balances between the investor and its associates or joint ventures should not be eliminated and, therefore, unsettled normal trading transactions should be included as current assets or liabilities. [FRS 9 para 36]. Similarly, with the exception of turnover, normal trading transactions between the group and its joint ventures or its associates do not require elimination. These principles are illustrated in the three examples that follow:

Example 1 – Elimination of intra-company trading – situation 1

A group sells goods to a distribution joint venture (owned 50/50) which in turn sells on to third parties at a margin. In the period the group makes sales of £10m to the joint venture which cost £5m to produce. The joint venture in turn sells the goods to third parties for £12m and it cost of sales is £10m.

The turnover required to be disclosed under the Companies Act is that of the group excluding its joint venture (that is, £10m) and the standard requires the group's share of its joint ventures' turnover to be shown. It would clearly be misleading to show a total group turnover including joint ventures of £16m. Hence, it is necessary to eliminate £5m relating to intra-group trading. The question then arises as to which figure of turnover to eliminate the £5m against. The £5m represents the group's share of the joint venture's cost of sales and it would be logical to eliminate this against the group's turnover reducing it to £5m and to show as share of joint venture's turnover £6m. This gives the correct total of, £11m, but does not comply with the Act's requirements, as the group's turnover, which must be disclosed under the Act, is £10m. Therefore, we suggest that the elimination is made against the share of the joint venture's turnover. This would result in the following presentation:

Consolidated profit and loss account (extract)	£m
Turnover including share of joint venture	11
Less: Share of joint venture	1
Group turnover	10
Cost of sales	5
Group operating profit	5
Share of operating profit of joint venture	1
Operating profit including share of joint venture	6

Depending on how material the group's share of its joint venture turnover is, it may be necessary to indicate that the reported share of joint venture turnover is stated after eliminating intra-group turnover of £5m.

An alternative presentation is to show the share of joint venture turnover before elimination of the £5m intra-group trading, with the intra-group element of the sales of the joint venture being shown separately. This would result in the following presentation.

Consolidated profit and loss account (extract)	£m
Turnover including share of joint venture	11
Less: Share of joint venture	(6)
Add: Sales to joint venture	5
Group turnover	10
Cost of sales	5
Group operating profit	5
Share of operating profit of joint venture	1
Operating profit including share of joint venture	6

This is the presentation adopted by Arcadia Group plc (see Table 27.9).

Table 27.9 — Arcadia Group plc — Report & Accounts — 25 August 2001

Consolidated profit and loss account (extract)

	2001	2000
For the financial year ended 25th August 2001	£m	£m
Turnover		
Total retail and joint ventures	1,896.8	1,955.3
Less: share of joint ventures	(21.6)	(30.3)
Add: sales to joint venture	14.6	20.0
Group	1,889.8	1,945.0

Example 2 – Elimination of intra-company trading – situation 2

The facts are the same as in example 1, except that the joint venture has sales of £9m and cost of sales of £7.5m, that is, a quarter of the goods purchased from the group by the joint venture remain unsold at the year end. The joint venture, therefore, has stock of £2.5m which was sold to it by the group at a profit of £1.25m. Since the joint venture is owned 50/50, 50% of that profit, £0.625m, should be treated as unrealised in the group's financial statements.

This would result in the following presentation.

Consolidated profit and loss account (extract)	£m
Turnover including share of joint venture (10 + 4.5 — 3.75)	10.750
Less: share of joint venture (4.5 — 3.75)	(0.750)
Group turnover	10.000
Cost of sales	5.625
Group operating profit	4.375
Share of operating profit of joint venture (50% × (9 — 7.5))	0.750
Operating profit including share of joint venture	5.125

The difference of £0.875m between the profit of £5.125m in this example and the profit of £6m in example 1 consists of two elements. First, in example 1 the group's results include its share of a profit on the additional £3m sales amounting to £0.25m. Secondly, in this example cost of sales has been increased by the reversal of the unrealised profit of £0.625m.

The group's share of the sales of the joint venture (50% × £9m = £4.5m), reduced by the group's share of the cost of sales of the joint venture (50% × £7.5m), reflects the group's share of incremental sales made by the joint venture to third parties. The turnover section of the profit and loss account now fairly represents the sales activity of the group and the group's share of joint venture combined. Similarly, the share of operating profit of the joint venture fairly reflects the profitability of the joint venture.

Consequently, the adjustment required to eliminate the unrealised profit in stock is best treated as an adjustment to cost of sales of the group.

The group's share of stock of the joint venture will be included in the share of gross assets shown on the face of the group balance sheet. This share of stock is £1.25m (50% × £2.5m) but since this includes the unrealised profit of £0.625m which requires elimination, the group's share of stock will be reduced to £0.625m. The double entry being – debit cost of sales and credit stock with £0.625m.

Example 3 – Elimination of intra-company trading – situation 3

A group has a 50% interest in a joint venture. The group charges the joint venture interest of £10,000 on a loan it has made to the joint venture. Therefore, the group has interest income in its profit and loss account of £10,000 and the joint venture has an interest expense of £10,000.

On consolidation the group would show for these items interest income of £10,000 and share of joint venture's interest payable of £5,000. Overall, therefore, the group has only recognised net income of £5,000, which represents the interest charged by the group to the other investor.

27.150 It can be seen from the examples that, with the exception of turnover, under equity accounting it is not necessary to eliminate inter-company trading on a line-by-line basis. Therefore, generally for trading transactions no consolidation adjustments are necessary as the group's share of the transaction is taken up in the share of its joint venture's or its associate's results. Consolidation adjustments are only necessary, as explained above, where profits and losses resulting from transactions between the investor and its joint venture, or its associate, are included in the carrying value of assets in either the group or the joint venture or associate and also to eliminate intra-group turnover.

Partnerships that are joint venture entities

27.151 Under the standard's provisions, a partnership may be either a joint venture entity or a joint arrangement that is not an entity. How to determine which type of joint arrangement an undertaking is, is considered from paragraph 27.177 below.

27.152 An issue arises with the accounting requirements for partnerships that are joint venture entities. In the group's consolidated financial statements, such partnerships should be equity accounted using the gross equity method. However, the question arises how the partnership should be accounted for in the investor's individual financial statements. The standard is silent as regards the treatment in the investor's own profit and loss account, but requires that, in the investor's own balance sheet, its interests in joint ventures should be treated as fixed asset investments and shown either at cost, less any amounts written off, or at valuation. It follows from this that in the company's profit and loss account only the investment income should be accounted for. Before the introduction of FRS 9, some partnerships of this nature were accounted for using proportional consolidation, or were equity accounted, in the investor's individual financial statements. Proportional consolidation is no longer possible following FRS 9's introduction. However, where there are no restrictions on the distribution of profits from the partnership, it may still be appropriate to record the investor's share of the results of its partnership. It could do this by showing its share of the results on one line representing its investment income rather than merely the distributions received from the partnership. In the balance sheet, the investment would be valued on the basis of the investor's share of the partnership's net assets. The accounting requirements that apply to partnerships that are joint arrangements are considered from paragraph 27.199 below.

Where the associate itself is a group

27.153 Where the associated undertaking (including joint ventures) is a group of undertakings, the Act requires that the net assets and the profits or losses that should be taken into account on equity accounting the associate should be those of the associate consolidated with its subsidiary undertakings. [CA85 4A Sch 22(2)]. This requirement is added to by FRS 9, which requires that the net assets and profits or losses to be dealt with should include the joint venture's or associate's share of the net assets and profits or losses of investments it may itself have in its own joint ventures or associates. [FRS 9 para 32].

Interests in losses and net liabilities

27.154 A problem may arise where a joint venture or an associate starts to make losses, particularly where those losses are such that the undertaking has net liabilities. Where this is so, the investing group should normally continue to record changes in carrying amounts of its joint ventures or associates in its consolidated balance sheet even where this results in recognising its share of any deficiency in a joint venture or an associate. [FRS 9 para 44]. This would apply, for example, where the investment is still regarded by the group as long-term (an essential condition of the definition of a joint venture or an associate).

27.155 The standard states that the only exception to equity accounting for such deficits is where there is sufficient evidence that an event has irrevocably changed the relationship between the investor and its investee, marking its irreversible withdrawal from its joint venture or associate. [FRS 9 para 44]. Consequently, where, for example, there is no intention to support the undertaking, then only the liabilities that the group will incur if the undertaking should cease to trade would need to be provided for in full in the consolidated financial statements. However, mere intention alone will not be adequate and the standard is looking for a demonstrable commitment to the withdrawal including a public statement to that effect. In particular, such a commitment will arise where the direction of the joint venture's or the associate's operating and financial policies has become the responsibility of its creditors (including bankers), for example where the joint venture or associate is in liquidation. Where the interest in a joint venture or an associate is in net liabilities, the amount recorded should be shown as a provision or a liability. [FRS 9 para 45].

Example – Interest in net liabilities

A company has an interest of 25% in an associate. The associate has net liabilities at the year end of £3.5m. The net liabilities include a loan of £2.5m from the investor. In the investor's individual financial statements a provision of £1.5m has been made against the loan.

In the group's consolidated financial statements, the investment in the associate is made up of its share of net liabilities together with any loan made to the associate. The group's share of the associate's net liabilities is £875,000 (that is, £3.5m × 25%). But of the net liabilities of £3.5m, the group has already made a provision of £1.5m against its loan. Consequently, it has, in effect, already made a provision against its share of net liabilities of £375,000 (that is, £1.5m × 25%) Therefore, the group only needs to provide for a further £500,000 on consolidation. This provision would also be made against the loan, giving a net investment in the associate of £500,000.

27.156 Often where a joint venture or an associate is making losses, there may be a significant diminution in the joint venture's or associate's value. Where there is any permanent diminution in value of any goodwill attributable to an investment in a joint venture or an associate, a provision should be made to write down that goodwill. [FRS 9 para 38]. A provision for any further impairment in the associate's net assets would not normally be required in the group's consolidated financial statements, because such an impairment in value would generally be reflected in the associate's net asset value. Where there is an impairment in goodwill, FRS 9 requires that the amount written off in the period should be separately disclosed. [CA85 4 Sch 19(2); FRS 9 para 38].

27.157 Where a group has an investment in an associate that has net liabilities, it is necessary to decide how to show the group's share of this deficit in the consolidated financial statements. It would not be appropriate to net the negative interest against other positive interests in associates. Positive interests should be shown within assets while negative interests should be shown within liabilities. The most appropriate caption in the balance sheet within which to show a negative interest is 'other provisions', although the standard states it can be shown as a provision or a liability. [FRS 9 para 45].

27.158 Table 27.10 shows a group that has treated its interest in negative net assets of an associate in a similar way to that described above.

Table 27.10 — Cordiant Communications Group plc — Annual report and accounts — 31 December 2000

Notes to the financial statements (extract)

21. Provisions (extract)
Provision for joint venture deficit

The Group share of net liabilities is as shown below:	**2000 £m**	**1999 £m**
Fixed assets	**2.1**	1.7
Current assets	**128.5**	84.4
Share of gross assets	**130.6**	86.1
Liabilities due within one year	**(142.6)**	(99.9)
Liabilities due after one year	**(0.1)**	(0.6)
Share of gross liabilities	**(142.7)**	(100.5)
Share of joint venture net liabilities	**(12.1)**	(14.4)

Joint and several liability

27.159 FRS 9 makes the important point that, where unincorporated undertakings are treated as joint ventures or associates, a liability could arise in excess of that taken into account when accounting for the group's share of the joint venture or associate. In this case it is important that all such liabilities with respect to that entity are reflected appropriately in the financial statements. [FRS 9 para 46] The example given in the standard is that of joint and several liability in a partnership. [FRS 9 para 47]. Where such a potential liability exists (or a similar type of support agreement exists) it is necessary to consider whether a provision should be made for the possibility that the other party to the agreement may be unable to meet its obligations under that agreement.

27.160 In circumstances where it is clear that the other party is able to honour such an agreement, it is still necessary under the Act, FRS 9 and FRS 12 for the group to disclose the existence of its potential commitment as a contingent liability and clearly explain the circumstances in which the liability might crystallise. [FRS 9 para 47, FRS 12 para 29]. Table 27.11 shows the extent of guarantees given in respect of bank borrowings and funding of associates.

Table 27.11 — Associated British Ports Holdings PLC — Annual report and accounts — 31 December 1998

Notes to the accounts (extract)

28 Contingent liabilities (extract)

	Group		Company	
Contingent liabilities under claims, indemnities and bank guarantees are as follows:	**1998**	1997	**1998**	1997
	£m	£m	**£m**	£m
Bank guarantees in respect of:				
— subsidiaries	—	—	**19.3**	22.7
— associated companies	—	0.1	—	0.1
Other guarantees and contingencies	**4.9**	0.6	—	—

The company has given guarantees of performance of contracts of work by one of its associated companies (Universal Pipe Coaters Limited) which totalled £18.5 million at 31 December 1998 (1997: £18.5 million). No claims had been notified under these guarantees at the year-end

Minority interests

27.161 Where the associate is held by a subsidiary that is partly held by a minority, the minority's share of the associate's results should be shown as part of minority interests in the consolidated financial statements.

Acquisitions and disposals

Effective date of acquisition or disposal

27.162 The effective date of acquisition of an associate is the date on which the investor begins to fulfil the two essential elements of the definition of an associate, that is, holding a participating interest and exercising significant influence. Similarly, the effective date for the acquisition of a joint venture interest is the date on which the investor begins to control that entity jointly with the other venturers. [FRS 9 para 40]. These requirements are equivalent to those in FRS 2, which states that for subsidiaries, the date on which an undertaking becomes a subsidiary is the date on which control passes to the parent. [FRS 2 para 45]. In addition, the investment must be a long-term interest, that is, it is not held for subsequent resale.

27.163 It follows, therefore, that the date on which an investment ceases to be an associate is the date on which it ceases to fulfil either element of the definition mentioned above. Similarly, the date on which an investment ceases to be a joint venture is the date on which the investor ceases to have joint control. [FRS 9 para 40].

27.164 Once the investment has qualified as a joint venture or an associate, minor temporary changes in the relationship between the investor and its joint venture or associate should not affect its status. In a similar way to the rules that apply to interests in subsidiaries, once the investor has accounted for its investments as associates or joint ventures, it should continue to equity account for them whether or not the investor intends to keep its interest or dispose of it. [FRS 9 paras 7, 43]. The investor should only stop equity accounting when the investment ceases to be a joint venture or an associate.

Acquisition rules

27.165 Often an investment in a joint venture or an associate is acquired in stages. Where this happens, FRS 9 states that the rules specified in paragraphs 50 to 52 of FRS 2 should be applied. [FRS 9 para 41]. These provisions require that where a group increases its interest in an undertaking that is already an associate or a joint venture, the identifiable assets and liabilities of that entity should be revalued to fair values and goodwill should be calculated only on the increase in interest by reference to those fair values. Consequently, a new fair value exercise will need to be carried out for each tranche of shares acquired, unless the difference between the fair values and the carrying amounts of the net assets attributable to the increase in stake is immaterial. For piecemeal acquisitions of subsidiaries, complying with FRS 2's requirements can conflict with the Act, because the Act requires the identifiable assets and liabilities of subsidiaries to be included in the consolidation at their fair value at the date of acquisition. This means that under the Act's provisions goodwill is calculated at the time the entity becomes a subsidiary, ignoring the effect of acquiring previous tranches. However, the conflict with the Act does not arise in accounting for piecemeal acquisitions of associates or joint ventures, because the Act does not deal with how to account for the acquisition of associates or joint ventures. Consequently, the rules in FRS 2 should be followed.

27.166 An undertaking might become an associate in a number of ways (whereas joint ventures tend to be set up as such from the outset), for example:

- The investing group acquires an additional investment in the undertaking to bring its voting rights to over 20 per cent.
- The investing group has an investment of over 20 per cent, but previously did not have board representation or significant influence over the financial or operating policy decisions of the undertaking. It has now gained significant influence.

27.166.1 Acquisitions of associates or joint ventures can also arise where a parent sells a subsidiary for shares in another undertaking, which results in that other undertaking becoming an associate or joint venture of the vendor. Therefore, at the same time as the acquisition there is a disposal. The accounting for such transactions is considered in UITF Abstract 31,

'Exchanges of businesses or other non-monetary assets for an interest in a subsidiary, joint venture or associate', which is dealt with in chapter 26.

27.167 The treatment of an investment becoming an associate is illustrated in the example that follows.

Example – Investment becomes an associate

A group made an investment of 10% in a company a few years ago. The investment cost £25,000 and has subsequently been revalued to £50,000. It makes a further investment of 15% to bring its total investment to 25%. The fair value of the consideration given for the additional investment is £250,000. The net assets of the investee stand in its own books at the date of the second acquisition at £800,000. A fair value exercise has been undertaken at the date of acquisition which shows a fair value of net assets of £1.1m (including capitalised goodwill in the associate of £100,000). The adjusted capital and reserves of the associate are, as a consequence, £200,000 share capital and £900,000 reserves (which includes a £200,000 revaluation reserve). The associate has goodwill recognised in its balance sheet of £100,000. The goodwill arising on acquisition and the balance sheet treatment in the group would be as follows:

Cost of acquisition	£'000
Original investment	25
Fair value of consideration given	250
Total consideration	275

Consolidation goodwill	£'000
Total consideration	275
Adjusted capital and reserves excluding capitalised goodwill of £100,000 (being, 25% × (£1.1m – £100,000 goodwill))	250
Goodwill	25

Balance sheet (extract)	£'000
Interest in associated undertakings	
Share of net assets excluding goodwill (being, 25% × £1m)	250
Goodwill on acquisition	25
	275

The only adjustments that would be required in this example are to reduce the value of the original investment from its market value to cost and to eliminate the goodwill recognised in the associate. Consequently, the entries on consolidation would be to debit the revaluation reserve of the investor with £25,000 and credit the investment £25,000 and in the associate to credit goodwill £100,000 and debit reserves with £100,000. The goodwill arising on acquisition of £25,000 would be dealt with in accordance with FRS 10 (see chapter 25).

Alternatively, the goodwill arising on the acquisition of the additional 15% interest can also be calculated separately.

Goodwill arising on acquisition of the additional 15% interest

	£'000
Fair value of consideration	250
Adjusted capital and reserves after elimination of goodwill arising in the associate (15% × (£1.1m – £100,000))	150
Goodwill	100

If goodwill of £100,000 is recognised, the difference between this amount and the goodwill of £25,000, being a credit of £75,000, calculated above represents a revaluation of the 10% interest and should be credited to the revaluation reserve. This calculation gives a fairer presentation of the goodwill arising on the increase in stake. At present, either method is acceptable.

27.168 In the example above, where an investment becomes an associate interest, it is possible to account for the increase in the investment in two ways. There are no specific rules in this area, so either method can be used. The technically correct method would be to calculate the goodwill arising on the acquisition of each tranche of the investment. However, this would generally not be practicable, because fair values would not necessarily be available at the time the original investment was made. The second method described above treats the increase in stake as a separate acquisition and gives a fairer result that the first method.

27.169 Although the second method described above is not required where an investment becomes an associate, it is necessary to consider each tranche separately where there is an increase in stake in an associate. FRS 2 requires that such a method is used for piecemeal acquisitions for subsidiaries and these same rules are applied *via* FRS 9 to increases in stake for associates. Consider the following example:

Example – Increase in stake in an associate

A group made an investment in an associate of 20% in 20X2. The investment cost £12m and the book value (also fair value) of the associate's net assets at that date was £50m. In 20X8 it makes a further investment in the company of 20% to bring its total investment to 40%. Goodwill on the original acquisition of the associate was written off directly against reserves in the year of acquisition (following the rules that applied before the introduction of FRS 10). The net assets of the associate stand in its books at £68m on the date of the increase in stake. The associate would be treated as follows up to the date of the original acquisition:

Acquisition of associate	£m
Original investment in company	12.0
Fair value of net assets acquired (20% × £50m)	10.0
Goodwill arising	2.0

The fair value of the consideration given for the additional 20% is £16m. The fair value exercise shows that the company's net assets are worth £75m, which is also the adjusted capital and reserves. The goodwill on acquisition of the increase in stake would be calculated as follows:

Increase in stake in associate	£m	£m
Cost of acquisition as shown in the investor's books		
Original investment in company		12
Fair value of consideration given for new investment		16
Total investment in associate		28
Consolidation goodwill		
Total consideration		28
Adjusted capital and reserves		
being 20% × £50m	10	
being 20% × £75m	15	25
Goodwill		3
Goodwill previously written off		2
New goodwill arising on the increase in stake		1

The goodwill figure that emerges is instinctively correct as it reflects the fact that a premium of £1m arises on the acquisition of the additional 20% (that is, £16m – (£75m × 20%)). The results since the date of acquisition of the associate are attributable to the group and as such are correctly treated as post-acquisition. The alternative calculation of considering the total investment of £28m compared to the total share of net assets of £30m (that is, £75m × 40%) gives a total figure of negative goodwill of £2m and, as a consequence, negative goodwill of £4m arising on the increase in stake. This method understates the goodwill arising on the increase in stake and is not the method specified in FRS 2, but nevertheless may be used where the difference between the net fair values and the carrying amounts of the assets and liabilities attributable to the increase in stake is not material.

Disposal rules

27.170 The standard states that where an interest in a joint venture or an associate is disposed of, the profit or loss arising on disposal should be calculated after taking into account any related goodwill that has not previously been written off through the profit and loss account. [FRS 9 para 40]. For example, there may be a balance of unamortised goodwill that relates to the joint venture or associate which is capitalised as part of the interest in the investment. Alternatively, under FRS 10's transitional provisions, goodwill arising on the acquisition of joint ventures or associates that arose before the introduction of that standard may still be written off directly against reserves. Where this is so, the goodwill that applies to the proportion of the investment disposed of should be brought into account in calculating the profit or loss arising on the disposal.

27.171 When an entity ceases to be either a joint venture or an associate, the investor may retain all or some of its interest in that entity simply as an investment. In this circumstance, it is necessary to determine the carrying value of any remaining interest in the undertaking. This should be based on the percentage retained of the final carrying amount for the joint venture or associate at the date the entity ceased to qualify as a subsidiary or an associate. The remaining interest should also include any related goodwill. [FRS 9 para 42]. For example, if goodwill arising on the original acquisition of a 24 per cent interest in an associate was £50,000, then if the investment decreases to 12 per cent and the entity is no longer an associate, the carrying value of the investment should include 50 per cent of the goodwill arising on the original investment, that is, £25,000. The new carrying amount of the investment is a surrogate cost (not based on any consideration paid) and should be reviewed and written down, if necessary, to its recoverable amount. [FRS 9 para 42].

Example – Disposal of associate

A group has had an investment of 40% in an associate for a number of years. At the beginning of the accounting period, the balance sheets of the group excluding the associate and the group including the associate are as follows:

Summarised balance sheets

	Group excluding associate	Associate	Group including associate
	£'000	£'000	£'000
Fixed assets	500	230	500
Investment in associate:			
Cost	110	–	–
Equity accounting			125
Current assets	300	150	300
Current liabilities	(250)	(80)	(250)
	660	300	675
Share capital	300	100	300
Share premium	220	50	220
Profit and loss reserve	40	100	55
Other reserves	100	50	100
	660	300	675

The net assets of the associate at the date of acquisition of the 40% interest were £250,000. The goodwill that arose on the original acquisition of the associate is £10,000 (that is, £110,000 – (£250,000 × 40%)). The goodwill was capitalised on the acquisition of the associate to accord with FRS 10's requirements and £5,000 has been amortised to the profit and loss account since acquisition. Consequently, the group's investment in the associate of £125,000 is made up of its share of net assets of £120,000 (that is, £300,000 × 40%) plus the balance of goodwill unamortised of £5,000.

The group's profit and loss reserve of £55,000 is made up of £40,000 less goodwill amortisation of £5,000 plus the share of the associate's post-acquisition reserves of £20,000 (that is, £50,000 × 40%).

During the year the group disposes of 50% of its investment in the associate and no longer has board representation. Consequently, the remaining interest of 20% is no longer considered to be that of an associate, but represents a simple investment. The proceeds received on the sale are £70,000 and the net asset value of the associate at the date of sale is £320,000. Consequently, up to the date of sale of part of the group's investment in the associate, it made a profit of £20,000. The associate, therefore, becomes an investment part way through the year. The profit and loss accounts of the group excluding the former associate, the former associate and the group adjusted to include the revised carrying amount of the investment in the former associate are given below:

Summarised profit and loss accounts

	Group excluding interest	Former associate	Group including interest
	£'000	£'000	£'000
Operating profit	40	30	40.0
Share of operating profit of associate (note (a))	–	–	8.0
Operating profit including associate	40	30	48.0
Profit on sale of interest in associate (note (b))	15	–	3.5
Profit for the financial year	55	30	51.5
Reserve brought forward	40	100	55.0
Reserve carried forward	95	130	106.5

(a) The income from interest in the associated undertaking of £8,000 is the group's share of the results of the undertaking before the disposal (that is, 40% × £20,000).

(b) The profit on the sale of the share of the associate in the company selling the interest is £15,000, which is calculated by deducting from the sale proceeds of £70,000 the cost of the investment of £55,000 (that is, £110,000 × 50%). The profit on sale to the group is £3,500, which is calculated by deducting from the sale proceeds of £70,000 a 20% share of the associate's net assets consolidated up to the date of sale of £64,000 (that is, £320,000 × 20%) and half of the balance of unamortised goodwill of £2,500 that arose on the original acquisition.

At the group's year end, the balance sheets of the group and the former associate, which is now an investment, are set out below:

Summarised balance sheets

	Group excluding interest	Former associate	Group including interest
	£'000	£'000	£'000
Fixed assets	530	250	530.0
Investment (cost)	55	–	66.5
Current assets	390	170	390.0
Current liabilities	(260)	(90)	(260.0)
	715	330	726.5
Share capital	300	100	300.0
Share premium	220	50	220.0
Profit and loss reserve	95	130	106.5
Other reserves	100	50	100.0
	715	330	726.5

The investment in the former associate of £66,500 represents the share of net assets and goodwill retained by the group at the date of disposal (that is, (£320,000 × 20%) + (£5,000 × 50%)). The share of goodwill remaining is shown as part of the investment. The result is curious, because the investment in the company holding the interest is shown at a cost to that company of £55,000, but the group shows a cost to the group for the investment of £66,500. The difference of £11,500 represents the results of the associate recorded by the group which include retained reserves of £14,000 (that is, (£320,000 – £250,000) × 20%) less goodwill amortisation of £2,500. It is necessary to ensure that the carrying value of the investment in the group is not impaired, but as long as this is not the case, it would be possible in the company to revalue the investment to £66,500 the same value as shown in the group and credit to the revaluation reserve with the difference of £11,500.

27.172 An example of a disposal of a part interest in an associate is given in Table 27.12.

Table 27.12 – Lonmin Plc – Annual Report – 30 September 2004

Notes to the accounts (extract)

11 Associate (extract)

The investment in associate of $4 million shown above in 2003 represented an investment of 44% in the ordinary share capital of Platinum Australia Limited, a company incorporated in Australia. This investment was reduced to 38% during the year and on 30 September 2004 it was transferred to fixed asset investments following the resignation of Lonmin representatives from the board of Platinum Australia. The Group no longer exercises significant influence over the operating and financial policies of Platinum Australia and it is the Group's intention to realise this investment. These factors rebut the presumption that a holding of 20% or more should be presumed to exercise a significant influence and consequently this holding is now included as a fixed asset investment.

A joint venture becomes an associate

27.173 An interest in an entity that ceases to be a joint venture may still qualify as an associate. In this case, a profit or loss will arise on disposal, but the same rules, that is, equity accounting, will apply to the remaining interest, albeit disclosure is no longer required of the share of the associate's gross turnover or gross assets and gross liabilities on the face of the balance sheet. In addition, a joint venture can become an associate where the investor does not dispose of any interest in the entity. This would arise where the degree of influence the investor has over its investee changes from joint control to mere significant influence. In this situation, there will be no change to the share to be equity accounted only the level of disclosure will decrease from the 'gross equity' requirements to the less detailed normal equity accounting disclosures.

A subsidiary becomes an associate

27.174 Acquisitions of associates are considered from paragraph 27.165 above, but an associate can also arise from the disposal of an interest in a subsidiary, for example:

- The investing group sells a share of a subsidiary company, which has reduced the group's shareholding to below 50 per cent of the undertaking's voting rights although the group has retained significant influence and, accordingly, it is now an associate.
- A subsidiary issues shares to a third party such that the investing group's shareholding reduces below 50 per cent of the undertaking's voting rights, although significant influence is retained.
- The investing group ceases to exercise or have the power to exercise dominant influence at, for example, the 40 per cent level, but continues to have significant influence.

27.175 The treatment of a subsidiary becoming an associate is illustrated in the example that follows.

Example – Subsidiary becomes an associate

A group has had an investment of 80% in a subsidiary for a number of years. At the beginning of the accounting period, the balance sheets of the group excluding the subsidiary and the group including the subsidiary are as follows:

Summarised balance sheets

	Group excluding sub £'000	Sub £'000	Group including sub £'000
Goodwill	–	–	10
Fixed assets	500	230	730
Investment in subsidiary	220	–	–
Current assets	300	150	450
Current liabilities	(250)	(80)	(330)
	770	300	860
Share capital	300	100	300
Share premium	220	50	220
Profit and loss reserve	150	100	180
Other reserves	100	50	100
Minority interests	–	–	60
	770	300	860

The goodwill that arose on the original acquisition of the subsidiary is £20,000 and is calculated as set out below. The goodwill was capitalised on the acquisition of the subsidiary to accord with the requirements of FRS 10 and £10,000 has been amortised to the profit and loss account since acquisition.

Cost of control account/goodwill

Investment	220,000	Share capital (80% × 100,000)	80,000
		Share premium (80% × 50,000)	40,000
		Pre-acq profit and loss reserve (80% × 50,000)	40,000
		Other reserves (80% × 50,000)	40,000
		Balance, *viz* goodwill	20,000
	220,000		220,000

The minority interests at the beginning of the year are calculated as follows:

Minority interests account

Minority interests	60,000	Share capital (20% × 100,000)	20,000
		Share premium (20% × 50,000)	10,000
		Profit and loss reserve (20% × 100,000)	20,000
		Other reserves (20% × 50,000)	10,000
	60,000		60,000

The group's profit and loss reserve of £180,000 is made up of £150,000 less goodwill amortisation of £10,000 plus the subsidiary's post-acquisition reserves of £40,000 (that is, £50,000 × 80%).

During the year the group disposes of 50% of its investment in the subsidiary. The proceeds received on the sale are £140,000 and the net asset value of the subsidiary at the date of sale is £320,000. Consequently, up to the date of sale of part of the group's investment in the subsidiary, it made a profit of £20,000. The subsidiary, therefore, becomes an associate part way through the year. The profit and loss accounts of the group excluding the associate, the associate, and the group including the associate using the equity method of accounting are given below:

Summarised profit and loss accounts

	Group excluding assoc £'000	Assoc £'000	Group including assoc £'000
Operating profit (note (a))	40	30	60
Share of operating profit of associate (note (b))	–	–	4
Operating profit including associate	40	30	64
Profit on sale of interest in subsidiary (note (c))	30	–	7
Operating profit	70	30	71
Minority interests (note (d))	–	–	(4)
Profit for the year	70	30	67
Reserve brought forward	150	100	180
Reserve carried forward	220	130	247

(a) The operating profit for the group of £60,000 represents the profit of the group of £40,000 (excluding the associate's profit), plus the profit of the subsidiary up to the date of sale of the 40% interest (which is £20,000).

(b) The income from interests in associated undertakings of £4,000 is the group's share of the results of the undertaking after it became an associate (that is, 40% × £10,000).

(c) The profit on the sale of the subsidiary in the company selling the interest is £30,000, which is calculated by deducting from the sale proceeds of £140,000 the cost of the investment of £110,000 (that is, £220,000 × 50%). The profit on sale to the group is £7,000, which is calculated by deducting from the sale proceeds of £140,000 a 40% share of the subsidiary's net assets consolidated up to the date of sale of £128,000 and half of the balance of unamortised goodwill that arose on the original acquisition of £5,000. The net assets of the subsidiary are made up of the net assets at the last balance sheet date of £300,000 plus the profit on ordinary activities to date of sale of £20,000. The group's share of those assets is £128,000 (that is, £320,000 × 40%).

(d) The minority interest figure of £4,000 is the minority's share of the profits of the subsidiary up to the date of sale of the 40% interest and is calculated by applying the minority's share of 20% to the profits recognised by the subsidiary in the period (that is, £20,000).

At the group's year end, the balance sheets of the group and the former subsidiary, which is now an associate, are set out below:

Summarised balance sheets

	Group excluding assoc	Assoc	Group including assoc
	£'000	£'000	£'000
Fixed assets	530	250	530
Investment in associate: Cost	110	—	—
Equity accounting	—	—	137
Current assets	460	170	460
Current liabilities	(260)	(90)	(260)
	840	330	867
Share capital	300	100	300
Share premium	220	50	220
Profit and loss reserve	220	130	247
Other reserves	100	50	100
Minority interest	—	—	—
	840	330	867

The investment in the associate of £137,000 represents the share of net assets and goodwill retained by the group at the date of sale (that is, (£320,000 × 40%) + (£10,000 × 50%)), together with the share of the associate's results that arose after the sale (that is, £10,000 × 40%). The goodwill is shown as part of the investment in the associate, but should also be separately disclosed in the notes to accord with FRS 9.

Equity accounting in a single company

27.176 How to account for investments in associates and joint ventures made by a single company is considered in chapter 6.

Joint arrangements

27.177 A 'joint arrangement' is a term which encompasses the following types of undertakings:

- A joint arrangement that has its own trade or business. This is a joint venture and should be gross equity accounted in accordance with the provisions of FRS 9, as explained earlier in this chapter.
- A 'joint arrangement that is not an entity'. This is a joint activity undertaken by two or more participants, whereby the activity does not amount to the carrying on of its own trade or business.
- A structure with the form, but not the substance, of a joint venture.

27.178 This section deals with the last two types of arrangement, which are referred to below as 'joint arrangements'. Joint arrangements of this type are required to be accounted for in a different way from associates and joint ventures; that is, interests in such arrangements should not be equity accounted. Both of these types of arrangement are somewhat similar in nature to joint ventures in that they will be formed by two or more participants and there will be an agreement covering the arrangement. But they differ from joint ventures in other respects.

Joint arrangement that is not an entity

27.179 A 'joint arrangement that is not an entity' is defined as:

> *"A contractual arrangement under which the participants engage in joint activities that do not create an entity because it would not be carrying on a trade or business of its own. A contractual arrangement where all significant matters of operating and financial policy are predetermined does not create an entity because the policies are those of its participants, not of a separate entity."* [FRS 9 para 4].

27.180 For this purpose, the term 'entity' is defined in FRS 9 to mean:

> *"A body corporate, partnership or unincorporated association carrying on a trade or business with or without a view to profit. The reference to carrying on a trade or business means a trade or business of its own and not just part of the trades or businesses of entities that have interests in it."* [FRS 9 para 4].

27.181 The term 'undertaking' in the Act uses identical wording to that in the first sentence of the definition of 'entity', but does not include the second qualifying sentence. Consequently, an undertaking can be a 'joint arrangement that is not an entity'. Appendix I to the standard, which includes a note on the legal requirements, says clearly that a joint arrangement may qualify as an undertaking under the Act, even where it does not carry on its own trade. It goes on to say that in such cases the undertaking acts merely as an agent for the venturers. [FRS 9 Appendix I para 6]. Therefore, a 'joint arrangement that is not an entity' can be an undertaking such as a limited company or a partnership or an unincorporated undertaking or may be a simple arrangement between the parties where a separate legal entity is not established, as it is the nature of its trading relationship that determines whether or not it will fall within the standard's definition, not how it is constituted. The term 'entity' is used to describe the substance rather than the legal form.

27.182 In contrast, for a joint arrangement to be a separate entity, that is, a joint venture, it must carry on a trade or business of its own and not just be part of its participants' trades or businesses. Such an entity will have some independence from its participants to pursue its own commercial strategy in buying and selling and will have access to the market in its own right for its main inputs and outputs. [FRS 9 para 8]. This independence must be allowed within the objectives set by the agreement governing the entity, for example, in the joint venture agreement. If, on the other hand, the objectives are predetermined in that agreement and in effect the business unwinds exactly as specified within that agreement, the undertaking is likely to be a joint arrangement.

27.183 As stated above, to be a joint arrangement the undertaking must not carry on a trade or business of its own. For this reason, cost-sharing or risk-sharing arrangements are likely to be classified as joint arrangements and the standard gives as examples the following types of arrangements:

- Joint marketing.
- Joint distribution.
- Shared production facilities.

For example, a joint marketing arrangement established by two parties whereby the participants fund a joint marketing campaign is likely to be a joint arrangement. In such a case, the joint arrangement does not have access to the market in its own right, but is merely an extension of each participant's trade.

27.184 It follows that a company will normally *only* be a joint arrangement where it acts as an agent for its joint venturers. In this circumstance, it will not have access to the market in its own right as it is merely acting on its principals' behalf. Consequently, in the example of the joint marketing arrangement mentioned above, if the joint marketing is conducted within a limited company, it would only amount to a joint arrangement where the company is acting as an agent for its principals, otherwise it will be a joint venture or an associate.

27.185 Repetition of buying and selling is indicative of an arrangement carrying on a trade or business. Conversely, where an arrangement carries out a single project, such as a single property joint development, the undertaking will not carry on a separate trade or business where it acts as an agent for its principals' businesses. The undertaking would fall to be treated as a joint arrangement. [FRS 9 para 9]. This would apply, for example, to a short-term property development undertaken as a partnership. However, it appears that where a short-term property development is undertaken in a limited company, then it will not be a joint arrangement, unless the company is acting as an agent for its principals. Where an agency arrangement does not exist, such a company would fall within the definitions of an associate or a joint venture even where, for example, it only runs for 18 months. This is because in this situation the investment would be deemed to be held for the long term. Long term is defined in the standard by reference to whether or not the investment is held with a view to subsequent resale and not in relation to the length of time the undertaking will exist to fulfil its purpose. [FRS 9 para 4].

27.186 The standard mentions two further examples of joint arrangements that are not entities. The first is where the participants derive their benefit from products or services taken in kind, rather than by receiving a share in the results of trading. [FRS 9 para 8(a)]. This could, for example, be a joint research arrangement, whereby each of the participants benefits from the research, but are not billed a royalty specifically by the research company for using that patented research. The participants would fund the research through some other means. In addition, the standard states that joint arrangements can cover situations where the participants take their share of the joint product in cash where that commodity is actively traded. [FRS 9 para 8(a)]. This might arise, for example, in the oil and gas industry where two or more producers form a joint distribution arrangement.

27.187 The second situation described in the standard is where each participant's share of the output or result of the joint activity is determined by its supply of key inputs to the process producing that output or result. [FRS 9 para 8(b)]. An example might be where it is possible to segregate the activities of the entity so that each of the participants' results can be separately seen. This is very similar to the standard's description of a joint arrangement that has the form, but not the substance, of a joint venture (see further para 27.191).

27.188 The nature of a joint arrangement might change over time. For example, it might start out as such an arrangement whereby it is just an extension of its participants' trades, such as with the development and use of an oil or gas pipeline. But if the joint arrangement starts to trade with third parties that are not participants in the joint arrangement, then it may well take on the form of a joint venture entity and require to be gross equity accounted. [FRS 9 para 9].

27.189 In practice, it will often be difficult to judge whether or not an undertaking is a joint arrangement or a joint venture. The following examples illustrate two different structures.

Example 1 – Difference between a joint arrangement and a joint venture

Three venturers form a company to supply IT services to a customer. The parties to the arrangement each own 33% of the company's shares. The venturers supply different IT products, with one supplying the software, another the hardware and the third supplying the systems expertise. The sole purpose for the company is to allow the parties to invoice the customer in one name. The supplier of the systems expertise manages the provision of the hardware and software supply and gives a performance guarantee to the customer. The hardware supply represents 50% of the company's turnover, the software accounts for 20% and the system development 30%. The operation of the company is governed by a shareholder agreement with the company and sub-contract agreements with the venturers. The company makes no margin on the on-billing of the hardware, software and systems development, any administrative expenses being recharged to the participants.

In this situation, it is clear that the financial and operating policies of the company are predetermined by the shareholder agreement and the other agreements surrounding the arrangement. In addition, the undertaking does not have access to the market in its own right as it is merely a facility through which the participants' businesses are conducted and, as a consequence, is acting as their agent. Therefore, the undertaking would be judged to be a joint arrangement rather than a joint venture under FRS 9's provisions.

Example 2 – Difference between a joint arrangement and a joint venture

Three venturers form a company to bid for the provision of healthcare services to a Health Trust under the Private Finance Initiative (PFI). The parties to the venture are a construction company, a service provider and an equity investment fund. Each of the venturers owns 33% of the company's shares. The company constructs a hospital, which is financed in part by the equity venturers and also by bank funding secured on the payments to be made by the Health Trust (that is, the unitary payment). In substance the construction and the service provision are sub-contracted to two of the venturers. The unitary payment made by the Health Trust varies depending upon the delivery performance under the terms of the PFI contract. The property has been judged to be on balance sheet of the company. There is a shareholder agreement with the company and sub-contract agreements with the venturers. Under the shareholder agreement, profits or losses of the company are shared equally between the venturers and all decisions have to have full agreement of the venturers (there are also arbitration procedures specified in the agreement). The amount the service provider receives is dependent upon its performance and this is detailed in its sub-contract agreement.

For the service provider, the arrangement could be either a joint venture or a joint arrangement. At first sight, the structure has many of the features of a joint arrangement. For example, most of the financial and operating policies are predetermined in the agreements (these include, the PFI agreement, the shareholder agreement, the loan agreement with the bank and the sub-contract agreements with the venturers). Also, it could be argued that the company does not have access to the market in its own right, because it only has one customer under the PFI agreement and its relationship with the Health Trust was established in the agreements. But this argument ignores the fact that the company is carrying on a business of its own, which is the provision of an *integrated* service to the Health Trust, and is not acting as an agent in this respect. In addition, the company could provide a similar service for other customers in the future and, as a consequence, has access to the market in its own right. Therefore, the facts of this case indicate that the undertaking falls within the definition of a joint venture, which should be accounted for under the gross equity accounting method by its venturers rather than falling to be treated as a joint arrangement.

27.190 Joint arrangements will often be agency type arrangements, where it is clear that the undertaking's business is just an extension of the separate businesses of its venturers and where it does not have access to the market in its own right.

Joint venture with the substance of a joint arrangement

27.191 Another type of joint arrangement identified in the standard is an undertaking that has the form of a joint venture, but not the substance of one. Such an arrangement would arise where the joint venture undertaking is used only as a means for each participant to carry on its own business. [FRS 9 para 24]. In this type of situation the venturers would operate their own businesses separately within the structure. The framework entity would act merely as an agent for each of the venturers, who are able to identify their own share of the assets, liabilities and cash flows within the framework. [FRS 9 para 25]. Where such an arrangement exists and is conducted through a limited company, the undertaking will only be a joint arrangement if it acts as an agent for its principals. [FRS 9 App I para 5].

27.192 Some securitisation special purpose vehicles work in this way. Each of the originators/participants in the special purpose vehicle will be able to identify the assets (such as, mortgage receivables) that it has contributed to the venture and its benefits and risks arise directly from those assets and their related finance.

Accounting for joint arrangements

27.193 FRS 9 requires the same accounting treatment for both the types of joint arrangements identified above. The only requirement specified in the standard is that the participants in such a joint arrangement should account for their own assets, liabilities and cash flows, measured according to the terms of the agreement governing the arrangement (for example see Table 27.13). [FRS 9 paras 18, 24].

Table 27.13 — Lonrho Plc — Annual Report and Accounts — 30 September 1998

Notes to the Accounts (extract)

Statement on accounting policies (extract)

Joint arrangements

The Group has certain contractual agreements with other participants to engage in joint activities that do not create an entity carrying on a trade or business of its own. The Group includes its share of assets, liabilities and cashflows in such joint arrangements, measured in accordance with the terms of each arrangement, which is usually pro-rata to the Group's interest in the joint arrangement.

27.194 In practice this requirement gives rise to a number of interpretation problems. First, the requirement does not specifically state that the participants must account also for the trading impact of those transactions, but this is implied because this will be the effect of accounting for the changes in assets and liabilities. In addition, appendix III to the standard says the accounting should be for the investor's *'own share of the assets, liabilities and cash flows'* as compared to the standard itself which makes no mention of the word 'share'. [FRS 9 App III para 8]. Consequently, how to account for the transactions might not be obvious. In most situations the amounts to be accounted for will not be governed by the participant's equity share, but will be dependent upon the economic sharing arrangements under the arrangement. For example, a joint billing arrangement might be conducted through an undertaking where the equity share is 50/50, but where one of the participants generates 80 per cent of the transactions, in which case it should recognise its own transactions undertaken by the joint arrangement. In this type of situation it will be necessary to consider carefully how any residual profit or loss in the joint arrangement is dealt with. In other situations, it might be more appropriate to account for the underlying transactions that specifically relate to the particular investor, rather than a share of the joint arrangement's transactions.

27.195 The paragraphs that follow consider how participants in different types of joint arrangement should account for their underlying transactions.

Joint agreements between participants

27.196 Joint arrangements that are merely agreements between the participants where there is no undertaking involved are easily dealt with under the standard's provisions. It is relatively simple for the participants to account for their share of the assets and liabilities and cash flows under the arrangement in their individual financial statements. Indeed, this is how transactions of this nature were accounted for before FRS 9 became standard practice.

27.197 Joint arrangements of this nature encompass jointly controlled operations and jointly controlled assets. These are dealt with in IAS 31, 'Interests in joint ventures', and FRS 9 follows the same path. Because IAS 31 has more detailed guidance than FRS 9, the explanation that follows draws heavily on IAS 31's provisions. In these types of arrangements, the venturers use their own assets and resources rather than establishing a company, partnership or other entity. Examples given in IAS 31 of jointly controlled operations include the manufacture, marketing and distribution jointly of a particular product, such as an aircraft. Different parts of the manufacturing process are carried out by the venturers, which bear their own costs and take a share of the revenues of the aircraft in accordance with the joint agreement. The accounting for jointly controlled operations under FRS 9 is the same as under IAS 31, with each of the venturers recognising in its individual financial statements and in its consolidated financial statements:

- The assets that it controls and the liabilities that it incurs.
- The expenses that it incurs and its share of the income that it earns from the sale of goods or services by the joint venture.

No consolidation adjustments or other consolidation procedures are necessary, because the assets, liabilities, income and expenses are already recognised in each of the joint venturers' financial statements. [IAS 31 para 16].

Example 1 – Joint arrangement accounting

Two companies decide to undertake a joint road construction project. They agree to supply different assets and staff to the joint arrangement. The joint arrangement has a separate bank account. The participants charge rental for their plant used in the project to the bank account and also have an agreed staff cost per hour, which is also charged to that account. The participants fund the account and invoice the customer in their joint names. Any surplus is shared 50/50.

The joint arrangement transactions that need to be reflected in each participant's accounts are unlikely to be a straight share of those transactions, but will depend on the costs that the participants have borne themselves. Therefore, although a participant is charging a rental to the joint arrangement for the use of its plant, that plant is already accounted for as a fixed asset in that participant's balance sheet and its profit and loss account will already bear a normal depreciation charge for the asset's use. The rental to the joint arrangement should be eliminated and in its place the share of the joint arrangement's income should be recognised. Similarly, the participant will have charged its actual staff costs in its profit and loss account, so it will need to eliminate any charge made to the joint arrangement on a different basis. The joint arrangement will bill its customers for the work undertaken by the venture and it would be appropriate for the participant to recognise its share (50% in this case) in its turnover. In order to arrive at the correct profit share in the participant's profit and loss account, it will be necessary to book an equalisation charge or credit in order to take into account that the actual costs incurred by the participant might be different from its share of the joint arrangement's costs. Consequently, the participant may in part be funding the costs of its joint arrangement partner (or *vice versa*).

Example 2 – Joint arrangement accounting

Company A and company B have entered into a joint arrangement to develop products for sale. The strategy of the joint arrangement is agreed jointly. The day to day management of the production is provided by company A who builds the product. Company A makes a 10% margin on the products it sells to the joint arrangement. Company B identified the opportunity and provided £40,000 investment capital. Company A provided £10,000 investment capital. Profits are shared 50/50.

The joint arrangement took out a loan of £100,000 and the interest charge for the year on this loan is £8,000. During the joint arrangement's first year, company A incurred costs of £70,000 in respect of work in progress, of which £50,000 was charged to the joint arrangement at £55,000. The joint arrangement made property sales to third parties of £40,000 and the cost of those sales in the joint arrangement was £30,000. There are no third party debtors or creditors at the year end as all transactions have been settled.

	Company A	JA	50% JA	Adjustments	Company A adjustments
	£'000	£'000	£'000	£'000	£'000
Balance sheet					
Investment	10.0	–	–	(10.0)(c)	–
Stock and work in progress					
Costs	70.0	55.0	27.5	(27.5)(a)	70.0
Tfr to cost of sales	(50.0)	(30.0)	(15.0)	25.0(b)	(40.0)
	20.0	25.0	12.5	(2.5)	30.0
Cash	(25.0)	127.0	63.5		38.5
	5.0	152.0	76.0	(12.5)	68.5
Loan	–	100.0	50.0		50.0
	5.0	52.0	26.0	(12.5)	18.5
Liability to company B	–	50.0	25.0	(10.0)(c)	15.0
Profit and loss account	5.0	2.0	1.0	(2.5)	3.5
	5.0	52.0	26.0	(12.5)	18.5
Profit and loss account					
Sales	55.0	400	20.0	(27.5)(a)	47.5
Cost of sales	(50.0)	(30.0)	(15.0)	25.0(b)	(40.0)
Gross profit	5.0	10.0	5.0	(2.5)	7.5
Interest	–	(8.0)	(4.0)		(4.0)
Net profit	5.0	2.0	1.0	(2.5)	3.5

(a) Half of company A's sales have in effect been made to company B and these can continue to be recognised by company A. But £27,500 of company A's sales need to be eliminated and replaced by its share of the sales made by the joint arrangement (that is, £20,000).

(b) Similarly, half of company A's cost of sales relates to sales made in effect to company B, the other half relate (that is, £25,000) to the goods sold to the joint arrangement at a profit margin of 10% and these need to be eliminated. The balance of stock of £30,000 is made up of company A's stock and work in progress together with the share outstanding in the joint arrangement of £12,500, less the profit element included in this stock of £2,500, which has been eliminated.

(c) There is a disparity in the amount of capital contributed by both of the parties to the joint arrangement. In effect this means that company A has an obligation under the arrangement to fund part of the repayment of company B's contribution out of its share of the resources of the joint arrangement. This obligation is likely to be settled eventually out of company A's share of the cash resources of the joint arrangement.

27.198 Many activities in the oil, gas and mineral extraction industries involve the use of jointly controlled assets. An often cited example is where a number of venturers jointly control and operate an oil pipeline. Typically in such arrangements, each venturer uses the pipeline to transport its own product, in return for which it bears an agreed proportion of the expenses of operating the pipeline. Again the accounting under FRS 9 for such ventures is the same as required under IAS 31. Each venturer shows in its individual financial statements and in its consolidated financial statements:

- Its share of the jointly controlled assets, classified according to the nature of the assets rather than as an investment. For example, a share of a jointly controlled oil pipeline is classified as property, plant and equipment.
- Any liabilities that it has incurred, for example, those incurred to finance its share of the asset.
- Its share of any liabilities incurred jointly with other venturers.
- Any income from the sale or use of its share of the output, together with its share of any expenses incurred.
- Any expenses which it has incurred in respect of its interest in the venture, for example those related to financing the venturer's interest in the assets and selling its share of the output.

As with joint operations, no consolidation adjustments or other consolidation procedures are necessary, because the assets, liabilities, income and expenses are already recognised in each of the joint venturers' financial statements. [IAS 31 para 22].

Joint arrangements in unincorporated undertakings including partnerships

27.199 FRS 9 goes further than IAS 31 and identifies that joint arrangements can arise in unincorporated undertakings, such as partnerships. FRS 9 requires that participants who enter into joint arrangements that are carried out in unincorporated undertakings and in partnerships should similarly account for their share of the assets, liabilities and cash flows under the arrangement in their individual financial statements and, as a consequence, these transactions will find their way into the group's consolidated financial statements.

27.200 Two legal issues arise from this accounting treatment. First, whether on consolidation the Companies Act allows a company to account for its joint arrangement entity's results in this way. Before the introduction of FRS 9, it was quite acceptable in the group's consolidated financial statements to proportionately consolidate the results of unincorporated joint ventures such as partnerships, as this is an option under the legislation (equity accounting also being permissible under the Act). The Act's rules remain unchanged following the introduction of FRS 9, so it would appear possible to continue to adopt proportional consolidation for such entities under the Act. To all intents and purposes in the group's consolidated financial statements, proportional consolidation gives the same result as FRS 9's requirement to account for the participant's share of the assets and liabilities and cash flows under the arrangements.

27.201 The second issue arises in the participant's individual financial statements. The issue is whether or not it is legal to include the appropriate share of the joint arrangement's transactions, which arise in a separate legal entity, in the financial statements of the participant, which will generally be a limited company. Where the joint venture entity is a partnership, it will be possible for the partners to record their share of the partnership's transactions in their individual financial statements. It is generally appropriate to do this, however, only where there is no restriction on the distribution of the partnership's profits and reserves. This basis of accounting is the same as that used prior to the introduction of FRS 9 for many partnership arrangements of this nature.

27.202 Furthermore, where the joint arrangement is acting as an agent of each of the participants (which might arise, for example, where the joint arrangement entity is on-billing goods for each participant), the share of the transactions should rightly be included in each principal's (that is, each participant's) books. Whether the transactions will be recorded in the agent's (that is, the joint arrangement entity's) books, or will be recorded at nil value, depends upon whether or not the entity is acting as a disclosed or an undisclosed agent (see chapter 9).

Joint arrangements in limited companies

27.203 Because of the definition of a joint arrangement, it is quite possible under FRS 9 for a limited company to be a joint arrangement. As for other joint arrangements FRS 9 requires that participants who invest in limited companies that are joint arrangements should account for their share of the assets and liabilities and cash flows under the arrangement in their individual financial statements and, as a consequence, in their group's consolidated financial statements.

27.204 As explained in paragraph 27.184 above, joint arrangements will not normally arise in a company, unless the undertaking acts as an agent of its participants. Consequently, where the joint arrangement company acts as either a disclosed agent or an undisclosed agent, the appropriate share of transactions undertaken by the agent should rightly be included in each principal's (that is, each participant's) books. Consequently, the participant's share of the joint arrangement's transactions would appear in its individual financial statements and, as a result, in its consolidated financial statements. This accounting treatment complies with FRS 9 and also with the Act. Furthermore, whether or not the transactions are also recorded in the agent's (that is, the joint arrangement undertaking's) books will depend on whether the joint arrangement is a disclosed agent or an undisclosed agent (see further chapter 9).

Joint arrangements versus quasi-subsidiaries

27.205 Following the FRRP ruling made against Associated Nursing Services plc there has been confusion concerning the distinction between a joint venture and a quasi-subsidiary and, therefore, concerning the entities that need to be consolidated in full or accounted for in some other way in the group's consolidated financial statements. The ruling was made in February 1997, before FRS 9's publication and that confusion has now been compounded by the advent of joint arrangements. The FRRP ruling noted that Associated Nursing Services had entered into joint ventures with two partners and it had treated the joint ventures as associated undertakings in its 1995 and 1996 financial statements under the rules in SSAP 1 prior to FRS 9's publication.

27.206 In one case, which involved a joint venture with a bank, the board of the joint venture company in question was 'deadlocked'. It was the FRRP's view that the financial and operating policies of that company were substantially predetermined by underlying agreements; and through its interest in the joint venture Associated Nursing Services gained benefits arising from the net assets of the company, such that it had control. In the other case a venture capital arrangement with five venture capital funds had been set up through an intermediary. In the FRRP's view the financial and operating policies of that company were again substantially predetermined by underlying agreements. Even though in that case Associated Nursing Services held only a minority of the ordinary share capital, the investor's interests were effectively limited and the FRRP took the view that Associated Nursing Services gained benefits arising from the company's net assets, such that it had control.

27.207 In the FRRP's view, therefore, the substance of the arrangements was that the joint venture companies were in fact quasi-subsidiaries as defined by FRS 5. Consequently, they should not have been accounted for by the equity method, but should have been treated, as FRS 5 requires, as if they were subsidiaries. The ruling hinges on paragraph 34 of FRS 5 which states that: *"where the financial and operating policies of a vehicle are in substance pre-determined, contractually or otherwise, the party possessing control will be the one that gains the benefits arising from the net assets of the vehicle"*.

27.208 The wording in paragraph 34 of FRS 5 uses similar terminology to that used in the definition of a 'joint arrangement that is not an entity' in paragraph 4 of FRS 9. Part of the joint arrangement definition says that:

> *"A contractual arrangement where all significant matters of operating and financial policy are predetermined does not create an entity because the policies are those of its participants not of a separate entity"*.

The feature which distinguishes a joint arrangement from a quasi-subsidiary seems to be that although in both a joint arrangement and a quasi-subsidiary the financial and operating policies may be predetermined, in a quasi-subsidiary the investor must gain the benefits arising from the net assets of the vehicle. This is because for an investment to meet the definition of a quasi-subsidiary the investment must give substantially the same benefits and risks to the investor as if it were an actual subsidiary.

Example – Joint arrangement versus quasi-subsidiary

An entity is established to undertake a property development. There are two parties to the arrangement each providing 50% of the equity. The property development activities of the venture are all predetermined in the agreements with the venturers setting up the undertaking and with the providers of finance, including the profit-sharing arrangements. Where the profit-sharing arrangements are 50/50 between the parties, this type of venture would seem to fall within the joint arrangement category of investment under FRS 9. The investor would then account for its share of the arrangement, as considered in the paragraphs above. However, where the profit-sharing arrangements are not in line with the venturers' equity investment and, for example, one of the parties is given (say) 90% of the profits generated by the business, then this would indicate that that party gains the benefits arising from the net assets of the vehicle. If this is the case, then the venture is a quasi-subsidiary of that investor and should be consolidated in its financial statements. Where the profit sharing arrangements are (say) 60:40, judgment will be needed to decide whether to account for the arrangement as a joint arrangement or as a quasi-subsidiary.

Chapter 28

Merger accounting

Chapter 28

Merger accounting

Introduction

28.1 Chapter 25 considers various matters concerning acquisition accounting. This chapter looks at the other accounting method a company must use in certain circumstances when preparing consolidated financial statements, namely merger accounting.

28.2 Although there are rare exceptions, a prerequisite for merger accounting is normally that shares issued as consideration for the combination must be eligible for merger relief or for group reconstruction relief. The legal provisions relating to these reliefs are described in chapter 23 and this chapter assumes knowledge of those provisions. Merger or group reconstruction relief may also be obtained where acquisition accounting rather than merger accounting is required for a combination. This is because the conditions for merger accounting are more restrictive than the conditions for obtaining merger or group reconstruction relief.

28.3 Schedule 6 to SI 2008/410, 'The Large and Medium-sized Companies and Groups (Accounts and Reports) Regulations' 2008, includes certain conditions that must apply to an acquisition before it can be accounted for as a merger in consolidated financial statements. Furthermore, Schedule 6 to SI 2008/410 includes certain additional disclosure requirements that apply where an acquisition is accounted for as a merger.

28.4 The provisions of both the Act and FRS 6, 'Acquisitions and mergers', are considered in detail in the paragraphs that follow.

28.5 Although the criteria for merger accounting in FRS 6 are stringent, international standard-setters do not consider 'true mergers' exist and can be distinguished from business combinations in which one entity obtains control of another entity (or entities). The IASB's IFRS 3 and IFRS 3 (revised, issued in January 2008) and the US GAAP business combination standards prohibit merger accounting. They require the use of acquisition accounting ('the purchase method') for all business combinations within their scope. As part of the ASB's programme of converging UK GAAP with IFRS in July 2005, the ASB issued FRED 36, 'Business combinations', proposing the introduction of IFRS 3 into UK GAAP to replace FRS 6 and FRS 7. This FRED has not been progressed to a standard, pending the overall reconsideration of UK GAAP and the adoption of IFRS for small and medium-sized entities (IFRS for SMEs) (see further chapter 2).

[The next paragraph is 28.9.]

Merger accounting conditions

28.9 The objectives of FRS 6 are:

- To ensure that merger accounting is used only for those business combinations that are not, in substance, the acquisition of one entity by another, but the formation of a new reporting entity as a substantially equal partnership where no party is dominant.
- To ensure the use of acquisition accounting for all other business combinations.
- To ensure that in either case the financial statements provide relevant information concerning the effect of the combination.

[FRS 6 para 1].

28.10 To this end the FRS defines a merger as:

> *"A business combination that results in the creation of a new reporting entity formed from the combining parties, in which the shareholders of the combining entities come together in a partnership for the mutual sharing of the risks and benefits of the combined entity, and in which no party to the combination in substance obtains control over any other, or is otherwise seen to be dominant, whether by virtue of the proportion of its shareholders' rights in the combined entity, the influence of its directors or otherwise."* [FRS 6 para 2].

28.11 If a business combination satisfies the conditions for merger accounting outlined in the Act and the combination meets the definition of a merger under FRS 6, the group must use merger accounting to account for it. To meet the definition of a merger in FRS 6 the combination *must* satisfy certain conditions which are described below. If the business combination fails to satisfy the conditions for merger accounting, the group *must* use acquisition accounting for the business combination. [SI 2008/410 6 Sch 8]. Situations may arise where the Act's conditions are satisfied, but those of FRS 6 are not. Where this arises, merger accounting should not be used. This is because the Act says the adoption of the merger method of accounting must accord with generally accepted accounting principles or practice (which currently means the conditions contained in FRS 6). [SI 2008/410 6 Sch 10(1)(d)]. Similarly, if FRS 6's conditions are satisfied, but those of the Act are not, merger accounting should not be used.

28.12 The conditions contained in the Act and FRS 6 require certain tests to be satisfied as follows:

- Offer to shareholders test.
- 90 per cent holding test.
- Immaterial cash or non-equity consideration test.

- No identifiable acquirer or acquiree test.
- Joint participation in management test.
- Relative size test.
- Full participation in future performance test.

28.13 Each of these tests is considered in the paragraphs that follow and the provisions of the Act and FRS 6 are contrasted.

Offer to shareholders test

28.14 The Act requires that the shares acquired as a result of the acquisition must be obtained by an arrangement providing for the issue of equity shares by the parent or any of its subsidiaries. [SI 2008/410 6 Sch 10(1)(b)]. Furthermore, FRS 6 requires that all but an immaterial proportion of the consideration must be in the form of equity shares. (See 'Immaterial cash or non-equity consideration test' below.) The definition of equity in FRS 6 is much more restrictive than the Act's definition. Equity shares include only those shares classified as equity in accordance with FRS 25, 'Financial instruments: Disclosure and presentation'. [FRS 6 para 2]. The reason for adopting the more restrictive definition in FRS 6 is to prevent the Act's condition, that the offer is satisfied by the issue of equity shares, being met by the use of shares that, although within the legal definition of equity, have nonetheless characteristics that are closer to non-equity shares. The difference between equity as defined in the Act and as defined in FRS 6 is described below.

28.15 Equity shares are defined in the Act as the issued share capital of a company excluding any part which, neither as respects dividends nor as respects capital, carries any right to participate beyond a specified amount in a distribution. [CA06 Sec 548]. Equity shares represent the residual interests in a company and as such confer on their holders the right to share in the net assets of the company (after settling any prior claims). Such shares are normally termed ordinary shares, but it is quite possible for a preference share to be constructed in such a way that it meets the Act's definition of equity. Non-equity shares as defined in the Act, by contrast, are shares which fall outside this definition.

28.16 FRS 6 provides its own definitions of equity and non-equity shares rather than adopting the Act's definitions. These are framed by reference to FRS 25, the result of which is that shares are classified as equity or non-equity based on their substance. [FRS 6 para 2].

28.17 It follows that under FRS 6, non-equity is a broader category than under the Act. The definition of non-equity shares in FRS 6 has been deliberately widely drawn so that, for instance, a right to a dividend or to a redemption payment that is for a limited amount will require the share to be treated as non-equity. Consequently, it is quite possible for a company to issue, for example, a preference share which is classified as equity share capital under the Act, but the preference share would be non-equity under FRS 6 for the purposes of determining whether all but an immaterial proportion of the consideration given in a business combination is in the form of equity shares.

28.18 This situation could arise, for instance, where a company issued as consideration for a business combination preference shares that had a fixed, non-discretionary dividend and unrestricted rights to distributions on winding up. The shares might have a right on liquidation to share in a fixed percentage of the balance on the company's share premium account. Whereas these shares would qualify under the Act as equity because the limitations on distributions apply only to dividends and not to capital, they would not qualify as equity under FRS 6, because fixed, non-discretionary payments of either dividends or capital means they are most likely non-equity under FRS 25. Therefore, although they qualify as equity for the purpose of obtaining merger relief under the Act, they do not count as equity under FRS 6 for the purpose of determining whether all but an immaterial proportion of the consideration is in the form of equity shares. (See 'Immaterial cash or non-equity consideration test' below.)

[The next paragraph is 28.21.]

Ninety per cent holding test

28.21 The Act requires that at least 90 per cent of the nominal value of the 'relevant shares' in an undertaking acquired (excluding any shares in the undertaking held as treasury shares) as a result of an arrangement must be held by or on behalf of the parent and its subsidiaries. [SI 2008/410 6 Sch 10(1)(a)]. In this context, 'relevant shares' means those shares in the acquired company that carry unrestricted rights to participate both in its distributions and in its assets upon liquidation. [SI 2008/410 6 Sch 10(2)]. This is in effect 'super-equity', and would include most ordinary share capital, but would exclude most other forms of participating preference shares (although these shares are often equity shares as defined in the Act). In this sense, therefore, the Act's definition of 'relevant shares' is similar to FRS 6's definition of equity.

28.22 The Act also states that the proportion referred to in paragraph 28.21, that is 90 per cent of the nominal value of the relevant shares, must be attained pursuant to an arrangement providing for the issue of equity shares. [SI 2008/410 6 Sch 10(b)]. However, this does not mean that, in order to merger account, the parent and its subsidiaries cannot hold more than 10 per cent of the nominal value of the relevant shares before the acquisition. It merely means that as a result of the offer, the company must have reached at least a 90 per cent holding in the relevant shares (taking into account any prior holdings). For this purpose, 'relevant shares' has the same meaning as explained in paragraph 28.21 above.

28.23 Similarly under FRS 6 there is no limit on prior holdings, although the nature of the consideration given for the prior holding *is* relevant. As an example, a company might hold 25 per cent of the relevant equity shares in another company that it acquired over two years before (see para 28.26 below) and might then obtain a further 65 per cent of the relevant shares of that other company as a result of an offer. In such a situation, and provided that all the other conditions for merger accounting were met, the existence of a prior holding of 25 per cent would not prevent merger accounting being adopted.

Immaterial cash or non-equity consideration test

28.24 Where merger accounting is adopted, the consideration given for the relevant shares can include other consideration such as debentures and cash. However, the provisions of the Act restrict significantly the other consideration that can be given where the merger accounting method is to be used. The fair value of such other consideration given by the parent and its subsidiaries cannot exceed more than 10 per cent of the *nominal value* of the equity shares issued as part of the consideration pursuant to the arrangement. [SI 2008/410 6 Sch 10(c)].

28.25 The provisions of the Act contrast with the requirement included in FRS 6 where the following conditions must apply:

- Under the terms of the combination or related arrangements, the consideration received by equity shareholders of each party to the combination, in relation to their equity shareholding, comprises primarily equity shares in the combined entity; and any non-equity consideration, or equity shares carrying substantially reduced voting or distribution rights, represents an immaterial proportion of the fair value of the consideration received by the shareholders.
- Where one of the combining entities has, within the period of two years before the combination, acquired equity shares in another of the combining entities, the consideration for this acquisition should be taken into account in determining whether this criterion (that is, the immaterial cash or non-equity consideration test) has been met.
- For the purposes of the above provisions, the consideration should not be taken to include the distribution to shareholders of:
  - an interest in a peripheral part of the business of the entity in which they were shareholders and that does not form part of the combined entity; or
  - the proceeds of the sale of such a business, or loan stock representing such proceeds.

A 'peripheral part of the business' is one which can be disposed of without having a material effect on the nature and focus of the entity's operations. [FRS 6 paras 9, 10].

28.26 Under these requirements in FRS 6, the fair value of the total consideration that the offeror gives should include also the fair value of the consideration that the offeror gave for shares that it acquired within two years before the offer. [FRS 6 para 9]. (In contrast, it is not necessary to take prior holdings into account in calculating the Act's limit mentioned in paragraph 28.21.)

28.27 It should be noted that the non-equity restriction in the Act relates to ten per cent of the *nominal* value of equity shares issued, whereas the restriction in FRS 6 relates to an immaterial proportion of the *fair* value of the consideration.

28.28 In some circumstances this may mean that the conditions of the Act are more restrictive than those of the standard as the following example demonstrates.

Example – Act cash restriction more onerous than FRS 6

A company issues equity shares in connection with a business combination, which have a nominal value of £100,000 together with £15,000 in cash. The fair value of the shares issued is £1,485,000. In this situation the business combination does not qualify for merger accounting under the Act, because the cash element is greater than 10% of the nominal value of the equity shares issued. The combination would however satisfy the condition in FRS 6, that not more than an immaterial proportion of the fair value of the consideration is in the form of non-equity consideration, because in this case it represents only 1% of the fair value. Because the Act's requirement also has to be satisfied, however, merger accounting would not be possible in this case.

If in the above example the consideration had been £100,000 nominal value of equity shares and £10,000 cash, the conditions of the Act would have been satisfied and merger accounting would be permitted under both the Act and FRS 6. This might be so even if the fair value of the consideration had been only £110,000, that is the fair value of each share was equal to its par value (the lowest possible amount for which they could be issued) because even then the cash element of the total fair value would have been less than 10% of the total fair value. This conclusion is based on the assumption that 'immaterial' in FRS 6 may be interpreted as less than 10%. However, interpretations may vary as discussed in paragraph 28.32 below.

28.29 Although the ten per cent condition in the Act appears more restrictive than the condition of FRS 6, the Act does not require holdings acquired before the offer, and which are not part of the arrangement through which the 90 per cent holding is acquired, to be taken into account in determining the cash or non-equity element of the consideration. In contrast, FRS 6 requires that any acquisition by one of the combining parties of equity shares in the other within two years before the combination should be taken into account in determining whether or not non-equity consideration represents more than an immaterial proportion of the total consideration. Where such acquisitions have taken place, the conditions of FRS 6 may be more restrictive than those of the Act, as the following example demonstrates.

Example – Treatment of holding prior to an offer

Company B has share capital of 1,000 £1 equity shares. Company A has previously acquired 100 shares in company B for £5,000 (that is, £50 per share). These shares were acquired entirely for cash 18 months ago and were not acquired as part of an arrangement to acquire over 90% of company B. Company A now wishes to acquire the remaining 900 shares in company B. The value of company B has decreased since company A acquired its previous holding and the 900 shares are valued at £45 per share. The consideration for these 900 shares is to be given entirely by an issue of company A's equity shares. A's equity shares to be issued have a nominal value of £20,000 and fair value of £40,500.

The fair value of the total consideration that company A will have given is:

	£
Cash	5,000
Fair value of Company A's shares (namely, 900 × £45)	40,500
Total consideration	45,500

Company A makes its offer for 90% of the relevant shares of company B and because this offer is wholly for shares, the Act's provisions on the cash limit explained above do not apply. It, therefore, does not matter that the £5,000 cash exceeds 10% of the £20,000 nominal value of the A shares that are issued. However, because the previous acquisition was made within two years of the current offer and the non-equity element represents 10.9% of the fair value of the total consideration given in the acquisition, the non-equity element is likely to be material. If the limit set out in FRS 6 is exceeded, merger accounting cannot be used.

28.30 As explained in paragraph 28.15 above, the definitions of equity in FRS 6 and the Act are different. When FRS 6 was issued, the ASB deliberately chose to adopt the meaning of 'equity' that was contained in FRS 4 to ensure that this test could not be avoided by the use of shares that are 'equity' under the Act, but are not so in substance. In 2004, the ASB issued FRS 25 such that, for years beginning on or after 1 January 2005, this definition was superseded. The principle remains, however, that for FRS 6 purposes the definition of 'equity' is based on substance rather than legal form. This difference between the definition included in FRS 6 and that in the Act may also affect the determination of whether the limitations placed on the proportion of non-equity consideration by the Act and FRS 6 have been exceeded. The following example illustrates how this might occur.

Example – Difference between 'equity' under the Act and FRS 6

Company A issues 100,000 ordinary shares and 250,000 participating preference shares as consideration for acquiring 100% of the equity shares of company B. The nominal values of the ordinary shares and the participating preference shares are £100,000 and £250,000, respectively, and their fair values are £1,000,000 and £250,000, respectively. The participating preference shares have the right to a fixed, non-discretionary dividend of 5%. In addition, they receive a proportion of the dividends paid on the ordinary shares. They qualify as equity under the Act, because they carry a right to participate beyond a specified amount in a distribution, but they do not qualify as equity under FRS 6. This is because one of the rights of the participating preference shares is to a fixed, non-discretionary dividend of 5% and, hence, is likely to be treated as a liability under FRS 25 and, therefore, as non-equity shares under FRS 6.

28.31 Under the Act, the whole of the consideration in this example qualifies as equity and, therefore, the ten per cent limitation for non-equity is not breached. Under FRS 6, however, the participating preference shares are non-equity. As they amount to 20 per cent of the total fair value of the consideration, the limit in FRS 6 that requires not more than an immaterial amount of the consideration to be in the form of non-equity is breached.

28.32 In the above examples, it has been suggested that the FRS 6 reference to immaterial might be interpreted as meaning less than ten per cent. No numerical figure is placed on the term 'immaterial' in FRS 6, but in practice, it is often assumed that amounts representing less than five per cent are not material, between five and ten per cent may or may not be material and over ten per cent are material. As the Act uses a ten per cent limit for non-equity consideration compared to the nominal value of equity shares, it seems reasonable to assume that in the context of the FRS 6 condition, a non-equity element that represents over ten per cent of the total fair value of the consideration should be regarded as material.

Disposal of peripheral part of business

28.33 The consideration for a business combination should not include the distribution to shareholders of an interest in a peripheral part of a business of an entity in which they were shareholders and that does not form part of the combined entity. Nor should it include the distribution of the proceeds of sale of such a business or loan stock representing such proceeds. The implication of this is that where such a distribution or sale is not peripheral, it should be counted as part of the consideration.

28.34 This situation might occur where two entities decide to merge, but there are certain businesses which do not fit in and the two parties decide should be disposed of prior to the merger taking place. FRS 6 makes it clear that the disposal of such businesses must not materially affect the nature and focus of the disposing entity's operations. This seems rather a harsh condition as a group might well wish to merge certain of its operations only with another entity whilst allowing its shareholders to receive shares in the remainder of the group by, for instance, a distribution in kind. Provided that the operations to be merged with the other entity have a proper track record and are independent of the rest of the group, there seems to be no good reason why the combination of that part of the group with another entity should not be eligible for merger accounting. However, FRS 6 would prohibit merger accounting in such a case, if the operations retained by the shareholders of the group and, therefore, excluded from the merger, materially affected the nature and focus of the original group's operations.

28.35 There is a similar prohibition in the Explanation section of FRS 6 which states that merger accounting is not appropriate for a combination where one entity divests itself of part of its business, which is then combined with another entity. The reason given in that section is that the divested business will not have been independent for a sufficient period to establish itself as being a party separate from its previous owner. The section continues that only once the divested business has established a track record of its own can it be considered as a party to a merger.

28.36 This condition is rather strange and appears over-restrictive. Many large groups have businesses that are run by their own management as quasi-independent entities under the group 'umbrella'. It is relatively straightforward to establish a trading record for such businesses. Evidence that this is so is the number of stock market flotations of businesses in recent years, which were hived off or demerged from larger groups.

Vendor placings and vendor rights

28.37 Under FRS 6, merger accounting is not allowed for a business combination where a vendor placing or a vendor rights was made to effect the combination. Vendor placings and vendor rights are described briefly below.

[The next paragraph is 28.39.]

28.39 A vendor placing normally works as follows. The acquiring company will offer its shares to the target company's shareholders in exchange for their shares in that company. If there are any shareholders of the target company who do not wish to retain the consideration shares of the acquiring company, the acquiring company will arrange for its financial adviser (for example, a merchant bank) to place those consideration shares. The financial adviser will put together a placing list (that will normally include institutions such as pension funds and insurance companies) so that the target company shareholders may dispose of their consideration shares in the acquiring company for cash.

28.40 After the vendor placing has occurred, cash has been transferred from the institutions, *via* the financial adviser (acting in his capacity as a broker), to some or all of the target company's shareholders. In return, the institutions now own shares in the acquiring company and the acquiring company now owns the target company. The acquiring company has issued shares, rather than paying cash, for the target company.

28.41 The vendor rights normally work as follows. The acquiring company will offer its shares to the target company's shareholders in exchange for their shares in that company. If any shareholders of the target company do not wish to retain their consideration shares of the acquiring company, the acquiring company will arrange for its financial adviser to place those consideration shares. Up to this point, the vendor rights method is the same as a vendor placing. However, as part of the placing agreement the acquiring company's shareholders will have an option to buy ('claw back') some of the consideration shares from the placees. They will be entitled to buy back at the placing price a certain proportion of the placed shares on a *pro rata* basis.

28.42 Therefore, after the vendor rights method is completed, cash has been transferred from the acquiring company's shareholders, *via* the financial adviser, to some or all of the target company's shareholders. In return, the acquiring company's shareholders now have a stake in a larger group, because the acquiring company now owns the target company. The acquiring company has issued shares, rather than paying cash, for the target company.

[The next paragraph is 28.44.]

28.44 FRS 6 follows the spirit of merger accounting and indicates that equity shareholders would be considered to have disposed of their shareholdings for cash where any arrangement is made in connection with the combination that enables them to exchange or redeem the shares they receive for cash or other non-equity consideration. Such arrangements will include a vendor placing or a vendor rights. All arrangements made in conjunction with the combination must be taken into account, but a normal market transaction or a privately arranged sale by a shareholder is not deemed to be made in conjunction with the combination and does not prevent the immaterial cash or non-equity consideration criterion being met. [FRS 6 para 71].

28.45 Any convertible shares or loan stock that are outstanding at the time of the offer should not normally be regarded as equity for the purposes of satisfying the merger conditions. The only exception to this is where the convertible stock is converted into equity as a result of the business combination. [FRS 6 para 12].

No identifiable acquirer or acquiree test

28.46 In order to qualify for merger accounting, a business combination must represent a genuine partnership between the combining entities in which none of the parties dominates the other party or parties. No party to the combination should be portrayed as either acquirer or acquiree either by its own board or management or by that of another party to the combination. [FRS 6 para 6]. This is the principle that underlies the definition of a merger in the standard (see para 28.10 above).

28.47 The standard sets out a number of factors that may be evident in a business combination and which could indicate that one or other party is dominant. It makes clear that for merger accounting to be possible, all of these factors must be absent.

28.48 The most straightforward of these factors is if one or other party is portrayed either by itself or by another party to the acquisition as the acquirer, or as having the subservient role of being acquired. One party's portrayal as acquirer or as acquiree is particularly likely to be a factor present in a contested bid, where one party attempts to gain control against the wishes of the other party's management.

28.49 As mentioned in paragraph 28.11 above, where all the conditions for merger accounting are satisfied the business combination must be accounted for as a merger. It is not an optional treatment. However, it is pointed out in paragraph 9 of the 'Development' section of FRS 6 that it would be relatively easy for merging parties to ensure that one of the conditions was not met, without fundamentally altering the commercial substance of the transaction, if they did not want to use merger accounting. This condition, that no party should be portrayed as an acquirer or as being acquired, seems to be probably the most susceptible to such manipulation.

28.50 FRS 6 lists a number of other aspects of a transaction that could indicate whether or not one party was dominant. These include:

- The form by which the combination was achieved.
- The plans for the combined entity's future operations (for instance whether any closures or disposals relate more to one party than to another).
- The proposed corporate image (such as name, logo, and location of headquarters and principal operations).
- In a publicly quoted company, the content of its communications with shareholders.

[FRS 6 para 62].

28.51 If any of these indicates that one party to the combination dominates the other or has the subservient role of being acquired, merger accounting is not permitted.

28.52 The standard indicates that where one party is seen to be paying a premium over the market value of the shares acquired, there is evidence that the party has assumed the role of acquirer, unless there is a clear explanation for the premium, other than it being a premium to acquire control. [FRS 6 para 61].

28.53 This condition is not always easy to put into operation. It appears to apply to cases where offers are made for listed companies which, at the date of the announcement of the offer, represent a substantial premium to the market price of the recipient of the offer at that date. During the course of the offer, the target company's share price will often rise to the offer price level or even above. However, we consider that the comparison with the market price of the recipient should be made as at the date the offer is announced, rather than at the later date when it goes unconditional, in order to determine whether or not it is a premium to market price and, if so, whether it is a premium to acquire control. If there is a substantial premium, it may be difficult to rebut the presumption that the premium is for control. As noted above, the standard requires that if that presumption is to be rebutted, there must be a clear explanation for the premium other than it being a premium for control.

Joint participation in management test

28.54 The FRS requires that the boards of all the combining parties or their appointees should participate in setting up the management structure for the combined entity and in selecting the management personnel. They should set up this structure and select the management personnel on the basis of consensus decisions between the combining parties rather than purely by exercise of voting rights. [FRS 6 para 7].

28.55 This does not mean that the management structure and personnel have to be equally divided between the combining parties. Indeed it could be that one party provides most of the management. This would not contravene the joint participation rule provided that it reflected the wishes of all the parties to the merger.

28.56 In determining whether the condition of joint participation is satisfied, consideration has to be given not just to the structure, but also to the identity of all persons involved in the main financial and operating decisions and the way in which the decision making process operates in practice. For instance, if all financial and operating decisions had to be approved by the managing director and only one of the parties to the combination could appoint the managing director, that party might be presumed to exert undue dominance over the management. As explained above, however, if that was in accordance with the wishes of all the parties it would not breach the 'joint participation' condition.

28.57 Sometimes there may be arrangements made at the date of combination whereby there is joint participation in management for a limited period only, with other arrangements being made thereafter. If at the outset there is such an agreement for short-term joint participation, but it is agreed that at the expiry of that period, one party may assume control of management whether or not the other party agrees, that arrangement would probably breach the joint participation rule and merger accounting would not be permitted. Where, however, arrangements for the period that followed a short period of joint participation provided that management should be selected on the basis of merit only, such arrangements would not breach the joint participation rule, provided that all parties agreed to the policy at the outset.

28.58 The standard makes clear that only decisions made about management structure and personnel at the outset of the merger need be considered in determining whether there is joint participation, but as illustrated above both the short-term and long-term consequences of those decisions need to be evaluated.

Relative size test

28.59 The standard requires that the relative sizes of the combining entities are not so disparate that one party dominates the combined entity by virtue of its relative size. [FRS 6 para 8].

28.60 As to what constitutes dominance in terms of size, the standard says that one party should be presumed to dominate if it is more than 50 per cent larger than each of the other parties to the combination. The test of size should be made by reference to the proportion of the equity of the combined entity attributable to each of the combining parties.

28.61 However the presumption of dominance, where one party is more than 50 per cent larger than each of the other parties, may be rebutted if it can be clearly shown that there is no such dominance. In some circumstances, for instance, there may be agreements between the parties that determine voting rights or other matters, such as powers of veto, which mean that the apparent dominance due to size is not effective in practice. Any such circumstances should be disclosed and explained.

Example 1 – Relative size test

Company A is listed and has 100 million equity shares of £1 in issue which have a market value of £1,000 million. Company B is also listed and has 100 million 5p equity shares in issue with a market value of £600 million. Company A makes an agreed offer for company B and the offer is valued at £750 million, that is company A will issue 75m shares.

In this situation if the relative sizes pre-merger are considered company A is more than 50% larger than company B. However, this is not relevant for determining whether or not the relative size test is satisfied. It is the relative proportions of equity of the combined entity that are relevant. Comparison of A's share of the combined equity of £1,750 million with B's share, shows that the company A shareholders own 100 million shares (that is, 57% of the combined entity), which is not more than 50% larger than that of company B shareholders' interest of 75 million shares (that is 43% of the combined entity). By reference to the size test alone, therefore, the combination would be entitled to be merger accounted. However, consideration would then have to be given as to whether the substantial premium of £150 million paid by company A was a premium to acquire control (see paras 28.52 and 28.53 above).

Example 2 – Relative size test

Company A is unlisted and has 15,000 equity shares in issue. There is no quoted market value available, but the company has net assets of £150,000. Company B is also unlisted and has 3,000 equity shares in issue. Its net assets are £50,000. Company A issues 5,000 equity shares to the shareholders of company B in consideration for their equity shares in that company.

A comparison of the respective holdings of the former shareholders of company A (15,000 shares) and the former shareholders of company B (5,000 shares) shows that the former shareholders of company A have a holding of 75% in the combined entity that is more than 50% larger than that of the former shareholders of company B who own 25%. Therefore, it is presumed that company A is dominant and merger accounting is not permitted (unless the presumption can be rebutted in some way).

Example 3 – Relative size test

Company A has 10,000 equity shares in issue that have a market value of £500,000. Company B has 1,000 equity shares in issue having a market value of £200,000. Company A is in a period of low profitability and its markets are mature and declining. The shares in company B are owned by a dynamic individual Mr X who also manages that company and has built its business up rapidly. Company A wishes to retain the services of that individual to run the combined business. In turn he wishes to retain an effective say in the running of the business whilst enjoying the benefits of a larger organisation. Company A issues 4,000 shares to acquire company B. At the same time, it enters into an agreement with Mr X as a shareholder in the combined entity. The agreement specifies that decisions on all major operational and financial matters must be agreed by shareholders representing at least 75% of the equity. In this way, control is effectively shared between the shareholders in the old company A and Mr X, the shareholder of the former company B.

In this situation, although the former shareholders of company A hold over 50% (71%) more of the enlarged equity than the former shareholder of company B (29%), the shareholders' agreement means that control is effectively divided equally between the two. In such a situation, the presumption that company A is dominant can be rebutted and if all the other conditions for merger accounting are satisfied, merger accounting would be required. The financial statements would have to disclose the reasons why company A was not considered to be dominant.

Full participation in future performance test

28.62 The FRS requires that no equity shareholders of any of the combining entities retain any material interest in the future performance of only part of the combined entity. [FRS 6 para 11].

28.63 A situation where different shareholders might retain material interests in different parts of a combined entity might be as follows:

Example 1 – Participation in future performance

Company A and company B combine by means of a new holding company, company C, issuing shares to the former shareholders of companies A and B. The shares issued to the former shareholders of company A (A shares) are entitled to 80% of the profits of the former company A businesses and the shares issued to the former shareholders of company B (B shares) are entitled to 80% of the profits of the former company B businesses. All other profits are shared equally between the two sets of shareholders. Assuming that there are an equal number of A and B shares and that the company A businesses make £100,000 in the first year and the company B businesses make £50,000, the A shares would be entitled to £80,000 of the profits from the company A businesses while the B shares would be entitled to £40,000 from the company B businesses. The balance of £30,000 of the total profits would be shared equally.

Because, in this example, certain of the equity shareholders retain a material interest in only part of the future performance of the combined entity, the condition of full participation in future performance would not be satisfied and merger accounting would not be permitted for the combination.

Similarly, where there is an earn out or similar performance related arrangement the condition would not be met.

Example 2 – Participation in future performance

Company A and company B combine by means of shares issued by company A to company B shareholders. Part of the consideration (to be settled in shares) is deferred and is contingent on the performance of the company B businesses over the next three years. The potential amount of the contingent consideration is material.

Because the shareholders of company B have a material interest in only one part of the combined business, the issue of further equity shares to them depends solely on the performance of the company B businesses.

It might be argued that once the earn out is completed, all shareholders will participate fully, but the standard appears to be concerned to ensure that the condition of full participation is satisfied based on conditions existing at the date of the combination.

An exception is where at the date of the combination there is uncertainty about the value of a specific asset or liability contributed by one of the parties, such as the eventual outcome of a legal action against one of the parties, or the eventual sales value of an asset owned by one of the parties. An agreement for the allocation of the consideration between the combining parties that depend on the eventual outcome of the uncertainty would not invalidate the full participation rule.

Example 3 – Participation in future performance

At the date of a business combination between company A and company B, company A has not resolved a claim made by it against various former customers who have failed to take delivery of goods manufactured for them under contract. No account of any potential gain has been taken in determining the consideration to be allocated to company A shareholders at the date of the combination, but it has been agreed that those shareholders will be entitled to 80% of any subsequent gain arising from the claim.

In these circumstances, the participation of the company A shareholders in any future gain arising from the claim would not infringe the condition of full participation, because the outcome does not depend on the future performance of the combined business, but rather on the outcome of an uncertainty existing at the date of the combination.

28.64 The full participation in future performance test is not met where there is a material minority, that is ten per cent or more, of shareholders of one of the combining parties that has not accepted the offer. This is because if there is such a minority, it retains an interest in only part of the combined entity and the condition that no equity shareholders of the combining entities should retain a material interest in the future performance of only part of the combined entity is not met. It is also unlikely that, if there was such a large minority, the other conditions for merger accounting could be met.

Merger accounting principles

28.65 The principles of acquisition accounting are explained in chapter 25 and the principles of merger accounting are considered in greater detail below.

28.66 When a group uses merger accounting to account for a business combination, the group does not need to incorporate into its consolidated financial statements the fair values of the subsidiary's assets and liabilities. [FRS 6 para 16]. Therefore, no goodwill arises in a merger and the group should incorporate into its consolidated financial statements the assets and liabilities at the amounts at which the subsidiary recorded them in its books before the combination. [SI 2008/410 6 Sch 11(2)].

28.67 One exception to this principle is that a group should adopt uniform group accounting policies for consolidation purposes in accordance with the Act and FRS 2. Consequently, if the acquired company's accounting policies are not the same as the acquiring company's, adjustments should be made to achieve uniformity. One way of doing this might be for the subsidiary to make these adjustments in its own records. It could restate the amount of its assets and liabilities in its books to reflect the change in accounting policy. Alternatively, if it is not practicable for the acquired company to change its accounting policies, adjustments may be made on consolidation to the values of the acquired company's assets and liabilities that are stated in its books.

28.67.1 An example of disclosure of adjustments to conform accounting policies is Table 28.1. It is worth noting that changes to the policies of either party to the merger may be made depending on which of the combining parties' policies the enlarged entity chooses to adopt.

Table 28.1 — Royal & Sun Alliance Insurance Group plc — Directors' Report and Accounts — 31 December 1996

Accounting policies (extract)

Effects of merger on Group financial statements

On 19th July 1996, Sun Alliance Group plc (Sun Alliance) was renamed Royal & Sun Alliance Insurance Group plc and became the Parent Company of the new Group formed by the merger of Royal Insurance Holdings plc (Royal Insurance) and Sun Alliance.

Merger accounting principles have been used and the results have been presented as if the new Group had been established throughout the current and prior years.

Alignment of accounting policies and presentation

The new Group's accounting policies are set out on pages 17 to 19. The process of aligning policies and presentation across the new Group has resulted in the following principal changes:

a) General business is accounted for on an annual basis. Previously Sun Alliance used a fund basis of accounting for London market marine and aviation business.

b) Overseas revenue transactions are translated at rates ruling at the year end. Previously Royal Insurance used average rates of exchange during the year to translate revenue transactions.

c) The reinsurers' share of technical provisions is presented on the assets side of the balance sheet. Previously Royal Insurance presented these amounts on the liabilities side of the balance sheet in arriving at net technical provisions.

d) Balances arising from insurance broking transactions are presented gross. Previously Sun Alliance took advantage of the transitional provision within Financial Reporting Standard 5 permitting the offset of balances between insurance brokers and the Group.

e) The value of long term business, being the value of the shareholders' interest in the long term funds in excess of that recognised under the modified statutory solvency basis of reporting long term business, is included within investments in the consolidated balance sheet. Previously Sun Alliance did not include this value in the financial statements but disclosed it in the Group Chief Executive's review.

f) British Aviation Insurance Company Ltd is accounted for as a subsidiary of the Group. Previously this company was an associated undertaking of both Royal Insurance and Sun Alliance.

g) Sun Alliance and Royal Insurance Australia Holdings Ltd is accounted for as a subsidiary of the Group. This company was previously an associated undertaking of Royal Insurance and a subsidiary of Sun Alliance.

h) Scrip acceptances received under the scrip dividend alternative are subsequently added back to reserves. Previously Sun Alliance made no adjustment to reserves for scrip dividend acceptances which were accounted as shares issued at a premium.

i) Goodwill arising on acquisitions is written off to other reserves in the consolidated balance sheet along with the merger reserve arising on consolidation of Royal Insurance and Sun Alliance. Previously Sun Alliance wrote goodwill off against the consolidated profit and loss account reserve.

[The next paragraph is 28.68.]

28.68 The results and cash flows of all the combining entities should be brought into the combined entity's consolidated financial statements from the beginning of the financial year in which the combination occurs, adjusted to achieve uniformity in accounting policies. [SI 2008/410 6 Sch 11(3); FRS 6 para 17]. That is to say, they should include the subsidiary's results for the part of the period before the business combination, as well as the results of the subsidiary for the part of the period after the business combination. These results should be consolidated on a line by line basis in the profit and loss account and the cash flow statement as if the subsidiary had always been part of the group. In addition, the corresponding amounts in the consolidated financial statements should be restated to include the results for all the combining entities for the previous period and also at the previous balance sheet date (as if the companies had been combined throughout the prior period), again adjusted to conform accounting policies. [SI 2008/410 6 Sch 11(4)].

28.69 The aim of the consolidated financial statements in merger accounting is to show the combined companies' results and financial positions as if they had always been combined. Consequently, even the share capital issued during the year for the purposes of the merger has to be shown as if it had always been issued.

Example – Treatment and disclosure of shares issued

In 20X1 company A and company B combine and the combination is eligible for merger accounting. The share capital of company A (which has remained unchanged since the beginning of 20X0) is 100,000 equity shares of £1 each prior to the merger and that of company B is 200,000 shares of 50p each. Company A issues 100,000 equity shares in consideration for the acquisition of company B, the fair value of which is £1 million, and incurs merger expenses of £10,000. Profits of company A for the year 20X0 were £150,000 and for 20X1 they were £200,000. Profits of company B for 20X0 were £190,000 and for 20X1 they were £100,000 to the date of merger and £75,000 for the post-merger period. There were no adjustments required to achieve uniformity of accounting policies.

The profits of the combined group would be presented as if company A and company B had always been combined. Thus the group profit and loss account would show profits for 20X0 of £340,000 (£150,000 + £190,000) and for 20X1 the profits would be £375,000 (£200,000 + £100,000 + £75,000), before merger expenses.

The share capital of company A would be adjusted so as to show the shares issued in respect of the merger as if they had been in existence at the start of 20X0. Therefore, company A's share capital at the beginning of 20X0 would be shown at £200,000. There would be no difference arising on consolidation as the nominal value of shares issued as consideration is equal to the nominal value of shares acquired. The merger expenses of £10,000 would be written off to the group profit and loss account for 20X1. (Although there might seem to be an argument for charging these expenses in 20X0, the standard specifically requires them to be charged at the date of the merger as reorganisation or restructuring expenses in accordance with paragraph 20 of FRS 3, that is as a post-operating profit exceptional item.)

28.70 The examples that follow illustrate some of the problems that can arise with the principles of merger accounting.

Example 1 – Treatment of tax losses

Company A combines with company B during the year and merger accounts for the combination. Company A has large tax losses and has never had a tax charge. Company B paid tax last year and it is proposed that the two companies' results should be combined and the tax charge of company B excluded from the comparatives on the basis that if the companies had always been combined, this tax charge would never have arisen.

In this type of situation, merger accounting would not allow the tax charge to be eliminated. The tax has been paid and cannot be recovered now that company B has joined the group. Consequently, the tax charge should be shown as a comparative in the merged profit and loss account. Company A could of course add a note to explain why the tax charge has arisen.

Example 2 – Non coterminous year ends

A company combines with another and will use merger accounting. The company's year end is 31 December and the subsidiary's year end is 30 June. The company wishes to know the impact of the difference in year ends.

The results of the loss-making subsidiaries should be included in the consolidation. Although technically they never become subsidiaries of the listed company, the spirit of FRS 6 requires that the merged companies should incorporate the unaltered results of the two companies for the full year. The results of the subsidiaries that are sold should, if material, be shown separately and disclosed as discontinued operations, but they should still be included in the consolidated profit and loss account of the merged companies.

Example 3 – Disposal of loss making subsidiary prior to merger

A listed company with a December year end combines with a company with a June year end. Merger accounting is to be used. The second company had a subsidiary that made losses to June, but it disposes of its loss-making subsidiary before the date of merger which is in November.

The results of the loss-making subsidiaries should be included in the consolidation. Although technically they never become subsidiaries of the listed company, the spirit of FRS 6 requires that the merged companies should incorporate the unaltered results of the two companies for the full year. The results of the subsidiaries that are sold should, if material, be shown separately and disclosed as discontinued operations, but they should still be included in the consolidated profit and loss account of the merged companies.

Applicability to business combinations achieved by using a new parent company

28.71 Often business combinations are effected by incorporating a new company which then issues shares to two or more combining companies. The accounting treatment in such cases will depend on the substance of the arrangement. This often means that the new parent should be ignored and the tests for merger accounting should be applied to the combining entities other than the new parent, (except insofar as it is necessary to bring in the new parent as, for instance, in satisfying the 'offer to shareholders', '90 per cent holding' and 'immaterial cash or non-equity consideration' tests).

28.72 If the substance is that a combination of the entities would have been a merger, merger accounting should be used. However, if the substance is that an acquirer can be identified, acquisition accounting should be used. In the latter case the new parent company and the acquirer should be accounted for by using merger accounting and then the other parties to the combination should be acquisition accounted. [FRS 6 para 14].

28.73 Where a new parent is used to effect a business combination and merger accounting is to be used, it is advisable to ensure that the accounting period of the new parent company is the same as that of the combining companies and that the new parent has been in existence for the whole of the combining companies' current accounting periods (see para 28.106 below).

Applicability to group reconstructions

28.74 Merger accounting may be used for group reconstructions, even where there is no business combination that meets the definition of a merger. However, this is conditional on:

- The use of merger accounting not being prohibited by companies legislation.
- The ultimate shareholders remaining the same and the rights of each such shareholder, relative to other shareholders, being unchanged.
- No minority's interest in the net assets of the group being altered by the combination.

[FRS 6 para 13].

28.74.1 The conditions for merger accounting under the Companies Act and FRS 6 have been discussed above from paragraph 28.12. In the case of a group reconstruction only the Act's requirements need to be met. The additional conditions imposed by FRS 6 for merger accounting are not required to be met. The Act's conditions which are explained in more detail from paragraph 28.12 above, are:

- At least 90 per cent of the nominal value of the relevant shares in the undertaking acquired (excluding any shares in the undertaking held as treasury shares) is held by or on behalf of the parent company and its subsidiary undertakings.
- The proportion referred to above was attained pursuant to an arrangement providing for the issue of equity shares by the parent company or one or more of its subsidiary undertakings.
- The fair value of any consideration other than the issue of equity shares given pursuant to the arrangement by the parent company and its subsidiary undertakings did not exceed ten per cent of the nominal value of the equity shares issued.
- Adoption of the merger method of accounting accords with generally accepted accounting principles or practice.

[SI 2008/410 6 Sch 10(1)].

[The next paragraph is 28.75.]

28.75 The definition of a group reconstruction in FRS 6 extends the meaning of the term to include several types of business combination which would not have been considered to be group reconstructions in the past. Indeed it includes several types of combination which would be eligible for merger relief rather than group reconstruction relief under the Act. The definition is:

"Group reconstruction:-

Any of the following arrangements:

(a) the transfer of a shareholding in a subsidiary undertaking from one group company to another;

(b) the addition of a new parent company to a group;

(c) the transfer of shares in one or more subsidiary undertakings of a group to a new company that is not a group company but whose shareholders are the same as those of the group's parent;

(d) the combination into a group of two or more companies that before the combination had the same shareholders."

[FRS 6 para 2].

28.76 Where any of the above forms of combination is planned, it will be necessary to determine whether group reconstruction relief or merger relief is applicable. These reliefs are explained in chapter 23.

Example 1 – Group reconstruction relief

Company A is the parent company of a group. It is proposed to form a new parent company, company B. Company B is formed as an independent company, not as a subsidiary of company A. Company B issues shares in exchange for all the shares in company A.

In this situation, company B does not qualify for group reconstruction relief, because it is not the wholly-owned subsidiary of company A, but it does qualify for merger relief.

Example 2 – Group reconstruction relief

Company A is the US parent company of a group which has a number of UK subsidiaries. It is proposed to form a new UK parent company for the UK subsidiaries. Company B is formed as a wholly-owned subsidiary of the US parent. It issues shares to the US parent in exchange for the US parent's holdings in the UK subsidiaries.

In this situation, company B is eligible for group reconstruction relief, because it is the wholly-owned subsidiary of the US parent and issues shares to that parent in exchange for the transfer to company B of the parent's holdings in the UK subsidiaries.

28.77 In both of the above situations merger accounting is permitted by law. The ultimate shareholders remain the same as do their rights, and there is no minority interest affected by the combination. Accordingly, merger accounting is permitted.

28.78 It is noticeable that FRS 6 does not make merger accounting compulsory in the case of group reconstructions, in contrast to other business combinations. However it is likely that, in most cases where there is a group reconstruction and the conditions set out above for merger accounting are satisfied, companies will wish to use merger accounting.

28.79 Example (d) in the definition of group reconstructions covers a situation where there is a so called 'horizontal' group. This is a group where the companies involved are not part of a legal group for Companies Act purposes, but are under the common ownership of an individual(s). Where this situation exists, it would clearly be somewhat severe if the combination had to satisfy all the stringent tests for merger accounting that apply to combinations other than group reconstructions. For instance, the 'relative size test' and the 'no identifiable acquirer or acquiree tests' are not really relevant in this situation.

Example – Group reconstruction with merger relief

Mr X and his family interests own the whole of the share capital of three companies — company A, company B and company C — which have net assets of 10, 100 and 1,000 respectively. It is decided that the three companies should be combined and company C issues shares to Mr X and his family interests in exchange for their shares in company A and company B. In this case, group reconstruction relief is not applicable, but company C is able to take merger relief. In addition, the combination is treated as a group reconstruction for the purposes of FRS 6 and the standard's conditions for merger accounting in the case of group reconstructions are satisfied. The conditions that FRS 6 sets out for business combinations that are not group reconstructions are not relevant. It does not matter if company C is portrayed as the acquirer or that company C is much larger than the other two parties to the combination.

28.80 One of the conditions for merger accounting for a group reconstruction is that no minority's interest in the net assets of the group is altered by the transfer. A minority's interest may be unaffected, for instance, where a subsidiary undertaking is transferred within a subgroup that has a minority shareholder, but is likely to be affected if a subsidiary is transferred into or out of such a group.

Example – Minority interest unchanged

Company B is the intermediate parent company of subsidiary companies C, D and E. There is a minority interest of 10% in company B the remainder of whose shares are owned by the ultimate parent company, company A. Company A has a further direct subsidiary company X. Company B enters into two transactions. First, it transfers ownership of company C to company E in exchange for shares in company E (which are issued to company B). Second, it transfers company E (which now owns company C) to company X for shares. Both company E and company X prepare consolidated financial statements.

Before construction

Stage 1

Stage 2

After stage 2, B holds an investment in X (which is not an associate or a subsidiary).

In the first transaction, the transfer of company C to company E, the minority interest is not affected because the composition of the subgroup headed by company B remains unchanged. In company E's consolidated financial statements, therefore, the combination with company C could be merger accounted.

In the second transaction company E and its subsidiary company C move out of the company B subgroup and company B's investment in company E (and its subsidiary company C) is replaced by an investment in company X (but company X does not thereby become a subsidiary of company B).

If the investment in company X is recorded in company B's consolidated financial statements at the same value as it had previously recorded the net assets of company E and company C (ignoring goodwill), the minority's share of net assets will be unchanged. In terms of the carrying values, this transaction might seem to satisfy the condition that the minority's interest in the net assets is not altered. However, the explanation section of the standard says:

> *"If a minority has effectively acquired, or disposed of, rights to part of the net assets of the group, the FRS requires the transfer to be accounted for by using acquisition accounting rather than merger accounting."* [FRS 6 para 79].

As the minority has indeed disposed of part of the company B group in this situation, it appears that company X must acquisition account for the combination with company E and company C. This would appear to be so because the 'group' referred to in quotation above must be the company B sub-group. This interpretation is reinforced by a further quotation from the explanation section of the standard:

> *"Thus the transfer of a subsidiary undertaking within a subgroup that has a minority shareholder may qualify for merger accounting; but acquisition accounting must be used for the transfer of a subsidiary undertaking out of, or into, such a subgroup."* [FRS 6 para 79].

Applicability to other forms of business combination

28.81 The provisions of FRS 6, which are framed in terms of an acquirer or issuing entity issuing shares as consideration for the transfer to it of shares in the other parties to a combination, should also be read as applying to other arrangements that achieve similar results. [FRS 6 para 15]. This provision of FRS 6 is presumably intended to cover arrangements other than those which involve a group reconstruction or straightforward merger, but which in substance amount to a merger.

28.82 The incidence of such arrangements is likely to be rare, as the merger accounting conditions are stringent and unlikely to be satisfied by unconventional arrangements.

Accounting treatment of the investment in an acquired company

28.83 The appendix to FRS 6 entitled 'Legal requirements' states that the FRS does not deal with the form of accounting to be used in the acquiring or issuing company's own financial statements. However, the Companies Act 2006 clarifies the accounting treatment of an investment in an acquired company that should be used in an issuing company's balance sheet where there is:

- Merger relief under section 612.
- Group reconstruction relief under section 611.

28.84 In these circumstances, the amount at which the issuing company carries its investment in the acquired company does not need to include an amount corresponding to the premium (or the part of the premium) that the issuing company has not credited to its share premium account. [CA06 Sec 615]. That is, the issuing company has a choice. Disregarding other considerations such as cash, the issuing company can record both the shares it issues and the investment in the new subsidiary at either:

- the nominal value of the shares issued and any section 611 minimum premium; or
- the fair value of the shares issued, with the premium in excess of any section 611 minimum premium credited to a merger reserve instead of to a share premium account.

28.85 The accounting treatment of the investment in an acquired company is considered further in chapter 23 which deals in detail with merger relief and group reconstruction relief.

28.86 Where merger accounting is adopted on consolidation and the investment shown in the holding company's balance sheet does not include the premium, it is debatable whether the investment should be described as being at cost, because the amount shown in the balance sheet may be quite different from the actual cost.

It could be argued that the 'true' cost of the shares issued is their fair value and not their nominal value. Consequently, the company may need to choose some appropriate wording other than 'cost' to describe the investment (for example, 'at nominal value of shares issued').

[The next paragraph is 28.92.]

Difference on consolidation

28.92 In merger accounting under the Act, the parent's balance sheet will generally show its investment in the subsidiary at the nominal value of the shares that it issued as consideration plus the fair value of any additional consideration.

28.93 A difference may then arise on consolidation between the value at which the parent carries its investment in the subsidiary and the aggregate of the nominal value of the subsidiary's shares that the parent acquires together with any share premium account and capital redemption reserve of the subsidiary (these being the parts of the subsidiary's shareholders' funds that need to be eliminated on consolidation, that is the subsidiary's distributable reserves flow through into the consolidated reserves). The value of the investment will represent the aggregate of the following:

- The nominal value of the 'qualifying shares' issued by the parent in consideration for the acquisition of the shares in the subsidiary. [SI 2008/410 6 Sch 11(5)(a)]. 'Qualifying shares' means those shares where merger relief is obtained and, consequently, no share premium has to be recorded on them or those shares where group reconstruction relief applies and where, consequently, the appropriate amount is the nominal value together with any minimum premium value as defined in section 611 of the Act. [SI 2008/410 6 Sch 11(7)].

- The fair value of any other consideration given for the acquisition determined at the date of acquisition. [SI 2008/410 6 Sch 11(5)(b)].

28.93.1 In the extract from the Movement in Shareholders' Funds statement given in Table 28.2 below, the difference arising on consolidation is shown as £494 million. This has been calculated as the difference between the nominal value of 706 million 25p shares issued by Sun Alliance, that is £176 million, and the share capital and share premium account of the subsidiary Royal Insurance amounting to £670 million.

Table 28.2 — Royal & Sun Alliance Insurance Group plc — Directors' Report and Accounts — 31 December 1996

Movement in Shareholders' Funds (extract)

	Notes	Share capital premium £m	Revaluation reserve £m	Other reserves (see below) £m	Profit and loss account £m	1996 £m	1995 £m
Shareholders' funds at 1st January as previously reported by							
Royal Insurance		670	991	(381)	1,396	**2,676**	1,882
Sun Alliance		377	1,752	–	511	**2,640**	1,768
Merger reserve adjustment		(494)	–	494	–	–	–
Accounting policy alignment	*1d*	–	869	(286)	287	**870**	702
Merged shareholders' funds at 1st January		553	3,612	(173)	2,194	**6,186**	4,352

Other reserves as restated at 1st January represent the cumulative amount of goodwill written off (adjusted for disposals) of £667m and the merger reserve of £494m arising as a result of the merger of Royal Insurance and Sun Alliance on 19th July 1996. As at 31st December 1996 the cumulative amount of goodwill written off (adjusted for disposals) is **£675m.**

Note 31 (extract)

On 14th June 1996 the authorised share capital was increased by the creation of 1,00,000,000 ordinary shares of 25p each. Pursuant to a scheme of arrangement, 706,252,430 shares were issued on 19th July 1996 to former shareholders of Royal Insurance on the basis of 1,067 ordinary shares of 25p each in the Company for every 1,000 Royal Insurance shares of 25p each held.

[The next paragraph is 28.94.]

28.94 On consolidation, the inclusion of the subsidiary's share premium account and capital redemption reserve in the set off reflects the fact that these accounts are effectively part of the capital of the subsidiary. Because these amounts are included in the set off, the effect is that the share premium and capital redemption reserve in the consolidated balance sheet will comprise only the amounts from the parent's balance sheet.

28.95 The group should adjust the differences arising on consolidation against other reserves on consolidation and should show the movement in reserves in the reconciliation of movements in shareholders' funds. [SI 2008/410 6 Sch 11(6); FRS 6 para 18].

28.96 Where the investment's carrying value is less than the nominal value of the shares (plus any share premium and capital redemption reserve of the subsidiary) that the parent company has acquired, the group should treat the difference as an 'other reserve' that arises on consolidation. Where the investment's carrying value is greater than the nominal value of the shares (again plus any share premium and capital redemption reserve) acquired, the difference represents the extent to which the group has effectively capitalised its reserves as a result of the merger. Consequently, the group should reduce its 'other reserves' by the amount of the difference.

28.97 The two examples that follow show how these consolidation differences arise and how they should be treated:

Example 1 – Where the carrying value is less than nominal value

Company A acquires all of company B's £200,000 nominal share capital. The purchase consideration consists of new shares that company A issues and these have a nominal value of £190,000. The business combination satisfies all the merger conditions and the group uses merger accounting. The respective balance sheets, after the merger, of the individual companies and the group are as follows:

	Co A	Co B	Group
	£'000	£'000	£'000
Net tangible assets	1,500	1,400	2,900
Investment in subsidiary	190		–
	1,690	1,400	2,900
Share capital	400	200	400
Profit and loss account	1,290	1,200	2,490
Difference on consolidation	–	–	10
	1,690	1,400	2,900

The difference on consolidation of £10,000 is calculated as follows:

	£'000
Nominal value of shares acquired	200
Parent company's carrying value of investment	190
Difference on consolidation	10

The group should treat the difference on consolidation as a reserve that arises on consolidation, because the investment's carrying value is less than the nominal value of the shares acquired.

Example 2 – Where the carrying value is greater than nominal value

The facts in this example are the same as those in example 1 above, except that the purchase consideration consists of new shares with a nominal value of £250,000. In this example, the respective balance sheets, after the merger, of the individual companies and the group are as follows:

	Co A	Co B	Group
	£'000	£'000	£'000
Net tangible assets	1,500	1,400	2,900
Investment in subsidiary	250	–	–
	1,750	1,400	2,900
Share capital	460	200	460
Profit and loss account	1,290	1,200	2,490
Other reserves	–	–	(50)
	1,750	1,400	2,900

The difference on consolidation of £50,000 is calculated as follows:

	£'000
Nominal value of shares acquired	200
Parent company's carrying value of investment	250
Difference on consolidation	(50)

The investment's carrying value is greater than the nominal value of the shares acquired, and so the group should reduce its reserves by the amount of the difference.

Merger expenses

28.98 Expenses of the merger must not be included in the calculation of the difference arising on consolidation. Merger expenses should instead be charged in the profit and loss account of the combined entity as reorganisation or restructuring expenses in accordance with paragraph 20 of FRS 3. [FRS 6 para 19]. This means that such expenses should be charged as a non-operating exceptional item, if material. An example of this is Table 28.3 which also shows exceptional operating costs arising from reorganisation as a pre-operating profit item.

Table 28.3 — United News & Media plc — Annual Report and Accounts — 31 December 1996

Group profit and loss account (extract)

	Notes	Before exceptional items 1996 £m	Exceptional items (note 4) 1996 £m	Total 1996 £m
Turnover	1			
Continuing operations		1,917.5		1,917.5
Acquisitions		21.0		21.0
		1,938.5		1,938.5
Discontinued operations		52.2		52.2
		1,990.7		1,990.7
Operating costs	2	(1,710.0)	(112.5)	(1,822.5)
Operating profit				
Continuing operations		268.9	(94.4)	174.5
Acquisitions		0.7	(18.1)	(17.4)
		269.6	(112.5)	157.1
Discontinued operations		11.1	–	11.1
		280.7	(112.5)	168.2
Income from interests in associated undertakings		21.2	(62.5)	(41.3)
Income from other fixed asset investments	3	2.2	–	2.2
Total operating profit	1	304.1	(175.0)	129.1
Continuing operations				
Merger expenses			(31.0)	(31.0)
Profit on the disposal of fixed asset investments			11.6	11.6
Discontinued operations				
Profit (loss) on sales and closure of businesses			138.0	138.0
Profit on ordinary activities before interest		304.1	(56.4)	247.7
Net interest expense	5	(13.9)	–	(13.9)
Profit on ordinary activities before tax		290.2	(56.4)	233.8
Tax on profit on ordinary activities	6	(88.6)	12.7	(75.9)
Profit on ordinary activities after tax		201.6	(43.7)	157.9
Minority interests		(5.5)	–	(5.5)
Profit for the year	7	196.1	(43.7)	152.4
Dividends	8			(115.3)
Retained profit for the year	23			37.1
Earnings per share after exceptional items	9			31.1p
Earnings per share before exceptional items	9			40.0p

28.99 The standard does not prohibit such expenses from being subsequently charged to share premium account by means of a reserve transfer from profit and loss account reserve to the share premium account provided the expenses are eligible to be charged to share premium account under section 610 of the Act. The relevant expenses that could be charged subsequently to the share premium account include, for example: the expenses of the issue of shares by the acquiring company; the preliminary expenses of any new parent company formed to effect the merger; and any commission paid on the issue of the shares.

28.100 The question of how merger expenses should be accounted for in the financial statements of the parent company that effects the combination is not dealt with in the standard. If the parent company has a share premium account and wishes to set eligible expenses against that account, it would seem reasonable that it should mirror the treatment on consolidation by passing the expenses through its own profit and loss account and then making a transfer from the profit and loss account reserve to the share premium account.

28.101 However, where there is no share premium account or the parent does not wish to write the eligible costs off against that account, there would appear to be a further alternative to writing these and other costs relating to the merger off to the profit and loss account. Because the parent has acquired an asset, the shares in the other party to the combination, it should record that asset at its purchase price and to the purchase price should be added any expenses incidental to its acquisition. [SI 2008/410 1 Sch 17, 27(1)].

28.102 The carrying value of the investment in the acquired entity may, therefore, be included in the parent company's balance sheet at the nominal value of shares issued plus the fair value of any other consideration given (where group reconstruction relief is obtained there may be some premium included) plus the expenses that are incidental to the merger. These expenses will of course have to be disregarded when comparing the carrying value of the investment with the nominal value of shares issued in order to determine the difference arising on consolidation that is discussed above. Also in the consolidated financial statements, the costs will be charged to the group profit and loss account.

28.103 Any difference between the treatment of merger expenses in the parent's financial statements and those of the group will need to be disclosed in a note to the financial statements together with the reasons for the difference. [SI 2008/410 6 Sch 4]. An example of such a note where such expenses have been capitalised in the parent is shown below.

Example – Merger expenses treatment – disclosure

Merger expenses of £5m have been included in the parent company's financial statements as part of the carrying value of the investment in X plc. On consolidation in accordance with the requirements of FRS 6, 'Acquisitions and mergers', these expenses have been charged to the consolidated profit and loss account. The difference in accounting treatment arises because such expenses may be included in the carrying value of the investment under the provisions of the Companies Act 2006, but must be written off to the profit and loss account on consolidation under the provisions of FRS 6.

28.104 Where relevant merger expenses are added to the carrying amount of investment in the parent's balance sheet, care will need to be taken to ensure that the resultant carrying amount does not exceed the investment's recoverable amount. If it did, a provision would be needed against the investment. This might occur if the expenses were very large in relation to the value of the entity with which the parent is combining. However, the fact that the shares issued are recorded at their nominal value, rather than at their fair value, should usually mean that the carrying value including expenses is well below the recoverable amount of the investment and thus, no provision will normally be needed.

28.105 The alternative treatment described above of costs that are eligible to be written off against share premium account, that is adding such costs to the carrying value of the investment, differs from the treatment of such costs prescribed by FRS 7 where acquisition accounting and fair valuing are required (see chapter 25). However, as the treatment of expenses on consolidation also differs between merger and acquisition accounting, this difference is considered acceptable.

Accounting periods

28.106 Where a new parent company is formed to effect a merger between two companies or to effect a group reconstruction whereby it becomes the parent company of an existing group, problems can arise if the accounting period of the new parent differs from that of the other combining entities. Three examples are given below and two other examples are given above in paragraph 28.70.

Example 1 – Different accounting periods

A new parent company is formed 1 July 20X1 and issues equity shares in exchange for the equity shares of company A. Company A's accounting reference period is the 12 months to December 20X1. The first reference period of the new parent company is fixed as the six months to 31 December 20X1. The combination satisfies the conditions for merger accounting.

The question arises as to what figures for company A should be included in the consolidated financial statements, which themselves must cover the period from 1 July to 31 December 20X1.

One argument would be that the consolidated financial statements should include the results of company A for the period from 1 July to 31 December 20X1 with comparatives for the period 1 July to 31 December 20X0. This treatment is the most obvious and is quite acceptable. However, this would mean that the group financial statements would omit the six months trading of company A from 1 January 20X1 to 30 June 20X1. It can also cause difficulties in obtaining figures for the 'stub period' of the combining entity. An alternative is that the consolidated financial statements would include the results of the new parent for the six months to 31 December 20X1 and the results of company A for the 12 months to December 20X1. The basis for this treatment is as follows:

Paragraph 2 of Schedule 6 to SI 2008/410 requires that the consolidated balance sheet and profit and loss account shall incorporate in full the information contained in the individual financial statements of the undertakings included in the consolidation. This is subject to the adjustments authorised or required by Schedule 6 to SI 2008/410 and to any other adjustments as may be appropriate in accordance with generally accepted accounting principles or practice.

Based on this provision of the Act and because there do not appear to be any adjustments that would be required by Schedule 6 to SI 2008/410 or generally accepted accounting principles or practice, we consider that in the situation described above, the results of company A may be included in the consolidated financial statements for the full accounting reference period of company A. Thus, the consolidated financial statements for the 6 months to 31 December 20X1 would include the results of the new parent for 6 months and the results of company A for 12 months. The comparative figures for the consolidated financial statements under merger accounting would comprise the profit and loss account, cash flow statement and balance sheet of the new subsidiary for the year to 31 December 20X0. An example of where a company has adopted the second approach is in Table 28.3A.

Table 28.3A — Allied Domecq PLC — Annual Report and Accounts — 31 August 1999

Accounting policies (extract)

Consolidation The group accounts consolidate the accounts of the company and its interests in subsidiaries. Interests in associates and joint ventures are equity accounted. During the year there was a capital reorganisation that required a new parent company for the group (refer to note 21). This has been accounted for using merger accounting principles.

Note 21 (extract)

Changes in authorised, allotted and issued ordinary share capital (extract)

Allied Domecq PLC was incorporated on 11 May 1999 as a public limited company with the name Allied Domecq 1999 PLC, which was changed to new Allied Domecq PLC ('the company') on 28 May 1999.

On 2 August 1999, the company acquired Allied Domecq PLC as part of the Scheme. Shares in Allied Domecq PLC were cancelled and in consideration shareholders received shares in the company, in the ratio of one share in the company for each share in Allied Domecq PLC. Allied Domecq PLC was renamed Allied Domecq (Holdings) PLC and new Allied Domecq PLC was renamed Allied Domecq PLC.

Group Profit and Loss Account (extract)
Year to 31 August 1999

		Year to 31 August 1999			Year to 31 August 1998		
		Before exceptional items	**Exceptional items**	**Total**	Before exceptional items	Exceptional items	Total
	Note	**£m**	**£m**	**£m**	£m	£m	£m
Continuing operations		**2,408**	–	**2,408**	2,398	–	2,398
Discontinued operations		**1,695**	–	**1,695**	1,910	–	1,910
Group turnover and share of turnover of joint venture undertaking	**1**	**4,103**	–	**4,103**	4,308	–	4,308
Less: share of turnover of joint venture – discontinued operation		**(624)**	–	**(624)**	–	–	–
Turnover		**3,479**	–	**3,479**	4,308	–	4,308
Operating costs	**3**	**(2,838)**	**(235)**	**(3,073)**	(3,609)	(87)	(3,696)
Continuing operations		**420**	**(220)**	**200**	415	(12)	403
Discontinued operations		**221**	**(15)**	**206**	284	(75)	209
Operating profit		**641**	**(235)**	**406**	699	(87)	612

Example 2 – Different accounting periods

A similar approach may be adopted if the new parent company were formed on 1 October 20X0 and had its first year end on 31 December 20X1, a 15 month accounting period.

In this case the consolidated financial statements for the 15 months to 31 December 20X1 would include the new parent for 15 months from 1 October 20X0 and company A's results for its accounting reference period of one year from 1 January 20X1 to 31 December 20X1. Comparative figures would most sensibly be for the year to December 20X0 as this would give a continuous record for the combined group. (There would be no duplication of the new parent company's results on the reasonable assumption that it will not have traded in the period to 31 December 20X0.)

28.107 As the above two examples demonstrate, the apparent problems that arise, where the accounting periods of the new parent and the other combining entity are different, can be overcome. It is obviously much simpler, however, to arrange that where a new parent company is to be formed and merger accounting is to be adopted it should have the same accounting period as the company that it combines with. Where a new top company is used to implement a merger, the forward planning should always seek to avoid the problems that can arise through having different accounting periods for the new parent and the other combining entity.

28.108 Where no new parent company is involved, but the year ends of the combining companies differ, again problems may arise.

Example – Different accounting periods

Company A, which has a year end of 31 December, combines with company B which has a year end of 30 September. Company A is preparing consolidated financial statements for the year ended 31 December 19X5, the year in which the merger took place. There are three apparent possibilities at first sight in respect of inclusion of company B's results.

(i) Include the results of company B for the year ended 31 December 19X5 based on interim accounts prepared by company B for the 12 months to that date. This is permitted by paragraph 2(2) of Schedule 6 to SI 2008/410 which states:

"If the financial year of a subsidiary undertaking included in the consolidation does not end with that of the parent company, the group accounts shall be made up —

(a) from the accounts of the subsidiary undertaking for its financial year last ending before the end of three the parent company's financial year, provided that year ended no more than three months before that of the parent company, or

(b) from interim accounts prepared by the subsidiary undertaking as at the end of the parent company's financial year."

The comparatives for the year ended 31 December 19X4 would similarly include the results of company B for the year ended on that date based on interim accounts for 12 months.

(ii) Include the results of company B for the 15 months ended 31 December 19X5 with the comparative figures for the year ended 31 December 19X4, including company B for the 15 months ended on that date again based on interim accounts. This approach is not appropriate as it would involve double counting of company B's results for the period from September 19X4 to December 19X4.

(iii) Include the results of company B for the 12 months to September 19X5 with the comparatives similarly including the results of company B for the 12 months to September 19X4. Although permitted by the Act (because the year end of company B is not more than three months before that of the parent), it should be noted that FRS 2 requires that interim accounts should be prepared to 31 December, the parent's year end, unless it is impracticable to do so. Therefore, this approach should only be adopted in the rare circumstances where it is impracticable to prepare interim accounts.

Of the three possibilities, (i) is the appropriate treatment in all cases except where it is impracticable, in which case (iii) would be adopted. The treatment in (ii) should not be adopted.

Comparison of acquisition accounting with merger accounting

28.109 FRS 6 highlights the following three main differences between acquisition accounting and merger accounting:

- In acquisition accounting, the consolidated financial statements reflect the acquired company's results from the date of acquisition only. However, in merger accounting, the consolidated financial statements incorporate the combined companies' results and cash flows as if the companies had always been combined. Consequently, under merger accounting, the consolidated financial statements reflect both companies' full year's results, even though the business combination may have occurred part of the way though the year. Under merger accounting, the corresponding amounts in the consolidated financial statements for the previous year should reflect the results of the combined companies, even though the business combination did not occur until the current year.

- In acquisition accounting, the acquiring group should account for the assets it acquired at the cost to the acquiring group. The acquiring group determines that cost by attributing a fair value to the assets and liabilities that it acquires. However, in merger accounting, the group does not restate any assets and liabilities at their fair values. Instead, the group incorporates the assets and liabilities at the amounts recorded in the books of the combining companies. As in the profit and loss account presentation, merger accounting shows the position of the combining companies as if the companies had always been combined.

- Acquisition accounting may give rise to goodwill on consolidation. However, goodwill does not arise in merger accounting. Merger accounting may lead to differences on consolidation. For example, in merger accounting, there may be a difference between the nominal value of the shares issued together with the fair value of any additional consideration given, and the nominal value of the other company's shares that have been acquired (see paras 28.92 to 28.97). However, such differences are not goodwill as defined in FRS 10, because they are not based on the fair values of both the consideration given and the identifiable assets and liabilities acquired.

28.110 The following example illustrates the difference between acquisition accounting and merger accounting. The example is somewhat artificial in that it shows both methods applying to the same situation whereas in practice, under FRS 6 there is no choice between the methods of accounting. The combination will either have to be acquisition accounted or it will have to be merger accounted. The method will depend on whether or not all the conditions for merger accounting in FRS 6 are met.

Example – Different between acquisition and merger accounting

Company H (the issuing company) acquires the whole of company A's equity share capital. The effect of the acquisition will be to merge the interests of company H and company A.

Company A's shareholders accept an offer from company H of 400,000 shares in company H for the 410,000 issued shares in company A as at 31 December 20X0. The value at 31 December of the 400,000 of company H's £1 shares that are offered to company A's shareholders is £6.4 million, (that is, £16 per share). The fair value of company A's net assets is £6.1 million (that is, £90,000 above their net book value). The difference of £300,000 is attributable to goodwill. On 31 December 20X0, before the acquisition, the summarised balance sheets of the two companies are as follows:

	Co H	Co A
	£'000	£'000
Net assets	5,000	6,010
Share capital (shares of £1 each)	500	410
Reserves	4,500	5,600
	5,000	6,010

The summarised consolidated balance sheets of the issuing company and its subsidiary under the two methods of accounting are as follows:

	Notes	Acquisition accounting £'000	Merger accounting £'000
Goodwill on consolidation	(a)	300	–
Net assets	(b)	11,100	11,010
		11,400	11,010
Share capital	(c)	900	900
Distributable reserves	(e)	4,500	10,100
Merger reserve	(d)	6,000	–
Other reserves	(f)	–	10
		11,400	11,010

Notes to the example above:

(a) Goodwill on consolidation is the amount by which the purchase consideration (that is, 400,000 shares at £16, or £6.4 million) exceeds the fair value of the underlying net assets acquired (that is, £6.1 million).

(b) Net assets are the two companies' total net assets. In acquisition accounting, the assets acquired are included at their fair value, as required by the Act and FRS 2. In merger accounting the assets of the combining companies are not fair valued.

(c) The share capital consists of the 500,000 shares originally in issue, together with the 400,000 shares allotted when company H combined with company A.

(d) The amount credited to the merger reserve taking merger relief under section 131 of the Act is £6 million (that is, 400,000 shares issued at a premium of £15 per share).

(e) Under merger accounting, there is no requirement to transfer to a merger reserve the premium on the shares allotted to the acquired company's shareholders. Consequently, both companies' distributable reserves are pooled. In accordance with the Act and paragraph 16 of FRS 6, the excess of the fair value of company A's net assets over their book value (that is, £90,000) need not be incorporated into the consolidated financial statements.

(f) Under merger accounting the difference between the nominal value of shares issued (that is, £400,000) and the nominal value of shares received as consideration (that is £410,000) is credited to other reserves. Had the carrying value of the investment exceeded the nominal value of the shares received as consideration the difference would be debited to reserves.

28.111 The example that follows illustrates the differences between using acquisition accounting and using merger accounting in a group reconstruction where the group reconstruction qualifies for relief under section 612.

Example – Acquisition and merger accounting compared where group reconstruction relief applies

In 19X1, company A acquired all of company C's issued share capital (100,000 £1 shares) for £390,000. Company C had no reserves at that time. On 31 December 19X5, another wholly-owned subsidiary (company B) allots 100,000 £1 shares to company A. In return for the allotment, company A transfers to company B the shares in company C that it owns. Subsequently, company A is to be liquidated, and its shareholders will receive shares in company B. At the time of the reconstruction, company B's shares that are issued to company A are worth £400,000 (that is, £4 per share) and the fair value of company C's recorded net assets is £360,000 (the difference of £40,000 being attributed to goodwill). The fair value of company A's and company B's net assets is equal to their book value.

Diagrammatically, the reconstruction is as follows:

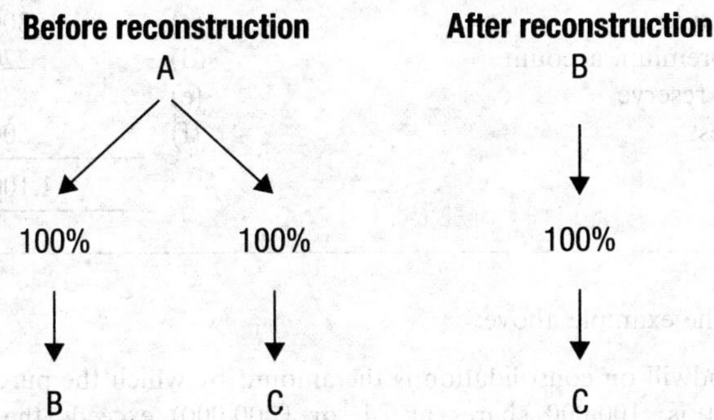

The individual balance sheets of the three companies as at 31 December 19X5 before the reconstruction are as follows:

	Co A £'000	Co B £'000	Co C £'000
Investment in B*	210	–	–
Investment in C*	320	–	–
Net assets	–	700	350
	530	700	350
Share capital (shares of 1 each)	150	200	100
Reserves	380	500	250
	530	700	350

*The investments are stated at the cost of shares to company A, reduced for company A's investment in company C by a write-down of £70,000 made in 19X2.

After the reconstruction, the summarised consolidated balance sheet of company B and its subsidiary company C is as follows:

	Notes	Acquisition accounting £'000	Merger accounting £'000
Goodwill on consolidation	(a)	40	–
Net assets	(b)	1,060	1,050
		1,100	1,050
Share capital	(c)	300	300
Share premium account	(d)	220	220
Merger reserve	(e)	80	–
Reserves	(f)	500	530
		1,100	1,050

Notes to the example above:

(a) Goodwill on consolidation is the amount by which the purchase consideration (that is, 100,000 shares at £4, or £400,000) exceeds the fair value of the underlying assets acquired (that is, £360,000). Under merger accounting, goodwill does not arise, because the net assets' fair value need not be incorporated in the consolidated financial statements.

(b) Company C's net assets are included at their fair value when they are accounted for as an acquisition. But when they are accounted for as a merger, they are included at their book value.

(c) The share capital consists of the 200,000 shares originally in issue, together with the 100,000 shares allotted on company B's acquisition of company C.

(d) Under section 612 of the Act, the issuing company is required to transfer to the share premium account only an amount equal to the minimum premium value. The minimum premium value is calculated as the amount by which the base value of the shares in company C, that are transferred from company A to company B, exceeds the aggregate nominal value of the shares that company B allots in consideration for the transfer. The amount of the transfer to the share premium account is calculated as follows:

	£'000	£'000
The base value of shares in company C is the lower of:		
The cost of the shares to company A	390	
The amount at which those shares are stated in company A's accounting records immediately before the transfer	320	
		320
Less: Nominal value of the shares company B allotted in respect of the transfer		100
Transfer to the share premium account		220

(e) The amount credited to the merger reserve under acquisition accounting is the amount of the premium that is not required to be taken to the share premium account because of section 612 relief (that is, 100,000 shares issued at a premium of £3, or £300,000 less £220,000 required to be taken to share premium under section 612).

(f) Under acquisition accounting, the amount to be included in other reserves is the amount of company B's reserves (that is, £500,000). Under section 612 of the Act (which gives the relief in respect of group reconstructions) other reserves are made up as follows:

	£'000
Reserves of company B	500
Reserves of company C less minimum premium value (that is, £250,000 — £220,000)	30
	530

Disclosure for merger accounting

Consolidated financial statements

28.112 The issuing company should disclose certain information in respect of all material mergers. The parent must disclose in the consolidated financial statements that deal with the period in which the merger occurs:

- The names of the merging companies (other than the reporting entity). [SI 2008/410 6 Sch 13(2)(a); FRS 6 para 21 (a)]. The Act goes on to add that where the issuing company has merged with a group of companies, only the name of the group's parent needs to be disclosed.

- Whether the acquisition has been accounted for by the acquisition or merger method of accounting. [SI 2008/410 6 Sch 13(2)(b); FRS 6 para 21(b)].
- The effective date of the merger. [FRS 6 para 21(c)].

28.113 In addition, further information is required to be disclosed for mergers. The FRS 6 disclosures listed below do not apply to group reconstructions (but the Act's disclosure requirements *do* apply even where they are the same as in FRS 6). [FRS 6 para 82]. These requirements are as follows:

- The composition and the fair value of the consideration given by the parent and its subsidiaries. [SI 2008/410 6 Sch 13(3); FRS 6 para 22(c)].
- A statement of any resulting adjustment to the consolidated reserves resulting from the merger (including a restatement of opening consolidated reserves). [SI 2008/410 6 Sch 13(4); FRS 6 para 22(f)].
- The nature and the amount of significant accounting adjustments made to the net assets of any party to the merger to achieve consistent accounting policies and an explanation of any other significant adjustments made to the net assets of any party to the merger as a consequence of the merger. [FRS 6 para 22(e)].
- The aggregate book value of the net assets of each party to the merger at the effective date of the merger. [FRS 6 para 22(d)].

28.114 If in the directors' opinion the disclosure of any of the information above that is required by the Act (relating to an undertaking established under the law of a country, or one that carries on a business, outside the UK) would be seriously prejudicial to the business of the undertaking, its parent or its fellow subsidiaries, it need not be given if the Secretary of State's permission is obtained. [SI 2008/410 6 Sch 16].

28.115 In addition, in respect of a material merger, other than a group reconstruction, the issuing company should disclose the following information in its financial statements that deal with a year in which a merger occurs:

- An analysis of the principal components of the current year's profit and loss account and statement of total recognised gains and losses into:
  - amounts relating to the merged entity for the period after the date of the merger; and
  - for each party to the merger, amounts relating to that party for the period up to the date of the merger.
- An analysis between the parties to the merger of the principal components of the profit and loss account and statement of total recognised gains and losses for the previous financial year.

[FRS 6 paras 22(a)(b)].

28.116 The standard specifies the headings that comprise the principal components of the profit and loss account and statement of total recognised gains and losses for the purposes of the disclosure requirements. These are:

- Turnover analysed between continuing operations (with acquisitions disclosed separately) and discontinued operations.
- Operating profit analysed in the same way as turnover.
- Exceptional items analysed in the same way as turnover.
- Profit before taxation.
- Taxation and minority interests.
- Extraordinary items (highly unlikely under FRS 3).

[FRS 6 para 22].

28.117 The principal components of the statement of total recognised gains and losses, whilst not specified in the FRS, would usually be:

- Profit for the financial year.
- Exchange gains or losses taken direct to reserves.
- Revaluation surpluses or deficits.
- Total recognised gains or losses.

28.118 In relation to the category of revaluation surpluses or deficits, the standard makes it clear that the requirement for disclosure does not mean that revaluations carried out at the end of a financial year would need to be repeated at the effective date of merger.

Example

An example of the extensive disclosure that might result from compliance with the requirements of the FRS and the Act is as follows:

XYZ plc merged with ABC plc on 30 June 20X1 and has accounted for the combination using merger accounting. The consideration was satisfied by the issue of £400,000 equity shares with a nominal value of £1 each. The fair value of the consideration was £5m based on the market price of XYZ plc shares at 30 June 20X1. No significant adjustments were made to the assets and liabilities of ABC plc which have been recorded at their book values immediately prior to the merger and no adjustments were made to the net assets of XYZ plc. The book value of net assets of XYZ plc and ABC plc at the date of the combination were £1.2m and £1m respectively. The difference of £50,000 arising on consolidation between the nominal value of XYZ plc shares issued (£400,000) and the nominal value of ABC plc shares acquired (£450,000) has been credited to reserves. ABC's financial year began on 1 January 20X1.

The analysis of the principal components of the profit and loss accounts and statements of total recognised gains and losses is as follows:

20X1	Combined post merger £m	XYZ plc pre merger £m	ABC plc pre merger £m	Total for the year £m
Profit and loss account				
Turnover				
Continuing	27	12	13	52
Acquisitions	4	–	1	5
Total continuing	31	12	14	57
Discontinued	1	1	–	2
	32	13	14	59
Operating profit				
Continuing	4	2	1	7
Acquisitions	1	–	–	1
Total continuing	5	2	1	8
Discontinued	(1)	–	–	(1)
	4	2	1	7
Exceptional items				
Discontinued operations				
Loss on sale of subsidiaries	(1)	–	–	(1)
Profit before taxation	3	2	1	6
Taxation	1	1	–	2
Profit after taxation and for the financial period	2	1	1	4
Total recognised gains and losses				
Profit after taxation and for the financial period	2	1	1	4
Exchange (losses)/gains	1	(1)	–	–
Revaluation surplus	3	–	–	3
Total recognised gains	6	–	1	7

The equivalent analysis for the previous year is as follows:

20X0	XYZ plc £m	ABC plc £m
Profit and loss account		
Turnover		
Continuing	20	23
Discontinued	3	–
	23	23
(There were no acquisitions in 20X0)		
Operating profit		
Continuing	3	4
Discontinued	(1)	–
	2	4
(there were no post operating profit exceptional items in 20X0)		
Profit before taxation	2	4
Taxation	–	1
Profit after tax and for the financial year	2	3
Total recognised gains and losses		
Profit after tax and for the financial year	2	3
Exchange (losses)/gains	(1)	1
Revaluation surpluses	3	4
Total recognised gains	4	8

[The next paragraph is 28.121.]

28.121 Interest has been ignored in the above example. Also the totals for 20X1 are not required as they appear in the profit and loss itself, but have been given above to enable the figures for the pre-acquisition and post-acquisition periods to be reconciled.

28.122 A further example of the disclosures described above is Table 28.4.

Table 28.4 — United News & Media plc — Annual Report and Accounts — 31 December 1996

Accounting policies (extract)

Merger with MAI plc On 8 February 1996, United News & Media plc (United) and MAI plc (MAI) announced plans for the merging of their respective businesses. The merger was to be effected by way of offers made by United for the whole of the issued share capital of MAI. These offers became unconditional on 2 April 1996. The merger has been accounted for using the merger accounting principles set out in Financial Reporting Standard 6. Accordingly, the financial information for the current period has been presented, and that for the prior year restated, as if MAI had been owned by United throughout the current and comparative accounting periods.

Note 24

24. Merger adjustments The merger adjustments reflect the alignment of accounting policies following the merger:

(a) Intangible assets—in previous periods publishing rights and titles had been stated at directors' valuation*. These are now stated at fair value on acquisition and are not revalued. The effect of this restatement is a debit adjustment to the revaluation reserve of £73 million. The comparative figures for 1995 have been restated.

(b) Consolidation—on acquisition of subsidiary undertakings, business or associated undertakings the purchase consideration is allocated between underlying assets on a fair value basis. Any goodwill arising is written off direct to reserves*. Previously in MAI the goodwill relating to certain associates was amortised over its expected economic life. The effect of this restatement is a debit adjustment to goodwill of £27.7 million. The comparative figures for 1995 have been restated.

Note 29

29. Business merger As explained in the accounting policies, on 8 February 1996, United and MAI announced plans for the merging of their respective businesses. The merger was to be effected by way of offers made by United for the whole of the issued share capital of MAI, being 332,718,123 ordinary shares of 5 pence each and 120,956,330 preference shares of 5 pence each, for a consideration of 242,090,550 ordinary shares of 25 pence each, the fair value of which amounted to £1,560.3 million. These offers became unconditional on 2 April 1996. The merger has been accounted for using the merger accounting principles set out in Financial Reporting Standard 6. Accordingly the financial information for the current period has been presented, and that for the prior periods restated, as if MAI had been owned by United throughout the current and prior accounting periods.

The book value of net assets at the time of the merger together with adjustments arising from the alignment of accounting policies were:

	£m
United	
Book value of net assets at time of merger	238.0
Merger adjustment (note 24)	(73.0)
Restated net assets at time of merger	165.0
MAI	
Book value of net assets at time of merger	224.6
Merger adjustment (note 24)	(27.7)
Restated net assets at time of merger	196.9

29. Business merger continued

An analysis of contribution to the profit attributable to shareholders made by the combining groups in the period prior to the merger date on 2 April 1996, the principal components of the profit and loss accounts and statements of total recognised gains and losses is as follows:

Profit and loss account	United pre merger £m	MAI pre merger £m	Combined post merger £m	Total £m
Turnover				
Continuing operations	268.8	196.9	1,451.8	1,917.5
Acquisitions	2.7	–	18.3	21.0
Discontinued operations	6.8	14.6	30.8	52.2
	278.3	211.5	1,500.9	1,990.7
Operating profit				
Continuing operations	21.4	23.5	129.6	174.5
Acquisitions	0.7	–	(18.1)	(17.4)
Discontinued operations	0.2	4.0	6.9	11.1
	22.3	27.5	118.4	168.2
Income from interests in associated undertakings	1.9	3.9	(47.1)	(41.3)
Income from other fixed asset investments	0.6	–	1.6	2.2
Total operating profit	24.8	31.4	72.9	129.1
Merger expenses	–	–	(31.0)	(31.0)
Profit on the disposal of fixed asset investments	–	11.6	–	11.6
Profit on sales and closure of businesses	–	–	138.0	138.0
Profit on ordinary activities before interest	24.8	43.0	179.9	247.7
Net interest expense	(4.0)	(1.0)	(8.9)	(13.9)
Profit before tax	20.8	42.0	171.0	233.8
Tax	(6.8)	(14.0)	(55.1)	(75.9)
Profit after tax	14.0	28.0	115.9	157.9
Minority interest	–	(0.2)	(5.3)	(5.5)
Profit for the year	14.0	27.8	110.6	152.4
Total recognised gains and losses				
Profit for the year	14.0	27.8	110.6	152.4
Exchange gains	–	–	1.4	1.4
	14.0	27.8	112.0	153.8

The equivalent analysis for the year ended 31 December 1995 is as follows:

Profit and loss account	United £m	MAI £m	Total £m
Turnover			
Continuing operations	1,032.9	768.2	1,801.1
Discontinued operations	37.7	52.6	90.3
	1,070.6	820.8	1,891.4
Operating profit			
Continuing operations	111.2	89.1	200.3
Discontinued operations	3.9	12.8	16.7
	115.1	101.9	217.0
Income from interests in associated undertakings	0.9	12.9	13.8
Income from other fixed asset investments	3.3	–	3.3
Total operating profit	119.3	114.8	234.1
Loss on sales and closures of businesses	(2.9)	–	(2.9)
Profit on ordinary activities before interest	116.4	114.8	231.2
Net interest expense	(11.9)	(4.0)	(15.9)
Profit before tax	104.5	110.8	215.3
Tax	(34.3)	(36.0)	(70.3)
Profit after tax	70.2	74.8	145.0
Minority interest	(1.5)	1.4	(0.1)
Profit for the year	68.7	76.2	144.9
Total recognised gains and losses			
Profit for the year	68.7	76.2	144.9
Exchange losses	(0.5)	–	(0.5)
	68.2	76.2	144.4

* Note that since the publication of FRS 10, carrying intangible assets at directors' valuation and writing goodwill off to reserves are not permitted.

Chapter 29

Related party disclosures

Page

Chapter 29

Related party disclosures

Introduction

29.1 FRS 8, Related party disclosures' is the UK equivalent of the international accounting standard, IAS 24 (revised), 'Related party disclosures'. Both standards aim to ensure that financial statements contain the disclosures necessary to draw attention to the possibility that the reported financial position and results have been affected by the existence of related parties and by transactions with them. Although FRS 8 is not an exact replica of IAS 24 (revised), they have a common definition of a 'related party' and, consequently, the disclosure requirements are very similar.

29.2 As the requirements of IAS 24 (revised) are very similar to those of FRS 8, the annex to this chapter reproduces the chapter from the Manual of Accounting – IFRS for the UK that deals with related party disclosures. Differences between the disclosure requirements of FRS 8 and IAS 24 (revised) are set out from paragraph 29.5 below.

29.3 In addition to the requirements of FRS 8, company law contains disclosure requirements. The interaction of FRS 8 with these disclosure requirements is discussed from paragraph 29.37 below.

Definition of related party

29.3.1 In November 2010, FRS 8 was amended to achieve greater consistency with IAS 24 (revised), following an amendment to that standard in November 2009. Since UK company law refers to the definition of a related party in IAS 24 (revised) in setting out legal disclosure requirements, a change to the IAS 24 (revised) definition required an amendment to FRS 8 to avoid inconsistency between the law and UK accounting standards. The amendment to FRS 8 is effective for accounting periods beginning on or after 1 January 2011, with earlier application permitted.

29.4 It is important to note that although most of the November 2010 amendments are clarifications of existing requirements, they also broaden the definition of related party and will mean that some entities will have additional disclosures to make. In particular:

- Where the reporting entity is a subsidiary, any joint venture or associate of any other member of the group is a related party.
- Where the reporting entity is a joint venture, any other joint venture or associate of any of the venturers is a related party.

- Where the reporting entity is an associate of an investor, any joint venture in which that investor is a venturer is a related party. Another associate of the investor is not, however, a related party of the reporting entity.

Significant differences between FRS 8 and IAS 24 (revised)

Wholly-owned subsidiaries

29.5 Unlike IAS 24 (revised), FRS 8 does not require disclosure of transactions entered into between two or more members of a group, provided that any subsidiary undertaking that is a party to the transaction is wholly-owned by a member of that group. [FRS 8 para 3(c)]. We believe that 'any subsidiary undertaking' should be taken to mean 'as many subsidiaries as there are' or 'all the subsidiaries that are relevant'. In addition, our view is that the term 'wholly-owned by a member of that group' encompasses situations where 100% ownership is achieved indirectly. This is illustrated in the following examples.

Example 1 – 100% ownership achieved indirectly

Entity A has two wholly-owned subsidiaries, entity B and entity C. Entity B owns 60% of entity D, while entity C owns 40% of entity D.

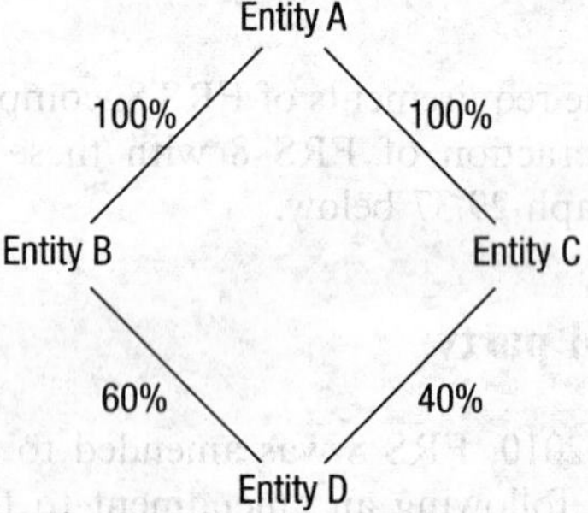

FRS 8 does not require disclosure of transactions between entities A and B, entities A and C or entities B and C, given that entities B and C are wholly-owned within entity A's group.

Indirectly, through entities B and C, entity D is also 100% owned within entity A's group. Hence, the disclosure exemption in paragraph 3(c) of FRS 8 may be applied to transactions entered into between entity D and entities A, B and C.

Example 2 – 100% ownership achieved indirectly as part of a wider group

Entity E owns 100% of entity F. Entity F owns 80% of entity G, the remaining 20% of entity G being held by entity E.

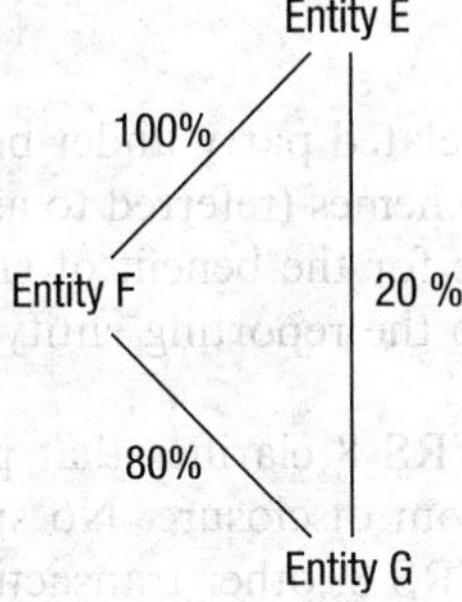

Entity E's financial statements

As explained in example 1 above, FRS 8 does not require disclosure of transactions between entity E and entity F, entity E and entity G, or entity F and entity G, given that entities F and G are wholly-owned within entity E's group.

Entity F's financial statements

In its financial statements, entity F may apply the exemption in paragraph 3(c) of FRS 8, in relation to transactions entered into with entity G. Entity G is 100% owned, indirectly, within entity E's group. We believe that the term 'group' in this situation may be taken to mean the wider E group (as opposed to only entity F's reporting group).

The exemption also applies to transactions between entity F and entity E, given that entity F is a wholly-owned member within entity E's group.

29.6 While FRS 8 does not specify that balances between two or more wholly-owned members of a group are exempt from disclosure, we believe that because transactions are exempt, by implication balances are also exempt.

29.7 As illustrated in the examples in paragraph 29.5 above, the exemption also covers parent entities, provided the subsidiaries with which they have transacted are wholly-owned.

29.8 However, certain information regarding subsidiaries needs to be provided, because the balance sheet formats under the Companies Act 2006 require the disclosure of amounts owed by and to group undertakings. The disclosure of control of the reporting entity is also required (see para 29.17).

29.9 Reporting entities taking advantage of the exemption in respect of transactions with wholly-owned subsidiaries are required to state that fact. [FRS 8 para 3]. The ASB considers disclosure of the fact that the exemption has been invoked is sufficient to alert the reader of the financial statements to the possible existence of related party transactions. Taking the exemption is, however, subject to the overriding requirement that the financial statements give a true and fair view (see from para 29.34).

Pension contributions

29.10 The definition of a related party under both FRS 8 and IAS 24 (revised) includes retirement benefit schemes (referred to as post-employment benefit plans in IAS 24 (revised)) that are for the benefit of employees of either the reporting entity or an entity related to the reporting entity. [FRS 8 para 2.5(v)].

29.11 Paragraph 3(d) of FRS 8 clarifies that pension contributions paid to a pension fund are exempt from disclosure. No such exemption exists in IAS 24 (revised). However, under FRS 8, other transactions and balances with the fund still need to be disclosed by the reporting entity, for instance refunds of contributions. In addition, any balances of pension contributions due but not paid at the year end are disclosable, as effectively they would constitute a loan from the pension fund.

Emoluments for services

29.12 Under FRS 8, no disclosure is required of emoluments in respect of services as an employee of the reporting entity. [FRS 8 para 3(e)]. This exemption covers payments 'in respect of services' and it, therefore, does not cover any *ex gratia* payment or other payment not in respect of services as an employee. For instance, payments under consultancy arrangements are not covered by the exemption. The exemption from disclosure of emoluments for services is not available under IAS 24 (revised) and emoluments for services paid to related parties are therefore disclosable by IFRS reporters.

29.13 Although it is not clear from FRS 8, it appears that the intention is to exclude from disclosure payments made or costs incurred in respect of persons employed under contracts *of* service, which are included in staff costs and disclosed in the profit and loss account or the notes. What constitutes staff costs is set out in section 411 of the Companies Act 2006 and is considered in chapter 5.

29.14 Key management personnel, including executive directors, who perform management functions, will usually have contracts *of* service; non-executive directors will usually have contracts *for* services. In each case it is a question of fact as to which type of contract an individual has. Amounts paid to directors under contracts for services should not be included in staff costs and, therefore, would seem to fall within the scope of FRS 8. Under IAS 24 (revised), an entity is required to disclose key management personnel compensation in total and for each of the following categories: short-term employee benefits, post-employment benefits, other long-term benefits, termination benefits and share-based payments. However, the FRS 8 exemption from disclosure of emoluments for services is, in effect, redundant in the case of directors. This is because extensive disclosure of directors' emoluments and their emoluments for services in connection with the management of the affairs of the company is already required, primarily, by Part I of Schedule 5 to SI 2008/410. These disclosures are likely to satisfy the disclosures that would be required by FRS 8 in respect of any directors' remuneration that is not covered by this exclusion. See further the Manual of Accounting – Narrative Reporting. The FRS 8 exemption would, however, be relevant and available in respect of the emoluments of those key managers that are not directors; under IAS 24 (revised), these emoluments would be included in the amounts reported as key management personnel compensation.

Duty of confidentiality

29.15 Related party disclosures are not required by FRS 8 if disclosure would conflict with the reporting entity's duties of confidentiality arising by operation of law (but not from contractual provisions relating to confidentiality). Thus, banks that, by law, have to observe a strict duty of confidentiality about their customers' affairs will not have to disclose details concerning related parties that would be in conflict with that duty. [FRS 8 para 16]. There is no such exemption in IAS 24 (revised).

Minor differences between FRS 8 and IAS 24 (revised)

29.16 There are differences between FRS 8, 'Related party disclosures', and IAS 24 (revised), Related party disclosures', that have little practical effect for UK GAAP reporters. These are described in paragraphs 29.17 to 29.33 below.

Ultimate parent, parent and subsidiaries

29.17 IAS 24 (revised) requires that relationships between a parent and its subsidiaries are disclosed irrespective of whether there have been transactions between them. An entity discloses the name of its parent and, if different, the ultimate controlling party. FRS 8 requires disclosure of the controlling party and ultimate controlling party but does not otherwise require disclosure of relationships between group companies. [FRS 8 para 5]. Under IAS 24 (revised), if neither the entity's parent nor the ultimate controlling party produces consolidated financial statements available for public use, the name of the next most senior parent that does so is disclosed. Although not all of the IAS 24 (revised) requirements as regards parents and subsidiaries are contained within FRS 8, the disclosure requirements of UK company law cover most of the same ground. These requirements are described in chapter 6.

Materiality

29.18 FRS 8 requires disclosure of *all* transactions with related parties provided they are *material* and gives specific guidance on how materiality should be interpreted in the context of related party transactions. IAS 24 (revised) is different in that it does not contain any reference to materiality, but IFRS disclosure requirements only apply to material items (see para 29.20 below).

Because potentially all related party transactions are disclosable, interpreting what is material in this context is particularly important. For the reasons described below, we believe that the assessment of materiality under FRS 8 is equivalent to that under IAS 24 (revised); that is, the difference in the level of guidance provided in the standards has no practical effect.

29.19 FRS 8 defines 'material' in the following way:

> *"Transactions are material when their disclosure might reasonably be expected to influence decisions made by the users of general purpose financial statements."* [FRS 8 para 20].

Whilst this does not explicitly say 'only disclose transactions that are abnormal', it does appear to exempt from disclosure those transactions that would be of no interest to users of financial statements.

29.20 Under IFRS, disclosure of related party transactions is required only if the transactions are material. IAS 1, 'Presentation of financial statements', assists with a definition of material: *"Omissions or misstatements of items are material if they could, individually or collectively, influence the economic decisions that users make on the basis of the financial statements. Materiality depends on the size and nature of the omission or misstatement judged in the surrounding circumstances. The size or nature of the item, or a combination of both, could be the determining factor".* [IAS 1 para 7].

29.21 In respect of disclosures, IAS 1 states: *"An entity need not provide a specific disclosure required by an IFRS if the information is not material".* [IAS 1 para 31].

29.22 FRS 8, however, goes on to provide that:

> *"The materiality of related party transactions is to be judged, not only in terms of their significance to the reporting entity, but also in relation to their significance to the other related party when that party is:*
>
> *(a) a director, key manager or other individual in a position to influence, or accountable for stewardship of, the reporting entity; or*
>
> *(b) a member of the close family of any individual mentioned in (a) above; or*
>
> *(c) an entity controlled by any individual mentioned in (a) or (b) above."*

[FRS 8 para 20].

29.23 FRS 8 explains that these words address the perspective that needs to be considered when a related party transaction has been undertaken directly or indirectly with an individual who is in a position to influence, or is accountable for stewardship of, the reporting entity. [FRS 8 App IV para 19]. Consequently, not only the significance to the entity, but the transaction's significance to the director would need to be considered in order to form a judgement as to whether the transaction was material. The transaction could be small to the entity, but a major investment for the director.

29.24 IAS 24 (revised) does not deal specifically with the situation where a transaction is immaterial in amount to the entity, but material to the person. The question is whether, under IFRS, the materiality of related party transactions should be judged from the person's perspective and/or from the entity's perspective. We believe that, despite the lack of specific guidance on the materiality of related party transactions, the intention of IAS 24 (revised) is that transactions that are material to the director are disclosable. (See from para 29A.89 of the annex to this chapter.) Therefore, although FRS 8 gives more guidance than IAS 24 (revised) on the materiality of related party transactions, we believe that the materiality considerations are similar under both standards.

Disclosure of transactions and balances

29.25 IAS 24 (revised) requires disclosure as follows:

"If an entity has had related party transactions during the periods covered by the financial statements, it shall disclose the nature of the related party relationship as well as information about those transactions and outstanding balances, including commitments, necessary for users to understand the potential effect of the relationship on the financial statements. These disclosure requirements are in addition to those in paragraph 17. At a minimum, disclosures shall include:

(a) the amount of the transactions;

(b) the amount of outstanding balances, including commitments, and:
  - *(i) their terms and conditions, including whether they are secured, and the nature of the consideration to be provided in settlement; and*
  - *(ii) details of any guarantees given or received;*

(c) provisions for doubtful debts related to the amount of outstanding balances; and

(d) the expense recognised during the period in respect of bad or doubtful debts due from related parties."

[IAS 24 (revised) para 18].

29.26 FRS 8 requires disclosure as follows:

"Financial statements should disclose material transactions undertaken by the reporting entity with a related party. Disclosure should be made irrespective of whether a price is charged. The disclosure should include:

(a) the names of the transacting related parties;

(b) a description of the relationship between the parties;

(c) a description of the transactions;

(d) the amounts involved;

(e) any other elements of the transactions necessary for an understanding of the financial statements;

(f) the amounts due to or from related parties at the balance sheet date and the provisions for doubtful debts due from such parties at that date; and

(g) amounts written off in the period in respect of debts due to or from related parties.

Transactions with related parties may be disclosed on an aggregated basis (aggregation of similar transactions by type of related party) unless disclosure of an individual transaction, or connected transactions, is necessary for an understanding of the impact of the transactions on the financial statements of the reporting entity or is required by law."

[FRS 8 para 6].

29.27 Although these disclosure requirements are expressed slightly differently, they will normally result in similar disclosures being made under FRS 8 and IAS 24 (revised). For example:

- FRS 8 requires disclosure of the name of the related party whereas IAS 24 (revised) does not. However, both standards require disclosure of the nature of the related party relationship and this will often mean that the related party is named. In addition, FRS 8 permits aggregation of disclosures by type of related party so that related parties are not always named individually.
- IAS 24 (revised) requires disclosure of *"outstanding balances, including commitments"*. Although FRS 8 makes no reference to the disclosure of commitments, it requires disclosure of *"any elements of the transactions necessary for an understanding of the financial statements"* and, in our view, this requirement would necessitate the disclosure of commitments.
- IAS 24 (revised) requires disclosure of the terms and conditions, including any secured balances or guarantees given. Again, although these disclosures are not specifically required in FRS 8, the requirement to disclose *"any elements of the transactions necessary for an understanding of the financial statements"* will mean that such information is disclosed by UK GAAP reporters.

Types of related party transactions

29.28 Both FRS 8 and IAS 24 (revised) provide examples of the types of related party transaction that require disclosure. [FRS 8 para 19, IAS 24 (revised) para 21]. These lists of examples are largely the same but there are some differences. FRS 8 does not include the following IAS 24 (revised) examples:

- Commitments to do something if a particular event occurs or does not occur in the future, including executory contracts (recognised and unrecognised).
- Settlement of liabilities on behalf of the entity or by the entity on behalf of that related party.

29.29 FRS 8 defines a related party transaction as *"the transfer of assets or liabilities or the performance of services by, to or for a related party irrespective of whether a price is charged"*. [FRS 8 para 2.6]. In our view, the types of transaction above would also require disclosure under FRS 8.

29.30 A commitment to do something in the future will usually transfer a liability (contingent or otherwise) to the reporting entity in which case it falls within the definition of a related party transaction. It may be an element of a larger transaction and be disclosable as part of the disclosures on that transaction because disclosure is necessary for an understanding of the financial statements. A commitment given in respect of another group company when all the subsidiaries within the group are wholly-owned would, in any event, be exempt from disclosure (see para 29.5 above). The settlement of liabilities, being in substance a transfer of liabilities, clearly falls within the definition of a related party transaction.

29.31 FRS 8 includes agency arrangements and management contracts as examples of types of transactions that should be disclosed. Although not specifically mentioned as examples in IAS 24 (revised), we believe they should also be disclosed under IFRS (see para 29A.86 of the annex to this chapter).

Government-related entities

29.32 IAS 24 (revised) provides a partial exemption from its disclosure requirements for government-related entities. FRS 8 contains no such exemption.

29.33 A *'government-related entity'* is an entity that is controlled, jointly controlled or significantly influenced by a government. The partial exemption reduces the disclosures that would otherwise be required in respect of related party transactions with that government or another entity that is a related party because the same government has control, joint control or significant influence over both the reporting entity and the other entity. This partial exemption was included in IAS 24 (revised) in response to concerns expressed by preparers in countries where government control is pervasive.

Overriding requirement to give a true and fair view

29.34 Section 393 of the Companies Act 2006 obliges the directors of a company to prepare individual (and, if prepared, consolidated financial statements) that give a true and fair view. The view expressed by the ASB in its Foreword to accounting standards is that the requirement to give a true and fair view may in special circumstances require a departure from accounting standards. However, it envisages that only in exceptional circumstances will such a departure be necessary in order for the financial statements to give a true and fair view. [ASB Foreword para 18]. Similar provisions are contained in IAS 1, 'Presentation of financial statements', which provides that in the extremely rare circumstances in which management concludes that compliance with a requirement in an IFRS would be so misleading that it would conflict with the objective of financial statements set out in the 'Framework for the preparation and presentation of financial statements', the entity should depart from that requirement. [IAS 1 para 19].

29.35 As discussed above, FRS 8 gives exemptions from disclosure that are not available under IAS 24 (revised). There may be circumstances, however, where, in order to give a true and fair view, it is necessary to give certain disclosures that would be exempt from disclosure under FRS 8. Such additional disclosure would not be a departure from the standard, because even though the standard may not specifically require the particular disclosure, it does not prohibit such disclosure being made.

29.36 Such a situation might arise where, in a group of companies suffering from financial difficulties, cheques are passed from one group company to another through a series of different banks (that is, by cheque kiting), in order to give the bankers the impression of high liquidity and of trading activities that do not actually exist. Because the subsidiaries are wholly-owned, the exemption in respect of intra-group transactions would apply to the financial statements of each member of the group. However, in order to give a true and fair view, it may, in our view, be necessary for the extent and nature of the artificial payments and receipts to be disclosed in the subsidiaries' financial statements.

Interaction with disclosures required by the Companies Act 2006

29.37 The disclosures that the Companies Act 2006 requires to be made concerning related party transactions are considered briefly in the paragraphs that follow. More detail is provided in the table appearing at the end of the annex to this chapter. The table also describes the disclosures that are required about group companies and investees regardless of whether there have been any transactions with these parties.

29.38 The Companies Act 2006 requires various disclosures to be made in relation to directors' remuneration. For the purposes of these disclosures, any amounts paid to or receivable by a person connected with the director are treated as being paid to or receivable by the director. [CA06 Sec 412]. A person connected with a director falls broadly into the following categories:

- Members of a director's family.
- A body corporate in which a director is interested, entitled to exercise or control the exercise of at least 20 per cent of the shares excluding any shares held as treasury shares.

- A trustee of a trust of which the director or any persons connected with him are beneficiaries.
- A partner of the director or of a person who is connected with him under the three scenarios above.
- A firm that is a legal person under the law by which it is governed and in which the director or a connected person is a partner.

See further the Manual of Accounting – Narrative Reporting.

29.39 The Companies Act 2006 allows certain transactions, such as loans, to be undertaken with directors subject to members' approval. [CA06 Sec 188 to 226]. In addition to triggering disclosures under the requirements of the Act, any such transactions may fall to be disclosed under IAS 24 (revised) as detailed above.

29.40 Where a company does not prepare consolidated financial statements, it is required to disclose details of advances and credits granted by the company to its directors and guarantees entered into by the company on behalf of its directors. Where a parent company prepares consolidated financial statements, it is required to disclose details of advances and credits granted to the parent company's directors, by that company or by any of its subsidiary undertakings and guarantees entered into on behalf of the parent company's directors, by that company or by any of its subsidiary undertakings. [CA06 Sec 413(1)(2)].

29.41 The details required to be disclosed in respect of an advance or credit are its amount, an indication of the interest rate, its main conditions and any amounts repaid. The details required in respect of a guarantee are its main terms, the amount of the maximum liability that may be incurred by the company (or its subsidiary) and any amount paid and any liability incurred by the company (or its subsidiary) for the purpose of fulfilling the guarantee (including any loss incurred by reason of enforcement of the guarantee). [CA06 Sec 413(3)(4)].

29.42 In respect of advances and credits to directors, the Companies Act 2006 also requires disclosure of the totals of amounts of advances and credits and the amounts repaid. In respect of guarantees entered into with directors, the Companies Act 2006 also requires disclosure of amounts of the maximum liability that may be incurred and of amounts paid and any liability incurred for the purpose of fulfilling the guarantee. [CA06 Sec 413(5)].

Annex

Related party disclosures

Introduction

A29.1 This chapter deals with IAS 24 (revised), 'Related party disclosures', issued by the IASB in November 2009. IAS 24 (revised) supersedes IAS 24, issued in 2003, and applies for annual periods beginning on or after 1 January 2011. Earlier application is permitted, in full or for part of the standard, as explained in paragraph A29.217.

A29.2 In summary, IAS 24 (revised) introduces two main changes to related party disclosures. It clarifies and simplifies the definition of a related party, but also enhances the definition such that some entities will be required to make additional disclosures to those given under the previous standard. The revised standard also removes the requirement for government-related entities to disclose details of all transactions with the government and other government-related entities and instead requires more limited disclosures of these transactions.

A29.3 Related party transactions can take a variety of forms. Many of them include transactions in the normal course of business, for example, purchases or sales of goods at market values. However, others can include significant one-off transactions that may be at a fair value on an arm's length basis or that may be at book value or some other amount that differs from market prices. The stated objective of IAS 24 (revised) is to ensure that financial statements contain the disclosures necessary to draw attention to the possibility that the reported financial position and results may have been affected by the existence of related parties and by transactions and outstanding balances, including commitments, with them. [IAS 24 (revised) para 1].

A29.4 The IASB has given an indication of its reasoning for requiring disclosure of related party transactions by explaining the effect on a reporting entity of the existence of related party relationships. This may be summarised as follows:

- The existence of related party relationships is a normal feature in business, because entities frequently carry out their activities through subsidiaries, joint ventures and associates. In such circumstances, the entity's ability to control, jointly control or influence the financial and operating policies of the related party means that it is able to affect the terms of transactions with the related party and how they are carried out.

- Related party transactions may affect the results and the financial position of an entity and its related parties in ways that transactions with unrelated parties might not. Also, related parties may enter into transactions that unrelated parties would not agree to enter. For example, a subsidiary might sell goods at cost to its parent or a fellow subsidiary, whereas it would not sell on such terms to a third party. Similarly, a parent might lend money to a subsidiary on an interest-free basis when it would not make loans to third parties on such terms.

- Even if there are no transactions between related parties, the results and financial position can still be affected. For example, a subsidiary might be required by its parent to stop doing business with a third party when its parent has acquired a new subsidiary that is a competitor of the third party. Similarly, a subsidiary might refrain from carrying out research and development if its parent told it not to do so.

- As a result, knowledge of related party transactions, outstanding balances including commitments, and relationships with related parties can affect how users of financial statements assess an entity's performance and financial position and the risks and opportunities facing the entity.

[IAS 24 (revised) paras 5-8].

A29.5 The above examples are relatively straightforward examples given in the standard. However, there are many more extreme examples where related party transactions (often concealed from shareholders) have significantly distorted results and financial position and led to the entity's collapse and subsequent investigation by regulatory bodies. Examples are:

- Borrowing by the entity from the entity's pension funds.
- Artificial sales and other transactions with 'special purpose entities' (SPEs) that are related to the entity.
- Loans to key management personnel.

The purpose of IAS 24 (revised) is to ensure that entities have a duty to make disclosure of all related party transactions and, thus, that stakeholders are aware that such transactions may have affected the financial performance and position.

> **UK.A29.5.1** The disclosures required by IAS 24 (revised) complement the UK statutory, Listing Rules and AIM Rules disclosure requirements for related parties, which still apply to UK companies reporting under EU-adopted IFRS. These rules are considered from paragraph UK.A29.217.1. IAS 24 (revised)'s perspective is somewhat broader in that it concentrates on the relevance of the information to the users of financial statements. It extends the amount of disclosure that has to be given in some instances and also requires disclosure of additional transactions and relationships. The Listing Rules and the AIM Rules use the term 'related party', but the definition of related parties in IAS 24 (revised) is different from those in either the Listing Rules or the AIM Rules. There are, however, related parties, such as directors and their families, which are common to all three definitions.

A29.6 Most related party transactions are carried out in the normal course of an entity's business, but companies do also sometimes act improperly or illegally through the medium of related parties and it is particularly in those circumstances that disclosure is important. Of course it would be naïve to think that an entity that indulged in improper or illegal activities would willingly disclose the fact. The disclosure requirements of IAS 24 (revised) cannot prevent illegal actions or fraud. However, the existence of rules in the standard gives authority to both employees involved in preparing the financial statements, and to auditors, to resist any suppression of disclosure. In addition, regulators and other authorities are able to use the standard's provisions when investigating and punishing any illegality revealed.

Scope

A29.7 IAS 24 (revised) is a disclosure standard. It sets out how related party relationships, transactions and balances, including commitments, should be identified and what disclosures should be made, and when. [IAS 24 (revised) para 2].

A29.8 The standard requires disclosure of related party transactions and balances, including commitments, in the separate financial statements of parent companies and subsidiaries. This means that intra-group transactions between such entities are disclosed, although generally such disclosures are likely to be aggregated by type due to their large number. For instance, a subsidiary would usually disclose aggregate sales to, and aggregate purchases from, its parent (see further from para A29.170). On consolidation, however, such transactions would be eliminated and would, therefore, not be disclosed in the consolidated financial statements. [IAS 24 (revised) paras 3, 4].

A29.9 The standard also requires disclosure of related party transactions and balances, including commitments, between a venturer or investor in a joint venture or an associate ('the investor') and its joint venture or associate ('the investee') to be disclosed in the separate financial statements of both the investor and the investee. [IAS 24 (revised) para 3]. As such, transactions and balances that are not eliminated on consolidation would also be disclosed in any consolidated financial statements produced by the investor.

A29.10 There are no exemptions from disclosure of intra-group transactions for subsidiaries, or for parent companies that produce consolidated financial statements with their separate financial statements. Nor is there any 'confidentiality' exemption, even in the situation where an entity has a duty of confidentiality imposed by law (see para A29.206). In relation to intra-group transactions between parents and subsidiaries, the IASB has stated that disclosure of related party transactions and balances is essential information for external parties who need to be aware of the level of support provided by related parties. [IAS 24 (revised) para BC14-17]. Many subsidiaries, for example, depend on financial support from their parents and those who advance credit to such subsidiaries need to be aware of the level of support available from the parent or of the lack of such support.

Related parties

The reporting entity

A29.11 IAS 24 (revised) requires transactions between a reporting entity and its related parties to be disclosed in the reporting entity's financial statements. The reporting entity will be the entity, where it is preparing its separate financial statements. However, if the entity is a parent entity and is preparing consolidated financial statements, the reporting entity will be the group headed by the parent entity. Under IAS 27, 'Consolidated and separate financial statements' (and IFRS 10, 'Consolidated financial statements', see chapter 24), a parent entity must prepare consolidated financial statements comprising itself and its subsidiaries. The criteria for establishing related party relationships between an entity and its related parties and the group and its related parties should, therefore, be applied at the separate entity level and, in the case of consolidated financial statements, at the group level.

Related party definition

A29.12 As mentioned in paragraph A29.2, IAS 24 (revised) removes inconsistencies in the definition of a related party that arose in applying the previous version of IAS 24. The inconsistencies meant, for example, that there were situations in which only one party to a transaction was required to make related party disclosures. The revised definition should, therefore, be simpler to apply and provide symmetry in disclosure.

A29.13 Some entities will, however, be required to make additional disclosures to those given under the previous standard. For example, a subsidiary applying IAS 24 (revised) is required to disclose transactions with an associate of its parent. An entity that is controlled by a person who is part of the key management personnel of another entity is required to disclose transactions with that second entity under IAS 24 (revised). The entities that are most likely to be affected are those that are part of a group that includes both subsidiaries and associates and entities with shareholders that are involved with other entities. The definition is discussed in further detail in the following sections.

A29.14 A related party can be a person, an entity, or an unincorporated business. The standard's definition is in two parts. The first part of the definition identifies general criteria that result in a *person,* or a close member of that person's family (see further from para A29.38), being a related party of the reporting entity. These general criteria are discussed from paragraph A29.15. The second part of the definition specifically identifies conditions that result in an *entity* being related to the reporting entity. These conditions are discussed from paragraph A29.42.

Relationships with persons — general criteria

A29.15 The general criteria state that a person, or a close member of that person's family (see further from para A29.38), is a related party of the reporting entity if that person:

- has control or joint control over the reporting entity;
- has significant influence over the reporting entity; or
- is a member of the key management personnel of the reporting entity or of a parent of the reporting entity.

[IAS 24 (revised) para 9(a)].

A29.16 The general criteria for persons involve the application of the terms 'control', 'joint control' and 'significant influence'. Such terms are familiar, because they are used elsewhere in IFRS in relation to consolidated financial statements (IAS 27, IFRS 10), joint ventures (IAS 31, IFRS 11) and associates (IAS 28). Each is discussed below in the context of how they should be applied for the purposes of IAS 24 (revised).

A29.17 Although this section primarily covers how to determine whether a person is related to an entity, the general criteria (control, joint control and significant influence) are also relevant in the context of entities. For example, the concept of 'control' is specifically referred to in the criteria to determine whether a person is related to an entity. In addition, 'control' is relevant in determining whether one entity is related to another in the context of parents and subsidiaries (see from para A29.43 below) and is specifically referred to in the criteria for determining whether an entity is a government-related entity (see from para A29.207 below). Furthermore, disclosures are required in relation to an entity's ultimate controlling party (see from para A29.102 below). Hence, the following paragraphs refer to control, as well as joint control and significant influence, in the context of both entities and persons.

Control

A29.18 IAS 24 (revised)'s definition of 'control' is identical to the definition of control found in paragraph 4 of IAS 27, 'Consolidated and separate financial statements'. The accounting concept of control is explained in IAS 27 in connection with identifying parents and subsidiaries in the context of consolidation. However, IAS 24 (revised) has broader application in that the ability to control can be held by a person as well as an 'entity'. 'Control' is defined as: *"the power to govern the financial and operating policies of an entity so as to obtain benefits from its activities"*. [IAS 24 (revised) para 9].

A29.19 The definition appears to have the effect that control exists, for the purpose of IAS 24 (revised), where, for example, another entity or a person holds more than half an entity's voting rights, whether or not that voting power is actually used to direct the entity's policies. There must also be some potential benefit for the controlling party as a result of this direction. For instance, venture capitalists with over 50 per cent of the shares with voting rights in an entity will generally have 'control' of that entity. Another example where control would exist would be where an entity or person has less than 50 per cent of voting rights, but has the power to control the financial and operating policies of an entity by, for example, agreement with the other shareholders. Based on paragraph 14 of IAS 27, the existence and effect of potential voting rights that are currently exercisable or convertible, including potential voting rights held by another entity or person, are considered when assessing whether an entity or person has the power to govern the financial and operating policies of another entity.

A29.19.1 IFRS 10, 'Consolidated financial statements', supersedes IAS 27 in respect of consolidated financial statements and applies to annual periods beginning on or after 1 January 2013 (early adoption permitted). IFRS 10 changes the definition of control; under IFRS 10, *"an investor controls an investee when the investor is exposed, or has rights, to variable returns from its involvement with the investee and has the ability to affect those returns through its power over the investee"*. [IFRS 10 App A]. 'Power' in this context is the current ability to direct the activities that significantly influence returns. IFRS 10 deletes the definitions of 'control', 'joint control' and 'significant influence' in IAS 24 and inserts cross references to those definitions in IFRS 10, IFRS 11, 'Joint arrangements', and IAS 28, 'Investments in associates and joint ventures'. Those entities that apply IFRS 10 will, therefore, apply the definitions in those standards in applying IAS 24 (revised). However, in most cases, the entities identified as controlled under IAS 27 will be the same as under IFRS 10. See chapter 24 for more details.

A29.20 The definition of control in IAS 24 (revised) encompasses control by persons and, for example, partnerships, as well as parent entities. An example of control by a partnership would be where a partnership controls over 50 per cent of the voting rights in a reporting entity. This is discussed further in paragraph A29.128. The question of control in relation to a trust is discussed from paragraph A29.120.

A29.21 Another issue that arises in practice is whether several shareholders acting together to control an entity should be viewed as one controlling party or whether they should be considered separately, despite the fact that they act together. This is discussed from paragraph A29.110.

A29.22 Where control exists, even though no transactions have taken place, IAS 24 (revised) requires disclosure of the parent entity and, if different, the ultimate controlling party. The disclosure requirements in relation to the ultimate controlling party are discussed below from paragraph A29.102.

UK.A29.22.1 Disclosure of the ultimate controlling party is in addition to the requirements of Schedule 4 to SI 2008/410, the 'Large and Medium-sized Companies and Groups (Accounts and Reports) Regulations 2008'. SI 2008/410 requires disclosure of the ultimate parent company (in addition to disclosure in respect of the parent undertaking of the largest group of undertakings for which group accounts are drawn up and the smallest such group of undertakings).

A29.23 Bearer shares cannot be issued to avoid disclosure of the controlling party. In addition to creating an auditing problem, it is difficult to see how this would be effective where the directors in practice know for whom they are working and to whom dividends are paid.

Joint control

A29.24 Joint control is defined in IAS 24 (revised) as *"the contractually agreed sharing of control over an economic activity"*. [IAS 24 (revised) para 9]. The definition in IAS 31, 'Interests in joint ventures', goes further to say that joint control exists only when the strategic financial and operating decisions relating to the activity require the unanimous consent of the parties sharing control (the venturers). (In IFRS 11, 'Joint arrangements', which supersedes IAS 31 for annual periods beginning on or after 1 January 2013, the definition of joint control is very similar: *"The contractually agreed sharing of control of an arrangement, which exists only when decisions about the relevant activities require the unanimous consent of the parties sharing control"*. [IFRS 11 App A].) The detail on the interpretation of joint control in IAS 31 is useful for the purpose of the IAS 24 (revised) definition and explains that:

- The existence of a contractual arrangement distinguishes interests that involve joint control from investments in associates in which the investor has significant influence. Activities that have no contractual arrangement to establish joint control are not joint ventures.
- The contractual arrangement may be evidenced in a number of ways, for example, by a contract between the venturers or minutes of discussions between the venturers. In some cases, the arrangement is incorporated in the articles or other by-laws of the joint venture. Whatever its form, the contractual arrangement is usually in writing and deals with such matters as:
  - The activity, duration and reporting obligations of the joint venture.
  - The appointment of the joint venture's board of directors or equivalent governing body and the voting rights of the venturers.
  - Any capital contributions by the venturers.
  - The sharing by the venturers of the output, income, expenses or results of the joint venture.

[IAS 31 paras 9, 10].

A29.25 This definition means that where the entity is a joint venture between two or more persons that share joint control over the entity, each of the persons, or close members of those persons' families, are related parties of the entity. The same principle may be applied where the venturers are entities; such entities are specifically identified as related parties of the joint venture – see paragraph A29.46 below.

Significant influence

A29.26 A person or close member of that person's family is related to the reporting entity if they have an interest in the reporting entity that gives them significant influence. Significant influence is defined in IAS 24 (revised) as *"the power to participate in the financial and operating policy decisions of an entity, but is not control over those policies. Significant influence may be gained by share ownership, statute or agreement"*. [IAS 24 (revised) para 9].

A29.27 This has the same meaning as the definition in IAS 28, 'Investments in associates'. IAS 28 gives more detail than IAS 24 (revised) on how the term should be interpreted. It states that the existence of significant influence is usually evidenced by one or more of the following:

- Representation on the board of directors or equivalent governing body of the investee.
- Participation in policy-making process, including participation in decisions about dividends or other distributions.
- Material transactions between the investor and the investee.
- Inter-change of managerial personnel.
- Provision of essential technical information.

[IAS 28 para 7].

A29.28 Significant influence may also arise as a result of contractual arrangements or management contracts between two parties. See further from paragraph A29.71.

A29.29 Where an entity has significant influence over another party, that other party is its associate. An associate is a specifically identified related party of the entity – see paragraph A29.46 below.

Key management personnel

A29.30 A member of the key management personnel of an entity or of a parent of the reporting entity, as well as a close member of that person's family, is a related party of the entity. The term 'key management personnel' is defined in IAS 24 (revised) as *"those persons having authority and responsibility for planning, directing and controlling the activities of the entity, directly or indirectly, including any director (whether executive or otherwise) of that entity"*. [IAS 24 (revised) para 9].

A29.31 The definition clearly includes directors and the term 'or otherwise' is intended to cover non-executive directors and supervisory boards as well as those who have responsibility for the management and direction of a significant part of the business without holding the title 'director'.

A29.32 Non-executive directors are related parties, even if their decisions are subject to approval at a higher level. This is illustrated in the example below.

Example – Non-executive directors' decisions are subject to governmental approval

The non-executive directors of entity A are appointed by a government minister. They are involved in planning and financing decisions, such as approval of budgets and contract negotiations, together with the executive directors. Final approvals are, however, required from the minister before their decisions can be executed.

Entity A's management should consider the non-executive directors whose decisions are subject to the approval by the minister as related parties of entity A under paragraph 9(a)(iii) of IAS 24 (revised). Even if their decisions are subject to the approval by the minister, non-executive directors have the authority and responsibility for planning, directing and controlling entity A's activities.

The minister would also be a related party as he/she is clearly involved in the approval of key planning and financing decisions.

UK.A29.32.1 In the UK, directors can be of three kinds: *de jure* directors (that is, directors who have been validly appointed as such – either as executive or non-executive); *de facto* directors (that is, directors who assume to act as directors without having been appointed validly or at all); and shadow directors. Under the Companies Act 2006 a shadow director is defined as a person in accordance with whose directions or instructions the directors of a company are accustomed to act. [CA06 Sec 251].

A29.33 'Key management personnel' includes directors of the entity. The term does not include directors of the entity's parent(s), subsidiaries or fellow subsidiaries, unless those directors have a role in directing the entity's affairs, for example, where the entity is a unit trust and its fellow subsidiary and its directors act as manager for the trust. See further from paragraph A29.35 below.

UK.A29.33.1 It should be noted that under the Listing Rules, a transaction between a company and a director of a subsidiary undertaking would be a transaction with a related party (see para UK.A29.217.13).

A29.34 Apart from directors, the term 'key management personnel' would include people who are not appointed directors, but whose activities encompass duties normally carried out by directors. Where management commentary refers to managers by name, entities should consider whether this indicates that they are key managers.

A29.35 As a reporting entity can be a group as well as a separate entity, key management personnel must also be considered in relation to directing or controlling the group's resources. Whilst the term 'key management personnel' in the group context could include a divisional director or the director of a subsidiary, such a person would need to direct or control a major part of the group's activities and resources in order to be key management personnel of the group. The following examples illustrate situations where the persons included in the IAS 24 (revised) key management personnel disclosures may include persons who are not directors of the entity.

Example 1 – Divisional managers

An entity has two equal-sized operating divisions. Each of the operating divisions is headed up by a 'divisional manager'. Neither divisional manager is a director of the entity: rather each is responsible for an operating division and reports to the board of directors on its performance.

Although the divisional managers are not directors of the entity, they would fall within the definition of 'key management personnel' in IAS 24 (revised), because they have authority and responsibility for planning, directing and controlling approximately half of the entity's activities.

Example 2 – Members of a management committee

A financial services entity has a board of directors that makes high level decisions about the markets in which the entity operates. It delegates decisions about the products that should be offered within those markets and the customers to whom those products should be marketed, to a management committee.

Because the management committee has authority for planning, directing and controlling the entity's activities, its members, together with the board of directors, are key management personnel.

Example 3 – Directors of subsidiaries as key management personnel of a group

A parent entity has three subsidiaries. The parent's main activity is to coordinate its subsidiaries' operations.

How should management disclose the remuneration of subsidiaries' directors in the consolidated financial statements?

A director of a subsidiary is not automatically a related party of the group. The director is a related party of the group if he is determined to be a member of the group's key management personnel.

Under IAS 24 (revised), the remuneration of any subsidiaries' directors who are identified as key management personnel of the group should be disclosed with the remuneration of the parent's directors in the consolidated financial statements.

Separate disclosure of the remuneration of the individual directors is not required under IAS 24 (revised) (although this may be required by local legislative requirements). Under IAS 24 (revised), this information may be aggregated.

UK.A29.35.1 In the UK, the Companies Act 2006 disclosure requirements include the emoluments of directors (including shadow and *de facto* directors) of the company and exclude the emoluments of any other key management personnel. In the examples above, the additional members of key management personnel are not shadow directors, because they do not influence the decisions of the directors.

A29.36 The term 'key management personnel' will also include people who have responsibilities for the administration or direction of reporting entities, such as trusts, which are not incorporated.

A29.37 A further example of key management personnel and related entities is provided in paragraph A29.56 below. The specific disclosure requirements for key management personnel compensation are dealt with from paragraph A29.129. Disclosure of other transactions with key management personnel is dealt with from paragraph A29.195.

Close family members

A29.38 A close family member of key management personnel of the entity or of a parent of the entity or of any person that controls, or has joint control or significant influence over the entity is a related party of the entity. [IAS 24 (revised) para 9(a)]. Close family members of a person are defined as those family members who may be expected to influence, or be influenced by, that person in their dealings with the entity. The standard notes that they include:

- The person's children and spouse or domestic partner.
- Children of the person's spouse or domestic partner.
- Dependants of the person or the person's spouse or domestic partner.

[IAS 24 (revised) para 9].

A29.39 The term 'domestic partner' would encompass any person, whether of a different sex or the same sex, who lives with the member of key management personnel as a partner in an enduring family relationship. In relation to children, it is worth noting that step-children are included in the definition and that the examples do not restrict the definition to infant children (or step-children). Dependants would include, for example foster children, and, where they are dependent on the person or the person's partner, could also include elderly and infirm parents, brothers, sisters, mothers-in-law or fathers-in-law, ex-partners receiving alimony and even more distant relatives such as cousins.

A29.40 The examples in the standard should not be taken to be complete, because the wider definition of a close family member makes it clear that anyone who is a member of the family (whether blood-related or not) is potentially a close family member for the purposes of the standard. They will be close family members if they may be expected to influence or be influenced by the person in their dealings with the entity.

UK.A29.40.1 The definition can be compared with similar provisions of the UK Listing Rules and the Companies Act 2006. Under the Listing Rules, 'family' in relation to a related party is defined as being their 'spouse, civil partner or child'. [LR 11.1.4R]. Section 253 of the Companies Act 2006 defines persons 'connected to the director'. Alongside the spouses and domestic partners and their minor children and step-children, , this definition also includes the director's parents, whether dependant or not, but does not include other dependants.. 'Close family' under IAS 24 (revised), is not limited to minor children and includes a wider range of dependants.

A29.41 An example showing where close family members are related to entities as a result of control and significant influence is provided in paragraph A29.56.

Relationships with other entities — specific criteria

A29.42 IAS 24 (revised) specifically identifies certain parties that are always treated as related parties under the standard. The following entities are related to each other:

- Members of the same group (which means that parents, subsidiaries and fellow subsidiaries are all related to each other) (see from para A29.43).
- An investor and its associate (as defined in IAS 28, 'Investments in associates') (or an entity and an associate of another member of a group of which the entity is a member) (see from para A29.46).
- A venturer and its joint venture (as defined in IAS 31, 'Interests in joint ventures') (or an entity and a joint venture of another member of a group of which the entity is a member) (see from para A29.46).
- Two joint ventures of the same third party (see from para A29.51).
- A joint venture of a third entity and an associate of that third entity (see from para A29.51).
- Where a person (or close member of that person's family):
  - controls or jointly controls an entity;
  - has significant influence over the entity; or
  - is a member of that entity's (or the entity's parent's) key management personnel,

  that entity is a related party of another entity controlled or jointly controlled by the same person (or close member of that person's family) (see from para A29.55).

- An entity and a post-employment benefit plan (such as a pension scheme) for the benefit of that entity's employees or employees of any other entity related to the entity. If the reporting entity is itself such a plan, the sponsoring employers are also related parties of that entity (see from para A29.64).

[IAS 24 (revised) para 9(b)].

Each of these related parties is discussed in the paragraphs below.

Parents, subsidiaries and fellow subsidiaries

A29.43 Members of the same group are related parties. This means that ultimate and intermediate parents, subsidiaries and fellow subsidiaries of the reporting entity are related parties. [IAS 24 (revised) para 9(b)(i)].

A29.44 There is no definition of parent and subsidiary in IAS 24 (revised), but they are defined in the Glossary of Terms in the IASB's handbook and it is reasonable to assume that the terms have the same meaning as in paragraph 4 of IAS 27, 'Consolidated and separate financial statements'. This defines a subsidiary (and by inference a parent) as *"an entity, including an unincorporated entity such as a partnership, that is controlled by another entity (known as the parent)"*. (IFRS 10, 'Consolidated financial statements', which supersedes IAS 27 for consolidated financial statements for annual periods beginning on or after 1 January 2013 defines a subsidiary as *"an entity that is controlled by another entity"*.) In addition, an entity is considered to be a fellow subsidiary of another entity if both are subsidiaries of the same parent (an example of 'common control' – see para A29.45). It should be noted that all entities in a group, whether unincorporated or incorporated, will be related parties. The concept of control is considered in more detail above from paragraph A29.18.

Common control

A29.45 Given the specific criterion identifying group members as related parties, as well as those entities that are controlled by the same person, entities subject to common control from the same source are effectively included in the definition of a related party. This is because of the potential effect of the common control on transactions between them and on their financial position. The most usual example of common control is within a group where fellow subsidiaries are both under the control of the parent. Common control can also occur in the investment management industry where various funds are controlled by the same fund manager (see from para A29.71). Common control also arises when two entities are subject to common control by a person (see further from para A29.54).

Associates, joint ventures and their investors and venturers

A29.46 Investors and their associates are related parties. Similarly, venturers and their joint ventures are related parties. [IAS 24 (revised) para 9(b)(ii)]. This extends to an associate or joint venture of a member of a group of which the reporting entity is a member. The definitions of associates and joint ventures in IAS 28 and IAS 31 (or IFRS 11, 'Joint arrangements', which supersedes IAS 31 for annual periods beginning on or after 1 January 2013) apply.

A29.47 Broadly, an associate is an entity (that is not a subsidiary or a joint venture) including an unincorporated entity, such as a partnership, over which the investor has significant influence. Significant influence is the power to participate in the financial and operating policy decisions of the investee, but is not control or joint control over those policies. [IAS 28 para 2]. Significant influence is presumed if the investor holds 20 per cent or more of the voting power, unless it can be clearly demonstrated that this is not the case. [IAS 28 para 6]. For an example of disclosure see Table A29.1. See also the example in paragraph A29.49 – similar principles may be applied where entity D is an associate rather than a joint venture as illustrated in that example. Further discussion on significant influence is given above from paragraph A29.26.

Table A29.1 – Transactions with associates and joint ventures

RTL Group S.A. – Annual Report and Accounts – 31 December 2010

10. RELATED PARTIES (extract)

10. 2. Transactions with associates and joint ventures

The following transactions were carried out with associates and joint ventures:

	2010 **€m**	2009 €m
Sales of goods and services to:		
Associates	**36**	48
Joint ventures	**23**	22
	59	70
Purchase of goods and services from:		
Associates	**5**	8
Joint ventures	**9**	10
	14	18

Sales and purchases to and from associates and joint ventures were carried out on commercial terms and conditions and at market prices.

Year-end balances arising from sales and purchases of goods and services are as follows:

	2010 **€m**	2009 €m
Trade accounts receivable from:		
Associates	**19**	28
Joint ventures	**5**	4
	24	32
Trade accounts payable to:		
Associates	**2**	1
RTL II is a party in legal proceedings with a subsidiary of RTL Group.	**2**	1

A29.48 A joint venture is an undertaking that an investing entity (the venturer) manages jointly with other venturers. Under IAS 31 a joint venture is defined as: *"a contractual arrangement whereby two or more parties undertake an economic activity that is subject to joint control"*. [IAS 31 para 3]. Table A29.3 above gives an example of disclosure of transactions and balances with joint ventures. Further discussion of joint control is given above from paragraph A29.24.

A29.49 The following example considers the situation where an entity is a joint venture of a member of a group of which the entity is a member.

Example – Joint venture of group member

Entity A owns 80% of entity B and 70% of entity C. Entity C has a 50% holding in a joint venture, entity D.

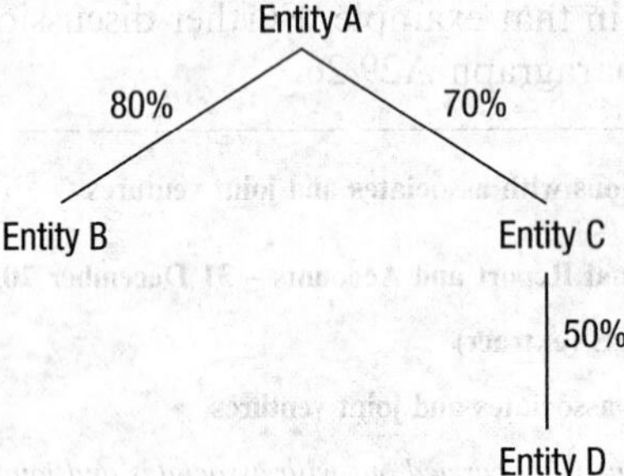

Entities A, B and C are members of the same group and, hence, are related parties of one another. [IAS 24 (revised) para 9(b)(i)]. As a joint venture of entity C, entity D is a related party of that entity. Entity D is also a related party of the other members of the group in which entity C sits, that is, entity D is a related party of both entity A and entity B. [IAS 24 (revised) para 9(b)(ii)]. Note that if entity D was an associate of entity C, it would, similarly, be a related party of entities A, B and C.

A29.50 IAS 24 (revised) confirms that where an entity has a joint venture, the joint venture's subsidiaries will be related parties of the entity. Similarly, where an entity has an associate, the associate's subsidiaries will be related parties of the entity. [IAS 24 (revised) para 12].

Group situations — subsidiaries, joint ventures and associates

A29.51 Where entity A has a subsidiary (entity B) and significant influence or joint control over another entity (entity C), entities B and C are both related parties of entity A. [IAS 24 (revised) para 9(b)(ii)]. Entity A would also be a related party of any subsidiary held by entity C. [IAS 24 (revised) para 12]. Entity B and entity C are also related parties of one another under the definitions in the standard. [IAS 24 (revised) para 9(b)(ii)]. This situation is illustrated in the following examples.

Example 1 – Control, significant influence or joint control from the same source

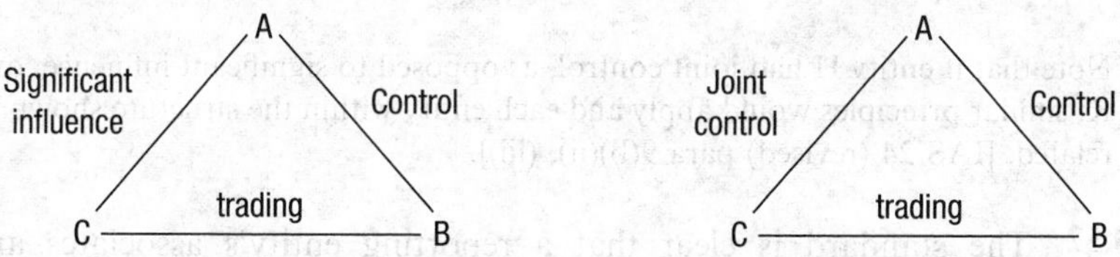

In each of the above scenarios, entities A and B are related parties under IAS 24 (revised). [IAS 24 (revised) para 9(b)(i)].

In each of the above scenarios, entities A and C are related parties under IAS 24 (revised). [IAS 24 (revised) para 9(b)(ii)].

In each of the above scenarios, entities B and C are related parties under the definitions in IAS 24 (revised). Entity B should disclose details of any transactions with entity C that have been entered into (together with any resulting balances). Similarly, entity C should include details of any transactions with entity B that have been entered into (together with any resulting balances). [IAS 24 (revised) para 9(b)(ii)].

Disclosure of transactions between entities B and C will be required in entity A's consolidated financial statements (even if the transactions were at arm's length) because these are related party transactions between an associate (or joint venture) and the entity A group (of which the entity controlled by entity A is a member) and the transactions are not eliminated on consolidation (see para A29.9)

However, entity A's management is not required to disclose the transactions between entity B and entity C as related party transactions in entity A's separate financial statements. IAS 24 (revised) defines a related party transaction as *"a transfer of resources, services or obligations between a reporting entity and a related party..."*. [IAS 24 (revised) para 9]. For its separate financial statements, entity A is the reporting entity and so transactions between entity B and entity C are not transactions with the reporting entity and are not, therefore, related party transactions.

Example 2 – Entity with joint control and significant influence

Entity H has joint control over entity J and significant influence over entity K.

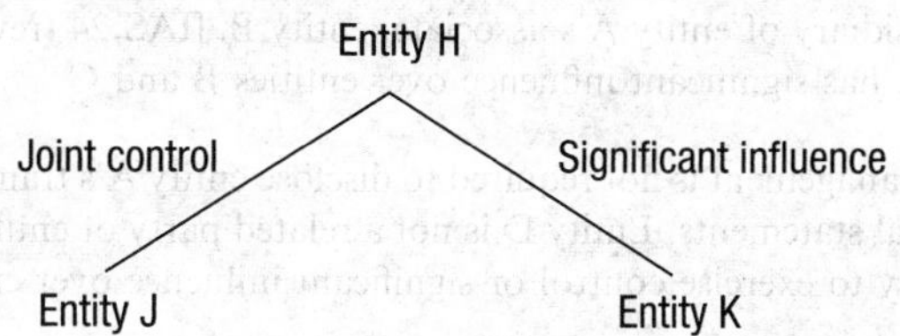

Entity H has a joint venture, entity J, and an associate, entity K. Therefore, both entities J and K are entity H's related parties. [IAS 24 (revised) para 9(b)(ii)].

For the purposes of entity J's financial statements, entities H and K are entity J's related parties. [IAS 24 (revised) para 9(b)(ii), (iv)].

Similarly, for the purposes of entity K's financial statements, entities H and J are entity K's related parties. [IAS 24 (revised) para 9(b)(ii), (iv)].

Note that if entity H had joint control, as opposed to significant influence, over entity K, similar principles would apply and each entity within the structure shown would be related. [IAS 24 (revised) para 9(b)(ii), (iii)].

A29.52 The standard is clear that a reporting entity's associates and joint ventures are its related parties. However, the question arises as to whether a reporting entity's transactions with the related parties of its associate or joint venture should be disclosed as related party transactions. This is considered in the examples below.

Example 1 – Transactions with the related parties of an associate or joint venture

Entity A owns 30% of the share capital of entity B and has the ability to exercise significant influence over it.

Entity B holds the following investments:

- 70% of the share capital of its subsidiary entity C; and
- 30% of the share capital of entity D, with the ability to exercise significant influence.

The structure is illustrated as follows:

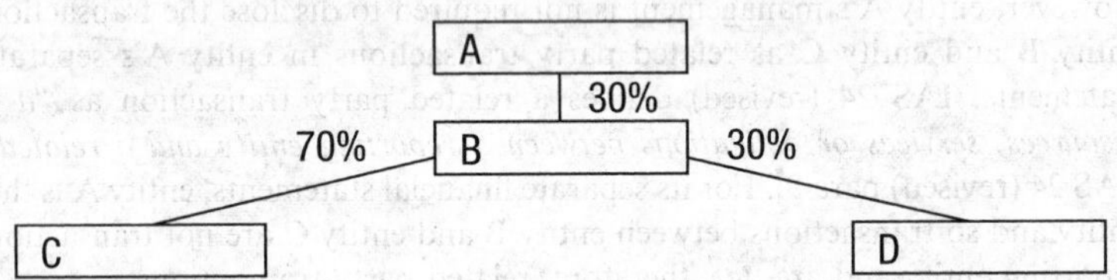

Entity A transacts with entities C and D. Should entity A disclose these transactions as related party transactions?

Entity A's management should disclose entity A's transactions with entity C in entity A's separate financial statements. Entity C is a related party of entity A, because entity C is the subsidiary of entity A's associate, entity B. [IAS 24 (revised) para 12]. Entity A, therefore, has significant influence over entities B and C.

Entity A's management is not required to disclose entity A's transactions with entity D in its financial statements. Entity D is not a related party of entity A, because entity A has no ability to exercise control or significant influence over entity D.

Consistent with the above, entity C is required to disclose its transactions with entity A in its financial statements, because, as explained above, entity A is a related party. Entity D is not required to disclose transactions with entity A, because they are not related parties.

Example 2 – Group holdings – subsidiaries and associates

Entity P has two wholly-owned subsidiaries – entity Q and entity R. Entity R has a wholly-owned subsidiary, entity S and a 30% holding in its associate, entity T. Entity P also has a 30% holding in its associate, entity U.

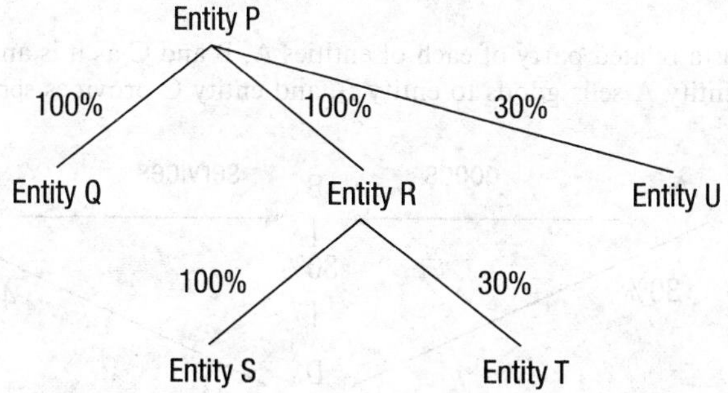

Entity P's consolidated and separate financial statements

Entities Q, R, S, T and U are all related parties of entity P for the purposes of entity P's separate financial statements. [IAS 24 (revised) para 9(b)(i), (ii)]. Entities T and U are related to entity P for the purposes of entity P's consolidated financial statements (while transactions between entity P and each of entities Q, R and S will be eliminated on consolidation and hence no related party disclosures would be required). [IAS 24 (revised) paras 9b(i), (ii), 4].

Financial statements of entities Q, R and S

All entities shown within the structure are related to one another for the purposes of each of subsidiary entities Q, R and S's separate financial statements. For example, entities P, R, S, T and U are all related parties of entity Q. [IAS 24 (revised) para 9b(i), (ii)].

Entity T's financial statements

Entity R is a related party of entity T and, therefore, the other entities (entities P, R and S) within entity R's group are also related parties of entity T. [IAS 24 (revised) para 9(b)(ii)]. However, entity U is not a related party of entity T because two associates of the same investor are not related parties simply by virtue of their common investor.

Entity U's financial statements

Entity P is a related party of entity U and, therefore, the other entities (entities Q, R and S) within entity P's group are also related parties of entity U. [IAS 24 (revised) para 9(b)(ii)]. However, entity T is not a related party of entity U.

A29.53 It might also be expected that the venturers that have joint control or investors that have significant influence over an entity are related parties of each other. However, the standard explains that this is *not necessarily* the case. [IAS 24 (revised) para 11(b)]. See further from paragraph A29.79 below. Applying similar principles, an investor in an associate or a joint venture is not necessarily a related party of other investors in the same associate or joint venture. This situation is illustrated in the following example.

Example – Transactions between different investors in an associate

Entity D is a related party of each of entities A, B and C as it is an associate of those entities. Entity A sells goods to entity B, and entity C provides services to entity B.

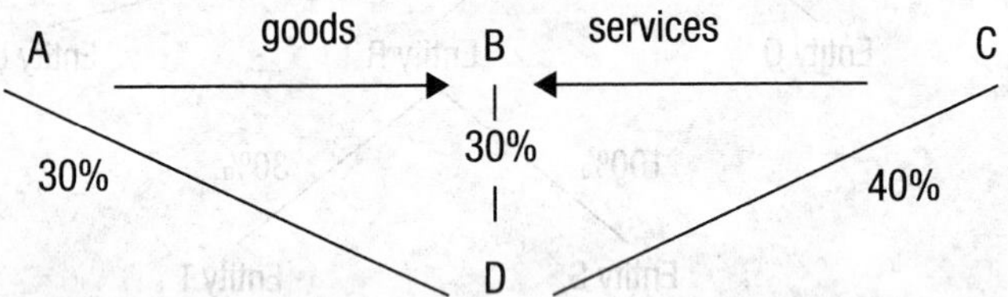

Entities A, B and C are related parties of entity D, but not necessarily related parties of each other. Consequently, unless there is some other relationship between entities A, B and C (other than the fact that they are all investees in entity D) that would make them related parties, the transactions between entities A and B and between entities C and B would not be disclosable in any of the financial statements of entities A, B, C or D. (If, for example entities A, B and C were all fellow subsidiaries of another entity they would be related parties of each other, but for a different reason than their investment in entity D). [IAS 24 (revised) paras 9(b)(i), 11(b)].

Entities in which related party persons have an interest

A29.54 As explained in paragraph A29.58, the standard specifically identifies the following related party relationships:

- Where a person (or close member of that person's family – see from para A29.38) controls or jointly controls an entity, that entity is a related party of another entity that is controlled or jointly controlled by the same person (or close member of that person's family).
- Where a person (or close member of that person's family) has significant influence over an entity, or is a member of that entity's (or a parent of that entity's) key management personnel, the entity is a related party of another entity that is controlled or jointly controlled by the same person (or a close member of that person's family).

[IAS 24 (revised) para 9(b)(vi), (vii)].

This section provides a number of practical examples to illustrate the definition.

A29.55 The following two examples concern persons with control, joint control and/or significant influence over more than one entity.

Example 1 – Investor controls one entity and has significant influence over another

Mr A owns 70% of entity B and 30% of entity C.

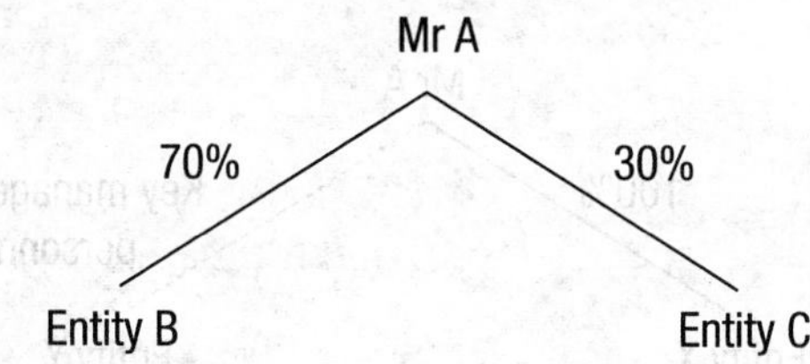

Mr A controls entity B and, therefore, is a related party of that entity. [IAS 24 (revised) para 9(a)(i)]. Mr A has significant influence over entity C and, therefore, is a related party of that entity. [IAS 24 (revised) para 9(a)(ii)]. Because Mr A has control over entity B and significant influence over entity C, entity B and entity C are related parties. [IAS 24 (revised) para 9(b)(vii)]. Therefore, entity B's financial statements should include details of transactions with Mr A and entity C. Entity C's financial statements should include details of transactions with Mr A and entity B.

Note that the position would be the same where Mr A had joint control, as opposed to control, over entity B. Mr A would be a related party of entity B and entity C while entities B and C would be related parties of one another.

Example 2 – Investor has significant influence over two entities

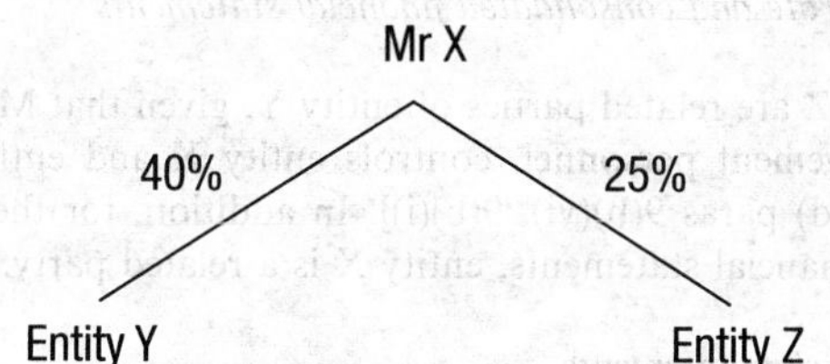

Mr X owns 40% of entity Y and 25% of entity Z.

Mr X has significant influence over entity Y and, therefore, is a related party of that entity. [IAS 24 (revised) para 9(a)(ii)]. Similarly, Mr X has significant influence over entity Z and, therefore, is a related party of that entity. [IAS 24 (revised) para 9(a)(ii)]. Entity Y and entity Z are not related to each other. Investees are not related just because they are subject to significant influence from the same investor. [IAS 24 (revised) para BC25].

A29.56 The following examples concern key management personnel and their close family members.

Example 1 – Key management personnel

Mr A owns all of the share capital of entity X. He is also a member of the key management personnel of entity Y. Entity Y owns all of the share capital of entity Z.

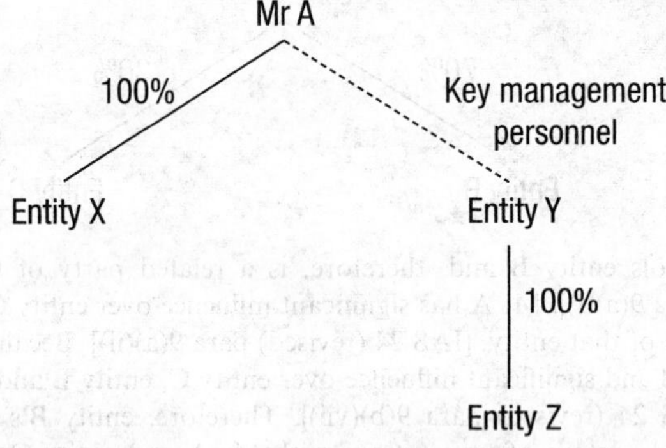

Entity X's financial statements

Entity Y is a related party of entity X because Mr A is a member of key management personnel of entity Y and he also controls entity X. [IAS 24 (revised) para 9(b)(vii).] Entity Z is also a related party of entity X, given that Mr A is a member of key management personnel of its parent, entity Y. [IAS 24 (revised) para 9(b)(vii)].

Entity Y's separate and consolidated financial statements

Entities X and Z are related parties of entity Y, given that Mr A, a member of entity Y's key management personnel, controls entity X and entity Y controls entity Z. [IAS 24 (revised) paras 9(b)(vi), 9(b)(i)]. In addition, for the purposes of entity Y's consolidated financial statements, entity X is a related party.

Entity Z's financial statements

Entity X is a related party of entity Z because Mr A controls entity X and he is also a member of entity Z's parent's key management personnel. [IAS 24 (revised) para 9(b)(vi)].

Example 2 – Close family members

Mr L's spouse is Mrs L. Mr L controls entity M. Mrs L has significant influence over entity N.

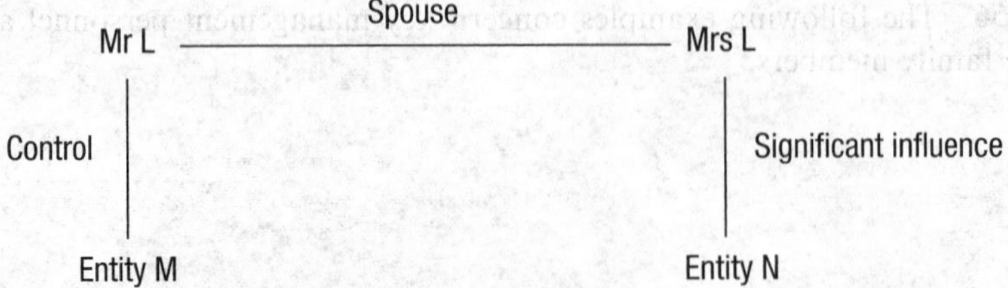

Given Mr L's control of entity M and Mrs L's significant influence over entity N, for the purposes of entity M's financial statements, entity N is a related party. [IAS 24 (revised) para 9(b)(vii)].

Similarly, for the purposes of entity N's financial statements, entity M is a related party. [IAS 24 (revised) para 9(b)(vi)].

A29.57 The definitions of control, joint control and significant influence are discussed from paragraph A29.18 above. A straightforward example of an entity controlled by a member of key management personnel is an entity in which a director has a controlling interest. This is quite common in relation to directors' remuneration where a director may set up an entity to receive his or her remuneration for tax planning purposes.

A29.58 There are sometimes other reasons for using connected entities, for example, to disguise or conceal transactions that are designed to benefit persons at the expense of the entity. These are the situations where it is particularly important to carefully consider the legal structure and the substance of arrangements (see further from para A29.77).

Example – Entities in which a director has an interest

Subsidiary S is owned by its parent P. Mr X, who works solely for entity S, is a director of entity S, but is not considered to be a member of key management personnel of entity P. Of Mr X's remuneration, some is paid by entity S and the remainder is paid by entity P. The remuneration is not paid directly to Mr X, rather it is paid to entity A, which is controlled by Mr X.

The disclosure of key management personnel compensation in the financial statements of entity S should include both the amounts paid by entity S and the amounts paid by entity P, as all Mr X's remuneration relates to services to entity S. This disclosure requirement is regardless of whether there is a cost recognised in entity S (for example, by way of a recharge) in respect of the amounts paid by entity P. The fact that the remuneration is paid to entity A and not directly to Mr X does not affect the disclosure.

A29.59 A member of key management personnel may also be a majority shareholder in an entity that trades with the reporting entity. Such relationships may also be captured by IAS 24 (revised), as illustrated in the following example.

Example – Director owns shares in a customer of the group

A parent has a wholly-owned subsidiary. One of the subsidiary's directors is the majority shareholder of an otherwise independent third party entity that sells goods on normal commercial terms to the subsidiary. The director is a member of the subsidiary's key management personnel.

How should transactions with the supplier be presented in:

(a) the subsidiary's financial statements;

(b) the consolidated financial statements; and

(c) the financial statements of the entity that sells the goods?

(a) The subsidiary's financial statements

The subsidiary's management should present the supplier as a related party of the subsidiary, because the director controls the supplier and, as a key manager, has influence over the subsidiary. [IAS 24 (revised) para 9(b)(vi)]. Management should disclose in the subsidiary's financial statements information related to the purchase of goods from this supplier, as well as the nature of the relationship between the subsidiary and the supplier.

(b) The consolidated financial statements

The parent's management should disclose the information set out under (a) above in the consolidated financial statements if it is determined that the director of the subsidiary is a member of the group's key management personnel. [IAS 24 (revised) para 9(a)(iii)].

(c) The financial statements of the entity that sells the goods

The subsidiary is a related party of the third party entity. The subsidiary's director, as majority shareholder, is a related party of the third party entity. The fact that the director is a member of key management personnel at the subsidiary also makes the subsidiary a related party of the entity that sells the goods. [IAS 24 (revised) para 9(b)(vii)]. Disclosure would, therefore, be required of sales made to the subsidiary, as well as the nature of the relationship with the subsidiary.

A29.60 Although trust arrangements are often used for genuine tax planning and other legitimate purposes, they can also be used for the purpose of secrecy and concealment. Trust arrangements are often difficult to evaluate in terms of whether a related party arrangement exists that should be disclosed. The following is an example of a situation where a trust is a related party of an entity because of the existence of a controlling interest by a related party (in this case, a director) of the entity.

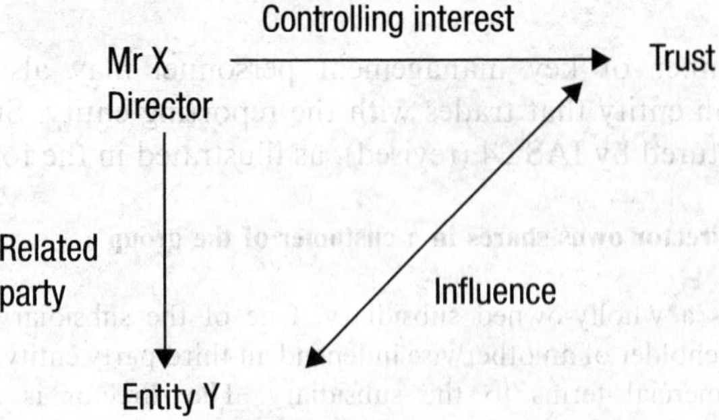

A29.61 Under IAS 24 (revised) paragraph 9(b)(vi) of the related party definition, the trust is a related party of entity Y because it is controlled by Mr X, a director of entity Y. In practice there may be difficulty in proving that Mr X has a controlling interest in the trust, because trustees will generally be legally obliged to act in the interests of beneficiaries, but the substance of the arrangement may be that Mr X in fact has control.

A29.62 The following example considers the implications for related party disclosures of a director's relationship with a trust.

Example – Director's relationship with a trust

Mr X, owns 95% of entity A and is also its director. He is also beneficiary of a trust that owns 100% of entity B, of which he is also a director.

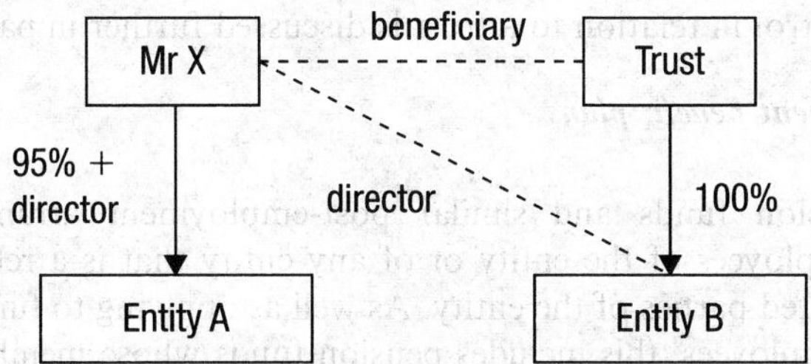

Entities A and B are related parties because the director controls entity A and is a member of the key management personnel of entity B. [IAS 24 (revised) para 9(b)(vii), (vi)]. Would the situation be any different if:

(a) Mr X transferred his 95% of entity A to the trust, but remained a director of entity A?

In this situation, if Mr X controls the trust, the two entities will be related under IAS 24 (revised). [IAS 24 (revised) para 9(b)(vi), (vii)].

(b) Mr X resigned as a director of entity A, but retained his 95% holding?

Whilst not (nominally) a director of entity A, Mr X continues to control entity A through his 95% holding. If Mr X controls the trust, entities A and B are related because Mr X controls entity A and also, through the trust, controls entity B. Entities A and B are controlled by the same person and so are related parties. [IAS 24 (revised) para 9(b)(vi)].

In addition, although not nominally a director of entity A, Mr X may still be 'key management personnel' (as this includes, but is not restricted to, directors, which include those who are executives 'or otherwise'). Therefore, even if he resigned as a director of entity A, the same answer as (a) above would be likely to apply. Hence, there are two reasons why entities A and B would continue to be related parties. [IAS 24 (revised) para 9(b)(vii)].

(c) Mr X resigned as a director of entities A and B and transferred the 95% holding in entity A to the trust?

If the director controls the trust, he controls entities A and B through the trust and they will, therefore, be related parties (see reasons in (b) above). [IAS 24 (revised) para 9(b)(vi)].

In addition, if, as seems likely, Mr X continues to direct the operating and financial policies of the two entities he should be regarded for the purpose of IAS 24 (revised) as being key management personnel (see also (b) above). [IAS 24 (revised) para 9(b)(vii)]. Note also that IAS 24 (revised) states in paragraph 10 that *"in considering each possible related party relationship, attention is directed to the substance of the relationship and not merely the legal form"*. If Mr X is regarded as key management personnel of, say, entity A then entity B is a related party, because he exercises control or significant influence over entity B by virtue of his control over the trust.

A29.63 Control in relation to a trust is discussed further in paragraph A29.120.

Post-employment benefit plans

A29.64 Pension funds and similar post-employment arrangements for the benefit of employees of the entity or of any entity that is a related party of the entity are related parties of the entity. As well as applying to funds for the benefit of all such employees, this includes pension funds whose membership is open to some, but not all, employees, for instance, those open to directors and senior managers only. On the other hand, industry-wide and state pension schemes that are not for the benefit of the entity's employees or for the benefit of employees of the entity's related parties would generally not be regarded as related parties of an entity under this definition.

A29.65 In contrast, a pension fund that is operated for the benefit of employees in a group is a related party of each entity within the group whose employees participate in the fund. This is because the entities and the fund are subject to control and influence from the same source.

A29.66 The fact that pension funds are related parties is not intended to call into question the independence of the trustees of the scheme. Transactions between the reporting entity and the pension fund may be in the interest of members, but nevertheless need to be reported in the reporting entity's financial statements.

A29.67 'Post-employment plans' is a broad term and is interpreted widely to include, for example, funds maintained by employers to pay pensions to employees disabled at work.

A29.68 It should be noted that it is not just pension funds for the benefit of employees in group companies that are related parties of the reporting entity. Instead, pension funds and similar post-employment arrangements for the benefit of employees of any entity that is a related party of the entity, are related parties of the entity. This is illustrated in the following example.

Example – Post employment plans of a related party outside the group

The wife of a member of entity A's key management personnel controls 25% of the voting power in entity B and has significant influence over entity B.

Entity A transacts with the pension fund set up for the benefits of all employees of entity B. Should entity A disclose these transactions?

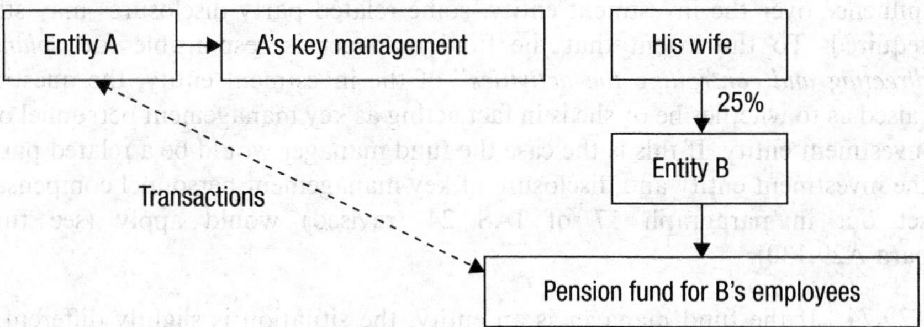

The pension fund is set up for the benefit of the employees of entity B and is, therefore, a related party of entity B. [IAS 24 (revised) para 9(b)(v)]. However, entity A is not a related party of entity B. Paragraph 11(a) of IAS 24 (revised) states that two entities are not related parties simply because a member of key management personnel of one entity has significant influence over the other entity.

Therefore, the pension fund is not a related party of entity A and the transactions between entity A and the pension fund do not need to be disclosed.

A29.69 As noted in the example above, the standard's definition makes clear that if the reporting entity itself is a post-employment benefit plan, the sponsoring employers are also related to the reporting entity. [IAS 24 (revised) para 9(b)(v)].

A29.70 Related party disclosures in respect of post-employment benefit plans are dealt with from paragraph A29.187.

Management contracts

A29.71 Paragraph 10 of IAS 24 (revised) specifies that the substance of relationships should be examined to determine whether a related party relationship exists. In some circumstances, management contracts may exist between entities that could indicate that the parties to the contract fit the definition of a related party. For example, in the investment management sector, it is common for an investment entity to outsource the day to day management of funds to a fund manager. The fund manager may be an entity or a person and may be working under a management contract for a fee. The question then arises as to whether the fund manager is a related party of the investment entity.

A29.72 In some cases, the fund manager may work for only one customer, the investment entity. If this is the case, it would be necessary to assess whether the fund manager (whether an entity or a person) has control, joint control or an interest that gives significant influence over the investment entity. To the extent that this is the case, the two parties would be related parties under IAS 24 (revised). Any transactions between the two parties, such as the fees, would need to be disclosed as related party transactions.

A29.73 If the fund manager is a person and it is established that he or she does not have control, joint control or an interest that gives him/her significant influence over the investment entity, some related party disclosures may still be required. To the extent that the fund manager is responsible for *"planning, directing and controlling the activities"* of the investment entity, the question is raised as to whether he or she is in fact acting as key management personnel of the investment entity. If this is the case the fund manager would be a related party of the investment entity and disclosure of key management personnel compensation set out in paragraph 17 of IAS 24 (revised) would apply (see further para A29.130).

A29.74 If the fund manager is an entity, the situation is slightly different. We consider that it is not possible for an entity to be a member of key management personnel; only persons can be members of key management personnel. However, in order to be key management personnel, a person does not have to be employed by the reporting entity. Therefore, if there are persons within the fund manager entity who are carrying out a role that involves planning, directing and controlling the activities of the investment entity, they will be considered key management personnel of the investment entity.

A29.75 Entities are required to disclose compensation paid to key management personnel under paragraph 17 of IAS 24 (revised). Clearly, in this case, the investment entity may not have access to relevant salary information regarding the persons employed by the fund manager. The way in which the investment entity pays for the key management personnel services is through the fees paid to the fund manager entity. Therefore, where the relevant salary information for such persons is not available, the investment entity should disclose the fees paid to the fund manager as a proxy for disclosing key management personnel compensation. A note should also be included stating that certain persons employed by the fund manager entity meet the definition of key management personnel. The investment entity should make it clear that its key management personnel compensation disclosure table does not include certain persons employed by the fund manager and cross-refer to the disclosure of fees paid to the fund manager.

A29.76 Where the fund manager does not exert significant influence, joint control or control over the investment entity and no persons within the fund manager are identified as key management personnel of the investment entity, there may be no related party relationship. Should this be the case, there will be no requirement to disclose transactions between the parties.

Substance of the relationship

A29.77 IAS 24 contains an important principle. It states that in considering each possible related party relationship, attention is directed to the substance of the relationship and not merely the legal form. [IAS 24 (revised) para 10].

A29.78 An example of how the substance principle might be applied to a situation involving common control is given below.

Example – Parties related in substance

Entity A is owned by Mr X who is its sole director and the entity is in financial difficulties. Entity A sells a property with a book value of C100,000 to entity B, which is owned by Mr Z who is also entity B's sole director, for C50,000. Entity B then sells the property for C50,000 to entity C which is also owned by Mr X, who is its sole director. Consider the disclosure in (i) entity A and (ii) entity C.

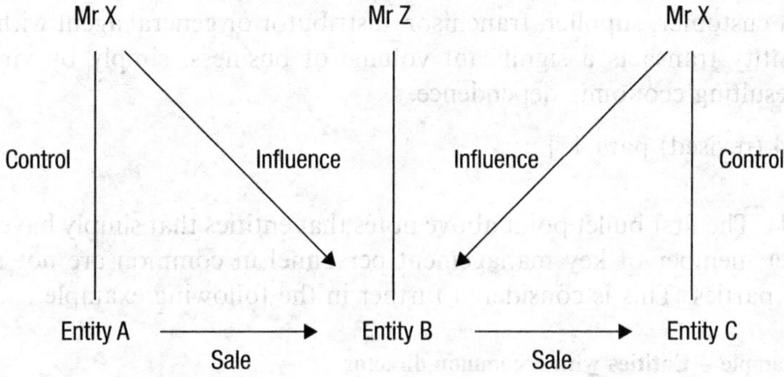

Entity A has ostensibly sold a property to a third party, unconnected to its director, at an amount below book value. On the basis that the entity is in financial difficulties it might be understandable that the sale is below book value as it might be a forced sale. However, entity B makes neither profit nor loss on the deal and appears to be an agent or intermediary for the transfer from entity A to entity C. Taking the transaction as a whole, the substance of this arrangement appears to be that a transaction has occurred between entity A and entity C. This has been facilitated via an intermediary – entity B. As entity A and entity C are subject to common control, they are related parties. In substance, a transaction has occurred between these two parties and the appropriate IAS 24 (revised) disclosures should, therefore, be made. It may also be necessary to consider whether Mr Z and entity B are also related parties of entity A and entity C. This is because entity B and Mr Z are unlikely to have agreed to participate in the transaction, unless they were controlled or influenced by Mr X. If this is the case, any transactions between entity A or entity C and Mr Z or entity B should also be disclosed.

In the financial statements of both entity A and entity C, details of the transaction should be disclosed alongside the fact that the transaction has been undertaken via an intermediary. If it is determined that Mr Z or entity B is a related party, disclosure should also be made of the fact that the intermediary company is a related party. This is because the standard requires disclosure of information *"necessary for users to understand the potential effect of the relationship on the financial statements"*. [IAS 24 (revised) para 18].

Parties that are not necessarily related

A29.79 IAS 24 (revised) states that the following are not related parties of an entity:

- Two entities simply because they have a director or other member of key management personnel in common, or because a member of key management personnel of one entity has significant influence over the other entity.
- Two venturers simply because they share joint control over a joint venture.
- Departments and agencies of a government that does not control, jointly control or significantly influence the reporting entity, providers of finance, trade unions and public utilities, simply by virtue of their normal dealings with an entity (even though they may affect the freedom of action of an entity or participate in its decision-making process).
- A customer, supplier, franchisor, distributor or general agent with whom an entity transacts a significant volume of business, simply by virtue of the resulting economic dependence.

[IAS 24 (revised) para 11].

A29.80 The first bullet point above notes that entities that simply have a director or other member of key management personnel in common are not necessarily related parties. This is considered further in the following example.

Example – Entities with a common director

A director (Mr X) of entity A is also a director of entity B. He does not control either entity. There are no other directors in common. Entity A has a trading relationship with entity B. Are entity A and entity B related parties?

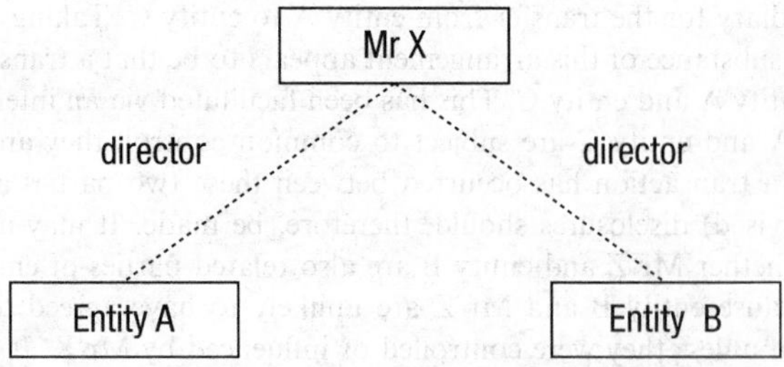

IAS 24 (revised) states that two entities are not related parties simply because they have a director or other member of key management personnel in common. [IAS 24 (revised) para 11(a)]. However, the standard indicates, through the words 'simply because', that even where two entities simply have a director in common, there is still a need to consider the possibility that the two entities are related.

As explained in paragraph A29.77, paragraph 10 of IAS 24 (revised) requires that in considering each possible related party relationship, attention should be directed to the substance of the relationship and not merely the legal form. The standard, therefore, places more emphasis on what actually happens in practice (substance) than on what the legal form is. If, for example, the director prevents one or other of the entities or both from pursuing its separate interests, the existence of the common director may mean that the director has control over one or both of the entities and, as such, paragraph 9(b)(vi) or (vii) in the related party definition in IAS 24 (revised) is applicable.

A29.81 The use of the phrase 'simply because' in paragraph 11 of IAS 24 (revised) implies that there is a possibility that such parties could be related, even if they have limited involvement with the entity. Normally, however, it would require some additional factor or unusual degree of involvement to make the parties related. An example of the former might be where a provider of finance was also a substantial shareholder (say over 20 per cent) in the entity. An example of the latter might be where a customer accounted for over 50 per cent of an entity's sales and was able to significantly influence the entity's production schedules and pricing such that the entity was not able freely to pursue its own separate interests.

A29.82 Where one of the above parties qualifies as a related party, we consider that all transactions with that related party are disclosable by the reporting entity, including any transactions that arise out of the related party's role as, for example, a supplier or a provider of finance. This is illustrated in the following examples.

Example 1 – Key supplier also has significant influence via a shareholding

A reporting entity might be heavily dependent on a supply of gas from a gas utility. But, as set out in paragraph 11(c)(iii) of IAS 24 (revised), that does not, by itself, result in the gas utility becoming a related party of the reporting entity.

If the gas utility has a 30% interest in the reporting entity, which it treats as an associate, this relationship causes the reporting entity and the gas utility to be related parties. [IAS 24 (revised) para 9(b)(ii)]. In the reporting entity's financial statements, transactions with the gas utility would be disclosable as they would not be eliminated on consolidation. The exemption in paragraph 11(c)(iii) of IAS 24 (revised) does not have any impact in this context, because the two are already related and the normal rules apply.

Example 2 – Financier has significant influence via a shareholding

A venture capitalist has helped to finance a management buyout. In addition to providing loan finance, it has taken a 30% equity stake in the MBO entity and placed a director on its board. The venture capitalist receives various payments from the entity, including management fees, interest and dividends. Can the MBO entity avoid disclosing these transactions by using the exemption in paragraph 11(c)(i) of IAS 24 (revised) in respect of transactions with providers of finance?

Paragraph 11(c) of IAS 24 (revised) states that providers of finance are *"not necessarily"* related parties simply by virtue of their normal dealings with an entity (even though they may affect the freedom of action of an entity or participate in its decision-making process).

A lending bank would not be treated as a related party simply because the terms of the loan enabled the bank to restrict the entity's borrowing or investing activities. However, the position is different where such parties are related for some other reason. In such circumstances, all material transactions with those related parties would be disclosable, including those relating to the provision of finance.

It is, therefore, necessary to consider whether the venture capitalist is a related party as a result of its 30% equity interest. Where an entity is an associate of an investor (as would often be the case where, as in this situation, the investor has an equity interest greater than 20%), IAS 24 (revised) states that the investor and the associate are related parties. [IAS 24 (revised) para 9(b)(ii)]. This is regardless of the manner in which the venture capitalist chooses to apply IAS 28 (see further chapter 27).

Therefore, if the venture capitalist's 30% voting power gave it significant influence then it would be a related party and disclosure of transactions and outstanding balances with the venture capitalist would be required in the investee's financial statements. Whilst providers of finance in the ordinary course of business are not related parties simply by virtue of the provision of that finance, the arrangement described in the question appears to amount to more than a simple financing arrangement as there is a separate related party relationship resulting from the venture capitalist's equity stake in the entity.

Related parties for only part of the year

A29.83 Questions arise as to what transactions are disclosable where the parties are related for only part of the year. Under IAS 24 (revised), disclosure is only required in respect of transactions during the period for which the entities are related. A related party transaction is a transaction between a reporting entity and a related party; it follows that a transaction with a party that is unrelated at the time of the transaction is not a related party transaction. This is considered further in paragraph A29.183 below.

Related party transactions

Definition of related party transactions

A29.84 A 'related party transaction' is defined in IAS 24 (revised) as: *"a transfer of resources, services or obligations between a reporting entity and a related party, regardless of whether a price is charged"*. [IAS 24 (revised) para 9].

Types of related party transactions

A29.85 The following are examples of related party transactions that require disclosure by a reporting entity in the period in which they occur:

- Purchases or sales of goods (finished or unfinished).
- Purchases or sales of property and other assets.
- Rendering or receiving of services.

- Leases.
- Transfers of research and development.
- Licence agreements.
- Provision of finance (including loans and equity contributions in cash or in kind).
- Guarantees and the provision of collateral security.
- Commitments to do something if a particular event occurs or does not occur in the future, including recognised and unrecognised executory contracts. Executory contracts are defined in IAS 37, 'Provisions, contingent liabilities and contingent assets', as contracts under which neither party has performed any of its obligations or both parties have partially performed their obligations to an equal extent.
- Settlement of liabilities on behalf of the entity or by the entity on behalf of that related party.
- Participation by a parent or subsidiary in a defined benefit plan that shares risks between group entities (see chapter 11).

[IAS 24 paras 21, 22].

A29.86 The above list is not exhaustive and there are a number of other transactions that should, in our view, also be disclosed. These could include:

- Agency arrangements.
- Management contracts (see from para A29.71).

A29.87 It is common, for example, for corporate reorganisations to take place whereby the business of a subsidiary is transferred to the parent, while the subsidiary continues to invoice customers as agent for its parent. In such circumstances it is important that the fact and details of the agency arrangement are disclosed in the financial statements of the individual entities involved (the transactions would be eliminated on consolidation, so disclosure in the consolidated financial statements would not be required) so that customers and others are aware of the role played by the subsidiary.

A29.88 The definition of a related party transaction (see para A29.84) envisages that some related party transactions might not be entered into an entity's accounting records or might not involve any consideration passing. Examples of such transactions are:

- Management services provided by one entity to another free of charge.
- Goods manufactured under a patent owned by a fellow subsidiary, which makes no charge.
- Guarantees given by directors (see para A29.197).

- Rent-free accommodation or the loan of vehicles or other assets at no charge.

Materiality

A29.89 As with other standards the disclosure of related party transactions is required only if the transactions are material. IAS 1, 'Presentation of financial statements', assists with a definition of material: *"Omissions or misstatements of items are material if they could, individually or collectively, influence the economic decisions that users make on the basis of the financial statements. Materiality depends on the size and nature of the omission or misstatement judged in the surrounding circumstances. The size or nature of the item, or a combination of both, could be the determining factor"*. [IAS 1 para 7].

A29.90 In respect of disclosures, IAS 1 states: *"An entity need not provide a specific disclosure required by an IFRS if the information is not material"*. [IAS 1 para 31].

A29.91 IAS 1 does not deal specifically with a situation that arises with related party transactions, particularly where such transactions involve a person. The issue is that whereas a transaction may be immaterial in amount to the entity, it may not be immaterial to the person and, therefore, the question is whether materiality should be judged from the person's perspective or from the entity's perspective.

A29.92 In a straightforward situation it may be clear that a transaction is immaterial to both the person and the entity, but often things are not straightforward. For example, a director buying a chocolate bar in the staff canteen is not of interest to users of financial statements, but the director or his close family buying a six-bedroom house from the entity at a price other than fair value certainly would be. Where the director bought the house from the entity at its fair value, the situation, interpreted by reference only to the above definition of materiality, would require further consideration as discussed below.

A29.93 In recent times there has been a considerable growth in shareholder interest in the rewards paid to persons, particularly directors. Much of this interest has been critical of large rewards paid in times when entities have not been performing well. Indeed, some jurisdictions have introduced legislation and corporate governance requirements designed to ensure that listed entities make full disclosure of policies for remuneration and take steps to minimise rewards for poor performance. It would be contradictory to think that this type of interest and concern would not extend to related party transactions with, for example, key management personnel of an entity or that shareholders and others would not consider such transactions to be material. The interest and concern has focussed both on the cost to the entity and on the benefit derived by the person. This implies that materiality should be judged from both the entity's and the person's perspective.

A29.94 Consequently, in the examples given above, not only the significance to the entity, but the transaction's significance to the director would need to be considered in order to form a judgement as to whether the transaction involving the purchase of the house was material. The transaction could be small to the entity, but a major investment for the director. We believe the intention of IAS 24 (revised) is that transactions of the type and size shown in the example in paragraph A29.92 that is, the purchase of a house, whether at market value or not, would be regarded as material to the director and, therefore, disclosable.

A29.95 Although it is clear that the purchase of a house is material from the director's point of view and that the purchase of a chocolate bar is not, there will in practice be transactions in between these two extremes whose materiality is borderline. It is not possible to be definitive about how materiality should be established, as much will depend on the facts of each case. However, a transaction being at arm's length and on normal commercial terms would contribute to its being regarded as immaterial. Equally, a transaction that is on terms advantageous to the director would contribute to its being regarded as material and, therefore, disclosable.

A29.96 In addition, if a director enters into several small transactions in a financial year, they will need to be aggregated in order to determine whether they are material from the director's point of view. If these transactions are material when aggregated, then they will need to be disclosed in accordance with the standard.

Disclosure requirements

Summary

A29.97 IAS 24 (revised) requires the following information about related parties to be disclosed in an entity's financial statements:

- Relationships between a parent and its subsidiaries, irrespective of whether there have been transactions between them (see from para A29.99).
- The name of its parent and, if different, the name of the ultimate controlling party (see from para A29.102).
- Key management personnel compensation (see from para A29.129).
- Details of transactions between the entity and any related parties (see from para A29.158).
- Details of balances due to, or from, related parties at the balance sheet date, including information on bad and doubtful debts (see from para A29.158).

[IAS 24 (revised) paras 13, 17, 18].

A29.98 There is no requirement in IAS 24 (revised) to disclose information about related party transactions in any specific note. However, it is likely to be more helpful to users to present the information in one comprehensive note, instead of including different aspects of related party disclosures in several notes to the financial statements. Where information is also required by other standards, then cross-references can be used, in order to avoid duplicated information.

Disclosure of control

Parents and subsidiaries

A29.99 As noted in paragraph A29.97 above, IAS 24 (revised) requires disclosure of relationships between a parent and its subsidiaries, irrespective of whether there have been transactions between them. [IAS 24 (revised) para 13].

A29.100 This disclosure is in addition to the requirements of IFRS 27, 'Consolidated and separate financial statements', which requires disclosure, in a parent's separate financial statements, of:

- A list of significant investments in subsidiaries, jointly controlled entities and associates, including the name, country of incorporation or residence, proportion of ownership interest and, if different, proportion of voting power held.
- A description of the method used to account for such investments.

[IAS 27 para 42].

A29.101 Under IAS 24 (revised), additional disclosures may be necessary in situations where:

- The subsidiary is dependent on the financial support of the parent and receives interest-free long-term loans.
- The subsidiary supplies the majority of its output to the parent or fellow subsidiaries at cost.
- The subsidiary acts as a disclosed or undisclosed agent of the parent.
- The subsidiary is a captive insurance entity for the group.
- The subsidiary is a finance entity that operates the group treasury function.
- The subsidiary is the property holding entity of the group.

Such disclosures would indicate the nature of the related party relationship by identifying the specific function that the subsidiary performs, by indicating the terms on which the subsidiary trades with the rest of the group or by disclosing the nature of the financial arrangements (including support arrangements) with the parent. The list above is not exhaustive and other disclosures may be necessary to describe additional features of the parent/subsidiary relationship.

Parent and ultimate controlling party

A29.102 An entity must disclose the name of its parent and, if different, the name of the ultimate controlling party. If neither the parent nor the ultimate controlling party produces consolidated financial statements available for public use, the name of the next most senior parent that does so must also be disclosed. [IAS 24 (revised) para 13]. This will be the first parent in the group above the immediate parent that produces consolidated financial statements available for public use. [IAS 24 (revised) para 16]. In addition, IAS 1 requires disclosure of the ultimate parent entity. [IAS 1 para 138(c)].

A29.103 The standard notes that related party relationships need to be disclosed where control exists, irrespective of whether there have been transactions between the parties. This is so that users may form a view about the effects of related party relationships on an entity. [IAS 24 (revised) para 14].

A29.104 In addition to the above requirements in IAS 24 (revised), there is a requirement in paragraph 138(c) of IAS 1, 'Presentation of financial statements', to disclose the name of the parent and the group's ultimate parent. In many cases, this disclosure will be the same as the IAS 24 (revised) disclosure, but will differ in situations where the ultimate controlling party is not an entity. The disclosure requirements are illustrated in the following example.

Example – Disclosure where the ultimate controlling party is not an entity

Entity XYZ Limited directly owns 100% of the shares of entity C and the ultimate controlling party of entity C is Mr A. Entity XYZ Limited does not publish financial statements available for public use.

Entity K is the immediate parent of XYZ Limited. Entity L is the immediate parent of entity K. Both entities K and L produce consolidated financial statements filed with the local stock exchange.

The following diagram shows the structure of the group:

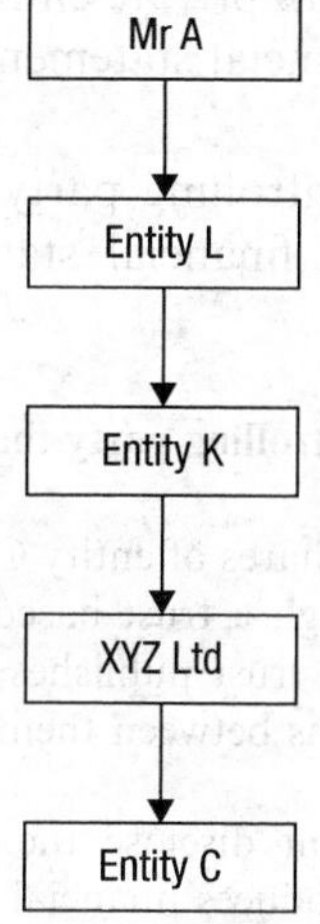

Which controlling parties need to be disclosed by entity C?

Entity C must disclose the name of XYZ Limited as the direct parent and Mr A as the ultimate controlling party, irrespective of whether there were transactions between them during the year. [IAS 24 (revised) para 13].

Entity K is also disclosed as the next most senior parent that produces consolidated financial statements available for public use. The next most senior parent is the first parent in the group above the immediate parent that produces consolidated financial statements available for public use. [IAS 24 (revised) para 16].

In addition to the above IAS 24 (revised) requirements, entity L must be disclosed as the ultimate parent entity of entity C, if this information is not disclosed elsewhere in the information published with the financial statements. [IAS 1 para 138(c)].

UK.A29.104.1 In the UK, disclosure of the name of the company regarded by the directors as the ultimate parent company is, in any event, required by Schedule 4 to SI 2008/410 and Schedule 2 to SI 2008/409. If the party disclosed as the ultimate parent company is also the ultimate controlling party, this should be made clear for the purposes of IAS 24 (revised). In addition, the same schedules require disclosure of the names of the parents of the largest and smallest groups in which the company is included in group financial statements.

A29.105 Whilst the term 'parent' relates to an entity, the term 'ultimate controlling party' could relate to a person, partnership or other entity. Alternatively, it could be a group of persons or entities acting together (see from para A29.110 below) if the persons or entities, although each with small shareholdings, actively co-operate to control the entity.

A29.106 Where the ultimate parent entity is, itself, controlled by, say, a person or a trust, the ultimate controlling party would be that person or trust. As a result, where a reporting entity is owned by, say, a US private entity, the name of any controlling shareholder of the US private entity will need to be given, even if not disclosed in the US entity's financial statements.

A29.107 Disclosure of the controlling party is required, regardless of whether the controlling party prepares financial statements. This is illustrated in the following example.

Example – Disclosure of a controlling party that does not prepare financial statements

Entity B directly owns 100% shares of entity C. Entity C's ultimate parent is entity A. Mr X controls entity A through a trust based in the British Virgin Islands. Neither entity B nor entity A nor the trust publishes financial statements. During the year, there have been no transactions between them and entity C.

Should entity C's management disclose the name of its parent and the ultimate controlling party if neither produces financial statements available for public use?

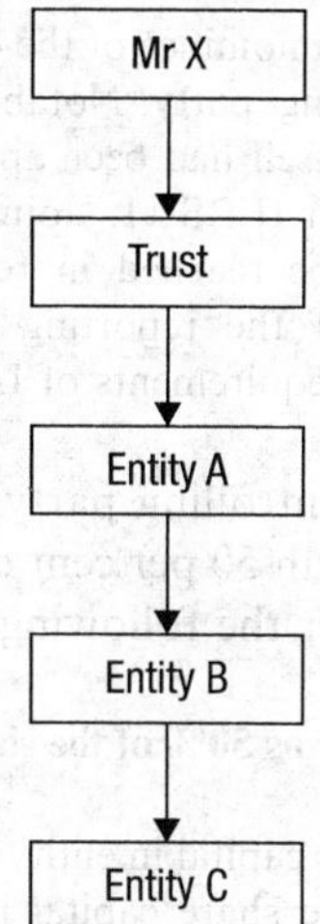

Yes. Entity C is obliged to disclose the name of entity B as the direct parent and Mr X as the ultimate controlling party, even if neither produces financial statements available for public use. [IAS 24 (revised) para 13]. The disclosure should be made irrespective of whether there were transactions between them during the year.

Entity C would also be required to disclose entity A as the ultimate parent entity. [IAS 1 para 138(c)].

A29.107.1 Where control is shared in the form of a joint venture, the question arises as to whether the venturers should be disclosed as a controlling party under IAS 24 (revised). This is considered in the following example.

Example – Controlling parties and joint control

An entity is owned 50% by one entity and 50% by another. It is a joint venture under the definition in IAS 31. Should the two venturers be treated as the controlling party, thus requiring them to be disclosed as such under IAS 24 (revised)?

IAS 24 (revised) does not deal with entities or persons working together to exercise joint control. Paragraph 11(b) of IAS 24 (revised) states that two venturers are not necessarily related parties simply because they share joint control over a joint venture.

If the venturers were acting together, however, and despite the lack of explicit reference to this situation in IAS 24 (revised), there would be a requirement to give disclosure, because of the general requirement in paragraph 13 of IAS 24 (revised) for disclosure of the ultimate controlling party. Paragraph 13 does not specifically limit disclosure to situations where the controlling party is a single person or entity.

In practice such a situation would be unusual and might indicate that one of the parties was in fact acting as a nominee for the other in order to disguise the fact that the other party actually had control. Paragraph 10 of IAS 24 (revised) requires that in considering each possible related party relationship attention should be directed to the substance of the relationship and not merely its legal form. If the substance was that one of the parties was in fact a nominee of the other, then only that other party would be disclosed as the controlling party. Notably, this might also call into question whether the reporting entity itself had been appropriately classified as a joint venture for the purposes of IAS 31 (or IFRS 11, 'Joint arrangements'). It would be expected that consistent conclusions be reached in relation to the control structure when considering the treatment of the reporting entity in the financial statements of investors and the disclosure requirements of IAS 24 (revised).

A29.108 Disclosure of the controlling party can be more complicated where a person indirectly owns more than 50 per cent of an entity's share capital, but does not control the entity. Consider the following example.

Example – Person indirectly owns 50% of the share capital but does not control an entity

Mr A owns 100% of the share capital in entity I and 20% of the share capital in entity P. The remaining 80% of the share capital in entity P is owned by 200 unrelated investors, who do not have a contractual arrangement to act together (see further from para A29.110).

Entities I and P own 49% and 51% respectively of the share capital in entity S. Assume one percentage shareholding constitutes one voting right and all investors of entity P are required to cast their votes for decisions relating to entity S.

The following diagram shows the structure of the group:

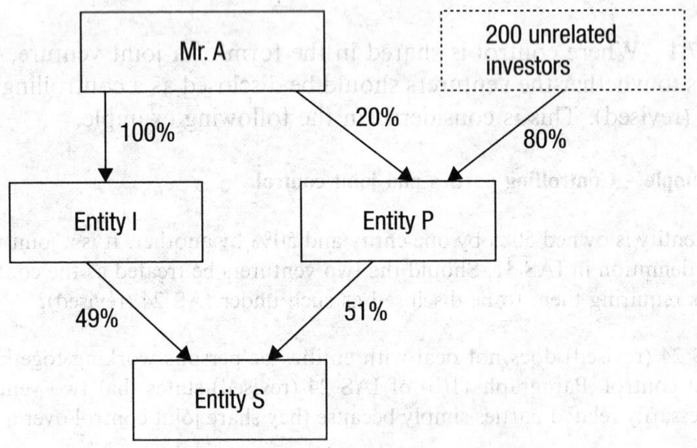

Should Mr A be disclosed as the ultimate controlling party?

Entity S's management should disclose entity P as the parent in entity S's financial statements, irrespective of whether there were transactions between them during the year. [IAS 24 (revised) para 13]. Entity P is also the ultimate controlling party of entity S, even though Mr A indirectly owns 59.2% ((100% × 49%) + (20% × 51%)) of the share capital in entity S.

Mr A is not the ultimate controlling party of entity S, because he is unable to exercise control over entity S. He does not control entity S's parent, entity P. He controls entity I, but entity I only has significant influence, as opposed to control, over entity S.

Mr A is still a related party of entity S, because his 100% interest in entity I gives him significant influence over entity S. In addition, he has significant influence over entity P which, in turn, controls entity S. If transactions have occurred between Mr A and entity S, the transactions should be disclosed as related party transactions in entity S's financial statements.

A29.109 Examples of disclosure of the name of a parent entity and ultimate controlling party are given in Table A29.2 and Table A29.3.

Table A29.2 – Disclosure of parent and ultimate controlling party

Associated British Foods Plc – Annual report – 18 September 2010

28. Related parties

The group has a controlling related party relationship with its parent company, which is also its ultimate parent company (see note 29). The group also has a related party relationship with its associates and joint ventures (see note 29) and with its directors. In the course of normal operations, related party transactions entered into by the group have been contracted on an arm's length basis.

Material transactions and year end balances with related parties were as follows:

	Sub note	2010 £000	2009 £000
Charges to Wittington Investments Limited in respect of services provided by the Company and its subsidiary undertakings		**240**	201
Dividends paid by ABF and received in a beneficial capacity by:			
(i) trustees of the Garfield Weston Foundation	1	**6,447**	6,142
(ii) directors of Wittington Investments Limited who are not trustees of the Foundation		**858**	806
(iii) directors of the Company who are not trustees of the Foundation and are not directors of Wittington Investments Limited	2	**7**	12
(iv) a member of the Weston family employed within the ABF group	3	**634**	596
Sales to fellow subsidiary undertakings on normal trading terms	4	**3,296**	2,246
Sales to a company with common key management personnel	5	**5,439**	4,448
Amounts due from fellow subsidiary undertakings on normal trading terms	4	**243**	193
Amounts due from a company with common key management personnel	5	**588**	508
Sales to joint ventures and associates on normal trading terms	6	**191,239**	328,915
Purchases from joint ventures and associates on normal trading terms	6	**264,225**	221,774
Amounts due from joint ventures and associates	6	**153,364**	95,068
Amounts due to joint ventures and associates	6	**23,092**	23,321

1. The Garfield Weston Foundation ('the Foundation') is an English charitable trust, established in 1958 by the late W Garfield Weston. The Foundation has no direct interest in the Company, but as at 18 September 2010 was the beneficial owner of 683,073 shares (2009 – 683,073 shares) in Wittington Investments Limited representing 79.2% (2009 – 79.2%) of that company's issued share capital and is, therefore, the Company's ultimate controlling party. At 18 September 2010 trustees of the Foundation comprised two children and two

grandchildren of the late W Garfield Weston and five children of the late Garry H Weston.
2. Details of the directors are given on pages 32 and 33. Their interests, including family interests, in the Company and its subsidiary undertakings are given on page 50. Key management personnel are considered to be the directors, and their remuneration is disclosed within the Remuneration report on page 48.
3. A member of the Weston family who is employed by the group and is not a director of the Company or Wittington Investments Limited and is not a trustee of the Foundation.
4. The fellow subsidiary undertaking is Fortnum and Mason plc.
5. The company with common key management personnel is George Weston Limited, in Canada.
6. Details of the group's principal joint ventures and associates are set out in note 29.
7. In 2009, sales were made by ACH to Stratas Foods under the transitional supply agreement entered into on creation of the joint venture. This agreement came to an end in February 2010.

Amounts due from joint ventures and associates comprise £20m (2009 – £19m) of finance lease receivables due from a joint venture (see note 14) and £126m (2009 – £50m) of loan receivables due from joint ventures. The remainder of the balance is trading balances. The loan receivables are all non-current, and all but £2m (2009 – £1m) of the finance lease receivables are non-current.

29. Group entities (extract)

Control of the group

The largest group in which the results of the Company are consolidated is that headed by Wittington Investments Limited, the accounts of which are available at Companies House, Crown Way, Cardiff CF14 3UZ. It is the ultimate holding company, is incorporated in Great Britain and is registered in England.

At 18 September 2010 Wittington Investments Limited together with its subsidiary, Howard Investments Limited, held 431,515,108 ordinary shares (2009 – 431,515,108) representing in aggregate 54.5% (2009 – 54.5%) of the total issued ordinary share capital of Associated British Foods plc.

Table A29.3 – Controlling party and ultimate controlling parties with joint control of parent

Imerys SA – Report and accounts – 31 December 2010

29 – Related parties (extract)

The related parties of Imerys are the Canadian group Power and the Belgian group Frère-CNP. These groups are the ultimate controlling parties of Imerys. Through their joint venture Parjointco, they exercise joint control on the Swiss group Pargesa that controls Imerys through a direct investment and an indirect investment in the Belgian group GBL; in this respect, Pargesa is a related party. The GBL group is a related party as it exercises a direct significant influence on Imerys. Imerys is not a party to any contract with its external related parties.

Joint control and significant influence exercised by groups of persons

A29.110 As noted in paragraph A29.105 above, the term 'ultimate controlling party' could relate to a group of persons acting together if the persons actively co-operated to control the entity. While rarely seen in some jurisdictions, this practice is seen, for example, in the UK.

A29.111 While IAS 24 (revised) provides no guidance on this point, guidance may be taken from paragraph 2 of Appendix B of IFRS 3, 'Business combinations', which states that *"a group of individuals shall be regarded as controlling an entity when, as a result of contractual arrangements, they collectively have the power to govern its financial and operating policies so as to obtain benefits from its activities"*. Thus, if two or more persons are contractually obliged to act together and by doing so in substance have control over the reporting entity, we consider that these persons are related parties of the reporting entity under paragraphs 9(a)(i) and 10 of IAS 24 (revised).

A29.112 The key consideration, particularly given the lack of guidance in the standard in this area, is substance. As noted in paragraph A29.77, paragraph 10 of IAS 24 (revised) states that *"in considering each possible related party relationship, attention is directed to the substance of the relationship and not merely the legal form"*. Therefore, each arrangement, should be assessed to determine the substance of relationships.

A29.113 It will also be necessary to consider local regulatory requirements as, even where no related party relationship exists in substance, regulation in some jurisdictions may mean that disclosure is still required. If the disclosure is only required by local legislation and not because a related party relationship exists, the disclosure should be clearly marked as separate to IAS 24 (revised)'s related party disclosures and an explanation for why it is necessary should be provided (for example, the name of the legal requirement should be given).

Table A29.4 – Disclosure of agreement to jointly exercise voting rights

Henkel AG & Co. KGaA – Annual Report and Accounts – 31 December 2010

(47) Information on voting rights/Related party transactions (extract)

The company has been notified that the share of voting rights of the parties to the Henkel share-pooling agreement at October 21, 2010 represents in total 53.21 percent of the voting rights (138,240,804 votes) in Henkel AG & Co. KGaA and is held by

- 111 members of the families of the descendants of Fritz Henkel, the company's founder,
- four foundations set up by members of those families,
- one civil-law partnership set up by members of those families, and
- eight private limited companies set up by members of those families, seven limited partnerships with a limited company as a general partner (GmbH & Co. KG) and one limited partnership (KG)

under the terms of a share-pooling agreement (agreement restricting the transfer of shares) pursuant to Section 22 (2) of the German Securities Trading Act [WpHG], whereby the shares held by the eight private limited companies, the seven limited partnerships with a limited company as a general partner and the one limited partnership representing a total of 14.02 percent (36,419,097 voting rights) are attributed (pursuant to Section 22 (1) no. 1 WpHG) to the family members who control those companies.

UK.A29.113.1 The Companies Act 2006 deals with similar arrangements in the context of interests in shares. Under section 825(1) of the 2006 Act, each party to an agreement is deemed to be interested in all the shares held by the other parties to the agreement. 'Agreement' includes undertakings, expectations or understandings operative under any arrangement. Existence of such an agreement in relation to a UK company would be strong evidence that the parties are in substance acting as one and that if they held sufficient voting rights to give them control or significant influence, they should be treated as a related party of the entity under IAS 24 (revised).

A29.114 The principle that a contractual arrangement between persons may result in them controlling the reporting entity may also be extended to situations where parties are contractually obliged to act together and by doing so in substance have joint control or significant influence over the reporting entity. In such a situation, we consider that the parties would be related parties of the reporting entity under paragraph 9(a)(i) and (ii) of the related party definition and paragraph 10 of IAS 24 (revised).

[The next paragraph is A29.116.]

A29.116 When considering whether or not a small group of shareholders is operating together such that joint control or significant influence exists, the specific circumstances need to be carefully examined. For example, the shares in an entity might be held by two (or three or four) brothers, or by two or more parties in a normal joint venture. In the absence of a contractual arrangement, the fact that they co-operate or vote the same way would not, in itself, make them related parties. They would just be shareholders working in the normal way for their collective benefit. A related party relationship will exist, however, where a contractual arrangement is in place, as illustrated in the following example.

Example – Persons together having joint control

Should a group of persons be disclosed as the ultimate controlling party when they have a contractual arrangement to act together?

Mr A, Mr B and Mr C have direct interests of 40%, 10% and 10% respectively, of trust T. The interest in the remaining 40% of trust T is held by 20 unrelated investors.

Mr A, Mr B and Mr C wish to control the trust and enter into a contractual arrangement to act together. In this situation, assume that a one per cent interest constitutes one voting right.

Entity S is a wholly-owned subsidiary of entity P. Entity P is wholly-owned by trust T.

The following diagram shows the structure of the group:

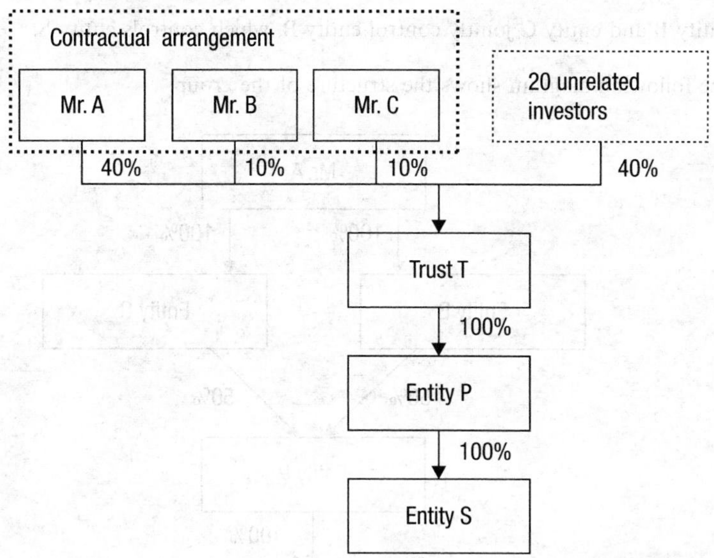

Entity S's management should disclose Mr A, Mr B and Mr C as the ultimate controlling party (as a group) of entity S when they have a contractual arrangement to act together, irrespective of whether there were transactions between them and entity S during the year. [IAS 24 (revised) para 13].

The agreement between Mr A, Mr B and Mr C provides them with a collective control over 60% (40% + 10% + 10%) of trust T's voting rights. Mr A, Mr B and Mr C form a group that controls trust T, which controls entities P and S.

In addition, trust T should be disclosed as the ultimate parent entity of entity S in the notes to the financial statements if this information is not disclosed elsewhere in information published with the financial statements. [IAS 1 para 138(c)].

If the contractual arrangement to act together did not exist, trust T would be the ultimate controlling party of entity S and only Mr A would be a related party of entity S. Mr A is related to entity S, because his 40% interest in trust T gives him significant influence over entity S. [IAS 24 (revised) para 9(a)(ii)].

[The next paragraph is A29.119.]

A29.119 Where investors in a joint venture act as intermediaries for an ultimate controlling party, then that party will be required to be disclosed, as shown in the following example.

Example – Ultimate control is exercised through a joint venture

Who should be disclosed as the ultimate controlling party when there is a joint venture whose investors act as intermediaries?

Mr A owns shares that entitle him to 100% of the voting rights in entity B and entity C.

Entity B and entity C jointly control entity P, which controls entity S.

The following diagram shows the structure of the group:

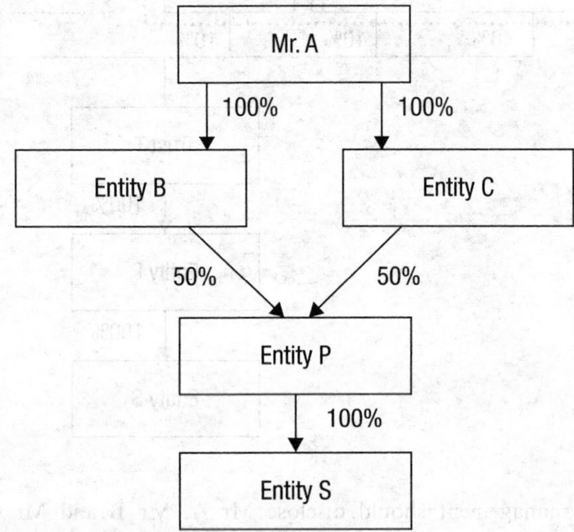

Entity S's management should disclose Mr A as the ultimate controlling party of entity S, irrespective of whether there were transactions between them during the year. [IAS 24 (revised) para 13].

Mr A controls entities B and C, which jointly control entities P and S. Entities B and C form a group which will vote according to Mr A's instruction.

Control by trusts

A29.120 In some cases, the disclosure requirements of IAS 1 regarding the parent entity or the group's ultimate parent are not applicable. This can happen for example, because the entity is directly controlled by, say, a person or a trust (rather than being owned by a parent entity as part of a group). In these situations, disclosure of the identity of the controlling party is still required by IAS 24 (revised). Where the controlling party is a trust, it will be necessary to consider whether the trust itself is controlled by a person or persons who will, therefore, need to be disclosed as the ultimate controlling party (see also para A29.107).

A29.121 The definition of control comprises two elements:

- the power to govern the financial and operating policies of an entity; and
- the ability to benefit from its activities.

[IAS 24 (revised) para 9].

Consequently, the question of establishing whether control exists is particularly difficult in relation to trusts. Trusteeship may be viewed as an example of where the two aspects of control are divided between two parties. The trustee has the power to deploy the trust assets: the beneficiary benefits from their deployment. In what may be called a pure trust, neither the trustee nor the beneficiary controls the trust. Not all vehicles created in the legal form of a trust will fall into the category of a pure trust and the rights and duties of the trustees and beneficiaries may be divided differently where the trust is not a pure trust. In fact, SIC 12, 'Consolidation – Special purpose entities', envisages situations where special purpose entities (SPEs) may take the form of trusts and where the decision-making powers of trustees are so limited that they operate on 'autopilot' (the term used in SIC 12). [SIC 12 para 1]. The interpretation notes that in such circumstances, control may exist for the sponsoring party or others with a beneficial interest, even though it may be particularly difficult to assess. It notes that the pre-determination of the activities of the SPE often provides evidence that the ability to control has been exercised by the party making the pre-determination for its own benefit at the formation of the SPE. [SIC 12 para 14]. In a pure trust, however, it is possible to argue that there is no controlling party of the trust, because neither the trustees nor the beneficiary have both elements of control. The question of whether or not control exists over a trust is one that will need particular care and scrutiny of the facts of each individual case.

A29.121.1 Similarly, IFRS 10, 'Consolidated financial statements', which supersedes SIC 12 for annual periods beginning on or after 1 January 2013 (early adoption permitted), recognises that in some circumstances an investee may be designed so that voting rights are not the dominant factor in deciding who controls the investee, such as when any voting rights relate to administrative tasks only and the relevant activities are directed by means of contractual arrangements. In such cases, the investor will need to assess those contractual arrangements to determine whether it has rights sufficient to give it power over the investee.

A29.122 Consequently, because of the above argument, where a 'pure trust' holds shares in the reporting entity it would follow that, other than disclosure of the trust as the controlling party, there would be no further requirement to disclose an ultimate controlling party.

A29.123 However, many trusts may not be set up along the lines of a 'pure trust'. In these circumstances, there are difficulties in determining whether the trustees or any outside parties have control over the reporting entity through the trust for the purposes of establishing its ultimate controlling party. In the case of some trusts, trustees may be acting on occasions in accordance with the wishes of the settlor, the beneficiaries or the entity's management. In others, the settlor may have the power to appoint or remove trustees in certain circumstances, or the trustees may need to refer to the settlor before doing certain things. If these matters do not interfere with the general independence of the trustees, it may not be necessary to regard the existence of those rights as giving the settlor (or any other party, as the case may be) control over the trustees, or the trust, in the sense that control (as opposed to influence) is used in the standard. Alternatively, there may be no evidence of the trustees having given independent consideration to matters relevant to the reporting entity in the light of independent advice. These circumstances may point to trustees allowing outside parties, such as settlors or beneficiaries, in a position to do so, to exercise unrestricted control. If they do exercise control, such parties would then need to be disclosed as the ultimate controlling party of the reporting entity.

A29.124 It would seem from the above that the following reasoning can be applied to ascertaining the party, if any, to be disclosed as the controlling party of a trust for the purposes of IAS 24 (revised). That is, the controlling party is likely to be the party that both:

- has the ability to direct the trust or to limit its powers (by pre-determination or otherwise), so as to ensure the implementation of its wishes concerning the trust's financial and operating policies; and
- derives the principal economic benefit, whether or not that party is a named beneficiary under the trust.

A29.125 Where a party controls a trust that holds shares in the reporting entity, that party will need to be disclosed as the ultimate controlling party (see the example below). The purpose for which a trust is established may, therefore, often indicate who the ultimate controlling party is, or whether there is one at all. For instance, where the reporting entity is a special purpose entity and a trust is established as a parent undertaking of the reporting entity as part of a securitisation, this will indicate that the trust and the reporting entity are probably controlled by one or other party to the securitisation.

Example – A trust as the ultimate controlling party

Entity B is controlled by Trust T.

Mr A has a direct interest in 100% of trust T and controls the trust. Trust T has signed an agreement with Mr A that prevents the trust from disclosing publicly the particulars of its controlling party, Mr A.

Who should entity B disclose as its controlling party, given trust T has signed an agreement prohibiting it from disclosing its relationship with Mr A?

Entity B's management should disclose Mr A as the controlling party of entity B, irrespective of whether there were transactions between them during the year. [IAS 24 (revised) para 13].

A legal agreement does not negate the requirement to disclose the controlling party. This is the case regardless of whether the agreement is between trust T and Mr A or between trust T and entity B. The financial statements should not be described as complying with IFRS, unless they comply with all the requirements of IFRS. [IAS 1 para 16].

The same principle applies to the disclosure of ultimate parent entity. The name of the ultimate parent entity should also be disclosed if it is not disclosed elsewhere in information published with the financial statements. [IAS 1 para 138(c)].

A29.126 Another complex situation would be where a director or other related party is a trustee of a trust that holds shares in the reporting entity (and the director or related party controls the trust). In such a situation, the shares held by the trust should be added to those held directly by the director for the purpose of establishing where control lies. Where a director or other related party – such as an adult or a minor child – is a beneficiary, but not a trustee, of a trust it would appear to be a question of establishing, on the facts of each case, whether the trustees administer the trust independently or whether the director or another related party controls it.

A29.127 An example that considers the implications for related party disclosures of a director's relationship with a trust is included in paragraph A29.62.

Partnerships

A29.128 Where a partnership in the form of a managed fund controls over 50 per cent of the shares with voting rights in a reporting entity, the question arises as to who controls the reporting entity. The partnership holds the majority of the voting rights in the reporting entity and would control it. One particular partner might be the reporting entity's controlling party, particularly where this partner has control over the management of the partnership and where it has a substantial partnership interest as well. However, this partner may, itself, have a parent undertaking or ultimate controlling party, which it discloses in its financial statements. This would mean that the reporting entity would have to disclose that party as its ultimate controlling party.

UK.A29.128.1 In the UK, such a situation commonly occurs where a general partner acts as manager of a limited partnership.

Key management personnel compensation

A29.129 A member of the key management personnel of an entity or its parent is a related party of the entity. The first step in the process of preparing the disclosure of key management personnel compensation is identifying the reporting entity's 'key management personnel'. The identification of key management personnel is dealt with from paragraph A29.30 above. This section considers the disclosure requirements for key management personnel compensation. Other transactions with key management personnel are considered from paragraph A29.195.

A29.130 Paragraph 17 of IAS 24 (revised) requires disclosure of key management personnel compensation in aggregate and for each of five specified categories (see para A29.134 below). The standard does not specifically state that the details of compensation should be given by individual director. As the amounts payable to individual directors are similar in nature it would appear, therefore, that details of compensation may normally be given in aggregate for directors and other key management personnel (see para A29.175 below).

A29.131 Paragraph 18 of IAS 24 (revised) requires disclosure of information about the transactions between related parties and any outstanding balances, including commitments (see para A29.158). The paragraph 18 disclosure requirements are in addition to the requirements in paragraph 17 to disclose key management personnel compensation. The paragraph 18 disclosure applies to all related party transactions and so, in principle, it applies to key management personnel compensation – although in some cases the requirement will be covered by the disclosure given under paragraph 17. However, where, for example, key managers are entitled to a bonus, but this is not payable until after the year end, then this would be an outstanding balance and would be disclosable under paragraph 18, in addition to the paragraph 17 disclosure.

A29.132 Although aggregation of compensation for key management personnel is generally appropriate, it may be necessary, under the general disclosure requirements in paragraph 18 of IAS 24 (revised), to disclose persons' compensation or elements of compensation where they are not similar in nature to other compensation. If, for example, a director is awarded a special bonus or special terms to accept office, such items may require separate disclosure.

Example – One-off elements of compensation

An entity discloses total compensation for key management personnel of C2,500,000 in the year. This is C500,000 higher than the remuneration for the same key management personnel in the previous year. The difference is a special bonus of C250,000 each paid to two members of key management personnel in respect of the disposal of a major subsidiary. In these circumstances the bonuses may need to be separately disclosed, because they are relevant to a user's understanding of the financial statements. It would not be necessary to separately identify the directors but it would be appropriate to include some disclosure specifying that two members of key management personnel received a special bonus on the disposal of a subsidiary.

A29.133 IAS 24 (revised) explains that compensation includes all employee benefits as defined in IAS 19, 'Employee benefits', and includes employee benefits to which IFRS 2, 'Share-based payment', applies. [IAS 24 (revised) para 9]. It includes all forms of compensation paid, payable or provided (for example, through benefits in kind) by the entity, or on its behalf, in return for services rendered to the entity. Also included is any such compensation paid on behalf of the entity's parent in respect of the entity. These requirements are illustrated in the following example and in the example in paragraph A29.143 below.

Example – Compensation paid by a parent entity

Entity S is a subsidiary of its parent, entity P. Entity S pays its key management personnel C100,000 in respect of their services to the entity. Entity S's key management personnel also receive bonuses that are paid by the parent in respect of their services to entity S. A group-wide employee share option scheme also grants options to key management personnel of the subsidiary and pension benefits are accrued in respect of such management through a group-wide pension scheme.

The remuneration paid directly by entity S forms part of the amounts to be disclosed by entity S. Each of the other amounts is also included because they are either paid by the parent in respect of services to entity S or provided on behalf of entity S or paid on behalf of the parent in respect of entity S.

Further guidance on disclosure of key management personnel compensation in a group situation is given from paragraph A29.147.

A29.134 The disclosure of compensation should be given in total and for each of the following categories:

- *Short-term employee benefits*. These include wages, salaries and social security contributions; holiday pay and sick pay; profit-sharing and bonuses payable within 12 months of the end of the period; and non-monetary benefits. Non-monetary benefits include medical care, housing, cars and free or subsidised goods and services.
- *Post-employment benefits*. These include pensions, other retirement rights, life insurance and medical care after employment ceases (see further para A29.140).
- *Other long-term benefits*. These include long-service or sabbatical leave or other long-service benefits, long-term disability benefits, profit-sharing, bonuses and deferred compensation not payable wholly within 12 months of the end of the period (see further para A29.141).
- *Termination benefits*. These include compensation for loss of office, ex-gratia payments, redundancy payments, enhanced retirement benefits and any related benefits-in-kind connected with a person leaving office or employment.
- *Share-based payment*. This includes share options and other grants of shares in respect of services to the entity (see further para A29.142).

[IAS 24 (revised) paras 17, 9].

UK.A29.134.1 The requirements in UK companies legislation to disclose aggregate directors' emoluments and for quoted companies to prepare directors' remuneration reports apply for companies reporting under IFRS. The requirements of IAS 24 (revised) set out above are unlikely to be met by disclosure of directors' remuneration in compliance with UK companies legislation. This is considered further from paragraph UK.A29.146.1.

A29.135 IAS 24 (revised) gives no further guidance regarding the amounts that should be included within each category. For certain types of key management personnel compensation (for example, short-term employee benefits payable in cash and termination benefits), we consider that the standard is clear and there should be no ambiguity over the amounts requiring disclosure.

A29.136 For some types of short-term employee benefits, where it is not clear what the cost of the benefit is, the disclosure will be more complicated, as illustrated in the example below.

Example – Benefits in kind

Mr A is a member of key management personnel of an entity. As part of his employment package, he has the benefit of staying in a residential property owned by the entity. The entity bought the residential property 30 years ago at a low price. The property is carried at cost and is still being depreciated. The value of the property has since increased significantly. The market rental of a similar property is also significantly higher than the depreciation charge on this property.

How should the housing benefits given to Mr A be disclosed?

The housing benefit is part of the compensation provided to Mr A. However, the amount of depreciation charge should not be included in the amount of short-term employee benefits compensation disclosed under paragraph 17(a) of IAS 24 (revised). Depreciation does not meet the definition of employee benefits compensation. Depreciation is also outside the scope of IAS 19, 'Employee benefits'.

Paragraph 18 of IAS 24 (revised) requires additional disclosure where necessary for users to understand the potential effect of the relationship on the financial statements. In this situation, it may be appropriate to disclose details such as the market rental of a similar property in narrative information below the key management personnel compensation table if the information is necessary for an understanding of the potential effect of the relationship on the financial statements. [IAS 24 (revised) para 18].

A29.137 Another benefit in kind frequently granted as key management personnel compensation is the use of a company car. Such cars may be leased or owned by the entity. If an entity owns the vehicle, there will be no cash cost to the business on an ongoing basis. Consistent with the example above, we do not consider it appropriate to include the depreciation charge on the car in the amount of short-term benefits compensation. It would be appropriate to show an estimation of the benefit to the employee in some narrative disclosure. This might, for example, be calculated with reference to the amount that the employee would have to pay to lease a similar vehicle. Care should be exercised if management are considering disclosing the taxable benefit in the narrative as being the benefit to the employee. In many jurisdictions, the taxable benefit may not be equal to the actual value of the benefit the employee is receiving. Alternatively, if the car is leased by the business, there will be a cash cost to the business. We consider that this cash cost should be included in the numerical information as a short-term benefit to the employee.

A29.138 For other types of key management personnel compensation (for example, post-employment benefits and share-based payment), the requirements are less clear. We consider that, for these categories, the principle underlying the standard is to disclose the cost of remunerating an entity's key management personnel for their services during the period covered by the financial statements. This would include the cost to the entity itself and any costs borne by other entities on its behalf (see para A29.144).

A29.139 For defined contribution post-employment benefit schemes, we consider that the most appropriate disclosure is of the aggregate contributions payable in the period by the entity to schemes for members of key management personnel.

A29.140 For defined benefit schemes, we consider that the most appropriate disclosure is of the total cost of the defined benefit scheme (including recognised actuarial gains and losses) calculated in accordance with IAS 19, 'Employee benefits', in respect of key management personnel. Where a defined benefit pension scheme is not operated solely for key management personnel, for example, an entity-wide scheme in which members of key management personnel participate, calculation of the total recognised cost in respect of key management personnel may not be practicable. Under these circumstances, we consider that disclosure of the current service cost attributable to key management personnel (calculated in line with IAS 19), is an acceptable alternative. There is also an argument for disclosing the value of benefits accrued in the scheme that could be transferred into another pension scheme (net of management's contributions), that is a net 'transfer value', where this information is available.

A29.141 For other long-term employee benefits that are accounted for in accordance with IAS 19, we consider that, like post-employment defined benefits, the most appropriate amount to be included in the disclosure of key management personnel compensation is the total cost (including advanced gains and losses) of the scheme (if the scheme is solely for key management personnel) or the relevant IAS 19 current service cost of the persons if the scheme extends beyond key management personnel. This is because it could be a reasonable indicator of the amount earned by the key management personnel in the period.

A29.142 We consider that the most appropriate amount to be disclosed in respect of compensation in the form of share-based payment is the expense in respect of the share-based payments, attributable to key management personnel, recognised by the entity in the period in accordance with IFRS 2, 'Share-based payment'. This is in addition to any additional disclosures that may be required under paragraph 18 of IAS 24 (revised) (details of transactions and outstanding balances – see para A29.158). It is also in addition to the other details that are required by IFRS 2 to be disclosed in respect of total awards in the notes to the financial statements, such as numbers of options granted and exercised in the period and options held at the beginning and end of the period. [IFRS 2 para 45]. IFRS 2 is dealt with in detail in chapter 12.

A29.143 As noted in paragraph A29.133 above, key management personnel compensation includes compensation provided on the entity's behalf for services rendered to the entity. This will apply, for instance, where share-based payment awards are made by an entity's owners.

Example – Share-based payment compensation funded by an entity's owners

Entity A is seeking a listing for its shares on a recognised stock exchange. Entity A's owners have donated shares in the entity to an employee trust and the shares are to be used to satisfy options granted to entity A's key management personnel that vest upon listing as a reward for their efforts in building up the entity's business.

The options should be included in the disclosure of key management personnel compensation under IAS 24 (revised), because the options represent compensation in respect of services provided by management to entity A and the options have been provided by the shareholders on entity A's behalf.

As explained in paragraph A29.142 above, the amount included in the disclosure will be the expense recognised by the entity in respect of the share-based payment.

A29.144 The disclosure of key management personnel compensation includes all forms of consideration paid in exchange for services to the entity. Therefore, disclosure will be required regardless of whether there is a cost to the reporting entity. Where an expense relating to employee service is recognised (for example, for equity-settled share-based payment as in the example in para A29.143 above), this will form the basis of the key management personnel compensation disclosure in line with the general principle in paragraph A29.138. However, where there is no expense in the reporting entity (for example, where cash payments are made by an entity's parent and are not required to be recognised in the entity), disclosure is still required under IAS 24 (revised). This is illustrated in paragraph A29.133 above.

A29.145 In some jurisdictions, it is common for directors to set up an entity to receive their compensation for tax purposes. Compensation paid indirectly to key management personnel would be captured by the requirements of paragraph 17 of IAS 24 (revised). See paragraph A29.57 for details.

A29.146 As noted in paragraph A29.134 above, IAS 24 (revised) also requires the total of the above categories of compensation to be given. This results in a sum that mixes disparate elements of compensation and is, arguably, not really meaningful in view of the differing nature and means of calculating the benefits. For instance, an amount for post-employment benefits has to be aggregated with short-term employee benefits such as salaries. However, it is required by the standard and so a total should be given. We consider that the elements included in the total should be made clear and, where necessary, the basis of calculation. We also consider that the disclosure given by entities should be on a consistent basis from one year to the next and, if it is necessary to change the basis, the reasons for this change should be given.

UK.A29.146.1 IAS 24 (revised)'s requirements are unlikely to be met by disclosure of directors' remuneration in compliance with the Companies Act 2006, either for a quoted company that prepares a directors' remuneration report or an unquoted company that does not. The key reasons for this are:

- Where both the consolidated and the parent's separate financial statements are being prepared in accordance with IFRS, disclosure is required in respect of the group's key management personnel for their services to the group and in respect of the parent's key management personnel for their services to the parent company. The Companies Act disclosures are of the parent company's directors' remuneration for services to the parent company and its subsidiaries, regardless of whether consolidated financial statements are prepared.
- The IAS 24 (revised) disclosure in respect of key management personnel may include persons who are not the company's directors, particularly when the 'entity' is a group preparing consolidated financial statements.
- The IAS 24 (revised) disclosures differ from those required by the Act (see the paragraphs below).

UK.A29.146.2 For UK companies, the extension of the disclosure requirement to include other members of key management personnel should not create many difficulties. However, the structure of the disclosures required by IAS 24 (revised) differs from that required by the Act, so even where the key management personnel of a company consists solely of its directors, separate analyses of their emoluments is usually required to satisfy each requirement.

UK.A29.146.3 Furthermore, under the Companies Act 2006, it is permitted for all directors' remuneration information (other than the aggregate gain on exercise of share options) to be disclosed outside the notes to the financial statements and it is common for companies preparing remuneration reports to include it in those reports. [SI 2008/410 5 Sch 3(6)]. IAS 24 (revised) is, however, specific that the information must be included in the notes to the financial statements.

UK.A29.146.4 The requirements of IAS 24 (revised) are in addition to the disclosure requirements contained in Schedule 5 and (for quoted companies) Schedule 8 of SI 2008/410, the 'Large and Medium-sized Companies and Groups (Accounts and Reports) Regulations 2008'. The Act's disclosure requirements are extensive and detailed and are not described here, but are dealt with in full in chapter 5 of the Manual of Accounting – Narrative Reporting.

UK.A29.146.5 Schedule 5 to the SI 2008/410 requires disclosure of 'aggregate remuneration paid to or receivable by directors for qualifying services'. [SI 2008/410 5 Sch 1(1)(a)]. This differs from the short-term employee benefits in the first bullet point in paragraph A29.134 in that IAS 24 (revised) requires social security contributions (in the UK, employers' national insurance contributions) to be included. Further, the Act does not rigidly divide bonuses between amounts *payable* within a year of the period end and amounts payable thereafter as the IAS 24 (revised) definitions do, but rather divides them by reference to the *period of service to which they relate*. That is, the Act divides them between the amounts payable in respect of the year and amounts not payable specifically in respect of the year.

UK.A29.146.6 For defined contribution (money purchase) schemes, Schedule 5 of SI 2008/410 requires disclosure of the aggregate contributions paid (or treated as paid) by the company to schemes for directors, which is consistent with the requirement of IAS 24 (revised). For defined benefit schemes, quoted companies have to disclose under Schedule 8 of SI 2008/410 the change in the accrued pension of each director in the year and the difference between its transfer value at the beginning and end of the year (less directors' contributions). It is arguable that the disclosures required by Schedule 8 of SI 2008/410 are not inconsistent with the requirement of IAS 24 (revised), but the disclosure will need to be extended to cover other members of key management personnel (either individually or in aggregate). Thus, we consider that, for the figure to be disclosed under IAS 24 (revised), there are arguments for the change in the transfer value of the accrued pension (net of key managers' contributions) to be disclosed in place of the total cost or current service cost attributable to key managers (where these are calculated using assumptions that are consistent with those used in the calculation of the IAS 19 accounting). We do not believe that disclosure of the change in the accrued pension alone meets the IAS 24 (revised) requirements, because that figure on its own does not tell the whole story. It does not convey the fact that any increase is payable for a number of years after retirement, so that the benefit is greater than simply the amount of any increase. However, the figure for the change in transfer value of the accrued pension reflects the fact that the change in the accrued pension is payable for a number of years.

UK.A29.146.7 SI 2008/410 requires disclosure of the amount of money and the value of other assets (other than share options) received under long-term incentive schemes. [SI 2008/410 5 Sch 1(1)(c)]. For companies that do not offer any of the other benefits described in the third bullet in paragraph A29.134 above, this is consistent with the disclosure requirement of IAS 24 (revised). However, where, for example, a bonus is payable more than 12 months after the period end, or the company's employees receive any other long-term benefits, there is inconsistency in the disclosure requirements.

UK.A29.146.8 SI 2008/410 also requires disclosure by unquoted companies of the aggregate compensation for loss of office (including benefits-in-kind) payable to directors (quoted companies have to give the information by individual director). [SI 2008/410 5 Sch 2(4); 8 Sch 7(1)(d)]. This is similar to the requirement in IAS 24 (revised) to disclose aggregate termination benefits, but under IAS 24 (revised) the requirement extends to all key management personnel as explained above. In addition, companies that have securities carrying voting rights admitted to trading on a regulated market at the end of their financial year are required to disclose, in their directors' reports, any agreements whereby compensation for loss of office or employment is payable to any directors or employee in the event of a takeover. [SI 2008/410 7 Sch 13(2)(k)]. See further chapter 2 of the Manual of Accounting – Narrative Reporting.

UK.A29.146.9 In respect of share-based payment, there is no present requirement under UK law to quantify the value of share options that are granted to directors. Quoted companies and those listed on AIM are required to disclose the aggregate gains made by directors on the exercise of share options and the amount of assets (including shares) receivable by directors under long-term incentive schemes. Other companies are required to disclose only the number of directors who exercised share options or who became entitled to receive shares under long-term incentive schemes during the period. Quoted companies are, however, required to give extensive disclosure in their remuneration report about the share option schemes and long-term incentive schemes in which the directors participate. See paragraph 29A.142 for the disclosure requirement under IAS 24 (revised).

UK.A29.146.10 SI 2008/410 requires separate disclosure by unquoted companies of aggregate sums paid to third parties in respect of directors' services (quoted companies must give the information by individual director). [SI 2008/410 5 Sch 2(5); SI 2008/410 8 Sch 7(16)]. This is consistent with the requirements of IAS 24 (revised) – see paragraph A29.144 above.

Group situations

A29.147 Common problems arise with the disclosure of key management personnel compensation in a group context. Consider the following examples where a director of a parent entity is also a director of one of its subsidiaries. In all the situations it is assumed that the director is compensated by the parent entity in connection with services to the parent entity. It is also assumed that all the relevant information concerning compensation is available to the reporting entity.

Example 1 – Subsidiary bears cost for services received

The subsidiary pays the director directly in respect of services as a director of the subsidiary, as well as the parent entity compensating the director for his/her services to the parent.

In this situation, the parent entity will need to disclose, within key management personnel compensation in its separate financial statements, the amount paid to the director in respect of services to the parent entity (which is the same as the amount paid by the parent entity). The subsidiary will need to disclose, within key management personnel compensation, the amount paid to the director by the subsidiary, that being the amount earned by the director in respect of services to the subsidiary.

Example 2 – Subsidiary bears cost indirectly via a management charge

The parent entity pays the director directly for his/her services as a director to both the subsidiary and the parent and recharges the subsidiary for the services as a director of the subsidiary.

The amount that needs to be disclosed, within key management personnel compensation, in the parent's separate financial statements is the same as in example 1. The notes to the subsidiary's financial statements must disclose, within key management personnel compensation, the amount receivable by the director for services to the subsidiary, that is, in this situation, the amount recharged by the parent in respect of the director's services.

Example 3 – Subsidiary bears no cost for services received

The parent entity pays the director directly for his/her services as a director to both the subsidiary as well as to the parent, but no recharge is made to the subsidiary.

Again, the amount that needs to be disclosed, within key management personnel compensation, in the parent's separate financial statements is the same as in example 1. The notes to the financial statements of the subsidiary, however, must include details of the compensation paid by the parent entity in respect of the director's services to the subsidiary. An explanation to the effect that the charge for director's compensation has been borne by the parent may be useful, although it is not required. In order to give this disclosure, it will be necessary to apportion the director's compensation between the parent and the subsidiary for disclosure purposes. Management of the entities may apportion it in any way they consider appropriate, although the method of apportionment should usually be consistent over time.

Example 4 – No significant services are received by subsidiary

In some cases, the parent entity may pay the director directly, but the director's role is to represent the parent's interests in the management of the subsidiary.

The director is a member of the subsidiary's key management personnel in accordance with paragraph 9 of IAS 24 (revised). Therefore, it will be necessary to consider the services for which the director is being compensated in order to allocate his/her compensation between that relating to services to the subsidiary and that relating to services to the parent. The substance of such an arrangement may be that, through a presence at board meetings of the subsidiary, the director is primarily performing services to the parent (representing the parent's interests) and not to the subsidiary. Thus, it could be argued that much of the compensation paid by the parent should be included in the disclosure in the parent's separate financial statements. It should be noted that the director will have certain fiduciary duties to the subsidiary and, therefore, some compensation may need to be allocated to the subsidiary even if there is no recharge made between the entities. The amount disclosed in the subsidiary's financial statements should reflect the compensation paid to the director relating to services rendered to the subsidiary.

UK.A29.147.1 In examples 1, 2 and 3 above, the disclosure in the parent's separate financial statements under IAS 24 (revised) differs from that required under UK companies legislation. The requirement in SI 2008/410 is to disclose the aggregate of the amount paid to the director in respect of his services to the parent company and the amount he receives in respect of his services to the subsidiary. [SI 2008/410 5 Sch 15(1); SI 2008/410 8 Sch 17(1)]. This will be the case even if the parent is not preparing consolidated financial statements. The disclosure under SI 2008/410 is dealt with in the section on group situations in chapter 5 of the Manual of Accounting – Narrative Reporting.

A29.148 Practical difficulties may arise in connection with disclosure of compensation in a subsidiary's financial statements where a member of the subsidiary's key management personnel is also:

- key management personnel or an employee of the parent and is paid by the parent; or
- key management personnel of another subsidiary and is paid by that other subsidiary.

A29.149 In such cases, it is often difficult to ascertain the compensation of the director that is paid to or receivable in respect of services to the subsidiary in question. This difficulty may be increased if there is no charge made to the subsidiary by the payer of the compensation. It may also sometimes be aggravated by a desire on the part of either the parent or the subsidiary to limit the amount of disclosure in the subsidiary's financial statements, if, for instance, the parent-appointed director is more highly rewarded than other members of key management personnel.

A29.150 Where there are difficulties in obtaining information, one or more of the steps described below might be taken.

A29.151 If the subsidiary is a party to the key manager's service agreement and that agreement stipulates what is paid in respect of services to the subsidiary, then those elements of the total compensation should be included within the disclosure in the subsidiary's financial statements.

A29.152 If the subsidiary is not a party to the service agreement (possibly because the agreement is with the parent or a fellow subsidiary), the subsidiary or its management should *make reasonable efforts* to obtain the information, for instance by asking the parent or fellow subsidiary for details of the terms of the service agreement, or by obtaining a detailed breakdown of any management charge.

A29.153 If the information needed is not obtainable by any of the above means, it is necessary to make an apportionment. This is relatively simple where the person performs services for only two or maybe three entities. It is less simple if the person is, for example, a director (and, hence, a member of key management personnel) of a large number of different subsidiaries. We suggest that where apportionment is relatively straightforward it may be the best way of determining the compensation to be disclosed in each entity. It should be noted that while an apportionment should be as accurate as possible, it need only be *reasonable*. Hence, situations where it is not possible should be rare.

A29.154 If, in rare circumstances, the necessary information is not available to an entity's management and a reasonable apportionment is not practicable, we consider that the financial statements would not give a true and fair view if no disclosure were made of the facts. Hence, in these circumstances some narrative information is required to ensure that the financial statements do, indeed, give a true and fair view.

A29.155 We suggest that appropriate notes for two situations that may arise where no information is available would be as follows:

Example 1 – Subsidiary cannot separately identify the cost of key management personnel compensation

A recharge is made to the subsidiary by the parent entity or fellow subsidiary, but the management charge includes other costs and the compensation cannot be separately identified.

> *"The above details of key management personnel compensation do not include Mr X's compensation, which is paid by the parent (fellow subsidiary) and recharged to the entity as part of a management charge. This management charge, which in 20XX amounted to C95,000 also includes a recharge of administration costs borne by the parent (fellow subsidiary) on behalf of the entity and it is not possible to identify separately the amount of Mr X's compensation."*

If Mr X was also a member of the key management personnel of the parent, it would be appropriate to disclose that his total compensation is disclosed in the parent's consolidated financial statements.

A29.156 It is envisaged that this situation would be very rare as normally a full breakdown of management charges should be possible.

Example 2 – No reasonable allocation of costs is practicable

The director is also a director of, and carries on work for, a number of other subsidiaries. The director is actively involved in the management of each subsidiary and is paid by the parent, which makes no recharge to the subsidiaries.

> *"Mr X's compensation is paid by the parent, which makes no recharge to the entity. Mr X is a director of the parent and a number of fellow subsidiaries and it is not possible to make a reasonable apportionment of his compensation in respect of each of the subsidiaries. Accordingly, the above details include no compensation in respect of Mr X. His total compensation is included in the aggregate of key management personnel compensation disclosed in the consolidated financial statements of the parent."*

A29.157 It is suggested that, where a similar situation applies but the compensation is paid by a fellow subsidiary, there should normally be a recharge. This is because the situation where a subsidiary pays compensation to other group directors normally only arises where the subsidiary is a group services entity and such an entity would usually recharge for these services. In this type of situation, the note would not be needed, because the appropriate amount to be disclosed should be ascertainable.

Disclosure of transactions and balances

Nature of information to be disclosed

A29.158 IAS 24 (revised) states that if there have been transactions between related parties, an entity should disclose the nature of the related party relationship, together with information about the transactions and outstanding balances. The information should be such as is necessary for an understanding of the potential effect of the relationship on the financial statements. The disclosures are additional to the disclosures referred to above in respect of key management personnel compensation. The information to be disclosed should, as a minimum, include the following:

- The legal, contractual or family relationship between the related parties, for example parent and subsidiary, key management personnel or domestic partner of key management personnel.
- A description of the transaction and balances between the related parties.
- The amount of the transactions.
- The amount of outstanding balances, including commitments, and:
  - the terms and conditions and whether the balances are secured, together with the type of consideration to be given in settlement; and
  - details of any guarantees given or received.
- Provisions against related party balances for doubtful debts and the amount of expense recognised in the period in respect of bad and doubtful debts.

[IAS 24 (revised) para 18].

A29.159 Other than for parent/subsidiary relationships (see from para A29.99), IAS 24 (revised) does not specifically require the disclosure of the names of the related parties. However this disclosure might be necessary, depending on the circumstances, in order to disclose the nature of the related party relationship and to provide an understanding of the potential effect of the relationship on the financial statements.

A29.160 The standard states that the elements of disclosure set out in paragraph A29.158 above represent a minimum. Other relevant facts should be disclosed where this is necessary to enable users to understand the effect of related party transactions or balances. For example, disclosure of the amount of a transaction involving a sale of assets to a related party may be insufficient if the amount is materially different from that obtainable on normal commercial terms. A statement giving an indication that such sales or purchases or other transfers have taken place at amounts materially different from that obtainable on normal commercial terms may then be necessary for an understanding of the financial statements.

A29.161 Where a related party transaction is carried out at market value, judgement will be needed to determine the information necessary for an understanding of the potential effect of the relationship on the financial statements. See the example below.

Example – Property sold at market value

A property is being transferred (for cash) from an entity to an associate at market value. Is the profit that will be made on the transaction an amount that needs to be disclosed under IAS 24 (revised)?

In the related party definition in IAS 24 (revised) paragraph 9(b)(ii), associates and their investors are included within the scope of related party relationships.

Paragraph 21(b) of IAS 24 (revised) states that the types of transactions that may lead to disclosures include *"purchases or sales of property and other assets"*.

Paragraph 18 of IAS 24 (revised) states that if there have been transactions between related parties, an entity should disclose the nature of the related party relationship as well as information about the transactions and outstanding balances necessary for an understanding of the relationship's potential effect on the financial statements.

The transaction price should normally be given, but whether or not the profit needs to be disclosed will depend on judgement as to whether a user would need this information in order to understand the potential effect of the relationship on the financial statements.

A29.162 Disclosure that transactions were carried out on an arm's length basis between related parties should not be made unless such arm's length terms can be substantiated. [IAS 24 (revised) para 23]. The term 'arm's length basis' is generally taken to mean that transactions have been undertaken on terms that could have been obtained in a transaction with an external party, in which each side bargained knowledgeably and freely, unaffected by any relationship between them. See the example below.

Example – Substantiating an arm's length transaction

Entity A earns part of its revenues from sales to related parties. Such sales are made at the same list price that is charged for sales to third parties. The sales are also processed by the same channel, using the same credit terms and other conditions as the sales to third parties.

Can management describe in entity A's financial statements that the sale transactions with related parties are on terms equivalent to those of an arm's length basis?

Under IAS 24 (revised), entities should disclose the fact that related party transactions were made on terms equivalent to those that prevail in arm's length transactions only if such terms can be substantiated. [IAS 24 (revised) para 23].

Entity A's management may state that the sales to related parties are made on terms equivalent to those of an arm's length basis. The fact that sales are made at the same price and terms as the sales to third parties, can be objectively verified and confirmed.

A29.163 The requirement to disclose balances between related parties arises independently of the requirement to disclose details of specific transactions undertaken during the year. For example, a balance may arise from a prior year transaction. If, after what may be an unusually long credit period, a balance due from a related party is written off, that information could be significant for users.

A29.164 Where an entity has provided against a balance owed to it by a related party, disclosure of the gross balance, the amount of the provision and the amount written off/provided in the period should be given. [IAS 24 (revised) para 18 (c)-(d)].

UK.A29.164.1 In addition, a UK company that has securities carrying voting rights admitted to trading on a regulated market at the end of its financial year is required to disclose, in its directors' report, details of any significant agreement (including any with related parties) that would be affected by a takeover of the company. This does not apply to an agreement if disclosure would be seriously prejudicial to the company and there is no other obligation to disclose it. [SI 2008/410 7 Sch 13(2)(k)]. This requirement is considered further in chapter 2 of the Manual of Accounting – Narrative Reporting.

Categories of disclosure

A29.165 The disclosures referred to in paragraphs A29.158 to A29.161 should be made separately in respect of each of the following:

- The parent.
- Entities that have joint control or significant influence over the entity.
- Subsidiaries
- Associates.
- Joint ventures.
- Key management personnel of the entity or of its parent.
- Other related parties.

[IAS 24 (revised) para 19].

A29.166 Whilst not specifically identified as a separate category in paragraph 19 of the standard, we consider that fellow subsidiaries could often be a further category for which separate disclosure should be made.

A29.167 Disclosure in respect of associates and joint ventures is considered in the examples below.

Example 1 – Separate disclosure of balances with associates and joint ventures

An entity shows in its balance sheet a combined figure for amounts owed to equity-accounted joint ventures and to associates. Should these amounts be split between amounts owed to joint ventures and amounts owed to associates?

Yes. Paragraph 19 of IAS 24 (revised) makes it clear that balances between the entity and its joint ventures and between the entity and its associates should be disclosed separately. IAS 24 (revised) explains that the classification of amounts payable to, and receivable from, related parties in the different categories as required in paragraph 19 is an extension of the disclosure requirement in IAS 1 for information to be presented either on the balance sheet or in the notes. The balance sheet categories are extended to provide a more comprehensive analysis of related party balances. [IAS 24 (revised) para 20]. This analysis of related party balances may be given on the face of the balance sheet (if this is relevant to an understanding of the entity's financial position) or in the notes.

Example 2 – Disclosure by a joint venture of balances with its investors

Should a joint venture's trading balances with its two investors be disclosed as amounts owed to group undertakings?

Paragraph 19 of IAS 24 (revised) makes it clear that balances between the entity and venturers, that is, entities with joint control over the entity, should be disclosed. They would not be described as amounts owed to 'group undertakings' as the venturers are not part of the entity's group.

A29.168 As noted in paragraph A29.165 above, paragraph 19 of the standard requires disclosures to be made separately for key management personnel of the entity or its parent. The definition of a related party in IAS 24 (revised) is clearer than the previous standard because it refers to *"key management personnel of the reporting entity or of a parent of the reporting entity"* as opposed to *"key management personnel of the entity or its parent"* under the previous standard, which could be interpreted as key management of only the entity's immediate parent. [IAS 24 (revised) para 9(a)(iii), IAS 24 para 9(d)]. It would be appropriate to provide separate disclosures for key management personnel of the entity or *any* parent of the entity (that is, not only the entity's immediate parent) as this is consistent with IAS 24 (revised)'s definition.

A29.169 Generally, related party transactions and balances will be disclosed in the notes, although major balances may need to be disclosed on the face of the balance sheet if that is necessary for a proper understanding of the financial position. For example, a major intra-group loan might be disclosed on the face of the balance sheet if it is the major source of finance for an entity and the entity is dependent on such support for it to be able to continue its operations.

Aggregation — general

A29.170 Clearly, related party transactions in many cases could be very extensive and in order to avoid excessive detail in the disclosures the standard permits aggregation of transactions and balances in certain circumstances. Aggregation is allowed for items of a similar nature, except when separate disclosure is necessary for an understanding of the effects of related party transactions on the financial statements. [IAS 24 (revised) para 24].

A29.171 Items of a similar nature should not be aggregated if:

- Separate disclosure of an item is required by law.
- Aggregation would obscure the importance of significant transactions. Material transactions should not be hidden or concealed by aggregation with other transactions. For, example the sale of a major item of property, plant and equipment to a related party should not be included in the aggregated disclosures for normal sales of trading inventory to that party, but instead should be separately disclosed.

A29.172 An example of aggregation is that purchases or sales of similar items, such as trading inventory, with other group entities may each be aggregated and described as such in the separate financial statements of a group entity. However, sales cannot be aggregated with purchases because they are not 'items of a similar nature' and, therefore, the netting of such transactions is not permitted.

A29.173 If intra-group transactions comprise different categories of transactions, for instance, purchases or sales of inventory, or purchases or sales of items of property, plant and equipment, individual balances for such categories of transactions will need to be separately disclosed.

A29.174 Where permitted, aggregation may be made by type of related party, provided that disclosure is given for each of the categories listed in paragraph A29.165. Within each of these categories, however the entity may aggregate similar transactions with the entities in that category. Where such aggregation is made, disclosure of the individual names of the related parties in that category would not necessarily be required. The extent of detail to be disclosed will depend on materiality.

Example 1 – Aggregation by counterparty

An entity has six associates and makes sales of goods to those associates. 50% of those sales are to two of the associates. If the amount of the sales is not material to the entity as a whole it may aggregate the sales to associates because they are similar in nature. However, it may be necessary to identify the two associates to which 50% of the sales are made and to disclose the extent of the sales (50%) to those associates. If, on the other hand, the sales to associates are a material proportion of the entity's sales as a whole, it may be necessary to disclose separately details of the transactions with the two associates to which the 50% of sales is made and the amounts of the sales transactions and accounts receivable balances for each of those associates. If the sales to the remaining four associates are not material to the entity as a whole, disclosure for those may continue to be given in aggregate. An example of aggregated disclosure is given in Table A29.1.

Example 2 – Aggregation by type of transaction and counterparty

Entity A enters into transactions with the following related parties:

Entity	Type of sale	Number of transactions	Value
Entity B	Security equipment	1	10,000
Entity C	Security services	10	5,000
Entity D	Security services	12	6,000
Entity D	Security equipment	1	10,000
Entity E	Security services	8	4,500

Entity C is an associate of entity A. Entities B, D and E are subsidiaries of entity G, a fellow subsidiary of entity A. The group structure is as follows:

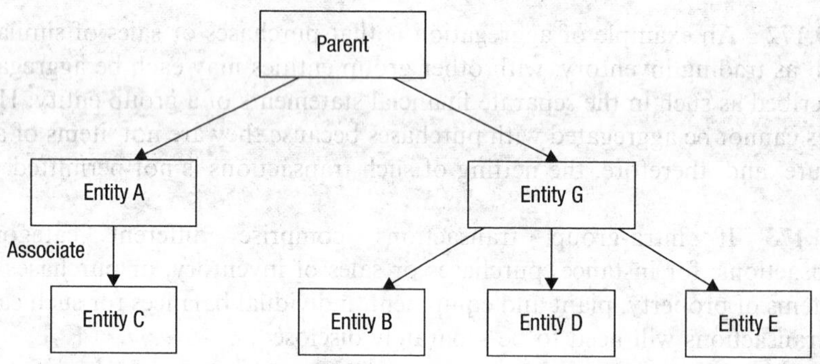

There have been no transactions between entity G and entity A. Other than the types of sale, all terms and conditions of the transactions are similar. How should management aggregate sales to related parties?

Like sales to a common related party may be aggregated. The following is a suggested aggregate disclosure in entity A's separate financial statements:

Sales of security equipment	
Subsidiaries (G group)	20,000
Sales of security services	
Associate (entity C)	5,000
Subsidiaries (G group)	10,500
	15,500

Aggregation — transactions with key management personnel

A29.175 Special considerations arise in connection with transactions with key management personnel and particularly with directors. Except for the disclosures in respect of compensation for services to the entity, IAS 24 (revised) would not generally permit the aggregation of other transactions with directors. This is because usually such transactions are not of a similar nature, but rather tend to be one-off transactions such as the purchase or sale of an asset. For example, separate disclosure is needed where a director of an entity buys a property from the entity.

A29.176 However, aggregation may be an acceptable approach in cases such as the following:

- A situation sometimes arises where all directors have material transactions with the entity. For example, where the entity is an association or co-operative serving all its members, the members may put all or most of their sales or purchases through the entity. Some of the members are elected directors for certain periods and they enter into similar transactions as all other members and on the same terms. Here it would be acceptable to aggregate the transactions for disclosure purposes. However, this approach cannot be used to conceal unusual transactions.
- In other circumstances, some or all directors may enter into transactions with the entity that are or may be material, but less material than the transactions described in the previous bullet point. An example would be insurance policies taken out by directors of insurance entities on normal or staff terms. Here again it seems reasonable to aggregate the transactions for disclosure purposes. However, this approach would not apply to unusual contracts or heavily discounted policies.

A29.177 In contrast to these two cases, consider the following example. Some directors of a house-building entity may, over a period of a few years, buy houses from that entity for their own or family use. However, given the nature of house purchases, they are likely to be less frequent than is the case with the insurance policy example. Moreover, they would be more clearly material to the directors. Hence, in this example we do not believe that aggregation is an appropriate approach, even where house-building is the entity's normal business and the transactions are on normal commercial terms.

Comparatives

A29.178 The standard is silent on comparatives. The rule in IAS 1, 'Presentation of financial statements', is that, except when a standard provides otherwise (which IAS 24 (revised) does not do), comparative information must be given for all amounts reported in the financial statements. Comparative information should be included for narrative and descriptive information when it is relevant to an understanding of the current period's financial statements. [IAS 1 para 38]. In the case of related party disclosure, comparative information is likely to be relevant for all narrative and descriptive information. This rule should, therefore, be applied to all financial statements to which IAS 1 applies.

A29.179 IAS 1 gives an example of narrative information from the previous period that continues to be relevant in the current period. The example is details of a legal dispute, the outcome of which was uncertain at the previous balance sheet date and which has yet to be resolved. Users benefit from information that the uncertainty existed in the previous period and from knowing what steps have been taken in the current period to resolve the uncertainty. [IAS 1 para 40]. In a similar way, if the parent or ultimate controlling party has changed in the current period, users may benefit from knowing that at the previous year end the entity was controlled by one party (comparative information about the name of the controlling party last year) and that during the year the controlling party has changed (current year information about the change and the name of the controlling party at the current year end).

Practical application

Transactions entered into by group companies

A29.180 An example of a transaction entered into by a group company is where a subsidiary of a group enters into a transaction with an associate of the group. The standard's related party definition specifically identifies the subsidiary and associate in this situation as related parties. See further from paragraph A29.51.

Transactions with minorities

A29.181 Where a group of companies includes a partially-owned subsidiary, the question arises as to whether transactions between the subsidiary and its minority investor are related party transactions from the group's perspective. This may depend on the subsidiary's significance to the whole group. This is considered in the following example.

Example – Transactions with minority shareholders

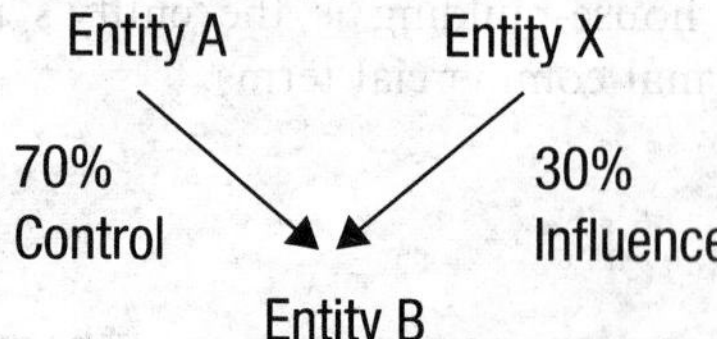

Entity A, which is a large trading company, owns 70% of the shares in a smaller company, entity B, which it consolidates. Entity X owns the remaining 30% of the shares in entity B. Entity B sells a property to entity X at its market value established by outside valuation.

Entity B's separate financial statements

If entity B is entity X's associate (and it would be presumed to be so as its interest exceeds 20 per cent), it is a related party of entity B. Entity B will, therefore, have to disclose details of the transaction in its financial statements, including any other elements of the transaction necessary for an understanding of the financial statements.

Entity A's separate financial statements

Entity A and entity X are not related parties simply because they both have an investment in entity B. They do not transact with one another and are not related parties if there is no other related party connection. Therefore, entity A is not required to disclose the transactions between entity B and entity X in its separate financial statements.

Entity A's consolidated financial statements

The question also arises as to whether entity X is a related party of entity A's group for the purpose of disclosing the transaction in the group's consolidated financial statements. The fact that entity A and entity X have an investment in the same entity, entity B, does not by itself make entity A and entity X related parties of each other as there would appear to be no related party relationship between them. Entity A's group and entity X will be related parties of each other only if there is some other connection whereby they fall within the definition of related parties in IAS 24 (revised) paragraph 9.

For instance, if entity A's group was significantly influenced by entity X such that entity X persuaded entity A's group to dispose of the property to entity X at below its market value (that is, entity X exerted significant influence over entity A's group), they would be related parties. This is a question of fact, but as the transaction was at market value, it is unlikely that entity X significantly influences entity A's group. Consequently, in this situation entity A's group and entity X would not be related parties and no disclosure would be necessary under IAS 24 (revised).

The position would differ if the parent entity did not itself trade and the subsidiary formed the bulk of the group. In this situation, management should disclose transactions between entity B and entity X as related party transactions in entity A's consolidated financial statements. As entity A is an investment holding company and the group's activity consists primarily of entity B's activities, the 30% interest in entity B gives entity X significant influence over entity A's group. Entity X is, therefore, a related party of entity A's group.

Example – Director holds a minority shareholding

The facts are as outlined in the example above, except that the minority shareholder is a person; Mr B. Mr B is a director of the subsidiary (entity B).

Entity B's separate financial statements

As director and shareholder of entity B, with significant influence over the entity, Mr B is a related party of entity B. [IAS 24 (revised) para 9(a)(ii), (iii)]. Management should, therefore, disclose details of the property sale in entity B's financial statements.

Entity A's consolidated financial statements

Entity A's management should disclose the property sale to Mr B in the consolidated financial statements if management considers that Mr B, in his role as a director of entity B, is a related party of A's group.

Mr B may be a related party of the A group if entity B forms a significant portion of the A group. This would be because the group's activities would mainly comprise the activities of entity B over which Mr B has significant influence. If this is the case, it is likely that Mr B would also be key management personnel of the A group.

Mr B and entity A are not related parties simply because they both have an investment in entity B. Entity A's management should assess whether Mr B is key management personnel of entity A's group by considering whether entity B constitutes a major activity or resource of entity A's group and whether, as a director of entity B, Mr B occupies a senior position with the necessary authority and responsibility in A's group.

A29.182 The implications where the minority investor is a director of the subsidiary (and possibly a key manager of the group) are considered in paragraph A29.199.

Subsidiaries acquired and disposed of in the year

A29.183 In practice, questions arise as to what transactions are disclosable in consolidated and separate financial statements where a group has acquired or disposed of a subsidiary during the year. It is considered that disclosure should be made on the following basis.

Consolidated financial statements

- Where a group has acquired a subsidiary, transactions between the members of the acquiring group and the acquired subsidiary prior to the date of acquisition are not disclosable in the consolidated financial statements. This is because an acquired subsidiary is deemed to be a related party of the group only for the period during which the related party relationship exists. Post-acquisition transactions would also not be disclosable in the consolidated financial statements as they are eliminated on consolidation.
- Where a group has disposed of a subsidiary during the year, post-disposal transactions between the members of the group and the subsidiary disposed of are not disclosable in the consolidated financial statements as the related party relationship ceases on disposal. As pre-disposal transactions are eliminated on consolidation, no disclosure is required.

Parent's separate financial statements

- Where an entity acquires a subsidiary, only transactions between the parent and the subsidiary after the date of acquisition are disclosable in the entity's separate financial statements. This is because it is this period during which the related party relationship exists.

- Where an entity disposes of a subsidiary, only transactions between the parent and the subsidiary up to the date of disposal are disclosable in the entity's separate financial statements. Again this is because it is this period during which the related party relationship exists.

Subsidiary's financial statements

- Where an entity is acquired in the period, only transactions after the date of acquisition are disclosable in its financial statements, because this is the period during which the related party relationship exists.

- Where a subsidiary is disposed of during the period, only transactions up to the date of disposal are disclosable in its financial statements, because this is the period during which the related party relationship exists.

Example – Parties are related for only part of the year

Entity A became a subsidiary of the B group on 1 February 20X5 and was sold on 30 November 20X5. Entity A is a regular supplier to the parent entity and during 20X5 it continued to supply goods to the parent.

How should the parent disclose transactions with entity A in its financial statements for the year ended 31 December 20X5, given that it was a related party for only part of the year?

Management should disclose in the parent's separate financial statements details of the transactions between entity A and the parent during the period that entity A met the definition of a related party. The period for which disclosure is required is, therefore, from 1 February 20X5 to 30 November 20X5. The transactions between entity A and the parent in the months of January and December 20X5 do not need to be disclosed, because entity A was not a related party of the parent during those periods.

Management does not need to disclose details of any outstanding balance at 31 December 20X4 and 20X5 with entity A. Entity A was not a related party of the group at those dates.

Similarly, in entity A's financial statements, transactions with the parent between 1 February 20X5 and 30 November 20X5 will be disclosable as related party transactions.

No disclosure will be required in the consolidated financial statements for the reasons given in the bullets above.

A29.184 It should be noted that disclosure of transactions with all shareholders, including those who clearly do not meet the standard's definition of a related party, would be confusing. Where such information is provided, it would be appropriate to clarify which disclosures are required by IAS 24 (revised) and which are provided as additional information.

A29.185 If an entity acquired and then disposed of an associate (or joint venture) during one financial period, the treatment in the entity financial statements of the parent and the associate (or joint venture) would be similar to that discussed in the example above. Transactions occurring during the period the parties were related would be disclosable as related party transactions by both entities. In this scenario however, disclosure of transactions between the parent and the associate (or joint venture) during the period the parties were related would also be disclosable in any consolidated financial statements prepared by the parent. This is because the transactions between the related parties would not eliminate on consolidation.

Special purpose entities

A29.186 Special purpose entities (SPEs) that are consolidated in accordance with SIC 12, 'Consolidation – Special purpose entities', should be treated for the purpose of IAS 24 (revised) in the same way as other entities that qualify as subsidiaries. (Under IFRS 10, 'Consolidated financial statements', which supersedes SIC 12 for annual periods beginning on or after 1 January 2013, entities that are controlled by the reporting entity are its subsidiaries.) That is, no disclosure is required of transactions that are eliminated on consolidation, but disclosure is required of related party transactions in the separate financial statements of the SPE and the controlling entity.

Pension funds

A29.187 Post-employment benefit plans, such as pension funds, are related parties of an entity if they are for the benefit of employees of the entity or of any entity that is a related party of the entity (see from para A29.64). Transactions with post-employment plans will be disclosable as related party transactions in the entity's financial statements. These will include contributions paid to the plan, although in practice for defined benefit schemes the amount of contributions is likely to be disclosed under the requirements of IAS 19, 'Employee benefits', as part of the reconciliation of movements in the net liability or asset recognised in the balance sheet. Other related party disclosures might include details of pension fund expenses charged to or recharged by the entity and more complex transactions, such as the sale and leaseback of property.

A29.188 An example of disclosure of transactions with pension schemes is given in Table A29.5.

Table A29.5 – Transactions with pension schemes

Nokia Corporation – Annual Report and Accounts – 31 December 2010

31. Related party transactions (extract)

At December 31, 2010, the Group had borrowings amounting to EUR 69 million (EUR 69 million in 2009 and EUR 69 million in 2008) from Nokia Unterstützungskasse GmbH, the Group's German pension fund, which is a separate legal entity. The loan bears interest at 6% annum and its duration is pending until further notice by the loan counterparts who have the right to terminate the loan with a 90 day notice period.

A29.189 IAS 24 (revised) also specifies that participation by a parent or subsidiary in a defined benefit plan that shares risks between group entities is a transaction between related parties. Paragraph 34B of IAS 19, 'Employee benefits', contains specific disclosure requirements in this situation. These are dealt with in chapter 11.

A29.190 The entity whose employees participate in a pension fund would not be a related party of the fund's *investment managers* by reason only of the investment managers acting for the fund. However, if the entity acted on behalf of the fund and paid the investment managers' fees, this would, if material, be disclosable by the entity as a related party transaction (because the fund is a related party of the entity under IAS 24 (revised)).

A29.191 Furthermore, the situation is more complicated where the investment manager of a pension scheme is a member of the group, as illustrated in the following example.

Example – Group entity is the fund manager of the group pension scheme

An entity's pension fund has investments that are managed by an investment manager that is a subsidiary of the entity. Does the entity, in its consolidated financial statements, have to disclose payments made by the pension fund to the investment manager?

IAS 24 (revised) specifically includes pension funds as related parties. [IAS 24 (revised) para 9(b)(v)].

Also, IAS 19, 'Employee benefits', states in paragraph 124:

> *"Where required by IAS 24, Related Party Disclosures, an entity discloses information about:*
>
> *(a) related party transactions with post-employment benefit plans; and*
>
> *(b) post-employment benefits for key management personnel."*

Therefore, transactions between the group and the pension fund should be disclosed in the consolidated financial statements. The transactions with the pension fund must also be disclosed in the subsidiary's financial statements as the fund is for the benefit of the employees of the subsidiary's parent (which is a related party of the subsidiary).

Shareholders

A29.192 Transactions with shareholders will be disclosable under IAS 24 (revised) if the shareholders meet the definition of a related party under IAS 24 (revised) (see further from para A29.15).

UK.A29.192.1 Transactions with shareholders are not disclosable as related party transactions under the Listing Rules if they are revenue transactions in the ordinary course of business or if they are very small transactions (see from para UK.A29.217.9). However, a listed company will need to comply in full with IAS 24 (revised).

A29.193 Table A29.6 illustrates disclosure of transactions with a 70 per cent shareholder.

Table A29.6 – Transactions with shareholder

H Lundbeck A/S – Annual Report and Accounts – 31 December 2010

28. Related Parties (extract)

Transactions and balances with the company's principal shareholder

Through its wholly owned subsidiary LFI a/s, the Lundbeck Foundation, which is the parent company's largest shareholder, held 137,351,918 shares at 31 December 2010 (137,351,918 shares at 31 December 2009), corresponding to approximately 70% of the shares and votes in H. Lundbeck A/S (approximately 70% in 2009). LFI a/s is the only shareholder who has notified the company that it holds more than 5% of the share capital. This was also the case at 31 December 2009.

There have been the following transactions and balances with the company's principal shareholder:

- Dividends
- Payment of provisional tax and residual tax of DKK 1 billion in 2010 (DKK 520 million in 2009) concerning the parent company and Danish subsidiaries.
- In 2009, sale of investments in the associate LifeCycle Pharma A/S and sale of investments in four small private equity funds.

LFI a/s / the Lundbeck Foundation has controlling influence in H. Lundbeck A/S.

A29.194 The example below considers whether transactions in shares are related party transactions.

Example – Transactions in shares

IAS 24 (revised) paragraph 9 defines a related party transaction as a transfer of resources, services or obligations between a reporting entity and a related party, regardless of whether a price is charged. Is disclosure required by IAS 24 (revised) in respect of the following transactions in shares by a related party (for example, a director)?

(a) The purchase or sale of shares in the market.

The transactions are between the related party and the market. As the entity is not a party to the transaction, no disclosure is required. IAS 24 (revised) requires only disclosure of transactions between the reporting entity and its related parties.

(b) Subscribing for shares in a rights issue.

Where a related party subscribes for shares in the entity under a rights issue, there is a transaction between the entity and the related party that meets the definition of a related party transaction. Therefore, disclosure would be required under IAS 24 (revised) if the transaction is material.

(c) Underwriting a rights issue and, as a result, subscribing for additional shares in respect of rights not taken up.

The underwriting of the rights issue is a separate arrangement from the rights issue. By underwriting the issue, the related party is performing a service for the entity. The underwriting arrangement and the subscription for additional shares would be disclosable related party transactions under IAS 24 (revised) (and would be presumed to be material, if they are unusual transactions).

(d) Subscribing for shares on exercise of share options granted under a senior executive long-term incentive scheme.

Directors' compensation is within the scope of IAS 24 (revised) and, accordingly, should be disclosed. See further from paragraph A29.129.

(e) Dividends paid to related parties.

Dividends paid to related parties are disclosable. Paragraph 11(c)(i) of IAS 24 (revised) has an exemption for transactions with providers of finance. However, if the counterparty receiving the dividend is a related party, by definition it cannot merely be a provider of finance. This may capture, for example, dividend payments made to shareholders who are members of key management personnel or investors with significant influence over the reporting entity. See paragraph A29.198 below.

Key management personnel

A29.195 Identifying key management personnel is dealt with from paragraph A29.30. Disclosure of key management personnel compensation is dealt with from paragraph A29.129. This section considers the disclosure of other transactions with key management personnel.

A29.196 Subscriptions for shares in an entity by a member of its key management personnel will be related party transactions and disclosable if the transactions are material. However, purchases and sales of an entity's shares in the market by a member of its key management personnel that do not involve the entity as a party to the transaction are not disclosable as related party transactions. See further paragraph A29.194 above.

A29.197 Guarantees are given as one of the examples of related party transactions in paragraph 21(h) of IAS 24 (revised). Personal guarantees by key management personnel of the reporting entity's borrowings would, therefore, be disclosable. It is probable that a key manager's personal guarantee is a material item both to the key manager and to the entity.

Example – Director guarantees a bank loan

An entity's director has given a bank a personal guarantee as security for his entity's overdraft facility. Does this have to be disclosed in the entity's financial statements?

Paragraph 21(h) of IAS 24 (revised) includes as an example of a related party transaction *"provision of guarantees or collateral"*. A director is a related party under IAS 24 (revised) as he/she is a member of the key management personnel of the entity or its parent. [IAS 24 (revised) para 9(a)(iii)]. Therefore, the guarantee would be disclosable as a related party transaction.

A29.198 Dividends paid to key managers are related party transactions. IAS 24 (revised) has an exemption for providers of finance (IAS 24 (revised) para 11(c)(i)), but this is *"... by virtue of their normal dealings with an entity ..."* and key managers are more than mere providers of finance. Therefore, dividends due to key managers or their close family should be disclosed under IAS 24 (revised). In some circumstances, it may be possible to derive the information regarding dividend payments to key management personnel from other information in the financial statements. For example, if disclosure is made of the number of shares held by key management personnel and, elsewhere in the financial statements, the dividend per share is given, the reader could recalculate the dividends paid to key management personnel. If this is the case, in our view, it would not be essential to include specific disclosure of dividend paid to key management personnel in the related parties note.

A29.199 Paragraph A29.181 above considers the situation where a group of companies includes a partially-owned subsidiary that enters into transactions with the minority investor. Where the minority investor is also a director of the subsidiary, it will be necessary to consider if he or she is part of the key management personnel of the group. This is illustrated in the example in paragraph A29.181 above.

A29.200 As noted from paragraph A29.42, an entity's related parties include entities controlled, jointly controlled, significantly influenced or over which significant voting power resides, directly or indirectly, by a member of the key management personnel of the entity or its parent (or their close family). This will have implications where an entity enters into trading transactions with another entity in which a key manager has an interest.

A29.201 Transactions with key managers are required to be disclosed if they are material. The concept of materiality is discussed from paragraph A29.89.

A29.202 In some cases, it may be appropriate to aggregate transactions when disclosing this management compensation. The aggregation of transactions with key management personnel is considered further from paragraph A29.175 above.

Close family

A29.203 Transactions with children and other 'close family' of key management personnel or of a person that controls, or that has joint control or significant influence over the entity will be disclosable, (see (a) in the example below). Entities controlled, jointly controlled or significantly influenced by any such party (described in the first sentence) are also related parties of the entity (see (b) in the example below).

Example – Parties that are related because of a family connection

Mr Y's father owns 100% of the shares in entity A. Mr and Mrs Y own 100% of the shares and are the only key management personnel of entity B. Mrs Y's sister provides book-keeping services from time to time to entity B, but is not an employee. Entity A has increased its loan of C150,000 to entity B to C200,000 during the year, for which entity A charges a below market rate of interest.

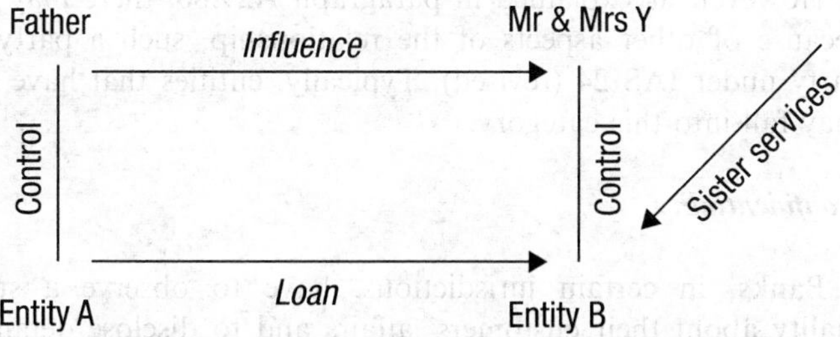

(a) Under IAS 24 (revised), Mr Y's father and Mrs Y's sister will be related parties of entity B, if they are 'close family' of either Mr or Mrs Y (key management personnel of entity B). They will be close family if they may be expected to influence, or be influenced by, Mr or Mrs Y in their dealings with entity B. It is assumed for this example that Mr Y's father does exert some influence over Mr and Mrs Y and so Mr Y's father is a related party of entity B.

(b) Mr Y's father has a controlling interest in entity A. It follows, therefore, that entity A will be a related party of entity B.

Both entities will need to disclose the necessary details regarding the increase in the loan to C200,000 in their financial statements. In addition, if any part of the existing loan of C150,000 and the additional loan of C50,000 is outstanding at the balance sheet date, entity A will need to disclose the amounts due to it from entity B on that date, together with any provisions and amounts written off. Entity B will need to disclose the amount it owes to entity A at the balance sheet date.

Entity B would have to disclose the transactions with the sister of Mrs Y if the sister might be expected to influence or be influenced by Mrs Y in her dealings with entity B. This is a matter of judgement based on the facts of the case.

Exemption from disclosure

Transactions eliminated on consolidation

A29.204 In consolidated financial statements, disclosure is not required of any transactions or balances between group entities that have been eliminated on consolidation. [IAS 24 (revised) para 4]. However, disclosure of control is not exempted and so relationships between parents and subsidiaries have to be disclosed irrespective of whether there have been transactions between those related parties (see para A29.99).

Parties that are not necessarily related

A29.205 As described from paragraph A29.79 there are certain parties that are regarded as not necessarily being related under IAS 24 (revised). Where such parties are so regarded, transactions with those parties are not required to be disclosed. However, as explained in paragraph A29.80, there may be situations where, because of other aspects of the relationship, such a party would be a related party under IAS 24 (revised). Typically, entities that have a controlling interest may fall into this category.

Duty of confidentiality

A29.206 Banks, in certain jurisdictions, have to observe a strict duty of confidentiality about their customers' affairs and to disclose details concerning related parties would potentially conflict with that duty. There is no exemption in IAS 24 (revised) from the disclosure requirements where such a duty of confidentiality exists. However, providers of finance are not necessarily related parties simply by virtue of their normal dealings with an entity (see from para A29.79). Therefore, normal banking transactions with the entity would not be disclosable, provided that there is no other related party relationship and, hence, there would normally be no conflict with any legal requirements as to confidentiality.

Government-related entities

A29.207 The previous version of IAS 24 did not contain any specific guidance for government-related entities. Such entities were, therefore, required to disclose transactions with the government and other government-related entities where these entities met the definition of related parties. This requirement was onerous in territories with pervasive government control and placed a significant burden on entities to identify related party transactions and collect the information required for disclosure. For example, a government-controlled railway was theoretically required to disclose details of its transactions with the government-controlled postal service. Such information is not necessarily useful to users of the financial statements and is costly and time-consuming to collect.

A29.208 In addition, the financial crisis widened the range of entities subject to government control and, hence, related party disclosure requirements. Financial support provided by governments to financial institutions in many countries means that the government now controls or significantly influences some of these entities. Under the previous version of IAS 24, for example, a government-controlled bank was required to disclose details of its transactions, deposits and commitments with all other government-controlled banks and with the central bank.

A29.209 IAS 24 (revised) introduces an exemption from the disclosure requirements of paragraph 18 (see para A29.158 above) in relation to related party transactions and outstanding balances, including commitments, with:

- a government that has control, joint control or significant influence over the reporting entity; and
- another entity that is a related party because the same government has control, joint control or significant influence over both the reporting entity and the other entity.

[IAS 24 (revised) para 25].

A29.210 IAS 24 (revised) defines 'government' as *"government, government agencies and similar bodies whether local, national or international"*. [IAS 24 (revised) para 9]. Government-related entities are those that are *"controlled, jointly controlled or significantly influenced by a government"*. [IAS 24 (revised) para 9].

A29.211 The following examples show situations where the exemption may be applied.

Example 1 – Government control

Government G, controls entity A. Entity A has a subsidiary, entity B. Government G also controls entity C. Entity C has a subsidiary, entity D.

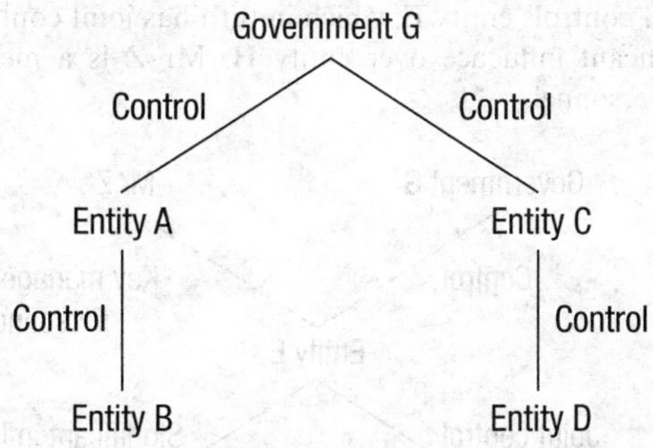

Entities A, B, C and D may take the exemption from disclosure for government-related entities set out in paragraph 25 of IAS 24 (revised). For example, entity A is not required to disclose details of its transactions with government G or with entities B, C and D. [IAS 24 (revised) para 25]. This is the conclusion in the illustrative example provided in the standard. [IAS 24 (revised) IE 1].

The rationale for this conclusion is as follows:

Entities A, B, C and D are exempt from the requirement to disclose transactions with government G because they are transactions with a government that has control. [IAS 24 (revised) para 25(a)].

Entities A and B are exempt from the requirement to disclose transactions with entities C and D, and *vice versa*. This is because they are transactions with another entity that is a related party because the same government has control. [IAS 24 (revised) para 25(b)].

The rationale for the position regarding transactions between entities A and B (or between entities C and D) is less clear. Paragraph 25(b) refers to transactions involving entities that are related *because* the same government has control. Entities A and B are controlled ultimately by the same government, but they are also related because entity A controls entity B.

However, the Basis for Conclusions section of the standard states:

> "*Some respondents reasoned that the exemption should not apply to transactions between members of a group that is controlled by a government, for example between a government-related entity and its parent or its fellow subsidiaries. Those respondents noted that the relationship within such a group might sometimes be closer and more influential than between government-related entities in an environment where government control is pervasive.*"

However, for reasons explained in the Basis of Conclusions, the Board concluded that the exemption should also apply within such groups. [IAS 24 (revised) para BC37].

Therefore, entities A and B are exempt from disclosing transactions with each other. (An equivalent exemption is available to entities C and D.)

Example 2 – Government control and member of key management personnel

Government G controls entity E, which in turn has joint control of entity F. Entity E also has significant influence over entity H. Mr Z is a member of entity E's key management personnel.

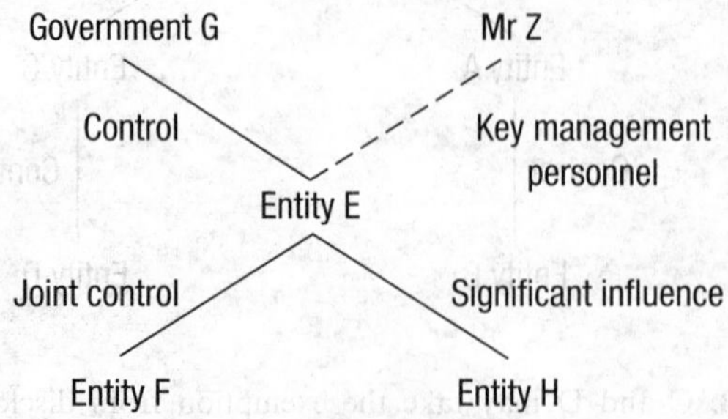

Entities E, F and H may take the exemption from disclosure for government-related entities set out in paragraph 25 of IAS 24 (revised), because government G has direct or indirect control, joint control or significant influence over each of them. For example, entity H is not required to disclose details of its transactions with government G and entities E and F. [IAS 24 (revised) para 25]. However, the exemption does not apply to transactions between entity E and Mr Z. Mr Z is not a related party of entities F and H since entity E is not a parent of either entity.

Example 3 – Government holding significant influence

Government G has significant influence over entity I. Entity I has significant influence over entity J and controls entity K.

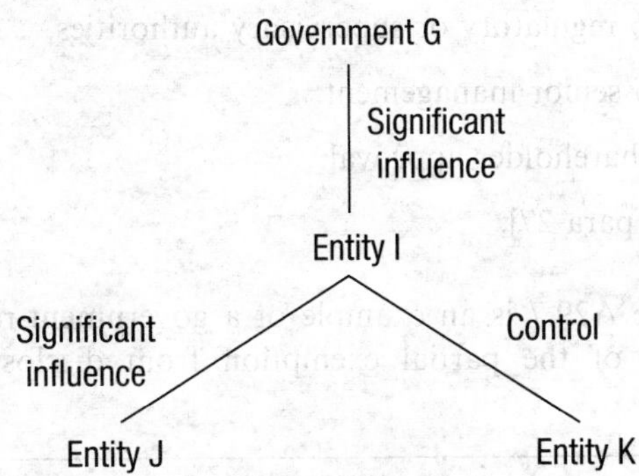

Entities I and K may take the exemption from disclosure for government-related entities set out in paragraph 25 of IAS 24 (revised), because government G has significant influence over entity I and entity K (as entity I controls entity K). [IAS 24 (revised) para 25]. However, the exemption does not extend to any transactions with entity J, because while, government G has significant influence over entity I, entity I's significant influence over entity J is not sufficient to assert that government G also has significant influence over entity J. Hence, transactions between entity J and entity I and between entity J and entity K are subject to the full disclosure requirements of IAS 24 (revised). [IAS 24 (revised) para 9(b)(ii)].

A29.212 If a reporting entity applies the exemption described in paragraph A29.209 above, it must disclose the following:

- the name of the government and the nature of its relationship with the reporting entity (that is, control, joint control or significant influence); and
- the following information in sufficient detail to enable users to understand the effect of related party transactions on the entity's financial statements:
  - the nature and amount of each individually significant transaction; and
  - the qualitative or quantitative extent of any collectively, but not individually, significant transactions (such as those set out in paragraph A29.172).

[IAS 24 (revised) para 26].

A29.213 The standard gives guidance on how to determine the level of detail to be disclosed in accordance with the requirements of the second bullet point in paragraph A29.212. It states that the closeness of the related party relationship, as well as other factors, should be considered. Other factors relevant in establishing the level of significance of the transaction include whether it is:

- Significant in terms of size.
- Carried out on non-market terms.
- Outside normal day-to-day business operations, such as the purchase and sale of businesses.
- Disclosed to regulatory or supervisory authorities.
- Reported to senior management.
- Subject to shareholder approval.

[IAS 24 (revised) para 27].

A29.213.1 Table A29.7 is an example of a government-related entity that has taken advantage of the partial exemption from disclosure of related party transactions.

Table A29.7 Partial exemption for government-related entities

Aer Lingus Group Plc – Annual Report – 31 December 2010

Note 2. Summary of significant accounting policies (extract)

2.1.1 Changes in accounting policy and disclosures (extract)

The accounting policies adopted are consistent with those of the previous financial year except as follows:

IAS 1 Presentation of Financial Statements (effective 1 January 2011) and IAS 24 (Revised) Related Party Disclosures (effective 1 January 2011) have been adopted early.

Note 31 Related party transactions (extract)

The Minister for Finance of Ireland holds 25.11% of the Group's issued share capital and is entitled to appoint three directors to the Board. The Group considers that, for the purpose of IAS 24 (2009) the government of Ireland is in a position to exercise significant influence over it, and therefore regards the government of Ireland and various of its bodies, including the Dublin Airport Authority (DAA), as related parties for the purpose of the disclosures required by IAS 24 (2009).

The Group incurs rental charges in respect of office space, check in facilities and other operational facilities at various Irish airports. The Group also incurs passenger, landing and other charges for the use of these airports. The Group incurs air navigation charges as a result of services provided by the Irish Aviation Authority.

The Group collects Airport Departure Tax and various payroll taxes on behalf of the Irish Revenue Commissioners and is liable to Irish Corporation Tax on profits earned, and to employer's PRSI on its payroll. The Group accounts for VAT in Ireland.

The Group sells seats on its scheduled services to various Government bodies in the normal course of its business and has banking relationships with institutions now controlled by the Irish government. As an airline, the Irish Department of Transport is the Group's principal regulator.

> The transactions described above are collectively but not individually significant to the financial statements.
>
> In June 2010, the Group signed a Heads of Agreement with the DAA under which it has agreed to surrender the leasehold interest in its Head Office Building site to the DAA. Further details are provided in Note 30.

Non-disclosure and the position of the auditor

A29.214 Where there is a material misstatement in the financial statements that relates to the non-disclosure of information (such as the ultimate controlling party), the auditor is guided by the requirements of ISA 705, 'Modifications to the opinion in the independent auditor's report', applicable for periods beginning on or after 15 December 2009. Paragraph 19 of ISA 705 states that where such circumstances arise, the auditor should:

- discuss the non-disclosure with those charged with governance;
- describe in the basis for modification paragraph the nature of the omitted information; and
- unless prohibited by law or regulation, include the omitted disclosures, provided it is practicable to do so and the auditor has obtained sufficient appropriate audit evidence about the omitted information.

[ISA 705 para 19].

A29.215 This means that qualified audit opinions will generally contain omitted disclosures (including, for example, details of the ultimate controlling party). This is a change from the previous auditing standard, applicable for periods beginning prior to 15 December 2009, where the auditor simply gave a qualified opinion and stated the company's failure to disclose the information.

A29.216 The ISA's application guidance describes circumstances where it would not be practicable to disclose the omitted information as follows:

- the disclosures have not been prepared by management or are not readily available to the auditor; or
- the auditor judges the disclosures to be unduly voluminous in relation to the auditor's report.

[ISA 705 para A19].

> **UK.A29.216.1** Requirements in the UK are consistent with those described above under international ISA 705. The APB's equivalent ISA, ISA (UK&I) 705, is applicable for periods ending on or after 15 December 2010.

Effective date and transition

A29.217 IAS 24 (revised) applies retrospectively for annual periods beginning on or after 1 January 2011. [IAS 24 (revised) para 28]. Early application is permitted, either for the whole standard, or for the partial exemption for government-related entities (see from para A29.207 above). If an entity applies either the whole standard or the partial exemption for government-related entities for a period beginning before 1 January 2011, it must disclose that fact.

Interaction with disclosures required by the Companies Act 2006

UK.A29.217.1 The disclosures that the Companies Act 2006 requires to be made concerning related party transactions are considered briefly in the paragraphs that follow. The annex to this chapter summarises the sections of the Companies Act 2006 that require disclosures to be made concerning related party transactions.

UK.A29.217.2 The Companies Act 2006 requires various disclosures to be made in relation to directors' remuneration. For the purposes of these disclosures, any amounts paid to or receivable by a person connected with the director are treated as being paid to or receivable by the director. [CA06 Sec 412]. A person connected with a director falls broadly into the following categories:

- Members of a director's family.
- A body corporate in which a director is interested, entitled to exercise or control the exercise of at least 20 per cent of the shares excluding any shares held as treasury shares.
- A trustee of a trust of which the director or any persons connected with him are beneficiaries.
- A partner of the director or of a person who is connected with him under the three scenarios above.
- A firm that is a legal person under the law by which it is governed and in which the director or a connected person is a partner.

See further the Manual of Accounting – Narrative Reporting.

UK.A29.217.3 The Companies Act 2006 allows certain transactions, such as loans, to be undertaken with directors subject to members' approval. [CA06 Sec 188 to 226]. In addition to triggering disclosures under the requirements of the Act, any such transactions may fall to be disclosed under IAS 24 (revised) as detailed above.

UK.A29.217.4 Where a company does not prepare consolidated financial statements, it is required to disclose details of advances and credits granted by the company to its directors and guarantees entered into by the company on behalf of its directors. Where a parent company prepares consolidated financial statements, it is required to disclose details of advances and credits granted to the directors of the parent company, by that company or by any of its subsidiary undertakings and guarantees entered into on behalf of the directors of the parent company, by that company or by any of its subsidiary undertakings. [CA06 Sec 413(1), (2)].

UK.A29.217.5 The details required to be disclosed in respect of an advance or credit are its amount, an indication of the interest rate, its main conditions, and any amounts repaid. The details required in respect of a guarantee are its main terms, the amount of the maximum liability that may be incurred by the company (or its subsidiary) and any amount paid and any liability incurred by the company (or its subsidiary) for the purpose of fulfilling the guarantee (including any loss incurred by reason of enforcement of the guarantee). [CA06 Sec 413(3), (4)].

UK.A29.217.6 In respect of advances and credits to directors, the Companies Act 2006 also requires disclosure of the totals of amounts of advances and credits and the amounts repaid. In respect of guarantees entered into with directors, the Companies Act 2006 also requires disclosure of amounts of the maximum liability that may be incurred and of amounts paid and any liability incurred for the purpose of fulfilling the guarantee. [CA06 Sec 413(5)].

Related party transactions under the Listing Rules

Usual requirements for transactions with related parties

UK.A29.217.7 Under chapter 11 of the Listing Rules, where a listed company (or any of its subsidiary undertakings) enters into a transaction with a related party, the usual requirements are as follows. Subject to certain exempted transactions (see from para UK.A29.217.16), the company must give the required details of the transaction to a Regulatory Information Service, send a circular to shareholders with the required information and obtain their approval to the transaction. [LR 11.1.7R, 11.1.3R]. If a circular is required, it must provide sufficient information to enable the recipient to evaluate the transaction's effect. The Listing Rules include specific requirements for related party circulars. [LR 13.3, 13.6]. Companies that do not have a primary listing of equity shares (or listed securities convertible into equity shares) do not have to comply with these provisions. Chapters 11, 15 and 16 apply to investment trusts (as well as to investment companies) and to venture capital trusts.

UK.A29.217.8 When related party transactions occur, details such as the identity of the related party, the value of consideration and other relevant circumstances should be disclosed in the financial statements. [LR 11.1.10R].

This requirement is, however, subject to various exemptions as discussed from paragraph UK.A29.217.16.

Definition of a related party transaction

UK.A29.217.9 The related party provisions in the Listing Rules include a definition of a *'related party transaction'*. [LR 11.1.5R]. This phrase means one of the following:

- A transaction (other than a transaction of a revenue nature in the ordinary course of business) between a company, or any of its subsidiary undertakings, and a related party.
- Any arrangements pursuant to which a listed company, or any of its subsidiary undertakings, and a related party each invests in, or provides finance to, another undertaking or asset.
- Any other similar transaction or arrangement (other than a transaction of a revenue nature in the ordinary course of business) between a company (or any of its subsidiary undertakings) and any other person (individual or legal entity), the purpose and effect of which is to benefit a related party.

[LR 11.1.5R, 11.1.3R].

UK.A29.217.10 Whilst the definition of a related party transaction under the Listing Rules is similar to that in IAS 24 (revised), there are some key differences. For example, the Listing Rules definition scopes out revenue transactions that occur in the ordinary course of business. The Listing Rules definition does, however, scope in certain additional transactions such as those where an entity co-invests in an undertaking or asset with a related party or indirect transactions where an entity transacts with a third party for the benefit of one of its related parties.

UK.A29.217.11 In assessing whether a transaction is in the ordinary course of business for the purpose of the related party provisions in the Listing Rules, the FSA has regard to the size and incidence of the transaction and also to whether the transaction's terms and conditions are unusual. [LR 11.1.5A G].

UK.A29.217.12 The provisions of the second bullet point in paragraph UK.A29.217.9 would be likely to catch arrangements where directors who are related parties and subsidiaries of the listed company both invest in a venture capital fund. However, such arrangements are excluded from the Listing Rules requirements both in relation to process and to disclosure. These are joint investment arrangements where the terms and circumstances of the investment by the company or any of its subsidiaries are, in the opinion of an independent adviser acceptable to the FSA, no less favourable than those applicable to the investment by the related party and the amount invested, or provided, by the related party is not more than 25 per cent of the amount invested, or provided, by the listed company or its subsidiary undertaking (as the case may be) and the listed company has advised the FSA in writing that this condition has been met. [LR 11 Annex para 8].

Definition of a related party

UK.A29.217.13 In the Listing Rules, a related party means:

- A substantial shareholder. This is any person who is, or was within the 12 months preceding the date of the transaction, entitled to exercise or control the exercise of ten per cent or more of votes able to be cast on all or substantially all matters at general meetings of the company (or of any company that is its parent, subsidiary or fellow subsidiary undertaking). Certain persons are excluded from this definition – see further paragraph UK.A29.217.14 below.
- A director (including a shadow director and a person who was a director or shadow director within the 12 months preceding the transaction) of the company or any company that is (and, if he has ceased to be such, was while he was a director or shadow director of such other company) its subsidiary undertaking or parent undertaking, or a fellow subsidiary undertaking of its parent undertaking.
- A person (individual or legal entity) exercising significant influence.
- An associate of a substantial shareholder, director or person exercising significant influence, as follows:
  - In relation to an individual, this includes the following:
    - An individual related party's spouse, civil partner or child (together 'the individual's family').
    - The trustees (acting as such) of a trust of which the individual or any of the individual's family is a beneficiary or discretionary object, other than certain trusts that are occupational pension schemes or employees' share schemes.
    - A company in whose equity shares the individual and/or members of the individual's family (taken together) have an interest that enables them (or would do so on the fulfilment of a condition or the occurrence of a contingency), directly or indirectly, to exercise or control the exercise of 30 per cent or more of votes at general meetings on all, or substantially all, matters; or appoint or remove directors holding a majority of voting rights at board meetings on all, or substantially all, matters.

For the purpose of the above bullet point, if more than one director of the listed company, its parent or any of its subsidiaries is interested in the equity securities of another company, then the interests of those directors and their associates are aggregated when determining whether that company is an associate of the director.

- In relation to a company, this includes the following:
  - Any other company that is its subsidiary undertaking or parent undertaking or fellow subsidiary undertaking.
  - Any company whose directors are accustomed to act in accordance with the substantial shareholder's or person exercising significant influence's directions or instructions.
  - Any company in the capital of which the substantial shareholder or person exercising significant influence and any other company that is an associate taken together, is (or would on the fulfilment of a condition or the occurrence of a contingency be) able to exercise or control the exercise of 30 per cent or more of votes at general meetings on all, or substantially all, matters; or appoint or remove directors holding a majority of voting rights at board meetings on all, or substantially all, matters.

[LR 11.1.4R].

UK.A29.217.14 The definition of a substantial shareholder disregards any voting rights that the person exercises (or controls the exercise of) independently in its capacity as bare trustee, investment manager, collective investment undertaking or a long-term insurer in respect of its linked long-term business if no associate of that person interferes by giving direct or indirect instructions, or in any other way, in the exercise of such voting rights (except to the extent any such person confers or collaborates with such an associate that also acts in its capacity as investment manager, collective investment undertaking or long term insurer). [LR App 1].

UK.A29.217.15 This dispensation is included in the definition to address concerns that a listed company would find it difficult to participate in normal commercial transactions with a financial services company that had a wholly-owned fund management subsidiary. This was on the basis that the subsidiary may hold substantial positions, often more than 10 per cent in listed companies and this would render the subsidiary and, consequently, the financial services company a related party without this dispensation. The definition, therefore, excludes situations where the substantial shareholder is only a related party of the listed company by virtue of managed funds held by a subsidiary of the substantial shareholder. In such situations, fiduciary duties are normally owed by the subsidiary to its clients, together with systems and controls in place, which the FSA believes ensure that no potential for influence by the substantial shareholder or its subsidiary on the listed company exists. The definition also excludes voting rights attained in the substantial shareholders' capacity as a long-term insurer.

Transactions exempted from disclosure under the Listing Rules

UK.A29.217.16 The rules in chapter 11 of the Listing Rules do not apply to a transaction the terms of which:

- were agreed at a time when no party to the transaction or person who was to receive the benefit of the transaction was a related party; and
- have not been amended, or required the exercise of discretion by the listed company under those terms, since the party or person become a related party.

[LR 11 Annex para 1A].

UK.A29.217.17 In addition, the rules in chapter 11 of the Listing Rules do not apply to a company where it proposes to enter into any of the following types of related party transactions, providing they do not have any unusual features:

- The take up by a related party of new securities or treasury shares under its entitlement in a pre-emptive offering.
- An issue of new securities made under the exercise of conversion or subscription rights attaching to a listed class of securities.
- Certain employees' share schemes and long-term incentive schemes.
- The granting of credit upon normal commercial terms or terms no more favourable than those offered to employees generally.
- The grant of an indemnity to, or maintenance of an insurance contract for, a director of the listed company or any of its subsidiary undertakings to the extent permitted by the Companies Act 2006. (This also applies to a listed company that is not subject to the Companies Act 2006 if the terms of the indemnity or contract of insurance are in accordance with those that would be specifically permitted under that Act (if it applied).)
- A transaction that consists of a loan or assistance to a director by a listed company or any of its subsidiary undertakings if the terms of the loan are in accordance with those specifically permitted to be given to a director under section 204 (exception for expenditure on company business) or section 205 (exception for expenditure on defending proceedings etc) of the Companies Act 2006.
- The underwriting by a related party of all or part of an issue of securities by the listed company (or any of its subsidiary undertakings) if the

consideration to be paid is no more than the usual commercial underwriting consideration and is the same as that to be paid to the other underwriters (if any). However, this exemption does not apply to the extent that a related party is underwriting securities that it is entitled to take up under an issue of securities.

- Certain joint investment arrangements (see para UK.A29.217.12).
- A transaction with an insignificant subsidiary. This will be exempt where the related party is a related party only by virtue of being a substantial shareholder or a director of a subsidiary undertaking of the company that has contributed less than 10 per cent of turnover and profits of, and has represented less than 10 per cent of the assets of, the listed company in each of the three financial years preceding the date of the transaction.

[LR 11.1.6(2)R, Annex paras 2 to 10].

UK.A29.217.18 In addition, the related party transaction rules do not apply to small transactions. These are transactions where each of the ratios based on gross assets, profits, consideration to market capitalisation and gross capital is equal to or less than 0.25 per cent. [LR 11 Annex para 1]. Where a company proposes to enter into a transaction with a related party where each of these ratios is less than five per cent, but one or more exceeds 0.25 per cent, it must inform the FSA in writing of details of the proposed transaction or arrangement. [LR 11.1.10R].

UK.A29.217.19 In addition, prior to completing any such transaction or arrangement the company must provide the FSA with written confirmation from an independent adviser acceptable to it that the terms of the proposed transaction or the arrangement with the related party are fair and reasonable so far as the shareholders are concerned. It must also undertake in writing to include details of the transaction or arrangement in its next financial statements, including the identity of the related party, the value of the consideration for the transaction or arrangement and all other relevant circumstances. [LR 11.1.10R]. The inclusion of these details in the financial statements is, in turn, required by paragraph 9.8.4R (3) of the Listing Rules.

Aggregation

UK.A29.217.20 The FSA requires all transactions to be aggregated which are entered into by the company (or any of its subsidiary undertakings) with the same related party (and any of its associates) in any twelve-month period. This would not apply where they have been approved by shareholders. If any percentage ratio is 5 per cent or more for the aggregated transactions or arrangements, the listed company must comply with the Listing Rules requirements for related parties (see para UK.A29.217.7) in respect of the latest transaction or arrangement. [LR 11.1.11R]. Details of aggregated transactions and arrangements are required to be included in a circular.

[LR 13.6.1R (8)]. If transactions or arrangements that are small transactions (see para UK.A29.217.18) are aggregated and for the aggregated small transactions each of the percentage ratios is less than 5 per cent, but one or more of the percentage ratios exceeds 0.25 per cent, modified requirements apply. [LR 11.1.11R (3)].

Other disclosures under Listing Rules

Contracts of significance

UK.A29.217.21 Particulars must be given of any contract of significance that subsisted during the period under review between the listed company, or one of its subsidiary undertakings, and a controlling shareholder. [LR 9.8.4R (10)(b)]. A contract of significance is one representing an amount equal to one per cent or more, calculated on a group basis where relevant, of:

- in the case of a capital transaction or transaction the principal purpose or effect of which is the granting of credit, the aggregate of the group's share capital and reserves; or
- in other cases, the total annual purchases, sales, payments or receipts, as the case may be, of the group.

[LR App 1.1].

UK.A29.217.22 In addition, particulars must be given of any contract subsisting during the period under review for the provision of services to the company or any of its subsidiary undertakings by a controlling shareholder. However, a contract need not be disclosed if:

- it is for the provision of services which it is the principal business of the shareholder to provide; and
- it is not a contract of significance.

[LR 9.8.4R (11)].

Directors' interests in contracts

UK.A29.217.23 The Listing Rules require a listed company's annual financial report to contain particulars of any contract of significance that existed during the period under review to which the company or one of its subsidiary undertakings was a party and in which a director of the company is or was materially interested. [LR 9.8.4R (10)(a)]. A 'contract of significance' is defined in paragraph UK.A29.217.21.

Interests in shares

UK.A29.217.24 A transaction in an entity's shares is not necessarily a related party transaction under IAS 24 (revised), as this will depend upon whether there has been a transaction with the entity (see further para A29.194). However, there are specific disclosure requirements for interests in shares in the Listing Rules.

UK.A29.217.25 The Listing Rules require a listed company's annual financial report to include a statement setting out all the interests of each person who is a director of the company as at the end of the period under review including:

- all changes in the interests of each director that have occurred between the end of the period under review and a date not more than one month prior to the date of the notice of the annual general meeting; or
- if there have been no changes in the interests of each director in the period described above, a statement that there have been no changes;

Interests of each director include the interests of connected persons of which the listed company is, or ought upon reasonable enquiry to become, aware.

[LR 9.8.6R (1)].

UK.A29.217.26 The Listing Rules also require a listed company's annual financial report to include a statement showing, as at a date not more than one month prior to the date of the notice of the AGM:

- all information disclosed to the company in accordance with DTR 5 (in respect of notifiable shareholdings); or
- that there have been no disclosures, if no disclosures have been made.

[LR 9.8.6R (2)].

UK.A29.217.27 Disclosure of directors' interests in shares and disclosure of major shareholdings are considered further in chapter 2 of the Manual of Accounting – Narrative Reporting.

Interim reports

UK.A29.217.28 The FSA's Disclosure and Transparency Rules include specific disclosure requirements for the interim management report in respect of related party transactions. An issuer of shares is required to disclose, as a minimum:

- Related party transactions that have taken place in the first six months of the current financial year and that have materially affected the entity's financial position or the performance during that period.
- Any changes in the related party transactions described in the last annual report that could have a material effect on the entity's financial position or performance in the first six months of the current financial year.

[DTR 4.2.8].

UK.A29.217.29 If an issuer of shares is *not* required to prepare consolidated financial statements, it is required to disclose, as a minimum, any transactions that have been entered into with related parties by the issuer, if such transactions are material and have not been concluded under normal market conditions. The disclosures required include the amount of such transactions, the nature of the related party relationship and other information about the transactions that is considered necessary for an understanding of the issuer's financial position. Information about such transactions may be aggregated according to their nature, except where separate information is necessary for an understanding of the effects of related party transactions on the issuer's financial position. [DTR 4.2.8].

UK.A29.217.30 Interim reports are dealt with in detail in chapter 31.

AIM companies

UK.A29.217.31 An AIM company must also notify transactions with related parties to a Regulatory Information Service as soon as the terms of the transaction are agreed. It must provide details of any transaction it enters into with a related party that exceeds five per cent in any of the class tests set out in Schedule 3 of the AIM Rules. These details include the name of the related party concerned, the nature and extent of the related party's interest in the transaction and the detailed information required by Schedule 4 of the AIM Rules. The notification must also include a statement from the directors of the AIM company (excluding any director who is involved in the transaction as a related party) that, in their opinion, having consulted with the company's nominated adviser, the terms of the transaction are fair and reasonable so far as the company's shareholders are concerned. [AIMR 13].

UK.A29.217.32 The annual financial statements of an AIM company must disclose any transaction with a related party, whether disclosed previously under the AIM Rules or not, where any of the class tests in Schedule 3 of the Rules exceed 0.25 per cent. The disclosure in the financial statements must specify the identity of the related party and the consideration for the transaction. [AIMR 19]. The definition of 'related party' in the AIM Rules is similar to the definition in the Listing Rules, but excludes specific reference to investment managers and controlling shareholders.

PLUS quoted companies

UK.A29.217.33 Entities quoted on PLUS must announce as soon as possible the agreed terms of any material transaction outside the ordinary course of business between the entity, or a subsidiary undertaking, and a related party. The announcement must contain the name of the related party and the nature of his or her relationship with the issuer. [PLUSR 35].

UK.A29.217.34 PLUS will consider that a transaction is not material where a reasonable investor would consider it to be of minor importance only and may include such matters as the grant of an unsecured loan or underwriting arrangements on usual commercial terms, the grant of a lawful indemnity, the payment of directors' remuneration, or participation in an employee saving or incentive scheme. [PLUSR GN35].

UK.A29.217.35 The definition of a related party given in the PLUS rules is *"A person who is a director, shadow director (including his or family and connected persons) or a controlling shareholder of an issuer, its subsidiary or parent undertaking, or subsidiary undertaking of its parent undertaking, or was during the 12 months preceding the transaction".*

Annex — Main disclosure requirements of the Companies Act 2006 and the Listing Rules

Disclosures regarding the related parties shown below include the following;

Related party	**Disclosures**	**Manual chapter No**
Directors and officers		
2006 Act		
Section 412	Notes to financial statements to contain details of directors' remuneration.	5 (NR)
SI 2008/410, Schedule 5 – Part I	Directors' emoluments, pensions and compensation.	5 (NR)
SI 2008/410, Schedule 5 – Part II	Details of highest paid director's emoluments and other disclosures specific to unquoted entities.	5 (NR)
Section 413	Details of advances and credits granted by the company (or its subsidiaries) to its directors.	
Section 413	Details of guarantees entered into by the company (or its subsidiaries) on behalf of its directors.	
	Directors' remuneration report to contain details of:	
2006 Act, SI 2008/410 Schedule 8	The company's remuneration policy and details of individual directors' remuneration packages.	5 (NR)
	Directors' report to state:	
2006 Act Section 416	Name of directors.	2 (NR)
2006 Act Section 992	Significant agreements that the company is a party to that will be affected by a change in control of the company, together with the effects of such agreements, other than agreements where disclosure would be seriously prejudicial and there is no other disclosure obligation.	2 (NR)
FSA	**Items to be included in annual report and accounts**	
LR 9.8.6R (1)	A statement setting out the beneficial and non-beneficial interests of each person who has been a director during (see para UK.A29.217.25) the period under review (including interests of connected persons), and any changes occurring between year end and a date not more than one month prior to date of notice of AGM.	2 (NR)

Related party	Disclosures	Manual chapter No
LR 9.8.4R (10)	Particulars of any contract of significance for a director involving the company or a subsidiary.	
LR 9.8.4R (5), (6)	Directors' emoluments waived or to be waived.	5 (NR)
LR.9.8.8R	The information required by LR 9.8.8R (on directors' remuneration) contained in a report to shareholders by the board.	5 (NR)
LR 9.8.4R (3)	Details of small related party transactions with directors.	
Substantial shareholders		
FSA	**Items to be included in annual report and accounts**	
LR 9.8.4R (12), (13)	Details of dividends waived or to be waived.	
LR 9.8.6R (2)	A statement showing, as at a date not more than one month prior to the date of the notice of the AGM, all information disclosed to the company in accordance with Part 22 of the Companies Act 2006 (information about interests in a company's shares) or DTR 5 (in respect of notifiable shareholdings).	29
LR 9.8.4R (10)	Particulars of contracts of significance with a controlling shareholder.	29
LR 9.8.4R (11)	Particulars of contract for provision of services by a controlling shareholder.	29
LR 9.8.4R (3)	Details of small related party transactions with shareholders.	29
2006 Act, SI 2008/410 4 Sch 9	Notes of subsidiary to disclose ultimate parent company.	24
Group companies and investees		
2006 Act		
Section 409	Notes to the financial statements to contain information about related undertakings.	24
SI 2008/410 4 Sch 9	Disclosure by subsidiary of ultimate *parent company*.	24
SI 2008/410 4 Sch 1-3, 15-17	Disclosure by parent of name and financial information for each *subsidiary undertaking*.	24
SI 2008/410 4 Sch 19	Disclosure details of investment of consolidated undertakings in and name of *associated undertakings* (20% plus of voting rights).	24

Related party	**Disclosures**	**Manual chapter No**
SI 2008/410 4 Sch 18	Name of and information on *joint ventures*.	24
SI 2008/410 4 Sch 4-6, 20-23	Name of and information on *significant holdings* of company or group in investees.	24
SI 2008/410 4 Sch 7	Details of membership of company or group in and name of unlimited company or partnership.	24
Section 410	Alternative disclosure where compliance with section 409 would result in information of excessive length.	24

Chapter 30

Cash flow statements

Chapter 30

Cash flow statements

Objectives and scope of FRS 1

Objectives

30.1 The success, growth and survival of every reporting entity depends on its ability to generate or otherwise obtain cash. Cash flow is a concept that everyone understands and with which they can identify. Reported profit is important to users of financial statements, but so too is an entity's cash flow generating potential. What enables an entity to survive is the tangible resource of cash not just profit, which is merely one indicator of financial performance. Thus, owners look for dividends, suppliers and lenders expect payments and repayments, employees receive wages for their services, and the tax authorities are legally entitled to tax revenues due.

30.2 The principal objective of FRS 1 is to require reporting entities falling within its scope to:

- Report their cash generation and cash absorption for a period by highlighting the significant components of cash flow in a way that facilitates comparison of the cash flow performances of different businesses.
- Provide information that assists in the assessment of their liquidity, solvency and financial adaptability.

[FRS 1 para 1].

30.3 The form of cash flow reporting required under FRS 1 provides useful information on liquidity, solvency and financial adaptability that is additional to that provided by the profit and loss account and balance sheet. A combination of profitability and liquidity data enables users of financial statements to view both perspectives when assessing corporate viability over time (business survival depends on both profits from operations and sound cash management). Reporting historical cash flows also helps management to discharge its stewardship function by showing an entity's past cash flows, solvency and liquidity performance. Although historical cash flow is not necessarily a good indicator of future cash flows, it may nevertheless help users to review the accuracy of their previous predictions and, therefore, act as a base for assessing future cash flow performance and liquidity.

30.4 The standard also sets out how cash flow information should be presented and how extensive it should be. A standard format results in uniform presentation of cash flow information and makes such information much more comparable among companies. This comparability should make the information useful to investors, creditors and other users of financial statements.

[The next paragraph is 30.22.]

Scope

30.22 There is no statutory requirement for companies to prepare a cash flow statement. However, FRS 1 requires all reporting entities that prepare financial statements intended to give a true and fair view of their financial position and profit or loss (or income and expenditure) to include a cash flow statement as a *primary* statement within their financial statements, unless specifically exempted. [FRS 1 paras 4, 5].

Available exemptions

30.23 The following entities are exempt from preparing a cash flow statement.

Subsidiary undertakings

30.24 A subsidiary undertaking, 90 per cent or more of whose voting rights are controlled within a group, is exempt from producing a cash flow statement, provided the consolidated financial statements in which the subsidiary undertaking is included are publicly available. There is no requirement for the parent undertaking's consolidated financial statements to be prepared under the same GAAP as that of the subsidiary or for the parent to prepare and make publicly available a consolidated cash flow statement that includes the cash flows of the subsidiary undertaking. [FRS 1 para 5(a)].

30.24.1 No definition is given in the FRS of the phrase 'publicly available', but it seems clear that it means available to the public in general and not, for instance, just to shareholders. Section 436 of the Companies Act 2006 refers to the publication of accounts and states:

> *"For the purposes of those sections a company is regarded as publishing a document if it publishes, issues or circulates it or otherwise makes it available for public inspection in a manner calculated to invite members of the public generally, or any class of members of the public, to read it."*

30.24.2 We consider that 'publicly available' may be interpreted in this way. However, the test should in practice be judged by reference to whether a copy of the consolidated financial statements can be acquired relatively easily. The financial statements may be on a public register, for example, but if the financial statements themselves cannot be easily obtained, they would not be regarded as publicly available. Where there is no public register but the address from which they may be obtained is given, the financial statements would be regarded as publicly available. See also the example below.

Example – Meaning of publicly available for the purpose of the cash flow statement exemption

A company is a 100% UK subsidiary of a US company. The company is aware of the exemption from preparing a cash flow statement in FRS 1 for over 90% owned subsidiaries, but notes that this is dependent on the parent's consolidated financial statements being publicly available. At present the US company's consolidated financial statements are not publicly available. However the US company is proposing to prepare non-statutory consolidated financial statements that it would make available to the public on request. If they stated in the UK company's financial statements that these consolidated financial statements of the US parent could be obtained from a particular address, could the UK company take the exemption?

The term 'publicly available' does not, we believe, mean that the US parent has to be SEC-listed and publish its financial statements widely. It does mean that the UK company should include in its financial statements wording to the effect that copies of the consolidated financial statements of the US parent are available from a stated address and that if someone writes to that address they will be sent those financial statements. As to what 'consolidated financial statements' means for the purpose of the FRS 1 exemption, in our view it does not need to be a full set of financial statements under US GAAP or UK GAAP. But what is provided must be reasonable, that is, at least a balance sheet and profit and loss account with reasonable detail, for example at least the UK legal format headings plus accounting policies etc. The consolidated financial statements do not need to be audited.

30.24.3 UK company legislation requires a company that is a subsidiary undertaking to give the name of the largest group and the smallest group of undertakings of which the company is a member and for which consolidated financial statements are drawn up. In addition, if copies of those financial statements are available to the public, the addresses from which they can be obtained must be stated in the notes to its financial statements. [SI 2008/410 4 Sch 8]. If no such address is given in its financial statements, it will be difficult for a subsidiary company to argue that consolidated financial statements in which it is included are publicly available.

30.24.4 A company that is part of a group where the parent company takes advantage of available exemptions in the Companies Act 2006, and does not prepare consolidated financial statements, will not be able to take advantage of the exemption in FRS 1 and will have to publish a cash flow statement in its own financial statements.

30.25 The following examples consider the practical application of the exemption from cash flow statements for subsidiary undertakings when there are changes in the group structure.

Example 1 – Availability of FRS 1 exemption when subsidiary is sold after the period end.

A subsidiary company was 100% owned by a US listed company at the balance sheet date of 31 December 20X6. Because of this it states in its financial statements that it has taken advantage of the exemption in FRS 1 not to prepare a cash flow statement.

The US company is selling the subsidiary to an individual and this is going to occur prior to the financial statements being signed, resulting in the subsidiary no longer qualifying as a 90% owned subsidiary on the date of signing. Does this mean that the subsidiary will have to prepare and disclose a cash flow statement and also disclose its transactions with the US company in the financial statements as at 31 December 20X6? That is, do the rules apply to the situation at the balance sheet date or at the date of signing?

A company that is wholly-owned at its year end (31 December 20X6) and consolidated into the parent's publicly available consolidated financial statements at that date is entitled to the exemptions in FRS 1. The fact that the company is subsequently sold by the parent does not affect the entitlement to the exemption in the company's financial statements for the year ended 31 December 20X6, that is, for the purpose of the exemption for subsidiary undertakings in paragraph 5(a) of FRS 1, the exemption applies to the situation at the balance sheet date.

Example 2 – Availability of FRS 1 exemption when subsidiary is acquired during the year

Company A was not a subsidiary at its last year end, 31 December 20X5, and under FRS 1, prepared a cash flow statement. In April 20X6 it was acquired by another company, company B, which is producing financial statements to 31 December 20X6. The financial statements of company B will be consolidated and will include company A from the date of acquisition in April 20X6. Does company A have to produce a cash flow statement for the year to 31 December 20X6 in its individual financial statements?

FRS 1 exempts subsidiaries, 90% or more of whose voting rights are controlled with in the group, from the requirement to present a cash flow statement provided that consolidated financial statements in which the company is included are publicly available. [FRS 1 para 5]. Although not specifically stated in the standard, for the purpose of the exemption for subsidiary undertakings in paragraph 5(a) of FRS 1, the year end position is the one we take and, therefore, if company A has 90% or more of its voting rights owned by company B at the year end and company B makes its consolidated financial statements publicly available, then company A can take the exemption and is not required to present a cash flow statement.

Mutual life assurance companies

30.26 Mutual life assurance societies that are owned by policy holders and friendly societies that carry on mutual life assurance business are exempt from producing a cash flow statement. [FRS 1 para 5(b)].

Pension schemes

30.27 Pension schemes are exempt from producing a cash flow statement. [FRS 1 para 5(c)]. The SORP, 'Financial reports of pension schemes', does not require pension schemes to produce a cash flow statement. This is because information about the cash flows of the scheme is normally provided by the fund account and net asset statement. Although the fund account adopts an accruals basis of accounting rather than a strict cash flow basis, re-presenting the information in the format of a cash flow statement would generally not provide any significant additional information for the readers of pension scheme financial statements.

Open-ended investment funds

30.28 The standard exempts open-ended investment funds from producing a cash flow statement provided certain conditions are satisfied. For this purpose, the standard defines an investment fund by using three of the four conditions for qualifying as an investment company as set out previously in section 266(2) of the Companies Act 1985 (now in section 833(2) of the Companies Act 2006). [FRS 1 para 2]. The fourth condition, which prohibits capital profits from being distributed, is intentionally left out of the standard's definition so as to allow unauthorised unit trust type vehicles (often used for unquoted or venture capital investments) and certain investment entities whose trust deeds or articles do not prohibit distribution of capital profits to claim the exemption from preparing a cash flow statement.

30.29 Clearly, the exemption is broad and means that a wide range of authorised and unauthorised investment vehicles will not have to prepare cash flow statements. However, the exemption is conditional on meeting all of the following criteria:

- Substantially all of the entity's investments are highly liquid.
- Substantially all of the entity's investments are carried at market value.
- The entity provides a statement of changes in net assets.

[FRS 1 para 5(d)].

[The next paragraph is 30.31.]

Small companies and groups

30.31 Small (but not medium-sized) companies entitled to file abbreviated financial statements with the Registrar under section 444 of the Companies Act 2006 need not prepare a cash flow statement. [FRS 1 para 5(f)]. Generally, a company qualifies as small if it meets the relevant conditions and the size criteria specified in the Act (see further chapter 32). A small company is not actually required to file abbreviated financial statements, but merely has to be entitled to do so in order to claim the exemption from preparing a cash flow statement. However, the exemption is not available where the small company is, or was at any time within the financial year to which the accounts relate, any one of the following:

- A public company.
- An authorised insurance company, banking company, e-money issuer, a MiFID investment firm or a UCITS management company (as defined by the Financial Services and Markets Act 2000).
- A company that carries on insurance market activity.
- A member of an ineligible group. A group is ineligible if any of its members is:
  - A public company.
  - A body corporate (other than a company) whose shares are admitted to trading on a regulated market in an EEA State.
  - A person (other than a small company) who has permission under Part 4 of the Financial Services and Markets Act 2000 to carry on a regulated activity.
  - A small company that is an authorised insurance company, a banking company, an e-money issuer, a MiFID investment firm or a UCITS management company.
  - A person who carries on insurance market activity.

[CA06 Sec 384(1)(2)].

30.32 The FRSSE encourages, but does not require, smaller entities to prepare a cash flow statement. Where a smaller entity voluntarily produces a cash flow statement, the statement should be prepared using the indirect method as discussed in paragraph 30.71. This is because the indirect method is helpful in understanding the connection between the cash generated during the period and the resulting profit.

30.33 Where a small company is also the parent company of a small group and the parent company opts not to prepare consolidated financial statements under section 398 of the Companies Act 2006, a consolidated cash flow statement need not be prepared. Although this would appear to be obvious, the exemption is not specifically mentioned in FRS 1 as it only makes reference in paragraph 5(f) of FRS 1 to the exemptions for *small companies when filing accounts with the Registrar*. Nevertheless, it will have the effect of applying in practice. This is because if a parent company of a small group can claim the exemption from having to prepare consolidated financial statements, then it is certain that the parent company and each of its subsidiary undertakings will qualify as small companies in their own right and will individually be exempt from preparing a cash flow statement. Consequently, a small parent will not have to include a consolidated cash flow statement or its own cash flow statement when preparing its individual financial statements.

30.34 Similarly, a consolidated cash flow statement is not required, for the reasons stated above, where the small group voluntarily prepares consolidated financial statements, although it may make sense to include a consolidated cash flow statement in this situation.

Medium-sized companies and groups

30.35 Medium-sized companies are not exempt from producing cash flow statements.

30.36 Under the Companies Act 2006, there is no exemption for medium-sized companies from producing consolidated financial statements. A consolidated cash flow statement is required in the group financial statements for a medium-sized group.

Small unincorporated entities

30.37 Entities that are unincorporated, but would satisfy the criteria for small company exemptions had they been incorporated under the relevant Companies Act are exempt from preparing a cash flow statement. [FRS 1 para 5(g)]. They are, nevertheless, encouraged to prepare one if they consider it appropriate on cost-benefit grounds.

Other entities

30.38 Except for the above exemptions, the provisions of the FRS apply across all industry groups since cash flow is relevant to all businesses. This means that banks, insurance companies and other financial institutions have to present cash flow information. Because of the special nature of their businesses, FRS 1 requires slightly different formats for banks and insurance companies. Appendix I to the standard provides illustrations of amended layouts for cash flow statements for a bank and an insurance group.

Listed subsidiary companies

30.39 If a UK company is a more than 90 per cent subsidiary of another company, the consolidated financial statements of which are publicly available, the subsidiary company would appear to qualify for an exemption from giving a cash flow statement under FRS 1 as more than 90 per cent of the voting rights are controlled by its parent. However, when a subsidiary is listed, this raises an additional consideration with regards to whether a cash flow statement must be presented as the subsidiary must also comply with the rules of the UK Listing Authority.

30.39.1 The Disclosure and Transparency Rules require companies to include audited financial statements in their annual report. For individual company financial statements, these audited financial statements must be prepared in accordance with national law (in this case under UK GAAP). [DTR para 4.1.6]. Paragraph 4.1 does not contain an overriding requirement to include information on cash flows in the financial statements. On this basis, there does not appear to be any requirement in the DTR that precludes listed subsidiaries reporting under UK GAAP in individual financial statements from taking the FRS 1 exemption and not producing a cash flow statement. Although there is no requirement to do so, companies may wish to include a cash flow statement in their annual report as this provides useful and relevant information to the users of the financial statements.

Preparation of cash flow statements

30.40 It is consistent with the objective stated in paragraph 30.5 above that a cash flow statement should focus on identifying the cash effects of transactions with parties that are external to the reporting entity and their impact on its cash position. Only those transactions that involve a *cash flow* should be reported in the cash flow statement [FRS 1 para 6]. *Cash flow* is defined as an increase or decrease in an amount of cash. [FRS 1 para 2].

Definition of cash

30.41 As the cash flow statement only reflects movements in cash, the definition of cash is central to its proper preparation. The standard does not define cash as used in common parlance, but extends the definition to include overdrafts that are repayable on demand. Overdrafts are included in the definition because they are generally viewed as negative cash balances and effectively repayable on demand. Thus cash includes:

- Cash in hand, and also deposits, including those denominated in foreign currencies, *repayable on demand* with any bank or other qualifying financial institutions.
- Overdrafts from any bank or qualifying financial institutions repayable on demand.

[FRS 1 para 2].

For this purpose, a qualifying financial institution is an entity that as part of its business receives deposits or other repayable funds and grants credits for its own account. [FRS 1 para 2].

30.42 One impact of the definition of cash is that monies transferred between deposits that qualify as cash do not result in cash inflows and outflows, but are merely movements within the overall cash balance. For instance, a transfer from a no-notice deposit account to reduce the company's overdraft would not be reflected in cash flows as it is an intra cash movement. However, all charges and credits on accounts qualifying as cash, such as bank interest, bank fees, deposits or withdrawals other than movements wholly within them, represent cash inflows and outflows of the reporting entity.

Meaning of 'repayable on demand'

30.43 In order to qualify as cash, deposits must be *'repayable on demand'*, which they are if they meet one of the following criteria:

- They can be withdrawn at any time or demanded without notice and without penalty.
- A period of notice of no more than 24 hours or one working day has been agreed.

[FRS 1 para 2].

30.43.1 *Without notice* implies that the instrument would be readily convertible into known amounts of cash on demand, that is, not subject to any time restriction. Therefore, monies deposited in a bank account for an unspecified period, but which can only be withdrawn by giving notice of more than 24 hours or one working day would not fall to be treated as cash under the definition. However, such funds often can be withdrawn early by paying a penalty. In some situations, this penalty payment may not be significant enough to cause any appreciable change in the capital amount withdrawn. Nevertheless, the standard makes it clear that cash is repayable on demand if it is in practice available within 24 hours *without penalty*. Therefore, repayable on demand implies both withdrawal without penalty and without notice, or if a notice period has been agreed it must not exceed 24 hours or one working day. If the deposits can be withdrawn immediately (that is, with no notice or, for example, with 24 hours notice) but with loss of interest earned then this is a penalty and so the deposits do not fall within the definition of cash. We interpret penalty to be wider than simply the loss of original capital invested, that is, it includes loss of interest.

Definition of liquid resources

30.44 The definition of cash is sufficiently narrow to exclude investments, however liquid or near maturity. Nevertheless, companies normally use a range of such investments like term deposits, gilts, money market instruments, listed equity securities and Euronotes, not for their investment potential, but for managing their overall cash or net debt position. If the focus of the cash flow statement is to report movements in pure cash, the question arises as to where in the cash flow statement movements in such investments, which do not qualify as cash, but which are nevertheless used increasingly in cash management and treasury operations, should be reported.

30.45 The heading 'management of liquid resources' differentiates investments that are effectively used in managing the entity's net debt or net funds position from those that are held for their investment potential. However, to qualify as a liquid resource, the investment must be held as a readily disposable store of value. To be held as a readily disposable store of value, the investment must be held as a current asset investment. Fixed asset investments do not qualify, because by definition these are held for use on a continuing basis and so are not readily disposable. For this purpose, a readily disposable investment is one that is not only disposable by the entity without curtailing or disrupting its business, but also satisfies either of the following criteria:

- It is readily convertible into known amounts of cash at or close to its carrying amount.
- It is traded in an active market.

[FRS 1 para 2].

30.46 The first criterion is particularly relevant for classifying investments in short-term deposits. Although a measure of liquidity, or a maturity period, is not specifically mentioned in the definition, the standard explains that the criterion that the deposit should be readily converted into cash at or near its carrying amount would tend to exclude any that are more than one year from maturity on acquisition. [FRS 1 para 52]. A period of one year would also be consistent with the investment's classification in the balance sheet as a current asset investment, a condition that is necessary for the investment to qualify as a liquid resource.

30.47 Liquid resources meeting the first condition are likely to encompass investments held with qualifying financial institutions that are short-dated and on which there are very little price fluctuation between the time the deposit was made and its ultimate conversion into cash. Therefore, it does not matter whether a term-deposit can be withdrawn by giving notice of more than 24 hours or whether the deposit can be withdrawn prior to its maturity by payment of a penalty, provided the penalty is not significant to cause any appreciable change in capital value. It does not also matter whether the maturity period is of a short duration (say three months) or medium duration (say six months to a year). As long as the deposit is readily convertible into a known amount of cash at or near its carrying amount and there are no restrictions as to the investor's ability to dispose of the investment without curtailing the business, it will qualify as a liquid resource. Deposits intended to be held for a long term, say between one and two years, are unlikely to qualify, even though they may be used by the entity in managing its overall cash or debt position. This is because, according to the definition, they are not sufficiently liquid. Therefore, any movements in them would fall to be reported under capital expenditure and financial investments.

30.48 The second condition allows current asset investments such as government securities, equity and debt instruments in other entities and derivative instruments to be treated as liquid resources, provided they are traded in an active market. Where an active market exists, the inference is that the instruments are easily exchangeable into known amount of cash and, hence, will represent readily disposable stores of value. Therefore, unlisted investments held as current assets are unlikely to qualify as liquid resources.

30.49 Provided they represent readily disposable stores of value, and meet either of the conditions set out in paragraph 30.45, a wide range of current asset investments will qualify as liquid resources. The emphasis is on a wider measure of liquidity rather than the type of the investment. The standard does not *require* all readily disposable investments to be classified as liquid resources. An entity can *choose* which of its current asset investments will be treated as liquid resources. However, it would need to explain its policy and any changes to its policy (see further para 30.106).

Treatment of borrowings

30.50 Borrowings, whether short or long-term, do not qualify as liquid resources, although bank overdrafts repayable on demand are included in cash (see para 30.41). It follows that, except for bank overdrafts, cash flows arising from all forms of borrowings, including commercial paper, should be included within the financing section of the cash flow statement.

30.50.1 A company may have an invoice discounting facility with a lending institution that is not a registered bank. Paragraph 2 of FRS 1 defines an overdraft as *'a borrowing facility repayable on demand that is used by drawing on a current account with a qualifying financial institution'*. To the extent that the lender meets the definition of a qualifying financial institution (that is it was an entity that as part of its business receives deposits or other repayable funds and grants credit for its own account) and the discounting facility is repayable on demand, the discounting facility would meet the definition of an overdraft. It would thus be classified as cash under FRS 1. The operating cash flow would occur when the debtors repay.

30.50.2 If the balance shown in the cash flow statement as 'cash' includes items that are otherwise classified in the balance sheet, a note should be presented reconciling the cash per the cash flow statement with the two or more relevant headings on the balance sheet.

Format of cash flow statements

30.51 The standard requires cash flows to be classified under the following standard headings:

- Operating activities.
- Dividends from joint ventures and associates.
- Returns on investments and servicing of finance.
- Taxation.
- Capital expenditure and financial investments.

- Acquisitions and disposals.
- Equity dividends paid.
- Management of liquid resources.
- Financing.

30.52 The cash flows for each of the headings should be listed in the order set out above. However, the last two headings may be combined under a single heading relating to the management of liquid resources and financing provided the cash flows relating to each are shown separately and separate subtotals are given. [FRS 1 para 7]. Some companies that manage their liquid investments and borrowings as an integrated treasury operation, making investments when rates are good and drawing down on borrowings when rates are low, and matching investments with borrowings, may find this ability to combine the two headings particularly useful (see Table 30.2).

30.53 Presenting a subtotal after any of the above headings is neither required nor prohibited. Therefore, it is possible to present a subtotal, for instance, after capital expenditure and before acquisitions and disposals. Indeed, some entities may consider it appropriate to highlight this figure as it indicates a measure of 'free cash flow' that their businesses have generated and over which they have discretionary spending ability. An example is given in Table 30.1 below. Although this measure does not necessarily distinguish between discretionary capital expenditure for expansion from that incurred for routine replacement and presumes that acquisitions and, more importantly, disposals are discretionary it may nevertheless be useful. Some may find it preferable to present a subtotal after equity dividends paid as indicated in Table 30.2 below. Others may find it useful to draw a sub-total before financing as shown in Table 30.3 below. The ability to present a subtotal at any level enables entities to highlight cash flows that they consider appropriate to their particular circumstances as illustrated in the examples below.

Table 30.1 – 'Free cash flow' sub-total in cash flow statement

Coats Viyella Plc – Annual Report and Accounts – 31 December 1998

Analysis of free cash flow

For the year ended 31 December 1998	1998 £m	1997 £m
Net cash inflow from operating activities	187.1	177.3
Returns on investments and servicing of finance	(43.5)	(54.9)
Tax paid	(25.2)	(45.9)
Capital expenditure and financial investment	(57.2)	(85.3)
Free cash flow	61.2	(8.8)

Table 30.2 – Sub-total after 'equity dividends' in cash flow statement

Bass PLC – Annual Report and Financial Statements – 30 September 1996

GROUP CASH FLOW STATEMENT

For the year ended 30 September 1996	Note	1996 £m	1996 £m	1995 £m	1995 £m
Operating activities	25		992		885
Interest paid		(127)		(128)	
Dividends paid to minority shareholders		(5)		(4)	
Interest received		51		57	
Returns on investments and servicing of finance			(81)		(75)
UK corporation tax paid		(92)		(112)	
Overseas corporate tax paid		(19)		(39)	
Taxation			(111)		(151)
Tangible fixed assets		(547)		(372)	
Trade loans		(60)		(65)	
Other fixed asset investments		(56)		(68)	
Paid		(663)		(505)	
Tangible fixed assets		24		97	
Trade loans		85		96	
Other fixed asset investments		45		28	
Received		154		221	
Capital expenditure and financial investment			(509)		(284)
Consideration for acquisitions	24	(246)		(306)	
Cash for overdrafts acquired		12		–	
Acquisitions			(234)		(306)
Equity dividends			(205)		(189)
Net cash flow	25		(148)		(120)
Management of liquid resources and financing	26		154		123
Movement in cash and overdrafts			6		3

Table 30.3 – Sub-total before 'financing' in cash flow statement

TI Group plc – Annual Report – 31 December 1997

CASH FLOW STATEMENT (extract)

FOR THE YEAR ENDED 31ST DECEMBER 1997 (extract)

	Notes	1997 £m	1996 £m
Net cash inflow from operating activities	**23**	**241.4**	218.1
Dividends received from joint ventures and associates	**23**	**10.6**	11.6
Returns on investments and servicing of finance	**24**	**(13.3)**	(4.7)
Taxation	**25**	**(73.5)**	(61.5)
Capital expenditure and financial investment	**26**	**(59.6)**	(50.0)
Acquisitions and disposals	**27**	**(13.7)**	(175.4)
Equity dividends paid		**(69.6)**	(55.2)
Management of liquid resources	**28**	**(94.0)**	60.8
Cash flow before financing		**(71.7)**	(56.3)
Issue of shares		**5.8**	12.8
Capital element of finance leases		**(0.4)**	(0.7)
Increase/(decrease) in loans		**26.7**	64.2
Financing		**32.1**	76.3
(Decrease)/increase in cash		**(39.6)**	20.0

30.54 There is also a degree of flexibility allowed in the reporting of the individual elements of cash inflows or outflows that make up each of the standard headings. Although the individual cash inflows or outflows should not be netted against each other, except in certain circumstances as explained in paragraph 30.59 below, they could either be reported gross on the face of the cash flow statement under the appropriate standard headings or shown in the notes. This means that it is acceptable to present the (net) totals for each of the above headings on the face of the cash flow statement. This may avoid clutter on the face of the cash flow statement and possibly make it easier to understand.

Classification of cash flows

30.55 A cash flow statement must classify cash receipts and cash payments under each of the nine standard headings. The classification of cash flows into reasonably distinct groups provides useful analysis about the relative importance of each of these groups and the inter-relationship between them. It should also provide useful information for comparison purposes across reporting entities.

30.56 The standard provides specific guidance for classifying cash flows. It sets out each individual element of cash inflows and outflows that should be included under a particular standard heading. Entities are required to disclose separately, where material, the individual categories of cash flows within each standard headings, either in the cash flow statement or in a note [FRS 1 para 8]. The way in which elements of cash flow are attributed to each standard heading is considered from paragraphs 30.67 below.

30.57 There are other elements of cash flows, not considered in the standard headings, that may cause classification difficulties. Clearly, it is not possible for the standard to provide an exhaustive list of all types of different cash flows. Consequently, the standard stipulates that where a cash flow is not specified in the categories set out in the standard headings, it should be shown under the most appropriate standard heading in accordance with the transaction's substance. [FRS 1 para 10]. Since the transaction's substance also determines the way in which it is normally reported in the profit and loss account and the balance sheet, it follows that there should be consistency of treatment in the cash flow statement and in the other primary statements. This requirement for consistency eliminates subjectivity in classifying cash flows not identified as specific items under the standard headings. [FRS 1 para 57]. Therefore, following this general principle, cash outflows relating to development expenditure that are capitalised in the balance sheet would fall to be shown under capital expenditure in the cash flow statement. Similarly, where the expenditure is written off as part of operating profit in the profit and loss account, the cash outflows would fall to be included in operating cash flows. Another example is the receipt of a government grant. To the extent that the grant is made as a contribution towards fixed assets, the substance argument would require the cash receipt to be shown under capital expenditure in the cash flow statement, irrespective of whether it is reported in the balance sheet as a deduction from the cost of the specific asset or included as deferred income and amortised over the expected useful economic life of the asset. Similarly grants given as a contribution towards revenue expenditure should be included in operating cash flows to match their treatment in the profit and loss account.

30.58 There is one situation where the general rule of classifying cash flows according to the transaction's substance is not considered appropriate. This applies to interest paid that is capitalised, for instance, as part of the construction cost of an asset in the balance sheet. Following the general rule would require reporting the interest paid under capital expenditure in the cash flow statement. However, all interest paid is specifically required to be shown under 'returns on investments and servicing of finance' heading, regardless of whether or not it is capitalised in the balance sheet. [FRS 1 para 10].

Gross or net cash flows

30.59 Generally cash inflows and outflows under each of the standard headings should be reported gross, whether on the face of the cash flow statement or in a note to it. However, there are some exceptions. These are as follows:

- The reporting of gross cash flows does not apply to operating activities where the indirect method is followed (see para 30.71).

- Cash inflows and outflows relating to the management of liquid resources or financing may be netted against each other provided the inflows and outflows meet either of the following conditions:
  - They relate in substance to a single financing transaction.
  - They are due to short maturities and high turnover occurring from rollover or reissue (for example, a commercial paper programme or short-term deposits).

[FRS 1 para 9].

30.60 The ability to net cash inflows and outflows relating to the management of liquid resources or financing allows a more reasonable presentation of transactions in many cases. Many large industrial and commercial companies raise funds by issuing commercial paper in the form of unsecured promissory notes with fixed maturity between seven and 364 days. Normally these are issued at a discount to the face value and provide a cheaper source of finance than other means of borrowing. A commercial paper programme may involve issues and redemptions throughout the financial year and often these are backed up by committed bank facilities. The reporting of these transactions as net may be considered to give a fairer representation of the transactions' substance.

[The next paragraph is 30.62.]

30.62 Similarly, short-term funds that are continuously rolled over by successive deposits and withdrawals will fall to be reported net under the second condition. A question arises as to whether netting is permissible in circumstances where withdrawals from short-term deposits and payments into short-term deposits are effected with different parties. The standard is silent on this point, but in practice, treasurers often withdraw funds from one party and place them on deposit with another party to increase the overall returns on those funds. Therefore, as long as the short-term deposit is constantly renewed or rolled over, whether with the same party or with a different party, it is acceptable to report the cash inflows and outflows on a net basis. The alternative of showing the gross amounts for raising and repaying money under a commercial paper programme or constantly renewable short-term deposits would not add very much to users' understanding of a company's treasury activities.

30.63 A further question can be raised with regards to the presentation of cash flows for a transaction where linked presentation is used in other primary statements by an entity that has not adopted FRS 26, 'Financial instruments: Recognition and measurement'.

Example – Cash flows where linked presentation is used

An entity may adopt linked presentation for a debt factoring arrangement when the requirements of FRS 5, 'Reporting the substance of transactions', are met and the entity has not adopted FRS 26. Should the cash flows be reported gross, with the proceeds from factoring as a source of financing, or net, with the movement in net debtors treated as an operating cash flow?

FRS 5 says that a scheme that qualifies for linked presentation is, in substance, a financing arrangement, but the non-returnable proceeds are not a liability, nor is the gross amount of the debtor an asset. These two statements may seem contradictory, but since the net amount is regarded as the asset, it is logical to show the non-returnable proceeds as operating cash flows. On this basis, the non-returnable proceeds should be treated as a partial collection of the debtors.

Additional classification

30.64 The individual items of cash inflows and outflows set out under each of the standard headings in FRS 1, other than operating activities, should not be regarded as depicting a rigid set of classification rules. The analysis under each heading merely refers to those items that would normally fall to be included under that heading and, hence, prescribe a minimum acceptable level of disaggregation of cash flow information. The individual items may be further sub-divided or new items added, if appropriate, to give a full description of the activities of the business or to provide segmental information. [FRS 1 para 8]. Indeed, the standard encourages entities to disclose additional information relevant to their particular circumstances. [FRS 1 para 56]. For example, repayments of amounts borrowed may be sub-divided further to show payments made on the redemption of debentures and other repayments of long-term borrowings. Another example would be to divide the cash flows from operating activities into those relating to continuing activities and those relating to discontinued operations (see further para 30.168).

30.65 Whatever level of detail is disclosed, it must be sufficient and relevant so that the user is able to understand the relationship between the entity's different activities and the way in which they generate and expend cash. On the other hand, too much information can cloud or obscure key issues. The problem is one of striking a balance between what the entity needs to report and how much explanation is required by the users. The amount of detail to be presented will be an area of judgement based upon the reporting entity's circumstances.

Departure from the standard presentation

30.66 Entities can add new items within each of the standard headings, but are not permitted to use a different heading, or depart from the format headings.

Classification of cash flows by standard headings

Cash flow from operating activities

30.67 Cash flows from operating activities generally include the cash effects of transactions and other events relating to the entity's operating or trading activities. The net cash flow from operating activities, therefore, represents the movements in cash resulting from the operations shown in the profit and loss account in arriving at operating profit. In addition, cash flows relating to any provision in respect of operating items, whether or not the provision was included in operating profit, should also be included as part of operating cash flows. For example, cash flows in respect of redundancy payments provided as part of the cost of a fundamental reorganisation or closure of operations that is reported outside operating profit in accordance with FRS 3, 'Reporting financial performance', will fall to be included in operating cash flows (see para 30.114). Similarly, operating cash flows will also include cash flows in respect of provision for integration costs following an acquisition [FRS 1 para 11].

[The next paragraph is 30.69.]

30.69 Operating cash flows may be reported on the gross or net basis (also known as the direct method and the indirect method respectively). [FRS 1 para 7]. Under the direct method, the major classes of gross operating cash receipts (for example, cash collected from customers) and gross operating cash payments (for example, cash paid to suppliers and employees) are reported on the face of the cash flow statement under operating activities. An example of the direct method of presentation for net operating cash flow is illustrated in Table 30.4.

Table 30.4 – Direct method of presentation

Marks and Spencer p.l.c. – Annual Report and Financial Statements – 31 March 1996

Consolidated cash flow statement (extract)

FOR THE YEAR ENDED 31 MARCH 1996

	Notes	**1996** **£m**	*1995* *£m*
OPERATING ACTIVITIES			
Received from customers		**7,046.0**	*6,665.0*
Payments to suppliers		**(4,741.9)**	*(4,426.3)*
Payments to and on behalf of employees		**(928.4)**	*(782.8)*
Other payments		**(566.9)**	*(547.1)*
Net cash inflow from operating activities	**24**	**808.8**	*908.8*

Notes to the financial statements (extract)

24 RECONCILIATION OF OPERATING PROFIT TO NET CASH INFLOW FROM OPERATING ACTIVITIES

	THE GROUP	
	1996	*1995*
	£m	*£m*
Operating profit	**940.2**	*896.5*
Depreciation	**160.4**	*150.7*
Increase in stocks	**(45.8)**	*(22.4)*
Increase in customer balances	**(190.2)**	*(144.5)*
Increase in other debtors	**(109.6)**	*(22.7)*
Increase in creditors	**53.8**	*51.2*
Net cash inflow from operating activities	**808.8**	*908.8*

Operating profit has increased by £43.7m whereas the net cash inflow from operating activities of £808.8m is £100.0m lower than last year. This reflects the £90.0m payment in respect of the pension scheme deficit (see note 10A) together with an increase of £45.7m in the movement of customer balances within Financial Services.

30.70 The standard allows, but does not require, reporting entities to provide information on gross operating cash flows. [FRS 1 para 58]. However, the standard makes it mandatory to provide a reconciliation between operating profit and net cash flow from operating activities as discussed in paragraph 30.72 below, *even where the direct method is adopted* as indicated in Table 30.4 above. For this reason and because of the additional burden of producing gross cash flow information, the direct method has not been commonly used in the UK.

30.71 Under the indirect method, the same operating cash flows as under the direct method are reported except that the net figure is produced by adjusting operating profit for non-cash items (such as depreciation), changes in working capital (such as accruals and prepayments) and bringing in cash flows relating to any provision in respect of operating items, whether or not the provision was included in operating profit. However, in keeping with the objective that a cash flow statement should only include items of pure cash flows, the standard requires that under the indirect method the cash flow statement should start with the net cash flow from operating activities.

Reconciliation of operating profit to net cash flow from operating activities

30.72 The reconciliation of operating profit to net cash flow from operating activities is not part of the cash flow statement. However, companies may choose whether to present the reconciliation as a supplementary note to the cash flow statement, or adjoining the cash flow statement. If the latter approach is adopted, the reconciliation statement should be separately identified and clearly labelled to maintain the distinction that it is not part of the primary cash flow statement. [FRS 1 para 12]. This is because the reconciling items are not themselves cash flows and to report them as part of the cash flow statement itself would be inappropriate.

30.72.1 The first example in Appendix 1 of FRS 1 presents the reconciliation statement immediately under the general heading 'Cash flow statement'. In this way, the reconciliation appears to be part of the cash flow statement itself, which is clearly not the intention. It may also be confusing to have two headings for cash flow statement on the same page. A way of dealing with this is to entitle the page something along the lines of 'Information on cash flows'. The term 'Cash flow statement' could then be used to describe the statement itself. A way of avoiding the problem is to position the reconciliation either under the cash flow statement or in a note.

30.73 The reconciliation should disclose separately the movements in stock, debtors and creditors related to operating activities and other differences (for example, depreciation or impairment of fixed assets included within operating profit, provisions, etc) between cash flow and operating results.

30.74 For the reconciliation to be properly carried out, it will be necessary to analyse the movements in opening and closing debtors and creditors in order to eliminate those movements that relate to items reported in the standard headings other than operating activities. For example, a company may purchase a fixed asset prior to the year end on credit. In this situation, the closing creditor balance would need to be adjusted to eliminate the amount owing for the fixed asset purchase before working out the balance sheet movements for operating creditors. It follows that movements in working capital included in the reconciliation would not be the same as the difference between the opening and the closing balance sheet amounts. Indeed, under FRS 1 this is rarely the case except in very simple situations. This is because the balance sheet movements in stock, debtors, and creditors may be affected by such items as acquisitions and disposals of subsidiaries during the year (see para 30.134), exchange differences on working capital of foreign subsidiaries (see example para 30.156) and other non-cash adjustments for opening and closing accruals of non-operating items.

30.75 A question arises as to whether the eliminated items within each balance sheet movement of working capital need to be reported separately so that the overall movement between the opening and closing balance sheet amounts is readily understandable. For example, a company could identify the total balance sheet movement in creditors and then separately itemise the operating element and the other movements. The standard is silent on this point and, in practice, this is rarely done, in the majority of cases only the operating movements are reported.

Dividends from joint ventures and associates

30.75.1 FRS 9 requires that the investor's share of the results of its equity accounted entities is included immediately *after* group operating profit rather than in group operating profit. Consistent with this treatment the cash flows relating to dividends received from joint ventures and associates are reported under a specific heading, between operating activities and returns on investment and servicing of finance. [FRS 1 para 12A].

Returns on investments and servicing of finance

30.76 'Returns on investments and servicing of finance' are receipts resulting from the ownership of an investment and payments to providers of finance, non-equity shareholders (for example, holders of preference shares) and minority interests, excluding those items that are specifically required by the standard to be classified under another heading. [FRS 1 para 13].

[The next paragraph is 30.78.]

30.78 Cash inflows in respect of returns on investments include the following items that should be separately disclosed:

- Interest received, including any related tax recovered.
- Dividends received net of any tax credits (except dividends from equity accounted entities).

[FRS 1 para 14].

30.79 Similarly, cash outflows from servicing of finance include:

- Interest paid (even if capitalised), including any tax deducted and paid to the relevant tax authority.
- Cash flows that are treated as finance costs (this will include issue costs on debt and non-equity share capital).
- The interest element of finance lease rental payments.
- Dividends paid on non-equity shares of the entity. Non-equity dividends are defined by FRS 1 as dividends relating to instruments classified as liabilities in accordance with FRS 25, 'Financial instruments: Presentation'.
- Dividends paid by subsidiaries to equity and non-equity minority interests.

[FRS 1 para 15].

This is consistent with FRS 25, which requires financial instruments that have the substance of debt, such as certain non-equity shares, to be classified as such on the balance sheet and the dividends paid on those shares to be recognised as interest in the profit and loss account.

30.80 Investment income included under this heading will include income from current asset investments, irrespective of whether they are regarded as liquid resources, and on fixed asset investments, other than equity accounted entities whose results are included as part of total operating profit.

30.81 The standard requires that the cash flow effect of any tax relating to interest should be shown as part of the interest. [FRS 1 para 15(a)] This applies to tax deducted at source on interest received as well as to tax withheld on interest paid. This means that the actual cash received (or paid) in respect of interest must be shown, but where tax has been deducted at source (or withheld) and is subsequently recovered (or paid), it should also be included under this heading as part of interest received (or paid) at the time of receipt (payment). For example, where there is a timing difference between the actual interest received (or paid) and the settlement of the tax, the net interest received (or paid) would fall to be shown in the period in which the cash is received (or paid), whereas the cash flow effect of any tax deducted at source (or withheld) would fall to be shown in the period in which the tax is recovered (or paid).

30.82 Interest paid should be the actual amount of interest paid during the period, irrespective of whether it is charged to the profit and loss account or capitalised in the balance sheet. Similarly, the interest paid on finance lease obligations should be reported under this heading.

[The next paragraph is 30.84.]

30.84 The cash flows relating to finance costs for debt (including shares classified as debt under FRS 25) should be reported under this heading. Therefore, in addition to reporting finance costs such as dividends paid on shares classified as liabilities and interest paid on debt instruments, this heading would also include any payments made for the issue of those shares and debt instruments. Furthermore, the cash flow effects of items such as discounts and premiums on such shares and debt instruments, which are treated as finance costs, would also fall to be included under this heading (see para 30.180).

30.85 The segregation of interest and dividends received and interest paid under the heading 'returns on investments and servicing of finance' is relevant particularly to non-financial companies, as these items are normally shown after operating profit. However, many investment companies and financial institutions show interest received and dividends received in their profit and loss account prior to arriving at their operating profit. Banks and insurance companies also include interest paid in operating profit. Where the special nature of the business requires the inclusion of items relating to interest and dividend in operating profit, the cash flows relating to these items should remain as part of the operating cash flows. If any interest paid clearly relates to financing, then it should be included under 'returns on investments and servicing of finance'. [FRS 1 para 60].

[The next paragraph is 30.87.]

Taxation

30.87 Reporting entities need to include under this heading the following items in respect of taxation relating to revenue and capital profits:

- Cash receipts from the relevant tax authority of tax rebates, claims or returns of overpayments.
- Cash payments for corporation tax.

For a subsidiary undertaking, payments received from or made to other members of the group for group relief should be included under this heading. [FRS 1 paras 17, 18].

30.88 It should be noted that cash flows relating to VAT or other sales taxes, employees income taxes, property taxes and any other taxes not assessed on revenue and capital profits should not be shown under the heading of 'taxation'. [FRS 1 para 16].

30.89 Generally, payments or receipts of VAT or other sales taxes should be netted against the cash flows that gave rise to them. For example, payments for fixed assets should be shown net of VAT under capital expenditure. However, where the VAT falls to be irrecoverable, because the entity carries on an exempt or partially exempt business, or incurs VAT on items that are disallowed (for example, VAT on purchase of motor vehicles), the cash flows should be shown gross of the irrecoverable tax. If this is not practicable for any reason, the irrecoverable tax should be included under the most appropriate standard heading. [FRS 1 para 39].

30.90 The net movement on the VAT payable, or receivable should be allocated to cash flows from operating activities unless it is more appropriate to allocate it to another heading. [FRS 1 para 39]. Generally, the majority of the VAT transactions would be relevant to operating activities, but where a significant proportion of the VAT payments (or receipts) relate to other cash flow headings, such as 'capital expenditure and financial investments' or 'acquisitions and disposals', it may be appropriate to include the net payment (or receipt) under that heading. The effect of including the net movement on the VAT account in operating cash flows means that there will be no need to eliminate the amount of VAT included in opening and closing debtors or creditors when carrying out the reconciliation between operating profit and net cash flow from operating activities.

30.91 Taxation cash flows excluding those in respect of tax on revenue and capital profits, VAT or other sales taxes should be included in the cash flow statement under the same standard headings as the cash flow that gave rise to the taxation cash flows. [FRS 1 para 40]. For example, employers' national insurance contributions and amounts paid in respect of PAYE to the tax authorities should be included in operating activities. Where the direct method is followed, they will be included in the amounts shown as paid to or on behalf of employees.

Capital expenditure and financial investment

30.92 The cash flows included in 'capital expenditure and financial investment' include the cash effects of transactions relating to the acquisition and disposal of any fixed asset (including investments) and current asset investments not regarded by the entity as liquid resources. For this purpose, fixed asset investments exclude a trade or business, or investment in an entity that is an associate, joint venture or a subsidiary undertaking. The cash flows relating to the acquisitions and disposals of these fixed asset investments are reported under 'acquisitions and disposals'. Therefore, cash flows relating to acquisitions and disposals of certain financial investments, for example long-term investments in gilts or other financial investments that are held purely for investment purposes and not for the management of liquid resources, would be reported under this heading, but returns on them would be reported under 'returns on investments and servicing of finance'. If no cash flows relating to financial investments fall to be included under this heading, the caption may be reduced to 'capital expenditure'. [FRS 1 para 19].

30.93 Cash inflows in respect of 'capital expenditure and financial investments' include the following items that should be separately disclosed:

- Receipts from sales or disposals of property, plant or equipment.
- Receipts from the repayment of the reporting entity's loans made to other entities or sale of other entities' debt instruments other than receipts forming part of an acquisition or disposal or a movement in liquid resources.

[FRS 1 para 20].

30.94 Cash outflows in respect of 'capital expenditure and financial investments' include the following items that should be separately disclosed:

- Payments to acquire property, plant or equipment.
- Loans made by the reporting entity and payments to acquire debt instruments of other entities other than payments forming part of an acquisition or disposal or a movement in liquid resources.

[FRS 1 para 21].

30.95 The amount paid in respect of tangible fixed assets during the year may not be the same as the amount of additions shown in the tangible fixed asset note. The difference may be due to a number of reasons. For example, tangible fixed assets may be purchased on credit, in which case the amounts for additions shown in the fixed asset note would need to be adjusted for the outstanding credit to arrive at the cash paid. Furthermore, the change in fixed asset creditors should be eliminated from the total change in creditors, to arrive at the movement in operating creditors, a figure needed for the reconciliation of operating profit to net cash flow from operating activities. Another example is where fixed assets have been acquired in foreign currencies. In this situation, the sterling equivalent of the foreign currency amount paid that is reported in the cash flow statement is not necessarily the same as the sterling equivalent of the cost recorded at the date of the transaction and included in the balance sheet, because of changes in exchange rates. In addition, where interest has been capitalised during the period, the figure for interest would need to be deducted to arrive at the correct amount of cash paid for the acquisition or construction of a fixed asset. The amount of interest capitalised and paid during the period would be shown under 'returns on investments and servicing of finance'.

30.96 A further example arises where assets have been acquired during the year under finance leases. Most companies do not show assets acquired under finance leases separately, but include them in the total additions figure for the year in their fixed assets movements note. Since assets acquired under finance leases do not involve any cash outlay at the inception of the lease, it will be necessary to eliminate the fair value of the leased assets that is included in the figure for fixed assets additions so that the true cash outflow for fixed assets actually purchased can be reflected in the cash flow statements. The finance lease rental payments should be analysed between interest and capital, with the interest element shown under 'returns on investments and servicing of finance' and the capital element shown under 'financing'.

[The next paragraph is 30.98.]

Acquisitions and disposals

30.98 As already discussed in paragraph 30.92 above cash flows included in, 'acquisitions and disposals' are those related to the acquisition or disposal of any trade, business or an entity that is an associate, joint venture or a subsidiary undertaking. [FRS 1 para 22].

30.99 Cash inflows from 'acquisitions and disposals' include:

- Receipts from sales of investments in subsidiary undertakings, showing separately any balances of cash and overdrafts transferred as part of the sale (see further para 30.133).
- Receipts from sales of investments in associates or joint ventures.
- Receipts from sales of trades or businesses.

[FRS 1 para 23].

30.100 Similarly, cash outflows from 'acquisitions and disposals' include:

- Payments to acquire investments in subsidiary undertakings, showing separately any balances of cash and overdrafts acquired (see further para 30.133).
- Payments to acquire investments in associates and joint ventures.
- Payments to acquire trades or businesses.

[FRS 1 para 24].

Cash flows arising under this standard heading are discussed from paragraph 30.132 onwards.

Equity dividends paid

30.101 Equity dividends paid by the reporting entity should be disclosed separately. These are dividends paid on the reporting entity's, or, in a group, the parent's equity shares. For this purpose, equity shares are those that fall to be treated as equity under FRS 25. The dividends paid should be the cash dividend paid. [FRS 1 para 25]. Dividends paid by subsidiaries to shareholders outside the group, both in respect of equity and non-equity interests must be reported under 'returns on investments and servicing of finance'. Therefore, equity dividends paid to minority interests should not be shown under this heading.

Management of liquid resources

30.102 The heading 'management of liquid resources' includes cash flows relating to items that the reporting entity uses to manage its liquidity (as opposed to earning returns from investments), but which fall outside the FRS 1 definition of cash. The type of liquid resources that should be reported under this heading are considered from paragraph 30.44.

30.103 Cash inflows in management of liquid resources include:

- Withdrawals from short-term deposits not qualifying as cash – to the extent that they do not relate to deposits that qualify for net reporting under a rollover or reissue transaction as explained in paragraph 30.59.
- Inflows from disposal or redemption of any other investments held as liquid resources.

[FRS 1 para 27].

30.104 Cash outflows in management of liquid resources include:

- Payments into short-term deposits not qualifying as cash to the extent that they do not relate to deposits that qualify for net reporting under a rollover or reissue transaction as explained in paragraph 30.59.
- Outflows to acquire any other investments held as liquid resources.

[FRS 1 para 28].

30.105 Cash flows relating to short-term deposits that are not repayable on demand and, therefore, do not meet the definition of cash would fall to be included under this heading. Generally, the gross cash inflows and outflows should be reported, unless the deposit is one that is continuously rolled over, in which case the net cash flows may be shown as explained further in paragraph 30.59.

30.106 Cash outflows and inflows relating to a wide range of other non-cash current investments would also fall to be reported under this heading provided they are easily and promptly convertible into cash through an active market without curtailing or disrupting the entities business as explained in paragraph 30.48. Although many such current asset investments may qualify as liquid resources, not all of them may be used in the entity's treasury activities. Some current asset investments may be held purely for investment purposes. Others may be held for trading purposes, although this would generally apply to banks and investment companies. Given that there is a choice as to which current asset investment can be used for managing the net funds or net debt position, the standard requires entities to explain what it includes as liquid resources and any changes in its policy. [FRS 1 para 26]. This is a sensible requirement as an investment initially acquired for investment purposes in one year could be designated as a liquid resource in the following year depending on the company's circumstances. A change in policy regarding the use of a particular investment would not give rise to any cash flows in the year of change, but would need to be reported as a non-cash movement in the reconciliation and analysis of net debt (see para 30.119). An example of a company that explains what it includes as liquid resources is given in Table 30.5 below.

Table 30.5 – Explanation of liquid resources

Unilever Group – Annual Accounts – 31 December 1996

Notes to the consolidated accounts (extract)

	£ million	
	1996	1995
23 Analysis of cash flows for headings netted in the cash flow statement (extract)		
Management of liquid resources		
Purchase of current investments	**(409)**	(383)
Sale of current investments	**342**	547
(Increase)/decrease in cash on deposit	**(226)**	94
	(293)	258
Financing		
Issue of ordinary share capital (employee share schemes)	**–**	3
Issue of shares by group companies to minority shareholders	**14**	14
Debt due within one year:		
Increases	**1 381**	1 529
Repayments	**(1 473)**	(1 790)
Debt due after one year:		
Increases	**507**	315
Repayments	**(135)**	(148)
	294	(77)

Included as liquid resources are term deposits of less than one year, government securities and AI/PI rated corporate commercial paper.

[The next paragraph is 30.108.]

Financing

30.108 Financing cash flows comprise receipts from or repayments to external providers of finance. [FRS 1 para 29]. They will generally include the cash effects of transactions relating to the manner in which the entity's operating and investing activities have been financed. However, only cash flows that relate to the principal amounts of finance are dealt with under this heading, since the cash flows relating to the servicing of finance (that is, dividends and interest) are dealt with under returns on investments and servicing of finance heading and equity dividends paid.

30.109 Cash inflows in respect of financing include the following items:

- Receipts from issuing shares or other equity instruments.
- Receipts from issuing debentures, loans, notes and bonds, and from other long and short-term borrowings (other than bank overdrafts).

[FRS 1 para 30].

30.110 Cash outflows in respect of financing include the following items:

- Repayments of amounts borrowed (other than overdrafts). The treatment of discounts and premiums on debt instruments is considered in paragraph 30.180 below.
- The capital element of finance lease rental payments.
- Payments to re-acquire or redeem the entity's shares.
- Payments of expenses or commissions on any issue of equity shares.

[FRS 1 para 31].

Table 30.6 shown below provides an illustration of the items that are normally included under this heading.

Table 30.6 – Cash flows classified as financing

Coats Viyella Plc – Annual Report and Accounts – 31 December 1998

32 Notes to the cash flow statement (extract)

		1998	1997
b Analysis of financing cash flows		£m	£m
Issue of ordinary share capital		0.3	0.1
Issue of shares to minorities		0.6	12.9
		0.9	13.0
(Decrease)/increase in			
borrowings:	– new long-term loans	0.4	–
	– new short-term loans	161.5	175.0
	– repayment of amounts borrowed	(212.7)	(162.8)
	– redemption of convertible debt	2.5	–
	– capital element of finance lease rental payments	(4.9)	(5.6)
		(58.2)	6.6
Net cash (outflow)/inflow from financing		(57.3)	19.6

30.111 The cash flows under financing can be shown in a single section with those under 'management of liquid resources', provided that separate subtotals for each are given. [FRS 1 para 29]. The flexibility to report cash flows relating to liquid resources and financing under a combined heading may appeal to a number of companies that manage their borrowings and liquid investments as an integrated treasury operation (See Table 30.2).

Exceptional and extraordinary cash flows

30.112 Where cash flows relate to items that are classed as exceptional, these exceptional cash flows should be shown under the appropriate standard heading, according to the nature of each item. The exceptional cash flows should be separately identified in the cash flow statement or a note to it and the relationship between the cash flows and the exceptional item should be explained. [FRS 1 para 37].

30.113 FRS 3 requires three exceptional items to be reported after operating profit:

- Profits or losses on the sale or termination of an operation.
- Profits or losses on sale of fixed assets.
- Costs of a fundamental reorganisation or restructuring.

The first two items are not themselves cash flows, but the net cash proceeds from the sale of operations will fall to be included under 'acquisitions and disposals', and those arising from the sale of fixed assets under 'capital expenditure and financial investment', irrespective of where the gain or loss is charged in the profit and loss account (see further para 30.182).

30.114 The disclosure of cash flows relating to costs of a fundamental reorganisation or restructuring that is reported outside operating profit is not so clear. In general, the cash outflows are likely to include an amalgam of items, such as:

- Redundancy costs.
- Costs associated with the elimination and reduction of product lines.
- Costs to consolidate or relocate plant facilities.
- Costs for new systems developments or acquisition.
- Costs to retrain employees to use newly deployed systems.
- Losses on asset impairments and disposal of assets.

However, as stated in paragraph 30.67 above, the standard makes it clear that the cash flows relating to any operating items should be reported in operating cash flow, whether or not the costs are included in operating profit. This means that the nature of each item included within the total reorganisation costs needs to be analysed, with the result that some cash flows fall to be reported under operating activities, some under capital expenditure and some under acquisitions and disposals. The cash flow effect of reorganisation provisions arising on an acquisition of a subsidiary is considered in paragraph 30.186 below.

[The next paragraph is 30.116.]

30.116 There may be instances where the cash flows are exceptional because of their size or incidence, but are not related to items that are treated as exceptional in the profit and loss account. These exceptional cash flows should also be disclosed and sufficient explanation given to explain their cause and nature. [FRS 1 para 38]. An example cited in the explanatory paragraph of the standard is that of a large prepayment against a pension liability which is not reported as part of an exceptional item in the profit and loss account. [FRS 1 para 63]. Disclosure of exceptional cash flows where there is no corresponding exceptional item in the profit and loss account is likely to arise where the provision to which the cash flows relates was reported as an exceptional item in a previous period.

30.117 Sufficient disclosure of the nature of the exceptional item and the related cash flows should also be given in a note to the cash flow statement so that users may gain an understanding of how these transactions have affected the reporting entity's cash flows.

30.118 Cash flows from extraordinary items would be reported in a similar manner. [FRS 1 paras 37]. In practice, however, such cash flows will rarely arise, if at all, following the virtual abolition of extraordinary items under FRS 3 (see further chapter 8).

Reconciliation with balance sheet figures

Reconciliation to net debt

30.119 One of the objectives of the cash flow statement is to provide information that is useful in assessing an entity's liquidity, solvency and financial adaptability.

30.120 The standard requires a note that reconciles the movement of cash in the period with the movement in *net debt* for the period. The changes in net debt should be analysed from the opening to the closing component amounts as shown in the opening and closing balance sheets. The reconciliation is not part of the cash flow statement and, if adjoining the cash flow statement (for example, presented at the foot of the statement), it should be clearly labelled and kept separate. [FRS 1 para 33]. For this purpose, net debt is defined to include the borrowings of the reporting entity (comprising debt as defined in FRS 25, together with related derivatives and obligations under finance leases), less cash (including overdrafts) and liquid resources. Where cash and liquid resources exceed the borrowings of the entity, reference should be made to 'net funds' rather than to 'net debt'. [FRS 1 para 2].

30.121 The reconciliation should begin with the increase or decrease in cash for the period as shown at the bottom of the cash flow statement. Because this movement in cash includes cash flows relating to management of liquid resources and cash flows relating to borrowings included in financing, these cash flows should be added back to give the total change in net debt resulting from cash flows during the period. These separate components of cash flows should be separately disclosed in the reconciliation where material. There may be other changes in net debt for the period that do not arise from cash flows. Typically these non-cash movements may relate to items such as exchange differences, acquisition of assets under finance leases, loans and finance leases acquired as part of an acquisition and other movements that have an effect on the closing figure for net debt. These non-cash changes in net debt should also be disclosed in the reconciliation, if material. [FRS 1 para 33].

30.122 The total change in net debt arising from both cash flows and non cash items should then be reconciled with the opening and closing net debt amounts. In particular, the standard requires the following reconciling items to be disclosed, where material:

- The cash flows relating to the separate component of net debt as explained above.
- The acquisition or disposal of subsidiary undertakings. These relate to borrowings acquired or transferred as part of the acquisition or disposal of a subsidiary undertaking because these are not reflected in the financing section of the cash flow statement, but have an effect on the closing amount of net debt.

- Other non-cash changes – an example being the acquisition of fixed assets under finance leases.

- The recognition of changes in market value and exchange rate movements. For example, changes in market values relating to current asset investments that are treated as liquid resources do not have any cash flow impact during the period, but may affect the carrying value of those investments at the balance sheet date (for example, if the company has a policy of carrying those investments at fair value). Similarly, exchange rate adjustments arising from the retranslation of opening foreign currency cash and borrowings and those arising from translating the cash flows of subsidiaries at rates other than the year end rate, do not give rise to any cash flows, but form part of the carrying values of cash and borrowings at the period end.

[FRS 1 para 33].

30.122.1 An example of a reconciliation required by the standard is given in Table 30.7 below.

Table 30.7 – Net funds reconciliation

Airtours plc – Annual Report and Accounts – 30 September 1996

Notes to the financial statements

25) **Reconciliation of net cash flow to movement in net funds**

	1996 £000	Restated 1995 £000
(Decrease)/increase in cash in the year	(26,310)	53,544
Cash outflow/(inflow) from decrease/(increase) in debt and lease financing	15,142	(83,459)
Cash outflow/(inflow) from increase/(decrease) in liquid resources	156,928	(41,801)
Changes in net debt resulting from cash flows	145,760	(71,716)
Loans and finance leases acquired with subsidiary undertakings	(15,040)	(1,606)
Transfer to accruals	–	29,641
New unsecured loan notes	–	(9,000)
Provisions	–	(38)
Exchange differences	(5,142)	2,074
Movement in net funds in the year	125,578	(50,645)
Net funds at 1st October	223,005	273,650
Net funds at 30th September	**348,583**	223,005

Analysis of changes in net debt

30.123 Where the opening and closing amounts of net debt shown in the above reconciliation are not readily apparent, because they are included under different balance sheet headings, sufficient details should be shown to enable the cash and other components of net debt to be respectively traced back to the amounts shown under the equivalent caption in the balance sheet. [FRS 1 para 33]. For example, bank loans and overdrafts included as a single figure within current liabilities would need to be identified separately because overdrafts, unlike other borrowings, are included within the cash component of net debt. Another example where separate identification may be necessary relates to the situation where some current asset investments are used for managing liquid resources, but others are not. This additional note is also necessary to enable the movements in net debt for the period to be readily understood. For example, the reclassification of an amount of debt from long-term to current categories in the balance sheet would not appear in the reconciliation to net debt, because it is a movement within the same component of net debt, but would need to be separately identified in the analysis of the changes in net debt for the closing amount of current and non-current debt to be readily identified with balance sheet figures. The ways in which an analysis of net funds or net debt can be presented are shown in Table 30.8 and Table 30.9 below.

Table 30.8 – Analysis of net funds

Airtours plc – Annual Report and Accounts – 30 September 1996

Notes to the financial statements
26) Analysis of net funds

	At 1st October 1995 £000	Cash flow £000	Acquisitions £000	Other non-cash changes £000	Exchange movements £000	30th September 1996 £000
Cash at bank and in hand	142,416	(26,378)	–	–	(4,491)	**111,547**
Term deposits	162,088	151,953	–	–	–	**314,041**
Overdrafts	(65)	68	–	–	(3)	–
Debt due within one year	(35,216)	130	–	(185)	44	**(35,227)**
Debt due after one year	(43,958)	–	–	185	13	**(43,760)**
Finance leases	(7,012)	15,012	(15,040)	–	(705)	**(7,745)**
Current asset investments	4,752	4,975	–	–	–	**9,727**
	223,005	145,760	(15,040)	–	(5,142)	**348,583**

Table 30.9 – Analysis of net debt

Bass PLC – Annual Report and Financial Statements – 30 September 1996

NOTES TO THE FINANCIAL STATEMENTS (extract)

29 Net debt	**Cash and overdrafts**			**Other borrowings**			
30 September 1996	**Cash at bank and in hand £m**	**Overdrafts £m**	**Total £m**	**Current asset investments £m**	**Due within one year £m**	**Due after one year £m**	**Total £m**
At 30 September 1995	69	(47)	22	684	(392)	(1,177)	(863)
Net cash flow (note 25)	(151)	3	(148)	–	–	–	(148)
Financing and liquid resources movement	154	–	154	(202)	69	7	28
Other borrowings acquired	–	–	–	–	(36)	(7)	(43)
Exchange adjustments	–	–	–	(1)	(4)	(4)	(9)
At 30 September 1996	**72**	**(44)**	**28**	**481**	**(363)**	**(1,181)**	**(1,035)**

30.124 The reconciliation to net debt and the corresponding analysis note is relevant only to non-financial companies. Banks and insurance companies are not required to give a reconciliation of net debt because the concept of net debt is not really applicable to them. Banks should, therefore, continue to give the notes reconciling the movements in cash and changes in financing with the related items in the opening and closing balance sheet. It should be noted that this requirement for banks is not explicitly stated in the standard, but is illustrated in example 3 in appendix I to FRS 1. Insurance companies, on the other hand, are required to give an equivalent note that analyses the movement in portfolio investments less financing, either adjoining the cash flow statement or in a note. [FRS 1 para 35]. A note linking the movements to the related balance sheet amounts for portfolio investments and financing is also required. [FRS 1 para 36].

Consolidated cash flow statements

30.125 The form and content of cash flow statements discussed above apply equally to any group of entities where consolidated financial statements are prepared. Therefore, a parent company of a group that is required to prepare a consolidated balance sheet and a consolidated profit and loss account should also prepare a consolidated cash flow statement reflecting the cash flows of the group. In preparing consolidated cash flow statements, adjustments should be made to eliminate those cash flows that are internal to the group. Only those cash receipts and payments that flow to and from the group as a whole should be included. [FRS 1 para 43].

Minority interests

30.126 Where there are minority interests in any subsidiary that is consolidated as part of a group, the treatment of the minority interest in the consolidated cash flow statement should be consistent with the overall approach followed in preparing the group's financial statements. Companies are required by law and FRS 2 to eliminate intra-group balances and intra-group transactions in the consolidated financial statements. Therefore, they should do the same in preparing a consolidated cash flow statement even where minority interests, which may be substantial, are involved. Intra-group transactions should be eliminated because the group, including partly owned subsidiaries, is a single entity for financial reporting purposes. Therefore, in this situation, only cash flows that are external to the group, which includes those with minorities, should be reflected in the cash flow statements. In particular, the standard requires dividends to minorities to be shown under the heading 'returns on investments and servicing of finance'.

30.127 FRS 25 requires minority interests to be shown as liabilities where the parent or any fellow subsidiary undertaking has guaranteed their dividends or redemption, or undertaken to purchase the minority shares if the subsidiary fails to make the expected payments. If minority interests are classified as liabilities, the dividends paid on those shares should be shown as part of the interest charge in the consolidated profit and loss account. It follows that, in the consolidated cash flow statement, the dividends paid should similarly be shown as interest paid and not as dividends to minorities; but they would still be included under the heading 'returns on investments and servicing of finance'.

30.127.1 When a partly-owned subsidiary company undertakes a rights issue, some of the cash flows generated will be internal to the group and some will be external. Only the external cash flows are presented in the consolidated cash flow statement. This is considered in the example in paragraph 30.192.

Investments accounted on the equity method

30.128 Where a group has investments in associates or joint ventures that are included in the consolidation under the equity method, the consolidated cash flow statement should include only the cash flows between the group and those entities, but not the cash flows of those entities. [FRS 1 para 44]. This means that only the following cash flows should be included:

- Cash flows from investments in, and dividends from, the associates or joint ventures.
- Cash flows from sales or purchases between the group and the associates or joint ventures.

The same treatment will apply to any non-consolidated subsidiaries that are included in the consolidation using the equity method.

30.129 Specifically, the following information should be disclosed separately for equity accounted entities:

- Dividends received from these entities should be shown under their own heading. [FRS 1 para 12A].
- Cash flows relating to acquisitions and divestments should be shown under acquisitions and disposals. [FRS 1 paras 23, 24].
- Financing cash flows received from or paid to equity accounted entities should be shown under financing. [FRS 1 para 32].

Investments in joint arrangements

30.130 As stated in chapter 27, a company may have an investment in a joint arrangement, which does not carry on a trade or business in its own right and is merely an extension of its participants' trades or businesses. In that situation, the participants in the joint arrangement should account for their own assets, liabilities and cash flows, measured according to the terms of the agreement governing the arrangement, that is, the investor's share of the relevant cash flows of the joint arrangement will be included in the related line items for the investing company. Adjustments may have to be made to eliminate cash transactions between the investor and the joint arrangement.

[The next paragraph is 30.132.]

Acquisitions and disposals of subsidiaries

30.132 When a parent undertaking acquires or disposes of a subsidiary undertaking during a financial year, the cash flows relating to the consideration should be reported under 'acquisitions and disposals' in the consolidated cash flow statement.

30.133 The standard specifies the treatment of cash and overdrafts acquired or transferred on acquisition, or disposal, of a subsidiary. It requires that the amounts of cash and overdrafts acquired or transferred to be shown separately along with the gross consideration paid or received for the acquisition or disposal. [FRS 1 paras 23(a), 24(a)]. An example is given in Table 30.10 below.

Table 30.10 – Net cash outflow from acquisition

Airtours plc – Annual Report and Accounts – 30 September 1996

Group cash flow statement (extract)

Year ended 30th September 1996	Notes	1996 £000	1996 £000	Restated 1995 £000
Acquisitions				
Purchase of subsidiary undertakings		**(18,350)**		(41,384)
Acquisition expenses		**(2,337)**		(786)
Cash at bank and in hand acquired with subsidiaries		**8,509**		5,931
Net cash outflow from acquisitions			**(12,178)**	(36,239)

30.134 Recording the gross consideration separately along with the cash and overdraft balances transferred means that any fixed assets, working capital excluding cash and overdrafts, and borrowings of the subsidiary at the date of acquisition or disposal would need to be eliminated so as to avoid double counting. For example, stock, debtors and creditors acquired or disposed of would need to be eliminated from the total balance sheet changes in stock, debtors and creditors in the reconciliation of operating profit to operating cash flows. Similarly, borrowings including finance lease obligations taken over or transferred would need to reflected in the reconciliation to net debt and the note that analyses the changes in net debt during the period.

30.135 Where the consideration for the acquisition or disposal has been discharged partly in *cash* and partly by the issue of *shares*, the cash flow statement would show only the cash element of the consideration paid or received. This would be shown as a single item (along with any cash and overdrafts of the subsidiary acquired or disposed of) under the heading 'acquisitions and disposals'. The shares that are issued as part of the consideration in exchange for net assets acquired do not give rise to any cash flows and, consequently, they should not be shown in the cash flow statement, but disclosed as a major non-cash transaction in a note to the cash flow statement (see para 30.165 below).

30.135.1 The classification of cash flows arising in connection with the acquisition of a subsidiary is considered in the following examples.

Example 1 – Cash flows related to the acquisition of a subsidiary

A parent company pays £20,000 in cash and issues shares with a fair value of £40,000 and £50,000 in loan notes to acquire a subsidiary with cash balances of £30,000, borrowings of £60,000 and other net assets including goodwill of £70,000.

In this situation, the cash flow statement would show a cash outflow of £20,000 and a cash inflow of £30,000 under acquisitions and disposals, despite it being an acquisition. The loan notes of £50,000 issued and the borrowings of £60,000 acquired would be reported in the reconciliation statement that analyses the changes in the balance sheet amounts making up net debt. The shares and loan notes would be disclosed in the note giving details of material non-cash transactions (see para 30.165). A note summarising the effects of the acquisition indicating how much of the consideration comprised cash is also required (see para 30.137).

Example 2 – Repayment of loan on acquisition of a subsidiary

A group acquired a subsidiary that had loans in its balance sheet. As part of the acquisition agreement, the acquiring group immediately repaid the loans. How is this treated in the cash flow statement?

If the repayment of loans is included as a financing outflow then 'loans acquired' would have to be shown as a non-cash movement in net debt. However, where the acquisition agreement requires the repayment of the loans as part of the overall consideration for the acquisition of the subsidiary (which would be referred to in the acquisitions note), then the repayment of the loans would be shown as an outflow in 'acquisitions' (with separate disclosure). In that case the loan obligations acquired would not be shown as a movement in net debt as they have not been considered to be part of the group's financing.

Example 3 – Payment of dividend to vendor shareholders

Company A acquired a subsidiary, company B. As part of the purchase agreement company B's shareholders authorised a dividend, pre-acquisition, that is payable to the former shareholders (the vendors). The purchase consideration payable by company A was reduced to take account of this. This dividend was paid to the vendor after the date of acquisition. Where should the cash flow resulting from the payment of the dividend be shown in the post-acquisition consolidated cash flow statement? Should it be under 'Acquisitions and disposals'?

Where there is a payment by the acquired company to the vendors which is, in substance, part of the vendor's proceeds and the purchaser's cost of acquisition, this should be accounted for as part of the fair value of the consideration paid for the acquisition. Because the payment in this case falls into this category and would be treated as part of the consideration in the fair value table, it should be shown under the acquisitions and disposals heading in the cash flow statement.

If, however, an acquired company had a normal dividend authorised prior to its acquisition, which was payable to the former shareholders, and this was not part of any arrangement with the purchaser, that dividend would be shown as a creditor in the fair value table in the normal way. It would not form part of the consideration paid. When the dividend was paid it would be included in the post-acquisition consolidated cash flow statement as part of cash inflow/outflow from operating activities as it would represent the settlement of a normal creditor (brought in on acquisition).

30.136 Where acquisitions and disposals take place during a financial year the cash flows of the group should include the cash flows of the subsidiary for the same period as the group profit and loss account includes the subsidiary's results (see further chapter 25). [FRS 1 para 43]. Care should be taken to eliminate all cash flows between the group and the subsidiary acquired or disposed of for the period that the subsidiary is included within the consolidated figures.

30.137 The standard also requires significant amounts of other disclosures to be made in respect of the cash flow effects of a subsidiary acquired or disposed of during the financial year. First, a note to the cash flow statement should show a summary of the effects of acquisitions and disposals indicating how much of the consideration comprised cash. [FRS 1 para 45]. In order to show the effects of the acquisition and disposal fully, it is necessary to disclose separately the assets and liabilities of the subsidiary acquired or disposed of. In practice, the summary of the effects of acquisitions and disposals required by the standard can be combined with that required by company law and FRS 6. An example of the relevant disclosures is given in Table 30.11.

30.138 Secondly, reporting entities are required to disclose, as far as practicable and where material, the extent to which the amounts reported under each of the standard headings have been affected by the cash flows of a subsidiary acquired or disposed of during the year. This information can be given by segregating cash flows between continuing and discontinued operations and acquisitions. [FRS 1 para 45]. Consequently, users of financial statements will be able to ascertain the amount of the contribution to the group's cash flows that has been made by acquired subsidiaries and how much the group's cash flows have been depleted as a result of a disposal. This information need only be given in the financial statements for the period in which the acquisition or disposal occurs. [FRS 1 para 48]. In practice, it may be difficult, if not impossible, to give this information, particularly where the business of the acquired subsidiary has been integrated with the group. Many companies, therefore, omit this disclosure on the basis that it is not practicable. An example where a company has been able to disclose the material effects of an acquisition on the amounts reported under each standard heading is shown in Tables 30.11 and 30.12.

Table 30.11– Cash flow effects of acquisitions and disposals

Bowater PLC – Annual Report – 31 December 1993

NOTES TO THE CASH FLOW STATEMENT (extract)

	Acquisitions		**Disposals**	
IV EFFECTS OF ACQUISITION AND DISPOSALS OF SUBSIDIARY UNDERTAKINGS AND BUSINESSES	**1993**	1992	**1993**	1992
	£m	£m	**£m**	£m
Tangible assets	**162.7**	144.6	**10.9**	11.2
Business for resale	**13.5**		**13.5**	
Associates	**1.3**	1.5	**0.1**	0.1
Associates goodwill eliminated		(0.7)		
Equity holding in associate	**(16.6)**			
Surplus properties	**0.2**			
Working capital	**44.2**	50.3	**(1.5)**	3.9
Current and deferred taxation	**8.5**	10.2		
Provisions	**(49.5)**	(65.2)	**1.1**	1.5
Cash and cash equivalents	**14.5**	(48.6)	**(2.3)**	(0.1)
Loan capital	**(89.6)**	(176.9)	**(3.0)**	
Finance leases	**(0.3)**	(3.6)		(0.8)
Minority interests	**(1.0)**	(0.3)		
Goodwill	**239.8**	326.0	**47.4**	16.9
Surplus/(deficiency) on disposal			**10.3**	(0.6)
	327.7	237.3	**76.5**	32.1
Consideration: cash	**312.3**	226.0	**76.5**	32.1
deferred	**26.7**	11.3		
Taxation relief	**(11.3)**			
	327.7	237.3	**76.5**	32.1

V ANALYSIS OF MOVEMENTS OF CASH AND CASH EQUIVALENTS IN RESPECT OF ACQUISITIONS AND DISPOSALS OF SUBSIDIARY UNDERTAKINGS AND BUSINESSES

	1993	1992	**1993**	1992
	£m	£m	**£m**	£m
Cash consideration	**312.3**	226.0	**76.5**	32.1
Cash and cash equivalents	**(14.5)**	48.6	**2.3**	0.1
	297.8	274.6	**78.8**	32.2

Table 30.12 – Effects of an acquisition on standard cash flow headings

Bowater PLC – Annual Report – 31 December 1993

NOTES TO THE CASH FLOW STATEMENT (extract)

III CASH FLOW MOVEMENTS ARISING FROM BUSINESSES ACQUIRED AND DISPOSED DURING THE YEAR

	1993	1992
Acquisitions:	**£m**	£m
Net cash inflow from operating activities	**56.4**	53.7
Returns on investments and servicing of finance	**(4.9)**	(3.2)
Taxation paid	**(1.4)**	(2.3)
Investing activities	**(20.2)**	(39.2)
Net cash inflow before financing	**29.9**	9.0

Disposals have not had a material impact.

Changes in stake

30.138.1 Paragraph 22 of FRS 1 says:

'The cash flows included in 'acquisitions and disposals' are those related to the acquisition or disposal of any trade or business, or of an investment in an entity that is, or, as a result of the transaction, becomes or ceases to be either an associate, a joint venture, or a subsidiary undertaking.'

The reference to an entity that *is* an associate, a joint venture or a subsidiary undertaking means that cash flows associated with changes in stake, even where there is no change in classification (say from associate to subsidiary) should be classified as 'acquisitions and disposals' in the cash flow statement.

Foreign currency

30.139 A company may engage in foreign currency operations in two main ways:

- First, it may enter directly into business transactions that are denominated in foreign currencies.
- Secondly, it may conduct its foreign operations through a subsidiary, associated company or branch whose operations are based in a country other than that of the investing company or whose assets and liabilities are denominated in a currency other than that of the investing company (a 'foreign entity').

30.140 The results of foreign currency transactions and the financial statements of the foreign entity will need to be translated into the currency in which the company reports. This translation process should produce results that are compatible with the effect of exchange rate changes on a company's cash flows and its equity. The accounting treatment of foreign currency operations in cash flow statements can be complex and there is little guidance on the subject. The guidance that follow deals with the treatment of exchange differences in individual companies first, followed by their treatment in consolidated financial statements.

Individual companies

30.141 Where an individual company has cash receipts or makes cash payments in a foreign currency, it is consistent with the objectives of cash flow statements that those receipts and payments should be translated into the reporting currency at the rate ruling at the date on which the receipt or payment is received or paid.

30.142 Exchange differences may, therefore, arise because of a rate change between the transaction date (the date at which the transaction is recorded) and the settlement date. Exchange differences also arise where a transaction remains unsettled (that is, not realised in cash) at the balance sheet date and is required to be retranslated at that date. Such differences relate to the retranslation of monetary assets and liabilities.

Settled transactions

30.143 Where a transaction is *settled* at an exchange rate which differs from that used when the transaction was initially recorded, the exchange difference will be recognised in the profit and loss account of the period in which the settlement takes place. To the extent that the settled transaction relates to operations, the gain or loss would be included in arriving at operating profit. This exchange gain or loss would also have the effect of increasing or decreasing the reporting currency equivalent of amounts paid or received in cash settlement. Consequently, no adjustment for the exchange gain or loss is necessary in the reconciliation of operating profit to operating cash flow. Consider the following example:

Example – Foreign exchange difference on a settled transaction

A UK company was set up in January 20X5 and raised £200,000 by issuing shares. It purchased goods for resale from overseas in February 20X5 for CU992,500 when the exchange rate was £1 = CU7.94. It entered the purchase in its stock records as: CU992,500 @ 7.94 = £125,000. Under the terms of the contract, the company settled the debt in October 20X5 when the exchange rate was £1 = CU8.58. The amount paid in settlement was: CU992,500 @ 8.58 = £115,676. The company would, therefore, record an exchange gain of £125,000 — £115,676 = £9,324 in arriving at its operating profit for the year.

Assuming that there are no other transactions during the year and the stock remained unsold at the balance sheet date at 31 December 20X5, a simplified cash flow statement is given below:

Cash flow statement		
	£	£
Net cash flow from operating activities		(115,676)
Financing		
Issue of shares		200,000
Increase in cash		84,324
Workings		
Proceeds of share issue	200,000	
Less: payment for stocks	(115,676)	
Increase in cash		84,324
Reconciliation of operating profit to net cash flow from operating activities		
Net operating profit		9,324
Increase in stocks		(125,000)
Net cash flow from operating activities		(115,676)

It is obvious that the net cash flow from operating activities comprises the payment of £115,676 for the stock. Because the outstanding creditor for £125,000 was settled during the year for £115,676, the exchange gain of £9,324 is already reflected in the payment and, therefore, no adjustment for the exchange gain is necessary in the reconciliation of operating profit to operating cash flow as illustrated above. Therefore, as a general rule, exchange differences on settled transactions relating to operations will not appear as a reconciling item in the reconciliation of operating profit to net cash flow from operating activities.

30.144 Where a settled transaction does not relate to operations and the exchange gain or loss is included in the profit and loss account, but not within operating profit, the exchange gain or loss will be included as part of the cash flows arising from the settlement. An example would be income receivable from a foreign investment. In this situation, the sterling equivalent of foreign cash actually received would be shown under 'returns on investments and servicing of finance', and would include any exchange gain or loss that arises at the time of receipt reported in the profit and loss account below operating profit.

Unsettled transactions

30.145 Where the transaction remains *outstanding* at the balance sheet date, an exchange difference arises as a consequence of recording the foreign currency transaction at the rate ruling at the date of the transaction (or when it was translated at a previous balance sheet date) and the subsequent retranslation to the rate ruling at the balance sheet date. This exchange difference will generally be included in the profit and loss account. Normally such exchange differences arise on monetary items (for example, foreign currency loans, debtors and creditors). In the context of an individual company's operations, these exchange gains or losses will ultimately be reflected in cash flows. However, the way in which they affect the cash flow statement will depend upon the nature of the monetary assets or liabilities, that is, whether they are short-term or long-term.

30.146 Where they relate to short-term monetary items such as debtors and creditors, no adjustment for the exchange difference arising on their retranslation at the balance sheet date is necessary in the reconciliation of operating profit to net cash flow from operating activities, even though they do not involve any cash flows. This is because increases or decreases in the debtor or creditor balances will include exchange differences on their retranslation at the balance sheet date, and the total movement in debtors and creditors would form an adjusting item in the reconciliation of operating profit to operating cash flows. The effect is that the net cash flow from operating activities will not be distorted by such retranslation differences as illustrated in the following example.

Example – Foreign exchange difference on an unsettled transaction

The facts are the same as in the previous example except that at the company's year end 31 December 20X5 the account had not been settled. At 31 December 20X5 the exchange rate was £1 = CU8.25 so that the original creditor for £125,000 would be retranslated at CU992,500 @ 8.25 = £120,303. The gain on exchange of £125,000 — £120,303 = £4,697 would be reported as part of operating profit for the year. The cash flow statement would be as follows:

Cash flow statement	£
Net cash flow from operating activities	Nil
Financing	
Issue of shares	200,000
Increase in cash	200,000
*Represented by closing cash balances	200,000
Reconciliation of operating profit to net cash flow from operating activities:	
Net operating profit	4,697
Increase in stocks	(125,000)
Increase in creditors	120,303
Net cash flow from operating activities	Nil

It is clear that the exchange difference included in operating profit and in the year end creditor balance cancels each other with the result that operating cash flows are not affected. Therefore, as a general rule balance sheet movements in foreign currency trade debtors and creditors, except where they relate to foreign subsidiaries (see example below), will include the impact of exchange differences reported in operating profit and no adjustments for such exchange differences are necessary in the reconciliation.

30.147 Exchange differences on long-term monetary items such as long-term loans would normally be reported as part of the profit or loss for the financial year. To the extent that such differences are included in operating profit, they need to be eliminated in arriving at the net cash flows from operating activities. This is because the actual movement on long-term monetary items which includes the relevant exchange difference is not reported in the reconciliation of operating profit to operating cash flow. Whether or not the exchange differences are reported within operating profit, they should, nevertheless, fall to be included in the reconciliation to net debt and the note that analyses the changes in the balance sheet amounts making up net debt. Consider the following example:

Example – Foreign exchange difference on a long-term loan

The opening balance sheet at 1 October 20X5 of a company consists of cash of £100,000 and share capital of £100,000. The company takes out a long-term loan on 31 March 20X6 of US$270,000 when the rate of exchange is £1 = US$1.8. The proceeds are immediately converted to sterling, that is, £150,000. There are no other transactions during the year. The exchange rate at the balance sheet date 30 September 20X6 is £1 = US$1.5.

The summarised balance sheet at 30 September 20X6	
	£'000
Cash	250
Long-term loan ($270,000 @ 1.5)	(180)
Net assets	70
Share capital	100
P&L account	(30)
	70

The foreign currency loan having been translated at the rate ruling at the date of receipt to £150,000 (US$270,000 @ 1.8), is retranslated at the balance sheet date to £180,000 (US$270,000 @ 1.5). The exchange loss of £30,000 is recognised in operating profit for the year. The cash is made up of £100,000 received from the share issue and £150,000 received on converting the currency loan immediately to sterling.

Simplified cash flow statement	
	£'000
Net cash flow from operating activities	–
Financing	
Receipt of foreign currency loan	150
Increase in cash	150
Notes to the cash flow statement	
Reconciliation of operating profit to net cash flow from operating activities	
Operating loss	(30)
Adjustment for exchange loss	30
Net cash flow from operating profit	–
Reconciliation on net cash flow to movement in net funds	
Increase in cash in the period	150
Cash inflow from increase in debt	(150)
Change in net funds resulting from cash flows	–
Net funds at 1 October 20X5	100
Exchange difference on loan	(30)
Net funds at 30 September 20X6	70

Analysis of net funds

	At 1 Oct 20X5 £'000	Cash Flows £'000	Exchange movement £'000	At 30 Sept 20X6 £'000
Cash	100	150	–	250
Loans	–	(150)	(30)	(180)
Total	100	–	(30)	70

It is apparent from the above illustration that the exchange loss of £30,000 does not have any cash flow effect and, therefore, needs to be eliminated from operating profit. A similar adjustment would be necessary if the loan remains outstanding at 30 September 20X7. However, if the exchange loss of £30,000 is included outside operating profit, for example in 'other interest receivable/payable and similar income/ expense', the exchange difference would only fall to be reported in the reconciliation and the analysis of net funds during the year.

30.148 Similarly, where exchange differences arise on the retranslation of foreign currency cash balances, they will not appear in the cash flow statement. This is because they are non-cash movements within the cash balances and will not form part of the increase or decrease in cash for the financial year. They do, however, form part of the reconciliation of opening to closing balances and will, therefore, appear in the reconciliation to net debt and the note that analyses the changes in net debt during the year.

Borrowings used for hedging equity investments

30.149 Where a company has used foreign currency borrowings either to finance, or to provide a hedge against, its foreign equity investments, exchange differences on the borrowings may have been taken directly to reserves in its individual financial statements in accordance with paragraph 51 of SSAP 20 (if the company has not adopted FRS 26). These exchange differences will have no cash flow impact and will not be included in the cash flow statement or in the reconciliation of operating profit to net cash flow from operating activities. They must, however, be included in the reconciliation to changes in net debt and the note that analyses the changes in net debt during the year (as illustrated in the example above). Similarly, the exchange difference on retranslating the hedged equity investment (taken to reserve) has no cash flow effect.

30.149.1 To the extent that exchange movements on the foreign borrowings are not subject to hedge accounting, their impact will be seen in the profit and loss account. Should this be the case, the exchange movements are treated as discussed in paragraphs 30.147 and 30.148 above.

Group companies

30.150 Where a group conducts part of its business through a foreign entity, different considerations arise from those for individual transactions discussed above. This is because the cash flows of the foreign entity are considered as a whole rather than as a series of single transactions. There are two commonly accepted methods of translation, the temporal method and the closing rate/net investment method. The latter method is generally used for translation purposes, unless the foreign entity's operations are regarded as being more dependent on the economic environment of the investing company's currency, when, under SSAP 20, the temporal method is used. Where a company is reporting in accordance with FRS 23, it is likely that such a foreign operation would have the same functional currency as the parent company and no retranslation gains or losses will occur. Foreign currency is considered further in chapter 7.

Temporal method

30.151 Under the temporal method, all non-monetary items and profit and loss account items of the foreign subsidiary or branch are translated at the rate ruling on the transaction date or at an average rate for a period if this is not materially different. Where the reporting entity uses the temporal method to translate the foreign entity's financial statements, then the only exchange differences that arise will be those relating to monetary items and these will be reported as part of operating profit.

30.152 By using the temporal method, the consolidated financial statements reflect the foreign entity's transactions as if they had been entered into by the reporting entity itself. Accordingly, the treatment of exchange differences in the consolidated cash flow statement will be similar to that explained above for exchange differences arising in individual companies.

Closing rate method

30.153 Under the closing rate/net investment method, the foreign entity's profit and loss account is translated at the rate ruling at the date of each transaction (which may, under certain circumstances, be approximated to an average rate) for companies reporting under FRS 23 and at either the closing rate or at an average rate for the period for companies reporting under SSAP 20. [SSAP 20 para 54, FRS 23 para 23]. FRS 1 requires that the rate that is used for translating the results of activities in the profit and loss account of the foreign subsidiary should also be used for translating the cash flows of those activities for inclusion in the consolidated cash flow statement. [FRS 1 para 41]. This means that *all* the cash flows of the foreign subsidiary (not just those arising from its operating activities) must be included in the consolidated cash flow statement using the same exchange rates as were used for translating the results of its activities in the consolidated profit and loss account.

30.154 Where the group uses the closing rate method of translating the foreign entity's financial statements, then all exchange differences relating to the retranslation of the foreign entity's opening net assets to the closing rate will have been taken directly to reserves. As such exchange differences have no actual or prospective cash flow effect, they will not be included in the consolidated cash flow statement. However, where the opening net assets include foreign currency cash, overdrafts and loan balances then, to that extent, the exchange difference arising on their retranslation at the closing rate for the current period will have been reflected in the closing balances. Such translation differences should not be reported in the cash flow statement itself, but should be included in the effect of exchange rate movements shown as part of the reconciliation to net debt. [FRS 1 para 33(d)].

30.155 Where the group translates the foreign entity's profit and loss account at either the transaction date rate or an average rate, a further translation difference between the result as translated at the average rate and the result translated at the closing rate will have been taken to reserves. This difference will include the exchange rate effect of the movement in foreign currency cash and overdrafts from the transaction date or average rate to the closing rate. Under FRS 1, this exchange difference will be included with the exchange differences arising on the retranslation of the opening foreign currency cash, overdrafts and loan balances (as stated in the preceding paragraph) in the note that provides a reconciliation between the movements of cash to net debt. [FRS 1 para 33(d)].

30.156 In summary, the treatment specified in the standard has the effect of removing all exchange differences from the cash flow statement that do not have any cash flow impact in the reporting period. The treatment of foreign currency exchange differences in the consolidated cash flow statement can be fairly complex.

30.156.1 In practice, a reporting entity will find it simpler to require each of its foreign subsidiaries to prepare a cash flow statement with supporting notes. Where the subsidiary's profit and loss account is translated using either the closing rate or the average rate, that cash flow statement could be prepared in the subsidiary's domestic currency and translated into the reporting entity's relevant local or functional currency at the rate used for translating the profit and loss account. Where, however, a transaction date rate is used (or, say, monthly average rates are used as a proxy for the transaction date rates), this will not be possible and the task is more complex. In such cases, it will be necessary for a cash flow statement in the reporting entity's relevant local or functional currency to be produced from the subsidiary's accounting records. The subsidiary's cash flow statement in that currency can then be consolidated with the reporting entity's cash flow statement after eliminating intra-group items such as dividends and inter-group loans.

30.157 Some companies will apply the closing rate method discussed in paragraphs 30.153 and 30.154 above. The following example illustrates the application of those principles.

Example – Cash flow statement prepared under the closing rate method

Company A, a UK company, whose accounting period ended on 30 September 20X5, has a wholly-owned US subsidiary, S Corporation, that was acquired for US$600,000 on 30 September 20X4. The fair value of the net assets at the date of acquisition was US$500,000. The exchange rate at 30 September 20X4 and 20X5 was £1 = US$2.0 and £1 = US$1.5 respectively. The average rate for the year ended 30 September 20X5 (which company A considers to be a good approximation for the transaction date rate) was £1 = US$1.65.

The summarised balance sheet at 30 September 20X4 and 20X5 and an analysis of the retained profit for the year ended 30 September 20X5 of S Corporation, extracted from the consolidation returns, in dollars and sterling equivalents, are as follows:

Balance sheets of S Corporation	**20X5 $'000**	20X4 $'000	**20X5 £'000 P&L closing**	**20X5 £'000 P&L average**	20X4 £'000
Exchange rate £1 =			**$1.50**	**$1.65**	$2.00
Fixed assets:					
Cost (20X5 additions: $30)	255	225	170.0	170.0	112.5
Depreciation (20X5 charge: $53)	98	45	65.3	65.3	22.5
Net book value	157	180	104.7	104.7	90.0
Current assets:					
Investments	250	100	166.6	166.6	50.0
Stocks	174	126	116.0	116.0	63.0
Debtors	210	145	140.0	140.0	72.5
Cash at bank	240	210	160.0	160.0	105.0
	874	581	582.6	582.6	290.5
Current liabilities:					
Bank overdraft	150	–	100.0	100.0	–
Trade creditors	125	113	83.3	83.3	56.5
Taxation	30	18	20.0	20.0	9.0
	305	131	203.3	203.3	65.5
Net current assets	569	450	379.3	379.3	225.0
Loan stock	150	130	100.0	100.0	65.0
Net assets	576	500	384.0	384.0	250.0
Share capital	300	300	150.0	150.0	150.0
Reserves:					
Pre acquisition	200	200	100.0	100.0	100.0
Post acquisition	76	–	50.7	46.1	–
Exchange difference					
Net assets ($500/1.5 — $500/2.0)	–	–	83.3	83.3	–
Increase ($76/1.5 — $76/1.65)	–	–	–	4.6	–
	576	500	384.0	384.0	250.0

Analysis of retained profit for year ended 30 September 20X5

		Closing rate	Average rate
	$'000	£'000	£'000
Operating profit	135	90.0	81.8
Interest paid	(15)	(10.0)	(9.0)
Taxation	(30)	(20.0)	(18.2)
Dividends paid in the year	(14)	(9.3)	(8.5)
Retained profit	76	50.7	46.1

It is further assumed that company A does not trade on its own and its only income is dividends received from S Corporation. The summarised balance sheet of company A at 30 September 20X4 and 20X5 is as follows:

Company A – Balance sheets	**20X5**	**20X4**
	£'000	**£'000**
Investments in subsidiary ($600,000 @ 2.0)	300	300
Cash	208	200
Net assets	508	500
Share capital	500	500
P&L account (dividend received: $14,000 @ 1.75*)	8	–
	458	500

* actual rate on date dividend received.

Where company A applies SSAP 20 and uses the closing rate/net investment method, it may use either the closing rate or the average rate for translating the results of S Corporation. The summarised consolidated profit and loss account for the year ended 30 September 20X5 drawn up on the two basis and the summarised consolidated balance sheet at that date are as follows:

Consolidated profit and loss account for the year ended 30 September 20X5

	£'000	**£'000**
	Closing rate	**Average rate**
Operating profit of S corporation	90.0	81.8
Operating profit of Company A	8.0	8.0
	98.0	89.8
Adjustment – inter company dividend	(9.3)	(8.5)
Retranslation of goodwill	16.7	16.7
Net operating profit	105.4	98.0
Interest paid	(10.0)	(9.0)
Taxation	(20.0)	(18.2)
Retained profit	75.5	70.8

Consolidated balance sheet as at 30 September 20X5

Fixed assets	104.7	104.7
Goodwill ($100,000 @ 1.5)	66.7	66.7
	171.4	171.4
Current assets:		
Investments	166.6	166.6
Stocks	116.0	116.0
Debtors	140.0	140.0
Cash (S Corporation: £160; Company A £208)	368.0	368.0
	790.6	790.6
Current liabilities:		
Bank overdraft	100.0	100.0
Trade creditors	83.3	83.3
Taxation	20.0	20.0
	203.3	203.3
Net current assets	587.3	587.3
Loan stocks	100.0	100.0
Net assets	658.7	658.7
Share capital	500.0	500.0
Reserves:		
Retained profit	75.5	70.8
Exchange difference on opening net assets	83.3	83.3
Exchange difference on P&L account	–	4.7
	658.8	658.8

In the above illustration, goodwill has been regarded as a currency asset which is retranslated at the closing rate. This is a treatment permitted by SSAP 20 and required by FRS 23. An alternative treatment that is permitted by SSAP 20 is to translate goodwill at the rate ruling on the date of acquisition on the grounds that it arises only on consolidation and is not part of the foreign entity's net assets.

Given the above information, the consolidated cash flow statement drawn up in accordance with the exchange rate used in the profit and loss account and the related notes to the cash flow statement are as follows:

Consolidated cash flow statement for the year ended 30 September 20X5

	£'000 Closing	£'000 Average
Net cash flow from operating activities	56.7	52.2
Returns on investments and servicing of finance		
Interest paid ($15,000 @ 1.5 and 1.65)	(10.0)	(9.1)
Taxation		
Overseas tax paid ($18,000* @ 1.5 and 1.65)	(12.0)	(10.9)
Capital expenditure		
Purchase of fixed assets ($30,000 @ 1.5 and 1.65)	(20.0)	(18.1)
Management of liquid resources		
Purchase of current asset investments ($150,000 @ 1.5 and 1.65)	(100.0)	(90.9)
Financing		
Issue of loan stock ($20,000 @ 1.5 and 1.65)	13.3	12.1
Decrease in cash	(72.0)	(64.7)

* Overseas tax paid relates to settlement of previous year's liability.

Reconciliation of net cash flow to movement in net funds

	£'000 Closing	£'000 Average
Decrease in cash for the period	(72.0)	(64.7)
Cash flow from increase in liquid resources	100.0	90.9
Cash flow from increase in debt	(13.3)	(12.1)
Change in net fund resulting from cash flows	14.7	14.1
Translation difference (see note 2)	29.9	30.5
Movement in net funds in the period	44.6	44.6
Net funds at 1 October 20X4	290.0	290.0
Net funds at 30 September 20X5	334.6	334.6

Notes to the cash flow statement

1 Reconciliation of operating profit to net cash inflow from operating activities

	Closing rate £'000	Average rate £'000
Operating profit	88.7	81.3
Depreciation ($53,000 @ 1.5 and 1.65)	35.3	32.1
Increase in stocks ($48,000 @ 1.5 and 1.65)	(32.0)	(29.1)
Increase in debtors ($65,000 @ 1.5 and 1.65)	(43.3)	(39.4)
Increase in creditors ($12,000 @ 1.5 and 1.65)	8.0	7.3
Net cash flow from operating activities	56.7	52.2

The movement in working capital in note 1 above could also be obtained by taking the difference between the closing and the opening balance sheet figures and adjusting the result to eliminate the non-cash effects of exchange rate adjustments. But this method is rather cumbersome as illustrated below for stocks:

	Closing rate £'000	Average rate £'000
Stocks at 30 September 20X5 ($174 @ 1.5)	116.0	116.0
Stocks at 30 September 20X4 ($126 @ 2.0)	63.0	63.0
Increase in stocks ($48)	53.0	53.0
Exchange difference:		
On opening balance ($126 @ 1.5 — $126 @ 2.0)	(21.0)	(21.0)
On movement ($48 @ 1.5 — $48 @ 1.65)	–	(2.9)
Increase in stocks included in reconciliation above	32.0	29.1

The effect of foreign exchange rate changes on net funds may be reconciled as follows:

2 Analysis of net funds – Closing rate method

	1 Oct 20X4 £'000	Cash flow £'000	Exchange difference £'000	30 Sep 20X5 £'000
Cash				
Cash at bank	305.0	28.0	35.0	368.0
Bank overdraft	–	(100.0)	–	(100.0)
	305.0	(72.0)	35.0	268.0
Liquid resources				
Current asset investments	50.0	100.0	16.6	166.6
Debt				
Loan stock	(65.0)	(13.3)	(21.7)	(100.0)
Net funds	290.0	14.7	29.9	334.6

Analysis of net funds – Average rate method

	1 Oct 20X4 £'000	Cash flow £'000	Exchange difference £'000	30 Sep 20X5 £'000
Cash				
Cash at bank	305.0	26.2	36.8	368.0
Bank overdraft		(90.9)	(9.1)	(100.0)
	305.0	(64.7)*	27.7	268.0
Liquid resources				
Current asset investments	50.0	90.9	25.7	166.6
Debt				
Loan stock	(65.0)	(12.1)	(22.9)	(100.0)
Net funds	290.0	14.1	30.5	334.6

*Note:

Movements in cash – (S Corp $30 @ 1.65 = £18.2 + A Ltd £8)	£26.2
Movement in overdraft (S corp $150 @ 1.65)	£90.9

See workings below for calculation of exchange differences

	Closing rate £'000	Average rate £'000
Cash at bank		
Opening balance ($210 @ 1.5 — $210 @ 2.0)	35.0	35.0
Increase in the period ($30 @ 1.5 — $30 @ 1.65)	–	1.8
	35.0	36.8
Bank overdraft:		
Opening balance	–	–
Increase in the period ($150 @ 1.5 — $150 @ 1.65)	–	(9.1)
	–	(9.1)
Liquid resources – current asset investment		
Opening balance ($100 @ 1.5 — $100 @ 2.0)	16.6	16.6
Increase in the period ($150 @ 1.5 — $150 @ 1.65)	–	9.1
	16.6	25.7
Debt – loan stock		
Opening balance ($130 @ 1.5 — $130 @ 2.0)	(21.7)	(21.7)
Increase in the period ($20 @ 1.5 — $20 @ 1.65)	–	(1.2)
	21.7	(22.9)

[The next paragraph is 30.158.]

Intra-group transactions

30.158 Transactions between members of a group located in different countries may not cancel out on consolidation because of exchange differences. As explained in chapter 7, these exchange differences are usually reported in the consolidated profit and loss account, particularly if they relate to intra-group trading transactions and dividends. Such exchange differences may have an effect on group cash flows. For consolidated cash flow statements, these intra-group cash flows may not cancel out unless the actual rate at the date of transfer is used for translation. In the previous example, the only intra-group transaction that took place between the parent and the subsidiary was in respect of a dividend payment. The consolidated operating profit after cancellation of the inter-company dividend is shown below for the two situations where the subsidiary's profit and loss account has been translated at the closing rate and the average rate.

Consolidated profit and loss account for the year ended 30 September 20X5	£'000 Closing rate	£'000 Average rate
Operating profit of S corporation	90.0	81.8
Operating profit of Company A	8.0	8.0
	98.0	89.8
Adjustment – inter company dividend	(9.3)	(8.5)
Net operating profit	88.7	81.3

30.159 As can be seen the amount of £9,300 and £8,500 is used to cancel the dividend paid by the subsidiary and not the £8,000 received by the parent. It would, therefore, appear that an exchange difference has been left in operating profit, which would need to be eliminated in the reconciliation of operating profit to operating cash flow. However, this is not the case. Deducting the amount for the dividend paid by the subsidiary in the consolidated profit and loss account at the same amount included in the subsidiary's profit and loss account translated at closing rate or average rate, cancels the dividend paid, and so ensures that the consolidated profit and loss account reflects the dividends received by the parent at the sterling amount received. In the consolidated cash flow statement, the same approach is adopted. In effect, the subsidiary's cash flows are reported at the closing rate or average rate, except that the dividend payment is reversed at that same rate and included at the sterling amount actually received by the parent. As a result, no further adjustment for the exchange difference is necessary in the reconciliation of operating profit to operating cash flow, or in the reconciliation to net debt. Indeed, this is to be expected as the transaction was settled during the year, any exchange difference already being reflected in cash flows. The standard, therefore, permits the use of an actual rate, or an approximation thereto, to translate intra-group cash flows in order to ensure that they cancel out in the preparation of the consolidated cash flow statement. [FRS 1 para 41].

30.160 If, on the other hand, the amount of £8,000 received by the parent had been used to cancel the intra-group dividend, the consolidated operating profit would have increased as shown below.

Consolidated profit and loss account for the year ended 30 September 20X5	**£'000 Closing rate**	**£'000 Average rate**
Operating profit of S corporation	90.0	81.8
Operating profit of Company A	8.0	8.0
	98.0	89.8
Adjustment – inter company dividend	(8.0)	(8.0)
Net operating profit	90.0	89.8

30.161 Using identical amounts to cancel the intra-group dividend in the consolidated profit and loss account does not mean that the exchange difference has been eliminated in the cash flow statement. The effect of using the actual amount received in the cancellation process means that the profits remitted by the subsidiary are being translated at the closing rate or the average rate. As a result the intra-group dividend paid and received does not cancel out in the consolidated cash flow statement. The difference of £1,300 for the closing rate or £500 for the average rate then needs to be eliminated. The standard states that if the rate used to translate intra-group cash flows is not the actual rate, any exchange rate differences should be included in the effect of the exchange rate movements shown as part of the reconciliation to net debt. [FRS 1 para 41]. It could be argued that it makes more sense to report this exchange rate difference in the reconciliation of operating profit to operating cash flows. This is because the subsidiary's cash has gone down by £9,300 and the holding company's cash has gone up by £8,000, resulting in a real economic loss to the group which normally falls to be recognised in the consolidated profit and loss account as explained in chapter 7. However, the treatment required by the standard ensures that the profit and loss account and the cash flow statement are treated in a consistent way. Because, in the above example, operating profit does not include any exchange difference on the intra-group dividend, it follows that no adjustment for the exchange difference is necessary in the reconciliation of operating profit to operating cash flows. The only other place to report this exchange difference is in the reconciliation to net debt.

Hedging transactions

30.162 Hedging transactions are normally undertaken by entities to protect themselves from financial loss, especially loss that would occur if prices or exchange rates were to vary. For example, an entity may purchase or sell a hedging instrument, such as a futures contract or a forward contract, in order to protect itself from price fluctuations that may arise in connection with the sale or purchase of stocks. The question arises as to how cash flows that result from the purchase or sale of the hedging instrument should be classified in the cash flow statement. Should these be shown under capital expenditure and financial investments or classified in the same category as the cash flows of the items being hedged, for example, under operating activities?

30.163 The standard provides that cash flows that result from transactions undertaken to hedge another transaction should be reported under the same standard heading as the transactions which are the subject of the hedge. [FRS 1 para 42]. The treatment required by the standard for hedging transactions applies only to futures contracts, forward contracts, options and swaps that are taken out as hedges of identifiable transactions or events. For example, the reporting entity may purchase a futures contract in order to reduce its exposure to increases in the price of a planned stock purchase and, therefore, any cash flows arising on the futures contract should be reported in operating cash flows.

30.164 The treatment required by the standard for hedged transactions cannot apply to situations where the reporting entity hedges a net investment in a foreign subsidiary with a borrowing that is denominated in the same currency as the net investment being hedged. Accounting for the borrowing as a hedge is incidental; it cannot change the basic fact that it is still a borrowing. Furthermore, the foreign subsidiary may have contributed to group cash flows reported under each of the standard headings. Since the cash flows from the borrowings cannot be identified with any specific cash flows from that subsidiary, it follows that the cash flows from the borrowing can only be classified in the cash flow statement under financing in the consolidated financial statements.

Notes to the cash flow statements

Specific disclosures

30.165 In addition to the cash flow statement itself, the standard requires a number of explanatory notes to the cash flow statements. The positioning of these notes within the financial statements varies from company to company, but in general they are either presented immediately after the cash flow statement itself or are included in the notes to the financial statements with appropriate cross-references to the cash flow statement. Many of the specific disclosures that are necessary to supplement the information presented in the cash flow statement have already been discussed and illustrated by practical examples, but are restated below for completeness.

- A note showing the reconciliation between operating profit and net cash flow from operating activities should be provided. This reconciliation should disclose all differences between operating cash flows and operating profits (see para 30.72). This reconciliation should be presented either adjoining the cash flow statement or in a note to the statement.
- A reconciliation of the movement in cash to the movement in net debt should be provided showing the changes in net debt during the year and the way in which such changes are related to the opening and closing balance sheet figures. This reconciliation, like the previous one, may be presented either adjoining the cash flow statement or in a note to the statement. Where several balance sheet items or parts thereof have to be combined to permit a reconciliation, sufficient detail should be shown to enable the movements to be understood. This detail should be given in a note to the statement (see para 30.123).
- Where a group acquires or disposes of a subsidiary undertaking, the notes to the cash flow statements should show a summary of the effects of the acquisition or disposal. Disclosure should also be made of the extent to which the amounts reported under each of the standard headings have been affected by the cash flows of the subsidiary acquired or disposed of during the year (see paras 30.137 and 30.138).
- Major non-cash transactions should also be disclosed. Such transactions do not involve any cash flow, but have the same effect as if several cash transactions were made together. For example, conversion of debt to equity can be viewed as the equivalent of repaying debt in cash and then receiving cash on the issue of new shares. Because there are no actual cash flows, the transaction would not feature in the cash flow statement. But important information would thereby remain undisclosed merely because, in effect, a notional cash outflow has been cancelled by an equal and opposite notional cash inflow. Therefore, in order to report an entity's activities in full, material non-cash transactions should be disclosed in a note to the cash flow statement if disclosure is necessary for an understanding of the underlying transactions.

Supplementary disclosures

30.166 In addition to the specific disclosures identified above, the standard *encourages* reporting entities to provide additional information relevant to their particular circumstances. [FRS 1 para 56]. The additional information that may be presented is considered below.

Reporting of gross operating cash flows

30.167 Entities are allowed to provide information on gross operating cash receipts and gross operating cash payments. [FRS 1 para 7]. Clearly, presentation of such information produces a cash flow statement in its purest form with new information that is not otherwise available from the profit and loss account or the balance sheet. The way in which such information should be presented is illustrated in Table 30.4.

Cash flows from discontinued operations

30.168 Entities are encouraged to distinguish between net cash flows from continuing operating activities and those arising from discontinued operations. [FRS 1 para 56]. Although not specifically required in the standard section of FRS 1, the analysis is given in example 2 of the illustrative examples included in the FRS. This disclosure is consistent with the separate disclosure in the profit and loss account of the results of continuing activities from those relating to discontinued operations required by FRS 3. Many companies have not given this analysis, but an example of a company that has separately analysed its net cash flows from operating activities between continuing and discontinued operations is shown in Table 30.13 below.

Table 30.13 – Analysis of cash flows from discontinued operations

Pearson plc – Directors' Report and Accounts – 31 December 1996
Notes to the Accounts (extract)

25 Notes to consolidated statement of cash flows

a) Reconciliation of operating profit to net cash inflow from operating activities	**Continuing 1996 £m**	**Discontinued 1996 £m**	**Total 1996 £m**	Continuing 1995 £m	Discontinued 1995 £m	Total 1995 £m
Operating profit	**146.0**	**35.3**	**181.3**	237.6	22.0	259.6
Depreciation charges	**56.8**	**6.4**	**63.2**	54.7	6.8	61.5
Share of profit of partnerships and associated undertakings	**(53.1)**	–	**(53.1)**	(43.3)	–	(43.3)
Dividends from partnerships and associated undertakings	**33.5**	–	**33.5**	30.7	–	30.7
Decrease/(increase) in stocks	**4.6**	**1.9**	**6.5**	(34.6)	(1.9)	(36.5)
Decrease/(increase) in debtors	**21.8**	**(1.0)**	**20.8**	(80.3)	(0.2)	(80.5)
Increase/(decrease) in creditors	**59.9**	**1.0**	**60.9**	20.2	(2.0)	18.2
(Decrease)/increase in operating provisions	**1.6**	**(3.5)**	**(1.9)**	29.2	(0.2)	29.0
Exchange adjustments	**(7.7)**	–	**(7.7)**	2.8	–	2.8
Other	**(10.6)**	**(1.7)**	**(12.3)**	(5.1)	–	(5.1)
Net cash inflow from operating activities*	**252.8**	**38.4**	**291.2**	211.9	24.5	236.4
Purchase of fixed assets and finance leases	**(85.9)**	**(5.0)**	**(90.9)**	(97.6)	(4.3)	(101.9)
Sale of operating tangible fixed assets	**6.5**	**0.4**	**6.9**	31.6	0.5	32.1
Other	**10.0**	**1.8**	**11.8**	(20.1)	–	(20.1)
Operating cash flow	**183.4**	**35.6**	**219.0**	125.8	20.7	146.5

* Cash inflow for 1996 includes a £20.9m outflow relating to exceptional items charged in 1996 and £12.5m outflow relating to exceptional items charged in prior years.

Undrawn facilities

30.169 There is no requirement in FRS 1 to disclose the amount of any undrawn borrowing facilities, for example, an undrawn loan facility agreed with the bank. However, for entities applying FRS 29, 'Financial instruments: Disclosures', this is covered by the liquidity risk disclosures required by that standard (see chapter 6). See also the discussion in paragraph 30.173 below on liquidity disclosures in the business review.

Commentary on cash flows in the business review

30.170 It is acknowledged that the assessment of liquidity, viability and financial adaptability of an entity requires more information than just a statement of cash flows. The Business Review (or Operating and Financial Review (OFR)), which is discussed further in chapter 2 of the Manual of Accounting – Management Reports and Governance, give opportunities for companies to provide a commentary on their cash flows. The ASB's 'Reporting statement: Operating and financial review', recommends discussion in the 'financial position' section of the statement concerning 'cash flows' and 'liquidity'. [RS (OFR) paras 68, 71]. Many companies use this opportunity to provide further information on their cash generating potential and liquidity position that goes beyond that required by FRS 1.

30.171 In discussing the cash generated from operations and other cash inflows during the period, the reporting statement encourages companies to disclose and discuss segmental cash flows where they are significantly out of line with segmental profits, because of the impact of capital expenditure. [RS (OFR) para 70]. In fact, FRS 1 also encourages entities to give a segmental breakdown of their cash flows, but does not specify how this information should be given. [FRS 1 para 8]. Many companies, following SSAP 25, 'Segmental reporting', already give segmental information about their operations in terms of turnover, profits, capital employed, etc. The extension of segmental information to cash flows enables users to understand the relationship between the cash flows of the business as a whole and those of its component parts.

30.172 The type of segmental cash flow information that should be reported is not specifically identified by FRS 1, or the reporting statement, but we consider that, as a minimum, an entity should give an analysis of the most important elements of operating cash flows between the major reportable segments. Clearly, there may be problems of allocation, such as common costs and interest, but they could be allocated between segments in the same way as other segmental information. Guidance on the allocation of common costs and interest is given in SSAP 25 and discussed in chapter 10. An example of a company that has given a segmental analysis of operating cash flows is shown in Table 30.14 below.

Table 30.14 – Segmental analysis of operating cash flows

Bass PLC – Annual Report and Financial Statements – 30 September 1996

NOTES TO THE FINANCIAL STATEMENTS (extract)

28 Operating cash flow		**1996 £m**	1995 £m
Hotels:	Holiday Inn Worldwide	**184**	115
Leisure retailing:	Bass Taverns	**114**	204
	Bass Leisure	**(22)**	19
Branded drinks:	Bass Brewers*	**139**	160
	Britvic Soft Drinks	**43**	41
Other activities*		**(9)**	24
		449	563

*Figures for 1995 have been restated to include in Bass Brewers operating cash flow related to its overseas brewing operations which was previously included in other activities; this restatement amounts to £28m outflow.

30.173 In discussing current liquidity, the reporting statement calls for disclosure and comments on the level of borrowings including seasonality, peak borrowing levels and maturity profile of both borrowings and committed borrowing facilities. [RS (OFR) para 71]. In addition, there are specific requirements in respect of liquidity risk disclosures for entities applying FRS 29, 'Financial instruments: Disclosures', (see chapter 6).

30.174 The discussion on borrowings suggested by the reporting statement should also refer to any restrictions on the ability of the group to transfer funds from one part of the group to another and restrictions and breaches of borrowing covenants. [RS (OFR) paras 71, 73, 74]. The disclosure of the amounts of cash that are not freely remittable to the parent company coupled with sufficient information on the restrictions (for example, exchange controls) provides useful information for users of financial statements to make an assessment of the probable future effect of the restriction on the company's cash flows. As discussed in paragraph 30.175, FRS 1 requires disclosures on the treatment of cash that is subject to restriction. Similarly, information on assets and liabilities denominated in foreign currencies, which incidentally is not directly relevant for supplementing information reported in the cash flow statement, may be useful for making assessments of a company's liquidity and financial viability. Information on any restrictive financial covenants on current borrowing agreements and breaches or likely breaches of covenants is equally important in assessing its viability and financial adaptability.

Restrictions on remittability

30.175 Sometimes cash may be held in a separate blocked account or an escrow account to be used only for a specific purpose, or held by subsidiaries operating in countries where exchange control restrictions are in force such that cash is not freely transferable around the group. The standard requires that where restrictions prevent the transfer of cash from one part of the business or group to another, a note to the cash flow statement should disclose the amount and explain the nature of the restriction. [FRS 1 para 47]. However, disclosure is required only in circumstances where the restriction is imposed by external factors outside the company's control. Restrictions arising from a specific purpose designated by the reporting entity need not be disclosed. A typical example of disclosure is where a foreign subsidiary is prevented from remitting funds to its overseas parent, because of local exchange control regulations. [FRS 1 para 68]. Other examples given in the standard where disclosure may be relevant, depending on the regulatory environment, relate to cash balances in escrow, deposited with a regulator or held within an employee share ownership trust. The treatment of cash subject to restriction is considered from paragraph 30.190.

Comparative figures

30.176 Comparative figures should be given for all items reported in the cash flow statements and in the supplementary notes. Comparative figures are required for the reconciliation of the movement of cash to the movement in net debt, but not for the note that analyses the changes in the balance sheet amounts making up net debt. Nor are comparative figures required for the amounts included under each of the standard headings in respect of the cash flows of subsidiaries acquired or disposed of during the year. [FRS 1 para 48].

Example – Requirement for comparatives when exemption applied in prior year

A company was a wholly-owned subsidiary of another company at the previous year end and took the exemption in FRS 1 from preparing a cash flow statement, which is available to 90% controlled subsidiaries. However, during the year the parent sold 20% of the company, so that it is less than 90% controlled at this year end and, therefore, has to produce a cash flow statement. Can the company just do a cash flow for the current year and not give comparatives, on the grounds that it was exempt last year?

No. Paragraph 48 of FRS 1 clearly states that comparatives are required for a cash flow statement and this applies even if the company was exempt in the prior year.

30.177 Normally, it is a relatively simple matter to provide comparative figures for all items reported in the cash flow statement itself. However, disclosure of comparative amounts for all items reported in the notes to the cash flow statement may cause some practical difficulties in interpreting this requirement. For example, the illustrative example in the standard provides a detailed breakdown of the assets and liabilities of subsidiaries acquired or disposed of during the year, together with an analysis of the net consideration paid or received in the transfer. Normally, such disclosures are also required by company law and by FRS 6, but only in the year of acquisition or disposal. If the strict wording of the standard is to be followed, then comparative figures would be required. Many companies do not provide such comparative information, although it is arguable that where an acquisition or disposal has taken place both in the current and the preceding year, the analysis of the net consideration should be given for both years in the notes as illustrated in Table 30.11.

Practical application of FRS 1

30.178 This section attempts to clarify some of the practical problems that may arise in interpreting and applying the standard.

Balance sheet cash versus FRS 1 cash

30.179 The strict definition of cash used for the purposes of cash flow reporting explained in paragraph 30.41 above is unlikely to accord with the interpretation of cash used in the balance sheet classification 'cash at bank and in hand'. Although some companies follow a narrow interpretation of cash by including only cash held in current accounts and short-term deposits repayable on demand under the balance sheet heading, others follow a wider interpretation by including the total amount of money on deposit with a bank or financial institution without regard to whether the deposit was short or long-term (see also chapter 4). If the wider interpretation is followed, the movements in cash as reported in the cash flow statement are unlikely to agree with the movements in cash as disclosed in the balance sheet caption. The differences are likely to be for those short-term deposits that are regarded as liquid resources and whose movements are reported under 'management of liquid resources' and for other long-term deposits that are not regarded as liquid resources whose movements are reported under 'capital expenditure and financial investment'.

Discounts and premiums

30.180 Where a deep discounted bond is redeemed or a premium is paid on the redemption of a debt security, the question sometimes arises as to where in the cash flow statement the premium should be reported. An intuitive response may be to include it within financing together with the other principal amount repaid on the instrument. However, under FRS 4 (or FRS 26, for companies applying that standard – see further chapter 6) the discount on issue and the redemption premium form part of the finance cost of the instruments, which is reported in the profit and loss account as interest expense over the life of the instruments. FRS 1 takes a similar approach. It requires that the cash flow effects of these items should be reported within 'returns on investments and servicing of finance' when the instruments are redeemed in order to provide a link between the profit and loss account and the cash flow statement as illustrated in the following example.

> **Example – Redemption of discounted bond**
>
> A company issues a ten year zero coupon bond with a face value of £100,000 at a discount of £61,446. Its issue price is, therefore, £38,554 and the effective yield is 10%. How should the transaction be reflected in the cash flow statement?

At the issue date, the proceeds of £38,554 would be shown as a cash inflow in financing. The discount of £61,446 represents a rolled-up interest charge which would be amortised to the profit and loss account as an interest expense over the life of the bond while the bond remains outstanding. However, there would be no cash flow in these periods, because no cash has been paid.

On maturity, the discount of £61,446, which is part of the finance cost under FRS 4 (and FRS 26), should be shown under 'returns on investments and servicing of finance' separately classified, if material, as premium paid on redemption of bond in accordance with paragraph 15(a) of the standard. The balance of £38,554 should be shown under financing as repayment of the bond. The result is that a decrease in cash of £100,000 would be reported at the end of the cash flow statement. It should be noted that although the discount has been accrued over the years when the bond was in issue, the repayment of the discount on redemption means that the accrual should be adjusted as a non-cash change in the reconciliation to net debt as shown below:

Reconciliation to net debt	£'000
Decrease in cash in the period	(100,000)
Cash flow from decrease in debt financing	38,554
Change in net debt from cash flows	(61,446)
Other non cash changes – reversal of accrual for discount	61,446
Movement in net debt for the period	–
Opening net funds (say cash of £150,000 less bond of £100,000)	50,000
Closing net funds (cash of £50,000)	50,000

It is clear from the above example that accruals for finance costs would need to be reported as other non-cash changes in the reconciliation to net debt. This adjustment should be made both in the year(s) in which the accrual arises (as an increase in net debt) and in the year in which it reverses, otherwise the movement in net debt for the period cannot be reconciled with the opening and closing component of net debt.

A similar treatment would apply to the investor. The investor should record the payment for the bond of £38,554 as part of cash outflow in financial investment. On maturity, the receipt of £100,000 should be split and shown as to £38,554 under financial investment and £61,446 under 'returns on investments and servicing of finance'.

30.181 Where debt instruments (including shares that are classified as liabilities) are redeemed at a premium, it will also be necessary to separate the principal and the interest element of the amounts paid on redemption. For example, where supplemental interest is paid on convertible bonds that are redeemed rather than converted, the whole amount of the supplemental interest accrued over the life of the bond and paid at redemption should be reported under 'returns on investments and servicing of finance'. See further chapter 6.

30.181.1 Note, issue costs of equity instruments (which are not amortised to the profit and loss account) are shown in the financing section of the cash flow statement and are separately disclosed (see para 30.110).

Gains and losses

30.182 It is consistent with the objective of cash flow reporting that gains and losses that do not give rise to any cash flows should be excluded from the cash flow statement. Gains and losses are reported in the profit and loss account or in the statement of total recognised gains and losses of the reporting entity. To the extent that these are included in arriving at operating profit, they should be adjusted (gains should be deducted and losses added) in the reconciliation to arrive at the net cash flow from operating activities. For example, a gain on the sale of plant and machinery that has been included in operating profit (as a depreciation adjustment) should be excluded from cash flow from operating activities. The gain is not a cash flow as such, but forms part of the proceeds from the sale that are disclosed under capital expenditure in the cash flow statement.

30.183 A similar treatment would apply to gains and losses on investments. However, where investments are used for trading activities (typically by a bank or a financial institution), any gain or loss arising on their disposal during the year would be included in operating profit. In this situation, operating profit need only be adjusted for the movement in investments and not for the gain or loss arising (which is realised) to arrive at the net cash flow from operating activities.

30.184 Gains and losses on current asset investments that are regarded as liquid resources, would need to be eliminated from operating profit, if the gain or loss is also reported as part of operating profit, to give the correct cash flow from operating activities. Irrespective of whether or not the gain or loss is reported within operating profit, the gain or loss would need to be reported as a non-cash item in the reconciliation to net debt.

30.185 In relation to debt securities, a further question arises as to whether a gain or loss that arises on the early settlement of a debt security issued by a reporting entity should be reported as part of the finance cost under 'returns on investments and servicing of finance' or as part of the capital repayment under 'financing'. Consider the following example.

Example – Loss on early redemption of bond

The facts are the same as in the previous example except that the company has decided to redeem the bond early at the beginning of year 4 for £55,000.

The carrying value of the bond in the balance sheet at the end of year 3 is calculated as follows:

	£'000	£'000
Proceeds at beginning of year 1		38,554
Interest accrued in year 1 – 10% on £38,554	3,854	
Interest accrued in year 2 – 10% on £42,408	4,241	
Interest accrued in year 3 – 10% on £46,649	4,665	12,760
Carrying value (capital value of bond £100,000 less unamortised discount of £61,446 – £12,760 = £48,686)		51,314
Loss on redemption:		
Redemption payment		55,000
Less carrying value		51,314
		3,686

The loss should be allocated to interest paid, giving £16,446 (£12,760 + £3,686) to be reported under returns on investments and servicing of finance and £38,554 to be reported as capital repayment under financing. This treatment is appropriate because the total cash cost of the finance is reflected in the cash flow statement. Under FRS 4 (and FRS 26, for companies applying that standard), the difference between the net proceeds of an instrument (in this example, £38,554) and the total amount of the payments made (£55,000) is finance cost (£16,446). As explained before, FRS 1 also requires the cash flow effect to be treated in a similar way. The alternative of reporting the loss incurred as part of the capital repayment, giving £42,240 (£38,554 + £3,686) to be reported under financing and £12,760 to be reported as interest paid under returns on investments and servicing of finance, is not considered acceptable.

Reorganisation costs following an acquisition

30.186 Where a company undertakes to reorganise the business of a recently acquired subsidiary, it may incur costs that are provided for in periods prior to the actual disbursement of cash. The question arises as to whether the subsequent cash outflow in respect of the amount provided should be disclosed as part of operating activities or 'acquisitions and disposals'.

30.187 FRS 7 requires such costs to be reported in the post-acquisition profit and loss account of the acquiring group. The cash outflows should, therefore, be reported under operating activities if such costs are also reported in the post-acquisition profit and loss account in arriving at operating profit. Where the costs are reported as a non-operating exceptional item in accordance with FRS 3 and FRS 6, 'Acquisition and mergers', (that is, if the reorganisation is fundamental to the enlarged group), the exceptional cash flows would also fall to be reported separately under operating activities as discussed in paragraph 30.114 above.

Refinancing of borrowings

30.188 Companies may renegotiate their existing borrowings on terms that are different from those that were in place prior to the renegotiation. For example, as part of the renegotiation, a significant part of the company's current overdraft balance may be converted into a long-term loan. The question arises as to how such a reclassification should be dealt with in the cash flow statement.

30.189 The answer depends on whether the renegotiation gives rise to any cash flows. If the renegotiation is undertaken with the same bankers, it is likely that no cash flows are involved. In that situation, the proper treatment would be to reclassify the relevant portion of the overdraft balance from cash to financing in the notes that analyse the changes in net debt during the year. On the other hand, if the refinancing is carried out with a different bank, such that the proceeds of the new loan are utilised to settle all or part of the old overdraft balance, a cash inflow and outflow have taken place. Consequently, the new loan would be shown in financing with the result that the net movement in the overdraft balance will automatically be reflected in the increase or decrease in cash for the period.

30.189.1 Even if the refinancing is carried out with the same bank, it is possible that cash flows have occurred. This may be the case if the old facilities have been repaid and new facilities put in place. The factors to be considered by both FRS 4 and FRS 26 users when determining whether a refinancing is a modification of pre-existing debt or the extinguishment of an old facility and inception of a new facility are considered separately in the relevant sections of chapter 6. If the refinancing is accounted for as an extinguishment of the old facility, it is consistent with the treatment in the balance sheet to show the repayment of this old facility as a financing outflow and the cash receipt from the new facility would be shown as an inflow. However, even where the refinancing is accounted for as a modification of pre-existing debt, if actual cash flows have occurred these should similarly be reflected in the cash flow statement, together with disclosure to explain the related accounting in the balance sheet.

Cash subject to restriction

30.190 The treatment of cash subject to restriction (sometimes called 'ring-fenced' cash) in the cash flow statement is not specifically covered by the standard, although disclosure is required, where access is severely restricted (see para 30.175). Nevertheless, the question arises as to how they should be dealt with in the cash flow statement itself. Consider the following example.

Example

A property company has secured development finance of £10m from its bankers during the year ended 31 December 20X5. The funds are held in a special blocked account to be used only for a specific development. Development on the property commenced during the year and by the end of its financial year the company had expended £2m. At 31 December 20X5, there was a balance of £8m in the blocked account.

The balance of £8m in the blocked account should not be included in cash, because to do so would create a distorted impression of the company's liquidity position. In that situation, the company would show the net cash outflow of £2m from operating activities, a cash inflow of £10m in financing with the balance of £8m as fixed deposits under capital expenditure and financial investment. Adequate disclosure on the restrictions should also be given in a note if funds can only be drawn down with the banker's permission.

It would not be appropriate to show the £8m balance as part of cash, as cash held in a special blocked deposit account does not meet the narrow definition of cash as set out in the standard (see para 30.41).

30.191 In general, the treatment of cash subject to restriction should depend on the nature of the item and the restriction in force. For example, client money is not generally available for business's own use and falls outside the definition of cash, even though it may be reported in the balance sheet along with the related liability. Another situation is where a company is required to give a bond or a guarantee to a third party, for example, a bond may be held by HM Revenue and Customs for the clearance of imported merchandise. In that situation, the payment to Customs would form part of operating cash flows. Where there are restrictions on the transfer of cash from a foreign subsidiary to the parent in the UK because of exchange control restrictions, the cash balances held in the foreign subsidiary would be treated as part of group cash in the cash flow statement, provided they meet the definition of cash in the foreign subsidiary that owns them. Furthermore, this restriction would need to be disclosed as stated in paragraph 30.175.

Proceeds of a rights issue by subsidiary

30.192 When a subsidiary company undertakes a rights issue, some of the cash flows generated will be internal to the group and, if there are minorities, some external cash flows may be generated. Only the external cash flows are presented in the consolidated cash flow statement.

Example – Rights issue to minority shareholders

A partly-owned subsidiary has made a rights issue of new equity shares *pro rata* to its parent and minority shareholders. How should the proceeds be shown in the group's cash flow statement? Does it make any difference if the new share issue is made to the minority shareholders only, assuming the subsidiary remains a subsidiary after the share issue?

In the subsidiary's own cash flow statement, the whole of the proceeds from the rights issue should be shown under the 'financing' section, which includes receipts from issuing shares. In the group's cash flow statement, the cash received from issuing shares to the parent will be eliminated on consolidation, leaving the receipt from the minority shareholders as a cash inflow to the group. Since there is no change in the group's interest in the subsidiary, this cash inflow should also be shown as financing.

In the second case, where the subsidiary issues new shares to the minority shareholders only, the receipts will again be shown as financing in the subsidiary's own cash flow statement. However, as far as the group is concerned, although the minority shareholders have injected new funds, the issue of shares outside the group gives rise to a reduction in the group's interest in the subsidiary. FRS 2, 'Accounting for subsidiary undertakings', refers to this as a deemed disposal. Deemed disposals are accounted for in consolidated financial statements in the same way as direct disposals of interests in subsidiaries. They may give rise to profits or losses on disposal in the consolidated profit and loss account.

FRS 1 encourages cash flows to be classified on a basis that is consistent with the treatment of the related items elsewhere in the financial statements. Receipts from sales of investments in subsidiaries are required to be shown under the 'acquisitions and disposals' section of the cash flow statement. It would be consistent for receipts relating to deemed disposals to be similarly classified.

Proceeds from sale and leaseback

30.193 FRS 1 has an overriding principle that each cash flow should be classified according to the substance of the transaction that gave rise to it. Where the treatment of a particular source of cash flow is not specified in the standard, the substance should prevail.

Example – Sale and leaseback of fixed assets

How should the sale and leaseback of fixed assets be dealt with in the cash flow statement?

If the sale and leaseback results in an operating lease, the proceeds would simply be shown as receipts from the sale of fixed assets, under the cash flow statement heading 'capital expenditure and financial investment'. Thereafter, the operating lease rentals would be included in operating cash flows.

If the leaseback is a finance lease, then under FRS 5, 'Reporting the substance of transactions', the transaction is in substance analogous to raising loan finance secured on the asset, and the asset has in substance never been disposed of. The guidance notes in SSAP 21, 'Accounting for leases and hire purchase contracts', discuss the substance in these terms and suggest leaving the asset unchanged on the balance sheet, setting up a creditor for the amount received on sale, and treating the lease payments partly as principal and partly as a finance charge. Application of FRS 5's principles would also result in this treatment. From a cash flow perspective, this means that the proceeds received would be treated as a financing inflow. The future cash payments (lease payments) would be allocated between repayment of that principal and interest payments as consistent with the treatment in the balance sheet and profit and loss account.

Chapter 31

Small and medium-sized companies and groups

Chapter 31

Small and medium-sized companies and groups

Introduction

31.1 In the UK, company law defines what is meant by 'small' and 'medium-sized' companies and groups. Subject to meeting certain criteria small and medium-sized companies and groups may be able to use specific exemptions in their accounting and reporting. This chapter sets out the criteria required to meet the definition of small or medium-sized in company law, explains the exemptions permitted and discusses the accounting framework options for small companies as set out in the Financial Reporting Standard for Smaller Entities (FRSSE).

31.1.1 A significant change as to how Company Law was written occurred when the Companies Act 2006 was being drafted. Previously the Companies Act 1985 was written to cover companies of all sizes with certain permitted exemptions being available if the criteria to be classified as small or medium-sized were met. As a change to this approach the Companies Act 2006 was written with a 'think small first' mind set. This resulted in separate legislation being brought in through separate statutory instruments for small and medium-sized companies being:

- SI 2008/409 The Small Companies and Groups (Accounts and Directors' Report) Regulations 2008 (referred to throughout this chapter as SI 2008/409).
- SI 2008/410 The Large and Medium-sized Companies and Groups (Accounts and Reports) Regulations 2008 (referred to throughout this chapter as SI 2008/410).

Previous versions of this chapter would have referred to exemptions being available to small or medium-sized companies. Owing to the change in the mind-set embedded in the legislation exemptions are no longer required as the legislation simply does not require small and medium-sized companies to comply with the more detailed requirements for large companies. The requirements for small and medium-sized companies are discussed in detail in this chapter. One of the objectives of the Companies Act 2006 in adopting the 'think small first' approach was to recognise that the vast majority of UK companies are small enterprises, often with limited accounting and legal expertise. Accordingly, the law has been structured to make it easier for small companies to interpret the law and comply with its provisions. Where practicable the Companies Act 2006 sets out the requirements for small companies first, then adds the requirements for larger companies.

Categorisation of small and medium-sized companies and groups

Excluded companies and groups

31.2 Companies excluded from the small or medium-sized companies regulations will not be able to avail themselves of the benefits that are available to small and medium-sized companies. These benefits include for example: small companies may prepare shorter-form financial statements for members; and small and medium-sized companies may file abbreviated financial statements. However, these concessions are not available to any company, regardless of its size, that is, or was at any time during a financial year, any one of the following:

Small company is ineligible if it was at any time within the financial year in question any one of the following: [CA06 Sec 384(1)].	Medium company is ineligible if it was at any time within the financial year in question any one of the following: [CA06 Sec 467(1)].
A public company.	A public company.
A company that is an authorised insurance company, a banking company, an e-money issuer, a MiFID (EU Markets in Financial Instruments Directive) investment firm or a UCITS management company (as defined by the Financial Services and Markets Act 2000).	
	A company that has permission under Part 4 of the Financial Services and Markets Act 2000 to carry on a regulated activity.
A company that carries on insurance market activity.	A company that carries on insurance market activity.
A member of an ineligible group.	A member of an ineligible group.
A group is ineligible if any of its members is: [CA06 Sec 384(2)].	A group is ineligible if any of its members is: [CA06 Sec 467(2)].
A public company.	A public company.
a body corporate (other than a company) whose shares are admitted to trading on a regulated market in an EEA state.	a body corporate (other than a company) whose shares are admitted to trading on a regulated market. (*Note: no reference is made here to the market having to be within an EEA state.*)

A person*, (other than a small company) that has permission under Part 4 of the Financial Services and Markets Act 2000 to carry on a regulated activity.	A person*, (other than a small company) that has permission under Part 4 of the Financial Services and Markets Act 2000 to carry on a regulated activity.
A small company that is an authorised insurance company, a banking company, an e-money issuer, [a MiFID investment firm] or a UCITS management company.	A small company that is an authorised insurance company, a banking company, an e-money issuer, [a MiFID investment firm] or a UCITS management company.
A person* who carries on insurance market activity.	A person* who carries on insurance market activity.

* As the criteria in the top half of the table relates to the individual company all references are made to that company. However in the bottom half of the table the references are widened to include all members of the group and as a consequence reference is made to 'person'. Within section 40 of the Financial Services and Markets Act 2000 a person refers to; an individual, a body corporate, a partnership or an unincorporated association.

31.2.1 A further change from the Companies Act 1985 is the relaxation in relation to body corporates (other than UK companies) with the power to issue shares to the public and for entities with certain listed securities. The Companies Act 2006 no longer focuses on a member of the group having the power to issue securities to the public, but instead on whether a member has actually done so. Hence a group is ineligible if there is within the group either a parent or a subsidiary undertaking that has any of its securities admitted to trading on a regulated market (and for a small group this confined to within an EEA state). However, the existence within a group of a UK public company, whether or not it is listed, still means that the group is ineligible.

31.2.1.1 When determining whether a company is a member of an ineligible group an obvious question is which group do you consider? The answer is that you need to look to the largest group of which the company is a member rather than any intermediate sub-group. In considering a group, all companies worldwide need to be included. This is the obvious conclusion when considering a company at the lowest level of the corporate chain, but when looking at an intermediate parent company it is easy to overlook the need to look up and/or across the corporate chain when the parent heads its own sub-group. This can sometime cause unexpected results in excluding UK companies from the small or medium-sized companies regulations as explained in paragraph 31.102.

31.2.2 If a company would have been considered small or medium if it were not a member of an ineligible group it may still avail of certain exemptions in relation to the directors' report – see paragraphs 31.60 and 31.95.

31.3 A company that is a subsidiary of a large *private* company and satisfies all the qualification criteria set out in paragraph 31.2 will not be excluded from qualifying as small. This point is further illustrated in paragraph 31.103.

[The next paragraph is 31.8.]

Small and medium-sized companies

Basic size tests

31.8 A company may qualify as small or medium-sized for a financial year if it satisfies *any two* of the three conditions under the applicable heading in the following table during that year:

	Small	Medium-sized
■ Annual turnover not exceeding	£6,500,000	£25,900,000
■ Balance sheet total not exceeding	£3,260,000	£12,900,000
■ Average number of employees not exceeding	50	250

[CA06 Secs 382(3), 465(3)].

31.9 The basic size parameters are subject to periodic amendment and are derived from limits laid down by the EU. The latest such amendment occurred in April 2008 when SI 2008/393 increased the annual turnover and balance sheet totals for small and medium-sized companies. It is important to ensure, therefore, that reference is made to the latest set of thresholds, and that advantage is taken of any transitional provisions that may apply.

[The next paragraph is 31.11.]

31.11 Where a company has not prepared its financial statements in respect of a 12 month period, the turnover thresholds must be proportionately adjusted in order to establish whether the appropriate conditions have been satisfied. [CA06 Secs 382(4), 465(4)]. For example, in the case of a company that prepares financial statements for a nine-month period, the turnover threshold will be less than £4,875,000 (that is, 9/12 × £6,500,000) for a small company, and less than £19,425,000 (that is, 9/12 × £25,900,000) for a medium-sized company. Neither the balance sheet threshold, nor the employee number threshold, is affected by shorter or longer accounting periods.

31.12 The 'balance sheet total' is the aggregate of the amounts shown as assets in the company's balance sheet.

31.13 The number of employees means the average number of persons employed by the company in the year, determined on a monthly basis. The method prescribed by the Act should be adopted for the calculation; that is, adding up those defined as employed for each month and dividing the total thereby derived by the number of months in the period. [CA06 Secs 382(6), 411(3)(4), 465(6)].

Further qualification criteria

31.14 The application of the criteria for small and medium-sized companies can prove complex, because, in addition to satisfying the basic size tests referred to above, companies must also satisfy other qualification criteria that may be more difficult to interpret.

31.15 The Act sets out the following additional criteria that must be applied in determining whether a company qualifies as small or medium-sized in relation to a financial year, for the purposes of filing abbreviated financial statements (small and medium-sized companies) or preparing shorter-form financial statements (small companies only):

- In respect of a company's first financial year, it will qualify as small or medium-sized, provided that it satisfies the appropriate size conditions under section 382(3) of the 2006 Act, for small companies, or under section 465(3) for medium-sized companies, in that year. [CA06 Secs 382(1), 465(1)].
- In subsequent years, a company will qualify as small or medium-sized, provided that it satisfies the appropriate size conditions under section 382(3) or section 465(3) of the 2006 Act in both the year in question and the preceding year. [CA06 Secs 382(2), 465(2)].
- A company that qualifies as small or medium-sized under sections 382(3) or 465(3) of the 2006 Act in one year will be treated as qualifying in the following year, even if it fails to satisfy the size conditions in that following year. However, if it does not satisfy the qualifying conditions in the year after that, then, for that third year, it must produce its financial statements in a format appropriate to its size. On the other hand, if the company reverts to satisfying the qualifying conditions in this third year, then it may continue to be classified as small or medium-sized as it had been in the second year. This test is required in every situation and not just in the initial years of incorporation as explained above. The aim of this legislation is to permit an occasional variation in the company's trading without requiring the company to be classified as a different sized entity. Therefore, a company will be required to trade at the same level for two consecutive years before any change in size classification is required. [CA06 Secs 382(2), 465(2)]

31.16 The application of these qualification criteria is best illustrated by way of an example:

Example

Consider the following details relating to two companies, S and M. While company S is incorporated on the first day of year 2, company M is a long-established entity that fulfilled the size conditions of a medium-sized company in the year immediately before year 1.

Company S	**Small criteria memo**	**Year 1**	**Year 2**	**Year 3**	**Year 4**
Turnover	£6.5m	—	£6.2m	£6.8m	£6.2m
Gross assets	£3.26m	—	£2.6m	£3.4m	£3.1m
Average number of employees	50	—	55	60	55

In year 2, its year of incorporation, company S fulfils the size criteria for qualification as a small company. This is because it fulfils the criteria both for turnover and gross assets, although not for average number of employees. As year 2 is its first financial year, company S qualifies as a small company by virtue of section 382(1) of the 2006 Act. As such, it can file abbreviated financial statements and prepare shorter-form financial statements for its members.

In year 3, company S has exceeded all three size criteria for small company qualification. However, by virtue of section 382(2) of the 2006 Act, it still qualifies as a small company, because it fulfilled the size conditions in the preceding year, which was its first financial year. It can, therefore, file abbreviated financial statements and prepare shorter-form financial statements for this year.

In year 4, company S satisfies the size criteria for qualification as a small company. Despite the fact that it did not satisfy the size conditions in year 3, it still qualifies as a small company by virtue of section 382(2) of the 2006 Act, because it was treated as so qualifying in year 3 and currently meets the qualifying criteria. It can, similarly, file abbreviated financial statements and prepare shorter-form financial statements for this year.

Company M	**Medium criteria**				
	memo	**Year 1**	**Year 2**	**Year 3**	**Year 4**
Turnover	£25.9m	£25.4m	£27.2m	£28.6m	£24.0m
Gross assets	£12.9m	£10.8m	£11.0m	£12.0m	£10.0m
Average number of employees	250	250	255	255	250

In year 1, company M fulfils all the size criteria that qualify it to be treated as a medium-sized company. Since it has fulfilled the size-conditions its first year, it can take advantage of the exemptions allowed to it to file abbreviated financial statements. As a medium-sized company it cannot prepare shorter-form financial statements as these are only available to small companies.

In year 2, company M ceases to fulfil the size conditions for a medium-sized company because both its turnover and its average number of employees exceed the specified thresholds. However, it still qualifies as a medium-sized company for abbreviated financial statements purposes by virtue of section 465(2) of the 2006 Act, in that it fulfilled the size criteria for qualification in the previous year.

In year 3, company M fails to meet the size criteria for a medium-sized company for a second consecutive year. Consequently, it no longer qualifies as a medium-sized company and cannot, therefore, file abbreviated financial statements for year 3.

In year 4, company M reverts to fulfilling the size conditions of a medium-sized company. However, it does not qualify as a medium-sized company for abbreviated financial statements purposes, because it has not fulfilled the size criteria for qualification for two consecutive years. Should it meet these criteria in year 5, it would then be able to revert to filing abbreviated financial statements.

31.17 A parent company should not be treated as qualifying as a small or medium-sized company in relation to a financial year, unless the group headed by it qualifies also as a small or medium-sized group. These rules are explained further from paragraph 31.98.

Small and medium-sized groups

Basic size tests

31.18 A group may qualify as small or medium-sized for a financial year (and for small groups, be exempt from the requirement to prepare consolidated financial statements) if it satisfies *any two* of the three conditions under the applicable heading in the following table during that year:

		Small	Medium-sized
■	Aggregate net turnover not exceeding	£6,500,000	£25,900,000
	or		
	Aggregate gross turnover not exceeding	£7,800,000	£31,100,000
■	Aggregate net balance sheet total not exceeding	£3,260,000	£12,900,000
	or		
	Aggregate gross balance sheet total not exceeding	£3,900,000	£15,500,000
■	Average number of employees not exceeding	50	250

[CA06 Secs 383(4), 466(4)].

31.19 For groups, the figures for turnover, balance sheet total and average number of employees are arrived at by adding together the relevant figures for each group company. The net figures refer to the relevant amounts after making consolidation adjustments for set-offs and other matters. As an alternative the gross figures can be applied to the relevant amounts before making such adjustments. [CA06 Secs 383(5)(6), 466(5)(6)]. A company may satisfy the qualifying criteria on the basis of gross or net figures and in any year it is permissible to mix the use of gross and net figures. Rather than having to eliminate group transactions, the gross size criteria should be checked first, and the net size criteria checked only if required.

31.20 If the financial year of a subsidiary company is not coterminous with that of the parent company, then the subsidiary's latest financial statements, for a year which immediately predates the financial year of the parent, should be used. [CA06 Secs 383(7), 466(7)]. However, if the subsidiary's figures cannot be ascertained without disproportionate expense or undue delay, the latest available figures should be used. [CA06 Secs 383(7), 466(7)].

Further qualification criteria

31.21 The other qualification criteria outlined in paragraph 31.15 of this chapter relating to small and medium-sized companies, are mirrored by similar criteria affecting small and medium-sized groups. [CA06 Secs 383(2)(3), 466(2)(3)]. Thus, a group qualifies as small or medium-sized in relation to a financial year, where:

- The size test conditions set out in section 383(4) (small companies) or section 466(4) (medium-sized companies) of the 2006 Act are met and it is the parent company's first financial year. [CA06 Secs 383(2), 466(2)].
- In any subsequent financial year the size test conditions are met and were met in the year immediately preceding. [CA06 Secs 383(3), 466(3)].
- The size test conditions were met in the preceding year, but are not met in the current year. [CA06 Secs 383(3), 466(3)].
- The size test conditions are met in the current year but were not met in the previous year, yet the group still qualified on that occasion. [CA06 Secs 383(3), 466(3)].

31.22 The application of the qualification criteria is complicated and is illustrated in the example in paragraph 31.16. Furthermore, if a group qualifies as small or medium-sized on, say, a net basis in a particular year, it is not required to apply the same basis in the following year. In each year, it may apply the net basis, the gross basis or a mixture of the two (see para 31.18).

[The next paragraph is 31.26.]

Small and medium-sized company financial statements

31.26A small company that prepares UK GAAP financial statements, as opposed to preparing IAS financial statements, has the following options in preparing its statutory financial statements.

- It may prepare and file full UK GAAP financial statements without taking any concessions, following full accounting standards and the Act's reporting rules and the Schedule 1 formats for large and medium-sized companies set out in SI 2008/410, as discussed in the main body of this Manual.
- It may prepare and file its annual financial statements in accordance with the special provisions available to small companies under Schedule 1 to SI 2008/409. The exemptions available when using this option are consistent with the requirements of the FRSSE.

31.26.1 In addition to preparing statutory financial statements for its members, a small company *must* file financial statements with the Registrar of Companies from the following range of options. Section 444 of the Companies Act 2006 states that the directors: *must* deliver to the Registrar for each financial year a copy of a balance sheet drawn up as at the last day of the financial year; they *may* in addition deliver a copy of the profit and loss account and the directors' report for that year. If the financial statements were audited then the audit report on the financial statements (and the directors' report if filed) *must* also be filed. The financial statements filed with the Registrar may be the annual financial statements of the company or 'abbreviated' financial statements prepared under Schedule 4 to SI 2008/409. When abbreviated accounts are filed, the audit report is the special audit report as detailed in section 449 of the Companies Act 2006. Therefore, a small company may file: abbreviated financial statements; full financial statements; or abbreviated or full financial statements but excluding the profit and loss account and the directors' report.

31.26.2 For a small company that prepares IAS individual financial statements, abbreviated accounts are not permitted to be filed. Such companies, as an alternative to filing full IAS financial statements, it may file just the balance sheet and notes from those financial statements together with the auditors' report on the full financial statements. The profit and loss account and the directors' report are not required to be filed.

31.26.3 Where a small company delivers full, as opposed to abbreviated accounts to the companies registrar and does not file the profit and loss account or the directors' report whether prepared under UK GAAP or IFRS, individual financial statements must include a prominent statement on the balance sheet that the accounts and reports have been prepared in accordance with the provisions applicable to companies subject to the small companies' regime. [CA06 Sec 444(5)].

31.26.4 While a small company may choose to prepare and file full accounts as discussed in paragraph 31.26 the following table summarises the filing options available for companies availing of exemptions within the small companies' regime.

	Full annual accounts	Full balance sheet only	Abbreviated accounts	Abbreviated balance sheet only
Format for Company Act accounts – SI 2008/409	Schedule 1	Schedule 1	Schedule 4	Schedule 4
Company Act accounts or IAS accounts	Option available for both	Option available for both	Not available for IAS accounts	Option available for both
Prominent statement on balance sheet (para 31.26.3)	Yes – required by CA 2006 Sec 414(3)	Yes – required by CA 2006 Sec 444(5)	Yes – required by SI 2008/ 409 Sch 4 para 2	Yes – required by CA 2006 Sec 444(5)
Copy of the full P&L account	Yes – required	No	No	No
Copy of the Directors' Report	Yes – required	No	No	No
Audit report (if audit exemption does not apply)	Yes – required by CA06 Sec 495	Yes – required by CA06 Sec 495	Yes – required by CA06 Sec 449 – special auditors' report	Yes – required by CA06 Sec 495
Requirement for accounting notes	Yes	Yes	Yes – but limited to those referred to in SI 2008/ 409 Sch 4	Yes – but limited to those referred to in SI 2008/ 409 Sch 4

31.27 Note that the financial statements prepared under Schedule 1 to SI 2008/409 are those that a company prepares for its members. If the company also prepares abbreviated financial statements under Schedule 4 this does not remove the requirement for the company to prepare full financial statements for its members. Therefore, if a small company wishes to file abbreviated full financial statements, then it must first prepare full financial statements as described in paragraph 31.26.

31.28 Financial statements prepared under the provisions of Schedule 1 to SI 2008/409, refer to the individual or group financial statements that small companies are permitted to prepare for members by virtue of the small company regime of the 2006 Act. In this chapter, such financial statements are referred to as 'shorter-form financial statements'. However, it should be noted that this term is not used in company law, but is used in this chapter purely for convenience, to avoid confusion with the term 'abbreviated financial statements'.

31.28.1 There is a fundamental difference between the 1985 and 2006 Acts in the way that they give relief from accounting rules and disclosures of small companies. The 1985 Act started from the premise that all companies would prepare full financial statements and a complex web of exemptions evolved that gave some relief from the rules. As a result, many of the sections dealing with small companies in the 1985 Act have become difficult to understand. The 2006 Act creates a 'small company regime' to which all eligible companies will belong, unless they choose to opt out of it.

31.29 'Abbreviated financial statements' means the individual financial statements that small and medium-sized companies are permitted to file by virtue of sections 444(1) and (3) or 445(3) of the 2006 Act. For small companies the provisions required are set out in Schedule 4 to SI 2008/409.

31.30 There are major differences between the form and content of shorter-form financial statements (Schedule 1 to SI 2008/409) and abbreviated financial statements (Schedule 4 to SI 2008/409). Shorter-form financial statements are prepared for members and are required to give a true and fair view. In contrast, abbreviated financial statements do not purport to give a true and fair view and on commercial or confidentiality grounds they exclude financial information that is integral to the true and fair view. Hence, the disclosure exemptions available in shorter-form financial statements are much less extensive than those available in respect of abbreviated financial statements in Schedule 4.

31.31 For shorter-form financial statements, the concessions from the detailed disclosure requirements for large and medium companies concerning the items to be disclosed in the formats and in the notes appear extensive. However, small companies may not have many of the items allowed to be aggregated under the rules and, hence, the concessions have less impact in practice. For example, under the heading of intangible assets, development costs, concessions, patents, licences, trade marks and similar rights and assets and payments on account are allowed to be aggregated under the single item 'other intangible assets'. Many small companies will not have such assets and, as a consequence, this concession has little impact. See paragraph 31.46.

Accounting standards

Small companies and groups

31.32 The ASB issued a Financial Reporting Standard for Smaller Entities (FRSSE) in November 1997, which has been revised regularly in the intervening years. The FRSSE contains relevant sections of the Companies Act in order to provide small companies with a 'one-stop-shop' standard incorporating accounting standards and legal requirements. The most recent version relates to accounting periods beginning on or after 6 April 2008, FRSSE (2008). Included in the Appendices to the standard is a summary of the main changes from the previous version. No accounting changes were introduced in the 2008 version, only changes in Company Law were included. It is designed to provide small companies with a single reporting standard that is focussed on their particular circumstances. The FRSSE is not compulsory, but where a small company chooses to adopt the FRSSE, the financial statements should state that they have been prepared in accordance with it. [FRSSE para 2.6]. This additional statement may be combined with the note of accounting policies, or for those companies taking advantage of the exemptions for small companies in company legislation, it may be included in the statement required by company legislation to be given on the balance sheet. An example of such a combined statement giving the disclosure required by the Act and the FRSSE is set out in paragraph 31.59. A company adopting the FRSSE is exempt from other accounting standards and UITF Abstracts, unless preparing consolidated financial statements, in which case certain other accounting standards apply, as set out in paragraph 31.109 below. Should a small company not adopt the FRSSE it will still be exempt from certain accounting standards and UITF Abstracts, such as FRS 1, 'Cash flow statements', (see chapter 30) and those standards listed in paragraph 31.37. A summary of the accounting requirements of the FRSSE is set out from 31.127 onwards.

31.33 The FRSSE imports disclosure rules from existing standards that are considered to be relevant to small companies. Section C of the FRSSE contains definitions of terms that apply to the accounting practices set out in the FRSSE. These terms have been imported from existing accounting standards suitably modified in certain cases.

31.34 Previously the FRSSE, in table format, contained an analysis of each paragraph of the FRSSE and explains the source and whether that source has been adopted in its entirety, or with minor amendments, or with major changes. In recent versions this derivation table has been excluded. However, the derivation table is freely available from the ASB web site (see derivation tables at www.frc.org.uk/asb/technical/frsse.cfm).

31.35 There may be circumstances where a small company enters into transactions on which accounting guidance is not provided in the FRSSE. It may be that guidance on such transactions is provided in the accounting standards applying to larger entities. In that situation, where a practice that has been clearly established and accepted, unless there are good reasons, a small company would normally follow it. Indeed, the FRSSE takes the view that for transactions and events not dealt with in the FRSSE, small companies should have regard to other accounting standards and UITF Abstracts, not as mandatory documents, but as a means of establishing current practice. [FRSSE App IV para 38]. In that situation, adequate disclosure should be made in the notes to the financial statements of the transaction or arrangement concerned and the treatment adopted. This requirement is implicit in paragraph 2.5 of the FRSSE. It follows that for transactions and events not dealt with in the FRSSE, but dealt with in other accounting standards and UITF Abstracts, a small company should have regard not only to the measurement rules, but also to any disclosure requirements relevant to those transactions.

31.36 The FRSSE is revised and updated periodically to reflect developments in financial reporting. The ASB has established a Committee on Accounting for Smaller Entities that recommends to the ASB how new standards or revisions to existing standards apply to smaller entities. The Committee is also responsible for reviewing the operation of the FRSSE. Any proposed changes to the FRSSE are subject to public consultation. Revisions of the FRSSE are formally approved and issued by the ASB. As UK GAAP continues to converge with IFRS it is uncertain as to how long the FRSSE will be permitted to remain, based on the current UK GAAP framework.

Medium-sized companies and groups

31.37 There are no special accounting standards for medium-sized companies and groups. Therefore, all accounting standards and UITF Abstracts apply to them except for the following:

- SSAP 13, 'Accounting for research and development', excludes private companies less than ten times the financial criteria defining a medium-sized company from profit and loss account disclosures (see chapter 15).
- SSAP 25, 'Segmental reporting', excludes private companies as in SSAP 13 above from some of the more detailed segmental disclosures (see chapter 10).
- FRS 13, 'Derivatives and other financial instruments: Disclosures', is applicable primarily to listed companies and banks (see chapter 6).
- FRS 22, 'Earnings per share', is applicable to listed companies only (see chapter 14).
- FRS 23, 'The effects of changes in foreign exchange rates', FRS 26, 'Financial instruments: Measurement' and the disclosure requirements of FRS 25, 'Financial instruments: Disclosure and presentation', and FRS 29, 'Financial instruments: Disclosures', all of which are mandatory primarily for listed companies and banks.

31.38 As can be seen from the above the exemptions allowed in SSAP 13 and SSAP 25 are based on size criteria, which serve to exempt companies larger than medium-sized from compliance.

31.38.1 A further point to stress is a recent change to FRS 2. Under Companies Act 1985 it was permissible for a medium-sized group to take an exemption from having to prepare consolidated financial statements. As the thresholds for small and medium-sized companies continued to increase in recent years it was decided that quite large groups were able to avail themselves of the exemption. The Companies Act 2006 changed the law in this regard, to make it mandatory for all groups, other than small groups, to prepare consolidated financial statements.

FRS 2 was revised to reflect this change in law which was effective for accounting periods commencing on or after 6 April 2008. As a consequence, a lot of medium-sized groups will have to prepare consolidated financial statements for the first time and comparative figures will also be required.

Summary

31.39 The options that are available to small and medium-sized companies in company law for the preparation and audit of financial statements for filing and for members are complex and are summarised in the annex to this chapter.

Form and content of shorter-form financial statements

31.40 The general provisions that relate to the form and content of small company financial statements are detailed in Schedule 1 to SI 2008/409. These provisions are supplemented by specific requirements of the FRSSE that provide a link with the Schedule 1 provisions. In preparing financial statements, a small company is permitted to comply with the provisions of Schedule 1, or it may comply instead with one or more of the corresponding provisions of Schedule 1 to SI 2008/410. Any reference in section 396 of the 2006 Act (Companies Act individual accounts) to compliance with the provisions of Schedule 1 to SI 2008/409 is then construed accordingly.

31.41 Section 411(1) gives further exemptions from the disclosure requirements of other schedules to the Act while sections 416(3) and 417(1) give exemptions from certain of the disclosures generally required in the directors' report. These exemptions are explained in paragraphs 31.61 and 31.95 respectively.

31.42 Three primary statements included within a small company's financial statements are:

- Profit and loss account.
- Statement of total recognised gains and losses.
- Balance sheet.

31.43 Schedule 1 to SI 2008/409, sets out two alternative formats for the balance sheet, which are a simplification of those set out in Schedule 1 to SI 2008/410 and four alternative formats for the profit and loss account, which are identical to those set out in Schedule 1 to SI 2008/410. It also lays down certain general guidelines to be followed. In addition, the Schedule requires small companies to give in the notes to the balance sheet and in the notes to the profit and loss account many of the disclosures that apply to the generality of companies.

31.44 The Act does not require companies to include in their financial statements a statement of total recognised gains and losses. This primary statement is required by FRS 3 or the FRSSE for all small companies' financial statements that are intended to give a true and fair view. However, where the only recognised gains and losses are the results included in the profit and loss account no separate statement to this effect is required. [FRSSE para 5.1].

31.45 There is no requirement in the Act for companies to prepare a cash flow statement. The FRSSE, like FRS 1, encourages, but does not require, small entities to prepare a cash flow statement. Section D of the FRSSE sets out the voluntary disclosures relating to cash flow information.

The balance sheet

Formats

31.46 The balance sheet formats set out in Schedule 1 to SI 2008/409 are simplifications of those set out in Schedule 1 SI 2008/410. The table below considers Format 1 of the balance sheet and indicates how the Schedule 1 to SI 2008/409 formats take those in Schedule 1 to SI 2008/410 and combine certain of the headings preceded by Arabic numerals. Format 2 allows identical combination of headings.

Items in italic in column 1 are combined under the item in italic shown opposite in column 2. The items with Roman numerals remain unchanged.

	Schedule 1 for the 'Large and Medium Companies and Groups (Accounts and Directors' Report) Regulations 2008', Format 1		**Schedule 1 for the 'Small Companies and Group (Accounts and Directors' Report) Regulations 2008', Format 1**
A	Called up share capital not paid	A	Called up share capital not paid
B	Fixed assets	B	Fixed assets
B 1	Intangible assets	B 1	Intangible assets
	3. Goodwill		1. Goodwill
	1. Development costs		*2. Other intangible assets*
	2. Concessions…		
	4. Payments on account		
B II	Tangible assets	B II	Tangible assets
	1. Land and buildings		1. Land and buildings
	2. Plant and machinery		*2. Plant and machinery, etc*
	3. Fixtures, fittings…		
	4. Payments on account…		

B III	Investments	B III	Investments
	1. Shares in group undertakings		*1. Shares in group undertakings and participating interests*
	3. Participating interests		
	2. Loans to group undertakings		*2. Loans to group undertakings and undertakings in which the company has a participating interest*
	4. Loans to undertakings, etc		
	5. Other investments other than loans		3. Other investments other than loans
	6. Other loans		*4. Other investments*
	7. Own shares		
C	Current assets	C	Current assets
C I	Stocks	C I	Stocks
	1. Raw materials, etc.		*1. Stocks*
	2. Work in progress		
	3. Finished goods/goods for resale		
	4. Payments on account		2. Payments on account
C II	Debtors	C II	Debtors
	1. Trade debtors		1. Trade debtors
	2. Amounts owed by group undertakings		*2. Amounts owed by group undertakings and undertakings in which the company has a participating interest*
	3. Amounts owed by undertakings in which the company has a participating interest		
	4. Other debtors		*3. Other debtors*
	5. Called up share capital not paid		
	6. Prepayments and accrued income		
C III	Investments	C III	Investments
	1. Shares in group undertakings		1. Shares in group undertakings
	2. Own shares		*2. Other investments*
	3. Other investments		
C IV	Cash at bank and in hand	C IV	Cash at bank and in hand
D	Prepayments and accrued income	D	Prepayments and accrued income

E	Creditors: amounts...within one year	E	Creditors: amounts...within one year
	2. Bank loans and overdrafts		1. Bank loans and overdrafts
	4. Trade creditors		2. Trade creditors
	6. Amounts owed to group undertakings		*3. Amounts owed to group undertakings and undertakings in which the company has a participating interest*
	7.Amounts owed to undertakings in which the company has a participating interest		
	1. Debenture loans		*4. Other creditors*
	3. Payments received on account		
	5. Bills of exchange payable		
	8. Other creditors including taxation and social security		
	9. Accruals and deferred income		
F	Net current assets (liabilities)	F	Net current assets (liabilities)
G	Total assets less current liabilities	G	Total assets less current liabilities
H	Creditors amounts...after one year	H	Creditors: amounts...after one year
	2. Bank loans and overdrafts		1. Bank loans and overdrafts
	4. Trade creditors		2. Trade creditors
	6. Amounts owed to group undertakings		*3. Amounts owed to group undertakings and undertakings in which the company has a participating interest*
	7. Amounts owed to undertakings in which the company has a participating interest		
	1. Debenture loans		*4. Other creditors*
	3. Payments received on account		
	5. Bills of exchange payable		
	8. Other creditors including taxation and social security		
	9. Accruals and deferred income		
I	Provision for liabilities	I	Provisions for liabilities
	1. Pensions and similar obligations		*(Items 1-3 need not be shown)*
	2. Taxation, etc		
	3. Other provisions		

J	Accruals and deferred income	J	Accruals and deferred income
K	Capital and reserves	K	Capital and reserves
KI	Called up share capital	KI	Called up share capital
KII	Share premium account	KII	Share premium account
KIII	Revaluation reserve	KIII	Revaluation reserve
KIV	Other reserves	KIV	Other reserves
	1. Capital redemption reserve		*(Items 1-4 need not be shown)*
	2. Reserve for own shares		
	3. Reserves provided for by articles		
	4. Other reserves		
KV	Profit and loss account	KV	Profit and loss account

31.47 The following additional exemptions are available:

- In the case of both Formats 1 and 2, a small company need not show amounts falling due after more than one year separately for each item included under debtors if it discloses the aggregate amount of debtors falling due after more than one year in the notes. [SI 2008/409 1 Sch (5)]. However, following UITF Abstract 4, in some instances where the amount of long-term debtors is so material the split might need to be given on the face of the balance sheet.
- In the case of Format 2, a small company need not show separately the amounts falling due within one year and after one year for each of the items included under creditors if it discloses the aggregate amount of creditors falling due within one year and the aggregate amount falling due after more than one year in the notes. [SI 2008/409 1 Sch (10)].
- Although the balance sheet formats do not include a separate line for creditors in respect of taxation and social security, this amount should be shown separately. [SI 2008/409 1 Sch (7)].

The profit and loss account

Formats

31.48 The Act permits small companies to use any one of the four alternative formats of the profit and loss account set out in Schedule 1 to SI 2008/409 and it leaves the choice between these formats to the company's directors. In addition, the Act attaches to the formats certain notes and comments on specific profit and loss account items. Since the formats and the related notes set out in Schedule 1 are the same as those set out in Schedule 1 to SI 2008/410, the discussions in chapter 4 relating to formats are relevant.

Notes to the financial statements

Notes to the balance sheet

31.49 Schedule 1 to SI 2008/409 requires small companies to disclose information which either supplements the information given with respect to any particular item shown in the balance sheet and the profit and loss account or is otherwise relevant to assessing the company's state of affairs in the light of the information so given. In order to provide a link between this chapter and the other chapters of this manual that deal with all the disclosure requirements of the Act, the paragraphs that follow specify the relevant paragraphs with which a small company need not comply and hence which are not included in Schedule 1 to SI 2008/409.

31.50 A small company need *not* give any of the information supplementing the balance sheet required by the following paragraphs of Schedule 1 to SI 2008/410.

- Paragraph 49 — particulars of any contingent right to the allotment of shares in the company.
- Paragraph 50 — information regarding issues of debentures.
- Paragraph 53 — details of the company's freehold and leasehold properties.
- Paragraph 56 — the fair value of derivatives not included in the balance sheet at fair value.
- Paragraph 60 — separate disclosure of the amount of any provision for deferred taxation (however, paras 9.10 and 9.11 of the FRSSE require this disclosure).
- Paragraph 61(2) — the terms of repayment and interest rates for debts.
- Paragraph 61(4)(b) — the nature of securities given for debts.
- Paragraph 64(2) — the aggregate amount of loans provided by way of permitted financial assistance for the purchase of own shares, such as under an employees' share scheme.

31.51 Further exemptions and modifications that are permitted in respect of balance sheet information are as follows:

- Where the carrying value of stocks and fungible assets included in the financial statements is calculated by a permitted approximation methodology, such as FIFO, and that value differs materially from their relevant alternative amount, in effect replacement cost, the amount of the difference need not be disclosed.
- Disclosure of debts repayable in more than five years need not be made for each item included in 'creditors', if the required information is given in aggregate for all items.

Notes to the profit and loss account

31.52 A qualifying small company also receives disclosure exemptions in respect of certain supplementary information to the profit and loss account normally required by Schedule 1 to SI 2008/410. Accordingly, it need *not* make separate disclosure of:

- Paragraph 66 — details of interest payable or similar charges.
- Paragraph 67 — particulars of tax, including details of corporation and income tax charges, and special circumstances affecting the tax charge (however, paragraph 9.2 of the FRSSE requires disclosure of the material components of the current and deferred tax charge).
- Paragraph 68 — segmental particulars of turnover. If, however, the company has supplied geographical markets outside the UK, the notes must state the percentage of turnover attributable to those markets. In giving this information, the directors must consider the manner in which the company's activities are organised.
- Section 11(1) – disclosure required in notes to annual accounts: particulars of staff. This includes details relating to the average number of employees and details relating to the analysis of wage costs split between; wages costs, social security and pension costs.

Other disclosure exemptions

31.53 Schedule 3 to SI 2008/409 does not include the disclosure requirements of other schedules relevant to medium and large companies. In particular, the following information regarding directors' emoluments need *not* be given:

- The numbers of directors exercising share options and receiving shares under long-term incentive schemes.
- Details of the highest paid director's emoluments.
- Details of directors' and past directors' excess retirement benefits.

31.54 In summary, therefore, the information which *must still be given* in respect of directors' emoluments is as follows:

- The aggregate amount of directors' remuneration, amounts receivable under long-term incentive schemes and contributions paid or treated as paid to a money purchase pension scheme. A small company may disclose a single figure, being the aggregate of these three items, rather than disclose the items separately. [SI 2008/409 3 Sch 1(1)].
- Number of directors to whom retirement benefits are accruing under each of money purchase and defined benefit schemes respectively. [SI 2008/409 3 Sch 1(2)].

- Aggregate compensation to directors for loss of office. [SI 2008/409 3 Sch 2].
- Sums paid to third parties for making available the services of directors. [SI 2008/409 3 Sch 3].

31.55 There is no requirement for small companies to disclose the information required by paragraph 12 of Schedule 4 to SI 2008/410 concerning financial years of subsidiary undertakings.

31.56 There is no exemption from disclosure in the notes in respect of audit fee disclosures required by Section 494 of the Act. However, qualifying small and medium-sized companies are not required to disclose the amounts paid to auditors for non-audit services. [SI 2008/489 Reg 4].

Additional statement required by company law and the FRSSE

31.57 Where the directors of a small company prepare shorter-form financial statements, those financial statements must contain a statement in a prominent position on the balance sheet, above the signature required by section 414 of the Act, that they are prepared in accordance with the special provisions of the Act relating to small companies. [CA06 Secs 414(3), 444(5), 450(3)].

31.58 There is also a similar requirement in the FRSSE for a statement that the financial statements have been prepared in accordance with the FRSSE. [FRSSE para 2.6].

31.59 A suitable wording that combines both the above statements is included by way of the following example.

> **Example – Basis of preparation statement**
>
> The financial statements have been prepared in accordance with the special provisions relating to companies subject to the small companies regime within Part 15 of the Companies Act 2006, 'The Small Companies and Groups (Accounts and Directors' Report) Regulations 2008' and with the Financial Reporting Standard for Smaller Entities (effective April 2008).

Directors' report

31.60 Where a small company prepares either full accounts in accordance with Schedule 1 to SI 2008/410 or shorter-form financial statements for members in accordance with Schedule 1 to SI 2008/409, it is also allowed to omit certain disclosures required in full financial statements from its directors' report. Even if a small company is a member of an ineligible group it is still able to take the following exemptions in relation to the directors' report and in addition they are not required to file the directors' report. [CA06 Sec 415A]. These exemptions are also available in the group directors' report where a small group prepares consolidated accounts either because it has to (exemptions from consolidation are not available under Secs 400 or 401) or it voluntarily does [CA06 Sec 416(2)].

Indeed, should a sub-group qualify as a small group even if it is contained within a larger ineligible group the exemptions relating to the directors' report are still available. As with the balance sheet and profit and loss account exemptions, these exemptions are not compulsory, so the company may give fuller disclosure if it so wishes.

31.61 Where advantage is taken of these exemptions, the directors' report need *not* disclose any of the information that is required by the following provisions:

- A business review. [CA06 Sec 417(1)].
- The dividends recommended by the directors. [CA06 Sec 416(3)].

31.62 The usefulness of the above exemptions will depend on the specific circumstances of the company concerned. Thus, a company that has little trading activity and no dividend payments, will benefit little from these exemptions. This contrasts with the situation of abbreviated financial statements, which are much shorter than either full financial statements or shorter-form financial statements and are, therefore, filed by many small companies to maintain business confidentiality.

31.63 Where the directors also take advantage any of the exemptions in respect of the preparation of the directors' report, they must make a statement in a prominent position above the signature on the directors' report that the report has been prepared in accordance either with SI 2008/409. [CA06 Sec 419(2)].

31.64 Suitable wording for such a statement is as follows:

> **Example – Directors' statement where advantage has been taken to exclude certain information**
>
> This report has been prepared in accordance with the special provisions relating to small companies within Part 15 of the Companies Act 2006.

Audit requirements

31.65 As a further complication, some (but not all) small companies and groups are exempt from the requirement for any external audit. This exemption is dealt with in chapter 8 of the Manual of Accounting – Management Reports and Governance. The following paragraphs discuss the requirements in the auditors' report when an audit is carried out on small and medium-sized companies.

Auditors' report

31.66 In general, shorter-form financial statements prepared in accordance with Schedule 1 to SI 2008/409 are capable of giving a true and fair view. However, there may be instances where the use of the exemptions means that the financial statements do not give a true and fair view. For example, a particular item may be of such significance that the auditors consider that it should be disclosed separately, but instead it is combined with other items using the available exemptions.

31.67 Where the shorter-form financial statements of a small company fail to give a true and fair view for any reason, including the use of the exemptions, the auditors will need to qualify their opinion in the same way as for a larger company.

31.68 The question also arises as to whether permitted non-compliance by small companies with the provisions of certain accounting standards affects the true and fair view. The following general guidance can be given:

- Where a matter of disclosure required by an accounting standard is specifically referred to in company law, and the law also allows exemption from that disclosure, it need not be given when preparing shorter-form financial statements for members.

- Where an accounting standard requires sub-analysis of an item which is exempted from disclosure under the law, that sub-analysis need not be given when preparing shorter-form financial statements for members.

31.69 Except for the above categories of item, all other disclosures required by accounting standards should be included when preparing shorter-form financial statements for the members of small companies.

31.70 As discussed in chapter 3 of the Manual of Accounting – Narrative Reporting, the directors are not required to comment on the re-appointment of the auditor, but it is customary to do so. If, when preparing the current year's audited financial statements, the directors become aware that the company will be eligible for audit exemption in the following year, the directors may wish to make an appropriate comment in the directors' report. Such a situation may arise when a company reduces in size and qualifies as a small company for the first time. In such a case suitable wording for such a statement may be:

'The directors do not propose to appoint an auditor at the AGM as the company will be eligible for audit exemption as permitted by section 477(1) of the Companies Act 2006] in the following year.'

31.71 However, note that audit exemption will not be available if members holding more than ten per cent of the company's nominal share capital deposit a notice at the registered office of the company demanding an audit.

31.72 Conversely, where a company had previously been exempt from audit but now finds it no longer satisfies the audit exemption thresholds, the in-coming auditor will be required to consider the reliability of the opening balances and may need to refer to this in the auditors' report. If the auditor is satisfied with the opening balances and the disclosure that the corresponding figures are unaudited, a suitable disclosure in the auditors' report may be:

'The financial statements of the company for the [year/period] ended XX/XX/20X8, forming the corresponding figures in the financial statements for the period ended XX/XX/20X9, are unaudited.'

In addition, some explanation should be included as to why the prior year's figures were unaudited (presumably because they were previously entitled to an audit exemption), in which case, the paragraph above could start with *'As explained in [note xx/the directors' report].....'*.

Abbreviated financial statements for filing

31.73 Abbreviated financial statements for small companies contain much less extensive financial information than shorter-form financial statements. (For a medium-sized company's abbreviated financial statements see para 31.89.) A *small* company may file abbreviated financial statements with the Registrar of Companies taking advantage of the following exemptions:

- It is not required to file a profit and loss account.
- It is not required to file a directors' report.
- It is permitted to file either an abbreviated or a shorter-form balance sheet and notes thereto. (See para 31.77.)

[CA06 Sec 444(1)(3)].

31.74 It is also permitted to omit certain other information normally required to be given in the notes to financial statements, including any information relating to remuneration, pensions and compensation for loss of office paid or payable to the directors. [SI 2008/409 Part 2 para 6(2)(b)].

31.75 The formats for an abbreviated balance sheet are set out in Schedule 4 to SI 2008/409. They adopt a similar layout to those in Schedule 1 (both Format 1 and Format 2), but disclose only those items preceded by either a letter or a Roman numeral. However, the aggregate amount of debtors and creditors falling due after more than one year must be shown separately from those falling due within one year, unless this information is given in the notes. [SI 2008/409 4 Sch Part 1 para (1)].

31.76 A Format 1 balance sheet from Schedule 4 to SI 2008/409 is shown in the table below.

Balance sheet – Format 1

A Called up share capital not paid

B Fixed assets

I Intangible assets

II Tangible assets

III Investments

C Current assets

I Stocks

II Debtors

III Investments

IV Cash at bank and in hand

D Prepayments and accrued income

E Creditors: amounts falling due within one year

F Net current assets (liabilities)

G Total assets less current liabilities

H Creditors: amounts falling due after more than one year

I Provisions for liabilities

J Accruals and deferred income

K Capital and reserves

I Called up share capital

II Share premium account

III Revaluation reserve

IV Other reserves

V Profit and loss account

31.77 A small company need only include the following information by way of notes to its abbreviated financial statements:

- Accounting policies. [SI 2008/409 4 Sch Part 2 para 3].
- Details of share capital. [SI 2008/409 4 Sch Part 2 para 4(1)].
- Particulars of allotments of shares. [SI 2008/409 4 Sch Part 2 para 4(2)].
- A fixed assets table, so far as it relates to items to which a letter or Roman number is assigned in the adopted balance sheet format. [SI 2008/409 4 Sch Part 2 para 6].
- Details of financial fixed assets. [SI 2008/409 4 Sch Part 2 para 7].
- Details of indebtedness. [SI 2008/409 4 Sch Part 2 paras 8(2), 8(1)(a)(b)].
- The basis used in translating foreign currency amounts into sterling. [SI 2008/409 4 Sch Part 2 para 9].
- Transactions with directors. [CA06 Sec 413].

- Details of ultimate control. [SI 2008/409 2 Sch Part 1 paras 9, 10].

[The next paragraph is 31.79.]

31.79 It is worth noting that a *small* company's abbreviated financial statements will not disclose the amount of its profit or loss for the year. As the company's profit and loss account will not be filed with the Registrar of Companies, it will not be available to the company's competitors. In fact, the best estimate available to a reader will be the difference between the profit and loss reserve in the balance sheet at both the beginning and the end of the period that the financial statements cover.

31.80 In view of the extensive range of exemptions allowed in abbreviated financial statements, they cannot give a true and fair view. Since they are not intended to present a true and fair view, there is no requirement for them to comply with the disclosure provisions contained in accounting and financial reporting standards, such as FRS 1, 'Cash flow statements', and FRS 8, 'Related party disclosures'. However, because abbreviated financial statements are based on full financial statements prepared for members, the measurement methods adopted will generally be consistent with those set out in accounting standards.

Directors' responsibilities

31.81 The provisions of company law regarding the signing of the copy of the full balance sheet delivered to the Registrar apply equally to abbreviated financial statements filed in their place. [CA06 Sec 414]. Therefore, where abbreviated financial statements are filed, the balance sheet must be signed on behalf of the board by a director. [CA06 Secs 444(6), 450(1)(2)].

31.82 Abbreviated financial statements filed by a small company must also contain a statement in a prominent position on the balance sheet, above the signature required by company law, that they are prepared in accordance with the 'Small Companies and Groups (Accounts and Directors' Report) Regulations 2008'. [CA06 Secs 414(3), 419(2), 444(5), 450(3)].

31.83 A suitable wording for such a statement is as follows:

> **Example**
>
> The abbreviated financial statements have been prepared in accordance with the special provisions relating to companies subject to the small companies regime within Part 15 of the Companies Act 2006 and SI 2008/409.

Auditors' responsibilities

31.84 Abbreviated financial statements prepared under the 2006 Act and delivered to the Registrar by a small company must be accompanied by a *special auditors' report*, unless the company is exempt from the requirement for an audit by virtue of sections of section 477(1) or section 480(1). This report must state that, in the auditors' opinion:

- The company is entitled to deliver abbreviated financial statements in accordance with the section in question.
- The abbreviated financial statements are properly prepared in accordance with regulations made under that section. (SI 2008/409 for small companies or SI 2008/410 for medium-sized companies.

[CA06 Secs 444(3)(4), 445(3)(4), 449(2)].

31.85 The above report assumes that the exemptions in respect of both directors' report and financial statements are taken (see para 31.73 and 31.74). If the exemptions in only one of the sections are taken the references in the report should be amended accordingly.

31.86 The full audit report required by section 475 of the 2006 Act need not be delivered with abbreviated financial statements. However, if the full audit report was qualified, then the special report must include the full text of that report, together with any further material necessary to understand the qualification. [CA06 Sec 449(3) to (5)]. If that audit report contained a statement under section 498(2) of the 2006 Act (accounts, records or returns inadequate or accounts not agreeing with records and returns) or section 498(3) of the 2006 Act (failure to obtain necessary information and explanations) then that statement should be reproduced in full. [CA06 Sec 449(3)(5)]. Section 503 of the 2006 Act (signature of auditors' report) apply to a special report as it applies to a full report under relevant section. [CA06 Sec 449(3)(5)]. The APB has issued a bulletin in relation to the special audit reports on abbreviated accounts – APB Bulletin 2008/04.

Full financial statements for filing

31.87 Under the 2006 Act, a small company follows the small company regime. It may, if it wishes, prepare and file full financial statements. If a company follows the small company regime, the financial statements must include the statements and special audit report discussed from paragraph 31.81. [CA06 Sec 449(1)].

Medium-sized companies

Accounting exemptions for medium-sized companies

31.88 The requirements applicable to medium-sized companies are greater than those for small companies. The legislation in the Companies Act 2006 is supplemented by SI 2008/410, which contains the detailed requirements for medium-sized companies. Concessions available to medium-sized companies are:

- The individual financial statements of a medium-sized company need not comply with the requirements of paragraph 45 of Schedule 1 to SI 2008/410, disclosure with respect to compliance with accounting standards.
- The individual financial statements of a medium-sized company need not comply with the requirements of paragraph 72 of Schedule 1 to SI 2008/410, related party transactions.
- The directors' report for the year need not comply with the requirements of section 417(6) of the 2006 Act business review to include analysis using key performance indicators so far as they relate to *non-financial* information. [CA06 Sec 417(7)].
- Medium-sized companies are entitled to file financial statements with the Registrar of Companies in an abbreviated format. However, this format differs from that available to small companies, since medium-sized companies are permitted very few disclosure exemptions. [SI 2008/410 4 Sch].
- Unlike small companies, medium-sized companies are not entitled to prepare shorter-form financial statements for members. Other than the exemption from paragraph 45 and 72 noted above, the financial statements prepared for the members must comply in full with Schedule 1 to SI 2008/410.

While the second bullet point above provides an exemption from disclosing related party transactions for medium-sized companies the requirements for FRS 8 will still need to be applied in order to ensure the accounts give a 'true and fair' view. (See paragraph 31.92 for abbreviated accounts.)

Abbreviated financial statements

31.89 The modifications that the Act permits in respect of the abbreviated financial statements that a medium-sized company may deliver to the Registrar of Companies relate principally to the profit and loss account. Consequently, the normal requirements for full directors' report, balance sheet and notes to the financial statements are generally unaffected.

31.90 The limited exemptions available to medium-sized companies allow the following profit and loss account items to be combined:

- In Format 1 (items 2, 3 and 6): the cost of sales, gross profit or loss and other operating income.
- In Format 2 (items 2 to 5): the change in stocks of finished goods and in work in progress, own work capitalised, other operating income, raw materials and consumables, and other external charges.
- In Format 3 (items A.1 and B.2): the cost of sales and other operating income.

- In Format 4 (items A.1, A.2 and B.2 to B.4): the reduction in stocks of finished goods and in work-in-progress, raw materials and consumables, and other external charges, increases in stocks of finished goods and work-in-progress, own work capitalised and other operating income.

[SI 2008/410 Reg 4(3)].

31.91 In addition, the notes to the financial statements may omit the segmental analysis of turnover that would otherwise be required by Regulation 4(3)(b) of SI 2008/410.

31.92 Since the concessions permitted to medium-sized companies by the Act are so limited, with the requirements for the balance sheet, related notes and the directors' report fundamentally the same as those for large companies, the additional cost of preparing abbreviated financial statements for medium-sized companies will tend to exceed the potential confidentiality benefits that might derive from them. It is clear that the abbreviated accounts of small companies prepared for filing and in accordance with Schedule 4 to SI 2008/409 contain insufficient information to enable them to give a true and fair view. It then follows that they do not need to include disclosures required only by accounting standards to those abbreviated accounts. It is less clear whether the same position applies to the abbreviated accounts of medium-sized companies. The concessions that a medium-sized company can take are restricted to those listed in paragraph 31.88, which allow omission of the disclosure of whether or not the accounts have been prepared in accordance with applicable accounting standards and allows some merging of items in the profit and loss account. As a matter of best practice a medium-sized entity should disclose all matters required in the Companies Act and accounting standards, unless an exemption is explicitly permitted. Such an exemption is given with regard to related party transactions and, therefore, medium-sized abbreviated accounts may exclude related party transaction disclosures. [SI 2008/410 Sch 1 para 72].

Statements to be made where advantage is taken of the exemptions

31.93 Where the directors of a medium-sized company file abbreviated financial statements, those financial statements must contain a statement in a prominent position on the balance sheet, above the signature required by company law, that they are prepared in accordance with the special provisions of the 2006 Act relating to medium-sized companies. [CA06 Sec 450(3)].

31.94 An example of such a statement would be:

> *'The abbreviated financial statements have been prepared in accordance with the special provisions relating to medium-sized companies within Part 15 of the Companies Act 2006 and the Large and Medium Companies and Groups (Accounts and Directors' Report) Regulations 2008.'*

Directors' report — medium-sized companies

31.95 Where the directors take advantage, in the directors' report, of the exemption in respect of non-disclosure of non-financial information from the business review, they must make a statement in a prominent position above the signature on the directors' report that the report has been prepared in accordance with the special provisions of the 2006 Act relating to medium-sized companies. [CA06 Sec 417(7)].

Suitable wording for such a statement is as follows:

> *'This report has been prepared in accordance with the special provisions relating to medium-sized companies within Part 15 of the Companies Act 2006.'*

Auditors' reports

31.96 The abbreviated financial statements filed by a medium-sized company must be accompanied by a special auditors' report. This report must state that, in the auditors' opinion:

- The company is entitled to deliver abbreviated financial statements.
- The abbreviated financial statements are properly prepared in accordance with regulations made under section 445(3) of the 2006 Act.

[CA06 Secs 445(4), 449(2)].

The matters discussed in paragraph 31.86 above, concerning qualification of the auditors' report on a small company's full financial statements, apply equally to medium-sized companies.

Small and medium-sized parent companies

31.97 The fact that a company qualifies as a small or a medium-sized company does not preclude it from also being the parent company of a group. Consequently, some consideration needs to be given to this category of entity and how it is affected by the shorter-form and the abbreviated financial statement exemptions. One of the main advantages of the small company regime is that if the group headed by the company qualifies as small, it is exempt from the requirement to prepare consolidated financial statements provided that the company is not part of a larger ineligible group. Previously this exemption was also available to medium-sized groups however, this was removed from Companies Act 2006 for years beginning on or after 6 April 2008.

31.98 The Act provides specific guidance in this area by stating that:

- A parent company shall not be treated as qualifying as a small company in relation to a financial year, unless the group headed by it qualifies as a small group.
- A parent company shall not be treated as qualifying as a medium-sized company in relation to a financial year, unless the group headed by it qualifies as a medium-sized group.

[CA06 Secs 383(1), 466(1)].

31.99 The criteria for determining small and medium-sized groups are considered from paragraph 31.18 and the exclusions thereto from paragraph 31.2. What they imply, however, is that parent companies that meet the general criteria for qualification as either small or medium-sized companies will need to undertake some form of partial group consolidation exercise in order to establish whether they meet the additional conditions set out in paragraph 31.98 above.

31.100 When considering the reporting position at an individual entity level, some guidance on interpretation may be of value:

- Where the group headed by a parent company (which qualifies as small) also qualifies as a small group, the parent may utilise the concessions generally available to small companies. Thus, it may opt to file abbreviated financial statements (Schedule 4 to SI 2008/409), prepare shorter-form financial statements (Schedule 1 to SI 2008/409) for members and no consolidation is required.
- Where the group headed by a small parent company does not qualify as a small group, but does qualify as a medium-sized group, the parent cannot take advantage of the concessions generally available to small companies.
- Where the group headed by a parent company fails to meet the criteria for determining small or medium-sized groups, the parent will not be allowed to avail itself of the exemptions generally available to small or medium-sized companies respectively. Thus, it cannot prepare shorter-form financial statements, nor can it file any form of abbreviated financial statements, nor take the exemption from preparing consolidated financial statements (para 31.102).
- Where the group headed by a medium-sized parent fails to meet the criteria for determining medium-sized groups, the parent will not be allowed to avail itself of any of the concessions generally available to medium-sized companies, in terms of filing abbreviated financial statements. Nor will it be able to take the exemption not to prepare consolidated financial statements (para 31.102). Refer to chapter 24 for general discussion on consolidation exemptions available for all companies.

Small and medium-sized groups

31.101 The 2006 Act assumes that the directors of parent companies within the small companies regime will not prepare consolidated financial statements, although section 398 allows them to opt to prepare them if they so desire. For all other parent companies there is a duty to prepare consolidated financial statements imposed in section 399 of the 2006 Act. In addition, FRS 2, 'Accounting for subsidiary undertakings', requires parent companies preparing financial statements intended to give a true and fair view of the financial position and profit or loss of the group, to prepare them in the form of consolidated financial statements. [FRS 2 para 18]. Furthermore, the standard (but not the Act) applies to *'all parent undertakings'* , a term designated to include not just corporate parents, but also partnerships and unincorporated associations.

31.101.1 In accordance with section 1161(5) of the Companies Act 2006, a group undertaking in relation to an entity is either a parent or subsidiary undertaking of that entity or a fellow subsidiary. A joint venture is not part of the same group as either of its investors. Therefore, in determining if a joint venture is a qualifying small or medium-sized company, there is no need to consider the investor entities. If, however, the joint venture is a parent company then the rules relating to parent companies will apply to the joint venture.

Example

Company A has a joint venture investment in which it holds a 50% interest. Company A would qualify as a small company if it were not a member of an ineligible group as its parent is a publicly listed UK company. A group is defined as a parent and its subsidiaries and so does not include joint venture companies. Therefore, the joint venture company is not a member of an ineligible group (that is, company A's group) and can hence prepare small company financial statements if all other criteria are met. The size of company A is not relevant.

Exemptions from consolidation

31.102 Under the Companies Act 2006 the availability of the exemption from the requirement to prepare consolidated financial statements is determined by reference to the combined size of the parent and its subsidiaries, not to the size of the group of which the parent is a member. Therefore, where the parent is itself a subsidiary the exemption for this sub-group will still be available. Both the Act and the standard allow specific exemptions from the general requirement to prepare consolidated financial statements. Included in these exemptions is the exemption allowed to a parent company not to prepare consolidated financial statements, if the group of which it is parent is a small group as defined in section 383 of the 2006 Act. Additionally, it must not be an ineligible group. [CA06 Sec 398]. The definitions of small and medium-sized groups and ineligible groups are covered from paragraph 31.2.

Example

Companies A to D are manufacturing companies. Company A is incorporated in the USA and company D is a public company. Company B is small in size, as is the sub-group of which it is parent. Companies B and C use UK GAAP.

As company B and company C are members of an ineligible group (the group contains D which is a public company, see para 31.2.1.1), company B and company C are not permitted to file abbreviated financial statements due to being members of an ineligible group. Company B will be required to prepare consolidated financial statements unless other exemptions are available (see para 31.97 and chapter 24 for exemptions to consolidation for companies, including intermediary companies). However, as companies B and C do qualify as small companies they may still take advantage of reduced disclosures in the directors' report and do not have to file the directors' report (see para 31.60).

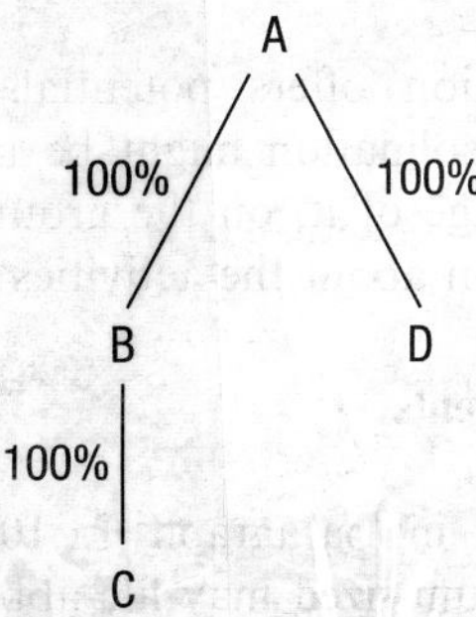

31.104 Company law requires the auditors to make a statement in their audit report where they consider the company's directors are not entitled to take advantage of the exemptions under the small companies' regime. [CA06 Sec 498(5)].

31.105 Where a parent company makes use of the exemption from consolidation, it is required to:

- Comply with the disclosure requirements of the Act in respect of parent companies not required to prepare consolidated financial statements. [SI 2008/410 Reg 7].
- State that its financial statements present information about it as an individual undertaking and not about its group. [FRS 2 para 22]. The statement should include or refer to the note giving the grounds on which the parent undertaking is exempt from preparing consolidated financial statements.

31.106 Set out below are two examples of an appropriate wording to be included in the accounting policies of a parent company or undertaking that uses the exemption from preparing consolidated financial statements for small groups:

Example 1 — parent company of a small group

The financial statements contain information about GAAP UK Limited as an individual company and do not contain consolidated financial information as the parent of a group. The company is not required to prepare consolidated financial statements under section 398 of the Companies Act 2006 as the group it heads qualifies as a small group.

Example 2 — unincorporated parent undertaking of small-sized group

The financial statements contain information about GAAP UK Co as an individual undertaking and do not contain consolidated financial information as the parent of a group. The partnership is exempt under paragraph 21(a) of Financial Reporting Standard No 2 from the requirement to prepare consolidated financial statements as the group it heads qualifies as a small-sized group.

31.107 While the exemption offers potential cost savings, particularly to complex groups where consolidation might be time consuming, directors may choose not to take advantage of it, on the grounds that the parent company's members require information about the activities of the group as a whole.

Abbreviated financial statements

31.108 As was discussed in paragraph 31.100 above, a parent company qualifying as small or medium-sized may file abbreviated financial statements if the group headed by it qualifies as a small or medium-sized group and is not ineligible. [CA06 Secs 384, 467]. However, for small companies/groups any abbreviated financial statements filed with the Registrar of Companies must be abbreviated individual company financial statements, because abbreviated consolidated financial statements are not permitted. In such instances, therefore, it is implicit that the parent company must take advantage of the exemption from consolidation which is available to small groups in respect of those abbreviated financial statements. Non-statutory consolidated financial statements may still be prepared for the members, but these must be accompanied by the appropriate statements set out in chapter 8 of the Manual of Accounting – Management Reports and Governance.

Consolidated shorter-form financial statements

31.109 Although a small parent company of a small group is exempt from preparing consolidated financial statements under section 398, it may nevertheless choose to prepare and file such consolidated financial statements. If it does, it may adopt the shorter-format that is available to small companies in preparing their individual financial statements and directors' report, as suitably modified for consolidated financial statements. [FRSSE para 16.2, 16.3; SI 2008/409 6 Sch].

31.110 Therefore, where a small parent company voluntarily prepares small group consolidated financial statements, it will have available to it the standard exemptions available to small companies. However, greater detail than that required by Schedule 1 to SI 2008/409 must be given in respect of investments and this is reflected in the FRSSE's requirements with respect to consolidated financial statements. Item B III (investments) in the balance sheet formats should be broken down as follows:

- Shares in group undertakings.
- Interests in associated undertakings.
- Other participating interests.
- Loans to group undertakings and undertakings in which a participating interest is held.
- Other investments other than loans.
- Others.

[FRSSE para 16.4; SI 2008/409 6 Sch 1(2)].

31.111 Small companies voluntarily preparing consolidated financial statements are also entitled to take advantage of the FRSSE's provisions as discussed from paragraph 31.127 onwards. In addition, consolidated financial statements prepared under the FRSSE should be prepared in accordance with the accounting practices and disclosure requirements set out in FRSs 2, 6, 7 and, as they apply in respect of consolidated financial statements, FRSs 5, 9, 10, 11 and 28. Where the reporting entity is part of a group that prepares publicly available consolidated financial statements, it is entitled to the exemptions given in FRS 8 paragraph 3(a)-(c). [FRSSE para 16.1].

31.112 As for individual company financial statements, the consolidated financial statements must include a statement in a prominent position above the signature on the balance sheet that they are prepared in accordance with the small companies regime of the 2006 Act (see paras 31.57 and 31.64) and (if applicable) in accordance with the FRSSE. [FRSSE para 16.5].

31.113 As medium-sized companies are not permitted to prepare shorter-form financial statements, it follows that medium-sized groups cannot prepare shorter-form consolidated financial statements.

[The next paragraph is 31.127.]

Financial Reporting Standard for Smaller Entities

31.127 The following sections summarise the accounting requirements of the FRSSE (effective 6 April 2008). Throughout this section mention of 'FRSSE' is to be understood to mean the 2008 version of the FRSSE. As discussed from paragraph 31.66, shorter-form financial statements are capable of giving a true and fair view and this will be the case if they comply fully with all relevant requirements of the FRSSE. There is generally no need to refer to other accounting standards, UITF abstracts or legislation to satisfy this requirement.

Tangible fixed assets and depreciation

31.128 Tangible fixed assets and depreciation are dealt with from paragraph 6.1 of the FRSSE.

31.129 The valuation bases and the depreciation rules discussed in chapter 16 are equally applicable to small companies, except for some simplifications, which are discussed below. Certain accounting treatments for tangible fixed assets have been simplified from the FRS 15 requirements:

- As is evident from the balance sheet formats at paragraph 31.46 above, small companies are permitted to sub-analyse tangible fixed assets into two categories of land and buildings and other tangible fixed assets in aggregate. [SI 2008/409 1 Sch].
- Where a small company adopts an accounting policy of revaluation in respect of tangible fixed assets, the basis for revaluation is market value or the best estimate thereof, unless judged inappropriate by the directors, in which case current value (lower of replacement cost and recoverable amount) can be used instead. [FRSSE para 6.23]
- The FRSSE allows the valuation to be performed by an experienced valuer, who does not necessarily need to be a qualified valuer as FRS 15 requires. [FRSSE para 6.24].
- Revaluation losses are taken to the profit and loss account irrespective of recoverable amounts, except when losses are caused only by a change in market value, where the losses are taken to the STRGL until the carrying amount reaches depreciated historical cost. [FRSSE para 6.25].
- Revaluation gains are recognised in the STRGL except to the extent (after adjusting for subsequent depreciation) that they reverse revaluation losses on the same asset that was previously recognised in the profit and loss account. To that extent they should be recognised in the profit and loss account. [FRSSE para 6.26].

31.130 The FRSSE does not provide any guidance for dealing with:

- Start-up or commissioning periods.
- When capitalisation of finance costs should begin.
- Construction of a tangible fixed asset being completed in parts.
- Major inspections or overhauls.
- Cases where it is impossible to obtain a reliable valuation.
- Insurance companies.

In these situations the accounting treatment in FRS 15 should be followed as current best practice. There is further discussion of this in paragraph 31.35 above. Start-up costs are dealt with in paragraph 31.137 below.

31.131 The Act's disclosure requirements for fixed assets are dealt with in paragraphs 48 and 49 of Schedule 1 to SI 2008/409. These disclosure requirements are a replica of the equivalent Schedule 1 to SI 2008/410 disclosure requirements, which are discussed in chapter 16. In addition, the FRSSE also requires the following information to be disclosed in respect of depreciation for each of the two categories of fixed assets mentioned in the first bullet point of paragraph 31.129 above:

- The depreciation methods used.
- The useful economic lives or the depreciation rates used.
- The financial effect, where material, of a change during the period in either the estimate of useful economic lives or the estimate of residual values.

[FRSSE para 6.42].

31.132 Any change in the depreciation method used and the effect, if material, should be disclosed in the period of change. The reason for the change should also be disclosed. [FRSSE para 6.43].

31.133 Certain accounting treatments in relation to depreciation and impairment have been simplified from the FRS 15 requirements:

- Residual values and useful economic lives for tangible fixed assets should be reviewed regularly rather than annually and revised when necessary rather than when expectations are significantly different from previous estimates.
- Disclosure of depreciation to be given for the two categories of land and buildings and other fixed assets in aggregate.
- There is no specific requirement for an annual impairment review where an asset's life exceeds 50 years or where depreciation is not charged as it is immaterial.
- The statement in FRS 15 that subsequent expenditure does not negate the need for depreciation is omitted.

31.134 The FRSSE does not provide any guidance for dealing with:

- Impairment and the basis on which residual values are priced.
- Renewals accounting.

In these cases the accounting treatment in FRS 15 should be followed as current best practice.

31.135 There is no requirement for small companies to disclose the investment revaluation reserve relating to investment properties on the face of the balance sheet as required by paragraph 15 of SSAP 19. The information can be given by way of a note to the balance sheet. However, the revaluation reserve is a separate line item in the balance sheet formats in Schedule 1 and 4 to SI 2008/409 and has to be shown on the face of the balance sheet.

[The next paragraph is 31.137.]

Start-up costs and pre-contract costs

31.137 Paragraph 8.15 of the FRSSE repeats the accounting requirement of the UITF Abstract 24, 'Accounting for start-up costs' for such costs to be accounted for on a basis consistent with similar costs incurred as part of an entity's on-going activities. Where there are no such similar costs, start-up costs that do not meet the criteria for recognition as assets under another specific requirement of the FRSSE should be written-off as incurred. They should not be carried forward as an asset. The FRSSE does not include any reference to the disclosures detailed in UITF Abstract 24.

31.138 The FRSSE also provides guidance in respect of pre-contract costs within paragraph 8.16 based on the requirements of UITF Abstract 34, 'Pre-contract costs'. Such costs should be written-off with the exception of directly attributable costs, which should only be recognised as an asset where it is virtually certain that a contract will be obtained and the present value of expected future net cash inflows expected to arise from the contract are not less than all amounts to be recognised as an asset. Costs incurred before the asset recognition criteria are met should not be recognised as an asset.

Leases

31.139 The FRSSE modifies the recognition rules for finance leases in SSAP 21 for small companies. Where a small company leases an asset on a finance lease, both the asset and the corresponding lease obligations should normally be recorded at the asset's fair value, rather than the present value of the minimum lease payments. [FRSSE para 7.2]. However, where the asset's fair value does not give a realistic estimate of the asset's cost to the lessee, because, for example, the lessee has benefited from grants and capital allowances that had the effect of reducing the aggregate minimum lease payments to below the fair value of the asset, the asset and the obligation should be recorded at the present value of the minimum lease payments. A negative finance charge should not be shown. [FRSSE para 7.3].

31.140 Where a small company is a lessor of assets under finance leases, the total gross earnings should be recognised on a systematic and rational basis. In most cases, this would be achieved by allocating gross earnings so as to give a constant periodic rate of return on the lessor's net investment. [FRSSE para 7.9].

31.141 The information to be disclosed by lessees and lessors is dealt with in paragraphs 7.16 to 7.18 of the FRSSE. They do not cover all the disclosure requirements given in SSAP 21 and discussed in chapter 19. In particular, small companies need *not* give the following information:

- For finance leased assets, the total depreciation for the period by major class of asset. This is because small companies are only required to analyse tangible fixed assets into land and buildings and other tangible fixed assets, rather than by major class of asset.
- Analysis of obligations under finance leases between amounts payable in the next year, amounts payable in the second to fifth years inclusive from the balance sheet date, and the aggregate amounts payable thereafter.
- Finance charges and operating lease rentals charged for the period.
- Analysis of operating lease commitments between land and buildings and other operating leases.
- Aggregate rentals receivable by lessors in the accounting period in relation to both finance and operating leases.

31.142 Paragraph 7.6 of the FRSSE deals with operating lease incentives, from both the lessee's and the lessor's perspective. It repeats the main principle from UITF Abstract 28, 'Operating lease incentives', that incentives should be spread on a straight-line basis over the lease term, or if shorter, over the period to the first review to market rental.

Investments

31.143 Paragraphs 6.30 to 6.33 of the FRSSE set out the requirements of the Companies Act 2006 in respect of disclosures required for fixed asset investments. Fixed asset investments should initially be carried at cost or market value as determined at the date of their last valuation or on any other basis as determined by the directors. Paragraphs 6.34 to 6.36 explain the accounting and disclosure requirements on the revaluation reserve of all fixed assets including investments.

31.144 Paragraphs 8.13 to 8.14 of the FRSSE consider the accounting and disclosure requirements for current asset investments. Such investments may be carried at the lower of cost or net realisable value or measured at their current cost.

Investment properties

31.145 The accounting requirements of investment properties are in line with SSAP 19. Such properties should be carried in the balance sheet at market value. Paragraphs 6.50 to 6.53 of the FRSSE set out these requirements and explains that the following points need to be disclosed:

- The name of the persons making the valuation, or particulars of their qualifications.
- The bases of the valuation used.
- If the person making the valuation is an employee or officer of the company or group that owns the property this fact need be disclosed.

Government grants

31.146 The requirements of SSAP 4 are included in the FRSSE in paragraphs 6.54 to 6.57. The FRSSE does not provide any guidance for dealing with grants made to give immediate financial support or assistance to an enterprise or to reimburse costs previously incurred. If a small company receives such a grant, it should follow the accounting treatment specified in paragraph 23 of SSAP 4 as current best practice.

Intangible fixed assets

31.147 Small companies need only classify intangible assets into goodwill and other intangible assets. Other intangible assets may include development expenditure. Paragraphs 6.3 to 6.10 of the FRSSE deal with the accounting and disclosure requirements for research and development expenditure, which are imported from SSAP 13 and discussed in detail in chapter 15.

31.148 Small companies are *not* required to disclose:

- The total amount of research and development expenditure charged to the profit and loss account.
- Movements on deferred development expenditure.

31.149 On goodwill, the FRSSE reflects the provisions of FRS 10. Paragraphs 6.11 to 6.17 of the FRSSE deal with other intangible assets and goodwill. The FRSSE imports none of the disclosure requirements of FRS 10, but does import most of the recognition and measurement rules with a number of exceptions, the key ones being:

- There is a requirement, rather than a presumption that useful economic lives are limited to 20 years.
- The exceptions in FRS 10 allowing recognition of internally generated intangible assets with a 'readily ascertainable' market value and revaluation of intangible assets with a 'readily ascertainable' market value are omitted in the FRSSE.
- Old goodwill previously eliminated against reserves should either be wholly reinstated or wholly left in reserves.

31.150 It is important to note that these exceptions only apply to goodwill and intangible assets arising in the financial statements of an individual entity. Consolidated financial statements should be based on FRS 10 in its entirety.

Write-downs to recoverable amount

31.151 The FRSSE reflects the principles of FRS 11, 'Impairment of fixed assets and goodwill'. However, the FRSSE only includes the key principle that assets held at above recoverable amount should be written down to recoverable amount and the conditions for recognising the reversal of write-downs. The rules are set out in paragraphs 6.44 to 6.49 of the FRSSE.

Stocks and long-term contracts

31.152 Many of the problems that small companies face in valuing stocks and long-term contracts are usually of a practical nature rather than matters of principle. The FRSSE recognises this and incorporates the whole of appendix I of SSAP 9 dealing with further practical considerations in appendix III. The valuation principles and the recognition rules relating to stocks and long-term contracts, which are dealt with in paragraphs 8.1 to 8.8 of the FRSSE, are consistent with SSAP 9 and are discussed in chapter 20. Consistent with the balance sheet formats, small companies are not required to sub-analyse the amount of stock stated in the balance sheet.

Consignment stock

31.153 Small companies are likely to enter into arrangements where goods are supplied to them on a consignment basis. Therefore, the FRSSE provides a table in appendix III, illustrating the factors that should be considered in deciding whether or not consignment stock is an asset. This table is a replica of the one contained in Application note A in FRS 5 and is reproduced in chapter 20 of this manual.

31.154 Where consignment stock is in substance an asset, a small company should recognise it in the balance sheet and show the amount due to the supplier, after deducting any deposits, as trade creditors. Where consignment stock is not in substance an asset, it should not be recognised. Any deposits paid should be shown in 'other debtors'. [FRSSE para 8.9].

Debt factoring

31.155 Debt factoring and invoice discounting arrangements provide an important source of finance for small companies. A small company will need to analyse whether or not it should continue to show factored debts as an asset in its balance sheet. Therefore, like consignment stocks, the FRSSE imports the table illustrating the considerations affecting the treatment of debt factoring from Application note C of FRS 5 into appendix III. This table is reproduced in chapter 3.

31.156 Paragraphs 8.10 to 8.12 of the FRSSE provide guidance on the three accounting treatments, *viz*, derecognition, linked presentation and separate presentation, that might apply to debt factoring arrangements. These issues are also considered in detail in paragraph 31.136.5.

Provisions, contingencies and post balance sheet events

31.157 Requirements relating to provisions and contingencies are dealt with in paragraphs 11.1 to 11.11, and those relating to post balance sheet events are dealt with in paragraphs 14.1 to 14.4 of the FRSSE.

31.158 The rules for provisions and contingencies are a simplification of the rules in FRS 12, 'Provisions, contingent liabilities and contingent assets', which are considered in chapter 21. The rules for post balance sheet events reflect those found in FRS 21, 'Events after the balance sheet date', although there is no requirement to disclose owners' or others' power to amend the financial statements after issue. FRS 21 is considered in detail in chapter 22.

31.159 Disclosure for provisions and contingencies has been simplified from FRS 12 with only the nature and financial effect of contingent liabilities (unless remote) and probable contingent assets being required.

31.160 In particular, the FRSSE does not provide guidance on and makes no reference to:

- Financial instruments, executory contracts, long-term contracts or insurance entities.
- Rare cases where it is not clear whether there is a present obligation.
- Risks, uncertainties and future events being taken into account in measuring a provision.
- Detailed rules relating to discount rates.
- Provisions and capitalising assets.
- Future operating losses, onerous contracts, restructuring or the sale of an operation.
- Non disclosure of information that is expected to prejudice seriously the position of the company in a dispute.
- Restriction on the amounts recognised as reimbursements not exceeding the related provision.

31.161 However, where the FRSSE is silent, small companies should refer to FRS 12 as a means of establishing current best practice.

Financial instruments

31.162 Financial instruments, other than shares, bank loans and overdrafts and leasing obligations, are unlikely to form a major source of finance for small companies. Accordingly, paragraphs 12.1 to 12.12 of the FRSSE deal with only the basic principles of FRS 4 and FRS 25 relating to debt, the treatment of dividends under FRS 21 and disclosure requirements relating to the company's share capital. The term 'debt' has been replaced in the FRSSE by borrowings, which are defined in the FRSSE to include all capital instruments that are classified as liabilities. [FRSSE Section C].

31.163 The FRSSE has included in appendix III new guidance on the FRS 25 requirement for the classification of capital instruments as debt or equity.

31.164 It is common for banks providing loans to small companies to charge arrangement fees. The accounting treatment of arrangement fees is not explicitly covered in FRS 4, so the FRSSE provides the following guidance:

- Where an arrangement fee is such as to represent a significant additional cost of finance when compared to the interest payable over the instrument's life, it should be allocated to periods over the term of the instrument at a constant rate on the carrying amount of the instrument.
- Where this is not the case, it should be charged immediately to the profit and loss account.

[FRSSE para 12.4].

31.165 In light of FRS 21 and FRS 25, the FRSSE mirrors the guidance with respect to dividends contained within these standards. As such, dividends relating to financial instruments or a component that is a financial liability should be recognised as an expense in the profit and loss account. Dividends relating to equity instruments should be debited to equity net of any related income tax benefit and any dividends declared after the balance sheet date should not be recognised as a liability at the balance sheet date. [FRSSE para 12.6]. The FRSSE also provides guidance with respect to fixed cumulative dividends on the company's shares. Where such dividends are in arrears, the amount of the arrears and the period for which each class of dividends is in arrears should be disclosed. [FRSSE para 12.8].

The effect of FRS 3

31.166 FRS 3 contains supplementary provisions relating to the format of the profit and loss account, but its effect on the profit and loss account formats for small companies is not significant. This is because the FRSSE does not include the FRS 3 requirements for small companies to analyse turnover, costs, results and exceptional items into continuing operations, acquisitions and discontinued operations. There is also no requirement for small companies to produce a note of historical cost profits and losses or a reconciliation of movements in shareholders' funds.

31.167 The FRSSE, nevertheless, requires small companies to show all exceptional items, other than the three items imported from paragraph 20 of FRS 3 and included in paragraph 3.6 of the FRSSE, under the statutory format headings to which they relate, either in the notes or on the face of the profit and loss account if this is necessary in order to give a true and fair view. [FRSSE para 3.5]. The FRS 3 paragraph 20 items are shown separately on the face of the profit and loss account after operating profit and before interest.

Revenue recognition

31.168 The FRSSE incorporates in full the requirements of FRS 5 Application note G with respect to revenue recognition so that small companies have definitive guidance in this area. These requirements are considered further in chapter 9.

31.169 Additional guidance, in line with UITF 40, 'Revenue recognition and service contracts', is included from paragraphs 4.10 to 4.15 of the FRSSE.

Taxation

31.170 Paragraphs 9.1 to 9.15 of the FRSSE deal with the measurement and disclosure relating to taxation. These paragraphs cover most of the measurement provisions of FRS 16 and FRS 19 dealt with in chapter 13 of this manual, but omit many of the disclosures required by those standards.

31.171 In particular, the FRSSE:

- Does not include the FRS 16 prohibition on adjustments to income and expenses to reflect notional tax.
- Makes no reference to tax rates (to be used for measuring current tax).
- Omits the detailed disclosure requirements of FRS 16 relating to the major components of the current tax charge.
- Omits the requirement in FRS 19 to provide deferred tax when assets are 'marked to market'.
- Omits the requirements of FRS 19 relating to unremitted earnings of subsidiaries, associates or joint ventures.
- States that discounting of deferred tax is not required (but if done, it should be done consistently) and makes no further reference to discounting except to say that the unwinding of the discount should be shown as a component of the tax charge and disclosed separately.
- Omits the presentational requirements of FRS 19.
- Omits the detailed disclosure requirements of FRS 19, except for the requirement relating to the unwinding of discount referred to above and those relating to revalued assets (disclosure of tax that would be payable or recoverable if the assets were sold at the values shown).

31.172 Although small companies are required to disclose any special circumstances that affect the overall tax charge or credit in accordance with paragraph 9.3 of the FRSSE, there is no specific reference in the FRSSE to disclose special circumstances affecting the tax attributable to the three non-operating exceptional items included in paragraph 3.6 of the FRSSE. In practice, however, it is likely that the explanation of the special circumstances affecting the overall tax charge or credit will include the tax effects of the three non-operating items.

31.173 Paragraph 9.15 of the FRSSE deals with disclosure of turnover and repeats the requirement of SSAP 5, 'Accounting for value added tax', that turnover should exclude VAT on taxable outputs. Irrecoverable VAT that can be allocated to fixed assets and to other items disclosed separately in the financial statements should be included in their cost where practicable and material.

Retirement benefits

31.174 Paragraphs 10.1 and 10.3 of the FRSSE deal with defined contribution schemes and repeat the requirements of FRS 17. Paragraph 10.2 deals with the Companies Act requirements with respect to disclosure of pension commitments. Appendix II of the FRSSE deals with defined benefit schemes.

[The next paragraph is 31.176.]

31.176 The requirements in paragraph 1 of Appendix II of the FRSSE are based on FRS 17, but with many of the disclosure requirements omitted. The accounting treatment is largely the same as FRS 17, but again has been simplified. The main simplifications are:

- No reference to multi-employer schemes.
- Omission of the requirement to attribute benefits according to the schemes benefit formula.
- Omission of the requirement to reflect expected future events in the actuarial assumptions.
- Omission of detailed requirements relating to the treatment of a scheme surplus.
- Omission of detailed requirements relating to the treatment of gains and losses.
- Omission of requirement relating to recognition of current tax relief on contributions.
- Omission of requirement relating to death-in-service and incapacity benefits.
- Omission of many of the detailed disclosure requirements including financial assumptions, analysis of fair value of assets by class and expected rates of return, analysis of amounts charged to profit and loss account and of amounts included in the STRGL and analysis of amounts included in reserves in respect of defined benefit assets or liabilities.

Share-based payments

31.177 For cash-settled share-based payment transactions the company should recognise the goods or services when it obtains them. The amount of the goods or services and the corresponding liability should be the best estimate of the expenditure required to settle the liability at the balance sheet date. The liability should be re-measured at each balance sheet date and at the date of settlement. Note that this is similar to FRS 20, but uses best estimate rather than fair value. [FRSSE paras 12.13 to 12.15].

31.178 For equity-settled share-based payment transactions only disclosure and no measurement or recognition is required. This is a significant difference to FRS 20.

Foreign currencies

31.179 Paragraphs 13.1 to 13.12 of the FRSSE cover most of the provisions relating to measurement, but none of the disclosure requirements of SSAP 20. Foreign currencies are dealt with in chapter 7.

Accounting policies and estimation techniques

31.180 Although there is no requirement for small companies to state whether the financial statements have been prepared in accordance with applicable accounting standards, both the Act and FRS 18 require disclosure of each material accounting policy and these requirements are incorporated into the FRSSE. [FRSSE paras 2.7, 2.8]. In addition, the FRSSE requires that the financial statements should state that they have been prepared in accordance with the FRSSE (effective April 2008).

31.181 The FRSSE incorporates the principal requirements of FRS 18, 'Accounting policies'. In addition to requiring disclosure of each material accounting policy it requires details to be given of any change in policy and a brief explanation of why each new policy is thought more appropriate. Prior period adjustments should be accounted for by restating comparatives and disclosing the cumulative effect at the foot of the STRGL. The effect of the change in the current and preceding period should be given, where practicable. [FRSSE para 2.15].

31.182 The FRSSE repeats the requirements of FRS 18 for accounting policies and estimation techniques to be the most appropriate for the purpose of giving a true and fair view, taking account of the objectives of relevance, reliability, comparability and understandability. It requires that the policies and techniques should be consistent with company legislation and the FRSSE's requirements. [FRSSE para 2.9].

31.183 Accounting policies should be reviewed regularly to ensure that they remain the most appropriate. Policies should be applied consistently within the same financial statements and from one financial year to the next. In judging whether a new policy is more appropriate due weight should be given to the impact on consistency and comparability. Changes in policy should be accounted for by a prior year adjustment. [FRSSE para 2.10].

31.184 Changes in estimation techniques are not accounted for as a prior year adjustment, but where the effect of such a change is material a description of the change and, where practicable, the effect on the results for the current period, should be given. [FRSSE para 2.7(c)].

31.185 A company is presumed to be carrying on business as a going concern. The financial statements should be prepared on this basis unless the directors determine after the balance sheet date either that they intend to liquidate the entity or to cease trading, or that they have no realistic alternative but to do so. When preparing financial statements directors should assess whether there are any significant doubts about the entity's ability to continue as a going concern. If there are material uncertainties they should be disclosed. Where the period considered by the directors in making this assessment is less than one year from the date of approval of the financial statements, that fact should be stated. [FRSSE para 2.12]. Companies will need to ensure that they have projections covering a sufficient period into the future for directors to give reasonable consideration to their assessment of going concern, if this disclosure is to be avoided.

31.186 The requirements relating to accounting policies, estimation techniques and prior year adjustments are contained in paragraphs 2.6 to 2.15 of the FRSSE and definitions are included in section C of the FRSSE. The FRSSE omits the following features and requirements of FRS 18:

- Reference to departures in exceptional circumstances from accounting standards or UITF Abstracts.
- Reference to preparation of financial statements on a going concern basis (but see para 31.185 above).
- Reference to preparation of financial statements on the accruals basis.
- Reference to selection of estimation techniques that enable the financial statements to give a true and fair view.
- Reference to constraints to be taken into account in judging the appropriateness of accounting policies.
- Requirement relating to accounting for changes in an estimation technique.
- Disclosure requirement relating to significant estimation techniques.
- Reference to SORPs.
- Reference to disclosures required when financial statements are not prepared on a going concern basis.
- Requirement to cross-refer disclosure of departures to disclosures required by companies legislation.

31.187 In addition to the above matters, paragraph 2.2 of the FRSSE requires that financial statements should give a true and fair view and that to achieve this, regard should be given to the substance of any arrangement or transaction that the entity has entered into.

Related party disclosures

31.188 Related party transactions are generally prevalent in small businesses. As a result, the FRSSE, recognising that the full requirements of FRS 8 would be unduly onerous for smaller entities, only requires disclosure of those related party transactions that are considered to be material to the small reporting entity. Without this concession, small companies would have been required to disclose related party transactions that were material in relation to the other related party, even when that related party was an individual. Such disclosures would have been unnecessarily burdensome for small companies. Since the FRSSE revises the requirements of FRS 8, the provisions of the FRSSE are considered in the paragraphs that follow.

31.189 Where a small reporting entity purchases, sells or transfers goods and other assets or liabilities; or renders or receives services; or provides or receives finance or financial support (irrespective of whether a price is charged) to, from or on behalf of a related party, then any such material transactions (materiality to be judged in terms of its significance to the reporting entity) should be disclosed, including:

- The names of the transacting related parties.
- A description of the relationship between the parties.
- A description of the transactions.
- The amounts involved.
- Any other elements of the transactions necessary to understand the financial statements.
- The amounts due to or from related parties at the balance sheet date and provisions for doubtful debts due from such parties at that date.
- Amounts written off in the period in respect of debts due to or from related parties.

[FRSSE para 15.1].

31.190 In addition, the FRSSE clarifies that personal guarantees given by directors in respect of borrowings by the reporting entity should be disclosed. [FRSSE para 15.2]. Transactions can be disclosed on an aggregated basis (aggregation of similar transactions by type of related party), unless disclosure of individual transactions or connected transactions is necessary to understand the impact of the transactions on the financial statements or is required by law. [FRSSE para 15.6]. FRS 8 does not require disclosure of related party transactions in certain circumstances which are considered in chapter 29. These circumstances are also listed in paragraph 15.7 of the FRSSE.

31.191 The FRSSE also incorporates the requirements of the Companies Act 2006 with respect to related party transactions. As such, where investment income, interest received or receivable, interest paid or payable and other similar income or charges relates to a group undertaking, they are required to be disclosed separately. [FRSSE para 15.3, 15.4]. Separate disclosure is also required of commitments that are undertaken on behalf of, or for the benefit of, any group undertaking. [FRSSE para 15.5].

31.192 Where the reporting entity is controlled by another party, disclosure should be made of:

- The name of the controlling party.
- If different, the name of the ultimate controlling party.

In both instances, the related party relationship should also be disclosed. These disclosures should also be made whether or not there have been any transactions between the parties. If the reporting party's controlling party or ultimate controlling party is not known, that fact should be disclosed. [FRSSE para 15.8]. The Companies Act 2006 requirements incorporated into the FRSSE also require disclosure of the ultimate parent company's country of incorporation. [FRSSE para 15.9].

31.193 The FRSSE also incorporates the Companies Act 2006 requirements to disclose transactions with directors. These requirements are discussed in chapter 29. In addition, the Companies Act 2006 requirements in relation to disclosure of holdings in subsidiary undertakings and related financial information as well as membership of qualifying undertakings are also incorporated within the FRSSE in full. These requirements are discussed further in chapter 6 (for individual financial statements) and chapter 24 (for consolidated financial statements).

True and fair override disclosures

31.194 The directors of a small company may depart from any of the Act's accounting provisions in order to give a true and fair view. In that situation, particulars of the departure, the reasons for it and its effect should be given in a note to the financial statements. The FRSSE uses the principles of FRS 18 in providing guidance on how the statutory disclosure requirements should be interpreted. [FRSSE para 2.2]. Where a departure continues in subsequent financial statements the disclosures should continue to be made and should include corresponding amounts. [FRSSE para 2.4].

Annex — Decision tables

Decision table 1 – Formats available for UK GAAP company (not consolidated)

Decision table 1 – Formats available for UK GAAP company (not consolidated)

Is the company a member of an ineligible group? — Yes → see third column. No ↓

Does the company satisfy the medium-size criteria? — Yes → see third column. No ↓

Does the company satisfy the small-size criteria? — No → see second column. Yes → see first column.

Options	Small-size criteria: Yes	Small-size criteria: No	Ineligible group or medium-size: Yes
For share-holders	SI 410 Sch 1 (full accounts) or SI 409 Sch 1 (shorter form accounts) A small company may reduce disclosures in its directors' report	SI 410 Sch 1 (full accounts)	SI 410 Sch 1 (full accounts) or A small company may reduce disclosures in its directors' report
For filing	SI 410 Sch 1 (full accounts) or SI 409 Sch 1 (shorter form accounts) or SI 409 Sch 4 (abbreviated accounts) or Copy balance sheet sent to shareholders under SI 409 or SI 410 with notes A small company does not need to file its directors' report	SI 410 Sch 1 (full accounts) or SI 410 Sch 1 (abbreviated accounts) (minimal exemptions)	SI 410 Sch 1 (full accounts) A small company does not need to file its directors' report

Decision table 2 – Formats available for UK GAAP company with subsidiaries (and not taking s400 or s401 consolidation exemptions)

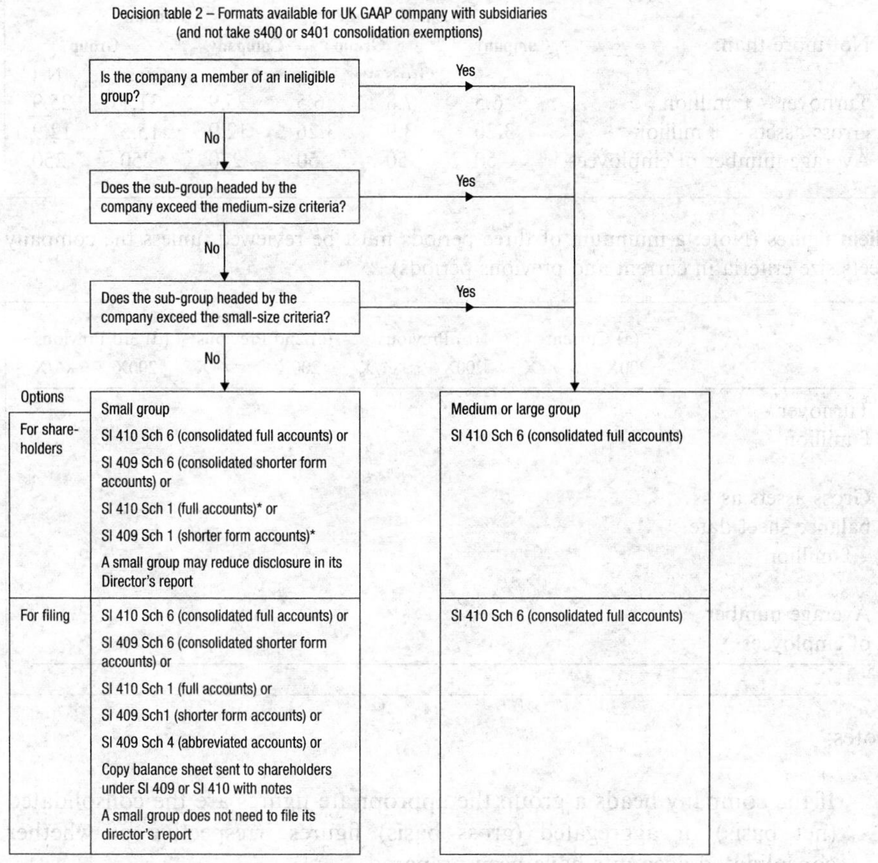

* If entity financial statements are filed, non-statutory consolidated financial statements may be prepared for the shareholders.

Decision table 3 — Eligibility

Size criteria

Not more than:	Small Company	Small Group Gross	Small Group Net	Medium Company	Medium Group Gross	Medium Group Net
Turnover – £ million	6.5	7.8	6.5	25.9	31.1	25.9
Gross assets – £ million	3.26	3.9	3.26	12.9	15.5	12.9
Average number of employees	50	50	50	250	250	250

Client figures (Note: a minimum of three periods must be reviewed, unless the company meets size criteria in current and previous periods)

	(a) Current 200X	✓/X	(b) Previous 200X	✓/X	(c) 2nd Previous 200X	✓/X	(d) 3rd Previous 200X	✓/X
Turnover – £ million								
Gross assets as balance sheet date – £ million								
Average number of employees								

Notes:

- If the company heads a group the appropriate figures are the consolidated (net basis) or aggregated (gross basis) figures irrespective of whether consolidated accounts have been prepared.
- Gross assets = fixed assets plus current assets without deduction for current or long term liabilities.
- There is a *pro rata* adjustment to turnover if the period is not 12 months.

Consideration of eligibility

Ensure that the company is not an ineligible company nor a member of a group that contains an ineligible company. Answering 'yes' to any to these items will make the reporting entity ineligible, without the need to look further at size:

		Circle which
■	Is the company a public company?	Yes/No
■	Does the company that have permission under Part 4 of the Financial Services and Markets Act 2000 to carry on a regulated activity?	Yes/No
■	Does the company that carry on an insurance market activity?	Yes/No
■	Does the group contain a body corporate that has power under its constitution to offer shares or debentures to the public and may lawfully exercise that power?	Yes/No
■	Does the company or group meet the size criteria in the current period?	Yes/No
■	Does the company or group meet the size criteria in the previous accounting period?	Yes/No
■	Does the company or group meet the size criteria in the 2nd previous accounting period?	Yes/No
■	Does the company or group meet the size criteria in the 3rd previous accounting period?	Yes/No
■	In the case of the company's first financial period does it qualify in that period?	Yes/No

Evaluations	**Tick which**
If Yes to (a) and (b) the company is eligible.	
If No to (a), but Yes to (b) and (c) the company is eligible.	
If No to (a), Yes to (b) and No to (c) the company is ineligible unless the 2 previous periods were Yes.	
If Yes to (a), No to (b) and No to (c) the company is ineligible.	
If Yes to (a), No to (b), Yes to (c) and Yes to (d) the company is eligible.	
If Yes to (a), No to (b), Yes to (c) and No to (d) the company is ineligible unless the 2 previous periods were Yes.	

Chapter 32

Overseas companies

Chapter 32

Overseas companies

Introduction

32.1 Companies incorporated outside the UK frequently establish trading operations in the UK. It is, therefore, necessary for the protection of the public that such companies are brought, to some extent, within the regulatory framework applicable to companies incorporated in the UK. This is done by requiring overseas companies to register with the Registrar of Companies and comply with certain aspects of the Companies Act 2006, but extending wide exemptions to them so as not to discourage them from operating in the UK.

32.2 Overseas companies (defined in para 32.6) are regulated by Part 34 of the Companies Act 2006 (Sections 1044-1059) and by SI 2009/1801, 'The Overseas Company Regulations 2009', which came into force from 1 October 2009. Prior to that date (and, in the case of financial statements, for periods commencing prior to that date), Part 1 of Schedule 21D of the Companies Act 1985, which sets out the requirements for delivery of reports and financial statements to the Registrar of Companies, remains applicable to 'oversea companies' (those incorporated outside the UK and Gibraltar but having a branch in Great Britain and that are not credit or financial institutions to which section 699A of the Companies Act 1985 applies).

32.3 The 1985 Act contained two regimes – the place of business regime and the branch registration regime – and required 'oversea companies' operating in Great Britain (a narrower definition than that of 'overseas companies' contained in the 2006 Act) to register with the Registrar of Companies under one or other of these regimes. As part of company law simplification, the 2006 Act no longer distinguishes between the two registration regimes. Instead, the Regulations provide for a single regime that applies to all overseas companies that establish a 'place of business' (which includes a branch) in the UK.

32.4 The 2006 Act and the Regulations provide for:

- Registration of overseas companies, including the regulation of names used by overseas companies and alteration of registered particulars.
- Preparation and filing of financial statements.
- Trading disclosures on documentation.
- Particulars to be delivered to the Registrar of Companies on winding up of an overseas company.
- Protection from disclosure of individuals' usual residential addresses.

32.5 The 2006 Act and the Regulations do distinguish between the financial reporting requirements for credit and financial institutions and for those companies other than credit or financial institutions. [CA06 Sec 1050]. This chapter deals primarily with the accounting and disclosure requirements for overseas companies that are not credit or financial institutions. Hence, references to an overseas company are to a company other than a credit or financial institution, unless stated otherwise. Furthermore, this chapter deals only with the first two bullet points mentioned in paragraph 32.4 above, the remainder being more secretarial in nature and separate from the financial reporting requirements for overseas companies.

Definition of an 'overseas company'

32.6 An 'overseas company' is defined in section 1044 of the 2006 Act as one that is incorporated outside the UK. However, it becomes clear from the Regulations that overseas companies are required to comply with the 2006 Act's requirements only if they open an 'establishment' in the UK.

32.7 For this purpose, an 'establishment' is defined as either:

- a branch within the meaning of the 11th Law Directive (89/666/EC); or
- a place of business that is not such a branch.

[SI 2009/1801 Reg 2(1)].

32.8 The concept of a 'branch' is one of EU law and has no ready counterpart in English law. Under the 1985 Act, when branches and places of business operated under different regimes, the distinction was important. However, under the 2006 Act, the definition of an establishment encompasses both structures so the distinction is, for this purpose at least, irrelevant.

Registration of overseas companies

32.9 There is no obligation upon a company incorporated outside the UK, to register in the UK unless it opens an 'establishment' in the UK.

32.10 Within one month of having opened an establishment in the UK, an overseas company must deliver a return to the Registrar of Companies specifying:

- The company's corporate name or an alternative name under which it proposes to carry on business in the UK (as permitted by section 1048 of the 2006 Act).
- The company's legal form.
- If it is registered in the country of its incorporation, the identity of the register in which it is registered and its registered number.

- A list of its directors and secretary, containing particulars as set out in Regulation 5 of SI 2009/1801 (which are not reproduced here and differ depending on whether the director or secretary is an individual or a company).
- The extent of the powers of the directors or secretary to represent the company in dealings with third parties or in legal proceedings, together with a statement as to whether they may act alone or must act jointly and, if jointly, the name of any other person concerned.
- Whether the company is a relevant credit or financial institution.
- The address of the establishment.
- The date on which the establishment was opened.
- The business carried on by the establishment.
- If different from the registered company name, the name of the establishment.
- The name and service address of every person resident in the UK authorised to accept service of documents on behalf of the company in respect of the establishment, or a statement that there is no such person.
- A list of every person authorised to represent the company as its permanent representative in respect of the establishment, containing his/her name (and former name where applicable), service address and usual residential address (or statement that it is the same as the service address) and the extent to which he/she is authorised to act alone or jointly together with the name of any other person with whom he/she is authorised to act.
- A statement of whether the overseas company (unless it is an unlimited company) intends to comply with the requirement to file financial statements in the UK (see para 32.29) in respect of the UK establishment to which the return relates or another UK establishment (giving its registered number).

[SI 2009/1801 Regs 4(1), 5, 6, 7].

32.11 If a company is incorporated in a country other than an EU Member State, the return must also specify:

- The law under which the company is incorporated.
- Where the company is required to prepare or disclose accounts under its parent law (see para 32.24), the period for which that law requires the accounts to be prepared and the period allowed for their preparation and public disclosure.
- The address of the company's principal place of business in its country of incorporation (or its registered office, if applicable).
- The company's objects.

- The amount of the company's issued share capital.

[SI 2009/1801 Reg 6(2)].

32.12 The company's return must be accompanied by:

- A certified copy of the company's constitution.
- If the company is required by its parent law to prepare, have audited and disclose financial statements or is incorporated in an EEA state and is required to prepare and disclose financial statements by its parent law, the latest disclosed financial statements.

[SI 2009/1801 Reg 8(1), 9(1)].

32.13 Where an overseas company already has another UK establishment and has delivered a return containing all the applicable information in respect of that establishment (and has no outstanding obligation to update that information, instead of filing the information about the company for a second time, it may state in the return that the particulars have been filed in respect of another UK establishment and give its registered number. [SI 2009/1801 Regs 5(2), 8(2), 9(3)]. See also paragraph 32.29.

32.14 The first time an overseas company registers a UK establishment, it is allocated a registered number by the Registrar of Companies. [CA06 Sec 1066]. A number is also allocated to every branch of an overseas company, which is known as the branch's registered number. [CA06 Sec 1067].

32.15 If an overseas company alters any of the particulars about the company identified in paragraphs 32.10 to 32.12 it must deliver an amended return to the Registrar containing details about the alteration. The details that must be included in the returns are:

- The particular(s) that have been altered.
- The particular(s) as altered.
- The effective date of the alteration.

[SI 2009/1801 Reg 3(4)].

32.16 The amended return must state the overseas company's name and registered number as well as the name (if different from the company's name) and registered number of every UK establishment to which the return relates. [SI 2009/1801 Reg 13(5)].

32.17 If the alteration is to the company's constitution, the return must state the date on which the constitution was altered and be accompanied by a certified copy of the company's constitution. [SI 2009/1801 Reg 14(1)(2)].

Accounting records

32.18 There are no provisions in the Act requiring an overseas company to keep adequate, or even any, accounting records. This is despite the detailed requirements to prepare and file financial statements considered in the paragraphs below. In practice, however, such records as are necessary for conducting the affairs of the overseas company are often kept.

Preparation and filing of financial statements

32.19 Every overseas company that has a UK establishment is required to file financial statements for the company with the Registrar of Companies. The requirements to prepare and file annual financial statements are dealt with in Part 5 of SI 2009/1801.

32.20 It is important to note that these financial statements are filed in respect of the company in its entirety and not just for the UK establishment.

32.21 Many companies see this as unattractive and may prefer instead to incorporate the UK operation as a UK company, governed by the Companies Act 2006. Although the administrative and disclosure burden may be higher, the financial statements filed in the UK would include only the transactions of the UK operation rather than of the overseas company. Furthermore, the company may be enable to take advantage of the small company exemptions available to UK companies, but not to overseas companies. Small company financial statements are considered in detail in chapter 31.

32.22 An overseas company that:

- is required by its parent law to prepare, have audited and disclose financial statements; or
- is incorporated in an EEA state (that is, an EU Member State and additionally, Norway, Lichtenstein or Iceland) and is required by its parent law to prepare and disclose financial statements, but is not required by its parent law to have its financial statements audited or deliver its financial statements;

must deliver a copy of those financial statements to the Registrar of Companies in relation to each financial period. [SI 2009/1801, Reg 31(1), 32(1)]

32.23 If the company does not fall within the scope of the above paragraph, that is, where an overseas company is not required to disclose financial statements under parent law, then the requirements imposed on it are somewhat more complex and described from paragraph 32.30.

Companies required to prepare and disclose accounts under parent law

32.24 The company is required to file with the Registrar of Companies "*a copy of all the accounting documents prepared in relation to a financial period of the company that are disclosed in accordance with its parent law*" for every financial period ending after its registration. [SI 2009/1801 Reg 32(1)]. For this purpose, the 'accounting documents' are:

- Its financial statements.
- Where the company has one or more subsidiaries, its consolidated financial statements. (For this purpose, *'consolidated financial statements'* and *'subsidiaries'* have the same definition as under the company's parent law.)
- Any directors' report for the period.
- Any auditors' report for the period, on either the financial statements or directors' report.

[SI 2009/1801 Reg 31(2)].

32.25 The accounting documents filed with the Registrar of Companies must state:

- The legislation under which the financial statements have been prepared and audited (where applicable).
- The name of the body that issued the GAAP in accordance with which the financial statements were prepared or a statement that they were not prepared in accordance with a set GAAP.
- The name of the body that issued the GAAS in accordance with which the financial statements were audited or a statement that the audit was not conducted in accordance with a set GAAS.
- Where the financial statements are unaudited, that no audit is required (if this is the case, for companies incorporated in EEA States only).

[SI 2009/1801 Reg 33].

32.26 If the overseas company is incorporated in an EEA State and is not required by its parent law to deliver accounting documents, it need not do so in the UK. [SI 2009/1801 Reg 32(3)]. Although, at face value, this seems inconsistent with the objective of protecting the UK public (see para 32.1), the imposition of additional requirements on EU companies operating in the UK is not permitted by EU law.

32.27 If the overseas company is permitted by its parent law to file documents in a modified form those may be filed with the Registrar of Companies in place of full financial statements. [SI 2009/1801 Reg 32(2)].

Filing deadline

32.28 An overseas company to which this section applies must file its financial statements with the Registrar within three months of it being required to disclose them by the law in its country of incorporation. [SI 2009/1801, Reg 34].

> **Example 1 – Filing deadline – end of month**
>
> An overseas company incorporated in an EEA State is required by the law of its country of incorporation to file its financial statements by 28 February. It is then required to file them with the Registrar of companies by 31 May (that is, three months later).

> **Example 2 – Filing deadline – during the month**
>
> The facts are the same as in example 1 but the filing deadline under local law is 5 February. It is required to file them with the Registrar of Companies by 5 May (that is, three months later).

More than one UK establishment

32.29 Where an overseas company has more than one UK establishment, it need not file the same financial statements for each one. On registration of a second or subsequent UK establishment, it may notify the Registrar of Companies that it intends to comply with the financial statement filing requirements in respect of an existing establishment, giving its UK registered number. If it has done so, the company may file the financial statements only in respect of that establishment, provided that they are filed before all relevant deadlines. [SI 2009/1801 Reg 32(6)].

> **Example 1 – Filing deadline – using registration of former establishment**
>
> An overseas company incorporated in an EEA State has two UK establishments, X and Y. The company is required by its local law to file its financial statements by 31 August. When it opened its second UK establishment (Y), it stated that it intended to comply with the financial statements filing requirements of establishment X, giving its registered number.
>
> The UK filing deadline for each of establishment X and establishment Y is 30 November (three months following disclosure under parent law). Establishment X filed the company's financial statements in the UK on 17 November and establishment Y need not, therefore, file anything.

> **Example 2 – Filing deadline – using registration for new establishment**
>
> The facts are the same as in example 1, except that X filed the company's financial statements in the UK on 17 December. Because this was after Y's filing deadline, the overseas company's entitlement to file them in respect of only one UK establishment falls away and Y must also file them in the UK.

Companies not required to prepare and disclose accounts under parent law

32.30 An overseas company that is not required to prepare and disclose its accounts under parent law (that is, one that falls outside the scope of para 32.23 above) is required to file financial statements with the Registrar of Companies for each financial year of the company. These overseas companies are known as 'relevant overseas companies'. [SI 2009/1801 Reg 38, 42].

32.31 The requirements to prepare and file financial statements for a relevant overseas company are very similar to those applying to a limited company that is formed and registered under the Companies Act 2006. In fact, the Overseas Company Regulations reproduces, with appropriate modifications, the equivalent sections of the Companies Act 2006 that are applicable to a limited company.

The company's financial year

32.32 Before an overseas company can consider the financial statements it must file in the UK, it must consider its financial year under the Act, as this may differ from the company's own financial year.

32.33 The rules determining an overseas company's financial year are similar to those determining that of a UK company, which are considered in detail in chapter 8.

32.34 The directors of a relevant overseas company must prepare financial statements for each financial year. [SI 2009/1801 Reg 38; CA06 Sec 394]. A company's first financial year begins on the day of its first accounting reference period and ends either with:

- the last day of the first accounting reference period; or
- another date determined by the directors that is not more than seven days before or after the end of that period.

[SI 2009/1801 Reg 37; CA06 Sec 390(2)].

32.35 Subsequent financial years begin with the day immediately following the end of the company's previous financial year and end either with:

- the last day of the first accounting reference period; or
- a date determined by the directors not more than seven days before or after the end of that period.

[SI 2009/1801 Reg 37; CA06 Sec 390(3)].

32.36 An overseas company's accounting reference period is determined by reference to its accounting reference date in each calendar year. [SI 2009/1801 Reg 37; CA06 Sec 391(1)].

32.37 An overseas company's accounting reference date is the last day of the month in which the anniversary of becoming a 'relevant overseas company' falls. [SI 2009/1801 Reg 37; CA06 Sec 391(2)]. This date is set without any regard to the company's own accounting reference date under its parent law.

32.38 An overseas company may give notice to the Registrar that it wishes to alter its accounting reference date in relation to the company's current and subsequent accounting reference periods or its previous accounting reference period and subsequent periods. 'Previous accounting reference period' means the period immediately preceding its current accounting reference period. [SI 2009/ 1801, Reg 37; CA06 Sec 392(1)].

32.39 An overseas company's first accounting period must end not less than six and not more than 18 months after the date on which it became a relevant overseas company (see para 32.30). [SI 2009/1801 Reg 37; CA06 Sec 391(3)]. If the overseas company does not change its accounting reference date, then its first accounting reference period will automatically be between a year and 13 months (depending on the precise date on which it became a relevant overseas company).

32.40 Subsequent accounting reference periods will have a year's duration, unless the overseas company changes its accounting reference date. [SI 2009/1801 Reg 37; CA06 Sec 391 (4)(5)].

32.41 The period may be shortened or extended any number of times without restriction. The prohibition on UK companies extending their accounting reference periods more than once in any five year period (unless certain conditions apply) has not been carried into SI 2009/1801.

32.42 A notice may not be given to change the accounting reference date in relation to a previous accounting reference period if the period allowed for filing financial statements in relation to that period has already expired . [SI 2009/1801 Reg 37; CA06 Sec 392(3)].

Example – Accounting reference period

A non-EEA company with no local audit requirement has a 31 December year end and prepares financial statements each year. On 8 March 20X0 it sets up and registers a UK establishment.

For the purposes of the Companies Act 2006 if it does nothing, then it will need to file financial statements with the Registrar of Companies that cover the period from 6 March 20X0 or (the date its directors have chosen which is no more than seven days before or after 31 March 20X1.

However, an overseas company that prepares its financial statements to 31 December each year is unlikely to want to incur the cost of preparing a new set of financial statements to 31 March each year so that its UK establishment can comply with the Regulations. Accordingly, the overseas company would need to give notice to change its accounting reference date to 31 December. Provided the notice is given before its filing deadline, it will need to file financial statements that cover the period from 8 March 20X0 to 31 December 20X0. Thereafter, it will be required to file financial statements for calendar years.

Duty to prepare individual financial statements

32.43 Every relevant overseas company is required to prepare financial statements for the company ('individual financial statements'). [SI 2009/1801 Reg 38; CA06 Sec 394].

32.44 These individual financial statements may be prepared in accordance with:

- Its parent law ('parent law financial statements') (see para 32.53).
- IAS ('IAS financial statements').
- Modified Companies Act 2006, based on section 396 of the Act ('overseas companies financial statements').

[SI 2009/1801 Reg 38 Sec 395(1)].

32.45 In principle, companies have a free choice over which framework they wish to apply in the preparation of their financial statement. However, there are restrictions that may have the effect of limiting that freedom for some overseas companies.

Duty to prepare consolidated financial statements

32.46 If the company was a parent company at the end of its financial year, the directors are required to prepare consolidated financial statements *instead of* individual financial statements. [SI 2009/180 Reg 38; CA06 Sec 399]. This differs from the obligation placed on UK parent companies that are required to prepare consolidated financial statements *as well as* individual financial statements.

32.47 The definition of a parent company for this purpose is the same as that contained in the 2006 Act. See further chapter 24.

32.48 An overseas company will be exempt from the requirement to prepare consolidated financial statements if:

- It prepares parent law financial statements and that parent law does not require the preparation of consolidated financial statements.
- It prepares IAS financial statements and is not required by IAS to prepare consolidated financial statements.
- It prepares overseas company financial statements and the exclusion of its subsidiaries is immaterial (both individually and in aggregate, where the company has more than one subsidiary).

[SI 2009/1801 Reg 38; CA06 Secs 402, 405(2)].

32.49 If an overseas parent company is, itself, the subsidiary of a holding company, the consolidated financial statements of that holding company may be deemed to satisfy the UK requirement for the overseas company to prepare group financial statements. [SI 2009/1801 Reg 38; CA06 Sec 402A]. This differs from the exemption from UK intermediate parent companies, which may be exempted from the requirement to prepare consolidated financial statements but which must, nonetheless, prepare individual financial statements. Overseas intermediate parent companies are required to prepare consolidated financial statements *instead of* individual financial statements (so the UK requirement to prepare those individual financial statements falls away) and may file their holding company consolidated financial statements in place of their own.

32.50 Although seemingly strange, this exemption recognises that a group of overseas companies has a choice about which company within that group opens a UK establishment. This permission enables this choice to be determined for commercial reasons rather than it being influenced by the need to prepare consolidated financial statements by the company that opens the UK establishment.

32.51 Once an overseas parent company has determined that it must prepare consolidated financial statements, those financial statements must be prepared in accordance with one of three frameworks:

- Its parent law ('parent law consolidated financial statements').
- IAS ('IAS consolidated financial statements').
- Modified Companies Act 2006, based on section 404 of the Act ('overseas companies consolidated financial statements').

[SI 2009/1801 Reg 38; CA06 Sec 403(1)].

32.52 Regardless of the framework applied in the preparation of the consolidated financial statements, the financial statements must include the parent company and all its subsidiary undertakings except where:

- Subsidiaries are immaterial to the consolidated financial statements (although for two or more subsidiaries to be excluded, they must be immaterial both individually and in aggregate).
- Subsidiaries operating under severe long-term restrictions substantially hinder the overseas parent company's ability to exercise its rights over the assets or management of the subsidiaries.
- The information necessary for the preparation of consolidated financial statements cannot be obtained without disproportionate expense or undue delay.
- Subsidiaries are held exclusively with a view to subsequent resale.

[SI 2009/1801 Reg 38; CA06 Sec 405(1)-(3)].

Parent law individual financial statements

32.53 A relevant overseas company (that does not prepare consolidated financial statements) may file with the Registrar of Companies individual financial statements prepared in accordance with the law of its country of incorporation.

32.54 This option is available if and only if those financial statements contain:

- A balance sheet as at the last day of the financial year and a profit and loss account (or equivalent statements), both of which must comply, as to content, with the provisions of Schedule 4 to SI 2009/1801 (see from para 32.65).
- Information in the notes to the financial statements set out in Schedule 4 to the Regulations (see from para 32.84).

[SI 2009/1801 Regs 38, 42; CA06 Secs 396, 474].

32.55 The financial statements must also state:

- That they have been prepared in accordance with the company's parent law.
- The name of the legislation under which the financial statements have been prepared'.
- The name of the body that issued the GAAP in accordance with which the financial statements were prepared or a statement that they were not prepared in accordance with a set GAAP.
- The name of the body that issued the GAAS in accordance with which the financial statements were audited (if applicable) or a statement that the financial statements were unaudited.

[SI 2009/1801 Reg 38; CA06 Sec 397(2)].

Parent law consolidated financial statements

32.56 A relevant overseas parent company may file with the Registrar of Companies consolidated financial statements prepared in accordance with the law of its country of incorporation.

32.57 This option is available to overseas companies if and only if the financial statements contain:

- A consolidated balance sheet as at the last day of the financial year and a consolidated profit and loss account, both of which must comply, as to content, with the provisions of Schedule 5 to SI 2009/1801 (see from para 32.86).
- Information in the notes to the financial statements set out in Schedule 5 to SI 2009/1801 (see from para 32.87).

[SI 2009/1801 Reg 38; CA06 Sec 404].

32.58 The consolidated financial statements must also state in the notes:

- That they have been prepared in accordance with the company's parent law.
- The name of the legislation under which the consolidated financial statements have been prepared.
- The name of the body that issued the GAAP in accordance with which the consolidated financial statements were prepared or a statement that they were not prepared in accordance with a set GAAP.
- The name of the body that issued the GAAS in accordance with which the consolidated financial statements were audited (if applicable) or a statement that the financial statements were unaudited.

[SI 2009/1801 Reg 38; CA06 Sec 406(2)].

IAS individual financial statements

32.59 An overseas company is permitted to prepare its individual financial statements in accordance with IAS. IAS means IASs within the meaning of Article 2 of the IAS Regulation (EC Regulation No 1606/2002). It includes all IASs, IFRSs, and related interpretations (SIC and IFRIC interpretations) issued by the IASB and adopted by the EU (including any subsequent amendments to those standards and interpretations). [SI 2009/1801 Reg 42; CA06 Sec 474].

32.60 The company's IAS financial statements must state:

- That they have been prepared in accordance with IAS.
- The name of the body that issued the GAAS with which the financial statements were audited (if applicable) or a statement that the financial statements were unaudited.

[SI 2009/1801 Reg 38; CA06 Sec 397(1)].

IAS consolidated financial statements

32.61 The company's IAS consolidated financial statements must state:

- That they have been prepared in accordance with IAS.
- The name body that issued the GAAS with which the financial statements were audited (if applicable) or a statement that the financial statements were unaudited.

[SI 2009/1801 Reg 38; CA06 Sec 406(1)].

Overseas companies financial statements

32.62 Overseas companies that do not prepare financial statements in accordance with parent law or IAS, must prepare financial statements in accordance with Schedule 4 to SI 2009/1801 as to the content of the balance sheet and the profit and loss account and any additional information provided in the notes.[SI 2009/1801 Reg 38; CA06 Sec 396]. The requirements surrounding the preparation of overseas companies financial statements are based on, and in many cases, similar to, the requirements imposed on UK companies by the 2006 Act. The main differences surround the structure of the balance sheet and profit and loss account (which are based on IFRS, rather than UK GAAP), the level of disclosure in the notes to the financial statements (which is lower than for UK companies) and the application of GAAP and GAAS. In other areas, additional guidance in the application of the law is available in this Manual of Accounting.

32.63 Where a relevant overseas company prepares its individual financial statements as stated above, these must state:

- That they have been prepared in accordance with section 396 as modified by SI 2009/1801.
- The name of the body that issued the GAAP in accordance with which the financial statements were prepared or a statement that they were not prepared in accordance with a set GAAP.
- The name of the body that issued the GAAS in accordance with which the financial statements were audited (if applicable) or a statement that the financial statements are unaudited.

[SI 2009/1801 Reg 38; CA06 Sec 397(3)].

32.64 A set of overseas company financial statements must comprise a balance sheet as at the last day of the financial year and a profit and loss account. [SI 2009/1801 Reg 38; CA06 Sec 396]. SI 2009/1801 recognises that different names are used around the world for these statements and defines each term so as to allow the use of equivalent statements with different names. [SI 2009/1801Reg 42; CA06 Sec 474].

32.65 Both the balance sheet and the profit and loss account must include each of the line items (as defined in IAS 1, 'Presentation of financial statements') that are, as a miniumum, required to be included in a balance sheet or profit and loss account (respectively) prepared in accordance with IAS. [SI 2009/1801 4 Sch 1(a)(b), 20].

32.66 That is, the balance sheet must include, as a minimum:

- Property, plant and equipment.
- Investment property.
- Intangible assets.
- Financial assets (excluding those shown under other categories).
- Investments accounted for using the equity method.

- Biological assets.
- Inventories.
- Trade and other receivables.
- Cash and cash equivalents.
- The total of assets classified as held-for-sale and assets included in disposal groups classified as held-for-sale in accordance with IFRS 5, 'Non-current assets held-for-sale and discontinued operations'.
- Trade and other payables.
- Provisions.
- Financial liabilities (excluding amounts shown in other categories).
- Liabilities and assets for current tax, as defined in IAS 12, 'Income taxes'.
- Deferred tax liabilities and deferred tax assets, as defined in IAS 12.
- Liabilities included in disposal groups classified as held-for-sale in accordance with IFRS 5.
- Non-controlling interest, presented within equity.
- Issued capital and reserves attributable to owners of the parent.

[IAS 1 (revised) para 54].

32.67 Although the line items that an overseas company is required to present on the face of its balance sheet as stated above refer to other IFRSs, we do not consider that the effect of that should be to determine the overseas company's accounting policies. SI 2009/1801 does not require overseas company financial statements to be prepared in accordance with any particular GAAP, so the above references to IAS 12 and IFRS 5 should not preclude the preparation of the overseas company financial statements in accordance with a GAAP that is inconsistent with either of those IAS standards. However, the principle that disclosure should be given on the face of the balance sheet for each of the following items should be followed:

- Assets classified as part of discontinued operations (or equivalent).
- Liabilities classified as part of discontinued operations (or equivalent).
- Current tax assets and liabilities.
- Deferred tax assets and liabilities.

32.68 Similarly, the profit and loss account must include the following line items, as a minimum:

- Revenue.
- Finance costs.

- Share of profits and losses of associates and joint ventures accounted for using the equity method.
- Tax expense.
- A single amount comprising the total of:
  - the post-tax profit or loss of discontinued operations; and
  - the post-tax gain or loss recognised on the measurement to fair value less costs to sell or on the disposal of the assets or disposal group(s) constituting the discontinued operation.
- Profit or loss.
- Allocations of profit or loss for the period:
- Profit or loss attributable to minority interest.
- Profit or loss attributable to owners of the parent.

[IAS 1 (revised) paras 82-84].

32.69 Although IAS 1 (revised) refers to the 'statement of comprehensive income' (which includes the items listed above as well as other items of comprehensive income) and not to the profit and loss account, it permits the items included in the list above to be presented as a separate statement. In effect, these line items become those required to be presented on the face of the profit and loss account.

32.70 Both the profit and loss account and the balance sheet must state the currency in which they are prepared. [SI 2009/1801 4 Sch 1(c)]. There is no requirement for this to be stated in any particular way.

32.71 Where the nature of the company's business requires it, the company's directors must adapt the line items in the balance sheet or profit and loss account. [SI 2009/1801 4 Sch 5(1)]. This is consistent with UK GAAP and is considered further in chapter 4.

32.72 The company's directors must, in determining how amounts are presented within items in the profit and loss account and balance sheet, have regard to the substance of the reported transaction or arrangement, in accordance with the GAAP applied in the preparation of the financial statements. [SI 2009/1801 4 Sch 9]. This is consistent with UK GAAP and is considered further in chapter 4.

32.73 Line items in the profit and loss account and balance sheet may be combined if they meet any of the following:

- They are of a similar nature.
- Their individual amounts are not material in assessing the company's state of affairs or profit or loss for the financial year in question. For this purpose, information is material if it supplements information that is included in the

balance sheet or profit and loss account or is relevant to an understanding of the overseas company's state of affairs.

- Their combination facilitates the assessment of the overseas company's state of affairs or profit and loss account (that is, it results in greater clarity). Where this applies, however, the detailed breakdown of the combined items must be given in the notes to the financial statements.

[SI 2009/1801 4 Sch 3, 4(2), 5(2)(3)].

This is consistent with UK GAAP and is considered further in chapter 4.

32.74 A line item need not be shown where there is no amount to be included for either the financial year in question or the immediately preceding financial year. [SI 2009/1801 4 Sch 6].

32.75 Whichever line items the directors use in the presentation of the profit and loss account and balance sheet, these should normally be consistent from year to year. Where the directors consider that there are special reasons for a change, particulars of the change and the reasons for it should be disclosed in the notes to the financial statements. [SI 2009/1801 4 Sch 2].

Corresponding amounts

32.76 Corresponding amounts for the year immediately preceding the year in question must be shown in respect of every line item in the balance sheet and profit and loss account. [SI 2009/1801 4 Sch 7(1)]. Although not specifically stated in SI 2009/1801, we consider that this applies even when no such item exists to be disclosed in respect of the current financial year.

32.77 Where the amount for the previous year is not comparable with the amount shown in respect of the current year, the previous year's amount must be adjusted. Where this applies, particulars of the adjustment and the reasons for it must be disclosed in the notes to the financial statements. [SI 2009/1801 4 Sch 7(2)].

32.78 This is consistent with UK GAAP and is considered further in chapter 4.

Offsetting

32.79 Asset and liability items may not be set off against each other. Similarly, income and expenditure items may not be set off against each other. [SI 2009/1801 4 Sch 7(8)].

32.80 The rule against offsetting assets and liabilities is also covered in IAS 32 and FRS 25, 'Financial instruments: Disclosure and presentation'. Both IAS 32 and FRS 25 set out conditions that must be met before debit and credit balances can be aggregated into a single net asset or liability, that is, where they do not constitute separate assets and liabilities. Although these standards are applicable only to financial statements prepared in accordance with IFRS and UK GAAP respectively, they may be used as indicative guidance for companies applying other GAAPs (see further Manual of Accounting – Financial instruments).

Accounting principles

32.81 The financial statements should be prepared in accordance with the following principles:

- Going concern – it is presumed that the overseas company is carrying on business as a going concern, but if this is not the case, then the following disclosure is required:
  - That the financial statements have not been prepared on the going concern basis.
  - The basis on which they have been prepared.
  - Why the overseas company is not a going concern.
- Consistency of accounting policies from one year to the next.
- Accruals – all income and expenses relating to a financial year must be recognised in that period, regardless of the date of receipt or payment.
- The carrying amount of each individual asset or liability must be calculated separately, prior to aggregation into the balance sheet line items.

[SI 2009/1801 4 Sch 11-14].

32.82 If the overseas company's directors believe that there are special reasons for departing from any of those principles in preparing the financial statements in respect of any financial year they may do so. However, disclosure must be given in the notes of the particulars of the departure, the reasons for it and its effect. [SI 2009/1801 4 Sch 10(2)].

32.83 These principles and departures from them are consistent with UK GAAP and are considered further in chapter 4.

Notes to the financial statements

32.84 The following information must be disclosed in the notes to the overseas company's financial statements, unless included in the profit and loss account or balance sheet:

- The accounting policies used to measure the amounts to be included in the line items in the balance sheet and profit and loss account (including such policies with respect to the depreciation and impairment of assets).
- The measurement basis (or bases) used in preparing the financial statements and any other accounting policies that are relevant to an understanding of the financial statements.

- Whether the financial statements have been prepared in accordance with the applicable GAAP and particulars of any material departure from the accounting standards that underpin that GAAP, together with the reasons for departure.

- Information relevant to assessing the state of the company's affairs including, as a minimum, information about:
  - Property, plant and equipment.
  - Investment property.
  - Intangible assets.
  - Financial assets.
  - Biological assets.
  - Inventories.
  - Trade and other receivables (and the amount falling due after more than one year must be shown separately for each item included under receivables).
  - Trade and other payables (and the amount falling due after more than one year must be shown separately for each item included under payables).
  - Provisions.
  - Financial liabilities.
  - Issued capital and reserves.
  - Finance costs.
  - Finance income.
  - Expenses and interest paid to group undertakings (this must be shown separately from expenses and interest paid to other entities).
  - Income and interest derived from group undertakings (this must be shown separately from income and interest derived from other sources).
  - Transactions with related parties.
  - Dividends.
  - Items described as other, sundry, miscellaneous or equivalent.
  - Guarantees.
  - Contingent liabilities.
  - Commitments.
  - Other off-balance sheet arrangements.
  - Financial instruments.

[SI 2009/1801 4 Sch 15-19].

Overseas companies consolidated financial statements

32.85 Where an overseas parent company prepares overseas companies consolidated financial statements, they must state in the notes:

- That they have been prepared in accordance with section 404 as modified by SI 2009/1801.
- The name of the body that issued the GAAP in accordance with which the financial statements were prepared or a statement that they were not prepared in accordance with a set GAAP.
- The name body that issued the GAAS in accordance with which the financial statements were audited (if applicable) or a statement that the financial statements are unaudited.

[SI 2009/1801 Reg 38; CA06 Sec 406(3)].

32.86 A set of overseas company financial statements must comprise a balance sheet as at the last day of the financial year, a profit and loss account and information by way of notes to the financial statements. [SI 2009/1801 Reg 38; CA06 Sec 404]. The line items that must be included in the balance sheet and profit and loss account are the same as for overseas individual financial statements (see from para 32.65). [SI 2009/1801 5 Sch 1(1)].

32.87 The notes to the consolidated overseas company financial statements must include:

- The information required to be disclosed in the notes to overseas company individual financial statements (see para 32.84).
- Information concerning investments accounted for using the equity method.
- Information concerning minority interest, presented within equity.

[SI 2009/1801 5 Sch 1(1)(2)].

32.88 The consolidated overseas company financial statements should be prepared as if all the entities included within the consolidation ('the group') were a single entity. [SI 2009/1801 5 Sch 1(1)]. They must incorporate, in full, the information included in the individual financial statements of the entities included in the consolidation, subject to adjustments permitted or required by either the GAAP under which they are prepared or SI 2009/1801. [SI 2009/1801 2 Sch 2]. This principle is consistent with the preparation of either UK GAAP or IFRS consolidated financial statements and is considered further in chapter 24.

Consistent accounting policies

32.89 Except in exceptional situations, which are explained below, (or when the resulting adjustments would be immaterial to the group financial statements, both individually and in aggregate) all assets and liabilities included in the consolidated financial statements should be measured using consistent accounting policies. Hence, on consolidation, adjustments might have to be made to the amounts that have been reported by subsidiaries in their individual financial statements if their accounting polices differ from those of the group. [SI 2009/1801 5 Sch 3(1)(3)].

32.90 However, in certain situations, the parent's directors might consider that there are special reasons for retaining the different accounting rules adopted by the subsidiary. Where this is so, SI 2009/1801 requires that particulars of the departure, the reasons for it and its effect should be disclosed in the notes to the consolidated financial statements. [SI 2009/1801 5 Sch 3(2)]. This principle is consistent with the preparation of either UK GAAP or IFRS consolidated financial statements and is considered further in chapter 24.

Elimination of group transactions

32.91 SI 2009/1801 requires '*debts and claims*' (that is, debtors and creditors) between group entities to be eliminated on consolidation. Similarly, profits and losses resulting from intra-group transactions that are included in the book value of assets or liabilities should be excluded. [SI 2009/1801 5 Sch 5(1)(2)]. The elimination, to the extent that are material, may be done in proportion to the group's interest in the shares of the subsidiaries. [SI2009/1801 5 Sch 5(3)(4)].

Business combinations

32.92 All business combinations must be accounted for using the 'acquisition' method of accounting (see further chapter 25) unless the GAAP under which the overseas company consolidated financial statements are prepared permits another method of accounting, in which case, that method must be disclosed in the notes to the financial statements. [SI 2009/1801 5 Sch 7].

Joint ventures and associates

32.93 A joint venture in which an overseas company has a financial interest may be (but need not be) accounted for in the consolidated financial statements, using the 'proportional consolidation' method of accounting. If this is applied, the principles of consolidation should be applied to the accounting for joint ventures. This is not permitted for subsidiaries (which must be fully consolidated) or for any joint venture that is a body corporate. [SI 2009/1801 5 Sch 9]. The option of proportionally consolidating a joint venture is not available under UK GAAP, but is considered in greater detail in Manual of Accounting – IFRS for the UK.

32.94 An associate as defined in paragraph 32.96 below should be accounted for using the equity method of accounting (see further chapter 27) unless the GAAP under which the overseas company financial statements are prepared permits another method of accounting, in which case, that method must be disclosed in the notes to the financial statements. [SI 2009/1801 5 Sch 11(1)(2)].

32.95 If the associate has subsidiaries, then the consolidated net assets and profits and losses of the associate (measured in accordance with SI 2009/1801) should be equity-accounted in the overseas company consolidated financial statements. [SI 2009/1801 5 Sch 11(3)].

32.96 An 'associate' is defined as an undertaking in which the overseas company has a 'participating interest' and over whose operating and financial policy it exercises a 'significant influence'. The definition excludes subsidiaries and joint ventures (see above). [SI 2009/1801 5 Sch 10].

32.97 In practice, under UK law, where an investing company holds more than 20 per cent of the voting rights in another undertaking, it is presumed to exercise significant influence, unless there is evidence to the contrary. [SI 2008/410 6 Sch 19(2)].

Approval and signing of financial statements

32.98 The relevant overseas company's annual financial statements (whether individual or consolidated and regardless of the framework under which they are prepared) must be approved by the directors and signed, on the balance sheet, by at least one director on behalf of them all. It is an offense to approve financial statements that do not comply with the Regulations. [SI 2009/1801 Reg 39; CA06 Sec 414].

32.99 In order to comply with this requirement, all directors of the overseas company should satisfy themselves that sufficient controls are in place to ensure compliance with UK law. An appropriate wording for inclusion at the foot of the balance sheet may be "*The financial statements were approved by the board of directors on [date] and signed on its behalf by:*" (followed by the name and signature of the signing director). [SI 2009/1801 Reg 40; CA06 Sec 441(2)].

Filing financial statements

32.100 Every overseas company is required to file a copy of its financial statements with the Registrar of Companies in respect of each UK establishment it operates (see para 32.104). [SI 2009/1801 Reg 40; CA06 Sec 441(3)].

32.101 The period that a company has for filing its financial statements is thirteen months from the end of its financial period. [SI 2009/1801 Reg 40; CA06 Sec 442(2)].

32.102 However, if the financial statements in question are for the overseas company's first financial period and that period lasts for more than a year, the financial statements must be filed within thirteen months of first anniversary of the overseas company becoming a relevant overseas company. [SI 2009/1801 Reg 40; CA06 Sec 442(3)].

32.103 Where an overseas company's financial period has been shortened, the filing deadline is the later of thirteen months from the end of the financial period and three months from the date on which notice of the shortened period was filed. [SI 2009/1801 Reg 40; CA06 Sec 442(4)]. This is similar to the provisions for UK companies and is illustrated by an example in chapter 8.

32.104 There are provisions that prevent an overseas company from the need to file the same information more than once. Where an overseas company has more than one UK establishment and the particulars of a UK establishment that were registered when it was established stated an intention to comply with the filing requirement for another UK establishment (giving the registered number of that establishment), the company need not file financial statements as long as the financial statements are filed before the expiry of the first UK establishment's filing deadline. [SI 2009/1801 Reg 40(4)].

Example 1 – Implications of filing before the deadline

A relevant overseas company has two UK establishments, X and Y. Establishment X was registered on 15 March 20X0, on which date the company became a relevant overseas company. Establishment Y was set up and registered on 27 September 20X2. In its registration documents for establishment Y, the company stated that it intended to comply with the financial statements filing requirements of establishment X, giving its registered number.

Establishment X is required to prepare its first financial statements in the UK covering the period from 16 March 20X0 to 31 March 20X1 (the last day of the month in which its anniversary of registration as a relevant overseas company falls). Establishment X must file these financial statements by 30 April 20X2 (thirteen months later).

The next financial statements that establishment X will need to file are for the year ended 31 March 20X2 and these must be filed by 30 April 20X3. As long as establishment X does so, the overseas company need not consider any filing requirement for establishment Y, as it has complied with its obligations by virtue of establishment X having done so.

Example 2 – Implications of filing after the deadline

The facts are the same as in example 1 except that establishment X files its financial statements for the year ended 31 March 20X2 on 15 May 20X3 (that is, after the deadline). Because this was after establishment Y's filing deadline, the overseas company's entitlement to file financial statements in respect of only one UK establishment falls away and financial statements must be filed by both establishment X and establishment Y.

Listed overseas companies

32.105 An overseas company that has obtained a listing on the Main Market of the London Stock Exchange or the Plus-listed market is bound by the requirements of the Financial Services Authority Listing Rules and Disclosure and Transparency Rules (LR and DTR). Such an overseas company should consider its obligations under DTR 4 (Periodic financial reporting), DTR 5 (Vote holder and issuer notification rules) and DTR 6 (Access to information). [LR.14.3.22].

32.106 An overseas company with a listing on the Main Market of the London Stock Exchange or on the Plus-listed market (classified as an EU regulated market) must publish annual financial statements and half yearly interim reports that comply with the requirements of DTR 4.16 and 4.2.4 (essentially, the annual financial statements must be prepared using IFRS and the condensed interim financial statements must comply with IAS 34 respectively). The annual financial statements must be audited.

32.107 A company whose registered office is in a non-EEA State whose relevant laws are considered equivalent by the FSA is exempted from the rules on annual financial reports (DTR 4.1), half-yearly financial reports (DTR 4.2) and interim management statements (DTR 4.3). [DTR 4.4.8]. The FSA maintains a list of non-EEA States that are judged to have laws that lay down requirements equivalent to those imposed on issuers by DTR 4. [DTR 4.4.9].

32.108 A LSE publication, 'Main market continuing obligations', can be downloaded from its web site and this document sets out in summary-checklist form the key continuing obligations for companies that have either a primary listing of equity or a secondary listing of equity or depositary receipts.

Overseas companies traded on AIM

32.109 The LSE requires EEA companies traded on its second market, AIM to publish annual and half yearly financial statements using IFRS. Where, at the end of the relevant financial period, such a company is not a parent company, it may prepare and present such financial information either in accordance with IAS or in accordance with the accounting and company legislation and regulations that are applicable to that company due to its country of incorporation. [AIM Rule 18, 19].

32.110 An AIM company incorporated in a non-EEA country must present its financial statements using either IFRS, US, Canadian, Australian GAAP or Japanese GAAP.

Index

Locators are:
paragraph numbers: 11.149, for Chapter 11, paragraph 149

Entries are in word-by-word alphabetical order, where a group of letters followed by a space is filed before the same group of letters followed by a letter, eg 'capital structure and treasury policy' will appear before 'capitalisation'. In determining alphabetical arrangement, initial articles, conjunctions and small prepositions are ignored.

Index